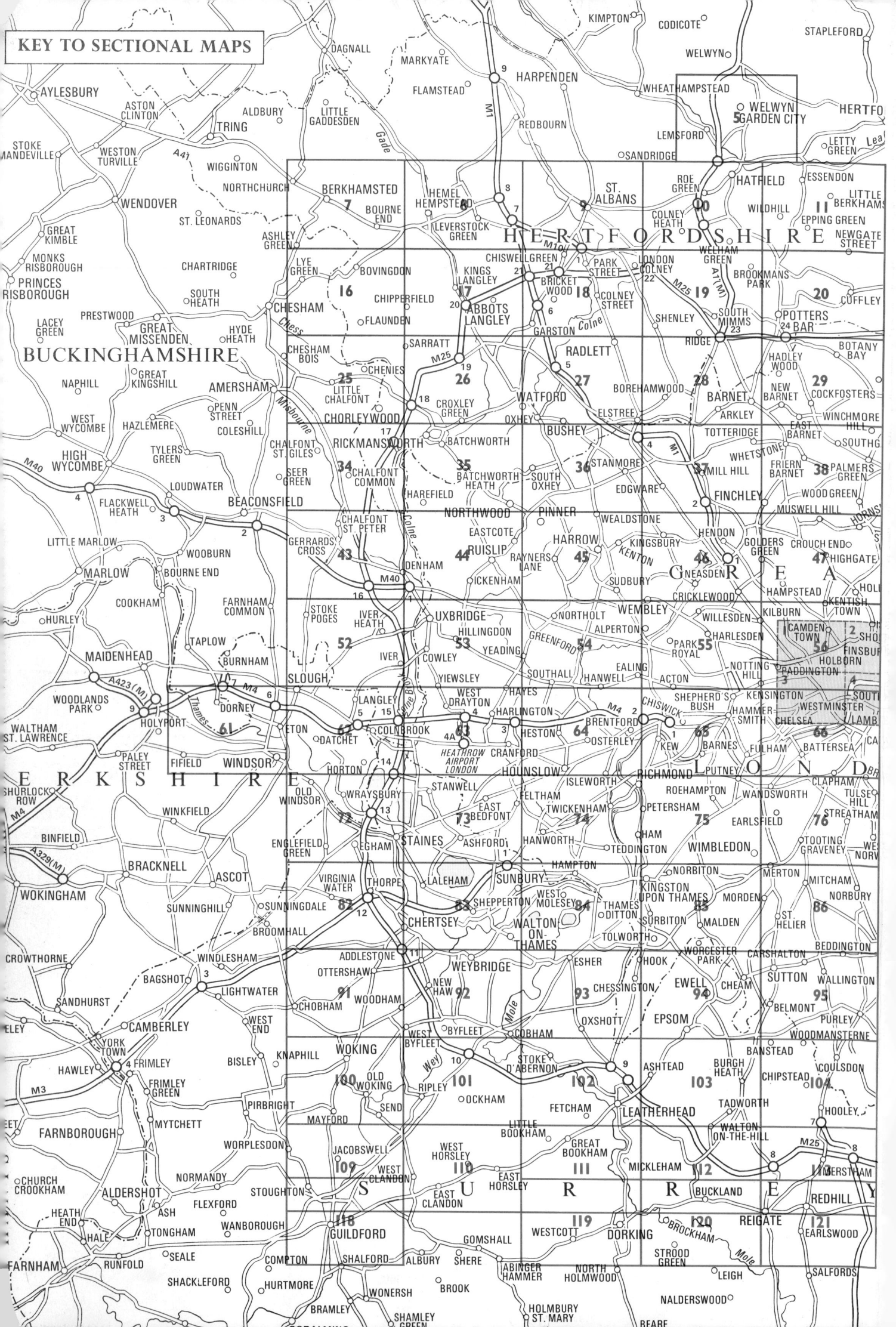

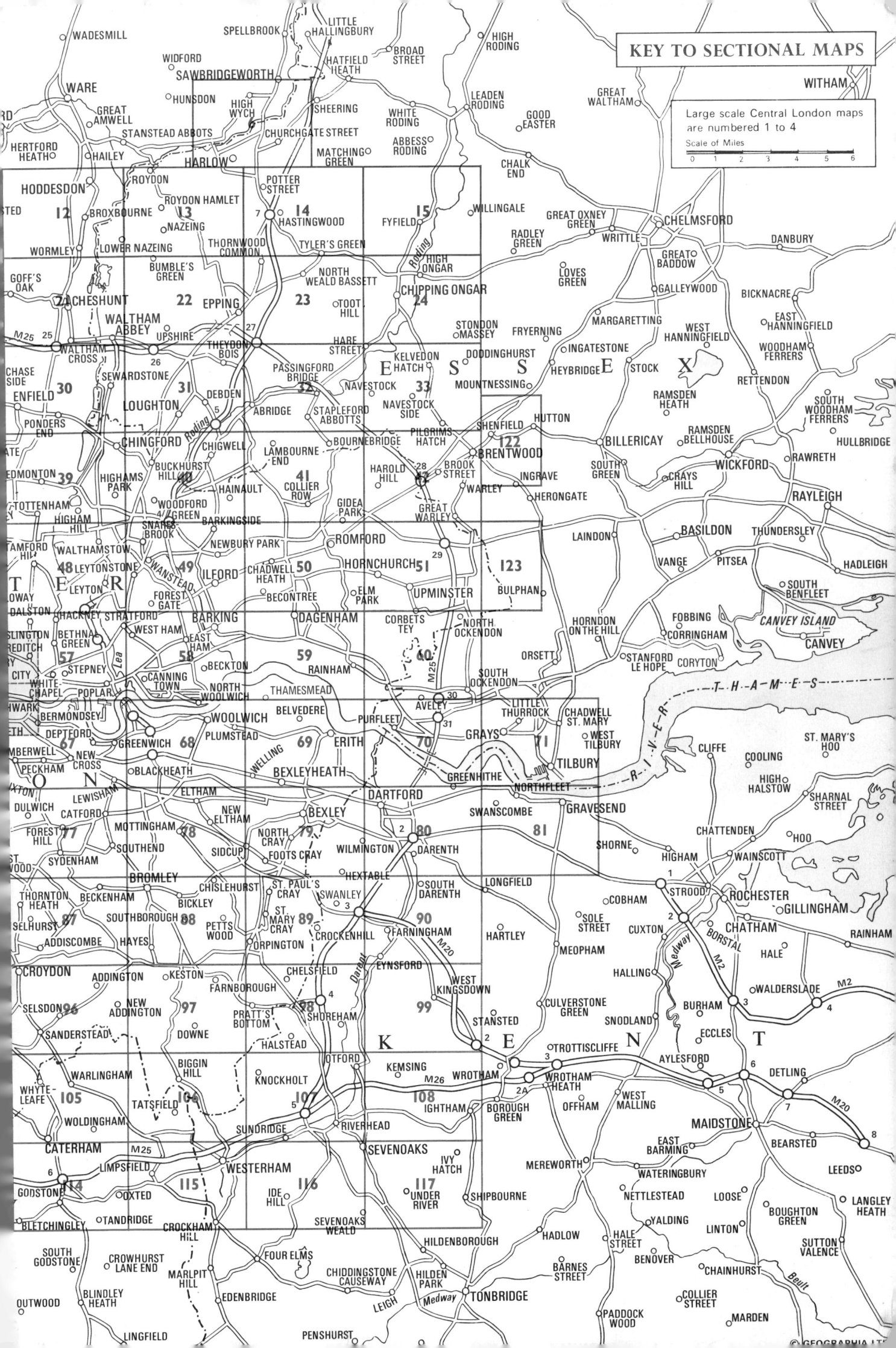

Published by

Nicholson
HarperCollins *Publishers* Ltd
77-85 Fulham Palace Road
London W6 8JB

© Copyright Nicholson 1992
First published by Geographia Ltd 1977
Seventh revised edition 1991
Reprinted 1992

Based upon the Ordnance Survey with the sanction
of the Controller of H.M. Stationery Office.
Crown Copyright Reserved.

The Ordnance Survey is not responsible for the
accuracy of the National Grid on this production.

Nicholson wishes to acknowledge the
co-operation of the Post Office in the preparation
of the postal information used in this atlas.

The greatest possible care and attention is taken in producing this atlas, but information can become out of date.
Although the publishers can accept no responsibility for errors and omissions, they are always grateful for corrections
and any other suggestions for improvement. Any information or queries relating to this atlas should be addressed
to:
   The Chief Cartographer
   Nicholson
   HarperCollins Publishers Ltd
   77-85 Fulham Palace Road
   London W6 8JB

London Underground map reproduced by
permission of London Regional Transport
LRT Registered User No 92/1496

Printed in Great Britain by
HarperCollins Manufacturing, Edinburgh

ISBN 0 7028 1254 4
91/1/210 EJ 5894 ENU

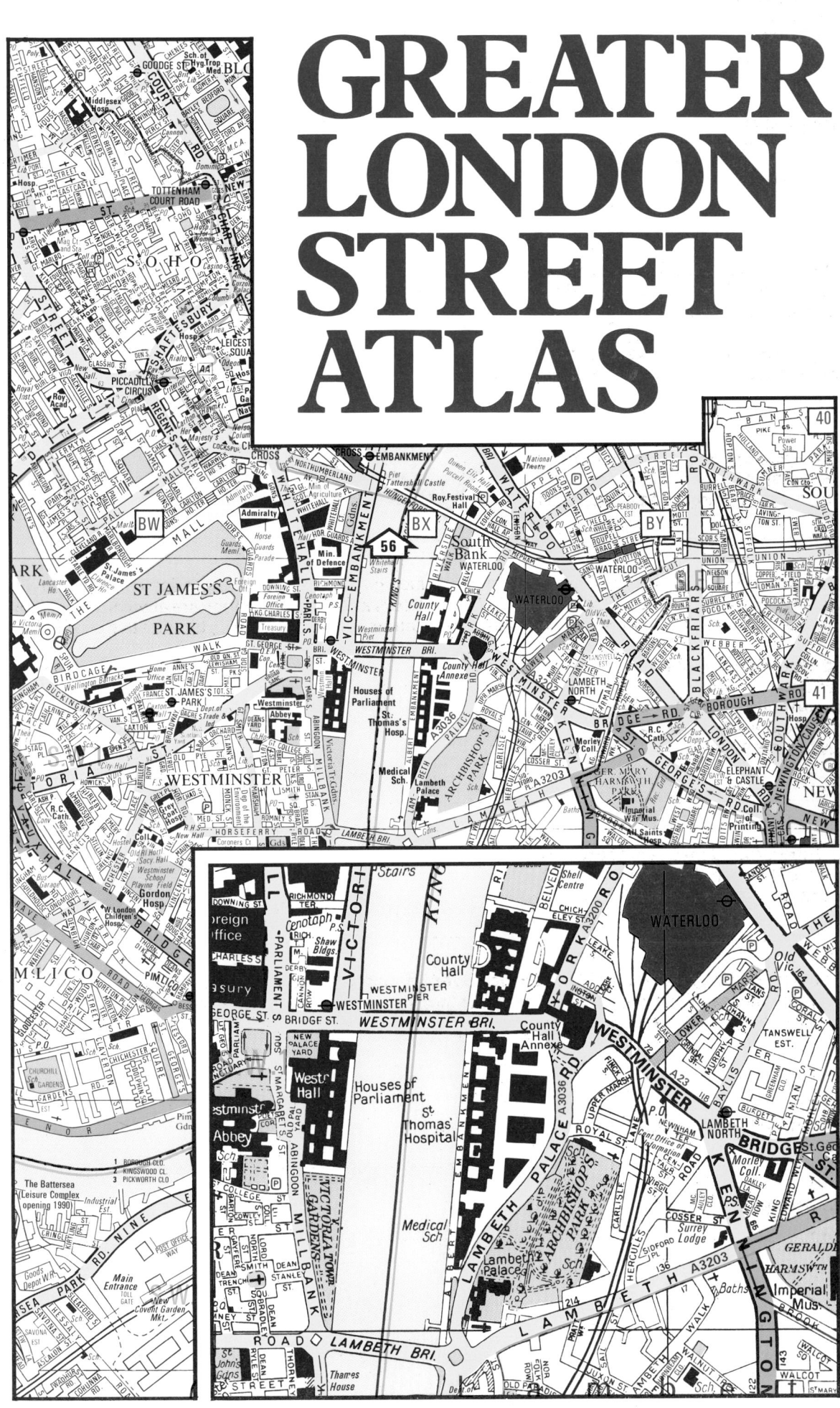

GREATER LONDON STREET ATLAS

GREATER LONDON STREET ATLAS

CONTENTS

Key to Sectional Maps .... inside front cover

Planning Maps

Inner London Route Map 4-5
London and M25 Route Map 6-7
M25 Junction-Mileage Planner 8

Street Maps

Legend
Central London .... Maps 1-4
Greater London .... Maps 5-123

Information

Underground Stations 256
Underground Map 257
British Rail Stations 258
Central London Theatres and Cinemas 260
Places of Interest 261

Indexes

Index to Place Names 263
Index to Street Names 267

Personal Information 410
Map of Administrative Areas .... inside back cover

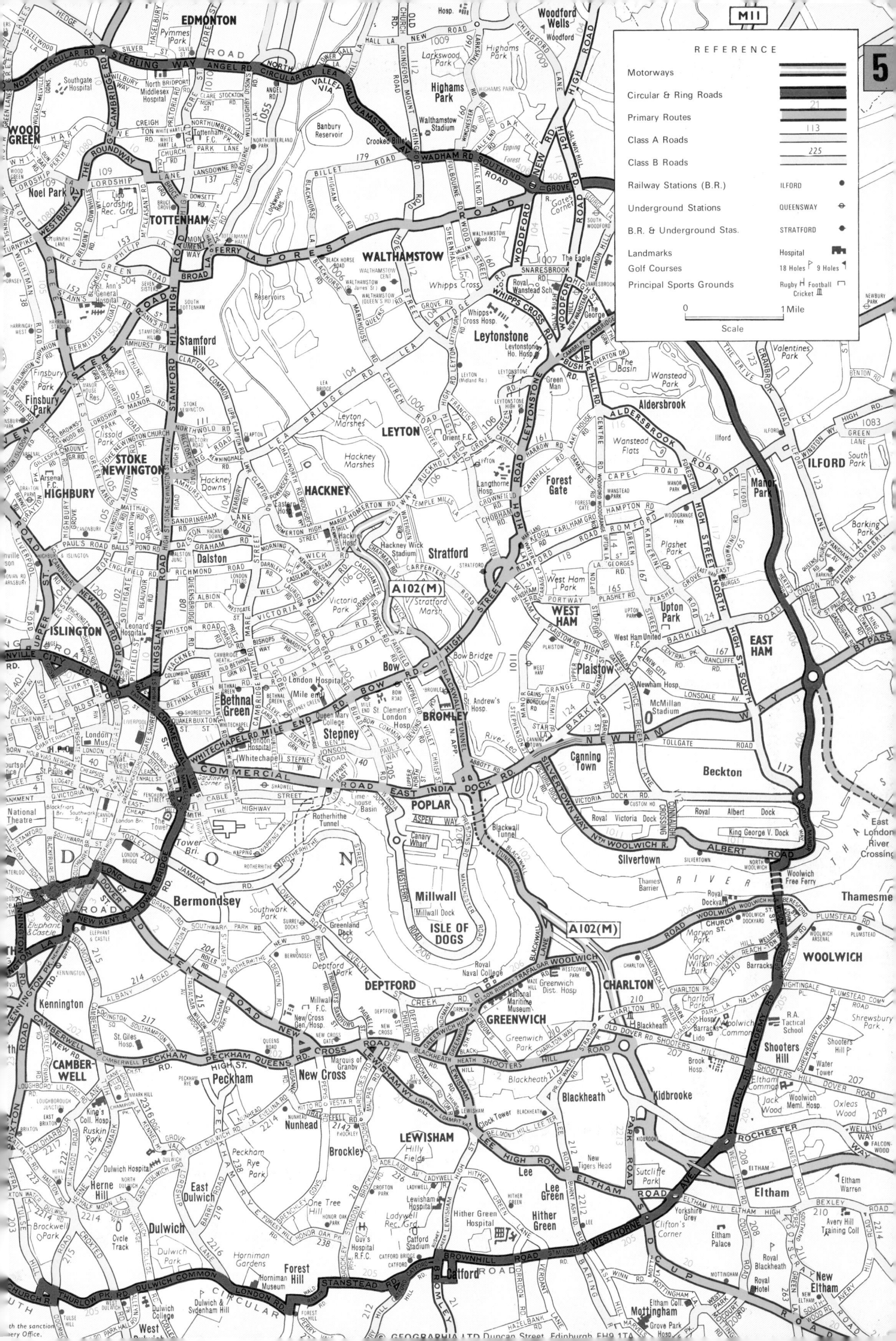

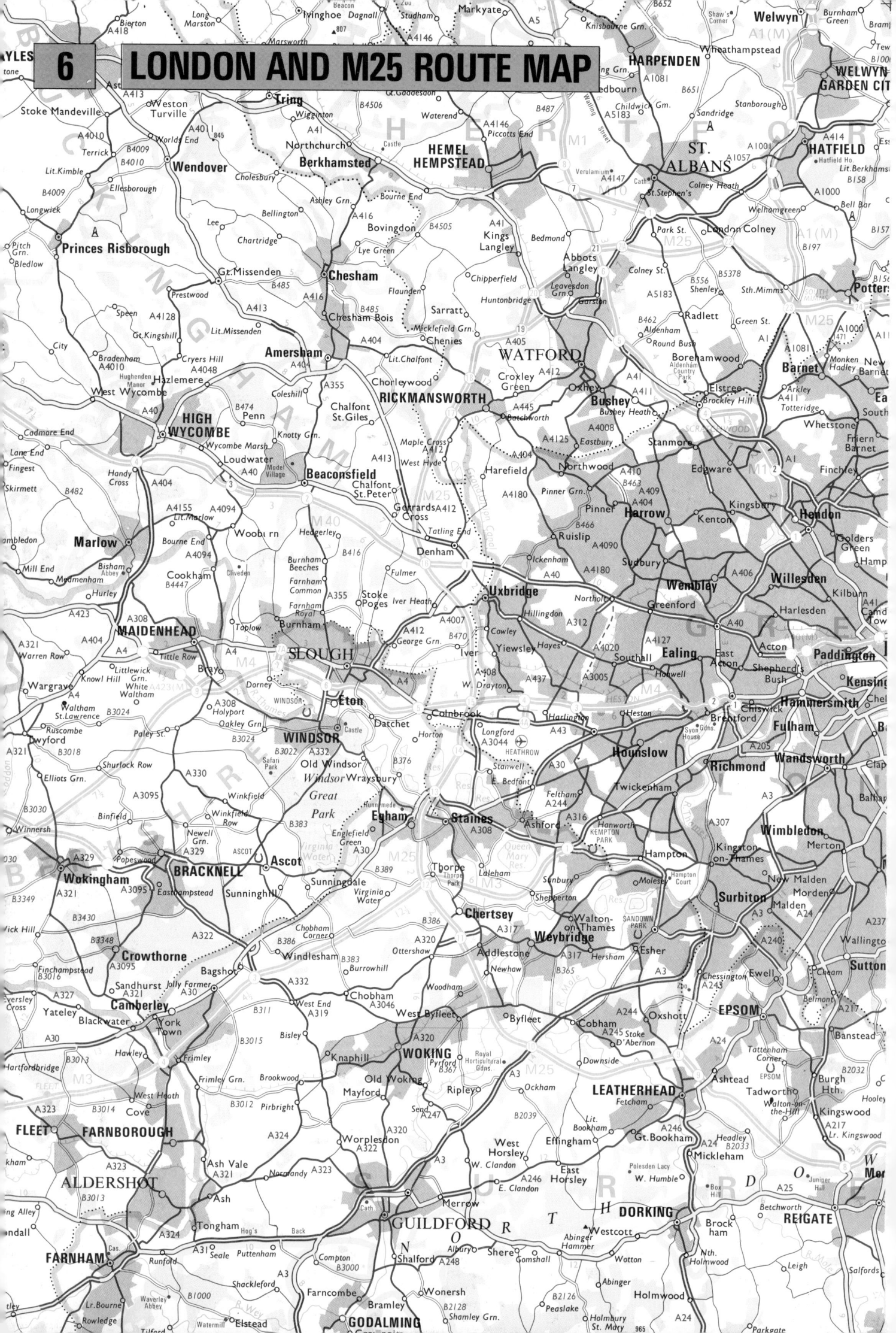

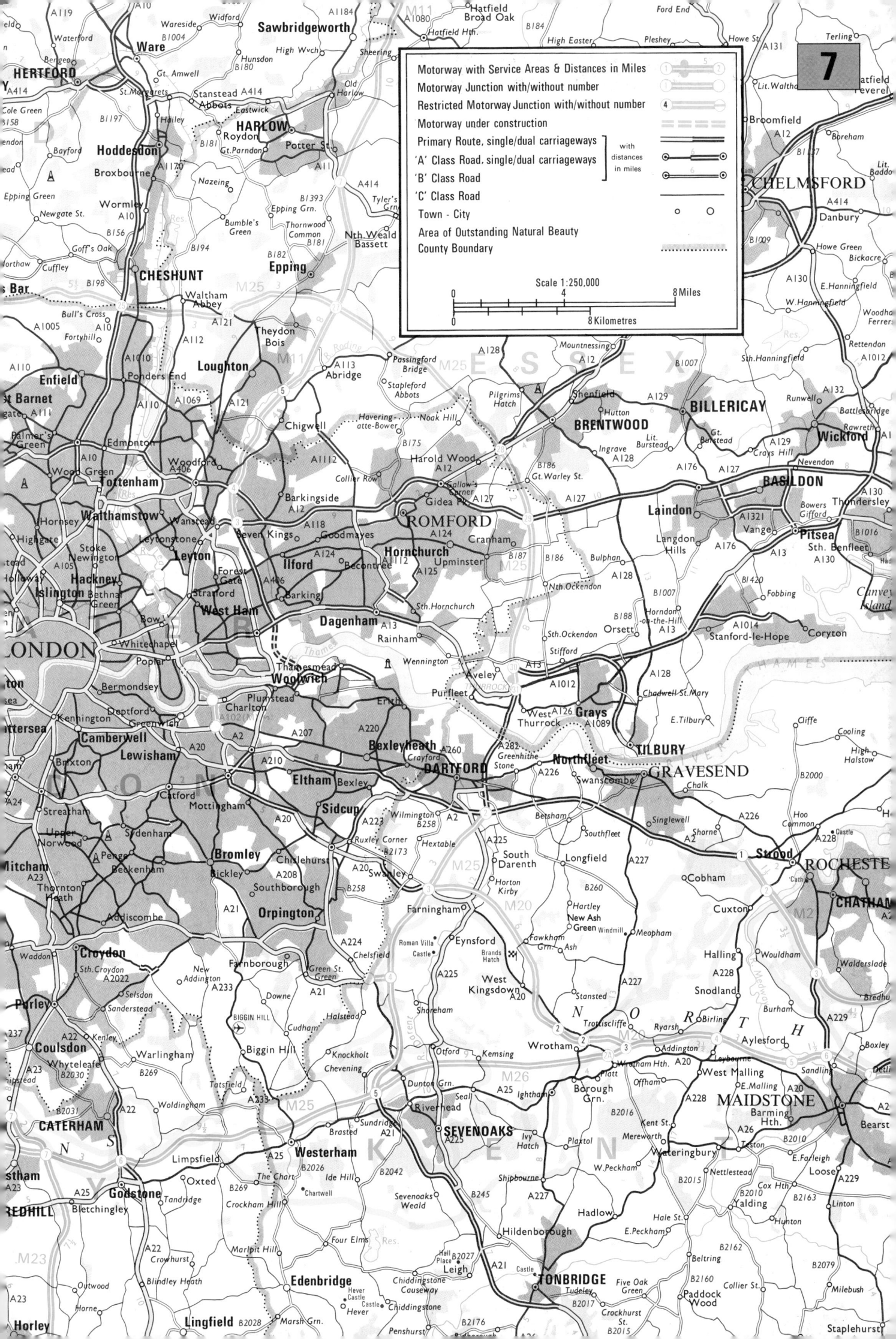

LEAVE MOTORWAY HERE (rows)
ENTER MOTORWAY HERE (columns)

Legend:
- 38 ... Mileage Clockwise
- 38 ... Mileage Anti-Clockwise

Junctions / locations:

1	DARTFORD
2	A2
3	M20
4	A21
5	M26
6	A22
7	M23
8	REIGATE
9	LEATHERHEAD
10	A3
11	CHERTSEY
12	M3
13	A30
14	HEATHROW 4
15	M4, HEATHROW 1–3
16	M40
17	RICKMANSWORTH
18	A404
19	WATFORD
20	A41
21	M1
22	ST. ALBANS
23	A1(M)
24	A111
25	A10
26	EPPING
27	M11
28	A12
29	A127
30	A13
31	A13

Shortest distance in miles between junctions (lower-triangular portion of the chart; the full chart is symmetric with colour indicating clockwise vs anti-clockwise):

Leave ↓ \ Enter →	1	2	3	4	5	6	7	8	9	10	11	12	13	14	15	16	17	18	19	20	21	22	23	24	25	26	27	28	29	30
2	4																													
3	4	3																												
4	8	7	4																											
5	12	11	8	4																										
6	22	21	18	14	10																									
7	25	24	21	17	13	3																								
8	28	27	24	20	16	6	3																							
9	35	34	31	27	23	13	10	7																						
10	41	40	37	33	29	19	16	13	6																					
11	46	45	42	38	34	24	21	18	11	5																				
12	48	47	44	40	36	26	23	20	13	7	2																			
13	51	50	47	43	39	29	26	23	16	10	5	3																		
14	53	52	49	45	41	31	28	25	18	12	7	5	2																	
15	55	54	51	47	43	33	30	27	20	14	9	7	4	2																
16	59	59	56	52	48	38	35	32	25	19	14	12	9	7	5															
17	53	54	57	58	54	48	45	42	35	29	24	21	18	16	11	6														
18	52	53	56	59	55	49	46	43	36	31	26	23	19	15	11	7	1													
19	49	50	53	57	58	52	49	46	39	32	27	24	21	14	12	9	4	3												
20	48	49	52	56	59	53	50	46	39	30	25	23	20	18	15	11	8	4	1											
21	45	46	49	53	57	55	50	44	38	33	28	26	24	21	18	16	13	8	4	3										
22	40	41	44	48	52	58	55	52	45	40	35	32	30	27	24	22	19	15	11	8	5									
23	37	38	41	45	49	59	59	56	49	43	39	36	34	32	30	27	24	20	16	13	9	6								
24	34	35	38	42	46	56	59	59	54	48	43	41	38	36	34	29	32	24	23	19	16	13	9							
25	28	29	32	36	40	50	53	56	59	54	49	47	44	42	40	35	38	32	28	24	20	15	12	9						
26	25	26	29	33	37	47	50	53	59	56	51	49	46	44	42	37	39	33	30	27	23	18	15	12	6					
27	21	22	25	29	33	43	46	49	56	57	52	50	47	45	43	38	40	34	31	28	24	19	16	13	7	4				
28	13	14	17	21	25	35	38	41	48	54	59	58	55	53	51	46	48	42	39	36	32	27	24	21	15	12	8			
29	10	11	14	18	22	32	35	38	45	51	56	58	59	57	55	50	52	46	43	40	36	31	28	25	19	16	12	8		
30	5	6	9	13	17	27	30	33	40	46	51	53	56	58	59	54	56	50	47	44	40	35	32	29	23	20	16	8	5	
31	4	5	8	12	16	26	29	32	39	45	50	52	55	57	59	55	57	51	48	45	41	36	33	30	24	21	17	9	6	1

Note: This chart shows the shortest distance in miles between junctions. The colours indicate whether the distance is clockwise or anti-clockwise. The total distance around the M25 is approx. 117 miles.

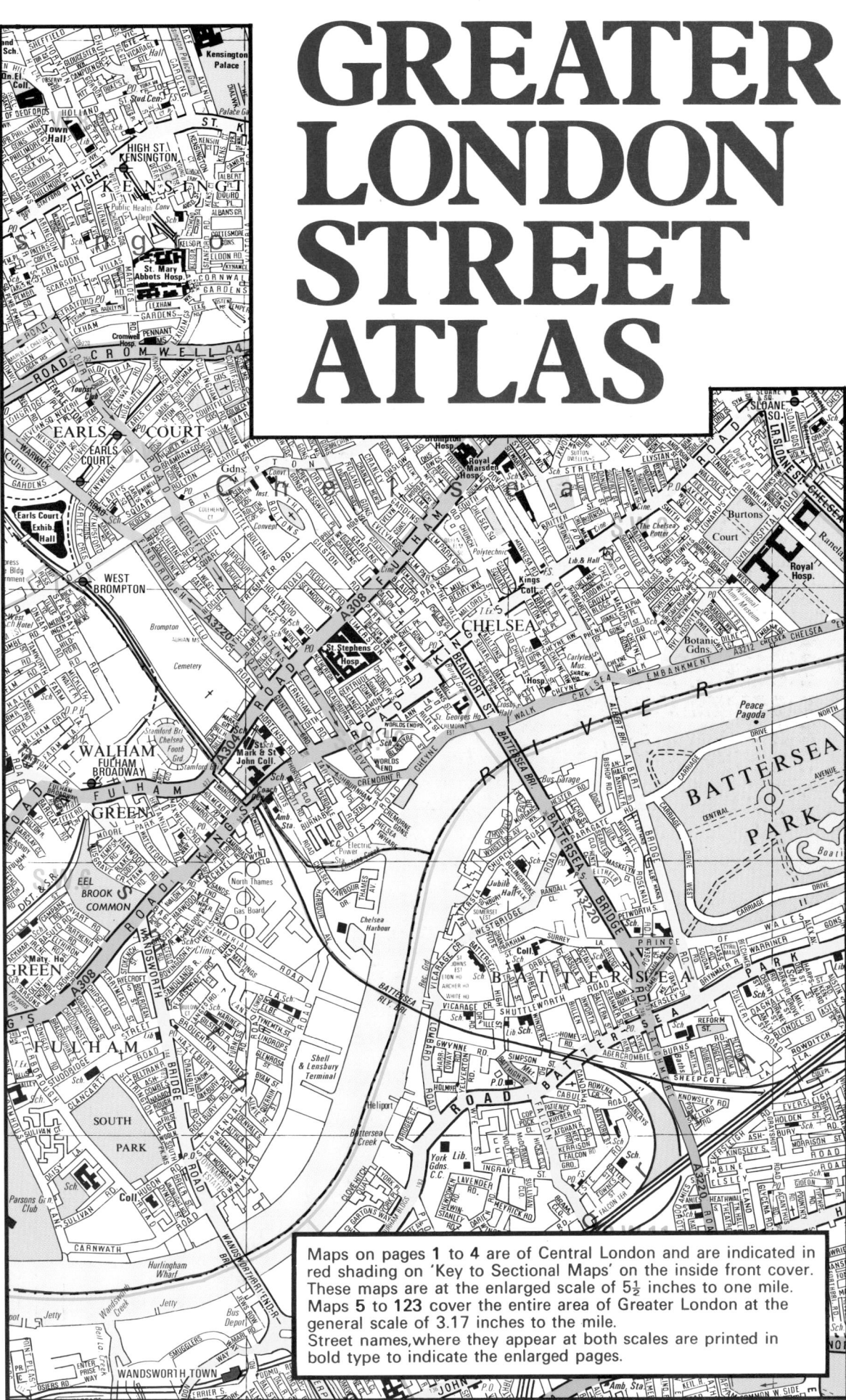

GREATER LONDON STREET ATLAS

Maps on pages **1** to **4** are of Central London and are indicated in red shading on 'Key to Sectional Maps' on the inside front cover. These maps are at the enlarged scale of 5½ inches to one mile.

Maps **5** to **123** cover the entire area of Greater London at the general scale of 3.17 inches to the mile.

Street names, where they appear at both scales are printed in bold type to indicate the enlarged pages.

LEGEND, INDEXING SYSTEM

Index to street names

The street name and postal district or locality of an entry is followed by a grid reference and number of the map on which the name will be found e.g. Abbey Rd. SW19 will be found in square **BT50** on map **76** and Norfolk Crescent, Sidcup in square **CN47** on map **78** (you will see from the map the latter location is in postcode boundary DA15)

The index contains some names for which there is insufficient space on the map. The adjoining thoroughfare to such roads is shown in italics e.g. Affleck Street, N1 is off *Pentonville Road* the later being found in square **BX37** on map **56**.

A strict alphabetical order is followed in which Avenue, Close, Gardens etc. although abbreviated, are read as part of the preceeding name.
For example Andrews Rd comes before Andrew St. and Abbey Orchard St. before Abbey Rd.

Legend

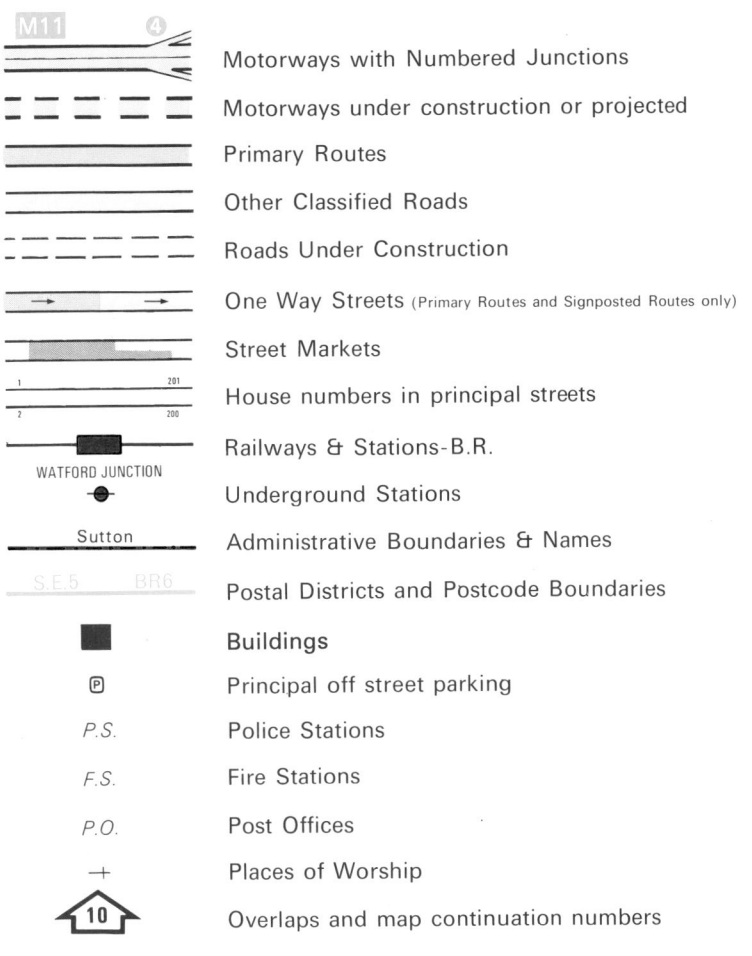

Motorways with Numbered Junctions

Motorways under construction or projected

Primary Routes

Other Classified Roads

Roads Under Construction

One Way Streets (Primary Routes and Signposted Routes only)

Street Markets

House numbers in principal streets

Railways & Stations-B.R.

Underground Stations

Administrative Boundaries & Names

Postal Districts and Postcode Boundaries

Buildings

Ⓟ Principal off street parking

P.S. Police Stations

F.S. Fire Stations

P.O. Post Offices

Places of Worship

Overlaps and map continuation numbers

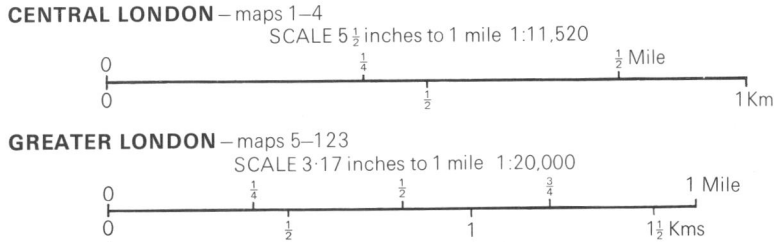

CENTRAL LONDON – maps 1–4
SCALE 5½ inches to 1 mile 1:11,520

GREATER LONDON – maps 5–123
SCALE 3·17 inches to 1 mile 1:20,000

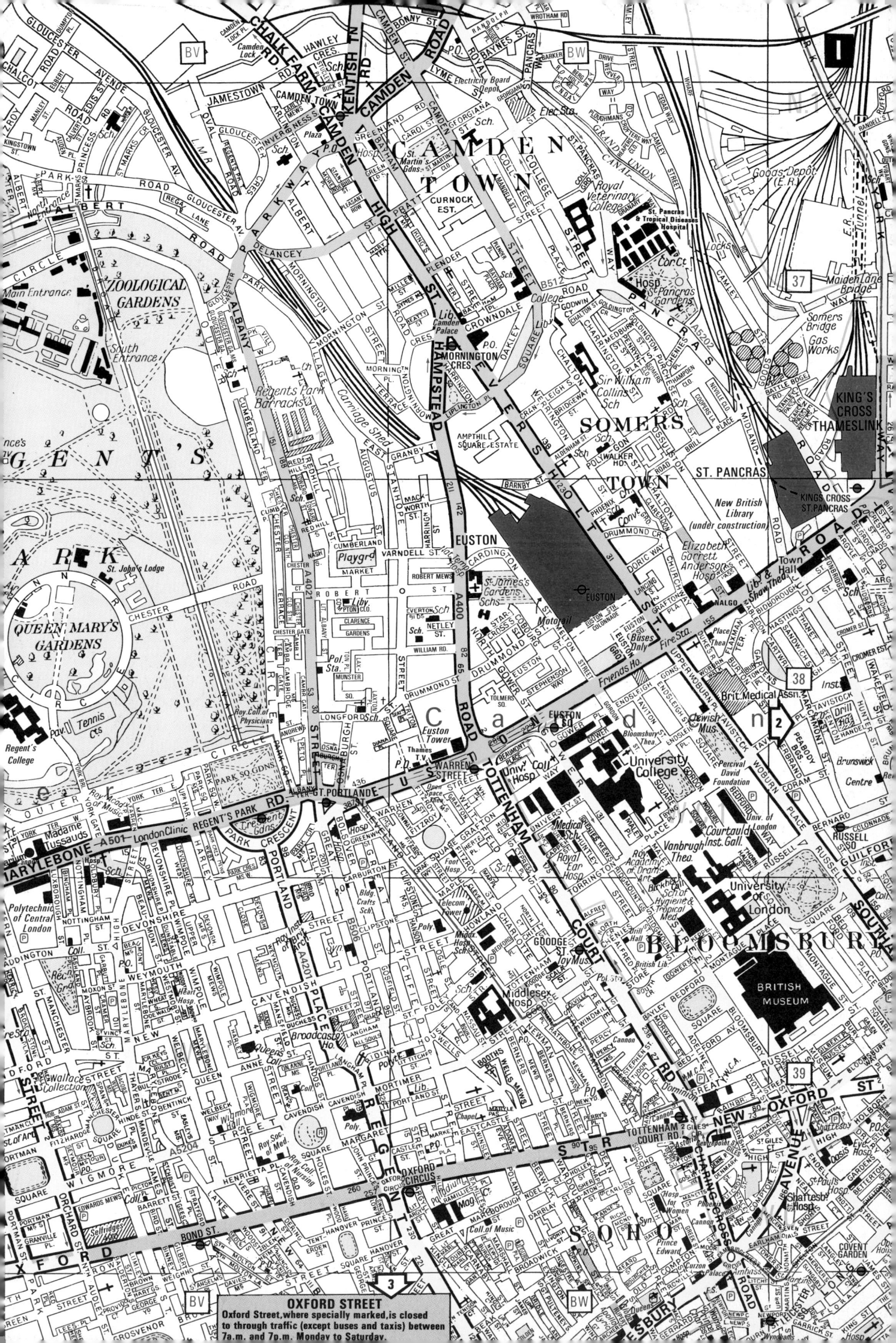

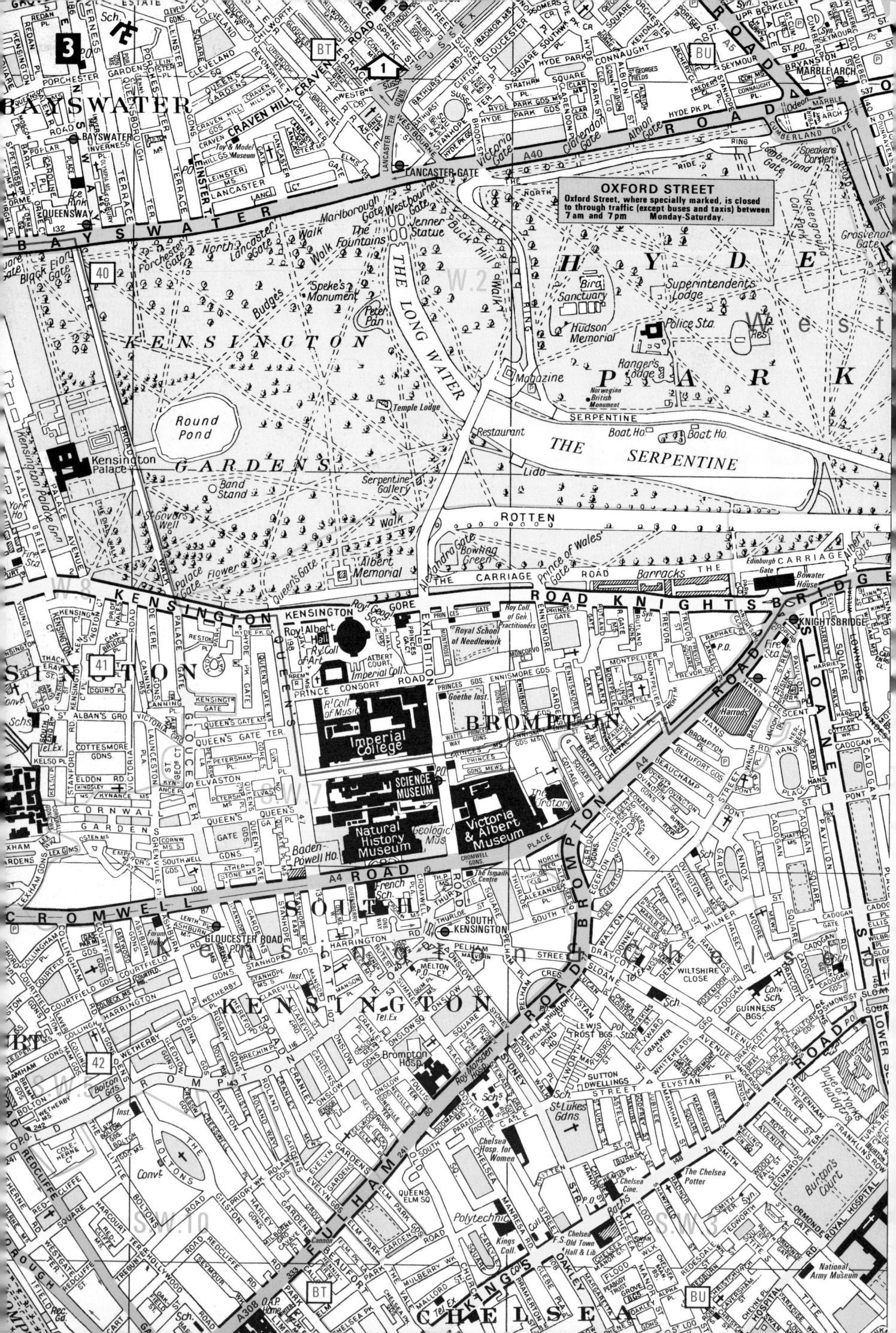

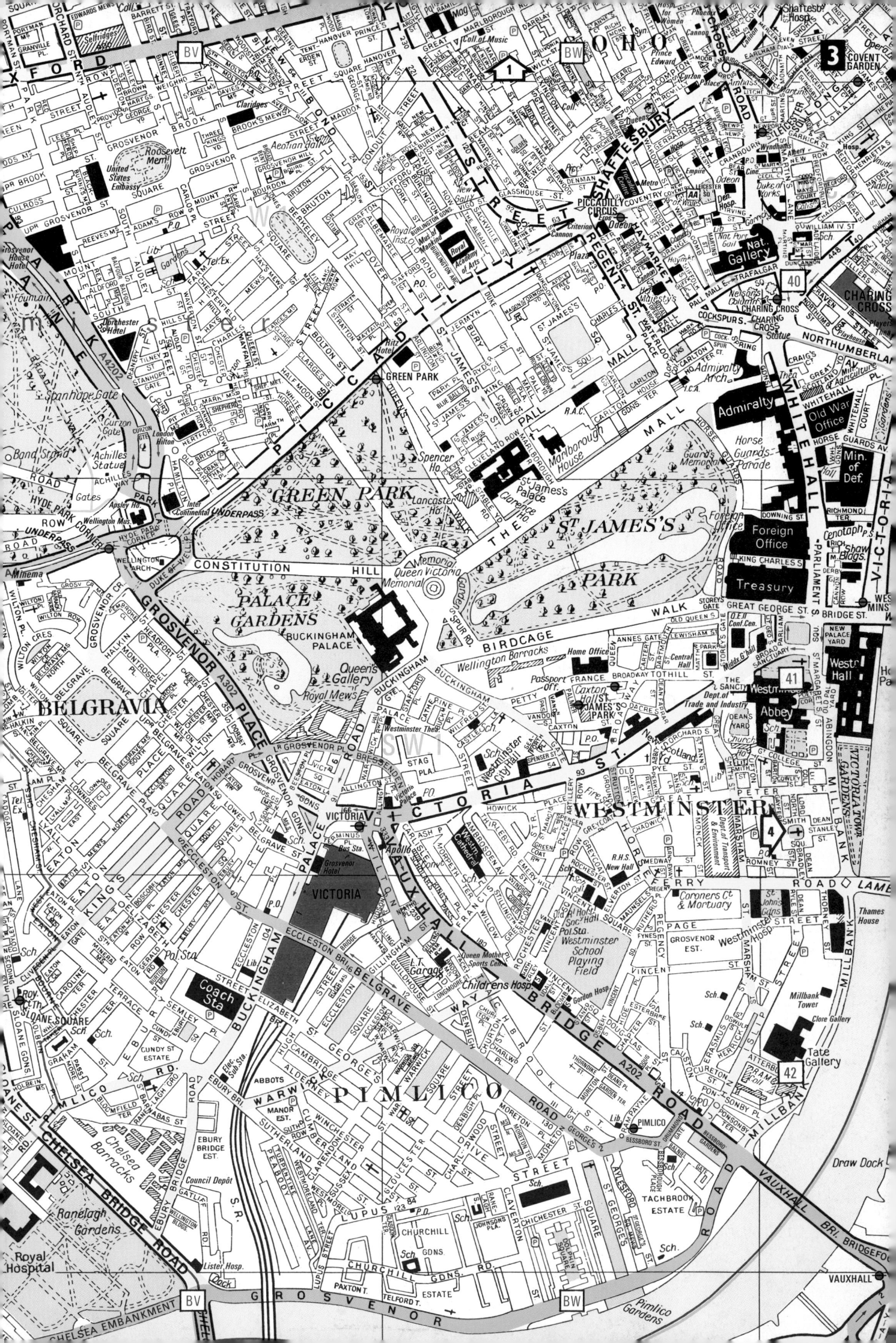

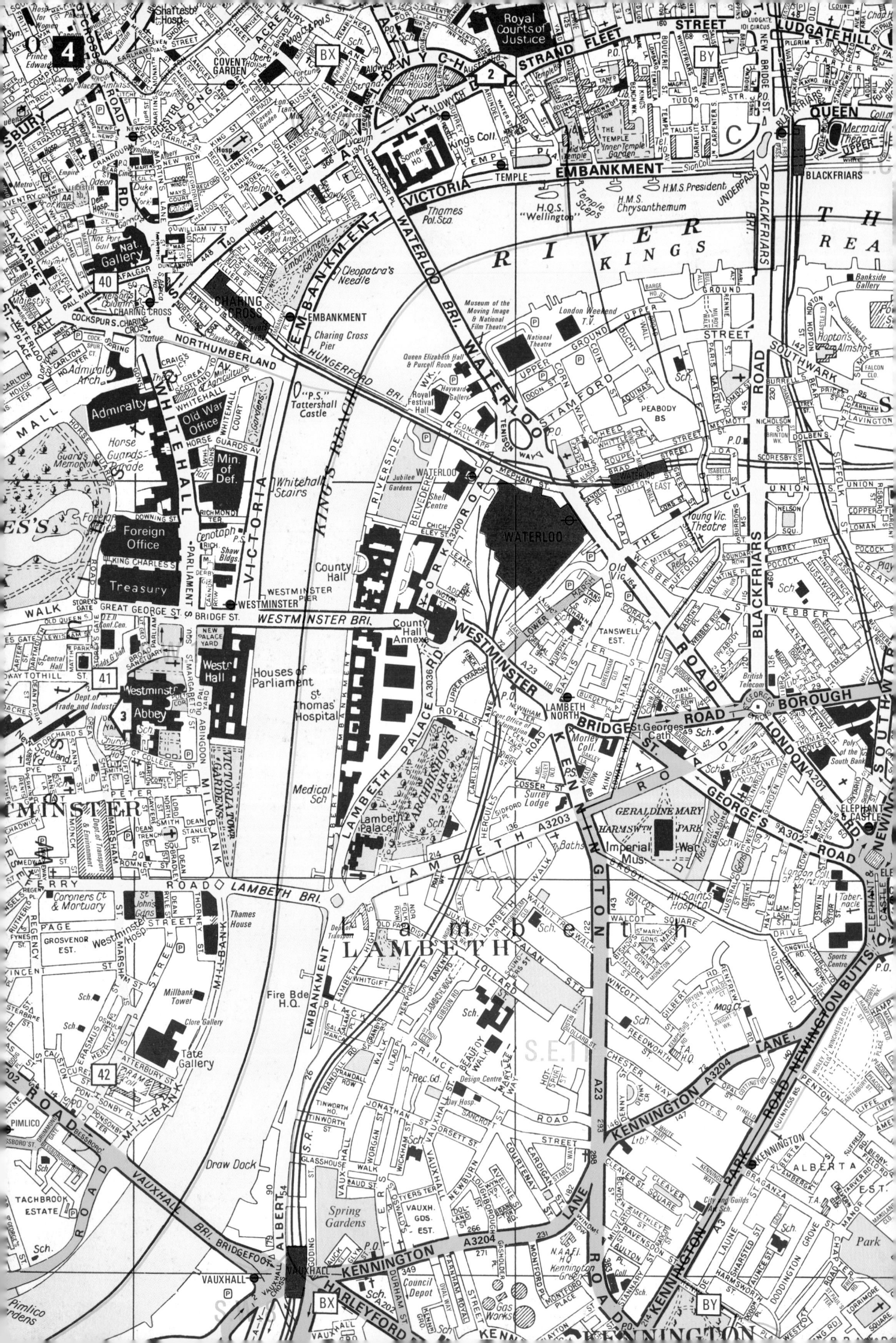

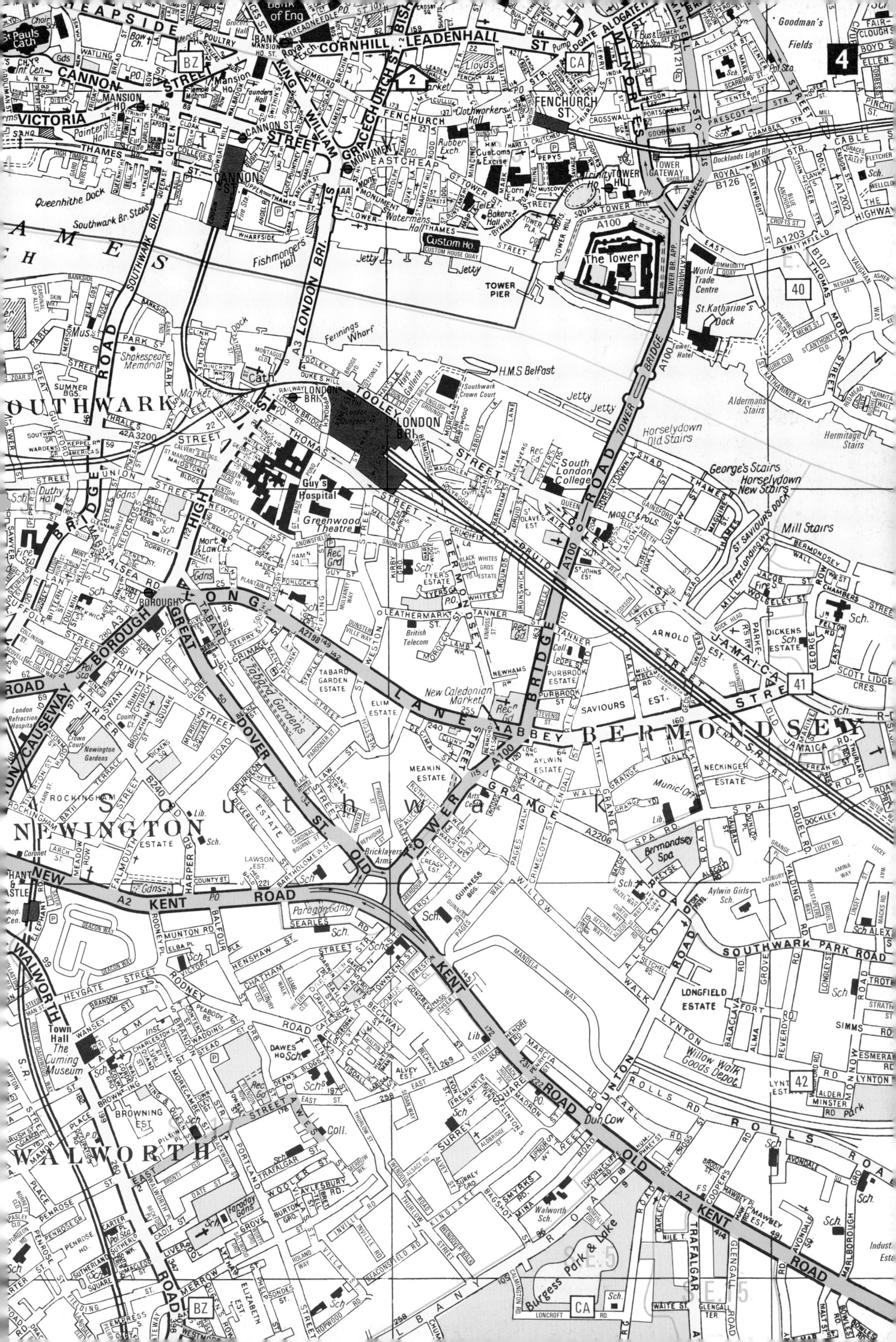

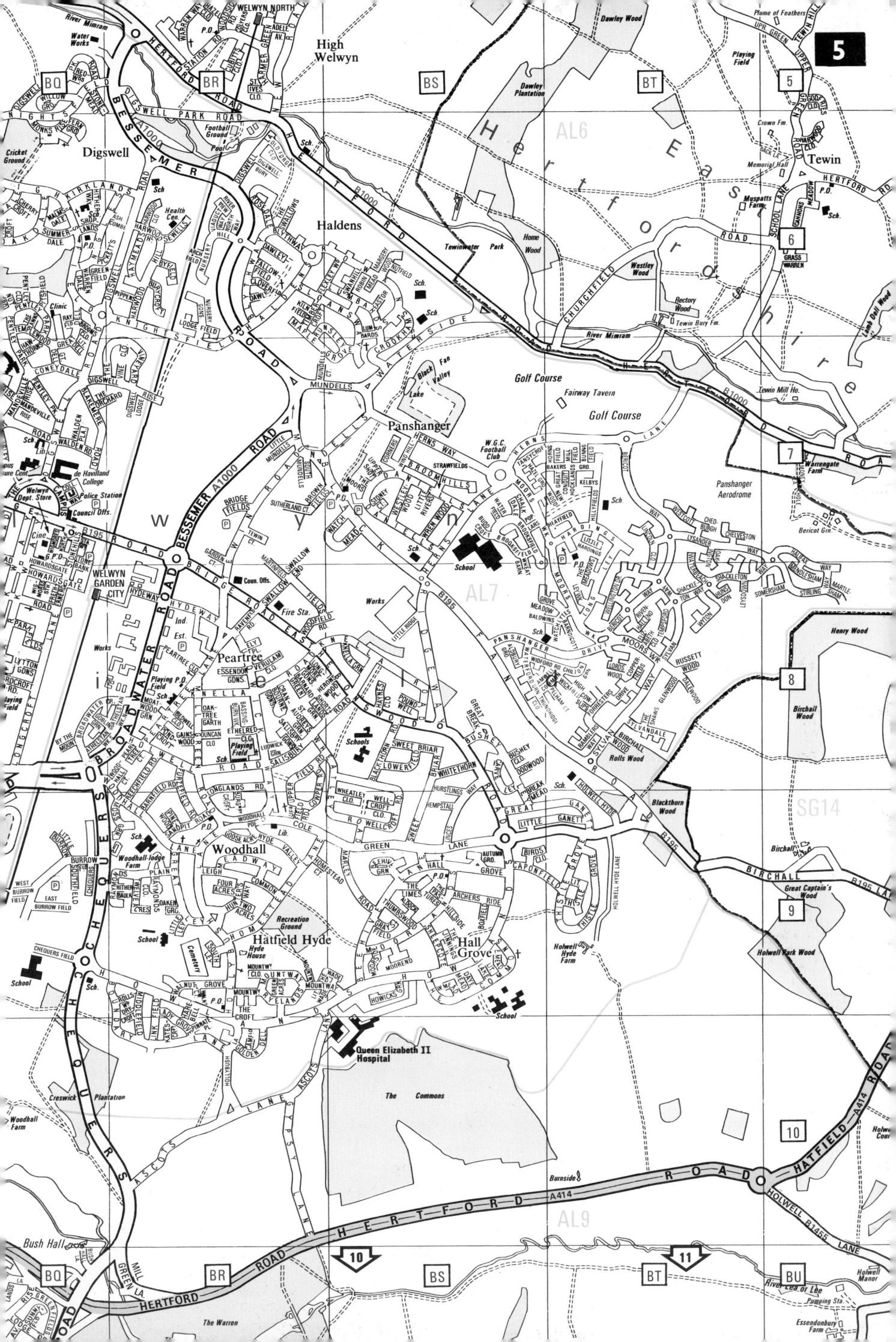

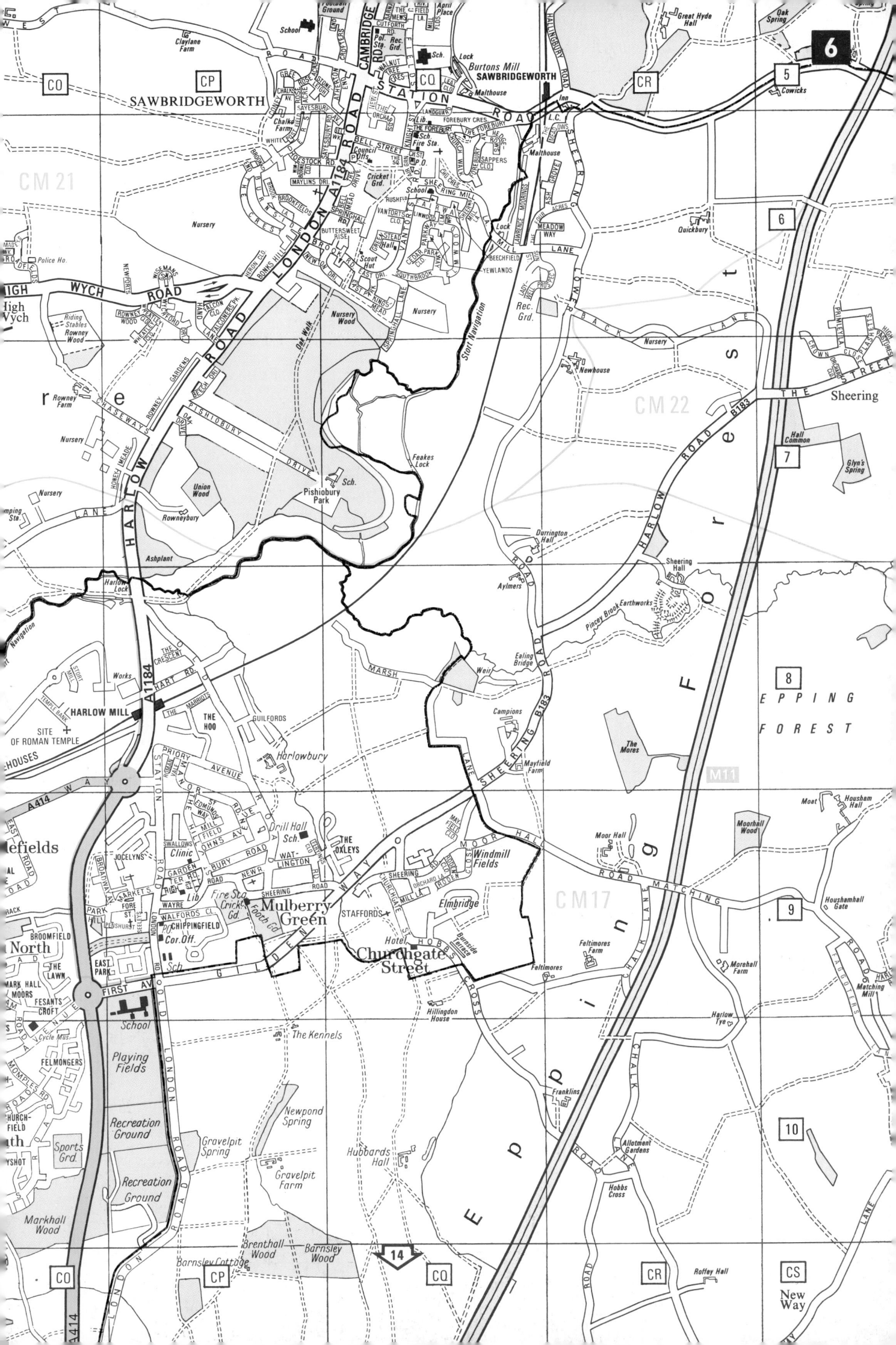

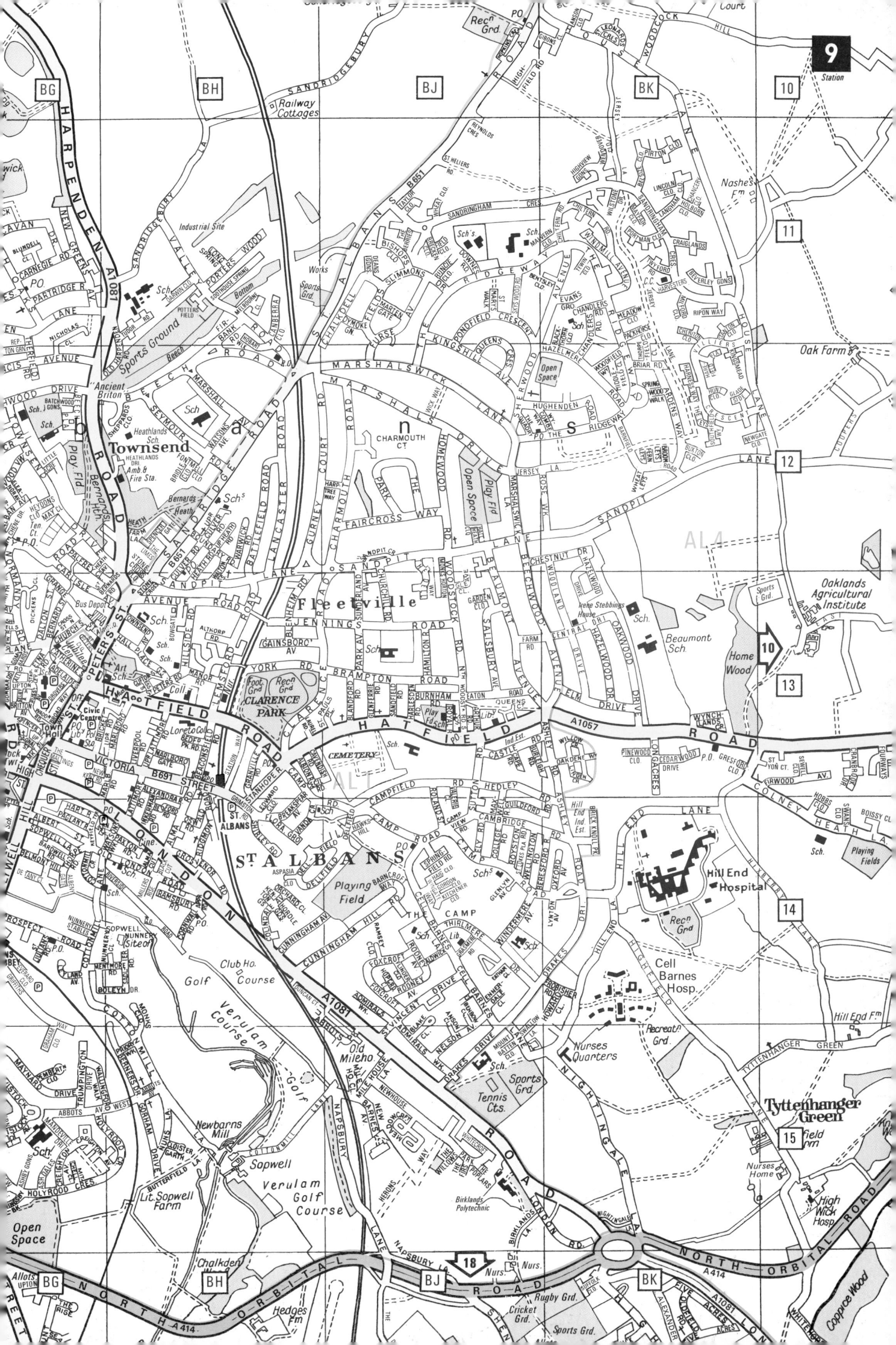

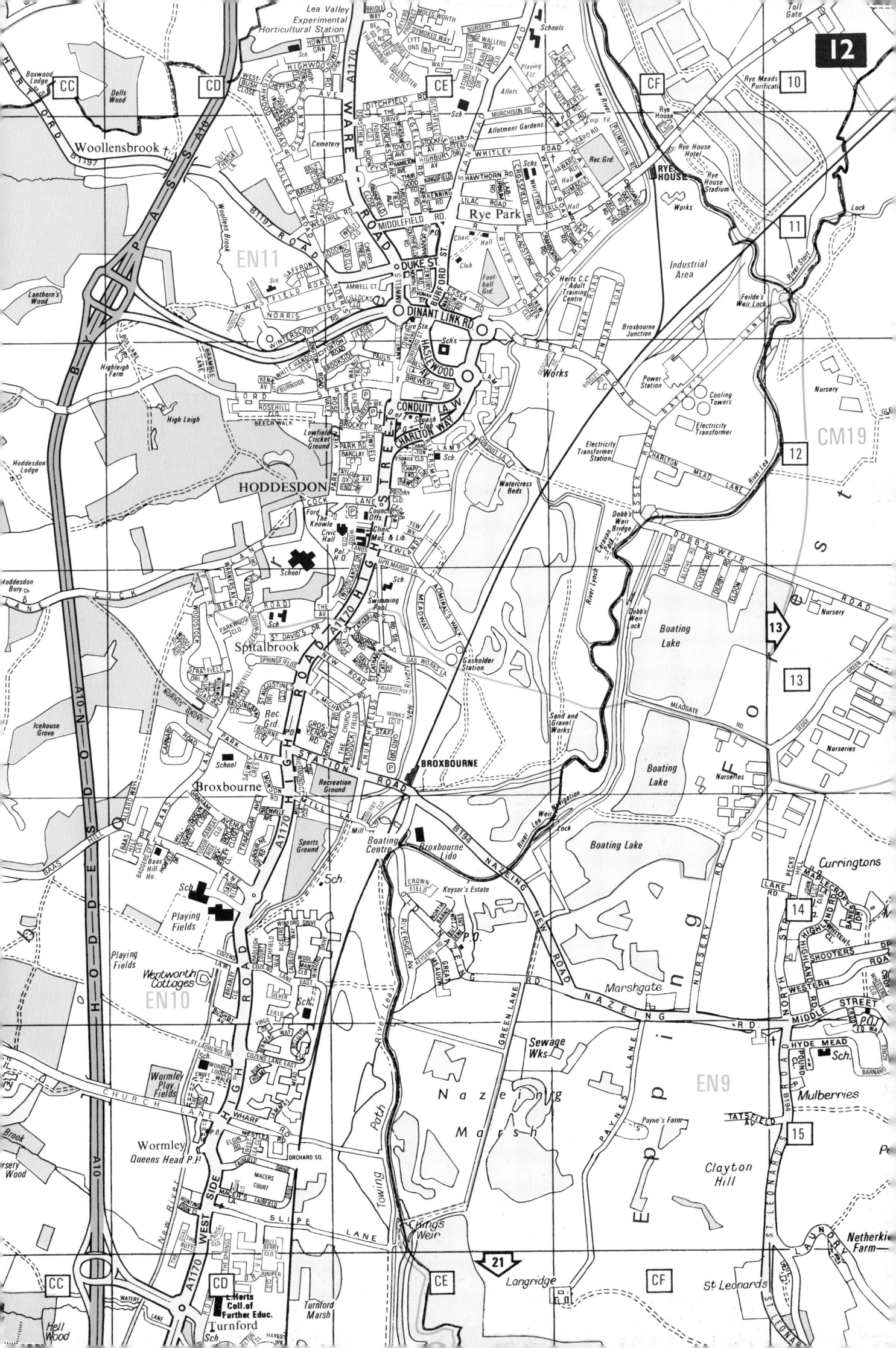

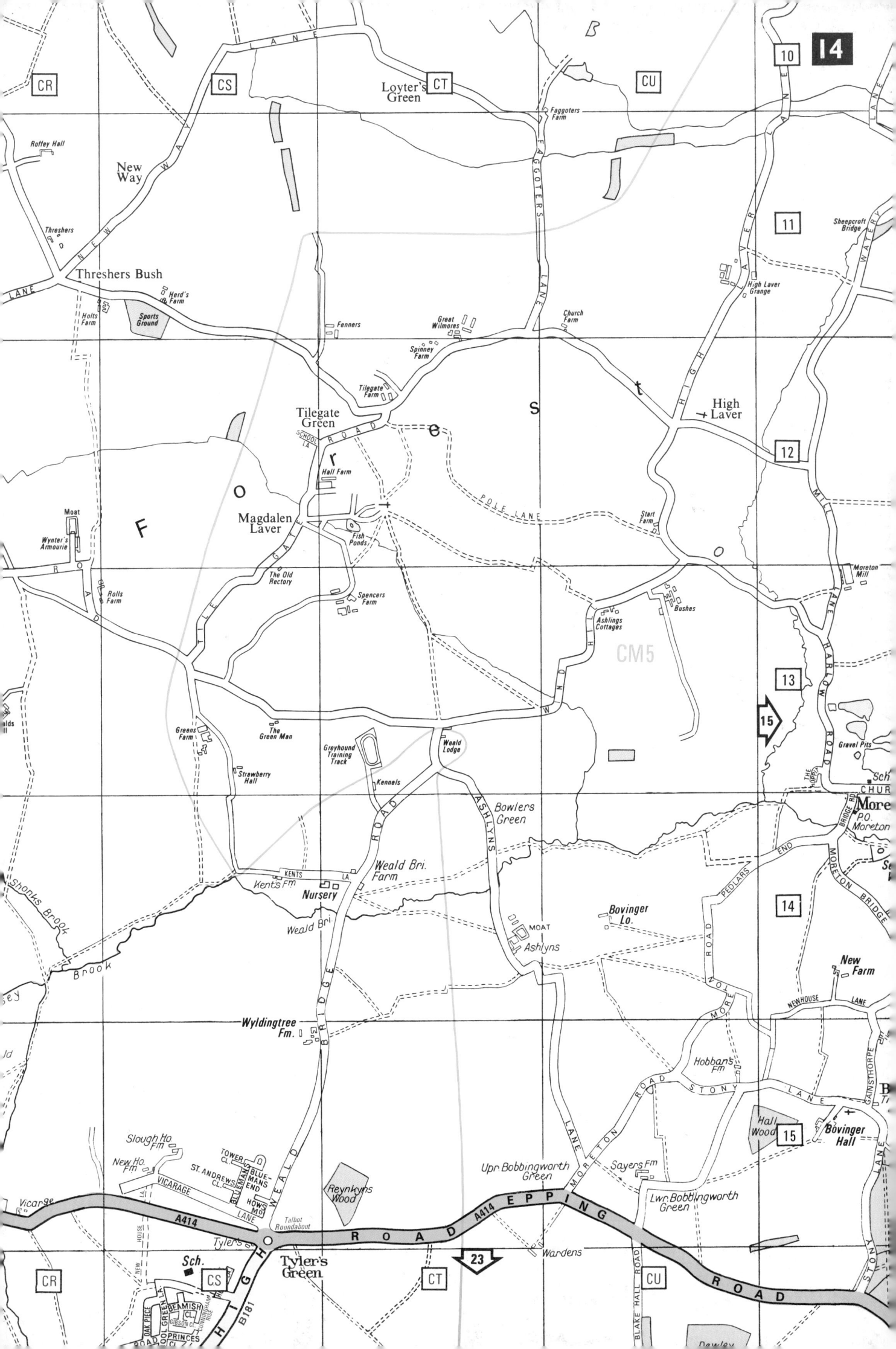

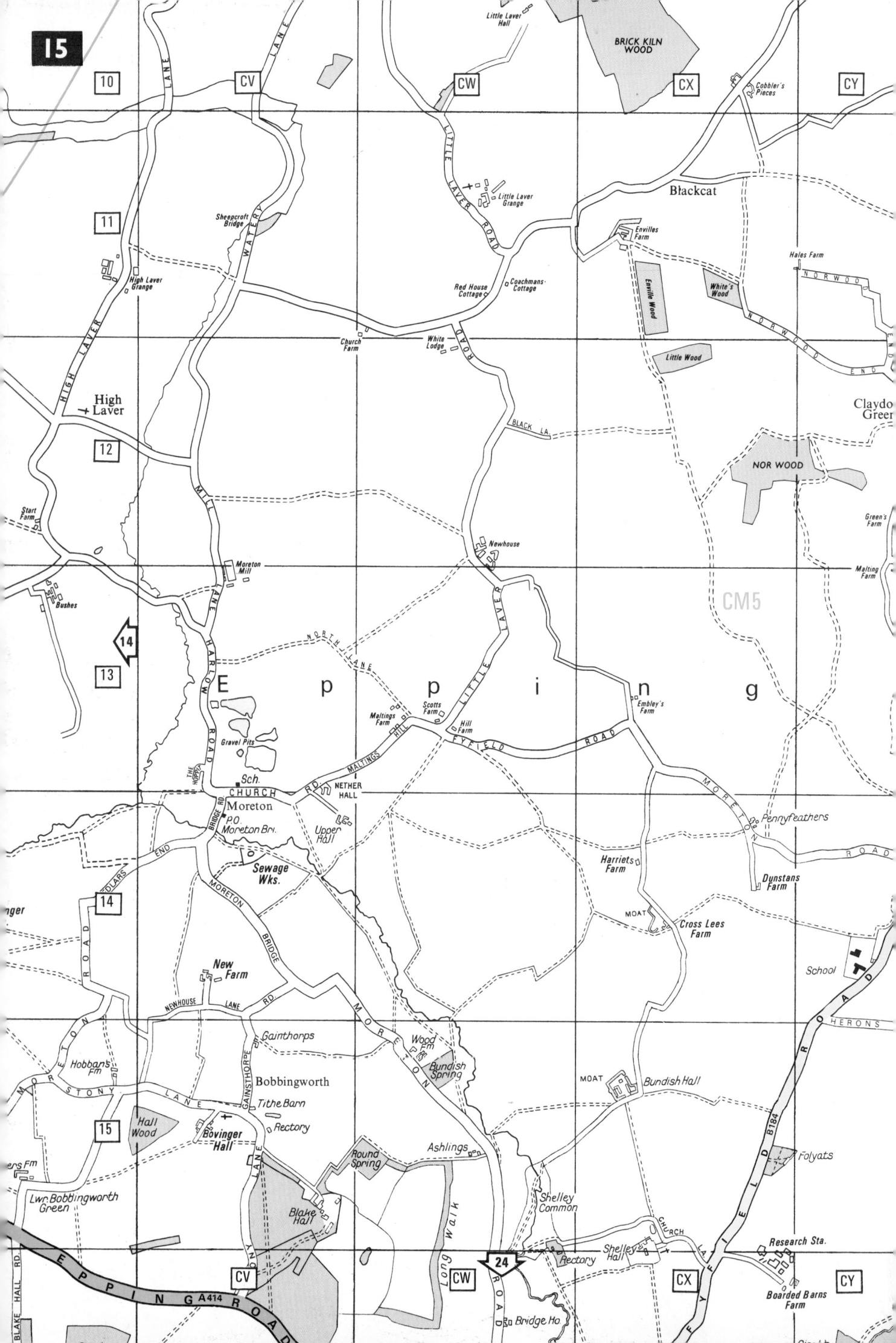

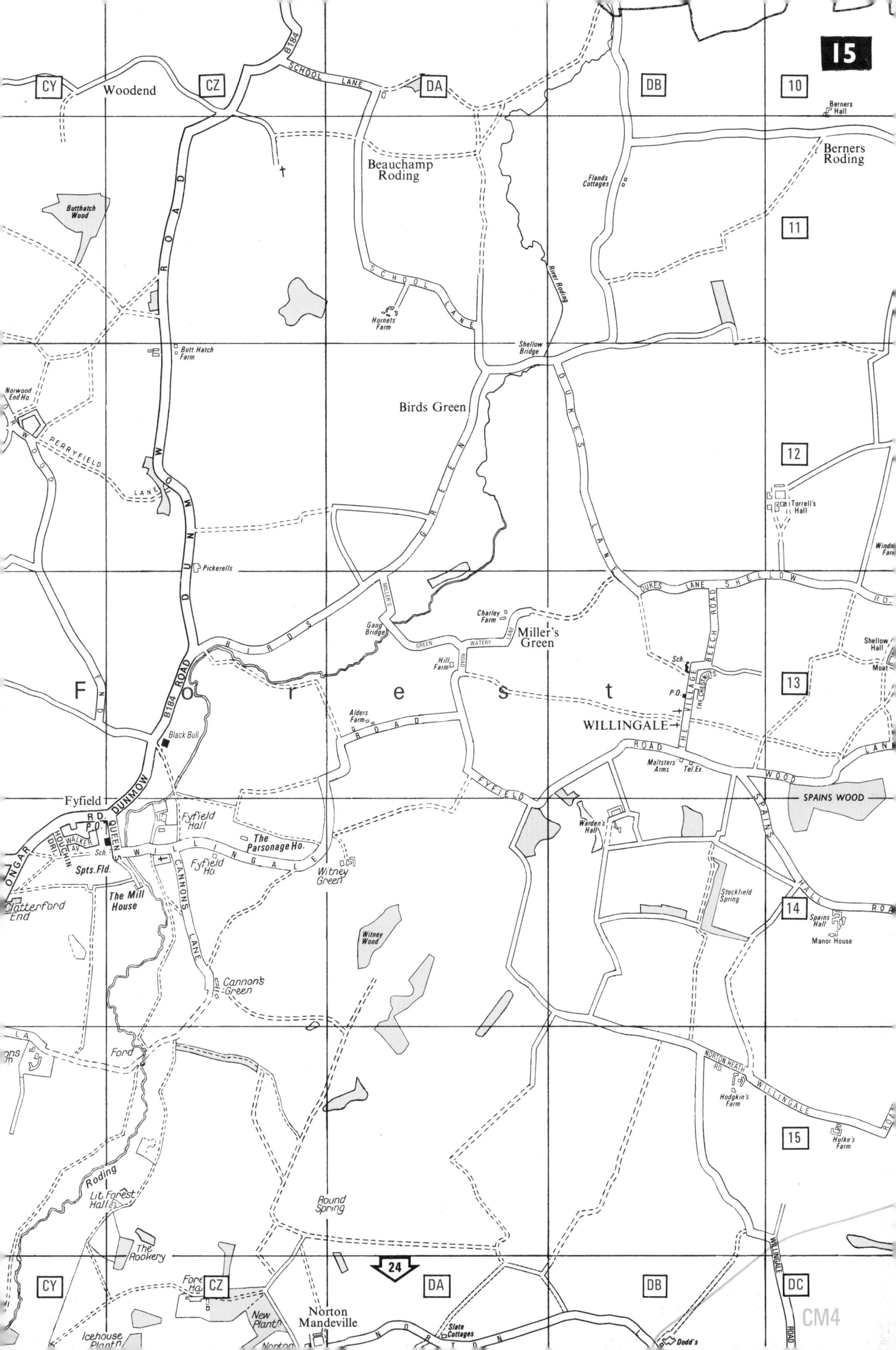

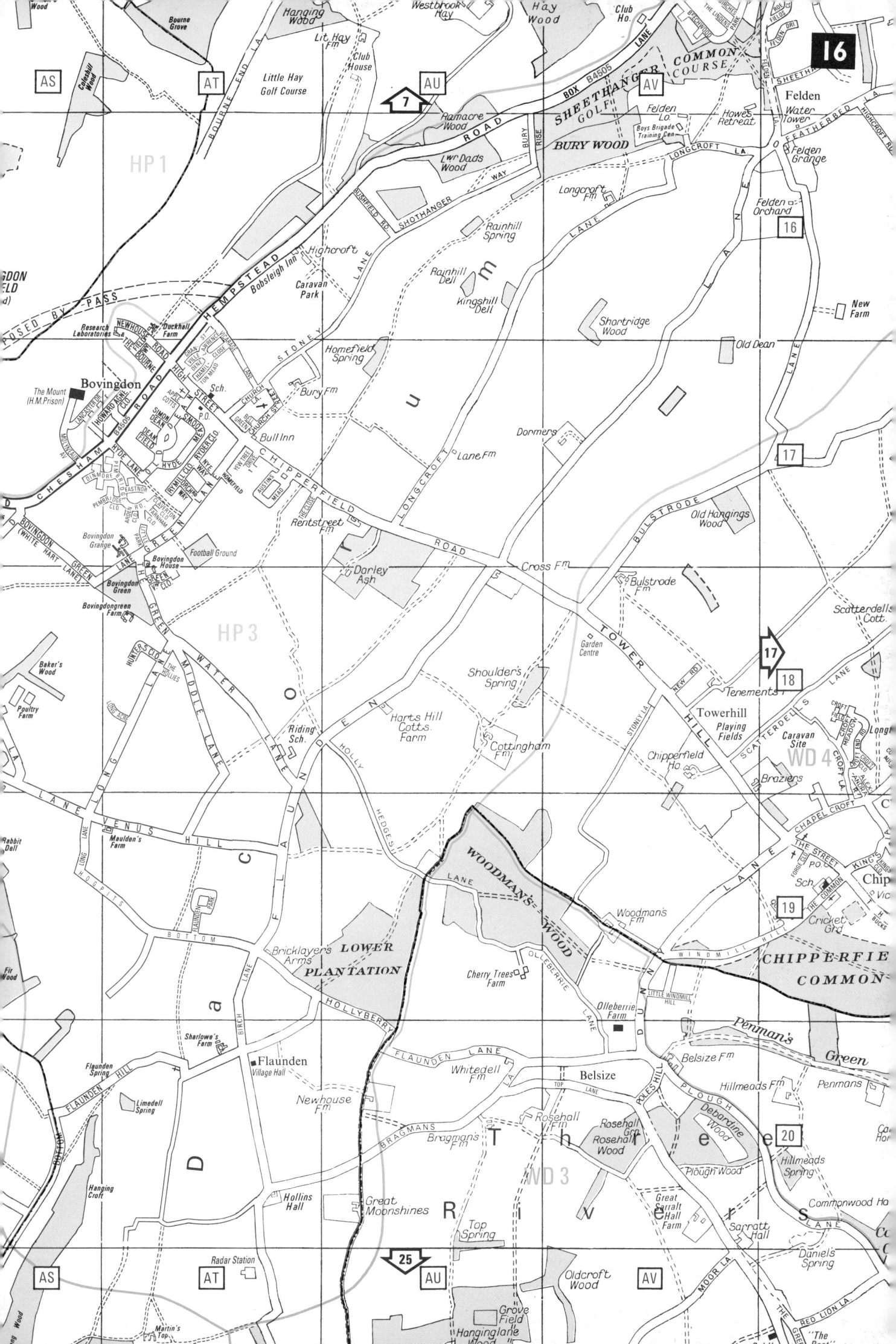

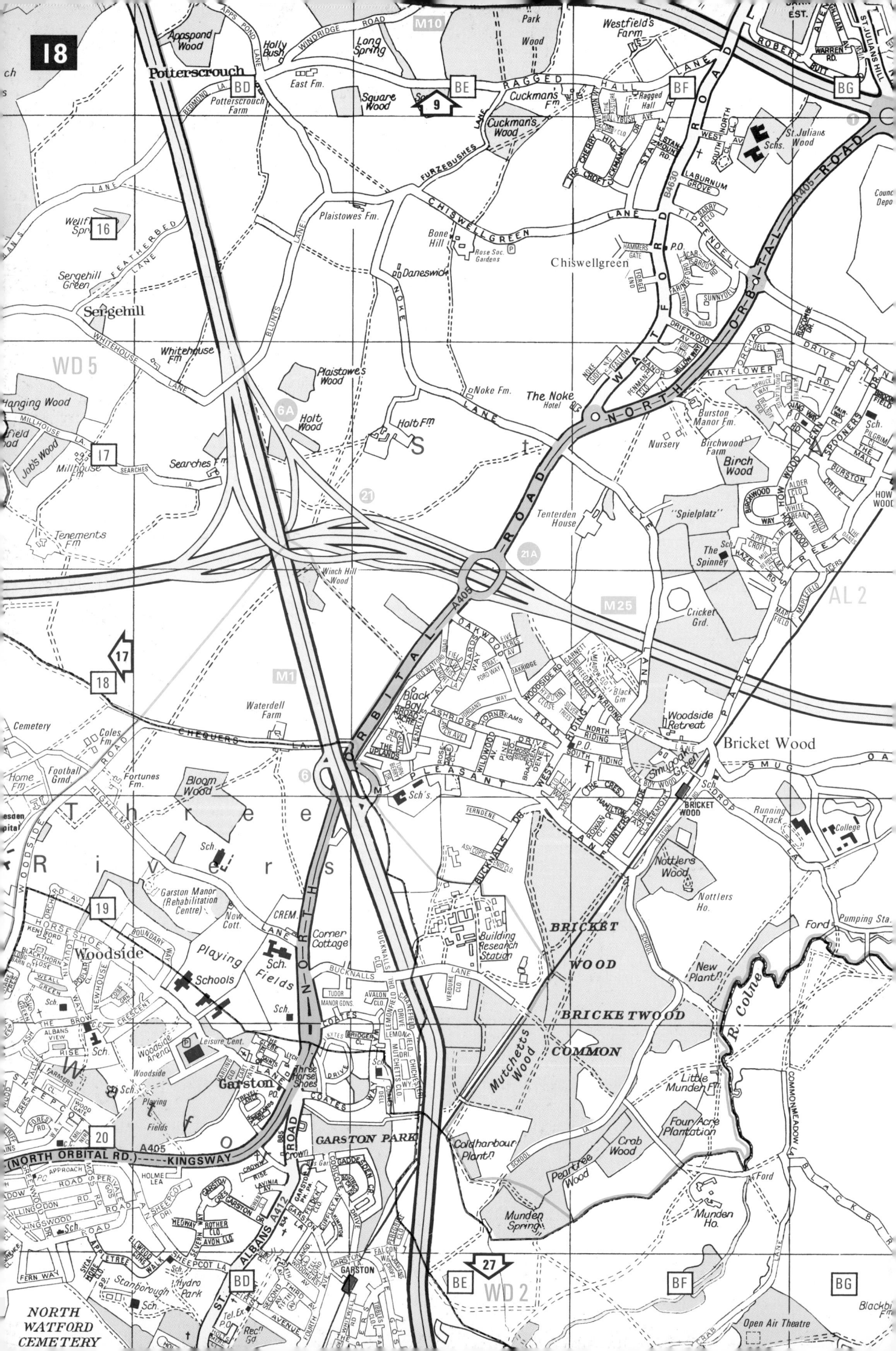

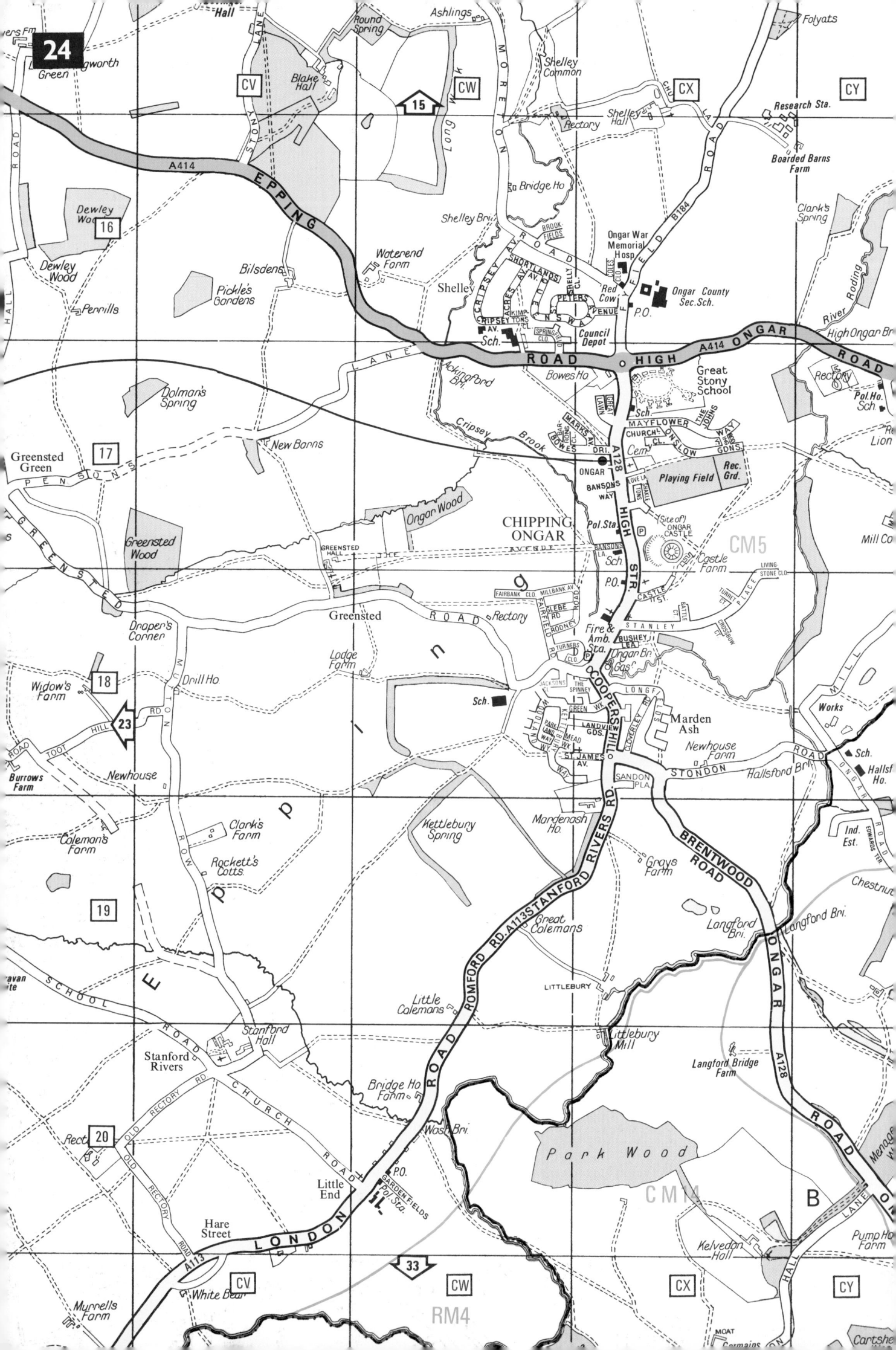

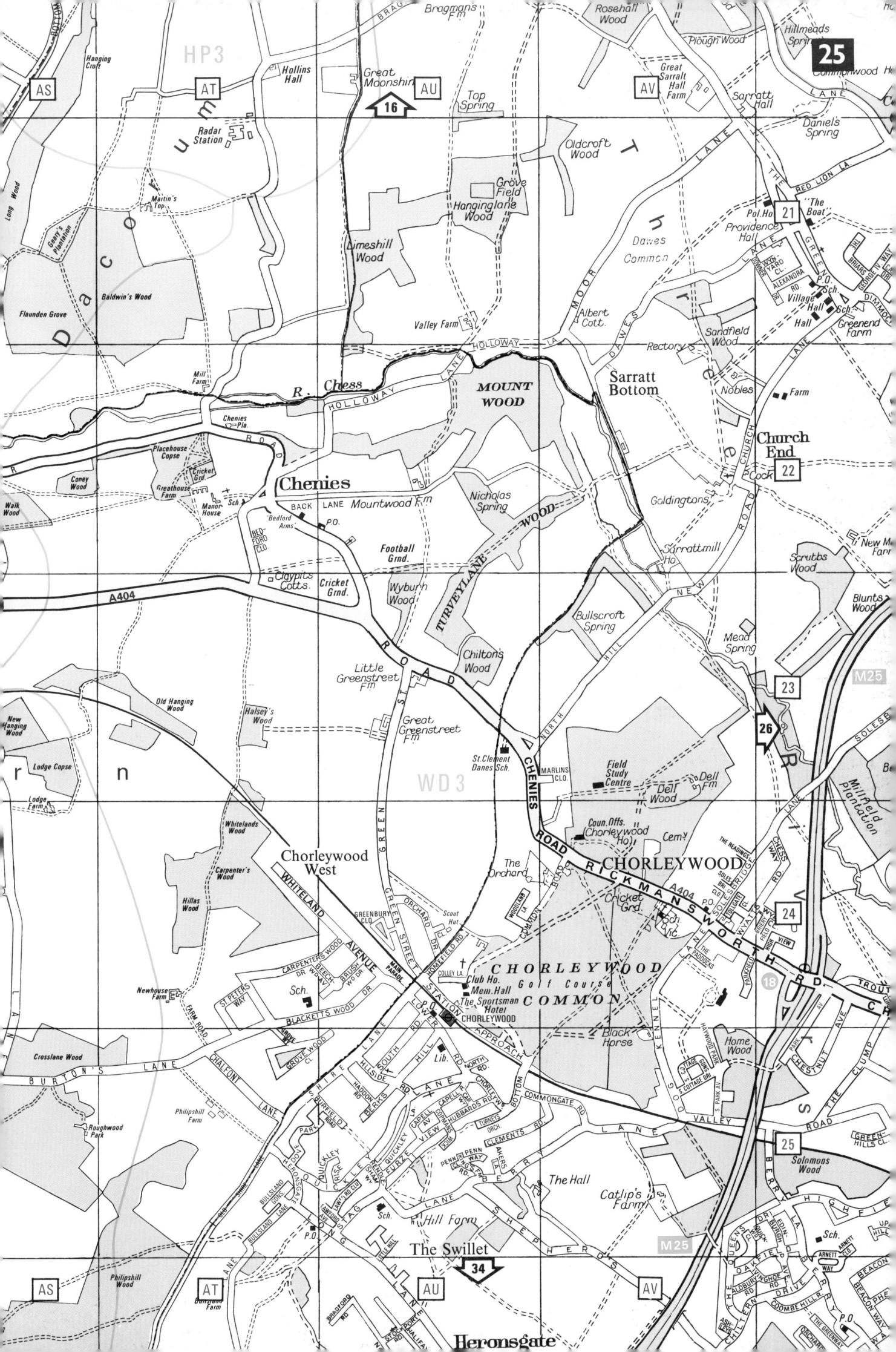

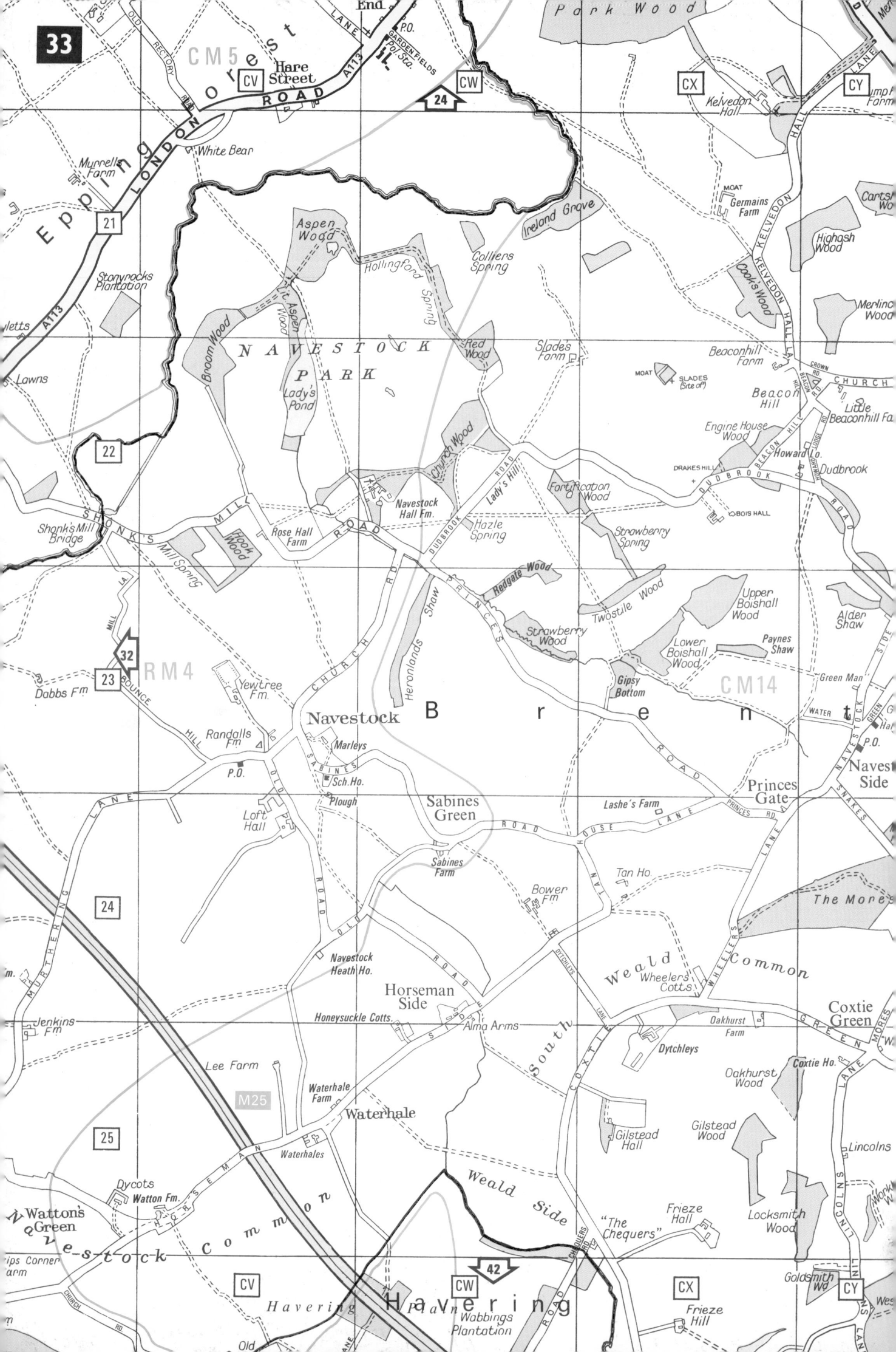

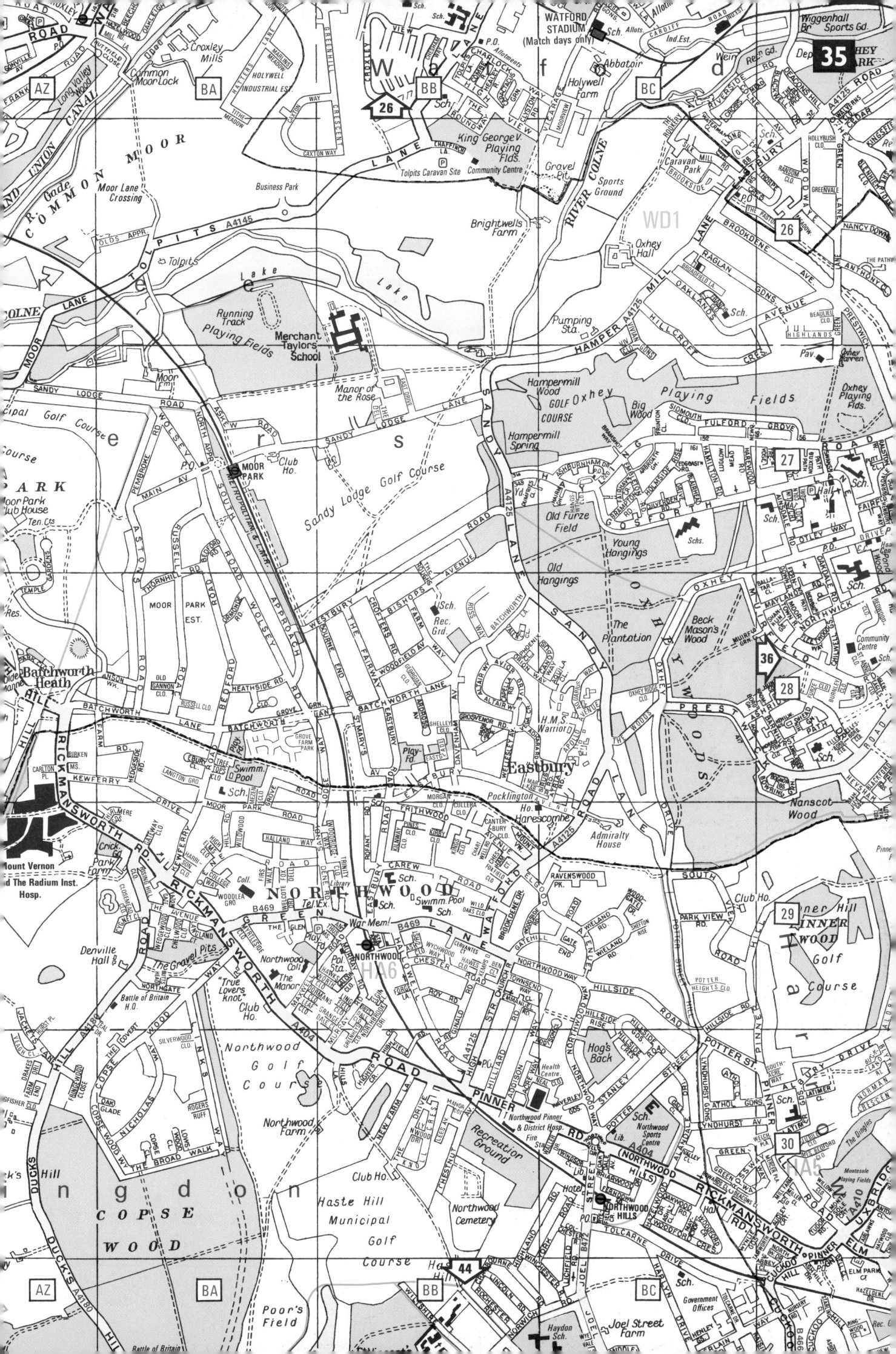

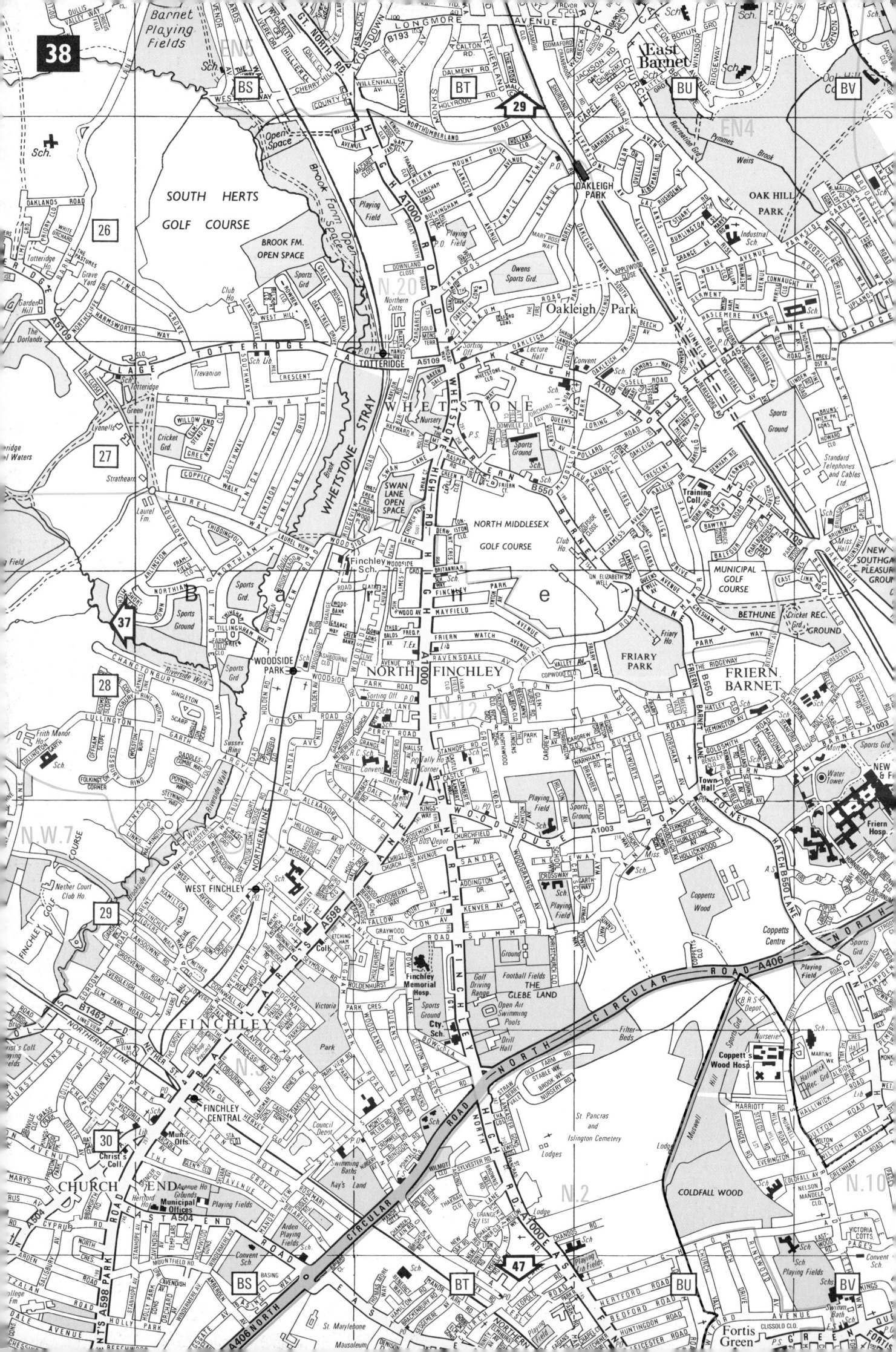

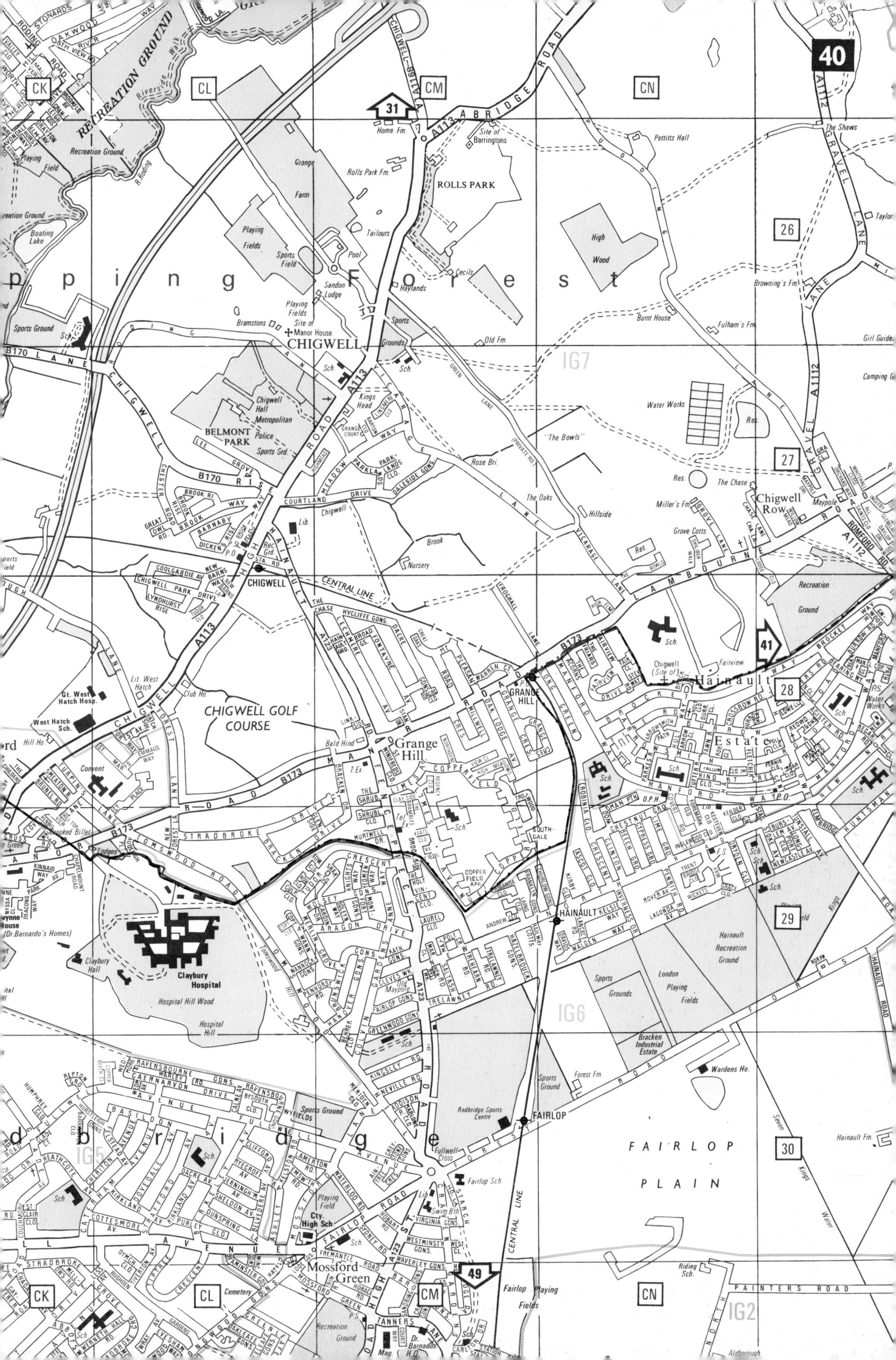

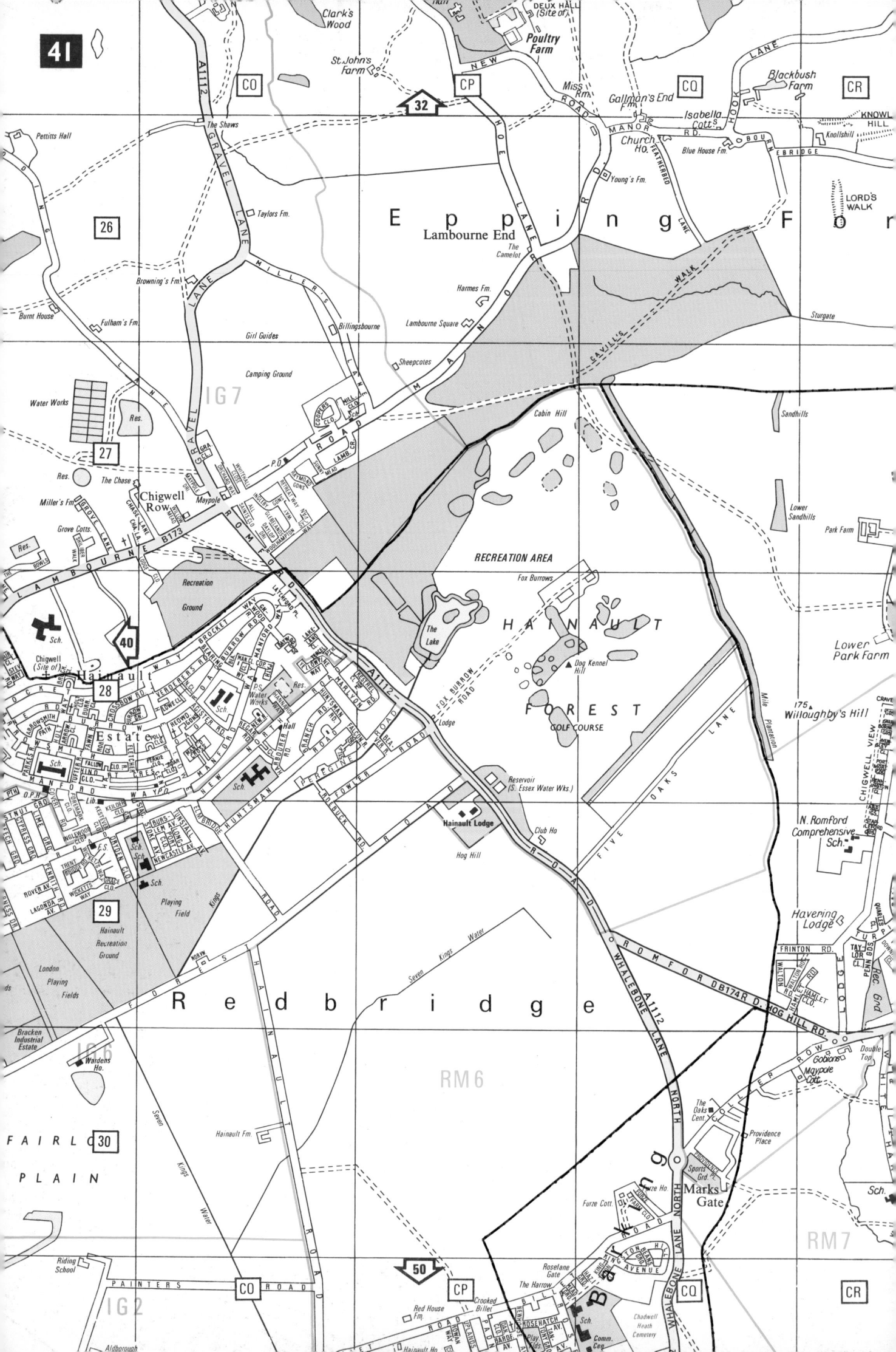

WEALD PARK
(Country Park)

Deer Park

The Forest

Fox Wd
Broom Wd
CY
Shepherd's Spinney
Larch Wood
Zoton's Wood
CZ

DA
33

DB

Bishops Hall Park
Sports Centre & Swimming Pool

BRENTWOOD A12 BY-PASS

CM15

Hall Wood

Pye Wood

26

A1023

Hallwood Cres.

Sawyers Hall Farm

Playing Field

Langtons

High Wood

High Wood Hospital

Calcott Hall

The Bogs

Play Flds

CAMP

Sandpits Lo.
Cricket Grd.

Halfway House Farm

Chalybeate Spring

Weald Hall
The Belvedere

hetts

South Weald
Almshouses
Sch. Tower Arms
P.O.

CM14

Vicarage Wood

Vicarage

FRONT PARK

Oaks

Lower Vicarage Wood

Sewage ks

Old Filter Beds

Sewage Works

Gibblings Shaw

Tylers Shaw

Tylehurst Hall

Jackson's Wood

St Faith's Hospital

Cemetery

Gov Bld

The Beeches

A1023 LONDON ROAD

Moat Ho. Hotel

Brook Street

162
Westbourne

BROOK A1023 ST.

M25

Mascalls

Boyles Court

Great Readings

Coombe Grn.

Coombe Lo.

Well Wood

Beredens

RM14

CZ
DA
51

Great Warley
P.O.

Stonyhills Farm

Thatchens Arms

Warley Place

Warley Lea Fm

The Chelmer Inst. of Higher Education
Amb. Sta.

Sports Grd.

Cricket Grd.

Brentwood Dis. Hosp.

Nuffield Nursing Home

Hunter Mem!

BRENTWOOD

Sports Ground

122

27

A128

Seven Arch Bri.

Seven Arches

THE BIRCHES

BRIDGE

Brentwood

ALEXA

Warley

28

Warley Hospital

Hart's Wood

Donkey Lane Plantation

Brentfield Club

Coun. Depot

Marillac Hospital

Barrack Wood

29

Reg. Mus.

Fords

Golf Range & Ski Slopes

Holden's Wood

Ellen's Wood

Devil's Ho. Plantation

Little Warley Common

Scrub Hill

Tennis Courts

Rustlings

Thornton Corner

Pump Farm

Little Warley Common

Warley Lodge

Rushy Piece

HOME PARK

Home Farm

CM13

30

GOLF COURSE

GREAT PARK

Fairstead

Warley Elms

Lodge

Reservoir (Dis)

Tooks Farm

Clapgate

Bluehouse Farm

Norman's

Little Wa

DB
DC

1	CANTERBURY WAY	7	EVELYN WALK
2	BIRCHWOOD CLO.	8	BUNYONS CLO.
3	ASHBEAM CLO.	9	GIBRALTAR CLO.
4	HAVENWOOD CLO.	10	GREENFIELDS CLO.
5	COVERLEY CLO.	11	FLEMINGS
6	WILMOT GREEN	12	MEADSWAY

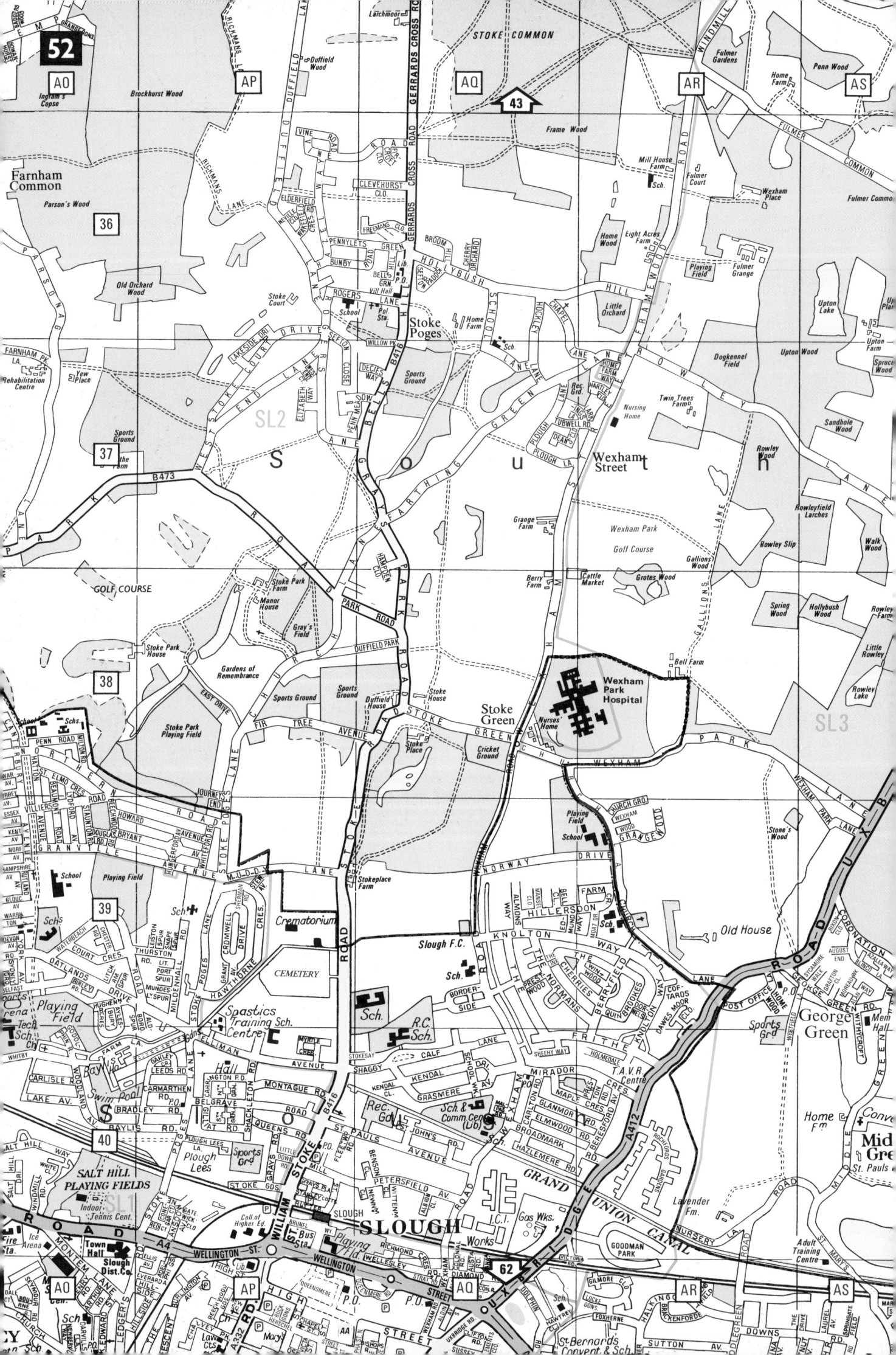

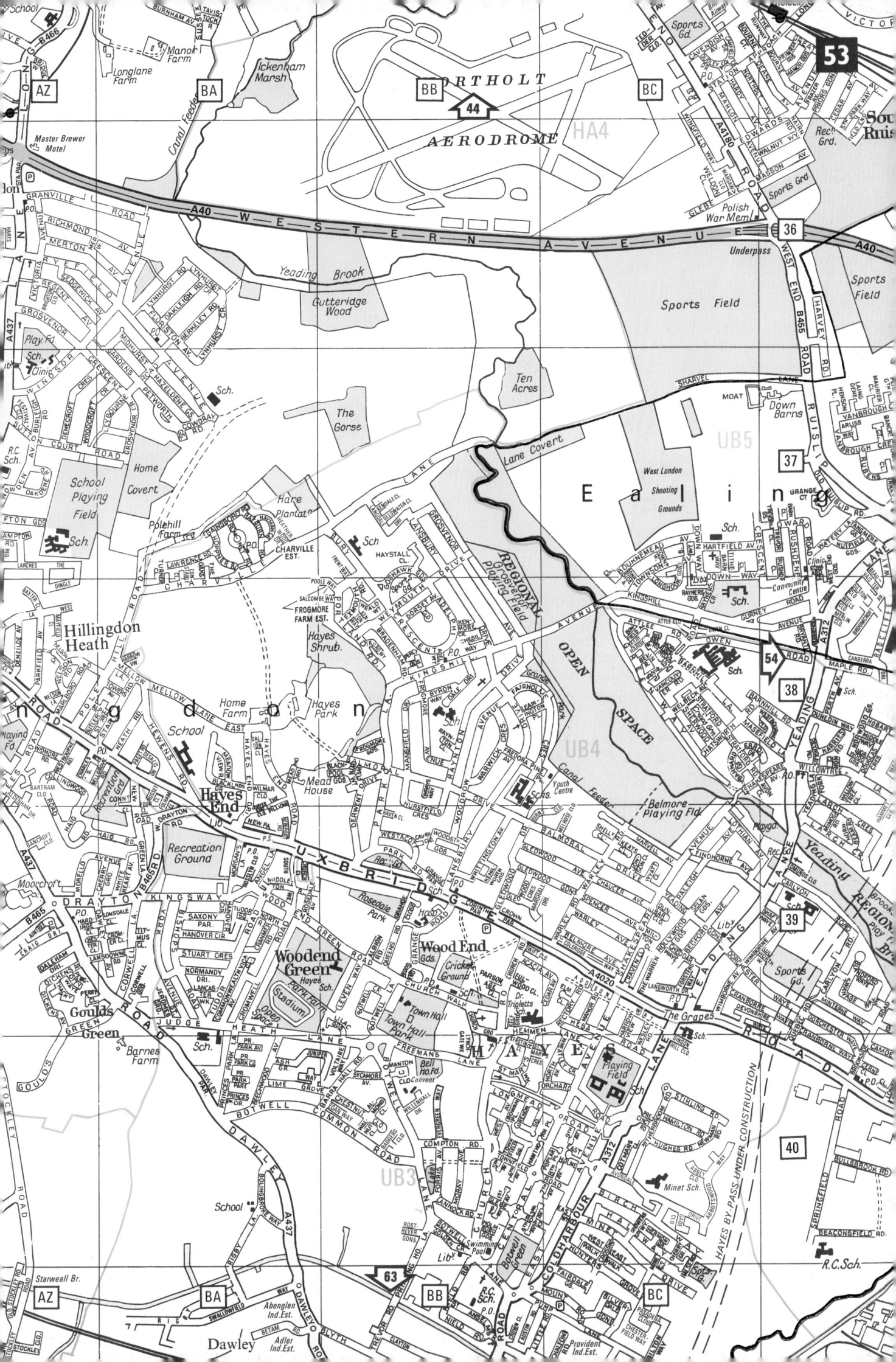

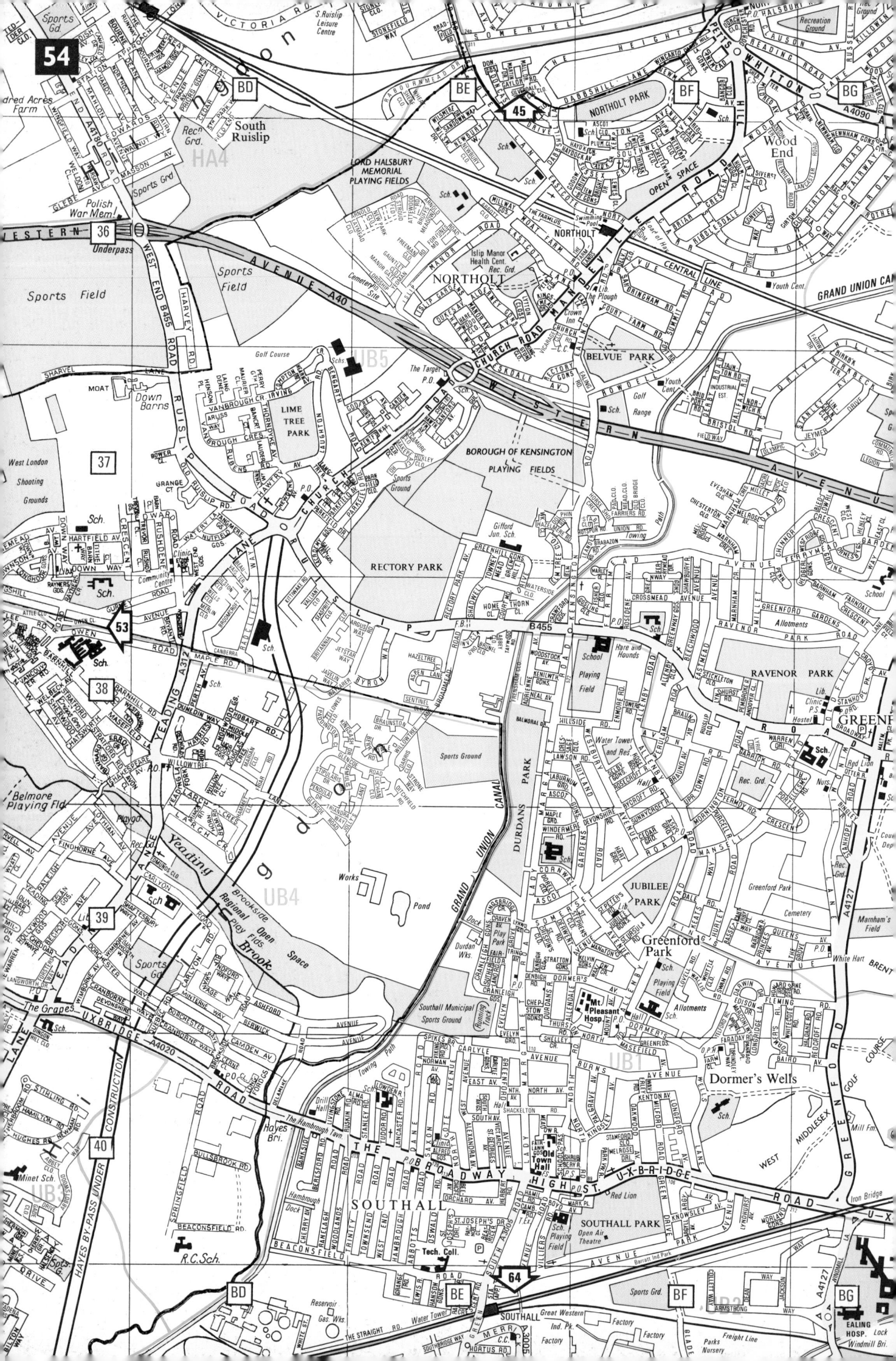

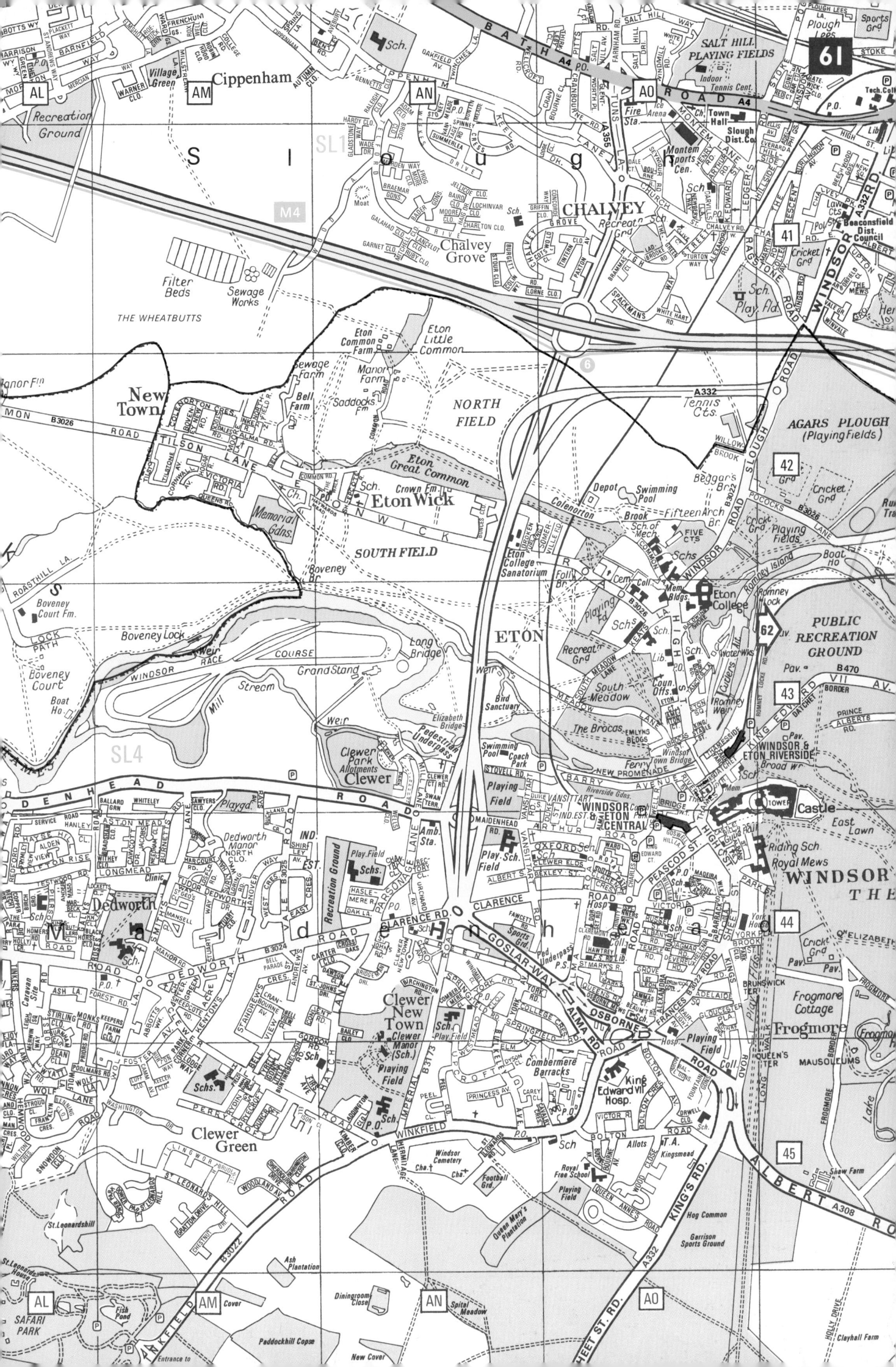

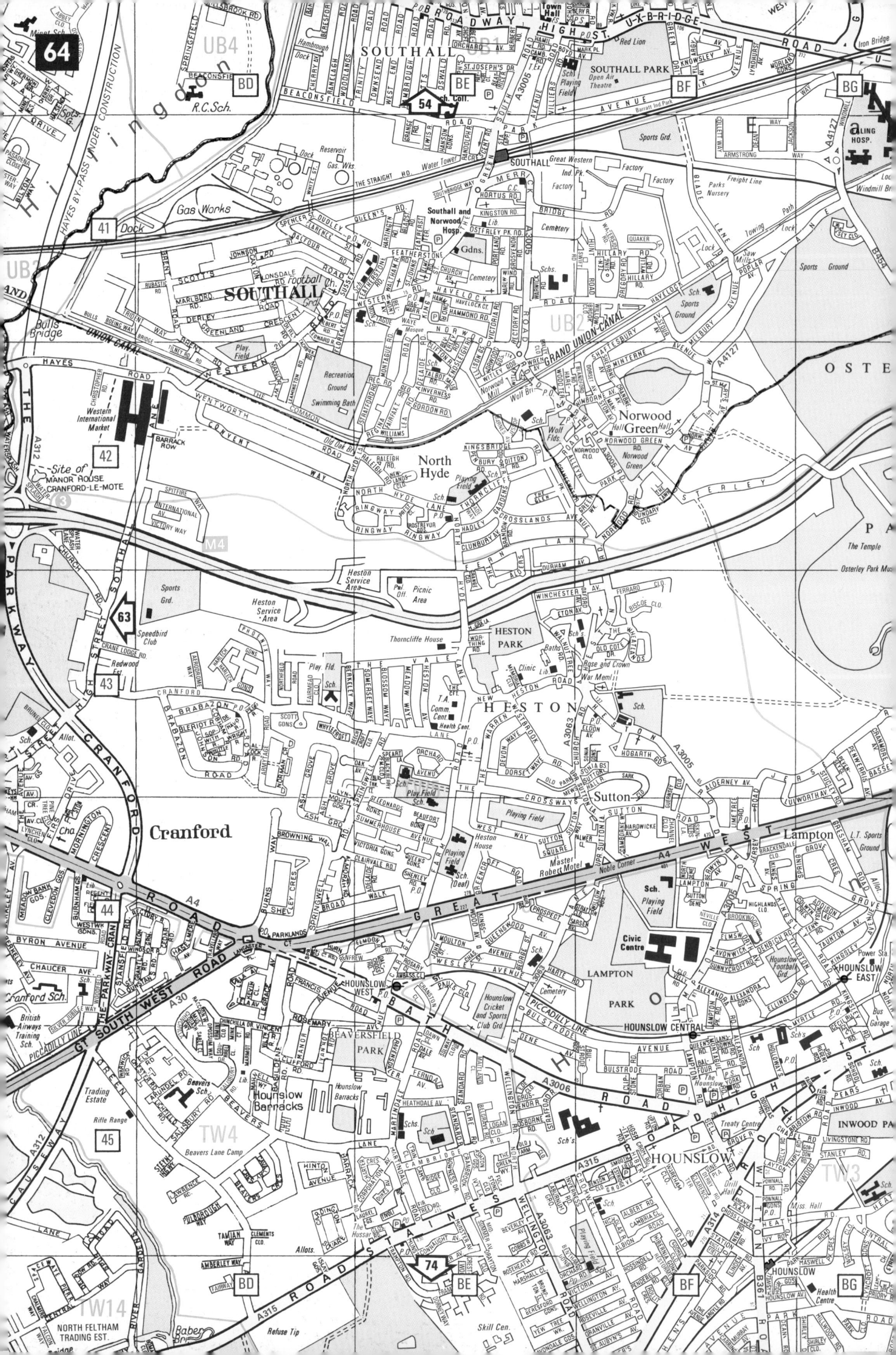

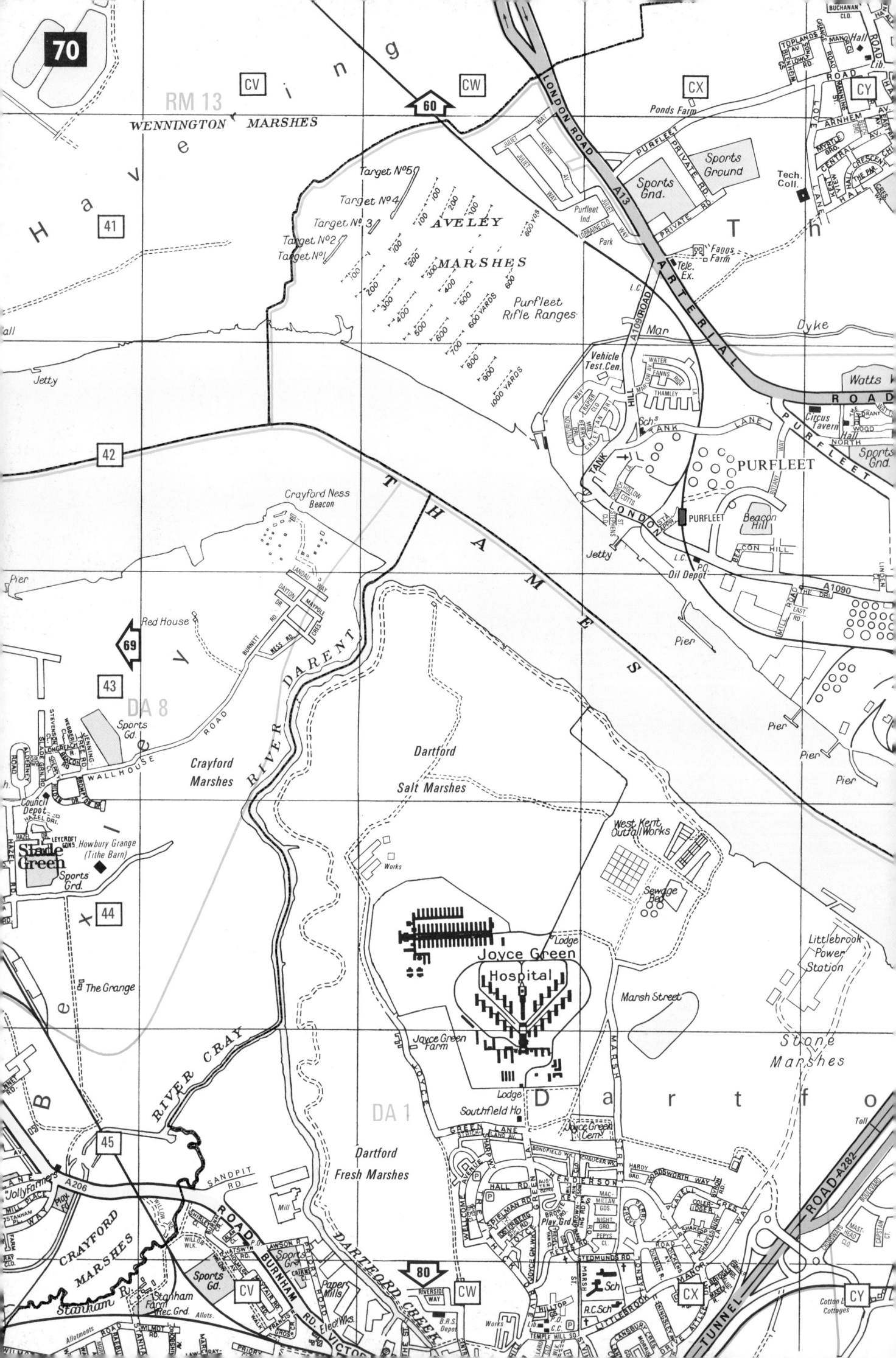

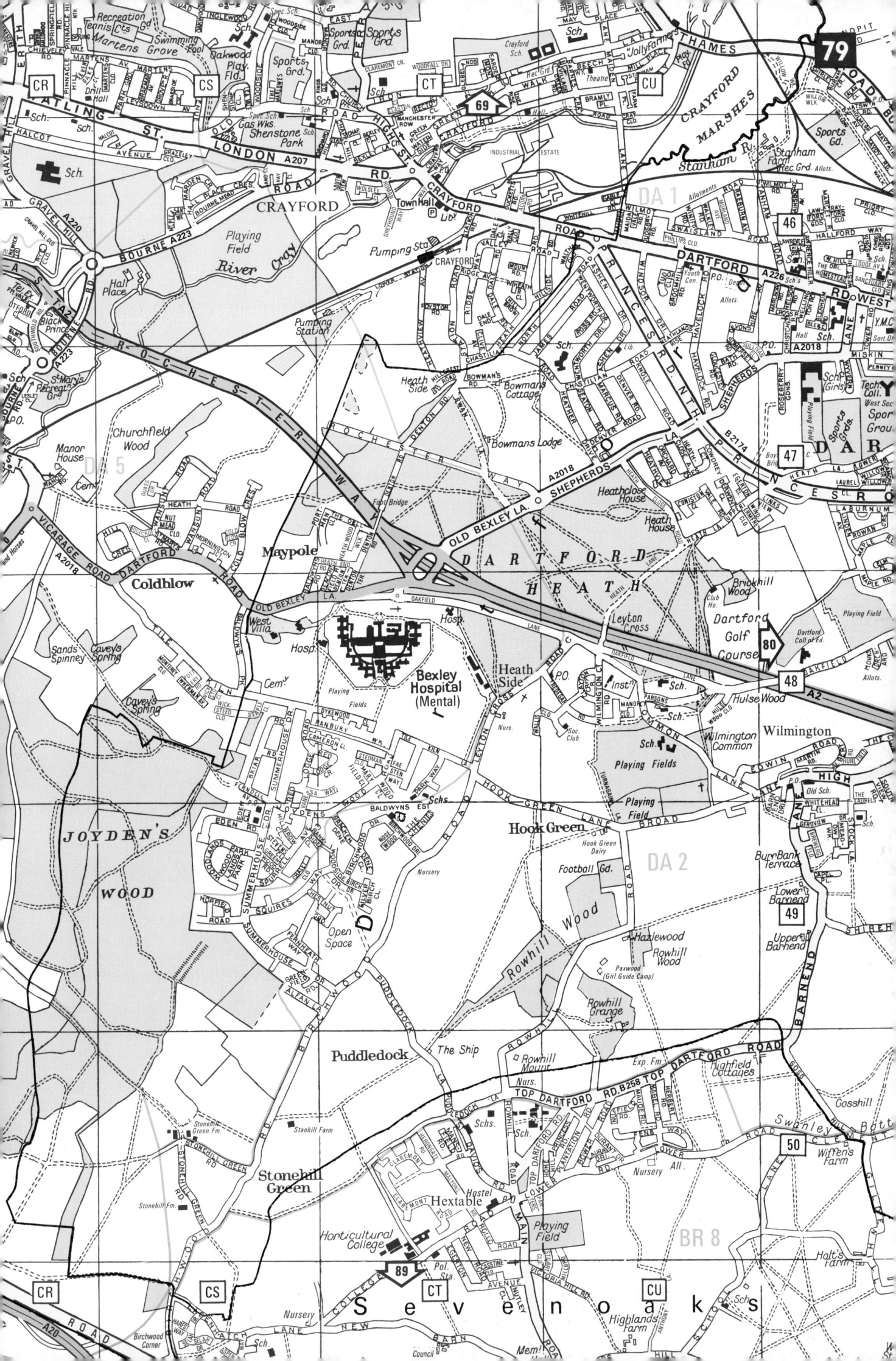

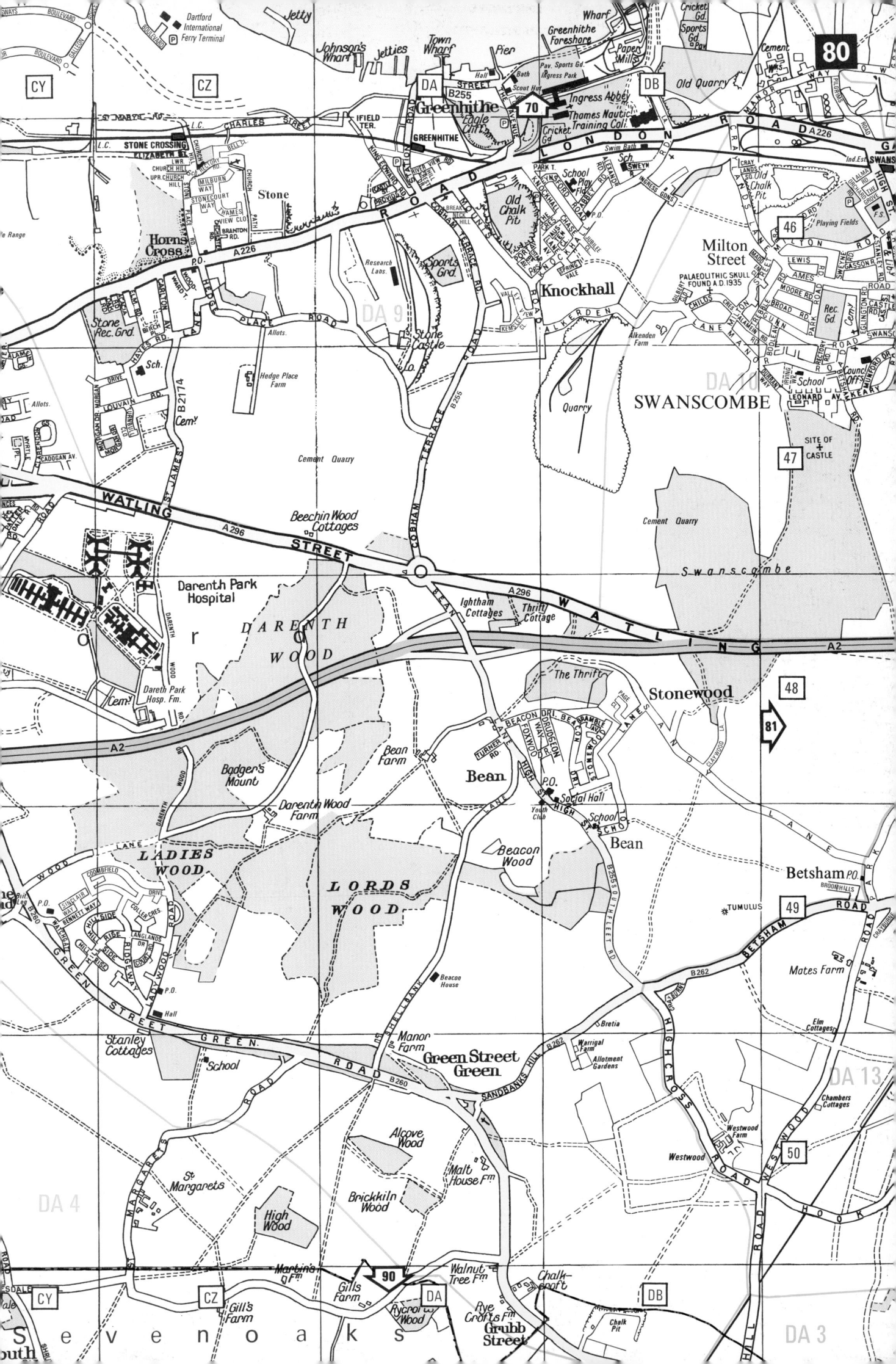

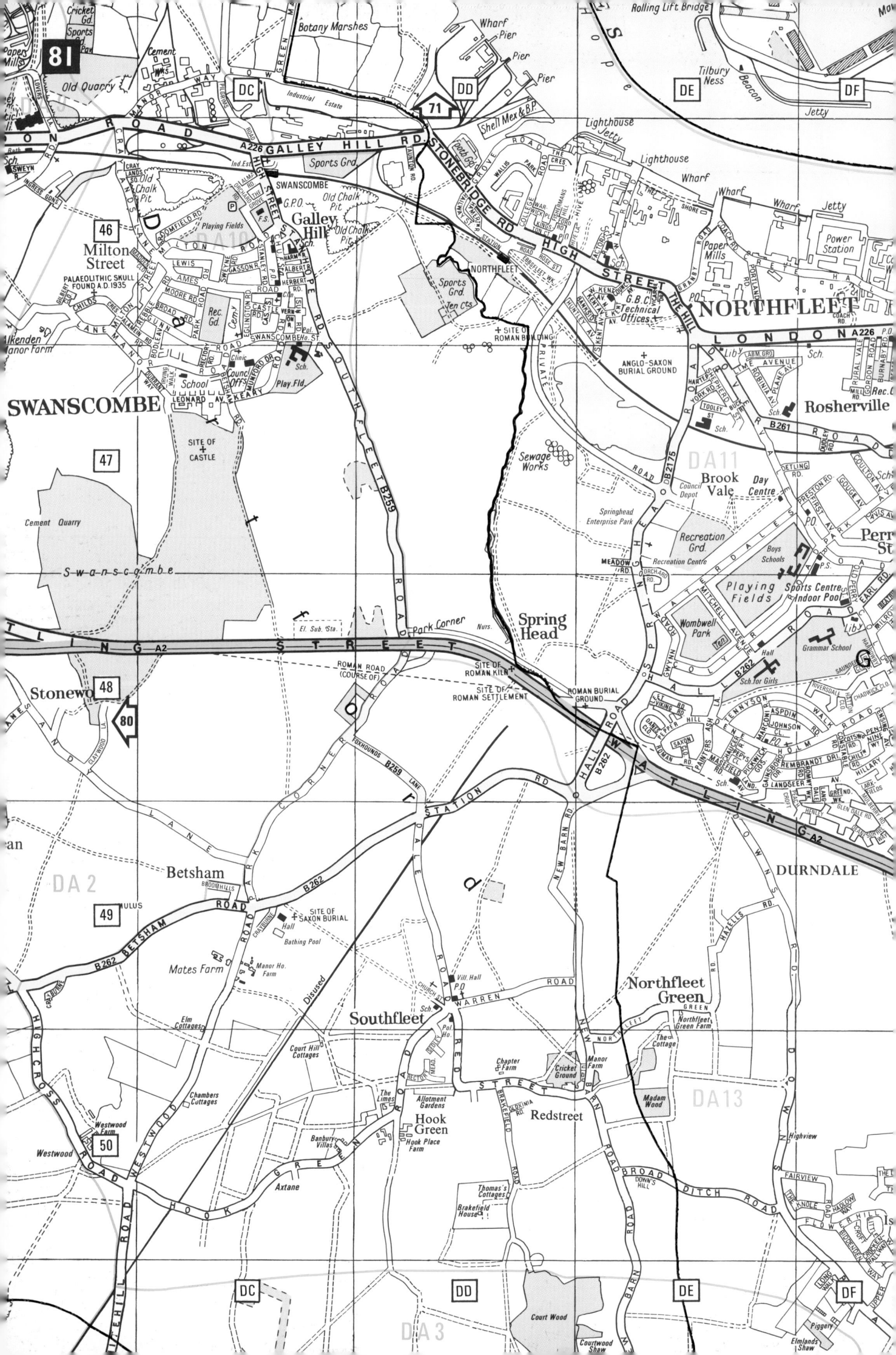

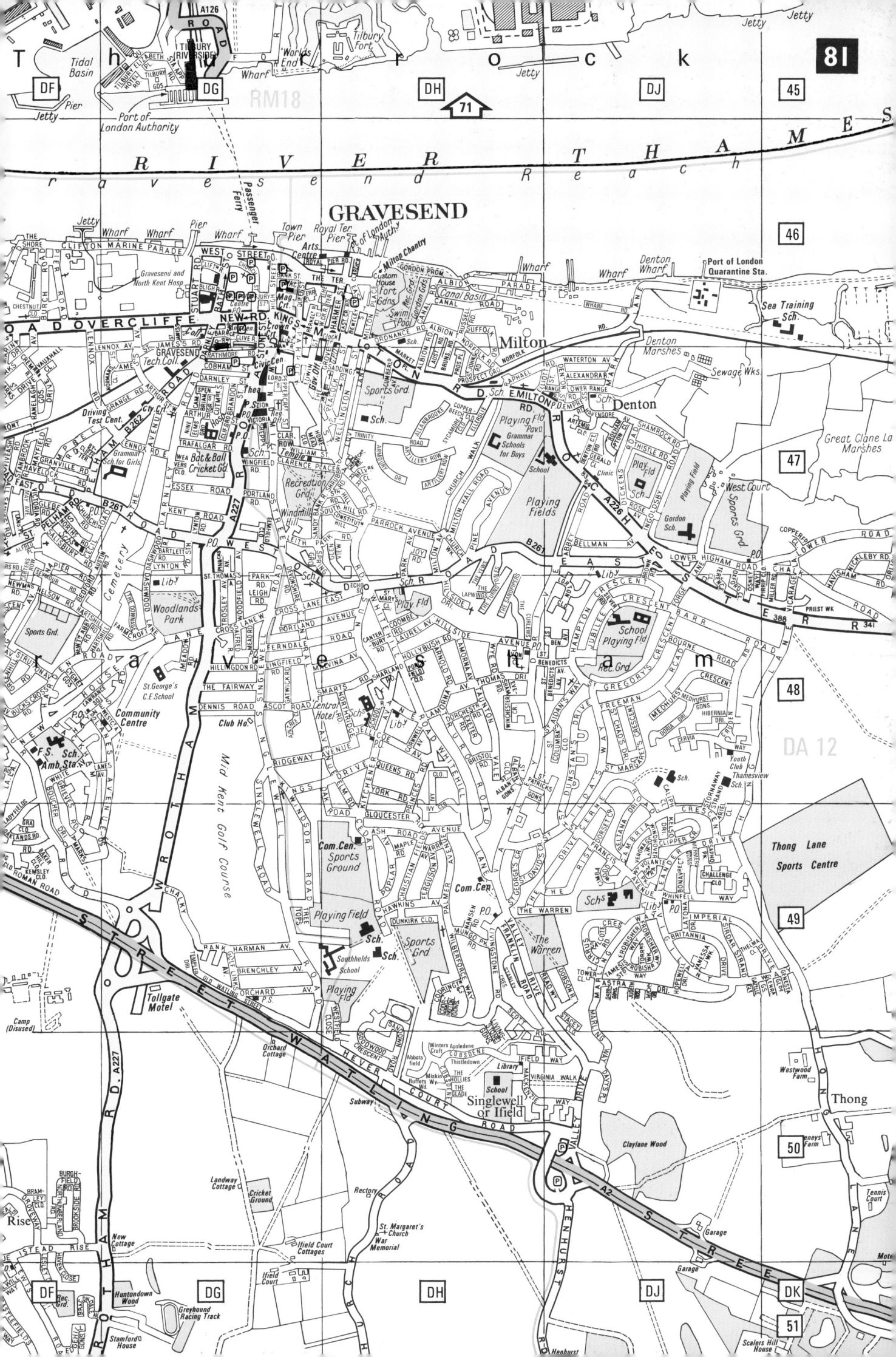

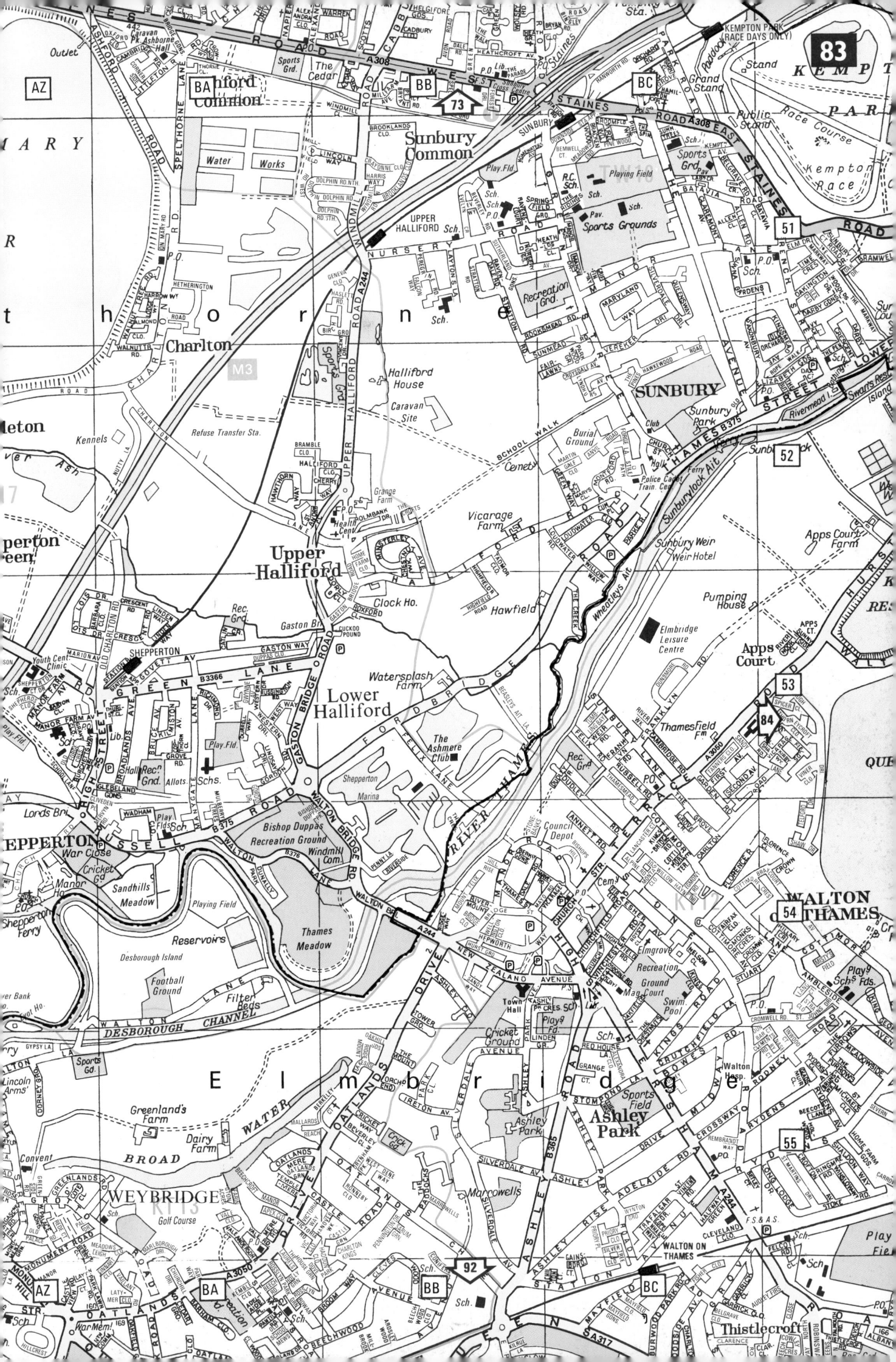

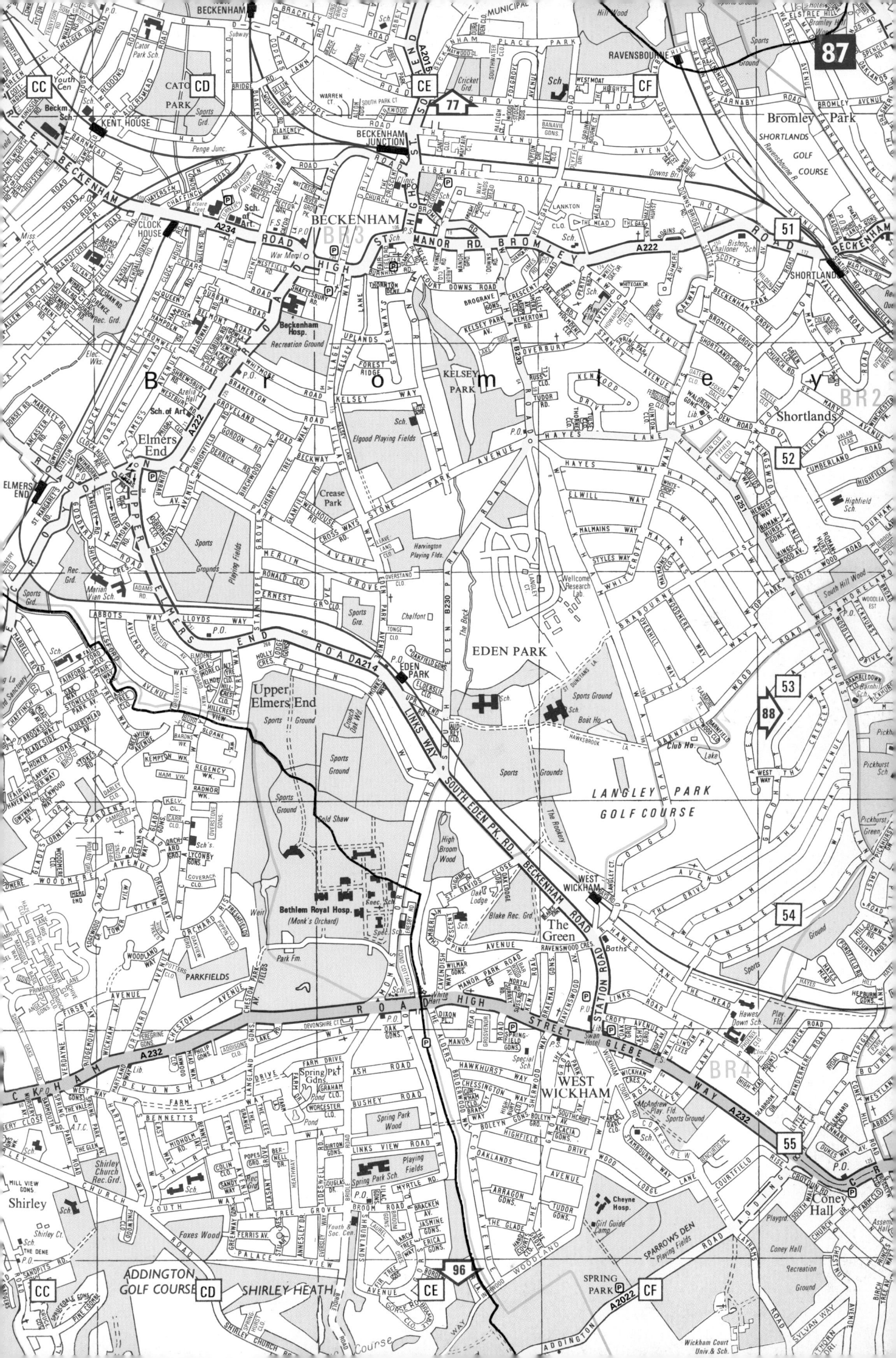

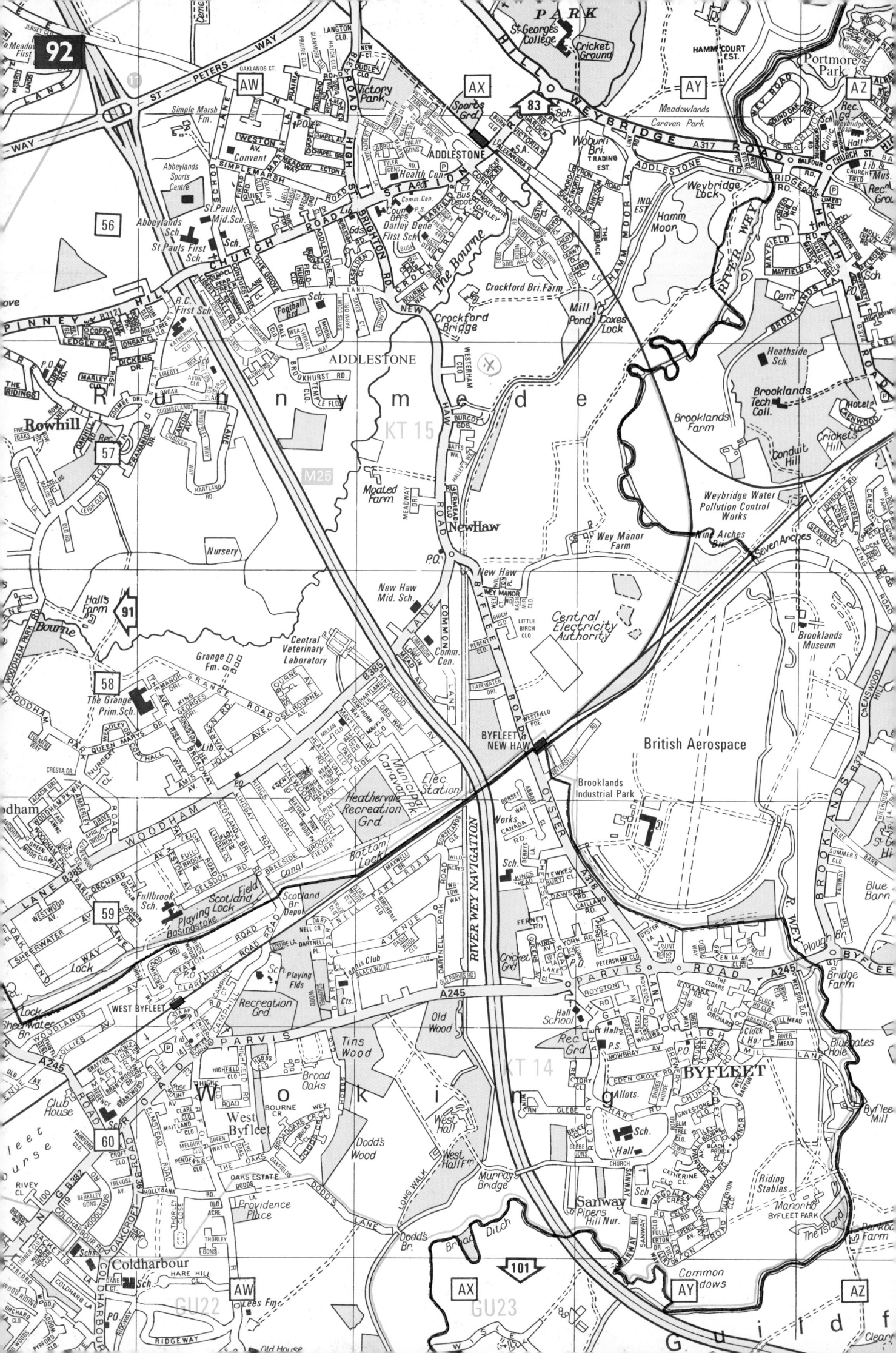

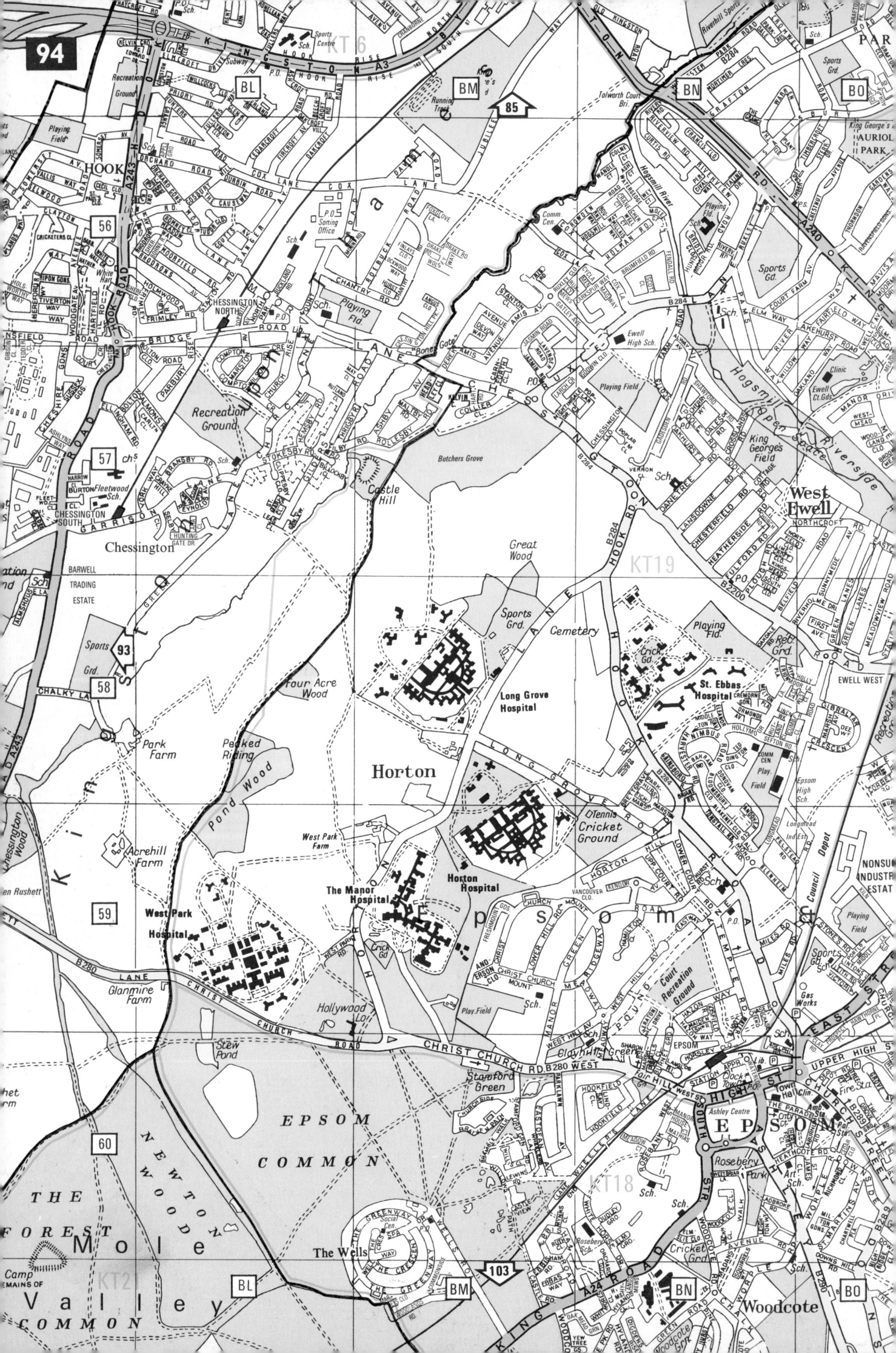

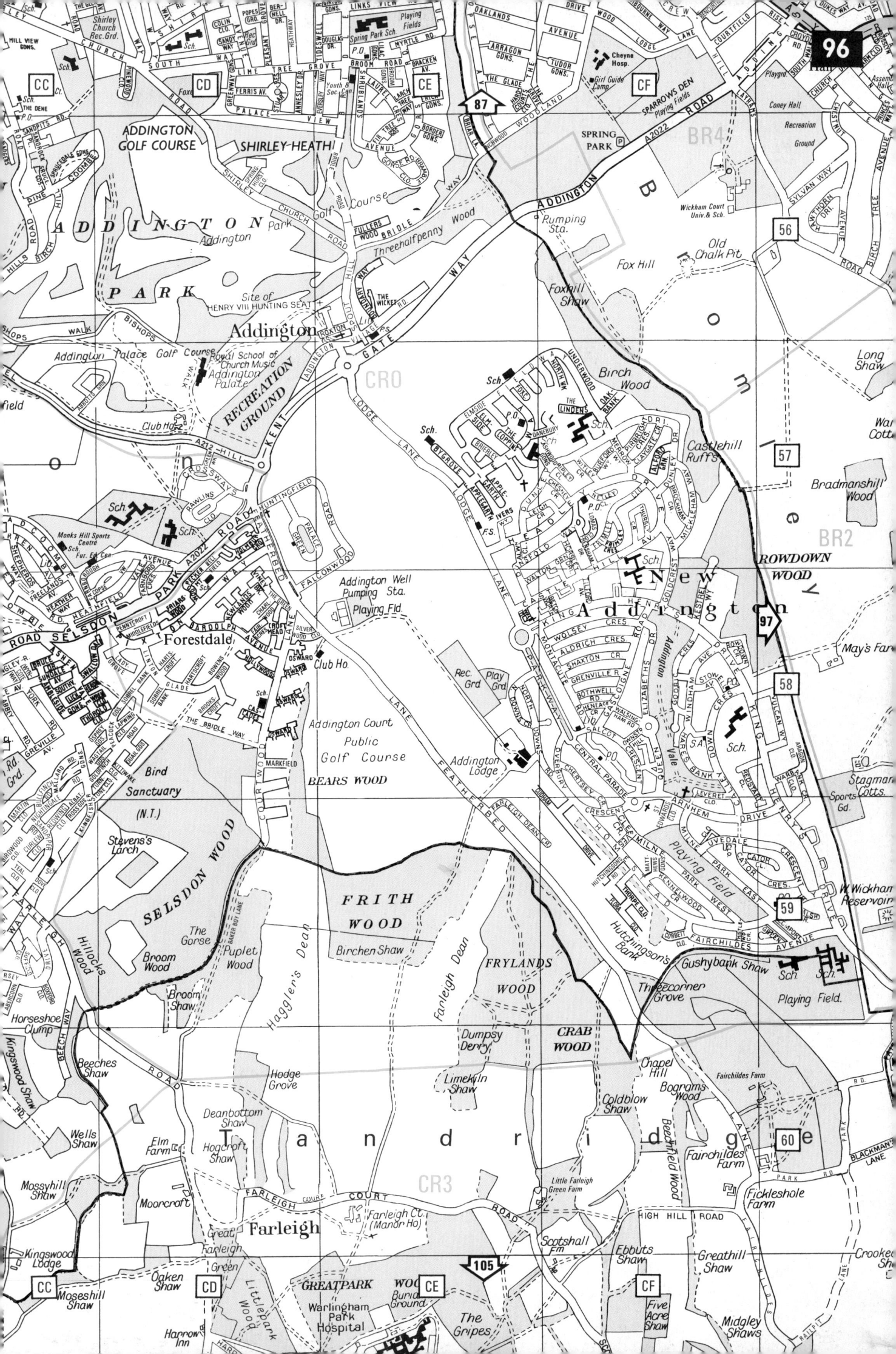

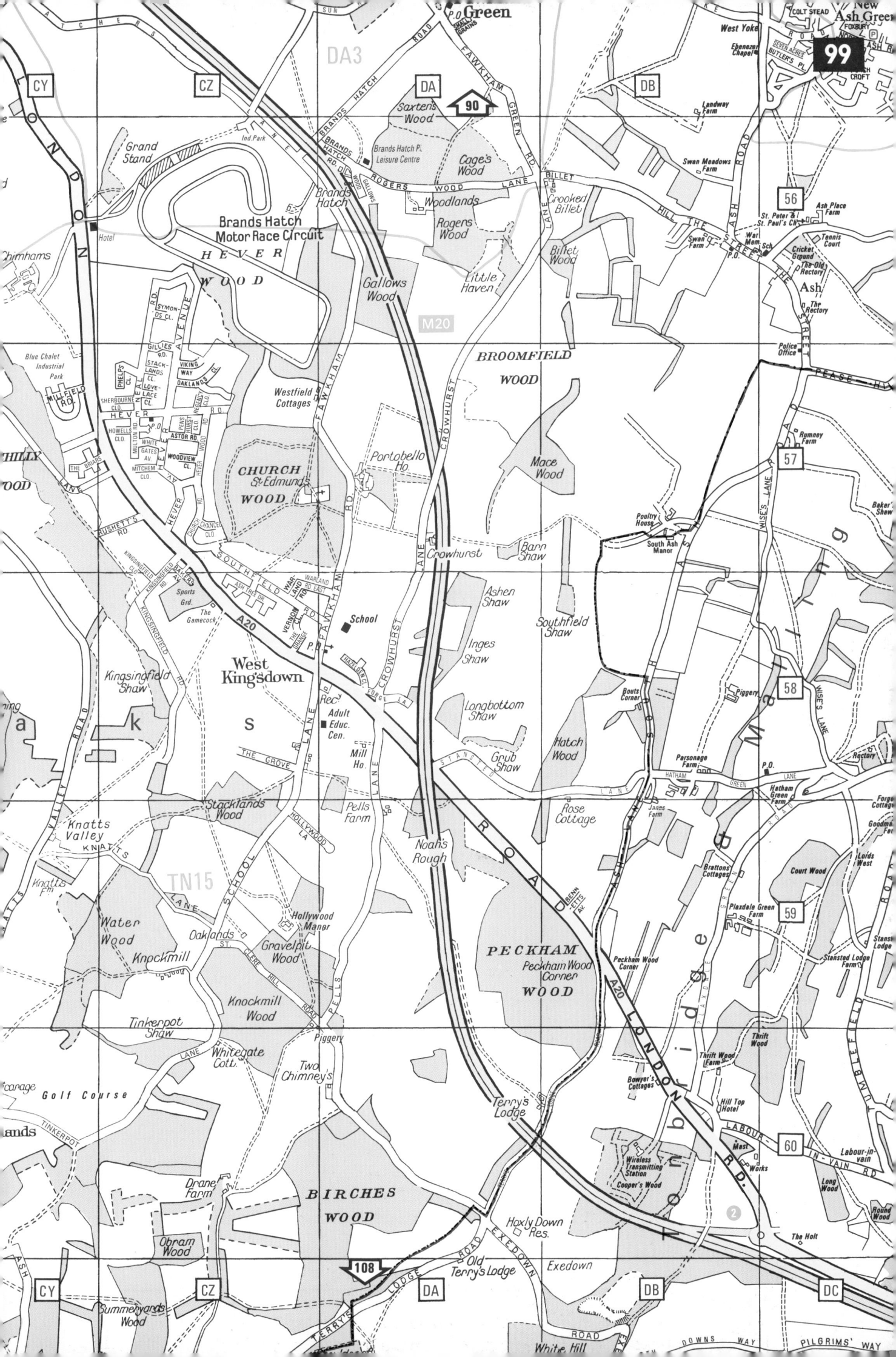

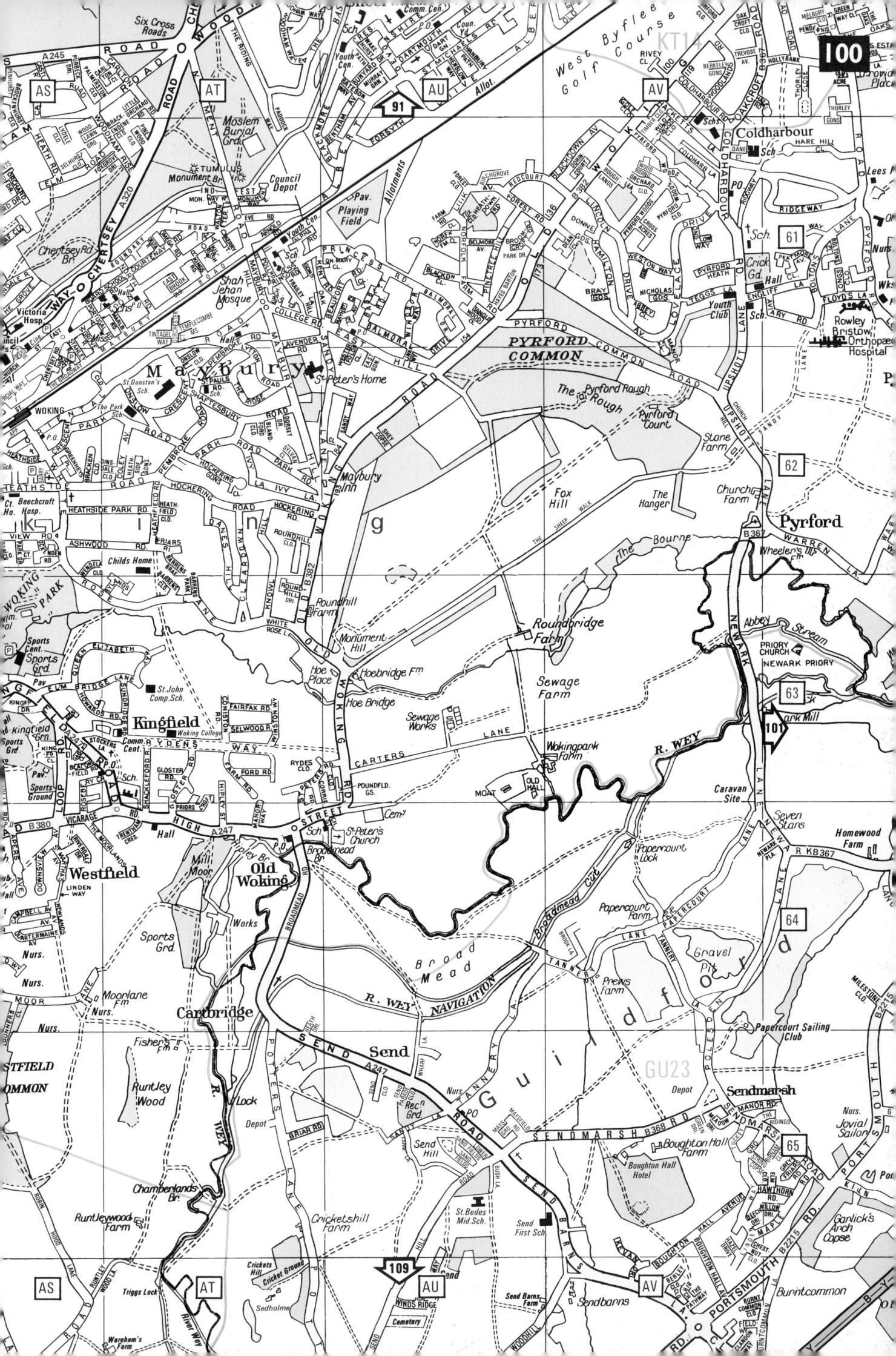

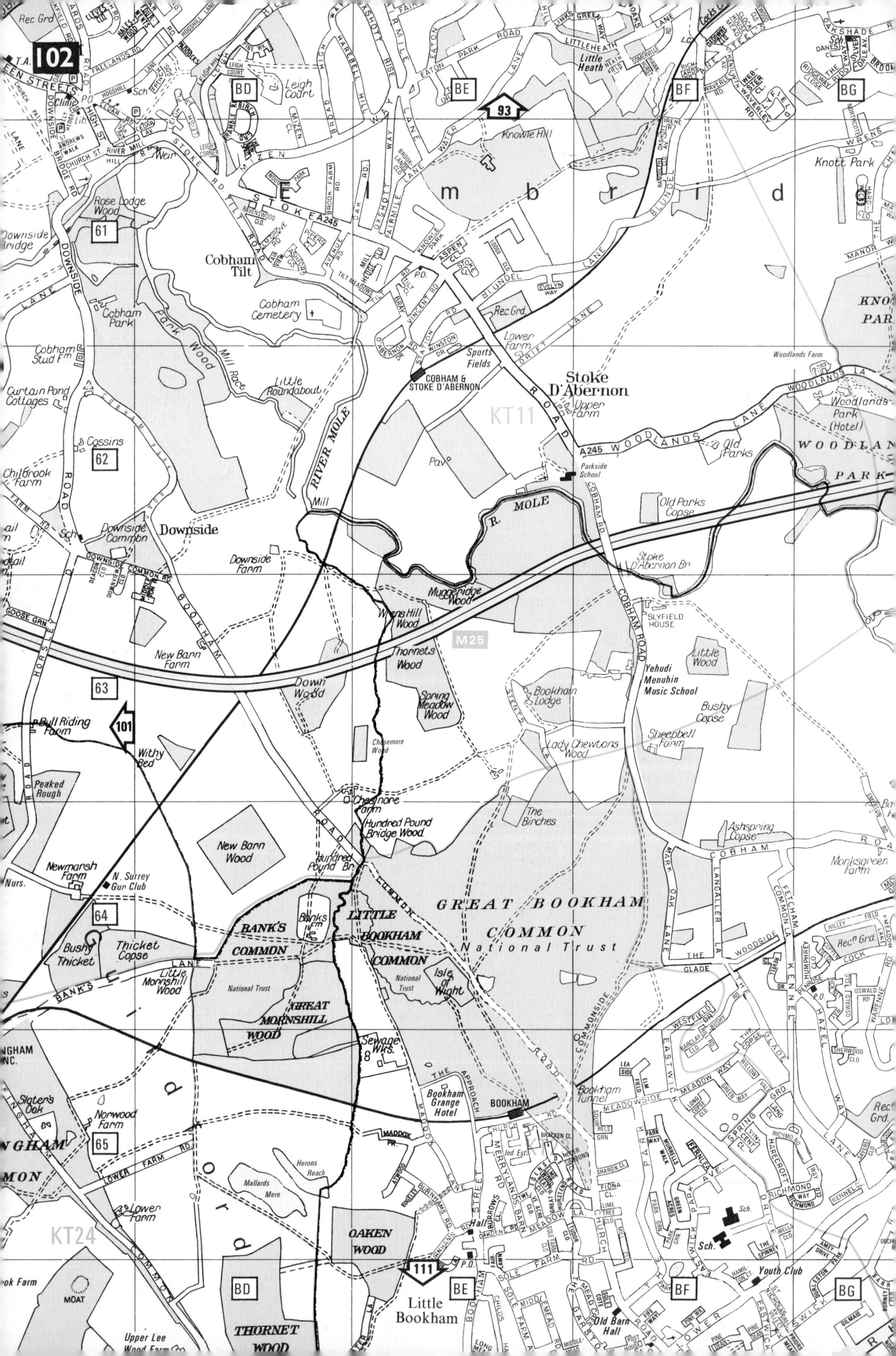

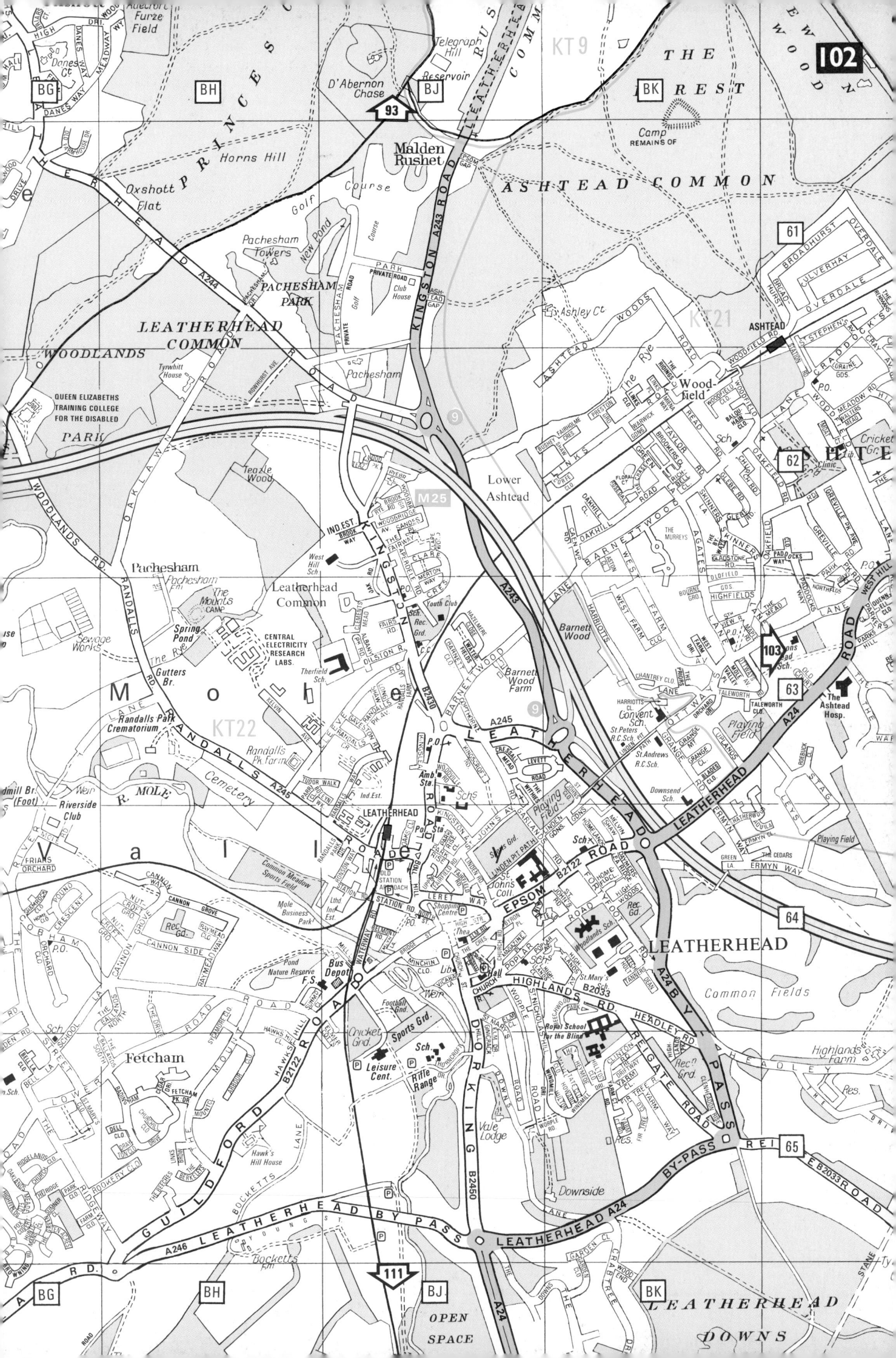

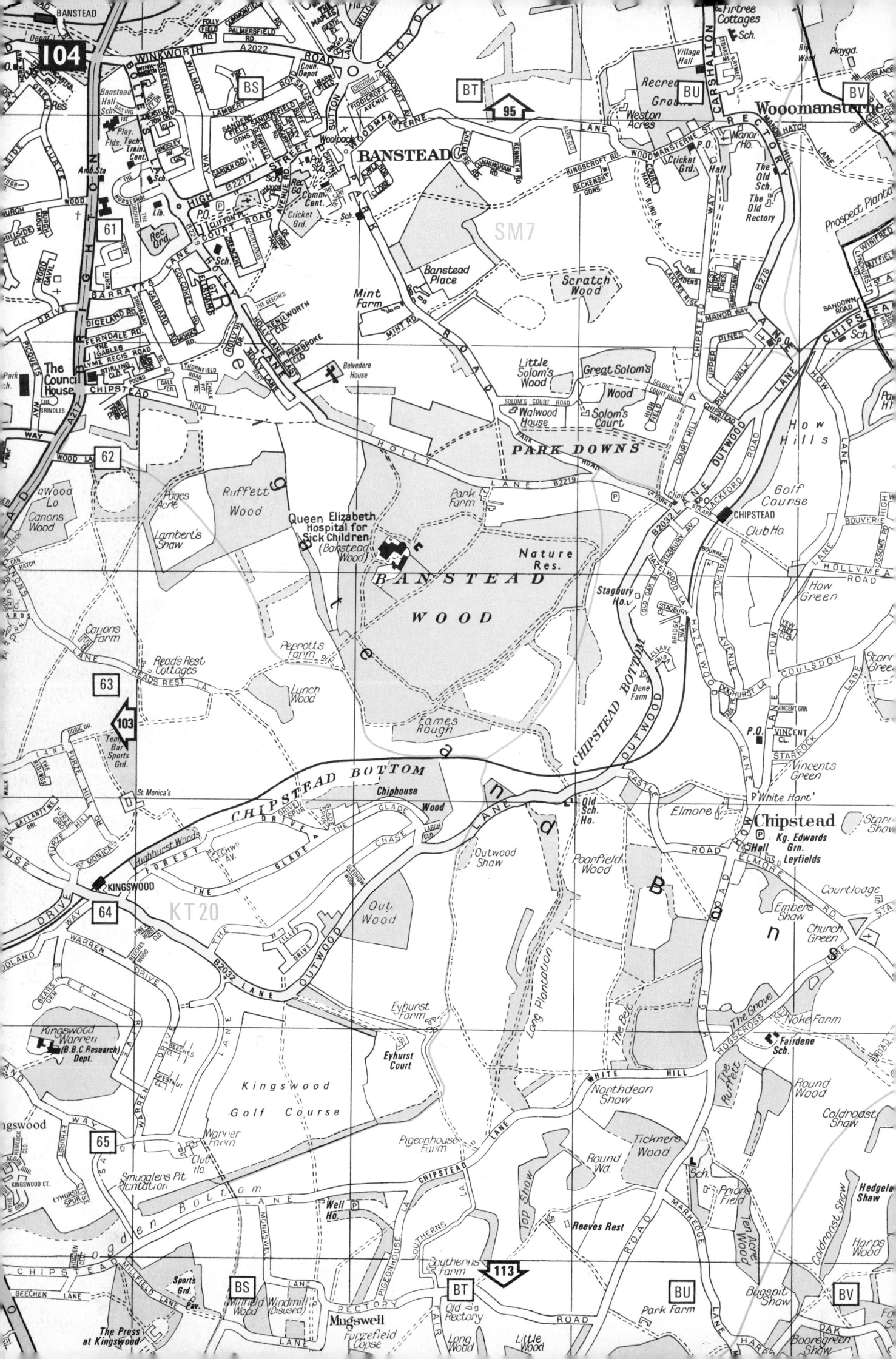

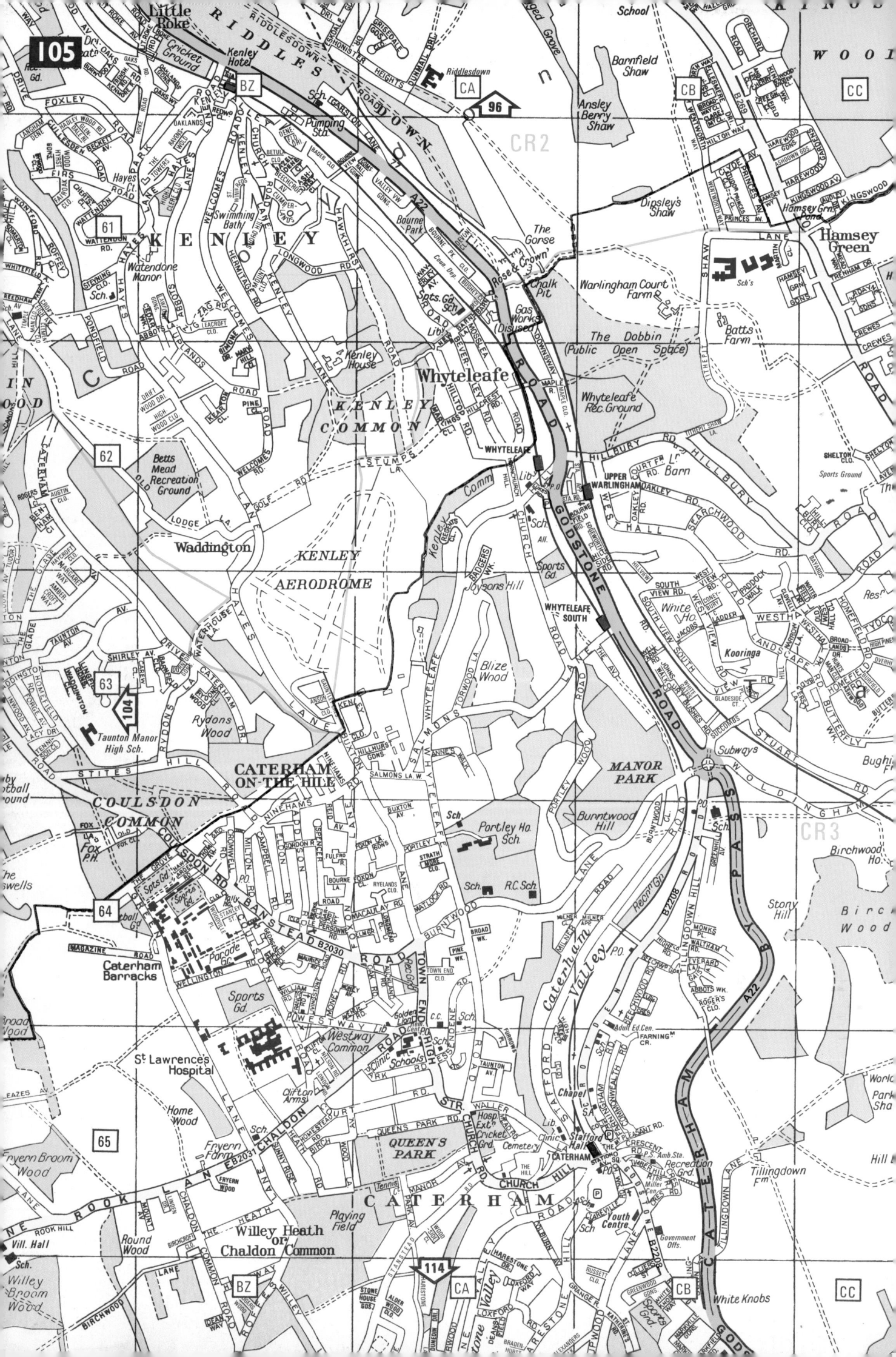

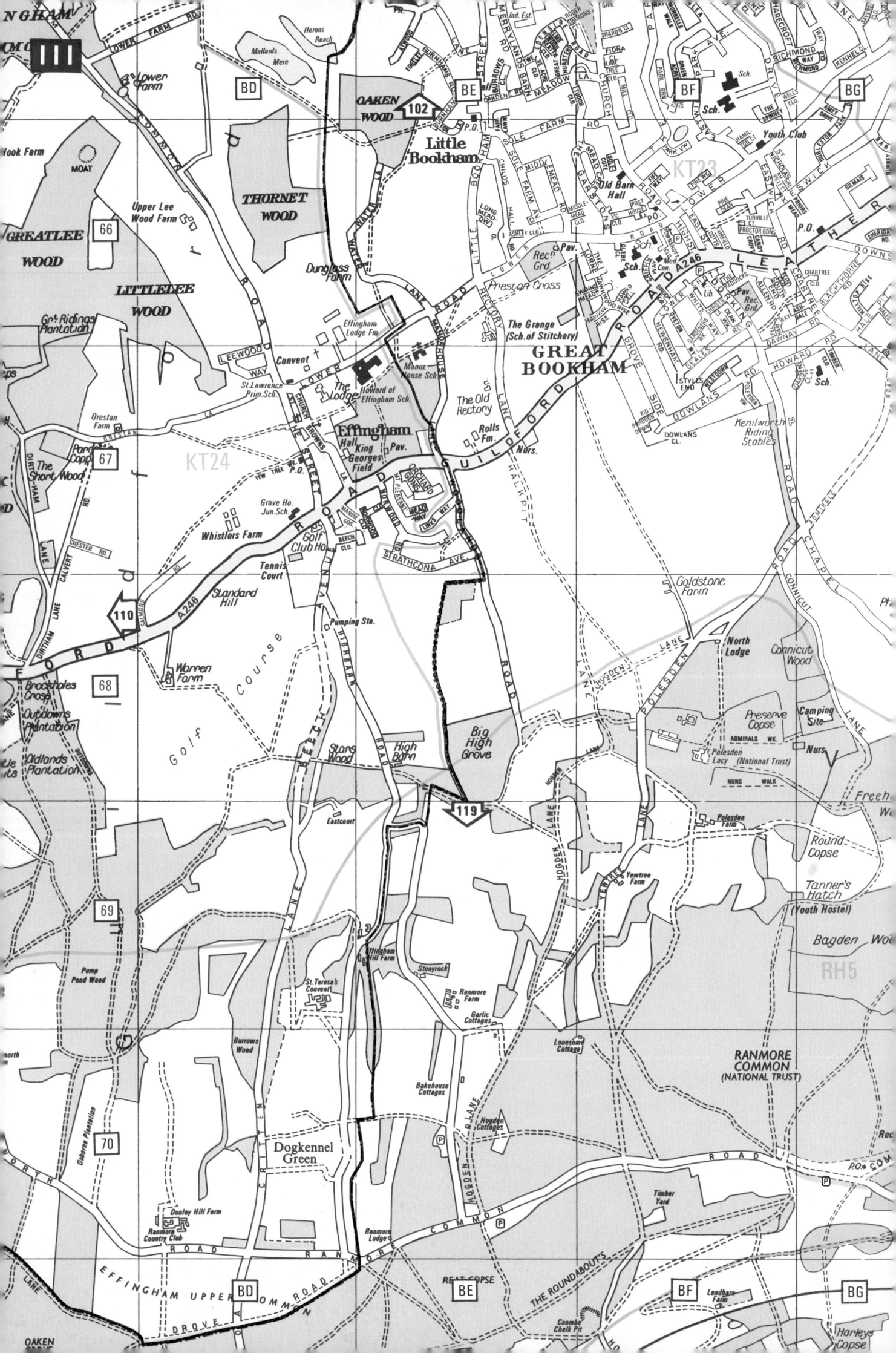

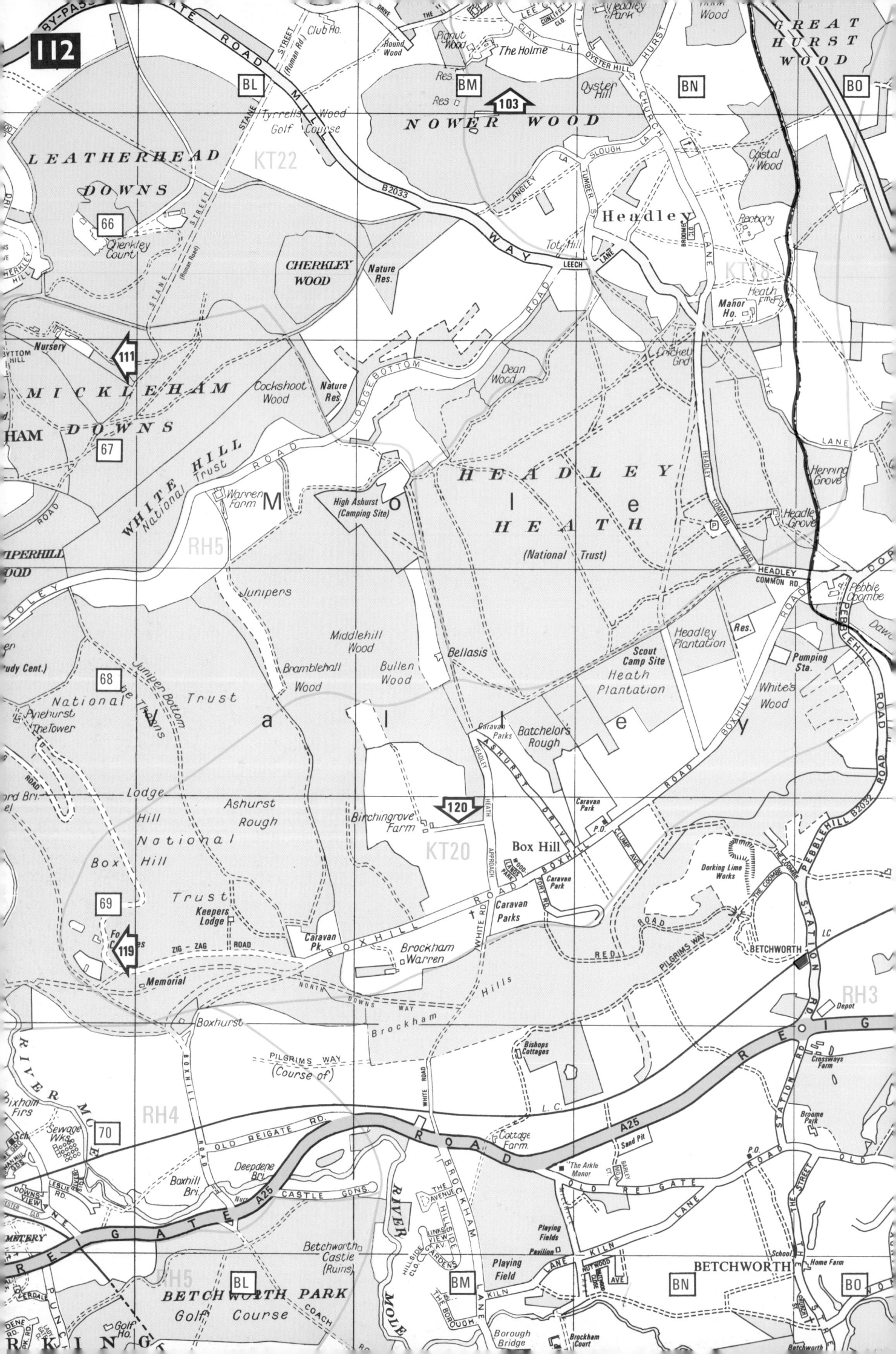

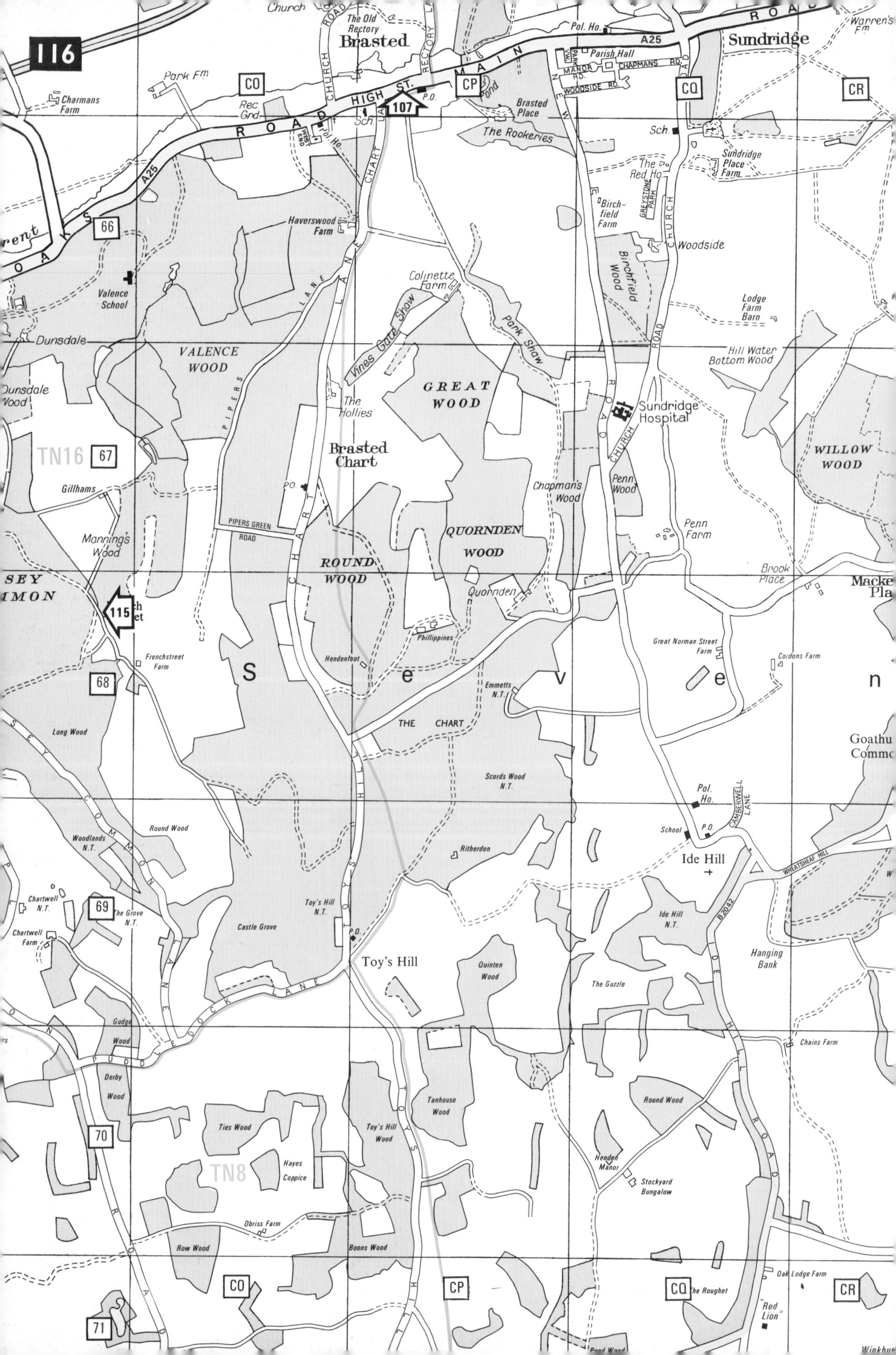

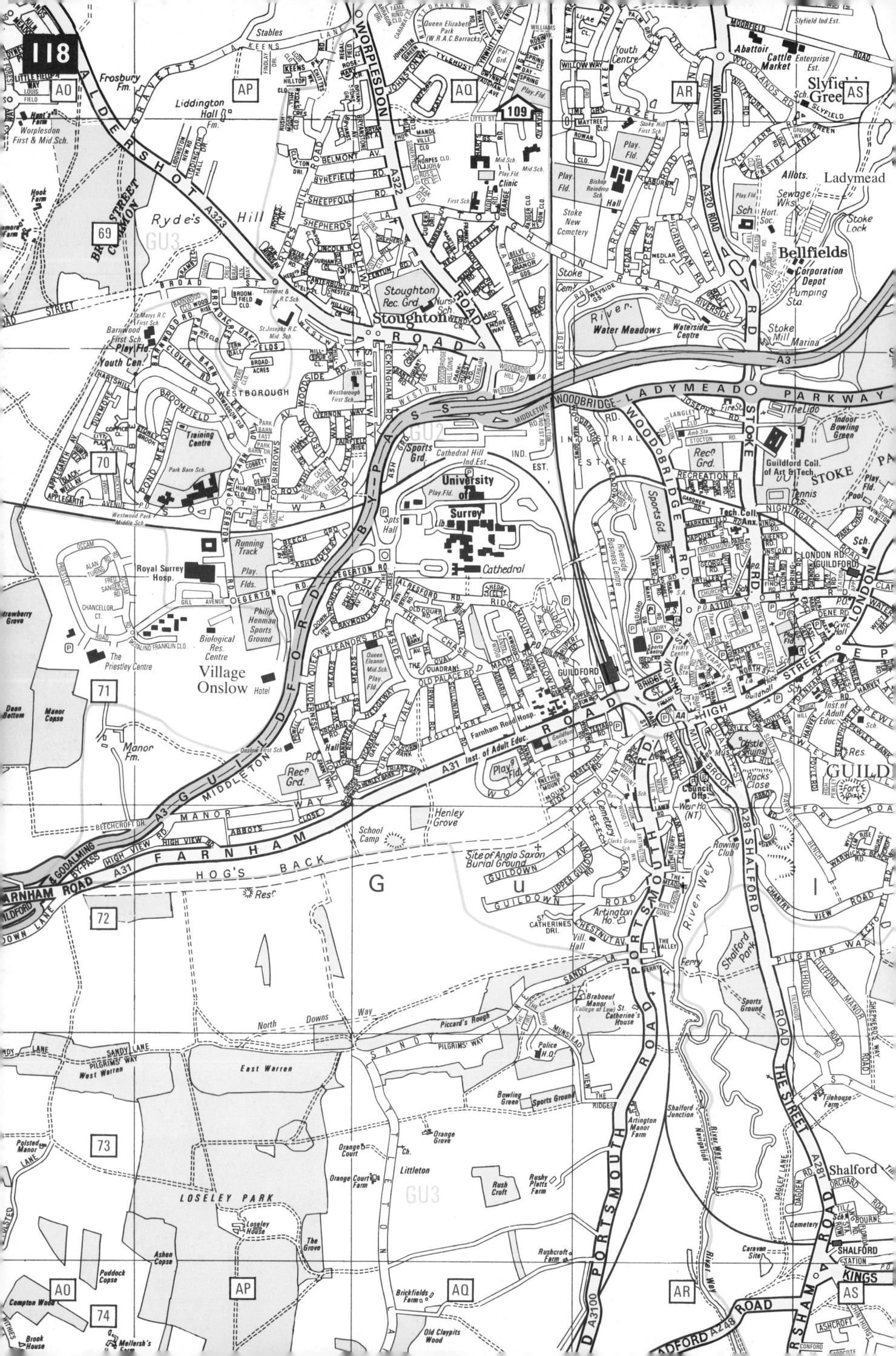

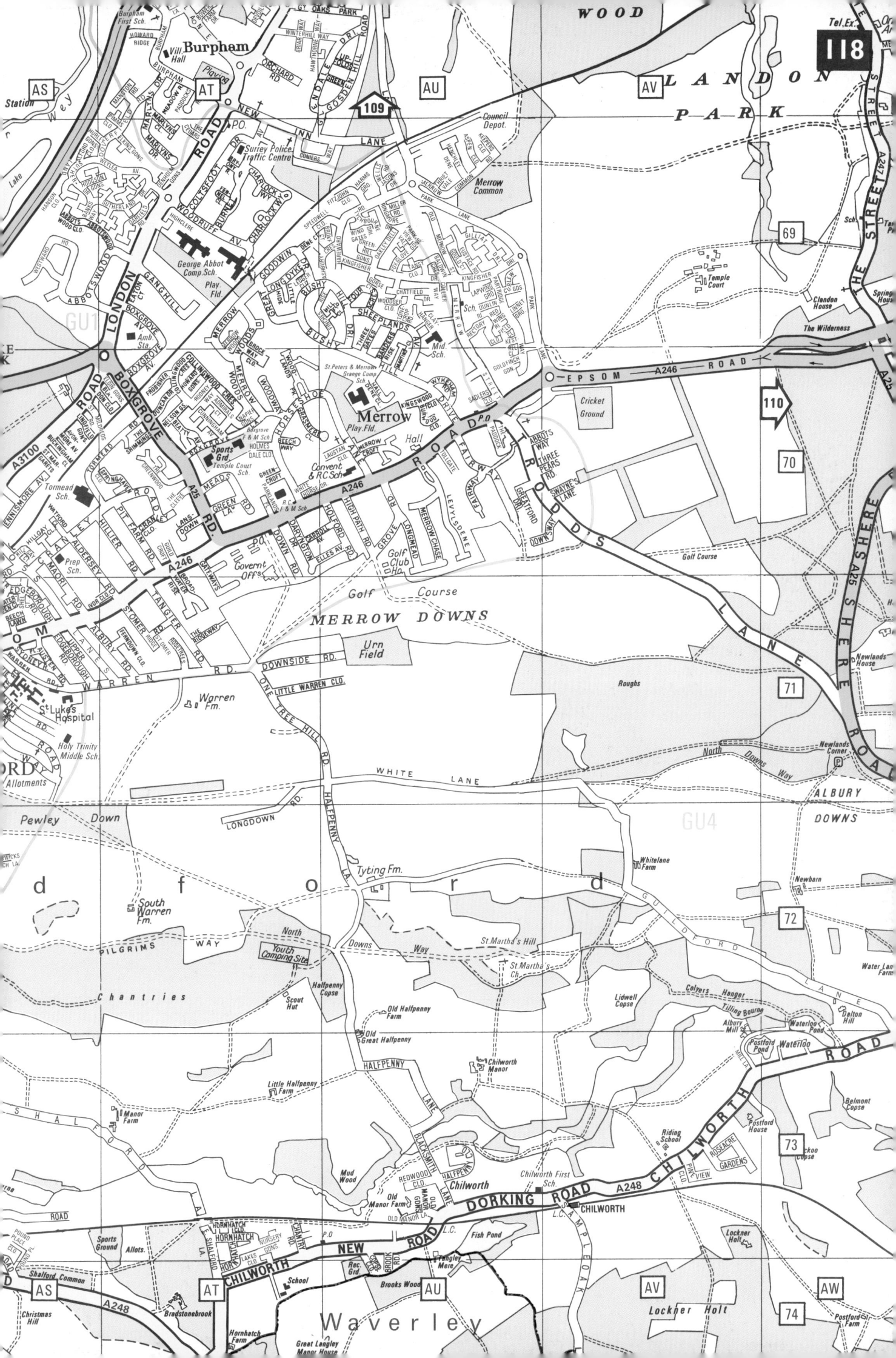

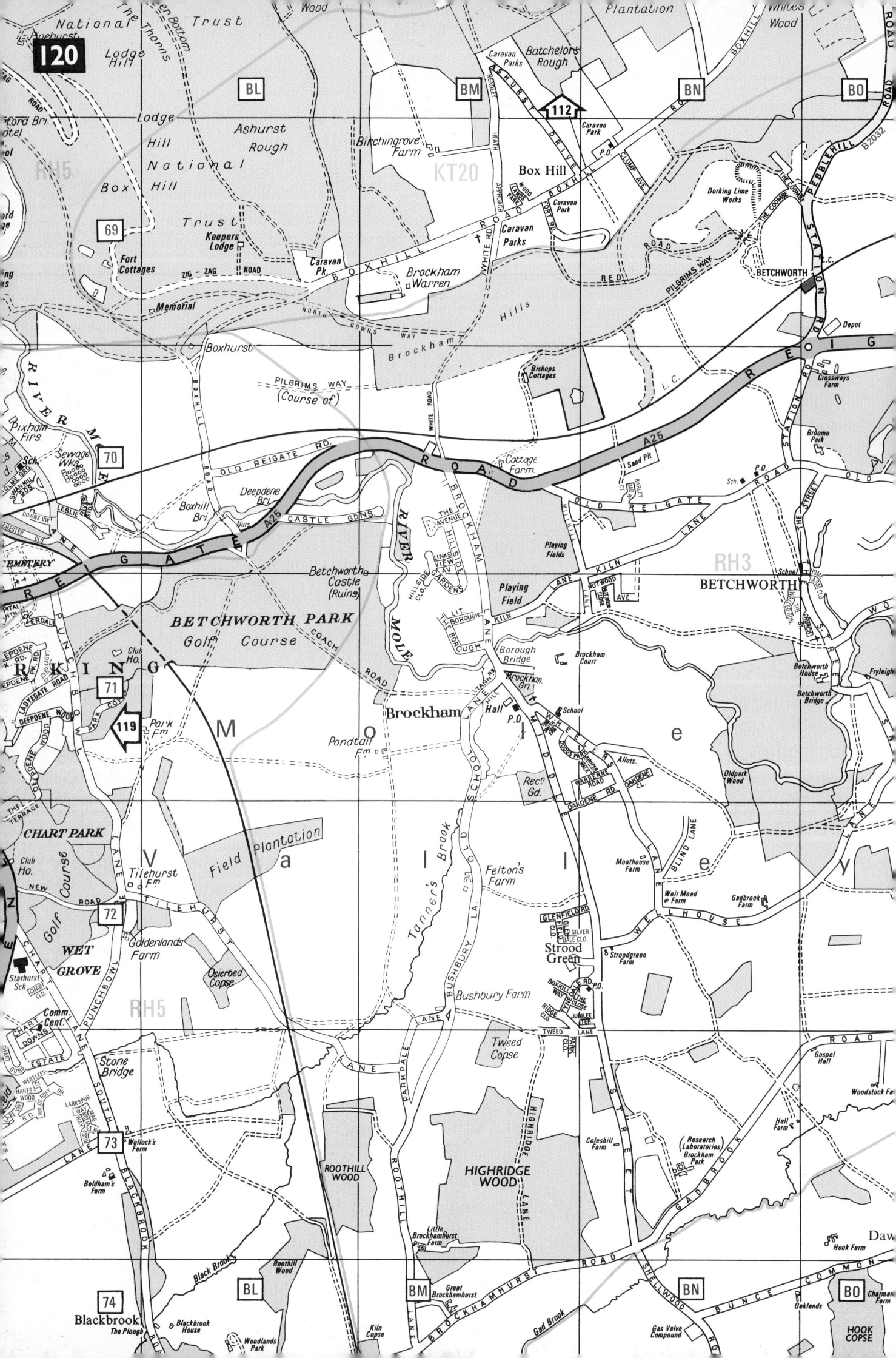

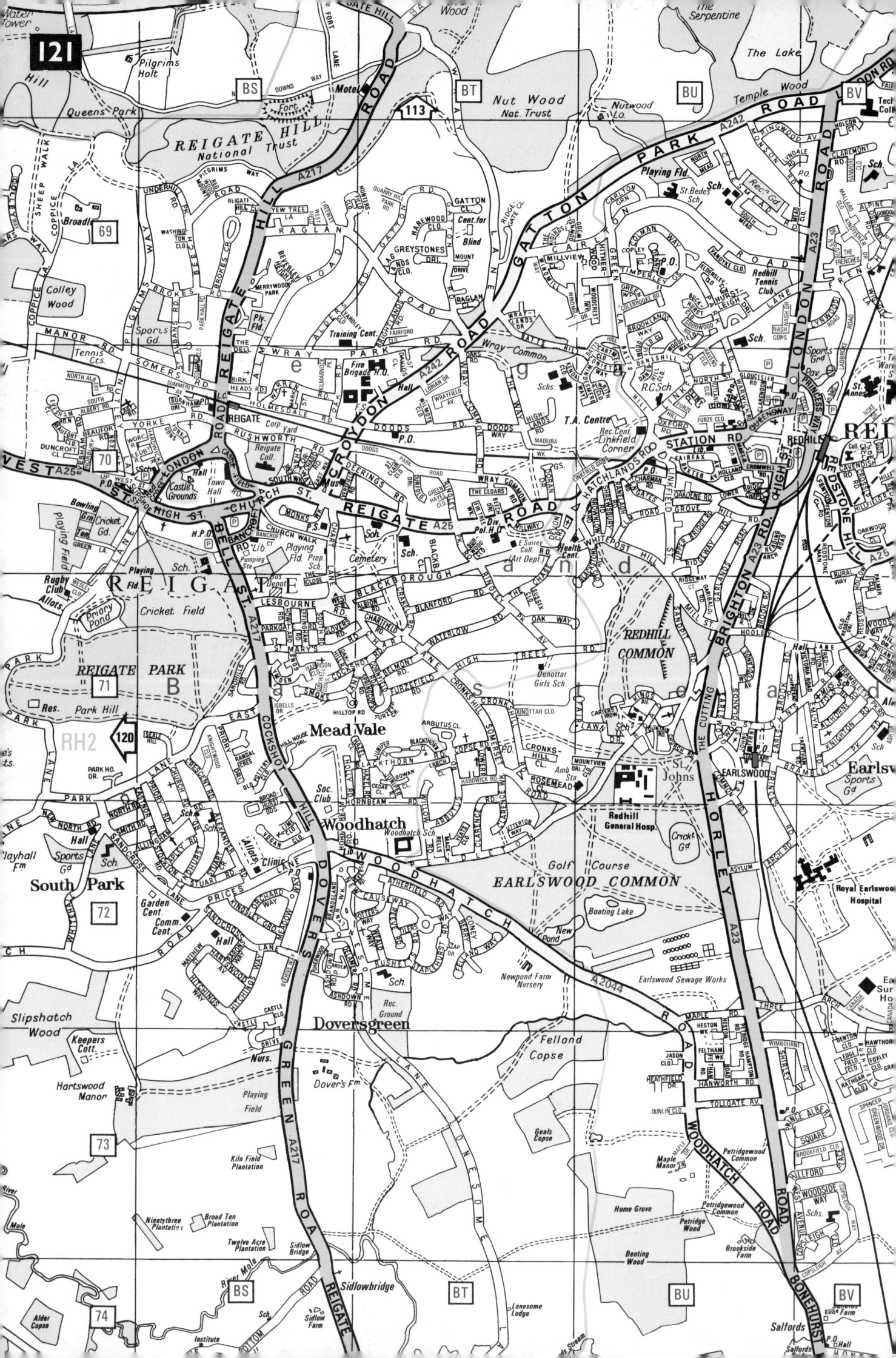

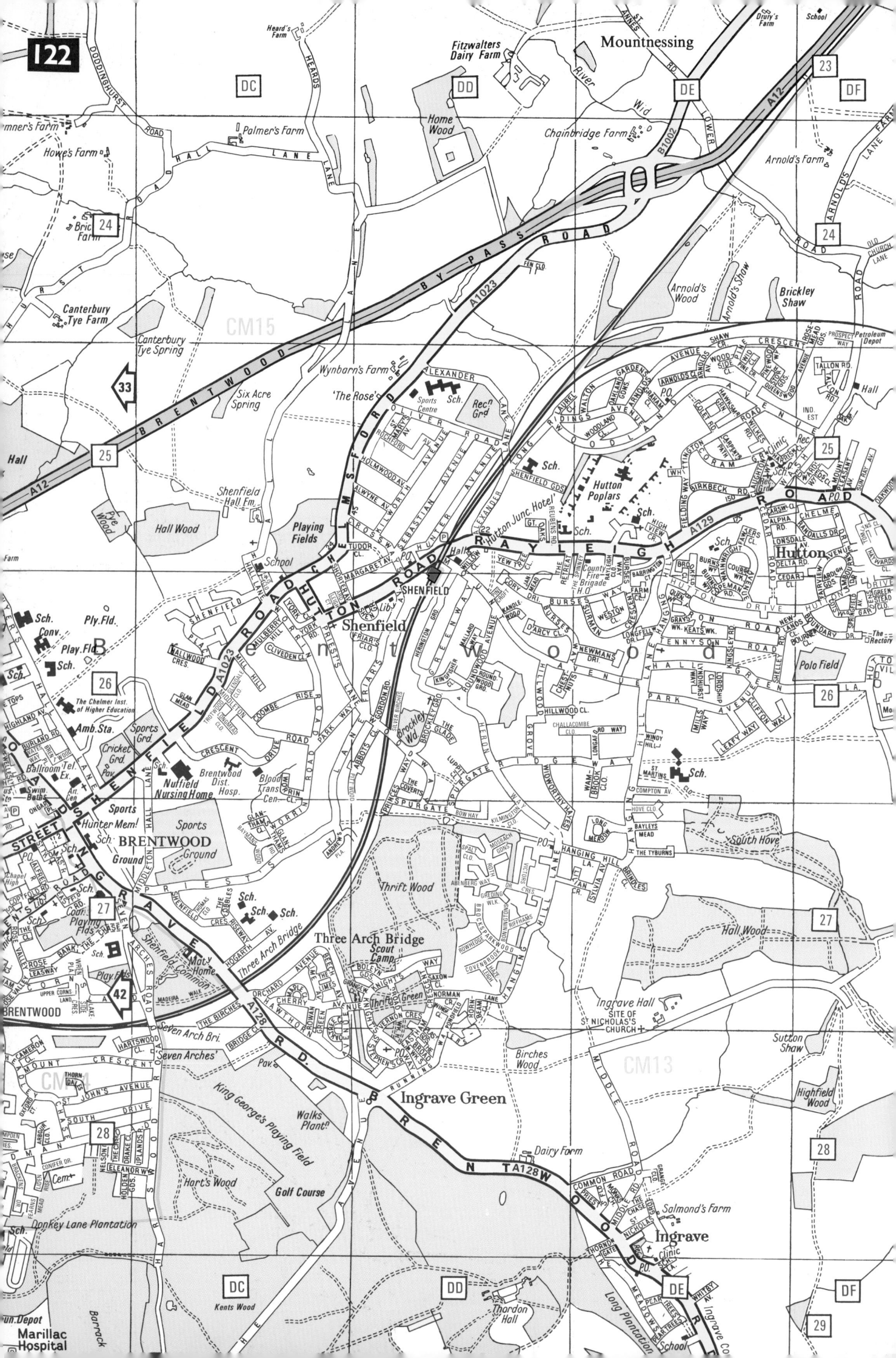

Acton Town *Dist & Picc* BM41 **65**
Aldgate *Met & Circle* CA39 **57**
Aldgate East *Dist & Met* CA39 **57**
Aldwych *Picc* BX40 **56**
Alperton *Picc* BL37 **55**
Amersham *Met* AO22 **25**
Angel *N'thn* BY37 **56**
Archway *N'thn* BW34 **47**
Arnos Grove *Picc* BW28 **38**
Arsenal *Picc* BY34 **47**

Baker Street *B'loo, Met, Circle & J'lee* BU38 **56**
Balham *N'thn* BV47 **76**
Bank *N'thn & Cent* BZ39 **57**
Barbican *Met & Circle* BZ39 **57**
Barking *Dist & Met* CM36 **58**
Barkingside *Cent* CM31 **49**
Barons Court *Dist & Picc* BR42 **65**
Bayswater *Dist & Circle* BS40 **56**
Becontree *Dist* CP36 **59**
Belsize Park *N'thn* BU35 **47**
Bethnal Green *Cent* CC38 **57**
Blackfriars *Dist & Circle* BY40 **56**
Blackhorse Road *Vic* CC31 **48**
Bond Street *Cent & J'lee* BV39 **56**
Borough *N'thn* BZ41 **67**
Boston Manor *Picc* BJ42 **64**
Bounds Green *Picc* BW29 **38**
Bow Road *Met & Dist* CE38 **57**
Brent Cross *N'thn* BQ33 **46**
Brixton *Vic* BY45 **66**
Bromley by Bow *Met & Dist* CF38 **57**
Buckhurst Hill *Cent* CJ27 **40**
Burnt Oak *N'thn* BN30 **37**

Caledonian Road *Picc* BX35 **47**
Camden Town *N'thn* BV37 **56**
Cannon Street *Dist & Circle* BZ40 **57**
Canons Park *J'lee* BL29 **37**
Chalfont & Latimer *Met* AR23 **25**
Chalk Farm *N'thn* BV36 **56**
Chancery Lane *Cent* BY39 **56**
Charing Cross *B'loo, N'thn & J'lee* BW40 **56**
Chesham *Mer* OUTSIDE ATLAS AREA
Chigwell *Cent* CL27 **40**
Chiswick Park *Dist* BN42 **65**
Chorleywood *Met* AU24 **25**
Clapham Common *N'thn* BW45 **66**
Clapham North *N'thn* BX45 **66**
Clapham South *N'thn* BV46 **76**
Cockfosters *Picc* BV24 **29**
Colindale *N'thn* BO31 **46**
Collier's Wood *N'thn* BT50 **76**
Covent Garden *Picc* BX40 **56**
Croxley *Met* AZ25 **26**

Dagenham East *Dist* CS36 **59**
Dagenham Heathway *Dist* CQ36 **59**
Debden *Cent* CM24 **31**
Dollis Hill *J'lee* BP35 **46**

Ealing Broadway *Dist & Cent* BK39 **54**
Ealing Common *Dist & Picc* BL40 **55**
Earl's Court *Dist & Picc* BS42 **66**
East Acton *Cent* BO39 **55**
Eastcote *Met & Picc* BD33 **45**
East Finchley *N'thn* BU31 **47**
East Ham *Dist & Met* CK36 **58**
East Putney *Dist* BR46 **75**
Edgware *N'thn* BM29 **37**
Edgware Road *Met, Dist, B'loo & Circle* BU39 **56**
Elephant and Castle *N'thn & B'loo* BY41 **66**
Elm Park *Dist* CU35 **50**
Embankment *B'loo, N'thn, Dist & Circle* BX40 **56**
Epping *Cent* CO19 **23**
Euston *N'thn & Vic* BW38 **56**
Euston Square *Circle & Met* BW38 **56**

Fairlop *Cent* CM30 **40**
Farringdon *Met & Circle* BY39 **56**
Finchley Central *N'thn* BS30 **38**
Finchley Road *Met & J'lee* BT36 **56**
Finsbury Park *Picc & Vic* BY34 **47**
Fulham Broadway *Dist* BS43 **66**

Gants Hill *Cent* CL32 **49**
Gloucester Road *Picc, Dist & Circle* BT42 **66**
Golders Green *N'thn* BS33 **47**
Goldhawk Road *Met* BQ41 **65**
Goodge Street *N'thn* NW39 **56**
Grange Hill *Cent* CM28 **40**
Great Portland Street *Met & Circle* BV38 **56**
Greenford *Cent* BG37 **54**
Green Park *Picc, Vic & J'lee* BV40 **56**
Gunnersbury *Dist* BM42 **65**

Hainault *Cent* CN29 **40**
Hammersmith *Met, Picc & Dist* BQ42 **65**
Hampstead *N'thn* BT35 **47**
Hanger Lane *Cent* BL38 **55**
Harlesden *B'loo* BN37 **55**
Harrow & Wealdstone *B'loo* BH31 **45**
Harrow-on-the-Hill *Met* BH32 **45**
Hatton Cross *Picc* BB45 **63**
Heathrow Central (Terminals 1, 2 & 3) *Picc* AZ45 **63**
Heathrow (Terminal 4) *Picc* BA46 **73**
Hendon Central *N'thn* BQ32 **46**
High Barnet *N'thn* BS24 **29**
Highbury and Islington *Vic* BY36 **56**
Highgate *N'thn* BV32 **47**
High Street Kensington *Dist & Circle* BS41 **66**
Hillingdon *Met & Picc* AZ35 **44**
Holborn *Cent & Picc* BX39 **56**
Holland Park *Cent* BR40 **56**
Holloway Road *Picc* BX35 **47**
Hornchurch *Dist* CV34 **51**

Hounslow Central *Picc* BF45 **64**
Hounslow East *Picc* BG44 **64**
Hounslow West *Picc* BE44 **64**
Hyde Park Corner *Picc* BV41 **66**

Ickenham *Met & Picc* BA35 **44**

Kennington *N'thn* BY42 **66**
Kensal Green *B'loo* BQ38 **55**
Kensington (Olympia) *Dist* BR41 **65**
Kentish Town *N'thn* BW35 **47**
Kenton *B'loo* BJ32 **45**
Kew Gardens *Dist* BM44 **65**
Kilburn *J'lee* BR36 **55**
Kilburn Park *B'loo* BS37 **56**
Kingsbury *J'lee* BM32 **46**
King's Cross, St Pancras *N'th, Picc, Met, Circle & Vic* BX38 **56**
Knightsbridge *Picc* BU41 **66**

Ladbroke Grove *Met* BR39 **55**
Lambeth North *B'loo* BY41 **66**
Lancaster Gate *Cent* BT40 **56**
Latimer Road *Met* BQ40 **55**
Leicester Square *N'thn & Picc* BW40 **56**
Leyton *Cent* CF34 **48**
Leytonstone *Cent* CG33 **49**
Liverpool Street *Met, Circle & Cent* CA39 **57**
London Bridge *N'thn* BZ40 **57**
Loughton *Cent* CK25 **31**

Maida Vale *B'loo* BS38 **56**
Manor House *Picc* BY33 **47**
Mansion House *Dist & Circle* BZ40 **57**
Marble Arch *Cent* BU39 **56**
Marylebone *B'loo* BU39 **56**
Mile End *Cent, Met & Dist* CD38 **57**
Mill Hill East *N'thn* BR29 **37**
Monument *Dist & Circle* BZ40 **57**
Moorgate *N'thn, Met & Circle* BZ39 **57**
Moor Park *Met* BA27 **35**
Morden *N'thn* BS52 **86**
Mornington Crescent *N'thn* BW37 **56**
Neasden *J'lee* BO35 **46**
Newbury Park *Cent* CM32 **49**
New Cross *E. Lon* CD43 **67**
New Cross Gate *E. Lon* CD43 **67**
North Acton *Cent* BN39 **55**
North Ealing *Picc* BL39 **55**
Northfields *Picc* BK41 **64**
North Harrow *Met* BF32 **45**
Northolt *Cent* BF36 **54**
North Weald *Cent* CR17 **23**
North Wembley *B'loo* BK34 **45**
Northwick Park *Met* BJ33 **45**
Northwood *Met* BB29 **35**
Northwood Hills *Met* BC30 **35**
Notting Hill Gate *Cent, Dist & Circle* BS40 **56**

Oakwood *Picc* BW25 **29**
Old Street *N'thn* BZ38 **57**
Ongar *Cent* CX17 **24**
Osterley *Picc* BG43 **64**
Oval *N'thn* BY43 **66**
Oxford Circus *B'loo, Cent & Vic* BW39 **56**

Paddington *B'loo, Met, Dist & Circle* BT39 **56**
Park Royal *Picc* BM38 **55**
Parsons Green *Dist* BS44 **66**
Perivale *Cent* BJ37 **54**
Piccadilly Circus *Picc & B'loo* BW40 **56**
Pimlico *Vic* BW42 **66**
Pinner *Met* BE31 **45**
Plaistow *Met & Dist* CG37 **58**
Preston Road *Met* BL33 **46**
Putney Bridge *Dist* BR45 **65**

Queensbury *J'lee* BL31 **46**
Queen's Park *B'loo* BR37 **55**
Queensway *Cent* BS40 **56**

Ravenscourt Park *Dist* BP42 **65**
Rayners Lane *Met & Picc* BE33 **45**
Redbridge *Cent* CJ32 **49**
Regent's Park *B'loo* BV38 **56**
Richmond *Dist* BL45 **65**
Rickmansworth *Met* AX26 **35**
Roding Valley *Cent* CJ28 **40**
Rotherhithe *E. Lon* CC41 **67**
Royal Oak *Met* BS39 **56**
Ruislip *Met & Picc* BB33 **44**
Ruislip Gardens *Cent* BC35 **44**
Ruislip Manor *Met & Picc* BC33 **44**
Russell Square *Picc* BX38 **56**

St. James's Park *Dist & Circle* BW41 **66**
St. John's Wood *J'lee* BT37 **56**
St. Paul's *Cent* BZ39 **57**
Seven Sisters *Vic* CA32 **48**
Shadwell *E. Lon* CB39 **57**
Shepherd's Bush *Cent & Met* BQ40 **55**
Shoreditch *E. Lon* CA38 **57**
Sloane Square *Dist & Circle* BV42 **66**
Snaresbrook *Cent* CH32 **49**
South Ealing *Picc* BK41 **64**
Southfields *Dist* BR47 **75**
Southgate *Picc* BW26 **38**
South Harrow *Picc* BG34 **45**
South Kensington *Picc, Dist & Circle* BT42 **66**
South Kenton *B'loo* BK33 **45**
South Ruislip *Cent* BD35 **45**
South Wimbledon *N'thn* BS50 **76**
South Woodford *Cent* CH31 **49**
Stamford Brook *Dist* BO42 **65**
Stanmore *J'lee* BK28 **36**
Stepney Green *Dist & Met* CC38 **57**
Stockwell *N'thn & Vic* BX44 **66**
Stonebridge Park *B'loo* BM36 **55**

Stratford *Cent* CF36 **57**
Sudbury Hill *Picc* BH35 **45**
Sudbury Town *Picc* BJ36 **54**
Surrey Quays *E. Lon* CC42 **67**
Swiss Cottage *J'lee* BT36 **56**

Temple *Circle & Dist* BX40 **56**
Theydon Bois *Cent* CN21 **31**
Tooting Bec *N'thn* BV48 **76**
Tooting Broadway *N'thn* BU49 **76**
Tottenham Court Road *Cent & N'thn* BW39 **56**
Tottenham Hale *Vic* CB31 **48**
Totteridge and Whetstone *N'thn* BT27 **38**
Tower Hill *Circle & Dist* CA40 **57**
Tufnell Park *N'thn* BW35 **47**
Turnham Green *Dist & Picc* BO42 **65**
Turnpike Lane *Picc* BY31 **47**

Upminster *Dist* CY34 **51**
Upminster Bridge *Dist* CX34 **51**
Upney *Dist* CN36 **58**
Upton Park *Dist & Met* CJ37 **58**
Uxbridge *Met & Picc* AX36 **53**

Vauxhall *Vic* BX43 **66**
Victoria *Circle, Dist & Vic* BV41 **66**

Walthamstow Central *Vic* CE32 **48**
Wanstead *Cent* CH32 **49**
Wapping *E. Lon* CC40 **57**
Warren Street *N'thn & Vic* BW38 **56**
Warwick Avenue *B'loo* BT38 **56**
Waterloo *N'thn & B'loo* BY41 **66**
Watford *Met* BB24 **26**
Wembley Central *B'loo* BL36 **55**
Wembley Park *Met & J'lee* BM34 **46**
West Acton *Cent* BM39 **55**
Westbourne Park *Met* BR39 **55**
West Brompton *Dist* BS42 **66**
West Finchley *N'thn* BS29 **38**
West Ham *Met & Dist* CG38 **58**
West Hampstead *J'lee* BS36 **56**
West Harrow *Met* BG32 **45**
West Kensington *Dist* BR42 **65**
Westminster *Circle & Dist* BX41 **66**
West Ruislip *Cent* BA34 **44**
Whitechapel *Met, Dist & E. Lon* CB39 **57**
White City *Cent* BQ40 **55**
Willesden Green *J'lee* BQ36 **55**
Willesden Junction *B'loo* BO38 **55**
Wimbledon *Dist* BR50 **75**
Wimbledon Park *Dist* BR48 **76**
Woodford *Cent* CH29 **40**
Wood Green *Picc* BY30 **38**
Woodside Park *N'thn* BS28 **38**

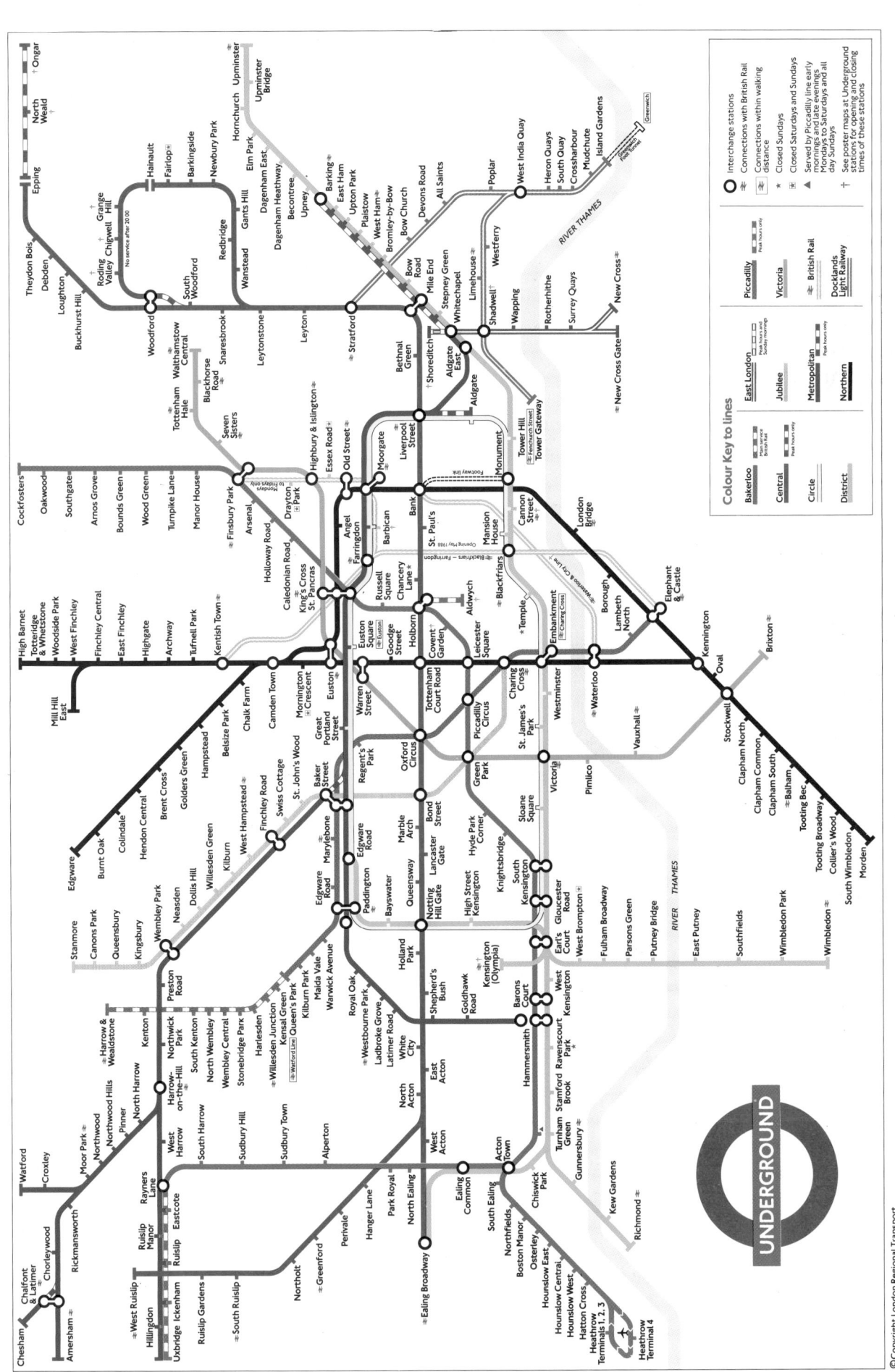

Abbey Wood   CP41 **69**
Acton Central   BN40 **55**
Acton Main Line
BN39 **55**
Addiscombe   CA54 **87**
Addlestone   AX56 **92**
Albany Park   CP48 **79**
Alexandra Palace
BX30 **38**
Amersham   AO22 **25**
Anerley   CB51 **87**
Angel Road   CC28 **39**
Apsley   AY16 **17**
Ashford   AY49 **73**
Ashtead   BL61 **103**

Balham   BV47 **76**
Bank   BZ39 **57**
Banstead   BR60 **94**
Barbican   BZ39 **57**
Barking   CM36 **58**
Barnehurst   CS44 **69**
Barnes   BP45 **65**
Barnes Bridge   BO44 **65**
Bat and Ball   CV64 **108**
Battersea Park   BV43 **66**
Bayford   BY12 **11**
Beckenham Hill
CF49 **77**
Beckenham Junction
CE51 **87**
Beddington Lane
BW53 **86**
Bellingham   CE48 **77**
Belmont   BS58 **95**
Belvedere   CR41 **69**
Berkhamsted   AR12 **7**
Berrylands   BM52 **85**
Betchworth   BO69 **120**
Bethnal Green   CB38 **57**
Bexley   CR47 **79**
Bexleyheath   CQ45 **69**
Bickley   CK52 **88**
Birkbeck   CC52 **87**
Blackfriars   BY40 **56**
Blackheath   CG44 **68**
Blackhorse Road
CC31 **48**
Bookham   BE65 **102**
Bowes Park   BX29 **38**
Boxhill and Westhumble
BJ69 **119**
Brentford   BK43 **64**
Brentwood   DB27 **42**
Bricket Wood   BF18 **18**
Brimsdown   CD24 **30**
Brixton   BY45 **66**
Brockley   CD45 **67**
Bromley North   CH51 **88**
Bromley South
CH52 **88**
Brondesbury   BR36 **55**
Brondesbury Park
BR37 **55**
Brookman's Park
BR16 **19**
Broxbourne   CE13 **12**
Bruce Grove   CA30 **39**
Bushey   BD25 **27**
Bush Hill Park   CA25 **30**
Byfleet and New Haw
AX58 **92**

Caledonian Road and
Barnsbury   BX36 **56**
Cambridge Heath
CB37 **57**
Camden Road
BW36 **56**

Canning Town
CG39 **58**
Cannon Street   BZ40 **57**
Canonbury   BZ35 **48**
Carpenders Park
BD27 **36**
Carshalton   BU56 **95**
Carshalton Beeches
BU57 **95**
Castle Bar Park
BH39 **54**
Caterham   CB65 **105**
Catford   CE47 **77**
Catford Bridge   CE47 **77**
Chadwell Heath
CP33 **50**
Chalfont & Latimer
AR23 **25**
Charing Cross   BX40 **56**
Charlton   CJ42 **68**
Cheam   BR57 **94**
Chelsfield   CO56 **98**
Chertsey   AV54 **82**
Cheshunt   CD18 **21**
Chessington North
BL56 **94**
Chessington South
BK57 **93**
Chilworth   AV73 **118**
Chingford   CG26 **40**
Chipstead   BU62 **104**
Chislehurst   CL51 **88**
Chiswick   BN43 **65**
Chorleywood   AU24 **25**
Clandon   AW68 **110**
Clapham   BW45 **66**
Clapham Junction
BU45 **65**
Clapton   CB34 **48**
Claygate   BH57 **93**
Clock House   CD51 **87**
Cobham and Stoke
D'Abernon   BE62 **102**
Coulsdon South
BW61 **104**
Crayford   CT46 **79**
Crews Hill   BX20 **20**
Cricklewood   BQ35 **46**
Crofton Park   CD46 **77**
Crouch Hill   BX33 **47**
Croxley Green   BA25 **26**
Crystal Palace   CB50 **77**
Cuffley   BX18 **20**
Custom House
CH40 **58**

Dagenham Dock
CQ38 **59**
Dalston (Kingsland)
CA36 **57**
Dartford   CW46 **80**
Datchet   AQ44 **62**
Denham   AW33 **44**
Denham Golf Club
AU33 **43**
Denmark Hill   BZ44 **67**
Deptford   CE43 **67**
Dorking   BK70 **119**
Dorking Deepdene
BK70 **119**
Dorking West   BH71 **119**
Drayton Green
BH39 **54**
Drayton Park   BY35 **47**
Dunton Green
CT63 **107**

Ealing Broadway
BK40 **54**

Earlsfield   BT47 **76**
Earlswood   BU71 **121**
East Croydon   BZ55 **87**
East Dulwich   CA45 **67**
East Tilbury   DK42 **71**
Eden Park   CE53 **87**
Effingham Junction
BC65 **101**
Egham   AT49 **72**
Elephant & Castle
BZ42 **67**
Elmers End   CC52 **87**
Elmstead Woods
CK50 **78**
Elstree and Borehamwood
BM24 **28**
Eltham   CK46 **78**
Emerson Park   CW33 **51**
Enfield Chase   BZ24 **30**
Enfield Lock   CD22 **30**
Enfield Town   CA24 **30**
Epsom   BN60 **94**
Epsom Downs   BP61 **103**
Erith   CT42 **69**
Esher   BG55 **84**
Essex Road   BZ36 **57**
Euston   BW38 **56**
Ewell East   BP58 **94**
Ewell West   BO58 **94**
Eynsford   CV56 **99**

Falconwood   CM45 **68**
Farningham Road
CX51 **90**
Farringdon   BY39 **56**
Feltham   BC47 **73**
Fenchurch Street
CA40 **57**
Finchley Road & Frognal
BT35 **47**
Finsbury Park   BY34 **47**
Forest Gate   CH35 **49**
Forest Hill   CC48 **77**
Fulwell   BG49 **74**

Garston (Herts)
BD21 **27**
Gerrards Cross
AS32 **43**
Gidea Park   CU31 **50**
Gipsy Hill   CA49 **77**
Goodmayes   CO33 **50**
Gordon Hill   BY23 **29**
Gospel Oak   BV35 **47**
Grange Park   BY25 **29**
Gravesend   DG46 **81**
Grays   DD43 **71**
Greenford   BG37 **54**
Greenhithe   DA46 **80**
Greenwich   CE43 **67**
Grove Park   CH48 **78**
Guildford   AR71 **118**
Gunnersbury   BM42 **65**

Hackbridge   BV55 **86**
Hackney Central
CB36 **57**
Hackney Downs
CB35 **48**
Hackney Wick   CE36 **57**
Hadley Wood   BT22 **29**
Hampstead Heath
BU35 **47**
Hampton   BF51 **84**
Hampton Court
BH52 **84**
Hampton Wick   BK51 **84**
Hanwell   BH40 **54**
Harlesden   BN37 **55**

Harlow Mill   CP8 **6**
Harlow Town   CM9 **6**
Harold Wood   CW30 **42**
Harringay   BY32 **47**
Harringay Stadium
BY32 **47**
Harrow and Wealdstone
BH31 **45**
Harrow-on-the-Hill
BH32 **45**
Hatch End   BF29 **36**
Hatfield   BQ12 **10**
Haydons Road   BT49 **76**
Hayes   CG54 **88**
Hayes and Harlington
BB41 **63**
Headstone Lane
BF30 **36**
Hemel Hemstead
AW15 **8**
Hendon   BP32 **46**
Herne Hill   BY46 **76**
Hersham   BE55 **84**
Highams Park   CF29 **39**
Highbury and Islington
BY36 **56**
Hinchley Wood
BH55 **84**
Hither Green   CG46 **78**
Homerton   CC36 **57**
Honor Oak Park
CC46 **77**
Hornsey   BX31 **47**
Horsley   BB66 **110**
Hounslow   BF46 **74**
How Wood   BG17 **18**
Hurst Green   CG69 **115**

Ilford   CL34 **49**
Isleworth   BH44 **64**
Iver   AV41 **62**

Kempton Park (Race days
only)   BC50 **73**
Kemsing   CY63 **108**
Kenley   BZ60 **96**
Kensal Green   BQ38 **55**
Kensal Rise   BQ37 **55**
Kensington Olympia
BR41 **65**
Kent House   CD51 **87**
Kentish Town
BW35 **47**
Kentish Town West
BV36 **56**
Kenton   BJ32 **45**
Kew Bridge   BL42 **65**
Kew Gardens   BM44 **65**
Kidbrooke   CH45 **68**
Kilburn High Road
BS37 **56**
Kings Road   DX37 **56**
Kings Cross Thameslink
BX38 **56**
Kings Langley   BA19 **17**
Kingston   BL51 **85**
Kingswood   BR64 **103**
Knockholt   CQ58 **98**

Ladywell   CE46 **77**
Langley (Bucks)
AT41 **62**
Leatherhead   BJ64 **102**
Lee   CH46 **78**
Lewisham   CF45 **67**
Leyton Midland Road
CF33 **48**

Leytonstone High Road CG34 **49**
Limehouse CD39 **57**
Liverpool Street CA39 **57**
London Bridge BZ40 **57**
London Fields CB36 **57**
London Road (Guildford) AS70 **118**
Longcross AP54 **82**
Longfield DC52 **90**
Loughborough Junction BY45 **66**
Lower Edmonton CB27 **39**
Lower Sydenham CD49 **77**

Malden Manor BO54 **85**
Manor Park CJ35 **49**
Maryland CG36 **58**
Marylebone BU38 **56**
Maze Hill CG43 **68**
Merstham BW67 **113**
Merton Park BS51 **86**
Mill Hill Broadway BO29 **37**
Mitcham BU52 **86**
Mitcham Junction BV53 **86**
Moorgate BZ39 **57**
Moor Park BA27 **35**
Morden Road BS51 **86**
Morden South BS53 **86**
Mortlake BN45 **65**
Motspur Park BP53 **85**
Mottingham CK47 **78**

New Barnet BT24 **29**
New Beckenham CD50 **77**
New Cross CD43 **67**
New Cross Gate CD43 **67**
New Eltham CL47 **78**
New Malden BO52 **85**
New Southgate BV28 **38**
Norbiton BM51 **85**
Norbury BX51 **86**
North Dulwich BZ46 **77**
Northfleet DD46 **81**
Northolt Park BF35 **45**
North Sheen BM45 **65**
Northumberland Park CB29 **39**
North Wembley BK34 **45**
North Woolwich CL41 **68**
Norwood Junction CB52 **87**
Nunhead CC45 **67**
Nutfield BX71 **121**

Oakleigh Park BU26 **38**
Ockendon DA38 **60**
Old Street BZ38 **57**
Orpington CN55 **88**
Otford CV61 **108**
Oxshott BG60 **93**
Oxted CG68 **115**

Paddington BT39 **56**
Palmers Green BX28 **38**
Park Street BG16 **18**
Peckham Rye CB44 **67**
Penge East CC50 **77**
Penge West CB50 **77**

Petts Wood CM53 **88**
Plumstead CM42 **68**
Ponders End CD25 **30**
Potters Bar BR19 **19**
Primrose Hill BV36 **56**
Purfleet CX42 **70**
Purley BY59 **95**
Purley Oaks BZ58 **96**
Putney BR45 **65**

Queens Park BR37 **55**
Queenstown Road (Battersea) BV44 **66**
Queens Road (Peckham) CC44 **67**

Radlett BJ21 **27**
Rainham CT38 **59**
Ravensbourne CF50 **77**
Raynes Park BQ51 **85**
Rectory Road CA34 **48**
Redhill BV70 **121**
Reedham BX60 **95**
Reigate BS70 **121**
Richmond BL45 **65**
Rickmansworth AX26 **35**
Riddlesdown BZ59 **96**
Romford CT32 **50**
Roydon CH10 **13**
Rye House CF11 **12**

St. Albans BH13 **9**
St. Albans Abbey BG14 **9**
St. Helier BS53 **86**
St. James Street CD32 **48**
St. John's CE44 **67**
St. Margaret's BJ46 **74**
St. Mary Cray CO52 **89**
St. Pancras BX38 **56**
Sanderstead BZ58 **96**
Sawbridgeworth CQ5 **6**
Seer Green AO29 **34**
Selhurst CA53 **87**
Seven Kings CN33 **49**
Sevenoaks CU65 **107**
Seven Sisters CA32 **48**
Shalford AS73 **118**
Shenfield DD26 **122**
Shepperton BA53 **83**
Shoreham CU59 **98**
Shortlands CG51 **88**
Sidcup CO48 **79**
Silver Street CA28 **39**
Silvertown & London City Airport CK40 **58**
Slade Green CU44 **69**
Slough AP40 **52**
Smitham BX61 **104**
South Acton BN41 **65**
Southall BE41 **64**
South Bermondsey CC42 **67**
Southbury CB24 **30**
South Croydon BZ56 **96**
South Greenford BH38 **54**
South Hampstead BT36 **56**
South Kenton BK33 **45**
South Merton BR52 **85**
South Ruislip BD35 **45**
South Tottenham CA32 **48**
Staines AW49 **73**
Stamford Hill CA33 **48**

Stoke Newington CA34 **48**
Stonebridge Park BM36 **55**
Stone Crossing CZ46 **80**
Stoneleigh BP56 **94**
Stratford CF36 **57**
Strawberry Hill BH48 **74**
Streatham BW49 **76**
Streatham Common BW50 **76**
Streatham Hill BX48 **76**
Sudbury and Harrow Road BJ35 **45**
Sudbury Hill Harrow BH35 **45**
Sunbury BC51 **83**
Sundridge Park CH50 **78**
Sunnymeads AS45 **62**
Surbiton BL53 **85**
Sutton BT57 **95**
Sutton Common BS55 **86**
Swanley CS52 **89**
Swanscombe DC46 **81**
Sydenham CC49 **77**
Sydenham Hill CA48 **77**
Syon Lane BJ43 **64**

Tadworth BQ64 **103**
Tattenham Corner BP62 **103**
Teddington BJ50 **74**
Thames Ditton BH54 **84**
Theobalds Grove CC19 **21**
Thornton Heath BZ52 **87**
Tilbury Riverside DG45 **71**
Tilbury Town DF44 **71**
Tolworth BM55 **85**
Tooting BU50 **76**
Tottenham Hale CB31 **48**
Tulse Hill BY48 **76**
Turkey Street CC22 **30**
Twickenham BJ47 **74**

Upminster CY34 **51**
Upper Halliford BB51 **83**
Upper Holloway BW34 **47**
Upper Warlingham CB62 **105**

Vauxhall BX42 **66**
Victoria BV42 **66**
Virginia Water AS53 **82**

Waddon BY56 **95**
Waddon Marsh BX54 **86**
Wallington BV57 **95**
Waltham Cross CD20 **21**
Walthamstow Central CE32 **48**
Walthamstow Queen's Road CD32 **48**
Walthamstow Wood Street CF31 **48**

Walton on Thames BC56 **92**
Wandsworth Common BU47 **76**
Wandsworth Road BW44 **66**
Wandsworth Town BS45 **66**
Wanstead Park CH35 **49**
Waterloo BY41 **66**
Watford High Street BD24 **27**
Watford Junction BD23 **27**
Watford North BD22 **27**
Watford Stadium (for football only) BC25 **26**
Watford West BB25 **26**
Welham Green BQ15 **10**
Welling CO44 **69**
Welwyn Garden City BQ8 **5**
Welwyn North BR5 **5**
Wembley Central BL36 **55**
Wembley Stadium BL35 **46**
Westbourne Park BR39 **55**
West Byfleet AW59 **92**
Westcombe Park CH42 **68**
West Croydon BZ54 **87**
West Drayton AY40 **53**
West Dulwich BZ47 **77**
West Ealing BJ40 **54**
West Ham CG38 **58**
West Hampstead BS36 **56**
West Horndon DE32 **123**
West Norwood BY49 **76**
West Ruislip BA34 **44**
West Sutton BS56 **95**
West Wickham CF54 **87**
Weybridge AZ57 **92**
White Hart Lane CA29 **39**
Whitton BG47 **74**
Whyteleaf CA62 **105**
Whyteleaf South CB63 **105**
Willesden Junction BO38 **55**
Wimbledon BR50 **75**
Wimbledon Chase BR51 **85**
Winchmore Hill BY26 **38**
Windsor and Eton Central AO44 **61**
Windsor and Eton Riverside AO43 **61**
Woking AS62 **100**
Woldingham CC64 **105**
Woodgrange Park CJ35 **49**
Woodmansterne BV61 **104**
Woodside CB53 **87**
Wood Street CF31 **48**
Woolwich Arsenal CL42 **68**
Woolwich Dockyard CK42 **68**
Worcester Park BP54 **85**
Worplesdon AQ65 **100**
Wraysbury AT46 **72**

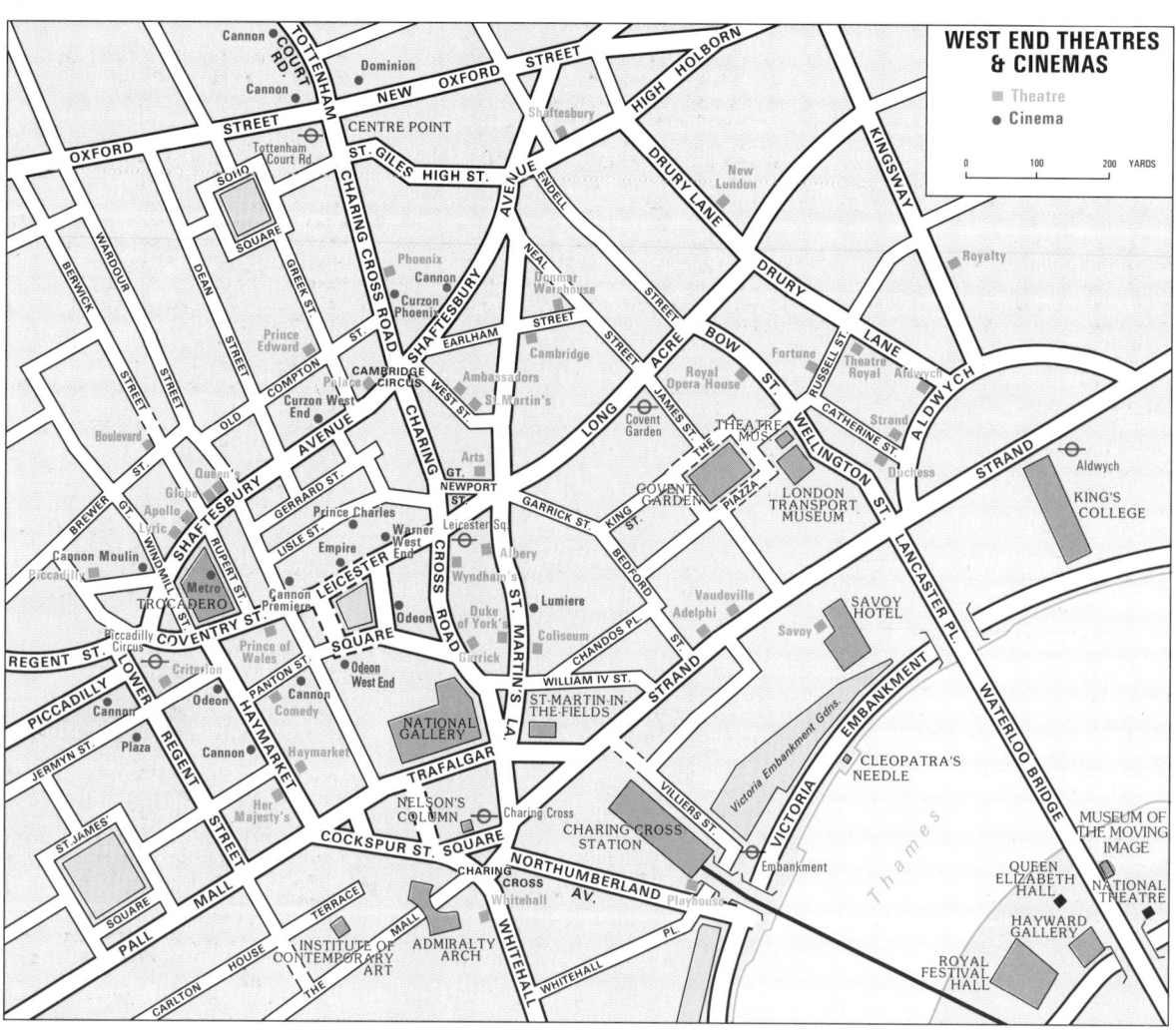

WEST END THEATRES & CINEMAS
- ■ Theatre
- ● Cinema

0   100   200   YARDS

Theatres

ADELPHI	The Strand	071 836 7611
ALBERRY	St. Martin's La,	071 836 3878
ALDWYCH	Aldwich	071 836 6404
*ALMEIDA	Almeida St. N1	071 359 4404
AMBASSADORS	West St.	071 836 6111
APOLLO	Shaftesbury	071 437 2663
*APOLLO VICTORIA	Wilton Rd. SW1	071 828 8665
ARTS	Gt. Newport St.	071 836 2132
*BARBICAN	Barbican Centre	071 638 8891
CAMBRIDGE	Earlham St.	071 379 5299
COMEDY	Panton St.	071 930 2578
CRITERION	Piccadilly	071 930 3216
DONMAR WAREHOUSE	Earlham St.	071 240 8230
*DRILL HALL	Chenies St. WC1	071 637 8270
DUCHESS	Catherine St.	071 839 1134
DUKE OF YORK'S	St. Martin's La.	071 836 5122
FORTUNE	Russel St.	071 836 2238
GARRICK	Charing Cross Rd.	071 379 6107
GLOBE	Shaftesbury Av.	071 437 3667
HAYMARKET	Haymarket	071 930 9832
(Theatre Royal)		
HER MAJESTY'S	Haymarket	071 839 3344
*LONDON PALLADIUM	Argyle St.	071 437 7373
LYRIC	Shaftesbury Av.	071 437 3686
*MAYFAIR	Stratton St. W1	071 629 3036
*MERMAID	Blackfriars EC4	071 236 5568
NATIONAL THEATRE	South Bank	071 928 2252
NEW LONDON	Drury La.	071 405 0072
*OLD VIC	Waterloo Rd. SE1	071 928 7616
*OPEN AIR THEATRE	Regents Park	071 486 2431
PALACE	Shaftesbury Av.	071 434 0909
PHOENIX	Charing Cross Rd.	071 836 2294
PICCADILLY	Denman St.	071 437 4506
PLAYHOUSE	Northumberland Av.	071 839 4401
QUEENS	Shaftesbury Av.	071 734 1166
PRINCE EDWARD	Old Compton St.	071 734 8951
PRINCE OF WALES	Coventry St.	071 839 5989
*ROYAL COURT	Sloane Sq. SW1	071 730 1745
ROYALTY	Kingsway	071 831 0660
SAVOY	Strand	071 836 8888
SHAFTESBURY	Shaftesbury Av.	071 379 5399
*SOHO POLY	Riding House St. W1	071 636 9050
ST. MARTINS	West St.	071 836 1443
STRAND	Aldwych	071 836 2660
THEATRE ROYAL	Drury La.	071 836 8108

VAUDEVILLE	Strand	071 836 9987
*VICTORIA PALACE	Victoria St. SW1	071834 1317
WHITEHALL	Whitehall	071 930 7765
WYNDHAM'S	Charing Cross Rd.	071 836 3028

Concert Halls, Opera and Ballet

*BARBICAN HALL	Barbican Centre	071 638 8891
COLISEUM	St. Martins La.	071 836 3161
QUEEN ELIZABETH HALL	South Bank	071 928 3191
ROYAL OPERA HOUSE	Covent Garden	071 240 1066
*SADLERS WELLS	Rosebery Av. EC1	071 278 8916

Cinemas

BOULEVARD	Berwick St.	071 437 2661
*CANNON	Baker St.	071 935 9772
*CANNON	Kings Rd. Chelsea	071 352 5096
*CANNON	Edgware Rd.	071 723 5901
CANNON	Fulham Rd.	071 370 2636
CANNON	Haymarket	071 839 1527
CANNON	Oxford St.	071 636 0310
CANNON	Panton St.	071 930 0631
CANNON	Piccadilly	071 437 3561
CANNON PREMIERE	Leicester Sq,	071 439 4470
CANNON	Shaftesbury Av.	071 836 6279
CANNON	Tottenham Court Rd.	071 636 6148
CANNON MOULIN	Gt. Windmill St.	071 437 1653
*CHELSEA	Kings Rd. SW3	071 351 3742
*CURZON	Curzon St. W1	071 499 3737
CURZON PHOENIX	Charing Cross Rd.	071 240 9661
CURZON WEST END	Shaftesbury Av.	071 439 4805
DOMINION	Tottenham Court Rd.	071 580 9562
EMPIRE	Leicester Sq.	071 240 7200
ODEON WEST END	Leicester Sq.	071 930 5252
LUMIERE	St. Martins La.	071 379 3014
METRO	Rupert St.	071 437 0757
*MINEMA	Knightsbridge	071 235 4225
ODEON	Haymarket	071 839 7697
*ODEON	Kensington	071 602 6644
ODEON	Leicester Sq.	071 930 6111
*ODEON	Marble Arch	071 723 2011
PLAZA	Piccadilly Circus	071 240 7200
PRINCE CHARLES	Leicester Sq.	071 437 8181
*RENOIR	Brunswick Sq.	071 837 8402
SCREEN	Baker St.	071 935 2772
WARNER WEST END	Leicester Sq,	071 439 0791

* NOT SHOWN ON THE MAP

The following is a comprehensive listing of the places of interest which appear on map pages 1-123

Abbey Mills Pumping Station CF37 57
Admiralty BW40 3
Admiralty Arch BW40 3
Aeolian Hall BV40 3
Albert Memorial BT41 3
Aldenham Reservoir BJ25 27
Alexandra Palace BW30 38
Annesley Lodge, Platts Lane, Hampstead BS34 47
Apsley House BV41 3
Arkley Manor, Barnet BP24 28
Arsenal Football Ground BY34 47
Australia House BX39 2
Avery Hill Park, Eltham CM46 78
Baden Powell House BT41 3
Baker Street BU38 1
Bakers Hall CA40 4
Bank of England BZ39 2
Bankside Gallery BY40 4
Banqueting House BX40 4
Barber Surgeons Hall BZ39 2
Barbican BZ39 2
Battersea Park BY43 66
Battersea Power Station BE43 66
Bayhurst Wood, Ruislip AY32 44
Belhus Park, Aveley CY39 60
Bentley Priory, Harrow BH27 36
Berkhamsted Castle AR12 7
Bethnal Green Museum of Childhood CB38 57
Biggin Hill Aerodrome CJ60 97
Birch Hall, Theydon Bois CM21 31
Black Charles, near Sevenoaks CX68 117
Black Park, near Slough AS37 52
Blackheath CG44 68
Bloomsbury Square BX39 2
Bow Church BZ39 2
Box Hill BK69 111
Brentford Football Ground BK43 64
Brewers Hall BZ39 2
British Museum BW39 1
British Travel Centre BW40 3
Brixton Windmill, Blenheim Gdns. BX46 76
Broadcasting House (BBC) BV39 1
Brockwell Park SE24 BY46 76
Brompton Oratory BU41 3
Bruce Castle Park, Tottenham CA30 39
Buckingham Palace BV41 3
Burgess Park SE5 CA42 4
Burlington Arcade BW40 3
Burlington House (Royal Academy) BW40 3
Bush House BX39 2
Bushy Park BJ51 84
Business Design Centre BY37 2
Camden Lock (Waterbuses) BV36 1
Camden Market (Antiques) BY37 2
Cannon Street Station BZ40 4
Canonbury Tower, Canonbury Pl. BY36 56
Carlyle's House BU43 66
Carnaby Street BW39 1
Cassiobury Park, Watford BB24 26
Cenotaph BX41 4
Central Criminal Court (Old Bailey) BY39 2
Central Hall, Westminster BW41 3
Centrepoint BW39 1
Chandos House, Chandos St. BV39 1
Charing Cross Road BW39 1
Charlton Athletic Football Ground CA52 87
Charlton House SE7 CJ43 68
Chartered Insurance Institutes Museum, Aldermanbury BZ39 2
Chartwell, near Westerham CN69 115
Chelsea Flower Show, Royal Hospital Grounds BV42 3
Chelsea Football Club BS43 66
Chelsea Old Town Hall BU42 3
Chelsea Physic Garden BU43 66
Chelsea Pottery BU42 66
Chenies Manor House AT22 25
Chertsey Museum AX54 83
Chessington Zoo BK58 93
Chevening Park CQ63 107
Chinatown, Gerrard St. BW40 3
Chiswick House BN43 65
Church Farm House Museum, Hendon BP31 46
Churchill's War Rooms BW41 3
Clandon Park, Surrey AV68 109
Clapham Common BV45 66
Clarence House BW41 3
Claridges BV40 3
Cleopatra's Needle BX40 4

Clissold Park N16 BZ34 48
Clore Gallery BX42 4
Clothworkers Hall CA40 4
Cobham Bus Museum BA60 92
College of Arms BY40 4
Commonwealth Institute BR41 65
Corn Exchange CA40 4
County Hall BX41 4
Courtauld Gallery BW38 1
Covent Garden BX40 4
Crafts Council, Waterloo Pl. BW40 3
Crystal Palace Football Ground CA52 87
Crystal Palace National Sport Centre CB50 77
Crystal Palace Park CB50 77
Cuming Museum BZ42 4
Custom House CA40 4
Cutty Sark CF43 67
Danson Park, Welling CP45 69
Dartford Heath CT47 79
Denham Aerodrome AV32 43
Denham Place AV33 43
Department of Trade & Industry BW41 3
Department of Transport & Environment BW41 3
Detillens, Limpsfield, Surrey CH68 115
Dickens' House BX38 2
Docklands Light Railway CA40 4
Doctor Johnson's House BY39 2
Dorchester Hotel BV40 3
Downe House, near Farnborough CL59 97
Downing Street BX41 4
Drapers Hall BZ39 2
Dulwich College Picture Library CA47 77
Dulwich Park CA47 77
Dulwich Picture Gallery CA47 77
Duthy Hall BZ41 4
Dyrham Park, near Barnet BP22 28
Ealing Common BL40 55
Earls Court Exhibition Hall BS42 66
Eel Pie Island BJ47 74
Elstree Aerodrome BH24 27
Eltham Palace CK46 78
Eltham Park SE9 CL45 68
Emmetts, near Sevenoaks CP68 116
Epping Forest CJ23 31
Epping Forest CG30 40
Epping Forest Museum CG26 40
Epsom Racecourse BP62 103
Eton College AO43 61
Eynsford Castle CW55 90
Fenton House, Hampstead BT34 47
Finsbury Park N4 BY33 47
Fishmongers Hall BZ40 4
Fitzroy Square W1 BW38 1
Flamstead House Museum, Greenwich CF43 67
Fleet Street BY39 2
Foreign Office BW41 3
Forty Hall & Museum, Enfield CA22 30
Founders Hall BZ40 4
Foundling Hospital Art Treasures BX38 2
Freemasons Hall BX39 2
Freud Museum, Maresfield Gdns. BT35 47
Fulham Football Club BQ44 65
Fulham Palace BR44 65
Geffryes Museum CA37 2
Geological Museum BT41 3
George Inn, Borough High St. BZ41 4
Girdlers Hall BZ39 2
Golders Hill Park NW11 BS34 47
Goldsmiths Hall BZ39 2
Gorhambury House, near St. Albans BD13 9
Grays Inn BX39 2
Great Bookham Common BE64 102
Green Park BV41 3
Greenwich Park CG43 68
Greenwich Pier CF43 67
Grocers Hall BZ39 2
Grosvenor House Hotel BV40 3
Guildhall Cathedral AQ70 118
Guildhall BZ39 2
Gunnersbury Park, Ealing BL41 65
Gypsy Moth IV CF43 67
Haberdashers Hall BZ39 2
Hackney Marshes CD34 48
Hainault Forest CP28 41
Hainault Forest CP40 41
Ham House BK47 74
Hammersmith Palais BQ42 65

Hammersmith Town Hall BP42 65
Hampstead Heath BT34 47
Hampton Court Palace BH52 84
Harrods BU41 3
Harrow School BH33 45
Hatchlands, Clandon, Surrey AY68 110
Hatfield House BQ12 10
Hayward Gallery BX40 4
Headley Heath, near Dorking BM67 112
Heathrow (London Airport) AZ45 63
Heinz Gallery, RIBA BV39 1
Historic Ships Collection CA40 4
HM Customs & Excise CA40 4
HMS 'Belfast' CA40 4
HMS 'Chrysanthemum' BY40 4
HMS 'President' BY40 4
Hogarths House, Hogarth La. BO43 65
Holiday Inn BU39 1
Holland House, Kensington BR41 65
Holland Park BR41 65
Holwood Park, near Farnborough, Kent CK57 97
Home Office BW41 3
Horniman Museum SE23 CB47 77
Horse Guards Parade BW40 3
Hounslow Heath BE46 74
Household Cavalry Museum, Windsor AO45 61
Houses of Parliament BX41 4
HQS 'Wellington' BY40 4
Hurlingham House BR45 65
Hyde Park BU40 3
Hyde Park Corner BV41 3
IBA Broadcasting Gallery, Brompton Rd. BU41 66
Ightham Mote DA67 117
Imperial College BT41 3
Imperial War Museum BY41 4
India House BX40 4
Institute of Contemporary Arts BW40 3
Inter Continental Hotel BV41 3
Ironmongers Hall BZ39 2
Ismaili Centre BT42 3
Jack Straw's Castle PH BT34 47
Jewel Tower, Old Palace Yard BX41 4
Jewish Museum BW38 1
Jordans Meeting House AP29 34
Jubilee Gardens BX40 4
Keats' House, Hampstead BU35 47
Kempton Park Racecourse BD50 74
Kensington Gardens BT40 3
Kensington Palace BS40 3
Kenwood House, Hampstead BU33 47
Kew Bridge Steam Museum BL42 65
Kew Gardens BL44 65
Kew Observatory BK45 64
Kings Road, Chelsea BU42 3
Knole House, Sevenoaks CW66 117
Knole Park, Sevenoaks CV67 117
Lambeth Palace BX41 4
Langley Park, Slough AS39 52
Leadenhall Market CA39 2
Leicester Square BW40 3
Leighton House, Holland Park Rd. BR41 65
Lesnes Abbey (remains) CP42 69
Leyton Orient Football Ground CE34 48
Limpsfield Common CH68 115
Lincolns Inn BX39 2
Linley Sambourne House, Stafford Ter. BS41 66
Little Venice (Waterbuses) BT39 1
Lloyds CA39 2
London Brass Rubbing Centre, St. Martin-in-the-Fields Church BX40 4
London Bridge BZ40 4
London Central Mosque, Regents Park BU38 1
London College of Printing BY41 4
London Diamond Centre, Hanover St. BV39 1
London Dungeon BZ40 4
London Hilton BV40 3
London Palladium BW39 1
London Peace Pagoda, Battersea Park BU43 66
London Transport Collection BK43 64
London Transport Museum BX40 4
London Zoo BV37 1
Lord's Cricket Ground & Museum BT38 1
Loseley Park, Guildford AP73 118
Lullingstone Castle CV56 99
Lullingstone Park, Eynsford, Kent CU56 98

Lullingstone Roman Villa   CU56 **98**
Lyceum Ballroom   BX40 **4**
Madame Tussauds   BV38 **1**
Mansion House   BZ39 **2**
Marble Arch   BU40 **4**
Marble Hill House, Twickenham   BK47 **74**
Marlborough House   BW40 **3**
Martinware Pottery Collection, Southall Library
BE41 **64**
Mercers Hall   BZ39 **2**
Merchant Taylors Hall   BZ39 **2**
Middlesex Guildhall   BW41 **3**
Millwall Football Ground   CC43 **67**
Milton's Cottage   AQ27 **34**
Ministry of Agriculture   BX40 **4**
Ministry of Defence   BX40 **4**
Monument, The   BZ40 **4**
Moor Park Golf Club   AZ27 **35**
Mordon College   CH44 **68**
Mosquito Aircraft Museum   BM18 **19**
Museum of Garden History, Lambeth Rd.
BX41 **4**
Museum of London   BZ39 **2**
Museum of Mankind   BW40 **3**
Museum of the Moving Image   BX40 **4**
Musical Museum, High St., Brentford
BL43 **65**
National Army Museum   BU42 **3**
National Gallery   BW40 **3**
National Maritime Museum   CF43 **67**
Old Limehouse Town Hall   CD39 **57**
National Physical Laboratory   BH50 **74**
National Portrait Gallery   BW40 **3**
National Postal Museum   BY39 **2**
Natural History Museum   BT41 **3**
Natwest Tower   CA39 **2**
Nelson's Column   BW40 **3**
New Scotland Yard   BW41 **3**
North Woolwich Station Museum   CL41 **68**
Northolt Aerodrome   BB35 **44**
Norwegian British Monument   BU40 **3**
Notting Hill Carnival, Ladbroke Gro.
BR40 **55**
Old Curiosity Shop   BX39 **2**
Old Deer Park, Richmond   BK45 **64**
Olympia   BR41 **65**
Opera House   BX39 **2**
Orleans House, Twickenham   BJ47 **74**
Osterley Park & Museum   BG42 **64**
Oval, The (Cricket Ground)   BX43 **66**
Oxford Circus   BW39 **1**
Oxford Street   BV39 **1**
Oxshott Heath   BF59 **93**
Painters Hall   BZ40 **4**
Pall Mall   BW40 **3**
Park Lane Hotel   BV40 **3**
Passmore Edwards Museum   CG36 **58**
Passport Office   BW41 **3**
Patent Office   BY39 **2**
Percival David Foundation   BW38 **1**
Petticoat Lane (Market)   CA39 **2**
Petts Wood   CM52 **88**
Pewterers Hall   BZ39 **2**
Photographers Gallery, Great Newport St.
BW40 **3**
Piccadilly Circus   BW40 **3**
Piccotts End, Hemel Hempstead   AX11 **8**
Pitshanger Manor Museum, Ealing   BK40 **54**
Plaisterers Hall   BZ39 **2**
Planetarium   BU38 **1**
Polesden Lacey   BF68 **111**
Pollocks Toy Museum   BW39 **1**
Primrose Hill Park   BU37 **1**
Prince Henry's Rooms, Fleet Street
BY39 **2**
PS 'Tattershall Castle'   BX40 **4**
Public Record Office   BY39 **2**
QPR Football Club   BP40 **55**
Quebec House (Wolfe's House)
Westerham, Kent   CM66 **115**
Queen Elizabeth II Conference Centre
BW41 **3**

Queen Elizabeth's Hunting Lodge,
Epping Forest   CG26 **40**
Queen's Gallery   BV41 **3**
Queen's Tower   BT41 **3**
Queens Club (Tennis Centre)   BR42 **65**
Queens Ice Rink   BS40 **3**
RAF Museum, Hendon   BO30 **37**
Ranmore Common, Dorking   BF70 **119**
Records Office   BY39 **2**
Regent Street   BW40 **3**
Regents Park   BU38 **1**
Richmond Palace (remains)   BK45 **64**
Richmond Park   BM47 **75**
Ritz, The   BW40 **3**
Roman Bath, Fleet St.   BY39 **2**
Rose Gardens, Royal National Rose Society,
St. Albans   BE16 **18**
Rotunda Museum of Artillery, Woolwich
CK42 **68**
Royal Academy of Arts   BW40 **3**
Royal Academy of Dramatic Art   BW38 **1**
Royal Albert Hall   BT41 **3**
Royal Botanic Gardens   BL44 **65**
Royal College of Art   BT41 **3**
Royal College of Music   BT41 **3**
Royal College of Surgeons   BX39 **2**
Royal Courts of Justice   BX39 **2**
Royal Exchange   BZ39 **2**
Royal Festival Hall   BX40 **4**
Royal Geographical Society   BT41 **3**
Royal Holloway College   AR50 **72**
Royal Horticultural Society (New Hall)
BW41 **3**
Royal Horticultural Society (Old Hall)
BW42 **3**
Royal Hospital, Chelsea   BV42 **3**
Royal Mews   BV41 **3**
Royal Naval College   CF42 **67**
Rubber Exchange   CA40 **4**
Rudolf Steiner Hall   BU38 **1**
Ruislip Lido   BA31 **44**
Runnymede   AS49 **72**
Saddlers Hall   BZ39 **2**
St. Albans Cathedral   BG13 **9**
St. Bartholomew the Great Church   BY39 **2**
St. Bride Printing Library, Bride La.   BY39 **2**
St. Brides Church, Fleet St.   BY39 **2**
St. Clement Church, Fleet St.   BY39 **2**
St. James's Palace   BW41 **3**
St. James's Park   BW41 **3**
St. John's Jerusalem, Sutton at Hone
CX50 **80**
St. Katharine's Dock   CA40 **4**
St. Lawrence Jewry Church, Gresham St.
BZ39 **2**
St. Martin-in-the-Fields Church, Trafalgar Sq.
BX40 **4**
St. Mary at Hill Church, Lovat La.   CA40 **4**
St. Paul's Cathedral   BZ39 **2**
Salisbury Hall, London Colney   BM18 **19**
Salters Hall   BZ39 **2**
Salvation Army HQ   BZ40 **4**
Sandown Park Racecourse   BG55 **84**
Savill Gardens, Windsor Great Park
AP50 **72**
Science Museum   BT41 **3**
Selfridges   BV39 **1**
Serpentine Gallery   BT41 **3**
Serpentine, The   BU40 **3**
Seymour Hall   BU39 **1**
Shakespeare Globe Museum, Bear Gdns.
BZ40 **4**
Shakespeare Memorial   BZ40 **4**
Shell Centre   BX41 **4**
Skinners Hall. Dowgate Hill   BZ40 **4**
Smithfield Market   BY39 **2**
Soane Museum   BX39 **2**
Somerset House   BX40 **4**
South Africa House   BX40 **4**
South London Art Gallery, Peckham Rd.
CA44 **67**
Southwark Cathedral   BZ40 **4**

Speakers Corner   BU40 **3**
Spitalfields Market   CA39 **2**
Squerryes Court   CM67 **115**
Stapleford Tawney Aerodrome   CR23 **32**
Stock Exchange   BZ39 **2**
Stockley Park   AZ40 **53**
Strand, The   BX40 **4**
Sutton Palace, near Guildford   AT67 **109**
Swakeley's   AZ35 **44**
Syon House, Brentford   BK44 **64**
Syon Park (Motor Museum)   BK44 **64**
Tate Gallery   BX42 **4**
Telecom Tower   BW39 **1**
Temple of Mithras   BZ40 **4**
Thames Flood Barrier   CJ41 **68**
Thames House   BX42 **4**
Theatre Museum   BX40 **4**
Thorndon Hall   DD29 **122**
Thorpe Park   AV52 **82**
Tottenham Hotspur Football Ground
CB29 **39**
Tower Hill   CA40 **4**
Tower of London   CA40 **4**
Tower Pier   CA40 **4**
Toy & Model Musem   BT40 **3**
Toynbee Hall   CA39 **2**
Trafalgar Square   BW40 **3**
Treasury   BW41 **3**
Trent Park, Enfield   BV23 **29**
Trinity House   CA40 **4**
Trocadero Centre   BW40 **3**
Twickenham Rugby Ground   BH46 **74**
University of London   BW39 **1**
US Embassy   BV40 **3**
Valley Gardens   AQ49 **72**
Verulamium   BF13 **9**
Verulamium Museum, St. Albans   BF13 **9**
Victoria & Albert Museum   BT41 **3**
Victoria Coach Station   BV42 **3**
Victoria Embankment Gardens   BX40 **4**
Victoria Park E9   CD37 **57**
Virginia Water   AP52 **82**
Wallace Collection   BV39 **1**
Waltham Abbey   CF20 **21**
Waterlow Park, Highgate   BV33 **47**
Watermens Hall   CA40 **4**
Watford Football Ground   BC25 **26**
Weald Park, Brentwood   CY26 **42**
Wellington Arch   BV41 **3**
Wellington Museum   BV41 **3**
Wembley Conference Centre   BM35 **46**
Wembley Stadium   BM35 **46**
Wentworth Golf Course   AP53 **82**
West Ham United Football Ground   CJ37 **58**
Westminster Abbey   BX41 **4**
Westminster Cathedral   BW41 **3**
Westminster City Hall   BW41 **3**
Westminster Pier   BX41 **4**
Weybridge Museum   AZ56 **92**
Whitbread Shirehorse Stables, Garret St.
BZ38 **2**
Whitechapel Art Gallery   CA39 **57**
Whitehall   BX40 **4**
William Morris Gallery, Lloyd Park E17
CE31 **48**
Wimbledon (All England Tennis Club)
BR48 **75**
Wimbledon Common   BP48 **75**
Wimbledon Football Club   BT49 **76**
Windsor Castle   AP43 **62**
Windsor Great Park   AP48 **72**
Windsor Safari Park   AM46 **61**
Wisley, Royal Horticultural Society Gardens
AY62 **101**
World of Motoring Exhibition   BK43 **64**
World Trade Centre   CA40 **4**
Wormwood Scrubs   BO39 **1**
YMCA   BW39 **1**
Zamana Gallery, Ismaili Centre   BT42 **3**

Abbey Wood SE2   CO42 **69**
Abbey Wood Estate SE2   CO41 **69**
Abbots Langley WD5   BB19 **17**
Abridge RM4   CO24 **32**
Acton W3   BM40 **55**
Addington CR0   CD56 **96**
Addiscombe CR0   CB54 **87**
Addlestone KT15   AW57 **92**
Addlestonemoor KT15   AW55 **83**
Adeyfield HP2   AZ13 **8**
Aldborough Hatch IG2   CN31 **49**
Aldenham WD2   BF22 **27**
Aldersbrook E12   CJ34 **49**
Alperton HA0   BL37 **55**
Amersham HP6   AP22 **25**
Amersham Common HP6   AP22 **25**
Anerley SE20   CB51 **87**
Anthonys GU21   AT59 **91**
Appleby Street EN7   CA16 **21**
Apps Court KT12   BC53 **83**
Apsley End HP3   AY15 **8**
Ardleigh Green RM11   CW31 **51**
Arkley EN5   BP25 **28**
Ash TN15   DC56 **99**
Ashford TW15   AZ49 **73**
Ashford Common TW15   BA50 **73**
Ashley Green HP5   AP15 **7**
Ashley Park KT12   BC55 **83**
Ashridge HP4   AP11 **7**
Ashtead KT21   BL62 **103**
Aveley RM15   CY41 **70**
Ayot Green AL6   BP6 **5**
Ayot St. Peter AL6   BO5 **5**
Bandon Hill SM6   BX56 **95**
Banstead SM7   BT61 **104**
Barking IG11   CM36 **58**
Barkingside IG6   CL31 **49**
Barnehurst DA7   CS45 **69**
Barnet EN5   BR24 **28**
Barnet Gate EN5   BO25 **28**
Barnsbury N1   BX36 **56**
Batchworth WD3   AY27 **35**
Batchworth Heath WD3   AZ28 **35**
Battersea SW11   BT44 **66**
Battlers Green WD7   BH22 **27**
Bayford SG13   BX12 **11**
Bayswater W2   BS40 **56**
Bean DA2   DB49 **80**
Beauchamp Roding CM5   DA11 **15**
Beckenham BR3   CE51 **87**
Beckton E6   CL39 **58**
Becontree RM8   CP34 **50**
Becontree Heath RM8   CR33 **50**
Beddington SM6   BW56 **95**
Beddington Corner CR4   BV54 **86**
Bedmond WD5   BB17 **17**
Belgravia SW1   BV41 **66**
Bell Bar AL9   BS15 **11**
Bellfields GU1   AR69 **118**
Belmont SM2   BS59 **95**
Belsize WD3   AV20 **16**
Belsize Park NW3   BT36 **56**
Belvedere DA17   CR42 **69**
Bennetts End HP3   AZ14 **8**
Bentley CM15   CY23 **33**
Bentley Heath EN5   BR21 **28**
Berkhamsted HP4   AR12 **7**
Bermondsey SE1   CA41 **67**
Berners Roding CM5   DC10 **15**
Berry's Green TN16   CL61 **106**
Bessel's Green TN13   CS65 **107**
Betchworth RH3   BN71 **120**
Bethnal Green E2   CB38 **57**
Betsham DA2   DC49 **81**
Bexley DA5   CR47 **79**
Bexleyheath DA7   CQ45 **69**
Bickley BR1   CK52 **88**
Biggin Hill TN16   CJ16 **106**
Birds Green CM5   DA12 **15**
Bishops Gate TW20   AP49 **72**
Blackbrook RH5   BK73 **119**
Blackcat CM5   CX11 **15**
Blackfen DA15   CO46 **79**
Blackheath SE3   CF44 **67**
Blackmore CM4   DB19 **24**
Blendon DA5   CP46 **79**
Bletchingley RH1   BZ70 **114**
Bloomsbury WC1   BW39 **56**
Bobbingworth CM5   CV15 **15**
Borehamwood WD6   BM24 **28**
Borough Green TN15   DC63 **108**
Botany Bay EN2   BW21 **29**
Botley HP5   AP18 **16**
Botleys KT16   AT55 **82**
Bourne End HP1   AU14 **7**
Bovingdon HP3   AS17 **16**
Bower Hill CM16   CO19 **23**
Bowes N13   BY29 **38**
Bowes Park N22   BX29 **38**
Bowmansgreen AL4   BL17 **19**
Box Hill KT20   BM69 **120**

Boxmoor HP1   AW14 **8**
Brand's Hill SL3   AT43 **62**
Brasted TN16   CO65 **107**
Brasted Chart TN14   CO67 **116**
Bray SL6   AH41 **61**
Bray Wick SL6   AG41 **61**
Brays Grove CM18   CO12 **14**
Brent, The DA1   CX47 **80**
Brentford TW8   BK43 **64**
Brentham W5   BK39 **54**
Brentwood CM15   DB27 **42**
Brickendon SG13   BZ12 **12**
Brickendon Green SG13   BY13 **11**
Bridge End GU23   AZ64 **101**
Bridgefoot EN6   BP20 **19**
Bridgen DA5   CQ47 **79**
Brimsdown EN3   CD23 **30**
Brixton SW2   BX46 **76**
Broadley Common EN9   CJ13 **13**
Brockham RH3   BM71 **120**
Brockley SE4   CD45 **67**
Bromley BR2   CG51 **88**
Bromley E3   CE38 **57**
Bromley Common BR2   CK55 **88**
Bromley Park BR2   CG51 **88**
Brompton SW7   BU41 **66**
Brondesbury NW2   BQ36 **55**
Brook Street CM14   DA28 **42**
Brook Vale DA11   DE47 **81**
Brookmans Park AL9   BS16 **20**
Broxbourne EN10   CD13 **12**
Buckhurst Hill IG9   CJ26 **40**
Buckland RH3   BP70 **120**
Buckshill WD4   AX20 **17**
Bull's Cross EN2   CB21 **30**
Bumble's Green EN9   CH15 **13**
Burgh Heath KT20   BR62 **103**
Burnt Oak HA8   BN29 **37**
Burpham GU4   AT68 **109**
Burwood Park KT12   BB56 **92**
Bury Street N9   CA26 **39**
Bush Hill N21   BZ25 **30**
Bush Hill Park EN1   CA25 **30**
Bushey WD2   BF26 **36**
Bushey Heath WD2   BG26 **36**
Button Street BR8   CV52 **90**
Byfleet KT14   AY60 **92**
Camberwell SE5   BZ43 **67**
Camden Town NW1   BW37 **56**
Canning Town E16   CG39 **58**
Carshalton SM1   BT56 **95**
Carshalton-on-the-Hill SM6   BU57 **95**
Cartbridge GU23   AT64 **100**
Castelnau SW13   BP43 **65**
Caterham CR3   CA65 **105**
Caterham-on-the-Hill CR3   BZ63 **105**
Catford SE6   CE47 **77**
Cattlegate EN2   BX19 **20**
Chadwell St. Mary RM16   DG42 **71**
Chaldon CR3   BX65 **104**
Chalfont Common SL9   AS28 **34**
Chalfont St. Giles HP8   AQ27 **34**
Chalfont St. Peter SL9   AR30 **34**
Chalvey SL1   AO41 **61**
Chalvey Grove SL1   AN41 **61**
Chandler's Cross WD3   AY22 **26**
Chapel Croft WD4   AW19 **17**
Charlton SE7   CJ43 **68**
Charlton TW17   BA52 **83**
Chart, The RH8   CK68 **115**
Chase Cross RM1   CT29 **41**
Chase Side EN2   BY23 **29**
Chaulden HP1   AV14 **7**
Cheam SM3   BR57 **94**
Cheam Common KT4   BQ55 **85**
Chelsea SW3   BT43 **66**
Chelsfield BR6   CQ56 **98**
Chelsham CR3   CD61 **105**
Chenies WD3   AT22 **25**
Chertsey KT16   AW54 **83**
Chesham HP5   AP18 **16**
Chesham Bois HP5   AP21 **25**
Cheshunt EN8   CD18 **21**
Chessington KT9   BK57 **94**
Chevening TN14   CR63 **107**
Chigwell IG7   CL26 **40**
Chigwell Row IG7   CO27 **41**
Childerditch CM13   DD31 **123**
Childs Hill NW2   BR34 **46**
Chingford E4   CF26 **40**
Chingford Hatch E4   CF28 **39**
Chipperfield WD4   AW19 **17**
Chipping Ongar CM5   CX18 **24**
Chipstead CR3   BU64 **104**
Chipstead TN13   CS65 **107**
Chislehurst BR7   CM51 **88**
Chislehurst West BR7   CL50 **78**
Chiswellgreen AL2   BE16 **18**
Chiswick W4   BN42 **65**
Chobham GU24   AP59 **91**
Chorleywood WD3   AV24 **25**
Chorleywood West WD3   AT24 **25**

Church End N3   BR30 **37**
Church End WD3   AW22 **26**
Church Town RH9   CC69 **114**
Churchgate EN8   CB18 **21**
Churchgate Street CM17   CQ9 **6**
Cippenham SL1   AM40 **61**
Clapham SW4   BV45 **66**
Clapham Park SW4   BW46 **76**
Clapton Park E5   CC35 **48**
Claremont Park KT10   BF57 **93**
Clay Hill EN2   BZ22 **30**
Claydon's Green CM5   CY12 **15**
Claygate KT10   BH57 **93**
Clement Street BR8   CV50 **80**
Clerkenwell EC1   BY38 **56**
Clewer SL4   AN43 **61**
Clewer Green SL4   AM45 **61**
Clewer New Town SL4   AN44 **61**
Cobbs Croft DA2   CX46 **80**
Cobham KT11   BC60 **92**
Cobham Tilt KT11   BD61 **102**
Cockfosters EN4   BV24 **29**
Coldblow DA5   CS48 **79**
Coldharbour GU22   AV61 **100**
Coldharbour TN11   CZ70 **117**
Colhan Green UB8   AY39 **53**
Collier Row RM7   CR30 **41**
Colliers Hatch CM16   CS18 **23**
Colliers Wood SW19   BT50 **76**
Colnbrook SL3   AU43 **62**
Colney Heath AL4   BN14 **10**
Colney Street AL2   BH18 **18**
Coney Hall BR4   CG55 **88**
Coombe KT2   BN50 **75**
Coopersale Common CM16   CP18 **23**
Coopersale Street CM16   CP19 **23**
Copthall Green EN9   CJ20 **22**
Corbet's Tey RM14   CX36 **60**
Cottenham Park SW20   BP51 **85**
Coulsdon CR3   BW61 **104**
Cowley UB8   AX38 **53**
Cowley Peachey UB8   AX39 **53**
Coxhill Green GU24   AQ60 **91**
Coxtie Green CM14   CY24 **33**
Cranbrook Park IG1   CK33 **49**
Cranford TW5   BD44 **64**
Cranham RM14   CY34 **51**
Crayford DA1   CS46 **79**
Creekmouth IG11   CN39 **58**
Cricklewood NW2   BQ35 **46**
Crockenhill BR8   CS53 **89**
Crockham Hill TN8   CM70 **115**
Crouch End N8   BW32 **47**
Crow Green CM15   DA24 **33**
Croxley Green WD3   AZ25 **26**
Croydon CR0   BY54 **86**
Cubitt Town E14   CF42 **67**
Cuckoo Hill HA5   BD31 **45**
Cudham TN14   CM61 **106**
Cuffley EN6   BW18 **20**
Cupid Green HP2   AZ11 **8**
Dagenham RM9   CQ36 **59**
Dalston E8   CA36 **57**
Dancers Hill EN5   BQ21 **28**
Darenth DA2   CY49 **80**
Dartford DA1   CV47 **80**
Dartmouth Park NW5   BV34 **47**
Datchet SL3   AR44 **62**
Datchet Common SL3   AR44 **62**
Dawesgreen RH2   BO73 **120**
Dawley UB3   BA41 **63**
Debden Estate IG10   CM24 **31**
Debden Green IG10   CL22 **31**
Dedworth SL4   AM44 **61**
Denham UB9   AW34 **44**
Denton DA12   DJ47 **81**
Deptford SE8   CD43 **67**
Digswell AL8   BQ6 **5**
Doddinghurst CM15   DB21 **33**
Dogkennel Green RH5   BD70 **119**
Dollis Hill NW2   BP35 **46**
Dorking RH5   BK71 **119**
Dormer's Wells UB1   BF40 **54**
Dorney SL4   AK42 **61**
Dorney Reach SL6   AJ41 **61**
Doversgreen RH2   BS72 **121**
Downe BR6   CK59 **97**
Downham BR1   CG49 **78**
Downham Estate BR1   CG48 **78**
Downs, The AL10   BP14 **10**
Downside KT11   BD62 **102**
Drayton Green W13   BJ39 **54**
Duckhall HP3   AW15 **8**
Duckland CM16   CP16 **23**
Dudswell HP4   AO11 **7**
Dulwich SE21   CA47 **77**
Dunton Green TN13   CS63 **107**
Durndale DA13   DE49 **81**
Earls Court SW5   BS42 **66**
Earlsfield SW18   BS47 **76**
Earlswood RH1   BV71 **121**
East Acton W3   BO40 **55**

East Barnet EN4   BU25 **29**
East Bedfont TW14   BA47 **73**
East Clandon GU4   AY69 **110**
East Dulwich SE22   CA46 **77**
East Finchley N2   BT31 **47**
East Hill TN15   CX59 **99**
East Horndon CM13   DF31 **123**
East Horsley KT24   BB68 **110**
East Molesey KT8   BG52 **84**
East Sheen SW14   BN45 **65**
East Wickham DA16   CO44 **69**
Eastbury HA6   BB28 **35**
Eastcote HA5   BC32 **44**
Eastly End TW20   AU51 **82**
Eastwick CM20   CL9 **6**
Eastworth KT16   AV54 **82**
Eden Park BR3   CE53 **87**
Edgware HA8   BM29 **37**
Edgware Bury HA8   BL26 **37**
Effingham KT24   BD67 **111**
Egham TW20   AT49 **72**
Egham Hythe TW18   AV49 **72**
Egham Wick TW20   AQ50 **72**
Elm Park RM12   CU35 **50**
Elmers End BR3   CD52 **87**
Elmstead BR7   CK50 **78**
Elstree WD6   BL25 **28**
Eltham SE9   CL46 **78**
Elthorne Heights W7   BG39 **54**
Emerson Park RM11   CW32 **51**
Enfield EN2   BZ37 **30**
Enfield Highway EN3   CC23 **30**
Enfield Lock EN3   CD21 **30**
Enfield Wash EN3   CC22 **30**
Englefield Green TW20   AQ49 **72**
Epping CM16   CO18 **23**
Epping Green CM16   CL15 **13**
Epping Green SG13   BW14 **11**
Epping Upland CM16   CM16 **22**
Epsom KT18   BN60 **94**
Erith DA8   CT42 **69**
Esher KT10   BG56 **93**
Essendon AL9   BU12 **11**
Eton SL4   AN43 **61**
Eton Wick SL4   AN42 **61**
Ewell KT17   BO58 **94**
Eynsford DA4   CV55 **90**
Fairmile KT11   BE59 **93**
Farleigh CR3   CD60 **96**
Farnborough BR6   CL56 **97**
Farningham DA4   CX53 **90**
Farthing Street BR6   CK58 **97**
Fawkham Green DA3   DA55 **90**
Felden HP3   AW15 **8**
Feltham TW13   BC47 **73**
Felthamhill TW16   BB49 **73**
Fetcham KT22   BH65 **102**
Fiddlers Hamlet CM16   CP19 **23**
Fifield SL6   AH44 **61**
Finchley N3   BS29 **38**
Finsbury Park N4   BY34 **47**
Flamstead End EN7   CB17 **21**
Flaunden HP3   AT20 **16**
Fleetville AL1   BH13 **9**
Folly, The WD7   BH21 **27**
Foots Cray DA14   CP49 **79**
Force Green TN16   CN65 **106**
Forest Gate E7   CH35 **49**
Forest Green SL6   AH44 **61**
Forest Hill SE23   CC47 **77**
Forestdale CR0   CD58 **96**
Fortis Green N2   BU31 **47**
Forty Hill EN1   CA22 **30**
Foster Street CM17   CQ12 **14**
Fox Hatch CM15   CZ22 **33**
French Street TN16   CN68 **115**
Friern Barnet N11   BU28 **38**
Frogmore AL2   BG17 **18**
Frogmore SL4   AP44 **62**
Frogmore End HP3   AX15 **8**
Fulham SW6   BS44 **66**
Fulmer SL3   AR35 **43**
Fulwell TW12   BG49 **74**
Fyfield CM5   CY14 **15**
Gadebridge HP1   AW12 **8**
Galley Hill DA10   DC46 **81**
Gallows Corner RM3   CV30 **42**
Ganwick Corner EN6   BS21 **29**
Garston WD2   BD20 **18**
Gatton RH2   BU67 **113**
George Green SL3   AS39 **52**
Gerrards Cross SL9   AS31 **43**
Giggs Hill KT7   BH54 **84**
Godden Green TN15   CX66 **117**
Godstone RH9   CB69 **114**
Goff's Oak EN7   BZ17 **21**
Goodmayes IG3   CO34 **50**
Goose Green EN11   CB11 **12**
Gorringe Park CR4   BV50 **76**
Gospel Oak NW3   BU35 **47**
Goulds Green UB8   AZ39 **53**
Grange Hill IG7   CM28 **40**

Grange Park N21   BY25 **29**
Gravesend DA12   DH46 **81**
Grays RM17   DD42 **71**
Great Bookham KT23   BE67 **111**
Great Parndon CM19   CL12 **13**
Great Warley CM13   DA30 **42**
Greatness TN14   CV63 **108**
Green Street WD6   BM22 **28**
Green Street Green BR6   CN57 **97**
Green Street Green DA2   DA50 **80**
Green, The BR4   CF54 **87**
Greenford UB6   BG38 **54**
Greenford Green UB6   BH36 **54**
Greenford Park UB1   BF39 **54**
Greenhithe DA9   DA45 **70**
Greensted CM5   CV18 **24**
Greensted Green CM5   CU17 **23**
Greenwich SE10   CF43 **67**
Grove Park SE12   CH48 **78**
Grove Park W4   BN43 **65**
Grubb Street DA4   DA51 **90**
Guildford GU1   AS71 **118**
Gunnersbury W4   BM42 **65**
Hackbridge SM6   BV54 **86**
Hackbridge Park SM6   BV54 **86**
Hackney E8   CB36 **57**
Hacton RM13   CW35 **51**
Hadley Wood EN4   BS22 **29**
Haggerston E2   CA37 **57**
Hainault IG7   CN28 **40**
Haldens AL7   BS26 **5**
Hale End IG8   CG29 **40**
Halfway Street DA15   CN47 **78**
Hall Grove AL7   BS9 **5**
Hallsgreen CM19   CJ12 **13**
Halstead TN14   CQ59 **98**
Ham TW10   BK48 **74**
Hammersmith W6   BP42 **65**
Hammond Street EN7   BZ16 **21**
Hampstead NW3   BT35 **47**
Hampstead NW6   BS36 **56**
Hampstead Garden Suburb NW11   BS32 **47**
Hampton TW12   BH50 **74**
Hampton Hill TW12   BG50 **74**
Hampton Wick KT1   BJ51 **84**
Hamsey Green CR3   CC61 **105**
Handside AL8   BP8 **5**
Hanwell W7   BH41 **64**
Hanworth TW13   BE49 **74**
Hare Street CM19   CL11 **13**
Hare Street CM5   CV20 **24**
Hare Street RM2   CU31 **50**
Harefield UB9   AX30 **35**
Harlesden NW10   BO37 **55**
Harlington UB3   BA43 **63**
Harlow CM18   CM11 **13**
Harmondsworth UB7   AX43 **63**
Harold Hill RM3   CW28 **42**
Harold Park RM3   CX29 **42**
Harold Wood RM3   CX30 **42**
Harrow HA1   BG33 **45**
Harrow Garden Village HA5   BE32 **45**
Harrow Weald HA3   BH29 **36**
Hartley DA3   DC53 **90**
Hastingwood CM17   CQ13 **14**
Hatch End HA5   BF29 **36**
Hatchford End GU23   BA63 **101**
Hatfield AL10   BP12 **10**
Hatfield Garden Village AL10   BO11 **10**
Hatfield Hyde AL7   BR9 **5**
Hatton TW14   BB46 **73**
Havering-Atte-Bower RM4   CT27 **41**
Hawley DA2   CX50 **80**
Hawley Fishery DA1   CX48 **80**
Hayes BR2   CH54 **88**
Hayes End UB4   BA38 **53**
Headley KT18   BN66 **112**
Heath Park RM11   CV32 **51**
Heath Side DA5   CT48 **79**
Heaverham TN15   CZ62 **108**
Hedgerley SL2   AO33 **43**
Hemel Hempstead HP1   AX13 **8**
Hendon NW4   BP31 **46**
Herne Hill SE2   BZ46 **77**
Heronsgate WD3   AU26 **34**
Hersham KT10   BE56 **93**
Heston TW5   BE43 **64**
Hextable BR8   CT50 **79**
High Beech IG10   CJ22 **31**
High Laver CM5   CU12 **14**
High Ongar CM5   CY17 **24**
High Welwyn AL6   BS5 **5**
High Wych CM21   CO6 **6**
High, The CM20   CM11 **13**
Higham Hill E17   CD30 **39**
Highams Park E4   CF28 **39**
Highbury N5   BY35 **47**
Highgate N6   BV33 **47**
Highwood Hill NW7   BO27 **37**
Hill End UB9   AW29 **35**
Hill Park TN16   CL65 **106**
Hillingdon UB10   AZ37 **53**

Hillingdon Heath UB10   AZ38 **53**
Hinchley Wood KT10   BH55 **84**
Hither Green SE13   CG46 **78**
Hobbs Cross CM16   CP21 **32**
Hoddesdon EN11   CD12 **12**
Holder's Hill NW4   BQ30 **37**
Holloway N7   BX35 **47**
Holmethorpe RH1   BV69 **121**
Holyfield EN9   CF17 **21**
Hook KT9   BK56 **93**
Hook Green DA13   DD50 **81**
Hook Green DA2   CT49 **79**
Hooley CR3   BV64 **104**
Hornchurch RM12   CV33 **51**
Horns Cross DA9   CZ46 **80**
Horns Green TN14   CN62 **106**
Hornsey N8   BX31 **47**
Horsell GU21   AR61 **100**
Horseman Side CM14   CW24 **33**
Horton KT19   BM58 **94**
Horton SL3   AT44 **62**
Horton Kirby DA4   CY52 **90**
Hosey Hill TN16   CN67 **115**
Hounslow TW3   BF45 **64**
Howell Hill SM2   BQ58 **94**
Hoxton N1   BZ37 **57**
Hulberry BR8   CU55 **89**
Hunton Bridge WD4   AZ20 **17**
Hutton CM13   DE25 **122**
Hyde, The NW9   BO32 **46**
Hythe End TW19   AT48 **72**
Ickenham UB10   AZ34 **44**
Ide Hill TN14   CQ69 **116**
Ifield or Singlewell DA12   DH50 **81**
Ightham TN15   DB64 **108**
Ilford IG1   CL34 **49**
Ingrave CM13   DE28 **122**
Ingrave Green CM13   DD28 **122**
Isle of Dogs E14   CF41 **67**
Isleworth TW7   BH45 **64**
Islington N1   BY37 **56**
Istead Rise DA13   DF50 **81**
Iver SL0   AW39 **53**
Iver Heath SL0   AV37 **52**
Ivy Chimneys CM16   CN19 **22**
Ivy Hatch TN15   DA66 **117**
Jordans HP9   AP29 **34**
Katherines CM19   CK12 **13**
Kelvedon Hatch CM14   CY22 **33**
Kemsing TN15   CX62 **108**
Kenley CR2   BZ61 **105**
Kennington SE11   BY43 **66**
Kensal Green NW10   BP38 **55**
Kensal Rise NW10   BP37 **55**
Kensington W8   BS41 **66**
Kentish Town NW5   BV36 **56**
Keston Mark BR2   CJ56 **97**
Kevington BR5   CQ53 **89**
Kew TW9   BM43 **65**
Kidbrooke SE3   CH44 **68**
Kilburn NW6   BR37 **55**
King's Langley WD4   AZ18 **17**
Kingfield GU22   AT63 **100**
Kingsbury NW9   BN34 **46**
Kingsmoor CM19   CL13 **13**
Kingston KT1   BL51 **85**
Kingston Hill KT2   BM50 **75**
Kingston Vale SW15   BO49 **75**
Kingswood KT20   BR65 **103**
Kippington TN13   CT66 **116**
Kirtley SE26   CD49 **77**
Knaphill GU21   AO61 **100**
Knockhall DA9   DB46 **80**
Knockholt TN14   CO61 **107**
Knockholt Pound TN14   CQ61 **107**
Ladymead GU1   AS69 **118**
Ladywell SE13   CE46 **77**
Laleham TW18   AX52 **83**
Lambeth SE11   BX42 **66**
Lambourne End RM4   CP26 **41**
Lamorbey DA15   CO47 **79**
Lampton TW3   BF44 **64**
Lane End DA2   CY49 **80**
Langley SL3   AS42 **62**
Langley Vale KT18   BO63 **103**
Latimer HP5   AS22 **25**
Latton Bush CM18   CO12 **14**
Lea Bridge E5   CC34 **48**
Leatherhead KT22   BK64 **102**
Leatherhead Common KT22   BH63 **102**
Leaves Green BR2   CJ59 **97**
Leavesden Green WD2   BB20 **17**
Lee SE13   CG45 **68**
Leigh RH2   BP74 **120**
Lemsford AL8   BO8 **5**
Letchmore Heath WD2   BH23 **27**
Leverstock Green HP2   BA14 **8**
Lewisham SE13   CE45 **67**
Ley Hill Common HP5   AQ18 **16**
Leyton E10   CE33 **48**
Leytonstone E11   CG33 **49**
Limehouse E14   CD39 **57**

Limpsfield RH8　CG67 **115**
Linford SS17　DK41 **71**
Little Berkhamsted SG13　BW13 **11**
Little Bookham KT23　BE66 **111**
Little Britain UB7　AW40 **53**
Little Bushey WD2　BG26 **36**
Little Chalfont HP8　AR23 **25**
Little Ealing W5　BK42 **64**
Little End CM5　CV20 **24**
Little Heath EN6　BS19 **20**
Little Heath IG2　CO31 **50**
Little Parndon CM20　CL10 **6**
Little Roke CR2　BZ60 **96**
Little Thurrock RM17　DE42 **71**
Little Warley CM13　DC30 **123**
Little Warley CM13　DC30 **42**
Little Woodcote SM5　BV59 **95**
Littleton TW17　AZ52 **83**
Locksbottom BR6　CK56 **97**
London Colney AL2　BL16 **19**
Long Ditton KT6　BK54 **84**
Longcross KT16　AQ55 **82**
Longfield DA3　DC51 **90**
Longford TN13　CS63 **107**
Longford UB7　AW44 **63**
Longlands DA15　CN48 **78**
Loughton IG10　CK24 **31**
Love Green SL0　AV39 **52**
Low Street RM18　DJ43 **71**
Lower Ashtead KT22　BJ62 **102**
Lower Cheam SM1　BR56 **94**
Lower Clapton E5　CC34 **48**
Lower Edmonton N9　CB27 **39**
Lower Feltham TW13　BB48 **73**
Lower Green KT10　BF55 **84**
Lower Halliford TW17　BB53 **83**
Lower Kingswood KT20　BS67 **113**
Lower Morden KT3　BQ53 **85**
Lower Nazeing EN9　CG14 **13**
Lower Streatham SW16　BW50 **76**
Lower Sydenham SE26　CD49 **77**
Loyter's Green CM17　CT10 **14**
Lucas End EN7　BZ17 **21**
Lullingstone DA4　CU56 **98**
Lye Green HP5　AP17 **16**
Lyne KT16　AT54 **82**
Mackerels Plain TN14　CR68 **116**
Magdalen Laver CM5　CS12 **14**
Maida Hill W9　BS38 **56**
Maida Vale W9　BS38 **56**
Malden KT4　BO54 **85**
Malden Rushet KT22　BJ61 **102**
Manor Park E12　CK35 **49**
Maple Cross WD3　AU28 **34**
Marden Ash CM5　CX18 **24**
Margery KT20　BS68 **113**
Mark Hall North CM20　CO9 **6**
Mark Hall South CM20　CO10 **6**
Marks Gate RM7　CQ30 **41**
Martyr's Green GU23　BA63 **101**
Maybury GU22　AT62 **100**
Mayford GU22　AS65 **100**
Maypole BR6　CQ57 **98**
Maypole DA5　CS47 **79**
Mead Vale RH2　BU71 **121**
Merrow GU1　AU70 **118**
Merry Hill WD2　BF26 **36**
Merstham RH1　BV67 **113**
Merton SW19　BS51 **86**
Mickleham RH5　BK67 **111**
Middle Green SL3　AS40 **52**
Middle Street EN9　CH15 **13**
Mile End E1　CC38 **57**
Mill End WD3　AW26 **35**
Mill Hill NW7　BO28 **37**
Miller's Green CM5　DA13 **15**
Millwall E14　CE41 **67**
Milton DA12　DH46 **81**
Milton Street DA10　DB46 **80**
Mitcham CR4　BU52 **86**
Mogador KT20　BR67 **112**
Moneyhill WD3　AX26 **35**
Monken Hadley EN4　BS23 **29**
Moorhouse Bank TN16　CL67 **115**
Morden SM4　BS53 **86**
Morden Common SM4　BQ54 **85**
Moreton CM5　CV14 **15**
Mossford Green IG6　CM31 **49**
Motspur Park KT3　BO53 **85**
Mottingham SE9　CJ48 **78**
Mount End CM16　CQ20 **23**
Mountnessing CM15　DE23 **122**
Muckingford SS17　DK41 **71**
Mugswell CR3　BS66 **113**
Mulberry Green CM17　CP9 **6**
Muswell Hill N10　BV31 **47**
Myrke SL1　AP42 **62**
Navestock RM4　CV23 **33**
Navestock Side CM14　CY23 **33**
Nazeing EN9　CJ14 **13**
Nazeing Gate EN9　CJ16 **22**
Nazeing Long Green EN9　CH16 **22**

Neasden NW10　BO35 **46**
Netteswell CM20　CN10 **6**
New Addington CR0　CF58 **96**
New Ash Green DA3　DC55 **90**
New Barnet EN5　BT24 **29**
New Beckenham BR3　CD50 **77**
New Beckton E6　CL39 **58**
New Cross SE14　CD43 **67**
New Denham UB9　AW36 **53**
New Eltham SE9　CL48 **78**
New Hanworth TW12　BF48 **74**
New Haw KT15　AX57 **92**
New Malden KT3　BO52 **85**
New Southgate N11　BW28 **38**
New Town DA1　CW46 **80**
New Town SL4　AM42 **61**
New Way CM17　CS11 **14**
Newbury Park IG2　CM32 **49**
Newgate Street SG13　BW16 **20**
Newington SE1　BZ41 **67**
Newyears Green UB9　AY32 **44**
Nine Ashes CM4　DB18 **24**
Noah's Ark TN15　CX63 **108**
Noak Hill RM4　CV27 **42**
Noel Park N22　BY30 **38**
Norbiton KT1　BM51 **85**
Norbury SW16　BX51 **86**
Nork KT18　BQ62 **103**
North Cheam SM3　BR54 **85**
North Cray DA14　CQ48 **79**
North End DA8　CT44 **69**
North End NW3　BT33 **47**
North Feltham TW14　BC46 **73**
North Finchley N12　BT28 **38**
North Hillingdon UB10　AZ36 **53**
North Holmwood RH4　BJ73 **119**
North Hyde UB2　BE42 **64**
North Kensington W10　BQ39 **55**
North Looe KT17　BQ60 **94**
North Ockendon RM14　DA35 **51**
North Sheen TW9　BM44 **65**
North Stifford RM16　DC40 **71**
North Stifford RM16　DC40 **60**
North Weald Bassett CM16　CR17 **23**
North Woolwich E16　CK41 **68**
Northaw EN6　BV18 **20**
Northchurch HP4　AP12 **7**
Northfleet DA11　DE46 **81**
Northfleet Green DA13　DE50 **81**
Northolt UB5　BE36 **54**
Northolt Park HA2　BE35 **45**
Northumberland Heath DA8　CS43 **69**
Northwood HA6　BA29 **35**
Norton Heath CM4　DC16 **24**
Norton Mandeville CM5　DA16 **24**
Norwood Green UB2　BF42 **64**
Notting Hill W11　BR40 **55**
Nunhead SE15　CC45 **67**
Nutfield RH1　BX70 **121**
Oakleigh Park N20　BT26 **38**
Oakley Green SL4　AK44 **61**
Ockham GU23　AZ64 **101**
Old Coulsdon CR3　BY62 **104**
Old Court RM14　AU12 **7**
Old Ford E3　CD37 **57**
Old Windsor SL4　AP46 **72**
Old Woking GU22　AT64 **100**
Oldbury TN15　DA64 **108**
Onslow Village GU3　AP71 **118**
Orpington BR6　CN54 **88**
Orsett Heath RM16　DF41 **71**
Osterley TW7　BG43 **64**
Otford TN14　CU61 **107**
Ottershaw KT16　AU56 **91**
Oxhey WD1　BE25 **27**
Oxshott KT22　BG60 **93**
Oxshott Heath KT22　BG58 **93**
Oxted RH8　CF68 **114**
Pachesham KT22　BH62 **102**
Paddington W2　BT39 **56**
Page Street NW7　BP29 **37**
Palmer's Green N14　BX27 **38**
Panshanger AL7　BS7 **5**
Park Royal NW10　BM38 **55**
Park Street AL2　BG16 **18**
Parsons Green SW6　BR44 **65**
Passingford Bridge RM4　CS23 **32**
Passmores CM18　CM12 **13**
Patchetts Green WD2　BF23 **27**
Peartree AL7　BR8 **5**
Peckham SE15　CB44 **67**
Penge SE20　CB50 **77**
Perivale UB6　BJ38 **54**
Perry Street DA11　DF47 **81**
Perry Street DA7　CT44 **69**
Petersham TW10　BK47 **74**
Petts Wood BR5　CN53 **88**
Piccotts End HP2　AX11 **8**
Pield Heath UB8　AY39 **53**
Pilgrim's Hatch CM14　CZ25 **33**
Pimlico SW1　BV42 **66**
Pimlico TN16　CK62 **106**

Pinnacles CM19　CK11 **13**
Pinner HA5　BE31 **45**
Plaistow BR1　CG50 **78**
Plaistow E13　CH38 **58**
Plaxtol TN15　DC67 **117**
Plumstead SE18　CM42 **68**
Ponder's End EN3　CC25 **30**
Pool End TW17　AZ53 **83**
Poplar E14　CE40 **57**
Portmore Park KT13　AZ55 **83**
Pot Kilns RM14　CY32 **51**
Potten End HP4　AT12 **7**
Potter Street CM17　CP11 **14**
Potters Bar EN6　BT20 **20**
Potterscrouch AL2　BD15 **9**
Poyle SL3　AV44 **62**
Pratt's Bottom BR6　CO58 **98**
Priest Hill KT17　BP59 **94**
Primrosehill WD4　AZ17 **17**
Princes Gate CM14　CX23 **33**
Puddledock DA2　CT50 **79**
Purfleet RM16　CX42 **70**
Purley CR2　BX59 **95**
Putney Vale SW15　BO48 **75**
Pye Corner CM20　CM8 **6**
Pyrcroft KT16　AV54 **82**
Pyrford GU22　AW62 **101**
Pyrford Green GU22　AW62 **101**
Queen's Park W10　BR38 **55**
Queensbury HA8　BL30 **37**
Radlett WD7　BH21 **27**
Rainham RM13　CU38 **59**
Redhill RH1　BV70 **121**
Redstreet DA13　DD50 **81**
Reigate RH2　BS71 **121**
Richings Park SL0　AU41 **62**
Richmond TW10　BL46 **75**
Richmond Hill TW10　BL46 **75**
Rickmansworth WD3　AX25 **26**
Ridge EN6　BO20 **19**
Ripley GU23　AW64 **101**
Rise Park RM1　CT29 **41**
Riverhead TN14　CT64 **107**
Roe Green AL10　BO13 **10**
Roe Green NW9　BM31 **46**
Roehampton SW15　BP47 **75**
Romney Street TN15　CW59 **99**
Rosherville DA11　DF47 **81**
Rotherhithe SE16　CC41 **67**
Round Bush WD2　BG22 **27**
Roupell Park SW2　BX47 **76**
Rowhill KT15　AV57 **91**
Roxeth HA2　BG34 **45**
Roydon CM19　CH10 **13**
Roydon Hamlet CM19　CJ13 **13**
Rucklers Green HP3　AY16 **17**
Ruislip HA4　BA33 **44**
Rush Green RM7　CT33 **50**
Rush Green UB9　AV35 **43**
Rushey Green SE6　CF47 **77**
Ruxley DA14　CQ50 **79**
Ryde, The AL9　BQ11 **10**
Rye Hill CM18　CN14 **13**
Rye Park EN11　CE11 **12**
Sabines Green RM4　CW24 **33**
Saint Albans AL1　BH14 **9**
Saint George's Hill KT13　AZ58 **92**
Saint Helier SM4　BS53 **86**
Saint John's TN13　CU65 **107**
Saint John's Wood NW8　BT37 **56**
Saint Johns RH1　BU71 **121**
Saint Margarets TW1　BJ46 **74**
Saint Mary Cray BR5　CO53 **89**
Saint Paul's Cray BR5　CP51 **89**
Saint Vincent's Hamlet CM14　CX26 **42**
Sanders's Corner EN2　BY20 **20**
Sanderstead CR2　BZ58 **96**
Sanway KT14　AY60 **92**
Sarratt WD3　AW21 **26**
Sarratt Bottoom WD3　AV22 **25**
Sawbridgeworth CM21　CP5 **6**
Seal TN15　CX64 **108**
Seer Green HP9　AO29 **34**
Selhurst CR0　BZ53 **87**
Selsdon CR2　CC58 **96**
Send GU23　AU65 **100**
Sendmarsh GU23　AV65 **100**
Sepham Heath TN14　CR60 **98**
Sergehill WD5　BC16 **17**
Seven Kings IG2　CM33 **49**
Sevenoaks TN13　CV66 **117**
Sevenoaks Weald TN14　CV69 **117**
Sewardstone E4　CF23 **30**
Sewardstonebury E4　CG25 **31**
Shadwell E1　CC40 **57**
Shalford GU4　AS73 **118**
Sheering CM22　CS7 **6**
Sheerwater GU21　AU60 **91**
Shelley CM5　CX15 **15**
Shenfield CM15　DC26 **122**
Shenley WD7　BM20 **19**
Shenleybury WD7　BK18 **18**

Shepherds Bush W12 BP40 **55**
Shepperton TW17 AZ54 **83**
Shepperton Green TW17 AZ52 **83**
Shipbourne TN11 DB68 **117**
Shirley CR0 CC56 **96**
Shirley CR0 CC55 **87**
Shooters Hill SE18 CL44 **68**
Shootersway HP4 AP13 **7**
Shoreditch EC2 BZ38 **57**
Shoreham TN14 CU59 **98**
Shortlands BR2 CG52 **88**
Shreding Green SL0 AU40 **52**
Sidcup DA14 CN49 **78**
Silvertown E16 CJ40 **58**
Single Street TN16 CL60 **97**
Singlewell or Ifield DA12 DH50 **81**
Sipson UB7 AZ43 **63**
Sipson Green UB3 BA43 **63**
Slade Green DA8 CU44 **69**
Slough SL2 AQ40 **52**
Slyfield Green GU1 AS68 **109**
Smug Oak AL2 BF18 **18**
Snaresbrook E11 CG32 **49**
Soho W1 BW39 **56**
Somers Town NW1 BW37 **56**
South Acton W3 BM41 **65**
South Bank SE1 BX40 **56**
South Beddington SM6 BW57 **95**
South Croydon CR2 BZ57 **96**
South Darenth DA4 CY51 **90**
South End SE9 CL47 **78**
South Hackney E9 CC37 **57**
South Harrow HA2 BF34 **45**
South Hatfield AL10 BP13 **10**
South Hornchurch RM13 CU37 **59**
South Kensington SW7 BT42 **66**
South Lambeth SW8 BX44 **66**
South Merstham RH1 BW68 **113**
South Mimms EN6 BO19 **19**
South Norwood BR3 CC52 **87**
South Nutfield RH1 BX71 **121**
South Ockendon RM15 DB38 **60**
South Oxhey WD1 BD27 **36**
South Park RH2 BR72 **120**
South Ruislip HA4 BD36 **54**
South Ruislip HA4 BD35 **45**
South Stifford RM16 DB42 **70**
South Street TN16 CK63 **106**
South Weald CM14 CZ27 **42**
South Wimbledon SW19 BS50 **76**
South Woodford E18 CG30 **40**
Southall UB1 BE40 **54**
Southall UB2 BD41 **64**
Southborough BR2 CK53 **88**
Southborough KT6 BK54 **84**
Southfields SW18 BR47 **75**
Southfleet DA13 DD49 **81**
Southgate N14 BW26 **38**
Southlea SL3 AQ44 **62**
Southwark SE1 BZ40 **57**
Spitalbrook EN10 CD13 **12**
Spitalfields E1 CA39 **57**
Spratts KT16 AU57 **91**
Spring Grove TW7 BH44 **64**
Spring Head DA11 DD48 **81**
Staines TW18 AW50 **73**
Stamford Hill N16 CA33 **48**
Stanborough AL8 BP10 **5**
Stanford Rivers CM5 CV20 **24**
Stanmore HA7 BJ28 **36**
Stanwell TW19 AX46 **73**
Stanwellmoor TW19 AV46 **72**
Stapleford Abbotts RM4 CR24 **32**
Stapleford Tawney RM4 CS21 **32**
Stepney E14 CD39 **57**
Steward's Green CM16 CO19 **23**
Stewards CM18 CN13 **13**
Stockwell SW9 BX44 **66**
Stoke D'Abernon KT11 BE62 **102**
Stoke Green SL2 AQ38 **52**
Stoke Newington N16 CA34 **48**
Stoke Poges SL2 AQ36 **52**
Stondon Massey CM15 DA20 **24**
Stone Street TN15 CZ66 **117**
Stonehill Green DA2 CS50 **79**
Stoneleigh KT17 BP56 **94**
Stonewood DA2 DB48 **80**
Stoughton GU2 AQ69 **118**
Strawberry Hill TW1 BH48 **74**
Streatham SW16 BW48 **76**
Stringers Common GU1 AR68 **109**
Strood Green RH3 BM72 **120**
Stroud Green N4 BX33 **47**
Stroude GU25 AS52 **82**
Styants Bottom TN15 CZ64 **108**
Sudbury HA0 BJ35 **45**
Sudbury Heights UB6 BJ36 **54**
Summerstown SW17 BS48 **76**
Sumners CM19 CL13 **13**
Sunbury TW16 BC52 **83**

Sunbury Common TW16 BB51 **83**
Sundridge TN14 CQ65 **107**
Sundridge Park BR1 CJ50 **78**
Surbiton KT5 BL53 **85**
Sutton SM2 BS57 **95**
Sutton TW5 BF43 **64**
Sutton at Hone DA4 CX50 **80**
Swallow Street SL0 AV39 **52**
Swanley BR8 CU52 **89**
Swanley Village BR8 CU51 **89**
Swanscombe DA10 DB47 **80**
Swillet, The WD3 AU25 **25**
Tadworth KT20 BP64 **103**
Tandridge RH8 CE70 **114**
Tatsfield TN16 CH64 **106**
Teddington TW11 BH49 **74**
Templefields CM20 CO9 **6**
Tewin AL6 BU6 **5**
Thames Ditton KT7 BH53 **84**
Thamesmead DA18 CQ41 **69**
Theydon Bois CM16 CM21 **31**
Theydon Garnon CM16 CP21 **32**
Theydon Mount CM16 CR21 **32**
Thistlecroft KT12 BC56 **92**
Thong DA12 DJ50 **81**
Thorney SL0 AW41 **63**
Thornton Heath CR4 BY52 **86**
Thornwood Common CM16 CO16 **23**
Thorpe TW20 AU52 **82**
Thorpe Green TW20 AT52 **82**
Thorpe Lea TW20 AT50 **72**
Three Arch Bridge CM13 DC27 **122**
Threshers Bush CM17 CR11 **14**
Tilbury RM18 DG44 **71**
Tilegate Green CM5 CS12 **14**
Timberden Bottom TN14 CT58 **98**
Titsey RH8 CH66 **115**
Tolworth KT6 BL54 **85**
Toot Hill CM5 CT18 **23**
Tooting Graveney SW17 BU49 **76**
Tottenham N17 CA30 **39**
Towerhill WD4 AV18 **16**
Townsend AL3 BH12 **9**
Toy's Hill TN14 CP69 **116**
Tufnell Park N7 BW35 **47**
Tulse Hill SW2 BY47 **76**
Turnford EN10 CD16 **21**
Twickenham TW1 BJ48 **74**
Two Waters HP3 AX15 **8**
Tye Green CM18 CN12 **13**
Tylers Causeway SG13 BW14 **11**
Tylers Green CM16 CS16 **23**
Tyttenhanger Green AL4 BL15 **10**
Underhill EN5 BR25 **28**
Underriver TN15 CX68 **117**
Upminster RM14 CX34 **51**
Upper Clapton E5 CB33 **48**
Upper Edmonton N9 CB28 **39**
Upper Elmers End BR3 CD53 **87**
Upper Halliford TW17 BA52 **83**
Upper Holloway N19 BW34 **47**
Upper Norwood SE19 BZ50 **77**
Upper Sydenham SE26 CB48 **77**
Upper Woodcote CR8 BW59 **95**
Upshire EN9 CJ20 **22**
Upton DA6 CQ46 **79**
Upton SL3 AQ41 **62**
Upton Park E13 CH37 **58**
Uxbridge UB8 AX37 **53**
Uxbridge Moor SL0 AW37 **53**
Virginia Water GU25 AR52 **82**
Waddington CR2 BZ62 **105**
Waddon CR0 BX55 **86**
Wake Arms IG10 CK21 **31**
Walham Green SW6 BS43 **66**
Walk End GU24 AO56 **91**
Wallington SM6 BW56 **95**
Waltham Abbey EN9 CF19 **21**
Waltham Cross EN8 CD20 **21**
Walthamstow E17 CD31 **48**
Walton on Thames KT12 BD54 **84**
Walton-on-the-Hill KT20 BO66 **112**
Walworth SE17 BZ42 **67**
Wandsworth SW18 BS46 **76**
Wanstead E11 CH32 **49**
Wapping E1 CB40 **57**
War Coppice Garden Village CR3 BZ67 **114**
Warley CM14 DB28 **42**
Warlingham CR3 CC62 **105**
Warner's End HP1 AV13 **7**
Warwick Wold RH1 BY68 **113**
Water End AL9 BP16 **19**
Waterend AL4 BN7 **5**
Waterhale CM14 CV25 **33**
Waterside HP5 AO20 **16**
Watford WD1 BC23 **26**
Watford Heath WD1 BE26 **36**
Watton's Green CM14 CU25 **32**
Wealdstone HA3 BH31 **45**
Welham Green AL9 BQ15 **10**

Well End WD6 BN22 **28**
Well Hill BR6 CR57 **98**
Welling DA16 CO45 **69**
Wells, The KT18 BL60 **94**
Welwyn Garden City AL8 BP8 **5**
Wembley HA9 BL35 **46**
Wembley Park HA9 BL33 **46**
Wennington RM13 CW40 **60**
Wentworth GU25 AP53 **82**
West Barnes KT3 BP53 **85**
West Bedfont TW19 AY46 **73**
West Byfleet KT14 AW60 **92**
West Clandon GU4 AW68 **110**
West Drayton UB7 AY41 **63**
West Dulwich SE21 BZ48 **77**
West Ealing W13 BJ40 **54**
West End AL9 BT12 **11**
West End KT10 BE56 **93**
West End UB3 BA43 **63**
West Ewell KT19 BO57 **94**
West Ham E5 CG37 **58**
West Hampstead NW6 BS35 **47**
West Heath DA17 CQ43 **69**
West Hendon NW9 BO33 **46**
West Horndon CM13 DE32 **123**
West Horsley KT24 BA67 **110**
West Humble RH5 BJ69 **119**
West Hyde WD3 AU29 **34**
West Kingsdown TN15 CZ58 **99**
West Molesey KT8 BF53 **84**
West Thurrock RM16 DA42 **70**
West Tilbury RM18 DJ43 **71**
West Wickham BR4 CF55 **87**
Westborough GU2 AP70 **118**
Westbourne Park W9 BS39 **56**
Westcott RH4 BG72 **119**
Westerham TN16 CM67 **115**
Westfield GU22 AS64 **100**
Westminster SW1 BW41 **66**
Weston Green KT7 BH54 **84**
Wexham Street SL3 AR37 **52**
Weybridge KT13 BA55 **83**
Whelpleyhill HP5 AR16 **16**
Whetstone N20 BT27 **38**
Whitechapel E1 CA39 **57**
Whiteley Village KT12 BB58 **92**
Whitton TW2 BF47 **74**
Whyteleafe CR3 CA62 **105**
Widmore BR1 CK52 **88**
Wildernesse TN15 CW64 **108**
Wildhill AL9 BT14 **11**
Willesden NW10 BO36 **55**
Willesden Green NW2 BP36 **55**
Willingale CM5 DB13 **15**
Willowbank UB9 AX35 **44**
Wilmington DA2 CV48 **80**
Wimbledon SW19 BR50 **75**
Winchmore Hill N21 BY26 **38**
Windsor SL4 AP44 **62**
Wisley GU23 AX61 **101**
Withybed Corner KT20 BP65 **103**
Woking GU21 AR62 **100**
Woldingham CR3 CD65 **105**
Woldingham Garden Village CR3 CD63 **105**
Wood End UB3 BB39 **53**
Wood End UB5 BF36 **54**
Wood Green N22 BX30 **38**
Woodcote KT18 BN61 **103**
Woodcote Green SM6 BV58 **95**
Woodend CM5 CZ10 **15**
Woodend Green UB3 BA39 **53**
Woodfield KT21 BK62 **102**
Woodford IG8 CH29 **40**
Woodford Bridge IG8 CK28 **40**
Woodford Green IG8 CG28 **40**
Woodford Wells IG8 CH28 **40**
Woodgreen EN9 CJ20 **22**
Woodhall AL7 BR9 **5**
Woodham KT15 AV59 **91**
Woodhatch CM16 CR19 **23**
Woodhatch RH2 BD72 **121**
Woodlands TN15 CY60 **99**
Woodmansterne CR3 BU60 **95**
Woodside CM16 CP16 **23**
Woodside SE25 CA53 **87**
Woodside WD2 BC19 **17**
Woollensbrook EN11 CC11 **12**
Woolwich SE18 CL42 **68**
Worcester Park KT4 BO55 **85**
Wormley EN10 CD15 **12**
Wormley West End EN10 CA14 **12**
Worplesdon GU3 AP67 **109**
Wotton RH5 BE73 **119**
Wraysbury TW19 AS47 **72**
Wrythe, The SM5 BU55 **86**
Wych Street GU22 AR63 **100**
Yiewsley UB7 AY39 **53**

Notes

The street name and postal district or locality of an entry is followed by a grid reference and number of the map on which the name will be found, e.g. Abbey Rd, SW19 will be found in square **BT50** on map **76** and Norfolk Crescent, Sidcup in square **CN47** on map **78** (you will see from the map the latter location is in postcode boundary DA15).

The index contains some names for which there is insufficient space on the map. The adjoining thoroughfare to such roads is shown in italics, e.g. Agar Place, NW1 is off *Agar Grove* the latter being found in square **BW36** on map **56**.

A strict alphabetical order is followed in which Avenue, Close, Gardens etc, although abbreviated, are read as part of the preceding name. For example, Andrews Rd comes before Andrew St, and Abbey Orchard St before Abbey Rd.

Certain streets named in the Index are to be found both in the Central London enlarged-scale section, maps 1 to 4, as well as in parts of maps 56, 57, 66 and 67. In order to distinguish between the two the name of the street which is duplicated is given first in **bold type** (indicating the Central London Section), followed immediately by the same name in ordinary type.

ADDENDUM see page 408

Abbreviations of District Names

Alp.	Alperton	Dor.	Dorking	Long.	Longfield	Sun.	Sunbury-on-Thames
Amer.	Amersham	E.Mol.	East Molesey	Loug.	Loughton	Surb.	Surbiton
Ashf.	Ashford	Eden.	Edenbridge	Lthd.	Leatherhead	Sutt.	Sutton
Ash.	Ashtead	Edg.	Edgware	Maid.	Maidenhead	S.at H.	Sutton at Hone
Bans.	Banstead	Egh.	Egham	Mitch.	Mitcham	Swan.	Swanley
Bark.	Barking	Enf.	Enfield	Mord.	Morden	Swans.	Swanscombe
Barn.	Barnet	Epp.	Epping	New A.G.	New Ash Green	Tad.	Tadworth
Beac.	Beaconsfield	Eyns.	Eynsford	N.Mal.	New Malden	Tedd.	Teddington
Beck.	Beckenham	Farn.	Farningham	Nthlt.	Northolt	T.Ditt.	Thames Ditton
Belv.	Belvedere	Fawk.	Fawkham	Nthwd.	Northwood	Th.Hth.	Thornton Heath
Berk.	Berkhamsted	Felt.	Feltham	Ong.	Ongar	Til.	Tilbury
Bet.	Betchworth	Ger.Cr.	Gerrards Cross	Orp.	Orpington	Ton.	Tonbridge
Bex.	Bexley	Gdse.	Godstone	Oxt.	Oxted	Twick.	Twickenham
Bexh.	Bexleyheath	Grav.	Gravesend	Pnr.	Pinner	Upmin.	Upminster
Bish.	Bishops Stortford	Grnf.	Greenford	Pot.B.	Potters Bar	Uxb.	Uxbridge
B.Wd.	Boreham Wood	Green.	Greenhithe	Pur.	Purley	Vir.W.	Virginia Water
Brent.	Brentford	Guil.	Guildford	Rad.	Radlett	Wall.	Wallington
Brwd.	Brentwood	Hmptn.	Hampton	Rain.	Rainham	Wal.Abb.	Waltham Abbey
Brom.	Bromley	Harl.	Harlow	Red.	Redhill	Wal.Cr.	Waltham Cross
Brox.	Broxbourne	Har.	Harrow	Reig.	Reigate	Walt.	Walton-on-Thames
Buck.H.	Buckhurst Hill	Hart.	Hartley	Rich.	Richmond	Warl.	Warlingham
Bush.	Bushey	Hat.	Hatfield	Rick.	Rickmansworth	Wat.	Watford
Cars.	Carshalton	Hav.	Havering-atte-Bower	Rom.	Romford	Well.	Welling
Cat.	Caterham	Hem.H.	Hemel Hempstead	Ruis.	Ruislip	Welw.	Welwyn
Ch.St.G.	Chalfont St.Giles	Hert.	Hertford	St.Alb.	St.Albans	Welw.G.C.	Welwyn Garden City
Cher.	Chertsey	Hodd.	Hoddesdon	Saw.	Sawbridgeworth	Wem.	Wembley
Chesh.	Chesham	Horn.	Hornchurch	Sev.	Sevenoaks	West Dr.	West Drayton
Chess.	Chessington	Hort.K.	Horton Kirby	Shep.	Shepperton	West.	Westerham
Chig.	Chigwell	Houns.	Hounslow	Sid.	Sidcup	W.Mol.	West Molesey
Chis.	Chislehurst	Ilf.	Ilford	Slou.	Slough	W.Wick.	West Wickham
Chsnt.	Cheshunt	Ing.	Ingatestone	Sthl.	Southall	Wey.	Weybridge
Cob.	Cobham	Islw.	Isleworth	S.Croy.	South Croydon	Whyt.	Whyteleafe
Couls.	Coulsdon	Ken.	Kenley	S.Dnth.	South Darenth	Wdf.Grn.	Woodford Green
Croy.	Croydon	Kes.	Keston	S.Ock.	South Ockendon	Wind.	Windsor
Cuff.	Cuffley	Kings L.	Kings Langley	Stai.	Staines	Wok.	Woking
Dag.	Dagenham	Kings.T.	Kingston on Thames	S.le H.	Stanford le Hope	Wor.Pk.	Worcester Park
Dart.	Dartford	Leyt.	Leytonstone	Stan.	Stanmore		

General Abbreviations

All.	Alley	Ct.	Court	La.	Lane	Rd.	Road
App.	Approach	Ctre.	Centre	Lo.	Lodge	S.	South
Arc.	Arcade	Dev.	Development	Mans.	Mansions	Shop.	Shopping
Av.	Avenue	Dr.	Drive	Mkt.	Market	Sq.	Square
Bdy.	Broadway	E.	East	Ms.	Mews	Sta.	Station
Bldgs.	Buildings	Embk.	Embankment	Mt.	Mount	St.	Street
Boul.	Boulevard	Esp.	Esplanade	N.	North	Ter.	Terrace
Bri.	Bridge	Est.	Estate	Par.	Parade	Trd.	Trading
Circ.	Circus	Gdns.	Gardens	Pass.	Passage	Vills.	Villas
Cft.	Croft	Gra.	Grange	Pk.	Park	Vw.	View
Clo.	Close	Grn.	Green	Pl.	Place	W.	West
Cor.	Corner	Gro.	Grove	Prom.	Promenade	Wf.	Wharf
Cotts.	Cottages	Ho.	House	Quad.	Quadrant	Wk.	Walk
Cres.	Crescent	Ind.	Industrial	Ri.	Rise	Yd.	Yard

A

Abberley Ms. SW4 BV45 66
Cedars Rd.
Abberton Wk., Rain. CT37 59
Abbess Clo. E6 CK39 58
Oliver Gdns.
Abbess Clo. SW2 BY47 76
Abbeville Rd. N8 BW31 47
Abbeville Rd. SW4 BW46 76
Abbey Av., St.Alb. BF15 9
Abbey Av., Wem. BL37 55
Abbey Clo., Hayes BC40 53
Abbey Clo., Nthlt. BE38 54
Abbey Clo., Pnr. BD31 45
Abbey Clo., Wok. AV61 100
Abbey Cres., Belv. CR42 69
Abbey Ct., Hmptn. BF51 84
Abbey Ct., St.Alb. BG14 9
Albert St.
Abbey Ct., Wal.Abb. CE20 21
Abbey Dr. SW17 BU49 76
Church La.
Abbey Dr., Stai. AX52 83
Abbey Gdns. Ms. NW8 BT37 1
Abbey Gdns. Ms. NW8 BT37 56
Abbey Gdns. NW8 BT37 1
Abbey Gdns. NW8 BT37 56
Abbey Gdns. W6 BR43 65
Abbey Gdns., Cher. AW53 83
Abbey Gro. SE2 CO42 69
Abbey La. E15 CF37 57
Abbey La., Beck. CE50 77
Abbey Mill End, St.Alb. BG14 9
Abbey Mill La., St.Alb. BG14 9
Abbey Ms. E17 CE32 48
Leamington Av.
Abbey Orchard St. SW1 BW41 3
Abbey Orchard St. SW1 BW41 66
Abbey Pk., Beck. CE50 77
Abbey Rd. E15 CF37 57
Abbey Rd. Est. NW8 BS37 1
Abbey Rd. Est. NW8 BS37 56
Abbey Rd. NW10 BM37 55
Abbey Rd. NW6 BS37 1
Abbey Rd. NW6 BS37 56
Abbey Rd. NW8 BT37 56
Abbey Rd. SE2 CP42 69
Abbey Rd. SW19 BT50 76
Abbey Rd., Bark. CL36 58
Abbey Rd., Belv. CP42 69
Abbey Rd., Bexh. CQ45 69
Abbey Rd., Cher. AW54 83
Abbey Rd., Croy. BY55 86
Abbey Rd., Enf. CA25 30
Abbey Rd., Grav. DJ47 81
Abbey Rd., Green. DB46 80
Abbey Rd., Ilf. CM32 49
Abbey Rd., S.Croy. CC58 96
Abbey Rd., Shep. AZ55 83
Abbey Rd., Vir.W. AR53 82
Abbey Rd., Wal.Cr. CD20 21
Abbey Rd., Wok. AR62 100
Abbey St. E13 CH38 58
Abbey St. SE1 CA41 4
Abbey St. SE1 CA41 67
Abbey Ter. NW10 BL37 55
Abbey Ter. SE2 CP42 69
Abbey Vw. NW7 BO27 37
Abbey Vw. Rd., St.Alb. BG13 9
Abbey Vw., Wal.Abb. CE20 21
Abbey Wk., E.Mol. BF52 84
Abbey Wood La., Rain. CV37 60
Abbey Wood Rd. SE2 CO42 69
Abbeydale Rd., Wem. BL37 55
Abbeyfield Gdns. SE16 CC42 67
Abbeyfield Rd. SE16 CC42 67
Abbeyfields Clo. NW10 BM37 55
Abbeyhill Rd., Sid. CP47 79
Abbot Clo., Stai. AX50 73
Bingham Dr.
Abbot Clo., Wey. AX59 92
Abbot Rd., Guil. AR71 118
Abbot St. E8 CA36 57
Kingsland High St.
Abbots Av. W., St.Alb. BG15 9
Abbots Av., St.Alb. BH15 9
Abbots Clo. N1 BZ36 57
Alwyne Rd.
Abbots Clo., Brwd. DD26 122
Abbots Clo., Guil. AP72 118
Abbots Clo., Orp. CM54 88
Abbots Clo., Rain. CV37 60
Abbots Clo., Ruis. BD34 45
Abbots Clo., Uxb. AX39 53
Abbots Cres., Enf. BY23 29
Abbots Dr., Vir.W. AQ53 82
Abbots Dr., Wal.Abb. CH20 22
Abbots Field, Grav. DH50 81
Abbots Ford Clo., Wok. AT62 100
Onslow Cres.
Abbots Gdns. N2 BT31 47
Abbots La. SE1 CA40 4
Abbots La. SE1 CA40 57
Abbots La., Ken. BZ61 105
Abbots Manor Est. SW1 BV42 3
Abbots Manor Est. SW1 BV42 66
Abbots Pk. SW2 BY47 76
Abbots Pk., St.Alb. BJ15 9
Abbots Pl. NW6 BS37 56
Abbots Rd. E6 CJ37 58
Abbots Rd., Edg. BN29 37
Abbots Rd., Wat. BA19 17
Abbots Ri., Kings L. AY16 17
Abbots Tilt, Walt. BE55 84
Abbots Vw., Kings L. AY17 17
Abbots Way, Beck. CD53 87
Abbots Way, Guil. AU70 118
Abbots Wk., Cat. CB64 105
Abbotsbury Clo. E15 CF37 57
Abbotsbury Clo. W14 BR41 65
Abbotsbury Gdns., Pnr. BD33 45
Abbotsbury Rd. W14 BR41 65
Abbotsbury Rd., Brom. CG55 88
Abbotsbury Rd., Mord. BS53 86
Abbotsfield, Grav. DH50 81
Abbotsford Av. N15 BZ31 48
Abbotsford Gdns., Wdf.Grn. CH30 40
Abbotsford Rd., Ilf. CO34 50
Abbotshall Av. N14 BW27 38
Abbotshall Rd. SE6 CF47 77
Abbotsleigh Clo., Sutt. BS57 95
Camborne Rd.
Abbotsleigh Rd. SW16 BW49 76
Abbotsmede Clo., Twick. BH48 74
Abbotstone Rd. SW15 BQ45 65
Abbotsweld, Harl. CN12 13
Abbotswell Rd. SE4 CD46 77
Abbotswood Clo., Belv. CQ41 69
Coptefield Dr.
Abbotswood Clo., Guil. AS69 118
Abbotswood Dr., Wey. BA59 92
Abbotswood Gdns., Ilf. CK31 49
Abbotswood Rd. SW16 BW48 76
Abbotswood Way, Hayes BC40 53
Abbotswood, Guil. AS69 118
Abbott Av. SW20 BQ51 85
Abbott Clo., Hmptn. BE50 74
Abbott Clo., Nthlt. BE36 54
Abbott Rd. E14 CF39 57
Abbotts Clo., Rom. CR31 50
Abbotts Clo., Swan. CU52 89
Abbotts Cres. E4 CF28 39
Abbotts Dr., Wem. BJ34 45
Abbotts Grn., S.Croy. CC57 96
Abbotts Park Rd. E10 CF33 48
Abbotts Rd., Barn. BS24 29
Abbotts Rd., Mitch. BW52 86
Abbotts Rd., Sthl. BE40 54
Abbotts Rd., Sutt. BR56 94
Abbotts Way, Slou. AL40 61
Abbotts Wk., Bexh. CP43 69
Abbotts Wk., Wind. AM44 61
Abbs Cross Gdns., Horn. CV33 51
Abbs Cross La., Horn. CV34 51
Abchurch La. EC4 BZ40 4
Abchurch La. EC4 BZ40 57
Abchurch Yd. EC4 BZ40 57
Abchurch La.
Abdale La., Hat. BP17 19
Abdale Rd. W12 BP40 55
Abel Clo., Hem.H. AZ13 8
Abels Bldgs. E1 CA40 4
Royal Mint St.
Abenbury Way, Brwd. DD27 122
Aberavon Rd. E3 CD38 57
Abercairn Rd. SW16 BW50 76
Aberconway Rd., Mord. BS52 86
Abercorn Clo. NW7 BR29 37
Abercorn Clo. NW8 BT38 1
Abercorn Clo. NW8 BT38 56
Abercorn Clo., S.Croy. CC59 96
Kersey Dr.
Abercorn Cres., Har. BF33 45
Abercorn Est., Wem. BK37 54
Abercorn Gdns., Har. BK33 45
Abercorn Gdns., Rom. CO32 50
Abercorn Gro., Ruis. BA31 44
Abercorn Pl. NW8 BT38 1
Abercorn Pl. NW8 BT38 56
Abercorn Rd. NW7 BR29 37
Abercorn Rd., Stan. BK29 36
Abercorn Way, Wok. AQ62 100
Abercrombie St. SW11 BU44 66
Abercrombie Way, Harl. CM12 13
Aberdale Gdns., Pot.B. BR19 19
Aberdare Clo., W.Wick. CF55 87
Aberdare Gdns. NW6 BS36 1
Aberdare Gdns. NW6 BS36 56
Aberdare Gdns. NW7 BQ29 37
Aberdare Rd., Enf. CB24 30
Aberdeen La. N5 BY35 47
Aberdeen Par. N18 CB28 39
Angel Rd.
Aberdeen Pk. N5 BY35 47
Aberdeen Pl. NW8 BT38 1
Aberdeen Pl. NW8 BT38 56
Aberdeen Rd. N18 CB28 39
Aberdeen Rd. N5 BZ35 48
Aberdeen Rd. NW10 BO35 46
Aberdeen Rd., Croy. BZ56 96
Aberdeen Rd., Har. BH30 36
Aberdeen Ter. SE3 CF44 67
Aberdour Rd., Ilf. CO34 50
Aberdour St. SE1 CA41 4
Aberdour St. SE1 CA41 67
Aberfeldy St. E14 CF39 57
Aberford Gdns. SE18 CK44 68
Aberford Rd., B.Wd. BM23 28
Aberfoyle Rd. SW16 BW50 76
Abergeldie Rd. SE12 CH46 78
Abernethy Rd. SE13 CG45 68
Abersham Rd. E8 CA35 48
Abery St. SE18 CN42 68
Abingdon Clo. NW1 BW36 56
Abingdon Clo. SE1 CA42 4
Bushwood Dr.
Abingdon Clo. SW19 BT50 76
Abingdon Clo., Uxb. AY37 53
Abingdon Clo., Wok. AQ62 100
Winnington Way
Abingdon Pl., Pot.B. BS19 20
Abingdon Rd. N3 BT30 38
Abingdon Rd. SW16 BX51 86
Abingdon Rd. W8 BS41 66
Abingdon St. SW1 BX41 4
Abingdon St. SW1 BX41 66
Abingdon Vill. W8 BS41 66
Abingdon Way, Orp. CO56 98
Abinger Av., Sutt. BQ58 94
Abinger Clo., Brom. CK52 88
Abinger Clo., Dor. BK73 119
Abinger Clo., Ilf. CO35 50
Abinger Clo., Wall. BX56 95
Abinger Gdns., Islw. BH45 64
Abinger Gro. SE8 CD43 67
Abinger La., Dor. BC73 119
Abinger Ms. W9 BS38 56
Warlock Rd.
Abinger Rd. W4 BO41 65
Abinger Way, Guil. AT68 109
Ablett St. SE16 CC42 67
Abourne St. W9 BS38 56
Amberley Rd.
Aboyne Dr. SW20 BP51 85
Aboyne Rd. NW10 BN34 46
Aboyne Rd. SW17 BT48 76
Abridge Clo., Wal.Cr. CC21 30
Abridge Gdns., Rom. CR29 41
Abridge Rd., Chig. CM25 31
Abridge Rd., Epp. CN22 31
Abridge Way, Bark. CO37 59
Abyssinia Clo. SW11 BU45 66
Cairns Rd.
Abyssinia Rd. SW11 BU45 66
Auckland Rd
Acacia Av. N17 BZ29 39
Acacia Av., Brent. BJ43 64
Acacia Av., Hayes BB39 53
Acacia Av., Horn. CT34 50
Acacia Av., Ruis. BC33 44
Acacia Av., Shep. AZ53 83
Acacia Av., Stai. AS45 62
Acacia Av., Wem. BL35 46
Acacia Av., West Dr. AY40 53
Acacia Av., Wok. AR63 100
Acacia Clo. SE20 CB51 87
Selby Rd.
Acacia Clo., Orp. CM53 88
Acacia Clo., Stan. BH29 36
Acacia Dr., Bans. BQ60 94
Acacia Dr., Sutt. BR54 85
Acacia Dr., Upmin. CX35 51
Acacia Dr., Wey. AV58 91
Acacia Gdns. NW8 BT37 1
Acacia Gdns., Upmin. CZ33 51
Acacia Gdns., W.Wick. CF55 87
Acacia Gro. SE21 BZ48 77
Acacia Gro., Berk. AQ13 7
Acacia Gro., N.Mal. BN52 85
Acacia Ms., West Dr. AX43 63
High St.
Acacia Ms., West Dr. AX43 63
High St., Harmondsworth
Acacia Pl. NW8 BT37 1
Acacia Pl. NW8 BT37 56
Acacia Rd. E11 CG34 49
Acacia Rd. E17 CD32 48
Acacia Rd. N22 BY30 38
Acacia Rd. NW8 BT37 1
Acacia Rd. NW8 BT37 56
Acacia Rd. SW16 BX51 86
Acacia Rd. W3 BN40 55
Acacia Rd., Beck. CD52 87
Acacia Rd., Dart. CV47 80
Acacia Rd., Enf. BZ23 30
Acacia Rd., Green. CZ46 80
Acacia Rd., Guil. AR70 118
Acacia Rd., Hmptn. BF50 74
Acacia Rd., Mitch. BV51 86
Acacia Rd., Stai. AW49 73
Acacia St., Hat. BP14 10
Acacia Wk., Swan. CS51 89
Walnut Way
Academy Gdns., Croy. CA54 87
Academy Gdns., Nthlt. BD37 54
Academy Rd. SE18 CK44 68
Acanthus Rd. SW11 BV45 66
Accommodation La., West Dr. AW44 63
Accommodation Rd. NW11 BR33 46
Accommodation Rd., Cher. AS56 91
Acer Av., Rain. CV38 60
Acer Rd., West. CJ61 106
Acers, St.Alb. BG17 18
Acfold Rd. SW6 BS44 66
Achilles Clo., Hem.H. AY12 8
Achilles Pl., Wok. AR61 100
Beggars La.
Achilles Rd. NW6 BS35 47
Achilles St. SE14 CD43 67
Achilles Way W1 BV40 3
Achilles Way W1 BV40 56
Acklam Rd. W10 BR39 55
Portobello Rd.
Acklington Dr. NW9 BO30 37
Ackmar Rd. SW6 BS44 66
Ackroyd Dr. E3 CD39 57
Ackroyd Rd. SE23 CC47 77
Ackroydon Est. SW19 BQ47 75
Ackworth Clo. N9 CC26 39
Turin Rd.
Acland Cres. SE5 BZ45 67
Acland Rd. NW2 BP36 55
Linacre Rd.
Acme Rd., Wat. BC22 26
Acol Cres., Ruis. BC35 44
Acol Rd. NW6 BS36 56
Acomb Rd., Dag. CO37 59
Aconbury Rd., Dag. CO37 59
Stamford Rd.
Acorn Clo. E4 CE28 39
The Lawns
Acorn Clo., Chis. CM49 78
Acorn Clo., Enf. BY23 29
Acorn Ct., Ilf. CN32 49
Acorn Gdns. SE19 CA51 87
Acorn Gdns. W3 BN39 55
Acorn Gro., Hayes BB43 63
Acorn Gro., Ruis. BB35 44
Acorn Gro., Tad. BR65 103
Acorn La., Cuff. BX18 20
Acorn Par. SE15 CB43 67
Acorn Pl., Wat. BC22 26
Acorn Rd., Dart. CT46 79
Acorn Rd., Hem.H. AZ14 8
Acorn Way SE23 CC48 77
Acorn Way, Orp. CL56 97
Starts Hill Rd.
Acorn Wk. SE16 CD40 57
Acorns Clo., Hmptn. BF50 74
Acorns Way, Esher BG56 93
Acorns, The, Chig. CN28 40
Acre La. SW2 BX45 66
Acre La., Cars. BV56 95
Acre Pass., Wind. AO44 61
Peascod St.
Acre Path, Nthlt. BE36 54
Arnold Rd.
Acre Rd. SW19 BT50 76
Acre Rd., Dag. CR36 59
Acre Rd., Kings.T. BL51 85
Acre Vw., Horn. CW31 51
Russetts
Acre Way, Nthwd. BB30 35
Acre Wd., Hem.H. AY14 8
Acrefield Rd., Ger.Cr. AR31 43
Acres Av., Ong. CW16 24
Acres End, Amer. AP23 25
Acres Gdns., Tad. BQ63 103
Acrewood Way, St.Alb. BL13 10
Acris St. SW18 BT46 76
Acton Clo., Chsnt. CD19 21
Russells Ride
Acton Est. E8 CA37 57
Acton La. NW10 BN38 55
Acton La. W3 BN41 65
Acton La. W4 BN42 65
Acton Ms. E8 CA37 2
Acton Pk. Ind. Est. W3 BN40 55
Acton St. WC1 BX38 2
Acton St. WC1 BX38 56
Acuba Rd. SW18 BS47 76
Ada Gdns. E14 CF39 57
Ada Gdns. E15 CG37 58
Ada Pl. E2 CB37 57
Ada Rd. SE5 CA43 67
Ada Rd., Wem. BK34 45
Ada St. E8 CB37 57
Adair Clo. SE25 CB52 87
Adair Rd. W10 BR38 55
Adam & Eve Ct. W1 BW39 1
Adam & Eve Ct. W1 BW39 56
Eastcastle St.
Adam & Eve Ms. W8 BS41 66
Adam Clo., Slou. AN40 61
Adam Pl. N16 CA34 48
High St.
Adam St. W1 BV39 1
Adam St. W1 BV39 56
Adam St. WC2 BX40 4
Adam St. WC2 BX40 56
Adam Wk. SW6 BQ43 65
Adams Clo. N3 BS29 38
Falkland Av.
Adams Clo. NW9 BM34 46
Adams Ct. EC2 BZ39 2
Old Broad St.
Adams Gdns. Est. SE16 CC41 67
Adams Pl. N7 BX35 47
Georges Rd.
Adams Rd. N17 CA30 39
Adams Rd., Beck. CD52 87
Adams Row W1 BV40 3
Adams Row W1 BV40 56
Adams Sq., Bexh. CP45 69
Adams Way, Croy. CA53 87
Adamsfield, Wal.Cr. CA16 21
Adamson Rd. E16 CH39 58
Adamson Rd. NW3 BT36 56
Adamsrill Clo., Enf. BZ25 30
Adamsrill Rd. SE26 CC49 77
Adare Wk. SW16 BX48 76
Adcock Wk., Orp. CN56 97
Adderley Gdns. SE9 CL49 78
Adderley Gro. SW11 BV46 76
Culmstock Rd.
Adderley Rd., Har. BH30 36
Adderley St. E14 CF39 57
Addington Clo., Wind. AN45 61
Addington Dr. N12 BT29 38
Addington Gro. SE26 CD49 77
Addington Rd. E16 CG38 58
Addington Rd. E3 CE38 57
Addington Rd. N4 BY32 47
Addington Rd., Croy. BY54 86
Addington Rd., S.Croy. CB59 96
Addington Rd., W.Wick. CG56 96
Addington Sq. SE5 BZ43 67
Addington St. SE1 BX41 4
Addington St. SE1 BX41 66
Addington Village Rd., Croy. CD57 96
Addis Clo., Enf. CC23 30
Addiscombe Av., Croy. CB54 87
Addiscombe Clo., Har. BK32 45
Addiscombe Court Rd., Croy. CA54 87
Addiscombe Gro., Croy. BZ55 87
Addiscombe Rd., Croy. BZ55 87
Addiscombe Rd., Wat. BC24 26
Addison Av. N14 BV25 29
Addison Av. W11 BR40 55
Addison Av., Houns. BG44 64
Addison Bridge Pl. W14 BR42 65
Addison Clo., Cat. BZ64 105
Addison Clo., Iver AV39 52
Dutton Way
Addison Clo., Nthwd. BB30 35
Addison Clo., Orp. CM53 88
Addison Cres. W14 BR41 65
Addison Dr. SE12 CH46 78
Addison Gdns. W14 BQ41 65
Addison Gdns., Grays DE42 71
Palmers Dr.
Addison Gdns., Surb. BL52 85
Addison Gro. W4 BO41 65
Addison Pl. SE25 CB52 87
Addison Rd.
Addison Pl. W11 BR40 55
Addison Pl., Sthl. BF40 54
Longford Av.
Addison Rd. E11 CH32 49
Addison Rd. E17 CE32 48
Addison Rd. SE25 CB52 87
Addison Rd. W14 BR41 65
Addison Rd., Brom. CJ53 88
Addison Rd., Cat. BZ64 105
Addison Rd., Enf. CC23 30
Addison Rd., Guil. AS71 118
Addison Rd., Ilf. CM30 40
Addison Rd., Tedd. BJ50 74
Addison Rd., Wok. AS62 100
Chertsey Rd.
Addison Way NW11 BR31 46
Addison Way, Hayes BC39 53
Addison Way, Nthwd. BB30 35
Addisons Clo., Croy. CD55 87
Addle Hill EC4 BY39 56
Addle Hill EC4 BY40 4
Addle St. EC2 BZ39 2
Wood St.
Addlestone Moor, Wey. AX55 83
Addlestone Pk., Wey. AW56 92
Liberty La.
Addlestone Rd., Wey. AY56 92
Adecroft Way, E.Mol. BG52 84
Adela Av., N.Mal. BP53 85
Adela St. W10 BR38 55
Kensal Rd.
Adelaide Av. SE4 CD45 67
Adelaide Clo., Enf. CA22 30
Adelaide Clo., Stan. BJ28 36
Adelaide Clo., Slou. AN41 61
Amerden Way
Adelaide Cotts. W7 BH40 54
Adelaide Gdns., Rom. CQ32 50
Adelaide Gro. W12 BP40 55
Adelaide Pl., Wey. BA56 92
Adelaide Rd. E10 CF34 48
Adelaide Rd. NW3 BT36 56
Adelaide Rd. W13 BJ40 54
Adelaide Rd., Ashf. AX49 73
Adelaide Rd., Chis. CL49 78
Adelaide Rd., Houns. BE44 64
Adelaide Rd., Ilf. CL34 49
Adelaide Rd., Rich. BL45 65
Adelaide Rd., Sthl. BE42 64
Adelaide Rd., Surb. BL53 85
Adelaide Rd., Tedd. BH50 74
Adelaide Rd., Til. DF44 71
Adelaide Rd., Walt. BC55 83
Adelaide Sq., Wind. AO44 61
Adelaide St. WC2 BX40 4
Adelaide St. WC2 BX40 56
William IV St.
Adelaide St., St.Alb. BG13 9
Adelaide Wk. SW9 BY45 66
Sussex Wk.
Adele Av., Welw.G.C. BR 5 5
Adelina Gro. E1 CC39 57
Adelina Ms. SW12 BW47 76
Kings Av.
Adeline Pl. WC1 BW39 1
Adeline Pl. WC1 BW39 56
Adelphi Cres., Hayes BB38 53
Adelphi Cres., Horn. CU34 50
Adelphi Gdns., Slou. AP41 62
Adelphi Rd., Epsom BN60 94
Adelphi Ter. WC2 BX40 4
Adelphi Ter. WC2 BX40 56
Adam St.
Adelphi Way, Hayes BB38 53
Aden Gro. N16 BZ35 48
Aden Lo. N16 BZ35 48
Aden Rd., Enf. CD24 30
Aden Rd., Ilf. CM33 49
Aden Ter. N5 BZ35 48
Adeney Clo. W6 BQ43 65
Adenmore Rd. SE6 CE47 77
Adeyfield Gdns., Hem.H. AY13 8
Adeyfield Rd., Hem.H. AX13 8
Adhara Rd., Nthwd. BB28 35
Adie Rd. W6 BQ41 65
Adine Rd. E13 CH38 58
Adingtons, Harl. CN10 6
Adler St. E1 CB39 2
Adler St. E1 CB39 57
Adlers La., Dor. BJ69 119
Adley St. E5 CD35 48
Admaston Rd. SE18 CM43 68
Admiral Seymour Rd. SE9 CK45 68
Admiral St. SE8 CE44 67
Admirals Clo. E18 CH31 49
Admirals Clo., St.Alb. BO15 10
Admirals Ct., Guil. AT70 118
Admirals Way E14 CE41 67
Admirals Wk. NW3 BT34 47
Admirals Wk., Couls. BX63 104
Admirals Wk., Hodd. CE13 12
Admirals Wk., St.Alb. BJ14 9
Admiralty Rd., Tedd. BH50 74
Adnams Wk., Rain. CT36 59
Adolf St. SE6 CE49 77
Adolphus Rd. N4 BY34 47
Adolphus St. SE8 CD43 67
Adomar Rd., Dag. CQ34 50
Adpar St. W2 BT39 1
Adpar St. W2 BT39 56
Adrian Clo., Uxb. AX30 35
Adrian Ms. SW10 BS43 66
Adrian Rd., Wat. BB19 17
Adrienne Av., Sthl. BE38 54
Adstock Way, Grays DC42 71
Adys Rd. SE15 CA45 67
Aerodrome Rd. NW9 BO30 37
Aerodrome Way, Houns. BD43 64
Aeroville, NW9 BO30 37
Affleck St. N1 BX37 2
Affleck St. N1 BX37 56
Pentonville Rd.
Afghan Rd. SW11 BU44 66
Afton Dr., S.Ock. DA39 60
Agamemnon Rd. NW6 BR35 46
Agar Clo., Surb. BL55 85
Agar Gro. Est. NW1 BW36 56
Agar Gro. NW1 BW36 56
Agar Pl. NW1 BW36 56
Agar St. WC2 BX40 4
Agar St. WC2 BX40 56
Chandos Pl.
Agars Plough, Eton AQ43 62
Agate Clo. E16 CJ39 58
Agate Rd. W6 BQ41 65
Agates La., Ash. BK62 102
Agatha Clo. E1 CC40 57
Agaton Rd. SE9 CM48 78
Agave Rd. NW2 BQ35 46
Agdon St. EC1 BY38 2
Agdon St. EC1 BY38 56
Agincourt Rd. NW3 BU35 47

Agister Rd., Chig. CO28 41
Agnes Av., Ilf. CL34 49
Agnes Clo. E6 CL39 58
Agnes Gdns., Dag. CP35 50
Agnes Rd. W3 BO40 55
Agnes Scott Ct., Wey. AZ55 83
Palace Dr.
Agnes St. E14 CD39 57
Agnew Rd. SE23 CC47 77
Agraria Rd., Guil. AQ71 118
Agricola Pl., Enf. CA25 30
Aidan Clo., Dag. CQ34 50
Aileen Wk. E15 CG36 58
Ailsa Av., Twick. BJ46 74
Ailsa Rd., Twick. BJ46 74
Ailsa St. E14 CF39 57
Ainger Ms. NW3 BU37 1
Ainger Rd.
Ainger Rd. NW3 BU36 56
Ainger Rd. NW3 BU37 1
Ainsdale Clo., Orp. CM54 88
Ainsdale Cres., Pnr. BF31 45
Ainsdale Rd. W5 BK38 54
Ainsdale Rd., Wat. BD27 36
Ainsdale Way, Wok. AQ62 100
Ainsley Av., Rom. CR32 50
Ainsley Clo. N9 CA26 39
Ainsley St. E2 CB38 57
Ainslie Wd. Cres. E4 CE28 39
Ainslie Wd. Gdns. E4 CE28 39
Ainslie Wd. Rd. E4 CE28 39
Ainslie Wk. SW12 BV47 76
Balham Gro.
Ainsty St. SE16 CC41 67
Brunel Rd.
Ainsworth Clo. NW2 BP34 46
Ainsworth Rd. E9 CC36 57
Ainsworth Rd., Croy. BY54 86
Ainsworth Way NW8 BT37 1
Ainsworth Way NW8 BT37 56
Aintree Av. E6 CK37 58
Aintree Clo., Grav. DG48 81
Aintree Clo., Slou. AV44 62
Aintree Clo., Uxb. AZ39 53
Aintree Cres., Ilf. CM30 40
Aintree Est. SW6 BR43 65
Aintree Gro., Upmin. CW34 51
Aintree Rd., Grnf. BJ37 54
Aintree St. SW6 BR43 65
Air St. W1 BW40 3
Air St. W1 BW40 56
Glasshouse St.
Airdrie Clo. N1 BX36 56
Airdrie Clo. N1 BX37 2
Airdrie Clo., Hayes BE39 54
Glencoe Rd.
Aire Dr., S.Ock. DA38 60
Airedale Av. S. W4 BO42 65
Netheravon Rd. S.
Airedale Av. W4 BO42 65
Airedale Rd. SW12 BU47 76
Airedale Rd. W5 BK41 64
Airedale, Hem.H. AY12 8
Airey Neave Ct., Grays DD41 71
Orchard Dr.
Airfield Way, Horn. CU36 59
Airlie Gdns. W8 BS40 56
Airlie Gdns., Ilf. CL33 49
Airport Way, Stai. AW45 63
Airthrie Rd., Ilf. CO34 50
Aisgill Av. W14 BR42 65
Aisher Rd. SE28 CP40 59
Aislibie Rd. SE12 CG45 68
Aitken Rd. SE6 CE48 77
Aitken Rd., Barn. BQ25 28
Ajax Av. NW9 BO31 46
Ajax Rd. NW6 BS35 47
Akehurst La., Sev. CV66 117
Akehurst St. SW15 BP46 75
Akeman Clo., St.Alb. BE15 9
Akenside Rd. NW3 BT35 47
Akerman Rd. SW9 BY44 66
Akerman Rd., Surb. BK53 84
Akers La., Rick. AU25 25
Alabama St. SE18 CM43 68
Alacross Rd. W5 BK41 64
Alamein Gdns., Dart. CY47 80
Alamein Rd., Swans. DB46 80
Alan Clo., Dart. CV45 70
Alan Dr., Barn. BR25 28
Alan Gdns., Rom. CR33 50
Alan Rd. SW19 BR49 75
Alan Tusing Rd., Guil. AO70 118
Alan Way., Slou. AS39 52
Alandale Dr., Pnr. BC30 35
Alanthus Clo. SE12 CG46 78
Alaska St. SE1 BY40 56
Cornwall Rd.
Alba Clo., Hayes BE38 54
Ramulis Dr.
Alba Gdns. NW11 BR32 46
Alba Pl. W11 BR39 55
Portobello Rd.
Albacore Cres. SE13 CE46 77
Albain Cres., Ashf. AY48 73
Alban Av., St.Alb. BG12 9
Alban Cres., B.Wd. BM23 28
Alban Cres., Farn. CX54 90
Alban Pk., St.Alb. BL13 10
Albans La. NW11 BS33 47
West Hth. Dr.
Albans Vw., Wat. BC20 17
Albany Clo. N15 BY31 47
Albany Clo. SW14 BM45 65
Albany Clo., Bex. CP47 79
Albany Clo., Bush. BG25 27
Albany Clo., Esher BF58 93
Albany Clo., Uxb. AZ35 44
Albany Cotts., Esher BE57 93
Albany Cres., Edg. BM29 37
Albany Cres., Esher BH57 93
Albany Ct. NW9 BN30 37
Albany Ct., Epp. CN18 22
Albany Mans. SW11 BU43 66
Albany Ms. SE17 BZ43 67
Albany Rd. SE5
Albany Ms., Kings.T. BK50 74
Albany Park Rd.
Albany Pass., Rich. BL46 75
Albany Pk. Av., Enf. CC23 30
Albany Pk. Rd., Kings.T. BK50 74
Albany Pk. Rd., Lthd. BJ63 102
Albany Pl. N7 BY35 47
Albany Pl., Brent. BK43 64
Albany Rd.
Albany Pl., Egh. AT49 72
Albany Rd. E10 CE33 48
Albany Rd. E12 CJ35 49
Albany Rd. E17 CD32 48
Albany Rd. N18 CC28 39
Albany Rd. N4 BY32 47
Albany Rd. SE5 BZ43 67
Albany Rd. SE5 CA43 4
Albany Rd. SW19 BS49 76
Albany Rd. W13 BJ39 54
Albany Rd., Belv. CQ43 69
Albany Rd., Bex. CP47 79
Albany Rd., Brent. BK43 64
Albany Rd., Brwd. DA25 33
Albany Rd., Chis. CL49 78
Albany Rd., Enf. CC22 30
Albany Rd., Horn. CU33 50
Albany Rd., N.Mal. BN52 85
Albany Rd., Old Windsor AQ46 72
Albany Rd., Rich. BL46 75
Albert Rd.
Albany Rd., Rom. CQ32 50
Albany Rd., Walt. BD56 93
Albany Rd., Wind. AO44 61
Albany Reach, Surb. BH53 84
Albany Row N2 BT31 47
The Causeway
Albany St. NW1 BV37 1
Albany St. NW1 BV37 56
Albany Ter. NW1 BV38 1
Albany Ter. NW1 BV38 56
Euston Rd.
Albany Vw., Buck.H. CH26 40
Albany, The W1 BW40 3
Albany, The W1 BW40 56
Vigo St.
Albany, The, Wdf.Grn. CG28 40
Albatross Gdns., S.Croy. CC59 96
Albatross St. SE18 CM43 68
Albatross Way SE16 CC41 67
Albemarle App., Ilf. CL32 49
Albemarle Av., Chsnt. CC17 21
Albemarle Av., Pot.B. BS19 20
Albemarle Clo., Grays DD41 71
Albemarle Gdns., Ilf. CL32 49
Albemarle Gdns., N.Mal. BN52 85
Albemarle Pk., Stan. BK28 36
Albemarle Rd., Barn. BU26 38
Albemarle Rd., Beck. CE51 87
Albemarle St. W1 BV40 3
Albemarle St. W1 BV40 56
Albemarle SW19 BQ48 75
Albemarle Way EC1 BY38 2
Albemarle Way EC1 BY38 56
Clerkenwell Rd.
Albeny Gate, St.Alb. BG14 9
Albermarle Av., Twick. BE47 74
Alberon Gdns., NW11 BR31 46
Albert Av. E4 CE28 39
Albert Av. SW8 BX43 66
Albert Av., Cher. AW52 83
Albert Av., Ilf. CM34 49
High Rd.
Albert Br. Rd. SW11 BU43 66
Albert Br. SW11 BU43 66
Albert Br. SW3 BU43 66
Albert Carr Gdns. SW16 BX49 76
Albert Clo. E9 CB37 57
Northiam St.
Albert Clo. N22 BW30 38
Albert Clo., Grays DE41 71
Albert Clo., Slou. AP41 62
Albert St.
Albert Cres. E4 CE28 39
Albert Ct. SW19 BR47 75
Albert Ct. SW7 BT41 3
Albert Ct. SW7 BT41 66
Albert Dr. SW19 BR48 75
Albert Dr., Wok. AU60 91
Albert Embankment SE1 BX42 4
Albert Embankment SE1 BX42 66
Albert Gate SW1 BU41 66
Rotten Row
Albert Gdns. E1 CC39 57
Albert Gro. SW20 BQ51 85
Albert Hall Ms. SW7 BT41 3
Albert Hall Ms. SW7 BT41 66
Prince Consort Rd.
Albert Mans. SW11 BU44 66
Albert Ms. W8 BT41 3
Albert Pl. N3 BS30 38
Popes Dr.
Albert Pl. W8 BS41 3
Albert Pl. W8 BS41 66
Albert Pl., Eton AN42 61
Common Rd.
Albert Rd. E10 CF34 48
Albert Rd. E16 CK40 58
Albert Rd. E17 CE32 48
Albert Rd. E18 CH31 49
Albert Rd. Est., Belv. CQ42 69
Albert Rd. N., Wat. BC24 26
Albert Rd. N15 CA32 48
Albert Rd. N22 BW30 38
Albert Rd. N4 BX33 47
Albert Rd. NW4 BQ31 46
Albert Rd. NW6 BR37 55
Albert Rd. NW7 BO28 37
Albert Rd. S., Wat. BC24 26
Albert Rd. SE20 CC50 77
Albert Rd. SE25 CB52 87
Albert Rd. SE9 CK48 78
Albert Rd. W5 BJ38 54
Albert Rd., Ash. BL62 103
Albert Rd., Ashf. AY49 73
Albert Rd., Barn. BT24 29
Albert Rd., Belv. CQ42 69
Albert Rd., Bex. CR47 79
Albert Rd., Brom. CJ53 88
Albert Rd., Buck.H. CJ27 40
Albert Rd., Dag. CQ33 50
Albert Rd., Dart. CV48 80
Albert Rd., Egh. AR50 72
Albert Rd., Epsom BO60 94
Albert Rd., Har. BG31 45
Albert Rd., Hayes BB41 63
Albert Rd., Hmptn. BG49 74
Albert Rd., Houns. BF45 64
Albert Rd., Ilf. CM34 49
Albert Rd., Kings.T. BL51 85
Albert Rd., Mitch. BU52 86
Albert Rd., N.Mal. BO52 85
Albert Rd., Orp. CO56 98
Albert Rd., Red. BW68 113
Albert Rd., Rich. BL46 75
Albert Rd., Rom. CT32 50
Albert Rd., St. Mary Cray CO53 89
Albert Rd., Sthl. BD41 64
Albert Rd., Sutt. BT56 95
Albert Rd., Swans. DC46 81
Albert Rd., Tedd. BH50 74
Albert Rd., Twick. BH47 74
Albert Rd., Warl. CD62 105
Albert Rd., West Dr. AY40 53
Albert Rd., Wey. AX55 83
Albert Rd., Wind. AP45 61
Albert Sq. E15 CG35 49
Albert Sq. SW8 BX43 66
Albert St. N12 BT28 38
Lodge La.
Albert St. NW1 BV37 1
Albert St. NW1 BV37 56
Albert St., Brwd. DB28 42
Albert St., Slou. AP41 62
Albert St., St.Alb. BG14 9
Albert St., Wat. BD24 27
Queens Rd.
Albert St., Wind. AN44 61
Albert Studios SW11 BU43 66
Albert Bridge Rd.
Albert Ter. Ms. NW1 BV37 1
Albert Ter. NW1 BV37 1
Albert Ter. NW1 BV37 56
Albert Ter. NW10 BN37 55
Albert Ter., Buck.H. CK27 40
Albert Wk. E16 CL41 68
Alberta Av., Sutt. BR56 94
Alberta Est. SE17 BY42 66
Alberta Rd., Enf. CA25 30
Alberta Rd., Erith CS44 69
Alberta St. SE17 BY42 4
Alberta St. SE17 BY42 66
Albion Av. N10 BV30 38
Albion Av. SW8 BW44 66
Albion Bldgs. EC1 BZ39 57
Bartholomew Clo.
Albion Clo. W2 BU40 3
Albion Clo. W2 BU40 56
Albion St.
Albion Clo., Rom. CS32 50
Albion Clo., Slou. AQ40 52
Albion Cres., Ch.St.G. AQ27 34
Albion Dr. E8 CA36 2
Albion Dr. E8 CA36 57
Albion Est. SE16 CC41 67
Albion Gate W2 BU40 56
Albion Gdns. W6 BP42 65
Albion Gro. N16 BZ35 48
Albion Hill SE13 CE44 67
Albion Hill, Hem.H. AX14 8
Albion Hill, Loug. CJ25 31
Albion Ms. N1 BY36 2
Albion Ms. N1 BY36 56
Albion Ms. W2 BU40 3
Albion Ms. W2 BU40 56
Albion Par., Grav. DH46 81
Albion Pk., Loug. CJ25 31
Albion Pl. EC1 BY39 2
London Wall
Albion Pl. EC1 BY39 56
Albion Pl. SE25 CB52 87
High St.
Albion Rd. E17 CF31 48
Albion Rd. N16 BZ34 48
Albion Rd. N17 CA30 39
Reform Row
Albion Rd., Bexh. CR45 69
Albion Rd., Ch.St.G. AQ27 34
Albion Rd., Grav. DH47 81
Albion Rd., Hayes BB39 53
Albion Rd., Houns. BF45 64
Albion Rd., Kings.T BN51 85
Albion Rd., Reig. BT71 121
Albion Rd., St.Alb. BH13 9
Albion Rd., Sutt. BT57 95
Albion Rd., Twick. BH47 74
Albion Sq. E8 CA36 2
Albion Sq. E8 CA36 57
Albion St. SE16 CC41 67
Albion St. W2 BU39 1
Albion St. W2 BU39 56
Albion St., Croy. BY54 86
Albion Ter. E8 CA36 57
Albion Ter., Grav. DH46 81
Albion Villas Rd. SE26 CC48 77
Albion Way SE13 CF45 67
Albion Way, Wem. BM34 46
Albrighton Rd. SE22 CA45 67
Albuhera Clo., Enf. BY23 29
Albury Av., Bexh. CQ44 69
Albury Av., Islw. BH43 64
Albury Av., Sutt. BQ58 94
Albury Clo., Cher. AQ55 82
Albury Clo., Hmptn. BF50 74
Albury Ct., Croy. BZ56 96
Albury Dr., Pnr. BD30 36
Albury Grove Rd., Chsnt. CC18 21
Albury Rd., Chess. BL56 94
Albury Rd., Guil. AS71 118
Albury Rd., Red. BW68 113
Albury Rd., Walt. BB57 92
Albury Ride, Chsnt. CC19 21
Albury St. SE8 CE43 67
Albury Wk., Chsnt. CC18 21
Albyfield, Brom. CK52 88
Albyn Rd. SE8 CE44 67
Albyns Clo., Rain. CU36 59
South End Rd.
Alcester Cres. E5 CB34 48
Alcester Rd., Wall. BV56 95
Alcock Clo., Wall. BW57 95
Alcock Rd., Houns. BD43 64
Alcocks Clo., Tad. BT63 103
Alcocks La., Tad. BR64 103
Alconbury Rd. E5 CB34 48
Alcorn Clo., Sutt. BS55 86
Alcott Clo. W7 BH39 54
Westcott Cres.
Aldam Pl. N16 CA34 48
High St.
Aldborough Rd. N., Ilf. CN32 49
Aldborough Rd. S., Ilf. CN33 49
Aldborough Rd., Dag. CS36 59
Aldborough Rd., Upmin. CW34 51
Aldborough Spur, Slou. AP39 52
Aldbourne Rd. W12 BO40 55
Aldbridge St. SE17 CA42 4
Aldbridge St. SE17 CA42 67
Aldbury Av., Wem. BM36 55
Aldbury Clo., St.Alb. BK11 9
Sandringham Cres.
Aldbury Clo., Wat. BD21 27
Aldbury Gro., Welw.G.C. BS 8 5
Aldbury Ms. N9 BZ26 39
Aldbury Rd., Rick. AV26 34
Aldebert Ter. SW8 BX43 66
Aldeburgh Clo. E5 CB34 48
Southwold Rd.
Aldeburgh Pl., Wdf.Grn. CH28 40
Aldeburgh St. SE10 CH42 68
Alden Av. E15 CG38 58
Alden Vw., Wind. AL44 61
Aldenham Av., Rad. BJ21 27
Aldenham Dr., Uxb. AZ38 53
Aldenham Gro., Rad. BJ20 18
Aldenham Rd., B.Wd. BJ24 27
Aldenham Rd., Bush. BE25 27
Aldenham Rd., Rad. BJ21 27
Aldenham Rd., Wat. BD25 27
Aldenham St. NW1 BW37 1
Aldenham St. NW1 BW37 56
Aldenholme, Wey. BB57 92
Aldensley Rd. W6 BP41 65
Alder Av., Upmin. CW35 51
Alder Cft., Couls. BX61 104
Alder Clo. SE15 CA43 67
Alder Clo., St.Alb. BG17 18
Alder Gro. NW2 BP34 46
Alder Ms. N19 BW34 47
Bredgar Rd.
Alder Rd. SW14 BN45 65
Alder Rd., Sid. CN48 78
Alder Rd., Uxb. AX36 53
Alder Way, Swan. CS51 89
Alderbourne La., Iver AT35 43
Alderbourne La., Slou. AR35 43
Alderbrook Rd. SW12 BV46 76
Alderbury Rd. SW13 BP43 65
Alderbury Rd. W., Slou. AS41 62
Alderbury Rd., Slou. AS41 62
Aldercoombe La., Cat. CA67 114
Aldercroft, Couls. BX61 104
Aldergrove Gdns., Houns. BE44 64
Bath Rd.
Aldergrove Wk., Horn. CV36 60
Airfield Way
Alderholt Way SE15 CA43 67
Alderley Ct., Berk. AR13 7
Alderman Av., Bark. CO38 59
Alderman Clo., Hat. BQ15 10
Alderman Judge Mall, Kings.T. BL51 85
Eden St.
Aldermanbury EC2 BZ39 2
Aldermanbury EC2 BZ39 57
Aldermanbury Sq. EC2 BZ39 2
Aldermanbury Sq. EC2 BZ39 57
Aldermanbury
Aldermans Hill N13 BX28 38
Aldermans Wk. EC2 CA39 57
Bishopsgate
Aldermary Rd., Brom. CH51 88
Aldermaston St. W10 BQ39 55
Alderminster Rd. SE1 CB42 4
Alderminster Rd. SE1 CB42 67
Aldermoor Rd. SE6 CD48 77
Alderney Av., Houns. BF43 64
Alderney Gdns., Nthlt. BE36 54
Alderney Rd. E1 CC38 57
Alderney Rd., Erith CU43 69
Alderney St. SW1 BV42 3
Alderney St. SW1 BV42 66
Alders Av., Wdf.Grn. CG29 40
Alders Clo. E11 CH34 49
Alders Clo. W5 BK41 64
South Ealing Rd.
Alders Clo., Edg. BN28 37
Alders Gro., E.Mol. BG53 84
Alders Rd., Edg. BN28 37
Alders Rd., Reig. BS69 121
Alders, The, Felt. BE49 74
Alders, The, Houns. BE42 64
Alders, The, N21 BY25 29
Alders, The, W.Wick. CE54 87
Aldersbrook Av., Enf. CA23 30
Aldersbrook Dr., Kings.T. BL50 75
Aldersbrook La. E12 CK34 49
Aldersbrook Rd. E11 CH34 49
Aldersbrook Rd. E12 CH34 49
Aldersey Gdns., Bark. CM36 58
Aldersey Rd., Guil. AS70 118
Aldersford Clo. SE4 CC46 77
Aldersgate St. EC1 BZ39 2
Aldersgate St. EC1 BZ39 57
Aldersgrove Av. SE9 CJ48 78
Aldersgrove, Wal.Abb. CG20 22
Roundhills
Aldershot Rd. NW6 BR37 55
Aldershot Rd., Guil. AO69 118
Aldershot Ter. SE18 CL43 68
Prince Imperial Way
Alderside Clo., Egh. AS49 72
Alderside Wk., Egh. AS49 72
Aldersmead Av., Croy. CC53 87
Aldersmead Rd., Beck. CD50 77
Alderson St. W10 BR38 55
Kensal Rd.
Alderstead La., Red. BW66 113
Alderton Clo. NW10 BN34 46
Alderton Clo., Brwd. DA25 33
Alderton Clo., Loug. CL24 31
Alderton Cres. NW4 BP32 46
Alderton Hall La., Loug. CL24 31
Alderton Hill, Loug. CK25 31
Alderton Rd. SE24 BZ45 67
Alderton Rd., Croy. CA54 87
Alderton Ri., Loug. CL24 31
Alderton Way NW4 BP32 46
Alderton Cres.
Alderton Way, Loug. CL25 31
Alderville Rd. SW6 BR44 65
Alderwick Dr., Houns. BG45 64
Alderwood Clo., Cat. CA66 114
Alderwood Dr., Rom. CO24 32
Alderwood Rd. SE9 CM46 78
Aldford St. W1 BV40 3
Aldford St. W1 BV40 56
Aldgate Av. E1 CA39 57
Aldgate EC3 CA39 2
Aldgate High St. EC3 CA39 2
Aldgate High St. EC3 CA39 57
Aldin Av. N., Slou. AQ41 62
Aldin Av. S., Slou. AQ41 62
Aldine Ct. W12 BQ41 65
Aldine Pl. W12 BQ41 65
Aldine St. W12 BQ41 65
Aldingham Gdns., Horn. CU35 50
Aldington Clo., Dag. CP33 50
Aldington Rd. SE18 CJ41 68
Aldis Ms. SW17 BU49 76
Aldis St.
Aldis St. SW17 BU49 76
Aldock, Welw.G.C. BS 9 5
Aldred Rd. NW6 BS35 47
Aldren Rd. SW17 BT48 76
Aldrich Cres., Croy. CF58 96
Aldrich Ter. SW18 BT48 76
Lidiard Rd.
Aldriche Way E4 CF29 39
Aldridge Av., Edg. BM27 37
Aldridge Av., Enf. CE22 30
Aldridge Av., Ruis. BD34 45
Aldridge Av., Stan. BL30 37
Aldridge Rd. Vill. W11 BR39 55
Aldridge Ri., N.Mal. BO54 85
Aldridge Wk. N14 BX26 38
Aldrington Rd. SW16 BW49 76
Aldsworth Clo. W9 BS39 56
Amberley Rd.
Aldwick Clo. SE9 CM48 78
Aldwick Ct., Hem.H. AX13 8
Aldwick Rd., Croy. BX55 86
Aldwick, St.Alb. BJ14 9
Aldworth Gro. SE13 CF46 77
Aldworth Rd. E15 CG36 58
Aldwych Av., Ilf. CM31 49
Aldwych Clo., Horn. CU34 50
Aldwych WC2 BX40 4
Aldwych WC2 BX40 56
Aldykes, Hat. BO12 10
Alers Rd., Bexh. CP46 79
Alestan Beck Rd. E16 CJ39 58
Alexander Av. NW10 BP36 55
Alexander Clo., Barn. BT24 29
Victoria Rd.
Alexander Clo., Brom. CH54 88
Alexander Clo., Sid. CN46 78
Alexander Clo., Twick. BH48 74
Alexander Godley Clo., Ash. BL63 103
Alexander La., Brwd. DD25 122
Alexander Lo., Wey. AZ56 92
Monument Hill
Alexander Ms. W2 BS39 56
Alexander St.
Alexander Pl. SW7 BU42 3
Alexander Pl. SW7 BU42 66
Alexander Rd. N19 BX34 47
Alexander Rd., Bexh. CP44 69
Alexander Rd., Chis. CL49 78
Alexander Rd., Couls. BV61 104
Alexander Rd., Green. DB46 80
Alexander Rd., Reig. BS72 121
Alexander Rd., St.Alb. BK16 18
Alexander Sq. SW3 BU41 66
Alexander Sq. SW3 BU42 3
Alexander St. W2 BS39 56
Alexander St., Chesh. AO18 16
Alexanders Wk., Cat. CA66 114
Alexandra Av. N22 BW30 38
Alexandra Av. SW11 BV44 66
Alexandra Av. W4 BN43 65
Alexandra Av., Har. BE33 45
Alexandra Av., Sthl. BE40 54
Alexandra Av., Sutt. BS55 86
Alexandra Av., Warl. CD62 105
Alexandra Clo., Ashf. BA50 73
Alexandra Clo., Grays DG41 71
Alexandra Clo., Har. BF34 45
Alexandra Clo., Stai. AX50 73
Alexandra Clo., Swan. CT51 89
Northview
Alexandra Clo., Walt. BC55 83
Alexandra Cotts. SE14 CD44 67
Alexandra Cres., Brom. CG50 78
Alexandra Ct. N14 BW25 29
Alexandra Ct. W9 BT38 1
Alexandra Ct., Wem. BL35 46
Alexandra Dr. SE19 CA49 77
Alexandra Dr., Surb. BM54 85
Alexandra Gdns. N10 BV31 47
Alexandra Gdns. W4 BO43 65
Alexandra Gdns., Cars. BU58 95

Alexandra Gdns., Houns. BF44 64
Alexandra Gro. N12 BS29 38
Alexandra Gro. N4 BY33 47
Alexandra Ms. N2 BU31 47
Fortis Grn.
Alexandra Pk. Rd. N10 BV30 38
Alexandra Pk. Rd. N22 BW30 38
Alexandra Pl. NW8 BT37 1
Alexandra Pl. NW8 BT37 56
Alexandra Pl. SE25 BZ53 87
Alexandra Pl., Croy. CA54 87
Alexandra Rd. E10 CF34 48
Alexandra Rd. E17 CD32 48
Alexandra Rd. E18 CH31 49
Alexandra Rd. E6 CL38 58
Alexandra Rd. N10 BV30 38
Alexandra Rd. N15 BZ32 48
Alexandra Rd. N8 BY31 47
Alexandra Rd. N9 CB26 39
King Edwards Rd.
Alexandra Rd. NW4 BQ31 46
Alexandra Rd. NW8 BT37 1
Alexandra Rd. NW8 BT37 56
Alexander Rd., Egh. AT49 72
Alexandra Rd. SE26 CC50 77
Alexandra Rd. SW14 BN45 65
Alexandra Rd. SW19 BR50 75
Alexandra Rd. W4 BN41 65
Alexandra Rd., Chipperfield AW18 17
Alexandra Rd., Chadwell Heath CP32 50
Alexandra Rd., Ashf. BA50 73
Alexandra Rd., B.Wd. BN22 28
Alexandra Rd., Brent. BK43 64
Alexandra Rd., Brwd. DB27 42
Alexandra Rd., Croy. CA54 87
Alexandra Rd., Egh. AR50 72
Alexandra Rd., Enf. CC24 30
Alexandra Rd., Epsom BO60 94
Alexandra Rd., Erith CT43 69
Alexandra Rd., Grav. DJ47 81
Alexandra Rd., Hem.H. AX13 8
Alexandra Rd., Houns. BF44 64
Alexandra Rd., Kings L. AZ18 17
Alexandra Rd., Kings.T. BM50 75
Alexandra Rd., Mitch. BU50 76
Alexandra Rd., Rain. CT37 59
Alexandra Rd., Rich. BL44 65
Alexandra Rd., Rick. AW21 26
Alexandra Rd., Rom. CT32 50
Alexandra Rd., Slou. AO41 61
Alexandra Rd., St.Alb. BH13 9
Alexandra Rd., T.Ditt. BH53 84
Alexandra Rd., Til. DF44 71
Alexandra Rd., Twick. BK46 74
Alexandra Rd., Uxb. AX37 53
Alexandra Rd., Warl. CD62 105
Alexandra Rd., Wat. BC23 26
Alexandra Rd., West. CH63 106
Alexandra Rd., Wey. AX56 92
Alexandra Rd., Wind. AO44 61
Alexandra Sq., Mord. BS53 86
Alexandra St. E16 CH39 58
Alexandra St. SE14 CD43 67
Alexandra Ter., Guil. AS71 118
Alexandra Way, Wal.Cr. CD20 21
Alexandra Wk. SE19 CA49 77
Alexandria Rd. W13 BJ40 54
Alexis St. SE16 CB42 4
Alexis St. SE16 CB42 67
Alf Lowne Ct., Grays DG41 71
Chilton Rd.
Alfan La., Dart. CS49 79
Alford Clo., Guil. AS69 109
Alford Grn., Croy. CF57 96
Alford Pl. N1 BZ37 57
Alford Rd. SW8 BW44 66
Union Gro.
Alford Rd., Erith CS42 69
Alfoxton Av. N15 BY31 47
Alfred Gdns., Sthl. BE40 54
Alfred Ms. W1 BW39 1
Alfred Ms. W1 BW39 56
Alfred Pl. WC1 BW39 1
Alfred Pl. WC1 BW39 56
Alfred Pl., Grav. DF47 81
Alfred Rd. E15 CG35 49
Alfred Rd. SE25 CB53 87
Alfred Rd. W2 BS39 56
Alfred Rd. W3 BN40 55
Alfred Rd., Belv. CQ42 69
Alfred Rd., Brwd. DB27 42
Alfred Rd., Buck.H. CJ27 40
Alfred Rd., Dart. CW49 80
Alfred Rd., Erith CT43 69
Alfred Rd., Felt. BD48 74
Alfred Rd., Grav. DG48 81
Alfred Rd., Kings.T. BL52 85
Alfred Rd., S.Ock. CY40 60
Alfred Rd., Sutt. BT56 95
Alfred St. E16 CG40 58
Dock Rd.
Alfred St. E3 CD38 57
Alfred St., Grays. DE43 71
Alfreda St. SW11 BV44 66
Alfreds Gdns., Bark. CN37 58
Alfreds Way, Bark. CM37 58
Alfreton Clo. SW19 BQ48 75
Alfriston Av., Croy. BX54 86
Alfriston Av., Har. BF32 5
Alfriston Clo., Surb. BL53 85
Alfriston Rd. SW11 BU45 66
Algar Clo., Islw. BJ45 64
Algar Rd.
Algar Clo., Stan. BH28 36
Algar Rd., Islw. BJ45 64
Algarve Rd. SW18 BS47 76
Algernon Rd. NW4 BP32 46
Algernon Rd. NW6 BS37 56
Algernon Rd. SE13 CE45 67
Algers Clo., Loug. CJ25 31
Algers Mead., Loug. CJ25 31
Algers Rd., Loug. CJ25 31
Algiers Rd. SE13 CE45 67
Alibon Gdns., Dag. CR35 50
Alibon Rd., Dag. CR35 50
Alice Gilliat Ct. W14 BR43 65
Alice Ruston Pl., Wok. AR63 100
Alice St. SE1 CA41 4
Alice St. SE1 CA41 67
Alicia Av., Har. BJ31 45
Alicia Clo., Har. BK31 45
Alicia Gdns., Har. BJ31 45
Alie St. E1 CA39 2
Alie St. E1 CA39 57
Alington Cres. NW9 BN33 46
Alington Gro., Wall. BW58 95
Alison Clo. E6 CL39 58
Alison Clo., Croy. CC54 87
Shirley Oaks Rd.
Alison Clo., Wok. AS60 100
Aliwal Rd. SW11 BU45 66
Alkerden La., Green. DB46 80
Alkerden Rd. W4 BO42 65
Alkham Rd. N16 CA33 48
All Hallows Rd. N17 CA30 39
The Roundway
All Saints Clo. N9 CB27 39
All Saints Clo., Brwd. DA21 33
All Saints Clo., Chig. CO27 41
All Saints Clo., Swans. DC46 81
High St.
All Saints Cres., Wat. BD20 18
All Saints Dr. SE3 CG44 68
Royal Par.
All Saints Dr., S.Croy. CA59 96
All Saints La., Rick. AZ25 26
All Saints Ms., Har. BH29 36
All Saints Pass. SW18 BS46 76
Wandsworth High St.
All Saints Rd. SW19 BT50 76
All Saints Rd. W11 BR39 55
All Saints Rd. W3 BN41 65
All Saints Rd., Grav. DF47 81
All Saints Rd., Sutt. BS55 86
All Saints St. N1 BX37 2
All Saints St. N1 BX37 56
All Souls Av. NW10 BP37 55
All Souls Pl. W1 BV39 1
All Souls Pl. W1 BV39 56
Langham Pl.
Allan Barclay Clo. N15 CA32 48
High Rd.
Allan Clo., Dart. CY47 80
Allan Clo., N.Mal. BN53 85
Allan Way W3 BN39 55
Allanbrooke, Grav. DH47 81
Allandale Av. N3 BR31 46
Allandale Cres., Pot.B. BR19 19
Allandale Pl., Orp. CP55 89
Allandale Rd., Enf. CC21 30
Allandale Rd., Hem.H. AX12 8
Allandale Rd., Horn. CT33 50
Allandale, Hem.H. AX12 8
Allandale, St.Alb. BF15 9
Allard Clo., Chsnt. CA17 21
Allard Clo., Orp. CP54 89
Allard Cres., Bush. BG27 36
Allard Way, Brox. CD14 12
Allardyce St. SW4 BX45 66
Allbrook Clo., Tedd. BH49 74
Allcot Clo., Felt. BB47 73
Allcroft Rd. NW5 BV35 47
Alldicks Rd., Hem.H. AY14 8
Allen Clo. SE26 CC49 77
Allen Clo., Sun. BC51 83
Allen Edwards Dr. SW8 BX44 66
Allen Rd. E3 CD37 57
Allen Rd. N16 CA35 48
Allen Rd., Beck. CC51 87
Allen Rd., Croy. BX54 86
Allen Rd., Lthd. BF66 111
Allen Rd., Rain. CV38 60
Allen Rd., Sun. BC51 83
Allen St. W8 BS41 66
Allenby Av., S.Croy. BZ58 96
Allenby Clo., Grnf. BF38 54
Allenby Cres., Grays DD42 71
Allenby Dr., Horn. CW33 51
Allenby Rd. SE23 CD48 77
Allenby Rd., Sthl. BF38 54
Allenby Rd., West. CK62 106
Allendale Av., Sthl. BF39 54
Allendale Clo. SE26 CC49 77
Trewsbury Rd.
Allendale Clo. SE5 BZ44 67
Love Wk.
Allendale Clo., Dart. CY47 80
Princes Rd.
Allendale Rd., Grnf. BJ36 54
Allens Rd., Enf. CC25 30
Allensbury Pl. NW1 BX36 56
Allenswood Rd. SE9 CK45 68
Allerford Ct., Har. BF32 45
Allerford Rd. SE6 CE48 77
Allerton Clo., B.Wd. BL22 28
Allerton Rd. N16 BZ34 48
Allerton Rd., B.Wd. BL22 28
Allerton Wk. N7 BX34 47
Durham Rd.
Allestree Rd. SW6 BR43 65
Alleyn Cres. SE21 BZ48 77
Alleyn Park Rd. SE21 BZ47 77
Alleyn Pk. Est. SE21 CA49 77
Alleyn Pk. SE21 BZ47 77
Alleyn Pk., Sthl. BE42 64
Alleyn Rd. SE21 BZ48 77
Alleyndale Rd., Dag. CP34 50
Allfarthing La. SW18 BS46 76
Allgood Clo., Mord. BQ53 85
Allgood St. E2 CA37 2
Allhallows La. EC4 BZ40 4
Allhallows La. EC4 BZ40 57
Allhallows Rd. E6 CK39 58
Allhusen Gdns., Slou. AS35 43
Alliance Rd. E13 CJ38 58
Alliance Rd. SE18 CO43 69
Alliance Rd. W3 BM38 55
Allingham Ct. NW3 BU35 47
Haverstock Hill
Allingham Rd., Reig. BS72 121
Allingham St. N1 BZ37 2
Allingham St. N1 BZ37 57
Allington Av. N17 CA29 39
Allington Clo. SW19 BQ49 75
Allington Clo., Grav. DJ47 81
Farley Rd.
Allington Ct., Enf. CC25 30
Allington Ct., Slou. AP40 52
Myrtle Cres.
Allington Rd. NW4 BP32 46
Allington Rd. W10 BR37 55
Allington Rd., Har. BG32 45
Allington Rd., Orp. CM55 88
Allington St. SW1 BV41 3
Allington St. SW1 BV41 66
Allison Clo. SE10 CF44 67
Allison Clo., Wal.Abb. CH19 22
Allison Gro. SE21 CA47 77
Allison Rd. N8 BY32 47
Allison Rd. W3 BN39 55
Allitsen Rd. NW8 BU37 1
Allitsen Rd. NW8 BU37 56
Allmains Clo., Wal.Abb. CH16 22
Allnutt Way SW4 BW46 76
Allnutts Rd., Epp. CO20 23
Alloa Rd. SE8 CC42 67
Alloa Rd., Ilf. CO34 50
Allonby Dr., Ruis. AZ32 44
Allonby Gdns., Wem. BK33 45
Allotment La., Sev. CV64 108
Alloway Clo., Wok. AQ62 100
Inglewood
Alloway Rd. E3 CD38 57
Allsop Pl. NW1 BU38 1
Allsop Pl. NW1 BU38 56
Allum Clo., B.Wd. BL24 28
Allum Gro., Tad. BP64 103
Allum La., B.Wd. BK25 27
Allum Way N20 BT27 38
Manus Way
Allwood Clo. SE26 CC49 77
Allyn Clo., Stai. AV50 72
Penton Rd.
Alma Av. E4 CF29 39
Alma Av., Horn. CW35 51
Alma Clo., Wok. AP62 100
Alma Cres., Sutt. BR56 94
Alma Cut., St.Alb. BH14 9
Alma Gro. SE1 CA42 4
Alma Gro. SE1 CA42 67
Alma Ho. E5 CB34 48
Downs Est.
Alma Pl. SE19 CA50 77
Church Rd.
Alma Pl., Th.Hth. BY53 86
Alma Rd. N10 BV29 38
Alma Rd. SW18 BT45 66
Alma Rd., Berk. AP12 7
Alma Rd., Cars. BU56 95
Alma Rd., Enf. CC25 30
Alma Rd., Esher BH54 85
Alma Rd., Eton AM42 61
Alma Rd., Har. BG30 36
Alma Rd., Orp. CP55 89
Alma Rd., Reig. BS70 121
Alma Rd., Sid. CO48 79
Alma Rd., St.Alb. BH14 9
Alma Rd., Sthl. BE40 54
Alma Rd., Swans. DC46 81
Alma Rd., Wind. AO44 61
Alma Sq. NW8 BT38 1
Alma Sq. NW8 BT38 56
Alma St. E15 CF36 57
Alma St. NW5 BV36 56
Alma Ter. SW18 BT47 76
Almack Rd. E5 CC35 48
Almeida St. N1 BY36 2
Almeida St. N1 BY36 56
Almer Rd. SW20 BP50 75
Almeric Rd. SW11 BU45 66
Almington St. N4 BX33 47
Almners Rd., Cher. AT54 82
Almond Av. W5 BL41 65
Almond Av., Buck.H. CH27 40
Almond Av., Cars. BU55 86
Almond Av., Uxb. AZ34 44
Almond Av., West Dr. AZ41 63
Almond Av., Wok. AR63 100
Almond Clo. SE15 CB44 67
Almond Clo., Brom. CL54 88
Almond Clo., Egh. AQ50 72
Almond Clo., Grays DG41 71
Almond Clo., Guil. AR69 118
Almond Clo., Hayes BB40 53
Almond Clo., Ruis. BB34 44
Almond Clo., Shep. BA51 83
Almond Clo., Wind. AN44 61
Green La.
Almond Dr., Swan. CS51 89
Almond Gro., Brent. BJ43 64
Almond Rd. N17 CB29 39
Trulock Rd.
Almond Rd. SE16 CB42 67
Almond Rd., Dart. CY47 80
Almond Rd., Epsom BN59 94
Almond Way, B.Wd. BM24 28
Whitehouse Av.
Almond Way, Brom. CL54 88
Almond Way, Har. BF30 36
Almond Way, Mitch. BW53 86
Almond Wk., Hat. BP14 10
Southdown Rd.
Almons Way, Slou. AQ39 52
Almorah Rd. N1 BZ36 2
Almorah Rd. N1 BZ36 57
Almorah Rd., Houns. BD44 64
Alms Heath, Wok. AZ64 101
Almshouse La., Chess. BK58 93
Almshouse La., Enf. CB22 30
Almworth Clo. SW15 BP46 75
Alnwick Gro., Mord. BS52 86
Abbotsbury Rd.
Alnwick Rd. E16 CJ39 58
Alnwick Rd. SE12 CH46 78
Alperton La., Wem. BK38 54
Alperton St. W10 BR38 55
Alpha Clo. NW1 BU38 1
Alpha Clo. NW1 BU38 56
Alpha Gdns. SW18 BS46 76
Alpha Gro. E14 CE41 67
Alpha Pl. NW6 BS37 56
Alpha Pl. SW3 BU43 3
Alpha Pl. SW3 BU43 66
Alpha Rd. E4 CE27 39
Alpha Rd. N18 CB29 39
Alpha Rd. SE14 CD44 67
Alpha Rd., Brwd. DE25 122
Alpha Rd., Chobham AP58 91
Alpha Rd., Croy. CA54 87
Alpha Rd., Enf. CD24 30
Alpha Rd., Surb. BL53 85
Alpha Rd., Tedd. BG49 74
Alpha Rd., Uxb. AZ38 53
Alpha Rd., Wok. AT61 100
Alpha St. N., Slou. AP41 62
Alpha St. S., Slou. AP41 62
Alpha St. SE15 CB44 67
Alphea Clo. SW19 BU50 76
Courtney Rd.
Alpine Av., Surb. BH55 85
Alpine Clo., Croy. CA55 87
Alpine Copse, Brom. CL51 88
Alpine Rd., Red. BV69 121
Alpine Rd., SE16 CC42 67
Alpine Rd., Walt. BC54 83
Alpine Way E6 CL39 58
Alpine Wk., Bush. BN27 36
Alresford Rd., Guil. AQ71 118
Alric Av. NW10 BN36 55
Alric Av., N.Mal. BO52 85
Alroy Rd. N4 BY33 47
Alsace Rd. SE17 CA42 4
Alsace Rd. SE17 CA42 67
Alscot Rd. SE1 CA42 4
Alscot Rd. SE1 CA42 67
Alscot Way SE1 CA42 4
Alsike Rd. SE2 CP41 69
Alsike Rd., Erith CP41 69
Alsom Av., Wor.Pk. BP56 94
Alston Clo., Surb. BJ54 84
Alston Rd. N18 CB28 39
Alston Rd. SW17 BT49 76
Alston Rd., Barn. BR24 28
Alston Rd., Hem.H. AW14 8
Alt Gro., SW19 BR50 75
Altair Clo. N17 CA29 39
Altair Way, Nthwd. BB28 35
Altash Way SE9 CK48 78
Altenburg Av. W13 BJ41 64
Altenburg Gdns. SW11 BU45 66
Alterton Clo., Wok. AQ62 100
Altham Grove, Harl. CN10 6
Altham Rd., Pnr. BE29 36
Althea St. SW6 BS44 66
Althorne Gdns. E18 CG31 49
Althorne Rd., Red. BV71 121
Althorne Way, Dag. CR34 50
Althorp Rd. SW17 BU47 76
Althorp Rd., St.Alb. BH13 9
Althorpe Gro. SW11 BT44 66
Westbridge Rd.
Althorpe Ms. SW11 BT44 66
Westbridge Rd.
Althorpe Rd. SW17 BU47 76
Althorpe Rd., Har. BG32 45
Altmore Av. E6 CK36 58
Alton Av., Stan. BH29 36
Alton Clo., Bex. CQ47 79
Alton Clo., Islw. BH44 64
Alton Ct., Stai. AV51 82
Aymer Dr.
Alton Gdns., Beck. CE50 77
Alton Gdns., Twick. BG47 74
Alton Rd. N17 BZ31 48
Alton Rd. SW15 BP47 75
Alton Rd., Croy. BY55 86
Alton Rd., Rich. BL45 65
Alton St. E14 CE39 57
Altyre Clo., Beck. CD53 87
Altyre Rd., Croy. BZ55 87
Altyre Way, Beck. CD53 87
Aluric Clo., Grays DG42 71
Alva Way, Wat. BD27 36
Alvanley Gdns. NW6 BS35 47
Alverstoke Rd., Rom. CW29 42
Alverston Gdns. SE25 CA52 87
Alverstone Av. SW19 BS48 76
Alverstone Av., Barn. BU26 38
Alverstone Gdns. SE9 CM47 78
Alverstone Rd. E12 CL35 49
Alverstone Rd. NW2 BQ36 55
Alverstone Rd., N.Mal. BO52 85
Alverstone Rd., Wem. BL33 46
Alverton St. SE8 CD42 67
Etta St.
Alverton, St.Alb. BG12 9
Alveston Av., Har. BJ31 45
Alvey Est. SE17 CA42 4
Alvey Est. SE17 CA42 67
Alvey St. SE17 CA42 4
Alvey St. SE17 CA42 67
Alvia Gdns., Sutt. BT56 95
Alvington Cres. E8 CA35 48
Alway Av., Epsom BN56 94
Alwen Gro., S.Ock. DA39 60
Alwood Cres. SE12 CH46 78
Alwyn Av. W4 BN42 65
Alwyn Clo., B.Wd. BL25 28
Alwyn Clo., Croy. CE57 96
Alwyn Gdns. W3 BM39 55
Noel Rd.
Alwyne Av., Brwd. DD25 122
Alwyne La. N1 BY36 56
Alwyne Pl. N1 BZ36 57
Alwyne Rd. N1 BZ36 57
Alwyne Rd. SW19 BR50 75
Alwyne Rd. W7 BH40 54
Alwyne Sq. N1 BZ36 57
Alwyne Vill. N1 BY36 56
Alwyns Clo., Cher. AW53 83
Alwyns La., Cher. AV53 82
Alyngton, Berk. AP11 7
Alyth Gdns., NW11 BS32 47
Amalgamated Dr., Brent. BJ43 64
Amanda Clo., Ilf. CM29 4
Amande Ct., Slou. AR41 6
Amazon St. E1 CB39 5
Hessel St.
Ambassador Clo., Houns. BE44 6
Ambassador Gdns. E6 CK39 5
Viscount Dr.
Ambassador Sq. E14 CE42 6
Cahir St.
Amber Av. E17 CD30 3
Amber St. E15 CF36 5
Salway Rd.
Ambercroft Way, Couls. BY63 10
Amberdeen Av. N3 BS31 4
Ambergate Ct., E5 CC35 4
Clapton Pk. Est.
Ambergate St. SE17 BY42 4
Ambergate St. SE17 BY42 6
Amberley Clo., Orp. CN56 9
Warnford Rd.
Amberley Clo., Pnr. BE31 4
Amberley Clo., Wok. AV66 10
Amberley Ct., Sid. CP49 7
Amberley Dr., Wey. AV59 91
Amberley Gdns., Enf. CA26 3
Amberley Gdns., Epsom BO56 9
Amberley Gro. SE26 CB49 7
Amberley Gro., Croy. CA54 8
Amberley Rd. E10 CE33 4
Amberley Rd. N13 BX27 3
Amberley Rd. SE2 CP43 6
Amberley Rd. W9 BS38 5
Amberley Rd., Buck.H. CJ26 4
Amberley Rd., Enf. CA26 3
Amberley Way, Houns. BD46 7
Amberley Way, Mord. BR54 8
Amberley Way, Rom. CR31 5
Amberley Way, Uxb. AY37 5
Amberry Ct., Harl. CM10 6
Amberwood Ri., N.Mal. BN53 8
Amblecote Clo. SE12 CH48 7
Amblecote Rd. SE12 CH48 7
Amblecote, Cob. BD59 9
Fair Acres
Ambler Rd. N4 BY34 4
Ambleside Av. SW16 BW49 7
Ambleside Av., Beck. CD53 8
Ambleside Av., Horn. CU35 5
Ambleside Av., Walt. BD54 8
Ambleside Clo. E9 CC35 4
Ambleside Cres., Enf. CC24 3
Ambleside Gdns., Ilf. CK31 4
Ambleside Gdns., S.Croy. CC58 9
Ambleside Gdns., Sutt. BT57 9
Ambleside Gdns., Wem. BK33 4
Ambleside Rd. NW10 BO36 5
Ambleside Rd., Bexh. CR44 6
Ambleside Way, Egh. AT50 7
Ambleside Wk., Uxb. AX37 5
High St.
Ambleside, Brom. CF50 77
Ambleside, Epp. CO19 23
Ambrey Way, Pur. BW58 95
Ambrooke Rd., Belv. CR42 69
Gertrude Rd.
Ambrosden Av. SW1 BW41 3
Ambrosden Av. SW1 BW41 66
Ambrose Av. NW11 BR33 46
Ambrose Clo. E6 CK39 58
Bondfield Rd.
Ambrose Clo., Orp. CN55 88
Ambrose Ms. SW11 BU44 66
Abercrombie St.
Ambrose St. SE16 CB42 67
Southwark Pk. Rd.
Ambrose Wk. E3 CE37 57
Malmesbury Rd.
Amelia St. SE17 BY42 4
Amelia St. SE17 BY42 66
Amen Cor. EC4 BY39 2
Amen Ct.
Amen Cor. SW17 BU50 76
Amen Ct. EC4 BY39 2
Amen Ct. EC4 BY39 56
Amerden Way, Slou. AN41 61
America Sq. EC3 CA40 4
America St. SE1 BZ40 4
America St. SE1 BZ40 57
Great Guildford St.
Amerland Rd. SW18 BR46 75
Amersham Av. N18 BZ29 39
Amersham By-pass, Amer. AO24 25
Amersham Clo., Rom. CW29 42
Amersham Dr., Rom. CW29 42
Amersham Gro. SE14 CD43 67
Amersham Pl., Amer. AR23 25
Amersham Rd. SE14 CD43 67
Amersham Rd., Chalfont Common AR28 34
Amersham Rd., Amer. AR23 25
Amersham Rd., Ch.St.G. AQ25 25
Amersham Rd., Croy. BZ53 87
Amersham Rd., Ger.Cr. AS31 43
Amersham Rd., Har. BH32 45
Amersham Rd., Rom. CW29 42
Amersham Vale SE14 CD43 67
Amersham Way, Amer. AS23 25
Amersham Wk., Rom. CW29 42
Amery Gdns. NW10 BP37 55
Amery Gdns., Rom CV31 51
Amery Rd., Har. BJ34 45
Ames Rd., Swans. DC46 81
Amesbury Av. SW2 BX48 76
Amesbury Clo., Epp. CN19 22
Amesbury Clo., Wor.Pk. BQ54 85
Amesbury Dr. E4 CE25 30
Amesbury Rd., Brom. CJ52 88
Amesbury Rd., Dag. CP36 59
Amesbury Rd., Epp. CN19 22
Amesbury Rd., Felt. BD48 74
Amesbury, Wal.Abb. CH19 22
Amethyst Rd. E15 CF35 48
Amey Dr., Lthd. BG65 102
Amherst Av. W13 BJ39 54
Amherst Clo., Orp. CO52 89
Amherst Dr., Orp. CN52 88

Amherst Gdns. W13 BK39 54
Amherst Rd.
Amherst Hill, Sev. CT64 107
Amherst Rd. W13 BK39 54
Amherst Rd., Sev. CU64 107
Amhurst Gdns., Islw. BH44 64
Amhurst Park Dev. N16 CA33 48
Amhurst Park N16 BZ33 48
Amhurst Pass. E8 CB35 48
Amhurst Rd. E8 CA35 48
Amhurst Rd. N16 CA35 48
Amhurst Ter. E8 CB35 48
Amhurst Wk. SE28 CO40 59
Pitfield Cres.
Amidas Gdns., Dag. CO35 50
Amiel St. E1 CC38 57
Colebert Av.
Amies St. SW11 BU45 66
Amina Way SE16 CB41 4
Amis Av., Epsom BM57 94
Amis Av., Wey. AW58 92
Amis Rd., Wok. AP63 100
Amity Gro. SW20 BQ51 85
Amity Rd. E15 CG37 58
Amner Rd. SW11 BV46 76
Amor Rd. W6 BQ41 65
Amott Rd. SE15 CB45 67
Amoy Pl. E14 CE40 57
Birchfield St.
Ampleforth Rd. SE2 CO41 69
Ampthill Sq. Est. NW1 BW37 1
Ampthill Sq. Est. NW1 BW37 56
Ampton Pl. WC1 BX38 2
Ampton Pl. WC1 BX38 56
Ampton St.
Ampton St. WC1 BX38 2
Ampton St. WC1 BX38 56
Amroth Clo. SE23 CB47 77
Amsterdam Rd. E14 CF41 67
Amwell Clo., Enf. BZ25 30
Amwell Common, Welw.G.C. BS8 5
Amwell Ct. N4 BZ33 48
Amwell Ct., Hodd. CE11 12
Amwell Ct., Wal.Abb. CG20 22
Amwell St. EC1 BY38 2
Amwell St. EC1 BY38 56
Amwell St., Hodd. CE11 12
Amy Rd., Oxt. CG68 115
Amyand Cotts., Twick. BJ46 74
Amyand Park Rd.
Amyand La., Twick. BJ46 74
Beaconsfield Rd.
Amyand Pk. Gdns., Twick. BJ46 74
Amyand Pk. Rd.
Amyand Pk. Rd., Twick. BJ47 74
Amyruth Rd. SE4 CE46 77
Analy St. SW11 BU44 66
Anatola Rd. N19 BW34 47
Ancaster Cres., N.Mal. BP53 85
Ancaster Rd., Beck. CC52 87
Ancaster St. SE18 CN43 68
Anchor & Hope La. SE7 CH41 68
Anchor Boul., Dart. CY45 70
Anchor Clo., Chsnt. CC17 21
Anchor Cres., Wok. AO62 100
Anchor Dr., Rain. CU38 59
Wentworth Way
Anchor Hill, Wok. AO62 100
Anchor La., Hem.H. AW14 8
Anchor Ms. SW12 BV46 76
Hazelbourne Rd.
Anchor St. SE16 CB42 67
Anchor Yd. EC1 BZ38 57
Old St.
Anchorage Clo. SW19 BS49 76
Ancill Clo. W6 BR43 65
Ancona Rd. NW10 BP37 55
Ancona Rd. SE18 CM42 68
Andalus Rd. SW9 BX45 66
Ander Clo., Wem. BK35 45
Andermass, Wind. AL44 61
Anderson Clo. W3 BN39 55
Cotton Av.
Anderson Clo., Epsom BM59 94
Anderson Clo., Uxb. AW30 35
Belfry Av.
Anderson Dr., Ashf. BA49 73
Anderson Pl., Houns. BF45 64
Anderson Rd. E9 CC36 57
Digby Rd.
Anderson Rd., Ilf. CJ31 49
Anderson Rd., Rad. BM20 19
Anderson Rd., Wey. BA55 83
Anderson St. SW3 BU42 3
Anderson St. SW3 BU42 66
Anderson St. W10 BR38 55
Kensal Rd.
Anderson Way, Belv. CR41 69
Anderton Clo. SE5 CA45 67
Andover Clo., Epsom BN58 94
Andover Clo., Grnf. BF38 54
Andover Clo., Uxb. AW37 53
Andover Ct., Wok. AR63 100
Andover Pl. NW6 BS37 56
Andover Rd. N7 BX34 47
Andover Rd., Orp. CN54 88
Andover Rd., Twick. BG47 74
Andre St. E8 CB35 48
Andrew Borde St. WC2 BW39 56
Charing Cross Rd.
Andrew Clo., Bex. CS46 79
Bourne Rd.
Andrew Clo., Ilf. CM29 40
Andrew Pl. SW8 BW44 66
Andrew St. E14 CF39 57
Andrewes Clo. E6 CK39 58
Linton Gdns.
Andrews Clo., Buck.H. CJ27 40
Andrews Clo., Epsom BO60 94
Andrews Clo., Har. BG33 45
Bessborough Rd.
Andrews Clo., Orp. CP51 89
Andrews Clo., Wor.Pk. BQ55 85
Andrews Crosse WC2 CM39 58
Bell Yd.
Andrews La., Chsnt. CB17 21
Andrews Pl. SE9 CL46 78
Andrews Rd. E8 CB37 57
Andrews Rd., Wal.Cr. CA17 21
Andrews Wk. SE17 BY43 66
John Ruskin St.
Andrewsfield, Welw.G.C. BT8 5
Rivenhall End
Androse Gdns., Brom. CJ51 88
Widmore Rd.
Andwell Clo. SE2 CO41 69
Anerley Gro. SE19 CA50 77
Anerley Hill SE19 CA50 77
Anerley Pk. Rd. SE20 CB50 77
Anerley Pk. SE20 CB50 77
Anerley Rd. SE19 CB50 77
Anerley Rd. SE20 CB50 77
Anerley St. SW11 BU44 66
Dagnall St.
Anerley Sta. Rd. SE20 CB51 87
Anerley Vale SE19 CA50 77
Anfield Clo. SW12 BW47 76
Angas Ct., Wey. BA56 92
Angel Alley E1 CA39 2
Whitechapel Rd.
Angel Clo. N18 CA28 39
Angel Ct. EC2 BZ39 2
Angel Ct. EC2 BZ39 57
Throgmorton St.
Angel Ct. SW1 BW40 3
Angel Ct. SW1 BW40 56
King St.
Angel Ct. SW17 BU49 76
Angel Hill Dr., Sutt. BS55 86
Angel Hill, Sutt. BS55 86
Angel La. E15 CF36 57
Angel La., Hayes BA39 53
Angel Ms. N1 BY37 2
Angel Ms. N1 BY37 56
Angel Pass. EC3 BZ40 57
Wharfside
Angel Pl. EC4 BZ40 4
Angel Pl. EC4 BZ40 57
Angel Pl. N18 CA28 39
Angel Clo.
Angel Pl. SE1 BZ41 4
Angel Pl. SE1 BZ41 67
Borough High St.
Angel Rd. N18 CB28 39
Angel Rd., Har. BH32 45
Angel Rd., T.Ditt. BJ54 84
Angel St. EC1 BZ39 57
Angel St. EC1. BZ39 2
Angel Way, Rom. CT32 50
Angel Wk. W6 BQ42 65
Angelfield, Houns. BF45 64
Angelica Gdns., Croy. CC54 87
Angell Pk. Gdns. SW9 BY45 66
Angell Rd. SW9 BY44 66
Angerstein La. SE3 CG43 68
Angle Clo., Uxb. AZ37 53
Angle Grn., Dag. CP33 50
Angle Pl., Berk. AQ13 7
Angle Rd., Grays DB43 70
Anglefield Rd., Berk. AQ13 7
Anglers Clo., Rich. BK49 74
Anglers La., NW5 BV36 56
Angles Rd. SW16 BX49 76
Anglesea Av. SE18 CL42 68
Anglesea Cent., Grav. DG46 81
New Rd.
Anglesea Pl., Grav. DG46 81
Clive Rd.
Anglesea Rd. SE18 CL42 68
Anglesea Rd., Kings T. BK52 84
Anglesea Rd., Orp. CO53 89
Anglesea St. E1 CB38 2
Anglesea St. E1 CB38 57
Anglesey Clo., Ashf. AZ48 73
Anglesey Ct. Rd., Cars. BV57 95
Anglesey Dr., Rain. CU38 59
Anglesey Gdns., Cars. BV57 95
Anglesey Rd., Enf. CB24 30
Anglesey Rd., Wat. BD28 36
Anglesmede Cres., Pnr. BF31 45
Anglesmede Way, Pnr. BF31 45
Anglia Wk. E6 CK37 58
Napier Rd.
Anglo Rd. E3 CD37 57
Angus Clo., Chess. BM56 94
Angus Dr., Ruis. BD35 45
Angus Gdns. NW9 BN30 37
Angus Rd. E13 CJ38 58
Angus St. SE14 CD43 67
Anhalt Rd. SW11 BU43 66
Ankerdine Cres. SE18 CL43 68
Anlaby Rd., Tedd. BH49 74
Anley Rd. W14 BQ41 65
Anmersh Gro., Stan. BK30 36
Ann La. SW10 BT43 66
Ann St. SE18 CM42 68
Anna Neagle Clo. E7 CH35 49
Dames Rd.
Annabel Clo. E14 CE39 57
Annalee Gdns., S.Ock. DA39 60
Annalee Rd., S.Ock. DA39 60
Annan Way, Rom. CS30 41
Annandale Gro., Uxb. BA34 44
Tweedale Gro.
Annandale Rd. SE10 CG42 68
Annandale Rd. W4 BO42 65
Annandale Rd., Croy. CB55 87
Annandale Rd., Guil. AQ71 118
Annandale Rd., Sid. CN47 78
Anne Boleyns Wk., Kings.T. BL49 75
Anne Boleyns Wk., Sutt. BR57 94
Anne of Cleves Rd., Dart. CB46 80
Anne St. E13 CH38 58
Anne Way, E.Mol. BF52 84
Anne Way, Ilf. CM29 40
Annes Wk., Cat. CA63 105
Annesley Av. NW9 BN31 46
Annesley Clo. NW10 BO34 46
Annesley Dr., Croy. CD55 87
Annesley Rd. SE3 CH44 68
Annesley Wk. N19 BW34 47
Macdonald Rd.
Annett Clo., Shep. BB52 83
Upper Halliford Rd.
Annett Rd., Walt. BC54 83
Annette Clo., Har. BH30 36
Spencer Rd.
Annette Cres. N1 BZ36 57
Essex Rd.
Annette Rd. N7 BX35 47
Annetts Gro. N1 BZ36 57
Essex Rd.
Annie Besant Clo. E3 CD37 57
Annifer Way, S.Ock. DA39 60
Anning St. EC2 CA38 57
New Inn Yd.
Annington Rd. N2 BU31 47
Annis Rd. E9 CD36 57
Anns Clo. SW1 BU41 3
Anns Clo. SW1 BV41 66
Kinnerton St.
Anns Pl. E1 CA39 2
Wentworth St.
Annsworthy Av., Th.Hth. BZ52 87
Annsworthy Cres. SE25 BZ51 87
Lenham Rd.
Ansdell Rd. SE15 CC44 67
Ansdell St. W8 BS41 3
Ansdell St. W8 BS41 66
St. Albans Gro.
Ansdell Ter. W8 BS41 3
Ansdell Ter. W8 BS41 66
Ansell Gro., Cars. BU54 86
Ansell Rd. SW17 BU48 76
Ansell Rd., Dor. BJ71 119
Anselm Clo., Croy. CA55 87
Anselm Rd. SW6 BS43 66
Anselm Rd., Pnr. BE29 36
Ansford Rd., Brom. CF49 77
Ansleigh Pl. W11 BQ40 55
Ansley Clo., S.Croy. CB60 96
Anslow Gdns., Iver AU37 52
Anson Clo., Hem.H. AS17 16
Lancaster Dr.
Anson Clo., Ken. BZ63 105
Anson Clo., Rom. CR30 41
Anson Clo., Sandridge BK10 9
Anson Clo., St.Alb. BJ14 9
Anson Rd. N7 BW35 47
Anson Rd. NW2 BQ35 46
Anson Ter., Nthlt. BF36 54
Anson Wk., Nthwd. BA28 35
Anstead Dr., Rain. CU37 59
Anstey Rd. SE15 CB45 67
Anstey Wk. N8 BY31 47
Anstice Clo. W4 BO43 65
Anstridge Rd. SE9 CM46 78
Antelope Av., Grays DD41 71
Antelope Rd. SE18 CK41 68
Anthony Clo. NW7 BO28 37
Anthony Clo., Sev. CT63 107
Anthony Clo., Wat. BD26 36
Anthony La., Swan. CU51 89
Anthony Rd. SE25 CB53 87
Anthony Rd., B.Wd. BL23 28
Anthony Rd., Grnf. BH37 54
Anthony Rd., Well. CO44 69
Anthony St., E1 CB39 57
Commercial Rd.
Anthorne Clo., Pot.B. BS19 20
Anthus Ms., Nthwd. BB29 35
Antill Rd. E3 CD38 57
Antill Rd. N15 CB31 48
Antill Ter. E1 CC39 57
Antlers Hill E4 CE25 30
Antoinette Ct., Wat. BB18 17
Dairy Way
Anton Cres., Sutt. BS55 86
Anton Rd., S.Ock. DA38 60
Anton St. E8 CB35 48
Antoneys Clo., Pnr. BD30 36
Antonine Gte., St.Alb. BF14 9
Antrim Gro. NW3 BU36 56
Antrim Mans. NW3 BU36 56
Antrim Rd. NW3 BU36 56
Antrobus Clo., Sutt. BR56 94
Antrobus Rd. W4 BN42 65
Anvil Clo., Hem.H. AT17 16
Anvil Ct., Slou. AT42 62
Blacksmith Row
Anvil La., Cob. BC60 92
Anvil Rd., Sun. BC52 83
Anworth Clo., Wdf.Grn. CH29 40
Anyards Rd., Cob. BC60 92
Apeldoorn Dr., Wall. BX58 95
Aperdele Rd., Lthd. BJ62 102
Aperfield Rd., Erith CT43 69
Aperfield Rd., West. CK62 106
Apers Av., Wok. AS64 100
Apex Clo., Beck. CF51 87
Apex Clo., Wey. BA55 83
Apley Rd., Reig. BS72 121
Aplin Way, Islw. BH44 64
Osterley Rd.
Apollo Av., Brom. CH51 88
Hawes Rd.
Apollo Av., Nthwd. BC28 35
Apollo Clo., Horn. CU34 50
Apollo Pl. SW10 BT44 66
Riley St.
Apollo Way SE28 CM41 68
Broadwater Rd.
Apollo Way, Hem.H. AY12 8
Apothecary St. EC4 BY39 56
New Bridge St.
Appach Rd. SW2 BY46 76
Appian Way Est., Erith CR42 69
Apple Cotts., Hem.H. AT17 16
Apple Garth, Brent. BK42 64
Apple Gro., Chess. BL56 94
Apple Gro., Enf. CA24 30
Apple Mkt., Kings.T. BK51 84
Apple Orchard, Hem.H. AY12 8
Apple Tree Av., Uxb. & West Dr. AY39 53
Apple Tree Yd. SW1 BW40 3
Apple Tree Yd. SW1 BW40 56
Duke of York St.
Appleby Clo. E4 CF29 39
Appleby Clo. N15 BZ32 48
Penrith Rd.
Appleby Clo., Twick. BG48 74
Appleby Dr., Rom. CV28 42
Appleby Grn., Rom. CV28 42
Appleby Rd. E16 CG39 58
Appleby Rd. E8 CB36 57
Appleby St. E2 CA37 2
Appleby St. E2 CA37 57
Appleby St., Chsnt. BZ16 21
Applecroft Rd., Welw.G.C. BP8 5
Applecroft, St.Alb. BF17 18
Appledore Av., Bexh. CS44 69
Appledore Av., Ruis. BC34 44
Appledore Clo. SW17 BU48 76
Appledore Clo., Brom. CG53 88
Appledore Clo., Edg. BM30 37
Appledore Clo., Rom. CV30 42
Appledore Cres., Sid. CN48 78
Appledore, Slou. AP36 52
Duffield La.
Appledown Ri., Couls. BW61 104
Applefield, Amer. AR23 25
Amersham Pl.
Appleford Clo., Hodd. CD11 12
Appleford Rd. W10 BR38 55
Applegarth Av., Guil. AO70 118
Applegarth Dr., Ilf. CN31 49
Applegarth Rd. SE28 CO40 59
Applegarth Rd. W14 BQ41 65
Applegarth, Croy. CE57 96
Applegarth, Esher BJ56 93
Applegate, Brwd. CZ25 33
Appleshaw Clo., Grav. DG49 81
Chalky Bank
Appleton Gdns., N.Mal. BP53 85
Appleton Rd. SE9 CK45 68
Appleton Rd., Loug. CL24 31
Appleton Way, Horn. CV34 51
Appletree Clo., Brwd. DB22 33
Appletree Cres.
Appletree Cres., Brwd. DB22 33
Appletree Ct., Guil. AU69 109
Old Merrow St.
Appletree Gdns., Barn. BU24 29
Appletree La., Slou. AR41 62
Appletree Wk., Chesh. AO20 16
Cresswell Rd.
Appletree Wk., Wat. BC20 17
Applewood Clo. N20 BU26 38
Applewood Clo. NW2 BP34 46
Appold St. EC2 CA39 2
Appold St. EC2 CA39 57
Appold St., Erith CT43 69
Apprentice Way E5 CB35 48
Clarence Rd.
Approach Clo. N16 CA35 48
Cowper Rd.
Approach Rd. E2 CC37 57
Approach Rd. SW20 BQ51 85
Approach Rd., Cockfosters BV24 29
Approach Rd., Ashf. BA49 73
Approach Rd., Barn. BT24 29
Approach Rd., E.Mol. BF53 84
Approach Rd., Pur. BY59 95
Approach Rd., St.Alb. BH14 9
Approach, The NW4 BQ32 46
Approach, The W3 BN39 55
Approach, The, Enf. CB23 30
Approach, The, Lthd. BE65 102
Approach, The, Orp. CN55 88
Approach, The, Pot.B. BR19 19
Approach, The, Upmin. CX34 51
Apps Ct., Walt. BD53 84
Apps Pond La., St.Alb. BC15 8
Aprey Gdns. NW4 BQ31 46
April Clo. W7 BH40 54
April Clo., Felt. BC48 73
April Clo., Orp. CN56 97
Briarswood Way
April Glen SE23 CC48 77
Mayow Rd.
April Wood Clo., Wey. AV59 91
Apsledene, Grav. DH50 81
Apsley Clo., Har. BG32 45
Apsley Rd. E17 CD32 48
Apsley Rd. SE25 CB52 87
Apsley Rd., N.Mal. BN52 85
Aquarius Way, Nthwd. BC28 35
Aquila Clo., Ash. BK64 102
Aquila Clo., Nthwd. BC28 35
Aquila St. NW8 BT37 1
Aquila St. NW8 BT37 56
Aquinas St. SE1 BY40 4
Aquinas St. SE1 BY40 56
Arabella Dr. SW15 BO45 65
Arabia Clo. E4 CF26 39
Arabin Rd. SE4 CD45 67
Araglen Av., S.Ock. DA39 60
Aragon Av., Epsom BP58 94
Aragon Av., T.Ditt. BH53 84
Aragon Clo., Brom. CK54 88
Seymour Dr.
Aragon Clo., Croy. CG58 96
Aragon Clo., Enf. BX22 29
Aragon Clo., Hem.H. BA11 8
Aragon Clo., Rom. CR29 41
Aragon Dr., Ilf. CM29 40
Aragon Dr., Ruis. BD33 45
Field End Rd.
Aragon Ms. E1 CB40 4
Aragon Ms. E1 CB40 57
Thomas More St.
Aragon Rd., Kings.T. BL49 75
Aragon Rd., Mord. BQ53 85
Arandora Cres., Rom. CO33 50
Arbery Rd. E3 CD38 57
Arbor Clo., Beck. CE51 87
Arbor Ct. N16 BZ34 48
Arbor Rd. E4 CF27 39
Arborfield Clo., Slou. AP41 62
Arbour Clo., Brwd. DB28 42
Arbour Clo., Lthd. BH65 102
Arbour Field, Wok. AS61 100
Arbour Rd., Enf. CC24 30
Arbour Sq. E1 CC39 57
Arbour View, Amer. AQ23 25
Bell La.
Arbour Way, Horn. CU35 50
Arbroath Grn., Wat. BC27 35
Arbroath Rd. SE9 CK45 68
Arbrook Clo., Orp. CO52 89
Arbrook La., Esher BG57 93
Arbury Ter. SE26 CB48 77
Wells Park Rd.
Arbuthnot La., Bex. CQ47 79
Arbuthnot Rd. SE14 CC44 67
Arbutus Clo., Red. BT71 121
Arbutus Rd., Red. BT72 121
Arbutus St. E8 CA36 57
Arbutus St. E8 CA37 2
Arcade Pl., Rom. CT32 50
Arcade, The E17 CE31 48
Hoe St.
Arcade, The EC2 CA39 2
Blomfield St.
Arcade, The EC2 CA39 57
Liverpool St.
Arcade, The SE9 CK46 78
Eltham High St.
Arcadia Av. N3 BS30 38
Arcadia St. E14 CE39 57
Arcadian Av., Bex. CQ46 79
Arcadian Clo., Bex. CQ46 79
Arcadian Gdns. N22 BX29 38
Arcadian Rd., Bex. CQ46 79
Arcany Rd., S.Ock. DA38 60
Arch Field, Welw.G.C. BR6 5
Arch Rd., Walt. BD55 84
Arch St. SE1 BZ41 4
Arch St. SE1 BZ41 67
Arch Way, Rom. CU29 41
Archangel St. SE16 CC41 67
Archates Av., Grays DD41 71
Archbishops Pl. SW2 BX47 76
Archdale Rd. SE22 CA46 77
Archel Rd. W14 BR43 65
Archer Clo., Kings L. AZ18 17
Archer Ho. SW11 BT44 66
Archer Ms., Hmptn. BG50 74
Archer Rd. SE25 CB52 87
Archer Rd., Orp. CO53 89
Archer St. W1 BW40 3
Archer St. W1 BW40 56
Rupert St.
Archer Ter., West Dr. AY40 53
Yew Av.
Archer Way, Swan. CU51 89
Archers Dr., Enf. CC23 30
Archers Ride, Welw.G.C. BS9 5
Archers, Harl. CL13 13
Archery Clo. W2 BU39 56
Archery Clo., Har. BH31 45
Archery Rd. SE9 CK46 78
Arches, The, Har. BG34 45
Archibald Ms. W1 BV40 3
Farm St.
Archibald Rd. N7 BW35 47
Archibald Rd., Rom. CX30 42
Archway Clo. N19 BW34 47
Archway Clo. SW19 BS49 76
Archway Mall N19 BW34 47
Archway Pl., Dor. BJ71 119
Archway Rd. N19 BV33 47
Archway Rd. N6 BU32 47
Archway St. SW13 BO45 65
Arcola St. E8 CA35 48
Arctic St. NW5 BV35 47
Arcus Rd., Brom. CG49 78
Ardbeg Rd. SE24 BZ46 77
Arden Clo., Bush. BH26 36
Arden Clo., Har. BG34 45
Arden Clo., Hem.H. AT17 16
Arden Clo., Reig. BS72 121
Arden Court Gdns. N2 BT33 47
Arden Cres. E14 CE42 67
Arden Cres., Dag. CP36 59
Arden Est. N1 CA38 57
Arden Gro., Orp. CL56 97
Pinecrest Gdns.
Arden Mhor, Pnr. BC31 44
Arden Rd. N3 BR31 46
Arden Rd. W13 BJ40 54
Ardens Way, St. Alb. BK12 9
Ardent Clo. SE25 CA52 87
Ardentinny, St. Alb. BH14 9
London Rd.
Ardfern Av. SW16 BY52 86
Ardfillan Rd. SE6 CF47 77
Ardgowan Rd. SE6 CG47 78
Ardilaun Rd. N5 BZ35 48
Ardleigh Clo., Horn. CV31 51
Ardleigh Ct. Brwd. DC26 122
Hutton Rd.
Ardleigh Gdns., Brwd. DF26 122
Ardleigh Gdns., Sutt. BS54 86
Ardleigh Grn. Rd., Horn. CV32 51
Ardleigh Ms., Ilf. CL34 49
Bengal Rd.
Ardleigh Rd. E17 CD30 39
Ardleigh Rd. N1 CA36 57
Ardley Clo. NW10 BO34 46
Ardley Clo. SE23 CD48 77
Ardley Clo., Ruis. BA33 44
Ardlui Rd. SE27 BZ48 77
Ardmay Gdns., Surb. BL53 85
Ardmere Rd. SE13 CF46 77
Ardmore Av., Guil. AQ69 118
Ardmore La., Buck.H. CH26 40
Ardmore Rd., S.Ock. DA38 60
Ardmore Way, Guil. AQ69 118
Ardoch Rd. SE6 CF48 77
Ardross Av., Nthwd. BB28 35
Ardrossan Gdns., Wor.Pk. BP55 85
Ardshiel Clo. SW15 BQ45 65
Bemish Rd.
Ardshiel Dr., Red. BU71 121
Fairlawn Dr.
Ardsley Wd., Wey. BB56 92

Ardwell Av., Ilf. CM32 49
Ardwell Rd. SW2 BX48 76
Ardwick Rd. NW2 BS35 47
Argall Av. E10 CC33 48
Argent St. SE1 BY41 4
Argent St., Grays DD43 71
Argon Ms. SW6 BS43 66
Argosy Gdns., Stai. AV50 72
Argosy La., Stai. AX47 73
Clare Rd.
Argus Clo., Rom. CR30 41
Lynton Av.
Argus Way, Nthlt. BE38 54
Argyle Av., Houns. BF46 74
Argyle Clo. W13 BJ38 54
Argyle Est. SW19 BQ48 75
Argyle Gdns., Upmin. CY35 51
Argyle Pass. N17 CB30 39
Argyle Rd.
Argyle Pl. W6 BP42 65
Argyle Rd. E1 CC38 57
Argyle Rd. E15 CG35 49
Argyle Rd. E16 CH39 58
Argyle Rd. N12 BS28 38
Argyle Rd. N17 CB30 39
Argyle Rd. N18 CB28 39
Argyle Rd. W13 BJ38 54
Argyle Rd., Barn. BQ24 28
Argyle Rd., Har. BF32 45
Argyle Rd., Houns. BF46 74
Argyle Rd., Ilf. CL34 49
Argyle Rd., Sev. CU66 116
Argyle Rd., Tedd. BH49 74
Argyle Sq. WC1 BX38 2
Argyle Sq. WC1 BX38 56
Argyle St. W1 BW39 1
Argyle St. WC1 BX38 2
Argyle St. WC1 BX38 56
Argyle Wk. WC1 BX38 2
Argyll Av., Sthl. BF40 54
Argyll Gdns., Edg. BM30 37
Argyll Rd. W8 BS41 66
Argyll Rd., Grays DD42 71
Argyll Rd., Hem.H. AY11 8
Argyll St. W1 BW39 56
Arica Rd. SE4 CD45 67
Ariel Clo., Grav. DJ49 81
Ariel Rd. NW6 BS36 56
Ariel Way W12 BQ40 55
Arisdale Av., S.Ock. DA39 60
Aristotle Rd. SW4 BW45 66
Ark Av., Grays DD41 71
Arkell Gro. SE19 BY50 76
Arkindale Rd. SE6 CF48 77
Arkley Cres. E17 CD32 48
Arkley Ct., Maid. AH42 61
Arkley Dr., Barn. BP24 28
Arkley La., Barn. BP24 28
Arkley Rd. E17 CD32 48
Arkley Rd., Hem.H. AZ11 8
Arkley Vw., Barn. BP24 28
Arklow Rd. SE14 CD43 67
Arkwright Rd. NW3 BT35 47
Arkwright Rd., S.Croy. CA58 96
Arkwright Rd., Slou. AV44 62
Arkwright Rd., Til. DG44 71
Arkwright St. E16 CG39 58
Arkwrights, Harl. CN10 6
Arlesford Rd. SW9 BX45 66
Arlesley Clo. SW15 BR46 75
Arlingford Ms. SW2 BY46 76
Arlingford Rd.
Arlingford Rd. SW2 BY46 76
Arlington Av. N1 BZ37 2
Arlington Av. N1 BZ37 57
Arlington Clo., Sid. CN47 78
Arlington Clo., Sutt. BS55 86
Arlington Clo., Twick. BK46 74
Arlington Cres., Wal.Cr. CD20 21
Arlington Ct., Hayes BB42 63
Arlington Dr., Cars. BU55 86
Arlington Dr., Ruis. BA32 44
Arlington Gdns. W4 BN42 65
Arlington Gdns., Ilf. CL33 49
Arlington Gdns., Rom. CW30 42
Arlington Lo. SW2 BX45 66
Arlington Ms., Twick. BK46 74
Arlington Rd.
Arlington N12 BS28 38
Arlington Pass., Tedd. BH49 74
Arlington Rd. N14 BV27 38
Arlington Rd. NW1 BV37 1
Arlington Rd. NW1 BV37 56
Arlington Rd. W13 BJ39 54
Arlington Rd., Ashf. AY49 73
Arlington Rd., Rich. BK48 74
Arlington Rd., Surb. BK53 84
Arlington Rd., Tedd. BH49 74
Arlington Rd., Twick. BK46 74
Arlington Rd., Wdf.Grn. CH30 40
Arlington Sq. N1 BZ37 2
Arlington Sq. N1 BZ37 57
Arlington St. SW1 BW40 3
Arlington St. SW1 BW40 56
Arlington Way EC1 BY38 2
Arlington Way EC1 BY38 56
Arliss Way, Nthlt. BD37 54
Arlow Rd. N21 BY26 38
Armada Ct. SE8 CE43 67
Watergate St.
Armada St. SE8 CE43 67
Armadale Clo. N15 CB31 48
Armadale Rd. SW6 BS43 66
Armadale Rd., Felt. BC46 73
Armadale Rd., Wok. AQ62 100
Armagh Rd. E3 CD37 57
Armand Clo., Wat. BB22 26
Armfield Clo., E.Mol. BE53 84
Armfield Cres., Mitch. BU51 86
Armfield Rd., Enf. BZ23 30
Arminger Rd. W12 BP40 55
Armitage Clo., Rick. AX24 26
Armitage Rd. NW11 BR33 46
Armitage Rd. SE10 CG42 68
Armor Rd., Grays CY42 70
Armour Clo. N7 BX36 56
Armoury Dr., Grav. DH47 81
Armoury Way SW18 BS46 76
Armstead Wk., Dag. CR36 59
Armstrong Av., Wdf.Grn. CG29 40
Armstrong Clo. E6 CK39 58
Armstrong Clo., Dag. CP33 50
Palmer Rd.
Armstrong Clo., Pnr. BC32 44
Armstrong Clo., Sev. CS61 107
Armstrong Clo., Walt. BC53 83
Armstrong Cres., Barn. BT24 29
Armstrong Pl., Hem.H. AX13 8
High St.
Armstrong Rd. W3 BO40 55
Armstrong Rd., Egh. AR50 72
Armstrong Rd., Felt. BE49 74
Armstrong Way, Sthl. BF41 64
Armytage Rd., Houns. BD43 64
Arnal Cres. SW18 BR47 75
Arndale Way, Egh. AT49 72
Arndale Wk. SW18 BS46 76
Arndale Centre
Arne Gro., Orp. CN55 88
Arne St. WC2 BX39 2
Arne Wk. SE3 CG45 68
Arnett Clo., Rick. AW25 26
Arnett Way, Rick. AW25 26
Arneway St. SW1 BW41 3
Arneway St. SW1 BW41 66
Horseferry Rd.
Arneways Av., Rom. CP31 50
Arnewood Clo. SW15 BP47 75
Arnewood Clo., Cob. BF60 93
Arneys La., Mitch. BV53 86
Arngask Rd. SE6 CF47 77
Arnhem Av., S.Ock. CY40 60
Arnhem Dr., Croy. CF59 96
Arnhem Way SE22 CA46 77
Dulwich Gro.
Arnison Rd., E.Mol. BG52 84
Arnold Av. E., Enf. CD22 30
Arnold Av. W., Enf. CD22 30
Arnold Cir. E2 CA38 2
Arnold Cir. E2 CA38 57
Arnold Clo., Har. BL33 46
Arnold Cres., Islw. BG46 74
Arnold Est. SE1 CA41 4
Arnold Est. SE1 CA41 67
Arnold Gdns. N13 BY28 38
Arnold Pl., Til. DG44 71
Kipling Av.
Arnold Rd. E3 CE38 57
Arnold Rd. N15 CA31 48
Arnold Rd. SW17 BU50 76
Arnold Rd., Dag. CQ36 59
Arnold Rd., Grav. DH48 81
Arnold Rd., Nthlt. BE36 54
Arnold Rd., Stai. AX50 73
Arnold Rd., Wok. AT61 100
Arnolds Av., Brwd. DE25 122
Arnolds Clo., Brwd. DE25 122
Arnolds Farm La., Brwd. CF24 122
Arnolds La., S.at H. CX50 80
Arnos Gro. N14 BW28 38
Arnos Rd. N11 BW28 38
Arnott Clo. SE28 CP40 59
Applegarth Rd.
Arnott Clo. W4 BN42 65
Arnould Av. SE5 BZ45 67
Arnsberg Rd., Erith CT43 69
Arnsberg Way, Bexh. CR45 69
Arnside Gdns., Wem. BK33 45
Arnside Rd., Bexh. CR44 69
Arnside St. SE17 BZ43 4
Arnside St. SE17 BZ43 67
Arnulf St. SE6 CE49 77
Arnulls Rd. SW16 BY50 76
Arodene Rd. SW2 BX46 76
Arragon Gdns. SW16 BX50 76
Arragon Gdns., W.Wick. CE55 87
Arragon Rd. E6 CJ37 58
Arragon Rd., Twick. BJ47 74
Arran Clo., Erith CS43 69
Arran Clo., Hem.H. BA14 8
Arran Clo., Wall. BW56 95
Arran Dr. E12 CJ33 49
Arran Dr., Stan. BK28 36
Arran Rd. SE6 CE48 77
Arran Way, Esher BF55 84
Arran Wk. N1 BZ36 57
Clephane Rd.
Arran Yews W5 BL40 55
Arras Av., Mord. BT53 86
Arretine Clo., St.Alb. BE14 9
Arrol Rd., Beck. CC52 87
Arrow Rd. E3 CE38 57
Arrowscout Wk., Nthlt. BD38 54
Wayfarer Rd.
Arrowsmith Clo., Chig. CN28 40
Arrowsmith Path, Chig. CN28 40
Arrowsmith Rd., Chig. CN28 40
Arrowsmith Rd., Loug. CK24 31
Arsenal Rd. SE9 CK44 68
Artemis Clo., Grav. DJ47 81
Arterberry Rd. SW20 BQ50 75
Arterial Av., Rain. CU38 59
Arterial Rd., Grays DA41 70
Artesian Clo., Horn. CT33 50
Artesian Rd. W2 BS39 56
Arthingworth St. E15 CG37 58
Arthur Ct. W2 BS39 1
Arthur Ct. W2 BS39 56
Queensway
Arthur Gro. SE18 CM42 68
Arthur Henderson Ho. SW6 BR44 65
Arthur Rd. E6 CK37 58
Arthur Rd. N7 BX34 47
Arthur Rd. N9 CA27 39
Arthur Rd. SW19 BS48 76
Arthur Rd., Kings.T. BM50 75
Arthur Rd., N.Mal. BP53 85
Arthur Rd., Rom. CP33 50
Arthur Rd., Slou. AO41 61
Arthur Rd., St.Alb. BJ13 9
Arthur Rd., West. CJ61 106
Arthur Rd., Wind. AO44 61
Arthur St. EC4 BZ40 4
Arthur St. EC4 BZ40 57
Arthur St. W., Grav. DG47 81
Arthur St., Bush. BD24 27
Arthur St., Erith CT43 69
Arthur St., Grav. DG47 81
Arthur St., Grays DE43 71
Arthur Toft Ho., Grays DD43 71
New Rd.
Arthurdon Rd. SE4 CE46 77
Arthurs Br. Rd., Wok. AR62 100
Artichoke Hill E1 CB40 57
Pennington St.
Artichoke Pl. SE5 BZ44 67
Camberwell Church St.
Artillery Clo., Ilf. CM32 49
Artillery La. E1 CA39 2
Artillery La. E1 CA39 57
Artillery Pass. E1 CA39 2
Artillery Pl. SE18 CK42 68
Artillery Rd., Guil. AR70 118
Artillery Row SW1 BW41 3
Artillery Row SW1 BW41 66
Artillery Row, Grav. DH47 81
Artillery Ter., Guil. AR70 118
Artillery Yd. EC2 CA38 57
Worship St.
Artington Clo., Orp. CM56 97
Artington Wk., Guil. AR72 118
Artizan St. E1 CA39 2
Artizan St. E1 CA39 57
Harrow Pl.
Arundel Av., Epsom BP58 94
Arundel Av., Mord. BR52 85
Arundel Av., S.Croy. CB58 96
Arundel Clo. E15 CG35 49
Arundel Clo. SW11 BU46 76
Arundel Clo., Bex. CQ46 79
Arundel Clo., Chsnt. CB17 21
Arundel Clo., Croy. BY55 86
Arundel Clo., Hem.H. AZ13 8
Arundel Clo., Hmptn. BF49 74
Arundel Ct., Slou. AR42 62
Arundel Dr., B.Wd. BN24 28
Arundel Dr., Har. BE35 45
Arundel Dr., Orp. CO56 98
Arundel Dr., Wdf.Grn. CH29 40
Arundel Gdns. N21 BY26 38
Arundel Gdns. W11 BR40 55
Arundel Gdns., Edg. BN29 37
Cressingham Rd.
Arundel Gdns., Ilf. CO34 50
Arundel Gro. N16 CA35 48
Arundel Pl. N1 BY36 56
Arundel Rd., Barn. BU24 29
Arundel Rd., Croy. BZ53 87
Arundel Rd., Dor. BJ71 119
Arundel Rd., Houns. BD45 64
Arundel Rd., Kings.T. BM51 85
Arundel Rd., Rom. CW30 42
Arundel Rd., Sutt. BR57 94
Arundel Rd., Uxb. AW37 53
Arundel Sq. N7 BY36 56
Arundel St. WC2 BX40 4
Arundel St. WC2 BX40 56
Arundel Ter. SW13 BP43 65
Arvon Rd. N5 BY35 47
Ascalon St. SW8 BW43 66
Ascension Rd., Rom. CS29 41
Ascham Dr. E4 CE29 39
Ascham End E17 CD30 39
Ascham St. NW5 BW35 47
Aschurch Rd., Croy. CA54 87
Ascot Clo., B.Wd. BM25 28
Ascot Clo., Ilf. CN29 40
Ascot Clo., Nthlt. BF36 54
Ascot Gdns., Enf. CC22 30
Ascot Gdns., Horn. CW35 51
Ascot Gdns., Sthl. BE39 54
Ascot Rd. E6 CK38 58
Ascot Rd. N15 BZ32 48
Ascot Rd. N18 CB28 39
Ascot Rd. SW17 BV50 76
Ascot Rd., Felt. AZ48 73
Ascot Rd., Grav. DG48 81
Ascot Rd., Maid. AG42 61
Ascot Rd., Orp. CN52 88
Ascot Rd., Wat. BB25 26
Ascots La., Hat. BR10 5
Ascott Av. W5 BL41 65
Ash Clo. E17 CD32 48
Ash Clo. SE20 CC51 87
Ash Clo., Brwd. CZ25 33
Ash Clo., Cars. BU55 86
Ash Clo., Edg. BN28 37
Ash Clo., Hat. BS16 20
Ash Clo., N.Mal. BN51 85
Ash Clo., Orp. CM53 88
Ash Clo., Red. BW68 113
Ash Clo., Rom. CR29 41
Ash Clo., Sid. CO48 79
Ash Clo., Slou. AT41 62
Ash Clo., Stan. BJ29 36
Ash Clo., Swan. CS51 89
Ash Clo., Uxb. AX30 35
Ash Clo., Wat. BA19 17
Ash Clo., Wok. AS63 100
Ash Ct., Epsom BN56 94
Ash Down Way SW17 BV48 76
Ash Dr., Hat. BP14 10
Ash Dr., Red. BV71 121
Ash Grn., Loug. CK23 31
Ash Grn., Uxb. AW36 53
Ash Gro. E8 CB37 57
Ash Gro. N13 BZ27 39
Ash Gro. NW2 BQ35 46
Ash Gro. SE20 CC51 87
Ash Gro. W5 BL41 65
Ash Gro., Enf. CA26 39
Ash Gro., Felt. BB47 73
Ash Gro., Guil. AQ70 118
Ash Gro., Hayes BA40 53
Ash Gro., Hem.H. AY15 8
Ash Gro., Houns. BD44 64
Ash Gro., Saw. CR6 6
Ash Gro., Stai. AX50 73
Ash Gro., Sthl. BF39 54
Ash Gro., Uxb. AX30 35
Ash Gro., W.Wick. CF55 87
Ash Gro., Wem. BJ35 45
Ash Gro., West.Dr. AY40 53
Ash Hill Clo., Bush. BF26 36
Ash Hill Dr., Pnr. BD31 45
Ash La., Croy. BY56 95
Ash La., Horn. CW31 51
Ash La., Rom. CU29 41
Ash La., Sev. DB59 99
Ash La., Wind. AL44 61
Ash Pl. SW1 BW41 3
Ash Platt Rd., Sev. CW63 108
Ash Rd. E15 CG35 49
Ash Rd., Croy. CE55 87
Ash Rd., Dart. CV47 80
Ash Rd., Grav. DH49 81
Ash Rd., Hart. DC52 90
Ash Rd., Hawley CW49 80
Ash Rd., Orp. CN57 97
Ash Rd., Sev. DB56 99
Ash Rd., Shep. AZ52 83
Ash Rd., Sutt. BR54 85
Ash Rd., West. CM66 115
Ash Rd., Wok. AS63 100
Ash Ride, Enf. BY21 29
Ash Row, Brom. CL54 88
Ash Tree Clo., Croy. CD53 87
Ash Tree Clo., Sev. CZ58 99
Ash Tree Dr.
Ash Tree Clo., Surb. BL54 85
Ash Tree Dell NW9 BN32 46
Ash Tree Dr., Sev. CZ58 99
Ash Tree Field, Harl. CL10 6
Ash Tree Way, Croy. CD53 87
Ash Vale, Rick. AU28 34
Ash View Gdns., Ashf. AY49 73
Ash Wk. SW2 BX47 76
Ashbeam Clo., Brwd. DA28 42
Ashborough Ter. SW19 BS50 76
Ashbourne Av. E18 CH31 49
Ashbourne Av. N20 BU27 38
Ashbourne Av. NW11 BR32 46
Ashbourne Av., Bexh. CQ43 69
Ashbourne Av., Har. BG34 45
Ashbourne Clo. N12 BS28 38
Ashbourne Clo. W5 BM39 55
Ashbourne Clo., Couls. BW62 104
Ashbourne Ct. E5 CC35 48
Clapton Park Est.
Ashbourne Gro. NW7 BN28 37
Ashbourne Gro. SE22 CA45 67
Ashbourne Gro. W4 BO42 65
Ashbourne Rd. W5 BL38 55
Ashbourne Rd., Brox. CD14 12
Ashbourne Rd., Mitch. BV50 76
Ashbourne Rd., Rom. CV28 42
Ashbourne Ri., Orp. CM56 97
Ashbourne Sq., Nthwd. BB29 35
Rofant Rd.
Ashbourne Ter. SW19 BR50 75
Ashbourne Way NW11 BR32 46
Ashbourne Av.
Ashbridge Rd. E11 CG33 49
Ashbridge St. NW8 BU38 56
Ashbrook Rd. N19 BW33 47
Ashbrook Rd., Dag. CR34 50
Ashbrook Rd., Wind. AQ47 72
Ashburn Gdns. SW7 BT42 3
Ashburn Gdns. SW7 BT42 66
Ashburn Ms. SW7 BT42 3
Ashburn Ms. SW7 BT42 66
Ashburn Pl. SW7 BT42 3
Ashburn Pl. SW7 BT42 66
Ashburnham Av., Har. BH32 45
Ashburnham Clo. N2 BT31 47
Ashburnham Clo., Wat. BC27 35
Ashburnham Dr.
Ashburnham Dr., Wat. BC27 35
Ashburnham Gdns., Upmin. CY33 51
Ashburnham Gdns., Har. BH32 45
Ashburnham Gro. SE10 CE43 67
Ashburnham Pk., Esher BG56 93
Ashburnham Pl. SE10 CE43 67
Ashburnham Rd. NW10 BQ38 55
Ashburnham Rd. SW10 BT43 66
Ashburnham Rd., Belv. CS42 69
Ashburnham Rd., Rich. BJ48 74
Ashburnham Retreat SE10 CE43 67
Ashburton Av., Croy. CB54 87
Ashburton Av., Ilf. CN35 49
Ashburton Clo., Croy. CB54 87
Ashburton Ct., Pnr. BD30 36
Ashburton Est. SW15 BQ46 75
Ashburton Gdns., Croy. CB55 87
Ashburton Gro. N7 BY35 47
Ashburton Rd. E16 CH39 58
Ashburton Rd., Croy. CB55 87
Ashburton Rd., Ruis. BC34 44
Ashburton Ter. E13 CH37 58
Grasmere Rd.
Ashbury Clo., Hat. BO12 10
St. Albans Rd. W.
Ashbury Cres., Guil. AU69 118
Ashbury Dr., Uxb. AZ34 44
Ashbury Gdns., Rom. CP32 50
Ashbury Rd. SW11 BU45 66
Ashby Av., Chess. BM57 94
Ashby Clo., Horn. CX33 51
Ashby Gdns., St.Alb. BG15 9
Ashby Gro. N1 BZ36 57
Ashby Ms. SE4 CD44 67
Ashby Rd. N15 CB32 48
Ashby Rd. SE4 CD44 67
Ashby Rd., Berk. AO11 7
Ashby Rd., Wat. BC22 26
Ashby St. EC1 BY38 2
Ashby St. EC1 BY38 56
Ashby Way, West Dr. AZ43 63
Ashby Wk., Croy. BZ53 87
Beulah Gro.
Ashchurch Gro. W12 BP41 65
Ashchurch Pk. Vill. W12 BP41 65
Ashchurch Ter. W12 BP41 65
Ashcombe Av., Surb. BK54 84
Ashcombe Gdns., Edg. BM28 37
Ashcombe Pk. NW2 BO34 4
Ashcombe Rd. SW19 BS49 7
Ashcombe Rd., Cars. BV57 9
Ashcombe Rd., Dor. BJ70 11
Ashcombe Rd., Red. BW67 11
Ashcombe Sq., N.Mal. BN52 8
Ashcombe St. SW6 BS44 6
Ashcombe Ter., Tad. BP63 10
Ashcombe, Welw.G.C. BR 6
Ashcroft Av., Sid. CO46 7
Ashcroft Clo., Guil. AS74 11
Ashcroft Cres., Sid. CO46 7
Ashcroft Dr., Uxb. AV32 4
Ashcroft Pk., Cob. BE59 9
Ashcroft Rd. E3 CD38 5
Ashcroft Rd., Chess. BL55 8
Ashcroft Ri., Couls. BX61 10
Ashcroft, Pnr. BF29 3
Ashdale Clo., Stai. AY47 7
Ashdale Clo., Twick. BF47 7
Ashdale Gro., Stan. BH29 3
Ashdale Rd. SE12 CH47 7
Ashdale Way, Twick. BF47 7
Ashdale Clo.
Ashdale, Lthd. BF66 11
Ashdales, St.Alb. BG15
Ashdene Clo., Ashf. BA50 7
Cambridge Rd.
Ashdene, Pnr. BD31 4
Ashdon Clo., Wdf.Grn. CH29 4
Ashdon Rd. NW10 BO37 5
Ashdon Rd., Bush. BD24 2
Ashdown Cres. NW5 BV35 4
Ashdown Cres., Chsnt. CD17 2
Ashdown Dr., B.Wd. BL23 2
Ashdown Gdns., S.Croy. CB61 10
Ashdown Rd., Enf. CC24 3
Ashdown Rd., Epsom BO60 9
Ashdown Rd., Kings.T. BL51 8
Ashdown Rd., Reig. BS72 12
Ashdown Rd., Uxb. AZ37 5
Ashdown Rd., Wat. BD28 3
Woodhall La.
Ashdown Way., Amer. AO22 2
Ashdown Wk. E14 CE42 6
Charnwood Gdns.
Ashdown Wk., Rom. CR30 4
Ashdowne Clo., Beck. CE51 8
Ashen Dr., Dart. CU46 7
Ashen Gro. SW19 BS48 7
Ashen Grove Rd., Sev. CX58 9
Ashen Vale, S.Croy. CC58 9
Ashenden Rd. E5 CC35 4
Ashenden Rd., Guil. AP70 11
Ashenden Wk., Slou. AO35 4
Ashendene Rd., Hert. BX13 1
Ashentree Ct. EC4 BY39 5
Whitefriars St.
Asher Way E1 CB40 4
Asher Way E1 CB40 5
Ashes La., Ton. DC70 11
Ashfield Av., Bush. BF26 3
Ashfield Av., Felt. BC47 7
Ashfield Clo., Rich. BL47 7
Ashfield La., Chis. CL50 7
Ashfield Par. N14 BW26 3
Ashfield Rd. N14 BW27 3
Ashfield Rd. N4 BZ32 4
Ashfield Rd. W3 BO40 5
Ashfield Rd., Chesh. AO18 1
Ashfield St. E1 CB39 5
Ashfields, Loug. CK23 3
Ashfields, Wat. BB21 2
Ashford Av. N8 BX31 4
Ashford Av., Ashf. AZ50 7
Ashford Av., Brwd. DA27 4
Ashford Av., Hayes BD39 5
Ashford Clo. E17 CD32 4
Ashford Clo., Ashf. AY49 7
Ashford Cres., Ashf. AY48 7
Ashford Cres., Enf. CC23 3
Ashford Gdns., Cob. BD61 10
Ashford Grn., Wat. BD28 3
Ashford La., Wind. AK41 6
Ashford Rd. E18 CH30 4
Ashford Rd. E6 CL36 5
Ashford Rd. NW2 BQ35 4
Ashford Rd., Ashf. BA50 7
Ashford Rd., Felt. BA49 7
Ashford Rd., Iver AU37 5
Ashford Rd., Stai. AX51 8
Ashford St. N1 CA38 2
Ashford St. N1 CA38 5
Ashgrove Rd., Ashf. BA49 7
Ashgrove Rd., Brom. CF50 7
Ashgrove Rd., Ilf. CN33 4
Ashgrove Rd., Sev. CU67 11
Ashingdon Clo. E4 CF27 3
Ashington Ct. SE26 CB49 7
Ashington Rd. SW6 BR44 6
Ashlake Rd. SW16 BX49 7
Ashland Pl. W1 BV39 1
Ashland Pl. W1 BV39 5
Ashlar Pl. SE18 CL42 6
Ashlea Rd., Ger.Cr. AS30 3
Ashleigh Av., Egh. AU50 7
Ashleigh Clo., Amer. AP23 2
Ashleigh Ct. N4 BZ32 4
Wiltshire Gdns.
Ashleigh Gdns., Sutt. BS55 8
Ashleigh Gdns., Upmin. CY35 5
Ashleigh Rd. SE20 CB52 8
Ashleigh Rd. SW14 BO45 6
Ashley Av., Epsom BN60 9
Ashley Rd.
Ashley Av., Ilf. CL30 4
Ashley Av., Mord. BS53 8
Ashley Clo. NW4 BQ30 3
Ashley Clo., Lthd. BE66 11
Ashley Clo., Pnr. BC30 3
Ashley Clo., Sev. CU65 10
Ashley Clo., Walt. BB54 8
Ashley Clo., Welw.G.C. BQ 7 5
Ashley Cres. N22 BY30 3
Ashley Cres. SW11 BV45 6
Ashley Dr., B.Wd. BN25 2
Ashley Dr., Bans. BS60 9

Ashley Dr., Islw. BH43 64
Ashley Dr., Twick. BF47 74
Ashley Dr., Walt. BC55 83
Ashley Gdns. N13 BZ28 39
Ashley Gdns., Grays DE40 71
Ashley Gdns., Orp. CN56 97
Ashley Gdns., Rich. BK48 74
Ashley Gdns., Wem. BL34 46
Ashley Green La., Chesh. AO17 16
Ashley Gro., Loug. CK24 31
Ashley La. NW4 BQ30 37
Ashley La., Croy. BY56 95
Ashley Park Av., Walt. BB55 84
Ashley Pk. Cres., Walt. BB54 83
Ashley Pk. NW4 BQ30 37
Ashley La.
Ashley Pk. Rd., Walt. BC55 83
Ashley Pl. SW1 BW41 66
Ashley Rd. E4 CE29 39
Ashley Rd. E7 CJ36 58
Ashley Rd. N17 CB31 48
Ashley Rd. N19 BX33 47
Ashley Rd. SW19 BS50 76
Ashley Rd., Dor. BG72 119
Ashley Rd., Enf. CC23 30
Ashley Rd., Epsom BN60 94
Ashley Rd., Hmptn. BF51 84
Ashley Rd., Rich. BL45 65
Jocelyn Rd.
Ashley Rd., Sev. CU65 107
Ashley Rd., St.Alb. BK13 9
Ashley Rd., T.Ditt. BH53 84
Ashley Rd., Th.Hth. BX52 86
Ashley Rd., Uxb. AW37 53
Ashley Rd., Walt. BB56 92
Ashley Rd., Wok. AP62 100
Ashley Ri., Walt. BB56 92
Ashley Wk. NW7 BQ29 37
Ashleys, Rick. AV26 34
Ashlin Rd. E15 CF35 48
Ashling Rd., Croy. CB54 87
Ashlone Rd. SW15 BQ45 65
Ashlyn Clo., Bush. BE24 27
Ashlyn Gro., Horn. CV31 51
Ashlyns Ct., Berk. AQ13 7
Ashlyns La., Epp. CT13 14
Ashlyns Pk., Cob. BE60 93
Ashlyns Rd., Berk. AQ13 7
Ashlyns Rd., Epp. CN18 22
Ashlyns Way, Chess. BK57 93
Ashmead Dr., Uxb. AW34 44
Ashmead La., Uxb. AW34 44
Ashmead N14 BW25 29
Ashmead Rd. SE8 CE44 67
Ashmead Rd., Felt. BC47 73
Ashmere Av., Beck. CF51 87
Ashmere Clo., Sutt. BQ56 94
Ashmere Gro. SW2 BX45 66
Ashmill St. NW1 BU39 1
Ashmill St. NW1 BU39 56
Ashmole Pl. SW8 BX43 66
Ashmole St. SW8 BX43 66
Ashmore Gdns., Hem.H. AZ14 8
Ashmore Gro., Well. CM45 68
Ashmore La., Kes. CJ59 97
Ashmore Rd. W9 BR38 55
Ashmount Rd. N15 CA32 48
Ashmount Rd. N19 BW33 47
Ashmour Gdns., Rom. CS30 41
Ashneal Gdns., Har. BG34 45
Ashness Gdns., Grnf. BJ36 54
Ashness Rd. SW11 BU46 76
Ashridge Clo., Har. BK32 45
Ashridge Clo., Hem.H. AS17 16
Pembridge Rd.
Ashridge Cres. SE18 CM43 68
Ashridge Dr., St.Alb. BE18 18
Ashridge Dr., Wat. BC28 35
Ashridge Gdns. N13 BW28 38
Ashridge Gdns., Pnr. BE31 45
Ashridge La., Chesh. AR19 16
Ashridge Ri., Berk. AP12 7
Ashridge Way, Mord. BR52 85
Ashridge Way, Sun. BC50 73
Ashtead Gap, Lthd. BJ61 102
Ashtead Rd. E5 CB33 48
Ashtead Woods Rd., Ash. BK62 102
Ashton Clo., Sutt. BR56 94
Gander Green La.
Ashton Clo., Wey. BC57 92
Ashton Gdns., Houns. BE45 64
Ashton Gdns., Rom. CQ32 50
Ashton Rd. E15 CF35 48
Ashton Rd., Enf. CD21 30
Ashton Rd., Rom. CV29 42
Ashton Rd., Wok. AP62 100
Ashton St. E14 CF40 57
Ashtree Av., Mitch. BT51 86
Ashtree Clo., Orp. CL56 97
Broadwater Gdns.
Ashtree Rd., Wat. BC21 26
Ashtree Way, Hem.H. AW14 8
Ashurst Clo. SE20 CB51 77
Ashurst Clo., Dart. CT45 69
Ashurst Clo., Ken. BZ61 105
Ashurst Clo., Nthwd. BB29 35
Ashurst Dr., Ilf. CL32 49
Ashurst Dr., Shep. AY52 83
Ashurst Dr., Tad. BM68 112
Ashurst Rd. N12 BU28 38
Ashurst Rd., Barn. BU25 29
Ashurst Wk., Croy. CB55 87
Ashvale Dr., Upmin. CZ34 51
Ashvale Gdns., Rom. CS28 41
Ashvale Gdns., Upmin. CZ34 51
Ashvale Rd. SW17 BU49 76
Ashville Rd. E11 CF34 48
Ashwater Rd. SE12 CH47 78
Ashwell Clo. E6 CK39 58
Northumberland Rd.
Ashwell St., St.Alb. BG13 9
Ashwells Rd., Brwd. CY24 33
Ashwells Way, Ch.St.G. AR27 34
Ashwin St. E8 CA36 57
Ashwindham Ct., Wok. AP62 100
Ashwood Av., Rain. CU38 59
Ashwood Av., Uxb. AZ39 53
Ashwood Gdns., Croy. CF57 96
Ashwood Gdns., Hayes BB42 63
Ashwood Pk., Lthd. BG65 102
Ashwood Rd. E4 CF27 39
Ashwood Rd., Egh. AQ50 72
Ashwood Rd., Pot.B. BS20 20
Ashwood Rd., Wok. AS62 100
Ashwood, Warl. CC63 105
Ashworth Pl., Guil. AP70 118
Ashworth Rd. W9 BS38 1
Ashworth Rd. W9 BS38 56
Aske St. N1 CA38 57
Pitfield St.
Askern Clo., Bexh. CP45 69
Askew Bldgs. W12 BP41 65
Askew Rd.
Askew Cres. W12 BO40 55
Askew Farm Rd., Grays DC42 71
Askew Rd. W12 BO40 55
Askew Rd., Nthwd. BA27 35
Askham Ct. W12 BP40 55
Askham Rd. W12 BP40 55
Askill Dr. SW15 BR46 75
Askwith Rd., Rain. CS38 59
Asland Rd. E15 CF37 57
Aslett St. SW18 BT47 76
Asmar Clo., Couls. BX61 104
Asmara Rd. NW2 BR35 46
Asmuns Hill NW11 BS32 47
Asmuns Pl. NW11 BR32 46
Aspasia Clo., St.Alb. BH14 9
Aspdin Rd., Grav. DE48 81
Aspect Row, Hem.H. AW12 8
Aspen Clo. N19 BW34 47
Hargrave Pk.
Aspen Clo. W5 BL41 65
Aspen Clo., Cob. BE61 102
Aspen Clo., Guil. AU69 118
Aspen Clo., Orp. CO56 98
Aspen Clo., Stai. AV49 72
Moormede Cres.
Aspen Clo., Swan. CS51 89
Aspen Clo., West Dr. AY40 53
Aspen Copse, Brom. CK51 88
Aspen Dr., Wem. BJ34 45
Aspen Gdns. W6 BP42 65
Bridge Av.
Aspen Gdns., Mitch. BV53 86
Aspen Grn., Erith CQ41 69
Aspen Gro., Upmin. CW35 51
Aspen La., Nthlt. BE38 54
Aspen Way E14 CE40 57
Aspen Way, Bans. BQ60 94
Aspen Way, Enf. CC21 30
Aspenlea Rd. W6 BQ43 65
Aspinall Rd. SE4 CC45 67
Aspinden Rd. SE16 CB42 67
Aspledene, Grav. DH50 81
Aspley Rd. SW18 BS46 76
Asplins Rd. N17 CB30 39
Asquith Clo., Dag. CP33 50
Crystal Way
Ass House La., Har. BF28 36
Assam St. E1 CB39 2
Assam St. E1 CB39 57
Assembly Pass. E1 CC39 57
Assembly Wk., Cars. BU54 86
Assher Rd., Walt. BE55 84
Astall Clo., Har. BH30 36
Astbury Rd. SE15 CC44 67
Aste St. E14 CF41 67
Astell St. SW3 BU42 3
Astell St. SW3 BU42 66
Aster Pl. SE1 BZ41 4
Aster Pl. SE1 BZ41 67
Asteys Row N1 BZ36 57
Asthall Gdns., Ilf. CM31 49
Astle St. SW11 BV44 66
Astleham Rd., Shep. AY52 83
Astley Av. NW2 BQ35 46
Astley Rd., Hem.H. AX13 8
Aston Av., Har. BK33 45
Aston Clo., Ash. BK62 102
Aston Clo., Sid. CO48 79
Aston Grn., Houns. BD44 64
Aston Mead, Wind. AM44 61
Aston Ms., Rom. CO33 50
Reynolds Av.
Aston Rd. SW20 BQ51 85
Approach Rd.
Aston Rd. W5 BK39 54
Aston Rd., Esher BH57 93
Aston St. E14 CD39 57
Aston Vw., Hem.H. AZ10 8
Aston Way, Epsom BO61 103
Aston Way, Pot.B. BT19 20
Astons Rd., Nthwd. BA27 35
Astonville St. SW18 BS47 76
Astor Av., Rom. CS32 50
Astor Clo., Kings.T. BM50 75
Astor Clo., Wey. AX56 92
Astor Rd., Sev. CZ57 99
Astoria Wk. SW9 BY45 66
Astra Clo., Horn. CU36 59
Astra Dr., Grav. DJ49 81
Astrop Ms. W6 BQ41 65
Astrop Ter. W6 BQ41 65
Astwick Av., Hat. BO11 10
Astwood Ms. SW7 BS42 3
Astwood Ms. SW7 BS42 66
Asylum Arch Rd., Red. BU72 121
Asylum Rd. SE15 CB43 67
Atalanta Clo., Pur. BY58 95
Atalanta St. SW6 BQ44 65
Atbara Ct., Tedd. BJ50 74
Atbara Rd., Tedd. BJ50 74
Atcham Rd., Houns. BG45 64
Atcost Rd., Bark. CO39 59
Atheldene Rd. SW18 BS47 76
Athelney St. SE6 CE48 77
Athelstan Clo., Rom. CW30 42
Athelstan Rd., Welw.G.C. BQ 8 5
Broadwater Cres.
Athelstan Rd., Har. BG30 36
Athelstan Rd., Kings.T. BL52 85
Villiers Rd.
Athelstan Rd., Rom. CW30 42
Athelstan Wk. N., Welw.G.C. BR 8 5
Athelstan Wk. S., Welw.G.C. BQ 8 5
Athelstane Gro. E3 CD37 57
Athelstane Ms. N4 BY33 47
Stroud Green Rd.
Athelstone Rd., Hem.H. AY15 8
Athena Clo., Har. BG34 45
Athena Pl., Nthwd. BB30 35
The Drive
Athenaeum Rd. N20 BT26 38
Athenlay Rd. SE15 CC46 77
Atherden Rd. E5 CC35 48
Atherfield Rd., Reig. BT72 121
Atherfold Rd. SW9 BX45 66
Atherley Way, Houns. BE47 74
Heath Side
Atherstone Ms. SW7 BT42 3
Atherstone Ms. SW7 BT42 66
Atherton Clo., Stai. AX46 73
Atherton Ct., Eton AO43 61
Atherton Dr. SW19 BQ49 75
Atherton End, Saw. CQ 5 6
Atherton Gdns., Grays DH42 71
Atherton Heights, Wem. BK36 54
Bridgewater Rd.
Atherton Ms. E7 CG36 58
Atherton Pl., Har. BG31 45
Atherton Pl., Sthl. BF40 54
Longford Av.
Atherton Rd. E7 CG35 49
Atherton Rd. SW13 BP43 65
Atherton Rd., Ilf. CK30 40
Atherton St. SW11 BU44 66
Athlon Rd., Wem. BK37 54
Athlone Clo. E5 CB35 48
Goulton Rd.
Athlone Clo., Esher BH57 93
Athlone Clo., Rad. BJ21 27
Athlone Gdns. W10 BR39 55
Faraday Rd.
Athlone Rd. SW2 BX47 76
Athlone Sq., Wind. AO44 61
Ward Royal
Athlone St. NW5 BV36 56
Athol Clo., Pnr. BC30 35
Athol Gdns., Pnr. BC30 35
Athol Rd., Erith CS42 69
Athol Sq. E14 CF39 57
Athol Way, Uxb. AZ38 53
Athole Gdns. Enf. CA25 30
Atholl Rd., Ilf. CO33 50
Atkins Clo., Wok. AQ62 100
Greythorne Rd.
Atkins Rd. E10 CE32 48
Atkins Rd. SW12 BW47 76
Atkinson Clo., Orp. CN56 97
Atkinson Rd. E16 CJ39 58
Atlantic Rd. SW9 BY45 66
Atlas Gdns. SE7 CJ42 68
Atlas Ms. N7 BX36 56
Atlas Rd. E13 CH37 58
Atlas Rd. NW10 BO38 55
Atlas Rd., Wem. BN35 46
Atley Rd. E3 CE37 57
Atley St. E3 CE37 57
Atney Rd. SW15 BR45 65
Atria Rd., Nthwd. BC28 35
Atterbury Rd. N4 BY32 47
Wightman Rd.
Atterbury St. SW1 BW42 3
Atterbury St. SW1 BX42 66
Attewood Av. NW10 BO34 46
Attewood Rd., Nthlt. BE36 54
Attfield Clo. N20 BT27 38
Attimore Clo., Welw.G.C. BP 8 5
Attimore Rd., Welw.G.C. BP 8 5
Attle Clo., Uxb. AZ37 53
Attlee Clo., Hayes BC38 53
Attlee Ct., Grays DD41 71
Lucas Rd.
Attlee Dr., Dart. CX46 80
Attlee Rd. SE28 CO40 59
Attlee Rd., Hayes BC38 53
Attlee Ter. E17 CE31 48
Attneave St. WC1 BY38 2
Attneave St. WC1 BY38 56
Attwood Clo., S.Croy. CB60 96
Atwater Clo. SW2 BY47 76
Atwell Clo. E10 CE32 48
Belmont Park Rd.
Atwell Rd. SE15 CB44 67
Atwood Av., Rich. BM44 65
Atwood Rd. W6 BP42 65
Atwood, Lthd. BE65 102
Atwoods Alley, Rich. BM44 65
Kew Gardens Rd.
Atworth St. E14 CF41 67
Auberon St. E16 CK40 58
Aubert Pk. N5 BY35 47
Aubert Rd. N5 BY35 47
Aubretia Clo., Rom. CW30 42
Sunflower Way
Aubrey Av., St.Alb. BK16 18
Aubrey Pl. NW8 BT37 1
Aubrey Pl. NW8 BT37 56
Aubrey Rd. E17 CE31 48
Aubrey Rd. N8 BX32 47
Aubrey Rd. W8 BR40 55
Aubrey Wk. W8 BR40 55
Aubreys Rd., Hem.H. AV14 7
Aubyn Hill SE27 BZ49 77
Aubyn Sq. SW15 BP46 75
Aubyns Rd. SE19 CA50 77
Auckland Av., Rain. CT38 59
Auckland Clo. SE19 CA51 87
Auckland Clo., Enf. CB22 30
Auckland Clo., Til. DG44 71
Auckland Gdns. SE19 CA51 87
Auckland Hill SE27 BZ49 77
Auckland Rd. E10 CE34 48
Auckland Rd. SE19 CA51 87
Auckland Rd. SW11 BU45 66
Auckland Rd., Cat. CA64 105
Auckland Rd., Ilf. CL33 49
Auckland Rd., Kings.T. BL52 85
Auckland Rd., Pot.B. BQ19 19
Auckland Ri. SE19 CA51 87
Auckland St. SE11 BX42 66
Kennington La.
Auden Pl. NW1 BV37 1
Auden Pl. NW1 BV37 56
Auden Pl., Cheam BQ56 94
Audleigh Pl., Chig. CL29 40
Audley Clo. SW11 BV45 66
Audley Clo., B.Wd. BM24 28
Audley Clo., Wey. AW56 92
Audley Ct. E18 CG31 49
Audley Ct., Pnr. BD30 36
Audley Ct., Twick. BG48 74
Audley Dr., Warl. CC61 105
Audley Firs, Walt. BD56 93
Audley Gdns., Ilf. CN34 49
Audley Gdns., Loug. CM23 31
Audley Gdns., Wal.Abb. CF20 21
Audley Pl., Sutt. BS57 95
Audley Rd. Enf. BY23 29
Audley Rd. NW4 BP32 46
Audley Rd. W5 BL39 55
Audley Rd., Rich. BL46 75
Audley Sq. W1 BV40 3
Audley Wk., Orp. CP53 89
Edmund Rd.
Audrey Clo., Beck. CE53 87
Audrey Gdns., Wem. BJ34 45
Audrey Rd., Ilf. CL34 49
Audrey St. E2 CB37 2
Audrey St. E2 CB37 57
Audric Clo., Kings.T. BM51 85
Audwick Clo., Chsnt. CD17 21
Ashdown Cres.
Augur Clo., Stai. AV49 72
Richmond Rd.
Augurs La. E13 CH38 58
August End, Slou. AS39 52
Augusta Rd., Twick. BG48 74
Augusta St. E14 CE39 57
Augustine Clo., Slou. AV45 62
Augustine Rd. W14 BQ41 65
Augustine Rd., Har. BG30 36
Augustine Rd., Orp. CP52 89
Augustus Clo., Brent. BK43 64
Augustus Clo., St.Alb. BF14 9
Augustus Ct. SW16 BW48 76
Augustus La., Orp. CO55 89
Augustus Rd. SW19 BQ47 75
Augustus St. NW1 BV37 1
Augustus St. NW1 BV37 56
Aukingford Gdns., Ong. CW17 24
Epping Rd.
Aulton Pl. SE11 BY42 4
Aultone Way, Cars. BU55 86
Aultone Way, Sutt. BS55 86
Aurelia Gdns., Croy. BX53 86
Aurelia Rd., Croy. BX53 86
Auriel Av., Dag. CS36 59
Auriga Ms. N16 BZ35 48
Auriol Clo., Wor.Pk. BO55 85
Auriol Dr., Grnf. BG36 54
Auriol Dr., Uxb. AZ36 53
Auriol Park Rd., Wor.Pk. BO55 85
Auriol Rd. W14 BR42 65
Aust Rd., Grav. DH47 81
Austell Gdns. NW7 BO27 37
Austen Clo. SE28 CO40 59
Austen Clo., Green. DB46 80
Austen Clo., Loug. CM24 31
Austen Clo., Til. DH44 71
Coleridge Rd.
Austen Gdns., Dart. CW45 70
Austen Pl., Guil. AS71 118
Austen Rd., Guil. AS71 118
Austen Rd., Har. BF34 45
Austenway, Ger.Cr. AR31 43
Austenwood Clo., Ger.Cr. AR30 34
Austenwood La., Ger.Cr. AR30 34
Austin Av., Brom. CK53 88
Austin Clo. SE6 CD47 77
Brockley Vw.
Austin Clo., Ken. BY62 104
Austin Clo., Twick. BK46 74
Austin Friars EC2 BZ39 2
Austin Friars EC2 BZ39 57
Austin Friars Pass. EC2 BZ39 57
Austin Friars
Austin Friars Sq. EC2 BZ39 2
Austin Friars
Austin Rd. SW11 BV44 66
Austin Rd., Grav. DF47 81
Austin Rd., Hayes BB41 63
Austin Rd., Orp. CO53 89
Austin St. E2 CA38 2
Austin St. E2 CA38 57
Austin Waye, Uxb. AX37 53
Austins La., Uxb. BA34 44
Austins Mead, Hem.H. AT17 16
Austins Pl., Hem.H. AX13 8
Austral Clo., Sid. CN48 78
Longlands Rd.
Austral Dr., Horn. CV33 51
Austral St. SE11 BY42 4
Austral St. SE11 BY42 66
Australia Rd. W12 BP40 55
Australia Rd., Slou. AQ41 62
Austyn Gdns., Surb. BM54 85
Autumn Clo., Enf. CB23 30
Autumn Clo., Slou. AM40 61
Autumn Glades, Hem.H. BA14 8
Autumn Gro., Welw.G.C. BS 9 5
Autumn St. E3 CE37 57
Auxiliaries Way, Uxb. AV32 43
Avalon Clo., Enf. BY23 29
Avalon Clo., Orp. CP55 89
Avalon Clo., Wat. BE19 18
Avalon Cres. W13 BJ39 54
Avalon Rd. SW6 BS44 66
Avalon Rd. W13 BJ38 54
Avalon Rd., Orp. CO55 89
Avard Gdns., Orp. CM56 97
Isabella Dr.
Avarn Rd. SW17 BU50 76
Ave Maria La. EC4 BY39 2
Avebury Pk., Surb. BK54 84
Avebury Rd. E11 CF33 48
Avebury Rd. SW19 BR51 85
Avebury Rd., Orp. CM55 88
Avebury St. N1 BZ37 2
Avebury, Slou. AN40 61
Aveley By-Pass, S.Ock. CY40 60
Aveley Clo., S.Ock. CY40 60
High St.
Aveley Rd., Rom. CS31 50
Aveley Rd., Upmin. CX36 60
Aveline St. SE11 BX42 4
Aveline St. SE11 BX42 66
Aveling Clo., Pur. BX60 95
Aveling Park Rd. E17 CE30 39
Avelon Rd., Rain. CU37 59
Avelon Rd., Rom. CS29 41
Avenell Rd. N5 BY34 47
Avening Rd. SW18 BS47 76
Avening Ter. SW18 BS46 76
Avenons Rd. E13 CH38 58
Avenue App., Kings L. AZ18 17
Avenue Clo. N14 BW25 29
Avenue Clo. NW2 BQ36 55
Avenue Clo. NW8 BU37 1
Avenue Clo. NW8 BU37 56
Avenue Clo., Houns. BC44 63
Avenue Clo., Rom. CW29 42
Avenue Clo., Tad. BP64 103
Avenue Clo., West.Dr. AX41 63
Avenue Cres. W3 BM41 65
Avenue Cres., Houns. BC43 63
Avenue Ct. N14 BW25 29
Avenue Rd.
Avenue Elmers, Surb. BL53 85
Avenue Gdns. SE25 CA51 87
Avenue Gdns. SW14 BO45 65
Avenue Gdns. W3 BM41 65
Avenue Gdns., Houns. BC43 63
Avenue Gdns., Tedd. BH50 74
Avenue Gte. SE21 CA49 77
Avenue Ms. N10 BV31 47
Queens Av.
Avenue Ms. NW6 BS35 47
Finchley Rd.
Avenue Pk. Rd. SE27 BY48 76
Avenue Rd. E7 CH35 49
Avenue Rd. N12 BT28 38
Avenue Rd. N14 BV26 38
Avenue Rd. N15 BZ32 48
Avenue Rd. N6 BW33 47
Avenue Rd. NW10 BO37 55
Avenue Rd. NW3 BT36 1
Avenue Rd. NW3 BT36 56
Avenue Rd. NW8 BU37 1
Avenue Rd. SE20 CC51 87
Avenue Rd. SE25 CA51 87
Avenue Rd. SW16 BW51 86
Avenue Rd. SW20 BP51 85
Avenue Rd. W3 BM41 65
Avenue Rd., Chadwell Heath CP33 50
Avenue Rd., Bans. BS61 104
Avenue Rd., Beck. CC51 87
Avenue Rd., Belv. CR42 69
Avenue Rd., Bexh. CQ45 69
Avenue Rd., Brent. BK42 64
Avenue Rd., Brwd. DB28 42
Avenue Rd., Cat. BZ64 105
Avenue Rd., Cob. BD61 102
Avenue Rd., Epp. CM21 31
Avenue Rd., Epsom BN60 94
Avenue Rd., Erith CS43 69
Avenue Rd., Felt. BB48 73
Avenue Rd., Harold Wood CW29 42
Avenue Rd., Hmptn. BF51 84
Avenue Rd., Hodd. CF13 12
Avenue Rd., Islw. BH44 64
Avenue Rd., Kings.T. BL52 85
Avenue Rd., Maid. AG40 61
Avenue Rd., N.Mal. BO52 85
Avenue Rd., Pnr. BE31 45
Avenue Rd., Sev. CV65 108
Avenue Rd., St.Alb. BH13 9
Avenue Rd., Stai. AU49 72
Avenue Rd., Sthl. BE40 54
Avenue Rd., Sutt. BS58 95
Avenue Rd., Tedd. BJ50 74
Avenue Rd., Wall. BW57 95
Avenue Rd., Wdf.Grn. CJ29 40
Avenue Rd., West. CK63 106
Avenue Ri., Bush. BF25 27
Avenue S., The, Surb. BL54 85
Avenue Ter., N.Mal. BN52 85
Avenue Ter., Wat. BE25 27
Avenue Vills., Red. BW68 113
Albury Rd.
Avenue, The E11 CH32 49
Avenue, The E4 CF29 39
Avenue, The N10 BW30 38
Avenue, The N11 BV28 38
Avenue, The N17 BZ30 39
Avenue, The N3 BS30 38
Avenue, The N8 BY31 47
Avenue, The NW6 BR36 55
Avenue, The SE10 CF43 67
Avenue, The SE7 CJ43 68
Avenue, The SW18 BU47 76
Avenue, The SW4 BV46 76
Avenue, The W13 BJ40 54
Avenue, The W4 BO41 65
Avenue, The, St. Paul's Cray CO50 79
Avenue, The, Amer. AO22 25
Avenue, The, Barn. BR24 28
Avenue, The, Beck. CE51 87
Avenue, The, Bet. BM70 120
Avenue, The, Bex. CP47 79
Avenue, The, Brom. CJ52 88
Avenue, The, Brwd. DC29 122
Avenue, The, Bush. BE24 27
Avenue, The, Cars. BV57 95

Avenue, The, Couls. BW61 104
Avenue, The, Cowley AX38 53
Avenue, The, Cranford BC44 63
Avenue, The, Croy. CA55 87
Avenue, The, Egh. AT49 72
Avenue, The, Epsom BQ57 94
Avenue, The, Esher BH57 93
Avenue, The, Grav. DG47 81
Avenue, The, Green. DA45 70
Avenue, The, Guil. AO74 118
Avenue, The, Har. BH30 36
Avenue, The, Harl. CM 9 6
Avenue, The, Hatch End BE29 36
Avenue, The, Hem.H. AV13 7
Avenue, The, Hmptn. BE50 74
Avenue, The, Hodd. CD13 12
Avenue, The, Horn. CV34 51
Avenue, The, Houns. BF46 74
Avenue, The, Ickenham AZ35 44
Avenue, The, Kes. CJ55 88
Avenue, The, Loug. CJ25 31
Avenue, The, Nthwd. BA29 35
Avenue, The, Orp. CN55 88
Avenue, The, Pnr. BE32 45
Avenue, The, Pot.B. BR18 19
Avenue, The, Rad. BJ20 18
Avenue, The, Red. BX72 121
Avenue, The, Rich. BL44 65
Avenue, The, Rom. CS31 50
Avenue, The, Stai. AW51 83
Avenue, The, Sun. BC51 83
Avenue, The, Sunnymeads AR45 62
Avenue, The, Surb. BL53 85
Avenue, The, Sutt. BR58 94
Avenue, The, Tad. BP64 103
Avenue, The, Twick. BJ46 74
Avenue, The, W.Wick. CF54 87
Avenue, The, Wat. BC23 26
Avenue, The, Wem. BL33 46
Avenue, The, West. CL65 106
Avenue, The, West.Dr. AY41 63
Avenue, The, Wey. AW58 92
Avenue, The, Whyt. CB63 105
Avenue, The, Wind. AQ46 72
Avenue, The, Wok. AP58 91
Avenue, The, Wor.Pk. BO55 85
Averil Gro. SW16 BY50 76
Averill St. W6 BQ43 65
Avern Gdns., E.Mol. BF52 84
Avern Rd., E.Mol. BF53 84
Avery Farm Row SW1 BV42 3
Cundy St.
Avery Gdns., Ilf. CK32 49
Avery Hill Rd. SE9 CM46 78
Avery Row W1 BV40 3
Avery Row W1 BV40 56
Avey La., Wal.Abb. CG22 31
Avia Clo., Hem.H. AX15 8
Aviary Clo. E16 CG39 58
Aviary Rd., Wok. AW61 101
Aviary St. E16 CG39 58
Lawrence St.
Aviemore Clo., Beck. CD53 87
Aviemore Way, Beck. CD53 87
Avignon Rd. SE4 CC45 67
Avington Clo., Guil. AS70 118
Avington Gro. SE20 CC50 77
Avington Way SE15 CA43 67
Avion Cres. NW9 BO30 37
Grahame Park Way
Avior Dr., Nthwd. BB28 35
Avis Sq. E1 CC39 57
Avoca Rd. SW17 BV49 76
Avocet Ms. SE28 CM41 68
Avon Clo., Grav. DH48 81
Avon Clo., Hayes BD38 54
Avon Clo., Sutt. BT56 95
Avon Clo., Wat. BD20 18
Avon Clo., Wey. AW57 92
Avon Clo., Wor.Pk. BP55 85
Avon Grn., S.Ock. DA39 60
Avon Ms., Pnr. BE29 36
Avon Path, S.Croy. BZ57 96
Avon Pl. SE1 BZ41 4
Avon Pl. SE1 BZ41 67
Avon Rd. E17 CF31 48
Avon Rd. SE4 CE45 67
Avon Rd., Grnf. BF38 54
Avon Rd., Sun. BB50 73
Avon Rd., Upmin. CY32 51
Avon Sq., Hem.H. AY11 8
Avon St. SE1 BZ41 67
Avon Way E18 CH31 49
Avondale Av. N12 BS28 38
Avondale Av. NW2 BO34 46
Avondale Av., Barn. BU26 38
Avondale Av., Esher BJ55 84
Avondale Av., Stai. AV50 72
Avondale Av., Wor.Pk. BO54 85
Avondale Clo., Loug. CK26 40
Avondale Clo., Walt. BD56 93
Avondale Cres., Enf. CD24 30
Avondale Cres., Ilf. CJ32 49
Avondale Ct. E16 CG39 58
Avondale Rd.
Avondale Ct. E18 CH30 40
Avondale Ct., St.Alb. BH13 9
Upper Lattimore Rd.
Avondale Dr., Hayes BC40 53
Avondale Dr., Loug. CK26 40
Avondale Gdns., Houns. BE46 74
Avondale Park Gdns. W11 BQ40 55
Avondale Park Rd. W11 BR40 55
Avondale Rd. E16 CG39 58
Avondale Rd. E17 CE33 48
Avondale Rd. N13 BY27 38
Avondale Rd. N15 BY32 47
Avondale Rd. N3 BT30 38
Avondale Rd. SE9 CK48 78
Avondale Rd. SW14 BN45 65
Avondale Rd. SW19 BS49 76
Avondale Rd., Ashf. AX48 73
Avondale Rd., Brom. CG50 78
Avondale Rd., Har. BH31 45
Avondale Rd., S.Croy. BZ57 96
Avondale Rd., Well. CP44 69
Avondale Ri. SE15 CA45 67
Avondale Sq. SE1 CB42 4
Avondale Sq. SE1 CB42 67
Avonley Rd. SE14 CC43 67
Avonmead, Wok. AR62 100
Silversmiths Way
Avonmore Av., Guil. AS70 118
Avonmore Pl. W14 BR42 65
Avonmore Rd.
Avonmore Rd. W14 BR42 65
Avonmouth St. SE1 BZ41 4
Avontar Rd., S.Ock. DA38 60
Avonwick Rd., Houns. BF44 64
Avril Way E4 CF28 39
Avro Way, Wall. BX57 95
Awlfield Av. N17 BZ30 39
Awliscombe Rd., Well. CN44 68
Axe St., Bark. CM37 58
Axholme Av., Edg. BM30 37
Axminster Cres., Well. CP44 69
Axminster Rd. N7 BX34 47
Axtaine Rd., Orp. CP54 89
Axtane Clo., S.at H. CY51 90
Millstone Clo.
Axwood, Epsom BN61 103
Aybrook St. W1 BV39 1
Aybrook St. W1 BV39 56
Aycliffe Clo., Brom. CK52 88
Aycliffe Dr., Hem.H. AY11 8
Aycliffe Rd. W12 BP40 55
Aycliffe Rd., B.Wd. BL23 28
Ayebridges Av., Egh. AU50 72
Ayelands La., New A.G. DC55 90
Aylands Rd., Enf. CC21 30
Ayles Rd., Hayes BC38 53
Aylesbury Clo. E7 CG36 58
Atherton Rd.
Aylesbury Cres., Slou. AO39 52
Aylesbury Rd. SE17 BZ42 4
Aylesbury Rd. SE17 BZ42 67
Aylesbury Rd., Brom. CH52 88
Aylesbury St. EC1 BY38 2
Aylesbury St. EC1 BY38 56
Aylesbury St. NW10 BN34 46
Aylesford Av., Beck. CD53 87
Aylesford St. SW1 BW42 3
Aylesford St. SW1 BW42 66
Aylesham La., Rom. CV28 42
Aylesham Rd., Orp. CN54 88
Aylestone Av. NW6 BQ36 55
Aylesworth Spur, Wind. AQ47 72
Ashbrook Rd.
Aylett Rd. SE5 CB52 87
Aylett Rd., Islw. BH44 64
Aylett Rd., Upmin. CY34 51
Ayley Cft., Enf. CB25 30
Ayliffe Clo., Kings.T. BM51 85
Cambridge Gdns.
Aylmer Clo., Stan. BJ28 36
Aylmer Dr., Stan. BJ28 36
Aylmer Rd. E11 CG33 49
Aylmer Rd. N2 BU32 47
Aylmer Rd. W12 BO41 65
Aylmer Rd., Dag. CQ34 50
Ayloffe Rd., Dag. CQ36 59
Ayloffs Clo., Horn. CW32 51
Ayloffs Wk., Horn. CV32 51
Aylsham Dr., Uxb. BA34 44
Aylsham Rd., Hodd. CF11 12
Aylton Est. SE16 CC41 67
Aylward Rd. SE23 CC48 77
Aylward Rd. SW20 BR51 85
Aylward St. E1 CC39 57
Aylwards Ri., Stan. BJ28 36
Aylwin Est. SE1 CA41 4
Aylwin Est. SE1 CA41 67
Aymer Clo., Stai. AV51 82
Aymer Dr., Stai. AV51 82
Aynho St., Wat. BC25 26
Aynhoe Rd. W14 BQ42 65
Aynscombe Angle, Orp. CO54 89
Aynscombe La. SW14 BN45 65
Aynscombe Path SW14 BN44 65
Thames Bank
Ayot Grn., Welw. BP 6 5
Ayot Little Grn., Welw. BO 6 5
Ayot Path, B.Wd. BM22 28
Ayot St. Peter Rd., Welw. BO 5 5
Ayr Ct. W3 BM39 55
Monks Dr.
Ayr Grn., Rom. CS29 41
Ayr Way, Rom. CT30 41
Ayres Clo. E13 CH38 58
Ayres Cres. NW10 BN36 55
Ayres St. SE1 BZ41 4
Ayres St. SE1 BZ41 67
Ayron Rd., S.Ock. DA38 60
Aysome Rd. N16 CA34 48
Aysgarth Pk., Maid. AG42 61
Aysgarth Rd. SE21 BZ46 77
Aytoun Rd. SW9 BX44 66
Azalea Clo. W7 BH40 54
Azalea Ct., Wok. AR63 100
Azalea Dr., Swan. CS52 89
Azalea Way, Slou. AS39 52
Azalea Wk., Pnr. BC32 44
Azenby Rd. SE15 CA44 67
Azof St. SE10 CG42 68

B

Baalbec Rd. N5 BY35 47
Baas Hill Clo., Brox. CD14 12
Baas Hill, Brox. CC14 12
Baas La., Brox. CD14 12
Babbacombe Clo., Chess. BK56 93
Babbacombe Gdns., Ilf. CK31 49
Babbacombe Rd., Brom. CH51 88
Baber Dr., Felt. BD46 74
Babington Rd. NW4 BP31 46
Babington Rd. SW16 BW49 76
Babington Rd., Dag. CP35 50
Babington Rd., Horn. CU33 50
Babington Ri., Wem. BM36 55
Babmaes St. SW1 BW40 3
Babmaes St. SW1 BW40 56
Jermyn St.
Babylon La., Tad. BS67 113
Bachelors Acre., Wind. AO44 61
Bachelors La., Wok. AY65 101
Baches St. N1 BZ38 2
Baches St. N1 BZ38 57
Back Alley EC3 CA39 2
Lloyds Av.
Back Alley, Dor. BJ71 119
Back Church La. E1 CB39 2
Back Church La. E1 CB39 57
Back Grn., Walt. BD57 93
Back Hill EC1 BY38 2
Back Hill EC1 BY38 56
Back La. N8 BX32 47
New Rd.
Back La. NW3 BT35 47
Flask Wk.
Back La., Bark. CM37 58
Broadway
Back La., Bex. CR47 79
Back La., Bish. CR 6 6
Back La., Brent. BK43 64
Back La., Brwd. DA21 33
Back La., Ch.St.G. AQ27 34
Back La., Edg. BN30 37
Back La., Grays DA41 70
Back La., Guil. AX69 110
Back La., Hert. BZ12 12
Back La., Ivy Hatch DB65 108
Back La., Mackerels Plain CR67 116
Back La., Plaxtol DC67 117
Back La., Rich. BK48 74
Back La., Rick. AT22 25
Back La., Rom. CP33 50
Station Rd.
Back La., Ton. DB69 117
Back La., Wal.Abb. CJ14 13
Back La., Wat. BH23 27
Back La., Welw. BT 6 5
Back Path, Red. BZ70 114
Back Rd., Sid. CO49 79
Back Row SW17 BU49 76
Totterdown St.
Back St. W3 BM40 55
Back Swan Yd. SE1 CA41 67
Bermondsey St.
Back, The, Berk. AT11 7
Backhouse Pl. SE17 CA42 4
Bacon Gro. SE1 CA41 4
Bacon Gro. SE1 CA41 67
Bacon La. NW9 BM31 46
Bacon La., Edg. BM30 37
Bacon Link, Rom. CR29 41
Bacon St. E1 CA38 2
Bacon St. E1 CA38 57
Bacon St. E2 CA38 2
Bacon St. E2 CA38 57
Bacons Dr., Cuff. BX18 20
Bacons La. N6 BV33 47
Bacons Mead, Uxb. AW34 44
Bacton St. E2 CC38 57
Digby St.
Badburgham Ct., Wal.Abb. CG20 22
Ninefields
Baddow Clo., Dag. CR37 59
Baddow Clo., Wdf.Grn. CJ29 40
Baddow Wk. N1 BZ37 57
Popham St.
Baden Clo., Stai. AW50 73
Baden Clo., Wey. BB57 92
Baden Pl. SE1 BZ41 4
Baden Pl. SE1 BZ41 67
Baden Powell Clo., Surb. BL55 85
Agar Clo.
Baden Powell Rd., Sev. CT64 107
Baden Rd. N8 BW31 47
Baden Rd., Guil. AQ69 118
Baden Rd., Ilf. CL35 49
Bader Clo., Ken. BZ61 105
Bader Clo., Welw.G.C. BT 8 5
Douglas Way
Bader Gdns., Slou. AN41 61
Bader Way, Rain. CU36 59
Bader Wk., Grav. DF48 81
Hillary Av.
Badger Clo., Guil. AQ69 118
Badger Clo., Houns. BD45 64
Chinchilla Dr.
Badger Way, Hat. BP13 10
Badgers Cft. N20 BR26 37
Badgers Cft. SE9 CL48 78
Badgers Cft., Brox. CD14 12
Badgers Cft., Hem.H. BA14 8
Pancake La.
Badgers Clo., Enf. BY24 29
Badgers Clo., Felt. BC49 73
Sycamore Clo.
Badgers Clo., Har. BG32 45
Badgers Clo., Hayes BB40 53
Badgers Clo., Wok. AQ62 100
St. Johns Rd.
Badgers Copse, Orp. CN55 88
Badgers Copse, Wor.Pk. BO55 85
Badgers Hill, Vir.W. AR53 82
Badgers Hole, Croy. CC56 96
Badgers La., Warl. CC63 105
Badgers Mt., Grays DF41 71
Badgers Rd., Sev. CR58 98
Badgers Ri., Sev. CR58 98
Badgers Wk., N.Mal. BO51 85
Badgers Wk., Pur. BW59 95
Badgers Wk., Whyt. CA63 105
Badgers Wood, Cat. BZ66 114
Badgers Wood, Slou. AO35 43
Badingham Dr., Lthd. BH65 102
Badlis Rd. E17 CD31 48
Badlow Clo., Erith CT43 69
Badminton Clo., B.Wd. BM23 28
Stratfield Rd.
Badminton Clo., Har. BH31 45
Badminton Clo., Nthlt. BF36 54
Badminton Pl., Brox. CD13 12
Badminton Rd. SW12 BV46 76
Badsworth Rd. SE5 BZ44 67
Bagden Hill, Dor. BG68 111
Bagley Clo., West Dr. AY41 63
Bagleys La. SW6 BS44 66
Bagleys Spring, Rom. CQ31 50
Bagot Clo., Ash. BL61 103
Bagshot Clo. SE18 CL44 68
Bagshot Rd., Egh. AR50 72
Bagshot Rd., Enf. CA26 39
Bagshot Rd., Guil. AO66 109
Bagshot Rd., Wok. AO65 100
Bagshot St. SE17 CA42 4
Bagshot St. SE17 CA42 67
Bahram Rd., Epsom BN58 94
Baildon St. SE8 CD43 67
Watsons St.
Bailey Clo., Grays CY42 70
Gabion Av.
Bailey Clo., Wind. AN44 61
Bailey Pl. SE26 CC50 77
Bailey Rd., Dor. BG72 119
Baillie Clo., Rain. CU38 59
Baillie Rd., Guil. AS71 118
Baillies Wk. W5 BK41 64
Bainbridge Rd., Dag. CQ35 50
Bainbridge St. WC1 BW39 1
Bainbridge St. WC1 BW39 56
Bainton Mead, Wok. AQ62 100
Baird Av., Sthl. BF40 54
Baird Clo. NW9 BN32 46
Baird Clo., Bush. BF25 27
Ashfield Av.
Baird Clo., Slou. AN41 61
Baird Gdns. SE21 CA49 77
Baird Rd., Enf. CB24 30
Baird St. EC1 BZ38 2
Bairstow Clo., B.Wd. BK23 27
Baizdon Rd. SE3 CG44 68
Bakeham La., Egh. AR50 72
Baker Boy La., Croy. CD59 96
Baker Ct., B.Wd. BM23 28
Brook Rd.
Baker Hill Clo., Grav. DF49 81
Baker La., Mitch. BV51 86
Baker Rd. NW10 BN37 55
Baker Rd. SE18 CK43 68
Baker St. NW1 BU38 1
Baker St. NW1 BU38 56
Baker St. W1 BU38 56
Baker St. W1 BU39 1
Baker St., Enf. BZ24 30
Baker St., Grays DF40 71
Baker St., Pot.B. BR21 28
Baker St., Wey. AZ56 92
Bakers Alley SE1 CA40 57
Abbots La.
Bakers Av. E17 CE32 48
Bakers Av., Sev. CZ57 99
Bakers End SW20 BR51 85
Bakers Field N7 BX35 47
Bakers Gro., Welw.G.C. BT 7 5
Bakers Hill E5 CB33 48
Bakers Hill, Barn. BT23 29
Bakers La. N6 BU32 47
North Hill
Bakers La. W5 BK40 54
The Grove
Bakers La., Epp. CN18 22
Bakers Mead, Gdse. CC68 114
Bakers Meadow, Brwd. DB22 33
Bakers Ms. W1 BV39 1
Bakers Ms. W1 BV39 56
Adam St.
Bakers Pass. NW3 BT35 47
Oriel Pl.
Bakers Rd., Chsnt. CB18 21
Bakers Rd., Uxb. AX36 53
Bakers Rents E2 CA38 2
Hackney Rd.
Bakers Row E15 CG37 58
Bakers Row EC1 BY38 2
Bakers Row EC1 BY38 56
Bakers Wood, Uxb. AU33 43
Bakerscroft, Wal.Cr. CD17 21
High St., Cheshunt
Bakery Clo., Harl. CJ11 13
Harlow Rd.
Bakewell Ct. E5 CC35 48
Clapton Park Est.
Bakewell Way, N.Mal. BO51 85
Balaam St. E13 CH38 58
Balaams La. N14 BW27 38
Balaclava Rd. SE1 CA42 4
Balaclava Rd. SE1 CA42 67
Balaclava Rd., Surb. BK54 84
Balben Rd. E9 CC36 57
Balcaskie Rd. SE9 CK46 78
Balchen Rd. SE3 CJ44 68
Balchier Rd. SE22 CB46 77
Balchins La., Dor. BF72 119
Balcombe St. NW1 BU38 1
Balcombe St. NW1 BU38 56
Balcon Way, B.Wd. BN23 28
Wilcox Clo.
Balcorne St. E9 CC36 57
Balder Ri. SE12 CH48 78
Balderton St. W1 BV39 1
Balderton St. W1 BV39 56
Baldock St. E3 CE37 57
Baldock Way, B.Wd. BL23 28
Baldocks Rd., Epp. CN21 31
Baldry Gdns. SW16 BX50 76
Baldwin Cres. SE5 BZ44 67
Baldwin Cres., Guil. AU69 118
Baldwin St. EC1 BZ38 2
Baldwin St. EC1 BZ38 57
Baldwin Ter. N1 BZ37 2
Baldwin Ter. N1 BZ37 57
Baldwins Gdns. EC1 BY39 2
Baldwins Gdns. EC1 BY39 56
Baldwins Hill, Loug. CK23 31
Baldwins La., Rick. AZ24 26
Baldwins Pond, Loug. CK23 31
Baldwins Shore, Wind. AO43 61
Baldwins, Welw.G.C. BS 8 5
Baldwyn Gdns. W3 BN40 55
Baldwyns Est., Dart. CT48 79
Baldwyns Pk., Bex. CS48 79
Baldwyns Rd., Bex. CS48 79
Balfe St. N1 BX37 2
Balfe St. N1 BX37 56
Balfern Gro. W4 BO42 65
Balfern St. SW11 BU44 66
Balfont Clo., S.Croy. CB60 96
Balfour App., Ilf. CL34 49
Balfour Rd.
Balfour Av. W7 BH40 54
Balfour Av., Wok. AS64 100
Balfour Gro. N20 BU27 38
Balfour Ho. W10 BQ39 55
Balfour Ms. N9 CB27 39
Bridge Rd.
Balfour Ms. W1 BV40 3
Balfour Pl. SW15 BP45 65
Balfour Pl. W1 BV40 3
Balfour Rd. N5 BZ35 48
Balfour Rd. N9 CB27 39
Victoria Rd.
Balfour Rd. SE25 CB52 87
Balfour Rd. SW19 BS50 76
Balfour Rd. W13 BJ41 64
Balfour Rd. W3 BN39 55
Balfour Rd., Brom. CJ53 88
Balfour Rd., Cars. BU57 95
Balfour Rd., Grays DE42 71
Balfour Rd., Har. BG32 45
Balfour Rd., Houns. BF45 64
Balfour Rd., Ilf. CL34 49
Balfour Rd., Sthl. BD41 64
Balfour Rd., Wey. AZ56 92
Balfour St. SE17 BZ42 4
Balfour St. SE17 BZ42 67
Balgonie Rd. E4 CF26 39
Balgores Cres., Rom. CU31 50
Balgores La., Rom. CU31 50
Balgores Sq., Rom. CU31 50
Balgowan Clo., N.Mal. BO52 85
Balgowan Rd., Beck. CD52 87
Balgowan St. SE18 CN42 68
Balham Gro. SW12 BV47 76
Balham High Rd. SW12 BV48 76
Balham High Rd. SW17 BV48 76
Balham Hill SW12 BV47 76
Balham New Rd. SW12 BV47 76
Balham Park Rd. SW12 BU47 76
Balham Rd. N9 CB27 39
Balham Station Rd. SW12 BV47 76
Balkan Wk. E1 CB40 57
Pennington St.
Ball Ct. EC3 BZ39 2
Cornhill
Ball La. N14 BW27 38
Balaams La.
Ballamore Rd., Brom. CH48 78
Ballance Rd. E9 CC36 57
Ballands N., The, Lthd. BH64 102
Ballands S., The, Lthd. BH65 102
Ballantine St. SW18 BT45 66
Ballantyne Dr., Tad. BR64 103
Ballard Clo., Kings.T. BN50 75
Ballard Grn., Wind. AM43 61
Ballards Av., S.Croy. CB57 96
Ballards Clo., Dag. CR37 59
Ballards Farm Rd., S.Croy. CB57 96
Ballards Grn., Tad. BR63 103
Ballards La. N12 BS30 38
Ballards La. N3 BS30 38
Ballards La., Oxt. CJ68 115
Ballards Ms., Edg. BM29 37
High St.
Ballards Rd. NW2 BP34 46
Ballards Rd., Dag. CR37 59
Ballards Ri., S.Croy. CB57 96
Ballards Way, Croy. CB57 96
Ballards Way, S.Croy. CB57 96
Ballast Quay SE10 CF42 67
Ballater Clo., Wat. BD28 36
Ballater Rd. SW2 BX45 66
Ballater Rd., S.Croy. CA56 96
Ballenger Ct., Wat. BC24 26
Halsey Rd.
Ballina St. SE23 CC47 77
Ballingdon Rd. SW11 BV46 76
Ballinger Ct., Berk. AQ13 7
Balliol Av. E4 CG28 40
Balliol Rd. N17 BZ30 39
Balliol Rd. W10 BQ39 55
Balliol Rd., Well. CO44 69
Balloch Rd. SE6 CF47 77
Ballogie Av. NW10 BO35 46
Ballow Clo. SE5 BZ43 67
Harris St.
Balls Pond Rd. N1 BZ36 57
Balmain Clo. W5 BK40 54
Balmer Rd. E3 CD37 57
Balmes Rd. N1 BZ37 2
Balmes Rd. N1 BZ37 57
Balmoral Av., Beck. CD52 87
Balmoral Clo. SW15 BQ46 75
Westleigh Av.
Balmoral Cres., E.Mol. BF52 84
Balmoral Dr., B.Wd. BN24 28
Balmoral Dr., Hayes BB38 53
Balmoral Dr., Sthl. BE38 54
Balmoral Dr., Wok. AU61 100
Balmoral Gdns. W13 BJ41 64
Balmoral Gdns., Bex. CQ47 79
Balmoral Gdns., Ilf. CN33 49
Balmoral Gdns., Wind. AO45 61
Balmoral Gro. N7 BX36 56
Brewery Rd.
Balmoral Ms. W12 BO41 65
Rylett Cres.
Balmoral Rd. E10 CE34 48
Balmoral Rd. E7 CJ35 49
Balmoral Rd. NW2 BP36 55
Balmoral Rd., Brwd. DA25 33
Balmoral Rd., Enf. CC21 30

Bal–Bar

Balmoral Rd., Har. BF35 45
Balmoral Rd., Horn. CV34 51
Balmoral Rd., Kings.T. BL52 85
Balmoral Rd., Rom. CU32 50
Balmoral Rd., S.at H. CX50 80
Balmoral Rd., Wat. BD22 27
Balmoral Rd., Wor.Pk. BP55 85
Balmoral Way, Sutt. BS58 95
Balmore Cres., Barn. BV25 29
Balmore St. N19 BV34 47
Balmuir Gdns. SW15 BQ45 65
Balnacraig Av. NW10 BO35 46
Balniel Gate SW1 BW42 3
Balniel Gate SW1 BW42 66
Balouhain Clo., Ash. BK62 102
Baltic Clo. SW19 BT50 76
Baltic St. EC1 BZ38 2
Baltic St. EC1 BZ38 57
Baltimore Pl., Well. CN44 68
Balvaird Pl. SW1 BW42 3
Bessborough Pl.
Balvernie Gro. SW18 BR47 75
Bamborough Gdns. W12 BQ41 65
Bamford Av., Wem. BL37 55
Bamford Ct. E15 CE35 48
Bamford Rd., Bark. CM36 58
Bamford Rd., Brom. CF49 77
Bamford Way, Rom. CR28 41
Bampfylde Clo., Wall. BW55 86
Bampton Rd. SE23 CC48 77
Bampton Rd., Rom. CW30 42
Bampton Way, Wok. AQ62 100
Banavie Gdns., Beck. CF51 87
Banbury Clo., Sutt. BS57 95
Banbury Ct. WC2 BX40 56
Long Acre
Banbury Rd. E9 CC36 57
Banbury St. SW11 BU44 66
Banbury St., Wat. BC25 26
Banbury Wk., Nthlt. BF37 54
Leander Rd.
Banchory Rd. SE3 CH43 68
Banckside, Long. DC52 90
Bancroft Av. N2 BU32 47
Bancroft Av., Buck.H. CH27 40
Bancroft Clo., Ashf. AZ49 73
Bancroft Ct., Nthlt. BD37 54
Bancroft Ct., Reig. BS70 121
Bancroft Gdns., Har. BG30 36
Bancroft Gdns., Orp. CN54 88
Bancroft Rd. E1 CC38 57
Bancroft Rd., Har. BG30 36
Bancroft Rd., Reig. BS70 121
Band La., Egh. AS49 72
Banders Ri., Guil. AU70 118
Bandon Ri., Wall. BW56 95
Banes Down, Wal.Abb. CG14 13
Bangalore St. SW15 BQ45 65
Bangor Clo., Nthlt. BF35 45
Bangor Rd., Brent. BL43 65
Bangors Clo., Iver AV39 52
Bangors Rd. N., Iver AU37 52
Bangors Rd. S., Iver AV38 52
Banim St. W6 BP42 65
Banister Rd. W10 BQ38 55
Bank Av., Mitch. BT51 86
Bank Ct., Dart. CW46 80
Bank Ct., Hem.H. AX14 8
Bank End SE1 BZ40 4
Bank La. SW15 BO46 75
Bank La., Kings.T. BL50 75
Bank La., Sev. CX69 117
Bank Mill La., Berk. AS13 7
Bank Mill, Berk. AS13 7
Bank Pl., Brwd. DB27 42
High St.
Bank St., Grav. DG46 81
Bank St., Sev. CU66 116
London Rd.
Bank, The N6 BV33 47
Bankfield Ct., Islw. BH44 64
Bankfoot Rd., Brom. CG49 78
Bankfoot, Grays DD42 71
Bankhurst Rd. SE6 CD47 77
Banks La., Bexh. CQ45 69
Banks La., Epp. CQ19 23
Banks La., Lthd. BC64 101
Banks Rd., B.Wd. BN23 28
Banks Spur, Slou. AN41 61
Cooper Way
Banks Way, Guil. AS69 118
Bankside Av., Nthlt. BC37 53
Bankside Clo., Bex. CS49 79
Bankside Clo., Cars. BU57 95
Bankside Clo., West. CJ62 106
Bankside Dr., T.Ditt. BJ54 84
Bankside SE1 BY40 4
Bankside SE1 BY40 56
Bankside Way SE19 CA50 77
Central Hill Est.
Bankside, Enf. BY23 29
Bankside, Grav. DE46 81
Bankside, S.Croy. CA57 96
Bankside, Sthl. BD40 54
Bankside, Wok. AQ62 100
Bankton Rd. SW2 BY45 66
Bankwell Rd. SE13 CG45 68
Bann Clo., S.Ock. DA40 60
Banner Clo., Grays CY42 70
Brimfield Rd.
Banner St. EC1 BZ38 2
Banner St. EC1 BZ38 57
Banning St. SE10 CG42 68
Bannister Clo. SW2 BY47 76
Bannister Clo., Har. BG35 45
Bannister Clo., Slou. AS41 62
Bannister Ho. E9 CC35 48
Bannisters Rd., Guil. AP71 118
Bannockburn Rd. SE18 CN42 68
Bansons La., Ong. CX17 24
Bansons Way, Ong. CX17 24
Banstead Gdns. N9 CA27 39
Banstead Rd. S., Sutt. BT59 95
Banstead Rd., Cars. BT58 95
Banstead Rd., Cat. BZ64 105
Banstead Rd., Epsom BP59 94
Banstead Rd., Pur. BY59 95
Banstead St. SE15 CC45 67
Banstead Way, Wall. BX56 95
Banstock Rd., Edg. BM29 37
Banton Clo., Enf. CB23 30
Bantry St. SE5 BZ43 67
Banyard Rd. SE16 CB41 67
Southwark Park Rd.
Banyards, Horn. CW32 51
Baptist Gdns. NW5 BV36 56
Queens Cres.
Barandon Wk. W11 BQ40 55
Lancaster Rd.
Barb Ms. W6 BQ41 65
Shepherds Bush Rd.
Barbara Clo., Shep. AZ53 83
Barbauld Rd. N16 CA34 48
Barbel Clo., Wal.Cr. CE20 21
Barbel St. SE1 BY41 4
Barber Clo. N21 BY26 38
Barberry Clo., Rom. CV29 42
Barberry Rd., Hem.H. AW13 8
Barbers All. E13 CH38 58
Barbers Rd. E15 CE37 57
Barbican Rd., Grnf. BF39 54
Barbican Site EC2 BZ39 57
Barbot Clo. N9 CB27 39
Barchard St. SW18 BS46 76
Barchester Clo. W7 BH40 54
Barchester Clo., Uxb. AX38 53
Barchester Rd., Har. BG30 36
Barchester Rd., Slou. AS41 62
Barchester St. E14 CE39 57
Barclay Clo. SW6 BS43 66
Barclay Clo., Lthd. BF65 102
Barclay Ct., Hodd. CE12 12
Barclay Oval, Wdf.Grn. CH28 40
Barclay Rd. E11 CG33 49
Barclay Rd. E13 CJ38 58
Barclay Rd. E17 CF32 48
Barclay Rd. N18 BZ29 39
Barclay Rd. SW6 BS43 66
Barclay Rd., Croy. BZ55 87
Barclay Way SE22 CB47 77
Wilkie Way
Barclay Way, Grays CZ42 70
Barcombe Av. SW2 BX48 76
Barcombe Clo., Orp. CN51 88
Petersham Dr.
Bard Rd. W10 BQ40 55
Barden Clo., Uxb. AX29 35
Barden St. SE18 CN43 68
Bardeswell Clo., Brwd. DB27 42
Bardfield Av., Rom. CP31 50
Bardney Rd., Mord. BS52 86
Bardolph Av., Croy. CD58 96
Bardolph Rd. N7 BX35 47
Bardolph Rd., Rich. BL45 65
St. Georges Rd.
Bardon Wk., Wok. AQ62 100
Bardsey Wk. N1 BZ36 57
Clephane Rd.
Bardsley Clo., Croy. CB55 87
Bardsley La. SE10 CF43 67
Bardwell Ct., St.Alb. BG14 9
Bardwell Rd.
Bardwell Rd., St.Alb. BG14 9
Barfett St. W10 BR38 55
Barfield Av. N20 BU27 38
Barfield Rd. E11 CG33 49
Barfield Rd., Brom. CL52 88
Barfield, S.at H. CX51 90
Barfields Cres., Red. BY70 121
Barfields Gdns., Loug. CL24 31
Barfields Path, Loug. CL24 31
Barfields, Loug. CL24 31
Barfolds, Hat. BQ15 10
Barford Clo. NW4 BP30 37
Barford St. N1 BY37 2
Barford St. N1 BY37 56
Barforth Rd. SE15 CB45 67
Barfreston Way SE20 CB51 87
Bargate Clo. SE18 CN42 68
Bargate Clo., N.Mal. BP54 85
Barge House Rd. E16 CL41 68
Barge House St. SE1 BY40 4
Barge House St. SE1 BY40 56
Barge Rd., E.Mol. BG52 84
Barge Wk., Kings.T. BK51 84
Bargery Rd. SE6 CE47 77
Bargrove Av., Hem.H. AW14 8
Bargrove Clo. SE19 CB50 77
Lullington Rd.
Bargrove Clo. SE20 CB50 77
Bargrove Cres. SE6 CD48 77
Elm La.
Barham Av., B.Wd. BL24 28
Barham Clo., Brom. CK54 88
Barham Clo., Chis. CL49 78
Barham Clo., Rom. CR30 41
Barham Clo., Wem. BJ36 54
Barham Clo., Wey. BA56 92
Barham Rd. SW20 BP50 75
Barham Rd., Chis. CL49 78
Barham Rd., Dart. CX47 80
Barham Rd., S.Croy. BZ56 96
Baring Clo. SE12 CH48 78
Baring Rd. SE12 CH47 78
Baring Rd., Barn. BT24 29
Baring Rd., Croy. CB54 87
Baring St. N1 BZ37 2
Baring St. N1 BZ37 57
Bark Burr Rd., Grays DC41 71
Bark Hart Rd., Orp. CO54 89
Bark Pl. W2 BS40 3
Bark Pl. W2 BS40 56
Barker Dr. NW1 BW36 1
Barker Dr. NW1 BW36 56
Barker Rd., Cher. AV54 82
Barker St. SW10 BT43 66
Barker Way SE22 CB47 77
Wilkie Way
Barker Wk. SW16 BW48 76
Barkham Rd. N17 BZ29 39
Barking By-pass, Bark. CM38 58
Barking Rd. E13 CG39 58
Barking Rd. E16 CG39 58
Barking Rd. E6 CJ37 58
Barkis Way SE16 CB42 67
Egan Way
Barkston Gdns. SW5 BS42 66
Barkston Path, B.Wd. BM22 28
Barkway Ct. N4 BZ34 48
Kings Crescent Est.
Barkworth Rd. SE16 CB42 67
Barlborough St. SE14 CC43 67
Barlby Gdns. W10 BQ38 55
Barlby Rd. W10 BQ39 55
Barle Gdns., S.Ock. DA39 60
Barley Cft., Harl. CM13 13
Barley Cft., Hem.H. BA13 8
Barley Clo., Bush. BF25 27
Barley Field, Brwd. CZ22 33
Barley La., Ilf. CO33 50
Barley La., Rom. CO33 50
Barley Mow Clo., Wok. AO62 100
Barley Mow Ct., Reig. BN70 120
Barley Mow La., St.Alb. BL14 10
Barley Mow La., Wok. AO61 100
Barley Mow Pass. W4 BN42 65
Heathfield Ter.
Barley Mow Rd., Egh. AR49 72
Barley Mow Way, Shep. AZ52 83
Petts La.
Barleycorn Way E14 CD40 57
Narrow St.
Barleycorn Way, Horn. CW32 51
Barleycroft Grn., Welw.G.C. BQ 8 5
Barleycroft Rd., Welw.G.C. BQ 8 5
Barleyfields Clo., Rom. CO32 50
Barleymow Pass. EC1 BY39 2
Cloth Fair
Barlow Clo., Wall. BX57 95
Redford Av.
Barlow Pl. W1 BV40 3
Barlow Pl. W1 BV40 56
Bruton La.
Barlow Rd. NW6 BR36 55
Barlow Rd. W3 BM40 55
Barlow Rd., Hmptn. BF50 74
Barlow St. SE17 BZ42 4
Barlow St. SE17 BZ42 67
Barlow Way, Rain. CS39 59
Barmeston Rd. SE6 CE48 77
Barmor Clo., Har. BF30 36
Barmouth Av., Grnf. BH37 54
Barmouth Rd. SW18 BT46 76
Barmouth Rd., Croy. CC55 87
Barn Clo., Ashf. AZ49 73
Barn Clo., Bans. BT61 104
Barn Clo., Hem.H. AY15 8
Barn Clo., Nthlt. BD37 54
Barn Clo., Rad. BJ21 27
Barn Clo., Welw.G.C. BQ 8 5
Barn Cres., Pur. BZ60 96
Barn Cres., Stan. BK29 36
Barn Ct., Saw. CQ 6 6
Station Rd.
Barn Elms Pk. SW15 BQ44 65
Barn Field, Epp. CO17 23
Barn Hill Av., Brom. CG53 88
Barn Hill, Harl. CH13 13
Barn Hill, Wem. BM33 46
Barn Lea, Rick. AW26 35
Barn Mead, Brwd. DB21 33
Barn Mead, Epp. CN21 31
Barn Mead, Harl. CN12 13
Barn Meadow Clo., Lthd. BE65 102
Barn Meadow La.
Barn Meadow La., Lthd. BE65 102
Barn Rd., Mitch. BV52 86
Barn Ri., Wem. BM34 46
Barn St. N16 CA34 48
Stoke Newington Church St.
Barn Way, Wem. BM33 46
Barnabas Rd. E9 CC35 48
Barnaby Clo., Har. BG34 45
Barnaby Way, Chig. CL27 40
Barnacre Clo., Uxb. AX39 53
Barnacres Cft., Hem.H. AZ15 8
Barnacres Rd., Hem.H. AY15 8
Barnard Acres, Wal.Abb. CG15 13
Barnard Clo. SE18 CL41 68
Barnard Clo., Chis. CM51 88
Barnard Clo., Hem.H. AY14 8
Barnard Clo., Sun. BC50 73
Barnard Clo., Wall. BW57 95
Barnard Ct., Wok. AP62 100
Ashwindham Ct.
Barnard Gdns., Hayes BC38 53
Barnard Gdns., N.Mal. BP52 85
Barnard Grn., Welw.G.C. BR 8 5
Barnard Gro. E15 CG36 58
Vicarage La.
Barnard Hill N10 BV30 38
Barnard Hill SW11 BU45 66
Barnard Rd.
Barnard Rd. SW11 BU45 66
Barnard Rd., Enf. CB23 30
Barnard Rd., Saw. CQ 5 6
Barnard Rd., Warl. CE63 105
Barnardo Dr., Ilf. CM31 49
Ashurst Dr.
Barnardo St. E1 CC39 57
Barnards Inn EC1 BY39 56
Fetter La.
Barnards Pl., Pur. BY58 95
Pampisford Rd.
Barnby Rd., Wok. AO62 100
Barnby St. E15 CG37 58
Barnby St. NW1 BW37 56
Barnby St. NW1 BW38 1
Barncroft Clo., Loug. CL25 31
Barncroft Clo., Uxb. AZ39 53
Barncroft Rd., Berk. AP13 7
Barncroft Rd., Loug. CL25 31
Barncroft Way, St.Alb. BJ14 9
Barndicott, Welw.G.C. BT 8 5
Barnehurst Av., Bexh. CS44 69
Barnehurst Av., Erith CS44 69
Barnehurst Clo., Erith CS44 69
Barnehurst Rd., Bexh. CR44 69
Barnend Dr., Dart. CV49 80
Barnend La., Dart. CV49 80
Barnes Alley, Hmptn. BG51 84
Barnes Av. SW13 BP43 65
Barnes Av., Chesh. AO18 16
Barnes Av., Sthl. BE42 64
Barnes Br. SW13 BO44 65
Barnes Br. W4 BO44 65
Barnes Clo. E12 CJ35 49
Barnes Cray Rd., Dart. CU45 69
Barnes Ct. E16 CJ39 58
Ridgewell Rd.
Barnes Ct. N22 BX29 38
Barnes Ct., Wdf.Grn. CJ28 40
Durham Av.
Barnes End, N.Mal. BP53 85
Barnes High St. SW13 BO44 65
Barnes La., Kings L. AW17 17
Barnes Pikle W5 BJ40 54
Mattock La.
Barnes Rd. N18 CC28 39
Barnes Rd., Ilf. CM35 49
Barnes Ri., Kings L. AY17 17
Barnes St. E14 CD39 57
Barnes Ter. SE8 CD42 67
Barnes Way, Iver AV40 52
Barnesbury Est. N1 BX37 2
Barnesdale Cres., Orp. CO53 89
Barnet By-pass, Barn. BO23 28
Barnet By-pass, Hat. BO12 10
Barnet Dr., Brom. CK55 88
Barnet Gate La., Barn. BO25 28
Barnet Gro. E2 CB38 2
Barnet Gro. E2 CB38 57
Barnet Hill, Barn. BR24 28
Barnet La. N20 BR26 37
Barnet La., B.Wd. BK25 27
Barnet Rd., Arkley BO25 28
Barnet Rd., Pot.B. BS21 29
Barnet Rd., St.Alb. BL17 19
Barnet Row., Guil. AR68 109
Barnet Way NW7 BN28 37
Barnet Wood Rd., Brom. CJ55 88
Barnett Clo., Erith CT44 69
Barnett Clo., Lthd. BJ63 102
Barnett St. E1 CB39 57
Kinder St.
Barnetts Shaw, Oxt. CF67 114
Barnettwood La., Lthd. BJ63 102
& Ash.
Barney Clo. SE7 CJ42 68
Barnfield Av., Croy. CC55 87
Barnfield Av., Kings.T. BK49 74
Barnfield Av., Mitch. BV52 86
Barnfield Clo. N4 BX33 47
Crouch Hill
Barnfield Clo., Couls. BZ63 105
Barnfield Clo., Hodd. CE11 12
Barnfield Clo., Swan. CS54 89
Barnfield Cres., Sev. CW62 108
Barnfield Gdns. Est. SE18 CL43 68
Barnfield Gdns., Kings.T. BL49 75
Barnfield Pl. E14 CE42 67
Barnfield Rd. SE18 CL43 68
Barnfield Rd. W5 BK38 54
Barnfield Rd., Welw.G.C. BR 9 5
Barnfield Rd., Belv. CQ43 69
Barnfield Rd., Edg. BN30 37
Barnfield Rd., Orp. CP52 89
Barnfield Rd., S.Croy. CA58 96
Barnfield Rd., Sev. CT65 107
Barnfield Rd., St.Alb. BK12 9
Barnfield Rd., West. CJ64 106
Barnfield Way, Oxt. CH70 115
Barnfield Wood Clo., Beck. CF53 87
Barnfield Wood Rd., Beck. CF53 87
Barnfield, Bans. BS60 95
Barnfield, Hem.H. AY15 8
Barnfield, Iver AV39 52
Barnfield, N.Mal. BN53 85
Barnfield, Slou. AL40 61
Barnham Rd., Grnf. BG38 54
Barnham St. SE1 CA41 4
Barnham St. SE1 CA41 67
Barnhill La., Hayes BC38 53
Barnhill Rd., Hayes BC38 53
Barnhill Rd., Wem. BN34 46
Barnhill, Pnr. BD32 45
Barnhurst Path., Wat. BD28 36
Barningham Way NW9 BN32 46
Barnlea Clo., Felt. BE48 74
Barnmead Gdns., Dag. CQ35 50
Barnmead Rd., Beck. CC51 87
Barnmead Rd., Dag. CQ35 50
Barnmead, Ong. CT18 23
Barnmead, Wok. AP58 91
Barnsbury Clo., N.Mal. BN52 85
Barnsbury Cres., Surb. BN54 85
Barnsbury Gro. N7 BX36 56
Roman Way
Barnsbury La., Surb. BM55 85
Barnsbury Ms. N1 BY36 56
Brooksby St.
Barnsbury Pk. N1 BY36 56
Barnsbury Rd. N1 BY37 2
Barnsbury Rd. N1 BY37 56
Barnsbury Sq. N1 BY36 56
Barnsbury St. N1 BY36 2
Barnsbury St. N1 BY36 56
Barnsbury Ter. N1 BX37 2
Barnsbury Ter. N1 BY36 56
Barnscroft SW20 BP52 85
Barnsdale Av. E14 CE42 67
Barnsdale Clo., B.Wd. BL23 28
Leeming Rd.
Barnsdale Rd. W9 BR38 55
Barnsdale Yd. W9 BR38 55
Barnsdale Rd.
Barnsfield Pl., Uxb. AX36 53
Barnside Ct., Welw.G.C. BQ 8 5
Barnsley Rd., Rom. CW29 42
Barnsley St. E1 CB38 57
Barnstaple La. SE13 CF45 67
Lewisham High St.
Barnstaple Path, Rom. CV28 42
Barnstaple Rd.
Barnstaple Rd., Rom. CV28 42
Barnstaple Rd., Ruis. BD34 45
Barnston Wk. N1 BZ37 57
Popham St.
Barnsway, Kings.L. AY17 17
Barnway, Egh. AR49 72
Barnwell Rd. SW2 BY46 76
Barnwood Clo. W9 BS38 1
Barnwood Clo. W9 BS38 56
Barnwood Clo., Guil. AP69 118
Barnwood Clo., Ruis. BA34 44
Barnwood Court Est. E16 CH40 58
Barnwood Ct. E16 CH40 58
Barnwood Rd., Guil. AP70 118
Barnyard, The, Tad. BP65 103
Baron Clo. N1 BY37 2
Baron St.
Baron Gdns., Ilf. CM31 49
Baron Gro., Mitch. BU52 86
Baron Rd., Dag. CP33 50
Baron St. N1 BY37 2
Baron St. N1 BY37 56
Baron Wk. E16 CG39 58
Baron Wk., Mitch. BU52 86
Baroness Rd. E2 CA38 2
Baroness Rd. E2 CA38 57
Baronet Gro. N17 CB30 39
Baronet Rd. N17 CB30 39
Barons Ct. NW9 BN32 46
Barons Ct. Rd. W14 BR42 65
Barons Gate, Barn. BU25 29
Barons Hurst, Epsom BN61 103
Barons Keep W14 BR42 65
Gliddon Rd.
Barons Mead, Har. BH31 45
Barons Pl. SE1 BY41 4
Barons Pl. SE1 BY41 66
Barons Way, Egh. AU50 72
Barons Way, Reig. BS72 121
Barons Wk., Croy. CD53 87
Barons, The, Twick. BJ46 74
Baronsfield Rd., Twick. BJ46 74
Baronsmead Rd. SW13 BP44 65
Baronsmede W5 BL41 65
Baronsmere Rd. N2 BU31 47
Barque Ms. SE8 CE43 67
Watergate St.
Barr Rd., Grav. DJ48 81
Barr Rd., Pot.B. BT20 20
Barra Clo., Hem.H. AZ15 8
Barra Hall Rd., Hayes BB40 53
Barrack La., Wind. AO44 61
Barrack Path, Wok. AP62 100
Barrack Rd., Guil. AQ69 118
Barrack Rd., Houns. BD45 64
Barrack Row, Grav. DG46 81
Barrack Row, Sthl. BD42 64
Barrards Way, Beac. AO29 34
Barrat Way, Har. BG31 45
Barratt Av. N22 BX30 38
Barratt Ind. Pk., Sthl. BF40 54
Barrenger Rd. N10 BU30 38
Barrens Brae, Wok. AT62 100
Barrens Clo., Wok. AT63 100
Barrens Pk., Wok. AT63 100
Barrett Rd. E17 CF31 48
Barrett Rd., Lthd. BG66 111
Barrett St. W1 BV39 1
Barrett St. W1 BV39 56
Barretts Green Rd. NW10 BN38 55
Barretts Gro. N16 CA35 48
Barretts Rd., Sev. CS63 107
Barrhill Rd. SW2 BX48 76
Barricane Clo., Wok. AQ63 100
Barrie Clo., Couls. BV61 104
Barrie Est. W2 BT40 56
Barriedale SE14 CD44 67
Barrier App. SE7 CJ41 68
Barringer Sq. SW17 BV49 76
Barrington Clo. NW5 BV35 47
Barrington Clo., Ilf. CK30 40
Barrington Clo., Loug. CM24 31
Barrington Ct. N10 BV30 38
Barrington Ct., Brwd. DE25 122
Barrington Ct., Dor. BJ72 119
Barrington Rd.
Barrington Grn., Loug. CM24 31
Barrington Lo., Wey. BA56 92
Princes Rd.
Barrington Park Gdns., Ch.St.G. AR26 34
Barrington Rd. E12 CL36 58
Barrington Rd. N8 BW32 47
Barrington Rd. SW9 BY45 66
Barrington Rd., Bexh. CP44 69
Barrington Rd., Dor. BJ72 119
Barrington Rd., Loug. CM24 31
Barrington Rd., Pur. BW59 95
Barrington Rd., Sutt. BS54 86
Barrington Vill. SE18 CL44 68
Barron Clo. WC1 BX39 2
Barrons Clo., Ong. CW17 24
Barrosa Dr., Hmptn. BF51 84
Oldfield Rd.
Barrow Av., Cars. BU57 95
Barrow Clo. N21 BY27 38
Barrow Green Rd., Oxt. CE68 114
Barrow Hedges Clo., Cars. BU57 95
Barrow Hedges Way, Cars. BU57 95
Barrow Hill Clo., Wor.Pk. BO55 85
Barrow Hill Est. NW8 BU37 1
Barrow Hill Est. NW8 BU37 56
Barrow Hill NW8 BU37 56
Barrow Hill Rd. NW8 BU37 1
Barrow Hill Rd. NW8 BU37 56
Barrow Hill, Wor.Pk. BO55 85
Barrow La., Chsnt. CA19 21
Barrow Point Av., Pnr. BE30 36
Barrow Point La., Pnr. BE30 36

Barrow Rd. SW16 BW50 76
Barrow Rd., Croy. BY57 95
Barrow Way N7 BX34 47
Barrow Wk., Brent. BK43 64
Glenhurst Rd.
Barrowdene Clo., Pnr. BE30 36
Paines La.
Barrowell Grn. N21 BY27 38
Barrowfield Clo. N9 CB27 39
Barrowgate Rd. W4 BN42 65
Barrows Rd., Harl. CK11 13
Barrowsfield, S.Croy. CB59 96
Barrs La., Wok. AO61 100
Barrs Rd. NW10 BN36 55
Barry Av. N15 CA32 48
Craven Park Rd.
Barry Av., Bexh. CQ43 69
Barry Av., Wind. AO43 61
Barry Clo., Grays DG41 71
Barry Clo., Orp. CN55 88
Barry Clo., St.Alb. BF16 18
Barry Pl., Wok. AS62 100
Barry Rd. E6 CK39 58
Barry Rd. NW10 BN36 55
Barry Rd. SE22 CA46 77
Bars, The, Guil. AR71 118
Barset Rd. SE15 CC45 67
Barson Clo. SE20 CC50 77
Barston Rd. SE27 BZ48 77
Barstow Cres. SW2 BX47 76
Bartel Clo., Hem.H. BA14 8
Barter St. WC1 BX39 2
Barter St. WC1 BX39 56
Barters Wk., Pnr. BE31 45
High St.
Barth Rd. SE18 CN42 68
Bartholomew Clo. EC1 BZ39 2
Bartholomew Clo. EC1 BZ39 57
Bartholomew Clo. SW18 BT45 66
Bartholomew La. EC2 BZ39 2
Bartholomew La. EC2 BZ39 57
Threadneedle St.
Bartholomew Pl. EC1 BZ39 2
Bartholomew Clo.
Bartholomew Rd. NW5 BW36 56
Bartholomew Sq. E1 CB38 57
Cudworth St.
Bartholomew Sq. EC1 BZ38 2
Bartholomew Sq. EC1 BZ38 57
Bartholomew St. SE1 BZ41 4
Bartholomew St. SE1 BZ41 67
Bartholomew Vill. NW5 BW36 56
Bartholomew Way, Swan. CT52 89
Bartle Av. E6 CK37 58
Bartle Rd. W11 BQ39 55
Bartlett Clo. E14 CE39 57
Bartlett Ct. EC4 BY39 2
Bartlett Ct. EC4 BY39 56
New Fetter La.
Bartlett Rd., Grav. DG47 81
Bartlett Rd., West. CM66 115
Croydon Rd.
Bartlett St., S.Croy. BZ56 96
Bartlow Gdns., Rom. CS30 41
Barton Av., Rom. CR33 50
Barton Clo. E6 CK39 58
Barton Clo. E9 CC35 48
Barton Clo. SE15 CB45 67
Barton Clo., Bexh. CQ46 79
Barton Clo., Chig. CM27 40
Barton Clo., Shep. AZ53 83
Barton Clo., Wey. AW57 92
Barton Grn., N.Mal. BN51 85
Barton Meadows, Ilf. CL31 49
Barton Rd. W14 BR42 65
Barton Rd., Horn. CU34 50
Barton Rd., S.at H. CX51 90
Barton Rd., Sid. CQ50 79
Barton Rd., Slou. AS41 62
Barton St. SW1 BX41 4
Barton St. SW1 BX41 66
Barton Way NW8 BT37 1
Barton Way NW8 BT37 56
Barton Way, B.Wd. BM23 28
Barton Way, Rick. AZ25 26
Barton, The, Cob. BD59 93
Bartons, The, B.Wd. BK25 27
Bartram Clo., Uxb. AZ38 53
Bartram Rd. SE4 CD46 77
Bartrams La., Barn. BT22 29
Bartrip St. E9 CD36 57
Wick Rd.
Barville Clo. SE4 CD45 67
St. Norbert Rd.
Barwell Trd. Est., Chess. BK58 93
Barwick Rd. E7 CH35 49
Barwood Av., W.Wick. CE54 87
Basden Gro., Felt. BF48 74
Basedale Rd., Dag. CO36 59
Baseing Clo. E6 CL39 58
Basford Way, Wind. AL45 61
Bashley Rd. NW10 BN38 55
Basil Av. E6 CK38 58
Basil Gdns., Croy. CC54 87
Basil St. SW3 BU41 3
Basil St. SW3 BU41 66
Basildene Rd., Houns. BD45 64
Basildon Av., Ilf. CL30 40
Basildon Clo., Sutt. BT58 95
Basildon Rd. SE2 CO42 69
Basildon Rd., Bexh. CQ44 69
Basildon Sq., Hem.H. AY11 8
Basin Rd. E16 CG40 58
Basing Clo., T.Ditt. BH54 84
Basing Ct. SE15 CA44 67
Basing Dr., Bex. CQ46 79
Basing Est. N3 BS31 47
Basing Hill NW11 BR33 46
Basing Hill, Wem. BL34 46
Basing House Yd. N1 CA38 57
Kingsland Rd.
Basing Pl. N1 CA38 2
Basing Rd., Bans. BR60 94
Basing Rd., Rick. AV26 34
Basing St. W11 BR39 55
Basing Way N3 BS31 47
Basing Way, T.Ditt. BH54 84
Basingdon Way SE5 BZ45 67
Basingfield Rd., T.Ditt. BH54 84
Basinghall Av. EC2 BZ39 2
Basinghall Av. EC2 BZ39 57
Basinghall Gdns., Sutt. BS58 95
Basinghall St. EC2 BZ39 2
Basinghall St. EC2 BZ39 57
Basire St. N1 BZ37 2
Basire St. N1 BZ37 57
Baskerville Rd. SW18 BU47 76
Basket Gdns. SE9 CK46 78
Baslow Clo., Har. BG30 36
Baslow Wk. E5 CC35 48
Clapton Park Est.
Basnett Rd. SW11 BV45 66
Bassano St. SE22 CA46 77
Bassant Rd. SE18 CN43 68
Bassein Park Rd. W12 BO41 65
Bassett Clo., Sutt. BS58 95
Bassett Clo., Wey. AW58 92
Bassett Gdns., Epp. CR16 23
Bassett Gdns., Islw. BG43 64
Bassett Rd. W10 BR39 55
Bassett Rd., Wok. AU61 100
Bassett St. NW5 BV35 47
Bassett Way, Grnf. BF39 54
Bassetts Clo., Orp. CL56 97
Bassetts Way, Orp. CL56 97
Bassil Rd., Hem.H. AX14 8
Bassingbourne Clo., Brox. CD13 12
Bassingburn Wk., Welw.G.C. BR 8 5
Bassingham Rd. SW18 BT47 76
Bassingham Rd., Wem. BK36 54
Bassishaw High Wk. EC2 BZ39 2
London Wall
Basswood Clo. SE15 CB45 67
Linden Gro.
Bastable Av., Bark. CN37 58
Bastion Rd. SE2 CO42 69
Baston Manor Rd., Brom. CH55 88
Baston Rd., Brom. CH54 88
Bastwick St. EC1 BY38 2
Bastwick St. EC1 BY38 56
Basuto Rd. SW6 BS44 66
Batavia Clo., Sun. BC51 83
Batavia Ms. SE14 CD43 67
Clifton Ri.
Batavia Rd. SE14 CD43 67
Batavia Rd., Sun. BC51 83
Batchelor St. N1 BY37 2
Batchelor St. N1 BY37 56
Batchelors Way, Amer. AO23 25
Batchwood Dr., St.Alb. BF12 9
Batchwood Gdns., St.Alb. BG12 9
Batchwood Grn., Orp. CO52 89
Batchwood Vw., St.Alb. BG12 9
Batchworth Heath Hill, Rick. AZ28 35
Batchworth Hill, Rick. AY27 35
Batchworth La., Nthwd. AZ28 35
Bate St. E14 CD40 57
Three Colt St.
Bateman Clo., Bark. CM36 58
Glenny Rd.
Bateman Rd. E4 CE29 39
Bateman Rd., Rick. AZ25 26
Bateman St. W1 BW39 1
Bateman St. W1 BW39 56
Dean St.
Batemans Bldgs. W1 BW39 1
Bateman St.
Batemans Row EC2 CA38 2
Batemans Row EC2 CA38 57
Bates Cres., Croy. BY56 95
Bates Hill, Sev. DB64 108
Bates Rd., Rom. CX29 42
Bates Wk., Wey. AX57 92
Bateson St. SE18 CN42 68
Gunning St.
Bateson Way, Wok. AU60 91
Batford Clo., Welw.G.C. BS 8 5
Waterford Grn.
Bath Clo. SE15 CB43 67
Bath Ct. EC1 BY38 2
Warner St.
Bath House Rd., Croy. BX54 86
Bath Pass., Kings.T. BK51 84
Bath Pl., Barn. BR24 28
Bath Rd. E7 CJ36 58
Bath Rd. N9 CB27 39
Bath Rd. W4 BO42 65
Bath Rd., Dart. CU47 79
Bath Rd., Hayes BC43 63
Bath Rd., Houns. BF45 64
Bath Rd., Mitch. BT52 86
Bath Rd., Poyle AV44 62
Bath Rd., Rom. CQ32 50
Bath Rd., Slou. AN40 61
Bath Rd., West.Dr. AX44 63
Bath St. EC1 BZ38 2
Bath St. EC1 BZ38 57
Bath St., Grav. DG46 81
Bath Ter. SE1 BZ41 4
Bath Ter. SE1 BZ41 67
Bathgate Rd. SW19 BQ48 75
Baths Rd., Brom. CJ52 88
Bathurst Av. SW19 BS51 86
Brisbane Av.
Bathurst Clo., Iver. AV41 62
Bathurst Gdns. NW10 BP37 55
Bathurst Ms. W2 BT40 3
Bathurst Ms. W2 BT40 56
Bathurst Rd., Hem.H. AX12 8
Bathurst Rd., Ilf. CL33 49
Bathurst St. W2 BT40 3
Bathurst St. W2 BT40 56
Bathurst Wk., Iver AV41 62
Bathway SE18 CL42 68
Market St.
Batley Rd. N16 CD34 48
Stoke Newington High St.
Batley Rd., Enf. BZ23 30
Batman Clo. W12 BP40 55
Batoum Gdns. W6 BQ41 65
Batson St. W12 BP41 65
Batsworth Rd., Mitch. BT52 86
Batten Av., Wok. AP63 100
Batten Clo. E6 CK39 58
Savage Gdns.
Batten St. SW11 BU45 66
Batterdale, Hat. BQ12 10
The Broadway
Battersby Rd. SE6 CF48 77
Battersea Bridge Rd. SW11 BU43 66
Battersea Bri. SW3 BT43 66
Battersea Church Rd. SW11 BT44 66
Battersea High St. SW11 BT44 66
Battersea Park Est. SW11 BV44 66
Dagnall St.
Battersea Park Rd. SW11 BU44 66
Battersea Park Rd. SW8 BU44 66
Battersea Ri. SW11 BT46 76
Battis, The, Rom. CT32 50
Battishill St. N1 BY36 56
Waterloo Ter.
Battle Bridge La. SE1 CA40 4
Battle Bridge La. SE1 CA40 57
Tooley St.
Battle Bridge Rd. NW1 BX37 2
Battle Bridge Rd. NW1 BX37 56
Battle Clo. SW19 BT50 76
North Rd.
Battle Ct., Ong. CX18 24
Battle Rd., Belv. CS42 69
Battle Rd., Erith CS42 69
Battlebridge La., Red. BV68 113
Battledean Rd. N5 BY35 47
Battlefield Rd., St.Alb. BH12 9
Battlefields Rd., Sev. DC61 108
Battlers Green Dr., Rad. BH21 27
Batts Hill, Reig. & Red. BU70 121
Batty St. E1 CB39 57
Baudwin Rd. SE6 CG48 78
Baugh Rd., Sid. CP49 79
Baulk, The SW18 BS47 76
Bavant Rd. SW16 BX51 86
Bavaria Rd. N19 BX34 47
Bavent Rd. SE5 BZ44 67
Bawdale Rd. SE22 CA46 77
Bawdsey Av., Ilf. CN31 49
Bawtree Clo., Sutt. BT58 95
Bawtree Rd. SE14 CD43 67
Bawtree Rd., Uxb. AX36 53
Bawtry Rd. N20 BU27 38
Baxendale N20 BT27 38
Baxendale St. E2 CB38 2
Baxendale St. E2 CB38 57
Baxter Av., Red. BU70 121
Baxter Clo., Uxb. AZ38 53
Baxter Rd. E16 CJ39 58
Baxter Rd. N1 BZ36 57
Baxter Rd. N17 CB31 48
Baxter Rd. N18 CB28 39
Baxter Rd. NW10 BO38 55
Baxter Rd., Ilf. CL35 49
Bay Ct., Berk. AQ13 7
Bay Manor La., Grays CZ43 70
Bay Path, Gdse. CC69 114
Bay Tree Clo., Brom. CJ51 88
Bay Tree Wk., Wat. BC22 26
Bayards, Warl. CC62 105
Bayeaux, Tad. BQ64 103
Bayes Clo. SE26 CC49 77
Bayfield Rd. SE9 CJ45 68
Bayford Clo., Hem.H. BA11 8
Bayford Grn., Hert. BY12 11
Bayford La., Hert. BX11 11
Bayford Rd. NW10 BQ38 55
Bayford St. E8 CB36 57
Bayham Pl. NW1 BW37 1
Bayham Pl. NW1 BW37 56
Bayham Rd. W13 BJ40 54
Bayham Rd. W4 BN41 65
Bayham Rd., Mord. BS52 86
Bayham Rd., Sev. CV65 108
Bayham St. NW1 BW37 1
Bayham St. NW1 BW37 56
Bayhurst Dr., Nthwd. BB29 35
Kings Clo.
Bayley St. WC1 BW39 1
Bayley St. WC1 BW39 56
Bayley Wk. SE2 CQ43 69
Bayleys Hill, Sev. CT69 116
Bayleys Mead, Brwd. DE27 122
Baylis Rd. SE1 BY41 4
Baylis Rd. SE1 BY41 66
Baylis Rd., Slou. AO40 52
Bayliss Av. SE28 CP40 59
Bayly Rd., Dart. CX46 80
Baymans Wood, Brwd. DC27 122
Bayne Clo. E6 CK39 58
Savage Gdns.
Bayne Hill, Beac. AO29 34
Baynes Clo., Enf. CB23 30
Baynes Ms. NW3 BT36 56
Belsize La.
Baynes St. NW1 BW36 1
Baynes St. NW1 BW36 56
Bayonne Rd. W6 BR43 65
Bayston Rd. N16 CA34 48
Bayswater Rd. W2 BS40 3
Bayswater Rd. W2 BS40 56
Baythorne St. E3 CD39 57
Baytree Clo., Sid. CN47 78
Larch Gro.
Baytree Rd. SW2 BX45 66
Baywood Sq., Chig. CO28 41
Bazalgette Clo., N.Mal. BN53 85
Bazalgette Gdns.
Bazalgette Gdns., N.Mal. BN53 85
Bazely St. E14 CF40 57
Bazes Shaw, Dart. DC55 90
Church Rd.
Bazile Rd. N21 BY25 29
Beach Gro., Felt. BF48 74
Beacham Clo. SE7 CJ42 68
Beachborough Rd., Brom. CF49 77
Beachcroft Ms. N19 BW33 47
Courtauld Rd.
Beachcroft Rd. E11 CG34 49
Beachcroft Way N19 BX33 47
Hornsey Ri.
Beachy Rd. E3 CE36 57
Beacon Clo., Bans. BQ61 103
Beacon Clo., Uxb. AX35 44
Beacon Dr., Dart. DA48 80
Beacon Gro., Cars. BV56 95
Beacon Hill N7 BX35 47
Beacon Hill Rd., Brwd. CX22 33
Beacon Hill, Brwd. CY22 33
Beacon Hill, Grays CX42 70
Beacon Hill, Wok. AQ63 100
Beacon Rd. SE13 CF46 77
Beacon Rd., Erith CU43 69
Beacon Rd., Houns. AZ46 73
Beacon Ri., Sev. CT66 116
Beacon Way, Bans. BQ61 103
Beacon Way, Rick. AW26 35
Beaconfields, Sev. CT66 116
Beacons Clo. E6 CK39 58
Oliver Gdns.
Beacons, The, Loug. CL22 31
Beaconsfield Av., Epp. CN18 22
Beaconsfield Clo. N11 BV28 38
Beaconsfield Clo. SE3 CH43 68
Beaconsfield Clo. W4 BN42 65
Beaconsfield Clo., Hat. BQ11 10
Beaconsfield Pl., Epsom BO59 94
Beaconsfield Rd. E10 CF34 48
Beaconsfield Rd. E16 CG38 58
Beaconsfield Rd. E17 CD32 48
Beaconsfield Rd. N11 BV27 38
Beaconsfield Rd. N15 CA31 48
Beaconsfield Rd. N9 CB27 39
Beaconsfield Rd. NW10 BO36 55
Beaconsfield Rd. SE17 CA42 67
Beaconsfield Rd. SE3 CG43 68
Beaconsfield Rd. SE9 CK48 78
Beaconsfield Rd. W4 BN41 65
Beaconsfield Rd. W5 BK41 64
Beaconsfield Rd., St.Alb. BH13 9
Beaconsfield Rd., Twick. BJ46 74
Beaconsfield Rd., Bex. CT48 79
Beaconsfield Rd., Brom. CJ52 88
Beaconsfield Rd., Croy. BZ53 87
Beaconsfield Rd., Enf. CC22 30
Beaconsfield Rd., Epp. CN18 22
Beaconsfield Rd., Epsom BN63 103
Beaconsfield Rd., Esher BH57 93
Beaconsfield Rd., Hat. BQ12 10
Beaconsfield Rd., Hayes BD40 54
Beaconsfield Rd., N.Mal. BN51 85
Beaconsfield Rd., Sthl. BD40 54
Beaconsfield Rd., Surb. BL54 85
Beaconsfield Rd., Twick. BJ46 74
Beaconsfield Rd., Wok. AS63 100
Beaconsfield Ter. W14 BR41 65
Maclise Rd.
Beaconsfield Ter., Rom. CQ32 50
Beaconsfield Way, Epp. CO18 23
Beaconsfield Wk. SW6 BR44 65
Parsons Green La.
Beacontree Av. E17 CF30 39
Beacontree Rd. E11 CG33 49
Beadles La., Oxt. CF68 114
Beadlow Clo., Cars. BT53 86
Olveston Wk.
Beadman St. SE27 BY49 76
Beadnell Rd. SE23 CC47 77
Beadon Rd. W6 BQ42 65
Beadon Rd., Brom. CH52 88
Beads Hall La., Brwd. DA24 33
Beadsfield E13 CH37 58
Valetta Gro.
Beaford Gro. SW20 BR52 85
Beagle Clo., Felt. BC49 73
Beagle Clo., Rad. BH22 27
Beagles Clo., Orp. CP55 89
Beak St. W1 BW40 3
Beak St. W1 BW40 56
Beal Clo., Well. CO44 69
Beal Rd., Ilf. CL34 49
Beale Clo. N13 BY28 38
Beale Pl. E3 CD37 57
Beale Rd. E3 CD37 57
Beales La., Wey. AZ55 83
Beales Rd., Lthd. BF67 111
Beam Av., Dag. CR37 59
Beam Way, Dag. CS36 59
Beaminster Gdns., Ilf. CL31 49
Beamish Clo., Epp. CS16 23
Beamish Dr., Bush. BG26 36
Beamish Rd. N9 CB26 39
Beamish Rd., Orp. CP54 89
Bean La., Dart. DA48 80
Bean Rd., Bexh. CP45 69
Beanacre Clo. E9 CD36 57
Mallard Clo
Beanshaw SE9 CL49 78
Beansland Gro., Rom. CQ30 41
Bear All. EC4 BY39 2
Bear All. EC4 BY39 56
Farringdon St.
Bear Clo., Rom. CR32 50
Fernden Way
Bear Gdns. SE1 BZ40 4
Bear Gdns. SE1 BZ40 57
Bear La. SE1 BY40 4
Bear La. SE1 BY40 56
Bear Rd., Felt. BD49 74
Bear St. WC2 BW40 3
Bear St. WC2 BW40 56
Long Acre
Beard Rd., Kings.T. BL49 75
Beardell St. SE19 CA50 77
Beardow Gro. N14 BW25 29
Beards Hill Clo., Hmptn. BF51 84
Beards Hill, Hmptn. BH51 84
Beards Rd., Ashf. BB50 73
Beardsfield E13 CH37 58
Valetta Gro.
Beardsley Way W3 BN41 65
Birkbeck Gro.
Bearfield Rd., Kings.T. BL50 75
Bearing Clo., Chig. CO28 41
Bearing Way, Chig. CO28 41
Bears Den, Tad. BR64 103
Bearstead Ri. SE4 CD64 77
Bearwood Clo., Pot.B. BT19 20
Bearwood Clo., Wey. AW57 92
Ongar Pl.
Beasleys Ait La., Sun. BB53 83
Beatrice Av. SW16 BX52 86
Beatrice Av., Wem. BL35 46
Beatrice Clo. E13 CH38 58
Chargeable La.
Beatrice Clo., Pnr. BC31 44
Beatrice Ct., Wem. BL35 46
Beatrice Gdns., Grav. DF48 81
Beatrice Rd. E17 CE32 48
Beatrice Rd. N4 BY33 47
Beatrice Rd. N9 CC26 39
Beatrice Rd. SE1 CB42 67
Beatrice Rd., Oxt. CG68 115
Beatrice Rd., Rich. BL46 75
Albert Rd.
Beatrice Rd., Sthl. BE40 54
Beatson Wk. SE16 CC40 57
Globe Pond Rd.
Beattie Clo., Lthd. BE65 102
Beattock Ri. N10 BV31 47
Beatty Av., Guil. AT70 118
Beatty Rd. N16 CA35 48
Beatty Rd., Stan. BK29 36
Beatty St. NW1 BW37 1
Beatty St. NW1 BW37 56
Beattyville Gdns., Ilf. CL31 49
Beauchamp Clo. W4 BN41 65
Church Path
Beauchamp Gdns., Rick. AW26 35
Beauchamp Pl. SW3 BU41 3
Beauchamp Pl. SW3 BU41 66
Beauchamp Rd. E7 CH36 58
Beauchamp Rd. SE19 BZ51 87
Beauchamp Rd. SW11 BU45 66
Beauchamp Rd., E.Mol. BF53 84
Beauchamp Rd., Sutt. BS56 95
Beauchamp Rd., Twick. BJ47 74
Beauchamp St. EC1 BY39 2
Beauchamp St. EC1 BY39 56
Leather La.
Beauchamp Ter. SW15 BP45 65
Dryburgh Rd.
Beauclare Clo., Ash. BK64 102
Hatherwood
Beauclerc Rd. W6 BP41 65
Beauclerk Clo., Felt. BC47 73
Florence Rd.
Beaudesert Ms., West.Dr. AY41 63
Beaufort Av., Har. BJ31 45
Beaufort Clo. E4 CE29 39
Higham Station Av.
Beaufort Clo. SW15 BP47 75
Seaton Clo.
Beaufort Clo. W5 BL39 55
Beaufort Clo., Epp. CR17 23
Wellington Rd.
Beaufort Clo., Reig. BR70 120
Beaufort Clo., Rom. CS31 50
Beaufort Clo., Wok. AU61 100
Beaufort Ct., Rich. BK49 74
Beaufort Dr. NW11 BS31 47
Beaufort Gdns. NW4 BQ32 46
Beaufort Gdns. SW16 BX50 76
Green La.
Beaufort Gdns. SW3 BU41 3
Beaufort Gdns. SW3 BU41 66
Beaufort Gdns., Houns. BE44 64
Beaufort Gdns., Ilf. CL33 49
Beaufort Pk. NW11 BS31 47
Beaufort Pl., Maid. AH41 61
Beaufort Rd. W5 BL39 55
Beaufort Rd., Kings.T. BL52 85
Beaufort Rd., Reig. BR70 120
Beaufort Rd., Rich. BK49 74
Beaufort Rd., Ruis. BA34 44
Lysander Rd.
Beaufort Rd., Twick. BK47 74
Beaufort Rd., Wok. AU61 100
Beaufort St. SW3 BT42 3
Beaufort St. SW3 BT43 66
Beaufort Way, Epsom BP57 94
Beauforts, Egh. AR49 72
Beaufoy Rd. N17 CA29 39
Beaufoy Rd. SW11 BV44 66
Beaufoy Wk. SE11 BX42 66
Beaulieu Av. SE26 CB49 77
Beaulieu Clo. NW9 BO31 46
Beaulieu Clo. SE5 BZ45 67
Beaulieu Clo., Mitch. BV51 86
Beaulieu Clo., Slou. AQ44 62
Beaulieu Clo., Twick. BK46 74
Beaulieu Clo., Wat. BD26 36
Beaulieu Dr., Pnr. BD32 45
Beaulieu Gdns. N21 BZ26 39
Beaulieu Pl. W4 BN41 65
Rothschild Rd.
Beauly Way, Rom. CT30 41
Beaumanor Gdns. SE9 CL49 78
Beanshaw
Beaumaris Dr., Wdf.Grn. CJ29 40
Beaumayes Clo., Hem.H. AW14 8
Beaumont Av. W14 BR42 65
Beaumont Av., Har. BF32 45
Beaumont Av., Rich. BL45 65
Beaumont Av., St.Alb. BJ12 9
Beaumont Av., Wem. BK35 45
Beaumont Clo., Rom. CV30 42
Beaumont Cres. W14 BR42 65
Beaumont Cres., Rain. CU36 59
Beaumont Dr., Ashf. BA49 73
Beaumont Dr., Grav. DF47 81
Beaumont Gdns. NW3 BS34 47

Beaumont Gdns., Brwd. DE25 122
Bannister Dr.
Beaumont Gro. E1 CC38 57
Beaumont Ms. W1 BV39 1
Beaumont Ms. W1 BV39 56
Marylebone High St.
Beaumont Pl. W1 BW38 1
Beaumont Pl. W1 BW38 56
Tottenham Court Rd.
Beaumont Pl., Barn. BR22 28
Beaumont Rd. E10 CE33 48
Beaumont Rd. E13 CH38 58
Beaumont Rd. SE19 BZ50 77
Beaumont Rd. SW19 BR47 75
Beaumont Rd. W4 BN41 65
Beaumont Rd., Brox. CA15 12
Beaumont Rd., Orp. CM53 88
Beaumont Rd., Pur. BY60 95
Beaumont Rd., Slou. AO38 52
Beaumont Rd., Wind. AO44 61
Beaumont Ri. N19 BW33 47
Beaumont Sq. E1 CC39 57
Beaumont St. W1 BV39 1
Beaumont St. W1 BV39 56
Beaumont Vw., Chsnt. BZ16 21
Pear Tree Wk.
Beaumont Wk. NW3 BU36 56
Adelaide Rd.
Beauvais Ter., Nthlt. BD37 54
Beauval Rd. SE22 CA46 77
Beaver Clo. SE20 CB50 77
Beaver Clo., Hmptn. BF51 84
Beaver Gro., Nthlt. BE38 54
Jetstar Way
Beaver Rd., Ilf. CP28 41
Beaverbank Rd. SE9 CM47 78
Beavercote Wk., Belv. CQ43 69
Osborne Rd.
Beavers Clo., Guil. AP70 118
Beavers Cres., Houns. BD45 64
Beavers La., Houns. BD45 64
Beaverwood Rd., Sid. CN49 78
Beavor La. W6 BP42 65
Bebbington Rd. SE18 CN42 68
Bebletts Clo., Orp. CN56 97
Bec Clo., Ruis. BD34 45
Beccles Dr., Bark. CN36 58
Beccles St. E14 CD39 57
Beck Clo. SE13 CE44 67
Beck La., Beck. CC52 87
Beck Rd. E8 CB37 57
Beck River Pk., Beck. CE51 87
Rectory Rd.
Beckenham Gdns. N9 CA27 39
Beckenham Gro., Brom. CF51 87
Beckenham Hill Rd. SE6 CE50 77
Beckenham Hill Rd., Beck. CE50 77
Beckenham La., Brom. CG51 88
Beckenham Place Pk., Beck. CE50 77
Beckenham Rd., Beck. CC51 87
Beckenham Rd., W.Wick. CE54 87
Beckenshaw Gdns., Bans. BT61 104
Beckers Est., The N16 CB34 48
Becket Av. E6 CL38 58
Becket Clo. SE25 CB53 87
Becket Clo., Brwd. DB29 42
Becket Fold, Har. BH32 45
Becket Rd. N18 CC28 39
Becket St. SE1 BZ41 4
Becket St. SE1 BZ41 67
Beckets Sq., Berk. AQ12 7
Bridle Way
Beckett Av., Ken. BY61 104
Beckett Clo. NW10 BN36 55
Beckett Clo. SW16 BW48 76
Beckett Clo., Belv. CQ41 69
Tunstock Way
Beckett Wk., Beck. CD50 77
Becketts Av., St.Alb. BG12 9
Becketts Clo., Houns. BC46 73
Harlington Rd. W.
Becketts Clo., Orp. CN55 88
Becketts Pl., Hmptn. BK51 84
Teddington Rd.
Beckford Pl. SE17 BZ42 4
Beckford Pl. SE17 BZ42 67
Walworth Rd.
Beckford Rd., Croy. CA53 87
Becklow Gdns. W12 BP41 65
Becklow Rd.
Becklow Rd. W12 BO41 65
Beckman Clo., Sev. CS61 107
Becks Rd., Sid. CO48 79
Beckton Rd. E16 CG39 58
Beckway Rd. SW16 BW51 86
Beckway St. SE17 BZ42 4
Beckway St. SE17 CA42 67
Beckway, Beck. CD52 87
Beckwith Rd. SE24 BZ46 77
Beclands Rd. SW17 BV50 76
Becmead Av. SW16 BW49 76
Becmead Av., Har. BJ32 45
Becondale Rd. SE19 CA49 77
Becontree Av., Dag. CO35 50
Bective Pl. SW15 BR45 65
Bective Rd. E7 CH35 49
Bective Rd. SW15 BR45 65
Becton Pl., Erith CR44 69
Bedale Rd., Enf. BZ22 30
Bedale Rd., Rom. CX28 42
Bedale St. SE1 BZ40 4
Bedale St. SE1 BZ40 57
Bedale Wk., Dart. CX47 80
Princes Av.
Beddingfield Rd. E15 CF35 48
Thornham Gro.
Beddington Farm Rd., Croy. BX54 86
Beddington Gdns., Wall. BV57 95
Beddington Grn., Orp. CN51 88
Beddington Gro., Wall. BW56 95
Beddington La., Croy. BW53 86
Beddington Path, Orp. CN51 88
Beddington Rd., Ilf. CN33 49
Beddington Rd., Orp. CN51 88
Beddlestead La., Warl. CG62 106
Bede Clo., Pnr. BD30 36
Bede Rd., Rom. CP32 50
Bedenham Way SE15 CA43 67
Hordle Prom. N.
Bedens Rd., Sid. CQ50 79
Bedfont Clo., Felt. BA46 73
Bedfont Ct., Stai. AW45 63
Bedfont La., Felt. BA47 73
Bedfont Rd., Felt. BA48 73
Bedfont La., Felt. BB47 73
Bedfont Rd., Stai. AY46 73
Bedford Av. WC1 BW39 1
Bedford Av. WC1 BW39 56
Bedford Av., Amer. AR23 25
Bedford Av., Barn. BR25 28
Bedford Av., Hayes BC39 53
Bedford Clo. N10 BV29 38
Bedford Clo., Rick. AT22 25
Bedford Cres., Enf. CD21 30
Bedford Ct. WC2 BX40 4
Bedford Ct. WC2 BX40 56
Bedford St.
Bedford Gdns. W8 BS40 56
Bedford Gdns., Horn. CV34 51
Bedford Hill SW12 BV47 76
Bedford Hill SW16 BV47 76
Bedford Pk. Mans. W4 BN42 65
Bedford Pk. Rd., St. Alb. BH13 9
Bedford Pk., Croy. BZ54 87
Bedford Pl. W1 BW39 1
Bedford Pl. W1 BW39 56
Bedford Pl. WC1 BX39 2
Bedford Pl. WC1 BX39 56
Bedford Pl., Croy. BZ54 87
Bedford Rd. E17 CE31 48
Bedford Rd. E18 CH30 40
Bedford Rd. E6 CL37 58
Bedford Rd. N15 CA31 48
Bedford Rd. N2 BU31 47
Bedford Rd. N22 BX30 38
Bedford Rd. N8 BW32 47
Bedford Rd. N9 CB26 39
Bedford Rd. NW7 BO27 37
Bedford Rd. SW4 BX45 66
Bedford Rd. W13 BJ40 54
Bedford Rd. W4 BN41 65
Bedford Rd., Brent. BL42 65
Clayponds La.
Bedford Rd., Dart. CX47 80
Bedford Rd., Grav. DF48 81
Bedford Rd., Grays DD42 71
Bedford Rd., Guil. AR71 118
Bedford Rd., Har. BG32 45
Bedford Rd., Ilf. CL34 49
Bedford Rd., Nthwd. BA27 35
Bedford Rd., Orp. CO55 89
Bedford Rd., Ruis. BB35 44
Bedford Rd., Sid. CN48 78
Bedford Rd., St.Alb. BH14 9
Bedford Rd., Twick. BG48 74
Bedford Rd., Wor.Pk. BQ55 85
Bedford Row WC1 BX39 2
Bedford Row WC1 BX39 56
Bedford Sq. WC1 BW39 1
Bedford Sq. WC1 BW39 56
Bedford St. WC2 BX40 4
Bedford St. WC2 BX40 56
Bedford St., Berk. AS13 7
George St.
Bedford St., Wat. BC23 26
Bedford Way WC1 BW38 1
Bedford Way WC1 BW38 56
Bedfordbury WC2 BX40 4
Bedfordbury WC2 BX40 56
Chandos Pl.
Bedgebury Gdns. SW19 BR47 75
Bedgebury Rd. SE9 CJ45 68
Bedivere Rd., Brom. CH48 78
Bedlow Way, Croy. BX56 95
Nicholas Rd.
Bedmond Grn., Wat. BB17 17
Bedmond Hill, Wat. BB16 17
Bedmond La., Potterscrouch BD15 9
Bedmond La., St.Alb. BE14 9
Bedmond Rd., Hem.H. BA14 8
Bedmond Rd., Wat. BB18 17
Bedonwell Rd. SE2 CQ43 69
Bedonwell Rd., Bexh. CQ44 69
Bedser Dr., Har. BG35 45
Bedster Gdns., E.Mol. BG51 84
Bedwardine Rd., SE19 CA50 77
Bedwell Av., Hat. BV12 11
Bedwell Gdns. E., Hayes BB42 63
Bedwell Gdns. W., Hayes BB42 63
Bedwell Rd. N17 CA30 39
Bedwell Rd., Belv. CQ42 69
Bedwin Way SE16 CB42 67
Bonamy Est. W.
Beeby Rd. E16 CH39 58
Beech Av. N20 BU26 38
Beech Av. W3 BO40 55
Beech Av., Brent. BJ43 64
Beech Av., Brwd. DC27 122
Beech Av., Buck.H. CH27 40
Beech Av., Enf. BY21 29
Beech Av., Lthd. BD68 111
Beech Av., Rad. BJ20 18
Beech Av., Ruis. BC33 44
Beech Av., S.Croy. BZ59 96
Beech Av., Sid. CO47 79
Beech Av., Swan. CT52 89
Beech Av., Upmin. CX35 51
Beech Av., West. CJ63 106
Beech Bottom, St.Alb. BG12 9
Beech Pl.
Beech Clo. N9 CB25 30
Beech Clo. SE8 CD43 67
Clyde St.
Beech Clo. SW15 BP47 75
Beech Clo. SW19 BQ50 75
Beech Clo., Ashf. BA49 73
Beech Clo., Cars. BU55 86
Beech Clo., Cob. BF59 93
Beech Clo., Dor. BH71 119
Beech Clo., Hat. BP13 10
Beech Clo., Horn. CU34 50
Beech Clo., Lthd. BD67 111
Beech Clo., Sun. BD51 84
Beech Clo., Walt. BD56 93
Beech Clo., West Dr. AZ41 63
Beech Clo., Wey. AY59 92
Beech Copse, Brom. CK51 88
Beech Copse, S.Croy. CB56 96
Beech Ct. SE9 CK46 78
Beech Ct., Cob. BE59 93
Beech Ct., Tedd. BK50 74
Broom Water
Beech Dell, Orp. CK56 97
Beech Dr. N2 BU30 38
Beech Dr. Saw. CP7 6
Beech Dr., B.Wd. BL23 28
Beech Dr., Berk. AR13 7
Beech Dr., Reig. BT70 121
Beech Dr., Tad. BR64 103
Beech Dr., Wok. AV65 100
Beech Farm Rd., Warl. CF63 105
Beech Field, Bans. BS60 95
Beech Gdns. W5 BL41 65
Beech Gdns., Dag. CR36 59
Beech Gdns., Wok. AR61 100
Beech Gro., Amer. AO23 25
Beech Gro., Cat. CA66 114
Beech Gro., Epsom BP62 103
Beech Gro., Guil. AP70 118
Beech Gro., Ilf. CN29 40
Beech Gro., Mitch. BW53 86
Beech Gro., N.Mal. BN52 85
Beech Gro., S.Ock. CY41 70
Beech Gro., Wey. AW56 92
Beech Gro., Wok. AR65 100
Beech Hall Cres. E4 CF29 39
Beech Hall Rd. E4 CF29 39
Beech Hill Av., Barn. BT23 29
Beech Hill Ct., Berk. AR13 7
Beech Hill Gdns., Wal.Abb. CH22 31
Beech Hill, Barn. BT22 29
Beech Hill, Wok. AR65 100
Beech Holt, Lthd. BK64 102
Beech House Rd., Croy. BZ55 87
Beech La., Beac. AP29 34
Beech La., Buck.H. CH27 40
Beech La., Guil. AR72 118
Beech Lawn, Guil. AS71 118
Beech Lawns N12 BT28 38
Beech Pk., Amer. AQ22 25
Beech Pl., Epp. CN19 22
Beech Pl., St.Alb. BG12 9
Beech Rd. N11 BX29 38
Beech Rd. SW16 BX51 86
Beech Rd., Dart. CV47 80
Beech Rd., Epsom BO61 103
Beech Rd., Felt. BB47 73
Beech Rd., Ong. DB13 15
Beech Rd., Orp. CO57 98
Beech Rd., Red. BW66 113
Beech Rd., Reig. BS69 121
Beech Rd., Sev. CU66 116
Beech Rd., Slou. AS41 62
Beech Rd., St.Alb. BH12 9
Beech Rd., Wat. BC22 26
Beech Rd., West. CH62 106
Beech Rd., Wey. BA56 92
Beech Row, Kings.T. BL49 75
Beech St. EC2 BZ39 2
Beech St. EC2 BZ39 57
Beech St., Rom. CS31 50
Beech Tree Clo., Stan. BK28 36
Beech Tree Glade E4 CG26 40
Beech Tree La., Stai. AW51 83
Beech Tree Pl., Sutt. BS56 95
West St.
Beech Way NW10 BN36 55
Beech Way, Croy. CC60 96
Beech Way, Epsom BO61 103
Beech Way, Guil. AT70 118
Beech Way, Twick. BF48 74
Beech Waye, Ger.Cr. AS33 43
Beech Wk. NW7 BN29 37
Beech Wk., Dart. CU45 69
Beech Wk., Epsom BP59 94
Beech Wk., Hodd. CD12 12
Beech Wood Av., Amer. AR22 25
Beechall, Cher. AU57 91
Beechcroft Av. NW11 BR33 46
Beechcroft Av., Bexh. CS44 69
Beechcroft Av., Har. BF33 45
Beechcroft Av., Ken. BZ61 105
Beechcroft Av., N.Mal. BN51 85
Beechcroft Av., Rick. BA25 26
Beechcroft Av., S.le H. DK42 71
Beechcroft Av., Sthl. BE40 54
Beechcroft Clo. Orp. CM56 97
Beechcroft Clo., Houns. BE43 64
Beechcroft Dr., Guil. AO72 118
Beechcroft Gdns., Wem. BL34 46
Beechcroft Manor, Wey. BA55 83
Beechcroft Rd. E18 CH30 40
Beechcroft Rd. SW14 BN45 65
Beechcroft Rd. SW17 BU48 76
Beechcroft Rd., Bush. BE25 27
Beechcroft Rd., Chess. BL55 85
Beechcroft Rd., Orp. CM56 97
Beechcroft, Ash. BL63 103
Beechcroft, Chis. CL50 78
Beechdale N21 BX27 38
Beechdale Rd. SW2 BX46 76
Beechdene, Tad. BP64 103
Beechen Cliff Way, Islw. BH44 64
Henley Clo.
Beechen Clo., Pnr. BE31 45
Beechen Gro., Wat. BC24 26
Beechen La., Tad. BR66 112
Beechen Pl. SE23 CC48 77
Hindsley Pl.
Beechenlea La., Swan. CU52 89
Beeches Av., The, Cars. BU57 95
Beeches Clo. SE20 CC51 87
Genoa Rd.
Beeches Clo., Tad. BS65 104
Beeches Rd. SW17 BU48 76
Beeches Rd., Sutt. BR54 85
Ridge Rd.
Beeches Wk., Cars. BT58 95
Beeches Wood, Tad. BR64 103
Beeches, The, Bans. BS61 104
Beeches, The, Brwd. DA27 42
Beeches, The, Lthd. BH65 102
Beeches, The, St.Alb. BG17 18
Sycamore Dr.
Beeches, The, Til. DG44 71
Beechfield Cotts., Brom. CJ51 88
Beechfield Gdns., Rom. CS33 50
Beechfield Rd. N4 BZ32 48
Beechfield Rd. SE6 CD47 77
Beechfield Rd., Welw.G.C. BR9 5
Beechfield Rd., Brom. CJ51 88
Beechfield Rd., Erith CT43 69
Beechfield Rd., Hem.H. AW14 8
Beechfield Wk., Wal.Abb. CF21 30
Beechfield, Kings L. AY18 17
Beechfield, Saw. CQ6 6
Beechhill Rd. SE9 CL46 78
Beechmont Av., Vir.W. AR53 82
Beechmont Clo., Brom. CG49 78
Beechmont Rd., Sev. CU68 116
Beechmore Gdns., Sutt. BQ55 85
Beechmore Rd. SW11 BU44 66
Beechmount Av. W7 BG39 54
Beecholme Av., Mitch. BV51 86
Beecholme Est. E5 CB34 48
Beecholme, Bans. BQ60 94
Beechpark Way, Wat. BB22 26
Beechtree Av., Egh. AQ50 72
Beechvale Clo. N12 BU28 38
Beechway, Bex. CP46 79
Beechwood Av. N3 BR31 46
Beechwood Av., Couls. BV61 104
Beechwood Av., Grnf. BF38 54
Beechwood Av., Har. BF34 45
Beechwood Av., Hayes BA40 53
Beechwood Av., Orp. CN56 97
Beechwood Av., Pot.B. BS20 20
Beechwood Av., Rich. BM44 65
Beechwood Av., Rick. AT24 25
Beechwood Av., Ruis. BB34 44
Beechwood Av., St.Alb. BJ12 9
Beechwood Av., Stai. AW50 73
Beechwood Av., Sun. BC50 73
Beechwood Av., Tad. BS64 104
Beechwood Av., Th.Hth. BY52 86
Beechwood Av., Uxb. AZ39 53
Beechwood Av., Wey. BA56 92
Beechwood Clo. NW7 BO28 37
Beechwood Clo., Amer. AR23 25
Beechwood Clo., Chsnt. CA16 21
Beechwood Clo., Surb. BK54 84
Beechwood Clo., Wey. BB56 92
Beechwood Clo., Wok. AP62 100
Beechwood Cres., Bexh. CP45 69
Beechwood Dr., Cob. BF59 93
Beechwood Dr., Kes. CJ56 97
Beechwood Dr., Wdf.Grn. CG28 40
Beechwood Gdns. NW10 BL38 55
St. Annes Gdns.
Beechwood Gdns., Cat. CB64 105
Beechwood Gdns., Har. BF34 45
Beechwood Gdns., Ilf. CK32 49
Beechwood Gdns., Rain. CU39 59
Beechwood Gdns., Slou. AP41 62
Beechwood Gro. W3 BO40 55
East Acton La.
Beechwood La., Warl. CC63 105
Beechwood Manor, Wey. BB56 92
Beechwood Ms. N9 CB27 39
Winchester Rd.
Beechwood Pk. E18 CH31 49
Beechwood Pk., Hem.H. AV15 7
Beechwood Pk., Lthd. BK64 102
Beechwood Rd. E8 CA36 57
Beechwood Rd. N8 BW31 47
Beechwood Rd., Cat. CB64 105
Beechwood Rd., S.Croy. BZ58 96
Beechwood Rd., Slou. AO39 52
Beechwood Rd., Vir.W. AQ54 82
Beechwood Rd., Wok. AP62 100
Beechwood Ri., Chis. CL49 78
Beechwood Ri., Wat. BC21 26
Beechwood Ter. E4 CF29 39
Larkshall Rd.
Beechwoods Ct. SE22 CA50 77
Crystal Palace Par.
Beechworth Clo. NW3 BS34 47
Beechy Lees Rd., Sev. CW61 108
Beecot La., Walt. BD55 84
Beecroft Rd. SE4 CD46 77
Beehive Chase, Brwd. DB21 33
Beehive Clo., B.Wd. BK25 27
Beehive Clo., Uxb. AY36 53
Honey Hill
Beehive Ct., Ilf. CK32 49
Beehive Grn., Welw.G.C. BS9 5
Beehive La., Ilf. CK32 49
Beehive La., Welw.G.C. BS9 5
Beehive Pass. EC3 CA39 2
Lime St.
Beehive Rd., Chsnt. BY17 20
Beehive Rd., Stai. AV49 72
Beehive Way, Reig. BS72 121
Beeken Dene, Orp. CM56 97
Beel Clo., Amer. AR23 25
Beeleigh Rd., Mord. BS52 86
Beesfield La., Farn. CX54 90
Beeston Clo. E8 CB35 48
Foxley Clo.
Beeston Clo., Wat. BD28 36
Beeston Dr., Wal.Cr. CC17 21
Beeston Pl. SW1 BV41 3
Beeston Pl. SW1 BV41 66
Beeston Rd., Barn. BT25 29
Berkeley Cres.
Beeston Way, Felt. BD46 74
Beethoven Rd., B.Wd. BK26 36
Beethoven St. W10 BR38 55
Beeton Clo., Pnr. BF29 36
Begbie Rd. SE3 CJ44 68
Beggars Bush La., Wat. BA25 26
Beggars Hill, Epsom BO57 94
Beggars Hollow, Enf. BZ22 30
Beggars La., West. CM65 106
Beggars La., Wok. AO59 91
Begonia Pl., Hmptn. BF50 74
Gresham Rd.
Begonia Wk. W12 BO39 55
Du Cane Rd.
Beira St. SW12 BV47 76
Bekesbourne St. E14 CD39 57
Ratcliffe La.
Belcher Rd., Hodd. CE11 12
Amwell St.
Belchers La., Wal.Abb. CJ15 13
Belcroft Clo., Brom. CG50 78
Hope Pk.
Beldam Haw, Sev. CR59 98
Beldham Gdns., E.Mol. BF52 84
Belfairs Dr., Rom. CP33 50
Belfairs Grn., Wat. BD28 36
Heysham Dr.
Belfast Av., Slou. AO39 52
Belfast Rd. N16 CA34 48
Belfast Rd. SE25 CB52 87
Belfield Rd., Epsom BN57 94
Belfont Wk. N7 BX35 47
Camden Rd.
Belford Gro. SE18 CL42 68
Belford Rd., B.Wd. BL22 28
Belfort Rd. SE15 CC44 67
Belfry Av., Uxb. AW29 35
Belfry La., Rick. AX26 35
Belgrade Rd. N16 CA35 48
Belgrade Rd., Hmptn. BF51 84
Belgrave Av., Rom. CV31 51
Belgrave Av., Wat. BB25 26
Belgrave Clo. N14 BW25 29
Belgrave Clo. W3 BM41 65
Avenue Rd.
Belgrave Clo., Orp. CP52 89
Sandway Rd.
Belgrave Clo., St.Alb. BK11 9
Portman Clo.
Belgrave Clo., Walt. BC56 92
Belgrave Cres., Sun. BC51 83
Belgrave Dr., Kings L. BA17 17
Belgrave Gdns. N14 BW24 29
Belgrave Gdns. NW8 BS37 1
Belgrave Gdns. NW8 BS37 56
Belgrave Gdns., Stan. BK28 36
Belgrave Grn. N., Slou. AP40 52
Belgrave Grn. S., Slou. AP40 52
Belgrave Manor, Wok. AS63 100
Brooklyn Rd.
Belgrave Ms. N. SW1 BV41 3
Belgrave Ms. N. SW1 BV41 66
Belgrave Ms. S. SW1 BV41 3
Belgrave Ms. S. SW1 BV41 66
Belgrave Ms. SW1 BV41 3
Belgrave Ms. SW1 BV41 66
Belgrave Ms. W. SW1 BV41 3
Belgrave Ms., Uxb. AX38 53
Belgrave Pl. SW1 BV41 3
Belgrave Pl. SW1 BV41 66
Belgrave Pl., Slou. AQ41 62
Clifton Rd.
Belgrave Rd. E10 CF33 48
Belgrave Rd. E11 CH34 49
Belgrave Rd. E13 CJ38 58
Belgrave Rd. E17 CE32 48
Belgrave Rd. SE25 CA52 87
Belgrave Rd. SW1 BV42 3
Belgrave Rd. SW1 BV42 66
Belgrave Rd. SW13 BO43 65
Belgrave Rd., Houns. BE45 64
Belgrave Rd., Ilf. CK33 49
Belgrave Rd., Mitch. BT52 86
Belgrave Rd., Slou. AP40 52
Belgrave Rd., Sun. BC51 83
Belgrave Sq. SW1 BV41 3
Belgrave Sq. SW1 BV41 66
Belgrave St. E1 CD39 57
Belgrave Ter., Wdf.Grn. CH27 40
Belgrave Wk., Mitch. BT52 86
Belgravia Gdns., Brom. CF50 77
Belgravia Ms., Kings.T. BK52 84
Belgrove St. WC1 BX38 2
Belgrove St. WC1 BX38 56
Belham Rd., Kings L. AY17 17
Belham Wk. SE5 BZ44 67
D'Eynsford Rd.
Belhaven Ct., B.Wd. BL23 28
Leeming Rd.
Belinda Rd. SW9 BY45 66
Belitha Vill. N1 BX36 56
Bell Av., Rom. CU30 41
Bell Av., West Dr. AY42 63
Bell Clo., Green. CZ46 80
Bell Clo., Pnr. BD30 36
Bell Clo., Ruis. BB34 44
Bell Clo., Slou. AQ39 52
Bell Clo., Wat. BC17 17
Bell Cor., Upmin. CY34 51
Bell Cres., Couls. BV64 104
Bell Ct., Surb. BM55 85
Bell Dr. SW18 BR47 75
Bell Farm Av., Dag. CS34 50
Bell Gate, Hem.H. AY12 8
Bathurst Rd.
Bell Gdns., Orp. CP53 89
Bell Grn. La. SE26 CD49 77
Bell Grn. SE26 CD49 77
Bell Grn., Hem.H. AT17 16
Bell Hill, Croy. BZ55 87
Crown Hill
Bell House Rd., Rom. CS33 50
Bell Inn Yd. EC3 BZ40 4
Gracechurch St.
Bell La. Clo., Lthd. BG65 102
Bell La. E1 CA39 2
Bell La. E1 CA39 57
Bell La. E16 CH40 58
Bell La. NW4 BQ31 46
Bell La., Amer. AQ23 25
Bell La., Berk. AP12 7

Bell La., Brox.	CD14	12
Bell La., Enf.	CC22	30
Bell La., Eton	AM42	61
Bell La., Hat.	BS15	11
Bell La., Hodd.	CE12	12
Bell La., Lthd.	BG65	102
Bell La., St.Alb.	BL18	19
Bell La., Twick.	BJ47	74
Bell La., Wat.	BB17	17
Bell Mead, Saw.	CQ6	6
Bell Meadow SE19	CA49	77
Dulwich Wood Av.		
Bell Meadow, Gdse.	CC69	114
Hickmans Clo.		
Bell Par., Wind.	AM44	61
Bell Rd., E.Mol.	BG53	84
Bell Rd., Enf.	BZ23	30
Bell Rd., Houns.	BF45	64
Bell St. NW1	**BU39**	**1**
Bell St. NW1	BU39	56
Bell St., Reig.	BS70	121
Bell St., Saw.	CQ6	6
Bell Vw. Clo., Wind.	AM44	61
Bell Vw., Wind.	AM45	61
Bell Water Gate SE18	CL41	68
Bell Wharf La. EC4	**BZ40**	**4**
Bell Wharf La. EC4	BZ40	57
Upper Thames St.		
Bell Wk., Saw.	CQ6	6
Bell Yard WC2	**BY39**	**2**
Bell Yard WC2	BY39	56
Bellamy Clo. SW5	BR42	65
Aisgill Av.		
Bellamy Clo., Uxb.	AZ34	44
Bellamy Clo., Wat.	BC23	26
Bellamy Dr., Stan.	BJ30	36
Bellamy Rd. E4	CE29	39
Bellamy Rd., Chsnt.	CD18	21
Bellamy Rd., Enf.	BZ23	30
Halifax Rd.		
Bellamy St. SW12	BV47	76
Bellasis Av. SW2	BX48	76
Bellclose Rd., West Dr.	AY41	63
Belle Vue Clo., Stai.	AW51	83
Belle Vue Est. NW4	BQ31	46
Belle Vue Rd., Bexh.	CQ46	79
Belle Vue Rd., Orp.	CL58	97
Standard Rd.		
Belle Vue Rd., Rom.	CS29	41
Belle Vue, Grnf.	BG37	54
Bellefield Rd., Orp.	CO53	89
Bellefields Rd. SW9	BX45	66
Bellegrove Clo., Well.	CN44	68
Bellegrove Rd., Well.	CN44	68
Bellenden Rd. SE15	CA45	67
Belleville Rd. SW11	BU46	76
Bellevue Gdns. SW9	BX44	66
Bellevue La., Bush.	BG26	36
Bellevue Ms. N11	BV28	38
Bellevue Rd.		
Bellevue Pk., Th.Hth.	BZ52	87
Bellevue Pl. E1	CC38	57
Bellevue Rd. E17	CF30	39
Bellevue Rd. N11	BV28	38
Bellevue Rd. NW4	BQ31	46
Bellevue Rd. SW13	BP44	65
Bellevue Rd. SW17	BU47	76
Bellevue Rd. W13	BJ38	54
Bellevue Rd., Horn.	CW33	51
Bellevue Rd., Kings.T.	BL52	85
Bellew St. SW17	BT48	76
Bellfield Av., Har.	BG29	36
Bellfield Rd., Guil.	AR69	118
Bellfield, Croy.	CD57	96
Bellfields Rd., Guil.	AR69	118
Bellflower Clo. E6	CK39	58
Sorrell Gdns.		
Bellflower Path, Rom.	CV29	42
Bellgate Ms. NW5	BV34	47
York Ri.		
Bellhouse La., Brwd.	CZ25	33
Bellingham Grn. SE6	CE48	77
Bellingham Rd. SE6	CE48	77
Bellman Av., Grav.	DJ47	81
Bellmarsh Rd., Wey.	AW56	92
Bellmount Wood Av., Wat.	BB23	26
Bellot St. SE10	CG42	68
Bellring Clo., Belv.	CR43	69
Bells All. SW6	BS44	66
Bells Gdns. Est. SE15	CB43	67
Bells Hill Grn., Slou.	AQ36	52
Bells Hill, Barn.	BQ25	28
Bells Hill, Slou.	AQ37	52
Bells La., Slou.	AT45	62
Bellstaines Pleasaunce E4	CE27	39
Bellswood La., Iver	AT39	52
Belltrees Gro. SW16	BX49	76
Bellvue Clo., Orp.	CL58	97
Bellweir Clo., Stai.	AT48	72
Wraysbury Rd.		
Bellwood Rd. SE15	CC45	67
Belmont Av. N13	BX28	38
Belmont Av. N17	BZ31	48
Belmont Av. N9	CB26	39
Belmont Av., Barn.	BU25	29
Belmont Av., Guil.	AP69	118
Belmont Av., N.Mal.	BP52	85
Belmont Av., Sthl.	BE41	64
Belmont Av., Upmin.	CX34	51
Belmont Av., Well.	CN44	68
Belmont Av., Wem.	BL37	55
Belmont Circle, Har.	BJ30	36
Belmont Clo. E4	CF28	39
Falmouth Av.		
Belmont Clo. N20	BS26	38
Belmont Clo. SW4	BW45	66
Belmont Clo., Barn.	BU24	29
Belmont Clo., Uxb.	AX36	53
Belmont Clo., Wdf.Grn.	CH28	40
Belmont Ct. NW11	BR32	46
Belmont Ct., St.Alb.	BG14	9
Belmont Hill		
Belmont Gro. SE13	CF45	67
Belmont Hall Ct. SE13	CF45	67
Belmont Hill SE13	CF45	67
Belmont Hill, St.Alb.	BG14	9
Belmont La., Chis.	CL49	78
Belmont La., Stan.	BK29	36
Belmont Pk. Clo. SE13	CF45	67
Belmont Pk.		
Belmont Pk. Rd. E10	CE32	48
Belmont Pk. SE13	CF45	67
Belmont Rd. N15	BZ31	48
Belmont Rd. N17	BZ31	48
Belmont Rd. SE25	CB53	87
Belmont Rd. SW4	BW45	66
Belmont Rd. W4	BN42	65
Belmont Rd., Beck.	CD51	87
Belmont Rd., Bush.	BE25	27
Belmont Rd., Chis.	CL49	78
Belmont Rd., Erith	CR43	69
Belmont Rd., Grays	DC43	71
Belmont Rd., Har.	BH31	45
Belmont Rd., Hem.H.	AY15	8
Belmont Rd., Horn.	CV34	51
Belmont Rd., Ilf.	CM34	49
Belmont Rd., Lthd.	BJ64	102
Belmont Rd., Reig.	BT71	121
Belmont Rd., Sev.	CU65	107
St. Botolphs Rd.		
Belmont Rd., Sutt.	BS58	95
Belmont Rd., Twick.	BG48	74
Belmont Rd., Uxb.	AX36	53
Belmont Rd., Wall.	BV56	95
Belmont Ri., Sutt.	BR57	94
Belmont St. NW1	BV36	56
Belmont Ter. W4	BN42	65
Belmont Rd.		
Belmor, B.Wd.	BM25	28
Belmore Av., Hayes	BC39	53
Belmore Av., Wok.	AU61	100
Belmore La. N7	BW35	47
Belmore St. SW8	BW44	66
Beloe Clo. SW15	BP45	65
Belper Ct. E5	CC35	48
Clapton Park Est.		
Belsham St. E9	CC36	57
Belsize Av. N13	BX29	38
Belsize Av. NW3	BT36	56
Belsize Av. W13	BJ41	64
Belsize Clo., Hem.H.	AZ14	8
Belsize Clo., St.Alb.	BK11	9
Belsize Cres. NW3	BT35	47
Belsize Gdns., Sutt.	BS56	95
Belsize Gro. NW3	BU36	56
Belsize La. NW3	BT36	56
Belsize Ms. NW3	BT35	47
Belsize La.		
Belsize Park Gdns. NW3	BU36	56
Belsize Park Ms. NW3	BT36	56
Belsize La.		
Belsize Pk. NW3	BT36	56
Belsize Pl. NW3	BT35	47
Belsize Rd. NW6	**BS37**	**1**
Belsize Rd. NW6	BS37	56
Belsize Rd., Har.	BG29	36
Belsize Rd., Hem.H.	AZ14	8
Belsize Sq. NW3	BT36	56
Belsize Ter. NW3	BT36	56
Belson Rd. SE18	CK42	68
Belswains Grn., Hem.H.	AY15	8
Belswains La.		
Belswains La., Hem.H.	AY15	8
Beltana Dr., Grav.	DJ49	81
Beltane Dr. SW19	BQ48	75
Belthorne Cres. SW12	BW47	76
Beltinge Rd., Rom.	CW31	51
Belton Rd. E11	CG35	49
Belton Rd. E7	CH36	58
Belton Rd. N17	CA31	48
Belton Rd. NW2	BP36	55
Belton Rd., Berk.	AQ12	7
Belton Rd., Sid.	CO49	79
Belton Way E3	CE39	57
Beltona Gdns., Chsnt.	CC17	21
Beltran Rd. SW6	BS44	66
Beltwood Rd., Belv.	CS42	69
Belvedere Av. SW19	BR49	75
Belvedere Av., Ilf.	CL30	40
Belvedere Bldgs. SE1	**BY41**	**4**
Belvedere Bldgs. SE1	BY41	66
Belvedere Clo., Esher	BF56	93
Belvedere Clo., Grav.	DH47	81
Belvedere Clo., Guil.	AQ69	118
Belvedere Clo., Tedd.	BH49	74
Belvedere Clo., Wey.	AZ56	92
Belvedere Ct. N2	BT32	47
Belvedere Ct. SW15	BQ45	65
Upper Richmond Rd.		
Belvedere Dr. SW19	BR49	75
Belvedere Gdns., E.Mol.	BE53	84
Belvedere Gro. SW19	BR49	75
Belvedere NW9	BO30	37
Belvedere Pl. SE1	**BY41**	**4**
Belvedere Pl. SE1	BY41	66
Borough Rd.		
Belvedere Rd. E10	CD33	48
Belvedere Rd. SE1	**BX41**	**4**
Belvedere Rd. SE1	BX41	66
Belvedere Rd. SE19	CA50	77
Belvedere Rd. SE2	CP40	59
Belvedere Rd. W7	BH41	64
Trumpers Way		
Belvedere Rd., Bexh.	CQ45	69
Belvedere Rd., Brwd.	CZ27	42
Belvedere Rd., West.	CK62	106
Belvedere Sq. SW19	BR49	75
Belvedere Way, Har.	BL32	46
Belvoir Clo. SE9	CK48	78
Nunnington Clo.		
Belvoir Lodge SE22	CB47	77
Underhill Rd.		
Belvoir Rd. SE22	CB47	77
Belvue Clo., Nthlt.	BF36	54
Belvue Rd., Nthlt.	BF36	54
Bembridge Clo. NW6	BQ36	55
Bembridge Ct., Slou.	AP41	62
Park St.		
Bembridge Gdns., Ruis.	BA34	44
Bemerton St. N1	**BX37**	**2**
Bemerton St. N1	BX37	56
Bemish Rd. SW15	BQ45	65
Bempton Dr., Ruis.	BC34	44
Bemsted Rd. E17	CD31	48
Bemwell Ct., Sun.	BC51	83
Ben Jonson Rd. E1	CC39	57
Ben Smith Way SE16	CB41	67
Jamaica Rd.		
Ben Tillet Clo., Bark.	CO36	59
Benares Rd. SE18	CN42	68
Benbow Clo., St.Alb.	BJ14	9
Benbow Rd. W6	BP41	65
Benbow St. SE8	CE43	67
Benbow Waye, Uxb.	AX39	53
Benbrick Rd., Guil.	AQ71	118
Benbury Clo., Brom.	CF49	77
Bence, The, Egh.	AT52	82
Bench Field, S.Croy.	CA57	96
Bench Manor Cres., Ger.Cr.	AR30	34
Bench, The, Rich.	BK48	74
Back La.		
Benchleys Rd., Hem.H.	AV14	7
Bencombe Rd., Pur.	BX60	95
Bencroft Rd. SW16	BW50	76
Bencroft, Chsnt.	CB16	21
Bencurtis Pk., W.Wick.	CF55	87
Bendall Ms. NW1	**BU39**	**1**
Bendall Ms. NW1	BU39	56
Bell St.		
Bendemeer Rd. SW15	BQ45	65
Bendish Rd. E6	CK36	58
Bendmore Av. SE2	CO42	69
Bendon Vall. SW18	BS47	76
Bendysh Rd., Bush.	BE24	27
Benedict Clo., Belv.	CQ41	69
Tunstock Way		
Benedict Clo., Orp.	CN55	88
Benedict Dr., Felt.	BA47	73
Benedict Rd. SW9	BX45	66
Stockwell Pk.		
Benedict Rd., Mitch.	BT52	86
Benedict Way N2	BT31	47
Benenden Grn., Brom.	CH53	88
Benenstock Rd., Stai.	AW46	73
Benets Rd., Horn.	CX33	51
Benett Gdns. SW16	BX51	86
Benfleet Clo., Cob.	BE59	93
Benfleet Clo., Sutt.	BT55	86
Benford Rd., Hodd.	CD13	12
Bengal Ct. EC3	**BZ39**	**2**
Birchin La.		
Bengal Rd., Ilf.	CL35	49
Bengarth Dr., Har.	BG30	36
Bengarth Rd., Nthlt.	BD37	54
Bengeworth Rd. SE5	BZ45	67
Bengeworth Rd., Har.	BJ34	45
Benhale Clo., Stan.	BJ28	36
Benham Clo. SW11	BT45	66
Hope St.		
Benham Clo., Couls.	BY62	104
Benham Gdns., Houns.	BE45	64
Benham Rd. W7	BH39	54
Benhams Pl. NW3	BT35	47
Holly Wk.		
Benhill Av., Sutt.	BS56	95
Benhill Rd. SE5	BZ43	67
Benhill Rd., Sutt.	BT55	86
Benhill Wood Rd., Sutt.	BT55	86
Benhilton Gdns., Sutt.	BS55	86
Benhurst Av., Horn.	CU35	50
Benhurst Clo., S.Croy.	CC58	96
Benhurst Ct. SW16	BY49	76
Benhurst Gdns., S.Croy.	CC58	96
Benhurst La. SW16	BY49	76
Benin St. SE13	CF47	77
Benison Ct., Slou.	AP41	62
Hencroft St.		
Benjafield Clo. N18	CB28	39
Brettenham Rd.		
Benjamin Clo., Rom.	CU32	50
Benjamin St. EC1	**BY39**	**2**
Benjamin St. EC1	BY39	56
Benledi St. E14	CF39	57
Benn St. E9	CD36	57
Bennerley Rd. SW11	BU46	76
Bennet St. SW1	**BW40**	**3**
Bennet St. SW1	BW40	56
Arlington St.		
Bennets Hill EC4	**BZ40**	**4**
Queen Victoria St.		
Bennett Clo., Kings.T.	BK51	84
Bennett Clo., Nthwd.	BB29	35
Bennett Clo., Well.	CO44	69
Bennett Gro. SE13	CE44	67
Bennett Pk. SE3	CG45	68
Bennett Rd. E13	CJ38	58
Bennett Rd. N16	CA35	48
Bennett Rd., Rom.	CQ32	50
Bennett St. W4	BO43	65
Bennett Way, Dart.	CY49	80
Bennett Way, Guil.	AW68	110
Bennetts Av., Croy.	CD55	87
Bennetts Av., Grnf.	BG37	54
Bennetts Av., Sev.	DB59	99
Bennetts Castle La., Dag.	CP35	50
Bennetts Clo. N17	CB29	39
Bennetts Clo., Cob.	BC60	92
Bennetts Clo., Slou.	AN41	61
Bennetts Clo., St.Alb.	BN15	10
Bennetts Copse, Chis.	CK50	78
Wood Dr.		
Bennetts End Clo., Hem.H.	AY14	8
Bennetts End Rd., Hem.H.	AZ14	8
Bennetts Gate, Hem.H.	AZ15	8
Bennetts End Rd.		
Bennetts Way, Croy.	CD55	87
Bennetts Yd. SW1	BX41	66
Marsham St.		
Bennetts, Chesh.	AO18	16
Benning Clo., Wind.	AL45	61
Benningholme Rd., Edg.	BO29	37
Bennington Rd. N17	CA30	39
Bennington Rd., Wdf.Grn.	CG29	40
Forest Dr.		
Bennions Clo., Horn.	CV36	60
Franklin Rd.		
Benns Wk., Rich.	BL45	65
Rosedale Rd.		
Benrek Clo., Ilf.	CM30	40
Bensbury Clo. SW15	BQ47	75
Bensham Clo., Th.Hth.	BZ52	87
Bensham Gro., Th.Hth.	BZ51	87
Bensham La., Croy.	BY54	86
Bensham Manor Rd., Th.Hth.	BZ52	87
Benskin Rd., Wat.	BC25	26
Benskins La., Hav.	CV26	42
Bensley Clo. N12	BU28	38
Benson Av. E6	CJ37	58
Benson Clo., Houns.	BF45	64
Benson Clo., Slou.	AQ40	52
Benson Clo., Uxb.	AY39	53
Benson Quay E1	CC40	57
Garnet St.		
Benson Rd. SE23	CC47	77
Benson Rd., Croy.	BY55	86
Benson Rd., Grays	DD43	71
Benston Clo., Houns.	BF45	64
Staines Rd.		
Bentfield Gdns. SE9	CJ48	78
Benthal Rd. N16	CB34	48
Benthall Gdns., Ken.	BZ62	105
Uplands Rd.		
Bentham Av., Wok.	AU61	100
Bentham Rd. E9	CC36	57
Bentham Rd. SE28	CO40	59
Bentham Wk. NW10	BN35	46
Lovett Way		
Bentinck Clo., Ger.Cr.	AR32	43
Bentinck Ms. W1	**BV39**	**1**
Bentinck Ms. W1	BV39	56
Marylebone La.		
Bentinck Rd., West.Dr.	AX40	53
Bentinck St. W1	**BV39**	**1**
Bentinck St. W1	BV39	56
Bentley Dr., Ilf.	CM32	49
Bentley Heath La., Barn.	BR21	28
Bentley Rd. N1	CA36	57
Tottenham Rd.		
Bentley Rd., Slou.	AN40	61
Bentley St., Grav.	DH46	81
Bentley Way, Stan.	BJ28	36
Bentley Way, Wdf.Grn.	CH27	40
Bentleys Meadow, Sev.	CW63	108
Benton Rd. E16	CJ40	58
Oriental Rd.		
Benton Rd., Ilf.	CM33	49
Benton Rd., Wat.	BD28	36
Bentons La. SE27	BZ49	77
Bentons Ri. SE27	BZ49	77
Bentry Clo., Dag.	CQ34	50
Bentry Rd., Dag.	CQ34	50
Bentsbrook Clo., Dor.	BJ73	119
Spook Hill		
Bentsbrook Pk., Dor.	BJ73	119
Bentsbrook Rd., Dor.	BJ73	119
Bentsley Clo., St.Alb.	BK11	9
Bentworth Rd. W12	BP39	55
Benwell Rd. N7	BY35	47
Benwick Clo. SE16	CB42	67
Aspinden Rd.		
Benworth St. E3	CD38	57
Benyon Path, S.Ock.	DB37	60
Benyon Rd. N1	**BZ37**	**2**
Benyon Rd. N1	BZ37	57
Berber Rd. SW11	BU46	76
Ashness Rd.		
Berberis Clo., Guil.	AR69	118
Cypress Rd.		
Berberis Wk., West Dr.	AY42	63
Berceau Wk., Wat.	BB23	26
Bercta Rd. SE9	CM48	78
Bere St. E1	CC40	57
Cranford St.		
Berecroft, Harl.	CM13	13
Beredens La., Upmin.	CZ31	51
Berenger Wk. SW10	BT43	66
Worlds End		
Berens Rd. NW10	BQ38	55
Berens Rd., Orp.	CP53	89
Berens Way, Chis.	CN52	88
Beresford Av. N20	BU27	38
Beresford Av. W7	BG39	54
Beresford Av., Slou.	AR40	52
Beresford Av., Surb.	BM54	85
Beresford Av., Twick.	BK46	74
Beresford Av., Wem.	BL37	55
Beresford Dr., Brom.	CK52	88
St. Michaels Clo.		
Beresford Dr., Wdf.Grn.	CJ28	40
Beresford Gdns., Enf.	CA24	30
Beresford Gdns., Houns.	BE46	74
Beresford Gdns., Rom.	CQ32	50
Beresford Rd. E17	CE30	39
Beresford Rd. E4	CG26	40
Beresford Rd. N2	BU31	47
Beresford Rd. N5	BZ35	48
Beresford Rd. N8	BY32	47
Beresford Rd., Dor.	BJ71	119
Beresford Rd., Grav.	DF47	81
Beresford Rd., Har.	BG32	45
Beresford Rd., Kings.T.	BL51	85
Beresford Rd., N.Mal.	BN52	85
Beresford Rd., Rick.	AV26	34
Beresford Rd., St.Alb.	BJ14	9
Beresford Rd., Sthl.	BD40	54
Beresford Rd., Sutt.	BR58	94
Beresford Sq. SE18	CL42	68
Beresford St. SE18	CL41	68
Beresford Ter. N5	BZ35	48
Berestede Rd. W6	BO42	65
Berger Clo., Orp.	CN53	88
Berger Rd. E9	CC36	57
Bergholt Av., Ilf.	CK32	49
Bergholt Cres. N16	CA33	48
Bergholt Ms. NW1	**BW37**	**1**
Bericot Way, Welw.G.C.	BT7	5
Bering Wk. E16	CJ39	58
Leyes Rd.		
Berkeley Av., Bexh.	CP44	69
Berkeley Av., Grnf.	BG36	54
Berkeley Av., Houns.	BC44	63
Berkeley Av., Ilf.	CL30	40
Berkeley Av., Rom.	CS29	41
Berkeley Clo., B.Wd.	BM25	28
Berkeley Clo., Brent.	BJ43	64
Berkeley Clo., Epsom	BN61	103
Berkeley Clo., Horn.	CX34	51
Berkeley Clo., Orp.	CN54	88
Buckingham Clo.		
Berkeley Clo., Pot.B.	BR19	19
Berkeley Clo., Ruis.	BC34	44
Berkeley Clo., Stai.	AU48	72
Moor La.		
Berkeley Clo., Wat.	BB19	17
Berkeley Cres., Barn.	BT25	29
Berkeley Cres., Dart.	CW47	80
Berkeley Ct. EC1	BY39	56
Briset St.		
Berkeley Ct. N14	BW25	29
Berkeley Ct., Guil.	AS70	118
Berkeley Ct., Wey.	BB55	83
Berkeley Dr., Horn.	CX34	51
Berkeley Gdns. N21	BZ26	39
Berkeley Gdns. W8	BS40	56
Brunswick Gdns.		
Berkeley Gdns., Esher	BJ57	93
Berkeley Gdns., Walt.	BB54	83
Berkeley Gdns., Wey.	AV60	91
Berkeley Ms. W1	**BU39**	**1**
Berkeley Ms. W1	BU39	56
Berkeley Pl. SW19	BQ50	75
Berkeley Rd. E12	CK35	49
Berkeley Rd. N15	BZ32	48
Berkeley Rd. N8	BW32	47
Berkeley Rd. NW9	BM31	46
Berkeley Rd. SW13	BP44	65
Berkeley Rd., Grav.	DG46	81
Berkeley Rd., Uxb.	BA36	53
Berkeley Sq. W1	**BV40**	**3**
Berkeley Sq. W1	BV40	56
Berkeley Sq., Hem.H.	BA10	8
Berkeley St. W1	**BV40**	**3**
Berkeley St. W1	BV40	56
Berkeley Waye, Houns.	BD43	64
Berkeley Wk. N7	BX34	47
Durham Rd.		
Berkeleys, The, Lthd.	BH65	102
Berkhampstead Rd., Belv.	CR42	69
Berkhamsted Av., Wem.	BL36	55
Berkhamsted Hill, Berk.	AS12	7
Berkhamsted La., Hat.	BU13	11
Berkhamsted Pl., Berk.	AQ12	7
Berkhamsted Rd., Hem.H.	AU12	7
Berkley Av., Wal.Cr.	CC20	21
Berkley Clo., St.Alb.	BK11	9
Portman Clo.		
Berkley Ct., Rick.	BA25	26
Mayfare		
Berkley Dr., E.Mol.	BE52	84
Berkley Gro. NW1	BU36	56
Berkley Rd.		
Berkley Rd. NW1	BU36	56
Berks Hill, Rick.	AU25	25
Berkshire Clo., Cat.	BZ64	105
Berkshire Gdns. N13	BY29	38
Berkshire Gdns. N18	CB28	39
Berkshire Rd. E9	CD36	57
Berkshire Sq., Mitch.	BX52	86
Berkshire Ter. E9	CD36	57
Berkshire Rd.		
Berkshire Way, Horn.	CX32	51
Berkshire Way, Mitch.	BX52	86
Bermans Clo., Brwd.	DD27	122
Hanging Hill La.		
Bermans Way NW10	BO35	46
Bermondsey Sq. SE1	**CA41**	**4**
Bermondsey Sq. SE1	CA41	67
Tower Bridge Rd.		
Bermondsey St. SE1	**CA40**	**4**
Bermondsey St. SE1	CA40	57
Bermondsey Wall E. SE16	CB41	67
Bermondsey Wall W. SE16	**CB41**	**4**
Bermondsey Wall W. SE16	CB41	67
Mill St.		
Bermuda Rd., Til.	DG44	71
Bernal Clo. SE28	CP40	59
Haldane Rd.		
Bernard Av. W13	BJ41	64
Bernard Cassidy St. E16	CG39	58
Morgan St.		
Bernard Gdns. SW19	BR49	75
Bernard Rd. N15	CA32	48
Bernard Rd., Rom.	CS33	50
Bernard Rd., Wall.	BV56	95
Bernard St. WC1	**BX38**	**2**
Bernard St. WC1	BX38	56
Bernard St., St.Alb.	BG13	9
Bernays Clo., Stan.	BK29	36
Bernays Gro. SW9	BX45	66
Berne Rd., Th.Hth.	BZ52	87
Bernell Dr., Croy.	CD55	87
Berner Est. E1	CB39	57
Berners Dr., St.Alb.	BH15	9
Berners Ms. W1	**BW39**	**1**
Berners Ms. W1	BW39	56
Berners Pl. W1	**BW39**	**1**
Berners Pl. W1	BW39	56
Berners Rd. N1	**BY37**	**2**
Berners Rd. N1	BY37	56
Berners Rd. N22	BY30	38
Berners St. W1	**BW39**	**1**
Berners St. W1	BW39	56
Berney Way, Brox.	CD15	12
Berney Rd., Croy.	BZ54	87
Cromwell Rd.		
Bernice Clo., Rain.	CV38	60
Arterial Av.		
Bernville Way, Har.	BL32	46
Kenton Rd.		
Bernwell Rd. E4	CG27	40
Berridge Est., Edg.	BL29	37
Berridge Grn., Edg.	BM29	37
Berridge Rd. SE19	BZ49	77

Berries, The, St.Alb. BJ11 9
Berriman Rd. N7 BX34 47
Berrin Way WC1 BX37 2
Berrin Way WC1 BX37 56
Berriton Rd., Har. BE33 45
Berry Av., Wat. BC21 26
Berry Clo. N21 BY26 38
Berry Clo. NW10 BO36 55
Berry Clo., Horn. CV36 60
Airfield Way
Berry Clo., Rick. AW26 35
Berry Gro. La., Bush. BE22 27
Berry Gro. La., Bush. BF23 27
Berry Hill, Stan. BK28 36
Berry Ho. Rd. SW11 BU44 66
Dagnall St.
Berry La. SE21 BZ49 77
Berry La., Guil. & Wok. AO65 100
Berry La., Rick. AU25 25
Berry La., Rick. AW25 26
Berry Meade, Ash. BL62 103
Berry Pl. EC1 BY38 2
Berry St. EC1 BY38 2
Berry St. EC1 BY38 56
Dallington St.
Berry Way W5 BL41 65
Berry Way, Rick. AW26 35
Berry Wk., Ash. BL63 103
Berrybank Clo. E4 CF27 39
Greenbank Clo.
Berrydale Rd., Hayes BE38 54
Berryfield Clo. E17 CE31 48
Berryfield Clo., Brom. CK51 88
Berryfield Rd. SE17 BY42 4
Berryfield Rd. SE17 BY42 66
Berryfield, Slou. AR39 52
Berryhill Gdns., SE9 CL45 68
Berryhill SE9 CL45 68
Berrylands Rd., Surb. BL53 85
Berrylands SW20 BQ52 85
Berrylands, Orp. CP55 89
Berrylands, Surb. BL53 85
Berryman Clo., Dag. CP34 50
Berrymans La. SE26 CC49 77
Berrymead Gdns. W3 BN41 65
Berrymead, Hem.H. AY12 8
Berrymede Rd. W4 BN41 65
Berrys Croft Rd., Stai. AX50 73
Berrys Grn. Rd., West. CL61 106
Berrys Hill, West. CL61 106
Berrys La., Wey. AX59 92
Bersham La., Grays DC42 71
Bert Rd., Th.Hth. BZ53 87
Bert Way, Enf. CA24 30
Bertal Rd. SW17 BT49 76
Berther Rd., Horn. CW33 51
Berthon St. SE8 CE43 67
Bertie Rd. NW10 BP36 55
Bertie Rd. SE26 CC50 77
Bertram Cott. SW19 BS50 76
Bertram Rd. Enf. CA24 30
Bertram Rd. NW4 BP32 46
Bertram Rd., Kings.T. BM50 75
Bertram St. N19 BV34 47
Bertram Way, Enf. CA24 30
Bertrand St. SE13 CE45 67
Bertrand Way SE28 CP40 59
Berwick Av., Hayes BD39 54
Berwick Clo., Stan. BH29 36
Gordon Av.
Berwick Clo., Wal.Cr. CE20 21
Queens Dr.
Berwick Cres., Sid. CN47 78
Berwick La., Ong. CT20 23
Berwick Pond Clo., Rain. CV37 60
Berwick Pond Rd., Rain. CW37 60
Berwick Rd. E16 CJ39 58
Berwick Rd. N22 BY30 38
Berwick Rd., B.Wd. BL22 28
Berwick Rd., Rain. CV37 60
Berwick Rd., Well. CO44 69
Berwick St. W1 BW39 1
Berwick St. W1 BW39 56
Berwick Way E17 CD31 48
High St.
Berwick Way, Orp. CO54 89
Vinson Clo.
Berwick Way, Sev. CU63 107
Cramptons Rd.
Berwyn Av., Houns. BF44 64
Berwyn Rd. SE24 BY47 76
Berwyn Rd., Rich. BM45 65
Beryl Av. E6 CK39 58
Beryl Rd. W6 BQ42 65
Berystede, Kings.T. BM50 75
Besant Ct. N1 BZ35 48
Mildmay Gro.
Besant Rd. NW2 BR35 46
Besant Way NW10 BN35 46
Besley St. SW16 BW50 76
Bessborough Gdns. SW1 BW42 3
Bessborough Pl. SW1 BW42 3
Bessborough Pl. SW1 BW42 66
Bessborough Rd. SW15 BP47 75
Bessborough Rd., Har. BG33 45
Bessborough St. SW1 BW42 3
Bessborough St. SW1 BW42 66
Bessels Grn. Rd., Sev. CS65 107
Bessels Meadows, Sev. CS65 107
Bessels Way
Bessels Way, Sev. CS65 107
Bessemer Rd. SE5 BZ44 67
Bessemer Rd., Welw.G.C. BR 7 5
Bessingby Rd., Ruis. BC34 44
Bessingham Wk. SE4 CD45 67
Frendsbury Rd.
Besson St. SE14 CC44 67
Bessy St. E2 CC38 57
Roman Rd.
Bestwood St. SE8 CC42 67
Beswick Mews NW6 BS36 56
Lymington Rd.
Beta Rd., Wok. AP58 91
Betam Rd., Hayes BA41 63
Betchworth Clo., Sutt. BT56 95
Turnpike La.
Betchworth Rd., Ilf. CN34 49
Betchworth Way, Croy. CF58 96
Betenson Av., Sev. CT64 107
Beth Rd., Wok. AT61 100
Princess Rd.
Betham Rd., Grnf. BG38 54
Bethany Waye, Felt. BB47 73
Bethecar Rd., Har. BH32 45
Bethel Rd., Sev. CV65 108
Bethel Rd., Well. CP45 69
Bethell Av. E16 CG38 58
Bethell Av., Ilf. CL33 49
Bethersden Clo., Beck. CD50 77
Bethnal Grn. Est. E2 CC38 57
Bethnal Grn. Rd. E1 CA38 2
Bethnal Grn. Rd. E1 CA38 57
Bethnal Grn. Rd. E2 CA38 2
Bethnal Grn. Rd. E2 CA38 57
Bethune Av. N11 BU28 38
Bethune Rd. N16 BZ33 48
Bethune Rd. NW10 BN38 55
Bethwin Rd. SE5 BY43 66
Betjeman Clo., Pnr. BF31 45
Pinner Rd.
Betjeman Way, Hem.H. AW12 8
Betley Ct., Walt. BC55 83
Betony Clo., Croy. CC54 87
Primrose La.
Betony Rd., Rom. CV29 42
Betoyne Av. E4 CG28 40
Betsham Rd., Erith CT43 69
Betsham Rd., Grav. DB49 80
Betsham Rd., Swans. DC47 81
Betstyle Rd. N11 BV28 38
Betterton Dr., Sid. CO48 79
Betterton Rd., Rain. CT38 59
Betterton St. WC2 BX39 2
Betterton St. WC2 BX39 56
Bettles Clo., Uxb. AX37 53
Bettons Pk. E15 CG37 58
New Plaistow Rd.
Bettridge Rd. SW6 BR44 65
Betts Clo., Beck. CD51 87
Kendall Rd.
Betts La., Wal.Abb. CJ14 13
Betts Rd. E16 CH40 58
Betts St. E1 CB40 57
Betts Way SE20 CB51 87
Anerley Rd.
Betts Way, Surb. BJ54 84
Betula Clo., Ken. BZ61 105
Betula Wk., Rain. CB38 60
Between Streets, Cob. BC60 92
Beulah Av., Th.Hth. BZ52 87
Beulah Rd.
Beulah Clo., Edg. BM27 37
Beulah Cres., Th.Hth. BZ51 87
Beulah Gro., Croy. BZ53 87
Beulah Hill SE19 BY50 76
Beulah Path E17 CE32 48
Addison Rd.
Beulah Rd. E11 CG34 49
Cathall Rd.
Beulah Rd. E17 CE32 48
Beulah Rd. SW19 BR50 75
Beulah Rd., Epp. CO18 23
Beulah Rd., Horn. CV34 51
Beulah Rd., Sutt. BS56 95
Beulah Rd., Th.Hth. BZ52 87
Beulah Wk., Cat. CD63 105
Beult Rd., Dart. CU45 69
Bev Callender Clo. SW8 BV45 66
Heath Rd.
Bevan Av., Bark. CO36 59
Bevan Clo., Hem.H. AX14 8
Bevan Ct., Croy. BY56 95
Bevan Est., Barn. BT24 29
Bevan Pl., Swan. CT52 89
Bevan Rd. SE2 CO42 69
Bevan Rd., Barn. BU24 29
Bevan St. N1 BZ37 2
Bevan St. N1 BZ37 57
Bevan Way, Horn. CW35 51
Bevenden St. N1 BZ38 2
Bevenden St. N1 BZ38 57
Beveridge Rd. NW10 BO36 55
Curzon Cres.
Beverley Av. SW20 BO51 85
Beverley Av., Houns. BE45 64
Beverley Av., Sid. CN47 78
Beverley Clo. N21 BZ26 39
Beverley Clo. SW11 BT45 66
Maysoule Rd.
Beverley Clo. SW13 BP44 65
Beverley Clo., AX56 92
Addlestone
Beverley Clo., Brox. CD14 12
Beverley Clo., Chess. BK56 93
Beverley Clo., Enf. CA24 30
Beverley Clo., Epsom BQ59 94
Beverley Clo., Horn. CW33 51
Beverley Clo., Wey. BB55 83
Beverley Cres., Wdf.Grn. CH30 40
Beverley Ct. N14 BW26 38
Beverley Ct. SE4 CD45 67
Beverley Ct., Slou. AQ41 62
Dolphin Rd.
Beverley Dr., Edg. BM31 46
Beverley Gdns. NW11 BR33 46
Beverley Gdns. SW13 BO45 65
Beverley Gdns., Chsnt. CB19 21
Beverley Gdns., Grnf. BH38 54
Western Av.
Beverley Gdns., Horn. CW33 51
Beverley Gdns., St.Alb. BK11 9
Beverley Gdns., Stan. BJ30 36
Beverley Gdns., Welw.G.C. BT 8 5
Wellington Dr.
Beverley Gdns., Wem. BL33 46
Beverley Gdns., Wor.Pk. BP54 85
Beverley Heights., Red. BT71 121
Cronks Hill
Beverley Heights., Reig. BS69 121
Beverley La., Kings.T. BO50 75
Beverley Ms. E4 CF29 39
Beverley Rd.
Beverley Path SW13 BO44 65
Beverley Rd. Bexh. CS44 69
Beverley Rd. E4 CF29 39
Beverley Rd. E6 CJ38 58
Beverley Rd. SE20 CB51 87
Beverley Rd. SW13 BO45 65
Beverley Rd. W4 BO42 65
Beverley Rd., Brom. CK55 88
Beverley Rd., Dag. CQ35 50
Beverley Rd., Kings.T. BK51 84
Beverley Rd., Mitch. BW52 86
Beverley Rd., N.Mal. BP52 85
Beverley Rd., Ruis. BC34 44
Beverley Rd., Sthl. BE42 64
Beverley Rd., Sun. BB51 83
Beverley Rd., Whyt. CA61 105
Beverley Rd., Wor.Pk. BO55 85
Beverley Way SW20 BO51 85
Beverley Way, N.Mal. BO51 85
Beversbrook Rd. N19 BW34 47
Beverstone Rd. SW2 BX46 76
Beverstone Rd., Th.Hth. BY52 86
Bevil Ct., Hodd. CE10 12
Molesworth
Bevil St. SE8 CE43 67
Frankham St.
Bevill Allen Clo. SW17 BU49 76
Bevin Clo. SE16 CD40 57
Stave Yard Rd.
Bevin Ct. WC1 BX38 2
Bevin Ct. WC1 BX38 56
Bevin Rd., Hayes BC38 53
Bevin Way WC1 BX38 2
Bevington Rd. W10 BR39 55
Bevington Rd., Beck. CE51 87
Bevington St. SE16 CB41 67
Bevis Clo., Dart. CY47 80
Bevis Marks EC3 CA39 2
Bevis Marks EC3 CA39 57
Bewcastle Gdns., Enf. BX24 29
Bewdley St. N1 BY36 56
Bewick St. SW8 BV44 66
Bewley Clo., Chsnt. CC19 21
Bewley La., Sev. DB66 117
Bewley St. E1 CC40 57
Bewlys Rd. SE27 BY49 76
Bexhill Clo., Felt. BH48 74
Bexhill Rd. N11 BW28 38
Bexhill Rd. SE4 CD46 77
Bexhill Rd. SW14 BN45 65
Bexhill Wk. E15 CG37 58
Manor Rd.
Bexley Clo., Dart. CT46 79
Bexley Gdns. N9 BZ27 39
Bexley La., Dart. CT46 79
Bexley La., Sid. CP49 79
Bexley Rd. SE9 CL46 78
Bexley Rd., Erith CS43 69
Bexley St., Wind. AN44 61
Beyers Gdns., Hodd. CE10 12
Beyers Prospect, Hodd. CE10 12
Beynon Rd., Cars. BU56 95
Bianca Ho. N1 CA37 57
Purcell St.
Bianca Rd. SE15 CA43 67
Bibsworth Rd. N3 BR30 37
Bibury Clo. SE15 CA43 69
St. Georges Way
Bicester Rd., Rich. BM45 65
Bickenhall St. W1 BU39 1
Bickenhall St. W1 BU39 56
Bickersteth Rd. SW17 BU50 76
Bickerton Rd. N19 BW34 47
Bickley Cres., Brom. CK52 88
Bickley Pk. Rd., Brom. CK52 88
Bickley Rd. E10 CE33 48
Bickley Rd., Brom. CJ51 88
Bickley St. SW17 BU49 76
Bicknell Rd. SE5 BZ45 67
Bickney Way, Lthd. BG65 102
Bicknoller Clo., Sutt. BS58 95
Cotswold Rd.
Bicknoller Rd., Enf. CA23 30
Bicknor Rd., Orp. CN54 88
Bidborough Clo., Brom. CG53 88
Bidborough St. WC1 BW38 56
Bidborough St. WC1 BW38 2
Biddenden Way SE9 CL49 78
Biddenden Way, Grav. DF50 81
Biddenham Turn, Wat. BD21 27
Bidder St. E16 CG38 58
Biddestone Rd. N7 BX35 47
Biddulph Rd. W9 BS38 1
Biddulph Rd. W9 BS38 56
Biddulph Rd., S.Croy. BZ58 96
Bideford Av., Grnf. BJ38 54
Bideford Clo., Edg. BM30 37
Bideford Clo., Felt. BE48 74
Bideford Clo., Rom. CV30 42
Bideford Gdns., Enf. CA26 39
Bideford Rd., Brom. CG48 78
Bideford Rd., Enf. CD22 30
Bideford Rd., Ruis. BC34 44
Bideford Rd., Well. CO43 69
Bidhams Cres., Tad. CO64 103
Bidwell Gdns. N11 BW29 38
Bidwell St. SE15 CB44 67
Big Common La., Red. BY70 121
Big Hill E5 CB33 48
Bigbury Clo. N17 CA29 39
Biggerstaff Rd. E15 CF37 57
Biggerstaff St. N4 BY34 47
Biggin Av., Mitch. BU51 86
Biggin Hill SE19 BY51 86
Biggin La., Grays DG43 71
Biggin Way SE19 BY50 76
Bigginwood Rd. SW16 BY50 76
Biggs Row SW15 BQ45 65
Felsham Rd.
Bigland St. E1 CB39 57
Bignell Rd. SE18 CL42 68
Bignold Rd. E7 CH35 49
Bigwood Ct. NW11 BS32 47
Bigwood Rd.
Bigwood Rd. NW11 BS32 47
Biko Clo., Uxb. AX39 53
Sefton Way
Bill Hamling Clo. CK48 78
SE9
Billet Clo., Rom. CP31 50
Billet Rd.
Billet Hill, Sev. DB56 99
Billet La., Berk. AQ12 7
Billet La., Horn. CV33 51
Billet La., Iver & Slou. AT38 52
Billet Rd. E17 CC30 39
Billet Rd., Rom. CO31 50
Billet Rd., Stai. AW48 73
Billing Pl. SW10 BS43 66
Billing Rd. SW10 BS43 66
Billing St. SW10 BS43 66
Billingford Clo. SE4 CC45 67
Billingsgate Rd. E14 CE40 57
Billingsgate St. SE10 CF43 67
Billington Pl. W3 BM40 55
Steyne Rd.
Billington Rd. SE14 CC43 67
Billiter Sq. EC3 CA39 57
Fenchurch Av.
Billiter St. EC3 CA39 2
Billiter St. EC3 CA39 57
Billockby Clo., Chess. BL57 94
Billson St. E14 CF42 67
Billy Lows La., Pot.B. BS19 20
Bilsby Gro. SE9 CJ49 78
Bilston Gro. SE16 CC42 67
Abbeyfield Gdns.
Bilton Clo., Slou. AV44 62
Colndale Rd.
Bilton Rd., Erith CU43 69
Bilton Rd., Grnf. BJ37 54
Bilton Way, Enf. CD23 30
Bilton Way, Hayes BC41 63
Bina Gdns. SW5 BT42 3
Bina Gdns. SW5 BT42 66
Bincote Rd., Enf. BX24 29
Binden Rd. W12 BO41 65
Bindon Grn., Mord. BS52 86
Bayham Rd.
Binfield Rd. SW4 BX44 66
Binfield Rd., S.Croy. CA56 96
Binfield Rd., Wey. AY59 92
Bingfield St. N1 BX37 2
Bingfield St. N1 BX37 56
Bingham Clo., S.Ock. DA39 60
Bingham Dr., Stai. AX50 73
Bingham Dr., Wok. AP62 100
Bingham Pl. W1 BV38 1
Bingham Pl. W1 BV38 56
Bingham Rd., Croy. CB54 87
Bingham St. N1 BZ36 57
Binghams, The, Maid. AG41 61
Bingley Rd. E16 CJ39 58
Bingley Rd., Grnf. BG38 54
Bingley Rd., Hodd. CF12 12
Bingley Rd., Sun. BC50 73
Binney St. W1 BV39 1
Binney St. W1 BV39 56
Binns Rd. W4 BO42 65
Binsey Wk. SE2 CP41 69
Binyon Cres., Stan. BH28 36
Birbetts Rd. SE9 CK48 78
Birch Av. N13 BZ27 39
Birch Av., Cat. BZ65 105
Birch Av., West Dr. AY39 53
Birch Clo. E16 CG39 58
Birch Clo. N19 BW34 47
Hargrave Pk.
Birch Clo. SE15 CB44 67
Bournemouth Rd.
Birch Clo., Brent. BJ43 64
Birch Clo., Buck.H. CJ27 40
Birch Clo., Rom. CR31 50
Birch Clo., Sendmarsh AV66 109
Birch Clo., Sev. CU65 107
Birch Clo., Tedd. BJ49 74
Birch Clo., Wey. AX58 92
Birch Clo., Wok. AR63 100
Birch Copse, St.Alb. BE18 18
Birch Cres., Horn. CW31 51
Birch Cres., Uxb. AY37 53
Birch Dr., Hat. BP13 10
Birch Dr., Rick. AU28 34
Birch Gdns., Dag. CS34 50
Birch Grn. NW9 BO29 37
Clayton Field
Birch Grn., Hem.H. AV12 7
Birch Grn., Stai. AV48 72
Birch Gro. SE12 CG47 78
Birch Gro. W3 BM40 55
Birch Gro., Cob. BD60 93
Birch Gro., Pot.B. BS19 20
Birch Gro., Shep. BB51 83
Birch Gro., Tad. BR65 103
Birch Gro., Well. CO45 69
Birch Gro., Wind. AL44 61
Birch Gro., Wok. AU61 100
Birch Hill, Croy. CC56 96
Birch La., Hem.H. AT20 16
Birch La., Pur. BX59 95
Birch Leys, Hem.H. AZ11 8
Hunters Oak
Birch Mead, Orp. CL55 88
Birch Pk., Har. BG29 36
Birch Pl., Green. CZ46 80
Birch Rd., Berk. AO11 7
Birch Rd., Felt. BE49 74
Birch Rd., Rom. CR31 50
Birch Row, Brom. CL54 88
Birch Tree Av., CG56 97
W.Wick.
Birch Tree Clo., Chesh. AQ18 16
Birch Tree Way, Croy. CB55 87
Birch Tree Wk., Wat. BB22 26
Birch Vale, Cob. BF59 93
Birch Vw., Epp. CO18 23
Ongar Rd.
Birch Way, Chesh. AO18 16
Birch Way, St.Alb. BK17 18
Birch Way, Warl. CD62 105
Birch Wk., B.Wd. BM23 28
Birch Wk., Erith CS43 69
Birch Wk., Mitch. BV51 86
Birch Wk., Wey. AW59 92
Birch Wood, Rad. BM20 19
Birchall La., Welw.G.C. BT 9 5
Birchall Wood, BT 8 5
Welw.G.C.
Bircham Path SE4 CD45 67
Frendsbury Rd.
Birchanger Rd. SE25 CB53 87
Birchcroft Clo., Cat. BZ65 105
Birchdale Clo., Wey. AX59 92
Birchdale Gdns., Rom. CP33 50
Birchdale Rd. E7 CJ35 49
Birchdale, Ger.Cr. AR33 43
Birchdene Dr. SE28 CO40 59
Birchen Clo. NW9 BN34 46
Birchend Clo., S.Croy. BZ57 96
Sussex Rd.
Birches Clo., Epsom BO61 103
Birches Clo., Pnr. BD32 45
Birches, The N21 BX25 29
Birches, The SE7 CH43 68
Birches, The, Brwd. DC27 122
Birches, The, Bush. BG25 27
Birches, The, Epp. CR16 23
Higham Vw.
Birches, The, Hem.H. AV15 7
Birches, The, Lthd. BB66 110
Birches, The, Orp. CL56 97
Birches, The, Swan. CT51 89
Birches, The, Wok. AS62 100
Commercial Way
Birchfield Clo., Couls. BX61 104
Birchfield Clo., Wey. AW56 92
Birchfield Gro., Epsom BO58 94
Birchfield Rd., Chsnt. CB18 21
Birchfield St. E14 CE40 57
Birchgate Ms., Tad. BQ64 103
Bidhams Cres.
Birchin Cross Rd., Sev. CW61 108
Birchin La. EC3 BZ39 2
Birchin La. EC3 BZ39 57
Birchington Clo., Bexh. CR44 69
Birchington Clo., Orp. CP54 89
Hart Dyke Rd.
Birchington Rd. N8 BW32 47
Birchington Rd. NW6 BS37 56
Birchington Rd., Surb. BL54 85
Birchington Rd., Wind. AN44 61
Birchlands Av. SW12 BU47 76
Birchmead Av., Pnr. BD31 45
Birchmead Clo., St.Alb. BG12 9
Birchmead, Wat. BB22 26
Birchmere Row SE3 CG44 68
Birchmore Wk. N5 BZ34 48
Birchville Ct., Bush. BH26 36
Birchway, Hat. BP11 10
Birchway, Hayes BC40 53
Birchway, Red. BV71 121
Birchwood Av. N10 BV31 47
Birchwood Av., Beck. CD52 87
Birchwood Av., Hat. BP11 10
Birchwood Av., Sid. CO48 79
Birchwood Av., Wall. BV55 86
Birchwood Clo., Brwd. DA28 42
Birchwood Clo., Hat. BP11 10
Birchwood Clo., Mord. BS52 86
Birchwood Cotts., Hert. BV15 11
Birchwood Ct. N13 BY28 38
Birchwood Ct., Edg. BN30 37
Birchwood Dr. NW3 BS34 47
Birchwood Dr., Dart. CT49 79
Birchwood Dr., Wey. AW59 92
Birchwood Gro., Hmptn. BF50 74
Birchwood La., Cat. BY66 113
Birchwood La., Esher BG58 93
Birchwood Pk. Av., Swan. CT52 89
Birchwood Rd. SW17 BV49 76
Birchwood Rd., Dart. CS50 79
Birchwood Rd., Orp. CM52 88
Birchwood Rd., Swan. CS51 89
Birchwood Rd., Wey. AW59 92
Birchwood Way., St.Alb. BF17 18
Birchwood, Wal.Abb. CG20 22
Roundhills
Bird La., Brwd. DB31 51
Bird La., Upmin. CY32 51
Bird La., Uxb. AX30 35
Bird St. W1 BV39 1
Bird St. W1 BV39 56
Bird Wk., Twick. BE47 74
Bird-in-bush Rd. SE15 CB43 67
Bird-in-hand La., Brom. CJ51 88
Bird-in-hand Pass. SE23 CC48 77
Dartmouth Rd.
Birdbrook Clo., Brwd. DE25 122
Poplar Dr.
Birdbrook Clo., Dag. CS36 59
Birdbrook Rd. SE3 CJ45 68
Birdcage Wk. SW1 BW41 3
Birdcage Wk. SW1 BW41 66
Birdcroft Rd., Welw.G.C. BQ 8 5
Birdham Clo., Brom. CK53 88
Birdhouse La., Orp. CL60 97
Birdhurst Av., S.Croy. BZ56 96
Birdhurst Gdns., S.Croy. BZ56 96
Birdhurst Rd. SW18 BT45 66
Birdhurst Rd. SW19 BU50 76
Birdhurst Rd., S.Croy. CA56 96
Birdhurst Rise, S.Croy. CA56 96
Birdlip Clo. SE15 CA43 67
St. Georges Way
Birds Clo., Welw.G.C. BS 9 5
Birds Farm Av., Rom. CR29 41
Birds Grn., Ong. CZ13 15
Birds Hill Dr., Lthd. BG60 93
Birds Hill Rd., Lthd. BG59 93
Birds Hill Ri., Lthd. BG60 93
Birds, Wok. AO63 100
Gorsewood Rd.
Birdswood Dr., Wok. AP63 100
Birdwood Clo., S.Croy. CC59 96
Birdwood Clo., Tedd. BH49 74
Birkbeck Av. W3 BN40 55
Birkbeck Av., Grnf. BG37 54
Birkbeck Gdns., Wdf.Grn. CH27 40
Birkbeck Gro. W3 BN41 65
Birkbeck Hill SE21 BY47 76
Birkbeck Pl. SE21 BZ47 77
Birkbeck Rd. E8 CA35 48
Birkbeck Rd. N12 BT28 38

Birkbeck Rd. N17 CA30 39
Birkbeck Rd. N8 BX31 47
Birkbeck Rd. NW7 BO28 37
Birkbeck Rd. SW19 BS49 76
Birkbeck Rd. W3 BN40 55
Birkbeck Rd. W5 BK42 64
Birkbeck Rd., Beck. CC51 87
Birkbeck Rd., Brwd. DE25 122
Birkbeck Rd., Enf. BZ23 30
Birkbeck Rd., Ilf. CM32 49
Birkbeck Rd., Rom. CS33 50
Birkbeck Rd., Sid. CO48 79
Birkbeck St. E2 CB38 57
Birkbeck Way, Grnf. BG37 54
Birkdale Av., Pnr. BF31 45
Birkdale Av., Rom. CW29 42
Birkdale Clo., Orp. CM54 88
Birkdale Gdns., Wat. BD27 36
Birkdale Pl., Orp. CM54 88
Birkdale Rd. SE2 CO42 69
Birkdale Rd. W5 BL38 55
Birken Ms., Nthwd. AZ28 35
Birkenhead Av., Kings.T. BL51 85
Birkenhead St. WC1 BX38 2
Birkenhead St. WC1 BX38 56
St. Chads St.
Birkett Way, Ch.St.G. AR24 25
Birkhall Rd. SE6 CF47 77
Birkheads Rd., Reig. BS70 121
Birklands La., St.Alb. BJ15 9
Birkwood Clo. SW12 BW47 76
Birley Rd. N20 BT27 38
Birley Rd., Slou. AO39 52
Birley St. SW11 BV44 66
Birling Rd., Erith CS43 69
Birnam Clo., Wok. AW65 101
Birnam Rd. N4 BX34 47
Birse Cres. NW10 BO35 46
Neasden La.
Birstall Grn., Wat. BD27 36
Birstall Rd. N15 CA32 48
Birtley Path, B.Wd. BL23 28
Darrington Rd.
Biscay Rd. W6 BQ42 65
Biscoe Clo., Houns. BF43 64
Biscoe Way SE13 CF45 67
Bisenden Rd., Croy. CA55 87
Bisham Clo., Cars. BU54 86
Bisham Gdns. N6 BV33 47
Bishop Craven Clo., Enf. BY23 29
Chasewood Av.
Bishop Duppas Pk., Shep. BA54 83
Bishop Hall Rd., Brwd. DA25 33
Bishop Ken Rd., Har. BH30 36
Bishop Kings Rd. W14 BR42 65
Bishop Rd. N14 BV26 38
Bishop Rd. SW11 BU43 66
Bishop St. N1 BZ37 2
Bishop St. N1 BZ37 57
Bishops Av. E13 CH37 58
Bishops Av. SW6 BQ44 65
Bishops Av., B.Wd. BL25 28
Bishops Av., Brom. CJ52 88
Bishops Av., Nthwd. BB28 35
Bishops Av., Rom. CP32 50
Bishops Av., The N2 BT33 47
Bishops Br. Rd. W2 BS39 1
Bishops Br. Rd. W2 BS39 56
Bishops Br. W2 BT39 56
Bishops Clo. E17 CE31 48
Bishops Clo. N19 BW34 47
Wyndham Cres.
Bishops Clo. SE9 CM48 78
Bishops Clo., Barn. BQ25 28
Bishops Clo., Couls. BY62 104
Bishops Clo., Enf. CB23 30
Bishops Clo., Hat. BO12 10
College La.
Bishops Clo., Rich. BK48 74
Bishops Clo., St.Alb. BJ11 9
Bishops Clo., Sutt. BS55 86
Bishops Clo., Uxb. AZ37 53
Bishops Ct. EC4 BY39 2
Bishops Ct. EC4 BY39 56
Old Bailey
Bishops Ct. WC2 BY39 2
Bishops Ct. WC2 BY39 56
Chancery La.
Bishops Dr., Felt. BA46 73
Bishops Farm Clo., Wind. AK44 61
Bishops Garth, St.Alb. BJ11 9
Bishops Clo.
Bishops Gro. N2 BU32 47
Bishops Gro., Hmptn. BF49 74
Bishops Hall, Kings.T. BK51 84
Thames St.
Bishops Hill, Walt. BC54 83
Bishops Mead, Hem.H. AW14 8
Bishops Pk. Rd. SW16 BX51 86
Bishops Pk. Rd. SW6 BQ44 65
Bishops Rd. N6 BV32 47
Bishops Rd. SW6 BR44 65
Bishops Rd. W7 BH41 64
Bishops Rd., Croy. BY54 86
Bishops Rd., Hayes BA39 53
Bishops Rd., Slou. AQ41 62
Bishops Ri., Hat. BO12 10
Bishops Ter. SE11 BY42 4
Bishops Ter. SE11 BY42 66
Bishops Way E2 CC37 57
Bishops Way NW10 BO36 55
Bishops Way, Egh. AU50 72
Bishops Wk., Chis. CM51 88
Bishops Wk., Croy. CC56 96
Bishops Wk., Pnr. BE31 45
High St.
Bishops Wood, Wok. AP62 100
Bishopsfield, Harl. CN12 13
Bishopsford Rd., Mord. BT54 86
Bishopsford, Cars. BU53 86
Bishopsgate Chyd. EC2 CA39 2
Bishopsgate Chyd. EC2 CA39 57
Bishopsgate EC2 CA39 2
Bishopsgate EC2 CA39 57
Bishopsgate Rd., Egh. AQ48 72
Bishopsmead Par., Lthd. BB67 110
Bishopsthorpe Rd. SE26 CC49 77
Bishopswood Rd. N6 BU33 47
Bisley Clo., Wal.Cr. CC20 21
Bisley Clo., Wor.Pk. BQ54 85
Bispham Rd. NW10 BL38 55
Bisson Rd. E15 CF37 57
Bisterne Av. E17 CF31 48
Bitchet Rd., Sev. CX67 117
Bittacy Clo. NW7 BQ29 37
Bittacy Hill NW7 BQ29 37
Bittacy Park Av. NW7 BQ29 37
Bittacy Rd. NW7 BQ29 37
Bittacy Ri. NW7 BQ29 37
Bittams La., Cher. AU56 91
Bittern Dr., Wok. AP61 100
Bittern St. SE1 BZ41 4
Bittern St. SE1 BZ41 67
Bittoms, The, Kings.T. BK52 84
Bixley Clo., Sthl. BE42 64
Black Acre Clo., Amer. AP23 25
Black Boy La. N15 BZ32 48
Black Boy Wd., St.Alb. BF18 18
Black Bush Clo., Sutt. BS57 95
Copse Hill
Black Cut, St.Alb. BH14 9
Black Ditch Rd., Wal.Abb. CF21 30
Black Fan Clo., Enf. BZ23 30
Black Fan Rd., Welw.G.C. BS7 5
Black Horse Av., Chesh. AO20 16
Black Horse Clo., Wind. AL44 61
Black Horse Ct. SE1 BZ41 4
Black Horse La., Epp. CS16 23
Black Horse Rd., Sid. CO49 79
Black Horse Yd. E1 CA39 57
Middlesex St.
Black Jacks La., Uxb. AW30 35
Black La., Ong. CW12 15
Black Lake Clo., Egh. AT51 82
Black Lion Hill, Rad. BL19 19
Black Lion La. W6 BP42 65
Black Lion Yd. E1 CB39 57
Old Montague St.
Black Path E10 CC33 48
Black Park Rd., Slou. AS37 52
Black Prince Clo., Wey. AY60 92
Black Prince Rd. SE1 BX42 66
Black Prince Rd. SE11 BX42 4
Black Prince Rd. SE11 BX42 66
Black Raven Alley EC4 BZ40 57
Wharfside
Black Swan Alley EC2 BZ39 2
London Wall
Black Swan Yd. SE1 CA41 4
Black Thorne Rd., West. CK61 106
Black Tree Mews SW9 BY45 66
Gresham Rd.
Blackacre Rd., Epp. CN22 31
Blackall St. EC2 CA38 2
Blackall St. EC2 CA38 57
Blackberry Clo., Shep. BB52 83
Cherry Way
Blackberry Farm Clo., Houns. BE43 64
Blackbird Hill NW9 BN34 46
Blackbird Yd. E2 CA37 2
Ravenscroft St.
Blackbird Yd. E2 CA38 57
Ravenscroft St.
Blackbirds La., Wat. BG20 18
Blackborne Rd., Dag. CR36 59
Blackborough Clo., Reig. BT70 121
Blackborough Rd., Reig. BT71 121
Blackbridge Rd., Wok. AR63 100
Blackbrook La., Brom. CK53 88
Blackbrook Rd., Dor. BK73 119
Blackburn Rd. NW6 BS36 56
Blackburn, The, Lthd. BE65 102
Little Bookham St.
Blackburnes Ms. W1 BV40 3
Blackburnes Ms. W1 BV40 56
Blackbury Clo., Pot.B. BT19 20
Quakers La.
Blackbush Av., Rom. CP32 50
Blackbush Spring, Harl. CO10 6
Blackdale, Chsnt. CB17 21
Blackdown Av., Wok. AV61 100
Blackdown Clo., Wok. AU61 100
Blackdown Ter. SE18 CK43 68
Blackett Clo., Stai. AV51 82
Blackett St. SW15 BQ45 65
Blacketts Wd. Dr., Rick. AT24 25
Blackfen Rd., Sid. CN46 78
Blackford Clo., S.Croy. BY58 95
Blackford Path SW15 BP47 75
Roehampton High St.
Blackford Pl., Pur. BY58 95
Pampisford Rd.
Blackford Rd., Wat. BD28 36
Blackfriars Br. EC4 BY40 4
Blackfriars Br. EC4 BY40 56
Blackfriars Br. SE1 BY40 56
Blackfriars Ct. EC4 BY40 4
Blackfriars Sta.
Blackfriars La. EC4 BY40 4
Blackfriars La. EC4 BY40 56
Blackfriars Pass. EC4 BY40 4
Blackfriars Pass. EC4 BY40 56
Blackfriars Rd. SE1 BY41 4
Blackfriars Rd. SE1 BY41 66
Blackhall La., Sev. CW65 108
Blackheath Av. SE10 CG43 68
Blackheath Gro. SE3 CG44 68
Blackheath Hill SE10 CE44 67
Blackheath Pk. SE3 CG45 68
Blackheath Rd. SE10 CE44 67
Blackheath Ri. SE13 CF44 67
Blackheath Vale SE3 CG44 68
Blackheath Vill. SE3 CG44 68
Blackhills, Esher BE58 93
Blackhorse Clo., Amer. AP22 25
Blackhorse Clo., Grays DE42 71
Richmond Rd.
Blackhorse Cres., Amer. AP22 25
Blackhorse La. E17 CC31 48
Blackhorse La., Croy. CB54 87
Blackhorse La., Pot.B. BO18 19
Blackhorse La., Reig. BS68 113
Blackhorse Rd. E17 CC31 48
Blackhorse Rd. SE8 CD43 67
Blackhorse Rd., Wok. AO63 100
Blacklands Dr., Hayes BA38 53
Blacklands Mead, Red. BX70 121
Blacklands Rd. SE6 CF49 77
Blacklands Ter. SW3 BU42 3
Blacklands Ter. SW3 BU42 66
Blackley Clo., Wat. BB22 26
Blackmans Clo., Dart. CV47 80
Blackmans La., War. CG60 97
Blackmoor La., Wat. BA25 26
Blackmore Av., Sthl. BG40 54
Blackmore Clo., Grays DE43 71
Richmond Rd.
Blackmore Cres., Wok. AU61 100
Blackmore Ct., Wal.Abb. CH20 22
Winters Way
Blackmore Mead, Ing. DC19 24
Blackmore Rd., Brwd. CZ22 33
Blackmore Rd., Buck.H. CK26 40
Blackmore Rd., Ing. DB18 24
Blackmore Way, Uxb. AX36 53
Blackmores Gro., Tedd. BJ50 74
Blackness La., Kes. CJ57 97
Blackness La., Wok. AS63 100
Blacknest Rd., Ascot AO52 82
Blackpool Gdns., Hayes BB38 53
Blackpool Rd. SE15 CB44 67
Blacks Rd. W6 BQ42 65
Blackshaw Pl. N1 CD36 57
Hertford Rd.
Blackshaw Rd. SW17 BT49 76
Blackshots La., Grays DE40 71
Blacksmith All., Ing. DC19 24
Blacksmith Clo., Ash. BL63 103
Rectory La.
Blacksmith La., Guil. AU73 118
Blacksmith Row, Slou. AT42 62
Blacksmiths Clo., Rom. CP32 50
Blacksmiths Hill, S.Croy. CB60 96
Blacksmiths Hill, Epp. CQ20 23
Blacksmiths La., Cher. AW54 83
London St.
Blacksmiths La., Orp. CP53 89
Blacksmiths La., Rain. CT37 59
Blacksmiths La., St. Alb. BF13 9
Blacksmiths La., Stai. AX52 83
Blacksmiths La., Uxb. AU34 43
Blackstock Ms. N4 BY34 47
Blackstock Rd.
Blackstock Rd. N4 BY34 47
Blackstock Rd. N5 BY34 47
Blackstone Clo., Red. BU70 121
Blackstone Hill, Red. BU70 121
Blackstone Rd. NW2 BQ35 46
Blackthorn Av., West Dr. AZ42 63
Blackthorn Clo., Reig. BT71 121
Blackthorn Clo., Sev. CZ58 99
Ash Tree Dr.
Blackthorn Clo., St.Alb. BK11 9
Blackthorn Clo., Wat. BC19 17
Blackthorn Ct., Houns. BE43 64
Blackthorn Dell, Slou. AR41 62
Hempson Av.
Blackthorn Gro., Bexh. CQ45 69
Blackthorn Rd., Grays DD40 71
Blackthorn Rd., Reig. BT71 121
Blackthorn Rd., Welw.G.C. BS8 5
Blackthorn St. E3 CE38 57
Blackthorn Way, Brent. DB28 42
Blackthorne Av., Croy. CC54 87
Blackthorne Clo., Hat. BO14 10
Blackthorne Dr. E4 CF28 39
Blackthorne Rd., Lthd. BG66 111
Blackthorne Rd., Slou. AV45 62
Blackwall La. SE10 CG41 68
Blackwall Tunnel Northern App. E14 CE37 57
Blackwall Tunnel App. SE10 CG41 68
Blackwall Way E14 CF40 57
Blackwater Clo., Rain. CS39 59
Blackwater La., Hem.H. BB15 8
Blackwater Rd., Sutt. BS56 95
High St.
Blackwater St. SE22 CA46 77
Blackwell Av., Guil. AO70 118
Blackwell Clo. E5 CC35 48
Clapton Pk. Est.
Blackwell Clo., Har. BG29 36
Blackwell Dr., Wat. BD25 27
Blackwell Gdns., Edg. BM27 37
Blackwell Hall La., Chesh. AQ21 25
Blackwell Rd., Kings L. AZ18 17
Blackwell St. SW9 BY43 66
Brixton Rd.
Blackwood Clo., Wey. AX59 92
Blackwood St. SE17 BZ42 4
Blackwood St. SE17 BZ42 67
Blade Ms. SW15 BR45 65
Deodar Rd.
Blades Clo., Lthd. BK63 102
Bladindon Dr., Bex. CP47 79
Bladon Clo., Guil. AT70 118
Bladon Gdns., Har. BF32 45
Blagdens Clo. N14 BW27 38
Blagdens La. N14 BW27 38
Blagdon Rd. SE13 CE46 77
Blagdon Rd., N.Mal. BO52 85
Blagdon Wk., Tedd. BK50 74
Blagrove Rd. W10 BR39 55
Blair Av. NW9 BO33 46
Blair Av., Esher BG55 84
Blair Clo. N1 BZ36 57
Blair Clo., Hem.H. AZ10 8
Braemar Turn
Blair Clo., Sid. CN46 78
Boundary Rd.
Blair Ct., Beck. CE51 87
The Knoll
Blair Dr., Sev. CU65 107
Blair St. E14 CF39 57
Blairderry Rd. SW2 BX48 76
Blairhead Dr., Wat. BC27 35
Blake Av., Bark. CN37 58
Blake Clo., Cars. BU54 86
Blake Clo., Rain. CT37 59
Blake Clo., St.Alb. BJ15 9
Blake Clo., Well. CN44 68
Blake Gdns. SW6 BS44 66
Blake Gdns., Dart. CW45 70
Blake Hall Cres. E11 CH33 49
Blake Hall Rd. E11 CH33 49
Blake Hall Rd., Ong. CU17 23
Blake Rd. E16 CG38 58
Blake Rd. N11 BW29 38
Blake Rd., Croy. CA55 87
Blake Rd., Mitch. BU52 86
Blake Way, Til. DH44 71
Coleridge Rd.
Blakeden Dr., Esher BH57 93
Blakehall Rd., Cars. BU57 95
Blakeley Bldgs. SE10 CF41 67
Blakeley Cotts. SE10 CF41 67
Blakemere Rd., Welw.G.C. BQ7 5
Blakemore Rd. SW16 BX48 76
Blakemore Rd., Th.Hth. BX53 86
Blakemore Way, Belv. CQ41 69
Halifield Dr.
Blakeney Av., Beck. CD51 87
Blakeney Clo. E8 CB35 48
Foxley Clo.
Blakeney Clo. N20 BT26 38
Blakeney Clo. NW1 BW37 1
Rossendale Way
Blakeney Clo., Epsom BN59 94
Blakeney Rd., Beck. CD50 77
Blakenham Rd. SW17 BU49 76
Blaker Ct. SE7 CJ43 68
Fairlawn
Blaker Rd. E15 CF37 57
Blaker Rd. SE15 CA43 67
Blakes Av., N.Mal. BO53 85
Blakes Grn., W.Wick. CF54 87
Blakes La., Guil. AY69 110
Blakes La., N.Mal. BO53 85
Blakes Ter., N.Mal. BP53 85
Blakes Way, Til. DH44 71
Coleridge Rd.
Blakesley Av. W5 BK39 54
Blakesware Gdns. N9 BZ26 39
Blakewood Clo., Felt. BD49 74
Blanch Clo. SE15 CC43 67
Clifton Way
Blanchard Clo. SE9 CK48 78
Shootery Clo.
Blanchard Way E8 CB36 57
Lansdowne Dr.
Blanchards Hill, Guil. AS67 109
Blanche La., Pot.B. BO20 19
Blanche St. E16 CG38 58
Blanchedowne SE5 BZ45 67
Blanchland Rd., Mord. BS53 86
Blanchmans Rd., Warl. CD63 105
Bland St. SE9 CJ45 68
Blandfield Rd. SW12 BV46 76
Blandford Av., Beck. CD51 87
Blandford Av., Twick. BF47 74
Blandford Clo. N2 BT32 47
Blandford Clo., Croy. BX55 86
Wandle Rd.
Blandford Clo., Wok. AT62 100
Blandford Clo., Rom. CR31 50
Blandford Clo., Slou. AR41 62
Blandford Rd. N.
Blandford Cres. E4 CF26 39
Blandford Ct., Slou. AR41 62
Blandford Rd. S.
Blandford Rd. N., Slou. AR41 62
Blandford Rd. S., Slou. AR41 62
Blandford Rd. W4 BO41 65
Blandford Rd. W5 BK41 64
Blandford Rd., Beck. CC51 87
Blandford Rd., St.Alb. BJ13 9
Blandford Rd., Sthl. BF42 64
Blandford Rd., Tedd. BG49 74
Blandford Sq. NW1 BU38 1
Blandford Sq. NW1 BU38 56
Blandford St. W1 BU39 1
Blandford St. W1 BU39 56
Blandford Waye, Hayes BD39 54
Blaney Cres. E6 CL38 58
Blanford Rd., Reig. BT71 121
Blanmerle Rd. SE9 CL47 78
Blann Clo. SE9 CJ46 78
Middle Pk. Av.
Blantyre St. SW10 BT43 66
Blantyre Wk. SW10 BT43 66
Worlds End
Blashford St. SE13 CF47 77
Blasker Wk. E14 CE42 67
Rainbow Av.
Blawith Rd., Har. BH31 45
Blaydon Clo. N17 CB29 39
Blaydon Clo., Ruis. BB33 44
Blays Clo. Egh. AR50 72
Blays La.
Blays La., Egh. AQ50 72
Bleak Hill La. SE18 CN43 68
Blean Gro. SE20 CC50 77
Bleasdale Av., Grnf. BH37 54
Blechynden St. W10 BQ40 55
Bramley Rd.
Bleddyn Clo., Bex. CP46 79
Bledlow Clo. SE28 CP40 59
Bledlow Ri., Grnf. BG37 54
Blegborough Rd. SW16 BW49 76
Blencarn Clo., Wok. AP61 100
Blendon Dr., Bex. CP46 79
Blendon Path, Brom. CG50 78
Hope Pk.
Blendon Rd., Bex. CP46 79
Blendon Row SE17 BZ42 4
Blendon Row SE17 BZ42 67
Blendon Ter. SE18 CM42 68
Blendworth Way SE15 CA43 67
Hordle Prom. N.
Blenheim Av., Ilf. CL32 49
Blenheim Clo. N21 BZ26 39
Blenheim Clo. SW20 BQ52 85
Blenheim Clo., Dart. CV46 80
Blenheim Clo., Grnf. BG37 54
Blenheim Clo., Rom. CS31 50
Blenheim Clo., Slou. AS40 52
Pickford Dr.
Blenheim Clo., Upmin. CZ33 51
Blenheim Clo., Wall. BW57 95
Blenheim Clo., Wat. BD26 36
Blenheim Clo., Wey. AV60 91
Madeira Rd.
Blenheim Cres. W11 BR40 55
Blenheim Cres., Ruis. BA34 44
Blenheim Cres., S.Croy. BZ57 96
Blenheim Ct. N19 BX34 47
Blenheim Ct., Sid. CM48 78
Blenheim Dr., Well. CN44 68
Blenheim Gdns. NW2 BQ35 46
Blenheim Gdns. SW2 BX46 76
Blenheim Gdns., Kings.T. BM50 75
Blenheim Gdns., S.Croy. CB59 96
Blenheim Gdns., S.Ock. CX40 60
Blenheim Gdns., Wall. BW57 95
Blenheim Gdns., Wem. BL34 46
Blenheim Gro. SE15 CA44 67
Blenheim Pass. NW8 BT37 56
Blenheim Pk. Rd., S.Croy. BZ58 96
Blenheim Pl. NW8 BT37 1
Blenheim Rd. E15 CG35 49
Blenheim Rd. E17 CC31 48
Blenheim Rd. E6 CJ38 58
Blenheim Rd. NW8 BT37 1
Blenheim Rd. NW8 BT37 56
Blenheim Rd. SE20 CC50 77
Blenheim Rd. SW20 BQ52 85
Blenheim Rd. W4 BO41 65
Blenheim Rd., Barn. BQ24 28
Blenheim Rd., Brom. CK52 88
Blenheim Rd., Brwd. DA25 33
Blenheim Rd., Dart. CV46 80
Blenheim Rd., Epsom BN59 94
Blenheim Rd., Har. BF32 45
Blenheim Rd., Nthlt. BF36 54
Blenheim Rd., Orp. CP55 89
Blenheim Rd., Sid. CP47 79
Blenheim Rd., Slou. AR42 62
Blenheim Rd., St.Alb. BH13 9
Blenheim Rd., Sutt. BS55 86
Blenheim St. W1 BV39 1
Blenheim St. W1 BV39 56
Blenheim Ter. NW8 BT37 1
Blenheim Ter. NW8 BT37 56
Blenheim Way, Epp. CR17 23
Blenkarne Rd. SW11 BU46 76
Blenkin Clo., St.Alb. BG11 9
Bleriot Rd., Houns. BD43 64
Blessbury Rd., Edg. BM30 37
Blessington Clo. SE13 CF45 67
Blessington Rd. SE13 CF45 67
Bletchingley Clo., Th.Hth. BY52 86
Nutfield Rd.
Bletchingley Clo., Red. BW68 113
Bletchingley Rd., South Merstham BW68 113
Bletchingley Rd., Gdse. CB69 114
Bletchingley Rd., Red. Nutfield BY70 121
Bletchley Ct. N1 BZ37 2
Bletchley Ct. N1 BZ37 57
Bletchley St. N1 BZ37 2
Bletchley St. N1 BZ37 57
Bletchmore Clo., Hayes BA42 63
Bletsoe Wk. N1 BZ37 57
Forston St.
Blewett St. SE17 BZ42 67
Sandford Row
Bligh St., Grav. DG46 81
Stuart Rd.
Blighs Rd., Sev. CU66 116
London Rd.
Blinco La., Slou. AS39 52
Blincoe Clo. SW19 BQ48 75
Thursley Gdns.
Blind La., Bans. BU61 104
Blind La., Bet. BN72 120
Blind La., Loug. CG23 31
Blind La., Maid. AG43 61
Blind La., St.Alb. BL17 19
Blind La., Wal.Abb. CJ20 22
Blindmans La., Chsnt. CC18 21
Bliss Cres. SE13 CE44 67
Blissett St. SE10 CF44 67
Blisworth Clo., Hayes BE38 54
Braunston Dr.
Blithbury Rd., Dag. CO36 59
Blithdale Rd. SE2 CO42 69
Blithfield St. W8 BS41 66
Stratford Rd.
Blockhouse Rd., Grays DE43 71
Blockley Rd., Wem. BJ34 45
Bloemfontein Av. W12 BP40 55
Bloemfontein Rd. W12 BP40 55
Blomfield Rd. W9 BS39 1
Blomfield Rd. W9 BS39 56
Blomfield St. EC2 BZ39 2
Blomfield St. EC2 BZ39 57
Blomfield Vill. W2 BS39 1
Blomfield Vill. W2 BS39 56
Blomville Rd., Dag. CQ34 50
Blondel St. SW11 BV44 66
Blondell Clo., West Dr. AX43 63
Blondin Av. W5 BK42 64
Blondin St. E3 CE37 57
Bloom Gro. SE27 BY48 76
Bloom Pk. Rd. SW6 BR43 65
Bloomburg St. SW1 BW42 66
Vincent Sq.
Bloomfield Cres., Ilf. CL32 49
Bloomfield Rd. N6 BV32 47
Bloomfield Rd. SE18 CL43 68
Bloomfield Rd., Kings.T. BL52 85
Bloomfield Rd., Brom. CJ53 88
Bloomfield Ter. SW1 BV42 3
Bloomfield Ter. SW1 BV42 66

Bloomfield Ter., West. CN66 115
Bloomhall Rd. SE19 BZ49 77
Bloomsbury Clo. W5 BL40 55
Bloomsbury Clo., Epsom BN58 94
Bloomsbury Ct., Pnr. BE31 45
Bloomsbury Pl. SW18 BT46 76
Fullerton Rd.
Bloomsbury Pl. WC1 BX39 2
Bloomsbury Pl. WC1 BX39 56
Southampton Row
Bloomsbury Sq. WC1 BX39 2
Bloomsbury Sq. WC1 BX39 56
Bloomsbury St. SW1 BW42 3
Bloomsbury St. WC1 BW39 1
Bloomsbury St. WC1 BW39 56
Bloomsbury Way WC1 BX39 2
Bloomsbury Way WC1 BX39 56
Blore Clo. SW8 BW44 66
Thessaly Rd.
Blossom Clo. W5 BL41 65
Blossom Clo., Croy. CA56 96
Blossom Clo., Dag. CQ37 59
Burdetts Rd.
Blossom La., Enf. BZ23 30
Blossom St. E1 CA38 2
Blossom St. E1 CA38 57
Blossom Way, Uxb. AY36 53
Blossom Way, West Dr. AZ42 63
Blossom Waye, Houns. BE43 64
Blount St. E14 CD39 57
Bloxam Gdns. SE9 CK46 78
Bloxhall Rd. E10 CD33 48
Bloxham Cres., Hmptn. BE50 74
Bloxworth Clo., Wall. BW55 86
Blucher Rd. SE5 BZ43 67
Comber Gro.
Blue Anchor All., Rich. BL45 65
Kew Rd.
Blue Anchor La. SE16 CB42 67
Blue Anchor La., Til. DH42 71
Blue Anchor Yd. E1 CA40 57
Blue Anchor Yd. E1 CB40 4
Blue Ball La., Egh. AS49 72
Blue Ball Yd. SW1 BW40 3
Blue Ball Yd. SW1 BW40 56
St. James St.
Blue Barn La., Wey. AZ59 92
Blue Cedars, Bans. BR60 94
Bluebell Clo. SE26 CA49 77
Bluebell Clo., Hem.H. AV14 7
Sundew Rd.
Bluebell Clo., Orp. CL55 88
Bluebell Ct., Wok. AR63 100
Blueberry Clo., St.Alb. BG11 9
New Greens Av.
Blueberry Gdns., Couls. BX61 104
Blueberry La., Sev. CP61 107
Bluebridge Av., Hat. BR17 19
Bluebridge Rd., Hat. BR17 19
Bluefield Clo., Hmptn. BF49 74
Bluehouse Hill, St.Alb. BF14 9
Bluehouse La., Oxt. CG67 115
Bluehouse Rd. E4 CG27 40
Bluemans End, Epp. CS15 14
Bluemans, Epp. CS15 14
Bluett Rd., St.Alb. BK17 18
Blundell Clo., St.Alb. BG11 9
Blundell La., Cob. BE61 102
Blundell Rd., Edg. BN30 37
Blundell St. N7 BX36 56
Blunden Clo., Dag. CP33 50
Blunesfield, Pot.B. BT19 20
Blunt Rd., S.Croy. BZ56 96
Blunts Av., West Dr. AZ44 63
Blunts La., St.Alb. BD16 18
Blunts Rd. SE9 CL46 78
Blurton Rd. E5 CC35 48
Blyth Clo. E14 CF42 67
Saunders Ness Rd.
Blyth Clo., B.Wd. BL23 28
Blyth Clo., Twick. BH47 74
Grimwood Rd.
Blyth Rd. E17 CD33 48
Blyth Rd. SE28 CP40 59
Blyth Rd., Brom. CG51 88
Blyth Rd., Hayes BB41 63
Blyth Wk., Upmin. CZ32 51
Blythe Clo. SE6 CD47 77
Blythe Clo., Iver AV39 52
Grange Way
Blythe Clo., Twick. BH47 74
Grimwood Rd.
Blythe Hill La. SE6 CD47 77
Blythe Hill SE6 CD47 77
Blythe Hill, Orp. CN51 88
Blythe Rd. W14 BR41 65
Blythe Rd., Hodd. CF13 12
Blythe St. E2 CB38 57
Blythe Vale SE6 CD47 77
Blythswood Rd., Ilf. CO33 50
Blythway, Welw.G.C. BR 6 5
Blythwood Rd. N4 BX33 47
Blythwood Rd., Pnr. BD30 36
Boades Ms. NW3 BT35 47
New End
Boadicea St. N1 BX37 2
Boadicea St. N1 BX37 56
Boakes Meadow, Sev. CT59 98
Boar Clo., Chig. CO28 41
Board School Rd., Wok. AS61 100
Boardman Av. E4 CE25 30
Boars Rd., Harl. CR11 14
Boathouse Wk. SE15 CA43 67
Bob Anker Clo. E13 CH38 58
Chesterton Rd.
Bob Marley Way SE24 BY45 66
Marcus Garvey Way
Bobbin Clo. SW4 BW45 66
Bobs La., Rom. CT30 41
Bocketts La., Lthd. BH65 102
Bockhampton Rd., Kings.T. BL50 75
Bocking St. E8 CB37 57
Boddicott Clo. SW19 BR48 75
Boddys Bri. SE1 BY40 56
Bodell Clo., Grays DD41 71
Bodiam Clo., Enf. BZ23 30
Bodiam Rd. SW16 BW50 76
Bodle Av., Swans. DC47 81
Bodley Clo., N.Mal. BO53 85
Bodley Rd., N.Mal. BN53 85
Bodley St. SE17 BZ42 67
Wansey St.
Bodmin Clo., Har. BE34 45
Bodmin Rd., Mord. BS53 86
Bodmin St. SW18 BS47 76
Bodnant Gdns. SW20 BP52 85
Bodney Rd. E8 CB35 48
Bodwell Clo., Hem.H. AW13 8
Bodwell Clo., Welw.G.C. BR 8 5
Boeing Way, Sthl. BC41 63
Bogey La., Orp. CK57 97
Bognor Gdns., Wat. BD28 36
Bognor Rd., Well. CP44 69
Bohemia Clo., Hem.H. AY13 8
Bohemia Pl. E8 CB36 57
Mare St.
Bohun Gro., Barn. BU25 29
Boileau Rd. SW13 BP43 65
Boileau Rd. W5 BL39 55
Bois Hall Rd., Wey. AX56 92
Bois Hill, Chesh. AP20 16
Bois La., Amer. AO21 25
Bois Moor Rd., Chesh. AO20 16
Bolden St. SE8 CE44 67
Boldero Pl. NW8 BU38 1
Gateforth St.
Bolderwood Way, W.Wick. CE55 87
Boldmere Rd., Pnr. BD33 45
Boleyn Av., Enf. CB23 30
Boleyn Av., Epsom BP58 94
Boleyn Clo., Hem.H. BA11 8
Boleyn Clo., Stai. AV49 72
Boleyn Dr., E.Mol. BE52 84
Boleyn Dr., Ruis. BD34 45
Boleyn Dr., Sev. CW62 108
Boleyn Dr., St.Alb. BG14 9
Boleyn Gdns., Brwd. DD27 122
Boleyn Gdns., Dag. CS36 59
Boleyn Gdns., W.Wick. CE55 87
Boleyn Gro., W.Wick. CE55 87
Boleyn Rd. E6 CJ37 58
Boleyn Rd. E7 CH36 58
Boleyn Rd. N16 CA35 48
Boleyn Way, Barn. BT24 29
Boleyn Way, Ilf. CM29 40
Boleyn Wk., Lthd. BH63 102
Bolina Rd. SE16 CC42 67
Bolingbroke Gro. SW11 BU46 76
Bolingbroke Rd. W14 BQ41 65
Bolingbroke Way, Hayes BA40 53
Bolingbroke Wk. SW11 BU44 66
Bollo Bridge Rd. W3 BM41 65
Bollo La. W3 BM41 65
Bollo La. W4 BM41 65
Bolney St. SW8 BX43 66
Bolney Way, Felt. BE48 74
Bolsover Gro., Red. BX68 113
Bolsover St. W1 BV38 1
Bolsover St. W1 BV38 56
Bolstead La., Mitch. BV51 86
Bolstead Pl., Mitch. BV51 86
Bolster Gro. N22 BW29 38
Bolt Cellar La., Epp. CN18 22
Bolt Ct. EC4 BY39 2
Bolt Ct. EC4 BY39 56
Gough Sq.
Bolters La., Bans. BR60 94
Boltmore Clo. NW4 BQ31 46
Bolton Av., Wind. AO45 61
Bolton Clo. SE20 CB51 87
Selby Rd.
Bolton Clo., Chess. BL57 94
Bolton Cres. SE5 BY43 66
Bolton Cres., Wind. AO45 61
Bolton Gdns. Ms. SW10 BS42 3
Bolton Gdns. Ms. SW10 BT42 66
Bolton Gdns. NW10 BQ37 55
Bolton Gdns. SW5 BS42 3
Bolton Gdns. SW5 BS42 66
Bolton Gdns., Brom. CG50 78
Bolton Gdns., Tedd. BJ50 74
Bolton Rd. E15 CG36 58
Bolton Rd. N18 CA28 39
Bolton Rd. NW10 BO37 55
Bolton Rd. NW8 BS37 1
Bolton Rd. NW8 BS37 56
Bolton Rd. W4 BN43 65
Bolton Rd., Chess. BK57 93
Bolton Rd., Har. BG31 45
Bolton Rd., Wind. AO45 61
Bolton St. W1 BV40 3
Bolton St. W1 BV40 56
Bolton Wk. N7 BX34 47
Durham Rd.
Boltons Clo., Wok. AW61 101
Boltons La., Hayes AZ44 63
Boltons La., Wok. AW61 101
Boltons, The SW10 BT42 3
Boltons, The SW10 BT42 66
Boltons, The, Wem. BH35 45
Bombay St. SE16 CB42 67
Bombers La., West. CM63 106
Bomer Clo., West Dr. AZ43 63
Bomore Rd. W11 BQ40 55
Bon Marche Ter. SE27 CA49 77
Gipsy Rd.
Bonamy Est. E. SE16 CB42 67
Bonamy Est. W. SE16 CB42 67
Bonar Pl., Chis. CK50 78
Bonar Rd. SE15 CB43 67
Bonavere Ct., Grav. DJ49 81
Bonchester Clo., Chis. CL51 88
Bonchurch Clo., Sutt. BS57 95
Ventnor Rd.
Bonchurch Rd. W10 BR39 55
Bonchurch Rd. W13 BJ40 54
Bond Clo., Sev. CP61 107
Bond Ct. EC3 BZ39 57
Walbrook
Bond Gdns., Wall. BW56 95
Bond Rd., Mitch. BU51 86
Bond Rd., Surb. BL55 85
Bond Rd., Warl. CC62 105
Bond St. E15 CG35 49
Bond St. W1 BV39 56
Bond St. W4 BO42 65
Chiswick Common Rd.
Bond St. W5 BK40 54
Bond St., Egh. AQ50 72
Bond St., Grays DE43 71
Bondfield Rd. E6 CK39 58
Bondfield Wk., Dart. CW45 70
Bonding Yard Wk. SE16 CD41 67
Finland St.
Bondway SW8 BX43 66
Bonehurst Rd., Red. BV74 121
Boneta Rd. SE18 CK41 68
Bonfield Av., Hayes BC38 53
Bonfield Rd. SE13 CF45 67
Bonham Gdns., Dag. CP34 50
Bonham Rd. SW2 BX46 76
Bonham Rd., Dag. CP34 50
Bonheur Rd. W4 BN41 65
Bonhill St. EC2 BZ38 2
Bonhill St. EC2 BZ38 57
Boniface Gdns., Har. BF29 36
Boniface Rd., Uxb. AZ34 44
Boniface Wk., Har. BF29 36
Bonks Hill, Saw. CP 6 6
Bonner Hill Rd., Kings.T. BL51 85
Bonner Rd. E2 CC37 57
Bonner St. E2 CC37 57
Bonners Clo., Wok. AS64 100
Bonnersfield Clo., Har. BH32 45
Bonnersfield La., Har. BH32 45
Bonneville Gdns. SW4 BW46 76
Bonney Gro., Chsnt. CB18 21
Bonney Way, Swan. CT51 89
Bonnington Rd., Horn. CV35 51
Bonnington Sq. SW8 BX43 66
Bonningtons, Brwd. DD27 122
Bonny St. NW1 BW36 1
Bonny St. NW1 BW36 56
Bonnys Rd., Reig. BQ71 120
Bonser Rd., Twick. BH48 74
Bonsey Clo., Wok. AS64 100
Bonsey La., Wok. AS64 100
Bonseys La., Wok. AS58 91
Bonseys Yd., Uxb. AX36 53
George Sq.
Bonsor Dr., Tad. BR64 103
Bonsor St. SE5 CA43 67
Bonville Rd., Brom. CG49 78
Book Ms. WC2 BW39 1
Flitcroft St.
Booker Rd. N18 CB28 39
Bookham Ct., Lthd. BE65 102
Church Rd.
Bookham Rd., Cob.. BD63 102
Boone St. SE13 CG45 68
Boones Rd. SE13 CG45 68
Boord St. SE10 CG41 68
Boot Alley, St.Alb. BG13 9
Chequer St.
Boot St. N1 CA38 2
Boot St. N1 CA38 57
Booth Clo. SE28 CO40 59
Booth Dr., Stai. AX50 73
Booth Rd. NW9 BN30 37
Booth Rd., Croy. BY55 86
Bourne St.
Boothby Rd. N19 BW34 47
Booths Clo., Hat. BQ15 10
Booths Pl. W1 BW39 1
Booths Pl. W1 BW39 56
Wells St.
Bordars Rd. W7 BH39 54
Bordars Wk. W7 BH39 54
Borden Av., Enf. BZ25 30
Border Cres. SE26 CB49 77
Border Gdns., Croy. CE56 96
Border Rd. SE26 CB49 77
Bordergate Est., Mitch. BU51 86
Bordergate, Mitch. BU51 86
Borders La., Loug. CL24 31
Borderside, Slou. AQ39 52
Bordesley Rd., Mord. BS53 86
Bordon Wk. SW15 BP47 75
Boreas Wk. N1 BY37 56
Nelson Pl.
Boreham Av. E16 CH39 58
Boreham Clo. E11 CF33 48
Hainault Rd.
Boreham Holt, B.Wd. BL24 28
Boreham Rd. N22 BZ30 39
Boreham St. E2 CA38 2
Borers Pass E1 CA39 2
Borers Pass. E1 CA39 57
Borgard Rd. SE18 CK42 68
Borkwood Pk., Orp. CN56 97
Borkwood Way, Orp. CM56 97
Borland Rd. SE15 CC46 77
Borland Rd., Tedd. BJ50 74
Borneo St. SW15 BQ45 65
Borough Clo. SW8 BX43 66
Kenchester Clo.
Borough Green Rd., Sev. DB64 108
Borough High St. SE1 BZ41 4
Borough High St. SE1 BZ41 67
Borough Hill, Croy. BY55 86
Borough Rd. SE1 BY41 4
Borough Rd. SE1 BY41 66
Borough Rd., Islw. BH44 64
Borough Rd., Kings.T. BM51 85
Borough Rd., Mitch. BU51 86
Borough Rd., West. CJ64 106
Borough Sq. SE1 BZ41 4
Borough Sq. SE1 BZ41 67
Great Suffolk St.
Borough Way, Pot.B. BR19 19
Borough, The, Bet. BM71 120
Borrett Clo. SE17 BZ42 4
Borrett Clo. SE17 BZ42 67
Borrodaile Rd. SW18 BS46 76
Borrowdale Av., Har. BJ30 36
Borrowdale Clo., S.Croy. CA60 96
Borrowdale Clo., Egh. AT50 72
Derwent Rd.
Borrowdale Clo., Ilf. CK31 49
Borrowdale Dr., S.Croy. CA59 96
Borrowdale, Hem.H. AY12 8
Lonsdale
Borthwick Ms. E15 CG35 49
Borthwick Rd.
Borthwick Rd. E15 CG35 49
Borthwick Rd. NW9 BO32 46
Borthwick St. SE8 CE42 67
Borwick Av. E17 CD31 48
Bosanquet Clo., Uxb. AX38 53
Bosanquet Rd., Hodd. CF11 12
Bosbury Rd. SE6 CF48 77
Boscastle Rd. NW5 BV34 47
Boscobel Pl. SW1 BV42 3
Boscobel Pl. SW1 BV42 66
Boscobel St. NW8 BT38 1
Boscobel St. NW8 BT38 56
Boscombe Av. E10 CF33 48
Boscombe Av., Grays DE42 71
Boscombe Av., Horn. CV33 51
Boscombe Clo. E5 CD35 48
Boscombe Clo., Egh. AU51 82
Boscombe Gdns., SW16 BX50 76
Boscombe Rd. SW17 BV50 76
Boscombe Rd. SW19 BS51 86
Boscombe Rd. W12 BP40 55
Boscombe Rd., Wor.Pk. BQ54 85
Bosgrove E4 CF26 39
Boss Rd. E9 CE36 57
Rothbury Rd.
Boss St. SE1 CA41 4
Boss St. SE1 CA41 67
Bostal Row, Bexh. CQ45 69
Bostall Hill Rd. SE2 CP43 69
Bostall Hill SE2 CO42 69
Bostall La. SE2 CO42 69
Bostall Manor Way SE2 CO42 69
Bostall Park Av., Bexh. CQ43 69
Bostall Rd., Orp. CO50 79
Boston Gdns. W4 BO43 65
Boston Gdns., Brent. BJ42 64
Boston Gro., Ruis. BA32 44
Boston Manor Rd., Brent. BJ42 64
Boston Park Rd., Brent. BK42 64
Boston Pl. NW1 BU38 1
Boston Pl. NW1 BU38 56
Boston Rd. E17 CE32 48
Boston Rd. E6 CK38 58
Boston Rd. W7 BH40 54
Boston Rd., Croy. BX53 86
Boston Rd., Edg. BN29 37
Boston Vale W7 BJ42 64
Bostonthorpe Rd. W7 BH41 64
Bosville Dr., Sev. CU65 107
Bosville Rd., Sev. CU65 107
Boswell Clo., Orp. CP54 89
Killewarren Way
Boswell Ct. WC1 BX39 2
Boswell Ct. WC1 BX39 56
Boswell Path, Hayes BB42 63
Boswell Rd., Th.Hth. BZ52 87
Boswell St. WC1 BX39 2
Boswell St. WC1 BX39 56
Boswick La., Berk. AO11 7
Bosworth Clo. E17 CD30 39
Bosworth Cres., Rom. CV29 42
Bosworth Rd. N11 BW29 38
Bosworth Rd. W10 BR38 55
Bosworth Rd., Barn. BS24 29
Bosworth Rd., Dag. CR35 50
Botany Bay La., Chis. CM51 88
Boteley Clo. E4 CF27 39
Boterys Cross, Red. BY70 121
Botha Rd. E13 CH39 58
Botham Clo., Edg. BM29 37
Pavilion Way
Bothwell Clo. E16 CG39 58
Bothwell Rd., Croy. CF58 96
Bothwell St. W6 BQ43 65
Delorme St.
Botley La., Chesh. AP18 16
Botley Rd., Hem.H. AZ11 8
Botolph Alley EC3 CA40 4
Botolph La.
Botolph La. EC3 BZ40 57
Botolph La. EC3 CA40 4
Botsford Rd. SW20 BR51 85
Botsom La., Sev. CY57 99
Bott Rd., Dart. CW49 80
Bottom House Farm La., Ch.St.G. AO27 34
Bottom La., Chesh. AP19 16
Bottom La., Rick. AW21 26
Bottrells La., Ch.St.G. AO27 34
Botts Ms. W2 BS39 56
Chepstow Rd.
Botwell Common Rd., Hayes BA40 53
Botwell Cres., Hayes BB39 53
Botwell La., Hayes BB40 53
Boucher Clo., Tedd. BH49 74
Boucher Dr., Grav. DF48 81
Bouchier Wk., Rain. CU36 59
Deere Av.
Boughton Av., Brom. CG54 88
Boughton Rd. SE28 CN41 68
Boulcott St. E1 CC39 57
Boulevard, The, Pnr. BE31 45
Boulevard, The, Wat. BA25 26
Boulmer Rd., Uxb. AX38 53
Boulogne Rd., Croy. BZ53 87
Boulter Gdns., Horn. CU36 59
Boulters Clo., Slou. AN41 61
Amerden Way
Boulthurst Way, Oxt. CH69 115
Boulton Rd., Dag. CQ34 50
Boultwood Rd. E6 CK39 58
Bounce Hill, Rom. CU23 32
Bounce, The, Hem.H. AX12 8
Bounces La. N9 CB27 39
Bounces Rd. N9 CB26 39
Boundaries Rd. SW12 BU48 76
Boundaries Rd., Felt. BD47 74
Boundary Clo. SE20 CB51 87
Haysleigh Gdns.
Boundary Clo., Ilf. CM35 49
Loxford La.
Boundary Clo., Kings.T. BM52 85
Boundary Clo., Sthl. BF42 64
Boundary Ct., Welw.G.C. BR10 5
Hollybush La.
Boundary Dr., Brwd. DF26 122
Boundary La. E13 CJ38 58
Boundary La. SE17 BZ43 67
Camberwell Rd.
Boundary La., Welw.G.C. BR 9 5
Boundary Ms. NW8 BS37 1
Boundary Rd.
Boundary Pass. E2 CA38 2
Boundary St.
Boundary Rd. E13 CJ37 58
Boundary Rd. E17 CD33 48
Boundary Rd. N22 BY31 47
Boundary Rd. N9 CC25 30
Boundary Rd. NW8 BS37 1
Boundary Rd. NW8 BS37 56
Boundary Rd. S., Wall. BV58 95
Boundary Rd. SW19 BT50 76
Boundary Rd., Ashf. AX49 73
Boundary Rd., Bark. CM37 58
Boundary Rd., Ger.Cr. AR29 34
Boundary Rd., Pnr. BD33 45
Boundary Rd., Rom. CU32 50
Boundary Rd., Sid. CN46 78
Boundary Rd., St.Alb. BH12 9
Boundary Rd., Upmin. CX34 51
Boundary Rd., Wall. BV57 95
Boundary Rd., Wok. AT61 100
Boundary Row SE1 BY41 4
Boundary Row SE1 BY41 66
Boundary St. E2 CA38 2
Boundary St. E2 CA38 57
Boundary St., Erith CT43 69
Boundary Way, Croy. CE56 96
Boundary Way, Wat. BD19 18
Boundary Yd., Wok. AT61 100
Boundary Rd.
Boundfield Rd. SE6 CG48 78
Bounds Green Rd. N11 BW29 38
Bounds Green Rd. N22 BX29 38
Bourchier Clo., Sev. CU66 116
Bourchier St. W1 BW40 3
Bourchier St. W1 BW40 56
Wardour St.
Bourdon Pl. W1 BV40 3
Bourdon Pl. W1 BV40 56
Bourdon St.
Bourdon Rd. SE20 CC51 87
Bourdon St. W1 BV40 3
Bourdon St. W1 BV40 56
Bourke Clo. NW10 BO36 55
Mayo Rd.
Bourke Clo. SW4 BX46 76
Bourke Hill, Couls. BU62 104
Bourlet Clo. W1 BW39 1
Bourlet Clo. W1 BW39 56
Riding House St.
Bourn Av. N15 BZ31 48
Bourn Av., Barn. BT25 29
Bournbrook Rd. SE3 CJ45 68
Bourne Av. N14 BX27 38
Bourne Av., Cher. AW52 83
Eastern Av.
Bourne Av., Hayes BA41 63
Bourne Av., Ruis. BD35 45
Bourne Av., Uxb. AZ38 53
Bourne Av., Wind. AO45 61
Bourne Clo., Brox. CD13 12
Bourne Cres., Wey. AW60 92
Bourne Ct., Ruis. BC35 44
Bourne Dr., Mitch. BT51 86
Bourne End La., Berk. AT15 7
Bourne End Rd., Nthwd. BB28 35
Bourne End, Horn. CX33 51
Bourne Est. EC1 BY39 2
Bourne Est. EC1 BY39 56
Bourne Gdns. E4 CE28 39
Bourne Gro., Ash. BK63 102
Bourne Hill Clo. N13 BX27 38
Bourne Hill N13 BX27 38
Bourne La., Cat. BZ64 106
Bourne La., Sev. DC66 117
Bourne Mead, Bex. CS46 79
Bourne Meadow, Cher. AT52 82
Bourne Park Clo., Ken. CA61 105
Bourne Pl. W4 BN42 65
Dukes Av.
Bourne Rd. E7 CG34 49
Bourne Rd. N8 BX32 47
Bourne Rd., Berk. AP12 7
Bourne Rd., Bex. CR47 79
Bourne Rd., Brom. CJ52 88
Bourne Rd., Bush. BF25 27
Bourne Rd., Grav. DJ48 81
Bourne Rd., Red. BW68 113
Bourne Rd., Slou. AO41 61
Bourne Rd., Vir.W. AR53 82
Bourne St. SW1 BV42 3
Bourne St. SW1 BV42 66
Bourne St., Croy. BY55 86
Bourne Ter. W2 BS39 1
Bourne Ter. W2 BS39 56
Bourne Vale, Brom. CG54 88
Bourne Vw., Grnf. BH36 54
Bourne Vw., Ken. BZ61 105
Bourne Way, Brom. CG55 88
Bourne Way, Epsom BN56 94
Bourne Way, Sutt. BR56 94
Bourne Way, Swan. CS52 89
Bourne Way, Wey. AX56 92
Bourne Way, Wok. AR54 100
Bourne, The N14 BW26 38
Bourne, The, Hem.H. AT17 16
Bournebridge Clo., Brwd. DF26 122
Bournebridge La., Rom. CQ26 41
Bournefield Rd., Whyt. CA62 105
Bournehall Av., Bush. BF25 27
Bournehall La., Bush. BF25 27
Bournehall Rd., Bush. BF25 27
Bournemead Av., Nthlt. BC37 53
Bournemead Clo., Nthlt. BC37 53
Bournemead Way, Nthlt. BC37 53

Bournemouth Rd. SE15 CB44 67
Bournemouth Rd. SW19 BS51 86
Bourneside Cres. N14 BW26 38
High St.
Bourneside Gdns. SE6 CF49 77
Bourneside Rd., Wey. AX56 92
Bourneside, Vir.W. AQ54 82
Bournevale Rd. SW16 BX49 76
Bournewood Rd. SE18 CO43 69
Bournewood Rd., Orp. CO54 89
Bournville Rd. SE6 CE47 77
Bournwell Clo., Barn. BU23 29
Bourton Clo., Hayes BC40 53
Avondale Dr.
Bousfield Rd. SE14 CC44 67
Bousley Ri., Cher. AU57 91
Boutflower Rd. SW11 BU45 66
Bouverie Gdns., Har. BK32 45
Bouverie Ms. N16 CA34 48
Bouverie Rd.
Bouverie Pl. W2 BT39 1
Bouverie Pl. W2 BT39 56
Bouverie Rd. N16 CA33 48
Bouverie Rd., Couls. BV62 104
Bouverie Rd., Har. BG32 45
Bouverie St. EC4 BY39 2
Bouverie St. EC4 BY39 56
Bouverie Way, Slou. AS42 62
Bouvier Rd., Enf. CC22 30
Bovay Pl. N7 BX35 47
Bovay St. N7 BX35 47
Boveney Clo., Slou. AN41 61
Amerden Way
Boveney New Rd., Eton AM42 61
Boveney Rd. SE23 CC47 77
Boveney Rd., Wind. AL42 61
Bovey Way, S.Ock. DA39 60
Bovill Rd. SE23 CC47 77
Bovingdon Av., Wem. BM36 55
Bovingdon Clo. N19 BW34 47
Bovingdon Cres., Wat. BD20 18
Bovingdon Green La., Hem.H. AS17 16
Bovingdon La. NW9 BO29 37
Bovingdon Rd. SW6 BS44 66
Bovingdon Sq., Mitch. BX52 86
Bow Arrow La., Dart. CX46 80
Bow Bridge Est. E3 CE38 57
Bow Churchyard EC4 BZ39 2
Cheapside
Bow Common La. E3 CD38 57
Bow Hay, Brwd. DD27 122
Bow La. EC4 BZ39 2
Bow La. EC4 BZ39 57
Bow La. N12 BT29 38
Bow La., Mord. BR53 85
Lower Morden La.
Bow Rd. E3 CD38 57
Bow Sprit, The, Cob. BD61 102
Bow St. E15 CG35 49
Bow St. WC2 BX39 2
Bow St. WC2 BX39 56
Bowater Clo. NW9 BN32 46
Bowater Clo. SW4 BX46 76
Loats Rd.
Bowater Pl. SE3 CH43 68
Bowater Rd. SE18 CJ41 68
Bowden Dr., Horn. CW33 51
Bowden St. SE11 BY42 4
Bowden St. SE11 BY42 66
Bowditch SE8 CD42 67
Bowdon Rd. E17 CE33 48
Bowen Dr. SE21 CA48 77
Bowen Rd., Har. BG33 45
Bowen St. E14 CE39 57
Bowens Wood, Croy. CD58 96
Bower Av. SE10 CG44 68
Bower Clo., Nthlt. BD37 54
Bower Clo., Rom. CS29 41
Bower Ct., Epp. CO19 23
Bower Ct., Wok. AT61 100
Princess Rd.
Bower Farm Rd., Hav. CS27 41
Bower Hill Clo., Red. BX72 121
Bower Hill, Epp. CO19 23
Bower La., Eyns. CX57 99
Bower Rd., Swan. CU50 79
Bower St. E1 CC39 57
Stepney Causeway
Bower Ter., Epp. CO19 23
Bower Vale, Epp. CO19 23
Bowerdean St. SW6 BS44 66
Bowerhill La., Red. BW71 121
Bowerman Av. SE14 CD43 67
Bowerman Rd., Grays DG42 71
Bowers Av., Grav. DF49 81
Mulberry Rd.
Bowers Clo., Guil. AT68 109
Cotts Wood Dr.
Bowers Farm Dr., Guil. AT68 109
Bowers La., Guil. AS68 109
Bowers Rd., Sev. CT59 98
Bowers Wk. E6 CK39 58
Northumberland Rd.
Bowes Clo., Sid. CO46 79
Bowes Dr., Ong. CW17 24
Bowes Rd. N11 BV28 38
Bowes Rd. N13 BV28 38
Bowes Rd. W3 BO40 55
Bowes Rd., Dag. CP35 50
Bowes Rd., Stai. AV50 72
Bowes Rd., Walt. BC55 83
Bowes-Lyon Clo., Wind. AO44 61
Ward Royal
Bowfell Rd. W6 BQ43 65
Bowford Av., Bexh. CQ44 69
Bowgate, St.Alb. BH13 9
Bowhay, Brwd. DD27 122
Bowhill Clo. SW9 BY43 66
Bowhill Ct. SW9 BY43 66
Bowie Clo. SW4 BW47 76
Plummer Rd.
Bowland Ct. E16 CG38 58
Beaconsfield Rd.
Bowland Rd. SW4 BW45 66
Bowland Rd., Wdf.Grn. CJ28 40
Bowland Yd. SW1 BU41 3
Kinnerton St.
Bowlers Orchard, Ch.St.G. AQ27 34
Bowles Grn., Enf. CB21 30
Bowles Rd. SE1 CB43 4
Bowles Rd. SE1 CB43 67
Bowley Clo. SE19 CA49 77
Bowley St. E14 CD40 57
Bowling Grn. Clo. SW15 BP47 75
Bowling Grn. Ct. N1 CA38 57
Bowling Grn. La. EC1 BY38 2
Bowling Grn. La. EC1 BY38 56
Bowling Grn. Pl. SE1 BZ41 4
Bowling Grn. Rd., Wok. AP58 91
Bowling Grn. Row SE18 CK42 68
Samuel St.
Bowling Grn. St. SE11 BY43 66
Bowling Grn. Wk. N1 CA38 2
Bowling Grn. Wk. N1 CA38 57
Bowls Clo., Stan. BJ28 36
Bowls, The, Chig. CN27 40
Bowman Av. E16 CG40 58
Bowman Ms. SW18 BR47 75
Standen Rd.
Bowmans Clo. W13 BJ40 54
Bowmans Clo., Pot.B. BT19 20
Bowmans Ct., Hem.H. AX12 8
Fletcher Way
Bowmans Grn., Wat. BE21 27
Bowmans Lea SE23 CC47 77
Dunoon Rd.
Bowmans Meadow, Wall. BV55 86
Bowmans Ms. E1 CB39 57
Hooper St.
Bowmans Ms. N7 BX34 47
Seven Sisters Rd.
Bowmans Pl. N7 BX34 47
Hercules St.
Bowmans Rd., Dart. CT47 79
Bowmead SE9 CK48 78
Bowmore Wk. NW1 BW36 56
Agar Gro.
Bown Clo., Til. DG45 71
Bowness Clo. E8 CA36 57
Rhodes Street Est.
Bowness Cres. SW15 BO49 75
Bowness Dr., Houns. BE45 64
Bowness Rd. SE6 CE47 77
Bowness Rd., Bexh. CR44 69
Bowness Way, Horn. CU35 50
Bowood Rd. SW11 BV45 66
Bowood Rd., Enf. CC23 30
Bowring Grn., Wat. BD28 36
Bowrons Av., Wem. BK36 54
Bowry Dr., Stai. AS46 72
Bowstridge La., Ch.St.G. AR27 34
Bowyer Clo. E6 CK39 58
Hallywell Cres.
Bowyer Cres., Uxb. AV32 43
Bowyer Pl. SE5 BZ43 67
Bowyer St. SE5 BZ43 67
Bowyers Clo., Ash. BL62 103
Bowyers, Hem.H. AX12 8
Bowzell Rd., Sev. CT70 116
Box La., Bark. CO37 59
Box La., Hem.H. AV15 7
Box La., Hodd. CD12 12
Box Ridge Av., Pur. BX59 95
Box Tree Clo., Chesh. AO20 16
Box Tree Wk., Orp. CP54 89
Boxall Rd. SE21 CA46 77
Boxall Rd., Dag. CQ35 50
Boxfield, Welw.G.C. BS 9 5
Boxford Clo., S.Croy. CC59 96
Boxgrove Av., Guil. AT69 118
Boxgrove La., Guil. AT70 118
Boxgrove Rd. SE2 CO41 69
Boxgrove Rd., Guil. AT70 118
Boxhill Rd., Dor. BL70 120
Boxhill Rd., Tad. BL69 120
Boxhill Way, Bet. BM72 120
Boxley Rd., Mord. BT52 86
Boxley St. E16 CH40 58
Boxmoor Rd., Har. BJ31 45
Boxmoor Rd., Rom. CS28 41
Boxted Clo., Buck.H. CK26 40
Boxted Rd., Hem.H. AV12 7
Boxtree La., Har. BG30 36
Boxtree Rd., Har. BG29 36
Boxwell Rd., Berk. AQ13 7
Boxwood Clo., West Dr. AY41 63
Boxwood Way, Warl. CC62 105
Boxworth Gro. N1 BX37 2
Boyard Rd. SE18 CL42 68
Boyce Clo., B.Wd. BL23 28
Boyce St. SE1 BX40 56
Mepham St.
Boyce Way E13 CH38 58
Boycroft Av. NW9 BN32 46
Boyd Av., Sthl. BE40 54
Boyd Clo., Kings.T. BM50 75
Crescent Rd.
Boyd Rd. SW19 BT50 76
Boyd St. E1 CB39 2
Boyd St. E1 CB39 57
Boydell Ct. NW8 BT37 56
Boyfield St. SE1 BY41 4
Boyfield St. SE1 BY41 66
Boyland Rd., Brom. CG49 78
Boyle Clo. W4 BN43 65
Burlington La.
Boyle Farm Rd., T.Ditt. BJ53 84
Boyle St. W1 BW40 56
Savile Row
Boyne Av. NW4 BQ31 46
Boyne Av., Stan. BJ29 36
Boyne Rd. SE13 CF45 67
Boyne Rd., Dag. CR34 50
Boyne Terrace Ms. W11 BR40 55
Boyseland Ct., Edg. BM27 37
Boyson Rd. SE17 BZ43 67
Boythorn Way SE16 CB42 67
Bonamy Estate E.
Boyton Clo. E1 CC38 57
Stayners Rd.
Boyton Clo. N8 BX31 47
Boyton Rd. N8 BX31 47
Brabant Ct. EC3 BZ40 57
Philpot La.
Brabant Rd. N22 BX30 38
Brabazon Av., Wall. BX57 95
Brabazon Rd., Houns. BD43 64
Brabazon Rd., Nthlt. BF37 54
Brabazon St. E14 CE39 57
Brabourn Gro. SE15 CC44 67
Brabourne Clo. SE19 CA49 77
Victoria Cres.
Brabourne Cres., Bexh. CQ43 69
Brabourne Ri., Beck. CF53 87
Bracewell Av., Grnf. BH35 45
Bracewell Rd. W10 BQ39 55
Bracewood Gdns., Croy. CA55 87
Bracey St. N4 BX33 47
Bracken Av. SW12 BV46 76
Bracken Av., Croy. CE55 87
Bracken Bridge Dr., Ruis. BD34 45
Bracken Clo. E6 CK39 58
Bracken Clo., Houns. BF47 74
Bracken Clo., Slou. AO35 43
Bracken Clo., Wok. AS62 100
Bracken Dene, Dart. CT49 79
Bracken Dr., Chig. CL29 40
Bracken End, Islw. BG46 74
Harvesters Clo.
Bracken Gdns. SW13 BP44 65
Bracken Hill Clo., Brom. CG51 88
Bracken Hill La., Brom. CG51 88
Bracken Hill, Cob. BF59 93
Bracken Hill, Ruis. BE35 45
Bracken Ms., Rom. CR32 50
Bracken Path, Epsom BM60 94
Bracken Way, Guil. AP69 118
Bracken Way, Wok. AP58 91
Bracken, The E4 CF26 30
Hortus Rd.
Brackenbury Gdns. W6 BP41 65
Brackenbury Rd. N2 BT31 47
Brackenbury Rd. W6 BP41 65
Brackendale Clo., Houns. BF44 64
Brackendale Ct., Beck. CE50 77
Brackendale Gdns., Upmin. CY35 51
Brackendale N21 BX26 38
Brackendale, Pot.B. BR20 19
Brackendene Clo., Wok. AT61 100
Brackendene, St.Alb. BE18 18
Brackenforde, Slou. AR41 62
Brackens Dr., Brwd. DB28 42
Brackens, The, Enf. CA26 39
Brackens, The, Orp. CO56 98
Brackenwood Rd., Wok. AO63 100
Brackenwood, Sun. BC51 83
Brackley Clo., Wall. BX57 95
Mollison Dr.
Brackley Rd. W4 BO42 65
Brackley Rd., Beck. CD50 77
Brackley Sq., Wdf.Grn. CJ29 40
Brackley St. EC1 BZ39 2
Brackley St. EC1 BZ39 57
Viscount St.
Brackley Ter. W4 BO42 65
Brackley, Wey. BA56 92
Bracklyn Ct. N1 BZ37 2
Bracklyn Ct. N1 BZ37 57
Bracklyn St. N1 BZ37 2
Bracknell Gate NW3 BS35 47
Bracknell Gdns. NW3 BS35 47
Bracknell Pl., Hem.H. AY11 8
Bracknell Way NW3 BS35 47
Brackwell Clo. N22 BY30 38
Bracondale Av., Grav. DF51 81
Bracondale Rd. SE2 CO42 69
Bracondale, Esher BG57 93
Brad St. SE1 BY40 4
Brad St. SE1 BY40 56
Bradbery, Rick. AU28 34
Bradbourne Park Rd., Sev. CU65 107
Bradbourne Rd., Bex. CR47 79
Bradbourne Rd., Grays DD43 71
Bradbourne Rd., Sev. CU64 107
Bradbourne St. SW6 BS44 66
Bradbourne Vale Rd., Sev. CT64 107
Bradbury Clo., Sthl. BE42 64
Blandford Rd.
Bradbury Gdns., Slou. AR35 43
Bradbury St. N16 CA35 48
Braddon Rd., Rich. BL45 65
Braddyll St. SE10 CG42 68
Braden St. W9 BS38 56
Bradenham Av., Well. CO45 69
Bradenham Rd., Har. BJ31 45
Bradenham Rd., Hayes BB38 53
Bradenhurst Clo., Cat. CA66 114
Bradfield Clo., Guil. AT69 118
Sutherland Dr.
Bradfield Clo., Wok. AS62 100
Bradfield Dr., Bark. CO35 50
Bradfield Rd. E16 CH41 68
Bradfield Rd., Ruis. BE35 45
Bradford Clo. SE26 CB49 77
Coombe Rd.
Bradford Clo., Brom. CK54 88
Bradford Dr., Epsom BO57 94
Bradford Rd. W3 BO41 65
Warple Way
Bradford Rd., Ilf. CM33 49
Bradford Rd., Rick. AU26 34
Bradgate Clo., Cuff. BW17 20
Bradgate Rd. SE6 CE46 77
Bradgate, Cuff. BW17 20
Brading Cres. E11 CH34 49
Brading Rd. SW2 BX47 76
Brading Rd., Croy. BX53 86
Bradiston Rd. W9 BR38 55
Bradleigh Av., Grays DD42 71
Bradley Clo. N7 BX36 56
Blundell St.
Bradley Gdns. W13 BJ39 54
Bradley La., Dor. BJ69 119
Bradley Ms. SW17 BU47 76
Bellevue Rd.
Bradley Rd. N22 BX30 38
Bradley Rd. SE19 BZ50 77
Bradley Rd., Enf. CD22 30
Bradley Rd., Slou. AO40 52
Bradleys Clo. N1 BY37 2
Bradleys Clo. N1 BY37 56
White Lion St.
Bradman Row, Edg. BM29 37
Pavilion Way
Bradmead SW8 BV43 66
Bradmore Grn., Hat. BR16 19
Bradmore La. W6 BQ42 65
Beadon Rd.
Bradmore La., Hat. BQ16 19
Bradmore Park Rd. W6 BP42 65
Bradmore Way, Couls. BX62 104
Bradmore Way, Hat. BR16 19
Bradshaw Clo., Wind. AM44 61
Bradshaw Rd., Wat. BD23 27
Bradshawe Rd., Grays DD40 71
Bradshawe Waye, Uxb. AY39 53
Bradshaws Clo. SE25 CB52 87
Bradshaws, Hat. BO14 10
Bradstock Rd. E9 CC36 57
Bradstock Rd. Est. E9 CC36 57
Bradstock Rd., Epsom BP57 94
Bradwell Av., Dag. CR34 50
Stour Rd.
Bradwell Clo. E18 CG31 49
Bradwell Clo., Horn. CU36 59
Bradwell Ms. N18 CB28 39
Lyndhurst Rd.
Bradwell Rd., Buck.H. CK26 40
Bradwell St. E1 CC38 57
Brady Av., Loug. CM23 31
Brady St. E1 CB38 57
Brae Ct., Kings.T. BM51 85
Wolverton Av.
Braefoot Ct. SW15 BQ46 75
Putney Hill
Braemar Av. N22 BX30 38
Braemar Av. NW10 BN34 46
Braemar Av. SW19 BS48 76
Braemar Av., Bexh. CS45 69
Braemar Av., S.Croy. BZ58 96
Braemar Av., Th.Hth. BY52 86
Braemar Av., Wem. BK36 54
Braemar Gdns. NW9 BN30 37
Braemar Gdns., Horn. CX32 51
Braemar Gdns., Sid. CM48 78
Braemar Gdns., Slou. AN41 61
Braemar Gdns., W.Wick. CF54 87
Braemar Rd. E13 CG38 58
Braemar Rd. N15 CA32 48
Braemar Rd., Brent. BK43 64
Braemar Rd., Wor.Pk. BP55 85
Braemar Turn, Hem.H. AZ10 8
Braes Mead, Red. BX71 121
Braes St. N1 BY36 56
Braeside Av. SW19 BR51 85
Braeside Av., Sev. CT65 107
Braeside Clo., Pnr. BF29 36
Braeside Clo., Sev. CT65 107
Braeside Cres., Bexh. CS45 69
Braeside Rd. SW16 BW50 76
Braeside, Beck. CE49 77
Braeside, Wey. AW59 92
Braesyde Clo., Belv. CQ42 69
Brafferton Rd., Croy. BZ56 96
Braganza St. SE17 BY42 4
Braganza St. SE17 BY42 66
Bragmans La., Rick. AU20 16
Braham St. E1 CA39 2
Braham St. E1 CA39 57
Braid Av. W3 BN39 55
Braid Clo., Felt. BE48 74
Braid, The, Chesh. AP18 16
Braidwood Rd. SE6 CF47 77
Braidwood St. SE1 CA40 4
Braidwood St. SE1 CA40 57
Brailsford Rd. SW2 BY46 76
Brain Clo., Hat. BP12 10
Brainton Av., Felt. BC47 73
Braintree Av., Ilf. CK32 49
Braintree Rd., Dag. CR34 50
Braintree Rd., Ruis. BC35 44
Braintree St. E2 CC38 57
Braithwaite Av., Rom. CR33 50
Braithwaite Gdns., Stan. BK30 36
Brakefield Rd., Grav. DD50 81
Brakey Hill, Red. CA70 114
Brakynbery, Berk. AP11 7
Brallings La., Ger.Cr. AT28 34
Bramah Grn. SW9 BY44 66
Eythorn Rd.
Bramalea Clo. N6 BV32 47
Bramall Clo. E15 CG35 49
Idmiston Rd.
Bramber Ct., Slou. AN40 61
Avebury
Bramber Rd. N12 BU28 38
Bramber Rd. W14 BR43 65
Bramble Av., Dart. DB48 80
Bramble Banks, Cars. BV58 95
Bramble Cft., Erith CS42 69
Bramble Clo., Brent. BJ43 64
Bramble Clo., Cat. CA64 105
Burntwood La.
Bramble Clo., Croy. CE56 96
Bramble Clo., Guil. AP69 118
Bramble Clo., Shep. BA52 83
Bramble Clo., Stan. BK30 36
Bramble Clo., Uxb. AY39 53
Bramble Clo., Wat. BC20 17
Bramble Down, Stai. AW51 83
Hereford Clo.
Bramble Farm Clo., Uxb. AZ38 53
Bramble Gdns. W12 BO40 55
Wallflower St.
Bramble La., Amer. AP24 25
Bramble La., Hodd. CD12 12
Bramble La., Sev. CU67 116
Bramble La., Upmin. CY37 60
Bramble Mead, Ch.St.G. AQ27 34
Bramble Rd., Hat. BN12 10
Bramble Ri., Cob. BD61 102
Bramble Ri., Harl. CM10 6
Hodings Rd.
Bramble Way, Wok. AV65 100
Linden Way
Bramble Wk., Epsom BM60 94
Bramblebury Rd. SE18 CM42 68
Brambledene Clo., Wok. AR62 100
Silversmiths Way
Brambledown Clo., W.Wick. CG53 88
Brambledown Rd., S.Croy. BZ57 96
Brambledown Rd., Cars. BV57 95
Bramblefield Clo., Long. DC52 90
Brambles, The, Chig. CM29 40
Brambles, The, West.Dr. AX42 63
Brambletye Park Rd., Red. BU71 121
Bramblewood Clo., Cars. BU54 86
Brambling Ri., Hem.H. AY11 8
Bramblings, The E4 CF28 39
Bramcote Av., Mitch. BU52 86
Bramcote Gro. SE16 CC42 67
Bramcote Rd. SW15 BP45 65
Bramdean Cres. SE12 CH47 78
Bramdean Gdns. SE12 CH47 78
Bramerton Rd., Beck. CD52 87
Bramerton St. SW3 BU43 3
Bramerton St. SW3 BU43 66
Bramfield Ct. N4 BZ34 48
Kings Crescent Est.
Bramfield Pl., Hem.H. AZ10 8
Elstree Rd.
Bramfield Rd. SW11 BU46 76
Bramford Ct. N14 BW27 38
Bramford Rd. SW18 BT45 66
Bramham Gdns. SW5 BS42 3
Bramham Gdns. SW5 BS42 66
Bramham Gdns., Chess. BK56 93
Bramhope La. SE7 CH43 68
Bramlands Clo. SW11 BU45 66
Bramleas, Wat. BB25 26
Bramley Av., Couls. BW61 104
Bramley Clo. E17 CD30 39
Bramley Clo. N14 BV25 29
Bramley Clo., Cher. AW54 83
Bramley Clo., Grav. DF50 81
Bramley Clo., Hayes BC40 53
Orchard Rd.
Bramley Clo., Orp. CL54 88
Bramley Clo., S.Croy. BY56 95
Bramley Clo., Stai. AX50 73
Kingston Rd.
Bramley Clo., Swan. CT52 89
Bramley Clo., Twick. BG46 74
Bramley Cres., Ilf. CL32 49
Bramley Ct., Well. CO44 69
Bramley Gdns., Wat. BD28 36
Bramley Hill, S.Croy. BY56 95
Bramley Par. N14 BW24 29
Bramley Pl., Dart. CU45 69
Bramley Rd. N14 BV25 29
Bramley Rd. W10 BQ40 55
Bramley Rd. W12 BQ40 55
Shalfleet Dr.
Bramley Rd. W5 BK41 64
Bramley Rd., Cheam BQ58 94
Bramley Rd., Sutt. BT56 95
Bramley Shaw, Wal.Abb. CG20 22
Bramley St. W10 BQ39 55
Bramley Way, Ash. BL62 103
Bramley Way, Houns. BE46 74
Bramley Way, W.Wick. CE55 87
Brammas Clo., Slou. AO41 61
Brampton Clo. E5 CB34 48
Comberton Rd.
Brampton Clo., Chsnt. CB17 21
Brampton Gdns. N15 BZ32 48
Brampton Rd.
Brampton Gdns., Walt. BD56 93
Brampton Gro. NW4 BP31 46
Brampton Gro., Har. BJ31 45
Brampton Gro., Wem. BL33 46
Brampton La. NW4 BQ31 46
Brampton Gro.
Brampton Park Rd. N8 BY31 47
High Rd.
Brampton Rd. E6 CJ38 58
Brampton Rd. N15 BZ32 48
Brampton Rd. NW9 BM31 46
Brampton Rd. SE2 CP43 69
Brampton Rd., Bexh. CP43 69
Brampton Rd., Croy. CA53 87
Brampton Rd., St.Alb. BJ13 9
Brampton Rd., Uxb. AZ37 53
Brampton Rd., Wat. BC27 35
Bramsham Gdns., Wat. BD28 36
Bramshaw Rd. E9 CC36 57
Bramshaw Ri., N.Mal. BO53 85
Bramshill Clo., Chig. CN28 40
Tine Rd.
Bramshill Gdns. NW5 BV34 47
Bramshill Rd. NW10 BO37 55
Bramshot Av. SE7 CH43 68
Bramshot Way, Wat. BC27 35
Bramston Rd. NW10 BP37 55
Bramwell Clo., Sun. BD51 84
Brancaster La., Pur. BZ58 96
Brancaster Rd. E12 CK35 49
Brancaster Rd. SW16 BX48 76
Brancaster Rd., Ilf. CM32 49
Brancepeth Gdns., Buck.H. CH27 40
Branch Clo., Hat. BQ11 10
Branch Hill NW3 BT34 47
Branch Pl. N1 BZ37 2
Branch Pl. N1 BZ37 57
Branch Rd. E14 CD40 57
Branch Rd., Ilf. CO28 41
Branch Rd., St.Alb. BF13 9
Branch Rd., Park Street BG17 18
Brancker Clo., Wall. BX57 95
Brancker Rd., Har. BK31 45
Brancroft Way, Enf. CD23 30
Brand St. SE10 CF43 67

Brandlehow Rd. SW15 BR45 65
Brandon Clo., Chsnt. CA16 21
Brandon Est. SE17 BY43 66
Brandon Rd. E17 CF31 48
Brandon Rd. N7 BX36 56
Brandon Rd., Dart. CX47 80
Brandon Rd., Sthl. BE42 64
Brandon Rd., Sutt. BS56 95
Brandon St. SE17 BZ42 4
Brandon St. SE17 BZ42 67
Brandon St., Grav. DG47 81
Brandram Rd. SE13 CG45 68
Brandreth Rd. E6 CK39 58
Brandreth Rd. SW17 BV48 76
Brandries, The, Wall. BW55 86
Brands Hatch Rd., Fawk. DA56 99
Brands Rd., Slou. AT43 62
Brandsland, Rei. BS72 121
Brandville Gdns., Ilf. CL31 49
Brandville Rd., W.Dray. AY41 63
Brandy Way, Sutt. BS57 95
Branfill Rd., Upmin. CX34 51
Brangbourne Rd., Brom. CF49 77
Brangton Rd. SE11 BX42 4
Brangton Rd. SE11 BX42 66
Loughborough St.
Brangwyn Cres. SW19 BT51 86
Branksea St. SW6 BR43 65
Branksome Av. N18 CA29 39
Branksome Clo., Hem.H. AZ13 8
Branksome Clo., Walt. BD54 84
Branksome Rd. SW19 BS51 86
Branksome Rd. SW2 BX45 66
Branksome Way, Har. BL32 46
Branksome Way, N.Mal. BN51 85
Bransby Rd., Chess. BL57 94
Branscombe Gdns. N21 BY26 38
Branscombe St. SE13 CE45 67
Bransdale Clo. NW6 BS37 56
West End La.
Bransell Clo., Swan. CS53 89
Bransgrove Rd., Edg. BL30 37
Branston Cres., Orp. CM54 88
Branstone Rd., Rich. BL44 65
Branton Rd., Green. CZ46 80
Brants Wk. W7 BH38 54
Brantwood Av., Erith CS43 69
Brantwood Av., Islw. BJ45 64
Brantwood Clo. E17 CE31 48
Brantwood Dr., Wey. AV60 91
Brantwood Gdns., Enf. BX24 29
Brantwood Gdns., Ilf. CK31 49
Brantwood Gdns., Wey. AV60 91
Brantwood Rd. N17 CA29 39
Brantwood Rd. SE24 BZ46 77
Brantwood Rd., Bexh. CR44 69
Brantwood Rd., S.Croy. BZ58 96
Brantwood Way, Orp. CP52 89
Brasher Clo., Grnf. BG35 45
Bedser Dr.
Brassey Rd. NW6 BR36 55
Brassey Rd., Oxt. CG68 115
Brassey Sq. SW11 BV45 66
Ashbury Rd.
Brassie Av. W3 BO39 55
Brasted Clo. SE26 CC49 77
Brasted Clo., Bexh. CP46 79
Brasted Clo., Orp. CO55 89
Brasted Hill Rd., West. CO64 107
Brasted Hill, Sev. CO63 107
Brasted La., Sev. CO63 107
Brasted Rd., Erith CT43 69
Brathway Rd. SW18 BS47 76
Bratley St. E1 CB38 2
Bratley St. E1 CB38 57
Weaver St.
Brattle Wood, Sev. CU68 116
Braund Av., Grnf. BF38 54
Braundton Av., Sid. CN47 78
Braunston Dr., Hayes BE38 54
Bravington Clo., Shep. AY53 83
Bravington Pl. W9 BR38 55
Bravington Rd.
Bravington Rd. W9 BR38 55
Braxfield Rd. SE4 CD45 67
Braxted Pk. SW16 BX50 76
Bray Clo., B.Wd. BN23 28
Denham Way
Bray Clo., Maid. AH41 61
Bray Cres. SE16 CC41 67
Marlow Way
Bray Ct., Maid. AH42 61
Bray Dr. E16 CG40 58
Bray Gdns., Wok. AV61 100
Bray Pass. E16 CG40 58
Bray Dr.
Bray Pl. SW3 BU42 3
Bray Pl. SW3 BU42 66
Bray Rd. NW7 BQ29 37
Bray Rd., Cob. BD61 102
Bray Rd., Guil. AQ71 118
Bray Rd., Maid. AG40 61
Brayards Rd. SE15 CB44 67
Braybank, Maid. AH41 61
Braybourne Clo., Uxb. AX36 53
Braybourne Dr., Islw. BH43 64
Braybrook St. W12 BO39 55
Braybrooke Gdns. SE19 CA50 77
Fox Hill
Brayburne Av. SW4 BW44 66
Braycourt Av., Walt. BC54 83
Braydon Rd. N16 CA33 48
Brayfield Rd., Maid. AH41 61
Brayfield Ter. N1 BY36 56
Lofting Rd.
Brays Mead, Harl. CN12 13
Brays Springs, Wal.Abb. CG20 22
Roundhills
Brayton Gdns., Enf. BW24 29
Braywood Av., Egh. AS50 72
Braywood Rd. SE9 CM45 68
Brazil Clo., Croy. BX54 86
Breach La., Dag. CR38 59
Breach La., Hert. BW12 11
Breach Rd., Grays CZ43 70
Bread & Cheese La., Chsnt. BZ16 21
Bread St. EC4 BZ39 2
Bread St. EC4 BZ39 57
Break Mead, Welw.G.C. BS 8 5
Breakfield, Couls. BX61 104
Breakneck Hill, Green. DA46 80
Breaks Rd., Hat. BP12 10
Breakspear Av., St.Alb. BH14 9
Breakspear Rd. S., Uxb. AY31 44
Breakspear Rd., Ruis. AZ32 44
Breakspear Rd., Uxb. AX30 35
Breakspear Way, Hem.H. BA13 8
Breakspeare Clo., Wat. BC22 26
Breakspeare Rd., Wat. BB19 17
Breakspears Dr., Orp. CO51 89
Breakspears Rd. SE4 CD45 67
Bream Gdns., E6 CL38 58
Bream St., E3 CE36 57
Breamore Clo. SW15 BP47 75
Breamore Ct., Ilf. CO34 50
Breamore Rd., Ilf. CN34 49
Breams Bldgs. EC4 BY39 2
Breams Bldgs. EC4 BY39 56
Breamwater Gdns., Rich. BJ48 74
Brearley Clo., Edg. BM29 37
Pavilion Way
Brearley Clo., Uxb. AY36 53
Breasley Clo. SW15 BP45 65
Brechin Pl. SW7 BT42 3
Brechin Pl. SW7 BT42 66
Brecken Clo., St.Alb. BJ11 9
Brecknock Rd. Est. N7 BW35 47
Brecknock Rd. N19 BW35 47
Brecknock Rd. N7 BW35 47
Brecon Clo., Mitch. BX52 86
Brecon Rd. W6 BR43 65
Brecon Rd., Enf. CC24 30
Brede Clo. E6 CL38 58
Bredgar Rd. N19 BW34 47
Bredhurst Clo. SE20 CC50 77
Bredon Rd. SE5 BZ45 67
Bredon Rd., Croy. CA54 87
Bredune, Ken. BZ61 105
Church Rd.
Breech La., Tad. BP66 112
Breer St. SW6 BS45 66
Breezers Hill E1 CB40 57
Pennington St.
Brember Rd., Har. BG34 45
Bremer Rd., Stai. AW48 73
Bremner Clo., Swan. CU52 89
Bremner Rd. SW7 BT41 3
Bremner Rd. SW7 BT41 66
Queens Gate
Brenchley Av., Grav. DG49 81
Brenchley Clo., Brom. CG53 88
Brenchley Clo., Chis. CL51 88
Brenchley Gdns. SE23 CC46 77
Brenchley Rd., Orp. CN51 88
Brenda Rd. SW17 BU48 76
Brendans Clo., Horn. CW33 51
Brende Gdns., E.Mol. BF52 84
Brendon Av. NW10 BO35 46
Brendon Clo., Erith CT44 69
Brendon Clo., Esher BG57 93
Brendon Clo., Hayes BA43 63
Brendon Dr., Esher BG57 93
Brendon Gdns., Har. BF35 45
Brendon Gdns., Ilf. CN32 49
Brendon Rd. SE9 CM48 78
Brendon Rd., Dag. CQ33 50
Brendon St. W1 BU39 1
Brendon St. W1 BU39 56
Brendon Way, Enf. CA26 39
Brenley Clo., Mitch. BV52 86
Brenley Gdns. SE9 CJ45 68
Brennan Rd., Til. DG44 71
Brent Clo., Bex. CQ47 79
Brent Clo., Dart. CX46 80
Brent Cres. NW10 BL37 55
Brent Cross Shop. Ctre. NW4 BQ33 46
Brent Ct. NW11 BQ33 46
Highfield Av.
Brent Grn. NW4 BQ32 46
Brent La., Dart. CW47 80
Brent Lea, Brent. BK43 64
Brent Park Rd. NW4 BP33 46
Brent Pl., Barn. BR25 28
Brent Rd. E16 CH39 58
Brent Rd. SE18 CL43 68
Brent Rd., Brent. BK43 64
Brent Rd., S.Croy. CB58 96
Brent Rd., Sthl. BD41 64
Brent Side, Brent. BK43 64
Brent St. NW4 BQ31 46
Brent Ter. NW2 BQ33 46
Brent View Rd. NW9 BP32 46
Brent Way N3 BS29 38
Brent Way, Brent. BK43 64
Brent Way, Dart. CX46 80
Brent Way, Wem. BM36 55
Brent, The, Dart. CX47 80
Brentcot Clo. W13 BJ38 54
Brentfield Clo. NW10 BN36 55
Brentfield Gdns. NW2 BQ33 46
Brentfield NW10 BM36 55
Brentfield Rd. NW10 BN36 55
Brentfield Rd., Dart. CX47 80
Brentford Clo., Hayes BD38 54
Paddington Clo.
Brentham Way W5 BK38 54
Brenthouse Rd. E9 CC36 57
Brenthurst Rd. NW10 BO36 55
Brentlands Dr., Dart. CX47 80
Brentmead Clo. W7 BH40 54
Brentmead Gdns. NW10 BL37 55
Brentmead Pl. NW11 BQ32 46
Brenton St. E14 CD39 57
Brentside Clo. W13 BJ38 54
Brentvale Av., Sthl. BG40 54
Brentvale Av., Wem. BL37 55
Brentwick Gdns., Brent. BL42 65
Brentwood By-pass, Brwd. DA25 33
Brentwood By-pass, Brwd. DA26 42
Brentwood Clo. SE9 CM47 78
Brentwood Pl., Brwd. DB26 42
Brentwood Rd., East Horndon DF30 123
Brentwood Rd., Brwd. DD28 122
Brentwood Rd., Grays DG42 71
Brentwood Rd., Ong. CX19 24
Brentwood Rd., Rom. CT32 50
Brereton Ct., Hem.H. AY14 8
Runham Rd.
Brereton Rd. N17 CA29 39
Bressenden Pl. SW1 BV41 3
Bressenden Pl. SW1 BV41 66
Bressey Gro. E18 CG30 40
Bretlands Rd., Cher. AV55 82
Brett Clo., Nthlt. BD38 54
Broomcroft Av.
Brett Cres. NW10 BN36 55
Brett Gdns., Dag. CQ36 59
Brett Pl., Wat. BC22 26
Brett Rd. E8 CB35 48
Brett Rd., Barn. BQ25 28
Brettell St. SE17 BZ42 4
Brettell St. SE17 BZ42 67
Merrow St.
Brettenham Av. E17 CE30 39
Brettenham Rd. E17 CD30 39
Brettenham Rd. N18 CB28 39
Brettgrave, Epsom BN58 94
Brevet Clo., Grays CY42 70
Brimfield Rd.
Brewer Pl. SE18 CL42 68
Charles Grindling Wk.
Brewer St. W1 BW40 3
Brewer St. W1 BW40 56
Brewer St., Red. BZ69 114
Brewers Fld., Dart. CV49 80
Brewers La., Rich. BK46 74
Brewery La., Twick. BH47 74
Brewery La., Wey. AX60 92
Brewery Rd. N7 BX36 56
Brewery Rd. SE18 CM42 68
Brewery Rd., Brom. CK54 88
Brewery Rd., Hodd. CE12 12
Brewery Rd., Wok. AR62 100
Brewhouse La. E1 CB40 57
Wapping La.
Brewhouse Rd. SE18 CK42 68
Red Barracks Rd.
Brewhouse St. SW15 BR45 65
Brewhouse Wk. SE16 CD40 57
Brewhouse Yd. EC1 BY38 2
Brewhouse Yd. EC1 BY38 56
Compton St.
Brewood Rd., Dag. CO36 59
Brewster Gdns. W10 BQ39 55
Brewster Rd. E10 CE33 48
Brian Av., S.Croy. CA59 96
Brian Clo., Horn. CU35 50
Brian Ct. N10 BV30 38
Brian Rd., Rom. CP32 50
Briane Rd., Epsom BN58 94
Briant St. SE4 CC44 67
Briants Clo., Pnr. BE30 36
Briar Av. SW16 BX50 76
Briar Banks, Cars. BV58 95
Briar Clo. N13 BZ27 39
Briar Clo. N2 BS31 47
Briar Clo., Berk. AT11 7
Briar Clo., Buck.H. CJ27 40
Briar Clo., Chsnt. CC18 21
Briar Clo., Hmptn. BE49 74
Briar Clo., Islw. BH46 74
Briar Clo., Wey. AW59 92
Briar Cres., Nthlt. BF36 54
Briar Gdns., Brom. CG54 88
Briar Gro., S.Croy. CB60 96
Briar Hill, Pur. BX59 95
Briar La., Cars. BV58 95
Briar La., Croy. CE56 96
Briar Pass. SW16 BX52 86
Briar Pl. SW16 BX52 86
Briar Rd. NW2 BQ35 46
Briar Rd. SW16 BX52 86
Briar Rd., Bex. CS48 79
Briar Rd., Har. BK32 45
Briar Rd., Rom. CV29 42
Briar Rd., Shep. AY53 83
Briar Rd., St.Alb. BK12 9
Briar Rd., Twick. BH47 74
Briar Rd., Wat. BC20 17
Briar Rd., Wok. AT65 100
Briar Way, Guil. AT68 109
Briar Way, West.Dr. AZ41 63
Briar Wk. SW15 BP45 65
Briar Wk. W10 BR38 55
Droop St.
Briar Wk., Edg. BN29 37
Briar Wk., Wey. AW59 92
Claremont Rd.
Briarbank Rd. W13 BJ39 54
Briardale Gdns. NW3 BS34 47
Briarfield Av. N3 BS30 38
Briarleas Gdns., Upmin. CZ33 51
Briarley Clo., Brox. CD14 12
Briars Clo. N17 CB29 39
Briars Clo., Hat. BP12 10
Briars Ct., Lthd. BG60 93
Briars La., Hat. BP12 10
Briars Wk., Rom. CW30 42
Briars Wood, Hat. BO12 10
Briars, The, Chsnt. CD19 21
Briars, The, Rick. AW21 26
Briars, The, Sev. CY57 99
Briars, The, Slou. AS42 62
Briarswood Way, Orp. CN56 97
Briarway, Berk. AR13 7
Briarwood Clo. NW9 BN32 46
Briarwood Dr., Nthwd. BC30 35
Briarwood Rd. SW4 BW46 76
Briarwood Rd., Epsom BP57 94
Briarwood Rd., Wok. AO63 100
Briarwood, Brwd. CZ22 33
Stockfield
Briary Clo. NW3 BU36 56
Fellows Rd.
Briary Ct., Sid. CO49 79
Briary Gdns., Brom. CH49 78
Briary La. N9 CA27 39
Brick Ct. EC4 BY39 56
Middle Temple La.
Brick Farm Clo., Rich. BM44 65
Brick Kiln Hill, Epp. CR21 32
Brick Kiln La., Oxt. CJ68 115
Brick Knoll Park, St.Alb. BK14 9
Brick La. E1 CA38 2
Brick La. E1 CA38 57
Brick La. E2 CA38 2
Brick La. E2 CA38 57
Brick La., Enf. CB23 30
Brick La., Stan. BK29 36
Honeypot La.
Brick St. W1 BV40 3
Brick St. W1 BV40 56
Brick Wall Clo., Welw. BP 7 5
Brick Yard La., Dor. BD74 119
Brickbarn Clo. SW10 BT43 66
Edith Gro.
Brickcroft, Brox. CD16 21
Brickenden Ct., Wal.Abb. CG20 22
Brickendon La., Hert. BZ12 12
Bricket Rd., St.Alb. BG13 9
Brickett Clo., Ruis. BA32 44
Brickfield Av., Hem.H. AZ14 8
Brickfield Clo., Brent. BK43 64
Brickfield Cotts. SE18 CN43 68
Brickfield Cotts., B.Wd. BL24 28
Brickfield Ct., Hat. BP14 10
Far End
Brickfield Farm Gdns., Orp. CL56 97
State Farm Av.
Brickfield La., Barn. BO25 28
Brickfield La., Wal.Abb. CF17 21
Brickfield Rd. E3 CE38 57
Brickfield Rd. SW19 BS49 76
Brickfield Rd., Epp. CP18 23
Brickfield Rd., Th.Hth. BY51 86
Brickfield, Hat. BP14 10
Brickfields La., Hayes BA43 63
Brickfields, Har. BG34 45
Brickmakers La., Hem.H. AZ14 8
Brickwall La., Ruis. BB33 44
Brickwood Clo. SE26 CB48 77
Kirkdale
Brickwood Rd., Croy. CA55 87
Bride Ct. EC4 BY39 2
Bride La.
Bride La. EC4 BY39 2
Bride La. EC4 BY39 56
Bride St. N7 BX36 56
Bridewell Pl. E1 CB40 57
Brewhouse La.
Bridewell Pl. EC4 BY39 2
Bridewell Pl. EC4 BY39 56
Tudor St.
Bridford Ms. W1 BV39 1
Bridford Ms. W1 BV39 56
Devonshire St.
Bridge App. NW1 BV36 56
Bridge Av. W6 BQ42 65
Bridge Av. W7 BG39 54
Bridge Av., Upmin. CX34 51
Bridge Clo., Brwd. DC28 122
Bridge Clo., Enf. CB23 30
Bridge Clo., Rom. CT32 50
Bridge Clo., Sun. BC52 83
Forge La.
Bridge Clo., Walt. BB54 83
Bridge Clo., Wey. AY59 92
Bridge Clo., Wok. AR62 100
Bridge Cotts., Surb. BJ54 84
Portsmouth Rd.
Bridge Ct. E10 CD33 48
Bridge Dr. N22 BY29 38
Bridge End E17 CF30 39
Bridge Gate N21 BZ26 39
Bridge Gdns., Ashf. BA50 73
Bridge Gdns., E.Mol. BG52 84
Bridge Hill Clo., Guil. AQ70 109
Aldershot Rd.
Bridge Hill, Epp. CN20 22
Bridge House Quay E14 CF40 57
Prestons Rd.
Bridge La. NW11 BR31 46
Bridge La. SW11 BU44 66
Bridge La., Vir.W. AS53 82
Bridge Path, Wat. BC23 26
Bridge Pl. SW1 BV42 3
Bridge Pl. SW1 BV42 66
Bridge Pl., Amer. AP22 25
Bridge Pl., Croy. BZ54 87
Bridge Pl., Wat. BD25 27
Bridge Rd. E., Welw.G.C. BR 8 5
Bridge Rd. E15 CF36 57
Bridge Rd. E17 CD33 48
Bridge Rd. E6 CK36 58
Bridge Rd. Ms. SW19 BS50 76
Bridge Rd.
Bridge Rd. N22 BX30 38
Bridge Rd. N9 CB27 39
Bridge Rd. NW10 BO36 55
Bridge Rd., Beck. CD50 77
Bridge Rd., Bexh. CQ45 69
Bridge Rd., Cher. AW54 83
Bridge Rd., Chess. BL56 94
Bridge Rd., Croy. BZ55 87
Bridge Rd., E.Mol. BG53 84
Bridge Rd., Epsom BO59 94
Bridge Rd., Erith CT44 69
Bridge Rd., Grays DD42 71
Bridge Rd., Grays DD43 71
Bridge Rd., Houns. BG45 64
Bridge Rd., Kings L. BA20 17
Bridge Rd., Ong. CV14 15
Bridge Rd., Orp. CO53 89
Bridge Rd., Rain. CU38 59
Bridge Rd., Sthl. BE41 64
Bridge Rd., Sutt. BS57 95
Bridge Rd., Twick. BJ46 74
Bridge Rd., Uxb. AX37 53
Bridge Rd., Wall. BW56 95
Bridge Rd., Welw.G.C. BQ 7 5
Bridge Rd., Wem. BM34 46
Bridge Rd., Wey. AY56 92
Bridge Row, Croy. BZ54 87
Cross Rd.
Bridge St. SW1 BX41 4
Bridge St. SW1 BX41 66
Bridge St. W4 BN42 65
Bridge St., Berk. AR13 7
Bridge St., Guil. AR71 118
Bridge St., Hem.H. AX14 8
Bridge St., Lthd. BJ64 102
Bridge St., Pnr. BE31 45
Bridge St., Rich. BK46 74
Bridge St., Slou. AU43 62
Bridge St., Stai. AV49 72
Bridge St., Walt. BB54 83
Bridge Ter. E15 CF36 57
Bridge Vw. W6 BQ42 65
Bridge Way N11 BW27 38
Bridge Way NW11 BR32 46
Bridge Way, Bark. CN36 58
Bridge Way, Couls. BU63 104
Bridge Way, Twick. BG47 74
Bridge Way, Uxb. AZ35 44
Bridge Way, Wem. BL36 55
Bridge Wharf, Cher. AX54 83
Bridge Rd.
Bridge Yd. SE1 BZ40 4
Bridge Yd. SE1 BZ40 57
Bridge, The W5 BK40 54
Bridge, The, Har. BH31 45
Bridgefield Clo., Bans. BQ61 103
Bridgefield Rd., Sutt. BS57 95
Bridgefields, Welw.G.C. BR 7 5
Bridgefoot La., Pot.B. BQ20 19
Bridgefoot SE1 BX42 4
Bridgefoot SE1 BX42 66
Bridgeham Clo., Wey. AZ56 92
Bridgehill Clo., Guil. AQ69 118
Aldershot Rd.
Bridgeland Rd. E16 CH40 58
Bridgeman Dr., Wind. AN44 61
Bridgeman Rd. N1 BX36 2
Bridgeman Rd. N1 BX36 56
Bridgeman Rd. W4 BN41 65
Bridgeman Rd., Tedd. BJ50 74
Bridgeman St. NW8 BU37 1
Bridgeman St. NW8 BU37 56
Bridgen Rd., Bex. CQ47 79
Bridgend Rd. SW18 BT45 66
Bridgend Rd., Enf. CC21 30
Bridgenhall Rd., Enf. CA23 30
Bridgeport Pl. E1 CB40 57
Asher Way
Bridger Clo., Wat. BE20 18
Bridges Ct. SW11 BT44 66
Bridges Dr., Dart. CX46 80
Bridges La., Croy. BX56 95
Bridges Pl. SW6 BR44 65
Bridges Rd. SW19 BS50 76
Bridges Rd., Stan. BH28 36
Bridgetown Clo. SE19 CA49 77
St. Kitts Road Ter.
Bridgewater Clo., Chis. CN52 88
Bridgewater Gdns., Edg. BL30 37
Bridgewater Rd., Berk. AQ11 7
Bridgewater Rd., Wem. BK36 54
Bridgewater Rd., Wey. BA57 92
Bridgewater Sq. EC2 BZ39 2
Bridgewater St. EC2 BZ39 2
Bridgewater St. EC2 BZ39 57
Viscount St.
Bridgewater Ter., Wind. AO44 61
Goswell Rd.
Bridgewater Way, Bush. BF26 36
Bridgeway St. NW1 BW37 1
Bridgeway St. NW1 BW37 56
Bridgewood Clo. SE20 CB50 77
Castledine Rd.
Bridgewood Rd. SW16 BW50 76
Bridgewood Rd., Wor.Pk. BP55 85
Bridgford St. SW18 BT48 76
Bridgwater Clo., Rom. CV28 42
Bridgwater Rd. E15 CF37 57
Bridgwater Rd., Rom. CV28 42
Bridgwater Rd., Ruis. BC35 44
Bridgwater Wk., Rom. CV28 42
Bridle Clo., Enf. CD22 30
Bridle Clo., Epsom BN56 94
Bridle Clo., Kings.T. BK52 84
Bridle Clo., St.Alb. BH12 9
Bridle Clo., Sun. BC52 83
Forge La.
Bridle End, Epsom BO60 94
Bridle La. W1 BW40 3
Bridle La. W1 BW40 56
Bridle Path, Croy. BX55 86
Bridle Path, The, Wdf.Grn. CG29 40
Bridle Rd., Croy. CE55 87
Bridle Rd., Epsom BO60 94
Bridle Rd., Esher BJ57 93
Bridle Rd., Pnr. BC32 44
Bridle Rd., The, Pur. BX58 95
Bridle Way S., Hodd. CE10 12
Bridle Way, Berk. AQ12 7
Bridle Way, Croy. CE56 96
Bridle Way, Hodd. CE10 12
Bridle Way, Orp. CL56 97
Broadwater Gdns.
Bridle Way, The, Croy. CD58 96
Bridle Way, The, Wall. BW56 95
Bridlebarn La., Wok. AR62 100
Bridlepath Way, Felt. BB47 73
Bridlington Clo., West. CH63 106
Bridlington Rd. N9 CB26 39
Bridlington Rd., Wat. BD27 36
Bridlington Spur, Slou. AN41 61
Scarborough Way
Bridport Av., Rom. CR32 50
Bridport Pl. N1 BZ37 2
Bridport Pl. N1 BZ37 57
Bridport Rd. N18 CA28 39
Bridport Rd., Grnf. BF37 54
Bridport Rd., Th.Hth. BY52 86
Bridstow Pl. W2 BS39 56
Brief St. SE5 BY44 66

Brier Lea, Tad. BR66 112
Brierley Av. N9 CC26 39
Brierley Clo. SE25 CB52 87
Brierley Clo., Horn. CU32 50
Brierley Rd. E11 CF35 48
Brierley Rd. SW12 BW48 76
Brierley, Croy. CE57 96
Brierly Clo., Guil. AQ69 118
Shepherds Hill
Brierly Gdns. E2 CC37 57
Cyprus St.
Brierly St. E2 CC38 57
Royston St.
Briery Ct., Hem.H. AZ13 8
Briery Field, Rick. AW24 26
Briery Rd., Hem.H. AZ12 8
Briery Way, Amer. AP22 25
Brigade St. SE3 CG44 68
Royal Par.
Brigadier Av., Enf. BZ23 30
Brigadier Hill, Enf. BZ22 30
Bright Clo., Belv. CP42 69
Bright Hill, Guil. AS71 118
Bright St. E14 CE39 57
Brightfield Rd. SE12 CG46 78
Brightlands Rd., Reig. BT69 121
Brightlands, Grav. DF49 81
Henley Deane
Brightling Rd. SE4 CD46 77
Brightlingsea Pl. E14 CD40 57
Brightman Rd. SW18 BT47 76
Brighton Av. E17 CD32 48
Brighton Clo., Uxb. AZ36 53
Brighton Clo., Wey. AW56 92
Burleigh Rd.
Brighton Dr., Nthlt. BF36 54
Brighton Gro. SE14 CD44 67
Brighton Rd. E6 CL38 58
Brighton Rd. N16 CA35 48
Brighton Rd. N2 BT30 38
Brighton Rd., Ban. BR60 94
Brighton Rd., Couls. BW62 104
Brighton Rd., Croy. BZ56 96
Brighton Rd., Hooley BV65 104
Brighton Rd., Pur. BX60 95
Brighton Rd., Red. BU71 121
Brighton Rd., Surb. BK53 84
Brighton Rd., Sutt. BT57 95
Brighton Rd., Tad. BR62 103
Brighton Rd., Wat. BC22 26
Brighton Rd., Wey. AX56 92
Brighton Ter. SW9 BX45 66
Brights Av., Rain. CU38 59
Brightside Av., Stai. AX50 73
Brightside Rd. SE13 CF46 77
Brightside, The, Enf. CC23 30
Brightwell Cres. SW17 BU49 76
Brightwell Rd., Wat. BC25 26
Brigstock Rd., Belv. CR42 69
Brigstock Rd., Couls. BV61 104
Brigstock Rd., Th.Hth. BY53 86
Brill Pl. NW1 BW37 1
Brill Pl. NW1 BW37 56
Brim Hill N2 BT31 47
Brimfield Rd., Grays CY42 70
Brimpsfield Clo. SE2 CO41 69
Brimsdown Av., Enf. CD23 30
Brimshot La., Wok. AP58 91
Brimstone Clo., Orp. CP57 98
Brindles Clo., Brwd. DE27 122
Brindles Clo., Til. DK42 71
Beechcroft Av.
Brindles, The, Bans. BR62 103
Brindley St. SE14 CD44 67
Brindley Way, Sthl. BF40 54
Brindwood Rd. E4 CD27 39
Brinkburn Clo. SE2 CO42 69
Brinkburn Clo., Edg. BM30 37
Brinkburn Gdns., Edg. BM31 46
Brinkley Rd., Wor.Pk. BP55 85
Brinklow Cres. SE18 CL43 68
Brinkworth Rd., Ilf. CK31 49
Brinkworth Way E9 CD36 57
Brinley Clo., Chsnt. CC19 21
Brinsdale Rd. NW4 BQ31 46
Brinsley Rd., Har. BG30 36
Brinsley St. E1 CB39 57
Watney St.
Brinsmead Rd., Rom. CX30 42
Brinsmead, Park Street BG17 18
Brinsworth Clo., Twick. BG47 74
Brinton Wk. SE1 BY40 4
Brion Pl. E14 CF39 57
Brisbane Av. SW19 BS50 76
Brisbane Ho., Til. DF44 71
Leicester Rd.
Brisbane Rd. E10 CE34 48
Brisbane Rd. W13 BJ40 54
Brisbane Rd., Ilf. CL33 49
Brisbane St. SE5 BZ43 67
Briscoe Clo. E11 CG34 49
Briscoe Clo., Hodd. CD11 12
Briscoe Rd. SW19 BT50 76
Briscoe Rd., Hodd. CD11 12
Briscoe Rd., Rain. CV37 60
Brise Cres. NW10 BO35 46
Neasden La.
Briset Rd. SE9 CJ45 68
Briset St. EC1 BY38 56
Briset St. EC1 BY39 2
Briset Way N7 BX34 47
Bristol Clo., Stai. AY46 73
Whitley Clo.
Bristol Gdns. W9 BS38 1
Bristol Gdns. W9 BS38 56
Bristol Ms. W9 BS38 1
Bristol Ms. W9 BS38 56
Bristol Park Rd. E17 CD31 48
Hervey Park Rd.
Bristol Rd. E7 CJ36 58
Bristol Rd., Grav. DH48 81
Bristol Rd., Grnf. BF37 54
Bristol Rd., Mord. BS53 86
Bristol Way, Slou. AP40 52
Stoke Gdns.
Bristow Rd. SE19 CA49 77
Bristow Rd., Bexh. CQ44 69
Bristow Rd., Croy. BX56 95
Bristow Rd., Houns. BF45 64
Britannia Clo. SW4 BW45 66
Clapham Cres.
Britannia Clo., Nthlt. BD38 54
Britannia Dr., Grav. DJ49 81
Britannia La., Twick. BG47 74
Britannia Rd. N12 BT27 38
Britannia Rd. SW6 BS43 66
Britannia Rd., Brwd. DB28 42
Britannia Rd., Ilf. CL34 49
Britannia Rd., Surb. BL54 85
Britannia Rd., Wal.Cr. CD20 21
Britannia Row N1 BY37 2
Britannia Row N1 BY37 56
Britannia St. WC1 BX38 2
Britannia St. WC1 BX38 56
Britannia Way NW10 BM38 55
Britannia Way SW6 BS43 66
Britannia Way, Stai. AX47 73
Britannia Wk. N1 BZ38 2
Britannia Wk. N1 BZ38 57
British Gro. Pass. W6 BO42 65
British Gro. S. W4 BO42 65
British Grove Pass.
British Gro. W4 BO42 65
British Legion Rd. E4 CG27 40
British St. E3 CD38 57
Briton Clo., S.Croy. CA59 96
Briton Cres., S.Croy. CA59 96
Briton Hill Rd., S.Croy. CA58 96
Brittain Rd., Dag. CQ34 50
Brittain Rd., Walt. BD56 93
Brittains La., Sev. CT65 107
Britten Clo. NW11 BS33 47
Britten Clo., B.Wd. BK25 27
Beehive Clo.
Britten Dr., Sthl. BE39 54
Thurston Rd.
Britten St. SW3 BU42 3
Britten St. SW3 BU42 66
Brittenden Clo., Orp. CN57 97
Brittens Clo., Guil. AQ68 109
Brittens Ct. E1 CB40 57
Britton Av., St.Alb. BG13 9
Britton St. EC1 BY38 56
Britton St. EC1 BY39 2
Brittons Ct. EC4 BY39 2
Whitefriars St.
Brixham Cres., Ruis. BC33 44
Brixham Gdns., Ilf. CN35 49
Brixham Rd. E16 CH39 58
Brixham Rd., Well. CP44 69
Brixham St. E16 CK40 58
Brixton Est., Edg. BM30 37
Brixton Hill Pl. SW2 BX47 76
Brixton Hill SW2 BX47 76
Brixton Oval SW2 BY45 66
Rushcroft Rd.
Brixton Rd. SW9 BY45 66
Brixton Rd., Wat. BC23 26
Brixton Station Rd. SW9 BY45 66
Brixton Water La. SW2 BX46 76
Broad Acre, St.Alb. BE18 18
Broad Acre, Stai. AW49 73
Cherry Orchard
Broad Acres, Hat. BO11 10
Broad Clo., Walt. BE55 84
Broad Ct. WC2 BX39 2
Broad Ct. WC2 BX39 56
Broad Ditch Rd., Grav. DE50 81
Broad Green Av., Croy. BY54 86
Broad Green Wood, Hert. BX11 11
Broad Grn., Hert. BX11 11
Broad High Way, Cob. BD61 102
Broad La. N15 CA31 48
Broad La. N8 BX32 47
Enfield Rd.
Broad La., Dart. CU49 79
Broad La., Hmptn. BE50 74
Broad Lawn SE9 CL48 78
Broad Meadow, Brwd. CZ22 33
Broad Oak Clo., Orp. CO51 89
Mickleham Rd.
Broad Oak, Wdf.Grn. CH28 40
Broad Oaks Way, Brom. CG53 88
Broad Oaks, Surb. BM54 85
Broadway
Broad Platts, Slou. AR41 62
Broad Rd., Swans. DC46 81
Broad Sanctuary SW1 BX41 4
Broad Sanctuary SW1 BX41 66
Broad St., Dag. CR36 59
Broad St., Guil. AO69 118
Broad St., Hem.H. AX13 8
Broad St., Tedd. BH49 74
Broad Street Av. EC2 CA39 2
Broad Street Av. EC2 CA39 57
Old Broad St.
Broad Street Bldgs. EC2 CA39 2
Liverpool St.
Broad Strood, Loug. CL22 31
Broad Vw. NW9 BM32 46
Broad Wk. La. NW11 BR33 46
Broad Wk. N., Brwd. DD27 122
Broad Wk. N21 BX27 38
Broad Wk. NW1 BV37 1
Broad Wk. NW1 BV37 56
Broad Wk. S., The, Brwd. DD28 122
Broad Wk. SE3 CJ44 68
Broad Wk. W1 BU40 3
Broad Wk., Burgh Heath BQ63 103
Broad Wk., Cat. CA64 105
Broad Wk., Couls. BV65 104
Broad Wk., Epsom BO62 103
Broad Wk., Har. BF31 45
Broad Wk., Harl. CM10 6
Broad Wk., Houns. BD44 64
Broad Wk., Orp. CP55 89
Broad Wk., Sev. CW67 117
Broad Wk., The W8 BS40 3
Broad Wk., The W8 BS40 56
Broad Wk., The, Nthwd. BA30 35
Broad Yd. EC1 BY38 2
Broad Yd. EC1 BY38 56
Broadacre Clo., Uxb. AZ34 44
Broadacres, Guil. AP69 118
Broadbent St. W1 BV40 3
Broadbent St. W1 BV40 56
Bourdon St.
Broadbridge Clo. SE3 CH43 68
Broadcoombe, S.Croy. CC57 96
Broadcroft Av., Stan. BK30 36
Broadcroft Rd., Orp. CM54 88
Broadfield Clo. NW2 BQ34 46
Broadfield Clo., Croy. BX55 86
Broadfield Clo., Rom. CT32 50
Broadfield Clo., Tad. BQ63 103
Broadfield Ct., Bush. BH27 36
Broadfield La. NW1 BX36 56
Broadfield La., Wat. BC26 35
Broadfield Pl., Welw.G.C. BP 8 5
Broadfield Rd. SE6 CG47 78
Broadfield Rd., Hem.H. AY13 8
Broadfield Sq., Enf. CB24 30
Broadfield Way, Buck.H. CJ28 40
Broadfield, Harl. CN10 6
Broadfields Av. N21 BY26 38
Broadfields Av., Edg. BM28 37
Broadfields, Chsnt. BY18 20
Broadfields, E.Mol. BG53 84
Broadfields, Har. BF30 36
Broadfields, Saw. CO 6 6
Broadford La., Wok. AP59 91
Broadford Rd., Guil. AR74 118
Broadgate Rd. E16 CJ39 58
Satanita Clo.
Broadgate, Wal.Abb. CG20 22
Broadgates Av., Barn. BS23 29
Broadgates Rd. SW18 BT47 76
Ellerton Rd.
Broadham Green Rd., Oxt. CF69 114
Broadhead Strand NW9 BO30 37
Broadheath Dr., Chis. CK49 78
Broadheath, Sev. CZ66 117
Broadhinton Rd. SW4 BV45 66
Broadhurst Av., Edg. BM28 37
Broadhurst Av., Ilf. CN35 49
Broadhurst Clo. NW6 BS36 56
Broadhurst Gdns.
Broadhurst Clo., Rich. BL46 75
Lower Grove Rd.
Broadhurst Gdns. NW6 BS36 56
Broadhurst Gdns., Chig. CM28 40
Broadhurst Gdns., Reig. BS72 121
Broadhurst Gdns., Ruis. BD34 45
Broadhurst Wk., Rain. CU36 59
Broadhurst, Ash. BL61 103
Broadlake Pl., St.Alb. BL17 19
Broadlands Av. SW16 BX48 76
Broadlands Av., Chesh. AO18 16
Broadlands Av., Enf. CB24 30
Broadlands Av., Shep. BA53 83
Broadlands Clo. N6 BV33 47
Broadlands Clo. SW16 BX48 76
Broadlands Clo., Enf. CB24 30
Broadlands Clo., Wal.Cr. CC20 21
Raglan Av.
Broadlands Dr., Warl. CC63 105
Broadlands Rd. N6 BU33 47
Broadlands Rd., Brom. CH49 78
Broadlands Way, N.Mal. BO53 85
Broadlands, Grays DC42 71
Broadlands, The, Felt. BE48 74
Broadlawns Clo., Har. BH30 36
Broadley Rd., Harl. CK13 13
Broadley St. NW8 BT39 1
Broadley St. NW8 BT39 56
Broadley Ter. NW1 BU38 1
Broadley Ter. NW1 BU38 56
Broadmark Rd., Slou. AQ40 52
Broadmead Av., Wor.Pk. BP54 85
Broadmead Clo., Hmptn. BF50 74
Broadmead Clo., Pnr. BE29 36
Broadmead Rd., Nthlt. BE38 54
Broadmead Rd., Wdf.Grn. CH29 40
Broadmead SE6 CE48 77
Broadmead, Ash. BL62 103
Broadoak Av., Enf. CC21 30
Broadoak Rd., Erith CS43 69
Broadoaks Cres., Wey. AW60 92
Broadoaks, Epp. CN19 22
Broadstone Pl. W1 BV39 1
Broadstone Pl. W1 BV39 56
Broadstone Rd., Horn. CU34 50
Broadview Av., Grays DE41 71
Broadview Rd. SW16 BW50 76
Broadwalk E18 CG31 49
Broadwall SE1 BY40 4
Broadwall SE1 BY40 56
Broadwater Clo., Stai. AS47 72
Broadwater Clo., Walt. BC56 92
Broadwater Clo., Wok. AU59 91
Woodham La.
Broadwater Cres., Welw.G.C. BQ 8 5
Broadwater Gdns., Orp. CL56 97
Broadwater Gdns., Uxb. AW31 44
Broadwater La., Uxb. AW31 44
Broadwater Pk., Maid. AJ42 61
Barn Dr.
Broadwater Rd. N., Walt. BC56 92
Broadwater Rd. N17 CA30 39
Broadwater Rd. S., Walt. BC56 92
Broadwater Rd. SE28 CM41 68
Broadwater Rd. SW17 BU49 76
Broadwater Rd., Welw.G.C. BR 8 5
Broadwater Rise, Guil. AT71 118
Broadwater SE28 CM41 68
Broadwater, Berk. AR12 7
Broadwater, Pot.B. BS18 20
Broadwaters Est. SE28 CN41 68
Broadway Av., Croy. BZ53 87
Broadway Av., Harl. CO 9 6
Broadway Av., Twick. BJ46 74
Broadway Clo., S.Croy. CB60 96
Broadway Clo., Wdf.Grn. CH29 40
Broadway Ct. E15 CF36 57
Broadway
Broadway Ct. SW19 BS50 76
Broadway E13 CH37 58
Broadway E15 CF36 57
Broadway Gdns., Mitch. BU52 86
Broadway Mkt. E8 CB37 57
Broadway Ms. N13 BX28 38
Elmdale Rd.
Broadway Ms. N21 BY26 38
Compton Rd.
Broadway N16 CA33 48
Broadway N20 BT27 38
Broadway SW1 BW41 3
Broadway SW1 BW41 66
Broadway SW16 BW49 76
Broadway W13 BJ40 54
Broadway W6 BQ42 65
Hammersmith Rd.
Broadway W7 BH40 54
Broadway, Bark. CM37 58
Broadway, Bexh. CQ45 69
Broadway, Edg. BM30 37
Broadway, Epsom BP56 94
Broadway, Grays DE43 71
Broadway, Grnf. BG38 54
Broadway, Hat. BQ12 10
Broadway, Rain. CU38 59
Broadway, Rom. CU30 41
Broadway, St.Alb. BG13 9
Broadway, Stai. AW49 73
Broadway, Surb. BM54 85
Broadway, Swan. CS53 89
Broadway, The E13 CH37 58
Broadway, The E4 CF29 39
Broadway, The N8 BX32 47
Broadway, The N9 CB27 39
Broadway, The NW7 BO28 37
Broadway, The SW14 BO44 65
The Terrace
Broadway, The SW19 BR50 75
Broadway, The W3 BM41 65
Gunnersbury La.
Broadway, The W5 BK40 54
Broadway, The, Croy. BX56 95
Broadway, The, Dag. CR34 50
Broadway, The, Har. BH30 36
Broadway, The, Hat. BQ12 10
Broadway, The, Horn. CU35 50
Broadway, The, Loug. CM24 31
Broadway, The, Pnr. BE29 36
Broadway, The, Stai. AX52 83
Broadway, The, Stan. BK28 36
Broadway, The, Sthl. BE40 54
Broadway, The, Surb. BH54 84
Broadway, The, Sutt. BR57 94
Broadway, The, Wat. BD24 27
Broadway, The, Wdf.Grn. CH29 40
Broadway, The, Wey. AW58 92
Broadway, The, Wok. AS62 100
Broadway, Til. DF44 71
Dock Rd.
Broadway, Wok. AO62 100
Broadwick St. W1 BW39 1
Broadwick St. W1 BW39 56
Broadwood Av., Ruis. BB32 44
Brocas Clo. NW3 BU36 56
Fellows Rd.
Brocas St., Eton AO43 61
Brock Grn., S.Ock. DA39 60
Brock Pl. E3 CE38 57
Brock Rd. E13 CH39 58
Brock St. SE15 CC45 67
Evelina Rd.
Brockdish Av., Bark. CN35 49
Brockenhurst Av., Wor.Pk. BO54 85
Brockenhurst Clo., Wok. AS60 91
Brockenhurst Gdns. NW7 BO28 37
Brockenhurst Gdns., Ilf. CM35 49
Brockenhurst Rd., Croy. CB54 87
Brockenhurst Way SW16 BW51 86
Brockenhurst, E.Mol BE53 84
Brocket Clo., Chig. CN28 40
Brocket Rd., Grays DG41 71
Cherry Wk.
Brocket Rd., Hodd. CE12 12
Brocket Rd., Welw.G.C. BO 9 5
Brocket Way, Chig. CN28 40
Brockett Clo., Welw.G.C. BP 8 5
Brockham Clo. SW19 BR49 75
Brockham Cres., Croy. CF57 96
Brockham Dr. SW2 BX47 76
Brockham Dr., Ilf. CM32 49
Brockham La., Bet. BM70 120
Brockham St. SE1 BZ41 4
Brockham St. SE1 BZ41 67
Brockhamhurst Rd., Bet. BM74 120
Brockhurst Clo., Stan. BH29 36
Brockhurst Rd., Chesh. AO18 16
Brockill Cres. SE4 CD45 67
Brocklebank Rd. SE7 CH42 68
Brocklebank Rd. SW18 BT47 76
Brocklehurst St. SE14 CC43 67
Brockles Mead., Harl. CM13 13
Brocklesbury Clo., Wat. BD24 27
Brocklesby Rd. SE25 CB52 87
Brockley Av. N., Stan. BL27 37
Brockley Av., Stan. BL27 37
Brockley Clo., Stan. BL28 37
Brockley Combe, Wey. BA56 92
Brockley Cres., Rom. CS29 41
Brockley Cross SE4 CD45 67
Brockley Footpath SE14 CC45 67
Brockley Gdns. SE4 CD44 67
Brockley Gro. SE4 CD46 77
Brockley Gro., Brwd. DD26 122
Brockley Hall Rd. SE4 CD46 77
Brockley Hill, Stan. BK26 36
Brockley Ms. SE4 CD46 77
Brockley Pk. SE23 CD47 77
Brockley Rd. SE4 CD45 67
Brockley Ri. SE23 CD47 77
Brockley Side, Stan. BL28 37
Brockley Ter. SE17 CA42 4
Brockley Ter. SE17 CA42 67
Alvey St.
Brockley Vw. SE23 CD47 77
Brockley Way SE4 CC46 77
Brockman Ri., Brom. CF49 77
Brocks Dr., Sutt. BR55 85
Brockshot Clo., Brent. BK43 64
Brocksparkwood, Brwd. DD27 122
Brockswood La., Welw.G.C. BP 7 5
Brockton Clo., Rom. CT31 50
Brockway Clo., Guil. AT70 118
Brockway, Vir.W. AR53 82
Brockwell Clo., Orp. CN53 88
Brockwell Ct. SW2 BY46 76
Brockwell Park Gdns. SE24 BY47 76
Brockworth Clo. SE15 CA43 67
St. Georges Way
Broderick Gro., Lthd. BF66 111
Broderick Rd. SE2 CO42 69
Brodewater Rd., B.Wd. BM23 28
Brodia Rd. N16 CA34 48
Brodie Rd. E4 CF26 39
Brodie Rd., Enf. BZ22 30
Brodie Rd., Guil. AS71 118
Brodie St. SE1 CA42 4
Brodie St. SE1 CA42 67
Brodlove La. E1 CC40 57
Brodrick Rd. SW17 BU48 76
Brograve Gdns., Beck. CE51 87
Brograve Rd. N17 CB31 48
Broke Ct., Guil. AU69 118
Broke Fm. Dr., Orp. CP58 98
Broken Furlong, Eton AN42 61
Broken Gate La., Uxb. AU33 43
Broken Wharf EC4 BZ40 4
High Timber St.
Broken Wharf EC4 BZ40 57
Brokes Cres., Reig. BS69 121
Brokes Rd., Reig. BS69 121
Brokesley St. E3 CD38 57
Bromar Rd. SE5 CA45 67
Bromborough Grn., Wat. BD28 36
Brome Rd. SE9 CK45 68
Bromefield Ct., Wal.Abb. CH20 22
Winters Way
Bromefield, Stan. BK30 36
Bromehead Rd. E1 CC39 57
Bromehead St. E1 CC39 57
Bromells Rd. SW4 BW45 66
Bromet Clo., Wat. BB22 26
Bromfelde Rd. SW4 BW45 66
Bromfelde Way SW4 BX44 66
Bromfield St. N1 BY37 2
Bromfield St. N1 BY37 56
Bromford Clo., Oxt. CH70 115
Bromhall Rd., Dag. CO36 59
Bromhedge SE9 CK48 78
Bromholm Rd. SE2 CO41 69
Bromleigh Clo., Chsnt. CD17 21
Ashdown Cres.
Bromley Av., Brom. CG50 78
Bromley Common, Brom. CJ52 88
Bromley Cres., Brom. CG51 88
Bromley Cres., Ruis. BB35 44
Bromley Gdns., Brom. CG51 88
Bromley Gro., Brom. CF51 87
Bromley Hall Rd. E14 CF39 57
Lochnagar St.
Bromley High St. E3 CE38 57
Bromley Hill, Brom. CG49 78
Bromley La., Chis. CM50 78
Bromley Rd. E10 CE32 48
Bromley Rd. E17 CE31 48
Bromley Rd. N17 CA30 39
Bromley Rd. N18 BZ28 39
Bromley Rd. SE6 CE47 77
Bromley Rd., Beck. CE51 87
Bromley Rd., Brom. CE47 77
Bromley Rd., Chis. CL51 88
Bromley St. E1 CC39 57
Brompton Clo. SE20 CB51 87
Selby Rd.
Brompton Clo., Houns. BE46 74
Brompton Dr., Erith CU43 69
Brompton Gro. N2 BU31 47
Brompton Park Cres. SW6 BS43 66
Brompton Park Rd. N8 BY31 47
High Rd.
Brompton Pl. SW3 BU41 3
Brompton Pl. SW3 BU41 66
Brompton Rd. SW1 BU42 66
Brompton Rd. SW3 BU42 3
Brompton Rd. SW3 BU42 66
Brompton Rd. SW7 BU42 66
Brompton Sq. SW3 BU41 3
Brompton Sq. SW3 BU41 66
Bromwich Av. N6 BV34 47
Bromyard Av. W3 BO40 55
Brondesbury Ct. NW2 BQ36 55
Brondesbury Pk. NW2 BP36 55
Brondesbury Pk. NW6 BP36 55
Brondesbury Rd. NW6 BR37 55
Brondesbury Vill. NW6 BR37 55
Bronhill Ter. N17 CB30 39
Lansdowne Rd.
Bronsart Rd. SW6 BR43 65
Bronsdon Way, Uxb. AV34 43
Bronson Rd. SW20 BQ51 85
Bronte Clo. E7 CH35 49
Bective Rd.
Bronte Clo., Ilf. CL31 49
Bronte Clo., Til. DH44 71
Coleridge Rd.
Bronte Cres., Hem.H. AZ10 8
Bronte Gro., Dart. CW45 70
Bronti Clo. SE17 BZ42 4
Bronti Clo. SE17 BZ42 67
Bronze St. SE8 CE43 67
Brook Av., Dag. CR36 59
Brook Av., Edg. BM29 37
Brook Av., Wem. BL34 46
Brook Clo. NW7 BR29 37
Brook Clo. SW20 BP52 85
Brook Clo., Chis. CL51 88
Brook Clo., Dor. BK70 119
Brook Clo., Rom. CT30 41
Brook Clo., Ruis. BB33 44
Brook Clo., Stai. AY47 73
Brook Cres. E4 CE28 39

Brook Cres. N9 CB28 39
Brook Ct., Edg. BM28 37
Brook Ct., Rad. BJ20 18
Watling St.
Brook Dr. SE11 BY41 4
Brook Dr. SE11 BY41 66
Brook Dr., Har. BG31 45
Brook Dr., Rad. BH20 18
Brook Dr., Ruis. BB33 44
Brook Dr., Sun. BB50 73
Brook End, Saw. CP 6 6
Brook Farm Rd., Cob. BD61 102
Brook Field, Sev. CW62 108
Brook Flds., Ong. CW16 24
Brook Gate W1 BU40 3
Brook Gdns. E4 CE28 39
Brook Gdns. SW13 BO45 65
Brook Gdns., Kings.T. BN51 85
Brook Grn. W6 BQ41 65
Brook Hill, Oxt. CF68 114
Brook House Gdns. E4 CG28 40
Brook La. N., Brent. BK42 64
Brook La. SE3 CH44 68
Brook La., Bex. CP46 79
Brook La., Brom. CH50 78
Brook La., Brwd. DB22 33
Brook La., Chobham AO59 91
Brook La., Saw. CP 6 6
Brook La., Wok. AV64 100
Brook Lane Field, Harl. CO12 14
Brook Meadow N12 BS28 38
Brook Ms. N. W2 BT40 3
Brook Ms. N. W2 BT40 56
Brook Par., Chig. CL27 40
Brook Pass. SW6 BS43 66
Moore Park Rd.
Brook Path, Loug. CK24 31
Brook Pl., Barn. BS25 29
Brook Rd. N22 BX31 47
Brook Rd. N8 BX31 47
Brook Rd. NW2 BO34 46
Brook Rd. S., Brent. BK43 64
Brook Rd., B.Wd. BM23 28
Brook Rd., Brwd. CZ27 42
Brook Rd., Buck.H. CH27 40
Brook Rd., Epp. CO20 23
Brook Rd., Grav. DF47 81
Brook Rd., Guil. AU73 118
Brook Rd., Ilf. CN32 49
Brook Rd., Loug. CK24 31
Brook Rd., Merstham BW68 113
Brook Rd., Red. BU71 121
Brook Rd., Rom. CT30 41
Brook Rd., Saw. CQ 6 6
Brook Rd., Surb. BL55 85
Brook Rd., Swan. CS52 89
Brook Rd., Th.Hth. BZ52 87
Brook Rd., Twick. BJ46 74
Brook Ri., Chig. CL27 40
Brook St. N17 CA30 39
High Rd.
Brook St. W1 BV40 3
Brook St. W1 BV40 56
Brook St. W2 BT40 3
Brook St. W2 BT40 56
Brook St., Belv. CR42 69
Brook St., Brwd. CY28 42
Brook St., Kings.T. BL51 85
Brook St., Wind. AO44 61
Brook Way SE3 CH45 68
Brook Way, Chig. CL27 40
Brook Way, Lthd. BJ62 102
Brook Way, Rain. CU39 59
Brook Wk. N2 BT30 38
Brook Wk., Edg. BN29 37
Brookbank Av. W7 BG39 54
Brookbank Rd. SE13 CE45 67
Brookdale Av., Upmin. CX34 51
Brookdale Clo., Upmin. CX34 51
Brookdale N11 BW28 38
Brookdale Rd. E17 CD31 48
Brookdale Rd. SE6 CE46 77
Brookdale Rd., Bex. CQ47 79
Brookdene Av., Wat. BC26 35
Brookdene Dr., Nthwd. BB29 35
Brookdene Rd. SE18 CN42 68
Brooke Av., Har. BG34 45
Brooke Clo., Bush. BG26 36
Brooke Rd. E17 CF31 48
Brooke Rd. E5 CA34 48
Brooke Rd. N16 CA34 48
Brooke Rd., Grays DD42 71
Brooke St. EC1 BY39 2
Brooke St. EC1 BY39 56
Brooke Way, Bush. BG26 36
Richfield Rd.
Brookehowse Rd. SE6 CE48 77
Brookend Rd., Sid. CN47 78
Brooker Rd., Wal.Abb. CF20 21
Brookers Clo., Ash. BK62 102
Brookes Ct. EC1 BY39 2
Brookes Ct. EC1 BY39 56
Baldwins Gdns.
Brookfield Av. E17 CF31 48
Brookfield Av. NW7 BP29 37
Brookfield Av. W5 BK38 54
Brookfield Av., Sutt. BT56 95
Brookfield Clo. NW7 BP29 37
Brookfield Clo., Brwd. DE25 122
Brookfield Clo., Red. BV73 121
Brookfield Cres. NW7 BP29 37
Brookfield Cres., Har. BK32 45
Brookfield Ct., Grnf. BG38 54
Brookfield Ct., Har. BK32 45
Brookfield Est. NW5 BV34 47
Brookfield Gdns., Chsnt. CC17 21
Brookfield Gdns., Esher BH57 93
Brookfield La., Chsnt. CB17 21
Brookfield N6 BV34 47
Brookfield Path, Wdf.Grn. CG29 40
Oak Hill
Brookfield Pk. NW5 BV34 47
Brookfield Rd. E9 CD36 57
Brookfield Rd. N9 CB27 39
Brookfield Rd. W4 BN41 65
Brookfield, Wok. AQ61 100
Brookfields Av., Mitch. BU53 86
Brookfields, Enf. CC24 30
Brookfields, Saw. CP 6 6
Brookhill Clo. SE18 CL42 68
Brookhill Clo., Barn. BU25 29
Brookhill Rd. SE18 CL42 68
Brookhill Rd., Barn. BT25 29
Brookhurst Rd., Wey. AW57 92
Brooking Rd. E7 CH35 49
Brookland Clo. NW11 BS31 47
Brookland Ri.
Brookland Garth NW11 BS31 47
Brookland Hill NW11 BS31 47
Brookland Ri. NW11 BS31 47
Brooklands App., Rom. CS31 50
Brooklands Av. SW19 BS48 76
Brooklands Av., Sid. CM48 78
Brooklands Clo., Cob. BE61 102
Brooklands Clo., Rom. CS31 50
Brooklands Clo., Sun. BB51 83
Brooklands Ct., Enf. BZ25 30
Bush Hill
Brooklands Dr., Grnf. BK37 54
Brooklands Gdns., Horn. CV32 51
Brooklands Gdns., Pot.B. BR19 19
Brooklands La., Rom. CS31 50
Brooklands La., Wey. AZ56 92
Brooklands Pk. SE3 CH45 68
Brooklands Rd., Rom. CS31 50
Brooklands Rd., T.Ditt. BH54 84
Brooklands Rd., Wey. AZ59 92
Brooklands St. SW8 BW44 66
Brooklands Way, Red. BU69 121
Brooklea Clo. NW9 BO30 37
Brookleys, Wok. AP58 91
Brooklyn Av. SE25 CB52 87
Brooklyn Av., Loug. CK24 31
Brooklyn Clo., Wok. AS63 100
Brooklyn Ct., Loug. CK24 31
High Rd.
Brooklyn Gro. SE25 CB52 87
Brooklyn Rd. SE25 CB52 87
Brooklyn Rd., Brom. CJ53 88
Brooklyn Rd., Wok. AS62 100
Brooklyn Way., West Dr. AX41 63
Brookmans Av., Grays DE40 71
Brookmans Av., Hat. BR16 19
Brookmans Clo., Upmin. CZ33 51
Brookmead Av., Brom. CK53 88
Brookmead Clo., Orp. CO54 89
Brookmead Rd., Croy. BW53 86
Brookmead Way, Orp. CO53 89
Brookmead, Epsom BO57 94
Brookmeads Est., Mitch. BU53 86
Brookmill Rd. SE8 CE44 67
Brooks Av. E6 CK38 58
Brooks Clo. SE9 CL48 78
Brooks Clo., Wey. AZ58 92
Brooks Ct. E15 CE35 48
Brooks La. W4 BM43 65
Brooks Ms. W1 BV40 3
Brooks Ms. W1 BV40 56
Brooks Rd. E13 CH37 58
Brooks Rd. W4 BM42 65
Brooks Way, Bush. BG26 36
Richfield Rd.
Brooks Way, Orp. CP51 89
Brooksbank St. E9 CC36 57
Brooksby St. N1 BY36 56
Brooksby Ms. N1 BY36 56
Brooksby St.
Brooksbys Wk. E9 CC35 48
Brookscroft Rd. E17 CE30 39
Brookscroft, Croy. CD58 96
Bowens Wood
Brooksfield, Welw.G.C. BS 7 5
Brookshill Av., Stan. BG28 36
Brookshill Dr., Har. BG28 36
Brookshill, Har. BG28 36
Brookside Av., Ashf. AX49 73
Brookside Av., Stai. AS45 62
Brookside Clo., Barn. BR25 28
Brookside Clo., Felt. BC48 73
Brookside Clo., Har. BE35 45
Brookside Clo., Kenton BK32 45
Brookside Cres., Cuff. BX17 20
Brookside Cres., Wor.Pk. BP54 85
Green La.
Brookside Gdns., Enf. CB22 30
Brookside N21 BX25 29
Brookside Rd. N19 BW34 47
Brookside Rd. N9 CB28 39
Brookside Rd. NW11 BR32 46
Brookside Rd., Grav. DF50 81
Brookside Rd., Hayes BD40 54
Brookside S., Barn. BV26 38
Brookside Way, Croy. CC53 87
Brookside Wk. NW11 BR31 46
Brookside, Barn. BU25 29
Brookside, Cars. BV56 95
Brookside, Cher. AV54 82
Brookside, Guil AR68 109
Brookside, Harl. CK12 13
Brookside, Hat. BN12 10
Brookside, Hodd. CE12 12
Brookside, Horn. CW32 51
Brookside, Ilf. CM29 40
Brookside, Orp. CN54 88
Brookside, Pot.B. BP19 19
Brookside, Slou. AU43 62
Brookside, Uxb. AY36 53
Brookside, Wal.Abb. CG19 22
Paternoster Hill
Brookside, Wat. BC26 35
Brooksville Av. NW6 BR37 55
Brookvale, Erith CR44 69
Brookview Rd. SW16 BV49 76
Brookville Rd. SW6 BR43 65
Brookwood Av. SW13 BO44 65
Brookwood Clo., Brom. CG52 88
Brookwood Lye Rd., Wok. AO63 100
Brookwood Rd. SW18 BR47 75
Brookwood Rd., Houns. BF44 64
Broom Av., Orp. CO51 89
Broom Clo., Brom. CK53 88
Broom Clo., Chsnt. CB17 21
Spicersfield
Broom Clo., Esher BF56 93
Broom Clo., Hat. BO14 10
Broom Clo., Tedd. BK50 74
Broom Ct., Rich. BM44 65
Lichfield Rd.
Broom Gdns., Croy. CE55 87
Broom Gro., Wat. BC22 26
Broom Hall Dr., Lthd. BG60 93
Broom Hall, Lthd. BG60 93
Broom Hill Ct., Wdf.Grn. CH29 40
Broom Hill, Hem.H. AV14 7
Broom Hill, Slou. AQ36 52
Broom La., Wok. AP57 91
Broom Leys, St.Alb. BK12 9
Broom Lock, Tedd. BK50 74
Broom Water
Broom Mead, Bexh. CR46 79
Broom Pk., Tedd. BK50 74
Broom Rd., Croy. CE55 87
Broom Rd., Tedd. BJ49 74
Broom Water W., Tedd. BK49 74
Broom Water, Tedd. BK50 74
Broom Way, Wey. BB56 92
Broomcroft Clo., Wok. AU61 100
Broomcroft Dr.
Broomcroft Dr., Wok. AU61 100
Broome Clo., Epsom BN66 112
Broome Pl., S.Ock. CY40 60
Park La.
Broome Rd., Hmptn. BE50 74
Broome Way SE5 BZ43 67
Broomfield Av. N13 BX28 38
Broomfield Av., Brox. CD16 21
Broomfield Av., Loug. CK25 31
Broomfield Av., Sev. CT64 107
Broomfield Clo., Guil. AP69 118
Broomfield Ct., Wey. AZ57 92
Broomfield E17 CD33 48
Broomfield La. N13 BX28 38
Broomfield Pk., Dor. BG72 119
Broomfield Pl. W13 BJ40 54
Mattock La.
Broomfield Rd. N13 BX28 38
Broomfield Rd. W13 BJ40 54
Broomfield Rd., Beck. CD52 87
Broomfield Rd., Bexh. CR46 79
Broomfield Rd., Rich. BL44 65
Broomfield Rd., Rom. CP33 50
Broomfield Rd., Surb. BL54 85
Broomfield Rd., Swans. DC46 81
Broomfield Rd., Tedd. BK50 74
Melbourne Rd.
Broomfield Rd., Wey. AW59 92
Broomfield Ri., Wat. BA19 17
Broomfield Ride, Lthd. BG80 93
Broomfield St. E14 CE39 57
Broomfield, Guil. AP70 118
Broomfield, Harl. CO 9 6
Broomfield, St.Alb. BG17 18
Broomfield, Sun. BC51 83
Broomfields, Esher BG56 93
Broomgrove Gdns., Edg. BM30 37
Broomgrove Rd. SW9 BX44 66
Broomhall End, Wok. AS61 100
Broomhall La.
Broomhall La., Wok. AS61 100
Broomhall Rd., S.Croy. BZ58 96
Broomhall Rd., Wok. AS61 100
Broomhill Rd. SW18 BS46 76
Broomhill Rd., Dart. CU46 79
Broomhill Rd., Ilf. CO34 50
Broomhill Rd., Orp. CO54 89
Broomhill Rd., Wdf.Grn. CH29 40
Broomhill Ri., Bexh. CR46 79
Broomhills, Grav. DC49 81
Broomhills, Welw.G.C. BS 7 5
Broomhouse Gdns. E4 CG28 40
Abbotts Cres.
Broomhouse La. SW6 BS44 66
Broomhouse Rd. SW6 BS44 66
Broomhurst Ct., Dor. BJ72 119
Ridgeway Rd.
Broomlands La., Oxt. CJ65 106
Broomloan La., Sutt. BS55 86
Brooms Clo., Welw.G.C. BQ 6 5
Broomsleigh St. NW6 BS35 47
Broomstick Hall Rd., Wal.Abb. CG20 22
Broomstick La., Chesh. AQ18 16
Broomwood Gdns., Brwd. DA25 33
Broomwood Rd. SW11 BU46 76
Broomwood Rd., Orp. CO51 89
Broseley Gdns., Rom. CW28 42
Broseley Gro. SE26 CD49 77
Broseley Rd., Rom. CW28 42
Broster Gdns. SE25 CA52 87
Brott St. E1 CC38 57
Mantus Rd.
Brougham Rd. E8 CB37 2
Brougham Rd. E8 CB37 57
Brougham Rd. W3 BN39 55
Broughinge Rd., B.Wd. BM23 28
Broughton Av. N3 BR31 46
Broughton Av., Rich. BK48 74
Broughton Ct. W13 BJ40 54
Broughton Rd.
Broughton Dr. SW9 BY45 66
Somerleyton Rd.
Broughton Gdns. N6 BW32 47
Broughton Hall Av., Wok. AV66 109
Broughton Rd. SW6 BS44 66
Broughton Rd. W13 BJ40 54
Broughton Rd., Orp. CM55 88
Broughton Rd., Sev. CU61 107
Broughton Rd., Th.Hth. BY53 86
Broughton St. SW8 BV44 66
Brouncker Rd. W3 BN41 65
Brow Clo., Orp. CP54 89
Brow Cres., Orp. CP54 89
Brow, The, Ch.St.G. AR27 34
Brow, The, Red. BV73 121
Spencer Way
Brow, The, Wat. BC19 17
Browells La., Felt. BC48 73
Brown Clo. SE17 BZ42 4
Brown Clo., Wall. BX57 95
Brown Fields, Welw.G.C. BR 7 5
Brown Hart Gdns. W1 BV40 3
Brown Hart Gdns. W1 BV40 56
Brown Rd., Grav. DJ47 81
Brown St. W1 BU39 1
Brown St. W1 BU39 56
Browne Clo., Rom. CR28 41
Brownfield St. E14 CF39 57
Browngraves Rd., Hayes BA43 63
Brownhill Rd. SE6 CE47 77
Browning Av. W7 BH39 54
Browning Av., Sutt. BU56 95
Browning Av., Wor.Pk. BP54 85
Browning Clo. W9 BT38 1
Randolph Av.
Browning Clo., Hmptn. BE49 74
Browning Clo., Well. CN44 68
Browning Est. SE17 BZ42 4
Browning Est. SE17 BZ42 67
Browning Ms. W1 BV39 1
Browning Ms. W1 BV39 56
New Cavendish St.
Browning Rd. E11 CG33 49
Browning Rd. E12 CK36 58
Browning Rd., Dart. CW45 70
Browning Rd., Enf. BZ22 30
Browning Rd., Lthd. BG66 111
Browning St. SE17 BZ42 4
Browning St. SE17 BZ42 67
Browning Way, Houns. BD44 64
Browning Wk., Til. DH44 71
Coleridge Rd.
Brownlea Gdns., Ilf. CO34 50
Brownlow Ms. WC1 BX38 2
Brownlow Ms. WC1 BX38 56
Brownlow Rd. E7 CH35 49
Woodford Rd.
Brownlow Rd. E8 CA37 2
Brownlow Rd. E8 CA37 57
Brownlow Rd. N11 BX29 38
Brownlow Rd. N3 BS29 38
Brownlow Rd. NW10 BO36 55
Brownlow Rd. W13 BJ40 54
Broadway
Brownlow Rd., B.Wd. BM24 28
Brownlow Rd., Berk. AR12 7
Brownlow Rd., Croy. CA56 96
Brownlow Rd., Red. BU70 121
Brownlow St. WC1 BX39 2
Brownlow St. WC1 BX39 56
Brownrigg Rd., Ashf. AZ49 73
Browns Bldgs. EC3 CA39 2
St. Marys Av.
Browns La. NW5 BV35 47
Browns La., Lthd. BD67 111
Browns Rd. E17 CE31 48
Browns Rd., Surb. BL54 85
Browns Spring, Berk. AU11 7
Brownspring Dr. SE9 CL49 78
Brownswell Rd. N2 BT30 38
Brownswood Rd. N4 BY34 47
Brox La., Cher. AU57 91
Brox Rd., Cher. AU57 91
Broxash Rd. SW11 BV46 76
Broxbourne Av. E18 CH31 49
Broxbourne Rd. E7 CH34 49
Broxbourne Rd., Orp. CN54 88
Broxburn Dr., S.Ock. DA39 60
Broxhill Rd., Hav. CT27 41
Broxholm Rd. SE27 BY48 76
Broxted Rd. SE6 CD48 77
Broxwood Way NW3 BU37 56
Broxwood Way, NW8 BU37 1
Bruce Av., Horn. CV34 51
Bruce Av., Shep. BA53 83
Bruce Castle Rd. N17 CA30 39
Bruce Clo., Slou. AN41 61
Bruce Clo., Well. CO44 69
Bruce Clo., Wey. AY60 92
Bruce Dr., S.Croy. CC58 96
Bruce Gdns. N20 BU27 38
Bruce Gro. N17 CA30 39
Bruce Gro., Orp. CO54 89
Bruce Gro., Wat. BD22 27
Bruce Hall Ms. SW17 BV49 76
Brudenell Rd.
Bruce Rd. E3 CE38 57
Bruce Rd. NW10 BN36 55
Bruce Rd. SE25 BZ52 87
Bruce Rd., Barn. BR24 28
Bruce Rd., Har. BH30 36
Bruce Rd., Mitch. BV50 76
Bruce Way, Wal.Cr. CC20 21
Bruce Wk., Wind. AL44 61
Tinkers La.
Bruces Wharf Rd., Grays DD43 71
Brudenell Rd. SW17 BU48 76
Brudenell, Wind. AM45 61
Bruffs Meadow, Nthlt. BE36 54
Bruges Pl. NW1 BW36 1
Brumana Clo., Wey. AZ57 92
Elgin Rd.
Brumfield Rd., Epsom BN56 94
Brummell Clo., Bexh. CS45 69
Brundall Clo., Hem.H. AX14 8
Brune St. E1 CA39 2
Brune St. E1 CA39 57
Brunel Clo. SE19 CA50 77
Aubyns Rd.
Brunel Clo., Houns. BC43 63
Brunel Clo., Nthlt. BE38 54
Brunel Clo., Til. DG45 71
Brunel Est. W2 BS39 56
Brunel Pl., Houns. BF39 54
Brunel Rd. SE16 CC41 67
Brunel Rd. W3 BO39 55
Brunel Rd., Wdf.Grn. CK28 40
Brunel St. E16 CG39 58
Brunel Way, Slou. AP40 52
Brunel Wk. N15 CA31 48
Brunel Wk., Houns. BF47 74
Mallard Clo.
Brunner Clo. NW11 BS32 47
Brunner Rd. E17 CD32 48
Brunner Rd. W5 BK38 54
Bruno Pl., Wem. BN34 46
Brunswick Av. N11 BV27 38
Brunswick Av., Upmin. CZ33 51
Brunswick Centre WC1 BX38 56
Brunswick Clo. EC1 BY38 2
Brunswick Clo. EC1 BY38 56
Brunswick Clo., Bexh. CP45 69
Brunswick Rd.
Brunswick Clo., Pnr. BE32 45
Brunswick Clo., T.Ditt. BH54 84
Brunswick Clo., Twick. BG48 74
Brunswick Cres. N11 BV27 38
Brunswick Ct. SE1 CA41 4
Brunswick Ct. SE1 CA41 67
Brunswick Ct., Walt. BD55 84
Brunswick Gdns. W5 BL38 55
Brunswick Gdns. W8 BS40 56
Brunswick Gdns., Ilf. CM29 40
Brunswick Gro. N11 BV27 38
Brunswick Gro., Cob. BD60 93
Brunswick Ms. SW16 BW50 76
Potters La.
Brunswick Ms. W1 BU39 1
Great Cumberland Pl.
Brunswick Pk. Gdns. N11 BV27 38
Brunswick Pk. Rd. N11 BV27 38
Brunswick Pk. SE5 BZ44 67
Brunswick Pl. N1 BZ38 2
Brunswick Pl. N1 BZ38 57
Brunswick Pl. SE19 CB50 77
Brunswick Pl., Grav. DH47 81
Brunswick Quay Gate SE16 CC41 67
Brunswick Quay
Brunswick Quay SE16 CC41 67
Brunswick Rd. E10 CF33 48
Brunswick Rd. E14 CF39 57
Brunswick Rd. W5 BK38 54
Brunswick Rd., Bexh. CP45 69
Brunswick Rd., Kings.T. BM51 85
Brunswick Rd., Sutt. BS56 95
Brunswick Sq. N17 CA29 39
Brunswick Sq. WC1 BX38 2
Brunswick Sq. WC1 BX38 56
Brunswick St. E17 CF32 48
Brunswick Ter., Wind. AO44 61
Brunswick Vill. SE5 CA43 67
Brunswick Way N11 BV28 38
Brunton Pl. E14 CD39 57
Brushfield St. E1 CA39 2
Brushfield St. E1 CA39 57
Brushwood Dr., Rick. AU24 25
Brushwood Rd., Chesh. AP18 16
Brussels Rd. SW11 BT45 66
Bruton Clo., Chis. CK50 78
Bullerswood Dr.
Bruton La. W1 BV40 3
Bruton La. W1 BV40 56
Bruton Pl. W1 BV40 3
Bruton Pl. W1 BV40 56
Bruton Rd., Mord. BT52 86
Bruton St. W1 BV40 3
Bruton St. W1 BV40 56
Bruton Way W13 BJ39 54
Bryan Av. NW10 BP36 55
Bryan Clo., Sun. BC50 73
Bryan Rd. SE16 CD41 67
Bryanston Av., Twick. BF47 74
Bryanston Clo., Sthl. BE42 64
Blandford Rd.
Bryanston Ms. E. W1 BU39 1
Bryanston Ms. W. W1 BU39 1
Bryanston Ms. W. W1 BU39 56
Bryanston Pl. W1 BU39 1
Bryanston Pl. W1 BU39 56
Bryanston Rd., Til. DH44 71
Bryanston Sq. W1 BU39 1
Bryanston Sq. W1 BU39 56
Bryanston St. W1 BU39 1
Bryanston St. W1 BU39 56
Bryanstone Av., Guil. AQ69 118
Bryanstone Clo., Guil. AP69 118
Bryanstone Gro., Guil. AP68 109
Bryanstone Rd. N8 BW32 47
Bryanstone Rd., Wal.Cr. CD20 21
Bryant Av., Rom. CV30 42
Bryant Av., Slou. AO39 52
Bryant Clo., Barn. BR25 28
Bryant Ct. E2 CA37 2
Bryant Rd., Nthlt. BD38 54
Bryant St. E15 CF36 57
Bryantwood Rd. N7 BY35 47
Bryce Rd., Dag. CP35 50
Brycedale Cres. N14 BW28 38
Bryden Clo. SE26 CD49 77
Bryden Gro. SE26 CD49 77
Brydges Pl. WC2 BX40 4
St. Martins La.
Brydges Rd. E15 CF35 48
Brydon Wk. N1 BX37 2
Brydon Wk. N1 BX37 56
Outram Pl.
Bryer Pl., Wind. AL45 61
Bryett Rd. N7 BX34 47
Brymay Clo. E3 CE37 57
Brympton Clo., Dor. BJ72 119
Bryn-y-Mawr Rd., Enf. CA24 30
Brynford Clo., Wok. AS61 100
Brynmaer Rd. SW11 BU44 66
Bryony Clo., Uxb. AY39 53
Bryony Rd. W12 BP40 55
Bryony Rd., Guil. AT69 118
Bubblestone Rd., Sev. CU61 107
Buccleuch Rd., Slou. AQ43 62
Buccleuch Ter. E5 CB33 48
Clapton Com.
Buchan Rd. SE15 CC45 67
Buchanan Clo., S.Ock. CY40 60
Buchanan Ct., B.Wd. BN23 28
Buchanan Gdns. NW10 BP37 55
Bucharest Rd. SW18 BT47 76
Buck Clo., Horn. CV32 51
Buck La. NW9 BN32 46
Buck Rd., Grav. DE47 81
Buck St. NW1 BV37 1
Buck Wk. E17 CF31 48
Buckbean Path, Rom. CV29 42
Buckden Clo. SE12 CG46 78

Buckden Clo. SE12 CG46 78
Upwood Rd.
Buckettsland La., B.Wd BN22 28
Buckfast Ct. W13 BJ40 54
Romsey Rd.
Buckfast Rd., Mord. BS52 86
Buckfast St. E2 CB38 2
Buckfast St. E2 CB38 57
Buckham Thorns Rd., West. CM66 115
Buckhold Rd. SW18 BS46 76
Buckhurst Av., Cars. BU54 86
Buckhurst Av., Sev. CV66 117
Buckhurst Clo., Red. BU69 121
Buckhurst La., Sev. CV66 117
Buckhurst Rd., West. CL64 106
Buckhurst St. E1 CB38 57
Buckhurst Way, Buck.H. CJ28 40
Buckingham Av. N20 BT26 38
Buckingham Av., E.Mol. BF52 84
Buckingham Av., Felt. BC46 73
Buckingham Av., Grnf. BJ37 54
Buckingham Av., Th.Hth. BY51 86
Buckingham Av., Well. CN45 68
Buckingham Clo. W5 BK39 54
Buckingham Clo., Enf. CA23 30
Buckingham Clo., Guil. AS70 118
Buckingham Clo., Hmptn. BE49 74
Buckingham Clo., Horn. CV32 51
Woodlands Av.
Buckingham Clo., Orp. CN54 88
Buckingham Ct. NW4 BP30 37
Buckingham Ct., Amer. AP22 25
Buckingham Dr., Chis. CL49 78
Buckingham Gdns., Th.Hth. BY51 86
Buckingham Gdns., E.Mol. BF51 84
Buckingham Gdns., Edg. BL29 37
Buckingham Gdns., Slou. AP41 62
Buckingham Gro., Uxb. AY37 53
Buckingham Gte. SW1 BV41 3
Buckingham Gte. SW1 BW41 66
Buckingham Hill Rd., S.le H. DK41 71
Buckingham La. SE23 CD47 77
Brockley Pk.
Buckingham Ms. NW10 BO37 55
Buckingham Ms. NW6 BS35 47
West End La.
Buckingham Palace Rd. SW1 BV42 66
Buckingham Palace Rd. SW1 BV42 3
Buckingham Pl. SW1 BW41 3
Buckingham Pl. SW1 BW41 66
Palace St.
Buckingham Rd. E10 CE34 48
Buckingham Rd. E11 CJ32 49
Buckingham Rd. E15 CG35 49
Buckingham Rd. E18 CG30 40
Buckingham Rd. N1 CA36 57
Buckingham Rd. N22 BX30 38
Buckingham Rd. NW10 BO37 55
Buckingham Rd., B.Wd. BN24 28
Buckingham Rd., Edg. BL29 37
Buckingham Rd., Har. BG32 45
Buckingham Rd., Hmptn. BE49 74
Buckingham Rd., Ilf. CM34 49
Buckingham Rd., Kings.T. BL52 85
Buckingham Rd., Mitch. BX53 86
Buckingham Rd., Rich. BK48 74
Buckingham Rd., Wat. BD22 27
Buckingham St. WC2 BX40 4
Buckingham St. WC2 BX40 56
Watergate Wk.
Buckingham Ter., Sthl. BF41 64
Havelock Rd.
Buckingham Way, Wall. BW58 95
Buckland Av., Slou. AQ42 62
Buckland Cres. NW3 BT36 56
Buckland Cres., Wind. AM44 61
Buckland La., Bet. BP68 112
Buckland La., Tad. BO68 112
Buckland Rd. E10 CF34 48
Buckland Rd., Chess. BL56 94
Buckland Rd., Orp. CN56 97
Buckland Rd., Reig. BQ70 120
Buckland Rd., Sutt. BQ58 94
Buckland Rd., Tad. BR67 112
Bucklands Rd., Tedd. BK50 74
Buckland Ri., Pnr. BD30 36
Buckland St. N1 BZ37 2
Buckland St. N1 BZ37 57
Buckland Way, Wor.Pk. BQ54 85
Buckland Wk., Mord. BT53 86
Buckle St. E1 CA39 2
Buckle St. E1 CA39 57
Bucklebury Clo., Maid. AH43 61
Buckleigh Av. SW20 BR52 85
Buckleigh Rd. SW16 BW50 76
Buckleigh Way SE19 CA50 77
Stambourne Way
Buckler Gdns. SE9 CK49 78
Bucklers All. SW6 BR43 65
Haldane Rd.
Bucklers Clo., Brox. CD14 12
Bucklers Ct., Brwd. DB28 42
Brackens Dr.
Bucklers Way, Cars. BU55 86
Bucklersbury EC4 BZ39 2
Bucklersbury EC4 BZ39 57
Walbrook
Buckles La., S.Ock. DB39 60
Buckles Way, Bans. BR61 103
Buckley Clo., Dart. CT44 69
Buckley Rd. NW6 BR36 55
Buckley St. SE1 BY48 56
Mepham St.
Buckmaster Rd. SW11 BU45 66
Bucknall St. WC2 BW39 1
Bucknall St. WC2 BW39 56
Bucknalls Clo., Wat. BE19 18
Bucknalls Dr., St.Alb. BE19 18
Bucknalls La., Wat. BD19 18
Bucknell Clo. SW2 BX45 66
Buckner Rd. SW2 BX45 66
Buckner St. W10 BR38 55
Bucknills Clo., Epsom BN60 94
Ebbisham Rd.
Buckrell Rd. E4 CF27 39
Bucks All., Hert. BW12 11
Bucks Av., Wat. BE26 36
Bucks Clo., Wey. AW60 92
Bucks Cross Rd., Grav. DF48 81
Bucks Cross Rd., Orp. CQ56 98
Bucks Hill Rd., Kings L. AW19 17
Bucks Hill, Kings L. AX20 17
Buckstone Clo. SE23 CC46 77
Buckstone Rd. N18 CB28 39
Buckters Rents SE16 CD40 57
Buckthorne Rd. SE4 CD46 77
Buckton Rd., B.Wd. BL22 28
Budd Cft., Welw.G.C. BS 7 5
Budd Clo. N12 BS28 38
Buddings Circ., Wem. BN34 46
Budebury Rd., Stai. AW49 73
Budge Row EC4 BZ40 4
Budge Row EC4 BZ40 57
Cannon St.
Budgen Dr., Red. BV69 121
Budgins Hill, Orp. CO59 98
Budleigh Cres., Well. CP43 69
Budoch Dr., Ilf. CO34 50
Buer Rd. SW6 BR44 65
Buff Av., Bans. BS60 95
Bug Hill, Warl. CC63 105
Bugsbys Way SE7 CH42 68
Bulbourne Clo., Berk. AP12 7
Bulbourne Clo., Hem.H. AW14 8
Bulganak Rd., Th.Hth. BZ52 87
Bulingford Clo. SE4 CD45 67
Frendsbury Rd.
Bulkeley Av., Wind. AN44 61
Bulkeley Clo., Egh. AR49 72
Bull All. SE1 BY40 4
Bull All., Well. CO45 69
Bull Hill, Lthd. BJ64 102
Bull Inn Ct. WC2 BX40 56
Strand
Bull La. N18 CA28 39
Bull La., Chis. CM50 78
Bull La., Dag. CR34 50
Bull La., Ger.Cr. AR31 43
Bull Rd. E15 CG37 58
Bull Stag Grn., Hat. BQ11 10
Bull Wharf La. EC4 BZ40 4
Bull Yd. N15 CA31 48
Stamford Hill High Rd.
Bullace Clo., Hem.H. AW13 8
Bullace La., Dart. CW46 80
Bullace Row SE5 BZ44 67
Camberwell Rd.
Bullards Pl. E2 CC38 57
Bullbanks Rd., Belv. CS42 69
Bullbeggars La., Berk. AS13 7
Bullbeggars La., Wok. AQ61 100
Bullbeggars Rd., Gdse. CC69 114
Bullen St. SW11 BU44 66
Bullens Grn. La., St.Alb. BO15 10
Buller Clo. SE15 CB43 67
Buller Rd. N17 CB30 39
Buller Rd. NW10 BQ38 55
Buller Rd., Bark. CN36 58
Buller Rd., Th.Hth. BZ51 87
Bullers Clo., Sid. CQ49 79
Bullers Rd. N22 BY30 38
Bullers Wood Dr., Chis. CK50 78
Bullescroft Rd., Edg. BM27 37
Bullfields, Saw. CQ 5 6
Bullfinch Clo., Sev. CS64 107
Bullfinch Dene, Sev. CS64 107
Bullfinch La., Sev. CS64 107
Bullfinch Rd., Croy. CC59 96
Bullhead Rd., B.Wd. BN23 28
Bullivant St. E14 CF39 57
Bullrush Cl., Hat. BP13 10
Bullrush Gro., Uxb. AX38 53
Iver La.
Bulls All. SW14 BN44 65
Bulls Bridge Rd., Sthl. BC41 63
Bulls Cross Ride, Wal.Cr. CB21 30
Bulls Cross, Enf. CB22 30
Bulls Gdns. SW3 BU42 3
Bulls Gdns. SW3 BU42 66
Walton St.
Bulls Head Pass. EC3 CA39 57
Gracechurch St.
Bulls La., Hat. BQ15 10
Bullsbrook Rd., Hayes BD40 54
Bullshead Pl. EC3 CA39 2
Bullsland Gdns., Rick. AT25 25
Bullsland La., Rick. AT25 25
Bullsmoor Clo., Wal.Cr. CC21 30
Bullsmoor Gdns., Wal.Cr. CB21 30
Bullsmoor La., Enf. CB21 30
Bullsmoor Ride, Wal.Cr. CC21 30
Bullsmoor Way, Wal.Cr. CB21 30
Bullwell Cres., Chsnt. CD18 21
Bulmer Gdns., Har. BK33 45
Bulmer Ms. W11 BS40 56
Kensington Pk. Rd.
Bulmer Pl. W11 BS40 56
Bulmer Wk., Rain. CV37 60
Bulow Ct. SW6 BS44 66
Bulstrode Av., Houns. BE44 64
Bulstrode Gdns., Houns. BF45 64
Bulstrode La., Kings L. AV17 16
Bulstrode Pl. W1 BV39 1
Bulstrode Pl. W1 BV39 56
Bulstrode Rd., Houns. BF45 64
Bulstrode St. W1 BV39 1
Bulstrode St. W1 BV40 56
Bulstrode Way, Ger.Cr. AR32 43
Bulwer Court Rd. E11 CF33 48
Bulwer Gdns., Barn. BT24 29
Bulwer Rd.
Bulwer Rd. E11 CF33 48
Bulwer Rd. N18 CA28 39
Bulwer Rd., Barn. BS24 29
Bulwer St. W12 BQ40 55
Bunby Rd., Slou. AP36 52
Bunce Common Rd., Reig. BN74 120
Buncefield La., Hem.H. AZ12 8
Bunces Clo., Eton AN42 61
Bunces La., Wdf.Grn. CG29 40
Bundys Way, Stai. AV50 72
Bungalow Rd., SE25 CA52 87
Bungalow Rd., Wok. AZ65 101
Bungalows, The SW16 BV50 76
Bungalows, The, Bush. BE24 27
Bunhill Row EC1 BZ38 2
Bunhill Row EC1 BZ38 57
Bunhouse Pl. SW1 BV42 66
Bourne St.
Bunkers Hill NW11 BT33 47
Bunkers Hill, Belv. CR42 69
Bunkers Hill, Sid. CQ48 79
Bunkers La., Hem.H. AZ16 17
Bunns Field, Welw.G.C. BT 7 5
Bunns La. NW7 BO29 37
Bunns La., Chesh. AQ20 16
Bunsen St. E3 CD37 57
Kenilworth Rd.
Bunten Meade, Slou. AN40 61
Bunting Clo., Mitch. BU53 86
Buntingbridge Rd., Ilf. CM32 49
Bunton St. SE18 CL41 68
Bunyan Rd. E17 CD31 48
Bunyans Clo., Brwd. DA28 42
Bunyans La., Wok. AO60 91
Bunyard Dr., Wok. AU60 91
Burbage Clo. SE1 BZ41 4
Burbage Clo. SE1 BZ41 67
Burbage Clo., Chsnt. CD19 21
Burbage Rd. SE21 BZ46 77
Burbage Rd. SE24 BZ46 77
Burberry Clo., N.Mal. BO51 85
Burbridge Rd., Shep. AZ52 83
Burbridge Way N17 CA30 39
Ladysmith Rd.
Burch Rd., Grav. DF46 81
Burcham St. E14 CE39 57
Burcharbro Rd. SE2 CP43 69
Burchell Ct., Bush. BG26 36
Burchell Rd. E10 CE33 48
Burchell Rd. SE15 CB44 67
Burchett Way, Rom. CQ32 50
Burchetts Way, Shep. AZ53 83
Burchwall Clo., Rom. CS29 41
Burcote Rd. SW18 BT47 76
Burcote, Wey. BA57 92
Burcott Gdns., Wey. AX57 92
Burcott Rd., Pur. BY60 95
Burden Clo., Brent. BK42 64
Burden Way E11 CH34 49
Burden Way, Guil. AQ68 109
Burdenshot Hill, Guil. AQ65 100
Burdenshott Av., Rich. BM45 65
Burder Clo. N1 CA36 57
Burder Rd.
Burder Rd. N1 CA36 57
Burdett Av. SW20 BP51 85
Burdett Clo., Sid. CQ49 79
Burdett Est. E14 CE39 57
Burdett Ms. NW3 BT36 56
Belsize Cres.
Burdett Ms. W2 BS39 1
Hatherley Gro.
Burdett Rd. E14 CD38 57
Burdett Rd. E3 CD38 57
Burdett Rd., Croy. BZ53 87
Burdett Rd., Rich. BL44 65
Burdett St. SE1 BY41 4
Burdett St. SE1 BY41 66
Pearman St.
Burdock Clo., Croy. CC54 87
Burdon La., Sutt. BR57 94
Burdon Pk., Sutt. BR58 94
Burfield Clo. SW17 BT49 76
Burfield Clo., Hat. BP11 10
Burfield Dr., Whyt. CC63 105
Burfield Rd., Rick. AU25 25
Burfield Rd., Wind. AQ46 72
Burford Clo., Dag. CP34 50
Burford Clo., Ilf. CM31 49
Burford Clo., Uxb. AY35 44
Burford Gdns. N13 BX27 38
Burford La., Epsom BQ59 94
Burford Pl., Hodd. CE12 12
Burford St.
Burford Rd. E15 CF37 57
Burford Rd. E6 CK38 58
Burford Rd. SE6 CD48 77
Burford Rd., Brent. BL42 65
Burford Rd., Brom. CK52 88
Burford Rd., Sutt. BS55 86
Burford Rd., Wor.Pk. BO54 85
Burford St., Hodd. CE12 12
Burford Way, Croy. CF57 96
Burgate Clo., Dart. CT45 69
Burges Clo., Horn. CW32 51
Burges Ct. E6 CL36 58
Burges Rd. E6 CK36 58
Burgess Av. NW9 BN32 46
Burgess Clo., Felt. BE49 74
Creswell Clo.
Burgess Hill NW2 BS35 47
Burgess Rd. E15 CG35 49
Burgess Rd., Sutt. BS56 95
Burgess St. E14 CE39 57
Burgett Rd., Slou. AN41 61
Burgh Heath Rd., Epsom BO60 94
Burgh Mt., Bans. BR61 103
Burgh St. N1 BY37 2
Burgh St. N1 BY37 56
Burgh Wood, Bans. BR61 103
Burghfield Rd., Grav. DF50 81
Burghfield, Epsom BO61 103
Burghill Rd. SE26 CC49 77
Burghley Av., B.Wd. BN25 28
Burghley Av., N.Mal. BN51 85
Burghley Rd. E11 CG33 49
Burghley Rd. N8 BY31 47
Burghley Rd. NW5 BV35 47
Burghley Rd. SW19 BQ49 75
Burgon St. EC4 BY39 56
Carter La.
Burgos Gro. SE10 CE44 67
Burgoyne Hatch, Harl. CO10 6
Burgoyne Rd. N4 BY32 47
Burgoyne Rd. SE25 CA52 87
Burgoyne Rd. SW9 BX45 66
Burgoyne Rd., Sun. BB50 73
Burgundy Cft., Welw.G.C. BR 9 5
Burham Clo. SE20 CC50 77
Blenheim Rd.
Burhill Gro., Pnr. BE30 36
Barrow Point La.
Burhill Rd., Walt. BC58 92
Burke Clo. SW15 BO45 65
Burke St. E16 CG39 58
Burland Rd. SW11 BU46 76
Burland Rd., Brwd. DB26 42
Burland Rd., Rom. CS29 41
Burlea Clo., Walt. BC56 92
Burleigh Av., Sid. CN46 78
Burleigh Av., Wall. BV55 86
Burleigh Clo., Wey. AW56 92
Burleigh Gdns. N14 BW26 38
Burleigh Gdns., Ashf. BA49 73
Burleigh Ho. W10 BQ39 55
Burleigh Mead, Hat. BQ11 10
Burleigh Pk., Cob. BE59 93
Burleigh Pl. SW15 BQ46 75
Cambalt Rd.
Burleigh Pl., Mitch. BU53 86
Burleigh Rd., Chsnt. CD19 21
Burleigh Rd., Enf. CA24 30
Burleigh Rd., Hem.H. BA14 8
Burleigh Rd., St.Alb. BJ13 9
Burleigh Rd., Sutt. BR54 85
Burleigh Rd., Uxb. AZ37 53
Burleigh Rd., Wey. AW56 92
Burleigh St. WC2 BX40 4
Burleigh St. WC2 BX40 56
Tavistock St.
Burleigh Way, Cuff. BX18 20
Burleigh Way, Enf. BZ24 30
Burley Clo. E4 CE28 39
Burley Clo. SW16 BW51 86
Burley Rd. E16 CJ39 58
Burlingham Clo., Guil. AU69 118
Gilliat Dr.
Burlings La., Sev. CN62 106
Burlington Arc. W1 BW40 3
Burlington Arc. W1 BW40 56
Burlington Gdns.
Burlington Av., Rich. BM44 65
Burlington Av., Rom. CS32 50
Burlington Av., Slou. AP41 62
Burlington Clo. E6 CK39 58
Northumberland Rd.
Burlington Clo. W9 BS38 56
Elgin Av.
Burlington Clo., Brom. CL55 88
Crofton Rd.
Burlington Clo., Felt. BA47 73
Burlington Clo., Orp. CL55 88
Burlington Gdns. W1 BW40 3
Burlington Gdns. W1 BW40 56
Burlington Gdns. W3 BN40 55
Burlington Gdns. W4 BN42 65
Burlington Gdns., Rom. CQ33 50
Burlington La. W4 BN43 65
Burlington Ms. E. W2 BS39 56
Shrewsbury Rd.
Burlington Ms. W. W2 BS39 56
Ledbury Rd.
Burlington Ms. W3 BO40 55
Burlington Gdns.
Burlington Pl., Wdf.Grn. CH27 40
Burlington Rd. N10 BV31 47
Tetherdown
Burlington Rd. N17 CB30 39
Burlington Rd. SW6 BR44 65
Burlington Rd. W4 BN42 65
Burlington Rd., Enf. BZ23 30
Burlington Rd., Islw. BG44 64
Burlington Rd., N.Mal. BO52 85
Burlington Rd., Slou. AP41 62
Burlington Rd., Th.Hth. BZ51 87
Burlington Ri., Barn. BU26 38
Burlington St. W1 BW40 56
Burma Ct. N5 BZ35 48
Green Lanes
Burma Rd. N16 BZ35 48
Burma Rd., Wok. AP53 82
Burman St. SE1 BY41 4
Burman St. SE1 BY41 66
Burmester Rd. SW17 BT48 76
Burn Brae Clo. N3 BS29 38
Burn Clo., Wat. BG24 27
Burn Clo., Wey. AX56 92
Burn Side N9 CC27 39
Burn Side, Ash. BL62 103
Burnaby Cres. W4 BN43 65
Burnaby Gdns. W4 BM43 65
Burnaby Rd., Grav. DF47 81
Burnaby St. SW10 BT43 66
Burnbury Rd. SW12 BW47 76
Burncroft Av., Enf. CC23 30
Burne Jones Ho. W14 BR42 65
Burne St. NW1 BU39 1
Burnell Av., Rich. BK49 74
Burnell Av., Well. CO44 69
Burnell Gdns., Stan. BK30 36
Burnell Rd., Sutt. BS56 95
Burnell Wk. SE1 CA42 4
Cadet Dr.
Burnell Wk., Brwd. DB29 42
Burnels Av. E6 CL38 58
Burness Clo. N7 BX36 56
Roman Way
Burness Clo., Uxb. AX37 53
Whitehall Rd.
Burnet Av., Guil. AT69 118
Burnet Gro., Epsom BN60 94
Burnett Clo. E9 CC35 48
Burnett Pk., Harl. CL13 13
Burnett Rd., Erith CV43 70
Burnetts Rd., Wind. AM44 61
Burney Av., Surb. BL53 85
Burney Clo. Lthd. BG66 111
Burney Dr., Loug. CL23 31
Burney Rd., Dor. BJ69 119
Burney St. SE10 CF43 67
Burnfoot Av. SW6 BR44 65
Burnham Av., Uxb. BA35 44
Burnham Clo. E11 CJ31 49
Burnham Clo. SE1 CA42 4
Bushwood Dr.
Burnham Clo., Enf. CA22 30
Burnham Clo., Wind. AL44 61
Burnham Clo., Wok. AO62 100
Burnham Cres., Dart. CV45 70
Burnham Ct. NW4 BQ31 46
Burnham Dr., Reig. BS70 121
Burnham Dr., Wor.Pk. BQ55 85
Burnham Gdns., Croy. CA54 87
Burnham Gdns., Hayes BA41 63
Burnham Gdns., Houns. BC44 63
Burnham Rd. E4 CD28 39
Burnham Rd., Dag. CO36 59
Burnham Rd., Dart. CV45 70
Burnham Rd., Mord. BS53 86
Burnham Rd., Rom. CS31 50
Burnham Rd., Sid. CQ48 79
Burnham Rd., St.Alb. BJ13 9
Burnham Rd., Wok. AO62 100
Burnham St. E2 CC38 57
Burnham St., Kings.T. BM51 85
Burnham Way W13 BJ41 64
Burnhams Rd., Lthd. BE65 102
Burnhill Rd., Beck. CE51 87
Burnley Clo., Wat. BD28 36
Burnley Rd. NW10 BO35 46
Burnley Rd. SW9 BX44 66
Burnley Rd., Grays DA43 70
Burns Av., Felt. BC46 73
Burns Av., Sid. CO46 79
Burns Av., Sthl. BF40 54
Burns Clo. SW19 BT50 76
North Rd.
Burns Clo., Cob. BG61 102
Burns Clo., Erith CT44 69
Burns Clo., Hayes BB39 53
Burns Clo., Well. CN44 68
Burns Dr., Hem.H. AZ10 8
Burns Pl., Til. DG44 71
Burns Rd. NW10 BO37 55
Burns Rd. SW11 BU44 66
Burns Rd. W13 BJ41 64
Burns Rd., Wem. BK37 54
Burns Way, Brwd. DE25 122
Burns Way, Houns. BD44 64
Burnsall St. SW3 BU42 3
Burnsall St. SW3 BU42 66
Burnside Clo. SE16 CC40 57
Burnside Clo., Barn. BS24 29
Meadway
Burnside Clo., Hat. BP11 10
Burnside Clo., Twick. BJ46 74
Burnside Cres., Wem. BK37 54
Burnside Rd., Dag. CP34 50
Burnside Ter., Harl. CQ 9 6
Burnside, Hodd. CD12 12
Burnside, Saw. CP 6 6
Burnt Ash Hill SE12 CG46 78
Burnt Ash La., Brom. CH50 78
Burnt Ash Rd. SE12 CH46 78
Burnt Common Clo., Wok. AV66 109
Burnt Farm Ride, Enf. BY20 20
Burnt Mill Clo., Harl. CM 9 6
Burnt Mill La.
Burnt Mill La., Harl. CM 9 6
Burnt Mill, Harl. CM 9 6
Burnt Oak Bdwy., Edg. BM30 37
Burnt Oak Fields, Edg. BM30 37
East Rd.
Burnt Oak La., Sid. CN46 78
Burntcommon La., Wok. AV66 109
Burnthouse La., Dart. CW49 80
Burnthwaite Rd. SW6 BR43 65
Burntmill La., Harl. CM 9 6
Burntwood Av., Horn. CV32 51
Burntwood Clo. SW18 BU47 76
Burntwood Clo., Brwd. DE32 123
Burntwood Clo., Cat. CB64 105
SW18
Burntwood Gro., Sev. CU67 116
Burntwood La. SW17 BT48 76
Burntwood La., Cat. CA64 105
Burntwood Rd., Sev. CU67 116
Burntwood, Brwd. DB27 42
Gerrard Cres.
Burnway, Horn. CW33 51
Burpham La., Guil. AT68 109
Burr Clo. E1 CB40 4
Burr Clo. E1 CB40 57
Burr Clo., Bexh. CQ45 69
Burr Clo., St.Alb. BL17 19
Burr Hill La., Wok. AP58 91
Burr Rd. SW18 BS47 76
Burrage Gro. SE18 CM42 68
Burrage Pl. SE18 CL42 68
Burrage Rd. SE18 CM42 68
Burrard Rd. E16 CH39 58
Burrard Rd. NW6 BS35 47
Burrell Clo., Croy. CD53 87
Burrell Clo., Edg. BM27 37
Burrell Row, Beck. CE51 87
High St.
Burrell St. SE1 BY40 4
Burrell St. SE1 BY40 56
Burrell, The, Dor. BG72 119
Burrells Wharf Sq. E14 CE42 67
Burrfield Dr., Orp. CP53 89
Burritt Rd., Kings.T. BM51 85
Burroughs Gdns. NW4 BP31 46
Burroughs, The NW4 BP31 46
Burrow Clo., Chig. CN28 40
Burrow Field, Welw.G.C. BQ 9 5
Burrow Grn., Chig. CN28 40
Burrow Hill Grn., Wok. AO58 91
Windlesham Rd.
Burrow Rd., Chig. CN28 40
Burrow Wk. SE24 BZ47 77
Rosendale Rd.
Burroway Rd., Slou. AT41 62
Burrows Clo., Lthd. BE65 102

Burrows Hill Clo., Houns. AX45 63
Burrows Hill La., Houns. AW45 63
Burrows Ms. SE1 BY41 4
Burrows Ms. SE1 BY41 66
Burrows Rd. NW10 BQ38 55
Bursar St. SE1 CA40 4
Tooley St.
Bursdon Clo., Sid. CN48 78
Burses Way, Brwd. DE25 122
Bursland Rd., Enf. CC24 30
Burslem Av., Ilf. CO29 41
Burslem St. E1 CB39 57
Burstead Clo., Cob. BD59 93
Burstock Rd. SW15 BR45 65
Burston Dr., St.Alb. BG17 18
Burston Rd. SW15 BQ45 65
Burstow Rd. SW20 BR51 85
Burt Rd. E16 CJ40 58
Burtenshaw Rd., T.Ditt. BJ53 84
Burtley Clo. N4 BZ33 48
Burton Av., Wat. BC24 26
Burton Clo. NW7 BQ28 37
Burton Clo., Chess. BK57 93
Burton Ct. SW3 BU42 3
Burton Ct. SW3 BU42 66
Burton Dr., Loug. CM24 31
Burton Gdns., Houns. BE44 64
Burton Gro. SE17 BZ42 4
Burton Gro. SE17 BZ42 67
Burton Hole La. NW7 BQ28 37
Burton La. SW9 BY44 66
Evandale Rd.
Burton La., Chsnt. CA18 21
Burton Ms. SW1 BV42 3
Burton Pl. WC1 BW38 1
Burton Pl. WC1 BW38 56
Burton St.
Burton Rd. E18 CH31 49
Burton Rd. NW6 BR36 55
Burton Rd. SW9 BY44 66
Burton Rd., Kings.T. BL50 75
Burton Rd., Loug. CM24 31
Burton St. WC1 BW38 1
Burton St. WC1 BW38 56
Burton Way, Wind. AM45 61
Burtons La., Ch.St.G. AR23 25
Burtons Rd., Hmptn. BF49 74
Burtons Way, Ch.St.G. AR23 25
Burtwell La. SE27 BZ49 77
Burwash Rd. SE18 CM42 68
Burway Cres., Cher. AW52 83
Western Av.
Burwell Av., Grnf. BH36 54
Burwell Clo. E1 CB39 57
Burwell Rd. E10 CD33 48
Burwell Wk. E3 CE38 57
Rounton Rd.
Burwood Av., Brom. CH55 88
Burwood Av., Ken. BY60 95
Burwood Av., Pnr. BC32 44
Burwood Clo., Guil. AU70 118
Burwood Clo., Reig. BT70 121
Burwood Clo., Surb. BM54 85
Burwood Clo., Walt. BD57 93
Burwood Gdns., Rain. CT38 59
Burwood Park Rd., Walt. BC56 92
Burwood Pl. W2 BU39 1
Burwood Pl. W2 BU39 56
Burwood Rd., Walt. BB57 92
Bury Av., Hayes BB37 53
Bury Av., Ruis. BA32 44
Bury Clo., Wok. AR61 100
Bury Ct. EC3 CA39 2
Bury Ct. EC3 CA39 57
Bury Green Rd., Chsnt. CB19 21
Bury Gro., Mord. BS53 86
Bury Hall Vill. N9 CA26 39
Bury Hill Clo., Hem.H. AX13 8
Bury Hill, Hem.H. AW13 8
Bury Holme, Brox. CD15 12
Bury La., Epp. CM17 22
Bury La., Rick. AX26 35
Bury La., Wok. AR61 100
Bury Meadows, Rick. AX26 35
Bury Pl. WC1 BX39 2
Bury Pl. WC1 BX39 56
Bury Rd. N22 BY31 47
Bury Rd., Dag. CR35 50
Bury Rd., Epp. CN19 22
Bury Rd., Harl. CP 9 6
Bury Rd., Hat. BQ12 10
Beaconsfield Rd.
Bury Rd., Hem.H. AX13 8
Bury Ri., Hem.H. AU16 16
Bury St. EC3 CA39 2
Bury St. EC3 CA39 57
Bury St. N9 CA26 39
Bury St. SW1 BW40 3
Bury St. SW1 BW40 56
Bury St. W. N9 BZ26 39
Bury St., Guil. AR71 118
Bury St., Ruis. BA32 44
Bury Wk. SW3 BU42 3
Bury Wk. SW3 BU42 66
Burycroft, Welw.G.C. BR 6 5
Burydell La., St.Alb. BG17 18
Buryfields, Guil. AT71 118
Busby Ms. NW5 BW36 56
Torriano Av.
Busby Pl. NW5 BW36 56
Busby St. E2 CA38 2
Chilton St.
Busch Cor., Islw. BJ44 64
Bush Clo., Ilf. CM32 49
Bush Clo., Wey. AX56 92
Bush Cotts. SW18 BS46 76
Putney Bridge Rd.
Bush Ct. N14 BW26 38
Bush Elms Rd., Horn. CU33 50
Bush Fair, Harl. CN12 13
Bush Gro. NW9 BN33 46
Bush Gro. Stan. BK29 36
Bush Hall La., Hat. BQ11 10
Bush Hill N21 BZ26 39
Bush Hill Rd. N21 BZ25 30
Bush Hill Rd., Har. BL32 46
Bush Industrial Est. NW10 BN38 55
Bush La. EC4 BZ40 4
Bush La. EC4 BZ40 57
Cannon St.
Bush La., Wok. AU65 100
Bush Rd. E11 CG33 49
Bush Rd. E8 CB37 57
Bush Rd. SE8 CC42 67
Bush Rd., Buck.H. CJ28 40
Bush Rd., Rich. BL43 65
Bush Rd., Shep. AY53 83
Bushbarns, Chsnt. CB18 21
Bushberry Rd. E9 CD36 57
Bushbury La., Bet. BM72 120
Bushby Av., Brox. CD14 12
Bushell Clo. SW2 BX48 76
Bushell Grn., Bush. BG27 36
Bushell St. E1 CB40 4
Bushell St. E1 CB40 57
Hermitage Wall
Bushell Way, Brom. CL47 78
Bushetts Gro., Red. BV68 113
Bushey Av. E18 CG31 49
Bushey Av., Orp. CM54 88
Bushey Cft., Harl. CN12 13
Bushey Cft., Oxt. CF68 114
High St.
Bushey Clo., Uxb. AZ34 44
Bushey Clo., Welw.G.C. BS 8 5
Bushey Clo., Whyt. CA61 105
Bushey Ct. SW20 BP51 85
Bushey Ct., Kings.T. BK50 74
Bushey Grn., Welw.G.C. BS 8 5
Bushey Ley
Bushey Grove Rd., Bush. BD24 27
Bushey Hall Dr., Bush. BE24 27
Bushey Hall Rd., Bush. BD24 27
Bushey Hill Rd. SE5 CA44 67
Bushey La., Sutt. BS56 95
Bushey Lea, Ong. CX18 24
Bushey Lees, Sid. CN46 78
Fen Gro.
Bushey Ley, Welw.G.C. BS 8 5
Bushey Mill Cres., Wat. BD22 27
Bushey Mill La., Bush. BE23 27
Bushey Mill La., Wat. BD22 27
Bushey Rd. E13 CJ37 58
Bushey Rd. N15 CA32 48
Bushey Rd. SW20 BP52 85
Bushey Rd., Croy. CE55 87
Bushey Rd., Hayes BB42 63
Bushey Rd., Sutt. BS56 95
Bushey Rd., Uxb. AZ34 44
Bushey Shaw, Ash. BK62 102
Bushey Way, Beck. CF53 87
Bushfield Clo., Edg. BM27 37
Bushfield Cres., Edg. BM27 37
Bushfield Dr., Red. BV73 121
Bushfield Rd., Hem.H. AU16 16
Bushfields, Loug. CL25 31
Bushgrove Rd., Dag. CP35 50
Bushmoor Cres. SE18 CL43 68
Bushnell Rd. SW17 BV48 76
Bushway, Dag. CP35 50
Bushwood Clo., Hat. BP15 10
Bushwood E11 CG33 49
Bushwood Rd., Rich. BM43 65
Bushy Down SW12 BV48 76
Bedford Hill
Bushy Hill Dr., Guil. AT69 118
Bushy Park Cotts., Tedd. BH50 74
Bushy Park Gdns., Tedd. BG49 74
Bushy Park Rd., Tedd. BJ50 74
Bushy Rd., Lthd. BF65 102
Bushy Rd., Tedd. BH50 74
Busk St. E2 CB37 57
Yorkton St.
Busty La., Sev. DB64 108
Butcher Row E14 CC40 57
Butchers Rd. E16 CH39 58
Bute Av., Rich. BL48 75
Bute Ct., Wall. BV56 95
Bute Rd.
Bute Gdns. W., Wall. BW56 95
Bute Gdns. W6 BQ42 65
Bute Gdns., Wall. BW56 95
Bute Rd., Croy. BY54 86
Bute Rd., Ilf. CL31 49
Bute Rd., Wall. BW56 95
Bute St. SW7 BT42 3
Bute St. SW7 BT42 66
Bute Wk. N1 BZ36 57
Clephane Rd.
Buthfield St. W8 BS41 66
Butler Av., Har. BG33 45
Butler Ho., Grays DD43 71
Hawkes Clo.
Butler Pl. SW1 BW41 3
Palmer St.
Butler Pl. SW1 BW41 66
Palmer St.
Butler Rd. NW10 BO36 55
Curzon Cres.
Butler Rd., Dag. CO35 50
Butler Rd., Har. BG33 45
Butler St. E2 CC38 57
Digby St.
Butler St., Uxb. AZ38 53
Butlers Clo., Wind. AL44 61
Butlers Dene Rd., Cat. CD63 105
Butlers Dr. E4 CF22 30
Butlers Hill, Lthd. AZ68 110
Butlers Pl., New A.G. DC55 90
Butt Field Vw., St.Alb. BG15 9
Butter Cross La., Epp. CO18 23
Butter Hill, Cars. BV55 86
Butter Hill, Wall. BV55 86
Buttercup Clo., Rom. CV30 42
Copperfields Way
Butterfield Clo., Twick. BH46 74
Butterfield La., St.Alb. BH15 9
Butterfield Sq. E6 CK39 58
Guildford Rd.
Butterfields E17 CF32 48
Butterfly La. SE9 CL46 78
Butterfly La., B.Wd. BJ24 27
Butterfly Wk., Warl. CC63 105
Butteridges Clo., Dag. CQ37 59
Buttermere Clo. SW20 BQ53 85
Buttermere Clo., Felt. BB47 73
Westmacott Dr.
Buttermere Clo., N.Mal. BQ53 85
Grand Dr.
Buttermere Dr. SW15 BR46 75
Buttermere Gdns., Pur. BZ60 96
Buttermere Rd., Orp. CP52 89
Buttermere Way, Egh. AT50 72
Keswick Way
Buttermere Wk. E8 BY36 56
Rhodes Dev.
Buttersweet Ri., Saw. CQ 6 6
Butterwick W6 BQ42 65
Butterwick, Wat. BE21 27
Buttesland St. N1 BZ38 2
Buttesland St. N1 BZ38 57
Buttfield Clo., Dag. CR36 59
Buttlehide, Rick. AU28 34
Buttmarsh Clo. SE18 CL42 68
Button St., Swan. CV53 90
Buttondene Cres., Brox. CE14 12
Butts Cotts., Felt. BE48 74
Butts Cres., Felt. BF48 74
Butts End, Hem.H. AW12 8
Butts Farm Est., Felt. BE48 74
Butts Green Rd., Horn. CV32 51
Butts Head, Nthwd. BA29 35
Butts Piece, Nthlt. BC37 53
Longhook Gdns.
Butts Rd., Brom. CG49 78
Butts Rd., Wok. AS62 100
Chobham Rd.
Butts, The, Brent. BK43 64
Butts, The, Brox. CD15 12
Butts, The, Sev. CU62 107
Butts, The, Sun. BD52 84
Buttsbury Rd., Ilf. CM35 49
Buxted Clo. E8 CA36 57
Buxted Rd. N12 BU28 38
Buxton Av., Cat. CA64 105
Buxton Clo., St.Alb. BK12 9
Buxton Clo., Wdf.Grn. CJ29 40
Buxton Cres., Sutt. BR56 94
Buxton Dr. E11 CG31 49
Buxton Dr., N.Mal. BN51 85
Buxton Gdns. W3 BM40 55
Buxton La., Cat. BZ63 105
Buxton Path, Wat. BD27 36
Buxton Rd. E15 CG35 49
Buxton Rd. E17 CD31 48
Buxton Rd. E4 CF26 39
Buxton Rd. E6 CK38 58
Buxton Rd. NW2 BP36 55
Buxton Rd. SW14 BO45 65
Buxton Rd., Ashf. AX49 73
Buxton Rd., Epp. CN21 31
Buxton Rd., Erith CS43 69
Buxton Rd., Grays DF41 71
Buxton Rd., Ilf. CN32 49
Buxton Rd., Th.Hth. BY53 86
Buxton Rd., Wal.Abb. CH20 22
Buxton St. E1 CA38 2
Buxton St. E1 CA38 57
By the Mount, Welw.G.C. BQ 8 5
By the Wood, Wat. BE27 36
By-ways, The, Ash. BK62 102
By-Wood End, Ger.Cr. AS28 34
Roberts Wood Dr.
Byam St. SW6 BT44 66
Byards Cft. SW16 BW51 86
Byatt Wk., Hmptn. BE50 74
Victors Dr.
Bychurch End, Tedd. BH49 74
Church Rd.
Bycliffe Ter., Grav. DF47 81
Bycroft Rd., Sthl. BF38 54
Bycroft St. SE20 CC50 77
Parish La.
Bycullah Av., Enf. BY24 29
Bycullah Rd., Enf. BY23 29
Bye Way, The, Har. BH30 36
Bye Ways, Twick. BF48 74
Bye, The W3 BO39 55
Byefield Ct., Brwd. DE32 123
Byegrove Rd. SW19 BT50 76
Byers Clo., Pot.B. BT20 20
Byeway, The SW14 BN45 65
Byeway, The, Rick. AY27 35
Byeways, The, Surb. BM53 85
Byfield Ct., Brwd. DE32 123
Byfield Ct., N.Mal. BP52 85
Byfield Gdns. SW13 BP44 65
Byfield Rd., Islw. BJ45 64
Byfield, Welw.G.C. BR 6 5
Byfleet Cor., Wey. AW60 92
Byfleet Rd., Cob. AZ59 92
Byfleet Rd., Wey. AX58 92
Byford Clo. E15 CG36 58
Bygrove St. E14 CE39 57
Bygrove, Croy. CE57 96
Byland Clo. N21 BX26 38
Byland Clo. SE2 CO41 69
Finchale Rd.
Byland Dr., Maid. AG42 61
Bylands Clo. SE16 CC40 57
Rotherhithe St.
Bylands, Wok. AT63 100
Byne Rd. SE26 CC50 77
Byne Rd., Cars. BU55 86
Bynes Rd., S.Croy. BZ57 96
Byng Dr., Pot.B. BS19 20
Byng Pl. WC1 BW38 1
Byng Pl. WC1 BW38 56
Byng Rd., Barn. BQ23 28
Byng St. E14 CE41 67
Bynghams, Harl. CK12 13
Bynon Av., Bexh. CQ45 69
Byrd Mead, Brwd. DA20 24
Byre Clo. N14 BV25 29
Byrefield Rd., Guil. AP69 118
Byrne Rd. SW12 BV47 76
Byron Av. E., Cars. BT56 95
Byron Av. E., N.Mal. BP52 85
Byron Av. E12 CK36 58
Byron Av. E18 CG31 49
Byron Av. NW9 BM31 46
Byron Av., B.Wd. BM25 28
Byron Av., Couls. BX61 104
Byron Av., Houns. BC44 63
Byron Av., Sutt. BT56 95
Byron Av., Wat. BD23 27
Byron Clo. E8 CA37 57
Brownlow Rd.
Byron Clo. E8 CB37 2
Byron Clo. SE28 CP40 59
Byron Clo., Hmptn. BE49 74
Byron Clo., Walt. BE54 84
Byron Clo., Wok. AP62 100
Byron Ct., Enf. BY23 29
Byron Ct., Rich. BK49 74
Byron Dr. N2 BT32 47
Byron Gdns., Sutt. BT56 95
Byron Gdns., Til. DH44 71
Byron Hill Rd., Har. BG33 45
Byron Pl., Hem.H. AZ10 8
Byron Pl., Lthd. BJ64 102
Byron Rd. E10 CE33 48
Byron Rd. E17 CE31 48
Byron Rd. NW2 BP34 46
Byron Rd. NW7 BP28 37
Byron Rd. W5 BL40 55
Byron Rd., Brwd. DE26 122
Byron Rd., Dart. CX45 70
Byron Rd., Har. BH32 45
Byron Rd., S.Croy. CB58 96
Byron Rd., Wealdstone BH30 36
Byron Rd., Wem. BK34 45
Byron Rd., Wey. AY56 92
Byron St. E14 CF39 57
Byron Ter. N9 CB26 39
Byron Ter., Har. BH32 45
St. Anns Rd.
Byron Way, Hayes BB38 53
Byron Way, Nthlt. BE38 54
Byron Way, Rom. CV30 42
Byron Way, West.Dr. AY42 63
Byron, Slou. AT42 62
Common Rd.
Bysouth Clo., Ilf. CL30 40
Bythorn St. SW9 BX45 66
Byton Rd. SW17 BU50 76
Byward Av., Felt. BD46 74
Byward St. EC3 CA40 4
Byward St. EC3 CA40 57
Bywater St. SW3 BU42 3
Bywater St. SW3 BU42 66
Byway, The, Epsom BO56 94
Byway, The, Pot.B. BS20 20
Byway, The, Sutt. BT58 95
Byways, Berk. AS12 7
Byways, The, T.Ditt. BM53 85
Bywood Av., Croy. CC53 87
Bywood Clo., Ken. BY61 104
Byworth Wk. N19 BX33 47
Nyton Clo.

C

Cabbell Pl., Wey. AX56 92
Cabbell St. NW1 BU39 1
Cabbell St. NW1 BU39 56
Cabell Rd., Guil. AO70 118
Cable Pl. SE10 CF43 67
Diamond Ter.
Cable St. E1 CB40 4
Cable St. E1 CB40 57
Cabot Way E6 CJ37 58
Parr Rd.
Cabrera Av., Vir.W. AR53 82
Cabrera Clo., Vir.W. AR53 82
Cabul Rd. SW11 BU44 66
Cackets La., Sev. CM61 106
Cactus Wk. W12 BO39 55
Du Cane Rd.
Cadbury Clo., Islw. BJ44 64
Cadbury Clo., Sun. BB50 73
Cadbury Rd., Sun. BB50 73
Cadbury Way SE16 CB41 4
Caddington Clo., Barn. BU25 29
Caddington Rd. NW2 BR34 46
Caddis Clo., Stan. BH29 36
Caddy Clo., Egh. AT49 72
Cade La., Sev. CV67 117
Cade Rd. SE10 CF44 67
Cadell Clo. E2 CA38 2
Shipton St.
Cader Rd. SW18 BT46 76
Cadet Pl. SE10 CG42 68
Cadiz Rd., Dag. CS36 59
Cadiz St. SE17 BZ42 4
Cadiz St. SE17 BZ42 67
Cadley Ter. SE23 CC48 77
Cadmer Clo., N.Mal. BO52 85
Cadmore La., Chsnt. CC17 21
Cadogan Av., Brwd. DE32 123
Cadogan Av., Dart. CY47 80
Cadogan Clo. E9 CD36 57
Cadogan Ter.
Cadogan Clo., Brom. CF51 87
Albermarle Rd.
Cadogan Clo., Har. BF35 45
Cadogan Clo., Maid. AG43 61
Cadogan Clo., Tedd. BH49 74
Cadogan Ct. SW3 BU42 66
Draycott Av.
Cadogan Ct., Sutt. BS57 95
Cadogan Gate SW1 BU42 3
Cadogan Gate SW1 BU42 66
Cadogan Gdns. E18 CH31 49
Cadogan Gdns. N21 BY25 29
Cadogan Gdns. N3 BS30 38
Cadogan Gdns. SW3 BU42 3
Cadogan Gdns. SW3 BU42 66
Cadogan La. SW1 BV41 3
Cadogan La. SW1 BV41 66
Cadogan Pl. SW1 BU41 3
Cadogan Pl. SW1 BU41 66
Cadogan Rd., Surb. BK53 84
Cadogan Sq. SW1 BU41 3
Cadogan Sq. SW1 BU41 66
Cadogan St. SW3 BU42 3
Cadogan St. SW3 BU42 66
Cadogan Ter. E9 CD36 57
Cadoxton Av. N15 CA32 48
Cadwallon Rd. SE9 CL48 78
Caedmon Rd. N7 BX35 47
Caen Wood Rd., Ash. BK62 102
Caenshill Rd., Wey. AZ57 92
Caenswood Hill, Wey. AZ58 92
Caenwood Clo., Wey. AZ57 92
Caerleon Clo., Sid. CP49 79
Caerleon Ter. SE2 CO42 69
Caernarvon Clo., Hem.H. AX13 8
Caernarvon Clo., Horn. CX34 51
Caernarvon Clo., Mitch. BX52 86
Caernarvon Dr., Ilf. CL30 40
Caesars Way, Shep. BA53 83
Nell Gwynne Av.
Caesars Wk., Mitch. BU53 86
Cage Pond Rd., Rad. BL20 19
Cage St. WC1 BX39 2
Cahill St. EC1 BZ38 2
Dufferin St.
Cahir St. E14 CE42 67
Caillard Rd., Wey. AY59 92
Cains La., Felt. BA46 73
Caird St. W10 BR38 55
Cairn Av. W5 BK40 54
Cairn Way, Stan. BH29 36
Cairndale Clo., Brom. CG50 78
Cairnfield Av. NW2 BO34 46
Cairngorm Clo., Tedd. BJ49 74
Vicarage Rd.
Cairngorm Pl., Slou. AO38 52
Northern Rd.
Cairns Av., Wdf.Grn. CK29 40
Cairns Clo., Dart. CV46 80
Cairns Rd. SW11 BU46 76
Cairo New Rd., Croy. BY55 86
Cairo Rd. E17 CE31 48
Caishowe Rd., B.Wd. BM23 28
Caistor Ms. SW12 BV47 76
Caistor Rd.
Caistor Park Rd. E15 CG37 58
Caistor Rd. SW12 BV47 76
Caithness Gdns., Sid. CN46 78
Caithness Rd. W14 BQ41 65
Caithness Rd., Mitch. BV50 76
Calabria Rd. N5 BY36 56
Calais St. SE5 BY44 66
Calbourne Av., Horn. CU35 50
Calbourne Rd. SW12 BU47 76
Calcott Clo., Brwd. DA26 42
Calcott Wk. SE9 CJ49 78
Calcutta Rd., Til. DF44 71
Caldbeck Av., Wor.Pk. BP55 85
Caldbeck, Wal.Abb. CF20 21
Caldecot Way, Brox. CD14 12
Caldecote Gdns., Bush. BH26 36
Caldecote La., Bush. BH26 36
Caldecot Rd. SE5 BZ44 67
Caldecott Way E5 CC34 48
Calder Av., Grnf. BH37 54
Calder Av., Hat. BS16 20
Calder Clo., Enf. CA24 30
Calder Ct., Slou. AS42 62
Ditton Park Rd.
Calder Gdns., Edg. BM31 46
Calder Way, Slou. AV45 62
Calderon Pl. W10 BQ39 55
St. Quintin Gdns.
Calderon Rd. E11 CF35 48
Caldervale Rd. SW4 BW46 76
Calderwood St. SE18 CL42 68
Caldew St. SE5 BZ43 67
Caldwell Rd., Wat. BD28 36
Caldwell St. SW9 BX43 66
Caldwell Yd. EC4 BZ40 4
Caldwell Yd. EC4 BZ40 57
Caldy Rd., Belv. CR41 69
Caldy Wk. N1 BZ36 57
Cale St. SW3 BU42 3
Cale St. SW3 BU42 66
Caleb St. SE1 BZ41 4
Caleb St. SE1 BZ41 67
Mint St.
Caledon Rd. E6 CK37 58
Caledon Rd., St.Alb. BK16 18
Caledon Rd., Wall. BV56 95
Caledonia Rd., Stai. AY47 73
Caledonia St. N1 BX37 2
Caledonia St. N1 BX37 56
Caledonian Rd. N1 BX37 2
Caledonian Rd. N1 BX37 56
Caledonian Rd. N7 BX37 56
Caledonian Rd. W10 BQ39 55
St. Quintin Gdns.
Caledonian Wf. E14 CF42 67
Caletock St. SE10 CG42 68
Lenthorp Rd.
Caletock Way SE10 CG42 68
Glenister Rd.
Calfstock La., S.Dnth. CW52 90
Caliban Tower N1 CA37 57
Purcell St.
Calico Row SW11 BT45 66
York Pl.
Calidore Clo. SW2 BX46 76
Endymion Rd.
California La., Bush. BG26 36
California Rd., N.Mal. BN52 85
Caliph Clo., Grav. DJ49 81
Callaby Ter. N1 BY36 56
St. Pauls Rd.
Callaghan Clo. SE13 CG45 68
Glenton Rd.
Callan Gro., S.Ock. DA40 60
Callander Rd. SE6 CE48 77
Callard Av. N13 BY28 38
Callcott Rd. NW6 BR36 55
Callcott St. W8 BS40 56

Calley Down Cres., Croy. CF59 96
Callis Farm Clo., Stai. AY46 73
Callis Rd. E17 CD32 48
Calliston Ct., Hem.H. AY12 8
Callow Fold., Pur. BY60 95
Higher Dr.
Callow Hill, Egh. AR51 82
Callow Hill, Vir.W. AR52 82
Callow St. SW3 BT43 3
Callow St. SW3 BT43 66
Calluna Ct., Wok. AS62 100
Heathside Rd.
Calmington Rd. SE5 CA43 4
Calmington Rd. SE5 CA43 67
Calmont Rd., Brom. CF50 77
Calmore Clo., Horn. CV35 51
Calne Av., Ilf. CL30 40
Calonne Rd. SW19 BQ49 75
Calshot Rd., Houns. AZ44 63
Calshot St. N1 BX37 2
Calshot St. N1 BX37 56
Calshot Way, Enf. BY24 29
Calshot Way, Houns. AZ44 63
Calshot Rd.
Calthorpe Gdns., Stan. BL28 37
Calthorpe Gdns., Sutt. BY55 86
Calthorpe St. WC1 BX38 2
Calthorpe St. WC1 BX38 56
Calton Av. SE21 CA46 77
Calton Rd., Barn. BT25 29
Calverley Clo., Beck. CE50 77
Calverley Cres., Dag. CR34 50
Calverley Gdns., Har. BK33 45
Calverley Gro. N19 BW33 47
Calverley Rd., Epsom BP57 94
Calvert Av. E2 CA38 2
Calvert Av. E2 CA38 57
Calvert Clo., Belv. CR42 69
Calvert Clo., Sid. CQ50 79
Calvert Cres., Dor. BJ70 119
Calvert Rd. SE10 CG42 68
Calvert Rd., Barn. BQ23 28
Calvert Rd., Dor. BJ70 119
Calvert Rd., Lthd. BC68 110
Calvert St. NW1 BV37 56
Chalcot Rd.
Calverton Rd. E6 CL37 58
Calverts Bldgs. SE1 BZ40 4
Calvin Clo., Orp. CP52 89
Calvin St. E1 CA38 2
Calvin St. E1 CA38 57
Calydon Rd. SE7 CH42 68
Calypso Way SE8 CD41 67
Cam Grn., S.Ock. DA39 60
Cam Rd. E15 CF37 57
Cam Ter., Chis. CL50 78
Mill Pl.
Camac Rd., Twick. BG47 74
Camartan Pl. SE1 CA41 4
Bermondsey St.
Cambalt Rd. SW15 BQ46 75
Camberley Av. SW20 BP51 85
Camberley Av., Enf. CA24 30
Camberley Rd., Houns. AZ45 63
Cambert Way SE3 CH45 68
Camberwell Church St. SE5 BZ44 67
Camberwell Glebe SE5 BZ44 67
Camberwell Grn. SE5 BZ44 67
Camberwell Gro. SE5 BZ44 67
Camberwell La., Sev. CQ69 116
Camberwell New Rd. SE5 BY43 66
Camberwell Pass. SE5 BZ44 67
Camberwell Rd.
Camberwell Rd. SE5 BZ43 67
Camberwell Station Rd. SE5 BZ44 67
Cambeys Rd., Dag. CR35 50
Camborne Av. W13 BJ41 64
Camborne Av., Rom. CV29 42
Camborne Clo., Houns. AZ45 63
Camborne Dr., Hem.H. AY11 8
Camborne Ms. W11 BR39 55
St. Marks Rd.
Camborne Rd. N., Houns. AZ45 63
Camborne Rd.
Camborne Rd. S., Houns. AZ45 63
Camborne Rd.
Camborne Rd. SW18 BS47 76
Camborne Rd., Croy. CB54 87
Camborne Rd., Houns. AZ45 63
Camborne Rd., Mord. BQ53 85
Camborne Rd., Sid. CP48 79
Camborne Rd., Sutt. BS57 95
Camborne Rd., Well. CN44 68
Camborne Way, Houns. AZ45 63
Camborne Rd.
Camborne Way, Houns. BF44 64
Camborne Way, Rom. CW29 42
Camborne Wk., Rich. BK46 74
Petersham Rd.
Cambourne Av. N9 CC26 39
Cambray Rd. SW12 BW47 76
Cambray Rd., Orp. CN54 88
Cambria Clo., Houns. BF45 64
Cambria Clo., Sid. CM47 78
Cambria Cres., Grav. DJ49 81
Cambria Ct., Felt. BC47 73
Cambria Ct., Slou. AR41 62
Turner Rd.
Cambria Gdns., Stai. AY47 73
Cambria Rd. SE5 BZ45 67
Cambria St. SW6 BS43 66
Cambrian Av., Ilf. CN32 49
Cambrian Clo. SE27 BY48 76
Cambrian Gro., Grav. DG47 81
Cambrian Rd. E10 CE33 48
Cambrian Rd., Rich. BL46 75
Cambrian Way, Hem.H. AY12 8
Cambridge Av. NW6 BS37 56
Cambridge Av., Grnf. BH35 45
Cambridge Av., N.Mal. BO52 85
Cambridge Av., Rom. CV30 42
Cambridge Av., Well. CN45 68
Cambridge Barracks Rd. SE18 CK42 68
Cambridge Cir. WC2 BW39 1
Cambridge Clo. SW20 BP51 85
Cambridge Clo., West Dr. AX43 63
Cambridge Clo., Chsnt. CC18 21
Cambridge Clo., Houns. BE45 64
Cambridge Clo., Wok. AP62 100
Cambridge Cotts., Rich. BM43 65
Cambridge Cres. E2 CB37 57
Cambridge Cres., Tedd. BJ49 74
Cambridge Cres., Wat. BD24 27
Cambridge Dr. SE12 CH46 78
Cambridge Dr., Pot.B. BQ19 19
Cambridge Dr., Ruis. BD34 45
Cambridge Gate Ms. NW1 BV38 1
Cambridge Gate Ms. NW1 BV38 56
Albany St.
Cambridge Gate NW1 BV38 1
Cambridge Gate NW1 BV38 56
Cambridge Gate SE17 BZ43 67
Walworth Rd.
Cambridge Gdns. N10 BV30 38
Sydney Rd.
Cambridge Gdns. N13 BY28 38
Cambridge Gdns. N17 BZ29 39
Great Cambridge Rd.
Cambridge Gdns. N21 BZ26 39
Cambridge Gdns. NW6 BS37 56
Cambridge Gdns. W10 BQ39 55
Cambridge Gdns., Kings.T. BM51 85
Cambridge Gdns., Enf. CB23 30
Cambridge Gdns., Grays DG42 71
Cambridge Grn. N9 CA26 39
Cambridge Grn. SE9 CL47 78
Cambridge Gro. Rd., Kings. T. BM52 85
Cambridge Gro. SE20 CB51 87
Cambridge Gro. W6 BP42 65
Cambridge Heath Rd. E1 CB39 57
Cambridge Ho., Wind. AO44 61
Ward Royal
Cambridge Ms. SW11 BU44 66
Cambridge Pde., Enf. CB23 30
Cambridge Pk. E11 CH33 49
Cambridge Pk. Est., Twick. BK46 74
Cambridge Pk. Rd. E11 CG33 49
Cambridge Pk., Twick. BK46 74
Cambridge Pl. NW6 BS38 56
Cambridge Rd.
Cambridge Pl. W8 BS41 3
Cambridge Pl. W8 BS41 66
Cambridge Rd. E11 CG32 49
Cambridge Rd. E4 CF26 39
Cambridge Rd. N. W4 BM42 65
Cambridge Rd. NW11 BF32 45
Cambridge Rd. NW6 BS38 56
Cambridge Rd. S. W4 BM42 65
Cambridge Rd. SE20 CB52 87
Cambridge Rd. SW11 BU44 66
Cambridge Rd. SW13 BO44 65
Cambridge Rd. SW20 BP51 85
Cambridge Rd. W7 BH41 64
Cambridge Rd., N.Mal. BN52 85
Cambridge Rd., Ashf. BA50 73
Cambridge Rd., Bark. CM36 58
Cambridge Rd., Brom. CH50 78
Cambridge Rd., Cars. BU57 95
Cambridge Rd., Hmptn. BE50 74
Cambridge Rd., Houns. BE45 64
Cambridge Rd., Ilf. CN33 49
Cambridge Rd., Kings.T. BL51 85
Cambridge Rd., Mitch. BV52 86
Cambridge Rd., Rich. BM43 65
Cambridge Rd., Saw. CQ 5 6
Cambridge Rd., Sid. CN49 78
Cambridge Rd., St.Alb. BJ14 9
Cambridge Rd., Sthl. BE40 54
Cambridge Rd., Tedd. BJ49 74
Cambridge Rd., Twick. BK46 74
Cambridge Rd., Uxb. AX36 53
Cambridge Rd., Walt. BC53 83
Cambridge Rd., Wat. BD24 27
Cambridge Row SE18 CL42 68
Cambridge Sq. W2 BU39 1
Cambridge Sq. W2 BU39 56
Cambridge St. SW1 BV42 3
Cambridge St. SW1 BV42 66
Cambridge Ter. Ms. NW1 BV38 1
Cambridge Ter. Ms. NW1 BV38 56
Albany St.
Cambridge Ter. N13 BY28 38
Cambridge Ter. N9 CA26 39
Bury St. W.
Cambridge Ter. NW1 BV38 1
Cambridge Ter. NW1 BV38 56
Outer Circle
Cambridge Ter., Berk. AR13 7
Cambus Clo., Hayes BE39 54
Kilpatrick Way
Cambus Rd. E16 CH39 58
Camdale Rd. SE18 CN43 68
Camden Av., Felt. BD48 74
Camden Av., Hayes BD40 54
Camden Clo. SW19 BR48 75
Victoria Dr.
Camden Clo., Chis. CM51 88
Camden Clo., Grays DG42 71
Camden Gdns., Sutt. BS56 95
Camden Gdns., Th.Hth. BY52 86
Camden Gro., Chis. CL50 78
Camden High St. NW1 BV36 56
Camden High St. NW1 BV37 1
Camden Hill Rd. SE19 CA50 77
Camden La. N7 BW35 47
Rowstock Gdns.
Camden Lock NW1 BV36 1
Camden Lock NW1 BV36 56
Camden Ms. NW1 BW36 56
Murray St.
Camden Pass. N1 BY37 2
Camden Pass. N1 BY37 56
Camden Pk. Rd. NW1 BW36 56
Camden Pk. Rd., Chis. CK50 78
Camden Rd. E11 CH32 49
Camden Rd. E17 CD32 48
Camden Rd. N7 BW36 56
Camden Rd. NW1 BV37 1
Camden Rd. NW1 BW36 56
Camden Rd., Bex. CQ47 79
Camden Rd., Cars. BU56 95
Camden Rd., Grays DC41 71
Camden Rd., Sev. CU64 107
Camden Rd., Sutt. BS56 95
Camden Row SE3 CG44 68
Camden Sq. NW1 BW36 56
Camden Sq. SE15 CA44 67
Chepstow Way
Camden St. NW1 BV36 1
Camden St. NW1 BW36 56
Camden Ter. NW1 BW36 56
North Vill.
Camden Way, Chis. CK50 78
Camden Way, Th.Hth. BY52 86
Camden Wk. N1 BY37 2
Camden Wk. N1 BY37 56
Camdenhurst St. E14 CD39 57
Camel Rd. E16 CJ40 58
Camelford Wk. W11 BQ40 55
Lancaster Rd.
Camellia Clo., Rom. CW30 42
Columbine Way
Camellia Pl., Twick. BF47 74
Camellia St. SW8 BX43 66
Camelot Clo. SE28 CM41 68
Camelot Clo. SW19 BR49 75
Camelot Clo., West. CJ61 106
Camelot St. SE15 CB43 67
Camera Pl. SW10 BT43 66
Cameron Clo. N18 CB28 39
Cameron Clo. N20 BT27 38
Cameron Clo., Bex. CS48 79
Cameron Clo., Brwd. DB28 42
Cameron Dr., Wal.Cr. CC20 21
Cameron Pl. E1 CB39 57
Cameron Rd. SE6 CD48 77
Cameron Rd., Brom. CH53 88
Cameron Rd., Chesh. AO18 16
Cameron Rd., Croy. BY53 86
Cameron Rd., Ilf. CN33 49
Camerton Clo. E8 CA36 57
Laurel St.
Camfield, Welw.G.C. BR10 5
Camilla Clo., Lthd. BF66 111
Pine Dean
Camilla Clo., Sun. BB50 73
Camilla Dr., Dor. BJ68 111
Camilla Rd. SE16 CB42 67
Camille Clo. SE25 CB52 87
Camlan Rd., Brom. CG49 78
Camlet St. E2 CA38 2
Camlet St. E2 CA38 57
Camlet Way, Barn. BS23 29
Camlet Way, St.Alb. BF13 9
Camley St. NW1 BW37 1
Camley St. NW1 BW37 56
Camm Av., Wind. AM45 61
Camm Gdns., Kings.T. BL51 85
Church Rd.
Camm Gdns., T.Ditt. BH54 84
Camomile Av., Mitch. BU51 86
Camomile St. EC3 CA39 2
Camomile St. EC3 CA39 57
Camp End Rd., Wey. BA59 92
Camp Rd. SW19 BP49 75
Camp Rd., Cat. CD64 105
Camp Rd., Ger.Cr. AR32 43
Camp Rd., St.Alb. BH13 9
Camp View Rd., St.Alb. BJ14 9
Camp Vw. SW19 BP49 75
Campana Rd. SW6 BS44 66
Campbell Av., Ilf. CL31 49
Campbell Av., Wok. AS64 100
Campbell Cft., Edg. BM28 37
Campbell Clo. SW16 BW49 76
Campbell Clo., Hav. CT29 41
Havering Rd.
Campbell Clo., Rom. CT29 41
Campbell Clo., Ruis. BC32 44
Campbell Clo., Twick. BG47 74
Campbell Ct. NW9 BN32 46
Campbell Est. SE18 CK44 68
Campbell Rd. E15 CG35 49
Trevelyan Rd.
Campbell Rd. E17 CD31 48
Campbell Rd. E3 CE38 57
Campbell Rd. E6 CK37 58
Campbell Rd. N17 CA30 39
Campbell Rd. W7 BH40 54
Campbell Rd., Cat. BZ64 105
Campbell Rd., Croy. BY54 86
Campbell Rd., E.Mol. BH52 84
Campbell Rd., Grav. DF47 81
Campbell Rd., Twick. BG47 74
Campbell Rd., Wey. AZ57 92
Campbell Wk. N1 BX37 2
Campdale Rd. N7 BW34 47
Campden Cres., Dag. CO35 50
Campden Cres., Wem. BJ34 45
Campden Gro. W8 BS41 66
Campden Hill Gdns. W8 BS40 56
Campden Hill Pl. W8 BR40 55
Campden Hill Rd. W8 BS40 56
Campden Hill Sq. W8 BR40 55
Campden Hill W8 BS41 66
Campden House Clo. W8 BS41 66
Hornton St.
Campden Rd., S.Croy. CA56 96
Campden Rd., Uxb. AY34 44
Campden St. W8 BS40 56
Campen Clo. SW19 BR48 75
Queensmere Rd.
Camperdown St. E1 CA39 2
Camperdown St. E1 CA39 57
Leman St.
Campfield Rd. SE9 CH47 78
Campfield Rd., St.Alb. BJ13 9
Campfield Wk. SW19 BT51 86
Brangwyn Cres.
Camphill Ct., Wey. AW59 92
Camphill Rd., Wey. AW59 92
Campion Clo. E6 CK40 58
Campion Clo., Croy. CA56 96
Campion Clo., Denham AW34 44
Campion Clo., Grav. DF49 81
Henley Deane
Campion Clo., Har. BL32 46
Campion Clo., Hillingdon AY39 53
Campion Clo., Grays DE43 71
Churchill Rd.
Campion Ho., Islw. BG43 64
Campion Pl. SE28 CO40 59
Campion Rd. SW15 BQ45 65
Campion Rd., Hem.H. AV14 7
Campion Rd., Islw. BH44 64
Campion Ter. NW2 BQ34 46
Campions Clo., B.Wd. BM22 28
Campions, Epp. CO17 23
Campions, Loug. CL22 31
Campions, The, B.Wd. BM22 28
Cample La., S.Ock. DA40 60
Camplin Rd., Har. BL32 46
Camplin St. SE14 CC43 67
Campsbourne Rd. N8 BX31 47
Campsbourne, The N8 BX31 47
Rectory Gdns.
Campsey Gdns., Dag. CO36 59
Campsey Rd., Dag. CO36 59
Campsfield Rd. N8 BX31 47
Campshill Pl. SE13 CF46 77
Campshill Rd.
Campshill Rd. SE13 CF46 77
Campus Rd. E17 CD32 48
Campus, The, Welw.G.C. BQ 7 5
Camrose Av., Edg. BL30 37
Camrose Av., Erith CR43 69
Camrose Av., Felt. BC49 73
Camrose Clo., Croy. CD54 87
Camrose Clo., Mord. BS52 86
Camrose St. SE2 CO42 69
Canada Av. N18 BZ29 39
Canada Av., Red. BV72 121
Canada Cres. W3 BN38 55
Canada Dr., Red. BV72 121
Canada Farm Rd., S.Dnth. DA52 90
Canada Gdns. SE13 CF46 77
Canada La., Brox. CD16 21
Canada Rd. W3 BN39 55
Canada Rd., Cob. BD60 93
Canada Rd., Slou. AQ41 62
Canada Rd., Wey. AX59 92
Canada St. SE16 CC41 67
Canada Way W12 BP40 55
Canadas, The, Brox. CD16 21
Rochford Clo.
Canadian Av. SE6 CE47 77
Canal App. SE8 CD42 67
Canal Clo. E1 CD38 57
Canal Gro. SE15 CB43 67
Canal Head SE15 CB44 67
Peckham High St.
Canal Rd. E3 CD38 57
Canal Rd., Grav. DH46 81
Canal St. SE5 BZ43 67
Canal Way NW1 BW36 56
Baynes St.
Canal Wharf, Slou. AT41 62
Canal Wk. N1 BZ37 2
Canal Wk. N1 BZ37 57
Canal Wk. SE26 CC49 77
Venner Rd.
Canary Wharf E14 CE40 57
Canberra Clo. NW4 BO31 46
Aerodrome Rd.
Canberra Clo., Dag. CS36 59
Canberra Clo., Horn. CV35 51
Canberra Clo., St.Alb. BH11 9
Canberra Cres., Dag. CS36 59
Canberra Rd. E6 CK37 58
Barking Rd.
Canberra Rd. SE7 CJ43 68
Canberra Rd., Bexh. CP43 69
Canberra Rd., Houns. AZ45 63
Canberra Sq., Til. DG44 71
Canbury Av., Kings.T. BL51 85
Canbury Ms. SE26 CB48 77
Wells Park Rd.
Canbury Park Rd., Kings.T. BL51 85
Canbury Pass., Kings.T. BK51 84
Canbury Path, Orp. CO52 89
Canbury Pl., Kings.T. BL51 85
Canbury Pass.
Cancell Rd. SW9 BY44 66
Candahar Rd. SW11 BU44 66
Cander Way, S.Ock. DA40 60
Candlefield Clo., Hem.H. AZ15 8
Candlefield Rd., Hem.H. AZ15 8
Candlefield Wk., Hem.H. AZ15 8
Candler St. N15 BZ32 48
Candover Clo., West.Dr. AX43 63
Candover Rd., Horn. CU33 50
Candover St. W1 BW39 1
Candover St. W1 BW39 56
Foley St.
Candy Cft., Lthd. BF66 111
Candy St. E3 CD37 57
Caneland Ct., Wal.Abb. CG20 22
Canes La., Harl. CQ14 14
Caney Ms. NW2 BQ34 46
Claremont Rd.
Canfield Dr., Ruis. BC35 44
Canfield Gdns. NW6 BS36 56
Canfield Pl. NW6 BT36 56
Canfield Rd., Rain. CT37 59
Canfield Rd., Wdf.Grn. CK29 40
Canford Av., Nthlt. BE37 54
Canford Clo., Enf. BY23 29
Canford Dr., Wey. AW55 83
Canford Gdns., N.Mal. BN53 85
Canford Rd. SW11 BV45 66
Cangels Clo., Hem.H. AV14 7
Canham Rd. SE25 CA52 87
Canham Rd. W3 BO41 65
Canmore Gdns., SW16 BW50 76
Cann Hall Rd. E11 CG35 49
Cann Hatch, Tad. BR62 103
Canning Cres. N22 BX30 38
Canning Cross SE5 BZ44 67
Grove La.
Canning Ms. W8 BT41 3
Canning Pass. W8 BT41 3
Canning Pass. W8 BT41 66
Victoria Rd.
Canning Pl. Ms. W8 BT41 66
Canning Pl.
Canning Pl. W8 BT41 3
Canning Pl. W8 BT41 66
Canning Rd. E15 CG37 58
Canning Rd. E17 CD31 48
Canning Rd. N5 BY34 47
Canning Rd., Croy. CA55 87
Canning Rd., Har. BH31 45
Cannington Rd., Dag. CP36 59
Cannizaro Rd. SW19 BQ50 75
Cannon Clo. SW20 BQ52 85
Cannon Clo., Hmptn. BF50 74
Cannon Cres., Wok. AP59 91
Cannon Dr. E14 CE40 57
Cannon Gro., Lthd. BH64 102
Cannon Hill La. SW20 BQ53 85
Cannon Hill Ms. N14 BX27 38
Cannon Hill
Cannon Hill N14 BX27 38
Cannon Hill NW6 BS35 47
Cannon La. NW3 BT34 47
Cannon La., Pnr. BE32 45
Cannon Mill Av., Chesh. AP20 16
Cannon Pl. NW3 BT34 47
Cannon Pl. SE7 CK42 68
Maryon Rd.
Cannon Rd. N14 BX27 38
Cannon Rd., Bexh. CQ44 69
Cannon Rd., Wat. BD25 27
Cannon Row SW1 BX41 4
Cannon Row SW1 BX41 66
Bridge St.
Cannon Side, Lthd. BH64 102
Cannon St. EC4 BZ39 2
Cannon St. EC4 BZ39 57
Cannon St. Rd. E1 CB39 57
Cannon St., St.Alb. BG13 9
Cannon Way, E. Mol. BF52 84
Cannon Way, Lthd. BH64 102
Cannonbury Av., Pnr. BD32 45
Cannons Cor., Edg. BL28 37
Cannons La., Ong. CZ14 15
Cannons Md., Brwd. DA20 24
Cannons Meadow, Welw. BU 6 5
Canon Av., Rom. CP32 50
Canon Beck Rd. SE16 CC41 67
Canon Ct., Edg. BL29 37
Stonegrove
Canon Hill Clo., Maid. AH42 61
Canon Hill Way, Maid. AG42 61
Canon Hill, Maid. AG41 61
Canon Mohan Clo. N14 BV25 29
Canon Murnane Rd. SE1 CA41 4
Grange Rd.
Canon Park Est., Stan. BK28 36
Canon Rd., Brom. CJ52 88
Canon St. N1 BZ37 2
Canon St. N1 BZ37 57
Prebend St.
Canonbie Rd. SE23 CC47 77
Canonbury Av. N1 BY36 56
Canonbury Rd.
Canonbury Gro. N1 BZ36 57
Canonbury La. N1 BY36 56
Canonbury Pk. N. N1 BZ36 57
Canonbury Pk. S. N1 BZ36 57
Canonbury Pl. N1 BY36 56
Canonbury Rd. N1 BY36 56
Canonbury Rd., Enf. CA23 30
Canonbury Sq. N1 BY36 56
Canonbury St. N1 BZ36 57
Canonbury Vill. N1 BY36 56
Canons Brook, Harl. CL11 13
Canons Clo. N2 BT33 47
Canons Clo., Edg. BL29 37
Canons Clo., Rad. BJ21 27
Canons Dr., Edg. BL29 37
Canons Gate, Harl. CL10 6
Canons Hatch, Tad. BR62 103
Canons Hill, Couls. BY62 104
Canons La., Tad. BR62 103
Canons Pk. Par., Edg. BL29 37
Canons Wk., Croy. CC55 87
Canonsleigh Rd., Dag. CO36 59
Canopus Way, Nthwd. BC28 35
Canopus Way, Stai. AY47 73
Canrobert St. E2 CB37 57
Cantelowes Rd. NW1 BW36 56
Canterbury Av., Ilf. CK33 49
Canterbury Av., Sid. CO48 79
Canterbury Av., Slou. AO38 52
Canterbury Av., Upmin. CZ34 51
Canterbury Clo. E6 CK39 58
Canterbury Clo., Amer. AP23 25
Canterbury Clo., Beck. CE51 87
Canterbury Clo., Brom. CE51 87
The Avenue
Canterbury Clo., Dart. CX47 80
Canterbury Clo., Grnf. BF39 54
Canterbury Clo., Nthwd. BB29 35
Canterbury Cres. SW9 BY45 66
Canterbury Gro. SE27 BY49 76
Canterbury Par., S.Ock. DB38 60
Canterbury Pl. SE17 BY42 4
Canterbury Rd. E10 CF33 48
Canterbury Rd. NW6 BS37 56
Canterbury Rd., B.Wd. BM23 28
Canterbury Rd., Croy. BX54 86
Canterbury Rd., Felt. BE48 74
Canterbury Rd., Grav. DH48 81
Canterbury Rd., Guil. AP69 118
Canterbury Rd., Har. BF32 45

Canterbury Rd., Mord. BS54 86
Canterbury Rd., Wat. BC23 26
Canterbury Ter. NW6 BC37 56
Canterbury Way, Brwd. DA28 42
Canterbury Way, Grays CZ42 70
Canterbury Way, Rick. BA24 26
Cantley Gdns. SE19 CA51 87
Cantley Gdns., Ilf. CM32 49
Cantley Rd. W7 BJ41 64
Canton St. E14 CE39 57
Cantrell Rd. E3 CD38 57
Cantwell Rd. SE18 CL43 68
Canute Gdns. SE16 CC42 67
Canvey St. SE1 BZ40 57
Zoar St.
Cape Clo., Bark. CL36 58
Cape Rd. N17 CB31 48
Cape Rd., St.Alb. BJ13 9
Cape Yd. E1 CB40 57
Asher Way
Capel Av., Wall. BX56 95
Capel Clo. N20 BT27 38
Capel Clo., Brom. CK54 88
Capel Ct. EC2 BZ39 2
Capel Ct. EC2 BZ39 57
Threadneedle St.
Capel Gdns., Ilf. CN35 49
Capel Gdns., Pnr. BE31 45
Capel Pl., Dart. CV49 80
Capel Rd. E12 CJ35 49
Capel Rd. E7 CH35 49
Capel Rd., Barn. BU25 29
Capel Rd., Enf. CB21 30
Capel Rd., Wat. BD25 27
Capel Vere Wk., Wat. BB23 26
Capell Av., Rick. AU25 25
Capell Rd., Rick. AU25 25
Capell Way, Rick. AU25 25
Capella Rd., Nthwd. BB28 35
Capeners Clo. SW1 BV41 66
Kinnerton St.
Capern Rd. SW18 BT47 76
Cargill Rd.
Capital Ho. SE6 CE46 77
Capital Interchange Way, Brent. BM42 65
Capitol Way NW9 BN31 46
Capland St. NW8 BT38 1
Capland St. NW8 BT38 56
Caple Rd. NW10 BO37 55
Capon Clo., Brwd. DA26 42
Caponfield, Welw.G.C. BS 9 5
Capper St. WC1 BW38 1
Caprea Clo., Hayes BD39 54
Triandra Way
Capri Rd., Croy. CA54 87
Capstan Clo., Rom. CO32 50
Capstan Ct., Dart. CY45 70
Capstan Rd. SE8 CD42 67
Capstan Ride, Enf. BY23 29
Capstan Sq. E14 CF41 67
Capstan Way SE16 CD40 57
Capstone Rd., Brom. CG49 78
Captain Cook Clo., Ch.St.G. AQ28 34
Captains Wk., Berk. AR13 7
Capthorne Av., Har. BE33 45
Capthorne Ct., Har. BE33 45
Capuchin Clo., Stan. BJ29 36
Temple Mead Clo.
Capworth St. E10 CE33 48
Caractacus Grn., Wat. BB25 26
Caradoc Clo. W2 BS39 56
Ledbury Rd.
Caradoc St. SE10 CG42 68
Caradon Clo. E11 CG34 49
Brockway Clo.
Caradon Clo., Wok. AQ62 100
Caradon Way N15 BZ31 48
Caravan La., Rick. AY26 35
Caravel Ms. SE8 CE43 67
Watergate St.
Caravelle Gdns., Nthlt. BD38 54
Javelin Way
Caraway Pl., Guil. AQ68 109
Carberry Rd. SE19 CA50 77
Carbery Av. W3 BL41 65
Carbis Clo. E4 CF26 39
Carbis Rd. E14 CD39 57
Carbone Hill, Cuff. BW17 20
Carburton St. W1 BV38 1
Carburton St. W1 BV38 56
Carbury Clo., Horn. CV36 60
Cardale St. E14 CF41 67
Plevna St.
Carden Rd. SE15 CB45 67
Cardiff Rd. W7 BJ41 64
Cardiff Rd., Enf. CB24 30
Cardiff Rd., Wat. BC25 26
Cardiff St. SE18 CN43 68
Cardigan Clo., Wok. AP62 100
Cardigan Gdns., Ilf. CO34 50
Cardigan Pl. NW6 BS38 56
Cardigan Rd. E3 CD37 57
Cardigan Rd. SW13 BP44 65
Cardigan Rd. SW19 BT50 76
Cardigan Rd., Rich. BL46 75
Cardigan St. SE11 BY42 4
Cardigan St. SE11 BY42 66
Cardigan Wk. N1 BZ36 57
Ashby Gro.
Cardinal Av., B.Wd. BM24 28
Cardinal Av., Kings.T BL49 75
Cardinal Av., Mord. BR53 85
Cardinal Bourne St. SE1 BZ41 4
Cardinal Bourne St. SE1 BZ41 67
Cardinal Cap Alley SE1 BZ40 4
Cardinal Clo., Chis. CM50 78
Cardinal Clo., Chsnt. CA16 21
Adamsfield
Cardinal Clo., Mord. BR53 85
Cardinal Clo., Wor.Pk. BP56 94
Cardinal Cres., N.Mal. BN51 85
Cardinal Dr., Ilf. CM29 40
Cardinal Dr., Walt. BD54 84
Cardinal Gro., St.Alb. BF14 9
Cardinal Pl. SW15 BQ45 65
Cardinal Rd., Felt. BC47 73
Cardinal Rd., Ruis. BD33 45
Cardinal Way, Har. BH31 45
Wolseley Rd.
Cardinal Way, Rain. CV37 60
Cardinals Way N19 BW33 47
Cardinals Wk., Hmptn. BG50 74
Cardinals Wk., Sun. BB50 73
Seymour Way
Cardingham, Wok. AQ62 100
Cardington Sq., Houns. BD45 64
Cardington St. NW1 BW38 1
Cardington St. NW1 BW38 56
Cardozo Rd. N7 BX35 47
Cardrew Av. N12 BT28 38
Cardrew Clo. N12 BT28 38
Cardross St. W6 BP41 65
Cardwell Rd. N7 BX35 47
Cardwell Rd. SE18 CL42 68
Cardwell Ter. N7 BX35 47
Cardwell Rd.
Cardy Rd., Hem.H. AW13 8
Carew Clo. N7 BX34 47
Carew Clo., Couls. BZ63 105
Carew Rd. N17 CB30 39
Carew Rd. W13 BK41 64
Carew Rd., Ash. BA50 73
Carew Rd., Mitch. BV51 86
Carew Rd., Nthwd. BB29 35
Carew Rd., Th.Hth. BY52 86
Carew Rd., Wall. BW57 95
Carew St. SE5 BZ44 67
Carey Clo., Wind. AN45 61
Carey Gdns. SW8 BW44 66
Stewarts Rd.
Carey La. EC2 BZ39 2
Carey La. EC2 BZ39 57
Gutter La.
Carey Pl., Wat. BD24 27
Clifford St.
Carey Rd., Dag. CQ35 50
Carey St. WC2 BX39 2
Carey St. WC2 BX39 56
Carfax Pl. SW4 BW45 66
Holwood Pl.
Carfax Rd., Hayes BB42 63
Carfax Rd., Horn. CT35 50
Carfax Sq. SW4 BW45 66
Clapham Pk. Rd.
Carfree Clo. N1 BY36 56
Bewdley St.
Cargill Rd. SW18 BS47 76
Cargreen Pl. SE25 CA52 87
Cargreen Rd.
Cargreen Rd. SE25 CA52 87
Carholme Rd. SE23 CD47 77
Carisbrook Av., Wat. BD23 27
Carisbrook Clo., Stan. BK30 36
Carisbrooke Av., Bex. CP47 79
Carisbrooke Clo., Enf. CA23 30
Carisbrooke Clo., Horn. CX34 51
Carisbrooke Ct., Slou. AP40 52
Carisbrooke Gdns. SE15 CA43 67
Commercial Way
Carisbrooke Rd. E17 CD31 48
Carisbrooke Rd., Brom. CJ52 88
Carisbrooke Rd., Brwd. DA25 33
Carisbrooke Rd., Mitch. BW52 86
Carisbrooke Rd., St.Alb. BF16 18
Carkers Lane NW5 BV35 47
Carleton Av., Wall. BW57 95
Carleton Clo., Esher BG54 84
Carleton Pl., Hort.K. CY52 90
Carleton Rd. N7 BW35 47
Carleton Rd., Chsnt. CC17 21
Carlile Clo. E3 CD37 57
Carlingford Gdns., Mitch. BU50 76
Carlingford Rd. N15 BY31 47
Carlingford Rd. NW3 BT35 47
Carlingford Rd., Mord. BQ53 85
Carlisle Av. EC3 CA39 2
Carlisle Av. EC3 CA39 57
Carlisle Av. W3 BO39 55
Carlisle Av., St.Alb. BG12 9
Carlisle Clo., Kings.T. BM51 85
Carlisle Gdns., Har. BK33 45
Carlisle Gdns., Ilf. CK32 49
Carlisle La. SE1 BX41 4
Carlisle La. SE1 BX41 66
Carlisle Ms., Kings.T. BM51 85
Carlisle Clo.
Carlisle Pl. N11 BV28 38
Carlisle Pl. SW1 BW41 3
Carlisle Pl. SW1 BW41 66
Carlisle Rd. E10 CE33 48
Carlisle Rd. N4 BY33 47
Scarborough Rd.
Carlisle Rd. NW6 BR37 55
Carlisle Rd. NW9 BN31 46
Carlisle Rd., Dart. CX46 80
Carlisle Rd., Hmptn. BF50 74
Carlisle Rd., Rom. CU32 50
Carlisle Rd., Slou. AO40 52
Carlisle Rd., Sutt. BR57 94
Carlisle St. W1 BW39 1
Carlisle St. W1 BW39 56
Soho Sq.
Carlisle Way SW17 BV49 76
Carlisle Wk. E8 CA36 57
Kirkland Wk.
Carlos Pl. W1 BV40 3
Carlos Pl. W1 BV40 56
Carlow St. NW1 BW37 56
Carlton Av. E., Wem. BK34 45
Carlton Av. N14 BW25 29
Carlton Av. W., Wem. BJ34 45
Carlton Av., Felt. BD46 74
Carlton Av., Green. CZ46 80
Carlton Av., Har. BJ32 45
Carlton Av., Hayes BB42 63
Carlton Av., S.Croy. BZ57 96
Carlton Clo. NW3 BS34 47
Carlton Clo., B.Wd. BN24 28
Carlton Clo., Chess. BL57 94
Carlton Clo., Edg. BM28 37
Carlton Clo., Grays DF41 71
Carlton Clo., Upmin. CX34 51
Carlton Clo., Wok. AT60 91
Carlton Cres., Sutt. BR56 94
Carlton Ct. W9 BS37 56
Carlton Dr. SW15 BQ46 75
Carlton Dr., Ilf. CM31 49
Carlton Gdns. SW1 BW40 3
Carlton Gdns. SW1 BW40 56
Carlton Gdns. W5 BK39 54
Carlton Grn., Red. BU69 121
Carlton Gro. SE15 CB44 67
Carlton Hill NW8 BS37 1
Carlton Hill NW8 BS37 56
Carlton Ho. Ter. SW1 BW40 3
Carlton Ho. Ter. SW1 BW40 56
Carlton Ms. SW1 BW40 3
Carlton Par., Orp. CO54 89
Carlton Pk. Av. SW20 BQ51 85
Carlton Pk., Sev. CV64 108
Carlton Pl., Nthwd. AZ28 35
Carlton Rd. E11 CG33 49
Carlton Rd. E12 CJ35 49
Carlton Rd. E17 CD30 39
Carlton Rd. N11 BV28 38
Carlton Rd. N4 BY33 47
Carlton Rd. SW14 BN45 65
Carlton Rd. W4 BN41 65
Carlton Rd. W5 BK40 54
Carlton Rd., Dart. CX47 80
Carlton Rd., Erith CR43 69
Carlton Rd., Grays DF41 71
Carlton Rd., N.Mal. BO51 85
Carlton Rd., Red. BT69 121
Carlton Rd., Rom. CT32 50
Carlton Rd., S.Croy. BZ57 96
Carlton Rd., Sid. CN49 78
Carlton Rd., Slou. AQ40 52
Carlton Rd., Sun. BB50 73
Carlton Rd., Walt. BC54 83
Carlton Rd., Well. CO45 69
Carlton Rd., Wok. AT60 91
Carlton Sq. E1 CC38 57
Carlton St. SW1 BW40 3
Carlton St. SW1 BW40 56
Regent St.
Carlton Ter. E11 CH32 49
Carlton Ter. E7 CJ36 58
Carlton Ter. N18 BZ27 39
Carlton Ter. SE26 CC48 77
Carlton Vale NW6 BS38 56
Carlwell St. SW17 BU49 76
Carlyle Av., Brom. CJ52 88
Carlyle Av., Sthl. BE40 54
Carlyle Clo. N2 BT32 47
Carlyle Clo. NW10 BN37 55
Carlyle Clo., E.Mol. BG51 84
Carlyle Gdns., Sthl. BE40 54
Carlyle Pl. SW15 BQ45 65
Lacy Rd.
Carlyle Rd. SE28 CO40 59
Carlyle Rd. W5 BK42 64
Carlyle Rd., Croy. CB55 87
Carlyle Rd., E12 CK35 49
Carlyle Rd., Stai. AW50 73
Carlyle Sq. SW3 BT42 3
Carlyle Sq. SW3 BT42 66
Carlyon Av., Har. BE35 45
Carlyon Clo., Wem. BL37 55
Carlyon Clo., Wok. AS62 100
Carlyon Rd., Hayes BD39 54
Carlyon Rd., Wem. BL37 55
Carmalt Gdns. SW15 BQ45 65
Carmalt Gdns., Walt. BD56 93
Carmarthen Pl. SE1 CA41 4
Bermondsey St.
Carmarthen Rd., Slou. AP40 52
Carmelite Clo., Har. BG30 36
Carmelite Rd., Har. BG30 36
Carmelite St. EC4 BY40 4
Carmelite St. EC4 BY40 56
Carmelite Way, Har. BG30 36
Carmelite Wk., Har. BG30 36
Carment St. E14 CE39 57
Carmichael Clo. SW11 BT45 66
Darien Rd.
Carmichael Clo., Ruis. BC35 44
Carmichael Ms. SW18 BT46 76
Heathfield Rd.
Carmichael Rd. SE25 CA53 87
Carminia Rd. SW17 BV48 76
Carnaby Rd., Brox. CD13 12
Carnaby St. W1 BW39 1
Carnaby St. W1 BW39 56
Carnac St. SE27 BZ48 77
Carnach Grn., S.Ock. DA40 60
Carnanton Rd. E17 CF30 39
Carnarvon Av., Enf. CA24 30
Carnarvon Dr., Hayes BA42 63
Carnarvon Rd. E10 CF32 48
Carnarvon Rd. E15 CG36 58
Carnarvon Rd. E18 CG30 40
Carnarvon Rd., Barn. BR24 28
Carnation St. SE2 CO42 69
Carnbrook Rd. SE3 CJ45 68
Carnecke Gdns. SE9 CK46 78
Carnegie Clo., Surb. BL55 85
Fullers Av.
Carnegie Pl. SW19 BQ48 75
Carnegie Rd., St.Alb. BG11 9
Carnegie St. N1 BX37 2
Carnegie St. N1 BX37 56
Carnforth Clo., Epsom BM57 94
Carnforth Gdns., Horn. CU35 50
Carnforth Rd. SW16 BW50 76
Carnoustie Dr. N1 BX36 2
Carnoustie Dr. N1 BX36 56
Carnwath Rd. SW6 BS45 66
Caro La., Hem.H. AZ14 8
Carol St. NW1 BW37 1
Carol St. NW1 BW37 56
Carolina Rd., Th.Hth. BY51 86
Caroline Clo. SW16 BX48 76
Caroline Clo., Croy. CA56 96
Brownlow Rd.
Caroline Clo., Islw. BH43 64
Osterley Rd.
Caroline Clo., West Dr. AX41 63
Old Farm Rd.
Caroline Ct., Ashf. AZ50 73
Caroline Ct., Stan. BJ29 36
The Chase
Caroline Gdns. N1 CA38 57
Kingsland Rd.
Caroline Gdns. SE15 CB43 67
Caroline Pl. Ms. W2 BS40 56
Orme La.
Caroline Pl. SW11 BV44 66
Caroline Pl. W2 BS40 3
Caroline Pl. W2 BS40 56
Caroline Pl., Wat. BE25 27
Caroline Pl., Hayes BB43 63
Nobel Dr.
Caroline Rd. SW19 BR50 75
Caroline St. E1 CC39 57
Caroline Ter. SW1 BV42 3
Caroline Ter. SW1 BV42 66
Carolyn Clo., Wok. AP63 100
Carolyn Dr., Orp. CO55 89
Caroon Dr., Rick. AW21 26
Carpenders Av., Wat. BE27 36
Carpenter Clo., Epsom BO58 94
West St.
Carpenter Gdns. N21 BY27 38
Carpenter Path, Brwd. DE25 122
Carpenter St. W1 BV40 3
Carpenters Arms La., Epp. CO16 23
Carpenters Clo. SW1 BU41 3
Carpenters Clo., Epsom BO58 94
West St.
Carpenters Ct., Twick. BH48 74
Hampton Rd.
Carpenters Pl. SW4 BW45 66
Carpenters Rd. E15 CE36 57
Carpenters Rd., Enf. CC21 30
Carpenters Way, Pot.B. BT20 20
Carpenters Wood Dr., Rick. AT24 25
Carr Rd. E17 CD30 39
Carr Rd., Nthlt. BF36 54
Carr St. E14 CD39 57
Carrara Wk. SW9 BY45 66
Somerleyton Dev.
Carriage Rd., The SW7 BT41 3
Carriage Rd., The SW7 BT41 66
Carriageway, The, Sev. CP65 107
Carrick Clo., Islw. BJ45 64
Byfield Rd.
Carrick Dr., Sev. CU65 107
Carrick Gate, Esher BG55 84
Carrick Gdns. N17 BZ30 39
Flexmere Rd.
Carrick Ms. SE8 CE43 67
Watergate St.
Carrill Way, Belv. CP42 69
Coptefield Dr.
Carrington Av., B.Wd. BM25 28
Carrington Av., Houns. BF46 74
Carrington Clo., B.Wd. BN25 28
Carrington Clo., Barn. BP25 28
Chartridge Clo.
Carrington Clo., Croy. CD54 87
Carrington Gdns. E7 CH35 49
Woodford Rd.
Carrington Ho. SE8 CE44 67
Carrington Rd., Dart. CW46 80
Carrington Rd., Rich. BM45 65
Carrington Rd., Slou. AP40 52
Carrington Sq., Har. BG29 36
Carrington St. W1 BV40 3
Carrington St. W1 BV40 56
Carrol Clo. NW5 BV35 47
Carroll Av., Guil. AT70 118
Carroll Clo. E15 CG35 49
Ash Rd.
Carroll Hill, Loug. CK24 31
Carron Clo. E14 CE39 57
Carronade Pl. SE28 CM41 68
Carroun Rd. SW8 BX43 66
Carrow Rd., Dag. CO36 59
Carrow Rd., Walt. BD55 84
Carroway La., Grnf. BG37 54
Cowgate Rd.
Carrs La. N21 BZ25 30
Carshalton Gro., Sutt. BT56 95
Carshalton Pk. Rd., Cars. BU57 95
Carshalton Pl., Cars. BV56 95
Carshalton Rd. W., Sutt. BS56 95
Carshalton Rd., Bans. BU60 95
Carshalton Rd., Mitch. BV52 86
Carshalton Rd., Sutt. BT56 95
Carsington Gdns., Dart. CV48 80
Carslake Rd. SW15 BQ46 75
Carson Rd. E16 CH38 58
Carson Rd. SE21 BZ47 77
Carson Rd., Barn. BU24 29
Carstairs Rd. SE6 CF48 77
Carston Clo. SE12 CG46 78
Carston Ms. SE12 CG46 78
Carswell Clo., Brwd. DE25 122
Carswell Clo., Ilf. CJ31 49
Carswell Rd. SE6 CF47 77
Cart Path, Wat. BD20 18
Cartel Clo., Grays CY42 70
Gabion Av.
Carter Clo., Rom. CR29 41
Carter Clo., Wall. BW57 95
Carter Clo., Wind. AN44 61
Carter Ct. EC4 BY39 56
Carter La.
Carter Dr., Rom. CR29 41
Carter La. EC4 BY39 2
Carter La. EC4 BY39 56
Carter Pl. SE17 BZ42 4
Carter Pl. SE17 BZ42 67
Carter Rd. E13 CH37 58
Carter Rd. SW19 BT50 76
Carter St. SE17 BZ43 4
Carter St. SE17 BZ43 67
Carteret St. SW1 BW41 3
Carteret St. SW1 BW41 66
Carteret Way SE8 CD42 67
Carterhatch La., Enf. CA22 30
Carterhatch Rd., Enf. CC23 30
Carters Clo., Loug. CL25 31
Carters Clo., Wor.Pk. BQ55 85
Carters Hill Clo. SE9 CJ47 78
Carters Hill SE9 CJ47 78
Carters Hill, Sev. CX67 117
Carters La. SE23 CD48 77
Carters La., Epp. CL15 13
Carters La., Wok. AU63 100
Carters Mead, Harl. CP12 14
Carters Rd., Epsom BO61 103
Carters Row, Grav. DF48 81
Carters Row, Red. BU71 121
Carters Yd. SW18 BS46 76
Wandsworth High St.
Cartersfield Rd., Wal.Abb. CF21 30
Carthew Rd. W6 BP41 65
Carthew Vill. W6 BP41 65
Carthouse La., Wok. AP60 91
Carthusian St. EC1 BZ39 2
Carting La. WC2 BX40 4
Carting La. WC2 BX40 56
Cartmel Clo. N18 CB29 39
Cartmel Clo., Red. BU70 121
Cartmel Rd., Bexh. CR44 69
Cartmell Gdns., Mord. BT53 86
Carton St. W1 BU39 1
Carton St. W1 BU39 56
Cartwright Gdns. WC1 BX38 2
Cartwright Gdns. WC1 BX38 56
Cartwright Rd., Dag. CQ36 59
Cartwright St. E1 CA40 4
Cartwright St. E1 CA40 57
Carve Ley, Welw.G.C. BS 8 5
Carver Rd. SE24 BZ46 77
Carville Cres., Brent. BL42 65
Carville St. N7 BY34 47
Durham Rd.
Carwell St. SW17 BU49 76
Cary Rd. E11 CG35 49
Carysfort Rd. N16 BZ34 48
Carysfort Rd. N8 BW32 47
Cascade Av. N10 BW31 47
Cascade Clo., Buck.H. CJ27 40
Cascade Rd.
Cascade Clo., Orp. CP52 88
Chalk Pit Av.
Cascade Rd., Buck.H. CJ27 40
Cascades, Croy. CD58 96
Caselden Clo., Wey. AW56 92
Casella Rd. SE14 CC43 67
Casewick Rd. SE27 BY49 76
Casimir Rd. E5 CC34 48
Casington Way, S.Ock. DA39 60
Casino Av. SE24 BZ46 77
Casket St. E2 CA38 57
Caslon Pl. E1 CB38 57
Cudworth St.
Caspian Clo. NW10 BO35 46
Caspian St. SE5 BZ43 67
Caspian Wk. E16 CJ39 58
King George Av.
Casselden Rd. NW10 BN36 55
Cassidy Rd. SW6 BS43 66
Cassilda Rd. SE2 CO42 69
Cassilis Rd., Twick. BJ46 74
Cassio Rd., Wat. BC24 26
Cassiobridge Rd., Wat. BB25 26
Cassiobury Av., Felt. BB46 73
Cassiobury Dr., Wat. BB22 26
Cassiobury Park Av., Wat. BB24 26
Cassiobury Rd. E17 CC32 48
Cassis Ct., Loug. CM24 31
Burton Dr.
Cassland Rd. E9 CC36 57
Cassland Rd., Th.Hth. BZ52 87
Casslee Rd. SE6 CD47 77
Cassocks Sq., Shep. BA54 83
Russell Rd.
Casson St. E1 CB39 2
Casson St. E1 CB39 57
Casstine Clo., Swan. CT51 89
Castalia Sq. E14 CF41 67
Plevna St.
Castalia St. E14 CF41 67
Castell Rd., Loug. CM23 31
Castellain Rd. W9 BS38 1
Castellain Rd. W9 BS38 56
Castellan Av., Rom. CU31 50
Castellane Clo., Stan. BH29 36
Daventer Dr.
Castello Av. SW15 BQ46 75
Castelnau Est. SW13 BP43 65
Castelnau Pl. SW13 BP43 65
Castelnau Row SW13 BP43 65
Lonsdale Rd.
Castelnau SW13 BP44 65
Casterbridge Rd. SE3 CH45 68
Castile Rd. SE18 CL42 68
Castillon Rd. SE6 CG48 78
Castlands Rd. SE6 CD48 77
Castle Av. E4 CF29 39
Castle Av., Epsom BP58 94
Castle Av., Rain. CT36 59
Castle Av., Slou. AQ43 62
Castle Av., West Dr. AY40 53
Castle Baynard St. EC4 BY40 4
Puddle Dock
Castle Clo. E9 CD35 48
Swinnerton St.
Castle Clo. SW19 BQ48 75
Castle Clo. W3 BM41 65
Park Rd. N.
Castle Clo., Brom. CG52 88
Castle Clo., Bush. BF25 27
Castle Clo., Hodd. CF10 12
Castle Clo., Red. BZ70 114
Castle Clo., Reig. BS72 121
Castle Clo., Sun. BB50 73
Millfarm Av.
Castle Ct. EC3 BZ39 57
Birchin La.
Castle Dr., Ilf. CK32 49
Castle Dr., Reig. BS72 121

Castle Dr., Sev. CW62 108
Castle Farm Rd., Sev. CT58 98
Castle Gate Way, Berk. AR12 7
Castle Gdns., Dor. BL70 120
Castle Grn., Wey. BB55 83
Castle Grove Rd., Wok. AP59 91
Castle Hill Av., Berk. AR12 7
Castle Hill Av., Croy. CE58 96
Castle Hill Clo., Berk. AR12 7
Castle Hill Rd., Egh. AQ48 72
Castle Hill, Berk. AR12 7
Castle Hill, Guil. AR71 118
Castle Hill, Hart. DB53 90
Castle Hill, Wind. AO44 61
Castle La. SW1 BW41 3
Castle La. SW1 BW41 66
Castle Mead, Hem.H. AW14 8
Castle Ms. N12 BT28 38
Castle Ms. NW1 BV36 56
Castle Rd.
Castle Pl. W4 BO42 65
Windmill Rd.
Castle Rd. Islw. BH44 64
Castle Rd. N12 BT28 38
Castle Rd. NW1 BV36 56
Castle Rd., Couls. BU63 104
Castle Rd., Dag. CO37 59
Castle Rd., Enf. CD23 30
Castle Rd., Epsom BM61 103
Castle Rd., Grays DC43 71
Castle Rd., Hodd. CE10 12
Castle Rd., Islw. BH44 64
Castle Rd., Nthlt. BF36 54
Castle Rd., Sev. CU57 98
Castle Rd., St.Alb. BJ13 9
Castle Rd., Sthl. BE41 64
Warwick Rd.
Castle Rd., Swans. DC46 81
Castle Rd., Wey. BB55 83
Castle Rd., Wok. AS60 91
Castle Sq., Guil. AR71 118
Castle Sq., Red. BZ70 114
Castle St. E6 CJ37 58
Castle St., Berk. AR13 7
Castle St., Green. DA46 80
Castle St., Guil. AR71 118
Castle St., Kings.T. BL51 85
Castle St., Ong. CX18 24
Castle St., Red. BY70 121
Castle St., Slou. AP41 62
Albert St.
Castle St., Swans. DC46 81
Castle View Rd., Slou. AR42 62
Castle View Rd., Wey. AZ56 92
Castle Vw., Epsom BM60 94
Castle Way SW19 BQ48 75
Castle Way, Epsom BP58 94
Castle Way, Felt. BD49 74
Castle Wk., Reig. BS70 121
High St.
Castle Wk., Sun. BD52 83
Elizabeth Gdns.
Castle Yd. SE1 BY40 4
Castle Yd., Rich. BK46 74
Hill St.
Castlebar Hill W5 BJ39 54
Castlebar Ms. W5 BJ39 54
Castlebar Pk. W5 BK39 54
Castlebar Rd. W5 BK39 54
Castlecombe Dr. SW19 BQ47 75
Castlecombe Rd. SE9 CK49 78
Castledine Rd. SE20 CB50 77
Castlefields Rd., Reig. BS70 121
Castlefields, Grav. DF51 81
Castleford Av. SE9 CL47 78
Castlegate, Rich. BL45 65
Castlehaven Rd. NW1 BV36 56
Castleleigh Ct., Enf. BZ25 30
Castlemaine Av., Epsom BP58 94
Castlemaine Av., S.Croy. CA56 96
Castlereagh St. W1 BU39 1
Castlereagh St. W1 BU39 56
Castleton Av., Bexh. CS44 69
Castleton Av., Wem. BL35 46
Castleton Clo., Bans. BS61 104
Castleton Dr., Bans. BS60 95
Castleton Rd. E17 CF30 39
Castleton Rd. SE9 CJ49 78
Castleton Rd., Ilf. CO33 50
Castleton Rd., Mitch. BW52 86
Castleton Rd., Ruis. BD33 45
Castletown Rd. W14 BR42 65
Castleview Gdns., Ilf. CK32 49
Castlewood Dr. SE9 CK44 68
Castlewood Rd. N15 CB32 48
Castlewood Rd. N16 CB32 48
Castlewood Rd., Barn. BT24 29
Castor La. E14 CE40 57
Castor St. E14 CE40 57
Cat Hill, Barn. BU25 29
Caterham Av., Ilf. CK30 40
Caterham By-pass, Cat. CB65 105
Caterham Ct., Wal.Abb. CG20 22
Caterham Dr., Couls. BY62 104
Caterham Rd. SE13 CF45 67
Catesby St. SE17 BZ42 67
Catford Bdy. SE6 CE47 77
Catford Hill SE6 CD48 77
Catford Rd. SE6 CE47 77
Cathall Rd. E11 CF34 48
Catham Clo., St.Alb. BJ14 9
Cathay St. SE16 CB41 67
Cathay Wk., Nthlt. BF37 54
Leander Rd.
Cathcart Dr., Orp. CN54 88
Cathcart Hill N19 BW34 47
Cathcart Rd. SW10 BS43 3
Cathcart Rd. SW10 BS43 66
Cathcart St. NW5 BV35 47
Cathedral Clo., Guil. AQ71 118
Cathedral Ct., St.Alb. BF14 9
Cathedral Pl. EC4 BY39 56
Newgate St.
Cathedral Pl. EC4 BZ39 2
Cathedral St. SE1 BZ40 4
Cathedral St. SE1 BZ40 57
Cathedral Vw., Guil. AP70 118
Catherall Rd. N5 BZ34 48
Catherine Clo., Brwd. DA25 33
Catherine Clo., Hem.H. AZ11 8
Catherine Clo., West Dr. AX41 63
Catherine Clo., Wey. AY60 92
Catherine Ct. N14 BW25 29
Catherine Dr., Sun. BB50 73
Catherine Gdns., Houns. BG45 64
Catherine Gro. SE10 CE44 67
Catherine Pl. SW1 BW41 3
Catherine Pl. SW1 BW41 66
Catherine Rd., Enf. CD21 30
Catherine Rd., Rom. CU32 50
Catherine Rd., Surb. BK53 84
Catherine St. WC2 BX40 4
Catherine St. WC2 BX40 56
Catherine St., St.Alb. BG13 9
Catherine Wheel All. E1 CA39 2
Middlesex St.
Catherine Wheel Rd., Brent. BK43 64
Cathles Rd. SW12 BV46 76
Cathnor Rd. W12 BP41 65
Catisfield Rd., Enf. CD22 30
Catkin Clo., Hem.H. AW13 8
Catlin Cres., Shep. BA53 83
Catlin St. SE16 CB42 67
Catlin St., Hem.H. AW15 8
Catling Clo. SE23 CC48 77
Dacres Rd.
Catlins La., Pnr. BC31 44
Cato Rd. SW4 BW45 66
Cato St. W1 BU39 1
Cato St. W1 BU39 56
Caton St. SE15 CA44 67
Cator Clo., Croy. CF59 96
Cator Cres., Croy. CF59 96
Cator La., Beck. CD51 87
Cator Rd. SE26 CC50 77
Cator Rd., Cars. BU56 95
Cator St. SE15 CA43 67
Catsey La., Bush. BG26 36
Catsey Woods, Bush. BG26 36
Catterick Way, B.Wd. BL23 28
Cattistock Rd. SE9 CK49 78
Cattle Market, Sev. CU65 107
Cattlegate Hill, Pot.B. BW19 20
Cattlegate Rd., Enf. BX20 20
Cattlegate Rd., Pot.B. BW19 20
Catton St. WC1 BX39 2
Catton St. WC1 BX39 56
Cattsdell, Hem.H. AY12 8
Caulfield Rd. E6 CK37 58
Caulfield Rd. SE15 CB44 67
Causeway Clo., Pot.B. BT19 20
Causeway Ct., Wok. AP62 100
Bingham Dr.
Causeway, The N2 BT31 47
Causeway, The SW18 BS46 76
Causeway, The SW19 BQ49 75
Causeway, The, Cars. BV55 86
Causeway, The, Chess. BL56 94
Causeway, The, Egh. & Stai. AU49 72
Causeway, The, Esher BH57 93
Causeway, The, Felt. BC45 63
Causeway, The, Pot.B. BT19 20
Causeway, The, St.Alb. BF14 9
Causeway, The, Sutt. BT58 95
Causeway, The, Tedd. BH50 74
Causey Pl., Wok. AS62 100
Causey Way
Causeyware Rd. N9 CB26 39
Causton Rd. N6 BV33 47
Causton St. SW1 BW42 3
Causton St. SW1 BW42 66
Cautley Av. SW4 BW46 76
Cavalier Clo., Rom. CP31 50
Cavalry Cres., Houns. BD45 64
Cavalry Cres., Wind. AN45 61
Cavalry Gdns. SW15 BR46 75
Upper Richmond Rd.
Cavan Dr., St.Alb. BG11 9
Cavaye Pl. SW10 BT42 3
Cavaye Pl. SW10 BT42 66
Fulham Rd.
Cave Rd. E13 CH37 58
Cave Rd., Rich. BK49 74
Cave St. N1 BX37 56
Cavell Cres., Dart. CX45 70
Cavell Dr., Enf. BY23 29
Cavell Rd. N17 BZ29 39
Cavell Rd., Chsnt. CA17 21
Cavell St. E1 CB39 57
Cavendish Av. N3 BS30 38
Cavendish Av. NW8 BT37 1
Cavendish Av. NW8 BT38 56
Cavendish Av. W13 BJ39 54
Cavendish Av., Erith CR43 69
Cavendish Av., Har. BG35 45
Cavendish Av., Horn. CU36 59
Cavendish Av., N.Mal. BP53 85
Cavendish Av., Ruis. BC35 44
Cavendish Av., Sev. CU64 107
Cavendish Av., Sid. CO47 79
Cavendish Av., Wdf.Grn. CH30 40
Cavendish Av., Well. CN45 68
Cavendish Clo. N18 CB28 39
Cavendish Clo. NW6 BR36 55
Cavendish Clo. NW8 BT38 1
Cavendish Clo. NW8 BT38 56
Cavendish Clo. SW15 BR46 75
St. Johns Av.
Cavendish Clo., Amer. AQ23 25
Cavendish Clo., Hayes BB39 53
Cavendish Clo., Sun. BB50 73
Cavendish Cres., B.Wd. BM24 28
Cavendish Cres., Horn. CU36 59
Cavendish Ct. EC3 CA39 57
Houndsditch
Cavendish Ct., Rick. BA25 26
Mayfare
Cavendish Dr. E11 CF33 48
Cavendish Dr., Edg. BL29 37
Cavendish Dr., Esher BH56 93
Cavendish Gdns., Bark. CN35 49
Cavendish Gdns., Ilf. CL33 49
Cavendish Gdns., Red. BV70 121
Cavendish Gdns., Rom. CQ32 50
Cavendish Ms. N. W1 BV39 56
Hallam St.
Cavendish Ms. S. W1 BV39 56
Hallam St.
Cavendish Pl. W1 BV39 1
Cavendish Pl. W1 BV39 56
Cavendish Rd. E4 CF29 39
Cavendish Rd. N18 CB28 39
Cavendish Rd. N4 BY32 47
Cavendish Rd. NW6 BR36 55
Cavendish Rd. SW12 BV46 76
Cavendish Rd. SW19 BT50 76
Cavendish Rd. W4 BN44 65
Cavendish Rd., Barn. BQ24 28
Cavendish Rd., Chesh. AO19 16
Cavendish Rd., Croy. BY54 86
Cavendish Rd., N.Mal. BO53 85
Cavendish Rd., Red. BV70 121
Cavendish Rd., St.Alb. BH13 9
Cavendish Rd., Sun. BB50 73
Cavendish Rd., Sutt. BT57 95
Cavendish Rd., Wey. AZ58 92
Cavendish Rd., Wok. AR63 100
Cavendish Sq. W1 BV39 1
Cavendish Sq. W1 BV39 56
Cavendish Sq., Long. DC52 90
Bramblefield Clo.
Cavendish St. N1 BZ37 2
Cavendish St. N1 BZ37 57
Cavendish St. W1 BV39 56
Cavendish Way, Hat. BO12 10
Cavendish Way, W.Wick. CE54 87
Cavenham Ct., Wok. AS63 100
Brooklyn Rd.
Cavenham Gdns., Horn. CV32 51
Cavenham Gdns., Ilf. CM34 49
Caverleigh Way, Wor.Pk. BP54 85
Caversham Av. N13 BY27 38
Caversham Av., Sutt. BR55 85
Caversham Rd. N15 BZ31 48
Caversham Rd. NW5 BW36 56
Caversham Rd., Kings.T. BL51 85
Fairfield N.
Caversham St. SW3 BU43 3
Caversham St. SW3 BU43 66
Caverswall St. W12 BQ39 55
Eynham Rd.
Caveside Clo., Chis. CL51 88
Cavills Wk., Rom. CQ27 41
Cawcott Dr., Wind. AM44 61
Cawdor Av., S.Ock. DA40 60
Cawdor Cres. W7 BJ41 64
Cawley Rd. E9 CC37 57
Cawnpore St. SE19 CA49 77
Cawsey Way, Wok. AS62 100
Caxton Av., Wey. AW57 92
Caxton Dr., Uxb. AX37 53
Caxton Gro. E3 CE38 57
Caxton La., Oxt. CK69 115
Caxton Rd. N22 BX30 38
Caxton Rd. SW19 BT49 76
Caxton Rd. W12 BQ40 55
Caxton Rd., Sthl. BD41 64
Caxton St. N. E16 CG39 58
Caxton St. S. E16 CG40 58
Caxton St. SW1 BW41 3
Caxton St. SW1 BW41 66
Caxton Way, Wat. BA25 26
Caygill Clo., Brom. CG52 88
Cayley Clo., Wall. BX57 95
Cayley St. E14 CD39 57
Cayman St. SE16 CB41 67
Cayton Pl. EC1 BZ38 57
Cayton St.
Cayton Rd., Grnf. BH37 54
Cayton St. EC1 BZ38 2
Cayton St. EC1 BZ38 57
Cazenove Rd. E17 CE30 39
Cazenove Rd. N16 CA34 48
Cearn Way, Couls. BX61 104
Cecil Av., Bark. CM36 58
Cecil Av., Enf. CA24 30
Cecil Av., Grays DC41 71
Cecil Av., Horn. CW31 51
Cecil Av., Wem. BL35 46
Cecil Clo., Ashf. BA50 73
Cecil Clo., Chess. BK56 93
Cecil Cres., Hat. BP11 10
Cecil Ct. WC2 BX40 56
St. Martins La.
Cecil Ct., Barn. BQ24 28
Cecil Ct., Croy. CA55 87
Cecil Pk., Pnr. BE31 45
Cecil Pl., Mitch. BU53 86
Cecil Rd. E11 CG34 49
Cecil Rd. E13 CH37 58
Cecil Rd. E17 CE30 39
Cecil Rd. N10 BV30 38
Cecil Rd. N14 BW26 38
Cecil Rd. NW10 BN37 55
Cecil Rd. NW9 BN31 46
Cecil Rd. SW19 BS50 76
Cecil Rd. W3 BN39 55
Cecil Rd., Ashf. BA50 73
Cecil Rd., Chsnt. CC19 21
Cecil Rd., Croy. BX53 86
Cecil Rd., Enf. BZ24 30
Cecil Rd., Grav. DF47 81
Cecil Rd., Har. BG31 45
Cecil Rd., Hodd. CF11 12
Cecil Rd., Houns. BG44 64
Cecil Rd., Ilf. CL35 49
Cecil Rd., Iver AV39 52
Cecil Rd., Pot.B. BP19 19
Cecil Rd., Reig. BV70 121
London Rd.
Cecil Rd., Rom. CP33 50
Cecil Rd., St.Alb. BH13 9
Cecil Rd., Sutt. BR57 94
Cecil St., Wat. BC22 26
Cecil Way, Brom. CH54 88
Cecile Pk. N8 BX32 47
Cecilia Clo. N2 BT31 47
Hamilton Rd.
Cecilia Rd. E8 CA35 48
Cedar Av., Barn. BU26 38
Cedar Av., Cob. BD61 102
Cedar Av., Enf. CC23 30
Cedar Av., Hayes BC39 53
Cedar Av., Rom. CQ32 50
Cedar Av., Ruis. BD35 45
Cedar Av., Sid. CN47 78
Cedar Av., Twick. BF46 74
Cedar Av., Upmin. CX35 51
Cedar Av., Wal.Cr. CC20 21
Cedar Av., West Dr. AY40 53
Cedar Clo. SE21 BZ47 77
Cedar Clo. SW15 BN49 75
Cedar Clo., B.Wd. BM24 28
Cedar Clo., Brom. CK55 88
Cedar Clo., Brwd. DE25 122
Cedar Clo., Buck.H. CJ27 40
Cedar Clo., Cars. BU57 95
Cedar Clo., Dor. BJ71 119
Cedar Clo., E.Mol. BH52 84
Cedar Clo., Epsom BO60 94
Cedar Clo., Esher BE57 93
Cedar Clo., Pot.B. BS18 20
Cedar Clo., Reig. BT71 121
Cedar Clo., Rom. CS31 50
Cedar Clo., Saw. CQ6 6
Cedar Clo., Stai. AW52 83
Cedar Clo., Swan. CS51 89
Cedar Clo., Warl. CD62 105
Cedar Copse, Brom. CK51 88
Cedar Cres., Brom. CK55 88
Cedar Ct. N10 BV30 38
Cedar Ct. SE9 CK46 78
Cedar Ct. SW19 BQ48 75
Cedar Ct., Egh. AT49 72
Cedar Ct., Epp. CO19 23
Cedar Ct., St.Alb. BK13 9
Cedarwood Dr.
Cedar Dr. N2 BU31 47
The Causeway
Cedar Dr., Lthd. BH65 102
Cedar Dr., Pnr. BF29 36
Cedar Dr., S.at H. CX51 90
Cedar Dr., Uxb. AY37 53
Cedar Gdns., Sutt. BT57 95
Cedar Gdns., Upmin. CY34 51
Cedar Grn., Hodd. CE12 12
Cedar Gro. W5 BL41 65
Cedar Gro., Amer. AO23 25
Cedar Gro., Bex. CP46 79
Cedar Gro., Sthl. BF39 54
Cedar Gro., Wey. BA56 92
Cedar Heights, Rich. BL47 75
Cedar Hill, Epsom BN61 103
Cedar Lawn Av., Barn. BR25 28
Cedar Lawn NW3 BT34 47
Cedar Ms. SW4 BV45 66
Cedar Mt. SE9 CJ47 78
Cedar Park Gdns., Rom. CP33 50
Cedar Park Rd., Enf. BZ22 30
Cedar Rd. N17 CA30 39
Cedar Rd. NW2 BQ35 46
Cedar Rd., Berk. AR13 7
Cedar Rd., Brom. CJ51 88
Cedar Rd., Brwd. DE25 122
Cedar Rd., Cob. BC60 92
Cedar Rd., Croy. BZ55 87
Cedar Rd., Dart. CV47 80
Cedar Rd., E.Mol. BG52 84
Cedar Rd., Enf. BY22 29
Cedar Rd., Erith CU44 69
Cedar Rd., Felt. BA47 73
Cedar Rd., Grav. DH49 81
Cedar Rd., Grays DG41 71
Cedar Rd., Hat. BP13 10
Cedar Rd., Horn. CV34 51
Cedar Rd., Houns. BD44 64
Cedar Rd., Rom. CS31 50
Cedar Rd., Sutt. BT57 95
Cedar Rd., Tedd. BJ49 74
Cedar Rd., Wat. BD25 27
Cedar Rd., Wey. AZ56 92
Cedar Rd., Wok. AQ63 100
Cedar Ri. N14 BV26 38
Cedar St. SW19 BQ48 75
Cedar Ter., Rich. BL45 65
Cedar Tree Gro. SE27 BY49 76
Cedar Way NW1 BW36 56
Cedar Way NW1 BW37 1
Cedar Way, Berk. AR13 7
Cedar Way, Guil. AR69 118
Cedar Way, Slou. AS42 62
Cedar Way, Sun. BB50 73
Cedar Wk., Hem.H. AX14 8
Cedar Wk., Ken. BZ61 105
Cedar Wk., Reig. BU68 113
Cedar Wk., Tad. BR63 103
Cedarcroft Rd., Chess. BL56 94
Cedarhurst Dr. SE9 CJ46 78
Cedarne Rd. SW6 BS43 66
Fulham Rd.
Cedars Av. E17 CE32 48
Cedars Av., Mitch. BV52 86
Cedars Av., Rick. AX26 35
Cedars Clo. NW4 BQ31 46
Cedars Clo., Ger.Cr. AS28 34
Cedars Ct. N9 CA27 39
Cedars Est., Mitch. BV52 86
Cedars Pl. SE7 CJ42 68
Charlton Church La.
Cedars Rd. E15 CG36 58
Cedars Rd. N21 BY27 38
Cedars Rd. N9 CB27 39
Cedars Rd. SW1 BO44 65
Cedars Rd. SW13 BO44 65
Cedars Rd. SW4 BV45 66
Cedars Rd. W4 BN43 65
Cedars Rd., Beck. CD51 87
Cedars Rd., Croy. BX55 86
Cedars Rd., Kings.T. BK51 84
Cedars Rd., Mord. BS52 86
Cedars Wk., Wal.Abb. CF20 21
Cedars, Bans. BU60 95
Cedars, The, Buck.H. CH26 40
Cedars, The, Guil. AT69 118
Cedars, The, Har. BG29 36
Cedars, The, Reig. BT70 121
Cedars, The, Tedd. BH50 74
Cedars, The, Wey. AY59 92
Cedarville Gdns. SW16 BX50 76
Cedarwood Dr., St.Alb. BK13 9
Cedra Ct. N16 CB33 48
Cedric Av., Rom. CT31 50
Cedric Rd. SE9 CM48 78
Celadon Clo., Enf. CD24 30
Celandine Clo. E14 CE39 57
Celandine Clo., S.Ock. DB38 60
Celandine Dr. SE28 CO40 59
Celandine Rd., Walt. BE56 93
Celandine Way E15 CG38 58
Memorial Av.
Celestial Gdns. SE13 CF45 67
Celia Cres., Ash. AX50 73
Celia Ho. N1 CA37 57
Purcell St.
Celia Rd. N19 BW35 47
Cell Barnes Clo., St.Alb. BJ14 9
Cell Barnes La., St.Alb. BJ14 9
Cell Farm Av., Wind. AQ46 72
Celtic Av., Brom. CG52 88
Celtic Rd., Wey. AY60 92
Celtic St. E14 CF39 57
Cement Block Cotts., Grays DE42 71
Cemetery Hill, Hem.H. AX14 8
Cemetery La. SE7 CK43 68
Cemetery La., Shep. AZ54 83
Cemetery La., Wal.Abb. CG16 22
Cemetery Rd. E7 CG35 49
Cemetery Rd. N17 CA29 39
Cemetery Rd. SE2 CO43 69
Cemmaes Court Rd., Hem.H. AX13 8
Cemmaes Mead, Hem.H. AX13 8
Cenacle Clo. NW3 BS34 47
Centaur St. SE1 BX41 4
Centaur St. SE1 BX41 66
Centaury Ct., Grays DE43 71
Churchill Rd.
Centenary Rd., Enf. CD24 30
Central Av. E11 CF34 48
Central Av. N2 BT30 38
Central Av. N9 CA27 39
Central Av. SW11 BU43 66
Central Av. W3 BN40 55
Central Av., E.Mol. BE52 84
Central Av., Enf. CB23 30
Central Av., Grav. DG48 81
Central Av., Grays CZ42 70
Central Av., Harl. CM11 13
Central Av., Hayes BB40 53
Central Av., Houns. BG45 64
Central Av., Pnr. BE32 45
Central Av., S.Ock. CY41 70
Central Av., Til. DG44 71
Central Av., Wal.Cr. CD20 21
Central Av., Well. CN45 68
Central Cir. NW4 BP32 46
Central Dr., Horn. CW34 51
Central Dr., St.Alb. BK13 9
Central Gdns., Mord. BS53 86
Central Hill Est. SE19 CA50 77
Central Hill SE19 BZ49 77
Central Mkts. EC1 BY39 2
Central Mkts. EC1 BY39 56
Central Par., Croy. CF58 96
Central Park Av., Dag. CR34 50
Central Park Rd. E6 CJ37 58
Central Pl. SE25 CB52 87
Central Rd., Dart. CW46 80
Central Rd., Harl. CO 9 6
Central Rd., Mord. BW53 86
Central Rd., Wem. BJ35 45
Central Rd., Wor.Pk. BP54 85
Central Sq. NW11 BS32 47
Central Sq., E.Mol. BE52 84
Central Sq., Wem. BL36 55
Station Gro.
Central St. EC1 BZ38 2
Central St. EC1 BZ38 57
Central St. NW1 BU39 56
Melcombe Pl.
Central Way SE28 CO40 59
Central Way, Cars. BU57 95
Central Way, Felt. BC46 73
Central Way, Oxt. CF67 114
Centre Av., Epp. CN19 22
Centre Clo., Epp. CN19 22
Centre Common Rd., Chis. CL50 78
Centre Dr., Epp. CN19 22
Centre Rd. E11 CH34 49
Centre Rd. E7 CH34 49
Centre Rd. SE18 CL42 68
Centre Rd., Dag. CR37 59
Centre Rd., New A.G. DC55 90
Ash Rd.
Centre St. E2 CB37 57
Centre Way E17 CF29 39
Centre Way N9 CC27 39
Centre Way, Wal.Abb. CF21 30
Centre, The, Felt. BC47 73
Centreway, Ilf. CM34 49
Centurion Clo. N7 BX36 56
Centurion Way, Erith CQ41 69
Centurion Way, Grays CW42 70
Century Rd. E17 CD31 48
Century Rd., Egh. AU49 72
Century Rd., Hodd. CE11 12
Cephas Av. E1 CC38 57
Cephas St. E1 CC38 57
Ceres Rd. SE18 CN42 68
Cerise Rd. SE15 CB44 67
Cerne Clo., Hayes BD40 54
Cerne Rd., Grav. DJ49 81
Cerne Rd., Mord. BT53 86
Cerney Ms. W2 BT40 56
Gloucester Ter.
Cerney Ms. W2 BY40 3
Cerotus Pl., Cher. AV54 83
Barker Rd.
Cervantes Ct., Nthwd. BB29 35

Cervia Way., Grav. DJ48 81
Cester St. E2 CB37 2
Cestreham Cres., Chesh. AO18 16
Ceylon Rd. W14 BQ41 65
Chace Av., Pot.B. BT19 20
Chad Grn. E13 CH37 58
Chadacre Av., Ilf. CK31 49
Chadacre Rd., Epsom BP57 94
Chadbourn St. E14 CE39 57
Chadd Dr., Brom. CK52 88
Chadfields, Til. DG43 71
Chadhurst Clo., Dor. BK73 119
Wildcroft Dr.
Chadville Gdns., Rom. CP32 50
Chadway, Dag. CP33 50
Chadwell Av., Chsnt. CC17 21
Chadwell Av., Rom. CO33 50
Chadwell By-pass, Grays DF42 71
Chadwell Heath La., Rom. CO31 50
Chadwell Hill, Grays DG42 71
Chadwell Rd., Grays DE42 71
Chadwell St. EC1 BY38 2
Chadwell St. EC1 BY38 56
Chadwick Av. E4 CF27 39
Chadwick Clo., Grav. DF48 81
Chadwick Clo., Tedd. BJ50 74
Chadwick Rd. E11 CG33 49
Chadwick Rd. NW10 BO36 55
Chadwick Rd. SE15 CA44 67
Chadwick Rd., Ilf. CL34 49
Chadwick St. SW1 BW41 3
Chadwick St. SW1 BW41 66
Chadwick Way SE28 CP40 59
Chadwin Rd. E13 CH39 58
Chadworth Way, Esher BG56 93
Chaffers Mead, Ash. BL61 103
Chaffinch Av., Croy. CC53 87
Chaffinch Clo., Croy. CC53 87
Chaffinch La., Wat. BB26 35
Chaffinch Rd., Beck. CD51 87
Chaffinches Grn., Hem.H. AZ15 8
Market Oak La.
Chafford Gdns., Brwd. DE32 123
Chafford Way, Grays DD40 71
Chafford Way, Rom. CP31 50
Chafford Wk., Rain. CV37 60
Chagford St. NW1 BU38 1
Chagford St. NW1 BU38 56
Chailey Av., Enf. CA23 30
Chailey Clo., Houns. BD44 64
Springwell Rd.
Chailey Pl., Walt. BE56 93
Chailey St. E5 CC34 48
Chairmans Av., Uxb. AV32 43
Chalbury Wk. N1 BX37 2
Chalbury Wk. N1 BX37 56
Eckford St.
Chalcombe Rd. SE2 CO41 69
Chalcot Clo., Sutt. BS57 95
Chalcot Cres. NW1 BU37 1
Chalcot Cres. NW1 BU37 56
Chalcot Gdns. NW3 BU36 56
Chalcot Gdns., Surb. BK54 84
Chalcot Rd. NW1 BV36 1
Chalcot Rd. NW1 BV36 56
Chalcot Sq. NW1 BV36 56
Chalcots Est. NW3 BT36 56
Chalcroft Rd. SE13 CG46 78
Chaldon Common Rd., Cat. BZ65 105
Chaldon Rd. SW6 BR43 65
Chaldon Rd., Cat. BZ65 105
Chaldon Way, Couls. BX62 104
Chale Rd. SW2 BX46 76
Chale Wk., Sutt. BS58 95
Hulverston Clo.
Chalet Clo., Berk. AP13 7
Chalet Clo., Bex. CS49 79
Chalfont Av., Amer. AR23 25
Chalfont Av., Wem. BM36 55
Chalfont Clo., Hem.H. AZ11 8
Chalfont Grn. N9 CA27 39
Chalfont La., Ger.Cr. AU29 34
Chalfont La., Rick. AT25 25
Chalfont Pl., St.Alb. BH13 9
Upper Lattimore Rd.
Chalfont Rd. N7 BY36 56
Sheringham Rd.
Chalfont Rd. N9 CA27 39
Chalfont Rd. SE25 CA52 87
Chalfont Rd., Beac. AO28 34
Chalfont Rd., Ger.Cr. AT27 34
Chalfont Rd., Hayes BC41 63
Chalfont Station Rd., Amer. AR23 25
Chalfont Way W13 BJ41 64
Chalfont Wk., Pnr. BD30 36
Willows Clo.
Chalford Clo., E.Mol. BF52 84
Chalford Rd. SE21 BZ49 77
Chalford Wk., Wdf.Grn. CJ30 40
Chalforde Gdns., Rom. CU31 50
Chalgrove Av., Mord. BS53 86
Chalgrove Cres., Ilf. CK30 40
Chalgrove Gdns. N3 BR31 46
Chalgrove Rd. E9 CC36 57
Morning La.
Chalgrove Rd. N17 CB30 39
Chalgrove Rd., Sutt. BT57 95
Chalice Clo., Wall. BW57 95
Chalice Way SW2 BX47 76
Chalk Dale, Welw.G.C. BS7 5
Chalk Farm Rd. NW1 BV36 1
Chalk Farm Rd. NW1 BV36 56
Chalk Hill Rd. W6 BQ42 65
Shortlands Ms.
Chalk Hill, St.Alb. BF15 9
Chalk Hill, Wat. BD25 27
Chalk La., Ash. BL63 103
Chalk La., Barn. BU24 29
Chalk La., Epsom BN61 103
Chalk La., Harl. CR9 6
Chalk La., Lthd. BB68 110
Chalk Paddock, Epsom BN61 103
Chalk La.
Chalk Pit Av., Orp. CP52 89
Chalk Pit Rd., Bans. BS62 104
Chalk Pit Rd., Epsom BN63 103
Chalk Pit Way, Sutt. BT56 95
Chalk Rd. E13 CH39 58
Chalk Rd., Grav. DK47 81
Chalkdell Fields, St.Alb. BJ11 9
Chalkenden Clo. SE20 CB50 77
Castledine Rd.
Chalkey Hill, Sev. CM60 97
Chalkhill Rd., Wem. BM34 46
Chalklands, The, Wem. BN34 46
Chalkpit La., Great Bookham BE67 111
Chalkpit La., Dor. BJ71 119
Chalkpit La., Oxt. CF66 114
Chalkpit Ter., Dor. BJ70 119
Chalkpit Wood, Oxt. CF67 114
Chalks Av., Saw. CP5 6
Chalkstone Clo., Well. CO44 69
Chalkwell Park Av., Enf. CA24 30
Chalky Bank, Grav. DG49 81
Chalky La., Chess. BK58 93
Challacombe Clo., Brwd. DD26 122
Challenge Clo., Grav. DJ49 81
Challenge Rd., Ashf. BA48 73
Challice Way SW2 BX47 76
Challin St. SE20 CC51 87
Challis Rd., Brent. BK42 64
Challock Clo., West. CJ61 106
Challoner Clo. N2 BT30 38
Challoner Cres. W14 BR42 65
Challoner St.
Challoner St. W14 BR42 65
Challoners Clo., E.Mol. BG52 84
Chalmers Ct., Rick. AY26 35
Chalmers La., Reig. BT67 113
Chalmers Rd. E., Ashf. BA49 73
Chalmers Rd., Ashf. AZ49 73
Chalmers Rd., Bans. BT61 104
Chalmers St. SW8 BW44 66
Chalmers Ter. N16 CA34 48
Victorian Rd.
Chalmers Way, Felt. BC46 73
Chalmers Wk. SE17 BY43 66
Hillingdon St.
Chalsey Rd. SE4 CD45 67
Chalton Dr. N2 BT32 47
Chalton St. NW1 BW37 1
Chalton St. NW1 BW37 56
Chalvey Gdns., Slou. AP41 62
Chalvey Rd. E.
Chalvey Gro., Slou. AN41 61
Chalvey Pk., Slou. AP41 62
Chalvey Rd. E., Slou. AP41 62
Chalvey Rd. W., Slou. AO41 61
Chamber St. E1 CA40 4
Chamber St. E1 CA40 57
Chamberlain Clo. SE28 CM41 68
Garrick Dr.
Chamberlain Cotts. SE5 BZ44 67
Camberwell Gro.
Chamberlain Cres., W.Wick. CE54 87
Chamberlain La., Pnr. BC31 44
Chamberlain Rd. N2 BT30 38
Chamberlain Rd. N9 CB27 39
Chamberlain Rd. W13 BJ41 64
Midhurst Rd.
Chamberlain Sq. N1 BY36 56
Lofting Rd.
Chamberlain St. NW1 BU36 56
Regents Park Rd.
Chamberlain Way, Pnr. BC31 44
Chamberlain Way, Surb. BL54 85
Chamberlain Wk., Felt. BD49 74
Swift Rd.
Chamberlayne Rd. NW10 BQ37 55
Chambers Gdns. N2 BT30 38
Chambers La. NW10 BP36 55
Chambers Rd. N7 BX35 47
Chambers St. SE16 CB41 4
Chambers St. SE16 CB41 67
Chambersbury La., Hem.H. AZ15 8
Chambersbury La., Hem.H. AZ16 17
Chambord St. E2 CA38 2
Chambord St. E2 CA38 57
Champion Cres. SE26 CD49 77
Champion Gdns. SE5 BZ44 67
Grove La.
Champion Gro. SE5 CA45 67
Champion Hill SE5 BZ45 67
Champion Pk. SE5 BZ44 67
Champion Rd. SE26 CD49 77
Champion Rd., Upmin. CX34 51
Champions Grn., Hodd. CE10 12
Bridle Way S.
Champions Way, Hodd. CE10 12
Lyttons Way
Champness Clo. SE27 BZ49 77
Pennington Clo.
Champneys Clo., Sutt. BR57 94
Chance St. E1 CA38 57
Chance St. E2 CA38 57
Chancel Clo., Sev. CZ57 99
Chancel St. SE1 BY40 4
Chancel St. SE1 BY40 56
Dolben St.
Chancellor Ct., Guil. AO71 118
Chancellor Gdns., S.Croy. BY58 95
Chancellor Gro. SE21 BZ48 77
Chancellor Way, Sev. CU64 107
Chancellors Rd. W6 BQ42 65
Chancellors St. W6 BQ42 65
Chancelot Rd. SE2 CO42 69
Chancery Clo., St.Alb. BK11 9
Chancery La. WC2 BX39 2
Chancery La. WC2 BX39 56
Chancery La., Beck. CE51 87
Chanctonbury Chase, Red. BV70 121
Chanctonbury Clo. SE9 CL48 78
Chanctonbury Gdns., Sutt. BS57 95
Chanctonbury Way N12 BR28 37
Chandler Av. E16 CH39 58
Chandler Clo., Hmptn. BF51 84
Chandler Rd., Loug. CL23 31
Chandler St. E1 CB40 57
Chandlers Clo., Felt. BB47 73
Chandlers Cor., Rain. CV38 60
Chandlers La., Rick. AY21 26
Chandlers Ms. E14 CE41 67
Chandlers Rd., St.Alb. BK11 9
Chandlers Way, Rom. CT32 50
Chandlers Wk., Brwd. CZ22 33
Windmill Way
Chandos Av. E17 CE30 39
Chandos Av. N14 BW27 38
Chandos Av. N20 BT26 38
Chandos Av. W5 BK42 64
Chandos Clo., Amer. AR22 25
Chandos Clo., Buck.H. CH27 40
Chandos Cres., Edg. BL29 37
Chandos Ct. N14 BW27 38
The Green
Chandos Pl. WC2 BX40 4
Chandos Pl. WC2 BX40 56
Chandos Rd. E15 CF35 48
Chandos Rd. N17 CA30 39
Chandos Rd. N2 BT30 38
Chandos Rd. NW10 BO38 55
Chandos Rd. NW2 BQ35 46
Chandos Rd., B.Wd. BL23 28
Chandos Rd., Har. BG32 45
Chandos Rd., Pnr. BD33 45
Chandos Rd., Stai. AU49 72
Chandos St. W1 BV39 1
Chandos St. W1 BV39 56
Chandos Way NW11 BS33 47
Chandrye Clo. SE9 CK46 78
Change All. EC3 BZ39 57
Birchin La.
Change St. E2 CA38 2
Chanlock Path, S.Ock. DA40 60
Carnach Grn.
Channel Clo., Houns. BF44 64
Channelsea Rd. E15 CF37 57
Channing Clo., Horn. CW33 51
Chant Sq. E15 CF36 57
Chant St. E15 CF36 57
Chanton Dr., Sutt. BQ58 94
Chantrey Clo., Ash. BK63 102
Chantrey Rd. SW9 BX45 66
Chantreywood, Brwd. DD27 122
Brocksparkwood
Chantry Av., Hart. DC53 90
Chantry Clo., Enf. BZ22 30
Chantry Clo., Har. BL32 46
Chantry Clo., Kings.L. AZ18 17
Chantry Clo., Sid. CQ49 79
Ellenborough La.
Chantry Clo., West.Dr. AX40 53
Chantry Clo., Wind. AN44 61
Chantry Ct., Hat. BP13 10
Chantry Hurst, Epsom BN61 103
Chantry La., Brom. CJ53 88
Chantry La., Hat. BO13 10
Chantry La., St.Alb. BK16 18
Chantry Pl., Har. BF30 36
Chantry Rd., Cher. AW54 83
Chantry Rd., Chess. BL56 94
Chantry Rd., Guil. AT73 118
Chantry Rd., Har. BF30 36
Chantry St. N1 BY37 2
Chantry St. N1 BY37 56
Chantry View Rd., Guil. AR72 118
Chantry Way, Rain. CS37 59
Chantry, The, Harl. CO9 6
Chantry, The, Uxb. AY38 53
Chapel All, Brent. BL43 65
High St.
Chapel Av., Wey. AW56 92
Chapel Cft., Kings L. AW19 17
Chapel Clo. N2 BU31 47
Chapel Ct.
Chapel Clo., Dart. CT46 79
Chapel Clo., Grays DA43 70
Credo Way
Chapel Clo., Wat. BC20 17
Chapel Crofts, Berk. AP12 7
Kite Field
Chapel Ct. N2 BU31 47
Chapel Ct. SE1 BZ41 67
Tennis St.
Chapel End, Hodd. CE12 12
Chapel Farm Rd. SE9 CK48 78
Chapel Fields, Harl. CP12 14
Chapel Gro., Epsom BQ63 103
Chapel Gro., Wey. AW56 92
Chapel High, Brwd. DB27 42
Chapel Hill Crossways, Lthd. BD67 111
Browns La.
Chapel Hill, Dart. CT46 79
Chapel Hill, Pnr. BC32 44
Chapel House Clo., Guil. AP70 118
Park Barn Dr.
Chapel House Pl. E14 CE42 67
Chapel House St. E14 CE42 67
Chapel La., Chig. CN27 40
Chapel La., Great Bookham BG68 111
Chapel La., Dor. BG72 119
Chapel La., Houns. BF45 64
Chapel La., Loug. CK24 31
Chapel La., Lthd. BG67 111
Chapel La., Ong. CV20 24
Chapel La., Pnr. BD31 45
Chapel La., Rom. CP33 50
Station Rd.
Chapel La., Slou. AQ36 52
Chapel La., Uxb. AZ39 53
Chapel Market N1 BY37 2
Chapel Market N1 BY37 56
Chapel Park Rd., Wey. AW56 92
Chapel Pl. N1 BY37 56
Chapel Market
Chapel Pl. N17 CA29 39
Chapel Pl. W1 BV39 1
Chapel Pl. W1 BV39 56
Chapel Rd. SE27 BY49 76
Chapel Rd. W13 BJ40 54
Chapel Rd., Bexh. CR45 69
Chapel Rd., Epp. CN18 22
Chapel Rd., Houns. BF45 64
Chapel Rd., Ilf. CL34 49
Chapel Rd., Mitch. BT52 86
Chapel Rd., Oxt. CJ68 115
Chapel Rd., Red. BU70 121
Chapel Rd., Sev. DB64 108
Chapel Rd., Tad. BQ65 103
Chapel Rd., Twick. BK47 74
Chapel Rd., Warl. CC62 105
Chapel Row, Uxb. AX30 35
Chapel Side W2 BS40 56
Chapel St. E15 CF36 57
Chapel St. NW1 BU39 1
Chapel St. NW1 BU39 56
Chapel St. SW1 BV41 3
Chapel St. SW1 BV41 66
Chapel St. W2 BS40 56
Chapel St., Berk. AR13 7
Chapel St., Enf. BZ24 30
Chapel St., Guil. AR71 118
Chapel St., Hem.H. AX13 8
Chapel St., Slou. AP41 62
Chapel St., Uxb. AX37 53
Cross St.
Chapel St., Wok. AS62 100
High St.
Chapel Stones N17 CA30 39
Kings Rd.
Chapel Vw., S.Croy. CC57 96
Chapel Way N7 BX34 47
Sussex Way
Chapel Way, Epsom BQ63 103
Chapel Wk. NW4 BP31 46
Chapel Wood Rd., Fawk. DC55 90
Chapel Wood, Dart. DC55 90
Chapel Yd. N18 CB29 39
Fore St.
Chapelmount Rd., Wdf.Grn. CK29 40
Chaplaincy Gdns., Horn. CW33 51
Allenby Dr.
Chaplin Clo. SE1 BY41 4
Chaplin Cres., Sun. BB50 73
Chaplin Rd. E15 CG37 58
Chaplin Rd. N17 CA31 48
Forster Rd.
Chaplin Rd. NW2 BP36 55
Chaplin Rd., Dag. CQ36 59
Chaplin Rd., Wem. BK36 54
Chapman Clo., West.Dr. AY41 63
Chapman Cres., Har. BL32 46
Chapman Rd. E9 CD36 57
Chapman Rd., Belv. CR42 69
Chapman Rd., Croy. BY54 86
Chapman St. E1 CB39 57
Chapmans La. SE2 CP42 69
Chapmans La., Belv. CP42 69
Abbey Rd.
Chapmans La., Orp. CP51 89
Chapmans Park Ind. Est. NW10 BO36 55
Chapmans Rd., Sev. CQ65 107
Chapples Clo., Loug. CM25 31
Chapter Clo. W4 BN41 65
Beaumont Rd.
Chapter Clo., Uxb. AY36 53
Chapter Rd. NW2 BP35 46
Chapter Rd. SE17 BY42 4
Chapter Rd. SE17 BY42 66
Chapter St. SW1 BW42 3
Chapter St. SW1 BW42 66
Chapter Way, Hmptn. BF49 74
Bishops Gro.
Chara Pl. W4 BN43 65
Charcroft Gdns., Enf. CC24 30
Chard Rd., Houns. AZ44 63
Calshot Rd.
Chardin Rd. W4 BO42 65
Elliott Rd.
Chardins Clo., Hem.H. AV13 7
Chardmore Rd. N16 CB33 48
Chardwell Clo. E6 CK39 58
Charecroft Way W12 BQ41 65
Charford Rd. E16 CH39 58
Chargate Clo., Walt. BB57 92
Chargeable La. E13 CG38 58
Chargeable St. E16 CG38 58
Chargrove Clo. SE16 CC41 67
Marlow Way
Charing Clo., Orp. CN56 97
Charing Cross Rd. WC2 BW39 1
Charing Cross Rd. WC2 BW39 56
Charing Cross WC2 BX40 4
Chariotts Pl. Wind. AO44 61
Peascod St.
Charlbert St. NW8 BU37 1
Charlbert St. NW8 BU37 56
Charlbury Av., Stan. BK28 36
Charlbury Clo., Rom. CV29 42
Charlbury Cres., Rom. CV29 42
Charlbury Gdns., Ilf. CN34 49
Charlbury Gro. W5 BK39 54
Charlbury Rd., Uxb. AY34 44
Charldane Rd. SE9 CL48 78
Charlecote Gro. SE26 CB48 77
Charlecote Rd., Dag. CQ34 50
Charlemont Rd. E6 CK38 58
Charles Barry Clo. SW4 BW45 66
Charles Burton Ct. E5 CD35 48
Meeson St.
Charles Clo., Sid. CO49 79
Charles Cres., Har. BG33 45
Charles Gdns., Slou. AQ39 52
Borderside
Charles Grindling Wk. SE18 CL42 68
Charles Ho. W14 BR42 65
Charles Ho., Wind. AO44 61
Ward Royal
Charles II St. SW1 BW40 3
Charles II St. SW1 BW40 56
Charles La. NW8 BU37 1
Charles La. NW8 BU37 56
Charles Mills Ct. SW16 BX50 76
Charles Pl. NW1 BW38 1
Drummond St.
Charles Rd. E7 CJ36 58
Charles Rd. SW19 BS51 86
Shelton Rd.
Charles Rd. W13 BJ39 54
Charles Rd., Dag. CS36 59
Charles Rd., Rom. CP33 50
Charles Rd., Sev. CR58 98
Charles Rd., Stai. AX50 73
Charles Sevright Dr. NW7 BQ28 37
Charles Sq. N1 BZ38 2
Charles Sq. N1 BZ38 57
Charles St. E16 CJ40 58
Charles St. SW13 BO45 65
Charles St. W1 BV40 3
Charles St. W1 BV40 56
Charles St. W5 BK40 54
Lancaster Rd.
Charles St., Berk. AQ13 7
Charles St., Cher. AV54 82
Charles St., Croy. BZ55 87
Charles St., Enf. CA25 30
Charles St., Epp. CO19 23
Charles St., Grays DD43 71
Charles St., Green. CZ46 80
Charles St., Hem.H. AX14 8
Charles St., Houns. BE44 64
Charles St., Uxb. AZ38 53
Charles St., Wind. AO44 61
Charlesfield SE9 CJ48 78
Charleston Clo., Felt. BC48 73
Charleston St. SE17 BZ42 4
Charleston St. SE17 BZ42 67
Charlesworth St. N7 BX36 56
Charleville Cir. SE26 CB49 77
Charlieville Rd., Erith CS43 69
Mill Rd.
Charlmont Rd. SW17 BU50 76
Charlock Way, Guil. AT69 118
Charlock Way, Wat. BB25 26
Charlotte Despard Av. SW11 BV44 66
Charlotte Gdns., Rom. CR29 41
Charlotte Ms. W1 BW39 56
Tottenham St.
Charlotte Ms. W14 BR42 65
Munden St.
Charlotte Pl. NW9 BN32 46
Uphill Dr.
Charlotte Pl. SW1 BW42 3
Wilton Rd.
Charlotte Pl. W1 BW39 1
Charlotte Pl. W1 BW39 56
Goodge St.
Charlotte Pl., Grays DA43 70
Credo Way
Charlotte Rd. EC2 CA38 2
Charlotte Rd. EC2 CA38 57
Charlotte Rd. SW13 BO44 65
Charlotte Rd., Dag. CR36 59
Charlotte Rd., Wall. BW57 95
Charlotte Row SW4 BW45 66
North St.
Charlotte Sq., Rich. BL46 75
Greville Rd.
Charlotte St. W1 BW39 1
Charlotte St. W1 BW39 56
Charlotte Ter. N1 BX37 2
Charlotte Ter. N1 BX37 56
Charlton Av., Walt. BC56 92
Charlton Church La. SE7 CJ42 68
Charlton Clo., Hodd. CE12 12
Charlton Clo., Slou. AN41 61
Charlton Clo., Uxb. AZ34 44
Charlton Cres., Bark. CN37 58
Charlton Dene SE7 CJ43 68
Charlton Dr., West. CJ62 106
Charlton Gdns., Couls. BW62 104
Charlton Kings Rd. NW5 BW35 47
Charlton Kings, Wey. BB55 83
Charlton La. SE7 CJ42 68
Charlton La., Shep. BA52 83
Charlton Mead La., Hodd. CF12 12
Charlton Pk. La. SE7 CJ43 68
Charlton Pk. Rd. SE7 CJ43 68
Charlton Pl. N1 BY37 2
Charlton Pl. N1 BY37 56
Charlton Pl., Wind. AL44 61
Charlton
Charlton Rd. N9 CC26 39
Charlton Rd. NW10 BO37 55
Charlton Rd. SE3 CH43 68
Charlton Rd. SE7 CH43 68
Charlton Rd., Har. BK31 45
Charlton Rd., Shep. BA52 83
Charlton Rd., Wem. BL33 46
Charlton Row, Wind. AL44 61
Charlton
Charlton Sq., Wind. AL44 61
Charlton
Charlton St., Grays DB43 70
Charlton Way SE10 CG44 68
Charlton Way SE3 CG43 68
Charlton Way, Hodd. CE12 12
Charlton Way, Wind. AL44 61
Charlton Wk., Wind. AL44 61
Charlton
Charlton, Wind. AL44 61
Charlwood Clo., Har. BH29 36
Charlwood Dr., Cob. BG61 102
Charlwood Pl. SW1 BW42 3
Charlwood Pl. SW1 BW42 66
Charlwood Rd. SW15 BQ45 65
Charlwood St. SW1 BW42 3
Charlwood St. SW1 BW42 66
Charlwood Ter. SW15 BQ45 65
Cardinal Pl.

Charlwood, Croy. CD58 96
Charman Rd., Red. BU70 121
Charmans La., Reig. BO74 120
Charmian Av., Stan. BK30 36
Charminster Av. SW19 BS51 86
Charminster Ct., Surb. BK54 84
Charminster Rd. SE9 CJ49 78
Charminster Rd., Wor.Pk. BQ54 85
Charmouth Ct., St.Alb. BJ12 9
Charmouth Rd., St.Alb. BJ12 9
Charmouth Rd., Well. CP44 69
Charmwood La., Orp. CO58 98
Charne, The, Sev. CU62 107
Charnock Ct. Cres., Swan. CT52 89
Charnock Rd. E5 CB34 48
Charnwood Av. SW19 BS51 86
Charnwood Clo., N.Mal. BO52 85
Charnwood Dr. E18 CH31 49
Charnwood Gdns. E14 CE42 67
Charnwood Pl. N20 BT27 38
Charnwood Rd. SE25 BZ53 87
Charnwood Rd., Enf. CB21 30
Charnwood Rd., Uxb. AZ37 53
Charnwood St. E5 CB34 48
Charrington Rd., Croy. BY55 86
Drayton Rd.
Charrington St. NW1 BW37 1
Charrington St. NW1 BW37 56
Charsley Clo., Amer. AR23 25
Charsley Rd. SE6 CE48 77
Chart Clo., Brom. CG51 88
Chart Clo., Croy. CC53 87
Chart Clo., Dor. BK72 119
Chart Downs Est., Dor. BK72 119
Chart Gdns., Dor. BK73 119
Chart La. S., Dor. BK72 119
Chart La., Dor. BK71 119
Chart La., Reig. BS70 121
Chart La., West. CO68 116
Chart St. N1 BZ38 2
Chart St. N1 BZ38 57
Chart Vw., Sev. CX62 108
Chart Way, Reig. BS70 121
Chartar Rd. E., Egh. AU50 72
Chartar Rd. S., Egh. AU50 72
Chartar Rd. W., Egh. AU50 72
Charter Av., Ilf. CM33 49
Charter Clo., Slou. AP41 62
Hencroft St.
Charter Cres., Houns. BE45 64
Charter Dr., Bex. CQ47 79
Charter Pl., Uxb. AX37 53
Cross St.
Charter Rd., Kings.T. BM52 85
Charter Rd., The, Wdf.Grn. CG29 40
Charter Sq., Kings.T. BM51 85
Charter Way N14 BW25 29
Charter Way N3 BR31 46
Regents Park Rd.
Charterhouse Av., Wem. BK35 45
Charterhouse Bldgs. EC1 BY38 56
Goswell Rd.
Charterhouse Dr., Sev. CU65 107
Charterhouse Ms. EC1 BY39 2
Charterhouse Rd., Orp. CO55 89
Charterhouse Sq. EC1 BY39 2
Charterhouse Sq. EC1 BY39 56
Charterhouse St. EC1 BY39 2
Charterhouse St. EC1 BY39 56
Charteris Rd. N4 BY33 47
Charteris Rd. NW6 BR37 55
Charteris Rd., Wdf.Grn. CH29 40
Charters Clo. SE19 CA49 77
Charters Cross, Harl. CM12 13
Chartfield Av. SW15 BP46 75
Chartfield Rd., Reig. BT71 121
Chartfield Sq. SW15 BQ46 75
Chartham Gro. SE27 BY48 76
Royal Circus
Chartham Rd. SE25 CB52 87
Chartley Av. NW2 BO34 46
Chartley Av., Stan. BH29 36
Charton Clo., Belv. CQ43 69
Chartridge Clo., Barn. BP25 28
Chartridge Way, Hem.H. BA13 8
Chartway, Sev. CV65 108
Chartwell Clo. SE9 CM48 78
Chartwell Clo., Wal.Abb. CG20 22
Mason Way
Chartwell Dr., Orp. CM56 97
Farnborough Hill
Chartwell Pl., Epsom BO60 94
Chartwell Pl., Sutt. BR55 85
Chartwell Rd., Nthwd. BB29 35
Chartwell Way SE20 CB51 77
Jasmine Gro.
Charville Est., Hayes BA37 53
Charville La. W., Uxb. AZ38 53
Charville La., Hayes BA38 53
Charville Rd. W14 BR42 65
Charwood SE27 BY49 76
Leigham Court Rd.
Chasden Rd., Hem.H. AV12 7
Chase Cross Rd., Rom. CS29 41
Chase Ct. Gdns., Enf. BZ24 30
Chase End, Epsom BN59 94
Chase Gdns. E4 CE28 39
Chase Gdns., Twick. BG46 74
Chase Grn. Av., Enf. BY23 29
Chase Grn., Enf. BZ24 30
Chase Hill, Enf. BZ24 30
Chase House Gdns., Horn. CW32 51
Great Nelmes Chase
Chase La., Chig. CN27 40
Chase La., Ilf. CM32 49
Chase Rd. E18 CG30 40
Chase Rd. N14 BW25 29
Chase Rd. NW10 BN38 55
Chase Rd. W3 BN39 55
Chase Rd., Brwd. DB27 42
Chase Rd., Epsom BN59 94
Chase Ridings, Enf. BY23 29
Chase Side Av. SW20 BR51 85
Chase Side Av., Enf. BZ23 30
Chase Side Clo., Rom. CT29 41
Chase Side Cres., Enf. BZ23 30
Chase Side N14 BV25 29
Chase Side Pl., Enf. BZ23 30
Cricketers Arms Rd.
Chase Side, Enf. BZ24 30
Chase Trd. Est., The NW10 BN38 55
Chase Way N14 BV27 38
Chase, The E12 CJ35 49
Chase, The SW16 BX50 76
Chase, The SW20 BR51 85
Chase, The SW4 BV45 66
Chase, The, Chadwell Heath CQ32 50
Chase, The, Ash. BK62 102
Chase, The, Bexh. CR45 69
Chase, The, Brom. CH52 88
Chase, The, Brook Street DA28 42
Cromwell Rd.
Chase, The, Brwd. DB27 42
Chase, The, Chig. CM28 40
Chase, The, Chsnt. BY17 20
Chase, The, Couls. BW60 95
Chase, The, East Horsley BG61 102
Chase, The, Eastcote BD32 45
Chase, The, Edg. BM30 37
Chase, The, Grays DB43 70
Chase, The, Guil. AQ71 118
Chase, The, Hem.H. AY14 8
Chase, The, Ingrave DE28 122
Chase, The, Oxshott BB66 110
Chase, The, Pnr. BE31 45
Chase, The, Rad. BH21 27
Chase, The, Reig. BT71 121
Chase, The, Rom. CT31 50
Chase, The, Rush Green CT34 50
Chase, The, Sev. CW61 108
Chase, The, Stan. BJ29 36
Chase, The, Sun. BC51 83
Staines Rd.
Chase, The, Tad. BS64 104
Chase, The, Upmin. CZ34 51
Chase, The, Uxb. AZ35 44
Chase, The, Wall. BX56 95
Chase, The, Wat. BB24 26
Chasefield Clo., Guil. AT69 118
Sutherland Dr.
Chasefield Rd. SW17 BU49 76
Chaseley St. E14 CD39 57
Chasemore Gdns., Croy. BY56 95
Chaseside Gdns., Cher. AW54 83
Chaseville Par. N21 BX25 29
Chaseville Park Rd.
Chaseville Pk. Rd. N21 BX25 29
Chaseways, Saw. CP 7 6
Chasewood Av., Enf. BY23 29
Chastillian Rd., Dart. CT47 79
Chaston St. NW5 BV35 47
Herbert St.
Chatfield Dr., Guil. AU69 118
Chatfield Pl. W5 BL39 55
Park View Rd.
Chatfield Rd. SW11 BT45 66
Chatfield Rd., Croy. BY54 86
Chatham Av. N1 BZ38 57
Nile St.
Chatham Av., Brom. CG54 88
Chatham Clo. NW11 BS32 47
Chatham Clo., Sutt. BR54 85
Chatham Hill Rd., Sev. CV64 108
Chatham Pl. E9 CC36 57
Chatham Rd. E17 CD31 48
Chatham Rd. E18 CG30 40
Grove Hill
Chatham Rd. SW11 BU46 76
Chatham Rd., Kings.T. BM51 85
Chatham Rd., Orp. CM56 97
Chatham St. SE17 BZ42 4
Chatham St. SE17 BZ42 67
Chatsfield, Epsom BP58 94
Cheam Rd.
Chatsworth Av. NW4 BQ30 37
Chatsworth Av. SW20 BR51 85
Chatsworth Av., Brom. CH49 78
Chatsworth Av., Sid. CO47 79
Chatsworth Av., Wem. BL35 46
Chatsworth Clo. NW4 BQ30 37
Chatsworth Clo., B.Wd. BM24 28
Chatsworth Clo., W.Wick. CG55 88
Deer Park Way
Chatsworth Cres., Houns. BG45 64
Chatsworth Ct. W8 BS42 66
Chatsworth Dr., Enf. CB26 39
Chatsworth Est. E5 CC35 48
Chatsworth Gdns. W3 BM40 55
Chatsworth Gdns., Har. BF33 45
Chatsworth Gdns., N.Mal BO53 85
Chatsworth Par., Orp. CM53 88
Chatsworth Pl., Mitch. BU52 86
Chatsworth Pl., Tedd. BJ49 74
Chatsworth Rd. E15 CG35 49
Chatsworth Rd. E5 CC34 48
Chatsworth Rd. NW2 BQ36 55
Chatsworth Rd. W4 BN43 65
Chatsworth Rd. W5 BL39 55
Chatsworth Rd., Croy. BZ55 87
Chatsworth Rd., Dart. CV45 70
Chatsworth Rd., Hayes BC38 53
Chatsworth Rd., Sutt. BQ56 94
Chatsworth Ri. W5 BL38 55
Chatsworth Way SE27 BY48 76
Chatteris Av., Rom. CV29 42
Chattern Hill, Ashf. AZ49 73
Chattern Rd., Ashf. BA49 73
Chatterton Rd. N4 BY34 47
Chatterton Rd., Brom. CJ52 88
Chatto Rd. SW11 BU46 76
Chaucer Av., Hayes BC39 53
Chaucer Av., Houns. BC44 63
Chaucer Av., Rich. BM44 65
Chaucer Av., Wey. AZ57 92
Chaucer Clo. N11 BW28 38
Chaucer Clo., Berk. AP12 7
Chaucer Clo., Til. DH44 71
Coleridge Rd.
Chaucer Gdns., Sutt. BS55 86
Chaucer Grn., Croy. CC54 87
Chaucer Rd. E11 CH32 49
Chaucer Rd. E17 CF30 39
Chaucer Rd. E7 CH36 58
Chaucer Rd. SE24 BY46 76
Chaucer Rd. W3 BN40 55
Chaucer Rd., Ashf. AY49 73
Chaucer Rd., Grav. DE48 81
Chaucer Rd., Rom. CU29 41
Chaucer Rd., Sid. CP47 79
Chaucer Rd., Sutt. BS56 95
Chaucer Rd., Well. CN44 68
Chaucer Way SW19 BT50 76
Chaucer Way, Dart. CX45 70
Chaucer Way, Wey. AW57 92
Chaucer Wk., Dart. CW45 70
Chaucer Wk., Hem.H. AZ10 8
Coleridge Cres.
Chaulden House Gdns., Hem.H. AV14 7
Chaulden La., Hem.H. AU14 7
Chaulden Ter., Hem.H. AV14 7
Chauncey Av., Pot.B. BT20 20
Chauncey Clo. N9 CB27 39
Chauntler Rd. E16 CH40 58
Victoria Dock Rd.
Chave Croft Ter., Tad. BQ63 103
Chave Rd., Dart. CW48 80
Chaworth Rd., Cher. AU57 91
Cheam Clo., Tad. BP64 103
Cheam Common Rd., Wor.Pk. BP55 85
Cheam Park Way, Sutt. BQ57 94
Cheam Rd., Epsom BP58 94
Cheam Rd., Sutt. BR57 94
Cheam St. SE15 CB45 67
Nunhead Gro.
Cheapside EC2 BZ39 2
Cheapside EC2 BZ39 57
Cheapside La., Uxb. AV34 43
Cheapside N18 BZ28 39
Taplow Rd.
Cheapside, Wok. AR61 100
Chedburgh, Welw.G.C. BT 7 5
Cheddar Rd., Houns. AZ45 63
Cromer Rd.
Cheddar Waye, Hayes BC39 53
Cheddington Rd. N18 CA27 39
Chedworth Clo. E16 CG39 58
Hallsville Rd.
Cheelson Rd., S.Ock. DB37 60
Cheeseman Clo., Hmptn. BE50 74
Victors Dr.
Cheffins Rd., Hodd. CD10 12
Chelford Rd., Brom. CF49 77
Chelmer Cres., Bark. CO37 59
Chelmer Dr., Brwd. DF25 122
Chelmer Rd. E9 CC35 48
Chelmer Rd., Grays DG42 71
Chelmer Rd., Upmin. CY32 51
Chelmsford Av., Rom. CS29 41
Chelmsford Clo. E6 CK39 58
Guildford Rd.
Chelmsford Clo. W6 BR43 65
Chelmsford Dr., Upmin. CW34 51
Chelmsford Gdns., Ilf. CK33 49
Chelmsford Rd. E11 CF33 48
Chelmsford Rd. E17 CE32 48
Chelmsford Rd. E18 CG30 40
Chelmsford Rd. N14 BW26 38
Chelmsford Rd., Brwd. DC25 122
Chelmsford Rd., Ing. DC19 24
Chelmsford Rd., Ong. CZ17 24
Chelmsford Sq. NW10 BQ37 55
Chelsea Br. Rd. SW1 BV42 3
Chelsea Br. Rd. SW1 BV42 66
Chelsea Br. SW1 & SW8 BV43 66
Chelsea Clo. NW10 BN37 55
Winchelsea Rd.
Chelsea Clo., Edg. BM30 37
Chelsea Clo., Hmptn. BG49 74
Chelsea Cloisters SW3 BU42 3
Chelsea Cloisters SW3 BU42 66
Makins St.
Chelsea Ct. SW3 BU43 66
Chelsea Embk. SW3 BU43 66
Chelsea Embk. SW3 BV43 3
Chelsea Gdns., Sutt. BR56 94
Chelsea Harbour Dr. SW10 BT44 66
Chelsea Manor Est. SW3 BU43 66
Alpha Pl.
Chelsea Manor Gdns. SW3 BU42 3
Chelsea Manor Gdns. SW3 BU42 66
Chelsea Manor St. SW3 BU42 3
Chelsea Manor St. SW3 BU42 66
Chelsea Park Gdns. SW3 BT43 3
Chelsea Park Gdns. SW3 BT43 66
Chelsea Sq. SW3 BT42 3
Chelsea Sq. SW3 BT42 66
Chelsea Wf. SW10 BT43 66
Chelsea Wk. SW3 BU43 66
Chelsfield Av. N9 CC26 39
Chelsfield Gdns. SE26 CC48 77
Chelsfield Grn. N9 CC26 39
Chelsfield Av.
Chelsfield Hill, Orp. CP58 98
Chelsfield La., Chelsfield CR57 98
Chelsfield La., Orp. CP54 89
Chelsfield Rd., Orp. CP53 89
Chelsham Clo., Warl. CD62 105
Chelsham Court Rd., Warl. CF63 105
Chelsham Rd. SW4 BW45 66
Chelsham Rd., S.Croy. BZ57 96
Chelsham Rd., Warl. CD62 105
Chelsing Ri., Hem.H. BA14 8
Chelston Rd., Ruis. BC33 44
Chelsworth Clo., Rom. CW30 42
Chelsworth Dr. SE18 CM43 68
Chelsworth Dr., Rom. CW30 42
Cheltenham Av., Twick. BJ47 74
Cheltenham Clo., Nthlt. BF36 54
Cheltenham Gdns. E6 CK37 58
Cheltenham Gdns., Loug. CK25 31
Cheltenham Pl. W3 BM40 55
Cheltenham Pl., Har. BL31 46
Cheltenham Rd. E10 CF32 48
Cheltenham Rd. SE15 CC45 67
Cheltenham Rd., Orp. CO55 89
Cheltenham Ter. SW3 BU42 3
Cheltenham Ter. SW3 BU42 66
Cheltenham Vill., Stai. AV46 72
Chelverton Rd. SW15 BQ45 65
Chelveston, Welw.G.C. BT 7 5
Chelwood Av., Hat. BP11 10
Chelwood Clo. E4 CE25 30
Chelwood Clo., Epsom BO59 94
Chelwood Clo., Nthwd. BA29 35
Chelwood Gdns. Pass., Rich. BM44 65
Pensford Av.
Chelwood Gdns., Rich. BM44 65
Chelwood Wk. SE4 CD45 67
Chenappa Clo. E13 CH38 58
Chenduit Way, Stan. BH28 36
Chene Dr., St.Alb. BG12 9
Cheney Rd. NW1 BX37 2
Cheney Rd. NW1 BX37 56
Cheney Row E17 CD30 39
Cheney St., Pnr. BD32 45
Cheneys Rd. E11 CG34 49
Chenies Av., Amer. AR23 25
Chenies Ct., Hem.H. AZ11 8
Chenies Ms. WC1 BW38 1
Chenies Ms. WC1 BW38 56
Chenies Par., Amer. AR23 25
Chenies Pl. NW1 BW37 1
Chenies Pl. NW1 BW37 56
Chenies Rd., Rick. AU23 25
Chenies St. WC1 BW39 1
Chenies St. WC1 BW39 56
Chenies, The, Dart. CT49 79
Chenies, The, Orp. CN53 88
Cheniston Clo., Wey. AV60 91
Cheniston Gdns. W8 BS41 66
Chennells, Hat. BO13 10
Chepstow Av., Horn. CW34 51
Chepstow Clo. SW15 BR46 75
Chepstow Cres. W11 BS40 56
Chepstow Cres., Ilf. CN32 49
Chepstow Gdns., Sthl. BE39 54
Chepstow Pl. W2 BS40 56
Chepstow Rd. W2 BS39 56
Chepstow Rd. W7 BJ41 64
Chepstow Rd., Croy. CA55 87
Chepstow Ri., Croy. CA55 87
Chepstow Vill. W11 BR40 55
Chepstow Way SE15 CA44 67
Chequer St. EC1 BZ38 2
Chequer St. EC1 BZ38 57
Chequer St., St.Alb. BG13 9
Chequer Tree Clo., Wok. AP61 100
Green Acre
Chequers Clo., Orp. CN52 88
Ravensbury Rd.
Chequers Clo., Tad. BP66 112
Chequers Field, Welw.G.C. BQ 9 5
Chequers Gdns. N13 BY28 38
Chequers Hill, Amer. AO23 25
Chequers La., Dag. CQ38 59
Chequers La., Tad. BP66 112
Chequers La., Wat. BD18 18
Chequers Orchard, Iver AV39 52
Chequers Pl., Dor. BJ71 119
Chequers Rd., Brwd. CW25 33
Chequers Rd., Loug. CL25 31
Chequers Rd., Rom. CW27 42
Chequers Sq., Uxb. AX36 53
High St.
Chequers Way N13 BY28 38
Chequers Wk., Wal.Abb. CG20 22
Mason Way
Chequers, Welw.G.C. BQ 9 5
Cherbury Clo. SE28 CP39 59
Cherbury Ct. N1 BZ37 2
Cherbury Ct. N1 BZ37 57
Cherbury St. N1 BZ37 2
Cherbury St. N1 BZ37 57
Cherchefelle Ms., Stan. BJ28 36
Green La.
Cherimoya Gdns., E.Mol. BF52 84
Cherington Rd. W7 BH40 54
Cheriton Av., Brom. CG53 88
Cheriton Av., Ilf. CK30 40
Cheriton Clo. W5 BK39 54
Queens Wk.
Cheriton Clo., St.Alb. BK11 9
Cheriton Ct., Walt. BD54 84
Stratton Clo.
Cheriton Dr. SE18 CM43 68
Cheriton Sq. SW17 BV48 76
Cherkley Hill, Lthd. BK66 111
Cherries, The, Slou. AQ39 52
Cherry Acre, Ger.Cr. AR28 34
Cherry Av., Brwd. DC27 122
Cherry Av., Slou. AR41 62
Cherry Av., Sthl. BD40 54
Cherry Av., Swan. CS52 89
Cherry Bounce, Hem.H. AX12 8
Cherry Cft., Welw.G.C. BQ 6 5
Cherry Clo. E17 CE32 48
Eden Rd.
Cherry Clo. W5 BK41 64
Cherry Clo., Bans. BQ60 94
Cherry Clo., Cars. BU55 86
Cherry Clo., Mord. BR52 85
Cherry Clo., Ruis. BB34 44
Cherry Cres., Brent. BJ43 64
Cherry Garth, Brent. BK42 64
Cherry Gdn. St. SE16 CB41 67
Cherry Gdns., Dag. CQ35 50
Cherry Gro., Hayes BC40 53
Cherry Gro., Uxb. AZ39 53
Cherry Hill Gdns., Croy. BX56 95
Cherry Hill, Barn. BS25 29
Cherry Hill, Rick. AW24 26
Cherry Hill, St.Alb. BF16 18
Cherry Hollow, Wat. BB19 17
Cherry La., West.Dr. AY42 63
Cherry Laurel Wk. SW2 BX46 76
Beechdale Rd.
Cherry Orchard Clo., Orp. CP53 89
Cherry Orchard Gdns., E.Mol. BE52 84
Cherry Orchard Gdns., Croy. CA54 87
Oval Rd.
Cherry Orchard La., Brom. CK55 88
Cherry Orchard Rd., E.Mol. BE52 84
Cherry Orchard Rd., Croy. BZ55 87
Cherry Orchard Rd., Brom. CK55 88
Cherry Orchard, West Dr. AY41 63
Cherry Orchard, Amer. AP22 25
Cherry Orchard, Ash. BM62 103
Cherry Orchard, Hem.H. AW12 8
Cherry Orchard, Slou. AQ36 52
Cherry Orchard, Stai. AW49 73
Cherry Rd., Enf. CC22 30
Cherry Ri., Ch.St.G. AR27 34
Cherry St., Rom. CS32 50
Cherry St., Wok. AS62 100
Cherry Tree Av., West Dr. AY39 53
Cherry Tree Av., Guil. AP70 118
Cherry Tree Av., St.Alb. BK16 18
Cherry Tree Av., Stai. AW50 73
Cherry Tree Clo., Grays DE43 71
Silverlocke Rd.
Cherry Tree Clo., Rain. CT37 59
Cherry Tree Clo., Wem. BH35 45
Cherry Tree Ct., Couls. BX62 104
Coulsdon Rd.
Cherry Tree Dr. SW16 BX48 76
Cherry Tree Gdns., Croy. BZ54 87
Oval Rd.
Cherry Tree Grn., S.Croy. CB60 96
Cherry Tree La., Ger.Cr. AR30 34
Cherry Tree La., Hem.H. BA11 8
Cherry Tree La., Iver AW37 53
Cherry Tree La., Pot.B. BS20 20
Cherry Tree La., Rain. CT38 59
Cherry Tree La., Rick. AU26 34
Cherry Tree La., Slou. AS36 52
Cherry Tree Rd. E15 CG35 49
Wingfield Rd.
Cherry Tree Rd. N2 BU31 47
Cherry Tree Rd., Hodd. CE11 12
Cherry Tree Rd., Wat. BC21 26
Cherry Tree Ri., Buck.H. CJ28 40
Cherry Tree Way, Stan. BJ28 36
Cherry Tree Wk. EC1 BZ38 2
Cherry Tree Wk., W.Wick. CG56 97
Cherry Tree Wk., Beck. CD52 87
Cherry Tree Wk., Chesh. AO17 16
Cherry Tree Wk., West. CJ61 106
Cherry Way, Epsom BN57 94
Cherry Way, Hat. BP14 10
Cherry Way, Shep. BB52 83
Cherry Way, Slou. AU45 62
Mill La.
Cherry Wk., Brom. CH54 88
Cherry Wk., Grays DG41 71
Cherry Wk., Rain. CT37 59
Cherry Wk., Rick. AX23 26
Cherrycot Hill, Orp. CM56 97
Cherrycot Ri., Orp. CM56 97
Cherrycroft Gdns., Pnr. BE29 36
Westfield Pk.
Cherrydale, Wat. BB24 26
Cherrydown Av. E4 CD27 39
Cherrydown Clo. E4 CD27 39
Cherrydown Rd., Sid. CP48 79
Cherrydown Wk., Rom. CR30 41
Cherrydown, Grays DE40 71
Cherrytree La., Iver AW37 53
Cherrywood Av., Egh. AQ50 72
Cherrywood Clo., Kings.T. BM50 75
Alexandra Rd.
Cherrywood Clo., Beac. AO28 34
Cherrywood Ct., Tedd. BJ49 74
Elmfield Av.
Cherrywood Dr. SW15 BQ46 75
Cherrywood Dr., Grav. DF49 81
Cherrywood La., Mord. BR52 85
Cherston Gdns., Loug. CL24 31
Cherston Rd., Loug. CL24 31
Chertsey Br. Rd., Cher. AX54 83
Chertsey Clo., Ken. BY61 104
Chertsey Cres., Croy. CF58 96
Chertsey Ct. SW14 BM45 65
Chertsey Dr., Sutt. BR55 85
Chertsey La., Cher. AV52 82
Chertsey La., Stai. AV49 72
Chertsey Rd. E11 CF34 48
Chertsey Rd. W4 BM42 65
Chertsey Rd., Addlestonemoor AW55 83
Chertsey Rd., Ash. & Sun. BA50 73
Chertsey Rd., Byfleet AX59 92
Chertsey Rd., Cher. AO56 91
Chertsey Rd., Chobham AP58 91
Chertsey Rd., Ilf. CM35 49
Chertsey Rd., Longcross AP55 82
Chertsey Rd., Shep. AY54 83
Chertsey Rd., Sun. & Felt. BB49 73
Chertsey Rd., Twick. BJ46 74
Chertsey Rd., Whitton BF48 74
Chertsey Rd., Wok. AS61 100

Chertsey Rd., Wok.	AS62	100
Chertsey St. SW17	BV49	76
Chertsey St., Guil.	AR71	118
Chervil Clo., Felt.	BC48	73
Charleston Clo.		
Chervil Ms. SE28	CO40	59
Cherwell Clo., Rick.	AZ25	26
Cherwell Clo., Slou.	AT43	62
Tweed Rd.		
Cherwell Ct., Epsom	BN56	94
Cherwell Gro., S.Ock.	DA40	60
Cherwell Way, Ruis.	BA32	44
Cheryls Clo. SW6	BS44	66
Cheselden Rd., Guil.	AS71	118
Cheseman St. SE26	CB48	77
Chesfield Rd., Kings.T.	BL50	75
Chesham Av., Orp.	CL53	88
Chesham Clo., Rom.	CS31	50
Chesham Clo., Sutt.	BR58	94
Chesham Cres. SE20	CC51	87
Chesham Ct., Berk.	AQ13	7
Ashlyns Rd.		
Chesham Ct., Nthwd.	BB29	35
Chesham La., Ch.St.G.	AS27	34
Chesham La., Ger.Cr.	AS28	34
Chesham Ms. SW1	**BV41**	**3**
Chesham Ms. SW1	BV41	66
Chesham Ms., Guil.	AS71	118
Chesham Rd.		
Chesham Pl. SW1	**BV41**	**3**
Chesham Pl. SW1	BV41	66
Chesham Rd. SE20	CC51	87
Chesham Rd. SW19	BT49	76
Chesham Rd., Berk.	AQ14	7
Chesham Rd., Guil.	AS71	118
Chesham Rd., Hem.H.	AS17	16
Chesham Rd., Kings.T.	BM51	85
Chesham St. NW10	BN34	46
Chesham St. SW1	**BV41**	**3**
Chesham St. SW1	BV41	66
Chesham Ter. W13	BJ41	64
Chesham Way, Wat.	BB25	26
Cheshire Clo. SE4	CD44	67
Malpas Rd.		
Cheshire Clo., Cher.	AU57	91
Cheshire Clo., Horn.	CX32	51
Cheshire Clo., Mitch.	BX52	86
Cheshire Ct. EC4	BY39	56
Fleet St.		
Cheshire Ct., Slou.	AQ41	62
Clements Clo.		
Cheshire Gdns., Chess.	BK57	93
Cheshire Rd. N22	BX29	38
Cheshire St. E2	**CA38**	**2**
Cheshire St. E2	CA38	57
Chesholm Rd. N16	CA34	48
Chesholm Rd., Ashf.	BA50	73
Cheshunt Gate Ho., Wal.Cr.	CB18	21
Cheshunt Pk., Chsnt.	CB17	21
Cheshunt Rd. E7	CH36	58
Cheshunt Rd., Belv.	CR42	69
Cheshunt Wash, Chsnt.	CD17	21
Chesil Way, Hayes	BB38	53
Chesilton Rd. SW6	BR44	65
Chesley Gdns. E6	CJ37	58
Chesney Cres., Croy.	CF57	96
Chesney St. SW11	BU44	66
Chesnut Gro. N17	CA31	48
Chesnut Rd.		
Chesnut Rd. N17	CA31	48
Chess Clo., Rick.	AX24	26
Chess Ct. E1	CA39	57
Old Castle St.		
Chess Hill, Rick.	AX24	26
Chess La., Rick.	AX24	26
Chess Vale Ri., Rick.	AY25	26
Chess Way, Rick.	AW24	26
Chessfield Pk., Amer.	AS22	25
Chessholme Ct., Sun.	BB50	73
Scotts Av.		
Chessington Av. N3	BR31	46
Chessington Av., Bexh.	CQ43	69
Chessington Clo., Epsom	BN57	94
Chessington Ct., Pnr.	BE31	45
Chessington Hall Gdns., Chess.	BK57	93
Harrow Clo.		
Chessington Hill Pk., Chess.	BM56	94
Chessington Par., Chess.	BK56	93
Chessington Rd., Epsom	BM57	94
Chessington Way, W.Wick.	CE55	87
Chessmount Ri., Chesh.	AO20	16
Chesson Rd. W14	BR43	65
Chesswood Way, Pnr.	BD30	36
Chester Av., Rich.	BL46	75
Chester Av., Twick.	BE47	74
Chester Av., Upmin.	CZ34	51
Chester Clo. N. NW1	**BV38**	**1**
Chester Clo. S. NW1	**BV38**	**1**
Chester Clo. SW1	**BV41**	**3**
Chester Clo. SW1	BV41	66
Chester Clo. SW13	BP45	65
Chester Clo., Ashf.	BA49	73
Chester Clo., Dor.	BK70	119
Chester Clo., Guil.	AP69	118
Chester Clo., Loug.	CM23	31
Chester Clo., Sutt.	BS55	86
Chester Clo., Uxb.	AZ39	53
Chester Cotts. SW1	BV42	66
Bourne St.		
Chester Cres. E8	CA35	48
Chester Ct. NW1	**BV38**	**1**
Chester Ct. NW5	BV35	47
Chester Ct. W3	BM39	55
Monks Dr.		
Chester Dr., Har.	BE32	45
Chester Gate NW1	**BV38**	**1**
Chester Gate NW1	BV38	56
Outer Circle		
Chester Gdns. W13	BJ39	54
Chester Gdns., Enf.	CB25	30
Chester Gdns., Mord.	BT53	86
Chester Grn., Loug.	CM23	31
Chester Gro. E2	CB38	57
Kelsey St.		
Chester Gro. SE18	CM42	68
Chester Ms. SW1	**BV41**	**3**
Chester Ms. SW1	BV41	66
Chester Path, Loug.	CM23	31
Chester Pl. NW1	**BV38**	**1**
Chester Pl. NW1	BV38	56
Chester Terrace Ms.		
Chester Rd. E11	CH32	49
Chester Rd. E16	CG38	58
Chester Rd. E17	CC32	48
Chester Rd. E7	CJ36	58
Chester Rd. N17	BZ31	48
Chester Rd. N19	BV34	47
Chester Rd. N9	CB26	39
Chester Rd. NW1	**BV38**	**1**
Chester Rd. NW1	BV38	56
Chester Rd. SW19	BQ50	75
Chester Rd., B.Wd.	BN24	28
Chester Rd., Chig.	CL27	40
Chester Rd., Heathrow	AZ45	63
Chester Rd., Houns.	BD45	64
Chester Rd., Ilf.	CN33	49
Chester Rd., Loug.	CL23	31
Chester Rd., Lthd.	BC67	110
Chester Rd., Nthwd.	BB29	35
Chester Rd., Sid.	CN46	78
Chester Rd., Slou.	AO39	52
Chester Rd., Wat.	BC25	26
Chester Row SW1	**BV42**	**3**
Chester Row SW1	BV42	66
Chester Sq. SW1	**BV42**	**3**
Chester Sq. SW1	BV42	66
Chester St. E11	CG34	49
Chester St. E2	CB38	57
Chester St. SW1	**BV41**	**3**
Chester St. SW1	BV41	66
Chester Ter. Ms. NW1	**BV38**	**1**
Chester Ter. Ms. NW1	BV38	56
Chester Ter. NW1	**BV38**	**1**
Chester Ter. NW1	BV38	56
Chester Way SE11	**BY42**	**4**
Chester Way SE11	BY42	66
Chesterfield Clo., Orp.	CQ52	89
Chesterfield Dr., Esher	BJ55	84
Chesterfield Dr., Sev.	CS64	107
Chesterfield Gdns. N4	BY32	47
Chesterfield Gdns. W1	**BV40**	**3**
Chesterfield Gdns. W1	BV40	56
Chesterfield Gro. SE22	CA46	77
Chesterfield Hill W1	**BV40**	**3**
Chesterfield Hill W1	BV40	56
Chesterfield Rd. E10	CF32	48
Chesterfield Rd. N3	BS29	38
Chesterfield Rd. W4	BN43	65
Chesterfield Rd., Ashf.	AX49	73
Chesterfield Rd., Barn.	BQ25	28
Chesterfield Rd., Enf.	CD22	30
Chesterfield Rd., Epsom	BN57	94
Chesterfield St. W1	**BV40**	**3**
Chesterfield St. W1	BV40	56
Chesterfield Way SE15	CC43	67
Chesterfield Way, Hayes	BC41	63
Chesterfield Wk. SE10	CF44	67
Chesterford Gdns. NW3	BS35	47
Chesterford Rd. E12	CK35	49
Chesters, The, N.Mal.	BO51	85
Chesterton Clo. SW18	BS46	76
Ericcson Clo.		
Chesterton Clo., Grnf.	BF37	54
Chesterton Dr., Red.	BX67	113
Chesterton Rd. E13	CH38	58
Chesterton Rd. W10	BQ39	55
Chesterton Ter. E13	CH38	58
Chesterton Ter., Kings.T.	BM51	85
Chesterton Way, Til.	DG44	71
Chesthunte Rd. N17	BZ30	39
Chestney St. SW11	BV44	66
Battersea Park Rd.		
Chestnut Av. E7	CH35	49
Chestnut Av. N. E17	CF31	48
Chestnut Av. N8	BX32	47
Chestnut Av. S. E17	CF32	48
Chestnut Av. SW14	BO45	65
Thornton Rd.		
Chestnut Av., Brent.	BK42	64
Chestnut Av., Buck.H.	CJ27	40
Chestnut Av., Chesh.	AP18	16
Chestnut Av., Edg.	BL29	37
Chestnut Av., Epsom	BO56	94
Chestnut Av., Esher	BG54	84
Chestnut Av., Grays	DD41	71
Chestnut Av., Guil.	AR72	118
Chestnut Av., Hmptn.	BF50	74
Chestnut Av., Horn.	CT34	50
Chestnut Av., Nthwd.	BB30	35
Chestnut Av., Rick.	AW25	26
Chestnut Av., Slou.	AS41	62
Chestnut Av., Tedd.	BH52	84
Chestnut Av., Vir.W.	AP52	82
Chestnut Av., W.Wick.	CG55	88
Chestnut Av., Walt.	BB58	92
Chestnut Av., Wem.	BJ35	45
Chestnut Av., West.	CK64	106
Chestnut Av., West.Dr.	AY40	53
Chestnut Av., Wey.	BA57	92
Chestnut Clo. N14	BW25	29
Chestnut Clo. N16	BZ34	48
Lordship Gro.		
Chestnut Clo. SE27	BY49	76
Leigham Court Rd.		
Chestnut Clo. SE6	CF49	77
Chestnut Clo., Amer.	AO22	25
Chestnut Clo., Ashf.	AZ49	73
Chestnut Clo., Berk.	AT12	7
Chestnut Clo., Buck.H.	CJ27	40
Chestnut Clo., Cars.	BU54	86
Chestnut Clo., Egh.	AQ50	72
Chestnut Clo., Ger.Cr.	AS30	34
Chestnut Clo., Grav.	DF46	81
Chestnut Clo., Hayes	BB40	53
Chestnut Clo., Horn.	CV35	51
Chestnut Clo., Orp.	CO56	98
Chestnut Clo., Red.	BV71	121
Haig Cres.		
Chestnut Clo., Sun.	BB50	73
Cavendish Rd.		
Chestnut Clo., Tad.	BS65	104
Chestnut Clo., West Dr.	AZ43	63
Chestnut Clo., Wey.	AX56	92
Chestnut Clo., Wok.	AV65	100
Chestnut Copse, Oxt.	CH69	115
Chestnut Ct., Amer.	AO22	25
Chestnut La.		
Chestnut Ct., N.Mal.	BO52	85
Chestnut Dr. E11	CH32	49
Chestnut Dr., Berk.	AR13	7
Chestnut Dr., Bexh.	CP45	69
Chestnut Dr., Egh.	AR50	72
Chestnut Dr., Har.	BH29	36
Chestnut Dr., Pnr.	BD32	45
Chestnut Dr., St.Alb.	BJ12	9
Chestnut Dr., Wind.	AM45	61
Chestnut Gdns., Sutt.	BS56	95
Elm Gro.		
Chestnut Glen, Horn.	CU34	50
Chestnut Grn., Stai.	AW49	73
Chestnut Gro. SW12	BV47	76
Chestnut Gro. W5	BK41	64
Chestnut Gro., Barn.	BU25	29
Chestnut Gro., Brwd.	DB27	42
Chestnut Gro., Dart.	CS49	79
Chestnut Gro., Ilf.	CN29	40
Chestnut Gro., Islw.	BJ45	64
Chestnut Gro., Mitch.	BW53	86
Chestnut Gro., N.Mal.	BN52	85
Chestnut Gro., S.Croy.	CB57	96
Chestnut Gro., Stai.	AX50	73
Chestnut Gro., Wem.	BJ35	45
Chestnut Gro., Wok.	AS63	100
Chestnut La. N20	BQ26	37
Chestnut La., Amer.	AO21	25
Chestnut La., Sev.	CU65	107
Chestnut La., Wey.	AZ56	92
Chestnut La., Wok.	AO57	91
Chestnut Manor Clo., Stai.	AW49	73
Chestnut Rd. Pass., Twick.	BH48	74
Chestnut Rd. SE27	BY48	76
Chestnut Rd. SW20	BQ51	85
Chestnut Rd., Ashf.	AZ49	73
Chestnut Rd., Dart.	CV47	80
Chestnut Rd., Enf.	CD21	30
Chestnut Rd., Guil.	AR70	118
Chestnut Rd., Kings.T.	BL50	75
Chestnut Rd., Twick.	BH48	74
Chestnut Ri. SE18	CM43	68
Chestnut Ri., Bush.	BF26	36
Chestnut Way, Felt.	BC48	73
Chestnut Wk., Ger.Cr.	AS29	34
Chestnut Wk., Sev.	CW67	117
Chestnut Wk., Shep.	BB53	83
Chestnut Wk., Walt.	BB58	92
Chestnut Wk., Wat.	BC22	26
Chestnut Wk., Wdf.Grn.	CH28	40
Chestnuts, Brwd.	DD26	122
Chestnuts, The, Hem.H.	AV15	7
Beechwood Pk.		
Chestnuts, The, Ong.	DB13	15
Chestnuts, The, Walt.	BC55	83
Cheston Av., Croy.	CD54	87
Chestwood Gro., Uxb.	AY37	53
Cheswick Clo., Dart.	CT45	69
Woodfall Dr.		
Chesworth Clo., Erith	CT44	69
Chettle Clo. SE1	**BZ41**	**4**
Chettle Clo. SE1	BZ41	67
Spurgeon St.		
Chetwode Dr., Epsom	BQ62	103
Chetwode Dr., Epsom	BQ63	103
Chetwode Rd. Epsom	BQ63	103
Chetwode Rd. SW17	BU48	76
Chetwood Wk. E6	CK39	58
Remington Rd.		
Chetwynd Av., Barn.	BU26	38
Chetwynd Dr., Uxb.	AY37	53
Chetwynd Rd. NW5	BV35	47
Cheval Pl. SW7	**BU41**	**3**
Cheval Pl. SW7	BU41	66
Cheval St. E14	CE41	67
Cheveley Clo., Rom.	CW30	42
Chevely Clo., Epp.	CP18	23
Cheveney Wk., Brom.	CH52	88
Marina Clo.		
Chevening La., Sev.	CQ61	107
Chevening Rd. NW6	BQ37	55
Chevening Rd. SE10	CG42	68
Chevening Rd. SE19	BZ50	77
Chevening Rd., Sev.	CQ65	107
Chevenings, The, Sid.	CO48	79
Cheverton Rd. N19	BW33	47
Chevet St. E9	CD35	48
Chevington Way, Horn.	CV35	51
Cheviot Clo., Bans.	BS61	104
Cheviot Clo., Bexh.	CT44	69
Cheviot Clo., Bush.	BG25	27
Cheviot Clo., Enf.	BZ23	30
Cheviot Clo., Sutt.	BY58	95
Cheviot Gate NW2	BR34	46
Cheviot Gdns. NW2	BQ34	46
Cheviot Rd. SE27	BY49	76
Cheviot Rd., Horn.	CU33	50
Cheviot Rd., Slou.	AT42	62
Cheviot Way, Grnf.	BJ37	54
Cheviot Way, Ilf.	CN32	49
Cheviots, Hat.	BP14	10
Cheviots, Hem.H.	AY12	8
Chewton Rd. E17	CD31	48
Cheyham Gdns., Sutt.	BQ58	94
Cheyham Way, Sutt.	BR58	94
Cheyne Av. E18	CG31	49
Cheyne Av., Twick.	BE47	74
Cheyne Clo. NW4	BQ32	46
Cheyne Clo., Amer.	AO21	25
Cheyne Clo., Brom.	CK55	88
Cheyne Clo., Ger.Cr.	AS33	43
Cheyne Ct. SW3	BU43	66
Flood St.		
Cheyne Ct., Bans.	BS61	104
Cheyne Gdns. SW3	BU43	66
Cheyne Hill, Surb.	BL52	85
Cheyne Ms. SW3	BU43	66
Cheyne Path W7	BH39	54
Copley Clo.		
Cheyne Pl. SW3	BU43	66
Cheyne Pl. SW3	**BU43**	**3**
Cheyne Rd., Ashf.	BA50	73
Napier Rd.		
Cheyne Row SW3	BU43	66
Cheyne Wk. N21	BY25	29
Cheyne Wk. NW4	BQ32	46
Cheyne Wk. SW10	BT43	66
Cheyne Wk. SW3	BT43	66
Cheyne Wk., Chesh.	AO18	16
Cheyne Wk., Croy.	CB55	87
Cheyneys Av., Edg.	BK29	36
Chichele Gdns., Croy.	CA56	96
Chichele Rd. NW2	BQ35	46
Chichele Rd., Oxt.	CG67	115
Chicheley Gdns., Har.	BG29	36
Chicheley Rd., Har.	BG29	36
Chicheley St. SE1	**BX41**	**4**
Chicheley St. SE1	BX41	66
Chichester Av., Ruis.	BA34	44
Chichester Clo. E6	CK39	58
Chichester Clo. SE3	CJ44	68
Chichester Clo., Dor.	BJ70	119
Chichester Clo., S.Ock.	CY40	60
Chichester Ct., Epsom	BO58	94
Old Schools La.		
Chichester Ct., Slou.	AQ41	62
Sussex Pl.		
Chichester Ct., Stan.	BL31	46
Chichester Dr., Pur.	BX59	95
Chichester Dr., Sev.	CT66	116
Chichester Gdns., Ilf.	CK33	49
Chichester Ms. SE27	BT49	76
Chichester Rd. E11	CG34	49
Chichester Rd. N9	CB26	39
Chichester Rd. NW6	BS37	56
Chichester Rd. W2	BS39	56
Chichester Rd., Croy.	CA55	87
Chichester Rd., Dor.	BJ70	119
Chichester Rd., Green.	CZ46	80
Chichester Rents WC2	**BY39**	**2**
Chichester Rents WC2	BY39	56
Chancery La.		
Chichester Ri., Grav.	DH49	81
Livingstone Rd.		
Chichester Row, Amer.	AO22	25
Chichester St. SW1	**BW42**	**3**
Chichester St. SW1	BW42	66
Chichester St. W2	**BS39**	**1**
Chichester Way E14	CF42	67
Chichester Way, Felt.	BD46	74
Chichester Way, Wat.	BE20	18
Chickabiddy Hill, Wok.	AO56	91
Chicksand Est. E1	**CB39**	**2**
Chicksand Est. E1	CB39	57
Chicksand St. E1	**CA39**	**2**
Chicksand St. E1	CA39	57
Chiddingfold N12	BS27	38
Chiddingstone Av., Bexh.	CQ43	69
Chiddingstone St. SW6	BS44	66
Chieftan Dr., Grays	CX42	70
Chieveley Rd., Bexh.	CR45	69
Chiffinch Gdns., Grav.	DF48	81
Riversdale		
Chignell Pl. W13	BJ40	54
Chigwell Hill E1	CB40	57
Pennington St.		
Chigwell Hurst Ct., Pnr.	BD30	36
Chigwell La., Loug.	CM24	31
Chigwell Pk. Dr., Chig.	CL28	40
Chigwell Rd. E18	CH31	49
Chigwell High Rd., Chig.	CL28	40
Chigwell Rd., Wdf.Grn.	CJ29	40
Chigwell Ri., Chig.	CL27	40
Chigwell Vw., Rom.	CR28	41
Chilberton Dr., Red.	BW69	121
Chilcot Clo. E14	CE39	57
Grundy St.		
Chilcote La., Amer.	AQ23	25
Chilcott Rd., Wat.	BB21	26
Childebert Rd. SW17	BV48	76
Childerditch La., Brwd.	DC29	42
Childerditch La., Brwd.	DD30	123
Childerditch St., Brwd.	DD30	123
Childeric Rd. SE14	CD43	67
Childerley St. SW6	BR44	65
Fulham Palace Rd.		
Childers St. SE8	CD43	67
Childers, The, Wdf.Grn.	CK28	40
Childs Clo., Horn.	CV32	51
Hill Cres.		
Childs Cres., Swans.	DB46	80
Childs Hall Rd., Lthd.	BE66	111
Childs La. SE19	CA50	77
Childs Pl. SW5	BS42	66
Childs St. SW5	BS42	66
Childs Way NW11	BR32	46
Childs Wk. SW5	BS42	66
Childs Pl.		
Childsbridge La., Sev.	CW62	108
Childsbridge Way, Sev.	CW63	108
Childwick Clo., Hem.H.	AZ15	8
Childwick Ct., Hem.H.	AZ15	8
Chilham Clo., Grnf.	BJ37	54
Horsenden La. S.		
Chilham Rd. SE9	CK49	78
Chilham Way, Brom.	CG54	88
Chillbrook Farm Rd., Cob.	BC62	101
Chillerton Rd. SW17	BV49	76
Chillingworth Gdns., Twick.	BH48	74
Tower Rd.		
Chillingworth Rd. N7	BY35	47
Chilmans Dr., Lthd.	BF66	111
Pine Dene		
Chilmark Gdns., N.Mal.	BP53	85
Chilmark Gdns., Red.	BX68	113
Chilmark Rd. SW16	BW51	86
Chilmead La., Red.	BW69	121
Chilsey Grn. Rd., Cher.	AV53	82
Chiltern Av., Amer.	AO22	25
Chiltern Av., Bush.	BG25	27
Chiltern Av., Twick.	BF47	74
Chiltern Clo., B.Wd.	BL23	28
Chiltern Clo., Berk.	AP12	7
Chiltern Clo., Bexh.	CT44	69
Chiltern Clo., Bush.	BF25	27
Chiltern Clo., Chsnt.	BY17	20
Chiltern Clo., Croy.	CB55	87
Chiltern Clo., Uxb.	AZ34	44
Chiltern Clo., Wok.	AR64	100
Chiltern Dene, Enf.	BX24	29
Chiltern Dr., Rick.	AV26	34
Chiltern Dr., Surb.	BM53	85
Chiltern Gdns. NW2	BQ34	46
Chiltern Gdns., Brom.	CG52	88
Chiltern Gdns., Horn.	CV34	51
Chiltern Hill, Ger.Cr.	AS30	34
Chiltern Pk. Av., Berk.	AQ12	7
Chiltern Rd. E3	CE38	57
Chiltern Rd., Grav.	DF48	81
Chiltern Rd., Ilf.	CN31	49
Chiltern Rd., Pnr.	BD32	45
Chiltern Rd., St.Alb.	BK11	9
Chiltern Rd., Sutt.	BS58	95
Chiltern St. W1	**BU39**	**1**
Chiltern St. W1	BV39	56
Chiltern Vw. Rd., Uxb.	AX37	53
Chiltern Way, Wdf.Grn.	CH27	40
Chilterns Clo., Bans.	BS61	104
High St.		
Chilterns, Berk.	AP12	7
Chilterns, Hat.	BP14	10
Chilterns, Hem.H.	AY12	8
Malvern Way		
Chilterns, The, Sutt.	BU58	95
Chilthorne Clo. SE6	CD47	77
Ravensbourne Park Cres.		
Chilton Av. W5	BK42	64
Chilton Ct., Walt.	BC56	92
Chilton Grn., Welw.G.C.	BT 8	5
Chilton Gro. SE8	CC42	67
Chilton Rd., Edg.	BM29	37
Chilton Rd., Grays	DG41	71
Chilton Rd., Rich.	BM45	65
Chilton St. E2	**CA38**	**2**
Chilton St. E2	CA38	57
Chiltons Clo., Bans.	BS61	104
High St.		
Chiltons, The E18	CH30	40
Grove Hill		
Chilver St. SE10	CG42	68
Chilwell Gdns., Wat.	BD28	36
Chilworth Ct. SW19	BQ47	75
Windlesham Gro.		
Chilworth Gdns., Sutt.	BT55	86
Chilworth Ms. W2	**BT39**	**1**
Chilworth Ms. W2	BT39	56
Chilworth New Rd., Guil.	AT74	118
Chilworth Rd., Guil.	AV73	118
Chilworth St. W2	**BT39**	**1**
Chilworth St. W2	BT39	56
Chimes Av. N13	BY28	38
China La., Upmin.	DE35	123
Chinbrook Cres. SE12	CH48	78
Chinbrook Rd.		
Chinbrook Rd. SE12	CH48	78
Chinchilla Dr., Houns.	BD44	64
Chindits La., Brwd.	DB28	42
Chine, The N10	BW31	47
Chine, The N21	BY25	29
Chine, The, Wem.	BJ35	45
Chingdale Rd. E4	CG27	40
Chingford Av. E4	CE27	39
Chingford La., Wdf.Grn.	CG28	40
Chingford Mt. Rd. E4	CE28	39
Chingford Rd. E4	CE29	39
Chingley Clo., Brom.	CG50	78
Chinnery Clo., Enf.	CA22	30
Chinnor Cres., Grnf.	BF37	54
Chinthurst La., Guil.	AS74	118
Chipka St. E14	CF41	67
Chipley St. SE14	CD43	67
Nynehead St.		
Chipmunk Gro., Nthlt.	BE38	54
Argus Way		
Chippen Clo., Pnr.	BB31	44
Chippendale All., Uxb.	AX37	53
Chippendale Rd., Orp.	CO51	89
Chippendale St. E5	CC34	48
Chippendale Waye, Uxb.	AX36	53
Chippenham Av., Wem.	BM35	46
Chippenham Clo., Rom.	CV28	42
Chippenham Gdns. NW6	BS38	56
Malvern Rd.		
Chippenham Gdns., Rom.	CV28	42
Chippenham Ms. W9	BS38	56
Chippenham Rd. W9	BS38	56
Chippenham Rd., Rom.	CV28	42
Chippenham Wk., Rom.	CV29	42
Chipperfield Clo., Upmin.	CZ33	51
Chipperfield Rd., Bovingdon	AT17	16
Chipperfield Rd., Hem.H.	AX15	8
Chipperfield Rd., Kings L.	AX18	17
Chipperfield Rd., Orp.	CO51	89
Chipping Clo., Barn.	BR24	28
Strafford Rd.		
Chippingfield, Harl.	CP 9	6
Chipstead Av., Th.Hth.	BY52	86
Chipstead Clo., Couls.	BV61	104
Chipstead Clo., Ger.Cr.	AR30	34
Chipstead Clo., Red.	BU71	121
Chipstead Clo., SE19	CA50	77
Chipstead Ct., Wok.	AP61	100
Creston Av.		
Chipstead Gdns. NW2	BP34	46
Chipstead La., Couls.	BT65	104
Chipstead La., Sev.	CS64	107
Chipstead La., Tad.	BR66	112
Chipstead Pk. Clo., Sev.	CS64	107
Chipstead Pk., Sev.	CS64	107
Chipstead Place Gdns., Sev.	CS64	107
Chipstead La.		

Chipstead Rd., Bans. BR62 103
Chipstead Rd., Erith CT43 69
Chipstead Rd., Houns. AZ45 63
Chipstead St. SW6 BS44 66
Chipstead Valley Rd., Couls. BV61 104
Chipstead Way, Bans. BU62 104
Chirk Clo., Hayes BE38 54
Chirton Wk., Wok. AQ62 100
Shilburn Way
Chisenhale Rd. E3 CD37 57
Chisholm Rd., Croy. CA55 87
Chisholm Rd., Rich. BL46 75
Chisledon Wk. E9 CD36 57
Trowbridge Est.
Chislehurst Av. N12 BT29 38
Chislehurst Rd., Brom. CJ51 88
Chislehurst Rd., Orp. CN52 88
Chislehurst Rd., Rich. BL46 75
Chislehurst Rd., Sid. CO49 79
Chislet Clo., Beck. CE50 77
Abbey La.
Chisley Rd. N15 CA32 48
Chiswell Sq. SE3 CH44 68
Brook La.
Chiswell St. EC1 BZ39 2
Chiswell St. EC1 BZ39 57
Chiswellgreen La., St.Alb. BE16 18
Chiswick Br. SW14 & W4 BN44 65
Chiswick Clo., Croy. BX55 86
Chiswick Common Rd. W4 BN42 65
Chiswick Ct., Pnr. BE31 45
Chiswick High Rd. W4 BM42 65
Chiswick La. S., W4 BO42 65
Chiswick La. W4 BO42 65
Chiswick Mall W4 BO43 65
Chiswick Quay W4 BN44 65
Chiswick Rd. N9 CB27 39
Chiswick Rd. W4 BN42 65
Chiswick Sq. W4 BO43 65
Hogarth Roundabout
Chiswick Staithe W4 BN44 65
Chiswick Vill. W4 BM43 65
Chitty St. W1 BW39 1
Chitty St. W1 BW39 56
Chittys La., Dag. CP34 50
Chittys Wk., Guil. AP68 109
Chivalry Rd. SW11 BU46 76
Chive Clo., Croy. CC54 87
Chivers Rd. E4 CE28 39
Chivers Rd., Brwd. CZ20 24
Choats Manor Way, Bark. CP38 59
Choats Rd., Dag. CQ38 59
Chobham Gdns. SW19 BQ48 75
Chobham La., Wok. AP55 82
Chobham Pk. La., Wok. AQ58 91
Chobham Pl., Wok. AO57 91
Chobham Rd. E15 CF35 48
Chobham Rd., Cher. AT57 91
Chobham Rd., Knaphill AO61 100
Chobham Rd., Horsell AR60 91
Chobham Rd., Wok. AS61 100
Choir Grn., Wok. AP62 100
Cholmeley Cres. N6 BV33 47
Cholmeley Pk. N6 BV33 47
Cholmley Gdns. NW6 BS35 47
Fortune Gr. Rd.
Cholmley Rd., T.Ditt. BJ53 84
Cholmondeley Av. NW10 BP37 55
Cholmondeley Wk., Rich. BK46 74
Choppins Ct. E1 CB40 57
Wapping La.
Chopwell Clo. E15 CG36 58
West Ham La.
Chorleywood Bottom, Rick. AU25 25
Chorleywood Clo., Rick. AX26 35
Nightingale Rd.
Chorleywood Cres., Orp. CN51 88
Chorleywood Rd., Rick. AW24 26
Choumert Gro. SE15 CB44 67
Choumert Rd. SE15 CA45 67
Choumert Sq. SE15 CB44 67
Chrichton St. SW8 BW44 66
Westbury St.
Chrislaine Clo., Stai. AX46 73
High Street, Stanwell
Chrisp St. E14 CE39 57
Christ Church Mt., Epsom BM59 94
Christ Church Rd. SW14 BM46 75
Christ Church Rd., Epsom BL59 94
Christchurch Av. N12 BT29 38
Christchurch Av. NW6 BQ37 55
Christchurch Av., Erith CT43 69
Christchurch Av., Har. BH31 45
Christchurch Av., Rain. CT38 59
Christchurch Av., Tedd. BJ49 74
Christchurch Av., Wem. BL36 55
Christchurch Clo. E9 CC37 57
Northiam St.
Christchurch Clo. N12 BT29 38
Christchurch Clo. SW19 BT50 76
Christchurch Clo., St.Alb. BG13 9
Worley Rd.
Christchurch Cres., Rad. BJ21 27
Christchurch Gdns., Har. BJ31 45
Christchurch Grn., Wem. BL36 55
Christchurch Hill NW3 BT34 47
Christchurch La., Barn. BR23 28
Christchurch Pass. NW3 BT34 47
Christchurch Hill
Christchurch Path, Hayes BA41 63
Christchurch Pk., Sutt. BT57 95
Christchurch Rd. N8 BX32 47
Christchurch Rd. SW19 BT51 86
Christchurch Rd. SW2 BX47 76
Christchurch Rd., Beck. CE51 87
Fairfield Rd.
Christchurch Rd., Dart. CV47 80
Christchurch Rd., Grav. DH47 81
Christchurch Rd., Hem.H. AX13 8
Christchurch Rd., Houns. AZ45 63
Christchurch Rd., Ilf. CL33 49
Christchurch Rd., Pur. BY58 95
Christchurch Rd., Sid. CN49 78
Christchurch Rd., Surb. BL54 85
Christchurch Rd., Til. DG44 71
Christchurch Rd., Vir.W. AQ52 82
Christchurch Sq. E2 CC37 57
Christchurch St. SW3 BU43 3
Christchurch St. SW3 BU43 66
Christchurch Ter. SW3 BU43 3
Christchurch St.
Christchurch Way SE10 CG42 68
Christchurch Way, Wok. AS62 100
Church St. E.
Christian Fields Av., Grav. DH49 81
Christian Fields SW16 BY50 76
Christian Sq., Wind. AO44 61
Ward Royal
Christian St. E1 CB39 57
Christie Ct. N19 BX34 47
Pine Gro.
Christie Gdns., Rom. CO32 50
Christie La., Lthd. BF66 111
Christie Rd. E9 CD36 57
Christina Sq. N4 BY33 47
Adolphus Rd.
Christina St. EC2 CA38 2
Christina St. EC2 CA38 57
Christopher Av. W7 BJ41 64
Christopher Clo. SE16 CC41 67
Christopher Clo., Horn. CV35 51
Chevington Way
Christopher Clo., Sid. CN46 78
Blackfen Rd.
Christopher Clo., Tad. BQ65 103
Christopher Ct., Hem.H. AX15 8
Seaton Rd.
Christopher Gdns., Dag. CP35 50
Wren Rd.
Christopher Ms. W11 BR40 55
Penzance St.
Christopher Pl. NW1 BW38 1
Chalton St.
Christopher Pl., St.Alb. BG13 9
Market Pl.
Christopher Rd., Sthl. BC42 63
Christopher St. EC2 BZ38 2
Christopher St. EC2 BZ38 57
Christy Rd., West. CJ61 106
Chryssell Rd. SW9 BY43 66
Chubworthy St. SE14 CD43 67
Chucks La., Tad. BP65 103
Chudleigh Cres., Ilf. CN35 49
Chudleigh Gdns., Sutt. BT55 86
Chudleigh Rd. NW6 BQ36 55
Chudleigh Rd. SE4 CD46 77
Chudleigh Rd., Rom. CW28 42
Chudleigh Rd., Twick. BH46 74
Chudleigh St. E1 CC39 57
Chudleigh Way, Ruis. BC33 44
Chulsa Rd. SE26 CB49 77
Chumleigh St. SE5 CA43 67
Chumleigh Wk., Surb. BL52 85
Church All., Brent. BK43 64
Church All., Croy. BY54 86
Church All., Wat. BG22 27
Church Alley EC2 BZ39 57
Basinghall St.
Church App. SE21 BZ48 77
Church App., Sev. CM61 106
Church App., Stai. AX46 73
Church Av. E4 CF29 39
Church Av. SW14 BN45 65
Church Av., Beck. CE51 87
Church Av., Nthlt. BE36 54
Church Av., Pnr. BE32 45
Church Av., Ruis. BA33 44
Church Av., Sid. CO49 79
Church Av., Sthl. BE41 64
Church Clo. N20 BU27 38
Church Clo. SE20 CC50 77
Laurel Gro.
Church Clo. W8 BS41 66
Church Clo., Brwd. CY22 33
Church Clo., Cuff. BX18 20
Church Clo., Edg. BN28 37
Church Clo., Hayes BA39 53
Church Clo., Hert. BW13 11
Church Clo., Loug. CK23 31
Church Clo., Lthd. BG65 102
Church Clo., Nthwd. BC29 35
Emmanuel Rd.
Church Clo., Stai. AX52 83
The Broadway
Church Clo., Tad. BR67 112
Church Clo., Uxb. AW37 53
Church Clo., West Dr. AY41 63
Church Clo., Wey. AW56 92
Church Clo., Wok. AR61 100
Church Cres. E9 CC36 57
Church Cres. N10 BV31 47
Church Cres. N20 BU27 38
Church Cres. N3 BR30 37
Church Cres., S.Ock. DB38 60
Church Cres., Saw. CQ 6 6
Church Cres., St.Alb. BG13 9
Church Ct., Rich. BK46 74
Church Dr. NW9 BN33 46
Church Dr., Har. BE32 45
Church Dr., Maid. AH41 61
Church Dr., Sev. CT66 116
Church Dr., W.Wick. CG55 88
Church Elm La., Dag. CR36 59
Church End E17 CE31 48
Church End NW4 BP31 46
Church End., Harl. CL12 13
Church Entry EC4 BY39 56
Carter La.
Church Farm Clo., Swan. CS53 89
Church Farm La., Sutt. BR57 94
Church Field Path, Chsnt. CC18 21
Church Field, Sev. CT64 107
Church Fields Rd., Beck. CC51 87
Church Fields, E.Mol. BF52 84
Church Fields., Loug. CK24 31
Church Gate SW6 BR45 65
Church Gdns. W5 BK41 64
Church Gdns., Wem. BJ35 45
Church Grn. SW9 BY44 66
Myatts Fields Dev.
Church Grn., Walt. BD57 93
Church Gro. SE13 CE45 67
Church Gro., Amer. AS23 25
Church Gro., Hayes BB39 53
Church Gro., Kings.T. BK51 84
Church Gro., Slou. AR39 52
Church Hill Clo., Warl. CC62 105
Church Hill E17 CE31 48
Church Hill N21 BX26 38
Church Hill Rd. E17 CE31 48
Church Hill Rd., Barn. BU26 38
Church Hill Rd., Surb. BL53 85
Church Hill Rd., Sutt. BQ55 85
Church Hill SE18 CK41 68
Church Hill SW19 BR49 75
Church Hill Wood, Orp. CN53 88
Church Hill, Barn. BU25 29
Church Hill, Cat. CA65 105
Church Hill, Crayford CT45 69
Church Hill, Dart. CV48 80
Church Hill, Epp. CO18 23
Church Hill, Green. CZ46 80
Church Hill, Har. BH33 45
Church Hill, Horsell AR61 100
Church Hill, Loug. CK24 31
Church Hill, Merstham BV66 113
Church Hill, Nutfield BX70 121
Church Hill, Orp. CO54 89
Church Hill, Pur. BX58 95
Church Hill, Pyrford AV62 100
Church Hill, Sev. CM61 106
Church Hill, Uxb. AX31 44
Church Hill, Welw.G.C. BO 8 5
Church Hill, West. CJ64 106
Church Hollow, Grays CX42 70
Church La.
Church Hyde SE18 CN43 68
Old Mill Rd.
Church La. Av., Couls. BV64 104
Church La. Clo., Stai. AX46 73
Church La. Dr., Couls. BV64 104
Church La. E11 CG33 49
Church La. E17 CE31 48
Church La. N17 CA30 39
Church La. N2 BT31 47
Church La. N8 BX31 47
Church La. N9 CA27 39
Church La. NW9 BN32 46
Church La. SW17 BU49 76
Church La. SW19 BR51 85
Church La. W5 BK41 64
Church La., Stapleford Abbotts CS24 32
Church La., Berk. AR13 7
Church La., Brom. CK54 88
Church La., Brox. CC14 12
Church La., Burgh Heath BQ62 103
Church La., Cat. BY65 104
Church La., Chelsham CF61 105
Church La., Chess. BL57 94
Church La., Chis. CM51 88
Church La., Chsnt. CC18 21
Church La., Couls. BV64 104
Church La., Dag. CR36 59
Church La., Doddinghurst DA22 33
Church La., Enf. BZ24 30
Church La., Epp. CR16 23
Church La., Gdse. CC69 114
Church La., Ger.Cr. AR30 34
Church La., Grays CX42 70
Church La., Great Warley DB32 51
Church La., Har. BH30 36
Church La., Hat. BQ12 10
Church La., Headley BN65 103
Church La., Hem.H. AT17 16
Church La., Hert. BX12 11
Church La., Kings L. AZ18 17
Church La., Loug. CK24 31
Church La., Maid. AH41 61
Church La., Ong. CX15 15
Church La., Oxt. CF68 114
Church La., Pnr. BE31 45
Church La., Pot.B. BV18 20
Church La., Red. BZ70 114
Church La., Rick. AV22 25
Church La., Rick. AW22 26
Church La., Rom. CP24 32
Church La., Send AT66 109
Church La., Worplesdon AP67 109
Church La., Rom. CT31 50
Church La., Sev. CX62 108
Heaverham Rd.
Church La., St.Alb. BM14 10
Church La., Stoke Poges AP38 52
Church La., T.Ditt. BJ53 84
Church La., Tedd. BH49 74
Church La., Twick. BJ47 74
Church La., Upmin. DA36 60
Church La., Uxb. AW37 53
Church La., Wall. BW55 86
Church La., Warl. CC62 105
Church La., Wennington CV39 60
Church La., West. CJ64 106
Church La., Wexham AQ38 52
Church Leys, Harl. CN11 13
Church Manor Way SE2 CN42 68
Church Manor Way, Erith CS42 69
Church Meadow, Surb. BK55 84
Church Mt. N2 BT32 47
Church Par., Ashf. AY49 73
Church Rd.
Church Pass. EC2 BZ39 57
Gresham St.
Church Pass., Rich. BK46 74
Red Lion St.
Church Pass., Surb. BL53 85
Church Path E11 CH32 49
Church Path E17 CE31 48
St. Mary Rd.
Church Path N12 BT28 38
Church Path N17 CA29 39
Church Path N20 BT28 38
Church Path N5 BY35 47
Church Path N5 BZ35 48
Church Path N8 BX32 47
Tottenham La.
Church Path NW10 BO36 55
Church Path SW14 BN45 65
North Worple Way
Church Path SW19 BR51 85
Church Path W4 BN41 65
Church Path W7 BH40 54
Church Path, Cob. BC60 92
Church Path, Couls. BY62 104
Church Path, Croy. BZ55 87
Church Path, Green. CZ46 80
Church Path, Maid. AH41 61
Church Path, Mitch. BU52 86
Church Path, Red. BV67 113
Church Path, Wok. AS62 100
High St.
Church Pl. SW1 BW40 3
Church Pl. SW8 BW44 66
Church Pl., Mitch. BU52 86
Church Pl., Shep. AZ54 83
Church Rd.
Church Rd. (Cobham), Grav. DH51 81
Church Rd. (Merton) SW19 BT51 86
Church Rd. (Wimbledon) SW19 BR49 75
Church Rd. E10 CE33 48
Church Rd. E12 CK35 49
Church Rd. E17 CD30 39
Church Rd. N17 CA30 39
Church Rd. N6 BV32 47
Church Rd. NW10 BO36 55
Church Rd. NW4 BP31 46
Church Rd. SE19 CA51 87
Church Rd. SE26 CB50 77
Church Rd. SW13 BO44 65
Church Rd. W3 BN40 55
Church Rd. W7 BG40 54
Church Rd., Sevenoaks Weald CU69 116
Church Rd., Stanford Rivers CV20 24
Church Rd., West Kingsdown CZ57 99
Church Rd., West Tilbury DJ43 71
Church Rd., Addlestone AW56 92
Church Rd., Ash. BK62 102
Church Rd., Ashf. AY48 73
Church Rd., Bark. CM36 58
Church Rd., Berk. AT12 7
Church Rd., Bexh. CQ45 69
Church Rd., Biggin Hill CJ62 106
Church Rd., Bookham BE65 102
Church Rd., Brasted CO65 107
Church Rd., Brom. CH51 88
Church Rd., Brwd. CY22 33
Church Rd., Buck.H. CH26 40
Church Rd., Byfleet AY60 92
Church Rd., Cat. CA65 105
Church Rd., Cowley AX38 53
Church Rd., Crockenhill CS54 89
Church Rd., Croy. BY55 86
Church Rd., E.Mol. BG52 84
Church Rd., Egh. AT49 72
Church Rd., Enf. CC25 30
Church Rd., Epsom BO59 94
Church Rd., Erith CS42 69
Church Rd., Esher BH57 93
Church Rd., Farnborough CM56 97
Church Rd., Felt. BD49 74
Church Rd., Foots Cray CP49 79
Church Rd., Grav. DF47 81
Church Rd., Guil. AR71 118
Church Rd., Halstead CQ59 98
Church Rd., Ham BK49 74
Church Rd., Harefield AX31 44
Church Rd., Harl. CP12 14
Church Rd., Harold Wood CX30 42
Church Rd., Hart. DC52 90
Church Rd., Hav. CV26 42
Church Rd., Hayes BB40 53
Church Rd., Hem.H. BA14 8
Church Rd., Hert. BW13 11
Church Rd., Heston BF43 64
Church Rd., Horsell AR61 100
Church Rd., Houns. BC42 63
Church Rd., Ilf. CN32 49
Church Rd., Islw. BG44 64
Church Rd., Iver AU38 52
Church Rd., Ken. BZ61 105
Church Rd., Kes. CJ57 97
Church Rd., Kings.T. BL51 85
Church Rd., Loug. CG24 31
Church Rd., Lthd. BJ64 102
Church Rd., Maid. AG40 61
Church Rd., Mitch. BT51 86
Church Rd., Moreton CV14 15
Church Rd., Navestock CV23 33
Church Rd., New A.G. DC55 90
Church Rd., Nthlt. BD37 54
Church Rd., Nthwd. BB29 35
Church Rd., Orp. CP57 98
Church Rd., Pot.B. BS18 20
Church Rd., Pur. BX58 95
Church Rd., Red. BU71 121
Church Rd., Reig. BS71 121
Church Rd., Rich. BL45 65
Church Rd., S.at H. CW50 80
Church Rd., Seal CW64 108
Church Rd., Shep. AZ54 83
Church Rd., Shortlands CG52 88
Church Rd., Sid. CO49 79
Church Rd., St. John's AQ63 100
Church Rd., Stan. BJ28 36
Church Rd., Sthl. BE41 64
Grosvenor Rd.
Church Rd., Stone Street CZ66 117
Church Rd., Sundridge CQ66 116
Church Rd., Surb. BK54 84
Church Rd., Sutt. BR57 94
Church Rd., Swan. CV51 90
Church Rd., Swans. DC46 81
Church Rd., Tedd. BH49 74
Church Rd., Til. DF44 71
Church Rd., Wall. BW55 86
Church Rd., Warl. CC62 105
Church Rd., Wat. BC23 26
Church Rd., Well. CO44 69
Church Rd., Welw.G.C. BQ 8 5
Church Rd., West Ewell BN57 94
Church Rd., West.Dr. AX41 63
Church Rd., Wey. AZ56 92
Church Rd., Whyt. CA62 105
Church Rd., Wind. AQ46 72
Church Rd., Woldingham CD65 105
Church Rd., Woldingham CD65 105
Church Rd., Wor.Pk. BO54 85
Church Ri. SE23 CC48 77
Church Ri., Chess. BL57 94
Church Row NW3 BT35 47
Church Row SW6 BS43 66
Moore Pk. Rd.
Church Row, Chis. CM51 88
Church SE17 BZ42 4
Church Side, Epsom BM60 94
Church Sq., Shep. AZ54 83
Church St. E., Wok. AS62 100
Church St. E15 CG37 58
Church St. E16 CL40 58
Church St. Est. NW8 BT38 1
Church St. Est. NW8 BT38 56
Church St. N. E15 CG37 58
Church St. N9 BZ26 39
Church St. NW8 BT39 1
Church St. NW8 BT39 56
Church St. Pass. E15 CG37 58
Church St. SE16 CC41 67
Church St. W., Wok. AS62 100
Church St. W2 BT39 1
Church St. W2 BT39 56
Church St. W4 BO43 65
Church St., Bet. BO71 120
Church St., Bovingdon AT17 16
Church St., Chalvey AO41 61
Church St., Cob. BC61 101
Church St., Croy. BY55 186
Church St., Dag. CR36 59
Church St., Dor. BJ71 119
Church St., Effingham BD67 111
Church St., Enf. BZ24 30
Church St., Epsom BO60 94
Church St., Esher BF56 93
Church St., Essendon BU12 11
Church St., Ewell BP58 94
Church St., Grav. DG46 81
Church St., Grays DE43 71
Church St., Hat. BQ12 10
Church St., Hem.H. AX12 8
Church St., Hmptn. BG51 84
Church St., Ing. DC19 24
Church St., Islw. BJ45 64
Church St., Kings.T. BK51 84
Clarence St.
Church St., Lthd. BJ64 102
Church St., Reig. BS70 121
Church St., Rick. AY26 35
Church St., Saw. CQ 6 6
Church St., Seal CX64 108
Church St., Shoreham CT59 98
Church St., Slou. AP41 62
Church St., Southfleet DD49 81
Church St., St.Alb. BG13 9
Church St., Stai. AV49 72
Church St., Sun. BC52 83
High St.
Church St., Sutt. BS56 95
Church St., Twick. BJ47 74
Church St., Wal.Abb. CF20 21
Church St., Walt. BC54 83
Church St., Wat. BC24 26
Church St., Wey. AZ56 92
Church St., Wok. AU64 100
Church Stretton Rd., Houns. BG46 74
Church Ter. N1 CA36 57
Mortimer Rd.
Church Ter. NE4 BP31 46
Church Ter. SE13 CG45 68
Church Ter. SW8 BW44 66
Union Gro.
Church Ter., Rich. BK46 74
Wakefield Rd.
Church Ter., Wind. AM44 61
Church Vale N2 BU31 47
Church Vale SE23 CC48 77
Church Vw., Brox. CD13 12
Church Vw., S.Ock. CY41 70
Church Vw., Upmin. CX34 51
Church Way N20 BU27 38
Church Way, Barn. BU24 29
Church Way, Edg. BM29 37
Church Way, Oxt. CG69 115
Church Way, S.Croy. CA58 96
Church Wk. N16 BZ35 48
Church Wk. N6 BV34 47
Swains La.
Church Wk. NW2 BR34 46
Church Wk. NW4 BQ31 46
Church Wk. NW9 BN34 46
Church Wk. SW13 BP44 65
Church Wk. SW16 BW51 86
Church Wk. SW20 BQ52 85
Church Wk., Brent. BK43 64
Church Wk., Brox. CD13 12
Church Wk., Cher. AW53 83
Church Wk., Dart. CV48 80
Church Wk., Grav. DH47 81
Church Wk., Hayes BB39 53
Church Wk., Lthd. BJ64 102
The Crescent
Church Wk., Red. BZ70 114
Church Wk., Reig. BS70 121
Church Wk., Rich. BK46 74
Church Wk., Saw. CQ 6 6

Church Wk., T.Ditt. BJ53 84
Church Wk., Walt. BC54 83
Church Wk., Wey. AZ55 83
Church Yard Row SE11 BY42 4
Church Yard Row SE11 BY42 66
Churchbury Clo., Enf. CA23 30
Churchbury La., Enf. BZ24 30
Churchbury Rd. SE9 CJ47 78
Churchbury Rd., Enf. CA23 30
Churchcroft Clo. SW12 BV47 76
Endlesham Rd.
Churchdown, Brom. CG49 78
Churchfield Av. N12 BT29 38
Churchfield Clo., Har. BG31 45
Churchfield Clo., Hayes BB40 53
West Av.
Churchfield Rd. W13 BJ40 54
Churchfield Rd. W3 BN40 55
Churchfield Rd. W7 BH41 64
Churchfield Rd., Ger.Cr. AR30 34
Churchfield Rd., Walt. BC54 83
Churchfield Rd., Well. CO45 69
Churchfield Rd., Welw. BT 6 5
Churchfield Rd., Wey. AZ56 92
Churchfield Way N12 BT29 38
Churchfield Av.
Churchfield, Harl. CO10 6
Churchfields Av., Wey. AZ56 92
Churchfields Av., Felt. BE48 74
Churchfields E18 CH30 40
Churchfields La., Brox. CE13 12
Churchfields Path, Wal.Cr. CC18 21
Churchfields, Brox. CE13 12
Churchfields, Dart. CV48 80
Churchfields, E.Mol. BF52 84
Churchfields, Guil. AT68 109
Churchgate Rd., Chsnt. CB18 21
Churchgate St., Harl. CQ 9 6
Churchgate, Chsnt. CB18 21
Churchill Av., Har. BJ32 45
Churchill Av., Uxb. AZ38 53
Churchill Clo., Lthd. BH65 102
Churchill Clo., Ong. CX17 24
Churchill Clo., Uxb. AZ38 53
Churchill Cres., Hat. BQ15 10
Churchill Dr., Wey. BA56 92
Churchill Gdns. Est. SW1 BW42 66
Churchill Gdns. Est. SW1 BW43 3
Churchill Gdns. Rd. SW1 BV42 3
Churchill Gdns. Rd. SW1 BV42 66
Churchill Gdns. W3 BM39 55
Churchill Pl., Har. BH31 45
Sandridge Clo.
Churchill Rd. E16 CJ39 58
Churchill Rd. NW2 BP36 55
Churchill Rd. NW5 BV35 47
Churchill Rd., Edg. BL29 37
Churchill Rd., Grays DE43 71
Churchill Rd., Guil. AS71 118
Churchill Rd., Hort.K. CY52 90
Churchill Rd., S.Croy. BZ58 96
Churchill Rd., Slou. AS42 62
Churchill Rd., St.Alb. BJ13 9
Churchill Ter. E4 CE27 39
Churchill Way, Sun. BC49 73
Churchill Wk. E9 CC35 48
Churchley Rd. SE26 CB49 77
Churchmead Clo., Barn. BU25 29
Churchmead Rd. NW10 BP36 55
Churchmore Rd. SW16 BW51 86
Churchside Clo., West. CJ62 106
Sunningvale Av.
Churchvale Ct. W4 BM42 65
Harvard Rd.
Churchview Rd., Twick. BG47 74
Churchway NW1 BW38 1
Churchway NW1 BW38 56
Churchwell Path E9 CC35 48
Churchyard Pass. SE5 BZ44 67
Camberwell Gro.
Churston Av. E13 CH37 58
Churston Dr., Mord. BQ53 85
Churston Gdns. N11 BW29 38
Churton Pl. SW1 BW42 3
Churton Pl. SW1 BW42 66
Churton St. SW1 BW42 3
Churton St. SW1 BW42 66
Chusan Pl. E14 CD39 57
Chuters Clo., Wey. AY60 92
High Rd.
Chuters Gro., Epsom BO59 94
Chyngton Clo., Sid. CN48 78
Priestlands Pk. Rd.
Cibber Rd. SE23 CC48 77
Cicada Rd. SW18 BT46 76
Cicely Rd. SE15 CB44 67
Cillocks Clo., Hodd. CE11 12
Cimba Wood, Grav. DJ49 81
Cinder Path, Wok. AR63 100
College La.
Cinderford Way, Brom. CG49 78
Cinnamon Gdns., Guil. AQ68 109
Oregano Way
Cinnamon Row SW11 BT45 66
Clove Hitch Quay
Cinnamon St. E1 CB40 57
Cintra Pk. SE19 CA50 77
Cippenham La., Slou. AN40 61
Circle Gdns. SW19 BS51 86
Circle Gdns., Wey. AY60 92
Circle Rd., Walt. BB58 92
Circle, The NW2 BO34 46
Circle, The NW7 BN29 37
Circle, The, Til. DG44 71
Circuits, The, Pnr. BD31 45
Circular Rd. N17 CA31 48
Circular Rd. SE1 BZ41 4
Circular Way SE18 CK43 68
Circus Pl. EC2 BZ39 2
Circus Pl. EC2 BZ39 57
London Wall
Circus Rd. NW8 BT38 1
Circus Rd. NW8 BT38 56
Circus St. SE10 CF43 67
Circus, The EC3 CA40 4
Circus, The EC3 CA40 57
Minories
Circus, The, Til. DG44 71
Cirencester St. W2 BS39 56
Cirrus Cres., Grav. DJ49 81
Cissbury Rd. N15 BZ32 48
Cissbury Ring N. N12 BR28 37
Cissbury Ring S. N12 BR28 37
Citizen Rd. N7 BY35 47
Citroen Ter. SE15 CB45 67
Nunhead Gro.
City Gdn. Row N1 BY37 2
City Gdn. Row N1 BY37 56
City Rd. EC1 BY37 2
City Rd. EC1 BY37 56
Civic Sq., Til. DG44 71
Civic Way, Ilf. CM31 49
Civic Way, Wok. AS62 100
Clabon Ms. SW1 BU41 3
Clabon Ms. SW1 BU41 66
Clack St. SE16 CC41 67
Clacton Path SE4 CD45 67
Frendsbury Rd.
Clacton Rd. E17 CD32 48
Clacton Rd. E6 CJ38 58
Claigmar Gdns. N3 BS30 38
Claire Ct. Clo. N12 BT28 38
Woodside Av.
Claire Ct., Pnr. BE29 36
Westfield Pk.
Claire Pl. E14 CE41 67
Tiller Rd.
Clairvale Rd., Houns. BE44 64
Clairvale, Horn. CW33 51
Clairview Rd. SW16 BV49 76
Clairville Ct., Reig. BT70 121
Wray Common
Clairy Gdns. W7 BH40 54
Clammas Waye, Uxb. AX39 53
Clamp Hill, Stan. BG28 36
Clancarty Rd. SW6 BS44 66
Clandon Av., Egh. AU50 72
Clandon Clo. W3 BM41 65
Avenue Rd.
Clandon Clo., Epsom BO57 94
Clandon Gdns. N3 BS31 47
Clandon Rd., Guil. AS71 118
Clandon Rd., Ilf. CN34 49
Clandon Rd., Wok. AV66 109
Clandon St. SE8 CE44 67
Clandon Way, Wok. AV66 109
Clanfield Way SE15 CA43 67
Hordle Prom. W.
Clanricarde Gdns. W2 BS40 56
Clapgate La., Wal.Abb. CF18 21
Clapgate Rd., Bush. BF25 27
Clapham Common North Side SW4 BU45 66
Clapham Common South Side SW4 BV46 76
Clapham Common West Side SW4 BU45 66
Clapham Cres. SW4 BW45 66
Clapham High St. SW4 BW45 66
Clapham Manor St. SW4 BW45 66
Clapham Pk. Est. SW2 BX47 76
Clapham Pk. Est. SW4 BW46 76
Clapham Pk. Rd. SW4 BW45 66
Clapham Rd. SW9 BX45 66
Clappers La., Wok. AO59 91
Claps Gate La., Bark. CL38 58
Clapton Common E5 CA33 48
Clapton Pk. Est. E5 CC35 48
Clapton Pass. E5 CC35 48
Lower Clapton Rd.
Clapton Sq. E5 CC35 48
Clapton Ter. N16 CB33 48
Clapton Way E5 CB35 48
Clara Pl. SE18 CL42 68
John Wilson St.
Clara Pl. SE18 CL42 68
Monk St.
Clare Clo., B.Wd. BL25 28
Clare Clo., Wey. AW60 92
Clare Cor. SE9 CL47 78
Clare Cotts., Red. BY70 121
Clare Cres., Lthd. BJ62 102
Clare Ct., Cat. CE65 105
Clare Gdns. E7 CH35 49
Clare Gdns. W11 BR39 55
Westbourne Park Rd.
Clare Gdns., Bark. CN36 58
Clare Gdns., Egh. AT49 72
Clare Gdns., Stan. BK28 36
Clare Hall Pl. SE16 CC42 67
Litlington St.
Clare La. N1 BZ36 57
Clare Lawn Av. SW14 BN46 75
Clare Mkt. WC2 BX39 2
Clare Mkt. WC2 BX39 56
Portugal St.
Clare Ms. SW6 BS43 66
Waterford Rd.
Clare Pk., Amer. AO23 25
Clare Pl. SW15 BO47 75
Minstead Gdns.
Clare Rd. E11 CF32 48
Clare Rd. NW10 BP36 55
Clare Rd. SE14 CD44 67
Clare Rd., Grnf. BG36 54
Clare Rd., Houns. BE45 64
Clare Rd., Stai. AX47 73
Clare St. E2 CB37 57
Clare Way, Bexh. CQ44 69
Clare Way, Sev. CB67 117
Clare Wood, Lthd. BJ62 102
Claredale St. E2 CB37 57
Clarehill Clo., Esher BF56 93
Clarehill Rd., Esher BF47 93
Claremont Av., Esher BE57 93
Claremont Av., Har. BL32 46
Claremont Av., N.Mal. BP53 85
Claremont Av., Sun. BC51 83
Claremont Av., Walt. BD56 93
Claremont Av., Wok. AS63 100
Claremont Clo. E16 CL40 58
Claremont Clo. N1 BY37 2
Claremont Clo. N1 BY37 56
Claremont Clo. SW2 BX47 76
Garden La.
Claremont Clo., Grays DE41 71
Premier Av.
Claremont Clo., Orp. CL56 97
Claremont Clo., S.Croy. CB60 96
Claremont Clo., Walt. BD56 93
Claremont Cres., Dart. CT45 69
Claremont Cres., Rick. BA25 26
Claremont Ct., Dor. BJ72 119
Rose Hill
Claremont Dr., Esher BF58 93
Claremont Dr., Wok. AS63 100
Claremont End, Esher BF57 93
Claremont Est. SW2 BX47 76
Claremont Gdns., Dart. CY47 80
Claremont Gdns., Ilf. CN34 49
Claremont Gdns., Surb. BL52 85
Claremont Gdns., Upmin. CY33 51
Claremont Gro. W4 BO43 65
Edensor Gdns.
Claremont Gro., Wdf.Grn. CJ29 40
Claremont La., Esher BF56 93
Claremont Pk. N3 BR30 37
Claremont Pk. Rd., Esher BF57 93
Claremont Rd. E11 CF34 48
Claremont Rd. E17 CD30 39
Claremont Rd. E7 CH35 49
Claremont Rd. N6 BV33 47
Claremont Rd. NW2 BQ33 46
Claremont Rd. W13 BJ39 54
Claremont Rd. W9 BR37 55
Claremont Rd., Barn. BT22 29
Claremont Rd., Brom. CK52 88
Claremont Rd., Croy. CB54 87
Claremont Rd., Esher BH57 93
Claremont Rd., Har. BH30 36
Claremont Rd., Horn. CU32 50
Claremont Rd., Red. BV69 121
Claremont Rd., Stai. AU49 72
Claremont Rd., Surb. BL53 85
Claremont Rd., Swan. CT50 79
Claremont Rd., Tedd. BH49 74
Claremont Rd., Twick. BJ46 74
Claremont Rd., Wey. AW59 92
Claremont Rd., Wind. AO44 61
Claremont Sq. N1 BY37 2
Claremont Sq. N1 BY37 56
Claremont St. E16 CL40 58
Claremont St. N18 CB29 39
Claremont St. SE10 CE43 67
Claremont Way NW2 BQ33 46
Claremont, Chsnt. CA18 21
Claremont, St.Alb. BF19 18
Claremount Gdns., Epsom BQ62 103
Clarence Av. SW4 BW47 76
Clarence Av., Brom. CK52 88
Clarence Av., Ilf. CL32 49
Clarence Av., N.Mal. BN51 85
Clarence Av., Upmin. CX34 51
Clarence Clo., Bush. BH26 36
Clarence Clo., Walt. BC56 92
Clarence Cres. SW4 BW46 76
Clarence Cres., Sid. CO48 79
Clarence Cres., Wind. AO44 61
Clarence Dr., Egh. AR49 72
Clarence Gdns. NW1 BV38 1
Clarence Gdns. NW1 BV38 56
Clarence La. SW15 BO46 75
Clarence Ms. E5 CB35 48
Clarence Pl.
Clarence Pass. NW1 BX37 2
Clarence Pl. E5 CB35 48
Clarence Pl., Grav. DG47 81
Clarence Rd. E12 CJ35 49
Clarence Rd. E16 CG38 58
Clarence Rd. E17 CC30 39
Clarence Rd. E5 CB35 48
Clarence Rd. N15 BZ32 48
Clarence Rd. N22 BX29 38
Clarence Rd. NW6 BR36 55
Clarence Rd. SE9 CK48 78
Clarence Rd. SW19 BS50 76
Clarence Rd. W4 BM42 65
Clarence Rd., Berk. AR13 7
Clarence Rd., Bexh. CQ45 69
Clarence Rd., Brom. CJ52 88
Clarence Rd., Brwd. DA25 33
Clarence Rd., Croy. BZ54 87
Clarence Rd., Enf. CB25 30
Clarence Rd., Grav. DH46 81
Clarence Rd., Grays DD42 71
Clarence Rd., Red. BT72 121
Clarence Rd., Rich. BL44 65
Clarence Rd., Sid. CO48 79
Clarence Rd., St.Alb. BH13 9
Clarence Rd., Sutt. BS56 95
Clarence Rd., Tedd. BH50 74
Clarence Rd., Wall. BV56 95
Clarence Rd., Walt. BC56 92
Clarence Rd., West CK62 106
Clarence Rd., Wind. AN44 61
Clarence Row, Grav. DG47 81
Clarence St., Egh. AS50 72
Clarence St., Kings.T. BK51 84
Clarence St., Rich. BL45 65
Clarence St., Stai. AV49 72
Clarence St., Sthl. BD41 64
Clarence Ter. NW1 BU38 1
Clarence Ter. NW1 BU38 56
Cornwall Ter.
Clarence Ter., Houns. BF45 64
Clarence Way Est. NW1 BV36 56
Clarence Way NW1 BV36 56
Clarence Wk. SW4 BX44 66
Clarence Wk., Red. BT72 121
Clarence Yd. SE17 BZ42 4
Clarendon Av. SE5 BZ43 67
Councillor St.
Clarendon Clo. W2 BU40 3
Clarendon Clo. W2 BU40 56
Clarendon Pl.
Clarendon Clo., Orp. CO52 89
Clarendon Cres., Twick. BG48 74
Clarendon Cross W11 BR40 55
Portland Rd.
Clarendon Ct. NW11 BR31 46
Finchley Rd.
Clarendon Ct., Slou. AQ40 52
Wexham Rd.
Clarendon Dr. SW15 BQ45 65
Clarendon Gdns. NW4 BP31 46
Clarendon Gdns. W9 BT38 1
Clarendon Gdns. W9 BT38 56
Clarendon Gdns., Dart. CY47 80
Clarendon Gdns., Ilf. CK33 49
Clarendon Gdns., Wem. BK35 45
Clarendon Grn., Orp. CO52 89
Clarendon Gro. NW1 BW38 1
Clarendon Gro. NW1 BW38 56
Phoenix Rd.
Clarendon Gro., Mitch. BU52 86
Clarendon Gro., Orp. CO52 89
Clarendon Ms. W2 BU40 3
Clarendon Ms. W2 BU40 56
Clarendon Pl.
Clarendon Par., Wal.Cr. CC18 21
Clarendon Path, Orp. CO52 89
Clarendon Pl. W2 BU40 3
Clarendon Pl. W2 BU40 56
Clarendon Rd. E11 CF33 48
Clarendon Rd. E17 CE32 48
Clarendon Rd. E18 CH31 49
Clarendon Rd. N15 BY31 47
Clarendon Rd. N18 CB29 39
Clarendon Rd. N22 BX30 38
Clarendon Rd. N8 BX31 47
Clarendon Rd. SW19 BU50 76
Clarendon Rd. W11 BR40 55
Clarendon Rd. W5 BL38 55
Clarendon Rd., Ashf. AY49 73
Clarendon Rd., B.Wd. BM24 28
Clarendon Rd., Chsnt. CC18 21
Clarendon Rd., Croy. BY55 86
Clarendon Rd., Har. BH32 45
Clarendon Rd., Hayes BB41 63
Clarendon Rd., Red. BU70 121
Clarendon Rd., Sev. CU66 116
Clarendon Rd., Wall. BW57 95
Clarendon Rd., Wat. BC24 26
Clarendon Ri. SE13 CF45 67
Clarendon St. SW1 BV42 3
Clarendon St. SW1 BV42 66
Clarendon Ter. W9 BT38 1
Clarendon Ter. W9 BT38 56
Maida Vale
Clarendon Way N21 BZ25 30
Clarendon Way, Chis. CN52 88
Clarendon Way, Orp. CN52 88
Clarendon Wk. W11 BQ40 55
Lancaster Rd.
Clarens St. SE6 CD48 77
Claret Gdns. SE25 CA52 87
Clareville Gro. SW7 BT42 3
Clareville Gro. SW7 BT42 66
Clareville Rd., Cat. CB65 105
Clareville Rd., Orp. CM55 88
Clareville St. SW7 BT42 3
Clareville St. SW7 BT42 66
Gloucester Rd.
Clarewood Mans. SW9 BY45 66
Coldharbour La.
Clarewood Wk. SW9 BY45 66
Somerleyton Rd.
Clarges Ms. W1 BV40 3
Clarges Ms. W1 BV40 56
Clarges St. W1 BV40 3
Clarges St. W1 BV40 56
Claribel Rd. SW9 BY44 66
Clarice Way, Pur. BX58 95
Claridge Rd., Dag. CP33 50
Clarina Rd. SE20 CC50 77
Clarissa Rd., Rom. CP33 50
Clarissa St. E8 CA37 2
Clarissa St. E8 CA37 57
Clark Clo., Erith CU44 69
Forest Rd.
Clark St. E1 CB39 57
Clark Way, Houns. BE43 64
Springwell Rd.
Clarkbourne Dr., Grays DE43 71
Clarke Path N16 CB33 48
Braydon Rd.
Clarke Rd. SE14 CD44 67
Clarke Way, Wat. BC21 26
Clarkes Av., Wor.Pk. BQ54 85
Clarkes Dr., Uxb. AY39 53
Clarkes Green Rd., Sev. CX60 99
Clarkes Rd., Hat. BP12 10
Clarkhill, Harl. CN12 13
Clarks Field, Rick. AW26 35
Church La.
Clarks La., Epp. CN19 22
Hemnall St.
Clarks La., Sev. CQ59 98
Clarks La., West. CG65 106
Clarks Mead, Bush BG26 36
Clarks Pl. EC2 CA39 2
Bishopsgate
Clarks Rd., Ilf. CM34 49
Clarkson Rd. E16 CG39 58
Clarkson St. E2 CB38 57
Clarksons, The, Bark. CM37 58
Claston Clo., Dart. CT45 69
Clatre Ct. N12 BT28 38
Claude Rd. E10 CF34 48
Claude Rd. E13 CH37 58
Claude Rd. SE15 CB44 67
Godman Rd.
Claude St. E14 CE42 67
Claudia Jones Way SW4 BX46 76
Loats Rd.
Claudia Pl. SW19 BR47 75
Augustus Rd.
Claudian Pl., St.Alb. BF14 9
Claudian Way, Grays DG41 71
Claughton Rd. E13 CJ37 58
Claughton Way, Brwd. DE25 122
Clausen Way, Grnf. BJ37 54
Clauson Av., Nthlt. BF35 45
Clave St. E1 CC40 57
Cinnamon St.
Claverdale Rd. SW2 BX47 76
Claverhambury Rd., Wal.Abb. CG18 22
Clavering Av. SW13 BP43 65
Clavering Clo., Twick. BJ49 74
Clavering Gdns., Brwd. DE32 123
Clavering Rd. E12 CJ33 49
Claverley Gro. N3 BS30 38
Claverley Vill. N3 BS30 38
Claverley Gro.
Claverton Clo., Hem.H. AT17 16
Claverton St. SW1 BW42 3
Claverton St. SW1 BW42 66
Claxton Gro. W6 BQ42 65
Clay Acre, Chesh. AO18 16
Clay Av., Mitch. BV51 86
Clay Cft., Welw.G.C. BS 7 5
Hazel Gro.
Clay Farm Rd. SE9 CM48 78
Clay Hill Clo., Reig. BP74 120
Clay Hill, Bush. BF25 27
Clay Hill, Enf. BY22 29
Clay La., Bush. BH26 36
Clay La., Edg. BM27 37
Clay La., Epsom BM65 103
Clay La., Guil. AR67 109
Clay La., Red. BW71 121
Clay La., Stai. AY47 73
Clay Rd., Epsom BO60 94
Clay Ride, Loug. CK25 31
Clay Side, Chig. CM28 40
Clay St. W1 BU39 1
Clay St. W1 BU39 56
Dorset St.
Clay Tye Rd., Upmin. DB35 51
Claybank Gro. SE13 CE45 67
Algernon Rd.
Claybourne Ms. SE19 CA50 77
Church Rd.
Claybridge Rd. SE12 CJ49 78
Claybrook Clo. N2 BT31 47
Long La.
Claybrook Rd. W6 BQ43 65
Clayburn Gdns., S.Ock. DA40 60
Claybury Broadway, Ilf. CK31 49
Claybury Rd., Wdf.Grn. CK29 40
Claybury, Bush. BF26 36
Claydon Dr., Croy. BX56 95
Claydon End, Ger.Cr. AS31 43
Claydon La., Ger.Cr. AS31 43
Claydon Rd., Wok. AQ61 100
Claygate Av., Ilf. CK31 49
Claygate Clo., Horn. CT35 50
Carfax Rd.
Claygate Cres., Croy. CF57 96
Claygate La., T.Ditt. BJ54 84
Claygate Lodge Clo., Esher BH57 93
Claygate Rd. W13 BJ41 64
Claygate Rd., Dor. BJ72 119
Clayhall Av., Ilf. CK30 40
Clayhall La., Reig. BQ72 120
Clayhall La., Wind. AP46 72
Clayhanger, Guil. AU69 118
Clayhill Cres. SE9 CJ49 78
Clayhill Rd., Reig. BP74 120
Claylands Pl. SW8 BY43 66
Claylands Rd. SW8 BX43 66
Claymore Clo., Mord. BS54 86
Claymore Rd., Hem.H. AY11 8
Claypit Hill, Loug. CJ22 31
Claypole Rd. E15 CF37 57
Clayponds Av., Brent. BL42 65
Clayponds Gdns. W5 BK42 64
Clayponds La., Brent. BL42 65
Clays La. Clo. E15 CE35 48
Clays La. E15 CE35 48
Clays La., Loug. CL23 31
Clayton Av., Upmin. CX35 51
Clayton Av., Wem. BL36 55
Clayton Clo. E6 CK39 58
Clayton Cres., Brent. BK42 64
Clayton Croft Rd., Dart. CU48 79
Clayton Dr., Guil. AP69 118
Clayton Field NW9 BO29 37
Clayton Rd. SE15 CB44 67
Clayton Rd., Chess. BK56 93
Clayton Rd., Epsom BO60 94
Clayton Rd., Hayes BB41 63
Clayton Rd., Islw. BH45 64
Clayton Rd., Rom. CS33 50
Clayton St. SE11 BY43 4
Clayton St. SE11 BY43 66
Clayton Waye, Uxb. AX38 53
Clayton Wk., Amer. AR23 25
Claywood Clo., Orp. CN54 88
Claywood La., Dart. DB48 80
Clayworth Clo., Sid. CO46 79
Cleall Av., Wal.Abb. CF20 21
Quaker La.
Cleanthus Rd. SE18 CL44 68
Clearbrook Way E1 CC39 57
West Arbour St.
Cleardene, Dor. BJ71 119
Cleardown, Wok. AT63 100
Clears, The, Reig. BR69 120
Clearwell Dr. W9 BS38 1
Clearwell Dr. W9 BS38 56
Cleave Av., Hayes BB42 63
Cleave Av., Orp. CN57 97
Cleave Prior, Couls. BU63 104
Cleaveland Rd., Surb. BK53 84
Cleaver Sq. SE11 BY42 4
Cleaver Sq. SE11 BY42 66
Cleaver St. SE11 BY42 4
Cleaver St. SE11 BY42 66
Cleaverholme Clo. SE25 CB53 87
Cleeve Ct., Wind. AM45 61
Firs Av.
Cleeve Hill SE23 CB47 77
Cleeve Park Gdns., Sid. CO48 79
Faraday Av.

Cle–Cob

Cleeve Rd., Lthd. BJ63 102
Cleeve, The, Guil. AT70 118
Cleeves Clo., Hem.H. AZ11 8
Cleeves Cres., Croy. CF59 96
Clegg St. E1 CB40 57
Prusom St.
Clegg St. E13 CH37 58
Cleland Path, Loug. CL23 31
Cleland Way, Ger.Cr. AR30 34
Clem Attlee Ct. SW6 BR43 65
Clematis Clo., Rom. CV29 42
Clematis St. W12 BP40 55
Clemence St. E14 CD39 57
Clement Av. SW4 BW45 66
Clement Clo. NW6 BQ36 55
Clement Clo. W4 BN41 65
Winston Wk.
Clement Clo., Pur. BY61 104
Clement Gdns., Hayes BB42 63
Clement Rd. SW19 BR49 75
Clement Rd., Beck. CC51 87
Clement Rd., Chsnt. CD17 21
Clement St., Swan. CV50 80
Clement Way, Upmin. CW34 51
Clementhorpe Rd., Dag. CP36 59
Clementina Rd. E10 CD33 48
Clements Av. E16 CH40 58
Clements Clo., Houns. BD45 64
Clements Clo., Slou. AQ41 62
Clements Inn Pass. WC2 BX39 2
Clements Inn WC2 BX39 2
Clements Inn WC2 BX39 56
Strand
Clements La. EC4 BZ40 4
Clements La. EC4 BZ40 57
Clements La., Ilf. CL34 49
Clements Mead, Lthd. BJ63 102
Clements Pl., Brent. BK42 64
Challis Rd.
Clements Rd. E6 CK36 58
Clements Rd. SE16 CB41 67
Clements Rd., Ilf. CL34 49
Clements Rd., Rick. AU25 25
Clements Rd., Walt. BC55 83
Clenches Farm La., Sev. CU66 116
Clenches Farm Rd., Sev. CU66 116
Clendon Way SE18 CM42 68
Clenheadon Ri., Lthd. BK65 102
Clennam St. SE1 BZ41 4
Clennam St. SE1 BZ41 67
Southwark Bridge Rd.
Clensham Ct., Sutt. BS55 86
Clensham La., Sutt. BS55 86
Clenston Ms. W1 BU39 1
Clenston Ms. W1 BU39 56
Seymour Pl.
Clephane Rd. N1 BZ36 57
Clere Pl. EC2 BZ38 2
Clere Pl. EC2 BZ38 57
Clere St.
Clere St. EC2 BZ38 2
Clere St. EC2 BZ38 57
Cleremont Rd. E9 CC37 57
Clerics Wk., Shep. BA54 83
Russell Rd.
Clerkenwell Clo. EC1 BY38 2
Clerkenwell Clo. EC1 BY38 56
Clerkenwell Grn. EC1 BY38 2
Clerkenwell Grn. EC1 BY38 56
Clerkenwell Rd. EC1 BY38 2
Clerkenwell Rd. EC1 BY38 56
Clerks Cft., Red. BZ70 114
Clerks Piece, Loug. CK24 31
Cleve Rd. NW6 BS36 56
Cleve Rd., Sid. CP48 79
Cleve Yd. SW1 BW40 3
Clevedon Clo. N16 CA34 48
Smalley Rd.
Clevedon Gdns., Hayes BA41 63
Clevedon Gdns., Houns. BC44 63
Clevedon Pass. N16 CA34 48
Stoke Newington High St.
Clevedon Rd. SE20 CC51 87
Clevedon Rd., Kings.T. BM51 85
Clevedon Rd., Twick. BK46 74
Clevedon St. N16 CA34 48
Stoke Newington High St.
Clevedon, Wey. BA56 92
Clevehurst Clo., Slou. AQ36 52
Cleveland Av. SW20 BR51 85
Cleveland Av. W4 BO42 65
Cleveland Av., Hmptn. BE50 74
Cleveland Clo., Walt. BC55 83
Cleveland Cres., B.Wd. BN25 28
Cleveland Ct. W13 BJ39 54
Kent Av.
Cleveland Dr., Stai. AW51 83
Cleveland Est. E1 CC38 57
Cleveland Gdns. N4 BZ32 48
Cleveland Gdns. NW2 BQ34 46
Cleveland Gdns. SW13 BO44 65
Cleveland Gdns. W13 BJ39 54
Argyle Rd.
Cleveland Gdns. W2 BT39 1
Cleveland Gdns. W2 BT39 56
Cleveland Gdns., Wor.Pk. BO55 85
Cleveland Gro. E1 CC38 57
Cleveland Way
Cleveland Ms. W1 BW39 1
Cleveland Ms. W1 BW39 56
Maple St.
Cleveland Park Av. E17 CE31 48
Cleveland Park Cres. E17 CE31 48
Cleveland Pl. SW1 BW40 56
King St.
Cleveland Rd. E18 CH31 49
Cleveland Rd. N1 BZ36 2
Cleveland Rd. N1 BZ36 57
Cleveland Rd. N9 CB26 39
Cleveland Rd. SW13 BO44 65
Cleveland Rd. W13 BJ39 54
Cleveland Rd. W4 BN41 65
Cleveland Rd., Ilf. CL34 49
Cleveland Rd., Islw. BJ45 64
Cleveland Rd., N.Mal. BO52 85
Cleveland Rd., Uxb. AX38 53
Cleveland Rd., Well. CN44 68
Cleveland Rd., Wor.Pk. BO55 85
Cleveland Ri., Mord. BQ54 85
Cleveland Row SW1 BW40 3
Cleveland Row SW1 BW40 56
Cleveland Sq. W2 BT39 1
Cleveland Sq. W2 BT39 56
Cleveland St. W1 BV38 1
Cleveland St. W1 BW38 56
Cleveland Ter. W2 BT39 1
Cleveland Ter. W2 BT39 56
Cleveland Way E1 CC38 57
Cleveland Way, Hem.H. AZ12 8
Cleveland, Hem.H. AZ12 8
Cleveley Clo. SE7 CJ42 68
Cleveley Cres. W5 BL37 55
Cleveleys Rd. E5 CB34 48
Cleverley Est. W12 BP40 55
Cleves Av., Epsom BP58 94
Cleves Clo., Cob. BC60 92
Cleves Clo., Hem.H. AZ11 8
Cleves Rd. E6 CJ37 58
Cleves Rd., Rich. BK48 74
Cleves Rd., Sev. CW62 108
Cleves Way, Hmptn. BE50 74
Cleves Way, Ruis. BD33 45
Cleves Wk., Ilf. CM29 40
Cleves Wood, Wey. BB56 92
Clewer Av., Wind. AN44 61
Clewer Court Rd., Wind. AN43 61
Clewer Cres., Har. BG30 36
Clewer Fields, Wind. AN44 61
Clewer Hill Rd., Wind. AM44 61
Clewer New Town, Wind. AN44 61
Clewer Pk., Wind. AN43 61
Clichy Est. E1 CC39 57
Clifden Rd. E5 CC35 48
Clifden Rd., Brent. BK43 64
Clifden Rd., Twick. BH47 74
Cliff End, Pur. BY60 95
Cliff Gro., Grav. DG47 81
Cliff Pl., S.Ock. DB38 60
Cliff Rd. NW1 BW36 56
Cliff St. E16 CG39 58
Trinity Gdns.
Cliff Ter. SE8 CE44 67
Cliff Vill. NW1 BW36 56
Cliff Wk. E16 CG39 58
Cliffe Rd., S.Croy. BZ56 96
Cliffe Wk., Sutt. BT56 95
Turnpike La.
Clifford Av. SW14 BM45 65
Clifford Av., Chis. CK50 78
Clifford Av., Ilf. CL30 40
Clifford Av., Wall. BW56 95
Clifford Clo., Nthlt. BE37 54
Clifford Ct. NW2 BO35 46
Clifford Dr. SW9 BY45 66
Clifford Gdns. NW10 BQ37 55
Clifford Gro. SE20 CC50 77
Clifford Gro., Ashf. AZ49 73
Clifford Manor Rd., Guil. AS72 118
Clifford Rd. E16 CG38 58
Clifford Rd. E17 CF30 39
Clifford Rd. N9 CC25 30
Clifford Rd. SE25 CB52 87
Clifford Rd., Barn. BS24 29
Clifford Rd., Grays DC41 71
Clifford Rd., Houns. BD45 64
Clifford Rd., Rich. BK48 74
Clifford Rd., Wem. BK36 54
Clifford St. W1 BW40 3
Clifford St. W1 BW40 56
Clifford St., Wat. BD24 27
Clifford Way NW10 BO35 46
Cliffords Inn EC4 BY39 56
Fleet St.
Cliffview Rd. SE13 CE45 67
Clifton Av. E17 CC31 48
Clifton Av. N3 BR30 37
Clifton Av. W12 BO41 65
Clifton Av., Felt. BD48 74
Clifton Av., Stan. BJ30 36
Clifton Av., Sutt. BS58 95
Clifton Av., Wem. BL36 55
Clifton Clo., Brwd. DE32 123
Clifton Clo., Cat. BZ65 105
Clifton Clo., Chsnt. CD18 21
Clifton Clo., Orp. CL56 97
Clifton Clo., Wey. AW55 83
Clifton Cres. SE15 CB43 67
Clifton Ct. NW8 BT38 1
Clifton Ct. NW8 BT38 56
Clifton Est. SE15 CB44 67
Clifton Gdns. N15 CA32 48
Clifton Gdns. NW11 BR32 46
Clifton Gdns. W4 BN42 65
Chiswick High Rd.
Clifton Gdns. W9 BT38 1
Clifton Gdns. W9 BT38 56
Clifton Gdns., Enf. BX24 29
Clifton Gdns., Uxb. AZ37 53
Clifton Gro. E8 CB36 57
Clifton Hill NW8 BS37 1
Clifton Hill NW8 BS37 56
Clifton Marine Par., Grav. DF46 81
Clifton Park Av. SW20 BQ51 85
Approach Rd.
Clifton Pl. SE2 CC41 67
Canon Beck Rd.
Clifton Pl. W2 BT40 56
Clifton Pl., Bans. BS61 104
Clifton Rd. E16 CG39 58
Clifton Rd. E7 CJ36 58
Clifton Rd. N22 BW30 38
Clifton Rd. N3 BT30 38
Clifton Rd. N8 BW32 47
Clifton Rd. NW10 BP37 55
Clifton Rd. SE25 BZ52 87
Clifton Rd. SW19 BQ50 75
Clifton Rd. W9 BT38 1
Clifton Rd. W9 BT38 56
Clifton Rd., Couls. BV61 104
Clifton Rd., Grav. DG48 81
Clifton Rd., Grnf. BG38 54
Clifton Rd., Har. BL32 46
Clifton Rd., Horn. CU32 50
Clifton Rd., Houns. AZ45 63
Conway Rd.
Clifton Rd., Ilf. CM32 49
Clifton Rd., Islw. BG44 64
Clifton Rd., Kings.T. BL50 75
Clifton Rd., Loug. CK24 31
Clifton Rd., Sid. CN49 78
Clifton Rd., Slou. AQ41 62
Clifton Rd., Sthl. BE42 64
Clifton Rd., Tedd. BH49 74
Clifton Rd., Wall. BV56 95
Clifton Rd., Wat. BC25 26
Clifton Rd., Well. CO45 69
Clifton Ri. SE14 CD43 67
Clifton Ri., Wind. AL44 61
Clifton St. EC2 CA39 2
Clifton St. EC2 CA39 57
Clifton St., E8 CB36 57
Graham Rd.
Clifton St., St.Alb. BH13 9
Clifton Ter. N4 BY34 47
Clifton Vills. W9 BS39 1
Clifton Vills. W9 BS39 56
Clifton Way SE15 CB43 67
Clifton Way, B.Wd. BL23 28
Clifton Way, Brwd. DE26 122
Clifton Way, Wem. BL37 55
Clifton Way, Wok. AP62 100
Cliftons La., Reig. BQ70 120
Cliftonville, Dor. BJ72 119
Climb, The, Rick. AW25 26
Clinch Ct. E16 CH39 58
Cline Rd. N11 BW29 38
Cline Rd., Guil. AS71 118
Clinger Ct. N1 CA37 2
Clink St. SE1 BZ40 4
Clink St. SE1 BZ40 57
Clinton Av., E.Mol. BG52 84
Clinton Av., Well. CN45 68
Clinton Clo., Wok. AO62 100
Clinton Cres., Ilf. CN29 40
Clinton Rd. E3 CD38 57
Clinton Rd. E7 CH35 49
Clinton Rd. N15 BZ31 48
Clinton Rd., Lthd. BK65 102
Clipper Boul., Dart. CY45 70
Clipper Clo. SE16 CC41 67
Kinburn St.
Clipper Cres., Grav. DJ49 81
Clipper Way SE13 CF45 67
Limes Gro.
Clippesby Clo., Chess. BL57 94
Clipstone Ms. W1 BW38 1
Clipstone Ms. W1 BW39 56
Clipstone Rd., Houns. BF45 64
Clipstone St. W1 BV39 56
Clissold Clo. N2 BU31 47
Clissold Cres. N16 BZ35 48
Clissold Ct. N16 BZ34 48
Clissold Rd. N16 BZ34 48
Clitheroe Av., Har. BF33 45
Clitheroe Gdns., Wat. BD27 36
Clitheroe Rd. SW9 BX44 66
Clitheroe Rd., Rom. CS28 41
Clitherow Av. W7 BJ41 64
Clitherow Rd., Brent. BJ42 64
Clitterhouse Cres. NW2 BQ33 46
Clitterhouse Rd. NW2 BQ33 46
Clive Av. N18 CB29 39
Clive Av., Dart. CT46 79
Clive Clo., Pot.B. BR19 19
Clive Ct., Slou. AO41 61
Clive Ct., Surb. BM55 85
Clive Pass. SE21 BZ48 77
Clive Rd.
Clive Pass. SE21 BZ48 77
Chalford Rd.
Clive Rd. SE21 BZ48 77
Clive Rd. SW19 BU50 76
Clive Rd., Belv. CQ42 69
Clive Rd., Brwd. DB29 42
Clive Rd., Enf. CB24 30
Clive Rd., Esher BF56 93
Clive Rd., Felt. BC46 73
Clive Rd., Grav. DG46 81
Clive Rd., Rom. CU32 50
Clive Rd., Twick. BJ49 74
Clive Way, Couls. BX62 104
Clive Way, Enf. CB24 30
Clive Way, Stai. AV51 82
Clive Way, Wat. BD23 27
Cliveden Clo. N12 BT28 38
Cliveden Clo., Brwd. DC26 122
Cliveden Pl. SW1 BV42 3
Cliveden Pl., Shep. AZ53 83
Cliveden Rd. SW19 BR51 85
Clivedon Rd. E4 CG28 40
Clivesdale Dr., Hayes BC40 53
Avondale Dr.
Cloak La. EC4 BZ40 4
Cloak La. EC4 BZ40 57
Clock House Clo., Wey. AY59 92
Clock House La., Sev. CU65 107
Clock House Mead, Lthd. BF60 93
Clock House Rd., Beck. CC52 87
Clock Pl. SE1 BY42 4
Clock Ter., Grav. DH46 81
Clock Tower Pl. N7 BX36 56
Clock Tower Rd., Islw. BH45 64
Clockhouse Av., Bark. CM37 58
Clockhouse Clo. SW19 BQ48 75
Clockhouse La. E., Egh. AT50 72
Clockhouse La. W., Egh. AT50 72
Clockhouse La., Ashf. & Felt. AZ48 73
Clockhouse La., Grays DC40 71
Clockhouse La., Rom. CR29 41
Clocktower Ms. N1 BZ37 2
Clocktower Ms. N1 BZ37 57
Arlington Av.
Clodhouse Hill, Wok. AO64 100
Cloister Clo., Rain. CU38 59
Cloister Garth, Berk. AR13 7
Priory Gdns.
Cloister Garth, St.Alb. BH15 9
Cloister Gdns. SE25 CB53 87
Cloister Gdns., Edg. BN28 37
Cloister Rd. NW2 BR34 46
Cloister Rd. W3 BN39 55
Cloister Wk., Hem.H. AX12 8
Townsend
Cloisters Av., Brom. CK53 88
Cloisters, The, Welw.G.C. BQ8 5
Parkway
Cloisters, The, Rick. AY26 35
Clonard Way, Pnr. BF29 36
Clonbrock Rd. N16 CA35 48
Cloncurry St. SW6 BQ44 65
Clonmel Clo., Har. BG33 45
Clonmel Rd. SW6 BR43 65
Clonmel Rd., Tedd. BG49 74
Clonmell Rd. N17 BZ31 48
Clonmore St. SW18 BR47 75
Cloonmore Av., Orp. CN56 97
Clorane Gdns., NW3 BS34 47
Close, The E4 CF29 39
Close, The N14 BY34 47
Close, The N20 BR27 37
Close, The SE3 CG45 68
Heath La.
Close, The, (Lyon Park Av.) Wem. BL36 55
Close, The, (Barnhill Rd.) Wem. BN34 46
Close, The, Barn. BU25 29
Close, The, Beck. CD52 87
Close, The, Bet. BM72 120
Close, The, Bex. CR47 79
Close, The, Brwd. DB27 42
Close, The, Bush. BF25 27
Close, The, Cars. BU58 95
Close, The, Dart. CV48 80
Close, The, Eastcote BD33 45
Close, The, Grays DD41 71
Close, The, Har. BG30 36
Close, The, Hat. BR16 19
Close, The, Hem.H. AT17 16
Close, The, Hillingdon AZ37 53
Close, The, Ightham DB63 108
Close, The, Islw. BG44 64
Close, The, Iver. AU38 52
Close, The, Mitch. BU52 86
Close, The, N.Mal. BN51 85
Close, The, Orp. CN53 88
Close, The, Pot.B. BS19 20
Close, The, Pur. BY58 95
Close, The, Rad. BH20 18
Close, The, Rayners Lane BE33 45
Close, The, Reig. BS71 121
Close, The, Rich. BM45 65
Close, The, Rick. AW26 35
Close, The, Rom. CQ32 50
Close, The, Russell Hill BX58 95
Close, The, Sev. CT65 107
Close, The, Sid. CO49 79
Close, The, Sutt. BR54 85
Close, The, Uxb. AY36 53
Close, The, Vir.W. AR53 82
Close, The, Wey. AW60 92
Closemead Clo., Nthwd. BA29 35
Cloth Ct. EC1 BY39 2
Cloth Fair
Cloth Fair EC1 BY39 2
Cloth Fair EC1 BY39 56
Cloth St. EC1 BZ39 2
Clothier St. E1 CA39 57
Cutler St.
Cloudberry Rd., Rom. CV29 42
Cloudesdale Rd. SW17 BV48 76
Cloudesley Pl. N1 BY37 2
Cloudesley Pl. N1 BY37 56
Cloudesley Rd. N1 BY37 2
Cloudesley Rd. N1 BY37 56
Cloudesley Rd., Bexh. CQ44 69
Cloudesley Rd., Erith CT44 69
Cloudesley Sq. N1 BY37 2
Cloudesley Sq. N1 BY37 56
Cloudesley St. N1 BY37 2
Cloudesley St. N1 BY37 56
Clouston Clo., Wall. BX56 95
Clova Rd. E7 CG36 58
Clove Hitch Quay SW18 BT45 66
Clove St. E13 CH38 58
Clovelly Av. NW9 BO31 46
Clovelly Av., Uxb. BA35 44
Clovelly Av., Warl. CB63 105
Clovelly Clo., Uxb. BA35 44
Clovelly Ct., Horn. CX34 51
Clovelly Gdns., Croy. CA51 87
Clovelly Gdns., Enf. CA26 39
Clovelly Gdns., Rom. CR30 41
Clovelly Rd. N8 BW31 47
Clovelly Rd. W4 BN41 65
Clovelly Rd. W5 BK41 64
Clovelly Rd., Bexh. CQ43 69
Clovelly Rd., Houns. BF44 64
Clovelly Way E1 CC39 57
Jamaica St.
Clovelly Way, Har. BE34 45
Clovelly Way, Orp. CN53 88
Cotswold Ri.
Clover Clo. E11 CF34 48
Clover Ct., Grays DE43 71
Churchill Rd.
Clover Ct., Wok. AR62 100
Clover Field, Harl. CO12 14
Clover Hill, Couls. BV64 104
Clover Leas, Epp. CN18 22
Clover Ms. SW3 BU43 3
Clover Ms. SW3 BU43 66
Clover Rd., Guil. AP69 118
Clover Way, Hem.H. AW13 8
Cloverdale Gdns., Sid. CN46 78
Cloverfield, Welw.G.C. BR6 5
Cloverland, Hat. BO14 10
Cloverley Rd., Ong. CX18 24
Clovers, The, Grav. DF49 81
Henley Deane
Clowders Rd. SE6 CD48 77
Clowser Clo., Sutt. BT56 95
Cloyster Wood, Edg. BK29 36
Cloysters Grn. E1 CB40 4
Thomas More St.
Club Gardens Rd., Brom. CH54 88
Club Row E1 & E2 CA38 2
Club Row E1 & E2 CA38 57
Clump Av., Tad. BN69 120
Clump, The, Rick. AW25 26
Clumps, The, Felt. BA49 73
Clunas Gdns., Rom. CV31 51
Clunbury Av., Sthl. BE42 64
Clunbury St. N1 BZ37 2
Clunbury St. N1 BZ37 57
Cluny Ms. SW5 BS42 66
Cluny Pl. SE1 CA41 4
Cluny Pl. SE1 CA41 67
Clutton St. E14 CE39 57
Clydach Rd., Enf. CA24 30
Clyde Av., S.Croy. CB61 105
Clyde Cir. N15 CA31 48
Clyde Clo., Red. BV70 121
Clyde Clo., Upmin. CZ32 51
Clyde Cres., Upmin. CZ32 51
Clyde Ct., Red. BV70 121
Clyde Clo.
Clyde Pl. E10 CE33 48
Clyde Pl. SE23 CC48 77
Clyde Rd. N15 CA31 48
Clyde Rd. N22 BW30 38
Clyde Rd., Croy. CA55 87
Clyde Rd., Hodd. CF13 12
Clyde Rd., Stai. AX47 73
Clyde Rd., Sutt. BS56 95
Clyde Rd., Wall. BW56 95
Clyde Sq., Hem.H. AY11 8
Clyde St. SE8 CD43 67
Clyde Ter. SE23 CC48 77
Clyde Vale SE23 CC48 77
Clyde Way, Rom. CT30 41
Clydesdale Av., Stan. BK31 45
Clydesdale Clo., B.Wd. BN25 28
Clydesdale Gdns., Rich. BM45 65
Clydesdale Path, B.Wd. BN25 28
Clydesdale Clo.
Clydesdale Rd. W11 BR39 55
Clydesdale Rd., Horn. CT33 50
Clydesdale Wk., Chsnt. CD16 21
Tarpan Way
Clydesdale, Enf. CC24 30
Clydon Clo., Erith CT43 69
Clyfford Rd., Ruis. BB35 44
Clyfton Clo., Brox. CD15 12
Clymping Dene, Felt. BC47 73
Clyston Rd., Wat. BB25 26
Clyston St. SW8 BW44 66
Coach & Horses Yd. W1 BW40 3
Coach & Horses Yd. W1 BW40 56
Old Burlington St.
Coach House La. N5 BY35 47
Highbury Hill
Coach House La. SW19 BQ48 75
Coach House Ms. SE23 CC47 77
Hengrave Rd.
Coach House Yd. NW3 BT35 47
Hampstead High St.
Coach Rd., Cher. AU57 91
Coach Rd., Dor. & Bet. BL71 120
Coach Rd., Sev. DA65 108
Coachhouse Ms. SE20 CB50 77
Coachlands Av., Guil. AP70 118
Coal Rd., Til. DJ42 71
Coal Wharf Rd. W12 BQ42 65
Coaldale Wk. SE24 BZ47 77
Rosendale Rd.
Coalecroft Rd. SW15 BQ45 65
Coaley Row, Dag. CQ37 59
Coast Hill La., Dor. BF72 119
Coast Hill, Dor. BE73 119
Coat Wicks, Beac. AO29 34
Coate St. E2 CB37 57
Coates Dell, Wat. BE20 18
Coates Hill Rd., Brom. CL51 88
Coates Rd., B.Wd. BK26 36
Coates St., Harl. CM11 13
Coates Way, Wat. BD20 18
Coates Wk., Brent. BL42 65
Burford Rd.
Cob Clo., B.Wd. BN25 28
Hunter Path
Cob Mead, Hat. BP11 10
Cobb Clo., Slou. AR44 62
Cobb Grn., Wat. BC19 17
Cobb Rd., Berk. AP13 7
Cobb St. E1 CA39 2
Cobb St. E1 CA39 57
Leyden St.
Cobbets Clo., Wok. AQ62 100
Cobbets Hill, Wey. AZ57 92
Cobbett Rd. SE9 CK45 68
Cobbett Rd., Twick. BF47 74
Cobbett, Guil. AP70 118
Cobbetts Av., Ilf. CJ32 49
Cobbins, The, Wal.Abb. CG19 22
Cobbinsend Rd., Wal.Abb. CJ18 22
Cobblers Wk., Tedd. BG50 74
Cobbles, The, Brwd. DC27 122
Cobbles, The, Upmin. CZ33 51
Cobblestone Pl., Croy. BZ54 87
Oakfield Rd.
Cobbold Est. NW10 BO36 55
Cobbold Rd. E11 CG34 49
Cobbold Rd. NW10 BO36 55
Cobbold Rd. W12 BO41 65
Cobbs Ct. EC4 BY39 2
Carter La.
Cobbs Rd., Houns. BE45 64
Cobden Clo., Uxb. AX37 53
Wellington Rd.
Cobden Hill, Rad. BJ21 27
Cobden Rd. E11 CG34 49
Cobden Rd. SE25 CB53 87
Cobden Rd., Orp. CM58 97
Cobden Rd., Sev. CV65 108
Cobham Av., N.Mal. BP53 85
Cobham Clo. SW11 BU46 76
Cobham Clo., Brom. CK54 88

Cobham Clo., Wall.	BX57	95
Redford Av.		
Cobham Park Rd., Cob.	BC62	101
Cobham Pl., Bexh.	CP46	79
Cobham Rd. E17	CF30	39
Cobham Rd. N22	BY31	47
Cobham Rd., Bark.	CM37	58
St. Margarets		
Cobham Rd., Cob. & Lthd.	BF62	102
Cobham Rd., Houns.	BD43	64
Cobham Rd., Ilf.	CN34	49
Cobham Rd., Kings.T.	BM51	85
Cobham Rd., Lthd.	BG64	102
Cobham St., Grav.	DG47	81
Cobham Terrace Rd., Green.	DA47	80
Cobham Way, Lthd.	BB66	110
Cobham, Grays	DD41	71
Cobill Clo., Horn.	CV31	51
Cobland Rd. SE12	CJ49	78
Coborn Rd. E3	CD37	57
Coborn St. E3	CD38	57
Cobourg Rd. SE5	CA43	67
Cobourg Rd. SE5	**CA45**	**4**
Cobourg St. NW1	**BW38**	**1**
Cobourg St. NW1	BW38	56
Cobs Clo., Sev.	BB64	108
Cobs Way, Wey.	AW58	92
Cobsdene, Grav.	DH50	81
Coburg Clo. SW1	**BW42**	**3**
Coburg Rd. N22	BX31	47
Coburgh Cres. SW2	BX47	76
Cochrane Clo. NW8	BT37	56
Cochrane Ms. NW8	BT37	56
Cochrane Rd. SW19	BR50	75
Cochrane St. NW8	**BT37**	**1**
Cochrane St. NW8	BT37	56
Cock Gro., Berk.	AO13	7
Cock Hill E1	CA39	57
New St.		
Cock La. EC1	**BY39**	**2**
Cock La. EC1	BY39	56
Cock La., Hodd.	CB13	12
Cock La., Lthd.	BG64	102
Cock Robins La., Harl.	CL7	6
Cock Robins La., Ware	CL6	6
Cock Yd. SE5	BZ44	67
Denmark Hill		
Cockayne Way SE8	CD42	67
Cocker Rd., Enf.	CB21	30
Cockerhurst Rd., Sev.	CS57	98
Cockett Rd., Slou.	AS41	62
Cockfosters Rd., Barn.	BU22	29
Cockmannings La., Orp.	CP54	89
Cockmannings Rd., Orp.	CP54	89
Cockpit Yd. WC1	**BX39**	**2**
Cockpit Yd. WC1	BX39	56
Northington St.		
Cocks Cres., N.Mal.	BO52	85
Cocksett Av., Orp.	CN57	97
Cockshot Hill, Reig.	BS71	121
Cockshot Rd., Reig.	BS71	121
Cockspur Ct. SW1	**BW40**	**3**
Cockspur Ct. SW1	BW40	56
Spring Gdns.		
Cockspur St. SW1	**BW40**	**3**
Cockspur St. SW1	BW40	56
Cocksure La., Sid.	CR48	79
Code St. E1	**CA38**	**2**
Code St. E1	CA38	57
Codham Hall La., Brwd.	DB31	51
Codicote Dr., Wat.	BD20	18
Codicote Rd., Welw.	BN5	5
Codicote Row, Hem.H.	AZ10	8
Codicote Ter. N4	BZ34	48
Codling Clo. E1	CB40	57
Vaughan Way		
Codling Way, Wem.	BK35	45
Codmore Cres., Chesh.	AP18	16
Codmore Wood Rd., Chesh.	AR20	16
Codrington Ct., Grav.	DH49	81
Codrington Ct., Wok.	AP62	100
Ashwindham Ct.		
Codrington Gdns., Grav.	DH49	81
Codrington Hill SE23	CD47	77
Codrington Ms. W11	BR39	55
Blenheim Cres.		
Cody Clo., Har.	BK31	45
Cody Clo., Wall.	BW57	95
Alcock Clo.		
Cody Clo., Wey.	AY59	92
Viscount Gdns.		
Cody Rd. E16	CF38	57
Coe Av. SE25	CB53	87
Coe Spur, Slou.	AN41	61
Cooper Way		
Cofers Circ., Wem.	BM34	46
Coftards, Slou.	AR39	52
Cogan Av. E17	CD30	39
Coin St. SE1	BY40	56
Coity Rd. NW5	BV36	56
Coke St. E1	CB39	57
Cokers La. SE21	BZ47	77
Perifield		
Cokes La., Ch.St.G.	AQ24	25
Colas Ms. NW6	BS37	56
Birchington Rd.		
Colbeck Ms. SW7	**BS42**	**3**
Colbeck Ms. SW7	BS42	66
Colbeck Rd., Har.	BG33	45
Colberg Pl. N16	CA33	48
Colborne Way, Wor.Pk.	BQ55	85
Colbrook Av., Hayes	BA41	63
Colbrook Clo., Hayes	BA41	63
Colburn Av., Cat.	CA65	105
Colburn Av., Pnr.	BE29	36
Colburn Cres., Guil.	AT69	118
Sutherland Dr.		
Colburn Way, Sutt.	BT55	86
Colby Rd. SE19	CA49	77
Colby Rd., Walt.	BC54	83
Colchester Av. E12	CK34	49
Colchester Dr., Pnr.	BD32	45
Colchester Rd. E10	CF33	48
Colchester Rd. E17	CE32	48
Colchester Rd., Edg.	BN30	37
Colchester Rd., Nthwd.	BC30	35
Colchester Rd., Rom.	CV30	42
Colcokes Rd., Bans.	BS61	104
Cold Arbor Rd., Sev.	CS65	107
Cold Blow Cres., Bex.	CS47	79
Cold Blows, Mitch.	BU52	86
Cold Harbour E3	CF40	57
Cold St. EC1	**BY38**	**2**
Coldbath Sq. EC1	BY38	56
Topham St.		
Coldbath St. SE13	CE44	67
Coldblow La. SE14	CC43	67
Coldershaw Rd. W13	BJ40	54
Coldfall Av. N10	BU30	38
Coldham Clo., Enf.	CD22	30
Standard Rd.		
Coldham Gro., Enf.	CD22	30
Standard Rd.		
Coldharbour Clo., Egh.	AV52	82
Coldharbour La.		
Coldharbour La. SE5	BZ45	67
Coldharbour La. SW9	BY45	66
Coldharbour La., Bush.	BF25	27
Coldharbour La., Dor.	BH74	119
Coldharbour La., Egh.	AU52	82
Coldharbour La., Hayes	BC40	53
Coldharbour La., Pur.	BY58	95
Coldharbour La., Red.	CA70	114
Coldharbour La., Ton.	CZ71	117
Coldharbour La., Wok.	AV61	100
Coldharbour Rd., Croy.	BY56	95
Coldharbour Rd., Grav.	DF48	81
Coldharbour Rd., Harl.	CK11	13
Coldharbour Rd., Wey.	AV60	91
Coldharbour Rd., Wok.	AV61	100
Coldharbour Way, Croy.	BY56	95
Coldshott, Oxt.	CH70	115
Coldstream Gdns. SW18	BR46	75
Cole Clo. SE28	CO40	59
Cole Gdns., Houns.	BC44	63
Sandringham Gdns.		
Cole Green La., Welw.G.C.	BR9	5
Cole Pk. Gdns., Twick.	BJ46	74
Cole Pk. Rd., Twick.	BJ46	74
Cole Rd., Twick.	BJ46	74
Cole Rd., Wat.	BC23	26
Cole St. SE1	**BZ41**	**4**
Cole St. SE1	BZ41	67
Cole St. SW11	BU44	66
Colebeck Ms. N1	BY36	56
Colebert Av. E1	CC38	57
Colebrook Av. W13	BJ39	54
Colebrook Clo. SW15	BQ47	75
Colebrook Dr. E11	CH33	49
Colebrook Gdns., Loug.	CM23	31
Colebrook La., Loug.	CL23	31
Colebrook Path, Loug.	CL23	31
Colebrook Rd. E17	CD31	48
Colebrook Rd. SW16	BX51	86
Colebrook Row N1	**BY37**	**2**
Colebrook Way N11	BV28	38
Colebrook Wk. E17	CD31	48
High St.		
Colebrook, Cher.	AU57	91
Colebrooke Rd., Reig.	BU69	121
Colebrooke Ri., Brom.	CG51	88
Colebrooke Row N1	BY37	56
Coleby Path SE5	BZ43	67
Harris St.		
Coledale Dr., Stan.	BK30	36
Coleford Rd. SW18	BT46	76
Colegrave Rd. E15	CF35	48
Colegrove Rd. SE15	CA43	67
Coleherne Ct. SW5	**BS42**	**3**
Coleherne Ct. SW5	BS42	66
Coleherne Ms. SW10	**BS42**	**3**
Coleherne Ms. SW10	BS42	66
Coleherne Rd. SW10	**BS42**	**3**
Coleherne Rd. SW10	BS42	66
Colehill Gdns. SW6	BR44	65
Fulham Palace Rd.		
Colehill La. SW6	BR44	65
Coleman Clo. E1	CC40	57
Garnet St.		
Coleman Ct. E1	CC40	57
Garnet St.		
Coleman Ct. SW18	BS47	76
Coleman Fields N1	**BZ37**	**2**
Coleman Fields N1	BZ37	57
Coleman Green La., St.Alb.	BM7	5
Coleman Rd. SE5	CA43	67
Coleman Rd., Belv.	CR42	69
Coleman Rd., Dag.	CQ36	59
Coleman St. EC2	**BZ39**	**2**
Coleman St. EC2	BZ39	57
Colemans Heath SE9	CL48	78
Colemans La., Wal.Abb.	CF16	21
Colenorton Cres., Eton	AM42	61
Colenso Rd. E5	CC35	48
Colenso Rd., Ilf.	CN33	49
Colepits Wood Rd. SE9	CM46	78
Coleraine Rd. N8	BY31	47
Coleraine Rd. SE3	CG43	68
Coleridge Av. E12	CK36	58
Coleridge Av., Sutt.	BU56	95
Coleridge Clo. SW8	BV44	66
Coleridge Clo., Brwd.	DE26	122
Byron Rd.		
Coleridge Cr., Hem.H.	AZ10	8
Coleridge Cres., Slou.	AV44	62
Coleridge Gdns. NW6	BT36	56
Coleridge La. N8	BX32	47
Coleridge Rd.		
Coleridge Rd. E17	CD31	48
Coleridge Rd. N12	BT28	38
Coleridge Rd. N4	BY34	47
Coleridge Rd. N8	BW32	47
Coleridge Rd., Ashf.	AY49	73
Coleridge Rd., Croy.	CC54	87
Coleridge Rd., Dart.	CX45	70
Coleridge Rd., Rom.	CU29	41
Coleridge Rd., Til.	DH44	71
Coleridge Way, Hayes	BC39	53
Coleridge Way, Orp.	CO53	89
Coleridge Way, West Dr.	AY42	63
Coleridge Wk. NW11	BS31	47
Coleridge Wk., Brwd.	DE26	122
Byron Rd.		
Coles Clo., Ong.	CX16	24
Coles Cres., Har.	BF34	45
Coles Grn. Ct. NW2	BP34	46
Coles Grn. Rd. NW2	BP33	46
Coles Grn., Bush.	BG26	36
Coles Grn., Loug.	CL23	31
Coles Hill, Hem.H.	AW12	8
Coles La., West.	CP65	107
Colesburg Rd., Beck.	CD52	87
Colescroft Hill, Pur.	BY61	104
Colesdale, Cuff.	BX18	20
Coleshill Rd., Tedd.	BH50	74
Colesmead Rd., Red.	BU69	121
Colestown St. SW11	BU44	66
Colet Gdns. W14	BQ42	65
Colet Rd., Brwd.	DE25	122
Colets Orchard, Sev.	CU61	107
Coley Av., Wok.	AT62	100
Coley St. WC1	**BX38**	**2**
Coley St. WC1	BX38	56
Colfe Rd. SE23	CD47	77
Colgrove, Welw.G.C.	BQ8	5
Colham Green Rd., Uxb.	AZ39	53
Colham Rd., Uxb.	AY38	53
Colham Rd., West Dr.	AY40	53
Colin Clo. NW9	BO31	46
Colin Clo., Croy.	CD55	87
Colin Clo., Dart.	CX46	80
Brent Clo.		
Colin Clo., W.Wick.	CG55	88
Colin Cres. NW9	BO31	46
Colin Dr. NW9	BO32	46
Colin Gdns. NW9	BO32	46
Colin Park Rd. NW9	BO31	46
Colin Rd. NW10	BP36	55
Colin Rd., Cat.	CB65	105
Colin St. SE1	**BY40**	**4**
Colin Way, Slou.	AN41	61
Colina Ms. N8	BW31	47
Park Rd.		
Colina Rd. N15	BY32	47
Colindale Av., Erith	CR43	69
Colindale Av., St.Alb.	BH14	9
Colindeep Gdns. NW4	BP31	46
Colindeep La. NW9	BN31	46
Colinette Rd. SW15	BQ45	65
Colinton Rd., Ilf.	CO34	50
Coliston Rd. SW18	BS47	76
Collage Clo., Twick.	BG47	74
Collamore Av. SW18	BU47	76
Collapit Clo., Har.	BF32	45
Collard Av., Loug.	CM23	31
Collard Grn., Loug.	CM23	31
College App. SE10	CF43	67
College Av., Egh.	AT50	72
College Av., Epsom	BO60	94
College Av., Grays	DD42	71
College Av., Har.	BH30	36
College Av., Slou.	AP41	62
College Clo. E9	CC35	48
College Clo. N18	CA28	39
College Clo., Grays	DD42	71
College Av.		
College Clo., Har.	BH29	36
College Cres. NW3	BT36	56
College Cres., Wind.	AN44	61
College Cross N1	BY36	56
College Ct., Chsnt.	CC18	21
College Dr., Ruis.	BC33	44
College Gate, Harl.	CM11	13
College Gdns. E4	CE26	39
College Gdns. N18	CA28	39
College Gdns. SE21	CA47	77
College Gdns. SW17	BU48	76
College Gdns., Enf.	BZ23	30
College Gdns., Ilf.	CK32	49
College Gdns., N.Mal.	BO53	85
College Grn. SE19	CA50	77
College Gro. NW1	**BW37**	**1**
College Hill EC4	**BZ40**	**4**
College Hill EC4	BZ40	57
College Hill Rd., Har.	BH29	36
College La. NW5	BV35	47
College La., Hat.	BO13	10
College La., Wok.	AR63	100
College Ms. SW18	BS46	76
St. Anns Hill		
College Park Clo. SE13	CF45	67
College Park Rd. N17	CA29	39
College Rd.		
College Pl. E17	CG31	49
College Pl. NW1	**BW37**	**1**
College Pl. NW1	BW37	56
College Pl., St.Alb.	BG13	9
College Rd. E17	CF32	48
College Rd. N17	CA29	39
College Rd. N21	BY27	38
College Rd. NW10	BQ37	55
College Rd. SE19	CA47	77
College Rd. SE21	CA47	77
College Rd. SW19	BT50	76
College Rd. W13	BJ39	54
College Rd., Brom.	CH51	88
College Rd., Chsnt.	CC18	21
College Rd., Croy.	BZ55	87
College Rd., Enf.	BZ23	30
College Rd., Epsom	BO60	94
College Rd., Grav.	DD46	81
College Rd., Grays	DE42	71
College Rd., Guil.	AR71	118
College Rd., Harrow Weald	BH30	36
College Rd., Harrow on the Hill	BH32	45
College Rd., Hodd.	CD11	12
College Rd., Islw.	BH44	64
College Rd., Slou.	AM40	61
College Rd., St.Alb.	BJ14	9
College Rd., Swan.	CT51	89
College Rd., Wat.	BB19	17
College Rd., Wem.	BK33	45
College Rd., Wok.	AT61	100
College Slip, Brom.	CH51	88
College St. EC4	**BZ40**	**4**
College St. EC4	BZ40	57
College St., St.Alb.	BG13	9
College Ter. E3	CD38	57
College Ter. N3	BR30	37
Hendon La.		
College Vw. SE9	CJ47	78
College Way, Nthwd.	BA29	35
College Way, Welw.G.C.	BQ7	5
College Wk., Kings.T.	BL52	85
Grange Rd.		
Collent St. E9	CC36	57
Coller Cres., Dart.	CZ49	80
Colless Rd. N15	CA32	48
Collet Clo., Chsnt.	CC17	21
Collet Gdns., Chsnt.	CC17	21
Collet Clo.		
Collet Rd., Sev.	CW62	108
Collett Rd. SE16	CB41	67
Collett Rd., Hem.H.	AX13	8
Collett Way, Sthl.	BF41	64
Colley Hill La., Slou.	AP34	43
Colley La., Reig.	BR70	120
Colley La., Rick.	AU24	25
Colley Manor Dr., Reig.	BQ70	120
Colley Way, Reig.	BR69	120
Collier Clo., Epsom	BM57	94
Collier Cres., Dart.	CZ49	80
Collier Dr., Edg.	BM30	37
Collier Row La., Rom.	CR29	41
Collier Row Rd., Rom.	CQ30	41
Collier St. N1	**BX37**	**2**
Collier St. N1	BX37	56
Collier Way, Guil.	AU69	118
Colliers Clo., Wok.	AQ62	100
Colliers Shaw, Kes.	CJ56	97
Colliers St., Cat.	CB66	114
Colliers Water La., Th.Hth.	BY53	86
Collindale Av. NW9	BN31	46
Collindale Av., Sid.	CO47	79
Collingbourne Rd. W12	BP40	55
Collingham Gdns. SW5	**BS42**	**3**
Collingham Gdns. SW5	BS42	66
Collingham Pl. SW5	**BS42**	**3**
Collingham Pl. SW5	BS42	66
Collingham Rd. SW5	**BS42**	**3**
Collingham Rd. SW5	BS42	66
Collings Clo. N22	BX29	38
Whittington Rd.		
Collington Clo., Grav.	DF47	81
Beresford Rd.		
Collingtree Av., Surb.	BN54	85
Collingtree Rd. SE26	CC49	77
Collingwood Av. N10	BV31	47
Collingwood Clo., SE20	CB51	77
Jasmine Gro.		
Collingwood Clo., Twick.	BF46	74
Collingwood Cres., Guil.	AT70	118
Collingwood Est. E1	CB38	57
Collingwood Pl. SE18	CL41	68
Rodney St.		
Collingwood Pl., Walt.	BC55	83
Trafalgar Dr.		
Collingwood Rd. E17	CE32	48
Collingwood Rd. N15	CA31	48
Collingwood Rd., Mitch.	BU51	86
Collingwood Rd., Sutt.	BR55	85
Collingwood Rd., Uxb.	AZ38	53
Collingwood St. E1	CB38	57
Collins Av., Stan.	BL30	37
Collins Dr., Ruis.	BD34	45
Collins Meadow, Harl.	CL11	13
Collins Rd. N5	BZ35	48
Collins Sq. SE3	CG44	68
Tranquil Vale		
Collins St. SE3	CG44	68
Collins Yd. N1	BY37	2
Collinson St. SE1	**BZ41**	**4**
Collinson St. SE1	BZ41	67
Collinson Wk. SE1	BZ41	67
Scovell Rd.		
Collinwood Av., Enf.	CC24	30
Collinwood Gdns., Ilf.	CK32	49
Collis Alley, Twick.	BH47	74
Albion Rd.		
Colls Rd. SE15	CC44	67
Collum Green Rd., Slou.	AP34	43
Collyer Av., Croy.	BX56	95
Collyer Clo. N1	BX37	56
Eckford St.		
Collyer Pl. SE15	CA44	67
Peckham High St.		
Collyer Rd., Croy.	BX56	95
Collyer Rd., St.Alb.	BK17	18
Colman Clo., Epsom	BP62	103
Colman Rd. E16	CJ39	58
Colman St. E2	CB38	57
Colman Way, Red.	BU69	121
Colmar Clo. E1	CC38	57
Alderney Rd.		
Colmer Pl., Har.	BG29	36
Colmer Rd. SW16	BX51	86
Colmore Rd., Enf.	CC24	30
Colnbrook By-pass, Slou.	AU43	62
Colnbrook By-pass, West Dr.	AW43	63
Colnbrook St. SE1	**BY41**	**4**
Colnbrook St. SE1	BY41	66
Colndale Rd., Slou.	AV44	62
Colne Av., Rick.	AW27	35
Colne Av., Wat.	BC25	26
Colne Av., West Dr.	AX41	63
Colne Dr., Rom.	CW29	42
Colne Dr., Walt.	BD55	84
Colne Gdns., St.Alb.	BL17	19
Colne Mead, Rick.	AW27	35
Uxbridge Rd.		
Colne Orchard, Iver	AV39	52
Colne Rd. E5	CD35	48
Colne Rd. N21	BZ26	39
Colne Rd., Twick.	BH47	74
Colne St. E13	CH38	58
Colne St., Epsom	BN56	94
Colne Valley, Upmin.	CZ32	51
Colne Vw. Ter., St.Alb.	BL15	10
Colne Way, Hem.H.	AY11	8
Colne Way, Stai.	AT48	72
Colne Way, Wat.	BE22	27
Colnebridge Clo., Stai.	AV49	72
Clarence St.		
Colnedale Rd., Uxb.	AX35	44
Colney Hatch La. N10	BV29	38
Colney Hatch La. N11	BU29	38
Colney Heath La., St.Alb.	BL13	10
Colney Rd., Dart.	CW46	80
Cologne Rd. SW11	BT45	66
Colomb St. SE10	CG42	68
Colombo Rd., Ilf.	CM33	49
Colombo St. SE1	**BY40**	**4**
Colombo St. SE1	BY40	56
Colonels La., Cher.	AW53	83
Colonels Wk., Enf.	BY24	29
Colonial Av., Twick.	BG46	74
Colonial Rd., Felt.	BB47	73
Colonial Rd., Slou.	AQ41	62
Colonial Way, Wat.	BD23	27
Colonnade WC1	**BX38**	**2**
Colonnade WC1	BX38	56
Herbrand St.		
Colson Gdns., Loug.	CL24	31
Colson Path, Loug.	CL24	31
Colson Rd., Croy.	CA55	87
Colson Rd., Loug.	CL24	31
Colson Way SW16	BW49	76
Colsterworth Rd. N15	CA31	48
Colston Av., Cars.	BU56	95
Colston Cres., Chsnt.	BY17	20
Colston Ct., Cars.	BU56	95
Colston Rd. E7	CJ36	58
Colston Rd. SW14	BN45	65
Colt Hatch, Harl.	CL10	6
Coltishall Rd., Horn.	CV36	60
Coltness Cres. SE2	CO42	69
Colton Gdns. N17	BZ31	48
Coltsfoot Ct., Grays	DE43	71
Coltsfoot Dr., Guil.	AT69	118
Coltsfoot Path, Rom.	CV29	42
Coltsfoot, The, Hem.H.	AV14	7
The Foxgloves		
Columbia Av., Edg.	BM30	37
Columbia Av., Wor.Pk.	BO54	85
Columbia Ct., N.Mal.	BO54	85
Columbia Rd. E13	CG38	58
Columbia Rd. E2	**CA38**	**2**
Columbia Rd. E2	CA38	57
Columbia Sq. E2	**CA38**	**2**
Columbia Sq. SW14	BN45	65
Upper Richmond Rd.		
Columbia Wharf Rd., Grays	DD43	71
Columbine Av. E6	CK39	58
Columbine Av., Croy.	BY57	95
Columbine Way SE13	CF44	67
Columbine Way, Rom.	CW30	42
Columbus Sq., Erith	CU43	69
Frobisher Rd.		
Colvestone Cres. E8	CA35	48
Colville Est. N1	BZ37	57
Colville Gdns. W11	BR39	55
Colville Ho. W11	BR39	55
Colville Ms. W11	BR39	55
Colville Pl. W1	**BW39**	**1**
Colville Pl. W1	BW39	56
Colville Rd. E11	CF34	48
Colville Rd. E17	CD30	39
Colville Rd. N9	CB26	39
Colville Rd. W11	BR39	55
Colville Rd. W3	BM41	65
Colville Sq. Ms. W11	BR39	55
Portobello Rd.		
Colville Sq. W11	BR39	55
Colville Ter. W11	BR39	55
Colvin Clo. SE26	CC49	77
Lawrie Park Rd.		
Colvin Gdns. E11	CH31	49
Colvin Gdns. E4	CF27	39
Colvin Gdns., Ilf.	CM30	40
Colvin Gdns., Wal.Cr.	CC21	30
Colvin Rd. E6	CK36	58
Colvin Rd., Th.Hth.	BY53	86
Colvin St. W6	BQ42	65
Glenthorne Rd.		
Colwell Rd. SE22	CA46	77
Colwick Clo. N6	BW33	47
Colwith Rd. W6	BQ43	65
Colwood Gdns. SW19	BT50	76
Colworth Gro. SE17	**BZ42**	**4**
Colworth Gro. SE17	BZ42	67
Browning St.		
Colworth Rd. E11	CG32	49
Colworth Rd., Croy.	CB54	87
Colwyn Av., Grnf.	BH37	54
Colwyn Cres., Houns.	BG44	64
Colwyn Rd. NW2	BP34	46
Colyer Clo. SE9	CL48	78
Colyer Rd., Grav.	DE48	81
Colyers Clo., Erith	CS44	69
Colyers Clo., Welw.G.C.	BR5	5
Colyers La., Erith	CS44	69
Colyers Wk., Erith	CT44	69
Colyton Clo., Well.	CP44	69
Colyton Clo., Wem.	BK36	54
Colyton Clo., Wok.	AR62	100
Winnington Way		
Colyton Rd. SE22	CB46	77
Colyton Way N18	CB28	39
Combe Av. SE3	CG43	68
Combe Bank Dr., Sev.	CQ64	107
Combe La., Walt.	BB58	92
Combe Lea., Brom.	CK52	88
Combe Ms. SE3	CG43	68
Combe Rd. N16	CD35	48
Trumans Rd.		
Combe Rd., Wat.	BB25	26
Combe St., Hem.H.	AX13	8
Combe Way, Wey.	AY59	92
Combedale Rd. SE10	CH42	68
Combemartin Rd. SW18	BR47	75
Comber Clo. NW2	BP34	46
Comber Gro. SE5	BZ43	67
Combermere Rd. SW9	BX45	66

Com–Cop

Combermere Rd., Mord. BS53 86
Comberton Rd. E5 CB34 48
Comberton Wk. E12 CL35 49
Landseer Av.
Combeside SE18 CN43 68
Combwell Cres. SE2 CO41 69
Comely Bank Rd. E17 CE32 48
Comeragh Clo., Wok. AQ63 100
Comeragh Ms. W14 BR42 65
Comeragh Rd.
Comeragh Rd. W14 BR42 65
Comerford Rd. SE4 CD45 67
Comet Clo., Grays CX42 70
Chieftan Dr.
Comet Clo., Wat. BB20 17
Comet House Pl. SE8 CE43 67
Watsons St.
Comet Pl. SE8 CE43 67
Comet St.
Comet Rd., Hat. BO12 10
Comet St. SE8 CE43 67
Comforts Fm. Av., Oxt. CG70 115
Comfrey Ct., Grays DE43 71
Commerce Rd. N22 BX30 38
Commerce Rd., Brent. BK43 64
Commerce Way, Croy. BX55 86
Commercial Dock Pass. SE16 CD41 67
Commercial Rd. E1 CB39 2
Commercial Rd. E1 CB39 57
Commercial Rd. E14 CD39 57
Commercial Rd. N18 CA29 39
Commercial Rd., Guil. AR71 118
Commercial Rd., Stai. AW50 73
Commercial St. E1 CA38 2
Commercial St. E1 CA38 57
Commercial Way NW10 BM37 55
Commercial Way SE15 CA43 67
Commercial Way, Wok. AS62 100
Commerell Pl. SE10 CG42 68
Blackwall La.
Commerell St. SE10 CG42 68
Commodity Quay E1 CA40 4
Commodore St. E1 CD38 57
Common Clo., Wok. AR60 91
Common Grn., Berk. AT12 7
Common La., Dart. CU48 79
Common La., Esher BJ57 93
Common La., Eton AO42 61
Common La., Kings L. AY17 17
Common La., Red. BZ69 114
Common La., Wat. BH23 27
Common La., Wey. AX58 92
Common Meadow La., Wat. BG20 18
Common Rd. SW13 BP45 65
Common Rd., Brwd. DE28 122
Common Rd., Dor. BG70 119
Common Rd., Esher BJ57 93
Common Rd., Eton AN42 61
Common Rd., Lthd. BE64 102
Common Rd., Red. BU71 121
Common Rd., Rick. AU24 25
Common Rd., Sev. DA65 108
Common Rd., Slou. AT42 62
Common Rd., Stan. BG28 36
Common Rd., Wal.Abb. CJ14 13
Common Rd., Wind. AL42 61
Common Way, Esher BG58 93
Common, The W5 BL40 55
Common, The, Berk. AS12 7
Common, The, Hat. BP12 10
Common, The, Kings L. AW19 17
Common, The, Rich. BK48 74
Common, The, Stan. BH27 36
Common, The, Sthl. BD42 64
Commondale SW15 BQ45 65
Commonfield La. SW17 BU49 76
Commonfield Rd., Bans. BS60 95
Commonfields, Harl. CN10 6
Commongate Rd., Rick. AU25 25
Commons La., Hem.H. AY13 8
Commons, The, Welw.G.C. BS 9 5
Commonside E., Mitch. BV52 86
Commonside Rd., Harl. CN13 13
Commonside W., Mitch. BU52 86
Commonside, Epsom BM61 103
Commonside, Harl. CN13 13
Commonside, Kes. CJ56 97
Commonside, Lthd. BF65 102
Commonside, Mitch. BW53 86
Commonwealth Av. W12 BP40 55
Commonwealth Av., Hayes BA39 53
Commonwealth Rd. N17 CB29 39
Commonwealth Rd., Cat. CB65 105
Commonwealth Way SE2 CO42 69
Community Clo., Uxb. AZ34 44
Long La.
Community Rd. E15 CF35 48
Community Rd., Grnf. BG37 54
Como Rd. SE23 CD48 77
Como St., Rom. CS31 50
Compass Hill, Rich. BL46 75
Petersham Rd.
Compayne Gdns. NW6 BS36 56
Comport Grn., Croy. CG59 97
Compton Av. E6 CJ37 58
Compton Av. N1 BY36 56
Compton Av. N6 BU33 47
Compton Av., Brwd. DE26 122
Compton Av., Rom. CU31 50
Compton Clo. NW1 BV38 1
Compton Clo. NW1 BV38 56
Robert St.
Compton Clo. W13 BH39 54
Compton Clo., Edg. BM29 37
Pavilion Way
Compton Clo., Esher BG56 93
Compton Cres. N17 BZ29 39
Compton Cres. W4 BN43 65
Compton Cres., Chess. BL57 94
Compton Cres., Nthlt. BD37 54
Compton Ct. SE19 CA49 77
Compton Gdns., St.Alb. BF16 18
Faringford Clo.
Compton Pass. EC1 BY38 2
Compton Pass. EC1 BY38 56
Compton St.
Compton Pl., Erith CT43 69
Compton Pl., Wat. BE28 36
Compton Rd. N1 BY36 56
Compton Rd. N21 BY26 38
Compton Rd. NW10 BQ38 55
Compton Rd. SW19 BR50 75
Compton Rd., Croy. CB54 87
Compton Rd., Hayes BB40 53
Compton Ri., Pnr. BE32 45
Compton Sq. N1 BY36 56
Canonbury Rd.
Compton St. E13 CH37 58
Compton St. EC1 BY38 2
Compton St. EC1 BY38 56
Compton Ter. N1 BY36 56
Comreddy Clo., Enf. BY22 29
Comus Pl. SE17 BZ42 4
Comus Pl. SE17 CA42 67
Comyn Rd. SW11 BU45 66
Comyne Rd., Wat. BB21 26
Comyns Clo. E16 CG39 58
Comyns Rd., Dag. CR36 59
Comyns, The, Bush. BG26 36
Conant Ms. E1 CB39 57
Back Church La.
Conaways Clo., Epsom BP58 94
Concanon Rd. SW2 BX45 66
Concert Hall App. SE1 BX40 4
Concert Hall App. SE1 BX40 56
Concord Clo., Nthlt. BD38 54
Britannia Clo.
Concord Rd. W3 BM38 55
Concord Rd., Enf. CB25 30
Concorde Clo., Houns. BF44 64
Lampton Rd.
Concorde Clo., Uxb. AY37 53
Concorde Dr. E6 CK39 58
Viscount Dr.
Concorde Dr., Hem.H. AX13 8
Concorde Way, Slou. AO41 61
Concourse, The N9 CB27 39
Concourse, The NW9 BO30 37
Long Mead
Condell Rd. SW8 BW44 66
Conder St. E14 CD39 57
Conderton Rd. SE5 BZ45 67
Bredon Rd.
Condor Path, Nthlt. BF37 54
Leander Rd.
Condor Rd., Stai. AX52 83
Condor Wk., Rain. CU36 59
Heron Flight Av.
Condover Cres. SE18 CL43 68
Condray Pl. SW11 BT44 66
Battersea Church Rd.
Condray St. SW11 BT44 66
Conduit Ct. WC2 BX40 56
Long Acre
Conduit La. E., Hodd. CE12 12
Conduit La. N18 BZ28 39
Hermitage La.
Conduit La. W., Hodd. CE12 12
Conduit La., Enf. CC26 31
Conduit La., S.Croy. CA56 96
Conduit La., Slou. AS42 62
Conduit Ms. W2 BT39 1
Conduit Ms. W2 BT39 56
Conduit Pl. W2 BT39 1
Conduit Pl. W2 BT39 56
London St.
Conduit Rd. SE18 CL42 68
Conduit St. W1 BV40 3
Conduit St. W1 BV40 56
Conduit Way NW10 BN36 55
Conegar Ct., Slou. AP40 52
Conewood Pl. N5 BY34 47
Conewood St.
Conewood St. N5 BY34 47
Coney Acre SE21 BZ47 77
Coney Berry, Reig. BT72 121
Coney Burrows E4 CG27 40
Wyemead Cres.
Coney Clo., Hat. BP13 10
Coney Gree, Saw. CP 5 6
Coney Gro., Uxb. AZ38 53
Coney Hill Rd., W.Wick. CG55 88
Coneybury Clo., Warl. CB63 105
Coneybury, Red. CA70 114
Coneydale, Welw.G.C. BQ 7 7
Coneygrove Path, Nthlt. BE36 54
Arnold Rd.
Conference Clo. E4 CF27 39
Greenbank Clo.
Conference Rd. SE2 CP42 69
Conford Dr., Guil. AS74 118
Congeton Gro. SE18 CM42 68
Congo Rd. SE18 CM42 68
Congress Rd. SE2 CP42 69
Congreve Rd. SE9 CK45 68
Congreve St. SE17 CA42 4
Congreve St. SE17 CA42 67
Congreve Wk. E16 CJ39 58
Fulmer Rd.
Conical Cor., Enf. BZ23 30
Coniers Way, Guil. AT69 118
Conifer Av., Hart. DC53 90
Conifer Av., Rom. CR28 41
Conifer Clo., Orp. CM56 97
Beechcroft Rd.
Conifer Clo., Reig. BS69 121
Reigate Hill
Conifer Dr., Brwd. DB28 42
Conifer Gdns. SW16 BX48 76
Conifer Gdns., Enf. CA25 30
Conifer Gdns., Sutt. BS55 86
Ashleigh Gdns.
Conifer La., Egh. AU49 72
Conifer Way, Hayes BC40 53
Longmead Rd.
Conifer Way, Swan. CS51 89
Conifers Clo., Tedd. BJ50 74
Conifers, Tedd. BK50 74
Conifers, The, Hem.H. AV15 7
Conifers, Wey. BB56 92
Coniger Rd. SW6 BS44 66
Coningham Ms. W12 BP40 55
Percy Rd.
Coningham Rd. W12 BP40 55
Coningsby Bank, St.Alb. BG15 9
Coningsby Clo., Hat. BQ15 10
Coningsby Cott. W5 BK41 64
Coningsby Rd.
Coningsby Dr., Pot.B. BT20 20
Coningsby Dr., Wat. BB23 26
Coningsby Gdns. E4 CE29 39
Coningsby La., Maid. AH44 61
Coningsby Rd. N4 BY33 47
Coningsby Rd. W5 BK41 64
Coningsby Rd., S.Croy. BZ58 96
Conington Rd. SE13 CE44 67
Conisbee Ct. N14 BW25 29
Conisborough Cres. SE6 CF48 77
Coniscliffe Rd. N13 BZ27 39
Conista Ct., Wok. AP61 100
Coniston Av., Bark. CN36 58
Coniston Av., Grnf. BJ38 54
Coniston Av., Upmin. CY35 51
Coniston Av., Well. CN45 68
Coniston Clo. N20 BT27 38
Coniston Clo. SW13 BO44 65
Lonsdale Rd.
Coniston Clo. SW20 BQ55 85
Coniston Clo. W4 BN43 65
Coniston Clo., Bark. CN36 58
Coniston Av.
Coniston Clo., Bexh. CS44 69
Coniston Clo., Dart. CU47 79
Coniston Clo., Erith CT43 69
Coniston Clo., Hem.H. BA14 8
Coniston Clo., N.Mal. BQ53 85
Grand Dr.
Coniston Ct., Wall. BV56 95
Danbury Mews
Coniston Gdns. N9 CC26 39
Coniston Gdns. NW9 BN32 46
Coniston Gdns., Ilf. CK31 49
Coniston Gdns., Pnr. BC32 44
Coniston Gdns., Sutt. BT57 95
Coniston Gdns., Wem. BK33 45
Coniston Rd. N10 BV30 38
Coniston Rd. N17 CB29 39
Coniston Rd., Bexh. CS44 69
Coniston Rd., Brom. CF50 77
Coniston Rd., Couls. BW61 104
Coniston Rd., Croy. CB54 87
Coniston Rd., Kings L. AY17 17
Coniston Rd., Twick. BF46 74
Coniston Rd., Wok. AT63 100
Coniston Way N7 BX36 56
Coniston Way, Chess. BL55 85
Coniston Way, Egh. AT50 72
Coniston Way, Horn. CU35 50
Coniston Wk. E9 CC35 48
Churchill Wk.
Conistone Way N7 BX36 56
Sutterton St.
Conistone Way, Red. BU70 121
Conlan St. W10 BR38 55
Conley Rd. NW10 BO36 55
Conley St. SE10 CG42 68
Connaught App. E16 CJ39 58
Baxter Rd.
Connaught Av. E4 CF26 39
Connaught Av. SW14 BN45 65
Connaught Av., Ashf. AX49 73
Connaught Av., Barn. BU26 38
Connaught Av., Enf. CA23 30
Connaught Av., Grays DD41 71
Connaught Av., Houns. BE45 64
Connaught Av., Loug. CJ24 31
Connaught Clo. E10 CD34 48
Connaught Clo. W2 BU39 1
Connaught Clo. W2 BU39 56
Connaught St.
Connaught Clo., Enf. CA23 30
Connaught Clo., Hem.H. AZ12 8
Connaught Clo., Sutt. BT55 86
Connaught Clo., Uxb. BA38 53
Connaught Crossing E16 CJ40 58
Connaught Dr. NW11 BS31 47
Connaught Gdns. N10 BW32 47
Connaught Gdns. N13 BY28 38
Connaught Gdns., Mord. BT53 86
Connaught Hill, Loug. CJ24 31
Connaught La., Ilf. CM34 49
Connaught Ms. W2 BU39 1
Connaught Ms. W2 BU39 56
Connaught Pl.
Connaught Pl. W2 BU40 3
Connaught Pl. W2 BU40 56
Connaught Rd. E11 CF33 48
Connaught Rd. E16 CJ40 58
Connaught Rd. E17 CE32 48
Connaught Rd. E4 CG26 40
Springfield Rd.
Connaught Rd. N4 BY33 47
Connaught Rd. NW10 BO37 55
Connaught Rd. SE18 CL42 68
Connaught Rd. W13 BJ40 54
Connaught Rd., Barn. BQ25 28
Connaught Rd., Har. BH30 36
Connaught Rd., Horn. CV34 51
Connaught Rd., Ilf. CM34 49
Connaught Rd., N.Mal. BO52 85
Connaught Rd., Rich. BL46 75
Albert Rd.
Connaught Rd., Slou. AQ41 62
Connaught Rd., St.Alb. BG12 9
Connaught Rd., Sutt. BT55 86
Connaught Rd., Tedd. BG49 74
Connaught Sq. W2 BU39 1
Connaught Sq. W2 BU39 56
Connaught St. W2 BU39 1
Connaught St. W2 BU39 56
Connaught Way N13 BY28 38
Connell Cres. W5 BL38 55
Connemara Clo., B.Wd. BN25 28
Percheron Rd.
Connicut La., Lthd. BF67 111
Connington Cres. E4 CF27 39
Connolly Rd. W7 BH40 54
Connop Rd., Enf. CC22 30
Connor Rd., Dag. CQ35 50
Connor St. E9 CC37 57
Lauriston Rd.
Connors Alley W6 BR43 65
Bayonne Rd.
Conquest Rd., Wey. AW56 92
Conrad Clo., Grays DD41 71
Conrad Gdns.
Conrad Dr., Wor.Pk. BQ54 85
Conrad Gdns., Grays DD41 71
Conrad St. E9 CC36 57
Cons St. SE1 BY41 4
Cons St. SE1 BY41 66
Windmill Wk.
Consfield Av., N.Mal. BP52 85
Consort Clo., Brwd. DB28 42
Queen St.
Consort Ms., Islw. BG46 74
Consort Rd. SE15 CB44 67
Constable Clo. NW11 BS32 47
Constable Clo., Hayes BA37 53
Constable Cres. N15 CB32 48
Constable Gdns., Edg. BM30 37
Constable Gdns., Islw. BG46 74
Constable Rd., Grav. DF48 81
Constable Wk. SE21 CA48 77
Constance Cres., Brom. CG54 88
Constance Rd., Croy. BY54 86
Constance Rd., Enf. CA25 30
Constance Rd., Sutt. BT56 95
Constance Rd., Twick. BF47 74
Constance St. E16 CK40 58
Constantine Rd. NW3 BU35 47
Constitution Hill SW1 BV41 3
Constitution Hill SW1 BV41 66
Constitution Hill, Grav. DH47 81
Constitution Hill, Wok. AS63 100
Constitution Rise SE18 CL44 68
Consul Gdns., Swan. CU50 79
Princess Rd.
Content St. SE17 BZ42 4
Content St. SE17 BZ42 67
Contessa Clo., Orp. CM56 97
Control Tower Rd., Houns. AZ45 63
Chester Rd.
Convair Wk., Nthlt. BD38 54
Kittiwake Rd.
Convent Est. SE19 BZ50 77
Convent Gdns. W11 BR39 55
Convent Gdns. W5 BK42 64
Convent Hill SE19 BZ50 77
Convent La., Cob. BB59 92
Convent Rd., Ashf. AZ49 73
Convent Rd., Wind. AM44 61
Convent Way, Sthl. BD42 64
Conway Clo., Rain. CU36 59
Conway Clo., Stan. BJ29 36
Conway Cres., Grnf. BH37 54
Conway Cres., Rom. CP33 50
Conway Dr., Ashf. BA50 73
Conway Dr., Hayes BA41 63
Conway Dr., Sutt. BS57 95
Conway Gdns., Enf. CA22 30
Conway Gdns., Grays DD43 71
Conway Gdns., Mitch. BW52 86
Conway Gdns., Wem. BK33 45
Conway Gro. W3 BN39 55
Conway Rd. N14 BX27 38
Conway Rd. N15 BY32 47
Conway Rd. NW2 BQ34 46
Conway Rd. SE18 CM42 68
Conway Rd. SW20 BQ51 85
Conway Rd., Felt. BD49 74
Conway Rd., Heathrow AZ45 63
Conway Rd., Houns. BE47 74
Conway St. E13 CH38 58
Philip St.
Conway St. W1 BW38 1
Conway St. W1 BW38 56
Conway Wk., Hmptn. BE50 74
Fearnley Cres.
Conybeare NW3 BU36 56
Quickswood
Conybury Clo., Wal.Abb. CH19 22
Conyer St. E3 CD37 57
Conyerd Rd., Sev. DC63 108
Conyers Clo., Walt. BD56 93
Conyers Clo., Wdf.Grn. CG29 40
Conyers Rd. SW16 BW49 76
Conyers Way, Loug. CL24 31
Cooden Clo., Brom. CH50 78
Plaistow La.
Cook Sq., Erith CT43 69
Cookes Clo. E11 CG34 49
Cookes La., Sutt. BR57 94
Church Rd.
Cookham Cres. SE16 CC41 67
Marlow Way
Cookham Dene Clo., Chis. CM51 88
Cookham Hill, Orp. CR55 89
Cookham Rd., Sid. CR50 79
Cookhill Rd. SE2 CO41 69
Cooks Clo., Rom. CS30 41
Cooks Hole Rd., Enf. BY22 29
Cooks Mead, Bush. BF25 27
Cooks Rd. E15 CE37 57
Cooks Rd. SE17 BY43 66
Cooks Spinney, Harl. CO10 6
Cooks Vennel, Hem.H. AW12 8
Cool Oak La. NW9 BO33 46
Coolfin Rd. E16 CH39 58
Coolgardie Av. E4 CF28 39
Coolgardie Av., Chig. CL27 40
Coolgardie Rd., Ashf. BA49 73
Coolhurst Rd. N8 BW32 47
Coomassie Rd. W9 BR38 55
Bravington Rd.
Coombe Av., Croy. CA56 96
Coombe Av., Sev. CU63 107
Coombe Bank., Kings.T. BO51 8
Coombe Clo., Edg. BL30 3
Coombe Clo., Houns. BF45 6
Coombe Cor. N21 BY26 3
Coombe Cres., Hmptn. BE50 7
Coombe Dr., Ruis. BC34 4
Coombe Dr., Wey. AV57 9
Coombe End, Kings.T. BN50 7
Coombe Gdns. SW20 BP51 8
Coombe Gdns., Berk. AP12
Coombe Gdns., N.Mal. BO52 8
Coombe Hill Glade, Kings.T. BO50 7
Coombe Hill Rd., Kings.T. BO50 7
Coombe Hill Rd., Rick. AW26 3
Coombe House Chase, N.Mal. BN51 8
Coombe La. W., Kings.T. BM51 8
Coombe La., Croy. CB56 9
Coombe La., Guil. AO67 10
Coombe La., Guil. AO67 10
Coombe Lea, Brom. CK52 8
Coombe Moor, Kings.T. BO50 7
Coombe Neville, Kings.T. BN50 7
Coombe Pk., Kings.T. BN49 7
Coombe Rd. NW10 BN34 4
Coombe Rd. SE26 CB49 7
Coombe Rd. W13 BJ41 6
Northcroft Rd.
Coombe Rd. W4 BO42 6
Coombe Rd., Bush. BG26 3
Coombe Rd., Croy. BZ56 9
Coombe Rd., Grav. DH48 8
Coombe Rd., Hmptn. BE50 7
Coombe Rd., Kings.T. BM51 8
Coombe Rd., N.Mal. BO51 8
Coombe Rd., Rom. CW31 5
Coombe Rd., Sev. CV61 10
Coombe Ri., Brwd. DC26 12
Coombe Ri., Kings.T. BN51 8
Coombe Ridings, Kings.T. BN49 7
Coombe Vale, Ger.Cr. AS33 4
Coombe Way, Wey. AY59 9
Green La.
Coombe Wk., Sutt. BS55 8
Coombe Wood Hill, Pur. BZ59 9
Coombe Wood Rd., Kings.T. BN49 7
Coombe, The, Bet. BN69 12
Coombefield Clo., N.Mal. BO53 8
Coombehurst Clo., Barn. BU23 2
Coombelands La., Wey. AW57 9
Coomber Way, Croy. BW54 8
Coombermere Clo., Wind. AN44 6
Coombes Rd., Dag. CQ37 5
Coombes Rd., St.Alb. BK16 1
Coombewood Dr., Rom. CR32 5
Coombfield Dr., Dart. CZ49 8
Coombs St. N1 BY37 2
Coombs St. N1 BY37 56
Remington St.
Coomer Rd. SW6 BR43 6
Cooms Wk., Edg. BM30 3
East Rd.
Cooper Av. E17 CD30 3
Cooper Clo. SE1 BY41 4
Morley St.
Cooper Cres., Cars. BU55 8
Cooper Ct. E15 CE35 4
Holt Ct.
Cooper Rd. NW10 BP35 4
Cooper Rd., Croy. BY56 9
Cooper Rd., Guil. AS71 11
Cooper St. E16 CG39 5
Coopers Clo. E1 CC38 5
Coopers Clo., Chig. CO27 4
Coopers Clo., S.Dnth. CY51 9
Paddock Clo.
Coopers Clo., Stai. AV49 7
Coopers Green La., St.Alb. BL12 1
Coopers Green La., Welw.G.C. BN10
Coopers Hill La., Egh. AR49 7
Coopers Hill Rd., Red. BX70 12
Coopers Hill Rd., Red. BY73 12
Coopers Hill, Ong. CX18 2
Coopers La. E10 CE33 4
Coopers La. N1 BW37 5
Coopers La. NW1 BW37 1
Coopers La. Rd., Pot.B. BU19 2
Coopers La. SE12 CH48 7
Coopers La., Pot.B. BT19 2
Coopers La., Til. DH43 7
Coopers Rd. NW4 BQ32 4
Renters Av.
Coopers Rd. SE1 CA42 4
Coopers Rd. SE1 CA42 67
Coopers Rd., Grav. DF47 8
Coopers Rd., Pot.B. BT18 2
Coopers Row EC3 CA40 4
Coopers Row EC3 CA40 57
Coopers Row, Iver AU38 52
Coopers Wk., Chsnt. CC17 21
Coopersale Clo., Wdf.Grn. CJ29 4
Coopersale Common, Epp. CP17 2
Coopersale La., Epp. CO22 3
Coopersale Rd. E9 CC35 4
Coopersale Rd., Epp. CO18 2
Coopersale St., Epp. CP19 2
Coote Gdns., Dag. CQ34 5
Coote Rd., Bexh. CQ44 6
Coote Rd., Dag. CQ34 5
Cope Pl. W8 BS41 66
Cope St. SE16 CC42 67
Copeland Dr. E14 CE42 67
Barnsdale Av.
Copeland Rd. E17 CE32 4
Copeland Rd. SE15 CB44 67
Copeman Clo. SE26 CC49 77

Copeman Rd., Brwd. DE26 122
Copenhagen Pl. E14 CD39 57
Copenhagen St. N1 BX37 2
Copenhagen St. N1 BX37 56
Copenhagen Way, Walt. BC55 83
Copers Cope Rd., Beck. CD50 77
Copeswood Rd., Wat. BC23 26
Copford Clo., Wdf.Grn. CK29 40
Green Wk.
Copford Wk. N1 BZ37 57
Popham St.
Copinger Wk., Edg. BM30 37
North Rd.
Copland Av., Wem. BK35 45
Copland Clo., Wem. BK35 45
Copland Rd., Wem. BL36 55
Copleigh Dr., Tad. BR63 103
Copleston Pass. SE5 CA45 67
Ivanhoe Rd.
Copleston Rd. SE15 CA45 67
Copley Clo. SE17 BY43 66
Hillingdon St.
Copley Clo. W7 BH39 54
Copley Clo., Red. BU69 121
Copley Clo., Wok. AP63 100
Copley Dene, Brom. CJ51 88
Copley Pk. SW16 BX50 76
Copley Rd., Stan. BK28 36
Copley St. E1 CC39 57
Copley Way, Tad. BQ63 103
Copmans Wick, Rick. AU25 25
Copnor Way SE15 CA43 67
Hordle Promenade W.
Coppelia Rd. SE3 CG45 68
Coppen Rd., Dag. CQ33 50
Copper Beech Clo., Hem.H. AV15 7
Copper Beech Clo., Orp. CP53 89
Rookery Gdns.
Copper Beech Clo., Ilf. CL30 40
Copper Beech Gro., Wind. AL44 61
Copper Beech Rd., S.Ock. DB38 60
Copper Clo. SE1 BY41 4
Copper Clo. SE19 CA50 77
Copper Mill La. SW17 BT49 76
Copper Mill Rd., Stai. AT46 72
Copper Ridge, Ger.Cr. AS28 34
Copperas St. SE8 CE43 67
Copperbeech Clo. NW3 BT35 47
Akenside Rd.
Copperbeech Clo., Grav. DH47 81
Copperdale Rd., Hayes BC41 63
Silverdale Gdns.
Copperfield App., Chig. CM29 40
Copperfield Av., Uxb. AZ39 53
Copperfield Clo., S.Croy. BZ59 96
Copperfield Clo., Grav. DK47 81
Copperfield Ct., Lthd. BJ64 102
Kingston Rd.
Copperfield Gdns., Brwd. DA26 42
Copperfield Ms. N18 CA28 39
Copperfield Orchard, Sev. CW62 108
Copperfields
Copperfield Rd. E3 CD38 57
Copperfield Rd. SE28 CP39 59
Copperfield Ri., Wey. AV56 91
Copperfield St. SE1 BY41 4
Copperfield St. SE1 BY41 66
Copperfield Way, Chis. CM50 78
Dickens Dr.
Copperfield Way, Pnr. BE31 45
Copperfield, Chig. CM28 40
Copperfields Way, Rom. CV30 42
Copperfields Wk., Sev. CW62 108
Copperfields, Lthd. BG64 102
Copperfields, Sev. CW62 108
Copperfields, Welw.G.C. BT 8 5
Coppergate Clo., Brom. CH51 88
Coppermead Clo. NW2 BQ34 46
Coppermill La. E17 CC32 48
Coppermill La., Rick. AV29 34
Coppermill La., Uxb. AW29 35
Coppetts Clo. N12 BU29 38
Coppetts Rd. N10 BU29 38
Coppice Clo. SW20 BQ52 85
Coppice Clo., Guil. AO70 118
Coppice Clo., Hat. BO14 10
Coppice Clo., Ruis. BA32 44
Coppice Dr. SW15 BP46 75
Coppice Dr., Stai. AR47 72
Coppice Est., Brom. CL53 88
Coppice La., Reig. BR69 120
Coppice Path, Chig. CO28 41
Coppice Row, Epp. CM21 31
Coppice Wk. E18 CG31 49
Coppice Wk. N20 BS27 38
Coppice, The, Ashf. AZ50 73
School Rd.
Coppice, The, Beac. AO29 34
School La.
Coppice, The, Brwd. CZ21 33
Coppice, The, Enf. BY24 29
Coppice, The, Hem.H. AZ13 8
Coppice, The, Wat. BD25 27
Coppice, The, West Dr. AY39 53
Coppies Gro. N11 BV28 38
Copping Clo., Croy. CA56 96
Coppings, The, Hodd. CE10 12
Coppins Clo., Berk. AP13 7
Coppins La., Iver AV39 52
Coppins, The, Croy. CE57 96
Coppins, The, Har. BH29 36
Coppock Clo. SW11 BU44 66
Copse Av., W.Wick. CE55 87
Copse Bank, Sev. CW63 108
Copse Clo. SE7 CH43 68
Copse Clo., Guil. AU73 118
Copse Clo., Nthwd. BA30 35
Copse Clo., West Dr. AX41 63
Copse Edge Av., Epsom BO60 94
Copse Glade, Surb. BK54 84
Copse Hill, Pur. BX60 95
Copse Hill, Sutt. BS57 95
Copse Hill, SW20 BP51 85
Copse La., Beac. AP29 34
Copse Rd., Cob. BC60 92
Copse Rd., Red. BT71 121
Copse Rd., Wok. AP62 100
Copse Side, Hart. DC52 90
Copse Vw., S.Croy. CC58 96
Copse Wood Way, Nthwd. BA30 35
Copse Wood, Iver AU37 52
Copse, The E4 CG26 40
Copse, The, Amer. AO22 25
Copse, The, Cat. CB66 114
Copse, The, Hem.H. AV12 7
Copse, The, Lthd. BF65 102
Copsem Dr., Esher BG57 93
Copsem La., Esher BG57 93
Copsem La., Lthd. BG59 93
Copsleigh Av., Red. BV74 121
Copsleigh Clo., Red. BV73 121
Copsleigh Way, Red. BV73 121
Copt Hall Rd., Sev. DA65 108
Coptefield Dr., Belv. CP41 69
Coptfold Rd., Brwd. DB27 42
Copthall Av. EC2 BZ39 2
Copthall Av. EC2 BZ39 57
Copthall Bldgs, EC2 BZ39 57
Telegraph St.
Copthall Clo. EC2 BZ39 2
Copthall Clo. EC2 BZ39 57
Copthall Clo., Ger.Cr. AS29 34
Copthall Cor., Ger.Cr. AS29 34
Copthall Ct. EC2 BZ39 57
Throgmorton St.
Copthall Dr. NW7 BP29 37
Copthall Gdns. NW7 BP29 37
Copthall Gdns., Twick. BH47 74
Copthall La., Ger.Cr. AS29 34
Copthall Rd. E., Uxb. AZ34 44
Copthall Rd. W., Uxb. AZ34 44
Copthall Way, Wey. AV58 91
Copthill La., Tad. BR63 103
Copthorn Clo., Shep. BA53 83
Copthorne Av. SW12 BW47 76
Copthorne Av., Brom. CK55 88
Copthorne Av., Ilf. CL29 40
Copthorne Clo., Ashf. AY49 73
Ford Rd.
Copthorne Clo., Ilf. CL29 40
Copthorne Clo., Rick. AY25 26
Copthorne Gdns., Horn. CX32 51
Copthorne Ms., Hayes BB42 63
Copthorne Rd., Lthd. BJ63 102
Copthorne Rd., Rick. AY25 26
Copthorne Ri., S.Croy. BZ60 96
Copthorpe Ct. NW8 BT38 56
Maida Vale
Coptic St. WC1 BX39 2
Coptic St. WC1 BX39 56
Copwood Clo. N12 BT28 38
Coral Clo., Rom. CP31 50
Coral House, Harl. CL10 6
Coral Row SW18 BT45 66
Gartons Way
Coral St. SE1 BY41 4
Coral St. SE1 BY41 66
Coralline Wk. SE2 CP41 69
Coram Clo., Berk. AR13 7
Coram Grn., Brwd. DE25 122
Coram St. WC1 BX38 2
Coram St. WC1 BX38 56
Coran Clo. N9 CC26 39
Corban Rd., Houns. BF45 64
Corbar Clo., Barn. BT23 29
Corbet Clo., Wall. BV55 86
Corbet Pl. E1 CA39 2
Corbet Pl. E1 CA39 57
Calvin St.
Corbet Rd., Epsom BO58 94
Corbets Av., Upmin. CX35 51
Corbets Tey Rd., Upmin. CX35 51
Corbett Clo., Croy. CF59 96
Corbett Gro. N22 BX29 38
Corbett Rd. E11 CJ32 49
Corbett Rd. E17 CF31 48
Corbett Rd. N22 BX29 38
Trinity Rd.
Corbett St. SW8 BX43 66
Corbetts Pass. SE16 CC42 67
Rotherhithe New Rd.
Corbicum E11 CG33 49
Corbiere Ct. SW19 BQ50 75
Thornton Rd.
Corbins La., Har. BF34 45
Corbridge Cres. E2 CB37 57
Corby Clo., St.Alb. BF16 18
Corby Cres., Enf. BX24 29
Corby Dr., Egh. AR50 72
Corby Rd. NW10 BN37 55
Corby Way E3 CE38 57
Knapp Rd.
Corbylands Rd., Sid. CN47 78
Corbyn St. N4 BX33 47
Corcorans, Brwd. DA25 33
Elizabeth Rd.
Cord Way E14 CE41 67
Mellish St.
Cordelia Gdns., Stai. AY47 73
Cordelia Rd., Stai. AY47 73
Cordelia St. E14 CE39 57
Cordell Clo., Chsht. CD17 21
Corder Clo., St.Alb. BF15 9
Cording St. E14 CE39 57
Cordingley Rd., Ruis. BA34 44
Cordons Clo., Ger.Cr. AR30 34
Cordova Rd. E3 CD38 57
Cordrey Gdns., Couls. BX61 104
Cordwainers Wk. E13 CH37 58
Turpin Est.
Cordwell Rd. SE13 CF46 77
Corelli Rd. SE3 CK44 68
Corfe Av., Har. BF35 45
Corfe Clo., Ash. BK62 102
Corfe Gdns., Slou. AN40 61
Avebury
Corfield St. E2 CB38 57
Corfton Rd. W5 BL39 55
Coriander Cres., Guil. AQ68 109
Oregano Way
Corinium Clo., Wem. BL35 46
Corinium Gate, St.Alb. BF14 9
Corinne Rd. N19 BW35 47
Corinth Par., Hayes BB39 53
Corinth Rd. N7 BX35 47
Corinthian Manorway, Erith CS42 69
Corinthian Rd., Erith CS42 69
Corinthian Way, Stai. AX47 73
Clare Rd.
Cork Sq. E1 CB40 57
Cork St. W1 BW40 3
Cork St. W1 BW40 56
Corker Wk. N7 BX34 47
Corkers Path, Ilf. CM34 49
Corkran Rd., Surb. BK54 84
Corkscrew Hill, W.Wick. CF55 87
Corlett St. NW1 BU39 1
Corlett St. NW1 BU39 56
Bell St.
Cormongers La., Red. BW70 121
Cormont Rd. SE5 BY44 66
Cormorant Wk., Rain. CU36 59
Heron Flight Av.
Corn Croft, Hat. BP11 10
Corn Mead, Welw.G.C. BQ 6 5
Corn Mill Dr., Orp. CN54 88
Cornbury Rd., Edg. BK29 36
Cornelia St. N7 BX36 56
Cornell Clo., Sid. CQ50 79
Cornell Way, Rom. CR28 41
Corner Grn. SE3 CH45 68
Corner Hall, Hem.H. AX14 8
Corner House St. WC2 BX40 4
Craven St.
Corner Mead NW9 BO30 37
Corner St. E16 CH39 58
Beckton Rd.
Corner Vw., Hat. BQ15 10
Dixons Hill Vw.
Cornerfield, Hat. BP11 10
Cornerhall Av., Hem.H. AX14 8
Corners, Welw.G.C. BS 7 5
Cornerside, Ashf. BA50 73
Corney Rd. W4 BO43 65
Cornfield Clo., Uxb. AX37 53
Cornfield Rd., Bush. BF24 27
Cornfield Rd., Reig. BT71 121
Cornfields, Hem.H. AW14 8
Cornflower La., Croy. CC54 87
Cornflower Ter. SE22 CB46 77
Cornflower Way, Rom. CW30 42
Cornford Clo., Brom. CH53 88
Cornford Gro. SW12 BV48 76
Cornhill Clo., Wey. AW55 83
Cornhill EC3 BZ39 2
Cornhill EC3 BZ39 57
Cornish Gro. SE20 CV51 87
Cornmill La. SE13 CF45 67
Cornmill, Wal.Abb. CE20 21
Cornshaw Rd., Dag. CP33 50
Cornsland, Brwd. DB27 42
Cornthwaite Rd. E5 CC34 48
Cornwall Av. E2 CC38 57
Cornwall Av. N22 BX30 38
Cornwall Av. N3 BS29 38
Cornwall Av., Esher BJ57 93
Cornwall Av., Sthl. BE39 54
Cornwall Av., Well. CN45 68
Cornwall Av., Wey. AY60 92
Cornwall Clo., Bark. CN36 58
Cornwall Clo., Eton AM42 61
Cornwall Clo., Horn. CX31 51
Cornwall Clo., Wal.Cr. CD20 21
Cornwall Cres. W11 BR40 55
Cornwall Dr., Orp. CP50 79
Cornwall Gate, Grays CX42 70
Water La.
Cornwall Gdns. Ms. SW7 BS41 66
Cornwall Gdns. NW10 BP36 55
Cornwall Gdns. SW7 BS41 3
Cornwall Gdns. SW7 BS41 66
Cornwall Gdns. Wk. SW7 BS41 3
Cornwall Gro. W4 BO42 65
Cornwall Lo., Kings.T. BM50 75
Cornwall Ms. S. SW7 BS41 3
Cornwall Ms. W. SW7 BS41 3
Cornwall Gdns.
Cornwall Rd. N15 BZ32 48
Cornwall Rd. N18 CB28 39
Cornwall Rd. N4 BY33 47
Cornwall Rd. SE1 BY40 4
Cornwall Rd. SE1 BY40 56
Cornwall Rd., Brwd. DA25 33
Cornwall Rd., Croy. BY55 86
Cornwall Rd., Har. BG32 45
Cornwall Rd., Pnr. BE29 36
Cornwall Rd., Ruis. BB34 44
Cornwall Rd., St.Alb. BH14 9
Cornwall Rd., Sutt. BS58 95
Cornwall Rd., Twick. BJ47 74
Cornwall Rd., Uxb. AX36 53
Cornwall St. E1 CB39 57
Watney St.
Cornwall Ter. NW1 BU38 1
Cornwall Ter. NW1 BU38 56
Cornwall Way, Stai. AV50 72
Cornwallis Av. N9 CB27 39
Cornwallis Av. SE9 CM48 78
Cornwallis Clo., Erith CU43 69
Frobisher Rd.
Cornwallis Gro. N9 CB27 39
Cornwallis Rd. E17 CC31 48
Cornwallis Rd. N19 BX34 47
Cornwallis Rd. N9 CB27 39
Cornwallis Rd., Dag. CP35 50
Cornwallis Wk. SE9 CK45 68
Cornwell Av., Grav. DH48 81
Cornwell Rd., Wind. AQ46 72
Cornwood Clo. N2 BT32 47
Cornwood Dr. E1 CC39 57
Cornworthy Rd., Dag. CP35 50
Corona Rd. SE12 CH47 78
Coronation Av., Slou. AS39 52
Coronation Av., Wind. AQ44 62
Coronation Clo., Bex. CP46 79
Coronation Clo., Ilf. CM31 49
Coronation Cres., Grays DG41 71
Loewen Rd.
Coronation Dr., Horn. CU35 50
Coronation Hill, Epp. CN18 22
Coronation Rd. E13 CJ38 58
Coronation Rd. Hayes BB42 63
Coronation Rd. NW10 BL38 55
Coronation Ter., West. CK62 106
Coronation Wk., Twick. BF47 74
Coroners Ct. W6 BQ42 65
Coronet St. N1 BA38 2
Coronet St. N1 CA38 57
Corporation Av., Houns. BE45 64
Corporation Row EC1 BY38 2
Corporation Row EC1 BY38 56
Corporation St. E15 CG37 58
Corporation St. N7 BX35 47
Corral Gdns., Hem.H. AY13 8
Corrall Rd. N7 BX36 56
Lough Rd.
Corran Way, S.Ock. DA40 60
Corrance Rd. SW2 BX45 66
Corri Av. N14 BW28 38
Corrib Dr., Cars. BU56 95
Corrie Gdns., Vir.W. AR54 82
Corrie Rd., Wey. AX56 92
Corrie Rd., Wok. AT63 100
Corrigan Av., Couls. BV61 104
Corringham Ct. NW11 BS33 47
Corringham Ct. St.Alb. BH13 9
Lemsford Rd.
Corringham Rd. NW11 BS33 47
Corringham Rd., Wem. BM34 46
Corrington Ms. W11 BR40 55
Blenheim Cres.
Corringway NW11 BS33 47
Corringway W5 BL39 55
Corsair Clo., Stai. AX47 73
Corsair Rd., Stai. AX47 73
Corscoombe Clo., Kings.T. BN49 75
Corsehill St. SW16 BW50 76
Corseley Way E9 CD36 57
Trowbridge Est.
Corsham St. N1 BZ38 2
Corsham St. N1 BZ38 57
Corsica St. N5 BY36 56
Cortayne Rd. SW6 BR44 65
Cortis Rd. SW15 BP46 75
Cortis Ter. SW15 BP46 75
Corunna Rd. SW8 BW44 66
Corunna Ter. SW8 BW44 66
Corve La., S.Ock. DA40 60
Corwell Gdns., Uxb. BA39 53
Corwell La., Uxb. BA39 53
Corwood Dr. E1 CC39 57
Cory Dr., Brwd. DD26 122
Coryton Path W9 BR38 55
Ashmore Rd.
Cosbycote Av. SE24 BZ46 77
Cosdach Av., Wall. BW57 95
Cosedge Cres., Croy. BY56 95
Cosgrove Clo. N21 BZ27 39
Cosgrove Clo., Hayes BD38 54
Kingsash Dr.
Cosmo Pl. WC1 BX39 2
Cosmo Pl. WC1 BX39 56
Southampton Row
Cosmur Clo. W12 BO41 65
Cossall Wk. SE15 CB44 67
Cosser St. SE1 BY41 4
Cosser St. SE1 BY41 66
Costa St. SE15 CB44 67
Costan Clo. SE4 CC45 67
Hainsford Clo.
Costead Manor Rd., Brwd. DA26 42
Costells Meadow, West. CM66 115
Coston Wk. SE4 CD45 67
Frendsbury Rd.
Costons Av., Grnf. BG38 54
Costons La., Grnf. BG38 54
Cosway St. NW1 BU39 1
Cosway St. NW1 BU39 56
Cotall St. E14 CE39 57
Coteford Clo., Loug. CL23 31
Coteford Clo., Pnr. BC32 44
Coteford St. SW17 BU49 76
Cotelands, Croy. CA55 87
Cotesbach Rd. E5 CC34 48
Cotesmore Gdns., Dag. CP35 50
Cotesmore Rd., Hem.H. AV14 7
Cotford Rd., Th.Hth. BZ52 87
Cotham St. SE17 BZ42 4
Cotham St. SE17 BZ42 67
Cotherstone Rd. SW2 BX47 76
Cotherstone, Epsom BN58 94
Cremorne Gdns.
Cotlandswick, St.Alb. BK16 18
Cotleigh Av., Bex. CP48 79
Cotleigh Rd. NW6 BS36 56
Cotleigh Rd., Rom. CS32 50
Cotman Clo. NW11 BT32 47
Cotman Clo. SW15 BQ46 75
Cotman Gdns., Edg. BM30 37
Cotmandene Cres., Orp. CO51 89
Cotmans Ash La., Sev. CX60 99
Cotmans Clo., Hayes BC40 53
Coton Rd., Well. CO45 69
Cotsford Av., N.Mal. BN53 85
Cotswold Av., Bush. BG25 27
Cotswold Clo., Bexh. CT44 69
Cotswold Clo., Kings.T. BN50 75
Cotswold Clo., Slou. AN41 61
Cotswold Clo., St.Alb. BK11 9
Chiltern Rd.
Cotswold Clo., Stai. AW49 73
Cotswold Clo., Uxb. AX37 53
Cotswold Gate NW2 BQ34 46
Cotswold Gdns.
Cotswold Gdns. E6 CJ38 58
Cotswold Gdns. NW2 BQ34 46
Cotswold Gdns., Brwd. DF26 122
Cotswold Gdns., Ilf. CM33 49
Cotswold Grn., Enf. BX24 29
Cotswold Way
Cotswold Ms. SW11 BT44 66
Battersea High St.
Cotswold Rd., Grav. DF48 81
Cotswold Rd., Hmptn. BF49 74
Cotswold Rd., Rom. CW30 42
Cotswold Rd., Sutt. BS58 95
Cotswold Ri., Orp. CN53 89
Cotswold St. SE27 BY49 76
Cotswold Way, Enf. BX24 29
Cotswold, Hem.H. AY12 8
Mendip Way
Cotswolds, Hat. BP13 10
Cottage Av., Brom. CK54 88
Cottage Clo., Cher. AU57 91
Cottage Clo., Ruis. BA33 44
Cottage Farm Way, Egh. AU52 82
Cottage Field Clo., Sid. CP47 79
Cottage Grn. SE5 BZ43 67
Cottage Gro. SE5 BZ43 67
Cottage Gro. SW9 BX45 66
Cottage Gro., Surb. BK53 84
Cottage Park Rd., Slou. AO34 43
Cottage Pl. SW3 BU41 3
Cottage Pl. SW3 BU41 66
Cottage Rd., Epsom BN57 94
Cottage St. E14 CE40 57
Cottage Wk. N16 CA34 48
Smalley Rd.
Cottage Wk. SE15 CA44 67
Sumner Est.
Cottage Wk. SW1 BU41 3
Cottage Wk. SW1 BU41 66
Cottage, The, Surb. BK54 84
Cottages, The, St.Alb. BH14 9
Cottenham Dr. SW20 BP50 75
Cottenham Par. SW20 BP51 85
Durham Rd.
Cottenham Pk. Rd. SW20 BP51 85
Cottenham Pl. SW20 BP50 75
Cottenham Rd. E17 CD31 48
Cotterells Hill, Hem.H. AX13 8
Cotterells, Hem.H. AX13 8
Cotterill Rd., Surb. BL55 85
Cottesbrook St. SE14 CD43 67
Nynehead St.
Cottesbrooke Clo., Slou. AU44 62
Cottesmore Av., Ilf. CL30 40
Cottesmore Gdns. W8 BS41 3
Cottesmore Gdns. W8 BS41 66
Cottimore Av., Walt. BC54 83
Cottimore Cres., Walt. BC54 83
Cottimore La., Walt. BC54 83
Cottimore Ter., Walt. BC54 83
Cottingham Chase, Ruis. BC34 44
Cottingham Rd. SE20 CC50 77
Cottingham Rd. SW8 BX43 66
Cottington Clo. SE11 BY42 4
Cottington Clo. SE11 BY42 66
Cottington Rd., Felt. BD49 74
Cottington St. SE11 BY42 4
Cottington St. SE11 BY42 66
Cotton Av. W3 BN39 55
Cotton Field, Hat. BP11 10
Cotton Hill, Brom. CF49 77
Cotton La., Green. CY46 80
Cotton Rd., Pot.B. BT19 20
Cotton Row SW18 BT45 66
York Pl.
Cotton St. E14 CF40 57
Cottongrass Clo., Croy. CC54 87
Cornflower La.
Cottonmill Cres., St.Alb. BG14 9
Cottonmill La., St.Alb. BG14 9
Cottons App., Rom. CS32 50
Pettley Gdns.
Cottons Gdns. E2 CA38 2
Cottons Gdns. E2 CA38 57
Hackney Rd.
Cottons La. SE1 BZ40 4
Cottons La. SE1 BZ40 57
Cottrill Rd. E8 CB36 57
Cotts Wood Dr., Guil. AT68 109
Couchmore Av., Esher BH55 84
Couchmore Av., Ilf. CK30 40
Coulgate St. SE4 CD45 67
Coulsdon Court Rd., Couls. BX61 104
Coulsdon La., Couls. BU63 104
Coulsdon Rd., Cat. BZ64 105
Coulsdon Rd., Couls. BX61 104
Coulsdon Ri., Couls. BX62 104
Coulser Clo., Hem.H. AW12 8
Coulson Clo., Dag. CP33 50
Gibson Rd.
Coulson St. SW3 BU42 3
Coulson St. SW3 BU42 66
Coulter Clo., Cuff. BW17 20
Coulter Clo., Hayes BE38 54
Berrydale Rd.
Coulter Rd. W6 BP41 65
Coulton Av., Grav. DF47 81
Council Av., Grav. DE46 81
Councillor St. SE5 BZ43 67
Counter St. SE1 CA40 4
Counter St. SE1 CA40 57
Counters Clo., Hem.H. AW13 8
Countess Clo., Uxb. AX30 35
Countess Rd. NW5 BW35 47
Countisbury Av., Enf. CA26 39
Countisbury Gdns., Wey. AW56 92
Addlestone Pk.
Country Way, Felt. BC50 73
County Gate SE9 CM48 78
County Gate, Barn. BS25 29
County Gdns., Bark. CN37 58
County Gro. SE5 BZ44 67
County Rd. E6 CL39 58
County Rd., Th.Hth. BY51 86
County St. SE1 BZ41 4
County St. SE1 BZ41 67
Coupland Pl. SE18 CM42 68

Courage Clo., Horn. CV32 51
Courage Wk., Brwd. DE25 122
Courcy Rd. N8 BY31 47
Courland Gro. SW8 BW44 66
Courland Rd., Wey. AW55 83
Courland St. SW8 BW44 66
Course, The SE9 CL48 78
Coursers Rd., St.Alb. BM17 19
Court Av., Belv. CQ42 69
Court Av., Couls. BY63 104
Court Av., Rom. CX29 42
Court Bushes Rd., Whyt. CB63 105
Court Clo., Har. BL31 46
Court Clo., Maid. AH42 61
Court Clo., Twick. BF48 74
Court Clo., Wall. BW57 95
Court Close Av., Twick. BF48 74
Court Cres., Chess. BK57 93
Court Cres., Slou. AO39 52
Court Downs Rd., Beck. CE51 87
Court Dr., Croy. BX56 95
Court Dr., Stan. BL28 37
Court Dr., Sutt. BU56 95
Court Dr., Uxb. AY37 53
Court Farm Av., Epsom BN56 94
Court Farm Rd. SE9 CK48 78
Court Farm Rd., Nthlt. BF36 54
Court Farm Rd., Warl. CB62 105
Court Green Heights, Wok. AR63 100
Fern Hill La.
Court Haw, Bans. BU61 104
Court Hill, Couls. BU62 104
Court Hill, S.Croy. CA59 96
Court House Gdns. N3 BS29 38
Court House Rd. N12 BS29 38
Court La. Gdns. SE21 CA47 77
Court La. SE21 CA46 77
Court La., Epsom BN60 94
Court La., Epsom BN60 94
West Hill
Court La., Iver AW40 53
Court La., Wind. AK41 61
Court Leas, Cob. BF60 93
Court Mead, Nthlt. BE38 54
Court Par., Wem. BJ34 45
Court Rd. SE25 CA51 87
Court Rd. SE9 CK48 78
Court Rd., Bans. BS61 104
Court Rd., Cat. BZ65 105
Court Rd., Dart. CZ49 80
Court Rd., Gdse. CC69 114
Court Rd., Orp. CO55 89
Court Rd., Sthl. BE42 64
Court Rd., Uxb. AZ35 44
Court Side N8 BW32 47
Court Side SE26 CC48 77
Round Hill
Court St. E1 CB39 57
Durward St.
Court St., Brom. CH51 88
South St.
Court Way NW9 BO31 46
Court Way W3 BN39 55
Court Way, Ilf. CM31 49
Court Way, Rom. CW30 42
Court Way, Twick. BH47 74
Court Wood Dr., Sev. CU65 107
Court Yard SE9 CK46 78
Court, The, Ruis. BE35 45
Court, The, Warl. CD62 105
Courtauld Clo. SE28 CO40 59
Pitfield Cres.
Courtauld Rd. N19 BW33 47
Courtaulds, Kings L. AW18 17
Courtenay Av. N6 BU33 47
Courtenay Av., Har. BG29 36
Courtenay Gdns., Har. BG30 36
Courtenay Gdns., Upmin. CY33 51
Courtenay Ms. E17 CD32 48
Courtenay Pl.
Courtenay Ms., Wok. AT61 100
North Rd.
Courtenay Pl. E17 CD32 48
Courtenay Rd. E11 CG34 49
Courtenay Rd. E17 CC31 48
Courtenay Rd., SE20 CC50 77
Courtenay Rd., Wok. AT61 100
Courtenay Rd., Wor.Pk. BQ55 85
Courtenay Sq. SE11 BY42 66
Courtenay St.
Courtenay St. SE11 BX42 4
Courtenay St. SE11 BY42 66
Courtfield Av., Har. BH32 45
Courtfield Cres., Har. BH32 45
Courtfield Gdns. SW5 BS42 3
Courtfield Gdns. SW5 BS42 66
Courtfield Gdns. W13 BJ39 54
Courtfield Gdns., Ruis. BB34 44
Courtfield Gdns., Uxb. AW34 44
Courtfield Ms. SW7 BT42 3
Courtfield Ms. SW7 BT42 66
Courtfield Rd. SW7 BS42 3
Courtfield Rd. SW7 BT42 66
Courtfield Rd., Ashf. AZ50 73
Courtfield Rise, W.Wick. CF55 87
Courthill Rd. SE13 CF45 67
Courthope Rd. NW3 BU35 47
Courthope Rd. SW19 BR49 75
Courthope Rd., Grnf. BG37 54
Courthope Vill. SW19 BR50 75
Courtland Av. E4 CG27 40
Courtland Av. NW7 BN27 37
Courtland Av., Ilf. CK34 49
Courtland Dr., Chig. CL27 40
Courtland Gro. SE28 CP40 59
Courtland Rd. E6 CK37 58
Harrow Rd.
Courtlands Av. Est. SE12 CH46 78
Courtlands Av. SE12 CH46 78
Courtlands Av. SW16 BX50 76
Courtlands Av., Brom. CG54 88
Courtlands Av., Esher BE57 93
Courtlands Av., Hmptn. BE50 74
Courtlands Av., Rich. BM44 65
Courtlands Av., Slou. AR42 62
Courtlands Clo., S.Croy. CA58 96
Courtlands Clo., Ruis. BB32 44
Courtlands Cres., Bans. BS61 104
Courtlands Dr., Epsom BO57 94
Courtlands Dr., Wat. BB22 26
Courtlands Rd., Surb. BM54 85
Courtlands, Rich. BM46 75
Courtleet Dr., Erith CR44 69
Alberta Rd.
Courtleigh Av., Barn. BT22 29
Courtleigh Gdns. NW11 BR31 46
Courtman Rd. N17 BZ29 39
Courtmead Clo. SE24 BZ46 77
Courtnell St. W2 BS39 56
Courtney Clo. SE19 CA50 77
Courtney Cres., Cars. BU57 95
Courtney Dr., Beck. CF51 87
Courtney Pl., Croy. BY55 86
Courtney Rd. N7 BY35 47
Courtney Rd. SW19 BU50 76
Courtney Rd., Croy. BY55 86
Courtney Rd., Grays DH41 71
Courtney Rd., Houns. AZ45 63
Courtney Way, Houns. AZ45 63
Courtney Rd.
Courtrai Rd. SE23 CD46 77
Courts, The SW16 BX50 76
Courtway, The, Wat. BE27 36
Courtway, Wdf.Grn. CJ28 40
Courtwood La., Croy. CD59 96
Courtyard, The N1 BY36 56
Barnsbury Ter.
Courtyards, The, Slou. AS41 62
Waterside Dr.
Cousin La. EC4 BZ40 4
Cousin La. EC4 BZ40 57
Cousins Clo., West Dr. AY40 53
Milburn Dr.
Couthurst Rd. SE3 CH43 68
Coutts Av., Chess. BL56 94
Coutts Cres. NW5 BV34 47
St. Albans Rd.
Coval Gdns. SW14 BM45 65
Coval La. SW14 BM45 65
Coval Pass. SW14 BN45 65
Upper Richmond Rd.
Coval Rd. SW14 BN45 65
Coveham Cres., Cob. BC60 92
Covenbrook, Brwd. DD27 122
Covent Gdn. WC2 BX40 4
Covent Gdn. WC2 BX40 56
Coventry Clo. E6 CK39 58
Harper Rd.
Coventry Clo. NW6 BS37 56
Coventry Cross Est. E3 CF38 57
Coventry Rd. E1 CB38 57
Coventry Rd. E2 CB38 57
Coventry Rd. SE25 CB52 87
Coventry Rd., Ilf. CL34 49
Coventry St. W1 BW40 3
Coventry St. W1 BW40 56
Coverack Clo. N14 BV25 29
Coverack Clo., Croy. CD54 87
Coverdale Clo., Stan. BJ28 36
Coverdale Gdns., Croy. CB55 87
Park Hill Rise
Coverdale Rd. NW2 BQ36 55
Coverdale Rd. W12 BP41 65
Coverdale, Hem.H. AY12 8
Coverdales, The, Bark. CM37 58
Coverley Clo. E1 CB39 2
Coverley Clo. E1 CB39 57
Coverley Clo., Brwd. DA28 42
Covert Clo., Berk. AO12 7
Covert Rd., Berk. AO11 7
Covert Rd., Chig. CN28 40
Covert Way, Barn. BT23 29
Covert, The, Nthwd. BA30 35
Covert, The, Orp. CN53 88
Coverton Rd. SW17 BU49 76
Coverts Rd., Lthd. BH58 93
Coverts, The, Brwd. DD26 122
Covington Gdns. SW16 BY50 76
Covington Way SW16 BX50 76
Cow La., Grnf. BG37 54
Cow La., Wat. BD21 27
Cowan Clo. E6 CK39 58
Oliver Gdns.
Cowbridge La., Bark. CL36 58
Cowbridge Rd., Har. BL31 46
Cowcross St. EC1 BY39 2
Cowcross St. EC1 BY39 56
Cowden Rd., Orp. CN54 88
Cowden St. SE6 CE49 77
Cowdenbeath Path N1 BX37 2
Cowdenbeath Path N1 BX37 56
Bemerton St.
Cowdray Rd., Uxb. BA37 53
Cowdray Way, Horn. CU35 50
Cowdrey Clo., Enf. CA23 30
Cowdrey Ct., Dart. CU47 79
Cowdrey Rd. SW19 BS49 76
Cowdry Rd. E9 CD36 57
Cowen Av., Har. BG34 45
Cowgate Rd., Grnf. BG37 54
Cowick Rd. SW17 BU49 76
Cowings Mead, Nthlt. BE36 54
Arnold Rd.
Cowland Av., Enf. CC24 30
Cowleaze Rd., Kings.T. BL51 85
Cowles, Chsnt. CA17 21
Cowley Av., Cher. AV54 82
Cowley Clo., S.Croy. CC58 96
Cowley Cres., Uxb. AX39 53
Cowley Cres., Walt. BD56 93
Cowley Hill, B.Wd. BM22 28
Cowley La. E11 CG34 49
Cathall Rd.
Cowley La., Cher. AV54 82
Cowley Mill Rd., Uxb. AW37 53
Cowley Rd. E11 CH32 49
Cowley Rd. SW14 BO45 65
Cowley Rd. SW9 BY44 66
Cowley Rd. W3 BO40 55
Cowley Rd., Ilf. CK33 49
Cowley Rd., Rom. CU29 41
Cowley Rd., Uxb. AX38 53
Cowley St. SW1 BX41 4
Cowley St. SW1 BX41 66
Little College St.
Cowling Clo. W11 BR40 55
Wilsham St.
Cowper Av. E6 CK36 58
Cowper Av., Sutt. BT56 95
Cowper Av., Til. DG44 71
Cowper Clo., Cher. AV53 82
Cowper Clo., Well. CO46 79
Cowper Ct., Wat. BC22 26
Cowper Gdns. N14 BV25 29
Cowper Gdns., Wall. BW57 95
Cowper Pl. EC2 BZ38 2
Cowper Rd. N14 BV26 38
Cowper Rd. N16 CA35 48
Cowper Rd. N18 CB28 39
Cowper Rd. SW19 BT50 76
Cowper Rd. W3 BN40 55
Cowper Rd. W7 BH40 54
Cowper Rd., Belv. CQ42 69
Cowper Rd., Berk. AQ13 7
Cowper Rd., Brom. CJ52 88
Cowper Rd., Hem.H. AW14 8
Cowper Rd., Kings.T. BL49 75
Cowper Rd., Rain. CU38 59
Cowper Rd., Welw.G.C. BR 9 5
Cowper St. EC2 BZ38 2
Cowper St. EC2 BZ38 57
Cowper Ter. W10 BQ39 55
St. Marks Rd.
Cowslip Clo., Uxb. AY36 53
Hyacinth Dr.
Cowslip La., Wok. AQ60 91
Cowslip Rd., E18 CH30 40
Cowslips, Welw.G.C. BT 8 5
Cowthorpe Rd. SW8 BW44 66
Cox La., Chess. BL56 94
Cox La., Epsom BM56 94
Coxdean, Epsom BQ63 103
Coxfield Clo., Hem.H. AY13 8
Coxley Rise, Pur. BZ60 96
Coxmount Rd. SE7 CJ42 68
Coxs La., Wok. AS64 100
Coxs Wk. SE21 CB47 77
Coxson Pl. SE1 CA41 4
Coxson Pl. SE1 CA41 67
Coxtie Green Rd., Brwd. CW25 33
Coxwell Rd. SE18 CM42 68
Coxwell Rd. SE19 CA50 77
Coxwold Path, Chess. BL57 94
Cozens La. E., Brox. CD14 12
Cozens La. W., Brox. CD14 12
Crab Hill La., Red. BX72 121
Crab Hill, Beck. CF50 77
Crab La., Wat. BF21 27
Crabbe Cres., Chess. AO18 16
Crabbs Croft Clo., Orp. CM56 97
Ladycroft Way
Crabtree Av., Rom. CP31 50
Crabtree Av., Wem. BL37 55
Crabtree Clo., Bush. BF25 27
Crabtree Clo., Hem.H. AX14 8
Crabtree Clo., Lthd. BG66 111
Crabtree Ct. E15 CE35 48
Crabtree Dr., Lthd. BK66 111
Crabtree La. SW6 BQ43 65
Crabtree La., Dor. BJ68 111
Crabtree La., Hem.H. AX14 8
Crabtree La., Lthd. BF66 111
Crabtree Manorway N. Belv. CS40 59
Crabtree Manorway S., Belv. CS41 69
Crabtree Rd., Egh. AU51 82
Crabtree Wk. SE15 CA44 67
Crabtree Wk., Croy. CA54 87
Addiscombe Rd.
Crace St. NW1 BW38 56
Drummond Cres.
Crackley Meadow, Hem.H. AZ11 8
Craddock Rd., Enf. CA24 30
Craddock St. NW5 BV36 56
Prince of Wales Rd.
Craddocks Av., Ash. BL62 103
Cradhurst Clo., Dor. BG72 119
Cradley Rd. SE9 CM47 78
Cragg Av., Rad. BH21 27
Craig Dr., Uxb. AZ39 53
Craig Gdns. E18 CG30 40
Craig Mt., Rad. BJ21 27
Craig Park Rd. N18 CB28 39
Craig Rd., Rich. BK49 74
Craigavon Rd., Hem.H. AY11 8
Craigdale Rd., Horn. CT32 50
Craigen Av., Croy. CB54 87
Craigerne Rd. SE3 CH43 68
Craigholm SE18 CL44 68
Craiglands, St.Alb. BK11 9
Craigmore Tower, Wok. AS63 100
Guildford Rd.
Craigmuir Pk., Wem. BL37 55
Craignair Rd. SW2 BX47 76
Craignish Av. SW16 BX51 86
Craigs Ct. SW1 BX40 4
Craigs Ct. SW1 BX40 56
Whitehall
Craigs Wk., Chsnt. CC17 21
Davison Dr.
Craigton Rd. SE9 CK45 68
Craigwell Av., Felt. BC48 73
Craigwell Av., Rad. BJ21 27
Craigwell Clo., Stan. BK28 36
Craigwell Dr., Stan. BK28 36
Craigwell Pl., Egh. AV50 72
Crail Row SE17 BZ42 4
Crail Row SE17 BZ42 67
Crakell Rd., Reig. BT71 121
Cramer St. W1 BV39 1
Cramer St. W1 BV39 56
Crammavill St., Grays DD40 71
Crammerville Wk., Rain. CV38 60
Deri Av.
Crammond Clo. W6 BR43 65
Abbey Gdns.
Crampshaw La., Ash. BL63 103
Crampton Rd. SE20 CC50 77
Crampton St. SE17 BY42 4
Crampton St. SE17 BZ42 67
Cramptons Rd., Sev. CU63 107
Cranberry Clo., Nthlt. BD37 54
Cranborne Av., Sthl. BF42 64
Cranborne Clo., Pot.B. BR19 19
Cranborne Cres., Pot.B. BR19 19
Cranborne Gdns., Upmin. CX34 51
Cranborne Rd., Bark. CM37 58
Cranborne Rd., Chsnt. CC19 21
Theobalds La.
Cranborne Rd., Hat. BP12 10
Cranborne Rd., Hodd. CE11 12
Cranborne Rd., Pot.B. BR19 19
Cranborne Waye, Hayes BC39 53
Cranbourn Pass. SE16 CB41 67
Wilson Gro.
Cranbourn St. WC2 BW40 3
Cranbourn St. WC2 BW40 56
Long Acre
Cranbourne Av. E11 CH31 49
Cranbourne Av., Surb. BM55 85
Cranbourne Av., Wind. AM44 61
Cranbourne Clo. SW16 BX52 86
Cranbourne Clo., Slou. AO40 61
Cranbourne Ct. E18 CH31 49
Cranbourne Dr., Pnr. BD32 45
Cranbourne Gdns. NW11 BR32 46
Cranbourne Gdns., Welw.G.C. BR 8 5
Cranbourne Gdns., Ilf. CM31 49
Cranbourne Rd. E12 CK35 49
Cranbourne Rd. E15 CF35 48
Cranbourne Rd. N10 BV30 38
Cranbourne Rd., Nthwd. BB31 44
Cranbourne Rd., Slou. AO40 61
Cranbrook Clo., Brom. CH53 88
Cranbrook Dr., Esher BG55 84
Cranbrook Dr., Rom. CU31 50
Cranbrook Dr., St.Alb. BL13 10
Cranbrook Dr., Twick. BF47 74
Cranbrook Est. E2 CC37 57
Cranbrook Ms. E17 CD32 48
Cranbrook Pk. N22 BX30 38
Cranbrook Rd. SE8 CE44 67
Cranbrook Rd. SW19 BR50 75
Cranbrook Rd. W4 BO42 65
Cranbrook Rd., Barn. BT25 29
Cranbrook Rd., Bexh. CQ44 69
Cranbrook Rd., Houns. BE45 64
Cranbrook Rd., Ilf. CL32 49
Cranbrook Rd., Th.Hth. BZ51 87
Cranbrook Ri., Ilf. CK32 49
Cranbrook St. E2 CC37 57
Roman Rd.
Cranbrook Ter. E2 CC37 57
Roman Rd.
Cranbury Rd. SW6 BS44 66
Crane Av. W3 BO40 55
Cumberland Pk.
Crane Av., Islw. BJ46 74
Crane Clo., Dag. CR36 59
Crane Ct. EC1 BY39 2
Fleet St.
Crane Ct., Epsom BN56 94
Crane Gdns., Hayes BB42 63
Crane Gro. N7 BY36 56
Furlong Rd.
Crane Lodge Rd., Houns. BC43 63
Crane Mead SE16 CC42 67
Crane Park Rd., Twick. BF48 74
Crane Rd., Twick. BH47 74
Crane St. SE10 CF42 67
Crane Way, Twick. BG47 74
Cranebrook, Twick. BG48 74
Craneford Clo., Twick. BH47 74
Craneford Way, Twick. BH47 74
Cranell Grn., S.Ock. DA40 60
Cranes Dr., Surb. BL52 85
Cranes Pk. Av., Surb. BL52 85
Cranes Pk. Cres., Surb. BL52 85
Cranes Pk., Surb. BL52 85
Cranes Water, Hayes BB43 63
Cranes Way, B.Wd. BN25 28
Craneswater Pk., Sthl. BE42 64
Cranewood Clo., Wok. AS63 100
Guildford Rd.
Cranfield Clo. SE27 BZ48 77
Dunelm Gro.
Cranfield Cres., Cuff. BX18 20
Cranfield Ct., Wok. AQ62 100
Martindale Rd.
Cranfield Dr. NW9 BO29 37
Cranfield Dr., Wat. BE19 18
Cranfield Rd. E., Cars. BV58 95
Cranfield Rd. SE4 CD45 67
Cranfield Rd. W., Cars. BV58 95
Cranfield Row SE1 BY41 4
Cranfield Vill. SE27 BZ49 77
Auckland Hill
Cranford Av. N13 BX28 38
Cranford Av., Stai. AY47 73
Cranford Clo. SW20 BP50 75
Cranford Clo., Stai. AY47 73
Cranford Cotts. E1 CC40 57
Cranford St.
Cranford Dr., Dart. CW47 80
Cranford Dr., Hayes BB42 63
Cranford La. Est., Houns. BC43 63
Cranford La., Felt. BB45 63
Cranford La., Hayes BA43 63
Cranford La., Houns. BD43 64
Cranford Parkway, The, Sthl. BC42 63
Cranford Pk. Rd., Hayes BB42 63
Cranford Rd., Hayes BB42 63
Cranford Ri., Esher BG56 93
Cranford St. E1 CC40 57
Cranham Gdns., Upmin. CZ33 51
Cranham Rd., Horn. CU32 50
Cranhurst Rd. NW2 BQ35 46
Cranleigh Clo. SE20 CB51 87
Cranleigh Clo., Bex. CR46 7
Cranleigh Clo., Chsnt. CB17 2
Valence Dr.
Cranleigh Clo., Orp. CN55 8
Cranleigh Clo., S.Croy. CB59 9
Cranleigh Dr., Swan. CT53 8
Cranleigh Dr., Wal.Cr. CB17 2
Cranleigh Gdns. N21 BY25 2
Cranleigh Gdns. SE25 CA52 8
Cranleigh Gdns., Kings.T. BL50 7
Cranleigh Gdns., S.Croy. CB59 9
Cranleigh Gdns., Bark. CM36 5
Cranleigh Gdns., Har. BL32 4
Cranleigh Gdns., Loug. CK25 3
Cranleigh Gdns., Sthl. BE39 5
Cranleigh Gdns., Sutt. BS55 8
Cranleigh Ms. SW11 BU44 6
Cabul Rd.
Cranleigh Rd. N15 BZ32 4
Cranleigh Rd. SW19 BR52 8
Cranleigh Rd., Esher BG54 8
Cranleigh Rd., Felt. BB49 7
Cranleigh St. NW1 BW37
Cranleigh St. NW1 BW37 5
Cranley Clo., Guil. AT70 11
Cranley Dr., Ilf. CM33 4
Cranley Dr., Ruis. BB34 4
Cranley Gdns. N10 BV31 4
Cranley Gdns. N13 BX27 3
Cranley Gdns. SW7 BT42
Cranley Gdns. SW7 BT42 6
Cranley Gdns., Wall. BW57 9
Cranley Gro., Walt. BB57 9
Cranley Ms. SW7 BT42
Cranley Ms. SW7 BT42 6
Cranley Ms., Ilf. CM32 4
Cranley Rd.
Cranley Pl. SW7 BT42 3
Cranley Pl. SW7 BT42 6
Cranley Rd. E13 CH39 5
Cranley Rd., Guil. AS70 11
Cranley Rd., Ilf. CM33 4
Cranley Rd., Walt. BB56 9
Cranmer Av. W13 BJ41 6
Cranmer Clo., Mord. BQ53 8
Cranmer Clo., Pot.B. BS18 2
Cranmer Clo., Ruis. BD33 4
Cranmer Clo., Stan. BK29 3
Cranmer Clo., Warl. CD62 105
Cranmer Gdns.
Cranmer Clo., Wey. AZ57 9
Cranmer Ct. SW3 BU42 3
Cranmer Ct. SW3 BU42 6
Cranmer Ct. SW4 BW45 6
Cranmer Ct., Hmptn. BF49 7
Cranmer Farm Clo., Mitch. BU52 8
Cranmer Gdns., Dag. CS35 5
Cranmer Gdns., Warl. CD62 10
Cranmer Rd. E7 CH35 4
Cranmer Rd. SW9 BY43 6
Cranmer Rd., Croy. BY55 8
Cranmer Rd., Edg. BM27 3
Cranmer Rd., Hayes BA39 5
Cranmer Rd., Hmptn. BF49 7
Cranmer Rd., Kings.T. BL49 7
Cranmer Rd., Mitch. BU52 8
Cranmer Rd., Sev. CT65 10
Cranmer Ter. SW17 BT49 7
Cranmore Av., Chis. CK49 7
Cranmore Av., Islw. BG43 6
Cranmore Ct., St.Alb. BH13 9
Avenue Rd.
Cranmore La., Lthd. AZ68 110
Cranmore Park Est., Chis. CK50 78
Cranmore Rd., Brom. CG48 78
Cranmore Way N10 BW31 47
Cranston Clo., Guil. AP68 109
Cranston Clo., Houns. BE44 64
Cranston Clo., Reig. BS71 121
Lymden Gdns.
Cranston Clo., Uxb. BA34 44
Cranston Est. N1 BZ37 57
Cranston Gdns. E4 CE28 39
Cranston Park Av., Upmin. CY35 51
Cranston Rd. SE23 CD47 77
Cranstoun Clo., Guil. AP68 109
Keens Park Rd.
Cranswick Rd. SE16 CB42 67
Crantock Rd. SE6 CE48 77
Cranwell Clo. E3 CE38 57
Cranwell Gro., Shep. AY52 83
Cranwell Rd., Houns. AZ44 63
Cranwich Av. N21 BZ26 39
Cranwich Rd. N16 BZ33 48
Cranwood St. EC1 BZ38 2
Cranwood St. EC1 BZ38 57
Cranworth Cres. E4 CF26 39
Cranworth Gdns. SW9 BY44 66
Craster Rd. SW2 BX47 76
Crathie Rd. SE12 CH46 78
Crathorn St. SE13 CF45 67
Cravan Av., Felt. BC48 73
Craven Av. W5 BK40 54
Craven Av., Sthl. BE39 54
Craven Clo., Hayes BC39 53
Craven Gdns. SW19 BS49 76
Craven Gdns., Collier Row CR28 41
Craven Gdns., Harold Wood CY29 42
Craven Gdns., Bark. CN37 58
Craven Gdns., Ilf. CM30 40
Craven Hill Gdns. W2 BT40 3
Craven Hill Gdns. W2 BT40 56
Craven Hill Ms. W2 BT40 3
Craven Hill Ms. W2 BT40 56
Craven Hill W2 BT40 3
Craven Hill W2 BT40 56
Craven Ms. SW11 BV46 76
Taybridge Rd.
Craven Park Ms. NW10 BN37 55
Craven Pass. WC2 BX40 4
Craven St.

Craven Pk. NW10 BN37 55
Craven Pk. Rd. N15 CA32 48
Craven Pk. Rd. NW10 BO37 55
Craven Pl. WC2 BX40 4
Craven Pl. WC2 BX40 56
Craven St.
Craven Rd. NW10 BN37 55
Craven Rd. W2 BT40 56
Craven Rd. W5 BK40 54
Craven Rd., Croy. CB54 87
Craven Rd., Kings.T. BL51 85
Craven Rd., Orp. CP55 89
Craven St. WC2 BX40 4
Craven St. WC2 BX40 56
Craven Ter. W2 BT40 3
Craven Ter. W2 BT40 56
Craven Wk. N16 CB33 48
Crawford Av., Grays DD40 71
Crawford Av., Wem. BK35 45
Crawford Clo., Islw. BH44 64
Crawford Compton Clo., Horn. CV36 60
Sarre Av.
Crawford Est. SE5 BZ44 67
Crawford Gdns. N13 BY27 38
Crawford Gdns., Nthlt. BE38 54
Crawford Ms. W1 BU39 1
York St.
Crawford Pass. EC1 BY38 2
Crawford Pass. EC1 BY38 56
Ray St.
Crawford Pl. W1 BU39 1
Crawford Pl. W1 BU39 56
Crawford Rd. SE5 BZ44 67
Crawford Rd., Hat. BP11 10
Crawford St. W1 BU39 1
Crawford St. W1 BU39 56
Crawfords, Swan. CT50 79
Dawson Dr.
Crawley Dr., Hem.H. AY11 8
Crawley Hatch, Harl. CK11 13
Crawley Rd. E10 CE33 48
Crawley Rd. N22 BZ30 39
Crawley Rd., Enf. CA26 39
Crawshaw Dr., Cher. AU57 91
Crawshaw Clo., Sev. CU65 107
Crawshay Rd. SW9 BY44 66
Crawthew Gro. SE22 CA45 67
Cray Av., Ash. BL61 103
Cray Av., Orp. CO54 89
Cray Clo., Dart. CU45 69
Cray Rd., Belv. CR43 69
Cray Rd., Sid. CP50 79
Cray Rd., Swan. CR53 89
Cray Valley Rd., Orp. CO53 89
Craybrooke Rd., Sid. CO49 79
Crayburne, Grav. DC49 81
Craybury End SE9 CM48 78
Craydene Rd., Erith CT44 69
Crayford Clo. E6 CJ39 58
Neatscourt Rd.
Crayford High St., Dart. CT45 69
Crayford Rd. N7 BW35 47
Crayford Rd., Dart. CT46 79
Crayford Rd., Erith CT43 69
Crayford Way, Dart. CT46 79
Crayke Hill, Chess. BL57 94
Craylands La., Swans. DB46 80
Craylands Sq., Swans. DB46 80
Craylands, Orp. CP52 89
Craymill Sq., Dart. CT45 69
Norris Way
Crayonne Clo., Sun. BB51 83
Crealock Gro., Wdf.Grn. CG28 40
Crealock St. SW18 BS46 76
Creasy Est. SE1 CA41 4
Creasy St. SE1 CA41 4
Creasy St. SE1 CA41 67
Webb St.
Crebor St. SE22 CB46 77
Creden Hall Dr., Brom. CK54 88
Lower Gravel Rd.
Credenhill St. SW16 BW50 76
Credenhill Way SE15 CB43 67
Ledbury St.
Crediton Hill NW6 BS35 47
Crediton Rd. E16 CH39 58
Crediton Rd. NW10 BQ37 55
Crediton Way, Esher BJ56 93
Credo Way, Grays DA43 70
Credon Rd. E13 CJ37 58
Credon Rd. SE16 CB42 67
Cree Way, Rom. CT29 41
Creechurch La. EC3 CA39 2
Creechurch La. EC3 CA39 57
Creed La. EC4 BY39 2
Creed La. EC4 BY39 56
Creek Br. SE10 CE43 67
Creek Rd. SE10 CE43 67
Creek Rd. SE8 CE43 67
Creek Rd., Bark. CN38 58
Creek Rd., E.Mol. BH52 84
Creek, The, Sun. BC53 83
Creekside SE8 CE43 67
Creekside, Rain. CT38 59
Creeland Gro. SE6 CD47 77
Catford Hill
Crefeld Clo. W6 BR43 65
Creffield Rd. W3 & W5 BL40 55
Creighton Av. E6 CJ37 58
Creighton Av. N10 BU30 38
Creighton Av. N2 BU31 47
Creighton Av., St.Alb. BG15 9
Creighton Rd. N17 CA29 39
Creighton Rd. NW6 BQ37 55
Creighton Rd. W5 BK41 64
Cremarne Rd., Grav. DF47 81
Cremer St. E2 CA37 2
Cremer St. E2 CA37 57
Cremorne Est. SW10 BT43 66
Cremorne Gdns. SW10 BT43 66
Cremorne Gdns., Epsom BN58 94
Cremorne Rd. SW10 BT43 66
Crescent Av., Grays DE42 71
Crescent Av., Horn. CT34 50
Crescent Ct., Surb. BK53 84
Crescent Dr., Brwd. DC26 122
Crescent Dr., Enf. CC22 30
Crescent Dr., Orp. CL53 88
Crescent E., Barn. BT22 29
Crescent Gdns. SW19 BS48 76
Crescent Gdns., Ruis. BC33 44
Crescent Gdns., Swan. CS51 89
Crescent Gro. SW4 BW45 66
Crescent Gro., Mitch. BU53 86
Crescent La. SW4 BW45 66
Crescent Ms. N22 BW30 38
Crescent Rd.
Crescent Pl. SW3 BU42 3
Crescent Pl. SW3 BU42 66
Crescent Rd. E10 CE34 48
Crescent Rd. E13 CH37 58
Crescent Rd. E18 CJ30 40
Crescent Rd. E4 CG26 40
Crescent Rd. E6 CJ37 58
Crescent Rd. N15 BY31 47
Carlingford Rd.
Crescent Rd. N22 BW30 38
Crescent Rd. N3 BR30 37
Crescent Rd. N8 BW32 47
Crescent Rd. N9 CB26 39
Crescent Rd. SE18 CL42 68
Crescent Rd. SW20 BQ50 75
Crescent Rd., Barn. BT24 29
Crescent Rd., Beck. CE51 87
Crescent Rd., Brom. CH50 78
Crescent Rd., Brwd. DA28 42
Crescent Rd., Cat. CB65 105
Crescent Rd., Dag. CR34 50
Crescent Rd., Enf. BY24 29
Crescent Rd., Erith CT43 69
Crescent Rd., Hem.H. AX13 8
Crescent Rd., Kings.T. BM50 75
Crescent Rd., Red. BZ70 114
Crescent Rd., Reig. BS71 121
Crescent Rd., S.Ock. CY41 70
Central Av.
Crescent Rd., Sev. CT63 107
Crescent Rd., Shep. BA53 83
Crescent Rd., Sid. CN48 78
Crescent Rd., Sthl. BE41 64
Crescent Ri. N22 BW29 38
Crescent Ri., Barn. BU25 29
Crescent Row EC1 BZ38 2
Crescent Row EC1 BZ38 57
Baltic St.
Crescent St. N1 BX36 56
Huntingdon St.
Crescent Stables SW15 BQ45 65
Upper Richmond Rd.
Crescent Vw., Loug. CJ25 31
Crescent W., Barn. BT22 29
Crescent Way N12 BU29 38
Crescent Way SE4 CE45 67
Crescent Way SW16 BX50 76
Crescent Way, Orp. CN56 97
Crescent Way, S.Ock. CY40 60
Crescent Wk., S.Ock. CY41 70
Crescent Wood Rd. SE26 CB48 77
Crescent, The E17 CD32 48
Crescent, The EC3 CA40 4
Crescent, The N11 BV28 38
Crescent, The NW2 BP34 46
Crescent, The SW13 BO44 65
Crescent, The SW19 BS48 76
Crescent, The W3 BN39 55
Crescent, The, Abbots Langley BB18 17
Crescent, The, Northfleet DD46 81
Crescent, The, Perry Street DF48 81
Crescent, The, Aldenham BF22 27
Crescent, The, Ashf. AY49 73
Crescent, The, Barn. BS23 29
Crescent, The, Beck. CE51 87
Crescent, The, Belmont BS59 95
Crescent, The, Bex. CP47 79
Crescent, The, Cat. CE65 105
Crescent, The, Cher. AW52 83
Crescent, The, Croy. BZ53 87
Crescent, The, E.Mol. BE52 84
Crescent, The, Egh. AS50 72
Crescent, The, Epp. CN19 22
Crescent, The, Epsom BM61 103
Crescent, The, Green. DB46 80
Crescent, The, Guil. AQ70 118
Crescent, The, Har. BG33 45
Crescent, The, Harl. CP 8 6
Crescent, The, Hayes BA43 63
Crescent, The, Ilf. CL32 49
Crescent, The, Long. DC52 90
Bramblefield Clo.
Crescent, The, Loug. CJ25 31
Crescent, The, Lthd. BJ64 102
Crescent, The, N.Mal. BN52 85
Crescent, The, Reig. BS70 121
Crescent, The, Rick. AZ25 26
Crescent, The, Sev. CV64 108
Crescent, The, Shep. BB53 83
Crescent, The, Sid. CN49 78
Crescent, The, Slou. AP41 62
Crescent, The, St.Alb. BF18 18
Crescent, The, Surb. BL53 85
Crescent, The, Sutt. BT56 95
Crescent, The, Upmin. CZ33 51
Crescent, The, W.Wick. CG53 88
Crescent, The, Wat. BD24 27
Crescent, The, Wem. BJ34 45
Crescent, The, Wey. AZ55 83
Cresfield Rd. SW6 BS45 66
Cresford Rd. SW6 BS44 66
Crespigny Rd. NW4 BP32 46
Cress End, Rick. AW27 35
Springwell Av.
Cress Rd., Slou. AN41 61
Cressage Av. W4 BM43 65
Cressage Clo., Sthl. BE38 54
Cressall Mead, Lthd. BJ63 102
Cresset Rd. E9 CC36 57
Cresset St. SW4 BW45 66
Cressfield Clo. NW5 BV35 47
Cressida Rd. N19 BW33 47
Cressingham Gdns. Est. SE24 BY47 76
Cressingham Gro., Sutt. BT56 95
Cressingham Rd. SE13 CF45 67
Cressingham Rd., Edg. BN29 37
Cressington Clo. N16 CA35 48
Wordsworth Rd.
Cresswell Gdns. SW5 BT42 3
Cresswell Gdns. SW5 BT42 66
Cresswell Gdns., Houns. BE45 64
Cresswell Pk. SE3 CG45 68
Cresswell Pl. SW10 BT42 3
Cresswell Pl. SW10 BT42 66
Cresswell Rd. SE5 CB52 87
Cresswell Rd., Chesh. AO20 16
Cresswell Rd., Felt. BE48 74
Cresswell Rd., Twick. BK46 74
Cresswell Way N21 BY26 38
Cresswells Mead, Maid. AG42 61
Cressy Ct. E1 CC39 57
Cressy Ct. W6 BP41 65
Cressy Pl. E1 CC39 57
Cressy Rd. NW3 BU35 47
Crest Av., Grays DD43 71
Crest Clo., Sev. CR59 98
Crest Dr., Enf. CC22 30
Crest Pk., Hem.H. BA13 8
Crest Rd. NW2 BO34 46
Crest Rd., Brom. CG54 88
Crest Rd., S.Croy. CB57 96
Crest St. N1 BX36 56
Huntingdon St.
Crest Vw., Pnr. BD31 45
Crest, The N13 BY28 38
Crest, The NW4 BQ32 46
Crest, The, Chsnt. BY17 20
Crest, The, Saw. CP 6 6
Crest, The, Surb. BM53 85
Cresta Clo., Wey. AV58 91
Cresta Ct. W5 BL38 55
Crestbrook Av. N13 BY27 38
Crestbrook Pl. N13 BY27 38
Crestfield St. WC1 BX38 2
Crestfield St. WC1 BX38 56
St. Chads St.
Cresthill Av., Grays DE42 71
Creston Av., Wok. AP61 100
Creston Way, Wor.Pk. BQ55 85
Crestview Dr., Orp. CL53 88
Crestway SW15 BP46 75
Crestwick Ct. W3 BM40 55
Crestwood, Houns. BE46 74
Creswick Ct., Welw.G.C. BQ 8 5
Goblins Grn.
Creswick Rd. E3 CE38 57
Creswick Rd. W3 BM40 55
Creswick Wk. E3 CE37 58
Malmesbury Rd.
Creswick Wk. NW11 BR31 46
Crete Hall Rd., Grav. DE46 81
Creton St. SE18 CL41 68
Crevington Way, Horn. CV35 51
Crewdson Rd. SW9 BY43 66
Crewe Pl. NW10 BO38 55
Crewes Av., Warl. CC61 105
Crewes Clo., Warl. CC62 105
Crewes Farm La., Warl. CC62 105
Crewes La., Warl. CC61 105
Crews Hill, Enf. BX20 20
Crews St. E14 CE42 67
Crewys Rd. NW2 BR34 46
Crewys Rd. SE15 CB44 67
Crichton Av., Wall. BW56 95
Crichton Gdns., Rom. CR33 50
Crichton Rd., Cars. BU57 95
Cricket Field Rd., Uxb. AX37 53
Cricket Grn., Mitch. BU52 86
Cricket Ground Rd., Chis. CL51 88
Cricket Hill, Red. BX71 121
Cricket La., Beck. CD50 77
Cricket Way, Wey. BB55 83
Cricketers Arms Rd., Enf. BZ23 30
Cricketers Clo. N14 BW26 38
Cricketers Clo., Chess. BK56 93
Cricketfield Rd. E5 CB35 48
Cricketfield Rd., West Dr. AX42 63
Cricklade Av. SW2 BX48 76
Cricklade Av., Rom. CV29 42
Cricklewood Broadway NW2 BQ35 46
Cricklewood La. NW2 BQ35 46
Cridland St. E15 CG37 58
Church St.
Crieff Ct., Tedd. BK50 74
Crieff Rd. SW18 BT46 76
Criffel Av. SW2 BW48 76
Crimp Hill Rd., Wind. AP47 72
Crimp Hill, Wind. AP47 72
Crimscott St. SE1 CA41 4
Crimscott St. SE1 CA41 67
Crimsworth Rd. SW8 BW44 66
Crinan St. N1 BX37 2
Crinan St. N1 BX37 56
Cringle St. SW8 BW43 66
Cripplegate St. EC1 BZ39 2
Cripsey Av., Ong. CW16 24
Crisp Rd. W6 BQ42 65
Crispen Rd., Felt. BE49 74
Crispian Clo. NW10 BO35 46
Neasden La.
Crispin Clo., Ash. BL62 103
Crispin Clo., Croy. BX55 86
Crispin Cres., Croy. BW55 86
Crispin Rd., Edg. BN29 37
Crispin St. E1 CA39 2
Crispin St. E1 CA39 57
Brushfield St.
Crispin Way, Slou. AO35 43
Criss Cres., Ger.Cr. AR30 34
Criss Gro., Ger.Cr. AR30 34
Cristowe Rd. SW6 BR44 65
Criterion Ms. N19 BW34 47
St. Johns Vill.
Critten La., Dor. BD70 119
Crockenhall Way, Grav. DF50 81
Crockenhill La., Dart. CV54 90
Crockenhill Rd., Orp. CP53 89
Crockenhill Rd., Swan. CQ53 89
Crockerton Rd. SW17 BU48 76
Crockery La., Guil. AY68 110
Crockford Clo., Wey. AX56 92
Crockford Park Rd.
Crockford Park Rd., Wey. AX56 92
Crockham Way SE9 CL49 78
Crocknorth Rd., Dor. BC70 110
Crocknorth Rd., Lthd. BB69 110
Crocus Clo., Croy. CC54 87
Primrose La.
Crocus Field, Barn. BR25 28
Croffets, Tad. BQ64 103
Croft Av., Dor. BJ70 119
Croft Av., W.Wick. CF54 87
Croft Clo. NW7 BO27 37
Croft Clo., Belv. CQ42 69
Croft Clo., Chis. CK49 78
Croft Clo., Hayes BA43 63
Croft Clo., Kings L. AW18 17
Croft Clo., Uxb. AZ36 53
Croft End Rd., Kings L. AW18 17
Croft Field, Hat. BP12 10
Croft Field, Kings L. AW18 17
Croft Gdns. W7 BJ41 64
Croft Gdns., Ruis. BB33 44
Croft La., Kings L. AW18 17
Croft Lodge Clo., Wdf.Grn. CH29 40
Croft Meadow, Kings L. AW18 17
Croft Rd. N17 CA29 39
Durban Rd.
Croft Rd. SW16 BY51 86
Croft Rd. SW19 BT50 76
Croft Rd., Brom. CH50 78
Croft Rd., Cat. CD64 105
Croft Rd., Enf. CD23 30
Croft Rd., Ger.Cr. AS30 34
Croft Rd., Sutt. BT56 95
Croft Rd., West. CL66 115
Croft St. SE8 CD42 67
Croft Way NW3 BS35 47
Croft Way, Sev. CT66 116
Croft Way, Sid. CN48 78
Croft Wk., Brox. CD15 12
Croft, The NW10 BO37 55
Croft, The W5 BL39 55
Croft, The, Barn. BQ24 28
Croft, The, Brox. CD15 12
Croft, The, Houns. BE43 64
Croft, The, Loug. CL23 31
Croft, The, Pnr. BE33 45
Croft, The, Ruis. BD35 45
Croft, The, St.Alb. BF16 18
Croft, The, Swan. CS51 89
Croft, The, Welw.G.C. BR 9 5
Croft, The, Wem. BK35 45
Croftdown Rd. NW5 BV34 47
Crofters Clo., Islw. BG46 74
Crofters End, Saw. CQ 5 6
Crofters Mead, Croy. CD58 96
Crofters Rd., Nthwd. BB28 35
Crofters Way NW1 BW37 1
Crofters Way NW1 BW37 56
Crofters, Stai. AQ46 72
Croftleigh Av., Pur. BY61 104
Crofton Av., Bex. CP47 79
Crofton Av., Orp. CM55 88
Crofton Av., Walt. BD55 84
Crofton Clo., Cher. AU57 91
Crofton Ct., Orp. CM54 88
Crofton La., Orp. CM55 88
Crofton Pk. Rd. SE4 CD46 77
Crofton Pound Hill, Orp. CM55 88
Crofton Rd. E13 CH38 58
Crofton Rd. SE5 CA44 67
Crofton Rd., Grays DF41 71
Crofton Rd., Orp. CL55 88
Crofton Ter. E5 CD35 48
Durrington Rd.
Crofton Ter., Rich. BL45 65
Crofton Way, Enf. BY23 29
Croftongate Way SE4 CD46 77
Crofts Path, Hem.H. AZ14 8
Crofts Rd., Har. BJ32 45
Crofts St. E1 CB40 4
Crofts, The, Hem.H. AZ14 8
Crofts, The, Shep. BB52 83
Croftway NW3 BS35 47
Croftway, Rich. BJ48 74
Crogsland Rd. NW1 BV36 56
Croham Clo., S.Croy. CA57 96
Croham Manor Rd., S.Croy. CA57 96
Croham Mt., S.Croy. CA57 96
Croham Pk. Av., S.Croy. CA56 96
Croham Rd., S.Croy. BZ56 96
Croham Valley Rd., S.Croy. CA57 96
Croindene Rd. SW16 BX51 86
Cromar Ct., Wok. AR61 100
Cromartie Rd. N19 BW33 47
Crombie Clo., Ilf. CK32 49
Crombie Rd., Sid. CM47 78
Crome St. SE10 CG42 68
Cromer Clo., Uxb. BA39 53
Cromer Est. WC1 BX38 2
Cromer Est. WC1 BX38 56
Cromer Hyde La., Welw.G.C. BN 8 5
Cromer Pl., Orp. CN54 88
Andover Rd.
Cromer Rd. E10 CF33 48
Cromer Rd. N17 CB30 39
Sherringham Av.
Cromer Rd. SE25 CB52 87
Cromer Rd. SW17 BV50 76
Cromer Rd. W., Houns. AZ45 63
Camberley Rd.
Cromer Rd., Barn. BT24 29
Cromer Rd., Chadwell Heath CQ32 50
Cromer Rd., Horn. CV33 51
Cromer Rd., Houns. AZ45 63
Cromer Rd., Rom. CS32 50
Cromer Rd., Wat. BD22 27
Cromer Rd., Wdf.Grn. CH28 40
Cromer St. WC1 BX38 2
Cromer St. WC1 BX38 56
Cromer Ter. E8 CB35 48
Foxley Clo.
Cromer Vill. Rd. SW18 BR46 75
Cromford Clo., Orp. CN55 88
Cromford Path E5 CC35 48
Clapton Park Est.
Cromford Rd. SW18 BS46 76
Cromford Way, N.Mal. BN51 85
Cromlix Clo., Chis. CL51 88
Crompton St. W2 BT38 1
Crompton St. W2 BT38 56
Cromwall Ct., Enf. CC25 30
Cromwell Av. N6 BV33 47
Cromwell Av. W6 BP42 65
Cromwell Av., Brom. CH52 88
Cromwell Av., Chsnt. CB18 21
Cromwell Av., N.Mal. BO53 85
Cromwell Clo. E1 CB40 4
Cromwell Clo. E1 CB40 57
Vaughan Way
Cromwell Clo. N2 BT31 47
Cromwell Clo. W3 BN40 55
Cromwell Clo., Brom. CH52 88
Cromwell Clo., Ch.St.G. AR27 34
Cromwell Clo., St.Alb. BK11 9
Langham Clo.
Cromwell Clo., Walt. BC54 83
Cromwell Cres. SW5 BS42 66
Cromwell Dr., Slou. AP39 52
Cromwell Gdns. SW7 BT41 3
Cromwell Gro. W6 BQ41 65
Cromwell Ms. SW7 BT42 3
Cromwell Ms. SW7 BT42 66
Cromwell Pl. N6 BV33 47
Cromwell Av.
Cromwell Pl. SW14 BN45 65
Cromwell Pl. SW7 BT42 3
Cromwell Pl. SW7 BT42 66
Cromwell Pl. W3 BN40 55
Grove Pl.
Cromwell Rd. E17 CF32 48
Cromwell Rd. E7 CJ36 58
Cromwell Rd. N10 BV29 38
Cromwell Rd. N3 BT30 38
Cromwell Rd. SW19 BS49 76
Cromwell Rd. SW5 BS42 3
Cromwell Rd. SW5 BS42 66
Cromwell Rd. SW7 BS42 66
Cromwell Rd. SW9 BY44 66
Cromwell Rd., B.Wd. BL23 28
Cromwell Rd., Beck. CD51 87
Cromwell Rd., Brwd. DA28 42
Cromwell Rd., Cat. BZ64 105
Cromwell Rd., Chsnt. CB17 21
Cromwell Rd., Croy. BZ54 87
Cromwell Rd., Felt. BC47 73
Cromwell Rd., Grays DD42 71
Cromwell Rd., Hayes BA39 53
Cromwell Rd., Kings.T. BL51 85
Cromwell Rd., Red. BU70 121
Cromwell Rd., Tedd. BJ50 74
Cromwell Rd., Walt. BC54 83
Cromwell Rd., Wem. BL37 55
Cromwell Rd., Wor.Pk. BN55 85
Cromwell St., Houns. BF45 64
Cromwells Mere, Rom. CS29 41
Crondace Rd. SW6 BS44 66
Crondall St. N1 BZ37 2
Crondall St. N1 BZ37 57
Cronks Hill, Red. BT71 121
Cronkshill Clo., Red. BT71 121
Cronkshill Rd., Red. BT71 121
Crook Log, Bexh. CP45 69
Crooke Rd. SE8 CC42 67
Crooked Billet SW19 BQ50 75
Crooked Billet Yard N1 CA38 57
Kingsland Rd.
Crooked Mile, Wal.Abb. CF18 21
Crooked Usage N3 BR31 46
Crooked Way, Wal.Abb. CG14 13
Crookham Rd. SW6 BR44 65
Fulham Rd.
Crookhams, Welw.G.C. BS 7 5
Crookston Rd. SE9 CL45 68
Croombs Rd. E16 CJ39 58
Crooms Hill Gro. SE10 CF43 67
Crooms Hill SE10 CF43 67
Crop Common, Hat. BP11 10
Cropley Ct. N1 BZ37 2
Cropley Ct. N1 BZ37 57
Cropley St. N1 BZ37 2
Cropley St. N1 BZ37 57
Croppath Rd., Dag. CR35 50
Cropthorne Ct. NW8 BT38 1
Crosby Clo., Felt. BE49 74
Crosby Ct. SE1 BZ41 4
Crosby Rd. E7 CH36 58
Crosby Rd. SE1 BZ41 67
Crosby Rd., Dag. CR37 59
Crosby Row SE1 BZ41 4
Crosby Sq. EC3 CA39 2
Crosby Sq. EC3 CA39 57
Crosby Wk. E8 CA36 57
Laurel St.
Crosier Way, Ruis. BB34 44
Crosland Pl. SW11 BV45 66
Taybridge Rd.
Cross Acres, Wok. AV61 100
Cross Deep Gdns, Twick. BH48 74
Cross Deep, Twick. BH48 74
Cross Keys Clo. W1 BV39 1
Cross Keys Clo. W1 BV39 56
Marylebone La.
Cross Keys Clo., Sev. CU67 116
Cross Keys Ct. EC2 BZ39 2
London Wall
Cross Keys Sq. EC1 BZ39 2
Little Britain
Cross Keys Sq. EC1 BZ39 57
Little Britain
Cross La. E., Grav. DG48 81

Cross La. EC3 CA40 4
St. Dunstans Hill
Cross La. N8 BX31 47
Cross La., Bex. CQ47 79
Cross La., Ches. AU57 91
Cross Lances Rd., Houns. BF45 64
Cross Lane Footpath, Cher. AT57 91
Cross Lanes Clo., Ger.Cr. AS28 34
Cross Lanes W., Grav. DG48 81
Cross Lanes, Ger.Cr. AS28 34
Cross Lanes, Guil. AS70 118
Cross Manorway SE28 CP40 59
Cross Oak Rd., Berk. AQ13 7
Cross Oaks, Wind. AN44 61
Cross Rd. E4 CF26 39
Cross Rd. N11 BV28 38
Cross Rd. N22 BY29 38
Cross Rd. SE5 CA44 67
Cross Rd. SW19 BS50 76
Cross Rd., South Harrow BF34 45
Cross Rd., Belmont BS58 95
Cross Rd., Brom. CK55 88
Cross Rd., Chadwell Hth. CP33 50
Cross Rd., Croy. BZ54 87
Cross Rd., Dart. CV46 80
Cross Rd., Enf. CA24 30
Cross Rd., Felt. BE49 74
Cross Rd., Grav. DF46 81
Burch Rd.
Cross Rd., Har. BG31 45
Cross Rd., Hawley CW49 80
Cross Rd., Kings.T. BL50 75
Cross Rd., Orp. CO53 89
Cross Rd., Pur. BY60 95
Cross Rd., Rom. CR31 50
Cross Rd., Sid. CO49 79
Cross Rd., Sutt. BT56 95
Cross Rd., Tad. BQ64 103
Cross Rd., Wal.Cr. CD20 21
Cross Rd., Wat. BE25 27
Cross Rd., Wdf.Grn. CK29 40
Cross Rd., Wealdstone BJ30 36
Cross Roads, Loug. CH23 31
Cross St. E1 CC39 57
Commercial Rd.
Cross St. E3 CE36 57
Monier Rd.
Cross St. N1 BY37 56
Cross St. N1 BY37 2
Cross St. N18 CB28 39
Wakefield St.
Cross St. SW13 BO44 65
Cross St., Erith CT43 69
Cross St., Harl. CM11 13
Cross St., Hmptn. BG49 74
Cross St., St.Alb. BG13 9
Spencer St.
Cross St., Uxb. AX37 53
Cross St., Wat. BD24 27
Cross Way, The SE9 CJ48 78
Cross Way, The, Har. BH30 36
Cross Ways Rd., Beck. CE52 87
Cross Ways, Berk. AP13 7
Cross Ways, Hem.H. AZ13 8
Crossbow Ct., Ong. CX18 24
Crossbow Rd., Chig. CN28 40
Crossbrook Rd. SE3 CK44 68
Crossbrook St., Chsnt. CC19 21
Crossbrook, Hat. BO13 10
Crossfell Rd., Hem.H. AZ14 8
Crossfield Clo., Berk. AP13 7
Crossfield Pl., Wey. AZ57 92
Crossfield Rd. N17 BZ31 48
Crossfield Rd. NW3 BT36 56
Crossfield Rd., Hodd. CE11 12
Crossfield Rd., Red. BV70 121
Crossfield St. SE8 CE43 67
Crossfields, Loug. CL25 31
Crossfields, St.Alb. BF15 9
Crossford St. SW9 BX44 66
Lingham St.
Crossgate, Edg. BM27 37
Crossgate, Grnf. BJ36 54
Crossing Rd., Epp. CO19 23
Crossland Rd., Th.Hth. BY53 86
Crosslands Av. W5 BL40 55
Crosslands Av., Sthl. BE42 64
Crosslands Rd., Epsom BN57 94
Crosslet Sq. SE17 BZ42 67
Townsend St.
Crosslet St. SE17 BZ42 4
Crossley Clo., West. CJ61 106
Crossley St. N7 BY36 56
Crossleys Hill, Ch.St.G. AR27 34
Crossleys, Ch.St.G. AR27 34
Crossmead Av., Grnf. BF38 54
Crossmead SE9 CK47 78
Crossmead, Wat. BC25 26
Crossness Footpath, Belv. CQ41 69
Crossness La. SE28 CQ40 59
Crossness Rd., Bark. CN38 58
Crossoaks La., South Mimms BN20 19
Crosspath, The, Rad. BJ21 27
Crossroads, The, Lthd. BD67 111
Manor Gdns.
Crossthwaite Av. SE5 BZ45 67
Crosswall EC3 CA40 4
Crosswall EC3 CA40 57
Crossway N12 BT29 38
Crossway N16 CA35 48
Crossway NW9 BO31 46
Crossway SE28 CP39 59
Crossway SW20 BQ52 85
Crossway, Chesh. AP18 16
Crossway, Dag. CP34 50
Crossway, Enf. CA26 39
Crossway, Hayes BC40 53
Crossway, Orp. CM52 88
Crossway, Pnr. BC30 35
Crossway, Ruis. BD35 45
Crossway, The N22 BY29 38
Crossway, The SE9 CJ48 78
Crossway, The W13 BJ38 54
Crossway, The, Uxb. AY37 53
Crossway, Walt. BC55 83
Crossway, Wdf.Grn. CJ28 40
Crossway, Welw.G.C. BQ6 5
Crossways Boul., Dart. CY45 70
Crossways La., Reig. BT67 113
Crossways N21 BZ25 30
Crossways Rd., Mitch. BV52 86
Crossways, Brwd. DD25 122
Crossways, Egh. AU50 72
Crossways, Guil. AP71 118
Crossways, Rom. CU31 50
Crossways, S.Croy. CD57 96
Crossways, Sun. BB50 73
Staines Rd. W.
Crossways, Sutt. BT57 95
Crossways, The, Couls. BX63 104
Crossways, The, Houns. BE43 64
Crossways, The, Red. BW68 113
Crossways, The, Wem. BM34 46
Crossways, West. CJ63 106
Crosswell Clo., Shep. BA51 83
Charlton Rd.
Croston St. E8 CB37 57
Crothall Clo. N13 BX27 38
Crouch Av., Bark. CO37 59
Crouch Cft. SE9 CL48 78
Crouch Clo., Beck. CE50 77
Abbey La.
Crouch End Hill N8 BW33 47
Crouch Hall Rd. N8 BW32 47
Crouch Hill N4 & N8 BX32 47
Crouch La., Chsnt. BZ17 21
Crouch Rd. NW10 BN36 55
Crouch Rd., Grays DG42 71
Crouch Valley, Upmin. CZ33 51
Crouchfield, Hem.H. AW14 8
Crouchmans Clo. SE26 CB48 77
Crouchoak La., Wey. AW56 92
Crow Clo., Warl. CD62 105
Crow Dr., Sev. CS61 107
Crow Green La., Brwd. DA25 33
Crow Green Rd., Brwd. CZ25 33
Crow La., Rom. CQ33 50
Crowborough Dr., Warl. CD62 105
Crowborough Path, Wat. BD27 36
Crowborough Rd. SW17 BV50 76
Crowden Way SE28 CP40 59
Crowder St. E1 CB40 57
Crowhurst Clo. SW9 BY44 66
Crowhurst La., Sev. DA58 99
Crowhurst Rd. SW9 BY44 66
Crowhurst Rd., Sev. DB65 108
Crowhurst Way, Orp. CP53 89
Crowland Av., Hayes BB42 63
Crowland Gdns. N14 BX26 38
Crowland Rd. N15 CA32 48
Crowland Rd., Th.Hth. BZ52 87
Crowland Ter. N1 BZ36 57
Crowland Wk., Mord. BS53 86
Crowlands Av., Rom. CR32 50
Crowley Cres., Croy. BY56 95
Crowlin Wk. N1 BZ36 57
Clephane Rd.
Crowmarsh Gdns. SE23 CC47 77
Tyson Rd.
Crown Ash Hill, West. CH60 97
Crown Ash La., West. CH61 106
Crown Clo. E3 CE37 57
Wick La.
Crown Clo. NW6 BS36 56
Lymington Rd.
Crown Clo. NW7 BO27 37
Crown Clo., Bish. CS7 6
Crown Clo., Hayes BB41 63
Crown Clo., Orp. CO56 98
Crown Clo., Walt. BD54 84
Crown Ct. EC2 BZ39 2
Cheapside
Crown Ct. EC2 BZ39 57
Cheapside
Crown Ct. N10 BV29 38
Crown Ct. SE12 CH46 78
Crown Ct. WC2 BX39 2
Crown Ct. WC2 BX39 56
Russell St.
Crown Ct., Brom. CK53 88
Crown Ct., Til. DG44 71
Newton Rd.
Crown Dale SE19 BY50 76
Crown Field, Brox. CE14 12
Crown Gate, Harl. CM11 13
Crown Hill Rd. NW10 BO37 55
Crown Hill, Croy. BZ55 87
Crown Hill, Wal.Abb. CK20 22
Crown La. N14 BW26 38
Crown La. Spur, Brom. CJ53 88
Crown La. SW16 BY49 76
Crown La., Brom. CJ53 88
Crown La., Chis. CM51 88
Crown La., Mord. BS52 86
Crown La., Vir.W. AR53 82
Crown Lane Gdns. SW16 BY49 76
Crown La.
Crown Office Row EC4 BY40 4
Crown Office Row EC4 BY40 58
Crown Par., Hayes BB39 53
Crown Pass. SW1 BW40 3
Crown Pass. SW1 BW40 56
King St.
Crown Pass., Wat. BD24 27
Crown Pl. NW5 BV36 56
Crown Point SE19 BY50 76
Crown Point, Sev. CZ64 108
Crown Rd. N10 BV29 38
Crown Rd., B.Wd. BM23 28
Crown Rd., Brwd. CY23 33
Crown Rd., Enf. CB24 30
Crown Rd., Grays DD43 71
Crown Rd., Ilf. CM31 49
Crown Rd., Mord. BS52 86
Crown Rd., N.Mal. BN51 85
Crown Rd., Orp. CO56 98
Crown Rd., Sev. CT58 98
Crown Rd., Sutt. BS56 95
Crown Rd., Twick. BJ46 74
Crown Rd., Vir.W. AR53 82
Crown Rd., West. CK63 106
Crown Ri., Wat. BD20 18
Crown St. SE5 BZ43 67
Crown St. W3 BM40 55
Crown St., Brwd. DB27 42
Crown St., Dag. CS36 59
Crown St., Egh. AT49 72
Crown St., Har. BG33 45
Crown Ter., Rich. BL45 65
Crown Way, West.Dr. AY40 53
Crown Wk., Uxb. AX36 53
High St.
Crown Wk., Wem. BL34 46
Crown Woods La. SE9 CL44 68
Crown Woods Way SE9 CM46 78
Crowndale Rd. NW1 BW37 1
Crowndale Rd. NW1 BW37 56
Crownfield Av., Ilf. CN32 49
Crownfield Rd. E15 CF35 48
Crownfields, Sev. CU66 116
Crownhill Rd., Wdf.Grn. CK29 40
Crownmead Way, Rom. CR31 50
Crownstone Rd. SW2 BY46 76
Crowntree Clo., Islw. BH43 64
Stags Way
Crows Rd. E15 CF38 57
Crows Rd., Bark. CL36 58
Crows Rd., Epp. CN18 22
Crowshott Av., Stan. BK30 36
Crowstone Rd., Grays DE41 71
Crowther Av., Brent. BL42 65
Crowther Rd. SE25 CB52 87
Crowthorne Clo. SW18 BR47 75
Crowthorne Rd. W10 BQ39 55
Croxdale Rd., B.Wd. BL23 28
Croxden Clo., Edg. BL31 46
Croxden Wk., Mord. BT53 86
Croxford Gdns. N22 BY29 38
Croxford Way, Rom. CS33 50
Croxley Clo., Orp. CO51 89
Croxley Grn., Orp. CO51 89
Croxley Rd. W9 BR38 55
Croxley Vw., Wat. BB25 26
Croxted Clo. SE21 BZ47 77
Croxted Rd. SE21 BZ47 77
Croxted Rd. SE24 BZ46 77
Croyde Av., Grnf. BG38 54
Croyde Av., Hayes BB42 63
Croyde Clo., Sid. CM47 78
Croydon Gro., Croy. BY54 86
Croydon La. S., Bans. BS60 95
Croydon La., Bans. BT60 95
Croydon Rd. E13 CG38 58
Croydon Rd. SE20 CB51 87
Croydon Rd., Beck. CC53 87
Croydon Rd., Brom. CJ55 88
Croydon Rd., Cat. CB65 105
Croydon Rd., Houns. AZ45 63
Croydon Rd., Mitch. BV52 86
Croydon Rd., Reig. BS70 121
Croydon Rd., W.Wick. CG55 88
Croydon Rd., Wall. BV56 95
Croydon Rd., Warl. CE63 105
Croydon Rd., West. CK65 106
Croyland Rd. N9 CB26 39
Croylands Dr., Surb BL54 85
Croysdale Av., Sun. BC52 83
Crozier Dr., S.Croy. CB58 96
Crozier Rd., Uxb. BA35 44
Crozier St. SE1 BX41 66
Crozier Ter. E9 CC35 48
Crucible Clo., Rom. CO32 50
Crucifix La. SE1 CA41 4
Crucifix La. SE1 CA41 67
Cruden Rd., Grav. DJ48 81
Cruden St. N1 BY37 2
Cruden St. N1 BY37 56
Cruick Av., S.Ock. DB39 60
Cruikshank Rd. E15 CG35 49
Cruikshank St. WC1 BY38 2
Cruikshank St. WC1 BY38 56
Crummock Gdns. NW9 BO32 46
Crumpsall St. SE2 CP42 69
Crundale Av. NW9 BM32 46
Crunden Rd., S.Croy. BZ57 96
Crusader Clo., Grays CX42 70
Centurian Way
Crusader Gdns., Croy. CA55 87
Crushes Clo., Brwd. DF25 122
Chelmer Dr.
Crusoe Rd., Erith CS42 69
Crusoe Rd., Mitch. BU50 76
Crutched Friars EC3 CA40 4
Crutched Friars EC3 CA40 57
Crutches La., Beac. AP29 34
Crutchfield La., Walt. BC55 83
Crutchley Rd. SE6 CG48 78
Crystal Av., Horn. CW35 51
Crystal Ct. SE19 CA49 77
Crystal Palace Par. SE19 CA50 77
Crystal Palace Park Rd. SE26 CB49 77
Crystal Palace Rd. SE22 CB45 67
Crystal Palace Sta. Rd. SE19 CB50 77
Crystal Ter. SE19 BZ50 77
Crystal View Ct., Brom. CF49 77
Crystal Way, Dag. CP33 50
Crystal Way, Har. BH32 45
Cuba Dr., Enf. CC23 30
Cuba St. E14 CE41 67
Cubitt St. WC1 BX38 2
Cubitt St. WC1 BX38 56
Cubitt St., Croy. BX56 95
Cubitt Ter. SW4 BW45 66
Cubitts Clo., Welw.G.C. BR5 5
Cubitts Cotts. SW18 BS47 76
Garratt La.
Cuckmans Dr., St.Alb. BF16 18
Cuckoo Av. W7 BH38 54
Cuckoo Dene W7 BG39 54
Cuckoo Hall La. N9 CC26 39
Cuckoo Hill Dr., Pnr. BD31 45
Cuckoo Hill Rd., Pnr. BD31 45
Cuckoo Hill, Pnr. BD31 45
Cuckoo La. W7 BH40 54
Cuckoo La., Grays DC40 71
Cuckoo Pound, Shep. BB53 83
Cucumber La., Hat. BU13 11
Cudas Clo., Epsom BO56 94
Cuddington Av., Wor.Pk. BO55 85
Cuddington Clo., Tad. BQ63 103
Cuddington Way, Sutt. BQ59 94
Cudham Dr., Croy. CF59 96
Cudham La. N., Sev. CM58 97
Cudham La. S., Sev. CM61 106
Cudham Park Rd., Sev. CM58 97
Cudham Rd., Orp. CL59 97
Cudham Rd., West. CK63 106
Cudham St. SE6 CF47 77
Cudworth St. E1 CB38 57
Cuff Cres. SE9 CJ46 78
Cuff Pl. E2 CA38 57
Angela St.
Cuffley Av., Wat. BD20 18
Cuffley Ct., Hem.H. BA11 8
Cuffley Hill, Chsnt. BY18 20
Culford Gdns. SW3 BU42 3
Culford Gdns. SW3 BU42 66
Culford Gro. N1 CA36 57
Culford Ms. N1 CA36 57
Southgate Rd.
Culford Rd. N1 CA36 57
Culford Rd., Grays DE41 71
Culgaith Gdns., Enf. BX24 29
Cullen Sq., S.Ock. DB40 60
Cullen Way NW10 BN38 55
Cullera Clo., Nthwd. BB29 35
Cullesden Rd., Ken. BY61 104
Culling Rd. SE16 CC41 67
Lower Rd.
Cullings Ct., Wal.Abb. CG20 22
Cullington Clo., Har. BJ31 45
Cullingworth Rd. NW10 BP35 46
Culloden Rd., Enf. BY23 29
Culloden St. E14 CF39 57
Cullum St. EC3 CA40 4
Cullum St. EC3 CA40 57
Culmington Rd. W13 BK40 54
Culmington Rd., S.Croy. BZ57 96
Culmore Cross SW12 BV47 76
Culmore Rd. SE15 CB43 67
Culmstock Rd. SW11 BV46 76
Culpeper Clo., Ilf. CL29 40
Culross Clo. N15 BZ31 48
Culross St. W1 BV40 3
Culross St. W1 BV40 56
Culsac Rd., Surb. BL55 85
Culver Dr., Oxt. CG68 115
Culver Gro., Stan. BK30 36
Culver Rd., St.Alb. BH12 9
Culverden Rd. SW12 BW48 76
Culverden Rd., Wat. BC27 35
Culverhay, Ash. BL61 103
Culverhouse Gdns. SW16 BX48 76
Culverlands Clo., Stan. BJ28 36
Culverley Rd. SE6 CE47 77
Culvers Av., Cars. BU55 86
Culvers Cft., Beac. AO29 34
Farmers Way
Culvers Retreat, Cars. BU54 86
Culvers Way, Cars. BU55 86
Culvers Yd., Brwd. DB27 42
High St.
Culverstone Clo., Brom. CG53 88
Culvert La., Uxb. AW37 53
Culvert Pl. SW11 BV44 66
Culvert Rd. N15 CA32 48
Culvert Rd. SW11 BU44 66
Culvey Clo., Hart. DC53 90
Culworth St. NW8 BU37 1
Culworth St. NW8 BU37 56
Cum Cum Hill, Hat. BU13 11
Cumberland Av. NW10 BM38 55
Cumberland Av., Grav. DH47 81
Cumberland Av., Guil. AQ68 109
Cumberland Av., Horn. CW34 51
Cumberland Av., Well. CN45 68
Cumberland Clo. E8 CA36 57
Forest Rd.
Cumberland Clo. SW20 BQ50 75
Cumberland Clo., Amer. AQ23 25
Cumberland Clo., Epsom BN59 94
Cumberland Clo., Hem.H. BB15 8
Cumberland Clo., Horn. CW34 51
Cumberland Dr.
Cumberland Clo., Twick. BJ46 74
Cumberland Cres. W14 BR42 65
Cumberland Ct., St.Alb. BH13 9
Carlisle Av.
Cumberland Dr., Bexh. CQ43 69
Cumberland Dr., Chess. BL55 85
Cumberland Dr., Dart. CW47 80
Cumberland Dr., Esher BJ55 84
Cumberland Gate W1 BU40 3
Cumberland Gate W1 BU40 56
Cumberland Gdns. NW4 BQ30 37
Cumberland Gdns. WC1 BX38 2
Cumberland Gdns. WC1 BX38 56
Cumberland Market Est. NW1 BV38 56
Cumberland Market NW1 BV38 1
Cumberland Market NW1 BV38 56
Cumberland Mills Sq. E14 CF42 67
Cumberland Pk. W3 BN40 55
Cumberland Pl. NW1 BV38 1
Cumberland Pl. NW1 BV38 56
Outer Circle
Cumberland Pl., Sun. BC52 83
Cumberland Rd. E12 CJ35 49
Cumberland Rd. E13 CH39 58
Cumberland Rd. E17 CD30 39
Cumberland Rd. N22 BX30 38
Cumberland Rd. N9 CC26 39
Cumberland Rd. SE25 CB53 87
Cumberland Rd. SW13 BO44 65
Cumberland Rd. W3 BN40 55
Cumberland Rd. W7 BH41 64
Cumberland Rd., Ashf. AX48 73
Cumberland Rd., Brom. CG52 8
Cumberland Rd., Har. BF32 4
Cumberland Rd., Rich. BM43 6
Cumberland Rd., Stan. BL31 4
Cumberland St. SW1 BV42
Cumberland St. SW1 BV42 6
Cumberland St., Stai. AU49 7
Cumberland Ter. Ms. NW1 BV37
Albany St.
Cumberland Ter. NW1 BV37
Cumberland Ter. NW1 BV37 5
Cumberlands, Ken. BZ61 10
Cumberlow Av. SE25 CA52 8
Cumberlow Pl., Hem.H. BA14
Cumbernauld Gdns., Sun. BB49 7
Cumberton Rd. N17 BZ30 3
Cumbrae Gdns., Surb. BK54 8
Cumbrian Av., Bexh. CT44 6
Cumbrian Gdns. NW2 BQ34 4
Cumbrian Way, Uxb. AX37 5
High St.
Cumley Rd., Epp. CT18 2
Cumming Est. N1 BZ37 5
Cumming St. N1 BX37
Cumming St. N1 BX37 5
Cummings Hall La., Rom. CV27 4
Cumnor Gdns., Epsom BP57 9
Cumnor Rd., Sutt. BT57 9
Cumnor Ri., Ken. BZ62 10
Hayes La.
Cunard Pl. EC3 CA39 5
Bury St.
Cunard Rd. NW10 BN38 5
Cunard St. SE5 CA43 6
Cunard Wk. SE16 CD42 6
Cundy Rd. E16 CJ39 5
Cundy St. Est. SW1 BV42
Cundy St. Est. SW1 BV42 6
Cundy St. SW1 BV42
Cundy St. SW1 BV42 6
Cunliffe Clo., Epsom BM65 10
Cunliffe Rd., Wor.Pk. BO56 9
Cunliffe St. SW16 BW50 7
Cunningham Av., Enf. CD21 3
Cunningham Av., Guil. AT70 11
Cunningham Av., St.Alb. BH14
Cunningham Clo., W.Wick. CE55 8
Cunningham Clo., Rom. CP32 5
Chadwell Heath La.
Cunningham Hill Rd., St.Alb. BH14
Cunningham Pk., Har. BG32 4
Cunningham Pl. NW8 BT38
Cunningham Pl. NW8 BT38 5
Cunningham Rd. N15 CB31 4
Cunningham Rd., Bans. BT61 10
Cunningham Rd., Chsnt. CD17 2
Cunningham Ri., Epp. CS16 2
Cunnington St. W4 BN41 6
Cupar Rd. SW11 BV44 6
Cupid Green La., Hem.H. AZ11
Cupola Clo., Brom. CH49 7
Powster Rd.
Cureton St. SW1 BW42
Cureton St. SW1 BW42 6
Curfew Yd., Wind. AO43 6
Datchet Rd.
Curie Gdns. NW9 BO30 3
Pasteur Clo.
Curlew Clo. SE28 CP40 5
Curlew Clo., Berk. AR13
Curlew Clo., Croy. CC59 9
Curlew Clo., S.Croy. CC58 9
Curlew Gdns., Guil. AU69 11
Curlew St. SE1 CA41
Curlew St. SE1 CA41 6
Curlews, The, Grav. DH48 8
Curling La., Grays DC42 7
Curling Vale, Guil. AQ71 11
Curnicks La. SE27 BZ49 7
Curnock Est. NW1 BW37
Curnock Est. NW1 BW37 5
Curran Av., Sid. CN46 7
Curran Av., Wall. BV55 8
Curran Clo., Uxb. AX38 5
Currey Rd., Grnf. BG36 5
Curricle St. W3 BO40 5
Currie Hill Clo. SW19 BR49 7
Curry Ri. NW7 BQ29 3
Cursitor St. EC4 BY39
Cursitor St. EC4 BY39 5
Curtain Rd. EC2 CA38
Curtain Rd. EC2 CA38 5
Curthwaite Gdns., Enf. BW24 2
Curtis Clo., Rick. AW26 3
Curtis Dr. W3 BN39 5
Cotton Av.
Curtis Field Rd. SW16 BX49 7
Curtis Gdns., Dor. BJ71 11
Curtis Rd.
Curtis Mill La., Rom. CT24 3
Curtis Rd., Dor. BJ71 11
Curtis Rd., Epsom BN56 9
Curtis Rd., Hem.H. BA14
Curtis Rd., Horn. CW33 5
Curtis Rd., Houns. BE47 7
Curtis St. SE1 CA42
Curtis St. SE1 CA42 6
Curtis Way SE1 CA42 6
Curtis Way SE28 CO40 5
Curtis Way, Berk. AR13
Curtismill Clo., Orp. CO52 8
Curtismill Way, Orp. CO52 8
Curvan Clo., Epsom BO58 9
Curve, The W12 BP40 5
Curwen Av. E7 CH35 4
Woodford Rd.
Curwen Rd. W12 BP41 6
Curzon Av., Enf. CC25 3
Curzon Av., Stan. BJ30 3
Curzon Clo., Orp. CM56 9
Curzon Clo., Wey. AZ56 9
Curzon Cres. NW10 BO36 5
Curzon Cres., Bark. CN37 5
Curzon Dr., Grays DD43 7

urzon Gate W1 BV40 3
urzon Ho. W5 BJ38 54
Castlebar Pk.
urzon Pl. W1 BV40 3
urzon Pl. W1 BV40 56
Curzon St.
urzon Pl., Pnr. BD32 45
urzon Rd. N10 BV30 38
urzon Rd. W5 BJ38 54
urzon Rd., Th.Hth. BX53 86
urzon Rd., Wey. AX56 92
urzon St. W1 BV40 3
urzon St. W1 BV40 56
usack Clo., Twick. BH49 74
ussons Clo., Chsnt. CB18 21
ustom House Wf. EC3 CA40 4
ustom House Wf. EC3 CA40 57
ut Throat La., Hodd. CD11 12
ut, The SE1 BY41 4
ut, The SE1 BY41 66
utcombe Rd. SE5 BZ44 67
utforth Rd., Saw. CQ 5 6
uthbert Gdns. SE25 CA52 87
Ross Rd.
uthbert Rd. E17 CF31 48
uthbert Rd. N18 CB28 39
uthbert Rd., Croy. BY55 86
uthbert St. W2 BT39 1
uthbert St. W2 BT39 56
uthbert St. W9 BT38 1
uthill Rd. SE5 BZ44 67
uthill Wk. SE5 BZ44 67
Grove La.
utler St. E1 CA39 2
utler St. E1 CA39 57
utlers Ter. N1 CA36 57
Balls Pond Rd.
utmere St., Grav. DG47 81
utmore Dr., St.Alb. BM14 10
utthroat All., Rich. BK48 74
utting, The, Red. BU71 121
uttsfield Ter., Hem.H. AV14 7
uxton Clo., Bexh. CQ46 79
yclamen Clo., Hmptn. BF50 74
Gresham Rd.
yclamen Rd., Swan. CS52 89
yclamen Way, Epsom BN56 94
ycle Track, Harl. CO11 14
yclops Ms. E14 CE41 67
Westferry Rd.
ygnet Av., Felt. BD47 74
ygnet Clo. NW10 BN36 55
Kingfisher Way
ygnet Clo., B.Wd. BN23 28
ygnet Clo., Nthwd. BA29 35
ygnet Gdns., Grav. DF48 81
ygnet St. E1 CA38 2
ygnet St. E1 CA38 57
Sclater St.
ygnet Vw., Grays CZ42 70
ygnets, The, Felt. BE49 74
ymbran Ct., Hem.H. AY11 8
ynthia St. N1 BX37 2
ynthia St. N1 BX37 56
yntra Pl. E8 CB36 57
Mare St.
ypress Av., Enf. BY21 29
ypress Av., Twick. BG47 74
ypress Clo., Wal.Abb. CF20 21
ypress Gro., Ilf. CN29 40
ypress Path, Rom. CV29 42
Cypress Pl. W1 BW38 1
ypress Pl. W1 BW38 56
Maple St.
Cypress Rd. SE25 CA51 87
Cypress Rd., Guil. AR69 118
Cypress Rd., Har. BG30 36
Cypress Rd., Sun. BB51 83
Harris Way
Cypress Way, Bans. BQ60 94
Cypress Wk., Egh. AQ50 72
Cyprus Av. N3 BR30 37
Cyprus Gdns. N3 BR30 37
Cyprus Pl. E2 CC37 57
Cyprus St.
Cyprus Pl. E6 CL40 58
Cyprus Rd. N3 BR30 37
Cyprus Rd. N9 CA27 39
Cyprus St. E2 CC37 57
Cyprus St. EC1 BY38 2
Cyprus St. EC1 BY38 56
Cyrena Rd. SE22 CA46 77
Cyril Mans. SW11 BU44 66
Cyril Rd., Bexh. CQ44 69
Cyril Rd., Orp. CO54 89
Czar St. SE8 CD43 67

D

D'Abernon Clo., Esher BF56 93
D'Abernon Dr., Cob. BD61 102
D'Arblay St. W1 BW39 1
D'Arblay St. W1 BW39 56
D'Arcy Clo., Brwd. DD26 122
D'Arcy Dr., Har. BK31 45
D'Arcy Gdns., Dag. CQ37 59
D'Arcy Gdns., Har. BK31 45
D'Arcy Pl., Ash. BL62 103
D'Arcy Rd., Ash. BL62 103
D'Arcy Rd., Sutt. BQ56 94
D'Eynsford Rd. SE5 BZ44 67
D'Oyley St. SW1 BV42 3
D'Oyley St. SW1 BV42 66
Da Palma Ct. SW6 BS43 66
Racton Rd.
Dabbshill La., Nthlt. BE35 45
Dabin Cres. SE10 CF44 67
Dacca St. SE8 CD43 67
Dace Rd. E3 CE36 57
Dacorum Way, Hem.H. AX13 8
Dacre Av., Ilf. CL30 40
Dacre Av., S.Ock. CY40 60
Dacre Clo., Chig. CM28 40
Dacre Clo., Grnf. BF37 54
Dacre Cres., S.Ock. CY40 60
Dacre Gdns. SE13 CG45 68
Dacre Gdns., B.Wd. BN25 28
Dacre Gdns., Chig. CM28 40
Dacre Pk. SE13 CG45 68
Dacre Pl. SE13 CG45 68
Dacre Rd. E11 CG33 49
Dacre Rd. E13 CH37 58
Dacre Rd., Croy. BX54 86
Dacre St. SW1 BW41 3
Dacre St. SW1 BW41 66
Dacres Clo. SE23 CC48 77
Dacres Rd. SE23 CC48 77
Dade Way, Sthl. BE42 64
Daerwood Clo., Brom. CK54 88
Daffodil Av., Brwd. DA25 33
Daffodil Clo., Croy. CC54 87
Primrose La.
Daffodil Pl., Hmptn. BF50 74
Gresham Rd.
Daffodil St. W12 BO40 55
Dafforne Rd. SW17 BU48 76
Dagden Rd., Guil. AS73 118
Dagenham Av., Dag. CQ37 59
Dagenham Rd. E10 CD33 48
Dagenham Rd., Dag. CR35 50
Dagenham Rd., Rain. CS36 59
Dagenham Rd., Rom. CS33 50
Dagger La., B.Wd. BJ25 27
Daggs Dell Rd., Hem.H. AV12 7
Dagley La., Guil. AR73 118
Dagmar Av., Wem. BL35 46
Dagmar Gdns. NW10 BQ37 55
Dagmar Pass. N1 BY37 2
Dagmar Pass. N1 BY37 56
Cross St.
Dagmar Rd. N15 BZ32 48
Cornwall Rd.
Dagmar Rd. N22 BW30 38
Dagmar Rd. N4 BY33 47
Dagmar Rd. SE25 CA52 87
Dagmar Rd. SE5 CA44 67
Dagmar Rd., Dag. CS36 59
Dagmar Rd., Kings.T. BL51 85
Dagmar Rd., Sthl. BE41 64
Dagmar Rd., Wind. AO44 61
Dagmar St. N1 BY37 2
Dagmar Ter. N1 BY37 56
Dagnall Cres., Uxb. AX39 53
Dagnall Pk. SE25 BZ53 87
Dagnall Rd. SE25 CA53 87
Dagnall St. SW11 BU44 66
Dagnam Park Clo., Rom. CX28 42
Dagnam Park Dr., Rom. CW28 42
Dagnam Park Gdns., Rom. CX29 42
Dagnam Park Sq., Rom. CX29 42
Dagnan Rd. SW12 BV47 76
Dagonet Gdns., Brom. CH48 78
Dagonet Rd., Brom. CH48 78
Dagwood La., Brwd. DA22 33
Dahlia Dr., Swan. CT51 89
Dahlia Gdns., Mitch. BW52 86
Dahlia Rd. SE2 CO42 69
Dahomey Rd. SW16 BW50 76
Daiglen Dr., S.Ock. DA40 60
Daimler Cotts. SE15 CA43 67
Cronin Rd.
Daimler Way, Wall. BX57 95
Daines Clo. E12 CK34 49
Daines Clo., S.Ock. DA38 60
Dainford Clo., Brom. CF49 77
Dainton Clo., Brom. CH51 88
Daintry Clo., Har. BJ31 45
Daintry Way E9 CD36 57
Dairsie Rd. SE9 CL45 68
Dairy Clo., S.at H. CX50 80
Dairy Clo., Th.Hth. BZ51 87
Dairy La., Eden. CL70 115
Dairy Ms. SW9 BX45 66
Andalus Rd.
Dairy Way, Wat. BB18 17
Dairy Wk. SW19 BR49 75
Dairymans Wk., Guil. AT68 109
Daisy Clo., Croy. CC54 87
Primrose La.
Daisy Dormer Ct. SW9 BX45 66
Trinity Gdns.
Daisy La. SW6 BS45 66
Daisy Rd. E18 CH30 40
Dakota Gdns., Nthlt. BE38 54
Argus Way
Dalberg Rd. SW2 BY45 66
Dalberg Way SE2 CP41 69
Lanridge Rd.
Dalby Rd. SW18 BT45 66
Dalby St. NW5 BV36 56
Dalcross Rd., Houns. BE44 64
Dale Av., Edg. BL30 37
Dale Av., Houns. BE45 64
Dale Clo. SE3 CH45 68
Dale Clo., Barn. BS25 29
Dale Clo., Dart. CT46 79
Dale Clo., Pnr. BC30 35
Dale Clo., S.Ock. DA39 60
Dale Clo., Wey. AW56 92
Dale Ct., Saw. CP 6 6
The Crest
Dale Ct., Slou. AO41 61
Dale Dr., Hayes BB38 53
Dale End, Dart. CT46 79
Dale Gdns., Wdf.Grn. CH28 40
Dale Green Rd. N11 BV27 38
Dale Gro. N12 BT28 38
Dale Park Av., Cars. BU55 86
Dale Park Rd. SE19 BZ51 87
Dale Rd. E16 CG38 58
Dale Rd. NW5 BV35 47
Grafton Rd.
Dale Rd. SE17 BY43 66
Hillingdon St.
Dale Rd. SE18 CL43 68
Dale Rd., Dart. CT46 79
Dale Rd., Grav. DD49 81
Dale Rd., Grnf. BF39 54
Dale Rd., Pur. BY59 95
Dale Rd., Sun. BB50 73
Dale Rd., Sutt. BR56 94
Dale Rd., Swan. CS51 89
Dale Rd., Walt. BB54 83
Dale Row W11 BR39 55
St. Marks Rd.
Dale Side, Ger.Cr. AS33 43
Dale St. W4 BO42 65
Dale View Av. E4 CF27 39
Dale View Cres. E4 CF27 39
Dale View Gdns. E4 CF27 39
Dale Vw., Epsom BM65 103
Dale Vw., Wok. AQ62 100
Dale Wk., Dart. CY47 80
Dale Wood Rd., Orp. CN54 88
Dale, The, Kes. CJ56 97
Dale, The, Wal.Abb. CG20 22
Dalebury Rd. SW17 BU48 76
Dalegarth Gdns., Pur. BZ60 96
Daleham Av., Egh. AS50 72
Daleham Dr., Uxb. AZ39 53
Daleham Gdns. NW3 BT36 56
Daleham Ms. NW3 BT36 56
Dales Path, B.Wd. BN25 28
Farriers Way
Dales Rd., B.Wd BN25 28
Daleside Clo., Orp. CO57 98
Daleside Dr., Pot.B. BR20 19
Daleside Gdns., Chig. CM27 40
Daleside Rd. SW16 BV49 76
Daleside Rd., Epsom BN57 94
Daleside, Orp. CO56 98
Daleview Rd. N15 CA32 48
Daleview, Erith CT44 69
Dalewood Clo., Horn. CW33 51
Dalewood Gdns., Wor.Pk. BP55 85
Dalewood, Welw.G.C. BT 8 5
Daley St. E9 CC36 57
Daley Thompson Way SW8 BV45 66
Dalgarno Gdns. W10 BQ39 55
Dalgarno Way W10 BQ38 55
Dalgleish St. E14 CD39 57
Daling Way E3 CD37 57
Dalkeith Gro., Stan. BK28 36
Dalkeith Rd. SE21 BZ47 77
Dalkeith Rd., Ilf. CM34 49
Dallas Rd. NW4 BP33 46
Dallas Rd. SE26 CB49 77
Dallas Rd. W5 BL39 55
Dallas Rd., Sutt. BR57 94
Dallas Ter., Hayes BB41 63
Dallin Rd. SE18 CL43 68
Dallin Rd., Bexh. CP45 69
Dalling Rd. W6 BP42 65
Dallinger Rd. SE12 CG46 78
Dallington Clo., Walt. BD57 93
Dallington St. EC1 BY38 2
Dallington St. EC1 BY38 56
Dalmain Rd. SE23 CC47 77
Dalmally Rd., Croy. CA54 87
Dalmeny Av. N7 BW35 47
Dalmeny Av. SW16 BY51 86
Dalmeny Clo., Wem. BK36 54
Dalmeny Cres., Houns. BG45 64
Dalmeny Rd. N7 BW34 47
Dalmeny Rd., Barn. BT25 29
Dalmeny Rd., Cars. BV57 95
Dalmeny Rd., Erith CR44 69
Dalmeny Rd., Wor.Pk. BP55 85
Dalmore Av., Esher BH57 93
Dalmore Rd. SE21 BZ48 77
Dalroy Clo., S.Ock. DA39 60
Dalrymple Rd. SE4 CD45 67
Dalston Gdns., Stan. BL30 37
Dalston La. E8 CA36 57
Dalton Av., Mitch. BU51 86
Dalton Clo., Dart. CT44 69
Dalton Clo., Hayes BA38 53
Dalton Clo., Orp. CN55 88
Dalton Rd., Har. BG30 36
Dalton St. SE27 BY48 76
Dalton St., St.Alb. BG13 9
Daltons Rd., Orp. CR55 89
Daltons Rd., Swan. CS54 89
Dalwood St. SE5 CA44 67
Daly Ct. E15 CE35 48
Holt Ct.
Dalyell Rd. SW9 BX45 66
Damascene Wk. SE21 BZ47 77
Lovelace Rd.
Damask Grn., Hem.H. AV14 7
Dame St. N1 BZ37 2
Dame St. N1 BZ37 57
Damer Ter. SW10 BT43 66
Ashburnham Rd.
Dames Rd. E7 CH34 49
Damien St. E1 CB39 57
Damon Clo., Sid. CO48 79
Damphurst Hollow, Dor. BF74 119
Damson Wood Clo., Sthl. BF41 64
Havelock Rd.
Dan Leno Wk. SW6 BS43 66
Britannia Rd.
Danbridge Clo. SE10 CG42 68
Chilvers St.
Danbrook Rd. SW16 BX51 86
Danbury Clo., Brwd. CZ25 33
Danbury Clo., Rom. CP31 50
Danbury Ms., Wall. BV56 95
Danbury Rd., Loug. CK26 40
Danbury Rd., Rain. CT37 59
Danbury St. N1 BY37 2
Danbury St. N1 BY37 56
Danbury Way, Wdf.Grn. CJ29 40
Danby St. SE15 CA45 67
Dancer Rd. SW6 BR44 65
Fulham Rd.
Dancer Rd., Rich. BM45 65
Dancers Hill Rd., Barn. BQ21 28
Dancers La., Barn. BQ21 28
Dando Cres. SE3 CH45 68
Dandridge Clo., Slou. AR42 62
Dane Clo., Amer. AP24 25
Dane Clo., Bex. CR47 79
Dane Clo., Orp. CM56 97
Dane Ct. N2 BT33 47
Dane Ct., Wok. AV60 91
Dane Pl. E3 CD37 57
Roman Rd.
Dane Rd. N18 CC28 39
Dane Rd. SW19 BT51 86
Dane Rd. W13 BK40 54
Dane Rd., Ashf. BA50 73
Dane Rd., Ilf. CM35 49
Dane Rd., Sev. CT62 107
Dane Rd., Sthl. BE40 54
Dane Rd., Warl. CC62 105
Dane St. WC1 BX39 2
Dane St. WC1 BX39 56
Red Lion Sq.
Danebury Av. SW15 BO46 75
Danebury, Croy. CF57 96
Daneby Rd. SE6 CE48 77
Danecourt Gdns., Croy. CA55 87
Danecroft Rd. SE24 BZ46 77
Danehill Wk., Sid. CO48 79
Hatherley Rd.
Danehurst Gdns., Ilf. CK32 49
Danehurst St. SW6 BR44 65
Daneland, Barn. BU25 29
Danemead Gdns., Nthlt. BF35 45
Danemead, Hodd. CE10 12
Danemere St. SW15 BQ45 65
Danes Clo., Grav. DE48 81
Danes Clo., Lthd. BG60 93
Danes Gate, Har. BH31 45
Danes Hill, Wok. AT62 100
Danes Rd., Rom. CS33 50
Danes Way, Brwd. DA25 33
Danes Way, Lthd. BG60 93
Danes, The, St.Alb. BG17 18
Park Street La.
Danesbury Rd., Felt. BC47 73
Danescombe SE12 CH47 78
Winn Rd.
Danescourt Cres., Sutt. BT55 86
Danescroft Av. NW4 BQ32 46
Danescroft Gdns. NW4 BQ32 46
Danescroft NW4 BQ32 46
Brent St.
Danesdale Rd. E9 CD36 57
Daneshill Clo., Red. BU70 121
Daneshill, Red. BU70 121
Daneswood Av. SE6 CF48 77
Daneswood Clo., Wey. BA56 92
Danethorpe Rd., Wem. BK36 54
Danetree Rd., Epsom BN57 94
Danette Gdns., Dag. CR34 50
Daneville Rd. SE5 BZ44 67
Dangan Rd. E11 CH32 49
Daniel Bolt Clo. E14 CE39 57
Daniel Clo. N18 CC28 39
Daniel Clo. SW17 BU50 76
Daniel Clo., Grays DG41 71
Daniel Gdns. SE15 CA43 67
Daniel Pl. NW4 BP32 46
Daniel Rd. W5 BL40 55
Daniells, Welw.G.C. BS 7 5
Daniels La., Warl. CD61 105
Daniels Rd. SE15 CC45 67
Danses Clo., Guil. AU69 118
Eustace Rd.
Dansington Rd., Well. CO45 69
Danson Cres., Well. CO45 69
Danson La., Well. CO45 69
Danson Mead, Well. CP45 69
Danson Rd. SE17 BY42 4
Danson Rd., Bex. CP46 79
Dante Pl. SE11 BY42 4
Dante Rd. SE11 BY42 4
Dante Rd. SE11 BY42 66
Danube St. SW3 BU42 3
Danube St. SW3 BU42 66
Danvers Rd. N8 BW31 47
Danvers St. SW3 BT43 66
Danyon Clo., Rain. CV38 60
Danziger Way, B.Wd. BN23 28
Dapdune Ct., Guil. AR70 118
Woodbridge Rd.
Dapdune Rd., Guil. AR70 118
Daphne Gdns. E4 CF27 39
Gunners Gro.
Daphne St. SW18 BT46 76
Daplyn St. E1 CB39 2
Daplyn St. E1 CB39 57
Darby Cres., Sun. BD51 84
Darby Dr., Wal.Abb. CF20 21
Sun St.
Darby Gdns., Sun. BD51 84
Darcy Av., Wall. BW56 95
Darcy Clo. N20 BT27 38
Darcy Clo., Chsnt. CD19 21
Darcy Clo., Couls. BY63 104
Darcy Rd. SW16 BW51 86
Dare Gdns., Dag. CQ34 50
Darell Rd., Rich. BM45 65
Darent Clo., Sev. CR64 107
Darent Mead, S.at H. CX51 90
Darenth Hill, Dart. CY49 80
Darenth La., S.Ock. DA39 60
Darenth La., Sev. CT64 107
Darenth Rd. N16 CA33 48
Darenth Rd., Dart. CW47 80
Darenth Rd., Well. CO44 69
Darenth Wood Rd., Dart. CZ48 80
Darfield Rd. SE4 CD46 77
Darfield Rd., Guil. AT69 118
Darfield Way W10 BQ40 55
Darfur St. SW15 BQ45 65
Dargate Clo. SE19 CA50 77
Chipstead Clo.
Darien Rd. SW11 BT45 66
Dark La., Brwd. CZ28 42
Dark La., Chsnt. CB18 21
Darkes La., Pot.B. BS19 20
Darlan Rd. SW6 BR43 65
Darlaston Rd. SW19 BQ50 75
Darley Clo., Croy. CD53 87
Darley Clo., Wey. AX56 92
Darley Dr., N.Mal. BN51 85
Darley Gdns., Mord. BT53 86
Darley Rd. N9 CA26 39
Darley Rd. SW11 BU46 76
Darling Rd. SE4 CE45 67
Darling Row E1 CB38 57
Darlington Clo., Amer. AO22 25
King George V Rd.
Darlington Gdns., Rom. CV28 42
Darlington Path, Rom. CV28 42
Darlington Rd. SE27 BY49 76
Darmaine Clo., S.Croy. BZ57 96
Churchill Rd.
Darnets Field, Sev. CT61 107
Darnhills, Rad. BH21 27
Darnicle Hill, Chsnt. BY16 20
Darnley Pk., Wey. AZ55 83
Portmore Park Rd.
Darnley Rd. E9 CB36 57
Darnley Rd., Grav. DG47 81
Darnley Rd., Grays DD43 71
Darnley Rd., Wdf.Grn. CH30 40
Darnley St., Grav. DG47 81
Darnley Ter. W11 BQ40 55
Darrell Clo., Slou. AS42 62
Darrell Rd. SE22 CB46 77
Darren Clo. N4 BX33 47
Darrick Wood Rd., Orp. CM55 88
Darrington Rd., B.Wd. BL23 28
Darris Clo., Hayes BE38 54
Darrs La., Berk. AO12 7
Darsley Dr. SW8 BW44 66
Dart Clo., Slou. AT43 62
Severn Cres.
Dart Clo., Upmin. CY32 51
Dart Grn., S.Ock. DA39 60
Dart St. W10 BR38 55
Dart, The, Hem.H. AZ11 8
Dartfields, Rom. CV29 42
Dartford Av. N9 CC25 30
Dartford By-pass, Dart. CU48 79
Dartford Rd., (The Brent) Dart. CX47 80
Dartford Rd., Bex. CS47 79
Dartford Rd., Dart. CU46 79
Dartford Rd., Farn. CW53 90
Dartford Rd., Sev. CV64 108
Dartford St. SE17 BZ43 4
Dartford St. SE17 BZ43 67
Dartford Tunnel App., Grays CZ43 70
Dartmoor Wk. E14 CE42 67
Charnwood Gdns.
Dartmouth Av., Wok. AU60 91
Dartmouth Clo. W11 BS39 56
Ledbury Rd.
Dartmouth Grn., Wok. AU60 91
Dartmouth Gro. SE10 CF44 67
Dartmouth Hill SE10 CF44 67
Dartmouth Park Av. NW5 BV34 47
Dartmouth Park Hill N19 BV33 47
Dartmouth Park Hill NW5 BV33 47
Dartmouth Park Rd. NW5 BV35 47
Dartmouth Path, Wok. AU60 91
Dartmouth Av.
Dartmouth Pl. SE23 CC48 77
Dartmouth Pl. W4 BO43 65
Dartmouth Rd. E16 CH39 58
Dartmouth Rd. NW2 BQ36 55
Dartmouth Rd. NW4 BP32 46
Dartmouth Rd. SE23 CC48 77
Dartmouth Rd. SE26 CB48 77
Dartmouth Rd., Brom. CH54 88
Dartmouth Rd., Ruis. BC34 44
Dartmouth Row SE10 CF44 67
Dartmouth St. SW1 BW41 3
Dartmouth St. SW1 BW41 66
Dartnell Av., Wey. AW59 92
Dartnell Cres., Wey. AW59 92
Dartnell Park Rd., Wey. AW59 92
Dartnell Pl., Wey. AW59 92
Dartnell Rd. SE5 CA43 67
Dartnell Rd. SE5 CA45 4
Dartnell Rd., Croy. CA54 87
Dartrey Wk. SW10 BT43 66
Worlds End
Dartview Clo., Grays DE42 71
Chadwell Rd.
Darvell Clo., Wok. AQ61 100
Darville Rd. N16 CA34 48
Darvills La., Slou. AO41 61
Darwell Clo. E6 CL37 58
Darwin Clo. N11 BV28 38
Darwin Clo., Hem.H. AZ10 8
Darwin Clo., Orp. CM56 97
Darwin Clo., St.Alb. BH11 9
Darwin Dr., Sthl. BF39 54
Darwin Gdns., Wat. BD28 36
Barnhurst Path
Darwin Pl. SE17 BZ42 4
Darwin Pl. SE17 BZ42 67
Darwin St.
Darwin Rd. N22 BY30 38
Darwin Rd. W5 BK42 64
Darwin Rd., Slou. AS41 62
Darwin Rd., Til. DF44 71
Darwin Rd., Well. CN45 68
Darwin St. SE17 BZ42 4
Darwin St. SE17 BZ42 67
Daryngton Dr., Grnf. BG37 54
Daryngton Dr., Guil. AT70 118
Dashes, The, Harl. CN10 6
Dashwood Clo., Bexh. CR46 79
Dashwood Clo., Slou. AR42 62
Dashwood Clo., Wey. AX59 92
Dashwood La., Grav. DG48 81
Dashwood Rd. N8 BX32 47
Dashwood Rd., Grav. DG47 81
Dassett Rd. SE27 BY49 76
Datchelor Pl. SE5 BZ44 67
Datchet Clo., Hem.H. AZ11 8
Datchet Pl., Slou. AQ44 62
Datchet Rd. SE6 CD48 77
Datchet Rd., Horton AS45 62
Datchet Rd., Old Windsor AQ45 62
Datchet Rd., Slou. AP42 62
Datchet Rd., Wind. AO43 61

Datchworth Ct. N4	BZ34	48
Kings Crescent Est.		
Datchworth Turn, Hem.H.	BA13	8
Date St. SE17	**BZ42**	**4**
Date St. SE17	BZ42	67
Daubeney Rd. E5	CD35	48
Daubeney Rd. N17	BZ29	39
Dault Rd. SW18	BT46	76
Davema Clo., Chis.	CL51	88
Brenchley Clo.		
Davenant Rd. N19	BW34	47
Davenant Rd., Croy.	BY56	95
Davenant St. E1	**CB39**	**2**
Davenant St. E1	CB39	57
Davenham Av., Nthwd.	BB28	35
Davenport Clo., Tedd.	BJ50	74
Udney Park Rd.		
Davenport Rd. SE6	CE46	77
Davenport Rd., Sid.	CP48	79
Daventer Dr., Stan.	BH29	36
Daventry Av. E17	CE32	48
Daventry Clo., Slou.	AV44	62
Rodney Way		
Daventry Gdns., Rom.	CV28	42
Daventry Grn., Rom.	CV28	42
Daventry Rd., Rom.	CV28	42
Daventry St. NW1	**BU39**	**1**
Daventry St. NW1	BU39	56
Daver Ct. W5	BK39	54
Mount Av.		
Davern Clo. SE10	CG42	68
Davey Clo. N7	BX36	56
Davey Rd. E9	CE36	57
Davey St. SE15	CA43	67
David Av., Grnf.	BH37	54
David Clo., Hayes	BB43	63
Nobel Dr.		
David Dr., Rom.	CX29	42
David Ms. W1	**BU39**	**1**
David Rd., Dag.	CQ34	50
David Rd., Slou.	AV44	62
David St. E15	CF36	57
Davidge St. SE1	**BY41**	**4**
Davidge St. SE1	BY41	66
King James St.		
Davids Rd. SE23	CC47	77
Davids Way, Ilf.	CN29	40
Davidson Gdns. SW8	BX43	66
Davidson La., Har.	BH33	45
Grove Hill		
Davidson Rd., Croy.	CA54	87
Davies Clo., Croy.	CB53	87
Davies Clo., Rain.	CV38	60
Davies La. E11	CG34	49
Davies Ms. W1	**BV40**	**3**
Davies Ms. W1	BV40	56
Davies St.		
Davies St. W1	**BV39**	**1**
Davies St. W1	BV39	56
Davies Way, Egh.	AU49	72
Davington Gdns., Dag.	CO35	50
Davington Rd., Dag.	CO36	59
Davinia Clo., Wdf.Grn.	CK29	40
Deacon Way		
Davis Av., Grav.	DF47	81
Davis Rd. W3	BO40	55
Davis Rd., Chess.	BM56	94
Davis Rd., S.Ock.	CY40	60
Davis St. E13	CH37	58
Davison Dr., Chsnt.	CC17	21
Davisville Rd. W12	BP41	65
Davos Clo., Wok.	AS63	100
Davys Pl., Grav.	DJ50	81
Dawell Dr., West.	CJ62	106
Dawes Av., Horn.	CV34	51
Dawes Av., Islw.	BJ45	64
Dawes Ct., Esher	BF56	93
Dawes Ho. SE17	**BZ42**	**4**
Dawes La., Rick.	AV22	25
Dawes Moor Clo., Slou.	AR39	52
Dawes Rd. SW6	BR43	65
Dawes Rd., Uxb.	AY37	53
Dawes St. SE17	**BZ42**	**4**
Dawes St. SE17	BZ42	67
Dawley Av., Uxb.	BA39	53
Dawley Ct., Hem.H.	AZ11	8
Dawley Grn., S.Ock.	DA39	60
Dawley Par., Hayes	BA40	53
Dawley Rd., Hayes	BA40	53
Dawley Ride, Slou.	AV44	62
Dawley, Welw.G.C.	BR 6	5
Dawlish Av. N13	BX28	38
Dawlish Av. SW18	BS48	76
Dawlish Av., Grnf.	BJ37	54
Dawlish Dr., Ilf.	CN35	49
Dawlish Dr., Pnr.	BE32	45
Dawlish Dr., Ruis.	BC34	44
Dawlish Rd. E10	CF33	48
Dawlish Rd. N17	CB31	48
Dawlish Rd. NW2	BQ36	55
Dawlish Wk., Rom.	CV30	42
Neave Cres.		
Dawn Clo., Houns.	BE45	64
Dawn Redwood Clo., Slou.	AT45	62
Dawnay Gdns. SW18	BT48	76
Dawnay Rd. SW18	BT48	76
Dawnay Rd., Lthd.	BF66	111
Dawpool Rd. NW2	BO34	46
Daws Hill E4	CF23	30
Daws La. NW7	BO28	37
Dawson Av., Bark.	CN36	58
Dawson Av., Orp.	CO51	89
Dawson Clo. SE18	CM42	68
Dawson Clo., Hayes	BA39	53
Dawson Clo., Wind.	AN44	61
Dawson Dr., Rain.	CU36	59
Dawson Gdns., Bark.	CN36	58
Dawson Av.		
Dawson Ho. SE5	CA44	67
Glebe Est.		
Dawson Pl. W2	BS40	56
Dawson Rd. E2	**CA37**	**2**
Dawson Rd. NW2	BQ35	46
Dawson Rd. SE17	BY42	66
Dawson Rd., Kings.T.	BL52	85

Dawson Rd., Wey.	AX59	92
Dawson St. E2	CA37	57
Dawson Ter. N9	CC26	39
St. Alphege Rd.		
Dax Ct., Sun.	BD52	84
Day Spring, Guil.	AQ68	109
Daybrook Rd. SW19	BS52	86
Daye Mead, Welw.G.C.	BS 9	5
Daylesford Av. SW15	BP45	65
Daylop Dr., Chig.	CO27	41
Daymer Gdns., Pnr.	BC31	44
Daymerslea Ridge, Lthd.	BK64	102
Days Acre, S.Croy.	CA58	96
Days Clo., Hat.	BO12	10
Days La., Brwd.	DA24	33
Days La., Sid.	CN47	78
Days Mead, Hat.	BO12	10
Daysbrook Rd. SW2	BX48	76
Dayton Dr., Erith	CV43	70
Dayton Gro. SE15	CC44	67
De Beauvoir Cres. N1	**CA37**	**2**
De Beauvoir Cres. N1	CA37	57
De Beauvoir Est. N1	**CA37**	**2**
De Beauvoir Est. N1	CA37	57
De Beauvoir Rd. N1	**CA37**	**2**
De Beauvoir Rd. N1	CA37	57
De Beauvoir Sq. N1	CA36	57
De Bohun Av. N14	BV25	29
De Burgh Pk., Bans.	BS61	104
De Burgh Rd. SW19	BT50	76
De Crespigny Pk. SE5	BZ44	67
De Frene Rd. SE26	CC49	77
De Haviland Rd., Houns.	BD43	64
De Havilland Way, Stai.	AX46	73
De Havilland Clo., Hat.	BO12	10
De Havilland Rd., Edg.	BM30	37
De Havilland Rd., Wall.	BX57	95
De Havilland Way, Wat.	BB19	17
De Lapre Clo., Orp.	CP54	89
De Lara Way, Wok.	AR62	100
De Laune St. SE17	BY42	66
De Laune St. SE17	**BY43**	**4**
De Luci Rd., Erith	CS42	69
De Montfort Rd. SW16	BX48	76
De Morgan Rd. SW6	BS45	66
De Quincy Rd. N17	BZ30	39
De Salis Rd., Uxb.	BA38	53
De Tany Ct., St.Alb.	BH14	9
De Vere Gdns. W8	**BT41**	**3**
De Vere Gdns. W8	BT41	66
De Vere Gdns., Ilf.	CK34	49
De Vere Wk., Wat.	BB23	26
De Walden St. W1	**BV39**	**1**
De Walden St. W1	BV39	56
Marylebone St.		
De'Arn Gdns., Mitch.	BU52	86
Deacon Clo., Cob.	BC63	101
Deacon Clo., St.Alb.	BG15	9
Creighton Av.		
Deacon Rd. NW2	BP35	46
Deacon Rd., Kings.T.	BL51	85
Deacon Way SE17	**BZ42**	**4**
Deacon Way SE17	BZ42	67
Deacon Way, Wdf.Grn.	CK29	40
Deacons Clo., B.Wd.	BM24	28
Deacons Clo., Pnr.	BC30	35
Deacons Heights, B.Wd.	BM25	28
Deacons Hill Rd., B.Wd.	BL24	28
Deacons Hill, Wat.	BD25	27
Deacons Leas, Orp.	CM56	97
Deacons Wk., Hmptn.	BF49	74
Deaconsfield Rd., Hem.H.	AY15	8
Deadhearn La., Ch.St.G.	AS26	34
Deadmans Ash La., Rick.	AW21	26
Deal Porters Way SE16	CC41	67
Deal Rd. SW17	BV50	76
Deal St. E1	**CB39**	**2**
Deal St. E1	CB39	57
Deal Tree Clo., Brwd.	DA21	33
Deal Wk. SW9	BY43	66
Mandela St.		
Deals Gateway SE10	CE44	67
Deptford Br.		
Dealtry Rd. SW15	BQ45	65
Dean Bradley St. SW1	**BX41**	**4**
Dean Bradley St. SW1	BX41	66
Dean Clo. E9	CC35	48
Dean Clo. SE16	CC40	57
Surrey Water Rd.		
Dean Clo., Uxb.	AY36	53
Dean Clo., Wind.	AL45	61
Dean Clo., Wok.	AV61	100
Dean Cross St. E1	CC39	57
Commercial Rd.		
Dean Ct., Wem.	BJ34	45
Dean Dr., Stan.	BL30	37
Dean Farrar St. SW1	**BW41**	**3**
Dean Farrar St. SW1	BW41	66
Tothill St.		
Dean Field, Hem.H.	AT17	16
Dean Gdns. E17	CF31	48
Dean La., Red.	BW65	104
Dean Rd. NW2	BQ36	55
Dean Rd., Croy.	BZ56	96
Dean Rd., Hmptn.	BF49	74
Dean Rd., Houns.	BF46	74
Dean Ryle St. SW1	**BX42**	**4**
Dean Ryle St. SW1	BX42	66
Dean St. E7	CH35	49
Dean St. W1	**BW39**	**1**
Dean St. W1	BW39	56
Dean Stanley St. SW1	**BX41**	**4**
Dean Stanley St. SW1	BX41	66
Dean Trench St. SW1	**BX41**	**4**
Dean Trench St. SW1	BX41	66
Tufton St.		
Dean Way, Cat.	BZ66	114
Dean Way, Ch.St.G.	AQ27	34
Dean Way, Sthl.	BF41	64
Dean Wk., Edg.	BN29	37
Dean Wk., Lthd.	BF66	111
Dean Wood Rd., Beac.	AO30	34
Deanacre Clo., Ger.Cr.	AS29	34
Deancroft Rd., Ger.Cr.	AS29	34
Deancross St. E1	CC39	57

Deane Av., Ruis.	BD35	45
Deane Croft Rd., Pnr.	BC32	44
Deane Way, Ruis.	BC32	44
Deanery Clo. N2	BU31	47
East Finchley Sta.		
Deanery Ms. W1	BV40	56
Deanery St.		
Deanery Rd. E15	CG36	58
Deanery Rd., Eden.	CM70	115
Deanery St. W1	**BV40**	**3**
Deanery St. W1	BV40	56
Deanhill Ct. SW14	BM45	65
Deanhill Rd. SW14	BM45	65
Deans Bldgs. SE17	BZ42	67
Deans Clo. W4	BM43	65
Whitehall Gdns.		
Deans Clo., Amer.	AP22	25
Deans Clo., Croy.	CB55	87
Deans Clo., Edg.	BN29	37
Deans Clo., Slou.	AQ37	52
Deans Clo., Tad.	BP65	103
Deans Clo., Wat.	BA19	17
Deans Ct. EC4	**BY39**	**2**
Deans Ct. EC4	BY39	56
St. Pauls Churchyard		
Deans Dr., Edg.	BN28	37
Deans Field, Cat.	CA66	114
Deans Gate Clo. SE23	CC48	77
Deans Gdns., St.Alb.	BJ11	9
Deans La., Edg.	BN29	37
Deans La., Tad.	BP66	112
Deans Ms. W1	**BV39**	**1**
Deans Ms. W1	BV39	56
Cavendish Sq.		
Deans Pl. SW1	**BW42**	**3**
Deans Pl. SW1	BW42	66
Deans Rd. W7	BH40	54
Deans Rd., Brwd.	DA28	42
Cromwell Rd.		
Deans Rd., Red.	BW68	113
Deans Rd., Sutt.	BS55	86
Deans Way, Edg.	BN28	37
Deans Wk., Couls.	BY62	104
Deans Yd. SW1	BW41	66
Deansbrook Clo., Edg.	BN29	37
Deansbrook Rd., Edg.	BM29	37
Deanscroft Av. NW9	BN34	46
Deansway N2	BT31	47
Deansway N9	BZ27	39
Deansway, Hem.H.	AY15	8
Dearne Clo., Stan.	BJ28	36
Deason St. E15	CF37	57
Debden Clo., Wdf.Grn.	CJ29	40
Debden La., Loug.	CM22	31
Debden Rd., Loug.	CL22	31
Debden Wk., Horn.	CU36	59
Debenham Rd., Chsnt.	CB17	21
Debnams Rd. SE16	CC42	67
Rotherhithe New Rd.		
Deborah Clo., Islw.	BH44	64
Osterley Rd.		
Deborah Cres., Ruis.	BA33	44
Debrabant Clo., Belv.	CS43	69
Decies Way, Slou.	AQ37	52
Decima St. SE1	**CA41**	**4**
Decima St. SE1	CA41	67
Deck Clo. SE16	CC41	67
Thame Rd.		
Decoy Av. NW11	BR32	46
Dedswell Dr., Guil.	AW68	110
Dedworth Dr., Wind.	AM44	61
Dedworth Rd., Wind.	AL44	61
Dee Clo., Upmin.	CZ32	51
Dee Rd. E13	CG38	58
Dee Rd., Rich.	BL45	65
Dee St. E14	CF39	57
Dee Way, Epsom	BO58	94
Dee Way, Rom.	CT29	41
Dee, The, Hem.H.	AY11	8
Deeley Rd. SW8	BW44	66
Deena Clo. W3	BL39	55
Deep Field, Slou.	AQ43	62
Deep Pool La., Wok.	AQ60	91
Deepdale Av., Brom.	CG52	88
Deepdale SW19	BQ49	75
Deepdene Av. Rd., Dor.	BK70	119
Deepdene Av., Croy.	CA55	87
Deepdene Av., Dor.	BK71	119
Deepdene Clo. E18	CH31	49
Deepdene Ct. N21	BY25	29
Deepdene Dr., Dor.	BK71	119
Deepdene Gdns. SW2	BX47	76
Deepdene Gdns., Dor.	BJ71	119
Deepdene Park Rd., Dor.	BK71	119
Deepdene Path, Loug.	CL24	31
Deepdene Rd. SE5	BZ45	67
Deepdene Rd., Loug.	CL24	31
Deepdene Rd., Well.	CO45	69
Deepdene Vale, Dor.	BK71	119
Deepdene W5	BL38	55
The Ridings		
Deepdene Wood, Dor.	BK71	119
Deepdene, Pot.B.	BQ19	19
Deepfield Way, Couls.	BX61	104
Deepwell Clo., Islw.	BJ44	64
Deepwood La., Grnf.	BG38	54
Deer Barn Rd., Guil.	AQ70	118
Deer Pk. Clo., Kings.T.	BM50	75
Crescent Rd.		
Deer Pk. Gdns., Mitch.	BT52	86
Deer Pk. Rd. SW19	BT51	86
Deer Pk. Way, W.Wick.	CG55	88
Deer Pk., Harl.	CL12	13
Deerbrook Rd. SE24	BY47	76
Deerdale Rd. SE24	BZ45	67
Deere Av., Rain.	CU36	59
Deerfield Cotts. NW9	BO32	46
Deerhurst Clo., Felt.	BC49	73
Deerhurst Rd. NW2	BQ36	55
Deerhurst Rd. SW16	BX49	76
Deerings Dr., Pnr.	BC32	44
Deerings Rd., Reig.	BS70	121
Deerleap Gro. E4	CE25	30
Deerleap Rd., Dor.	BF72	119
Deerswood Av., Hat.	BP13	10
Deeside Rd. SW17	BT48	76
Deeves Hall La., Pot.B.	BO20	19

Defiance Wk. SE18	CK41	68
Antelope Rd.		
Defiant Way, Wall.	BX57	95
Defoe Av., Rich.	BM43	65
Defoe Clo. SW17	BU50	76
Defoe Clo., Erith	CT44	69
Selkirk Dr.		
Defoe Par., Grays	DG41	71
Defoe Rd. N16	CA34	48
Defoe Way, Rom.	CR29	41
Degema Rd., Chis.	CL49	78
Dehar Cres. NW4	BP33	46
Deimos Dr., Hem.H.	AZ12	8
Dekker Rd. SE21	CA46	77
Delabole Rd., Red.	BX68	113
Delacourt Rd. SE3	CH43	68
Old Dover Rd.		
Delafield Rd. SE7	CH42	68
Delafield Rd., Grays	DE42	71
Delaford Clo., Iver	AV39	52
Delaford Rd. SE16	CB42	67
Delaford St. SW6	BR43	65
Delagarde Rd., West.	CM66	115
Delahay Ri., Berk.	AQ12	7
Delamare Rd., Chsnt.	CD18	21
Delamere Cres. SW9	BX45	66
Brighton Ter.		
Delamere Cres., Croy.	CC53	87
Delamere Gdns. NW7	BN29	37
Delamere Rd. SW20	BQ51	85
Delamere Rd. W5	BL40	55
Delamere Rd., B.Wd.	BM23	28
Delamere Rd., Hayes	BD40	54
Delamere Rd., Reig.	BS72	121
Delamere St. W2	**BS39**	**1**
Blomfield Vills.		
Delamere Ter. W2	**BS39**	**1**
Delamere Ter. W2	BS39	56
Delancey St. NW1	**BV37**	**1**
Delancey St. NW1	BV37	56
Delaporte, Epsom.	BO59	94
Hawthorne Pl.		
Delargy Clo., Grays	DG41	71
Longhouse Rd.		
Delaware Rd. W9	BS38	56
Delawyk Cres. SE24	BZ46	77
Delbow Rd., Felt.	BC46	73
Delcombe Av., Wor.Pk.	BQ54	85
Delderfield, Ash.	BK64	102
Hatherwood		
Delft Way SE22	CA46	77
Dulwich Gro.		
Delhi Rd., Enf.	CA26	39
Delhi St. N1	**BX37**	**2**
Delhi St. N1	BX37	56
Delia St. SW18	BS47	76
Delius Clo., B.Wd.	BK25	27
Dell Clo. E15	CF37	57
Dell Clo., Dor.	BK67	111
Dell Clo., Lthd.	BH65	102
Dell Clo., Wall.	BW56	95
Dell Clo., Wdf.Grn.	CH27	40
Dell Farm Rd., Ruis.	BA32	44
Dell La., Epsom	BP56	94
Dell Lees, Beac.	AO29	34
Dell Meadow, Hem.H.	AY15	8
Dell Rd., Berk.	AO11	7
Dell Rd., Enf.	CC22	30
Dell Rd., Epsom	BP57	94
Dell Rd., Grays	DD42	71
Dell Rd., Wat.	BC22	26
Dell Rd., West Dr.	AY42	63
Dell Ri., St.Alb.	BF17	18
Dell Side, Wat.	BC22	26
Dell Way W13	BK39	54
Dell Wk., N.Mal.	BO51	85
Dell, The SE19	CA51	87
Dell, The SE2	CO42	69
Dell, The, Bex.	CT47	79
Dell, The, Brent.	BK43	64
Boston Manor Rd.		
Dell, The, Brwd.	DA29	42
Dell, The, Felt.	BC47	73
Dell, The, Ger.Cr.	AS29	34
Dell, The, Nthwd.	BB27	35
Dell, The, Pnr.	BD30	36
Dell, The, Rad.	BJ21	27
Dell, The, Reig.	BS70	121
Dell, The, St.Alb.	BJ12	9
Dell, The, Tad.	BQ64	103
Fairacres		
Dell, The, Wall.	BW56	95
Dell, The, Wdf.Grn.	CH27	40
Dell, The, Wem.	BJ35	45
Dell, The, Wok.	AR62	100
Della Path E5	CB34	48
Downs Est.		
Dellcott Clo., Welw.G.C.	BP 7	5
Dellcut Rd., Hem.H.	AZ12	8
Dellfield Av., Berk.	AQ12	7
Dellfield Clo., Berk.	AQ12	7
Dellfield Clo., Brom.	CS50	77
Foxgrove Rd.		
Dellfield Clo., Rad.	BH21	27
Dellfield Clo., Wat.	BC23	26
Dellfield Cres., Uxb.	AX38	53
Dellfield Rd., Hat.	BP12	10
Dellfield, St.Alb.	BH14	9
Dellmeadow, Wat.	BB19	17
Dellors Clo., Barn.	BQ25	28
Dellow Clo., Ilf.	CM33	49
Dellow St. E1	CB40	57
Dells, The, Hem.H.	AZ14	8
Dellside, Uxb.	AX32	44
Dellsome Gdns., St.Alb.	BO15	10
Dellsome La., Hat.	BP15	10
Dellsome Par., Hat.	BQ15	10
Dellsome La.		
Dellwood Clo., Rick.	AW26	35
Dellwood Gdns., Ilf.	CL31	49
Delmar Av., Hem.H.	BA14	8
Delmare Clo. SW9	BX45	66
Brighton Ter.		
Delme Cres. SE3	CH44	68
Delmey Clo., Croy.	CA55	87
Deloraine St. SE8	CE44	67

Delorme St. W6	BQ43	6
Delphian Ct. SW16	BY49	7
Leigham Court Rd.		
Delsa Ct. NW2	BP34	4
Delta Clo., Wok.	AP58	9
Delta Clo., Wor.Pk.	BO55	8
Delta Gain, Wat.	BD27	3
Delta Gro., Nthlt.	BD38	5
Kittiwake Rd.		
Delta Rd., Brwd.	DE25	12
Delta Rd., Chobham	AP58	9
Delta Rd., Wok.	AT61	10
Delta Rd., Wor.Pk.	BO55	8
Delta St. E2	**CB38**	
Delta St. E2	CB38	5
Wellington Row		
Deltaway, Egh.	AU51	8
Delvers Mead, Dag.	CS35	5
Felhurst Cres.		
Delverton Rd. SE17	**BY42**	
Delverton Rd. SE17	BY42	6
Delves, Tad.	BQ64	10
Delvino Rd. SW6	BS44	6
Demesne Rd., Wall.	BW57	9
Demeta Clo., Wem.	BN34	4
Dempster Clo., Surb.	BK54	8
Dempster Rd. SW18	BT45	6
Den Clo., Beck.	CF52	8
Den Rd., Brom.	CF52	8
Denberry Dr., Sid.	CO48	7
Denbigh Clo. NW10	BO36	5
Denbigh Clo. W11	BR40	5
Denbigh Clo., Chis.	CK50	7
Denbigh Clo., Horn.	CW31	5
Denbigh Clo., Ruis.	BB34	4
Denbigh Clo., Sid.	CQ48	7
Riverside Rd.		
Denbigh Clo., Sthl.	BE39	5
Denbigh Clo., Sutt.	BT56	9
Denbigh Dr., Hayes	BA41	6
Denbigh Gdns., Rich.	BL46	7
Denbigh Ms. SW1	**BW42**	
Denbigh St.		
Denbigh Pl. SW1	**BW42**	
Denbigh Pl. SW1	BW42	6
Denbigh Rd. E6	CJ38	5
Denbigh Rd. W11	BR40	5
Denbigh Rd. W13	BJ40	5
Denbigh Rd., Houns.	BF44	6
Denbigh Rd., Sthl.	BE39	5
Denbigh St. SW1	**BW42**	
Denbigh St. SW1	BW42	6
Denbigh Ter. W11	BR40	5
Denbridge Rd., Brom.	CK51	8
Denby Rd., Cob.	BD59	9
Dendridge Clo., Enf.	CB22	3
Dendy St. SW12	BV47	7
Dene Av., Houns.	BE45	6
Dene Av., Sid.	CO47	7
Dene Clo. SE4	CD45	6
Dene Clo., Brom.	CG54	8
Dene Clo., Dart.	CT49	7
Dene Clo., Wor.Pk.	BO55	8
Dene Ct., Guil.	AT69	11
Dene Dr., Orp.	CO55	8
Dene Gdns., Stan.	BK28	3
Dene Gdns., T.Ditt.	BJ55	84
Dene Holm Rd., Grav.	DE48	8
Dene Path, S.Ock.	DA39	6
Dene Pl., Wok.	AQ62	10
Caradon Clo.		
Dene Rd. NW11	BU26	3
Dene Rd., Ash.	BL63	10
Dene Rd., Buck.H.	CJ26	4
Dene Rd., Dart.	CW47	8
Dene Rd., Guil.	AS71	11
Dene Rd., Nthwd.	BA29	3
Dene St. Gdns., Dor.	BJ71	11
Dene St., Dor.	BJ71	11
Dene Wk., Long.	DC52	9
Dene, The W13	BJ39	54
Templewood		
Dene, The, Croy.	CC55	87
Dene, The, Dor.	BC73	119
Dene, The, E.Mol.	BE53	84
Dene, The, Sev.	CU66	116
Dene, The, Sutt.	BR59	94
Dene, The, Wem.	BL35	46
Denecroft Cres., Uxb.	AZ37	53
Denecroft Gdns., Grays	DE41	71
Denefield Dr., Ken.	BZ61	105
Denehurst Gdns. NW4	BQ32	46
Denehurst Gdns. W3	BM40	55
Denehurst Gdns., Wdf.Grn.	CH28	40
Denehurst Gdns., Rich.	BM45	65
Denehurst Gdns., Twick.	BG47	74
Denes, The, Hem.H.	AY15	8
Denewood Clo., Wat.	BB22	26
Denewood Rd. N6	BU32	47
Denewood, Barn.	BT25	29
Denfield, Dor.	BJ72	119
Denford Rd. SE10	CG42	68
Glenforth St.		
Dengie Wk. N1	BZ37	57
Basire St.		
Denham Av., Uxb.	AV34	43
Denham Clo., Hem.H.	AZ11	8
Sarratt Av.		
Denham Clo., Uxb.	AW34	44
Denham Clo., Well.	CP45	69
Park View Rd.		
Denham Cres., Mitch.	BU52	86
Denham Ct. SE26	CB48	77
Halifax St.		
Denham Dr., Esher	BJ57	93
Denham Dr., Ilf.	CM32	49
Denham Green Clo., Uxb.	AW33	44
Denham Green La., Uxb.	AV32	43
Denham La., Ger.Cr.	AS29	34
Denham Rd. N20	BU27	38
Denham Rd. SE10	CH42	68
Denham Rd., Egh.	AT49	72
Denham Rd., Epsom	BO59	94
Denham Rd., Felt.	BD46	74
Denham Rd., Iver & Uxb.	AU37	52

Denham Way, B.Wd.	BN23	28
Denham Way, Bark.	CN37	58
Denham Way, Rick.	AV29	34
Denham Way, Uxb.	AW34	44
Denham Wk., Ger.Cr.	AS29	34
Denholm Gdns., Guil.	AT69	118
Denholme Rd. W9	BR38	55
Denholme Wk., Rain.	CT36	59
Denis Way SW4	BW45	66
Denison Clo. N2	BT31	47
Denison Rd. SW19	BT50	76
Denison Rd. W5	BK38	54
Denison Rd., Felt.	BB49	73
Deniston Av., Bex.	CQ47	79
Denleigh Gdns. N21	BY26	38
Denleigh Gdns., T.Ditt.	BH53	84
Denman Dr. N. NW11	BS32	47
Denman Dr. NW11	BS32	47
Denman Dr. S. NW11	BS32	47
Denman Dr., Ashf.	AZ50	73
Denman Rd. SE15	CA44	67
Denman St. W1	**BW40**	**3**
Denman St. W1	BW40	56
Denmark Av. SW19	BR50	75
Denmark Ct., Mord.	BS53	86
Denmark Gdns., Cars.	BU55	86
Denmark Gro. N1	**BY37**	**2**
Denmark Gro. N1	BY37	56
Denmark Hill Dr. NW9	BP31	46
Denmark Hill SE5	BZ44	67
Denmark Pl. N8	BY31	47
Denmark Rd.		
Denmark Pl. WC2	**BW39**	**1**
Denmark Rd. N8	BY31	47
Denmark Rd. NW6	BR37	55
Denmark Rd. SE25	CB53	87
Denmark Rd. SE5	BZ44	67
Denmark Rd. SW19	BQ50	75
Denmark Rd. W13	BJ40	54
Denmark Rd., Brom.	CH51	88
Denmark Rd., Cars.	BU55	86
Denmark Rd., Guil.	AS71	118
Denmark Rd., Kings.T.	BL52	85
Denmark Rd., Twick.	BG48	74
Denmark St. E13	CH39	58
Denmark St. N17	CB30	39
Denmark St. WC2	**BW39**	**1**
Denmark St. WC2	BW39	56
Denmark St., Wat.	BC23	26
Denmark Wk. SE27	BZ49	77
Denmead Clo., Ger.Cr.	AS33	43
Denmead Rd., Croy.	BY54	86
Denmead Way SE15	CA43	67
Hordle Promenade S.		
Dennan Rd., Surb.	BL54	85
Denner Rd. E4	CE27	39
Dennets, Wok.	AP62	100
Staveley Way		
Dennett Rd., Croy.	BY54	86
Dennetts Gro. SE14	CC44	67
Dennetts Rd. SE14	CC44	67
Dennettsland Rd., Eden.	CM70	115
Denning Av., Croy.	BY56	95
Denning Clo. NW8	**BT38**	**1**
Denning Clo. NW8	BT38	56
Denning Clo., Hmptn.	BE49	74
Denning Rd. NW3	BT35	47
Dennington Clo. E5	CB34	48
Southwold Rd.		
Dennington Park Rd. NW6	BS36	56
Dennis Av., Wem.	BL35	46
Dennis Clo., Ashf.	BA50	73
Chertsey Rd.		
Dennis Clo., Red.	BU69	121
Dennis Gdns., Stan.	BK28	36
Dennis La. Est., Stan.	BJ28	36
Dennis La., Stan.	BJ27	36
Dennis Park Cres. SW20	BR51	85
Dennis Rd., E.Mol.	BG52	84
Dennis Rd., Grav.	DG48	81
Dennis Rd., Grnf.	BJ37	54
Dennis Rd., S.Ock.	DA37	60
Dennis Reeve Clo., Mitch.	BU51	86
Dennises La., Upmin.	CZ37	60
Denny Av., Wal.Abb.	CF20	21
Denny Clo. E6	CK39	58
Linton Gdns.		
Denny Cres. SE11	**BY42**	**4**
Denny Cres. SE11	BY42	66
Denny St.		
Denny Gdns., Dag.	CO36	59
Denny Rd. N9	CB26	39
Denny Rd., Slou.	AS42	62
Churchill Rd.		
Denny St. SE11	**BY42**	**4**
Denny St. SE11	BY42	66
Dens Pl., Wok.	AQ62	100
Densham Rd. E15	CG37	58
Densley Clo., Welw.G.C.	BQ 7	5
Densole Clo., Beck.	CD51	87
Kings Hall Rd.		
Densor Gdns. Est. W9	BS39	56
Densworth Gro. N9	CC27	39
Dent Clo., S.Ock.	DA39	60
Dunning Clo.		
Denton Clo., Barn.	BQ25	28
Denton Clo., Red.	BV73	121
Denton Court Rd., Grav.	DJ47	81
Denton Gro., Walt.	BE55	84
Denton Rd. N18	CA28	39
Denton Rd. N8	BX32	47
Denton Rd. NW10	BN36	55
Denton Rd., Bex.	CT48	79
Denton Rd., Twick.	BK46	74
Denton Rd., Well.	CP43	69
Denton St. SW18	BS46	76
Denton St., Grav.	DJ47	81
Denton Ter., Bex.	CT48	79
Denton Way E5	CC34	48
Denton Way, Wok.	AP62	100
Dents Gro., Tad.	BR67	112
Dents Rd. SW11	BU46	76
Denvale Wk., Wok.	AQ62	100
Muirfield Rd.		
Denver Clo., Orp.	CN53	88
Denver Rd. N16	CA33	48
Denver Rd., Dart.	CU47	79
Denyer St. SW3	**BU42**	**3**
Denyer St. SW3	BU42	66
Denzil Rd. NW10	BO35	46
Denzil Rd., Guil.	AQ71	118
Denziloe Av., Uxb.	AZ38	53
Deodar Rd. SW15	BR45	65
Deodora Clo. N20	BU27	38
Oakleigh Rd. N.		
Depot Rd., Epsom	BO60	94
Depot Rd., Houns.	BG45	64
Depot St. SE5	BZ43	67
Deptford Br. SE8	CE44	67
Deptford Broadway SE8	CE44	67
Deptford Church St. SE8	CE43	67
Deptford Ferry Rd. E14	CE42	67
Deptford Grn. SE8	CE43	67
Deptford High St. SE8	CE43	67
Deptford Strand SE8	CD42	67
Deptford Wf. SE8	CD42	67
Derby Arms Rd., Epsom	BO62	103
Derby Av. N12	BT28	38
Derby Av., Har.	BG30	36
Derby Av., Rom.	CS32	50
Derby Av., Upmin.	CW35	51
Derby Clo., Epsom	BP63	103
Derby Ct. E5	CC35	48
Clapton Park Est.		
Derby Gate SW1	**BX41**	**4**
Derby Gate SW1	BX41	66
Derby Hill Cres. SE23	CC48	77
Derby Hill Est. SE23	CC48	77
Derby Hill SE23	CC48	77
Derby Rd. E18	CG30	40
Derby Rd. E7	CJ36	58
Derby Rd. E9	CC37	57
Derby Rd. N15	BY31	47
Derby Rd. N18	CB28	39
Derby Rd. SW14	BM45	65
Derby Rd. SW19	BS50	76
Derby Rd., Croy.	BY54	86
Derby Rd., Enf.	CB25	30
Derby Rd., Grays	DD43	71
Derby Rd., Grnf.	BF37	54
Derby Rd., Guil.	AP70	118
Derby Rd., Hodd.	CF13	12
Derby Rd., Surb.	BM54	85
Derby Rd., Sutt.	BR57	94
Derby Rd., Uxb.	AX37	53
Derby Rd., Wat.	BD24	27
Derby St. W1	**BV40**	**3**
Derby St. W1	BV40	56
Curzon St.		
Derby Stables Rd., Epsom	BO62	103
Derbyshire St. E2	CB38	57
Dereham Pl. EC2	**CA38**	**2**
Dereham Pl. EC2	CA38	57
Dereham Rd., Bark.	CN35	49
Derek Av., Epsom	BM57	94
Derek Av., Wall.	BV56	95
Derek Av., Wem.	BM36	55
Derham Gdns., Upmin.	CY34	51
Deri Av., Rain.	CU38	59
Dericote Rd. E8	CB37	57
Croston St.		
Deridene Clo., Stai.	AY46	73
Derifall Clo. E6	CK39	58
Hallywell Cres.		
Dering Pl., Croy.	BZ56	96
Dering Rd., Croy.	BZ56	96
Dering St. W1	**BV39**	**1**
Dering St. W1	BV39	56
Dering Yd. W1	**BV39**	**1**
New Bond St.		
Derinton Rd. SW17	BU49	76
Derley Rd., Sthl.	BD41	64
Dermody Gdns. SE13	CF46	77
Dermody Rd. SE13	CF46	77
Deronda Rd. SE24	BY47	76
Deroy Clo., Cars.	BU57	95
Derrick Av., S.Croy.	BZ58	96
Derrick Gdns. SE7	CJ41	68
Derrick Rd., Beck.	CD52	87
Derry Av., S.Ock.	DA39	60
Derry Down, Wok.	AR64	100
Derry Downs, Orp.	CP53	89
Derry Rd., Croy.	BX55	86
Derry St. W8	BS41	66
Dersingham Av. E12	CK35	49
Dersingham Rd. NW2	BR34	46
Derwent Av. N18	BZ28	39
Derwent Av. NW7	BN29	37
Derwent Av. NW9	BO32	46
Derwent Av. SW15	BO49	75
Derwent Av., Barn.	BU26	38
Derwent Av., Pnr.	BE29	36
Derwent Av., Uxb.	AZ34	44
Derwent Clo., Dart.	CU47	79
Derwent Clo., Esher	BH57	93
Derwent Clo., Felt.	BB47	73
Derwent Clo., Wey.	AX56	92
Derwent Cres. N20	BT27	38
Derwent Cres., Bexh.	CR44	69
Derwent Cres., Stan.	BK30	36
Derwent Dr., Hayes	BB39	53
Derwent Dr., Orp.	CM54	88
Derwent Dr., Pur.	BZ60	96
Derwent Gdns., Ilf.	CK31	49
Derwent Gdns., Wem.	BK33	45
Derwent Gro. SE22	CA45	67
Derwent Par., S.Ock.	DA39	60
Derwent Rd. N13	BX28	38
Derwent Rd. SE20	CB51	87
Derwent Rd. SW20	BQ53	85
Derwent Rd. W5	BK41	64
Derwent Rd., Egh.	AT50	72
Derwent Rd., N.Mal.	BQ53	85
Grand Dr.		
Derwent Rd., S.Croy.	BZ60	96
Derwent Rd., Sthl.	BE39	54
Derwent Rd., Twick.	BF46	74
Derwent Ri. NW9	BO32	46
Derwent St. SE10	CG42	68
Derwent Way, Horn.	CU35	50
Derwent Wk., Wall.	BV57	95
Woodbourne Gdns.		
Derwentwater Rd. W3	BN40	55
Derwentwater Rd., Hem.H.	BA14	8
Desborough Clo., Shep.	AZ54	83
Ferry La.		
Desborough St. W2	BS39	56
Cirencester St.		
Desenfans Rd. SE21	CA46	77
Desford Ct., Ashf.	AY48	73
Desford Rd. E16	CG38	58
Desford Way, Ashf.	AY48	73
Desmond Rd., Wat.	BB21	26
Desmond St. SE14	CD43	67
Despard Av. SW11	BV44	66
Despard Rd. N19	BW33	47
Detillens La., Oxt.	CH68	115
Detling Clo., Horn.	CV35	51
Detling Rd., Brom.	CH49	78
Detling Rd., Erith	CS43	69
Detling Rd., Grav.	DE47	81
Deva Clo., St.Alb.	BF14	9
Devalls Clo. E6	CL39	58
Devana End, Cars.	BU55	86
Devas Rd. SW20	BQ51	85
Devas St. E3	CE38	57
Devenay Rd. E15	CG36	58
Devenish Rd. SE2	CO41	69
Deventer Cres. SE22	CA46	77
Dulwich Gro.		
Deverell St. SE1	**BZ41**	**4**
Deverell St. SE1	BZ41	67
Devereux Ct. EC4	BY40	56
Fountain Ct.		
Devereux Dr., Wat.	BB22	26
Devereux Rd. SW11	BU46	76
Devereux Rd., Wind.	AO44	61
Deveron Gdns., S.Ock.	DA39	60
Deveron Way, Rom.	CT30	41
Devils La., Egh.	AU50	72
Devitt Clo., Ash.	BM61	103
Devizes St. N1	**BZ37**	**2**
Devlan Clo. SE18	CL43	68
Llanover St.		
Devoil Clo., Guil.	AT68	109
Devoke Way, Walt.	BD55	84
Devon Av., Slou.	AO39	52
Devon Av., Twick.	BG47	74
Devon Bank, Guil.	AR72	118
Portsmouth Rd.		
Devon Clo. N17	CA31	48
Devon Clo., Buck.H.	CH27	40
Devon Clo., Grnf.	BK37	54
Devon Clo., Ken.	CA61	105
Devon Cres., Grnf.	BK37	54
Devon Cres., Red.	BT70	121
Devon Ct. W3	BM39	55
Links Rd.		
Devon Ct., Dart.	CX51	90
Darent Mead		
Devon Ct., Hmptn.	BF50	74
Devon Ct., St.Alb.	BH14	9
Old London Rd.		
Devon Gdns. N4	BY32	47
Devon Rd., Bark.	CN37	58
Devon Rd., Red.	BW68	113
Devon Rd., S.at H.	CX51	90
Devon Rd., Sutt.	BR58	94
Devon Rd., Walt.	BD56	93
Devon Rd., Wat.	BD23	27
Devon Rise N2	BT31	47
Devon St. SE15	CB43	67
Devon Way, Chess.	BK56	93
Devon Way, Epsom	BM56	94
Devon Waye, Houns.	BE43	64
Devon Waye, Uxb.	AY37	53
Devoncroft Gdns., Twick.	BJ47	74
Oak La.		
Devonia Gdns. N18	BZ29	39
Devonia Rd. N1	**BY37**	**2**
Devonia Rd. N1	BY37	56
Devonport Gdns., Ilf.	CK32	49
Devonport Ms. W12	BP41	65
Devonport Pass. E1	CC39	57
Devonport Rd. W12	BP40	55
Devonport St. E1	CC39	57
Devons Est. E3	CE38	57
Devons Rd. E3	CE38	57
Devonshire Av., Dart.	CU46	79
Devonshire Av., Sutt.	BT57	95
Devonshire Av., Wok.	AU60	91
Devonshire Clo. E15	CG35	49
Devonshire Clo. N13	BY27	38
Devonshire Clo. W1	**BV39**	**1**
Devonshire Clo. W1	BV39	56
Devonshire Cres. NW7	BQ29	37
Devonshire Ct., Croy.	CD54	87
Devonshire Ct., Rich.	BL44	65
Holmesdale Rd.		
Devonshire Dr. SE10	CE43	67
Devonshire Dr., Surb.	BK54	84
Devonshire Gdns. N17	BZ29	39
Devonshire Gdns. N21	BZ26	39
Devonshire Gdns. W4	BN43	65
Devonshire Gdns., S.le H.	DK41	71
Somerset Rd.		
Devonshire Gro. SE15	CB43	67
Devonshire Hill La. N17	BY29	38
Devonshire Ms. N. W1	BV38	56
Park Crescent Ms. W.		
Devonshire Ms. S. W1	**BV39**	**1**
Devonshire Ms. S. W1	BV39	56
Devonshire Ms. W. W1	**BV38**	**1**
Devonshire Ms. W. W1	BV38	56
Devonshire Ms. W4	BO42	65
Glebe St.		
Devonshire Pl. Ms. W1	**BV38**	**1**
Devonshire Pl. Ms. W1	BV38	56
Devonshire Pl. NW2	BS34	47
Devonshire Pl. W1	**BV38**	**1**
Devonshire Pl. W1	BV38	56
Devonshire Pl. W4	BO42	65
Devonshire Rd. E15	CG35	49
Devonshire Rd. E16	CH39	58
Devonshire Rd. E17	CE32	48
Devonshire Rd. N13	BX28	38
Devonshire Rd. N17	BZ29	39
Devonshire Rd. N9	CC26	39
Devonshire Rd. NW7	BQ29	37
Devonshire Rd. SE23	CC47	77
Devonshire Rd. SE9	CK48	78
Devonshire Rd. SW19	BU50	76
Devonshire Rd. W4	BO42	65
Devonshire Rd. W5	BK41	64
Devonshire Rd., Hatch End	BE30	36
Devonshire Rd., Bexh.	CQ45	69
Devonshire Rd., Cars.	BV56	95
Devonshire Rd., Croy.	BZ54	87
Devonshire Rd., Eastcote	BD32	45
Devonshire Rd., Felt.	BE48	74
Devonshire Rd., Grav.	DG48	81
Devonshire Rd., Grays	DC42	71
Devonshire Rd., Har.	BG32	45
Devonshire Rd., Horn.	CV34	51
Devonshire Rd., Ilf.	CM33	49
Devonshire Rd., Orp.	CO54	89
Devonshire Rd., Sthl.	BF39	54
Devonshire Rd., Sutt.	BT57	95
Devonshire Rd., Wey.	AZ56	92
Devonshire Row EC2	**CA39**	**2**
Devonshire Row EC2	CA39	57
Devonshire Row Ms. W1	**BV39**	**1**
Devonshire St.		
Devonshire Sq. EC2	**CA39**	**2**
Devonshire Sq. EC2	CA39	57
Devonshire Sq., Brom.	CH52	88
Masons Hill		
Devonshire St. W1	**BV39**	**1**
Devonshire St. W1	BV39	56
Devonshire St. W4	BO42	65
Devonshire Ter. W2	**BT39**	**1**
Devonshire Ter. W2	BT39	56
Devonshire Way, Croy.	CD55	87
Devonshire Way, Hayes	BC39	53
Dewar St. SE15	CB45	67
Dewberry Gdns. E6	CK39	58
Yarrow Cres.		
Dewberry St. E14	CF39	57
Dewey Rd. N1	**BY37**	**2**
Dewey Rd. N1	BY37	56
Dewey Rd., Dag.	CS36	59
Dewey St. SW17	BU49	76
Dewgrass Gro., Wal.Cr.	CC21	30
Holmesdale		
Dewhurst Rd. W14	BQ41	65
Dewhurst Rd., Chsht.	CB18	21
Dewlands Av., Dart.	CX47	80
Dewlands, Gdse.	CC69	114
Dewport St. W6	BR43	65
Field Rd.		
Dewsbury Clo., Pnr.	BE32	45
Dewsbury Clo., Rom.	CW29	42
Dewsbury Ct. W4	BN42	65
Chiswick Rd.		
Dewsbury Gdns., Rom.	CW29	42
Dewsbury Gdns., Wor.Pk.	BP55	85
Dewsbury Rd. NW10	BP35	46
Dewsbury Rd., Rom.	CW29	42
Dewsbury Ter. NW1	BV36	56
Camden High St.		
Dexter Clo., Grays	DD41	71
Dexter Rd. SE24	BY45	66
Dexter Rd., Barn.	BQ25	28
Deyncourt Gdns., Upmin.	CY34	51
Deyncourt Rd. N17	BZ30	39
Deynecourt Gdns. E11	CJ31	49
Diadem Ct. W1	**BW39**	**1**
Great Chapel St.		
Dial Wk., The SW7	**BS41**	**3**
Dial Wk., The W8	BS41	66
Diamedes Av., Stai.	AX47	73
Diamedes Cres., Stai.	AX47	73
Diameter Rd., Orp.	CL54	88
Diamond Clo. E7	CH35	49
Stracey Rd.		
Diamond Clo., Dag.	CP33	50
Diamond Rd., Ruis.	BE35	45
Diamond Rd., Slou.	AQ41	62
Diamond Rd., Wat.	BC22	26
Diamond St. SE15	CA43	67
Diamond Ter. SE10	CF43	67
Diana Clo. E18	CH30	40
Diana Clo., Slou.	AS39	52
Blinco La.		
Diana Gdns., Surb.	BL55	85
Diana Pl. NW1	**BV38**	**1**
Diana Pl. NW1	BV38	56
Diana Rd. E17	CD31	48
Dianthus Clo. SE2	CO42	69
Carnation St.		
Dianthus Ct., Wok.	AR62	100
Diban Av., Horn.	CU35	50
Dibden Hill, Ch.St.G.	AQ28	34
Dibden La., Sev.	CT66	116
Dibden St. N1	**BY37**	**2**
Dibden St. N1	BZ37	57
Dibdens Cotts. SE27	BY49	76
Crown La.		
Dibdin Clo., Sutt.	BS55	86
Dibdin Ho. NW6	BS38	56
Dibdin Ho. W9	**BS37**	**1**
Dibdin Rd. NW6	BS37	56
Dibdin Rd. SE1	BY41	66
Gerridge St.		
Dibdin Rd., Sutt.	BS55	86
Dibna Clo., Slou.	AS39	52
Blinco La.		
Diceland Rd., Bans.	BR61	103
Dicey Av. NW2	BQ35	46
Dick Turpin Way, Felt.	BB45	63
Dickens Av. N3	BT30	38
Dickens Av., Dart.	CX45	70
Dickens Av., Til.	DG44	71
Dickens Av., Uxb.	AZ39	53
Dickens Clo., Hart.	DC53	90
Dickens Clo., Hayes	BB42	63
Croyde Av.		
Dickens Clo., Rich.	BL48	75
Dickens Clo., St.Alb.	BG13	9
Dickens Clo., Wal.Cr.	CB17	21
Dickens Ct., Hem.H.	AZ10	8
Dickens Dr., Chis.	CM50	78
Dickens Dr., Wey.	AW56	92
Dickens Est. SE1	CB41	67
Dickens Est. SE16	**CB41**	**4**
Dickens La. N18	CA28	39
Dickens Rd. E6	CJ37	58
Dickens Rd., Grav.	DJ47	81
Dickens Ri., Chig.	CL27	40
Dickens Sq. SE1	**BZ41**	**4**
Dickens Sq. SE1	BZ41	67
Dickens St. SW8	BV44	66
Dickenson Rd. N8	BX33	47
Dickenson Rd., Felt.	BD49	74
Dickenson St. NW5	BV36	56
Dalby St.		
Dickensons La. SE25	CB53	87
Dickensons Pl. SE25	CB53	87
Dickerage La., N.Mal.	BN52	85
Dickerage Rd., N.Mal.	BN51	85
Dickins Clo., Chsht.	CB17	21
Spicersfield		
Dickinson Av., Rick.	AZ25	26
Dickinson Sq., Rick.	AZ25	26
Dickson Rd. SE9	CK45	68
Dickson, Chsht.	CA17	21
Dicksons Fold, Pnr.	BD31	45
Didcot St. SW11	BT45	66
Didsbury Clo. E6	CK37	58
Barking Rd.		
Digby Cres. N4	BZ34	48
Digby Est. E2	CC38	57
Digby Gdns., Dag.	CR37	59
Digby Pl., Croy.	CA55	87
Digby Rd. E9	CC35	48
Digby Rd., Bark.	CN36	58
Digby St. E2	CC38	57
Digby Way, Wey.	AY59	92
Digby Wk., Horn.	CV35	51
Digdag Hill, Chsht.	CA17	21
Digdens Ri., Epsom	BN61	103
Diggon St. E1	CC39	57
Dighton Rd. SW18	BT46	76
Dignum St. N1	**BY37**	**2**
Dignum St. N1	BY37	56
Digswell Clo., B.Wd.	BM22	28
Digswell Ct., Welw.G.C.	BQ 7	5
Digswell Ri.		
Digswell Hl., Welw.G.C.	BP 6	5
Digswell House Ms., Welw.G.C.	BQ 6	5
Monks Ri.		
Digswell La., Welw.G.C.	BR 6	5
Digswell Lodge, Welw.G.C.	BR 7	5
Digswell Park Rd., Welw.G.C.	BQ 5	5
Digswell Rd., Welw.G.C.	BQ 7	5
Digswell Ri., Welw.G.C.	BQ 7	5
Digswell St. N7	BY36	56
Holloway Rd.		
Digswellbury, Welw.G.C.	BR 6	5
Dilhorne Clo. SE12	CH48	78
Dilke St. SW3	BU43	66
Dillon Pl. N7	BX34	47
Dillwyn Clo. SE26	CD49	77
Dilston Clo., Nthlt.	BD38	54
Yeading La.		
Dilston Gro. SE16	CC42	67
Abbeyfield Rd.		
Dilston Rd., Lthd.	BJ63	102
Dilton Gdns. SW15	BP47	75
Dimes Pl. W6	BP42	65
King St.		
Dimmock Dr., Har.	BG35	45
Dimmocks La., Rick.	AW21	26
Dimond Clo. E7	CH35	49
Stracey Rd.		
Dimsdale Dr. NW9	BN33	46
Dimsdale Dr., Enf.	CB25	30
Dimsdale Wk. E13	CG37	58
Dinant Link Rd., Hodd.	CE11	12
Dingle Clo., Barn.	BO25	28
Dingle Gdns. E14	CE40	57
Dingle Rd., Ashf.	AZ49	73
Dingle, The, Uxb.	AZ38	53
Dingley La. SW16	BW48	76
Dingley Pl. EC1	**BZ38**	**2**
Dingley Pl. EC1	BZ38	57
Dingley Rd.		
Dingley Rd. EC1	**BZ38**	**2**
Dingley Rd. EC1	BZ38	57
Dingon Hill Clo., Hayes	BC40	53
Dingwall Av., Croy.	BZ55	87
Dingwall Gdns. NW11	BS32	47
Dingwall Pl., Croy.	BZ55	87
Dingwall Rd. SW18	BT47	76
Dingwall Rd., Cars.	BU58	95
Dingwall Rd., Croy.	BZ54	87
Dinmont Est. E2	CB37	57
Dinmont St. E2	CB37	57
Dinmore, Hem.H.	AS17	16
Dinsdale Clo., Wok.	AT62	100
Dinsdale Gdns. SE25	CA52	87
Dinsdale Gdns., Barn.	BS25	29
Dinsdale Rd. SE3	CG43	68
Dinsmore Rd. SW12	BV47	76
Dinton Rd. SW19	BT50	76
Dinton Rd., Kings.T.	BL50	75
Dione Rd., Hem.H.	AY12	8
Diploma Way N2	BU31	47
Dippers Clo., Sev.	CW62	108
Dirdene Clo., Epsom	BO59	94
Dirdene Gdns., Epsom	BO59	94
Dirdene Gro., Epsom	BO59	94
Dirleton Rd. E15	CG37	58
Dirtham La., Lthd.	BC67	110
Disbrowe Rd. W6	BR43	65
Discovery Wk. E1	CB40	57
Dishforth La. NW9	BO30	37
Disney Pl. SE1	**BZ41**	**1**
Disney Pl. SE1	BZ41	67
Disney St.		
Disney St. SE1	**BZ41**	**4**
Disney St. SE1	BZ41	67

Dison Clo., Enf. CC23 30
Disraeli Clo. SE28 CP40 59
Disraeli Clo. W4 BN41 65
Winston Wk.
Disraeli Ct., Slou. AT43 62
Sutton Pl.
Disraeli Gdns. SW15 BR45 65
Fawe Park Rd.
Disraeli Rd. E7 CH36 58
Disraeli Rd. NW10 BN37 55
Disraeli Rd. SW15 BQ45 65
Disraeli Rd. W5 BK40 54
Diss St. E2 CA38 2
Diss St. E2 CA38 57
Distaff La. EC4 BZ39 57
Cannon St.
Distaff La. EC4 BZ40 4
Distillery La. W6 BQ42 65
Distillery Rd. W6 BQ42 65
Distillery Wk., Brent. BL43 65
Pottery Rd.
District Rd., Wem. BJ35 45
Ditch Alley SE10 CE44 67
Ditchburn St. E14 CF40 57
Ditches La., Couls. BX63 104
Ditchfield Rd., Hayes BE38 54
Ditchfield Rd., Hodd. CE10 12
Dittisham Rd. SE9 CK49 78
Ditton Clo., T.Ditt. BJ54 84
Ditton Grange Clo., Surb. BK54 84
Ditton Grange Dr., Surb. BK54 84
Ditton Hill Rd., Surb. BK54 84
Ditton Lawn, T.Ditt. BJ54 84
Ditton Park Rd., Slou. AS43 62
Ditton Pl. SE20 CB51 87
Ditton Rd., Bexh. CP46 79
Ditton Rd., Slou. AR44 62
Ditton Rd., Slou. AS43 62
Ditton Rd., Sthl. BE42 64
Ditton Rd., Surb. BK55 84
Ditton Reach, T.Ditt. BS53 84
Divis Way SW15 BP46 75
Dover Pk. Dr.
Dixon Clo. E6 CK39 58
Brandreth Rd.
Dixon Pl., W.Wick. CE54 87
Dixon Rd. SE14 CD44 67
Dixon Rd. SE25 CA52 87
Dixons Alley SE16 CB41 67
West La.
Dixons Hill Clo., Hat. BP16 19
Dixons Hill Rd., Hat. BP16 19
Dobbin Clo., Har. BJ30 36
Dobbs Weir Rd., Hodd. CF12 12
Dobell Rd. SE9 CK46 78
Dobree Av. NW10 BP36 55
Dobson Clo. NW6 BT36 56
Belsize Rd.
Dobson Rd., Grav. DJ49 81
Dock App. Rd., Grays DF43 71
Dock Rd. E16 CG40 58
Dock Rd., Brent. BK43 64
Dock Rd., Grays DE43 71
Dock Rd., Til. DF44 71
Dock St. E1 CB40 4
Dock St. E1 CB40 57
Dockers Tanner Rd. E14 CE42 67
Dockett Eddy La., Shep. AY54 83
Dockhead SE1 CA41 67
Jamaica Rd.
Dockhill Av. SE16 CC41 67
Dockland St. E16 CL40 58
Dockley Rd. SE16 CB41 4
Dockley Rd. SE16 CB41 67
Dockwell Clo., Felt. BC45 63
Doctor Johnsons Av. SW17 BV48 76
Doctor Williams Wk., Guil. AQ68 109
Doctors Clo. SE26 CC49 77
Lawrie Peak Rd.
Doctors Commons Rd., Berk. AQ13 7
Doctors La., Cat. BY65 104
Docwras Bldgs. N1 BZ36 57
Dod St. E14 CD39 57
Dodbrooke Rd. SE27 BY48 76
Doddinghurst Rd., Doddinghurst DB22 33
Doddinghurst Rd., Brwd. DB26 42
Doddington Gro. SE17 BY43 4
Doddington Gro. SE17 BY43 66
Doddington Pl. SE17 BY43 4
Doddington Pl. SE17 BY43 66
Kennington Pk. Pl.
Dodds Cres., Wey. AW60 92
Dodds La., Ch.St.G. AQ27 34
Dodds La., Hem.H. AX11 8
Dodds La., Wey. AW60 92
Dodds Pk., Bet. BM71 120
Dodsley Pl. N9 CB27 39
Dodson St. SE1 BY41 4
Dodson St. SE1 BY41 66
Dodwood, Welw.G.C. BS 8 5
Doel Cl. SW19 BT50 76
Dog Kennel Hill SE22 CA45 67
Dog Kennel La., Hat. BP12 10
Dog Kennel La., Rick. AV25 25
Dog La. NW10 BO35 46
Dog Wood Clo., Grav. DF49 81
Doggets Clo., Barn. BU25 29
Doggett Rd. SE6 CE47 77
Doggetts Cor., Horn. CW34 51
Doggetts Farm Rd., Uxb. AU33 43
Doggetts Way, St.Alb. BG15 9
Doggetts Wood Clo., Ch.St.G. AQ24 25
Doggetts Wood La., Ch.St.G. AQ24 25
Doghurst Av., Hayes AZ43 63
Doghurst Dr., West Dr. AZ43 63
Doghurst La., Couls. BU63 104
Dognell Grn., Welw.G.C. BP 7 5
Doherty Rd. E13 CH38 58
Dolben St. SE1 BY40 4
Dolben St. SE1 BY40 56
Dolby Rd. SW6 BR44 65
Ewald Rd.
Dole St. NW7 BQ29 37
Dolland St. SE11 BX42 4
Dolland St. SE11 BX42 66
Dollis Av. N3 BR30 37
Dollis Brook Wk., Barn. BR25 28
Alan Dr.
Dollis Cres., Ruis. BD33 45
Dollis Hill Av. NW2 BP34 46
Dollis Hill Est. NW2 BP34 46
Dollis Hill La. NW2 BO35 46
Dollis Ms. N3 BS30 38
Dollis Pk.
Dollis Pk. N3 BR30 37
Dollis Rd. N3 BR29 37
Dollis Rd. NW7 BR30 37
Dollis Valley Way, Barn. BR25 28
Dolman Rd. W4 BN42 65
Dolman St. SW4 BX45 66
Dolphin App., Rom. CT31 50
Dolphin Clo. SE16 CC41 67
Kinburn St.
Dolphin Clo. SE28 CP39 59
Watersmeet Way
Dolphin Clo., Surb. BK53 84
Dolphin Ct., Slou. AQ41 62
Dolphin Rd.
Dolphin Ct., Stai. AW48 73
Dolphin La. E14 CE40 57
Dolphin Rd. N., Sun. BB51 83
Dolphin Rd. S., Sun. BB51 83
Dolphin Rd. W., Sun. BB51 83
Dolphin Rd., Nthlt. BE37 54
Dolphin Rd., Slou. AQ41 62
Dolphin Rd., Sun. BB51 83
Dolphin Sq. SW1 BW42 3
Dolphin Sq. SW1 BW42 66
Dolphin St., Kings.T. BL51 85
Wood St.
Dombey St. WC1 BX39 2
Dombey St. WC1 BX39 56
Dome Hill Peak, Cat. CA66 114
Dome Hill Pk. SE26 CA49 77
Dome Hill, Cat. CA67 114
Dome Way, Red. BU70 121
Domett Clo. SE5 BZ45 67
Domingo St. EC1 BZ38 57
Baltic St.
Dominic Dr. SE9 CL49 78
Dominion Dr., Rom. CR29 41
Dominion Rd., Croy. CA54 87
Dominion Rd., Sthl. BE41 64
Featherstone Rd.
Dominion St. EC2 BZ39 2
Dominion St. EC2 BZ39 57
Dominion Way, Rain. CU38 59
Domitian Pl., Enf. CA25 30
Domville Clo. N20 BT27 38
Domville Gro. SE5 CA42 4
Domville Gro. SE5 CA42 67
Don Phelan Clo. SE5 BZ44 67
Don Way, Rom. CT29 41
Donald Dr., Rom. CP32 50
Donald Rd. E13 CH37 58
Donald Rd., Croy. BX54 86
Donaldson Rd. NW6 BR37 55
Donaldson Rd. SE18 CL44 68
Doncaster Dr., Nthlt. BE35 45
Doncaster Gdns. N4 BY32 47
Stanhope Gdns.
Doncaster Gdns. Nthlt. BE35 45
Doncaster Rd. N9 CB26 39
Doncaster Way, Upmin. CW34 51
Donegal St. N1 BX37 2
Donegal St. N1 BX37 56
Doneraile St. SW6 BQ44 65
Dongola Rd. E13 CH38 58
Dongola Rd. N17 CA31 48
Dongola Rd. W. E13 CH38 58
Donington Av., Ilf. CM32 49
Donkey All. SE22 CB47 77
Donkey La., Enf. CB23 30
Donkey La., Farn. CX55 90
Donkey La., West Dr. AX42 63
Donne Gdns., Wok. AV61 100
Donne Pl. SW3 BU42 3
Donne Pl. SW3 BU42 66
Donne Pl., Mitch. BV52 86
Donne Rd., Dag. CP34 50
Donnefield Av., Edg. BL29 37
Donnington Rd. NW10 BP36 55
Donnington Rd., Har. BK32 45
Donnington Rd., Sev. CS63 107
Donnington Rd., Wor.Pk. BP55 85
Donnybrook Rd. SW16 BW50 76
Donovan Av. N10 BV30 38
Donovan Clo., Epsom BN58 94
Doods Park Rd., Reig. BT70 121
Doods Rd., Reig. BT70 121
Doods Way, Reig. BT70 121
Doon St. SE1 BY40 4
Doon St. SE1 BY40 56
Doone Clo., Tedd. BJ50 74
Dora Rd. SW19 BS49 76
Dora St. E14 CD39 57
Dorado Gdns., Orp. CP55 89
Doral Way, Cars. BU56 95
Carshalton Park Rd.
Doran Dr., Reig. BT70 121
Doran Gdns., Reig. BT70 121
Doran Gro. SE18 CM43 68
Doran Mans. N2 BU32 47
Doran Wk. E15 CF36 57
Dorcas Ct., St.Alb. BH14 9
Old London Rd.
Dorchester Av. N13 BZ28 39
Dorchester Av., Bex. CP47 79
Dorchester Av., Har. BF32 45
Dorchester Av., Hodd. CE11 12
Dorchester Clo., Dart. CW47 80
Dorchester Clo., Nthlt. BF35 45
Dorchester Clo., Orp. CO50 79
Grovelands Rd.
Dorchester Ct. N14 BV26 38
Dorchester Ct. SE24 BZ46 77
Dorchester Ct., Rick. BA25 26
Mayfare
Dorchester Ct., Wok. AT61 100
Dorchester Dr. SE24 BZ46 77
Dorchester Dr., Felt. BB46 73
Dorchester Gdns. NW11 BS31 47
Dorchester Gdns. E4 CE28 39
Dorchester Gro. W4 BO43 65
Dorchester Rd., Grav. DH48 81
Dorchester Rd., Mord. BS54 86
Dorchester Rd., Nthlt. BF35 45
Dorchester Rd., Wey. AZ55 83
Dorchester Rd., Wor.Pk. BQ54 85
Dorchester Way, Har. BL32 46
Dorchester Waye, Hayes BC39 53
Dorcis Av., Bexh. CQ44 69
Dordrecht Rd. W3 BO40 55
Dore Av. E12 CL35 49
Dore Gdns., Mord. BS54 86
Doreen Av. NW9 BN33 46
Dorell Clo., Sthl. BE39 54
Doria Dr., Grav. DJ48 81
Doria Rd., SW6 BR44 65
Dorian Rd., Horn. CU33 50
Doric Dr., Tad. BR63 103
Doric Way NW1 BW38 1
Doric Way NW1 BW38 56
Dorien Rd. SW20 BQ51 85
Dorin Ct., Wok. AV61 100
Dorinda St. N7 BY36 56
Dorinium Clo., Wem. BL35 46
Lea Gdns.
Doris Av., Erith CS44 69
Doris Rd. E7 CH36 58
Doris Rd., Ashf. BA50 73
Doris St. SE11 BY42 66
Tracey St.
Dorking Clo. SE8 CD43 67
Dorking Clo., Wor.Pk. BQ55 85
Dorking Gdns., Rom. CV28 42
Dorking Rd.
Dorking Glen, Rom. CW28 42
Dorking Rd., Great Bookham BF66 111
Dorking Rd., Ash. BM61 103
Dorking Rd., Epsom BM61 103
Dorking Rd., Guil. AU73 118
Dorking Rd., Lthd. BJ64 102
Dorking Rd., Rom. CV28 42
Dorking Rd., Tad. BO67 112
Dorking Ri., Rom. CV28 42
Dorking Wk., Rom. CV28 42
Dorkins Way, Upmin. CZ33 51
Dorlcote Rd. SW18 BT47 76
Dorling Dr., Epsom BO59 94
Dorly Clo., Shep. BB53 83
Dorman Pl. N9 CB27 39
Balham Rd.
Dorman Way NW8 BT37 56
Dorman Wk. NW10 BN36 55
Garden Way
Dormans Clo., Nthwd. BA29 35
Dormay St. SW18 BS46 76
Dormer Clo. E15 CG36 58
Dormer Clo., Barn. BQ25 28
Dormers Av., Sthl. BE39 54
Dormers Ri., Sthl. BF40 54
Dormers Wells La., Sthl. BF39 54
Dormie Clo., St.Alb. BG12 9
Dormy Wood, Ruis. BB32 44
Dornbergh Clo. SE3 CH43 68
Dornberry Rd. SE3 CH43 68
Banchory Rd.
Dorncliffe Rd. SW6 BR44 65
Dornels, Slou. AR39 52
Dorney Gro., Wey. AZ55 83
Dorney Reach Rd., Maid. AJ41 61
Dorney Ri., Orp. CN53 88
Dorney Way, Houns. BE46 74
Dornfell St. NW6 BR35 46
Dornford Gdns., Couls. BZ63 105
Dornton Rd. SW12 BV48 76
Dornton Rd., S.Croy. BZ57 96
Dorothy Av., Wem. BL36 55
Dorothy Evans Clo., Bexh. CR45 69
Dorothy Gdns., Dag. CO35 50
Dorothy Rd. SW11 BU45 66
Dorriens Cft., Berk. AP12 7
Dorrington Gdns., Horn. CV33 51
Dorrington St. EC1 BY39 2
Dorrington St. EC1 BY39 56
Dorrit Cres., Guil. AP69 118
Dorrit Ms. N18 CA28 39
Dorrit St. SE1 BZ41 4
Dorrit Way, Chis. CM50 78
Dickens Dr.
Dorrofield Clo., Rick. BA25 26
Dors Clo. NW9 BN33 46
Dorset Av., Hayes BB38 53
Dorset Av., Rom. CS31 50
Dorset Av., Sthl. BF42 64
Dorset Av., Well. CN45 68
Dorset Bldgs. EC4 BY39 56
Dorset Ri.
Dorset Clo. NW1 BU39 1
Dorset Clo. NW1 BU39 56
Dorset Clo., Berk. AP12 7
Dorset Clo., Hayes BB38 53
Dorset Cres., Grav. DJ49 81
Dorset Dr., Edg. BL29 37
Dorset Dr., Wok. AT62 100
Dorset Est. E2 CA38 57
Dorset Gdns., Mitch. BX52 86
Dorset Gdns., S.le H. DK41 71
Somerset Rd.
Dorset Ms. SW1 BV41 3
Dorset Ms. SW1 BV41 66
Wilton St.
Dorset Pl. E15 CF36 57
Dorset Pl. SW1 BW42 3
Dorset Pl. SW1 BW42 66
Rampayne St.
Dorset Rd. E7 CJ36 58
Dorset Rd. N15 BZ31 48
Dorset Rd. N22 BX30 38
Dorset Rd. SE9 CK48 78
Dorset Rd. SW19 BS51 86
Dorset Rd. SW8 BX43 66
Dorset Rd. W5 BK41 64
Dorset Rd., Ashf. AX48 73
Dorset Rd., Beck. CC52 87
Dorset Rd., Har. BG32 45
Dorset Rd., Mitch. BU51 86
Dorset Rd., Sutt. BS58 95
Dorset Rd., Wind. AO44 61
Dorset Ri. EC4 BY39 2
Dorset Ri. EC4 BY39 56
Dorset Sq. NW1 BU38 1
Dorset Sq. NW1 BU38 56
Dorset Sq., Epsom BN58 94
Hollymoor La.
Dorset St. W1 BU39 1
Dorset St. W1 BU39 56
Dorset Way, Twick. BG47 74
Dorset Way, Wey. AX59 92
Dorset Waye, Houns. BE43 64
Dorset Waye, Uxb. AY37 53
Dorville Cres. W6 BP41 65
Dorville Rd. SE12 CG46 78
Dothill Rd. SE18 CM43 68
Douai Gro., Hmptn. BG51 84
Doubleday Rd., Loug. CM24 31
Doughty Ms. WC1 BX38 2
Doughty Ms. WC1 BX38 56
Roger St.
Doughty St. WC1 BX38 2
Doughty St. WC1 BX38 56
Douglas Av. E17 CE30 39
Douglas Av., N.Mal. BP52 85
Douglas Av., Rom. CW30 42
Douglas Av., Wat. BD22 27
Douglas Av., Wem. BL36 55
Douglas Clo., Guil. AR67 109
Douglas Clo., Stan. BJ28 36
Douglas Clo., Wall. BX57 95
Mollison Dr.
Douglas Cres., Hayes BD38 54
Douglas Dr., Croy. CE55 87
Douglas Est. N1 BZ36 57
Douglas Gdns., Berk. AP12 7
Douglas La., Stai. AS46 72
Douglas Pl. E14 CF42 67
Douglas Pl. SW1 BW42 3
Douglas Rd. E16 CH39 58
Douglas Rd. E4 CG26 40
Douglas Rd. N1 BZ36 57
Douglas Rd. N22 BY30 38
Douglas Rd. NW6 BR37 55
Douglas Rd., Esher BF55 84
Douglas Rd., Horn. CT32 50
Douglas Rd., Houns. BF45 64
Douglas Rd., Ilf. CO33 50
Douglas Rd., Kings.T. BM52 85
Douglas Rd., Slou. AO39 52
Douglas Rd., Stai. AX46 73
Douglas Rd., Surb. BL55 85
Douglas Rd., Well. CO44 69
Douglas Rd., Wey. AW55 83
Douglas Robinson Ct. SW16 BX50 76
Douglas Sq., Mord. BS53 86
Douglas St. SW1 BW42 3
Douglas St. SW1 BW42 66
Douglas Way SE8 CD43 67
Douglas Way, Welw.G.C. BT 8 5
Doulton Ms. NW6 BS36 56
Lymington Rd.
Dounesforth Gdns. SW18 BS47 76
Dounsell Ct., Brwd. DA25 33
Douro Pl. W8 BS41 3
Douro Pl. W8 BS41 66
Douro St. E3 CE37 57
Douthwaite Sq. E1 CB40 57
Torrington Pl.
Dove App. E6 CK39 58
Dove Clo., S.Croy. CC59 96
Dove Ct., Hat. BP13 10
Dove House Gdns. E4 CE27 39
Dove La., Pot.B. BS20 20
Dove Ms. SW5 BT42 3
Dove Ms. SW5 BT42 66
Dove Pk., Pnr. BF29 36
Dove Pk., Rick. AT25 25
Dove Rd. N1 BZ36 57
Dove Row E2 CB37 2
Dove Row E2 CB37 57
Dove Wk., Rain. CU36 59
Dovecote Av. N22 BY31 47
Dovecote Clo., Wey. AZ55 83
Dovecott Gdns. SW14 BN45 65
North Worple Way
Dovedale Av., Har. BK32 45
Dovedale Av., Ilf. CL30 40
Dovedale Clo., Uxb. AX30 35
Dovedale Clo., Well. CO44 69
Dovedale Rd. SE22 CB46 77
Dovedale Rd., Dart. CY47 80
Dovedale Ri., Mitch. BU50 76
Dovedon Clo. N14 BX27 38
Dovehouse Cft., Harl. CO10 6
Dovehouse Grn., Wey. BA56 92
Dovehouse Mead., Bark. CM37 58
Dovehouse St. SW3 BT42 3
Dovehouse St. SW3 BT42 66
Doveney Clo., Orp. CP52 89
Dover Clo., Rom. CS30 41
Dover House Rd. SW15 BP45 65
Dover Park Dr. SW15 BP46 75
Dover Rd. E., Grav. DF47 81
Dover Rd. E12 CJ34 49
Dover Rd. N9 CC27 39
Dover Rd. SE19 BZ50 77
Dover Rd. W1 BW40 3
Dover Rd., Grav. DE47 81
Dover Rd., Rom. CQ32 50
Dover St. W1 BV40 3
Dover St. W1 BV40 56
Dover Way, Rick. BA24 26
Dover Yd. W1 BU39 56
Berkeley St.
Dovercourt Av., Th.Hth. BY53 86
Dovercourt Gdns., Stan. BL28 3
Dovercourt La., Sutt. BT55 8
Dovercourt Rd. SE22 CA46 7
Doverfield Rd. SW2 BX46 7
Doverfield Rd., Guil. AT69 11
Doverfield, Wal.Cr. BZ18 2
Doveridge Gdns. N13 BY28 3
Dovers Cor., Rain. CT38 5
Dovers Grn. Rd., Reig. BS73 12
Dovers Grn., Rad. BN19 1
Doversmead, Wok. AP61 10
Doves Clo., Brom. CK55 8
Doveton Rd., S.Croy. BZ56 9
Doveton St. E1 CC38 5
Dowanhill Rd. SE6 CF47 7
Dowdells La., Welw. BN 5
Dowdeswell Clo. SW15 BO45 6
Dowding Pl., Stan. BJ29 3
Dowding Rd., Uxb. AY36 5
Dowding Rd., West. CJ61 10
Dowding Wk., Grav. DF48 8
Durndale La.
Dower Av., Wall. BV58 9
Dower Pk., Wind. AM45 6
Dowgate Hill EC4 BZ40
Dowgate Hill EC4 BZ40 5
Dowland Clo. N20 BT26 3
Dowland St. W10 BR38 5
Dowlans Clo., Lthd. BF67 11
Dowlans Rd., Lthd. BF67 11
Dowlas St. SE5 CA43 6
Dowlerville Rd., Orp. CN57 9
Dowling Ct., Hem.H. AY14
Woodman Rd.
Dowlings Par., Wem. BK37 5
Bridgewater Rd.
Dowman Clo. SW19 BS51 8
Nelson Green Rd.
Down Ct., Hat. BP14 1
Down Edge, St.Alb. BF13
Down End SE18 CL43 6
Moordown
Down Hall Rd., Kings.T. BK51 8
Down La., Guil. AO72 11
Down Pl. W6 BP42 6
Bridge Av.
Down Pl., Wind. AK43 6
Down Rd., Guil. AT70 11
Down Rd., Tedd. BJ50 7
Down St. W1 BV40
Down St. W1 BV40 5
Down St., E.Mol. BF53 8
Down Street Ms. W1 BV40
Down St.
Down Way Clo., Nthlt. BC37 5
Down Way, Nthlt. BC37 5
Downage NW4 BQ30 3
Downage, The, Grav. DG48 8
Downalong, Bush. BG26 3
Downbank Av., Bexh. CS44 6
Downbarns Rd., Ruis. BD35 4
Downbury Ms. SW18 BS46 7
Merton Rd.
Downderry Rd., Brom. CF48 7
Downe Av., Sev. CM59 9
Downe Clo., Well. CP43 6
Downe Rd., Kes. CK58 9
Downe Rd., Mitch. BU51 8
Downe Rd., Sev. CM60 9
Downer Dr., Rick. AW21 2
Downers Cotts. SW4 BW45 6
Downes Clo., Twick. BJ46 7
St. Margarets Rd.
Downes Ct. N21 BY26 3
Downes Rd., St.Alb. BJ11
Downes Ter., Rich. BL46 7
Richmond Hill
Downfield Clo. W9 BS38 5
Downfield Rd., Chsnt. CD19 2
Downfield, Wor.Pk. BO54 8
Downfields, Welw.G.C. BP 9
Downham Clo., Rom. CR29 4
Downham Rd. N1 BZ36
Downham Rd. N1 BZ36 5
Downham Way, Brom. CG49 7
Downhills Av. N17 BZ31 4
Downhills Park Rd. N17 BZ31 4
Downhills Way N17 BZ31 4
Downhills Way N22 BZ30 3
Downhurst Av. NW7 BN28 3
Downing Av., Guil. AP71 11
Downing Clo., Har. BG31 4
Downing Dr., Grnf. BG37 5
Downing Rd., Dag. CQ37 5
Downing St. SW1 BX41 6
Downing St. SW1 BX41
Downings Wood, Rick. AU28 3
Downland Clo., Couls. BV60 9
Downland Clo., Epsom BP62 10
Downland Gdns., Epsom BP62 10
Downland Way, Epsom BP62 10
Downlands Rd., Pur. BX60 9
Downlands, Wal.Abb. CG20 2
Downleys Clo. SE9 CK48 7
Downman Rd. SE9 CK45 6
Downs Av., Chis. CK49 7
Downs Av., Dart. CX47 8
Downs Av., Epsom BO60 9
Downs Av., Pnr. BE32 4
Downs Br. Rd., Beck. CG51 8
Downs Ct. Rd., Pur. BY59 9
Downs Ct. SW20 BQ50 7
Downs Hill Rd., Epsom BO60 9
Downs Hill, Beck. CF50 7
Downs Hill, Grav. DE50 8
Downs House Rd., Tad. BO62 10
Downs La., Lthd. BJ65 10
Downs Park Rd. E5 CA35 4
Downs Rd. E14 CF39 5
Dewberry St.
Downs Rd. E5 CB35 4
Downs Rd., Beck. CE51 8
Downs Rd., Couls. BW62 10
Downs Rd., Dor. BK68 11
Downs Rd., Enf. CA24 3
Downs Rd., Epsom BO60 9
Downs Rd., Grav. DE49 8

Downs Rd., Pur. BY59 95
Downs Rd., Slou. AR41 62
Downs Rd., Sutt. BS58 95
Downs Rd., Th.Hth. BZ51 87
Downs Side, Sutt. BR59 94
Downs Valley, Long. DC52 90
Downs View Rd., Lthd. BG67 111
Downs Vw., Islw. BH44 64
Downs Vw., Tad. BP64 103
Downs Way Clo., Tad. BP64 103
Downs Way, Epsom BO61 103
Downs Way, Lthd. BG66 111
Downs Way, Orp. CN56 97
Downs Way, Oxt. CG67 115
Downs Way, Tad. BP64 103
Downs Wood, Epsom BP62 103
Downs, The SW20 BQ50 75
Downs, The, Harl. CN11 13
Downs, The, Hat. BP13 10
Downs, The, Lthd. BJ66 111
Downsell Rd. E15 CF35 48
Downsfield Rd. E17 CD32 48
Downsfield, Hat. BP14 10
Sandfield
Downshall Av., Ilf. CN32 49
Downshire Hill NW3 BT35 47
Downside Br. Rd., Cob. BC60 92
Downside Clo. SW19 BT50 76
Downside Common Rd., Cob. BC62 101
Downside Cres. NW3 BU35 47
Downside Cres. W13 BJ38 54
Downside Rd., Cob. BC61 101
Downside Rd., Guil. AT71 118
Downside Rd., Sutt. BT57 95
Downside Wk., Nthlt. BD38 54
Invicta Gro.
Downside, Cher. AV54 82
Downside, Epsom BO60 94
Downside, Hem.H. AY13 8
Downside, Sun. BC51 83
Downside, Twick. BH48 74
Downsland Dr., Brwd. DB27 42
Downsview Av., Wok. AS64 100
Downsview Clo., Orp. CP58 98
Downsview Clo., Swan. CT52 89
Downsview Gdns. SE19 BY50 76
Downsview Rd. SE19 BZ50 77
Downsview Rd., Sev. CT66 116
Downsview, Dor. BK70 119
Downsway, Guil. AV70 118
Downsway, S.Croy. CA59 96
Downsway, The, Sutt. BS58 95
Downsway, Whyt. CA61 105
Downswood, Reig. BT69 121
Downton Av. SW2 BX48 76
Downtown Rd. SE16 CD41 67
Downview Clo., Cob. BC63 101
Downway N12 BU29 38
Dowrey St. N1 BY37 56
Richmond Av.
Dowsett Rd. N17 CA30 39
Dowson Clo. SE5 BZ45 67
Doyce St. SE1 BZ41 4
Doyce St. SE1 BZ41 67
Southwark Bridge Rd.
Doyle Clo., Erith CT44 69
Doyle Gdns. NW10 BP37 55
Doyle Rd. SE25 CB52 87
Doyle Way, Til. DH44 71
Coleridge Rd.
Doynton St. N19 BV34 47
Draco St. SE17 BZ43 4
Draco St. SE17 BZ43 67
Dragmire La., Mitch. BT52 86
Dragon La., Wey. AZ58 92
Dragoon Rd. SE8 CD42 67
Dragor Rd. NW10 BN38 55
Drake Av., Slou. AR42 62
Drake Av., Stai. AV49 72
Drake Clo. SE16 CC41 67
Middleton Dr.
Drake Clo., Brwd. DB28 42
Drake Ct., Har. BE34 45
Drake Rd. SE4 CE45 67
Drake Rd., Chess. BM56 94
Drake Rd., Croy. BX54 86
Drake Rd., Grays DC41 71
Drake Rd., Har. BE34 45
Drake Rd., Mitch. BV53 86
Drake St. WC1 BX39 2
Drake St. WC1 BX39 56
Theobalds Rd.
Drake St., Enf. BZ23 30
Drakefell Rd. SE14 CC44 67
Drakefell Rd. SE4 CD45 67
Drakefield Rd. SW17 BV48 76
Drakely Ct. N5 BY35 47
Highbury Hill
Drakes Clo., Chsnt. CC17 21
Drakes Clo., Esher BF56 93
Drakes Dr., Nthwd. AZ30 35
Drakes Dr., St.Alb. BJ15 9
Drakes Grn., Esher BF56 93
Drakes Rd., Amer. AP23 25
Drakes Way, Wok. AR64 100
Drakes Wk. E6 CK37 58
Drakewood Rd. SW16 BW50 76
Draper Clo., Belv. CQ42 69
Drapers Rd. E15 CF35 48
Drapers Rd. N17 CA31 48
Drapers Rd., Enf. BY23 29
Drappers Way SE16 CB42 67
St. James's Rd.
Draw Dock Rd. SE10 CF40 57
Drawell Clo. SE18 CN42 68
Drax Av. SW20 BP50 75
Draxmont App. SW19 BR50 75
Dray Gdns. SW2 BX46 76
Draycot Rd. E11 CH32 49
Draycot Rd., Surb. BM55 85
Draycott Av. SW3 BU42 3
Draycott Av. SW3 BU42 66
Draycott Av., Har. BJ32 45
Draycott Clo., Har. BJ32 45
Draycott Pl. SW3 BU42 3
Draycott Pl. SW3 BU42 66
Draycott Ter. SW3 BU42 3
Draycott Ter. SW3 BU42 66
Drayford Clo. W9 BR38 55
Drayson Ms. W8 BS41 66
Drayton Av. W13 BJ40 54
Drayton Av., Loug. CK26 40
Drayton Av., Orp. CL54 88
Drayton Av., Pot.B. BR19 19
Drayton Bridge Rd. W13 BJ39 54
Drayton Bridge Rd. W7 BH40 54
Drayton Clo., Houns. BE46 74
Drayton Clo., Lthd. BH65 102
Drayton Gdns. N21 BY26 38
Drayton Gdns. SW10 BT42 3
Drayton Gdns. SW10 BT42 66
Drayton Gdns. W13 BJ40 54
Drayton Gdns., West Dr. AY41 63
Drayton Grn. Rd. W13 BJ40 54
Drayton Grn. W13 BJ40 54
Drayton Gro. W13 BJ40 54
Drayton Pk. N5 BY34 47
Drayton Rd. E11 CF33 48
Drayton Rd. N17 CA30 39
Drayton Rd. NW10 BO37 55
Drayton Rd. W13 BJ39 54
Drayton Rd., B.Wd. BM24 28
Drayton Rd., Croy. BY55 86
Drayton Waye, Har. BJ32 45
Dreadnought St. SE10 CG41 68
Drenon Sq., Hayes BB40 53
Dresden Clo. NW6 BS36 56
Lymington Rd.
Dresden Rd. N19 BW33 47
Dresden Way, Wey. AZ56 92
Dressington Av. SE4 CE46 77
Chudleigh Rd.
Drew Av. NW7 BQ29 37
Drew Gdns., Grnf. BH36 54
Drew Rd. E16 CK40 58
Drewstead Rd. SW16 BW48 76
Drey, The, Ger.Cr. AS28 34
Driffield Rd. E3 CD37 57
Drift La., Cob. BE62 102
Drift Rd., Wind. AG45 61
Drift, The, Kes. CJ55 88
Drifts Way, Slou. AU44 62
Driftway, Hem.H. AY13 8
Driftway, The, Bans. BQ61 103
Driftway, The, Lthd. BK65 102
Driftway, The, Mitch. BV51 86
Driftwood Av., St.Alb. BF16 18
Driftwood Dr., Ken. BZ62 105
Drill Hall Rd., Cher. AW54 83
Drinkwater Est., Felt. BC46 73
Drinkwater Rd., Har. BF34 45
Drive Mead, Couls. BX60 95
Drive Rd., Couls. BW63 104
Drive Rd., Rick. AX26 35
Drive Spur, Tad. BS64 104
Drive, The E17 CE31 48
Drive, The E18 CH31 49
Drive, The E4 CF26 39
Drive, The N11 BW29 38
Drive, The N2 BU32 47
Drive, The N3 BS29 38
Drive, The N7 BX36 47
Drive, The NW11 BR33 46
Drive, The SW16 BX52 86
Drive, The SW20 BQ50 75
Drive, The SW6 BR44 65
Drive, The W3 BN39 55
Drive, The, Harold Wood CW30 42
Drive, The, Onslow Village AP71 118
Drive, The, Amer. AO22 25
Drive, The, Ashf. BA50 73
Drive, The, Bans. BR62 103
Drive, The, Bark. CN30 40
Drive, The, Bark. CN36 58
Drive, The, Barn. BR24 28
Drive, The, Beck. CE51 87
Drive, The, Bex. CP47 79
Drive, The, Brwd. DB29 42
Drive, The, Buck.H. CJ26 40
Drive, The, Chis. CN52 88
Drive, The, Chsnt. BY17 20
Drive, The, Cob. BE60 93
Drive, The, Couls. BX60 95
Drive, The, Datchet AQ44 62
Drive, The, Edg. BM28 37
Drive, The, Enf. BZ23 30
Drive, The, Epsom BO57 94
Drive, The, Erith CR43 69
Drive, The, Esher BG54 84
Drive, The, Felt. BC47 73
Drive, The, Fetcham BH64 102
Drive, The, Ger.Cr. AS29 34
Drive, The, Grav. DH49 81
Drive, The, Grays CX43 70
Drive, The, Guil. AP70 118
Beech Gro.
Drive, The, Guil. AQ72 118
Drive, The, Har. BF32 45
Drive, The, Harl. CN10 6
Drive, The, Hat. BS16 20
Drive, The, Headley BM65 103
Drive, The, Hodd. CE11 12
Drive, The, Houns. BG44 64
Drive, The, Ilf. CK32 49
Drive, The, Kings.T. BN51 85
Drive, The, Loug. CK24 31
Drive, The, Lthd. BL65 103
Drive, The, Mord. BT53 86
Drive, The, New Barnet BT25 29
Drive, The, Nthwd. BB30 35
Drive, The, Orp. CN55 88
Drive, The, Pot.B. BR20 19
Drive, The, Rad. BJ20 18
Drive, The, Rick. AW25 26
Drive, The, Rom. CS29 41
Drive, The, Saw. CQ 6 6
Drive, The, Sev. CU65 107
Drive, The, Sid. CO48 79
Drive, The, Slou. AS41 62
Drive, The, Stai. AR46 72
Drive, The, Surb. BL54 85
Drive, The, Sutt. BR59 94
Drive, The, Th.Hth. BZ52 87
Drive, The, Uxb. AY35 44
Drive, The, Vir.W. AS53 82
Drive, The, W.Wick. CF54 87
Drive, The, Wall. BW58 95
Drive, The, Wat. BB22 26
Drive, The, Wem. BN34 46
Drive, The, Wok. AQ63 100
Driveway, The, Cuff. BX17 20
Driveway, The, Hem.H. AW14 8
Anchor La.
Droitwich Clo. SE26 CB48 77
Dromey Gdns., Har. BH29 36
Dromore Rd. SW15 BR46 75
Dronfield Gdns., Dag. CP35 50
Drood Yd. E1 CB40 57
Pennington St.
Droop St. W10 BQ38 55
Drop La., St.Alb. BF18 18
Drove Rd., Dor. BC71 119
Drove Way, Loug. CL23 31
Drover La. SE15 CB43 67
Drovers Rd., S.Croy. BZ56 96
Drovers Way, Beac. AO29 34
Drovers Way, Hat. BP11 10
Drovers Way, St.Alb. BG13 9
Droveway, The, Grav. DF50 81
Druce Rd. SE21 CA46 77
Drudgeon Way, Dart. DB48 80
Druid St. SE1 CA41 4
Druid St. SE1 CA41 67
Druids Clo., Ash. BL63 103
Druids Way, Brom. CF52 87
Drum St. E1 CA39 112
Drumaline Ridge, Wor.Pk. BO55 85
Drummond Av., Rom. CS31 50
Drummond Clo., Erith CT44 69
Drummond Cres. NW1 BW38 1
Drummond Cres. NW1 BW38 56
Drummond Dr., Stan. BH29 36
Drummond Gate SW1 BW42 66
Drummond Pl., Twick. BJ46 74
Drummond Rd. E11 CH32 49
Drummond Rd. SE16 CB41 67
Drummond Rd., Croy. BZ55 87
Drummond Rd., Guil. AR70 118
Drummond Rd., Rom. CS31 50
Drummond St. NW1 BW38 1
Drummond St. NW1 BW38 56
Drummonds, The, Buck.H. CH27 40
Drummonds, The, Epp. CO18 23
Hartland Rd.
Drury Cres., Croy. BY55 86
Drury La. WC2 BX39 2
Drury La. WC2 BX39 56
Drury Rd., Har. BG33 45
Drury Way NW10 BN35 46
Dryad St. SW15 BQ45 65
Dryburgh Gdns. NW9 BM31 46
Dryburgh Rd. SW15 BP45 65
Drycroft, Welw.G.C. BR 9 5
Dryden Av. W7 BH39 54
Dryden Clo., Ilf. CN29 40
Dryden Ct., Guil. AS71 118
Lower Edgeborough Rd.
Dryden Ho. SE5 CA44 67
Glebe Est.
Dryden Pl., Til. DG44 71
Fielding Av.
Dryden Rd. SW19 BT50 76
Dryden Rd., Enf. CA25 30
Dryden Rd., Har. BH30 36
Dryden Rd., Well. CN44 68
Dryden St. WC2 BX39 2
Dryden Way, Orp. CO54 89
Dryfield Clo. NW10 BN36 55
Dryfield Rd., Edg. BN29 37
Dryfield Wk. SE8 CE43 67
New King St.
Dryhill La., Sev. CR65 107
Dryhill Rd., Belv. CQ43 69
Dryland Av., Orp. CN56 97
Drylands Rd. N8 BX32 47
Drynham Pk., Wey. BB55 83
Drysdale Av. E4 CE26 39
Drysdale Clo., Nthwd. BB29 35
Drysdale Pl. N1 CA38 2
Drysdale Pl. N1 CA38 57
Drysdale St.
Drysdale St. N1 CA38 2
Drysdale St. N1 CA38 57
Du Cane Clo. W12 BQ39 55
Du Cane Rd.
Du Cane Ct. SW17 BV47 76
Du Cane Rd. W12 BP39 55
Du Cros Dr., Stan. BK29 36
Du Cros Rd. W3 BO40 55
Duboyne Rd. NW5 BU35 47
Dubrae Clo., St.Alb. BF14 9
Ducal St. E2 CA38 2
Ducal St. E2 CA38 57
Brick La.
Ducat St. E2 CA38 57
Duchess Ms. W1 BV39 1
Duchess Ms. W1 BV39 56
Duchess St.
Duchess of Bedfords Wk. W8 BS41 66
Duchess St. W1 BV39 1
Duchess St. W1 BV39 56
Duchy Rd., Barn. BT22 29
Duchy St. SE1 BY40 4
Duchy St. SE1 BY40 56
Ducie St. SW4 BX45 66
Duck La. W1 BW39 1
Duck La. W1 BW39 56
Broadwick St.
Duck La., Epp. CP16 23
Duck Lees La., Enf. CD24 30
Duckett Rd. N4 BY32 47
Duckett St. E1 CC38 57
Ducketts Rd., Dart. CT46 79
Ducking Stool Ct., Rom. CT31 50
Market Link
Duckling La., Saw. CQ 6 6
Fair Grn.
Ducks Hill Rd., Nthwd. AZ31 44
Ducks Hill, Nthwd. AZ30 35
Ducks Wk., Twick. BK46 74
Ducksfoot La. EC4 BZ40 57
Upper Thames St.
Dudbrook Rd., Rom. CW22 33
Dudden Hill La. NW10 BO35 46
Duddington Clo. SE9 CJ49 78
Dudley Av., Har. BK31 45
Dudley Av., Wal.Cr. CC19 21
Dudley Clo., Hem.H. AT16 16
Dudley Clo., Wey. AW55 83
Dudley Ct. NW11 BR31 46
Dudley Ct., Slou. AQ41 62
Upton Rd.
Dudley Dr., Mord. BR54 85
Dudley Dr., Ruis. BC35 44
Dudley Gdns. W13 BJ41 64
Dudley Gdns., Har. BG33 45
Dudley Gdns., Rom. CV29 42
Dudley Gro., Epsom BN60 94
Dudley Rd. E17 CE31 48
Dudley Rd. N3 BS30 38
Dudley Rd. NW6 BR37 55
Dudley Rd. SW19 BS50 76
Dudley Rd., Ashf. AY49 73
Dudley Rd., Felt. BA47 73
Dudley Rd., Grav. CF47 81
Dudley Rd., Har. BG34 45
Dudley Rd., Ilf. CL35 49
Dudley Rd., Kings.T. BL52 85
Dudley Rd., Rich. BL44 65
Dudley Rd., Rom. CV29 42
Dudley Rd., Sthl. BD41 64
Dudley Rd., Walt. BC53 83
Dudley St. W2 BT39 1
Dudlington Rd. E5 CC34 48
Dudmaston Ms. SW3 BT42 3
Dudmaston Ms. SW3 BT42 66
Dudsbury Rd., Dart. CU46 79
Dudsbury Rd., Sid. CO49 79
Dudset La., Houns. BC44 63
Dudswell La., Berk. AO10 7
Duff St. E14 CE39 57
Dufferin Av. EC1 BZ38 2
Dufferin St.
Dufferin St. EC1 BZ38 2
Dufferin St. EC1 BZ38 57
Duffield Clo., Har. BH32 45
Duffield La., Slou. AP35 43
Duffield Pk., Slou. AQ38 52
Duffield Rd. SW11 BU45 66
Batten St.
Duffield Rd., Tad. BP65 103
Duffins Orchard, Cher. AU57 91
Dufours Pl. W1 BW39 1
Dufours Pl. W1 BW39 56
Broadwick St.
Dugdale Hill La., Pot.B. BR20 19
Dugdales, Rick. AZ24 26
Duke Gdns., Ilf. CM31 49
Duke Rd.
Duke Humphrey Rd. SE3 CG44 68
Duke of Cambridge Clo., Twick. BG46 74
Duke of Edinburgh Rd., Sutt. BT55 86
Duke of Wellington Pl. SW1 BV41 3
Duke of Wellington Pl., SW1 BV41 66
Duke of York St. SW1 BW40 3
Duke of York St. SW1 BW40 56
Duke Rd. W4 BN42 65
Duke Rd., Ilf. CM31 49
Duke Shore Pl. E14 CD40 57
Narrow St.
Duke St. Hill SE1 BZ40 4
Duke St. Hill SE1 BZ40 57
Duke St. Ms. NW8 BU38 56
Lisson Gro.
Duke St. SW1 BW40 3
Duke St. SW1 BW40 56
Duke St. W1 BV39 1
Duke St. W1 BV39 56
Duke St., Hodd. CE11 12
Duke St., Rich. BK46 74
Duke St., Sutt. BT56 95
Duke St., Wat. BD24 27
Duke St., Wind. AO44 61
Duke St., Wok. AS62 100
Dukes Av. N10 BW31 47
Dukes Av. N3 BS30 38
Dukes Av. W4 BN42 65
Dukes Av., Edg. BL29 37
Dukes Av., Epp. CN21 31
Dukes Av., Grays DD41 71
Dukes Av., Har. BE32 45
Dukes Av., Houns. BE45 64
Dukes Av., N.Mal. BO52 85
Dukes Av., Nthlt. BE36 54
Dukes Av., Rich. BK49 74
Dukes Av., Wealdstone BH31 45
Dukes Clo., Ashf. BA49 73
Dukes Clo., Epp. CR17 23
Dukes Clo., Ger.Cr. AR33 43
Dukes Clo., Hmptn. BE49 74
Dukes Clo., Kings.T. BK49 74
Dukes Ct. E6 CL37 58
Dukes Hill, Warl. CD63 105
Dukes Kiln Rd., Ger.Cr. AR34 43
Dukes La. W8 BS41 66
Dukes La., Ger.Cr. AR33 43
Dukes La., Ong. DB12 15
Dukes Lodge, Nthwd. BB28 35
Eastbury Av.
Dukes Meadows W4 BN44 65
Dukes Ms. N10 BV31 47
Dukes Av.
Dukes Ms. W1 BV39 1
Dukes Ms. W1 BV39 56
Duke St.
Dukes Orchard, Bex. CS47 79
Dukes Pass. E17 CF31 48
Marlowe Rd.
Dukes Pl. EC3 CA39 2
Dukes Pl. EC3 CA39 57
Dukes Pl., Brwd. DB26 42
Wellesley Rd.
Dukes Rd. E6 CL37 58
Dukes Rd. W3 BM38 55
Dukes Rd. WC1 BW38 1
Dukes Rd. WC1 BW38 56
Dukes Rd., Walt. BD56 93
Dukes Ride, Dor. BK73 119
Dukes Ride, Ger.Cr. AS33 43
Dukes Ride, Uxb. AY35 44
The Drive
Dukes Way, Berk. AQ12 7
Dukes Way, W.Wick. CG55 88
Dukes Wood Av., Ger.Cr. AS33 43
Dukes Wood Dr., Ger.Cr. AR33 43
Dukes Yd. W1 BV39 1
Binney St.
Dukesthorpe Rd. SE26 CC49 77
Dulas St. N4 BX33 47
Everleigh St.
Dulford St. W11 BR40 55
Dulka Rd. SW11 BU46 76
Dulton Clo., Hem.H. AX14 8
Dulverton Rd. SE9 CM48 78
Dulverton Rd., Rom. CV29 42
Dulverton Rd., Ruis. BC33 44
Dulverton Rd., S.Croy. CC58 96
Dulwich Common SE21 CA47 77
Dulwich Gate SE21 CA47 77
Dulwich Gro. SE22 CA46 77
Dulwich Lawn Clo. SE22 CA46 77
Colwell Rd.
Dulwich Rd. SE24 BY46 76
Dulwich Village SE21 CA46 77
Dulwich Way, Rick. AZ25 26
Dulwich Wood Av. SE19 CA49 77
Dulwich Wood Pk. SE19 CA49 77
Dumbarton Av., Wal.Cr. CC20 21
Raglan Av.
Dumbarton Rd. SW2 BX46 76
Dumbleton Clo., Kings.T. BM51 85
Gloucester Rd.
Dumbreck Rd. SE9 CK45 68
Dumfries Clo., Wat. BB27 35
Dumont Rd. N16 CA34 48
Dumpton Pl. NW1 BV36 56
Dunally Pk., Shep. BA54 83
Dunbar Av. SW16 BY51 86
Dunbar Av., Beck. CD52 87
Dunbar Av., Dag. CR34 50
Dunbar Clo., Hayes BC39 53
Dunbar Ct., Walt. BD55 84
Dunbar Gdns., Dag. CR35 50
Dunbar Rd. E7 CH36 58
Dunbar Rd. N22 BY30 38
Dunbar Rd., N.Mal. BN52 85
Dunbar St. SE27 BZ48 77
Dunblane Rd. SE9 CK45 68
Dunboe Pl., Shep. BA54 83
Russell Rd.
Dunboyne Rd. NW3 BU35 47
Dunbridge St. E2 CB38 57
Duncan Clo., Barn. BT24 29
Duncan Clo., Welw.G.C. BR 8 5
Duncan Ct., St.Alb. BH14 9
Duncan Dr., Guil. AT70 118
Duncan Gro. W3 BO39 55
Duncan Rd. E8 CB37 57
Duncan Rd., Rich. BL45 65
Duncan Rd., Tad. BR63 103
Duncan St. N1 BY37 2
Duncan St. N1 BY37 56
Duncan Ter. N1 BY37 2
Duncan Ter. N1 BY37 56
Duncan Way, Bush. BE23 27
Duncannon Cres., Wind. AL45 61
Duncannon St. WC2 BX40 4
Duncannon St. WC2 BX40 56
Willian IV St.
Dunch St. E1 CB39 57
Watney St.
Duncombe Clo., Amer. AP22 25
Duncombe Hill SE23 CD47 77
Duncombe Rd. N19 BW33 47
Duncombe Rd., Berk. AP12 7
Duncrievie Rd. SE13 CF46 77
Duncroft Clo., Reig. BR70 120
Duncroft SE18 CN43 68
Duncroft, Wind. AM45 61
Dundalk Rd. SE4 CD45 67
Dundas Gdns., E.Mol. BF52 84
Dundas Rd. SE15 CC44 67
Dundee Rd. E13 CH37 58
Dundee Rd. SE25 CB53 87
Dundee St. E1 CB40 57
Green Bank
Dundela Gdns., Wor.Pk. BP56 94
Dundon Gdns. SE23 CC47 77
Dundonald Clo. E6 CK39 58
Northumberland Rd.
Dundonald Rd. NW10 BQ37 55
Dundonald Rd. SW19 BR51 85
Dundrey Cres., Red. BX68 113
Dunedin Dr., Cat. CA66 114
Dunedin Rd. E10 CE34 48
Dunedin Rd., Ilf. CM33 49
Dunedin Rd., Rain. CT38 59
Dunedin Way, Hayes BD38 54
Dunelm Gro. SE27 BZ48 77
Dunelm St. E1 CC39 57
Dunfee Way, Wey. AY59 92
Viscount Gdns.
Dunfield Gdns. SE6 CE49 77
Dunfield Rd. SE6 CE49 77
Dunford Rd. N7 BX35 47
Dungarvan Av. SW15 BP45 65
Dungates La., Bet. BP70 120
Dunheved Clo., Th.Hth. BT53 86
Dunheved Rd. N., Th.Hth. BY53 86
Dunheved Rd. S., Th.Hth. BY53 86
Dunheved Rd. W., Th.Hth. BY53 86

Dunholme Grn. N9	CA27	39
Dunholme La. N9	CA27	39
Dunholme Rd.		
Dunholme Rd. N9	CA27	39
Dunkeld Rd. SE25	BZ52	87
Dunkeld Rd., Dag.	CO34	50
Dunkellin Gro., S.Ock.	DA39	60
Dunkellin Way, S.Ock.	DA39	60
Dunkery Rd. SE9	CH49	78
Dunkin Rd., Dart.	CX45	70
Dunkirk Clo., Grav.	DH49	81
Waring St.		
Dunlace Rd. E5	CC35	48
Dunleary Clo., Houns.	BE47	74
Dunley Dr., Croy.	CE57	96
Dunlin Clo., Reig. & Red.	BU73	121
Dunlin Ri., Guil.	AU69	118
Dunlin, Hem.H.	AY11	8
Dunloe Av. N17	BZ31	48
Dunloe Pl. E2	**CA37**	**2**
Dunloe St. E2	**CA37**	**2**
Dunloe St. E2	CA37	57
Dunlop Pl. SE16	**CA41**	**4**
Dunlop Pl. SE16	CA41	67
Dunlop Rd., Til.	DF44	71
Dunmail Dr., Pur.	CA60	96
Dunmore Rd. NW6	BR37	55
Dunmore Rd. SW20	BQ51	85
Dunmore, Guil.	AO70	118
Dunmow Clo., Felt.	BE49	74
Dunmow Clo., Loug.	CK25	31
Dunmow Clo., Rom.	CP32	50
Dunmow Dr., Rain.	CT37	59
Dunmow Gdns., Brwd.	DE32	123
Dunmow Rd. E15	CF35	48
Dunmow Rd., Ong.	CZ14	15
Dunmow Wk. N1	BZ37	57
Popham St.		
Dunn Mead NW9	BO29	37
Dunn St. E8	CA35	48
Dunnents, Wok.	AP62	100
Staveley Way		
Dunning Clo., S.Ock.	DA39	60
Dunningford Clo., Horn.	CT35	50
Dunnings La., Brwd.	DC33	123
Dunnings La., Upmin.	DD34	123
Dunnock Clo., B.Wd.	BM24	28
Goldfinch Way		
Dunnock Rd. E6	CK39	58
Dunny La., Kings L.	AV19	16
Dunnymans Rd., Bans.	BR61	94
Basing Rd.		
Dunollie Pl. NW5	BW35	47
Dunollie Rd.		
Dunollie Rd. NW5	BW35	47
Dunoon Gdns. SE23	CC47	77
Devonshire Rd.		
Dunoon Rd. SE23	CC47	77
Dunottar Clo., Red.	BT71	121
Dunraven Dr., Enf.	BY23	29
Dunraven Rd. W12	BP40	55
Dunraven St. W1	BU40	56
Green St.		
Dunraven St. W1	**BV40**	**3**
Dunsany Rd. W14	BQ41	65
Dunsbury Clo., Sutt.	BS58	95
Nettlecombe Clo.		
Dunsdon Av., Guil.	AQ71	118
Dunsfold Ri., Couls.	BW60	95
Dunsfold Way, Croy.	CE58	96
Dunsford Cres. SW18	BS47	76
Merton Rd.		
Dunsford Way SW15	BP46	75
Dover Park Dr.		
Dunsley Pl. SE13	CE45	67
Dunsmore Clo., Bush.	BG25	27
Dunsmore Clo., Hayes	BD38	54
Kingsash Dr.		
Dunsmore Clo., Bush.	BG25	27
Dunsmore Rd., Walt.	BC53	83
Dunsmore Way, Bush.	BG25	27
Dunsmure Rd. N16	CA33	48
Dunspring La., Ilf.	CL30	40
Dunstable Clo., Rom.	CV29	42
Dunstable Ms. W1	**BV39**	**1**
Dunstable Ms. W1	BV39	56
Dunstable Rd., E.Mol.	BE52	84
Dunstable Rd., Rich.	BL45	65
Dunstable Rd., Rom.	CV29	42
Dunstall Rd. SW20	BP50	75
Dunstall Way, E.Mol.	BF52	84
Dunstalls, Harl.	CL13	13
Dunstan Clo. N2	BT31	47
Thomas More Way		
Dunstan Rd. NW11	BR33	46
Dunstan Rd., Couls.	BW62	104
Dunstans Gro. SE22	CB46	77
Dunstans Rd. SE22	CB47	77
Dunster Av. SW15	BP46	75
Dunster Av., Mord.	BQ54	85
Dunster Clo., Barn.	BQ24	28
Dunster Clo., Rom.	CS30	41
Dunster Clo., Uxb.	AW30	35
Dunster Cres., Horn.	CX34	51
Dunster Ct. EC3	**CA40**	**4**
Dunster Dr. NW9	BN33	46
Dunster Gdns. NW6	BR36	55
Dunster Way, Har.	BE34	45
Dunsterville Way SE1	**BZ41**	**4**
Dunsterville Way SE1	BZ41	67
Dunston Rd. E8	**CA37**	**2**
Dunston Rd. E8	CA37	57
Dunston Rd. SW11	BV44	66
Dunston Rd., Hem.H.	AZ10	8
Dunston St. E8	**CA37**	**2**
Dunston St. E8	CA37	57
Dunton Clo., Surb.	BK54	84
Malcolm Dr.		
Dunton Rd. E10	CE33	48
Dunton Rd. SE1	**CA42**	**4**
Dunton Rd. SE1	CA42	67
Dunton Rd., Rom.	CT31	50
Duntshill Rd. SW18	BS47	76
Dunvegan Clo., E.Mol.	BF52	84
Dunvegan Rd. SE9	CK45	68
Dunwich Rd., Bexh.	CQ44	69
Dunworth Ms. W11	BR40	55
Portobello Rd.		
Duplex Ride SW1	**BU41**	**3**
Kinnerton St.		
Dupont Rd. SW20	BQ51	85
Dupont St. E14	CD39	57
Duppas Av., Croy.	BY56	95
Violet La.		
Duppas Clo., Shep.	BA53	83
Duppas Hill La., Croy.	BY56	95
Duppas Hill Rd., Croy.	BY56	95
Duppas Hill Ter., Croy.	BY55	86
Duppas La., Croy.	BY55	86
Duppas Rd., Croy.	BY55	86
Dupree Rd. SE7	CH42	68
Dura Den Clo., Beck.	CE50	77
Durand Clo., Cars.	BU54	86
Durand Gdns. SW9	BX44	66
Durand Way NW10	BN36	55
Durant Dr., Swan.	CU50	79
Durant St. E2	**CB37**	**2**
Durant St. E2	CB37	57
Durants Park Av., Enf.	CC24	30
Durants Rd., Enf.	CC24	30
Durban Gdns., Dag.	CS36	59
Durban Ho. E7	CJ36	58
Durban Rd. E., Wat.	BC24	26
Durban Rd. E15	CG38	58
Durban Rd. E17	CD30	39
Durban Rd. N17	CA29	39
Durban Rd. SE27	BZ49	77
Durban Rd. W., Wat.	BC24	26
Durban Rd., Beck.	CD51	87
Durban Rd., Felt.	BC48	73
Durban Rd., Ilf.	CN33	49
Durbin Rd., Chess.	BL56	94
Durdans Rd., Sthl.	BE39	54
Durell Gdns., Dag.	CP35	50
Durell Rd., Dag.	CP35	50
Durfold Dr., Reig.	BT70	121
Durford Cres. SW15	BP47	75
Durham Av., Brom.	CG52	88
Durham Av., Houns.	BE42	64
Durham Av., Rom.	CV31	51
Durham Av., Wdf.Grn.	CJ28	40
Durham Bldgs. SW11	BT45	66
Durham Clo. SW20	BP51	85
Durham Clo., Guil.	AP69	118
Durham Hill, Brom.	CG49	78
Durham House St. WC2	**BX40**	**4**
Durham House St. WC2	BX40	56
Strand		
Durham Pl. SW3	**BU42**	**3**
Durham Pl. SW3	BU42	66
Durham Rd. E12	CJ35	49
Durham Rd. E16	CG38	58
Durham Rd. N2	BU31	47
Durham Rd. N7	BX34	47
Durham Rd. N9	CB27	39
Durham Rd. SW20	BP51	85
Durham Rd. W5	BK41	64
Durham Rd., B.Wd.	BN24	28
Durham Rd., Brom.	CG52	88
Durham Rd., Dag.	CS35	50
Durham Rd., Felt.	BD47	74
Durham Rd., Har.	BF32	45
Durham Rd., Sid.	CO49	79
Durham Ri. SE18	CM42	68
Durham Row E1	CC39	57
Stepney High St.		
Durham St. SE11	BX42	66
Durham St. SE11	**BX43**	**4**
Durham Ter. W2	BS39	56
Durleston Park Dr., Lthd.	BG66	111
Durley Av., Pnr.	BE33	45
Durley Gdns., Orp.	CO55	89
Durley Rd. N16	CA33	48
Durlston Rd. E5	CB34	48
Durlston Rd., Kings.T.	BL50	75
Durndale La., Grav.	DF49	81
Durnell Way, Loug.	CL24	31
Durnford St. N15	CA32	48
Durnford St. SE10	CF43	67
Greenwich Church St.		
Durning Rd. SE19	BZ49	77
Durnsford Av. SW19	BS48	76
Durnsford Rd. N11	BW30	38
Durnsford Rd. SW19	BS48	76
Duro Pl. W8	BS42	66
Durrant Way, Orp.	CM56	97
Durrant Way, Swans.	DC47	81
Durrants Clo., Rain.	CV37	60
Durrants Dr., Rick.	BA24	26
Durrants Hill Rd., Hem.H.	AX15	8
Durrants La., Berk.	AP13	7
Durrants La., Rick.	AY24	26
Durrants Rd., Berk.	AP12	7
Durrell Rd. SW6	BR44	65
Durrell Way, Shep.	BA53	83
Durrington Av. SW20	BQ50	75
Durrington Park Rd. SW20	BQ51	85
Durrington Rd. Dev. E5	CD35	48
Durrington Rd. E5	CD35	48
Dursley Clo. SE3	CJ44	68
Dursley Gdns. SE3	CJ44	68
Dursley Rd. SE3	CJ44	68
Durward St. E1	CB39	57
Durweston Ms. W1	BV39	56
Crawford St.		
Durweston St. W1	BV39	56
York St.		
Dury Falls Clo., Horn.	CX33	51
Dury Rd., Barn.	BR23	28
Dutch Barn Clo., Stai.	AX46	73
Douglas Rd.		
Dutch Yd. SW18	BS46	76
Wandsworth High St.		
Dutton St. SE10	CF44	67
Dutton Way, Iver	AV39	52
Duxford Clo., Horn.	CV36	60
Duxons Turn, Hem.H.	AZ13	8
Dyall Ho., Grays	DD43	71
Hawkes Clo.		
Dye House La. E3	CE37	57
Dyers Bldgs. EC1	BY39	56
Holborn		
Dyers Hall Rd. E11	CF34	48
Dyers La. SW15	BP45	65
Dyers Way, Rom.	CU29	41
Dyke Dr., Orp.	CP54	89
Dykes Path, Wok.	AU61	100
Bentham Av.		
Dykes Way, Brom.	CG52	88
Dykewood Clo., Bex.	CT48	79
Dylan Clo., Brwd.	BK26	36
Sullivan Way		
Dylan Rd., Belv.	CR41	69
Dylways SE5	BZ45	67
Dymchurch Clo., Ilf.	CL30	40
Dymchurch Clo., Orp.	CN56	97
Dymes Path SW19	BR48	75
Queensmere Rd.		
Dymock St. SW6	BS45	66
Dymoke Grn., St.Alb.	BJ11	9
Dymoke Rd., Horn.	CT33	50
Dymokes Way, Hodd.	CE10	12
Dyne Rd. NW6	BR36	55
Dyneley Rd. SE12	CJ49	78
Dynes Rd., Sev.	CW62	108
Dynevor Pl., Guil.	AO68	109
Dynevor Rd. N16	CA34	48
Dynevor Rd., Rich.	BL46	75
Dynham Rd. NW6	BS36	56
Dyott St. WC1	**BW39**	**1**
Dyott St. WC1	BW39	56
Dyrham La., Barn.	BP21	28
Dysart Av., Kings.T.	BK49	74
Dysart St. EC2	**BZ38**	**2**
Dysart St. EC2	BZ38	57
Dyson Clo., Wind.	AN45	61
Dyson Rd. E11	CG32	49
Dyson Rd. E15	CG36	58
Dysons Clo., Wal.Cr.	CC19	21
Dysons Rd. N18	CB29	39
Dytchleys La., Brwd.	CW24	33

E

Eade Rd. N4	BZ33	47
Eagans Clo. N2	BT31	47
Eagle Av., Rom.	CQ32	50
Eagle Clo., Enf.	CC24	30
Eagle Clo., Rain.	CU36	59
Eagle Ct. EC1	**BY39**	**2**
Eagle Ct. EC1	BY39	56
Albion Pl.		
Eagle Hill SE19	BZ50	77
Eagle La. E11	CH31	49
Eagle La., Brwd.	CZ22	33
Eagle Pl. SW1	**BW40**	**3**
Eagle Pl. SW1	BW40	56
Jermyn St.		
Eagle Rd., Guil.	AR70	118
Eagle Rd., Wem.	BK36	54
Eagle St. WC1	**BX39**	**2**
Eagle St. WC1	BX39	56
High Holborn		
Eagle Ter., Wdf.Grn.	CH29	40
Eagle Way, Brwd.	DA29	42
Eagle Way, Hat.	BP13	10
Eagle Wharf Rd. N1	**BZ37**	**2**
Eagle Wharf Rd. N1	BZ37	57
Eagles Dr., West.	CJ62	106
Ricketts Hill		
Eagles, The N6	BU34	47
Eaglesfield Rd. SE18	CL44	68
Eaglet Pl. E1	CC38	57
Mile End Rd.		
Ealdham Sq. SE9	CJ45	68
Ealing Clo., B.Wd.	BN23	28
Ealing Grn. W5	BK40	54
Ealing Park Gdns. W5	BK42	64
Ealing Park Ms. W5	BK41	64
Ealing Rd.		
Ealing Rd., Brent.	BK42	64
Ealing Rd., Nthlt.	BF37	54
Ealing Rd., Wem.	BL36	55
Ealing Vill. W5	BL39	55
Eamont Clo., Ruis.	AZ33	44
Allonby Dr.		
Eamont St. NW8	**BU37**	**1**
Eamont St. NW8	BU37	56
Eardemont Clo., Dart.	CT45	69
Eardley Cres. SW5	BS42	66
Eardley Rd. SW16	BW49	76
Eardley Rd., Belv.	CR42	69
Eardley Rd., Sev.	CU65	107
Earl Cotts. SE1	**CA42**	**4**
Earl Cotts. SE1	CA42	67
Earl Rd. SE1	**CA42**	**4**
Earl Rd. SE1	CA42	67
Earl Rd. SW14	BN45	65
Earl Rd., Grav.	DF48	81
Earl Ri. SE18	CM42	68
Earl St. EC2	**BZ39**	**2**
Earl St. EC2	BZ39	57
Earl St., Wat.	BD24	27
Earldom Rd. SW15	BQ45	65
Earle Gdns., Kings.T.	BL50	75
Earlham Gro. E7	CG35	49
Earlham Gro. N22	BX29	38
Earlham St. WC2	**BW39**	**1**
Earlham St. WC2	BW39	56
Earls Cres., Har.	BH31	45
Earls Ct. Gdns. SW5	BS42	66
Earls Ct. Rd. SW5	BS41	66
Earls Ct. Rd. W8	BS41	66
Earls Ct. Sq. SW5	BS42	66
Earls La., Pot.B.	BO19	19
Earls Path, Loug.	CJ23	31
Earls Ter. W8	BR41	65
Earls Wk. W8	BS41	66
Earls Wk., Dag.	CO35	50
Earlsbrook Rd., Red.	BU71	121
Earlsferry Clo. N1	BX36	56
Earlsferry Clo. N1	**BX37**	**2**
Earlsferry Way N1	BX36	56
Earlsferry Clo.		
Earlsfield Rd. SW18	BT47	76
Earlsfield, Maid.	AH42	61
Earlshall Rd. SE9	CK45	68
Earlsmead Rd. N15	CA32	48
Earlsmead Rd. NW10	BQ38	55
Earlsmead, Har.	BE35	45
Earlsthorpe Ms. SW12	BV46	76
Nightingale La.		
Earlsthorpe Rd. SE26	CC49	77
Earlstoke St. EC1	**BY38**	**2**
Spencer St.		
Earlstoke St. EC1	BY38	56
Spencer St.		
Earlstone Gro. E9	CB37	57
Victoria Pk. Rd.		
Earlswood Av., Th.Hth.	BY53	86
Earlswood Clo. SE10	CG42	68
Earlswood St.		
Earlswood Gdns., Ilf.	CL31	49
Earlswood Rd., Red.	BU71	121
Earlswood St. SE10	CG42	68
Earlswood, Cob.	BD59	93
Early Ms. NW1	BV37	56
Arlington Rd.		
Earnshaw St. WC2	**BW39**	**1**
Earnshaw St. WC2	BW39	56
Earsby St. W14	BR42	65
Easby Cres., Mord.	BS53	86
Easebourne Rd., Dag.	CP35	50
Easedale Dr., Horn.	CU35	50
Easington Pl., Guil.	AS71	118
Maori Rd.		
Easington Way, S.Ock.	DA39	60
Easleys Ms. W1	**BV39**	**1**
Easleys Ms. W1	BV39	56
Wigmore St.		
East Acton La. W3	BO40	55
East Arbour St. E1	CC39	57
East Av. E12	CK36	58
East Av. E17	CE31	48
East Av., Hayes	BB40	53
East Av., Sthl.	BE40	54
East Av., Wall.	BX56	95
East Av., Walt.	BB58	92
East Bank N16	CA33	48
East Barnet Rd., Barn.	BT24	29
East Brook Clo., Wok.	AT61	100
East Burrow Fld., Welw.G.C.	BQ 9	5
East Churchfield Rd. W3	BN40	55
East Clo. W5	BM38	55
East Clo., Barn.	BV24	29
East Clo., Grnf.	BG37	54
East Clo., Rain.	CU38	59
East Common, Ger.Cr.	AS32	43
East Cres. N11	BU28	38
East Cres. Rd., Grav.	DH46	81
East Cres., Enf.	CA25	30
East Cres., Wind.	AM44	61
East Cross Route E3	CD36	57
East Ct., Wem.	BK34	45
East Dr. SW11	BV43	66
East Dr., Cars.	BU58	95
East Dr., Nthwd.	BB27	35
East Dr., Orp.	CO53	89
East Dr., Saw.	CQ 6	6
East Dr., Slou.	AP38	52
East Dr., St.Alb.	BL13	10
East Dr., Vir.W.	AQ53	82
East Dr., Wat.	BC21	26
East Dulwich Est. SE22	CA45	67
East Dulwich Gro. SE22	CA46	77
East Dulwich Rd. SE22	CA45	67
East End Rd. N2	BS30	38
East End Rd. N3	BS30	38
East End Way, Pnr.	BE31	45
East Entrance, Dag.	CR37	59
East Ferry Rd. E14	CE42	67
East Ferry Rd. E14	CF41	67
East Flint, Hem.H.	AV13	7
East Gate, Harl.	CM10	6
East Gdn., Wok.	AU62	100
East Gdns. SW17	BU50	76
East Glade, Pnr.	BE31	45
East Grn., Hem.H.	AY16	17
East Hall Rd., Orp.	CQ54	89
East Ham Manor Way E6	CL39	58
East Harding St. EC4	**BY39**	**2**
East Harding St. EC4	BY39	56
East Heath Rd. NW3	BT34	47
East Hill Dr., Dart.	CW47	80
East Hill Rd., Oxt.	CG68	115
East Hill SW18	BS46	76
East Hill, Dart.	CW47	80
East Hill, Oxt.	CG68	115
East Hill, S.Croy.	CA58	96
East Hill, S.Dnth.	CY51	90
East Hill, Sev.	CX59	99
East Hill, Wem.	BM34	46
East Hill, West.	CH62	106
East Hill, Wok.	AU61	100
East Holme, Erith	CS44	69
East Holme, Hayes	BC40	53
East India Dock Rd. E14	CE39	57
East India Dock Wall Rd. E14	CF40	57
East Kent Av., Grav.	DE46	81
East La. SE16	**CB41**	**4**
East La. SE16	CB41	67
East La., Kings.T.	BK52	84
High St.		
East La., Lthd.	BA66	110
East La., Wat.	BC18	17
East La., Wem.	BJ34	45
East Leigh Clo., Sutt.	BS57	95
East Lodge La., Enf.	BW21	29
East Mead Clo., Brom.	CK51	88
East Mead, Welw.G.C.	BS 9	5
East Mead, Wok.	AQ62	100
East Meads, Guil.	AQ71	118
East Milton Rd., Grav.	DH47	81
East Mount St. E1	CB39	57
East Park Clo., Rom.	CQ32	50
East Pass. EC1	**BZ39**	**2**
Cloth St.		
East Pk., Harl.	CO 9	6
East Pk., Saw.	CQ 6	6
East Pl. SE27	BZ49	77
Pilgrim Hill		
East Poultry Av. EC1	**BY39**	**2**
East Ramp, Houns.	AZ44	63
East Rd. E11	CH32	49
East Rd. E15	CH37	58
East Rd. N1	**BZ38**	**2**
East Rd. N1	BZ38	57
East Rd. SW19	BT50	76
East Rd., Chadwell Heath	CQ31	50
East Rd., Barn.	BV26	38
East Rd., Belv.	CQ41	69
East Rd., Edg.	BM30	37
East Rd., Enf.	CC22	30
East Rd., Felt.	BA47	73
East Rd., Grays	CX43	70
East Rd., Harl.	CO 9	6
East Rd., Kings.T.	BL51	85
East Rd., Reig.	BR70	112
East Rd., Rush Green	CS33	50
East Rd., Well.	CO44	69
East Rd., West Dr.	AY42	63
East Rd., Wey.	BA57	92
East Ridgeway, Cuff.	BX17	20
East Rochester Way, Sid.	CM45	68
East Rochester Way, Bex.	CQ46	79
East Row W10	BR38	55
East Shalford La., Guil.	AS73	118
East Sheen Av. SW14	BN46	75
East Smithfield E1	**CA40**	**4**
East Smithfield E1	CA40	57
East Sq. SE18	CL42	68
East St. EC2	**BZ39**	**2**
East St. EC2	BZ39	57
Blomfield St.		
East St. SE17	**BZ42**	**4**
East St. SE17	BZ42	67
East St., South Stifford	DC43	71
East St., Bark.	CM36	58
East St., Bexh.	CR45	69
East St., Brent.	BK43	64
East St., Brom.	CH51	88
East St., Epsom	BO59	94
East St., Grays	DE43	71
East St., Hem.H.	AX13	8
East St., Lthd.	BF66	111
East Surrey Gro. SE15	CA43	67
Commercial Way		
East Tenter St. E1	**CA39**	**2**
East Tenter St. E1	CA39	57
East Ter., Grav.	DH46	81
East Thurrock Rd., Grays	DD43	71
East Tilbury Rd., S.le H.	DJ40	71
East Towers, Pnr.	BD32	45
East Vw. E4	CF28	39
East Vw. NW3	BT34	47
East Vw., Barn.	BR23	28
East Vw., Hat.	BU12	11
East Way E11	CH32	49
East Way, Brom.	CH54	88
East Way, Croy.	CD55	87
East Way, Guil.	AP70	118
East Way, Hayes	BC40	53
East Way, Wal.Abb.	CF21	30
East Wk., Barn.	BV26	38
East Wk., Hayes	BC40	53
East Wk., Reig.	BS70	121
East Woodside, Bex.	CQ47	79
Eastbank Rd., Hmptn.	BG49	74
Eastbourne Av. W3	BN39	55
Eastbourne Gdns. SW14	BN45	65
Eastbourne Ms. W2	**BT39**	**1**
Eastbourne Ms. W2	BT39	56
Eastbourne Rd. E15	CG37	58
Eastbourne Rd. E6	CL38	58
Eastbourne Rd. N15	CA32	48
Eastbourne Rd. SW17	BV50	76
Eastbourne Rd. W4	BN43	65
Eastbourne Rd., Brent.	BK42	64
Eastbourne Rd., Felt.	BD48	74
Eastbourne Rd., Gdse.	CC69	114
Eastbourne Ter. W2	BT39	1
Eastbourne Ter. W2	BT39	56
Eastbournia Av. N9	CB27	39
Eastbridge, Slou.	AQ40	52
Victoria Rd.		
Eastbrook Av. N9	CC26	39
Eastbrook Av., Dag.	CS35	50
Eastbrook Dr., Rom.	CT34	50
Eastbrook Rd. SE3	CH43	68
Eastbrook Rd., Wal.Abb.	CG20	22
Eastbury Av., Bark.	CN37	58
Eastbury Av., Enf.	CA23	30
Eastbury Av., Nthwd.	BB28	35
Eastbury Ct., St.Alb.	BH13	9
Lemsford Rd.		
Eastbury Gro. W4	BO43	65
Eastbury Rd.		
Eastbury Pl., Nthwd.	BB28	35
Eastbury Av.		
Eastbury Rd. E6	CL38	58
Eastbury Rd. W4	BO42	65
Eastbury Rd., Kings.T.	BL50	75
Eastbury Rd., Nthwd.	BB28	35
Eastbury Rd., Orp.	CM53	88
Eastbury Rd., Rom.	CS32	50
Eastbury Rd., Wat.	BC26	35
Eastbury Sq., Bark.	CN37	58
Eastbury Ter. E1	CC38	57
Eastcastle St. W1	**BW39**	**1**
Eastcastle St. W1	BW39	56
Eastcheap EC3	**BZ40**	**4**
Eastcheap EC3	CA40	57
Eastchurch Rd., Houns.	BB44	63
Eastcombe Av. SE7	CH43	68
Eastcote Av., E.Mol.	BE53	84
Eastcote Av., Grnf.	BJ35	45

Eastcote Av., Har. BF34 45
Eastcote Gdns., Well. CM44 68
Eastcote High Rd., Pnr. BC32 44
Eastcote La. N., Nthlt. BE36 54
Eastcote La., Har. BE35 45
Eastcote La., Nthlt. BE35 45
Eastcote Rd., Har. BG34 45
Eastcote Rd., Pnr. BD32 45
Eastcote Rd., Ruis. BB33 44
Eastcote Rd., Well. CM44 68
Eastcote St. SW9 BX44 66
Eastcote Vw., Pnr. BD31 45
Eastcote, Orp. CN54 88
Eastcroft Rd., Epsom BO57 94
Eastdean Av., Epsom BM60 94
Eastdene Dr., Rom. CV28 42
Eastdown Pk. SE13 CF45 67
Eastern Av. E., Rom. CT30 41
Eastern Av. W., Ilf. CQ31 50
Eastern Av., Cher. AW52 83
Eastern Av., Grays CZ42 70
Eastern Av., Ilf. CH32 49
Eastern Av., Pnr. BD33 45
Eastern Av., Rom. CQ31 50
Eastern Av., S.Ock. CY41 70
Eastern Av., Wal.Cr. CD20 21
Eastern Ind. Est., Belv. CR41 69
Eastern Perimeter Rd., Houns. BB44 63
Eastern Rd. E13 CH37 58
Eastern Rd. E17 CF32 48
Eastern Rd. N2 BU31 47
Eastern Rd. N22 BX30 38
Eastern Rd. SE4 CE45 67
Eastern Rd., Grays DE42 71
Eastern Rd., Rom. CT32 50
Eastern Vw., West. CJ61 106
Eastern Way SE28 CO41 69
Eastern Way, Erith CQ40 59
Eastern Way, Grays DD42 71
Easternville Gdns., Ilf. CM32 49
Eastfield Av., Wat. BD23 27
Eastfield Clo., Slou. AQ41 62
Eastfield Ct., St.Alb. BK12 9
Southfield Way
Eastfield Gdns., Dag. CR35 50
Eastfield Par., Pot.B. BT19 20
Forbes Av.
Eastfield Rd. E17 CE31 48
Eastfield Rd. N8 BX31 47
Eastfield Rd., Brwd. DB27 42
Eastfield Rd., Dag. CQ35 50
Eastfield Rd., Enf. CC22 30
Eastfield Rd., Wal.Cr. CD19 21
Eastfields Rd. W3 BN39 55
Eastfields Rd., Mitch. BV51 86
Eastfields St. E14 CD39 57
Eastfields, Pnr. BD22 45
Eastgate Clo. SE28 CP39 59
Eastgate Gdns., Guil. AS71 118
Eastgate, Bans. BR60 94
Eastglade, Nthwd. BB28 35
Easthall La., Rain. CV39 60
Eastham Cres., Brwd. DD28 122
Eastholm NW11 BS31 47
Eastington Pl., Guil. AS71 118
Maori Rd.
Eastlake Rd. SE5 BZ44 67
Eastlands Clo., Oxt. CF67 114
Eastlands Cres. SE21 CA46 77
Eastlands Way, Oxt. CF67 114
Eastlea Av., Wat. BE22 27
Eastleigh Av., Har. BF34 45
Eastleigh Clo. NW2 BO34 46
Eastleigh Rd., Bexh. CS45 69
Eastleigh Rd., Felt. BB45 63
Eastleigh Wk. SW15 BP47 75
Eastman Rd. W3 BN40 55
The Vale
Eastman St. E1 CB38 57
Eastman Way, Hem.H. AZ12 8
Eastmead Av., Grnf. BF38 54
Eastmead, Ruis. BD34 45
Eastmearn Rd. SE21 BZ48 77
Eastminster E1 CA40 4
Eastminster E1 CA40 57
Royal Mint St.
Eastmont Rd., Esher BH55 84
Eastmoor Pl. SE7 CJ41 68
Eastmoor St.
Eastmoor St. SE7 CJ41 68
Eastney Rd., Croy. BY54 86
Eastney St. SE10 CF42 67
Eastnor Rd. SE9 CM47 78
Eastnor Rd., Reig. BS71 121
Eastnor, Hem.H. AT17 16
Easton Clo. SW1 BV42 3
Easton Gdns., B.Wd. BO24 28
Easton St. WC1 BY38 2
Easton St. WC1 BY38 56
Eastor, Welw.G.C. BS 6 5
Eastry Av., Brom. CG53 88
Eastry Rd., Erith CR43 69
Eastside Rd. NW11 BR31 46
Eastview Av. SE18 CN43 68
Eastville Av. NW11 BR32 46
Eastway E9 CD36 57
Eastway, Epsom BN59 94
Eastway, Mord. BQ53 85
Eastway, Ruis. BC33 44
Eastway, Wall. BW56 95
Eastwell Clo., Beck. CD51 87
Kings Hall Rd.
Eastwick Cres., Rick. AV27 34
Eastwick Dr., Lthd. BF65 102
Eastwick Hall La., Harl. CL 8 6
Eastwick Pk. Av., Lthd. BF65 102
Eastwick Rd., Harl. CM 9 6
Eastwick Rd., Lthd. BF66 111
Eastwick Rd., Walt. BC57 92
Eastwick Rd., Ware CK 9 6
Eastwick Row, Hem.H. AZ14 8
Eastwood Clo. E18 CH30 40
Eastwood Ct., Hem.H. AZ13 8
Eastwood Dr., Rain. CU39 59
Eastwood Est. SW15 BP46 75
Eastwood Rd. E18 CH30 40
Eastwood Rd. N10 BV30 38
Eastwood Rd., Ilf. CO33 50
Eastwood St. SW16 BW50 76
Eastworth Rd., Cher. AW54 83
Eatington Rd. E10 CF32 48
Eaton Clo. SW1 BV42 66
Eaton Clo., Stan. BJ28 36
Eaton Ct., Guil. AT69 118
Eaton Dr. SW9 BY45 66
Eaton Dr., Kings.T. BM50 75
Eaton Dr., Rom. CR29 41
Eaton Gate SW1 BV42 3
Eaton Gate SW1 BV42 66
Eaton Gate, Nthwd. BA29 35
Eaton Gdns., Dag. CQ36 59
Eaton La. SW1 BV41 3
Eaton La. SW1 BV41 66
Eaton Ms. N. SW1 BV41 66
Eaton Ms. N. SW1 BV42 3
Eaton Ms. S. SW1 BV42 3
Eaton Ms. S. SW1 BV42 66
Eaton Ms. SW1 BV42 3
Eaton Ms. W. SW1 BV42 3
Eaton Ms. W. SW1 BV42 66
Eaton Park Rd. N13 BY27 38
Eaton Park Rd., Cob. BE60 93
Eaton Pk., Cob. BE60 93
Eaton Pl. SW1 BV41 3
Eaton Pl. SW1 BV41 66
Eaton Rd. E11 CJ32 49
Eaton Rd. NW4 BQ32 46
Eaton Rd. SW9 BY45 66
Eaton Rd., Enf. CA24 30
Eaton Rd., Hem.H. AZ12 8
Eaton Rd., Houns. BG45 64
Eaton Rd., Sid. CP48 79
Eaton Rd., St.Alb. BJ13 9
Eaton Rd., Sutt. BT57 95
Eaton Ri. W5 BK39 54
Eaton Row SW1 BV41 3
Eaton Row SW1 BV41 66
Eaton Sq. SW1 BV42 3
Eaton Sq. SW1 BV42 66
Eaton Ter. Ms. SW1 BV42 3
Eaton Ter.
Eaton Ter. SW1 BV42 3
Eaton Ter. SW1 BV42 66
Eaton Wk. SE15 CA44 67
Sumner Est.
Eatons Mead E4 CE27 39
Eatonville Rd. SW17 BU48 76
Eatonville Vill. SW17 BU48 76
Eatonville Rd.
Ebbas Way, Epsom BM61 103
Ebberns Rd., Hem.H. AY15 8
Ebbisham Clo., Dor. BJ71 119
Ebbisham Dr. SW8 BX43 66
Ebbisham La., Tad. BP64 103
Ebbisham Rd., Epsom BM60 94
Ebbisham Rd., Wor.Pk. BQ55 85
Ebbsfleet Rd. NW2 BR35 46
Ebbsfleet Wk., Grav. DD46 81
Ebdon Way SE3 CH45 68
Ebenezer Rd. NW2 BS34 47
Ebenezer St. N1 BZ38 2
Ebenezer St. N1 BZ38 57
Ebenezer Wk. SW16 BW51 86
Ebley Clo. SE15 CA43 67
St. Georges Way
Ebner St. SW18 BS46 76
Ebor St. E1 CA38 2
Ebor St. E1 CA38 57
Ebrington Rd., Har. BK32 45
Ebsworth St. SE23 CC47 77
Eburne Rd. N7 BX34 47
Ebury App., Rick. AX26 35
Ebury Rd.
Ebury Br. Est. SW1 BV42 3
Ebury Br. Est. SW1 BV42 66
Ebury Br. Rd. SW1 BV42 3
Ebury Br. Rd. SW1 BV42 66
Ebury Br. SW1 BV42 3
Ebury Br. SW1 BV42 66
Ebury Clo., Kes. CK55 88
Ebury Clo., Nthwd. BA28 35
Ebury Ms. E. SW1 BV41 3
Ebury Ms. SW1 BV42 3
Ebury Ms. SW1 BV42 66
Ebury Rd., Rick. AX26 35
Ebury Rd., Wat. BD24 27
Ebury Sq. SW1 BV42 3
Ebury Sq. SW1 BV42 66
Ebury St. SW1 BV42 3
Ebury St. SW1 BV42 66
Eccles Hill, Dor. BK73 119
Eccles Rd. SW11 BU45 66
Ecclesbourne Clo. N13 BY28 38
Ecclesbourne Gdns. N13 BY28 38
Ecclesbourne Rd. N1 BZ36 57
Ecclesbourne Rd. N1 BZ38 2
Ecclesbourne Rd., Th.Hth. BZ53 87
Eccleston Br. SW1 BV42 3
Eccleston Br. SW1 BV42 66
Eccleston Clo., Barn. BU24 29
Carson Rd.
Eccleston Clo., Orp. CM54 88
Eccleston Cres., Rom. CO33 50
Eccleston Ct., Wem. BL35 46
Eccleston Ms. SW1 BV41 3
Eccleston Ms. SW1 BV41 66
Eccleston Ms., Wem. BL35 46
Eccleston Pl. SW1 BV42 3
Eccleston Pl. SW1 BV42 66
Eccleston Pl., Wem. BL35 46
Eccleston Rd. W13 BJ40 54
Eccleston Sq. Ms. SW1 BV42 3
Eccleston Sq. Ms. SW1 BW42 66
Warwick Pl. N.
Eccleston Sq. SW1 BV42 3
Eccleston Sq. SW1 BV42 66
Eccleston St. SW1 BV41 3
Eccleston St. SW1 BV41 66
Echelforde Dr., Ashf. AZ49 73
Echo Heights E4 CE26 39
Mount Echo Dr.
Echo Pit Rd., Guil. AS72 118
Echo Sq., Grav. DH48 81
Eckersley St. E1 CA38 2
Eckersley St. E1 CA38 57
Eckford St. N1 BY37 2
Eckford St. N1 BY37 56
Eckington Gdns. SE14 CC43 67
Monsoon Rd.
Eckstein Rd. SW11 BU45 66
Eclipse Rd. E13 CH39 58
Ecob Clo., Guil. AP68 109
Ecton Rd., Wey. AW56 92
Ector Rd. SE6 CG48 78
Edbrooke Rd. W9 BS38 56
Eddington St. N4 BY33 47
Everleigh St.
Eddiscombe Rd. SW6 BR44 65
Eddy Clo., Rom. CR32 50
Eddy St., Berk. AQ12 7
Eddystone Rd. SE4 CD46 77
Eddystone Wk., Stai. AY47 73
Clare Rd.
Ede Clo., Houns. BE45 64
Eden Clo. W8 BS41 66
Adam & Eve Ms.
Eden Clo., Bex. CS49 79
Eden Clo., Slou. AT42 62
Eden Clo., Wem. BK37 54
Eden Clo., Wey. AW58 92
Eden Ct. W5 BL39 55
Station Rd.
Eden Grn., S.Ock. DA39 60
Eden Gro. E17 CE32 48
Eden Gro. N7 BX35 47
Eden Grove Rd., Wey. AY60 92
Eden Ms. SW17 BT48 76
Huntspill St.
Eden Park Av., Beck. CD52 87
Eden Rd. E17 CE32 48
Eden Rd. SE27 BY49 76
Eden Rd., Beck. CD52 87
Eden Rd., Bex. CS49 79
Eden Rd., Croy. BZ56 96
Eden St., Kings.T. BL51 85
Eden Way, Beck. CD53 87
Eden Way, Warl. CD62 105
Edenbridge Clo., Orp. CP52 89
Edenbridge Rd. E9 CC36 57
Edenbridge Rd., Enf. CA25 30
Edencourt Rd. SW16 BV50 76
Edendale Rd., Bexh. CS44 69
Edendale W3 BM40 55
Julian Av.
Edenfield Gdns., Wor.Pk. BO55 85
Edenhall Clo., Hem.H. BA14 8
Edenhall Clo., Rom. CV28 42
Edenhall Rd.
Edenhall Glen, Rom. CV28 42
Edenhall Rd.
Edenhall Rd., Rom. CV28 42
Edenham Way W10 BR39 55
Elkstone Rd.
Edenhurst Av. SW6 BR45 65
Edenside Rd., Lthd. BE65 102
Edensor Gdns. Est. W9 BS40 56
Edensor Gdns. W4 BO43 65
Edensor Rd. W4 BO43 65
Edenvale Rd., Mitch. BV50 76
Edenvale St. SW6 BS44 66
Ederline Av. SW16 BX52 86
Edgar Clo., Swan. CT52 89
Edgar Rd. E3 CE38 57
Edgar Rd., Houns. BE47 74
Edgar Rd., Rom. CP33 50
Edgar Rd., S.Croy. BZ58 96
Edgar Rd., Sev. CW62 108
Edgar Rd., West Dr. AY40 53
Edgar Rd., West. CJ64 106
Edgarley Ter. SW6 BR44 65
Edgars Ct., Welw.G.C. BQ 8 5
Broadwater Cres.
Edgbaston Rd., Wat. BC27 35
Edge Clo., Wey. AZ57 92
Edge Field Clo., Red. BV73 121
Edge Hill Av. N3 BS31 47
Edge Hill Ct. SW19 BQ50 75
Edge Hill SE18 CL43 68
Edge Hill SW19 BQ50 75
Edge St. W8 BS40 56
Edgeborough Way, Brom. CJ51 88
Edgebury Est., Chis. CM49 78
Edgebury Wk., Chis. CM49 78
Edgebury, Chis. CL49 78
Edgecombe Clo., Kings.T. BN50 75
Edgecombe Rd. E11 CG33 49
Harvey Rd.
Edgecombe, S.Croy. CC57 96
Edgecot Gro. N15 CA32 48
Edgefield Av., Bark. CN36 58
Edgefield Clo., Dart. CX47 80
Edgehill Ct., Walt. BD54 84
Rodney Rd.
Edgehill Gdns., Dag. CR35 50
Edgehill Gdns., Grav. DF51 81
Edgehill Rd. W13 BJ39 54
Edgehill Rd., Chis. CM48 78
Edgehill Rd., Mitch. BV51 86
Edgehill Rd., Pur. BY58 95
Edgel St. SW18 BS45 66
Ferrier St.
Edgeley La. SW4 BW45 66
Edgeley Rd. SW4 BW45 66
Edgeley, Lthd. BE65 102
Edgell Clo., Vir.W. AS52 82
Edgell Rd., Stai. AV49 72
Edgepoint Clo. SE27 BY49 76
Knights Hill
Edgewood Dr., Orp. CN58 97
Edgewood Grn., Croy. CC54 87
Edgeworth Av. NW4 BP32 46
Edgeworth Clo. NW4 BP32 46
Edgeworth Clo., Whyt. CB62 105
Edgeworth Cres. NW4 BP32 46
Edgeworth Rd. SE9 CJ45 68
Edgeworth Rd., Barn. BU24 29
Edgington Rd. SW16 BW50 76
Edgware Ct., Edg. BM29 37
Edgware Rd. NW2 BP33 46
Edgware Rd. NW9 BN30 37
Edgware Rd. W2 BT38 1
Edgware Rd. W2 BT38 56
Edgware Way, Edg. BK26 36
Edgwarebury Gdns., Edg. BM28 37
Edgwarebury La., B.Wd. BL26 37
Edgwarebury La., Edg. BM28 37
Edinburgh Av., Rick. AW25 26
Edinburgh Clo., Uxb. AZ35 44
Edinburgh Cres., Wal.Cr. CD20 21
Edinburgh Ct. SW20 BQ53 85
Edinburgh Dr., Stai. AX50 73
Edinburgh Dr., Denham AV32 43
Edinburgh Dr., Ickenham AZ35 44
Edinburgh Gate SW1 BU41 3
Edinburgh Gate SW1 BU41 66
Edinburgh Gdns., Wind. AO44 61
Edinburgh Ms., Til. DG44 71
London Rd.
Edinburgh Pl., Harl. CO 9 6
Edinburgh Rd. E13 CH37 58
Edinburgh Rd. E17 CD32 48
Edinburgh Rd. N18 CB28 39
Edinburgh Rd. W7 BH41 64
Edinburgh Rd., Sutt. BT55 86
Edinburgh Way, Harl. CN 9 6
Edington Rd. SE2 CO41 69
Edington Rd., Enf. CC23 30
Edis St. NW1 BV37 1
Edis St. NW1 BV37 56
Edison Av., Horn. CT33 50
Edison Clo., Horn. CT33 50
Edison Dr., Sthl. BF39 54
Edison Gro. SE18 CN43 68
Edison Rd. N8 BW32 47
Edison Rd., Brom. CH51 88
Church Rd.
Edison Rd., Well. CN44 68
Edith Dr. N11 BW29 38
Edith Gdns., Surb. BM54 85
Edith Gro. SW10 BT43 66
Edith Ms. SW6 BS44 66
Edith Row
Edith Nesbitt Gdns. SE12 CH46 78
Osberton Rd.
Edith Rd. E15 CF35 48
Edith Rd. E6 CJ36 58
Edith Rd. SE25 BZ53 87
Edith Rd. SW19 BS50 76
Edith Rd. W14 BR42 65
Edith Rd., Orp. CO56 98
Edith Rd., Rom. CP33 50
Edith Row SW6 BS44 66
Edith St. E2 CA37 57
Edith Ter. SW10 BT43 66
Edith Yd. SW10 BT43 66
Worlds End
Edithna St. SW9 BX45 66
Ediths Rd., Sev. CX62 108
Edlyn Clo., Berk. AP12 7
Edmansons Clo. N17 CA30 39
Bruce Gro.
Edmondscote W13 BJ39 54
Cleveland Rd.
Edmund Beaufort Dr., St.Alb. BH12 9
Harpenden Rd.
Edmund Rd., Mitch. BU52 86
Edmund Rd., Orp. CP53 89
Edmund Rd., Rain. CT38 59
Edmund Rd., Well. CO45 69
Edmund St. SE5 BZ43 67
Edmund Way, Slou. AQ39 52
Edmunds Av., Orp. CP52 89
Edmunds Clo., Hayes BD39 54
Edmunds Wk. N2 BU31 47
Edna Rd. SW20 BQ51 85
Edna St. SW11 BU44 66
Edric Rd. SE14 CC43 67
Edrick Rd., Edg. BN29 37
Edrick Wk., Edg. BN29 37
Edridge Clo., Bush. BG25 27
Edridge Clo., Horn. CV35 51
Edridge Rd., Croy. BZ55 87
Edulf Rd., B.Wd. BM23 28
Edward Av. E4 CE29 39
Edward Av., Mord. BT53 86
Edward Clo. N9 CA26 39
Edward Clo., Hmptn. BG49 74
Edward Clo., Nthlt. BD37 54
Edward Clo., Rom. CV31 51
Edward Clo., St.Alb. BH14 9
Edward Clo., Wat. BB19 17
Edward Ct. E16 CH39 58
Alexandra St.
Edward Ct., Hem.H. AX15 8
King Edward St.
Edward Ct., Stai. AX50 73
Elizabeth Av.
Edward Ct., Wal.Abb. CG20 22
Ninefields
Edward Gro., Barn. BT25 29
Edward II Av., Wey. AY60 92
Edward Ms. NW1 BV38 1
Edward Ms. W1 BV39 1
Edward Pl. SE8 CD43 67
Edward Rd. E17 CC31 48
Edward Rd. SE20 CC50 77
Edward Rd., Barn. BT24 29
Edward Rd., Brom. CH50 78
Edward Rd., Chis. CL49 78
Edward Rd., Couls. BW61 104
Edward Rd., Croy. CA54 87
Edward Rd., Felt. BA46 73
Edward Rd., Har. BG31 45
Edward Rd., Hmptn. BG49 74
Edward Rd., Nthlt. BD37 54
Edward Rd., Rom. CQ32 50
Edward Rd., West. CK62 106
Edward Sq. N1 BX37 2
Edward Sq. N1 BX37 56
Edward St. E16 CH38 58
Edward St. SE14 CD43 67
Edward St. SE8 CD43 67
Edward Temme Av. E15 CG36 58
Edward Way, Ashf. AY48 73
Edwardes Sq. W8 BR41 65
Edwards Av., Ruis. BC36 53
Edwards Clo., Brwd. DF25 122
Edwards Clo., Wor.Pk. BQ55 85
Edwards Cotts. N1 BY36 56
Compton Av.
Edwards Ct., Slou. AP41 62
Chalvey Pk.
Edwards Gdns., Swan. CS52 89
Edwards La. N16 BZ34 48
Edwards Rd., Belv. CR42 69
Edwards Ter., Ong. CY19 24
Edwards Way, Brwd. DF25 122
Edwin Av. E6 CL38 58
Edwin Clo., Bexh. CQ43 69
Edwin Clo., Rain. CT38 59
Edwin Rd., Dart. CU48 79
Edwin Rd., Edg. BN29 37
Edwin Rd., Lthd. BA66 110
Edwin Rd., Twick. BH47 74
Edwin St. E1 CC38 57
Edwin St. E16 CH39 58
Edwin St., Grav. DG47 81
Edwina Gdns., Ilf. CK32 49
Edwins Mead E9 CD35 48
Kings Mead Est.
Edwyn Clo., Barn. BQ25 28
Effie Pl. SW6 BS43 66
Effie Rd. SW6 BS43 66
Effingham Clo., Sutt. BS57 95
Effingham Ct., Wok. AS62 100
Constitution Hill
Effingham Rd. N8 BY32 47
Effingham Rd. SE12 CG46 78
Effingham Rd., Croy. BX54 86
Effingham Rd., Reig. BS71 121
Effingham Rd., Surb. BJ54 84
Effort St. SW17 BU49 76
Effra Clo. SW19 BS50 76
Effra Par. SW2 BY46 76
Effra Rd. SW19 BS50 76
Effra Rd. SW2 BY45 66
Egan Way SE16 CB42 67
Bonamy Est. E.
Egan Way, Hayes BB40 53
Egbert St. NW1 BV36 56
Egdean Wk., Sev. CV65 108
Egerton Av., Swan. CT50 79
Egerton Clo., Dart. CU47 79
Egerton Clo., Pnr. BC31 44
Egerton Cres. SW3 BU42 3
Egerton Cres. SW3 BU42 66
Egerton Ct. E11 CF33 48
Egerton Dr. SE10 CE44 67
Egerton Gdns. Ms. SW3 BU41 66
Egerton Gdns. NW10 BQ37 55
Egerton Gdns. NW4 BP31 46
Egerton Gdns. SW3 BU41 3
Egerton Gdns. SW3 BU41 66
Egerton Gdns. W13 BJ39 54
Egerton Gdns., Ilf. CN34 49
Egerton Pl. SW3 BU41 3
Egerton Pl. SW3 BU41 66
Egerton Pl., Wey. BA57 92
Egerton Rd. N16 CA33 48
Egerton Rd. SE25 CA52 87
Egerton Rd., Berk. AQ12 7
Egerton Rd., Guil. AP70 118
Egerton Rd., N.Mal. BO52 85
Egerton Rd., Twick. BH46 74
Egerton Rd., Wem. BL36 55
Egerton Rd., Wey. BA57 92
Egerton Ter. SW3 BU41 3
Egerton Ter. SW3 BU41 66
Egg Hall, Epp. CO18 23
Eggpie La., Sev. & Ton. CV70 117
Egham By-pass, Egh. AS49 72
Egham Clo. SW19 BR48 75
Frimley Clo.
Egham Clo., Sutt. BR55 85
Egham Cres., Sutt. BQ55 85
Egham Hill, Egh. AR50 72
Egham Rd. E13 CH39 58
Egham Clo. SW19 BR48 75
Winterfold Clo.
Eglantine La., Hort.K. CX54 90
Eglantine Rd. SW18 BT46 76
Egleston Rd., Mord. BS53 86
Egley Dr., Wok. AR64 100
Egley Rd., Wok. AR64 100
Eglington Ct. SE17 BZ43 67
Carter St.
Eglington Rd. E4 CF26 39
Eglington Rd., Swans. DC48 81
Eglinton Hill SE18 CL43 68
Eglinton Rd. SE18 CL43 68
Eglise Rd., Warl. CD62 105
Egliston Ms. SW15 BQ45 65
Egliston Rd. SW15 BQ45 65
Eglon Ms. NW1 BU36 56
Berkley Rd.
Egmont Av., Surb. BL54 85
Egmont Park Rd., Tad. BP66 112
Egmont Rd., N.Mal. BO52 85
Egmont Rd., Surb. BL54 85
Egmont Rd., Sutt. BT57 95
Egmont Rd., Walt. BC54 83
Egmont St. SE14 CC43 67
Egmont Way, Tad. BR63 103
Egremont Rd. SE27 BY48 76
Eider St. SE17 BZ42 67
Rodney Rd.
Eighth Av. E12 CK35 49
Eighth Av., Hayes BC40 53
Eileen Rd. SE25 BZ53 87
Eisenhower Dr. E6 CK39 58
Elaine Gro. NW5 BV35 47
Elam Clo. SE5 BY44 66
Elam St. SE5 BY44 66
Elan Rd., S.Ock. DA39 60
Eland Rd. SW11 BU45 66
Eland Rd., Croy. BY55 86

Elba Pl. SE17 BZ42 4
Elba Pl. SE17 BZ42 67
Rodney Pl.
Elbe St. SW6 BT44 66
Elberon Av., Croy. BW53 86
Elborough Rd. SE25 CB53 87
Elborough St. SW18 BS47 76
Elbow La., Hert. CB11 12
Elbow Meadow, Slou. AV44 62
Elbury Dr. E16 CH39 58
Elby Clo. E6 CK39 58
Linton Gdns.
Elcho St. SW11 BU43 66
Elcom St. W10 BR39 55
Kensal Rd.
Elcot Av. SE15 CB43 67
Elder Av. N8 BX32 47
Elder Clo., Guil. AT69 118
Sutherland Dr.
Elder Ct., Bush. BH27 36
Elder Oak Clo. SE20 CB51 87
Elder Rd. SE27 BZ49 77
Elder St. E1 CA39 2
Elder St. E1 CA39 57
Elder Way, Dor. BK73 119
Elder Way, Rain. CV38 60
Elder Way, Slou. AS41 62
Waterside Dr.
Elder Wk. N1 BY37 56
Essex Rd.
Elderbeck, Chsnt. CB18 21
Elderberry Gro. SE27 BZ49 77
Linton Gro.
Elderberry Rd. W5 BL41 65
Elderfield Rd. E5 CC35 48
Elderfield Rd., Slou. AP36 52
Elderfield Wk. E11 CH32 49
Eldersley Clo., Red. BU69 121
Elderslie Clo., Beck. CE53 87
Elderslie Rd. SE9 CL46 78
Elderton Rd. SE26 CD49 77
Eldertree Pl., Mitch. BV51 86
Eldertree Way, Mitch. BV51 86
Elderwood Pl. SE27 BZ49 77
Eldon Av., B.Wd. BM23 28
Eldon Av., Croy. CC55 87
Eldon Av., Houns. BF43 64
Eldon Gro. NW3 BT35 47
Eldon Pk. SE25 CB52 87
Eldon Rd. E17 CD31 48
Eldon Rd. N22 BY30 38
Eldon Rd. N9 CC27 39
Eldon Rd. NW3 BT35 47
Eldon Rd. W8 BS41 3
Eldon Rd. W8 BS41 66
Eldon Rd., Cat. BZ64 105
Eldon Rd., Hodd. CF13 12
Eldon St. EC2 BX39 57
Eldon St. EC2 BZ39 2
Eldon Way NW10 BM37 55
Eldred Dr., Orp. CP54 89
Eldred Gdns., Upmin. CZ33 51
Eldred Rd., Bark. CM37 58
Eldridge Clo., Felt. BC47 73
Eleanor Av., Epsom BN58 94
Eleanor Av., St.Alb. BG12 9
Eleanor Clo. SE16 CC41 67
Eleanor Cres. NW7 BQ28 37
Eleanor Cross Rd., Wal.Cr. CD20 21
Eleanor Gdns., Barn. BQ25 28
Chesterfield Rd.
Eleanor Gdns., Dag. CQ34 50
Eleanor Gro. SW13 BO45 65
Eleanor Gro., Uxb. AZ34 44
Eleanor Rd. E15 CG36 58
Eleanor Rd. E8 CB36 57
Eleanor Rd. N11 BX29 38
Eleanor Rd., Ger.Cr. AR30 34
Eleanor Rd., Wal.Cr. CD20 21
Eleanor St. E3 CE38 57
Eleanor Way, Brwd. DB28 42
Eleanor Wk. SE18 CK42 68
Samuel St.
Electric Av. SW9 BY45 66
Electric La. SW9 BY45 66
Electric Par., Surb. BK53 84
Elephant & Castle SE1 BY42 4
Elephant & Castle SE1 BY42 66
Elephant La. SE16 CC41 67
Elephant Rd. SE17 BZ42 4
Elephant Rd. SE17 BZ42 67
Elers Rd. W13 BK41 64
Elers Rd., Hayes BA42 63
Eleven Acre Ri., Loug. CK24 31
Eley Rd. N18 CC28 39
Eleys Est. N18 CC28 39
Elf Row E1 CC40 57
Elfin Gro., Tedd. BH49 74
Elfin Rd. SE5 BY43 66
Warrior Rd.
Elfindale Rd. SE24 BZ46 77
Elford Clo. SE3 CJ45 68
Elfort Rd. N5 BY34 47
Elfrida Cres. SE6 CE49 77
Elfrida Rd., Wat. BD25 27
Elfwine Rd. W7 BH39 54
Elgal Clo., Orp. CL56 97
Orchard Rd.
Elgar Av. NW10 BN36 55
Mitchellbrook Way
Elgar Av. SW16 BX52 86
Elgar Av. W5 BL41 65
Elgar Av., Surb. BM54 85
Elgar Clo. SE8 CE43 67
Elgar Clo., B.Wd. BK26 36
Sullivan Way
Elgar Clo., Uxb. AZ34 44
Elgar Gdns., Til. DG44 71
Elgar St. SE16 CD41 67
Elgin Av. W9 BS38 1
Elgin Av. W9 BS38 56
Elgin Av., Ashf. BA50 73
Elgin Av., Har. BJ30 36
Elgin Av., Rom. CX29 42
Elgin Clo., Nthwd. BB29 35
Elgin Cres. W11 BR40 55
Elgin Cres., Cat. CB64 105
Elgin Cres., Houns. BB44 63
Eastern Perimeter Rd.
Elgin Gdns., Guil. AT70 118
Bladon Clo.
Elgin Ms. N. W9 BS38 1
Elgin Ms. N. W9 BS38 56
Elgin Ms. S. W9 BS38 1
Elgin Ms. S. W9 BS38 56
Elgin Ms. W11 BR39 55
Elgin Rd. N22 BW30 38
Elgin Rd., Brox. CD15 12
Elgin Rd., Chsnt. CC18 21
Elgin Rd., Croy. CA55 87
Elgin Rd., Ilf. CN33 49
Elgin Rd., Sutt. BT55 86
Elgin Rd., Wall. BW57 95
Elgin Rd., Wey. AZ56 92
Elgin Ter. W11 BR40 55
Elgood Av., Nthwd. BB29 35
Elgood Clo. W11 BR40 55
Avondale Park Rd.
Elham Clo., Brom. CJ50 78
Romney Dr.
Elia Ms. N1 BY37 2
Elia Ms. N1 BY37 56
Elia St. N1 BY37 2
Elia St. N1 BY37 56
Elias Pl. SW8 BY43 66
Elibank Rd. SE9 CK45 68
Elim Est. SE1 BZ41 4
Elim Est. SE1 CA41 67
Elim Way E13 CG38 58
Eliot Bank SE23 CB48 77
Eliot Cotts. SE3 CG44 68
Eliot Dr., Har. BF34 45
Eliot Gdns. SW15 BP45 65
Eliot Hill SE13 CF44 67
Eliot Pk. SE13 CF44 67
Eliot Pl. SE3 CG44 68
Eliot Rd., Dag. CP35 50
Eliot Rd., Dart. CX46 80
Eliot Vale SE3 CF44 67
Elizabeth Av. N1 BZ37 2
Elizabeth Av. N1 BZ37 57
Elizabeth Av., Amer. AQ23 25
Elizabeth Av., Enf. BY24 29
Elizabeth Av., Ilf. CM34 49
Elizabeth Av., Stai. AX50 73
Elizabeth Br. SW1 BV42 3
Elizabeth Br. SW1 BV42 66
Elizabeth Clo. E14 CE39 57
Grundy St.
Elizabeth Clo. W9 BT38 1
Randolph Av.
Elizabeth Clo., Welw.G.C. BT 8 5
Elizabeth Clo., Wal.Abb. CF15 12
Nazeing Rd.
Elizabeth Clo., Barn. BQ24 28
Elizabeth Clo., Rom. CR30 41
Elizabeth Clo., Til. DG44 71
London Rd.
Elizabeth Clyde Clo. N15 CA31 48
Lawrence Rd.
Elizabeth Cotts., Rich. BL44 65
Elizabeth Ct., Mord. BR54 85
Dudley Dr.
Elizabeth Ct., St.Alb. BK12 9
Villiers Cres.
Elizabeth Ct., Wat. BB22 26
Elizabeth Dr., Epp. CN21 31
Elizabeth Est. SE17 BZ43 4
Elizabeth Est. SE17 BZ43 67
Elizabeth Gdns. W3 BO40 55
Elizabeth Gdns., Stan. BK29 36
Elizabeth Gdns., Sun. BC52 83
Elizabeth Ms. NW3 BU36 56
Elizabeth Pl. N15 BZ31 48
Elizabeth Rd. E6 CJ37 58
Elizabeth Rd. N15 CA32 48
Elizabeth Rd., Brwd. DA25 33
Elizabeth Rd., Grays DC41 71
Elizabeth Ride N9 CB26 39
Elizabeth St. SW1 BV42 3
Elizabeth St. SW1 BV42 66
Elizabeth St., Green. CZ46 80
Elizabeth Ter. SE9 CK46 78
Elizabeth Way SE19 BZ51 87
Elizabeth Way, Felt. BD49 74
Elizabeth Way, Harl. CK11 13
Elizabeth Way, Orp. CP53 89
Elizabeth Way, Slou. AP37 52
Elizabethan Clo., Stai. AX47 73
Elizabethan Way, Stai. AX47 73
Elkington Rd. E13 CH38 58
Elkins Gdns., Guil. AT69 118
Elkins Rd., Slou. AP34 43
Elkins, The, Rom. CT30 41
Elkstone Rd. W10 BR39 55
Ella Rd. N8 BX33 47
Ellaline Rd. W6 BQ43 65
Ellanby Cres. N18 CB28 39
Elland Rd. SE15 CC45 67
Ellement Clo., Pnr. BD32 45
Ellen Clo., Brom. CJ52 88
Ellen Ct. N9 CC27 39
Densworth Gro.
Ellen St. E1 CB39 2
Ellen St. E1 CB39 57
Ellenborough Pl. SW15 BP45 65
Ellenborough Rd. N22 BY30 38
Ellenborough Rd., Sid. CP50 79
Ellenbridge Way, S.Croy. CA58 96
Ellenbrook Cres., Hat. BN12 10
Ellenbrook La., Hat. BN12 10
Elleray Rd., Tedd. BH50 74
Ellerby St. SW6 BQ44 65
Ellerdale Clo. NW3 BT35 47
Ellerdale Rd. NW3 BT35 47
Ellerdale St. SE13 CE45 67
Ellerdine Rd., Houns. BG45 64
Ellerker Gdns., Rich. BL46 75
Ellerman Av., Twick. BE47 74
Ellerman Rd., Til. DF44 71
Church Rd.
Ellerslie Gdns. NW10 BP37 55
Ellerslie Rd. W12 BP40 55
Ellerslie Sq. SW4 BX46 76
Ellerslie, Grav. DH47 81
Ellerton Gdns., Dag. CP36 59
Ellerton Rd. SW13 BP44 65
Ellerton Rd. SW18 BT47 76
Ellerton Rd. SW20 BP50 75
Ellerton Rd., Dag. CP36 59
Ellerton Rd., Surb. BL55 85
Ellery Rd. SE19 BZ50 77
Ellery St. SE15 CB44 67
Elles Av., Guil. AU70 118
Ellesborough Clo., Wey. BD28 36
Ellesmere Av. NW7 BN27 37
Ellesmere Av., Beck. CE51 87
Ellesmere Clo. E11 CG32 49
Ellesmere Clo., Ruis. BA33 44
Ellesmere Ct. W4 BN42 65
Great West Rd.
Ellesmere Dr., S.Croy. CB60 96
Ellesmere Gdns., Ilf. CK32 49
Ellesmere Gro., Barn. BR25 28
Ellesmere Rd. E3 CD37 57
Ellesmere Rd. NW10 BP35 46
Ellesmere Rd. W4 BN43 65
Ellesmere Rd., Berk. AR13 7
Ellesmere Rd., Grnf. BG38 54
Ellesmere Rd., Twick. BK46 74
Ellesmere Rd., Wey. BA57 92
Ellesmere St. E14 CE39 57
Ellice Rd., Oxt. CG68 115
Elliman Av., Slou. AP40 52
Ellingfort Rd. E8 CB36 57
Ellingham Clo., Hem.H. AZ12 8
Ellingham Rd. E15 CF35 48
Ellingham Rd. W12 BP41 65
Ellingham Rd., Chess. BK57 93
Ellingham Rd., Hem.H. AY13 8
Ellington Rd. N10 BV31 47
Ellington Rd., Felt. BB49 73
Ellington Rd., Houns. BF44 64
Ellington St. N7 BY36 56
Elliot Clo. E15 CG36 58
Elliot Rd. NW4 BP32 46
Elliot Rd., Stan. BJ29 36
Elliott Clo., Wem. BL34 46
Elliott Gdns., Rom. CU30 41
Elliott Gdns., Shep. AZ52 83
Elliott Rd. SW9 BY43 66
Elliott Rd. W4 BO42 65
Elliott Rd., Brom. CJ52 88
Elliott Rd., Th.Hth. BY52 86
Elliott St., Grav. DH47 81
Elliotts Ct. EC4 BY39 56
Old Bailey
Elliotts Pl. N1 BY37 56
St. Peters St.
Elliotts Row SE11 BY42 4
Elliotts Row SE11 BY42 66
Ellis Av., Ger.Cr. AS30 34
Ellis Av., Guil. AP71 118
Ellis Av., Rain. CU39 59
Ellis Av., Slou. AP41 62
Ellis Clo. SE9 CM48 78
Ellis Clo., Couls. BX63 104
Ellis Farm Clo., Wok. AR64 100
Ellis Ms. SE7 CJ43 68
Ellis Rd., Couls. BX63 104
Ellis Rd., Mitch. BU53 86
Ellis St. SW1 BU42 3
Ellis St. SW1 BU42 66
Elliscombe Rd. SE7 CJ42 68
Ellisfield Dr. SW15 BP47 75
Ellison Clo., Wind. AM45 61
Ellison Gdns., Sthl. BE42 64
Ellison Rd. SW13 BO44 65
Ellison Rd. SW16 BW50 76
Ellison Rd., Sid. CM47 78
Ellmore Clo., Rom. CU30 41
Ellora Rd. SW16 BW49 76
Ellsworth St. E2 CB38 57
Ellwood Gdns., Wat. BC20 17
Ellwood Ri., Ch.St.G. AR27 34
Elm Av. W5 BL40 55
Elm Av., Ruis. BC33 44
Elm Av., Upmin. CX34 51
Elm Av., Wat. BE26 36
Elm Bank Av., Guil. AQ71 118
Elm Bank Dr., Brom. CJ51 88
Sundridge Av.
Elm Bank Gdns. SW13 BO44 65
Elm Cft., Slou. AR44 62
Elm Clo. E11 CH32 49
Elm Clo. N19 BW34 47
Hargrave Pk.
Elm Clo. NW4 BQ32 46
Elm Clo. SW20 BQ52 85
Elm Clo., Amer. AO22 25
Elm Clo., Buck.H. CJ27 40
Elm Clo., Cars. BU54 86
Elm Clo., Dart. CV47 80
Elm Clo., Epp. CL15 13
Elm Clo., Har. BF32 45
Elm Clo., Hayes BC39 53
Elm Clo., Lthd. BJ64 102
Elm Clo., Rom. CR30 41
Elm Clo., S.Croy. BZ57 96
Elm Clo., Sendmarsh AW65 101
Elm Clo., Surb. BN54 85
Elm Clo., Twick. BF48 74
Elm Clo., Wal.Abb. CF20 21
Elm Clo., Warl. CC62 105
Elm Clo., Wok. AR61 100
Elm Cres. W5 BL40 55
Elm Cres., Kings.T. BL51 85
Elm Croft Dr., Ashf. AZ49 73
Elm Ct. N3 BR30 37
Elm Ct., Mitch. BU51 86
Elm Ct., Wok. AO62 100
Beechwood Rd.
Elm Dr., Chsnt. CD17 21
Elm Dr., Har. BF32 45
Elm Dr., Hat. BP13 10
Elm Dr., Lthd. BJ64 102
Elm Dr., St.Alb. BK13 9
Elm Dr., Sun. BD51 84
Elm Dr., Swan. CS51 89
Elm Dr., Wok. AP58 91
Elm Field, Lthd. BF65 102
Elm Friars Wk. NW1 BW36 56
Maiden La.
Elm Gdns. N2 BT31 47
Elm Gdns., Enf. BZ22 30
Elm Gdns., Epp. CR16 23
Elm Gdns., Epsom BQ63 103
Elm Gdns., Esher BH57 93
Elm Gdns., Mitch. BW52 86
Elm Gdns., Welw.G.C. BP 8 5
Elm Grn. W3 BO39 55
Elm Grn., Hem.H. AV12 7
Elm Gro. N8 BX32 47
Elm Gro. NW2 BQ35 46
Elm Gro. SE15 CA44 67
Elm Gro. SW19 BR50 75
Elm Gro., Berk. AR13 7
Elm Gro., Cat. CA64 105
Elm Gro., Epsom BN60 94
Elm Gro., Erith CS43 69
Elm Gro., Har. BF33 45
Elm Gro., Horn. CW32 51
Elm Gro., Kings.T. BL51 85
Elm Gro., Orp. CN54 88
Elm Gro., Sutt. BS56 95
High St.
Elm Gro., Wat. BC22 26
Elm Gro., Wdf.Grn. CG28 40
Elm Gro., West.Dr. AY40 53
Elm Grove Clo., Wok. AO63 100
Elm Grove Rd. SW13 BP44 65
Elm La. SE6 CD48 77
Elm La., Ripley AY63 101
Elm Lawn Clo., Uxb. AY36 53
Elm Ms. W2 BT41 66
Elm Ms., Rich. BL46 75
Grove Rd.
Elm Nursery Est., Mitch. BV51 86
Elm Park Av. N15 CA32 48
Elm Park Av., Horn. CU35 50
Elm Park Ct., Pnr. BD31 45
Elm Park Gdns. NW4 BQ32 46
Elm Park Gdns. SW10 BT42 3
Elm Park Gdns. SW10 BT42 66
Elm Park Gdns. W3 BN39 55
Noel Rd.
Elm Park Gdns., S.Croy. CC58 96
Elm Park La. SW3 BT42 3
Elm Park La. SW3 BT42 66
Elm Park Mans. SW10 BT43 3
Elm Park Mans. SW10 BT43 66
Elm Park Par. W3 BN39 55
Noel Rd.
Elm Park Rd. E10 CD33 48
Elm Park Rd. N21 BZ26 39
Elm Park Rd. N3 BR29 37
Elm Park Rd. SE25 CA52 87
Elm Park Rd. SW3 BT43 3
Elm Park Rd. SW3 BT43 66
Elm Park Rd., Pnr. BD30 36
Elm Pk. SW2 BX46 76
Elm Pk., Stan. BJ28 36
Elm Pl. SW7 BT42 3
Elm Pl. SW7 BT42 66
Elm Rd. E11 CF34 48
Elm Rd. E17 CF32 48
Elm Rd. E7 CG36 58
Elm Rd. N22 BY30 38
Elm Rd. SW14 BN45 65
Elm Rd. W., Sutt. BR54 85
Elm Rd., Barn. BR24 28
Elm Rd., Beck. CD51 87
Elm Rd., Chess. BK56 93
Elm Rd., Dart. CV47 80
Elm Rd., Epsom BO57 94
Elm Rd., Erith CU44 69
Elm Rd., Esher BH57 93
Elm Rd., Felt. BA47 73
Elm Rd., Grav. DH48 81
Elm Rd., Grays DE43 71
Elm Rd., Green. CZ46 80
Elm Rd., Hodd. CE12 12
Elm Rd., Horsell AS61 100
Elm Rd., Houns. BE44 64
Elm Rd., Kings.T. BL51 85
Elm Rd., Lthd. BJ64 102
Elm Rd., N.Mal. BN52 85
Elm Rd., Orp. CO57 98
Elm Rd., Pur. BY60 95
Elm Rd., Red. BU70 121
Elm Rd., Rom. CR30 41
Elm Rd., S.Ock. CY40 60
Elm Rd., Sid. CO49 79
Elm Rd., Th.Hth. BZ52 87
Elm Rd., Wall. BV54 86
Elm Rd., Warl. CC62 105
Elm Rd., Wem. BL35 46
Elm Rd., West. CM66 115
Elm Rd., Wind. AN45 61
Elm Rd., Wok. AR62 100
Elm Row NW3 BT34 47
Elm St. WC1 BX38 2
Elm St. WC1 BX38 56
Elm Ter. NW2 BS34 47
Hermitage La.
Elm Ter. NW3 BU35 47
South End Grn.
Elm Ter. SE9 CL46 78
Elm Ter., Grays DA43 70
Elm Ter., Har. BG29 36
Elm Tree Clo. NW8 BT38 1
Elm Tree Clo. NW8 BT38 56
Elm Tree Clo., Ashf. AZ49 73
Elm Tree Clo., Cher. AV55 82
Elm Tree Clo., Nthlt. BE37 54
Elm Tree Clo., Wey. AY60 92
Elm Tree Gdns., Nthlt. BE37 54
Elm Tree Clo.
Elm Tree Rd. NW8 BT38 1
Elm Tree Rd. NW8 BT38 56
Elm Way N11 BV29 38
Elm Way NW10 BO35 46
Elm Way NW3 BS33 47
West Heath Rd.
Elm Way, Brwd. DA28 42
Elm Way, Epsom BN56 94
Elm Way, Rick. AW26 35
Elm Way, Wor.Pk. BQ55 85
Elm Wk. NW3 BS34 47
Elm Wk. SW20 BQ52 85
Elm Wk., Orp. CK55 88
Elm Wk., Rad. BH21 27
Elm Wk., Rom. CU31 50
Elmar Rd. N15 BZ31 48
Elmbank Av., Barn. BQ24 28
Elmbank Av., Egh. AQ50 72
Elmbank N14 BX26 38
Elmbank Way W7 BG39 54
Elmbourne Dr., Belv. CR42 69
Elmbourne Rd. SW17 BV48 76
Elmbridge Av., Surb. BM53 85
Elmbridge Clo., Ruis. BC32 44
Elmbridge Dr., Ruis. BB32 44
Elmbridge La., Wok. AS63 100
Elmbridge Rd., Ilf. CO29 41
Elmbridge Wk. E8 CB36 57
Wilman Gro.
Elmbrook Clo., Sun. BC51 83
The Avenue
Elmbrook Gdns. SE9 CK45 68
Elmbrook Rd., Sutt. BR56 94
Elmcote, Rick. AY25 26
Elmcourt Rd. SE27 BY48 76
Elmcroft Av. E11 CH32 49
Elmcroft Av. N9 CB25 30
Elmcroft Av. NW11 BR33 46
Elmcroft Av., Sid. CN46 78
Elmcroft Clo. E11 CH31 49
Elmcroft Clo. W5 BK39 54
Elmcroft Clo., Chess. BL55 85
Elmcroft Clo., Felt. BB46 73
Elmcroft Cres. NW11 BQ33 46
Elmcroft Cres., Har. BF31 45
Elmcroft Dr., Chess. BL55 85
Elmcroft Gdns. NW9 BM32 46
Elmcroft Rd., Orp. CO54 89
Elmcroft St. E5 CC35 48
Elmdale Rd. N13 BX28 38
Elmdene Av., Horn. CW32 51
Elmdene Clo., Beck. CD53 87
Elmdene Est., Beck. CD53 87
Elmdene Rd. SE18 CL42 68
Elmdene, Surb. BN54 85
Elmdon Rd., Hatton Cross BB45 63
Elmdon Rd., Houns. BE44 64
Elmer Av., Hav. CT27 41
Elmer Clo., Enf. BX24 29
Elmer Clo., Rain. CU36 59
Elmer Cotts., Lthd. BJ64 102
Elmer Gdns., Edg. BM29 37
Elmer Gdns., Islw. BG45 64
Elmer Gdns., Rain. CU36 59
Elmer Rd. SE6 CF47 77
Elmers Dr., Tedd. BJ50 74
Elmers End Rd. SE20 CC51 87
Elmers End Rd., Beck. CC51 87
Elmers Rd. SE25 CB54 87
Elmerside Rd., Beck. CD52 87
Elmfield Av. N8 BX32 47
Elmfield Av., Mitch. BV51 86
Elmfield Av., Tedd. BH49 74
Elmfield Clo., Grav. DG47 81
Elmfield Clo., Har. BG34 45
Mount Park Av.
Elmfield Clo., Pot.B. BR20 19
Elmfield Pk., Brom. CH52 88
Elmfield Rd. E17 CC32 48
Elmfield Rd. E4 CF27 39
Elmfield Rd. N2 BT31 47
Elmfield Rd. SW17 BV48 76
Elmfield Rd., Brom. CH51 88
Elmfield Rd., Pot.B. BR19 19
Elmfield Rd., Sthl. BE41 64
Elmfield Way, S.Croy. CA58 96
Elmgate Av., Felt. BC48 73
Elmgate Gdns., Edg. BN28 37
Elmgreen Clo. E15 CG37 58
Church St. N.
Elmgrove Cres., Har. BH32 45
Elmgrove Gdns., Har. BJ32 45
Elmgrove Par., Wall. BV55 86
Elmgrove Rd. W5 BL41 65
Elmgrove Rd., Cob. BD61 102
Elmgrove Rd., Croy. CB54 87
Elmgrove Rd., Har. BH32 45
Elmgrove Rd., Wey. AZ55 83
Elmhall Gdns. E11 CH32 49
Elmhurst Av. N2 BT31 47
Elmhurst Av., Mitch. BV50 76
Elmhurst Ct., Guil. AS71 118
Lower Edgeborough Rd.
Elmhurst Dr. E18 CH30 40
Elmhurst Dr., Dor. BJ72 119
Elmhurst Dr., Horn. CV33 51
Elmhurst Gdns. E18 CH30 40
Elmhurst Rd. E7 CH36 58
Elmhurst Rd. N17 CA30 39
Elmhurst Rd. SE9 CK48 78
Elmhurst Rd., Enf. CC22 30
Elmhurst Rd., Slou. AT41 62
Elmhurst St. SW4 BW45 66
Elmhurst Way, Loug. CK26 40
Elmhurst, Belv. CQ43 69
Elmington Clo., Bex. CR46 79
Elmington Est. SE5 BZ43 67
Elmington Rd. SE5 BZ44 67
Elmira St. SE13 CE45 67
Elmlea Dr., Hayes BB39 53
Grange Rd.
Elmlee Clo., Chis. CK50 78
Elmley Clo. E6 CK39 58
Northumberland Rd.
Elmley St. SE18 CM42 68
Elmore Rd. E11 CF34 48
Elmore Rd., Couls. BU64 104
Elmore Rd., Enf. CC22 30
Elmore St. N1 BZ36 57
Elmores, Loug. CL24 31
Elmroyd Av., Pot.B. BR20 19

Elmroyd Clo., Pot.B. BR20 19
Elms Av. N10 BV31 47
Elms Av. NW4 BQ32 46
Elms Cres. SW4 BW46 76
Elms Ct., Wem. BJ35 45
Elms Farm Rd., Horn. CV35 51
Elms Gdns., Dag. CQ35 50
Elms Gdns., Wem. BJ35 45
Elms La., Wem. BJ34 45
Elms Ms. W2 BT40 3
Elms Ms. W2 BT40 56
Elms Park Av., Wem. BJ35 45
Elms Rd. SW4 BW46 76
Elms Rd., Ger.Cr. AS29 34
Elms Rd., Har. BH29 36
Elms Wood, Lthd. BE65 102
Elms, The SW13 BO45 65
Elms, The, Mord. BR54 85
Elms, The, Ong. CX18 24
Coopers Hill
Elms, The, Slou. AV44 62
Elmscott Gdns. N21 BZ25 30
Elmscott Rd., Brom. CG49 78
Elmscroft Gdns., Pot.B. BR19 19
Elmsdale Rd. E17 CD31 48
Elmshaw Rd. SW15 BP46 75
Elmshorn, Epsom BQ61 103
Elmshott La., Slou. AM40 61
Elmshurst Cres. N2 BT31 47
Elmshurst Est. N2 BT31 47
Elmside Rd., Wem. BM34 46
Elmside, Croy. CE57 96
Elmside, Guil. AQ71 118
Elmsleigh Av., Har. BJ31 45
Elmsleigh Ct., Sutt. BS55 86
Elmsleigh Rd., Stai. AV49 72
Elmsleigh Rd., Twick. BG48 74
Elmslie Clo., Epsom BN60 94
Elmslie Clo., Wdf.Grn. CK29 40
Gwynne Park Av.
Elmstead Av., Chis. CK49 78
Elmstead Av., Wem. BL33 46
Elmstead Clo. N20 BS27 38
Elmstead Clo., Epsom BO56 94
Elmstead Clo., Sev. CT64 107
Elmstead Gdns., Wor.Pk. BP55 85
Elmstead Glade, Chis. CK50 78
Elmstead La., Chis. CK50 78
Elmstead Rd., Erith CT44 69
Elmstead Rd., Ilf. CN34 49
Elmstead Rd., Wey. AW60 92
Elmsted Cres., Well. CP43 69
Elmstone Rd. SW6 BS44 66
Elmsway, Ashf. AY49 73
Elmsworth Av., Houns. BF44 64
Elmtree Av., Brwd. CZ22 33
Elmtree Av., Esher BG54 84
Elmtree Rd., Tedd. BH49 74
Elmway, Grays DE40 71
Elmwood Av. N13 BX28 38
Elmwood Av., B.Wd. BM24 28
Elmwood Av., Felt. BC48 73
Elmwood Av., Har. BJ32 45
Elmwood Clo., Ash. BK62 102
Woodfield
Elmwood Clo., Epsom BP57 94
Elmwood Clo., Wall. BV55 86
Elmwood Cres. NW9 BN31 46
Elmwood Ct., Wem. BJ34 45
Elmwood Dr., Bex. CQ47 79
Elmwood Dr., Epsom BP57 94
Elmwood Gdns. W7 BH39 54
Elmwood Pk., Ger.Cr. AS33 43
Elmwood Rd. SE24 BZ46 77
Elmwood Rd. W4 BN43 65
Elmwood Rd., Croy. BY54 86
Elmwood Rd., Mitch. BU52 86
Elmwood Rd., Red. BV69 121
Elmwood Rd., Slou. AQ40 52
Elmwood Rd., Wok. AO63 100
Elmwood, Saw. CQ 6 6
Elmwood, Welw.G.C. BP 8 5
Elmworth Gro. SE21 BZ48 77
Elnathan Ms. W9 BS38 1
Elnathan Ms. W9 BS38 56
Elphinstone Rd. E17 CD30 39
Elphinstone St. N5 BY34 47
Elrick Clo., Erith CT43 69
Queen St.
Elrington Rd. E8 CB36 57
Elruge Clo., West Dr. AX41 63
Elsa Rd., Well. CO44 69
Elsa St. E14 CD39 57
Elsdale St. E9 CC36 57
Elsden Ms. E2 CC37 57
Old Ford Rd.
Elsden Rd. N17 CA30 39
Elsdon Rd., Wok. AQ62 100
Elsenham Rd. E12 CK35 49
Elsenham St. SW18 BR47 75
Elsham Rd. E11 CG34 49
Elsham Rd. W14 BR41 65
Elsham Ter. W14 BR41 65
Elsie Rd. SE22 CA45 67
Elsiedene Rd. N21 BZ26 39
Elsiemaud Rd. SE4 CD46 77
Elsinge Rd., Enf. CB22 30
Elsinore Av., Stai. AY47 73
Elsinore Gdns. NW2 BQ34 46
Cricklewood Trd. Est.
Elsinore Rd. SE23 CD47 77
Elsley Rd. SW11 BU45 66
Elspeth Rd. SW11 BU45 66
Elspeth Rd., Wem. BL35 46
Elsrick Av., Mord. BS53 86
Elstan Way, Croy. CD54 87
Elsted St. SE17 BZ42 4
Elsted St. SE17 BZ42 67
Elstow Clo. SE9 CL46 78
Elstow Clo., Ruis. BD33 45
Elstow Gdns., Dag. CQ37 59
Elstow Rd., Dag. CQ36 59
Elstree Gdns. N9 CB26 39
Elstree Gdns., Belv. CQ42 69
Elstree Gdns., Ilf. CM35 49
Elstree Hill N., B.Wd. BK25 27
Elstree Hill S., B.Wd. BK26 36
Elstree Hill, Brom. CG50 78
Elstree Rd., B.Wd. BJ25 27
Elstree Rd., Bush. BG26 36
Elstree Rd., Hem.H. AZ10 8
Elstree Rd., Stan. BK27 36
Elstree Rd., Wat. BH23 27
Elstree Way, B.Wd. BM23 28
Elswick Rd. SE13 CE44 67
Elswick St. SW6 BT44 66
Elsworthy Rd. NW3 BT37 1
Elsworthy Rd. NW3 BT37 56
Elsworthy Ri. NW3 BU36 56
Elsworthy Ter. NW3 BU36 56
Elsworthy, T.Ditt. BH53 84
Elsynge Rd. SW18 BT46 76
Eltham Green Rd. SE9 CJ45 68
Eltham Grn. SE9 CJ46 78
Eltham High St. SE9 CK46 78
Eltham Hill SE9 CJ46 78
Eltham Palace Rd. SE9 CJ46 78
Eltham Park Gdns. SE9 CL45 68
Eltham Pl., Guil. AP69 118
Eltham Rd. SE12 CG46 78
Eltham Rd. SE9 CG46 78
Elthiron Rd. SW6 BS44 66
Elthorne Av. W7 BH41 64
Elthorne Ct., Felt. BD47 74
Elthorne Park Rd. W7 BH41 64
Elthorne Rd. N19 BW34 47
Elthorne Rd. NW9 BN33 46
Elthorne Rd., Uxb. AX37 53
Elthorne Way NW9 BN32 46
Elthruda Rd. SE13 CF46 77
Eltisley Rd., Ilf. CL35 49
Elton Av., Barn. BR25 28
Elton Av., Grnf. BH36 54
Elton Av., Wem. BJ35 45
Elton Clo., Kings.T. BK50 74
Normansfield Av.
Elton Clo., Tedd. BK50 74
Elton Pk., Wat. BC23 26
Langley Rd.
Elton Pl. N16 CA35 48
Elton Rd., Kings.T. BL51 85
Elton Rd., Pur. BW59 95
Elton St. N16 CA35 48
Matthias Rd.
Elton Way, Bush. BF23 27
Eltringham St. SW18 BT45 66
Petergate
Elvaston Ms. SW7 BT41 3
Elvaston Ms. SW7 BT41 66
Elvaston Pl. SW7 BT41 3
Elvaston Pl. SW7 BT41 66
Elvaston Ter. SW7 BT42 66
Elveden Clo., Wok. AW62 101
Elveden Pl. NW10 BM37 55
Elveden Rd. NW10 BM37 55
Elvendon Rd. N13 BX29 38
Elver Gdns. E2 CB38 57
Avebury Est.
Elverson Rd. SE8 CE44 67
Elverton St. SW1 BW42 3
Elverton St. SW1 BW42 66
Elvet Av., Rom. CV31 51
Elvington Grn., Brom. CG53 88
Elvington La. NW9 BO30 37
Elvino Rd. SE26 CC49 77
Elvis Rd. NW2 BQ36 55
Elwell Clo., Egh. AT50 72
Elwell Rd. SW4 BX44 66
Elwick Rd., S.Ock. DB39 60
Elwill Way, Beck. CF52 87
Elwill Way, Grav. DF51 81
Elwin St. E2 CA38 57
Elwin St. E2 CB38 2
Elwood St. N5 BY34 47
Elwyn Gdns. SE12 CH47 78
Ely Clo., Amer. AP23 25
Ely Clo., Erith CT44 69
Ely Clo., Hat. BO12 10
Ely Clo., N.Mal. BO51 85
Ely Cotts. SW8 BX43 66
Ely Gdns., B.Wd. BN25 28
Ely Gdns., Dag. CS34 50
Ely Pl. EC1 BY39 2
Ely Pl. EC1 BY39 56
Ely Pl., Wdf.Grn. CL29 40
Ely Pl., Welw.G.C. BR 8 5
Ely Rd. E10 CF32 48
Ely Rd., Croy. BZ53 87
Ely Rd., Houns. BB44 63
Eastern Perimeter Rd.
Ely Rd., Houns. BD45 64
Ely Rd., St.Alb. BJ14 9
Elyne Rd. N4 BY32 47
Elysian Av., Orp. CN53 88
Elysium Pl. SW6 BR44 65
Fulham Park Gdns.
Elysium St. SW6 BR44 65
Fulham Park Gdns.
Elystan Clo., Wall. BV57 95
Elystan Pl. SW3 BU42 3
Elystan Pl. SW3 BU42 66
Elystan St. SW3 BU42 3
Elystan St. SW3 BU42 66
Elystan Wk. N1 BY37 2
Elystan Wk. N1 BY37 56
Emanuel Av. W3 BN39 55
Emba St. SE16 CB41 67
Embankment Gdns. SW3 BU43 66
Embankment Pl. WC2 BX40 4
Embankment Pl. WC2 BX40 56
Villiers St.
Embankment, The SW15 BQ44 65
Embankment, The, Stai. AR47 72
Embankment, The, Twick. BJ47 74
Embassy Ct., Sid. CO48 79
Ember Clo., Orp. CM54 88
Ember Clo., Wey. AX56 92
Ember Farm Av., E.Mol. BG53 84
Ember Farm Way, E.Mol. BG53 84
Ember Gdns., T.Ditt. BH53 84
Ember La., E.Mol. BG54 84
Ember La., Esher BG54 84
Ember Rd., Slou. AT41 62
Embercourt Rd., T.Ditt. BH53 84
Emberson Way, Epp. CR16 23
Embleton Rd. SE13 CE45 67
Embleton Rd., Wat. BC27 35
Embley Point E5 CB34 48
Downs Est.
Embry Clo., Stan. BJ28 36
Embry Dr., Stan. BJ29 36
Embry Way, Stan. BJ28 36
Emden St. SW6 BS44 66
Emerald Clo. E16 CJ39 58
Emerald Ct., Slou. AP41 62
Chalvey Rd. E.
Emerald Gdns., Dag. CR33 50
Emerald St. WC1 BX39 2
Emerald St. WC1 BX39 56
Emerson Dr., Horn. CV33 51
Emerson Gdns., Har. BL32 46
Emerson Rd., Ilf. CL33 49
Emerson St. SE1 BZ40 4
Emerson St. SE1 BZ40 57
Emerton Clo., Bexh. CQ45 69
Emerton Ct., Berk. AP11 7
Emerton Garth
Emerton Garth, Berk. AP11 7
Emerton Rd., Lthd. BG64 102
Emery Hill St. SW1 BW41 3
Emery Hill St. SW1 BW41 66
Emery St. SE1 BY41 4
Morley St.
Emery St. SE1 BY41 66
Morley St.
Emes Rd., Erith CS43 69
Emily Pl. N7 BY35 47
Emily Rd., Wey. AW55 83
Emily St. E16 CG39 58
Jude St.
Emlyn Gdns. W12 BO41 65
Emlyn La., Lthd. BJ64 102
Emlyn Rd. W12 BO41 65
Emlyn Rd., Red. BV71 121
Emma Rd. E13 CG37 58
Emma St. E2 CB37 57
Emma Ter. E11 CG34 49
Montague Rd.
Emmanuel Clo., Guil. AQ69 118
Shepherds Hill
Emmanuel Clo., Nthwd. BB29 35
Emmanuel Rd. SW12 BW47 76
Emmanuel Rd., Nthwd. BB29 35
Emmaus Way, Chig. CL28 40
Emmott Av., Ilf. CM32 49
Emmott Clo. E1 CD38 57
Emmott Clo. NW11 BT32 47
Emmott St. E1 CD38 57
Emnetts Clo., Wok. AR52 100
Kirby Rd.
Emperors Gate SW7 BS41 3
Emperors Gate SW7 BS41 66
Empire Av. N18 BZ28 39
Empire Ct., Wem. BM34 46
Empire Par. N18 BZ29 39
Empire Pl. SE8 CD43 67
Watsons St.
Empire Rd., Grnf. BJ37 54
Empire Way, Wem. BL35 46
Empire Wharf Rd. E14 CF42 67
Empire Yd. N7 BX34 47
Empress Av. E12 CJ34 49
Empress Av. E4 CE29 39
Empress Av., Ilf. CK34 49
Empress Av., Wdf.Grn. CG29 40
Empress Dr., Chis. CL50 78
Empress Pl. SW6 BS42 66
Empress Rd., Grav. DJ47 81
Empress St. SE17 BZ43 4
Empress St. SE17 BZ43 67
Empson St. E3 CE38 57
Emsworth Clo. N9 CC26 39
Emsworth Rd., Ilf. CL30 40
Emsworth St. SW2 BX48 76
Emu Rd. SW8 BV44 66
Ena Rd. SW16 BX52 86
Enborne Grn., S.Ock. DA39 60
Enbrook St. W10 BR38 55
Endale Clo., Cars. BU55 86
Endeavour Rd., Chsnt. CD17 21
Endeavour Way SW19 BS49 76
Endeavour Way, Bark. CO37 59
Endeavour Way, Croy. BW54 86
Endell St. WC2 BX39 2
Endell St. WC2 BX39 56
Enderley Clo., Har. BH30 36
Enderley Rd., Har. BH30 36
Enderley St. SE10 CG42 68
Endersby Rd., Barn. BQ25 28
Endersleigh Gdns. NW4 BP31 46
Endlebury Rd. E4 CE27 39
Endlesham Rd. SW12 BV47 76
Endsleigh Clo., S.Croy. CC58 96
Endsleigh Gdns. WC1 BW38 1
Endsleigh Gdns. WC1 BW38 56
Endsleigh Gdns., Ilf. CK34 49
Endsleigh Gdns., Surb. BK53 84
Endsleigh Gdns., Walt. BC56 92
Endsleigh Pl. WC1 BW38 1
Endsleigh Pl. WC1 BW38 56
Endsleigh Rd. W13 BJ40 54
Endsleigh Rd., Red. BW68 113
Endsleigh Rd., Sthl. BE42 64
Endsleigh St. WC1 BW38 1
Endsleigh St. WC1 BW38 56
Endway, Surb. BM54 85
Endwell Rd. SE4 CD44 67
Endymion Rd. N4 BY33 47
Endymion Rd. SW2 BX46 76
Endymion Rd., Hat. BQ12 10
Enfield Clo., Uxb. AX37 53
Enfield Rd. E., Brent. BK42 64
Enfield Rd. N1 CA36 2
Enfield Rd. N1 CA36 57
Enfield Rd. N8 BX32 47
Enfield Rd. W3 BM41 65
Enfield Rd., Brent. BK42 64
Enfield Rd., Enf. BW24 29
Enfield Rd., Houns. BB44 63
Eastern Perimeter Rd.
Enford St. W1 BU39 1
Enford St. W1 BU39 56
Engadine Clo., Croy. CA55 87
Engadine St. SW18 BR47 75
Engate St. SE13 CF45 67
Engayne Gdns., Upmin. CX33 51
Engel Pk. NW7 BQ29 37
Engineer Clo. SE18 CL43 68
Engineers Dr., Bush. BF24 27
Engineers Way, Wem. BM35 46
Englands La. NW3 BU36 56
Englands La., Loug. CL23 31
Englefield Clo., Croy. BZ53 87
Queens Rd.
Englefield Clo., Enf. BY23 29
Englefield Clo., Orp. CN53 88
Englefield Cres., Orp. CN52 88
Englefield Path, Orp. CN52 88
Englefield Rd. N1 BZ36 57
Englefield Rd., Wok. AO62 100
Englefield Wk., Egh. AR50 72
Alexandra Rd.
Engleheart Dr., Felt. BB46 73
Engleheart Rd. SE6 CE47 77
Englehurst, Egh. AR50 72
Englewood Rd. SW12 BV46 76
Engliff La., Wok. AV61 100
English Gdns., Stai. AR46 72
English Grounds SE1 CA40 4
English Grounds SE1 CA40 57
English St. E3 CD38 57
Enid Clo., St.Alb. BE19 18
Enid St. SE16 CA41 4
Enid St. SE16 CA41 67
Enkel St. N7 BX34 47
Enmore Av. SE25 CB53 87
Enmore Gdns. SW14 BN46 75
Enmore Rd. SE25 CB53 87
Enmore Rd. SW15 BQ45 65
Enmore Rd., Sthl. BF38 54
Ennerdale Av., Horn. CU35 50
Ennerdale Av., Stan. BK31 45
Ennerdale Clo., Cheam BR56 94
Elmbrook Rd.
Ennerdale Clo., Felt. BB47 73
Westmacott Dr.
Ennerdale Clo., St.Alb. BJ14 9
Ennerdale Dr. NW9 BN32 46
Ennerdale Gdns., Wem. BK33 45
Ennerdale Rd., Bexh. CR44 69
Ennerdale Rd., Rich. BL44 65
Ennersdale Rd. SE13 CF46 77
Ennis Rd. N4 BY33 47
Ennis Rd. SE18 CM43 68
Ennismore Av. W4 BO42 65
Ennismore Av., Grnf. BH36 54
Ennismore Av., Guil. AS70 118
Ennismore Gdns. Ms. SW7 BU41 3
Ennismore Gdns. Ms. SW7 BU41 66
Ennismore Gdns. SW7 BT41 3
Ennismore Gdns. SW7 BU41 66
Ennismore Gdns., T.Ditt. BH53 84
Ennismore Ms. SW7 BU41 3
Ennismore Ms. SW7 BU41 66
Ennismore St. SW7 BU41 66
Ennismore Gdns.
Ensign Clo., Pur. BY58 95
Ensign Clo., Stai. AX47 73
Ensign Dr. N13 BZ27 39
Ensign St. E1 CB40 4
Ensign St. E1 CB40 57
Ensign Way, Stai. AX47 73
Enslin Rd. SE9 CL46 78
Ensor Ms. SW7 BT42 3
Ensor Ms. SW7 BT42 66
Cranley Gdns.
Enstone Rd., Enf. CD24 30
Enstone Rd., Uxb. AY34 44
Enterprise Clo., Croy. BY54 86
Enterprise Way NW10 BP38 55
Hythe Rd.
Enterprise Way SW18 BS45 66
Enterprise Way, Tedd. BJ50 74
Station Rd.
Enterprize Way SE8 CD42 67
Envis Way, Guil. AO69 118
Envis Way, Guil. AQ69 118
Epirus Ms. SW6 BS43 66
Epirus Rd. SW6 BR43 65
Epping Clo. E14 CE42 67
Charnwood Gdns.
Epping Clo., Rom. CR31 50
Epping Glade E4 CF25 30
Epping Grn., Hem.H. AZ11 8
Epping La., Rom. CO23 32
Epping New Rd., Buck.H. CH27 40
Epping New Rd., Loug. CH25 31
Epping Pl. N1 BY36 56
Liverpool Rd.
Epping Rd., Colliers Hatch CS18 23
Epping Rd., Epping Forest CP17 23
Epping Rd., Epping Green CL14 13
Epping Rd., Theydon Bois CL21 31
Epping Rd., Epp. CM19 22
Epping Rd., Harl. CJ12 13
Epping Rd., Ong. CT15 14
Epping Way E4 CE25 30
Epple Rd. SW6 BR44 65
Epsom Clo., Bexh. CR45 69
Epsom Clo., Nthlt. BE35 45
Epsom Gap, Lthd. BJ61 102
Epsom La. S., Tad. BQ64 103
Epsom La., Epsom BP63 103
Epsom Rd. E10 CF32 48
Epsom Rd., Ash. BL62 103
Epsom Rd., Croy. BY56 95
Epsom Rd., East Clandon AX69 110
Epsom Rd., Epsom BO59 94
Epsom Rd., Guil. AS71 118
Epsom Rd., Ilf. CN32 49
Epsom Rd., Lthd. BJ64 102
Epsom Rd., Mord. BR54 85
Epsom Rd., Sutt. BR54 85
Epsom Sq., Houns. BB44 63
Eastern Perimeter Rd.
Epsom Way, Horn. CW35 51
Epstein Rd. SE28 CO40 59
Epworth Pl. EC2 BZ38 57
Epworth St.
Epworth Rd., Islw. BJ43 64
Epworth St. EC2 BZ38 2
Epworth St. EC2 BZ38 57
Erasmus St. SW1 BW42 3
Erasmus St. SW1 BW42 66
Erconwald St. W12 BO39 55
Eresby Pl. NW6 BS36 56
Kingsgate Rd.
Eresby Rd. NW6 BS36 56
Eresby Rd., Beck. CE54 87
Eric Clo. E7 CH35 49
Eric Rd. E7 CH35 49
Eric Rd., Rom. CP33 50
Eric St. E3 CD38 57
Erica Ct., Wok. AR62 100
Erica Gdns., Croy. CE55 87
Erica St. W12 BP40 55
Ericcson Clo. SW18 BS46 76
Eridge Rd. W4 BN41 65
Erin Clo., Brom. CG50 78
Erindale SE18 CM43 68
Erindale Ter. SE18 CM43 68
Eriswell Cres., Walt. BB57 92
Eriswell Rd., Walt. BB56 92
Erith Cres., Rom. CS30 41
Erith Ct., Grays CX42 70
Erith Rd., Belv. CR42 69
Erith Rd., Bexh. CR45 69
Erith Rd., Erith CR44 69
Erkenwald Clo., Cher. AV53 82
Erlanger Rd. SE14 CC44 67
Erlesmere Gdns. W13 BJ41 64
Ermine Clo., Chsnt. CB19 21
Ermine Clo., Houns. BD45 64
Ermine Clo., St.Alb. BF14 9
Ermine Rd. N15 CA32 48
Ermine Rd. SE13 CE45 67
Ermine Side, Enf. CB25 30
Ermington Rd. SE9 CM48 78
Ermyn Clo., Lthd. BK64 102
Ermyn Way, Lthd. BK64 102
Ernald Av. E6 CK37 58
Ernan Clo., S.Ock. DA39 60
Ernan Rd., S.Ock. DA39 60
Erncroft Way, Twick. BH46 74
Ernest Av. SE27 BY49 76
Ernest Gdns. W4 BM43 65
Ernest Gro. Clo., Beck. CE53 87
Ernest Gro., Beck. CD53 87
Ernest Rd., Horn. CW32 51
Ernest Rd., Kings.T. BM51 85
Ernest Sq., Kings.T. BM51 85
Ernest St. E1 CC38 57
Ernle Rd. SW20 BP50 75
Ernshaw Pl. SW15 BR46 75
Carlton Dr.
Erpingham Rd. SW15 BQ45 65
Erridge Rd. SW19 BS51 86
Erriff Dr., S.Ock. CZ39 60
Errington Clo., Grays DG41 71
Cedar Rd.
Errington Rd. W9 BR38 55
Errol Gdns., Hayes BC38 53
Errol Gdns., N.Mal. BP52 85
Errol St. EC1 BZ38 2
Errol St. EC1 BZ38 57
Erroll Rd., Rom. CT31 50
Erskine Clo., Sutt. BU55 86
Erskine Cres. N15 CB31 48
Erskine Hill NW11 BS32 47
Erskine Ms. NW3 BU36 56
Ainger Rd.
Erskine Rd. E17 CD31 48
Erskine Rd. NW3 BU36 56
Erskine Rd., Sutt. BT56 95
Erwood Rd. SE7 CK42 68
Esam Way SW16 BY49 76
Escombe Dr., Guil. AQ68 109
Escot Way, Barn. BQ25 28
Escott Gdns. SE9 CK49 78
Escott Pl., Cher. AU57 91
Escreet Gro. SE18 CL42 68
Esdaile Gdns., Upmin. CY33 51
Esdaile La., Hodd. CE12 12
Esher Av., Rom. CS32 50
Esher Av., Sutt. BQ55 85
Esher Av., Walt. BC54 83
Esher Clo., Bex. CQ47 79
Esher Clo., Esher BF56 93
Esher Cres., Houns. BB44 63
Eastern Perimeter Rd.
Esher Gdns. SW19 BQ48 75
Esher Grn., Esher BF56 93
Esher Ms., Mitch. BU52 86
Esher Park Av., Esher BF56 93
Esher Place Av., Esher BF56 93
Esher Rd., E.Mol. BG53 84
Esher Rd., Ilf. CN34 49
Esher Rd., Walt. BE56 93
Esk Rd. E13 CH38 58
Esk Way, Rom. CS29 41
Eskdale Av., Chesh. AO18 16
Eskdale Av., Nthlt. BE37 54
Eskdale Clo., Dart. CY47 80
Eskdale Clo., Wem. BK34 45
Eskdale Gdns., Maid. AG42 61
Eskdale Gdns., Pur. BZ60 96
Eskdale Rd., Bexh. CR44 69
Eskdale Rd., Uxb. AW37 53
Eskdale, Hem.H. AY12 8
Lonsdale
Eskdale, St.Alb. BL17 19
Thamesdale
Eskley Gdns., S.Ock. DA39 60
Eskmont Ridge SE19 CA50 77
Esmar Cres. NW9 BP33 46
Esmeralda Rd. SE1 CB42 4
Esmeralda Rd. SE1 CB42 67
Esmond Clo., Rain. CU36 59

Esmond Gdns. W5 BK41 64
St. Marys Rd.
Esmond Rd. NW6 BR37 55
Esmond Rd. W4 BN42 65
Esmond St. SW15 BR45 65
Esparto St. SW18 BS47 76
Essenden Clo., Belv. CR42 69
Essenden Rd., Belv. CR42 69
Essenden Rd., S.Croy. BZ57 96
Essendene Rd., Cat. CA65 105
Essendine Rd. W9 BS38 56
Essendon Clo., Hat. BU12 11
Essendon Gdns., Welw.G.C. BR8 5
Essendon Hill, Hat. BU12 11
Essendon Rd., Hert. BV11 11
Essex Av., Islw. BH45 64
Essex Av., Slou. AO39 52
Essex Clo. E17 CC31 48
Essex Clo., Mord. BQ54 85
Essex Clo., Rom. CR31 50
Essex Clo., Ruis. BD33 45
Essex Clo., Wey. AX56 92
Garfield Rd.
Essex Ct. EC4 BY39 2
Essex Ct. EC4 BY39 56
Middle Temple La.
Essex Ct. SW13 BO44 65
Essex Gdns. N4 BY32 47
Rutland Gdns.
Essex Gdns., Horn. CX32 51
Essex Gdns., S.le H. DK41 71
Somerset Rd.
Essex Gro. SE19 BZ50 77
Essex La., Kings L. BA20 17
Essex Mead, Hem.H. AY10 8
Essex Pk. Ms. W3 BO40 55
Essex Pk. N3 BS29 38
Essex Pl. W4 BN42 65
Essex Rd. E10 CF32 48
Essex Rd. E12 CK35 49
Essex Rd. E17 CD32 48
Essex Rd. E18 CH30 40
Essex Rd. E4 CG26 40
Essex Rd. N1 BY37 2
Essex Rd. N1 BY37 56
Essex Rd. NW10 BO36 55
Essex Rd. S. E11 CF33 48
Essex Rd. W3 BN40 55
Essex Rd. W4 BN42 65
Belmont Rd.
Essex Rd., B.Wd. BM24 28
Essex Rd., Bark. CM36 58
Essex Rd., Dag. CS35 50
Essex Rd., Dart. CV46 80
Essex Rd., Enf. BZ24 30
Essex Rd., Grav. DG47 81
Essex Rd., Grays DA43 70
Essex Rd., Hodd. CE11 12
Essex Rd., Long. DB51 90
Essex Rd., Chadwell Heath CP33 50
Essex Rd., Rom. CR31 50
Essex Rd., Wat. BC23 26
Essex St. E7 CH35 49
Essex St. WC2 BY39 56
Essex St. WC2 BY40 4
Essex St., St.Alb. BH13 9
Essex Ter. EC4 BY40 4
Essex Vill. W8 BS41 66
Essex Way, Brwd. DB29 42
Essex Wf. E10 CC34 48
Essian St. E1 CD39 57
Essoldo Way, Edg. BL31 46
Queensbury Sta. Par.
Estate Way E10 CE33 48
Estcourt Rd. SE25 CB53 87
Estcourt Rd. SW6 BR43 65
Estcourt Rd., Wat. BD24 27
Este Rd. SW11 BU45 66
Estella Av., N.Mal. BP52 85
Estelle Rd. NW3 BU35 47
Esterbrooke St. SW1 BW42 3
Esterbrooke St. SW1 BW42 66
Esther Clo. N21 BY26 38
Esther Rd. E11 CG33 49
Estreham Rd. SW16 BW50 76
Estridge Clo., Houns. BF45 64
Eswyn Rd. SW17 BU49 76
Etchingham Ct. N12 BS29 38
Etchingham Park Rd. N3 BS29 38
Etchingham Rd. E15 CF35 48
Eternit Wk. SW6 BQ44 65
Etfield Gro., Sid. CO49 79
Ethel Rankin Ct. SW6 BR44 65
Fulham Rd.
Ethel Rd. E16 CH39 58
Ethel Rd., Ashf. AY49 73
Ethel St. SE17 BZ42 4
Ethel Ter., Orp. CP58 98
Ethelbert Clo., Brom. CH52 88
Ethelbert Gdns., Ilf. CK32 49
Ethelbert Rd. SW20 BQ51 85
Ethelbert Rd., Brom. CH52 88
Ethelbert Rd., Dart. CW49 80
Ethelbert Rd., Erith CS43 69
Hengist Rd.
Ethelbert Rd., Orp. CP52 89
Ethelbert St. SW12 BV47 76
Fernlea Rd.
Ethelburga Rd., Rom. CW30 42
Ethelburga St. SW11 BU44 66
Ethelden Rd. W12 BP40 55
Etheldene Av. N10 BW31 47
Ethelred Clo., Welw.G.C. BR8 5
Etheridge Grn., Loug. CM24 31
Etheridge Rd. NW4 BQ33 46
Prince Charles Dr.
Etheridge Rd., Loug. CL23 31
Etherley Rd. N15 BZ32 48
Etherow St. SE22 CB46 77
Etherstone Grn. SW16 BX49 76
Etherstone Rd. SW16 BY49 76
Ethnard Rd. SE15 CB43 67
Ethorpe Clo., Ger.Cr. AS32 43
Ethronvi Rd., Bexh. CQ45 69
Etloe Rd. E10 CE34 48
Wiseman Rd.
Etna Rd., St.Alb. BG13 9
Eton Av. N12 BT29 38
Eton Av. NW3 BT36 56
Eton Av., Barn. BU25 29
Eton Av., Houns. BE43 64
Eton Av., N.Mal. BN53 85
Eton Av., Wem. BJ35 45
Eton Clo., Slou. AQ43 62
Eton College Rd. NW3 BU36 56
Eton Ct., Eton AO43 61
Eton Ct., Stai. AV49 72
Eton Ct., Wem. BK35 45
Eton Garages NW3 BU36 56
Lambolle Pl.
Eton Gro. N19 BW34 47
Wedmore St.
Eton Gro. NW9 BM31 46
Eton Gro. SE13 CG45 68
Eton Ho. SW11 BT44 66
Eton Pl. NW3 BU36 56
Eton Rd. NW3 BU36 56
Eton Rd., Hayes BB43 63
Eton Rd., Ilf. CM35 49
Eton Rd., Orp. CO56 98
Eton Rd., Slou. AP42 62
Eton Sq., Eton AO43 61
Eton St., Rich. BL46 75
Eton Vill. NW3 BU36 56
Eton Wick Rd., Eton AN42 61
Etta St. SE8 CD43 67
Etton Clo., Horn. CW34 51
Ettrick St. E14 CF39 57
Ettringham St. SW11 BT45 66
Petergate
Etwell Pl., Surb. BL53 85
Euclid Way, Grays CZ42 70
Eugene Clo., Rom. CV31 51
Eugenia Rd. SE16 CC42 67
Eunice Gro., Chesh. AO19 16
Eureka Rd., Kings.T. BM51 85
Europa Pl. EC1 BZ38 2
Europa Pl. EC1 BZ38 57
Lever St.
Europa Rd., Hem.H. AY12 8
Europe Rd. SE18 CK41 68
Eustace Pl. SE18 CK42 68
Eustace Rd. E6 CK38 58
Eustace Rd. SW6 BS43 66
Eustace Rd., Guil. AU69 118
Eustace Rd., Rom. CP33 50
Euston Av., Wat. BB25 26
Euston Gro. NW1 BW38 1
Euston Gro. NW1 BW38 56
Euston Rd. NW1 BV38 1
Euston Rd. NW1 BW38 56
Euston Rd., Croy BX54 86
Euston Sq. NW1 BW38 1
Euston Sq. NW1 BW38 56
Euston St. NW1 BW38 1
Euston St. NW1 BW38 56
Euston Station BW38 1
Colonnade NW1
Eva Rd., Rom. CP33 50
Evandale Rd. SW9 BY44 66
Evangelist Rd. NW5 BV35 47
Evans Av., Wat. BB21 26
Evans Clo. E8 CA36 57
Forest Rd.
Evans Clo., Rick. AZ25 26
Evans Dale, Rain. CT38 59
Evans Gro., Felt. BF48 74
Evans Gro., St.Alb. BK11 9
Evans Rd. SE6 CG48 78
Evanston Av. E4 CF29 39
Evanston Gdns., Ilf. CK32 49
Eve Rd. E11 CG35 49
Eve Rd. E15 CG37 58
Eve Rd. N17 CA31 48
Eve Rd., Islw. BJ45 64
Eve Rd., Wok. AT61 100
Evelina Clo. SE20 CC50 77
Evelina Rd. SE15 CC45 67
Evelina Rd. SE20 CC50 77
Eveline Rd., Mitch. BU51 86
Evelyn Av. NW9 BN31 46
Evelyn Av., Ruis. BB33 44
Evelyn Clo., Twick. BF47 74
Evelyn Clo., Wok. AR63 100
Evelyn Cres., Sun. BB51 83
Evelyn Ct. N1 BZ37 2
Evelyn Ct. N1 BZ37 57
Evelyn Dennington Rd. E6 CK39 58
Evelyn Dr., Pnr. BD29 36
Evelyn Gdns. SW7 BT42 3
Evelyn Gdns. SW7 BT42 66
Evelyn Gdns., Gdse. CC68 114
Evelyn Gdns., Rich. BL45 65
Kew Rd.
Evelyn Gro. W5 BL40 55
Evelyn Gro., Sthl. BE39 54
Evelyn Rd. E16 CH40 58
Evelyn Rd. E17 CF31 48
Evelyn Rd. SW19 BS49 76
Evelyn Rd. W4 BN41 65
Evelyn Rd., Barn. BU24 29
Evelyn Rd., Ham BK48 74
Evelyn Rd., Rich. BL45 65
Evelyn Rd., Sev. CV61 108
Evelyn Sharp Clo., Rom. CV31 51
Evelyn St. SE8 CD42 67
Evelyn Ter., Rich. BL45 65
Evelyn Way, Cob. BD61 102
Evelyn Way, Sun. BB51 83
Evelyn Way, Wall. BW56 95
Evelyn Wk. Brwd. DA28 42
Evelyn Wk. N1 BZ37 2
Evelyn Wk. N1 BZ37 57
Evelyn Yd. W1 BW39 1
Evelyns Clo., Uxb. AZ39 53
Evening Hill, Brom. CF50 77
Evenwood Clo. SW15 BR46 75
Everard Av., Brom. CH54 88
Everard Av., Slou. AP41 62
Everard Clo., St.Alb. BG14 9
Everard La., Cat. CB64 105
Everard Way, Wem. BL34 46
Everatt Clo. SW18 BR46 75
Amerland Rd.
Everdon Rd. SW13 BP43 65
Everest Clo., Grav. DF48 81
Everest Ct., Wok. AP61 100
Everest Pl. E14 CF39 57
Everest Pl., Swan. CS52 89
Everest Rd. SE9 CK46 78
Everest Rd., Stai. AX47 73
Everest Way, Hem.H. AZ13 8
Everett Clo., Pnr. BB31 44
Wiltshire La.
Everett Wk., Belv. CQ43 69
Osborne Rd.
Everglade Strand NW9 BO30 37
Everglade, West. CJ62 106
Evergreen Oak Av., Wind. AQ45 62
Evergreen Way, Hayes BB40 53
Everilda St. N1 BX37 2
Everilda St. N1 BX37 56
Evering Rd. E5 CB34 48
Evering Rd. N16 CA34 48
Everington Rd. N10 BU30 38
Everington St. W6 BQ43 65
Everitt Rd. NW10 BN38 55
Everlands Clo., Wok. AS62 100
Everlasting La., St.Alb. BG13 9
Everleigh St. N4 BX33 47
Eversfield Gdns. NW7 BO29 37
Eversfield Rd., Reig. BS70 121
Eversfield Rd., Rich. BL44 65
Eversham Wk. SW9 BY44 66
Myatts Fields Dev.
Eversholt St. NW1 BW37 1
Eversholt St. NW1 BW37 56
Evershot Rd. N4 BX33 47
Eversleigh Gdns., Upmin. CY33 51
Eversleigh Rd. E6 CJ37 58
Eversleigh Rd. N3 BR29 37
Eversleigh Rd. SW11 BU45 66
Eversleigh Rd., Barn. BT25 29
Eversley Av., Bexh. CS44 69
Eversley Av., Wem. BM34 46
Eversley Clo. N21 BX25 29
Eversley Clo., Egh. AU51 82
Eversley Cres. N21 BX25 29
Eversley Cres., Islw. BG44 64
Eversley Cres., Ruis. BB34 44
Eversley Cross, Bexh. CT44 69
Eversley Mt. N21 BX25 29
Eversley Park Rd. N21 BX25 29
Eversley Pk. SW19 BP49 75
Eversley Rd. SE19 BZ50 77
Eversley Rd. SE7 CH43 68
Eversley Rd., Surb. BL52 85
Eversley Way, Croy. CE55 87
Everthorpe Rd. SE15 CA45 67
Everton Bldgs. NW1 BW38 1
Everton Bldgs. NW1 BW38 56
Stanhope St.
Everton Dr., Stan. BL31 46
Everton Rd., Croy. CB54 87
Evesham Av. E17 CE30 39
Evesham Clo., Grnf. BF37 54
Evesham Clo., Reig. BR70 120
Evesham Clo., Sutt. BS57 95
Evesham Grn., Mord. BS53 86
Evesham Rd. E15 CG37 58
Evesham Rd. N., Reig. BR70 120
Evesham Rd. N11 BW28 38
Evesham Rd., Felt. BD46 74
Evesham Rd., Grav. DH48 81
Evesham Rd., Mord. BS53 86
Evesham Rd., Reig. BR70 120
Evesham St. W11 BQ40 55
Evesham Way SW11 BV44 66
Evesham Way, Ilf. CL31 49
Evesham Wk. SE5 BY44 66
Love Wk.
Evreham Rd., Iver AV39 52
Evry Rd., Sid. CP50 79
Ewald Rd. SW6 BR44 65
Ewanrigg Ter., Wdf.Grn. CJ28 40
Ewart Gro. N22 BX30 38
Ewart Rd. SE23 CC47 77
Ewe Clo. N7 BX36 56
Ewell By-pass, Epsom BP58 94
Ewell Court Av., Epsom BO56 94
Ewell Downs Rd., Epsom BP59 94
Ewell House Gro., Epsom BO58 94
Ewell Park Way, Epsom BP57 94
Ewell Rd., Long Ditton BJ54 84
Ewell Rd., Surb. BL53 85
Ewell Rd., Sutt. BQ57 94
Ewellhurst Rd., Ilf. CK30 40
Ewelme Rd. SE23 CC47 77
Ewen Cres. SW2 BY47 76
Ewer St. SE1 BZ40 4
Ewer St. SE1 BZ40 57
Ewhurst Av., S.Croy. CA58 96
Ewhurst Clo., Sutt. BQ58 94
Ewhurst Rd. SE4 CD46 77
Ewing St. E3 CD38 57
Maidman St.
Exbury Rd. SE6 CD48 77
Excelsior Clo., King.T. BM51 85
Washington Rd.
Excelsior Gdns., SE13 CF44 67
Lewisham Rd.
Exchange Bldgs. E1 CA39 57
Cutler St.
Exchange Ct. WC2 BX40 4
Strand
Exchange Rd., Wat. BC24 26
Exchange St. EC1 BZ38 2
Exchange St. EC1 BZ38 57
Dingley Rd.
Exchange St., Rom. CT32 50
Exedown Rd., Sev. DB61 108
Exeforde Av., Ashf. AZ49 73
Exeter Clo. E6 CK39 58
Exeter Gdns., Ilf. CK33 49
Exeter Ho. SW15 BQ46 75
Exeter Pl., Guil. AP69 118
Exeter Rd. E16 CH39 58
Exeter Rd. E17 CE32 48
Exeter Rd. N14 BV26 38
Exeter Rd. N9 CC27 39
Exeter Rd. NW2 BR35 46
Exeter Rd. SE15 CA44 67
Exeter Rd., Croy. CA54 87
Exeter Rd., Dag. CR36 59
Exeter Rd., Enf. CC24 30
Exeter Rd., Felt. BE48 74
Exeter Rd., Grav. DH48 81
Exeter Rd., Har. BE34 45
Exeter Rd., Well. CN44 68
Exeter St. WC2 BX40 4
Exeter St. WC2 BX40 56
Exeter Way SE14 CD43 67
New Cross Sta.
Exford Gdns. SE12 CH47 78
Exford Rd. SE12 CH48 78
Exhibition Clo. W12 BQ40 55
White City Clo.
Exhibition Rd. SW7 BT41 3
Exhibition Rd. SW7 BT41 66
Exmoor St. W10 BQ39 55
Exmouth Mkt. EC1 BY38 2
Exmouth Mkt. EC1 BY38 56
Exmouth Ms. NW1 BW38 1
Drummond St.
Exmouth Rd. E17 CD32 48
Exmouth Rd., Brom. CH52 88
Exmouth Rd., Grays DD43 71
Exmouth Rd., Hayes BB38 53
Exmouth Rd., Ruis. BD34 45
Exmouth Rd., Well. CO43 69
Exmouth St. E1 CC39 57
Exning Rd. E16 CG38 58
Exon St. SE17 CA42 4
Exon St. SE17 CA42 67
Explorer Av., Stai. AY47 73
Exton Cres. NW10 BN36 55
Exton Gdns., Dag. CP35 50
Exton St. SE1 BY40 4
Exton St. SE1 BY40 56
Eyebright Clo., Croy. CC54 87
Primrose La.
Eyethorne Rd. SW9 BY44 66
Eyhurst Av., Horn. CU34 50
Eyhurst Clo. NW2 BP34 46
Eyhurst Clo., Tad. BR65 103
Eyhurst Spur, Tad. BR65 103
Eylewood Rd. SE27 BZ49 77
Eynella Rd. SE22 CA47 77
Eynham Rd. W12 BQ39 55
Eynsford Clo., Orp. CN54 88
Eynsford Cres., Bex. CP47 79
Eynsford Rd., Farn. CW54 90
Eynsford Rd., Green. DB46 80
Eynsford Rd., Ilf. CN34 49
Eynsford Rd., Sev. CU59 98
Eynsford Rd., Swan. CS53 89
Eynsford Ri., Eyns. CV56 99
Eynsford Ter., West Dr. AY39 53
Royal La.
Eynsham Br. SE2 CO42 69
Eynsham Dr. SE2 CO41 69
Eynswood Dr., Sid. CO49 79
Eyot Gdns. W6 BO42 65
Eyre Clo. NW8 BT37 56
Eyre Clo., Rom. CV31 51
Eyre Ct. NW8 BT37 1
Eyre St. Hill EC1 BY38 2
Eyre St. Hill EC1 BY38 56
Eythorpe Rd. SW9 BY44 66
Eywood Rd., St.Alb. BG14 9
Ezra Rd. SE5 BZ44 67
Harvey Rd.
Ezra St. E2 CA38 2
Ezra St. E2 CA38 57

F

Faber Gdns. NW4 BP32 46
Fabian Rd. SW6 BR43 65
Fabian St. E6 CK38 58
Fackenden La., Sev. CU60 98
Factory La. N17 CA30 39
Factory La., Croy. BY54 86
Factory Path, Stai. AV49 72
Factory Pl. E14 CF42 67
Factory Rd. E16 CK40 58
Factory Rd., Grav. DE46 81
Factory Sq. SW16 BX50 76
Factory Yd. W7 BH40 54
Faesten Way, Bex. CT48 79
Faggoters La., Harl. CS9 6
Faggoters La., Ong. CT11 14
Faggots Clo., Rad. BJ21 27
Faggs Rd., Felt. BB45 63
Fagus Av., Rain. CV38 60
Fair Acre, Hem.H. AY15 8
Fair Acres, Wind. AL44 61
Fair Clo., Bush. BF26 36
Fair Grn., Saw. CQ6 6
Fair La., Couls. BT66 113
Fair Lawn, Lthd. BE65 102
Fair Lawns, Wey. AV59 91
Fair St. SE1 CA41 4
Popham St.
Fair St. SE1 CA41 67
Fair St., Houns. BG45 64
Fair Vw., Cob. BD61 102
Fairacre, Islw. BG44 64
Fairacre, N.Mal. BO52 85
Fairacres Clo., Pot.B. BR20 19
Fairacres SW15 BP45 65
Fairacres, Brom. CH53 88
Fairacres, Cob. BD59 93
Fairacres, Croy. CD58 96
Fairacres, Ruis. BB33 44
Fairacres, Tad. BQ64 103
Fairbairn Clo., Pur. BY60 95
Beaumont Rd.
Fairbairn Grn. SW9 BY44 66
Fairbairn Rd. SW9 BY44 66
Fairbank Av., Orp. CL55 88
Fairbank Clo., Ong. CW18 24
Fairbanks Rd. N17 CA31 48
Fairbourne Clo., Wok. AQ62 100
Shilburn Way
Fairbourne Rd. N17 CA31 48
Fairbourne, Cob. BD60 93
Fairbridge Rd. N19 BW34 47
Fairbrook Clo. N13 BY28 38
Fairbrook Rd. N13 BY29 38
Tottenhall Rd.
Fairburn Clo., B.Wd. BM23 28
Fairby La., Hart. DC53 90
Fairby Rd. SE12 CH46 78
Fairchild St. EC2 CA38 2
Fairchildes Av., Croy. CF59 96
Fairchildes Rd., Warl. CF60 96
Fairchildes, Warl. CG60 97
Fairclough St. E1 CB39 2
Fairclough St. E1 CB39 57
Faircross Av., Bark. CM36 58
Faircross Av., Rom. CS29 41
Faircross Way, St.Alb. BJ12 9
Fairdale Gdns. SW15 BP45 65
Fairdale Gdns., Hayes BC40 53
Fairdene Rd., Couls. BW62 104
Fairey Av., Hayes BB42 63
Fairfax Av., Epsom BP58 94
Fairfax Av., Red. BU70 121
Fairfax Clo., Walt. BC54 83
Fairfax Gdns. SE3 CJ44 68
Fairfax Pl. NW6 BT36 56
Fairfax Rd. N8 BY31 47
Fairfax Rd. NW6 BT36 1
Fairfax Rd. NW6 BT36 56
Fairfax Rd. W4 BO41 65
Fairfax Rd., Grays DD42 71
Fairfax Rd., Tedd. BJ50 74
Fairfax Rd., Til. DF44 71
Fairfax Rd., Wok. AT63 100
Fairfax Ter., Sthl. BE42 64
Fairfield App., Stai. AR46 72
Fairfield Av. NW4 BP32 46
Fairfield Av., Edg. BM29 37
Fairfield Av., Grays DE40 71
Fairfield Av., Ruis. BA33 44
Fairfield Av., Slou. AR43 62
Fairfield Av., Stai. AV49 72
Fairfield Av., Twick. BF47 74
Fairfield Av., Upmin. CY35 51
Fairfield Av., Wat. BD27 36
Fairfield Clo. N12 BT28 38
Fairfield Clo., Dor. BJ70 119
Fairfield Clo., Enf. CD25 30
Scotland Grn. Rd. N.
Fairfield Clo., Hat. BQ11 10
Lockley Cres.
Fairfield Clo., Nthwd. BA29 35
Rickmansworth Rd.
Fairfield Clo., Rad. BH22 27
Fairfield Clo., Rom. CU33 50
Fairfield Clo., Sid. CN46 78
Fairfield Clo., Slou. AR43 62
Fairfield Cotts., Lthd. BF66 111
Fairfield Cres., Edg. BM29 37
Fairfield Ct. NW10 BP37 55
Longstone Av.
Fairfield Ct., Wdf.Grn. CH29 40
Fairfield Rd.
Fairfield Dr. SW18 BS46 76
Fairfield Dr., Brox. CD15 12
Fairfield Dr., Dor. BJ70 119
Fairfield Dr., Grnf. BK37 54
Fairfield Dr., Har. BG31 45
Fairfield E., Kings.T. BL51 85
Fairfield Gdns. N8 BX32 47
Elder Av.
Fairfield Gro. SE7 CJ43 68
Fairfield N., Kings.T. BL51 85
Fairfield Path, Croy. CA55 87
Fairfield Pl., Kings.T. BL52 85
Fairfield Rd. E17 CD30 39
Fairfield Rd. E3 CE37 57
Fairfield Rd. N18 CB28 39
Fairfield Rd. N8 BX32 47
Fairfield Rd. W7 BJ41 64
Fairfield Rd., Beck. CE51 87
Fairfield Rd., Bexh. CQ44 69
Fairfield Rd., Brom. CH50 78
Fairfield Rd., Brwd. DB27 42
Fairfield Rd., Croy. BZ55 87
Fairfield Rd., Epp. CO18 23
Fairfield Rd., Hodd. CE11 12
Fairfield Rd., Ilf. CL36 58
Fairfield Rd., Kings.T. BL51 85
Fairfield Rd., Lthd. BJ64 102
Fairfield Rd., Ong. CW18 24
Fairfield Rd., Orp. CM54 88
Fairfield Rd., Sev. DC63 108
Fairfield Rd., Stai. AR46 72
Fairfield Rd., Sthl. BE39 54
Fairfield Rd., Uxb. AX36 53
Fairfield Rd., Wdf.Grn. CH29 40
Fairfield Rd., West.Dr. AY40 53
Fairfield Ri., Guil. AP70 118
Fairfield S., Kings.T. BL52 85
Fairfield St. SW18 BS46 76
Fairfield W., Kings.T. BL51 85
Fairfield Way, Barn. BS25 29
Fairfield Way, Couls. BW60 95
Fairfield Way, Epsom BO56 94
Fairfield Wk., Chsnt. CD17 21
Fairfield, Lthd. BF66 111
Fairfields Clo. NW9 BN32 46
Fairfields Cres. NW9 BN31 46
Fairfields Rd., Houns. BG45 64
Fairfolds, Wat. BE21 27
Fairfoot Rd. E3 CE38 57
Fairford Av., Bexh. CS44 69
Fairford Av., Croy. CC53 87
Fairford Clo., Croy. CC53 87
Fairford Clo., Reig. BT69 121
Fairford Clo., Rom. CX29 42

Fairford Clo., Wey. AV60 91
Fairford Gdns., Wor.Pk. BO55 85
Fairford Way, Rom. CX29 42
Fairgreen E., Barn. BU24 29
Fairgreen Rd., Th.Hth. BY53 86
Fairgreen, Barn. BU24 29
Fairham Av., S.Ock. DA40 60
Fairhaven Av., Croy. CC53 87
Fairhaven Cres., Wat. BC27 35
Fairhaven Rd., Red. BV68 113
Fairhaven, Egh. AS49 72
Fairhazel Gdns. NW6 BS36 56
Fairhazel Gdns. NW6 BT36 1
Fairholme Av., Rom. CU32 50
Fairholme Clo. N3 BR31 46
Fairholme Cres. Hayes BB38 53
Fairholme Cres., Ash. BK62 102
Fairholme Gdns. N3 BR31 46
Fairholme Gdns., Upmin. CZ33 51
Fairholme Rd. W14 BR42 65
Fairholme Rd., Ashf. AY49 73
Fairholme Rd., Croy. BY54 86
Fairholme Rd., Har. BH32 45
Fairholme Rd., Ilf. CK32 49
Fairholme Rd., Sutt. BR57 94
Fairholme, Felt. BA47 73
Fairholt Clo. N16 CA33 48
Fairholt Rd. N16 BZ33 48
Fairholt St. SW7 BU41 3
Fairholt St. SW7 BU41 66
Montpelier Wk.
Fairkytes Av., Horn. CV33 51
Fairland Rd. E15 CG36 58
Fairlands Av., Buck.H. CH27 40
Fairlands Av., Sutt. BS55 86
Fairlands Av., Th.Hth. BX52 86
Fairlands Rd., Guil. AO68 109
Fairlawn Av. N2 BU31 47
Fairlawn Av. W4 BN42 65
Fairlawn Av., Bexh. CP44 69
Fairlawn Clo. N14 BW25 29
Fairlawn Clo., Esher BH57 93
Fairlawn Clo., Felt. BE49 74
Fairlawn Clo., Kings.T. BN50 75
Fairlawn Ct. SE7 CJ43 68
Fairlawn
Fairlawn Ct. W4 BN42 65
Cunnington St.
Fairlawn Dr., Red. BJ71 121
Fairlawn Dr., Wdf.Grn. CH29 40
Fairlawn Gdns., Sthl. BE40 54
Fairlawn Gro. W4 BN42 65
Fairlawn Gro., Bans. BT60 95
Fairlawn Pk. SE26 CD49 77
Fairlawn Rd. SW19 BR50 75
Fairlawn Rd., Sutt. BT59 95
Fairlawn SE7 CJ43 68
Fairlawn, Lthd. BE66 111
Fairlawn, Wat. BB22 26
Langley Rd.
Fairlawn, Wdf.Grn. CK29 40
Vicarage Rd.
Fairlawn, Wey. BB56 92
Fairlawns Clo., Horn. CW33 51
Herbert Rd.
Fairlawns Clo., Stai. AW50 73
Kingston Rd.
Fairlawns SW15 BQ46 75
Putney Hill
Fairlawns, Pnr. BD30 36
Fairlawns, Sun. BC52 83
Fairlawns, Twick. BK46 74
Fairlea Pl. W5 BK38 54
Fairley Way, Chsnt. CB17 21
Fairlie Gdns. SE23 CC47 77
Fairlight Av. E4 CF27 39
Fairlight Av. NW10 BO37 55
Fairlight Av., Wdf.Grn. CH29 40
Fairlight Av., Wind. AO44 61
Fairlight Clo. E4 CF27 39
Fairlight Clo., Wor.Pk. BQ56 94
Fairlight Dr., Uxb. AX36 53
Fairlight Rd. SW17 BT49 76
Fairlop Clo., Horn. CU36 59
Fairlop Gdns., Ilf. CM29 40
Fairlop Pl. NW8 BT38 1
Fairlop Pl. NW8 BT38 56
Fairlop Rd. E11 CF33 48
Fairlop Rd., Ilf. CM30 40
Fairmark Dr., Uxb. AZ36 53
Fairmead Clo., Brom. CK52 88
Fairmead Clo., Houns. BD43 64
Fairmead Clo., N.Mal. BN52 85
Fairmead Cres., Edg. BN27 37
Fairmead Gdns., Ilf. CJ32 49
Fairmead Rd. N19 BW34 47
Fairmead Rd., Croy. BX54 86
Fairmead Rd., Loug. CH25 31
Fairmead Side, Loug. CJ25 31
Fairmead, Brom. CK52 88
Fairmead, Surb. BM54 85
Fairmead, Wok. AR62 100
Fairmeads, Cob. BE60 93
Fairmile Av. SW16 BW49 76
Fairmile Av., Cob. BE60 93
Fairmile La., Cob. BD59 93
Fairmile Pk. Rd., Cob. BE59 93
Fairmont Clo., Belv. CQ43 69
Albany Rd.
Fairmount Rd. SW2 BX46 76
Fairoak Clo., Ken. BY61 104
Fairoak Clo., Lthd. BG59 93
Fairoak Clo., Orp. CL54 88
Fairoak Dr. SE9 CM46 78
Fairoak Gdns., Rom. CT30 41
Fairoak La., Lthd. BG59 93
Fairs Rd., Lthd. BJ63 102
Fairseat Clo., Bush. BH27 36
Hive Rd.
Fairshot Ct., St.Alb. BK10 9
Fairstead Wk. N1 BZ37 57
Fairthorn Rd. SE7 CH42 68
Fairtrough Rd., Orp. CO60 98
Fairview Av., Brwd. DF26 122
Fairview Av., Rain. CV37 60
Fairview Av., Wem. BK36 54
Fairview Clo. E17 CD30 39
Fairview Clo., Chig. CN28 40
Fairview Clo., Epsom BQ59 94
Fairview Cres., Har. BF33 45
Fairview Dr., Chig. CN28 40
Fairview Dr., Orp. CM56 97
Fairview Dr., Shep. AY53 83
Fairview Dr., Wat. BB21 26
Fairview Gdns., Wdf.Grn. CH30 40
Fairview Pl. SW2 BX47 76
Holmewood Gdns.
Fairview Rd. N15 CA32 48
Fairview Rd. SW16 BX51 86
Fairview Rd., Chig. CN28 40
Fairview Rd., Enf. BX23 29
Fairview Rd., Epsom BO59 94
Fairview Rd., Grav. DE50 81
Fairview Rd., Sutt. BT56 95
Fairview Way, Edg. BM28 37
Fairview, Epsom BR57 94
Fairview, Erith CT43 69
Fairview, Pot.B. BS18 20
Fairwall Ho. SE5 CA44 67
Glebe Est.
Fairwater Av., Well. CO45 69
Fairwater Dr., Wey. AX58 92
Fairway Av. NW9 BM31 46
Fairway Av., B.Wd. BM23 28
Fairway Av., West Dr. AX40 53
Fairway Clo. NW11 BT33 47
Fairway Clo., Croy. CD53 87
Fairway Clo., Epsom BN55 85
Riverview Rd.
Fairway Clo., Houns. BD46 74
Fairway Clo., St.Alb. BG17 18
Fairway Clo., West Dr. AX40 53
Fairway Clo., Wok. AQ63 100
Fairway Ct., Hem.H. AY15 8
Fairway
Fairway Dr., Dart. CX47 80
Fairway Dr., Grnf. BG36 54
Fairway Gdns., Ilf. CM35 49
Fairway SW20 BQ52 85
Fairway, Bexh. CQ46 79
Fairway, Cars. BT59 95
Fairway, Cher. AW54 83
Fairway, Grays DD40 71
Fairway, Guil. AU70 118
Fairway, Hem.H. AY15 8
Fairway, Orp. CM53 88
Fairway, Saw. CQ 6 6
Fairway, The N13 BZ27 39
Fairway, The N14 BV25 29
Fairway, The NW7 BN27 37
Fairway, The W3 BO39 55
Fairway, The, Barn. BS25 29
Fairway, The, Brom. CK53 88
Fairway, The, E.Mol. BF52 84
Fairway, The, Grav. DG48 81
Fairway, The, Lthd. BJ62 102
Fairway, The, N.Mal. BN51 85
Fairway, The, Nthlt. BG36 54
Fairway, The, Nthwd. BB28 35
Fairway, The, Ruis. BD35 45
Fairway, The, Upmin. CY33 51
Fairway, The, Uxb. AY37 53
Fairway, The, Wat. BA19 17
Fairway, The, Wem. BJ34 45
Fairway, The, Wey. AZ59 92
Fairway, Vir.W. AR53 82
Fairway, Wdf.Grn. CJ28 40
Fairways, Ashf. AZ50 73
Fairways, Ken. BZ62 105
Hayes La.
Fairways, Stai. AW49 73
Knowle Grn.
Fairways, Stan. BL30 37
Fairways, Tedd. BK50 74
Fairways, The, Harl. CO12 14
Fairways, Wal.Abb. CG20 22
Fairways, Wal.Cr. CC16 21
Fairweather Clo. N15 CA31 48
Lawrence Rd.
Fairweather Rd. N16 CB32 48
Fairwell La., Lthd. AZ67 110
Fairwood Ct. E11 CF33 48
Fairwyn Rd. SE26 CD49 77
Falaise, Egh. AS49 72
Falcon Av., Brom. CK52 88
Falcon Av., Grays DD43 71
Falcon Clo. SE1 BY40 4
Falcon Clo., Dart. CW46 80
Falcon Clo., Hat. BP13 10
Falcon Clo., Nthwd. BB29 35
Falcon Clo., Saw. CP 6 6
Falcon Cres., Enf. CC25 30
Falcon Dr., Stai. AX46 73
Falcon Gro. SW11 BU45 66
Falcon La. SW11 BU45 66
Falcon Pl. N16 CA34 48
Stoke Newington Church St.
Falcon Rd. SW11 BU44 66
Falcon Rd., Enf. CC25 30
Falcon Rd., Guil. AR71 118
Falcon Rd., Hmptn. BE50 74
Falcon Ridge, Berk. AR13 7
Falcon St. E13 CG38 58
Falcon Ter. SW11 BU45 66
Falcon Trd. Est. NW10 BO35 46
Falcon Way E11 CH31 49
Falcon Way E14 CE42 67
Undine Rd.
Falcon Way, Felt. BC46 73
Falcon Way, Har. BL32 46
Falcon Way, Rain. CU36 59
Falcon Way, Sun. BB51 83
Falcon Way, Wat. BE20 18
Falconberg Ms. W1 BW39 1
Falconberg Ms. W1 BW39 56
Sutton Row
Falconer Rd., Bush. BE25 27
Falconer Rd., Ilf. CO28 41
Falconer Wk. N7 BX34 47
Andover Est.
Falconers Pk., Saw. CP 6 6
Falconwood Av., Well. CM44 68
Falconwood Par., Well. CN45 68
Falconwood Rd., Croy. CD58 96
Falcourt Clo., Sutt. BS56 95
Robin Hood La.
Falkholt St. SW7 BU42 66
Rutland St.
Falkirk Clo., Horn. CX34 51
Falkirk Gdns., Wat. BD28 36
Falkirk St. N1 CA37 2
Falkirk St. N1 CA37 57
Falkland Av. N11 BV28 38
Falkland Av. N3 BS29 38
Falkland Gdns., Dor. BJ72 119
Falkand Gro.
Falkland Gro., Dor. BJ71 119
Vincents La.
Falkland Park Av. SE25 CA52 87
Falkland Pl. NW5 BW35 47
Falkland Rd.
Falkland Rd. N8 BY31 47
Falkland Rd. NW5 BW35 47
Falkland Rd., Barn. BR23 28
Falkland Rd., Dor. BJ72 119
Fallaize Av., Ilf. CL35 49
Riverdene Rd.
Falling La., West Dr. AY40 53
Falloden Way NW11 BS31 47
Fallow Clo., Chig. CN28 40
Fallow Court Av. N12 BT29 38
Fallow Hurst Path N3 BT29 38
Park Cres.
Fallowfield Clo., Uxb. AX30 35
Northwood Rd.
Fallowfield Ct., Stan. BJ27 36
Fallowfield Wk., Hem.H. AW12 8
Fallowfield, Stan. BJ27 36
Fallowfield, Welw.G.C. BR 6 5
Fallsbrook Rd. SW16 BV50 76
Falmer Rd. E17 CE31 48
Falmer Rd. N15 BZ32 48
Falmer Rd., Enf. CA24 30
Falmouth Av. E4 CF28 39
Falmouth Clo. N22 BX29 38
Falmouth Clo. SE12 CG46 78
Taunton Rd.
Falmouth Gdns., Ilf. CJ31 49
Falmouth Rd. SE1 BZ41 4
Falmouth Rd. SE1 BZ41 67
Falmouth Rd., Walt. BD56 93
Falmouth St. E15 CF35 48
Falstaff Gdns., St.Alb. BG15 9
Falstaff Ho. N1 CA37 57
Purcell St.
Falstone, Wok. AQ62 100
Fambridge Clo. SE26 CD49 77
Fambridge Rd., Dag. CR33 50
Famet Av., Pur. BZ60 96
Famet Clo., Pur. BZ60 96
Famet Wk., Pur. BZ60 96
Fane St. W14 BR43 65
Fann St. EC1 BZ38 2
Fann St. EC1 BZ38 57
Fanns Ri., Grays CX42 70
Fanshaw St. N1 CA38 2
Fanshaw St. N1 CA38 57
Fanshawe Av., Bark. CM36 58
Fanshawe Cres., Dag. CQ35 50
Fanshawe Cres., Horn. CV32 51
Fanshawe Rd., Grays DG41 71
Fanshawe Rd., Rich. BK49 74
Fanshaws La., Hert. BZ12 12
Fanthorpe St. SW15 BQ45 65
Far End, Hat. BP14 10
Faraday Av., Sid. CO48 79
Faraday Clo. N7 BX36 56
Faraday Clo., Wat. BB25 26
Faraday Rd. E15 CG36 58
Faraday Rd. SE7 CJ41 68
Faraday Rd. SW19 BS50 76
Faraday Rd. W10 BR39 55
Faraday Rd. W3 BN40 55
Faraday Rd., E.Mol. BF52 84
Faraday Rd., Sthl. BF39 54
Faraday Rd., Well. CO45 69
Faraday Way, Orp. CO52 89
Fareham Rd., Felt. BD46 74
Fareham St. W1 BW39 1
Dean St.
Farewell Pl., Mitch. BT51 86
Faringdon Av., Brom. CL54 88
Faringdon Av., Rom. CV30 42
Faringford Clo., St.Alb. BF16 18
Faringford Clo., Pot.B. BT19 20
Penshurst Rd.
Faringford Rd. E15 CG36 58
Farington Acres, Wey. BA55 83
Faris La., Wey. AV59 91
Farisbarn Dr., Wey. AV59 91
Farjeon Rd. SE3 CJ44 68
Farland Rd., Hem.H. AZ13 8
Farleigh Av., Brom. CG53 88
Farleigh Ct. Rd., Warl. CD60 96
Farleigh Dean Cres., Croy. CE59 96
Farleigh Pl. N16 CA35 48
Farleigh Rd. N16 CA35 48
Farleigh Rd., Warl. CC62 105
Farleigh Rd., Wey. AW59 92
Farleton Clo., Wey. BA57 92
Farley Cft., West. CM66 115
Farley Dr., Ilf. CN33 49
Farley Pk., Oxt. CF68 114
Farley Pl. SE25 CB52 87
Farley Rd. SE6 CE46 77
Farley Rd., S.Croy. CB58 96
Farleys Clo., Lthd. BA66 110
Farlington Pl. SW15 BP47 75
Farlow Clo., Grav. DF48 81
Grieves Rd.
Farlow Rd. SW15 BQ45 65
Farlton Rd. SW18 BS47 76
Farm Av. NW2 BR34 46
Farm Av. SW16 BX49 76
Farm Av., Har. BE33 45
Farm Av., Orp. CM54 88
Farm Av., Swan. CS52 89
Farm Av., Wem. BK36 54
Farm Clo., East Horsley BB67 110
Farm Clo., Amer. AR23 25
Farm Clo., Barn. BP25 28
Farm Clo., Brwd. DE26 122
Farm Clo., Buck.H. CJ27 40
Farm Clo., Cher. AT53 82
Farm Clo., Chsnt. CC18 21
Great Cambridge Rd.
Farm Clo., Cuff. BW17 20
Farm Clo., Dag. CS36 59
Farm Clo., Fetcham BG65 102
Farm Clo., Guil. AR69 118
Farm Clo., Maid. AH42 61
Farm Clo., Shep. AZ54 83
Farm Clo., Stai. AV49 72
Farm Clo., Sthl. BF40 54
Farm Clo., Sutt. BT57 95
Farm Clo., W.Wick. CG55 88
Farm Clo., Wall. BW58 95
Farm Clo., Welw.G.C. BQ 8 5
Farm Cres., Slou. AR39 52
Farm Ct. NW4 BP31 46
Farm Ct., Uxb. AZ34 44
Farm Dr., Croy. CD55 87
Farm Dr., Pur. BW59 95
Farm End E4 CG25 31
Farm End, Nthwd. AZ30 35
Farm Field, Wat. BB22 26
Farm Fields, S.Croy. CA59 96
Farm Hill Rd., Wal.Abb. CF20 21
Farm House Clo., Brox. CD16 21
Farm House Clo., Wok. AU61 100
Farm La. SW6 BS43 66
Farm La., Ash. BM61 103
Farm La., Beac. AO29 34
Farm La., Croy. CD55 87
Farm La., Lthd. BB67 110
Farm La., Pur. BW58 95
Farm La., Rick. AX24 26
Farm La., Slou. AO40 52
Farm La., Wok. AU65 100
Farm Pl. W8 BS40 56
Farm Pl., Berk. AP12 7
Farm Pl., Dart. CU45 69
Farm Rd. N21 BY26 38
Farm Rd., Edg. BM29 37
Farm Rd., Esher BF54 84
Farm Rd., Grays DF41 71
Farm Rd., Hmptn. BE47 74
Farm Rd., Houns. BE47 74
Farm Rd., Mord. BS53 86
Farm Rd., Nthwd. BA28 35
Farm Rd., Rain. CV38 60
Farm Rd., Rick. AT24 25
Farm Rd., Sev. CV63 108
Farm Rd., St.Alb. BJ13 9
Farm Rd., Stai. AW50 73
Farm Rd., Sutt. BT57 95
Farm Rd., Warl. CD63 105
Farm Rd., Wok. AT63 100
Farm Rd., Wraysbury AU46 72
Farm St. W1 BV40 3
Farm St. W1 BV40 56
Farm Vale, Bex. CR46 79
Farm Way, Buck.H. CJ28 40
Farm Way, Bush. BF24 27
Farm Way, Horn. CU35 50
Farm Way, Nthwd. BB28 35
Farm Way, Stai. AV46 72
Farm Way, Wor.Pk. BQ55 85
Farm Wk. NW11 BR32 46
Farm Wk., Guil. AP71 118
Farm, The SW19 BQ47 75
Princes Way
Farman Gro., Nthlt. BD38 54
Wayfarer Rd.
Farmborough Clo., Har. BG33 45
Pool Rd.
Farmcote Rd. SE12 CH47 78
Farmcroft, Grav. DG48 81
Farmdale Rd. SE10 CH42 68
Farmdale Rd., Cars. BU57 95
Farmer Ct., Wal.Abb. CH20 22
Winters Way
Farmer Rd. E10 CE33 48
Farmer St. W8 BS40 56
Farmers Clo., Wat. BC20 17
Farmers Rd. SE5 BY43 66
Farmers Rd., Stai. AV49 72
Farmers Way, Beac. AO29 34
Farmfield Clo. N12 BS28 38
Farmfield Rd., Brom. CF49 77
Farmhouse Rd. SW16 BW50 76
Farmilo Rd. E17 CD33 48
Farmington Av., Sutt. BT55 86
Farmland Wk., Chis. CL49 78
Farmlands, Enf. BY23 29
Farmlands, Pnr. BC31 44
Farmlands, The, Nthlt. BE36 54
Farmleigh Gro., Walt. BB56 92
Farmleigh N14 BW26 38
Farmstead Rd. SE6 CE49 77
Farmstead Rd., Har. BG30 36
Farmway, Dag. CP34 50
Farn Yd., Wind. AO43 61
Farnaby Dr., Sev. CU66 116
Farnaby Rd. SE9 CJ45 68
Farnaby Rd., Brom. CF50 77
Farnan Av. E17 CE30 39
Farnan Rd. SW16 BX49 76
Farnborough Av. E17 CD31 48
Farnborough Av., S.Croy. CC58 96
Farnborough Clo., Wem. BM34 46
Farnborough Common, Orp. CK55 88
Farnborough Cres., S.Croy. CD58 96
Farnborough Hill, Orp. CM56 97
Farnborough Way SE15 CA43 67
Farnborough Way, Orp. CL56 97
Farncombe St. SE16 CB41 67
Farndale Av. N13 BY27 38
Farndale Cres, Grnf. BG38 54
Farndon Mill La., Harl. CL 9 6
Farnell Ms. SW5 BS42 66
Farnell Point E5 CB34 48
Downs Est.
Farnell Rd., Islw. BG45 64
Farnell Rd., Stai. AW48 73
Farnes Dr., Rom. CV30 42
Farnham Clo. N20 BT26 38
Farnham Clo., Hem.H. AT17 16
Farnham Gdns. SW20 BP51 85
Farnham Park La., Slou. AO37 52
Farnham Pl. SE1 BY40 4
Farnham Pl. SE1 BY40 56
Farnham Rd., Guil. AO72 118
Farnham Rd., Ilf. CN33 49
Farnham Rd., Rom. CV28 42
Farnham Rd., Slou. AO40 61
Farnham Rd., Well. CP44 69
Farnham Royal SE11 BX42 4
Farnham Royal SE11 BX43 66
Farningham Cres., Cat. CB65 105
Farningham Hill Rd., Farn. CV53 90
Farningham Rd. N17 CB29 39
Farningham Rd., Cat. CB65 105
Farnley Rd. E4 CG26 40
Farnley Rd. SE25 BZ52 87
Farnley, Wok. AP62 100
Clifton Way
Farnol Rd., Dart. CX46 80
Faro Clo., Brom. CL51 88
Faroe Rd. W14 BQ41 65
Farorna Wk., Enf. BY23 29
Farquhar Rd. SE19 CA49 77
Farquhar Rd. SW19 BS48 76
Farquharson Rd., Croy. BZ54 87
Farr Av., Bark. CO37 59
Maybury Rd.
Farr Rd., Enf. BZ23 30
Farraday Clo., St.Alb. BH11 9
Darwin Clo.
Farraline Rd., Wat. BC24 26
Farrance Est. E14 CE39 57
Farrance Rd., Rom. CQ32 50
Farrance St. E14 CE39 57
Farrans Ct., Har. BJ33 45
Farrant Av. N22 BY30 38
Farrant Clo., Orp. CN57 97
Farrant Way, B.Wd. BL23 28
Farren Rd. SE23 CD48 77
Farrer Rd. N8 BW31 47
Farrer Rd., Har. BL32 46
Farrier Clo., Sun. BC52 83
Anvil Rd.
Farrier St. NW1 BW36 56
Farriers Clo., Grav. DJ47 81
Lower Higham Rd.
Farriers End, Brox. CD16 21
Tarpan Way
Farriers Rd., Nthlt. BF37 54
Farriers Way, B.Wd. BN25 28
Farringdon La. EC1 BY38 2
Farringdon La. EC1 BY38 56
Farringdon Rd. EC1 BY38 2
Farringdon Rd. EC1 BY38 56
Farringdon St. EC4 BY39 2
Farringdon St. EC4 BY39 56
Farrington Av., Orp. CO52 89
Farrins Rents SE16 CD40 57
Farrow Gdns., Grays DD40 71
Farrow Pl. SE16 CD41 67
Farthing Alley SE1 CB41 67
Wolseley St.
Farthing Barn La., Orp. CK58 97
Farthing Clo., Dart. CW45 70
Farthing Fields E1 CB40 57
Raine St.
Farthing Green La., Slou. AQ37 52
Farthing St., Orp. CK57 97
Farthings Clo. E4 CG27 40
Farthings Clo., Pnr. BC32 44
Farthings, The, Kings.T. BM51 85
Brunswick Rd.
Farthings, Wok. AP61 100
Mead Ct.
Farwell Rd., Sid. CO48 79
Farwig La., Brom. CG51 88
Fashion St. E1 CA39 2
Fashion St. E1 CA39 57
Fashoda Rd., Brom. CJ52 88
Fassett Rd. E8 CB36 57
Fassett Rd., Kings.T. BL52 85
Fassett Sq. E8 CB36 57
Fauconberg Rd. W14 BN43 65
Faulkner Clo., Dag. CP33 50
Palmer Rd.
Faulkner St. SE14 CC44 67
Kender St.
Faulkners Alley EC1 BY39 2
Cowcross St.
Faulkners Rd., Walt. BD56 93
Fauna Clo., Rom. CP32 50
Faunce St. SE17 BY42 66
Faunce St. SE17 BY43 4
Favart Rd. SW6 BS44 66
Faversham Av. E4 CG26 40
Faversham Av., Enf. BZ25 30
Faversham Clo., Chig. CO27 41
Faversham Rd. SE6 CD47 77
Faversham Rd., Beck. CD51 87
Croydon Rd.
Faversham Rd., Mord. BS53 86
Fawcett Clo. SW11 BT44 66
Wye St.
Fawcett Est. E5 CB33 48
Fawcett Rd. NW10 BO37 55
Fawcett Rd., Croy. BZ55 87
Fawcett Rd., Wind. AN44 61
Fawcett St. SW10 BT43 66
Fawcus Clo., Esher BH57 93
Fawe Park Rd. SW15 BR45 65
Fawe St. E14 CE39 57
Fawke Common Rd., Sev. CX66 117
Fawkham Green Rd., Fawk. DA55 90
Fawkham Rd., S.Dnth. DB52 90
Fawkham Rd., Sev. CZ57 99

Fawkon Wk., Hodd. CE12 12
Fawley Rd. NW6 BS35 47
Fawn Ct., Hat. BQ11 10
Fawn Rd. E13 CJ37 58
Fawn Rd., Chig. CN28 40
Fawnbrake Av. SE24 BY46 76
Fawns Manor Clo., Felt. BA47 73
Bedfont Rd.
Fawns Manor Rd., Felt. BA47 73
Fawood Av. NW10 BN36 55
Fawsley Clo., Slou. AV44 62
Coleridge Cres.
Fawters Clo., Brwd. DE25 122
Fay Grn., Wat. BA20 17
Fayerfield, Pot.B. BT19 20
Blunesfield
Faygate Cres., Bexh. CR46 79
Faygate Rd. SW2 BX48 76
Fayland Av. SW16 BW49 76
Fayland Est. SW16 BW49 76
Faymore Gdns., S.Ock. DA39 60
Feacey Down, Hem.H. AW12 8
Fearn Clo., Lthd. BB68 110
Fearney Mead, Rick. AW26 35
Hall Clo.
Fearnley Cres., Hmptn. BE49 74
Fearnley Rd. SE5 CA44 67
Lettsom St.
Fearnley Rd., Welw.G.C. BQ 8 5
Fearnley St., Wat. BC24 26
Fearns Mead, Brwd. DB28 42
Fearon St. SE10 CH42 68
Feather Dell, Hat. BO12 10
Featherbed La., Croy. CD57 96
Featherbed La., Hem.H. AW16 17
Featherbed La., Rom. CQ26 41
Featherbed La., Wat. BC16 17
Feathers La., Stai. AT48 72
Feathers Pl. SE10 CF43 67
Featherstone Av. SE23 CB48 77
Featherstone Clo., Pot.B. BT19 20
Featherstone Ct. EC1 BZ38 57
Featherstone St.
Featherstone Gdns., B.Wd. BN24 28
Featherstone Rd. NW7 BP29 37
Featherstone Rd., Sthl. BE41 64
Featherstone St. EC1 BZ38 2
Featherstone St. EC1 BZ38 57
Featherstone Ter., Sthl. BE41 64
Featley Rd. SW9 BY45 66
Angell Rd.
Federal Rd., Grnf. BK37 54
Federal Way, Wat. BD22 27
Federation Rd. SE2 CO42 69
Fee Farm Rd., Esher BH57 93
Feenan Highway, Til. DG43 71
Felbridge Av., Stan. BJ30 36
Felbridge Clo. SW16 BY49 76
Felbridge Clo., Sutt. BS58 95
Felbrigge Rd., Ilf. CN34 49
Felcott Clo., Walt. BD55 84
Felcott Rd., Walt. BD55 84
Felday Rd. SE13 CE46 77
Felden Clo., Pnr. BE29 36
Felden Clo., Wat. BD20 18
Felden Dr., Hem.H. AW15 8
Felden La., Hem.H. AW15 8
Felden Rd., Hem.H. AX15 8
Felden St. SW6 BR44 65
Feldman Clo., N16 CB33 48
Oldhill St.
Feldwick Pl., Red. BV70 121
Ladbroke Rd.
Felgate Ms. W6 BP42 65
Felhampton Rd. SE9 CL48 78
Felhurst Cres., Dag. CR35 50
Felicia Way, Grays DG42 71
Felix Av. N8 BX32 47
Felix Dr., Guil. AW67 110
Felix La., Shep. BB53 83
Felix Rd. W13 BJ40 54
Felix Rd., Walt. BD53 83
Felixstowe Rd. N17 CA31 48
Felixstowe Rd. N9 CB27 39
Felixstowe Rd. NW10 BP38 55
Felixstowe Rd. SE2 CO41 69
Fell Path, B.Wd. BN25 28
Fell Rd., Croy. BZ55 87
Felland Way, Reig. BT72 121
Fellbrigg Rd. SE22 CA46 77
Fellbrigg St. E1 CB38 57
Headlam St.
Fellbrook, Rich. BJ48 74
Fellowes Clo., Hayes BD38 54
Fellowes La., St.Alb. BO15 10
Fellowes Rd., Cars. BU55 86
Fellows Ct. E2 CA37 2
Fellows Ct. E2 CA37 57
Fellows Rd. NW3 BT36 56
Felltram Way SE7 CH42 68
Felmersham Clo. SW4 BW45 66
Haselrigge Rd.
Felmingham Rd. SE20 CC51 87
Felmongers, Harl. CO10 6
Felnex Est. NW10 BN38 55
Fels Clo., Dag. CR34 50
Fels Farm Av., Dag. CS34 50
Felsberg Rd. SW2 BX46 76
Felsham Rd. SW15 BQ45 65
Felspar Clo. SE18 CN42 68
Felstead Av., Ilf. CL30 40
Felstead Clo., Brwd. DE25 122
Bannister Dr.
Felstead Gdns. E14 CF42 67
Ferry St.
Felstead Rd. E11 CH33 49
Felstead Rd., Epsom BN59 94
Felstead Rd., Loug. CK26 40
Felstead Rd., Orp. CO55 89
Felstead Rd., Rom. CS29 41
Felstead Rd., Wal.Cr. CD19 21
Felstead St. E9 CD36 57
Felsted Rd. E16 CJ39 58
Feltham Av., E.Mol. BH52 84
Feltham Hill Rd., Ashf. AZ49 73

Feltham Rd., Ashf. AZ49 73
Feltham Rd., Mitch. BV51 86
Feltham Rd., Red. BU73 121
Feltham Wk., Red. BU73 121
Felthambrook Way, Felt. BC49 73
Felthamhill Rd., Felt. BC49 73
Felton Clo., B.Wd. BL22 28
Felton Clo., Brom. CL53 88
Felton Clo., Brox. CD16 21
Felton Gdns., Bark. CN37 58
Felton Rd.
Felton Lea., Sid. CN49 78
Felton Rd. W13 BK41 64
Camborne Av.
Felton Rd., Bark. CN37 58
Felton St. N1 BZ37 2
Felton St. N1 BZ37 57
Fen Clo., Brwd. DE24 122
Fen Ct. EC3 CA39 57
Fen Gro., Sid. CN46 78
Fen La., Upmin. DB35 51
Fen La., Upmin. DD35 123
Fen Pond Rd., Sev. DB62 108
Fen St. E16 CG40 58
Caxton St. N.
Fencepiece Rd., Chig. CM28 40
Fencepiece Rd., Ilf. CM30 40
Fenchurch Av. EC3 CA39 2
Fenchurch Av. EC3 CA39 57
Fenchurch Bldgs. EC3 CA39 2
Fenchurch Bldgs. EC3 CA39 57
Fenchurch Ct. EC3 CA39 2
Fenchurch Ct. EC3 CA39 57
Fenchurch Pl. EC3 CA40 4
Fenchurch St. EC3 BZ40 57
Fenchurch St. EC3 CA40 4
Fendall Rd., Epsom BN56 94
Fendall St. SE1 CA41 4
Fendall St. SE1 CA41 67
Fendt Clo. E16 CG40 58
Bowman Av.
Fendyke Rd., Belv. CP42 69
Fenelon Pl. W14 BR42 65
Fengates Rd., Red. BU70 121
Fenham Rd. SE15 CB43 67
Fenman Ct. N17 CB30 39
Shelbourne Rd.
Fenn Clo., Brom. CH50 78
Fenn St. E9 CC35 48
Fennel Clo., Croy. CC54 87
Primrose La.
Fennel Clo., Guil. AT69 118
Fennel St. SE18 CL43 68
Fennells Mead, Epsom BO58 94
Fennels, Harl. CM13 13
Fenner Sq. SW11 BT45 66
Thomas Baines Rd.
Fenning St. SE1 CA41 4
Fenning St. SE1 CA41 67
St. Thomas St.
Fennings, The, Amer. AO21 25
Fenns Way, Wok. AS61 100
Fennycroft Rd., Hem.H. AV12 7
Fens Way, Swan. CU50 79
Fensomes All., Hem.H. AX13 8
Fenstanton Av. N12 BT29 38
Fentiman Rd. SW8 BX43 66
Fentiman Way, Horn. CW33 51
Fenton Av., Stai. AX50 73
Fenton Clo. SW9 BX44 66
Stockwell La.
Fenton Clo., Brom. CK49 78
Fenton Clo., Red. BV70 121
Fenton House Est. NW3 BT34 47
Fenton Rd. N17 BZ29 39
Fenton Rd., Red. BV70 121
Fenton St. E1 CB39 57
Commercial Rd.
Fentons Av. E13 CH37 58
Fentum Rd., Guil. AQ69 118
Fenwick Clo. SE18 CL43 68
Ritter St.
Fenwick Clo., Wok. AQ62 100
Fenwick Gro. SE15 CB45 67
Fenwick Path, B.Wd. BL22 28
Berwick Rd.
Fenwick Pl. SW9 BX45 66
Fenwick Rd. SE15 CB45 67
Ferdinand Est. NW1 BV36 56
Ferdinand Pl. NW1 BV36 56
Ferdinand St.
Ferdinand St. NW1 BV36 56
Fergus Rd. N5 BY35 47
Calabria Rd.
Ferguson Av., Grav. DH49 81
Ferguson Av., Rom. CV30 42
Ferguson Av., Surb. BL53 85
Ferguson Clo., Brom. CF52 87
Ferguson Cres., Rom. CV30 42
Ferguson Ct., Rom. CV30 42
Ferme Pk. Rd. N4 BX32 47
Ferme Pk. Rd. N8 BX32 47
Fermor Rd. SE23 CD47 77
Fermoy Rd. W9 BR38 55
Fermoy Rd., Grnf. BF38 54
Fern Av., Mitch. BW52 86
Fern Cft., St.Alb. BG15 9
Fern Clo., Brox. CD15 12
Cozens La. E.
Fern Clo., Warl. CD62 105
Fern Ct., Berk. AQ13 7
Charles St.
Fern Dale, Guil. AP69 118
Fern Dells, Hat. BO13 10
Fern Dene W13 BJ39 54
Templewood
Fern Dr., Felt. BC47 73
Fern Dr., Hem.H. AY14 8
Fern Gro., Felt. BC47 73
Fern Gro., Welw.G.C. BQ 6 5
Fern Hill La., Wok. AR63 100
Fern Hill, Lthd. BG30 93
Fern La., Houns. BE42 64
Fern Leys, St.Alb. BK12 9
Fern St. E3 CE38 57
Fern Way, Wat. BC21 26
Fern Wk., Ashf. AX49 73

Fernbank Av., Horn. CV35 51
Fernbank Av., Walt. BE54 84
Fernbank Av., Wem. BH35 45
Fernbank Rd., Wey. AW56 92
Fernbank, Buck.H. CH26 40
Fernbrook Av., Sid. CN46 78
Fernbrook Cres. SE13 CG46 78
Fernbrook Dr., Har. BF33 45
Fernbrook Rd. SE13 CG46 78
Ferncliff Rd. E8 CB35 48
Ferncroft Av. N12 BU29 38
Ferncroft Av. NW3 BS34 47
Ferncroft Av., Ruis. BD34 45
Ferndale Av. E17 CF32 48
Ferndale Av., Cher. AV55 82
Ferndale Av., Houns. BE45 64
Ferndale Cres., Uxb. AX38 53
Ferndale Ct. SE3 CG43 68
Ferndale Ct. SW9 BX45 66
Ferndale Rd. E11 CG34 49
Ferndale Rd. E7 CH36 58
Ferndale Rd. N15 CA32 48
Ferndale Rd. SE25 CB53 87
Ferndale Rd. SW4 BX45 66
Ferndale Rd. SW9 BX45 66
Ferndale Rd., Ashf. AX49 73
Ferndale Rd., Bans. BR61 103
Ferndale Rd., Enf. CD22 30
Ferndale Rd., Grav. DG48 81
Ferndale Rd., Rom. CS30 41
Ferndale Rd., Wok. AS61 100
Ferndale St. E6 CL40 58
Ferndale Ter., Har. BH31 45
Ferndale Way, Orp. CM56 97
Ferndale, Brom. CJ51 88
Ferndell Av., Bex. CS48 79
Fernden Way, Rom. CR32 50
Ferndene Rd. SE24 BZ45 67
Fernden, St.Alb. BE19 18
Ferndown Av., Orp. CN54 88
Ferndown Clo., Guil. AT71 118
Ferndown Clo., Pnr. BE29 36
Ferndown Clo., Sutt. BF57 95
Ferndown Gdns., Cob. BD60 93
Ferndown Rd. SE9 CJ47 78
Ferndown Rd., Nthwd. BC30 35
Ferndown Rd., Wat. BD27 36
Ferndown, Horn. CW32 51
Fernecroft, St.Alb. BG15 9
Fernery, The, Stai. AV49 72
Fernes Clo., Uxb. AX39 53
Ferney Clo., Byfleet AX59 92
Ferney Rd.
Ferney Rd., Barn. BV26 38
Ferney Rd., Wey. AX59 92
Fernhall Dr., Ilf. CJ32 49
Fernhall La., Wal.Abb. CJ19 22
Fernham Rd., Th.Hth. BZ52 87
Fernhead Rd. W9 BR38 55
Fernhead Yd. W9 BR39 55
Fernhead Rd.
Fernheath Way, Dart. CS49 79
Fernhill Clo., Wok. AR63 100
Fernhill Ct. E17 CF30 39
Fernhill Ct., Kings.T. BK49 74
Fernhill Gdns., Kings.T. BK49 74
Fernhill La., Harl. CN13 13
Fernhill Pk., Wor.Pk. AR63 100
Fernhill St. E16 CK40 58
Fernhill, Harl. CN13 13
Fernhills, Kings L. BA20 17
Fernholme Rd. SE15 CC46 77
Fernhurst Gdns., Edg. BM29 37
Fernhurst Rd. SW6 BR44 65
Fernhurst Rd., Ashf. BA49 73
Fernhurst Rd., Croy. CB54 87
Fernie Clo., Chig. CO28 41
Fernlands Clo., Cher. AV55 82
Fernlea Rd. SW12 BV47 76
Fernlea Rd., Mitch. BV51 86
Fernlea, Lthd. BF65 102
Fernleigh Clo., Croy. BY56 95
Stafford Rd.
Fernleigh Ct., Har. BF30 36
Fernleigh Ct., Wem. BL34 46
Fernleigh Rd. N21 BY27 38
Ferns Clo., Enf. CD21 30
Ferns Clo., S.Croy. CB58 96
Ferns Rd, E15 CG36 58
Fernsbury St. WC1 BY38 2
Fernsbury St. WC1 BY38 56
Margery St.
Fernshaw Rd. SW10 BT43 66
Fernside Av. NW7 BN27 37
Fernside Av., Felt. BC49 73
Fernside La., Sev. CV68 117
Fernside NW3 BS34 47
Fernside NW4 BQ30 37
Fernside Rd. SW12 BU47 76
Fernside, Buck.H. CH26 40
Fernsleigh Clo., Ger.Cr. AS29 34
Fernthorpe Rd. SW16 BW50 76
Ferntower Rd. N5 BZ35 48
Fernville La., Hem.H. AX13 8
Fernways, Ilf. CL35 49
Cecil Rd.
Fernwood Av. SW16 BW49 76
Fernwood Av., Wem. BK36 54
Fernwood Clo., Brom. CJ51 88
Fernwood Cres. N20 BU27 38
Ferny Hill, Enf. BU22 29
Ferranti Clo. SE7 CJ42 68
Ferraro Clo., Houns. BF43 64
Ferrers Av., Wall. BW56 95
Ferrers Av., West Dr. AX41 63
Ferrers Rd. SW16 BW49 76
Ferrestone Rd. N8 BX31 47
Ferriby Clo. N1 BY36 56
Bewdley St.
Ferrier St. SW18 BS45 66
Ferriers Way, Epsom BQ63 103
Ferring Clo., Har. BG33 45
Ferrings SE21 CA48 77
Ferris Av., Croy. CD55 87
Ferris Rd. SE22 CB45 67

Ferro Rd., Rain. CU38 59
Ferron Rd. E5 CB34 48
Ferry App. SE18 CL41 68
Ferry Av., Stai. AV50 72
Ferry La. N17 CB31 48
Ferry La. SW13 BO43 65
Ferry La., Brent. BL43 65
Ferry La., Guil. AR72 118
Ferry La., Hythe End AT48 72
Ferry La., Laleham AX52 83
Ferry La., Rain. CT39 59
Ferry La., Rich. BL43 65
Ferry La., Shep. AZ54 83
Ferry Path, Cher. AW53 83
Ferry Pl. SE18 CL41 68
Ferry Rd. SW13 BP43 65
Ferry Rd., E.Mol. BF52 84
Ferry Rd., Maid. AH41 61
Ferry Rd., Surb. BJ53 84
Ferry Rd., Tedd. BJ49 74
Ferry Rd., Til. DG45 71
Ferry Rd., Twick. BJ47 74
Ferry Sq., Brent. BK43 64
Ferry Sq., Shep. AZ54 83
Church Sq.
Ferry St. E14 CF42 67
Ferryhills Clo., Wat. BD27 36
Ferrymead Av., Grnf. BF38 54
Ferrymead Dr., Grnf. BF37 54
Ferrymead Gdns., Grnf. BF37 54
Ferrymoor, Rich. BJ48 74
Feryby Rd., Grays DG41 71
Feryings Clo., Harl. CP 9 6
Fesants Cft., Harl. CO 9 6
Festing Rd. SW15 BQ45 65
Festival Clo., Bex. CP47 79
Festival Clo., Erith CT43 69
Festival Clo., Uxb. AZ37 53
Fetcham Common La., Lthd. BF64 102
Fetcham Park Dr., Lthd. BH65 102
Fetter La. EC4 BY39 2
Fetter La. EC4 BY39 56
Ffinch St. SE8 CE43 67
Fiddicroft Av., Bans. BS60 95
Fiddle Bridge La., Hat. BO12 10
Fidler Pl., Bush. BF26 36
Ashfield Av.
Field Clo. E4 CE29 39
Field Clo., Brom. CJ51 88
Field Clo., Buck.H. CJ27 40
Field Clo., Chesh. AP17 16
Field Clo., Chess. BK57 93
Field Clo., E.Mol. BF53 84
Field Clo., Guil. AU69 118
Field Clo., Hayes BA43 63
Field Clo., Houns. BC44 63
Field Clo., Rom. CO24 32
Field Clo., Ruis. BA33 44
Field Clo., S.Croy. CB60 96
Field Clo., St.Alb. BJ11 9
Field Clo., Uxb. AZ34 44
Field Ct. WC1 BX39 2
Field Ct. WC1 BX39 56
Field Ct., Oxt. CG67 115
Field End Clo., Wat. BE26 36
Field End Rd., Pnr. BC32 44
Field End Rd., Ruis. BD33 45
Field End, Barn. BP24 28
Field End, Couls. BW60 95
Field End, Nthlt. BD36 54
Arnold Rd.
Field End, Ruis. BD36 54
Field End, Twick. BH49 74
Field Gate La., Mitch. BU52 86
Field La., Brent. BK43 64
Field La., Tedd. BJ49 74
Field Mead NW9 BO29 37
Field Park Cres., Rom. CP32 50
Field Pl. EC1 BY37 2
Field Pl. EC1 BY37 56
St. John St.
Field Pl., N.Mal. BO53 85
Field Rd. E17 CE31 48
Field Rd. E7 CG35 49
Field Rd. N17 BZ31 48
Field Rd. NW10 BQ38 55
Field Rd. W6 BR42 65
Field Rd., Felt. BC46 73
Field Rd., Hem.H. AZ14 8
Field Rd., S.Ock. CY40 60
Field Rd., Uxb. AV35 43
Field Rd., Wat. BE25 27
Field St. WC1 BX38 2
Field St. WC1 BX38 56
Field View Rd., Pot.B. BS20 20
Field View Ri., St.Alb. BE18 18
Field Vw., Egh. AU49 72
Field Vw., Felt. BA49 73
Field Way NW10 BN36 55
Field Way, Berk. AS14 7
Field Way, Dag. CO35 50
Field Way, Ger.Cr. AR29 34
Field Way, Grnf. BF37 54
Field Way, Hem.H. AT17 16
Field Way, Rick. AW26 35
Field Way, Ruis. BA33 44
Field Way, Wok. AV66 109
Burntcommon La.
Field Waye, Uxb. AX38 53
Fieldcommon La., Walt. BE54 84
Fieldend Rd. SW16 BW51 86
Fielders Clo., Har. BG33 45
Dudley Gdns.
Fielders Grn., Guil. AT70 118
Springhaven Clo.
Fieldfare Rd. SE28 CP40 59
Fieldgate St. E1 CB39 2
Fieldgate St. E1 CB39 57
Fieldhouse Rd. SW12 BW47 76
Fieldhurst Clo., Wey. AW56 92
Fieldhurst, Slou. AS42 62
The Briars
Fielding Av., Til. DG44 71
Fielding Av., Twick. BG48 74
Fielding Rd. W14 BQ41 65

Fielding Rd. W4 BN41 6
Fielding St. SE17 BZ43
Fielding St. SE17 BZ43 6
Fielding Ter. W5 BL40 5
Uxbridge Rd.
Fielding Way, Brwd. DE25 12
Fieldings Rd., Chsnt. CD18 2
Fieldings, The SE23 CC47 7
Fieldman Clo. N16 CC33 4
Oldhill St.
Fields Ct., Pot.B. BT20 2
Fields End La., Hem.H. AU12
Fields Est. E8 CB36 5
Fieldsend Rd., Sutt. BR56 9
Fieldside Clo., Orp. CL56 9
State Farm Av.
Fieldside Rd., Brom. CF49 7
Fieldview SW18 BT47 7
Fieldway Cres. N5 BY35 4
Fieldway, Croy. CE57 9
Fieldway, Grays DD40 7
Fieldway, Orp. CM53 8
Fieldway, Wok. AV66 10
Fiennes Clo., Dag. CP33 5
Fife Ct. W3 BM39 5
Links Rd.
Fife Rd. E16 CH39 5
Fife Rd. N22 BY29 3
Fife Rd. SW14 BN46 7
Fife Rd., Kings.T. BL51 8
Fife Ter. N1 BX37 5
Wynford Rd.
Fife Way, Brom. CH51 8
White Hart Slip
Fifehead Clo., Ashf. AY50 7
Fifeway, Lthd. BF66 11
Fifield La., Wind. AH45 6
Fifield Path SE23 CC48 7
Bampton Rd.
Fifield Rd., Maid. AH43 6
Fifield Rd., Wind. AH44 6
Fifth Av. E12 CK35 4
Fifth Av. W10 BR38 5
Fifth Av., Enf. CA25 3
Fifth Av., Grays DA43 7
Fifth Av., Harl. CM 9
Fifth Av., Hayes BB40 5
Fifth Av., Wat. BD21 2
Fifth Cross Rd., Twick. BG48 7
Fifth Way, Wem. BM35 4
Fig St., Sev. CT67 11
Fig Tree Hill, Hem.H. AX13
Figgs Rd., Mitch. BV50 7
Filby Rd., Chess. BL57 9
Filey Av. N16 CB33 4
Filey Clo., Sutt. BT57 9
Filey Clo., West. CH63 10
Filey Spur, Slou. AN41 6
Scarborough Way
Filey Waye, Ruis. BC34 4
Fillebrook Av., Enf. CA23 3
Fillebrook Rd. E11 CF33 4
Filmer La., Sev. CW64 10
Filmer Rd. SW6 BR44 6
Filmer Rd., Wind. AL44 6
Filston La., Sev. CS61 10
Filston Rd., Erith CR42 6
Riverdale Rd.
Finborough Rd. SW10 BS42 6
Finborough Rd. SW17 BU50 7
Finch Av. SE27 BZ49 7
Finch Clo. NW10 BN36 5
Brentfield Rd.
Finch Clo., Barn. BS25 2
Finch Clo., Hat. BP13 1
Finch Clo., Wok. AO62 10
Finch Dr., Felt. BD47 7
Finch La. EC3 BZ39
Finch La. EC3 BZ39 5
Finch La., Amer. AP24 2
Finch La., Bush. BE24 2
Finch Rd., Berk. AQ12
Finch Rd., Guil. AR70 11
Finchale Rd. SE2 CO41 6
Fincham Clo., Uxb. BA34 4
Aylsham Dr.
Finchdale, Hem.H. AW14
Finchdean Way SE15 CA43 6
Finches Ri., Guil. AU69 11
Finchingfield Av., Wdf.Grn. CJ29 4
Finchley Clo., Dart. CX46 8
Finchley Ct. N3 BS29 3
Finchley La. NW4 BQ31 4
Finchley Pk. N12 BT28 3
Finchley Pl. NW8 BT37
Finchley Pl. NW8 BT37 5
Finchley Rd. NW11 BR31 4
Finchley Rd. NW2 BS34 4
Finchley Rd. NW3 BS35 4
Finchley Rd. NW8 BT37
Finchley Rd. NW8 BT37 5
Finchley Rd., Grays DD43 7
Finchley Way N3 BS29 3
Finchmoor, Harl. CM12 1
Finck St. SE1 BX41
Finck St. SE1 BX41 6
Finden Rd. E7 CH35 4
Findhorn St. E14 CF39 5
Aberfeldy St.
Findhorne Av., Hayes BC39 5
Findlay Dr., Guil. AP68 10
Findon Clo. SW18 BS46 7
Findon Clo., Har. BF34 4
Findon Gdns., Rain. CU39 5
Findon Rd. N9 CB26 3
Findon Rd. W12 BP41 6
Fine Bush La., Uxb. AZ32 4
Fingal St. SE10 CG42 6
Fingrith Hall La., Ing. DC17 2
Finians Clo., Uxb. AY36 5
Finland Pl. SE16 CD41 6
Finland Rd. SE4 CD45 6
Finland St. SE16 CD41 6
Finlay Gdns., Wey. AX56 9
Finlay St. SW6 BQ44 6
Finlays Clo., Chess. BM56 9

Finnart Clo., Wey. BA56 92
Meadows Leigh Clo.
Finnis St. E2 CB38 57
Finnymore Rd., Dag. CQ36 59
Finsbury Av. EC2 BZ39 2
Eldon St.
Finsbury Cir. EC2 BX39 2
Finsbury Cir. EC2 BZ39 57
Finsbury Cotts. N22 BX29 38
Finsbury Mkt. EC2 CA38 2
Finsbury Mkt. EC2 CA38 57
Finsbury Park Rd. N4 BY34 47
Finsbury Pavement EC2 BZ39 2
Finsbury Pavement EC2 BZ39 57
Finsbury Rd. N22 BX29 38
Finsbury Sq. EC2 BZ38 2
Finsbury Sq. EC2 BZ38 57
Finsbury St. EC2 BZ39 2
Finsbury St. EC2 BZ39 57
Finsen Rd. SE5 BZ45 67
Finstock Rd. W10 BQ39 55
Finucane Dr., Orp. CP54 89
Finucane Gdns., Rain. CU36 59
Finucane Ri., Bush. BG27 36
Finway Rd., Hem.H. AZ11 8
Fiona Clo., Lthd. BF65 102
Fir Clo., Walt. BC54 83
Fir Dene, Orp. CK55 88
Fir Grange Av., Wey. AZ56 92
Fir Gro., N.Mal. BO53 85
Fir Gro., Wok. AQ63 100
Fir Pk., Harl. CL12 13
Fir Rd., Felt. BD49 74
Fir Rd., Sutt. BR54 85
Fir Tree Av., Slou. AP38 52
Fir Tree Clo. SW16 BW49 76
Fir Tree Clo. W5 BL39 55
Fir Tree Clo., Stoneleigh BO56 94
Fir Tree Clo., Epsom BQ61 103
Fir Tree Clo., Esher BG56 93
Fir Tree Clo., Grays DE43 71
Lawn Cres.
Fir Tree Clo., Hem.H. AZ14 8
Fir Tree Clo., Lthd. BK65 102
Fir Tree Clo., Rom. CT31 50
Fir Tree Ct., Brwd. BL24 28
Fir Tree Gdns., Croy. CE56 96
Fir Tree Hill, Rick. AY22 26
Fir Tree Pl., Ashf. AZ49 73
Fir Tree Rd., Bans. BR60 94
Fir Tree Rd., Epsom BP61 103
Fir Tree Rd., Guil. AR69 118
Fir Tree Rd., Houns. BE45 64
Fir Tree Rd., Lthd. BK65 102
Fir Tree Wk., Enf. BZ24 30
Fir Tree Wk., Reig. BT70 121
Fir Trees, Epp. CO18 23
Tidys La.
Fir Wk., Sutt. BQ57 94
Firbank Clo. E16 CJ39 58
Firbank Clo., Enf. BZ24 30
Gladbeck Way
Firbank Dr., Wat. BE26 36
Firbank Dr., Wok. AQ63 100
Firbank La., Wok. AQ63 100
Firbank Pl., Egh. AQ50 72
Firbank Rd. SE15 CB44 67
Firbank Rd., Rom. CR28 41
Firbank Rd., St.Alb. BH11 9
Fircroft Av., Chess. BL56 94
Fircroft Clo., Slou. AQ36 52
Fircroft Clo., Wok. AS62 100
Ockenden Rd.
Fircroft Gdns., Har. BH34 45
Fircroft Rd. SW17 BU48 76
Firdene, Surb. BN54 85
Fire Bell All., Surb. BL53 85
Firecrest Dr. NW3 BS34 47
Firefly Clo., Wall. BX57 95
Firfield Rd., Wey. AW56 92
Firham Park Av., Rom. CX29 42
Firhill Rd. SE6 CE49 77
Firlands, Wey. BB57 92
Firmin Rd., Dart. CV46 80
Firs Av. N10 BV31 47
Firs Av. N11 BV29 38
Firs Av. SW14 BN45 65
Firs Av., Wind. AM45 61
Firs Clo. N10 BV31 47
Firs Av.
Firs Clo. SE23 CD47 77
Firs Clo., Dor. BJ72 119
Firs Clo., Esher BH57 93
Firs Clo., Hat. BP13 10
Firs Clo., Mitch. BV51 86
Firs Dr., Houns. BC44 63
Firs Dr., Loug. CK23 31
Firs La. N13 BZ27 39
Firs La. N21 BZ27 39
Firs La., Pot.B. BS20 20
Firs Park Av. N21 BZ26 39
Firs Park Gdns. N21 BZ26 39
Firs Rd., Ken. BY61 104
Firs Way, Guil. AQ70 118
Firs Wk., Nthwd. BA29 35
Firs Wk., Wdf.Grn. CH28 40
Firs, The N20 BT26 38
Athenaeum Rd.
Firs, The SW20 BP50 75
Firs, The W5 BK39 54
Firs, The, Bex. CS47 79
Dartford Rd.
Firs, The, Brwd. DA25 33
Ongar Rd.
Firs, The, Grays DE40 71
Firs, The, Guil. AQ72 118
Firs, The, St.Alb. BJ15 9
Firs, The, Welw.G.C. BQ 6 5
Firsby Av., Croy. CC54 87
Firsby Rd. N16 CA33 48
Firscroft N13 BZ27 39
Firsdene Clo., Cher. AU57 91
Firsgrove Cres., Brwd. DA28 42
Firsgrove Rd., Brwd. DA28 42
Firside Clo., Sid. CN47 78
First Av. E12 CK35 49
First Av. E13 CH38 58
First Av. E17 CE32 48
First Av. N18 CC28 39
First Av. NW4 BQ31 46
First Av. SW14 BO45 65
First Av. W10 BR38 55
First Av. W3 BO40 55
First Av., Amer. AO23 25
First Av., Brwd. DB20 24
First Av., Dag. CR37 59
First Av., E.Mol. BE52 84
First Av., Enf. CA25 30
First Av., Epsom BO58 94
First Av., Grav. DF47 81
First Av., Grays DA43 70
First Av., Harl. CM10 6
First Av., Hayes BB40 53
First Av., Rom. CP32 50
First Av., Walt. BC53 83
First Av., Wat. BD21 27
First Av., Well. CP43 69
First Av., Wem. BK34 45
First Clo., E.Mol. BG52 84
First Cross Rd., Twick. BH48 74
First St. SW3 BU42 3
First St. SW3 BU42 66
First Way SW20 BQ51 85
First Way, Wem. BM35 46
Firswood Av., Epsom BO56 94
Firth Gdns. SW6 BR44 65
Firtree Av., Mitch. BV51 86
Firtree Av., West Dr. AZ41 63
Firtree Clo. SE16 CD40 57
Firtree Clo., Orp. CN56 97
Firtree Gro., Cars. BU57 95
Firtree Wk., Dag. CS34 50
Firwood Av., St.Alb. BL13 10
Firwood Clo., Wok. AP63 100
Firwood Rd., Vir.W. AP53 82
Fish Street Hill EC3 BZ40 4
Fish Street Hill EC3 BZ40 57
Lower Thames St.
Fisher Clo., Croy. CA54 87
Lower Addiscombe Rd.
Fisher Clo., Grnf. BF38 54
Fisher Clo., Kings L. AZ18 17
Fisher Clo., Wal.Cr. CE20 21
Fisher Clo., Walt. BC56 92
Fisher Rd., Har. BH30 36
Fisher St. E16 CH39 58
Fisher St. WC1 BX39 2
Fisher St. WC1 BX39 56
Fisherman Clo., Rich. BK49 74
Fishermans Dr. SE16 CC41 67
Fishermans Hill, Grav. DD46 81
Fishers Ct. SE14 CC44 67
Fishers Hatch, Harl. CN10 6
Fishers Hill, Wok. AP64 100
Fishers La. W4 BN42 65
Fishers La., Epp. CN19 22
Fishers Way, Belv. CS40 59
Fishersdene, Esher BJ57 93
Kilnside
Fisherton St. Est. NW8 BT38 1
Fisherton St. Est. NW8 BT38 56
Fisherton St. NW8 BT38 1
Fisherton St. NW8 BT38 56
Fishery Pl., Hem.H. AW14 8
Fishery Rd., Hem.H. AW14 8
Fishery Rd., Maid. AH40 61
Fishmongers Hall St. EC4 BZ40 57
Wharfside
Fishponds Rd. SW17 BU49 76
Fishponds Rd., Kes. CJ56 97
Fishpool St., St.Alb. BF13 9
Fitz Wygram Clo., Hmptn. BG49 74
Fitzalan Rd. N3 BR31 46
Fitzalan Rd., Esher BH57 93
Fitzalan St. SE11 BY42 4
Fitzalan St. SE11 BY42 66
Fitzgeorge Av. W14 BR42 65
Fitzgeorge Av., N.Mal. BN51 85
Fitzgerald Av. SW14 BO45 65
Fitzgerald Rd. E11 CH32 49
Fitzgerald Rd. SW14 BN45 65
Fitzgerald Rd., T.Ditt. BJ53 84
Fitzhardinge St. W1 BV39 1
Fitzhardinge St. W1 BV39 56
Fitzhugh Gro. SW18 BT46 76
Fitzilian Av., Rom. CW30 42
Fitzjames Av. W14 BR42 65
Fitzjames Av., Croy. CB55 87
Fitzjohn Av., Barn. BR25 28
Fitzjohn Clo., Guil. AU69 109
Fitzjohns Av. NW3 BT35 47
Fitzmaurice Pl. W1 BV40 3
Fitzmaurice Pl. W1 BV40 56
Curzon St.
Fitzneal St. W12 BO39 55
Fitzrobert Pl., Egh. AT50 72
Fitzroy Clo., Har. BH30 36
Fitzroy Gdns. SE19 CA50 77
Fitzroy Ms. W1 BW38 1
Fitzroy Ms. W1 BW38 56
Cleveland St.
Fitzroy Pk. N6 BU33 47
Fitzroy Rd. NW1 BU37 1
Fitzroy Rd. NW1 BV37 56
Fitzroy Sq. W1 BW38 1
Fitzroy Sq. W1 BW38 56
Fitzroy St. W1 BW38 1
Fitzroy St. W1 BW38 56
Fitzstephen Rd., Dag. CO35 50
Fitzwarren Gdns. N19 BW33 47
Fitzwilliam Av., Rich. BL44 65
Fitzwilliam Rd. SW4 BW45 66
Five Acre NW9 BO30 37
Five Acre Wk., Welw.G.C. BR 8 5
Salisbury Rd.
Five Acres Av., St.Alb. BE18 18
Five Acres, Chesh. AO20 16
Five Acres, Harl. CN12 13
Five Acres, Kings L. AY18 17
Five Acres, St.Alb. BK16 18
Five Elms Rd., Brom. CJ55 88
Five Elms Rd., Dag. CQ34 50
Five Oaks Clo., Wok. AP63 100
Five Oaks La., Chig. CQ29 41
Five Oaks, Wey. AV47 91
Five Ways Rd. SW9 BY44 66
Fiveacre Clo., Croy. BY53 86
Fiveash Rd., Grav. CF47 81
Fivewents, Swan. CU51 89
Fladbury Rd. N15 BZ32 48
Fladgate Rd. E11 CG32 49
Flag Clo., Croy. CC54 87
Primrose La.
Flag Wk., Pnr. BC32 44
Flags, The, Hem.H. AZ13 8
Flambard Rd., Har. BJ32 45
Flamborough Clo., West. CH63 106
Flamborough Rd., Ruis. BC34 44
Flamborough St. E14 CD39 57
Flamborough Wk. E14 CD39 57
Flamborough St.
Flamingo Gdns., Nthlt. BE38 54
Jetstar Way
Flamingo Wk., Rain. CU36 59
Fulmar Rd.
Flamstead End Rd., Chsnt. CB17 21
Flamstead End Relief Rd. Wal.Cr. CA18 21
Flamstead Est. SE10 CG42 68
Flamstead Gdns., Dag. CP36 59
Flamstead Rd. SE7 CK42 68
Flamstead Rd., Dag. CP36 59
Flamsted Av., Wem. BM36 55
Flanchford Rd. W12 BO41 65
Flanchford Rd., Reig. BP73 120
Flanders Cres. SW17 BU50 76
Flanders Ct., Egh. AU49 72
Mullens Rd.
Flanders Rd. E6 CK37 58
Flanders Rd. W4 BO42 65
Flanders Way E9 CC36 57
Flanders Wk., Egh. AU49 72
Mullens Rd.
Flank St. E1 CB40 4
Flank St. E1 CB40 57
Dock St.
Flash La., Enf. BY22 29
Flask Wk. NW3 BT35 47
Flatfield Rd., Hem.H. AZ14 8
Flaunden Bottom, Chesh. AS21 25
Flaunden Bottom, Hem.H. AS20 16
Flaunden Hill, Hem.H. AS20 16
Flaunden La., Hem.H. AT19 16
Flaunden La., Rick. AU20 16
Flaunden Pk., Hem.H. AT19 16
Flavian Clo., St.Alb. BE15 9
Flaxley Rd., Mord. BS54 86
Flaxman Ct. W1 BW39 1
Wardour St.
Flaxman Ct. W1 BW39 56
Wardour St.
Flaxman Rd. SE5 BY45 66
Flaxman Ter. WC1 BW38 1
Flaxman Ter. WC1 BW38 56
Flaxmore Pl., Beck. CF53 87
Flaxton Rd. SE18 CM44 68
Flecker Clo., Stan. BH28 36
Fleece Rd., Surb. BK54 84
Fleece Wk. N7 BX36 56
Fleeming Clo. E17 CD30 39
Pennant Ter.
Fleeming Rd. E17 CD30 39
Fleet Av., Dart. CY47 80
Fleet Av., Upmin. CY32 51
Fleet Clo., E.Mol. BF53 84
Fleet Clo., Upmin. CY32 51
Fleet La. EC4 BY39 2
Fleet La. EC4 BY39 56
Fleet La., E.Mol. BE53 84
Fleet Rd. NW3 BU35 47
Fleet Rd., Dart. CY47 80
Fleet Rd., Grav. DE48 81
Fleet Side, E.Mol. BE53 84
Fleet St. EC4 BY39 2
Fleet St. EC4 BY39 56
Fleet Street Hill E1 CB38 2
Fleet Street Hill E1 CB38 57
Weaver St.
Fleet Way, Egh. AU52 82
Fleetdale Par., Dart. CY47 80
Swaledale Rd.
Fleethall Gro., Grays DD40 71
Fleetwood Clo. E16 CJ39 58
Fleetwood Clo., Ch.St.G. AQ28 34
Fleetwood Clo., Chess. BK57 93
Fleetwood Clo., Croy. CA55 87
Chepstow Ri.
Fleetwood Clo., Tad. BQ63 103
Fleetwood Ct. E6 CK39 58
Pembroke Rd.
Fleetwood Ct., Wey. AW60 92
Madeira Rd.
Fleetwood Rd. NW10 BP35 46
Fleetwood Rd., Kings.T. BM52 85
Fleetwood Rd., Slou. AP40 52
Fleetwood Sq., Kings.T. BM52 85
Fleetwood St. N16 CA34 48
Fleetwood Way, Wat. BD28 36
Fleming Clo. E17 CD30 39
Pennant Ter.
Fleming Clo., Chsnt. CB17 21
Spicersfield
Fleming Ct. W2 BT39 56
St. Marys Ter.
Fleming Ct., Croy. BY56 95
Fleming Gdns., Til. DH44 71
Fielding Av.
Fleming Mead, Mitch. BU50 76
Fleming Rd. SE17 BY43 4
Fleming Rd. SE17 BY43 66
Fleming Rd., Sthl. BF39 54
Fleming Way SE28 CP40 59
Fleming Way, Islw. BH45 64
Fleming Wk. NW9 BO30 37
Pasteur Clo.
Flemings, Brwd. DA28 42
Flemish Fields, Cher. AW54 83
Flempton Rd. E10 CD33 48
Fletcher Clo., Cher. AV57 91
Fletcher La. E10 CF33 48
Fletcher Path SE8 CE43 67
New Butt La.
Fletcher Rd. W4 BN41 65
Fletcher Rd., Cher. AU57 91
Fletcher Rd., Chig. CN28 40
Fletcher St. E1 CB40 4
Fletcher St. E1 CB40 57
Fletcher Way, Hem.H. AX12 8
Fletchers Clo., Brom. CH52 88
Fletching Rd. E5 CC34 48
Fletching Rd. SE7 CJ42 68
Lansdowne La.
Fletton Rd. N11 BX29 38
Fleur de Lis St. E1 CA38 2
Fleur de Lis St. E1 CA38 57
Fleur Gates SW19 BQ47 75
Princes Way
Flexley Wood, Welw.G.C. BR 6 5
Flexmere Rd. N17 BZ30 39
Flimwell Clo., Brom. CG49 78
Flinder Clo., St.Alb. BJ14 9
Flint Clo., Lthd. BF66 111
Flint Clo., Red. BU70 121
Flint Hill Clo., Dor. BJ73 119
Flint Hill, Dor. BJ73 119
Flint St. Grays DA43 70
Flint St. SE17 BZ42 4
Flint St. SE17 BZ42 67
Flint Way, St.Alb. BG11 9
Flintlock Clo., Stai. AW45 63
Flintmill Cres. SE3 CK44 68
Flinton St. SE17 CA42 4
Flinton St. SE17 CA42 67
Flitcroft St. WC2 BW39 1
Flitcroft St. WC2 BW39 56
Flockton St. SE16 CB41 67
George Row
Flodden Rd. SE5 BZ44 67
Flood Pass. SE18 CK42 68
Samuel St.
Flood St. SW3 BU42 3
Flood St. SW3 BU42 66
Flood Wk. SW3 BU43 3
Flood Wk. SW3 BU43 66
Flora Clo. E14 CE39 57
Flora Clo., Croy. CF59 96
Flora Gdns. Est. W6 BP42 65
Flora Gdns., Rom. CP32 50
Flora Gro., St.Alb. BH14 9
Flora St., Belv. CQ42 69
Floral Ct., Ash. BK62 102
Floral Dr., St.Alb. BK16 18
Floral St. WC2 BX40 4
Floral St. WC2 BX40 56
Florence Av., Enf. BZ24 30
Florence Av., Mord. BT53 86
Florence Av., Wey. AW59 92
Florence Clo., Grays DC43 71
Florence Clo., Harl. CP12 14
London Rd.
Florence Clo., Horn. CW34 51
Florence Clo., Walt. BD54 84
Florence Clo., Wat. BC21 26
Florence Ct. NW4 BP32 46
Vivian Av.
Florence Ct. NW8 BT38 1
Florence Dr., Enf. BZ24 30
Florence Gdns. W4 BN43 65
Florence Gdns., Stai. AW50 73
Florence Rd. E13 CG38 58
Florence Rd. E6 CJ37 58
Florence Rd. N4 BX33 47
Florence Rd. SE14 CD44 67
Florence Rd. SE2 CP42 69
Florence Rd. SW19 BS50 76
Florence Rd. W4 BN41 65
Florence Rd. W5 BL40 55
Florence Rd., Beck. CC51 87
Florence Rd., Brom. CH51 88
Florence Rd., Felt. BC47 73
Florence Rd., Kings.T. BL50 75
Florence Rd., S.Croy. BZ58 96
Florence Rd., Sthl. BD42 64
Florence Rd., Walt. BC54 83
Florence St. E16 CG38 58
Florence St. N1 BY36 2
Florence St. N1 BY36 56
Florence St. NW4 BQ31 46
Florence Ter. SE14 CD44 67
Florian Av., Sutt. BT56 95
Florian Rd. SW15 BR45 65
Florida Clo., Bush. BG27 36
Florida Rd., Guil. AS73 118
Florida Rd., Th.Hth. BY51 86
Florida St. E2 CB38 57
Floriston Av., Uxb. BA36 53
Floriston Clo., Stan. BJ30 36
Floriston Gdns., Stan. BJ30 36
Florys Ct. SW19 BR47 75
Floss St. SW15 BQ44 65
Flower & Dean St. E1 CA39 57
Flower Cres., Cher. AT57 91
Flower La. NW7 BO28 37
Flower La., Gdse. CC68 114
Flower Wk., Guil. AR72 118
Flowerfield, Sev. CT62 107
Flowerhill Way, Grav. DF50 81
Flowers Ms. N19 BW34 47
St. Johns Way
Flowersmead SW17 BV48 76
Floyd Rd. SE7 CJ42 68
Floyds La., Wok. AW61 101
Fludyer St. SE13 CG45 68
Fluys La., Epp. CO20 23
Brook Rd.
Folair Way SE16 CB42 67
Bonamy St. W.
Fold Cft., Harl. CL10 6
Fold Rd., Red. BV71 121
Foley Rd., Esher BH57 93
Foley Rd., West. BQ53 106
Foley St. W1 BW39 1
Foley St. W1 BW39 56
Folgate St. E1 CA39 2
Folgate St. E1 CA39 57
Foliot St. W12 BO39 55
Folk La. NW9 BN30 37
Folkes La., Upmin. CZ31 51
Folkestone Gdns. SE8 CD43 67
Trundleys Rd.
Folkestone Rd. E17 CE31 48
Folkestone Rd. E6 CL37 58
Folkestone Rd. N18 CB28 39
Folkingham La. NW9 BO30 37
Folkington Cor. N12 BR28 37
Follett Clo., Wind. AQ46 72
Follett Dr., Wat. BB19 17
Follett St. E14 CF39 57
Folly Av., St.Alb. BG13 9
Folly Clo., Rad. BH21 27
Folly La. E17 CD30 39
Folly La., St.Alb. BG13 9
Folly Ms. W11 BR39 55
Kensington Pk.
Folly Pathway, Rad. BH21 27
Folly Wall E14 CF41 67
Follyfield Rd., Bans. BS60 95
Fontaine Rd. SW16 BX50 76
Fontarabia Rd. SW11 BV45 66
Fontayne Av., Chig. CM28 40
Fontayne Av., Rain. CT36 59
Fontayne Av., Rom. CT30 41
Fontenoy Rd. SW12 BV48 76
Fonteyne Gdns., Wdf.Grn. CJ30 40
Fonthill Clo. SE20 CB51 87
Selby Rd.
Fonthill Ms. N4 BX34 47
Lennox Rd.
Fonthill Rd. N4 BX33 47
Fontley Way SW15 BP47 75
Fontmell Clo., Ashf. AZ49 73
Fontmell Clo., St.Alb. BH12 9
Fontmell Pk., Ashf. AY49 73
Fonts Hill N2 BT30 38
Fontwell Clo., Har. BH29 36
Fontwell Clo., Nthlt. BF36 54
Fontwell Dr., Brom. CK53 88
Fontwell Park Gdns., Horn. CW35 51
Football La., Har. BH33 45
Footbury Hill Rd., Orp. CO54 89
Foots Cray High St., Sid. CP50 79
Foots Cray La., Sid. CP47 79
Foots Cray Rd. SE9 CL46 78
Forbes Av., Pot.B. BT20 20
Forbes St. E1 CB39 57
Forburg Rd. N16 CB33 48
Ford Bridge Clo., Cher. AW54 83
Ford Clo., Ashf. AY50 73
Ford Clo., Bush. BG24 27
Ford Clo., Croy. BY53 86
Ford Clo., Har. BG33 45
Ford Clo., Rain. CT36 59
Ford Clo., Shep. AZ52 83
Ford End, Wdf.Grn. CH29 40
Ford La., Iver AW39 53
Ford La., Rain. CT36 59
Ford Rd. E3 CD37 57
Ford Rd., Ashf. AY49 73
Ford Rd., Cher. AW54 83
Ford Rd., Dag. CQ36 59
Ford Rd., Grav. DD46 81
Ford Rd., Wok. AT63 100
Ford Sq. E1 CB39 57
Cavell St.
Ford St. E16 CG39 58
Ford St. E3 CD37 57
Fordbridge Rd., Ashf. AY50 73
Fordbridge Rd., Shep. BB53 83
Fordbridge Rd., Sun. BB53 83
Fordcroft Rd., Orp. CO53 89
Forde Av., Brom. CJ52 88
Fordel Rd. SE6 CF47 77
Fordham Clo., Barn. BU24 29
Fordham Clo., West Dr. AY39 53
Fordham Rd., Barn. BT24 29
Fordham St. E1 CB39 57
Fordhook Av. W5 BL40 55
Fordingley Rd. W9 BR38 55
Fordington Rd. N6 BU32 47
Fordland St. SE18 CM42 68
Fordmill Rd. SE6 CE48 77
Fords Gro. N21 BZ26 39
Fords Park Rd. E16 CH39 58
Fordwater Rd., Cher. AW54 83
Fordwich Clo., Orp. CN54 88
Fordwich Rd., Welw.G.C. BQ 8 5
Fordwych Cres. NW2 BR35 46
Fordwych Rd. NW2 BR35 46
Fordyce Rd. SE13 CF46 77
Fordyke Rd., Dag. CQ34 50
Fore St. EC2 BZ39 2
Fore St. EC2 BZ39 57
Fore St. N18 CA29 39
Fore St. N9 CA29 39
Fore St., Harl. CP 9 6
Fore St., Hat. BQ12 10
Fore St., Pnr. BB31 44
Fore Street Av. EC2 BZ39 2
Fore Street Av. EC2 BZ39 57
Forebury Av., Saw. CQ 6 6
Forebury Cres., Saw. CQ 6 6
Forebury, The, Saw. CQ 6 6
Forefield, St.Alb. BF17 18
Foreland Ct. NW4 BR30 37
Foreland St. SE18 CM42 68
Plumstead Rd.
Foreman Ct. W6 BQ42 65
Foremark Clo., Chig. CN28 40
Foreshore SE8 CD42 67
Forest App., Wdf.Grn. CG29 40
Forest Av. E4 CG26 40
Forest Av., Chig. CL28 40
Forest Av., Hem.H. AY14 8
Forest Clo. E11 CG32 49
Forest Clo., Chis. CL51 88
Caveside Clo.

Forest Clo., Lthd. BB66 110
Forest Clo., Wal.Abb. CH22 31
Forest Clo., Wdf.Grn. CH28 40
Forest Clo., Wok. AU61 100
Forest Cres., Ash. BM61 103
Forest Ct. E11 CG31 49
Forest Ct. E4 CG26 40
Forest Dr. E. E11 CF33 48
Forest Dr. E12 CJ34 49
Forest Dr. W. E11 CF33 48
Forest Dr., Epp. CN21 31
Forest Dr., Kes. CK56 97
Forest Dr., Sun. BB50 73
Forest Dr., Tad. BS64 104
Forest Dr., Wdf.Grn. CF29 39
Forest Edge, Buck.H. CJ28 40
Forest Gate NW9 BO32 46
Forest Gdns. N17 CA30 39
Bruce Gro.
Forest Glade E11 CG32 49
Forest Glade E4 CG28 40
Forest Glade, Epp. CQ17 23
Forest Green Rd., Maid. AG44 61
Forest Gro. E8 CA36 57
Forest Hill Rd. SE22 CB46 77
Forest Hill Rd. SE23 CB46 77
Forest La. E15 CH35 49
Forest La. E7 CG35 49
Forest La., Chig. CL28 40
Forest La., Lthd. BB65 101
Forest Mount Rd., Wdf.Grn. CF29 39
Forest Rd. E11 CF33 48
Forest Rd. E17 CC31 48
Forest Rd. E7 CH35 49
Forest Rd. E8 CA36 57
Forest Rd. N17 CC31 48
Forest Rd. N9 CB26 39
Forest Rd., Chsnt. CC18 21
Forest Rd., Enf. CD21 30
Forest Rd., Erith CU44 69
Forest Rd., Felt. BD48 74
Forest Rd., Ilf. CM30 40
Forest Rd., Loug. CJ24 31
Forest Rd., Lthd. BB66 110
Forest Rd., Rich. BM43 65
Forest Rd., Rom. CR31 50
Forest Rd., Sutt. BS54 86
Forest Rd., Wat. BC20 17
Forest Rd., Wdf.Grn. CH27 40
Forest Rd., Wind. AL44 61
Forest Rd., Wok. AU61 100
Forest Ri. E17 CF31 48
Forest Ridge, Beck. CE52 87
Forest Ridge, Kes. CK56 97
Forest Side E4 CG26 40
Forest Side E7 CH35 49
Capel Rd.
Forest Side, Buck.H. CJ26 40
Forest Side, Epp. CM20 22
Forest Side, Wal.Abb. CJ21 31
Forest Side, Wor.Pk. BO54 85
Forest St. E7 CH35 49
Forest View Av. E10 CF32 48
Forest View Rd. E12 CK35 49
Forest View Rd. E17 CF30 39
Forest View Rd., Loug. CJ24 31
Forest Vw. E11 CG33 49
Forest Vw. E4 CF25 30
Forest Way N19 BW34 47
Hargrave Pk.
Forest Way, Ash. BL62 103
Forest Way, Loug. CK24 31
Forest Way, Orp. CN53 88
Forest Way, Sid. CM47 78
Forest Way, Wdf.Grn. CH28 40
Forest Wk., Bush. BE23 27
Forest Wk., Wey. AZ56 92
Hanger Hill
Forest, The E11 CG31 49
Forestdale N14 BW28 38
Forester Rd. SE15 CB45 67
Forester St. E3 CD38 57
Foresters Clo., Wall. BW57 95
Foresters Clo., Wok. AP62 100
Foresters Cres., Bexh. CR45 69
Foresters Dr. E17 CF31 48
Foresters Dr., Wall. BW57 95
Forestholme Clo. SE23 CC48 77
Taymount Ri.
Forfar Rd. N22 BY30 38
Forfar Rd. SW11 BV44 66
Forge Av., Couls. BY63 104
Forge Clo., Brom. CH54 88
Forge Clo., Hayes BA43 63
Forge Clo., Kings L. AW19 17
Forge Dr., Esher BJ57 93
Forge End, St.Alb. BF16 18
Forge End, Wok. AS62 100
Forge La., Felt. BE49 74
Forge La., Grav. DJ48 81
Forge La., Hort.K. CY52 90
Forge La., Nthwd. BB29 35
Forge La., Sev. DA58 99
Forge La., Sun. BC52 83
Forge La., Sutt. BR57 94
Forge Pl. NW1 BV36 56
Forge Way, Sev. CT59 98
Forgefield, West. CJ61 106
Forlong Path, Nthlt. BE36 54
Ridgeway Wk.
Forman Pl. N16 CA35 48
Farleigh Rd.
Formby Av., Stan. BK31 45
Formosa St. W9 BS38 56
Formosa St. W9 BS39 1
Formunt Clo. E16 CG39 58
Forres Clo., Hodd. CE11 12
Forres Ct. SE19 CA49 77
Forres Gdns. NW11 BS32 47
Forrest Gdns. SW16 BX52 86
Forrester Path SE26 CC49 77
Queensthorpe Rd.
Forresters Dr., Welw.G.C. BT 8 5
Forris Av., Hayes BB40 53
Forset St. W1 BU39 1
Forset St. W1 BU39 56
Forstal Clo., Brom. CG52 88
Forster Rd. E17 CD32 48
Forster Rd. N17 CA31 48
Forster Rd. SW2 BX47 76
Forster Rd., Beck. CD52 87
Forster Rd., Croy. BZ53 87
Windmill Rd.
Forsters Clo., Rom. CQ32 50
Forsters Way, Hayes BC39 53
Forston St. N1 BZ37 2
Forston St. N1 BZ37 57
Forsyte Cres. SE19 CA51 87
Forsyth Gdns. SE17 BY43 66
Forsyth Path, Wok. AU60 91
Forsyth Pl., Enf. CA25 30
Forsyth Rd., Wok. AU61 100
Forsythe Av., Hodd. CE11 12
Fort La., Reig. BS68 113
Fort Pass. SE16 CA42 4
Fort Pass. SE16 CA42 67
Fort Pass. SE18 CL42 68
Sandy Hill Rd.
Fort Rd. SE1 CA42 4
Fort Rd. SE1 CA42 67
Fort Rd., Guil. AS72 118
Fort Rd., Nthlt. BF36 54
Fort Rd., Sev. CS61 107
Fort Rd., Tad. BM69 120
Fort Rd., Til. DG45 71
Fort St. E1 CA39 2
Fort St. E16 CH40 58
Forterie Gdns., Ilf. CO34 50
Fortescue Av. E8 CB36 57
Mentmore Ter.
Fortescue Av., Twick. BG48 74
Fortescue Rd. SW19 BT50 76
Fortescue Rd., Edg. BN30 37
Fortescue Rd., Wey. AY56 92
Fortess Gro. NW5 BW35 47
Fortess Rd.
Fortess Rd. NW5 BW35 47
Fortess Wk. NW5 BV35 47
Fortess Rd.
Forth Rd., Upmin. CY32 51
Forthbridge Rd. SW11 BV45 66
Fortin Clo., S.Ock. DA40 60
Fortin Path, S.Ock. DA40 60
Fortin Way
Fortin Way, S.Ock. DA40 60
Fortis Clo. E16 CJ39 58
Fortis Green Av. N2 BU31 47
Fortis Green Rd. N10 BV31 47
Fortis Grn. N2 BU31 47
Fortismere Av. N10 BV31 47
Fortnam Rd. N19 BW34 47
Fortnums Acre, Stan. BH29 36
Fortrose Gdns. SW2 BX47 76
New Park Rd.
Fortuna Clo. N7 BX36 56
Roman Way
Fortune Gate Rd. NW10 BO37 55
Fortune Green Rd. NW6 BS35 47
Fortune La., B.Wd. BL25 28
Fortune St. EC1 BZ38 2
Fortune St. EC1 BZ38 57
Fortune Way NW10 BP38 55
Fortune Wk. SE28 CM41 68
Garrick Dr.
Fortunes Mead, Nthlt. BE36 54
Fortunes, The, Harl. CN12 13
Forty Acre La. E16 CH39 58
Forty Av., Wem. BL34 46
Forty Clo., Wem. BL34 46
Forty Hall Est., Enf. CA22 30
Forty Hill, Enf. CA22 30
Forty La., Wem. BM34 46
Fortyfoot Rd., Lthd. BK64 102
Forum Pl., Hat. BO12 10
Fiddle Bridge La.
Forum, The, E.Mol. BF52 84
Forum, The, Edg. BM29 37
Forval Clo., Mitch. BU53 86
Forward Dr., Har. BJ31 45
Fosbury Ms. W2 BS40 3
Fosbury Ms. W2 BS41 66
Inverness Ter.
Foscote Ms. W9 BS39 56
Amberley Rd.
Foscote Rd. NW4 BP32 46
Foskett Rd. SW6 BR44 65
Foss Av., Croy. BY56 95
Foss Rd. SW17 BT49 76
Fossdene Rd. SE7 CH42 68
Fossdyke Clo., Hayes BE39 54
Telford Way
Fosse Way W13 BJ39 54
Fosse, The, St.Alb. BE13 9
Fossil Rd. SE13 CE45 67
Fossington Rd., Belv. CP42 69
Fossway, Dag. CP34 50
Foster Av., Wind. AM45 61
Foster La. EC2 BZ39 2
Foster La. EC2 BZ39 57
Foster La., Wok. AO62 100
Foster Rd. E13 CH38 58
Foster Rd. W3 BO40 55
Foster Rd. W4 BN42 65
Foster Rd., Hem.H. AW14 8
Foster St. NW4 BQ31 46
Foster St., Harl. CQ12 14
Foster Wk. NW4 BQ31 46
Fosterdown, Gdse. CB68 114
Fosters Clo. E18 CH30 40
Latchett Rd.
Fosters Clo., Chis. CK49 78
Fothergill Clo. E13 CG37 58
Fotheringham Rd., Enf. CA24 30
Fotherley Rd., Rick. AV26 34
Fouberts Pl. W1 BW39 1
Fouberts Pl. W1 BW39 56
Foulden Rd. N16 CA35 48
Foulis Ter. SW7 BT42 3
Foulis Ter. SW7 BT42 66
Foulser Rd. SW17 BU48 76
Foulsham Rd., Th. Hth. BZ52 87
Founders Ct. EC2 BZ39 2
Lothbury
Founders Dr., Uxb. AV32 43
Queen Mother Dr.
Founders Gdns. SE19 BZ50 77
Hermitage Rd.
Foundry Clo. SE16 CD40 57
Foundry La., Slou. AT45 62
Fount St. SW8 BW43 66
Fountain Clo., Uxb. BA39 53
Fountain Ct. EC4 BY40 4
Fountain Ct. EC4 BY40 56
Fountain Ct. SE26 CC50 77
Fountain Dr. SE19 CA49 77
Fountain Farm, Harl. CN12 13
Fountain Gdns., Wind. AO45 61
Fountain La., Sev. CZ64 108
Fountain Ms. N5 BZ35 48
Kelross Rd.
Fountain Pl. SW9 BY44 66
Fountain Pl., Wal.Abb. CF20 21
Fountain Rd. SW17 BT49 76
Fountain Rd., Red. BU71 121
Fountain Rd., Th.Hth. BZ51 87
Fountain St. E2 CA38 2
Fountain St. E2 CA38 57
Columbia Rd.
Fountain Wk., Grav. DF46 81
Fountains Av., Felt. BE48 74
Fountains Clo., Felt. BE48 74
Fountains Cres. N14 BX26 38
Fountayne Rd. N15 CB31 48
Fountayne Rd. N16 CB34 48
Four Acres Dr., Hem.H. AY14 8
Four Acres Wk., Hem.H. AY14 8
Four Acres, Cob. BE60 93
Four Acres, Guil. AU69 118
Four Acres, Saw. CQ 6 6
Four Acres, Welw.G.C. BR 9 5
Four Seasons Cres., Sutt. BR55 85
Four Tubs, Bush. BG26 36
Fouracres, Enf. CD23 30
Fouracres, Kings.T. BN50 75
Fourfield Clo., Epsom BN64 103
Fourland Wk., Edg. BN29 37
Fournier St. E1 CA39 2
Fournier St. E1 CA39 57
Fourth Av. E12 CK35 49
Fourth Av. W10 BR38 55
Fourth Av., Enf. CA25 30
Fourth Av., Grays DA43 70
Fourth Av., Harl. CK11 13
Fourth Av., Hayes BB40 53
Fourth Av., Rom. CS33 50
Fourth Av., Wat. BD21 27
Fourth Cross Rd., Twick. BG48 74
Fourth Dr., Couls. BW61 104
Fourth Way, Wem. BN35 46
Fourways, Hat. BQ15 10
Fourways, St.Alb. BL13 10
Fourwents, Cob. BD60 93
Fowell St. W11 BQ40 55
Fowey Av., Ilf. CJ32 49
Fowey Clo. E1 CB40 57
Kennet St.
Fowler Clo., Sid. CQ49 79
Fowler Rd. E7 CH35 49
Fowler Rd. N1 BY37 2
Fowler Rd., Ilf. CO28 41
Fowler Rd., Mitch. BV51 86
Priestley Rd.
Fowlers Clo. SW11 BT45 66
Plough Rd.
Fowlers Mead, Wok. AP58 91
Fowlers Wk. W5 BK38 54
Fowley Clo., Wal.Cr. CE20 21
Longcroft Dr.
Fownes St. SW11 BU45 66
Fox & Knot St. EC1 BY39 2
Charterhouse St.
Fox Burrow Rd., Chig. CP28 41
Fox Clo. E1 CC38 57
Colebert Av.
Fox Clo. E16 CH39 58
Fox Clo., B.Wd. BK25 27
Rodgers Clo.
Fox Clo., Orp. CO56 98
Fox Clo., Rom. CR28 41
Fox Clo., Wey. BA56 92
Fox Clo., Wok. AU61 100
Fox Covert, Lthd. BG65 105
High Fields
Fox Ct. EC1 BY39 2
Fox Ct. EC1 BY39 56
Brooke St.
Fox Dell, Nthwd. BA29 35
Fox Hatch, Brwd. CZ22 33
Fox Hill Gdns. SE19 CA50 77
Fox Hill SE19 CA50 77
Fox Hill, Kes. CJ56 97
Fox Hills Clo., Cher. AT57 91
Fox Hills, Wok. AR62 100
Parley Dr.
Fox Hollows, Hat. BP11 10
Fox House Rd., Belv. CR42 69
Fox La. N., Cher. AV54 82
Fox La. N13 BX27 38
Fox La. S., Cher. AV54 82
Fox La. W5 BL38 55
Fox La., Cat. BY64 104
Fox La., Kes. CH56 97
Fox La., Lthd. BE66 111
Fox Rd. E16 CG39 58
Fox Rd., Slou. AR42 62
Foxberry Rd. SE4 CD45 67
Foxborough Clo., Slou. AT42 62
Foxborough Gdns. SE4 CE46 77
Foxbourne Rd. SW17 BV48 76
Foxburrows Av., Guil. AP70 118
Foxbury Av., Chis. CM50 78
Foxbury Clo., Brom. CH50 78
Foxbury Clo., Orp. CO56 98
Foxbury Dr., Orp. CO57 98
Foxbury Rd., Brom. CH50 78
Foxcombe Clo. E6 CJ37 58
Boleyn Rd.
Foxcombe Rd. SW15 BP47 75
Foxcombe, Croy. CE57 96
Foxcroft Rd. SE18 CL44 68
Foxcroft, St.Alb. BJ14 9
Foxdell Way, Ger.Cr. AS28 34
Foxearth Clo., West. CK62 107
Foxearth Rd., S.Croy. CB58 96
Foxearth Spur, S.Croy. CC58 96
Foxenden Rd., Guil. AS71 118
Foxes Dale SE3 CH45 68
Foxes Dale, Brom. CF52 87
Foxes Grn., Grays DG41 71
Foxfield Clo., Nthwd. BB29 35
Foxfield Rd., Orp. CM55 88
Foxglove Clo., Hat. BP13 10
Foxglove Gdns., Guil. AU69 118
Foxglove Gdns., Pur. BX59 95
Foxglove La., Chess. BM56 94
Foxglove Rd., S.Ock. DB39 60
Foxglove St. W12 BO40 55
Foxgloves, The, Hem. H. AV14 7
Foxgrove Av., Beck. CE50 77
Foxgrove Dr., Wok. AT61 100
Foxgrove N14 BX27 38
Foxgrove Path. Wat. BD28 36
Foxgrove Rd., Beck. CE50 77
Foxhall Rd., Upmin. CY35 51
Foxham Rd. N19 BW34 47
Foxherne, Slou. AR41 62
Foxhills Rd., Cher. AT56 91
Foxhills Rd., Grays DE40 71
Brookmans Av.
Foxhole Rd. SE9 CK46 78
Foxholes, Wey. BA56 92
Foxhollow Dr., Bexh. CP45 69
Foxholme Clo., Chis. CL50 78
Foxholt Gdns. NW10 BN36 55
Foxhounds La., Grav. DD48 81
Foxlake Rd., Wey. AY59 92
Foxlands Cres., Dag. CS35 50
Foxlands Rd., Dag. CS35 50
Foxley Clo. E8 CB35 48
Foxley Clo., Loug. CL24 31
Foxley Clo., Red. BY73 121
Foxley Gdns., Pur. BY60 95
Foxley Hill Rd., Pur. BY59 95
Foxley La., Pur. BW59 95
Foxley Rd. SW9 BY43 66
Foxley Rd., Ken. BY60 95
Foxley Rd., Th.Hth. BY52 86
Foxleys, Wat. BE27 36
Foxmanor Way, Grays DA43 70
Foxmead Clo., Enf. BX24 29
Foxmore St. SW11 BU44 66
Foxoak Hill, Walt. BB58 92
Foxon Clo., Cat. CA64 105
Foxon La., Cat. BZ64 105
Foxon Lane Gdns., Cat. CA64 105
Foxs La., Hat. BQ15 10
Foxs Path, Mitch. BT51 86
Foxton Rd., Grays DB43 70
Foxton Rd., Hodd. CE12 12
Foxwarren, Esher BH58 93
Foxwell St. SE4 CD45 67
Foxwood Clo., Felt. BC48 73
Foxwood Dr., Dart. DA48 80
Foxwood Rd. SE3 CG45 68
Foyle Dr., S.Ock. DA39 60
Foyle Rd. N17 CB30 39
Foyle Rd. SE3 CG43 68
Frailey Clo., Wok. AT61 100
Frailey Hill, Wok. AT61 100
Framewood Rd., Slou. AR36 52
Framfield Clo. N12 BS27 38
Framfield Rd. N5 BY35 47
Framfield Rd. W7 BH39 54
Framfield Rd., Mitch. BV50 76
Framlingham Clo. E5 CB34 48
Southwold Rd.
Framlingham Cres. SE9 CK49 78
Frampton Clo., Sut. BS57 95
Frampton Park Est. E9 CC36 57
Frampton Park Rd. E9 CC36 57
Frampton Rd., Epp. CO17 23
Frampton Rd., Houns. BE45 64
Frampton Rd., Pot.B. BT18 20
Frampton St. NW8 BT38 1
Frampton St. NW8 BT38 56
Francemary Rd. SE4 CE46 77
Frances Gdns., S.Ock. CZ39 60
Frances Rd. E4 CE29 39
Frances Rd., Wind. AO44 61
Frances St. SE18 CK42 68
Frances St., Chesh. AO18 16
Franche Court Rd. SW17 BT48 76
Francis Av., Bexh. CR44 69
Francis Av., Felt. BC48 73
Francis Av., Har. BJ32 45
Francis Av., Ilf. CM34 49
Francis Av., St.Alb. BG12 9
Francis Barber Clo. SW16 BX49 76
Valley Rd.
Francis Chichester Way, SW11 BV44 66
Francis Clo. E14 CF42 67
Saunders Ness Rd.
Francis Clo., Epsom BN56 94
Francis Clo., Shep. AZ52 83
Francis Gro. SW19 BR50 75
Francis Rd. E10 CF33 48
Francis Rd. N2 BU31 47
Lynmouth Rd.
Francis Rd., Cat. BZ64 105
Francis Rd., Croy. BY53 86
Francis Rd., Dart. CV46 80
Francis Rd., Grnf. BJ37 54
Francis Rd., Har. BJ32 45
Francis Rd., Houns. BD44 64
Francis Rd., Ilf. CM34 49
Francis Rd., Orp. CP52 89
Francis Rd., Pnr. BD32 45
Francis Rd., Wall. BW57 95
Francis Rd., Wat. BC24 26
Francis St. E15 CG35 49
Francis St. SW1 BW42 3
Francis St. SW1 BW42 66
Francis St., Ilf. CM34 49
Francis Ter. N19 BW34 47
Francis Wk. N1 BX37 2
Bingfield St.
Franciscan Rd. SW17 BU49 76
Francklyn Gdns., Edg. BM27 37
Francombe Gdns., Rom. CU32 50
Franconia Rd. SW4 BW46 76
Frank Bailey Wk. E12 CK35 49
Gainsborough Av.
Frank Dixon Clo. SE21 CA47 77
Frank Dixon Way SE21 CA47 77
Frank St. E13 CH38 58
Frankfurt Rd. SE24 BZ46 77
Frankham St. SE8 CE43 67
Frankland Clo. SE16 CB41 67
Wardale Clo.
Frankland Clo., Rick. AZ26 35
Frankland Clo., Wdf.Grn. CJ28 40
Frankland Rd. E4 CE28 39
Frankland Rd., Rick. AZ25 26
Franklands Dr., Wey. AW57 92
Franklin Av., Chsnt. CB18 21
Franklin Clo. N20 BT26 38
Franklin Clo. SE27 BY48 76
Franklin Clo., Hem.H. AY15 8
Franklin Clo., Kings.T. BM52 85
Willingham Way
Franklin Clo., St.Alb. BO14 10
Franklin Cres., Mitch. BW52 86
Franklin Pass. SE9 CK45 68
Franklin Rd. SE20 CC50 77
Franklin Rd., Bexh. CQ44 69
Franklin Rd., Grav. DH49 81
Franklin Rd., Horn. CV36 60
Franklin Rd., Wat. BC23 26
Franklin Sq. SW5 BR42 65
Marchbank Rd.
Franklin St. E3 CE38 57
Bromley High St.
Franklin St. N15 CA32 48
Franklins Ms., Har. BG34 45
Franklins Row SW3 BU42 3
Franklins Row SW3 BU42 66
Franklyn Clo., Dag. CS36 59
Franklyn Cres., Wind. AL45 61
Franklyn Gdns., Ilf. CM29 40
Franklyn Rd. NW10 BO36 55
Franklyn Rd., Walt. BC53 83
Franklyns, Harl. CM11 13
Franks Av., N.Mal. BN52 85
Franks La., Hort.K. CX53 90
Franks Rd., Guil. AQ69 118
Franks Wood Av., Orp. CL53 88
Frankswood Av., West Dr. AY39 53
Franlaw Cres. N13 BZ28 39
Franmil Rd., Horn. CU33 50
Fransfield Gro. SE26 CB48 77
Frant Clo. SE20 CC50 77
Frant Rd., Th.Hth. BY53 86
Franthorne Way SE6 CE48 77
Randlesdown Rd.
Fraser Clo. E6 CK39 58
Linton Gdns.
Fraser Clo., Bex. CS48 79
Dartford Rd.
Fraser Gdns., Dor. BJ71 119
Fraser Rd. E17 CE32 48
Fraser Rd. N9 CB27 39
Fraser Rd., Chsnt. CD17 21
Fraser Rd., Erith CS42 69
Fraser Rd., Grnf. BJ37 54
Fraser St. W4 BO42 65
Frating Cres., Wdf.Grn. CH29 40
Frays Av., West Dr. AX41 63
Frays Clo., West Dr. AX41 63
Frays Lea, Uxb. AX37 53
Frays Waye, Uxb. AX37 53
Frazer Av., Ruis. BD35 45
Frazier St. SE1 BY41 4
Frazier St. SE1 BY41 66
Frean St. SE16 CB41 4
Frean St. SE16 CB41 67
Frederic St. E17 CD32 48
Frederica Rd. E4 CF26 39
Frederica St. N7 BX36 56
Caledonian Rd.
Frederick Andrews Ct., Grays DE43 71
Silverlocke Rd.
Frederick Clo. W2 BU39 56
Frederick Clo. W2 BU40 3
Frederick Clo., Sutt. BR56 94
Frederick Cres. SW9 BY43 66
Frederick Cres., Enf. CC23 30
Frederick Gdns., Sutt. BR56 94
Frederick Pl. SE18 CL42 68
Frederick Rd. SE17 BY43 4
Frederick Rd. SE17 BY43 66
Frederick Rd., Rain. CS37 59
Frederick Rd., Sutt. BR56 94
Frederick Sanger Rd., Guil. AO70 118
Frederick St. WC1 BX38 2
Frederick St. WC1 BX38 56
Frederick Ter. E8 CA36 2
Frederick Ter. E8 CA36 57
Fredericks Pl. EC2 BZ39 57
Old Jewry
Fredericks Pl. N12 BT28 38
Fredericks Row EC1 BY38 2
Sidney Gro.
Fredora Av., Hayes BB38 53
Free Prae Rd., Cher. AW54 83
Freeborne Gdns., Rain. CU36 59
Mungo Park Rd.
Freedom St. SW11 BU44 66
Freedown La., Sutt. BT60 95
Freegrove Rd. N7 BX35 47
Freeland Pk. NW4 BR30 37
Freeland Rd. W5 BL40 55
Freeland Way, Erith CU44 69
Freelands Av., S.Croy. CC58 96
Freelands Gro., Brom. CH51 88
Freelands Rd., Brom. CH51 88

Freelands Rd., Cob. BC60 92
Freeling St. N1 BX36 2
Freeman Clo., Nthlt. BE36 54
Freeman Clo., Shep. BB52 83
The Crofts
Freeman Ct., Chesh. AO18 16
Barnes Av.
Freeman Rd., Grav. DJ48 81
Freeman Rd., Mord. BT53 86
Freeman Way, Horn. CW32 51
Freemans Clo., Slou. AQ36 52
Freemans La., Hayes BB40 53
Freemantle Av., Enf. CC25 30
Freemantle Rd., Belv. CR42 69
Freemantle St. SE17 CA42 4
Freemasons Rd. E16 CH39 58
Freemasons Rd., Croy. CA54 87
Freesia Clo., Orp. CN56 97
Briarswood Way
Freethorpe Clo. SE19 BZ20 77
Freke Rd. SW11 BV45 66
Fremantle Ho., Til. DG44 71
Leicester Rd.
Fremantle Rd., Ilf. CM30 40
Fremantle St. SE17 CA42 67
Fremont St. E9 CC37 57
French Gdns., Cob. BD60 93
French Horn La., Hat. BP12 10
French Row, St.Alb. BG13 9
Market Pl.
French St., Sun. BD51 84
French Wells, Wok. AQ62 100
Frencham Ct., Mitch. BT52 86
Belgrave Rd.
Frenchaye, Wey. AX56 92
Frenches Dr., Red. BV69 121
The Frenches
Frenches Rd., Red. BV69 121
Frenches, The, Red. BV69 121
Frenchlands Hatch, Lthd. BB67 110
Frenchum Gdns., Slou. AM40 61
Frendsbury Rd. SE4 CC45 67
Frensham Clo., Sthl. BE38 54
Frensham Dr. SW15 BO48 75
Frensham Dr., Croy. CF57 96
Frensham Rd. SE9 CM48 78
Frensham Rd., Ken. BY60 95
Frensham St. SE15 CB43 67
Frensham Way, Epsom BQ61 103
Frensham, Chsnt. CA17 21
Frere St. SW11 BU44 66
Fresh Wharf Est., Bark. CL37 58
Fresh Wharf Rd., Bark. CL37 58
Freshborough Ct., Guil. AS71 118
Lower Edgeborough Rd.
Freshfield Clo. SE13 CF45 67
Marischal Rd.
Freshfield Dr. N14 BV26 38
Freshfields Av., Upmin. CX35 51
Freshfields, Croy. CD54 87
Freshford St. SW18 BT48 76
Freshmount Gdns., Epsom BM59 94
Freshwater Clo. SW17 BV50 76
Freshwater Rd. SW17 BV50 76
Freshwater Rd., Dag. CP33 50
Freshwaters, Harl. CN10 6
Freshwell Av., Rom. CP31 50
Freshwell Gdns., Brwd. DE32 123
Freshwood Clo., Beck. CE51 87
Freshwood Way, Wall. BV57 95
Fresley Clo. N15 BZ31 48
Clinton Rd.
Freston Gdns., Barn. BV25 29
Freston Pk. N3 BR30 37
Freston Rd. W10 BQ40 55
Freta Rd., Bexh. CQ46 79
Fretherne Rd., Welw.G.C. BQ 8 5
Frewin Rd. SW18 BT47 76
Friar Ms. SE27 BY48 76
Prioress Rd.
Friar Rd., Hayes BD38 54
Friar Rd., Orp. CO53 89
Friar St. EC4 BY39 2
Friar St. EC4 BY39 56
Carter La.
Friars Av. N20 BU27 38
Friars Av. SW15 BO48 75
Friars Av., Brwd. DD26 122
Friars Clo. N2 BT31 47
Friars Clo., Brwd. DD26 122
Friars Clo., Nthlt. BD38 54
Broomcroft Av.
Friars Field, Berk. AP11 7
Herons Elm
Friars Gate Clo., Wdf.Grn. CH28 40
Friars Gate, Guil. AQ71 118
Friars Gdns. W3 BN40 55
St. Dunstans Av.
Friars La., Rich. BK46 74
Friars Mead E14 CF41 67
Friars Ms. SE9 CL46 78
Friars Orchard, Lthd. BG64 102
Friars Place La. W3 BN40 55
Friars Rd. E6 CJ37 58
Friars Rd., Vir.W. AR52 82
Friars Ri., Wok. AT62 100
Friars Stile Pl., Rich. BL46 75
Friars Stile Rd.
Friars Stile Rd., Rich. BL46 75
Friars Way W3 BN39 55
Friars Way, Bush. BE23 27
Friars Way, Cher. AV53 82
Friars Way, Kings L. AZ18 17
Friars Wk. N14 BV26 38
Friars Wk. SE2 CP42 69
Friars Wk., Har. BH29 36
Friars Wood, Croy. CD58 96
Friars, The, Chig. CN28 40
Friars, The, Harl. CL12 13
Friarscroft, Brox. CE13 12
Friary Br., Guil. AR71 118
Friary Clo. N12 BU28 38
Friary Est. SE15 CB43 67
Friary La., Wdf.Grn. CH28 40
Friary Rd. N12 BT28 38
Friary Rd. SE15 CB43 67
Friary Rd. W3 BN39 55
Friary Rd., Stai. AR47 72
Friary St., Guil. AR71 118
Friary Way N12 BU28 38
Friary, The, Wind. AR46 72
Friday Hill E4 CG27 40
Friday Hill W. E4 CG27 40
Friday Hill, Belv. CR42 69
Friday Rd., Erith CS42 69
Friday Rd., Mitch. BU50 76
Friday St. EC4 BZ39 57
Cannon St.
Friday St. EC4 BZ40 4
Frideswide Pl. NW5 BW35 47
Islip St.
Friend St. EC1 BY38 2
Friend St. EC1 BY38 56
Friendly St. Ms. SE8 CE44 67
Friendly St. SE8 CE44 67
Friends Rd., Croy. BZ55 87
Friends Rd., Pur. BY59 95
Friendship Wk., Nthlt. BD38 54
Wayfarer Rd.
Friern Barnet La. N11 BT27 38
Friern Barnet La. N20 BT27 38
Friern Barnet Rd. N11 BU28 38
Friern Ct. N20 BT27 38
Friern Mount Dr. N20 BT26 38
Friern Pk. N12 BT28 38
Friern Rd. SE22 CB47 77
Friern Watch Av. N12 BT28 38
Frieze Hill, Brwd. CX26 42
Frigate Ms. SE8 CE43 67
Watergate St.
Frimley Av., Horn. CX33 51
Frimley Clo. SW19 BR48 75
Frimley Clo., Croy. CF57 96
Frimley Cres., Croy. CF57 96
Frimley Ct., Sid. CP49 79
Frimley Gdns., Mitch. BU52 86
Frimley Rd., Chess. BL56 94
Frimley Rd., Hem.H. AV13 7
Frimley Rd., Ilf. CN34 49
Frimley St. E1 CC38 57
Frimley Way
Frimley Vw., Wind. AL44 61
Frimley Way E1 CC38 57
Fringewood Clo., Nthwd. AZ30 35
Frinsted Clo., Orp. CP52 89
Frinsted Rd., Erith CS43 69
Frinton Clo., Wat. BC27 35
Frinton Dr., Wdf.Grn. CF29 39
Frinton Mews, Ilf. CL32 49
Bramley Cres.
Frinton Rd. E6 CJ38 58
Frinton Rd. N15 CA32 48
Frinton Rd. SW17 BV50 76
Frinton Rd., Rom. CQ29 41
Frinton Rd., Sid. CQ48 79
Friston Path, Chig. CN28 40
Manford Way
Friston St. SW6 BS44 66
Frith Ct. NW7 BR29 37
Frith Gdns. SW6 BR45 65
Frith Knowle, Walt. BC57 92
Frith La. NW7 BR29 37
Frith Rd. E11 CF35 48
Frith Rd., Croy. BZ55 87
Frith St. W1 BW39 1
Frith St. W1 BW39 56
Fritham Clo., N.Mal. BO53 85
Frithe, The, Slou. AR40 52
Friths Dr., Reig. BS69 121
Raglan Rd.
Frithsden Copse, Berk. AS11 7
Frithville Gdns. W12 BQ40 55
Frithwald Rd., Cher. AV54 82
Frithwood Av., Nthwd. BB28 35
Frizlands La., Dag. CR35 50
Frobisher Clo., Ken. BZ62 105
Hayes La.
Frobisher Clo., Pnr. BD33 45
Frobisher Cres., Stai. AY47 73
Frobisher Ct. SE23 CB48 77
Sydenham Ri.
Frobisher Gdns., Guil. AT70 118
Frobisher Gdns., Stai. AY47 73
Frobisher Rd. E6 CK39 58
Frobisher Rd. N8 BY31 47
Frobisher Rd., Erith CU43 69
Frobisher Rd., St.Alb. BK14 9
Frobisher St. SE10 CG43 68
Frobisher Way, Grav. DJ49 81
Frog La., Guil. AS66 109
Frog St., Brwd. CZ23 33
Froggy La., Uxb. AU34 43
Froghall La., Chig. CM28 40
Froghole La., Eden. CN70 115
Frogley Rd. SE22 CA45 67
Frogmoor La., Rick. AX27 35
Frogmore Av., Hayes BB38 53
Frogmore Clo., Slou. AN41 61
Frogmore Clo., Sutt. BQ55 85
Frogmore Ct., Rick. AX27 35
Frogmore La.
Frogmore Ct., Sthl. BF42 64
Norwood Rd.
Frogmore Dr., Wind. AP44 62
Frogmore Farm Est., Hayes BA38 53
Frogmore Gdns., Hayes BB38 53
Frogmore Gdns., Sutt. BQ56 94
Frogmore Rd., Hem.H. AX15 8
Frogmore SW18 BS46 76
Frognal Av., Har. BH31 45
Frognal Av., Sid. CO50 79
Frognal Clo. NW3 BT35 47
Frognal Ct. NW3 BT36 56
Frognal Gdns. NW3 BT35 47
Frognal La. NW3 BS35 47
Frognal NW3 BT35 47
Frognal Par. NW3 BT36 56
Frognal Ct.
Frognal Pl., Sid. CO50 79
Frognal Rd. NW3 BT36 56
Frognal Ri. NW3 BT34 47
Frognal Way NW3 BT35 47
Froissart Rd. SE9 CJ46 78
Frome Sq., Hem.H. AY11 8
Frome St. N1 BZ37 2
Frome St. N1 BZ37 57
Fromondes Rd., Sutt. BR56 94
Front La., Upmin. CZ33 51
Front, The, Berk. AT11 7
Frostic Pl. E1 CA39 57
Hopetown
Frostic Wk. E1 CA39 57
Chicksand St.
Froude St. SW8 BW44 66
Robertson St.
Frowick Clo., Hat. BP15 10
Frowyke Cres., Pot.B. BP19 19
Fruen Rd., Felt. BB47 73
Fry Clo., Rom. CR28 41
Fry Rd. E6 CJ36 58
Fry Rd. NW10 BO37 55
Fry Rd., Ashf. AX49 73
Fryatt Rd. N17 BZ29 39
Fryatt St. E14 CG39 58
Fryent Clo. NW9 BM32 46
Fryent Cres. NW9 BO32 46
Fryent Fields NW9 BO32 46
Fryent Gro. NW9 BO32 46
Fryent Way NW9 BM32 46
Fryer Clo., Chesh. AO20 16
Fryern Wood, Cat. BZ64 105
Frying Pan All. E1 CA39 2
Frying Pan All. E1 CA39 57
Bell La.
Fryston Av., Couls. BV60 95
Fryston Av., Croy. CB55 87
Fryth Mead, St.Alb. BF13 9
Fuchsia St. SE2 CO42 69
Fulbeck Dr. NW9 BO30 37
Fulbeck Way, Har. BG30 36
Fulbourne Est. E1 CB38 57
Fulbourne Rd. E17 CF30 39
Fulbourne St. E1 CB39 57
Durward St.
Fulbrook La., S.Ock. CZ40 60
Fulbrook Rd. N19 BW35 47
Junction Rd.
Fuley Rd., West. CJ62 106
Fulford Gro., Wat. BC27 35
Fulford Rd., Cat. BZ64 105
Fulford Rd., Epsom BN57 94
Fulford St. SE16 CB41 67
Fulham Broadway SW6 BS43 66
Fulham Clo., Uxb. BA38 53
Fulham Ct. SW6 BS44 66
Fulham Est. SW6 BR43 65
Fulham High St. SW6 BR44 65
Fulham Palace Rd. SW6 BQ43 65
Fulham Palace Rd. W6 BQ42 65
Fulham Park Gdns. SW6 BR44 65
Fulham Park Rd. SW6 BR44 65
Fulham Rd. SW10 BR44 65
Fulham Rd. SW10 BT42 3
Fulham Rd. SW3 BR44 65
Fulham Rd. SW6 BR44 65
Fulham Rd. SW8 BR44 65
Fullarton Cres., S.Ock. DA40 60
Fullbrook Av., Wey. AW59 92
Fullbrooks Av., Wor.Pk. BO54 85
Fuller Clo., Orp. CN56 97
Fuller Gdns., Wat. BC22 26
Fuller Rd., Dag. CO34 50
Fuller Rd., Wat. BC22 26
Fuller St. E2 CB38 2
Fuller St. E2 CB38 57
Cheshire St.
Fuller St. NW4 BQ31 46
Fuller Way, Hayes BB42 63
Fuller Way, Rick. AZ25 26
Fullers Av., Surb. BL55 85
Fullers Av., Wdf.Grn. CG29 40
Fullers Clo., Rom. CS29 41
Fullers Clo., Wal.Abb. CH20 22
Fullers Hill, West. CM66 115
High St.
Fullers La., Rom. CS29 41
Fullers Mead, Harl. CP11 14
Fullers Rd. E18 CG30 40
Fullers St., Sev. CX63 108
Fullers Way N., Surb. BL55 85
Fullers Way S., Chess. BL56 94
Fullers Wood La., Red. BW71 121
Fullers Wood, Croy. CE56 96
Fullerton Clo., Wey. AY60 92
Fullerton Dr., Wey. AY60 92
Fullerton Rd. SW18 BT46 76
Fullerton Rd., Cars. BU58 95
Fullerton Rd., Croy. CA54 87
Fullerton Rd., Wey. AY60 92
Fullerton Way, Wey. AY60 92
Fullmer Way, Wey. AV58 91
Fullwell Av., Ilf. CK30 40
Fullwoods Ms. N1 BZ38 2
Fullwoods Ms. N1 BZ38 57
Bevenden St.
Fulmar Cres., Hem.H. AW14 8
Fulmar Rd., Rain. CU36 59
Fulmead St. SW6 BS44 66
Fulmer Clo., Hmptn. BE49 74
Fulmer Common Rd., Slou. & Iver AR36 52
Fulmer Dr., Ger.Cr. AR34 43
Fulmer La., Ger.Cr. AS34 43
Fulmer Rd. E15 CJ39 58
Fulmer Rd., Ger.Cr. AS33 43
Fulmer Way W13 BJ41 64
Fulmer Way, Ger.Cr. AS32 43
Fulready Rd. E10 CF32 48
Fulstone Clo., Houns. BE45 64
Fulthorp Rd. SE3 CG44 68
Fulton Ms. W2 BT40 3
Fulton Ms. W2 BT40 56
Porchester Ter.
Fulton Rd., Wem. BM34 46
Fulton St. E16 CG39 58
George St.
Fulwell Pk. Av., Twick. BF48 74
Fulwell Rd., Tedd. BG49 74
Fulwich Rd., Dart. CW46 80
Fulwood Av., Wem. BL37 55
Fulwood Clo., Hayes BB39 53
Fulwood Gdns. Twick. BJ46 74
Fulwood Pl. WC1 BX39 2
Fulwood Pl. WC1 BX39 56
Fulwood Wk. SW19 BR47 75
Furber St. W6 BP41 65
Furham Flds., Pnr. BF29 36
Furley Pl. N1 BY36 56
Islington Park St.
Furley Rd. SE15 CB44 67
Furlong Clo., Wall. BV54 86
Furlong Rd. N7 BY36 56
Furlong Rd., Dor. BG72 119
Furlongs, Hem.H. AW13 8
Furmage St. SW18 BS47 76
Furmingers Rd., Orp. CR56 98
Furneaux Av., SE27 BY49 76
Furner Clo., Dart. CT45 69
Furness Clo., Grays DG42 71
St. Johns Rd.
Furness Pl., Wind. AL44 61
Furness
Furness Rd. NW10 BP37 55
Furness Rd. SW6 BS44 66
Furness Rd., Har. BF33 45
Furness Rd., Mord. BS54 86
Furness Row, Wind. AL44 61
Furness
Furness Sq., Wind. AL44 61
Furness
Furness Way, Horn. CU35 50
Furness Way, Wind. AL44 61
Furness Wk., Wind. AL44 61
Furness
Furness, Wind. AL44 61
Furnival Clo., Vir.W. AR53 82
Furnival St. EC4 BY39 2
Furnival St. EC4 BY39 56
Furrow La. E9 CC35 48
Furrowfield, Hat. BP11 10
Crop Common
Furrows Pl., Cat. CA65 105
Furrows, The, Uxb. AX32 44
Furrows, The, Walt. BD55 84
Fursby Av. N3 BS29 38
Furse Av., St.Alb. BJ11 9
Further Acre NW9 BO37 37
Further Green Rd. SE6 CG47 78
Furtherfield Clo., Croy. BY53 86
Boston Rd.
Furtherfield, Wat. BB19 17
Furtherground, Hem.H. AY13 8
Wood Farm Rd.
Furze Clo., Red. BU70 121
Furze Clo., Wat. BD28 36
Furze Farm Clo., Rom. CQ30 41
Furze Field, Lthd. BH60 93
Furze Gro., Tad. BR64 103
Furze Hill, Pur. BX59 95
Furze Hill, Red. BU70 121
Furze Hill, Tad. BR64 103
Furze La., Pur. BX59 95
Furze Rd., Hem.H. AV14 7
Furze Rd., Th.Hth. BZ52 87
Furze Rd., Wey. AV57 91
Furze St. E3 CE39 57
Furze Vw., Rick. AU25 25
Furze Wood, Sun. BC51 83
Furzebushes La., St.Alb. BE16 18
Furzedown Dr. SW17 BV49 76
Furzedown Rd. SW17 BV49 76
Furzedown Rd., Sutt. BT59 95
Furzefield Clo., Chis. CL50 78
Furzefield Cres., Reig. BT71 121
Furzefield Rd. SE3 CH43 68
Furzefield Rd., Welw.G.C. BR 8 5
Furzefield Rd., Reig. BT71 121
Furzefield, Chsnt. CB17 21
Flamstead End Rd.
Furzeham Rd., West Dr. AY41 63
Furzehill Par., B.Wd. BM24 28
Furzehill Rd.
Furzehill Rd., B.Wd. BM24 28
Furzen Cres., Hat. BO14 10
Fusedale Way, S.Ock. CZ40 60
Fyfe Ter. N1 BX37 2
Fyfe Way, Brom. CH51 88
Lownds Av.
Fyfield Clo., Brom. CF52 87
Fyfield Clo., Brwd. DE32 123
Fyfield Ct. E7 CH36 58
Fyfield Rd. E17 CF31 48
Fyfield Rd. SW9 BY45 66
Fyfield Rd., Enf. CA24 30
Fyfield Rd., Moreton CW13 15
Fyfield Rd., Ong. CX16 24
Fyfield Rd., Rain. CT37 59
Fyfield Rd., Wdf.Grn. CJ29 40
Fyfield Rd., Willingale DA13 15
Fynes St. SW1 BW42 66
Regency St.
Fynes St. W1 BW42 3

G

Gabion Av., Grays CY42 70
Gable Clo., Dart. CU46 79
Gable Clo., Pnr. BF29 36
Gable Clo., Wat. BB19 17
Gable Ct. SE26 CB49 77
Gables Av., Ashf. AY49 73
Gables Av., B.Wd. BL24 28
Gables Clo. SE12 CH47 78
Gables Clo., Ger.Cr. AS28 34
Gables Clo., Slou. AQ43 62
Gables Clo., Wok. AS63 100
Gables, The, Bans. BR62 103
Gables, The, Grays DC42 71
Gables, The, Lthd. BG59 93
Gabriel Clo., Felt. BD49 74
Gabriel Clo., Rom. CS29 41
Gabriel Spring Rd., Dart. CZ55 90
Gabriel St. SE23 CC47 77
Gabrielle Clo., Wem. BL34 46
Gabriels Gdns., Grav. DJ49 81
Gadbrook Rd., Bet. BN73 120
Gaddesden Av., Wem. BL36 55
Gaddesden Cres., Wat. BD20 18
Gaddesdon Gro., Welw.G.C. BT 8 5
Chilton Grn.
Gade Av., Wat. BB24 26
Gade Bk., Rick. BA24 26
Gade Clo., Hayes BC40 53
Gade Clo., Hem.H. AW12 8
Gade Vall. Clo., Kings L. AZ17 17
Gade View Gdns., Kings L. BA19 17
Gade View Rd., Hem.H. AX15 8
Gadebridge La., Hem.H. AW12 8
Gadebridge Rd., Hem.H. AW12 8
Gadesden Rd., Epsom BN57 94
Gadeside, Wat. BA21 26
Gadsden Clo., Upmin. CZ32 51
Gadwall Way SE28 CM41 68
Gadwell Clo., Wat. BE21 27
Gage Rd. E16 CG39 58
Gage St. WC1 BX39 56
Boswell St.
Gainford St. N1 BY37 2
Gainford St. N1 BY37 56
Gains Av. E11 CF34 48
Gains Sq., Bexh. CP45 69
Gainsborough Av. E12 CL35 49
Gainsborough Av., St.Alb. BH13 9
Gainsborough Av., Dart. CV46 80
Gainsborough Av., Til. DG44 71
Gainsborough Clo., Esher BH54 84
Gainsborough Clo., Beck. CD50 77
Brackley Rd.
Gainsborough Ct., Walt. BC55 83
Gainsborough Dr., S.Croy CB60 96
Gainsborough Dr., Grav. DE48 81
Gainsborough Dr., S.Croy. CB60 96
Gainsborough Gdns. NW11 BR33 46
Gainsborough Gdns. NW3 BT34 47
Gainsborough Gdns., Islw. BG46 74
Gainsborough Gdns., Grnf. BH35 45
Gainsborough Gdns., Edg. BL30 37
Gainsborough Ms. SE26 CB48 77
Panmure Rd.
Gainsborough Rd. E11 CG33 49
Gainsborough Rd. E15 CG38 58
Gainsborough Rd. N12 BS28 38
Gainsborough Rd. W4 BO42 65
Gainsborough Rd., N.Mal. BN53 85
Gainsborough Rd., Wdf.Grn. CK29 40
Gainsborough Rd., Dag. CO35 50
Gainsborough Rd., Epsom BN58 94
Gainsborough Rd., Hayes BA37 53
Gainsborough Rd., Rain. CU37 59
Gainsborough Rd., Rich. BL44 65
Gainsborough Sq., Bexh. CP45 69
Regency Way
Gainsford Rd. E17 CD31 48
Gainsford St. SE1 CA41 4
Gainsford St. SE1 CA41 67
Gainsthorpe Rd., Ong. CV15 15
Gainswood, Welw.G.C. BR 8 5
Gairloch Rd. SE5 CA44 67
Gaisford St. NW5 BW36 56
Gaist Av., Cat. CB64 105
Gaitskell Rd. SE9 CM47 78
Galahad Clo., Slou. AN41 61
Mitchell Clo.
Galahad Rd., Brom. CH48 78
Galata Rd. SW13 BP43 65
Galatia Sq. SE15 CB45 67
Scylla Rd.
Galbraith St. E14 CF41 67
Galdana Av., Barn. BT24 29
Gale Clo., Hmptn. BE50 74
Gale Clo., Mitch. BT52 86
Gale Cres., Bans. BS62 104
Gale Grn., S.Ock. DA39 60
Gale St. E3 CE39 57
Gale St., Dag. CP37 59
Galeborough Av., Wdf.Grn. CF29 39
Galen Pl. WC1 BX39 2
Galen Pl. WC1 BX39 56
Bury Pl.
Galena Rd. W6 BP42 65
Gales Clo., Guil. AU69 118
Gilliat Dr.
Gales Gdns. E2 CB38 57
Bethnal Green Rd.
Galesbury Rd. SW18 BT46 76
Galesway, Wdf.Grn. CK29 40
Galey Grn., S.Ock. DA39 60
Galgate Clo. SW19 BR47 75
Gallants Farm Rd., Barn. BU26 38
Galleon Boul., Dart. CY45 70
Galleon Clo. SE16 CC41 67
Kinburn St.
Gallery Gdns., Nthlt. BD37 54
Gallery Rd. SE21 BZ47 77
Galley Hill Rd., Grav. DC46 81
Galley Hill, Hem.H. AV12 7
Galley La., Barn. BP23 28

Galleyhill Rd., Wal.Abb. CG19 22
Galleymead Rd., Slou. AV44 62
Galleywall Rd. SE16 CB42 67
Galleywood Cres., Rom. CS29 41
Gallia Rd. N5 BY35 47
Calabria Rd.
Galliard Clo. N9 CC25 30
Galliard Rd. N9 CB26 39
Gallions Clo., Bark. CO38 59
Gallions La., Slou. AR38 52
Gallions Rd. E16 CL40 58
Gallions Rd. SE7 CH42 68
Gallon Clo. SE7 CJ42 68
Gallop, The, S.Croy. CB57 96
Gallop, The, Sutt. BT58 95
Gallop, The, Wind. AO47 72
Gallosson Rd. SE18 CN42 68
Galloway Clo., Brox. CD16 21
Galloway Rd. W12 BP40 55
Gallows Cor., Rom. CV30 42
Gallows Hill La., Wat. BA19 17
Gallows Hill, Kings L. BA19 17
Gallows Wood, Fawk. DA56 99
Gallus Clo. N21 BX25 29
Gallus Sq. SE3 CH45 68
Gallys Rd., Wind. AL44 61
Galpins Rd., Th.Hth. BX53 86
Galsworthy Av., Rom. CO33 50
Galsworthy Clo. SE28 CO40 59
Galsworthy Cres. SE3 CJ44 68
Merriman Rd.
Galsworthy Rd. NW2 BR35 46
Galsworthy Rd., Cher. AW54 83
Galsworthy Rd., King.T. BM50 75
Galsworthy Rd., Til. DH44 71
Galton St. W10 BR38 55
Galva Clo., Barn. BV24 29
Galveston Rd. SW15 BR46 75
Galvins Clo., Guil. AQ69 118
Galway St. EC1 BZ38 2
Gambetta St. SW8 BV44 66
Gambia St. SE1 BY40 4
Gambia St. SE1 BY40 56
Gambles La., Wok. AX65 101
Gambole Rd. SW17 BU49 76
Games Rd., Barn. BU24 29
Gamlen Rd. SW15 BQ45 65
Gammon Clo., Hem.H. AZ14 8
Bennets End Rd.
Gammons Farm Clo., Wat. BB21 26
Gammons La., Brox. CA16 21
Gammons La., Wat. BB21 26
Gander Green La., Sutt. BR56 94
Ganders Ash, Wat. BC20 17
Gane Clo., Wall. BX57 95
Gangers Hill, Gdse. CD67 114
Ganghill, Guil. AT69 118
Gant Ct., Wal.Abb. CG20 22
Ganton St. W1 BW40 3
Ganton St. W1 BW40 56
Kingly St.
Gantshill Cres., Ilf. CL32 49
Gantshill Cross, Ilf. CL32 49
Ganymede Pl., Hem.H. AY12 8
Gap Rd. SW19 BS49 76
Garage Rd. W3 BM39 55
Garbrand Wk., Epsom BO58 94
Lyncroft Gdns.
Garbutt Pl. W1 BV39 1
Garbutt Pl. W1 BV39 56
Garbutt Rd., Upmin. CY34 51
Gard St. EC1 BY38 2
Moreland St.
Gard St. EC1 BY38 56
Masons Pl.
Garden Av., Bexh. CR45 69
Garden Av., Hat. BP14 10
Garden Av., Mitch. BV50 76
Garden City, Edg. BM29 37
Garden Clo. E4 CE28 39
Garden Clo. SE12 CH48 78
Garden Clo. SW15 BP47 75
Bristol Gdns.
Garden Clo., Ashf. BA50 73
Garden Clo., Bans. BS61 104
Garden Clo., Barn. BQ24 28
Garden Clo., Hmptn. BE49 74
Garden Clo., Lthd. BK66 111
Garden Clo., Nthlt. BE37 54
Garden Clo., Ruis. BB34 44
Garden Clo., St.Alb. BJ13 9
Garden Clo., Wall. BX56 95
Garden Clo., Wat. BB23 26
Garden Clo., Wey. AX56 92
Garden Cotts., Epsom BO59 94
East St.
Garden Ct. EC4 BY40 4
Fountain Ct.
Garden Ct. EC4 BY40 56
Fountain Ct.
Garden Ct. SE15 CA44 67
Sumner Est.
Garden Ct., Rich. BL44 65
Garden Ct., Welw.G.C. BR7 5
Garden End, Amer. AP22 25
Garden Fields, Ong. CW20 24
Garden La. SW2 BX47 76
Garden La., Brom. CH50 78
Garden Ms. W2 BS40 56
Linden Gdns.
Garden Pl., Dart. CV48 80
Garden Rd. NW8 BT38 1
Garden Rd. NW8 BT38 56
Garden Rd. SE20 CC51 87
Garden Rd., Brom. CH50 78
Garden Rd., Rich. BM45 65
Garden Rd., Sev. CV64 108
Garden Rd., Walt. BC53 83
Garden Rd., Wat. BB19 17
Garden Reach, Ch.St.G. AR24 25
Garden Row SE1 BY41 4
Garden Row SE1 BY41 66
Garden Row, Grav. DF48 81
Haynes Rd.
Garden St. E1 CC39 57
Garden Ter. Rd., Harl. CP9 6
Garden Ter. SW1 BW42 3
Garden Ter. SW1 BW42 66
Moreton St.
Garden Way NW10 BN36 55
Garden Way, Cat. BZ64 105
Garden Way, Loug. CL22 31
Garden Wk. EC2 CA38 2
Garden Wk. EC2 CA38 57
Rivington St.
Garden Wk., Beck. CP51 87
Hayne Rd.
Garden Wk., Couls. BV65 104
Gardeners Rd. E3 CC37 57
Gardeners Rd., Croy. BY54 86
Albion St.
Gardenia Rd., Enf. CA25 30
Gardens, The N16 CA33 48
Gardens, The N8 BX31 47
Rectory Gdns.
Gardens, The SE22 CB45 67
Gardens, The, Beck. CF51 87
Gardens, The, Brwd. DA21 33
Gardens, The, Esher BF56 93
Gardens, The, Felt. BA46 73
Gardens, The, Har. BG32 45
Gardens, The, Hat. BR17 19
Gardens, The, Pnr. BE32 45
Gardens, The, Wat. BB23 26
Gardiner Av. NW2 BQ35 46
Gardiner Clo., Orp. CP51 89
Gardner Clo. E11 CH32 49
Gardner Gro., Felt. BE48 74
Gardner Rd. E13 CH38 58
Gardner Rd., Guil. AR70 118
Gardners La., EC4 BZ40 4
Gardners Wk. Lthd. BF66 111
Gardnor Rd. NW3 BT35 47
Flask Wk.
Garendon Gdns., Mord. BS54 86
Garendon Rd., Mord. BS54 86
Gareth Clo., Wor.Pk. BW55 85
Burnham Dr.
Gareth Gro., Brom. CH49 78
Garfield Pl., Wind. AO44 61
Albany Rd.
Garfield Rd. E13 CG38 58
Garfield Rd. E4 CF26 39
Garfield Rd. SW11 BV45 66
Garfield Rd. SW19 BT49 76
Garfield Rd., Enf. CC24 30
Garfield Rd., Twick. BJ47 74
York St.
Garfield Rd., Wey. AX56 92
Garfield St., Wat. BC22 26
Garford St. E14 CE40 57
Garganey Wk. SE28 CP40 59
Garibaldi Rd., Red. BU71 121
Garibaldi St. SE18 CN42 68
Garland Clo., Hem.H. AX13 8
Allandale
Garland Rd. SE18 CM43 68
Garland Rd., Stan. BL30 37
Garland Way, Horn. CW31 51
Garlands Rd., Lthd. BJ64 102
Garlands Rd., Red. BU71 121
Garlands, Ton. CY71 117
Garlichill Rd., Epsom BP62 103
Garlick Hill EC4 BZ40 4
Garlick Hill EC4 BZ40 57
Queen Victoria St.
Garlies Rd. SE23 CD48 77
Garlinge Rd., NW2 BR36 55
Garman Rd. N18 CC29 39
Garnault Ms. EC1 BY38 2
Garnault Ms. EC1 BY38 56
Hardwick St.
Garnault Pl. EC1 BY38 2
Garnault Pl. EC1 BY38 56
Myddleton St.
Garnault Rd., Enf. CA22 30
Garner Dr., Brox. CD16 21
Garner Rd. E17 CF30 39
Garner St. E2 CB37 57
Coate St.
Garners Clo., Ger.Cr. AS29 34
Garners End, Ger.Cr. AS29 34
Garners Rd., Ger.Cr. AS29 34
Garnet Clo., Slou. AN41 61
Garnet Rd. NW10 BO36 55
Garnet Rd., Th.Hth. BZ52 87
Garnet St. E1 CC40 57
Garnet Wk. E6 CK39 58
Kingfisher St.
Garnett Clo. SE9 CK45 68
Garnett Clo., Wat. BD22 27
Garnett Dr., St.Alb. BF18 18
Garnett Rd. NW3 BU35 47
Garnett Way E17 CD30 39
McEntee Av.
Garnham Clo. N16 CA34 48
Smalley Rd.
Garnham St. N16 CA34 48
High St.
Garnies Clo. SE15 CA43 67
Thruxton Rd.
Garnon Mead, Epp. CP17 23
Garrads Rd. SW16 BW48 76
Garrard Clo., Bexh. CR45 69
Garrard Clo., Chis. CL49 78
Garrard Rd., Bans. BS61 104
Garratt Clo., Croy. BX56 95
Croydon Rd.
Garratt La. SW18 BS46 76
Garratt Rd., Edg. BM29 37
Garratt Ter. SW17 BU49 76
Garratts La., Bans. BR61 103
Garratts Rd., Bush. BG26 36
Garrett St. EC1 BZ38 2
Garrett St. EC1 BZ38 57
Garrick Av. NW11 BR32 46
Garrick Clo. SW18 BT45 66
Garrick Clo. W5 BL38 55
Garrick Clo., Rich. BK46 74
The Green
Garrick Clo., Stai. AW50 73
Garrick Clo., Walt. BC56 92
Garrick Cres., Croy. CB55 86
Garrick Dr. NW4 BQ30 37
Garrick Dr. SE18 CM41 68
Garrick Gdns., E.Mol. BF52 84
Garrick Pk. NW4 BQ30 37
Garrick Rd. NW9 BO32 46
Garrick Rd., Grnf. BF38 54
Garrick Rd., Rich. BM44 65
Garrick St. WC2 BX40 4
Garrick St. WC2 BX40 56
Garrick Way NW4 BQ31 46
Garrison Clo. SE18 CL44 68
Red Lion La.
Garrison La., Chess. BK57 93
Garrod St., Grav. DG46 81
New Rd.
Garron La., S.Ock. CZ40 60
Garry Clo., Rom. CT29 41
Garry Way, Rom. CT29 41
Garside Clo. SE28 CM41 68
Goosander Way
Garside Clo., Hmptn. BF50 74
Garsington Ms. SE4 CD45 67
Garsmouth Way, Wat. BD21 27
Garson La., Stai. AR47 72
Garson Rd., Esher BE56 93
Garston Cres., Wat. BD20 18
Garston Dr., Wat. BD20 18
Garston La., Ken. BZ60 96
Garston La., Wat. BD20 18
Garston Park Par., Wat. BD20 18
Garstons, The, Lthd. BF66 111
Garth Clo., Kings.T. BL49 75
Garth Clo., Mord. BQ54 85
Garth Clo., Ruis. BD33 45
Garth Ct. W4 BO42 65
Garth Rd.
Garth Ms. W5 BL38 55
Greystoke Gdns.
Garth Rd. NW2 BR34 46
Garth Rd. W4 BN43 65
Garth Rd., King.T. BL49 75
Garth Rd., Mord. BQ53 85
Garth Rd., S.Ock. DB38 60
Garth Rd., Sev. CV67 117
Garth, The, Cob. BE60 93
Garth, The, Har. BL32 46
Garth, The, Hmptn. BF50 74
Garth, The, Wat. BA20 17
Garthland Dr., Barn. BP25 28
Garthorne Rd. SE23 CC47 77
Garthside, Rich. BL49 75
Garthway N12 BU29 38
Gartlett Rd., Wat. BD25 27
Gartmoor Gdns. SW19 BR47 75
Gartmore Rd., Ilf. CN34 49
Garton Pl. SW18 BT46 76
Gartons Clo., Enf. CC24 30
Garfield Rd.
Gartons Way SW11 BT45 66
Garvary Rd. E16 CH39 58
Garvock Dr., Sev. CU66 116
Kippington Rd.
Garway Rd. W2 BS39 56
Gas La., Maid. AG41 61
Hibbert Rd.
Gas Works La., Brox. CE13 12
Gas Works Rd., Sthl. BE41 64
Gascoigne Gdns., Wdf.Grn. CG29 40
Gascoigne Pl. E2 CA38 2
Gascoigne Pl. E2 CA38 57
Gascoigne Rd., Bark. CM37 58
Gascoigne Rd., Croy. CF58 96
Gascoigne Rd., Wey. AZ55 83
Gascony Av. NW6 BS36 56
Gascoyne Clo., Pot.B. BP19 19
Gascoyne Dr., Dart. CT45 69
Gascoyne Est. E9 CD36 57
Gascoyne Rd. E9 CC36 57
Gaselee St. E14 CF40 57
Gasholder Pl. SE11 BX42 4
Gasholder Pl. SE11 BX42 66
Gaskarth Rd. SW12 BV46 76
Gaskarth Rd., Edg. BN30 37
Gaskell Rd. N6 BU32 47
Gaskell St. SW4 BX44 66
Gaskin St. N1 BY37 2
Gaskin St. N1 BY37 56
Gaspar Ms. SW5 BS42 3
Gaspar Ms. SW5 BS42 66
Courtfield Gdns.
Gassiot Rd. SW17 BU49 76
Gassiot Way, Sutt. BT55 86
Gasson Rd., Swans. DC46 81
Gastein Rd. W6 BQ43 65
Gaston Bell Clo., Rich. BL45 65
Gaston Bridge Rd., Shep. BA53 83
Gaston Rd., Mitch. BV52 86
Gaston Way, Shep. BA53 83
Gataker St. SE16 CB41 67
Gatcombe Rd. N19 BW34 47
Gate Clo., B.Wd. BN23 28
Danziger Way
Gate End, Nthwd. BC29 35
Gate St. WC2 BX39 2
Gate St. WC2 BX39 56
Kingsway
Gateforth St. NW8 BU38 1
Gateforth St. NW8 BU38 56
Gatehill Rd., Nthwd. BB29 35
Gatehope Dr., S.Ock. CZ39 60
Gatehouse Clo., Kings.T. BN51 85
Gately Rd. SW9 BX45 66
Gates Green Rd., W.Wick. CG55 88
Gatesborough St. EC2 CA38 2
Phipp St.
Gatesborough St. EC2 CA38 57
Phipp St.
Gatesby St. SE17 BZ42 4
Gatesby St. SE17 BZ42 67
Gatesden Rd., Lthd. BG65 102
Gateshead Rd., B.Wd. BL23 28
Gateside Rd. SW17 BU48 76
Gatestone Rd. SE19 CA50 77
Gateway Av. N1 BY37 2
Islington High St.
Gateway Av. N1 BY37 56
Islington High St.
Gateway Clo., Nthwd. BA29 35
Gateway SE17 BZ43 4
Gateway SE17 BZ43 67
Gateway Trd. Est. NW10 BO38 55
Gateway, The, Wok. AU60 91
Gateway, Wey. AZ55 83
Palace Dr.
Gateways, Guil. AT70 118
Gateways, Surb. BL53 85
Surbiton Hill Rd.
Gateways, The SW3 BU42 3
Gateways, The SW3 BU42 66
Whiteheads Gro.
Gatewick Clo., Slou. AP40 52
Gatfield Gro., Felt. BF48 74
Gathorne Rd. N22 BY30 38
Gathorne St. E2 CC37 57
Gatley Av., Epsom BM56 94
Gatliff Rd. SW1 BV42 3
Gatliff Rd. SW1 BV42 66
Gatling Rd. SE2 CO42 69
Gatting Clo., Edg. BM29 37
Pavilion Way
Gatting Way, Uxb. AY36 53
Gatton Bottom, Red. BU67 113
Gatton Clo., Reig. BT69 121
Gatton Clo., Sutt. BS58 95
Gatton Park Rd., Reig. & Red. BT69 121
Gatton Rd. SW17 BU49 76
Gatton Rd., Reig. BT69 121
Gattons Way, Sid. CQ49 79
Gatward Clo. N21 BY25 29
Gatward Grn. N9 CA27 39
Gatwick Rd. SW18 BR47 75
Gatwick Rd., Grav. DG48 81
Gatwick Way, Horn. CW34 51
Gauden Clo. SW4 BW44 66
Gauden Rd. SW4 BW44 66
Gaumont App., Wat. BC24 26
Gaunt St. SE1 BY41 4
Gaunt St. SE1 BZ41 67
Newington Causeway
Gauntlet Clo., Nthlt. BE36 54
Gauntlet Cres., Ken. BZ63 105
Gauntlett Ct., Wem. BJ35 45
Gauntlett Rd., Sutt. BT56 95
Gautrey Rd. SE15 CC44 67
Gautrey Sq. E6 CK39 58
Truesdale Rd.
Gavel St. SE17 BZ42 4
Gavel St. SE17 BZ42 67
Mason St.
Gavell Rd., Cob. BC60 92
Gavenny Path, S.Ock. CZ39 60
Gaveston Dr., Berk. AQ12 7
Gaveston Rd., Lthd. BJ63 102
Gavestone Clo., Wey. AY60 92
Gavestone Rd. SE12 CH47 78
Gavin St. SE18 CN42 68
Gavina Clo., Mord. BT53 86
Gaviots Clo., Ger.Cr. AS33 43
Gaviots Grn., Ger.Cr. AS33 43
Gaviots Way, Ger.Cr. AS33 43
Gawber St. E2 CC38 57
Gawsworth Clo. E15 CG35 49
Gawthorne Av. NW7 BR28 37
Gay Clo. NW2 BP35 46
Gay Gdns., Dag. CS35 50
Gay Rd. E15 CF37 57
Gay St. SW15 BQ45 65
Gaydon La. NW9 BO30 37
Gayfere Rd., Epsom BP56 94
Gayfere Rd., Ilf. CK31 49
Gayfere St. SW1 BX41 4
Gayfere St. SW1 BX41 66
Great Peter St.
Gayford Rd. W12 BO41 65
Gayhurst Rd. E8 CB36 57
Gaylor Rd., Nthlt. BE35 45
Gaylor Rd., Til. DF44 71
Gaynes Ct., Upmin. CX35 51
Gaynes Hill Rd., Wdf.Grn. CK29 40
Gaynes Park Rd., Upmin. CX35 51
Gaynes Parkway, Upmin. CW34 51
Gaynes Rd., Upmin. CX34 51
Gaynesford Rd. SE23 CC48 77
Gaynesford Rd., Cars. BU57 95
Gays La., Maid. AG43 61
Gaysham Av., Ilf. CL32 49
Gayton Clo., Amer. AP21 25
Gayton Cres., NW3 BT35 47
Gayton Rd. NW3 BT35 47
Gayton Rd. SE2 CP42 69
Wilton Rd.
Gayton Rd., Har. BH32 45
Gayville Rd. SW11 BU46 76
Gaywood Av., Chsnt. CC18 21
Gaywood Clo. SW2 BY47 76
Gaywood Est. SE1 BY41 66
Gaywood Rd. E17 CE31 48
Gaywood Rd., Ash. BL62 103
Gaywood St. SE1 BY41 4
Gaywood St. SE1 BY41 66
Gaza St. SE17 BY42 4
Gaza St. SE17 BY42 66
Gazeley Ct. SE19 CA49 77
Gipsy Hill
Gazelle Glade, Grav. DJ49 81
Gean Wk., Hat. BP14 10
Southdown Rd.
Geariesville Gdns., Ilf. CL31 49
Geary Ct., Brwd. DB26 42
Geary Dr.
Geary Dr., Brwd. DB26 42
Geary Rd. NW10 BP35 46
Geary St. N7 BX35 47
Geddes Rd., Bush. BG24 27
Geddings Rd., Hodd. CE12 12
Gedeney Rd.N17 BZ30 39
Gedling Pl. SE1 CA41 4
Gedling Pl. SE1 CA41 67
Abbey St.
Gee St. EC1 BY38 2
Gee St. EC1 BY38 56
Geere Rd. E15 CG37 58
Gees Ct. W1 BV39 1
Gees Ct. W1 BV39 56
Barrett St.
Geffrye Ct. N1 CA37 2
Geffrye Ct. N1 CA37 57
Geffrye St. E2 CA37 2
Geffrye St. E2 CA37 57
Geisthorp Ct., Wal.Abb. CH20 22
Winters Way
Geldart Rd. SE15 CB43 67
Geldeston Rd. E5 CB34 48
Gell Clo., Uxb. AY35 44
Gellatly Rd. SE14 CC44 67
Gelsthorpe Rd., Rom. CR29 41
Gemini Gro., Nthlt. BD38 54
Javelin Way
General Gordon Pl. SE18 CL42 68
General Wolfe Rd. SE10 CF44 67
Generals Wk., The, Enf. CD22 30
Genesta Glade, Grav. DJ49 81
Genesta Rd. SE18 CL43 68
Geneva Clo., Shep. BB51 83
Haslett Rd.
Geneva Ct. N16 BZ33 48
Geneva Dr. SW9 BY45 66
Geneva Gdns., Rom. CQ32 50
Geneva Rd. SW9 BY45 66
Geneva Rd., Kings.T. BL52 85
Geneva Rd., Th.Hth. BZ53 87
Geneva Ter. SW9 BY45 66
Genever Clo. E4 CE28 39
Genista Rd. N18 CB28 39
Angel Rd.
Genoa Av. SW15 BQ46 75
Genoa Rd. SE20 CC51 87
Genotin Rd., Enf. BZ24 30
Genotin Ter., Enf. BZ24 30
Genotin Rd.
Gentian Row SE13 CF44 67
Sparta St.
Gentlemans Row, Enf. BZ24 30
Gentry Gdns. E13 CH38 58
Genyn Rd., Guil. AQ71 118
Geoffrey Av., Rom. CX29 42
Geoffrey Clo. SE5 BZ44 67
Lilford Rd.
Geoffrey Gdns. E6 CK37 58
Geoffrey Rd. SE4 CD45 67
George Avey Cft., Epp. CR16 23
Church La.
George Beard Rd. SE8 CD42 67
George Comberton Wk. E12 CL35 49
Gainsborough Av.
George Cres. N10 BV29 38
George Crooks Ho., Grays DD43 71
New Rd.
George Ct. WC2 BX40 56
Strand
George Downing Est. N16 CA34 48
George Green Rd., Slou. AS39 52
George Inn Yd. SE1 BZ40 4
George Inn Yd. SE1 BZ40 57
Borough High St.
George IV Way, Rick. AW21 26
George La. SE13 CE46 77
George La., Brom. CH54 88
George Lands, Ripley AW64 101
George Ms., Enf. BZ24 30
Sydney Rd.
George Rd. E4 CE29 39
George Rd., Guil. AR70 118
George Rd., Kings.T. BM50 75
George Rd., N.Mal. BO52 85
George Row SE16 CB41 4
George Row SE16 CB41 67
George Sq. SW19 BR52 85
George Sq., Uxb. AX36 53
George St. E16 CG39 58
George St. EC4 BZ40 4
George St. W1 BU39 1
George St. W1 BU39 56
George St. W7 BH40 54
George St., Bark. CM36 58
George St., Berk. AR13 7
George St., Chesh. AO18 16
George St., Croy. BZ55 87
George St., Grays DD43 71
George St., Hem.H. AX13 8
George St., Houns. BE44 64
George St., Rich. BK46 74
George St., Rom. CT32 50
George St., St.Alb. BG13 9
George St., Stai. AV49 72
George St., Sthl. BE42 64
George St., Sutt. BS56 95
High St.
George St., Uxb. AX36 53
George St., Wat. BD24 27
George Tilbury Ho., Grays DG41 71
George V Av., Pnr. BE30 36
George V Clo., Pnr. BF31 45
George V Way, Grnf. BJ37 54
George Wyver Clo. SW18 BR47 75
Beaumont Rd.
George Yd. EC3 BZ39 57
Lombard St.
George Yd. W1 BV40 3
George Yd. W1 BV40 56
Georges Clo., Orp. CP52 89
Georges Dr., Brwd. CZ25 33
Georges Mead, B.Wd. BL25 28
Georges Rd. N7 BX36 56
Georges Rd., West. CJ63 106
Georges Sq. SW6 BR43 65
Georges Ter., Cat. BZ64 105
Georges Wood Rd., Hat. BS16 20
Georgetown Clo. SE19 CA49 77
St. Kitts Road Ter.
Georgette Pl. SE10 CF43 67

Georgeville Gdns., Ilf. CL31 49
Georgewood Rd., Hem.H. AY16 17
Georgia Rd., N.Mal. BN52 85
Georgia Rd., Th.Hth. BY51 86
Georgian Clo., Brom. CH54 88
Georgian Clo., Nthwd. BB28 35
Georgian Clo., Stai. AW49 73
Georgian Clo., Stan. BJ29 36
Georgian Clo., Uxb. AX35 44
Georgian Ct. NW4 BP32 46
Foscote Rd.
Georgian Ct., Wem. BM36 55
Georgian Way, Har. BG34 45
Georgiana St. NW1 BW37 1
Georgiana St. NW1 BW37 56
Georgina Gdns. E2 CA38 2
Georgina Gdns. E2 CA38 57
Columbia Rd.
Geraint Rd., Brom. CH48 78
Gerald Clo., Grav. DJ47 81
Gerald Rd. E16 CG38 58
Gerald Rd. SW1 BV42 3
Gerald Rd. SW1 BV42 66
Gerald Rd., Dag. CQ34 50
Geraldine Rd. SW18 BT46 76
Geraldine Rd. W4 BM43 65
Geraldine St. SE11 BY41 4
Geraldine St. SE11 BY41 66
St. Georges Rd.
Geralds Gro., Bans. BQ60 94
Gerard Av., Houns. BF47 74
Gerard Gdns., Rain. CT37 59
Gerard Rd. SW13 BO44 65
Gerard Rd., Har. BJ32 45
Gerards Clo. SE16 CB42 67
Varcoe Rd.
Gerda Rd. SE9 CL48 78
Gerdview Dr., Dart. CV49 80
Germander Way E15 CG38 58
Gernon Clo., Rain. CV37 60
Gernon Rd. E3 CD37 57
Geron Way NW2 BP33 46
Gerpins La., Upmin. CW37 60
Gerrard Cres., Brwd. DB27 42
Gerrard Gdns., Pnr. BC32 44
Gerrard Pl. WC2 BW40 56
Gerrard St.
Gerrard Rd. N1 BY37 2
Gerrard Rd. N1 BY37 56
Gerrard St. W1 BW40 3
Gerrard St. W1 BW40 56
Gerrards Clo. N14 BW25 29
Gerrards Cross Rd., Slou. AQ36 52
Gerrards Mead, Bans. BR61 103
Garratts La.
Gerridge St. SE1 BY41 4
Gerridge St. SE1 BY41 66
Gerry Raffles Sq. E15 CF36 57
Salway Rd.
Gertrude Rd., Belv. CR42 69
Gertrude St. SW10 BT43 66
Gervase Clo., Wem. BN34 46
Chalkhill Rd.
Gervase Rd., Edg. BN30 37
Gervase St. SE15 CB43 67
Gews Cor., Chsnt. CC18 21
Ghent St. SE6 CE48 77
Ghent Way E8 CA36 57
Ramsgate St.
Giant Tree Hill, Bush. BG26 36
Gibbins Rd. E15 CF36 57
Gibbon Rd. SE15 CC45 67
Gibbon Rd. W3 BN40 55
Gibbon Rd., Kings.T. BL51 85
Gibbon Wk. SW15 BP45 65
Swinburne Rd.
Gibbons Clo., B.Wd. BL23 28
Gibbons Rd. NW10 BN36 55
Gibbs Av. SE19 BZ49 77
Gibbs Brook La., Oxt. CF71 114
Gibbs Clo. SE19 BZ49 77
Gibbs Clo., Chsnt. CC18 21
Gibbs Couch, Wat. BD27 36
Gibbs Grn. W14 BR42 65
Gibbs Grn., Edg. BN28 37
Gibbs Rd. N18 CC28 39
Gibbs Sq. SE19 BZ49 77
Gibons Clo., St.Alb. BK10 9
Gibraltar Clo., Brwd. DA28 42
Gibraltar Cres., Epsom BO58 94
Gibraltar Gdns. E2 CA38 2
Gibraltar Gdns. E2 CA38 57
Bethnal Green Rd.
Gibraltar Wk. E2 CA38 2
Gibraltar Wk. E2 CA38 57
Gibson Clo. E1 CC38 57
Colebert Av.
Gibson Clo., Chess. BK56 93
Mansfield Rd.
Gibson Clo., Epp. CS16 23
Gibson Clo., Islw. BH45 64
Gibson Ct., Slou. AS42 62
Gibson Gdns. N16 CA34 48
Gibson Pl., Stai. AX46 73
Gibson Rd. SE11 BX42 4
Gibson Rd. SE11 BX42 66
Gibson Rd., Dag. CP33 50
Gibson Rd., Sutt. BS56 95
Robin Hood Rd.
Gibson Rd., Uxb. AY35 44
Gibson Sq. N1 BY37 2
Gibson Sq. N1 BY37 56
Gibson St. SE10 CG42 68
Gibsons Hill SW6 BY50 76
Gidd Hill, Couls. BV61 104
Gidea Av., Rom. CU31 50
Gidea Clo., Rom. CU31 50
Gidea Clo., S.Ock. DB37 60
Gidean Ct., St.Alb. BG17 18
Gideon Clo., Belv. CR42 69
Gideon Rd. SW11 BV45 66
Giesbach Rd. N19 BW34 47
Giffard Rd. N18 CA28 39
Giffin St. SE8 CE43 67
Gifford Gdns. W7 BG39 54
Gifford Pl., Brwd. DB28 42
Blackthorn Way
Gifford St. N1 BX36 2
Gifford St. N1 BX36 56
Giffordside, Grays DG42 71
Gift La. E15 CG37 58
Giggs Hill Gdns., T.Ditt. BJ54 84
Giggs Hill Rd., T.Ditt. BJ54 84
Giggs Hill, Orp. CO51 89
Gilbert Clo., Swans. DB46 80
Gilbert Gro., Edg. BN30 37
Gilbert Ho. SE8 CE43 67
Gilbert Pl. WC1 BX39 2
Gilbert Pl. WC1 BX39 56
Gilbert Rd. SE11 BY42 4
Gilbert Rd. SE11 BY42 66
Gilbert Rd. SW19 BT50 76
Gilbert Rd., Belv. CR41 69
Gilbert Rd., Brom. CH50 78
Gilbert Rd., Pnr. BD31 45
Gilbert Rd., Rom. CT31 50
Gilbert Rd., Uxb. AX30 35
Gilbert St. E15 CG35 49
Gilbert St. W1 BV39 1
Gilbert St. W1 BV39 56
Gilbert St., Enf. CC22 30
Gilbert St., Houns. BG45 64
High St.
Gilbert Way, Berk. AQ13 7
Gilbey Clo., Uxb. AZ35 44
Gilbey Rd. SW17 BU49 76
Gilbourne Rd. SE18 CN43 68
Gilda Av., Enf. CD25 30
Gilda Cres. N16 CB33 48
Gilda Ct. NW7 BP30 37
Gildea St. W1 BV39 1
Gildea St. W1 BV39 56
Great Portland St.
Gilden Clo., Harl. CQ 9 6
Sheering Rd.
Gilden Cres. NW5 BV35 47
Gilden Way, Harl. CP 9 6
Gildenhill Rd., Swan. CV50 80
Gilder St. W1 BV39 56
Portland St.
Gilders Rd., Chess. BL57 94
Gilders, Saw. CP 6 6
Giles Clo., Rain. CV37 60
Giles Coppice SE19 CA49 77
Giles Travers Clo., Egh. AU52 82
Gilfrid Clo., Uxb. AZ39 53
Craig Dr.
Gilhams Av., Bans. BQ59 94
Gilkes Cres. SE21 CA46 77
Gilkes Pl. SE21 CA46 77
Gill Av. E16 CH39 58
Gill Av., Guil. AP71 118
Gill Cres., Grav. CD48 81
Packham Rd.
Gill St. E14 CD40 57
Gillam Way, Rain. CU36 59
Gillan Grn., Bush. BG27 36
Gillender St. E3 CF38 57
Gillespie Rd. N5 BY34 47
Gillett Av. E6 CK37 58
Gillett Pl. N16 CA35 48
Gillett St.
Gillett Rd., Th.Hth. BZ52 87
Gillett St. N16 CA35 48
Gillham Ter. N17 CB29 39
Gilliam Clo., Pur. BY58 95
Gillian Av., St.Alb. BG15 9
Gillian Cres., Rom. CV30 42
Gillian Park Rd., Sutt. BR54 85
Gillian St. SE13 CE46 77
Gilliat Dr., Guil. AU69 118
Gilliat Rd., Slou. AP40 52
Gilliatt Clo., Iver AV39 52
Dutton Way
Gillies Rd., Sev. CZ57 99
Gillies St. NW5 BV35 47
Gilling Ct. NW3 BU36 56
Gillingham Ms. SW1 BV42 3
Gillingham Ms. SW1 BV42 66
Gillingham St.
Gillingham Rd. NW2 BR34 46
Gillingham Row SW1 BW42 3
Gillingham Row SW1 BW42 66
Vauxhall Bridge Rd.
Gillingham St. SW1 BV42 3
Gillingham St. SW1 BW42 66
Gillman Dr. E15 CG37 58
Gillmans Rd., Orp. CO54 89
Gills Hill La., Rad. BH21 27
Gills Hill, Rad. BH21 27
Gills Hollow, Rad. BH21 27
Gillum Clo., Barn. BU26 38
Gilmais, Lthd. BG66 111
Gilman Cres., Wind. AL45 61
Gilmore Clo., Slou. AR41 62
Gilmore Clo., Uxb. AZ34 44
Gilmore Cres., Ashf. AZ49 73
Gilmore Rd. SE13 CF45 67
Gilmour Clo., Enf. CB21 30
Gilpin Av. SW14 BN45 65
Gilpin Clo., Mitch. BU51 86
Lowry Cres.
Gilpin Cres. N18 CA28 39
Gilpin Cres., Twick. BF47 74
Gilpin Rd. E5 CD35 48
Gilpin Way, Hayes BA43 63
Gilpins Ride, Berk. AR12 7
Gilroy Clo., Rain. CT36 59
Gilroy Way, Orp. CO54 89
Gilsand Rd., Th.Hth. BZ52 87
Gilsand, Wal.Abb. CG21 31
Gilstead Rd. SW6 BS44 66
Gilston Rd. SW10 BT42 3
Gilston Rd. SW10 BT42 66
Gilton Rd. SE6 CG48 78
Giltspur St. EC1 BY39 2
Giltspur St. EC1 BY39 56
Gilwell Clo. E4 CE25 30
Antlers Hill
Gilwell La. E4 CF24 30
Gimcrack Hill, Lthd. BJ64 102
Gippeswyck Clo., Pnr. BD30 36
Uxbridge Rd.
Gipsy Hill SE19 CA49 77
Gipsy La. SW15 BP45 65
Gipsy La., Grays DE43 71
Gipsy Rd. Gdns. SE27 BZ49 77
Gipsy Rd. SE27 BZ49 77
Gipsy Rd., Well. CP44 69
Giralda Clo. E16 CJ39 58
Fulmer Rd.
Giraud St. E14 CE39 57
Girdlers Rd. W14 BQ42 65
Girdlestone Est. N19 BW34 47
Girdlestone Wk. N19 BW34 47
Girdwood Rd. SW18 BR47 75
Girling Way, Felt. BC45 63
Gironde Rd. SW6 BR43 65
Girtin Rd., Bush. BF24 27
Girton Av. NW9 BM31 46
Girton Clo., Nthlt. BF36 54
Girton Gdns., Croy. CE55 87
Girton Ms. N1 BY36 56
Lofting Rd.
Girton Rd. SE26 CC49 77
Girton Rd., Nthlt. BG36 54
Girton Way, Rick. BA25 26
Gisborne Gdns., Rain. CT38 59
Gisburn Rd. N8 BX31 47
Gissing Wk. N1 BY36 2
Gissing Wk. N1 BY36 56
Lofting Rd.
Given Wilson Wk. E13 CG37 58
Stride Rd.
Givons Gro., Lthd. BK66 111
Gladbeck Way, Enf. BZ24 30
Gladding Rd. E12 CJ35 49
Glade Clo., Surb. BK55 84
Glade Ct., Ilf. CK30 40
Glade Gdns., Croy. CD54 87
Glade La., Sthl. BF41 64
Glade Spur, Tad. BS64 104
Glade, The N21 BX26 38
Glade, The SE7 CJ43 68
Glade, The, Brom. CJ51 88
Glade, The, Brwd. DD26 122
Glade, The, Couls. BY63 104
Glade, The, Croy. CC53 87
Glade, The, Enf. BY24 29
Glade, The, Epsom BP57 94
Glade, The, Ger.Cr. AR33 43
Glade, The, Ilf. CK30 40
Glade, The, Lthd. BF64 102
Glade, The, Sev. CU65 107
Glade, The, Stai. AW50 73
Glade, The, Sutt. BR58 94
Glade, The, Tad. BS64 104
Glade, The, Upmin. CY35 51
Glade, The, W.Wick. CE55 87
Glade, The, Wdf.Grn. CH27 40
Glade, The, Welw.G.C. BQ 7 5
Glades, The, Brom. CH51 88
Glades, The, Grav. BH50 81
Glades, The, Hem.H. AV13 7
The Shrubbery
Gladeside Clo., Chess. BK57 93
Gladeside Ct., Warl. CB63 105
Gladeside N21 BX25 29
Gladeside, Croy. CC53 87
Gladeside, St.Alb. BK12 9
Gladesmore Rd. N15 CA32 48
Gladeswood Rd., Belv. CR42 69
Gladeway, The, Wal.Abb. CF20 21
Gladiator St. SE23 CD47 77
Glading Ter. N16 CA34 48
Gladioli Clo., Hmptn. BF50 74
Gresham Rd.
Gladsdale Dr., Pnr. BC31 44
Gladsmuir Clo., Walt. BD55 84
Gladsmuir Rd. N19 BW33 47
Gladsmuir Rd., Barn. BR23 28
Gladstone Av. E12 CK36 58
Gladstone Av. N22 BY30 38
Gladstone Av., Felt. BC46 73
Gladstone Av., Twick. BG47 74
Gladstone Clo W4 BN41 65
Gladstone Ms. N22 BY30 38
Pelham Rd.
Gladstone Ms. SE20 CC50 77
Graveney Gro.
Gladstone Park Gdns. NW2 BP35 46
Gladstone Pl. E3 CD37 57
Roman Rd.
Gladstone Pl., Barn. BQ24 28
Gladstone Rd. E15 CG36 58
Gladstone Rd. SW19 BS50 76
Gladstone Rd., Ash. BK62 102
Gladstone Rd., Buck.H. CH26 40
Gladstone Rd., Croy. BZ54 87
Gladstone Rd., Dart. CW46 80
Gladstone Rd., Hodd. CE11 12
Gladstone Rd., Kings.T. BM52 85
Gladstone Rd., Orp. CM56 97
Gladstone Rd., Sthl. BE41 64
Gladstone Rd., Surb. BK55 84
Gladstone Rd., Wat. BD24 27
Gladstone St. N22 BY30 38
Pelham Rd.
Gladstone St. SE1 BY41 4
Gladstone St. SE1 BY41 66
Gladstone Ter. SE27 BZ49 77
Gladstone Ter. SW8 BV44 66
Gladstone Way, Har. BH31 45
Palmerston Rd.
Gladstone Way, Slou. AN41 61
Gladwell Rd. N8 BX32 47
Gladwell Rd., Brom. CH50 78
Gladwyn Rd. SW15 BQ45 65
Gladys Rd. NW6 BS36 56
Glaisyer Way, Iver AU37 52
Glamis Clo., Chsnt. CB18 21
Glamis Clo., Hem.H. AZ10 8
Dunster Rd.
Glamis Cres., Hayes BA41 63
Glamis Dr., Horn. CW33 51
Glamis Pl. E1 CC40 57
Glamis Rd. E1 CC40 57
Glamis Way, Nthlt. BG36 54
Glamorgan Clo., Mitch. BX52 86
Glamorgan Rd., Kings.T. BK50 74
Glanfield Rd., Beck. CD52 87
Glanfield, Hem.H. AY12 8
Glanleam Rd., Stan. BK28 36
Glanmead, Brwd. DC26 122
Glanmor Rd., Slou. AQ40 52
Glanthams Clo., Brwd. DC27 122
Glanthams Rd., Brwd. DC27 122
Glanty, The, Egh. AT49 72
Glanville Dr., Horn. CW34 51
Glanville Rd. SW2 BX46 76
Glanville Rd., Brom. CH52 88
Glasbrook Av., Twick. BE47 74
Glasbrook Rd. SE9 CJ47 78
Glaserton Rd. N16 CA33 48
Glasford St. SW17 BU50 76
Glasgow Rd. E13 CH37 58
Glasgow Rd. N18 CB28 39
Glasgow Ter. SW1 BW42 3
Glasgow Ter. SW1 BW42 66
Lupus St.
Glass House Yd. EC1 BZ39 2
Glass House Yd. EC1 BZ39 57
Aldersgate St.
Glass St. E2 CB38 57
Coventry Rd.
Glass Yd. SE18 CL41 68
Woolwich High St.
Glasshill St. SE1 BY41 4
Glasshill St. SE1 BY41 66
Glasshouse Fields E1 CC40 57
Glasshouse St. W1 BW40 3
Glasshouse St. W1 BW40 56
Glasshouse Wk. SE11 BX42 4
Glasshouse Wk. SE11 BX42 66
Glasslyn Rd. N8 BW32 47
Glassmill La., Brom. CG51 88
Glasson Clo., West Dr. AY41 63
Glastonbury Av., Wdf.Grn. CJ29 40
Glastonbury Rd. N9 CB26 39
Chichester Rd.
Glastonbury Rd., Mord. BS54 86
Glastonbury St. NW6 BR35 46
Glaucus St. E3 CE39 57
Glazbury Rd. W14 BR42 65
Glazebrook Clo. SE21 BZ48 77
Glazebrook Rd., Tedd. BH50 74
Gleave Clo., St.Alb. BJ13 9
Glebe Av., Enf. BY24 29
Glebe Av., Har. BL31 46
Glebe Av., Mitch. BU51 86
Glebe Av., Ruis. BC36 53
Glebe Av., Uxb. BA35 44
Glebe Av., Wdf.Grn. CH29 40
Glebe Clo. W4 CO42 69
Glebe St.
Glebe Clo., Ger.Cr. AR29 34
Glebe Clo., Hat. BU12 11
Glebe Clo., Hem.H. AY15 8
Glebe Clo., Lthd. BF66 111
Glebe Clo., Maid. AJ41 61
Glebe Clo., S.Croy. CA59 96
Glebe Clo., Uxb. BA35 44
Glebe Cotts., Felt. BF48 74
Glebe Cotts., Guil. AW69 110
Glebe Cotts., Hat. BU12 11
Glebe Cres. NW4 BQ31 46
Glebe Cres., Har. BL31 46
Glebe Ct. W7 BG40 54
Glebe Ct., Hat. BP12 10
Brian Clo.
Glebe Ct., Mitch. BU52 86
Glebe Ct., Stan. BK28 36
Glebe Est. SE5 CA44 67
Glebe Gdns., N.Mal. BO54 85
Glebe Gdns., Wey. AY60 92
Glebe House Dr., Brom. CH54 88
Glebe Hyrst SE19 CA49 77
Giles Coppice
Glebe Hyrst, S.Croy. CA59 96
Glebe La., Barn. BP25 28
Glebe La., Har. BL31 146
Glebe La., Sev. CU66 116
Glebe Path, Mitch. BU52 86
Glebe Pl. SW3 BU43 3
Glebe Pl. SW3 BU43 66
Glebe Pl., Hort.K. CY52 90
Glebe Rd. E8 CA36 57
Glebe Rd. N3 BT30 38
Glebe Rd. N8 BX31 47
Glebe Rd. NW10 BP36 55
Glebe Rd. SW13 BP44 65
Glebe Rd., Ash. BK62 102
Glebe Rd., Brom. CH51 88
Glebe Rd., Cars. BU57 95
Glebe Rd., Dag. CR36 59
Church St.
Glebe Rd., Dor. BH71 119
Glebe Rd., Egh. AU49 72
Glebe Rd., Ger.Cr. AR30 34
Glebe Rd., Grav. DF47 81
Glebe Rd., Hayes BB40 53
Glebe Rd., Maid. AG40 61
Glebe Rd., Ong. CW18 24
Glebe Rd., Rain. CU38 59
Glebe Rd., Red. BV65 104
Glebe Rd., Sev. CU69 116
Glebe Rd., Stai. AW49 73
Glebe Rd., Stan. BK28 36
Glebe Rd., Sutt. BR58 94
Glebe Rd., Uxb. AX37 53
Glebe Rd., Warl. CC62 105
Glebe Rd., Wind. AQ46 72
Glebe Side, Twick. BH46 74
Glebe St. W4 BN42 65
Glebe Ter. E3 CE38 57
Glebe Way, Amer. AO21 25
Glebe Way, Erith CT43 69
Glebe Way, Felt. BF48 74
Glebe Way, S.Croy. CA59 96
Glebe Way, W.Wick. CF55 87
Glebe, The SE3 CG45 68
Glebe, The SW16 BW49 76
Prentis Rd.
Glebe, The, Chis. CM51 88
Glebe, The, Kings L. AZ18 17
Glebe, The, Reig. BP74 120
Glebe, The, Wat. BD20 18
Glebe, The, West Dr. AY42 63
Glebe, The, Wor.Pk. BO54 85
Glebefields, The, Sev. CT64 107
Shoreham La.
Glebeland Gdns., Shep. BA53 83
Glebeland, Hat. BQ12 10
Glebelands Av. E18 CH30 40
Glebelands Av., Ilf. CM33 49
Glebelands Clo. SE5 CA45 67
Grove Hill Rd.
Glebelands Rd., Felt. BC47 73
Glebelands, Chig. CO27 41
Glebelands, Dart. CT45 69
Glebelands, E.Mol. BF53 84
Glebelands, Esher BH58 93
Glebelands, Harl. CN11 13
Glebeway, Horn. CW33 51
Glebeway, Wdf.Grn. CJ28 40
Gledhow Gdns. SW5 BT42 3
Gledhow Gdns. SW5 BT42 66
Gledhow Wood, Tad. BS64 104
Gledstanes Rd. W14 BR42 65
Gledwood Av., Hayes BB39 53
Gledwood Cres., Hayes BB39 53
Gledwood Dr., Hayes BB39 53
Gledwood Gdns., Hayes BB39 53
Gleed Av., Bush. BG27 36
Gleeson Dr., Orp. CN56 97
Glegg Pl. SW15 BQ45 65
Glen Albyn Rd. SW19 BQ48 75
Glen Av., Ashf. AZ49 73
Glen Clo., Shep. AZ52 83
Glen Clo., Tad. BR64 103
Glen Cres., Wdf.Grn. CH29 40
Glen Dale Rd., Grav. DF49 81
Glen End Rd., Wall. BV58 95
Glen Faba Rd., Harl. CG12 13
Glen Gdns., Croy. BY55 86
Glen Hazel, Brwd. DB21 33
Glen Rd. E13 CJ38 58
Glen Rd. E17 CD32 48
Glen Rd., Chess. BL55 85
Glen Ri., Wdf.Grn. CH29 40
Glen Vw., Grav. DH47 81
Glen Way, Wat. BB22 26
Glen Wk., Islw. BG46 74
Glen Wood, Dor. BK72 119
Glen, The, Croy. CC55 87
Glen, The, Eastcote BC32 44
Glen, The, Enf. BY24 29
Glen, The, Hem.H. AY11 8
Glen, The, Nthwd. BA29 35
Glen, The, Orp. CK55 88
Glen, The, Pnr. BE33 45
Glen, The, Rain. CV38 60
Glen, The, Slou. AR42 62
Glen, The, Sthl. BE42 64
Glen, The, Wem. BK35 45
Glen, The, Wey. AV56 91
Glena Mt., Sutt. BT56 95
Glenaffric Av. E14 CF42 67
Glenalla Rd., Ruis. BB33 44
Glenalmond Rd., Har. BL31 46
Glenalyon Way SE18 CK42 68
Glenarm Rd. E5 CC35 48
Glenavon Clo., Esher BJ57 93
Glenavon Gdns., Slou. AR42 62
Glenavon Rd. E15 CG36 58
Glenbarr Clo. SE9 CL45 68
Glenbow Rd., Brom. CG50 78
Glenbrook N., Enf. BX24 29
Glenbrook Rd. NW6 BS35 47
Glenbrook S., Enf. BX24 29
Glenbuck Ct., Surb. BL53 85
Glenbuck Rd., Surb. BK53 84
Glenburnie Rd. SW17 BU48 76
Glencairn Dr. W5 BJ38 54
Glencairn Rd. SW16 BX51 86
Glencairne Clo. E16 CJ39 58
Glencoe Av., Ilf. CM33 49
Glencoe Dr., Dag. CR35 50
Glencoe Rd., Bush. BF25 27
Glencoe Rd., Wey. AZ55 83
Glencourse Grn., Wat. BD28 36
Coldwell Rd.
Glendale Av. N22 BY29 38
Glendale Av., Edg. BM28 37
Glendale Av., Rom. CP33 50
Glendale Clo. SE9 CL45 68
Glendale Clo., Brwd. DC26 122
Glendale Clo., Wok. AR62 100
Glendale Dr. SW19 BR49 75
Glendale Dr., Guil. AU68 109
Glendale Gdns., Hem.H. AW13 8
Glendale Gdns., Wem. BK33 45
Glendale Ms., Beck. CE51 87
Westgate Rd.
Glendale Rd., Erith CS42 69
Glendale Ri., Pur. BY61 104
Glendale Way SE28 CP40 59
Glendale Wk., Chsnt. CD18 21
Glendale, Swan. CT53 89
Glendall St. SW9 BX45 66
Glendarvon St. SW15 BQ45 65
Glendene Av., Lthd. BB66 110
Glendish Rd. N17 CB30 39
Glendor Gdns. NW7 BN28 37
Glendower Cres., Orp. CO53 89
Glendower Gdns. SW14 BN45 65
Glendower Rd.
Glendower Pl. SW7 BT42 3
Glendower Pl. SW7 BT42 66
Harrington Rd.
Glendower Rd. E4 CF26 39
Glendower Rd. SW14 BN45 65
Glendown Rd. SE2 CO42 69
Glendun Ct. W3 BO40 55
Glendun Rd.
Glendun Rd. W3 BO40 55
Gleneagle Ms. SW16 BW49 76
Ambleside Av.
Gleneagle Rd. SW16 BW50 76
Gleneagles Clo., Orp. CM54 88

Gleneagles Clo., Rom. CW29 42
Gleneagles Clo., Stai. AX46 73
Park Rd.
Gleneagles Clo., Stan. BJ29 36
Gleneagles Clo., Wat. BD28 36
Gleneagles Grn., Orp. CM54 88
Gleneagles Clo.
Gleneagles, Stan. BJ29 36
Gordon Av.
Gleneldon Ms. SW16 BX49 76
Gleneldon Rd. SW16 BX49 76
Glenelg Rd. SW2 BX46 76
Glenesk Rd. SE9 CL45 68
Glenester Clo., Hodd. CE10 12
Glenfarg Rd. SE6 CF47 77
Glenferrie Rd., St.Alb. BJ13 9
Glenfield Clo., Bet. BM72 120
Glenfield Cres., Ruis. BA33 44
Glenfield Rd. SW12 BW47 76
Glenfield Rd. W13 BJ41 64
Glenfield Rd., Ashf. AZ50 73
Glenfield Rd., Bans. BS61 104
Glenfield Rd., Bet. BM72 120
Glenfield Ter. W13 BJ40 54
Glenfinlas Way SE5 BY43 66
Glenforth St. SE10 CG42 68
Glengall Causeway E14 CE41 67
Glengall Gro. E14 CE41 67
Glengall Ms. SE1 CA42 67
Glengall Rd. NW6 BR37 55
Glengall Rd. SE15 CA42 4
Glengall Rd. SE15 CA42 67
Glengall Rd., Bexh. CQ45 69
Glengall Rd., Edg. BM27 37
Glengall Rd., Wdf.Grn. CH29 40
Glengall Ter. SE15 CA43 4
Glengall Ter. SE15 CA43 67
Glengarnock Av. E14 CF42 67
Glengarry Rd. SE22 CA46 77
Glenham Dr., Ilf. CL32 49
Glenhaven Av., B.Wd. BM24 28
Glenhead Clo. SE9 CL45 68
Glenhill Clo. N3 BS30 38
Glenhouse Rd. SE9 CL46 78
Glenhurst Av. NW5 BV35 47
Glenhurst Av., Bex. CQ47 79
Glenhurst Av., Ruis. BA33 44
Glenhurst Rd. N12 BT28 38
Glenhurst Rd., Brent. BK43 64
Glenhurst Ri. SE19 BZ50 77
Glenilla Rd. NW3 BU36 56
Glenista Rd. N18 CB28 39
Glenister Park Rd. SW16 BW50 76
Glenister Rd. SE10 CG42 68
Glenister St. E16 CL40 58
Glenlea Rd. SE9 CK46 78
Glenloch Rd. NW3 BU36 56
Glenloch Rd., Enf. CC23 30
Glenluce Rd. SE3 CH43 68
Glenlyn Av., St.Alb. BJ14 9
Glenlyon Rd. SE9 CL46 78
Glenmere Av. NW7 BP29 37
Glenmill, Hmptn. BE49 74
Glenmore Clo., Wey. AW55 83
Glenmore Rd. NW3 BU36 56
Glenmore Rd., Well. CN43 68
Glenmore Way, Bark. CO37 59
Glenmount Path SE18 CM42 68
Raglan Rd.
Glenn Av., Pur. BY59 95
Glennie Rd. SE27 BY48 76
Glenny Rd., Bark. CM36 58
Glenorchy Clo., Hayes BE39 54
Kilpatrick Way
Glenparke Rd. E7 CH36 58
Glenrosa Gdns., Grav. DK49 81
Glenrosa St. SW6 BT44 66
Glenroy St. W12 BQ39 55
Glensdale Rd. SE4 CD45 67
Glenshee Clo., Nthwd. BA29 35
Merrows Clo.
Glenshiel Rd. SE9 CL46 78
Glenside Cotts., Slou. AP41 62
Upton Clo.
Glenside Rd. SE18 CN42 68
Glenside, Chig. CM29 40
Glentanner Way SW17 BT48 76
Aboyne Rd.
Glentham Gdns. SW13 BP43 65
Glentham Rd.
Glentham Rd. SW13 BP43 65
Glenthorn Gdns., Ilf. CL31 49
Glenthorne Av., Croy. CB54 87
Glenthorne Clo., Sutt. BS54 86
Glenthorne Gdns., Sutt. BS54 86
Glenthorne Rd. E17 CD32 48
Glenthorne Rd. N11 BU28 38
Glenthorne Rd. W6 BP42 65
Glenthorne Rd., Kings.T. BL52 85
Glenthorpe Rd., Mord. BQ53 85
Glenton Clo., Rom. CT29 41
Glenton Rd. SE13 CG45 68
Glenton Way, Rom. CT29 41
Glentrammon Av., Orp. CN57 97
Glentrammon Clo., Orp. CN56 97
Glentrammon Gdns., Orp. CN57 97
Glentrammon Rd., Orp. CN57 97
Glentworth Pl., Slou. AO40 61
Glentworth St. NW1 BU38 1
Glentworth St. NW1 BU38 56
Glenure Rd. SE9 CL46 78
Glenview Rd., Brom. CJ51 88
Glenview Rd., Hem.H. AW13 8
Glenview SE2 CP43 69
Glenville Av., Enf. BZ22 30
Glenville Clo., Surb. BN54 85
Glenville Gro. SE8 CD43 67
Glenville Ms. SW18 BS47 76
Glenville Rd., Kings.T. BM51 85
Glenwood Av. NW9 BN33 46
Glenwood Av., Rain. CU38 59
Glenwood Clo., Har. BH32 45
Glenwood Dr., Rom. CU31 50
Glenwood Gdns., Ilf. CL32 49
Glenwood Gro. NW9 BN33 46
Glenwood Rd. N15 BY32 47
Glenwood Rd. NW7 BO27 37
Glenwood Rd. SE6 CD47 77
Glenwood Rd., Epsom BP57 94
Glenwood Rd., Houns. BG45 64
Glenwood Way, Croy. CC53 87
Glenwood, Brox. CD13 12
Glenwood, Welw.G.C. BT8 5
Glenworth Av. E14 CF42 67
Glevum Clo., St.Alb. BE14 9
Gliddon Rd. W14 BR42 65
Glimpsing Grn., Belv. CQ41 69
Glisson Rd., Uxb. AZ37 53
Gload Cres., Orp. CP55 89
Global App. E3 CF38 57
Globe Cres. E15 CG35 49
Globe La. SE18 CL41 68
Globe Pond Rd. SE16 CD40 57
Globe Rd. E15 CG35 49
Globe Rd. E2 CC38 57
Globe Rd., Horn. CU32 50
Globe Rd., Wdf.Grn. CJ29 40
Globe St. SE1 BZ41 4
Globe St. SE1 BZ41 67
Globe Ter. E2 CC38 57
Globe Rd.
Glory Mead, Dor. BJ73 119
Glossop Rd., S.Croy. BZ58 96
Gloster Rd., N.Mal. BO52 85
Gloster Rd., Wok. AT63 100
Gloucester Av. NW1 BV36 1
Gloucester Av. NW1 BV36 56
Gloucester Av., Grays DE41 71
Gloucester Av., Horn. CW31 51
Gloucester Av., Sid. CN48 78
Gloucester Av., Slou. AO39 52
Gloucester Av., Wal.Cr. CD20 21
Gloucester Av., Well. CN45 68
Gloucester Cir. SE10 CF43 67
Gloucester Clo. NW10 BN36 55
Gloucester Clo., S.Ock. DB38 60
South Rd.
Gloucester Clo., T.Ditt. BJ54 84
Gloucester Cres. NW1 BV37 1
Gloucester Cres. NW1 BV37 56
Gloucester Cres., Stai. AX50 73
Gloucester Ct. EC3 CA40 4
Tower Hill
Gloucester Ct. EC3 CA40 57
Tower Hill
Gloucester Ct. W3 BM39 55
Links Rd.
Gloucester Ct., Rich. BM43 65
Gloucester Dr. N4 BY34 47
Gloucester Dr. NW11 BS31 47
Gloucester Dr., Stai. AU48 72
Gloucester Gate Ms. NW1 BV37 1
Gloucester Gate Ms. NW1 BV37 56
Gloucester Gate
Gloucester Gate NW1 BV37 1
Gloucester Gate NW1 BV37 56
Gloucester Gdns. NW11 BR33 46
Gloucester Gdns. W2 BT39 1
Gloucester Gdns. W2 BT39 56
Gloucester Gdns., Barn. BV24 29
Gloucester Gdns., Ilf. CK33 49
Gloucester Gdns., Sutt. BS55 86
Gloucester Gro., Edg. BN30 37
Gloucester Ms. NW1 BV37 56
Albany St.
Gloucester Ms. W. W2 BT39 1
Gloucester Ms. W. W2 BT39 56
Gloucester Ms. W2 BT39 1
Gloucester Ms. W2 BT39 56
Gloucester Par., Sid. CO46 79
Gloucester Pl. Ms. W1 BU39 1
Gloucester Pl. Ms. W1 BU39 56
Gloucester Pl. NW1 BU38 1
Gloucester Pl. NW1 BU38 56
Gloucester Pl., Wind. AO44 61
Gloucester Rd. E10 CE33 48
Gloucester Rd. E11 CH32 49
Gloucester Rd. E12 CK35 49
Gloucester Rd. E17 CC30 39
Gloucester Rd. N17 BZ30 39
Gloucester Rd. N18 CA28 39
Gloucester Rd. SW7 BT41 3
Gloucester Rd. SW7 BT41 66
Gloucester Rd. W3 BN41 65
Gloucester Rd. W5 BK41 64
Gloucester Rd., Kings.T. BM51 85
Gloucester Rd., Barn. BS25 29
Gloucester Rd., Belv. CQ42 69
Gloucester Rd., Brwd. DA25 33
Gloucester Rd., Croy. BZ54 87
Gloucester Rd., Dart. CU47 79
Gloucester Rd., Enf. BZ22 30
Gloucester Rd., Felt. BD47 74
Gloucester Rd., Grav. DG49 81
Gloucester Rd., Guil. AP69 118
Gloucester Rd., Har. BF32 45
Gloucester Rd., Hmptn. BF50 74
Gloucester Rd., Houns. BE45 64
Gloucester Rd., Red. BU70 121
Gloucester Rd., Rich. BM43 65
Gloucester Rd., Rom. CT32 50
Gloucester Rd., Tedd. BH49 74
Gloucester Rd., Twick. BG47 74
Gloucester Sq. W2 BT39 1
Gloucester Sq. W2 BT39 56
Gloucester Sq., Wok. AS62 100
Civic Way
Gloucester St. SW1 BW42 3
Gloucester St. SW1 BW42 66
Gloucester Ter. NW1 BV37 56
Outer Circle
Gloucester Ter. W2 BS39 1
Gloucester Ter. W2 BS39 56
Gloucester Way EC1 BY38 2
Gloucester Way EC1 BY38 56
Gloucester Wk. W8 BS41 66
Glover Rd., Pnr. BD32 45
Glovers Field, Brwd. CZ22 33
Glovers Gro., Ruis. AZ33 44
Glovers La., Harl. CQ13 14
Glovers Rd., Reig. BS71 121
Gloxinia Rd., Grav. DD50 81
Gloxinia Wk., Hmptn. BF50 74
The Avenue
Glycena Rd. SW11 BU45 66
Glyn Av., Barn. BT24 29
Glyn Clo. SE25 CA51 87
Grange Hill
Glyn Clo., Epsom BP58 94
Glyn Ct. SE27 BY48 76
Glyn Dr., Sid. CO49 79
Glyn Rd. E5 CC34 48
Glyn Rd., Enf. CC24 30
Glyn Rd., Wor.Pk. BQ55 85
Glyn St. SE11 BX42 4
Glyn St. SE11 BX42 66
Glynde Ms. SW3 BU41 3
Glynde Ms. SW3 BU41 66
Yeomans Row
Glynde Rd., Bexh. CP45 69
Glynde St. SE4 CD46 77
Glyndebourne Pk., Orp. CL55 88
Glyndon Rd. SE18 CM42 68
Glynfield Rd. NW10 BO36 55
Glynswood, Ger.Cr. AS29 34
Glynwood Ct. SE26 CC48 77
Glynwood Dr.
Glynwood Dr. SE26 CC48 77
Goat House Br. SE25 CB52 87
Goat La., Enf. CA22 30
Goat La., Surb. BJ55 84
Goat Rd., Mitch. BU54 86
Goat St. SE1 CA41 4
Lafone St.
Goat St. SE1 CA41 67
Lafone St.
Goatsfield Rd., West. CJ63 106
Gobions Av., Rom. CS29 41
Gobions Way, Pot.B. BS17 20
Gobions, Rom. CR30 41
Goblins Grn., Welw.G.C. BQ8 5
Godalming Av., Wall. BX56 95
Godalming By-pass, Guil. AR70 118
Godalming Rd. E14 CE39 57
Chrisp St.
Godbold Av. E15 CG38 58
Goddard Clo., Shep. AY52 83
Magdalene Rd.
Goddard Rd., Beck. CC52 87
Goddard Rd., Grays DD40 71
Goddards Clo., Hert. BW13 11
Goddington Chase, Orp. CO56 98
Goddington La., Orp. CO55 89
Godfrey Av., Nthlt. BE37 54
Godfrey Av., Twick. BG47 74
Godfrey Hill SE18 CK42 68
Godfrey Rd. SE18 CK42 68
Godfrey St. E15 CF37 57
Godfrey St. SW3 BU42 3
Godfrey St. SW3 BU42 66
Godfrey Way, Houns. BE47 74
Godfries Clo., Welw. BU5 5
Goding St. SE11 BX42 4
Goding St. SE11 BX42 66
Godley Rd. SW18 BT47 76
Godley Rd., Wey. AY60 92
Godliman St. EC4 BY39 2
Godliman St. EC4 BY39 56
Godman Rd. SE15 CB44 67
Godman Rd., Grays DG41 71
Godolphin Clo., Sutt. BR58 94
Godolphin Rd. W12 BP40 55
Godolphin Rd., Beac. AO29 34
Godolphin Rd., Slou. AO40 52
Godolphin Rd., Wey. BA57 92
Godric Cres., Croy. CF58 96
Godson Rd., Croy. BY55 86
Godson St. N1 BY37 2
Godson St. N1 BY37 56
Godstone By-pass, Gdse. CD69 114
Godstone Hill, Gdse. CB67 114
Godstone Rd., Cat. CB65 105
Godstone Rd., Oxt. CE69 114
Godstone Rd., Pur. BY59 95
Godstone Rd., Red. CA70 114
Godstone Rd., Sutt. BT56 95
Godstone Rd., Twick. BJ46 74
Godstow Rd. SE2 CO41 69
Godwin Clo., Epsom BN57 94
Godwin Ct. NW1 BW37 1
Godwin Ct. NW1 BW37 56
Chalton St.
Godwin Rd. E7 CH35 49
Godwin Rd., Brom. CJ52 88
Goffers Rd. SE3 CG44 68
Goffs Cres., Chsnt. BZ18 21
Goffs La., Chsnt. BZ18 21
Goffs Oak Av., Chsnt. BZ17 21
Goffs Rd., Ashf. BA50 73
Gogmore Farm Clo., Cher. AV53 82
Gogmore La., Cher. AW54 83
Goidel Clo., Wall. BW56 95
Golborne Gdns. W10 BR38 55
Golborne Rd.
Golborne Ms. W10 BR39 55
Portobello Rd.
Golborne Rd. W10 BR39 55
Gold Cft., Hem.H. AZ14 8
Gold Hill E., Ger.Cr. AR30 34
Gold Hill N., Ger.Cr. AR30 34
Gold Hill W., Ger.Cr. AR30 34
Gold Hill, Edg. BN29 37
Gold La., Edg. BN29 37
Golda Clo., Barn. BQ25 28
Goldbeaters Gro., Edg. BQ29 37
Goldcliff Clo., Mord. BS54 86
Goldcrest Clo. E16 CJ39 58
Goldcrest Clo. SE28 CP40 59
Goldcrest Way, Bush. BG26 36
Goldcrest Way, Croy. CF58 96
Goldcrest Way, Pur. BW58 95
Great Woodcote Dr.
Golden Cres., Hayes BB40 53
Golden Ct., Rich. BK46 74
George St.
Golden Dell, Welw.G.C. BR10 5
Golden La. EC1 BZ38 2
Golden La. EC1 BZ38 57
Golden La. Est. EC1 BZ38 57
Golden Manor W7 BH40 54
Golden Sq. W1 BW40 3
Golden Sq. W1 BW40 56
Golders Clo. Edg. BM28 37
Golders Gdns. NW11 BR33 46
Golders Grn. Cres. NW11 BR33 46
Golders Grn. Rd. NW11 BR32 46
Golders Manor Dr. NW4 BQ32 46
Golders Park Clo. NW11 BS33 47
Golders Ri. NW4 BQ32 46
Golders Way NW11 BR33 46
Goldfinch Clo., Orp. CO56 98
Goldfinch Gdns., Guil. AU70 118
Goldfinch Rd. SE28 CM41 68
Goldfinch Rd., S.Croy. CC58 96
Goldfinch Way, B.Wd. BM24 28
Goldford Pl. NW1 BU38 1
Goldfort Wk., Wok. AP61 100
Langmans Way
Goldhawk Rd. W12 BP41 65
Goldhawk Rd. W6 BO42 65
Goldhaze Clo., Wdf.Grn. CJ29 40
Goldhurst Ter. NW6 BS36 1
Goldhurst Ter. NW6 BS36 56
Golding Rd., Sev. CV64 108
Golding St. E1 CB39 57
Goldingham Av., Loug. CM23 31
Goldings Cres., Hat. BP12 10
Goldings Hill, Loug. CK21 31
Goldings Rd., Loug. CL23 31
Goldings Ri., Loug. CL23 31
Goldington Clo., Hodd. CD10 12
Goldington Cres. NW1 BW37 1
Goldington Cres. NW1 BW37 56
Goldington St. NW1 BW37 1
Goldington St. NW1 BW37 56
Goldman Clo. E2 CB38 2
Goldman Clo. E2 CB38 57
Goldney Rd. W9 BS38 56
Goldrings Rd., Lthd. BF60 93
Goldsborough Cres. E4 CE27 39
Goldsborough Rd. SW8 BW44 66
Goldsdown Clo., Enf. CD23 30
Goldsdown Rd., Enf. CC23 30
Goldsell Rd., Swan. CS53 89
Goldsmid St. SE18 CN42 68
Sladedale Rd.
Goldsmith Av. E12 CK36 58
Goldsmith Av. NW9 BO32 46
Goldsmith Av. W3 BN40 55
Goldsmith Av., Rom. CR33 50
Goldsmith Clo. W3 BN40 55
East Acton La.
Goldsmith Clo., Har. BF33 45
Goldsmith La. NW9 BM31 46
Goldsmith Rd. E10 CE33 48
Goldsmith Rd. E17 CC30 39
Goldsmith Rd. N11 BU28 38
Goldsmith Rd. SE15 CB44 67
Goldsmith Rd. W3 BN40 55
Goldsmith St. EC2 BZ39 57
Gutter La.
Goldsmiths Clo., Wok. AR62 100
Goldsmiths Row E2 CB37 2
Goldsmiths Row E2 CB37 57
Goldsmiths Sq. E2 CB37 57
Goldsworth Orch., Wok. AQ62 100
Goldsworth Rd., Wok. AR62 100
Goldsworth Relief Rd., Wok. AR62 100
Goldsworthy Gdns. SE16 CC42 67
Goldwell Rd., Th.Hth. BX52 86
Goldwin Clo. SE15 CC44 67
Pomeroy St.
Golf Clo., Bush. BD23 27
Golf Clo., Stan. BK29 36
Golf Clo., Wok. AV60 91
Golf Club Dr., Kings.T. BN50 75
Golf Club Rd., Wey. AZ58 92
Golf Club Rd., Wok. AQ63 100
Golf Links Av., Grav. DG49 81
Golf Rd. W5 BL39 55
Boileau Rd.
Golf Rd., Brom. CL52 88
Golf Rd., Ken. BZ62 105
Golf Ride, Enf. BY21 29
Golf Side, Sutt. BR59 94
Golf Side, Twick. BG48 74
Golfe Rd., Ilf. CM34 49
Golfside Clo. N20 BU27 38
Golfside Clo., N.Mal. BO51 85
Goliath Clo., Wall. BX57 95
Gollogly Ter. SE7 CJ42 68
Nadine St.
Gombards All., St.Alb. BG13 9
Gombards, St.Alb. BG13 9
Gomer Gdns., Tedd. BJ50 74
Gomer Pl., Tedd. BJ49 74
Gomm Rd. SE16 CC41 67
Gomshall Av., Wall. BX56 95
Gomshall Gdns., Ken. BZ61 105
Gomshall Rd., Sutt. BQ58 94
Gondar Gdns. NW6 BR35 46
Gonnerston, St.Alb. BF13 9
Kings Rd.
Gonson Pl. SE8 CE43 67
Gonson St. SE8 CE43 67
Gonston Clo. SW19 BR48 75
Bodicott Clo.
Gonville Av., Rick. AZ25 26
Gonville Cres., Nthlt. BF36 54
Gonville Rd., Th.Hth. BX53 86
Gonville St. SW6 BR45 65
Putney Bridge App.
Good Clo., Couls. BY63 104
Goodall Rd. E11 CF35 48
Goodbury Rd., Sev. CX60 99
Gooden Ct., Har. BH34 45
Goodenough Rd. SW19 BR50 75
Goodenough Way, Couls. BX63 104
Gooderham Ho., Grays DG41 71
Goodge Pl. W1 BW39 1
Goodge Pl. W1 BW39 56
Goodge St.
Goodge St. W1 BW39 1
Goodge St. W1 BW39 56
Goodhall St. NW10 BO38 55
Goodhart Way, W.Wick. CG54 88
Goodhew Rd., Croy. CB53 87
Gooding Ho. SE7 CJ42 68
Goodinge Clo. N7 BX35 47
North Rd.
Goodinge Rd. N7 BX36 56
Goodlake Ct., Uxb. AV33 43
Goodley Stock Rd., West. CL67 115
Goodman Cres. SW2 BX48 76
Goodman Pk., Slou. AR40 52
Goodman Pl., Stai. AV49 72
High St.
Goodman Rd. E10 CF33 48
Goodman St. E1 CB39 2
Goodmans Fields E1 CB39 57
Goodmans Stile E1 CB39 2
Goodmans Stile E1 CB39 57
Commercial Rd.
Goodmans Yd. E1 CA40 57
Goodmayes Av., Ilf. CO33 50
Goodmayes La., Ilf. CO35 50
Goodmayes Rd., Ilf. CO33 50
Goodmead Rd., Orp. CO54 89
Goodrich Clo., Wat. BC21 26
Goodrich Rd. SE22 CA46 77
Goods Way NW1 BW37 56
Goods Way NW1 BX37 2
Goodson Rd. NW10 BO36 55
Goodstone Rd., Whyt. CA62 105
Goodway Gdns. E14 CF39 57
Goodwin Clo., Mitch. BT52 86
Phipps Bridge Rd.
Goodwin Dr., Sid. CP48 79
Goodwin Gdns., Croy. BY57 95
Goodwin Rd. N9 CC26 39
Goodwin Rd. W12 BP41 65
Goodwin Rd., Croy. BY57 95
Goodwin St. N4 BY34 47
Goodwins Ct. WC2 BX40 4
Goodwins Ct. WC2 BX40 56
St. Martins La.
Goodwood Av., Enf. CC22 30
Goodwood Av., Horn. CW35 51
Goodwood Av., Wat. BB21 26
Goodwood Clo., Hodd. CE11 12
Goodwood Clo., Mord. BS52 86
Goodwood Clo., Stan. BK28 36
Marsh La.
Goodwood Cres., Grav. DH50 81
Goodwood Dr., Nthlt. BF36 54
Goodwood Par., Wat. BB21 26
Goodwood Path, B.Wd. BM23 28
Stratfield Rd.
Goodwood Rd. SE14 CD43 67
Goodwood Rd., Red. BU69 121
Goodwyn Av. NW7 BO28 37
Goodwyns Farm Est., Dor. BJ73 119
Goodwyns Rd., Dor. BJ73 119
Goodwyns Vale N10 BV30 38
Goodyear Pl. SE5 BZ43 67
Addington Sq.
Goodyear Ter., Grays DA43 70
Goodyers Av., Rad. BH20 18
Goodyers Gdns. NW4 BQ32 46
Brent Grn.
Goosander Way SE28 CM41 68
Goose Acre, Chesh. AQ18 16
Goose Acre, Welw.G.C. BR9 5
Goose Croft, Hem.H. AV13 7
Goose Grn. Clo., Orp. CO51 89
Goose Grn., Cob. BC63 101
Goose La., Wok. AQ64 100
Goose Rye Rd., Guil. AO66 109
Goose Sq. E6 CK39 58
Harper Rd.
Goose Yd. EC1 BY37 2
Goose Yd. EC1 BY37 56
St. John St.
Gooseacre La., Har. BK32 45
Goosefield, E.Mol. BF52 84
Gooseley La. E6 CL38 58
Gooshays Dr., Rom. CW28 42
Gooshays Gdns., Rom. CW29 42
Goossens Clo., Sutt. BT56 95
Turnpike La.
Gophir La. EC4 BZ40 57
Bush La.
Gopsall St. N1 BZ37 2
Gopsall St. N1 BZ37 57
Goral Mead, Rick. AX26 35
Gordon Av. E4 CG29 40
Gordon Av. SW14 BO45 65
Gordon Av., Horn. CT34 50
Gordon Av., S.Croy. BZ58 96
Gordon Av., Stan. BH29 36
Gordon Av., Twick. BJ46 74
Gordon Clo. E17 CE32 48
Lennox Rd.
Gordon Clo. N19 BW33 47
Highgate Hill
Gordon Clo., Cher. AV55 82
Gordon Clo., St.Alb. BJ14 9
Gordon Clo., Stai. AW50 73
Gordon Cres., Croy. CA54 87
Gordon Cres., Hayes BC41 63
Gordon Ct. W12 BP39 55
Du Cane Rd.
Gordon Dr., Cher. AV55 82
Gordon Dr., Shep. BA53 83
Gordon Gdns., Edg. BM30 37
Gordon Gro. SE5 BY44 66
Gordon Hill, Enf. BZ23 30
Gordon House Rd. NW5 BV35 47
Gordon Pl. W8 BS41 66
Gordon Prom., Grav. DH46 81
Gordon Rd. E11 CH32 49
Gordon Rd. E12 CL34 49
Gordon Rd. E15 CF35 48
Gordon Rd. E17 CD32 48
Gordon Rd. E18 CH30 40
Gordon Rd. E4 CG26 40
Gordon Rd. N11 BW29 38
Gordon Rd. N3 BR29 37

Gordon Rd. N9 CB27 39
Gordon Rd. NW6 BS38 56
Gordon Rd. SE15 CB44 67
Gordon Rd. W13 BJ40 54
Gordon Rd. W4 BM43 65
Gordon Rd. W5 BK40 54
Gordon Rd., Ashf. AY48 73
Gordon Rd., Bark. CN37 58
Gordon Rd., Beck. CC51 87
Gordon Rd., Beck. CD52 87
Gordon Rd., Belv. CS42 69
Gordon Rd., Brwd. DD26 122
Gordon Rd., Cars. BU57 95
Gordon Rd., Cat. BZ64 105
Gordon Rd., Chesh. AO19 16
Gordon Rd., Dart. CV47 80
Gordon Rd., Enf. BZ23 30
Gordon Rd., Esher BH57 93
Gordon Rd., Grav. DF47 81
Gordon Rd., Grays DF41 71
Gordon Rd., Har. BH31 45
Gordon Rd., Houns. BG45 64
Gordon Rd., Ilf. CM34 49
Gordon Rd., Kings.T. BL51 85
Gordon Rd., Red. BV69 121
Gordon Rd., Rich. BL44 65
Gordon Rd., Rom. CQ32 50
Gordon Rd., Sev. CU66 116
Gordon Rd., Shep. BA53 83
Gordon Rd., Sid. CM46 78
Gordon Rd., Stai. AU49 72
Gordon Rd., Sthl. BE42 64
Gordon Rd., Surb. BL54 85
Gordon Rd., Wal.Abb. CE20 21
Gordon Rd., West Dr. AY40 53
Gordon Rd., Wind. AM44 61
Gordon Sq. WC1 BW38 1
Gordon Sq. WC1 BW38 56
Gordon St. E13 CH38 58
Gordon St. WC1 BW38 1
Gordon St. WC1 BW38 56
Gordon St., Twick. BJ46 74
Gordon Way, Barn. BR24 28
Gordon Way, Ch.St.G. AQ27 34
Gordonbrock Rd. SE4 CE46 77
Gordondale Rd. SW19 BS48 76
Gordons Way, Oxt. CF67 114
Gore Cotts., Dart. CX49 80
Gore Ct. NW9 BM32 46
Gore Rd. E9 CC37 57
Gore Rd. SW20 BQ51 85
Gore Rd., Dart. CY47 80
Gore St. SW7 BT41 3
Gore St. SW7 BT41 66
Gorefield Pl. NW6 BS37 56
Gorelands La., Ch.St.G. AR26 34
Goresbrook Rd., Dag. CO37 59
Gorham Dr., St.Alb. BH15 9
Gorham Pl. W11 BR40 55
Mary Pl.
Gorhambury Dr., St.Alb. BE12 9
Goring Clo., Rom. CS30 41
Goring Gdns., Dag. CP35 50
Goring Rd. N., Dag. CS36 59
Goring Rd. N11 BX29 38
Goring Rd., Dag. CS36 59
Goring Rd., Stai. AV49 72
Goring St. EC3 CA39 2
Goring St. EC3 CA39 57
Houndsditch
Goring Way, Grnf. BG37 54
Gorings Sq., Stai. AV49 72
Gorle Clo., Wat. BC21 26
Gorleston Rd. N15 BZ32 48
Gorleston St. W14 BR42 65
Gorman Rd. SE18 CK42 68
Gorringe Av., S.Dnth. CY51 90
Gorringe Park Av., Mitch. BU50 76
Gorse Clo., Hat. BO14 10
Gorse Ct., Guil. AU69 118
Gorse Hill La., Vir.W. AR52 82
Gorse Hill Rd., Vir.W. AR52 82
Gorse Hill, Farn. CX54 90
Gorse La., Wok. AP57 91
Windsor Rd.
Gorse Mead, Slou. AN40 61
Weekes Dr.
Gorse Rd., Croy. CE56 96
Gorse Rd., Orp. CQ54 89
Gorse Ri. SW17 BV49 76
Gorse Way, Rom. CT33 50
Gorse Wk., West Dr. AY39 53
Gorselands Clo., Wey. AX59 92
Gorsewood Rd., Wok. AO63 100
Gorst Rd. NW10 BN38 55
Gorst Rd. SW11 BU46 76
Gorsuch Pl. E2 CA38 2
Gorsuch St. E2 CA38 2
Gorsuch St. E2 CA38 57
Gosberton Rd. SW12 BU47 76
Gosbury Hill, Chess. BL56 94
Gosden Hill Rd., Guil. AU68 109
Gosfield Rd., Dag. CR34 50
Gosfield Rd., Epsom BN59 94
Gosfield St. W1 BV39 1
Gosfield St. W1 BW39 56
Gosford Gdns., Ilf. CK32 49
Gosforth La., Wat. BC27 35
Goshawk Gdns., Hayes BB38 53
Goslar Way, Wind. AN44 61
Goslett Yd. WC2 BW39 1
Goslett Yd. WC2 BW39 56
Charing Cross Rd.
Gosling Clo., Grnf. BF38 54
Gosling Grn., Slou. AS41 62
Gosling Rd.
Gosling Rd., Slou. AS41 62
Gosling Way SW9 BY44 66
Gospatrick Rd. N17 BZ29 39
Gospel Oak Est. NW5 BU35 47
Gosport Dr., Horn. CV36 60
Gosport Rd. E17 CD32 48
Gosport Way SE15 CA43 67
Goss Hill, Swan. CV50 80
Gossage Rd. SE18 CM42 68
Ancona Rd.
Gossage Rd., Uxb. AY36 53
Gossamers, The, Wat. BE21 27
Gosset St. E2 CA38 2
Gosset St. E2 CA38 57
Gosshill Rd., Brom. CL51 88
Gossington Clo., Chis. CL49 78
Beechwood Ri.
Gossoms End, Berk. AQ12 7
Gossoms Ryde, Berk. AQ12 7
Victory Rd.
Gosterwood St. SE8 CD43 67
Gostling Rd., Twick. BF47 74
Goston Gdns., Th.Hth. BY52 86
Goswell Hill, Wind. AO44 61
Goswell Pl. EC1 BY38 2
Goswell Pl. EC1 BY38 56
Goswell Rd.
Goswell Rd. EC1 BY37 2
Goswell Rd. EC1 BY37 56
Goswell Rd., Wind. AO44 61
Gothic Clo., Dart. CW48 80
Gothic Ct., Hayes BA43 63
Sipson La.
Gothic Rd., Twick. BG48 74
Goudhurst Rd., Brom. CG49 78
Gouge Av., Grav. DF47 81
Gough Rd. E15 CG35 49
Gough Rd., Enf. CB23 30
Gough Sq. EC4 BY39 2
Gough Sq. EC4 BY39 56
Gough St. WC1 BX38 2
Gough St. WC1 BX38 56
Gough Wk. E14 CE39 57
Gould Clo., Hat. BP15 10
Gould Ct. SE19 CA49 77
Gould Ct., Guil. AU69 109
Eustace Rd.
Gould Rd., Felt. BB47 73
Gould Rd., Twick. BH47 74
Goulds Grn., Uxb. AZ40 53
Goulston St. E1 CA39 2
Goulston St. E1 CA39 57
Goulton Rd. E5 CB35 48
Gourley Pl. N15 CA32 48
Gourley St.
Gourley St. N15 CA32 48
Gourock Rd. SE9 CL46 78
Govan St. E2 CB37 2
Govan St. E2 CB37 57
Whiston Rd.
Government Row, Enf. CE22 30
Governors Av., Uxb. AV32 43
Govett Av., Shep. BA53 83
Govier Clo. E15 CG36 58
Gowan Av. SW6 BR44 65
Gowan Rd. NW10 BP36 55
Gowar Field, Pot.B. BP19 19
Gower Clo. E15 CG36 58
Gower Ct. WC1 BW38 1
Gower Ct. WC1 BW38 56
Gower St.
Gower Ms. WC1 BW39 1
Gower Ms. WC1 BW39 56
Gower Pl. WC1 BW38 1
Gower Pl. WC1 BW38 56
Gower Rd. E7 CH36 58
Gower Rd., Islw. BH43 64
Gower Rd., Wey. BA57 92
Gower St. WC1 BW38 1
Gower St. WC1 BW38 56
Gower, The, Egh. AT52 82
Gowers La., Grays DF41 71
Gowers Wk. E1 CB39 2
Gowers Wk. E1 CB39 57
Gowers, The, Amer. AP22 25
Gowers, The, Harl. CO10 6
Gowland Pl., Beck. CD51 87
Gowlett Rd. SE15 CB45 67
Gowrie Rd. SW11 BV45 66
Graburn Way, E.Mol. BG52 84
Grace Av., Bexh. CQ44 69
Grace Clo. SE9 CJ49 78
Dunkery Rd.
Grace Clo., Edg. BM29 37
Pavilion Way
Grace Clo., Ilf. CN29 40
Grace Jones Clo. E8 CB36 57
Parkholme Rd.
Grace Path SE26 CC49 77
Silverdale Rd.
Grace Rd., Croy. BZ53 87
Grace St. E3 CE38 57
Gracechurch St. EC3 BZ40 4
Gracechurch St. EC3 BZ40 57
Gracedale Rd. SW16 BV49 76
Gracefield Gdns. SW16 BX48 76
Graces Alley E1 CB40 4
Graces Alley E1 CB40 57
Ensign St.
Graces Ms. SE5 BZ44 67
Graces Rd. SE5 CA44 67
Gracious La., Sev. CU68 116
Gracious Pond Rd., Wok. AQ57 91
Gradient, The SE26 CB49 77
Graeme Rd., Enf. BZ23 30
Graemes Dyke Rd., Berk. AQ13 7
Graemesdyke Av. SW14 BM45 65
Grafton Clo. W13 BJ39 54
Grafton Clo., Houns. BE47 74
Grafton Clo., Slou. AS39 52
Grafton Clo., Wey. AV60 91
Grafton Clo., Wor.Pk. BO55 85
Grafton Cres. NW1 BV36 56
Grafton Gdns. N4 CB32 48
Rutland Gdns.
Grafton Gdns., Dag. CQ34 50
Grafton Ms. W1 BW38 1
Grafton Ms. W1 BW38 56
Grafton Park Rd., N.Mal. BO55 85
Grafton Pl. NW1 BW38 1
Grafton Pl. NW1 BW38 56
Grafton Rd. NW5 BV35 47
Grafton Rd. W3 BN40 55
Grafton Rd., Croy. BY54 86
Grafton Rd., Dag. CQ34 50
Grafton Rd., Enf. BX24 29
Grafton Rd., Har. BG32 45
Grafton Rd., N.Mal. BO52 85
Grafton Rd., Wor.Pk. BN55 85
Grafton Sq. SW4 BW45 66
Grafton St. NW3 BS34 47
Hermitage La.
Grafton St. W1 BV40 3
Grafton St. W1 BV40 56
Grafton Ter. NW2 BS34 47
Hermitage La.
Grafton Ter. NW5 BU35 47
Grafton Way W1 BW38 56
Grafton Way W1 & WC1 BW38 1
Grafton Way WC1 BW38 56
Grafton Yd. NW5 BV36 56
Prince of Wales Rd.
Graham Av. W13 BJ41 64
Graham Av., Brox. CD14 12
Graham Av., Mitch. BV51 86
Graham Clo., Brwd. DE25 122
Graham Clo., Croy. CE55 87
Graham Clo., St.Alb. BG15 9
Graham Gdns., Surb. BL54 85
Graham Rd. E13 CH38 58
Graham Rd. E8 CB36 57
Graham Rd. N15 BY31 47
Graham Rd. NW4 BP32 46
Graham Rd. SW19 BR50 75
Graham Rd. W4 BN41 65
Graham Rd., Bexh. CQ45 69
Graham Rd., Har. BG31 45
Graham Rd., Hmptn. BF49 74
Graham Rd., Mitch. BV51 86
Graham Rd., Pur. BY60 95
Graham St. N1 BY37 2
Graham St. N1 BY37 56
Graham Ter. SW1 BV42 3
Graham Ter. SW1 BV42 66
Grahame Park Est. NW9 BO30 37
Grahame Park Way NW9 BO30 37
Grainger Clo., Nthlt. BG35 45
Grainger Rd. N22 BZ30 39
Grainger Rd., Islw. BH44 64
Grainges Yd., Uxb. AX36 53
Windsor St.
Gramer Clo. E11 CF34 48
Norman Rd.
Grampian Clo., Orp. CN53 89
Cotswold Ri.
Grampian Gdns. NW2 BR33 46
Grampian Way, Hayes BA43 63
Pennine Way
Grampian Way, Slou. AT42 62
Granada St. SW17 BU49 76
Granard Av. SW15 BP46 75
Granard Rd. SW12 BU47 76
Turin Rd.
Granary Clo. N9 CC26 39
Granary Meadow, Brwd. DC21 33
Granary Way NW1 BW37 1
Granary Way NW1 BW37 56
Granby Park Rd., Chsnt. CB17 21
Granby Rd. SE9 CK44 68
Granby Rd., Grav. DE46 81
Granby Row E2 CA38 2
Granby St.
Granby St. E2 CA38 2
Granby St. E2 CA38 57
Granby Ter. NW1 BW37 1
Granby Ter. NW1 BW37 56
Granbys Bldgs. SE11 BX42 4
Granbys Bldgs. SE11 BX42 66
Salamanca St.
Grand Av. E., Wem. BM35 46
Grand Av. EC1 BY39 2
Grand Av. EC1 BY39 56
Charterhouse St.
Grand Av. N10 BV31 47
Grand Av., Surb. BM53 85
Grand Av., Wem. BM35 46
Grand Central Wk. SE19 CB50 77
Grand Depot Rd. SE18 CL42 68
Grand Dr. SW20 BQ52 85
Grand Par., Surb. BM54 85
Grand Par., The NW3 BT35 47
Finchley Rd.
Grand Par., Wem. BM34 46
Grand Parade Ms. SW15 BR46 75
Upper Richmond Rd.
Grand Sq. SE10 CF42 67
Grand Stand Rd., Epsom BO62 103
Grand Union Ind. Est. NW10 BM37 55
Grand View Av., West. CJ62 106
Grand Wk. E1 CD38 57
Solebay St.
Granden Rd. SW16 BX51 86
Grandfield Av., Wat. BC23 26
Grandis Cotts., Wok. AW64 101
Grandison Rd. SW11 BU45 66
Grandison Rd., Wor.Pk. BQ55 85
Granfield St. SW11 BT44 66
Grange Av. N12 BT28 38
Grange Av. N20 BR26 37
Grange Av. SE25 CA51 87
Grange Av., Barn. BU26 38
Grange Av., Stan. BJ30 36
Grange Av., Twick. BH48 74
Grange Av., Wdf.Grn. CH29 40
Grange Clo., Brwd. DE28 122
Grange Clo., E.Mol. BF52 84
Grange Clo., Edg. BN28 37
Grange Clo., Ger.Cr. AS30 34
Grange Clo., Guil. AQ68 109
Grange Clo., Hayes BB39 53
Grange Clo., Hem.H. AZ14 8
Grange Clo., Houns. BE43 64
Grange Clo., Lthd. BK63 102
Grange Clo., N.Mal. BP53 85
Grange Clo., Red. BV67 113
Grange Clo., Sid. CO48 79
Grange Clo., Stai. AS46 72
Grange Clo., Wdf.Grn. CH29 40
Grange Clo., West. CM66 115
Grange Cres. SE28 CP39 59
Grange Cres., Chig. CM28 40
Grange Ct. Rd. N16 CA33 48
Grange Ct. WC2 BX39 2
Grange Ct. WC2 BX39 56
Grange Ct., Chig. CM27 40
Grange Ct., Loug. CJ25 31
Grange Ct., Nthlt. BD37 54
Grange Ct., Shep. AZ52 83
Watersplash Rd.
Grange Ct., St.Alb. BG13 9
Grange St.
Grange Ct., Wal.Abb. CE20 21
Grange Ct., Walt. BC55 83
Grange Dr., Chis. CK50 78
Grange Dr., Orp. CP59 98
Grange Dr., Red. BV67 113
Grange Dr., Wok. AS61 100
Grange Est. N2 BT30 38
Grange Farm Clo., Har. BG34 45
Grange Fields, Ger.Cr. AS30 34
Grange Gdns. N14 BW26 38
Grange Gdns. NW3 BS34 47
Templewood Av.
Grange Gdns. SE25 CA51 87
Grange Gdns., Bans. BS60 95
Grange Gdns., Pnr. BE31 45
Grange Gdns., Slou. AO35 43
Grange Gro. N1 BY36 56
Grange Hill SE25 CA51 87
Grange Hill, Edg. BN28 37
Grange La. SE21 CA48 77
Grange La., Harl. CJ11 13
Grange Meadow, Bans. BS60 95
Grange Mt., Lthd. BK63 102
Grange Par., Hayes BB39 53
Grange Pk. Av. N21 BZ25 30
Grange Pk. Pl. SW20 BP50 75
Thurstan Rd.
Grange Pk. Rd. E10 CE33 48
Grange Pk. Rd., Th.Hth. BZ52 87
Grange Pk. W5 BL40 55
Grange Pk., Wok. AS61 100
Grange Pl. NW6 BS37 56
Grange Pl. SE16 CB41 4
Grange Pl. SE16 CB41 67
Yalding Rd.
Grange Pl., Stai. AW51 83
Grange Rd. E10 CE33 48
Grange Rd. E13 CG38 58
Grange Rd. E17 CD32 48
Grange Rd. N17 CB29 39
Grange Rd. N6 BU32 47
Grange Rd. NW10 BP36 55
Grange Rd. SE1 CA41 67
Grange Rd. SE19 BZ51 87
Grange Rd. SW13 BP44 65
Grange Rd. W4 BM42 65
Grange Rd. W5 BK40 54
Grange Rd., B.Wd. BL25 28
Grange Rd., Bush. BE25 27
Grange Rd., Cat. CA66 114
Grange Rd., Chess. BL55 85
Grange Rd., E.Mol. BF53 84
Grange Rd., Edg. BN29 37
Grange Rd., Egh. AS49 72
Grange Rd., Ger.Cr. AS30 34
Grange Rd., Grav. DG47 81
Grange Rd., Grays DD43 71
Grange Rd., Guil. AQ68 109
Grange Rd., Har. BG34 45
Grange Rd., Har. BJ32 45
Grange Rd., Hayes BB39 53
Grange Rd., Ilf. CL35 49
Grange Rd., Kings.T. BL52 85
Grange Rd., Lthd. BK63 102
Grange Rd., Orp. CM55 88
Grange Rd., Rom. CU29 41
Grange Rd., S.Croy. BZ58 96
Grange Rd., S.Ock. CV40 60
Grange Rd., Sev. CU67 116
Grange Rd., Sthl. BE41 64
Grange Rd., Sutt. BS57 95
Grange Rd., Th.Hth. BZ52 87
Grange Rd., Walt. BE56 93
Grange Rd., Wey. AW58 92
Grange Rd., Wok. AS60 91
Grange St. N1 BZ37 2
Grange St., St.Alb. BG13 9
Grange Vale, Sutt. BS57 95
Grange View Rd. N20 BT26 38
Grange Way N12 BS28 38
Grange Way, Erith CU43 69
Grange Way, Iver AV39 52
Grange Wk. SE1 CA41 4
Grange Wk. SE1 CA41 67
Grange Yd. SE1 CA41 4
Grange Yd. SE1 CA41 67
Grange, The N20 BT26 38
Grange, The NW3 BS34 47
Grange, The SE1 CA41 4
Grange, The SE1 CA41 67
Grange, The SW19 BQ49 75
Grange, The, Croy. CD55 87
Grange, The, Dart. CY51 90
Grange, The, N.Mal. BP53 85
Grange, The, Sev. CZ58 99
Grange, The, Wem. BM36 55
Grange, The, Wind. AQ46 72
Grange, The, Wor.Pk. BN55 85
Grangecliffe Gdns. SE25 CA51 87
Grangedale Clo., Nthwd. BB29 35
Grangefields Rd., Guil. AR67 109
Grangehill Pl. SE9 CK45 68
Grangehill Rd. SE9 CK45 68
Grangemill Rd. SE6 CE48 77
Grangemill Way SE6 CE48 77
Granger Way, Rom. CU32 50
Grangeway Gdns., Ilf. CK32 49
Grangeway NW6 BS36 56
Messina Av.
Grangeway, The N21 BY25 29
Grangeway, Wdf.Grn. CJ28 40
Grangeways Clo., Grav. DF49 81
Grangewood Av., Grays DF41 71
Grangewood Av., Rain. CV38 60
Grangewood Clo., Brwd. DD27 122
Grangewood Clo., Pnr. BC32 44
Grangewood Dr., Sun. BB50 73
Forest Dr.
Grangewood La., Beck. CD50 77
Grangewood St. E6 CJ37 58
Grangewood, Bex. CQ47 79
Hurst Rd.
Grangewood, Pot.B. BS18 20
Grangewood, Slou. AR39 52
Granham Gdns. N9 CA27 39
Granite St. SE18 CN42 68
Granleigh Rd. E11 CG34 49
Gransden Av. E8 CB36 57
London La.
Gransden Rd. W12 BO41 65
Wendell Rd.
Grant Av., Slou. AP39 52
Grant Clo. N14 BW26 38
Grant Clo., Shep. AZ53 83
Grant Pl., Croy. CA54 87
Grant Rd. SW11 BT45 66
Grant Rd., Croy. CA54 87
Grant Rd., Har. BH31 45
Grant St. E13 CH38 58
Grant St. N1 BY37 2
Grant St. N1 BY37 56
Chapel Market
Grant Way, Islw. BJ43 64
Grantbridge St. N1 BY37 2
Grantbridge St. N1 BY37 56
Grantchester Clo., Har. BH34 45
Grantham Clo., Edg. BL27 37
Grantham Gdns., Rom. CQ32 50
Grantham Grn., B.Wd. BN25 28
Grantham Pl. W1 BV40 3
Grantham Pl. W1 BV40 56
Old Park La.
Grantham Rd. E12 CL34 49
Grantham Rd. SW9 BX44 66
Grantham Rd. W4 BO43 65
Grantham Way, Grays DD40 71
Grantley Gdns., Guil. AQ70 118
Grantley Rd., Guil. AQ70 118
Grantley Rd., Houns. BC44 63
Grantley St. E1 CC38 57
Grantock Rd. E17 CF30 39
Granton Av., Upmin. CW34 51
Granton Rd. SW16 BW51 86
Granton Rd., Ilf. CO33 50
Granton Rd., Sid. CP50 79
Grants Clo. NW7 BQ29 37
Grants La., Oxt. CJ70 115
Grantully Rd. W9 BS38 56
Grantwood Clo., Red. BV73 121
Granville Av. N9 CC27 39
Granville Av., Felt. BC48 73
Granville Av., Houns. BF46 74
Granville Av., Slou. AO39 52
Granville Clo., Croy. CB55 87
Granville Clo., Wey. AY60 92
Church Rd.
Granville Clo., Wey. BA57 92
Granville Dene, Hem.H. AT17 16
Granville Gdns. SW16 BX51 86
Granville Gdns. W5 BL40 55
Granville Gro. SE13 CF45 67
Granville Ms. NW2 BR34 46
Granville Pk. SE13 CF45 67
Granville Pl. N12 BT29 38
High Rd. N. Finchley
Granville Pl. W1 BV39 1
Granville Pl. W1 BV39 56
Granville Rd. E17 CE32 48
Granville Rd. E18 CH30 40
Granville Rd. N12 BS29 38
Granville Rd. N13 BX29 38
Granville Rd. N22 BY30 38
Granville Rd. N4 BX32 47
Granville Rd. NW2 BR34 46
Granville Rd. NW6 BS37 56
Granville Rd. SW18 BR47 75
Granville Rd. SW19 BS50 76
Granville Rd., Barn. BQ24 28
Granville Rd., Berk. AP12 7
Granville Rd., Epp. CO18 23
Granville Rd., Grav. DF47 81
Granville Rd., Hayes BB42 63
Granville Rd., Ilf. CL33 49
Granville Rd., Oxt. CG68 115
Granville Rd., Sev. CU65 107
Granville Rd., Sid. CO49 79
Granville Rd., St.Alb. BH13 9
Granville Rd., Uxb. AZ36 53
Granville Rd., Wat. BD24 27
Granville Rd., Well. CP45 69
Granville Rd., West. CM66 115
Granville Rd., Wey. BA57 92
Granville Rd., Wok. AS63 100
Granville Sq. SE15 CA43 67
Blakes Rd.
Granville Sq. WC1 BX38 2
Granville Sq. WC1 BX38 56
Granville St. WC1 BX38 2
Granville St. WC1 BX38 56
Wharton St.
Grape St. WC2 BX39 56
High Holborn
Grasdene Rd. SE18 CO43 69
Grasmere Av. SW15 BN49 75
Grasmere Av. SW19 BS51 86
Grasmere Av. W3 BN40 55
Grasmere Av., Houns. BF46 74
Grasmere Av., Orp. CL55 88
Grasmere Av., Ruis. BA33 44
Grasmere Av., Slou. AQ40 52
Grasmere Av., Wem. BK33 45
Grasmere Clo., Egh. AT50 72
Keswick Way
Grasmere Clo., Felt. BB47 73
Derwent Clo.
Grasmere Clo., Guil. AT70 118
Grasmere Clo., Hem.H. AZ14 8
Grasmere Clo., Loug. CK23 31
Grasmere Ct. N22 BX29 38
Palmerston Rd.
Grasmere Gdns., Har. BJ30 36
Grasmere Gdns., Ilf. CK32 49
Grasmere Gdns., Orp. CL55 88
Grasmere Rd. E13 CH37 58
Grasmere Rd. N10 BV30 38

Grasmere Rd. N17 CB29 39
Grasmere Rd. SE25 CB53 87
Grasmere Rd. SW16 BX49 76
Grasmere Rd., Bexh. CS44 69
Grasmere Rd., Brom. CG51 88
Grasmere Rd., Horn. CW31 51
Grasmere Rd., Orp. CL55 88
Grasmere Rd., Pur. BY59 95
Grasmere Rd., St.Alb. BJ14 9
Grasmere Way, Wey. AY59 92
Grass Mt. SE23 CB48 77
Grass Pk. N3 BR30 37
Grass Warren, Welw. BU 6 5
Grassfield Clo., Couls. BW63 104
Grassingham End, Ger.Cr. AS29 34
Grassingham Rd., Ger.Cr. AS29 34
Grassington Clo., St.Alb. BF18 18
West Riding
Grassington Rd., Sid. CO49 79
Grassmount SE23 CB48 77
Grassmount, Pur. BW58 95
Grassway, Wall. BW56 95
Grassy Clo., Hem.H. AW13 8
Grassy La., Sev. CU66 116
Grasvenor Av., Barn. BS25 29
Grateley Way SE15 CA43 67
Hordle Promenade N.
Gratton Bottom, Reig. BT68 113
Gratton Dr., Wind. AM45 61
Gratton Rd. W14 BR41 65
Gratton Ter. NW2 BQ34 46
Gratton Way W1 BW38 56
Gravel Clo., Chig. CO27 41
Gravel Hill Clo., Bexh. CR46 79
Gravel Hill N3 BR30 37
The Broadway
Gravel Hill Ter., Hem.H. AW14 8
Gravel Hill, Bexh. CR46 79
Gravel Hill, Ger.Cr. AS29 34
Gravel Hill, Hem.H. AW13 8
Gravel Hill, Loug. CH23 31
Gravel Hill, Lthd. BJ64 102
Kingston Av.
Gravel Hill, S.Croy. CC57 96
Gravel Hill, Uxb. AX35 44
Gravel La. E1 CA39 2
Gravel La. E1 CA39 57
Gravel La., Chig. CO26 41
Gravel La., Hem.H. AW13 8
Gravel Path, Berk. AR13 7
Gravel Path, Hem.H. AW13 8
Gravel Pit La. SE9 CM46 78
Gravel Pit Way, Orp. CO55 89
Gravel Rd., Brom. CK55 88
Gravel Rd., Twick. BH47 74
Gravel St. E1 CC40 57
Gravel Wood Clo., Chis. CM48 78
Graveley Av., B.Wd. BN24 28
Graveley Ct., Hem.H. BA14 8
Graveley Dell, Welw.G.C. BS 8 5
Waterford Grn.
Gravelly Hill, Cat. CA67 114
Gravelly Ride SW19 BP49 75
Graveney Gro. SE20 CC50 77
Graveney Rd. SW17 BU49 76
Gravesend Rd. W12 BP40 55
Gravetts La., Guil. AP68 109
Gray Av., Dag. CQ33 50
Gray Gdns., Rain. CU36 59
Gray St. SE1 BY41 4
Gray St. SE1 BY41 66
Grayburn Clo., Ch.St.G. AQ27 34
Grayburne, Grav. DB49 80
Graydon St. SE18 CL43 68
Grayfield Ter. N1 BY37 2
Grayford Clo. E6 CJ39 58
Neatscourt Rd.
Grayham Cres., N.Mal. BN52 85
Grayham Rd., N.Mal. BN52 85
Grayland Clo., Brom. CJ51 88
Graylands Clo., Wok. AS61 100
Horsell Pk.
Graylands La., Swans. DB46 60
Graylands Sq., Swans. DB46 60
Graylands, Epp. CM22 31
Graylands, Wok. AS61 100
Grayling Rd. N16 BZ34 48
Grayling Sq. E2 CB38 57
Avebury Est.
Graylings, The, Wat. BA20 17
Grays End Clo., Grays DD41 71
Grays Farm Rd., Orp. CO51 89
Grays Inn Rd. WC1 BX38 2
Grays Inn Rd. WC1 BX38 56
Grays Inn Sq. WC1 BY39 2
Grays Inn Sq. WC1 BY39 56
Grays La., Ash. BL63 103
Grays La., Ashf. AZ49 73
Grays Park Rd., Slou. AQ37 52
Grays Pl., Slou. AP40 52
Grays Rd., Slou. AP40 52
Grays Rd., Uxb. AY36 53
Grays Rd., West. CL64 106
Grays Wk., Brwd. DE26 122
Grayscroft Rd. SW16 BW50 76
Graysfield, Welw.G.C. BS 9 5
Grayshot Rd. SW11 BU44 66
Grayswood Gdns. SW20 BP51 85
Graywood Ct. N12 BT29 38
Grazebrook Rd. N16 BZ34 48
Grazeley Clo., Bexh. CS46 79
Grazings, The, Hem.H. AZ12 8
Great Acre Ct. SW4 BW45 66
Clapham Park Rd.
Great Bell Alley EC2 BZ39 2
Moorgate
Great Bell Alley EC2 BZ39 57
Moorgate
Great Benty, West Dr. AY42 63
Great Braitch La., Hat. BO10 5
Great Brays, Harl. CO11 14
Great Break, Welw.G.C. BS 8 5
Great Brownings SE21 CA29 77
Great Bushey Dr. N20 BS26 38
Great Cambridge Rd. N17 BZ30 39
Great Cambridge Rd., Enf. CB25 30
Great Cambridge Rd., Chsnt. CC19 21
Great Castle St. W1 BV39 1
Great Castle St. W1 BV39 56
Great Central Av., Ruis. BD35 45
Great Central St. NW1 BU39 1
Great Central St. NW1 BU39 56
Melcombe Sq.
Great Chapel St. W1 BW39 1
Great Chapel St. W1 BW39 56
Great Chertsey Rd. W4 BN44 65
Great Chertsey Rd., Felt. BE48 74
Great Church La. W6 BQ42 65
Great College St. SW1 BX41 4
Great College St. SW1 BX41 66
Great Conduit, Welw.G.C. BT 7 5
Great Cross Av. SE10 CG43 68
Great Cullings, Rom. CT34 50
Great Cumberland Ms. W1 BU39 1
Great Cumberland Ms. W1 BU39 56
Seymour Pl.
Great Cumberland Pl. W1 BU39 1
Great Cumberland Pl. W1 BU39 56
Great Dell, Welw.G.C. BQ 7 7
Great Dover St. SE1 BZ41 4
Great Dover St. SE1 BZ41 67
Great Eastern Rd. E15 CF36 57
Great Eastern Rd., Brwd. DB28 42
Great Eastern St. EC2 CA38 2
Great Eastern St. EC2 CA38 57
Great Eastern Way NW10 BN35 46
Great Ellshams, Bans. BS61 104
Great Elms Rd., Brom. CJ52 88
Great Elms Rd., Hem.H. AY15 8
Great Field NW9 BO30 37
Great Fox Meadow, Brwd. CZ22 33
Great Ganett, Welw.G.C. BS 9 5
Great Gardens Rd., Horn. CU32 50
Great George St. SW1 BW41 3
Great George St. SW1 BW41 66
Great Goodwin Dr., Guil. AT69 118
Great Gro., Bush. BF24 27
Great Guildford St. SE1 BZ40 4
Great Guildford St. SE1 BZ40 57
Great Harry Dr. SE9 CL48 78
Great Heath, Hat. BP11 10
Great Hurstend, Lthd. BE65 102
Great James St. WC1 BX39 2
Great James St. WC1 BX39 56
Great Lawn, Ong. CX17 24
Great Ley, Welw.G.C. BR 9 5
Great Leylands, Harl. CO11 14
Great Marlborough St. W1 BW39 1
Great Marlborough St. W1 BW39 56
Great Maze Pond SE1 BZ41 4
Great Maze Pond SE1 BZ41 67
St. Thomas St.
Great Meadow, Brox. CE14 12
Great Nelmes Chase, Horn. CW32 51
Great New St. EC4 BY39 2
Great New St. EC4 BY39 56
East Harding St.
Great Newport St. WC2 BX40 4
Great Newport St. WC2 BX40 56
Upper St. Martins La.
Great North Rd. N2 BU31 47
Great North Rd., Barn. BS25 29
Great North Rd., Hat. BP13 10
Great North Rd., Pot.B. BT18 20
Great North Way NW4 BP30 37
Great Oaks Pk., Guil. AT68 109
Great Oaks, Brwd. DD25 122
Great Oaks, Chig. CM28 40
Great Ormond St. WC1 BX39 2
Great Ormond St. WC1 BX39 56
Great Owl Rd., Chig. CL27 40
Great Palmers, Hem.H. AY11 8
Great Parndon, Harl. CL12 13
Great Percy St. WC1 BX38 2
Great Percy St. WC1 BX38 56
Great Peter St. SW1 BW41 3
Great Peter St. SW1 BX41 66
Great Pk., Kings L. AY18 17
Great Plumtree, Harl. CN10 6
Great Portland St. W1 BV38 1
Great Portland St. W1 BV38 56
Great Pulteney St. W1 BW40 3
Great Pulteney St. W1 BW40 56
Great Quarry, Guil. AR71 118
Great Queen St. WC2 BX39 2
Great Queen St. WC2 BX39 56
Great Queen St., Dart. CW47 80
Great Rd., Hem.H. AY13 8
Great Ropers La., Brwd. DA29 42
Great Russell St. WC1 BW39 1
Great Russell St. WC1 BW39 56
Great Scotland Yd. SW1 BX40 4
Great Scotland Yd. SW1 BX40 56
Great Slades, Pot.B. BR20 19
Great Smith St. SW1 BW41 3
Great Smith St. SW1 BW41 66
Great South West Rd., Felt. BA47 73
Great Spilmans SE22 CA46 77
Great St. Helens EC3 CA39 2
Great St. Helens EC3 CA39 57
Great St. Thomas Apostle EC4 BZ40 4
Great St. Thomas Apostle EC4 BZ40 57
Queen St.
Great Strand NW9 BO30 37
Great Sturgess Rd., Hem.H. AV13 7
Great Suffolk St. SE1 BY40 4
Great Suffolk St. SE1 BY40 56
Great Sutton St. EC1 BY38 2
Great Sutton St. EC1 BY38 56
Great Swan All. EC2 BZ39 2
Great Swan All. EC2 BZ39 57
Great Tattenhams, Epsom BP62 103
Great Thrift, Orp. CM52 88
Great Titchfield St. W1 BV38 1
Great Titchfield St. W1 BV38 56
Great Tower St. EC3 CA40 57
Great Trinity La. EC4 BZ40 4
Great Trinity La. EC4 BZ40 57
Queen Victoria St.
Great Turnstile WC2 BX39 2
Great Turnstile WC2 BX39 56
High Holborn
Great Warley St., Brwd. DA30 42
Great West Rd., Houns. BE44 64
Great Western Rd. W9 BR38 55
Great Whites Rd., Hem.H. AY14 8
Great Winchester St. EC2 BZ39 2
Great Winchester St. EC2 BZ39 57
Great Windmill St. W1 BW40 3
Great Windmill St. W1 BW40 56
Great Woodcote Dr., Pur. BW58 95
Great Woodcote Pk., Pur. BW58 95
Greatdown Rd. W7 BH38 54
Greatfield Av. E6 CK38 58
Greatfield Clo. N19 BW34 47
Warrender Rd.
Greatfield Clo. SE4 CE45 67
Greatfields Dr., Uxb. AZ39 53
Greatfields Rd., Bark. CM37 58
Greatford Dr., Guil. AU70 118
Greatham Rd., Bush. BD24 27
Greatham Wk. SW15 BP47 75
Bessborough Rd.
Greatheart, Hem.H. AY12 8
Greatness La., Sev. CV64 108
Greatness Rd., Sev. CV64 108
Greatorex St. E1 CB39 2
Greatorex St. E1 CB39 57
Greatwood Clo., Cher. AU58 91
Greatwood, Chis. CL50 78
Greaves Clo., Bark. CN36 58
Norfolk Rd.
Greaves Pl. SW17 BU49 76
Grecian Cres. SE19 BY50 76
Greding Wk., Brwd. DD27 122
Greek Ct. W1 BW39 1
Greek Ct. W1 BW39 56
Old Compton St.
Greek St. W1 BW39 1
Greek St. W1 BW39 56
Green Acre Clo., Barn. BR22 28
Green Acre, Wind. AM44 61
Green Acre, Wok. AP61 100
Mead Ct.
Green Acres, Croy. CA55 87
Green Acres, Hem.H. BA14 8
Green Acres, Lthd. BF65 102
Green Acres, Welw.G.C. BR 9 5
Green Arbour Ct. EC4 BY39 56
Old Bailey
Green Av. NW7 BN28 37
Green Av. W13 BJ41 64
Green Bank Clo., Rom. CV27 42
Green Bank E1 CB40 57
Green Bank N12 BS28 38
Green Banks, Upmin. CZ34 51
Green Cft., Hat. BP11 10
Green Clo. NW11 BT33 47
Green Clo. NW9 BN32 46
Green Clo., Brom. CG52 88
Green Clo., Cars. BU55 86
Green Clo., Chsnt. CD19 21
Green Clo., Epp. CL15 13
Green Clo., Felt. BE49 74
Green Clo., Hat. BR16 19
Green Ct. Av., Croy. CB55 87
Green Ct. Gdns., Croy. CB54 87
Green Ct. Rd., Swan. CS53 89
Green Ct., Edg. BM29 37
Green Curve, Bans. BR60 94
Green Dale Clo. SE22 CA46 77
Green Dale
Green Dale NW7 BO28 37
Green Dale SE22 BZ45 67
Green Dell Way, Hem.H. AZ13 8
Green Dene, Lthd. BA70 110
Green Dr., Slou. AS42 62
Green Dr., Sthl. BF40 54
Green Dr., Wok. AV65 100
Green Dragon La. N21 BY25 29
Green Dragon La., Brent. BL42 65
Green Dragon Yd. E1 CB39 2
Green Dragon Yd. E1 CB39 57
Old Montague St.
Green East Rd., Beac. AP29 34
Green End La., Hem.H. AV13 7
Green End N21 BY27 38
Green End Rd., Hem.H. AW14 8
Green End, Chess. BK56 93
Green Field Rd., Berk. AR13 7
Green Gdns., Orp. CM56 97
Green Glade, Epp. CN22 31
Green Hayes Clo., Reig. BT70 121
Green Hill La., Warl. CD62 105
Green Hill SE18 CK42 68
Green Hill Ter. SE18 CK42 68
Green Hill, Buck.H. CJ26 40
Green Hill, Orp. CK59 97
Green Hundred Rd. SE15 CB43 67
Green La. Av., Walt. BD56 93
Green La. Clo., Amer. AO21 25
Green La. Clo., Cher. AV55 82
Green La. Clo., Wey. AY56 92
Green La. E4 CF24 30
Green La. Gdns., Th.Hth. BZ51 87
Green La. NW4 BQ31 46
Green La. SE20 CC50 77
Green La. SE9 CL47 78
Green La. SW16 BX50 76
Green La. W7 BH41 64
Green La., Amer. AO21 25
Green La., Amer. AP22 25
Green La., Ash. BK62 102
Green La., Bov. AT17 16
Green La., Brox. CE15 12
Green La., Brwd. CY23 33
Green La., Brwd. DA26 42
Green La., Brwd. DB25 33
Green La., Cat. BZ64 105
Green La., Cher. AV55 82
Green La., Chesh. AQ20 16
Green La., Chess. BK58 93
Green La., Chig. CM26 40
Green La., Chis. CL49 78
Green La., Cob. BE59 93
Green La., Dag. CM34 49
Green La., Dag. CP34 50
Green La., Datchet AQ44 62
Green La., E.Mol. BF53 84
Green La., Edg. BL28 37
Green La., Egh. AT49 72
Green La., Felt. BE49 74
Green La., Fifield AG44 61
Green La., Guil. AT70 118
Green La., Guil. AW67 110
Green La., Har. BH34 45
Green La., Harl. CR11 14
Green La., Hem.H. BA14 8
Green La., Houns. BC45 63
Green La., Ilf. CM34 49
Green La., Ing. DB19 24
Green La., Lthd. BK64 102
Green La., Maid. AG40 61
Green La., Mord. BS53 86
Green La., N.Mal. BN53 85
Green La., Nthwd. BA29 35
Green La., Pur. BW59 95
Green La., Red. BU69 121
Green La., Red. BV73 121
Green La., Red. CA68 114
Green La., Reig. BR70 120
Green La., Rick. AY25 26
Green La., Shep. BA53 83
Green La., St.Alb. BG12 9
Green La., Stan. BJ28 36
Green La., Sun. BB50 73
Green La., Tad. BR66 112
Green La., Th.Hth. BX50 76
Green La., Thorpe AU51 82
Green La., Upmin. CY37 60
Green La., Uxb. BA39 53
Green La., Wal.Abb. CJ20 22
Green La., Walt. BC57 92
Green La., Warl. CD62 105
Green La., Warley DA29 42
Green La., Wat. BD26 36
Green La., West. CM65 106
Green La., Wey. AY59 92
Green La., Wind. AN44 61
Green La., Wok. AP58 91
Green La., Wok. AQ64 100
Green La., Wok. AR62 100
Green La., Wok. AZ65 101
Green La., Wor.Pk. BP54 85
Green Lane W., Wok. AZ66 100
Green Lanes N13 BX29 38
Green Lanes N16 BZ34 48
Green Lanes N21 BY27 38
Green Lanes N8 BY31 47
Green Lanes, Epsom BO58 94
Green Lanes, Welw.G.C. BO 9 5
Green Lawns, Ruis. BD33 45
Green Leas, Sun. BB50 73
Green Leas, Wal.Abb. CF20 21
Green Man Gdns. W13 BJ40 54
Green Man La. W13 BJ40 54
Green Man La., Felt. BC45 63
Green Manor Way, Grav. DC45 71
Green Mead, Esher BE57 93
Green Meadow, Pot.B. BS18 20
Green Moor Link N21 BY26 38
Green North Rd., Beac. AP29 34
Green Pk., Stai. AV48 72
Vicarage Rd.
Green Pl., Dart. CT46 79
Green Pond Rd. E17 CD31 48
Green Rd. N14 BV25 29
Green Rd. N20 BT27 38
Green Rd., Egh. AT52 82
Green Ride, Epp. CM20 22
Green Ride, Loug. CH25 31
Green Slade Av., Ash. BM63 103
Green St. E13 CJ37 58
Green St. E7 CH36 58
Green St. W1 BV40 3
Green St. W1 BV40 56
Green St., Enf. CC23 30
Green St., Hat. BS13 11
Green St., Rad. BM21 28
Green St., Rick. AU24 25
Green St., Sun. BC51 83
Green Street Green Rd., Dart. CX48 80
Green Ter. EC1 BY38 2
Green Ter. EC1 BY38 56
Green Vale Rd., Wok. AO62 100
Southwood Av.
Green Vale W5 BL39 55
Green Vale, Bexh. CP46 79
Green Verges, Stan. BK29 36
Green View Clo., Hem.H. AT18 16
Green Vw., Chess. BL57 94
Green Way SE9 CJ46 78
Green Way, Brom. CK53 88
Green Way, Hart. DC53 90
Green Way, Red. BU69 121
Green Way, Sun. BC52 83
Green Way, The, Houns. BE45 64
Green West Rd., Beac. AP29 34
Green Wk. E4 CF26 39
Green Wk. NW4 BQ31 46
Green Wk. SE1 CA41 4
Green Wk. SE1 CA41 67
Green Wk., Dart. CT46 79
Green Wk., Hmptn. BE50 74
Orpwood Clo.
Green Wk., Ong. CW18 24
Green Wk., Ruis. BB33 44
Green Wk., S.Croy. CD57 96
Green Wk., Sthl. BF42 64
Green Wk., Wdf.Grn. CK29 40
Green Wrythe La., Cars. BT53 86
Green Yd., Wal.Abb. CF21 21
Green, The E11 CH32 49
Green, The E15 CG36 58
Green, The E4 CF26 39
Green, The N14 BW27 38
Green, The N21 BY26 38
Green, The N9 CB27 39
Green, The W3 BO39 55
Green, The W5 BK40 54
Green, The, Amer. AO22 25
Green, The, Bexh. CR44 69
Green, The, Brom. CH48 78
Green, The, Brom. CH54 88
Green, The, Cat. CE65 105
Green, The, Chsnt. CC17 21
Green, The, Croy. CD58 96
Green, The, Epp. CM21 31
Green, The, Epsom BP59 94
Green, The, Felt. BC48 73
Browells La.
Green, The, Gdse. CB69 114
Green, The, Hem.H. AT18 16
Green, The, Houns. BF43 64
Heston Rd.
Green, The, Ing. DC19 24
Green, The, Lthd. BG65 102
Green, The, Mord. BR52 85
Green, The, N.Mal. BN52 85
Green, The, Orp. CO50 79
Green, The, Orp. CP58 98
Green, The, Rain. CW40 60
Green, The, Rich. BK46 74
Green, The, Rick. AW21 26
Green, The, Rick. AY25 26
Green, The, Sev. CV64 108
Green, The, Shep. BB52 83
The Crofts
Green, The, Sid. CO49 79
Green, The, Slou. AO41 61
Green, The, Slou. AQ43 62
Green, The, St.Alb. BK17 18
Green, The, Stai. AS46 72
Green, The, Sthl. BE41 64
Green, The, Sthl. BE41 64
Green, The, Sutt. BS55 86
Green, The, Tad. BR63 103
Green, The, Twick. BH47 74
Green, The, Wal.Abb. CF20 21
Mile Rd.
Green, The, Walt. BB58 92
Green, The, Wat. BC22 26
Green, The, Wdf.Grn. CH28 40
Green, The, Well. CN45 68
Green, The, Wem. BJ34 45
Green, The, West Dr. AX41 63
Green, The, West. CM66 115
Greenacre Clo., Rain. CW38 60
Greenacre Clo., Swan. CT52 89
Greenacre Sq. SE16 CC41 67
Fishermans Dr.
Greenacre Wk. N14 BX27 38
Cannon Hill
Greenacre, Dart. CV48 80
Greenacres Av., Uxb. AY34 44
Greenacres Clo., Orp. CL56 97
State Farm Av.
Greenacres Ct., Egh. AR50 72
South Rd.
Greenacres Dr., Stan. BJ29 36
Greenacres SE9 CL46 78
Greenacres, Bush. BG27 36
Greenacres, Epp. CN17 22
Lindsey St.
Greenacres, Oxt. CG67 115
Greenall Clo., Chsnt. CD18 21
Roundmoor Dr.
Greenaway Gdns. NW3 BS35 47
Greenbank Av., Wem. BJ35 45
Greenbank Clo. E4 CF27 39
Greenbank Cres. NW4 BR31 46
Greenbank Rd., Wat. BA21 26
Greenbank, Chsnt. CB17 21
Greenbanks, Dart. CW48 80
Greenbanks, St.Alb. BH14 9
Colindale Av.
Greenbay Rd. SE7 CJ43 68
Greenberry St. NW8 BU37 1
Greenberry St. NW8 BU37 56
Greenbrook Av., Barn. BT23 29
Greenbury Clo., Rick. AU24 25
Greencoat Pl. SW1 BW42 3
Greencoat Pl. SW1 BW42 66
Greencoat Row SW1 BW41 3
Greencoat Row SW1 BW41 66
Francis St.
Greencourt Av., Edg. BM30 37
Greencourt Rd., Orp. CM53 88
Greencrest Pl. NW2 BP34 46
Dollis Hill La.
Greencroft Av., Ruis. BD34 45
Greencroft Clo. E6 CJ39 58
Neatscourt Rd.
Greencroft Gdns. NW6 BS36 56
Greencroft Gdns., Enf. CA24 30
Greencroft Rd., Houns. BE44 64
Greencroft, Guil. AT70 118
Greendale Ms., Slou. AQ40 52
St. Pauls Av.
Greendale Wk., Grav. DF48 81
Greene Wk., Berk. AR13 7
Greenefielde End, Stai. AX50 73
Greenend Rd. W4 BO41 65
Greenfarm Clo., Orp. CN57 97
Greenfell St. SE10 CG41 68
Greenfield Av., Surb. BM54 85
Greenfield Av., Wat. BE27 36
Greenfield End, Ger.Cr. AS29 34

Greenfield Gdns, Orp. CM54 88
Greenfield Gdns. NW2 BR34 46
Greenfield Gdns., Dag. CP37 59
Greenfield Link, Couls. BX61 104
Greenfield Rd. E1 CB39 2
Greenfield Rd. E1 CB39 57
Greenfield Rd. N15 CA32 48
Greenfield Rd., Dag. CP37 59
Greenfield Rd., Dart. CS49 79
Greenfield St., Wal.Abb. CF20 21
Greenfield Way, Har. BF31 45
Greenfield, Welw.G.C. BQ6 5
Greenfields Clo., Brwd. DA28 42
Greenfields Clo., Loug. CL24 31
Greenfields NW7 BO27 37
Lawrence St.
Greenfields, Hat. BQ11 10
Greenfields, Loug. CL24 31
Greenfields, Sthl. BF40 54
Greenford Av. W7 BH38 54
Greenford Av., Sthl. BE40 54
Greenford Gdns., Grnf. BF38 54
Greenford Rd., Har. BH35 45
Greenford Rd., Sthl. BG40 54
Greenford Rd., Sutt. BS56 95
St. Nicholas Way
Greengate St. E13 CH37 58
Greengate, Grnf. BJ36 54
Greenglades, Horn. CW32 51
Greenhalgh Wk. N2 BT31 47
Greenham Clo. SE1 BY41 4
Greenham Clo. SE1 BY41 66
Frazier St.
Greenham Rd. N10 BV30 38
Greenham Wk., Wok. AR62 100
Greenhayes Av., Bans. BS60 95
Greenhayes Gdns., Bans. BS61 104
Greenheys Clo., Nthwd. BB30 35
Greenheys Dr. E18 CG31 49
Greenheys Pl., Wok. AS62 100
Greenhill Av., Cat. CB64 105
Greenhill Cres., Wat. BB25 26
Greenhill Gdns., Guil. AU69 118
Greenhill Gdns., Nthlt. BE37 54
Greenhill Gro. E12 CK35 49
Greenhill NW3 BT35 47
Hampstead High St.
Greenhill Pk. NW10 BO37 55
Greenhill Pk., Barn. BS25 29
Greenhill Rd. NW10 BO37 55
Greenhill Rd., Grav. DF48 81
Greenhill Rd., Har. BH32 45
Greenhill Rd., Sev. CV61 108
Greenhill Ter., Nthlt. BE37 54
Greenhill Way, Har. BH32 45
Greenhill Way, Wem. BM34 46
Greenhill, Sutt. BT55 86
Greenhill, Wem. BM34 46
Greenhills Clo., Rick. AW25 26
Greenhills Rents EC1 BY39 56
Cowcross St.
Greenhills Ter. N1 BZ36 57
Baxter Rd.
Greenhills, Harl. CN11 13
Greenhithe Clo., Sid. CN47 78
Greenholm Rd. SE9 CL46 78
Greenhurst La., Oxt. CH69 115
Greenhurst Rd. SE27 BY49 76
Greening St. SE2 CP42 69
Greenland Cres., Sthl. BD41 64
Greenland Gate SE16 CC42 67
Greenland Ms. SE8 CC42 67
Trundleys Rd.
Greenland Pl. NW1 BV37 1
Greenland Rd.
Greenland Pl. NW1 BV37 56
Greenland Rd.
Greenland Quay SE16 CC42 67
Greenland Rd. NW1 BV37 1
Greenland Rd. NW1 BV37 56
Greenland Rd., Barn. BQ25 28
Greenland St. NW1 BV37 1
Greenland St. NW1 BV37 56
Camden High St.
Greenlands Rd., Sev. CX63 108
Greenlands Rd., Stai. AW49 73
Greenlands Rd., Wey. AZ55 83
Greenlaw Gdns., N.Mal. BO54 85
Greenlaw St. SE18 CK41 68
Greenleaf Rd. E17 CD31 48
Greenleaf Rd. E6 CJ37 58
Greenleafe Dr., Ilf. CL31 49
Greenman St. N1 BZ36 2
Greenman St. N1 BZ36 57
Greenmeads, Wok. AS64 100
Greenmoor Rd., Enf. CC23 30
Greeno Cres., Shep. AZ53 83
Greenoak Ri., West. CJ62 106
Greenoak Way SW19 BQ50 75
Greenock Rd. SW16 BW51 86
Greenock Rd. W3 BM41 65
Corville Rd.
Greenock Way, Rom. CT29 41
Greenpark Ct., Wem. BK36 54
Greens Clo., The, Loug. CL23 31
Greens End SE18 CL42 68
Greensand Rd., Red. BV69 121
Noke Dr.
Greenshaw, Brwd. DA26 42
Greenside Clo., Guil. AU69 118
Foxglove Gdns.
Greenside Rd. W12 BP41 65
Greenside Rd., Croy. BY54 86
Greenside Rd., Wey. AZ55 83
Kings Rd.
Greenside Wk., West. CJ62 106
Kings Rd.
Greenside, B.Wd. BM22 28
Greenside, Bex. CQ47 79
Greenside, Dag. CP33 50
Greenside, Rich. BK46 74
Greenside, Swan. CS51 89
Greenstead Av., Wdf.Grn. CJ29 40
Greenstead Clo., Wdf.Grn. CJ29 40
Greenstead Clo., Brwd. DF26 122
Greenstead Gdns. SW15 CP46 75
Greenstead Gdns., Wdf.Grn. CJ29 40
Greenstead, Saw. CQ6 6
Greensted Rd., Loug. CK26 40
Greensted Rd., Ong. CU17 23
Greenstone Ms. E18 CH32 49
Voluntary Pl.
Greensward, Bush. BF26 36
Ashfield Av.
Greentiles La., Uxb. AV33 43
Greenvale Rd. SE9 CK45 68
Greenvale Rd., Wok. AO62 100
Greenvale, Wat. BD26 36
Greenview Av., Croy. CD53 87
Greenview Ct., Ashf. AY49 73
Greenville Clo., Cob. BD60 93
Greenway Av. E17 CF31 48
Greenway Clo. N11 BV29 38
Poplar Gro.
Greenway Clo. N20 BS27 38
Greenway Clo. N4 BZ34 48
Greenway Clo. NW9 BN30 37
Greenway Clo., Wey. AW60 92
Greenway Dr., Stai. AX51 83
Greenway Gdns. NW9 BN30 37
Greenway Gdns., Croy. CD55 87
Greenway Gdns., Grnf. BF38 54
Greenway Gdns., Har. BH30 36
Greenway N14 BX27 38
Greenway N20 BS27 38
Greenway SW20 CQ52 85
Greenway, Berk. AQ13 7
Greenway, Brwd. DD26 122
Greenway, Chis. CL49 78
Greenway, Dag. CP34 50
Greenway, Har. BL32 46
Greenway, Hayes BC38 53
Greenway, Hem.H. AZ13 8
Greenway, Lthd. BF65 102
Greenway, Pnr. BC30 35
Greenway, Rom. CX29 42
Greenway, The NW9 BN30 37
Greenway, The, Enf. CC21 30
Greenway, The, Epsom BM61 103
Greenway, The, Ger.Cr. AR31 43
Greenway, The, Har. BH30 36
Greenway, The, Orp. CO53 89
Greenway, The, Oxt. CH70 115
Greenway, The, Pnr. BE32 45
Greenway, The, Pot.B. BS20 20
Greenway, The, Rick. AW26 35
Greenway, The, Slou. AL40 61
Greenway, The, Uxb. AX37 53
Greenway, The, Uxb. AZ34 44
Greenway, Wall. BW56 95
Greenway, Wdf.Grn. CJ28 40
Greenway, West. CJ63 106
Greenways Est. E2 CC38 57
Greenways, Beck. CE52 87
Greenways, Chsnt. BY18 20
Greenways, Egh. AS50 72
Greenways, Esher BH56 93
Greenways, Tad. BP66 112
Greenways, Wat. BB19 17
Greenwell St. W1 BV38 1
Greenwell St. W1 BV38 56
Greenwich Church St. SE10 CF43 67
Greenwich Cres. E6 CK39 58
Swann App.
Greenwich High Rd. SE10 CE44 67
Greenwich Mkt. SE10 CF43 67
Greenwich Park St. SE10 CF42 67
Greenwich South St. SE10 CE44 67
Greenwich View Pl. E14 CE41 67
Greenwood Av., Chsnt. CB19 21
Greenwood Av., Dag. CR35 50
Greenwood Av., Enf. CD23 30
Greenwood Clo., Chsnt. CB19 21
Greenwood Clo., Amer. AP22 25
Greenwood Clo., Beac. AO29 34
Farmers Way
Greenwood Clo., Bush. BH26 36
Langmead Dr.
Greenwood Clo., Mord. BR52 85
Greenwood Clo., Orp. CN53 88
Greenwood Clo., Sid. CO48 79
Greenwood Clo., T.Ditt. BJ54 84
Greenwood Clo., Wey. AV59 91
Greenwood Dr. E4 CF28 39
Avril Way
Greenwood Dr., Red. BV73 121
Greenwood Dr., Wat. BC20 17
Greenwood Gdns. N13 BY27 38
Greenwood Gdns., Cat. CB66 114
Greenwood Gdns., Ilf. CM29 40
Greenwood Ho., Grays DD43 71
Hawkes Clo.
Greenwood La., Hmptn. BF49 74
Greenwood Pk., Kings.T. BO50 75
Greenwood Pl. NW5 BV35 47
Highgate Rd.
Greenwood Rd. E13 CG37 58
Maud Rd.
Greenwood Rd. E8 CB36 57
Greenwood Rd., Bex. CS49 79
Greenwood Rd., Chig. CO28 41
Greenwood Rd., Croy. BY53 86
Greenwood Rd., Islw. BH45 64
Greenwood Rd., Mitch. BW52 86
Greenwood Rd., T.Ditt. BJ54 84
Greenwood Rd., Wok. AP63 100
Greenwood Ter. NW10 BN37 55
Greenwood Way, Sev. CT66 116
Greenwood, The, Guil. AT70 118
Greenwrythe Cres., Cars. BU54 86
Greer Rd., Har. BG30 36
Greet St. SE1 BY40 4
Greet St. SE1 BY41 66
Gregor Ms. SE3 CH43 68
Gregory Av., Pot.B. BT20 20
Gregory Cres. SE9 CJ47 78
Gregory Dr., Stai. AQ46 72
Gregory Pl. W8 BS41 66
Gregory Rd. Sthl. BF41 64
Gregory Rd., Rom. CP31 50
Gregory Rd., Slou. AO34 43
Greig Clo. N8 BX32 47
Greig Ter. SE17 BY43 66
Lorrimore Sq.
Grena Gdns., Rich. BL45 65
Grena Rd., Rich. BL45 65
Grenaby Av., Croy. BZ54 87
Grenaby Rd., Croy. BZ54 87
Grenada Rd. SE7 CJ43 68
Grenade St. E14 CD40 57
Grenadier St. E16 CK40 58
Grendon Gdns., Wem. BM34 46
Grendon St. NW8 BU38 1
Grendon St. NW8 BU38 56
Grenfell Av., Horn. CT33 50
Grenfell Clo., West. CJ59 97
Grenfell Gdns., Har. BL33 46
Grenfell Rd. W11 BQ40 55
Grenfell Rd., Mitch. BU50 76
Grenfell Wk. W11 BQ40 55
Lancaster Rd.
Grennell Clo., Sutt. BT55 86
Grennell Rd., Sutt. BT55 86
Grenoble Gdns., N13 BY29 38
Grenville Av., Brox. CD14 12
Grenville Clo. N3 BR30 37
Grenville Clo., Wal.Cr. CC19 21
Grenville Gdns., Wdf.Grn. CJ30 40
Grenville Ms. SW7 BT42 3
Grenville Ms. SW7 BT42 66
Grenville Ms., Hmptn. BF49 74
Grenville Pl. NW7 BN28 37
Grenville Pl. SW7 BT41 3
Grenville Pl. SW7 BT41 66
Grenville Rd. N19 BX33 47
Grenville Rd., Croy. CG58 96
Grenville St. WC1 BX38 2
Grenville St. WC1 BX38 56
Guilford St.
Gresford Clo., St.Alb. BK13 9
Gresham Av., N20 BU28 38
Gresham Av., Warl. CD62 105
Gresham Clo., Bex. CQ46 79
Gresham Clo., Enf. BZ24 30
Gladbeck Way
Gresham Ct., Berk. AQ13 7
Ashlyns Rd.
Gresham Dr., Rom. CO32 50
Gresham Gdns. NW11 BR33 46
Gresham Ms. W4 BN41 65
Reynolds Rd.
Gresham Rd. E16 CH39 58
Gresham Rd. E6 CK37 58
Gresham Rd. NW10 BN35 46
Gresham Rd. SE25 CB52 87
Gresham Rd. SW9 BY45 66
Gresham Rd., Beck. CD51 87
Gresham Rd., Brwd. DB27 42
Gresham Rd., Edg. BL29 37
Gresham Rd., Hmptn. BF50 74
Gresham Rd., Houns. BG44 64
Gresham Rd., Oxt. CG68 115
Gresham Rd., Stai. AV49 72
Gresham Rd., Uxb. AZ37 53
Gresham St. EC2 BZ39 2
Gresham St. EC2 BZ39 57
Gresley Ct., Pot.B. BS18 20
Heathfield Clo.
Gresley Rd. N19 BW33 47
Gresse St. W1 BW39 1
Gresse St. W1 BW39 56
Gressenhall Rd. SW18 BR46 75
Greswell Clo., Sid. CO48 79
Greswell Rd. SW6 BQ44 65
Greta Bank, Lthd. BA66 110
Gretton Rd. N17 CA29 39
Beaufoy Rd.
Greville Av., S.Croy. CC58 96
Greville Clo., Ash. BL63 103
Greville Clo., Guil. AP70 118
Greville Clo., Hat. BQ15 10
Greville Clo., Twick. BJ47 74
Greville Ct., Lthd. BF66 111
Greville Hall NW6 BS37 1
Greville Hall NW6 BS37 56
Greville Ms. NW6 BS37 1
Greville Rd.
Greville Ms. NW6 BS37 56
Greville Rd.
Greville Pk. Av., Ash. BL62 103
Greville Pk. Rd., Ash. BL62 103
Greville Pl. NW6 BS37 1
Greville Pl. NW6 BS37 56
Greville Rd. E17 CF31 48
Greville Rd. NW6 BS37 1
Greville Rd. NW6 BS37 56
Greville Rd., Rich. BL46 75
Greville St. EC1 BY39 2
Greville St. EC1 BY39 56
Grey Alders, Bans. BQ60 94
High Beeches
Grey Clo. NW11 BT32 47
Grey Eagle St. E1 CA39 2
Grey Eagle St. E1 CA39 57
Grey St. E16 CJ40 58
Grey Towers Av., Horn. CV33 51
Grey Towers Gdns., Horn. CV33 51
Greycaine Rd., Wat. BD22 27
Greycoat Pl. SW1 BW41 3
Greycoat Pl. SW1 BW41 66
Greycoat St. SW1 BW41 3
Greycoat St. SW1 BW41 66
Greycott Rd., Beck. CE49 77
Greyfell Clo., Stan. BJ28 36
Coverdale Clo.
Greyfields Clo., Pur. BY60 95
Partridge Knoll
Greyfriars Pass. EC1 BY39 2
Greyfriars Pass. EC1 BY39 56
Newgate St.
Greyfriars Rd., Wok. AW65 101
Greygoose Pk., Harl. CL12 13
Greyhound Ct. WC2 BX40 4
Milford La.
Greyhound Ct. WC2 BX40 56
Milford La.
Greyhound Hill NW4 BP31 46
Greyhound La. SW16 BW50 76
Greyhound La., Grays DG41 71
Greyhound La., Pot.B. BP20 19
Greyhound Rd. N17 CA31 48
Greyhound Rd. NW10 BP38 55
Greyhound Rd. W6 BQ43 65
Greyhound Rd., Sutt. BT56 95
Greyhound Ter. SW16 BW51 86
Greyhound Way, Dart. CT46 79
Stadium Way
Greyladies Gdns. SE10 CF44 67
Wat Tyler Rd.
Greys Park Clo., Kes. BJ56 97
Greystead Rd. SE23 CC47 77
Greystoke Av., Pnr. BF31 45
Greystoke Clo., Berk. AQ13 7
Greystoke Dr., Ruis. AZ33 44
Greystoke Gdns. W5 BL38 55
Greystoke Gdns., Enf. BW24 29
Greystoke Lo. W5 BL38 55
Hanger La.
Greystoke Park Ter. W5 BK38 54
Greystoke Pl. EC4 BY39 56
Cursitor St.
Greystone Clo., Croy. CC59 96
Greystone Gdns., Har. BK32 45
Greystone Gdns., Ilf. CM30 40
Greystone Pk., Sev. CQ66 116
Greystones Clo., Red. BT71 121
Hardwicke Rd.
Greystones Clo., Sev. CW62 108
Greystones Dr., Reig. BT69 121
Greyswood St. SW16 BV50 76
Greythorne Rd., Wok. AQ62 100
Grice Av., West. CH60 97
Grid Iron Pl., Upmin. CX34 51
Gridland St. E15 CG37 58
Church St.
Grierson Rd. SE23 CC47 77
Grieves Rd., Grav. DF48 81
Griffin Av., Upmin. CZ32 51
Griffin Clo. NW10 BP35 46
Griffin Clo., Slou. AN41 61
Griffin Manor Way SE28 CM41 68
Griffin Rd. N17 CA30 39
Griffin Rd. SE18 CM42 68
Griffin Way, Lthd. BF66 111
Griffin Way, Sun. BC51 83
Griffins, The, Grays DD41 71
Griffith Clo., Dag. CP33 50
Gibson Rd.
Griffiths Clo., Wor.Pk. BP55 85
Griffiths Rd. SW19 BS50 76
Griffiths Way, St.Alb. BG14 9
Griggs App., Ilf. CM34 49
Griggs Pl. SE1 CA41 4
Griggs Pl. SE1 CA41 67
Grange Rd.
Griggs Rd. E10 CF32 48
Grilse Clo. N9 CB28 39
Parr Clo.
Grimsby St. E2 CA38 2
Grimsby St. E2 CA38 57
Grimsdells La., Amer. AO22 25
Grimsdyke Cres., Barn. BQ24 28
Grimsdyke Rd., Pnr. BE29 36
Grimsel Path SE17 BY43 66
Brandon Est.
Grimshaw Clo. N6 BV33 47
Grimston Rd. SW6 BR44 65
Grimston Rd., St.Alb. BH14 9
Grimstone Clo., Rom. CR29 41
Grimthorpe Clo., St.Alb. BG12 9
Grimthorpe Ho. EC1 BY38 2
Grimwade Av., Croy. CB55 87
Grimwade Cres. SE15 CC45 67
Grimwood Rd., Twick. BH47 74
Grindal St. SE1 BY41 4
Grindal St. SE1 BY41 66
Lower Marsh
Grindall Clo., Croy. BY56 95
Hillside Rd.
Grinling Pl. SE8 CE43 67
Grinstead Rd. SE8 CD42 67
Grisedale Clo., Pur. CA60 96
Grisedale Gdns., Pur. CA60 96
Grittledon Rd. W9 BS38 56
Grittleton Av., Wem. BM36 55
Grizedale Ter. SE23 CB48 77
Grocers Hall Ct. EC2 BZ39 2
Grocers Hall Ct. EC2 BZ39 57
Poultry
Grogan Clo., Hmptn. BE50 74
Groom Cres. SW18 BT47 76
Groom Pl. SW1 BV41 3
Groom Pl. SW1 BV41 66
Chapel St.
Groom Rd., Brox. CD16 21
Groom Wk., Guil. AR69 118
Groombridge Clo., Walt. BC56 92
Groombridge Clo., Well. CO46 79
Groombridge Rd. E9 CC36 57
Groomfield Clo. SW17 BV49 76
Grooms Cotts., Chesh. AQ18 16
Grooms Dr., Pnr. BC32 44
Fore St.
Grosmont Rd. SE18 CN43 68
Grosse Way, SW15 BP46 75
Dover Pk. Dr.
Grosvenor Av. N5 BZ35 48
Grosvenor Av. SW14 BO45 65
Grosvenor Av., Cars. BU57 95
Grosvenor Av., Har. BF33 45
Grosvenor Av., Hayes BB37 53
Grosvenor Av., Kings L. BA17 17
Grosvenor Av., Rich. BL46 75
Grosvenor Rd.
Grosvenor Clo., Iver AU38 52
Grosvenor Clo., Loug. CL23 31
Grosvenor Cres. Ms. SW1 BV41 3
Grosvenor Cres. Ms. SW1 BV41 66
Grosvenor Cres. NW9 BM31 46
Grosvenor Cres. SW1 BV41 3
Grosvenor Cres. SW1 BV41 66
Grosvenor Cres., Dart. CV46 80
Grosvenor Cres., Uxb. AZ36 53
Grosvenor Ct. N14 BW26 38
Grosvenor Ct., Guil. AT69 118
Oakley Dell
Grosvenor Ct., Mord. BS52 86
Grosvenor Ct., Rick. BA25 26
Mayfare
Grosvenor Ct., Wey. BA57 92
Grosvenor Dr., Horn. CV33 51
Grosvenor Dr., Loug. CL23 31
Grosvenor Est. SW1 BW42 3
Grosvenor Est. SW1 BW42 66
Grosvenor Gardens Ms. S. SW1 BV41 3
Grosvenor Gardens Ms. S. SW1 BV41 666
Ebury St.
Grosvenor Gate W1 BV40 3
Grosvenor Gdns. E6 CJ38 58
Grosvenor Gdns. Ms. N. SW1 BV41 3
Grosvenor Gdns. Ms. N. SW1 BV41 66
Ebury St.
Grosvenor Gdns. N10 BW31 47
Grosvenor Gdns. N14 BW24 29
Grosvenor Gdns. NW11 BR32 46
Grosvenor Gdns. NW2 BQ36 55
Grosvenor Gdns. SW1 BV41 3
Grosvenor Gdns. SW1 BV41 66
Grosvenor Gdns. SW14 BO45 65
Grosvenor Gdns., Kings.T. BK50 74
Grosvenor Gdns., Wdf.Grn. CH29 40
Grosvenor Gdns., Upmin. CY33 51
Grosvenor Gdns., Wall. BW57 95
Grosvenor Hill SW19 BR50 75
Grosvenor Hill W1 BV40 3
Grosvenor Hill W1 BV40 56
Grosvenor Path, Loug. CM23 31
Grosvenor Pk. Rd. E17 CE32 48
Grosvenor Pk. SE5 BZ43 67
Grosvenor Pl. SW1 BV41 3
Grosvenor Pl. SW1 BV41 66
Grosvenor Rd. E10 CF33 48
Grosvenor Rd. E11 CH32 49
Grosvenor Rd. E6 CJ37 58
Grosvenor Rd. E7 CH36 58
Grosvenor Rd. N10 BV30 38
Grosvenor Rd. N3 BR29 37
Grosvenor Rd. N9 CB26 39
Grosvenor Rd. SE25 CB52 87
Grosvenor Rd. SW1 BV43 3
Grosvenor Rd. SW1 BV43 66
Grosvenor Rd. W4 BM42 65
Grosvenor Rd. W7 BJ40 54
Grosvenor Rd., B.Wd. BM24 28
Grosvenor Rd., Belv. CQ43 69
Grosvenor Rd., Bexh. CP46 79
Grosvenor Rd., Brent. BK43 64
Grosvenor Rd., Brox. CD13 12
Grosvenor Rd., Dag. CQ33 50
Grosvenor Rd., Epsom BN63 103
Grosvenor Rd., Houns. BE45 64
Grosvenor Rd., Ilf. CM34 49
Grosvenor Rd., Nthwd. BB28 35
Grosvenor Rd., Orp. CN53 88
Grosvenor Rd., Rich. BL46 75
Grosvenor Rd., Rom. CS33 50
Grosvenor Rd., St.Alb. BH14 9
Grosvenor Rd., Stai. AW50 73
Grosvenor Rd., Sthl. BE41 64
Grosvenor Rd., Twick. BJ47 74
Grosvenor Rd., W.Wick. CE55 87
Grosvenor Rd., Wall. BV57 95
Grosvenor Rd., Wat. BD24 27
Grosvenor Rd., Wok. AO60 91
Grosvenor Ri. E. E17 CE32 48
Grosvenor Sq. W1 BV40 3
Grosvenor Sq. W1 BV40 56
Grosvenor Sq., Long. DC52 90
Bramblefield Clo.
Grosvenor St. W1 BV40 3
Grosvenor St. W1 BV40 56
Grosvenor Ter., Hem.H. AW14 8
Grosvenor Vale, Ruis. BB34 44
Grosvenor Wharf Rd. E14 CF42 67
Grotes Bldgs. SE3 CG44 68
Grotes Pl. SE3 CG44 68
Groton Rd. SW18 BS48 76
Grotto Pass. W1 BV39 1
Paddington St.
Grotto Pass. W1 BV39 56
Paddington St.
Grotto Rd., Wey. AZ55 83
Grotto Rd., Twick. BH48 74
Ground La., Hat. BP11 10
Grove Av. N10 BW30 38
Grove Av. N3 BS29 38
Grove Av. W7 BH39 54
Grove Av., Epsom BO60 94
Grove Av., Pnr. BE32 45
Grove Av., Sutt. BS57 95
Grove Av., Twick. BH47 74
Grove Bldgs. SW3 BU43 3
Grove Bldgs. SW3 BU43 66
Grove Clo. SE23 CD47 77
Grove Clo., Brom. CH55 88
Grove Clo., Felt. BE49 74
Grove Clo., Ger.Cr. AR30 34
Grove Clo., Kings.T. BL52 85
Grove Clo., Lthd. BF67 111
Groveside Clo.
Grove Clo., Slou. AQ41 62
Grove Clo., Uxb. AZ35 44
Grove Clo., Wind. AQ47 72
Grove Cor., Lthd. BF66 111
Lower Shott
Grove Cres. E18 CG30 40
Grove Cres. NW9 BN31 46
Grove Cres. Rd. E15 CF36 57
Grove Cres. SE5 CA44 67
Grove Cres., Felt. BE49 74

Grove Cres., Kings.T. BL52 85
Grove Cres., Rick. AZ24 26
Grove Cres., Walt. BC54 83
Grove Ct. SE3 CH44 68
Grove Ct., E.Mol. BG53 84
Grove Ct., Tedd. BJ49 74
Cambridge Rd.
Grove Ct., Wal.Abb. CE20 21
Grove End La., Esher BG54 84
Grove End Rd. NW8 BT38 1
Grove End Rd. NW8 BT38 56
Grove End., Ger.Cr. AR30 34
Grove Est. SE5 CA44 67
Grove Est., Pnr. BE32 45
Grove Farm Pk., Nthwd. BA28 35
Grove Foot Path, Surb. BL52 85
Grove Gdns. E15 CG36 58
Grove Gdns. NW4 BP31 46
Grove Gdns. NW8 BU38 1
Grove Gdns. NW8 BU38 56
Grove Gdns., Dag. CS34 50
Grove Gdns., Enf. CC23 30
Grove Gdns., Tedd. BJ49 74
Grove Grn. Rd. E11 CF34 48
Grove Grn., Nthwd. BA28 35
Grove Hall Ct. NW8 BT38 1
Grove Hall Ct. NW8 BT38 56
Grove Heath N., Wok. AW64 101
Grove Heath Rd., Ripley AW65 101
Grove Hill E18 CG30 40
Grove Hill Rd. SE5 CA45 67
Grove Hill Rd., Har. BH33 45
Grove Hill Rd., Red. BU70 121
Grove Hill, Ger.Cr. AR29 34
Grove Hill, Har. BH33 45
Grove House Rd. N8 BX31 47
Grove La. SE5 BZ44 67
Grove La., Chesh. AQ17 16
Grove La., Chig. CN27 40
Grove La., Couls. BU59 95
Grove La., Ger.Cr. AQ30 34
Grove La., King.T. BL52 85
Grove La., Uxb. AY38 53
Grove Lea, Hat. BP14 10
Grove Market Pl. SE9 CK46 78
Grove Mead, Hat. BO12 10
Grove Meadow, Welw.G.C. BS 8 5
Grove Mill La., Wat. BA22 26
Grove Ms. W6 BQ41 65
Grove Park Av. E4 CE29 39
Grove Park Br. W4 BN43 65
Grove Park Ms. W4 BN43 65
Grove Park Br.
Grove Pass. E2 CB37 57
Grove Pass., Tedd. BJ49 74
Grove Path, Chsnt. CB19 21
Grove Pk. E11 CH32 49
Grove Pk. Gdns. W4 BM43 65
Grove Pk. NW9 BN31 46
Grove Pk. Rd. N15 CA31 48
Grove Pk. Rd. SE9 CJ48 78
Grove Pk. Rd. W4 BM43 65
Grove Pk. Rd., Rain. CU37 59
Grove Pk. SE5 CA44 67
Grove Pk. Ter. W4 BM43 65
Grove Pl. NW3 BT34 47
Christchurch Hill
Grove Pl. W3 BN40 55
Grove Pl. W5 BK40 54
Grove Pl., Bark. CM36 58
Clockhouse Av.
Grove Pl., Hat. BQ15 10
Dixons Hill Rd.
Grove Pl., Wat. BF23 27
Grove Pl., Wey. BA56 92
Grove Rd. E11 CG33 49
Grove Rd. E17 CE32 48
Grove Rd. E3 CD37 57
Grove Rd. E4 CE28 39
Grove Rd. E9 CC37 57
Grove Rd. N11 BV28 38
Grove Rd. N12 BT28 38
Grove Rd. N15 CA32 48
Grove Rd. NW2 BQ36 55
Grove Rd. SW13 BO44 65
Grove Rd. SW19 BT50 76
Grove Rd. W., Enf. CC22 30
Grove Rd. W3 BN40 55
Grove Rd. W5 BK40 54
Grove Rd., Amer. AP22 25
Grove Rd., Ash. BL62 103
Grove Rd., B.Wd. BM23 28
Grove Rd., Barn. BU24 29
Grove Rd., Belv. CQ43 69
Grove Rd., Bexh. CS45 69
Grove Rd., Brent. BK42 64
Grove Rd., Cher. AV53 82
Grove Rd., Croy. BY52 86
Grove Rd., E.Mol. BG52 84
Grove Rd., Edg. BM29 37
Grove Rd., Epsom BO60 94
Grove Rd., Grav. DD46 81
Grove Rd., Grays DE43 71
Grove Rd., Guil. AU70 118
Grove Rd., Hem.H. AW14 8
Grove Rd., Houns. BF45 64
Grove Rd., Islw. BH44 64
Grove Rd., Mitch. BV51 86
Grove Rd., Nthwd. BA29 35
Grove Rd., Oxt. CF70 114
Grove Rd., Pnr. BE32 45
Grove Rd., Rich. BL46 75
Grove Rd., Rick. AW27 35
Grove Rd., Rom. CO33 50
Grove Rd., Seal CX64 108
Grove Rd., Sev. CV64 108
Grove Rd., Shep. BA53 83
Grove Rd., St.Alb. BG14 9
Grove Rd., Surb. BK53 84
Grove Rd., Sutt. BS57 95
Grove Rd., Twick. BG48 74
Grove Rd., Uxb. AX36 53
Grove Rd., West. CJ63 106
Grove Rd., Wind. AO44 61
Grove Rd., Wok. AS61 100
Grove Shaw, Tad. BR65 103
Grove Side, Lthd. BF66 111
Grove St. N18 CA28 39
Grove St. SE8 CD42 67
Grove Stile Waye, Felt. BA47 73
Grove Ter. NW5 BV34 47
Highgate Rd.
Grove Ter., Tedd. BJ49 74
Grove Vale SE22 CA45 67
Grove Vale, Chis. CL50 78
Grove Vills. E14 CE40 57
Grove Way, Dag. CP35 50
Grove Way, Esher BG54 84
Grove Way, Rick. AT25 25
Grove Waye, Uxb. AX36 53
Grove Wk. N1 CA38 2
Grove Wood Clo., Rick. AT25 25
Grove Wood Hill, Couls. BW60 95
Grove, The E15 CG36 58
Grove, The N13 BY28 38
Grove, The N14 BW25 29
Chase Rd.
Grove, The N3 BS30 38
Grove, The N4 BX33 47
Grove, The N6 BV33 47
Grove, The N8 BW32 47
Grove, The NW11 BR33 46
Grove, The NW9 BN32 46
Grove, The SE21 CA47 77
Grove, The SW16 BW49 76
Grove, The W5 BK40 54
Grove, The, Amer. AO21 25
Grove, The, Bexh. CP45 69
Grove, The, Brwd. CZ28 42
Grove, The, Cat. BZ64 105
Grove, The, Chesh. AR21 25
Grove, The, Couls. BW61 104
Grove, The, Edg. BM28 37
Grove, The, Egh. AT49 72
Grove, The, Enf. BY23 29
Grove, The, Epsom BO60 94
Grove, The, Esher BF54 84
Grove, The, Ewell BO58 94
Grove, The, Grav. DH47 81
Grove, The, Grnf. BG39 54
Grove, The, Hat. BS17 20
Grove, The, Islw. BH44 64
Grove, The, Pot.B. BT19 20
Grove, The, Rad. BJ20 18
Grove, The, Sev. CZ58 99
Grove, The, Sid. CQ49 79
Grove, The, Slou. AQ41 62
Grove, The, Swans. DC46 81
Grove, The, Tedd. BJ49 74
Grove, The, Upmin. CX35 51
Grove, The, Uxb. AZ35 44
Grove, The, W.Wick. CE55 87
Grove, The, Walt. BC53 83
Grove, The, West. CJ62 106
Grove, The, Wey. AW56 92
Grove, The, Wok. AS61 100
Grovebarns, Stai. AW50 73
Grovebury Clo., Erith CT43 69
Grovebury Ct. N14 BW26 38
Grovebury Rd. SE2 CO41 69
Grovedale Clo., Chsnt. CA18 21
Grovedale Rd. N19 BW34 47
Grovehall Rd., Bush. BE24 27
Groveland Av. SW16 BX50 76
Groveland Ct. EC4 BZ39 2
Bow La.
Groveland Ct. EC4 BZ39 57
Bow La.
Groveland Rd., Beck. CD52 87
Groveland Way, N.Mal. BN53 85
Grovelands Clo. SE5 CA44 67
Grovelands Clo., Har. BF34 45
Grovelands Ct. N14 BW26 38
Grovelands Rd. N13 BX28 38
Grovelands Rd. N15 CB32 48
Grovelands Rd., Orp. CO50 79
Grovelands Rd., Pur. BX59 95
Grovelands Way, Grays DC42 71
Grovelands, St.Alb. BF17 18
Grovelands, W.Mol. BF52 84
Groveley Rd., Sun. BB49 73
Grover Clo., Hem.H. AX13 8
Grover Rd., Wat. BD26 36
Groveside Clo. W3 BM39 55
Groveside Clo., Lthd. BF67 111
Grove Side
Groveside Rd. E4 CG27 40
Groveway SW9 BX44 66
Groveway, Wem. BM35 46
Grovewood Rd., Rich. BM44 65
Sandycombe Rd.
Grubb St., Oxt. CJ67 115
Grubbs La., Hat. BS14 11
Grummant Rd. SE15 CA44 67
Grundy St. E14 CE39 57
Gruneisen Rd. N3 BS29 38
Guards Rd., Wind. AL44 61
Guards Wk., Wind. AL44 61
Guardsman Clo., Brwd. DB28 42
Woodman Rd.
Gubbins La., Rom. CW29 42
Gubyon Av. SE24 BY46 76
Guerin Sq. E3 CE37 58
Malmesbury Rd.
Guerin St. E3 CD38 57
Guernsey Clo., Guil. AT68 109
Cotts Wood Dr.
Guernsey Clo., Houns. BF44 64
Guernsey Farm Dr., Wok. AR61 100
Guernsey Gro. SE24 BZ47 77
Guernsey Rd. E11 CF33 48
Guessens Ct., Welw. G.C. BQ 8 5
Guessens Gro., Welw. G.C. BQ 8 5
Guessens Rd., Welw. G.C. BQ 8 5
Guessens Wk., Welw. G.C. BQ 7 5
Guibal Rd. SE12 CH47 78
Guild Cft., Guil. AT70 118
Guild Rd. SE7 CJ42 68
Guild Rd., Erith CT43 69
Guildables La., Eden. CK70 115
Guildersfield Rd. SW16 BX50 76
Guildford & Godalming By-pass, Guil. AO72 118
Guildford Av., Felt. BB48 73
Guildford Gdns., Rom. CW29 42
Guildford Gro. SE10 CE44 67
Guildford La., Guil. AU71 118
Guildford Lo. Ri., Lthd. BB68 110
Guildford Pk. Av., Guil. AQ71 118
Guildford Pk. Rd., Guil. AQ71 118
Guildford Pl., Wok. AS63 100
Guildford Rd. E17 CF30 39
Guildford Rd. E6 CK39 58
Guildford Rd. N1 CA36 2
Guildford Rd. SW8 BX44 66
Guildford Rd., East Horsley BB68 110
Guildford Rd., Great Bookham BE67 111
Guildford Rd., Cher. AU57 91
Guildford Rd., Cher. AV54 82
Guildford Rd., Croy. BZ53 87
Guildford Rd., Dor. BC73 119
Guildford Rd., Dor. BF72 119
Guildford Rd., Guil. AR66 109
Guildford Rd., Ilf. CN34 49
Guildford Rd., Lthd. BH65 102
Guildford Rd., Rom. CW29 42
Guildford Rd., St.Alb. BJ14 9
Guildford Rd., Wok. AS63 100
Guildford St., Cher. AV54 82
Guildford St., Stai. AW50 73
Guildford Vills., Surb. BL53 85
Guildford Way, Wall. BX56 95
Guildhall Bldgs. EC2 BZ39 2
Guildhall Bldgs. EC2 BZ39 57
Guildhall Yd. EC2 BZ39 2
Guildhall Yd. EC2 BZ39 57
Gresham St.
Guildhouse St. SW1 BW42 3
Guildhouse St. SW1 BW42 66
Guildown Av. N12 BS28 38
Guildown Av., Guil. AQ72 118
Guildown Rd., Guil. AQ72 118
Guilds Way E17 CD30 39
Guileshill La., Wok. AY65 101
Guilford Av., Surb. BL53 85
Guilford Pl. WC1 BX38 2
Guilford Pl. WC1 BX38 56
Guilford St. WC1 BX38 2
Guilford St. WC1 BX38 56
Guilfords, Harl. CP 9 6
Guilsborough Clo. NW10 BO36 55
Guinne Clo., Hayes BA41 63
Guinness Bldgs. E2 CB37 2
Guinness Bldgs. SE1 CA42 67
Guinness Bldgs. SE11 BY42 4
Guinness Bldgs. SE11 BY42 66
Guinness Bldgs. SW3 BU42 3
Guinness Bldgs. SW3 BU42 66
Guinness Bldgs. W6 BQ42 65
Fulham Palace Rd.
Guinness Clo. E9 CD36 57
Guinness Clo., Hayes BA41 63
Bourne Av.
Guinness Ct., Wok. AP62 100
Ivergh Rd.
Guinness Sq. SE1 CA42 4
Guinness Sq. SE1 CA42 67
Pages Wk.
Guinness Trust Bldgs. SW10 CN44 68
Guinness Trust Dwellings N16 CA33 48
Guinness Trust SE24 BY45 66
Guion Rd. SW6 BR44 65
Gull Clo., Wall. BX57 95
Gull Wk., Rain. CU36 59
Fulmar Rd.
Gulland Clo., Bush. BG25 27
Gulland Wk. N1 BZ36 57
Gullbrook, Hem.H. AW13 8
Gullet Wood Rd., Wat. BC21 17
Rushton Av.
Gulliver Clo., Nthlt. BE37 54
Gulliver Rd., Sid. CN48 78
Gulliver St. SE16 CD41 67
Gumleigh Rd. W5 BK42 64
Gumley Gdns., Islw. BJ45 64
Gumley Rd., Grays DB43 70
Gumping Rd., Orp. CM55 88
Gun Hill, Til. DH43 71
Gun St. E1 CA39 2
Gundulph Rd., Brom. CJ52 88
Gunfleet Clo., Grav. DJ47 81
Roehampton Clo.
Gunmakers La. E3 CD37 57
Gunn Rd., Swans. DC46 81
Gunner La., SE18 CL42 68
Gunners Gro. E4 CF27 39
Gunners Rd. SW18 BT48 76
Gunnersbury Av. W5 BL40 55
Gunnersbury Cres. W3 BM41 65
Gunnersbury Ct. W3 BM41 65
Bollo La.
Gunnersbury Dr. W5 BL41 65
Gunnersbury Gdns. W3 BM41 65
Gunnersbury La. W3 BM41 65
Gunnersbury Ms., Brent BM42 65
Gunning St. SE18 CN42 68
Gunpowder Sq. EC4 BY39 2
Wine Office Ct.
Gunstor Rd. N16 CA35 48
Gunter Gro. SW10 BT43 66
Gunter Gro., Edg. BN30 37
Gunterstone Rd. W14 BR42 65
Gunthorpe St. E1 CA39 2
Gunthorpe St. E1 CA39 57
Wentworth St.
Gunton Rd. E5 CB34 48
Gunton Rd. SW17 BV50 76
Gunwhale Clo. SE16 CC40 57
Surrey Water Rd.
Gurdon Rd. SE7 CH42 68
Gurnard Clo., West Dr. AX40 53
Trout Rd.
Gurnell Gro. W13 BH38 54
Gurney Clo. E15 CG35 49
Gurney Rd.
Gurney Clo., Bark. CL36 58
Gurney Cres., Croy. BX54 86
Gurney Ct. Rd., St.Alb. BH12 9
Gurney Dr. N2 BT31 47
Gurney Rd. E15 CG35 49
Gurney Rd., Cars. BU56 95
Gurney Rd., Nthlt. BC38 53
Guthrie St. SW3 BU42 3
Guthrie St. SW3 BU42 66
Cale St.
Gutter La. EC2 BZ39 2
Gutter La. EC2 BZ39 57
Guy Rd., Wall. BW55 86
Guy St. SE1 BZ41 4
Guy St. SE1 BZ41 67
Guyatt Gdns., Mitch. BV51 86
Ormerod Gdns.
Guyscliff Rd. SE13 CF46 77
Guysfield Clo., Rain. CU37 59
Guysfield Dr., Rain. CU37 59
Gwalior Rd. SW15 BQ45 65
Felsham Rd.
Gwendolen Av. SW15 BQ45 65
Gwendolen Clo. SW15 BQ46 75
Gwendoline Av. E13 CH37 58
Gwendwr Rd. W14 BR42 65
Gwent Clo., Wat. BD20 18
Gwillim Clo., Sid. CO46 79
Gwydor Rd., Beck. CC52 87
Gwydyr Rd., Brom. CG52 88
Gwyn Clo. SW6 BT43 66
Gwynn Rd., Grav. DE48 81
Gwynne Av., Croy. CC54 87
Gwynne Clo., Wind. AM44 61
Cawcott Dr.
Gwynne Park Av., Wdf.Grn. CK29 40
Gwynne Pl. WC1 BX38 56
Kings Cross Rd.
Gwynne Rd. SW11 BT44 66
Gwynne Vaughan Av., Guil. AQ68 109
Gyfford Wk., Wal.Cr. CB19 21
Hawthorne Clo.
Gylcote Clo. SE5 BZ45 67
Gyles Pk., Stan. BK29 36
Gyllyngdune Gdns., Ilf. CN34 49
Gypsy La., Kings L. BA20 17
Gypsy La., Slou. AP35 43
Gypsy La., Welw.G.C. BR10 5
Gypsy La., Wey. AZ55 83

H

Ha-Ha Rd. SE18 CK43 68
Haarlem Rd. W14 BQ41 65
Haberdasher St. N1 BZ38 2
Haberdasher St. N1 BZ38 57
Habet Rd. W2 BT39 1
Habet Rd. W2 BT39 56
Habgood Rd., Loug. CK24 31
Hackbridge Park Gdns., Cars. BU55 86
Hackbridge Rd., Wall. BV55 86
Hacketts La., Wok. AV60 91
Hackford Rd. SW9 BX44 66
Hackforth Clo., Barn. BP25 28
Hackington Cres., Beck. CE50 77
Hackney Clo., B.Wd. BN25 28
Hackney Gro. E8 CB36 57
Hackney Rd. E2 CA38 2
Hackney Rd. E2 CA38 57
Hacombe Rd. SW19 BT50 76
Hacton Dr., Horn. CV35 51
Hacton La., Horn. CW34 51
Hacton Parkway, Upmin. CW35 51
Hadden Rd. SE28 CN41 68
Hadden Way, Grnf. BG36 54
Haddington Rd., Brom. CF48 77
Haddo St. SE10 CE43 67
Haddon Clo., B.Wd. BM23 28
Haddon Clo., Enf. CB25 30
Haddon Clo., Hem.H. AZ14 8
Haddon Clo., N.Mal. BO53 85
Cromwell Av.
Haddon Clo., Wey. BA55 83
Haddon Gro., Sid. CN47 78
Haddon Rd., Orp. CP53 89
Haddon Rd., Rick. AU25 25
Haddon Rd., Sutt. BS56 95
Thorncroft Rd.
Haden Ct. N4 BY34 47
Hadfield Rd., Stai. AX47 73
Hadleigh Clo. E1 CC38 57
Martus Rd.
Hadleigh Ct., Brox. CD14 12
Hadleigh Rd. N9 CB26 39
Hadleigh St. E2 CC38 57
Hadleigh Wk. E6 CK39 58
Dunnock Rd.
Hadley Clo. N21 BY25 29
Hadley Clo., B.Wd. BL25 28
Hadley Common, Barn. BS23 29
Hadley Gdns. W4 BN42 65
Hadley Gdns., Sthl. BE42 64
Hadley Grn. Rd., Barn. BR23 28
Hadley Grn. W., Barn. BR23 28
Hadley Gro., Barn. BR23 28
Hadley Highstone, Barn. BR23 28
Hadley Rd., Barn. BS24 29
Hadley Rd., Belv. CQ42 69
Hadley Rd., Enf. BW22 29
Hadley Rd., Mitch. BW52 86
Hadley Ridge, Barn. BR24 28
Hadley St. NW1 BV36 56
Hadley Way N21 BY25 29
Hadley Wood Ri., S.Croy. BY61 104
Hadlow Ct., Slou. AO40 61
Hadlow Pl. SE19 CB50 77
Hadlow Rd., Sid. CO49 79
Hadlow Rd., Well. CP43 69
Hadlow Way, Grav. DF50 81
Hadrian Clo., Stai. AY47 73
Hadrian Clo., Wall. BX57 95
Hadrian Est. E2 CB37 57
Hadrian St. SE10 CG42 68
Hadrian Way, Stai. AX47 73
Hadrians Clo., St.Alb. BE15 9
Hadrians Ride, Enf. CA25 30
Hadyn Park Rd. W12 BP41 65
Hafer Rd. SW11 BU45 66
Hafton Rd. SE6 CG47 78
Hagden La., Wat. BB25 26
Haggard Rd., Twick. BJ47 74
Haggerston Est. E8 CA37 2
Haggerston Est. E8 CA37 57
Haggerston Rd. E8 CA36 2
Haggerston Rd. E8 CA36 57
Haggerston Rd., B.Wd. BL22 28
Hague St. E2 CB38 57
Derbyshire St.
Haig Clo., St.Alb. BJ14 9
Haig Dr., Slou. AN41 61
Haig Rd. E. E13 CJ38 58
Haig Rd. W. E13 CJ38 58
Haig Rd., Grays DG41 71
Haig Rd., Stan. BK28 36
Haig Rd., Uxb. AZ39 53
Haig Rd., West. CK62 106
Haigh Cres., Red. BV71 121
Haigville Gdns., Ilf. CL31 49
Hailes Clo. SW19 BT50 76
North Rd.
Hailey Rd., Erith CR41 69
Haileybury Av., Enf. CA25 30
Haileybury Rd., Orp. CO56 98
Hailsham Av. SW2 BX48 76
Hailsham Clo., Rom. CV28 42
Hailsham Clo., Surb. BK54 84
Hailsham Dr., Har. BH31 45
Hailsham Gdns., Rom. CV28 42
Hailsham Rd. SW17 BV50 76
Hailsham Rd., Rom. CV28 42
Hailsham Ter. N18 BZ28 39
Haimo Rd. SE9 CJ46 78
Hainault Ct. E17 CF31 48
Hainault Gore, Rom. CQ32 50
Hainault Gro., Chig. CM28 40
Hainault Rd. E11 CF33 48
Hainault Rd., Chig. CL27 40
Hainault Rd., Rom. CO29 41
Hainault Rd., Rom. CQ32 50
Hainault Rd., Rom. CS30 41
Hainault St. SE9 CL47 78
Hainault St., Ilf. CM34 49
Haines Ct., Wey. BA56 92
Haines Way, Wat. BC20 17
Hainford Clo. SE4 CD45 67
Frendsbury Rd.
Haining Clo., Brent. BM42 65
Wellesley Rd.
Hainsford Clo. SE4 CC45 67
Hainthorpe Rd. SE27 BY48 76
Hainton Path E1 CB39 57
Watney Market
Halberd Ms. E5 CB34 48
Knightland Rd.
Halbutt Gdns., Dag. CQ34 50
Halbutt St., Dag. CQ34 50
Halcomb St. N1 CA37 2
Halcomb St. N1 CA37 57
Orsman Rd.
Halcot Av., Bexh. CR46 79
Halcrow St. E1 CB39 57
Halcyon Way, Horn. CW33 51
Haldan Rd. E4 CF29 39
Haldane Clo. N10 BV29 38
Haldane Pl. SW18 BS47 76
Haldane Rd. E6 CJ38 58
Haldane Rd. SE28 CP40 59
Haldane Rd. SW6 BR43 65
Haldane Rd., Sthl. BG40 54
Haldens, Welw.G.C. BR 6 5
Haldon Clo., Chig. CN28 40
Arrowsmith Rd.
Haldon Rd. SW18 BR46 75
Hale Clo. E4 CF27 39
Hale Clo., Edg. BN28 37
Hale Clo., Orp. CM56 97
Broadwater Gdns.
Hale Ct., Edg. BN28 37
Hale Dr. NW7 BN29 37
Hale End Clo., Ruis. BC32 44
Hale End Rd. E17 CF30 39
Hale End Rd. E4 CF29 39
Hale End Rd., Wdf.Grn. CF29 39
Hale End, Rom. CU29 41
Hale Gdns. N17 CB31 48
High Cross Rd.
Hale Gdns. W3 BM40 55
Hale Grove Gdns. NW7 BN28 37
Hale La. NW7 BN28 37
Hale La., Edg. BM28 37
Hale La., Sev. CT62 107
Hale Oak Rd., Sev. CU70 116
Hale Path SE27 BY49 76
Hale Pit Rd., Lthd. BG66 111

Hale Rd. E6 CK38 58
Hale St. E14 CE40 57
Hale St., Stai. AV49 72
Hale Wk. W7 BH39 54
Hale, The E4 CF29 39
Hale, The N17 CB31 48
Halefield Rd. N17 CB30 39
Hales Oak, Lthd. BG66 111
Hales Park Clo., Hem.H. BA13 8
Hales Pk., Hem.H. BA13 8
Hales St. SE8 CE43 67
Halesowen Rd., Mord. BS54 86
Haleswood Rd., Hem.H. AZ13 8
Haleswood, Cob. BC60 83
Halesworth Clo. E5 CB34 48
Southwold Rd.
Halesworth Clo., Rom. CW29 42
Halesworth Rd. SE13 CE45 67
Halesworth Rd., Rom. CW29 42
Haley Rd. NW4 BQ32 46
Half Acre Hill, Ger.Cr. AS30 34
Half Acre Rd. W7 BH40 54
Half Acre, Brent. BK43 64
Half Moon Cres. N1 BX37 2
Half Moon Cres. N1 BX37 56
Half Moon Ct. EC1 BZ39 2
Bartholomew Clo.
Half Moon Ct. EC1 BZ39 57
Bartholomew Clo.
Half Moon La. SE24 BZ46 77
Half Moon Meadow, Hem.H. AZ11 8
Half Moon Pass. E1 CA39 2
Half Moon Pass. E1 CA39 57
Braham St.
Half Moon St. W1 BV40 3
Half Moon St. W1 BV40 56
Halfhide La., Chsnt. CC16 21
Halfhides, Wal.Abb. CF20 21
Halfield Est. W2 BT40 56
Halford Rd. E10 CF32 48
Halford Rd. SW6 BS43 66
Halford Rd., Rich. BL46 75
Halford Rd., Uxb. AZ35 44
Halfpenny Clo., Guil. AU73 118
Halfpenny La., Guil. AU71 118
Halfway Ct., Grays CX42 70
Halfway Grn., Walt. BC55 83
Halfway St., Sid. CM47 78
Haliburton Rd., Twick. BJ46 74
Haliday Wk. N1 BZ36 57
Mildmay St.
Halidon Clo. E9 CC35 48
Halidon Ri., Rom. CX29 42
Halifax Rd., Enf. BZ23 30
Halifax Rd., Grnf. BF37 54
Halifax Rd., Rick. AU26 34
Halifax St. SE26 CB49 77
Halifax Way, Welw.G.C. BU 7 5
Halifield Dr., Belv. CQ41 69
Haling Gro., S.Croy. BZ57 96
Haling Park Gdns., S.Croy. BY57 95
Haling Rd., S.Croy. BZ57 96
Halings La., Uxb. AU31 43
Halkin Arc. SW1 BV41 3
Halkin Arc. SW1 BV41 66
Motcomb St.
Halkin Ms. SW1 BV41 66
Motcomb St.
Halkin Pl. SW1 BV41 3
Halkin Pl. SW1 BV41 66
Halkin St. SW1 BV41 3
Halkin St. SW1 BV41 66
Halkingcroft, Slou. AR41 62
Hall Av., S.Ock. CY40 60
Hall Clo. W5 BK39 54
Regal Clo.
Hall Clo. W5 BL39 55
Hall Clo., Rick. AW26 35
Hall Cres., S.Ock. CY41 70
Hall Ct., Slou. AQ43 62
Hall Dene Clo., Guil. AU70 118
Hall Dr. SE26 CB49 77
Hall Dr. W7 BH39 54
Hall Dr., Uxb. AX29 35
Hall Farm Clo., Stan. BJ27 36
Hall Farm Dr., Twick. BG47 74
Hall Gate NW8 BT38 1
Hall Gate NW8 BT38 56
Hall Rd.
Hall Gdns. E4 CD28 39
Hall Gdns., St.Alb. BN15 10
Hall Green La., Brwd. DE26 122
Hall Gro., Welw.G.C. BS 9 5
Hall Heath Clo., St.Alb. BJ12 9
Hall Hill, Oxt. CF69 114
Hall Hill, Sev. CX65 108
Hall La. E4 CD28 39
Hall La. NW4 BP30 37
Hall La., Brwd. DC25 122
Hall La., Hayes BA43 63
Hall La., S.Ock. DB37 60
Hall La., Upmin. CY30 42
Hall Oak Wk. NW6 BR36 55
Maygrove Rd.
Hall Pk. Gate, Berk. AS14 7
Hall Pk. Hill, Berk. AS14 7
Hall Pk. Rd., Upmin. CY35 51
Hall Pk., Berk. AS13 7
Hall Pl. Cres., Bex. CS46 79
Hall Pl. Dr., Wey. BB56 92
Hall Pl. Gdns., St.Alb. BH13 9
Hall Pl. W2 BT38 1
Hall Pl. W2 BT38 56
Hall Pl., Wok. AT61 100
North Rd.
Hall Rd. E15 CF35 48
Hall Rd. E6 CK37 58
Hall Rd. NW8 BT38 1
Hall Rd. NW8 BT38 56
Hall Rd., Dart. CW45 70
Hall Rd., Grav. DE48 81
Hall Rd., Hem.H. AZ12 8
Hall Rd., Islw. BG46 74
Hall Rd., Rom. CP32 50
Hall Rd., Rom. CV31 51
Hall Rd., S.Ock. CY41 70
Hall Rd., Wall. BV58 95
Hall St. EC1 BY38 2
Hall St. EC1 BY38 56
Hall St. N12 BT28 38
Hall Ter., S.Ock. CY41 70
Hall Vw. SE9 CJ48 78
Hall Way, Pur. BY60 95
Hall, The SE3 CH45 68
Hallam Clo., Brwd. DA22 33
Hallam Clo., Chis. CK49 78
Hallam Gdns., Pnr. BE29 36
Hallam Ms. W1 BV39 1
Hallam St.
Hallam Ms. W1 BV39 56
Hallam St.
Hallam Rd. N2 BY31 47
Hallam St. W1 BV38 1
Hallam St. W1 BV38 56
Halland Way, Nthwd. BA29 35
Halley Gdns. SE13 CF45 67
Halley Rd. E7 CJ36 58
Halley St. E14 CD39 57
Halleys App., Wok. AQ62 100
Halleys Wk., Wey. AX57 92
Hallfield Est. W2 BS39 1
Hallfield Est. W2 BT39 56
Hallford Way, Dart. CV46 80
Halliford Clo., Shep. BB52 83
Halliford Rd., Shep. BB53 83
Halliford Rd., Sun. BB52 83
Halliford St. N1 BZ36 2
Halliford St. N1 BZ36 57
Halling Hill, Harl. CN10 6
Hallingbury Rd., Saw. CR 5 6
Hallington Clo., Wok. AQ62 100
Halliwell Rd. SW2 BX46 76
Halliwick Rd. N10 BV30 38
Hallmead, Sutt. BS55 86
Hallmores, Brox. CE13 12
Hallowell Av., Croy. BX56 95
Hallowell Clo., Mitch. BV52 86
Hallowell Cres., Wat. BC27 35
Hayling Rd.
Hallowell Rd., Nthwd. BB29 35
Halls Farm Clo., Wok. AO62 100
Hallside Rd., Enf. CA22 30
Hallsville Rd. E16 CG39 58
Hallswelle Rd. NW11 BR32 46
Hallwood Cres., Brwd. DC26 122
Hallywell Cres. E6 CK39 58
Halons Rd. SE9 CL47 78
Halpin Pl. SE17 BZ42 4
Halpin Pl. SE17 BZ42 67
Halsbrook Rd. SE3 CJ45 68
Halsbury Clo., Stan. BJ28 36
Halsbury Rd. E., Nthlt. BG35 45
Halsbury Rd. W., Nthlt. BF35 45
Halsbury St. W12 BP40 55
Halsend, Hayes BC41 63
Halsey Pl., Wat. BC22 26
Halsey Rd., Wat. BC24 26
Halsey St. SW3 BU42 3
Halsey St. SW3 BU42 66
Halsham Cres., Bark. CN35 49
Halsmere Rd. SE5 BY44 66
Halstead Gdns. N21 BZ26 39
Halstead Hill, Chsnt. CA18 21
Halstead Rd. E11 CH22 49
Halstead Rd. N21 BZ26 39
Halstead Rd., Enf. CA24 30
Halstead Rd., Erith CT44 69
Halston Clo. SW11 BU46 76
Northcote Rd.
Halstow Rd. NW10 BQ38 55
Halstow Rd. SE10 CH42 68
Halsway, Hayes BC40 53
Halt Dr., S.le H. DK42 71
Halt Robin La., Belv. CR42 69
Halt Robin Rd.
Halt Robin Rd., Belv. CR42 69
Halter Clo., B.Wd. BN25 28
Clydesdale Clo.
Halton Cross St. N1 BY36 56
Halton Rd.
Halton Pl. N1 BZ37 57
Dibden St.
Halton Rd. N1 BY36 2
Halton Rd. N1 BY36 56
Halton Rd., Grays DG41 71
Haltside, Hat. BO13 10
Crossbrook
Halyons, The, Shep. BA53 83
Gordon Rd.
Ham Clo., Rich. BK48 74
Ham Farm Rd., Rich. BK49 74
Ham Gate Av., Rich. BK48 74
Ham La., Egh. AQ49 72
Ham La., Old Windsor AQ46 72
Ham La., Wind. AR45 62
Ham Park Rd. E15 CG36 58
Ham Ridings, Rich. BL49 75
Ham Shades Clo., Sid. CO48 79
Ham St., Rich. BK47 74
Ham Vw., Croy. CD53 87
Ham Yd. W1 BW40 3
Windmill St.
Ham Yd. W1 BW40 56
Windmill St.
Ham, The, Brent. BK43 64
Hambalt Rd. SW4 BW46 76
Hamberlins La., Berk. AO11 7
Hamble Clo., Ruis. BB34 44
Hamble Clo., Wok. AQ62 100
Denton Way
Hamble La., S.Ock. CZ39 60
Hamble St. SW6 BS45 66
Hamble Wk., Nthlt. BF37 54
Leander Rd.
Hamble Wk., Wok. AQ62 100
Denton Way
Hambledon Clo., Uxb. AZ38 53
Aldenham Dr.
Hambledon Hill, Epsom BN61 103
Hambledon Rd. SW18 BR47 75
Hambledon Rd., Sid. CM47 78
Hambledon Vale, Epsom BN61 103
Hambleton Gdns. SE25 CA52 87
Hambro Av., Brom. CH54 88
Hambro Rd. SW16 BW50 76
Hambro Rd., Brwd. DB27 42
Ingrave Rd.
Hambrook Rd. SE25 CB52 87
Hambrough Rd., Sthl. BE40 54
Hamden Cres., Dag. CR34 50
Hamelin St. E14 CF39 57
Hamerton Rd., Grav. DD46 81
Hameway E6 CL38 58
Hamfield Clo., Oxt. CF67 114
Hamfrith Rd. E15 CG36 58
Hamilton Av. N9 CB26 39
Hamilton Av., Cob. BC60 92
Hamilton Av., Hodd. CE11 12
Hamilton Av., Ilf. CL31 49
Hamilton Av., Rom. CS30 41
Hamilton Av., Surb. BM55 85
Hamilton Av., Sutt. BR54 85
Hamilton Av., Wok. AV61 100
Hamilton Clo. N17 CA31 48
Hamilton Clo. NW8 BT38 1
Hamilton Clo. NW8 BT38 56
Hamilton Clo. SE16 CD41 67
Somerford Rd.
Hamilton Clo., Barn. BU24 29
Hamilton Clo., Cher. AV54 82
Hamilton Clo., Epsom BN59 94
Hamilton Clo., Felt. BB49 73
Hamilton Clo., Guil. AQ68 109
Oregano Way
Hamilton Clo., Pot.B. BP20 19
Hamilton Clo., St.Alb. BF19 18
Hamilton Clo., Stan. BH27 36
Hamilton Cres. N13 BY28 38
Hamilton Cres., Brwd. DB28 42
Hamilton Cres., Har. BE34 45
Hamilton Cres., Houns. BF46 74
Hamilton Ct. W5 BL40 55
Hamilton Rd.
Hamilton Ct. W9 BT38 1
Hamilton Ct. W9 BT38 56
Hamilton Ct., Lthd. BF66 111
Hamilton Dr., Guil. AQ68 109
Hamilton Dr., Rom. CW30 42
Hamilton Gdns. NW8 BT38 1
Hamilton Gdns. NW8 BT38 56
Hamilton La. N5 BY35 47
Hamilton Mead, Hem.H. AT17 16
Hamilton Pk. N5 BY35 47
Hamilton Pk. W. N5 BY35 47
Hamilton Pl. W1 BV40 3
Hamilton Pl. W1 BV40 56
Hamilton Pl., Guil. AQ68 109
Oregano Way
Hamilton Pl., Sun. BC50 73
Hamilton Rd. E15 CG38 58
Hamilton Rd. E17 CD30 39
Hamilton Rd. N2 BT31 47
Hamilton Rd. N9 CB26 39
Hamilton Rd. NW10 BP35 46
Hamilton Rd. NW11 BQ33 46
Hamilton Rd. SE27 BZ49 77
Hamilton Rd. SW19 BS50 76
Hamilton Rd. W4 BO41 65
Hamilton Rd. W5 BL40 55
Hamilton Rd., Barn. BU24 29
Hamilton Rd., Berk. AQ13 7
Hamilton Rd., Bexh. CQ44 69
Hamilton Rd., Brent. BK43 64
Hamilton Rd., Felt. BB49 73
Hamilton Rd., Har. BH32 45
Hamilton Rd., Hayes BC40 53
Hamilton Rd., Ilf. CL35 49
Hamilton Rd., Kings L. BA20 17
Hamilton Rd., Rom. CU32 50
Hamilton Rd., Sid. CO49 79
Hamilton Rd., St.Alb. BJ13 9
Hamilton Rd., Sthl. BE40 54
Hamilton Rd., Th.Hth. BZ52 87
Hamilton Rd., Twick. BH47 74
Hamilton Rd., Uxb. AX38 53
Hamilton Rd., Wat. BC27 35
Hamilton Sq. SE1 BZ41 4
Hamilton Sq. SE1 BZ41 67
Kipling St.
Hamilton St. SE8 CE43 67
Deptford High St.
Hamilton St., Wat. BD25 27
Hamilton Ter. NW8 BS37 1
Hamilton Ter. NW8 BS37 56
Hamilton Way N13 BY28 38
Hamilton Cres.
Hamilton Way N3 BS29 38
Hamilton Way, Wall. BW58 95
Hamilton Wk., Erith CT43 69
Hamish St. SE11 BX42 4
Hamish St. SE11 BX42 66
Lambeth Wk.
Hamlea Clo. SE12 CH46 78
Hamlet Clo., Rom. CR29 41
Hamlet Clo., Wdf.Grn. CH29 40
Hamlet Gdns. W6 BP42 65
Hamlet Hill, Harl. CH13 13
Hamlet Lodge SE13 CG45 68
Old Rd.
Hamlet Rd. SE19 CA50 77
Hamlet Rd., Rom. CQ29 41
Hamlet Sq. NW2 BQ34 46
Cricklewood Trd. Est.
Hamlet, The SE5 BZ45 67
Hamlet, The, Berk. AT11 7
Hamlets Way E3 CD38 57
Hamlin Cres., Pnr. BD32 45
Hamlin Rd., Sev. CT64 107
Hamlyn Clo., Edg. BL27 37
Hamlyn Gdns. SE19 CA50 77
Hamm Moor La., Wey. AY56 92
Hammarskjold Rd., Harl. CM10 6
Hammelton Rd., Brom. CG51 88
Hammer La., Hem.H. AY13 8
Hammers Gate, St.Alb. BF16 18
Hammers La. NW7 BP28 37
Hammersmith Br. Rd. W6 BQ42 65
Hammersmith Gro. W6 BQ41 65
Hammersmith Rd. W6 BQ42 65
Hammersmith Ter. W6 BP42 65
Hammet Clo., Hayes BD39 54
Hammett St. EC3 CA40 57
Minories
Hammond Av., Mitch. BV51 86
Hammond Clo., Barn. BR25 28
Hammond Clo., Chsnt. CA16 21
Hammond Clo., Har. BG35 45
Lilian Board Way
Hammond Clo., Hmptn. BF51 84
Hammond Clo., Wok. AR61 100
Hammond Rd., Enf. CS23 30
Hammond Rd., Sthl. BE41 64
Hammond Rd., Wok. AR61 100
Hammond St. NW5 BW36 56
Hammond Street Rd., Chsnt. BZ16 21
Hammond Way SE28 CO40 59
Hammonds La., Brwd. DA29 42
Hammonds La., Hat. BM 9 5
Hamonde Clo., Edg. BM27 37
Hampden Av., Beck. CD51 87
Hampden Clo. NW1 BW37 1
Hampden Clo. NW1 BW37 56
Hampden Clo., Epp. CR17 23
Wellington Rd.
Hampden Clo., Slou. AQ38 52
Hampden Cres., Brwd. DB28 42
Hampden Cres., Chsnt. CB19 21
Hampden Ct. N10 BV29 38
Hampden Gurney St. W1 BU39 1
Hampden Gurney St. W1 BU39 56
Seymour Pl.
Hampden La. N17 CA30 39
Hampden Rd. N10 BV29 38
Hampden Rd. N17 CB30 39
Hampden Rd. N19 BW34 47
Holloway Rd.
Hampden Rd. N8 BY31 47
Hampden Rd., Beck. CD51 87
Hampden Rd., Ger.Cr. AR30 34
Hampden Rd., Grays DD42 71
Hampden Rd., Har. BG30 36
Hampden Rd., Kings.T. BM51 85
Hampden Rd., Rom. CR29 41
Hampden Rd., Slou. AS41 62
Hampden Sq. N14 BV26 38
Hampden Way N14 BV26 38
Hampden Way, Wat. BB21 26
Hampdon Pl., St.Alb. BH18 18
Hamper Mill La., Wat. BC26 35
Hampshire Av., Slou. AO39 52
Hampshire Clo. N18 CB28 39
Berkshire Gdns.
Hampshire Gdns., S.le H. DK41 71
Somerset Rd.
Hampshire Rd. N22 BX29 38
Hampshire Rd., Horn. CX31 51
Hampshire St. NW5 BW36 56
Torriano Av.
Hampson Way SW8 BX44 66
Hampstead Clo. SE28 CO40 59
Hampstead Gdns. NW11 BS32 47
Hampstead Gdns. NW3 BU35 47
Rosslyn Hill
Hampstead Gro. NW3 BT34 47
Hampstead High St. NW3 BT35 47
Hampstead Hill Gdns. NW3 BT35 47
Hampstead La. NW3 BT33 47
Hampstead La., Dor. BH72 119
Hampstead Rd. NW1 BW37 1
Hampstead Rd. NW1 BW37 56
Hampstead Rd., Dor. BJ72 119
Hampstead Sq. NW3 BT34 47
Hampstead Way NW11 BS32 47
Hampton Clo. NW6 BS38 56
Hampton Clo. SW20 BQ50 75
Hampton Cres., Grav. DJ48 81
Hampton Ct. Av., E.Mol. BG53 84
Hampton Ct. N1 BY36 56
Upper St.
Hampton Ct. Rd., Kings.T. BH52 84
Hampton Ct. Rd., Hmptn. BG51 84
Hampton Ct. Way, E.Mol. BH53 84
Hampton Gro. NW3 BU35 47
Pond St.
Hampton Gro., Epsom BO59 94
Hampton La., Felt. BE49 74
Hampton Mead, Loug. CL24 31
Hampton Pl. NW6 BS39 56
Hampton Rd. E., Felt. BE48 74
Hampton Rd. E11 CF33 48
Hampton Rd. E4 CD28 39
Hampton Rd. E7 CH35 49
Hampton Rd. NW6 BS38 56
Hampton Rd. W., Felt. BE48 74
Hampton Rd., Croy. BZ53 87
Hampton Rd., Ilf. CL35 49
Hampton Rd., Red. BU73 121
Hampton Rd., Tedd. BG49 74
Hampton Rd., Twick. BG48 74
Hampton Rd., Wor.Pk. BP55 85
Hampton Ri., Har. BL32 46
Hampton St. SE17 BY42 4
Hampton St. SE17 BY42 66
Hamsey Green Gdns., Warl. CB61 105
Hamsey Way, S.Croy. CB61 105
Hamshades Clo., Sid. CN48 78
Hamstel Rd., Harl. CM10 6
Hanameel St. E16 CH40 58
Hanbury Clo., Chsnt. CC18 21
Hanbury Dr., West. CH60 97
Hanbury La., Hat. BU12 11
Hanbury Ms. N1 BZ37 2
Hanbury Ms. N1 BZ37 57
Mary St.
Hanbury Path, Wok. AU60 91
Hanbury Rd. N17 CB30 39
Hanbury Rd. W3 BM41 65
Hanbury St. E1 CA39 2
Hanbury St. E1 CB39 57
Hanbury Wk., Bex. CS48 79
Hancock Ct., B.Wd. BN23 28
Hancock Rd. E3 CF38 57
Hancock Rd. SE19 BZ50 77
Hand Ct. WC1 BX39 2
Hand Ct. WC1 BX39 56
Sandland St.
Hand La., Saw. CP 6 6
Handa Clo., Hem.H. AZ15 8
Handa Wk. N1 BZ36 57
Handcroft Rd., Croy. BY54 86
Handel Clo., Edg. BL29 37
Handel Cres., Til. DG43 71
Handel Pl. NW10 BN36 55
Mitchellbrook Way
Handel St. WC1 BX38 2
Handel St. WC1 BX38 56
Handel Way, Edg. BM29 37
Handen Rd. SE12 CG46 78
Handforth Rd. SW9 BY43 66
Handforth Rd., Ilf. CL34 49
Winston Way
Handley Rd. E9 CC37 57
Victoria Park Rd.
Handpost Hill, Cuff. BV17 20
Hands Wk. E16 CH39 58
Butchers Rd.
Handside Clo., Welw.G.C. BQ 8 5
Handside Clo., Wor.Pk. BQ54 85
Handside Grn., Welw.G.C. BQ 7 5
Handside La., Welw.G.C. BP 9 5
Handsworth Av. E4 CF29 39
Handsworth Clo., Wat. BC27 35
Handsworth Rd. N17 BZ31 48
Handtrough Way, Bark. CL37 58
Fresh Wharf Rd.
Hanford Clo. SW18 BS47 76
Hanford Rd., S.Ock. CY40 60
Hanford Row SW19 BQ50 75
Hangar Ruding, Wat. BE27 36
Hanger Ct. W5 BL38 55
Heathcroft
Hanger Grn. W5 BM38 55
Hanger Hill, Wey. AZ57 92
Hanger La. W5 BL37 55
Hanger Vale La. W5 BL39 55
Hanger View Way W3 BL39 55
Hanger Vale La.
Hanging Hill La., Brwd. DD27 122
Hangrove Hill, Orp. CL60 97
Hankey Pl. SE1 BZ41 4
Hankey Pl. SE1 BZ41 67
Hankins La. NW7 BO27 37
Hanks Vw., Cob. BE60 93
Hanley Clo., Wind. AL44 61
Hanley Rd. N4 BX33 47
Hanmer Wk. N7 BX34 47
Newington Way
Hannah Clo. NW10 BN35 46
Hannards Way, Chig. CO28 41
Hannell Rd. SW6 BR43 65
Hannen Rd. SE27 BY48 76
Hannibal Rd. E1 CC39 57
Hannibal Rd., Stai. AX47 73
Hannibal Way, Croy. BX56 95
Hannington Rd. SW4 BV45 66
Hanover Av., Felt. BC47 73
Hanover Cir., Hayes BA39 53
Hanover Clo., Egh. AQ50 72
Blays La.
Hanover Clo., Red. BW67 113
Hanover Clo., Rich. BM43 65
Hanover Clo., Slou. AQ41 62
Yew Tree Rd.
Hanover Clo., Sutt. BR56 94
Hanover Ct. W12 BP40 55
Hanover Ct., Dor. BH71 119
Hanover Dr., Chis. CL49 78
Beechwood Ri.
Hanover Gate Ms. NW1 BU38 1
Hanover Gate NW1 BU38 1
Hanover Gate NW1 BU38 56
Hanover Gdns. SE11 BY43 66
Hanover Gdns., Ilf. CM29 40
Hanover Grn., Hem.H. AW14 8
Hanover Mead, Maid. AH41 61
Hanover Pk. SE15 CB44 67
Hanover Pl. WC2 BX40 56
Long Acre.
Hanover Pl., Egh. AR50 72
Blays La.
Hanover Rd. N15 CA31 48
Hanover Rd. NW10 BQ36 55
Hanover Rd. SW19 BT50 76
Hanover Sq. W1 BV39 1
Hanover Sq. W1 BV39 56
Hanover St. W1 BV39 1
Hanover St. W1 BV39 56
Hanover St., Croy. BY55 86
Latimer Rd.
Hanover Ter. Ms. NW1 BU38 1
Hanover Ter. Ms. NW1 BU38 56
Hanover Ter. NW1 BU38 1
Hanover Ter. NW1 BU38 56
Hanover Way, Bexh. CP45 69
Hanover Way, Wind. AM44 61
Hanover West Ind. Est. NW10 BN38 55

Hanover Wk., Hat. BO14 10
Tudor Clo.
Hanover Wk., Wey. BB55 83
Hanover Yd. N1 BY37 56
Noel Rd.
Hans Cres. SW1 BU41 3
Hans Cres. SW1 BU41 66
Hans Pl. SW1 BU41 3
Hans Pl. SW1 BU41 66
Hans Rd. SW3 BU41 3
Hans Rd. SW3 BU41 66
Hans St. SW1 BU41 3
Hans St. SW1 BU41 66
Pavilion Rd.
Hansard Ms. W14 BQ41 65
Hansart Way, Enf. BY23 29
Hanselin Clo., Stan. BH28 36
Chenduit Way
Hansells Mead, Harl. CH11 13
Hanshaw Dr., Edg. BN30 37
Hansler Gro. E.Mol. BG53 84
Hansler Rd. SE22 CA46 77
Hansol Rd., Bexh. CQ46 79
Hanson Clo. SW12 BV47 76
Hanson Clo., Guil. AS69 118
Hanson Clo., Loug. CM23 31
Hanson Dr., Loug. CM23 31
Hanson Gdns., Sthl. BE41 64
Hanson Grn., Loug. CM23 31
Hanson St. W1 BW39 1
Hanson St. W1 BW39 56
Hanway Pl. W1 BW39 1
Hanway Pl. W1 BW39 56
Hanway St.
Hanway Rd. W7 BG39 54
Hanway St. W1 BW39 1
Hanway St. W1 BW39 56
Hanworth Clo., Felt. BE49 74
Hanworth La., Cher. AV54 82
Hanworth Rd., Felt. BC47 73
Hanworth Rd., Hmptn. BE49 74
Hanworth Rd., Houns. BE47 74
Hanworth Rd., Red. BU73 121
Hanworth Rd., Sun. BC50 73
Hanworth Ter., Houns. BF45 64
Whitton Rd.
Hanworth Trading Est., Felt. BE48 74
Hanworth Trd. Est., Cher. AV54 82
Hanyards End., Cuff. BW17 20
Hill Rise
Hanyards La., Cuff.. BW17 20
Hapgood Clo., Har. BG35 45
Harads Pl. E1 CB40 57
Ensign St.
Harben Rd. NW6 BT36 56
Harberson Rd. E15 CG37 58
Harberson Rd. SW12 BV47 76
Harbert Rd. E4 CC28 39
Harberton Rd. N19 BW33 47
Harberts Rd., Harl. CL11 13
Harbet Rd. W2 BT39 1
Harbet Rd. W2 BT39 56
Harbex Clo., Bex. CR47 79
Harbinger Rd. E14 CE42 67
Harbledown Pl., Orp. CP52 89
Okemore Gdns.
Harbledown Rd. SW6 BS44 66
Harbledown Rd., S.Croy. CB59 96
Harbord St. SW6 BQ44 65
Harborough Av., Sid. CN47 78
Harborough Clo., Slou. AL40 61
Harborough Rd. SW16 BX49 76
Harbour Av. SW10 BT44 66
Harbour Exchange Sq. E14 CE41 67
Harbour Rd. SE5 BZ45 67
Harbourer Clo., Ilf. CO28 41
Harbourer Rd., Ilf. CO28 41
Harbourfield Rd., Bans. BS61 104
Harbridge Av. SW15 BO47 75
Harbury Rd., Cars. BU58 95
Harbut Rd. SW11 BT45 66
Harcombe Rd. N16 CA34 48
Harcourt Av. E12 CK35 49
Harcourt Av., Edg. BN27 37
Harcourt Av., Sid. CP46 79
Harcourt Av., Wall. BV56 95
Harcourt Clo., Egh. AU50 72
Harcourt Clo., Islw. BJ45 64
Silverhall St.
Harcourt Field, Wall. BV56 95
Harcourt La., Maid. AJ41 61
Harcourt Rd. E15 CG37 58
Harcourt Rd. N22 BW30 38
Harcourt Rd. SE4 CD45 67
Harcourt Rd. SW19 BS50 76
Russell Rd.
Harcourt Rd., Bexh. CQ45 69
Harcourt Rd., Bush. BF25 27
Harcourt Rd., Maid. AJ41 61
Harcourt Rd., Th.Hth. BX53 86
Harcourt Rd., Wall. BV56 95
Harcourt Rd., Wind. AM44 61
Harcourt St. W1 BU39 1
Harcourt St. W1 BU39 56
Harcourt Ter. SW10 BS42 3
Harcourt Ter. SW10 BS42 66
Hardcastle Clo. SE25 CA53 87
Adams Way
Hardcourts Clo., W.Wick. CE55 87
Hardel Ri. SW2 BY47 76
Hardell Clo., Egh. AT49 72
Harden Rd., Grav. DF48 81
Harden St. SE18 CK42 68
Hardens Manor Way SE7 CJ41 68
Harders Rd. SE15 CB44 67
Harders Road Ms. SE15 CB44 67
Hardess St. SE24 BZ45 67
Herne Hill Rd.
Hardie Clo. NW10 BN35 46
Hardie Rd., Dag. CS34 50
Harding Clo., Wat. BD20 18
Harding Rd., Bexh. CQ44 69
Harding Rd., Chesh. AO18 16
Harding Rd., Epsom BO63 103
Harding Rd., Grays DG41 71
Hardinge Clo., Uxb. AZ39 53
Hardinge Rd. N18 CA29 39
Hardinge Rd. NW10 BP37 55
Hardinge St. E1 CC39 57
Hardings La. SE20 CC50 77
Hardings Row, Iver AU38 52
Hardings, Welw.G.C. BT 7 5
Hardley Cres., Horn. CV31 51
Hardman Rd. SE7 CH42 68
Hardman Rd., Kings.T. BL51 85
Hardness St. SE24 BY45 67
Herne Hill Rd.
Hardwick Clo., Stan. BK28 36
Marsh La.
Hardwick Grn. W13 BJ39 54
Templewood
Hardwick La., Cher. AU54 82
Hardwick Rd., Red. BT71 121
Hardwick St. EC1 BY38 2
Hardwick St. EC1 BY38 56
Hardwicke Av., Houns. BF44 64
Hardwicke Clo., Cob. BG61 102
Hardwicke Gdns., Amer. AP22 25
Green La.
Hardwicke Pl., St.Alb. BK17 18
Hardwicke Rd. N13 BX29 38
Hardwicke Rd. W4 BN42 65
Hardwicke Rd., Reig. BS70 121
Hardwicke Rd., Rich. BK49 74
Hardwicke St., Bark. CM37 58
Hardwicks Way SW18 BS46 76
Hardwidge St. SE1 CA41 4
Hardwidge St. SE1 CA41 67
Snows Fields
Hardy Av., Grav. DF48 81
Hardy Av., Ruis. BC35 44
Hardy Clo. SE16 CC41 67
Middleton Dr.
Hardy Clo., Dor. BJ73 119
Hardy Clo., Pnr. BD33 45
Hardy Clo., Slou. AN40 61
Hardy Gro., Dart. CX45 70
Hardy Pass. N22 BY30 38
Cranbrook Pk.
Hardy Rd. SE3 CG43 68
Hardy Rd. SW19 BS50 76
Hardy Rd., Hem.H AY13 8
Hardy Way, Enf. BY23 29
Hare & Billet Rd. SE3 CF44 67
Hare Cres., Wat. BC19 17
Hare Ct. EC4 BY40 4
Middle Temple La.
Hare Ct. EC4 BY40 56
Middle Temple La.
Hare Hall La., Rom. CU31 50
Hare Hill Clo., Wok. AW61 101
Hare Hill, Wey. AV57 91
Hare La., Esher BH57 93
Hare La., Hat. BP13 10
Hare Marsh E2 CB38 2
Hare Marsh E2 CB38 57
Cheshire St.
Hare Park Clo., Hem.H. AV13 7
Hare Pl. EC4 BY39 2
Hare Pl. EC4 BY39 56
Fleet St.
Hare Row E2 CB37 57
Cambridge Heath Rd.
Hare St. SE18 CL41 68
Hare St. Springs, Harl. CL11 13
Hare Wk. N1 CA37 2
Hare Wk. N1 CA37 57
Harebell Hill, Cob. BD60 93
Harebell Way, Rom. CV29 42
Harebell, Welw.G.C. BR 9 5
Harebreaks, The, Wat. BC21 26
Harecastle Clo., Hayes BE38 54
Braunston Dr.
Harecourt Rd. N1 BZ36 57
Harecroft, Dor. BK73 119
Harecroft, Lthd. BF65 102
Haredale Rd. SE24 BZ45 67
Haredon Clo. SE23 CC47 77
Harefield Av., Sutt. BQ58 94
Harefield Clo., Enf. BY23 29
Hunters Way
Harefield Grn. NW7 BQ29 37
Harefield Ms. SE4 CD45 67
Harefield Pl. Est., Uxb. AY35 44
Harefield Pl., St.Alb. BK12 9
Harefield Rd. N8 BW32 47
Harefield Rd. SE4 CD45 67
Harefield Rd. SW16 BX50 76
Harefield Rd., Rick. AX27 35
Harefield Rd., Sid. CP48 79
Harefield Rd., Uxb. AX36 53
Harefield, Esher BH55 84
Harefield, Harl. CO10 6
Harelands Clo., Wok. AR62 100
Harelands La., Wok. AQ62 100
Harendon, Tad. BQ64 103
Hares Bank, Croy. CF58 96
Haresfield Rd., Dag. CR36 59
Harestone Dr., Cat. CA65 105
Harestone Hill, Cat. CA66 114
Harestone La., Cat. CA66 114
Harestone Valley Rd., Cat. CA66 114
Hareward Rd., Guil. AU69 109
Harewood Av. NW1 BU38 1
Harewood Av. NW1 BU38 56
Harewood Av., Nthlt. BE36 54
Harewood Clo., Nthlt. BE36 54
Harewood Clo., Reig. BT69 121
Harewood Dr., Ilf. CK30 40
Harewood Gdns., S.Croy. CB61 105
Harewood Hill, Epp. CN21 31
Harewood Pl. W1 BV39 1
Harewood Pl. W1 BV39 56
Hanover Sq.
Harewood Pl., Slou. AQ41 62
Harewood Rd. SW19 BU50 76
Harewood Rd., Brwd. DA25 33
Harewood Rd., Ch.St.G. AR24 25
Harewood Rd., Islw. BH43 64
Harewood Rd., S.Croy. CA57 96
Harewood Rd., Wat. BC27 35
Harewood Row NW1 BU39 1
Harewood Row NW1 BU39 56
Harewood Av.
Harewood Ter., Sthl. BE42 64
Harewood, Rick. AX25 26
Harfield Gdns. SE5 CA45 67
Harfield Rd., Sun. BD51 84
Harford Clo. E4 CE26 39
Harford Dr., Wat. BB22 26
Harford Rd. E4 CE26 39
Harford St. E1 CD38 57
Harford Wk. N2 BT31 47
Harfst Way, Swan. CS51 89
Hargood Clo., Har. BL32 46
Hargood Rd. SE3 CJ44 68
Hargrave Pk. N19 BW34 47
Hargrave Pl. N7 BW35 47
Brecknock Rd.
Hargrave Rd. N19 BW34 47
Hargreaves Av., Chsnt. CB18 21
Hargreaves Clo., Chsnt. CB19 21
Hargwyne St. SW9 BX45 66
Haringey Pass. N4 BY31 47
Haringey Pk. N8 BX32 47
Haringey Rd. N8 BX31 47
Harington Ter. N18 BZ27 39
Harkett Clo., Har. BH30 36
Church La.
Harkness Clo., Epsom BQ61 103
Harkness Clo., Rom. CW28 42
Harkness, Chsnt. CB18 21
Harland Av., Croy. CA55 87
Harland Av., Sid. CM48 78
Harland Rd. SE12 CH47 78
Harlands Gro., Orp. CL56 97
Pinecrest Gdns.
Harlech Gdns., Houns. BD43 64
Harlech Rd. N14 BX27 38
Harlequin Av., Brent. BJ43 64
Harlequin Rd., Tedd. BJ50 74
Harlescott Rd. SE15 CC45 67
Harlesden Clo., Rom. CW29 42
Harlesden Gdns. NW10 BO37 55
Harlesden Rd. NW10 BP36 55
Harlesden Rd., Rom. CW29 42
Harlesden Rd., St.Alb. BJ13 9
Harlesden Wk., Rom. CW29 42
Harleston Clo. E5 CB34 48
Southwold Rd.
Harley Clo., Wem. BK36 54
Harley Cres., Har. BG31 45
Harley Ct., Har. BG31 45
Harley Ct., St.Alb. BK11 9
Villiers Cres.
Harley Gdns. SW10 BT42 3
Harley Gdns. SW10 BT42 66
Harley Gdns., Orp. CN56 97
Harley Gro. E3 CD38 57
Harley Pl. W1 BV39 1
Harley Pl. W1 BV39 56
Harley Rd. NW10 BO37 55
Harley Rd. NW3 BT36 1
Harley Rd. NW3 BT36 56
Harley Rd., Har. BG31 45
Harley St. W1 BV38 1
Harley St. W1 BV38 56
Harleyford Rd. SE11 BX43 4
Harleyford Rd. SE11 BX43 66
Harleyford St. SE11 BY43 66
Harleyford, Brom. CJ51 88
Harlington Clo., Hayes BA43 63
Harlington High St., Hayes BA43 63
Harlington Rd. E., Felt. BC47 73
Harlington Rd. W., Felt. BC46 73
Harlington Rd., Uxb.& Hayes AZ38 53
Harlington Rd., Bexh. CQ45 69
Harlow Common Rd., Harl. CP12 14
Harlow Gdns., Rom. CS29 41
Harlow Rd. N13 BZ27 39
Harlow Rd., Bish. CR 7 6
Harlow Rd., Ong. CV13 15
Harlow Rd., Rain. CT37 59
Harlow Rd., Saw. CP 7 6
Harlow St., Hem.H. AZ11 8
Harlowe Clo. E8 CB37 57
Brougham Rd.
Harlton Ct., Wal.Abb. CG20 22
Harlyn Dr., Pnr. BC31 44
Harman Av., Grav. DG49 81
Harman Av., Wdf.Grn. CG29 40
Harman Clo. E4 CF28 39
Harman Clo. NW2 BR35 46
Harman Dr. NW2 BR35 46
Harman Dr., Sid. CN46 78
Harman Est. N1 CA37 2
Harman Est. N1 CA37 57
Harman Rd., Enf. CA25 30
Harmer Grn. La., Welw.G.C. BR 5 5
Harmer Rd., Swans. DC46 81
Harmer St., Grav. DH46 81
Harmondsworth La., West Dr. AY43 63
Harmondsworth Rd., West Dr. AY42 63
Harmony Clo. NW11 BR32 46
Harmony Clo., Pur. BX58 95
Harmood Gro. NW1 BV36 56
Clarence Way
Harmood St. NW1 BV36 56
Harms Gro., Guil. AU69 109
Harmsworth St. SE17 BY42 4
Harmsworth St. SE17 BY42 66
Harmsworth Way N20 BR26 37
Harnage Rd., Brent. BL42 65
Harness Rd. SE28 CO41 69
Harness Way, St.Alb. BK12 9
Harold Av., Belv. CQ42 69
Harold Av., Hayes BB41 63
Harold Cres., Wal.Abb. CF19 21
Harold Ct. Rd., Rom. CX29 42
Harold Est., Wal.Abb. CF19 21
Harold Gibbons Ct. SE7 CJ43 68
Harold Hill Ind. Est., Rom. CV29 42
Harold Rd. E11 CG33 49
Harold Rd. E13 CH37 58
Harold Rd. E4 CF27 39
Harold Rd. N15 CA32 48
Harold Rd. N8 BX32 47
Harold Rd. NW10 BN38 55
Harold Rd. SE19 BZ50 77
Harold Rd., Dart. CW49 80
Harold Rd., Sutt. BT56 95
Harold Rd., Wdf.Grn. CH30 40
Harold Vw., Rom. CW30 42
Heath Rd.
Harolds Clo., Harl. CK11 13
Harolds Rd.
Harolds Rd., Harl. CK11 13
Haroldstone Rd. E17 CC32 48
Harp All. EC4 BY39 2
Harp All. EC4 BY39 56
St. Bride St.
Harp La. EC3 CA40 4
Harp La. EC3 CA40 57
Lower Thames St.
Harp Rd. W7 BH38 54
Harpenden Rd. E12 CJ34 49
Harpenden Rd. SE27 BY48 76
Harpenden Rd., St.Alb. BG11 9
Harper La., Rad. BJ19 18
Harper Rd. E6 CK39 58
Harper Rd. SE1 BZ41 4
Harper Rd. SE1 BZ41 67
Harpers La., B.Wd. DB22 33
Harpers Yd. N17 CA30 39
Ruskin Rd.
Harpesford Av., Vir.W. AQ53 82
Harpley Sq. E1 CC38 57
Harpour Rd., Bark. CM36 58
Harps Oak La., Red. BU66 113
Harpsden St. SW11 BV44 66
Harpsfield Bdwy., Hat. BO12 10
Harptree Way, St.Alb. BJ12 9
Harpur St. WC1 BX39 2
Harpur St. WC1 BX39 56
Dombey St.
Harpurs, Tad. BQ64 103
Harraden Rd. SE3 CJ44 68
Harrap Chase, Grays DC42 71
Harrier Clo., Rain. CU36 59
Harrier Ms. SE28 CM41 68
Harrier Way E6 CK39 58
Harriers Clo. W5 BL40 55
Harries Rd., Hayes BD38 54
Harriescourt, Wal.Abb. CH19 22
Harriet Clo. E8 CB37 57
Harriet Clo. E8 CB37 2
Harriet Gdns., Croy. CB55 87
Harriet St. SW1 BU41 3
Harriet St. SW1 BU41 66
Sloane St.
Harriet Way, Bush. BG26 36
Harriet Wk. SW1 BU41 3
Harriet Wk. SW1 BU41 66
Harringay Gdns. N15 BY31 47
Harringay Rd. N15 BY32 47
Harrington Clo., Croy. BX55 86
Harrington Clo., Reig. BP74 120
Harrington Clo., Wind. AM45 61
Harrington Gdns. SW7 BS42 3
Harrington Gdns. SW7 BS42 66
Harrington Hill E5 CB33 48
Harrington Pl., Reig. BS69 121
Reigate Hill
Harrington Rd. E11 CG33 49
Harrington Rd. SE25 CB52 87
Harrington Rd. SW7 BT42 3
Harrington Rd. SW7 BT42 66
Harrington Sq. NW1 BW37 1
Harrington Sq. NW1 BW37 56
Harrington St. NW1 BW38 1
Harrington St. NW1 BW38 56
Harrington Way SE18 CJ41 68
Harriott Clo. SE10 CG42 68
Tunnel Av.
Harriotts Clo., Ash. BK63 102
Harriotts La., Ash. BK63 102
Harris Clo., Enf. BY23 29
Harris Clo., Grav. DF48 81
Harris Clo., Houns. BF44 64
Willow Gdns.
Harris La., Rad. BM20 19
Harris Rd., Bexh. CQ44 69
Harris Rd., Dag. CQ35 50
Harris Rd., Wat. BC21 26
Harris St. E17 CD33 48
Harris St. SE5 BZ43 67
Harris Way, Sun. BB51 83
Harrison Clo., Brwd. DE25 122
Harrison Clo., Nthwd. BA29 35
Harrison Clo., Reig. BS71 121
Harrison Ct., Shep. AZ53 83
Harrison Dr., Epp. CR16 23
High Rd.
Harrison Rd., Dag. CR36 59
Harrison St. WC1 BX38 2
Harrison St. WC1 BX38 56
Harrison Way, Sev. CU64 107
Harrison Way, Slou. AL40 61
Harrison Wk., Chsnt. CC18 21
Harrisons Ri., Croy. BY55 86
Harrogate Ct., Slou. AT42 62
Harrogate Rd., Wat. BD27 36
Harrold Rd., Dag. CO35 50
Harrow Av., Enf. CA25 30
Harrow Bottom Rd., Vir.W. AS53 82
Harrow Clo., Chess. BK57 93
Harrow Clo., Dor. BJ72 119
Harrow Clo., Wey. AW55 83
Harrow Cotts., Felt. AZ48 73
Harrow Cres., Rom. CU29 41
Harrow Dr. N9 CA26 39
Harrow Dr., Horn. CU33 50
Harrow Gdns., Orp. CO56 98
Harrow Gdns., Warl. CD61 105
Harrow La. E14 CF40 57
Harrow Manorway SE2 CP40 59
Harrow Pk., Har. BH34 45
Harrow Pl. E1 CA39 2
Harrow Pl. E1 CA39 57
Harrow Rd. E., Dor. BJ72 119
Harrow Rd. E11 CG34 49
Harrow Rd. E6 CK37 58
Harrow Rd. NW10 BP38 55
Harrow Rd. W., Dor. BJ72 119
Harrow Rd. W10 BR38 55
Harrow Rd. W2 BT39 1
Harrow Rd., Bark. CN37 58
Harrow Rd., Cars. BU57 95
Harrow Rd., Felt. AZ48 73
Harrow Rd., Ilf. CM35 49
Harrow Rd., Sev. CQ61 107
Harrow Rd., Slou. AS41 62
Harrow Rd., Warl. CD61 105
Harrow Rd., Wem. BM35 55
Harrow Vw. Rd. W5 BJ38 54
Harrow Vw., Har. BG31 45
Harrow Vw., Hayes BC39 53
Harrow Vw., Uxb. BA38 53
Harrow Way, Shep. BA51 83
Harrow Way, Wat. BE27 36
Harrow Weald Pk., Har. BG29 36
Harrow Weald, Har. BG29 36
Harroway Rd. SW11 BT44 66
Harrowby Gdns., Grav. DF48 81
Harrowby St. W1 BU39 1
Harrowby St. W1 BU39 56
Harrowdene Clo., Wem. BK35 45
Harrowdene Gdns., Tedd. BJ50 74
Harrowdene Rd., Wem. BK34 45
Harrowes Meade, Edg. BM27 37
Harrowfields Gdns., Har. BH34 45
Sudbury Hill
Harrowgate Rd. E9 CD36 57
Hart Cres., Chig. CN28 40
Hart Dyke Cres., Swan. CS52 89
Hart Dyke Rd., Orp. CP54 89
Hart Dyke Rd., Swan. CS52 89
Hart Gro. Clo. W5 BM40 55
Hart Gro.
Hart Gro. W5 BM40 55
Hart Gro., Sthl. BF39 54
Hart Rd., Dor. BJ71 119
Hart Rd., Harl. CP 8 6
Hart Rd., St.Alb. BG14 9
Hart Rd., Wey. AY60 92
Hart St. EC3 CA40 4
Hart St. EC3 CA40 57
Mark La.
Hart St. WC2 BX39 2
Hart St., Brwd. DB27 42
Harte Rd., Houns. BE44 64
Hartfield Av., B.Wd. BM25 28
Hartfield Av., Nthlt. BC37 53
Hartfield Clo., B.Wd. BM25 28
Hartfield Cres. SW19 BR50 75
Hartfield Cres., W.Wick. CH55 88
Hartfield Gro. SE20 CB51 87
Hartfield Rd. SW19 BR50 75
Hartfield Rd., W.Wick. CH56 97
Hartfield Rd., Chess. BK56 93
Hartfield Ter. E3 CE37 57
Hartford Av., Har. BJ31 45
Hartford Pl., Grav. DE47 81
Hartford Rd., Bex. CR46 79
Hartford Rd., Epsom BM57 94
Hartforde Rd., B.Wd. BM25 28
Harthall La., Hem.H. AZ17 17
Hartham Clo. N7 BX35 47
Hartham Clo., Islw. BJ44 64
Hartham Rd. N17 CA30 39
Hartham Rd. N7 BX35 47
Hartham Rd., Islw. BH44 64
Hartin Clo., Uxb. AY37 53
Harting Rd. SE9 CK49 78
Hartington Clo., Har. BH35 45
Hartington Ct. W4 BM43 65
Hartington Pl., Reig. BS69 121
Reigate Hill Rd.
Hartington Rd. E16 CH39 58
Hartington Rd. E17 CD32 48
Hartington Rd. SW8 BX44 66
Hartington Rd. W13 BJ40 54
Hartington Rd. W4 BM43 65
Hartington Rd., Sthl. BE41 64
Hartington Rd., Twick. BJ46 74
Hartismere Rd. SW6 BR43 65
Hartlake Rd. E9 CC36 57
Hartland Clo., Edg. BM27 37
Hartland Clo., Slou. AO40 52
Bath Rd.
Hartland Clo., Wey. AX58 92
Hartland Dr., Edg. BM27 37
Hartland Dr., Ruis. BC34 44
Hartland Gro. NW1 BV36 56
Hartland Rd.
Hartland Rd. E15 CG36 58
Hartland Rd. N11 BU28 38
Hartland Rd. NW1 BV36 56
Hartland Rd. NW6 BR37 55

Hartland Rd., Chsnt. CC18 21
Hartland Rd., Epp. CO19 23
Hartland Rd., Hmptn. BF49 74
Hartland Rd., Horn. CU34 50
Hartland Rd., Islw. BJ45 64
Hartland Rd., Mord. BS54 86
Hartland Rd., Wey. AW57 92
Hartland St. NW1 BV36 56
Hartland Way, Croy. CD55 87
Hartland Way, Mord. BR54 85
Hartley Av. E6 CK37 58
Hartley Av. NW7 BO28 37
Hartley Clo. NW7 BO28 37
Hartley Clo. W3 BM40 55
Uxbridge Rd.
Hartley Clo., Brom. CK51 88
Hartley Clo., Slou. AR37 52
Hartley Down Rd., Pur. BX61 104
Hartley Farm Est., Pur. BX61 104
Hartley Hill, Pur. BX61 104
Hartley Old Rd., Pur. BX61 104
Hartley Rd. E11 CG33 49
Hartley Rd. West. CM66 115
Hartley Rd., Croy. BY54 86
Hartley Rd., Long. DC51 90
Hartley Rd., Well. CP43 69
Hartley St. E2 CC38 57
Hartley Way, Pur. BX61 104
Hartmann Rd. E16 CJ40 58
Hartnoll St. N7 BX35 47
Eden Gro.
Harton Clo., Brom. CJ51 88
Harton Rd. N9 CB27 39
Harton St. SE8 CE44 67
Harts Clo., Bush. BF23 27
Harts Gdns., Guil. AQ69 118
Harts Hill Clo., Uxb. AZ36 53
Harts La. SE14 CC43 67
Harts La., Bark. CL36 58
Hartsbourne Av., Bush. BG27 36
Hartsbourne Clo., Bush. BG27 36
Hartsbourne Rd., Bush. BG27 36
Hartsbourne Way, Hem.H. BA14 8
Hartscroft, Croy. CD58 96
Hartshill Rd., Grav. DF48 81
Hartshill Wk., Wok. AQ61 100
Hartshill, Guil. AO70 118
Hartshorn All. EC3 CA39 2
Leadenhall St.
Hartshorn All. EC3 CA39 57
Leadenhall St.
Hartshorn Gdns. E6 CL38 58
Hartslands Rd., Sev. CV65 108
Hartslock Dr. SE2 CP41 69
Hartsmead Rd. SE9 CK48 78
Hartspring La., Bush. BF23 27
Hartsway, Enf. CC24 30
Hartswood Av., Reig. BS72 121
Hartswood Clo., Brwd. DB28 42
Hartswood Rd. W12 BO41 65
Hartswood Rd., Brwd. DC28 122
Hartswood, Dor. BK73 119
Hartsworth Clo. E13 CG37 58
Rudolph Rd.
Hartville Rd. SE18 CN42 68
Hartwell Dr. E4 CF29 39
Hartwell St. E8 CA36 57
Dalston La.
Harty Clo., Grays DD40 71
Harvard Ct. NW6 BS35 47
West End La.
Harvard Hill W4 BM43 65
Wolseley Gdns.
Harvard La. W4 BN42 65
Harvard Rd.
Harvard Rd. SE13 CF46 77
Harvard Rd. W4 BM42 65
Harvard Rd., Islw. BH44 64
Harvard Wk., Horn. CU35 50
Harvel Cres. SE2 CP42 69
Harvest Bank Rd., W.Wick. CG55 88
Harvest End, Wat. BD21 27
Harvest Mead, Hat. BP12 10
Crop Common
Harvest Rd., Bush. BF24 27
Harvest Rd., Egh. AR49 72
Harvest Rd., Felt. BC48 73
Harvest Way, Swan. CS54 89
Harvester Rd., Epsom BN58 94
Harvesters Clo., Islw. BG46 74
Harvesters, St.Alb. BK11 9
Harvey Centre, Harl. CM11 13
Harvey Fields, Wal.Abb. CF20 21
Harvey Gdns. E11 CG33 49
Harvey Rd.
Harvey Gdns. SE7 CJ42 68
Harvey Gdns., Loug. CL24 31
Harvey Rd. E11 CG33 49
Harvey Rd. N8 BX32 47
Harvey Rd. SE5 BZ44 67
Harvey Rd., Guil. AS71 118
Harvey Rd., Houns. BE47 74
Harvey Rd., Ilf. CL35 49
Harvey Rd., Nthlt. BD36 54
Harvey Rd., Rick. AZ25 26
Harvey Rd., Slou. AT41 62
Harvey Rd., St.Alb. BK16 18
Harvey Rd., Uxb. AZ37 53
Harvey Rd., Walt. BC54 83
Harvey St. N1 BZ37 2
Harvey St. N1 BZ37 57
Harvey, Grays DD41 71
Harveys La., Rom. CS34 50
Harvil Rd., Uxb. AX31 44
Harvill Rd., Sid CP49 79
Harvington Wk. E8 CB36 57
Wilman Gro.
Harvist Rd. NW6 BQ37 55
Harwater Dr., Loug. CK23 31
Harwell Clo., Ruis. BA33 44
Harwell Pass. N2 BU31 47
Harwood Av., Brom. CH51 88
Harwood Av., Horn. CW31 51
Harwood Av., Mitch. BU52 86
Harwood Clo., Welw.G.C. BR 6 5
Harwood Clo., Welw.G.C. BU 6 5
Harwood Clo., Wem. BK34 45
Harrowdene Rd.
Harwood Ct. SW15 BQ45 65
Upper Richmond Rd.
Harwood Gdns., Wind. AQ47 72
Harwood Hall La., Upmin. CX36 60
Harwood Hill, Welw.G.C. BR 6 5
Harwood Rd. SW6 BS43 66
Harwood Ter. SW6 BS44 66
Harwoods Rd., Wat. BC24 26
Harwoods Yd. N21 BY26 38
Wades Hill
Hascombe Ter. SE5 BZ44 67
Hasedines Rd., Hem.H. AW13 8
Haselbury Rd. N18 CA28 39
Haseldene Rd., St.Alb. BK16 18
Haseldine Meadows, Hat. BO13 10
Haseley End SE23 CC47 77
Tyson Rd.
Haselmere Av., Houns. BD44 64
Haselrigge Rd. SW4 BW45 66
Haseltine Rd. SE26 CD49 77
Green La.
Haselwood Dr., Enf. BY24 29
Haskard Rd., Dag. CP35 50
Hasker St. SW3 BU42 3
Hasker St. SW3 BU42 66
Haslam Av., Sutt. BR54 85
Haslam Clo. N1 BY36 56
Haslam Clo., Uxb. BA34 44
Haslemere Av. NW4 BQ32 46
Haslemere Av. SW18 BS48 76
Haslemere Av. W7 BJ41 64
Haslemere Av., Barn. BU26 38
Haslemere Av., Houns. BD44 64
Haslemere Av., Mitch. BT51 86
Haslemere Clo., Hmptn. BE49 74
Haslemere Clo., Wall. BX56 95
Haslemere Gdns. N3 BR31 46
Haslemere Rd. N21 BY27 38
Haslemere Rd. N8 BW33 47
Haslemere Rd., Bexh. CQ44 69
Haslemere Rd., Th.Hth. BY53 86
Haslemere Rd., Wind. AN44 61
Hasler Clo. SE28 CP40 59
Haslet Rd., Wat. BC24 26
Haslett Rd., Shep. BB51 83
Haslewood Av., Hodd. CE12 12
Hasluck Gdns., Barn. BT25 29
Hassard St. E2 CA37 2
Hassard St. E2 CA37 57
Hassendean Rd. SE3 CH43 68
Hassett Rd. E9 CC36 57
Hassock Wd., Kes. CJ56 97
Hassocks Clo. SE26 CB48 77
Hassocks Rd. SW16 BW51 86
Hassop Rd. NW2 BQ35 46
Hassop Wk. SE9 CK49 78
Hasted Rd. SE7 CJ42 68
Hastings Av., Ilf. CL31 49
Hastings Clo. SE15 CB43 67
Bells Gdns.
Hastings Clo., Barn. BT24 29
Leicester Rd.
Hastings Clo., Maid. AH42 61
Hastings Rd. N11 BW28 38
Hastings Rd. W13 BJ40 54
Hastings Rd., Brom. CK54 88
Hastings Rd., Croy. CA54 87
Hastings Rd., Rom. CU32 50
Hastings St. WC1 BX38 2
Hastings St. WC1 BX38 56
Hastings Way, Bush. BE24 27
Hastings Way, Rick. BA24 26
Hastingwood Rd., Harl. CP13 14
Hastoe Clo., Hayes BD38 54
Kingsash Dr.
Hatch Clo., Wey. AW55 83
Hatch End, Pnr. BE29 36
Hatch Gdns., Tad. BQ63 103
Hatch Gro., Rom. CQ31 50
Hatch La. E4 CF28 39
Hatch La., Bans. BU61 104
Hatch La., West Dr. AX43 63
Hatch La., Wind. AN45 61
Hatch La., Wok. AZ63 101
Hatch Pl., King.T. BL49 75
Hatch Rd. SW16 BX51 86
Hatch Rd., Brwd. DA25 33
Hatch Side, Chig. CL28 40
Hatch, The, Enf. CC23 30
Hatch, The, Wind. AL43 61
Hatcham Park Ms. SE14 CC44 67
Hatcham Park Rd.
Hatcham Park Rd. SE14 CC44 67
Hatcham Rd. SE15 CC43 67
Hatchard Rd. N19 BW34 47
Hatchcroft NW4 BP31 46
Hatchett Rd., Felt. BA47 73
Hatchlands Rd., Red. BU70 121
Hatchwood Clo., Wdf.Grn. CG28 40
Sunset Av.
Hatcliffe Clo. SE3 CG45 68
Hatcliffe St. SE10 CG42 68
Hatfield Clo. SE14 CC43 67
Hatfield Clo., Brwd. DE26 122
Hutton Dr.
Hatfield Clo., Horn. CV35 51
Hatfield Clo., Ilf. CL31 49
Hatfield Clo., Mitch. BT52 86
Hatfield Cres., Hem.H. AY11 8
Hatfield Mead, Mord. BS53 86
Hatfield Rd. E15 CG35 49
Hatfield Rd. W13 BJ40 54
Hatfield Rd. W4 BN41 65
Hatfield Rd., Ash. BL62 103
Hatfield Rd., Dag. CQ36 59
Hatfield Rd., Hat. BU10 5
Hatfield Rd., Pot.B. BT19 20
Hatfield Rd., Slou. AQ41 62
Hatfield Rd., St.Alb. BH13 9
Hatfield Rd., St.Alb. BL13 10
Hatfield Rd., Wat. BC23 26
Hatfields Rd., Loug. CL24 31
Hatfields SE1 BY40 4
Hatfields SE1 BY40 56
Hatham Green La., Sev. DB58 99
Hatham Rd., Grays DH41 71
Hathaway Clo., Brom. CK54 88
Seymour Dr.
Hathaway Clo., Ruis. BB35 44
Stafford Rd.
Hathaway Clo., Stan. BJ28 36
Uxbridge Rd.
Hathaway Cres. E12 CK36 58
Hathaway Ct., St.Alb. BL13 10
Hatfield Rd.
Hathaway Gdns. W13 BJ39 54
Hathaway Gdns., Grays DD41 71
Hathaway Rd.
Hathaway Gdns., Rom. CP32 50
Hathaway Rd., Croy. BY54 86
Hathaway Rd., Grays DD41 71
Hatherleigh Clo., Chess. BK56 93
Hatherleigh Clo., Mord. BS52 86
Hatherleigh Gdns., Pot.B. BT19 20
Hatherleigh Rd., Ruis. BC34 44
Hatherleigh Way, Rom. CV30 42
Hatherley Cres., Sid. CO48 79
Hatherley Gdns. E6 CJ37 58
Hatherley Gdns. N8 BX32 47
Hatherley Gro. W2 BS39 1
Hatherley Gro. W2 BS39 56
Hatherley Ms. E17 CE31 48
Hatherley Rd.
Hatherley Rd. E17 CD31 48
Hatherley Rd., Rich. BL44 65
Hatherley Rd., Sid. CO49 79
Hatherley St. SW1 BW42 3
Hatherley St. SW1 BW42 66
Vincent Sq.
Hathern Gdns. SE9 CL49 78
Hatherop Rd., Hmptn. BE50 74
Hatherwood, Ash. BK64 102
Hathorne Clo. SE15 CC44 67
Hathway St. SE15 CC44 67
Gibbon Rd.
Hathway Ter. SE14 CC44 67
Gibbon Rd.
Hatley Av., Ilf. CM31 49
Hatley Clo. N11 BU28 38
Hatley Rd. N4 BX34 47
Hatteraick St. SE16 CC41 67
Church St.
Hatters La., Wat. BA25 26
Hattersfield Clo., Belv. CQ42 69
Hatton Av., Slou. AO38 52
Hatton Clo. SE18 CM43 68
Hatton Clo., Grav. DF48 81
Hatton Ct. E5 CC35 48
Clapton Park Est.
Hatton Gdn. EC1 BY39 2
Hatton Gdn. EC1 BY39 56
Hatton Gdns., Mitch. BU53 86
Hatton Grn., Felt. BC45 63
Hatton Pl. EC1 BY39 2
Hatton Pl. EC1 BY39 56
Hatton Wall
Hatton Rd. N., Houns. BA44 63
Hatton Rd. N., West Dr. AX40 53
Hatton Rd. S., Felt. BB45 63
Hatton Cres.
Hatton Rd., Chsnt. CC18 21
Hatton Rd., Croy. BY54 86
Hatton Rd., Felt. BA47 73
Hatton Row NW8 BT38 1
Hatton St. NW8 BT38 1
Hatton St. NW8 BT38 56
Hatton Wall EC1 BY39 2
Hatton Wall EC1 BY39 56
Haunch of Venison Yd. W1 BV39 1
Haunch of Venison Yd. W1 BV39 56
Brook St.
Havana Clo., Rom. CT32 50
Havana Rd. SW19 BS48 76
Havannah St. E14 CE41 67
Havant Rd. E17 CF31 48
Havant Way SE15 CA43 67
Landport Way
Havelius Clo. SE10 CG42 68
Flamstead Est.
Havelock Ct., Sthl. BE41 64
Havelock Pl. SE18 CL42 68
Anglesea Rd.
Havelock Pl., Har. BH32 45
Havelock Rd. N17 CB30 39
Havelock Rd. SW19 BT49 76
Havelock Rd., Belv. CQ42 69
Havelock Rd., Brom. CJ52 88
Havelock Rd., Croy. CA55 87
Havelock Rd., Dart. CU46 79
Havelock Rd., Grav. DF47 81
Havelock Rd., Har. BH31 45
Havelock Rd., Kings L. AY17 17
Havelock Rd., Sthl. BE41 64
Havelock St. N1 BX37 56
Havelock St., Ilf. CL34 49
Havelock Ter. SW8 BV43 66
Havelock Wk. SE23 CC47 77
Haven Clo. SE9 CK48 78
Mottingham Rd.
Haven Clo. SW19 BQ48 75
Haven Clo., Grav. CF50 81
Haven Clo., Hat. BP12 10
Haven Clo., Hayes BB39 53
Haven Clo., Sid. CP50 79
Haven Clo., Swan. CT51 89
Haven Grn. Ct. W5 BK39 54
Haven Grn.
Haven Grn. W5 BK39 54
Haven La. W5 BK39 54
Haven Pl. W5 BK40 54
The Broadway
Haven Pl., Grays DE41 71
Haven Rd., Ashf. AZ49 73
Reedsfield Rd.
Haven St. NW1 BV36 56
Castlehaven Rd.
Haven Ter. W5 BK40 54
The Broadway
Haven, The, Grays DG42 71
Haven, The, Rich. BM45 65
Havengore Av., Grav. DJ47 81
Havenhurst Ri., Enf. BY23 29
Havensfield, Kings L. AW19 17
Nunfield
Havenwood Clo., Brwd. DA28 42
Havenwood, Wem. BM34 46
Havercroft Clo., St.Alb. BF14 9
Haverfield Gdns., Rich. BM43 65
Haverfield Rd. E3 CD38 57
Haverford Way, Edg. BL30 37
Haverhill Rd. E4 CF26 39
Pretoria Rd.
Haverhill Rd. SW12 BW47 76
Havering Dr., Rom. CT31 50
Havering Gdns., Rom. CP32 50
Havering Pl., Hav. CS27 41
Havering Rd., Rom. CS30 41
Havering St. E1 CC39 57
Havering Way, Bark. CO38 59
Havers Av., Walt. BD56 93
Haversham Clo., Twick. BK46 74
Haversham Gra., Twick. BK46 74
Haverstock Hill NW3 BU35 47
Haverstock Rd. NW5 BU35 47
Haverstock St. N1 BY37 2
Haverstock St. N1 BY37 56
Haverthwaite Rd., Orp. CM55 88
Havil St. SE5 CA43 67
Havisham Pl. SE19 BY50 76
Havisham Rd., Grav. DK48 81
Haward Rd., Hodd. CF11 12
Hawarden Av., Wal.Cr. CC20 21
Hawarden Gro. SE24 BZ47 77
Hawarden Hill NW2 BP34 46
Hawarden Rd. E17 CC31 48
Hawarden Rd., Cat. BZ64 105
Hawbridge Rd. E11 CF33 48
Hawes Clo., Nthwd. BB29 35
Hawes La. E4 CF22 30
Hawes La., W.Wick. CF54 87
Hawes Rd. N18 CB29 39
Hawes Rd., Brom. CH51 88
Hawes Rd., Tad. BQ63 103
Hawes St. N1 BY36 2
Hawes St. N1 BY36 56
Hawfield Bank, Orp. CP55 89
Hawfield Gdns., St.Alb. BG16 18
Hawgood St. E3 CE39 57
Hawkdene E4 CE25 30
Hawke Park Rd. N22 BY31 47
Hawke Pl. SE16 CC41 67
Middleton Dr.
Hawke Rd. SE19 BZ50 77
Hawkenbury, Harl. CL12 13
Hawker Clo., Wall. BX57 95
Hawkes Clo., Grays DD43 71
Hawkes Ms. SE10 CF43 67
Luton Pl.
Hawkes Rd., Mitch. BU51 86
Hawkesbury Rd. SW15 BP46 75
Hawkesfield Rd. SE23 CD48 77
Hawkesley Clo., Twick. BJ49 74
Hawkewood Rd., Sun. BC52 83
Hawkfield Ct., Islw. BH44 64
Hawkhirst Rd., Ken. BZ61 105
Hawkhurst Gdns., Chess. BL56 94
Orchard Rd.
Hawkhurst Gdns., Rom. CS29 41
Hawkhurst Rd. SW16 BW51 86
Hawkhurst Way, N.Mal. BN53 85
Hawkhurst Way, W.Wick. CE55 87
Hawkhurst, Cob. BF60 93
Hawkinge Way, Horn. CV36 60
Hawkinge Wk., Orp. CO52 89
Robin Way
Hawkins Av., Grav. DH49 81
Hawkins Clo., B.Wd. BN23 28
Hawkins Clo., Har. BG33 45
Hawkins Rd., Tedd. BJ50 74
Hawkley Gdns. SE27 BY48 76
Hawkridge Clo., Rom. CP32 50
Hawks Hill Clo., Lthd. BH64 102
Hawks Hill, Lthd. BH65 102
Hawks Mews SE10 CF43 67
Luton Pl.
Hawks Rd., Kings.T. BL51 85
Hawksbrook La., Beck. CF53 87
Hawkshaw Clo. SW2 BX47 76
Hawkshead Clo., Brom. CG50 78
Coniston Rd.
Hawkshead La., Hat. BQ17 19
Hawkshead Rd. NW10 BO36 55
Hawkshead Rd. W4 BO41 65
Hawkshead Rd., Pot.B. BS18 20
Hawkshill Clo., Esher BF57 93
Hawkshill Dr., Hem.H. AV15 7
Hawkshill Way, Esher BF57 93
Hawkshill, St.Alb. BJ14 9
Hawkslade Rd. SE15 CC46 77
Hawksley Rd. N16 BZ34 48
Hawksmead Clo., Enf. CC21 30
Hawksmoor Clo. E6 CK39 58
Allhallows Rd.
Hawksmoor Grn., Brwd. DE25 122
Hawksmoor Ms. E1 CB40 57
Cable St.
Hawksmoor St. W6 BQ43 65
Hawksmoor, Rad. BM20 19
Hawksmouth E4 CF26 39
Hawkstone Rd. SE16 CC42 67
Hawksway, Stai. AV48 72
Hawkswell Clo., Wok. AP62 100
Hawkswell Wk., Wok. AP62 100
Hawkswood Est., Chis. CM52 88
Hawkswood Gro., Slou. AS36 52
Hawkswood La., Ger.Cr. AS35 43
Hawksworth Clo., Nthwd. BB29 35
Hawkwell Wk. N1 BZ37 57
Basire St.
Hawkwood Cres. E4 CE25 30
Hawkwood Dell, Lthd. BF66 111
Hawkwood La., Chis. CM51 88
Hawkwood Mt. E5 CB33 48
Hawkwood Ri., Lthd. BF66 111
Hawlands Dr., Pnr. BE33 45
Hawley Clo., Hmptn. BE50 74
Hawley Cres. NW1 BV36 1
Hawley Cres. NW1 BV36 56
Hawley Ms. NW1 BV36 56
Hawley St.
Hawley Rd. NW1 BV36 56
Hawley Rd., Dart. CW48 80
Hawley St. NW1 BV36 56
Hawley Way, Ashf. AZ49 73
Haws La., Stai. AW46 73
Hawstead La., Orp. CQ56 98
Hawstead Rd. SE6 CE46 77
Hawsted, Buck.H. CH26 40
Hawthorn Av. N13 BX28 38
Hawthorn Av., Brwd. DC27 122
Hawthorn Av., Cars. BV57 95
Hawthorn Av., Rain. CU38 59
Hawthorn Clo., Hmptn. BF49 74
Hawthorn Clo., Orp. CM53 88
Hawthorn Clo., Oxt. CH70 115
Holland La.
Hawthorn Clo., Red. BV73 121
Hawthorn Clo., Wat. BB22 26
Hawthorn Clo., Wok. AS63 100
Hawthorn Cres. SW17 BV49 76
Hawthorn Cres., Croy. CC59 96
Hawthorn Ct., Sutt. BS56 95
Hawthorn Dr., Har. BE32 45
Hawthorn Dr., Uxb. AX36 53
Hawthorn Dr., W.Wick. CG56 97
Hawthorn Gdns. W5 BK41 64
Hawthorn Gro., Barn. BO25 28
Hawthorn Gro., Enf. BZ22 30
Hawthorn Gro., SE20 CB51 87
Hawthorn Hatch, Brent. BJ43 64
Hawthorn La., Hem.H. AV13 7
Hawthorn La., Sev. CT64 107
Hawthorn Ms. NW7 BQ30 37
Holders Hill Rd.
Hawthorn Pl., Erith CS42 69
Hawthorn Pl., Hayes BB40 53
Hawthorn Rd. E17 CE31 48
Hawthorn Rd. N18 CA29 39
Hawthorn Rd. N8 BW31 47
Hawthorn Rd. NW10 BP36 55
Hawthorn Rd., Sendmarsh AV65 100
Hawthorn Rd., Bexh. CQ46 79
Hawthorn Rd., Brent. BJ43 64
Hawthorn Rd., Buck.H. CJ28 40
Hawthorn Rd., Dart. CV47 80
Hawthorn Rd., Hodd. CE11 12
Hawthorn Rd., Stai. AU49 72
Hawthorn Rd., Sutt. BT56 95
Hawthorn Rd., Wall. BV57 95
Hawthorn Rd., Wok. AR63 100
Hawthorn Way N9 CA27 39
Hawthorn Way, Chesh. AO18 16
Hawthorn Way, Shep. BA52 83
Hawthorn Way, St.Alb. BF16 18
Hawthorn Way, Wey. AW58 92
Hawthorn Wk. W10 BR38 55
Droop St.
Hawthorndene Clo., Brom. CG55 88
Hawthorndene Rd., Brom. CG55 88
Hawthorne Av., Mitch. BT51 86
Hawthorne Av., Th.Hth. BY51 86
Hawthorne Av., Chsnt. CB19 21
Hawthorne Av., Har. BJ32 45
Hawthorne Av., Ruis. BC33 44
Hawthorne Av., West. CJ61 106
Hawthorne Clo. N1 CA36 57
Hawthorne Clo., Chsnt. CB19 21
Hawthorne Clo., Brom. CK52 88
Hawthorne Clo., Sutt. BT55 86
Hawthorne Cres., West D. AY41 63
Hawthorne Cres., S.Croy. CC58 96
Hawthorne Cres., Slou. AP39 52
Hawthorne Farm Av., Nthlt. BE37 54
Hawthorne Gro. NW9 BN33 46
Hawthorne Pl., Epsom BO59 94
Hawthorne Rd., Brom. CK52 88
Hawthorne Rd., Rad. BJ20 18
Hawthorne Way, Guil. AT69 109
Hawthornes, Hat. BO13 10
Hawthorns, Rick. AU28 34
Hawthorns, The, Berk. AQ12 7
Hawthorns, The, Hem.H. AV15 7
Beechwood Pk.
Hawthorns, The, Loug. CL24 31
Hawthorns, The, Slou. AV44 62
Raymond Clo.
Hawthorns, Wdf.Grn. CH27 40
Hawthorns, Welw.G.C. BQ 7 5
Hawtrees, Rad. BH21 27
Hawtrey Av., Nthlt. BD37 54
Hawtrey Clo., Slou. AQ41 62
Hawtrey Dr., Ruis. BC33 44
Hawtrey Rd. NW3 BT36 56
Hawtrey Rd., Wind. AO44 61
Haxtead Rd., Brom. CH51 88
Hay Clo. E15 CG36 58
Hay Clo., B.Wd. BN23 28
Hay Currie St. E14 CE39 57
Hay Green La., Brwd. DB21 33
Hay Hill W1 BV40 3
Hay Hill W1 BV40 56
Hay La. NW9 BN31 46
Hay La., Slou. AR35 43
Hay St. E2 CB37 2
Haybourn Mead, Hem.H. AW14 8
Hayburn Way, Horn. CT33 50
Haycroft Clo., Ken. BY62 104

Street	Grid	Page
Haycroft Gdns. NW10	BP37	55
Haycroft Rd. SW2	BX46	76
Haycroft Rd., Surb.	BK55	84
Hayday Rd. E16	CH39	58
Hayden Ct., Wey.	AW59	92
Hayden Pl., Guil.	AR71	118
Hayden Way, Rom.	CS30	41
Haydens Clo., Orp.	CP54	89
Haydens Pl. W11	BR39	55
Haydens Rd., Harl.	CM11	13
Haydn Av., Pur.	BY60	95
Haydns Ms. W3	BN39	55
Haydock Av., Nthlt.	BE36	54
Haydock Clo., Horn.	CW35	51
Haydock Grn., Nthlt.	BF36	54
Haydon Clo. NW9	BN31	46
Haydon Clo., Enf.	BZ25	30
Mortimer Dr.		
Haydon Dr., Pnr.	BC31	44
Haydon Park Rd. SW19	BS49	76
Haydon Rd., Dag.	CP34	50
Haydon Rd., Wat.	BE25	27
Haydon Sq. E1	CA39	57
Haydon St. EC1	**CA40**	**4**
Haydon St. EC1	CA40	57
Haydons Rd. SW19	BS49	76
Hayes Barton, Wok.	AV61	100
Hayes Chase, W.Wick.	CF53	87
Hayes Clo., Brom.	CH55	88
Hayes Clo., Grays	DB43	70
Hayes Cres. NW11	BR32	46
Hayes Cres., Sutt.	BQ56	94
Hayes Ct. SW2	BX47	76
Hayes Dr., Rain.	CU36	59
Hayes End Clo., Hayes	BA38	53
Hayes End Dr., Hayes	BA38	53
Hayes End Rd., Hayes	BA38	53
Hayes Gdns., Brom.	CH55	88
Hayes Hill Rd., Brom.	CG54	88
Hayes Hill, Brom.	CG54	88
Hayes La., Beck.	CF52	87
Hayes La., Brom.	CH54	88
Hayes La., Ken.	BY61	104
Hayes Mead, Brom.	CG54	88
Hayes Pl. NW1	BU39	56
Hayes Rd., Brom.	CH52	88
Hayes Rd., Green.	CZ47	80
Hayes Rd., Sthl.	BC42	63
Hayes St., Brom.	CH54	88
Hayes Way, Beck.	CF52	87
Hayes Wd. Av., Brom.	CH54	88
Hayes Wk., Brox.	CD16	21
Hayes Wk., Pot.B.	BS20	20
Willow Way		
Hayes, The, Epsom	BN63	103
Hayesford Park Dr., Brom.	CG53	88
Hayesford Park Est., Brom.	CH53	88
Hayfield Clo., Bush.	BF24	27
Hayfield Pass. E1	CC38	57
Hayfield Rd., Orp.	CO53	89
Haygarth Pl. SW19	BQ49	75
Haygreen Clo., Kings.T.	BM50	75
Hayland Clo. NW9	BN31	46
Hayles St. SE11	**BY42**	**4**
Hayles St. SE11	BY42	66
Hayling Av., Felt.	BC48	73
Hayling Rd., Wat.	BC27	35
Haymaker Clo., Uxb.	AY36	53
Honey Hill		
Hayman Cres., Hayes	BA37	53
Hayman St. N1	**BY37**	**2**
Haymarket SW1	**BW40**	**3**
Haymarket SW1	BW40	56
Haymeads Dr., Esher	BG57	93
Haymeads Hill, Welw.G.C.	BR 6	5
Haymeads, Welw.G.C.	BR 6	5
Haymer Gdns., Wor.Pk.	BP55	85
Haymerle Rd. SE15	CB43	67
Hayne Rd., Beck.	CD51	87
Hayne St. EC1	**BY39**	**2**
Hayne St. EC1	BY39	56
Haynes Clo. N17	CB29	39
Haynes Clo. SE3	CG45	68
Haynes Clo., Slou.	AS42	62
Haynes Clo., Welw.G.C.	BS 8	5
Haynes La. SE19	CA50	77
Haynes Mead, Berk.	AQ12	7
Haynes Rd., Grav.	DF48	81
Haynes Rd., Horn.	CV32	51
Haynes Rd., Wem.	BL36	55
Haynt Wk. SW20	BR52	85
Hays La. SE1	**BZ40**	**4**
Hays La. SE1	CA40	57
Hays Ms. W1	**BV40**	**3**
Hays Ms. W1	BV40	56
Hays Wk., Sutt.	BQ58	94
Hayse Hl., Wind.	AL44	61
Haysleigh Gdns. SE20	CB51	87
Haysoms Clo., Rom.	CT31	50
Ingrave Rd.		
Haystall Clo., Hayes	BB37	53
Hayter Rd. SW2	BX46	76
Hayton Clo. E8	CA36	57
Forest Rd.		
Haywains, Oxt.	CF68	114
Hayward Clo. SW19	BS51	86
Hayward Clo., Bex.	CS46	79
Bourne Rd.		
Hayward Gdns. SW15	BQ46	75
Hayward Rd. N20	BT27	38
Haywards Clo., Brwd.	DF25	122
Haywards Clo., Dart.	CS46	79
Haywards Mead, Eton	AN42	61
Haywards Pl. EC1	BY38	56
Sekforde St.		
Haywood Ct., Wal.Abb.	CG20	22
Haywood Pk., Rick.	AV25	25
Haywood Rd., Brom.	CJ52	88
Haywood Ri., Orp.	CN56	97
Haywoods Clo., Pnr.	BD30	36
Haywoods Pl. EC1	**BY38**	**2**
Haywoods Pl. EC1	BY38	56
Sekforde St.		
Hayworth Clo., Enf.	CD23	30
Hazel Av., Guil.	AR68	109
Hazel Av., West Dr.	AZ41	63
Hazel Bnk., Surb.	BN54	85
Hazel Cft., Pnr.	BF29	36
Hazel Clo. N13	BZ27	39
Hazel Clo. N19	BW34	47
Hargrave Pk.		
Hazel Clo. SE15	CB44	67
Hazel Clo., Brent.	BJ43	64
Hazel Clo., Croy.	CC54	87
Hazel Clo., Egh.	AQ50	72
Hazel Clo., Horn.	CU34	50
Hazel Clo., Mitch.	BW52	86
Hazel Clo., Reig.	BT71	121
Hazel Clo., Twick.	BG47	74
Hazel Clo., Welw.G.C.	BR 5	5
Hazel Clo., Wem.	BL37	55
Carlyon Rd.		
Hazel Dr., Erith	CU44	69
Hazel Dr., Wok.	AV65	100
Hazel End, Swan.	CT53	89
Hazel Gdns., Edg.	BM28	37
Hazel Gdns., Grays	DF41	71
Hazel Gro. SE26	CC49	77
Hazel Gro., Enf.	CB25	30
Dimsdale Dr.		
Hazel Gro., Hat.	BO14	10
Hazel Gro., Orp.	CL55	88
Hazel Gro., Rom.	CQ31	50
Hazel Gro., Stai.	AW50	73
Hazel Gro., Welw.G.C.	BS 7	5
Hazel Gro., Wem.	BL37	55
Carlyon Rd.		
Hazel La., Rich.	BL48	75
Hazel Mead, Barn.	BP25	28
Hazel Mead, Epsom	BP58	94
Hazel Rd. E15	CG35	49
Wingfield Rd.		
Hazel Rd. NW10	BQ38	55
Hazel Rd., Berk.	AR13	7
Hazel Rd., Dart.	CV47	80
Hazel Rd., Erith	CU44	69
Hazel Rd., Reig.	BT71	121
Hazel Rd., St.Alb.	BF17	18
Hazel Rd., Wey.	AV60	91
Hazel Ri., Horn.	CV32	51
Hazel Tree Rd., Wat.	BC22	26
Hazel Way E4	CD29	39
Hazel Way SE1	CA42	67
Alscot Rd.		
Hazel Way, Lthd.	BG64	102
Hazel Way, Slou.	AP36	52
Hazel Wk., Brom.	CL53	88
Hazel Wk., Dor.	BK73	119
Homesdale Rd.		
Hazelbank Rd. SE6	CF48	77
Hazelbank Rd., Cher.	AX54	83
Hazelbourne Rd. SW12	BV46	76
Hazelbrouck Gdns., Ilf.	CM29	40
Hazelbury Av., Wat.	BA19	17
Hazelbury Grn. N9	CA27	39
Hazelbury La. N9	CA27	39
Hazelcroft Clo., Uxb.	AY36	53
Blossom Way		
Hazeldean Rd. NW10	BN36	55
Hazeldean Rd., Croy.	BZ55	87
Hazeldell Link, Hem.H.	AV14	7
Lindlings		
Hazeldell Rd., Hem.H.	AV14	7
Hazelden Clo., Sev.	DA58	99
Hazeldene Clo., Wey.	AX56	92
Crockford Pk. Rd.		
Hazeldene Ct., Ken.	BZ61	105
Hazeldene Dr., Pnr.	BD31	45
Hazeldene Gdns., Uxb.	BA37	53
Hazeldene Rd., Ilf.	CO34	50
Hazeldene Rd., Well.	CP44	69
Hazeldene Wey.	AX56	92
Crockford Park Rd.		
Hazeldene, Wey.	AX56	92
Hazeldon Rd. SE4	CD46	77
Hazeleigh Gdns., Wdf.Grn.	CK28	40
Hazeleigh, Brwd.	DD27	122
Hazelgreen Clo. N21	BY26	38
Hazelhurst Clo., Guil.	AT68	109
Weybrook Dr.		
Hazelhurst Rd. SW17	BT49	76
Hazelhurst, Beck.	CF51	87
Hazell Cres., Rom.	CR29	41
Hazell Pk., Amer.	AO23	25
Hazells Rd., Grav.	DD49	81
Hazellville Rd. N19	BW33	47
Hazelmere Clo., Felt.	BA46	73
Hazelmere Clo., Lthd.	BJ63	102
Hazelmere Clo., Nthlt.	BE37	54
Hazelmere Dr., Nthlt.	BE37	54
Hazelmere Rd.		
Hazelmere Gdns., Horn.	CU32	50
Hazelmere Rd. NW6	BT37	55
Hazelmere Rd., Nthlt.	BE37	54
Hazelmere Rd., Orp.	CM52	88
Hazelmere Rd., St.Alb.	BK12	9
Hazelmere Way, Brom.	CH53	88
Hazelmere Wk., Nthlt.	BE37	54
Hazeltree La., Nthlt.	BE38	54
Hazelwood Av., Mord.	BS52	86
Hazelwood Clo. W5	BL41	65
Hazelwood Clo., Chesh.	AO18	16
Hazelwood Clo., Har.	BF31	45
Hazelwood Cres. N13	BY28	38
Hazelwood Cres. W10	BR38	55
Hazelwood Ct., Surb.	BL53	85
Hazelwood Dr., Pnr.	BC30	35
Hazelwood Dr., St.Alb.	BK12	9
Hazelwood Gdns., Brwd.	DA25	33
Hazelwood Ho. SE8	CD42	67
Hazelwood La. N13	BY28	38
Hazelwood La., Couls.	BU63	104
Hazelwood La., Wat.	BA19	17
Hazelwood Rd. E17	CD32	48
Hazelwood Rd., Enf.	CA25	30
Hazelwood Rd., Oxt.	CH69	115
Hazelwood Rd., Rick.	BA25	26
Hazelwood Rd., Sev.	CM59	97
Hazelwood Rd., Wok.	AO62	100
Southwood Av.		
Hazelwood, S.le H.	DK42	71
Hazlebury Rd. SW6	BS44	66
Hazledene Rd. W4	BN43	65
Hazledene, Wal.Cr.	CC19	21
Eastfield Rd.		
Hazlemere Clo., Lthd.	BJ63	102
Hazlemere Gdns., Wor.Pk.	BP54	85
Hazlemere Rd., Ilf.	CN34	49
Hazlemere Rd., Slou.	AQ40	52
Hazlewell Rd. SW15	BP46	75
Hazlewood Cres. W10	BR39	55
Hazlewood Gro., S.Croy.	CB60	96
Hazlewood, Loug.	CJ25	31
Hazlitt Rd. W14	BR41	65
Hazon Way, Epsom	BN59	94
Heacham Av., Uxb.	BA34	44
Head St. E1	CC39	57
Headcorn Pl., Th.Hth.	BX52	86
Headcorn Rd. N17	CA29	39
Tenterden Rd.		
Headcorn Rd., Brom.	CG49	78
Headcorn Rd., Th.Hth.	BX52	86
Headfort Pl. SW1	**BV41**	**3**
Headfort Pl. SW1	BV41	66
Heading St. NW4	BQ31	46
Headingley Clo., Chsnt.	CA16	21
Holbeck La.		
Headingley Clo., Ilf.	CN29	40
Wickets Way		
Headington Rd. SW18	BT47	76
Headlam Rd. SW4	BW46	76
Headlam St. E1	CB38	57
Headley App., Ilf.	CL32	49
Headley Av., Wall.	BX56	95
Headley Chase, Brwd.	DB28	42
Headley Clo., Epsom	BM57	94
Headley Common Rd., Epsom	BN67	112
Headley Dr., Croy.	CE57	96
Headley Dr., Epsom	BP63	103
Headley Dr., Ilf.	CL32	49
Headley Gro., Tad.	BP63	103
Headley Heath App., Tad.	BM69	112
Headley Rd., Dor.	BK68	111
Headley Rd., Epsom	BM62	103
Headley Rd., Epsom	BN64	103
Headley Rd., Lthd.	BK64	102
Headley St. SE15	CB44	67
Gordon Rd.		
Heads Ms. W2	BS39	56
Artesian Rd.		
Headstone Dr., Har.	BG31	45
Headstone Gdns., Har.	BG31	45
Headstone La., Har.	BF31	45
Headstone Rd., Har.	BG32	45
Headway, The, Epsom	BO58	94
Heald St. SE8	CE44	67
Heston St.		
Healey Dr., Orp.	CN56	97
Healey Rd., Wat.	BB25	26
Healey St. NW1	BV36	56
Heanor Ct. E5	CC35	48
Clapton Park Est.		
Heards La., Brwd.	DC23	122
Hearn Rd., Rom.	CT32	50
Hearn Ri., Nthlt.	BD37	54
Hearn St. EC2	**CA38**	**2**
Hearn St. EC2	CA38	57
Curtain Rd.		
Hearne Ct., Ch.St.G.	AQ27	34
Gordon Way		
Hearne Rd. W4	BM42	65
Hearnes Clo., Beac.	AO28	34
Hearnes Mead, Beac.	AO28	34
Hearns Bldgs. SE17	**BZ42**	**4**
Hearns Bldgs. SE17	BZ42	67
Elsted St.		
Hearns Clo., Orp.	CP52	89
Hearns Rd., Orp.	CP52	89
Hearns Ri., Orp.	CP52	89
Hearnville Rd. SW12	BV47	76
Heath Av., Bexh.	CP43	69
Heath Av., St.Alb.	BG12	9
Heath Brow, Hem.H.	AX14	8
Heath La.		
Heath Cft. NW11	BS33	47
Heath Clo. NW11	BS33	47
Heath Clo. W5	BL38	55
Heath Clo., Bans.	BS60	95
Heath Clo., Hayes	BA43	63
Heath Clo., Hem.H.	AX14	8
Heath Clo., Orp.	CP54	89
Heath Clo., Pot.B.	BS18	20
Heath Clo., Rom.	CU31	50
Heath Clo., Stai.	AX46	73
Heath Clo., Vir.W.	AR52	82
Heath Close Rd., Dart.	CU47	79
Heath Ct. W5	BL38	55
Heath Dr. NW3	BS35	47
Heath Dr. SW20	BQ52	85
Heath Dr., Epp.	CN21	31
Heath Dr., Pot.B.	BS18	20
Heath Dr., Rom.	CU30	41
Heath Dr., Sutt.	BT58	95
Heath Dr., Tad.	BP66	112
Heath Dr., Wok.	AT64	100
Heath Edge SE26	CB48	77
Heath End Rd., Bex.	CT47	79
Heath Farm Ct., Wat.	BA22	26
Grove Mill La.		
Heath Farm La., St.Alb.	BH12	9
Heath Gdns., Twick.	BH47	74
Heath Gro. SE20	CC50	77
Heath Hill, Dor.	BJ71	119
Heath House La., Wok.	AO64	100
Heath Hurst Rd. NW3	BT35	47
Keats Gro.		
Heath La. SE3	CF44	67
Heath La., Dart.	CU48	79
Heath La., Hem.H.	AX14	8
Heath Lane Lower, Dart.	CV47	80
Heath Lane Upper, Dart.	CU47	79
Heath Park Ct., Rom.	CU32	50
Heath Park Dr., Brom.	CK52	88
Heath Park Rd., Rom.	CU32	50
Heath Rd. SW8	BV44	66
Heath Rd., Bex.	CS47	79
Heath Rd., Cat.	BZ65	105
Heath Rd., Dart.	CT46	79
Heath Rd., Grays	DF40	71
Heath Rd., Har.	BG33	45
Heath Rd., Houns.	BF45	64
Heath Rd., Lthd.	BG59	93
Heath Rd., Pot.B.	BS18	20
Heath Rd., Rom.	CP33	50
Heath Rd., St.Alb.	BH12	9
Heath Rd., Th.Hth.	BZ52	87
Heath Rd., Twick.	BH47	74
Heath Rd., Uxb.	BA38	53
Heath Rd., Wat.	BD26	36
Heath Rd., Wey.	AZ56	92
Heath Rd., Wok.	AS61	100
Heath Ri. SW15	BQ46	75
Heath Ri., Brom.	CG53	88
Heath Ri., Dor.	BG72	119
Heath Ri., Vir.W.	AR52	82
Heath Ri., Wok.	AW65	101
Heath Ridge Grn., Cob.	BF60	93
Heath Side NW3	BT35	47
Heath Side, Houns.	BE47	74
Heath Side, Orp.	CM54	88
Heath St. NW3	BT34	47
Heath St., Bark.	CM37	58
Heath St., Dart.	CV47	80
Heath Vills. SE18	CN42	68
Heath Vw. Clo. N2	BT31	47
Heath Vw. Gdns., Grays	DE41	71
Heath Vw. N2	BT31	47
Heath Vw. Rd., Grays	DE41	71
Heath Vw., Lthd.	BB66	110
Heath Way, Erith	CS44	69
Heath Way, West Dr.	AX40	53
Heath, The W7	BH40	54
Lower Boston Rd.		
Heath, The, Cat.	BZ65	105
Heath, The, Rad.	BJ20	18
Heatham Pk., Twick.	BH47	74
Heathbourne Rd., Bush.	BH26	36
Heathbrow NW3	BT34	47
North End Way		
Heathcote Av., Hat.	BP11	10
Heathcote Av., Ilf.	CK30	40
Heathcote Gro. E4	CF27	39
Heathcote Rd., Epsom	BN60	94
Heathcote Rd., Twick.	BJ46	74
Heathcote St. WC1	**BX38**	**2**
Heathcote St. WC1	BX38	56
Heathcote Way, West Dr.	AX40	53
Tavistock Rd.		
Heathcote, Tad.	BQ64	103
Heathcroft Av., Sun.	BB50	73
Heathcroft Grn., Sun.	BB50	73
Heathcroft W5	BL38	55
Heathdale Av., Houns.	BE45	64
Heathdene Dr., Belv.	CR42	69
Heathdene Rd. SW16	BX50	76
Heathdene Rd., Wall.	BV57	95
Heathdene, Tad.	BR62	103
Canons La.		
Heathdown Rd., Wok.	AU61	100
Heathend Rd., Bex.	CT47	79
Heather Av., Rom.	CS30	41
Heather Clo. Brwd.	DB25	42
Heather Clo. E6	CL39	58
Heather Clo. SW8	BV45	66
Heather Clo., Brwd.	DA25	33
Heather Clo., Hmptn.	BE51	84
Heather Clo., Islw.	BG46	74
Heather Clo., Rom.	CS30	41
Heather Clo., Tad.	BR64	103
Heather Clo., Uxb.	AY39	53
Heather Clo., Wey.	AW58	92
Heather Clo., Wok.	AR61	100
Heather Dr., Dart.	CU47	79
Heather Dr., Enf.	BY23	29
Chasewood Av.		
Heather Dr., Rom.	CS30	41
Heather Gdns. NW11	BR32	46
Heather Gdns., Rom.	CS30	41
Heather Gdns., Sutt.	BS57	95
Heather Glen, Rom.	CS30	41
Heather La., West Dr.	AY39	53
Heather Park Dr., Wem.	BM36	55
Heather Pl., Esher	BF56	93
Heather Rd. NW2	BO34	46
Heather Rd. SE12	CH48	78
Heather Rd., Welw.G.C.	BQ 9	5
Heather Ri., Bush.	BE23	27
Heather Way, Hem.H.	AX13	8
Heather Way, Pot.B.	BR19	19
Heather Way, Rom.	CS30	41
Heather Way, S.Croy.	CC58	96
Heather Way, Stan.	BH29	36
Heather Way, Wok.	AP57	91
Heather Wk. W10	BR38	55
Droop St.		
Heather Wk., Edg.	BM28	37
Heather Wk., Houns.	BF47	74
Stephenson Rd.		
Heather Wk., Walt.	BB58	92
Heatherbank SE9	CK44	68
Heatherbank, Chis.	CL51	88
Heatherdale Clo., Kings.T.	BM50	75
Heatherdean Clo., Mitch.	BT52	86
Heatherden Grn., Iver	AU37	52
Heatherdene, Lthd.	BA66	110
Heatherlands, Sun.	BC50	73
Heatherley Dr., Ilf.	CK31	49
Heathers Land, Dor.	BK73	119
Heathers, The, Stai.	AY47	73
Heatherset Gdns. SW16	BX50	76
Heatherside Dr., Vir.W.	AQ53	82
Heatherside Gdns., Slou.	AO34	43
Heatherside Rd., Epsom	BN57	94
Heatherside Rd., Sid.	CP48	79
Bexley La.		
Heatherton Ter. N3	BS30	38
Squires La.		
Heathervale Rd., Wey.	AW58	92
Heatherwood Clo. E12	CJ34	49
Heatherwood Dr., Hayes	BA37	53
Heathfield Av. SW18	BT47	76
Heathfield Clo. E16	CJ39	58
Heathfield Clo., Hert.	BS18	20
Church Rd.		
Heathfield Clo., Kes.	CJ56	97
Heathfield Clo., Pot.B.	BS18	20
Heathfield Clo., Wok.	AT62	100
Heathfield Ct. W4	BN42	65
Heathfield Ter.		
Heathfield Ct., St.Alb.	BH13	9
Avenue Rd.		
Heathfield Dr., Red.	BU73	121
Heathfield E4	CF27	39
Heathfield Gdns. NW11	BQ32	46
Heathfield Gdns. SW18	BT46	76
Heathfield Gdns. W4	BN42	65
Heathfield Gdns., Croy.	BZ56	96
Heathfield Rd.		
Heathfield La., Chis.	CL50	78
Heathfield N., Twick.	BH47	74
Heathfield Pk. NW2	BQ36	55
Heathfield Rd. SW18	BT46	76
Heathfield Rd. W3	BM41	65
Heathfield Rd., Bexh.	CQ45	69
Heathfield Rd., Brom.	CG50	78
Heathfield Rd., Bush.	BE24	27
Heathfield Rd., Croy.	BZ56	96
Heathfield Rd., Kes.	CJ56	97
Heathfield Rd., Sev.	CT64	107
Heathfield Rd., Walt.	BE56	93
Heathfield Rd., Wok.	AT62	100
Heathfield Ri., Ruis.	BA33	44
Heathfield S., Twick.	BH47	74
Heathfield Sq. SW18	BT47	76
Heathfield St. W11	BR40	55
Portland Rd.		
Heathfield SW17	BU47	76
Burntwood Grange Rd.		
Heathfield Ter. SE18	CN43	68
Heathfield Ter. W4	BN42	65
Heathfield Vale, S.Croy	CC58	96
Heathfield Way, Ger.Cr.	AR32	43
Heathfield, Chis.	CM50	78
Heathfield, Cob.	BF60	93
Heathfields Ct., Houns.	BE46	74
Heathlands Way		
Heathgate NW11	BS32	47
Heathland Rd. N16	CA33	48
Heathlands Clo., Sun.	BC51	83
Heathlands Clo., Twick.	BH47	74
Heathlands Dr., St.Alb.	BH12	9
Heathlands NW3	BT34	47
Heathlands Ri., Dart.	CU46	79
Heathlands Way, Houns.	BE46	74
Heathlands, The, Tad.	BR64	103
Heathlee Rd. SE3	CG45	68
Heathley End, Chis.	CM50	78
Heathmans Yd. SW6	BR44	65
Heathmead SW19	BQ48	75
Heathrow Clo., West.Dr.	AW44	63
Heaths Clo., Enf.	CA23	30
Heathside Av., Bexh.	CQ44	69
Heathside Clo., Esher	BH55	84
Heathside Clo., Nthwd.	BA28	35
Heathside Cres., Wok.	AS62	100
Heathside Gdns., Wok.	AT62	100
Heathside Pk. Rd., Wok.	AS62	100
Heathside Rd., Nthwd.	BA28	35
Heathside Rd., Wok.	AS62	100
Heathside, Esher	BH55	84
Heathside, Wey.	AZ56	92
Heathstan Rd. W12	BP39	55
Heathurst Rd., S.Croy.	BZ58	96
Heathview Av., Dart.	CT47	79
Heathview Cres., Dart.	CU47	79
Heathview Dr. SE2	CP43	69
Heathview Gdns. SW15	BQ47	75
Heathview Rd., Th.Hth.	BT52	86
Heathville Rd. N19	BX33	47
Heathwall St. SW11	BU45	66
Heathway SE3	CH43	68
Heathway, Cat.	BZ66	114
Heathway, Croy.	CD55	87
Heathway, Dag.	CQ34	50
Heathway, Iver	AU37	52
Heathway, Lthd.	BB65	101
Heathway, Wdf.Grn.	CJ28	40
Heathwood Gdns. SE7	CK42	68
Heathwood Gdns. Swan.	CS51	89
Heathwood Wk., Bex.	CT47	79
Heaton Av., Rom.	CU29	41
Heaton Clo., Rom.	CV29	42
Heaton Grange Rd., Rom.	CT30	41
Heaton Pl. E15	CF35	48
Heaton Rd. SE15	CB45	67
Heaton Rd., Mitch.	BV50	76
Heaton Way, Rom.	CV29	42
Heaver Clo. SW11	BT45	66
Heaver Rd. SW11	BT45	66
Wye St.		
Heaverham Rd., Sev.	CX62	108
Heavitree Rd. SE18	CM42	68
Heayfield, Welw.G.C.	BT 7	5
Hebden Ct. E2	**CA37**	**2**
Hebdon Rd. SW17	BU48	76
Heber Rd. SE22	CA46	77
Heber Rd., NW2	BQ35	46
Hebron Rd. W6	BP41	65
Hecham Clo. E17	CD30	39
Heckfield Pl. SW6	BS43	66
Fulham Rd.		
Heckford St. E1	CC40	57
The Highway		
Hector St. SE18	CN42	68
Heddon Clo., Islw.	BJ45	64
Heddon Ct. Av., Barn.	BU25	29
Heddon Rd., Barn.	BU25	29
Heddon St. W1	**BW40**	**3**
Heddon St. W1	BW40	56
Hedge Brooms, Welw.G.C.	BT 7	5
New Wood		
Hedge Hill, Enf.	BY23	29
Hedge La. N13	BY27	38
Hedge Pl. Rd., Green.	CZ46	80

Hedge Row, Ger.Cr. AS29 34
Hedge Wk. SE6 CE49 77
Lushington Rd.
Hedgeley St. SE12 CG46 78
Hedgeley, Ilf. CK31 49
Hedgemans Rd., Dag. CP36 59
Hedgemans Way, Dag. CQ36 59
Hedgerley Ct., Wok. AR62 100
Hedgerley Gdns., Grnf. BG37 54
Hedgerley Hill, Slou. AO34 43
Hedgerley La., Slou. AP32 43
Hedgerows, Saw. CQ 6 6
Hedgers Gro. E9 CD36 57
Hedges Clo., Hat. BP12 10
Stonecross Rd.
Hedgeside Rd., Nthwd. BA28 35
Hedgeside, Berk. AT11 7
Hedgeway, Guil. AQ71 118
Hedgewood Gdns., Ilf. CL31 49
Hedingham Clo. N1 BZ36 57
Poplar Rd.
Hedingham Clo. N1 BZ37 2
Popham Rd.
Hedingham Clo. N1 BZ37 57
Popham Rd.
Hedingham Rd., Dag. CO35 50
Hedingham Rd., Horn. CX33 51
Hedley Av., Grays DB43 70
Hedley Rd., Houns. BF47 74
Hedley Rd., St.Alb. BJ13 9
Hedley Row N5 BZ35 48
Poets Rd.
Hedworth Av., Wal.Cr. CC20 21
Heenan Clo., Bark. CM36 58
Glenny Rd.
Heene Rd., Enf. BZ23 30
Heideck Gdns., Brwd. DD27 122
Victors Cres.
Heigham Rd. E6 CJ36 58
Heighams, Harl. CK12 13
Heighton Gdns., Croy. BY56 95
Heights Clo., Bans. BR61 103
Heights Clo., SW20 BP50 75
Heights, The SE7 CJ42 68
Heights, The, Beck. CF50 77
Heights, The, Hem.H. AY12 8
Saturn Way
Heights, The, Loug. CK23 31
Heights, The, Nthlt. BE35 45
Heiron St. SE17 BZ43 67
John Ruskin St.
Helby Rd. SW4 BW46 76
Helder Gro. SE12 CG47 78
Helder St., S.Croy. BZ57 96
Heldmann Clo., Islw. BG45 64
Helen Av., Felt. BC47 73
Helen Clo. N2 BT31 47
Thomas More Way
Helen Clo., Dart. CU47 79
Havelock Rd.
Helen Clo., E.Mol. BF52 84
Helen Rd., Horn. CV31 51
Helen St. SE18 CL42 68
Helena Clo., Barn. BT22 29
Helena Clo., Wall. BX57 95
Helena Ct. W5 BK39 54
Eaton Ri.
Helena Rd. E13 CG37 58
Helena Rd. E17 CE32 48
Helena Rd. NW10 BP35 46
Helena Rd. W5 BK39 54
Helena Rd., Wind. AO44 61
Helena St. WC1 BY38 56
Fernsbury St.
Helens Pl. E2 CC38 57
Roman Rd.
Helenslea Av. NW11 BR33 46
Helford Clo., Ruis. BB34 44
Chichester Av.
Helford Ct., S.Ock. DA40 60
Cample La.
Helford Way, Upmin. CY32 51
Helford Wk., Wok. AQ62 100
Muirfield Rd.
Helgiford Gdns., Sun. BB50 73
Helions Rd., Harl. CL11 13
Helix Gdns. SW2 BX46 76
Helix Rd. SW2 BX46 76
Helleborine, Grays DC42 71
Helling St. E1 CB40 4
Helling St. E1 CB40 57
Hermitage Wall
Helme Clo. SW19 BR49 75
Helmet Row EC1 BZ38 2
Helmet Row EC1 BZ38 57
Helmsdale Clo., Hayes BE38 54
Berrydale Rd.
Helmsdale Clo., Rom. CT29 41
Helmsdale Rd. SW16 BW51 86
Helmsdale Rd., Rom. CT29 41
Helmsdale, Wok. AQ62 100
Winnington Way
Helmsley St. E8 CB36 57
Helston Clo., Pnr. BE29 36
Helston Dene, Hem.H. AX11 8
Washington Av.
Helston Gro., Hem.H. AX11 8
Helston Pl., Wat. BB19 17
Helvellyn Clo., Egh. AU50 72
Helvetia St. SE6 CD48 77
Hemans St. SW8 BX43 66
Wandsworth Rd.
Hemberton Rd. SW9 BX45 66
Hemel Hempstead Rd., Wat. BA21 26
Hemel Hempstead Rd., Hem.H. BB14 8
Hemel Hempstead Rd., St. Alb. BD14 9
Heming Rd., Edg. BM29 37
Hemingford Rd. N1 BX37 2
Hemingford Rd. N1 BX37 56
Hemingford Rd., Sutt. BQ56 94
Hemingford Rd., Wat. BB21 26
Hemington Av. N11 BU28 38
Hemlock Clo., Tad. BR65 103
Hemlock Rd. W12 BO40 55

Hemmen La., Hayes BB39 53
Hemming Clo., Hmptn. BF51 84
Hemming St. E1 CB38 57
Hemming Way, Wat. BC21 26
Hemmings, The, Berk. AP13 7
Hemnall St., Epp. CN19 22
Hemp Wk. SE17 BZ42 4
Hemp Wk. SE17 BZ42 67
Chatham St.
Hempshaw Av., Bans. BU61 104
Hempson Av., Slou. AR41 62
Hempstall, Welw.G.C. BS 9 5
Hempstead Clo., Buck.H. CH27 40
Hempstead Rd. E17 CF31 48
Hempstead Rd., Berk. AT12 7
Hempstead Rd., Hem.H. AT16 16
Hempstead Rd., Kings L. AY16 17
Hemsby Rd., Chess. BL57 94
Hemstal Rd. NW6 BS36 56
Hemsted Rd., Erith CT43 69
Hemswell Dr. NW9 BO30 37
Hemsworth Ct. N1 CA37 2
Hemsworth Ct. N1 CA37 57
Hemsworth St.
Hemsworth St. N1 CA37 2
Hemsworth St. N1 CA37 57
Hemus Pl. SW3 BU42 3
Hemus Pl. SW3 BU42 66
Chelsea Manor St.
Hemwood Rd., Wind. AL45 61
Hen & Chickens Ct. EC4 BY39 56
Fleet St.
Hen Grove Cres., Ashf. AX48 73
Henbane Path, Rom. CV29 42
Clematis Clo.
Henbit Clo., Tad. BP63 103
Henbury Way, Wat. BD27 36
Henchley Dene, Guil. AU69 118
Henchman St. W12 BO39 55
Hencroft St., Slou. AP41 62
Hendale Av. NW4 BP31 46
Henderson Av., Guil. AQ68 109
Henderson Clo. NW10 BN36 55
Henderson Clo., St.Alb. BG11 9
Henderson Dr. NW8 BT38 56
Henderson Dr., Dart. CW45 70
Henderson Pl., Wat. BB17 17
Henderson Rd. E7 CJ36 58
Henderson Rd. N9 CB26 39
Henderson Rd. SW18 CU47 76
Henderson Rd., Croy. BZ53 87
Henderson Rd., West. CJ59 97
Hendham Rd. SW17 BU48 76
Hendon Av. N3 BR30 37
Hendon Gdns., Rom. CS29 41
Hendon La. N3 BR31 46
Hendon Park Mans. NW4 BQ32 46
Hendon Park Row NW11 BR32 46
Hendon Rd. N9 CB27 39
Hendon Way NW4 BP32 46
Hendon Way, Stai. AX46 73
Hendon Wood La. NW7 BO26 37
Hendons Way, Maid. AG42 61
Hendre Rd. SE1 CA42 4
Hendre Rd. SE1 CA42 67
Hendren Clo., Har. BG35 45
Dimmock Dr.
Hendrick Av. SW12 BU47 76
Hendricks Ter. N17 CB31 48
Heneage Cres., Croy. CF58 96
Heneage La. EC3 CA39 2
Heneage La. EC3 CA39 57
Bevis Marks
Heneage St. E1 CA39 2
Heneage St. E1 CA39 57
Henfield Clo. N19 BW33 47
Henfield Clo., Bex. CR46 79
Henfield Rd. SW19 BR51 85
Hengeld Gdns., Mitch. BT52 86
Hengist Rd. Erith CR43 69
Hengist Rd. SE12 CH47 78
Hengist Way, Brom. CF52 87
Hengrave Rd. SE23 CC46 77
Hengrove Ct., Bex. CQ47 79
Hurst Rd.
Henhurst Rd., Grav. DJ50 81
Henley Av., Sutt. BR55 85
Henley Bank, Guil. AQ71 118
Henley Clo. SW11 CA44 67
Henley Clo., Grn. BG37 54
Henley Clo., Islw. BH44 64
Henley Ct. N14 BW26 38
Henley Deane, Grav. DF49 81
Henley Dr., Kings.T. BO50 75
Henley Gdns., Pnr. BC31 44
Henley Gdns., Rom. CQ32 50
Henley Rd. E16 CK41 68
Henley Rd. N18 CA28 39
Henley Rd. NW10 BQ37 55
Henley Rd., Ilf. CM35 49
Henley St. SW11 BV44 66
Henley Way, Felt. BD49 74
Hennel Clo., SE23 CC48 77
Henniker Gdns. E6 CJ38 58
Henniker Ms. SW3 BT42 3
Henniker Ms. SW3 BT44 66
Callow St.
Henniker Rd. E15 CF35 48
Henning St. SW11 BU44 66
Shuttleworth Rd.
Henningham Rd. N17 BZ30 39
Henrietta Ms. WC1 BX38 2
Henrietta Ms. WC1 BX38 56
Brunswick Sq.
Henrietta Pl. W1 BV39 1
Henrietta Pl. W1 BV39 56
Henrietta St. E15 CF35 48
Henrietta St. WC2 BX40 4
Henrietta St. WC2 BX40 56
Henriques St. E1 CB39 57
Henry Cooper Way SE9 CJ49 78
Dunkery Rd.
Henry Darlot Dr. NW7 BQ28 37
Henry Dickens Ct. W11 BQ40 55
Henry Jackson Rd. SW15 BQ45 65
Henry Rd. E6 CK37 58
Henry Rd. N4 BY33 47

Henry Rd., Barn. BT25 29
Henry Rd., Slou. AO41 61
Henry St., Brom. CH51 88
Henry St., Hem.H. AX15 8
Henry Wells Sq., Hem.H. AY11 8
Henrys Av., Wdf.Grn. CG28 40
Henrys Ter., Brwd. DA20 24
Henrys Wk., Ilf. CM29 40
Henryson Rd. SE4 CD46 77
Hensford Gdns. SE26 CB48 77
Wells Park Rd.
Henshall St. N1 BZ36 57
Henshaw St. SE17 BZ42 4
Henshaw St. SE17 BZ42 67
Henshawe Rd., Dag. CP34 50
Henslow Way, Wok. AU60 91
Henslowe Rd. SE22 CB46 77
Henson Av. NW2 BQ35 46
Henson Clo., Orp. CL55 88
Henson Path, Har. BK31 45
Henson Pl., Nthlt. BD37 54
Henstridge Pl. NW8 BU37 1
Henstridge Pl. NW8 BU37 56
Hensworth Rd., Ashf. AX49 73
Henty Clo. SW11 BU43 66
Henty Wk. SW15 BP46 75
Henville Rd., Brom. CH51 88
Henwick Rd. SE9 CJ45 68
Henwood Rd. SE16 CC41 67
Henwood Side, Wdf.Grn. CK29 40
Hepburn Gdns., W.Wick. CG54 88
Hepburn Ms. SW11 BU46 76
Webbs Rd.
Hepple Clo., Islw. BJ44 64
Hepplestone Clo. SW15 BP46 75
Dover Park Dr.
Hepscott Rd. E9 CE36 57
Hepworth Gdns., Bark. CO35 50
Hepworth Rd. SW16 BX50 76
Hepworth Way, Walt. BB54 83
Heracles Clo., Wall. BX57 95
Herald St. E2 CB38 57
Herald Wk., Dart. CW46 80
Heralds Pl. SE11 BY42 4
Gilbert Rd.
Heralds Pl. SE11 BY42 66
Gilbert Rd.
Herbal Hill EC1 BY38 2
Herbal Hill EC1 BY38 56
Ray St.
Herbert Cres. SW1 BU41 3
Herbert Cres. SW1 BU41 66
Pavilion Rd.
Herbert Cres., Wok. AP62 100
Herbert Gdns. NW10 BP37 55
Herbert Gdns. W4 BM43 65
Magnolia Rd.
Herbert Gdns., Rom. CP33 50
Herbert Rd. E12 CK35 49
Herbert Rd. E17 CD33 48
Herbert Rd. N11 BX29 38
Herbert Rd. N15 CA32 48
Herbert Rd. NW9 BP32 46
Herbert Rd. SE18 CL43 68
Herbert Rd. SW19 BR50 75
Herbert Rd., Bexh. CQ44 69
Herbert Rd., Brom. CJ53 88
Herbert Rd., Horn. CW33 51
Herbert Rd., Ilf. CN34 49
Herbert Rd., Kings.T. BL52 85
Herbert Rd., Sthl. BE40 54
Herbert Rd., Swan. CU50 79
Herbert Rd., Swans. DC46 81
Herbert St. E13 CH37 58
Herbert St. NW5 BV35 47
Herbert St., Hem.H. AX13 8
Herbert St., Wat. BD24 27
Herbrand St. WC1 BX38 2
Herbrand St. WC1 BX38 56
Hercies Rd., Uxb. AY36 53
Hercules Pl. N7 BX34 47
Hercules St.
Hercules Rd. SE1 BX41 4
Hercules Rd. SE1 BX41 66
Hercules St. N7 BX34 47
Hercules Yd. N7 BX34 47
Hercules St.
Hereford Av., Barn. BU26 38
Hereford Clo., Epsom BN60 94
Hereford Clo., Guil. AP69 118
Hereford Clo., Stai. AW51 83
Hereford Clo., Wok. AQ63 100
Hereford Gdns. SE13 CF46 77
Longhurst Rd.
Hereford Gdns., Ilf. CK33 49
Hereford Gdns., Pnr. BE32 45
Hereford Gdns., Twick. BG47 74
Hereford Ms. W2 BS39 56
Hereford Rd.
Hereford Rd. E11 CH32 49
Hereford Rd. W2 BS39 56
Hereford Rd. W3 BM40 55
Hereford Rd. W5 BK41 64
Hereford Rd., Felt. BD47 74
Hereford Retreat SE15 CB43 67
Bird-in-Bush Rd.
Hereford Sq. SW7 BT42 3
Hereford Sq. SW7 BT42 66
Hereford St. E2 CB38 2
Hereford St. E2 CB38 57
Hereford Way, Chess. BK56 93
Herent Dr., Ilf. CK31 49
Hereward Av., Pur. BY59 95
Hereward Clo., Wal.Abb. CF19 21
Hereward Gdns. N13 BY28 38
Hereward Rd. SW17 CU49 76
Herga Ct., Har. BH34 45
Herga Ct., Wat. BC23 26
Herga Rd., Har. BH31 45
Herington Gro., Brwd. DD26 122
Heriot Av. E4 CD27 39
Heriot Pl. NW5 BV35 47
Mansfield Rd.
Heriot Rd. NW4 BQ32 46
Heriot Rd., Cher. AW54 83
Heriots Clo., Stan. BJ28 36

Heritage Clo., St.Alb. BG13 9
High St.
Heritage Clo., Uxb. AX38 53
Heritage Hl., Kes. CJ56 97
Heritage Vw., Har. BH34 45
Herkomer Clo., Bush. BF25 27
Herkomer Rd., Bush. BF25 27
Herlwyn Av., Ruis. BB34 44
Herlwyn Gdns. SW17 BU49 76
Hermes St. N1 BY37 56
Hermes Way, Wall. BW57 95
Hermes Wk., Nthlt. BF37 54
Leander Rd.
Hermiston Av. N8 BX32 47
Hermit Rd. E16 CG39 58
Hermit St. EC1 BY38 2
Hermit St. EC1 BY38 56
Hermitage Clo. E18 CG31 49
Hermitage Clo., Enf. BY23 29
Hermitage Clo., Esher BJ57 93
Hermitage Clo., Pot.B. BT20 20
Hermitage Clo., Shep. AZ52 83
Hermitage Clo., Slou. AR41 62
Hermitage Ct. E18 CH31 49
Hermitage Ct., Pot.B. BT20 20
Southgate Rd.
Hermitage Gdns. NW2 BS34 47
Hermitage Gdns. SE19 BZ50 77
Hermitage La. N18 BZ28 39
Hermitage La. NW2 BS34 47
Hermitage La. SE25 CB53 87
Hermitage La. SW16 BX50 76
Hermitage La., Wind. AN45 61
Hermitage Rd. N15 BZ32 48
Hermitage Rd. N4 BZ33 48
Hermitage Rd. SE19 BZ50 77
Hermitage Rd., Ken. BZ61 105
Hermitage Rd., Wok. AO63 100
Hermitage St. W2 BT39 1
Hermitage Wall E1 CB40 4
Hermitage Wall E1 CB40 57
Hermitage Way, Stan. BJ30 36
Hermitage Wk. E18 CG31 49
Hermitage Wk. SW16 BX51 86
Acacia Rd.
Hermitage Woods Cres., Wok. AO63 100
Hermitage, The SE23 CC47 77
Hermitage, The SW13 BO44 65
Hermitage, The, Felt. BB48 73
St. Dunstans Rd.
Hermitage, The, Rich. BL46 75
Hermitage, The, Uxb. AX36 53
Hermon Clo., Wok. AS62 100
Mount Hermon Rd.
Hermon Gro., Hayes BC40 53
Hermon Hill E11 CH32 49
Herndon Rd. SW18 BT46 76
Herne Clo. NW10 BN35 46
Herne Hill Rd. SE24 BZ45 67
Herne Hill SE24 BZ46 77
Herne Ms. N18 CB28 39
Herne Pl. SE24 BY46 76
Herne Rd., Bush. BF25 27
Herne Rd., Surb. BK55 84
Herneshaw, Hat. BO13 10
Herns La., Welw.G.C. BS 7 5
Herns Way, Welw.G.C. BS 7 5
Heron Clo. E17 CD30 39
Heron Clo. NW10 BO36 55
Heron Clo., Buck.H. CH26 40
Heron Clo., Guil. AQ69 118
Heron Clo., Rick. AX27 35
Heron Clo., Saw. CP 6 6
Heron Clo., Uxb. AX36 53
Heron Cres., Sid. CN48 78
Heron Ct., Brom. CJ52 88
Heron Ct., Rich. BK46 74
Bridge St.
Heron Dale, Wey. AX56 92
Heron Flight Av., Rain. CU36 59
Heron Hill, Belv. CQ42 69
Heron Ms., Ilf. CL34 49
Heron Quay E14 CE40 57
Heron Rd. SE24 BZ45 67
Heron Rd., Croy. CA54 87
Heron Rd., Twick. BJ45 64
Heron Sq., Rich. BK46 74
Whittaker Av.
Heron Way, Brwd. DD26 122
Heron Way, Grays DA42 70
Heron Way, Hat. BP13 10
Heron Way, Upmin. CZ33 51
Herondale Av. SW18 BT47 76
Herondale, S.Croy. CC58 96
Heronfield, Egh. AQ50 72
Heronfield, Pot.B. BT18 20
Herongate Rd. E12 CJ34 49
Herongate Rd., Chsnt. CD17 21
Herongate Rd., Swan. CT50 79
Heronry, The, Walt. BC57 92
Herons Cft., Wey. BA57 92
Herons Elm, Berk. AP11 7
Herons La., Ong. CY14 15
Herons Ri., Barn. BU24 29
Herons Way, St.Alb. BJ15 9
Herons Wood, Harl. CL10 6
Herons, The E11 CG32 49
Heronsforde W13 BK39 54
Heronsgate, Edg. BM28 37
Heronsgate, Rick. AT25 25
Heronslea Dr., Stan. BL28 37
Heronslea, Wat. BD21 27
Heronswood Pl., Welw.G.C. BS 8 5
Heronswood Rd., Welw.G.C. BS 8 5
Heronswood, Wal.Abb. CG20 22
Roundhills
Heronway, Brwd. DD26 122
Heronway, Wdf.Grn. CJ28 40
Herrick Rd. N5 BZ34 48
Herrick St. SW1 BW42 3
Herrick St. SW1 BW42 66
Herries St. W10 BR37 55
Herring St. SE5 CA43 67
Herringham Rd. SE7 CJ41 68

Herrings La., Cher. AW53 83
Herrongate Clo., Enf. CA23 30
Hersant Clo. NW10 BP37 55
Herschel Park Dr., AP41 62
Albert St.
Herschel St., Slou. AP41 62
Herschell Rd. SE23 CC47 77
Hersham By-pass, Walt. BC56 92
Hersham Clo. SW15 BP47 75
Hersham Rd., Walt. BC55 83
Hersham Trd. Est., Walt. BE55 84
Hertford Av. SW14 BN46 75
Hertford Clo., Barn. BT24 29
Hertford Pl. W1 BW38 1
Hertford Pl. W1 BW38 56
Whitfield St.
Hertford Rd. N1 CA37 2
Hertford Rd. N1 CA37 57
Hertford Rd. N2 BU31 47
Hertford Rd. N9 CB27 39
Hertford Rd., Bark. CL36 58
Hertford Rd., Barn. BT24 29
Hertford Rd., Enf. CC24 30
Hertford Rd., Hat. BQ11 10
Hertford Rd., Hodd. CC10 12
Hertford Rd., Ilf. CN32 49
Hertford Rd., Tewin BU 6 5
Hertford Rd., Welw.G.C. BR 5 5
Hertford Sq., Mitch. BX52 86
Hertford St. W1 BV40 3
Hertford St. W1 BV40 56
Hertford Way, Mitch. BX52 86
Hertford Wk., Belv. CR42 69
Hood Rd.
Hertslet Rd. N7 BX34 47
Hervey Clo. N3 BS30 38
Hervey Park Rd. E17 CD31 48
Hervey Rd. SE3 CH44 68
Hervey Way N3 BS30 38
Hervey Clo.
Hesa Rd., Hayes BC39 53
Heseltine Rd. SE26 CD49 77
Green La.
Hesham Rd., Berk. AP15 7
Hesiers Hill, Warl. CG62 106
Hesiers Rd., Warl. CG61 106
Hesketh Av., Dart. CX47 80
Hesketh Pl. W11 BR40 55
Hesketh Rd. E7 CH34 49
Heslop Rd. SW12 BU47 76
Hesper Ms. SW5 BS42 3
Hesper Ms. SW5 BS42 66
Hesperus Cres. E14 CE42 67
Hessel Rd. W13 BJ41 64
Hessell St. E1 CB39 57
Hesselyn Dr., Rain. CU36 59
Hessle Gro., Epsom BO59 94
Hester Rd. N18 CB28 39
Hester Rd. SW11 BU43 66
Hestercombe Av. SW6 BR44 65
Heston Av., Houns. BE43 64
Heston Grange La., Houns. BE43 64
Heston Grn., Houns. BE43 64
Walnut Tree Rd.
Heston Ho. SE8 CD44 67
Heston Rd., Houns. BF43 64
Heston Rd., Red. BU72 121
Heston St. SE8 CD44 67
Heston Wk., Red. BU72 121
Hetchleys, Hem.H. AW12 8
Hetherington Rd. SW4 BX45 66
Hetherington Rd., Shep. BA51 83
Hetherington Way, Uxb. AY35 44
Hetley Gdns. SE19 CA50 77
Fox Hill
Hetley Rd. W12 BP40 55
Hetton St. W6 BQ42 65
Glenthorne Rd.
Heusden Way, Ger.Cr. AS33 43
Hevelius Clo. SE10 CG42 68
Hever Av., Sev. CZ57 99
Hever Cft. SE9 CL49 78
Hever Court Rd., Grav. DH50 81
Hever Gdns., Brom. CL51 88
Hever Rd., Sev. CZ57 99
Hever Wood Rd., Sev. CZ57 99
Heverham Rd. SE18 CN42 68
Heversham Rd., Bexh. CR44 69
Hewens Rd., Uxb. BA38 53
Hewer St. W10 BQ39 55
Hewers Way, Tad. BQ63 103
Hewett Clo., Stan. BJ28 36
Hewett Pl., Swan. CS52 89
Hewett Rd., Dag. CP35 50
Hewett St. EC2 CA38 2
Hewett St. EC2 CA38 57
Curtain Rd.
Hewish Rd. N18 CA28 39
Hewitt Av. N22 BY30 38
Hewitt Rd. N8 BY32 47
Hewitts Rd., Orp. CQ57 98
Hewlett Rd. E3 CD37 57
Hexagon, The N6 BU33 47
Hexal Rd. SE6 CG48 78
Hexham Gdns., Islw. BJ43 64
Hexham Rd. SE27 BZ48 77
Hexham Rd., Barn. BS24 29
Hexham Rd., Mord. BS54 86
Hextalls La., Red. BZ67 114
Heybourne Rd. N17 CB29 39
Heybridge Av. SW16 BX50 76
Heybridge Dr., Ilf. CM31 49
Heybridge Way E10 CD33 48
Heydons Clo., St.Alb. BG12 9
Heyford Av. SW20 BR52 85
Heyford Av. SW8 BX43 66
Heyford Rd., Mitch. BU51 86
Heyford Rd., Rad. BJ21 27
Heygate St. SE17 BZ42 4
Heygate St. SE17 BZ42 67
Heylyn Sq. E3 CE37 58
Malmesbury Rd.
Heymede, Lthd. BK65 102
Heynes Rd., Dag. CP35 50
Heysham Dr., Wat. BD28 36

Heysham Rd. N15 BZ32 48
Heythorpe Clo., Wok. AP62 100
Kenton Way
Heythorpe St. SW18 BR47 75
Heywood Av. NW9 BO30 37
Heyworth Rd. E15 CG35 49
Heyworth Rd. E5 CB35 48
Hibbert Av., Wat. BD22 27
Hibbert Rd. E17 CD33 48
Hibbert Rd., Har. BH30 36
Hibbert Rd., Maid. AG41 61
Hibbert St. SW11 BT45 66
Hibberts Alley, Wind. AO44 61
Peascod St.
Hibernia Dr., Grav. DJ48 81
Hibernia Gdns., Houns. BF45 64
Hibernia Rd., Houns. BF45 64
Hichisson Rd. SE15 CC46 77
Hickin Clo. SE7 CJ42 68
Hickin St. E14 CF41 67
Plevna St.
Hickling Rd., Ilf. CL35 49
Hickman Av. E4 CF28 39
Hickman Clo. E16 CJ39 58
Hickman Rd., Rom. CP33 50
Hickmans Clo., Gdse. CC69 114
Hickmore Wk. SW4 BW45 66
Belmont Clo.
Hicks Av., Grnf. BG37 54
Hicks Clo. SW11 BU45 66
Hicks St. SE8 CD42 67
Hidalgo Ct., Hem.H. AY12 8
Hide Pl. SW1 BW42 3
Hide Pl. SW1 BW42 66
Hide Rd., Har. BG31 45
Hides St. N7 BX36 56
Sheringham Rd.
Hides, The, Harl. CM10 6
Higgs Row SW15 BQ45 65
Felsham Rd.
High Acres, Wat. BA19 17
High Banks Rd., Pnr. BF29 36
High Beech Rd., Loug. CK24 31
High Beech, S.Croy. CA57 96
High Beeches Clo., Wall. BW58 95
High Beeches, Bans. BQ60 94
High Beeches, Ger.Cr. AR33 43
High Beeches, Orp. CO57 98
High Beeches, Sid. CQ49 79
High Bois La., Amer. AO21 25
High Bridge SE10 CF42 67
High Bridge St., Wal.Abb. CE20 21
High Canons, B.Wd. BN22 28
High Cedar Dr. SW20 BQ50 75
High Clo., Rick. AX25 26
High Cross Rd. N17 CB31 48
High Cross Rd., Sev. DA66 117
High Cross, Wat. BG22 27
High Ct., Wdf.Grn. CH29 40
Higham Rd.
High Dells, Hat. BO13 10
High Dr., Cat. CE64 105
High Dr., Lthd. BG60 93
High Dr., N.Mal. BN51 85
High Elms Clo., Nthwd. BA29 35
High Elms Rd., Orp. CL59 97
High Elms, Chig. CN28 40
High Elms, Upmin. CZ33 51
High Elms, Wdf.Grn. CH28 40
High Field, Bans. BU62 104
High Field, Wind. AM45 61
High Firs, Swan. CT52 89
High Foleys, Esher BJ57 93
High Gables, Loug. CJ25 31
High Garth, Esher BG57 93
High Gro. SE18 CM43 68
High Gro., Welw.G.C. BQ 7 5
High Hill Est. E5 CB33 48
High Hill Rd., Warl. CF60 96
High Holborn WC1 BX39 2
High Holborn WC1 BX39 56
High House La., Grays DH41 71
High La. W7 BG39 54
High La., Warl. CD62 105
High Laver La., Ong. CU12 14
High Level Dr. SE25 CB49 77
High Mead, Har. BH32 45
High Mead, W.Wick. CF55 87
High Meadow Clo., Dor. BJ72 119
High Meadow Clo., Pnr. BC31 44
High Meadow Cres. NW9 BN32 46
High Meadows, Chig. CM28 40
High Meads Rd. E16 CJ39 58
Alestan Beck Rd.
High Moor, Amer. AO23 25
High Oaks Rd., Welw.G.C. BP 7 5
High Oaks, Enf. BX22 29
High Oaks, St.Alb. BG11 9
High Ongar Rd., Ong. CX17 24
High Park Av., Lthd. BB66 110
High Park Av., Rich. BM44 65
High Park Rd., Rich. BM44 65
High Pastures, Bish. CS 7 6
High Path Rd., Guil. AU70 118
High Path SW19 BS51 86
High Pewley, Guil. AS71 118
High Pine Clo., Wey. BA56 92
High Pines, Warl. CC63 105
High Point SE9 CL48 78
High Point, Wey. AZ56 92
High Rd. E. Finchley N2 BT30 38
High Rd. E11 CG34 49
High Rd. E18 CG29 40
High Rd. Leytonstone E15 CG35 49
High Rd. N. Finchley N12 BT28 38
High Rd. N11 BV28 38
High Rd. N15 CA32 48
High Rd. N17 CA30 39
High Rd. N20 BT26 38
High Rd. N22 BX29 38
High Rd. NW10 BP36 55
High Rd., Brox. CD15 12
High Rd., Buck.H. CH27 40
High Rd., Bush. BG26 36
High Rd., Chig. CL28 40
High Rd., Epp. CO15 14
High Rd., Epp. CO17 23
High Rd., Epp. CR16 23
High Rd., Grays DC40 71
High Rd., Harrow Weald BH29 36
High Rd., Hat. BU12 11
High Rd., Ickenham AZ34 44
High Rd., Ilf. CL34 49
High Rd., Leavesden BB20 17
High Rd., Leyt. CF34 48
High Rd., Loug. CJ25 31
High Rd., Reig. BY67 113
High Rd., Rom. CO33 50
High Rd., Uxb. AX39 53
High Rd., Wdf.Grn. CG29 40
High Rd., Wem. BK35 45
High Rd., Wey. AY59 92
High Rd., Willesden Grn. NW10 BO36 55
High Rd., Wilmington CV48 80
High Ridge Clo., Epsom BO60 94
High Ridge N10 BV30 38
High Ridge Rd., Hem.H. AX16 17
High Ridge, Cuff. BX17 20
High Silver, Loug. CJ24 31
High St, Oxshott BG60 93
High St. E11 CH32 49
High St. E13 CH37 58
High St. E15 CF37 57
High St. E17 CD32 48
High St. Grn., Hem.H. AZ12 8
High St. Ms. SW19 BR49 75
Courthope Rd.
High St. N. E12 CK35 49
High St. N. E6 CK36 58
High St. N14 BW26 38
High St. N8 BX31 47
High St. NW10 BO37 55
High St. NW7 BP28 37
High St. S. E6 CK37 58
High St. S., Norwood SE25 CA52 87
High St. SE20 CB50 77
High St. SW19 BQ49 75
High St. SW6 BR45 65
High St. W3 BM40 55
High St. W5 BK40 54
High St., Abbots Langley BB19 17
High St., Addlestone AW56 92
High St., Aveley CY40 60
High St., Bans. BS61 104
High St., Barkingside CM31 49
High St., Barn. BR24 28
High St., Bean DA48 80
High St., Beck. CE51 87
High St., Bedmond BB17 17
High St., Berk. AP11 7
High St., Bex. CR47 79
High St., Bletchingley BX70 121
High St., Bovingdon AT17 16
High St., Bray AH41 61
High St., Brent. BK43 64
High St., Brom. CG51 88
High St., Brwd. DB27 42
High St., Bush. BE25 27
High St., Cars. BU56 95
High St., Ch.St.G. AR27 34
High St., Chalvey AO41 61
High St., Cheam BR57 94
High St., Chipstead CS64 107
High St., Chis. CL50 78
High St., Chobham AP59 91
High St., Chsnt. CC18 21
High St., Chsnt. CD20 21
High St., Claygate BH57 93
High St., Cob. BC61 101
High St., Colliers Wood SW19 BT50 76
High St., Colnbrook AU43 62
High St., Colney Heath BN14 10
High St., Cowley AX39 53
High St., Cranford BC43 63
High St., Crayford CT46 79
High St., Croy. BZ55 87
High St., Dart. CW46 80
High St., Datchet AQ44 62
High St., Dor. BJ71 119
High St., Downe CL59 97
High St., E.Mol. BF52 84
High St., Edg. BM29 37
High St., Egh. AS49 72
High St., Elstree BK25 27
High St., Enf. CC25 30
High St., Epp. CN19 22
High St., Epsom BN60 94
High St., Erith CT42 69
High St., Esher BF56 93
High St., Eton AO43 61
High St., Ewell BO58 94
High St., Eyns. CW55 90
High St., Farn. CW53 90
High St., Farnborough CL56 97
High St., Felt. BC48 73
High St., Ger.Cr. AS30 34
High St., Grav. DD46 81
High St., Grays DD43 71
High St., Great Bookham BF66 111
High St., Green Street Green. CN57 97
High St., Green. DA45 70
High St., Guil. AR71 118
High St., Hampton Wick BK51 84
High St., Har. BH33 45
High St., Harefield AX30 35
High St., Harl. CP 9 6
High St., Hem.H. AX13 8
High St., Hmptn. BG51 84
High St., Hodd. CE13 12
High St., Horn. CV33 51
High St., Horsell AR61 100
High St., Houns. BF45 64
High St., Iver AV39 52
High St., Kemsing CX62 108
High St., Kings L. AZ18 17
High St., Kings.T. BK52 84
High St., Limpsfield CH67 115
High St., London Colney BK16 18
High St., Lthd. BJ64 102
High St., Merstham BU70 121
High St., Northfleet DD46 81
High St., Nthwd. BB30 35
High St., Nutfield BV67 113
High St., Old Woking AT64 100
High St., Ong. CX17 24
High St., Orp. CO55 89
High St., Otford CU61 107
High St., Oxt. CF68 114
High St., Plaxtol DC67 117
High St., Pnr. BE31 45
High St., Ponders End CC25 30
High St., Pot.B. BT19 20
High St., Pur. BY59 95
High St., Red. BZ70 114
High St., Reig. BS70 121
High St., Rick. AX26 35
High St., Ripley AW64 101
High St., Rom. CT32 50
High St., Roydon CH10 13
High St., Ruis. BB33 44
High St., S.Ock. DB38 60
High St., Seal CW64 108
High St., Sev. CV66 117
High St., Shep. AZ54 83
High St., Shoreham CT58 98
High St., Sid. CP50 79
High St., Slou. AP41 62
High St., Southgate N14 BW26 38
High St., St. Mary Cray CP53 89
High St., St.Alb. BG13 9
High St., Stai. AV49 72
High St., Stanwell AX46 73
High St., Sthl. BE40 54
High St., Sutt. BS56 95
High St., Swan. CT52 89
High St., Swans. DC46 81
High St., T.Ditt. BJ53 84
High St., Tad. BQ65 103
High St., Tedd. BJ49 74
High St., Th.Hth. BZ52 87
High St., Uxb. AX36 53
High St., W.Wick. CE54 87
High St., Walt. BC54 83
High St., Wat. BD24 27
High St., Wealdstone BH30 36
High St., Well. CO45 69
High St., Wem. BL35 46
High St., West Dr. AX43 63
High St., West. CM67 115
High St., Wey. AZ56 92
High St., Whitton BG47 74
High St., Wind. AO44 61
High St., Wok. AS62 100
High St., Wraysbury AS46 72
High St., Yiewsley AX40 53
High Timber St. EC4 BZ40 4
High Timber St. EC4 BZ40 57
Broken Wharf
High Tor Clo., Brom. CH50 78
Babbacombe Rd.
High Tree Clo., Wey. AW56 92
High Tree Ct. W7 BH40 54
High Trees Clo., Cat. CA64 105
High Trees Rd., Reig. BT71 121
High Trees SW2 BY47 76
High Trees, Barn. BU25 29
High Trees, Croy. CD54 87
High View Av., Grays DE42 71
High View Clo. SE19 CA51 87
High View Clo., Loug. CJ25 31
High View Clo., Pot.B. BT20 20
High View Gdns.
High View Gdns., Pot.B. BT20 20
High View Rd. E18 CG31 49
High View Rd. SE19 BZ50 77
High View Rd., Guil. AO72 118
High View Rd., Orp. CL58 97
High View Rd., Sid. CO49 79
High Vw., Hat. BO13 10
High Vw., Rick. AW24 26
High Vw., Sutt. BR59 94
High Vw., Wat. BB25 26
High Wickfield, Welw.G.C. BT 8 5
High Worple, Har. BE33 45
High Wych La., Saw. CO 6 6
High Wych Rd., Harl. CN 7 6
Higham Av., Hem.H. AX14 8
Higham Hill Rd. E17 CD30 39
Higham La., Ton. DC70 117
Higham Pl. E17 CD31 48
Higham Rd. E17 CD30 39
Higham Rd. N17 BZ31 48
Higham Rd., Wdf.Grn. CH29 40
Higham St. E17 CD31 48
Higham Station Av. E4 CE29 39
Higham Vw., Epp. CR16 23
Highams Hill, War. CH59 97
Highams Pk., The, Wdf.Grn. CG28 40
Highash Clo., S.le H. DK42 71
Highbanks Clo., Well. CO43 69
Highbarn Rd., Lthd. BD68 111
Highbarns Rd., Hem.H. AZ16 17
Highbarrow Rd., Croy. CA54 87
Highbridge Rd., Bark. CL37 58
Highbrook Rd. SE3 CJ45 68
Highbroom Cres., W.Wick. CE54 87
Highbury Av., Hodd. CE11 12
Highbury Av., Th.Hth. BY51 86
Highbury Clo., W.Wick. CE55 87
Highbury Cor. N5 BY36 56
Highbury Cres. N5 BY35 47
Highbury Gdns., Ilf. CN34 49
Highbury Gra. N5 BY35 47
Highbury Gro. N5 BY36 56
Highbury Gro., N.Mal. BN52 85
Highbury Hill N5 BY35 47
Highbury Ms. N5 BY35 47
Ronalds Rd.
Highbury New Pk. N5 BZ34 48
Highbury Pk. N5 BY35 47
Highbury Pl. N5 BY36 56
Highbury Quadrant Est. N5 BZ34 48
Highbury Quadrant N5 BY34 47
Highbury Rd. SW19 BR49 75
Highbury Station Rd. N1 BY36 56
Highbury Ter. Ms. N5 BY35 47
Ronalds Rd.
Highbury Ter. N5 BY35 47
Highclere Clo., Ken. BZ61 105
Highclere Ct., St.Alb. BH13 9
Avenue Rd.
Highclere Dr., Hem.H. AZ15 8
Highclere Gdns., Wok. AO62 100
Highclere Rd., N.Mal. BN52 85
Highclere Rd., Wok. AO62 100
Highclere St. SE26 CD49 77
Highclere, Guil. AT69 118
Highcliffe Dr. SW15 BO46 75
Highcliffe Gdns., Ilf. CK32 49
Highcombe Clo. SE9 CJ47 78
Highcombe SE7 CH43 68
Highcotts La., Wok. AV66 109
Highcroft Av., Wem. BL36 55
Highcroft Gdns. NW11 BR32 46
Highcroft NW9 BO32 46
Highcroft Rd. N19 BX33 47
Highcroft Rd., Hem.H. AW16 17
Highcross Rd., Grav. DB49 80
Highcross Way SW15 BP47 75
Bessborough Rd.
Highdaun Dr. SW16 BX52 86
Highdown Rd. SW15 BP46 75
Highdown, Wor.Pk. BO55 85
Highelms La., Wat. BC18 17
Higher Dr., Bans. BQ59 94
Higher Dr., Lthd. BB67 110
Higher Dr., Pur. BY60 95
Higher Grn., Epsom BP60 94
Highfield Av. NW11 BQ33 46
Highfield Av. NW9 BN32 46
Highfield Av., Erith CR43 69
Highfield Av., Grnf. BH35 45
Highfield Av., Orp. CN56 97
Highfield Av., Pnr. BE32 45
Highfield Av., Wem. BL34 46
Highfield Clo. NW9 BN32 46
Highfield Clo., Amer. AO22 25
Highfield Clo., Egh. AR50 72
Highfield Clo., Nthwd. BB30 35
Highfield Clo., Rom. CS29 41
Highfield Clo., Surb. BK54 84
Highfield Clo., Wey. AW60 92
Highfield Cres., Horn. CW34 51
Highfield Cres., Nthwd. BB30 35
Highfield Ct. N14 BW25 29
Highfield Dr., Brom. CG52 88
Highfield Dr., Brox. CD14 12
Highfield Dr., Epsom BO57 94
Highfield Dr., Uxb. AY34 44
Highfield Dr., W.Wick. CE55 87
Highfield Gdns. NW11 BR32 46
Highfield Gdns., Grays DE41 71
Highfield Grn., Epp. CN19 22
Highfield Hill SE19 BZ50 77
Highfield La., Hem.H. AY12 8
Highfield La., St.Alb. BK14 9
Highfield Link, Rom. CS29 41
Highfield Pl., Epp. CN19 22
Highfield Rd. N21 BY26 38
Highfield Rd. NW11 BR32 46
Highfield Rd. S., Dart. CV47 80
Highfield Rd. W3 BM39 55
Highfield Rd., Berk. AR13 7
Highfield Rd., Bexh. CQ46 79
Highfield Rd., Brom. CK52 88
Highfield Rd., Bush. BE25 27
Highfield Rd., Cat. CB64 105
Highfield Rd., Cher. AW54 83
Highfield Rd., Chis. CN52 88
Highfield Rd., Chsnt. CA16 21
Highfield Rd., Dart. CV47 80
Highfield Rd., Felt. BC47 73
Highfield Rd., Horn. CW34 51
Highfield Rd., Islw. BH44 64
Highfield Rd., Nthwd. BB30 35
Highfield Rd., Pur. BX58 95
Highfield Rd., Rom. CS29 41
Highfield Rd., Sev. CW61 108
Highfield Rd., St.Alb. BJ10 9
Highfield Rd., Sun. BB53 83
Highfield Rd., Surb. BN54 85
Highfield Rd., Sutt. BU56 95
Highfield Rd., Walt. BC54 83
Highfield Rd., Wdf.Grn. CK29 40
Highfield Rd., West. CJ62 106
Highfield Rd., Wey. AW60 92
Highfield Way, Horn. CW34 51
Highfield Way, Pot.B. BS19 20
Highfield Way, Rick. AW25 26
Highfield, Ch.St.G. AR26 34
Highfield, Harl. CO11 14
Highfield, Kings L. AY17 17
Highfield, Rom. CS29 41
Highfields, Ash. BK63 102
Highfields, Cuff. BX17 20
Highfields, East Horsley BB67 110
Highfields, Lthd. BG65 102
Highgate Av. N6 BV33 47
Highgate Clo. N6 BV33 47
Highgate Gro, Saw. CP 6 6
White Post Field
Highgate High St. N6 BV33 47
Highgate Hill N19 BV33 47
Highgate Rd. NW5 BV34 47
Highgate West Hill N6 BV33 47
Highgrove Clo., Chis. CK51 88
Logs Hill
Highgrove Rd., Dag. CP35 50
Highgrove Way, Ruis. BC33 44
Highland Av. W7 BH39 54
Highland Av., Brwd. DB26 42
Highland Av., Dag. CS34 50
Highland Av., Loug. CK25 31
Highland Cft., Beck. CE50 77
Highland Cotts., Wall. BV56 95
Highland Dr., Bush. BG26 36
Highland Dr., Hem.H. AZ13 8
Highland Pk., Felt. BB49 73
Highland Rd. SE19 CA50 77
Highland Rd., Amer. AO23 25
Highland Rd., Bexh. CR46 79
Highland Rd., Brom. CG51 88
Highland Rd., Nthwd. BB31 44
Highland Rd., Pur. BY60 95
Highland Rd., Sev. CR59 98
Highland Rd., Wal.Abb. CG14 13
Highlands Av. W3 BN40 55
Highlands Av., Lthd. BK64 102
Highlands Clo. N4 BX33 47
Mount View Rd.
Highlands Clo., Ger.Cr. AS29 34
Highlands Clo., Houns. BF44 64
Highlands Clo., Lthd. BJ64 102
Highlands End, Ger.Cr. AS29 34
Highlands Gdns., Ilf. CK33 49
Highlands Heath Clo. SW15 BQ47 75
Highlands Heath SW15 BQ47 75
Bristol Gdns.
Highlands Hill, Swan. CU51 89
Highlands La., Ger.Cr. AS29 34
Highlands Pk., Lthd. BK65 102
Highlands Pk., Sev. CW64 108
Highlands Rd., Barn. BS25 29
Highlands Rd., Beac. AO28 34
Highlands Rd., Lthd. BJ64 102
Highlands Rd., Orp. CO54 89
Highlands Rd., Reig. BT70 121
Highlands, Hat. BQ11 10
Highlands, The, Edg. BM30 37
Highlands, The, Lthd. BB66 110
Highlands, The, Pot.B. BT18 20
Highlands, The, Rick. AW26 35
Highlands, Wat. BD26 36
Highlands, Wok. AS64 100
Highlea Clo. NW9 BO30 37
Highlever Rd. W10 BQ39 55
Highmead Cres., Wem. BL36 55
Highmead SE18 CN43 68
Highmead, Chig. CL27 40
Highmore Rd. SE3 CG43 68
Highover Pk., Amer. AO23 25
Highridge La., Bet. BM73 120
Highridge Pl., Enf. BY23 29
The Ridgeway
Highshore Rd. SE15 CA44 67
Highstead Cres., Erith CT43 69
Highstone Av. E11 CH32 49
Highstone E11 CG32 49
Highview Av., Edg. BN28 37
Highview Av., Wall. BX56 95
Highview Cres., Brwd. DE25 122
Highview Gdns. N11 BW28 38
Highview Gdns. N3 BR31 46
Highview Gdns., Edg. BN28 37
Highview Gdns., St.Alb. BK11 9
Highview Gdns., Upmin. CX34 51
Highview Pk., Bans. BS61 104
Highview Rd. W13 BJ39 54
Highview, Pnr. BD31 45
Highway, The E1 CB40 4
Highway, The E1 CB40 57
Highway, The, Orp. CO56 98
Highway, The, Stan. BH30 36
Highway, The, Sutt. BT58 95
Highwold, Couls. BV62 104
Highwood Av. N12 BT28 38
Highwood Av., Bush. BE23 27
Highwood Clo., Brwd. DA26 42
Highwood Clo., Ken. BZ62 105
Highwood Clo., Orp. CM55 88
Highwood Dr., Orp. CM55 88
Highwood Gdns. Ilf. CK32 49
Highwood Gro. NW7 BN28 37
Highwood Hill NW7 BO27 37
Highwood La., Loug. CL25 31
Highwood Rd. N19 BX34 47
Highwood Rd., Hodd. CD10 12
Highwoods, Cat. CA66 114
Highwoods, Lthd. BK64 102
Highworth Rd. N11 BW29 38
Highwych Way, Hem.H. AZ10 8
Elstree Rd.
Hilary Av., Mitch. BV52 86
Hilary Clo. SW6 BS43 66
Hilary Clo., Erith CR44 69
Hilary Clo., Horn. CV35 51
Hilary Rd. W12 BO39 55
Hilary Rd., Slou. AS41 62
Hilbert Rd., Sutt. BQ55 85
Hilborough Way, Orp. CM56 97
Hilda May Av., Swan. CT52 89
Hilda Rd. E16 CG38 58
Hilda Rd. E6 CJ36 58
Hilda Ter. SW9 BY44 66
Myatts Fields Dev.
Hilda Vale Clo., Orp. CL56 97
Hilda Vale Rd., Orp. CL56 97
Hilden Dr., Erith CU43 69
Hildenborough Gdns., Brom. CG50 78
Hildenlea Pl., Brom. CG51 88
Hildenley Clo., Red. BW67 113
Malmstone Av.
Hildens, The, Dor. BG72 119
Hilders, The, Ash. BM62 103
Hildreth St. SW12 BV47 76
Hildyard Rd. SW6 BS43 66
Hiley Rd. NW10 BQ38 55
Hilfield La. S., Bush. BH25 27
Hilfield La., Wat. BF23 27
Hilgrove Rd. NW6 BT36 1
Hilgrove Rd. NW6 BT36 56
Hiliard Rd., Nthwd. BC30 35
Hiliary Gdns., Stan. BK30 36
Hiljon Cres., Ger.Cr. AS30 34
Hill Barn, S.Croy. CA59 96
Hill Brow, Brom. CJ51 88
Hill Brow, Dart. CT46 79
Hill Clo. NW11 BS32 47
Hill Clo. NW2 BP34 46
Hill Clo., Barn. BQ25 28
Hill Clo., Chis. CL49 78

Hill Clo., Grav. DF50 81
Hill Clo., Har. BH34 45
Hill Clo., Pur. BZ60 96
Hill Clo., Rom. CV28 42
Hill Clo., Stan. BJ28 36
Hill Clo., Wok. AR61 100
Hill Common, Hem.H. AZ15 8
Hill Cres. N20 BS27 38
Hill Cres., Bex. CS47 79
Hill Cres., Har. BJ32 45
Hill Cres., Horn. CV32 51
Hill Cres., Surb. BL53 85
Hill Cres., Wor.Pk. BQ55 85
Hill Crest Dr., Green. DA46 80
Hill Crest Gdns. N3 BR31 46
Hill Crest, Pot.B. BT20 20
Hill Crest, Sev. CU64 107
Hill Crest, Sid. CO47 79
Hill Ct. SW15 BQ46 75
Putney Hill
Hill Ct. W5 BL38 55
The Ridings
Hill Dr. NW9 BN33 46
Hill Dr. SW16 BX52 86
Hill End La., St.Alb. BK14 9
Hill End Rd., Uxb. AX29 35
Hill End, Orp. CN55 88
Hill Farm Av., Wat. BC20 17
Hill Farm Clo., Wat. BC20 17
Hill Farm La., Ch.St.G. AQ26 34
Hill Farm Rd. W10 BQ39 55
Hill Farm Rd., Chesh. AO20 16
Hill Farm Rd., Uxb. BA35 44
Hill Gdns., Wey. AV56 91
Hill Gro., Rom. CT31 50
Hill House Av., Stan. BH29 36
Hill House Clo. N21 BY26 38
Hill House Clo., Ger.Cr. AS29 34
Rickmansworth La.
Hill House Dr., Reig. BS71 121
Hill House Rd. SW16 BX49 76
Hill La., Ruis. BA33 44
Hill La., Tad. BR64 103
Hill Ley, Hat. BO12 10
Bishops Ri.
Hill Leys, Cuff. BX17 20
Homewood Av.
Hill Path SW16 BX49 76
Hill Rd. N10 BU30 38
Hill Rd. NW8 BT38 1
Hill Rd. NW8 BT38 56
Hill Rd., Amer. AO22 25
Hill Rd., Brwd. DA27 42
Hill Rd., Cars. BU57 95
Hill Rd., Dart. CW48 80
Hill Rd., Epp. CN22 31
Hill Rd., Har. BJ32 45
Hill Rd., Hem.H. AV14 7
Hill Rd., Lthd. BF64 102
Hill Rd., Mitch. BV51 86
Hill Rd., Nthwd. BA29 35
Hill Rd., Pnr. BE32 45
Hill Rd., Pur. BX59 95
Hill Rd., Sutt. BS56 95
Hill Rd., Wem. BJ34 45
Hill Ri. Cres., Ger.Cr. AS30 34
Hill Ri. N9 CB25 30
Hill Ri. NW11 BS31 47
Hill Ri. SE23 CB47 77
Hill Ri., Cuff. BW17 20
Hill Ri., Dart. CY49 80
Hill Ri., Dor. BJ70 119
Hill Ri., Esher BJ55 84
Hill Ri., Ger.Cr. AR30 34
Hill Ri., Grnf. BG36 54
Hill Ri., Pot.B. BT20 20
Hill Ri., Rich. BK46 74
Hill Ri., Rick. AW26 35
Hill Ri., Ruis. BA33 44
Hill Ri., Slou. AT43 62
Hill Ri., Upmin. CX34 51
Hill Ri., Walt. BB54 83
Hill Side Rd., Sev. CV65 108
Hill Side, Surb. BK54 84
Hill St. W1 BV40 3
Hill St. W1 BV40 56
Hill St., Rich. BK46 74
Hill St., St.Alb. BG13 9
Hill Ter., Wat. BB19 17
Hill Top Clo., Berk. AR13 7
Hill Top Clo., Guil. AP68 109
Hill Top Clo., Loug. CL24 31
Hill Top NW11 BS31 47
Hill Top Rd., Berk. AR13 7
Hill Top Vw., Chig. CK29 40
Hill Top, Loug. CL24 31
Hill View Clo., Pnr. BE29 36
Hill View Clo., Tad. BQ64 103
Shelvers Way
Hill View Cres., Guil. AP69 118
Hill View Cres., Ilf. CK32 49
Hill View Cres., Orp. CN54 88
Hill View Dr., Well. CN44 68
Hill View Gdns. NW9 BN32 46
Hill View Rd. NW7 BQ28 37
Hill View Rd., Esher BJ57 93
Hill View Rd., Orp. CN54 88
Hill View Rd., Pnr. BE29 36
Hill View Rd., Stai. AR46 72
Hill View Rd., Twick. BJ46 74
Hill View Rd., Wok. AS62 100
Hill Vw., Wok. AS62 100
Hill View Rd.
Hill Waye, Ger.Cr. AS32 43
Hill, The, Cat. CA65 105
Hill, The, Grav. DE46 81
Hill, The, Harl. CP 9 6
Hillars Heath Rd., Couls. BX61 104
Hillary Av., Grav. DF48 81
Hillary Cres., Walt. BD54 84
Hillary Rd., Hem.H. AZ13 8
Hillary Rd., Sthl. BF41 64
Hillary Ri., Barn. BS24 29
Hillbeck Clo. SE15 CC43 67
Hillbeck Way, Grnf. BG37 54
Hillborne Clo., Hayes BC42 63
Hillborough Av., Sev. CV64 108
Hillborough Clo. SW19 BT50 76
Hillbrook Rd. SW17 BU48 76
Hillbrow Clo., Bex. CS49 79
Hillbrow Ct., Gdse. CC69 114
Hickmans Clo.
Hillbrow Rd., Brom. CG50 78
Hillbrow Rd., Esher BG56 93
Hillbrow, N.Mal. BO52 85
Hillbury Av., Har. BJ32 45
Hillbury Clo., Warl. CC62 105
Hillbury Rd. SW17 BV48 76
Hillbury Rd., Whyt. CB62 105
Hillbury, Hat. BO13 10
Hillcote Av. SW16 BY50 76
Hillcourt Av. N12 BS29 38
Hillcourt Est. N16 BZ33 48
Hillcourt Rd. SE22 CB46 77
Hillcrest Av. NW11 BR32 46
Hillcrest Av., Cher. AV55 82
Hillcrest Av., Edg. BM28 37
Hillcrest Av., Grays DA43 70
Hillcrest Av., Pnr. BD31 45
Hillcrest Clo. SE26 CB49 77
Hillcrest Clo., Beck. CD53 87
Hillcrest Clo., Epsom BO61 103
Treadwell Rd.
Hillcrest Gdns. NW2 BP34 46
Hillcrest Gdns., Esher BH55 84
Hillcrest Gdns., Ruis. BD34 45
Hillcrest N21 BY26 38
Hillcrest N6 BV33 47
Hillcrest Rd. E17 CF30 39
Hillcrest Rd. E18 CG30 40
Hillcrest Rd. W3 BM40 55
Hillcrest Rd. W5 BL39 55
Hillcrest Rd., Brom. CH49 78
Hillcrest Rd., Dart. CT47 79
Hillcrest Rd., Epp. CT18 23
Hillcrest Rd., Guil. AP70 118
Hillcrest Rd., Horn. CU33 50
Hillcrest Rd., Loug. CJ25 31
Hillcrest Rd., Orp. CO55 89
Hillcrest Rd., Pur. BX58 95
Hillcrest Rd., Rad. BM20 19
Hillcrest Rd., West. CJ61 106
Hillcrest Rd., Whyt. CA62 105
Hillcrest Vw., Beck. CD53 87
Hillcrest Way, Epp. CO19 23
Bower Hill
Hillcrest Waye, Ger.Cr. AS32 43
Hillcrest, Hat. BO12 10
Hillcrest, St.Alb. BF14 9
Hillcrest, Wey. AZ56 92
Hillcroft Av., Pnr. BE32 45
Hillcroft Av., Pur. BW60 95
Hillcroft Cres. W5 BK39 54
Hillcroft Cres., Ruis. BD34 45
Hillcroft Cres., Wat. BC26 35
Hillcroft Cres., Wem. BL35 46
Hillcroft Rd. E6 CL39 58
Hillcroft Rd., Chesh. AO18 16
Hillcroft, Loug. CL23 31
Hillcroome Rd., Sutt. BT57 95
Hillcross Av., Mord. BQ53 85
Hilldale Rd., Sutt. BR56 94
Hilldene Av., Rom. CV29 42
Hilldene Clo., Rom. CV28 42
Hilldene Av.
Hilldown Rd. SW16 BX50 76
Hilldown Rd., Brom. CG54 88
Hilldown Rd., Hem.H. AW12 8
Hilldrop Cres. N7 BW35 47
Hilldrop Est. N7 BW35 47
Hilldrop La. N7 BW35 47
Hilldrop Rd. N7 BW35 47
Hilldrop Rd., Brom. CH50 78
Hillend SE18 CL44 68
Hillerdon Av., Edg. BL28 37
Hillers Av., Uxb. AZ38 53
Hillersdon Av. SW13 BP44 65
Hillersdon, Slou. AQ39 52
Hillery Clo. SE17 BZ42 4
Hillery Clo. SE17 BZ42 67
Catesby St.
Hilley Field La., Lthd. BG64 102
Hillfarm Rd., Ger.Cr. AS29 34
Hillfield Av. N8 BX32 47
Hillfield Av. NW9 BO32 46
Hillfield Av., Mitch. BU53 86
Hillfield Av., Wem. BL36 55
Hillfield Clo., Guil. AU69 118
Hillfield Clo., Har. BG31 45
Hillfield Clo., Red. BV70 121
Hillfield Ct. NW3 BU35 47
Belsize Av.
Hillfield Ct., Esher BF56 93
Hillfield Pk. Ms. N10 BV31 47
Hillfield Pk.
Hillfield Pk. N10 BV31 47
Hillfield Pk. N21 BY27 38
Hillfield Rd. NW6 BR35 46
Hillfield Rd., Ger.Cr. AS29 34
Hillfield Rd., Hem.H. AX13 8
Hillfield Rd., Hmptn. BE50 74
Hillfield Rd., Red. BV70 121
Hillfield Rd., Sev. CT63 107
Hillfield Sq., Ger.Cr. AS29 34
Hillfield, Hat. BQ11 10
Hillfoot Av., Rom. CS30 41
Hillfoot Rd., Rom. CS30 41
Hillford Pl., Red. BV73 121
Hillgate Pl. W8 BS40 56
Hillgate St. W8 BS40 56
Hillgay Clo., Guil. AS70 118
Hillgay Ct., Guil. AS70 118
Hillgrove, Ger.Cr. AS30 34
Hillhouse La., Wey. AZ58 92
Hillhouse Rd., Dart. CY47 80
Hillhouse, Wal.Abb. CG20 22
Hillhurst Gdns., Cat. CA63 105
Hilliard Rd., Nthwd. BB30 35
Hilliards Ct. E1 CC40 57
Hilliards Rd., Uxb. AX39 53
Hillier Clo., Barn. BS25 29
Hillier Rd. SW11 BU46 76
Hillier Rd., Guil. AT70 118
Hilliers La., Croy. BX55 86
Hillingdale, West. CH62 106
Hillingdon Av., Sev. CV64 108
Hillingdon Av., Stai. AY47 73
Hillingdon Cir., Uxb. AZ36 53
Hillingdon Hill, Uxb. AY37 53
Hillingdon Rd., Bexh. CS44 69
Hillingdon Rd., Grav. DG48 81
Hillingdon Rd., Uxb. AX37 53
Hillingdon Rd., Wat. BC20 17
Hillingdon Ri., Sev. CV64 108
Hillingdon St. SE17 BY43 66
Hillington Gdns., Wdf.Grn. CJ30 40
Hillman Clo., Horn. CV31 51
Stafford Av.
Hillman Clo., Uxb. AY35 44
Hillman St. E8 CB36 57
Hillmarton Rd. N7 BX35 47
Hillmay Dr., Hem.H. AW14 8
Hillmead Dr. SW9 BY45 66
Hillmead, Berk. AQ13 7
Hillmont Rd., Esher BH55 84
Hillmore Gro. SE26 CC49 77
Hillreach SE18 CK42 68
Hillrise Av., Wat. BD22 27
Hillrise Est. N19 BX33 47
Hillrise Rd.
Hillrise Rd. N19 BX33 47
Hillrise Rd., Rom. CS29 41
Hills Chace, Brwd. DB28 42
Hills La., Nthwd. BB30 35
Hills Pl. W1 BW39 1
Hills Pl. W1 BW39 56
Ramillies Pl.
Hills Rd., Buck.H. CH26 40
Hillsborough Grn., Wat. BC27 35
Ashburnham Dr.
Hillsborough Rd. SE22 CA46 77
Hillside Av. N11 BU29 38
Hillside Av., B.Wd. BM24 28
Hillside Av., Chsnt. CC19 21
Hillside Av., Grav. DH48 81
Hillside Av., Pur. BY60 95
Hillside Av., Wdf.Grn. CJ28 40
Hillside Av., Wem. BL35 46
Hillside Clo. NW8 BT37 56
Carlton Hill
Hillside Clo., Bans. BR61 103
Hillside Clo., Bet. BM71 120
Hillside Clo., Ch.St.G. AQ27 34
Hillside Clo., Ger.Cr. AS29 34
Hillside Clo., Mord. BR52 85
Hillside Clo., Wat. BB19 17
Hillside Clo., Wdf.Grn. CJ28 40
Hillside Clo., Wok. AO62 100
Hillside Cres., Chsnt. CC19 21
Hillside Cres., Enf. BZ22 30
Hillside Cres., Har. BG33 45
Hillside Cres., Nthwd. BC30 35
Hillside Cres., Wat. BD25 27
Hillside Ct. NW4 BQ30 37
Hillside Ct., St.Alb. BH13 9
Hillside Rd.
Hillside Dr., Edg. BM28 37
Hillside Dr., Grav. DH48 81
Hillside Est. N15 CA32 48
Hillside Gdns. E17 CF31 48
Hillside Gdns. Est. SW2 BY48 76
Hillside Gdns. N1 BW29 38
Hillside Gdns. N6 BV32 47
Hillside Gdns., Barn. BR25 28
Hillside Gdns., Berk. AR13 7
Hillside Gdns., Bet. BM70 120
Hillside Gdns., Edg. BL28 37
Hillside Gdns., Har. BL33 46
Hillside Gdns., Nthwd. BC29 35
Hillside Gdns., Wall. BW57 95
Hillside Gdns., Wey. AV56 91
Hillside Gro. N14 BW26 38
Hillside Gro. NW7 BP29 37
Hillside La., Brom. CG55 88
Hillside NW10 BN37 55
Hillside NW9 BN31 46
Hillside Rd. N15 CA33 48
Hillside Rd. W5 BL39 55
Hillside Rd., Ash. BL62 103
Hillside Rd., Brom. CG52 88
Hillside Rd., Bush. BE25 27
Hillside Rd., Couls. BX62 104
Hillside Rd., Croy. BY56 95
Hillside Rd., Dart. CT46 79
Hillside Rd., Epsom BQ58 94
Hillside Rd., Nthwd. BC29 35
Hillside Rd., Rad. BJ21 27
Hillside Rd., Rick. AU25 25
Hillside Rd., Sev. CV65 108
Hillside Rd., St.Alb. BH13 9
Hillside Rd., Sthl. BE38 54
Hillside Rd., Surb. BM52 85
Hillside Rd., Sutt. BR57 94
Hillside Rd., West. CK63 106
Hillside Rd., Whyt. CB62 105
Hillside Ri., Nthwd. BC29 35
Hillside SW19 BQ50 75
Hillside SW2 BX49 76
Hillside Wk., Brwd. CZ27 42
Hillside, Bans. BR61 103
Hillside, Barn. BT25 29
Hillside, Dart. CY49 80
Hillside, Erith CS42 69
Hillside, Farn. CW54 90
Hillside, Grays DE42 71
Hillside, Harl. CP12 14
Hillside, Hat. BP12 10
Hillside, Hodd. CD11 12
Hillside, Slou. AP41 62
Hillside, Slou. AR41 62
Hillside, The, Orp. CO58 98
Hillside, Uxb. AX32 44
Hillside, Vir.W. AR53 82
Hillside, Welw.G.C. BS 9 5
Hillside, Wok. AR63 100
Hillsleigh Rd. W8 BR40 55
Hillsmead Way, S.Croy. CB60 96
Hillspur Clo., Guil. AP70 118
Hillspur Rd., Guil. AP70 118
Hillstowe St. E5 CC34 48
Hilltop Clo., Chsnt. CA16 21
Hilltop Clo., Loug. CL24 31
Hilltop Clo., Lthd. BK65 102
Hilltop Gdns. NW4 BP30 37
Hilltop Gdns., Dart. CW46 80
Hilltop Gdns., Orp. CN55 88
Hilltop La., Cat. BY66 113
Hilltop Rd. NW6 BS36 56
Hilltop Rd., Grays DA43 70
Hilltop Rd., Kings L. BA17 17
Hilltop Rd., Reig. BS71 121
Hilltop Rd., Whyt. CA62 105
Hilltop Ri., Lthd. BG66 111
Hilltop Way, Stan. BJ27 36
Hilltop, Loug. CL24 31
Hilltop, Mord. BS53 86
Hilltop, Sutt. BR54 85
Hillview Av., Har. BL32 46
Hillview Av., Horn. CV32 51
Hillview Clo., Pur. BY59 95
Hillview Dr., Red. BV71 121
Hillview Gdns. NW4 BQ31 46
Hillview Gdns., Chsnt. CD17 21
Hillview Gdns., Har. BF31 45
Hillview Rd., Chis. CL49 78
Hillview Rd., Sutt. BT55 86
Hillview SW20 BP50 75
Heights Clo.
Hillview, Whyt. CB62 105
Hillway NW6 BV34 47
Hillway NW9 BO33 46
Hillwood Clo., Brwd. DD26 122
Hillwood Gro., Brwd. DD26 122
Hillworth Rd. SW2 BY47 76
Hilly Field, Harl. CO13 14
Hilly Fields Cres. SE4 CE45 67
Hillyard Rd. W7 BH39 54
Hillyard St. SW9 BX44 66
Hillydeal Rd., Sev. CV61 108
Hillyfields E17 CD30 39
Hillyfields Est., Loug. CL23 31
Hillyfields, Loug. CL23 31
Hillyfields, Welw.G.C. BT 7 5
Hilperton Rd., Slou. AP41 62
Burlington Av.
Hilsea St. E5 CC35 48
Hilton Av. N12 BT28 38
Hilton Clo., Uxb. AW37 53
Hilton Way, S.Croy. CB61 105
Hilversum Cres. SE22 CA46 77
Dulwich Gro.
Himley Rd. SW17 BU49 76
Hinchcliffe Clo., Wall. BX57 95
Hinchley Clo., Esher BH55 84
Hinchley Dr., Esher BH55 84
Hinchley Way, Esher BJ55 84
Hinckley Rd. SE15 CB45 67
Hind Clo., Chig. CN28 40
Hind Cres., Erith CS43 69
Hind Ct. EC4 BY39 2
Hind Ct. EC4 BY39 56
Gough Sq.
Hind Gro. E14 CE39 57
Hinde St. W1 BV39 1
Hinde St. W1 BV39 56
Hindes Rd., Har. BG32 45
Hindhead Clo. N16 CA33 48
Hindhead Clo., Uxb. AZ38 53
Aldenham Dr.
Hindhead Gdns., Nthlt. BE37 54
Hindhead Grn., Wat. BD28 36
Hindhead Way, Wall. BX56 95
Hindman Way, Dag. CQ38 59
Hindmans Rd. SE22 CB46 77
Hindmarsh Clo. E1 CB40 57
Cable St.
Hindrey Rd. E5 CB35 48
Hindrey Road Est. E5 CB35 48
Pembury Rd.
Hindsley Pl. SE23 CC48 77
Hinkler Clo., Wall. BX57 95
Hinkler Rd., Har. BK31 45
Hinkley Clo., Uxb. AX31 44
Hinksey Clo., Slou. AT41 62
Hinksey Path SE2 CP41 69
Hinstock Rd. SE18 CM43 68
Hinton Av., Houns. BD45 64
Hinton Clo. SE9 CK47 78
Hinton Rd. N18 CA28 39
Hinton Rd. SE24 BZ45 67
Hinton Rd., Uxb. AX37 53
Hinton Rd., Wall. BW57 95
Hintons, Harl. CL13 13
Hipley St., Wok. AT63 100
Hippodrome Pl. W11 BR40 55
Portland Rd.
Hiroshima Wk. SE7 CH41 68
Hitcham Rd. E17 CD33 48
Hitchcock Clo., Shep. AY52 83
Studios Rd.
Hitchen Hatch La., Sev. CU65 107
Hitchens Clo., Hem.H. AV13 7
Hitchin Clo., Rom. CV28 42
Hitchin Sq. E3 CD37 57
Hitchings Way, Reig. BS72 121
Hither Green La. SE13 CF46 77
Hither Meadow, Ger.Cr. AS30 34
Hither Way, Welw.G.C. BQ 6 5
Hither Wood Dr. SE19 CA49 77
Hitherbaulk, Welw.G.C. BR 9 5
Hitherbroom Rd., Hayes BC40 53
Hitherbury Clo., Guil. AR72 118
Hitherfield Rd. SW16 BX48 76
Hitherfield Rd., Dag. CQ34 50
Hithermoor Rd., Stai. AV46 72
Hitherwell Dr., Har. BG30 36
Hitherwood Clo., Horn. CV35 51
Swanbourne Dr.
Hitherwood Clo., Reig. BU69 121
Hive Clo., Bush. BG27 36
Hive La., Grav. DD46 81
Hive Rd., Bush. BG27 36
Hixberry La., St.Alb. BL14 10
Hoadly Rd. SW16 BW48 76
Hobart Clo. N20 BU27 38
Hobart Gdns., Th.Hth. BZ52 87
Hobart Pl. SW1 BV41 3
Hobart Pl. SW1 BV41 66
Belgrave St.
Hobart Pl., Rich. BL47 75
Chisholm Rd.
Hobart Rd., Dag. CP35 50
Hobart Rd., Hayes BD38 54
Hobart Rd., Ilf. CM30 40
Hobart Rd., Til. DF44 71
Hobart Rd., Wor.Pk. BP55 85
Hobart Wk., St.Alb. BH11 9
Hobarts Dr., Uxb. AV32 43
Queen Mothers Dr.
Hobbayne Rd. W7 BG39 54
Hobbes Wk. SW15 BP46 75
Sunnymead Rd.
Hobbs Clo., Chsnt. CC18 21
Hobbs Clo., St.Alb. BL13 10
Hobbs Clo., Wey. AW60 92
Hobbs Cross Rd., Epp. CP21 32
Hobbs Cross Rd., Harl. CQ 9 6
Hobbs Grn. N2 BT31 47
Hobbs Rd. SE27 BZ49 77
Hobbs Way, Welw.G.C. BQ 8 5
Hobbshill Rd., Hem.H. AY15 8
Hobday St. E14 CE39 57
Hobhouse Ct. SW1 BW40 56
Suffolk St.
Hobill Wk., Surb. BL53 85
Hoblands End, Chis. CN50 78
Hobletts Rd., Hem.H. AY13 8
Hobsons Clo., Hodd. CD10 12
Hobtoe Rd., Harl. CL10 6
Hobury St. SW10 BT43 66
Hockenden La., Swan. CR52 89
Hocker St. E2 CA38 2
Hocker St. E2 CA38 57
Arnold Circus
Hockering Clo., Wok. AT62 100
Hockering Gdns., Wok. AT62 100
Hockering Rd., Wok. AT62 100
Hockett Clo. SE8 CD42 67
Hocklands, Welw.G.C. BT 7 5
Hockley Av. E6 CK37 58
Hockley Dr., Rom. CU30 41
Hockley La., Slou. AQ36 52
Hocroft Av. NW2 BR34 46
Hocroft Rd. NW2 BR35 46
Hodder Dr., Grnf. BH37 54
Hoddesdon By-pass, Brox. CC14 12
Hoddesdon Rd., Belv. CR42 69
Hodds Wood Rd., Chesh. AO20 16
Hodford Rd. NW11 BR33 46
Hodgkin Clo. SE28 CP40 59
Fleming Way
Hodgson Gdns., Guil. AS69 118
Hodings Rd., Harl. CL10 6
Hodister Clo. SE5 BZ43 67
Comber Gro.
Hodnet Gro. SE16 CC42 67
Suffolk Gro.
Hodsoll Ct., Orp. CP53 89
Hodson Clo., Har. BE34 45
Hodson Cres., Orp. CP53 89
Hoe Cft., Wal.Abb. CG14 13
Hoe La., Enf. CB22 30
Hoe La., Rom. CO24 32
Hoe La., Wal.Abb. CG14 13
Hoe St. E17 CE31 48
Hoe, The, Wat. BD27 36
Hoestock Rd., Saw. CP 6 6
Hofland Rd. W14 BR41 65
Hog Hill Rd., Rom. CQ29 41
Hog La., Chesh. AO14 7
Hogan Ms. W2 BT39 1
Hogarth Av., Ashf. BA50 73
Hogarth Av., Brwd. DC27 122
Hogarth Clo. E16 CJ39 58
Hogarth Clo. W5 BL39 55
Hillcrest Rd.
Hogarth Cres. SW19 BT51 86
Hogarth Cres., Croy. BZ54 87
Hogarth Ct. EC3 CA40 4
Fenchurch St.
Hogarth Ct. EC3 CA40 57
Fenchurch St.
Hogarth Ct. SE19 CA49 77
Fountain Dr.
Hogarth Ct., Bush. BF26 36
Steeplands
Hogarth Est. W4 BO42 65
Hogarth Gdns., Houns. BF43 64
Hogarth Hill NW11 BR31 46
Hogarth La. W4 BO43 65
Hogarth Pl. SW5 BS42 66
Hogarth Rd.
Hogarth Rd. SW5 BS42 66
Hogarth Rd., Edg. BM30 37
Hogarth Reach, Loug. CK25 31
Hogarth Way, Hmptn. BG51 84
Hogarths Rd., Grays DD40 71
Hogden Clo., Tad. BR66 112
Hogden La., Dor. BE70 119
Hogden La., Dor. BF68 111
Hogg End La., Hem.H. & St.Alb. BB12 8
Hogg La., B.Wd. BJ24 27
Hogg La., Grays DD41 71
Hogpits Bottom, Hem.H. AT19 16
Hogs Back, Guil. AO72 118
Hogscross La., Couls. BU65 104
Hogsden Clo. N1 BZ37 57
Forston St.
Hogshead Pass. E1 CB40 57
Pennington St.
Hogshill La., Cob. BC60 92
Hogsmill Way, Epsom BN56 94
Hogtrough Hill, West. CN64 106
Hogtrough La., Oxt. CE67 114
Hogtrough La., Red. BW71 121
Holbeach Gdns., Sid. CN46 78
Holbeach Ms. SW12 BV47 76
Harberson Rd.
Holbeach Rd. SE6 CE47 77
Holbeck La., Chsnt. CA16 21

Holbeck Row SE15 CB43 67
Holbein Ms. SW1 BV42 3
Holbein Ms. SW1 BV42 66
Holbein Pl. SW1 BV42 3
Holbein Pl. SW1 BV42 66
Holberton Gdns. NW10 BP38 55
Holborn Cir. EC1 BY39 2
Holborn Cir. EC1 BY39 56
Holborn Clo., St.Alb. BK11 9
Holborn EC1 BY39 2
Holborn EC1 BY39 56
Holborn Rd. E13 CH38 58
Holborn Viaduct EC1 BY39 2
Holborn Viaduct EC1 BY39 56
Holbrook Clo. N19 BV33 47
Dartmouth Park Hill
Holbrook Clo., Enf. CA23 30
Holbrook La., Chis. CM50 78
Holbrook Rd. E15 CG37 58
Holbrook Way, Brom. CK53 88
Holbrooke Ct. N7 BX35 47
Holbrooke Pl., Rich. BK46 74
Hill Ri.
Holburne Clo. SE3 CJ44 68
Holburne Gdns. SE3 CJ44 68
Holburne Rd. SE3 CJ44 68
Holcombe Dale NW7 BP27 37
Holcombe Hill NW7 BP27 37
Holcombe Rd. N17 CA31 48
Holcombe Rd., Ilf. CL33 49
Holcombe St. W6 BP42 65
Holcon Ct., Red. BV69 121
Holcote Clo., Belv. CQ41 69
Blakemore Way
Holcroft Rd. E9 CC36 57
Holdbrook N., Wal.Cr. CD20 21
Holdbrook S., Wal.Cr. CD20 21
Holdbrook Way, Rom. CW30 42
Gubbins La.
Holdbrook, Wal.Cr. CD20 21
Holden Av. N12 BS28 38
Holden Av. NW9 BN33 46
Holden Gdns., Brwd. DB28 42
Holden Rd. N12 BS28 38
Holden Rd., Dag. CO34 50
Holden St. SW11 BV44 66
Holden Way, Upmin. CY33 51
Holdenby Rd. SE4 CD46 77
Holdenhurst Av. N12 BT29 38
Holderness Way SE27 BY49 76
Holdernesse Rd. SW17 BU48 76
Holders Hill Av. NW4 BQ30 37
Holders Hill Cir. NW4 BR29 37
Holders Hill Cres. NW4 BQ30 37
Holders Hill Dr. NW4 BQ31 46
Holders Hill Gdns. NW4 BR30 37
Holders Hill Rd. NW4 BQ30 37
Holdgate St. SE7 CJ41 68
Westmoor St.
Holdings, The, Hat. BQ11 10
Hole Cft., Wal.Abb. CG20 22
Roundhills
Hole Farm La., Brwd. DA30 42
Holehill La., Dor. BF71 119
Holford Pl. WC1 BY38 2
Holford Pl. WC1 BY38 56
Holford Rd. NW3 BT34 47
Hampstead Sq.
Holford Rd., Guil. AU70 118
Holford Rd., S.le H. DH42 71
Holford St. WC1 BY38 2
Holford St. WC1 BY38 56
Holgate Av. SW11 BT45 66
Holgate Ct., Edg. BL28 37
Holgate Gdns., Dag. CR35 50
Holgate Rd., Dag. CR35 50
Holland Av. SW20 BO51 85
Holland Av., Sutt. BS57 95
Holland Clo., Barn. BT26 38
Holland Clo., Brom. CG55 88
Holland Clo., Red. BU70 121
Holland Clo., Stan. BJ28 36
Holland Cres., Oxt. CH70 115
Holland Dr. SE23 CD48 77
Queenswood Rd.
Holland Gdns. W14 BR41 65
Holland Gdns., Egh. AV51 82
Holland Gdns., Wat. BD21 27
Holland Gro. SW9 BY43 66
Holland Gro., Barn. BT25 29
Holland La. W14 BR41 65
Holland La., Oxt. CH70 115
Holland Pass. N1 BZ37 57
Basire St.
Holland Pk. Av. W11 BR40 55
Holland Pk. Av., Ilf. CN32 49
Holland Pk. Gdns. W14 BR41 65
Holland Pk. Ms. W11 BR40 55
Holland Pk. Rd. W14 BR41 65
Holland Pk. W11 BR40 55
Holland Rd. E15 CG38 58
Holland Rd. E6 CK37 58
Holland Rd. NW10 BP37 55
Holland Rd. SE25 CB53 87
Holland Rd. W14 BQ41 65
Holland Rd., Oxt. CH70 115
Holland Rd., Wem. BK36 54
Holland St. SE1 BY40 4
Holland St. SE1 BY40 56
Holland St. W8 BS41 66
Holland Villas Rd. W14 BR41 65
Holland Way, Brom. CG55 88
Holland Wk. N19 BW33 47
Holland Wk. W8 BS41 66
Holland Wk., Stan. BJ28 36
Hollands, The, Wor.Pk. BO54 85
Hollar Rd. N16 CA34 48
Stoke Newington High St.
Hollen St. W1 BW39 1
Hollen St. W1 BW39 56
Wardour St.
Holles Clo., Hmptn. BF49 74
Holles St. W1 BV39 1
Holles St. W1 BV39 56
Cavendish Sq.
Holley Rd. W12 BO41 65
Hollickwood Av. N12 BU29 38
Holliday St., Berk. AR13 7
Hollidge Way, Dag. CR36 59
Hollier Ct., Hat. BP12 10
Holliers Way, Hat. BP12 10
Hollies Av., Sid. CN48 78
Hollies Av., Wey. AV60 91
Hollies Clo. SW16 BY50 76
Hollies Clo., Twick. BH48 74
Hollies Ct., Wey. AX56 92
Hollies End NW7 BP28 37
Hollies Rd. W5 BK42 64
Hollies St. W1 BV39 56
Cavendish Sq.
Hollies Way SW12 BV47 76
Bracken Av.
Hollies Way, Pot.B. BT19 20
Hollies, The, Grav. DH50 81
Hollies, The, Hem.H. AT18 16
Hollies, The, Ilf. CH32 49
New Wanstead
Holligrave Rd., Brom. CH51 88
Hollingbourne Av., Bexh. CQ44 69
Hollingbourne Gdns. W13 BJ39 54
Hollingbourne Rd. SE24 BZ46 77
Hollingsworth Rd., Croy. CB57 96
Hollingsworth St. N7 BX35 47
Hollington Cres., N.Mal. BO53 85
Hollington Rd. E6 CK38 58
Hollington Rd. N17 CB30 39
Sherringham Av.
Hollingworth Rd., Brom. CL53 88
Hollingworth Way, West. CM66 115
Quebec Av.
Hollis Pl., Grays DD42 71
Hollman Gdns. SW16 BY50 76
Hollow Cotts., Grays CX42 70
Hollow Hill La., Iver AT40 52
Hollow La., Dor. BD73 119
Hollow La., Vir.W. AR52 82
Hollow Way La., Amer. AP21 25
Hollow, The, Wdf.Grn. CG28 40
Holloway Arc. N7 BX34 47
Holloway Rd.
Holloway Clo., West Dr. AY42 63
Holloway Hill, Cher. AU55 82
Holloway La., Rick. AU22 25
Holloway La., West Dr. AY43 63
Holloway Rd. E11 CF34 48
Holloway Rd. E6 CK38 58
Holloway Rd. N19 BW34 47
Holloway Rd. N7 BX34 47
Holloway Rd. SW11 BT45 66
Holloway St., Houns. BF45 64
Holloways La., Hat. BQ15 10
Hollowfield Av., Grays DE42 71
Hollowfield Wk., Nthlt. BE36 54
Hollows, The, Brent. BL43 65
Holly Av., Stan. BL30 37
Holly Av., Walt. BD54 84
Holly Av., Wey. AW58 92
Holly Bank Rd., Wok. AQ64 100
Holly Bush Clo., Sev. CV65 108
Holly Bush Hill NW3 BT35 47
Holly Bush Hill, Berk. AU11 7
Holly Bush La., Hmptn. BE50 74
Holly Bush La., Sev. CV65 108
Holly Bush Vale NW3 BT35 47
Heath St.
Holly Bush Wk. SW9 BY45 66
Holly Clo. NW10 BO36 55
Holly Clo., Buck.H. CJ27 40
Holly Clo., Cher. AQ55 82
Holly Clo., Egh. AQ50 72
Holly Clo., Felt. BE49 74
Holly Clo., Hat. BO13 10
Holly Clo., Wok. AQ63 100
Holly Cres., Beck. CD53 87
Holly Cres., Wdf.Grn. CF29 39
Holly Cres., Wind. AL44 61
Holly Dr. E4 CE26 39
Holly Dr., Berk. AR13 7
Holly Dr., Pot.B. BS20 20
Holly Dr., Wind. AP46 72
Holly Field, Harl. CM12 13
Holly Gdns. West D. AY41 63
Holly Grn., Wey. BA56 92
Holly Gro. NW9 BN33 46
Holly Gro. SE15 CA44 67
Holly Gro., Bush. BG26 36
Holly Hedges La., Hem.H. AU18 16
Holly Hill Dr., Bans. BS61 104
Holly Hill N21 BX25 29
Holly Hill NW3 BT35 47
Holly Hill Rd., Belv. CR42 69
Holly La. E., Bans. BS61 104
Holly La. W., Bans. BS62 104
Holly La., Bans. BS61 104
Holly La., Guil. AO68 109
Holly Lea, Guil. AR67 109
Holly Ms. SW10 BT42 66
Drayton Gdns.
Holly Mt. NW3 BT35 47
Holly Bush Hill
Holly Park Gdns. N3 BS31 47
Holly Park Rd. N11 BV28 38
Holly Park Rd. W7 BH40 54
Holly Pk. N3 BR31 46
Holly Pk. N4 BX33 47
Holly Rd. E11 CG33 49
Holly Rd., Dart. CV47 80
Holly Rd., Enf. CC21 30
Holly Rd., Hmptn. BG50 74
Holly Rd., Houns. BF45 64
Holly Rd., Orp. CO57 98
Holly Rd., Reig. BS71 121
Holly Rd., Twick. BH47 74
Holly St. E1 CB39 57
Holly St. E8 CA36 57
Holly Street Est. E8 CA36 57
Holly Ter. N20 BT27 38
Holly Tree Clo., Chesh. AQ19 16
Holly Way, Mitch. BW52 86
Holly Wk. NW3 BT35 47
Holly Wk., Enf. BZ24 30
Holly Wk., Welw.G.C. BQ 6 5
Hollybank Clo., Hmptn. BF49 74
Hollybank Rd., Wey. AW60 92
Hollyberry La. NW3 BT35 47
Holly Wk.
Hollyberry, Hem.H. AU19 16
Hollybrake Clo., Chis. CM50 78
Hollybush Av., St.Alb. BF15 9
Hollybush Clo. E11 CH32 49
Woodford Rd.
Hollybush Clo., Berk. AU11 7
Hollybush Clo., Har. BH30 36
Hollybush Clo., Wat. BD26 36
Hollybush Gdns. E2 CB38 57
Hollybush Hill E11 CG33 49
Hollybush Hill, Slou. AQ36 52
Hollybush La., Welw.G.C. BR10 5
Hollybush La., Amer. AO21 25
Hollybush La., Hem.H. AV12 7
Hollybush La., Iver AT39 52
Hollybush La., Orp. CR57 98
Hollybush La., Uxb. AU34 43
Hollybush Rd., Wok. AX63 101
Hollybush Pl. E2 CB38 57
Bethnal Green Rd.
Hollybush Rd., Grav. DH48 81
Hollybush Rd., Kings.T. BL49 75
Hollybush St. E13 CH37 58
Hollybush Wk. SW9 BY45 66
Somerleyton Rd. Dev.
Hollycombe, Egh. AR49 72
Hollycroft Av. NW3 BS34 47
Hollycroft Av., Wem. BL34 46
Hollycroft Clo., West Dr. AZ43 63
Hollycroft Gdns., West Dr. AZ43 63
Hollydale Dr., Brom. CK55 88
Hollydale Rd. SE15 CC44 67
Hollydene SE15 CB44 67
Hollydown Way E11 CF34 48
Hollyfield Av. N11 BU28 38
Hollyfield Rd., Surb. BL54 85
Hollyfield, Hat. BP14 10
Hollyfields, Brox. CD16 21
Hollyhedge Rd., Cob. BC60 92
Hollyhedge Ter. SE13 CF46 77
Dermody Rd.
Hollylodge Gdns. N6 BV33 47
Hollymead Rd., Couls. BV62 104
Hollymead, Cars. BU56 95
Hollymeoak Rd., Couls. BV62 104
Hollymoor La., Epsom BN58 94
Hollymount Clo. SE10 CF44 67
Hollymount Rd. SE10 CF44 67
Blackheath Hill
Hollytree Av., Swan. CT51 89
Hollytree Clo. SW19 BQ47 75
Hollytree Clo., Ger.Cr. AS28 34
Hollytree, Ger.Cr. AS28 34
Monument La.
Hollywood Gdns., Hayes BC39 53
Hollywood La., Sev. CZ59 99
Hollywood Rd. E4 CD28 39
Hollywood Rd. SW10 BT42 3
Hollywood Rd. SW10 BT43 66
Hollywood Way, Wdf.Grn. CF29 39
Hollywoods, Croy. CD58 96
Holm Clo., Wey. AV59 91
Holm Gro., Uxb. AZ36 53
Holm Oak Clo. SW18 BR46 75
West Hill
Holm Oak Ms. SW4 BX46 76
Kings Av.
Holm Wk. SE3 CH44 68
Blackheath Pk.
Holman Ct., Epsom BP58 94
Holman Hunt Ho. W14 BR42 65
Field Rd.
Holman Rd. SW11 BT44 66
Holman Rd., Epsom BN56 94
Holmbank Dr., Shep. BB52 83
Holmbridge Gdns., Enf. CC24 30
Holmbrook Dr. NW4 BQ32 46
Holmbury Ct. SW17 BU48 76
Holmbury Dr., Dor. BK73 119
Holmbury Gdns., Hayes BB40 53
Holmbury Gro., Croy. CD57 96
Holmbury Pk., Brom. CK50 78
Holmbury Vw. E5 CB33 48
Holmbush Rd. SW15 BR46 75
Holmcote Gdns. N5 BZ35 48
Highbury New Pk.
Holmcroft Way, Brom. CK53 88
Holmcroft, Tad. BP66 112
Holmdale Clo., B.Wd. BL23 28
Holmdale Gdns. NW4 BQ32 46
Holmdale Lodge Ct. W3 BM40 55
Whitehall Gdns.
Holmdale Rd. NW6 BS35 47
Holmdale Rd., Chis. CM49 78
Holmdale Ter. N15 CA33 48
Holmdene Av. NW7 BP29 37
Holmdene Av. SE24 BZ46 77
Holmdene Av., Har. BF31 45
Holmdene Clo., Beck. CF51 87
Holme Chase, Mord. BR53 85
Holme Chase, Wey. BA57 92
Holme Clo., Chsnt. CD19 21
Holme Clo., Hat. BO11 10
Holme Lacey Rd. SE12 CG46 78
Holme Lea, Wat. BD20 18
Holme Pk., B.Wd. BL23 28
Holme Rd. E6 CK37 58
Holme Rd., Hat. BO11 10
Holme Rd., Horn. CX33 51
Holmead Rd. SW6 BS43 66
Holmebury Clo., Bush. BH27 36
Holmecote Gdns. N5 BZ35 48
Holmedale, Slou. AR40 52
Holmes Av. E17 CD31 48
Holmes Av. NW7 BR28 37
Holmes Meadow, Harl. CL14 13
Holmes Rd. NW5 BV36 56
Holmes Rd. SW19 BT50 76
Holmes Rd., Twick. BH48 74
Holmes Ter. SE1 BY41 4
Waterloo Rd.
Holmes Ter. SE1 BY41 66
Waterloo Rd.
Holmes Way, Stan. BH29 36
Holmesdale Av. SW14 BM45 65
Holmesdale Clo. SE25 CA52 87
Holmesdale Clo., Guil. AT70 118
Holmesdale Hill, S.Dnth. CY51 90
Holmesdale Rd. N6 BV32 47
Holmesdale Rd., Bexh. CP44 69
Holmesdale Rd., Croy. BZ53 87
Holmesdale Rd., Dor. BK73 119
Holmesdale Rd., Red. BX71 121
Holmesdale Rd., Reig. BS70 121
Holmesdale Rd., Rich. BL44 65
Holmesdale Rd., S.Dnth. CY51 90
Holmesdale Rd., Tedd. BK50 74
Holmesdale, Wal.Cr. CC21 30
Holmeshaw Clo. SE26 CD49 77
Holmesley Rd. SE23 CD46 77
Holmethorpe Av., Red. BV69 121
Holmewood Gdns. SW2 BX47 76
Holmewood Rd. SE25 CA52 87
Holmewood Rd. SW2 BX47 76
Holmfield Av. NW4 BQ32 46
Holmfield Ct., NW3 BU35 47
Holmhurst Rd., Belv. CR42 69
Holmlea Rd., Slou. AR44 62
Holmlea Wk., Slou. AR44 62
Holmleigh Av., Dart. CV45 70
Holmleigh Rd. N16 CA33 48
Holmsdale Clo., Iver AV40 52
Thorney La. N.
Holmsdale Gro., Bexh. CT44 69
Holmsdale Rd. N11 BV28 38
Holmsdale Rd., Sev. CV65 108
Holmshaw Clo. SE26 CD49 77
Holmshill La., B.Wd. BO21 28
Holmside Rd. SW12 BV46 76
Holmside Ri., Wat. BC27 35
Holmsley Clo., N.Mal. BO53 85
Holmstall Av., Edg. BN30 37
Holmwood Av., Brwd. DD25 122
Holmwood Av., S.Croy. CA60 96
Holmwood Clo., Har. BG31 45
Holmwood Clo., Lthd. BB67 110
Holmwood Clo., Nthlt. BF36 54
Holmwood Clo., Sutt. BQ58 94
Holmwood Clo., Wey. AW56 92
Holmwood Gdns. N3 BS30 38
Holmwood Gdns., Wall. BV57 95
Holmwood Gro. NW7 BN28 37
Holmwood Rd., Chess. BL56 94
Holmwood Rd., Enf. CC21 30
Holmwood Rd., Ilf. CN34 49
Holmwood Rd., Sutt. BQ58 94
Holne Chase N2 BT32 47
Holness Rd. E15 CG36 58
Holroyd Clo., Esher BJ58 93
Holroyd Rd. SW15 BQ45 65
Holroyd Rd., Lthd. BH58 93
Holstein Av., Wey. AZ56 92
Holstein Way, Erith CP41 69
Holstock Rd., Ilf. CM34 49
Holsworth Clo., Har. BG32 45
Holsworthy Way, Chess. BK56 93
Holt Clo. N10 BV31 47
Holt Clo. SE28 CO40 59
Holt Clo., B.Wd. BL24 28
Holt Clo., Chig. CN28 40
Holt Ct. E15 CE35 48
Holt Rd. E16 CK40 58
Holt Rd., Wem. BJ34 45
Holt Way, Chig. CN28 40
Holt, The, Hem.H. AY14 8
Holt, The, Ilf. CM29 40
Holt, The, Wall. BW56 95
Holt, The, Welw.G.C. BT 8 5
Sylvandale
Holton St. E1 CC38 57
Holtsmere Clo., Wat. BD21 27
Holtwhites Av., Enf. BZ23 30
Holtwhites Hill, Enf. BY23 29
Holtwood Rd., Lthd. BG60 93
Holwell Ct., Hat. BU10 11
Holwell Hyde La., Welw.G.C. BT 9 5
Holwell Hyde, Welw.G.C. BT 8 5
Holwell La., Hat. BU10 5
Holwell Pl., Pnr. BE31 45
Holwell Rd., Welw.G.C. BR 8 5
Holwood Clo., Walt. BD55 84
Holwood Park Av., Orp. CK56 97
Holwood Pl. SW4 BW45 66
Holy Cross Hill, Brox. CB15 12
Holy Wk., Brox. CE13 12
St. Catharines Rd.
Holybourne Av. SW15 BP47 75
Holyfield Rd., Wal.Abb. CF18 21
Holyhead Clo. E3 CE38 57
Campbell Rd.
Holyoak Rd. SE11 BY42 4
Holyoak Rd. SE11 BY42 66
Holyoake Av., Wok. AR62 100
Holyoake Cres., Wok. AR62 100
Holyoake Ter., Sev. CU65 107
Holyoake Wk. N2 BT31 47
Holyoake Wk. W5 BK38 54
Holyport Rd. SW6 BQ43 65
Holyport Rd., Maid. AG43 61
Holyport St., Maid. AG43 61
Holyrood Av., Har. BE35 45
Holyrood Cres., St.Alb. BG15 9
Holyrood Gdns., Edg. BM31 46
Holyrood Gdns., Grays DH42 71
Holyrood Rd., Barn. BT25 29
Holyrood St. SE1 CA41 4
Holyrood St. SE1 CA41 67
Bermondsey St.
Holywell Clo. SE3 CH43 68
Holywell Clo., Stai. AY47 73
Holywell Hill, St.Alb. BG14 9
Holywell La. EC2 CA38 2
Holywell La. EC2 CA38 57
Holywell Rd., Wat. BC25 26
Holywell Row EC2 CA38 2
Holywell Row EC2 CA38 57
Scrutton St.
Holywell Way, Stai. AY47 73
Home Clo., Brox. CD15 12
Home Clo., Cars, BU55 86
Home Clo., Harl. CN11 13
Home Clo., Lthd. BG64 102
Home Clo., Nthlt. BE38 54
Home Ct., Felt. BC47 73
Home Farm Clo., Bet. BO71 120
Home Farm Clo., Epsom BQ62 103
Home Farm Clo., Esher BF57 93
Home Farm Clo., Shep. BB52 83
Home Farm Clo., T.Ditt. BH54 84
Home Farm Gdns., Walt. BD55 84
Home Farm Rd., Berk. AO11 7
Home Farm Rd., Brwd. DC30 42
Home Farm Rd., Rick. AZ28 35
Home Farm Way, Slou. AR37 52
Home Gdns., Dag. CS34 50
Home Gdns., Dart. CW46 80
Home Hill, Swan. CT50 79
Home Lea., Orp. CN56 97
Osgood Av.
Home Mead Clo., Grav. DG47 81
Home Mead, Stan. BK30 36
Home Orchard, Dart. CW46 80
Home Park Rd. SW19 BR49 75
Home Park Wk., Kings.T. BK52 84
Home Pk., Oxt. CH69 115
Home Rd. SW11 BU44 66
Home Way, Rick. AV26 34
Home Wood La., Pot.B. BW17 20
Homecroft Gdns., Loug. CL24 31
Homecroft Rd. N22 BY30 38
Homecroft Rd. SE26 CC49 77
Homedean Rd., Sev. CS64 107
Homefarm Clo., Cher. AT57 91
Homefarm Rd. W7 BH39 54
Homefield Av., Ilf. CN32 49
Homefield Clo. NW10 BN36 55
Homefield Clo., Epp. CO18 23
Homefield Clo., Hem.H. AZ13 8
Homefield Clo., Lthd. BK64 102
Homefield Clo., Swan. CT52 89
Homefield Clo., Wey. AV59 91
Homefield Gdns. N2 BT31 47
Stanley Rd.
Homefield Gdns., Mitch. BT51 86
Homefield Gdns., Tad. BQ63 103
Homefield Pk., Sutt. BS57 95
Sutton Park Rd.
Homefield Rd. SW19 BQ50 75
Homefield Rd. W4 BO42 65
Homefield Rd., Brom. CJ51 88
Homefield Rd., Bush. BF25 27
Homefield Rd., Couls. BY63 104
Homefield Rd., Edg. BN29 37
Homefield Rd., Rad. BH22 27
Homefield Rd., Rick. AU24 25
Homefield Rd., Sev. CT64 107
Homefield Rd., Walt. BE54 84
Homefield Rd., Warl. CC63 105
Homefield Rd., Wem. BJ35 45
Homefield Ri., Orp. CO54 89
Homefield Sq. N1 CA37 2
Homefield St. N1 CA37 57
Regan Way
Homefield, Berk. AT11 7
Homefield, Hem.H. AT17 16
Homefield, Wal.Abb. CH19 22
Homefield, Walt. BD56 93
Homeland Dr., Sutt. BS58 95
Homelands Dr. SE19 CA50 77
Homelands, Lthd. BK64 102
Homeleigh Rd. SE15 CC46 77
Homemead Rd., Brom. CK53 88
Homemead Rd., Croy. BW53 86
Homemead, Hat. BP11 10
Homer Clo., Bexh. CS44 69
Homer Dr. E14 CE42 67
Homer Rd. E9 CD36 57
Homer Rd., Croy. CC53 87
Homer Row W1 BU39 1
Homer Row W1 BU39 56
Homer St. W1 BU39 1
Homer St. W1 BU39 56
Homerfield, Welw.G.C. BQ 7 5
Homers Rd., Wind. AL44 61
Homersham Rd., Kings.T. BM51 85
Homerswood La., Welw. BP 6 5
Homerton Gro. E9 CC35 48
Homerton High St. E9 CC35 48
Homerton Rd. E9 CD35 48
Homerton Row E9 CC35 48
Homerton Ter. E9 CC36 57
Homesdale Clo., Ilf. CH32 49
New Wanstead
Homesdale Rd., Brom. CJ52 88
Homesdale Rd., Cat. BZ65 105
London Rd.
Homesdale Rd., Orp. CN54 88
Homesfield NW11 BS32 47
Homestall Rd. SE22 CC46 77
Homestall, Guil. AO70 118
Homestead Ct., Welw.G.C. BR 9 5
Homestead Gdns., Esher BH56 93
Homestead La., Welw.G.C. BR 9 5
Homestead Paddock N14 BV25 29
Homestead Pk. NW2 BO34 46
Homestead Rd. SW6 BR43 65
Homestead Rd., Cat. BZ65 105
Homestead Rd., Dag. CQ34 50
Homestead Rd., Hat. BP11 10
Homestead Rd., Orp. CO57 98
Homestead Rd., Rick. AX26 35
Homestead Rd., Stai. AW50 73
Homestead Way, Croy. CF59 96
Homestead, The, Dart. CV46 80
Homewater Av., Sun. BB51 83
Homeway, Rom. CX29 42
Homewillow Clo. N21 BY25 29
Homewood Av., Cuff. BX17 20

Homewood Clo., Hmptn. BE49 74
Fearnley Cres.
Homewood Cres., Chis. CN50 78
Homewood Rd., St.Alb. BJ12 9
Homewood, Slou. AR39 52
Honduras St. EC1 BZ38 2
Honduras St. EC1 BZ38 57
Baltic St.
Hone Par. SE11 BX42 66
Lambeth Wk.
Honey Cft., Welw.G.C. BQ8 5
Honey Clo., B.Wd. DB21 33
Honey Hill, Uxb. AY36 53
Honey La. EC2 BZ39 2
Honey La. EC2 BZ39 57
Cheapside
Honey La., Wal.Abb. CG20 22
Honeybourne Rd. NW6 BS35 47
Honeybourne Way, Orp. CM54 88
Honeybrook Rd. SW12 BW47 76
Honeybrook, Wal.Abb. CG20 22
Honeycrock La., Red. BV74 121
Honeycroft Hill, Uxb. AY36 53
Honeycroft, Loug. CL24 31
Honeycross Rd., Hem.H. AV14 7
Honeyden Rd., Sid. CQ50 79
Honeyhill, Harl. CN13 13
Honeyman Clo. NW6 BQ36 55
Honeymeade, Saw. CP7 6
Honeypot Clo. NW9 BL31 46
Honeypot La. NW9 BL31 46
Honeypot La., Brwd. DA27 42
Honeypot La., Sev. CX63 108
Honeypot La., Stan. BK29 36
Honeypots Rd., Wok. AR64 100
Honeysett Rd. N17 CA30 39
Reform Row
Honeysuckle Bottom, Lthd. BB70 110
Honeysuckle Clo., Brwd. DA25 33
Honeysuckle Clo., Rom. CV29 42
Cloudberry Rd.
Honeysuckle Gdns., Croy. CC54 87
Primrose La.
Honeysuckle Gdns., Hat. BP13 10
Honeysuckle La. N22 BZ30 39
Crawley Rd.
Honeysuckle La., Dor. BK73 119
Honeywell Rd. SW11 BU46 76
Honeywood Clo., Pot.B. BT20 20
Honeywood Rd. NW10 BO37 55
Honeywood Rd., Islw. BJ45 64
Honeywood Wk., Cars. BU56 95
Honister Clo., Stan. BJ29 36
Honister Gdns., Stan. BJ29 36
Honister Heights, Pur. BZ60 96
Honister Pl., Stan. BJ30 36
Honiton Rd. NW6 BR37 55
Honiton Rd., Rom. CS32 50
Honiton Rd., Well. CN44 68
Honley Rd. SE6 CE47 77
Honnor Rd., Stai. AX50 73
Bingham Dr.
Honor Oak Est. SE4 CD45 67
Honor Oak Pk. SE23 CC46 77
Honor Oak Rd. SE23 CC47 77
Honor Oak Ri. SE23 CC46 77
Hoo, The, Harl. CP8 6
Hood Av. N14 BW25 29
Hood Av. SW14 BN46 75
Hood Av., Orp. CO53 89
Hood Clo., Croy. BY54 86
Parsons Mead
Hood Rd. SW20 BO50 75
Hood Rd., Rain. CT37 59
Hood Wk., Rom. CR30 41
Hoodcote Gdns. N21 BY26 38
Hook End La., B.Wd. DB20 24
Hook End Rd., B.Wd. DA21 33
Hook Farm Rd., Brom. CJ53 88
Hook Fields, Grav. DF48 81
Hook Gate, Enf. CB21 30
Hook Green La., Dart. CT48 79
Hook Green Rd., Grav. DC50 81
Hook Heath Av., Wok. AQ63 100
Hook Heath Gdns., Wok. AQ64 100
Hook Heath Rd., Wok. AP64 100
Hook Hill La., Wok. AQ64 100
Hook Hill Pk., Wok. AQ64 100
Hook Hill, S.Croy. CA58 96
Hook La., Pot.B. BU19 20
Hook La., Rom. CQ25 32
Hook La., Well. CN46 78
Hook Rd., Chess. BK56 93
Hook Rd., Epsom BN57 94
Hook Ri. N., Surb. BL55 85
Hook Ri. S., Surb. BL55 85
Hook Wk., Edg. BN29 37
Hook, The, Barn. BT25 29
Hooke Rd., Lthd. BB66 110
Hookers Rd. E17 CC31 48
Hookfield, Epsom BN60 94
Hookfield, Harl. CN12 13
Hooking Grn., Har. BF32 45
Hooks Clo. SE15 CB44 67
Wood Rd.
Hooks Hall Dr., Dag. CS34 50
Hooks Way SE22 CB47 77
Dulwich Common
Hookstone Way, Wdf.Grn. CJ29 40
Hookwood Rd., Orp. CP59 98
Hooley La., Red. BU71 121
Hoop La. NW11 BR33 46
Hooper Rd. E16 CH39 58
Hooper St. E1 CB39 57
Hoopers Ct. SW3 BU41 3
Hoopers Ct. SW3 BU41 66
Basil St.
Hoopers Ms. W3 BM40 55
Churchfield Rd.
Hoopers Yd., Sev. CV66 117
Hop Fields, Wok. AS61 100
Hop Gdns. WC2 BX40 56
Bedfordbury
Hopcroft Rd. NW2 BR35 46
Hope Clo. SE12 CH48 78
Hope Clo., Sutt. BT56 95
Hope Clo., Wdf.Grn. CJ29 40
West Gro.
Hope Grn., Wat. BC20 17
Hope Pk., Brom. CG50 78
Hope Rd., Swans. DC46 81
High St.
Hope St. SW11 BT45 66
Hopedale Rd. SE7 CH43 68
Hopefield Av. NW6 BR37 55
Hopetown St. E1 CA39 2
Hopetown St. E1 CA39 57
Hopewell Dr., Grav. DJ49 81
Hopewell St. SE5 BZ43 67
Hopfield Av., Wey. AY59 92
Hopgarden La., Sev. CU67 116
Hopgood St. W12 BQ40 55
Macfarlane Rd.
Hopground Clo., St.Alb. BJ14 9
Hopkins Cres., St.Alb. BJ10 9
Hopkins St. W1 BW39 1
Hopkins St. W1 BW39 56
Hopkinsons Pl. NW1 BV37 1
Fitzroy Rd.
Hopkinsons Pl. NW1 BV37 56
Fitzroy Rd.
Hopland Rd. W14 BR42 65
Hoppers Rd. N21 BY27 38
Hoppett Rd. E4 CG27 40
Hoppety, The, Tad. BQ64 103
Hopping La. N1 BY36 56
St. Marys Gro.
Hoppingwood Av., N.Mal. BO52 85
Hoppit Rd., Wal.Abb. CE19 21
Hoppitt, The, Ong. CV13 15
Hoppner Rd., Hayes BA37 53
Hopton Gdns., N.Mal. BP53 85
Hopton Rd. SW16 BX49 76
Hopton St. SE1 BY40 56
Hopwood Rd. SE17 BZ43 67
Hopwood Wk. E8 CB36 57
Wilman Gro.
Horace Av., Rom. CS33 50
Horace Rd. E7 CH35 49
Horace Rd., Ilf. CM31 49
Horace Rd., Kings.T. BL52 85
Horatio St. E2 CA37 2
Horatio St. E2 CA37 57
Horatius Way, Croy. BX57 95
Horbury Cres. W11 BS40 56
Horbury Ms. W11 BR40 55
Horder Rd. SW6 BR44 65
Hordle Gdns., St.Alb. BH14 9
Hordle Prom. E. SE15 CA43 67
Hordle Prom. N. SE15 CA43 67
Hordle Prom. S. SE15 CA43 67
Hordle Prom. W. SE15 CA43 67
Horizon Way SE7 CH42 68
Horley Clo., Bexh. CR46 79
Horley Rd. SE9 CK49 78
Horley Rd., Red. BU71 121
Hormead Rd. W9 BR38 55
Horn Hill La., Ger.Cr. AS28 34
Horn La. SE10 CH42 68
Horn La. W3 BN40 55
Horn La., Bexh. CS44 69
Horn La., Wdf.Grn. CH29 40
Horn Park Clo. SE12 CH46 78
Horn Park La. SE12 CH46 78
Hornbeam Av., Upmin. CX35 51
Hornbeam Clo. SE11 BY42 4
Hornbeam Clo., B.Wd. BM23 28
Hornbeam Clo., Brwd. DD27 122
Hornbeam Clo., Buck.H. CJ27 40
Hornbeam Rd.
Hornbeam Clo., Nthlt. BE35 45
Dabbs Hill La.
Hornbeam Cres., Brent. BJ43 64
Hornbeam Gdns., Slou. AQ41 62
Upton Rd.
Hornbeam Gro. E4 CG27 40
Hornbeam La. E4 CG25 31
Hornbeam La., Bexh. CS44 69
Hornbeam La., Hat. BU14 11
Hornbeam Rd., Buck.H. CJ27 40
Hornbeam Rd., Epp. CM22 31
Hornbeam Rd., Guil. AR69 118
Hornbeam Rd., Hayes BD39 54
Hornbeam Rd., Reig. BS71 121
Hornbeam Way, Brom. CL53 88
Hornbeam Wk., Walt. BB58 92
Hornbeams Av., Enf. CC21 30
Hornbeams Ri. N11 BV29 38
Hornbeams, St.Alb. BE18 18
Hornbeams, The, Harl. CM10 6
Hornbill Clo., Uxb. AX39 53
Hornbuckle Clo., Har. BG34 45
Hornby Clo. NW3 BT36 56
Horncastle Clo. SE12 CH47 78
Horncastle Rd. SE12 CH47 78
Hornchurch Hill, Whyt. CA62 105
Hornchurch Rd., Horn. CT33 50
Horndean Clo. SW15 BP47 75
Bessborough Rd.
Horndon Clo., Rom. CS30 41
Horndon Grn., Rom. CS30 41
Horndon Rd., Rom. CS30 41
Horne Rd., Shep. AZ52 83
Horne Way SW15 BQ44 65
Horner La., Mitch. BT51 86
Hornets, The, Wat. BC24 26
Hornfair Rd. SE7 CJ43 68
Hornford Way, Rom. CT33 50
Hornhatch Clo., Guil. AT73 118
Hornhatch, Guil. AT73 118
Hornhill Rd., Rick. AU28 34
Horniman Dr. SE23 CB47 77
Horning Clo. SE9 CK49 78
Hornminster Glen., Horn. CX34 51
Horns End Pl., Pnr. BD32 45
Horns Field, Welw.G.C. BT7 5
Horns Rd., Ilf. CM32 49
Hornsby La., Grays DG41 71
Hornsey La. Est. N19 BW33 47
Hornsey La. Gdns. N6 BW33 47
Hornsey La. N6 BV33 47
Hornsey Park Rd. N8 BX31 47
Hornsey Rd. N19 BX33 47
Hornsey Ri. Gdns. N19 BW33 47
Hornsey Ri. N19 BW33 47
Hornsey St. N7 BX35 47
Hornshay St. SE15 CC43 67
Hornton Pl. W8 BS41 66
Hornton St.
Hornton St. W8 BS41 66
Horsa Rd. SE12 CJ47 78
Horsa Rd., Erith CR43 69
Horsbury Cres. W11 BS40 56
Horscroft, Bans. BS62 104
Horse Fair, Kings.T. BK51 84
Horse Fair, Kings.T. BL51 85
Wood St.
Horse Guards Av. SW1 BX40 4
Horse Guards Av. SW1 BX40 56
Horse Guards Rd. SW1 BW40 3
Horse Guards Rd. SW1 BW40 56
Horse Hill, Chesh. AR19 16
Horse Shoe Cres., Nthlt. BF37 54
Horse Yd. N1 BY37 2
Horse Yd. N1 BY37 56
Essex Rd.
Horsecroft Clo., Harl. CK11 13
Horsecroft Clo., Orp. CO54 89
Horsecroft Rd., Edg. BN29 37
Horsecroft Rd., Harl. CK11 13
Horsecroft Rd., Hem.H. AW14 8
Horseferry Pl. SE10 CF43 67
Horseferry Rd. SW1 BW41 3
Horseferry Rd. SW1 BW41 66
Horselers, Hem.H. AY15 8
Horsell Birch, Wok. AQ61 100
Horsell Common Rd., Wok. AR60 91
Horsell Ct., Cher. AW54 83
Horsell Moor, Wok. AR62 100
Horsell Pk. Clo., Wok. AR61 100
Horsell Pk., Wok. AS61 100
Horsell Rd. N5 BY35 47
Horsell Rd., Orp. CO51 89
Horsell Ri. Clo., Wok. AR61 100
Horsell Ri., Wok. AR61 100
Horsell Vale, Wok. AS61 100
Horsell Way, Wok. AR61 100
Horselydown La. SE1 CA41 4
Horselydown La. SE1 CA41 67
Horseman Side, B.Wd. CV25 33
Horsemondon Clo., Orp. CN54 88
Horsemoor Clo., Slou. AT42 62
Parlaunt Rd.
Horsenden Av., Grnf. BH35 45
Horsenden Cres., Grnf. BH35 45
Horsenden La. N., Grnf. BH36 54
Horsenden La. S., Grnf. BJ37 54
Horseshoe All. SE1 BZ40 4
Bankside
Horseshoe All. SE1 BZ40 57
Bankside
Horseshoe Clo. E14 CF42 67
Ferry St.
Horseshoe Clo. NW2 BP34 46
Horseshoe Grn., Sutt. BS55 86
Horseshoe Hill, Wal.Abb CJ19 22
Horseshoe La. N20 BQ26 37
Horseshoe La., Enf. BZ24 30
Chase Side
Horseshoe La., Guil. AT70 118
Horseshoe La., Wat. BC19 17
Horseshoe, The, Bans. BR61 103
Horseshoe, The, Couls. BW60 95
Horseshoe, The, Hem.H BA14 8
Horsfield Gdns. SE9 CK46 78
Horsfield Rd. SE9 CJ46 78
Horsford Rd. SW2 BX46 76
Horsham Av. N12 BU28 38
Horsham Rd., Bexh. CR46 79
Horsham Rd., Dor. BJ72 119
Horsham Rd., Felt. BA46 73
Horsham Rd., Guil. AS74 118
Horsley Clo., Epsom BN60 94
Horsley Dr., Croy. CF57 96
Horsley Rd. E4 CF27 39
Horsley Rd., Brom. CH51 88
Horsley Rd., Cob. BC64 101
Horsley St. SE17 BZ43 4
Horsley St. SE17 BZ43 67
Horsleys, Rick. AU28 34
Long Croft Rd.
Horsmonden Rd. SE4 CD46 77
Hortensia Rd. SW10 BT43 66
Horticultural Pl. W4 BN42 65
Heathfield Ter.
Horton Av. NW2 BR35 46
Horton Bridge Rd., West Dr. AY40 53
Horton Clo., West Dr. AY40 53
Horton Gdns., Hem.H. AZ10 8
Elstree Rd.
Horton Hill, Epsom BN59 94
Horton La., Epsom BM59 94
Horton La., West Dr. AY40 53
Horton Rd. E8 CB36 57
Horton Rd., Datchet AQ43 62
Horton Rd., Hort.K. CY52 90
Horton Rd., Slou. AT44 62
Horton Rd., Slou. AU45 62
Horton Rd., Stai. AW46 73
Horton Rd., West Dr. AY40 53
Horton St. SE13 CE45 67
Horton Way, Farn. CW54 90
Hortons Way, West. CM66 115
Hortus Rd. E4 CF26 39
Hortus Rd., Sthl. BE41 64
Horvath Clo., Wey. BA56 92
Rosslyn Pk.
Hosack Rd. SW17 BU47 76
Hoselands Vw., Hart. DC52 90
Hoser Av. SE12 CH48 78
Hosey Common La., Eden. CM70 115
Hosey Common Rd., West. CM67 115
Hosier La. EC1 BY39 2
Hosier La. EC1 BY39 56
Hoskins Clo. E16 CJ39 58
Hoskins Clo., Hayes BB42 63
Hoskins Rd., Oxt. CG68 115
Hoskins St. SE10 CF42 67
Hospital Bridge Rd., Twick. BF47 74
Hospital Hill, Chesh. AO19 16
Hospital La., Islw. BH46 74
Hospital Rd., Houns. BF45 64
Hospital Rd., Sev. CV64 108
Hotham Clo., E.Mol. BF52 84
Hotham Clo., S.at H. CX50 80
Hotham Rd. SW15 BQ45 65
Hotham Rd. SW19 BT50 76
Hotham St. E15 CG37 58
Hothfield Pl. SE16 CC41 67
Hotspur Rd., Nthlt. BF37 54
Hotspur St. SE11 BY42 4
Hotspur St. SE11 BY42 66
Hottsfield, Hart. DC52 90
Houblon Rd., Rich. BL46 75
Houblons Hill, Epp. CP19 23
Houchin Dr., Ong. CY14 15
Hough St. SE18 CL41 68
Houghton Clo. E8 CA36 57
Forest Rd.
Houghton Clo., Hmptn. BE50 74
Houghton Rd. N15 CA31 48
Houghton St. WC2 BX39 2
Houghton St. WC2 BX39 56
Houlder Cres., Croy. BY57 95
Houndsden Rd. N21 BX25 29
Houndsditch EC3 CA39 2
Houndsditch EC3 CA39 57
Houndsfield Rd. N9 CB26 39
Hounslow Av., Houns. BF46 74
Hounslow Gdns., Houns. BF46 74
Hounslow Rd., Felt. BC47 73
Hounslow Rd., Felt. BE48 74
Hounslow Rd., Twick. BF46 74
House La., St.Alb. BK10 9
Houseman Way SE5 BZ43 67
Bantry St.
Housewood End, Hem.H. AW12 8
Houston Rd. SE23 CD48 77
Hove Av. E17 CD32 48
Hove Clo., Brwd. DE27 122
Hove Gdn., Sutt. BS54 86
Hove St. SE15 CC43 67
Culmore Rd.
Hoveden Rd. NW2 BQ35 46
Hoveton Rd. SE28 CP40 59
How La., Couls. BU63 104
How Wood, St.Alb. BF17 18
Howard Agne Clo., Hem.H. AT17 16
Howard Av., Bex. CP47 79
Howard Av., Epsom BP58 94
Howard Av., Slou. AO39 52
Howard Clo. N11 BV27 38
Howard Clo. NW2 BR35 46
Marnham Av.
Howard Clo. W3 BM39 55
Howard Clo., Ash. BL62 103
Howard Clo., Bush. BH26 36
Howard Clo., Hmptn. BG50 74
Howard Clo., Horsley BA66 110
Howard Clo., Lthd. BK65 102
Howard Clo., St.Alb. BK14 9
Howard Clo., Sun. BB50 73
Howard Clo., Tad. BO66 112
Howard Clo., Wat. BC22 26
Howard Cres., Beac. AO28 34
Howard Dr., B.Wd. BN24 28
Howard Gdns. SE25 CB53 87
Howard Gdns., Guil. AT70 118
Howard Lodge Rd., B.Wd. CY22 33
Howard Ms. N5 BY35 47
Hamilton Pk.
Howard Pl. SW1 BW41 66
Vauxhall Bridge Rd.
Howard Rd. E11 CG34 49
Howard Rd. E17 CE31 48
Howard Rd. E6 CK37 58
Howard Rd. N15 CA32 48
Howard Rd. N16 BZ35 48
Howard Rd. NW2 BQ35 46
Howard Rd. SE20 CC51 87
Howard Rd. SE25 CB53 87
Howard Rd., Ashf. AX49 73
Howard Rd., Bark. CM37 58
Howard Rd., Beac. AO28 34
Howard Rd., Brom. CG50 78
Howard Rd., Couls. BW61 104
Howard Rd., Dart. CX46 80
Howard Rd., Dor. BJ71 119
Howard Rd., Great Bookham BF67 111
Howard Rd., Ilf. CL35 49
Howard Rd., Islw. BH45 64
Howard Rd., Lthd. BC64 101
Howard Rd., N.Mal. BO52 85
Howard Rd., Reig. BS71 121
Howard Rd., Sthl. BF39 54
Howard Rd., Surb. BL53 85
Howard Rd., Upmin. CY34 51
Howard Ridge, Guil. AT68 109
Howard St., T.Ditt. BJ54 84
Howard Way SE2 CB47 77
Wilkie Way
Howard Way, Harl. CN9 6
Howard Wk. N2 BT31 47
Howards Clo., Pnr. BC30 35
Howards Crest Clo., Beck. CF51 87
Howards Dr., Hem.H. AW12 8
Howards La. SW15 BP45 65
Howards La., Wey. AV57 91
Howards Rd. E13 CH38 58
Howards Rd., Wok. AS63 100
Howards Thicket, Ger.Cr. AR33 43
Howards Wood Dr., Ger.Cr. AR34 43
Howards Yd. SE18 CL41 68
Powis St.
Howardsgate, Welw.G.C. BQ8 5
Howarth Ct. E15 CE35 48
Howarth Rd. SE2 CO42 69
Howberry Clo., Edg. BK29 36
Howberry Rd., Edg. BK29 36
Howberry Rd., Th.Hth. BZ51 87
Howbury La., Erith CT44 69
Howbury Rd. SE15 CC45 67
Howcroft Cres. N3 BS29 38
Howcroft La., Grnf. BG37 54
Cowgate Rd.
Howden Clo. SE28 CP40 59
Howden Rd. SE25 CA51 87
Howden St. SE15 CB45 67
Howe Clo., Rom. CR30 41
Howe Dell, Hat. BP12 10
Howe Rd., Hem.H. AZ15 8
Howell Clo., Rom. CP32 50
Howell Hill Clo., Epsom BQ59 94
Howell Hill Gro., Epsom BQ58 94
Howell Wk. SE1 BY42 4
Howell Wk. SE1 BY42 66
Howells Clo., Sev. CZ57 99
Howes Clo. N3 BS31 47
Mountfield Rd.
Howfield Grn., Hodd. CD10 12
Howgate Rd. SW14 BN45 65
Howick Pl. SW1 BW41 3
Howick Pl. SW1 BW41 66
Howicks Grn., Welw.G.C. BS9 5
Howie St. SW11 BU43 66
Howitt Rd. NW3 BU36 56
Howland Garth, St.Alb. BG15 9
Howland Ms.E. W1 BW39 1
Howland Ms.E. W1 BW39 56
Howland St.
Howland Ms.W. W1 BW39 1
Howland Ms.W. W1 BW39 56
Howland St.
Howland St. W1 BW39 1
Howland St. W1 BW39 56
Howland Way SE16 CD41 67
Howlands, Welw.G.C. BQ9 5
Howletts La., Ruis. BA32 44
Howletts Rd. SE24 BZ46 77
Howley Pl. W2 BT39 1
Howley Pl. W2 BT39 56
Howley Rd., Croy. BY55 86
Hows Clo., Uxb. AX37 53
Hows Mead, Epp. CS15 14
Hows Rd., Uxb. AX37 53
Hows St. E2 CA37 2
Hows St. E2 CA37 57
Howsman Rd. SW13 BP43 65
Howson Rd. SE4 CD45 67
Howson Ter., Rich. BL46 75
Howton Pl., Bush. BG26 36
Hoxton Mkt. N1 CA38 57
Boot St.
Hoxton Sq. N1 CA38 2
Hoxton Sq. N1 CA38 57
Hoxton St. N1 CA37 2
Hoxton St. N1 CA37 57
Hoy St. E16 CG40 58
Caxton St. N.
Hoylake Cres., Uxb. AZ34 44
Hoylake Gdns., Mitch. BW52 86
Hoylake Gdns., Rom. CW30 42
Hoylake Gdns., Ruis. BC33 44
Hoylake Gdns., Wat. BD28 36
Hoylake Rd. W3 BO39 55
Hoyland Clo. SE15 CB43 67
Commercial Way
Hoyle Rd. SW17 BU49 76
Hoyle St. W1 BW40 3
Hoyle St. W1 BW40 56
Savile Row
Hubbard Rd. SE27 BZ49 77
Hubbard St. E15 CG37 58
Hubbards Chase, Horn. CX32 51
Hubbards Clo., Horn. CX32 51
Hubbards Hill, Sev. CU68 116
Hubbards Rd., Rick. AU25 25
Hubert Gro. SW9 BX45 66
Hubert Rd. E6 CJ38 58
Hubert Rd., Brwd. DA27 42
Hubert Rd., Rain. CT38 59
Hubert Rd., Slou. AR42 62
Hucknall Clo., Rom. CW29 42
Petersfield Av.
Huddart St. E3 CD39 57
Huddleston Rd. N7 BW34 47
Huddlestone Cres., Red. BW67 113
Huddlestone Rd. E7 CG35 49
Huddlestone Rd. NW2 BP36 55
Hudson Clo., Wat. BB21 26
Hudson Pl. SE18 CM42 68
Hudson Pl. SW1 BV42 3
Hudson Pl. SW1 BW42 66
Hudson Rd., Bexh. CQ44 69
Hudson Rd., Hayes BA43 63
Hudsons, Tad. BQ64 103
Huggin Ct. EC4 BZ40 4
Huggin Hill
Huggin Hill EC4 BZ40 4
Huggin Hill EC4 BZ40 57
Queen Victoria St.
Huggins La., Hat. BQ15 10
Hugh Ms. SW1 BV42 3
Hugh Ms. SW1 BV42 66
Hugh St.
Hugh St. SW1 BV42 3
Hugh St. SW1 BV42 66
Hughan Rd. E15 CF35 48
Hughenden Av., Har. BJ32 45
Hughenden Gdns., Nthlt. BD38 54
Hughenden Rd., Slou. AO39 52
Hughenden Rd., St.Alb. BK12 9
Hughenden Rd., Wor.Pk. BP54 85
Hughendon Ter. E15 CF35 48
Hughes Rd., Ashf. BA50 73

Hughes Rd., Grays DG41 71
Hughes Rd., Hayes BC40 53
Hughes Wk., Croy. BZ54 87
St. Saviours Rd.
Hugo Gdns., Rain. CU36 59
Hugo Rd. N19 BW35 47
Hugon Rd. SW6 BS45 66
Huguenot Pl. SW18 BT46 76
Huguenot Sq. SE15 CB45 67
Scylla Rd.
Huitt Sq. SW11 BT45 66
Winstanley Rd.
Hull Clo. SE16 CC40 57
Hull Gro., Harl. CL13 13
Hull Pl. SE18 CN42 68
Hull Rd., Rom. CQ32 50
Hull St. EC1 BZ38 2
Hull St. EC1 BZ38 57
Hullbridge Ms. N1 BZ37 2
Hulletts La., Brwd. CZ24 33
Hulse Av., Bark. CM36 58
Hulse Av., Rom. CR30 41
Hulsewood Clo., Dart. CU48 79
Hulton Clo., Lthd. BK65 102
Hulverston Clo., Sutt. BS58 95
Humber Av., S.Ock. CZ39 60
Humber Dr., Upmin. CY32 51
Humber Rd. NW2 BP34 46
Humber Rd. SE3 CG43 68
Humber Way, Slou. AT42 62
Humberstone Rd. E13 CJ38 58
Humberton Clo. E9 CD35 48
Swinnerton St.
Humbolt Clo., Guil. AP70 118
Humbolt Rd. W6 BR43 65
Hume Av., Til. DG44 71
Hume Way, Ruis. BC32 44
Humes Av. W7 BH41 64
Hummer Rd., Egh. AT49 72
Humphrey Clo., Ilf. CK30 40
Humphrey Clo., Lthd. BG64 102
Humphrey St. SE1 CA42 4
Humphrey St. SE1 CA42 67
Humphries Clo., Dag. CQ35 50
Hundred Acre NW9 BO30 37
Hundred Acres La., Amer. AO23 25
Hungerdown E4 CF26 39
Hungerford Av., Slou. AP39 52
Hungerford Bridge WC2 BX40 4
Hungerford La. WC2 BX40 56
Craven St.
Hungerford Rd. N7 BW36 56
Hungerford Sq., Wey. BA56 92
Rosslyn Pk.
Hungerford St. E1 CB39 57
Commercial Rd.
Hungry Hill, Wok. AX66 110
Hunsdon Clo., Dag. CQ36 59
Hunsdon Dr., Sev. CU65 107
Hunsdon Est. E5 CB34 48
Hunsdon Rd. SE14 CC43 67
Hunsdon, Welw.G.C. BT 8 5
Hunslett St. E2 CC37 57
Royston St.
Hunston Rd., Mord. BS54 86
Hunt Clo., St.Alb. BK12 9
Hunt Rd., Grav. DF48 81
Hunt Rd., Sthl. BF41 64
Hunt St. W11 BQ40 55
Hunt Way SE22 CB47 77
Hunter Av., Brwd. DD25 122
Hunter Clo. SE1 BZ41 4
Hunter Clo. SE1 BZ41 67
Hunter Clo. SW12 BV47 76
Balham Park Rd.
Hunter Clo., B.Wd. BN25 28
Hunter Clo., Pot.B. BS20 20
Hunter Dr., Horn. CV35 51
Hunter Rd. SW20 BQ51 85
Hunter Rd., Guil. AS71 118
Hunter Rd., Ilf. CL35 49
Hunter Rd., Th.Hth. BZ52 87
Hunter St. WC1 BX38 2
Hunter St. WC1 BX38 56
Hunter Wk. E13 CH37 58
Hunter Wk., B.Wd. BN25 28
Huntercombe Gdns., Wat. BD28 36
Huntercombe La., Maid. AK40 61
Hunters Clo. SW12 BV47 76
Balham Park Rd.
Hunters Clo., Epsom BN60 94
Burnet Gro.
Hunters Clo., Hem.H. AT18 16
Hunters Gro., Har. BK31 45
Hunters Gro., Hayes BC40 53
Hunters Gro., Orp. CL56 97
State Farm Av.
Hunters Gro., Rom. CR28 41
Hunters Hall Rd., Dag. CR35 50
Hunters Hill, Ruis. BD34 45
Hunters La., Wat. BB20 17
Hunters Meadow SE19 CA49 77
Dulwich Wood Av.
Hunters Oak, Hem.H. AZ11 8
Hunters Pk., Berk. AS12 7
Hunters Rd., Chess. BL55 85
Hunters Reach, Wal.Cr. CB18 21
Hunters Ride, St.Alb. BF19 18
Hunters Sq., Dag. CR35 50
Hunters Way, Enf. BY23 29
Hunters Way, Welw.G.C. BR 9 5
Hunters Wk., Sev. CQ60 98
Huntersfield Clo., Reig. BS69 121
Hunting Clo., Esher BF56 93
Hunting Gate Clo., Enf. BY24 29
Slades Ri.
Hunting Gate Dr., Chess. BL57 94
Hunting Gate Ms., Sutt. BS55 86
Hunting Gate Ms., Twick. BH47 74
Colne Rd.
Hunting Gate, Hem.H. AY11 8
Huntingdon Clo., Brox. CD15 12
Huntingdon Clo., Mitch. BX52 86
Huntingdon Gdns., Wor.Pk. BQ55 85
Huntingdon Rd. N2 BU31 47
Huntingdon Rd. N9 CC26 39
Huntingdon Rd., Red. BU70 121
Cromwell Rd.
Huntingdon Rd., Wok. AP62 100
Huntingdon St. E16 CG39 58
Huntingdon St. N1 BX36 56
Huntingdon Way, Croy. CA56 96
Huntingfield Rd. SW15 BP45 65
Huntingfield Way, Egh. AU50 72
Huntingfield, Croy. CD57 96
Huntings Rd., Dag. CR36 59
Huntland Clo., Rain. CU39 59
Beechwood Gdns.
Huntley Av., Grav. DD46 81
Huntley Dr. N3 BS29 38
Nether St.
Huntley St. WC1 BW38 1
Huntley St. WC1 BW38 56
Huntley Way SW10 BP51 85
Huntly Rd. SE25 CA52 87
Hunton St. E1 CB38 57
Hunton St. E1 CB39 2
Huntonbridge Hill, Kings.L. BA20 17
Hunts Clo. SE3 CH44 68
Hunts Clo., Guil. AO70 118
Hunts Ct. WC2 BW40 3
Charing Cross Rd.
Hunts Ct. WC2 BW40 56
Charing Cross Rd.
Hunts La. E15 CF37 57
Hunts Mill Rd., Hem.H. AV14 7
Hunts Slip Rd. SE21 CA48 77
Huntsman Clo., Warl. CC63 105
Huntsman Dr., Upmin. CY35 51
Huntsman Rd., Ilf. CO29 41
Huntsman St. SE17 BZ42 4
Huntsman St. SE17 BZ42 67
Barlow St.
Huntsmans Clo., Felt. BC49 73
Huntsmans Clo., Lthd. BG65 102
The Green
Huntsmead Clo., Chis. CK50 78
Bullerswood Dr.
Huntsmead, Enf. CC24 30
Huntsmoor Rd., Epsom BN56 94
Huntspill St. SW17 BT48 76
Huntsworth Ms. NW1 BU38 1
Huntsworth Ms. NW1 BU38 56
Hurley Clo., Walt. BC55 83
Hurley Cres. SE16 CC41 67
Marlow Way
Hurley Gdns., Guil. AT69 109
Hurley Rd., Grnf. BF39 54
Hurlfield, Dart. CV48 80
Hurlford, Wok. AQ62 100
Hurlingham Ct. SW6 BR45 65
Hurlingham Gdns. SW6 BR45 65
Hurlingham Rd. SW6 BR44 65
Hurlingham Rd., Bexh. CQ43 69
Hurlock St. N5 BY34 47
Hurlstone Rd. SE25 BZ53 87
Hurn Court Rd., Houns. BD44 64
Hurnford Clo., S.Croy. CA58 96
Huron Rd. SW17 BV48 76
Hurren Clo. SE3 CG45 68
Hurry Clo. E15 CG36 58
Hursley Rd., Chig. CN28 40
Hart Cres.
Hurst Av. E4 CE28 39
Hurst Av. N6 BW32 47
Hurst Cft., Guil. AS72 118
Hurst Clo, Brom. CG54 88
Hurst Clo. E4 CE27 39
Hurst Clo. NW11 BS32 47
Hurst Clo., Chess. BM56 94
Hurst Clo., Nthlt. BE35 45
Hurst Clo., Welw.G.C. BT 8 5
Sylvandale
Hurst Clo., Wok. AR63 100
Hurst Dr., Tad. BP66 112
Hurst Dr., Wal.Cr. CC20 21
Hurst Farm Rd., Sev. CU69 116
Hurst Grn. Rd., Oxt. CG69 115
Hurst Grn., Oxt. CG69 115
Hurst Gro., Walt. BB54 83
Hurst La. SE2 CP42 69
Hurst La., E.Mol. BG52 84
Hurst La., Egh. AT51 82
Hurst La., Epsom BH65 103
Hurst Park Av., Horn. CW35 51
Hurst Pl., Nthwd. AZ30 35
Hurst Place Est. SE2 CP42 69
Hurst Rd. E17 CE31 48
Hurst Rd. N21 BY26 38
Hurst Rd., Bex. CP47 79
Hurst Rd., Buck.H. CJ26 40
Hurst Rd., E.Mol. BF52 84
Hurst Rd., Epsom BN59 94
Hurst Rd., Erith CS44 69
Hurst Rd., Orp. BZ56 96
Hurst Rd., S.Croy. BZ56 96
Hurst Rd., Sid. CO48 79
Hurst Rd., Tad. BP65 103
Hurst Rd., Walt. BD53 84
Hurst Ri., Barn. BS24 29
Hurst Springs, Bex. CQ47 79
Hurst St. SE24 BY46 76
Hurst St. W11 BQ40 55
Hurst View Rd., S.Croy. CA57 96
Hurst Way, S.Croy. CA57 96
Hurst Way, Sev. CV57 117
Hurst Way, Wok. AV60 91
Hurstbourne Gdns., Bark. CN36 58
Hurstbourne Rd. SE23 CD47 77
Hurstbourne, Esher BH57 93
Hurstcourt Rd., Sutt. BS55 86
Hurstdene Av., Brom. CG54 88
Hurstdene Av., Stai. AW50 73
Hurstdene Gdns. N15 CA32 48
Hurstfield Cres., Hayes BB39 53
Hurstfield Rd., E.Mol. BF52 84
Hurstfield, Brom. CH53 88
Hursthead Ct., Edg. BM28 37
Hurstlands Clo., Horn. CV32 51
Hurstlands, Oxt. CH69 115
Hurstleigh Clo., Red. BU69 121
Hurstleigh Dr., Red. BU69 121
Hurstleigh Gdns., Ilf. CK30 40
Hurstlings, Welw.G.C. BS 8 5
Hurstway Wk. W11 BQ40 55
Lancaster Rd.
Hurstwood Av. E18 CH31 49
Hurstwood Av., Bex. CQ47 79
Hurstwood Av., Brwd. DA26 42
Hurstwood Av., Erith CT44 69
Hurstwood Ct. N12 BU29 38
Woodleigh Av.
Hurstwood Ct. NW11 BR31 46
Hurstwood Dr., Brom. CK52 88
Hurstwood Rd. NW11 BR31 46
Hurtwood Rd., Walt. BE54 84
Hurworth Rd., Slou. AR41 62
Huson Clo. NW3 BU36 56
Husseywell Cres., Brom. CH54 88
Hutchings St. E14 CE41 67
Hutchings Wk. NW11 BS31 47
Hutchingsons Rd., Croy. CF59 96
Hutchins Clo. E15 CG36 57
Gibbins Rd.
Hutchinson Ter., Wem. BK34 45
Hutton Clo., Har. BG35 45
Mary Peters Dr.
Hutton Clo., Wdf.Grn. CH28 40
Hutton Dr., Brwd. DE26 122
Hutton Gdns., Har. BG29 36
Hutton Gro. N12 BS28 38
Hutton La., Har. BG29 36
Hutton Rd., Brwd. DC26 122
Hutton Row, Edg. BM29 37
Pavilion Way
Hutton St. EC4 BY39 56
Dorset Ri.
Hutton Vill., Brwd. DF26 122
Hutton Wk., Har. BG29 36
Huxbear St. SE4 CD46 77
Huxley Clo. E10 CF34 48
Huxley Clo., Nthlt. BE37 54
Huxley Clo., Uxb. AX38 53
Huxley Dr., Rom. CO33 50
Huxley Gdns. NW10 BL38 55
Huxley Par. N18 BZ28 39
Huxley Pl. N13 BY27 38
Huxley Rd. E10 CF34 48
Huxley Rd. N18 BZ28 39
Huxley Rd., Well. CN45 68
Huxley S. N18 BZ28 39
Huxley Sayze N18 BZ28 39
Huxley St. W10 BR38 55
Hyacinth Clo., Hmptn. BF50 74
Gresham Rd.
Hyacinth Ct., Pnr. BD31 45
Nursery Rd.
Hyacinth Dr., Uxb. AY36 53
Hyacinth Rd. SW15 BP47 75
Hyburn Clo., St.Alb. BE18 18
Hycliffe Gdns., Chig. CM28 40
Hyde Av., Pot.B. BS20 20
Hyde Clo. E13 CH37 58
Turpin Est.
Hyde Clo., Barn. BR24 28
Hyde Cres. NW9 BO32 46
Hyde La. SW11 BU44 66
Battersea Bridge Rd.
Hyde La., Bovingdon AT17 16
Hyde La., Hem.H. AZ17 17
Hyde La., St.Alb. BG17 18
Hyde La., Wok. AZ63 101
Hyde Mead, Wal.Abb. CG15 13
Hyde Meadows, Hem.H. AT17 16
Hyde Park Av. N21 BZ26 39
Hyde Park Corner W1 BV41 3
Hyde Park Corner W1 BV41 66
Hyde Park Cres. W2 BU39 1
Hyde Park Cres. W2 BU39 56
Hyde Park Gate Ms. SW7 BT41 66
Hyde Park Gate SW7 BT41 1
Hyde Park Gate SW7 BT41 66
Hyde Park Gdns. Ms. W2 BT40 3
Hyde Park Gdns. Ms. W2 BT40 56
Hyde Park Gdns. N21 BZ26 39
Hyde Park Gdns. W2 BT40 3
Hyde Park Gdns. W2 BT40 56
Hyde Park Mans. NW1 BU39 1
Hyde Park Mans. NW1 BU39 56
Edgeware Rd.
Hyde Park Ms. SW7 BT41 3
Hyde Park Ms. SW7 BT41 66
Hyde Park Pl. W2 BU40 3
Hyde Park Pl. W2 BU40 56
Bayswater Rd.
Hyde Park Sq. W2 BU39 1
Hyde Park Sq. W2 BU39 56
Hyde Park St. W2 BU39 1
Hyde Park St. W2 BU39 56
Hyde Pl. N1 BY36 56
Compton Av.
Hyde Rd. N1 BZ37 2
Hyde Rd. N1 BZ37 57
Hyde Rd., Bexh. CQ44 69
Hyde Rd., Rich. BL46 75
Albert Rd.
Hyde Rd., S.Croy. BZ60 96
Hyde Rd., Wat. BC23 26
Hyde St. SE8 CE43 67
Deptford High St.
Hyde Ter., Ashf. BB50 73
Hyde Vale SE10 CF43 67
Hyde Vall., Welw.G.C. BR 9 5
Hyde Way N9 CA27 39
Hyde Way, Hayes BB42 63
Hyde Way, Welw.G.C. BR 8 5
Hyde Wk., Mord. BS54 86
Hyde, The NW9 BO31 46
Hydefield Clo. N21 BZ26 39
Hydefield Ct. N9 CA27 39
Hyder Rd., Grays DH41 71
Hydes Pl. N1 BY36 56
Compton Av.
Hydeside Gdns. N9 CA27 39
Hydethorpe Av. N9 CA27 39
Hydethorpe Rd. SW12 BW47 76
Hyland Clo., Horn. CU33 50
Hyland Way, Horn. CU33 50
Hylands Clo., Epsom BN61 103
Hylands Ms., Epsom BN61 103
Hylands Rd. E17 CF30 39
Hylands Rd., Epsom BN61 103
Hylle Clo., Wind. AM44 61
Cawcott Dr.
Hylton St. SE18 CN42 68
Hyndewood SE23 CC48 77
Bampton Rd.
Hyndman St. SE15 CB43 67
Hynton Rd., Dag. CP34 50
Hyperion Ct., Hem.H. AY12 8
Hyperion Pl., Epsom BN58 94
Hyrons Clo., Amer. AP22 25
Hyrons La., Amer. AO22 25
Hyrst Dene, S.Croy. BY56 95
Hyson Rd. SE16 CB42 67
Hythe Av., Bexh. CQ43 69
Hythe Clo. N18 CB28 39
Hythe Clo., Orp. CP52 89
Hythe End Rd., Stai. AT48 72
Hythe Field Av., Egh. AU50 72
Hythe Park Rd., Egh. AV49 72
Hythe Rd. NW10 BP38 55
Hythe Rd. Stai. AU49 72
Hythe Rd., Th.Hth. BZ51 87
Hythe St., Dart. CW46 80
Hythe, The, Stai. AV49 72
Hyver Hill NW7 BN26 37

I

Ian Sq., Enf. CC23 30
Ibbetson Path, Loug. CL24 31
Ibbotson Av. E16 CG39 58
Ibbott St. E1 CC38 57
Mantus Rd.
Iberian Av., Wall. BW56 95
Ibis La. W4 BN44 65
Ibscott Clo., Dag. CS36 59
Ibsley Gdns. SW15 BP47 75
Ibsley Way, Barn. BU24 29
Icehouse Wood, Oxt. CG69 115
Iceland Rd. E3 CE37 57
Ickburgh Est. E5 CB34 48
Ickburgh Rd. E5 CB34 48
Ickenham Clo., Ruis. BA34 44
Ickenham Rd., Ruis. BA33 44
Ickenham Rd., Uxb. BA34 44
Ickleton Rd. SE9 CK49 78
Icklingham Rd., Cob. BD59 93
Icknield Clo., St.Alb. BE15 9
Icknield Dr., Ilf. CL32 49
Ickworth Park Rd. E17 CD31 48
Ida Rd. N15 BZ32 48
Ida St. E14 CF39 57
Ide Hill Rd., Sev. CQ69 116
Ide Hill Rd., Sev. CS67 116
Ide Hill, Sev. CS65 107
Iden Clo., Brom. CG52 88
Idenden Cotts. SE10 CG41 68
Idlecombe Rd. SW17 BV50 76
Idmiston Rd. E15 CG35 49
Idmiston Rd. SE27 BZ48 77
Idmiston Rd., Wor.Pk. BO54 85
Idmiston Sq., Wor.Pk. BO54 85
Idol La. EC3 CA40 4
Idol La. EC3 CA40 57
Idonia St. SE8 CD43 67
Iffley Clo., Uxb. AX36 53
Iffley Rd. W6 BP41 65
Ifield Rd. SW10 BS43 66
Ifield Ter., Green. DA46 80
Ifield Way, Grav. DH50 81
Ightham By-pass, Sev. DB64 108
Ightham Mote, Sev. DA67 117
Ightham Rd., Erith CR43 69
Ightham Rd., Sev. DB64 108
Ikona Ct., Wey. BA56 92
Ilbert St. W10 BQ38 55
Ilchester Gdns. W2 BS40 56
Ilchester Pl. W14 BR41 65
Ilchester Rd., Dag. CO35 50
Ildersley Gro. SE21 BZ48 77
Ilderton Rd. SE15 CC43 67
Ilex Clo., Egh. AQ50 72
Ilex Clo., Sun. BD51 83
Ilex Ct., Berk. AQ13 7
Angle Pl.
Ilex Rd. NW10 BO36 55
Ilex Way SW16 BY49 76
Ilford Hill, Ilf. CL34 49
Ilford La., Ilf. CL34 49
Ilfracombe Cres., Horn. CV35 51
Ilfracombe Gdns., Rom. CO33 50
Ilfracombe Rd., Brom. CG48 78
Iliffe St. SE17 BY42 4
Iliffe St. SE17 BY42 66
Iliffe Yd. SE17 BY42 4
Iliffe Yd. SE17 BY42 66
Amelia St.
Ilkeston Ct. E5 CC35 48
Clapton Park Est.
Ilkley Clo. SE19 BZ50 77
Rockmount Rd.
Ilkley Rd. E16 CJ39 58
Ilkley Rd., Wat. BD28 36
Illingworth Clo., Mitch. BT52 86
Illingworth Way, Enf. CA25 30
Illingworth, Wind. AM45 61
Ilmington Rd., Har. BK32 45
Ilminster Gdns. SW11 BU45 66
Imber Clo. N14 BW26 38
Imber Ct., E.Mol. BG54 84
Imber Gro., Esher BG54 84
Imber Park Rd., Esher BG54 84
Imber St. N1 BZ37 2
Imber St. N1 BZ37 57
Poole St.
Imperial Av. N16 CA35 48
Imperial Clo., Har. BF32 45
Imperial Dr., Grav. DJ49 81
Imperial Dr., Har. BF33 45
Imperial Ms. E6 CJ37 58
Imperial Rd. N22 BX30 38
Imperial Rd. SW6 BS44 66
Imperial Rd., Felt. BB47 73
Imperial Rd., Wind. AN45 61
Imperial Sq. SW6 BS44 66
Imperial St. E3 CF38 57
Imperial Way SE18 CK43 68
Imperial Way, Chis. CM48 78
Imperial Way, Croy. BY57 95
Imperial Way, Har. BL32 46
Imperial Way, Wat. BD23 27
Inca Dr. SE9 CL47 78
Ince Rd., Watt. BB57 92
Inchmery Rd. SE6 CE48 77
Inchwood, Croy. CE56 96
Indells, Hat. BO13 10
Independents Rd. SE3 CG45 68
Inderwick Rd. N8 BX32 47
Indescon Ct. E14 CE41 67
India Rd., Slou. AQ41 62
India St. EC3 CA39 2
India St. EC3 CA39 57
Jewry St.
India Way W12 BP40 55
Indus Rd. SE7 CJ43 68
Industrial Est., Grnf. BF37 54
Industrial Est., Iver AV40 52
Industrial Est., Mitch. BU53 86
Ingal Rd. E13 CH38 58
Ingate Pl. SW8 BV44 66
Ingatestone Rd. E12 CJ33 49
Ingatestone Rd. SE25 CB52 87
Ingatestone Rd., Wdf.Grn. CH29 40
Ingatestone Rd., Ing. DC19 24
Ingelow Rd. SW8 BV44 66
Ingels Mead, Epp. CN18 22
Ingersoll Rd. W12 BP40 55
Ingersoll Rd., Enf. CC22 30
Ingestre Pl. W1 BW39 1
Ingestre Pl. W1 BW39 56
Ingestre Rd. E7 CH35 49
Ingestre Rd. NW5 BV35 47
Ingford St. N1 BY37 2
Ingham Clo., S.Croy. CC58 96
Ingham Rd. NW6 BS35 47
Ingham Rd., S.Croy. CC56 96
Ingle Clo., Pnr. BE31 45
Inglebert St. EC1 BY38 2
Inglebert St. EC1 BY38 56
Ingleboro Dr., Pur. BZ60 96
Ingleby Clo., Dag. CR36 59
Ingleby Dr., Har. BG34 45
Ingleby Gdns., Chig. CO27 41
Ingleby Rd. N7 BX34 47
Ingleby Rd., Dag. CR36 59
Ingleby Rd., Grays DG41 71
Ingleby Rd., Ilf. CL33 49
Ingleby Way, Chis. CL49 78
Ingleby Way, Wall. BW57 95
Ingledew Rd. SE18 CM42 68
Ingleglen, Horn. CX33 51
Inglehurst Gdns., Ilf. CK32 49
Inglehurst, Wey. AW58 92
Inglemere Rd. SE23 CC48 77
Inglemere Rd., Mitch. BU50 76
Ingles, Welw.G.C. BQ 6 5
Inglesham Wk. E9 CD36 57
Trowbridge Est.
Ingleside Clo., Beck. CE50 77
Ingleside Gro. SE3 CG43 68
Ingleside, Slou. AV44 62
Bath Road
Inglethorpe St. SW6 BQ44 65
Ingleton Av., Well. CO46 79
Ingleton Rd. N18 CB29 39
Ingleton Rd., Cars. BU58 95
Ingleway N12 BT29 38
Inglewood Clo. E14 CE42 67
Barnsdale Av.
Inglewood Clo., Chig. CN29 40
Inglewood Clo., Horn. CV35 51
Inglewood Copse, Brom. CK51 88
Inglewood Rd. NW6 BS35 47
Inglewood Rd., Bexh. CS45 69
Inglewood, Cher. AV55 82
Inglewood, Wok. AQ62 100
Inglis Rd. W5 BL40 55
Inglis Rd., Croy. CA54 87
Inglis St. SE5 BY44 66
Knatchbull Rd.
Ingoldsby Rd., Grav. DJ47 81
Ingram Av. NW11 BT33 47
Ingram Clo. SE11 BX42 4
Ingram Clo. SE11 BX42 66
Juxon St.
Ingram Clo., Stan. BK28 36
Ingram Rd. N2 BU31 47
Ingram Rd., Dart. CW47 80
Ingram Rd., Grays DE42 71
Ingram Rd., Th.Hth. BZ51 87
Ingram Way, Grnf. BG37 54
Ingrams Clo., Walt. BD56 93
Ingrave Rd., Brwd. DB27 42
Ingrave Rd., Rom. CS31 50
Ingrave St. SW11 BT45 66
Ingrebourne Gdns., Upmin. CY33 51
Ingrebourne Rd., Rain. CU38 59
Ingress Gdns., Green. DB46 80
Ingreway, Rom. CX29 42
Inholms La., Dor. BJ73 119
Inigo Jones Rd. SE7 CJ43 68
Inkerman Rd. NW5 BV36 56
Inkerman Rd., Eton AM42 61
Inkerman Rd., St.Alb. BH14 9
Inkerman Rd., Wok. AP62 100
Inkerman Ter., Chesh. AO20 16
Inkerman Way, Wok. AP62 100
Inks Grn. E4 CE28 39
Inman Rd. NW10 BO37 55
Inman Rd. SW18 BT47 76
Inmans Row, Wdf.Grn. CH28 40
Inner Circ. NW1 BV38 1

Inner Circ. NW1 BV38 56
Inner Park Rd. SW19 BQ47 75
Inner Ring E., Houns. AZ45 63
Conway Rd.
Inner Ring W., Houns. AZ45 63
Chester Rd.
Inner Staithe W4 BN43 65
Upper Staithe
Inner Temple La. EC4 BY39 2
Fleet St.
Inner Temple La. EC4 BY39 56
Fleet St.
Innes Clo. SW20 BR51 85
Innes Ct., Hem.H. AX15 8
Seaton Rd.
Innes Gdns. SW15 BP46 75
Innes Lo. SE23 CC48 77
Innes Yd., Croy. BZ55 87
Whitgift St.
Inniskilling Rd. E13 CJ37 58
Inskip Clo. E10 CE34 48
Inskip Dr., Horn. CW33 51
Inskip Rd., Dag. CP33 50
Institute Pl. E8 CB35 48
Amhurst Rd.
Institute Rd., Epp. CP18 23
Institution Rd., Dor. BG72 119
Instone Clo., Pur. BY58 95
Instone Clo., Wall. BX57 95
Instone Rd., Dart. CV47 80
Instow Pl. N7 BY35 47
Queensland Rd.
Insurance St. WC1 BY38 2
Insurance St. WC1 BY38 56
Margery St.
Integer Gdns. E11 CF33 48
Forest Rd.
International Av., Houns. BD42 64
Inver Clo. E5 CB34 48
Southwold Rd.
Inverarey Pl. SE18 CM43 68
Inverclyde Gdns., Rom. CP31 50
Inveresk Gdns., Wor.Pk. BO55 85
Inverforth Clo. NW3 BT34 47
North End Way
Inverforth Rd. N11 BV28 38
Inverine Rd. SE7 CH42 68
Invermore Pl. SE18 CM42 68
Inverna Gdns. W8 BS42 66
Inverness Av., Enf. CA23 30
Inverness Ct. W3 BM39 55
Links Rd.
Inverness Dr., Ilf. CN29 40
Inverness Gdns. W8 BS40 56
Inverness Ms. W2 BS40 3
Inverness Ms. W2 BS40 56
Inverness Ter.
Inverness Pl. W2 BS40 3
Inverness Pl. W2 BS40 56
Inverness Ter.
Inverness Rd. N18 CB28 39
Inverness Rd., Houns. BE45 64
Inverness Rd., Sthl. BE42 64
Inverness Rd., Wor.Pk. BQ54 85
Inverness St. NW1 BV37 1
Inverness St. NW1 BV37 56
Inverness Ter. W2 BS39 56
Inverton Rd. SE15 CC45 67
Invicta Clo., Chis. CL49 78
Invicta Gro., Nthlt. BE38 54
Invicta Rd. SE3 CH43 68
Invicta Rd., Dart. CX46 80
Inville Rd. SE1 BZ42 67
Inwood Av., Couls. BY63 104
Inwood Av., Houns. BG45 64
Inwood Clo., Croy. CD55 87
Inwood Ct., Walt. BD55 84
Inwood Rd., Houns. BF45 64
Inworth St. SW11 BU44 66
Inworth Wk. N1 BZ37 57
Popham St.
Ion Sq. E2 CB37 2
Ion Sq. E2 CB37 57
Hackney Rd.
Iona Clo. SE6 CD47 77
Ionian Way, Hem.H. AY12 8
Ipswich Rd. SW17 BV50 76
Ireland Pl. N22 BX29 38
Whittington Rd.
Ireland Yd. EC4 BY39 2
Ireland Yd. EC4 BY39 56
St. Andrews Hill
Irene Rd. SW6 BS44 66
Irene Rd., Cob. BF61 102
Irene Rd., Orp. CN54 88
Ireton Av., Walt. BB55 83
Ireton Pl., Grays DD42 71
Irford Clo. SE4 CD45 67
St. Norbert Rd.
Iris Av., Bex. CQ46 79
Iris Clo., Brwd. DA25 33
Iris Clo., Croy. CC54 87
Iris Clo., Surb. BL54 95
Iris Cres., Bexh. CQ43 69
Iris Ct., Pnr. BD31 45
Nursery Rd.
Iris Path, Rom. CV29 42
Iris Rd., Epsom BM56 94
Iris Way E4 CD29 39
Irkdale Av., Enf. CA23 30
Iron Bridge Rd., West Dr. AZ40 53
Iron Mill La., Dart. CT45 69
Iron Mill Pl. SW18 BS46 76
Garratt La.
Iron Mill Pl., Dart. CT45 69
Iron Mill Rd. SW18 BS46 76
Irongate Wharf Rd. W2 BT39 56
Ironmonger La. EC2 BZ39 2
Ironmonger La. EC2 BZ39 57
Ironmonger Row EC1 BZ38 2
Ironmonger Row EC1 BZ38 57
Ironmongers Pl. E14 CE42 67
Spindrift Av.
Irons Bottom Rd., Reig. BS74 121
Irons Way, Rom. CS29 41
Ironside Clo. SE16 CC41 67
Kinburn St.
Irvine Av., Har. BJ31 45
Irvine Clo. N20 BU27 38
Irvine Gdns., S.Ock. CZ39 60
Irvine Way, Orp. CN54 88
Irving Av., Nthlt. BD37 54
Irving Gro. SW9 BX44 66
Irving Rd. W14 BQ41 65
Irving St. WC2 BW40 3
Irving St. WC2 BW40 56
Leicester Sq.
Irving Way NW9 BO32 46
Irving Way, Swan. CS51 89
Irving Wk., Swans. DC47 81
Irwin Av. SE18 CN43 68
Irwin Gdns. NW10 BP37 55
Irwin Rd., Guil. AQ71 118
Isabel St. SW9 BX44 66
Isabella Dr., Orp. CM56 97
Isabella Rd. E9 CC35 48
Isabella St. SE1 BY40 4
Isabella St. SE1 BY40 56
Joan St.
Isambard Clo., Uxb. AX38 53
Isambard Ms. E14 CF41 67
Isambard Pl. SE16 CC41 67
Rotherhithe St.
Isbell Gdns., Rom. CT29 41
Isbells Dr., Reig. BS71 121
Isel Way SE22 CA46 77
Dulwich Gro.
Isenburg Way, Hem.H. AX11 8
Isham Rd. SW16 BX51 86
Isis Clo. SW15 BQ45 65
Isis Clo., Ruis. BA32 44
Thames Dr.
Isis Dr., Upmin. CZ32 51
Isis St. SW18 BT48 76
Isla Rd. SE18 CM43 68
Island Clo., Stai. AV49 72
Island Farm Av., E.Mol. BF53 84
Island Farm Rd., E.Mol. BE53 84
Island Rd., Mitch. BU50 76
Island Row E14 CD39 57
Island, The, Stai. AT48 72
Islay Gdns., Houns. BD46 74
Islay Wk. N1 BZ36 57
Isledon Rd. N7 BY34 47
Islehurst Clo., Chis. CL51 88
Summer Hill
Islington Grn. N1 BY37 2
Islington Grn. N1 BY37 56
Upper St.
Islington High St. N1 BY37 2
Islington High St. N1 BY37 56
Islington Park St. N1 BY36 56
Islip Gdns., Edg. BN29 37
Islip Gdns., Nthlt. BE36 54
Islip Manor Rd., Nthlt. BE36 54
Islip St. NW5 BW35 47
Ismailia Rd. E7 CH36 58
Ismay Ct., Slou. AP39 52
Ismays Rd., Sev. DA66 117
Isom Clo. E13 CJ38 58
Belgrave Rd.
Istead Ri., Grav. DF50 81
Itchingwood Common Rd., Oxt. CJ70 115
Ivanhoe Clo., Uxb. AX39 53
Ivanhoe Dr., Har. BJ31 45
Ivanhoe Rd. SE5 CA45 67
Ivanhoe Rd., Houns. BD45 64
Ivatt Pl. W14 BR42 65
Ivatt Way N17 BZ31 48
Ive Farm Clo. E10 CE34 48
Ive Farm La. E10 CE34 48
Iveagh Av. NW10 BM37 55
Iveagh Clo. E9 CC37 57
Iveagh Clo. NW10 BM37 55
Iveagh Clo., Nthwd. AZ30 35
Iveagh Rd., Guil. AQ71 118
Iveagh Rd., Wok. AP62 100
Ivedon Rd., Well. CP44 69
Iveley Rd. SW4 BW44 66
Iver La., Iver & Uxb. AW39 53
Iver Rd., Brwd. DA25 33
Harewood Rd.
Iverdale Clo., Iver AU40 52
Ivere Dr. Barn. BS25 29
Iverhurst Clo., Bexh. CP46 79
Iverna Ct. W8 BS41 66
Iverna Gdns.
Iverna Gdns. W8 BS41 66
Iverna Gdns., Felt. BA46 73
Ivers Way, Croy. CE57 96
Iverson Rd. NW6 BR36 55
Ives Gdns., Rom. CT31 50
Ives Rd. E16 CG39 58
Ives Rd., Slou. AS41 62
Ives St. SW3 BU42 3
Ives St. SW3 BU42 66
Ivestor Ter. SE23 CC47 77
Ivimey St. E2 CB38 2
Barnet Gro.
Ivimey St. E2 CB38 57
Barnet Gro.
Ivinghoe Clo., Enf. BZ23 30
Ivinghoe Clo., St.Alb. BK11 9
Highview Gdns.
Ivinghoe Clo., Wat. BD21 27
Ivinghoe Rd., Bush. BG26 36
Ivinghoe Rd., Dag. CO35 50
Ivinghoe Rd., Rick. AV26 34
Ivor Clo., Guil. AT71 118
Ivor Gro. SE9 CL47 78
Ivor Pl. NW1 BU38 1
Ivor Pl. NW1 BU38 56
Ivor St. NW1 BW36 56
Ivory Sq. SW18 BT45 66
Gartons Way
Ivorydown, Brom. CH49 78
Ivy Bower Clo., Green. DA46 80
Riverview Rd.
Ivy Clo., Dart. CX47 80
Ivy Clo., Grav. DH49 81
Ivy Clo., Har. BE35 45
Ivy Clo., Pnr. BD33 45
Ivy Clo., Sun. BD51 84
Ivy Cotts. E14 CE40 57
Grove Villas
Ivy Cres. W4 BN42 65
Ivy Dene Clo., Red. BV73 121
Ivy Gdns. N8 BX32 47
Ivy Gdns., Mitch. BW52 86
Ivy House La., Berk. AR13 7
Ivy House La., Sev. CS62 107
Ivy La., Houns. BE45 64
Ivy La., Wok. AT62 100
Ivy Lea, Rick. AW27 35
Springwell Av.
Ivy Lodge La., Rom. CX30 42
Ivy Mill Clo., Gdse. CB69 114
Ivy Mill La., Gdse. CB69 114
Ivy Pl., Surb. BL53 85
Ivy Rd. E16 CH39 58
Ivy Rd. E17 CE32 48
Ivy Rd. N14 BW26 38
Ivy Rd. NW2 BQ35 46
Ivy Rd. SE4 CD45 67
Ivy Rd., Houns. BF45 64
Ivy Rd., Surb. BM54 85
Ivy St. N1 CA37 2
Ivy St. N1 CA37 57
Ivy Ter., Hodd. CF11 12
Ivy Wk., Dag. CQ36 59
Ivybridge Clo., Twick. BJ46 74
Ivybridge La. W12 BX40 56
Savoy Pl.
Ivybridge, Brox. CE13 12
Ivychimneys Rd., Epp. CN20 22
Ivychurch Clo. SE20 CB50 77
Laurel Gro.
Ivychurch La. SE17 CA42 4
Kinglake St.
Ivychurch La. SE17 CA42 67
Kinglake St.
Ivydale Rd. SE15 CC46 77
Ivydale Rd., Cars. BU55 86
Ivyday Gro. SW16 BX48 76
Ivydene Clo., Sutt. BT56 95
Ivydene Rd. E8 CB36 57
Ivydene, E.Mol. BE53 84
Ivyhouse Rd., Dag. CP36 59
Ivyhouse Rd., Uxb. AZ34 44
Ivymount Rd. SE27 BY48 76
Ixworth Pl. SW3 BU42 3
Ixworth Pl. SW3 BU42 66
Izane Rd., Bexh. CQ45 69

J

Jack Barnett Way N22 BX30 38
Mayes Rd.
Jack Cornwell St. E12 CL35 49
Jack Stevens Clo., Harl CP12 14
Hillside
Jack Walker Ct. N7 BY35 47
Jackass La., Kes. CH57 97
Jackass La., Oxt. CD69 114
Jackdaws, Welw.G.C. BT8 5
Grove Meadow
Jackets La., Nthwd. AZ29 35
Jacketts Fld., Wat. BB18 17
Jacklin Grn., Wdf.Grn CH28 40
Jackman Ms. NW10 BO34 46
North Circular Rd.
Jackman St. E8 CB37 57
Jackmans La., Wok. AQ63 100
Jacks La., Ubx. AW30 35
Jackson Clo., Epsom BN60 94
Jackson Clo., Uxb. AY36 53
St. Lukes Rd.
Jackson Rd. N7 BX35 47
Jackson Rd., Bark. CM37 58
Jackson Rd., Barn. BU25 29
Jackson Rd., Brom. CK55 88
Jackson Rd., Grnf. BJ37 54
Sindall Rd.
Jackson Rd., Uxb. AY36 53
St. Lukes Rd.
Jackson St. SE18 CL43 68
Jackson Way, Sthl. BF41 64
Jacksons Clo., Ong. CW18 24
Jacksons Dr., Wal.Cr. CB17 21
Jacksons La. N6 BV33 47
Jacksons Pl., Croy. BZ54 87
Jacob St. SE1 CA41 4
Jacob St. SE1 CB41 67
Jacobs Clo., Wind. AM44 61
Jacobs Ladder, Hat. BQ12 10
The Broadway
Jacobs Ladder, Warl. CB63 105
Jacobs Well Ms. W1 BV39 1
Jacobs Well Ms. W1 BV39 56
George St.
Jacobs Well Rd., Guil. AR68 109
Jacqueline Clo., Nthlt. BE37 54
Jade Clo. E16 CJ39 58
Jade Clo., Dag. CP33 50
Jaffray Pl. SE27 BY49 76
Jaffray Rd., Brom. CJ52 88
Jaggard Way SW12 BU47 76
Nightingale La.
Jago Clo. SE18 CM43 68
Jago Wk. SE5 BZ43 67
Lomond Gro.
Jail La., Biggin Hill CJ61 106
Jamaica Rd. SE1 CA41 4
Jamaica Rd. SE1 CA41 67
Jamaica Rd. SE16 CB41 67
Jamaica Rd., Th.Hth. BY53 86
Jamaica St. E1 CC39 57
James Av. NW2 BQ35 46
James Av., Dag. CQ33 50
James Bedford Clo., Pnr. BD30 36
James Boswell Clo., SW16 BX49 76
Curtis Field Rd.
James Clo. E13 CH37 58
Turpin Est.
James Clo., Bush. BE25 27
James Clo., Rom. CU32 50
James Collins Clo. W9 BR38 55
Fermoy Rd.
James Cotts., Rich. BM43 65
Kew Rd.
James Ct. N1 BZ36 57
Morton Rd.
James Ct. N1 BZ36 57
Morton Rd.
James Ct. N1 BZ37 2
James Gdns. N22 BY29 38
James Gdns. SE27 BZ49 77
James La. E10 CF33 48
James Newman Ct. SE9 CL49 78
James Pass. N17 CA29 39
Church Rd.
James Rd., Dart. CT47 79
James St. W1 BV39 1
James St. W1 BV39 56
James St. W1 BW40 3
James St. W1 BW40 56
Brewer St.
James St. WC2 BX39 2
James St. WC2 BX40 56
Long Acre
James St., Bark. CM36 58
James St., Enf. CA25 30
James St., Epp. CO17 23
James St., Houns. BG45 64
James St., Wind. AO44 61
Peascod St.
James's Cott., Rich. BM43 65
Kew Rd.
Jameson Ct., St.Alb. BH13 9
Avenue Rd.
Jameson St. W8 BS40 56
Jamestown Rd. NW1 BV37 1
Jamestown Rd. NW1 BV37 56
Jamnagar Clo., Stai. AV50 72
Jan Mead, Brwd. DD26 122
Jane Clo., Hem.H. AZ11 8
Jane Pl., Uxb. AX36 53
Vine St.
Jane St. E1 CB39 57
Commercial Rd.
Janet St. E14 CE41 67
Janeway Pl. SE16 CB41 67
Janeway St.
Janeway St. SE16 CB41 67
Janice Ms., Ilf. CL34 49
Oakfield Rd.
Janoway Hill La., Wok. AR63 100
Jansen Wk. SW11 BT45 66
Wayland Rd.
Janson Clo. E15 CG35 49
Janson Rd.
Janson Clo. NW10 BN34 46
Janson Rd. E15 CG35 49
Jansons Rd. N15 CA31 48
Japan Cres. N4 BX33 47
Japan Rd., Rom. CP32 50
Japonica Clo., Wok. AR62 100
Silversmiths Way
Jarman Clo., Hem.H. AY14 8
Jarrah Cotts., Grays CY43 70
Jarrett Clo. SW2 BY47 76
Abbess Clo.
Jarrow Clo., Mord. BS53 86
Jarrow Rd. N15 CB31 48
Jarrow Rd. SE16 CC42 67
Jarrow Rd., Rom. CP32 50
Jarrow Way E9 CD35 48
Kings Mead Est.
Jarvis Cleys, Chsnt. CA16 21
Jarvis Clo., Barn. BQ25 28
Jarvis Rd. SE22 CA45 67
Melbourne Gro.
Jarvis Rd., S.Croy. BZ57 96
Jasmin Clo., Nthwd. BB30 35
Pinner Rd.
Jasmin Rd., Epsom BM57 94
Jasmine Clo., Orp. CL55 88
Jasmine Clo., Red. BV73 121
Jasmine Clo., Wok. AP61 100
Jasmine Gdns., Croy. CE55 87
Jasmine Gdns., Har. BF34 45
Sandringham Cres.
Jasmine Gro. SE20 CB51 87
Jasmine Ter., West Dr. AZ41 63
Jasmine Way, E.Mol. BH52 84
Jason Clo. E15 CG35 49
Jason Rd.
Jason Clo., Brwd. CZ27 42
Jason Clo., Red. BU73 121
Jason Clo., Wey. BA56 92
Jason Wk. SE9 CL49 78
Jasons Dr., Guil. AU69 118
Jasons Hill, Chesh. AQ18 16
Jasper Clo., Enf. CC22 30
Jasper Pass. SE19 CA50 77
Jasper Rd. E16 CJ39 58
Jasper Rd. SE19 CA50 77
Javelin Way, Nthlt. BD38 54
Jay Bldgs. W1 BX37 56
Rodney St.
Jay Ms. SW7 BT41 3
Jay Ms. SW7 BT41 66
Jaycroft, Enf. BY23 29
Hansart Way
Jebb Av., SW2 BX46 76
Jebb St. E3 CE37 57
Jedburgh Rd. E13 CJ38 58
Jedburgh St. SW11 BV45 66
Jeddo Rd. W12 BO41 65
Jefferson Clo. W13 BJ41 64
Jefferson Clo., Ilf. CL32 49
Jefferson Clo., Slou. AT42 62
Swabey Rd.
Jefferson Wk. SE18 CL43 68
Kempt St.
Jeffreys Pl. NW1 BW36 56
Jeffreys St.
Jeffreys Rd. SW4 BX44 66
Jeffreys Rd., Enf. CD24 30
Jeffreys St. NW1 BW36 56
Jeffreys Wk. SW4 BX44 66
Jeffries Rd., Lthd. BA68 110
Jeffs Clo., Hmptn. BF50 74
Uxbridge Rd.
Jeffs Rd., Sutt. BR56 94
Jeken Rd. SE9 CJ45 68
Jelf Rd. SW2 BY46 76
Jellicoe Av., Grav. DH48 81
Jellicoe Clo., Slou. AN41 61
Jellicoe Gdns., Stan. BJ29 36
Jellicoe Rd. E13 CH38 58
Jutland Rd.
Jellicoe Rd. N17 BZ29 39
Jengar Clo. BS56
Jengar Clo., Sutt. BS56 95
Jenkins Av., St.Alb. BE18 18
Jenkins La., Bark. CL37 58
Jenkins Rd. E13 CH38 58
Jenner Pl. SW13 BP43 65
Jenner Rd. N16 CA34 48
Jenner Rd., Guil. AS71 118
Jennett Rd., Croy. BY55 86
Jennifer Rd., Brom. CG48 78
Jenningham Dr., Grays. DD40 71
Jennings Rd. SE22 CA46 77
Jennings Rd., St.Alb. BH13 9
Jennings Way, Barn. BQ24 28
Jenningtree Rd., Erith CU43 69
Jenningtree Way, Belv. CS41 69
Jenny Hammond Clo. E11 CG34 49
Newcomen Rd.
Jenny Path, Rom. CV29 42
Jenson Way SE19 CA50 77
Fox Hill
Jenton Av., Bexh. CQ44 69
Jephson Rd. E7 CJ36 58
Jephson St. SE5 BZ44 67
Grove La.
Jephtha Rd. SW18 BS46 76
Jeppos La., Mitch. BU52 86
Jerdan Pl. SW6 BS43 66
Fulham Broadway
Jeremiah St. E14 CE39 57
Jeremys Grn. N18 CB28 39
Jericho Pl., Ing. DC19 24
Jermyn St. SW1 BW40 3
Jermyn St. SW1 BW40 56
Jerningham Av., Ilf. CL30 40
Jerningham Rd. SE14 CD44 67
Jerome Cres. NW8 BU38 1
Jerome Cres. NW8 BU38 56
Jerome Dr., St.Alb. BF15 9
Jerome Pl. SE17 BZ43 4
Jerome Pl. SE17 BZ43 67
Hillingdon St.
Jerome St. E1 CA38 2
Jerome St. E1 CA38 57
Calvin St.
Jerounds, Harl. CL12 13
Jerrard St. N1 CA37 2
Jerrard St. N1 CA37 57
Stanway St.
Jerrard St. SE13 CE45 67
Jersey Av., Stan. BJ30 36
Jersey Clo., Cher. AV55 82
Jersey Clo., Guil. AT68 109
Weybrook Dr.
Jersey Clo., Hodd. CE11 12
Jersey Dr., Orp. CM53 88
Jersey La., St.Alb. BJ12 9
Jersey Rd. E11 CF33 48
Jersey Rd. E16 CH39 58
Jersey Rd. SW17 BV50 76
Jersey Rd. W7 BJ41 64
Jersey Rd., Houns. BF44 64
Jersey Rd., Ilf. CL35 49
Jersey Rd., Rain. CU36 59
Jersey St. E2 CB38 57
Bethnal Green Rd.
Jerusalem Pass. EC1 BY38 2
Jerusalem Pass. EC1 BY38 56
Jerusalem Pl. EC1 BY38 2
Aylesbury St.
Jerusalem Pl. EC1 BY38 56
Aylesbury St.
Jervis Av., Enf. CD21 30
Jerviston Gdns. SW16 BY50 76
Jesmond Av., Wem. BL36 55
Jesmond Rd., Croy. CA54 87
Jesmond Rd., Grays DE40 71
Jesmond Way, Stan. BL28 37
Jessam Av. E5 CB33 48
Jessamine Pl., Dart. CW48 80
Jessamine Pl., Dart. CY47 80
Jessamine Rd. W7 BH40 54
Jessamy St., Wey. AZ55 83
Jesse Rd. E10 CF33 48
Jessel Dr., Loug. CM23 31
Jessica Rd. SW18 BT46 76
Jessiman Ter., Shep. AZ53 83
Jessop Av., Sthl. BE42 64
Jessop Rd. SE24 BZ45 67
Jessops Way, Mitch. BW53 86
Jessup Clo. SE18 CM42 68
Jetstar Way, Nthlt. BD38 54
Jetty Wk., Grays DD43 71
Jevington Way SE12 CH47 78
Jewel Rd. E17 CE31 48
Jewels Hill, West. CH60 97
Jewry St. EC3 CA39 2
Jewry St. EC3 CA39 57
Jews Row SW18 BS45 66
Jews Wk. SE26 CB49 77
Jeymer Av. NW2 BP35 46
Jeymer Dr., Grnf. BG37 54
Jeypore Rd. SW18 BT46 76
Jillian Clo., Hmptn. BF50 74
Jim Bradley Clo. SE18 CL42 68
John Wilson St.
Jinnings, The, Welw.G.C. BS 9 5
Joan Cres. SE9 CJ47 78

Joan Gdns., Dag. CQ34 50
Joan Rd., Dag. CQ34 50
Joan St. SE1 BY40 4
Joan St. SE1 BY40 56
Jocelyn Rd., Rich. BL45 65
Jocelyns, Harl. CP 9 6
Jocketts Hill, Hem.H. AV14 7
Jocketts Rd., Hem.H. AV14 7
Jockeys Fields WC1 BX39 2
Jockeys Fields WC1 BX39 56
Jodrell Rd. E3 CD37 57
Jodrell Way., Grays CZ42 70
Joe Hunt Ct. SE27 BY49 76
Cedar Tree Gro.
Joel St., Nthwd. BC31 44
Johanna St. SE1 BY41 4
Johanna St. SE1 BY41 66
John Adam St. WC2 BX40 4
John Adam St. WC2 BX40 56
Villiers St.
John Aird Ct. W2 BT39 56
Howley Pl.
John Ashby Clo. SW2 BX46 76
John Barnes Wk. E15 CG36 58
John Bradshaw Rd. N14 BW26 38
John Burns Dr., Bark. CN36 58
John Campbell Rd. N16 CA35 48
John Carpenter St. EC4 BY40 4
John Carpenter St. EC4 BY40 56
John Clay Gdns., Grays DD40 71
Whitmore Av.
John Clynge Ct. SW15 BP45 65
Woodborough Rd.
John Cobb Rd., Wey. AZ57 92
John Ct., Hodd. CE10 12
Molesworth
John Dwight Ho. SW6 BS45 66
John Eliot Clo., Wal.Abb. CG14 13
John Felton Rd. SE16 CB41 4
John Felton Rd. SE16 CB41 67
John Fisher St. E1 CB40 4
John Fisher St. E1 CB40 57
John Gooch Dr., Enf. BY23 29
John Islip St. SW1 BW42 3
John Islip St. SW1 BW42 66
John Parker Clo., Dag. CR36 59
John Parker Sq. SW11 BT45 66
Thomas Baines Rd.
John Penn St. SE13 CE44 67
John Perrin Pl., Har. BL33 46
John Princes St. W1 BV39 1
John Princes St. W1 BV39 56
John Rennie Wk. E1 CB40 57
John Ruskin St. SE5 BY43 66
John Russell Clo., Guil. AQ69 118
John Spencer Sq. N1 BY36 56
John St. E15 CG37 58
John St. SE25 CB52 87
John St. WC1 BX38 2
John St. WC1 BX38 56
John St., Enf. CA25 30
John St., Grays DE43 71
John St., Houns. BE44 64
John Taylor Ct., Slou. AO40 61
Tuns La.
John Wilson St. SE18 CL41 68
John Woolley Clo. SE13 CF45 67
Johnby Cl., Enf. CD22 30
Manly Dixon Dr.
Johns Av. NW4 BQ31 46
Johns Clo., Ashf. BA49 73
Johns Gro., Rich. BL45 65
Kew Foot Rd.
Johns La., Chesh. AP14 7
Johns La., Mord. BT53 86
Johns Ms. WC1 BX38 2
Johns Ms. WC1 BX38 56
Johns Pl. E1 CB39 57
Nelson St.
Johns Rd., West. CJ63 106
Johns Ter., Croy. CA54 87
Johns Wk., Whyt. CB63 105
Johns, The, Ong. CX17 24
Johnsdale, Oxt. CG68 115
Johnson Clo., Grav. DE48 81
Johnson Clo., Mitch. BV52 86
Johnson Ct., Hem.H. AY14 8
Woodman Rd.
Johnson Rd., Brom. CJ53 88
Johnson Rd., Houns. BD43 64
Johnson St. E1 CC40 57
Johnson St., Sthl. BD41 64
Johnson Way NW10 BM38 55
Johnsons Av., Sev. CR58 98
Johnsons Clo., Cars. BU55 86
Johnsons Ct. EC4 BY39 2
Fleet St.
Johnsons Dr., Hmptn. BG51 84
Johnsons Pl. SW1 BW42 3
Johnsons Pl. SW1 BW42 66
Claverton St.
Johnston Grn., Guil. AQ68 109
Johnston Rd., Croy. BZ54 87
Johnston Rd., Wdf.Grn. CH29 40
Johnston Ter. NW2 BQ34 46
Johnston Wk., Guil. AQ68 109
Johnstone Rd. E6 CK38 58
Joiner St. SE1 BZ40 4
Joiner St. SE1 BZ40 57
Joiners Clo., Chesh. AQ18 16
Joiners Clo., Ger.Cr. AS29 34
Joiners La., Ger.Cr. AS30 34
Joiners Way, Ger.Cr. AS29 34
Jolleys La., Har. BG33 45
Jolliffe Rd., Red. BW66 113
Jollys La., Hayes BD39 54
Jonathan St. SE11 BX42 4
Jonathan St. SE11 BX42 66
Jones Rd. E13 CH38 58
Holborn Rd.
Jones Rd., Chsnt. BY18 20
Jones St. W1 BV40 3
Jones St. W1 BV40 56
Bourdon St.
Jones Way, Slou. AO34 43
Jones Wk., Rich. BL46 75
Ryland Rd.
Jonquil Gdns., Hmptn. BF50 74
Partridge Rd.
Jonson Clo., Hayes BC39 53
Joram Way SE16 CB42 67
The Bonamy Est. E.
Jordan Clo., Dag. CR35 50
Muggeridge Rd.
Jordan Clo., Har. BE34 45
Jordan Clo., Islw. BH44 64
Jordan Rd., Grnf. BJ37 54
Jordans Clo., Guil. AT70 118
Beatty Av.
Jordans Clo., Red. BV73 121
Jordans Clo., S.Croy. CA59 96
Jordans Clo., Stai. AX47 73
Jordans Clo., Wat. BB21 26
Jordans La., Beac. AP29 34
Jordans Way, Beac. AP29 34
Jordans Way, Rain. CV37 60
Jordans Way, St.Alb. BE18 18
Jordon Dr., Red. BV73 121
Joseph Powell Clo. SW12 BW46 76
Hazelbourne Rd.
Joseph St. E3 CD38 57
Josephine Av. SW2 BX46 76
Josephine Av., Tad. BR67 112
Josephs Rd., Guil. AR70 118
Joshua St. E14 CF39 57
Joslin Rd., Grays CY42 70
Joubert St. SW11 BU44 66
Journeys End, Slou. AP38 52
Jowett St. SE15 CA43 67
Joy Rd., Grav. DH47 81
Joyce Av. N18 CA28 39
Joyce Ct., Wal.Abb. CF20 21
Joyce Dawson Way SE28 CO40 59
Joyce Green La., Dart. CW45 70
Joyce Green Wk., Dart. CW46 80
Joyce Page Clo. SE7 CJ43 68
Lansdowne La.
Joycroft, Enf. BY23 29
Hansart Way
Joydens Wood Rd., Bex. CS48 79
Joydon Dr., Rom. CO32 50
Joyes Clo., Rom. CV28 42
Troopers Dr.
Joyners Clo., Dag. CQ35 50
Connor Rd.
Joyners Field, Harl. CM13 13
Jubilee Av. E4 CF28 39
Jubilee Av., Rom. CR32 50
Jubilee Av., Twick. BG47 74
Jubilee Clo. NW9 BN32 46
Jubilee Clo., Green. DB46 80
Jubilee Clo., Pnr. BD30 36
Jubilee Clo., Rom. CR32 50
Jubilee Clo., Stai. AX47 73
Lauser Rd.
Jubilee Cres. E14 CF41 67
Manchester Rd.
Jubilee Cres. N9 CB26 39
Jubilee Cres., Grav. DJ48 81
Jubilee Cres., Sev. DB64 108
Jubilee Cres., Wey. AX56 92
Jubilee Ct., Hat. BP11 10
Northfield
Jubilee Ct., Th.Hth. BY52 86
Jubilee Dr., Ruis. BD35 45
Jubilee Gdns., Sthl. BF39 54
Jubilee Pl. SW3 BU42 3
Jubilee Pl. SW3 BU42 66
Jubilee Rd., Grays. DA43 70
Jubilee Rd., Grnf. BJ37 54
Jubilee Rd., Orp. CQ57 98
Jubilee Rd., St.Alb. BK16 18
Jubilee Rd., Sutt. BQ57 94
Jubilee Rd., Wat. BC22 26
Jubilee Ri., Sev. CW46 108
Jubilee St. E1 CC39 57
Jubilee Ter., Bet. BN72 120
Jubilee Ter., Dor. BJ71 119
Jubilee Way SW19 BS51 86
Jubilee Way, Chess. BM56 94
Jubilee Way, Sid. CO48 79
Judd St. WC1 BX38 2
Judd St. WC1 BX38 56
Jude St. E16 CG39 58
Judeth Gdns., Grav. DJ49 81
Judge Heath La., Hayes BA39 53
Judge St., Wat. BC22 26
Judge Wk., Esher BH57 93
Judges Hill, Pot.B. BU18 20
Judges Wk. NW3 BT34 47
Judith Ann Ct., Upmin. CZ34 51
Judith Av., Rom. CR29 41
Juer St. SW11 BU43 66
Jug Hill, West. CG61 106
Juglans Rd., Orp. CO54 89
Julia Gdns., Bark. CP37 59
Julia St. NW5 BV35 47
Oak Village
Julian Av. W3 BM40 55
Julian Clo., Barn. BS24 29
Julian Clo., Wok. AR62 100
Silversmiths Way
Julian Clo., Wok. AR62 100
Julian Hill, Har. BH34 45
Julian Hill, Wey. AZ57 92
Julian Pl. E14 CE42 67
Julian Rd., Orp. CO57 98
Julian Taylor Path SE23 CB48 77
Eliot Bank
Julians Clo., Sev. CU67 116
Julians Way, Sev. CU67 116
Julien Rd. W5 BK42 64
Julien Rd., Couls. BW61 104
Juliet Ho. N1 CA37 57
Purcell St.
Juliet Way, Grays CW41 70
Junction App. SE13 CF45 67
Junction App. SW11 BU45 66
Junction Ms. W2 BU39 1
Junction Ms. W2 BU39 56
Sale Pl
Junction Rd. E., Rom. CQ33 50
Kenneth Rd.
Junction Rd. E13 CH37 58
Junction Rd. N17 CB31 48
Junction Rd. N19 BW34 47
Junction Rd. N9 CB26 39
Junction Rd. W., Rom. CQ33 50
Junction Rd. W5 BK42 64
Junction Rd., Ashf. BA49 73
Junction Rd., Brwd. DB28 42
Junction Rd., Dart. CV46 80
Junction Rd., Dor. BJ71 119
Junction Rd., Har. BG32 45
Junction Rd., Rom. CT31 50
Junction Rd., S.Croy. BZ57 96
June Clo., Couls. BV60 95
June La., Red. BV74 121
Junewood Clo., Wey. AV59 91
Juniper Av., St.Alb. BF19 18
Juniper Clo., Brox. CD16 21
Juniper Clo., Guil. AR68 109
Juniper Clo., Reig. BT71 121
Juniper Clo., Rick. AX27 35
Juniper Clo., Wem. BM35 46
Juniper Clo., West. CK62 106
Juniper Ct., Slou. AQ41 62
Nixey Clo.
Juniper Gate, Rick. AX27 35
Juniper Gdns., Mitch. BW51 86
Leonard Rd.
Juniper Grn., Hem.H. AV13 7
Juniper Gro., Wat. BC22 26
Juniper La. E6 CK39 58
Northumberland Rd.
Juniper Rd., Ilf. CL35 49
Riverdene Rd.
Juniper Rd., Reig. BT71 121
Juniper St. E1 CC40 57
Juniper Way, Hayes BA40 53
Juniper Way, Rom. CW30 42
Juniper Wk., Bet. BN71 120
Juno Rd., Hem.H. AY12 8
Juno Way SE14 CC43 67
Jupiter Dr., Hem.H. AY12 8
Jupiter Way N7 BX36 56
Jupp Rd. E15 CF36 57
Jupp Rd. W. E15 CF37 57
Jurgens Rd., Grays CY43 70
Jury St., Grav. DG46 81
Church St.
Justice Wk. SW3 BU43 66
Lawrence St.
Justin Clo., Brent. BK43 64
Justin Rd. E4 CD29 39
Jute La., Enf. CD24 30
Jutland Gdns., Couls. BX63 104
Jutland Pl., Egh. AU49 72
Mullens Rd.
Jutland Rd. E13 CH38 58
Jutland Rd. SE6 CF47 77
Jutsums Av., Rom. CR32 50
Jutsums La., Rom. CR32 50
Juxon Clo., Har. BF30 36
Juxon St. SE11 BX42 4
Juxon St. SE11 BX42 66

K

Kaduna Clo., Pnr. BC32 44
Kale Rd., Erith CQ41 69
Kambala Clo. SW11 BT45 66
Wye St.
Kambala Rd. SW11 BT44 66
Kandlewood, Brwd. DD26 122
Kangley Bridge Rd. SE26 CD49 77
Karen Clo., Brwd. DB26 42
Karen Clo., Rain. CT37 59
Karen Ct. SE4 CD44 67
Karen Ct., Brom. CG51 88
Karen Ter. E11 CG34 49
Montague Rd.
Karl House, Harl. CN13 13
Karoline Gdns., Grnf. BG37 54
Kashgar Rd. SE18 CN42 68
Kashmir Clo., Wey. AX58 92
Kashmir Rd. SE7 CJ43 68
Kassala Rd. SW11 BU44 66
Kates Clo., Barn. BP25 28
Kates Croft, Welw.G.C. BR10 5
Katharine Rd., Twick. BJ47 74
London Rd.
Katharine St., Croy. BZ55 87
Katherine Clo., Hem.H. AY15 8
Newell Rd.
Katherine Clo., Wey. AW57 92
Katherine Gdns. SE9 CJ45 68
Katherine Gdns., Ilf. CM29 40
Katherine Rd. E6 CJ36 58
Katherine Rd. E7 CJ35 49
Katherine Sq. W11 BQ40 55
Wilsham St.
Katherines Way, Harl. CL12 13
Kathleen Av. W3 BN39 55
Kathleen Av., Wem. BL36 55
Kathleen Rd. SW11 BU45 66
Katrine Sq., Hem.H. AX11 8
Kavanaghs Rd., Brwd. DA27 42
Kavanaghs Ter., Brwd. DA27 42
Kavanaghs Rd.
Kavanaghs Ter., Brwd. DA27 42
Kay Rd. SW9 BX44 66
Kay St. E15 CF36 57
New Mk. St.
Kay St. E2 CB37 2
Kay St. E2 CB37 57
Kay St., Well. CO44 69
Kayemoor Rd., Sutt. BT57 95
Kaywood Clo., Slou. AR41 62
Kean St. WC2 BX39 2
Kean St. WC2 BX39 56
Kearton Clo., Ken. BZ62 105
Keary Rd., Swans. DC47 81
Keatings, The, Brwd. CZ22 33
Mill La.
Keats Av., Rom. CU30 41
Keats Clo. NW3 BU35 47
Keats Gro.
Keats Clo. SW19 BT50 76
North Rd.
Keats Clo., Chig. CM29 40
Keats Clo., Hayes BC39 53
Keats Clo., Hem.H. AZ10 8
Bronte Cres.
Keats Clo., SE1 CA42 67
Milton Clo.
Keats Gdns., Til. DG44 71
Keats Gro. NW3 BT35 47
Keats La., Wind. AO43 61
Keats Pl. EC2 BZ39 2
Keats Rd., Belv. CS41 69
Keats Rd., Well. CN44 68
Keats Way, Croy. CC53 87
Keats Way, Grnf. BF39 54
Keats Way, West Dr. AY42 63
Keats Wk., Brwd. DE26 122
Keble Clo., Nthlt. BG35 45
Keble Clo., Wor.Pk. BO54 85
Keble St. SW17 BT49 76
Keble Ter., Wat. BB19 17
Kechill Gdns., Brom. CH54 88
Kedeston Ct., Sutt. BS55 86
Kedleston Ct. E5 CC35 48
Clapton Park Est.
Kedleston Dr., Orp. CN53 88
Kedleston Wk. E2 CB38 57
Kedward Rd., Rom. CT32 50
Victoria Rd.
Keedonwood Rd., Brom. CG49 78
Keefield, Harl. CL13 13
Keel Clo. SE16 CC40 57
Hull Clo.
Keel Dr., Slou. AN40 61
Keeler Clo., Wind. AM45 61
Keeley Rd., Croy. BZ55 87
Keeley St. WC2 BX39 2
Keeley St. WC2 BX39 56
Keeling Rd. SE9 CJ46 78
Keely Clo., Barn. BU25 29
Keemor Clo. SE18 CL43 68
Llanover St.
Keens La., Guil. AP68 109
Keens Park Rd., Guil. AP68 109
Keens Rd., Croy. BZ56 96
Keens Yd. N1 BY36 56
St. Pauls Rd.
Keensacre, Iver AU37 52
Keep, The, Kings.T. BL50 75
Keep, The, SE3 CH44 68
Keepers Clo., Guil. AU69 118
Keepers Farm Clo., Wind. AM44 61
Keepers Wk., Vir.W. AR53 82
Keetons Rd. SE16 CB41 67
Keevil Dr. SW19 BQ47 75
Keighley Clo. N7 BX35 47
Penn Rd.
Keighley Rd., Rom. CW29 42
Keightley Dr. SE9 CK47 78
Keilder Clo., Chig. CN29 40
Keilder Clo., Uxb. AZ37 53
Charnwood Rd.
Keildon Rd. SW11 BU45 66
Keir Hardie Est. E5 CB33 48
Keir Hardie Ho. W6 BQ43 65
Keir Hardie Way, Bark. CO36 59
Keir Hardie Way, Hayes BC38 53
Keir, The SW19 BQ49 75
Keith Av., S.at H. CX50 80
Keith Connor Clo. SW8 BV45 66
Heath Rd.
Keith Gro. W12 BP41 65
Keith Park Cres., West. CH59 97
Keith Park Rd., Uxb. AY36 53
Keith Rd. E17 CD30 39
Keith Rd., Bark. CM37 58
Keith Rd., Hayes BB41 63
Keiths Rd., Hem.H. AZ14 8
Keithway, Horn. CW33 51
Kelbrook Rd. SE3 CK44 68
Kelburn Way, Rain. CT38 59
Kelby Path SE9 CL48 78
Kelbys, Welw.G.C. BT 7 5
Kelceda Clo. NW2 BP34 46
Kelf Gro., Hayes BB39 53
Kelfield Gdns. W10 BQ39 55
Kell St. SE1 BY41 4
Kell St. SE1 BY41 66
Borough Rd.
Kelland Clo. N8 BW32 47
Kelland Rd. E13 CH38 58
Kellaway Rd. SE3 CJ44 68
Kellerton Rd. SE13 CG46 78
Kellett Rd. SW2 BY45 66
Kelling Gdns., Croy. BY54 86
Kellino St. SW17 BU49 76
Kelliwell Ct. SE22 CB46 77
Kellner Rd. SE28 CN41 68
Kellway Pl. W14 BR42 65
Kelly Clo., Shep. BB51 83
Geneva Clo.
Kelly Rd. NW7 BR29 37
Kelly St. NW1 BV36 56
Kelly Way, Rom. CQ32 50
Kelman Clo. SW4 BW44 66
Kelmore Gro. SE22 CB45 67
Kelmscott Clo. E17 CD30 39
Kelmscott Clo., Wat. BC25 26
Kelmscott Cres., Wat. BC25 26
Kelmscott Gdns. W12 BP41 65
Kelmscott Rd. SW11 BU46 76
Kelross Pass. N5 BZ35 48
Kelross Rd.
Kelross Rd. N5 BY35 47
Kelsall Clo. SE3 CH44 68
Kelsey La., Beck. CE52 87
Kelsey Park Av., Beck. CE51 87
Kelsey Park Rd., Beck. CE51 87
Kelsey Rd., Orp. CO51 89
Kelsey St. E2 CB38 57
Kelsey Way, Beck. CE52 87
Kelshall Ct. N4 BZ34 48
Kings Cres. Est.
Kelshall, Wat. BE21 27
Kelsie Way, Ilf. CN29 40
Kelsmore La., Chsnt. CC18 21
Kelso Dr., Grav. DJ49 81
Kelso Pl. W8 BS41 3
Kelso Pl. W8 BS41 66
Kelso Rd., Cars. BT54 86
Kelston Rd., Ilf. CL30 40
Kelvedon Av., Watt. BB57 92
Kelvedon Clo., Brwd. DF26 122
Lambourne Dr.
Kelvedon Clo., Kings.T. BM50 75
Kelvedon Grn., B.Wd. CZ22 33
Kelvedon Hall La., B.Wd. CX21 33
Kelvedon Rd. SW6 BR43 65
Kelvedon Way., Wdf.Grn. CK29 40
Kelvedon Wk., Rain. CT37 59
Kelvin Av. N13 BX29 38
Kelvin Av., Lthd. BH63 102
Kelvin Av., Tedd. BH50 74
Kelvin Clo., Epsom BM57 94
Kelvin Cres., Har. BH29 36
Kelvin Dr., Twick. BJ46 74
Kelvin Gdns., Sthl. BF39 54
Kelvin Gro. SE26 CB48 77
Kelvin Gro., Chess. BK55 84
Kelvin Par., Orp. CN54 88
Kelvin Rd. N5 BZ35 48
Kelvin Rd., Til. DG44 71
Kelvin Rd., Well. CO45 69
Kelvinbrook, E.Mol. BF52 84
Kelvington Clo., Croy. CD53 87
Kelvington Rd. SE15 CC46 77
Kelway Pl. W14 BR43 65
Kember St. N1 BX36 56
Carnoustie Dr.
Kemble Clo., Pot.B. BT20 20
Kemble Clo., Wey. BA56 92
Kemble Dr., Brom. CK55 88
Kemble Par., Pot.B. BT19 20
High St.
Kemble Rd. N17 CB30 39
Kemble Rd. SE23 CC47 77
Kemble Rd., Croy. BY55 86
Kemble St. WC2 BX39 2
Kemble St. WC2 BX39 56
Kembleside Rd., West. CJ62 106
Kings Rd.
Kemerton Rd. SE5 BZ45 67
Kemerton Rd., Beck. CE51 87
Kemerton Rd., Croy. CA54 87
Kemeys St. E9 CD35 48
Kemnal Rd., Chis. CM50 78
Kemp Gdns., Croy. BZ53 87
St. Saviours Rd.
Kemp Pl., Bush. BF25 27
Kemp Rd., Dag. CP33 50
Kempe Clo., St.Alb. BG15 9
Kempe Rd. NW6 BQ37 55
Kempe Rd., Enf. CB21 30
Kempis Way SE22 CA46 77
Dulwich Gro.
Kemplay Rd. NW3 BT35 47
Kempley Ct., Grays DE43 71
Dock Rd.
Kemps Dr. E14 CE40 57
Morant St.
Kemps Dr., Nthwd. BB29 35
Kemps Gdns. SE13 CF46 77
Thornford Rd.
Kempsford Gdns. SW5 BS42 66
Kempsford Rd. SE11 BY42 4
Kempshead Rd. SE5 CA42 4
Kempshead Rd. SE5 CA42 67
Kempshott Rd. SW16 BW50 76
Kempson Rd. SW6 BS43 66
Kempt St. SE18 CL43 68
Kempthorne Rd. SE8 CD42 67
Kempton Av., Horn. CW35 51
Kempton Av., Nthlt. BF36 54
Kempton Av., Sun. BC51 83
Kempton Clo., Erith CS43 69
Kempton Clo., Uxb. BA35 44
Lawrence Dr.
Kempton Rd. E6 CK37 58
Kempton Rd., Hmptn. BE51 84
Kempton Wk., Croy. CD53 87
Kemsing Clo., Bex. CQ47 79
Kemsing Clo., Brom. CG55 88
Bourne Way
Kemsing Clo., Th.Hth. BZ52 87
Kemsing Rd. SE10 CH42 68
Kemsing Rd., Sev. DA62 108
Kemsley Clo., Grav. DF49 81
Kemsley Clo., Green. DA46 80
Kemsley Rd., West. CJ63 106
Ken Way, Wem. BN34 46
Kenbury Clo., Uxb. AZ34 44
Kenbury St. SE5 BZ44 67
Kenchester Clo. SW8 BX43 66
Kencot Way, Erith CQ41 69
Kendal Av. N18 BZ28 39
Kendal Av. W3 BM39 55
Kendal Av., Bark. CN37 58
Kendal Av., Epp. CO19 23
Kendal Cft., Horn. CU35 50
Kendal Clo. SW9 BY43 66
Foxley Rd.
Kendal Clo., Reig. BT70 121
Kendal Clo., Slou. AQ40 52
Kendal Clo., Wdf.Grn. CG27 40
Kendal Dr., Slou. AQ40 52
Kendal Gdns. N18 BZ28 39
Kendal Pl. SW15 BR46 75
Upper Richmond Rd.
Kendal Rd. NW10 BP35 46
Kendal St. W2 BU39 1
Kendal St. W2 BU39 56
Kendale Clo., Hayes BB37 53
Kendale Rd., Brom. CG49 78

Kendale, Grays DG41 71
Godman Rd.
Kendale, Hem.H. AZ14 8
Kendall Av. S., S.Croy. BZ58 96
Kendall Av., Beck. CD51 87
Kendall Av., S.Croy. BZ58 96
Kendall Gdns., Sutt. BT55 86
Kendall Pl. W1 BV39 1
Kendall Pl. W1 BV39 56
George St.
Kendall Rd., Beck. CD51 87
Kendall Rd., Islw. BJ44 64
Kendals Clo., Rad. BH21 27
Kender Est. SE14 CC44 67
Kender St. SE14 CC44 67
Kendoa Rd. SW4 BW45 66
Kendon Clo. E11 CH32 49
The Avenue
Kendor Av., Epsom BN59 94
Kendra Hall Rd., S.Croy. BY57 95
Kendrey Gdns., Twick. BH46 74
Kendrick Ms. SW7 BT42 3
Kendrick Ms. SW7 BT42 66
Reece Ms.
Kendrick Pl. SW7 BT42 3
Reece Ms.
Kendrick Pl. SW7 BT42 66
Reece Ms.
Kendrick Rd., Slou. AQ41 62
Kenelm Clo., Har. BJ34 45
Kenerne Dr., Barn. BR25 28
Kenford Clo., Wat. BC19 17
Kenia Wk., Grav. DJ48 81
Cervia Way
Kenilford Rd. SW12 BV47 76
Kenilworth Av. E17 CE30 39
Kenilworth Av. SW19 BS49 76
Kenilworth Av., Cob. BF60 93
Kenilworth Av., Har. BE35 45
Kenilworth Av., Rom. CX29 42
Kenilworth Clo., B.Wd. BN24 28
Kenilworth Clo., Bans. BS61 104
Kenilworth Clo., Slou. AP41 62
Kenilworth Clo., Wal.Cr. CC20 21
Kenilworth Cres., Enf. CA23 30
Kenilworth Ct. SW15 BQ45 65
Kenilworth Ct., Twick. BG48 74
Kenilworth Ct., Wat. BC23 26
Kenilworth Dr., B.Wd. BN24 28
Kenilworth Dr., Rick. AZ24 26
Kenilworth Dr., Walt. BD55 84
Kenilworth Gdns. SE18 CL44 68
Kenilworth Gdns., Hayes BB39 53
Kenilworth Gdns., Horn. CV34 51
Kenilworth Gdns., Ilf. CN34 49
Kenilworth Gdns., Loug. CK25 31
Kenilworth Gdns., Stai. AX49 73
Kenilworth Gdns., Sthl. BE38 54
Kenilworth Gdns., Wat. BD28 36
Kenilworth Rd. E3 CD37 57
Kenilworth Rd. NW6 BR37 55
Kenilworth Rd. SE20 CC51 87
Kenilworth Rd. W5 BL40 55
Kenilworth Rd., Ashf. AX48 73
Kenilworth Rd., Edg. BN27 37
Kenilworth Rd., Epsom BP56 94
Kenilworth Rd., Orp. CM53 88
Kenilworth Way, Slou. AP41 62
Mere Rd.
Kenley Av. NW9 BO30 37
Kenley Clo., Bex. CR47 79
Kenley Clo., Cat. BZ63 105
Kenley Clo., Chis. CN52 88
Kenley Gdns., Horn. CW34 51
Kenley Gdns., Th.Hth. BY52 86
Kenley La., Ken. BZ61 105
Kenley Rd. SW19 BR51 85
Kenley Rd., Kings.T. BM51 85
Kenley Rd., Twick. BJ46 74
Kenley Wk. W11 BR40 55
Kenley Wk., Sutt. BQ56 94
Kenlor Rd. SW17 BT49 76
Kenmare Dr., Mitch. BU50 76
Kenmare Gdns. N13 BZ28 39
Kenmare Rd., Th.Hth. BX53 86
Kenmere Gdns., Wem. BM37 55
Kenmere Rd., Well. CP44 69
Kenmont Gdns. NW10 BP38 55
Kenmore Av., Har. BJ32 45
Kenmore Clo., Rich. BM43 65
Kent Rd.
Kenmore Cres., Hayes BB38 53
Kenmore Gdns., Edg. BM30 37
Kenmore N2 BT33 47
Kenmore Rd., Har. BK31 45
Kenmore Rd., Ken. BY60 95
Kenmure Rd. E8 CB35 48
Kennal La., Lthd. BF64 102
Kennard Rd. E15 CF36 57
Kennard Rd. N11 BU28 38
Kennard St. E16 CK40 58
Kennard St. SW11 BV44 66
Kenneally Clo., Wind. AL44 61
Kenneally
Kenneally Pl., Wind. AL44 61
Kenneally
Kenneally Wk., Wind. AL44 61
Kenneally
Kenneally, Wind. AL44 61
Kennedy Av., Enf. CC25 30
Kennedy Av., Hodd. CD12 12
Kennedy Clo. E13 CH37 58
Kennedy Clo., Chsnt. CD17 21
High St.
Kennedy Clo., Orp. CM54 88
Kennedy Clo., Pnr. BE29 36
Kennedy Gdns., Sev. CV65 108
Kennedy Rd. W7 BH39 54
Kennedy Rd., Bark. CN37 58
Kennel Clo., Lthd. BG65 102
Kennel La., B.Wd. CY23 33
Kennel Wood La., Hat. BP12 10
Kennelwood Cres., Croy. CF59 96
Kenners La., Wal.Abb. CK13 13
Kennet Cl. SW11 BT45 66
Maysoule Rd.
Kennet Clo., Upmin. CZ32 51
Kennet Grn., S.Ock. DA40 60
Cawdor Av.
Kennet Rd. W9 BR38 55
Kennet Rd., Dart. CU45 69
Kennet Rd., Islw. BH45 64
Kennet St. E1 CB40 4
Kennet St. E1 CB40 57
Kennet Wharf La. EC4 BZ40 4
Upper Thames St.
Kennet Wharf La. EC4 BZ40 57
Upper Thames St.
Kenneth Av., Ilf. CL35 49
Kenneth Cres. NW2 BP35 46
Kenneth Gdns., Stan. BJ29 36
Kenneth More Rd., Ilf. CL34 49
Oakfield Rd.
Kenneth Rd., Bans. BT61 104
Kenneth Rd., Rom. CP33 50
Kennett Rd., Slou. AT41 62
Kenning Rd., Hodd. CE11 12
Kenning St. SE16 CC41 67
Kenning Ter. N1 CA37 2
Kenning Ter. N1 CA37 57
Branch Pl.
Kenninghall Rd. E5 CB34 48
Kenninghall Rd. N18 CC28 39
Kennings Est. SE11 BY42 66
Kennings Way SE11 BY42 4
Kennings Way SE11 BY42 66
Kennington Gro. SE11 BX43 4
Kennington Gro. SE11 BX43 66
Kennington La. SE11 BX42 4
Kennington La. SE11 BX42 66
Kennington Oval SE11 BX43 66
Kennington Pk. Est. SE11 BY43 66
Kennington Pk. Gdns. SE11 BY43 66
Kennington Pk. Pl. SE11 BY43 4
Kennington Pk. Pl. SE11 BY43 66
Kennington Pk. Rd. SE11 BY43 4
Kennington Pk. Rd. SE11 BY43 66
Kennington Rd. SE1 BY41 4
Kennington Rd. SE1 BY41 66
Kenny Rd. NW7 BR29 37
Kennyland Ct. NW4 BP32 46
Kenrick Pl. W1 BV39 1
Kenrick Pl. W1 BV39 56
Dorset St.
Kenrick Sq., Red. CA70 114
Kensal Rd. W10 BQ38 55
Kensington Av. E12 CK36 58
Kensington Av., Th.Hth. BY51 86
Kensington Av., Wat. BB24 26
Kensington Church St. W8 BS40 56
Kensington Church Wk. W8 BS41 66
Holland St.
Kensington Ct. Ms. W8 BS41 66
Kensington Court Pl.
Kensington Ct. Pl. W8 BS41 3
Kensington Ct. Pl. W8 BS41 66
Kensington Ct. W8 BS41 3
Kensington Ct. W8 BS41 66
Kensington Dr., Wdf.Grn CJ30 40
Kensington Gate W8 BT41 3
Kensington Gate W8 BT41 66
Kensington Gdns. Sq. W2 BS39 56
Kensington Gdns., Ilf. CK33 49
Kensington Gore SW7 BT41 3
Kensington Gore SW7 BT41 66
Kensington High St. W8 BR41 65
Kensington Mall W8 BS40 56
Kensington Palace Gdns. W8 BS40 56
Kensington Pk. Gdns. W11 BR40 55
Kensington Pk. Ms. W11 BR39 55
Kensington Pk. Rd. W11 BR39 55
Kensington Pl. W8 BS40 56
Kensington Rd. SW7 BT41 66
Kensington Rd. W8 BS41 3
Kensington Rd. W8 BT41 66
Kensington Rd., Brwd. DA25 33
Kensington Rd., Nthlt. BF38 54
Kensington Rd., Rom. CS32 50
Kensington Sq. W8 BS41 3
Kensington Sq. W8 BS41 66
Kensington Ter., S.Croy. BZ57 96
Kent Av. W13 BJ39 54
Kent Av., Dag. CR39 59
Kent Av., Slou. AO39 52
Kent Av., Well. CN46 78
Kent Clo., B.Wd. BN22 28
Kent Clo., Mitch. BX52 86
Kent Clo., Orp. CN57 97
Kent Clo., Stai. AX50 73
Kent Clo., Uxb. AX36 53
Kent Dr., Barn. BV24 29
Kent Dr., Horn. CV35 51
Kent Dr., Tedd. BH49 74
Kent Gate Way, Croy. CD57 96
Kent Gdns. W13 BJ39 54
Kent Gdns., Ruis. BC32 44
Kent Hatch Rd., Oxt. CJ68 115
Kent House La., Beck. CD50 77
Kent House Rd., Beck. CD50 77
Kent Pass. NW1 BU38 1
Kent Pass. NW1 BU38 56
Kent Rd. N15 CA32 48
Kent Rd. N21 BZ26 39
Kent Rd. SE1 CA42 4
Kent Rd. W4 BN41 65
Kent Rd., Dag. CR35 50
Kent Rd., Dart. CV46 80
Kent Rd., E.Mol. BG52 84
Kent Rd., Grav. DG47 81
Kent Rd., Grays DE43 71
Kent Rd., Kings.T. BK52 84
Kent Rd., Long. DB51 90
Kent Rd., Orp. CO53 89
Kent Rd., Rich. BM43 65
Kent Rd., W.Wick. CE54 87
Kent Rd., Wok. AT61 100
Kent St. E13 CH38 58
Kent St. E2 CA37 2
Kent St. E2 CA37 57
Kent Ter. NW1 BU38 1
Kent Ter. NW1 BU38 56
Kent Vw. Gdns., Ilf. CN34 49
Kent Vw., S.Ock. CY41 70
Kent Way SE15 CA44 67
Sumner Est.
Kent Way, Surb. BL55 85
Kent Wk. SW9 BY45 66
Kent Yd. SW7 BU41 3
Rutland Gdns.
Kent Yd. SW7 BU41 66
Rutland Gdns.
Kentford Way, Nthlt. BE37 54
Kentish Bldgs. SE1 BZ41 4
Kentish Bldgs. SE1 BZ41 67
Borough High St.
Kentish La., Hat. BT16 20
Kentish Rd., Belv. CR42 69
Kentish Town Rd. NW1 BV36 56
Kentish Town Rd. NW1 BV37 1
Kentish Way, Brom. CH51 88
Kentmere Rd. SE18 CN42 68
Kenton Av., Har. BH33 45
Kenton Av., Sthl. BF40 54
Kenton Av., Sun. BD51 84
Kenton Ct., Har. BJ32 45
Kenton Gdns., Har. BK32 45
Kenton Gdns., St.Alb. BH14 9
Kenton La., Har. BH29 36
Kenton Park Av., Har. BK31 45
Kenton Park Clo., Har. BK32 45
Kenton Park Cres., Har. BK31 45
Kenton Park Rd., Har. BK31 45
Kenton Rd. E9 CC36 57
Kenton Rd., Har. BH33 45
Kenton St. WC1 BX38 2
Kenton St. WC1 BX38 56
Kenton Way, Hayes BB38 53
Kenton Way, Wok. AP61 100
Kentons La., Wind. AM44 61
Kents Av., Hem.H. AX15 8
Kents La., Epp. CS14 14
Kents Pass., Hmptn. BE51 84
Kentwell Clo. SE4 CD46 77
Turnham Rd.
Kentwode Grn. SW13 BP43 65
Kentwyns Ri., Red. BX71 121
Kenver Av. N12 BT29 38
Kenward Rd. SE9 CJ46 78
Kenway Clo., Rain. CV38 60
Kenway Dr., Amer. AQ23 25
Kenway Rd. SW5 BS42 66
Kenway Wk., Rain. CV38 60
Kenway, Rain. CV38 60
Kenway, Rom. CS30 41
Kenwood Av. N14 BW25 29
Kenwood Av. SE14 CC44 67
Briant St.
Kenwood Clo. NW3 BT33 47
Kenwood Clo., West Dr. AZ43 63
Kenwood Dr., Beck. CF52 87
Kenwood Dr., Rick. AV27 34
Kenwood Dr., Walt. BC57 92
Kenwood Gdns. E18 CH31 49
Kenwood Gdns., Ilf. CL31 49
Kenwood Pk., Wey. BA57 92
Kenwood Rd. N6 BU32 47
Kenwood Rd. N9 CB26 39
Kenwood Ridge, Ken. BY62 104
Kenworthy Rd. E9 CD35 48
Kenwyn Dr. NW2 BO34 46
Kenwyn Rd. SW20 BQ51 85
Kenwyn Rd. SW4 BW45 66
Kenya Rd. SE7 CJ43 68
Kenyngton Dr., Sun. BC49 73
Kenyngton Pl., Har. BK32 45
Kenyon St. SW6 BQ44 65
Kenyons, Lthd. AZ67 110
Keogh Rd. E15 CG36 58
Kepler Rd. SW4 BX45 66
Keppel Rd. E6 CK36 58
Keppel Rd., Dag. CQ35 50
Keppel Row SE1 BZ40 4
Keppel Row SE1 BZ40 57
Great Guildford St.
Keppel Spur, Wind. AQ47 72
Keppel St. WC1 BW39 1
Keppel St. WC1 BW39 56
Malet St.
Keppel St., Wind. AO44 61
Helena Rd.
Keppell Rd., Dor. BJ70 119
Kerbela St. E2 CB38 2
Kerbela St. E2 CB38 57
Kerbey St. E14 CE39 57
Kerdistone Clo., Pot.B. BS18 20
Kerfield Cres. SE5 BZ44 67
Grove La.
Kerfield Pl. SE5 BZ44 67
Kernick Clo. N7 BX36 56
Sutterton St.
Kernow Clo., Horn. CW34 51
Kerrill Av., Couls. BY63 104
Kerrison Pl. W5 BK40 54
Kerrison Rd. E15 CF37 57
Kerrison Rd. SW11 BU45 66
Kerrison Rd. W5 BK40 54
Kerry Av., Grays CW41 70
Kerry Av., Stan. BK28 36
Kerry Clo. E16 CH39 58
Kerry Clo., Barn. BQ24 28
Kerry Clo., Upmin. CZ33 51
Kerry Dr., Upmin. CZ33 51
Kerry Path SE14 CD43 67
Kerry Rd. SE14 CD43 67
Kerry Rd., Grays DE40 71
Kerry Ter., Wok. AT61 100
Kersey Dr., S.Croy. CC59 96
Kersey Gdns. SE9 CK49 78
Kersey Gdns., Rom. CW29 42
Kersfield Rd. SW15 BQ46 75
Kershaw Clo. SW18 BT46 76
Kershaw Rd., Dag. CR34 50
Kersley Ms. SW11 BU44 66
Kersley Rd. N16 CA34 48
Kersley St. SW11 BU44 66
Kerstin Clo., Hayes BB40 53
Kerswell Cres. N15 CA32 48
Kerwick Clo. N7 BX36 56
Blundell St.
Keslake Rd. NW6 BQ37 55
Kessock Clo. N15 CB32 48
Kesters Rd., Chesh. AO19 16
Kesteven Clo., Ilf. CN29 40
Keston Av., Couls. BY63 104
Keston Av., Kes. CJ56 97
Keston Av., Wey. AW59 92
Keston Clo. N18 BZ27 39
Keston Clo., Well. CP43 69
Keston Gdns., Kes. CJ56 97
Keston Ms., Wat. BC23 26
Keston Park Clo., Kes. CK55 88
Keston Rd. N17 BZ31 48
Keston Rd. SE15 CB45 67
Keston Rd., Th.Hth. BX53 86
Kestrel Av. E6 CK39 58
Swann App.
Kestrel Av. SE24 BZ46 77
Kestrel Av., Stai. AV48 72
Kestrel Clo. NW10 BN36 55
Kingfisher Way
Kestrel Clo., Berk. AR13 7
Kestrel Clo., Guil. AV69 118
Kestrel Clo., Ilf. CP28 41
Kestrel Clo., Rain. CU36 59
Kestrel Ct. E17 CC30 39
Kestrel Grn., Hat. BP13 10
Kestrel Way, Croy. CF58 96
Keswick Av. SW15 BO49 75
Keswick Av. SW19 BS51 86
Keswick Av., Horn. CV33 51
Keswick Clo., Sutt. BT56 95
Keswick Ct., Slou. AP40 52
Stoke Rd.
Keswick Dr., Enf. CC22 30
Keswick Gdns., Ilf. CK31 49
Keswick Gdns., Ruis. BA32 44
Keswick Gdns., Wem. BL35 46
Keswick Ms. W5 BK40 54
Keswick Rd. SW15 BR46 75
Keswick Rd., Bexh. CR44 69
Keswick Rd., Egh. AT50 72
Keswick Rd., Lthd. BF66 111
Keswick Rd., Orp. CN54 88
Keswick Rd., Twick. BG46 74
Keswick Rd., W.Wick. CG55 88
Kett Gdns. SW2 BX46 76
Kettering Rd., Enf. CC22 30
Kettering Rd., Rom. CW29 42
Kettering St. SW16 BV50 76
Kettlebaston Rd. E10 CD33 48
Kettlebury Way, Ong. CW18 24
Kettlewell Clo., Swan. CT51 89
Kettlewell Clo., Wok. AR61 100
Kettlewell Dr., Wok. AS60 91
Kettlewell Hill, Wok. AS60 91
Ketton Grn., Red. BW67 113
Malmstone Av.
Kevan Dr., Wok. AV65 100
Kevelioc Rd. N17 BZ30 39
Kevin Clo., Houns. BD44 64
Kevington Clo., Orp. CO52 89
Kevington Dr., Brom. CN52 88
Kevington Dr., Chis. CN52 88
Kevington Dr., Orp. CN52 88
Kew Bridge Ct. W4 BM42 65
Kew Bridge Rd., Brent. BL43 65
Kew Clo. E1 CC38 57
Cambridge Heath Rd.
Kew Cres., Sutt. BR55 85
Kew Foot Rd., Rich. BL45 65
Kew Gardens Rd., Rich. BL43 65
Kew Grn., Rich. BL43 65
Kew Meadows Path, Rich. BM44 65
Kew Palace, Rich. BL43 65
Kew Rd., Rich. BL45 65
Keway Ct., Berk. AQ13 7
Cross Oak Rd.
Kewferry Dr., Nthwd. AZ28 35
Kewferry Rd., Nthwd. BA29 35
Key Clo. E1 CC38 57
Keyes Rd. NW2 BQ35 46
Keyes Rd., Dart. CW45 70
Keyfield Ter., St.Alb. BG14 9
Keymer Clo., West. CJ61 106
Keymer Rd. SW2 BX48 76
Keynes Clo. N2 BU31 47
Keynsham Av., Wdf.Grn. CG28 40
Keynsham Gdns. SE9 CK46 78
Keynsham Rd. SE9 CJ46 78
Keynsham Rd., Mord. BS54 86
Keynsham Wk., Mord. BS54 86
Keys, The, Brwd. DB29 42
Eagle Way
Keyse Rd. SE1 CA41 4
Keyse Rd. SE1 CA41 67
Grange Rd.
Keysers Rd., Brox. CE14 12
Keysham Av., Houns. BC43 63
Keystone Cres. N1 BX37 2
Keystone Cres. N1 BX37 56
Caledonian Rd.
Keywood Dr., Sun. BC50 73
Keyworth St. SE1 BY41 4
Keyworth St. SE1 BY41 66
Kezia St. SE8 CC42 67
Trundleys Rd.
Khama Rd. SW17 BU49 76
Khartoum Rd. E13 CH38 58
Khartoum Rd. SW17 BT49 76
Khartoum Rd., Ilf. CL35 49
Khyber Rd. SW11 BU44 66
Kibworth St. SW8 BX43 66
Dorset Rd.
Kidborough Down, Lthd. BF67 111
Kidbrooke Gdns. SE3 CH44 68
Kidbrooke Gro. SE3 CH44 68
Kidbrooke La. SE9 CK45 68
Kidbrooke Park Clo. SE3 CH44 68
Kidbrooke Park Rd. SE3 CH44 68
Kidbrooke Way SE3 CH44 68
Kidd Pl. SE7 CK42 68
Kidderminster Rd., Croy. BY54 86
Kidderpore Av. NW3 BS35 47
Kidderpore Gdns. NW3 BS35 47
Kidlington Way NW9 BO30 37
Kidrow Way E9 CC37 57
Cleremont Rd.
Kielder Clo., Ilf. CN29 40
New North Rd.
Kiffen St. EC2 BZ38 2
Kiffen St. EC2 BZ38 57
Clere St.
Kilbride Ct., Hem.H. AY11 8
Kilburn Bldgs. NW6 BS37 56
Kilburn High St.
Kilburn Gate NW6 BS37 1
Kilburn Gate NW6 BS37 56
Kilburn High Rd. NW6 BR36 55
Kilburn La. W10 BQ38 55
Kilburn Park Rd. NW6 BS38 56
Kilburn Pl. NW6 BS37 56
Kilburn Priory NW6 BS37 56
Kilburn Sq. NW6 BS37 56
Kilburn Vale NW6 BS37 56
Belsize Rd.
Kilby Clo., Wat. BD20 18
Kilcorral Clo., Epsom BP60 94
Kildare Clo., Ruis. BD33 45
Kildare Gdns. W2 BS39 56
Kildare Rd. E16 CH39 58
Kildare Ter. W2 BS39 56
Kildare Wk. E14 CE39 58
Farrance St.
Kildonan Clo., Wat. BB23 26
Kildoran Rd. SW2 BX46 76
Kildowan Rd., Ilf. CO33 50
Kilfillan Gdns., Berk. AQ13 7
Kilgour Rd. SW23 CD46 77
Kilgowan Rd., Ilf. CO33 50
Kilkie St. SW6 BT44 66
Killarney Rd. SW18 BT46 76
Killearn Rd. SE6 CF47 77
Killester Gdns., Wor.Pk. BP56 94
Killewarren Way, Orp. CP54 89
Killick St. N1 BX37 2
Killick St. N1 BX37 56
Killieser Av. SW2 BX48 76
Killip Clo. E16 CG39 58
Killowen Av., Nthlt. BG35 45
Killowen Rd. E9 CC36 57
Killy Hill, Wok. AP57 91
Killyon Rd. SW8 BW44 66
Kilmaine Rd. SW6 BR43 65
Kilmarnock Gdns., Dag. CP34 50
Lindsey Rd.
Kilmarnock Pk., Reig. BS70 121
Kilmarnock Rd., Wat. BD28 36
Woodhall La.
Kilmarsh Rd. W6 BQ42 65
Kilmartin Av. SW16 BX52 86
Kilmartin Rd., Ilf. CO34 50
Kilmartin Way, Horn. CU35 50
Kilmeston Way SE15 CA43 67
Kilmington Clo., Brwd. DD27 122
Kilmington Rd. SW13 BP43 65
Kilmiston Av., Shep. BA53 83
Kilmorey Gdns., Twick. BJ46 74
Kilmorey Rd., Twick. BJ45 64
Kilmorie Rd. SE23 CD47 77
Kiln Av., Amer. AR22 25
Kiln Clo., Hayes BA43 63
Kiln Field, Brwd. DB21 33
Kiln Field, Welw.G.C. BR6 5
Kiln Ground, Hem.H. AZ14 8
Kiln La., Bet. BN70 120
Kiln La., Chesh. AQ19 16
Kiln La., Epsom BO59 94
Kiln La., Slou. AO33 43
Kiln La., Wok. AO68 109
Kiln Meadows, Guil. AO68 109
Kiln Pl. NW5 BV35 47
Kiln Rd., Epp. CR17 23
Kiln Way, Grays DC42 71
Kilncroft, Hem.H. AZ14 8
Kilndown, Grav. DH50 81
Kilner St. E14 CE39 57
Kilnside, Esher BJ57 93
Kilnway Clo., Nthwd. BB29 35
Kilnwood, Sev. CQ60 98
Kilravock St. W10 BR38 55
Kilrue La., Walt. BB56 92
Kilrush Ter., Wok. AT61 100
Kilsby Wk., Dag. CO36 59
Rugby Rd.
Kilsha Rd., Walt. BD53 84
Kilvinton Dr., Enf. BZ22 30
Kilworth Av., Brwd. DD25 122
Kimbell Gdns. SW6 BR44 65
Kimber Clo., Wind. AN45 61
Kimber Ct., Guil. AU69 118
Gilliat Dr.
Kimber Rd. SW18 BS47 76
Kimberley Av. E6 CK37 58
Kimberley Av. SE15 CB44 67
Kimberley Av., Ilf. CM33 49
Kimberley Av., Rom. CS32 50
Kimberley Clo., Slou. AS42 62
Kimberley Dr., Sid. CP48 79
Kimberley Gdns. N4 BY32 47
Kimberley Gdns., Enf. CA24 30
Kimberley Pl., Pur. BY59 95
Brighton Rd.
Kimberley Rd. E11 CF34 48
Kimberley Rd. E16 CG38 58
Kimberley Rd. E17 CD30 39
Kimberley Rd. E4 CG26 40
Kimberley Rd. N17 CB30 39
Kimberley Rd. N18 CB29 39
Kimberley Rd. NW6 BR37 55
Kimberley Rd. SW9 BX44 66
Kimberley Rd., Beck. CC51 87
Kimberley Rd., Croy. BY53 86
Kimberley Rd., St.Alb. BG13 9

Kimberley Ride, Cob. BF60 93
Kimberley Way E4 CG26 40
Kimble Cres., Bush. BG26 36
Kimble Rd. SW19 BT50 76
Kimbolton Clo. SE12 CG46 78
Kimbolton Grn., Brwd. BN24 28
Kimbolton Row SW3 BU42 66
Fulham Rd.
Kimmeridge Gdns. SE9 CK49 78
Kimmeridge Rd. SE9 CK49 78
Kimps Way, Hem.H. AZ15 8
Kimpton Av., Brwd. DA26 42
Kimpton Clo., Hem.H. AZ11 8
Kimpton Clo., Wat. BD20 18
Kimpton Rd. SE5 BZ44 67
Kimpton Rd., Sutt. BR55 85
Kimptons Clo., Ong. CW16 24
Kimptons Clo., Pot.B. BQ19 19
Kimptons Mead, Pot.B. BQ19 19
Kinburn St. SE16 CC41 67
Kincaid Rd. SE15 CB43 67
Kinch Gro., Har. BL33 46
Kincraig Dr., Sev. CU65 107
Kinder Clo. SE28 CP40 59
Kinder Scout, Hem.H. AZ14 8
Crofts Path
Kinder St. E1 CB39 57
Kindersley Way, Wat. BA19 17
Kinfauns Av., Horn. CV32 51
Kinfauns Rd. SW2 BY48 76
Kinfauns Rd., Ilf. CO33 50
King & Queen St. SE17 BZ42 4
King & Queen St. SE17 BZ42 67
King Alfred Av. SE6 CE49 77
King Alfred Rd., Rom. CW30 42
King Arthur Clo. CC43 67
SE15
King Charles Cres., BL54 85
Surb.
King Charles Rd., Surb. BL53 85
King Charles St. SW1 BW41 3
King Charles St. SW1 BW41 66
King Charles Wk. SW13 BR47 75
Princes Way
King Craig Dr., Sev. CU65 107
King David La. E1 CC40 57
King Edward Av., Dart. CV46 80
King Edward Av., Rain. CV37 60
King Edward Ct., Wind. AO44 61
King Edward Dr., Chess. BK55 84
King Edward Dr., Grays DF42 71
King Edward Ms. BP44 65
SW13
Byfield Gdns.
King Edward Rd. E10 CF33 48
King Edward Rd. E17 CD31 48
King Edward Rd., Barn. BS24 29
King Edward Rd., Brwd. DB27 42
King Edward Rd., Green. DA46 80
King Edward Rd., Rad. BL20 19
King Edward Rd., Rom. CT32 50
King Edward Rd., Wal.Cr. CD20 21
King Edward Rd., Wat. BE25 27
King Edward St. EC1 BZ39 2
King Edward St. EC1 BZ39 57
King Edward St., Hem.H. AX15 8
King Edward St., Slou. AO41 61
King Edward VII Av., AO43 61
Wind.
King Edward Wk. SE1 BY41 4
King Edward Wk. SE1 BY41 66
King Edwards Gdns. W3 BM40 55
King Edwards Gro., BJ50 74
Tedd.
King Edwards Rd. E9 CB37 57
King Edwards Rd. N9 CB26 39
King Edwards Rd., Bark. CM37 58
King Edwards Rd., Enf. CC24 30
King Edwards Rd., Rom. CT32 50
Victoria Rd.
King Edwards Rd., Ruis. BA33 44
King Gdns., Croy. BY56 95
King George Av. E16 CJ39 58
King George Av., Bush. BF25 27
King George Av., Walt. BD54 84
King George Clo., Rom. CS31 50
King George Rd., CF20 21
Wal.Abb.
King George Sq., Rich. BL46 75
King George St. SE10 CF43 67
King George V Rd., AO22 25
Amer.
King George VI Av., BU52 86
Mitch.
King George VI Av., CJ61 106
West.
King Georges Av., Wat. BB24 26
King Georges Dr., Sthl. BE39 54
Lady Margaret Rd.
King Georges Dr., Wey. AW58 92
King Georges Rd., Brwd. DA25 33
King Harolds Way, Bexh. CP43 69
King Harry La., St.Alb. BF14 9
King Harry St., Hem.H. AX13 8
King Henry Ms., Orp. CN56 97
Osgood Av.
King Henry St. N16 CA35 48
King Henrys Dr., Croy. CF58 96
King Henrys Ms., Enf. CE22 30
King Henrys Rd. NW3 BU36 1
King Henrys Rd. NW3 BU36 56
King Henrys Rd., BM52 85
Kings.T.
King Henrys Wk. N1 CA36 57
King James Av., Cuff. BX18 20
King James St. SE1 BY41 4
King James St. SE1 BY41 66
King John Ct. EC2 CA38 2
King John Ct. EC2 CA38 57
New Inn Yd.
King John St. E1 CC39 57
King Johns Clo., Stai. AR46 72
King Johns Wk. SE9 CJ47 78
King St. E13 CH38 58
King St. EC2 BZ39 2
King St. EC2 BZ39 57
King St. N2 BT31 47
King St. SW1 BW40 3
King St. SW1 BW40 56
King St. W3 BM40 55
King St. W6 BO42 65
King St. WC2 BX40 4
King St. WC2 BX40 56
King St. Wk., Grays DD43 71
Argent St.
King St., Cher. AV54 82
King St., Grav. DG46 81
King St., Ong. CZ17 24
King St., Rich. BK46 74
King St., Sthl. BE41 64
King St., Twick. BJ47 74
King St., Wat. BD24 27
King Stairs Clo. SE16 CC41 67
Elephant La.
King William IV Gdns., CC50 77
SE20
St. Johns Rd.
King William La. SE10 CG42 68
Orlop St.
King William St. EC4 BZ39 2
King William St. EC4 BZ39 57
King William Wk. SE10 CF43 67
Kingaby Gdns., Rain. CU36 59
Kingcup Clo., Croy. CC54 87
Primrose La.
Kingdon Rd. NW6 BS36 56
Kingfield Clo., Wok. AS63 100
Kingfield Dr., Wok. AS63 100
Kingfield Gdns., Wok. AS63 100
Kingfield Rd. W5 BK38 54
Kingfield Rd., Wok. AS63 100
Kingfield St. E14 CF42 67
Kingfisher Clo. SE28 CP40 59
Kingfisher Clo., Brwd. DD26 122
Kingfisher Clo., Nthwd. AZ30 35
Kingfisher Clo., Orp. CP52 89
Sandpiper Way
Kingfisher Clo., Walt. BE56 93
Kingfisher Dr., Guil. AU69 118
Kingfisher Dr., Red. BV69 121
Kingfisher Dr., Rich. BK49 74
Kingfisher Dr., Stai. AV49 72
Kingfisher Gdns., CC59 96
S.Croy.
Kingfisher Lure, AZ18 17
Kings L.
Kingfisher Lure, Rick. AW24 26
Kingfisher Rd., Upmin. CZ33 51
Kingfisher Sq. SE8 CD43 67
Dorking Clo.
Kingfisher St. E6 CK39 58
Kingham Clo. SW18 BT47 76
Kingham Clo. W11 BR41 65
Kinghorn St. EC1 BZ39 2
Kinglake Ct., Wok. AP62 100
William Russel Ct.
Kinglake Est. SE17 CA42 4
Kinglake Est. SE17 CA42 67
Kinglake St. SE17 CA42 4
Kinglake St. SE17 CA42 67
Kingly Ct. W1 BW40 3
Kingly Ct. W1 BW40 56
Beak St.
Kingly St. W1 BW39 1
Kingly St. W1 BW39 56
Kings Arbour, Sthl. BE42 64
Ringway
Kings Arms Ct. E1 CB39 2
Kings Arms Ct. E1 CB39 57
Kings Arms Yd. EC2 BZ39 2
Kings Arms Yd. EC2 BZ39 57
Kings Arms Yd. SW18 BS46 76
Wandsworth High St.
Kings Arms Yd., Rom. CT32 50
Quadrant Arc.
Kings Av. N10 BV31 47
Kings Av. N21 BY26 38
Kings Av. SW4 & SW12 BW47 76
Kings Av. W5 BK39 54
Kings Av., Brom. CG50 78
Kings Av., Buck.H. CJ27 40
Kings Av., Cars. BU57 95
Kings Av., Grnf. BF39 54
Kings Av., Hem.H. AY15 8
Kings Av., Houns. BF44 64
Kings Av., N.Mal. BO52 85
Kings Av., Red. BU71 121
Kings Av., Rom. CQ32 50
Kings Av., Sun. BB49 73
Kings Av., Wat. BB25 26
Kings Av., Wdf.Grn. CH29 40
Kings Av., Wey. AX59 92
Kings Bench St. SE1 BY41 4
Kings Bench St. SE1 BY41 66
Kings Bench Wk. EC4 BY40 4
Kings Brook, Lthd. BJ62 102
Kingston Rd.
Kings Cft., Welw.G.C. BS 7 5
Hazel Gro.
Kings Chase, Brwd. DB27 42
Kings Chase, E.Mol. BG52 84
Kings Clo. E10 CE33 48
Kings Clo. NW4 BQ31 46
Kings Clo., Ch.St.G. AR27 34
Kings Clo., Dart. CT45 69
Kings Clo., Kings L. AW19 17
Kings Clo., Nthwd. BB29 35
Kings Clo., Stai. AX50 73
Kings Clo., Walt. BC54 83
Kings Clo., Wat. BD24 27
Exchange Rd.
Kings College Rd. NW3 BT36 56
Kings College Rd., Ruis. BB32 44
Kings Cres. Est. N4 BZ34 48
Kings Cres. N4 BZ34 48
Kings Cross Rd. WC1 BX38 2
Kings Cross Rd. WC1 BX38 56
Kings Ct. E13 CH37 58
Kings Ct. SE1 BZ41 4
Kings Ct. SE1 BZ41 67
Great Suffolk St.
Kings Ct. SW19 BS50 76
Kings Ct. W5 BK39 54
Castlebar Pk.
Kings Ct. W6 BP42 65
Kings Ct., Berk. AR12 7
Lower Kings Rd.
Kings Ct., Har. BF34 45
Kings Ct., Tad. BP64 103
Kings Ct., Wem. BM34 46
Kings Dr., Edg. BL28 37
Kings Dr., Grav. DG48 81
Kings Dr., Surb. BM54 85
Kings Dr., T.Ditt. BJ53 84
Kings Dr., Tedd. BG49 74
Kings Dr., Walt. BB58 92
Kings Dr., Wem. BM34 46
Kings Farm Av., Rich. BM45 65
Kings Farm Rd., Rick. AU25 25
Kings Gdns., Ilf. CM33 49
Kings Gdns., Upmin. CZ33 51
Kings Grn., Loug. CK24 31
Kings Gro. SE15 CB44 67
Kings Gro., Rom. CU32 50
Kings Hall Rd., Beck. CD50 77
Kings Head Ct. EC3 BZ40 57
Fish St. Hill
Kings Head Ct., Saw. CQ 6 6
London Rd.
Kings Head Hill E4 CE26 39
Kings Head Pass. SW4 BW45 66
Clapham Park Rd.
Kings Head Yd. SE1 BZ40 4
Kings Head Yd. SE1 BZ40 57
Borough High St.
Kings Henrys Ms., Enf. CE22 30
Kings Highway SE18 CN43 68
Kings Hill, Loug. CK23 31
Kings La., Egh. AQ49 72
Kings La., Kings L. AW19 17
Kings La., Sutt. BT56 95
Kings Lynn Clo., Rom. CV29 42
Kings Lynn Dr., Rom. CV29 42
Kings Lynn Path, Rom. CV29 42
Kings Lynn Dr.
Kings Mead Est. E9 CD35 48
Kings Mead Pk., Esher BH57 93
Kings Mead Way E9 CD35 48
Kings Meadow, Kings L. AZ17 17
Kings Mill La., Red. BW73 121
Kings Ms. SW4 BX46 76
Kings Ms. WC1 BX38 2
Kings Ms. WC1 BX38 56
Kings Orch. SE9 CK46 78
Kings Pass., Kings.T. BK51 84
Kings Pl. SE1 BZ41 4
Kings Pl. SE1 BZ41 67
Kings Pl. W4 BN42 65
Kings Pl., Buck.H. CJ27 40
Kings Rd. E11 CG33 49
Kings Rd. E4 CF26 39
Kings Rd. E6 CJ37 58
Kings Rd. N17 CA30 39
Kings Rd. N18 CB28 39
Kings Rd. N22 BX30 38
Kings Rd. NW10 BP36 55
Kings Rd. SE25 CB52 87
Kings Rd. SW1 BV42 3
Kings Rd. SW1 BV42 66
Kings Rd. SW10 BT43 66
Kings Rd. SW14 BN45 65
Kings Rd. SW19 BS50 76
Kings Rd. SW3 BS43 66
Kings Rd. SW3 BT43 3
Kings Rd. SW6 BS44 66
Kings Rd. W5 BK39 54
Kings Rd., Bark. CM36 58
North St.
Kings Rd., Barn. BQ24 28
Kings Rd., Berk. AQ13 7
Kings Rd., Brwd. DB27 42
Kings Rd., Ch.St.G. AR27 34
Kings Rd., Egh. AT49 72
Kings Rd., Felt. BD47 74
Kings Rd., Guil. AR70 118
Kings Rd., Har. BE34 45
Kings Rd., Kings.T. BL51 85
Kings Rd., Mitch. BV52 86
Kings Rd., Orp. CN56 97
Kings Rd., Rich. BL46 75
Kings Rd., Rom. CU32 50
Kings Rd., Slou. AP41 62
Kings Rd., St.Alb. BF13 9
Kings Rd., St.Alb. BK16 18
Kings Rd., Surb. BK54 84
Kings Rd., Sutt. BS58 95
Kings Rd., Tedd. BG49 74
Kings Rd., Twick. BJ46 74
Kings Rd., Uxb. AX37 53
Kings Rd., Wal.Cr. CD20 21
Kings Rd., Walt. BC55 83
Kings Rd., West Dr. AY41 63
Kings Rd., West. CJ62 106
Kings Rd., Wey. AW58 92
Kings Rd., Wind. AO45 61
Kings Rd., Wok. AT61 100
Kings Ride Gate, Rich. BM45 65
Kings Scholars Pass. BW41 3
SW1
Kings Scholars Pass. BW41 66
SW1
Carlisle Pl.
Kings Sq. EC1 BZ38 2
Kings Sq. EC1 BZ38 57
Lever St.
Kings Sq. Est. EC1 BY38 56
Kings Ter. NW1 BW37 1
Kings Ter. NW1 BW37 56
Plender St.
Kings Ter., Islw. BJ45 64
Kings Way, Har. BH31 45
Kings Wk., Grays DD43 71
West St.
Kings Wk., Kings.T. BK51 84
Kings Wk., S.Croy. CB60 96
Kingsand Rd. SE12 CH48 78
Kingsash Dr., Hayes BD38 54
Kingsbridge Av. W3 BL41 65
Kingsbridge Cir., Rom. CW29 42
Kingsbridge Clo., Rom. CW29 42
Kingsbridge Cres., Sthl. BE39 54
Kingsbridge Rd. W10 BQ39 55
Kingsbridge Rd., Bark. CM37 58
Kingsbridge Rd., Mord. BQ53 85
Kingsbridge Rd., Rom. CW29 42
Kingsbridge Rd., Sthl. BE42 64
Kingsbridge Rd., Walt. BC54 83
Kingsbridge Way, Hayes BB38 53
Weymouth Dr.
Kingstable St., Wind. AO43 61
Kingsbury Av., St.Alb. BG13 9
Kingsbury Cir. NW9 BM32 46
Kingsbury Dr., Wind. AQ47 72
Kingsbury Rd. N1 CA36 57
Kingsbury Rd. NW9 BM32 46
Kingsbury Ter. N1 CA36 57
Kingsclere Clo. SW15 BP47 75
Kingscliffe Gdns. SW19 BR47 75
Kingscote Rd. W4 BN41 65
Kingscote Rd., Croy. CB54 87
Kingscote Rd., N.Mal. BN52 85
Kingscote St. EC4 BY40 4
Kingscote St. EC4 BY40 56
Tudor St.
Kingscourt Rd. SW16 BW48 76
Kingscroft Rd. NW2 BR36 55
Kingscroft Rd., Bans. BT61 104
Kingscroft Rd., Lthd. BJ63 102
Kingscross La., Red. BW71 121
Kingsdale Est. SE18 CN43 68
Kingsdale Gdns. W11 BQ40 55
Kingsdale Rd. SE18 CN43 68
Kingsdale Rd. SE20 CC50 77
Kingsdale Rd., Berks. AQ13 7
Kingsdene, Tad. BP64 103
Kingsdon La., Harl. CP11 14
Kingsdown Av. W13 BJ41 64
Kingsdown Av. W3 BO40 55
Kingsdown Av., S.Croy. BY58 95
Kingsdown Clo. W10 BQ39 55
Kingsdown Clo., Grav. DJ47 81
Farley Rd.
Kingsdown Rd. E11 CG34 49
Kingsdown Rd. N19 BX34 47
Kingsdown Rd., Epsom BP60 94
Kingsdown Rd., Sutt. BR56 94
Kingsdown Way, Brom. CH53 88
Kingsdowne Rd., Surb. BL54 85
Kingsend, Ruis. BA33 44
Kingsfield Av., Har. BF31 45
Kingsfield Dr., Enf. CC21 30
Kingsfield Rd., Har. BG33 45
Kingsfield Rd., Wat. BD26 36
Kingsfield Ter., Dart. CV46 80
Kingsfield Ter., Har. BG33 45
Kingsfield Way, Enf. CC21 30
Kingsfield, Hodd. CE11 12
Kingsfield, Wind. AL44 61
Kingsford Av., Wall. BX57 95
Kingsford St. NW5 BU35 47
Southampton Rd.
Kingsgate Av. N3 BS31 47
Kingsgate Clo., Bexh. CQ44 69
Kingsgate Clo., Orp. CP52 89
Main Rd.
Kingsgate Pl. NW6 BS36 56
Kingsgate Rd. NW6 BS36 56
Kingsgate Rd., Kings.T. BL51 85
Kingsgate, Wem. BM34 46
Kingsground SE9 CK47 78
Kingshead La., Wey. AX59 92
Kingshill Av., Har. BJ31 45
Kingshill Av., Hayes BB38 53
Kingshill Av., Nthlt. BD38 54
Kingshill Av., Rom. CS29 41
Kingshill Av., St.Alb. BJ11 9
Kingshill Av., Wor.Pk. BP54 85
Kingshill Dr., Har. BK30 36
Kingshill Rd. E2 CA38 57
Kingshill Way, Berk. AQ14 7
Kingshold Est. E9 CC37 57
Kingshold Rd. E9 CC36 57
Kingsholm Gdns. SE9 CJ45 68
Kingshurst Rd. SE12 CH47 78
Kingsingfield Clo., Sev. CZ57 99
Kingsingfield Rd., Sev. CZ58 99
Kingsland Est. E2 CA37 2
Kingsland Est. E2 CA37 57
Kingsland Grn. N16 CA36 57
Kingsland High St. E8 CA36 57
Kingsland Pass. E8 CA36 57
Kingsland Grn.
Kingsland Rd. E13 CJ38 58
Kingsland Rd. E2 CA38 2
Kingsland Rd. E2 CA38 57
Kingsland Rd., Hem.H. AW14 8
Kingsland, Harl. CM12 13
Kingslawn Clo. SW15 BP46 75
Kingslea, Lthd. BJ63 102
Kingsleigh Pl., Mitch. BU52 86
Whitford Gdns.
Kingsleigh Wk., Brom. CG52 88
Stamford Dr.
Kingsley Av. W13 BJ39 54
Kingsley Av., Bans. BS61 104
Kingsley Av., Brwd. BL23 28
Kingsley Av., Chsnt. CB18 21
Kingsley Av., Dart. CX46 80
Kingsley Av., Houns. BG44 64
Kingsley Av., Sthl. BF40 54
Kingsley Av., Sutt. BT56 95
Kingsley Clo. N2 BT32 47
Kingsley Clo., Dag. CR35 50
Kingsley Dr., Egh. AQ50 72
Kingsley Dr., Wor.Pk. BO55 85
Badgers Copse
Kingsley Gdns. E4 CE28 39
Kingsley Gdns., Horn. CV31 51
Kingsley Gro., Reig. BS72 121
Kingsley Ms. E1 CB40 57
Wapping La.
Kingsley Ms. W8 BS41 3
Kingsley Ms. W8 BS41 66
Stanford Rd.
Kingsley Pl. N6 BV33 47
Kingsley Rd. E17 CF30 39
Kingsley Rd. E7 CH36 58
Kingsley Rd. N13 BY28 38
Kingsley Rd. NW6 BR37 55
Kingsley Rd. SW19 BS49 76
Kingsley Rd., Brwd. DE26 122
Kingsley Rd., Croy. BY54 86
Kingsley Rd., Har. BG35 45
Kingsley Rd., Houns. BF44 64
Kingsley Rd., Ilf. CM30 40
Kingsley Rd., Loug. CM24 31
Kingsley Rd., Orp. CN57 97
Kingsley Rd., Pnr. BE31 45
Kingsley St. SW11 BU45 66
Kingsley Way N2 BT32 47
Kingsley Wk., Grays DG42 71
Kingsley Wood Dr. SE9 CK48 78
Kingslyn Cres. SE19 CA51 87
Kingsman St. SE18 CK41 68
Kingsmead Av. N9 CB26 39
Kingsmead Av. NW9 BN33 46
Kingsmead Av., Mitch. BW52 86
Kingsmead Av., Rom. CT32 50
Kingsmead Av., Sun. BD51 84
Kingsmead Av., Surb. BM55 85
Kingsmead Av., Wor.Pk. BP55 85
Kingsmead Clo., Epsom BN57 94
Kingsmead Clo., Harl. CH11 13
Kingsmead Clo., Sid. CO48 79
Kingsmead Clo., Tedd. BJ50 74
Kingsmead Dr., Nthlt. BE36 54
Kingsmead Rd. SW2 BY48 76
Kingsmead, Barn. BS24 29
Kingsmead, Cuff. BX17 20
Kingsmead, Rich. BL46 75
Kingsmead, Saw. CQ 6 6
Kingsmead, St.Alb. BK12 9
Kingsmead, West. CJ61 106
Kingsmere Clo. SW15 BR45 65
Weimar St.
Kingsmere Pk. NW9 BM33 46
Kingsmere Rd. SW19 BQ48 75
Kingsmill Gdns., Dag. CQ35 50
Kingsmill Rd., Dag. CQ35 50
Kingsmill Ter. NW8 BT37 1
Kingsmill Ter. NW8 BT37 56
Kingsmoor Rd., Harl. CL12 13
Kingsnympton Pk., BM50 75
Kings.T.
Kingspark Ct. E18 CH31 49
Kingspark Ct., Ilf. CK33 49
The Drive
Kingsridge Gdns., Dart. CV46 80
Kingsridge SW19 BR48 75
Kingstable St., Eton AO43 61
Kingsthorpe Rd. SE26 CC49 77
Kingston Av., Felt. BB46 73
Kingston Av., Lthd. BB66 110
Kingston Av., Lthd. BJ64 102
Kingston Av., Sutt. BR55 85
Kingston Av., West Dr. AY40 53
Kingston Br., Kings.T. BK51 84
Kingston By-pass, Esher BH55 84
Kingston By-pass, N.Mal. BO53 83
Kingston By-pass, Surb. BL55 85
Kingston By-pass, SW15 BO49 75
Kingston By-pass, SW20 BP51 85
Kingston Clo., Nthlt. BE36 54
Kingston Clo., Rom. CQ31 50
Kingston Clo., Tedd. BJ50 74
Kingston Cres., Ashf. AX49 73
Kingston Cres., Beck. CD51 87
Kingston Ct. N4 BZ32 48
Wiltshire Gdns.
Kingston Ct., Grav. DD46 81
Kingston Gdns., Croy. BX55 86
Wandle Rd.
Kingston Hall Rd., BK52 84
Kings.T.
Kingston Hill Av., Rom. CQ30 41
Kingston Hill, Kings.T. BM51 85
Kingston House Gdns., BJ64 102
Lthd.
Upper Fairfield Rd.
Kingston La., Lthd. AZ67 110
Kingston La., Tedd. BJ49 74
Kingston La., Uxb. AY38 53
Kingston La., West Dr. AY41 63
Kingston Park Est., BM50 75
Kings.T.
Kingston Pl., Har. BH29 36
Richmond Gdns.
Kingston Rd. N9 CB27 39
Kingston Rd. SW15 BP48 75
Kingston Rd. SW20 BQ51 85
Kingston Rd., Ashf. AY50 73
Kingston Rd., Barn. BT25 29
Kingston Rd., Epsom BO57 94
Kingston Rd., Ilf. CL35 49
Kingston Rd., Kings.T. BM52 85
Kingston Rd., Lthd. BJ62 102
Kingston Rd., N.Mal. BN52 85
Kingston Rd., Rom. CT31 50
Kingston Rd., Stai. & AW49 73
Ashf.
Kingston Rd., Sthl. BE41 64
Kingston Rd., Surb. BM55 85
Kingston Rd., Tedd. BJ49 74
Kingston Ri., Wey. AW58 92
Kingston Sq. SE19 BZ49 77
Kingston Vale SW15 BN49 75
Kingstown St. NW1 BV37 56
Kingswater Pl. SW11 BT44 66
Battersea Church Rd.
Kingsway Av., S.Croy. CC58 96
Kingsway Av., Wok. AR62 100
Kingsway Cres., Har. BG31 45
Kingsway Ind. Est. N18 CC29 39
Kingsway N12 BT29 38
Kingsway NW8 BU37 56
Kingsway Rd., Sutt. BR57 94
Kingsway SW14 BM45 65
Kingsway WC2 BX39 2
Kingsway WC2 BX39 56
Kingsway, Croy. BX56 95
Kingsway, Cuff. BX18 20
Kingsway, Enf. CB25 30
Kingsway, Ger.Cr. AS30 34
Kingsway, Hayes BA39 53
Kingsway, Iver AV39 52

Kingsway, N.Mal. BQ52 85
Kingsway, Orp. CM53 88
Kingsway, Stai. AX47 73
Kingsway, The, Epsom BP59 94
Kingsway, W.Wick. CG55 88
Kingsway, Wat. BB21 26
Kingsway, Wat. BD20 18
Kingsway, Wdf.Grn. CJ28 40
Kingsway, Wem. BL35 46
Kingsway, Wok. AR62 100
Kingswear Rd. NW5 BV34 47
Kingswear Rd., Ruis. BC34 44
Kingswell Ride, Cuff. BX18 20
Kingswood Av. NW6 BR37 55
Kingswood Av., Belv. CQ42 69
Kingswood Av., Brom. CG52 88
Kingswood Av., Hmptn. BF50 74
Kingswood Av., Houns. BE44 64
Kingswood Av., S.Croy. CB61 105
Kingswood Av., Swan. CT52 89
Kingswood Av., Th.Hth. BY53 86
Kingswood Clo. N20 BT26 38
Kingswood Clo. SW8 BX43 66
Kenchester Clo.
Kingswood Clo., Dart. CV46 80
Kingswood Clo., Egh. AR49 72
Kingswood Clo., Guil. AU70 118
Kingswood Clo., N.Mal. BO53 85
Motspur Pk.
Kingswood Clo., Orp. CM54 88
Woodcote Rd.
Kingswood Clo., Surb. BL54 85
Kingswood Clo., Wey. AZ57 92
Kingswood Creek, Stai. AR46 72
Kingswood Ct., Rich. BL46 75
Marchmont Rd.
Kingswood Ct., Tad. BR65 103
Kingswood Dr. SE19 CA49 77
Kingswood Dr., Cars. BU54 86
Kingswood Est. SE21 CA49 77
Kingswood La., Warl. CC61 105
Kingswood Pk. N3 BR30 37
Kingswood Pl. SE13 CG45 68
Kingswood Rd. SE20 CC50 77
Kingswood Rd. SW19 BR50 75
Kingswood Rd. SW2 BX46 76
Kingswood Rd. W4 BN41 65
Kingswood Rd., Brom. CF52 87
Kingswood Rd., Ilf. CO33 50
Kingswood Rd., Sev. CT64 107
Kingswood Rd., Tad. BP64 103
Kingswood Rd., Wat. BC20 17
Kingswood Ri., Egh. AR49 72
Kingswood Way, Croy. CC60 96
Kingswood Way, Wall. BX56 95
Kingsworth Clo., Beck. CD52 87
Shirley Cres.
Kingsworthy Clo., Kings.T. BL52 85
Dawson Rd.
Kingthorpe Rd. NW10 BN36 55
Kingthorpe Ter. NW10 BN36 55
Kingwell Rd., Barn. BT22 29
Kingwood Rd. SW6 BR44 65
Kinlet Clo., SE18 CM44 68
Kinlet Rd.
Kinlet Rd. SE18 CL44 68
Kinloch Dr. NW9 BN33 46
Kinloch St. N7 BX34 47
Kinloss Ct. N3 BR31 46
Kinloss Gdns.
Kinloss Gdns. N3 BR31 46
Kinloss Rd., Cars. BT54 86
Kinnaid Way, Wdf.Grn. CK29 40
Kinnaird Av. W4 BN43 65
Kinnaird Av., Brom. CG50 78
Kinnaird Clo., Brom. CG50 78
Kinnear Rd. W12 BO41 65
Kinnersley Wk., Reig. BS72 121
Castle Dr.
Kinnerton Pl. N. SW1 BU41 3
Kinnerton Pl. N. SW1 BU41 66
Kinnerton St.
Kinnerton Pl. S. SW1 BU41 3
Kinnerton Pl. S. SW1 BU41 66
Kinnerton St.
Kinnerton St. SW1 BU41 3
Kinnerton St. SW1 BV41 66
Kinnoul Rd. W6 BR43 65
Kinross Av., Wor.Pk. BP55 85
Kinross Clo., Har. BL32 46
Kinross Clo., Sun. BB49 73
Kinross Dr., Sun. BB49 73
Kinross St. SE1 CA41 4
Kinross St. SE1 CA41 67
Tanner St.
Kinsale Rd. SE15 CB45 67
Kinsfield, Hodd. CE11 12
Kintore St. SE1 CA42 4
Kintore St. SE1 CA42 67
Kintore Way SE1 CA42 4
Kintore Way SE1 CA42 67
Alscot Rd.
Kintyre Clo. SW16 BX51 86
Kinveachy Gdns. SE7 CK42 68
Kinver Rd. N. SE26 CC49 77
Kinver Rd. S. SE26 CC49 77
Kipings, Tad. BQ64 103
Kipling Av., Til. DG44 71
Kipling Dr. SW19 BT50 76
Kipling Gro., Hem.H. AZ10 8
Kipling Pl., Stan. BH29 36
Kipling Rd., Bexh. CQ44 69
Kipling Rd., Dart. CX46 80
Kipling St. SE1 BZ41 4
Kipling St. SE1 BZ41 67
Kipling Ter. N9 BZ27 39
Kippington Clo., Sev. CT65 107
Kippington Dr. SE9 CJ47 78
Kippington Rd., Sev. CU65 107
Kirby Clo., Epsom BO56 94
Kirby Clo., Ilf. CN29 40
Kirby Clo., Loug. CK26 40
Kirby Clo., Nthwd. BB29 35
Kirby Est. SE16 CB41 67
Kirby Gro. SE1 CA41 4
Kirby Gro. SE1 CA41 67
Kirby Rd., Dart. CY47 80
Kirby Rd., Wok. AR61 100
Kirby St. EC1 BY39 2
Kirby St. EC1 BY39 56
Kirby Way, Walt. BD53 84
Kircaldy Grn., Wat. BD27 36
Trevose Way
Kirchen Rd. W13 BJ40 54
Kirk Ct., Sev. CU65 107
Kirk La. SE18 CM43 68
Kirk Rd. E17 CD32 48
Kirk Ri., Sutt. BS55 86
Kirkdale Rd. E11 CG33 49
Kirkdale SE26 CB48 77
Kirkham Rd. E6 CK39 58
Kirkham St. SE18 CN43 68
Kirkland Av., Ilf. CL30 40
Kirkland Av., Wok. AP61 100
Kirkland Clo., Sid. CN46 78
Kirkland Pl. SE10 CG41 68
Kirkland Way, Orp. CP52 89
Kirkland Wk. E8 CA36 57
Laurel St.
Kirklands, Welw.G.C. BQ 6 5
Kirklees Rd., Surb. BL54 85
Kirklees Rd., Th.Hth. BX52 86
Kirkley Rd. SW19 BS50 76
Kirkly Clo., S.Croy. CA58 96
Kirkmichael Rd. E14 CF39 57
Kirks Pl. E14 CD39 57
Rhodeswell Rd.
Kirkside Rd. SE3 CH43 68
Kirkstall Av. N17 BZ31 48
Kirkstall Gdns. SW2 BW47 76
Kirkstall Rd. SW2 BW47 76
Kirkstead Ct. E5 CC35 48
Clapton Park Est.
Kirksted Rd., Mord. BS54 86
Kirkstone Way, Brom. CG50 78
Kirkton Clo. W4 BN42 65
Dolman Rd.
Kirkton Gdns. E2 CA38 57
Chambord St.
Kirkton Rd. N15 CA32 48
Kirkwall Pl. E2 CC38 57
Kirkwood Rd. SE15 CB44 67
Kirn Rd. W13 BJ40 54
Kirchen Rd.
Kirtley Rd. SE26 CD49 77
Kirtling St. SW8 BW43 66
Kirton Clo. W4 BN42 65
Dolman Rd.
Kirton Clo., Horn. CV36 60
Sarre Av.
Kirton Rd. E13 CJ37 58
Kirton Wk., Edg. BN29 37
Kirwyn Way SE5 BZ43 67
Kitchener Av., Grav. DH48 81
Kitchener Clo., St.Alb. BJ14 9
Kitchener Rd. E17 CE30 39
Kitchener Rd. E7 CH36 58
Kitchener Rd. N17 BZ31 48
Kitchener Rd. N2 BU31 47
Kitchener Rd., Dag. CR36 59
Kitchener Rd., Th.Hth. BZ52 87
Kitcheners La., Red. CA70 114
Kite Field, Berk. AP12 7
Kitkat Ter. E3 CE38 57
Kitley Gdns. SE19 CA51 87
Kitsbury Rd., Berk. AQ13 7
Kitsbury Ter., Berk. AQ13 7
Kitsmead La., Cher. AR54 82
Kitson Rd. SE5 BZ43 67
Kitson Rd. SW13 BP44 65
Kitson Way, Harl. CM10 6
Kitswell Way, Rad. BH20 18
Kittiwake Clo., S.Croy. CD58 96
Kittiwake Rd., Nthlt. BD38 54
Kitto Rd. SE14 CC44 67
Kitts End Rd., Barn. BQ21 28
Kiver Rd. N19 BW34 47
Klea Av. SW4 BW46 76
Knapdale Clo. SE23 CB48 77
Knapmill Rd. SE6 CE48 77
Knapmill Way SE6 CE48 77
Knapp Clo. NW10 BO36 55
Knapp Rd. E3 CE38 57
Knappe Rd., Ashf. AY49 73
Knaresborough Pl. SW5 BS42 3
Knaresborough Pl. SW5 BS42 66
Knaresborough Rd. SW5 BS43 66
Knatchbull Rd. NW10 BN37 55
Knatchbull Rd. SE5 BY44 66
Knatts La., Sev. CY59 99
Knatts Valley Rd., Sev. CY59 99
Knavewood Rd., Sev. CW62 108
Knavewood Rd., Sev. CW62 108
Knebworth Av. E17 CE30 39
Knebworth Path, Brwd. BN24 28
Knebworth Rd. N16 CA35 48
Knee Hill Cres. SE2 CP42 69
Knee Hill SE2 CP42 69
Knella Grn., Welw.G.C. BS 8 5
Knella Rd., Welw.G.C. BR 8 5
Kneller Gdns., Islw. BG46 74
Kneller Rd. SE4 CD45 67
Kneller Rd., N.Mal. BN54 85
Kneller Rd., Twick. BG46 74
Knight St., Saw. CQ 6 6
Knighten St. E1 CB40 57
Knightland Rd. E5 CB34 48
Knighton Clo., Rom. CS32 50
Knighton Clo., S.Croy. BY57 95
Knighton Clo., Wdf.Grn. CH28 40
Knighton Dr., Wdf.Grn. CH28 40
Knighton La., Buck.H. CH27 40
Knighton Park Rd. SE26 CC49 77
Knighton Rd. E7 CH34 49
Knighton Rd., Red. BV71 121
Knighton Rd., Rom. CS32 50
Knighton Rd., Sev. CT61 107
Knighton Way La., Uxb. AW36 53
Knightrider Ct. EC4 BZ40 4
Knightrider St.
Knightrider Ct. EC4 BZ40 57
Knightrider St.
Knightrider St. EC4 BZ39 57
Godliman St.
Knightrider St. EC4 BZ40 4
Knights Av. W5 BL41 65
Knights Clo. E9 CC35 48
Churchill Wk.
Knights Clo., Egh. AU50 72
Knights Clo., Winds. AL44 61
Knights Ct., Kings.T. BL52 85
Knights Hill SE27 BY49 76
Knights Hill Sq. SE27 BY49 76
Knights Hill
Knights La. N9 CB27 39
Knights Manor Way, Dart. CW46 80
Knights Pk., Kings.T. BL52 85
Knights Rd. E16 CH41 68
Knights Rd., Stan. BK28 36
Knights Ridge, Orp. CO56 98
Stirling Dr.
Knights Way, Brwd. DD27 122
Knights Way, Ilf. CM29 40
Knights Wk., Rom. CO24 32
Knightsbridge Clo. SW1 BU41 3
Knightsbridge Clo. SW1 BU41 66
Knightsbridge
Knightsbridge Cres., Stai. AW50 73
Knightsbridge Gdns., Rom. CS32 50
Knightsbridge Grn. SW1 BU41 3
Knightsbridge Grn. SW1 BU41 66
Knightsbridge
Knightsbridge SW7 BU41 3
Knightsbridge SW7 BU41 66
Knightsbridge Way, Hem.H. AY13 8
Knightsfield, Welw.G.C. BQ 5 5
Knightswood Clo., Edg. BN27 37
Knightswood, Wok. AP62 100
Knightwood Clo., Reig. BS71 121
Knightwood Cres., N.Mal. BO53 85
Knipp Hill, Cob. BE60 93
Knivett Rd. SW6 BS43 66
Knobs Hill Rd. E15 CE37 57
Knockhall Chase, Green. DB46 80
Knockhall Rd., Green. DB46 80
Knockholt Main Rd., Sev. CN63 106
Knockholt Rd. SE9 CJ46 78
Knockholt Rd., Sev. CO61 107
Knole Clo., Croy. CC53 87
Knole La., Sev. CV66 117
Knole Rd., Dart. CU47 79
Knole Rd., Sev. CV65 108
Knole Way, Sev. CV66 117
Knole, The SE9 CL49 78
Knole, The, Grav. DF50 81
Knoll Cres., Nthwd. BB30 35
Knoll Dr. N14 BV26 38
Knoll Gate, Sid. CN48 78
Woodside Cres.
Knoll Rd. SW18 BT46 76
Knoll Rd., Bex. CR47 79
Knoll Rd., Dor. BJ72 119
Knoll Rd., Sid. CO49 79
Knoll Ri., Orp. CN54 88
Knoll, The W13 BK39 54
Knoll, The, Beck. CE51 87
Knoll, The, Brom. CH55 88
Knoll, The, Cob. BF60 93
Knolles Cres., Hat. BP15 10
Knollmead, Surb. BN54 85
Knolls Clo., Wor.Pk. BP55 85
Knolls, The, Epsom BQ61 103
Knollys Clo. SW16 BY48 76
Knollys Rd. SW16 BX48 76
Knolton Way, Slou. AQ39 52
Knottisford St. E2 CC38 57
Knotts Green Rd. E10 CE32 48
Knotts Pl., Sev. CU65 107
Knowl Hill, Wok. AT63 100
Knowl Way, B.Wd. BL24 28
Knowle Av., Bexh. CQ43 69
Knowle Clo. SW9 BY45 66
Knowle Gdns., Wey. AV60 91
Madeira Rd.
Knowle Grn., Stai. AW49 73
Knowle Gro. Clo., Vir.W. AR54 82
Knowle Gro., Vir.W. AR54 82
Knowle Hill, Vir.W. AR54 82
Knowle Pk. Av., Stai. AW50 73
Knowle Pk., Cob. BE61 102
Knowle Rd., Brom. CK55 88
Knowle Rd., Twick. BH47 74
Knowle, The, Hodd. CE12 12
Cock La.
Knowle, The, Tad. BQ64 103
Knowles Hill Cres. SE13 CF46 77
Knowles Wk. SW4 BW45 66
Knowlton Grn., Brom. CG53 88
Knowsley Av., Sthl. BF40 54
Knowsley Rd. SW11 BU44 66
Knox Rd. E7 CG36 58
Knox Rd., Guil. AQ68 109
Knox St. W1 BU39 1
Knox St. W1 BU39 56
Knoyle St. SE14 CD43 67
Chubworthy St.
Knutsford Av., Wat. BD22 27
Koh-i-noor Av., Bush. BF25 27
Kohat Rd. SW19 BS49 76
Koonowla Clo., West. CJ61 106
Dowding Rd.
Korda Clo., Shep. AY52 83
Kossuth St. SE10 CG42 68
Kramer Ms. SW5 BS42 66
Kreisel Wk., Rich. BL43 65
Kuala Gdns. SW16 BX51 86
Bush Rd.
Kuhn Way E7 CH35 49
Kydbrook Clo., Orp. CM54 88
Kylemore Clo. E6 CJ37 58
Parr Rd.
Kylemore Rd. NW6 BS36 56
Kymberley Rd., Har. BH32 45
Kyme Rd., Rom. CT32 50
Kynance Clo., Rom. CV28 42
Kynance Gdns., Stan. BK30 36
Kynance Ms. SW7 BS41 3
Kynance Ms. SW7 BS41 66
Kynance Pl. SW7 BT41 3
Kynance Pl. SW7 BT41 66
Kynaston Av. N16 CA34 48
Dynevor Rd.
Kynaston Av., Th.Hth. BZ53 87
Kynaston Clo., Har. BG29 36
Kynaston Cres., Th.Hth. BZ53 87
Kynaston Rd. N16 CA34 48
Kynaston Rd., Brom. CH49 78
Kynaston Rd., Enf. BZ23 30
Kynaston Rd., Orp. CO54 89
Kynaston Rd., Th.Hth. BZ53 87
Kynaston Wd., Har. BG29 36
Kynnersley Clo., Cars. BU55 86
William St.
Kynock Rd. N18 CC28 39
Kyrle Rd. SW11 BU46 76
Kytes Dr., Wat. BD20 18
Kyverdale Rd. N16 CA33 48

L

La Plata Gro., Brwd. DA27 42
La Roche Clo., Slou. AR41 62
Hempson Av.
La Tourne Gdns., Orp. CM55 88
Labour-in-Vain Rd., Sev. DB60 99
Laburnham Av., West Dr. AY40 53
Laburnham Clo., Upmin. DA33 51
Laburnham Ct., Stan. BK28 36
Laburnham Gdns., Croy. CC54 87
Primrose La.
Laburnham Gdns., Upmin. CZ33 51
Laburnham Rd., Epp. CP18 23
Laburnum Av. N17 BZ29 39
Laburnum Av. N9 CA27 39
Laburnum Av., Dart. CV47 80
Laburnum Av., Horn. CT34 50
Laburnum Av., Sutt. BU55 86
Laburnum Av., Swan. CS52 89
Laburnum Clo. E4 CD29 39
Maple Av.
Laburnum Clo. N11 BV29 38
Laburnum Clo. SE15 CC43 67
Clifton Way
Laburnum Clo., Chsnt. CC19 21
Laburnum Clo., Guil. AR69 118
Laburnum Cres., Sun. BC51 83
Laburnum Ct. E2 CA37 2
Laburnum Ct. E2 CA37 57
Laburnum St.
Laburnum Gdns. N21 BZ27 39
Laburnum Gro. N21 BZ27 39
Laburnum Gro. NW9 BN33 46
Laburnum Gro., Grav. DE47 81
Laburnum Gro., Houns. BE45 64
Laburnum Gro., N.Mal. BN51 85
Laburnum Gro., Ruis. BA32 44
Laburnum Gro., Slou. AT43 62
Laburnum Gro., St.Alb. BF16 18
Laburnum Gro., Sthl. BE38 54
Laburnum Pl. SE9 CL46 78
Laburnum Pl., Egh. AQ50 72
Laburnum Rd. SW19 BT50 76
Laburnum Rd., Cher. AW54 83
Laburnum Rd., Epsom BO60 94
Laburnum Rd., Hayes BB42 63
Laburnum Rd., Hodd. CE11 12
Laburnum Rd., Mitch. BV51 86
Laburnum Rd., Wok. AR63 100
Laburnum St. E2 CA37 2
Laburnum St. E2 CA37 57
Laburnum Way, Brom. CL54 88
Laburnum Way, Chsnt. BY17 20
Laburnum Way, Stai. AY47 73
Laburnum Wk., Horn. CV35 51
Lacey Av., Couls. BY63 104
Lacey Clo. N9 CB27 39
Balham Rd.
Lacey Clo., Egh. AU50 72
Lacey Dr., Edg. BL28 37
Lacey Dr., Hmptn. BE51 84
Lacey Grn., Couls. BY63 104
Lacey Wk. E3 CE37 57
Lackford Rd., Couls. BU62 104
Lackington St. EC2 BZ39 2
Lackington St. EC2 BZ39 57
Lackmore Rd., Enf. CC21 30
Lacock Clo. SW19 BT50 76
Lacock Ct. W13 BJ40 54
Lacon Rd. SE22 CB45 67
Lacy Dr., Couls. BY63 104
Lacy Rd. SW15 BQ45 65
Ladas Rd. SE27 BZ49 77
Ladbroke Clo. W11 BR39 55
Ladbroke Gro.
Ladbroke Cres. W11 BR39 55
Ladbroke Gro.
Ladbroke Gdns. W11 BR40 55
Ladbroke Gro. W10 BQ38 55
Ladbroke Gro., Red. BV70 121
Ladbroke Ms. W11 BR40 55
Ladbroke Rd.
Ladbroke Rd. W11 BR40 55
Ladbroke Rd., Enf. CA25 30
Ladbroke Rd., Epsom BN60 94
Ladbroke Rd., Red. BV70 121
Ladbroke Sq. Gdns. W11 BR40 55
Ladbroke Sq. W11 BR40 55
Ladbroke Ter. W11 BR40 55
Ladbroke Wk. W11 BR40 55
Ladbrook Clo., Pnr. BE32 45
Ladbrook Rd. SE25 BZ52 87
Ladbrooke Clo., Pot.B. BS19 20
Strafford Gate
Ladbrooke Cres., Sid. CP48 79
Ladbrooke Dr., Pot.B. BS19 20
Ladbrooke Rd., Slou. AO41 61
Ladders Wood Way N11 BW28 38
Palmers Rd.
Ladderstile Ride, Kings.T. BN49 75
Ladds Way, Swan. CS52 89
Ladenhatch La., Swan. CS51 89
Ladies Gro., St.Alb. BF13 9
Lady Amhersts Dr., Sev. CR69 116
Lady Booth Rd., Kings.T. BL51 85
Eden St.
Lady Gro., Welw.G.C. BR 9 5
Lady Hay, Wor.Pk. BO55 85
Lady Margaret Rd. NW5 BW35 47
Lady Margaret Rd., Sthl. BE40 54
Lady Shaw Ct. N13 BX27 38
St. Georges Rd.
Lady Somerset Rd. NW5 BV35 47
Lady Spencer Gro., St.Alb. BG14 9
Lady Vane Clo., Ton. DB68 117
Ladybower Ct. E5 CC35 48
Clapton Park Est.
Ladycroft Gdns., Orp. CM56 97
Ladycroft Rd. SE13 CE45 67
Ladycroft Way, Orp. CM56 97
Ladycroft Wk., Stan. BK30 36
Ladyday Pl., Slou. AO40 61
Glentworth Pl.
Ladyegate Clo., Dor. BK71 119
Ladyegate Rd., Dor. BK71 119
Ladyfield Clo., Loug. CL24 31
Ladyfields
Ladyfields, Grav. DF49 81
Ladyfields, Loug. CL24 31
Ladygate La., Ruis. AZ32 44
Ladygrove Dr., Guil. AT68 109
Ladygrove, Croy. CD58 96
Ladymead Parkway, Guil. AR70 118
Ladymeadow, Kings L. AX17 17
Ladys Clo., Wat. BD24 27
Ladyshot, Harl. CO10 6
Ladysmith Av. E6 CK37 58
Ladysmith Av., Ilf. CM33 49
Ladysmith Rd. E16 CG38 58
Ladysmith Rd. N17 CB30 39
Ladysmith Rd. N18 CB28 39
Ladysmith Rd. SE9 CL46 78
Ladysmith Rd., Enf. CA24 30
Ladysmith Rd., Har. BH30 36
Ladysmith Rd., St.Alb. BG13 9
Ladythorne Clo., Wey. AW56 92
Church Rd.
Ladywalk, Rick. AV28 34
Ladywell Prospect, Bish. CR 6 6
Ladywell Rd. SE13 CE46 77
Ladywell St. E15 CG37 58
Ladywood Av., Orp. CN53 88
Ladywood Clo., Rick. AX24 26
Ladywood Rd., Dart. CZ49 80
Ladywood Rd., Surb. BM55 85
Lafone Av., Felt. BD48 74
Lafone St. SE1 CA41 4
Lafone St. SE1 CA41 67
Lagado Ms. SE16 CC40 57
Lagger Clo., Ch.St.G. AQ27 34
Lagger, The, Ch.St.G. AQ27 34
Laglands Clo., Reig. BT69 121
Lagonda Av., Ilf. CN29 40
Lagonda Clo., Wey. AY59 92
Viscount Gdns.
Lagoon Rd., Orp. CO53 89
Lahore Rd., Croy. BZ53 87
Sydenham Rd.
Laidon Sq., Hem.H. AX11 8
Laindon Av. E15 CG35 49
Leytonstone Rd.
Laing Clo., Ilf. CM29 40
Laing Dene, Nthlt. BD37 54
Laings Av., Mitch. BU51 86
Lainlock Pl., Houns. BF44 64
Spring Grove Rd.
Lainson St. SW18 BS47 76
Laird Av., Grays DE41 71
Lairdale Clo. SE21 BZ47 77
Lairs Clo. N7 BX35 47
Laitwood Rd. SW12 BV47 76
Lake Av., Brom. CH50 78
Lake Av., Rain. CV37 60
Lake Av., Slou. AO40 52
Lake Clo. SW19 BR49 75
Lake Rd.
Lake Clo., Wey. AX59 92
Lake End Rd., Maid. AK40 61
Lake Gdns., Dag. CR35 50
Lake Gdns., Rich. BJ48 74
Lake Gdns., Wall. BV55 86
Lake House Rd. E11 CH34 49
Lake Rd. SW19 BR49 75
Lake Rd., Croy. CD55 87
Lake Rd., Rom. CP31 50
Lake Rd., Vir.W. AQ52 82
Lake Rd., Wal.Abb. CG14 13
Lake Ri., Grays DA42 70
Lake Ri., Rom. CT30 41
Lake Vw., Dor. BK73 119
Lake Vw., Edg. BL28 37
Lake Vw., Pot.B. BT20 20
Lake, The, Bush. BG26 36
Lakedale Rd. SE18 CN43 68
Lakefield Rd. N22 BY30 38
Lakefields Clo., Rain. CV37 60
Lakehall Gdns., Th.Hth. BY53 86
Lakehall Rd., Th.Hth. BY53 86
Lakehurst Rd., Epsom BO56 94
Lakeland Clo., Chig. CO28 41
Lakeland Clo., Har. BG29 36
Lakenheath N14 BW25 29
Laker Pl. SW15 BR46 75
Lakers Ri., Bans. BU61 104
Lakes Clo., Guil. AT73 118
Lakes Rd., Kes. CJ56 97
Lakeside Av., Ilf. CJ31 49
Lakeside Clo. SE25 CA51 87
Lakeside Clo., Ruis. BA31 44
Lakeside Clo., Sid. CP46 79
Lakeside Clo., Wok. AP63 100

Lakeside Cres., Barn.	BU25	29
Lakeside Cres., Brwd.	DB27	42
Lakeside Ct., B.Wd.	BM24	28
Lakeside Dr., Brom.	CK55	88
Lakeside Dr., Esher	BG57	93
Lakeside Dr., Slou.	AP37	52
Lakeside Pl., St.Alb.	BK17	18
Lakeside Rd. N13	BX28	38
Lakeside Rd. W14	BQ41	65
Lakeside Rd., Chsnt.	CC17	21
Lakeside Rd., Slou.	AW43	63
Lakeside W13	BK39	54
Edge Hill Rd.		
Lakeside Way, Wem.	BM35	46
Lakeside, Beck.	CE52	87
Lakeside, Enf.	BW24	29
Lakeside, Rain.	CW37	60
Lakeside, Red.	BV69	121
Kingfisher Dr.		
Lakeside, Wall.	BV56	95
Lakeside, Wey.	BB55	83
Lakeside, Wok.	AP63	100
Lakeswood Rd., Orp.	CL53	88
Lakeview Rd. SE27	BY49	76
Lakeview Rd., Sev.	CU65	107
Lakeview Rd., Well.	CO45	69
Lakis Clo. NW3	BT53	47
Flask Wk.		
Laleham Av. NW7	BN27	37
Laleham Ct., Wok.	AS61	100
Chobham Rd.		
Laleham Rd. SE6	CF47	77
Laleham Rd., Shep.	AY52	83
Laleham Rd., Stai.	AV49	72
Lalor St. SW6	BR44	65
Lamb Clo., Hat.	BP13	10
Lamb Clo., Til.	DH44	71
Coleridge Rd.		
Lamb La. E8	CB36	57
Lamb Ms. N1	**BY37**	**2**
Lamb Ms. N1	BY37	56
Camden Wk.		
Lamb St. E1	**CA39**	**2**
Lamb St. E1	CA39	57
Lamb Wk. SE1	**CA41**	**4**
Lamb Wk. SE1	CA41	67
Lamb Yd., Wat.	BD24	27
Lambarde Av. SE9	CL49	78
Lambarde Dr., Sev.	CU65	107
Lambarde Rd., Sev.	CU64	107
Lambardes Clo., Orp.	CP58	98
The Green		
Lamberhurst Clo., Orp.	CP54	89
Lamberhurst Rd. SE27	BY49	76
Lamberhurst Rd., Dag.	CQ33	50
Lambert Av., Rich.	BM45	65
Lambert Av., Slou.	AS41	62
Lambert Clo., West.	CJ61	106
Sunningvale Av.		
Lambert Ct., Bush.	BD24	27
Lambert Rd. E16	CH39	58
Lambert Rd. N12	BT28	38
Lambert Rd. SW2	BX46	76
Lambert Rd., Bans.	BS60	95
Lambert St. N1	BY36	56
Lambert Way N12	BT28	38
Lambert Wk., Wem.	BK34	45
Hutchinson Ter.		
Lamberton Ct., B.Wd.	BL23	28
Lamberts Pl., Croy.	BZ54	87
Lamberts Rd., Surb.	BL53	85
Lambeth Bridge SW1	**BX42**	**4**
Lambeth High St. SE1	**BX42**	**4**
Lambeth High St. SE1	BX42	66
Lambeth Hill EC4	BZ40	57
Upper Thames St.		
Lambeth Ms. SE11	**BX42**	**2**
Lambeth Ms. SE11	BX42	66
Lambeth Palace Rd. SE1	**BX41**	**4**
Lambeth Palace Rd. SE1	BX41	66
Lambeth Rd. SE1	**BX41**	**4**
Lambeth Rd. SE1	BX41	66
Lambeth Rd., Croy.	BY54	86
Lambeth St. E1	**CB39**	**2**
Lambeth St. E1	CB39	57
Lambeth St. N1	**BY37**	**2**
Lambeth Wk. N1	BX37	56
Outram St.		
Lambeth Wk. SE11	**BX42**	**4**
Lambeth Wk. SE11	BX42	66
Lamble St. NW5	BV35	47
Lambley Rd., Dag.	CO36	59
Lambolle Ms. NW3	BU36	56
Lambolle Rd.		
Lambolle Pl. NW3	BU36	56
Lambolle Rd. NW3	BU36	56
Lambourn Chase, Rad.	BH21	27
Lambourn Clo. W7	BH41	64
Lambourn Rd. SE17	**BZ42**	**4**
Lambourn Rd. SE17	BZ43	67
Lambourn Rd. SW4	BV45	66
Lambourne Av. SW19	BR49	75
Lambourne Cres., Chig.	CO27	41
Lambourne Cres., Wok.	AU60	91
Lambourne Dr., Brwd.	DF26	122
Lambourne Gdns. E4	CE27	39
Lambourne Gdns., Bark.	CN36	58
Lambourne Rd.		
Lambourne Gdns., Enf.	CA23	30
Lambourne Gdns., Horn.	CV34	51
Lambourne Gro., Kings.T.	BM51	85
Gloucester Rd.		
Lambourne Pl. SE3	CH44	68
Shooters Hill Rd.		
Lambourne Rd. E11	CF33	48
Lambourne Rd., Bark.	CN36	58
Lambourne Rd., Chig.	CN28	40
Lambourne Rd., Ilf.	CN34	49
Lambrook Ter. SW6	BR44	65
Lambs Bldgs. EC1	**BZ38**	**2**
Lambs Bldgs. EC1	BZ38	57
Errol St.		
Lambs Clo. N9	CB27	39
Winchester Rd.		
Lambs Clo., Cuff.	BX18	20
Lambs Conduit Pass. WC1	**BX39**	**2**
Lambs Conduit Pass. WC1	BX39	56
Red Lion Sq.		
Lambs Conduit St. WC1	**BX38**	**2**
Lambs Conduit St. WC1	BX38	56
Lambs Croft Way, Ger.Cr.	AS30	34
Lambs La., Rain.	CU39	59
Lambs Meadow, Wdf.Grn.	CJ30	40
Lambs Ms. N1	**BY37**	**2**
Lambs Ms. N1	BY37	56
Colebrook Row		
Lambs Pass. EC1	**BZ39**	**2**
Lambs Pass. EC1	BZ39	57
Lambs Pass., Brent.	BL42	65
Lambs Ter. N9	BZ27	39
Lambs Wk., Enf.	BZ23	30
Lambscroft Av. SE9	CJ48	78
Lambton Av., Wal.Cr.	CC19	21
Lambton Pl. W11	BS40	56
Lambton Rd. N19	BX33	47
Lambton Rd. SW20	BQ51	85
Lamerock Rd., Brom.	CG49	78
Lamerton Rd., Ilf.	CL30	40
Lamerton St. SE8	CE43	67
Lamford Clo. N17	BZ29	39
Lamington St. W6	BP42	65
Lamlash St. SE11	**BY42**	**4**
Lamlash St. SE11	BY42	66
Hayles St.		
Lammas Av., Mitch.	BV51	86
Lammas Ct., Stai.	AU48	72
Lammas Ct., Wind.	AO44	61
Lammas Dr., Stai.	AU49	72
Lammas Grn. SE26	CB48	77
Lammas Hill, Esher	BF56	93
Lammas La., Esher	BF56	93
Lammas Mead, Brox.	CD15	12
Lammas Park Gdns. W5	BK40	54
Lammas Park Rd. W5	BK40	54
Lammas Rd. E10	CD33	48
Lammas Rd. E9	CC36	57
Lammas Rd., Rich.	BK49	74
Lammas Rd., Wat.	BD25	27
Lammermoor Rd. SW12	BV47	76
Lamont Rd. SW10	BT43	66
Lamorbey Clo., Sid.	CN47	78
Lamorna Av., Grav.	DH48	81
Lamorna Clo., Orp.	CO54	89
Lamorna Clo., Rad.	BJ20	18
Lamorna Gro., Stan.	BK30	36
Lampard Gro. N16	CA33	48
Lampern Sq. E2	CB38	57
Nelson Gdns.		
Lampeter Clo., Wok.	AS62	100
Lampeter Sq. W6	BR43	65
Humbolt Rd.		
Lampits, Hodd.	CE12	12
Lamplighter Clo. E1	CC38	57
Cleveland Way		
Lamplighters Clo., Dart.	CW46	80
Tufnail Rd.		
Lampmead Rd. SE12	CG46	78
Lamport Clo. SE18	CK42	68
Lampton Av., Houns.	BF44	64
Lampton House Clo. SW19	BQ49	75
Lampton Park Rd., Houns.	BF44	64
Lampton Rd., Houns.	BF44	64
Lamsey Rd., Hem.H.	AX14	8
Lamson Rd., Rain.	CT39	59
Lanacre Av. NW9	BO30	37
Lanark Clo. W5	BK39	54
Lanark Pl. W9	**BT38**	**1**
Lanark Pl. W9	BT38	56
Lanark Rd. W9	**BS37**	**1**
Lanark Rd. W9	BS37	56
Lanark Sq. E14	CE41	67
Selsdon Way		
Lanark Sq. E14	CE41	67
Pepper St.		
Lanata Wk., Hayes	BD38	54
Ramulis Dr.		
Lanbury Rd. SE15	CC45	67
Lancashire Gate W1	BV40	56
Avery Row		
Lancashire Rd. E17	CD30	39
Lancaster Av. E18	CH31	49
Lancaster Av. SE27	BY48	76
Lancaster Av. SW19	BQ49	75
Lancaster Av., Bark.	CN36	58
Lancaster Av., Barn.	BT22	29
Lancaster Av., Mitch.	BX53	86
Lancaster Clo. N17	CB29	39
Park La.		
Lancaster Clo. SE27	BZ48	77
Lancaster Clo., Kings.T.	BK49	74
Lancaster Clo., Brom.	CG52	88
Lancaster Clo., Brwd.	DA25	33
Lancaster Clo., Wall.	BX55	86
Beddington La.		
Lancaster Cotts., Rich.	BL46	75
Lancaster Pk.		
Lancaster Ct. SW6	BR43	65
Lancaster Ct. W2	**BT40**	**3**
Lancaster Ct. W2	BT40	56
Lancaster Ct., Bans.	BR60	94
Lancaster Ct., Walt.	BC54	83
Lancaster Dr. E14	CF40	57
Prestons Rd.		
Lancaster Dr. NW3	BU36	56
Lancaster Dr., Hem.H.	AS17	16
Lancaster Dr., Horn.	CU35	50
Lancaster Gate W2	**BT40**	**3**
Lancaster Gate W2	BT40	56
Lancaster Gdns. NW3	BU36	56
Lambolle Pl.		
Lancaster Gdns. SW19	BR49	75
Lancaster Gdns. W13	BJ40	54
Lancaster Gdns. W2	BT40	56
Lancaster Gdns., Kings.T.	BK49	74
Lancaster Gro. NW3	BT36	56
Lancaster Ms. W2	**BT40**	**3**
Lancaster Ms. W2	BT40	56
Lancaster Ms., Rich.	BL46	75
Richmond Hill		
Lancaster Pk., Rich.	BL46	75
Lancaster Pl. SW19	BQ49	75
Lancaster Pl. WC2	**BX40**	**4**
Lancaster Pl. WC2	BX40	56
Lancaster Pl., Houns.	BD44	64
Lancaster Pl., Twick.	BJ47	74
Lancaster Rd. E11	CG34	49
Lancaster Rd. E17	CC30	39
Lancaster Rd. E7	CH36	58
Lancaster Rd. N11	BW29	38
Lancaster Rd. N18	CA28	39
Lancaster Rd. N4	BY33	47
Lancaster Rd. NW10	BP35	46
Lancaster Rd. SE25	CA51	87
Lancaster Rd. SW19	BQ49	75
Lancaster Rd. W10	BQ41	65
Lancaster Rd. W11	BQ40	55
Lancaster Rd., Barn.	BT24	29
Lancaster Rd., Enf.	BZ23	30
Lancaster Rd., Epp.	CR16	23
Lancaster Rd., Har.	BF32	45
Lancaster Rd., Nthlt.	BG36	54
Lancaster Rd., St.Alb.	BH12	9
Lancaster Rd., Sthl.	BE40	54
Lancaster Rd., Uxb.	AX36	53
Lancaster St. SE1	**BY41**	**4**
Lancaster St. SE1	BY41	66
Lancaster Stables NW3	BU36	56
Lambolle Pl.		
Lancaster Ter. W2	**BT40**	**3**
Lancaster Ter. W2	BT40	56
Lancaster Way, Wat.	BB19	17
Wadham Rd.		
Lancaster Way, Welw.	BQ 5	5
Lancaster Wk., Hayes	BA39	53
Lance Rd., Har.	BG33	45
Lancefield St. W10	BR38	55
Lancell St. N16	CA34	48
Lancelot Av., Wem.	BK35	45
Lancelot Clo., Slou.	AN41	61
Mitchell Clo.		
Lancelot Cres., Wem.	BK35	45
Lancelot Gdns., Barn.	BV26	38
Lancelot Pl. SW7	**BU41**	**3**
Lancelot Pl. SW7	BU41	66
Lancelot Rd., Ilf.	CN29	40
Lancelot Rd., Well.	CO45	69
Lancelot Rd., Wem.	BK35	45
Lancey Clo. SE7	CJ42	68
Cleveley Clo.		
Lanchester Rd. N6	BU32	47
Lancing Gdns. N9	CA26	39
Lancing Rd. W13	BJ40	54
Drayton Green Rd.		
Lancing Rd., Croy.	BX54	86
Lancing Rd., Felt.	BB48	73
Lancing Rd., Ilf.	CM32	49
Lancing Rd., Orp.	CO55	89
Lancing Rd., Rom.	CW29	42
Lancing St. NW1	**BW38**	**1**
Lancing St. NW1	BW38	56
Lancing Way, Rick.	AZ25	26
Lancresse Clo., Uxb.	AX36	53
Landau Way, Brox.	CD16	21
Landau Way, Erith	CV43	70
Landcroft Rd. SE22	CA46	77
Landells Rd. SE22	CA46	77
Lander Rd., Grays	DE42	71
Landfold Clo., Rick.	AY27	35
Landford Rd. SW15	BQ45	65
Landgrove Rd. SW19	BS49	76
Landguard, Saw.	CQ 6	6
Landmann Way SE14	CC42	67
Landmead Rd., Chsnt.	CD18	21
Landon Pl. SW1	**BU41**	**3**
Landon Pl. SW1	BU41	66
Landon Way, Ashf.	BA50	73
Landon Wk. E1	CE40	57
Shirbutt St.		
Landon Wk. E14	CE40	57
Cottage St.		
Landons Clo. E14	CF40	57
Landor Ct. N16	CA35	48
Arundel Gro.		
Landor Rd. SW9	BX45	66
Landor Wk. W12	BP41	65
Landport Way SE15	CA43	67
Landra Gdns. N21	BY25	29
Landridge Rd. SW6	BR44	65
Landrock Rd. N8	BX32	47
Lands End, Bush.	BK25	27
Landsbury Dr., Hayes	BC38	53
Landscape Rd., Warl.	CB63	105
Landscape Rd., Wdf.Grn.	CH29	40
Landseer Av. E12	CL35	49
Landseer Av., Grav.	DE48	81
Landseer Clo. SW19	BT51	86
Brangwyn Cres.		
Landseer Clo., Edg.	BM30	37
Landseer Rd. N19	BX34	47
Landseer Rd., Enf.	CB25	30
Landseer Rd., N.Mal.	BN54	85
Landseer Rd., Sutt.	BS57	95
Landstead Rd. SE18	CM43	68
Landview Gdns., Ong.	CX18	24
Landway, The, Orp.	CP52	89
Landway, The, Sev.	CW63	108
Landway, The, Sev.	CX62	108
Lane App. NW7	BR28	37
Lane Av., Green.	DB46	80
Lane Clo. NW2	BP34	46
Lane Clo., Wey.	AW56	92
Lane Ct. SW11	BU46	76
Thurleigh Rd.		
Lane End, Bexh.	CR45	69
Lane End, Epsom	BN60	94
Lane End, Hat.	BO14	10
Lane Gdns., Bush.	BH26	36
Lane Way SW15	BP46	75
Sunnymead Rd.		
Lane, The NW8	**BT37**	**1**
Lane, The NW8	BT37	56
Lane, The SE3	CH45	68
Lane, The, Cher.	AW52	83
Lane, The, Vir.W.	AS52	82
Lanefield Wk., Welw.G.C.	BQ 8	5
Lanercost Clo. SW2	BY48	76
Lanercost Gdns. N14	BX26	38
Lanercost Rd. SW2	BY48	76
Lanes Av., Grav.	DF48	81
Laneside Av., Dag.	CQ33	50
Laneside, Chis.	CL49	78
Laneside, Edg.	BN28	37
Lanewood Clo., Amer.	AP23	25
Lanfranc Rd. E3	CD37	57
Lanfrey Pl. W14	BR42	65
North End Rd.		
Lang Clo., Lthd.	BF65	102
Lang Mead SE27	BY49	76
Lang St. E1	CC38	57
Langafel Clo., Long.	DC51	90
Langaller La., Lthd.	BF64	102
Langbourne Av. N6	BV34	47
Langbourne Way, Esher	BJ56	93
Langbrook Rd. SE3	CJ45	68
Langcroft Clo., Cars.	BU55	86
Langdale Av., Mitch.	BU52	86
Langdale Clo. SE17	**BY43**	**4**
Langdale Clo. SE17	BY44	66
Olney St.		
Langdale Clo., Orp.	CL55	88
Grasmere Gdns.		
Langdale Clo., Wok.	AR61	100
Langdale Cres., Bexh.	CR43	69
Langdale Ct., Hem.H.	AY12	8
Langdale Dr., Hayes	BB37	53
Langdale Gdns., Grnf.	BJ38	54
Langdale Gdns., Horn.	CU35	50
Langdale Gdns., Wal.Cr.	CC21	30
Langdale Rd. SE10	CE43	67
Langdale Rd., Th.Hth.	BY52	86
Langdale St. E1	CB39	57
Langdale Wk., Grav.	DF48	81
Langdon Cres. E6	CL37	58
Langdon Ct. NW10	BO37	55
Langdon Dr. NW9	BN33	46
Langdon Park Rd. N6	BW33	47
Langdon Pl. SW14	BN45	65
Rosemary La.		
Langdon Rd. E6	CL37	58
Langdon Rd., Brom.	CH52	88
Langdon Rd., Mord.	BT53	86
Langdon Shaw, Sid.	CN49	78
Langford Clo. E8	CB35	48
Ferncliffe Est.		
Langford Clo. E8	CB35	48
Ferncliff Rd.		
Langford Clo. NW8	**BT37**	**1**
Langford Clo. NW8	BT37	56
Langford Cres., Barn.	BU24	29
Langford Ct. NW8	BT37	56
Langford Grn. SE5	CA45	67
Champion Hill		
Langford Pl. NW8	**BT37**	**1**
Langford Pl. NW8	BT37	56
Langford Pl., Sid.	CO48	79
Langford Rd. SW6	BS44	66
Langford Rd., Barn.	BU24	29
Langford Rd., Wdf.Grn.	CJ29	40
Langfords, Buck.H.	CJ27	40
Langham Clo. N15	BY31	47
Langham Rd.		
Langham Clo., St.Alb.	BK11	9
Langham Ct., Horn.	CV33	51
Langham Dene, Ken.	BY61	104
Langham Dr., Rom.	CO32	50
Langham Gdns. N21	BY25	29
Langham Gdns. W13	BJ40	54
Langham Gdns., Edg.	BN29	37
Langham Gdns., Rich.	BK49	74
Langham Gdns., Wem.	BK34	45
Langham House Clo., Rich.	BK49	74
Langham Pl. N15	BY31	47
Langham Pl. W1	**BV39**	**1**
Langham Pl. W1	BV39	56
Langham Pl. W4	BO43	65
Hogarth Roundabout		
Langham Pl., Egh.	AS49	72
Langham Rd. N15	BY31	47
Langham Rd. SW20	BQ51	85
Langham Rd., Edg.	BN29	37
Langham Rd., Tedd.	BJ49	74
Langham St. W1	**BV39**	**1**
Langham St. W1	BV39	56
Langhedge Clo. N18	CA29	39
Langhedge La. N18	CA28	39
Langholme, Bush.	BG26	38
Sparrows Herne		
Langhorne Rd., Dag.	CR36	59
Langland Cres. E., Stan.	BK30	36
Langland Cres. N., Stan.	BK30	36
Langland Cres. S., Stan.	BL31	46
Langland Cres. W., Stan.	BK30	36
Langland Ct., Nthwd.	BA29	35
Langland Dr., Pnr.	BE29	36
Langland Gdns. NW3	BS35	47
Langland Gdns., Croy.	CD55	87
Langland Ri., Epsom	BN60	94
Langlands Dr., Dart.	CZ49	80
Langler Rd. NW10	BQ37	55
Langley Av., Hem.H.	AY15	8
Langley Av., Ruis.	BC34	44
Langley Av., Surb.	BK54	84
Langley Av., Wor.Pk.	BQ54	85
Langley Broom, Slou.	AS42	62
Langley Clo., Epsom	BN63	103
Langley Clo., Guil.	AR70	118
Langley Clo., Rom.	CV29	42
Faringdon Av.		
Langley Cres. E11	CH33	49
Langley Cres., Dag.	CP36	59
Langley Cres., Edg.	BN27	37
Langley Cres., Hayes	BB43	63
Langley Cres., Kings L.	AZ18	17
Langley Cres., St.Alb.	BG12	9
Langley Ct. SE9	CL46	78
Langley Ct. WC2	**BX40**	**4**
Langley Ct. WC2	BX40	56
Long Acre		
Langley Ct., Beck.	CE53	87
Langley Ct., W.Wick.	CF54	87
Langley Dr. E11	CH33	49
Langley Dr. W3	BM41	65
Langley Dr., Brwd.	DA27	42
Langley Gdns., Brom.	CJ52	88
Langley Gdns., Dag.	CP36	59
Langley Gdns., Orp.	CL53	88
Langley Gro., N.Mal.	BO51	85
Langley High St., Slou.	AT42	62
Langley Hill Clo., Kings L.	AZ18	17
Langley Hill, Kings L.	AY18	17
Langley La. SW8	BX43	66
Langley La., Epsom	BM66	112
Langley La., Wat.	BB19	17
Langley Lodge La., Kings L.	AZ19	17
Langley Meadows, Loug.	CM23	31
Langley Oaks Av., S.Croy.	CB58	96
Langley Pk. NW7	BO29	37
Langley Pk. Rd., Slou. & Iver	AT40	52
Langley Pk. Rd., Sutt.	BT56	95
Langley Quay, Slou.	AS41	62
Waterside Dr.		
Langley Rd. SW19	BR51	85
Langley Rd., Beck.	CC52	87
Langley Rd., Islw.	BH44	64
Langley Rd., Kings L.	AW18	17
Langley Rd., S.Croy.	CC58	96
Langley Rd., Slou.	AR41	62
Langley Rd., Stai.	AV50	72
Langley Rd., Surb.	BL54	85
Langley Rd., Wat.	BB19	17
Langley Rd., Wat.	BB22	26
Langley Rd., Well.	CP43	69
Langley St. WC2	**BX39**	**2**
Langley St. WC2	BX39	56
Langley Vale Rd., Epsom	BN63	103
Langley Vale Rd., Epsom	BO62	103
Langley Way, W.Wick.	CF54	87
Langley Way, Wat.	BB23	26
Langley Wk., Wok.	AS63	100
Midhope Rd.		
Langleybury La.	AZ22	26
Langmans Way, Wok.	AP61	100
Langmead Dr., Bush.	BH26	36
Langmead St. SE27	BY49	76
Langport Ct., Walt.	BD54	84
Langroyd Rd. SW17	BU48	76
Langshott Clo., Wey.	AV59	91
Langside Av. SW15	BP45	65
Langside Cres. N14	BW27	38
Langston Rd., Loug.	CM25	31
Langtay Wk. NW8	BS37	56
Abbey Rd.		
Langthorn Ct. EC2	**BZ39**	**2**
Copthall Av.		
Langthorn Ct. EC2	BZ39	57
Copthall Av.		
Langthorne Cres., Grays	DE42	71
Langthorne Rd. E11	CF34	48
Langthorne St. SW6	BQ43	65
Langton Av. E6	CL38	58
Langton Av. N20	BT26	38
Langton Av., Epsom	BO59	94
Langton Clo. WC1	**BX38**	**2**
Langton Clo. WC1	BX38	56
Wren St.		
Langton Clo., Wey.	AW55	83
Langton Clo., Wok.	AP62	100
Langton Gro., Nthwd.	BA28	35
Langton Rd. NW2	BQ34	46
Langton Rd. SW9	BY43	66
Langton Rd., E.Mol.	BG53	84
Langton Rd., Har.	BG29	36
Langton Rd., Hodd.	CD12	12
Langton Ri. SE23	CB47	77
Langton St. SW10	BT43	66
Langton Way SE3	CG44	68
Langton Way, Croy.	CA55	87
Langton Way, Egh.	AU50	72
Langton Way, Grays	DH42	71
Langtry Rd. NW8	**BS37**	**1**
Langtry Rd. NW8	BS37	56
Langtry Rd., Nthlt.	BD37	54
Langtry Wk. NW8	**BT37**	**1**
Langtry Wk. NW8	BT37	56
Ainsworth Est.		
Langwood Chase, Tedd.	BK50	74
Langwood Gdns., Wat.	BC23	26
Langworth Clo., Dart.	CV48	80
Langworth Dr., Hayes	BC39	53
Langworthy End., Maid.	AG43	61
Langworthy La., Maid.	AG43	61
Lanhill Rd. W9	BS38	56
Lanier Rd. SE13	CF46	77
Lankaster Gdns. N2	BT30	38
Lankers Dr., Har.	BE32	45
Lankton Clo., Beck.	CF51	87
Lannock Rd., Hayes	BB40	53
Lannoy Rd. SE9	CM47	78
Lanrick Rd. E14	CF39	57
Lanridge Rd. SE2	CP41	69
Lansbury Av. N18	BZ28	39
Lansbury Av., Bark.	CO36	59
Lansbury Av., Felt.	BC46	73
Lansbury Av., Rom.	CQ32	50
Lansbury Clo. NW10	BN35	46
Lansbury Cres., Dart.	CX46	80
Lansbury Dr., Hayes	BB37	53
Lansbury Est. E14	CE39	57
Lansbury Gdns. E14	CF39	57
Lansbury Gdns., Til.	DG44	71
Central Av.		
Lansbury Rd., Enf.	CC23	30
Lansbury Way N18	CA28	39
Lansbury Av.		
Lansdell Rd., Mitch.	BV51	86
Lansdown Clo., Walt.	BD54	84
St. Johns		
Lansdown Clo., Wok.	AP63	100

Lansdown Pl., Grav. DF47 81
Lansdown Rd. E7 CJ36 58
Lansdown Rd., Ger.Cr. AR30 34
Lansdown Rd., Sid. CO48 79
Lansdown, Guil. AT70 118
Lansdowne Av., Bexh. CP43 69
Lansdowne Av., Orp. CL54 88
Lansdowne Av., Slou. AP40 52
Lansdowne Clo. SW20 BQ50 75
Lansdowne Clo., Twick. BH47 74
Lansdowne Clo., Wat. BD21 27
Lansdowne Cres. W11 BR40 55
Lansdowne Ct., Pur. BY58 95
Lansdowne Ct., Slou. AP40 52
Lansdowne Av.
Lansdowne Ct., Wor.Pk. BP55 85
Lansdowne Dr. E8 CB36 57
Lansdowne Gdns. SW8 BX44 66
Lansdowne Gdns. W11 BR41 65
Lansdowne Green Est. SW8 BX44 66
Lansdowne Gro. NW10 BO35 46
Lansdowne Hill SE27 BY48 76
Lansdowne La. SE7 CJ43 68
Lansdowne Ms. SE7 CJ42 68
Lansdowne Ms. W11 BR40 55
Lansdowne Rd.
Lansdowne Pl. SE1 BZ41 4
Lansdowne Pl. SE1 BZ41 67
Lansdowne Pl. SE19 CA50 77
Lansdowne Rd. E11 CG34 49
Lansdowne Rd. E17 CE32 48
Lansdowne Rd. E18 CH31 49
Lansdowne Rd. E4 CE27 39
Lansdowne Rd. N10 BW30 38
Lansdowne Rd. N17 CB30 39
Lansdowne Rd. N3 BR29 37
Lansdowne Rd. SW20 BQ50 75
Lansdowne Rd. W11 BR40 55
Lansdowne Rd., Brom. CH50 78
Lansdowne Rd., Croy. BZ55 87
Lansdowne Rd., Epsom BN57 94
Lansdowne Rd., Har. BH33 45
Lansdowne Rd., Houns. BF45 64
Lansdowne Rd., Ilf. CN33 49
Lansdowne Rd., Pur. BX59 95
Lansdowne Rd., Stai. AW50 73
Lansdowne Rd., Stan. BK29 36
Lansdowne Rd., Til. DF44 71
Lansdowne Rd., Uxb. AZ39 53
Lansdowne Ri. W11 BR40 55
Lansdowne Row W1 BV40 3
Lansdowne Row W1 BV40 56
Berkeley St.
Lansdowne Ter. WC1 BX38 2
Lansdowne Ter. WC1 BX38 56
Lansdowne Way SW8 BW44 66
Lansdowne Wk. W11 BR40 55
Lansdowne Wood Clo. SE27 BY48 76
Lansdowne Hill
Lansfield Av. N18 CB28 39
Lanstead Rd. SE18 CM43 68
Lant St. SE1 BZ41 4
Lant St. SE1 BZ41 67
Lantern Clo. SW15 BP45 65
Lantern Clo., Wem. BK35 45
Lanterns Ct. E14 CE41 67
Lanvanor Rd. SE15 CC44 67
Lapford Clo. W9 BR38 55
Lapponum Wk., Hayes BD39 54
Jollys La.
Lapse Wood Wk. SE23 CB48 77
Lapstone Gdns., Har. BK32 45
Lapwing Clo., Hem.H. AY11 8
Lapwing Clo., S.Croy. CD58 96
Lapwing Gro., Guil. AU69 118
Lapwings, The, Grav. DH48 81
Lapworth Clo., Orp. CP55 89
Woodley Rd.
Lara Clo. SE13 CF46 77
Lara Clo., Chess. BL57 94
Larbert Rd. SW16 BW50 76
Larby Pl., Epsom BO58 94
Larch Av. W3 BO40 55
Larch Av., Guil. AR69 118
Larch Av., St.Alb. BE18 18
Larch Clo. N11 BV29 38
Larch Clo. SE8 CD43 67
Clyde St.
Larch Clo. SW12 BV47 76
Larch Clo., Red. BT71 121
Larch Clo., Tad. BT64 104
Larch Clo., Warl. CD63 105
Larch Cres., Epsom BM57 94
Larch Cres., Hayes BD38 54
Larch Grn. NW9 BO29 37
Clayton Field
Larch Gro., Sid. CN47 78
Larch Ms. N19 BW34 47
Bredgar Rd.
Larch Rd. NW2 BQ35 46
Larch Rd., Dart. CV47 80
Larch Tree Way, Croy. CE55 87
Larch Way, Brom. CL54 88
Larchdene, Orp. CL55 88
Larches Av. SW14 BN45 65
Larches Av., Enf. CC21 30
Larches, The N13 BZ27 39
Larches, The, Berk. AO12 7
Larches, The, Uxb. AZ38 53
Larches, The, Wat. BE25 27
Larchwood Av., Rom. CR29 41
Larchwood Clo., Bans. BR61 103
Larchwood Clo., Rom. CS29 41
Larchwood Dr., Egh. AQ50 72
Larchwood Gdns., Brwd. DA25 33
Larchwood Rd. SE9 CL48 78
Larchwood Rd., Hem.H. AY12 8
Larchwood Wk., Wok. AO63 100
Gorsewood Rd.
Larcom St. SE17 BZ42 4
Larcom St. SE17 BZ42 67
Larcombe Clo., Croy. CA56 96
Larden Rd. W3 BO40 55
Lardo Av. SW6 BR45 65
Largewood Av., Surb. BL55 85
Largo Wk., Erith CT44 69
Drummond Clo.
Larissa St. SE17 BZ42 4
Larissa St. SE17 BZ42 67
Tisdall Pl.
Lark Av., Stai. AV48 72
Lark Field, Cob. BC60 92
Lark Fields, Grav. DF48 81
Lark Ri., Hat. BP13 10
Lark Ri., Lthd. BB69 100
Lark Row E3 CC37 57
Larkbere Rd. SE26 CD49 77
Larken Dr., Bush. BG26 36
Larkfield Av., Har. BJ31 45
Larkfield Clo., Brom. CH55 88
Station Hill
Larkfield Rd., Rich. BL45 65
Larkfield Rd., Sev. CS65 107
Larkfield Rd., Sid. CN48 78
Larkhall Clo., Walt. BD56 93
Larkhall Est. SW8 BW44 66
Larkhall La. SW4 BW44 66
Larkhall Ri. SW4 BW44 66
Larkin Clo., Brwd. DE26 122
Grays Wk.
Larkings La., Slou. AR37 52
Larkins Clo., Brwd. DE26 122
Grays Wk.
Larks Field, Hart. DC52 90
Larks Gro., Bark. CN36 58
Larks Ri., Chesh. AO20 16
Larksfield Gro., Enf. CB23 30
Larksfield, Egh. AR50 72
Larkshall Cres. E4 CF28 39
Larkshall Rd. E4 CF28 39
Larkspur Clo. E6 CK39 58
Larkspur Clo. N17 BZ29 39
Larkspur Clo., Orp. CP55 89
Berrylands
Larkspur Clo., S.Ock. DB38 60
Larkspur Way, Dor. BK73 119
Larkspur Way, Epsom BN56 94
Larkswood Rd. E4 CE28 39
Larkswood Ri., Pnr. BD31 45
Larkswood Ri., St.Alb. BK11 9
Sandringham Cres.
Larkswood, Harl. CP12 14
Larkway Clo. NW9 BN31 46
Larmans Rd., Enf. CC21 30
Larnach Rd. W6 BQ43 65
Larne Rd., Ruis. BB33 44
Larner Rd., Erith CT43 69
Larpent Av. SW15 BQ45 65
Larsen Dr., Wal.Abb. CF20 21
Larwood Clo., Har. BG35 45
Lascelles Av., Har. BG33 45
Lascelles Clo. E11 CF34 48
Lascelles Clo., Brwd. DA25 33
Lascelles Rd., Slou. AQ42 62
Lascotts Rd. N22 BX29 38
Lassa Rd. SE9 CK46 78
Lassell St. SE10 CF42 67
Lasswade Rd., Cher. AV54 82
Latchett Rd. E18 CH30 40
Latchford Pl., Chig. CO28 41
Latching Clo., Rom. CV28 42
Troopers Dr.
Latchington Gdns., Wdf.Grn. CK29 40
Latchmere Clo. SW11 BU44 66
Battersea Park Rd.
Latchmere Clo., Rich. BL49 75
Latchmere Ho., Kings.T. BL49 75
Latchmere La., Kings.T. BL50 75
Latchmere Pass. SW11 BU44 66
Cabul Rd.
Latchmere Rd. SW11 BU44 66
Latchmere Rd., Kings.T. BL50 75
Latchmere St. SW11 BU44 66
Burns Rd.
Latchmoor Av., Ger.Cr. AR31 43
Latchmoor Way, Ger.Cr. AR31 43
Late Braxton Rd. SW16 BX50 76
Westwell Rd.
Lateward Rd., Brent. BK43 64
Latham Clo., Twick. BJ47 74
Latham Clo., West. CJ61 106
Latham Rd., Bexh. CR46 79
Latham Rd., Twick. BH47 74
Lathams Way, Croy. BX54 86
Lathkill Clo., Enf. CA26 39
Lathom Clo. E6 CK39 58
Oliver Gdns.
Lathom Rd. E6 CK36 58
Latima Clo., Wok. AT61 100
Alpha Rd.
Latimer Av. E6 CK37 58
Latimer Clo., Amer. AR23 25
Latimer Clo., Hem.H. AZ11 8
Latimer Clo., Pnr. BD30 36
Latimer Clo., Wor.Pk. BP56 94
Latimer Gdns., Pnr. BD30 36
Latimer Ms. W10 BQ39 55
Latimer Pl. W10 BQ39 55
Latimer Rd. E7 CH35 49
Latimer Rd. N15 CA32 48
Latimer Rd. SW19 BS50 76
Latimer Rd. W10 BQ39 55
Latimer Rd. W11 BO40 55
Latimer Rd., Barn. BS24 29
Latimer Rd., Chesh. AP20 16
Latimer Rd., Tedd. BH49 74
Latimer St. E1 CC39 57
Latona Dr., Grav. DJ49 81
Latona Rd. SE15 CA43 67
Lattimore Rd., St.Alb. BH14 9
Latton Clo., Esher BF56 93
Latton Clo., Walt. BE54 84
Latton Common Rd., Harl. CO12 14
Latton Grn., Harl. CN13 13
Latton Hall Clo., Harl. CO10 6
Burgoyne Hatch
Latton Ho., Harl. CO12 14
Latymer Clo., Wey. BA56 92
Latymer Ct. W6 BQ42 65
Latymer Rd. N9 CA26 39
Latymer Way N9 CA27 39
Laud St. SE11 BX42 4
Laud St. SE11 BX42 66
Laud St., Croy. BZ55 87
Lauder Clo., Nthlt. BD37 54
Lauderdale Dr., Rich. BK48 74
Lauderdale Rd. W9 BS38 1
Lauderdale Rd. W9 BS38 56
Laudersdale Rd., Kings L. BA20 17
Laughedge La. N18 CA28 39
Laughton Rd., Nthlt. BD37 54
Launcelot Rd., Brom. CH49 78
Launcelot St. SE1 BY41 4
Launceston Clo., Rom. CV30 42
Launceston Gdns., Grnf. BK37 54
Launceston Pl. W8 BT41 3
Launceston Pl. W8 BT41 66
Launceston Rd., Grnf. BK37 54
Launch St. E14 CF41 67
Launders La., Rain. CW39 60
Laundry La., Wal.Abb. CG15 13
Laundry Rd. E4 CF26 39
Station Rd.
Laundry Rd. W6 BR43 65
Laundry Rd., Guil. AR71 118
Laura Clo., Enf. CA25 30
Private Rd.
Laura Clo., Ilf. CJ32 49
Laura Dr., Swan. CU50 79
Laura Pl. E5 CC35 48
Lauradale Rd. N2 BU31 47
Laurel Av., Egh. AQ49 72
Laurel Av., Grav. DH48 81
Lauradale Rd. N2 BU31 47
Laurel Av., Egh. AQ49 72
Laurel Av., Grav. DH48 81
Laurel Av., Pot.B. BR19 19
Laurel Av., Slou. AS41 62
Laurel Av., Twick. BH47 74
Laurel Bank Gdns. SW6 BR44 65
New Kings Rd.
Laurel Bank Rd., Enf. BZ23 30
Laurel Clo. N19 BW34 47
Hargrave Pk.
Laurel Clo., Brwd. DD25 122
Laurel Clo., Dart. CV47 80
Laurel Clo., Hem.H. AY13 8
Laurel Clo., Ilf. CM29 40
Laurel Clo., Sid. CO48 79
Laurel Clo., Slou. AV44 62
Laurel Cres., Croy. CE55 87
Laurel Cres., Rom. CT33 50
Laurel Cres., Wok. AU60 91
Laurel Dene, Tedd. BG49 74
Laurel Dr. N21 BY26 38
Laurel Dr., Oxt. CG69 115
Laurel Gdns. E4 CE26 39
Laurel Gdns. NW7 BN27 37
Laurel Gdns. W7 BH40 54
Laurel Gdns., Houns. BE45 64
Laurel Gro. SE20 CB50 77
Laurel Gro. SE26 CC49 77
Laurel La., West Dr. AY42 63
Laurel Lodge La., Barn. BQ21 28
Laurel Pk., Har. BH29 36
Kenton La.
Laurel Rd. SW13 BP44 65
Laurel Rd. SW20 BP51 85
Laurel Rd., Ger.Cr. AR30 34
Laurel Rd., St.Alb. BH13 9
Laurel Rd., Tedd. BG49 74
Laurel St. E8 CA36 57
Laurel Vw. N12 BS27 38
Laurel Way N20 BS27 38
Laurel Way, Ilf. CG31 49
Laurels Rd., Iver AU37 52
Laurels, The, Berk. AU12 7
Laurels, The, Dart. CV49 80
Stock La.
Laurels, The, Har. BH29 36
Kenton La.
Laurels, The, Wey. BA55 83
Laurence Blds. N16 CA34 48
Brook Rd.
Laurence Ms. W12 BP41 65
Askew Rd.
Laurence Pountney Hill EC4 BZ40 4
Laurence Pountney Hill EC4 BX40 57
Cannon St.
Laurence Pountney La. EC4 BZ40 4
Laurence Pountney La. EC4 BZ40 57
Laurie Gdns. W7 BH39 54
Laurie Gro. SE14 CD44 67
Laurie Rd. W7 BH39 54
Laurie Wk., Rom. CT32 50
Laurier Rd. NW5 BV34 47
Laurier Rd., Croy. CA54 87
Lauries La., Hem.H. AU14 7
Laurimel Clo., Stan. BJ29 36
September Way
Lauriston Clo., Wok. AO62 100
Victoria Rd.
Lauriston Rd. E9 CC36 57
Lauriston Rd. SW19 BQ50 75
Lausanne Rd. N8 BY31 47
Lausanne Rd. SE15 CC44 67
Lauser Rd., Stai. AX47 73
Laustan Clo., Guil. AU70 118
Lavell St. N16 BZ35 48
Albion Rd.
Lavender Av. NW9 BN33 46
Lavender Av., Brwd. DA25 33
Lavender Av., Mitch. BU51 86
Lavender Av., Wor.Pk. BQ55 85
Lavender Clo. SW3 BU43 66
Danvers St.
Lavender Clo., Cars. BV56 95
Lavender Rd.
Lavender Clo., Chsnt. CA17 21
Peakes Way
Lavender Clo., Couls. BW63 104
Starrock Rd.
Lavender Clo., Red. BV73 121
Lavender Clo., Rom. CV29 42
Lavender Gdns. SW11 BU45 66
Lavender Gdns., Enf. BY22 29
Lavender Gro. E8 CA36 57
Lavender Gro., Mitch. BU51 86
Lavender Hill SW11 BU45 66
Lavender Hill, Enf. BY23 29
Lavender Hill, Swan. CS52 89
Lavender Park Rd., Wey. AW60 92
Lavender Rd. SE16 CD40 57
Lavender Rd. SW11 BT45 66
Lavender Rd., Cars. BV56 95
Lavender Rd., Croy. BX53 86
Lavender Rd., Enf. BX23 30
Lavender Rd., Epsom BM57 94
Lavender Rd., Sutt. BT56 95
Parkhurst Rd.
Lavender Rd., Uxb. AY39 53
Lavender Rd., Wok. AT61 100
Lavender Ri., West Dr. AZ41 63
Lavender St. E15 CG36 58
Lavender Sweep SW11 BU45 66
Lavender Ter. SW11 BU45 66
Falcon Rd.
Lavender Vale, Wall. BW57 95
Lavender Way, Croy. CC53 87
Lavender Wk. SW11 BU45 66
Lavender Hill
Lavender Wk., Mitch. BV52 86
Lavengro Rd. SE27 BZ48 77
Lavenham Rd. SW18 BR48 75
Lavernock Rd., Bexh. CR44 69
Lavers Rd. N16 CA34 48
Laverstoke Gdns. SW15 BO47 75
Laverton Pl. SW5 BS42 3
Laverton Pl. SW5 BS42 66
Courtfield Gdns.
Lavidge Rd. SE9 CK48 78
Lavie Ms. W10 BR38 55
Portobello Rd.
Lavina Gro. N1 BX37 2
Lavina Gro. N1 BX37 56
Wharfdale Rd.
Lavington Rd. W13 BJ40 54
Lavington Rd., Croy. BX55 86
Lavington St. SE1 BY40 4
Lavington St. SE1 BY40 56
Lavinia Av., Wat. BD20 18
Lavinia Rd., Dart. CW46 80
Lavrock La., Rick. AY26 35
Law St. SE1 BZ41 4
Law St. SE1 BZ41 67
Lawdons Gdns., Croy. BY56 95
Lawford Av., Rick. AU25 25
Lawford Clo., Horn. CV35 51
Lawford Clo., Wall. BX58 95
Lawford Gdns., Dart. CV46 80
Lawford Gdns., Ken. BZ61 105
Lawford Rd. Clo., Rick. AU25 25
Lawford Rd. N1 CA36 2
Lawford Rd. N1 CA36 57
Lawford Rd. NW5 BW36 56
Lawford Rd. W4 BN43 65
Lawless St. E14 CE40 57
Lawley Rd. N14 BV26 38
Lawley St. E5 CC35 48
Lawn Av., West Dr. AX41 63
Lawn Clo. N9 CA26 39
Lawn Clo., Brom. CH50 78
Lawn Clo., N.Mal. BO51 85
Lawn Clo., Ruis. BB34 44
Lawn Clo., Slou. AR43 62
Lawn Clo., Swan. CS51 89
Lawn Cres., Rich. BL44 65
Lawn Ct., Wem. BM34 46
The Avenue
Lawn Farm Gro., Rom. CQ31 50
Lawn Gdns. W7 BH40 54
Lawn La. SW8 BX43 66
Lawn La., Hem.H. AX14 8
Lawn Pl. SE15 CA44 67
Sumner Est.
Lawn Rd. NW3 BU35 47
Lawn Rd., Beck. CD50 77
Lawn Rd., Grav. DE46 81
Lawn Rd., Guil. AR72 118
Lawn Rd., Uxb. AX36 53
Lawn Ter. SE3 CG45 68
Lawn Vale, Pnr. BD30 36
Lawn, The, Harl. CO 9 6
Lawn, The, Houns. BF44 64
Lawn, The, Sthl. BF42 64
Lawnfield NW6 BQ36 55
Lawns Cres., Grays DE43 71
Lawns Dr., The, Brox. CD14 12
High Rd.
Lawns Est., The SE19 BZ51 87
Lawns, The E4 CE28 39
Lawns, The SE19 BZ51 87
Lawns, The SE3 CG45 68
Lawns, The, Brwd. DC28 122
Uplands Rd.
Lawns, The, Hem.H. AV13 7
Lawns, The, Pnr. BF29 36
Lawns, The, Sid. CO49 79
Lawns, The, Slou. AV44 62
Bath Rd.
Lawns, The, St.Alb. BG13 9
Lawns, The, Sutt. BR57 94
Lawns, The, Welw.G.C. BQ 6 5
Lawnside SE3 CG45 68
Lawnsway, Rom. CS29 41
Lawrance Rd., St.Alb. BG11 9
Lawrance Sq., Grav. DF48 81
Lawrence Av. E12 CL35 49
Lawrence Av. E17 CC30 39
Lawrence Av. N13 BY28 38
Lawrence Av. NW7 BO28 37
Lawrence Av., N.Mal. BN53 85
Lawrence Av., N.Mal. BO54 85
Lawrence Campe Clo. N20 BT27 38
Friern Barnet La.
Lawrence Clo. E3 CE37 58
Malmesbury Rd.
Lawrence Clo. N15 CA31 48
Lawrence Clo., Guil. AT68 109
Ladygrove Dr.
Lawrence Cres., Dag. CR34 50
Lawrence Cres., Edg. BM30 37
Lawrence Ct. NW7 BO28 37
Lawrence Dr., Uxb. BA35 44
Lawrence Fairweather Pl. N15 CA31 48
Lawrence Rd.
Lawrence Gdns. NW7 BO27 37
Lawrence Gdns., Chsnt. CC17 21
Lawrence Gdns., Ken. BZ61 105
Lawrence Gdns., Til. DG43 71
Lawrence Hill E4 CE27 39
Lawrence Hill Gdns., Dart. CV46 80
Lawrence Hill Rd., Dart. CV46 80
Lawrence La. EC2 BZ39 2
Lawrence La. EC2 BZ39 57
Trump St.
Lawrence La., Bet. BP69 120
Lawrence Moorings, Saw. CQ 6 6
Lawrence Pl. N1 BX37 2
Delhi St.
Lawrence Pl. N1 BX37 56
Delhi St.
Lawrence Rd. E13 CH37 58
Lawrence Rd. E6 CK37 58
Lawrence Rd. N15 CA31 48
Lawrence Rd. N18 CB28 39
Lawrence Rd. SE25 CA52 87
Lawrence Rd. W5 BK42 64
Lawrence Rd., Houns. BD45 64
Lawrence Rd., W.Wick. CH56 97
Lawrence Rd., Hayes BA37 53
Lawrence Rd., Hmptn. BE50 74
Lawrence Rd., Pnr. BD32 45
Lawrence Rd., Rich. BK49 74
Lawrence Rd., Rom. CU32 50
Lawrence St. E16 CG39 58
Lawrence St. NW7 BO28 37
Lawrence St. SW3 BU43 66
Lawrence Way, Grnf. BJ37 54
Lawrie Park Av. SE26 CB49 77
Lawrie Park Cres. SE26 CB49 77
Lawrie Park Gdns. SE26 CB49 77
Lawrie Park Rd. SE26 CB50 77
Lawson Clo. SW19 BQ48 75
Lawson Est. SE1 BZ41 4
Lawson Gdns., Pnr. BC31 44
Tolcarne Dr.
Lawson Rd., Dart. CV45 70
Lawson Rd., Enf. CC23 30
Lawson Rd., Sthl. BE38 54
Lawsons Clo. E16 CJ39 58
Lawton Rd. E10 CF33 48
Lawton Rd. E3 CD38 57
Lawton Rd. N22 BX30 38
Lawton Rd., Barn. BT24 29
Lawton Rd., Loug. CL23 31
Laxey Rd., Orp. CN57 97
Laxley Clo. SE5 BY43 66
Laxton Gdns., Red. BW67 113
Laxton Pl. NW1 BV38 1
Layard Rd. SE16 CB42 67
Layard Rd., Enf. CA23 30
Layard Rd., Th.Hth. BZ51 87
Layard Sq. SE16 CB41 67
Laybrook Clo., St.Alb. BJ11 9
The Berries
Layburn Cres., Slou. AT43 62
Laycock St. N1 BY36 56
Layer Gdns. W3 BM40 55
Layfield Clo. NW4 BP33 46
Layfield Cres. NW4 BP33 46
Layfield Pl. E14 CF39 57
Byron St.
Layfield Rd. NW4 BP33 46
Layhams Rd., Kes. CG59 97
Laymarsh Clo., Belv. CQ41 69
Laymead Clo., Nthlt. BE36 54
Laystall St. EC1 BY38 2
Laystall St. EC1 BY38 56
Layters Av. S., Ger.Cr. AR30 34
Layters Av., Ger.Cr. AR30 34
Layters Clo., Ger.Cr. AR30 34
Layters End, Ger.Cr. AR30 34
Layters Green La., Ger.Cr. AQ30 34
Layters Way, Ger.Cr. AR32 43
Layton Cotts., Brent. BL43 65
Kew Bridge Rd.
Layton Cres., Croy. BY56 95
Layton Ct., Wey. AZ56 92
Layton La., Sun. BB51 83
Layton Rd. N1 BY37 2
Layton Rd. N1 BY37 56
Layton Rd., Brent. BK42 64
Layton Rd., Houns. BF45 64
Laytons Bldgs. SE1 BZ41 4
Borough High St.
Layzell Wk. SE9 CJ47 78
Mottingham La.
Lazar Wk. N7 BX34 47
Briset Way
Le May Av. SE12 CH48 78
Le Personne Rd., Cat. BZ64 105
Lea Bridge Rd. E5 CB34 48
Lea Bushes, Wat. BE21 27
Lea Clo., Bush. BF25 27
Lea Cres., Ruis. BB35 44
Lea Gdns., Wem. BL35 46
Lea Hall Rd. E10 CE33 48
Lea Rd., Beck. CD51 87
Lea Rd., Enf. BZ23 30
Lea Rd., Grays DG42 71
Lea Rd., Hodd. CF11 12
Lea Rd., Sev. CV67 117
Lea Rd., Sthl. BE42 64
Lea Rd., Wal.Abb. CE20 21
Lea Side, Lthd. BF65 102
Lea Vale, Dart. CS45 69
Lea Valley Rd., Enf. CD25 30
Lea Vw. Ho. E5 CB33 48
Lea Vw., Wal.Abb. CE20 21

Lea, The, Egh. AV51 82
Leabank Clo., Har. BH34 45
Leabank Vw. N15 CB32 48
Leabourne Rd. N16 CB32 48
Leachcroft, Ger.Cr. AQ30 34
Leacroft Av. SW12 BU47 76
Leacroft Clo., Ken. BZ61 105
Leacroft Clo., Stai. AW49 73
Leacroft Clo., West Dr. AY39 53
Leacroft Rd., Iver AV39 52
Leacroft, Stai. AW49 73
Leadale Av. E4 CD27 39
Leadale Rd. N15 & N16 CB32 48
Leadenhall Mkt. EC3 CA39 2
Leadenhall Pl.
Leadenhall Pl. EC3 CA39 2
Leadenhall Pl. EC3 CA39 57
Lime St.
Leadenhall St. EC3 CA39 2
Leadenhall St. EC3 CA39 57
Leadenham Ct. E3 CE38 57
Campbell Rd.
Leader Av. E12 CL35 49
Leadings, The, Wem. BN34 46
Leaf Clo., E.Mol. BH53 84
Leaf Clo., Nthwd. BA29 35
Leaf Gro. SE27 BY49 76
Leafield Clo. SW16 BY50 76
Leafield Clo., Wok. AQ62 100
Winnington Way
Leafield La., Sid. CQ49 79
Leafield Rd. SW20 BR52 85
Leafield Rd., Sutt. BS55 86
Leaford Cres., Wat. BB22 26
Leafy Gro., Kes. CJ56 97
Leafy Oak Rd. SE12 CJ49 78
Leafy Way, Brwd. DE26 122
Leafy Way, Croy. CB55 87
Leagrave St. E5 CC34 48
Leaholme Waye, Ruis. BA32 44
Leahurst Rd. SE13 CF46 77
Leake Ct. SE1 BX41 4
Leake Ct. SE1 BX41 66
Addington St.
Leake St. SE1 BX41 4
Leake St. SE1 BX41 66
Lealand Rd. N15 CA32 48
Leamead Av., Nthlt. BE36 54
Leamington Av., Brom. CJ49 78
Leamington Av., Mord. BR52 85
Leamington Av., Orp. CN56 97
Leamington Av.E17 CE32 48
Leamington Clo. E12 CK35 49
Leamington Clo., Brom. CJ49 78
Leamington Clo., Houns. BG46 74
Leamington Clo., Rom. CX29 42
Leamington Cres., Har. BE34 45
Leamington Gdns., Ilf. CN34 49
Leamington Pk. W3 BN39 55
Leamington Pl., Hayes BB38 53
Leamington Rd. Vills. W11 BR39 55
Leamington Rd., Rom. CX29 42
Leamington Rd., Sthl. BD42 64
Leamore St. W6 BQ42 65
Leamouth Rd. E14 CF39 57
Leamouth Rd. E6 CK39 58
Leander Dr., Grav. DJ49 81
Leander Gdns., Wat. BE22 27
Eastlea Av.
Leander Rd. SW2 BX46 76
Leander Rd., Nthlt. BF37 54
Leander Rd., Th.Hth. BX52 86
Leapale La., Guil. AR71 118
Leapale Rd., Guil. AR71 118
Learoyd Gdns. E6 CL39 58
Leas Clo., Chess. BL57 94
Leas Dale SE9 CL48 78
Leas Dr., Iver AV39 52
Leas Grn., Chis. CN50 78
Leas La., Warl. CC62 105
Leas Rd., Guil. AR71 118
Leas Rd., Warl. CC62 105
Leas, The, Bush. BE23 27
Leas, The, Hem.H. AZ16 17
Leas, The, Upmin. CY33 51
Leaside Av. N10 BV31 47
Leaside Rd. E5 CB33 48
Leaside, Hem.H. BA14 8
Leasowes Rd. E10 CE33 48
Leasway, Brwd. DB27 42
Leasway, Grays DE40 71
Leasway, Upmin. CY35 51
Leat Clo., Saw. CQ5 6
Leather Bottle Grn., Erith CQ41 69
Leather Bottle La., Belv. CQ42 69
Leather Clo., Mitch. BV51 86
Leather Gdns. E15 CG37 58
Leather La. EC1 BY38 56
Leather La. EC1 BY39 2
Leatherdale St. E1 CC38 57
Portelet Rd.
Leatherhead By-pass, Lthd. BH65 102
Leatherhead Clo. N16 CA33 48
Leatherhead Rd., Lthd. BF66 111
Leatherhead Rd., Lthd. BG60 93
Leatherhead Rd., Chess. BK59 93
Leatherhead Rd., Cob. BG61 102
Leatherhead Rd., Lthd. & Ash. BK64 102
Leathermarket St. SE1 CA41 4
Leathermarket St. SE1 CA41 67
Leathsail Rd., Har. BF34 45
Leathwaite Rd. SW11 BU45 66
Leathwell Rd. SE8 CE44 67
Leaveland Clo., Beck. CE52 87
Leaver Gdns., Grnf. BH37 54
Leaves Green Cres., Kes. CJ59 97
Leaves Green Rd., Kes. CJ58 97
Leavesden Rd., Stan. BJ29 36
Leavesden Rd., Wat. BC22 26
Leavesden Rd., Wey. AZ56 92
Leaway E10 CC33 48
Leazes Av., Cat. BY65 104
Lebanon Av., Felt. BD49 74
Lebanon Clo., Wat. BA21 26
Lebanon Ct., Twick. BJ47 74
Lebanon Dr., Cob. BF60 93
Lebanon Gdns. SW18 BS46 76
Lebanon Gdns., West. CJ62 106
Lebanon Pk., Twick. BJ47 74
Lebanon Rd. SW18 BS46 76
Lebanon Rd., Croy. CA54 87
Lebrun Sq. SE3 CH45 68
Lechmere Av., Chig. CM28 40
Lechmere Av., Wdf.Grn. CJ30 40
Lechmere Rd. NW2 BP36 55
Leckford Rd. SW18 BT47 76
Leckwith Av., Bexh. CQ43 69
Lecky St. SW7 BT42 3
Lecky St. SW7 BT42 66
Leconfield Av. SW13 BO45 65
Leconfield Rd. N5 BZ35 48
Leconfield Wk., Horn. CV36 60
Airfield Way
Lectern La., St.Alb. BG15 9
Creighton Av.
Leda Av., Enf. CC22 30
Leda Rd. SE18 CK41 68
Ledbury Ms. N. W11 BS40 56
Ledbury Ms. W. W11 BS40 56
Ledbury Pl., Croy. BZ56 96
Ledbury Rd. W11 BR39 55
Ledbury Rd., Croy. BX56 96
Ledbury Rd., Reig. BS70 121
Ledbury St. SE15 CB43 67
Ledger Clo., Guil. AT69 118
Ledger Dr., Wey. AV56 91
Ledger La., Maid. AH44 61
Ledgers Rd., Slou. AO41 61
Ledgers Rd., Warl. CE62 105
Ledrington Rd. SE19 CA50 77
Ledway Dr., Wem. BL33 46
Lee Av., Rom. CQ32 50
Lee Br. SE13 CF45 67
Lee Church St. SE13 CG45 68
Lee Clo. E17 CC30 39
Lee Conservancy Rd. E9 CD35 48
Lee Farm Clo., Chesh. AQ18 16
Lee Gdns. Av., Horn. CX33 51
Lee Green Bri. SE12 CG45 68
Lee Grn. La., Epsom BM65 103
Lee Grn. SE12 CG45 68
Lee Grn., Orp. CO53 89
Lee Gro., Chig. CL27 40
Lee High Rd. SE12 CG45 68
Lee High Rd. SE13 CF45 67
Lee Pk. SE3 CG45 68
Lee Pk. Way N18 CC28 39
Lee Rd. NW7 BQ29 37
Lee Rd. SE3 CG45 68
Lee Rd. SW19 BS51 86
Lee Rd., Enf. CB25 30
Lee Rd., Grnf. BK37 54
Lee St. E8 CA37 2
Lee St. E8 CA37 57
Lee Ter. SE3 CG45 68
Lee Valley Trd. Est. E4 CC28 39
Lee Vw., Enf. BY23 29
Leech La., Lthd. BM66 112
Leechcroft Av., Sid. CN46 78
Leechcroft Av., Swan. CT52 89
Leechcroft Rd., Wall. BV55 86
Leecroft Rd., Barn. BR24 28
Leeds Clo., Orp. CP55 89
Leeds Pl. N4 BX33 47
Leeds Rd., Ilf. CM33 49
Leeds Rd., Slou. AP40 52
Leeds St. N18 CB28 39
Leefern Rd. W12 BP41 65
Leegate Ho. SE12 CG46 78
Leeke St. WC1 BX38 2
Leeke St. WC1 BX38 56
Leeland Rd. W13 BJ40 54
Broadway
Leeland Ter. W13 BJ40 54
Leeland Way NW10 BO35 46
Leeming Rd., B.Wd. BL22 28
Leemount Clo. NW4 BQ31 46
Leerdam Dr. E14 CF41 67
Lees Av., Nthwd. BB30 35
Lees Pl. W1 BV40 3
Lees Pl. W1 BV40 56
Lees Rd., Uxb. AZ38 53
Lees, The, Croy. CD55 87
Leeside Cres. NW11 BR32 46
Leeside Rd. N18 CC29 39
Leeside, Barn. BR25 28
Leeson Rd. SE24 BY45 66
Mayall Rd.
Leesons Hill, Chis. CN52 88
Leesons Way, Orp. CN51 88
Leeward Gdns. SW19 BR49 75
Leeway Clo., Pnr. BE29 36
Wood Ridings Clo.
Leeway SE8 CD42 67
Leewood Pl., Swan. CS52 89
Leewood Way, Lthd. BD67 111
Lefevre Wk. E3 CD37 57
Lefroy Rd. W12 BO41 65
Legard Rd. N5 BY34 47
Legatt Rd. SE9 CJ46 78
Leggatt Rd. E15 CF37 57
Leggatts Clo., Wat. BB21 26
Leggatts Ri., Wat. BC21 26
Leggatts Way, Wat. BB21 26
Leggatts Wood Av., Wat. BC21 26
Legge St. SE13 CF46 77
Leggfield Ter., Hem.H. AV13 7
Leghorn Rd. NW10 BO37 55
Leghorn Rd. SE18 CM42 68
Legion Clo. N1 BY36 56
Legion Ct., Mord. BS53 86
Legion Rd., Grnf. BG37 54
Legon Av., Rom. CS33 50
Legrace Av., Houns. BD44 64
Leicester Av., Mitch. BX52 86
Leicester Clo., Wor.Pk. BQ56 94
Leicester Ct. WC2 BW40 3
Leicester Ct. WC2 BW40 56
Cranbourn St.
Leicester Gdns., Ilf. CN33 49
Leicester Pl. WC2 BW40 3
Leicester Pl. WC2 BW40 56
Lisle St.
Leicester Rd. E11 CH32 49
Leicester Rd. N2 BU31 47
Leicester Rd. NW10 BN36 55
Leicester Rd., Barn. BS25 29
Leicester Rd., Croy. CA54 87
Leicester Rd., Til. DF44 71
Leicester Sq. WC2 BW40 3
Leicester Sq. WC2 BW40 56
Leicester St. WC2 BW40 3
Leicester St. WC2 BW40 56
Lisle St.
Leigh Av., Ilf. CJ31 49
Leigh Clo., N.Mal. BN52 85
Leigh Clo., Wey. AV57 91
Leigh Common, Welw.G.C. BR 9 5
Leigh Corner, Cob. BD61 102
Leigh Cres., Croy. CE57 96
Leigh Ct. Clo., Cob. BD60 93
Leigh Ct., Har. BH33 45
Leigh Dr., Rom. CV28 42
Leigh Gdns. NW10 BQ37 55
Leigh Hill Rd., Cob. BD60 93
Leigh Hunt St. SE1 BZ41 4
Leigh Hunt St. SE1 BZ41 67
Lant La.
Leigh Orchard Clo. SW16 BX48 76
Ivyday Gro.
Leigh Pk., Slou. AQ43 62
Leigh Pl. La., Gdse. CC69 114
Leigh Pl. Rd., Reig. BP73 120
Leigh Pl., Cob. BD61 102
Leigh Pl., Well. CO44 69
Leigh Rd. E10 CF33 48
Leigh Rd. E6 CL36 58
Leigh Rd. N5 BY35 47
Leigh Rd., Cob. BC60 92
Leigh Rd., Grav. DG48 81
Leigh Rd., Houns. BG45 64
Leigh Rood, Wat. BE27 36
Leigh Sq., Wind. AL44 61
Leigh St. WC1 BX38 2
Leigh St. WC1 BX38 56
Leigh Ter., Orp. CO52 89
Leigham Av. SW16 BX48 76
Leigham Court Rd. SW16 BX48 76
Leigham Dr., Islw. BH43 64
Leigham Vale SW16 BX48 76
Leighton Av. E12 CL35 49
Leighton Av., Pnr. BE31 45
Leighton Buzzard Rd., Hem.H. AW10 8
Leighton Clo., Edg. BM30 37
Leighton Cres. NW5 BW35 47
Leighton Gro.
Leighton Gdns. NW10 BP37 55
Leighton Gdns., S.Croy. CB60 96
Leighton Gdns., Til. DG43 71
Leighton Gro. NW5 BW35 47
Leighton Ho. W14 BR41 65
Leighton Pl. NW5 BW35 47
Leighton Rd.
Leighton Rd. NW5 BW35 47
Leighton Rd. W13 BJ41 64
Leighton Rd., Enf. CA25 30
Leighton Rd., Har. BG30 36
Leighton St. E., Croy. BY54 86
Leighton St. W., Croy. BY54 86
Leighton Way, Epsom BN60 94
Leinster Av. SW14 BN45 65
Leinster Gdns. W2 BT39 1
Leinster Gdns. W2 BT39 56
Leinster Ms. W2 BT40 3
Leinster Ms. W2 BT40 56
Leinster Pl. W2 BT39 1
Leinster Pl. W2 BT39 56
Leinster Rd. N10 BV31 47
Leinster Sq. W2 BS40 56
Leinster Ter. W2 BT40 3
Leinster Ter. W2 BT40 56
Leiston Spur, Slou. AP39 52
Leisure La., Wey. AW59 92
Leith Clo. NW9 BN33 46
Leith Hill Grn., Orp. CO51 89
Leith Hill
Leith Hill, Orp. CN51 88
Leith Park Rd., Grav. DG47 81
Leith Rd. N22 BY30 38
Leith Rd., Epsom BO59 94
Leith Vw., Dor. BK73 119
Leithcote Gdns. SW16 BX49 76
Leithcote Path SW16 BX48 76
Ivyday Gro.
Lela Av., Houns. BD44 64
Leman Pl. E1 CB39 2
Leman St. E1 CA39 2
Leman St. E1 CA39 57
Lemark Clo., Stan. BK28 36
Lemmon Rd. SE10 CG43 68
Lemna Rd. E11 CG33 49
Lemonfield Dr., Wat. BE20 18
Lemonwell Ct. SE9 CM46 78
Lemsford Clo. N15 CB32 48
Lemsford Ct. N4 BZ34 48
Kings Crescent Est.
Lemsford Ct., B.Wd. BN24 28
Lemsford La., Welw.G.C. BP 8 5
Lemsford Rd., Hat. BP11 10
Lemsford Rd., St.Alb. BH13 9
Lemsford Village, Welw.G.C. BO 8 5
Lena Gdns. W6 BQ41 65
Lena Kennedy Clo. E4 CE29 39
Lendal Ter. SW4 BX45 66
Lenelby Rd., Surb. BM54 85
Lenham Rd. SE12 CG45 68
Lenham Rd., Bexh. CQ43 69
Lenham Rd., Sutt. BS56 95
Lenham Rd., Th.Hth. BZ51 87
Lenmore Av., Grays DE41 71
Lennard Av., W.Wick. CG55 88
Lennard Clo., W.Wick. CG55 88
Lennard Rd. SE20 CC50 77
Lennard Rd., Beck. CD50 77
Lennard Rd., Brom. CK54 88
Lennard Rd., Croy. BZ54 87
Lennard Rd., Sev. CT63 107
Lennard Row, S.Ock. CY40 60
Lennon Rd. NW2 BQ36 55
Lennox Av. E17 CE32 48
Lennox Av., Grav. DF47 81
Lennox Clo., Rom. CT32 50
Lennox Gdns. Ms. SW1 BU41 3
Lennox Gdns. Ms. SW1 BU41 66
Lennox Gdns. NW10 BO35 46
Lennox Gdns. SW1 BU41 3
Lennox Gdns. SW1 BU41 66
Lennox Gdns., Croy. BY56 95
Violet La.
Lennox Gdns., Ilf. CK33 49
Lennox Rd. E., Grav. DG47 81
Lennox Rd. E17 CD32 48
Lennox Rd. N4 BX34 47
Lennox Rd., Grav. DF46 81
Lenor Clo., Bex. CQ45 69
Lens Rd. E7 CJ36 58
Lensbury Clo., Chsnt. CD17 21
Lensbury Way SE2 CP41 69
Lenthall Av., Grays DD41 71
Lenthall Pl. SW7 BT42 66
Gloucester Rd.
Lenthall Rd. E8 CA36 57
Lenthall Rd., Loug. CM24 31
Lenthorp Rd. SE10 CG42 68
Lentmead Rd., Brom. CG48 78
Lenton Ri., Rich. BL45 65
Evelyn Ter.
Lenton St. SE18 CM42 68
Lenton Ter. N4 BY34 47
Lennox Rd.
Lenville Way SE16 CB42 67
The Bonamy Est. W.
Leo St. SE15 CB43 67
Leo Yd. EC1 BY38 2
Leo Yd. EC1 BY38 56
Great Sutton St.
Leof Cres. SE6 CE49 77
Leominster Rd., Mord. BT53 86
Leominster Wk., Mord. BT53 86
Leonard Av., Mord. BT53 86
Leonard Av., Rom. CS33 50
Leonard Av., Sev. CU61 107
Leonard Av., Swans. DC47 81
Leonard Rd. E4 CE29 39
Leonard Rd. E7 CH35 49
Leonard Rd. N9 CA27 39
Leonard Rd. SW16 BW51 86
Leonard Rd., Sthl. BD41 64
Leonard Robbins Path SE28 CO40 59
Tawney Rd.
Leonard St. E16 CK40 58
Leonard St. EC2 BZ38 2
Leonard St. EC2 BZ38 57
Leonard Way, Brwd. CZ28 42
Leontine Clo. SE15 CB43 67
Leopold Av. SW19 BR49 75
Leopold Rd. E17 CE32 48
Leopold Rd. N18 CB28 39
Albany Rd.
Leopold Rd. N2 BT31 47
Leopold Rd. NW10 BO36 55
Leopold Rd. SW19 BR49 75
Leopold Rd. W5 BL40 55
Leopold St. E3 CD39 57
Lepe Clo., Brom. CG49 78
Leppoc Rd. SW4 BW46 76
Leret Way, Lthd. BJ64 102
Leroy St. SE1 CA42 4
Leroy St. SE1 CA42 67
Lesbourne Rd., Reig. BS71 121
Lescombe Clo. SE23 CD48 77
Lescombe Rd. SE23 CD48 77
Lesley Clo., Bex. CR47 79
Lesley Clo., Grav. DF50 81
Lesley Clo., Swan. CS52 89
Leslie Gdns., Sutt. BS57 95
Leslie Gro., Croy. BZ54 87
Leslie Park Rd., Croy. CA54 87
Leslie Rd. E11 CF35 48
Leslie Rd. E16 CH39 58
Leslie Rd. N2 BT31 47
Leslie Rd., Dor. BK70 119
Leslie Rd., Wok. AP58 91
Leslie Smith Sq. SE18 CL43 68
Nightingale Vale
Lesney Farm Est., Erith CT43 69
Lesney Pk. Rd., Erith CS43 69
Lesney Pk., Erith CS43 69
Lessar Av. SW4 BV46 76
Lessing St. SE23 CD47 77
Lessingham Av. SW17 BU49 76
Lessingham Av., Ilf. CL31 49
Lessington Av., Rom. CS32 50
Lessness Av., Bexh. CP43 69
Lessness Pk., Belv. CQ42 69
Lessness Rd., Belv. CR43 69
Stapley Rd.
Lessness Rd., Mord. BT53 86
Lester Av. E15 CG38 58
Leston Clo., Rain. CU38 59
Leswin Pl. N16 CA34 48
Leswin Rd.
Leswin Rd. N16 CA34 48
Letchfield, Chesh. AQ19 16
Letchford Cotts., Har. BF30 36
Letchford Gdns. NW10 BP38 55
Letchford Ms. NW10 BP38 55
Letchford Gdns.
Letchmore Heath Rd., Wat. BG22 27
Letchmore Rd., Rad. BJ21 27
Letchworth Av., Felt. BB47 73
Letchworth Clo., Brom. CH53 88
Letchworth Clo., Wat. BD29 36
Letchworth Dr., Brom. CH53 88
Letchworth St. SW17 BU49 76
Lethbridge Clo. SE13 CF44 67
Lett Rd. E15 CF36 57
Letter Box La., Sev. CV68 117
Letterstone Rd. SW6 BR43 65
Varna Rd.
Lettice St. SW6 BR44 65
Lettsom St. SE5 CA44 67
Lettsom Wk. E13 CH37 58
Hunter Wk.
Leucha Rd. E17 CD32 48
Levana Clo.SW19 BQ47 75
Victoria Dr.
Levehurst Way SW4 BX44 66
Paradise Rd.
Leven Clo., Wat. BD28 36
Leven Dr., Wal.Cr. CC20 21
Leven Rd. E14 CF39 57
Leven Way, Hayes BB39 53
Leven Way, Hem.H. AX11 8
Lomond Rd.
Levendale Rd. SE23 CD48 77
Lever Sq., Grays DF42 71
Lever St. EC1 BY38 2
Lever St. EC1 BY38 56
Leveret Clo., Croy. CF58 96
Leveret Clo., Wat. BC20 17
Leverett Pl. SW3 BU42 66
Denyer St.
Leverett St. SW3 BU42 66
Denyer St.
Leverholme Gdns. SE9 CL49 78
Leverington Pl. N1 BZ38 2
Leverington Pl. N1 BZ38 57
Charles Sq.
Leverson St. SW16 BW50 76
Leverstock Grn. Rd., Hem.H. AZ13 8
Leverstock Grn. Way, Hem.H. BA13 8
Leverstock Grn., Hem.H. AZ13 8
Leverton Pl. NW5 BW35 47
Leverton St.
Leverton St. NW5 BW35 47
Leverton Way, Wal.Abb. CF20 21
Leveson Rd., Grays DG41 71
Levett Gdns., Ilf. CN35 49
Levett Rd., Bark. CN36 58
Levett Rd., Lthd. BJ63 102
Levine Gdns., Bark. CP37 59
Levison Way N19 BW33 47
Ashbrook Rd.
Levylsdene, Guil. AU70 118
Lewes Clo., Nthlt. BF36 54
Lewes Rd. N12 BU28 38
Lewes Rd., Brom. CJ51 88
Lewes Rd., Rom. CV28 42
Lewes Way, Rick. BA24 26
Lewesdon Clo. SW19 BQ47 75
Leweston Pl. N16 CA33 48
Lewgars Av. NW9 BN32 46
Lewin Rd. SW14 BN45 65
Lewin Rd. SW16 BW50 76
Lewin Rd., Bexh. CQ46 79
Lewins Rd., Epsom BM60 94
Lewins Rd., Ger.Cr. AR31 43
Lewis Av. E17 CE30 39
Lewis Clo., Brwd. DC26 122
Lewis Clo., Wey. AX56 92
Cabbell Pl.
Lewis Cres. NW10 BN35 46
Lewis Gdns. N2 BT30 38
Lewis Gro. SE13 CF45 67
Lewis La., Ger.Cr. AS30 34
Lewis Rd., Grav. DF51 81
Lewis Rd., Horn. CV32 51
Lewis Rd., Mitch. BT51 86
Lewis Rd., Rich. BK46 74
Red Lion St.
Lewis Rd., Sid. CP48 79
Lewis Rd., Sthl. BE41 64
Lewis Rd., Sutt. BS55 86
Lewis Rd., Swans. DC46 81
Lewis Rd., Well. CP45 69
Lewis St. NW1 BV36 56
Lewis Trust Bldgs. SW3 BU42 3
Lewis Trust Bldgs. SW3 BU42 66
Lewisham High St. SE13 CE46 77
Lewisham Hill SE13 CF44 67
Lewisham Pk. SE13 CE46 77
Lewisham Rd. SE13 CE44 67
Lewisham St. SW1 BW41 3
Lewisham St. SW1 BW41 66
Lewisham Way SE4 & SE14 CD44 67
Lewville Way SE16 CB42 67
The Bonamy Est. W.
Lexden Dr., Rom. CO32 50
Lexden Rd. W3 BM40 55
Lexden Rd., Mitch. BW52 86
Lexham Clo., Nthlt. BE36 54
Lexham Gdns. Ms. W8 BS41 3
Lexham Gdns. Ms. W8 BS41 66
Lexham Gdns. W8 BS41 3
Lexham Gdns. W8 BS42 66
Lexham Gdns., Amer. AO22 25
Lexham Ms. W8 BS42 66
Lexham Wk. W8 BS41 3
Lexham Wk. W8 BS41 66
Lexington Clo., B.Wd. BL23 28
Lexington Clo., Pur. BZ58 96
Lexington St. W1 BW39 56
Lexington St. W1 BW40 3
Lexington Way, Barn. BQ24 28
Lexington Way, Upmin. CZ32 51
Lexton Gdns. SW12 BW47 76
Ley Hill Rd., Hem.H. AR18 16
Ley St., Ilf. CL34 49
Ley Wk., Welw.G.C. BT 8 5
Leyborne Av. W13 BJ41 64
Leyborne Pk., Rich. BM44 65
Leybourne Av., Wey. AY60 92
Leybourne Clo., Brom. CH53 88
Leybourne Clo., Wey. AY60 92
Leybourne Rd. E11 CG33 49
Leybourne Rd. NW1 BV36 56
Leybourne Rd. NW9 BM32 46
Leybourne Rd., Uxb. BA37 53

Leybourne St. NW1 BV36 56
Hawley St.
Leybridge Ct. SE12 CH46 78
Leyburn Clo. E17 CE31 48
Leyburn Cres., Rom. CW29 42
Leyburn Gdns., Croy. CA55 87
Leyburn Gro. N18 CB29 39
Leyburn Rd. N18 CB29 39
Leyburn Rd., Rom. CW29 42
Leycroft Clo., Loug. CL25 31
Leycroft Gdns., Erith CU44 69
Leyden St. E1 CA39 2
Leyden St. E1 CA39 57
Leydon Clo. SE16 CC40 57
Lagado Ms.
Leyes Rd. E16 CJ39 58
Leyfield, Wor.Pk. BO54 85
Leyhill Clo., Swan. CT53 89
Leyland Av., Enf. CD23 30
Leyland Av., St.Alb. BG14 9
Leyland Clo., Chsnt. CC17 21
Leyland Gdns., Wdf.Grn. CJ28 40
Leyland Rd. SE12 CG46 78
Leylands La., Slou. AV45 62
Leylang Rd. SE14 CC43 67
Leys Av., Dag. CS37 59
Leys Clo., Dag. CS36 59
Leys Clo., Har. BG32 45
Leys Clo., Uxb. AX30 35
Leys Gdns., Barn. BV25 29
Leys Rd. E., Enf. CD23 30
Leys Rd. W., Enf. CD23 30
Leys Rd., Hem.H. AY14 8
Leys Rd., Lthd. BG59 93
Leys, The N2 BT31 47
Leys, The, Har. BL32 46
Leys, The, St.Alb. BK12 9
Leysdown Av., Bexh. CS45 69
Leysdown Rd. SE9 CK48 78
Leysdown, Welw.G.C. BT 8 5
Leysfield Rd. W12 BP41 65
Leyspring Rd. E11 CG33 49
Leyswood Dr., Ilf. CN32 49
Leythe Rd. W3 BN41 65
Leyton Cross Rd., Dart. CT48 79
Leyton Grange E10 CE34 48
Leyton Green Rd. E10 CF32 48
Leyton Park Rd. E10 CF34 48
Leyton Rd. E15 CF35 48
Leyton Rd. SW19 BT50 76
Leyton Way E11 CG33 49
Leytonstone Rd. E15 CG36 58
Leywick St. E15 CG37 58
Leywood Clo., Amer. AO23 25
Lezayre Rd., Orp. CN57 97
Liardet St. SE14 CD43 67
Liberia Rd. N5 BY36 56
Liberty Av. SW19 BT51 86
Liberty Hall Rd., Wey. AW56 92
Liberty La., Wey. AW57 92
Liberty Ms. SW12 BV46 76
Liberty Ri., Wey. AW57 92
Liberty St. SW9 BX44 66
Liberty, The, Rom. CT32 50
Libra Rd. E13 CH37 58
Libra Rd. E3 CD37 57
Library Hill, Brwd. DB27 42
Queens Rd.
Library Pl. E1 CB40 57
Library St. SE1 BY41 4
Library St. SE1 BY41 66
Lichfield Clo., Upmin. CZ34 51
Lichfield Gdns., Rich. BL45 75
Lichfield Gro. N3 BS30 38
Lichfield Rd. E3 CD38 57
Lichfield Rd. E6 CJ38 58
Lichfield Rd. N9 CB27 39
Winchester Rd.
Lichfield Rd. NW2 BR35 46
Lichfield Rd., Dag. CO35 50
Lichfield Rd., Houns. BD45 64
Lichfield Rd., Nthwd. BC31 44
Lichfield Rd., Rich. BL44 65
Lichfield Rd., Wdf.Grn. CG28 40
Lichfield Ter., Upmin. CZ34 51
Lichfield Way, Brox. CD14 12
Lichfield Way, S.Croy. CC58 96
Lichlade Clo., Orp. CN56 97
Lidbury Rd. NW7 BR29 37
Liddall Way, West Dr. AY40 53
Liddell Clo., Har. BK31 45
Liddell Gdns. NW10 BQ37 55
Liddell Pl., Wind. AL45 61
Liddell
Liddell Rd. NW6 BS36 56
Liddell Sq., Wind. AL45 61
Liddell
Liddell Way, Wind. AL45 61
Liddell
Liddell, Wind. AL45 61
Lidding Rd., Har. BK32 45
Liddington Hall Dr., Guil. AP69 118
Liddington New Rd., Guil. AP69 118
Liddington Rd. E15 CG37 58
Liddon Rd. E13 CH38 58
Liddon Rd., Brom. CJ52 88
Lidfield Rd. N16 BZ35 48
Lidiard Rd. SW18 BT48 76
Lidlington Pl. NW1 BW37 56
Lidstone Clo., Wok. AQ62 100
Lidyard Rd. N19 BW33 47
Liffler Rd. SE18 CM42 68
Lifford St. SW15 BQ45 65
Liffords Pl. SW13 BO44 65
Barnes High St.
Lightcliffe Rd. N13 BY28 38
Lightermans Rd. E14 CE41 67
Lightfoot Rd. N8 BX31 47
Lightley Clo., Wem. BL36 55
Stanley Av.
Ligonier St. E2 CA38 2
Ligonier St. E2 CA38 57
Lila Pl., Swan. CS52 89
Azalea Dr.
Lilac Av., Wok. AR63 100
Lilac Clo. E4 CD29 39
Lilac Clo., Brwd. DB25 33
Magnolia Way
Lilac Clo., Chsnt. CB19 21
Greenwood Av.
Lilac Clo., Guil. AR68 109
Lilac Gdns. W5 BK41 64
Lilac Gdns., Croy. CE55 87
Lilac Gdns., Hayes. BB39 53
Lilac Gdns., Rom. CT33 50
Lilac Gdns., Swan. CS52 89
Lilac Pl. SE11 BX42 4
Lilac Pl. SE11 BX42 66
Lilac Rd., Hodd. CE11 12
Lilac St. W12 BP40 55
Lilacs Av., Enf. CC21 30
Lilburne Gdns. SE9 CK46 78
Lilburne Rd. SE9 CK46 78
Lilburne Wk. NW10 BN36 55
Lile Cres. W7 BH39 54
Lilestone Est. NW8 BT38 1
Lilestone Est. NW8 BT38 56
Lilestone St. NW8 BU38 1
Lilestone St. W1 BU38 56
Lilford Rd. SE5 BY44 66
Lilian Board Way, Har. BG35 45
Lilian Clo. N16 CA34 48
Barbauld Rd.
Lilian Cres., Brwd. DE27 122
Lillechurch Rd., Dag. CO36 59
Lilleshall Rd., Mord. BT53 86
Lilley Clo., Brwd. CZ28 42
Lilley Dr., Tad. BS64 104
Lilley La. NW7 BN28 37
Lillian Av. W3 BM41 65
Lillian Gdns., Wdf.Grn. CH30 40
Lillian Rd. SW13 BP43 65
Lillian Rd. SW16 BW51 86
Lillie Br. Ms. SW6 BS43 66
Lillie Rd. SW6 BQ43 65
Lillie Rd., West. CJ62 106
Lillie Yd. SW6 BS43 66
Lillieshall Rd. SW4 BV45 66
Lilliput Av., Nthlt. BE37 54
Lilliput Rd., Rom. CS33 50
Lily Clo. W14 BR42 65
Lily Gdns., Wem. BK37 54
Lily Rd. E17 CE32 48
Lily Wk., Grnf. BK37 54
Lilyville Rd. SW6 BR44 65
Limbourne Av., Dag. CQ33 50
Limburg Rd. SW11 BU45 66
Lime Av., Brwd. DC27 122
Lime Av., Grav. DE47 81
Lime Av., Upmin. CX35 51
Lime Av., West Dr. AY40 53
Lime Clo. E1 CB40 57
Lime Clo., Brom. CK52 88
Lime Clo., Buck.H. CJ27 40
Lime Clo., Cars. BU55 86
Lime Clo., Guil. AW67 110
Lime Clo., Reig. BS72 121
Lime Clo., Rom. CS31 50
Lime Clo., S.Ock. DB38 60
Lime Clo., Wat. BD26 36
Lime Cres., Sun. BD51 84
Lime Gro. N20 BR26 37
Lime Gro. Rd., Guil. AW67 110
Lime Gro. W12 BQ41 65
Lime Gro., B.Wd. DB22 33
Lime Gro., Guil. AR68 109
Lime Gro., Hayes BA40 53
Lime Gro., Ilf. CN29 40
Lime Gro., N.Mal. BN52 85
Lime Gro., Orp. CL55 88
Lime Gro., Ruis. BC33 44
Lime Gro., Sid. CN46 78
Lime Gro., Twick. BJ46 74
Lime Gro., Warl. CD62 105
Lime Gro., Wey. AW56 92
Lime Gro., Wok. AS64 100
Lime Meadow Av., S.Croy. CB60 96
Lime Pass. EC3 CA39 57
Lime St.
Lime Pit La., Sev. CS62 107
Lime Rd., Epp. CN19 22
Lime Rd., Erith CQ41 69
Northwood Pl.
Lime Rd., Rich. BL45 65
St Marys Gro.
Lime Rd., Swan. CS52 89
Lime Row, Erith CQ41 69
Northwood Pl.
Lime St. E17 CD31 48
Lime St. EC3 CA40 4
Lime St. EC3 CA40 57
Lime St. Pass. EC3 CA39 57
Lime St.
Lime Ter. W7 BH40 54
Lime Tree Clo. SW2 BX47 76
Lime Tree Clo., Lthd. BE65 102
Lime Tree Gro., Croy. CD55 87
Lime Tree Pl., Mitch. BV51 86
Lime Tree Wk., Amer. AP23 25
Lime Tree Wk., Bush. BH26 36
Lime Tree Wk., Enf. BZ22 30
Lime Tree Wk., Rick. AW25 26
Lime Tree Wk., Sev. CU66 116
Lime Tree Wk., W.Wick. CG56 97
Lime Way Ter., Dor. BJ70 119
Lime Wk. E15 CG37 58
Church St. N.
Lime Wk., Hem.H. AY14 8
Lime Wk., Uxb. AX35 44
Lime Works Rd., Red. BW66 113
Limebush Clo., Wey. AX58 92
Limecroft Clo., Epsom BN57 94
Limedene Clo., Pnr. BD30 36
Limeharbour E14 CE41 67
Limehouse Causeway E14 CD40 57
Limehouse Fields Est. E14 CD39 57
Limerick Clo. SW12 BW47 76
Limerick Gdns., Upmin. CZ33 51
Limerston St. SW10 BT43 66
Limes Av. E11 CH31 49
Limes Av. N12 BT28 38
Limes Av. NW11 BR33 46
Limes Av. NW7 BO29 37
Limes Av. SE20 CB50 77
Limes Av. SW13 BO44 65
Limes Av., Cars. BU54 86
Limes Av., Chig. CM28 40
Limes Av., Croy. BX55 86
Limes Av., The N11 BW28 38
Limes Clo., Ashf. AZ49 73
Limes Gdns. SW18 BS46 76
Limes Gro. SE13 CF45 67
Limes Pl., Croy. BZ53 87
Limes Rd., Beck. CE51 87
Limes Rd., Chsnt. CC19 21
Limes Rd., Croy. BZ53 87
Limes Rd., Egh. AS49 72
Limes Rd., Wey. AZ56 92
Limes Row, Orp. CL56 97
Orchard Rd.
Limes Wk. SE15 CC45 67
Limes Wk. W5 BM41 65
Chestnut Gro.
Limes, The, Brom. CK55 88
Limes, The, Brwd. DC27 122
Limes, The, Grays CX42 70
Limes, The, St.Alb. BH12 9
Limes, The, Welw.G.C. BS 9 5
Limesdale Gdns., Edg. BN30 37
Limesfield Rd. SW14 BO45 65
White Hart La.
Limesford Rd. SE15 CC45 67
Limestone Wk., Erith CP41 69
Yarnton Way
Limetree Av. SE20 CB51 87
Limetree Av., T.Ditt. BG54 84
Limetree Rd., Houns. BF44 64
Limetree Wk. SW17 BV49 76
Limewood Clo. W13 BJ39 54
St. Stephens Rd.
Limewood Clo., Wok. AO63 100
Limewood Rd., Erith CS43 69
Limpsfield Av. SW19 BQ47 75
Limpsfield Av., Th.Hth. BX53 86
Limpsfield Rd., S.Croy. CB59 96
Limpsfield Rd., Warl. CC62 105
Linacre Ct. W6 BQ42 65
Colet Gdns.
Linacre Rd. NW2 BP36 55
Linberry Wk. SE8 CD42 67
Carteret Way
Lince La., Dor. BG71 119
Linces Way, Welw.G.C. BS 9 5
Linchfield Rd., Slou. AR44 62
Linchmere Rd. SE12 CG47 78
Lincoln Av. N14 BW27 38
Lincoln Av. SW19 BQ48 75
Lincoln Av., Rom. CT34 50
Lincoln Av., Twick. BG48 74
Lincoln Clo. SE25 CB53 87
Lincoln Clo., Erith CT44 69
Lincoln Clo., Grnf. BG37 54
Lincoln Clo., Har. BE32 45
Lincoln Clo., Horn. CX32 51
Lincoln Clo., St.Alb. BK11 9
Lincoln Clo., Welw.G.C. BT 7 5
Lincoln Cres., Enf. CA25 30
Lincoln Ct. N16 BZ33 48
Lincoln Ct., B.Wd. BN25 28
Lincoln Dr., Rick. AZ24 26
Lincoln Dr., Wat. BD27 36
Lincoln Dr., Wok. AV61 100
Lincoln Est. E3 CE38 57
Lincoln Gdns., Ilf. CK33 49
Lincoln Green Rd., Orp. CN53 88
Lincoln Ms. NW6 BR37 55
Lincoln Ms. SE21 BZ47 77
Lincoln Park, Amer. AP23 25
Lincoln Rd. E13 CH38 58
Lincoln Rd. E18 CH30 40
Lincoln Rd. E7 CJ36 58
Lincoln Rd. N17 CB31 48
Lincoln Rd. N2 BU31 47
Lincoln Rd. SE25 CB52 87
Lincoln Rd., Dor. BK70 119
Lincoln Rd., Enf. CA24 30
Lincoln Rd., Erith CT44 69
Lincoln Rd., Felt. BE48 74
Lincoln Rd., Ger.Cr. AS30 34
Lincoln Rd., Guil. AP69 118
Lincoln Rd., Har. BE32 45
Lincoln Rd., Mitch. BX53 86
Lincoln Rd., N.Mal. BN52 85
Lincoln Rd., Nthwd. BB31 44
Lincoln Rd., Sid. CO49 79
Lincoln Rd., Wem. BK36 54
Lincoln Rd., Wor.Pk. BP54 85
Lincoln St. E11 CG34 49
Lincoln St. SW3 BU42 3
Lincoln St. SW3 BU42 66
Lincoln Way, Enf. CB25 30
Lincoln Way, Rick. AZ24 26
Lincoln Way, Sun. BB51 83
Lincoln Wk., Epsom BN58 94
Hollymoor La.
Lincolnes, The NW7 BO27 37
Lincolns Field, Epp. CN18 22
Lincolns Inn Fields WC2 BX39 2
Lincolns Inn Fields WC2 BX39 56
Lincolns Inn WC2 BX39 2
Lincolns Inn WC2 BX39 56
Lincolns La., Brwd. CY26 42
Lincombe Rd., Brom. CG48 78
Lind Rd., Sutt. BT56 95
Lind St. SE8 CE44 67
Lindal Cres., Enf. BX24 29
Lindal Rd. SE4 CD46 77
Lindale Clo., Vir.W. AP52 82
Lindales, The N17 CA29 39
Brantwood Rd.
Lindbergh Rd., Wall. BX57 95
Lindbergh, Welw.G.C. BT 8 5
Wellington Dr.
Linden Av. NW10 BQ37 55
Linden Av., Couls. BV61 104
Linden Av., Dart. CV47 80
Linden Av., Enf. CB23 30
Linden Av., Houns. BF46 74
Linden Av., Ruis. BC33 44
Linden Av., Th.Hth. BY52 86
Linden Av., Wem. BL35 46
Linden Chase Rd., Sev. CU64 107
Linden Clo. N14 BW25 29
Linden Clo., Grays CY42 70
Linden Clo., Maid. AG43 61
Linden Clo., Orp. CO56 98
Linden Clo., Ruis. BC33 44
Linden Clo., Stan. BJ28 36
Linden Clo., T.Ditt. BJ54 84
Linden Clo., Wey. AW59 92
Linden Cres., Grnf. BH36 54
Linden Cres., Kings.T. BL51 85
Linden Cres., St.Alb. BK13 9
Linden Cres., Wdf.Grn. CH29 40
Linden Ct. W12 BQ40 55
Linden Ct., Egh. AQ50 72
Linden Ct., Lthd. BJ64 102
Linden Rd.
Linden Dr., Cat. BZ65 105
Linden Gdns. W2 BS40 56
Linden Gdns. W4 BO42 65
Linden Gdns. W9 BS41 66
Linden Gdns., Enf. CB23 30
Linden Gdns., Lthd. BK64 102
Linden Glade, Hem.H. AW14 8
Wrensfield
Linden Gro. Est. SE15 CB45 67
Linden Gro. SE15 CB45 67
Linden Gro. SE26 CC50 77
Linden Gro., N.Mal. BO52 85
Linden Gro., Tedd. BH49 74
Linden Gro., Walt. BB55 83
Linden Gro., Warl. CD62 105
Linden Lawns, Wem. BL35 46
Linden Lea N2 BT32 47
Linden Lea, Dor. BK72 119
Linden Lea, Wat. BC20 17
Linden Lees, W.Wick. CF55 87
Linden Ms. N1 BZ35 48
Linden Ms. W2 BS40 56
Linden Gdns.
Linden Pit Path, Lthd. BJ64 102
Linden Rd. E17 CD32 48
Linden Rd. N10 BV31 47
Linden Rd. N11 BV27 38
Linden Rd. N15 BZ31 48
Linden Rd., Guil. AR70 118
Linden Rd., Hmptn. BF50 74
Linden Rd., Lthd. BJ64 102
Linden Rd., Wey. BA58 92
Linden Ri., Brwd. DB28 42
Blackthorn Way
Linden Sq., Sev. CT64 107
London Rd.
Linden St., Rom. CS31 50
Linden Way N14 BW25 29
Linden Way, Pur. BW58 95
Linden Way, Shep. BA53 83
Linden Way, Wok. AS64 100
Linden Way, Wok. AV65 100
Lindenfield, Chis. CL51 88
Lindens Clo., Lthd. BE67 111
Mt. Pleasant
Lindens, The N12 BT28 38
Lindens, The W4 BN44 65
Hartington Rd.
Lindens, The, Croy. CF57 96
Lindens, The, Hem.H. AV15 7
Lindens, The, Loug. CL25 31
Lindent Ct. W12 BQ40 55
Lindfield Gdns. NW3 BT35 47
Lindfield Gdns., Guil. AS70 118
Lindfield Rd. W5 BK38 54
Lindfield Rd., Croy. CA53 87
Lindfield Rd., Rom. CW28 42
Lindfield St. E14 CE39 57
Lindisfarne Clo., Grav. DJ48 81
St. Benedicts Av.
Lindisfarne Rd. SW20 BP50 75
Lindisfarne Rd., Dag. CP34 50
Lindisfarne SW20 BP50 75
Lindisfarne Way E9 CD35 48
Kings Mead Est.
Lindley Est. SE15 CB43 67
Lindley Rd. E10 CE34 48
Lindley Rd., Gdse. CC68 114
Lindley Rd., Walt. BE55 84
Lindley St. E1 CC39 57
Lindlings, Hem.H. AV14 7
Lindore Rd. SW11 BU45 66
Lindores Rd., Cars. BT54 86
Lindores Rd., Maid. AG43 61
Lindrop St. SW6 BT44 66
Lindsay Clo., Chess. BL57 94
Hunting Gate Dr.
Lindsay Clo., Epsom BN60 94
Lindsay Clo., Stai. AX46 73
Lindsay Dr., Har. BL32 46
Lindsay Dr., Shep. BA53 83
Lindsay Rd., Hmptn. BF49 74
Lindsay Rd., Wey. AW58 92
Lindsay Rd., Wor.Pk. BP55 85
Lindsell Rd., Bark. CM37 58
Lindsell St. SE10 CF44 67
Lindsey Clo., Brom. CK52 88
Clarence Rd.
Lindsey Clo., Brwd. DA28 42
Lindsey Clo., Mitch. BX52 86
Lindsey Dr. W5 BK39 54
Regal Clo.
Lindsey Gdns., Felt. BA47 73
Natalie Clo.
Lindsey Ms. N1 BZ36 57
Elmore St.
Lindsey Rd., Dag. CP35 50
Lindsey Rd., Uxb. AW34 44
Lindsey St. EC1 BY39 2
Lindsey St. EC1 BY39 56
Lindsey St., Epp. CN17 22
Lindsey Way, Horn. CV32 51
Lindum Pl., St.Alb. BF14 9
Lindum Rd., Tedd. BK50 74
Lindway SE27 BY49 76
Lindwood Clo. E6 CK39 58
Northumberland Rd.
Linfield Clo., Walt. BC56 92
Linfields, Amer. AR23 25
Linford Clo., Harl. CL12 13
Linford End, Harl. CM12 13
Linford Rd. E17 CF31 48
Linford Rd., Grays CD42 71
Linford St. SW8 BW44 66
Ling Rd. E16 CH39 58
Ling Rd., Erith CS43 69
Lingards Rd. SE13 CF45 67
Lingey Clo., Sid. CN48 78
Lingfield Av., Dart. CX47 80
Lingfield Av., Kings.T. BL52 85
Lingfield Av., Upmin. CW34 51
Lingfield Clo., Enf. CA25 30
Lingfield Clo., Nthwd. BB29 35
Lingfield Cres. SE9 CM45 68
Lingfield Gdns. N9 CB26 39
Lingfield Gdns., Couls. BY63 104
Lingfield Rd. SW19 BQ49 75
Lingfield Rd., Grav. DG48 81
Lingfield Rd., Wor.Pk. BQ55 85
Lingham St. SW9 BX44 66
Lingholm Way, Barn. BQ24 28
Lingmere Clo., Chig. CM27 40
Lingrove Gdns., Wdf.Grn. CH27 40
Beech La.
Lings Coppice SE21 BZ48 77
Lingwell Rd. SW17 BU48 76
Lingwood Gdns., Islw. BH43 64
Lingwood Rd. E5 CB33 48
Linhope St. NW1 BU38 1
Linhope St. NW1 BU38 56
Link Av., Wok. AU61 100
Link Dr., Hat. BP12 10
Link Field, Welw.G.C. BR10 5
Link La., Wall. BW57 95
Link Rd. N11 BV28 38
Link Rd., Bush. BD23 27
Link Rd., Dag. CR37 59
Link Rd., Felt. BB47 73
Link Rd., Slou. AR44 62
Link Rd., Wall. BV54 86
Link Rd., Wey. AY56 92
Link St. E9 CC35 48
Link Way, Brom. CK53 88
Link Way, Dag. CP35 50
Link Way, Guil. AP70 118
Link Way, Pnr. BD30 36
Link Way, Stai. AW50 73
Link Way, Uxb. AW32 44
Link Way, Wok. AU62 100
Link, The W3 BM40 55
Saxon Dr.
Link, The, Enf. CD23 30
Link, The, Pnr. BD33 45
Link, The, Slou. AQ39 52
Link, The, Wem. BK33 45
Nathans Rd.
Linkfield Gdns., Red. BU70 121
Linkfield La., Red. BU70 121
Linkfield Rd., Islw. BH44 64
Linkfield St., Red. BU70 121
Linkfield, Brom. CH53 88
Linkfield, E.Mol. BF52 84
Linklea Clo. NW9 BO29 37
Links Av., Mord. BS45 86
Links Av., Rom. CU30 41
Links Brow, Lthd. BH65 102
Links Clo., Ash. BK62 102
Links Dr. N20 BS26 38
Links Dr., B.Wd. BL24 28
Links Dr., Rad. BH20 18
Links Gdns. SW16 BY50 76
Links Green Way, Cob. BE60 93
Links Pl., Ash. BK62 102
Links Rd. NW2 BO34 46
Links Rd. SW17 BU50 76
Links Rd. W3 BM39 55
Links Rd., Ash. BK62 102
Links Rd., Ashf. AY49 73
Links Rd., Epsom BP60 94
Links Rd., W.Wick. CF54 87
Links Rd., Wdf.Grn. CH28 40
Links Side, Enf. BX24 29
Links Vw. Av., Bet. BM70 120
Links Vw. Clo., Stan. BJ29 36
Links Vw. N2 BU31 47
Great North Rd.
Links Vw. N3 BR29 37
Links Vw. Rd., Croy. CE55 87
Links Vw. Rd., Hmptn. BG49 74
Links Vw., Dart. CU47 79
Links Vw., St.Alb. BF12 9
Links Way, Beck. CE53 87
Links Way, Lthd. BE67 111
Links Way, Nthwd. BA29 35
Links Way, Rick. BA24 26
Links, The E17 CD31 48
Links, The, Chsnt. CC16 21
Links, The, Walt. BC55 83
Links, The, Welw.G.C. BP 8 5
Valley Rd.
Linkscroft Av., Ashf. AZ50 73
Linkside Clo., Enf. BX24 29
Linkside Gdns., Enf. BX24 29
Linkside N12 BR29 37
Linkside, Chig. CM28 40
Linkside, N.Mal. BO51 85
Linksway NW4 BQ30 37
Linksway, Stan. BJ29 36
May Tree La.
Linkway N4 BZ33 48
Vale Rd.
Linkway Rd., Brwd. CZ27 42
Linkway SW20 BP52 85
Linkway, Horn. CW33 51
Linkway, Rich. BJ48 74
Linkway, The, Barn. BS25 29
Linkway, The, Sutt. BT58 95
Linley Cres., Rom. CR31 50
Linley Rd. N17 CA30 39
Linnell Clo. NW11 BS32 47
Linnell Dr. NW11 BS32 47

Linnell Rd. N18 CB28 39
Linnell Rd. SE5 CA44 67
Linnell Rd., Red. BV71 121
Linnet Clo. SE28 CP40 59
Linnet Clo., Bush. BG26 36
Linnet Clo., S.Croy. CC58 96
Mallard Rd.
Linnet Gro., Guil. AU69 118
Linnet Ms. SW12 BV47 76
Linnet Wk., Hat. BP13 10
Lark Ri.
Linnett Clo. E4 CF28 39
Linnington Av., Chesh. AQ18 16
Linom Rd. SW4 BX45 66
Linscott Rd. E5 CC35 48
Linsey Clo., Hem.H. AZ15 8
Linsey St. SE16 CB42 4
Linsey St. SE16 CB42 67
Linslade Clo., Houns. BE46 74
Heathlands Way
Linslade Clo., Pnr. BC31 44
Linslade Rd., Orp. CO57 98
Linstead Ct. SE9 CN46 78
Linstead St. NW6 BS36 56
Linstead Way SW18 BR47 75
Linster Gro., B.Wd. BN25 28
Lintaine Clo. W6 BR43 65
Moylan Rd.
Linthorpe Av., Wem. BK36 54
Linthorpe Rd. N16 CA33 48
Linthorpe Rd., Barn. BU24 29
Linton Av., B.Wd. BL23 28
Linton Clo., Well. CO44 69
Anthony Rd.
Linton Ct., Rom. CT30 41
Rise Park Par.
Linton Ct., Stai. AX46 73
High St.
Linton Gdns. E6 CK39 58
Linton Glade, Croy. CD58 96
Linton Gro. SE27 BZ49 77
Linton Rd., Bark. CM36 58
Linton St. N1 BZ37 2
Linton St. N1 BZ37 57
Lintons La., Epsom BO59 94
Lintott Ct., Stai. AX46 73
Stanwell Clo.
Linver Rd. SW6 BS44 66
Linwood Clo. E6 CK39 58
Northumberland Rd.
Linwood Way SE15 CA43 67
Linwood, Saw. CQ 6 6
Linx Hill, Lthd. BB67 110
Linzee Rd. N8 BX31 47
Lion Av., Twick. BH47 74
Lion Clo., Shep. AY52 83
Lion Ct., B.Wd. BN23 28
Lion Gate Gdns., Rich. BL45 65
Lion Green Rd., Couls. BW61 104
Lion Rd. E6 CK39 58
Lion Rd. N9 CB27 39
Lion Rd., Bexh. CQ45 69
Lion Rd., Croy. BZ53 87
Lion Rd., Twick. BH47 74
Lion Way, Brent. BK43 64
Lion Wharf Rd., Islw. BJ45 64
Lionel Gdns. SE9 CJ46 78
Lionel Ms. W10 BR39 55
Telford Rd.
Lionel Oxley Ho., Grays DD43 71
New Rd.
Lionel Rd. SE9 CJ46 78
Lionel Rd., Brent. BL41 65
Lions Clo. SE12 CJ49 78
Lionsdale Clo. SE9 CJ49 78
Dunkery Rd.
Liphook Clo., Horn. CT35 50
Petworth Way
Liphook Cres. SE23 CC47 77
Liphook Rd., Wat. BD28 36
Liplington Pl. NW1 BW37 1
Lippitts Hill, Loug. CG23 31
Lipsham Clo., Bans. BT60 95
Lipton Clo. SE28 CP40 59
Lipton Rd. E1 CC39 57
Lisbon Av., Twick. BG48 74
Lisburne Rd. NW3 BU35 47
Lisford St. SE15 CA44 67
Lisgar Ter. W14 BR42 65
Liskeard Clo., Chis. CM50 78
Liskeard Ct., Cat. CB66 114
Liskeard Gdns. SE3 CH44 68
Lisle Pl., Grays DD41 71
Lisle St. WC2 BW40 3
Lisle St. WC2 BW40 56
Lismore Cir. NW5 BV35 47
Lismore Clo., Islw. BJ44 64
Lismore Rd. N17 BZ31 48
Lismore Rd., S.Croy. CA57 96
Lismore Wk. N1 BZ36 57
Marquess Est.
Lismore, Hem.H. BA14 8
Liss Way SE15 CA43 67
Hordle Promenade S.
Lissenden Gdns. NW5 BV35 47
Lissoms Rd., Couls. BV62 104
Lisson Green Est. NW8 BT39 56
Lisson Gro. NW1 BT38 1
Lisson Gro. NW1 BT38 56
Lisson St. NW1 BU39 1
Lisson St. NW1 BU39 56
Lister Ct. N16 CA34 48
Lister Ct. NW9 BO30 37
Pasteur Clo.
Lister Gdns. N18 BZ28 39
Lister Ms. N7 BX35 47
Lister Rd. E11 CG33 49
Lister Rd., Til. DG45 71
Lister St. E13 CH38 58
Sewell St.
Lister Wk. SE28 CP40 59
Haldane Rd.
Liston Rd. N17 CB30 39
Liston Rd. SW4 BW45 66
Liston Way, Wdf.Grn. CJ29 40
Listowel Rd., Dag. CR34 50
Listria Pk. N16 CA34 48
Litcham Spur, Slou. AO39 52
Litchfield Av. E15 CG36 58
Litchfield Av., Mord. BR54 85
Litchfield Gdns. NW10 BP36 55
Litchfield Rd., Sutt. BT56 95
Litchfield St. WC2 BW40 3
Litchfield St. WC2 BW40 56
Litchfield Way NW11 BS32 47
Litchfield Way, Guil. AP71 118
Lithgows Rd., Felt. BB45 63
Lithos Rd. NW3 BS36 56
Litlington St. SE16 CB42 67
Little Acre, Beck. CE52 87
Little Acre, St.Alb. BG12 9
Little Albany St. NW1 BV38 1
Little Albany St. NW1 BV38 56
Little Argyll St. W1 BW39 1
Little Argyll St. W1 BW39 56
Argyll St.
Little Aston Rd., Rom. CW30 42
Little Belhus Clo., S.Ock. DA38 60
Little Benty, West Dr. AX42 63
Little Birch Clo., Wey. AX56 92
Little Birches, Sid. CN48 78
Little Boltons, The SW10 BS42 3
Little Boltons, The SW10 BS42 66
Little Bookham St., Lthd. BE66 111
Little Bornes SE21 CA49 77
Little Borough, Bet. BM71 120
Little Brays, Harl. CO11 14
Little Bridge Rd., Berk. AR13 7
Little Britain EC1 BY39 2
Little Britain EC1 BY39 56
Little Brownings SE23 CB48 77
Little Buntings, Wind. AM45 61
Little Burrow, Welw.G.C. BQ 9 5
Little Bury St. N9 BZ26 39
Little Bushey La., Bush. BF23 27
Little Cattins, Harl. CK13 13
Little Cedars N12 BT28 38
Woodside Av.
Little Chester St. SW1 BV41 3
Little Chester St. SW1 BV41 66
Wilton Ms.
Little College La. EC4 BZ40 57
College St.
Little College St. SW1 BX41 4
Little College St. SW1 BX41 66
Little Common La., Red. BY69 121
Little Court Rd., Sev. CU65 107
Little Cranmore La., Lthd. AZ67 110
Little Ct., W.Wick. CG55 88
Little Dell, Welw.G.C. BQ 7 5
Little Dimocks SW12 BV48 76
Little Dorrit Ct. SE1 BZ41 4
Little Dorrit Ct. SE1 BZ41 67
Little Ealing La. W5 BK42 64
Little Edward St. NW1 BV38 1
Little Edward St. NW1 BV38 56
Redhill St.
Little Elms, Hayes BA43 63
Little Ferry Rd., Twick. BJ47 74
Ferry Rd.
Little Friday Hill E4 CG27 40
Little Friday Rd. E4 CG27 40
Little Ganett, Welw.G.C. BS 9 5
Little Gaynes Gdns., Upmin. CX35 51
Little Gaynes La., Upmin. CX35 51
Little Gearies, Ilf. CL31 49
Little George St. SW1 BX41 4
Little George St. SW1 BX41 66
Great George St.
Little Gerpins La., Upmin. CW37 60
Little Graylings, Wat. BB20 17
Little Green, Rich. BK45 64
Little Gregories La., Epp. CM21 31
Little Grn. La., Cher. AV55 82
Little Grn. La., Rick. AZ24 26
Little Grn. St. NW5 BV35 47
College La.
Little Grn., Rick. AZ24 26
Little Gro., Barn. BU25 29
Little Gro., Bush. BF24 27
Little Grove Field, Harl. CM11 13
Little Hardings, Welw.G.C. BT 7 5
Little Hayes, Kings L. AZ18 17
High St.
Little Heath La., Berk. AT14 7
Little Heath Rd., Bexh. CQ44 69
Little Heath Rd., Wok. AP58 91
Little Heath SE7 CK43 68
Little Heath, Rom. CO31 50
Little Hide, Guil. AT69 118
Little Hill, Rick. AU25 25
Little Holt E11 CH32 49
Little How Croft, Wat. BA19 17
Little Ilford La. E12 CK35 49
Little John Rd. W7 BH39 54
Little Julian Hill, Sev. CU67 116
Little Lake, Welw.G.C. BS 9 5
Little Laver Rd., Ong. CW11 15
Little Ley, Welw.G.C. BR 9 5
Little Many Gates SW12 BV48 76
Little Marlborough St. W1 BW39 1
Little Marlborough St. W1 BW39 56
Kingly St.
Little Martins, Bush. BF25 27
Little Mead, Hat. BP11 10
Little Moss La., Pnr. BE30 36
Little Mundells, Welw.G.C. BR 7 5
Little New St. EC4 BY39 2
Little New St. EC4 BY39 56
Little Newport St. WC2 BW40 56
Charing Cross Rd.
Little Orchard Clo., Pnr. BE30 36
Little Orchard Rd., Wok. AT60 91
Little Orchard, Wey. AV59 91
Little Oxhey La., Wat. BE28 36
Little Park Dr., Felt. BD48 74
Little Park Gdns., Enf. BZ24 30
Little Park, Hem.H. AT17 16
Little Pastures, Brwd. CZ28 42
River Rd.
Little Pipers Clo., Chsnt. BZ18 21
Little Platt, Guil. AO71 118
Little Pluckets Way Buck.H. CJ26 40
Little Port Spur, Slou. AP39 52
Little Portland St. W1 BV39 1
Little Portland St. W1 BW39 56
Little Potters, Bush. BG26 36
Little Pynchons, Harl. CN12 13
Little Queen St., Dart. CW47 80
Little Queens Rd., Tedd. BH50 74
Little Rd., Hayes BB41 63
Little Rd., Hem.H. AY13 8
Little Redlands, Brom. CK51 88
Little Reeves Av., Amer. AP23 25
Little Ridge, Welw.G.C. BS 8 5
Little Rivers, Welw.G.C. BS 7 5
Little Rogues La. SE16 CC41 67
Lower Rd.
Little Roke Av., Ken. BY60 95
Little Roke Rd., Ken. BZ60 96
Little Russell St. WC1 BX39 2
Little Russell St. WC1 BX39 56
Little Sanctuary SW1 BW41 3
Little Sanctuary SW1 BX41 66
Broad Sanctuary
Little Smith St. SW1 BW41 3
Little Smith St. SW1 BW41 66
Great Smith St.
Little Somerset St. E1 CA39 2
Little Somerset St. E1 CA39 57
Little St James St. SW1 BW40 3
Little St James St. SW1 BW40 56
Little St. Leonards SW14 BN45 65
Little St., Guil. AQ68 109
Little Strand NW9 BO30 37
Little Stream Clo., Nthwd. BB28 35
Eastbury Av.
Little Sutton La., Slou. AU42 62
Little Thistle, Welw.G.C. BT 9 5
Little Thrift, Orp. CM52 88
Little Titchfield St. W1 BW39 1
Little Titchfield St. W1 BW39 56
Great Titchfield St.
Little Trinity La. EC4 BZ40 2
Little Trinity La. EC4 BZ40 57
Queen Victoria St.
Little Turnstile WC1 BX39 2
Little Turnstile WC1 BX39 56
High Holborn
Little Wade, Welw.G.C. BR 9 5
Little Warley Hall La., B.Wd. DC30 123
Little Warren Clo., Guil. AT71 118
Little Windmill Hill, Kings La. AV19 16
Little Wk., Harl. CM11 13
Little Woodcote La., Cars. BV59 95
Little Youngs, Welw.G.C. BQ 8 5
Littlebrook Clo., Croy. CC53 87
Littlebrook Gdns., Chsnt. CC18 21
Littlebrook Manor Way, Dart. CX46 80
Littlebury Ct., B.Wd. CZ22 33
Kelvedon Grn.
Littlebury Rd. SW4 BW45 66
Littlecombe Clo. SW15 BQ46 75
Lytton Gro.
Littlecombe SE7 CH43 68
Littlecote Clo. SW19 BR47 75
Littlecote Pl., Pnr. BE30 36
Littlecroft Rd., Egh. AS49 72
Littlecroft SE9 CL45 68
Littlecroft, Grav. DF50 81
Littledale SE2 CO43 69
Littledown Rd., Slou. AP40 52
Littlefield Clo. N19 BW35 47
Junction Rd.
Littlefield Clo., Guil. AO68 109
Littlefield Ct., West Dr. AX43 63
Littlefield Rd., Edg. BN29 37
Littlefield Way, Guil. AO68 109
Littleheath La., Cob. BF60 93
Littleheath Rd., S.Croy. CB58 96
Littlejohn Rd., Orp. CO53 89
Littlemead, Esher BG56 93
Littlemede SE9 CK48 78
Littlemore Rd. SE2 CO41 69
Littlemore Rd., Ilf. CM34 49
Littlers Clo. SW19 BT51 86
Littlestone Clo., Beck. CE50 77
Abbey La.
Littleton Av. E4 CG26 40
Valance Av.
Littleton Cres., Har. BH34 45
Littleton Gdns., Ashf. BA50 73
Littleton La., Guil. AQ73 118
Littleton La., Reig. BQ71 120
Littleton La., Shep. AX54 83
Littleton Rd., Ashf. BA50 73
Littleton Rd., Har. BH34 45
Littleton St. SW18 BT48 76
Littlewick Rd., Wok. AP61 100
Littlewick Rd., Wok. AR60 91
Littlewood Clo. W13 BJ41 64
Littlewood Rd., Sev. CV64 108
Littlewood SE13 CF46 77
Littleworth Av., Esher BG56 93
Littleworth Common Rd., Esher BG55 84
Littleworth La., Esher BG56 93
Littleworth Pl., Esher BG56 93
Littleworth Rd., Esher BG56 93
Livermere Rd. E8 CA37 2
Liverpool Gro. SE17 BZ42 4
Liverpool Gro. SE17 BZ42 67
Liverpool Rd. E10 CF32 48
Liverpool Rd. E16 CG38 58
Liverpool Rd. N1 BY36 2
Liverpool Rd. N1 BY36 56
Liverpool Rd. N7 BY35 47
Liverpool Rd. W5 BK41 64
Liverpool Rd., Kings.T. BM50 75
Liverpool Rd., St.Alb. BH13 9
Liverpool Rd., Th.Hth. BZ52 87
Liverpool Rd., Wat. BC25 26
Liverpool St. EC2 CA39 2
Liverpool St. EC2 CA39 57
Livesey Pl. SE15 CB43 67
Peckham Park Rd.
Livingstone Clo., Ong. CX18 24
Livingstone Gdns., Grav. DH49 81
Livingstone Pl. E14 CF42 67
Ferry St.
Livingstone Rd. E15 CF37 57
Livingstone Rd. E17 CE32 48
Livingstone Rd. N13 BX29 38
Livingstone Rd. SW11 BT45 66
Winstanley Rd.
Livingstone Rd., Cat. BZ64 105
Livingstone Rd., Grav. DH49 81
Livingstone Rd., Houns. BG45 64
Livingstone Rd., Sthl. BD40 54
Livingstone Rd., Th.Hth. BZ51 87
Livingstone Ter., Rain. CT37 59
Livingstone Wk. SW11 BT45 66
Plough Rd.
Livingstone Wk., Hem.H. AY11 8
Livonia St. W1 BW39 1
Livonia St. W1 BW39 56
Berwick St.
Lizard St. EC1 BZ38 2
Lizard St. EC1 BZ38 57
Lizban St. SE3 CH43 68
Llanbury Clo., Ger.Cr. AS29 34
Llanelly La. NW2 BR34 46
Llanelly Rd. NW2 BR34 46
Crewys Rd.
Llanover Rd., Wem. BK34 45
Llanover St. SE18 CL43 68
Llanthony Rd., Mord. BT53 86
Llanvanor Rd. NW2 BR34 46
Llewellyn St. SE16 CB41 67
Chambers St.
Lloyd Av. SW16 BX51 86
Lloyd Av., Couls. BV60 95
Lloyd Baker St. WC1 BX38 2
Lloyd Baker St. WC1 BX38 56
Lloyd Ct., Pnr. BD32 45
Lloyd Park Av., Croy. CA56 96
Lloyd Rd. E17 CC31 48
Lloyd Rd. E6 CK37 58
Lloyd Rd., Dag. CQ36 59
Lloyd Rd., Wor.Pk. BQ55 85
Lloyd Sq. WC1 BY38 2
Lloyd Sq. WC1 BY38 56
Lloyd St. WC1 BY38 2
Lloyd St. WC1 BY38 56
Lloyds Av. EC3 CA39 2
Lloyds Av. EC3 CA39 57
Lloyds Pl. SE3 CG44 68
Lloyds Row EC1 BY38 2
Lloyds Row EC1 BY38 56
Lloyds Way, Beck. CD53 87
Loampit Hill SE13 CE44 67
Loampit Vale SE13 CE45 67
Loanda Clo. E8 CA37 2
Clarissa St.
Loanda Clo. E8 CA37 57
Clarissa St.
Loates La., Wat. BD24 27
Loats Rd. SW4 BX46 76
Lobelia Clo. E6 CK39 58
Sorrell Gdns.
Local Board Rd., Wat. BD25 27
Locarno Rd. W3 BO41 65
High St.
Locarno Rd., Grnf. BG38 54
Lochaber Rd. SE13 CG45 68
Lochaline St. W6 BQ43 65
Lochinvar Clo., Slou. AN41 61
Lochinvar St. SW12 BV47 76
Lochmere Clo., Erith CR43 69
Lochnagar St. E14 CF39 57
Lochnell Rd., Berk. AP12 7
Lock Chase SE3 CG45 68
Lock Clo., Wok. AV60 91
Lock La., Wok. AW61 101
Lock Path, Wind. AL43 61
Lock Rd., Guil. AR69 118
Lock Rd., Rich. BK49 74
Lock St. W10 BQ40 55
Locke Clo., Rain. CT36 59
Locke Gdns., Slou. AR41 62
Locke King Clo., Wey. AZ57 92
Locke King Rd., Wey. AZ57 92
Lockers Park La., Hem.H. AW13 8
Lockesfield Pl. E14 CE42 67
Lockesley Dr., Orp. CN53 88
Lockesley Sq., Surb. BK53 84
Locket Rd., Har. BH30 36
Lockets Clo., Wind. AL44 61
Lockfield Av., Enf. CD23 30
Lockfield Dr., Wok. AP61 100
Lockhart Clo. N7 BX36 56
Lockhart Rd., Cob. BD60 93
Lockhart St. E3 CD38 57
Lockhurst Rd. E5 CC35 48
Lockie Pl. SE25 CB52 87
Lockier Wk., Wem. BK34 45
Hutchinson Ter.
Lockington Rd. SW8 BV44 66
Lockley Cres., Hat. BP11 10
Lockmead Rd. N15 CB32 48
Lockmead Rd. SE13 CF45 67
Locks La., Mitch. BU51 86
Locksley Est. E14 CD39 57
Locksley St. E14 CD39 57
Locksmeade Rd., Rich. BK49 74
Lockwood Clo. SE26 CC49 77
Mayow Rd.
Lockwood Path, Wok. AV60 91
Lockwood Rd., Ilf. CM34 49
Lockwood Sq. SE16 CB41 67
Southwark Park Rd.
Lockwood Way, Chess. BM56 94
Lockwood Wk., Rom. CT32 50
Lockyer Rd., Grays CY43 70
Lockyer St. SE1 BZ41 4
Lockyer St. SE1 BZ41 67
Kipling St.
Locton Est. E3 CD37 57
Loddiges Rd. E9 CC36 57
Loddon Spur, Slou. AO39 52
Oatlands Dr.
Loder Clo., Wok. AU60 91
Loder St. SE15 CC43 67
Lodge Av. SW14 BN45 65
South Worple Way
Lodge Av., B.Wd. BL25 28
Lodge Av., Croy. BX55 86
Lodge Av., Dag. CO37 59
Lodge Av., Dart. CV46 80
Lodge Av., Hart. BL31 46
Lodge Av., Rom. CT32 50
Lodge Clo. N18 BZ28 39
Lodge Clo., Chig. CO27 41
Lodge Clo., Cob. BE61 102
Lodge Clo., Dor. BK73 119
Lodge Clo., Edg. BL29 37
Lodge Clo., Egh. AR49 72
Lodge Clo., Epsom BW58 94
Lodge Clo., Islw. BJ44 65
London Rd.
Lodge Clo., Lthd. BG64 102
Lodge Clo., Orp. CO54 89
Lodge Clo., Slou. AO41 61
Lodge Clo., Uxb. AX38 53
Lodge Clo., Wall. BV54 86
Lodge Cres., Orp. CO54 89
Lodge Cres., Wal.Abb. CC20 21
Lodge Ct., Horn. CW34 51
Lodge Dr. N13 BY28 38
Lodge Dr., Hat. BQ11 10
Lodge Dr., Rick. AX24 26
Lodge End, Rad. BJ20 18
Lodge Field, Welw.G.C. BR 6 5
Lodge Gdns., Beck. CD53 87
Lodge Hall, Harl. CN13 13
Lodge Hill, Ilf. CK31 49
Lodge Hill, Pur. BY61 104
Lodge Hill, Well. CO43 69
Lodge La. N12 BT28 38
Lodge La., Bex. CP46 79
Lodge La., Ch.St.G. AS23 25
Lodge La., Croy. CE57 96
Lodge La., Grays DC41 71
Lodge La., Grays DD41 71
Lodge La., Rom. CR29 41
Lodge La., Wal.Abb. CF21 30
Lodge La., West. CM67 115
Lodge Ms. N5 BZ35 48
Aberdeen Pk.
Lodge Pl., Sutt. BS56 95
Lodge Rd. NW4 BQ31 46
Lodge Rd. NW8 BT38 1
Lodge Rd. NW8 BT38 56
Lodge Rd., Brom. CH50 78
Lodge Rd., Croy. BY53 86
Lodge Rd., Epp. CL20 22
Lodge Rd., Lthd. BG64 102
Lodge Rd., Sutt. BS56 95
Throwley Way
Lodge Rd., Wall. BV56 95
Lodge Vill., Wdf.Grn. CG29 40
Lodge Way, Ashf. AY48 73
Lodge Way, Shep. BA51 83
Lodge Way, Wind. AM45 61
Lodgebottom Rd., Lthd. BL67 112
Lodgehill Park Clo., Har. BF34 45
Lodore Gdns. NW9 BN32 46
Lodore Grn., Uxb. AY34 44
Lodore St. E14 CF39 57
Loewen Rd., Grays DG41 71
Loftie St. SE16 CB41 67
Chambers St.
Lofting Rd. N1 BX36 2
Lofting Rd. N1 BX36 56
Loftus Rd. W12 BP40 55
Logan Clo., Enf. CC23 30
Logan Clo., Houns. BE45 64
Logan Ms. W8 BS42 66
Logan Pl. W8 BS42 66
Logan Rd. N9 CB27 39
Logan Rd., Wem. BK34 45
Loggetts, The SE21 CA48 77
Alleyn Pk.
Logmore La., Dor. BF72 119
Logs Hill Clo., Chis. CK51 88
Logs Hill, Chis. CK51 88
Lois Dr., Shep. BA53 83
Lolesworth St. E1 CA39 2
Lolesworth St. E1 CA39 57
Wentworth St.
Lollard St. SE11 BX42 4
Lollard St. SE11 BX42 66
Lollesworth La., Lthd. BA66 110
Loman Path, S.Ock. CZ39 60
Loman St. SE1 BY41 4
Loman St. SE1 BY41 66
Lomas Clo., Croy. CF57 96
Lomas St. E1 CB39 57
Lombard Av., Enf. CC23 30
Lombard Av., Ilf. CN33 49
Lombard Ct. EC3 BZ40 4
Gracechurch St.
Lombard Ct. EC3 BZ40 57
Gracechurch St.
Lombard La. EC4 BY39 2

Lombard La. EC4 BY39 56
Lombard Rd. N11 BW28 38
Lombard Rd. SW11 BT44 66
Lombard Rd. SW19 BS51 86
Lombard St. EC3 BZ39 2
Lombard St. EC3 BZ39 57
Lombard Wall SE7 CH41 68
Lombards Chase, Brwd. DE32 123
Station La.
Lombardy Clo., Hem.H. BA14 8
Lombardy Clo., Wok. AP62 100
Nethercote Av.
Lombardy Dr., Berk. AR13 7
Lombardy Pl. W2 BS40 56
Bark Pl.
Lombardy Way, B.Wd. BL23 28
Lomond Clo. N15 CA31 48
Kirton Rd.
Lomond Clo., Wem. BL36 55
Lomond Gro. SE5 BZ43 67
Lomond Rd., Hem.H. AX11 8
Loncin Mead Av., Wey. AX58 92
Loncroft Rd. SE5 CA43 4
Londesborough Rd. N16 CA35 48
London Bridge EC4 BZ40 4
London Bridge EC4 BZ40 57
London Bridge St. SE1 BZ40 4
London Bridge St. SE1 BZ40 57
London Bridge Wk. SE1 BZ40 4
Tooley St.
London Bridge Wk. SE1 BZ40 57
Tooley St.
London Colney By-pass, St.Alb. BL16 19
London Fields E8 CB37 57
London Fields East Side E8 CB36 57
London Fields West Side E8 CB36 57
London La. E8 CB36 57
London La., Brom. CG50 78
London La., Lthd. BC68 110
London La., Uxb. AZ38 53
London Ms. W2 BT39 1
London Ms. W2 BT39 56
London St.
London Rd. E., Amer. AP24 25
London Rd. E13 CH37 58
London Rd. N., Red. BW67 113
London Rd. S., Red. BV68 113
London Rd. SE1 BY41 4
London Rd. SE1 BY41 66
London Rd. SE23 CB47 77
London Rd. SW16 BX51 86
London Rd. SW17 BU53 86
London Rd. W., Amer. AO23 25
London Rd., Bark. CL36 58
London Rd., Berk. AS13 7
London Rd., Brom. CG50 78
London Rd., Brwd. CZ28 42
London Rd., Bush. BE25 27
London Rd., Cat. BZ65 105
London Rd., Ch.St.G. AR27 34
London Rd., Croy. BY52 86
London Rd., Dart. CX47 80
London Rd., Dart. CS46 79
London Rd., Dor. BJ71 119
London Rd., Enf. BZ25 30
London Rd., Epsom BP58 94
London Rd., Grav. DE46 81
London Rd., Grays DB42 70
London Rd., Green. DB46 80
London Rd., Guil. AS71 118
London Rd., Har. BH34 45
London Rd., Harl. CP 9 6
London Rd., Harl. CP11 14
London Rd., Harl. CP14 14
London Rd., Hem.H. AX15 8
London Rd., Houns. BG45 64
London Rd., Islw. BH44 64
London Rd., Kings.T. BL51 85
London Rd., Mitch. BU53 86
London Rd., Mitch. BV53 86
London Rd., Mord. BS53 86
London Rd., Ong. CV20 24
London Rd., Purfleet CX42 70
London Rd., Rad. BL20 19
London Rd., Red. BU70 121
London Rd., Reig. BS70 121
London Rd., Rick. AY27 35
London Rd., Rom. CO24 32
London Rd., Rom. CR32 50
London Rd., Rom. CS23 32
London Rd., Saw. CP 6 6
London Rd., Sev. CQ58 98
London Rd., Sev. CR59 98
London Rd., Sev. CS62 107
London Rd., Sev. CU66 116
London Rd., Sev. CY56 99
London Rd., Sev. & Ton. CW70 117
London Rd., Slou. AQ43 62
London Rd., Slou. AR41 62
London Rd., St.Alb. BH14 9
London Rd., Stai., Ashf.& Felt. AW49 73
London Rd., Stan. BK28 36
London Rd., Sutt. BQ55 85
London Rd., Swan. CS51 89
London Rd., Swan. CU52 89
London Rd., Swans. DC46 81
London Rd., Th.Hth. & Croy. BX51 86
London Rd., Til. DG44 71
London Rd., Twick. BJ47 74
London Rd., Vir.W. AQ51 82
London Rd., Wall. BV55 86
London Rd., Welw. BQ 5 5
London Rd., Wem. BL35 46
London Rd., West. CM66 115
London Rd., Wok. AU67 109
London St. EC3 CA40 4
London St. EC3 CA40 57
Fenchurch St.
London St. W2 BT39 1
London St. W2 BT39 56
London St., Cher. AW54 83
London Stile W4 BM42 65
Wellesley Rd.
London Ter. EC3 CA40 4
London Tilbury Rd., Rain. CV38 60
London Wall EC2 BX39 2
London Wall EC2 BZ39 57
Londons Clo., Upmin. CY35 51
Londrina Ter., Berk. AR13 7
Lonesome La., Reig. BS72 121
Lonfield, Saw. CQ 6 6
Brook Rd.
Long Acre WC2 BX40 4
Long Acre WC2 BX40 56
Long Acre, Hem.H. AT18 16
Long Acre, Orp. CP55 89
Long Arrotts, Hem.H. AW12 8
Long Banks, Harl. CM12 13
Long Barn Clo., Wat. BC19 17
Long Barn Rd., Sev. CU70 116
Long Chaulden, Hem.H. AV13 7
Long Copse Clo., Lthd. BF65 102
Long Croft Rd., Rick. AU28 34
Long Croft, Wat. BC26 35
Long Ct., Grays CX42 70
Long Deacon Rd. E4 CG26 40
Long Dr. W3 BO39 55
Long Dr., Grnf. BF37 54
Long Dr., Ruis. BD35 45
Long Dyke, Guil. AT69 118
Long Elmes, Har. BF30 36
Long Elms Clo., Wat. BA20 17
Long Elms
Long Elms, Wat. BA20 17
Long Fallow, St.Alb. BF17 18
Long Field NW9 BO30 37
Long Grn., Chig. CN28 40
Long Gro. Rd., Epsom. BM58 94
Long Gro., Beac. AO29 34
Long Hill, Cat. CC64 105
Long John, Hem.H. AY14 8
Long La. EC1 BY39 2
Long La. EC1 BY39 56
Long La. N3 BS30 38
Long La. SE1 BZ41 4
Long La. SE1 BZ41 67
Long La., Bexh. CP43 69
Long La., Croy. CB53 87
Long La., Grays DD41 71
Long La., Hem.H. AS19 16
Long La., Rick. AU25 25
Long La., Rick. AV27 34
Long La., Stai. AY48 73
Long La., Uxb. AZ35 44
Long Ley, Harl. CO11 14
Long Ley, Welw.G.C. BT 8 5
Long Leys E4 CE29 39
Long Lodge Dr., Walt. BD55 84
Long Mark Rd. E16 CJ39 58
Long Mead NW9 BO30 37
Long Mead, Hat. BP11 10
Long Meadow NW5 BW35 47
Long Meadow, Brwd. DE27 122
Long Meadow, Lthd. BE66 111
Long Moor, Wal.Cr. CD18 21
Long Pk., Amer. AO21 25
Long Pond Rd. SE3 CG44 68
Long Reach Rd., Bark. CN38 58
Long Reach, Wok. AZ65 101
Long Ride, The, Hat. BR11 10
Long Ridings Av., Brwd. DD25 122
Long Shaw, Lthd. BJ63 102
Long Spring, St.Alb. BH11 9
Long St. E2 CA38 2
Long St. E2 CA38 57
Long St., Wal.Abb. CK19 22
Long Vw., Berk. AQ12 7
Long Wall E15 CF38 57
Long Wk. SE1 CA41 4
Long Wk. SE1 CA41 67
Long Wk. SE18 CL43 68
Long Wk. SW13 BO44 65
The Terrace
Long Wk., Ch.St.G. AR24 25
Long Wk., Epsom BQ63 103
Long Wk., Grav. DF51 81
Long Wk., Guil. AY68 110
Long Wk., N.Mal. BN52 85
Long Wk., The, Wind. AO47 72
Long Wk., Wal.Abb. CE18 21
Long Wood Dr., Beac. AP29 34
Long Yd. WC1 BX38 2
Long Yd. WC1 BX38 56
Longacre Pl., Cars. BV57 95
Longacre Rd. E17 CF30 39
Longacres, St.Alb. BK13 9
Longaford Way, Brwd. DE26 122
Longbeach Rd. SW11 BU45 66
Longberrys Rd. NW2 BR34 46
Longbottom La., Beac. AO29 34
Longbourne Way, Cher. AV53 82
Longbridge Rd., Berk. CM36 58
Longbridge Way SE13 CF46 77
Longbridge Way, Uxb. AW37 53
Longbury Clo., Orp. CO52 89
Longbury Dr., Orp. CO52 89
Longcliffe Path, Wat. BC27 35
Gosforth La.
Longcroft Av., Bans. BT60 95
Longcroft Dr., Wal.Cr. CD20 21
Longcroft Grn., Welw.G.C. BQ 9 5
Stanborough La.
Longcroft La., Welw.G.C. BQ 8 5
Longcroft La., Hem.H. AU17 16
Longcroft Rd. SE5 CA43 67
Longcroft Rd., Edg. BK29 36
Longcroft Ri., Loug. CL25 31
Longcroft SE9 CK48 78
Longcrofts, Wal.Abb. CG20 22
Roundhills
Longcross Rd., Cher. AP55 82
Longdean Pk., Hem.H. AZ16 17
Longdon Wd., Kes. CK56 97
Longdown La. N., Epsom BP60 94
Longdown La. S., Epsom BP61 103
Longdown Rd. SE6 CE49 77
Longdown Rd., Epsom BP60 94
Longdown Rd., Guil. AT72 118
Longfellow Dr., Brwd. DE26 122
Longfellow Rd. E17 CD32 48
Longfellow Rd., Wor.Pk. BP54 85
Longfield Av. E17 CD31 48
Longfield Av. NW7 BP29 37
Longfield Av. W5 BK40 54
Longfield Av., Enf. CC22 30
Longfield Av., Horn. CT33 50
Longfield Av., Wall. BV54 86
Longfield Av., Wem. BL33 46
Longfield Cres. SE26 CC48 77
Longfield Cres., Tad. BQ63 103
Longfield Dr. SW14 BM46 75
Longfield Est. SE1 CA42 4
Longfield Est. SE1 CA42 67
Longfield La., Chsnt. CB17 21
Longfield Rd. W5 BK40 54
Longfield Rd., Dor. BH72 119
Longfield St. SW18 BS47 76
Longfield Wk. W5 BK39 54
Longfield, Brom. CG51 88
Longfield, Harl. CO12 14
Longfield, Hem.H. AZ14 8
Longfield, Loug. CJ25 31
Longfield, Slou. AO34 43
Longfields, Ong. CX18 24
Longford Av., Felt. BB46 73
Longford Av., Stai. AY47 73
Longford Av., Sthl. BF40 54
Longford Clo. N15 CA32 48
Longford Clo., Hayes BD40 54
Longford Clo., Hmptn. BF49 74
Longford Ct. E5 CC35 48
Clapton Park Est.
Longford Ct., Epsom BN56 94
Watersedge
Longford Gdns., Hayes BD40 54
Longford Gdns., Sutt. BT55 86
Longford Rd., Twick. BF47 74
Longford St. NW1 BV38 1
Longford St. NW1 BV38 56
Longford Way, Stai. AY47 73
Longhayes Av., Rom. CP31 50
Longheath Gdns., Croy. CC53 87
Longhedge St. SW11 BV44 66
Rowditch La.
Longhill Rd. SE6 CF48 77
Longhook Gdns., Nthlt. BC38 53
Longhouse Rd., Grays DG41 71
Longhurst Rd. SE13 CF46 77
Longhurst Rd., Croy. CB53 87
Longhurst Rd., Lthd. BB68 110
Longland Dr. N20 BS27 38
Longlands Av., Couls. BV60 95
Longlands Clo., Chsnt. CC19 21
Longlands Ct. W11 BR40 55
Westbourne Gro.
Longlands Park Cres., Sid. CN48 78
Longlands Rd., Welw.G.C. BR 8 5
Longlands Rd., Sid. CN48 78
Longlands, Hem.H. AY13 8
Longleat Ms., Orp. CP52 89
Star La.
Longleat Rd., Enf. CA25 30
Longleat Way, Felt. BA47 73
Longlees, Rick. AU28 34
Long Croft Rd.
Longleigh Ho. SE5 CA44 67
Glebe Est.
Longleigh La. SE2 CP43 69
Longley Av., Wem. BL37 55
Longley Rd. SW17 BU50 76
Longley Rd., Croy. BY54 86
Longley Rd., Har. BG32 45
Longley St. SE1 CB42 4
Longley St. SE1 CB42 67
Longley Way NW2 BQ34 46
Longmarsh Vw., S.at H. CX51 90
Longmead Clo., Brwd. DC26 122
Longmead Clo., Cat. CA64 105
Longmead Dr., Sid. CP48 79
Longmead Rd. SW17 BU49 76
Longmead Rd., Epsom BN59 94
Longmead Rd., Hayes BB40 53
Longmead Rd., T.Ditt. BH54 84
Longmead, Chis. CL51 88
Longmead, Guil. AU70 118
Longmead, Wind. AM44 61
Longmeadow Rd., Sid. CN47 78
Longmere Gdns., Tad. BQ63 103
Longmoor, Chsnt. CD18 21
Longmoore St. SW1 BW42 3
Longmoore St. SW1 BW42 66
Longmore Av., Barn. BT25 29
Longmore Clo., Rick. AV28 34
Longmore Gdns., Welw.G.C. BR 8 5
Longmore Rd., Walt. BE56 93
Longmore St. SW1 BW42 66
Longnor Rd. E1 CC38 57
Longport Clo., Ilf. CO29 41
Longreach Rd., Erith CU43 69
Longridge Gro., Wok. AV60 91
Woking Rd.
Longridge La., Sthl. BF40 54
Longridge Rd. SW5 BS42 66
Longs Clo., Wok. AW61 101
Longshaw Rd. E4 CF27 39
Longshore SE8 CD42 67
Longside Clo., Egh. AU51 82
Longspring, Wat. BC22 26
Longstaff Cres. SW18 BS46 76
Longstaff Rd. SW18 BS46 76
Longstone Av. NW10 BO36 55
Longstone Rd. SW17 BV49 76
Longstone Rd., Iver AU37 52
Longthornton Rd. SW16 BW51 86
Longton Av. SE26 CB49 77
Longton Gro. SE26 CB49 77
Longtown Clo., Rom. CV28 42
Longtown Rd., Rom. CV28 42
Longview Way, Rom. CS30 41
Longville Rd. SE11 BY42 4
Longville Rd. SE11 BY42 66
Longways, Stai. AV51 82
Longwood Clo., Upmin. CY35 51
Longwood Dr. SW15 BP46 75
Longwood Gdns., Ilf. CK31 49
Longwood La., Amer. AO23 25
Longwood Rd., Ken. BZ61 105
Longworth Clo. SE28 CP39 59
Loning, The NW9 BO31 46
Loning, The, Enf. CC22 30
Lonsdale Av. E6 CJ38 58
Lonsdale Av., Brwd. DE25 122
Lonsdale Av., Rom. CS32 50
Lonsdale Av., Wem. BL35 46
Lonsdale Clo. E6 CK38 58
Lonsdale Clo. SE9 CJ49 78
Lonsdale Clo., Edg. BL28 37
Lonsdale Clo., Pnr. BE29 36
Lonsdale Clo., Uxb. BA39 53
Lonsdale Cres., Dart. CY47 80
Lonsdale Cres., Ilf. CL32 49
Lonsdale Dr. N., Enf. BX25 29
Lonsdale Dr., Enf. BW24 29
Lonsdale Gdns., Th.Hth. BX52 86
Lonsdale Ms. W11 BR39 55
Lonsdale Rd.
Lonsdale Ms., Rich. BL44 65
Lonsdale Pl. N1 BY36 56
Lonsdale Pl. N1 BY37 2
Lonsdale Rd. E11 CG33 49
Lonsdale Rd. NW6 BR37 55
Lonsdale Rd. SE25 CB52 87
Lonsdale Rd. SW13 BO44 65
Lonsdale Rd. W11 BR39 55
Lonsdale Rd. W4 BO42 65
Lonsdale Rd., Bexh. CQ44 69
Lonsdale Rd., Dor. BJ71 119
Lonsdale Rd., Sthl. BD41 64
Lonsdale Rd., Wey. AZ57 92
Lonsdale Sq. N1 BY36 2
Lonsdale Sq. N1 BY36 56
Lonsdale Way, Maid. AH42 61
Springfield Pk.
Lonsdale, Hem.H. AY12 8
Loobert Rd. N15 CA31 48
Looe Gdns., Ilf. CL31 49
Loom La., Rad. BH22 27
Loom Pl., Rad. BJ21 27
Loop Rd., Chis. CL50 78
Loop Rd., Epsom BN61 103
Loop Rd., Wal.Abb. CE19 21
Loop Rd., Wok. AS64 100
Lopen Rd. N18 CA28 39
Loraine Clo., Enf. CC25 30
Loraine Gdns., Ash. BL62 103
Loraine Rd. N7 BX35 47
Loraine Rd. W4 BM43 65
Lord Av. Ilf. CK31 49
Lord Chancellor Wk., Kings.T. BN51 85
Lord Gdns., Ilf. CK31 49
Lord Hills Br. W2 BS39 56
Lord Hills Rd. W2 BS39 1
Lord Hills Rd. W2 BS39 56
Lord Holland La. SW9 BY44 66
Myatts Fields Dev.
Lord Knyvett Clo. AX46 73
Lord Napier Pl. W6 BP42 65
Upper Mall
Lord North St. SW1 BX41 4
Lord North St. SW1 BX41 66
Lord Roberts Ms. SW6 BS43 66
Moore Park Rd.
Lord Roberts Ter. SE18 CL42 68
Lord St. E16 CK40 58
Lord St., Grav. DG47 81
Lord St., Hodd. CB12 12
Lord St., Wat. BD24 27
Loates La.
Lord Warwick St. SE18 CK41 68
Lorden Wk. E2 CB38 2
Lorden Wk. E2 CB38 57
Lords Clo. SE21 BZ47 77
Lords Clo., Felt. BE48 74
Lords Wood, Welw.G.C. BT 8 5
Lordsbury Fld., Wall. BW58 95
Lordship Clo., Brwd. DE26 122
Lordship Gro. N16 BZ34 48
Lordship La. N22 BY30 38
Lordship La. SE22 CA46 77
Lordship Pk. N16 BZ34 48
Lordship Pl. SW3 BU43 66
Cheyne Row
Lordship Rd. N16 BZ33 48
Lordship Rd., Chsnt. CB18 21
Lordship Rd., Nthlt. BE36 54
Lordship Ter. N16 BZ34 48
Lordsmead Rd. N17 CA30 39
Lordswood Clo., Dart. CZ49 80
Coombfield Dr.
Lorenzo St. WC1 BX38 2
Lorenzo St. WC1 BX38 56
Loretto Gdns., Har. BL31 46
Lorian Av. N12 BS28 38
Holden Rd.
Lorian Clo. N12 BS28 38
Guildown Av.
Lorian Dr., Reig. BT70 121
Loring Rd. N20 BU27 38
Loring Rd., Berk. AR13 7
Loring Rd., Islw. BH44 64
Loring Rd., Wind. AM44 61
Loris Rd. W6 BQ41 65
Lorn Rd. SW9 BX44 66
Lorne Av., Croy. CC54 87
Lorne Clo. NW8 BU38 1
Lorne Clo. NW8 BU38 56
Park Rd.
Lorne Clo., Slou. AN41 61
Lorne Gdns. E11 CJ31 49
Lorne Gdns. W11 BQ41 65
Lorne Gdns. W14 BQ32 46
Lorne Gdns., Croy. CC54 87
Lorne Rd. E17 CE32 48
Lorne Rd. E7 CH35 49
Lorne Rd. N4 BX33 47
Lorne Rd., Brwd. DB28 42
Lorne Rd., Har. BH30 36
Lorne Rd., Rich. BL46 75
Albert Rd.
Lorne, The, Lthd. BF66 111
Lorraine Clo., Grays CX41 70
Lorraine Pk., Har. BH29 36
Lorrimore Rd. SE17 BY43 66
Lorrimore Sq. SE17 BY43 4
Lorrimore Sq. SE17 BY43 66
Lorton Clo., Grav. DJ48 81
Losberne Way SE16 CB42 67
Bonamy Est. W.
Loseberry Rd., Esher BG56 93
Losfield Rd., Wind. AM44 61
Lossie Dr., Iver AU40 52
Lothair Rd. N. N4 BY32 47
Lothair Rd. S. N4 BY33 47
Lothair Rd. W5 BK41 64
Lothbury EC2 BZ39 2
Lothbury EC2 BZ39 57
Lothian Av., Hayes BC39 53
Lothian Clo., Wem. BJ35 45
St. Andrews Clo.
Lothian Ms. SW9 BY44 66
Lothian Rd.
Lothian Rd. SW9 BY44 66
Lothian Wd., Tad. BP64 103
Lothrop St. W10 BR38 55
Lots Rd. SW10 BT43 66
Lotus Rd., West. CK62 106
Loubet St. SW17 BU50 76
Loudhams Rd., Amer. AR23 25
Loudhams Wood La., Ch.St.G. AR23 25
Loudoun Av., Ilf. CL32 49
Loudoun Rd. NW8 BT36 56
Loudoun Rd. NW8 BT37 1
Loudwater Clo., Sun. BC52 83
Loudwater Dr., Rick. AX24 26
Loudwater Heights, Rick. AW24 26
Loudwater Hill, Rick. AX25 26
Loudwater La., Rick. AX24 26
Loudwater Rd., Sun. BC52 83
Loudwater Ridge, Rick. AX24 26
Lough Rd. N7 BX35 47
Loughborough Est. SW9 BY44 66
Loughborough Pk. Dev. SW9 BY44 66
Loughborough Pk. SW9 BY45 66
Loughborough Rd. SW9 BY44 66
Loughborough St. SE11 BX42 4
Loughborough St. SE11 BX42 66
Loughton Ct., Wal.Abb. CH20 22
Loughton La., Epp. CM22 31
Loughton Way, Buck.H. CJ26 40
Louis Field, Guil. AO68 109
Louisa Gdns. E1 CC38 57
Louisa St.
Louisa St. E1 CC38 57
Louise Gdns., Rain. CT38 59
Louise Rd. E15 CG36 58
Louisville Rd. SW17 BV48 76
Lourdon Rd. Ms. NW8 BT37 56
Lourdon Rd.
Lousehall La., Wal.Abb. CF16 21
Louvain Rd., Green. CZ47 80
Louvain Way, Wat. BC19 17
Louvaine Rd. SW11 BT45 66
Lovage App. E6 CK39 58
Lovat Clo. NW2 BO34 46
Lovat La. EC3 CA40 4
Lovat La. EC3 CA40 57
Lovat Wk., Houns. BE43 64
Cranford La.
Lovatt Clo., Edg. BM29 37
Lovatt Dr., Ruis. BB32 44
Lovatts, Rick. AZ24 26
Love Green La., Iver AV39 52
Love Hill La., Slou. AT40 52
Love La. EC2 BZ39 2
Love La. EC2 BZ39 57
Love La. N17 CA29 39
Love La. SE18 CL42 68
Love La. SE25 CB52 87
Love La., Bex. CQ46 79
Love La., Brom. CH51 88
Love La., Gdse. CC69 114
Love La., Grav. CH47 81
Love La., Hat. BP17 19
Love La., Iver AU39 52
Love La., Kings L. AY18 17
Love La., Mitch. BU52 86
Love La., Mord. BS54 86
Love La., Ong. CX17 24
Love La., Pnr. BE31 45
Love La., S.Ock. CY40 60
Love La., Surb. BK55 84
Love La., Sutt. BR57 94
Love La., Tad. BO67 112
Love La., Wat. BB18 17
Love La., Wdf.Grn. CK29 40
Love Wk. SE5 BZ44 67
Loveday Rd. W13 BJ40 54
Lovegrove St. SE1 CB43 67
Lovegrove Wk. E14 CF40 57
Lovejoy La., Wind. AL44 61
Lovekyn Clo., Kings.T. BL51 85
Lovel Av., Well. CO44 69
Lovel Clo., Hem.H. AW13 8
Lovel End, Ger.Cr. AR29 34
Lovel Mead, Ger.Cr. AR29 34
Lovel Rd., Ger.Cr. AR29 34
Lovelace Av., Brom. CL53 88
Lovelace Clo., Lthd. BC65 101
Lovelace Clo., Sev. CZ57 99
Lovelace Dr., Wok. AV61 100
Lovelace Gdns., Bark. CO35 50
Lovelace Gdns., Surb. BK54 84
Lovelace Gdns., Walt. BD56 93
Lovelace Grn. SE9 CK45 68
Lovelace Rd. SE21 BZ48 77
Lovelace Rd., Barn. BU26 38
Lovelace Rd., Surb. BK54 84
Lovelands La., Tad. BS67 113
Lovelands La., Wok. AO60 91

Lovelinch Clo. SE14 CC43 67
Lovell Pl. SE16 CD41 67
Lovell Rd., Enf. CB21 30
Lovell Rd., Rich. BK48 74
Lovell Rd., Sthl. BF39 54
Lovell Wk., Rain. CT36 59
Loveridge Ms. NW6 BR36 55
Loveridge Rd.
Loveridge Rd. NW6 BR36 55
Lovers La., Green. DB45 70
Lovers Wk. N3 BS29 38
Lovers Wk. SE10 CF43 67
Lovers Wk., Rom. CS28 41
Lovet Rd., Harl. CL11 13
Lovett Dr., Cars. BT54 86
Lovett Rd., Egh. AT49 72
Lovett Rd., Uxb. AX31 44
Lovett Way NW10 BN35 46
Lovetts Pl. SW18 BS45 66
York Rd.
Lovibonds Av., Orp. CL56 97
Lovibonds Av., West Dr. AY39 53
Low Cross Wood La. SE21 CA48 77
Low Hall Clo. E4 CE26 39
Low Hall La. E17 CD32 48
Low Hill Rd., Harl. CG12 13
Low Hill, Harl. CG12 13
Low Rd., Hat. BU11 11
Low Street La., Til. DJ43 71
Lowbell La., St.Alb. BL17 19
Lowbrook Rd., Ilf. CL35 49
Lowburys, Dor. BJ73 119
Lowdell Clo., West Dr. AY39 53
Lowden Rd. N9 CB26 39
Lowden Rd. SE24 BY45 66
Lowden Rd., Sthl. BE40 54
Lowe Av. E16 CH39 58
Watford Rd.
Lowe Clo., Chig. CO28 41
Lowe, The, Chig. CO28 41
Lowell St. E14 CD39 57
Lowen Rd., Rain. CS37 59
Lower Addiscombe Rd., Croy. CA54 87
Lower Addison Gdns. W14 BR41 65
Lower Barn Rd., Pur. BZ59 96
Lower Barn, Hem.H. AY15 8
Lower Bedfords Rd., Rom. CT29 41
Lower Belgrave St. SW1 BV41 3
Lower Belgrave St. SW1 BV41 66
Lower Boston Rd. W7 BH40 54
Lower Bridge Rd., Red. BU70 121
Lower Broad St., Dag. CR37 59
Lower Bury La., Epp. CN19 22
Lower Camden, Chis. CK50 78
Lower Cft., Swan. CT52 89
Lower Church Hill, Green. CZ46 80
Lower Church St., Croy. BY55 86
Waddon New Rd.
Lower Cippenham La., Slou. AM40 61
Lower Clapton Rd. E5 CB34 48
Lower Clarendon Wk. W11 BQ40 55
Lancaster Rd.
Lower Common S. SW15 BP45 65
Lower Coombe St., Croy. BZ56 96
Lower Court Rd., Epsom BN59 94
Lower Cres., S.le H. DK41 71
Lower Dagnal St., St.Alb. BG13 9
Lower Derby Rd., Wat. BD24 27
Lower Downs Rd. SW20 BQ51 85
Lower Drayton Pl., Croy. BY55 86
Drayton Rd.
Lower Dunnymans Ms., Bans. BR60 94
Basing Rd.
Lower Edgeborough Rd., Guil. AS71 118
Lower Emms, Hem.H. AZ11 8
Hunters Oak
Lower Farm Rd., Lthd. BC65 101
Lower George St., Rich. BK46 74
George St.
Lower Gravel Rd., Brom. CK54 88
Lower Green Rd., Esher BF55 84
Lower Green W., Mitch. BU52 86
Lower Grosvenor Pl. SW1 BV41 3
Lower Grosvenor Pl. SW1 BV41 66
Lower Grove Rd., Rich. BL46 75
Lower Guildford Rd., Wok. AO62 100
Lower Hall La. E4 CD28 39
Lower Ham Rd., Kings.T. BK50 74
Lower Hampton Rd., Sun. BD52 84
Lower Hatfield Rd., Hert. BX11 11
Lower Higham Rd., Grav. DJ47 81
Lower Hill Rd., Epsom BM59 94
Lower Hythe St., Dart. CW46 80
Lower James St. W1 BW40 3
Lower James St. W1 BW40 56
Brewer St.
Lower John St. W1 BW40 3
Lower John St. W1 BW40 56
Brewer St.
Lower Kenwood Av., Enf. BW25 29
Lower Kings Rd., Berk. AR13 7
Lower Maidstone Rd. N11 BW29 38
Lower Mall W6 BP42 65
Lower Mardyke Av., Rain. CS37 59
Lower Marsh La., Kings.T. BL52 85
Lower Marsh SE1 BY41 4
Lower Marsh SE1 BY41 66
Lower Mead, Iver AU38 52
Lower Meadow, Harl. CN13 13
Lower Merton Ri. NW3 BU36 1
Lower Merton Ri. NW3 BU36 56
Lower Morden La., Mord. BQ53 85
Lower Mortlake Rd., Rich. BL45 65
Lower Newport St. WC2 BW40 3
Lower Noke Clo., Rom. CW27 42
Lower Northfield Rd., Bans. BR60 94
Basing Rd.
Lower Paddock Rd., Wat. BE25 27
Lower Park Rd. N11 BW28 38
Lower Park Rd., Bans. BU62 104
Lower Park Rd., Belv. CR41 69
Lower Park Rd., Loug. CJ25 31
Lower Paxton Rd., St.Alb. BH14 9
Paxton Rd.
Lower Peryers, Lthd. BB67 110
Lower Pillory Downs, Cars. BV60 95
Lower Plantation, Rick. AX24 26
Lower Pyrford Rd., Wok. AW61 101
Lower Queens Rd., Buck.H. CJ27 40
Lower Range Rd., Grav. DJ47 81
Lower Rd. E13 CH38 58
Lower Rd. SE16 CC41 67
Lower Rd., Belv. CR41 69
Lower Rd., Brwd. DE23 122
Lower Rd., Erith CS42 69
Lower Rd., Ger.Cr. AS31 43
Lower Rd., Grav. DC45 71
Lower Rd., Grav. DK47 81
Lower Rd., Har. BG34 45
Lower Rd., Hem.H. AZ16 17
Lower Rd., Ken. BY60 95
Lower Rd., Loug. CL23 31
Lower Rd., Lthd. BD67 111
Lower Rd., Lthd. BG65 102
Lower Rd., Orp. CO54 89
Lower Rd., Red. BT71 121
Lower Rd., Rick. AU24 25
Lower Rd., Sutt. BT56 95
Lower Rd., Swan. CT50 79
Lower Rd., Uxb. AU33 43
Lower Richmond Rd. SW14 BM45 65
Lower Richmond Rd. SW15 BP45 65
Lower Richmond Rd., Rich. BM45 65
Lower Sales, Hem.H. AV14 7
Lower Sandfields, Wok. AU65 100
Lower Sawley Wood, Bans. BR60 94
Basing Rd.
Lower Shott Clo., Lthd. BF66 111
Lower Shott
Lower Shott, Chsnt. CA16 21
Adamsfield
Lower Shott, Lthd. BF66 111
Lower Sloane St. SW1 BU42 3
Lower Sloane St. SW1 BV42 66
Lower Sq., Islw. BJ45 64
Lower Staithe W4 BN44 65
Lower Station Rd., Crayford CT46 79
Lower Strand NW9 BO30 37
Lower Sunbury Rd., Hmptn. BE51 84
Lower Swaines, Epp. CN18 22
Lower Tail, Wat. BE27 36
Lower Teddington Rd., Kings.T. BK50 74
Lower Ter. NW3 BT34 47
Lower Thames St. EC3 BZ40 4
Lower Thames St. EC3 BZ40 57
Lower Trinity La. EC4 BZ40 4
Lower Tub, Bush. BG26 36
Lower Wood Rd., Esher BJ57 93
Lower Yott, Hem.H. AY13 8
Lowerfield, Welw.G.C. BS8 5
Lowestoft Clo. E5 CB34 48
Southwold Rd.
Lowestoft Rd., Wat. BC23 26
Loweswater Clo., Wem. BK34 45
Carlton Av. E.
Lowfield La., Hodd. CE12 12
Lowfield Rd. NW6 BS36 56
Lowfield Rd. W3 BM39 55
Lowfield St., Dart. CW48 80
Lowfield, Saw. CQ6 6
Brook Rd.
Lowick Rd., Har. BH31 45
Lowlands Gdns., Rom. CR32 50
Lowlands Rd., Har. BH33 45
Lowlands Rd., Pnr. BD33 45
Lowlands Rd., S.Ock. CX40 60
Lowlands, Hat. BQ11 10
Lowman Rd. N7 BX35 47
Lowndes Clo. SW1 BV41 3
Lowndes Clo. SW1 BV41 66
Lowndes Pl. SW1 BV41 3
Lowndes Pl. SW1 BV41 66
Lowndes Sq. SW1 BU41 3
Lowndes Sq. SW1 BU41 66
Lowndes St. SW1 BU41 3
Lowndes St. SW1 BU41 66
Lowood St. E1 CB40 57
Lowry Cres., Mitch. BU51 86
Lowshoe La., Rom. CR30 41
Lowson Gro., Wat. BE26 36
Lowswood Clo., Nthwd. BA30 35
Lowth Rd. SE5 BZ44 67
Lowther Clo., B.Wd. BL25 28
Lowther Dr., Enf. BX24 29
Lowther Hill SE23 CD47 77
Lowther Rd. E17 CD30 39
Lowther Rd. N7 BY35 47
Mackenzie Rd.
Lowther Rd. SW13 BO44 65
Lowther Rd., Kings.T. BL51 85
Lowther Rd., Stan. BL31 46
Lowthorpe, Wok. AQ62 100
Shilburn Way
Loxford Av. E6 CJ37 58
Loxford La., Ilf. CM35 49
Loxford Rd., Bark. CL36 58
Loxham Rd. E4 CE29 39
Loxham St. WC1 BX38 2
Loxham St. WC1 BX38 56
Cromer St.
Loxley Clo. SE26 CC49 77
Trewsbury Rd.
Loxley Rd. SW18 BT47 76
Loxley Rd., Berk. AP12 7
Loxley Rd., Hmptn. BE49 74
Loxton Rd. SE23 CC47 77
Loxwood Clo., Orp. CP55 89
Chelsfield La.
Loxwood Rd. N17 CA31 48
Lubbock Rd., Chis. CK50 78
Lubbock St. SE14 CC43 67
Lucan Dr., Stai. AX50 73
Bingham Dr.
Lucan Pl. SW3 BU42 3
Lucan Pl. SW3 BU42 66
Lucan Rd., Barn. BR24 28
Lucas Av. E13 CH37 58
Lucas Av., Har. BF34 45
Lucas Ct., Har. BF34 45
Lucas Ct., Wal.Abb. CG20 22
Lucas Rd. SE20 CC50 77
Lucas Rd., Grays DD41 71
Lucas St. SE8 CD44 67
Lucerne Clo. N13 BX27 38
Lucerne Clo., Wok. AS63 100
Claremont Av.
Lucerne Ct., Erith CQ41 69
Middle Way
Lucerne Gro. E17 CF31 48
Lucerne Ms. W8 BS40 56
Kensington Mall
Lucerne Rd. N5 BY35 47
Lucerne Rd., Orp. CN54 88
Lucerne Rd., Th.Hth. BY52 86
Lucerne Way, Rom. CV29 42
Lucey Rd. SE16 CB41 4
Lucey Rd. SE16 CB41 67
Lucey Way SE16 CB41 4
Lucey Way SE16 CB41 67
Linsey St.
Lucie Av., Ashf. AZ50 73
Lucien Rd. SW17 BV49 76
Lucien Rd. SW19 BS48 76
Lucknow St. SE18 CN43 68
Lucks Hill, Hem.H. AV13 7
Lucorn Clo., SE12 CG46 78
Luctons Av., Buck.H. CJ26 40
Lucy Cres. W3 BN39 55
Lucy Gdns., Dag. CQ34 50
Luddesdon Rd., Erith CR43 69
Luddington Av., Vir.W. AS51 82
Ludford Clo. NW9 BO30 37
Ludford Clo., Croy. BY55 86
Warrington Rd.
Ludgate Bdwy. EC4 BY39 2
Pilgrim St.
Ludgate Bdwy. EC4 BY39 56
Pilgrim St.
Ludgate Cir. EC4 BY39 2
Ludgate Cir. EC4 BY39 56
Ludgate Ct. EC4 BY39 2
Ludgate Hill
Ludgate Ct. EC4 BY39 56
Ludgate Hill
Ludgate Hill EC4 BY39 2
Ludgate Hill EC4 BY39 56
Ludgate Sq. EC4 BY39 2
Ludgate Sq. EC4 BY39 56
Creed La.
Ludham Clo. SE28 CP40 59
Rollesby Way
Ludlow Clo., Brom. CH52 88
Aylesbury Rd.
Ludlow Clo., Har. BE35 45
Ludlow Mead, Wat. BC27 35
Ludlow Pl., Grays DD41 71
Ludlow Rd. W5 BK38 54
Ludlow Rd., Felt. BB48 73
Ludlow Rd., Guil. AQ71 118
Ludlow St. EC1 BZ38 2
Gee St.
Ludlow St. EC1 BZ38 57
Gee St.
Ludlow Way N2 BT31 47
Ludlow Way, Rick. BA24 26
Ludovik Wk. SW15 BO45 65
Ludwick Grn., Welw.G.C. BR8 5
Ludwick Ms. SE14 CD43 67
Ludwick Rd. SE14 CD43 67
Ludwick Way, Welw.G.C. BR8 5
Luff Clo., Wind. AM45 61
Luffield Rd. SE2 CO41 69
Luffman Rd. SE12 CH48 78
Lugard Rd. SE15 CB44 67
Lugg App. E12 CL34 49
Luke St. EC2 CA38 57
Lukin Cres. E4 CF27 39
Lukin St. E1 CC39 57
Lullarook Clo., West. CJ61 106
Lullingstone Av., Swan. CT52 89
Lullingstone Clo., Orp. CO50 79
Lullingstone Cres., Orp. CO50 79
Lullingstone La., Eyns. CV55 90
Lullingstone Rd., Belv. CQ43 69
Barnfield Rd.
Lullington Garth N12 BR28 37
Lullington Garth, B.Wd. BM25 28
Lullington Garth, Brom. CG50 78
Lullington Rd. SE20 CB50 77
Lullington Rd., Dag. CQ36 59
Lulot Gdns. N6 BV34 47
Lulworth Av., Chsnt. BY18 20
Lulworth Av., Houns. BF44 64
Lulworth Av., Wem. BK33 45
Lulworth Clo., Har. BE34 45
Lulworth Dr., Pnr. BD33 45
Lulworth Dr., Rom. CR28 41
Lulworth Gdns., Har. BE34 45
Lulworth Rd. SE15 CB44 67
Lulworth Rd. SE9 CK48 78
Lulworth Rd., Well. CN44 68
Lulworth Waye, Hayes BC39 53
Lumbards, Welw.G.C. BS6 5
Lumley Clo., Belv. CR43 69
Lumley Ct. WC2 BX40 4
Strand
Lumley Ct. WC2 BX40 56
Strand
Lumley Gdns., Sutt. BR56 94
Lumley Rd., Sutt. BR57 94
Lumley St. W1 BV39 1
Lumley St. W1 BV39 56
Luna Rd., Th.Hth. BZ52 87
Lunar Clo., West. CJ61 106
Lundin Wk., Wat. BD28 36
Lundy Dr., Hayes BB42 63
Lundy St. W6 BR43 65
Field Rd.
Lundy Wk. N1 BZ36 57
Marquess Est.
Lunedale Rd., Dart. CX47 80
Lunghurst Rd., Cat. CD63 105
Lunham Rd. SE19 CA50 77
Luntly Pl. E1 CA39 57
Chicksand St.
Luntly Pl. E1 CB39 2
Lupin Clo. SW2 BY48 76
Palace Rd.
Lupin Clo., Croy. CC54 87
Lupin Clo., West Dr. AX42 63
Luppit Clo., Brwd. DD26 122
Lupton Clo., Brom. CH49 78
Lupton St. NW5 BW35 47
Lupus St. SW1 BV42 66
Lupus St. SW1 BV43 3
Luralda Gdns. E14 CF42 67
Lurgan Av. W6 BQ43 65
Lurline Gdns. SW11 BV44 66
Luscombe Way SW8 BX43 66
Lushes Rd., Loug. CL25 31
Lushington Dr., Cob. BC60 92
Lushington Rd. NW10 BP37 55
Lushington Rd. SE6 CE49 77
Lusted Hall La., West. CH63 106
Lusted Rd., Sev. CT63 107
Lusteds Clo., Dor. BK73 119
Luther Clo., Edg. BN27 37
Luther King Rd., Harl. CM11 13
Luther Rd., Tedd. BH49 74
Lutheran Pl. SW2 BX47 76
Upper Tulse Hill
Luthers Clo., Brwd. CZ22 33
Luton Pl. SE10 CF43 67
Luton Rd. E17 CD31 48
Luton Rd., Sid. CP48 79
Luton St. NW8 BT38 1
Luton St. NW8 BT38 56
Luton Ter. NW3 BT35 47
Flask Wk.
Luttrell Av. SW15 BP46 75
Lutwyche Rd. SE6 CD48 77
Luxborough La., Chig. CK27 40
Luxborough Pl. W1 BV38 56
Luxborough St. W1 BV38 1
Luxborough St. W1 BV39 56
Luxemburg Gdns. W6 BQ42 65
Luxfield Rd. SE9 CK47 78
Luxford St. SE16 CC42 67
Luxmore Gdns. SE4 CD44 67
Luxmore St. SE4 CC44 67
Luxor St. SE5 BZ44 67
Luxted Rd., Orp. CL59 97
Lyal Rd. E3 CD37 57
Lyall Av. SE21 CA48 77
Lyall Ms. E. SW1 BV41 3
Lyall Ms. E. SW1 BV41 66
Lyall Ms. W. SW1 BV41 3
Lyall Ms. W. SW1 BV41 66
Lyall St.
Lyall St. SW1 BV41 66
Lycaste Clo., St.Alb. BJ14 9
Dellfield
Lycett Pl. W12 BP41 65
Vespan Rd.
Lych Gate Rd., Orp. CO54 89
Lych Gate Wk., Hayes BB40 53
Lych Gate, Wat. BD20 18
Lych Way, Wok. AR61 100
Lyconby Gdns., Croy. CD54 87
Lycrome La., Chesh. AO17 16
Lycrome Rd., Chesh. AP17 16
Lydd Clo., Sid. CN48 78
Lydd Rd., Bexh. CQ43 69
Lydden Ct. SE9 CN46 78
Lydden Gro. SW18 BS47 76
Lydden Rd. SW18 BS47 76
Lydeard Rd. E6 CK36 58
Lydele Clo., Wok. AS61 100
Lydford Av., Slou. AO38 52
Lydford Rd. NW2 BQ36 55
Lydford Rd. W9 BR38 55
Lydhurst Av. SW2 BX48 76
Lydia Ms., Hat. BQ15 10
Lydia Rd., Erith CT43 69
Lydney Clo. SE15 CA43 67
Blakes Rd.
Lydney Clo. SW15 BR48 75
Princes Way
Lydon Rd. SW4 BW45 66
Lydstep Rd., Chis. CL49 78
Lye Green Rd., Chesh. AP18 16
Lye La., St.Alb. BF17 18
Lye Rd., Wok. AO63 100
Lye, The, Tad. BQ65 103
Lyell Pl. E., Wind. AL45 61
Lyell
Lyell Pl. W., Wind. AL45 61
Lyell
Lyell Wk. E., Wind. AL45 61
Lyell
Lyell Wk. W., Wind. AL45 61
Lyell
Lyell, Wind. AL45 61
Lyfield, Cob. BF60 93
Lyford Rd. N15 BZ32 48
Lyford Rd. SW18 BT47 76
Lyford St. SE18 CK42 68
Lygon Pl. SW1 BV41 3
Lyham Clo. SW2 BX46 76
Lyham Rd. SW2 BX46 76
Lyle Clo., Mitch. BV54 86
Lyle Pk., Sev. CU65 107
Lymbourne Clo., Sutt. BS58 95
Lymden Gdns., Reig. BS71 121
Lyme Av., Berk. AO11 7
Lyme Farm Rd. SE12 CH45 68
Lyme Rd., Well. CO44 69
Lyme Regis Rd., Bans. BR62 103
Lyme St. NW1 BW36 1
Lyme St. NW1 BW36 56
Lyme Ter. NW1 BW36 56
Royal College St.
Lymer Av. SE19 CA49 77
Lymescote Gdns., Sutt. BS55 86
Lyminge Clo., Sid. CN48 78
Lyminge Gdns. SW18 BU47 76
Lymington Av. N22 BY30 38
Lymington Clo. SW16 BW51 86
Lymington Dr., Ruis. BA34 44
Lymington Gdns., Epsom BO56 94
Lymington Rd. NW6 BS36 56
Lymington Rd., Dag. CP33 50
Lympstone Gdns. SE15 CB43 67
Lyn Rd., Vir.W. AS53 82
Lynbridge Gdns. N13 BY28 38
Lynbrook Clo. SE15 CA43 67
Blakes Rd.
Lynbrook Clo., Rain. CS37 59
Lynceley Gra., Epp. CO18 23
Lynch Clo., Uxb. AX36 53
The Lynch
Lynch Place, The, Uxb. AX36 56
Lynch, The, Uxb. AX36 53
Lynchen Clo., Houns. BC44 63
Lyncott Cres. SW4 BV45 66
Cedars Rd.
Lyncroft Av., Pnr. BE32 45
Lyncroft Gdns. NW6 BS35 47
Lyncroft Gdns. W13 BK41 64
Lyncroft Gdns., Epsom BO58 94
Lyncroft Gdns., Houns. BG46 74
Lyncross Clo., Rom. CW30 42
Lyndale Av. NW2 BR34 46
Lyndale Clo. SE3 CG43 68
Lyndale Ct., Wey. AW60 92
Parvis Rd.
Lyndale NW2 BR35 46
Lyndale Rd., Red. BU69 121
Lyndale, Brwd. CZ22 33
Stock Fld.
Lynden Way, Swan. CS52 89
Lyndhurst Av. N12 BU29 38
Lyndhurst Av. NW7 BO29 37
Lyndhurst Av. SW16 BW51 86
Lyndhurst Av., Pnr. BC30 35
Lyndhurst Av., Sthl. BF40 54
Lyndhurst Av., Sun. BC52 83
Lyndhurst Av., Surb. BM54 85
Lyndhurst Av., Twick. BE47 74
Lyndhurst Clo. NW10 BN34 46
Lyndhurst Clo., Bexh. CR45 69
Lyndhurst Clo., Croy. CA55 87
Selborne Rd.
Lyndhurst Clo., Orp. CL56 97
Broadwater Gdns.
Lyndhurst Clo., Wok. AR61 100
Lyndhurst Ct. E18 CH30 40
Lyndhurst Dr. E10 CF33 48
Lyndhurst Dr., Horn. CV33 51
Lyndhurst Dr., N.Mal. BO53 85
Lyndhurst Dr., Sev. CT65 107
Lyndhurst Gdns. N3 BR30 37
Lyndhurst Gdns. NW3 BT35 47
Lyndhurst Gdns., Bark. CN36 58
Lyndhurst Gdns., Enf. CA24 30
Lyndhurst Gdns., Ilf. CM32 49
Lyndhurst Gdns., Pnr. BC30 35
Lyndhurst Gro. SE15 CA44 67
Lyndhurst Rd. E4 CF29 39
Lyndhurst Rd. N18 CB28 39
Lyndhurst Rd. N22 BX29 38
Lyndhurst Rd. NW3 BT35 47
Lyndhurst Rd., Bexh. CR45 69
Lyndhurst Rd., Couls. BV61 104
Lyndhurst Rd., Grnf. BF38 54
Lyndhurst Rd., Reig. BS72 121
Lyndhurst Rd., Th.Hth. BY52 86
Lyndhurst Ri., Chig. CL28 40
Lyndhurst Sq. SE15 CA44 67
Lyndhurst Ter. NW3 BT35 47
Lyndhurst Way SE15 CA44 67
Lyndhurst Way, Brwd. DE26 122
Lyndhurst Way, Cher. AV55 82
Lyndhurst Way, Grav. DF51 81
Lyndhurst Way, Sutt. BS58 95
Lyndon Av., Pnr. BE29 36
Lyndon Av., Sid. CN46 78
Lyndon Av., Wall. BV55 86
Lyndon Rd., Belv. CR42 69
Lyndwood Dr., Wind. AQ46 72
Lyne Clo., Vir.W. AS53 82
Lyne Cres. E17 CD30 39
Lyne Crossing Rd., Cher. AT53 82
Lyne La., Vir.W. AT53 82
Lyne Way, Hem.H. AV12 7
Lynegrove Av., Ashf. BA49 73
Lyneham Wk. E5 CD35 48
Durrington Rd.
Lyneham Wk. E5 CD35 48
Boscombe Clo.
Lyneham Wk., Pnr. BB31 44
Lynett Rd., Dag. CP34 50
Lynette Av. SW4 BV46 76
Lynford Clo., Edg. BN29 37
Lynford Gdns., Edg. BM27 37
Lynford Gdns., Ilf. CN34 49
Lynford Ter. N9 CA26 39
Lynhurst Cres., Uxb. BA36 53
Lynhurst Rd., Uxb. BA36 53
Lynmere Rd., Well. CO44 69
Lynmouth Av., Enf. CA25 30
Lynmouth Av., Mord. BQ53 85
Lynmouth Dr., Ruis. BC34 44
Lynmouth Gdns., Grnf. BJ37 54
Lynmouth Gdns., Houns. BD43 64
Lynmouth Rd. E17 CD32 48
Lynmouth Rd. N16 CA33 48
Lynmouth Rd. N2 BU31 47

Lynmouth Rd., Grnf. BJ37 54
Lynmouth Ri., Orp. CO52 89
Lynn Clo., Ashf. BA49 73
Lynn Clo., Har. BG30 36
Lynn Rd. E11 CG34 49
Lynn Rd. SW12 BV47 76
Lynn Rd., Ilf. CM33 49
Lynn St., Enf. BZ23 30
Lynn Wk., Reig. BS72 120
Lynne Clo., Orp. CN57 97
Lynne Clo., S.Croy. CC58 96
Lynne Way, Nthlt. BD37 54
Lynne Way, NW10 BO36 55
Lynne Wk., Esher BG56 93
Lynscott Way, S.Croy. BY58 95
Lynsted Clo., Bexh. CR46 79
Lynsted Clo., Brom. CJ51 88
Lynsted Gdns. SE9 CJ45 68
Lynton Av. N12 BT28 38
Lynton Av. NW9 BO31 46
Lynton Av. W13 BJ39 54
Lynton Av., Orp. CO52 89
Lynton Av., Rom. CR30 41
Lynton Av., St.Alb. BK14 9
Lynton Clo., Chess. BL56 94
Lynton Clo., Islw. BH45 64
Lynton Cres., Ilf. CL32 49
Lynton Crest, Pot.B. BS19 20
Strafford Gate
Lynton Gdns. N11 BW29 38
Lynton Gdns., Enf. CA26 39
Lynton Mead, N20 BS27 38
Lynton Par., Wal.Cr. CC18 21
Turners Crossbrook St.
Lynton Rd. E11 CF35 48
Toronto Rd.
Lynton Rd. E4 CE28 39
Lynton Rd. N8 BW32 47
Lynton Rd. NW6 BR37 55
Lynton Rd. S., Grav. DG47 81
Lynton Rd. SE1 CA42 4
Lynton Rd. SE1 CA42 67
Lynton Rd. W3 BM40 55
Lynton Rd., Croy. BY53 86
Lynton Rd., Dag. CP34 50
Lynton Rd., Grav. DG47 81
Lynton Rd., Har. BE34 45
Lynton Rd., N.Mal. BN53 85
Lynton Wk., Hayes BB38 53
Exmouth Rd.
Lynwood Av., Couls. BV61 104
Lynwood Av., Egh. AS50 72
Lynwood Av., Epsom. BO60 94
Lynwood Av., Slou. AR41 62
Lynwood Clo. E18 CJ30 40
Lynwood Clo., Har. BE34 45
Lynwood Clo., Rom. CR29 41
Lynwood Clo., Wok. AU60 91
Lynwood Dr., Nthwd. BB30 35
Lynwood Dr., Rom. CR29 41
Lynwood Dr., Wor.Pk. BP55 85
Lynwood Gdns., Croy. BX56 95
Lynwood Gdns., Sthl. BE39 54
Lynwood Gro. N21 BY26 38
Lynwood Gro., Orp. CN54 88
Lynwood Heights, Rick. AW25 26
Lynwood Rd. SW17 BU49 76
Lynwood Rd. W5 BK38 54
Lynwood Rd., Epsom BO60 94
Lynwood Rd., Red. BV69 121
Lynwood Rd., T.Ditt. BH55 84
Lynwood, Guil. AQ71 118
Lyon Meade, Stan. BK30 36
Lyon Park Av., Wem. BL36 55
Lyon Rd. SW19 BT51 86
Lyon Rd., Har. BH32 45
Lyon Rd., Rom. CT33 50
Lyon Rd., Walt. BE55 84
Lyon St. N1 BX36 56
Caledonian Rd.
Lyon Way, Grnf. BH37 54
Lyon Way, St.Alb. BM13 10
Lyons Ct., Dor. BJ71 119
High St.
Lyons Dene, Tad. BR67 112
Lyons Dr., Guil. AQ68 109
Lyons Pl. NW8 BT38 1
Lyons Pl. NW8 BT38 56
Lyons Wk. W14 BR42 65
Blythe Rd.
Lyonsdown Av., Barn. BT25 29
Lyonsdown Rd., Barn. BT25 29
Lyoth Rd., Orp. CM55 88
Lyric Dr., Grnf. BF38 54
Lyric Rd. SW13 BO44 65
Lysander Clo., Hem.H. AS17 16
Lancaster Dr.
Lysander Gro. N19 BW33 47
Lysander Rd., Croy. BX57 95
Lysander Rd., Ruis. BA34 44
Lysander Way, Orp. CM55 88
Lysander Way, Welw.G.C. BT7 5
Lysia St. SW6 BQ43 65
Lysias Rd. SW12 BV46 76
Lysons Wk. SW15 BP46 75
Swinburne Rd.
Lytchet Way, Enf. CC23 30
Lytchett Rd., Brom. CH50 78
Lytchgate Clo., S.Croy. CA57 96
Lytcott Gro. SE22 CA46 77
Lytham Av., Wat. BD28 36
Lytham Gro. W5 BL38 55
Lytham St. SE17 BZ42 4
Lytham St. SE17 BZ42 67
Lyton Gdns., Wall. BW56 95
Lyttelton Clo. NW3 BU36 56
Lyttelton Ct. N2 BT32 47
Lyttelton Rd. E10 CE34 48
Lyttelton Rd. N2 BT32 47
Lyttleton Rd. N8 BY31 47
Lytton Av. N13 BY27 38
Lytton Av., Enf. CD22 30
Lytton Clo. N2 BT32 47
Lytton Clo., Loug. CM24 31
Lytton Clo., Nthlt. BE36 54
Lytton Gdns., Welw.G.C. BQ8 5
Lytton Gro. SW15 BQ46 75
Lytton Rd. E11 CG33 49
Lytton Rd., Barn. BT24 29
Lytton Rd., Grays DG42 71
Lytton Rd., Pnr. BE29 36
Lytton Rd., Rom. CU32 50
Lytton Rd., Wok. AT61 100
Lytton Strachey Path SE28 CO40 59
Curtis Way
Lyttons Way, Hodd. CE10 12
Bridleway S.
Lyveden Rd. SE3 CH43 68
Lyvedon Rd. SW17 BU50 76
Lywood Clo., Tad. BQ64 103

M

M1 Motorway NW4 BN28 37
M1 Motorway NW7 BN28 37
M1 Motorway, Edg. BL26 37
M1 Motorway, Wat. BE21 27
M4 Motorway, Hayes BC42 63
Mabbits Clo., St.Alb. BE18 18
Jenkins Av.
Mabbotts, Tad. BQ64 103
Mabel Rd., Swan. CU50 79
Mabel St., Wok. AR62 100
Maberley Cres. SE19 CB50 77
Maberley Rd. SE19 CA51 87
Maberley Rd., Beck. CC52 87
Mabeys Wk. Saw. CO6 6
Mabledon Pl. WC1 BW38 1
Mabledon Pl. WC1 BW38 56
Mablethorpe Rd. SW6 BR43 65
Mabley St. E9 CD35 48
Mabyn Rd. SE18 CN42 68
Macaret Clo. N20 BT26 38
Macarthur Ter. SE7 CJ43 68
Charlton La.
Macaulay Ct. SW4 BV45 66
Macaulay Rd. SW4 BV45 66
Macaulay Rd., Cat. CA64 105
Macaulay Sq. SW4 BV45 66
Macaulay Way SE28 CO40 59
Macauley Av., Esher BH55 84
Macauley Ms. SE13 CF44 67
Macauley Rd. E6 CJ37 58
Macbean St. SE18 CL41 68
Macbeth Ho. N1 CA37 57
Purcell St.
Macbeth St. W6 BP42 65
Macclesfield Br. NW1 BU37 56
Macclesfield Rd. EC1 BZ38 2
Macclesfield Rd. EC1 BZ38 57
Macclesfield Rd. SE25 CB53 87
Macclesfield St. W1 BW40 3
Macclesfield St. W1 BW40 56
Gerrard St.
Macdonald Av., Dag. CR34 50
Macdonald Av., Horn. CW31 51
Macdonald Clo., Amer. AO21 25
Macdonald Clo., Horn. CW31 51
Macdonald Rd. E17 CF30 39
Macdonald Rd. E7 CH35 49
Macdonald Rd. N11 BU28 38
Macdonald Rd. N19 BW34 47
Macdonald Way, Horn. CW31 51
Macdonell Gdns., Wat. BB21 26
High Rd.
Macduff Rd. SW11 BV44 66
Mace Clo. E1 CB40 57
Kennet St.
Mace Ct., Grays DF43 71
Medlar Rd.
Mace La., Sev. CM60 97
Mace St. E2 CC37 57
Macers Ct., Brox. CD15 12
Macers La., Brox. CD15 12
Macfarlane Rd. W12 BQ40 55
Macfarren Pl. NW1 BV38 1
Macgregor Rd. E16 CJ39 58
Machell Rd. SE15 CC45 67
Macintosh La. E9 CC35 48
High St.
Mackay Rd. SW4 BV45 66
Mackennal St. NW8 BU37 1
Mackennal St. NW8 BU37 56
Mackenzie Mall, Slou. AP41 62
Mackenzie Rd. N7 BX36 56
Mackenzie Rd., Beck. CC51 87
Mackenzie St., Slou. AP41 62
High St.
Mackenzie Way, Grav. DH50 81
Mackeson Rd. NW3 BU35 47
Mackie Rd. SW2 BY47 76
Macklin St. WC2 BX39 2
Macklin St. WC2 BX39 56
Mackrells Rd., Red. BT72 121
Mackrow Wk. E14 CF40 57
Macks Rd. SE16 CB42 4
Macks Rd. SE16 CB42 67
Mackworth St. NW1 BW38 1
Mackworth St. NW1 BW38 56
Maclean Rd. SE23 CD46 77
Maclennan Av., Rain. CV38 60
Macleod Clo., Grays DE42 71
Palmers Dr.
Macleod St. SE17 BZ42 4
Macleod St. SE17 BZ42 67
Maclise Rd. W14 BR41 65
Macmillan Gdns., Dart. CX45 70
Macoma Rd. SE18 CM43 68
Macoma Ter. SE18 CM43 68
Macon Way, Upmin. CZ32 51
Maconochies Rd. E14 CE42 67
Macquarie Way, E14 CE42 67
Macready Pl. N7 BX35 47
Macroom Rd. W9 BR38 55
Mada Rd., Orp. CL55 88
Madan Rd., West. CM66 115
Madans Wk., Epsom BN61 103
Maddams St. E3 CE38 57
Maddells, Epp. CN19 22
Madden Clo., Swans. DB46 80
Maddison Clo., Tedd. BH50 74
Maddison Way, Sev. CT65 107
Maddock Way SE17 BY43 66
Maddocks Clo., Sid. CQ49 79
Maddox La., Lthd. BE65 102
Maddox Pk., Lthd. BF65 102
Maddox Rd., Harl. CN10 6
Maddox Rd., Hem.H. AZ13 8
Maddox St. W1 BV40 3
Maddox St. W1 BV40 56
Madeira Av., Brom. CG50 78
Madeira Clo., Wey. AW60 92
Brantwood Gdns.
Madeira Cres., Wey. AW60 92
Brantwood Gdns.
Madeira Gro., Wdf.Grn. CJ29 40
Madeira Rd. E11 CF33 48
Madeira Rd. N13 BY28 38
Madeira Rd. SW16 BX49 76
Madeira Rd., Mitch. BU52 86
Madeira Rd., Wey. AV60 91
Madeira Wk., Brwd. DC27 122
Madeira Wk., Reig. BT70 121
Madeira Wk., Wind. AO44 61
Madeley Clo., Amer. AO21 25
Madeley Rd. W5 BK39 54
Madeline Rd. SE20 CB50 77
Madewell Lodge, B.Wd. BL23 28
Theobald St.
Madison Cres., Bexh. CP43 69
Madison Gdns., Bexh. CP43 69
Madison Gdns., Brom. CG52 88
Madras Pl. N7 BY36 56
Madras Rd., Ilf. CL35 49
Madrid Rd. SW13 BP44 65
Madrid Rd., Guil. AQ71 118
Madron St. SE17 CA42 4
Madron St. SE17 CA42 67
Maesmaur Rd., West. CJ64 106
Mafeking Av. E6 CK37 58
Mafeking Av., Brent. BK43 64
Mafeking Av., Ilf. CM33 49
Mafeking Rd. E16 CG38 58
Mafeking Rd. N17 CB30 39
Mafeking Rd., Enf. CA24 30
Mafeking Rd., Stai. AT48 72
Magazine Pl., Lthd. BJ64 102
Magazine Rd., Cat. BY64 104
Magdala Av. N19 BV34 47
Magdala Rd., Islw. BJ45 64
Magdala Rd., S.Croy. BZ57 96
Magdalen Clo., Wey. AY60 92
Magdalen Cres., Wey. AY60 92
Magdalen Gdns., Brwd. DF26 122
Hutton Dr.
Magdalen Gro., Orp. CO56 98
Magdalen Pass. E1 CA40 4
Chamber St.
Magdalen Rd. SW18 BT47 76
Magdalen St. SE1 CA40 4
Magdalen St. SE1 CA40 57
Magdalene Clo. SE15 CB44 67
Heaton Rd.
Magdalene Gdns. E6 CL38 58
Homeway
Magdalene Rd., Shep. AZ52 83
Magee St. SE11 BY43 66
Magna Carta La., Stai. AR47 72
Magna Rd., Egh. AQ50 72
Magnaville Rd., Bush. BH26 36
Magnet Rd., Grays DB43 70
Magnolia Clo., Kings.T. BM50 75
Magnolia Ct., Har. BL33 46
Magnolia Dr., West. CJ61 106
Magnolia Gdns., Slou. AR41 62
Appletree La.
Magnolia Pl. SW4 BX45 66
Kings Av.
Magnolia Rd. W4 BM43 65
Magnolia St., West Dr. AX42 63
Magnolia Way, Brwd. DA25 33
Magnolia Way, Dor. BK73 119
Magnolia Way, Epsom BN56 94
Magnum Clo., Rain. CV39 60
The Glen
Magpie All. EC4 BY39 2
Magpie All. EC4 BY39 56
Whitefriars St.
Magpie Clo., Couls. BW62 104
Magpie Hall Clo., Brom. CK53 88
Magpie Hall La., Brom. CK54 88
Magpie Hall Rd., Bush. BH27 36
Magpie La., Brwd. DB30 42
Magpie La., Sev. CW60 99
Magpie Wk., Hat. BP13 10
Lark Ri.
Magpies, The, Epp. CL15 13
Magri Wk. E1 CC39 57
Ashfield St.
Maguire Dr., Rich. BK49 74
Maguire St. SE1 CA41 4
Maguire St. SE1 CA41 67
Mahlon Av., Ruis. BC35 44
Mahogany Clo. SE16 CD40 57
Mahon Clo., Enf. CA23 30
Maid of Honour Row, Rich. BK46 74
The Green
Maida Av. E4 CE26 39
Maida Av. W2 BT39 1
Maida Av. W2 BT39 56
Maida Rd. W2 BT40 56
Maida Rd., Belv. CR41 69
Maida Vale Rd., Dart. CU46 79
Maida Vale W9 BS37 1
Maida Vale W9 BS37 56
Maida Way E4 CE26 39
Maiden Erlegh Av., Bex. CQ47 79
Maiden La. N7 BW36 56
Maiden La. NW1 BW36 56
Maiden La. WC2 BX40 4
Maiden La. WC2 BX40 56
Bedford St.
Maiden La., Dart. CU45 69
Maiden Rd. E15 CG36 58
Maidenhead Rd., Wind. AL44 61
Maidenshaw Rd., Epsom BN59 94
Maidenstone Hill SE10 CF44 67
Maidman St. E3 CD38 57
Maidstone Av., Rom. CS30 41
Maidstone Bldgs. SE1 BZ40 4
Maidstone Bldgs. SE1 BZ40 57
Maidstone Rd. N11 BW29 38
Maidstone Rd., Grays DD43 71
Maidstone Rd., Sev. CT64 107
Maidstone Rd., Sid. CP50 79
Maidstone St. SE15 CB43 67
Mail Coach Yd. N1 CA38 57
Kingsland Rd.
Main Av., Enf. CA25 30
Main Av., Nthwd. BA27 35
Main Dr., Ger.Cr. AR32 43
Main Dr., Houns. BG43 64
Main Par., Rick. AU24 25
Main Rd., Eden. CM70 115
Main Rd., Farn. CW53 90
Main Rd., Long. DB51 90
Main Rd., Orp. CP51 89
Main Rd., Rom. CT31 50
Main Rd., S.at H. CX50 80
Main Rd., Sev. CP65 107
Main Rd., Sid. CM48 78
Main Rd., Swan. CT50 79
Main Rd., West. CJ62 106
Main St., Felt. BD49 74
Mainridge Rd., Chis. CL49 78
Maisemore St. SE15 CB43 67
Peckham Park Rd.
Maisie Webster Clo., Stai. AX47 73
Lauser Rd.
Maitland Clo. SE10 CE43 67
Maitland Clo., Houns. BE45 64
Maitland Clo., Wey. AW60 92
Maitland Pk. Est. NW3 BU36 56
Maitland Pk. Rd. NW3 BU36 56
Maitland Pk. Vill. NW3 BU35 56
Maitland Pl. E5 CB35 48
Clarence Rd.
Maitland Rd. E15 CG36 58
Maitland Rd. SE26 CC50 77
Maize Row E14 CD40 57
Maizey Ct., Brwd. DA25 33
Danes Way
Majendie Rd. SE18 CM42 68
Majestic Way, Mitch. BU51 86
St. Marks Rd.
Major Rd. E15 CF35 48
Major Rd. SE16 CB41 67
Majors Farm Rd., Slou. AR43 62
Makepeace Av. N6 BV34 47
Makepeace Rd., Nthlt. BE37 54
Makins St. SW3 BU42 3
Makins St. SW3 BU42 66
Malabar St. E14 CE41 67
Malacca Farm Rd., Guil. AW67 110
Malam Gdns. E14 CE40 57
Wades Pl.
Malan Clo., West. CK62 106
Malan Sq., Rain. CU36 59
Malay St. E1 CC40 57
Malbrook Rd. SW15 BP45 65
Malby Ct., B.Wd. BL23 29
Leeming Rd.
Malcolm Cres. NW4 BP32 46
Malcolm Ct. W5 BL38 55
Malcolm Ct., Stan. BK28 36
Malcolm Dr., Surb. BK54 84
Malcolm Pl. E2 CC38 57
Malcolm Rd. E1 CC38 57
Malcolm Rd. SE20 CC50 77
Malcolm Rd. SE25 CB53 87
Malcolm Rd. SW19 BR50 75
Malcolm Rd., Couls. BW61 104
Malcolm Rd., Uxb. AY35 44
Malcolm Way E11 CH31 49
Malcomb Ho. N1 CA37 57
Purcell St.
Malden Av. SE25 CB52 87
Malden Av., Grnf. BH35 45
Malden Cres. NW1 BV36 56
Malden Ct. N4 BZ32 48
Finsbury Park Av.
Malden Ct., N.Mal. BP52 85
Malden Green Av., Wor.Pk. BO54 85
Malden High St., N.Mal. BO52 85
Malden Hill Gdns., N.Mal. BO52 85
Malden Hill, N.Mal. BO52 85
Malden Manor, The, N.Mal. BO54 85
Malden Pk., N.Mal. BO53 85
Malden Pl. NW5 BV35 47
Grafton Ter.
Malden Rd. NW5 BV35 47
Malden Rd., B.Wd. BM24 28
Malden Rd., N.Mal. BO53 85
Malden Rd., Sutt. BQ56 94
Malden Rd., Wat. BC23 26
Malden Rd., Wor.Pk. BO54 85
Malden Way, N.Mal. BN53 85
Maldon Clo. N1 BZ37 57
Popham St.
Maldon Clo. SE5 CA45 67
Maldon Ct., N.Mal. BP52 85
Maldon Rd. N9 CA27 39
Maldon Rd. W3 BN40 55
Maldon Rd., Rom. CS33 50
Maldon Rd., Wall. BV56 95
Maldon Wk., Wdf.Grn. CJ29 40
Malet Clo., Egh. AU50 72
Malet Pl. WC1 BW38 1
Malet Pl. WC1 BW38 56
Malet St. WC1 BW38 1
Malet St. WC1 BW38 56
Maley Av. SE27 BY48 76
Malford Ct. E18 CH30 40
Malford Gro. E18 CG31 49
Malfort Rd. SE5 CA45 67
Malham Rd. SE23 CC47 77
Malins Clo., Barn. BP25 28
Mall Rd. W6 BP42 65
Mall, The E15 CF36 57
Mall, The N14 BX27 38
Mall, The SW1 BW41 3
Mall, The SW1 BW41 66
Mall, The SW14 BN46 75
Mall, The W5 BK40 54
Mall, The, Brom. CH52 88
Mall, The, Dag. CR36 59
Mall, The, Har. BL33 46
Mall, The, St.Alb. BG17 18
Mall, The, Surb. BK53 84
Mallams Ms. SW9 BY45 66
St.James Cres.
Mallard Clo. E9 CD36 57
Mallard Clo., Barn. BT25 29
Mallard Clo., Dart. CW46 80
Mallard Clo., Houns. BF47 74
Mallard Clo., Red. BV69 121
Mallard Clo., Upmin. CZ33 51
Mallard Ct. NW9 BN33 46
Mallard Path SE28 CM41 68
Tom Cribb Rd.
Mallard Pl., Twick. BJ48 74
Mallard Rd., S.Croy. CC58 96
Mallard Way NW9 BN33 46
Mallard Way, Brwd. DD26 122
Mallard Way, Nthwd. BA29 35
Ducks Hill Rd.
Mallard Way, Wat. BE21 27
Mallard Wk., Sid. CP50 79
Cray Rd.
Mallards Rd., Wdf.Grn. CH29 40
Mallards Reach, Wey. BA55 83
Mallards, The, Stai. AW51 83
Beech Tree La.
Mallet Dr., Nthlt. BE35 45
Mallet Rd. SE13 CF46 77
Malling Clo., Croy. CC53 87
Stockbury Rd.
Malling Gdns., Mord. BT53 86
Malling Way, Brom. CG54 88
Mallinson Rd. SW11 BU46 76
Mallinson Rd., Croy. BW55 86
Mallion Ct., Wal.Abb. CG20 22
Mallord St. SW3 BT43 66
Mallord St. SW3 BT43 3
Mallory Clo. SE4 CD45 67
Mallory Gdns., Barn. BV26 38
Mallory St. NW8 BU38 1
Mallory St. NW8 BU38 56
Mallow Clo., Croy. CC54 87
Primrose La.
Mallow Clo., Grav. DF49 81
Sorrel Way
Mallow Ct., Grays DE43 71
Mallow Mead NW7 BR29 37
Mallow St. EC1 BZ38 2
Mallow St. EC1 BZ38 57
Mallows Grn., Harl. CL13 13
Mallows, The, Uxb. AZ34 44
Malm Clo., The, Rick. AX27 35
Malmains Clo., Beck. CF53 87
Malmains Way, Beck. CF52 87
Malmesbury Clo., Pnr. BB31 44
Malmesbury Rd. E16 CG39 58
Malmesbury Rd. E18 CG30 40
Malmesbury Rd. E3 CD38 57
Malmesbury Rd., Mord. BT54 86
Malmesbury Ter. E16 CG39 58
Malmescroft, Hem.H. BA14 8
Malmsdale, Welw.G.C. BQ6 5
Malmstone Av., Red. BW67 113
Malpas Dr., Pnr. BD32 45
Malpas Rd. E8 CB36 57
Malpas Rd. SE4 CD44 67
Malpas Rd., Dag. CP36 59
Malpas Rd., Grays DH41 71
Malpas Rd., Slou. AQ40 52
Malpin Pl. SE17 BZ42 4
Malt Hill, Egh. AS49 72
Malt House Clo., Wind. AQ47 72
Malt House Pass. SW13 BO44 65
The Terrace
Malt La., Rad. BJ21 27
Malt St. SE1 CB43 4
Malt St. SE1 CB43 67
Malta Rd. E10 CE33 48
Malta Rd., Til. DF44 71
Malta St. EC1 BY38 2
Malta St. EC1 BY38 56
Maltby Clo., Orp. CO54 89
Vinson Clo.
Maltby Dr., Enf. CB22 30
Maltby Rd., Chess. BM57 94
Maltby St. SE1 CA41 4
Maltby St. SE1 CA41 67
Malthouse Ct., Guil. AS73 118
The Street
Malthouse Ct., St.Alb. BG14 9
Sopwell La.
Malthouse Dr., Felt. BD49 74
Malthus Path SE28 CP40 59
Owen Clo.
Malting La., Epp. CO18 23
Maltings Clo. SW13 BO44 65
Cleveland Gdns.
Maltings Dr., Epp. CO18 23
High St.
Maltings Hill, Ong. CV13 15
Maltings Ms., Sid. CO48 79
Station Rd.
Maltings Pl. SW6 BS44 66
Maltings, The, Kings L. BA20 17
Maltings, The, Orp. CN54 88
Elm Gro.
Maltings, The, Oxt. CG69 115
Maltings, The, St.Alb. BG13 9
Maltings, The, Wey. AY60 92
Brewery La.
Maltmans La., Ger.Cr. AR31 43
Maltmans Pk., Grnf. BG38 54
Malton Ms. W10 BR39 55
Cambridge Gdns.
Malton Rd. W10 BR39 55
Malton St. SE18 CN43 68
Maltravers St. WC2 BX40 4

Maltravers St. WC2 BX40 56
Arundel St.
Malus Clo., Hem.H. AZ13 8
Malus Clo., Wey. AV57 91
Malus Dr., Wey. AV57 91
Malva Clo. SW18 BS46 76
Malva Rd.
Malva Rd. SW18 BS46 76
Malvern Av. E4 CF29 39
Malvern Av., Bexh. CQ43 69
Malvern Av., Har. BE34 45
Malvern Clo. SE20 CB51 87
Derwent Rd.
Malvern Clo. W10 BR39 55
Malvern Clo., Cher. AU57 91
Chobham Rd.
Malvern Clo., Hat. BO11 10
Malvern Clo., Mitch. BW52 86
Malvern Clo., St.Alb. BK11 9
Malvern Clo., Surb. BL54 85
Malvern Clo., Uxb. AZ34 44
Malvern Ct. SW7 BT42 3
Malvern Ct. SW7 BT42 66
Malvern Ct., Slou. AT43 62
Malvern Dr., Felt. BD49 74
Malvern Dr., Ilf. CN35 49
Malvern Dr., Wdf.Grn. CJ28 40
Malvern Gdns. NW2 BR34 46
Malvern Gdns. NW6 BR37 55
Canterbury Rd.
Malvern Gdns., Har. BL31 46
Malvern Gdns., Loug. CK25 31
Malvern Ms. NW6 BS38 56
Malvern Pl. W9 BR38 55
Malvern Rd. E11 CG34 49
Malvern Rd. E6 CK37 58
Malvern Rd. E8 CB36 2
Malvern Rd. E8 CB36 57
Malvern Rd. N17 CB31 48
Malvern Rd. N8 BX31 47
Malvern Rd. NW6 BS38 56
Malvern Rd., Enf. CD22 30
Malvern Rd., Grays DF42 71
Malvern Rd., Hayes BB43 63
Malvern Rd., Hmptn. BF50 74
Malvern Rd., Horn. CU33 50
Malvern Rd., Orp. CO56 98
Malvern Rd., Surb. BL55 85
Malvern Rd., Th.Hth. BY52 86
Malvern Ter. N1 BY37 2
Malvern Ter. N1 BY37 56
Malvern Ter. N9 CA26 39
Malvern Way W13 BJ39 54
Malvern Way, Hem.H. AY12 8
Malvern Way, Rick. AZ25 26
Malvina Av., Grav. DG48 81
Malwood Rd. SW12 BV46 76
Malyons Rd. SE13 CE46 77
Malyons Rd., Swan. CT50 79
Malyons Ter. SE13 CE46 77
Managers St. E14 CF40 57
Manan Clo., Hem.H. BA14 8
Manaton Clo. SE15 CB45 67
Manaton Clo. W., B.Wd. BK25 27
Manaton Cres., Sthl. BF39 54
Manbey Gro. E15 CG36 58
Manbey Park Rd. E15 CG36 58
Manbey Rd. E15 CG36 58
Manbey St. E15 CG36 58
Manborough Av. E6 CK38 58
Manbre Rd. W6 BQ43 65
Manchester Dr. W10 BR38 55
Manchester Est. E14 CF42 67
Manchester Gro. E14 CF42 67
Manchester Ms. W1 BV39 1
Manchester St.
Manchester Ms. W1 BV39 56
Manchester St.
Manchester Rd. E14 CF41 67
Manchester Rd. N15 BZ32 48
Manchester Rd., Th.Hth. BZ52 87
Manchester Row, Dart. CT45 69
Manchester Sq. W1 BV39 1
Manchester Sq. W1 BV39 56
Manchester St. W1 BV39 1
Manchester St. W1 BV39 56
Manchester Way, Dag. CR35 50
Manchuria Rd. SW11 BV46 76
Manciple St. SE1 BZ41 4
Manciple St. SE1 BZ41 67
Mancroft Rd., Hem.H. AY14 8
Mandalay Rd. SW4 BW46 76
Mandarin St. E14 CE40 57
Salter St.
Mandela Clo. NW10 BN36 55
Mandela Rd. E16 CH39 58
Mandela St. NW1 BW37 1
Mandela St. NW1 BW37 56
Mandela St. SW9 BY43 66
Mandela Way SE1 CA42 4
Mandela Way SE1 CA42 67
Mandelyns, Berk. AP11 7
Mandeville Clo. SE3 CG43 68
Vanbrugh Pk.
Mandeville Clo. SW20 BR51 85
Mandeville Clo., Brox. CD13 12
Mandeville Clo., Guil. AQ69 118
Mandeville Clo., Harl. CP12 14
Mandeville Clo., Wat. BB22 26
Mandeville Ct. E4 CD28 39
Lower Hall La.
Mandeville Ct., Egh. AT49 72
Mandeville Dr., St.Alb. BG15 9
Mandeville Dr., Surb. BK54 84
Mandeville Houses N1 BY37 56
Mandeville Pl. W1 BV39 1
Mandeville Pl. W1 BV39 56
Mandeville Rd. N14 BV27 38
Mandeville Rd., Enf. CC21 30
Mandeville Rd., Islw. BJ44 64
Mandeville Rd., Nthlt. BE36 54
Mandeville Rd., Pot.B. BT19 20
Mandeville Rd., Shep. AZ53 83
Mandeville Ri., Welw.G.C. BQ 7 5
Mandeville St. E5 CD34 48
Mandeville Wk., Brwd. DF26 122
Hutton Dr.
Mandon St. E14 CE40 57
Salter St.
Mandrake Rd. SW17 BU48 76
Mandrell Rd. SW2 BX46 76
Manette St. W1 BW39 1
Manette St. W1 BW39 56
Charing Cross Rd.
Manford Clo., Chig. CO28 41
Manford Cross, Chig. CO28 41
Manford Way, Chig. CN28 40
Manfred Ct. SW15 BR46 75
Manfred Rd.
Manfred Rd. SW15 BR46 75
Manger Rd. N7 BX36 56
Mangles Rd., Guil. AR69 118
Mangold Way, Erith CP41 69
Mangrove La., Hert. CA10 12
Manilla St. E14 CE41 67
Manister Rd. SE2 CO41 69
Manlays Yd. SW11 BU44 66
Manley Ct. N16 CA34 48
Stoke Newington High St.
Manley Rd., Hem.H. AY13 8
Manley St. NW1 BV37 1
Manley St. NW1 BV37 56
Manly Dixon Dr., Enf. CD22 30
Mannicotts, Welw.G.C. BP 8 5
Mannin Rd., Rom. CO33 50
Manning Gdns., Har. BK33 45
Manning Rd. E17 CC32 48
Manning Rd., Dag. CR36 59
Manning Rd., Orp. CP53 89
Manning St., S.Ock. CY40 60
Manningford Clo. EC1 BY38 2
Manningford Clo. EC1 BY38 56
Manningtree Clo. SW18 BR47 75
Manningtree Rd., Ruis. BC35 44
Manningtree St. E1 CB39 2
Manningtree St. E1 CB39 57
Mannock Dr., Loug. CM23 31
Mannock Rd. N22 BY31 47
Manns Clo., Islw. BH46 74
Manns Rd., Edg. BM29 37
Manoel Rd., Twick. BG48 74
Manor Alley W4 BO42 65
Devonshire Rd.
Manor Av. Par., Chig. CM28 40
Grange Cres.
Manor Av. SE4 CD44 67
Manor Av., Cat. CA65 105
Manor Av., Hem.H. AX15 8
Manor Av., Horn. CV32 51
Manor Av., Houns. BD45 64
Manor Av., Nthlt. BE36 54
Manor Chase, Wey. AZ56 92
Manor Clo. NW7 BN28 37
Manor Dr.
Manor Clo. NW9 BM31 46
Manor Clo. S., S.Ock. CY40 60
Manor Clo.
Manor Clo. SE28 CP39 59
Manor Clo., Barn. BR24 28
Wood St.
Manor Clo., Berk. AR13 7
Manor Clo., Crayford CS45 69
Manor Clo., Dag. CS36 59
Manor Clo., Hat. BO11 10
Manor Clo., Lthd. BB67 110
Manor Clo., Rom. CU32 50
Manor Rd.
Manor Clo., Ruis. BB33 44
Manor Clo., S.Ock. CY40 60
Manor Clo., Warl. CD62 105
Manor Clo., Wilmington CU48 79
Manor Clo., Wok. AV61 100
Manor Clo., Wor.Pk. BO54 85
Manor Cott., Nthwd. BB30 35
Manor Cotts. N2 BT30 38
Manor Cres., Beac. AO28 34
Manor Cres., Guil. AQ69 118
Manor Cres., Horn. CV32 51
Manor Cres., Surb. BM53 85
Manor Cres., Wey. AY60 92
Manor Ct. N14 BW27 38
Manor Ct. N2 BU32 47
Manor Ct. Rd. W7 BH40 54
Manor Ct. SW16 BX48 76
Streatham Ct.
Manor Ct. W3 BM42 65
Manor Gdns.
Manor Ct., Enf. CB21 30
Manor Ct., Wey. AZ56 92
Manor Dr. N., N.Mal. BN54 85
Manor Dr. N., Wor.Pk. BO54 85
Manor Dr. N14 BV26 38
Manor Dr. N20 BU28 38
Manor Dr. NW7 BN28 37
Manor Dr., Epsom BO57 94
Manor Dr., Esher BH55 84
Manor Dr., Felt. BD49 74
Manor Dr., St.Alb. BF17 18
Manor Dr., Sun. BC51 83
Manor Dr., Surb. BL53 85
Manor Dr., The, Wor.Pk. BO54 85
Manor Dr., Wem. BL35 46
Manor Dr., Wey. AW58 92
Manor Farm Av., Shep. AZ53 83
Manor Farm Clo., Wind. AM45 61
Manor Farm Dr. E4 CG27 40
Manor Farm Dr., Enf. CB21 30
Manor Farm Est., Stai. AR46 72
Manor Farm La., Egh. AT49 72
Manor Farm Rd. SW16 BY51 86
Manor Farm Rd., Enf. CB21 30
Manor Farm Rd., Wem. BK37 54
Manor Farm Way, Beac. AO29 34
Manor Farm, Farn. CW54 90
Manor Fields SW15 BQ46 75
Manor Gate, Nthlt. BE36 54
Manor Gdns. N7 BX34 47
Manor Gdns. SW20 BR51 85
Manor Gdns. W3 BM42 65
Manor Gdns., Guil. AQ69 118
Manor Gdns., Hmptn. BF50 74
Manor Gdns., Lthd. BD67 111
Manor Gdns., Rich. BL45 65
Manor Gdns., Ruis. BD35 45
Manor Gdns., S.Croy. CA57 96
Manor Gdns., Sun. BC51 83
Manor Green Rd., Epsom BM60 94
Manor Gro. SE15 CC43 67
Manor Gro., Beck. CE51 87
Manor Gro., Lthd. BB67 110
Manor Gro., Maid. AH43 61
Manor Gro., Rich. BM45 65
Manor Hall Av. NW4 BQ30 37
Manor Hall Dr. NW4 BQ30 37
Manor Hall Gdns. E10 CE33 48
Manor Hatch Clo., Harl. CO11 14
Tumbler Rd.
Manor Hatch, Harl. CO12 14
Manor Hill, Bans. BU60 95
Manor Ho., Chis. CM51 88
Manor Ho., Surb. BK55 84
Manor Ho., Wor.Pk. BN54 85
Manor House Ct., Epsom BN60 94
Manor House Ct., Shep. AZ54 83
Church Rd.
Manor House Dr. NW6 BQ36 55
Manor House Gdns., Wat. BA19 17
Manor House La., Slou. AQ43 62
Manor House Way, Islw. BJ45 64
Church St.
Manor La. SE12 CG46 78
Manor La. SE13 CG45 68
Manor La. Ter. SE13 CG45 68
Manor La., Fawk. DB54 90
Manor La., Felt. BC48 73
Manor La., Ger.Cr. AR33 43
Manor La., Hayes BA43 63
Manor La., Sun. BC51 83
Manor La., Sutt. BS56 95
Manor La., Tad. BS68 113
Manor Leaze, Egh. AT49 72
Manor Ms. NW6 BS37 56
Cambridge Av.
Manor Ms. SE4 CD44 67
Lewisham Way
Manor Mt. SE23 CC47 77
Manor Par., Hat. BO11 10
Manor Par., Hayes BA43 63
Manor Park Clo., W.Wick. CE54 87
Manor Park Cres., Edg. BM29 37
Manor Park Dr., Har. BF31 45
Manor Park Gdns., Edg. BM28 37
Manor Park Par. SE13 CF45 67
Lee High Rd.
Manor Park Rd. E12 CJ35 49
Manor Park Rd. N2 BT31 47
Manor Park Rd. NW10 BO37 55
Manor Park Rd., Chis. CM51 88
Manor Park Rd., Sutt. BT56 95
Manor Park Rd., W.Wick. CE54 87
Manor Pk. SE13 CF45 67
Manor Pk., Chis. CM51 88
Manor Pk., Hat. BO11 10
Manor Pk., Rich. BL45 65
Manor Pl. SE17 BY42 4
Manor Pl. SE17 BY42 66
Manor Pl., Chis. CM51 88
Manor Pl., Dart. CV47 80
Manor Pl., Felt. BC47 73
Manor Pl., Mitch. BW52 86
Manor Pl., Stai. AW49 73
Manor Pl., Sutt. BS56 95
Manor Rd. E10 CE33 48
Manor Rd. E15 CG37 58
Manor Rd. E16 CG38 58
Manor Rd. E17 CD30 39
Manor Rd. N., Esher BH55 84
Manor Rd. N., T.Ditt. BJ54 84
Manor Rd. N., Wall. BV56 93
Manor Rd. N16 BZ34 48
Manor Rd. N17 CB30 39
Manor Rd. N22 BX29 38
Manor Rd. S., Esher BH55 93
Manor Rd. SE25 CB52 87
Manor Rd. SW20 BR51 85
Manor Rd. W13 BJ40 54
Manor Rd., Lambourne End CP27 41
Manor Rd., West Thurrock DB43 70
Manor Rd., Ashf. AY49 73
Manor Rd., Bark. CN36 58
Manor Rd., Barn. BR25 28
Manor Rd., Beac. AO28 34
Manor Rd., Beck. CE51 87
Manor Rd., Bex. CR47 79
Manor Rd., Chadwell Hth. CP32 50
Manor Rd., Chig. CK29 40
Manor Rd., Dag. CS36 59
Manor Rd., Dart. CT45 69
Manor Rd., E.Mol. BG52 84
Manor Rd., Enf. BZ23 30
Manor Rd., Erith CT43 69
Manor Rd., Grays DE43 71
Manor Rd., Guil. AQ69 118
Manor Rd., Har. BJ32 45
Manor Rd., Harl. CP 8 6
Manor Rd., Hat. BM10 5
Manor Rd., Hayes BC39 53
Manor Rd., High Beech CH22 31
Manor Rd., Hodd. CE11 12
Manor Rd., London Colney BK16 18
Manor Rd., Loug. CH25 31
Manor Rd., Mitch. BW52 86
Manor Rd., Pot.B. BR19 19
Manor Rd., Red. BW68 113
Manor Rd., Reig. BR69 120
Manor Rd., Rich. BL45 65
Manor Rd., Rom. CU32 50
Manor Rd., Ruis. BA33 44
Manor Rd., Sendmarsh AV65 100
Manor Rd., Sev. CP65 107
Manor Rd., Sid. CN48 78
Manor Rd., St.Alb. BH13 9
Manor Rd., Sutt. BR57 94
Manor Rd., Swans. DB46 80
Manor Rd., Tedd. BJ49 74
Manor Rd., Til. DG44 71
Manor Rd., Twick. BG48 74
Manor Rd., W.Wick. CE55 87
Manor Rd., Wal.Abb. CF20 21
Manor Rd., Wall. BV56 95
Manor Rd., Walt. BB54 83
Manor Rd., Wat. BC23 26
Manor Rd., Wdf.Grn. CK29 40
Manor Rd., West. CK63 106
Manor Rd., Wind. AM44 61
Manor Rd., Wok. AR61 100
Manor Sq., Dag. CP34 50
Manor St., Berk. AR13 7
Manor Vale, Brent. BK42 64
Manor Vw. N3 BS30 38
Manor Vw., Beck. CE51 87
High St.
Manor Way E4 CF28 39
Manor Way NW9 BO31 46
Manor Way SE3 CG45 68
Manor Way, (Bridge Rd.) Grays DD43 71
Manor Way, (Manor Rd.) Grays DE43 71
Manor Way, B.Wd. BN23 28
Manor Way, Bans. BU61 104
Manor Way, Beck. CE51 87
Manor Way, Bex. CR47 79
Manor Way, Bexh. CS45 69
Manor Way, Brom. CK53 88
Manor Way, Brwd. DA27 42
Manor Way, Chesh. AO18 16
Manor Way, Chsnt. CD18 21
Manor Way, Egh. AS50 72
Manor Way, Guil. AO72 118
Manor Way, Har. BF31 45
Manor Way, Lthd. BG61 102
Manor Way, Maid. AG43 61
Manor Way, Mitch. BW52 86
Manor Way, Orp. CM53 88
Manor Way, Pot.B. BS18 20
Manor Way, Rain. CT39 59
Manor Way, Rick. AZ24 26
Manor Way, Ruis. BB33 44
Manor Way, S.Croy. CA57 96
Manor Way, Sthl. BD42 64
Manor Way, Swans. DB45 70
Manor Way, The, Pur. BX59 95
Manor Way, Wall. BV56 95
Manor Way, Wok. AT64 100
Manor Way, Wor.Pk. BO54 85
Manor Waye, Uxb. AX37 53
Manor Wk., Wey. AZ56 92
Manor Wood Rd., Pur. BX60 95
Manorbrook SE3 CH45 68
Manorcroft Rd., Egh. AT50 72
Manordene Clo., T.Ditt. BJ54 84
Manordene Rd. SE28 CP39 59
Manorfield Clo. N19 BW35 47
Tufnell Park Rd.
Manorgate Rd., Kings.T. BM51 85
Manorhouse La., Lthd. BE66 111
Manorside Clo. SE2 CP42 69
New Rd.
Manorside, Barn. BR24 28
Manorville Rd., Hem.H. AX15 8
Manorway, Enf. CA26 39
Manorway, Grays DD43 71
Manorway, Wdf.Grn. CJ28 40
Manresa Rd. SW3 BT42 3
Manresa Rd. SW3 BU42 66
Mansard Beeches SW17 BV49 76
Mansard Clo., Horn. CU34 50
Mansard Clo., Pnr. BD31 45
Manscroft Rd., Hem.H. AW12 8
Manse Clo., Hayes BA43 63
Manse Rd. N16 CA34 48
Manse Way, Swan. CU52 89
Mansel Clo., Guil. AQ68 109
Mansel Clo., Slou. AQ39 52
Mansel Gro. E17 CE30 39
Mansel Rd. SW19 BR50 75
Mansell Clo., Wind. AM44 61
Mansell Rd. W3 BN41 65
Mansell Rd., Grnf. BF39 54
Mansell St. E1 CA39 2
Mansell St. E1 CA39 57
Manser Rd., Rain. CT38 59
Mansfield Av. N15 BZ31 48
Mansfield Av., Barn. BU25 29
Mansfield Clo. N9 CB25 30
Mansfield Clo., Orp. CP54 89
Mansfield Clo., Wey. AZ56 92
Mansfield Dr., Hayes BB38 53
Mansfield Dr., Red. BW67 113
Mansfield Gdns., Horn. CV34 51
Mansfield Hill E4 CE26 39
Mansfield Ms. W1 BV39 1
Mansfield Ms. W1 BV39 56
Duchess St.
Mansfield Pl. NW3 BT35 47
Streatley Pl.
Mansfield Pl., S.Croy. BZ57 96
Mansfield Rd. E11 CH32 49
Mansfield Rd. E17 CD31 48
Mansfield Rd. NW3 BU35 47
Mansfield Rd. W3 BM38 55
Mansfield Rd., Chess. BK56 93
Mansfield Rd., Ilf. CL33 49
Mansfield Rd., S.Croy. BZ57 96
Mansfield Rd., Swan. CT50 79
Mansfield St. W1 BV39 1
Mansfield St. W1 BV39 56
Mansfield, Saw. CO 6 6
Mansford St. E2 CB37 57
Manship Rd., Mitch. BV50 76
Mansion Gdns. NW3 BS34 47
Firecrest Dr.
Mansion House Pl. EC4 BZ39 2
George St.
Mansion La., Iver AU40 52
Manson Ms. SW7 BT42 3
Manson Ms. SW7 BT42 66
Manson Pl. SW7 BT42 3
Manson Pl. SW7 BT42 66
Manstead Clo., Rain. CU39 59
Mansted Gdns., Rom. CP33 50
Manston Av., Sthl. BF42 64
Manston Clo. SE20 CC51 87
Manston Clo., Chsnt. CC18 21
Elgin Rd.
Manston Rd., Guil. AT68 109
Manston Rd., Harl. CN11 13
Manston Way, Horn. CU36 59
Manstone Rd. NW2 BR35 46
Manthorp Rd. SE18 CM42 68
Mantilla Rd. SW17 BV49 76
Mantle Rd. SE4 CD45 67
Manton Av. W7 BH41 64
Manton Clo., Hayes BB40 53
Manton Rd. SE2 CO42 69
Mantua Clo. SW11 BT45 66
Wye St.
Mantua Rd. SW11 BT45 66
Mantus Clo. E1 CC38 57
Mantus Rd.
Mantus Rd. E1 CC38 57
Manus Way N20 BT27 38
Manville Gdns. SW17 BV48 76
Manville Rd. SW17 BV48 76
Manwood Rd. SE4 CD46 77
Manwood St. E16 CK40 58
Many Gates SW12 BV48 76
Manygate La., Shep. BA54 83
Maori Rd., Guil. AS70 118
Mape St. E2 CB38 57
Mapesbury Rd. NW2 BR36 55
Maple Av. E4 CD28 39
Maple Av. W3 BO40 55
Maple Av., Har. BF34 45
Maple Av., St.Alb. BG11 9
Maple Av., Upmin. CX35 51
Maple Av., West Dr. AY40 53
Maple Clo. SW4 BW46 76
Maple Clo., Brwd. DC27 122
Maple Clo., Buck.H. CJ27 40
Maple Clo., Bush. BE23 27
Maple Clo., Hat. BP13 10
Maple Clo., Horn. CU34 50
Maple Clo., Mitch. BV51 86
Maple Clo., Orp. CM53 88
Maple Clo., Ruis. BC32 44
Maple Clo., Swan. CT51 89
Maple Clo., Whyt. CA62 105
Maple Cres., Sid. CO46 79
Maple Cres., Slou. AQ40 52
Maple Ct., Egh. AQ50 72
Maple Ct., N.Mal. BO52 85
Maple Ct., Wok. AR61 100
Maple Dr., Red. BU73 121
Maple Gdns., Edg. BO29 37
Maple Gdns., Stai. AY48 73
Maple Grn., Hem.H. AV12 7
Maple Gro. NW9 BN33 46
Maple Gro. W5 BK41 64
Maple Gro., Brent. BJ43 64
Maple Gro., Guil. AR69 118
Maple Gro., Sthl. BE39 54
Maple Gro., Wat. BC23 26
Maple Gro., Welw.G.C. BR 6 5
Maple Gro., Wok. AS64 100
Maple Hill, Hem.H. AR18 16
Maple Ho. SE8 CD43 67
Idonia St.
Maple Leaf Dr., Sid. CN47 78
Maple Leaf Sq. SE16 CC41 67
St. Elmos Rd.
Maple Ms. NW6 BS37 56
Kilburn Park Rd.
Maple Ms. SW16 BX49 76
Maple Pl. E1 CB39 57
Maple Pl. W1 BW38 1
Maple Pl. W1 BW38 56
Maple St.
Maple Pl., Bans. BQ60 94
Maple Pl., West Dr. AY40 53
Maple Rd. E11 CG32 49
Maple Rd. SE20 CB51 87
Maple Rd., Ash. BK63 102
Maple Rd., Dart. CV47 80
Maple Rd., Grav. DH49 81
Maple Rd., Grays DE43 71
Maple Rd., Hayes BD38 54
Maple Rd., Red. BU72 121
Maple Rd., Surb. BK53 84
Maple Rd., Whyt. CA62 105
Maple Rd., Wok. AV65 100
Maple Springs, Wal.Abb. CH20 22
Maple St. W1 BW39 1
Maple St. W1 BW39 56
Maple St., Rom. CS31 50
Maple Ter., Rick. AV28 34
Maple Way, Couls. BV64 104
Maple Way, Felt. BC48 73
Maple Wk. W10 BR38 55
Droop St.
Maple Wk., Sutt. BS58 95
Cotswold Rd.
Maplecroft Clo. E6 CK39 58
Allhallows Rd.
Maplecroft La., Wal.Abb. CG14 13
Mapledale Av., Croy. CB55 87
Mapledene Rd. E8 CA36 57
Mapledene, Chis. CM50 78
Maplefield La., Ch.St.G. AQ24 25
Maplefield, St.Alb. BF18 18
Maplehurst Clo., Kings.T. BL52 85
Surbiton Rd.
Mapleleafe Gdns., Ilf. CL31 49
Maplelodge Clo., Rick. AV28 34
Maples Pl. E1 CB39 57
Raven Row
Maples, The, Bans. BS60 95
Maples, The, Cher. AU57 91
Maples, The, Harl. CL13 13
Maplescombe La., Farn. CX55 90
Maplestead Rd. SW2 BX47 76
Maplestead Rd., Dag. CO37 59
Maplethorpe Rd., Th.Hth. BY52 86
Mapleton Clo., Brom. CH53 88
Mapleton Cres. SW18 BS46 76
Mapleton Rd.
Mapleton Cres., Enf. CC22 30
Mapleton Rd. E4 CF27 39
Mapleton Rd. SW18 BS46 76

Mapleton Rd., Enf. CB23 30
Mapleton Rd., West. CN68 115
Maplin Clo. N21 BX25 29
Maplin Rd. E16 CH39 58
Maplin St. E3 CD38 57
Mapperley Dr., Wdf.Grn. CG29 40
Forest Dr.
Mar Rd., S.Ock. DB38 60
Maran Way, Erith CP41 69
Marban Rd. W9 BR38 55
Marbeck Clo., Wind. AL44 61
Marble Arch W1 BU40 3
Marble Arch W1 BU40 56
Marble Clo. W3 BM40 55
Gunnersbury La.
Marble Hill Clo., Twick. BJ47 74
Marble Hill Gdns., Twick. BJ47 74
Marble Hill River Path, Twick. BK47 74
Orleans Rd.
Marble Quay E1 CB40 4
Marbles Way, Tad. BQ63 103
Marbrook Ct. SE12 CJ48 78
Marcellina Way, Orp. CN55 88
Marcet Rd., Dart. CV46 80
March Rd., Twick. BJ47 74
March Rd., Wey. AZ56 92
Marchant Rd. E11 CF34 48
Marchant St. SE14 CD43 67
Sanford St.
Marchbank Rd. SW5 BR43 65
Marchmant Clo., Horn. CV34 51
Connaught Rd.
Marchmont Rd., Rich. BL46 75
Marchmont Rd., Wall. BW57 95
Marchmont St. WC1 BX38 2
Marchmont St. WC1 BX38 56
Marchside Clo., Houns. BD44 64
Springwell Rd.
Marchwood Clo. SE5 CA43 67
Marchwood Cres. W5 BK39 54
Marcia Rd. SE1 CA42 4
Marcia Rd. SE1 CA42 67
Marcilly Rd. SW18 BT46 76
Marco Rd. W6 BP41 65
Marcon Pl. E8 CB35 48
Marconi Rd., Grav. DE48 81
Marconi Way, Sthl. BF39 54
Marcus Ct. E15 CG37 58
Marcus Garvey Way SE24 BY45 66
Marcus Rd., Dart. CU47 79
Marcus St. E15 CG37 58
Marcus St. SW18 BS46 76
Marcus Ter. SW18 BS46 76
Denton St.
Mardale Dr. NW9 BN32 46
Mardell Rd., Croy. CC53 87
Marden Av., Brom. CG53 88
Marden Clo., Chig. CO27 41
Marden Cres., Bex. CS46 79
Marden Cres., Croy. BX53 86
Marden Rd. N17 CA30 39
The Avenue
Marden Rd., Croy. BX53 86
Marden Rd., Rom. CT32 50
Marden Sq. SE16 CB41 67
Marder Rd. W13 BJ41 64
Mardyke Rd., Harl. CO10 6
Mardyke St. SE17 BZ42 4
Mardyke St. SE17 BZ42 67
Townsend St.
Mare St. E8 CB37 57
Marechal Niel Av., Sid. CM48 78
Mares Field, Croy. CA55 87
Mareschal Rd., Guil. AR71 118
Maresfield Gdns. NW3 BT35 47
Marfield Ct., N.Mal. BO54 85
Marford Rd., Welw.G.C. BN 8 5
Margaret Av. E4 CE25 30
Margaret Av., Brwd. DC26 122
Margaret Av., St.Alb. BG12 9
Margaret Bldgs. N16 CA33 48
Margaret Rd.
Margaret Bondfield Av., Bark. CO36 59
Margaret Clo., Epp. CN18 22
Margaret Rd.
Margaret Clo., Pot.B. BT20 20
Margaret Clo., Rom. CU32 50
Margaret Clo., Stai. AX50 73
Margaret Clo., Wal.Abb. CF20 21
Moremead
Margaret Clo., Wat. BB19 17
Margaret Ct. W1 BW39 56
Margaret St.
Margaret Dr., Horn. CW33 51
Margaret Gardner Dr. SE9 CK48 78
Bowmead
Margaret Rd. N16 CA33 48
Margaret Rd., Barn. BT24 29
Margaret Rd., Bex. CP46 79
Margaret Rd., Epp. CO18 23
Margaret Rd., Guil. AR71 118
Margaret Rd., Rom. CU32 50
Margaret St. W1 BV39 1
Margaret St. W1 BV39 56
Margaret St., Uxb. AX36 53
Cross St.
Margaret Way, Couls. BY62 104
Margaret Way, Ilf. CJ32 49
Margaretta Ter. SW3 BU43 3
Margaretta Ter. SW3 BU43 66
Margaretting Rd. E12 CJ34 49
Margate Rd. SW2 BX46 76
Margeholes, Wat. BE27 36
Margery Gro., Tad. BR68 112
Margery La., Tad. BR68 112
Margery Park Rd. E7 CH36 58
Margery Rd., Dag. CP34 50
Margery St. WC1 BY38 2
Margery St. WC1 BY38 56
Margery Wood, Welw.G.C. BS 6 5
Margin Dr. SW19 BQ49 75
Margravine Gdns. W6 BQ42 65
Margravine Rd. W6 BQ42 65
Marham Gdns. SW18 BU47 76
Marham Gdns., Mord. BT53 86
Maria Clo. SE1 CB42 67
Beatrice Rd.
Maria Ter. E1 CC38 57
Maria Theresa Clo., N.Mal. BN53 85
Mariam Gdns., Horn. CW34 51
Marian Clo., Grays DC40 60
Marian Clo., Hayes BD38 54
Marian Ct., Sutt. BS56 95
Marian Pl. E2 CB37 57
Marian Rd. SW16 BW51 86
Marian Sq. E2 CB37 57
Marian Way NW10 BO36 55
Maricas Av., Har. BG29 36
Marie Lloyd Wk. E8 CA36 57
Forest Rd.
Mariette Way, Pur. BX58 95
Marigold St. SE16 CB41 67
Marigold Way, Croy. CC54 87
Marina App., Hayes BE39 54
West Quay Dr.
Marina Av., N.Mal. BP53 85
Marina Clo., Brom. CG52 88
Marina Dr., Dart. CW47 80
Marina Dr., Grav. DF47 81
Marina Dr., Well. CN44 68
Marina Gdns., Chsnt. CC18 21
Marina Gdns., Rom. CS32 50
Marina Pl. SW8 BX44 66
Priory Gro.
Marina Way, Iver AV40 52
Marina Way, Tedd. BK50 74
Fairways
Marine Dr. SE18 CK42 68
Marine St. SE16 CB41 4
Marine St. SE16 CB41 67
Enid St.
Marinefield Rd. SW6 BS44 66
Mariner Gdns., Rich. BJ48 74
Ashburnham Rd.
Mariner Rd. E12 CL35 49
Mariner Way, Hem.H. AZ14 8
Mariners Ms. E14 CF42 67
Sextant Av.
Mariners Wk., Erith CU43 69
Frobisher Rd.
Marion Av., Shep. AZ53 83
Marion Clo., Bush. BE23 27
Marion Clo., Ilf. CM29 40
Marion Cres., Orp. CO53 89
Marion Gro., Wdf.Grn. CG28 40
Marion Rd. NW7 BP28 37
Marion Rd., Th.Hth. BZ53 87
Marischal Rd. SE13 CF45 67
Marisco Clo., Grays DG42 71
Marish La., Uxb. AU31 43
Maritime St. E3 CD38 57
Marius Pass. SW17 BV48 76
Marius Rd.
Marius Rd. SW17 BV48 76
Marjorams Av., Loug. CL23 31
Marjorie Gro. SW11 BU45 66
Mark Av. E4 CE25 30
Mark Clo., Bexh. CQ44 69
Mark Clo., Sthl. BF40 54
Mark Dr., Ger.Cr. AR28 34
Mark Grn., Wat. BD28 36
Mark Hall Moors, Harl. CO 9 6
Mark La. EC3 CA40 4
Mark La. EC3 CA40 57
Mark La., Grav. DJ47 81
Mark Oak La., Lthd. BF64 102
Mark Pl., Sthl. BF40 54
Mark Rd. N22 BY30 38
Mark Rd., Hem.H. AZ12 8
Mark St. E15 CG36 58
Mark St. EC2 CA38 2
Mark St. EC2 CA38 57
Mark St., Reig. BS70 121
Mark Way, Swan. CU53 89
Markab Rd., Nthwd. BB28 35
Marke Clo., Kes. CK56 97
Markedge La., Couls. BU65 104
Markedge La., Red. BU66 113
Markenfield Rd., Guil. AR70 118
Market Ct. W1 BW39 56
Market Pl.
Market Hill SE18 CL41 68
Market La., Slou. AU42 62
Market Link, Rom. CT31 50
Market Meadow Pl., Orp. CP52 89
Market Ms. W1 BV40 3
Market Ms. W1 BV40 56
Market Oak La., Hem.H. AZ15 8
Market Par. SE15 CB44 67
Market Pl. N2 BU31 47
Market Pl. NW11 BS31 47
Market Pl. SE16 CB42 67
Southwark Park Rd.
Market Pl. W1 BW39 1
Market Pl. W1 BW39 56
Market Pl. W3 BN40 55
Market Pl., Abridge CO24 32
Market Pl., Brent. BK43 64
Market Pl., Dart. CW47 80
Market St.
Market Pl., Dor. BJ71 119
Market Pl., Enf. BZ24 30
Market Pl., Ger.Cr. AR30 34
Market Pl., Grav. DH47 81
Market Pl., Grays DD43 71
Market Pl., Hat. BP12 10
Market Pl., Kings.T. BK51 84
Market Pl., Rom. CT32 50
Market Pl., St.Alb. BG13 9
Market Pl., Wat. BD24 27
Market Rd. E14 CE40 57
Market Rd. N7 BX36 56
Market Rd., Rich. BM45 65
Market Row SW9 BY45 66
Atlantic Rd.
Market Sq., Brom. CH51 88
Market Sq., Hem.H. AX13 8
Market Sq., Stai. AV49 72
Clarence St.
Market Sq., Uxb. AX36 53
High St.
Market Sq., Wal.Abb. CF20 21
Market Sq., Wok. AS62 100
Market St. E6 CK37 58
Market St. SE18 CL42 68
Market St., Dart. CW47 80
Market St., Guil. AR71 118
Market St., Harl. CP 9 6
Market St., Wat. BC24 26
Market Way E14 CE39 57
Market Way, West. CM66 115
Costells Meadows
Market, The, Cars. BT54 86
Markfield Gdns. E4 CE26 39
Markfield Rd. N15 CB31 48
Markfield Rd., Cat. CB66 114
Markfield, Croy. CB58 96
Markham Sq. SW3 BU42 3
Markham Sq. SW3 BU42 66
Markham St. SW3 BU42 3
Markham St. SW3 BU42 66
Markhole Clo., Hmptn. BE50 74
Markhouse Av. E17 CD32 48
Markhouse Rd. E17 CD32 48
Markmanor Av. E17 CD33 48
Marks Av., Ong. CW17 24
Marks Rd., Rom. CS32 50
Marks Rd., Warl. CD62 105
Marks Sq., Grav. DF49 81
Marks St. E1 CA39 57
Marksbury Av., Rich. BM45 65
Markville Gdns., Cat. CB66 114
Markway, Sun. BD51 84
Markwell Clo. SE26 CB49 77
Taylors La.
Markyate Rd., Dag. CO35 50
Marl Rd. SW18 BS45 66
Marland Ms. N1 BY36 56
Lofting Rd.
Marlands Rd., Ilf. CK31 49
Marlborough Av. E8 CB37 2
Marlborough Av. E8 CB37 57
Marlborough Av. N14 BW27 38
Marlborough Av., Edg. BM27 37
Marlborough Av., Ruis. BA32 44
Marlborough Bldgs. SW3 BU42 3
Marlborough Bldgs. SW3 BU42 66
Marlborough Clo. N20 BU27 38
Marlborough Clo. SE17 BY42 4
Marlborough Clo. SE17 BY42 66
Marlborough Clo. SW19 BU50 76
Marlborough Clo., Grays DE41 71
Marlborough Clo., Orp. CN54 88
Marlborough Clo., Upmin. CZ33 51
Marlborough Clo., Walt. BD55 84
Marlborough Cres. W4 BN41 65
Marlborough Cres., Sev. CT65 107
Marlborough Ct. W1 BW39 1
Marlborough Ct. W8 BS42 66
Marlborough Dr., Ilf. CK31 49
Marlborough Dr., Wey. BA55 83
Marlborough Gate, St.Alb. BH13 9
Marlborough Gdns. N20 BU27 38
Marlborough Gdns., Upmin. CY33 51
Marlborough Gdns., Surb. BK54 84
Marlborough Gro. SE1 CB42 4
Marlborough Gro. SE1 CB42 67
Marlborough Hill NW8 BT37 1
Marlborough Hill NW8 BT37 56
Marlborough Hill, Dor. BJ71 119
Marlborough Hill, Har. BG32 45
Marlborough La. SE7 CJ43 68
Marlborough Park Av., Sid. CO47 79
Marlborough Pl. NW8 BT37 1
Marlborough Pl. NW8 BT37 56
Marlborough Rd. E15 CG35 49
Borthwick Rd.
Marlborough Rd. E18 CH31 49
Marlborough Rd. E4 CE29 39
Marlborough Rd. E7 CJ36 58
Marlborough Rd. N19 BW34 47
Marlborough Rd. N22 BX29 38
Marlborough Rd. N9 CA26 39
Marlborough Rd. SW1 BW40 3
Marlborough Rd. SW1 BW40 56
Marlborough Rd. SW19 BT50 76
Marlborough Rd. W4 BN42 65
Marlborough Rd. W5 BK41 64
Marlborough Rd., Ashf. AX49 73
Marlborough Rd., Bexh. CP45 69
Marlborough Rd., Brom. CJ52 88
Marlborough Rd., Brwd. DA25 33
Marlborough Rd., Dag. CO35 50
Marlborough Rd., Dart. CV46 80
Marlborough Rd., Dor. BJ71 119
Marlborough Rd., Felt. BD48 74
Marlborough Rd., Har. BH31 45
Marlborough Rd., Hmptn. BF50 74
Marlborough Rd., Islw. BJ44 64
Marlborough Rd., Rich. BL46 75
Marlborough Rd., Rom. CR31 50
Marlborough Rd., S.Croy. BZ57 96
Marlborough Rd., Slou. AR42 62
Marlborough Rd., St.Alb. BH13 9
Marlborough Rd., Sthl. BD41 64
Marlborough Rd., Sutt. BS55 86
Marlborough Rd., Uxb. AZ38 53
Marlborough Rd., Wat. BC24 26
Marlborough Rd., Wok. AT61 100
Marlborough Ri., Hem.H. AY12 8
Marlborough St. SW3 BU42 3
Marlborough St. SW3 BU42 66
Marlborough Yd. N19 BW34 47
Marlborough Rd.
Marld, The, Ash. BL62 103
Marle Gdns., Wal.Abb. CF19 21
Marler Rd. SE23 CD47 77
Marlescroft Way, Loug. CL25 31
Marley Av., Bexh. CP43 69
Marley Clo., Grnf. BF37 54
Marley Clo., Wey. AV57 91
Marley Rd., Welw.G.C. BS 9 5
Marlin Clo., Berk. AP12 7
Marlin Sq., Wat. BB19 17
Marling Way, Grav. DJ49 81
Marlingdene Clo., Hmptn. BF50 74
Marlings Clo., Chis. CN52 88
Marlings Clo., Whyt. CA62 105
Marlings Park Av., Chis. CN52 88
Marlins Clo., Rick. AV23 25
Marlins Clo., Sutt. BT56 95
Turnpike La.
Marlins Meadow, Wat. BA25 26
Marlins Turn, Hem.H. AW12 8
Marlins, The, Nthwd. BB28 35
Eastbury Av.
Marloes Clo. W8 BS41 66
Marloes Clo., Wem. BK35 45
Marloes Rd. W8 BS41 66
Marlow Av., Grays CX42 70
Marlow Clo. SE20 CB52 87
Marlow Cres., Twick. BH46 74
Marlow Ct. NW6 BQ36 55
Marlow Dr., Sutt. BQ55 85
Marlow Gdns., Hayes BA41 63
Marlow Gdns., Rom. CV30 42
Marlow Rd. E6 CK38 58
Marlow Rd. SE20 CB52 87
Marlow Rd., Sthl. BE41 64
Marlow Way SE16 CC41 67
Marlowe Clo., Chis. CM50 78
Marlowe Clo., Ilf. CM30 40
Marlowe Gdns. SE9 CL46 78
Foots Cray Rd.
Marlowe Gdns., Rom. CV30 43
Shenstone Gdns.
Marlowe Rd. E17 CF31 48
Marlowe Sq., Mitch. BV52 86
Marlowe Way, Croy. BX55 86
Marlowes, Hem.H. AX14 8
Marlowes, The, Dart. CS45 69
Marlowes, The, NW8 BT37 1
Marlowes, The, NW8 BT37 56
Marlpit Av., Couls. BX62 104
Marlpit La., Couls. BW61 104
Marlton St. SE10 CG42 68
Marlyns Clo., Guil. AT68 109
Marlyns Dr., Guil. AT68 109
Marlyon Rd., Ilf. CO28 41
Marmadon Rd. SE18 CN42 68
Marmion App. E4 CE28 39
Marmion Clo.
Marmion Av. E4 CD28 39
Marmion Clo. E4 CE28 39
Marmion Ms. SW11 BV45 66
Taybridge Rd.
Marmion Rd. SW11 BV45 66
Marmont Rd. SE15 CB44 67
Marmora Rd. SE22 CC46 77
Marmot Rd., Houns. BD45 64
Marne Av. N11 BV28 38
Marne Av., Well. CO45 69
Marne St. W10 BR38 55
Marnell Way, Houns. BD45 64
Marney Rd. SW11 BV45 66
Marneys Clo., Epsom BM61 103
Marnham Av. NW2 BR35 46
Marnham Cres., Grnf. BF37 54
Marnham Ri., Hem.H. AW12 8
Marnock Rd. SE4 CD46 77
Maroon St. E14 CD39 57
Maroons Way SE6 CE49 77
Marquess Gro. N1 BZ36 57
Marquess Rd.
Marquess Rd. N1 BZ36 57
Marquis Clo., Wem. BL36 55
Marquis Rd. N22 BX29 38
Marquis Rd. N4 BX33 47
Marquis Rd. NW1 BW36 56
Marram Ct., Grays DF43 71
Medlar Rd.
Marrick Clo. SW15 BP45 65
Marrilyne Av., Enf. CD22 30
Marriot Rd., Barn. BQ24 28
Marriots Clo. NW9 BO32 46
Marriots, The, Harl. CP 8 6
Marriott Clo., Felt. BA46 73
Marriott Lodge Clo., Wey. AX56 92
Marriott Rd. E15 CG37 38
Marriott Rd. N10 BU30 38
Marriott Rd. N4 BX33 47
Marriott Rd., Dart. CW47 80
Waldeck Rd.
Marrowells, Wey. BB55 83
Marryat Pl. SW19 BR49 75
Marryat Rd. SW19 BQ49 75
Marryat Rd., Enf. CB21 30
Marsala Rd. SE13 CE45 67
Marsden Clo., Welw.G.C. BP 9 5
Marsden Grn., Welw.G.C. BP 8 5
Marsden Rd. N9 CB27 39
Marsden Rd. SE15 CA45 67
Marsden Rd., Welw.G.C. BP 8 5
Marsden St. NW5 BV36 56
Marsden Way, Orp. CN55 88
Stapleton Rd.
Marsh Av., Epsom BO58 94
Marsh Av., Loug. CM23 31
Marsh Av., Mitch. BU51 86
Marsh Clo. NW7 BO27 37
Marsh Clo., Wal.Cr. CD20 21
Marsh Dr. NW9 BO32 46
Marsh Farm Rd., Twick. BH47 74
Marsh Green Rd., Dag. CR37 59
Marsh Hill E9 CD35 48
Marsh Hill, Wal.Abb. CG17 22
Marsh La. E10 CE34 48
Marsh La. NW7 BN28 37
Marsh La. W17 CB30 39
Marsh La., Harl. CQ 8 6
Marsh La., Maid. AJ40 61
Marsh La., Stan. BK28 36
Marsh La., Wey. AW56 92
Marsh Rd., Pnr. BE31 45
Marsh Rd., Wem. BK37 54
Marsh St. E14 CE42 67
Marsh St., Dart. CX45 70
Marsh Wall E14 CE41 67
Marsh Way, Rain. CS39 59
Marshall Av., St.Alb. BH12 9
Marshall Clo. SW18 BT46 76
Allfarthing La.
Marshall Clo., Houns. BE46 74
Marshall Dr., Hayes BB39 53
Marshall Gdns. SE1 BY41 66
London Rd.
Marshall Path SE28 CO40 59
Titmuss Av.
Marshall Rd. N17 BZ30 39
Marshall St. W1 BW39 1
Marshall St. W1 BW39 56
Marshalls Clo. N11 BV28 38
Marshalls Clo., Epsom BN60 94
Marshalls Dr., Rom. CT31 50
Marshalls Gro. SE18 CK42 68
Marshalls Pl. SE16 CA41 67
Marshalls Rd., Rom. CS31 50
Marshalls Rd., Sutt. BS56 95
High St.
Marshals Dr., St.Alb. BJ12 9
Marshalsea Rd. SE1 BZ41 4
Marshalsea Rd. SE1 BZ41 67
Marshalswick La., St.Alb. BJ12 9
Marsham Clo., Chis. CL49 78
Marsham La., Ger.Cr. AS32 43
Marsham St. SW1 BW41 3
Marsham St. SW1 BW41 66
Marsham Way, Ger.Cr. AS32 43
Marshbrooke Clo. SE3 CJ45 68
Marshcroft Dr., Chsnt. CD18 21
Southmead Cres.
Marshe Clo., Pot.B. BT19 20
Marshfield St. E14 CF41 67
Marshfoot Rd., Grays DF42 71
Marshgate La. E15 CE37 57
Marshgate Path SE28 CM41 68
Tom Cribb Rd.
Marshgate, Harl. CN 9 6
Marshmoor Cres., Hat. BQ15 10
Marshmoor La., Hat. BQ14 10
Marsland Clo. SE17 BY42 4
Marsland Clo. SE17 BY42 66
Marsland Rd. SE17 BY42 4
Marston Av., Chess. BL57 94
Marston Av., Dag. CR34 50
Marston Clo. NW6 BT36 56
Marston Clo., Dag. CR34 50
Marston Clo., Hem.H. AZ14 8
Marston Ct., Walt. BD54 84
St. Johns Dr.
Marston Dr., Warl. CD62 105
Marston Rd., Hodd. CE11 12
Marston Rd., Ilf. CK30 40
Marston Rd., Tedd. BJ49 74
Marston Rd., Wok. AQ62 100
Marston Way SE19 BY50 76
Marston, Epsom BN58 94
Marsworth Av., Pnr. BD30 36
Mart St. WC2 BX40 4
Mart St. WC2 BX40 56
Floral St.
Martaban Rd. N16 CA34 48
Listria Pk.
Martell Rd. SE21 BZ48 77
Martello St. E8 CB36 57
Marten Gate, St.Alb. BJ11 9
Marten Rd. E17 CE30 39
Martens Av., Bexh. CR45 69
Martens Clo., Bexh. CS45 69
Martha Ct. E2 CB37 57
Cambridge Heath Rd.
Martha Rd. E15 CG36 58
Martha St. E1 CB39 57
Martham Clo. SE28 CP40 59
Surlingham Clo.
Marthorne Cres., Har. BG30 36
Martian Av., Hem.H. AZ12 8
Martin Bowes Rd. SE9 CK45 68
Martin Clo., Hat. BP13 10
Martin Clo., S.Croy. CC59 96
Martin Clo., Warl. CB61 105
Martin Clo., Wind. AL44 61
Martin Cres., Croy. BY54 86
Martin Dene, Bexh. CQ46 79
Martin Dr., Nthlt. BE35 45
Martin Dr., Rain. CU38 59
Martin Gdns., Dag. CP35 50
Martin Gro., Mord. BS52 86
Martin La. EC4 BZ40 4
Martin La. EC4 BZ40 57
Martin Rd., Dag. CP35 50
Martin Rd., Dart. CV48 80
Martin Rd., Guil. AQ69 118
Martin Rd., S.Ock. CY40 60
Martin Rd., Slou. AP41 62
Martin Ri., Bexh. CQ46 79
Martin Way SW20 BR52 85
Martin Way, Mord. BR52 85
Martin Way, Wok. AQ62 100
Martindale Av. E16 CH40 58
Bridgeland Rd.
Martindale Av., Orp. CN56 97
Martindale Clo., Guil. AU69 109
Gilliat Dr.
Martindale Rd. SW12 BV47 76
Martindale Rd., Hem.H. AV13 7
Martindale Rd., Houns. BE45 64
Martindale Rd., Wok. AQ62 100
Martindale SW14 BN46 75
Martineau Clo., Esher DG56 93
Martineau Dr., Dor. BJ72 119
Martineau Est. E1 CC40 57
Martineau Rd. N5 BY35 47
Martineau St. E1 CC39 57
Lukin St.
Martinfield, Welw.G.C. BR 8 5
Martingale Clo., Rich. BK48 74
Martingale Clo., Sun. BC52 83
Martins Bldgs. SW18 BS46 76
Frogmore
Martins Clo., Guil. AU70 118
Martins Clo., Orp. CP52 89
Martins Ct., St.Alb. BJ15 9
Swallow La.
Martins Dr., Chsnt. CD17 21

Martins Mt., Barn. BS24 29
Martins Rd., Brom. CG51 88
Martins Shaw, Sev. CT64 107
Martins Wk. M10 BV30 38
Martins Wk., B.Wd. BM24 28
Goldfinch Way
Martins, The SE26 CB49 77
Lawrie Park Gdns.
Martlesham Clo., Horn. CV35 51
Martlesham, Welw.G.C. BU 8 5
Martlet Gro., Nthlt. BS38 54
Javelin Way
Martlett Ct. WC2 BX39 2
Martlett Ct. WC2 BX39 56
Drury La.
Martley Dr., Ilf. CL32 49
Martock Clo., Har. BJ31 45
Marton Clo. SE6 CE48 77
Martyr Clo., St.Alb. BG15 9
Creighton Av.
Martyr Rd., Guil. AR71 118
Martyrs La., Wok. AT59 91
Martys Yd. NW3 BT35 47
Hampstead High St.
Marvell Av., Hayes BC39 53
Marvels Clo. SE12 CH48 78
Marvels La. SE12 CH48 78
Marville Rd. SW6 BR43 65
Marvin St. E8 CB36 57
Sylvester Rd.
Marwell Clo., W.Wick. CG55 88
Deer Park Way
Marwell, West. CM66 115
Farley Cft.
Marwood Clo., Kings L. AY18 17
Marwood Clo., Well. CO45 69
Marwood Way SE16 CB42 67
Bonamy Est. W.
Mary Adelaide Clo. SW15 BO49 75
Kingston Vale
Mary Ann Gdns. SE8 CE43 67
Mary Burrows Gdn., Sev. CX62 108
Church La.
Mary Clo., Har. BL31 46
Mary Datchelor Clo. SE5 BZ44 57
Vicarage Gro.
Mary Hill Clo., Ken. BZ62 105
Mary Kingsley Pl. N6 BV33 47
Mary Lawrenson Pl. SE3 CH43 68
Heathway
Mary Macarthur Ho. W14 BR43 65
Mary Peters Dr., Har. BG35 45
Mary Pl. W11 BR40 55
Mary Rd., Guil. AR71 118
Mary Rose Clo., Hmptn. BF51 84
Ashley Rd.
Mary Rose Mall E6 CK39 58
Frobisher Rd.
Mary Rose Way N20 BT26 38
Mary Seacole Clo. E8 CA37 2
Clarissa St.
Mary Seacole Clo. E8 CA37 57
Clarissa St.
Mary St. N1 BZ37 2
Mary St. N1 BZ37 57
Mary Ter. NW1 BV37 1
Mary Ter. NW1 BV37 56
Maryatt Av., Har. BF34 45
Marybank SE18 CK42 68
Frances St.
Maryfield Clo., Bex. CT48 79
Maryland Pk. E15 CG35 49
Maryland Rd. E15 CF35 48
Maryland Rd. N22 BX29 38
Maryland Rd., Th.Hth. BY51 86
Maryland Sq. E15 CG35 49
Maryland St. E15 CF35 48
Maryland Way, Sun. BC51 83
Maryland Wk. N1 BZ37 2
Popham St.
Maryland Wk. N1 BZ37 57
Popham St.
Maryland, Hat. BO13 10
Marylands Rd. W9 BS38 56
Marylebone Cir. NW1 BU38 56
Marylebone Cir. NW1 BU39 1
Marylebone High St. W1 BV39 1
Marylebone High St. W1 BV39 56
Marylebone La. W1 BV39 1
Marylebone La. W1 BV39 56
Marylebone Ms. W1 BV39 1
Marylebone Ms. W1 BV39 56
Marylebone Pass. W1 BW39 1
Marylebone Rd. NW1 BU39 1
Marylebone Rd. NW1 BU39 56
Marylebone St. W1 BV39 1
Marylebone St. W1 BV39 56
Marylee Way SE11 BX42 4
Marylee Way SE11 BX42 66
Maryon Gro. SE7 CK42 68
Maryon Ms. NW3 BU35 47
South End Rd.
Maryon Rd. SE7 CK42 68
Marys Ter., Twick. BJ47 74
Maryside, Slou. AS41 62
Masbro Rd. W14 BQ41 65
Mascalls Ct. SE7 CJ43 68
Victoria Way
Mascalls Gdns., Brwd. CZ28 42
Mascalls La., Brwd. CZ28 42
Mascalls Rd. SE7 CJ43 68
Mascotte Rd. SW15 BQ45 65
Felsham Rd.
Mascotts Clo. NW2 BP34 46
Masefield Av., B.Wd. BM25 28
Masefield Av., Stan. BH28 36
Masefield Av., Sthl. BF40 54
Masefield Clo., Erith CT44 69
Masefield Clo., Rom. CU30 41
Masefield Cres. N14 BV25 29
Masefield Cres., Rom. CV30 42
Masefield Dr., Upmin. CY33 51
Masefield Gdns. E6 CL38 58
Masefield La., Hayes BC38 53
Masefield Rd., Dart. CX46 80
Masefield Rd., Grav. DE48 81
Masefield Rd., Grays DF41 71
Masefield Rd., Hmptn. BE49 74
Masefield Vw., Orp. CM55 88
Mashie Rd. W3 BO39 55
Mashiters Hill, Rom. CS30 41
Mashiters Wk., Rom. CT31 50
Maskall Clo. SW2 BY47 76
Maskell Rd. SW17 BT48 76
Maskelyn Clo. SW11 BU44 66
Mason Clo. E16 CH40 58
Mason Clo., B.Wd. BN23 28
Mason Clo., Bexh. CR45 69
Mason Clo., Hmptn. BE51 84
Mason Pl., Mitch. BU51 86
Mason Rd., Wdf.Grn. CG28 40
Mason St. SE17 BZ42 4
Mason St. SE17 BZ42 67
Mason Way, Wal.Abb. CG20 22
Masonic Hall Rd., Cher. AV53 82
Masons Arms Ms. W1 BV40 3
Masons Arms Yd. W1 BV40 56
Maddox St.
Masons Av. EC2 BZ39 2
Masons Av. EC2 BZ39 57
Masons Av., Croy. BZ55 87
Masons Av., Har. BH31 45
Masons Bridge Rd., Red. BV73 121
Masons Ct., Wem. BM34 46
Masons Green La. W3 BM38 55
Masons Hill SE18 CL42 68
Masons Hill, Brom. CH52 88
Masons Paddock, Dor. BJ70 119
Masons Pl. EC1 BY38 2
Masons Pl. EC1 BY38 56
Masons Rd., Enf. CB21 30
Masons Rd., Hem.H. AZ13 8
Masons Yd. SW1 BW40 3
Masons Yd. SW1 BW40 56
Duke St.
Massey Clo. N11 BV28 38
Grove Rd.
Massie Rd. E8 CB36 57
Graham Rd.
Massinger St. SE17 CA42 4
Massinger St. SE17 CA42 67
Massingham St. E1 CC38 57
Masson Av., Ruis. BD36 54
Mast House Ter. E14 CE42 67
Master Gunner Pl. SE18 CK43 68
Masterman Rd. E6 CK38 58
Masters St. E1 CC39 57
Masthead Clo., Dart. CY45 70
Mastmaker Rd. E14 CE41 67
Maswell Park Cres., Houns. BG46 74
Maswell Park Rd., Houns. BF46 74
Matcham Rd. E11 CG34 49
Matching Rd., Harl. CR 9 6
Matchless Dr. SE18 CL44 68
Red Lion La.
Matfield Clo., Brom. CH53 88
Matfield Rd., Belv. CR43 69
Matham Gro. SE22 CA45 67
Matham Rd., E.Mol. BG53 84
Matheson Pl. W14 BR42 65
Matheson Rd. W14 BR42 65
Mathews Av. E6 CL37 58
Mathews La., Stai. AV49 72
Mathews Yd. WC2 BX39 56
Short Gdns.
Mathias Clo., Epsom BN60 94
Matilda Ho. E1 CB40 4
Matilda St. N1 BX37 2
Matilda St. N1 BX37 56
Matlock Clo. SE24 BZ45 67
Matlock Cres., Sutt. BR55 85
Matlock Cres., Wat. BD27 36
Matlock Ct. SE5 BZ45 67
Matlock Gdns., Horn. CW34 51
Matlock Gdns., Sutt. BR56 94
Matlock Pl., Sutt. BR56 94
Matlock Rd. E10 CF32 48
Matlock Rd., Cat. CA64 105
Matlock St. E14 CD39 57
Matlock Way, N.Mal. BN51 85
Matrimony Pl. SW8 BW44 66
Wandsworth Rd.
Matthew Arnold Clo., Cob. BC60 92
Matthew Clo. W10 BQ38 55
Matthew Parker St. SW1 BW41 3
Matthew Parker St. SW1 BW41 66
Matthew St. SW11 BU44 66
Matthew St., Reig. BS72 121
Matthews Av. E6 CL37 58
Folkestone Rd.
Matthews Clo., Hav. CW30 42
Oak Rd.
Matthews Gdns., Croy. CF59 96
Matthews Park Av. E15 CG36 58
Matthews Rd., Har. BG35 45
Matthews St. SW11 BU44 66
Matthias Rd. N16 BZ35 48
Mattingley Way SE15 CA43 67
Mattison Rd. N4 BY32 47
Mattock La. W13 BJ40 54
Mattock La. W5 BK40 54
Mattock Rd. W5 BK40 54
Mattock La.
Maud Gdns. E13 CG37 58
Maud Gdns., Bark. CN37 58
Maud Rd. E10 CF34 48
Maud Rd. E13 CG37 58
Maud St. E16 CG39 58
Maude Cres., Wat. BC22 26
Maude Rd. E17 CD32 48
Maude Rd. SE5 CA44 67
Maude Rd., Swan. CU50 79
Maude Ter. E17 CD31 48
Maudesville Cotts. W7 BH40 54
Maudlins Grn. E1 CB40 57
Burr Clo.
Maudslay Rd. SE9 CK45 68
Mauleverer Rd. SW2 BX46 76
Maunder Rd. W7 BH40 54
Maunsel St. SW1 BW42 3
Maunsel St. SW1 BW42 66
Maurice Av. N22 BY30 38
Maurice Av., Cat. BZ64 105
Maurice Brown Clo. NW7 BQ28 37
Maurice Wk. NW11 BT31 47
Maurier Clo., Nthlt. BD37 54
Mauritius Rd. SE10 CG42 68
Maurne St. W12 BP39 55
Maury Rd. N16 CB34 48
Mauve St. E14 CF39 57
St. Leonards Av.
Mavelstone Clo., Brom. CK51 88
Mavelstone Rd., Brom. CJ51 88
Maverton Rd. E3 CE37 57
Mavis Av., Epsom BO56 94
Mavis Clo., Epsom BO56 94
Mavis Gro., Horn. CW34 51
Mavis Wk. E6 CK39 58
Tollgate Rd.
Mawbey Est. SE1 CA42 4
Mawbey Est. SE1 CB42 67
Mawbey Pl. SE1 CA42 4
Mawbey Pl. SE1 CA42 67
Mawbey Rd.
Mawbey Rd. SE1 CA42 4
Mawbey Rd. SE1 CA42 67
Mawbey Rd. SW8 BX43 66
Mawbey Rd., Cher. AU57 91
Mawney Clo., Rom. CR30 41
Mawney Rd., Rom. CR30 41
Mawson Clo. SW20 BR51 85
Mawson Ho. EC1 BY39 56
Baldwins Gdns.
Mawson La. W4 BO43 65
Maxey Gdns., Dag. CQ35 50
Maxey Rd. SE18 CM42 68
Maxey Rd., Dag. CQ35 50
Maxilla Wk. W10 BQ39 55
Bartle Rd.
Maxim Rd. N21 BY25 29
Maxim Rd., Dart. CT46 79
Roman Way
Maxim Rd., Erith CS42 69
Maximfeldt Rd., Erith CT42 69
Maxted Clo., Hem.H. AZ12 8
Maxted Pk., Har. BH33 45
Maxted Rd. SE15 CA45 67
Maxted Rd., Hem.H. AZ12 8
Maxwell Clo., Rick. AW27 35
Maxwell Dr., Wey. AX59 92
Maxwell Gdns., Orp. CN55 88
Maxwell Rd. SW6 BS43 66
Maxwell Rd., Ashf. BA50 73
Maxwell Rd., B.Wd. BN23 28
Maxwell Rd., Nthwd. BA29 35
Maxwell Rd., St.Alb. BJ14 9
Maxwell Rd., Well. CO45 69
Maxwell Rd., West Dr. AY42 63
Maxwell Ri., Wat. BE26 36
Maxwelton Av. NW7 BN28 37
Maxwelton Clo. NW7 BN28 37
May Av., Grav. DF47 81
May Av., Orp. CO53 89
May Clo., Chess. BL57 94
May Clo., St.Alb. BG12 9
May Ct., Grays DE43 71
Medlar Rd.
May Ct., Hem.H. AX13 8
May Gdns., Wem. BK37 54
May Place La. SE18 CL43 68
May Rd. E13 CH37 58
May Rd. E4 CE29 39
May Rd., Dart. CW49 80
May Rd., Twick. BH47 74
May Tree La., Stan. BJ29 36
May Wk. E13 CH37 58
Maya Rd. N2 BT31 47
Mayall Rd. SE24 BY46 76
Maybank Av. E18 CH30 40
Maybank Av., Horn. CU35 50
Maybank Av., Wem. BH35 45
Maybank Gdns., Pnr. BC32 44
Maybank Rd. E18 CH30 40
Maybank Vill., Ilf. CO33 50
Mayberry Pl., Surb. BL54 85
Maybourne Clo. SE26 CB49 77
Maybourne Ri., Wok. AR65 100
Maybrick Rd., Horn. CV32 51
Maybrook Meadow Est., Bark. CO36 59
Maybury Av., Chsnt. CB17 21
Maybury Av., Dart. CY47 80
Maybury Clo., Orp. CL53 88
Maybury Clo., Tad. BR63 103
Maybury Gdns. NW10 BP36 55
Maybury Hill, Wok. AT61 100
Maybury Rd. E13 CJ38 58
Maybury Rd., Bark. CN37 58
Maybury Rd., Wok. AS62 100
Maybury St. SW17 BU49 76
Maybush Rd., Horn. CW33 51
Maychurch Clo., Stan. BK29 36
Maycock Gro., Nthwd. BB29 35
Carew Rd.
Maycroft Av., Grays DE42 71
Maycroft Gdns., Grays DE42 71
Maycroft Rd., Chsnt. CA16 21
Maycroft, Pnr. BC30 35
Maycross Av., Mord. BR52 85
Mayday Gdns. SE3 CK44 68
Mayday Rd., Th.Hth. BY53 86
Mayell Clo., Lthd. BK65 102
Mayerne Rd. SE9 CJ46 78
Mayes Clo., Swan. CU52 89
Mayes Clo., Warl. CC62 105
Mayes Rd. N22 BX30 38
Mayesbrook Rd., Bark. CN37 58
Mayesbrook Rd., Dag. CO34 50
Mayesbrook Rd., Ilf. CO34 50
Mayesford Rd., Rom. CP33 50
Mayeswood Rd. SE12 CJ48 78
Mayfair Av., Bexh. CP44 69
Mayfair Av., Ilf. CK34 49
Mayfair Av., Rom. CP32 50
Mayfair Av., Twick. BG47 74
Mayfair Av., Wor.Pk. BP54 85
Mayfair Clo., Beck. CE51 87
Mayfair Clo., St.Alb. BK11 9
Mayfair Clo., Surb. BL54 85
Mayfair Ct., Beck. CE51 87
Mayfair Gdns. N17 BZ29 39
Mayfair Gdns., Wdf.Grn. CH29 40
Mayfair Pl. W1 BV40 3
Mayfair Pl. W1 BV40 56
Mayfair Rd., Dart. CV46 80
Mayfair Ter. N14 BW26 38
Mayfare, Rick. BA25 26
Mayfield Av. N12 BT28 38
Mayfield Av. N14 BW27 38
Mayfield Av. W13 BJ41 64
Mayfield Av. W4 BO42 65
Mayfield Av., Ger.Cr. AR31 43
Mayfield Av., Har. BJ32 45
Mayfield Av., Orp. CN54 88
Mayfield Av., Wdf.Grn. CH29 40
Mayfield Av., Wey. AW58 92
Mayfield Clo. E8 CA36 57
Forest Rd.
Mayfield Clo. SE20 CB51 87
Anerley Rd.
Mayfield Clo. SW4 BW46 76
Mayfield Clo., Ashf. AZ50 73
Mayfield Clo., Harl. CQ 9 6
Mayfield Clo., Red. BV73 121
Brookfield Clo.
Mayfield Clo., T.Ditt. BJ54 84
Mayfield Clo., Uxb. AZ38 53
Mayfield Clo., Walt. BC56 92
Mayfield Clo., Wey. AW58 92
Mayfield Cres. N9 CB25 30
Mayfield Cres., Th.Hth. BX52 86
Mayfield Dr., Pnr. BE31 45
Mayfield Gdns. NW4 BQ32 46
Mayfield Gdns. W7 BG39 54
Mayfield Gdns., Brwd. DA26 42
Mayfield Gdns., Stai. AV50 72
Mayfield Gdns., Walt. BC56 92
Mayfield Rd. E13 CG38 58
Mayfield Rd. E17 CD30 39
Mayfield Rd. E4 CF27 39
Mayfield Rd. E8 CA36 57
Mayfield Rd. N8 BX32 47
Mayfield Rd. SW19 BR51 85
Mayfield Rd. W12 BO41 65
Mayfield Rd. W3 BM40 55
Mayfield Rd., Belv. CS42 69
Mayfield Rd., Brom. CK53 88
Mayfield Rd., Dag. CP33 50
Mayfield Rd., Enf. CC23 30
Mayfield Rd., Grav. DF47 81
Mayfield Rd., S.Croy. BZ58 96
Mayfield Rd., Sutt. BT57 95
Mayfield Rd., Th.Hth. BX52 86
Mayfield Rd., Walt. BC56 92
Mayfield Rd., Wey. AZ56 92
Mayfield, Bexh. CQ45 69
Church Rd.
Mayfield, Wal.Abb. CF20 21
Roundhills
Mayfield, Welw.G.C. BQ 6 5
Mayfields Clo., Wem. BM34 46
Mayfields, Grays DE41 71
Mayfields, Wem. BM34 46
Mayflower Av., Hem.H. AX13 8
Mayflower Clo., Ruis. BA32 44
Mayflower Clo., S.Ock. DB38 60
Mayflower Clo., Wal.Abb. CG15 13
Crooked Way
Mayflower Path, Brwd. DB29 42
Mayflower Rd. SW9 BX44 66
Mayflower Rd., St.Alb. BF17 18
Mayflower St. SE16 CC41 67
St. Mary Church St.
Mayflower Way, Ong. CX17 24
Mayflower Way, Slou. AO35 43
Mayfly Gdns., Nthlt. BD38 54
Valliant Clo.
Mayford Clo. SW12 BU47 76
Mayford Clo., Beck. CC52 87
Gwydor Rd.
Mayford Clo., Wok. AR64 100
Mayford Rd. SW12 BU47 76
Mayford, Wok. AR64 100
Maygold Wk., Amer. AR23 25
Maygood St. N1 BX37 2
Maygood St. N1 BY37 56
Maygoods Clo., Uxb. AX39 53
Maygoods Grn., Uxb. AX39 53
Maygoods La., Uxb. AX39 53
Maygoods Vw., Uxb. AX39 53
Maygreen Cres., Horn. CU33 50
Maygrove Rd. NW6 BR36 55
Mayhew Clo. E4 CE27 39
Mayhill Rd. SE7 CH43 68
Mayhill Rd., Barn. BR25 28
Mayhurst Av., Wok. AU61 100
Mayhurst Clo., Wok. AU61 100
Mayhurst Av.
Mayhurst Cres., Wok. AU61 100
Mayhurst Av.
Maylands Av., Hem.H. AZ12 8
Maylands Av., Horn. CU35 50
Maylands Dr., Sid. CP48 79
Maylands Dr., Uxb. AX36 53
Maylands Rd., Wat. BD28 36
Maylands Way, Rom. CY29 42
Maylins Dr., Saw. CP 6 6
Maynard Clo. N15 CA31 48
Brunswick Rd.
Maynard Clo. SW6 BS43 66
Cambria St.
Maynard Clo., Erith CT43 69
Maynard Ct., Wal.Abb. CG20 22
Maynard Dr., St.Alb. BG15 9
Maynard Pl., Cuff. BX18 20
Station Rd.
Maynard Rd. E17 CE32 48
Maynard Rd., Hem.H. AX14 8
Maynards Quay E1 CC40 57
Garnet St.
Maynards, Horn. CW33 51
Clairvale
Mayne Av., St.Alb. BF14 9
Mayo Clo., Chsnt. CC17 21
Mayo Rd. NW10 BO36 55
Mayo Rd., Croy. BZ53 87
Mayo Rd., Walt. BB54 83
Mayola Rd. E5 CC35 48
Mayow Rd. SE26 CC49 77
Mayplace Av., Dart. CU45 69
Mayplace Clo., Bexh. CR45 69
Mayplace Rd. E., Bexh. CR45 69
Mayplace Rd. W., Bexh. CR45 69
Maypole Cres., Erith CV43 70
Maypole Cres., Ilf. CM29 40
Maypole Dr., Chig. CO27 41
Maypole Rd., Orp. CQ56 98
Mayroyd Av., Surb. BM55 85
Mays Bldgs. Ms. SE10 CF43 67
Crooms Hill
Mays Ct. WC2 BX40 4
Mays Ct. WC2 BX40 56
St. Martins La.
Mays Gro., Wok. AU65 100
Mays Hill Rd., Brom. CG51 88
Mays La. E4 CF27 39
Mays La., Barn. BP26 37
Mays Pl. SE15 CB45 67
Scylla Rd.
Mays Rd., Tedd. BG49 74
Maysfield Rd., Wok. AU65 100
Maysgrove, Wok. AU65 100
Maysfield Rd.
Maysoule Rd. SW11 BT45 66
Mayswood Gdns., Dag. CS36 59
Maythorn Clo., Wat. BB24 26
Mayton St. N7 BX34 47
Maytree Clo., Edg. BN27 37
Maytree Clo., Guil. AR68 109
Maytree Clo., Rain. CT37 59
Maytree Cres., Wat. BB21 26
Maytree Wk. SW2 BY48 76
Mayville Est. N16 CA35 48
Mayville Rd. E11 CG34 49
Mayville Rd., Ilf. CL35 49
Mayville St. N16 CD35 48
Woodville Rd.
Maywards Ho. SE5 CA44 67
Glebe Est.
Maywater Clo., S.Croy. BZ59 96
Maywin Dr., Horn. CW33 51
Maywood Clo., Beck. CE50 77
Maze Hill SE10 CG43 68
Maze Hill SE3 CG43 68
Maze Rd., Rich. BM43 65
Mazenod Av. NW6 BS36 56
McAdam Clo., Hodd. CE11 12
McAdam Dr., Enf. BY23 29
McAll Clo. SW4 BX44 66
McAuley Clo. SE1 BY41 4
McAuley Clo. SE1 BY41 66
McAuley Clo. SE9 CL46 78
McCall Cres. SE7 CK42 68
McCarthy Rd., Felt. BD49 74
McCoid Way SE1 BZ41 4
McCoid Way SE1 BZ41 67
Borough Rd.
McCoid Wk. SE1 BZ41 67
Scovell Rd.
McCrone Ms. NW3 BT36 56
Belsize La.
McDermott Clo. SW11 BU45 66
McDermott Rd. SE15 CB45 67
McDonough Clo., Chess. BL56 94
Hook Rd.
McDowall Rd. SE5 BZ44 67
McDowell Clo. E16 CH39 58
McEntee Av. E17 CD30 39
McEwan Way E15 CF37 57
McGrath Rd. E15 CG35 49
McGredy, Chsnt. CB18 21
McGregor Rd. W11 BR39 55
McIntosh Clo., Rom. CT31 50
McIntosh Clo., Wall. BX57 95
Redford Av.
McIntosh Rd., Rom. CT31 50
McKay Rd. SW20 BP50 75
McKellar Clo., Bush. BG27 36
McKenzie Rd., Brox. CD13 12
McKerrell Rd. SE15 CB44 67
McLeod Rd. SE2 CO42 69
McLeods Ms. SW7 BS41 3
McLeods Ms. SW7 BS41 66
McMillan St. SE8 CE43 67
McNeil Rd. SE5 CA44 67
Mead Av., Slou. AT41 62
Mead Clo., Egh. AT50 72
Mead Clo., Grays DD41 71
Mead Clo., Har. BG30 36
Mead Clo., Red. BU69 121
Mead Clo., Rom. CU30 41
Mead Clo., Slou. AT41 62
Mead Clo., Swan. CU53 89
Mead Clo., Uxb. AW34 44
Mead Cres. E4 CF28 39
Mead Cres., Dart. CV47 80
Mead Cres., Lthd. BF66 111
Mead Cres., Sutt. BU56 95
Mead Ct. NW9 BN32 46
Mead Ct., Wal.Abb. CE20 21
Mead Ct., Wok. AP61 100
Mead End., Ash. BL62 103
Mead Gro., Rom. CP31 50
Mead House Rd., Hayes BA38 53
Mead La., Cher. AW54 83
Mead Path SW17 BT49 76
Mead Path SW19 BT49 76
Mead Pl. E9 CC36 57
Mead Pl., Croy. BY54 86
Mead Pl., Rick. AW26 35
Mead Plat NW10 BN36 55
Mead Rd., Cat. CA65 105
Mead Rd., Chis. CM50 78
Mead Rd., Dart. CV47 80
Mead Rd., Grav. DG48 81
Mead Rd., Rich. BK48 74
Mead Rd., Uxb. AX36 53
Mead Rd., Walt. BE56 93
Mead Row SE1 BY41 4
Mead Row SE1 BY41 66
Westminster Bridge Rd.

Mead Way NW10 BN36 55
Mead Way, Beck. CF51 87
Mead Way, Brom. CG53 88
Mead Way, Bush. BE23 27
Mead Way, Croy. CD55 87
Mead Way, St.Alb. BN15 10
Mead Way, The, Sev. CT64 107
Mead Way, Warl. CC61 105
Mead Wk., Ong. CW18 24
Mead Wk., Slou. AT41 62
Mead, The N2 BT30 38
Mead, The W13 BJ39 54
Templewood
Mead, The, Ash. BL63 103
Mead, The, Beck. CF51 87
Mead, The, Chsnt. CC18 21
Mead, The, Rom. CO24 32
Mead, The, Uxb. AZ34 44
Mead, The, W.Wick. CF54 87
Mead, The, Wall. BW57 95
Mead, The, Wat. BE27 36
Meadcroft Rd. SE11 BY43 66
St. Agnes Pl.
Meade Clo. W4 BM43 65
Meadfield Av., Slou. AT41 62
Meadfield Grn., Edg. BM27 37
Meadfield Rd., Slou. AT41 62
Meadfield, Edg. BM27 37
Meadfoot Rd. SW16 BW50 76
Meadgate Av., Wdf.Grn. CK28 40
Meadgate Rd., Epp. CF13 12
Meadhurst Rd., Cher. AW54 83
Meadlands Dr., Rich. BK48 74
Meadow Av., Croy. CC53 87
Meadow Bank N21 BX25 29
Meadow Bank, Lthd. BB67 110
Meadow Bank, Oxt. CF68 114
Meadow Bank, Sev. CZ58 99
Ash Tree Dr.
Meadow Bank, Wat. BD26 36
Meadow Cft., Hat. BO12 10
Meadow Clo. E4 CE26 39
Meadow Clo. SE6 CE49 77
Meadow Clo. SW20 BQ52 85
Meadow Clo., BF18 18
Bricket Wood
Meadow Clo., BK11 9
London Colney
Meadow Clo., Barn. BR25 28
Meadow Clo., Brwd. DE29 122
The Meadows
Meadow Clo., Chis. CL49 78
Meadow Clo., Enf. CD22 30
Meadow Clo., Esher BH55 84
Meadow Clo., Hat. BQ15 10
Meadow Clo., Houns. BF46 74
Meadow Clo., Nthlt. BF37 54
Meadow Clo., Pur. BW60 95
Meadow Clo., Rich. BL47 75
Meadow Clo., Ruis. BB32 44
Meadow Clo., S.le H. DK41 71
Lower Cres.
Meadow Clo., St.Alb. BK17 18
Meadow Clo., Sutt. BT55 86
Meadow Clo., Walt. BE56 93
Meadow Clo., Wind. AQ46 72
Meadow Cross, Wal.Abb. CG20 22
Meadow Ct., Epsom BN60 94
Meadow Ct., Harl. CN13 13
Meadow Ct., Stai. AV48 72
Moor La.
Meadow Dell, Hat. BO12 10
Meadow Dr. N10 BV31 47
Meadow Dr. NW4 BQ30 37
Meadow Dr., Amer. AP22 25
Meadow Dr., Sev. CU65 107
Lambarde Rd.
Meadow Dr., Wok. AV65 100
Meadow Garth NW10 BN36 55
Meadow Gdns., Edg. BM29 37
Meadow Gdns., Stai. AU49 72
Meadow Grn., Welw.G.C. BQ 8 5
Meadow Hill, N.Mal. BO53 85
Meadow Hill, Pur. BW60 95
Meadow La., Eton AO43 61
Meadow La., Lthd. BG64 102
Meadow Mead, Rad. BH20 18
Meadow Ms. SW8 BX43 66
Meadow Pl. SW8 BX43 66
Meadow Rd. SW19 BT50 76
Meadow Rd. SW8 BX43 66
Meadow Rd., Ash. BL62 103
Meadow Rd., Ashf. BA49 73
Meadow Rd., B.Wd. BM23 28
Meadow Rd., Bark. CN36 58
Meadow Rd., Berk. AQ12 7
Meadow Rd., Brom. CG51 88
Meadow Rd., Bush. BF25 27
Meadow Rd., Dag. CQ36 59
Meadow Rd., Epp. CN18 22
Meadow Rd., Esher BH57 93
Meadow Rd., Felt. BE48 74
Meadow Rd., Grav. DG48 81
Meadow Rd., Grays DD40 71
Meadow Rd., Guil. AT68 109
Meadow Rd., Hem.H. AZ16 17
Meadow Rd., Loug. CK25 31
Meadow Rd., Northfleet DE47 81
Meadow Rd., Pnr. BE31 45
Meadow Rd., Rom. CS33 50
Meadow Rd., Slou. AS42 62
Meadow Rd., Sthl. BE40 54
Meadow Rd., Sutt. BU56 95
Meadow Rd., Vir.W. AP53 82
Meadow Rd., Wat. BC20 17
Meadow Ri., Couls. BW60 95
Meadow Ri., Ing. DC19 24
Meadow Row SE1 BZ41 4
Meadow Row SE1 BZ41 67
Meadow Stile, Croy. BZ55 87
High St.
Meadow Vw. Rd., Hayes BA38 53
Meadow Vw. Rd., Th.Hth. BY53 86
Meadow Vw., Ch.St.G. AQ27 34
Meadow Vw., Orp. CP52 89
Meadow Vw., Sid. CO47 79
Meadow Way NW9 BN32 46
Meadow Way, Bookham BF65 102
Meadow Way, Chess. BL56 94
Meadow Way, Chig. CM27 40
Meadow Way, Dart. CY47 80
Meadow Way, AJ41 61
Dorney Reach
Meadow Way, Fifield AH44 61
Meadow Way, Hem.H. AW15 8
Meadow Way, Horsley BA66 110
Meadow Way, Kings L. AZ18 17
Meadow Way, Orp. CL55 88
Meadow Way, Pot.B. BS20 20
Meadow Way, Reig. BS72 121
Meadow Way, Rick. AX26 35
Meadow Way, Ruis. BC33 44
Meadow Way, Saw. CR 6 6
Meadow Way, Tad. BR62 103
Meadow Way, The, Har. BH30 36
Meadow Way, Upmin. CY35 51
Meadow Way, Wat. BB17 17
Meadow Way, Wem. BK35 45
Meadow Way, Wey. AW56 92
Meadow Way, Wind. AQ46 72
Meadow Waye, Houns. BE43 64
Meadow Wk. E18 CH31 49
Meadow Wk., Dag. CQ36 59
Meadow Wk., Dart. CV49 80
Meadow Wk., Epsom BO57 94
Meadow Wk., Tad. BP65 103
Meadow Wk., Wall. BV55 86
Meadow, The, Chis. CM50 78
Meadowbank Clo. SW6 BQ43 65
Meadowbank Gdns., BC44 63
Houns.
Meadowbank NW3 BU36 1
Meadowbank NW3 BU36 56
Meadowbank Rd. NW9 BN33 46
Meadowbank SE3 CG45 68
Meadowbank, Surb. BL53 85
Meadowbank, Twick. BK47 74
Meadowbanks, Barn. BP25 28
Meadowbrook Clo., Slou. AV44 62
Meadowbrook Rd., Dor. BJ71 119
Meadowcourt Rd. SE3 CG45 68
Meadowcroft Clo. N13 BY27 38
Meadowcroft Rd. N13 BY27 38
Meadowcroft, Brom. CK52 88
Meadowcroft, Bush. BF25 27
Clay Hill
Meadowcroft, Ger.Cr. AR30 34
Meadowcroft, St.Alb. BJ15 9
Meadowlands, Cob. BC60 92
Meadowlands, Guil. AW68 110
Meadowlands, Horn. CW33 51
Meadowlands, Oxt. CH70 115
Meadowlands, Sev. CW63 108
Meadows Clo. E10 CE34 48
Meadows Clo., Brwd. DE29 122
The Meadows
Meadows End, Sun. BC51 83
Meadows Leigh Clo., BA55 83
Wey.
Meadows, The, Amer. AP23 25
Meadows, The, Brwd. DE29 122
Meadows, The, Guil. AR72 118
Meadows, The, Orp. CP57 98
Meadows, The, Saw. CR 6 6
Meadows, The, Sev. CQ60 98
Meadows, The, Welw. BT 8 5
G.C.
Meadowside Rd., Sutt. BR58 94
Meadowside Rd., Upmin. CY35 51
Meadowside SE9 CJ45 68
Meadowside, Beac. AP29 34
Meadowside, Dart. CW47 80
Meadowside, Lthd. BF65 102
Meadowside, Twick. BK47 74
Meadowside, Walt. BD55 84
Meadowsweet Clo. E16 CJ39 58
Monarch Dr.
Meadowview Rd. SE6 CD49 77
Meadowview Rd., Bex. CQ46 79
Meadowview Rd., Epsom BO58 94
Meadowview, Shep. BA54 83
Russell Rd.
Meads La., Ilf. CN33 49
Meads Rd. N22 BY30 38
Meads Rd., Edg. BM29 37
Meads Rd., Enf. CD23 30
Meads Rd., Guil. AT70 118
Meads, The, Berk. AP12 7
Meads, The, Edg. BN29 37
Meads, The, St.Alb. BF18 18
Meads, The, Sutt. BO55 85
Meads, The, Upmin. CZ34 51
Meads, The, Uxb. AY38 53
Meadsway, Brwd. DA28 42
Meadvale Rd. W5 BJ38 54
Meadvale Rd., Croy. CA54 87
Meadway Clo. NW11 BS32 47
Meadway Clo., Barn. BS24 29
Meadway Clo., Pnr. BF29 36
High Banks Rd.
Meadway Clo., Stai. AW50 73
Meadway Clo., Twick. BK49 74
Meadway Ct. NW11 BS32 47
Meadway Dr., Wey. AX57 92
Meadway Dr., Wok. AR61 100
Meadway Gate NW11 BS32 47
Meadway Gdns., Ruis. BA32 44
Meadway N14 BW27 38
Meadway NW11 BS32 47
Meadway Pk., Ger.Cr. AR33 43
Meadway SW20 BQ52 85
Meadway, Ashf. AZ49 73
Meadway, Barn. BR24 28
Meadway, Berk. AS12 7
Meadway, Bookham BE67 111
Meadway, Couls. BX62 104
Meadway, Enf. CC21 30
Meadway, Epsom BM59 94
Meadway, Esher BF58 93
Meadway, Grays DE42 71
Meadway, Guil. AU68 109
Meadway, Hodd. CE13 12
Meadway, Ilf. CN35 49
Meadway, Oxshott BH60 93
Meadway, Rich. BG47 74
Meadway, Rom. CT30 41
Meadway, Ruis. BA32 44
Meadway, Sev. CQ60 98
Meadway, Stai. AW50 73
Meadway, Surb. BN54 85
Meadway, Wall. BV56 95
Meadway, The SE3 CF44 67
Meadway, The, Buck.H. CJ26 40
Meadway, The, Cuff. BX18 20
Meadway, The, Loug. CK25 31
Meadway, The, Orp. CO56 98
Meadway, Wdf.Grn. CJ28 40
Meadway, Welw.G.C. BR 9 5
Meaford Way SE20 CB50 77
Meakin Est. SE1 CA41 4
Meakin Est. SE1 CA41 67
Meald St. SE14 CD44 67
Meanley Rd. E12 CK35 49
Meard St. W1 BW39 1
Meard St. W1 BW39 56
Meare Clo., Tad. BQ65 103
Meath Clo., Orp. CO53 89
Meath Rd. E15 CG37 58
Meath Rd., Ilf. CM34 49
Meath St. SW11 BV44 66
Meautys, St.Alb. BF15 9
Mechanics Pass. SE8 CE43 67
Mecklenburgh Pl. WC1 BX38 2
Mecklenburgh Pl. WC1 BX38 56
Guilford St.
Mecklenburgh Sq. WC1 BX38 2
Mecklenburgh Sq. WC1 BX38 56
Medburn St. NW1 BW37 1
Medburn St. NW1 BW37 56
Medcalf Rd., Enf. CD22 30
Medcroft Gdns. SW14 BN45 65
Mede Clo., Stai. AR47 72
Mede Fld., Lthd. BG65 102
Highfields
Medebourne Clo. SE3 CH45 68
Medesenge Way N13 BY29 38
Wolves La.
Medfield St. SW15 BP47 75
Medhurst Clo. E3 CD37 57
Medhurst Cres., Grav. DJ48 81
Medhurst Gdns., Grav. DJ48 81
Medhurst Rd. E3 CD37 57
Arbery Rd.
Median Rd. E5 CC35 48
Medick Ct., Grays DF43 71
Medlar Rd.
Medina Av., Esher BH55 84
Medina Gro. N7 BY34 47
Medina Rd. N7 BY34 47
Medina Rd., Grays DE42 71
Medlake Rd., Egh. AU50 72
Medland Clo., Wall. BV54 86
Medlar Clo., Guil. AR69 118
Medlar Clo., Nthlt. BD37 54
Medlar Rd., Grays DF43 71
Medlar St. SE5 BZ44 67
Medley Rd. NW6 BS36 56
Medman Clo., Uxb. AX37 53
Chiltern View Rd.
Medora Rd. SW2 BX47 76
Medora Rd., Rom. CS31 50
Medusa Rd. SE6 CE47 77
Medway Bldgs. E3 CD37 57
Medway Rd.
Medway Clo., Croy. CC53 87
Medway Clo., Ilf. CM35 49
Loxford La.
Medway Dr., Grnf. BH37 54
Medway Gdns., Wem. BJ35 45
Medway Ms. E3 CD37 57
Medway Rd.
Medway Par., Grnf. BH37 54
Welland Gdns.
Medway Rd. E3 CD37 57
Medway Rd., Dart. CU45 69
Medway Rd., Hem.H. AY11 8
Medway St. SW1 BW41 3
Medway St. SW1 BW41 66
Medway, Wat. BD20 18
Medwick Ms., Hem.H. AZ11 8
Hunters Oak
Medwin St. SW4 BX45 66
Meek St. SW10 BT43 66
Ulverdale Rd.
Meerbrook Rd. SE3 CJ45 68
Meeson Rd. E15 CG37 58
Meeson St. E5 CD35 48
Meesons La., Grays DC42 71
Meeting Fields Path E9 CC36 57
Homerton Ter.
Meeting House La. SE15 CB44 67
Meetinghouse Alley E1 CB40 57
Chandler St.
Megg La., Kings L. AW18 17
Meggs Pl. E1 CB39 57
Kingward St.
Mehetabel Rd. E9 CC35 48
Melanda Clo., Chis. CK49 78
Melanie Clo., Bexh. CQ44 69
Melba Gdns., Til. DG43 71
Melba Way SE13 CE44 67
Melbourne Av. N13 BX29 38
Melbourne Av. W13 BJ40 54
Melbourne Av., Pnr. BF31 45
Melbourne Clo. E5 CC35 48
Clapton Park Est.
Melbourne Clo., Orp. CN54 88
Melbourne Clo., St.Alb. BH11 9
Melbourne Clo., Uxb. AZ35 44
Melbourne Clo., Wall. BW56 95
Melbourne Ct. SE20 CB50 77
Melbourne Ct., Welw.G.C. BP 8 5
Melbourne Flds. SW9 BY44 66
Melbourne Gdns., Rom. CQ31 50
Melbourne Gro. SE22 CA45 67
Melbourne Ms. SE6 CF47 77
Laleham Rd.
Melbourne Ms. SW9 BY44 66
Melbourne Pl. WC2 BX40 56
Melbourne Rd. E10 CE33 48
Melbourne Rd. E17 CD31 48
Melbourne Rd. E6 CK37 58
Melbourne Rd. SW19 BS51 86
Melbourne Rd., Bush. BF25 27
Melbourne Rd., Ilf. CL33 49
Melbourne Rd., Tedd. BK50 74
Melbourne Rd., Til. DF44 71
Melbourne Rd., Wall. BV56 95
Melbourne Sq. SW9 BY44 66
Brixton Rd.
Melbourne Ter. SW6 BS43 66
Britannia Rd.
Melbourne Way, Enf. CA25 30
Melbury Av., Sthl. BF41 64
Melbury Clo., Cher. AW54 83
London St.
Melbury Clo., Chis. CK50 78
Melbury Clo., Esher BJ57 93
Melbury Clo., Wey. AW60 92
Melbury Ct. W8 BR41 65
Melbury Dr. SE5 CA43 67
Sedgmoor Pl.
Melbury Gdns. SW20 BP51 85
Melbury Rd. W14 BR41 65
Melbury Rd., Har. BL32 46
Melbury Ter. NW1 BU38 56
Harewood Av.
Melcombe Gdns., Har. BL32 46
Melcombe Pl. NW1 BU39 1
Melcombe Pl. NW1 BU39 56
Melcombe St. NW1 BU38 1
Melcombe St. NW1 BU38 56
Meldon Clo. SW6 BS44 66
Meldrum Clo., Orp. CP54 89
Killewarren Way
Meldrum Clo., Oxt. CG69 115
Meldrum Rd., Ilf. CO34 50
Melfield Gdns. SE6 CF49 77
Melford Av., Bark. CN36 58
Melford Rd. E11 CG34 49
Melford Rd. E13 CH38 58
Melford Rd. E17 CD31 48
Melford Rd. E6 CK38 58
Melford Rd. SE22 CB47 77
Melford Rd., Ilf. CM34 49
Melfort Av., Th.Hth. BY52 86
Melfort Rd., Th.Hth. BY52 86
Melgund Rd. N5 BY35 47
Melina Clo., Hayes BA39 53
Middleton Rd.
Melina Pl. NW8 BT38 1
Melina Pl. NW8 BT38 56
Melina Rd. W12 BP41 65
Melior Pl. SE1 CA41 4
Snowsfields
Melior St. SE1 BZ41 4
Melior St. SE1 BZ41 67
Weston St.
Meliot Rd. SE6 CF48 77
Melksham Clo., Rom. CW29 42
Melksham Dr., Rom. CW29 42
Melksham Gdns., Rom. CW29 42
Melksham Grn., Rom. CW29 42
Mell St. SE10 CG42 68
Meller Clo., Croy. BX55 86
Melling St. SE18 CN43 68
Mellings, The, Hem.H. AZ11 8
Mellish Clo., Bark. CN37 58
Mellish St. E14 CE41 67
Mellison Rd. SW17 BU49 76
Mellitus St. W12 BO39 55
Mellor Clo., Walt. BE54 84
Mellow Clo., Bans. BS60 95
Mellow La. E., Hayes BA38 53
Mellow La., Uxb. BA38 53
Mellows Rd., Ilf. CK31 49
Mellows Rd., Wall. BW56 95
Mells Cres. SE9 CK49 78
Melody Rd. SW18 BT46 76
Melody Rd., West. CH62 106
Melon Pl. W8 BS41 66
Kensington Church St.
Melon Rd. SE15 CA44 67
Melrose Av. N22 BY30 38
Melrose Av. NW2 BP35 46
Melrose Av. SW16 BX52 86
Melrose Av. SW19 BR48 75
Melrose Av., B.Wd. BM25 28
Melrose Av., Grnf. BF37 54
Melrose Av., Mitch. BV50 76
Melrose Av., Pot.B. BS19 20
Melrose Av., Twick. BF47 74
Melrose Clo. SE12 CH47 78
Melrose Clo., Grnf. BF37 54
Melrose Clo., Hayes BC39 53
Melrose Cres., Orp. CM56 97
Melrose Ct. W13 BJ40 54
Broadway
Melrose Dr., Sthl. BF40 54
Melrose Gdns. W6 BQ41 65
Melrose Gdns., Edg. BM30 37
Melrose Gdns., N.Mal. BN52 85
Melrose Gdns., Walt. BD56 93
Melrose Pl., Wat. BB22 26
Melrose Rd. SW13 BO44 65
Melrose Rd. SW18 BR46 75
Melrose Rd. SW19 BS51 86
Melrose Rd. W3 BM41 65
Melrose Rd., Couls. BV61 104
Melrose Rd., Pnr. BE31 45
Melrose Rd., West. CJ61 106
Melrose Rd., Wey. AZ56 92
Melrose Ter. W6 BQ41 65
Melsa Rd., Mord. BT53 86
Melsted Rd., Hem.H. AW13 8
Melstock Av., Upmin. CY35 51
Meltham Way SE16 CB42 67
Egan Way
Melthorne Dr., Ruis. BD34 45
Melthorpe Gdns. SE3 CJ44 68
Melton Clo., Ruis. BD33 45
Melton Ct. SW7 BT42 3
Melton Ct. SW7 BT42 66
Melton Fields, Epsom BN58 94
Melton Pl.
Melton Gdns., Rom. CT33 50
Melton Pl., Epsom BN58 94
Melton Rd., Red. BW68 113
Melton St. NW1 BW38 1
Melton St. NW1 BW38 56
Melville Av. SW20 BP50 75
Melville Av., Grnf. BH35 45
Melville Av., S.Croy. CA56 96
Melville Clo., Uxb. BA34 44
Melville Ct. W12 BP41 65
Melville Gdns. N13 BY28 38
Melville Rd. E17 CD31 48
Melville Rd. N1 BZ37 2
Essex Rd.
Melville Rd. NW10 BN36 55
Melville Rd. SW13 BP44 65
Melville Rd., Rain. CU38 59
Melville Rd., Rom. CR29 41
Melville Rd., Sid. CP48 79
Melville St. N1 BZ36 2
Melville St. N1 BZ36 57
Essex Rd.
Melville Villas Rd. W3 BO40 55
Melvin Rd. SE20 CC51 87
Melvin Shaw, Lthd. BK64 102
Melvyn Clo., Chsnt. BY17 20
Melyn Clo. N19 BW35 47
Anson Rd.
Memel Ct. EC1 BZ38 2
Baltic St.
Memel St. EC1 BZ38 57
Baltic St.
Memess Path SE18 CL43 68
Engineer Clo.
Memorial Av. E15 CG38 58
Memorial Clo., Houns. BF43 64
Mendip Clo. SE26 CC49 77
Peak Hill Av.
Mendip Clo. SW19 BR48 75
Queensmere Rd.
Mendip Clo., Hayes BA43 63
Pennine Way
Mendip Clo., Slou. AT42 62
Mendip Clo., St.Alb. BK11 9
Chiltern Rd.
Mendip Cres. SW11 BT45 66
Mendip Dr. NW2 BQ34 46
Mendip Rd. SW11 BT45 66
Mendip Rd., Bexh. CT44 69
Mendip Rd., Bush. BG25 27
Mendip Rd., Horn. CU33 50
Mendip Rd., Ilf. CN32 49
Mendip Way, Hem.H. AY12 8
Mendlesham, Welw.G.C. BU 8 5
Mendora Rd. SW6 BR43 65
Mendoza Clo., Horn. CW32 51
Menelik Rd. NW2 BR35 46
Menlo Gdns. SE19 BZ50 77
Menotti St. E2 CB38 57
Dunbridge St.
Menthone Pl., Horn. CV33 51
North St.
Mentmore Clo., Har. BK32 45
Mentmore Rd., St.Alb. BG14 9
Mentmore Ter. E8 CB36 57
Meon Clo., Tad. BP64 103
Meon Rd. W3 BN41 65
Meopham Rd., Mitch. BW51 86
Mepham Cres., Har. BG29 36
Mepham Gdns., Har. BG29 36
Mepham St. SE1 BX40 4
Mepham St. SE1 BX40 56
Mera Dr., Bexh. CR45 69
Merbury Clo. SE13 CF46 77
Hither Green La.
Mercator Rd. SE13 CF45 67
Mercer Av. WC2 BX39 2
Endell St.
Mercer Clo., T.Ditt. BJ54 84
Mercer Pl., Pnr. BD30 36
Mercer St. WC2 BX39 2
Mercer St. WC2 BX39 56
Mercer Wk., Uxb. AX36 53
High St.
Merceron St. E1 CB38 57
Mercers Clo. SE10 CG42 68
Tunnel Av.
Mercers Pl. W6 BQ42 65
Mercers Rd. N19 BW34 47
Mercers Row, St.Alb. BG14 9
Mercers, Harl. CL12 13
Mercers, Hem.H. AY12 8
Merchant St. E3 CD38 57
Merchiston Rd. SE6 CF48 77
Merchland Rd. SE9 CM47 78
Mercia Gro. SE13 CF45 67
Mercia Wk., Wok. AS62 100
Church St. W.
Mercian Way, Slou. AL40 61
Mercier Rd. SW15 BR46 75
Mercury Gdns., Rom. CT31 50
Mercury Rd., Brent. BK42 64
Mercury Way SE14 CC43 67
Mercury Wk., Hem.H. AY12 8
Mercy Ter. SE13 CE45 67
Mere Clo. SW19 BQ47 75
Mere Clo., Orp. CL55 88
Mere End, Croy. CC54 87
Mere Rd., Shep. AZ53 83
Mere Rd., Slou. AP41 62
Mere Rd., Tad. BP65 103
Mere Rd., Wey. BA55 83
Mere Side, Orp. CL55 88
Mere, The, Slou. AP41 62
Mere Rd.
Merebank La., Wall. BX56 95
Meredith Av. NW2 BQ35 46
Meredith Clo., Pnr. BD29 36
Meredith Rd., Grays DG42 71
Meredith St. E13 CH38 58
Meredith St. EC1 BY38 2
Meredith St. EC1 BY38 56
Meredyth Rd. SW13 BP44 65
Merefield Gdns., Tad. BQ63 103
Merefield, Saw. CQ 6 6
Brook Rd.
Mereside Pl., Vir.W. AQ54 82
Meretone Clo. SE4 CD45 67
Meretune Ct., Mord. BR52 85
Merevale Cres., Mord. BT53 86
Mereway Rd., Twick. BG47 74

Merewood Clo., Brom. CL51 88
Merewood Rd., Bexh. CS44 69
Mereworth Clo., Brom. CG53 88
Mereworth Dr. SE18 CL43 68
Merganser Gdns. SE28 CM41 68
Avocet Ms.
Meriden Clo., Brom. CJ51 88
Meriden Clo., Ilf. CM30 40
Meriden Way, Wat. BE21 27
Meridian Est. SE7 CH42 68
Meridian Rd. SE7 CJ43 68
Meridian Wk. N18 CA29 39
Merifield Rd. SE9 CJ45 68
Merino Pl., Sid. CO46 79
Merivale Rd. SW15 BR45 65
Merivale Rd., Har. BG33 45
Merland Grn., Tad. BQ63 103
Merland Ri., Epsom BQ63 103
Merle Av., Uxb. AW30 35
Merlewood Clo., Cat. BZ63 105
Ninehams Rd.
Merlewood Dr., Chis. CK51 88
Merlewood, Sev. CU65 107
Merley Ct. NW9 BN33 46
Merlin Clo., Croy. CA55 87
Merlin Clo., Ilf. CP28 41
Merlin Clo., Rom. CS29 41
Merlin Clo., Slou. AT43 62
Merlin Cres., Edg. BL29 37
Merlin Gdns., Brom. CH48 78
Merlin Gdns., Rom. CS29 41
Merlin Gro., Beck. CD52 87
Merlin Gro., Ilf. CL29 40
Merlin Rd. E12 CJ34 49
Merlin Rd. N., Well. CO45 69
Merlin Rd., Rom. CS29 41
Merlin Rd., Well. CO45 69
Merlin St. WC1 BY38 2
Merlin St. WC1 BY38 56
Wilmington St.
Merling Cft., Berk. AP11 7
Kite Field
Merling Cft., Berk. AP12 7
Kite Field
Merlins Av., Har. BE34 45
Mermagen Dr., Rain. CU36 59
Mermaid Ct. SE1 BZ41 4
Mermaid Ct. SE1 BZ41 67
Mermers Gdns., Grav. DJ49 81
Merredene St. SW2 BX46 76
Merrick Rd., Sthl. BE41 64
Merrick Sq. SE1 BZ41 4
Merrick Sq. SE1 BZ41 67
Merridene N21 BY25 29
Merrielands Cres., Bark. CQ37 59
Merrilands Rd., Wor.Pk. BQ54 85
Merrilees Rd., Sid. CN47 78
Merrilyn Clo., Esher BJ57 93
Merriman Rd. SE3 CJ44 68
Merrington Rd. SW6 BS43 66
Merrion Av., Stan. BK28 36
Merritt Rd. SE4 CD46 77
Merritt Wk., Hat. BP15 10
Dellsome La.
Merrivale Av., Ilf. CJ31 49
Merrivale Gdns., Wok. AR62 100
Merrivale Ms., West Dr. AX40 53
Merrivale N14 BW25 29
Merrow Chase, Guil. AU70 118
Merrow Common Rd., Guil. AU69 118
Merrow Copse, Guil. AT70 118
Boxgrove La.
Merrow Croft, Guil. AU70 118
Merrow Dr., Hem.H. AV13 7
Merrow La., Guil. AU68 109
Merrow Rd., Sutt. BA58 94
Merrow St. SE17 BZ43 4
Merrow St. SE17 BZ43 67
Merrow St., Guil. AU69 118
Merrow Way, Croy. CF57 96
Merrow Wk. SE17 BZ42 4
Merrow Woods, Guil. AT69 109
Merrows Clo., Nthwd. BA29 35
Rickmansworth Rd.
Merry Hill Mt., Bush. BF26 36
Merry Hill Rd., Bush. BE25 27
Merrydown Way, Chis. CK51 88
Merryfield Gdns., Stan. BK28 36
Merryfield SE3 CG44 68
Merryfields, Uxb. AX37 53
Merryhill Clo. E4 CE26 39
Merryhills Clo., West. CJ61 106
Merryhills Dr., Enf. BW24 29
Merrylands Ct., Lthd. BE65 102
Merrylands Rd.
Merrylands Rd., Lthd. BE65 102
Merrylands, Cher. AV55 82
Merrymeet, Bans. BU60 95
Merrywood Pk., Reig. BS69 121
Mersey Av., Upmin. CY32 51
Mersey Pl., Hem.H. AY11 8
Mersey Rd. E17 CD31 48
Mersey Wk., Nthlt. BF37 54
Leander Rd.
Mersham Dr. NW9 BM32 46
Mersham Pl. SE20 CB51 87
Mersham Rd., Th.Hth. BZ52 87
Merstham Rd., Red. BY68 113
Merten Rd., Rom. CQ33 50
Merthyr Ter. SW13 BP43 65
Mertins Rd. SE15 CC46 77
Ivydale Rd.
Merton Abbey Sta. Rd. SW19 BT51 86
Merton Av. W4 BO42 65
Merton Av., Hart. DC52 90
Merton Av., Nthlt. BG35 45
Merton Av., Uxb. AZ36 53
Merton Gdns., Orp. CL53 88
Merton Gdns., Tad. BQ63 103
Merton Hall Gdns. SW20 BR51 85
Merton Hall Rd. SW19 BR50 75
Merton High St. SW19 BT50 76
Merton La. N6 BU34 47
Merton Mans. SW20 BQ51 85
Merton Pl. SE10 CF44 67
Merton Pl., Grays DG42 71
Merton Rd. E17 CF32 48
Merton Rd. SE25 CB53 87
Merton Rd. SW18 BS46 76
Merton Rd. SW19 BS50 76
Merton Rd., Bark. CN36 58
Merton Rd., Enf. BZ22 30
Merton Rd., Har. BG33 45
Merton Rd., Ilf. CN33 49
Merton Rd., Slou. AQ41 62
Merton Rd., Wat. BC24 26
Merton Ri. NW3 BU36 56
Merton Spur SW20 BP52 85
Bushey Rd.
Merton Way, E.Mol. BF52 84
Merton Way, Lthd. BJ63 102
Merton Way, Uxb. AZ36 53
Merton Wk., Lthd. BJ62 102
Merton Way
Merttins Rd. SE15 CC46 77
Mervan Rd. SW2 BY45 66
Mervyn Av. SE9 CM48 78
Mervyn Rd. W13 BJ41 64
Mervyn Rd., Shep. AZ54 83
Merwin Way, Wind. AL45 61
Meryfield Clo., B.Wd. BL23 28
Mesne Way, Sev. CT59 98
Messaline Av. W3 BN39 55
Messent Rd. SE9 CJ46 78
Messeter Pl. SE9 CL46 78
Messina Av. NW6 BS36 56
Metcalf Rd., Ashf. AZ49 73
Metcalf Wk., Felt. BE49 74
Creswell Clo.
Meteor St. SW1 BV45 66
Meteor Way, Wall. BX57 95
Metheringham Way NW9 BO30 37
Methley St. SE11 BY42 4
Methley St. SE11 BY42 66
Methuen Clo., Edg. BM29 37
Methuen Pk. N10 BV30 38
Methuen Rd., Belv. CR42 69
Methuen Rd., Bexh. CQ45 69
Methuen Rd., Edg. BM29 37
Methwold Rd. W10 BQ39 55
Meux Clo., Chsnt. CB19 21
Mews End, West. CJ62 106
Mews Pl., Wdf.Grn. CH28 40
Mews St. E1 CB40 4
Mews, The N1 BZ37 2
St. Paul St.
Mews, The N1 BZ37 57
St Paul St.
Mews, The, Harl. CN13 13
Commonside Rd.
Mews, The, Ilf. CJ32 49
Mews, The, Long. DC52 90
Bramblefield Clo.
Mews, The, Rom. CT31 50
Mews, The, Saw. CQ5 6
Mews, The, Slou. AP41 62
Mews, The, Twick. BJ46 74
Bridge Rd.
Mexfield Rd. SW15 BR46 75
Meyer Grn., Enf. CB22 30
Meyer Rd., Erith CS43 69
Meymott St. SE1 BY40 4
Meymott St. SE1 BY40 56
Meynell Cres. E9 CC36 57
Meynell Rd. E9 CC36 57
Meynell Rd., Rom. CU29 41
Meyrick Clo., Wok. AP61 100
Creston Av.
Meyrick Rd. NW10 BP36 55
Meyrick Rd. SW11 BT45 66
Mezen Clo., Nthwd. BA29 35
Miall Wk. SE26 CD49 77
Dillwyn Clo.
Micawber Av., Uxb. AZ39 53
Micawber St. N1 BZ38 2
Micawber St. N1 BZ38 57
Michael Faraday Ho. SE17 BZ42 4
Michael Faraday Ho. SE17 BZ42 67
Michael Gaynor Clo. W7 BH40 54
Michael Gdns., Grav. DJ49 81
Michael Gdns., Horn. CV31 51
Michael Rd. E11 CG33 49
Michael Rd. SE25 CA52 87
Michael Rd. SW6 BS44 66
Michaels Clo. SE13 CG45 68
Micheldever Rd. SE12 CG46 78
Michelham Down N12 BR28 37
Michelham Gdns., Tad. BQ63 103
Michelham Gdns., Twick. BJ48 74
Michels Row, Rich. BL45 65
Kew Foot Rd.
Michigan Av. E12 CK35 49
Micholls Av., Ger.Cr. AS28 34
Micklefield Rd., Hem.H. BA13 8
Micklefield Way, B.Wd. BL22 28
Mickleham By-pass, Dor. BJ67 111
Mickleham Clo., Orp. CN51 88
Mickleham Rd.
Mickleham Dr., Lthd. BK66 111
Mickleham Gdns., Sutt. BR57 94
Mickleham Rd., Orp. CN51 88
Mickleham Way, Croy. CF57 96
Micklem Dr., Hem.H. AV13 7
Micklethwaite Rd. SW6 BS43 66
Mid Croft, Ruis. BB33 44
Mid Cross La., Ger.Cr. AS28 34
Mid St., Red. BX72 121
Midcot Way, Berk. AP12 7
Middle Boy, Rom. CP24 32
Middle Clo., Amer. AP22 25
Middle Clo., Couls. BY63 104
Middle Clo., Epsom BO59 94
Middle Cres., Uxb. AU33 43
Middle Dene NW7 BN27 37
Middle Field NW8 BT37 56
Middle Fielde W13 BJ39 54
Templewood
Middle Furlong, Bush. BF24 27
Middle Grn. La., Surb. BL54 85
Alpha Rd.
Middle Grn., Brwd. DB22 33
Middle Grn., Slou. AS40 52
Middle Grn., Stai. AX50 73
Middle Hill, Egh. AR49 72
Middle Hill, Hem.H. AV13 7
Middle La. Ms. N8 BX32 47
Middle La.
Middle La. N8 BX32 47
Middle La., Epsom BO59 94
Middle La., Hem.H. AT18 16
Middle La., Tedd. BH50 74
Middle Meadow, Ch.St.G. AR27 34
Middle Ope, Wat. BC22 26
Middle Park Av. SE9 CJ46 78
Middle Path, Har. BG33 45
Middle Rd. E13 CH37 58
London Rd.
Middle Rd. SW16 BW51 86
Middle Rd., Barn. BU25 29
Middle Rd., Berk. AQ13 7
Middle Rd., Brwd. DE28 122
Middle Rd., Har. BG34 45
Middle Rd., Lthd. BJ64 102
Upper Fairfield Rd.
Middle Rd., Uxb. AU33 43
Middle Rd., Wal.Abb. CE19 21
Middle Row Pl. WC1 BY39 56
High Holborn
Middle Row W10 BR38 55
Middle St. EC1 BZ39 2
Middle St. EC1 BZ39 57
Bartholomew Clo.
Middle St., Bet. BM71 120
Middle St., Croy. BZ55 87
Middle St., Wal.Abb. CG14 13
Middle Temple La. EC4 BY39 2
Middle Temple La. EC4 BY39 56
Middle Way SW16 BW51 86
Middle Way, Erith CQ41 69
Middle Way, Hayes BD38 54
Middle Way, The, Har. BH30 36
Middle Way, Wat. BC22 26
Middle Wk., Wok. AS62 100
Church St. W.
Middlefield Av., Hodd. CE11 12
Middlefield Clo., St.Alb. BK12 9
Middlefield Gdns., Ilf. CL32 49
Middlefield NW8 BT37 56
Boundary Rd.
Middlefield Rd., Hodd. CE11 12
Middlefield, Hat. BP12 10
Lemsford Rd.
Middlefield, Welw.G.C. BR9 5
Middlefields, Croy. CD58 96
Middlegreen Rd., Slou. AR41 62
Middleham Gdns. N18 CB29 39
Middleham Rd. N18 CB29 39
Middleknights Hill, Hem.H. AW12 8
Middlemead Clo., Lthd. BE66 111
Middlemead Rd., Lthd. BE66 111
Middlesborough Rd. N18 CB29 39
Middlesex Rd., Mitch. BX53 86
Middlesex St. E1 CA39 2
Middlesex St. E1 CA39 57
Middlesex Wharf E5 CC34 48
Middleton Av. E4 CD28 39
Middleton Av., Grnf. BG37 54
Middleton Av., Sid. CO50 79
Middleton Bldgs. W1 BW39 56
Langham St.
Middleton Clo. E4 CD27 39
Middleton Dr. SE16 CC41 67
Middleton Dr., Pnr. BC31 44
Middleton Gdns., Ilf. CL32 49
Middleton Gro. N7 BX35 47
Middleton Hall La., Brwd. DC27 122
Middleton Industrial Estate Rd., Guil. AQ70 118
Middleton Ms. N7 BX35 47
Middleton Gro.
Middleton Pass. EC1 BY38 2
Middleton Rd. E8 CA36 57
Middleton Rd. NW11 BS33 47
Middleton Rd., Brwd. DC26 122
Middleton Rd., Cob. BD63 102
Middleton Rd., Epsom BN58 94
Eleanor Av.
Middleton Rd., Hayes BA39 53
Middleton Rd., Mord. BS53 86
Middleton Rd., N.Mal. BN51 85
Middleton Rd., Rick. AW26 35
Middleton St. E2 CB38 57
Canrobert St.
Middleton Way SE13 CF45 67
Middleton, Guil. AP71 118
Middleway NW11 BS32 47
Middlings Ri., Sev. CT66 116
Middlings Wood, Sev. CT66 116
Middlings, The, Sev. CT66 116
Midfield Av., Bexh. CS45 69
Midfield Pl. W1 BW38 1
Midfield Way, Orp. CO51 89
Midford Pl. W1 BW38 56
Tottenham Court Rd.
Midholm Clo. NW11 BS31 47
Midholm NW11 BS31 47
Midholm Rd., Croy. CD55 87
Midholm, Wem. BM33 46
Midhope Clo., Wok. AS63 100
Midhope Rd.
Midhope Gdns., Wok. AS63 100
Midhope Rd.
Midhope Rd., Wok. AS63 100
Midhope St. WC1 BX38 2
Midhope St. WC1 BX38 56
Argyle Wk.
Midhurst Av. N10 BV31 47
Midhurst Av., Croy. BY54 86
Midhurst Clo., Horn. CU35 50
Cowdray Way
Midhurst Gdns., Uxb. BA37 53
Midhurst Hill, Bexh. CR46 79
Midhurst Rd. W13 BJ41 64
Midland Pl. E14 CF42 67
Ferry St.
Midland Rd. E10 CF33 48
Midland Rd. NW1 BW37 1
Midland Rd. NW1 BW37 56
Midland Rd., Hem.H. AX13 8
Midland Ter. NW10 BO38 55
Midland Ter. NW2 BQ34 46
Midlothian Rd. E3 CD38 57
Burdett Rd.
Midmoor Rd. SW12 BW47 76
Midmoor Rd. SW19 BQ50 75
Midship Clo. SE16 CC40 57
Surrey Water Rd.
Midstrath Rd. NW10 BO35 46
Balnacraig Av.
Midsummer Av., Houns. BE45 64
Midway Av., Egh. AT52 82
Midway, St.Alb. BF15 9
Midway, Sutt. BR54 85
Midway, Walt. BC55 83
Midwood Clo. NW2 BP34 46
Miena Way, Ash. BK62 102
Miers Clo. E6 CL37 58
Mighell Av., Ilf. CJ32 49
Milberry Grn., Warl. CF62 105
Milborne Gro. SW10 BT42 3
Milborne Gro. SW10 BT42 66
Gilston Rd.
Milborne St. E9 CC36 57
Well St.
Milborough Cres. SE12 CG46 78
Milbourne La., Esher BG57 93
Milbrook, Esher BG57 93
Milburn Way, Green. CZ46 80
Milburn Wk., Epsom BO61 103
Milcombe Clo., Wok. AQ62 100
Inglewood
Milcote St. SE1 BY41 4
Milcote St. SE1 BY41 66
Mildenhall Rd. E5 CB35 48
Mildenhall Rd., Slou. AP39 52
Mildmay Av. N1 BZ36 57
Mildmay Gro. N1 BZ35 48
Mildmay Pk. N1 BZ35 48
Mildmay Pl., Sev. CT59 98
Mildmay Rd. N1 BZ35 48
Mildmay Rd., Ilf. CL34 49
Mildmay Rd., Rom. CS32 50
Mildmay St. N1 BZ36 57
Mildred Av., B.Wd. BM24 28
Mildred Av., Hayes BA42 63
Mildred Av., Nthlt. BF35 45
Mildred Av., Wat. BB24 26
Mildred Clo., Dart. CX46 80
Mildred Rd., Erith CS42 69
Mildreds Ct. EC4 BZ39 2
Poultry
Mile Clo., Wal.Abb. CF19 21
Mile End Pl. E1 CC38 57
Mile End Rd. E1 CC38 57
Mile End Rd. E3 CD38 57
Mile End, The E17 CC30 39
Mile House Clo., St.Alb. BJ15 9
Mile House La., St.Alb. BJ15 9
Mile Path, Wok. AQ63 100
Mile Rd., Wall. BV54 86
Miles Clo., Harl. CL11 13
Miles La. EC4 BZ40 4
Miles La. EC4 BZ40 57
Arthur St.
Miles La., Cob. BE60 93
Miles Pl. NW1 BT39 56
Miles Pl., Surb. BL52 85
Miles Rd. N8 BX31 47
Miles Rd., Epsom BN59 94
Miles Rd., Mitch. BT52 86
Miles St. SW8 BX43 66
Miles Way N20 BU27 38
Milespit Hill NW7 BP28 37
Milestone Clo., Sutt. BT57 95
Milestone Clo., Wok. AW64 101
Milestone Rd. SE19 CA50 77
Milestone Rd., Dart. CX47 80
Milfoil St. W12 BP40 55
Milford Clo. SE2 CQ43 69
Milford Clo., St.Alb. BK11 9
Milford Ct., Slou. AQ41 62
Wexham Rd.
Milford Gdns., Edg. BM29 37
Milford Gdns., Wem. BK35 45
Milford Gro., Sutt. BT56 95
Milford La. WC2 BX40 56
Milford La. WC2 BX40 4
Milford Ms. SW16 BX49 76
Milford Rd. W13 BJ40 54
Milford Rd., Grays DE40 71
Milford Rd., Sthl. BF40 54
Milford Way SE15 CA44 67
Sumner Estate
Milk St. E16 CL40 58
Milk St. EC2 BZ39 2
Milk St. EC2 BZ39 57
Milk St., Brom. CH50 78
Milk Yd. E1 CC40 57
Milking La., Kes. CJ59 97
Milkwell Gdns., Wdf.Grn. CH29 40
Milkwell Yd. SE5 BZ44 67
Denmark Hill
Milkwood Rd. SE24 BY46 76
Mill Av., Uxb. AX37 53
Mill Brook Rd., Orp. CP52 89
Mill Clo., Apsley End AZ16 17
Mill Clo., Cars. BV55 86
Mill Clo., Chesh. AP20 16
Mill Clo., Lthd. BF65 102
Mill Clo., Piccotts End AW11 8
Mill Clo., Wal.Cr. CD17 21
Mill Clo., Welw.G.C. BP8 5
Mill Clo., West Dr. AX41 63
Mill Corner, Barn. BR23 28
Mill Farm Clo., Pnr. BD30 36
Mill Farm Cres., Houns. BE47 74
Mill Field, Berk. AR12 7
Mill Field, Harl. CP9 6
Mill Field, Welw.G.C. BT7 5
Mill Fields, Saw. CQ5 6
Mill Gdns. SE26 CB49 77
Mill Green Rd., Mitch. BU54 86
Mill Grn. La., Hat. BR11 10
Mill Grn. Rd., Welw.G.C. BR8 5
Mill Hedge Clo., Cob. BE61 102
Mill Hill Gr. NW7 BO28 37
Mill Hill Gro. W3 BN40 55
Mill Hill Rd. SW13 BP44 65
Mill Hill Rd. W3 BM41 65
Mill Hill Ter. W3 BM40 55
Mill Hill, Brwd. DC26 122
Mill House Clo., Farn. CW54 90
Mill House La., Cher. AT52 82
Mill La. E4 CE24 30
Mill La. NW6 BR35 46
Mill La. SE18 CL42 68
Mill La., Brox. CD14 12
Mill La., Cars. BU56 95
Mill La., Ch.St.G. AQ27 34
Mill La., Chadwell Heath CQ32 50
Mill La., Chilworth AV73 118
Mill La., Chsnt. CG28 40
Mill La., Croy. BX55 86
Mill La., Doddinghurst DB21 33
Mill La., Dor. BJ71 119
Mill La., Downe CL58 97
Mill La., Egh. AU52 82
Mill La., Epsom BO58 94
Mill La., Eyns. CW54 90
Mill La., Ger.Cr. AS32 43
Mill La., Grays DB41 70
Mill La., Guil. AR71 118
Millbrook
Mill La., Harl. CQ9 6
Mill La., Ightham DB64 108
Mill La., Kelvedon Hatch CZ22 33
Mill La., Kings L. AZ18 17
Mill La., Kings.T. BL52 85
Mill La., Longham CT64 107
Mill La., Lthd. BJ64 102
Mill La., Moreton CV12 15
Mill La., Navestock CU23 32
Mill La., Ong. CY18 24
Mill La., Oxt. CG69 115
Mill La., Red. BW69 121
Mill La., Rick. BA25 26
Mill La., Saw. CQ6 6
Mill La., Sev. CV64 108
Mill La., Shoreham CT58 98
Mill La., Slou. AT45 62
Mill La., St. Mary Cray CO52 89
Mill La., The Chart CK69 115
Mill La., Ton. CX71 117
Mill La., Toot Hill CT18 23
Mill La., Underriver CY69 117
Mill La., Wal.Cr. CD17 21
Mill La., West. CM67 115
Mill La., Wey. AY60 92
Mill La., Wind. AN43 61
Mill La., Wok. AX63 101
Mill Lane Clo., Brox. CD14 12
Mill Mead Rd. N17 CB31 48
Mill Mead, Stai. AV49 72
Mill Mead, Wey. AY59 92
Mill Park Av., Horn. CW34 51
Mill Pl. E14 CD39 57
Mill Pl., Chis. CL51 88
Mill Pl., Dart. CU45 69
Mill Pl., Kings.T. BL52 85
Mill Pl., Slou. AR44 62
Mill Plat Av., Islw. BJ44 64
Mill Plat, Islw. BJ44 64
Mill Pond Rd., Dart. CW46 80
Mill Rd. E16 CH40 58
Mill Rd. SE13 CF45 67
Loampit Vale
Mill Rd. SW19 BT50 76
Mill Rd., Dart. CW49 80
Mill Rd., Epsom BO59 94
Mill Rd., Erith CS43 69
Mill Rd., Esher BF55 84
Mill Rd., Grav. DF47 81
Mill Rd., Grays CX43 70
Mill Rd., Ilf. CL34 49
Mill Rd., S.Ock. CY40 60
Mill Rd., Tad. BQ65 103
Mill Rd., Twick. BG48 74
Mill Rd., West Dr. AX41 63
Mill Ridge, Edg. BL28 37
Mill Row N1 CA37 2
Mill Row N1 CA37 57
Mill Row W4 BN42 65
Belmont Rd.
Mill Shaw, Oxt. CG69 115
Mill Shot Clo. SW6 BQ44 65
Mill St. SE1 CA41 4
Mill St. SE1 CA41 67
Mill St. W1 BV40 3
Mill St. W1 BV40 56
Mill St., Berk. AR13 7
Mill St., Colnbrook AU43 62
Mill St., Harl. CQ12 14
Mill St., Hem.H. AX15 8
Mill St., Kings T. BL52 85
Mill St., Red. BU71 121
Mill St., Slou. AP40 52
Mill St., West. CM67 115
Mill Vale, Brom. CG51 88
Mill View Gdns., Croy. CC55 87
Mill Way, Bush. BE23 27
Mill Way, Felt. BC46 73
Mill Way, Rick. AV26 34
Mill Yd. E1 CB40 4
Millais Av. E12 CL35 49
Millais Gdns., Edg. BM30 37
Millais Pl., Til. DG43 71
Millais Rd. E11 CF35 48
Millais Rd., Enf. CA25 30
Millais Rd., N.Mal. BO53 85
Millais Way, Epsom BN56 94
Millan Clo., Wey. AW58 92
Millard Ter., Dag. CR36 59
Millbank Av., Ong. CW18 24
Millbank SW1 BW42 3
Millbank SW1 BW42 66
Millbank Way SE12 CH46 78
Osberton Rd.
Millbourne Rd., Felt. BE49 74
Millbro, Swan. CU51 89

Millbrook Av., Well.	CM45	68
Millbrook Ct. SW15	BR46	75
Keswick Rd.		
Millbrook Gdns., Chadwell Heath	CQ32	50
Millbrook Gdns., Rom.	CT30	41
Millbrook Gdns., Wey.	AZ57	92
Millbrook Rd. N9	CB26	39
Millbrook Rd. SW9	BY45	66
Millbrook Rd., Bush.	BE23	27
Millbrook Way, Slou.	AV44	62
Mathisen Way		
Millbrook, Guil.	AR71	118
Millbrook, Wey.	BB56	92
Millcrest Rd., Chsnt.	BY17	20
Millender Wk. SE16	CC42	67
Miller Clo., Pnr.	BD30	36
Miller Rd. SW19	BT50	76
Miller Rd., Croy.	BX54	86
Miller Rd., Grav.	DK48	81
Miller Rd., Guil.	AU69	118
Miller St. NW1	**BW37**	**1**
Miller St. NW1	BW37	56
Miller Wk. SE11	**BY40**	**4**
Aquinas St.		
Millers Av. E8	CA35	48
Millers Clo. NW7	BP28	37
Millers Clo., Chig.	CO27	41
Millers Copse, Epsom	BN63	103
Millers Ct. W6	BO42	65
Millers Green Clo., Enf.	BY24	29
Millers Green Rd., Ong.	DA13	15
Millers La., Chig.	CO26	41
Millers La., Wind.	AP46	72
Millers Ri., St.Alb.	BH14	9
Millers Ter. E8	CA35	48
Millers Way W12	BQ41	65
Millersdale, Harl.	CL13	13
Millet Rd., Grnf.	BF38	54
Millfarm Av., Sun.	BB50	73
Millfield Av. E17	CD30	39
Millfield La. N6	BU34	47
Millfield La., New.A.G.	DC55	90
Millfield La., Tad.	BR66	112
Millfield Pl. N6	BV34	47
Millfield Rd., Edg.	BN30	37
Millfield Rd., Houns.	BE47	74
Millfield Rd., Sev.	CY57	99
Millfield Wk., Hem.H.	AZ15	8
Millfield, Sun.	BA51	83
Millfields Clo., Orp.	CO52	89
Millfields Rd. E5	CC35	48
Millfields, Ong.	CY17	24
Millford, Wok.	AQ62	100
Millgrove St. SW11	BV44	66
Millharbour E14	CE41	67
Millhaven Clo., Rom.	CO32	50
Millhill La., Bet.	BM70	120
Millhoo Ct., Wal.Abb.	CG20	22
Millhouse La., Wat.	BB17	17
Millhouse Pl. SE27	BY49	76
Millicent Rd. E10	CD33	48
Milligan St. E14	CD40	57
Milling Rd., Edg.	BN29	37
Millman St. WC1	**BX38**	**2**
Millman St. WC1	BX38	56
Millmans Ms. WC1	BX38	56
Millmark Gro. SE14	CD44	67
Millmarsh La., Enf.	CD23	30
Millmead Ter., Guil.	AR71	118
Millmead Way, Loug.	CK23	31
Millmead, Guil.	AR71	118
Millpond Est. SE16	CB41	67
Mills Clo., Uxb.	AZ37	53
Mills Cres., Sev.	CW62	108
Mills Ct. E11	CG34	49
Harrow Rd.		
Mills Ct. EC2	**CA38**	**2**
Mills Gro. E14	CF39	57
Mills Gro. NW4	BQ31	46
Mills Pl. NW8	**BT39**	**1**
Mills Rd., Walt.	BD56	93
Mills Row, W4	BN42	65
Bridge St.		
Mills Spur, Wind.	AQ47	72
Mills Way, Brwd.	DE26	122
Millshot Dr., Amer.	AO23	25
Millside Clo., Islw.	BJ44	64
Millside, Cars.	BU55	86
Millsom Clo. N20	BT27	38
Damville Clo.		
Millstead Clo., Tad.	BP65	103
Spindlewoods		
Millstone Clo., S.at H.	CY51	90
Millstream La., Slou.	AM40	61
Millstream Rd. SE1	**CA41**	**4**
Millstream Rd. SE1	CA41	67
Millthorn Clo., Rick.	AY25	26
Millview Clo., Reig.	BT69	121
Millwall Dock Rd. E14	CE41	67
Tiller St.		
Millward St. W10	BQ40	55
Charles Sq.		
Millwards, Hat.	BP14	10
Millway Gdns., Nthlt.	BE36	54
Millway NW7	BO28	37
Millway, Reig.	BT70	121
Millwell Cres., Chig.	CM28	40
Millwood Rd., Houns.	BG46	74
Millwood Rd., Orp.	CP52	89
Millwood St. W10	BQ39	55
Chesterton Rd.		
Milman Clo., Pnr.	BD30	36
Milman Rd. NW6	BQ37	55
Milmans St. SW10	BT43	66
Milne Est. SE18	CK42	68
Milne Field, Pnr.	BF29	36
Milne Gdns. SE9	CK46	78
Milne Pk. E., Croy.	CF59	96
Milne Pk. W., Croy.	CF59	96
Milne Way, Uxb.	AW30	35
Milner App., Cat.	CB64	105
Milner Clo., Cat.	CA64	105
Milner Clo., Wat.	BC20	17
Milner Ct., Bush.	BF26	36
Bridgewater Way		
Milner Dr., Cob.	BE59	93
Milner Dr., Twick.	BR47	74
Milner Pl. N1	**BY37**	**2**
Milner Pl. N1	BY37	56
Milner Rd. E15	CG38	58
Milner Rd. SW19	BS51	86
Milner Rd., Cat.	CA64	105
Milner Rd., Dag.	CP34	50
Milner Rd., Kings.T.	BK52	84
Milner Rd., Mord.	BT53	86
Milner Rd., Th.Hth.	BZ52	87
Milner Sq. N1	**BY36**	**2**
Milner Sq. N1	BY36	56
Milner St. EC1	**BY38**	**2**
Milner St. SW3	**BU42**	**3**
Milner St. SW3	BU42	66
Milnthorpe Rd. W4	BN43	65
Milo Rd. SE22	CA46	77
Milroy Av., Grav.	DF48	81
Milroy Wk. SE1	**BY40**	**4**
Milroy Wk. WC2	BY40	56
Rennie St.		
Milson Rd. W14	BQ41	65
Milstead Clo., Tad.	BP64	103
The Avenue		
Milton Av. E6	CJ36	58
Milton Av. N6	BW33	47
Milton Av. NW10	BN37	55
Milton Av. NW9	BM31	46
Milton Av., Barn.	BR25	28
Milton Av., Croy.	BZ54	87
Milton Av., Dor.	BG72	119
Milton Av., Ger.Cr.	AR31	43
Milton Av., Grav.	DH47	81
Milton Av., Horn.	CT34	50
Milton Av., Sev.	CR58	98
Milton Av., Sutt.	BT55	86
Milton Clo. N2	BT32	47
Milton Clo., Hayes	BC39	53
Milton Clo., Pnr.	BE29	36
Milton Clo., Slou.	AT45	62
Milton Clo., Sutt.	BT55	86
Milton Court Rd. SE14	CD43	67
Milton Cres., Ilf.	CM33	49
Milton Ct. EC2	**BZ39**	**2**
Milton Ct. EC2	BZ39	57
Milton St.		
Milton Ct., Kings.T.	BL49	75
Milton Ct., Uxb.	AZ34	44
Milton Ct., Wal.Abb.	CF20	21
Milton St.		
Milton Dene, Hem.H.	AZ10	8
Coleridge Cres.		
Milton Dr., B.Wd.	BM25	28
Milton Dr., Shep.	AY52	83
Milton Flds., Ch.St.G.	AQ27	34
Milton Gdns., Epsom	BO60	94
Milton Gdns., Til.	DG44	71
Milton Gro. N11	BW28	38
Milton Gro. N16	BZ35	48
Milton Hall Rd., Grav.	DH47	81
Milton Hill, Ch.St.G.	AQ27	34
Milton Lawns, Amer.	AO21	25
Milton Pk. N6	BW33	47
Milton Pl. N7	BY35	47
Georges Rd.		
Milton Pl., Grav.	DH46	81
Milton Rd. E17	CE31	48
Milton Rd. N15	BY31	47
Milton Rd. N6	BW33	47
Milton Rd. NW7	BP28	37
Milton Rd. NW9	BP33	46
Milton Rd. SE24	BY46	76
Milton Rd. SW14	BN45	65
Milton Rd. SW19	BT50	76
Milton Rd. W3	BN40	55
Milton Rd. W7	BH40	54
Milton Rd., Belv.	CR42	69
Milton Rd., Brwd.	DA28	42
Milton Rd., Cat.	BZ64	105
Milton Rd., Croy.	BZ54	87
Milton Rd., Egh.	AS49	72
Milton Rd., Grav.	DG46	81
Milton Rd., Grays	DD42	71
Milton Rd., Har.	BH31	45
Milton Rd., Hmptn.	BF50	74
Milton Rd., Mitch.	BV50	76
Milton Rd., Rom.	CU32	50
Milton Rd., Sev.	CT64	107
Milton Rd., Slou.	AO38	52
Milton Rd., Sutt.	BS55	86
Milton Rd., Swans.	DC46	81
Milton Rd., Uxb.	AZ35	44
Milton Rd., Wall.	BW57	95
Milton Rd., Walt.	BD55	84
Lindley Rd.		
Milton Rd., Well.	CN44	68
Milton Rd., Wey.	AW57	92
Milton St. E13	CH37	58
Greenwood Rd.		
Milton St. EC2	**BZ39**	**2**
Milton St. EC2	BZ39	57
Milton St., Dor.	BG72	119
Milton St., Swans.	DB46	80
Milton St., Wal.Abb.	CF20	21
Woollard St.		
Milton St., Wat.	BC22	26
Milton Way, West Dr.	AY42	63
Miltoncourt La., Dor.	BH71	119
Milverton Dr., Uxb.	BA35	44
Milverton Gdns., Ilf.	CN34	49
Milverton Rd. NW6	BQ36	55
Milverton St. SE11	**BY42**	**4**
Milverton St. SE11	BY42	66
Milverton Way SE9	CL49	78
Milward St. E1	CB39	57
Milward Wk. SE18	CL43	68
Spearman St.		
Milwards, Harl.	CL13	13
Mimas Rd., Hem.H.	AY12	8
Mimms Hall Rd., Pot.B.	BQ19	19
Mimms La., Pot.B.	BN19	19
Mimms La., Rad.	BM20	19
Mimosa Clo., Brwd.	DA25	33
Mimosa Clo., Orp.	CP55	89
Berrylands		
Mimosa Clo., Rom.	CV29	42
Mimosa Rd., Hayes	BD39	54
Mimosa Rd., Rom.	CV29	42
Mimosa St. SW6	BR44	65
Mina Av., Slou.	AR41	62
Mina Rd. SE17	**CA42**	**4**
Mina Rd. SE17	CA42	67
Mina Rd. SW19	BS51	86
Minard Rd. SE6	CG47	78
Minchen Rd., Harl.	CO10	6
Minchenden Cres. N14	BW27	38
Minchin Clo., Lthd.	BJ64	102
Mincing La. EC3	**CA40**	**4**
Mincing La. EC3	CA40	57
Mincing La., Wok.	AP58	91
Minden Rd. SE20	CB51	87
Minden Rd., Sutt.	BR55	85
Minehead Ct., Har.	BF34	45
Minehead Rd. SW16	BX49	76
Minehead Rd., Har.	BF34	45
Minera Ms. SW1	**BV42**	**3**
Minera Ms. SW1	BV42	66
Mineral St. SE18	CM42	68
Minerva Clo. SW9	BY43	66
Minerva Clo., Sid.	CN49	78
Minerva Dr., Wat.	BB21	26
Minerva Est. E2	CB37	57
Minerva Rd. E4	CE29	39
Minerva Rd. NW10	BN38	55
Minerva Rd., Kings.T.	BL51	85
Minerva St. E2	CB37	57
Minet Av. NW10	BO37	55
Minet Dr., Hayes	BC40	53
Minet Gdns. NW10	BO37	55
Minet Gdns., Hayes	BC40	53
Minet Rd. SW9	BY44	66
Minford Gdns. W14	BQ41	65
Minford Ho. W14	BQ41	65
Ming St. E14	CE40	57
Mingard Wk. N7	BX34	47
Ministry Way SE9	CK48	78
Miniver Pl. EC4	BZ40	57
Queen Victoria St.		
Mink Ct., Houns.	BD45	64
Minnersley Wk., Reig.	BS73	121
Castle Dr.		
Minniedale, Surb.	BL53	85
Minnow St. SE17	**CA42**	**4**
Minnow St. SE17	CA42	67
Minorca Rd., Wey.	AZ56	92
Minories EC3	**CA39**	**2**
Minories EC3	CA39	57
Minshull St. SW8	BW44	66
Wandsworth Rd.		
Minson Rd. E9	CC37	57
Minstead Gdns. SW15	BO46	75
Minstead Way, N.Mal.	BO53	85
Minster Av., Sutt.	BS55	86
Minster Clo., Hat.	BP13	10
Minster Dr., Croy.	CA56	96
Minster Gdns., E.Mol.	BE52	84
Minster Rd. NW2	BR35	46
Minster Rd., Brom.	CH50	78
Minster Way, Horn.	CW33	51
Minster Way, Slou.	AS41	62
Minster Wk. N8	BX31	47
Minsterley Av., Shep.	BB53	83
Minstrel Gdns., Surb.	BL52	85
Mint Gdns., Dor.	BJ71	119
Mint Rd., Bans.	BT61	104
Mint Rd., Wall.	BV56	95
Mint St. SE1	**BZ41**	**4**
Mint St. SE1	BZ41	67
Mint Wk., Croy.	BZ55	87
High St.		
Mint Wk., Warl.	CC62	105
Mint Wk., Wok.	AP62	100
Staveley Way		
Mintern Clo. N13	BY27	38
Mintern St. N1	**BZ37**	**2**
Mintern St. N1	BZ37	57
Minterne Av., Sthl.	BF42	64
Minterne Rd., Har.	BL32	46
Minterne Way, Hayes	BD39	54
Minton Ms. NW6	BS36	56
Lymington Rd.		
Mirabel Rd. SW6	BR43	65
Mirador Cres., Slou.	AQ40	52
Miramar Way, Horn.	CV35	51
Chevington Way		
Miranda Ho. N1	CA37	57
Purcell St.		
Miranda Rd. N19	BW33	47
Mirfield St. SE7	CJ41	68
Miriam Rd. SE18	CN42	68
Mirrie La., Uxb.	AU32	43
Mirror Path SE9	CJ48	78
Charlesfield		
Misbourne Av., Ger.Cr.	AR28	34
Misbourne Clo., Ger.Cr.	AS28	34
Misbourne Rd., Uxb.	AZ37	53
Misbourne Vale, Ger.Cr.	AR28	34
Miskin Rd., Dart.	CV47	80
Miskin Way, Grav.	DH50	81
Missden Dr., Hem.H.	BA14	8
Missenden Gdns., Mord.	BT53	86
Mission Gro. E17	CD32	48
Mission Pl. SE15	CB44	67
Mission Sq., Brent.	BL43	65
Pottery Rd.		
Mistletoe Clo., Croy.	CC54	87
Marigold Way		
Mistley Rd., Harl.	CO10	6
Mistys Field, Walt.	BD54	84
Mitcham Garden Vill., Mitch.	BV53	86
Mitcham Ind. Est., Mitch.	BV51	86
Mitcham La. SW16	BV50	76
Mitcham Pk., Mitch.	BU52	86
Mitcham Rd. E6	CK38	58
Mitcham Rd. SW17	BU49	76
Mitcham Rd., Croy.	BW53	86
Mitcham Rd., Ilf.	CN33	49
Mitchell Av., Grav.	DE48	81
Mitchell Clo. SE2	CP42	69
Mitchell Clo., Belv.	CS41	69
Mitchell Clo., Dart.	CW48	80
Mitchell Clo., Hem.H.	AS17	16
Lancaster Dr.		
Mitchell Clo., Orp.	CN55	88
Stapleton Rd.		
Mitchell Clo., Slou.	AN41	61
Mitchell Clo., St.Alb.	BG15	9
Mitchell Clo., Welw.G.C.	BT 8	5
Wellington Dr.		
Mitchell Rd. N13	BY28	38
Mitchell Rd., Orp.	CN56	97
Mitchell St. EC1	**BZ38**	**2**
Mitchell St. EC1	BZ38	57
Mitchell Way NW10	BN36	55
Mitchell Way, Brom.	CH51	88
Tweedy Rd.		
Mitchell Wk. E6	CK39	58
Oliver Gdns.		
Mitchell Wk., Amer.	AP22	25
Mitchell Wk., Swans.	DC47	81
Manor Rd.		
Mitchellbrook Way NW10	BN36	55
Mitchem Clo., Sev.	CZ57	99
Mitcheners La., Red.	CA70	114
Mitchison Rd. N1	BZ36	57
Mitchley Av., Pur.	BZ60	96
Mitchley Gro., S.Croy.	CB60	96
Mitchley Hill, S.Croy.	CA60	96
Mitchley Rd. N17	CB31	48
Mitchley Vw., S.Croy.	CB60	96
Mitford Rd. N19	BX34	47
Mitre Clo., Shep.	BA53	83
Gordon Dr.		
Mitre Clo., Sutt.	BT57	95
Mitre Ct. EC2	**BZ39**	**2**
Mitre Ct. EC2	BZ39	57
Wood St.		
Mitre Rd. E15	CG37	58
Mitre Rd. SE1	**BY41**	**4**
Mitre Rd. SE1	BY41	66
Mitre St. EC3	**CA39**	**2**
Mitre St. EC3	CA39	57
Mitre Way NW10	BP39	55
Mitre, The E14	CD40	57
Mixbury Gro., Wey.	BA57	92
Bridgewater Rd.		
Mixnams La., Cher.	AW52	83
Mizen Clo., Cob.	BD61	102
Mizen Way, Cob.	BD61	102
Moat Clo., Brwd.	DB21	33
Moat Clo., Bush.	BF25	27
Moatfield Rd.		
Moat Clo., Orp.	CN57	97
Moat Cres. N3	BS31	47
Basing Way		
Moat Ct., Ash.	BL62	103
Moat Dr. E13	CJ37	58
Boundary Rd.		
Moat Dr., Har.	BG31	45
Moat Dr., Ruis.	BB33	44
Moat Dr., Slou.	AR39	52
Moat Farm Rd., Nthlt.	BE36	54
Moat Gdns. SE28	CP40	59
Moat La., Erith	CU44	69
Moat Pl. SW9	BX45	66
Moat Pl. W3	BM39	55
Moat Side, Enf.	CC24	30
Durants Pk.		
Moat, The, N.Mal.	BO51	85
Moat, The, Ong.	CT18	23
Moatfield Rd., Bush.	BF25	27
Moats La., Red.	BY73	121
Moatside, Felt.	BD49	74
Moatwood Grn., Welw.G.C.	BR 8	5
Moberley Rd. SW4	BW47	76
Modbury Gdns. NW5	BV36	56
Queens Cres.		
Modder Pl. SW15	BQ45	65
Cardinal Pl.		
Model Bldgs. WC1	**BX38**	**2**
Model Cotts. SW14	BN45	65
Upper Richmond Rd.		
Model Cotts. W13	BJ41	64
Glenfield Rd.		
Model Farm Clo. SE9	CK48	78
Modena St. W10	BR39	55
Kensal Rd.		
Modern Ct. EC4	BY39	56
Farringdon St.		
Moelyn Ms., Har.	BJ32	45
Moffat Gdns., Mitch.	BT52	86
Moffat Rd. N13	BX29	38
Moffat Rd. SW17	BU49	76
Moffat Rd., Th.Hth.	BZ51	87
Moffats Clo., Hat.	BS16	20
Moffats La., Hat.	BR17	19
Moffatt Ct. SW19	BS49	76
Gap Rd.		
Mogador Rd., Tad.	BR67	112
Mogden La., Islw.	BH46	74
Moiety Rd. E14	CE41	67
Moir Clo., S.Croy.	CB58	96
Moira Clo. N17	CA30	39
Moira Rd. SE9	CK45	68
Moiravale, Kings.T.	BK51	84
Moland Mead SE16	CC42	67
Crane Mead		
Molash Rd., Orp.	CP52	89
Molasses Row SW18	BT45	66
Clove Hitch Quay		
Mole Abbey Gdns., E.Mol.	BF52	84
Mole Ct., Epsom	BN56	94
Mole Rd., Walt.	BD56	93
Mole Valley Pl., Ash.	BK63	102
Molember Ct., E.Mol.	BH52	84
Molember Rd., E.Mol.	BH53	84
Moles Hill, Lthd.	BG59	93
Molescroft SE9	CM48	78
Molesey Av., E.Mol.	BE53	84
Molesey Clo., Walt.	BE56	93
Molesey Dr., Sutt.	BR55	85
Molesey Park Av., E.Mol.	BF53	84
Molesey Park Clo., E.Mol.	BG53	84
Molesey Park Rd., E.Mol.	BF53	84
Molesey Rd., E.Mol.	BE53	84
Molesey Rd., Walt.	BD56	93
Molesford Rd. SW6	BS44	66
Molesham Clo., E.Mol.	BF52	84
Molesham Way, E.Mol.	BF52	84
Molesworth Rd., Cob.	BC60	92
Pennyfield		
Molesworth St. SE13	CF45	67
Molesworth, Hodd.	CE10	12
Mollands La., S.Ock.	DB38	60
Mollison Av., Enf.	CD25	30
Mollison Dr., Wall.	BW57	95
Mollison Way, Edg.	BM30	37
Molly Huggins Clo. SW12	BW47	76
Molteno Rd., Wat.	BC23	26
Molyneaux Av., Hem.H.	AS17	16
Molyneux Rd., Wey.	AZ56	92
Molyneux St. W1	**BU39**	**1**
Molyneux St. W1	BU39	56
Momples Rd., Harl.	CO10	6
Mona Rd. SE15	CC44	67
Mona St. E16	CG39	58
Monahan Av., Pnr.	BX59	95
Monarch Clo., Felt.	BB47	73
Monarch Clo., Til.	DG44	71
Monarch Clo., W.Wick.	CG56	97
Monarch Ct. N2	BT32	47
Monarch Dr. E16	CJ39	58
Monarch Ms. SW16	BY49	76
Monarch Rd., Belv.	CR41	69
Ambrooke Rd.		
Monarchs Way, Ruis.	BA33	44
Monarchs Way, Wal.Cr.	CD20	21
Monastery Gdns., Enf.	BZ23	30
Monaveen Gdns., E.Mol.	BF52	84
Monck St. SW1	**BW41**	**3**
Monck St. SW1	BW41	66
Monclar Rd. SE5	BZ45	67
Moncorvo Clo. SW7	**BU41**	**3**
Moncorvo Clo. SW7	BU41	66
Ennismore Gdns.		
Moncrieff Clo. E6	CK39	58
Linton Gdns.		
Moncrieff St. SE15	CB44	67
Monega Rd. E12	CJ36	58
Monega Rd. E7	CJ36	58
Money Av., Cat.	BZ64	105
Money Hill Rd., Rick.	AX26	35
Money Hole La., Welw.G.C.	BU 7	5
Money La., West Dr.	AX41	63
Money Rd., Cat.	BZ64	105
Mongers La., Epsom	BO58	94
Monica Clo., Wat.	BD23	27
Monier Rd. E3	CE36	57
Monivea Rd., Beck.	CD50	77
Monk Dr. E16	CG39	58
Monk Pass. E16	CG40	58
Monk Dr.		
Monk St. SE18	CL42	68
Monkchester Clo., Loug.	CK23	31
Monkey Island La., Maid.	AJ42	61
Monkfrith Av. N14	BV25	29
Monkfrith Clo. N14	BV26	38
Monkfrith Way N14	BV26	38
Monkhams Av., Wdf.Grn.	CH28	40
Monkhams Dr., Wdf.Grn.	CH28	40
Monkhams La., Wdf.Grn.	CH28	40
Monkleigh Rd., Mord.	BR52	85
Monks Av., Barn.	BT25	29
Monks Av., E.Mol.	BE53	84
Monks Chase, Brwd.	DE28	122
Monks Clo. SE2	CP42	69
New Rd.		
Monks Clo., Brox.	CE13	12
Monks Clo., Enf.	BZ23	30
Monks Clo., Ruis.	BD35	45
Monks Clo., St.Alb.	BH14	9
Monks Cres., Walt.	BC54	83
Monks Dr. W3	BM39	55
Monks Grn., Lthd.	BG64	102
Monks Gro., Loug.	CL25	31
Monks Horton Way, St.Alb.	BJ12	9
Monks Orchard Rd., Beck.	CE54	87
Monks Orchard, Dart.	CV48	80
Monks Pk. Gdns., Wem.	BM36	55
Monks Pk. Par., Wem.	BM36	55
Monks Pk., Wem.	BM36	55
Monks Pl., Cat.	CB64	105
Monks Rd., Bans.	BS61	104
Monks Rd., Enf.	BY23	29
Monks Rd., Vir.W.	AR52	82
Monks Rd., Wind.	AL44	61
Monks Ri., Welw.G.C.	BQ 6	5
Monks Way, Beck.	CE53	87
Monks Way, Orp.	CM54	88
Monks Way, Stai.	AX50	73
Bingham Dr.		
Monks Way, West Dr.	AY43	63
Monks Wk., Egh.	AV52	82
Monks Wk., Grav.	DD50	81
Rectory Meadow		
Monks Wk., Reig.	BS70	121
Monks Wk., Welw.G.C.	BQ 6	5
Monksdene Gdns., Sutt.	BS55	86
Monksmead, B.Wd.	BN24	28
Monkswell Ct. N10	BV30	38
Monkswell La., Couls.	BS65	104
Monkswick Rd., Harl.	CN10	6
Monkswood Av., Wal.Abb.	CF20	21
Monkswood Gdns., B.Wd.	BN24	28
Monkswood Gdns., Ilf.	CL31	49
Monkswood, Welw.G.C.	BQ 6	5
Monkton Rd., Well.	CN44	68
Monkton St. SE11	**BY42**	**4**
Monkton St. SE11	BY42	66
Monkville Av. NW11	BR31	46
Monkwell Sq. EC2	**BZ39**	**2**
Monkwell Sq. EC2	BZ39	57
Monmouth Av. E18	CH31	49
Monmouth Av., Kings.T.	BK50	74
Monmouth Clo., Mitch.	BX52	86
Monmouth Clo., Well.	CO45	69
Monmouth Pl. W2	BS39	56
Monmouth Rd. E6	CK38	58
Monmouth Rd. N9	CB27	39
Monmouth Rd. W2	BS39	56

Monmouth Rd., Dag. CQ35 50
Monmouth Rd., Hayes BB42 63
Monmouth Rd., Wat. BC24 26
Monmouth St. WC2 BX39 2
Monmouth St. WC2 BX39 56
Monnery Rd. N19 BW34 47
Monnow Grn., S.Ock. CY40 60
Monnow Rd.
Monnow Rd. SE1 CB42 4
Monnow Rd. SE1 CB42 67
Monnow Rd., S.Ock. CY40 60
Monnow Ter., Wok. AQ62 100
Mono La., Felt. BC48 73
Monoux Gro. E17 CD30 39
Monro Gdns., Har. BH29 36
Monroe Cres., Enf. CB23 30
Monroe Dr. SW14 BM46 75
Mons Way, Brom. CK53 88
Monsal Ct. E5 CC35 48
Clapton Park Est.
Monsell Gdns., Stai. AV49 72
Monsell Rd. N4 BY34 47
Monsey St. E1 CD38 57
Monson Rd. NW10 BP37 55
Monson Rd. SE14 CC43 67
Monson Rd., Brox. CD13 12
Monson Rd., Red. BU69 121
Montacre Clo. SE26 CB49 77
Montacute Rd. SE6 CD47 77
Montacute Rd., Bush. BH26 36
Montacute Rd., Croy. CF58 96
Montacute Rd., Mord. BT53 86
Montagu Cres. N18 CB28 39
Montagu Gdns. N18 CB28 39
Montagu Gdns., Wall. BW56 95
Montagu Mans. W1 BU39 1
Montagu Mans. W1 BU39 56
Montagu Ms. N. W1 BU39 1
Montagu Ms. S. W1 BU39 1
Montagu Ms. W. W1 BU39 1
Montagu Ms. W1 BU39 56
Montagu Pl. W1 BU39 1
Montagu Pl. W1 BU39 56
Montagu Rd. N18 CB28 39
Montagu Rd. N9 CC27 39
Montagu Rd. NW4 BP32 46
Montagu Row W1 BU39 1
Montagu Row W1 BU39 56
Montagu Sq. W1 BU39 56
Montagu St. W1 BU39 1
Montagu St. W1 BU39 56
Montague Av. SE4 CD45 67
Montague Av. W7 BH40 54
Montague Av., S.Croy. CA59 96
Montague Clo. SE1 BZ40 4
Montague Clo. SE1 BZ40 57
Montague Clo., Walt. BC54 83
Montague Ct. EC1 BZ39 57
Bartholomew Clo.
Montague Gdns. W3 BM40 55
Montague Ind. Est. N18 CC28 39
Montague Ms. W. W1 BU39 1
Montague Ms. W1 BU39 1
Montague Pl. WC1 BW39 1
Montague Pl. WC1 BW39 56
Montague Rd. E11 CG34 49
Montague Rd. E8 CB35 48
Montague Rd. N15 CB31 48
Montague Rd. N8 BX32 47
Montague Rd. SW19 BS50 76
Montague Rd. W13 BJ39 54
Montague Rd. W7 BH40 54
Montague Rd., Berk. AQ13 7
Montague Rd., Croy. BY54 86
Montague Rd., Datchet AQ44 62
Montague Rd., Houns. BF45 64
Montague Rd., Rich. BL46 75
Montague Rd., Slou. AP40 52
Montague Rd., Sthl. BE42 64
Montague Rd., Swan. CT52 89
Montague Rd., Uxb. AX36 53
Montague Sq. SE15 CC43 67
Montague St. WC1 BX39 2
Montague St. WC1 BX39 56
Montague Waye, Sthl. BE41 64
Montalt Rd., Wdf.Grn. CG28 40
Montana Clo., Croy. BZ58 96
Montana Rd. SW17 BV49 76
Montana Rd. SW20 BQ51 85
Montayne Rd., Chsnt. CC19 21
Montbelle Rd. SE9 CL48 78
Montcalm Clo., Brom. CH53 88
Montcalm Clo., Hayes BC38 53
Ayles Rd.
Montcalm Rd. SE7 CJ43 68
Montclare St. E2 CA38 2
Montclare St. E2 CA38 57
Monteagle Av., Bark. CM36 58
Monteagle Way E5 CB34 48
Downs Est.
Monteagle Way SE15 CB45 67
Montefiore St. SW8 BV44 66
Monteith Rd. E3 CD37 57
Montem La., Slou. AO40 61
Montem Rd. SE23 CD47 77
Montem Rd., N.Mal. BO52 85
Montem St. N4 BX33 47
Montenotte Rd. N8 BW32 47
Monterey Clo., Bex. CS48 79
Montesole Ct., Pnr. BD30 36
Montford Pl. SE11 BY42 4
Montford Pl. SE11 BY42 66
Montford Rd., Sev. CW62 108
Montford Rd., Sun. BC52 83
Montford St. E1 CB39 2
Montford St. E1 CB39 57
Montfort Gdns., Ilf. CM29 40
Montfort Pl. SW19 BQ47 75
Montgolfier Wk., Nthlt. BD38 54
Montgomerie Clo., Berk. AQ12 7
Mortain Dr.
Montgomerie Dr., Guil. AQ68 109
Montgomery Av., Esher BH55 84
Montgomery Av., Hem.H. AZ13 8
Montgomery Clo., Grays DE41 71
Montgomery Clo., Mitch. BX52 86
Montgomery Clo., Sid. CN46 78
Montgomery Cres., Rom. CV28 42
Montgomery Dr., Chsnt. CD17 21
Montgomery Rd. W4 BN42 65
Montgomery Rd., Edg. BL29 37
Montgomery Rd., S.Dnth. CY51 90
Montgomery Rd., Wok. AS62 100
Montholme Rd. SW11 BU46 76
Monthope Rd. E1 CB39 2
Montolieu Gdns. SW15 BP46 75
Montpelier Av. N3 BT30 38
Montpelier Av. W5 BK39 54
Montpelier Av., Bex. CP47 79
Montpelier Clo., Uxb. AZ37 53
Montpelier Gdns. E6 CJ38 58
Montpelier Gdns. NW5 BW35 47
Montpelier Gdns., Rom. CP33 50
Montpelier Gro. NW5 BW35 47
Montpelier Ms. SW7 BU41 3
Montpelier Pl. SW7 BU41 3
Montpelier Pl. SW7 BU41 66
Montpelier Rd. SE15 CB44 67
Montpelier Rd. W5 BK39 54
Montpelier Rd., Pur. BY58 95
Montpelier Rd., Sutt. BT56 95
Montpelier Ri. NW11 BR33 46
Montpelier Ri., Wem. BK33 45
Montpelier Row SE3 CG44 68
Montpelier Row, Twick. BK47 74
Montpelier Sq. SW7 BU41 3
Montpelier Sq. SW7 BU41 66
Montpelier St. SW7 BU41 3
Montpelier St. SW7 BU41 66
Montpelier Ter. SW7 BU41 3
Montpelier Ter. SW7 BU41 66
Montpelier Vale SE3 CG44 68
Montpelier Way NW11 BR33 46
Montpelier Wk. SW7 BU41 3
Montpelier Wk. SW7 BU41 66
Montrave Rd. SE20 CC50 77
Montreal Pl. WC2 BX40 4
Montreal Pl. WC2 BX40 56
Aldwych
Montreal Rd., Ilf. CM33 49
Montreal Rd., Sev. CT65 107
Montreal Rd., Til. DG45 71
Montrell Rd. SW2 BX47 76
Montrose Av. NW6 BR37 55
Montrose Av., Edg. BN30 37
Montrose Av., Rom. CV30 42
Montrose Av., Sid. CO47 79
Montrose Av., Slou. AR43 62
Montrose Av., Twick. BF47 74
Montrose Av., Well. CM45 68
Montrose Clo., Ash. BA50 73
Montrose Clo., Wdf.Grn. CH28 40
Montrose Clo., Well. CN45 68
Montrose Cres. N12 BT29 38
Montrose Cres., Wem. BL36 55
Montrose Ct. NW11 BR31 46
Addison Way
Montrose Ct. NW9 BN30 37
Montrose Ct. SW7 BT41 3
Montrose Gdns., Lthd. BH59 93
Montrose Gdns., Mitch. BU51 86
Montrose Gdns., Sutt. BS55 86
Montrose Pl. SW1 BV41 3
Montrose Pl. SW1 BV41 66
Montrose Rd., Felt. BA46 73
Montrose Rd., Har. BH30 36
Montrose Way SE23 CC47 77
Rockbourne Rd.
Montrose Way, Slou. AR43 62
Montrose Wk. Wey. AZ55 83
Montrouge Cres., Epsom BQ61 103
Montserrat Av., Wdf.Grn. CF29 39
Montserrat Clo. SE19 BZ49 77
Berridge Rd.
Montserrat Rd. SW15 BR45 65
Monument Gdns. SE13 CF46 77
Monument Grn., Wey. AZ55 83
Monument Hill, Wey. AZ56 92
Monument La., Ger.Cr. AS29 34
Monument Rd., Wey. AZ56 92
Monument Rd., Wok. AT60 91
Monument St. EC3 BZ40 4
Monument St. EC3 BZ40 57
Monument Way E., Wok. AT61 100
Monument Way N17 CA31 48
Monument Way W., Wok. AT61 100
Monza St. E1 CC40 57
Moodkee St. SE16 CC41 67
Moody La., Dart. CX46 80
Moody St. E1 CC38 57
Moon Ct. SE12 CH45 68
Lyme Farm Rd.
Moon La., Barn. BR24 28
Moon St. N1 BY37 2
Moon St. N1 BY37 56
Moonrakers, St.Alb. BN14 10
High St.
Moor End Rd., Hem.H. AX14 8
Moor End, Maid. AH42 61
Moor Hall Rd., Harl. CQ9 6
Moor Holme, Wok. AS63 100
Moor La. EC2 BZ39 2
Moor La. EC2 BZ39 57
Moor La., Chess. BL56 94
Moor La., Rick. AY27 35
Moor La., Sarratt AV21 25
Moor La., Stai. AV48 72
Moor La., Upmin. CZ33 51
Moor La., West Dr. AX43 63
Moor La., Wok. AS64 100
Moor Mead Rd., Twick. BJ46 74
Moor Mill La., St.Alb. BH18 18
Moor Park Est., Nthwd. BA28 35
Moor Park Rd., Nthwd. BA29 35
Moor Pl. EC2 BZ39 2
Moorfields
Moor Rd., Chesh. AO20 16
Moor St. W1 BW39 1
Moor St. W1 BW39 56
Old Compton St.
Moor Vw., Wat. BC25 26
Moorcroft La., Uxb. AZ39 53
Moorcroft Rd. SW16 BW48 76
Moorcroft Way, Pnr. BE32 45
Moordown SE18 CL43 68
Moore Av., Grays DC42 71
Moore Av., Til. DG44 71
Moore Clo. SW14 BN45 65
Little St. Leonards
Moore Clo., Mitch. BV51 86
Moore Clo., Slou. AN41 61
Moore Clo., Wall. BX57 95
Moore Clo., Wey. AW56 92
Moore Cres., Dag. CO37 59
Moore Grove Cres., Egh. AS50 72
Moore Park Rd. SW6 BS43 66
Moore Rd. SE19 BY50 76
Moore Rd., Berk. AP12 7
Moore Rd., Swans. DC46 81
Moore St. SW3 BU42 3
Moore St. SW3 BU42 66
Moore Way SE22 CB47 77
Wilkie Way
Moore Wk. E7 CH35 49
Stracey Rd.
Moorefield Rd. N17 CA30 39
Moorehead Way SE3 CH45 68
Mooreland Rd., Brom. CG50 78
Moorend, Welw.G.C. BS 9 5
Moores La., Eton AM42 61
Moores Pl., Brwd. DB27 42
High St.
Moores Rd., Dor. BJ71 119
Moorescroft, Brwd. CZ22 33
Moorey Clo. E15 CG37 58
Stephens Rd.
Moorfield Av. W5 BK38 54
Moorfield Highbank EC2 BZ39 57
St. Alphages Gdns.
Moorfield Rd., Chess. BL56 94
Moorfield Rd., Denham AW33 44
Moorfield Rd., Enf. CC23 30
Moorfield Rd., Guil. AR68 109
Moorfield Rd., Orp. CO54 89
Moorfield Rd., Uxb. AX39 53
Moorfield, Harl. CM13 13
Moorfields Clo., Stai. AV51 82
Moorfields EC2 BZ39 2
Moorfields EC2 BZ39 57
Moorfields High Wk. EC2 BZ39 2
St. Alphage Gdns.
Moorgate EC2 BZ39 2
Moorgate EC2 BZ39 57
Moorgate Pl. EC2 BZ39 2
Great Swan Alley
Moorhall Rd., Uxb. AW32 44
Moorhayes Dr., Stai. AX52 83
Moorhouse Rd. W2 BS39 56
Moorhouse Rd., Har. BK31 45
Moorhouse Rd., Oxt. CK69 115
Moorhurst Av., Chsnt. BY18 20
Moorland Clo., Houns. BF47 74
Moorland Clo., Mitch. BU52 86
Church Rd.
Moorland Clo., Rom. CR29 41
Moorland Rd. SW9 BY45 66
Moorland Rd., Har. BL32 46
Moorland Rd., Hem.H. AW14 8
Moorland Rd., West Dr. AX43 63
Moorlands Av. NW7 BP29 37
Moorlands, St.Alb. BH17 18
Radlett Rd.
Moorlands, The, Wok. AS64 100
Moorlands, Welw.G.C. BS 9 5
Moormead Dr., Epsom BO56 94
Moormede Cres., Stai. AV49 72
Moors Rd., Sev. CU63 107
Moors Wk., Welw.G.C. BS 7 5
Moors, The, Welw.G.C. BS 7 5
Moorside Rd., Brom. CG48 78
Moorside, Welw.G.C. BS 9 5
Moorsom Way, Couls. BW62 104
Moortown Rd., Wat. BD28 36
Moot Ct. NW9 BM32 46
Mora Rd. NW2 BQ35 46
Mora St. EC1 BZ38 2
Mora St. EC1 BZ38 57
Morant Gdns., Rom. CR28 41
Morant Path E14 CE40 57
Pennyfields
Morant Pl. N22 BX30 38
Morant Rd., Grays DG41 71
Morant St. E14 CE40 57
Morants Court Rd., Sev. CS62 107
Morat St. SW9 BX44 66
Moravian Pl. SW10 BT43 66
Milmans St.
Moravian St. E2 CC38 57
Gawber St.
Moray Av., Hayes BB40 53
Moray Clo., Rom. CT29 41
Moray Ms. N4 BX34 47
Durham Rd.
Moray Rd. N4 BX34 47
Moray St. E2 CC38 57
Cyprus St.
Moray Way, Rom. CS29 41
Morcote Clo., Guil. AS74 118
Mordaunt Gdns., Dag. CQ36 59
Mordaunt Rd. NW10 BN37 55
Mordaunt St. SW9 BX45 66
Morden Clo. SE13 CF44 67
Morden Clo., Tad. BQ63 103
Morden Ct., Mord. BS52 86
Morden Gdns., Grnf. BH35 45
Morden Gdns., Mitch. BT52 86
Morden Hall Rd., Mord. BS52 86
Morden Hill SE13 CF44 67
Morden La. SE13 CF44 67
Morden Lo., Mord. BT52 86
Morden Rd. Ms. SE3 CH44 68
Morden Rd. SE3 CH44 68
Morden Rd. SW19 BS51 86
Morden Rd., Mitch. BT52 86
Morden Rd., Rom. CQ33 50
Morden St. SE13 CE44 67
Morden Way, Sutt. BS54 86
Morden Wharf Rd. SE10 CG41 68
Mordon Rd., Ilf. CN33 49
Mordred Rd. SE6 CG48 78
More Clo. E16 CG39 58
More Clo. W14 BQ42 65
More Clo., Pur. BY59 95
More La., Esher BF55 84
Moreau Wk., Slou. AS39 52
Alan Way
Morecambe Clo. E1 CC39 57
Morecambe Clo., Horn. CU35 50
Morecambe Gdns., Stan. BK28 36
Morecambe St. SE17 BZ42 4
Morecambe St. SE17 BZ42 67
Morecambe Ter. N18 BZ28 39
Morecoombe Clo., Kings.T. BM50 75
Kingston Hill
Moree Way N18 CB28 39
Moreland Av., Grays DE41 71
Victoria Av.
Moreland Av., Slou. AU43 62
Moreland Clo. NW11 BS33 47
Moreland St. EC1 BY38 2
Moreland St. EC1 BY38 56
Moreland Way E4 CE27 39
Morelands Dr., Ger.Cr. AS32 43
Morell Clo., Barn. BT24 29
Galdana Av.
Morella Clo., Vir.W. AR52 82
Morella Rd. SW12 BU47 76
Morello Av., Uxb. AZ39 53
Moremead Rd. SE6 CD49 77
Moremead, Wal.Abb. CF20 21
Morena St. SE6 CE47 77
Mores La., Brwd. CY25 33
Moresby Av., Surb. BM54 85
Moresby Rd. E5 CB33 48
Moresby Wk. SW8 BV45 66
Heath Rd.
Moretaine Rd., Ashf. AX48 73
Moreton Av., Islw. BG44 64
Moreton Br., Ong. CV14 15
Moreton Clo. E5 CC34 48
Moreton Clo. N15 BZ32 48
Moreton Clo. NW7 BQ29 37
Moreton Clo., Chsnt. CB17 21
Moreton Clo., Swan. CT51 89
Moreton Gdns., Wdf.Grn. CK28 40
Moreton Pl. SW1 BW42 3
Moreton Pl. SW1 BW42 66
Moreton Rd. N15 BZ32 48
Moreton Rd., Fifield CX13 15
Moreton Rd., Ong. CW15 15
Moreton Rd., S.Croy. BZ56 96
Moreton Rd., Wor.Pk. BP55 85
Moreton St. SW1 BW42 3
Moreton St. SW1 BW42 66
Moreton Ter. SW1 BW42 3
Moreton Ter. SW1 BW42 66
Moreton Terrace Ms. N. SW1 BW42 3
Moreton Terrace Ms. S. SW1 BW42 3
Moreton Way, Slou. AL40 61
Morewood Clo., Sev. CT65 107
Morford Clo., Ruis. BC33 44
Morford Way, Ruis. BC33 44
Morgan Av. E17 CF31 48
Morgan Clo. W10 CR36 59
Morgan Clo., Nthwd. BB28 35
Morgan Cres., Epp. CM21 31
Morgan Dr., Green. CZ47 80
Morgan Rd. N7 BY35 47
Morgan Rd. W10 BR39 55
Morgan Rd., Brom. CG50 78
Morgan St. E16 CG39 58
Morgan St. E3 CD38 57
Morgan Way, Rain. CV38 60
Morgan Way, Wdf.Grn. CK29 40
Morgans La. SE1 CA40 4
Morgans La. SE1 CA40 57
Morgans La., Hayes BA39 53
Morgans Wk. SW11 BU43 66
Morice Rd., Hodd. CD11 12
Morie St. SW18 BS45 66
Ferrier St.
Morieux Rd. E10 CD33 48
Moring Rd. SW17 BV49 76
Morkyns Wk. SE21 CA48 77
Morland Av., Croy. CA54 87
Morland Av., Dart. CU46 79
Morland Clo., Hmptn. BE49 74
Morland Clo., Mitch. BU52 86
Morland Gdns. NW10 BN36 55
Morland Gdns., Sthl. BF40 51
Morland Ms. N1 BY37 2
Morland Rd. E17 CC32 48
Morland Rd. SE20 CC50 77
Morland Rd., Croy. CA54 87
Morland Rd., Dag. CR36 59
Morland Rd., Ilf. CL34 49
Morland Rd., Sutt. BT56 95
Morland Way, Chsnt. CD17 21
Morley Av. E4 CF29 39
Morley Av. N18 CB28 39
Morley Av. N22 BY30 38
Morley Clo., Orp. CL55 88
Morley Clo., Slou. AS41 62
Morley Cres. E., Stan. BK30 36
Morley Cres. W., Stan. BK30 36
Morley Cres., Edg. BN27 37
Morley Cres., Ruis. BD34 45
Morley Gro., Harl. CM10 6
Morley Hill, Enf. BZ22 30
Morley Ho. E5 CB34 48
Morley Rd. E10 CF33 48
Morley Rd. E15 CG37 58
Morley Rd. SE13 CF45 67
Morley Rd., Bark. CM37 58
Morley Rd., Chis. CM51 88
Morley Rd., Rom. CQ32 50
Morley Rd., S.Croy. CA58 96
Morley Rd., Sutt. BR54 85
Morley Rd., Twick. BK46 74
Morley Sq., Grays DG42 71
Morley St. SE1 BY41 4
Morley St. SE1 BY41 66
Morleys Rd., Sev. CV70 117
Morna Rd. SE5 BZ44 67
Morning La. E9 CC36 57
Morning Ri., Rick. AX24 26
Morningside Est. E9 CC36 57
Morningside Rd., Wor.Pk. BP55 85
Mornington Av. W14 BR42 65
Mornington Av., Brom. CJ52 88
Mornington Av., Ilf. CL33 49
Mornington Clo., Wdf.Grn. CH28 40
Mornington Clo., West. CJ62 106
Mount Pleasant
Mornington Cres. NW1 BW37 1
Mornington Cres. NW1 BW37 56
Mornington Cres., Houns. BC44 63
Mornington Ct., Bex. CS47 79
Mornington Gro. E3 CE38 57
Mornington Ms. SE5 BZ44 67
County Gro.
Mornington Pl. NW1 BV37 1
Mornington Pl. NW1 BV37 56
Mornington Ter.
Mornington Rd. E11 CG33 49
Mornington Rd. E4 CF26 39
Mornington Rd. SE8 CD43 67
Mornington Rd., Ashf. BA49 73
Mornington Rd., Grnf. BF39 54
Mornington Rd., Loug. CM24 31
Mornington Rd., Rad. BJ20 18
Mornington Rd., Wdf.Grn. CG28 40
Mornington St. NW1 BV37 1
Mornington St. NW1 BV37 56
Mornington Ter. NW1 BV37 1
Mornington Ter. NW1 BV37 56
Mornington Wk., Rich. BK49 74
Morningtons, Harl. CM13 13
Morocco St. SE1 CA41 4
Morocco St. SE1 CA41 67
Morpeth Av., B.Wd. BL22 28
Morpeth Gro. E9 CC37 57
Morpeth Rd. E9 CC37 57
Morpeth St. E2 CC38 57
Morpeth Ter. SW1 BW41 3
Morpeth Ter. SW1 BW41 66
Morrab Gdns., Ilf. CN34 49
Morrice Clo., Slou. AS42 62
Morris Av. E12 CK35 49
Morris Clo., Ger.Cr. AS30 34
Morris Clo., Orp. CN55 88
Morris Ct., Wal.Abb. CG20 22
Morris Gdns. SW18 BS47 76
Morris Gdns., Dart. CX46 80
Morris Pl. N4 BY34 47
Morris Rd. E14 CE39 57
Morris Rd. E15 CG35 49
Morris Rd., Dag. CQ34 50
Morris Rd., Islw. BH45 64
Morris Rd., Red. BX71 121
Morris Rd., Rom. CU29 41
Morris St. E1 CB39 57
Morris Way, St.Alb. BK16 18
Morrish Rd. SW2 BX47 76
Morrison Av. N17 CA31 48
Morrison Rd., Bark. CQ37 59
Morrison Rd., Hayes BC38 53
Morrison St. SW11 BV45 66
Morriston Clo., Wat. BD28 36
Morse Clo. E13 CH38 58
Morshead Rd. W9 BS38 56
Morston Clo., Tad. BP63 103
Morston Gdns. SE9 CK49 78
Mortain Dr., Berk. AP12 7
Morten Clo. SW4 BW46 76
Morten Gdns., Uxb. AW33 44
Mortens Wood, Amer. AO23 25
Morteyne Rd. N17 BZ30 39
Mortgramit Sq. SE18 CL41 68
Hare St.
Mortham St. E15 CG37 58
Mortimer Clo. NW2 BR34 46
Garth Rd.
Mortimer Clo. SW16 BW48 76
Mortimer Clo., Bush. BF26 36
Ashfield Av.
Mortimer Cres. NW6 BS37 1
Mortimer Cres. NW6 BS37 56
Mortimer Cres., Wor.Pk. BN55 85
Mortimer Dr., Enf. BZ25 30
Mortimer Est. NW6 BS37 1
Mortimer Est. NW6 BS37 56
Mortimer Mkt. WC1 BW38 1
Mortimer Mkt. WC1 BW38 56
Mortimer Pl. NW6 BS37 1
Mortimer Pl. NW6 BS37 56
Mortimer Rd. E6 CK38 58
Mortimer Rd. N1 CA36 2
Mortimer Rd. N1 CA36 57
Mortimer Rd. NW10 BQ38 55
Mortimer Rd. W13 BK39 54
Mortimer Rd., Erith CS43 69
Mortimer Rd., Mitch. BU51 86
Mortimer Rd., Orp. CO55 89
Mortimer Rd., Slou. AR41 62
Stile Rd.
Mortimer Rd., West. CJ59 97
Mortimer Sq. W11 BQ40 55
St. Anns Rd.
Mortimer St. W1 BV39 1
Mortimer St. W1 BW39 56
Mortimer Ter. NW5 BV35 47
Mortlake Clo., Croy. BX55 86
Mortlake High St. SW14 BN45 65
Mortlake Rd. E16 CH39 58
Mortlake Rd., Ilf. CM35 49
Mortlake Rd., Rich. BM43 65
Mortlock Clo. SE15 CB44 67
Morton Clo., Wok. AR61 100
Morton Cres. N14 BW28 38
Morton Gdns., Wall. BW56 95
Morton Pl. SE1 BY41 4
Morton Pl. SE1 BY41 66
Morton Rd. E15 CG36 58
Morton Rd. N1 BZ36 2
Morton Rd. N1 BZ36 57
Morton Rd., Mord. BT53 86
Morton Rd., Wok. AR61 100
Morton Way N14 BW27 38
Morton, Tad. BQ64 103
Morval Rd. SW2 BY46 76

Morvale Clo., Belv. CQ42 69
Morven Clo., Pot.B. BT19 20
Morven Rd. SW17 BU48 76
Morville St. E3 CE37 57
Morwell St. WC1 BW39 1
Morwell St. WC1 BW39 56
Mosbach Gdns., Brwd. DD27 122
Moscow Pl. W2 BS40 3
Moscow Pl. W2 BS40 56
Moscow Rd.
Moscow Rd. W2 BS40 56
Mosedale St. SE5 BZ44 67
Moselle Av. N22 BY30 38
Moselle Clo. N8 BX31 47
Moselle Pl. N17 CA29 39
High Rd.
Moselle Rd., West. CK62 106
Moselle St. N17 CA29 39
Mospey Cres., Epsom BO61 103
Moss Clo. E1 CB39 57
Moss Clo., Pnr. BE30 36
Moss Clo., Rick. AX27 35
Heron Clo.
Moss Gdns., Felt. BC48 73
Rose Gdns.
Moss Gdns., S.Croy. CC57 96
Warren Av.
Moss Grn., Welw.G.C. BR 9 5
Moss La., Pnr. BE30 36
Moss La., Rom. CT32 50
Moss Rd., Dag. CR36 59
Moss Rd., S.Ock. DB39 60
Moss Rd., Wat. BC20 17
Moss Side, St.Alb. BE18 18
Mossborough Clo. N12 BS29 38
Mossbury Rd. SW11 BU45 66
Mossdown Clo., Belv. CR42 69
Mossendew Clo., Uxb. AX30 35
Mossfield, Cob. BC60 92
Mossford Grn., Ilf. CL31 49
Mossford La., Ilf. CL30 40
Mossford St. E3 CD38 57
Mosshall Cres. N12 BS29 38
Mosshall Gro. N12 BS29 38
Mossington Gdns. SE16 CC42 67
Abbeyfield Rd.
Mosslea Rd. SE20 CC50 77
Mosslea Rd., Brom. CJ53 88
Mosslea Rd., Orp. CL55 88
Mosslea Rd., Whyt. CA61 105
Mossop St. SW3 BU42 3
Mossop St. SW3 BU42 66
Mossville Gdns., Mord. BR52 85
Moston Clo., Hayes BB42 63
Mostyn Av., Wem. BL35 46
Mostyn Gdns. NW10 BQ37 55
Mostyn Gro. E3 CD37 57
Mostyn Rd. E3 CD37 57
Mostyn Rd. SW19 BR51 85
Mostyn Rd. SW9 BY44 66
Mostyn Rd., Bush. BG25 27
Mostyn Rd., Edg. BN29 37
Mostyn Ter., Red. BV71 121
Mosul Way, Brom. CK53 88
Mosyer Dr., Orp. CP55 89
Motcomb St. SW1 BU41 3
Motcomb St. SW1 BV41 66
Mote Rd., Lthd. BG64 102
Mote Rd., Sev. CZ68 117
Motherwell Way, Grays DA42 70
Motspur Pk., N.Mal. BO53 85
Mott St. E4 CF22 30
Mott St., Loug. CG23 31
Mottingham Gdns. SE9 CJ47 78
Mottingham La. SE12 CJ47 78
Mottingham La. SE9 CJ47 78
Mottingham Rd. N9 CC26 39
Mottingham Rd. SE9 CK48 78
Mottisfont Rd. SE2 CO41 69
Motts Hill La., Tad. BP65 103
Mottscroft Clo., Loug. CL25 31
Mouchotte Clo., West. CH59 97
Moulins Rd. E9 CC36 57
Moultain Hill, Swan. CU52 89
Moulton Av., Houns. BE44 64
Moultrie Way, Upmin. CZ33 51
Mound, The SE9 CL48 78
William Barefoot Dr.
Moundfield Rd. N16 CB32 48
Mount Adon Pk. SE22 CB47 77
Mount Angelus Rd. SW15 BO47 75
Mount Ararat Rd., Rich. BL46 75
Mount Ararat SW20 BQ50 75
Mount Ash Rd. SE26 CB48 77
Mount Av. E4 CE27 39
Mount Av. W5 BK39 54
Mount Av., Brwd. DD25 122
Mount Av., Rom. CY29 42
Mount Av., Sthl. BF39 54
Mount Clo. SE19 CA49 77
Mount Clo. W5 BM39 55
Mount Av.
Mount Clo., Barn. BV24 29
Mount Clo., Brom. CK51 88
Mount Clo., Cars. BV58 95
Mount Clo., Hem.H. AV13 7
Mount Clo., Ken. BZ61 105
Mount Clo., Lthd. BH65 102
Mount Clo., Sev. CT65 107
Mount Clo., The, Vir.W. AR53 82
Mount Clo., Wok. AQ64 100
Mount Cres., Brwd. DB28 42
Mount Ct., W.Wick. CG55 88
Mount Culver Av., Sid. CP50 79
Mount Culver Par., Sid. CP50 79
Maidstone Rd.
Mount Dr., Bexh. CQ46 79
Mount Dr., Har. BE32 45
Mount Dr., Reig. BT69 121
Mount Dr., St.Alb. BG16 18
Mount Dr., Wem. BN34 46
Mount Echo Av. E4 CE26 39
Mount Echo Dr. E4 CE26 39
Mount Ephraim La. SW16 BW48 76
Mount Ephraim Rd. SW16 BW48 76
Mount Est., The E5 CB34 48
Mount Felix, Walt. BB54 83
Mount Gdns. SE26 CB48 77
Mount Gro., Edg. BN27 37
Mount Harry Rd., Sev. CU65 107
Mount Hermon Clo., Wok. AS62 100
Mount Hermon Rd.
Mount Hermon Rd., Wok. AR63 100
Mount Hill La., Ger.Cr. AQ33 43
Mount Hill, Sev. CO62 107
Mount La., Uxb. AU34 43
Mount Lee, Egh. AS49 72
Mount Mills EC1 BY38 56
Seward St.
Mount Nod Rd. SW16 BX48 76
Mount Pk. Av., Har. BG34 45
Mount Pk. Av., S.Croy. BY58 95
Mount Pk. Cres. W5 BK39 54
Mount Pk. Rd. W5 BK39 54
Mount Pk. Rd., Har. BG34 45
Mount Pk. Rd., Pnr. BC32 44
Mount Pk., Cars. BV57 95
Mount Pleasant Av., Brwd. DF25 122
Mount Pleasant Clo., Hat. BQ11 10
Mount Pleasant Cres. N4 BX33 47
Mount Pleasant Hill E5 CB34 48
Mount Pleasant La. E5 CB33 48
Mount Pleasant La., St.Alb. BE18 18
Mount Pleasant La., Hat. BQ11 10
Mount Pleasant NW4 BP31 46
Church End
Mount Pleasant Rd. NW10 BQ36 55
Mount Pleasant Rd. E17 CD30 39
Mount Pleasant Rd. N17 CA30 39
Mount Pleasant Rd. SE13 CE46 77
Mount Pleasant Rd. W5 BK38 54
Mount Pleasant Rd., N.Mal. BN52 85
Mount Pleasant Rd., Chig. CM28 40
Mount Pleasant Rd., Dart. CW46 80
Mount Pleasant Rd., Cat. CB65 105
Mount Pleasant Rd., Rom. CS29 41
Mount Pleasant Rd., Sev. CU70 116
Mount Pleasant SE27 BZ49 77
Hubbard Rd.
Mount Pleasant Vill. N4 BX33 47
Mount Pleasant WC1 BY38 2
Mount Pleasant WC1 BY38 56
Mount Pleasant Wk., Bex. CS46 79
Mount Pleasant, Effingham BE67 111
Mount Pleasant, Barn. BU24 29
Mount Pleasant, Epsom BO58 94
Mount Pleasant, Guil. AR71 118
Mount Pleasant, Horsley AZ68 110
Mount Pleasant, Ruis. BD34 45
Mount Pleasant, St.Alb. BF13 9
Mount Pleasant, Uxb. AW30 35
Mount Pleasant, Wem. BL37 55
Mount Pleasant, West. CJ62 106
Mount Pleasant, Wey. AZ55 83
Mount Rd. NW2 BP34 46
Mount Rd. NW4 BP32 46
Mount Rd. SE19 BZ50 77
Mount Rd. SW19 BS48 76
Mount Rd., Barn. BU25 29
Mount Rd., Bexh. CP46 79
Mount Rd., Chess. BL56 94
Mount Rd., Chobham AQ59 91
Mount Rd., Dag. CQ33 50
Mount Rd., Dart. CT46 79
Mount Rd., Epp. CP19 23
Mount Rd., Felt. BE48 74
Mount Rd., Hayes BC41 63
Mount Rd., Ilf. CL35 49
Mount Rd., Mitch. BT51 86
Mount Rd., N.Mal. BN52 85
Mount Rd., Wok. AQ64 100
Mount Row W1 BV40 3
Mount Row W1 BV40 56
Mount Side, Guil. AQ71 118
Mount Sq., The NW3 BT34 47
Heath St.
Mount St. W1 BV40 3
Mount St. W1 BV40 56
Mount St., Dor. BJ71 119
Mount Stewart Av., Har. BK33 45
Mount Ter. E1 CB39 57
Mount Vernon NW3 BT35 47
Mount Vills. SE27 BY48 76
Canterbury Gro.
Mount Vw. NW7 BN27 37
Mount Vw. Rd. E4 CF26 39
Mount Vw. Rd. N4 BX33 47
Mount Vw. Rd. NW9 BN32 46
Mount Vw. W5 BK38 54
Mount Vw., Enf. BX22 29
Mount Vw., Rick. AW26 35
Mount Vw., St.Alb. BL17 19
Mount Way, Cars. BV58 95
Mount, The N20 BT27 38
Mount, The NW3 BT34 47
Heath St.
Mount, The, Brwd. DB27 42
St. James Rd.
Mount, The, Chsnt. BZ16 21
Pear Tree Wk.
Mount, The, Couls. BV61 104
Mount, The, Esher BF57 93
Mount, The, Ewell BO58 94
Mount, The, Guil. AR72 118
Mount, The, Lthd. BH65 102
Mount, The, N.Mal. BO52 85
Mount, The, Pot.B. BS18 20
Mount, The, Rick. AX25 26
Mount, The, Rom. CV27 42
Mount, The, Stoneleigh BP56 94
Mount, The, Tad. BR66 112
Mount, The, Wem. BN34 46
Mount, The, Wey. BB55 83
Mount, The, Wok. AR62 100
Elm Rd.
Mountacre Clo. SE26 CB49 77
Mountague Pl. E14 CF40 57
Mountbatten Clo. SE18 CN43 68
Mountbatten Clo. SE19 CA49 77
Sainsbury Rd.
Mountbatten Clo., Slou. AQ41 62
Yew Tree Rd.
Mountbatten Clo., St.Alb. BJ15 9
Mountbatten Clo., Buck.H. CJ27 40
Lower Queens Rd.
Mountbatten Ms. SW18 BT47 76
Inman Rd.
Mountbatten Sq., Wind. AO44 61
Ward Royal
Mountbell Rd., Stan. BJ30 36
Mountcombe Clo., Surb. BL54 85
Mountearl Gdns. SW16 BX48 76
Mountfield Rd. E6 CK37 58
Mountfield Rd. N3 BS31 47
Mountfield Rd. W5 BK39 54
Mountfield Rd., Hem.H. AY13 8
Mountfield Way, Orp. CP52 89
Mountford St. E1 CB39 2
Mountford St. E1 CB39 57
Adler St.
Mountfort Ter. N1 BY36 56
Barnsbury Sq.
Mountgrace Rd., Pot.B. BS19 20
Mountgrove Rd. N5 BY34 47
Mounthurst Rd., Brom. CG54 88
Mountington Park Clo. BK32 45
Donnington Rd.
Mountjoy Clo. SE2 CO41 69
Mountnessing La., Brwd. DB22 33
Mounts Pond Rd. SE3 CF44 67
Mounts Rd., Green. DA46 80
Mountsfield Clo., Stai. AW46 73
Benenstock Rd.
Mountsfield Ct. SE13 CF46 77
Mountside, Felt. BE48 74
Mountside, Stan. BH30 36
Mountview Ct. N8 BY31 47
Mountview Dr., Red. BU71 121
Mountview Rd., Chsnt. CA16 21
Mountview Rd., Esher BJ57 93
Mountview Rd., Orp. CO54 89
Mountview, Nthwd. BB29 35
Mountway Clo., Welw.G.C. BR 9 5
Mountway, Pot.B. BS18 20
Mountway, Welw.G.C. BR 9 5
Mountwood Clo., S.Croy. CB58 96
Mountwood, E.Mol. BF52 84
Move St. E2 CB37 57
Movers La., Bark. CM37 58
Mowatt Clo. N19 BW33 47
Mowbray Av., Wey. AY60 92
Mowbray Cres., Egh. AT49 72
Mowbray Gdns., Dor. BJ70 119
Mowbray Rd. NW6 BR36 55
Mowbray Rd. SE19 CA51 87
Mowbray Rd., Barn. BT24 29
Mowbray Rd., Edg. BM28 37
Mowbray Rd., Harl. CN10 6
Mowbray Rd., Rich. BK48 74
Mowbrays Clo., Rom. CS30 41
Mowbrays Rd., Rom. CS30 41
Mowbrey Gdns., Loug. CM23 31
Mowlem St. E2 CB37 57
Mowll St. SW9 BY43 66
Moxon Clo. E13 CG37 58
Whitelegg Rd.
Moxon St. W1 BV39 1
Moxon St. W1 BV39 56
Moxon St., Barn. BR24 28
Moye Clo. E2 CB37 2
Moye Clo. E2 CB37 57
Moyers Rd. E10 CF33 48
Moylan Rd. W6 BR43 65
Moyne Ct., Wok. AP62 100
Iveagh Rd.
Moyne Pl. NW10 BM37 55
Moyser Rd. SW16 BV49 76
Mozart Sq. SW1 BV42 66
Ebury Bridge Rd.
Mozart St. W10 BR38 55
Muchelney Rd., Mord. BT53 86
Muckhatch La., Egh. AT52 82
Muckingford Rd., Til. DJ42 71
Mud La. W5 BK39 54
Muddy La., Slou. AP39 52
Mudlarks Way SE7 & SE10 CH41 68
Muggeridge Rd., Dag. CR35 50
Muir Rd. E5 CB35 48
Muir St. E16 CK40 58
Muirdown Av. SW14 BN45 65
Muirfield Clo., Wat. BD28 36
Muirfield Grn., Wat. BC28 35
Muirfield Rd., Wat. BD28 36
Muirfield Rd., Wok. AP62 100
Muirfield W3 BO39 55
Muirkirk Rd. SE6 CF47 77
Mulberry Av., Stai. AY47 73
Mulberry Clo. E4 CE27 39
Mulberry Clo. NW3 BT35 47
Hampstead High St.
Mulberry Clo. NW4 BQ31 46
Mulberry Clo. SE7 CJ43 68
Mulberry Clo. SW16 BW49 76
Mulberry Clo., Barn. BT24 29
Margaret Rd.
Mulberry Clo., Brox. CD15 12
Mulberry Clo., Nthlt. BD37 54
Mulberry Clo., Rom. CV31 51
Mulberry Clo., St.Alb. BF17 18
Mulberry Clo., Wey. AZ55 83
Mulberry Clo., Wok. AS60 91
Mulberry Cres., Brent. BJ43 64
Mulberry Cres., West Dr. AZ41 63
Mulberry Ct., Bark. CN36 58
Westrow Dr.
Mulberry Dr., Grays CW42 70
Mulberry Dr., Slou. AS42 62
Mulberry Gdns. NW4 BQ31 46
Mulberry Hill, Brwd. DC26 122
Mulberry La., Croy. CA54 87
Mulberry Ms., Wall. BW57 95
Clarendon Rd.
Mulberry Rd., Grav. DF48 81
Mulberry St. E1 CB39 2
Mulberry St. E1 CB39 57
Mulberry Trees, Shep. BA54 83
Mulberry Way E18 CH30 40
Mulberry Way, Belv. CS41 69
Mulberry Way, Ilf. CM31 49
Mulberry Wk. SW3 BT43 3
Mulberry Wk. SW3 BT43 66
Mulgrave Rd. NW10 BO35 46
Mulgrave Rd. SW6 BR43 65
Mulgrave Rd. W5 BK38 54
Mulgrave Rd., Croy. BZ55 87
Mulgrave Rd., Har. BJ34 45
Mulgrave Rd., Sutt. BR57 94
Mulgrave Way, Wok. AP62 100
Mulholland Clo., Mitch. BV51 86
Mulkern Rd. N19 BW33 47
Mull Wk. N1 BZ36 57
Marquess Est.
Mullein Ct., Grays DE43 71
Mullens Rd., Egh. AT49 72
Muller Rd. SW4 BW46 76
Mullet Gdns. E2 CB38 57
St. Peters Clo.
Mullins Path SW14 BN45 65
North Worple Way
Mullion Clo., Har. BF30 36
Mullion Wk., Wat. BD28 36
Mulready St. NW8 BU38 1
Mulready St. NW8 BU38 56
Multi-way W3 BO41 65
Valetta Rd.
Multon Rd. SW18 BT47 76
Multon Rd., Sev. CZ57 99
Mulvaney Way SE1 BZ41 4
Mumford Ct. EC2 BZ39 57
Milk St.
Mumford Rd. SE24 BY46 76
Mumfords La., Ger.Cr. AQ31 43
Muncaster Clo., Ashf. AZ49 73
Muncaster Rd. SW11 BU45 66
Muncaster Rd., Ashf. AZ49 73
Muncies Ms. SE6 CF48 77
Mund St. W14 BR42 65
Mundania Rd. SE22 CB46 77
Munday Rd. E16 CH40 58
Mundells Ct., Welw.G.C. BR 7 5
Mundells, Welw.G.C. BR 7 5
Munden Gro., Wat. BD22 27
Munden Pl. W14 BR42 65
Munden St.
Munden St. W14 BR42 65
Mundesley Spur, Slou. AP39 52
Mundford Rd. E5 CC34 48
Mundon Gdns., Ilf. CM33 49
Mundy St. N1 CA38 2
Mundy St. N1 CA38 57
Hoxton Sq.
Munford Dr., Swans. DC47 81
Mungo Park Clo., Bush. BG27 36
Mungo Park Rd., Grav. DH49 81
Mungo Park Rd., Rain. CU36 59
Mungo Park Way, Orp. CP54 89
Munnery Way, Orp. CL55 88
Munnings Gdns., Islw. BG46 74
Munro Dr. N11 BW29 38
Munro Ms. W10 BR39 55
Munro Rd., Bush. BF25 27
Munro Ter. SW10 BT43 66
Riley St.
Munstead Vw., Guil. AQ72 118
Munster Av., Houns. BE45 64
Munster Gdns. N13 BY28 38
Munster Rd. SW6 BR43 65
Munster Rd., Tedd. BJ50 74
Munster Sq. NW1 BV38 1
Munster Sq. NW1 BV38 56
Munton Rd. SE17 BZ42 4
Munton Rd. SE17 BZ42 67
Murchison Av., Bex. CP47 79
Murchison Rd. E10 CF34 48
Murchison Rd., Hodd. CE10 12
Murdoch Clo., Stai. AW49 73
Cherry Orch.
Murdock Clo. E16 CG39 58
Rogers Rd.
Murdock Cotts. E3 CD38 57
Clinton Rd.
Murdock St. SE15 CB43 67
Murfett Clo. SW19 BR48 75
Victoria Dr.
Murfitt Way, Upmin. CX35 51
Muriel Av., Wat. BD25 27
Muriel St. N1 BX37 2
Muriel St. N1 BX37 56
Murillo Rd. SE13 CF45 67
Murphy St. SE1 BY41 4
Murphy St. SE1 BY41 66
Murray Av., Brom. CH52 88
Murray Av., Houns. BF46 74
Murray Cres., Pnr. BD30 36
Murray Grn., Wok. AU60 91
Murray Gro. N1 BZ37 2
Murray Gro. N1 BZ37 57
Murray Ms. NW1 BW36 56
Murray Rd. SW19 BQ50 75
Murray Rd. W5 BK42 64
Murray Rd., Berk. AR12 7
Murray Rd., Cher. AU57 91
Murray Rd., Nthwd. BB29 35
Murray Rd., Orp. CO52 89
Murray Rd., Rich. BJ48 74
Murray Sq. E16 CH39 58
Murray St. NW1 BW36 56
Murray Ter. NW3 BT35 47
Flask Wk.
Murray Yd. SE18 CL42 68
Powis St.
Murrells Wk., Lthd. BF65 102
Murreys, The, Ash. BK62 102
Murthering La., Rom. CT25 32
Murton Ct., St.Alb. BH13 9
Althorp Rd.
Murton St. EC1 BZ38 57
Lever St.
Murtwell Dr., Chig. CM29 40
Musard Rd. W6 BR43 65
Musbury St. E1 CC39 57
Muscatel Pl. SE5 CA44 67
Dalwood St.
Muschamp Rd. SE15 CA45 67
Muschamp Rd., Cars. BT55 86
Muscovy St. EC3 CA40 4
Muscovy St. EC3 CA40 57
Seething La.
Museum Pass. E2 CC38 57
Victoria Park Sq.
Museum St. WC1 BX39 2
Museum St. WC1 BX39 56
Musgrave Clo., Barn. BT23 29
Musgrave Cres. SW6 BS43 66
Musgrave Rd., Islw. BH44 64
Musgrove Rd. SE14 CC44 67
Musjid Clo. SW11 BT45 66
Wye St.
Musjid Rd. SW11 BT44 66
Musk Hill, Hem.H. AV14 7
Muskalls Clo., Chsnt. CB17 21
Spicersfield
Muskham Rd., Harl. CO 9 6
Musquash Way, Houns. BD44 64
Mussenden La., Hort.K. CY53 90
Mustard Mill Rd., Stai. AV49 72
Muston Rd. E5 CB34 48
Muswell Av. N10 BV30 38
Muswell Hill Broadway N10 BV31 47
Muswell Hill Est. N10 BU30 38
Muswell Hill N10 BV31 47
Muswell Hill Pl. N10 BV31 47
Muswell Hill Rd. N10 BV32 47
Muswell Hill Rd. N6 BV32 47
Muswell Ms. N10 BV31 47
Muswell Rd.
Muswell Rd. N10 BV31 47
Mutchetts Clo., Wat. BE20 18
Mutrix Rd. NW6 BS37 56
Mutton La., Pot.B. BQ19 19
Mutton Pl. NW1 BV36 56
Harmood St.
Mutton Row, Ong. CV18 24
Muybridge Rd., N.Mal. BN51 85
Myatt Rd. SW9 BY44 66
Myatts Fields Dev. SW9 BY44 66
Myburn Clo., Hem.H. AZ14 8
Mycenae Rd. SE3 CH43 68
Mychurch La. SE7 CA42 67
Myddelton Av, Enf. CA22 30
Myddelton Clo., Enf. CA22 30
Myddelton Av.
Myddelton Gdns. N21 BY26 38
Myddelton Pass. EC1 BY38 56
Myddelton Pk. N20 BT27 38
Myddelton Rd. N8 BX31 47
Myddelton Sq. EC1 BY38 2
Myddelton Sq. EC1 BY38 56
Myddelton St. EC1 BY38 2
Myddelton St. EC1 BY38 56
Myddelton Path, Chsnt. CB19 21
Myddleton Rd. N22 BX29 38
Myddleton Rd., Uxb. AX37 53
Mygrove Clo., Rain. CV37 60
Mygrove Gdns., Rain. CV37 60
Mygrove Rd., Rain. CV37 60
Mylis Clo. SE26 CB49 77
Mylne St. EC1 BY37 2
Mymms Dr., Hat. BS16 20
Mynns Clo., Epsom BM60 94
Myra St. SE2 CO42 69
Myrdle St. E1 CB39 57
Myrke, The, Slou. AP42 62
Myrna Clo., Mitch. BU50 76
Myron Pl. SE13 CF45 67

N

Nadine St. SE7 CJ42 68
Nagasaki Wk. SE7 CJ41 68
Nagle Clo. E17 CF30 39
Nags Head Ct. EC1 BZ38 2
Banner St.
Nags Head Est. E2 CA37 57
Nags Head Est. E2 CB37 2
Nags Head La., Brwd. CZ28 42
Nags Head La., Upmin. CY30 42
Nags Head La., Well. CO45 69
Nags Head Rd., Enf. CC24 30
Nags Head St. E2 CA37 2
Nailsworth Cres., Red. BW68 113
Nailzee Clo., Ger.Cr. AS33 43
Nairn Grn., Wat. BC27 35
Nairn Rd., Ruis. BD35 45
Nairn St. E14 CF39 57
Nairne Gro. SE24 BZ45 67
Naish Ct. N1 BX37 2
Naish Ct. N1 BX37 56
Nalders Rd., Chesh. AO18 16
Nallhead Rd., Felt. BD49 74
Namton Dr., Th.Hth. BX52 86
Nan-Clarks La. NW7 BO27 37
Nancy Downs, Wat. BD26 36
Nankin St. E14 CE39 57
Nansen Rd. SW11 BV45 66
Nansen Rd., Grav. DH49 81
Nant Rd. NW2 BR34 46
Nant St. E2 CB38 57
Nantes Clo. SW18 BT45 66
Nantes Pass. E1 CA39 57
Lamb St.
Nap, The, Kings L. AZ18 17
Napier Av. E14 CE42 67

Napier Av. SW6 BR45 65
Napier Clo. SE14 CD43 67
Amersham Vale
Napier Clo. W14 BR41 65
Napier Rd.
Napier Clo., West Dr. AY41 63
Napier Ct. SW6 BR45 65
Napier Dr., Bush. BE24 27
Napier Gdns., Guil. AT70 118
Napier Gro. N1 BZ37 2
Napier Gro. N1 BZ37 57
Napier Pl. W14 BR41 65
Napier Rd. E11 CG35 49
Napier Rd. E15 CG37 58
Napier Rd. E6 CL37 58
Napier Rd. N17 CA31 48
Napier Rd. NW10 BP38 55
Victor Rd.
Napier Rd. SE25 CB52 87
Napier Rd. W14 BR41 65
Napier Rd., Ashf. BA50 73
Napier Rd., Belv. CQ42 69
Napier Rd., Brom. CH52 88
Napier Rd., Enf. CC25 30
Napier Rd., Grav. DF47 81
Napier Rd., Houns. AX44 63
Napier Rd., Islw. BJ45 64
Napier Rd., S.Croy. BZ57 96
Napier Rd., Wem. BK35 45
Napier St. N1 BY36 2
Napier Ter. N1 BY36 56
Napoleon Rd., Twick. BJ47 74
Napsbury Av., St.Alb. BK16 18
Napsbury La., St.Alb. BJ15 9
Napton Clo., Hayes BD38 54
Kingsash Dr.
Narbonne Av. SE4 BW46 76
Narborough Clo., Uxb. BA34 44
Narborough St. SW6 BS44 66
Narcissus Rd. NW6 BS35 47
Narcot La., Ch.St.G. AQ27 34
Narcot Rd., Ch.St.G. AQ27 34
Narcot Way, Ch.St.G. AQ28 34
Nare Rd., S.Ock. CY40 60
Narford Rd. E5 CB34 48
Narrow La., Warl. CB63 105
Narrow St. E14 CD40 57
Narrow St. W3 BM40 55
Steyne Rd.
Narrow Way, Brom. CK53 88
Nascot Pl., Wat. BC23 26
Nascot Rd., Wat. BC23 26
Nascot St. W12 BQ39 55
Nascot St., Wat. BC23 26
Nascot Wood Rd., Wat. BB22 26
Naseby Clo. NW6 BT36 56
Naseby Clo., Islw. BH44 64
Naseby Ct., Walt. BD55 84
Naseby Rd. SE19 BZ50 77
Naseby Rd., Dag. CR34 50
Naseby Rd., Ilf. CK30 40
Nash Cft., Grav. DF49 81
Henley Deane
Nash Clo., B.Wd. BL24 28
Nash Clo., Hat. BQ15 10
Nash Dr., Red. BU69 121
Nash Gdns., Red. BU70 121
Nash Grn., Brom. CH50 78
Nash Grn., Hem.H. AZ16 17
Nash La., Kes. CH57 97
Nash Mills La., Hem.H. AY16 17
Nash Rd. N9 CC27 39
Nash Rd. SE4 CD45 67
Nash Rd., Rom. CP31 50
Nash Rd., Slou. AS42 62
Nash St. NW1 BV38 1
Nash St. NW1 BV38 56
Nashleigh Hill, Chesh. AO17 16
Nasmyth St. W6 BP41 65
Nassau Path SE28 CP40 59
Disraeli Clo.
Nassau Rd. SW13 BO44 65
Nassau St. W1 BW39 1
Nassau St. W1 BW39 56
Nassington Rd. NW3 BU35 47
Natal Rd. N11 BW29 38
Natal Rd. SW16 BW50 76
Natal Rd., Ilf. CL35 49
Natal Rd., Th.Hth. BZ52 87
Natalie Clo., Felt. BA47 73
Nathan Way SE28 CO41 69
Nathans Rd., Wem. BK33 45
Naval Row E14 CF40 57
Naval Wk., Brom. CH51 88
High St.
Navarino Gro. E8 CB36 57
Navarino Rd. E8 CB36 57
Navarre Gdns., Rom. CR28 41
Navarre Rd. E6 CK37 58
Navarre St. E2 CA38 2
Navarre St. E2 CA38 57
Navenby Wk. E3 CE38 57
Rounton Rd.
Navestock Clo. E4 CF27 39
Mapleton Rd.
Navestock Cres., Wdf.Grn. CJ29 40
Navestock Side, Brwd. CY23 33
Navy St. SW4 BW45 66
Naylor Gro., Enf. CC25 30
South St.
Naylor Rd. N20 BT27 38
Naylor Rd. SE15 CB43 67
Nazeing Common, Wal.Abb. CJ15 13
Nazeing New Rd., Brox. CE14 12
Nazeing Rd., Wal.Abb. CF14 12
Nazeing Wk., Rain. CT37 59
Nazrul St. E2 CA38 2
Neagle Clo., B.Wd. BN23 28
Neal Av., Sthl. BE38 54
Neal Clo., Ger.Cr. AT33 43
Neal Clo., Nthwd. BB30 35
Neal Rd., Sev. CZ57 99
Neal St. WC2 BX39 2
Neal St. WC2 BX39 56
Neal St., Wat. BD25 27
Nealden St. SW9 BX45 66
Neale Clo. N2 BT31 47
Neals Rd., Erith CS43 69
Brook St.
Neals Yd. WC2 BX39 2
Shorts Gdns.
Near Acre NW9 BO30 37
Neasden Clo. NW10 BO35 46
Neasden La. N. NW10 BN34 46
Neasden La. NW10 BO35 46
Neasham Rd., Dag. CO35 50
Neat Clo., Wal.Abb. CG20 22
Hillhouse
Neate St. SE5 CA43 67
Neath Gdns., Mord. BT53 86
Neathouse Pl. SW1 BW42 3
Neathouse Pl. SW1 BW42 66
Vauxhall Bridge Rd.
Neats Acre, Ruis. BA33 44
Neatscourt Rd. E6 CJ39 58
Neave Cres., Rom. CV30 42
Neb Corner Rd., Oxt. CF69 114
Nebraska St. SE1 BZ41 4
Nebraska St. SE1 BZ41 67
Neckinger Est. SE16 CA41 4
Neckinger Est. SE16 CA41 67
Neckinger SE16 CA41 4
Neckinger SE16 CA41 67
Neckinger St. SE1 CA41 4
Nectarine Way SE13 CE44 67
Needham Clo., Wind. AM44 61
Needham Rd. W2 BS39 56
Artesian Rd.
Needham Ter. NW2 BQ34 46
Needleman St. SE16 CC41 67
Neela Clo., Uxb. AZ35 44
Neeld Cres. NW4 BP32 46
Neeld Cres., Wem. BM35 46
Neil Clo., Ashf. BA49 73
Nelgarde Rd. SE6 CE47 77
Nell Gwynne Av., Shep. BA53 83
Green La.
Nella Rd. W6 BQ43 65
Nelldale Rd. SE16 CC42 67
Nellgrove Rd., Uxb. AZ38 53
Nello James Gdns. SE27 BZ49 77
Hamilton Rd.
Nelmes Clo., Horn. CW32 51
Nelmes Cres., Horn. CW32 51
Nelmes Rd., Horn. CW33 51
Nelmes Way, Horn. CV31 51
Nelson Av., St.Alb. BJ15 9
Nelson Clo., Brwd. DB28 42
Nelson Clo., Croy. BY54 86
Nelson Clo., Rom. CR30 41
Lynton Av.
Nelson Clo., Slou. AR42 62
Nelson Clo., Uxb. AZ38 53
Nelson Clo., Walt. BC54 83
Nelson Clo., West. CK62 106
Nelson Est. SE17 BZ42 4
Nelson Gdns. E2 CB38 57
Nelson Gdns., Guil. AT70 118
Nelson Gdns., Houns. BF46 74
Nelson Gro. Rd. SW19 BW51 86
Nelson La., Uxb. AZ38 53
Nelson Mandela Clo. N10 BV30 38
Nelson Mandela Rd. SE3 CJ45 68
Nelson Pass. EC1 BZ38 2
Mora St.
Nelson Pl. N1 BY37 2
Nelson Pl. N1 BY37 56
Nelson Pl. NW6 BS38 56
Percy Rd.
Nelson Pl. W3 BM40 55
Steyne Rd.
Nelson Pl., Sid. CO49 79
Nelson Rd. E11 CH31 49
Nelson Rd. E4 CE29 39
Nelson Rd. N15 CA31 48
Nelson Rd. N8 BX32 47
Nelson Rd. N9 CB27 39
Nelson Rd. SE10 CF43 67
Nelson Rd. SW19 BS50 76
Nelson Rd., Ashf. AY49 73
Nelson Rd., Belv. CQ42 69
Nelson Rd., Brom. CJ52 88
Nelson Rd., Cat. BZ65 105
Nelson Rd., Dart. CV46 80
Nelson Rd., Enf. CC25 30
Nelson Rd., Grav. DF48 81
Nelson Rd., Har. BH33 45
Nelson Rd., Heathrow AY44 63
Nelson Rd., Houns. BF46 74
Nelson Rd., N.Mal. BN53 85
Nelson Rd., Rain. CT37 59
Nelson Rd., S.Ock. DB37 60
Nelson Rd., Sid. CO49 79
Nelson Rd., Stan. BK29 36
Nelson Rd., Uxb. AZ38 53
Nelson Rd., Wind. AM45 61
Nelson Sq. SE1 BY41 4
Nelson Sq. SE1 BY41 66
Nelson St. E1 CB39 57
Nelson St. E16 CG40 58
Caxton St. N.
Nelson St. E6 CK37 58
Nelson Ter. N1 BY37 2
Nelson Wk. SE16 CD40 57
Nelsons Row SW4 BW45 66
Nelwyn Av., Horn. CW32 51
Nemoure Rd. W3 BN40 55
Nene Gdns., Felt. BE48 74
Nene Rd., Houns. AZ44 63
Nepaul Rd. SW11 BU44 66
Nepean St. SW15 BP46 75
Neptune Dr., Hem.H. AY12 8
Neptune Rd., Har. BG32 45
Neptune St. SE16 CC41 67
Nesbit Clo. SE3 CG45 68
Hurren Clo.
Nesbit Rd. SE9 CJ45 68
Nesham St. E1 CB40 4
Nesham St. E1 CB40 57
Ness Rd., Erith CV43 70
Ness St. SE16 CB41 4
Ness St. SE16 CB41 67
Spa Rd.
Nesta Rd., Wdf.Grn. CG29 40
Nestles Av., Hayes BB41 63
Neston Rd., Wat. BD22 27
Nestor Av. N21 BY25 29
Nethan Dr., S.Ock. CY40 60
Nether Clo. W3 BS29 38
Nether Mount, Guil. AQ71 118
Nether St. N12 BS29 38
Nether St. N3 BS30 38
Netheravon Rd. S. W4 BO42 65
Netheravon Rd. W4 BO42 65
Netheravon Rd. W7 BH40 54
Netherbury Rd. W5 BK41 64
Netherby Gdns., Enf. BX24 29
Netherby Rd. SE23 CC47 77
Nethercote Av., Wok. AP62 100
Clifton Way
Nethercourt Av. N3 BS29 38
Netherfield Gdns., Bark. CM36 58
Netherfield Rd. N12 BS28 38
Netherfield St. W11 BR40 55
Portland Rd.
Netherford Rd. SW4 BW44 66
Netherhall Gdns. NW3 BT36 56
Netherhall Rd., Harl. CG12 13
Netherhall Way NW3 BT35 47
Netherhall Gdns.
Netherland Rd. SW17 BV48 76
Netherland Rd., Barn. BT25 29
Netherlands, The, Couls. BW63 104
Netherleigh Clo. N6 BW33 47
Netherleigh Pk., Red. BX72 121
Nethern Court Rd., Cat. CE65 105
Netherne La., Couls. BW65 104
Netherpark Dr., Rom. CT30 41
Netherton Gro. SW10 BT43 66
Netherton Rd., Twick. BJ46 74
Netherway, St.Alb. BF15 9
Netherwood Rd. W14 BQ41 65
Netherwood St. Est. NW6 BR36 55
Netherwood St. NW6 BR36 55
Netley Clo., Croy. CF57 96
Netley Clo., Sutt. BQ56 94
Netley Dr., Walt. BE54 84
Netley Gdns., Mord. BT54 86
Netley Rd. E17 CD32 48
Netley Rd. W., Houns. BA44 63
Netley Rd., Brent. BL43 65
Netley Rd., Ilf. CM32 49
Netley Rd., Mord. BT54 86
Netley St. NW1 BW38 1
Nettle Cft., Welw.G.C. BS 7 5
Hazel Gro.
Nettlecombe Clo., Sutt. BS58 95
Nettlecroft, Hem.H. AW14 8
Nettleden Av., Wem. BM36 55
Nettleden Rd., Berk. AS12 7
Nettlefold Pl. SE27 BY48 76
Nettles Ter., Guil. AR70 118
Nettlestead Clo., Beck. CD50 77
Nettleton Rd. SE14 CC44 67
Nettleton Rd., Houns. AZ44 63
Nettleton Rd., Uxb. AY35 44
Nettlewood Rd. SW16 BW50 76
Neuchatel Rd. SE6 CD48 77
Nevada Clo., N.Mal. BN52 85
Georgia Rd.
Nevada St. SE10 CF43 67
Nevell Rd., Grays DG41 71
Brentwood Rd.
Nevern Pl. SW5 BS42 66
Nevern Rd. SW5 BS42 66
Nevern Sq. SW5 BS42 66
Nevill Gro., Wat. BC23 26
Nevill Rd. N16 CA34 48
Nevill Way, Loug. CK26 40
Neville Av., N.Mal. BN51 85
Neville Clo. E11 CG34 49
Cobbold Rd.
Neville Clo. NW1 BW37 1
Neville Clo. NW1 BW37 56
Neville Clo. NW6 BR37 55
Neville Clo. SE15 CB43 67
Neville Clo. W3 BN41 65
Acton La.
Neville Clo., Esher BE57 93
Neville Clo., Houns. BF44 64
Neville Clo., Pot.B. BR19 19
Neville Clo., Sid. CN49 78
Neville Dr. N2 BT32 47
Neville Gdns., Dag. CP34 50
Neville Rd.
Neville Gill Clo. SW18 BS46 76
Neville Pl. NW6 BR37 55
Neville Rd. E7 CH36 58
Neville Rd. NW6 BR37 55
Neville Rd. W5 BK38 54
Neville Rd., Croy. BZ54 87
Neville Rd., Dag. CP34 50
Neville Rd., Ilf. CM30 40
Neville Rd., Kings.T. BM51 85
Neville Rd., Rich. BK48 74
Neville St. SW7 BT42 3
Neville St. SW7 BT42 66
Neville Ter. SW7 BT42 3
Neville Ter. SW7 BT42 66
Neville Way, Houns. BF44 64
Neville Wk., Cars. BU54 86
Green Wrythe La.
Nevilles Ct. NW2 BP34 46
Nevin Dr. E4 CE26 39
Nevis Clo., Rom. CT29 41
Nevis Rd. SW17 BV48 76
New Ash Clo. N2 BT31 47
Oakridge Dr.
New Barn La., Sev. CM62 106
New Barn La., West. CM62 106
New Barn La., Whyt. CA61 105
New Barn Rd., Grav. DD49 81
New Barn Rd., Swan. CT51 89
New Barn St. E13 CH39 58
New Barnes Av., St.Alb. BJ15 9
New Barns Av., Mitch. BW52 86
New Barns Way, Chig. CL27 40
New Battlebridge La., Red. BV68 113
New Bond St. W1 BV39 56
New Bond St. W1 BV40 3
New Brent St. NW4 BQ32 46
New Bridge St. EC4 BY39 2
New Bridge St. EC4 BY39 56
New Bridge, Erith CS42 69
New Broad St. EC2 BZ39 2
New Broad St. EC2 BZ39 57
New Broadway W5 BK40 54
New Burlington Ms. W1 BW40 3
New Burlington Ms. W1 BW40 56
Regent St.
New Burlington Pl. W1 BW40 3
New Burlington St. W1 BW40 3
New Burlington St. W1 BW40 56
New Bury La., Walt. BD56 93
New Butt La. SE8 CE43 67
New Causeway, Reig. BS72 121
New Cavendish St. W1 BV39 1
New Cavendish St. W1 BV39 56
New Change EC4 BZ39 2
New Change EC4 BZ39 57
New Chapel Sq., Felt. BC47 73
New Church Rd. SE5 BZ43 67
New City Rd. E13 CJ38 58
New Clo. Est., Mitch. BT51 86
New Clo. SW19 BT51 86
New Clo., Felt. BE49 74
New College Ms. N1 BY36 56
College Cross
New Compton St. WC2 BW39 1
New Compton St. WC2 BW39 56
New Coventry St. W1 BW40 3
New Coventry St. W1 BW40 56
Coventry St.
New Crane Pl. E1 CC40 57
Garnet St.
New Cross Gate SE14 CC44 67
New Cross Rd. SE14 CC43 67
New Cross Rd., Guil. AQ69 118
New Ct. WC2 BX39 2
New Ct., Dart. CW46 80
New Ct., Nthlt. BF35 45
Dorchester Clo.
New Ct., Uxb. AX39 53
New Ct., Wey. AX55 83
New End NW3 BT35 47
New End Sq. NW3 BT35 47
New England St., St.Alb. BG13 9
New Euston Ct. NW1 BW38 1
New Farm Av., Brom. CH52 88
New Farm Dr., Rom. CP24 32
New Farm La., Nthwd. BB30 35
New Fetter La. EC4 BY39 2
New Fetter La. EC4 BY39 56
New Ford Rd., Wal.Cr. CD20 21
New Forest La., Chig. CL29 40
New Goulston St. E1 CA39 2
New Goulston St. E1 CA39 57
Middlesex St.
New Greens Av., St.Alb. BG11 9
New Hall Clo., Hem.H. AT17 16
High St.
New Hall Dr., Rom. CW30 42
New Haw Rd., Wey. AX56 92
New Heston Rd., Houns. BE43 64
New Hill Rd., Orp. CK58 97
New House La., Epp. CS16 23
New House La., Grav. DF48 81
New House La., Sev. DC61 108
New Inn La., Guil. AT68 109
New Inn St. EC2 CA38 2
New Inn Yd. EC2 CA38 2
New Inn Yd. EC2 CA38 57
New Inn, Broadway EC2 CA38 57
New Inn Yd.
New James Ct. SE15 CB45 67
New James St. SE15 CB45 67
Scylla Rd.
New Kent Rd. SE1 BZ41 4
New Kent Rd. SE1 BZ41 67
New Kent Rd., St.Alb. BG13 9
New King St. SE8 CE43 67
New Kings Rd. SW6 BR44 65
New La., Guil. AS66 109
New La., Wok. & Guil. AS64 100
New Lodge Dr., Oxt. CG67 115
New London St. EC3 CA40 57
Hart St.
New Lydenbergh St. CJ41 68
New Meadows Path, Rich. BM44 65
Townmead Rd.
New Mill Rd., Orp. CP51 89
New Mount St. E15 CF36 57
New North Pl. EC2 CA38 2
New North Pl. EC2 CA38 57
Luke St.
New North Rd. N1 BZ36 2
New North Rd. N1 BZ36 57
New North Rd., Ilf. CM29 40
New North Rd., Reig. BR72 120
New North St. WC1 BX39 2
New North St. WC1 BX39 56
New Oak Rd. N2 BT30 38
New Orleans Wk. N19 BW33 47
New Oxford St. WC1 BW39 1
New Oxford St. WC1 BW39 56
New Oxford St. WC1 BX39 2
New Palace Yd. SW1 BX41 4
New Par., Ashf. AY49 73
Church Rd.
New Park Av. N13 BZ27 39
New Park Clo., Nthlt. BE36 54
New Park Ct. SW2 BX47 76
New Park Dr., Hem.H. AZ13 8
New Park Rd. SW2 BW47 76
New Park Rd., Ashf. BA49 73
New Park Rd., Hert. BW15 11
New Park Rd., Uxb. AX30 35
New Peachey La. Clo., Uxb. AX39 53
New Peachey La., Uxb. AX39 53
New Place Gdns., Upmin. CY34 51
New Place Sq. SE16 CB41 67
Southwark Park Rd.
New Plaistow Rd. E15 CG37 58
New Pond Rd., Guil. AO74 118
New Quebec St. W1 BU39 1
New Quebec St. W1 BU39 56
New Rd. E1 CB39 57
New Rd. E16 CG39 58
New Rd. E4 CE28 39
New Rd. N17 CA30 39
New Rd. N22 BZ30 39
New Rd. N8 BX32 47
New Rd. N9 CB27 39
New Rd. NW7 BO26 37
(Barnet Gate)
New Rd. NW7 BR29 37
(Mill Hill E.)
New Rd. SE2 CP42 69
New Rd., Amer. AP22 25
New Rd., B.Wd. BK25 27
High St.
New Rd., Berk. AS11 7
New Rd., Brent. BK43 64
New Rd., Brox. CD13 12
New Rd., Brwd. DB27 42
Coptfold Rd.
New Rd., Ch.St.G. AS24 25
New Rd., Church End AV23 25
New Rd., Dag. CR37 59
New Rd., Datchet AR44 62
New Rd., Dor. BK72 119
New Rd., E.Mol. BF52 84
New Rd., East Bedfont BA46 73
New Rd., Epp. CR19 23
New Rd., Esher BG55 84
New Rd., Felt. BC47 73
New Rd., Grav. DG46 81
New Rd., Grays DD43 71
New Rd., Guil. AY69 110
New Rd., Hanworth BE49 74
New Rd., Har. BH35 45
New Rd., Harl. CP 9 6
New Rd., Hayes BA43 63
New Rd., Hextable CT50 79
New Rd., High Welwyn BR 5 5
New Rd., Houns. BF45 64
New Rd., Ilf. CN34 49
New Rd., Kings L. AV18 16
New Rd., Kings.T. BM50 75
New Rd., Langley AT41 62
New Rd., Lechmore Heath BH23 27
New Rd., Lthd. BH59 93
New Rd., Maid. AG43 61
New Rd., Mord. BU54 86
New Rd., Northchurch AP12 7
New Rd., Orp. CO54 89
New Rd., Oxt. CH68 115
New Rd., Pot.B. BP20 19
New Rd., Rad. BH21 27
New Rd., Rain. CS37 59
New Rd., Rich. BK49 74
New Rd., Rick. AZ25 26
New Rd., Rom. CP25 32
New Rd., S.Dnth. CY51 90
New Rd., Shep. AZ52 83
New Rd., South Mimms BM20 19
New Rd., Stai. AU49 72
New Rd., Swan. CT52 89
New Rd., Tad. BQ65 103
New Rd., Uxb. BA38 53
New Rd., Wat. BD24 27
New Rd., Well. CO44 69
New Rd., Welw.G.C. BP 9 5
New Rd., Wey. BA56 92
New River Clo., Hodd. CE11 12
New River Cres. N13 BY28 38
New River Ct. N5 BZ35 48
New River Ct., Wal.Cr. CB19 21
New River Gdns. N22 BY29 38
New River Wk. N1 BZ36 57
New Row WC2 BX40 4
New Row WC2 BX40 56
New Scotland Yd. SW1 BX41 66
Derby Gate
New Spring Gardens Wk. SE11 BX42 4
Albert Embankment
New Spring Gdns., Brent. BK43 64
Albany Rd.
New Sq. WC2 BX39 2
New Sq. WC2 BX39 56
New Sq., Slou. AP41 62
New St. EC2 CA39 2
New St. EC2 CA39 57
New St. Hill EC4 BY39 56
Little New St.
New St. Hill, Brom. CH49 78
New St. Sq. EC4 BY39 2
New St. Sq. EC4 BY39 56
New St., Berk. AR13 7
New St., Saw. CQ 5 6
New St., Stai. AW49 73
New St., Wat. BD24 27
Church St.
New St., West. CM67 115
New Street Hill EC4 BY39 2
Little New St.
New Street Sq. EC4 BY39 2
New Trinity Rd. N2 BT31 47
New Union Clo. E14 CF41 67
New Union St. EC2 BZ39 2
New Wanstead E11 CG32 49
New Way La., Harl. CR11 14
New Way Rd. NW9 BO31 46
New Wharf N1 BX37 2
New Wharf Rd. N1 BX37 56
New Wickham La., Egh. AT50 72
New Windsor St., Uxb. AX37 53
New Wk., Sev. DC61 108
Battlefields Rd.
New Wood, Welw.G.C. BT 7 5
New Years La., Sev. CN61 106
New Zealand Av., Walt. BB54 83
New Zealand Way W12 BP40 55
New Zealand Way, Rain. CT38 59
Newall Rd., Houns. BA44 63
Newark Clo., Guil. AT68 109
Dairymans Wk.
Newark Cres. NW10 BN38 55

Newark Ct., Walt. BD54 84
Stratton Clo.
Newark Grn., B.Wd. BN24 28
Newark La., Wok. AV63 100
Newark Pl., Wok. AW64 101
Newark Rd., S.Croy. BZ57 96
Newark St. E1 CB39 57
Newark Way NW4 BP31 46
Newbarn La., Beac. AP28 34
Newberries Av., Rad. BJ21 27
Newberry Cres., Wind. AL44 61
Newberry Est. N1 BZ36 57
Newbery Rd., Erith CT44 69
Newbery Way, Slou. AO41 61
Newbiggin Path, Wat. BD28 36
Newbolt Av., Sutt. BQ56 94
Newbolt Rd., Stan. BH28 36
Newborough Grn., N.Mal. BN52 85
Newburgh Rd. W3 BN40 55
Newburgh St. W1 BW39 1
Newburgh St. W1 BW39 56
Fouberts Pl.
Newburn St. SE11 BX42 4
Newburn St. SE11 BX42 66
Newbury Av., Enf. CD22 30
Newbury Clo., Nthlt. BE36 54
Newbury Clo., Rom. CV29 42
Newbury Ct. E11 CH31 49
Newbury Gdns., Epsom BO56 94
Newbury Gdns., Rom. CV29 42
Newbury Gdns., Upmin. CW34 51
Newbury Ms. NW5 BV36 56
Malden Rd.
Newbury Rd. E4 CF29 39
Newbury Rd., Brom. CH52 88
Newbury Rd., Houns. AY44 63
Newbury Rd., Ilf. CN32 49
Newbury Rd., Rom. CV28 42
Newbury St. EC1 BZ39 2
Newbury St. EC1 BZ39 57
Newbury Way, Nthlt. BE36 54
Newbury Wk., Rom. CV28 42
Newby Clo., Enf. CA23 30
Newby Pl. E14 CF40 57
Newby St. SW8 BV45 66
Newcastle Av., Ilf. CO29 41
Newcastle Ct. EC4 BY39 2
Newcastle Ct. EC4 BY39 56
Farringdon St.
Newcastle Pl. W2 BT39 1
Newcastle Pl. W2 BT39 56
Newcastle Row EC1 BY38 2
Clerkenwell Clo.
Newcastle St. W8 BS41 66
Newcombe Pk. NW7 BO28 37
Newcombe Pk., Wem. BL37 55
Newcombe Rd., Rad. BM20 19
Newcombe St. W8 BS40 56
Newcome Path, Rad. BM20 19
Newcomen Rd. E11 CG34 49
Newcomen Rd. SW11 BT45 66
Newcomen St. SE1 BZ41 4
Newcomen St. SE1 BZ41 67
Newcourt St. NW8 BU37 1
Newcourt St. NW8 BU37 56
Newcroft Clo., Uxb. AY39 53
Newdales Clo. N9 CB27 39
Balham Rd.
Newdene Av., Nthlt. BD37 54
Newdigate Grn., Uxb. AX30 35
Newdigate Rd. E., Uxb. AX30 35
Newdigate Rd., Uxb. AX30 35
Newell Rd., Hem.H. AY15 8
Newell St. E14 CD39 57
Newenham Rd., Lthd. BF66 111
Newent Clo. SE15 CA43 67
Newent Clo., Cars. BU54 86
Newfield Clo., Hmptn. BF51 84
Newfield La., Hem.H. AY13 8
Newfield Ri. NW2 BP34 46
Newfields, Welw.G.C. BP 8 5
Newford Clo., Hem.H. AZ13 8
Newgale Gdns., Edg. BL30 37
Newgate Clo., Felt. BE48 74
Newgate Clo., St.Alb. BK12 9
Newgate St. E4 CG27 40
Newgate St. EC1 BY39 2
Newgate St. EC1 BY39 56
Newgate St., Hert. BW15 11
Newgate Street Rd., Chsnt. BY16 20
Newgate Street Village, Hert. BX16 20
Newgate, Croy. BZ54 87
Newhall Ct., Wal.Abb. CG20 22
Newham Rd., Houns. BA44 63
Newall Rd.
Newham Way E16 CJ39 58
Newham Way E6 CL38 58
Newham Way, Har. BL31 46
Newhams Clo., Brom. CK52 88
Newhams Row SE1 CA41 4
Newhams Row SE1 CA41 67
Newhaven Clo., Hayes BB42 63
Newhaven Cres., Ashf. BA49 73
Newhaven Gdns. SE9 CJ45 68
Newhaven Rd. SE25 BZ53 87
Newhouse Av., Rom. CP31 50
Newhouse Clo., N.Mal. BO54 85
Newhouse Cres., Wat. BC19 17
Newhouse La., Ong. CV14 15
Newhouse Pk., St.Alb. BJ15 9
Newhouse Rd., Hem.H. AT16 16
Newhouse Way, Mord. BT54 86
Newick Clo., Bex. CR46 79
Newick Rd. E5 CB34 48
Newing Grn., Brom. CJ50 78
Newington Barrow Way N7 BX34 47
Andover Est.
Newington Butts SE1 BY42 4
Newington Butts SE1 BY42 66
Newington Causeway SE1 BY41 4
Newington Causeway SE1 BY41 66
Newington Grn. N16 BZ35 48
Newington Grn. Rd. N1 BZ35 48
Newington Way N7 BX34 47
Newland Clo., Pnr. BE29 36
Newland Clo., St.Alb. BJ15 9
Mile House Clo.
Newland Dr., Enf. CB23 30
Newland Gdns. W13 BJ41 64
Newland Rd. N8 BX31 47
Newland St. E16 CK40 58
Newlands Av., Rad. BH20 18
Newlands Av., T.Ditt. BH54 84
Newlands Av., Wok. AS64 100
Newlands Clo., Brwd. DE26 122
Newlands Clo., Edg. BL27 37
Newlands Clo., Sthl. BE42 64
Newlands Clo., Walt. BE56 93
Newlands Clo., Wem. BK36 54
Newlands Ct., Wem. BM34 46
Newlands Dr., Slou. AV45 62
Newlands Est. SW17 BV49 76
Newlands Pk. SE26 CC50 77
Newlands Pl., Barn. BQ25 28
Newlands Quay E1 CC40 57
Newlands Rd. SW16 BX51 86
Newlands Rd., Hem.H. AV13 7
Newlands Rd., Wdf.Grn. CG27 4C
Newlands Way, Chess. BK56 93
Newlands Way, Pot.B. BS18 20
Osborne Rd.
Newlands Wood, Croy. CD58 96
Newlands Wk., Wat. BD20 18
Newlands, Hat. BQ11 10
Old Hertford Rd.
Newlands, The, Wall. BW57 95
Newling Clo. E6 CK39 58
Newling Est. E2 CA38 57
Newlyn Clo., St.Alb. BE18 18
Newlyn Clo., Uxb. AZ39 53
Newlyn Gdns., Har. BE33 45
Newlyn Rd. N17 CA30 39
Newlyn Rd. NW2 BQ33 46
Newlyn Rd., Barn. BR24 28
Newlyn Rd., Well. CN44 68
Newman Clo., Horn. CW32 51
Newman Pass. W1 BW39 1
Newman Pass. W1 BW39 56
Newman St.
Newman Rd. E13 CH38 58
Newman Rd. E17 CC32 48
Newman Rd., Brom. CH51 88
Newman Rd., Croy. BX54 86
Newman Rd., Hayes BC40 53
Newman Rd., Houns. AZ44 63
Nimrod Rd.
Newman St. W1 BW39 1
Newman St. W1 BW39 56
Newman Yd. W1 BW39 1
Newmans Clo., Loug. CL24 31
Newmans Ct. EC3 BZ39 2
Cornhill
Newmans Dr., Brwd. DE26 122
Newmans La., Loug. CL24 31
Newmans Rd., Grav. DF48 81
Newmans Row WC2 BX39 2
Newmans Row WC2 BX39 56
Great Turnstile
Newmans Way, Barn. BT23 29
Newmarket Av., Nthlt. BF35 45
Newmarket Grn. SE9 CJ47 78
Newmarket Way, Horn. CW35 51
Newminster Rd., Mord. BT53 86
Newnes Path SW15 BP45 65
Newnham Av., Ruis. BD33 45
Newnham Clo., Loug. CJ25 31
Newnham Clo., Nthlt. BG36 54
Newnham Clo., Slou. AQ40 52
Newnham Clo., Th.Hth. BZ51 87
Newnham Gdns., Nthlt. BG36 54
Newnham Ms. N22 BX30 38
Newnham Rd.
Newnham Par., Wal.Cr. CC18 21
Newnham Pl., Grays DG42 71
Newnham Rd. N22 BX30 38
Newnham St. E1 CA39 2
Newnham Ter. SE1 BY41 4
Newnham Ter. SE1 BY41 66
Newnhams Clo., Brom. CK52 88
Newnton Clo. N4 BZ33 48
Newpiece, Loug. CL24 31
Newport Av. E13 CH38 58
Palmer Rd.
Newport Clo., Enf. CD21 30
Mandeville Rd.
Newport Ct. WC2 BW40 3
Newport Ct. WC2 BW40 56
Charing Cross Rd.
Newport Mead, Wat. BD28 36
Newport Pl. WC2 BW40 3
Newport Pl. WC2 BW40 56
Shaftesbury Av.
Newport Rd. E10 CF34 48
Newport Rd. E17 CD31 48
Newport Rd. SW13 BP44 65
Newport Rd., Hayes BA39 53
Newport Rd., Houns. AY44 63
Newbury Rd.
Newport St. SE11 BX42 4
Newport St. SE11 BX42 66
Newport St. WC2 BW40 3
Newport St. WC2 BW41 66
Charing Cross Rd.
Newports, Saw. CP 6 6
Newports, Swan. CS54 89
Newquay Cres., Har. BE34 45
Newquay Gdns., Wat. BC27 35
Newquay Rd. SE6 CE48 77
Newry Rd., Twick. BJ46 74
Newsam Av. N15 BZ32 48
Newsham Rd., Wok. AP62 100
Newstead Av., Orp. CM55 88
Newstead Rd. SE12 CG47 78
Newstead Ri., Cat. CB66 114
Newstead Way SW19 BQ49 75
Newstead Wk., Cars. BT54 86
Newstead, Hat. BO14 10
Newteswell Dr., Wal.Abb. CF19 21
Newton Abbot Rd., Grav. DF48 81
Newton Av. N10 BV30 38
Newton Av. W3 BN41 65
Newton Clo., Slou. AS41 62
Newton Ct., Stai. AQ46 72
Newton Dr., Saw. CP 6 6
Newton Gro. N1 BZ37 2
Newton Gro. N1 BZ37 57
Northport St.
Newton Gro. W4 BO41 65
Newton La., Wind. AQ46 72
Newton Rd. E15 CF35 48
Newton Rd. N15 CA32 48
Newton Rd. NW2 BQ35 46
Newton Rd. SW19 BR50 75
Newton Rd. W2 BS39 56
Newton Rd., Chig. CO28 41
Newton Rd., Har. BH30 36
Newton Rd., Houns. AY44 63
Newton Rd., Islw. BH44 64
Newton Rd., Pur. BW59 95
Newton Rd., Til. DG44 71
Newton Rd., Well. CO45 69
Newton Rd., Wem. BL36 55
Newton St. WC2 BX39 2
Newton St. WC2 BX39 56
Newton Way N18 BZ28 39
Newton Wk., Edg. BM30 37
North Rd.
Newton Wood Rd., Ash. BL61 103
Newtons Clo., Rain. CT36 59
Newtons Cor., Rain. CT36 59
Newtons Yd. SW18 BS46 76
Wandsworth High St.
Newtown Rd., Uxb. AW36 53
Newtown St. SW11 BV44 66
Strasburg Rd.
Newyears Green La., Uxb. AY32 44
Niagara Av. W5 BK42 64
Niagara Clo., Chsnt. CC18 21
Forest Rd.
Nibthwaite Rd., Har. BH32 45
Nichol Clo. N14 BW26 38
Nichol La., Brom. CH50 78
Nicholas Clo., Grnf. BF37 54
Nicholas Clo., S.Ock. DB38 60
Nicholas Clo., St.Alb. BG11 9
Nicholas Clo., Wat. BC22 26
Nicholas Dr., Sev. CV66 117
Nicholas Gdns. W5 BK40 54
Nicholas Gdns., Wok. AV61 100
Nicholas La. EC4 BZ40 4
Nicholas La. EC4 BZ40 57
Nicholas Rd. E1 CC38 57
Nicholas Rd., B.Wd. BL25 28
Nicholas Rd., Croy. BX56 95
Nicholas Rd., Dag. CQ34 50
Nicholas Rd., Houns. BF45 64
Nicholas Way, Hem.H. AY12 8
Nicholas Way, Nthwd. BA30 35
Nicholay Rd. N19 BW33 47
Calverland Gro.
Nicholl Rd., Epp. CN19 22
Nicholls Av., Uxb. AZ38 53
Nicholls Field, Harl. CO11 14
Nicholls, Wind. AL45 61
Nichollsfield Wk. N7 BX35 47
Nichols Grn. W5 BK39 54
Montpelier Rd.
Nicholson Dr., Bush. BG26 36
Nicholson Dr., Egh. AT49 72
Nicholson Ms., Egh. AT49 72
Nicholson Dr.
Nicholson Rd., Croy. CA54 87
Nicholson St. SE1 BY40 4
Nicholson St. SE1 BY40 56
Nicholson Way, Sev. CV64 108
Nickelby Clo. SE28 CP39 59
Nickelby Clo., Uxb. AZ39 53
Thackeray Clo.
Nickelby Rd., Grav. DK47 81
Nickols Wk. SW18 BS45 66
Nicol Clo., Twick. BJ46 74
Nicol End, Ger.Cr. AR30 34
Nicol Rd., Ger.Cr. AR30 34
Nicola Clo., Har. BG30 36
Nicola Clo., S.Croy. BZ57 96
Nicolas Wk., Grays DG41 71
Godman Rd.
Nicoll Pl. NW4 BP32 46
Nicoll Rd. NW10 BO37 55
Nicoll Way, B.Wd. BN24 28
Nicolson Rd., Orp. CP54 89
Nicosia Rd. SW18 BU47 76
Niddersdale, Hem.H. AY12 8
Niederwald Rd. SE26 CD49 77
Nield Rd., Hayes BB41 63
Nigel Clo., Nthlt. BE37 54
Church Rd.
Nigel Ms., Ilf. CL35 49
Nigel Playfair Av. W6 BP42 65
Nigel Rd. E7 CJ35 49
Nigel Rd. SE15 CB45 67
Nigeria Rd. SE7 CJ43 68
Nightingale Av. E4 CG28 40
Nightingale Av., Lthd. BA65 101
Nightingale Av., Upmin. CZ33 51
Nightingale Clo. E4 CF28 39
Nightingale Clo. W4 BN43 65
Nightingale Clo., Cars. BV55 86
Nightingale Clo., Cob. BD59 93
Nightingale Clo., Grav. DF49 81
Mulberry Rd.
Nightingale Clo., Ruis. BD32 45
Nightingale Cres. SW11 BU46 76
Blenkarne Rd.
Nightingale Cres., Lthd. BA65 101
Nightingale Dr., Epsom BM57 94
Nightingale Gro. SE13 CF46 77
Nightingale Gro., Dart. CX45 70
Nightingale La. E11 CH32 49
Nightingale La. N6 BU33 47
Nightingale La. N8 BX31 47
Nightingale La. SW12 BV47 76
Nightingale La. SW4 BV46 76
Nightingale La., St.Alb. BK15 9
Nightingale La., Brom. CJ51 88
Nightingale La., Rich. BL47 75
Nightingale La., Sev. CR68 116
Nightingale Pl. SE18 CL43 68
Nightingale Pl., Rick. AX26 35
Nightingale Rd.
Nightingale Rd. E5 CB34 48
Nightingale Rd. N22 BX29 38
Nightingale Rd. N9 CC26 39
Nightingale Rd. NW10 BO37 55
Nightingale Rd. W7 BH40 54
Nightingale Rd., Bush. BF25 27
Nightingale Rd., Cars. BU55 86
Nightingale Rd., Croy. CC59 96
Nightingale Rd., E.Mol. BF53 84
Nightingale Rd., Esher BE56 93
Nightingale Rd., Guil. AR70 118
Nightingale Rd., Hmptn. BF49 74
Nightingale Rd., Lthd. BB66 110
Nightingale Rd., Orp. CM53 88
Nightingale Rd., Rick. AX26 35
Nightingale Rd., S.Croy. CC58 96
Nightingale Rd., Sev. CW62 108
Nightingale Sq. SW12 BV47 76
Nightingale Vale SE18 CL43 68
Nightingale Way E6 CK39 58
Nightingale Way, Swan. CT52 89
London Rd.
Nightingale Way, Uxb. AV33 43
Nightingale Wk. SW4 BV46 76
Nightingale Wk., Hem.H. BA10 8
Nightingales La., Ch.St.G. AR24 25
Nightingales, Wal.Abb. CG20 22
Roundhills
Nijmegen Way SE22 CA46 77
Dulwich Gro.
Nile Path SE18 CL43 68
Jackson St.
Nile Rd. E13 CJ37 58
Nile St. N1 BZ38 2
Nile St. N1 BZ38 57
Nile Ter. SE15 CA42 4
Nile Ter. SE15 CA42 67
Nimbus Rd., Epsom BN58 94
Nimmo Dr., Bush. BG26 36
Nimrod Clo., Nthlt. BD38 54
Britannia Clo.
Nimrod Rd. SW17 BV50 76
Nimrod Rd., Houns. AZ44 63
Nimrod Way, Houns. AZ44 63
Nimrod Rd.
Nine Acres Clo. E12 CK35 49
Nine Ashes Rd., Brwd. DA20 24
Nine Ashes Rd., Ing. DC18 24
Nine Elms Av., Uxb. AX39 53
Nine Elms Clo., Uxb. AX39 53
Nine Elms Gro., Grav. DG47 81
Nine Elms La. SW8 BW43 66
Nine Stiles Clo., Uxb. AW36 53
Nineacres Way, Couls. BX61 104
Ninefields, Wal.Abb. CG20 22
Ninehams Clo., Cat. BZ63 105
Ninehams Gdns., Cat. BZ63 105
Ninehams Rd.
Ninehams Rd., Cat. BZ64 105
Ninehams Rd., West. CH64 106
Nineteenth Rd., Mitch. BX52 86
Carisbrooke Rd.
Ninhams Wood, Orp. CK56 97
Ninian Rd., Hem.H. AY11 8
Ninnings Rd., Ger.Cr. AS29 34
Ninnings Way, Ger.Cr. AS29 34
Ninth Av., Hayes BC40 53
Nisbet Ho. E9 CC35 48
Nita Rd., Brwd. DB28 42
Nithdale Rd. SE18 CL43 68
Nithsdale Gro., Uxb. BA34 44
Tweeddale Gro.
Niton Clo., Barn. BQ25 28
Niton Rd., Rich. BM45 65
Niton St. SW6 BQ43 65
Nixey Clo., Slou. AQ41 62
Nizels La., Ton. CW71 117
Nizels Rd., Ton. CW70 117
Noahs Ark, Sev. CX62 108
Noak Hill Rd., Rom. CV28 42
Nobel Rd. N18 CC28 39
Noble Cor., Houns. BF44 64
Noble St. EC2 BZ39 2
Noble St. EC2 BZ39 57
Nobles Way, Egh. AS50 72
Noel Park Rd. N22 BY30 38
Noel Rd. E6 CK38 58
Noel Rd. N1 BY37 2
Noel Rd. N1 BY37 56
Noel Rd. W3 BM40 55
Noel Sq., Dag. CP35 50
Noel St. W1 BW39 1
Noel St. W1 BW39 56
Noel Ter. SE23 CC48 77
Dartmouth Rd.
Noke Dr., Red. BV70 121
Noke La., St.Alb. BE16 18
Noke Side, St.Alb. BF17 18
Nokes, The, Hem.H. AW12 8
Nolan Way E5 CB35 48
Nolton Pl., Edg. BL30 37
Nonsuch Clo., Ilf. CL29 40
Nonsuch Court Av., Epsom BP58 94
Nonsuch Wk., Sutt. BQ58 94
Nora Gdns. NW4 BQ31 46
Nora Ter., Har. BH33 45
Norah St. E2 CB38 57
Norbiton Av., Kings.T. BM51 85
Norbiton Common Rd., Kings.T. BM52 85
Norbiton Hall, Kings.T. BL51 85
Norbiton Rd. E14 CD39 57
Norbreck Gdns. NW10 BL38 55
Norbreck Par. NW10 BL38 55
Norbroke St. W12 BO40 55
Norburn St. W10 BR39 55
Chesterton Rd.
Norbury Av. SW16 BX51 86
Norbury Av., Houns. BG45 64
Norbury Av., Th.Hth. BY51 86
Norbury Clo. SW16 BY51 86
Norbury Cres. SW16 BX51 86
Norbury Cross SW16 BX52 86
Norbury Ct. E5 CC35 48
Clapton Park Est.
Norbury Ct. Rd. SW16 BX52 86
Norbury Gdns., Rom. CP32 50
Norbury Gro. NW7 BO27 37
Norbury Hill SW16 BY50 76
Norbury Ms. SW16 BX51 86
Norbury Cres.
Norbury Rd. E4 CE28 39
Norbury Rd., Reig. BR70 120
Norbury Rd., Th.Hth. BZ51 87
Norbury Ri. SW16 BX52 86
Norbury Way, Lthd. BG66 111
Norcombe Gdns., Har. BK32 45
Norcott Clo., Hayes BD38 54
Norcott Rd. N16 CB34 48
Norcroft Gdns. SE22 CB47 77
Norcutt Rd., Twick. BH47 74
Nordenfeldt Rd., Erith CS42 69
Norfield Rd., Bex. CS49 79
Norfolk Av. N13 BY29 38
Norfolk Av. N15 CA32 48
Norfolk Av., S.Croy. CA58 96
Norfolk Av., Slou. AO39 52
Norfolk Av., Wat. BD22 27
Norfolk Clo. N13 BY29 38
Norfolk Clo. N2 BU31 47
Park Rd.
Norfolk Clo., Barn. BV24 29
Norfolk Clo., Twick. BJ46 74
Norfolk Cres. W2 BU39 1
Norfolk Cres. W2 BU39 56
Norfolk Cres., Sid. CN47 78
Norfolk Est. E1 CC38 57
Norfolk Farm Clo., Wok. AU61 100
Norfolk Farm Rd., Wok. AU61 100
Norfolk Gdns., B.Wd. BN24 28
Norfolk Gdns., Bexh. CQ44 69
Norfolk House Rd. SW16 BW48 76
Norfolk Pl. W2 BT39 1
Norfolk Pl. W2 BT39 56
Norfolk Pl., Well. CO44 69
Norfolk Rd. E17 CC30 39
Norfolk Rd. E6 CK37 58
Norfolk Rd. NW10 BO36 55
Norfolk Rd. NW8 BT37 1
Norfolk Rd. NW8 BT37 56
Norfolk Rd. SW19 BU50 76
Norfolk Rd., Bark. CN36 58
Norfolk Rd., Barn. BS24 29
Norfolk Rd., Dag. CR35 50
Norfolk Rd., Dor. BJ71 119
Norfolk Rd., Enf. CB25 30
Norfolk Rd., Esher BH56 93
Norfolk Rd., Felt. BD47 74
Norfolk Rd., Grav. DH47 81
Norfolk Rd., Har. BF32 45
Norfolk Rd., Ilf. CN33 49
Norfolk Rd., Rick. AY26 35
Norfolk Rd., Rom. CS32 50
Norfolk Rd., Th.Hth. BZ52 87
Norfolk Rd., Upmin. CX34 51
Norfolk Rd., Uxb. AX36 53
Norfolk Row SE11 BX42 4
Norfolk Sq. W2 BT39 1
Norfolk Sq. W2 BT39 56
Norfolk St. E7 CH35 49
Norfolk Ter. W6 BR42 65
Norgrove St. SW12 BV47 76
Norheads La., West. CJ61 106
Norheads, West. CH62 106
Norhyrst Av. SE25 CA52 87
Nork Gdns., Bans. BR60 94
Nork Ri., Bans. BQ61 103
Nork Way, Bans. BQ61 103
Norland Pl. W11 BR40 55
Princedale Rd.
Norland Rd. W11 BQ40 55
Norland Sq. W11 BR40 55
Norlands Cres., Chis. CL51 88
Norlands La., Egh. AV51 82
Norley Rd. SE13 CF45 67
Norley Vale SW15 BP47 75
Norlington Rd. E10 CF33 48
Norlington Rd. E11 CF33 48
Norman Av. N22 BY30 38
Norman Av., Epsom BO59 94
Norman Av., Felt. BE48 74
Norman Av., S.Croy. BZ58 96
Norman Av., Sthl. BE40 54
Norman Av., Twick. BJ47 74
Norman Clo. N22 BZ30 39
Norman Av.
Norman Clo., Dart. CW47 80
Norman Clo., Orp. CM55 88
Norman Clo., Rom. CR30 41
Norman Clo., Wal.Abb. CF20 21
Norman Cres., Brwd. DD27 122
Norman Cres., Houns. BD43 64
Norman Cres., Pnr. BD30 36
Norman Ct. N4 BY33 47
Norman Ct., Pot.B. BT19 20
Norman Gro. E3 CD37 57
Norman Ho., Felt. BE48 74
Norman Hurst, Ashf. AZ49 73
Norman Rd. E11 CF34 48
Norman Rd. E6 CK38 58
Norman Rd. N15 CA32 48
Norman Rd. SE10 CE43 67
Norman Rd. SW19 BT50 76
Norman Rd., Ashf. BA50 73
Norman Rd., Belv. CR41 69
Norman Rd., Dart. CW47 80
Norman Rd., Horn. CU33 50
Norman Rd., Ilf. CL35 49
Norman Rd., Sutt. BS56 95
Norman Rd., Th.Hth. BY53 86
Norman St., Welw.G.C. BP 5 5
Norman St. EC1 BZ38 2
Norman St. EC1 BZ38 57
Norman Way N14 BX27 38
Norman Way W3 BM39 55

Normanby Clo. SW15 BR46 75
Manfred Rd.
Normanby Rd. NW10 BO35 46
Normand Ms. W14 BR43 65
Normand Rd. W14 BR43 65
Normandy Av., Barn. BR25 28
Normandy Dr., Berk. AQ12 7
Normandy Dr., Hayes BA39 53
Normandy Pl., Egh. AU49 72
Normandy Rd. SW9 BY44 66
Normandy Rd., St.Alb. BG12 9
Normandy Ter. E16 CH39 58
Coolfin Rd.
Normandy Way, Erith CT44 69
Normanhurst Av., Bexh. CP44 69
Normanhurst Dr., Twick. BJ46 74
St. Margarets Rd.
Normanhurst Rd. SW2 BX48 76
Normanhurst Rd., Orp. CO51 89
Normanhurst Rd., Walt. BD55 84
Normans Bldgs. EC1 BZ38 2
Normans Bldgs. EC1 BZ38 57
Normans Clo. NW10 BN36 55
Normans Clo., Grav. DG47 81
Normans Clo., Uxb. AY39 53
Normans Mead NW10 BN36 55
Normans, The, Slou. AQ39 52
Normansfield Av., Tedd. BK50 74
Normansfield Clo., Bush. BF26 36
Normansfield, Tedd. BK50 74
Normanshire Av. E4 CF28 39
Normanshire Dr. E4 CE28 39
Normanton Av. SW19 BS48 76
Normanton Pk. E4 CG27 40
Normanton Rd., S.Croy. CA57 96
Normanton St. SE23 CC48 77
Normington Clo. SW16 BY49 76
Norrels Dr., Lthd. BB66 110
Norrels Ride, Lthd. BB66 110
Norrice Lea N2 BT32 47
Norris Gro., Brox. CD13 12
Norris La., Hodd. CE11 12
Norris Rd., Hodd. CE12 12
Norris Rd., Stai. AV49 72
Norris Ri., Hodd. CD11 12
Norris St. SW1 BW40 3
Norris St. SW1 BW40 56
Haymarket
Norris Way, Dart. CT45 69
Norroy Rd. SW15 BQ45 65
Norrys Clo., Barn. BU24 29
Norrys Rd., Barn. BU24 29
Norseman Ct., Brwd. CZ22 33
Kelvedon Grn.
Norseman Way, Grnf. BF37 54
Olympic Way
Norstead Pl. SW15 BP48 75
Norsted La., Orp. CO59 98
North Access Rd. E17 CC32 48
North Acre NW9 BO30 37
North Acre, Bans. BR61 103
North Acton Rd. NW10 BN37 55
North Albert Rd., Reig. BR70 120
North App., Nthwd. BA27 35
North App., Wat. BC20 17
North Ash Rd., New.A.G. DC55 90
North Audley St. W1 BV39 56
North Audley St. W1 BV40 3
North Av. N18 CB28 39
North Av. W13 BJ39 54
North Av., Cars. BU57 95
North Av., Har. BF32 45
North Av., Hayes BC40 53
North Av., Rich. BM44 65
Sandycombe Rd.
North Av., Sthl. BE40 54
North Av., Walt. BB58 92
North Bank NW8 BU38 1
North Bank NW8 BU38 56
North Barns, Brox. CE14 12
North Birkbeck Rd. E11 CF34 48
North Bridge Rd., Berk. AP12 7
North Church Rd., Wem. BM36 55
North Circular Rd. E18 CG30 40
North Circular Rd. E4 CD28 39
North Circular Rd. N12 BU29 38
North Circular Rd. N13 BY28 38
North Circular Rd. N3 BS31 47
North Circular Rd. NW10 BL38 55
North Circular Rd. NW11 BQ32 46
North Circular Rd. NW2 BO34 46
North Clo., Barn. BQ25 28
North Clo., Bexh. CP45 69
North Clo., Chig. CO28 41
North Clo., Dag. CR37 59
North Clo., Dor. BK73 119
North Clo., Felt. BA46 73
North Rd.
North Clo., Mord. BR52 85
North Clo., St.Alb. BF16 18
North Clo., Wind. AM44 61
North Common Rd. W5 BL40 55
North Common Rd., Uxb. AX35 44
North Common, Wey. BA56 92
North Countess Rd. E17 CD30 39
North Cray Rd., Bex. CR48 79
North Cray Rd., Sid. CQ50 79
North Cres. N3 BR30 37
North Cres. WC1 BW39 1
North Cres. WC1 BW39 56
Store St.
North Cross Rd. SE22 CA46 77
North Cross Rd., Ilf. CM31 49
North Ct. W1 BW39 1
North Ct. W1 BW39 56
Chitty St.
North Dene NW7 BN27 37
North Dene, Houns. BF44 64
North Down La., Guil. AS72 118
North Down Rd., Ger.Cr. AS29 34
North Down Rd., Sutt. BS58 95
North Down, S.Croy. CA59 96
North Downs Cres., Croy. CE58 96
North Downs Rd., Croy. CE58 96
North Downs Way, Bet. BP68 112
North Downs Way, Dor. BD72 119
North Downs Way, Red. BW67 113
North Downs Way, Sev. DB61 108
North Downs Way, Tad. BS68 113
North Downs Way, West. CL65 106
North Dr. SW11 BU43 66
North Dr. SW16 BW49 76
North Dr., Houns. BG44 64
North Dr., Orp. CN56 97
North Dr., Rom. CV31 51
North Dr., Ruis. BB33 44
North Dr., Vir.W. AP53 82
North End Av. NW3 BT34 47
North End Cres. W14 BR42 65
North End Ho. W14 BR42 65
North End La., Orp. CL58 97
North End NW3 BT34 47
North End Par. W14 BR42 65
North End Rd.
North End Rd. NW11 BS33 47
North End Rd. W14 BR42 65
North End Rd., Wem. BM34 46
North End Ri. SW6 BR43 65
North End W14 BR43 65
North End Way NW3 BT34 47
North End, Buck.H. CJ26 40
North End, Croy. BZ54 87
North Eyot Gdns. W6 BO42 65
Berestead Rd.
North Eyot St. W6 BP42 65
St. Peters Sq.
North Feltham Trading Estate, Felt. BC46 73
North Gate Path, B.Wd. BL22 28
North Gate. Harl. CM10 6
North Gdns. SW19 BT50 76
North Glade, The, Bex. CQ47 79
North Gower St. NW1 BW38 1
North Gower St. NW1 BW38 56
North Grn. NW9 BO29 37
Clayton Field
North Grn., Slou. AP40 52
North Gro. N15 BZ32 48
North Gro. N6 BV33 47
North Gro., Cher. AV53 82
North Gro., Harl. CO11 14
North Harrow Est., Har. BF31 45
North Hill Av. N6 BU32 47
North Hill Dr., Rom. CV27 42
North Hill Grn., Rom. CV28 42
North Hill N6 BU32 47
North Hill, Rick. AV23 25
North Hyde Gdns., Hayes BC42 63
North Hyde La., Houns. BE42 64
North Hyde La., Sthl. BD42 64
North Hyde Rd., Hayes BB41 63
North Kent Av., Grav. DE46 81
North Kent Rd., St.Alb. BG13 9
North La., Tedd. BH50 74
North Lodge Clo. SW15 BQ46 75
Westleigh Av.
North Lodge W5 BK40 54
North Mall N9 CB27 39
North Mead, Reig. BU69 121
North Moors, Guil. AS68 109
North Ms. WC1 BX38 2
North Ms. WC1 BX38 56
North Ockham Rd. S., Lthd. BA66 110
North Orbital Rd., St.Alb. BE18 18
North Orbital Rd., Hat. BP10 5
North Orbital Rd., Uxb. AV33 43
North Orbital Rd., Wat. BC20 17
North Par., Chess. BL56 94
North Pass. SW18 BS46 76
North Pk. La., Gdse. CB68 114
North Pk. SE9 CK46 78
North Pk., Ger.Cr. AS31 43
North Pk., Iver AU41 62
North Pl., Mitch. BU50 76
North Pl., Tedd. BH50 74
North Pl., Wal.Abb. CE20 21
North Pole La., Kes. CG57 97
North Pole Rd. W10 BQ39 55
North Quay E1 CB40 57
North Rd. Av., Brwd. DB26 42
North Rd. N6 BV33 47
North Rd. N7 BX36 56
North Rd. N9 CB26 39
North Rd. SE18 CN42 68
North Rd. SW19 BT50 76
North Rd. W5 BK41 64
North Rd., Amer. AO21 25
North Rd., Belv. CR41 69
North Rd., Berk. AQ13 7
North Rd., Brent. BL43 65
North Rd., Brom. CH51 88
North Rd., Brwd. DB26 42
North Rd., Dart. BT46 79
North Rd., Edg. BM30 37
North Rd., Felt. BA46 73
North Rd., Grays CY42 70
North Rd., Guil. AQ69 118
North Rd., Hav. CT27 41
North Rd., Hayes BA39 53
North Rd., Hodd. CE11 12
North Rd., Ilf. CN34 49
North Rd., Reig. BR72 120
North Rd., Rich. BM45 65
North Rd., Rick. AU25 25
North Rd., Rom. CQ32 50
North Rd., S.Ock. DA37 60
North Rd., Sthl. BF40 54
North Rd., Surb. BK53 84
North Rd., W.Wick. CE54 87
North Rd., Wal.Cr. CD20 21
North Rd., Walt. BD56 93
North Rd., West Dr. AY41 63
North Rd., Wok. AT61 100
North Ride W2 BU40 3
North Ride W2 BU40 56
North Riding, St.Alb. BF18 18
North Row W1 BU40 3
North Row W1 BU40 56
North Service Rd., Brwd. DB27 42
North Several SE3 CF44 67
North Side SW18 BT46 76
North Sq. N9 CB27 39
North Sq. NW11 BS32 47
North St. E13 CH37 58
North St. NW4 BQ32 46
Heriot Rd.
North St. Pass. E13 CH37 58
North St. SW4 BW45 66
North St., Bark. CL36 58
North St., Bexh. CR45 69
North St., Brom. CH51 88
North St., Cars. BU55 86
North St., Dart. CV47 80
Heath St.
North St., Dor. BJ71 119
North St., Egh. AS49 72
North St., Guil. AR71 118
North St., Horn. CV33 51
North St., Islw. BJ45 64
North St., Lthd. BJ64 102
North St., Red. BU70 121
North St., Rom. CS31 50
North St., Rom. CT32 50
North St., Wal.Abb. CG14 13
North St., Westcott BG72 119
North Station App., Red. BX71 121
North Tenter St. E1 CA39 2
North Tenter St. E1 CA39 57
North Ter. SW3 BU41 3
North Ter. SW3 BU41 66
North Verbena Gdns. W6 BP42 65
St. Peters Sq.
North Vill. NW1 BW36 56
North Vw. Av., Til. DG44 71
North Vw. Cres., Epsom BP62 103
North Vw. Cres., NW10 BO35 46
North Vw. Dr., Wdf.Grn. CJ30 40
North Vw. Rd. N8 BW31 47
North Vw. SW19 BP49 75
North Vw. W5 BK38 54
North Vw., Ilf. CO29 41
North Vw., Pnr. BD33 45
North Way N9 CC27 39
North Way NW9 BM31 46
North Way, Mord. BR52 85
North Way, Pnr. BD31 45
North Way, Uxb. AY36 53
North Way, Welw.G.C. BR6 5
North Western Av., Wat. BB21 26
North Western Av., Wat. BD21 27
North Wharf Rd. W2 BT39 1
North Wharf Rd. W2 BT39 56
North Wk., Croy. CF57 96
North Woolwich Rd. E16 CH40 58
North Worple Way SW14 BN45 65
Northall Rd., Bexh. CS44 69
Northallerton Way, Rom. CV28 42
Northampton Gro. N1 BZ35 48
St. Pauls Pl.
Northampton Pk. N1 BZ36 57
Northampton Rd. EC1 BY38 2
Northampton Rd. EC1 BY38 56
Northampton Rd., Croy. CB55 87
Northampton Rd., Enf. CD25 30
Northampton Row EC1 BY38 2
Exmouth Mkt.
Northampton Sq. EC1 BY38 2
Northampton Sq. EC1 BY38 56
Northampton St. N1 BZ36 57
Northanger Rd. SW16 BX50 76
Northaw Clo., Hem.H. AZ11 8
Northaw Rd. E., Cuff. BW19 20
Northaw Rd. W., Pot.B. BU18 20
Northbank Rd. E17 CF30 39
Northborough Rd. SW16 BW52 86
Northbourne Rd. SW4 BW45 66
Northbourne, Brom. CH54 88
Northbrook Dr., Nthwd. BB30 35
Northbrook Rd. N22 BX29 38
Northbrook Rd. SE13 CF46 77
Northbrook Rd., Barn. BR25 28
Northbrook Rd., Croy. BZ53 87
Northbrook Rd., Ilf. CL34 49
Northbrooks, Harl. CM11 13
Northburgh St. EC1 BY38 2
Northburgh St. EC1 BY38 56
Northchurch Rd. N1 BZ36 57
Northchurch Ter. N1 CA36 57
De Beauvoir Rd.
Northcliffe Clo., Wor.Pk. BO55 85
Auriol Park Rd.
Northcliffe Dr. N20 BR26 37
Northcliffe Rd., Grav. DF47 81
Northcote Av. W5 BL40 55
Northcote Av., Islw. BJ46 74
Northcote Av., Sthl. BE40 54
Northcote Av., Surb. BM54 85
Northcote Clo., Lthd. BA66 110
Northcote Cres., Lthd. BA66 110
Northcote Rd. E17 CD31 48
Northcote Rd. NW10 BO36 55
Northcote Rd. SW11 BU46 76
Northcote Rd., Croy. BZ53 87
Northcote Rd., Lthd. BA66 110
Northcote Rd., N.Mal. BN52 85
Northcote Rd., Sid. CN49 78
Northcote Rd., Twick. BJ46 74
Northcote, Lthd. BG60 93
Northcote, Wey. AX56 92
Northcott Av. N22 BX30 38
Northcourt, Rick. AW27 35
Springwell Av.
Northcroft Clo., Egh. AQ49 72
Northcroft Gdns., Egh. AQ49 72
Northcroft Rd. W13 BJ41 64
Northcroft Rd., Egh. AQ49 72
Northcroft Rd., Epsom BN57 94
Northcroft Vill., Egh. AQ49 72
Northdene Gdns. N15 CA32 48
Northdene, Chig. CM28 40
Northdon Clo., Ruis. BB34 44
Northdown Gdns., Ilf. CN32 49
Northdown Rd., Cat. CE65 105
Northdown Rd., Hat. BP14 10
Northdown Rd., Horn. CU33 50
Northdown Rd., Long. DB51 90
Northdown Rd., Sev. CW62 108
Northdown Rd., Well. CO44 69
Northdown St. N1 BX37 2
Northdown St. N1 BX37 56
Northeast Pl. N1 BY37 56
Chapel Mkt.
Northend Rd., Erith CT44 69
Northend, Brwd. DB28 42
Northend, Hem.H. AZ14 8
Northern Av. N9 CA27 39
Northern Perimeter Rd., Houns. AX44 63
Northern Rd. E13 CH37 58
Northern Rd., Slou. AO38 52
Northernhay Wk., Mord. BR52 85
Northey Av., Sutt. BQ58 94
Northey St. E14 CD40 57
Northfield Av. W13 BJ40 54
Northfield Av. W5 BK41 64
Northfield Av., Orp. CP53 89
Northfield Av., Pnr. BD31 45
Northfield Clo., Brom. CK51 88
Logs Hill
Northfield Clo., Hayes BB41 63
Northfield Cres., Sutt. BR56 94
Abbotts Rd.
Northfield Ct., Stai. AW51 83
Northfield Gdns., Dag. CQ35 50
Northfield Gdns., Wat. BD22 27
Northfield Ind. Est., Wem. BM37 55
Northfield Path, Dag. CQ34 50
Northfield Pk., Hayes BB41 63
Northfield Pl., Wey. AZ57 92
Northfield Rd. N16 CA33 48
Northfield Rd. W13 BJ41 64
Northfield Rd., B.Wd. BM23 28
Northfield Rd., Barn. BU24 29
Northfield Rd., Cob. BC60 92
Northfield Rd., Dag. CQ35 50
Northfield Rd., E6 CK36 58
Northfield Rd., Enf. CB25 30
Northfield Rd., Eton AM42 61
Northfield Rd., Houns. BD43 64
Northfield Rd., Stai. AW51 83
Northfield Rd., Wal.Cr. CD19 21
Northfield, Hat. BP11 10
Northfields Rd. W3 BM39 55
Northfields SW18 BS45 66
Northfields, Ash. BL63 103
Northfields, Grays DE42 71
Northfleet Green Rd., Grav. DE50 81
Northgate Dr. NW9 BO32 46
Snowdon Dr.
Northgate, Nthwd. BA29 35
Northiam N12 BS28 38
Northiam St. E8 CB37 57
Northington St. WC1 BX38 2
Northington St. WC1 BX38 56
Northlands Av., Orp. CM56 97
Northlands St. SE5 BZ44 67
Northlands, Pot.B. BT19 20
Northolm, Edg. BN28 37
Northolme Clo., Grays DE41 71
Premier Av.
Northolme Gdns., Edg. BM30 37
Northolme Rd. N5 BY35 47
Northolme Ri., Orp. CN55 88
Northolt Av., Ruis. BC35 44
Northolt Gdns., Grnf. BH35 45
Northolt Rd., Har. BF35 45
Northolt Rd., Houns. AX44 63
Northolt Way, Horn. CV36 60
Northover, Brom. CG48 78
Northport St. N1 BZ37 2
Northport St. N1 BZ37 57
Northridge Rd., Grav. DH48 81
Northridge Way, Hem.H. AV14 7
Northrop Rd., Houns. BB44 63
Northside Rd., Brom. CH51 88
Tweedy Rd.
Northspur Rd., Sutt. BS55 86
Northstead Rd. SW2 BY48 76
Northumberland All. EC3 CA39 2
Northumberland All. EC3 CA39 57
Northumberland Av. WC2 BX40 4
Northumberland Av. WC2 BX40 56
Northumberland Av. E12 CJ33 49
Northumberland Av., Islw. BH44 64
Northumberland Av., Well. CM45 68
Northumberland Av., Horn. CV32 51
Northumberland Av., Enf. CB22 30
Northumberland Clo., Stai. AY46 73
Northumberland Clo., Erith CS43 69
Northumberland Cres., Felt. BB46 73
Northumberland Gdns. N9 CA27 39
Northumberland Gdns., Mitch BW53 86
Northumberland Gro. N17 CB29 39
Northumberland Pk. Clo. N17 CB29 39
Northumberland Pk.
Northumberland Pk. N17 CA29 39
Northumberland Pk., Erith CR43 69
Northumberland Pl. W2 BS39 56
Northumberland Pl., Rich. BK46 74
Hill Ri.
Northumberland Rd. E17 CE33 48
Northumberland Rd. E6 CK39 58
Northumberland Rd., Barn. BT26 38
Northumberland Rd., Grav. DF50 81
Northumberland Rd., S.Le H. DJ41 71
Northumberland Rd., Har. BE32 45
Northumberland Row, Twick. BH47 74
Colne Rd.
Northumberland St. WC2 BX40 4
Northumberland St. WC2 BX40 56
Northumberland Way, Erith CS44 69
Northumbria St. E14 CE39 57
Northview Rd., Sev. CV64 108
Northview, Swan. CT51 89
Northway Cir. NW7 BN28 37
Northway Cres. NW7 BN28 37
Northway N11 BW29 38
Northway NW11 BS32 47
Northway Rd. SE5 BZ45 67
Northway Rd., Croy. CA53 87
Northway, Guil. AQ69 118
Northway, Rick. AX26 35
Northway, Wall. BW56 95
Northways NW3 BT36 56
College Cres.
Northwest Pl. N1 BY37 2
Northwest Pl. N1 BY37 56
Chapel Mkt.
Northwick Av., Har. BJ32 45
Northwick Circle, Har. BK32 45
Northwick Clo. NW8 BT38 1
Northwick Clo. NW8 BT38 56
Norwood Cres.
Northwick Pk. Rd., Har. BH32 45
Northwick Rd., Wat. BD28 36
Northwick Rd., Wem. BK37 54
Northwick Sq., Houns. BA44 63
Northwick Ter. NW8 BT38 1
Northwick Ter. NW8 BT38 56
Northwick Wk., Har. BH33 45
Northwold Dr., Pnr. BD30 36
Northwold Est. E5 CB34 48
Northwold Rd. E5 CB34 48
Northwold Rd. N16 CA34 48
Northwood Av., Horn. CU35 50
Northwood Av., Pur. BY59 95
Northwood Av., Wok. AO62 100
Northwood Gdns. N12 BT28 38
Northwood Gdns., Grnf. BH35 45
Northwood Gdns., Ilf. CL31 49
Northwood Hills Cir., Nthwd. BC30 35
Northwood Hills, Nthwd. BC30 35
Northwood Pl., Erith CQ41 69
Northwood Rd. N6 BV33 47
Northwood Rd., Cars. BV57 95
Northwood Rd., Houns. AX44 63
Northwood Rd., SE23 CD47 77
Northwood Rd., Th.Hth. BY51 86
Northwood Rd., Uxb. AX30 35
Northwood Way, Nthwd. BB29 35
Northwood Way, SE19 CA50 77
Central Hill Est.
Northwood Way, Uxb. AX30 35
Northwood, Grays DG41 71
Northwood, Welw.G.C. BT8 5
Shackleton Way
Nortoft Rd., Ger.Cr. AS29 34
Norton Av., Surb. BM54 85
Norton Clo. E4 CE28 39
Norton Clo., B.Wd. BM23 28
Norton Clo., Enf. CB23 30
Norton Folgate E1 CA39 2
Norton Folgate E1 CA39 57
Norton Gdns. SW16 BX51 86
Norton Heath Rd., Ong. DB15 15
Norton La., Cob. BB63 101
Norton La., Ong. DA16 24
Norton Rd. E10 BX33 47
Dagenham Rd.
Norton Rd., Dag. CS36 59
Norton Rd., Uxb. AX38 53
Norton Rd., Wem. BK36 54
Norval Grn. SW9 BY44 66
Myatts Fields Dev.
Norval Rd., Wem. BJ34 45
Norway Dr., Slou. AQ39 52
Norway Gate SE16 CD41 67
Norway Pl. E14 CD39 57
Norway St. SE10 CE43 67
Norway Wk., Rain. CV39 60
The Glen
Norwich Ms., Ilf. CO33 50
Ashgrove Rd.
Norwich Rd. E7 CH35 49
Norwich Rd. E8 CB37 57
Norwich Rd., Dag. CR37 59
Norwich Rd., Grnf. BF37 54
Norwich Rd., Nthwd. BB31 44
Norwich Rd., Th.Hth. BZ52 87
Norwich St. EC4 BY39 2
Norwich St. EC4 BY39 56
Norwich Way, Rick. AZ24 26
Norwich Wk., Edg. BN29 37
Norwood Av., Rom. CT33 50
Norwood Av., Wem. BL37 55
Norwood Clo., Lthd. BE67 111
Norwood Clo., Sthl. BF42 64
Norwood Cres., Houns. BA44 63
Norwood Dr., Har. BE32 45
Norwood End, Ong. CX11 15
Norwood Gdns., Hayes BD38 54
Norwood Gdns., Sthl. BE42 64
Norwood Grn. Rd., Sthl. BF42 64
Norwood High St. SE27 BY48 76
Norwood La., Iver AU38 52
Norwood Park Rd. SE27 BZ49 77
Norwood Rd. SE24 BY47 76
Norwood Rd. SE27 BY47 76
Norwood Rd., Lthd. BE67 111
Norwood Rd., SE17 BZ43 4
Norwood Rd., Sthl. BE41 64
Norwood Ter., Sthl. BF42 64
Notley End, Egh. AR50 72
Notley St. SE5 BZ43 67
Notre Dame Est. SW4 BW46 76
Notson Rd. SE25 CB52 87
Nott Ct. WC2 BX39 56
Shorts Gdns.
Notting Barn Rd. W10 BQ38 55

Notting Hill Gate W11 BS40 56
Nottingham Av. E16 CJ39 58
Nottingham Clo., Wat. BC20 17
Nottingham Clo., Wok. AP62 100
Nottingham Ct. WC2 BX39 2
Nottingham Pl. W1 BV38 1
Nottingham Pl. W1 BV38 56
Nottingham Rd. E10 CF32 48
Nottingham Rd. SW17 BU47 76
Nottingham Rd. W10 BQ38 55
Nottingham Rd., Islw. BH44 64
Nottingham Rd., Rick. AU26 34
Nottingham Rd., S.Croy. BZ56 96
Nottingham St. W1 BV39 1
Nottingham St. W1 BV39 56
Nottingham Ter. NW1 BV38 1
Nottingham Ter. NW1 BV38 56
Allsop Pl.
Nottingsdale Sq. W11 BR40 55
Wilsham St.
Nova Mews, Sutt. BR54 85
Nova Rd., Croy. BY54 86
Novar Clo., Orp. CN54 88
Novar Rd. SE9 CM47 78
Novello St. SW6 BS44 66
Nowell Rd. SW13 BP43 65
Nower Hill, Pnr. BE31 45
Nower Rd., Dor. BJ71 119
Nower, The, Sev. CN63 106
Noyna Rd. SW17 BU48 76
Nuding Clo. SE13 CE45 67
Nuding Rd. SE13 CE45 67
Nuffield Rd., Swan. CU50 79
Nugent Rd. N19 BX33 47
Nugent Rd. SE25 CA52 87
Nugent Ter. NW8 BT37 1
Nugent Ter. NW8 BT38 56
Nugents Ct., Pnr. BE30 36
Nugents Pk., Pnr. BE30 36
Nunappleton Way, Oxt. CH69 115
Nuneaton Rd., Dag. CP36 59
Nunfield, Kings L. AW19 17
Nunhead Cres. SE15 CB45 67
Nunhead Grn. SE15 CB45 67
Nunhead Gro. SE15 CB45 67
Nunhead La. SE15 CB45 67
Nunhead Pass. SE15 CB45 67
Peckham Rye
Nunnery Clo., St. Alb. BH14 9
Nunnery Stables, St.Alb. BG14 9
Nunnington Clo. SE9 CK48 78
Nunns Rd., Enf. BZ23 30
Nunns Way, Grays DE42 71
Nunns Wk., Egh. AU49 72
Nuns La., St.Alb. BH15 9
Nuns Wk., Vir.W. AR53 82
Nunsbury Dr., Brox. CD16 21
Nupton Dr., Barn. BQ25 28
Nursery Av. N3 BT30 38
Nursery Av., Bexh. CQ45 69
Nursery Av., Croy. CC55 87
Nursery Clo. SW15 BQ45 65
Nursery Clo., Amer. AP23 25
Nursery Clo., Croy. CC55 87
Nursery Clo., Dart. CY47 80
Nursery Clo., Enf. CC23 30
Nursery Clo., Epsom BO58 94
Nursery Clo., Felt. BC47 73
Nursery Clo., Orp. CO54 89
Nursery Clo., Rom. CP32 50
Nursery Clo., S.Ock. DB38 60
Nursery Clo., Sev. CV64 108
Nursery Clo., Swan. CS51 89
Nursery Clo., Tad. BP66 112
Nursery Clo., Wdf.Grn. CH28 40
Nursery Clo., Wey. AV58 91
Nursery Clo., Wok. AR61 100
Nursery Gdns., Enf. CC23 30
Nursery Gdns., Guil. AT73 118
Nursery Gdns., Stai. AW50 73
Nursery Gdns., Sun. BB51 83
Nursery Gdns., Welw.G.C. BR 6 5
Nursery Hill, Welw.G.C. BR 6 5
Nursery La. E7 CH36 58
Nursery La. Rd., Slou. AR40 52
Nursery La. W10 BQ39 55
Highlever Rd.
Nursery La., Uxb. AX38 53
Nursery Pl., Sev. CS65 107
Nursery Rd. N14 BW26 38
Nursery Rd. N2 BT30 38
Nursery Rd. SW19 BR50 75
Nursery Rd. SW9 BX45 66
Nursery Rd., Brox. CD16 21
Nursery Rd., Brwd. DB20 24
Nursery Rd., High Beech CH23 31
Nursery Rd., Hodd. CE10 12
Nursery Rd., Loug. CJ25 31
Nursery Rd., Pnr. BD31 45
Nursery Rd., Sun. BB51 83
Nursery Rd., Sutt. BT56 95
Nursery Rd., Tad. BP66 112
Nursery Rd., Th.Hth. BZ52 87
Nursery Rd., Wal.Abb. CF14 12
Nursery Rd., Wok. AO62 100
Nursery St. N17 CA29 39
Nursery St. SW4 BV45 66
Heath Rd.
Nursery Way, Stai. AR46 72
Nursery Waye, Uxb. AX37 53
Nursery Wk. NW4 BP31 46
Nursery Wk., Rom. CS32 50
Nursery, The, Erith CT43 69
Nursery, The, West. CM67 115
Nurstead Rd., Erith CR43 69
Nut Gro., Welw.G.C. BQ 6 5
Nut Tree Clo., Orp. CP55 89
Nutberry Av., Grays DD41 71
Nutberry Clo., Grays DD41 71
Nutbourne St. W10 BR38 55
Nutbrook St. SE15 CA45 67
Nutbrowne Rd., Dag. CQ37 59
Nutcombe La., Dor. BH71 119
Nutcroft Gro., Lthd. BH64 102
Nutcroft Rd. SE15 CB43 67
Nutfield Clo. N18 CB29 39
Fore St.
Nutfield Clo., Cars. BT54 86
Wrythe La.
Nutfield Gdns., Ilf. CO34 50
Nutfield Gdns., Nthlt. BD37 54
Nutfield Marsh Rd., Red. BW69 121
Nutfield Pl., Th.Hth. BY52 86
Nutfield Rd. E15 CF35 48
Nutfield Rd. SE22 CA45 67
Nutfield Rd., BW68 113
South Merstham
Nutfield Rd., Couls. BV61 104
Nutfield Rd., NW2 BP34 46
Nutfield Rd., Red. BV70 121
Nutfield Rd., Th.Hth. BY52 86
Nutfield Way, Orp. CL55 88
Nutfield, Welw.G.C. BS 6 5
Nutford Pl. W1 BU39 1
Nutford Pl. W1 BU39 56
Nuthatch Gdns. SE28 CM41 68
Harrier Ms.
Nuthurst Av. SW2 BX48 76
Nutley Clo., Swan. CT51 89
Nutley Gro., Reig. BR70 120
Nutley La., Reig. BR70 120
Nutley Ter. NW3 BT36 56
Nutmead Clo., Bex. CS47 79
Nutmeg La. E14 CF39 57
Nutt Gro., Stan. BK27 36
Nutt St. SE15 CA43 67
Sumner Rd.
Nuttall St. N1 CA37 2
Nuttall St. N1 CA37 57
Nutter La. E11 CH32 49
Nuttfield Clo., Rick. AZ25 26
Nutty La., Shep. BA52 83
Nutwell St. SW17 BU49 76
Nutwood Av., Bet. BN71 120
Nutwood Clo., Bet. BN71 120
Nuxley Rd., Belv. CQ43 69
Nyanza St. SE18 CM43 68
Nye Bevan Est. E5 CC34 48
Nye Way, Hem.H. AT17 16
Nyefield Pk., Tad. BP66 112
Nylands Av., Rich. BM44 65
Nymans Gdns. SW20 BP51 85
Nynehead St. SE14 CD43 67
Nyon Gro. SE6 CD48 77
Nyssa Clo., Wdf.Grn. CK29 40
Nyth Clo., Upmin. CY32 51
Nyton Clo. N19 BX33 47

O

O'Leary Sq. E1 CC39 57
Adelina Gro.
O'Meara St. SE1 BZ40 4
O'Meara St. SE1 BZ40 57
O'Neill Path SE18 CL43 68
Kempt St.
O'Shea Gro. E3 CD37 57
Oak Av. N10 BV29 38
Oak Av. N17 BZ29 39
Oak Av. N8 BX31 47
Oak Av., Croy. CE54 87
Oak Av., Egh. AU50 72
Oak Av., Enf. BX22 29
Oak Av., Hmptn. BE49 74
Oak Av., Houns. BE43 64
Oak Av., Sev. CU67 116
Oak Av., St.Alb. BF18 18
Oak Av., Upmin. CX35 51
Oak Av., Uxb. AZ34 44
Oak Av., West Dr. AZ41 63
Oak Bank, Wok. AS63 100
Oak Clo. N14 BV26 38
Oak Clo., Dart. CT45 69
Oak Clo., Hem.H. AY15 8
Oak Clo., Sutt. BT55 86
Oak Clo., Wal.Abb. CF20 21
Oak Clo., West Dr. AZ41 63
Oak Common W3 BO39 55
Common La.
Oak Corner, Berk. AO13 7
Oak Cottage Clo. SE6 CG47 78
Verdant La.
Oak Cres. E16 CG39 58
Oak Ct. N1 CA38 2
Oak Ct., Barn. BU25 29
Oak Dene W13 BJ39 54
The Dene
Oak Dene, Tad. BR63 103
Oak Dr., Berk. AR13 7
Oak Dr., Saw. CP 7 6
Oak End Way, Wey. AV59 91
Oak End, Harl. CN12 13
Oak Farm, B.Wd. BN25 28
Oak Gdns., Croy. CE54 87
Oak Gdns., Edg. BN30 37
Oak Glade, Nthwd. BA30 35
Oak Glen, Horn. CW31 51
Oak Grange Rd., Guil. AW68 110
Oak Green Way, Wat. BB19 17
Oak Grn., Wat. BB19 17
Oak Gro. NW2 BQ35 46
Oak Gro., Hat. BO12 10
Oak Gro., Ruis. BC33 44
Oak Gro., Sun. BC50 73
Oak Gro., W.Wick. CF55 87
Oak Hill Av. NW3 BS35 47
Oak Hill Clo., Wdf.Grn. CF29 39
Oak Hill Cres., Wdf.Grn. CF29 39
Oak Hill Ct. SE23 CC46 77
Oak Hill Ct., Wdf.Grn. CF29 39
Oak Hill Park Ms. NW3 BS35 47
Oak Hill Pk. NW3 BS35 47
Oak Hill Rd., Beck. CF51 87
Oak Hill Rd., Orp. CN54 88
Oak Hill Rd., Rom. CS26 41
Oak Hill Rd., Sev. CU65 107
Oak Hill Way NW3 BT35 47
Oak Hill, Epsom BN61 103
Oak Hill, Guil. AU68 109
Oak Hill, Wdf.Grn. CF29 39
Oak La. E14 CD40 57
Oak La. N11 BW29 38
Oak La. N2 BT30 38
Oak La., Cuff. BX17 20
Oak La., Egh. AR48 72
Oak La., Islw. BH45 64
Oak La., Sev. CT68 116
Oak La., Twick. BJ47 74
Oak La., Wdf.Grn. CG28 40
Oak La., Wind. AN44 61
Oak La., Wok. AT61 100
Oak Lodge Av., Chig. CM28 40
Oak Lodge Clo., Stan. BK28 36
Oak Lodge Clo., Walt. BD56 93
Oak Lodge Dr., W.Wick. CE54 87
Oak Path, Bush. BF26 36
Ashfield Av.
Oak Piece, Epp. CS16 23
Oak Pk., Wey. AV60 91
Oak Rd. W5 BK40 54
Oak Rd., Cat. CA64 105
Oak Rd., Cob. BE61 102
Oak Rd., Epp. CN18 22
Oak Rd., Erith CS43 69
Oak Rd., Grav. DH48 81
Oak Rd., Grays DE43 71
Oak Rd., Green. CZ46 80
Oak Rd., Lthd. BJ63 102
Oak Rd., N.Mal. BN51 85
Oak Rd., Orp. CO57 98
Oak Rd., Reig. BS70 121
Oak Rd., Rom. CW30 42
Oak Rd., Slade Green CU44 69
Oak Rd., West. CM66 115
Oak Ri., Buck.H. CJ27 40
Oak Ridge, Dor. BJ73 119
Oak Row, Mitch. BW51 86
Oak Side, Uxb. AW36 53
Oak St., Hem.H. AY15 8
Oak St., Rom. CS31 50
Oak Stubbs La., Maid. AJ41 61
Oak Tree Clo. W13 BK39 54
Pinewood Gro.
Oak Tree Clo., AR67 109
Stringers Common
Oak Tree Clo., Brwd. DC28 122
Oak Tree Clo., Burpham AU68 109
Oak Tree Clo., Hat. BP12 10
Oak Tree Clo., Stan. BK29 36
Oak Tree Clo., Vir.W. AR53 82
Oak Tree Clo., Wal.Cr. BY17 20
Oak Tree Ct., B.Wd. BK25 27
Oak Tree Dell NW9 BN32 46
Oak Tree Dr. N20 BS26 38
Oak Tree Dr., Egh. AR49 72
Oak Tree Dr., Guil. AR68 109
Oak Tree Gdns., Brom. CH49 78
Oak Tree Rd. NW8 BT38 56
Oak Tree Rd. NW8 BU38 1
Oak Village NW5 BV35 47
Oak Way N14 BV26 38
Oak Way W3 BO40 55
Oak Way, Ash. BM61 103
Oak Way, Croy. CC53 87
Oak Way, Felt. BB47 73
Oak Way, Reig. BT71 121
Oak Wk., Saw. CP 7 6
Oak Wood Chase, Horn. CW32 51
Oak Wood Dr., Lthd. BB67 110
Oak Wood, Berk. AP13 7
Oakapple Clo., S.Croy. CB60 96
Cherry Tree Grn.
Oakbank Av., Walt. BE54 84
Oakbank Gro. SE24 BZ45 67
Oakbank, Brwd. DF25 122
Oakbank, Croy. CF57 96
Oakbrook Clo., Brom. CH49 78
Ridgeway Dr.
Oakbury Rd. SW6 BS44 66
Oakcombe Clo., N.Mal. BO51 85
Traps La.
Oakcroft Clo., Wey. AV60 91
Oakcroft Rd. SE13 CF44 67
Oakcroft Rd., Chess. BL56 94
Oakcroft Rd., Wey. AV60 91
Oakcroft Vill., Chess. BL56 94
Oakdale Av., Har. BL32 46
Oakdale Av., Nthwd. BC30 35
Oakdale Clo., Wat. BD28 36
Oakdale Ct. E4 CF28 39
Oakdale La., Eden. CM70 115
Oakdale N14 BV26 38
Oakdale Rd. E11 CF34 48
Oakdale Rd. E18 CH30 40
Oakdale Rd. E7 CH36 58
Oakdale Rd. N4 BZ32 48
Oakdale Rd. SE15 CC45 67
Ivydale Rd.
Oakdale Rd. SW16 BX49 76
Oakdale Rd., Epsom BN57 94
Oakdale Rd., Wat. BD27 36
Oakdale Rd., Wey. AZ55 83
Oakdale Way, Mitch. BV54 86
Wolseley Rd.
Oakdale, Welw.G.C. BQ 6 5
Oakden St. SE11 BY42 4
Oakden St. SE11 BY42 66
Oakdene Av., Chis. CL49 78
Oakdene Av., Erith CS43 69
Oakdene Av., T.Ditt. BJ54 84
Oakdene Clo., Bet. BN71 120
Oakdene Clo., Horn. CU32 50
Oakdene Clo., Lthd. BF67 111
Oakdene Clo., Pnr. BE29 36
Oakdene Dr., Surb. BN54 85
Oakdene Pk. N3 BR29 37
Oakdene Rd., Bet. BM72 120
Oakdene Rd., Cob. BC60 92
Oakdene Rd., Hem.H. AY15 8
Oakdene Rd., Lthd. BE65 102
Oakdene Rd., Orp. CN53 88
Oakdene Rd., Red. BU70 121
Oakdene Rd., Sev. CU64 107
Oakdene Rd., Uxb. AZ37 53
Oakdene Rd., Wat. BC21 26
Oakdene Way, St.Alb. BK13 9
Oakdene, Chsnt. CD18 21
Oakdene, Wok. AP58 91
Oaken Coppice La., Ash. BM63 103
Oaken Dr., Esher BH57 93
Oaken Gro., Welw.G.C. BR 9 5
Oaken La., Esher BH56 93
Oakend Way, Ger.Cr. AS32 43
Oakenshaw Clo., Surb. BL54 85
Oakes Clo. E6 CK39 58
Savage Gdns.
Oakes Gro. E4 CG27 40
Oakeshott Av. N6 BV34 47
Oakey La. SE1 BY41 66
Oakfield Av., Har. BJ31 45
Oakfield Av., Slou. AN40 61
Oakfield Clo., N.Mal. BO53 85
Oakfield Ct. N8 BX33 47
Oakfield Ct. NW2 BQ33 46
Oakfield Dr., Reig. BS69 121
Reigate Hill Rd.
Oakfield Gdns. N18 CA28 39
Oakfield Gdns. SE19 CA49 77
Oakfield Gdns., Beck. CE53 87
Oakfield Gdns., Cars. BU54 86
Oakfield Gdns., Grnf. BG38 54
Oakfield Glade, Wey. BA56 92
Oakfield La., Dart. CV48 80
Oakfield La., Kes. CJ56 97
Oakfield Pk. Rd., Dart. CV48 80
Oakfield Pl., Dart. CV48 80
Oakfield Rd. E17 CD30 39
Oakfield Rd. E6 CK37 58
Oakfield Rd. N14 BX27 38
Oakfield Rd. N3 BS30 38
Oakfield Rd. N4 BY32 47
Oakfield Rd. SE20 CB51 87
Oakfield Rd. SW19 BQ48 75
Oakfield Rd., Ash. BL62 103
Oakfield Rd., Ashf. AZ49 73
Oakfield Rd., Croy. BZ54 87
Oakfield Rd., Ilf. CL34 49
Oakfield Rd., Orp. CO54 89
Oakfield St. SW10 BT43 3
Oakfield St. SW10 BT43 66
Oakfield, Rick. AV26 34
Oakfield, Wok. AP61 100
Oakfields Rd. NW11 BR32 46
Oakfields, Guil. AP69 118
Oakfields, Sev. CU66 116
Oakfields, Walt. BC54 83
Oakfields, Wey. AW60 92
Oakford Rd. NW5 BW35 47
Oakgrove Rd. SE20 CC51 87
Oakhall Ct. E11 CH32 49
Cambridge Pk.
Oakhall Dr., Sun. BB49 73
Oakhall Rd. E11 CH32 49
Oakham Clo. SE6 CD48 77
Rutland Wk.
Oakham Dr., Brom. CG52 88
Oakhampton Rd. NW7 BQ29 37
Oakhill Av., Pnr. BE30 36
Oakhill Clo., Ash. BK62 102
Oakhill Cres., Surb. BL54 85
Oakhill Dr., Surb. BL54 85
Oakhill Gdns., Wdf.Grn. CG30 40
Oakhill Gdns., Wey. BB55 83
Oakhill Gro., Surb. BL53 85
Oakhill Path, Surb. BL53 85
Oakhill Pl. SW15 BS46 76
Oakhill Rd.
Oakhill Rd. SW15 BR46 75
Oakhill Rd. SW16 BX51 86
Oakhill Rd., Ash. BK62 102
Oakhill Rd., Reig. BS71 121
Oakhill Rd., Rick. AU28 34
Oakhill Rd., Surb. BL53 85
Oakhill Rd., Sutt. BS55 86
Oakhill Rd., Wey. AV57 91
Oakhill, Esher BJ57 93
Oakhill, Surb. BL54 85
Oakhouse Rd., Bexh. CR46 79
Oakhurst Av., Barn. BU26 38
Oakhurst Av., Bexh. CQ44 69
Oakhurst Clo. E17 CG31 49
Oakhurst Gdns. E17 CG31 49
Oakhurst Gdns. E4 CG26 40
Oakhurst Gdns., Bexh. CQ43 69
Oakhurst Gro. SE22 CB45 67
Oakhurst Rd., Enf. CC21 30
Oakhurst Rd., Epsom BN57 94
Oakhurst Ri., Cars. BU58 95
Oakhurst, Wok. AP58 91
Oakington Av., Amer. AS23 25
Oakington Av., Har. BF33 45
Oakington Av., Hayes BA42 63
Oakington Av., Wem. BL34 46
Oakington Dr., Sun. BD51 84
Oakington Manor Dr., BM35 46
Wem.
Oakington Rd. W9 BS38 56
Oakington Way N8 BX32 47
Oakington, Welw.G.C. BT 7 5
Oakland Gdns., Brwd. DE25 122
Oakland Way, Epsom BN57 94
Oaklands Av. N9 CB25 30
Oaklands Av., Esher BG54 84
Oaklands Av., Hat. BR17 19
Oaklands Av., Islw. BH43 64
Oaklands Av., Rom. CT31 50
Oaklands Av., Sid. CN47 78
Oaklands Av., Th.Hth. BY52 86
Oaklands Av., W.Wick. CE55 87
Oaklands Av., Wat. BC26 35
Oaklands Clo., Bexh. CQ46 79
Oaklands Clo., Orp. CN53 88
Oaklands Clo., Sev. CZ57 99
Oaklands Ct. SE26 CB49 77
Oaklands Ct., Wat. BC23 26
Oaklands Ct., Wem. BK35 45
Oaklands Ct., Wey. AW55 83
Oaklands Dr., Red. BV71 121
Oaklands Dr., S.Ock. DB39 60
Oaklands Est. SW4 BW46 76
Oaklands Gate, Nthwd. BA29 35
Green La.
Oaklands Gdns., Ken. BZ60 96
Oaklands Gro. W12 BP40 55
Oaklands La., Barn. BP24 28
Oaklands La., St.Alb. BM13 10
Oaklands La., West. CH60 97
Oaklands N21 BX27 38
Oaklands Park Av., Ilf. CM34 49
Oaklands Pl. SW4 BW45 66
Oaklands Rd. N20 BR26 37
Oaklands Rd. NW2 BQ35 46
Oaklands Rd. SW14 BN45 65
Oaklands Rd. W7 BH41 64
Oaklands Rd., Bexh. CQ45 69
Oaklands Rd., Brom. CG50 78
Oaklands Rd., Chsnt. CA16 21
Oaklands Rd., Dart. CX47 80
Oaklands Rd., Grav. DF49 81
Oaklands Way, Tad. BQ64 103
Oaklands Way, Wall. BW57 95
Oaklands, Ken. BZ61 105
Oaklands, Lthd. BG65 102
Oaklands, Twick. BG47 74
Oaklawn Rd., Lthd. BH62 102
Oaklea Pass., Kings.T. BK52 84
Oakleafe Gdns., Ilf. CL31 49
Oakleigh Av. N29 BT27 38
Oakleigh Av., Edg. BM30 37
Oakleigh Av., Surb. BM54 85
Oakleigh Clo. N20 BU27 38
Oakleigh Clo., Swan. CT52 89
Oakleigh Cres. N20 BU27 38
Oakleigh Ct., Edg. BN30 37
Oakleigh Dr., Rick. BA25 26
Oakleigh Gdns. N20 BT26 38
Oakleigh Gdns., Edg. BL28 37
Oakleigh Gdns., Orp. CN56 97
Oakleigh Pk. Av., Chis. CL51 88
Oakleigh Pk. N. N20 BT27 38
Oakleigh Pk. S. N20 BU26 38
Oakleigh Rd. N. N20 BT27 38
Oakleigh Rd. S. N11 BV27 38
Oakleigh Rd., Pnr. BE29 36
Oakleigh Rd., Uxb. BA36 53
Oakleigh Ri., Epp. CP19 23
Oakleigh Way, Mitch. BV51 86
Oakleigh Way, Surb. BM54 85
Oakley Av. W5 BM40 55
Oakley Av., Bark. CN36 58
Oakley Av., Croy. BX56 95
Oakley Clo. E4 CF27 39
Mapleton Rd.
Oakley Clo. E6 CK39 58
Northumberland Rd.
Oakley Clo. W7 BH40 54
Oakley Clo., Grays DB43 70
Oakley Clo., Islw. BG44 64
Oakley Clo., Wey. AX56 92
Oakley Cres. N1 BY37 56
City Rd.
Oakley Cres., Slou. AP40 52
Oakley Ct., Mitch. BV54 86
Oakley Dell, Guil. AU69 118
Oakley Dr., Brom. CK55 88
Oakley Dr., Rom. CX28 42
Oakley Dr., Sid. CM47 78
Oakley Gdns. N8 BX32 47
Oakley Gdns. SW3 BU43 3
Oakley Gdns. SW3 BU43 66
Oakley Gdns., Bans. BS61 104
Oakley Green Rd., AK44 61
Wind.
Oakley Ho. W5 BM40 55
Oakley La. SE1 BY41 4
Oakley Pk., Bex. CP47 79
Oakley Pl. SE1 CA42 4
Oakley Pl. SE1 CA42 67
Oakley Rd. N1 BZ36 57
Oakley Rd. SE25 CB53 87
Oakley Rd., Brom. CK55 88
Oakley Rd., Har. BH32 45
Oakley Rd., Warl. CB62 105
Oakley Sq. NW1 BW37 1
Oakley Sq. NW1 BW37 56
Oakley St. SW3 BU42 3
Oakley St. SW3 BU42 66
Oakmead Av., Brom. CH53 88
Oakmead Gdns., Edg. BN28 37
Oakmead Grn., Epsom BM61 103
Oakmead Rd. SW12 BV47 76
Oakmead Rd., Croy. BW53 86
Oakmeade, Pnr. BF29 36
Oakmere Av., Pot.B. BT20 20
Oakmere Clo., Pot.B. BT19 20
Oakmere La., Pot.B. BT19 20
Oakmere Rd. SE2 CO43 69
Oakmoor Way, Chig. CN28 40
Parkes Rd.
Oakmount Pl., Orp. CM54 88
Oakridge Av., Rad. BH20 18
Oakridge La., Rad. BH20 18
Oakridge La., Wat. BG21 27
Oakridge Rd., Brom. CF49 77
Oakridge, St.Alb. BE18 18
Oakroyd Av., Pot.B. BR20 19
Oakroyd Clo., Pot.B. BR20 19
Oaks Av. SE19 BZ49 77
Oaks Av., Felt. BE48 74
Oaks Av., Rom. CS30 41
Oaks Av., Wor.Pk. BP55 85
Oaks Clo., Lthd. BJ64 102
Oaks Clo., Rad. BH21 27
Oaks Est., West Byfleet AW60 92
Oaks La., Croy. CB56 96
Oaks La., Croy. CC55 87
Oaks La., Ilf. CN31 49
Oaks Rd., Croy. CB56 96
Oaks Rd., Ken. BY60 95
Oaks Rd., Reig. BT70 121
Oaks Rd., Stai. AX46 73
Oaks Rd., Wok. AS62 100
Oaks Way, Cars. BU57 95
Oaks Way, Epsom BP63 103
Oaks Way, Ken. BZ60 96
Oaks Way, Surb. BK55 84
Oaks, The SE18 CM42 68
Oaks, The, Berk. AQ13 7
Oaks, The, Epsom BO60 94
Oaks, The, Hayes BA37 53

Oaks, The, Ruis. BB33 44
Oaks, The, Stai. AV49 72
Moormede Cres.
Oaks, The, Swan. CT51 89
The Spinney
Oaks, The, Wdf.Grn. CG29 40
Oaks, The, Wey. AW60 92
Oaksford Av. SE26 CB49 77
Oakshade Rd., Brom. CF49 77
Oakshade Rd., Lthd. BG60 93
Oakshaw Rd. SW18 BS47 76
Oakshaw, Oxt. CF67 114
Oakside, Uxb. AW35 44
Oakthorpe Rd. N13 BY28 38
Oaktree Av. N13 BY27 38
Oaktree Clo., Brwd. DC28 122
Oaktree Garth, Welw.G.C. BR 8 5
Oakview Gdns. N2 BT31 47
Oakview Gro., Croy. CD54 87
Oakview Rd. SE6 CE49 77
Oakway Clo., Bex. CQ46 79
Oakway SW20 BQ52 85
Oakway, Brom. CF51 87
Oakway, Grays DD40 71
Oakway, Wok. AP63 100
Oakways SE9 CL46 78
Oakwood Av. N14 BW26 38
Oakwood Av., B.Wd. BM24 28
Oakwood Av., Beck. CF51 87
Oakwood Av., Brom. CH52 88
Oakwood Av., Brwd. DF25 122
Oakwood Av., Mitch. BT51 86
Oakwood Av., Pur. BY59 95
Oakwood Av., Sthl. BF40 54
Oakwood Clo. N14 BW25 29
Oakwood Clo., South Nutfield BX71 121
Oakwood Clo., Chis. CK50 78
Oakwood Clo., Dart. CX47 80
Oakwood Clo., Lthd. BB67 110
Oakwood Clo., Red. BV70 121
Oakwood Clo., Wdf.Grn. CK29 40
Oakwood Cres. N21 BX25 29
Oakwood Cres., Grnf. BJ36 54
Oakwood Ct. W14 BR41 65
Oakwood Dr. SE19 CA50 77
Central Hill Est.
Oakwood Dr., Bexh. CS45 69
Oakwood Dr., Edg. BN29 37
Oakwood Dr., Lthd. BB67 110
Oakwood Dr., St.Alb. BK13 9
Oakwood Gdns., Ilf. CN34 49
Oakwood Gdns., Orp. CM55 88
Oakwood Gdns., Sutt. BS55 86
Oakwood Hill, Loug. CK25 31
Oakwood La. W14 BR41 65
Oakwood Par., Enf. CA25 30
Queen Annes Pl.
Oakwood Park Rd. N14 BW26 38
Oakwood Pl., Croy. BY53 86
Oakwood Rd. NW11 BS31 47
Oakwood Rd. SW20 BP51 85
Oakwood Rd., Croy. BY53 86
Oakwood Rd., Orp. CM55 88
Oakwood Rd., Pnr. BC30 35
Oakwood Rd., Red. BY68 113
Oakwood Rd., St.Alb. BE18 18
Oakwood Rd., Vir.W. AR53 82
Oakwood Rd., Wok. AP63 100
Oakwood Ri., Long. DC52 90
Oakwood Vw. N14 BW25 29
Oakwood, Guil. AQ68 109
Tarragon Dr.
Oakwood, Wal.Abb. CF20 21
Oakwood, Wall. BV58 95
Oakworth Rd. W10 BQ39 55
Oast House Clo., Stai. AS47 72
Oast Rd., Oxt. CG69 115
Oast Way, Hart. DC53 90
Oasthouse Way, Orp. CO52 89
Oat La. EC2 BZ39 2
Oat La. EC2 BZ39 57
Oates Clo., Brom. CF52 87
Oates Rd., Rom. CR28 41
Oatfield Rd., Orp. CN54 88
Oatfield Rd., Tad. BP64 103
Oatland Ri. E17 CD30 39
Oatlands Av., Wey. BA56 92
Oatlands Chase, Wey. BB55 83
Oatlands Clo., Wey. BA56 92
Oatlands Dr., Slou. AO39 52
Oatlands Dr., Wey. AZ56 92
Oatlands Grn., Wey. BA55 83
Oatlands Mere, Wey. BA55 83
Oatlands Rd., Enf. CC23 30
Oatlands Rd., Tad. BR63 103
Oban Ho. E14 CF39 57
Oban Rd. E13 CJ38 58
Oban Rd. SE25 BZ52 87
Oban St. E14 CF39 57
Obelisk Par. SE13 CF45 67
Loampit Vale
Obelisk Ride, Egh. AP50 72
Oberon Clo., Shep. AY52 82
Oberon Ho. N1 CA37 57
Purcell St.
Oberstein Rd. SW11 BT45 66
Oborne Clo. SE24 BY46 76
Observatory Gdns. W8 BS41 66
Observatory Rd. SW14 BN45 65
Occam Rd., Guil. AO70 118
Occupation La. SE18 CL44 68
Occupation La. W5 BK42 64
Occupation Rd. SE17 BZ42 4
Occupation Rd. SE17 BZ42 67
Manor Pl.
Occupation Rd. W7 BJ42 64
Occupation Rd., Belv. CQ41 69
Occupation Rd., Wat. BC25 26
Ocean Est. E1 CC38 57
Ocean St. E1 CC39 57
Masters St.
Ockenden Clo., Wok. AS62 100
Ockenden Rd.
Ockenden Rd. N1 BZ36 57
Ockenden Rd., Upmin. CY35 51
Ockenden Rd., Wok. AS62 100
Ockham Dr., Orp. CO50 79
Ockham La., Cob. BA63 101
Ockham Rd. N., Ripley AY63 101
Ockham Rd. N., Wok. AZ64 101
Ockham Rd. S., Lthd. BB67 110
Ockley Rd. SW16 BX49 76
Ockley Rd., Croy. BX54 86
Ockleys Mead, Gdse. CC68 114
Octagon Rd., Walt. BB58 92
Octavia Clo., Mitch. BU53 86
Octavia Rd., Islw. BH45 64
Octavia St. SW11 BU44 66
Octavia Way SE28 CO40 59
Octavia Way, Stai. AW50 73
Octavius St. SE8 CE43 67
Odard Rd., E.Mol. BF52 84
Oddesey Rd., B.Wd. BM23 28
Odell St. SE5 CA42 4
Odell St. SE5 CA42 67
Odeon Par. N7 BX34 47
Holloway Rd.
Odessa Rd. E7 CG35 49
Odessa Rd. NW10 BP37 55
Odessa St. SE16 CD41 67
Odger St. SW11 BU44 66
Offa Rd., St.Alb. BG13 9
Offas Mead E9 CD35 48
Kings Mead Est.
Offenham Rd. SE9 CK49 78
Offerton Rd. SW4 BW45 66
Offham Slope N12 BR28 37
Offley Rd. SW9 BY43 66
Offord Clo. N17 CB29 39
Offord Rd. N1 BX36 56
Offord St. N1 BX36 56
Ogard Rd., Hodd. CF11 12
Ogilby St. SE18 CK42 68
Oglander Rd. SE15 CA45 67
Ogle St. W1 BW39 1
Ogle St. W1 BW39 56
Oglethorpe Rd., Dag. CQ34 50
Ohio Rd. E13 CG38 58
Oil Mill La. W6 BP42 65
Okeburn Rd. SW17 BV49 76
Okehampton Clo. N12 BT28 38
Okehampton Cres., Well. CO43 69
Okehampton Rd. NW10 BQ37 55
Okehampton Rd., Rom. CV29 42
Okehampton Sq., Rom. CV29 42
Okemore Gdns., Orp. CP52 89
Olaf St. W11 BQ40 55
Old Acre, Wey. AW60 92
Old Av., West Byfleet AV60 91
Old Av., Wey. BA57 92
Old Avenue Clo., Wey. AV60 91
Old Bailey EC4 BY39 2
Old Bailey EC4 BY39 56
Old Barn Clo., Sutt. BR57 94
Old Barn La., Rick. AY25 26
Old Barn La., Whyt. CA61 105
Old Barn Rd., Epsom BN62 103
Old Barn Way, Bexh. CS45 69
Old Barrack Yd. SW1 BV41 3
Old Barrowfield E15 CG37 58
New Plaistow Rd.
Old Bethnal Green Rd. E2 CB38 57
Old Bexley La., Bex. CS48 79
Old Bexley La., Dart. CT47 79
Old Bond St. W1 BW40 3
Old Bond St. W1 BW40 56
Old Brewery Ms. NW3 BT35 47
Hampstead High St.
Old Bridge Clo., Nthlt. BF37 54
Old Bridge St., Kings.T. BK51 84
Thames St.
Old Broad St. EC2 BZ39 2
Old Broad St. EC2 BZ39 57
Old Bromley Rd., Brom. CF49 77
Old Brompton Rd. SW5 BS42 3
Old Brompton Rd. SW5 BS42 66
Old Brompton Rd. SW7 BT42 66
Old Burlington St. W1 BW40 3
Old Burlington St. W1 BW40 56
Old Carriageway, The, Sev. CS64 107
High St.
Old Castle St. E1 CA39 2
Old Castle St. E1 CA39 57
Old Cavendish St. W1 BV39 1
Old Cavendish St. W1 BV39 56
Old Change Ct. EC4 BZ39 2
Old Change Ct. EC4 BZ39 57
Peters Hill
Old Chapel Rd., Swan. CS54 89
Old Charlton Rd., Shep. BA53 83
Old Chertsey Rd., Wok. AQ58 91
Old Cheshire St. E2 CA38 2
Old Chestnut Av., Esher BF57 93
Old Church La. NW9 BN34 46
Old Church La., Brwd. DF24 122
Old Church La., Grnf. BJ38 54
Perivale La.
Old Church La., Stan. BJ28 36
Old Church Rd. E1 CC39 57
Old Church Rd. E4 CE28 39
Old Church St. SW3 BT42 3
Old Church St. SW3 BT42 66
Old Claygate La., Esher BJ57 93
Old Clem Sq. SE18 CL43 68
Kempt St.
Old Coach Rd., Cher. AV53 82
Old Coach Rd., Sev. DC60 99
Old Common Rd., Cob. BC60 92
Old Compton St. W1 BW40 3
Old Compton St. W1 BW40 56
Old Cote Dr., Houns. BF43 64
Old Court Pl. W8 BS41 66
Old Court Rd., Guil. AQ71 118
Old Crabtree La., Hem.H. AY14 8
Old Crown La., Brwd. CY23 33
Old Crown Rd., Brwd. CY23 33
Old Ct. W5 BL39 55
Hillcrest Rd.
Old Ct., Ash. BL63 103
Old Dartford Rd., Farn. CW53 90
Old Dean, Hem.H. AT17 16
Old Deer Park Gdns., Rich. BL45 65
Old Devonshire Rd. SW12 BV47 76
Old Dock Approach Rd., Grays DF42 71
Old Dock Clo., Rich. BM43 65
Old Dock Ct., Rich. BM43 65
Bushwood Rd.
Old Dover Rd. SE3 CH43 68
Old Downs, Hart. DC53 90
Old Drive, The, Welw.G.C. BP 8 5
Old Esher Clo., Walt. BD56 93
Old Esher Rd., Walt. BD56 93
Old Farleigh Rd., S.Croy. CC58 96
Old Farleigh Rd., Warl. CD62 105
Old Farm Av. N14 BW26 38
Old Farm Av., Sid. CM47 78
Old Farm Clo., Houns. BE45 64
Old Farm Gdns., Swan. CT52 89
Old Farm Pass., Hmptn. BG51 84
Old Farm Rd. E., Sid. CO48 79
Old Farm Rd. N2 BT30 38
Old Farm Rd. W., Sid. CN48 78
Old Farm Rd., Guil. AR69 118
Old Farm Rd., Hmptn. BE50 74
Old Farm Rd., West.Dr. AX41 63
Old Farmhouse Dr., Lthd. BG61 93
Old Ferry Dr., Stai. AR46 72
Old Fishery Cut, Hem.H. AV15 7
Old Fishery La., Hem.H. AV14 7
Old Fold Clo., Barn. BR23 28
Old Fold La., Barn. BR23 28
Old Fold Vw., Barn. BQ24 28
Old Ford Rd. E2 CC37 57
Old Ford Rd. E3 CD37 57
Old Forge Clo., Welw.G.C. BR 6 5
Old Forge Clo., Stan. BJ28 36
Old Forge Clo., Wat. BC20 17
Old Forge Cres., Shep. AZ53 83
Old Forge Ms. W12 BP41 65
Goodwin Rd.
Old Forge Rd., Enf. CA22 30
Old Forge Way, Sid. CO49 79
Old Fox Clo., Cat. BY64 104
Old Fox Footpath, S.Croy. CA58 96
Old French Horn La., Hat. BP12 10
Old Gannon Clo., Nthwd. BA28 35
Old Garden Ct., St.Alb. BG13 9
Mount Pleasant
Old Garden, The, Sev. CS65 107
Old Gloucester St. WC1 BX39 2
Old Gloucester St. WC1 BX39 56
Old Hall Clo., Pnr. BE30 36
Old Hall Dr., Pnr. BE30 36
Old Harpenden Rd., St.Alb. BH12 9
Old Harrow La., West. CM63 106
Old Hatch Manor, Ruis. BB33 44
Old Hertford Rd., Hat. BQ11 10
Old Highway, Hodd. CE10 12
Old Hill, Chis. CL51 88
Old Hill, Orp. CM57 97
Old Hill, Wok. AR63 100
Old Homesdale Rd., Brom. CJ52 88
Old House Cft., Harl. CN10 6
Old House Clo. SW19 BR49 75
Old House Clo., Epsom BO58 94
Old House Ct., Hem.H. AY13 8
Old House La., Wal.Abb. CG15 13
Old House Rd., Hem.H. AY13 8
Old Jamaica Rd. SE16 CB41 4
Old Jamaica Rd. SE16 CB41 67
Old James St. SE15 CB45 67
Old Jewry EC2 BZ39 2
Old Jewry EC2 BZ39 57
Old Kent Rd. SE1 CA42 4
Old Kent Rd. SE1 CA42 67
Old Kent Rd. SE15 CB43 67
Old Kenton La. NW9 BM32 46
Old Kingston Rd., Wor.Pk. BN55 85
Old La., Cob. AZ62 101
Old La., Sev. DA65 108
Old La., West. CJ64 106
Old Lambeth Palace Rd. SE1 BX41 66
Old Lane Gdns., Cob. BB64 101
Old Leys, Hat. BP14 10
Old Lodge La., Pur. BX60 95
Old Lodge Pl., Twick. BJ46 74
Old Lodge Way, Stan. BJ28 36
Old London Rd., Dor. BK67 111
Old London Rd., Epsom BP62 103
Old London Rd., Harl. CP10 6
Old London Rd., Lthd. BC66 110
Old London Rd., Sev. CQ61 107
Old London Rd., St.Alb. BH14 9
Old Maidstone Rd., Sid. CQ50 79
Old Malden La., Wor.Pk. BN55 85
Old Malt Way, Wok. AR62 100
Old Manor Dr., Islw. BG46 74
Old Manor Gdns., Guil. AU73 118
Old Manor La., Guil. AU73 118
Old Manor Rd., Til. DG45 71
Old Manor Way, Bexh. CS44 69
Old Manor Way, Chis. CK49 78
Old Manor Yd. SW5 BS42 66
Earls Court Rd.
Old Maple, Hem.H. AY10 8
Old Marsh La., Maid. AJ41 61
Old Marylebone Rd. NW1 BU39 1
Old Marylebone Rd. NW1 BU39 56
Old Mead, Ger.Cr. AS29 34
Old Merrow St., Guil. AU69 118
Old Mill Clo., Eyns. CW54 90
Old Mill Ct. E18 CJ31 49
Old Mill Gdns., Berk. AR13 7
London Rd.
Old Mill La. W6 BP42 65
Upper Mall
Old Mill La., Maid. AH41 61
Old Mill La., Red. BV67 113
Old Mill La., Uxb. AW39 53
Old Mill Rd. SE18 CM43 68
Old Mill Rd., Kings L. BA20 17
Old Mill Rd., Uxb. AW34 44
Old Montague St. E1 CA39 57
Old Montague St. E1 CB39 2
Old Ms., Har. BH32 45
Old Nazeing Rd., Brox. CE14 12
Old Nichol St. E2 CA38 2
Old Nichol St. E2 CA38 57
Old North St. WC1 BX39 2
Old North St. WC1 BX39 56
Theobalds Rd.
Old Oak Av., Couls. BU63 104
Old Oak Common La. NW10 BO39 55
Old Oak Common La. W3 BO39 55
Old Oak Common Way W3 BO40 55
Old Oak Est. W12 BO40 55
Old Oak La. NW10 BO38 55
Old Oak Rd. W3 BO40 55
Old Orchard, Harl. CM12 13
Old Orchard, St.Alb. BG16 18
Old Orchard, Sun. BD51 84
Old Orchard, The NW3 BU35 47
Nassington Rd.
Old Orchard, Wey. AY59 92
Old Otford Rd., Sev. CU62 107
Old Palace La., Rich. BK46 74
Old Palace Rd., Croy. BY55 86
Old Palace Rd., Guil. AQ71 118
Old Palace Rd., Wey. AZ55 83
Old Palace Yd. SW1 BX41 4
Old Palace Yd., Rich. BK46 74
Old Paradise St. SE11 BX42 4
Old Paradise St. SE11 BX42 66
Old Park Av. SW12 BV46 76
Old Park Av., Enf. BZ24 30
Old Park Gdns. SW19 BQ47 75
Old Park Gro., Enf. BZ24 30
Old Park La. W1 BV40 3
Old Park La. W1 BV40 56
Old Park Ms., Houns. BE43 64
Old Park Rd. N13 BX28 38
Old Park Rd. S., Enf. BY24 29
Old Park Rd. SE2 CO42 69
Old Park Rd., Enf. BY24 29
Old Park Ride, Wal.Cr. BY19 20
Old Park Ridings N21 BY25 29
Old Park Vw., Enf. BY24 29
Old Parkbury La., St.Alb. BH18 18
Old Parvis Rd., Wey. AX59 92
Old Perry St., Chis. CN50 78
Old Perry St., Grav. DF47 81
Old Portsmouth Rd., Guil. AR74 118
Old Pottery Clo., Reig. BS71 121
Old Pye St. SW1 BW41 3
Old Pye St. SW1 BW41 66
Old Quebec St. W1 BU39 1
Old Quebec St. W1 BU39 56
Old Queen St. SW1 BW41 3
Old Queen St. SW1 BW41 66
Old Rd. E., Grav. DG47 81
Old Rd. SE13 CG45 68
Old Rd. W., Grav. DF47 81
Old Rd., Brwd. CV24 33
Old Rd., Dart. CS46 79
Old Rd., Enf. CC23 30
Old Rd., Harl. CP 8 6
Old Rd., Rom. CV23 33
Old Rd., Wey. AV57 91
Old Rectory Clo., Tad. BP65 103
Old Rectory Dr., Hat. BP12 10
Old Rectory Gdns., Edg. BM29 37
Old Rectory Ho. SW19 BR49 75
Old Rectory La., Lthd. BB66 110
Old Rectory La., Uxb. AV33 43
Old Rectory Rd., Ong. CV20 24
Old Redding, Har. BF28 36
Old Redstone Dr., Red. BV71 121
Old Reigate Rd., Bet. BM70 120
Old Reigate Rd., Dor. BL70 120
Old Rope Wk., Sun. BC52 83
Old Ruislip Rd., Nthlt. BD37 54
Old School Clo. SW19 BS51 86
Old School Ct., Stai. AS47 72
Old School La., Bet. BM72 120
Old School La., Epsom BO58 94
Old School Ms., Wey. BA56 92
Old Seacoal La. EC4 BY39 2
Old Shire La., Rick. AT25 25
Old Shire La., Wal.Abb. CH21 31
Old Slade La., Iver AV41 62
Old Sopwell Gdns., St.Alb. BG14 9
Cottonmill La.
Old South Clo., Pnr. BD30 36
Old South Lambeth Rd. SW8 BX43 66
Old Sq. WC2 BX39 2
Old St. E13 CH37 58
Old St. EC1 BZ38 2
Old St. EC1 BZ38 57
Old Station App., Lthd. BJ64 102
Old Station La., Stai. AS46 72
Old Station Rd., Knockholt CQ58 98
Old Station Rd., Hayes BB41 63
Old Station Rd., Loug. CK25 31
Old Stockley Rd., West Dr. AZ41 63
Old Swan Yd., Cars. BU56 95
Old Terrys Lodge Rd., Sev. CZ61 108
Old Town SW4 BW45 66
Old Town, Croy. BY55 86
Old Tye Av., West. CK61 106
Old Uxbridge Rd., Rick. AV29 34
Old Watford Rd., St.Alb. BE18 18
Old Watling St., Grav. DG49 81
Old Westhall Clo., Warl. CC63 105
Old Wk., The, Sev. CV62 108
Old Woking Rd., Wok. AT63 100
Old Woolwich Rd. SE10 CF43 67
Oldacre Ms. SW12 BV47 76
Balham Gro.
Oldberry Rd., Edg. BN29 37
Oldborough Rd., Wem. BK34 45
Oldbury Clo., Cher. AV54 82
Oldbury Rd
Oldbury Clo., Orp. CP52 89
Oldbury Clo., Sev. DA64 108
Oldbury La., Sev. DA64 108
Oldbury Pl. W1 BV38 1
Oldbury Pl. W1 BV38 56
Oldbury Rd., Cher. AV54 82
Oldbury Rd., Enf. CB23 30
Oldchurch Gdns., Rom. CS33 50
Oldchurch Rd., Rom. CS33 50
Oldchurch Ri., Rom. CT33 50
Olden La., Pur. BY59 95
Oldershaw Rd. N7 BX36 56
Oldfield Cir., Nthlt. BG36 54
Oldfield Clo., Amer. AS23 25
Oldfield Clo., Brom. CK52 88
Oldfield Clo., Chsnt. CD17 21
Oldfield Clo., Grnf. BH35 45
Oldfield Clo., Stan. BJ28 36
Oldfield Dr., Chsnt. CD17 21
Oldfield Farm Gdns., Grnf. BG37 54
Oldfield Gdns., Ash. BK63 102
Oldfield Gro. SE16 CC42 67
Oldfield La. N., Grnf. BG36 54
Oldfield La. S., Grnf. BG38 54
Oldfield Rd. N16 CA34 48
Oldfield Rd. NW10 BO36 55
Oldfield Rd. SW19 BR50 75
Oldfield Rd., Bexh. CQ44 69
Oldfield Rd., Brom. CK52 88
Oldfield Rd., Hem.H. AV14 7
Oldfield Rd., Hmptn. BE51 84
Oldfield Rd., St.Alb. BK16 18
Oldfields Rd., Sutt. BR55 85
Oldhams Ter. W3 BN40 55
Oldhill Pl. N16 CB33 48
Oldhill St. N16 CB33 48
Oldhouse La., Harl. CJ12 13
Oldhouse La., Kings L. AY21 26
Oldridge Rd. SW12 BV47 76
Olds Approach, Wat. BA26 35
Oldstead Rd., Brom. CF49 77
Oldway La., Slou. AL40 61
Oleander Clo., Orp. CM56 97
Olevedon Pass. N16 CA34 48
Brooke Rd.
Oley Pl. E1 CC39 57
Olga St. E3 CD37 57
Conyer St.
Olinda Rd. N16 CA32 48
Oliphant St. W10 BQ38 55
Olive Rd. E13 CJ38 58
Olive Rd. NW2 BQ35 46
Olive Rd. SW19 BT50 76
Olive Rd. W5 BK41 64
Olive Rd., Dart. CV47 80
Olive St., Rom. CS31 50
Olive Taylor Ct., Hem.H. AY11 8
Stevenage Ri.
Oliver Av. SE25 CA52 87
Oliver Clo. E10 CE34 48
Oliver Clo. W4 BM43 65
Oliver Clo., Grays CZ43 70
Oliver Clo., Hem.H. AY15 8
Oliver Clo., St.Alb. BG17 18
Oliver Clo., Wey. AW56 92
Oliver Cres., Farn. CW54 90
Oliver Gdns. E6 CK39 58
Oliver Goldsmith Est. SE15 CB44 67
Oliver Gro. SE25 CA52 87
Oliver Rd. E10 CE34 48
Oliver Rd. E17 CF32 48
Oliver Rd., Brwd. DD25 122
Oliver Rd., Grays DA43 70
Oliver Rd., Hem.H. AY15 8
Oliver Rd., N.Mal. BN51 85
Oliver Rd., Rain. CT37 59
Oliver Rd., Sutt. BT56 95
Oliver Rd., Swan. CS52 89
Olivers Av., Berk. AU11 7
Olivers Mill, Dart. DC55 90
Olivers Yd. EC2 BZ38 2
Olivers Yd. EC2 BZ38 57
City Rd.
Olivette St. SW15 BW45 65
Felsham Rd.
Ollards Gro., Loug. CJ24 31
Olleberrie La., Rick. AU19 16
Ollerton Grn. E3 CD37 57
Ollerton Rd. N11 BW28 38
Olley Clo., Wall. BX57 95
Redford Av.
Ollgar Clo. W12 BP40 55
Olliffe St. E14 CF41 67
Olmar St. SE1 CB43 4
Olmar St. SE1 CB43 67
Olney Rd. SE17 BY43 66
Olron Cres., Bexh. CP46 79
Olven Rd. SE18 CM43 68
Olveston Wk., Cars. BT53 86
Olyffe Av., Well. CO44 69
Olyffe Dr., Brom. CF51 87
Olympia Ms. W2 BS40 3
Olympic Way, Grnf. BF37 54
Olympic Way, Wem. BM34 46
Olympus Sq. E5 CB34 48
Downs Est.
Oman Av. NW2 BP35 46
Omega Pl. N1 BX37 2
Omega Pl. N1 BX37 56
Caledonian Rd.
Omega Rd., Wok. AT61 100
Omega St. SE14 CD44 67
Ommaney Rd. SE14 CC44 67
On The Hill, Wat. BE27 36
Ondine Rd. SE15 CA45 67

One Pin La., Slou. AO35 43
One Tree Clo. SE23 CC46 77
One Tree Hill Rd., Guil. AT71 118
Onega Gate SE16 CD41 67
Ongar Clo., Rom. CP32 50
Ongar Clo., Wey. AV56 91
Ongar Hill, Wey. AW57 92
Ongar Pl., Brwd. DB27 42
Ongar Pl., Wey. AW57 92
Ongar Rd. SW6 BS43 66
Ongar Rd., Pilgrim's Hatch CY24 33
Ongar Rd., Brwd. DA26 42
Ongar Rd., Epp. CO18 23
Ongar Rd., Ong. CY14 15
Ongar Rd., Rom. CO24 32
Ongar Rd., Stondon Massey CZ20 24
Ongar Rd., Wey. AW56 92
Ongar Way, Rain. CT37 59
Onra Rd. E17 CE33 48
Onslow Av., Rich. BL46 75
Onslow Av., Sutt. BR58 94
Onslow Clo. E4 CF27 39
Onslow Clo., Hat. BP12 10
Onslow Clo., Surb. BH54 84
Onslow Way
Onslow Clo., Wok. AT62 100
Onslow Cres. SW7 BT42 66
Old Brompton Rd.
Onslow Cres., Chis. CL51 88
Onslow Cres., Wok. AT62 100
Onslow Dr., Sid. CP48 79
Onslow Gdns. E18 CH31 49
Onslow Gdns. N10 BV32 47
Onslow Gdns. N21 BY25 29
Onslow Gdns. SW7 BT42 3
Onslow Gdns. SW7 BT42 66
Onslow Gdns., Ong. CX17 24
Onslow Gdns., S.Croy. CB59 96
Onslow Gdns., T.Ditt. BH54 84
Onslow Gdns., Wall. BW57 95
Onslow Ms. E. SW7 BT42 3
Onslow Ms. W. SW7 BT42 3
Onslow Ms. W. SW7 BT42 66
Cranley Pl.
Onslow Rd., Croy. BX54 86
Onslow Rd., Guil. AR70 118
Onslow Rd., N.Mal. BP52 85
Onslow Rd., Rich. BL46 75
Onslow Rd., Walt. BB56 92
Onslow Sq. SW7 BT42 3
Onslow Sq. SW7 BT42 66
Onslow St. EC1 BY38 56
Clerkenwell Rd.
Onslow St. EC1 BY39 2
Onslow St., Guil. AR71 118
Onslow Way, T.Ditt. BH54 84
Onslow Way, Wok. AV61 100
Ontario St. SE1 BY41 4
Ontario St. SE1 BY41 66
Opal Clo. E16 CJ39 58
Opal Ms., Ilf. CL34 49
Ley St.
Opal St. SE11 BY42 4
Opal St. SE11 BY42 66
Openshaw Rd. SE2 CO42 69
Openview SW18 BT47 76
Ophelia Gdns. NW2 BQ34 46
Cricklewood Trd. Est.
Ophir Ter. SE15 CB44 67
Opossum Way, Houns. BD45 64
Oppidans Ms. NW3 BU36 56
Oppidans Rd. NW3 BU36 1
Oppidans Rd. NW3 BU36 56
Oram Pl., Hem.H. AX15 8
Orange Court La., Orp. CL58 97
Orange Ct. E1 CB40 57
Hermitage Wall
Orange Hill Rd., Edg. BN29 37
Orange Pl. SE16 CC41 67
Orange St. WC2 BW40 3
Orange St. WC2 BW40 56
Orange Tree Hill, Hav. CS28 41
Orangery La. SE9 CK46 78
Orangery, The, Rich. BK48 74
Orb St. SE17 BZ42 4
Orb St. SE17 BZ42 67
Orbain Rd. SW6 BR43 65
Orbel St. SW11 BU44 66
Orbital 1, Dart. CX48 80
Orbital Cres., Wat. BB21 26
Orchard Av. N14 BW26 38
Orchard Av. N20 BT27 38
Orchard Av. N3 BS31 47
Orchard Av., Ashf. BA50 73
Orchard Av., Belv. CQ43 69
Orchard Av., Berk. AQ13 7
Orchard Av., Brwd. DC27 122
Orchard Av., Croy. CD54 87
Orchard Av., Dart. CU47 79
Orchard Av., Felt. BA46 73
Orchard Av., Grav. DG49 81
Orchard Av., Houns. BE43 64
Orchard Av., Mitch. BV54 86
Orchard Av., N.Mal. BO51 85
Orchard Av., Rain. CV38 60
Orchard Av., Sthl. BE40 54
Orchard Av., T.Ditt. BJ54 84
Orchard Av., Wat. BC19 17
Orchard Av., Wey. AV59 91
Orchard Av., Wind. AN44 61
Orchard Clo. NW2 BP34 46
Orchard Clo. SE23 CC46 67
Brenchley Gdns.
Orchard Clo. SW20 BQ52 85
Orchard Clo. W10 BR39 55
Wornington Rd.
Orchard Clo., Ashf. BA50 73
Orchard Clo., B.Wd. BL24 28
Orchard Clo., Bans. BS60 95
Orchard Clo., Bexh. CQ44 69
Orchard Clo., Bish. CS 7 6
Orchard Clo., Bush. BG26 36
Orchard Clo., Cuff. BX17 20
Orchard Clo., Edg. BL29 37
Orchard Clo., Effingham BB65 101
Orchard Clo., Egh. AT49 72
Orchard Clo., Fetcham BG64 102
Orchard Clo., Hem.H. AZ12 8
Orchard Clo., Hert. BW13 11
Orchard Clo., Rad. BH22 27
Orchard Clo., Rick. AU24 25
Orchard Clo., Ruis. BA33 44
Orchard Clo., S.Ock. DB38 60
Orchard Clo., Sev. CV63 108
Orchard Clo., St.Alb. BH14 9
Orchard Clo., Surb. BJ54 84
Orchard Clo., Uxb. AW36 53
Orchard Clo., Walt. BC53 83
Garden Rd.
Orchard Clo., Wat. BB23 26
Orchard Clo., Wem. BL36 55
Orchard Clo., Wok. AT61 100
Orchard Cotts., Brwd. DC32 123
Orchard Cres., Edg. BN28 37
Orchard Cres., Enf. CA23 30
Orchard Croft, Harl. CO10 6
Orchard Ct., Edg. BL28 37
Orchard Ct., Hem.H. AT17 16
Apple Cotts.
Orchard Ct., Islw. BG44 64
Thornbury Av.
Orchard Ct., Wor.Pk. BP54 85
Orchard Dr. SE3 CF44 67
Orchard Dr., Ash. BK63 102
Orchard Dr., Edg. BL28 37
Orchard Dr., Epp. CN21 31
Orchard Dr., Grays DD41 71
Orchard Dr., Rick. AU24 25
Orchard Dr., St.Alb. BF17 18
Orchard Dr., Uxb. AX38 53
Orchard Dr., Wat. BB23 26
Orchard Dr., Wok. AS61 100
Orchard End Av., Amer. AP23 25
Orchard End, Cat. CA64 105
Town End Clo.
Orchard End, Lthd. BG65 102
Orchard End, Ong. CW16 24
Springfield Clo.
Orchard End, Wey. BB55 83
Orchard Est. SE13 CE44 67
Orchard Gate NW9 BO31 46
Orchard Gate, Esher BG54 84
Orchard Gate, Grnf. BJ36 54
Orchard Gdns., Chess. BL56 94
Orchard Gdns., Epsom BN60 94
Orchard Gdns., Lthd. BE67 111
Orchard Gdns., Sutt. BS56 95
Orchard Gdns., Wal.Abb. CF20 21
Orchard Grn., Orp. CN55 88
Orchard Gro. SE20 CB50 77
Orchard Gro., Croy. CD54 87
Orchard Gro., Edg. BM30 37
Orchard Gro., Ger.Cr. AR30 34
Orchard Gro., Har. BL32 46
Orchard Gro., Orp. CN55 88
Orchard Hill SE13 CE44 67
Coldbath St.
Orchard Hill, Cars. BU56 95
Orchard Hill, Dart. CT46 79
Orchard La. SW20 BP51 85
Orchard La., Amer. AO22 25
Orchard La., Brwd. CZ25 33
Orchard La., E.Mol. BG53 84
Orchard La., Harl. CQ 9 6
Orchard La., Wdf.Grn. CJ28 40
Orchard Lea Clo., Wok. AV61 100
Orchard Leigh, Chesh. AQ17 16
Orchard Mains, Wok. AR63 100
Orchard Mead, Hat. BO12 10
Orchard Ms. N1 BZ36 2
Orchard Ms. N1 BZ36 57
Southgate Gro.
Orchard Par., Pot.B. BQ19 19
Mutton La.
Orchard Piece, Ing. DC18 24
Orchard Pl. E14 CG40 58
Orchard Pl. N17 CA29 39
Orchard Pl., Brom. CH51 88
Orchard Rd. N6 BV33 47
Orchard Rd. SE18 CM42 68
Orchard Rd. SE3 CG44 68
Orchard Rd., Barn. BR24 28
Orchard Rd., Beac. AO28 34
Orchard Rd., Belv. CR42 69
Orchard Rd., Farnborough CL56 97
Orchard Rd., Pratt's Bottom CP58 98
Orchard Rd., Brent. BK43 64
Orchard Rd., Brom. CJ51 88
Orchard Rd., Burpham AT68 109
Orchard Rd., Ch.St.G. AR27 34
Orchard Rd., Chess. BL56 94
Orchard Rd., Dag. CR37 59
Orchard Rd., Dor. BJ72 119
Orchard Rd., Enf. CC25 30
Orchard Rd., Grav. DE48 81
Orchard Rd., Guil. AP71 118
Orchard Rd., Hayes BC40 53
Orchard Rd., Hmptn. BE50 74
Orchard Rd., Houns. BE46 74
Orchard Rd., Kings.T. BL52 85
Orchard Rd., Mitch. BV54 86
Orchard Rd., Otford CT61 107
Orchard Rd., Reig. BS70 121
Orchard Rd., Rich. BM45 65
Orchard Rd., Riverhead CT64 107
Orchard Rd., Rom. CR30 41
Orchard Rd., S.Croy. CB60 96
Orchard Rd., S.Ock. DB38 60
Orchard Rd., Shalford AS73 118
Orchard Rd., Sid. CN49 78
Orchard Rd., Sun. BC50 73
Orchard Rd., Sutt. BS56 95
Orchard Rd., Swans. DC46 81
Orchard Rd., Twick. BJ46 74
Orchard Rd., Well. CO45 69
Orchard Rd., Wind. AQ46 72
Orchard Ri. E., Sid. CN46 78
Orchard Ri. W., Sid. CN45 68
Orchard Ri., Croy. CD54 87
Orchard Ri., Kings.T. BN51 85
Orchard Ri., Rich. BM46 75
Orchard Sq. W14 BR42 65
Sun Rd.
Orchard Sq., Brox. CD15 12
Orchard St. E17 CD31 48
Orchard St. W1 BV39 1
Orchard St. W1 BV39 56
Orchard St., Dart. CW46 80
Orchard St., Hem.H. AX15 8
Orchard St., St.Alb. BG14 9
Orchard Ter., Enf. CB25 30
Orchard Vw., Uxb. AX38 53
Orchard Way, Ashf. AY48 73
Orchard Way, Chig. CO27 41
Orchard Way, Chsnt. BY17 20
Orchard Way, Croy. CD54 87
Orchard Way, Dart. CV48 80
Orchard Way, Dor. BJ72 119
Orchard Way, Enf. CA24 30
Orchard Way, Esher BG57 93
Orchard Way, Hem.H. AT17 16
Orchard Way, Oxt. CH70 115
Orchard Way, Pot.B. BS18 20
Orchard Way, Reig. BS72 121
Orchard Way, Rick. AW26 35
Orchard Way, Sev. CX62 108
Orchard Way, Slou. AS40 52
Firs Dr.
Orchard Way, Sutt. BT56 95
Orchard Way, Tad. BR66 112
Orchard Way, Wey. AW56 92
Orchard Way, Wok. AU66 109
Orchard Waye, Uxb. AX37 53
Orchard, The N21 BZ25 30
Orchard, The NW11 BS32 47
Orchard, The SE3 CF44 67
Orchard, The W4 BN42 65
Orchard, The W5 BK39 54
Orchard, The, Bans. BS61 104
Orchard, The, Dor. BK73 119
Orchard, The, Epsom BO57 94
Orchard, The, Houns. BG44 64
Orchard, The, Kings L. AZ18 17
Orchard, The, Sev. CT64 107
Milton Rd.
Orchard, The, Swan. CS51 89
Orchard, The, Vir.W. AS53 82
Orchard, The, Welw.G.C. BQ 7 5
Orchard, The, Wok. AS64 100
Orchardleigh Av., Enf. CC23 30
Orchardleigh, Lthd. BJ64 102
St Nicholas Hill
Orchardmede N21 BZ25 30
Orchards N., The, Epp. CO19 23
Orchards S., The, Epp. CO19 23
Orchards, The, Saw. CQ 6 6
Orchardson St. NW8 BT38 1
Orchardson St. NW8 BT38 56
Orchehill Av., Ger.Cr. AR31 43
Orchehill Ri., Ger.Cr. AS32 43
Orchid Clo. E6 CK38 58
Orchid Rd. N14 BW26 38
Orchid St. W12 BP40 55
Orchis Gro., Grays DC42 71
Orchis Way, Rom. CW29 42
Orde Hall St. WC1 BX39 2
Orde Hall St. WC1 BX39 56
Ordell Rd. E3 CD37 57
Ordnance Clo., Felt. BC48 73
Ordnance Cres. SE10 CG41 68
Ordnance Hill NW8 BT37 1
Ordnance Hill NW8 BT37 56
Ordnance Ms. NW8 BT37 1
Ordnance Rd. E16 CG39 58
Ordnance Rd. SE18 CL43 68
Ordnance Rd., Enf. CC22 30
Ordnance Rd., Grav. DH46 81
Oregano Way, Guil. AQ68 109
Oregon Av. E12 CK35 49
Oregon Clo., N.Mal. BN52 85
Georgia Rd.
Oregon Sq., Orp. CM54 88
Orestan La., Lthd. BC67 110
Orestes Ms. NW6 BS35 47
Aldred Rd.
Oreston Rd., Rain. CV38 60
Orewell Gdns., Reig. BS71 121
Orford Ct. SE27 BY48 76
Orford Gdns., Twick. BH48 74
Orford Rd. E17 CE32 48
Orford Rd. E18 CH31 49
Organ Hall Rd., B.Wd. BK23 27
Organ La. E4 CF27 39
Oriel Clo., Mitch. BW52 86
Holly Way
Oriel Ct., Mitch. BW52 86
Oriel Gdns., Ilf. CK31 49
Oriel Pl. NW3 BT35 47
Oriel Rd. E9 CC36 57
Oriel Way, Nthlt. BF36 54
Orient Rd., Til. DG45 71
Orient St. SE11 BY42 4
Orient St. SE11 BY42 66
West Sq.
Orient Way E5 CC34 48
Oriental Clo., Wok. AS62 100
Oriental Rd. E16 CJ40 58
Oriental Rd., Wok. AS62 100
Oriole Way SE28 CO40 59
Orion Pk. W7 BJ41 64
Orion Way, Nthwd. BB28 35
Orissa Rd. SE18 CN42 68
Orkney St. SW11 BV44 66
Orlando Gdns., Epsom BN58 94
Ormonde Av.
Orlando Rd. SW4 BW45 66
Orleans Rd. SE19 BZ50 77
Orleans Rd., Twick. BJ47 74
Orleston Ms. N7 BY36 56
Orleston Rd. N7 BY36 56
Orlestone Gdns., Orp. CQ56 98
Orley Farm Rd., Har. BH34 45
Orlick Rd., Grav. DK48 81
Orlop St. SE10 CG42 68
Ormanton Rd. SE26 CB49 77
Orme Ct. Ms. W2 BS40 56
Orme La.
Orme Ct. W2 BS40 3
Orme Ct. W2 BS40 56
Orme La. W2 BS40 3
Orme La. W2 BS40 56
Orme Ms. W2 BS40 56
Orme Ct.
Orme Rd., Kings.T. BM51 85
Orme Sq. W2 BS40 3
Orme Sq. W2 BS40 56
Ormeley Rd. SW12 BV47 76
Ormerod Gdns., Mitch. BV51 86
Ormesby Clo. SE28 CP40 59
Wroxham Rd.
Ormesby Dr., Pot.B. BQ19 19
Ormesby Gdns., Grnf. BG37 54
Ormesby Way, Har. BL32 46
Ormiston Gro. W12 BP40 55
Ormiston Rd. SE10 CH42 68
Ormond Av., Hmptn. BF51 84
Ormond Av., Rich. BK46 74
Ormond Rd.
Ormond Clo. WC1 BX39 2
Ormond Cres., Hmptn. BF51 84
Ormond Dr., Hmptn. BF50 74
Ormond Ms. WC1 BX38 2
Ormond Ms. WC1 BX38 56
Guilford St.
Ormond Rd. N19 BX33 47
Ormond Rd., Rich. BK46 74
Ormond Yd. SW1 BW40 3
Ormond Yd. SW1 BW40 56
Duke of York St.
Ormonde Av., Epsom BN58 94
Ormonde Av., Orp. CM55 88
Ormonde Ct. SW15 BQ45 65
Upper Richmond Rd.
Ormonde Gate SW3 BU42 3
Ormonde Gate SW3 BU42 66
Ormonde Pl. SW1 BV42 66
Bourne St.
Ormonde Rd. SW14 BM45 65
Ormonde Rd., Nthwd. BA28 35
Ormonde Rd., Wok. AR61 100
Ormonde Ri., Buck.H. CJ26 40
Ormonde Ter. NW8 BU37 1
Ormonde Ter. NW8 BU37 56
Ormsby Pl. N16 CD34 48
Victorian Gro.
Ormsby St. E2 CA37 2
Ormsby St. E2 CA37 57
Ormside St. SE15 CC43 67
Ormside Way, Red. BV69 121
Ormskirk Rd., Wat. BD28 36
Ornan Rd. NW3 BU35 47
Oronsay Wk. N1 BZ36 57
Oronsay, Hem.H. AZ14 8
Orphanage Rd., Wat. BD23 27
Orpheus St. SE5 BZ44 67
Orpin Rd., Red. BV68 113
Orpington By-Pass, Orp. CP56 98
Orpington Gdns. N18 CA27 39
Orpington Rd. N21 BY26 38
Orpington Rd., Chis. CN51 88
Orpwood Clo., Hmptn. BE50 74
Orris Ms. W6 BQ42 65
Beadon Rd.
Orsett Heath Cres., Grays DG41 71
Orsett Rd., Grays DD42 71
Orsett St. SE11 BX42 4
Orsett St. SE11 BX42 66
Orsett Ter. W2 BS39 1
Orsett Ter. W2 BS39 56
Orsett Ter., Wdf.Grn. CJ29 40
Orsman Rd. N1 CA37 2
Orsman Rd. N1 CA37 57
Orton St. E1 CB40 4
Orton St. E1 CB40 57
Hermitage Wall
Orville Rd. SW11 BT44 66
Orwell Clo., Rain. CS39 59
Orwell Clo., Wind. AO45 61
Orwell Ct. N5 BZ35 48
Orwell Rd. E13 CJ37 58
Osbaldeston Rd. N16 CA34 48
Osbert St. SW1 BW42 3
Osbert St. SW1 BW42 66
Vincent Sq.
Osberton Rd. SE12 CH46 78
Osborn Clo. E8 CB37 2
Osborn Clo. E8 CB37 57
Osborn Gdns. NW7 BQ29 37
Osborn La. SE23 CD47 77
Brockley Pk.
Osborn St. E1 CA39 2
Osborn St. E1 CA39 57
Osborn Ter. SE3 CG45 68
Osborne Av., Stai. AY47 73
Osborne Clo., Beck. CD52 87
Osborne Clo., Felt. BD49 74
Osborne Clo., Horn. CU32 50
Osborne Clo., Sutt. BT56 95
Albert Rd.
Osborne Gdns., Pot.B. BS18 20
Osborne Rd.
Osborne Gdns., Th.Hth. BZ51 87
Osborne Gro. E17 CD32 48
Osborne Ms., Wind. AO44 61
Osborne Pl., Sutt. BT56 95
Albert Rd.
Osborne Rd. E10 CE34 48
Osborne Rd. E7 CH35 49
Osborne Rd. E9 CD36 57
Osborne Rd. N13 BY27 38
Osborne Rd. N4 BY33 47
Osborne Rd. NW2 BP36 55
Osborne Rd. W3 BM41 65
Osborne Rd., Belv. CQ42 69
Osborne Rd., Brox. CE13 12
Osborne Rd., Brwd. DA25 33
Osborne Rd., Buck.H. CH26 40
Osborne Rd., Dag. CQ35 50
Osborne Rd., Egh. AS50 72
Osborne Rd., Enf. CD23 30
Osborne Rd., Horn. CU32 50
Osborne Rd., Houns. BE45 64
Osborne Rd., Kings.T. BL50 75
Osborne Rd., Pot.B. BS18 20
Osborne Rd., Red. BV69 121
Osborne Rd., Sthl. BF39 54
Osborne Rd., Th.Hth. BZ51 87
Osborne Rd., Uxb. AX36 53
Oxford Rd.
Osborne Rd., Wal.Cr. CD17 21
Osborne Rd., Walt. BC54 83
Osborne Rd., Wat. BD22 27
Osborne Rd., Wind. AO44 61
Osborne Sq., Dag. CQ35 50
Osborne St. SE17 BZ42 4
Osborne St. SE17 BZ42 67
Osborne St., Slou. AP41 62
Osbourne Av., Kings L. AY17 17
Oscar St. SE8 CE44 67
Oseney Cres. NW5 BW35 47
Osgood Av., Orp. CN56 97
Osgood Gdns., Orp. CN56 97
Osidge La. N14 BV26 38
Osier St. E1 CC38 57
Cephas Av.
Osier Way E10 CE34 48
Osier Way, Bans. BR60 94
Osier Way, Mitch. BU53 86
Osiers Rd. SW18 BS45 66
Oslac Rd. SE6 CE49 77
Oslo Ct. NW8 BU37 1
Oslo Ct. NW8 BU37 56
Osman Clo. N15 BZ32 48
Tewkesbury Rd.
Osman Rd. N9 CB27 39
Osmond Clo., Har. BG34 45
Osmond Gdns., Wall. BW56 95
Osmund St. W12 BO39 55
Braybrook St.
Osnaburgh St. NW1 BV38 1
Robert St.
Osnaburgh St. NW1 BV38 56
Osnaburgh Ter. NW1 BV38 1
Osnaburgh Ter. NW1 BV38 56
Osnaburgh St.
Osney Way, Grav. DJ48 81
Osney Wk., Cars. BT53 86
Osprey Clo. E11 CH31 49
Osprey Clo. E6 CK39 58
Dove App.
Osprey Clo., West Dr. AY41 63
Osprey Gdns., S.Croy. CC58 96
Osprey Ms., Enf. CB25 30
Derby Rd.
Ospringe Clo. SE20 CC51 87
Ospringe Ct. SE9 CM46 78
Ospringe Rd. NW5 BW35 47
Osric Path N1 CA37 2
Osric Path N1 CA37 57
Ossian Rd. N4 BX33 47
Ossington Bldgs. W1 BV39 56
Moxon St.
Ossington Clo. W2 BS40 56
Ossington St.
Ossington St. W2 BS40 56
Ossory Rd. SE1 CB42 67
Ossory Rd. SE1 CB43 4
Ossulston Est. NW1 BW38 1
Ossulston Est. NW1 BW38 56
Ossulston St. NW1 BW37 1
Ossulston St. NW1 BW37 56
Ossulton Pl. N2 BT31 47
Ossulton Way
Ossulton Way N2 BT31 47
Ostade Rd. SW2 BX47 76
Osten Ms. SW7 BS41 3
Osten Ms. SW7 BS41 66
Ostend Pl. SE17 BZ42 4
Sayer St.
Oster St., St.Alb. BG13 9
Osterberg Rd., Dart. CW45 70
Osterley Av., Islw. BG43 64
Osterley Clo., Orp. CO51 88
Leith Hill
Osterley Cres., Islw. BH44 64
Osterley Ct., Islw. BG44 64
Osterley Gdns., Th.Hth. BZ51 87
Osterley La., Sthl. BF42 64
Osterley Park Rd., Sthl. BE41 64
Osterley Park View Rd. W7 BH41 64
Osterley Rd. N16 CA35 48
Osterley Rd., Islw. BH43 64
Oswald Clo., Lthd. BG64 102
Oswald Rd., Lthd. BG64 102
Oswald Rd., St.Alb. BH14 9
Oswald Rd., Sthl. BE40 54
Oswald Ter. NW2 BQ34 46
Stoll Clo.
Oswalds Mead E9 CD35 48
Kings Mead Est.
Osward Pl. N9 CB27 39
Osward Rd. SW17 BU48 76
Osward, Croy. CD58 96
Oswin St. SE11 BY42 4
Oswin St. SE11 BY42 66
Oswyth Rd. SE5 CA44 67
Otford Clo., Bex. CR46 79
Otford Clo., Brom. CL52 88
Otford Cres. SE4 CD46 77
Otford La., Sev. CQ59 98
Otford Rd., Sev. CU63 107
Othello Clo. SE11 BY42 66
Otis St. E3 CF38 57
Otley App., Ilf. CL32 49
Otley Dr., Ilf. CL32 49
Otley Rd. E16 CJ39 58
Otley Rd., Chesh. AP18 16
Otley Ter. E5 CC34 48
Otley Way, Wat. BD27 36
Otlinge Clo., Orp. CP52 89
Ottawa Gdns., Dag. CS36 59
Ottawa Rd., Til. DG44 71
Ottaway St. E5 CB34 48
Otter Gdns., Hat. BP13 10
Otter Rd., Grnf. BG38 54
Otterbourne Rd. E4 CF27 39
Otterbourne Rd., Croy. BY55 86
Ruskin Rd.
Otterburn Gdns., Islw. BJ43 64

Otterburn St. SW17	BU50	76
Otterden Clo., Orp.	CN56	97
Otterden St. SE6	CE49	77
Otterfield Rd., West Dr.	AY40	53
Ottermead La., Cher.	AU57	91
Otterspool La., Wat.	BE22	27
Otterspool Way, Wat.	BE23	27
Ottesbrook St. SE14	CD43	67
Otto Clo. SE26	CB48	77
Sydenham Hill		
Otto St. SE17	BY43	66
Ottoman Ter., Wat.	BD24	27
Ebury Rd.		
Ottways Av., Ash.	BK63	102
Ottways La., Ash.	BK63	102
Otways Clo., Pot.B.	BS19	20
Oulton Clo. E5	CB34	48
Southwold Rd.		
Oulton Clo. SE28	CP40	59
Rollesby Way		
Oulton Cres, Bark.	CN35	49
Oulton Cres., Pot.B.	BQ19	19
Oulton Rd. N15	BZ32	48
Oulton Rd., Pot.B.	BQ19	19
Oulton Way, Wat.	BE28	36
Oundle Av., Bush.	BG25	27
Ousden Clo., Chsnt.	CD18	21
Ousden Dr., Chsnt.	CD18	21
Ouseley Rd. SW12	BU47	76
Ouseley Rd., Wind.	AR47	72
Outer Circle NW1	**BV38**	**1**
Outer Circle NW1	BV38	56
Outfield Rd., Ger.Cr.	AR29	34
Outgate Rd. NW10	BO36	55
Outings La., Brwd.	DA21	33
Outram Pl. N1	**BX37**	**2**
Outram Pl. N1	BX37	56
Outram Pl., Wey.	BA56	92
St. Georges Av.		
Outram Rd. E6	CK37	58
Outram Rd. N22	BW30	38
Outram Rd., Croy.	CA55	87
Outram St. N1	BX37	56
Outwich St. EC3	CA39	57
Houndsditch		
Outwood La., Couls.	BU63	104
Outwood La., Red.	BZ71	114
Outwood La., Tad.	BS64	104
Oval Ct., Edg.	BM29	37
Pavilion Way		
Oval Gdns., Grays	DE41	71
Oval Pl. SW8	BX43	66
Oval Rd. N., Dag.	CR37	59
Oval Rd. NW1	**BV37**	**1**
Oval Rd. NW1	BV37	56
Oval Rd. S., Dag.	CR37	59
Oval Rd., Croy.	BZ55	87
Oval Way SE11	**BX42**	**4**
Oval Way SE11	BX42	66
Oval Way, Ger.Cr.	AS31	43
Oval, The E2	CB37	57
Oval, The, Bans.	BS60	95
Oval, The, Brox.	CD15	12
Oval, The, Guil.	AQ71	118
Oval, The, Sid.	CO47	79
Ovenden Rd., Sev.	CP63	107
Over Brae, Beck.	CE50	77
Over The Misbourne, Ger.Cr.	AT32	43
Overbrook Wk., Edg.	BM29	37
Chandos Cres.		
Overbrook, Lthd.	AZ68	110
Overbury Av., Beck.	CE52	87
Overbury Cres., Croy.	CF58	96
Overbury Rd. N15	BZ32	48
Overbury St. E5	CC35	48
Overcliff Rd. SE13	CE45	67
Overcliff Rd., Grays	DE42	71
Overcliffe, Grav.	DF46	81
Overcourt Clo., Sid.	CO46	79
Blackfen Rd.		
Overdale Av., N.Mal.	BN51	85
Overdale Rd. W5	BK41	64
Overdale, Ash.	BL61	103
Overdale, Dor.	BK71	119
Overdale, Red.	BZ70	114
Overdown Rd. SE6	CE49	77
Overhill Gdns. SE22	CB47	77
Overhill Rd. SE22	CB47	77
Overhill Rd., Pur.	BY58	95
Overhill Way, Beck.	CF53	87
Overhill, Whyt.	CC63	105
Overlea Rd. E5	CB33	48
Overmead, Sid.	CM47	78
Overmead, Swan.	CT53	89
Overstand Clo., Beck.	CE53	87
Overstone Gdns., Croy.	CD54	87
Overstone Rd. W6	BQ41	65
Overstream, Rick.	AW24	26
Overthorpe Clo., Wok.	AP62	100
Overton Clo. NW10	BN36	55
Overton Clo., Islw.	BH44	64
Overton Dr. E11	CH33	49
Overton Dr., Rom.	CP33	50
Overton Rd. E. SE2	CP41	69
Overton Rd.		
Overton Rd. E10	CD33	48
Overton Rd. N14	BX25	29
Overton Rd. SE2	CP41	69
Overton Rd. SW9	BY44	66
Overton Rd., Sutt.	BS57	95
Overtons Yd., Croy.	BZ55	87
Overy Liberty, Dart.	CW47	80
Overy St., Dart.	CW46	80
Ovesdon Av., Har.	BE33	45
Oveton Way, Lthd.	BF66	111
Ovett Clo. SE19	CA50	77
Childs La.		
Ovex Clo. E14	CF41	67
Ovington Ct., Wok.	AP61	100
Roundthorne Way		
Ovington Gdns. SW3	**BU41**	**3**
Ovington Gdns. SW3	BU41	66
Ovington Ms. SW3	**BU41**	**3**
Ovington Ms. SW3	BU41	66
Ovington Sq. SW3	**BU41**	**3**
Ovington Sq. SW3	BU41	66

Ovington St. SW3	**BU42**	**3**
Ovington St. SW3	BU42	66
Owen Clo. SE28	CP40	59
Owen Clo., Hayes	BC38	53
Owen Gdns., Wdf.Grn.	CK29	40
Owen Pl., Lthd.	BJ64	102
Church Rd.		
Owen Rd. N13	BZ28	39
Owen Rd., Hayes	BC38	53
Owen St. EC1	**BY37**	**2**
Owen Way NW10	BN35	46
Owen Wk. SE20	CB51	87
Sycamore Gro.		
Owenite St. SE2	CO42	69
Owens Ct. EC1	**BY38**	**2**
Owens Ct. EC1	BY38	56
Goswell Rd.		
Owens Rd. EC1	BY38	56
St. John St.		
Owens Row EC1	**BY38**	**2**
Owens Way SE23	CD47	77
Brockley Pk.		
Owens Way, Rick.	AZ24	26
Owgan Clo. SE5	BZ43	67
Benhill Rd.		
Owl Clo., S.Croy.	CC58	96
Kingfisher Gdns.		
Owlets Hall Clo., Rom.	CW31	51
Ownstead Gdns., S.Croy.	CA59	96
Ownstead Hill, Croy.	CF58	96
Ox La., Epsom	BP58	94
Oxberry Av. SW6	BR44	65
Oxdowne Clo., Cob.	BF60	93
Oxenden Dr., Hodd.	CE12	12
Oxenden Wood Rd., Orp.	CO57	98
Oxendon St. SW1	**BW40**	**3**
Oxendon St. SW1	BW40	56
Oxenford St. SE15	CA45	67
Oxenhill Rd., Sev.	CW62	108
Oxenpark Av., Wem.	BL33	46
Oxestalls Rd. SE8	CD42	67
Oxfield Clo., Berk.	AQ13	7
Oxford Av. SW20	BR51	85
Oxford Av., Grays	DG42	71
Oxford Av., Hayes	BB43	63
Oxford Av., Horn.	CX31	51
Oxford Av., Houns.	BF43	64
Oxford Av., St.Alb.	BK14	9
Oxford Circus W1	**BV39**	**1**
Oxford Clo. N9	CB27	39
Oxford Clo., Ashf.	BA50	73
Oxford Clo., Chsnt.	CC18	21
Oxford Clo., Grav.	DJ48	81
Oxford Clo., Mitch.	BW52	86
Oxford Cres., N.Mal.	BN53	85
Oxford Ct., Brwd.	DB28	42
Oxford Ct., Felt.	BD49	74
Oxford Dr., Ruis.	BD34	45
Oxford Gdns. N20	BT26	38
Oxford Gdns. N21	BZ26	39
Oxford Gdns. W10	BQ39	55
Oxford Gdns. W4	BM42	65
Oxford Gdns., Uxb.	AW34	44
Oxford La., Guil.	AR71	118
Oxford Ms., Bex.	CR47	79
Bexley High St.		
Oxford Rd. E15	CF36	57
Oxford Rd. N. W4	BM42	65
Oxford Rd. N4	BY33	47
Oxford Rd. N9	CB27	39
Oxford Rd. NW6	BS37	56
Oxford Rd. S. W4	BM42	65
Oxford Rd. SE19	BZ50	77
Oxford Rd. SW15	BR45	65
Oxford Rd. W5	BK40	54
Oxford Rd., Cars.	BU57	95
Oxford Rd., Cat.	CA66	114
Oxford Rd., Denham	AW34	44
Oxford Rd., Enf.	CB25	30
Oxford Rd., Ger.Cr.	AO31	43
Oxford Rd., Guil.	AR71	118
Oxford Rd., Har.	BG32	45
Oxford Rd., Ilf.	CM35	49
Oxford Rd., Red.	BU70	121
Oxford Rd., Rom.	CW29	42
Oxford Rd., Sid.	CO49	79
Oxford Rd., Tedd.	BG49	74
Oxford Rd., Uxb.	AX36	53
Oxford Rd., Wall.	BW56	95
Oxford Rd., Wdf.Grn.	CJ28	40
Oxford Sq. W2	**BU39**	**1**
Oxford Sq. W2	BU39	56
Oxford St. W1	**BV39**	**1**
Oxford St. W1	BV39	56
Oxford St., Bark.	CL36	58
Oxford St., Wat.	BC25	26
Oxford Way, Cat.	CA66	114
Oxford Way, Felt.	BD49	74
Oxgate Gdns. NW2	BP34	46
Oxgate La. NW2	BP34	46
Oxhawth Cres., Brom.	CL53	88
Oxhey Av., Wat.	BD26	36
Oxhey Dr., Nthwd.	BC28	35
Oxhey La., Wat.	BE26	36
Oxhey Rd., Wat.	BD25	27
Oxhey Ridge Clo., Nthwd.	BC28	35
Oxleas Clo., Well.	CM44	68
Oxlease Dr., Hat.	BP13	10
Oxleay Av., Har.	BF33	45
Oxleay Ct., Har.	BF33	45
Oxleigh Clo., N.Mal.	BO53	85
Oxley Clo., Rom.	CV30	42
Oxleys Rd. NW2	BP34	46
Oxleys Rd., Wal.Abb.	CH20	22
Oxleys, The, Harl.	CQ 9	6
Oxlip Clo., Croy.	CC54	87
Marigold Way		
Oxlow La., Dag.	CQ35	50
Oxonian St. SE22	CA45	67
Oxshott Av., Cob.	BF61	102
Oxshott Ri., Cob.	BE60	93
Oxshott Way, Cob.	BE61	102
Oxted Clo., Mitch.	BT52	86
Oxted Rd., Gdse.	CC68	114
Oxtoby Way SW16	BW51	86
Oyster Hill, Epsom	BN65	103
Oyster La., Wey.	AY59	92

Oyster Row E1	CC39	57
Ozaling Wk. E16	CG39	58

P

Pace Pl. E1	CB39	57
Pachesham Dr., Lthd.	BH61	102
Pachesham Pk., Lthd.	BJ61	102
Pacific Rd. E16	CH39	58
Packe Cres., Ruis.	BA32	44
Bury St.		
Packet Boat La., Uxb.	AX39	53
Packham Clo., Orp.	CP55	89
Berrylands		
Packham Rd., Grav.	DF48	81
Packhorse Clo., St.Alb.	BK11	9
Packhorse La., B.Wd.	BN20	19
Packhorse La., B.Wd.	BO22	28
Packhorse La., Pot.B.	BN18	19
Packhorse Path, Stai.	AV49	72
South St.		
Packhorse Rd., Ger.Cr.	AS31	43
Packhorse Rd., Sev.	CS65	107
Packington Sq. N1	**BZ37**	**2**
Packington Sq. N1	BZ37	57
Packington St. N1	**BY37**	**2**
Packington St. N1	BY37	56
Packmores Rd. SE9	CM46	78
Padbrook, Oxt.	CH68	115
Padbury Ct. E2	**CA38**	**2**
Padbury Ct. E2	CA38	57
Padcroft Rd., West Dr.	AX40	53
Paddenswick Ct. W6	BP41	65
Paddenswick Rd.		
Paddenswick Rd. W6	BP41	65
Paddick Clo., Hodd.	CD11	12
Paddington Basin W2	**BT39**	**1**
Paddington Clo., Hayes	BD38	54
Paddington Grn. W2	**BT39**	**1**
Paddington Grn. W2	BT39	56
Paddington St. W1	**BV39**	**1**
Paddington St. W1	BV39	56
Paddock Clo. SE26	CC49	77
Paddock Clo. SE3	CH44	68
Paddock Clo., Har.	BF35	45
Paddock Clo., Nthlt.	BF37	54
Paddock Clo., Orp.	CL56	97
State Farm Av.		
Paddock Clo., Oxt.	CG69	115
Paddock Clo., S.Dnth.	CY51	90
Paddock Clo., Wor.Pk.	BO54	85
Paddock Gdns. SE19	CA50	77
Paddock Mead, Harl.	CM13	13
Paddock Rd. NW2	BP34	46
Paddock Rd., Bexh.	CQ45	69
Paddock Rd., Ruis.	BD34	45
Paddock Way, Chis.	CM50	78
Paddock Way, Hem.H.	AV13	7
Paddock Way, Oxt.	CG69	115
Paddock Way, Wok.	AT60	91
Paddock Wk., Warl.	CB63	105
Paddock, The, Brox.	CE13	12
Paddock, The, Dor.	BG72	119
Paddock, The, Ger.Cr.	AS28	34
Paddock, The, Guil.	AU70	118
Paddock, The, Hat.	BP11	10
Lemsford Rd.		
Paddock, The, Slou.	AQ44	62
Paddock, The, Uxb.	AZ35	44
Paddock, The, West.	CM66	115
Paddocks Clo., Ash.	BL62	103
Paddocks Clo., Orp.	CP55	89
Paddocks Mead, Wok.	AP61	100
Paddocks Rd., Guil.	AT68	109
Paddocks Way, Ash.	BL62	103
Paddocks Way, Cher.	AW54	83
Paddocks, Cob.	BD60	93
Paddocks, The, Barn.	BU24	29
Paddocks, The, Croy.	CE56	96
Addington Village Rd.		
Paddocks, The, Lthd.	BF66	111
Leatherhead Rd.		
Paddocks, The, Lthd.	BF66	111
Paddocks, The, Rick.	AV24	25
Paddocks, The, Welw.G.C.	BS 7	5
Brooksfield		
Paddocks, The, Wem.	BM34	46
Paddocks, The, Wey.	BB55	83
Padfield Rd. SE5	BZ45	67
Padgets, The, Wal.Abb.	CG20	22
Honey La.		
Padnall Rd., Rom.	CP31	50
Padstow Clo., Slou.	AS41	62
St. Marys Rd.		
Padstow Rd., Enf.	BY23	29
Padua Rd. SE20	CC51	87
Pagden St. SW8	BV44	66
Page Clo., Dart.	DB48	80
Page Clo., Har.	BL32	46
Page Clo., Hmptn.	BE50	74
Page Cres., Croy.	BY57	95
Page Cres., Erith	CT43	69
Page Gdns., Chis.	CL51	88
Page Green Rd. N15	CB32	48
Page Green Ter. N15	CA32	48
Page Heath La., Brom.	CJ52	88
Page Heath Vill., Brom.	CJ52	88
Page Meadow NW7	BP29	37
Page Rd., Felt.	BA46	73
Page St. NW7	BP29	37
Page St. SW1	**BW42**	**3**
Page St. SW1	BW42	66
Pageant Clo., Til.	DG44	71
Pageant Rd., St.Alb.	BG14	9
Pageant Wk., Croy.	CA55	87
Pagehurst Rd., Croy.	CB54	87
Pages Cft., Berk.	AQ12	7
Pages Hill N10	BV30	38
Pages La. N10	BV30	38
Pages La., Uxb.	AX36	53
Pages Wk. SE1	**CA42**	**4**
Pages Wk. SE1	CA42	67

Pages Yd. W4	BO43	65
Church St.		
Paget Av., Sutt.	BT55	86
Paget Clo., Hmptn.	BG49	74
Paget La., Islw.	BH45	64
Paget Rd. N16	BZ33	48
Paget Rd., Ilf.	CL35	49
Paget Rd., Slou.	AS42	62
Paget Rd., Uxb.	BA38	53
Paget Ri. SE18	CL43	68
Paget St. EC1	**BY38**	**2**
Paget St. EC1	BY38	56
Paget Ter. SE18	CL43	68
Pagette Way, Grays	DD42	71
Paglesfield, Brwd.	DE25	122
Rayleigh Rd.		
Pagnell St. SE14	CD43	67
Pagoda Av., Rich.	BL45	65
Pagoda Gdns. SE3	CF44	67
Paignton Rd. N15	CA32	48
Paignton Rd., Ruis.	BC34	44
Paines Brook Rd., Rom.	CW29	42
Paines Brook Way, Rom.	CW29	42
Paines Clo., Pnr.	BE31	45
Paines Hill, Oxt.	CJ69	115
Paines La., Pnr.	BE30	36
Pains Clo., Mitch.	BV51	86
Painsthorpe Rd. N16	CA34	48
Oldfield Rd.		
Painters Ash La., Grav.	DE48	81
Painters La., Enf.	CD21	30
Painters Rd., Ilf.	CN31	49
Paisley Rd. N22	BY30	38
Paisley Rd., Cars.	BT54	86
Pakeman St. N7	BX34	47
Pakenham Clo. SW12	BV47	76
Balham Park Rd.		
Pakenham St. WC1	**BX38**	**2**
Pakenham St. WC1	BX38	56
Pakes Way, Epp.	CN22	31
Palace Av. W8	BS40	56
Palace Av. W8	**BS41**	**3**
Palace Clo., Kings L.	AY18	17
Palace Court Gdns. N10	BW30	38
Palace Ct. W2	BS40	56
Palace Ct., Brom.	CH51	88
Palace Ct., Har.	BL32	46
Palace Ct., Twick.	BH47	74
Palace Dr., Wey.	AZ55	83
Palace Gate W8	**BT41**	**3**
Palace Gate W8	BT41	66
Palace Gates Rd. N22	BW30	38
Palace Gdns. Ms. W8	BS40	56
Palace Gdns. Ter. W8	BS40	56
Palace Gdns., Buck.H.	CJ26	40
Palace Gdns., Enf.	BZ24	30
Palace Grn. W8	**BS41**	**3**
Palace Grn., Croy.	CD57	96
Palace Gro. SE19	CA50	77
Palace Gro., Brom.	CH51	88
Palace Ms., Enf.	BZ24	30
Palace Gdns.		
Palace Pl. SW1	**BV41**	**3**
Palace Pl. SW1	BW41	66
Palace St.		
Palace Rd. N11	BW29	38
Palace Rd. N8	BW32	47
Palace Rd. SE19	CA50	77
Palace Rd. SW2	BX47	76
Palace Rd., Brom.	CH51	88
Palace Rd., E.Mol.	BG52	84
Palace Rd., Kings.T.	BK52	84
Palace Rd., Ruis.	BE35	45
Palace Rd., West.	CL64	106
Palace Sq. SE19	CA50	77
Palace St. SW1	**BW41**	**3**
Palace St. SW1	BW41	66
Palace Vw. Rd. E4	CE28	39
Palace Vw. SE12	CH48	78
Palace Vw., Brom.	CH52	88
Palace Vw., Croy.	CD55	87
Palace Way, Wey.	BA55	83
Palace Dr.		
Palamos Rd. E10	CE33	48
Palatine Rd. N16	CA35	48
Palermo Rd. NW10	BP37	55
Palestine Gro. SW19	BT51	86
Palewell Clo., Orp.	CO51	89
Palewell Common Dr., SW14	BN46	75
Palewell Pk. SW14	BN46	75
Paley Gdns., Loug.	CL24	31
Palfrey Clo., St.Alb.	BG12	9
Palfrey Pl. SW8	BX43	66
Palgrave Av., Sthl.	BF40	54
Palgrave Rd. W12	BO41	65
Palins Way, Grays	DD40	71
Palissy St. E2	**CA38**	**2**
Palissy St. E2	CA38	57
Pall Mall E. SW1	**BW40**	**3**
Pall Mall E. SW1	BW40	56
Pall Mall Pl. SW1	**BW40**	**3**
Pall Mall Pl. SW1	BW40	56
Pall Mall SW1	**BW40**	**3**
Pall Mall SW1	BW40	56
Pallas Rd., Hem.H.	AY12	8
Paller Way SE18	CJ44	68
Tellson Av.		
Palliser Rd. W14	BR42	65
Palliser Rd., Ch.St.G.	AQ27	34
Palm Av., Sid.	CP50	79
Palm Gro. W5	BL41	65
Palm Gro., Guil.	AR68	109
Palm Rd., Rom.	CS32	50
Palmar Cres., Bexh.	CR45	69
Palmar Rd., Bexh.	CR44	69
Palmarsh Clo., Orp.	CP52	89
Palmeira Rd., Bexh.	CP45	69
Palmer Av., Bush.	BF25	27
Palmer Av., Grav.	DH49	81
Palmer Av., Sutt.	BO56	94
Palmer Clo., Houns.	BF44	64
Palmer Clo., Red.	BV71	121
Palmer Cres., Cher.	AU57	91
Palmer Cres., Kings.T.	BL52	85
Palmer Pl. N7	BY35	47
Palmer Rd. E13	CH38	58
Palmer Rd., Dag.	CP33	50

Palmer St. SW1	**BW41**	**3**
Palmer St. SW1	BW41	66
Palmer St. W10	BQ40	55
Palmers Av., Grays	DE42	71
Palmers Dr., Grays	DE42	71
Palmers Gdns., Barn.	BQ25	28
Palmers Gro., E.Mol.	BF52	84
Palmers Gro., Wal.Abb.	CG14	13
Palmers La., Enf.	CB23	30
Palmers Moor La., Iver	AW38	53
Palmers Orchard, Sev.	CT59	98
Palmers Pass. SW14	BN45	65
Palmers Rd.		
Palmers Rd. E2	CC37	57
Palmers Rd. N11	BW28	38
Palmers Rd. SW14	BN45	65
Palmers Rd. SW16	BX51	86
Palmers Rd., B.Wd.	BM23	28
Palmers Way, Chsnt.	CD18	21
Palmersfield Rd., Bans.	BS60	95
Palmerston Av., Slou.	AQ41	62
Palmerston Clo., Welw.G.C.	BQ 8	5
Palmerston Clo., Wok.	AS60	91
Palmerston Cres. N13	BX28	38
Palmerston Cres. SE18	CM43	68
Palmerston Ct. E17	CD31	48
Palmerston Rd.		
Palmerston Gdns., Grays	DB42	70
Palmerston Gro. SW19	BS50	76
Palmerston Rd. NW6	BS36	56
Palmerston Rd. E17	CD31	48
Palmerston Rd. E7	CH35	49
Palmerston Rd. N22	BX29	38
Palmerston Rd. SE18	CM43	68
Palmerston Rd. SW14	BN45	65
Palmerston Rd. SW19	BS50	76
Palmerston Rd. W3	BN41	65
Palmerston Rd., Buck.H.	CH27	40
Palmerston Rd., Cars.	BU56	95
Palmerston Rd., Grays	DB43	70
Palmerston Rd., Har.	BH31	45
Palmerston Rd., Orp.	CM56	97
Palmerston Rd., Rain.	CV37	60
Palmerston Rd., Sutt.	BT56	95
Palmerston Rd., Th.Hth.	BZ53	87
Palmerston Rd., Twick.	BH46	74
Palmerston Way SW8	BV43	66
Bradmead		
Pamber St. W10	BQ39	55
Pamela Av., Hem.H.	AY15	8
Pamela Gdns., Pur.	BC32	44
Pampisford Rd., Pur.	BY59	95
Pams Way, Epsom	BN56	94
Pancake La., Hem.H.	BA14	8
Pancras La. EC4	**BZ39**	**2**
Pancras La. EC4	BZ39	57
Queen Victoria St.		
Pancras Rd. NW1	**BW37**	**1**
Pancras Rd. NW1	BW37	56
Pancroft, Rom.	CO24	32
Pandora Rd. NW6	BS36	56
Panfield Ms., Ilf.	CL32	49
Panfield Rd. SE2	CO41	69
Pangbourne Av. W10	BQ39	55
Pangbourne Dr., Stan.	BL28	37
Pankhurst Clo. SE14	CC44	67
Briant St.		
Panmuir Rd. SW20	BP51	85
Panmure Clo. N5	BY35	47
Panmure Rd. SE26	CB48	77
Pannard Pl., Sthl.	BF40	54
Panshanger Dr., Welw.G.C.	BS 8	5
Pansy Gdns. W12	BP40	55
Panters, Swan.	CT50	79
Pantile Rd., Wey.	BA56	92
Pantile Row, Slou.	AT42	62
Pantile Wk., Uxb.	AX36	53
High St.		
Pantiles Clo., Wok.	AQ62	100
Pantiles, The NW11	BR31	46
Pantiles, The, Bexh.	CQ43	69
Pantiles, The, Brom.	CJ52	88
Pantiles, The, Bush.	BG26	36
The Butts		
Panton St. SW1	**BW40**	**3**
Panton St. SW1	BW40	56
Haymarket		
Panxworth Rd., Hem.H.	AX14	8
Panyer Alley EC4	**BY39**	**2**
Panyer Alley EC4	BY39	56
Newgate St.		
Paper Ms., Dor.	BJ71	119
Papercourt La., Wok.	AU64	100
Papillons Wk. SE3	CH45	68
Papworth Gdns. N7	BX35	47
Chill Rd.		
Papworth Way SW2	BY47	76
Parade Mans. NW4	BP32	46
Parade Ms. SW2	BY48	76
Norwood Rd.		
Parade, The N4	BY33	47
Stroud Green La.		
Parade, The NW6	BS37	56
Kilburn High Rd.		
Parade, The, Brwd.	DB27	42
King Edward Rd.		
Parade, The, Dart.	CT46	79
Crayford Way		
Parade, The, Epsom	BN60	94
Parade, The, Esher	BH57	93
Parade, The, Guil.	AQ68	109
Parade, The, Hat.	BQ11	10
Parade, The, S.Ock.	CY41	70
Parade, The, Sun.	BB50	73
Parade, The, Wind.	AL44	61
Paradise Clo. W8	BS41	66
Adam & Eve Ms.		
Paradise Clo., Chsnt.	CB17	21
Paradise Cotts., Rich.	BL46	75
Paradise Rd.		
Paradise Hill, Brox.	CB16	21
Paradise Pass. N7	BY35	47
Paradise Pl. SE18	CK42	68
Samuel St.		
Paradise Rd. SW4	BX44	66

Paradise Rd., Rich. BK46 74
Paradise Row E2 CB38 57
Bethnal Green Rd.
Paradise Row, Wal.Abb. CF20 21
Paradise St. SE16 CB41 67
Paradise Wk. SW3 BU43 3
Paradise Wk. SW3 BU43 66
Paradise Wood La., Hem.H. AX14 8
Paragon All. SE1 CA41 4
Webb St.
Paragon Gro., Surb. BL53 85
Paragon Ms. SE1 BZ42 4
Searles Rd.
Paragon Pl. SE3 CG44 68
Paragon Pl., Surb. BL53 85
Paragon Rd. E9 CB36 57
Paragon Row SE17 BZ42 67
Paragon, The SE3 CG44 68
Parbury Rd. SE23 CD46 77
Parbury Ri., Chess. BL57 94
Parchment Clo., Amer. AP22 25
Chestnut La.
Parchmore Rd., Th.Hth. BY51 86
Parchmore Way, Th.Hth. BY51 86
Pardon St. EC1 BY38 2
Pardon St. EC1 BY38 56
Dallington St.
Pardoner St. SE1 BZ41 4
Pardoner St. SE1 BZ41 67
Pares Clo., Wok. AR61 100
Parfett St. E1 CB39 57
Parfour Dr., Ken. BZ61 105
Abbots La.
Parfrey St. W6 BQ43 65
Parham Dr., Ilf. CL32 49
Parham Way N10 BW30 38
Paringdon Rd., Harl. CL13 13
Paris Gdn. SE1 BY40 4
Paris Gdn. SE1 BY40 56
Parish Clo., Horn. CU34 50
Steed Clo.
Parish Gate Dr., Sid. CN46 78
Parish La. SE20 CC50 77
Parish La., Slou. AO34 43
Parish Ms. SE20 CC50 77
Parish La.
Park App., Well. CO45 69
Park Av. E., Epsom BP57 94
Park Av. E15 CG36 58
Park Av. E6 CL37 58
Park Av. Ms., Mitch. BV50 76
Park Av.
Park Av. N. N8 BW31 47
Park Av. N. NW10 BP35 46
Park Av. N13 BY27 38
Park Av. N18 CB28 39
Park Av. N22 BX30 38
Park Av. N3 BS30 38
Park Av. NW10 BL37 55
Park Av. NW11 BS33 47
Park Av. NW2 BP36 55
Park Av. Rd. N17 CB29 39
Park Av. S. N8 BW31 47
Park Av. SW14 BN45 65
Park Av. W., Epsom BP57 94
Park Av., Bark. CM36 58
Park Av., Barn. BT25 29
Park Av., Brom. CG50 78
Park Av., Brwd. DE26 122
Park Av., Bush. BD24 27
Park Av., Cars. BV57 95
Park Av., Cat. CA65 105
Park Av., Egh. AU50 72
Park Av., Enf. BZ25 30
Park Av., Farnborough CK55 88
Park Av., Grav. DH47 81
Park Av., Grays DA43 70
Park Av., Harl. CP12 14
Park Av., Houns. BF46 74
Park Av., Ilf. CL33 49
Park Av., Mitch. BV50 76
Park Av., Orp. CO55 89
Park Av., Perry Street DF47 81
Park Av., Pot.B. BT20 20
Park Av., Rad. BJ20 18
Park Av., Rick. AW25 26
Park Av., Ruis. BA32 44
Park Av., St.Alb. BJ13 9
Park Av., Stai. AV50 72
Park Av., Sthl. BE41 64
Park Av., Sunnymeads AR46 72
Park Av., Upmin. CZ33 51
Park Av., W.Wick. CF55 87
Park Av., Wat. BC24 26
Park Av., Wdf.Grn. CH28 40
Park Barn Dr., Guil. AP69 118
Park Barn E., Guil. AP70 118
Park Boul., Rom. CT30 41
Park Chase, Guil. AS70 118
Park Chase, Wem. BL35 46
Park Clo. NW10 BL38 55
Park Clo. NW2 BP34 46
Park Clo. SW1 BU41 3
Park Clo. SW1 BU41 66
Park Clo. W14 BR41 65
Park Clo., Brookmans Park BS16 20
Park Clo., Bet. BM73 120
Park Clo., Bush. BD24 27
Park Clo., Cars. BU57 95
Park Clo., Epp. CR17 23
Park Clo., Esher BF57 93
Park Clo., Har. BH30 36
Park Clo., Hat. BQ12 10
Park Clo., Hmptn. BG51 84
Park Clo., Houns. BG46 74
Park Clo., Lthd. BG65 102
Park Clo., Rick. AZ28 35
Park Clo., Walt. BB55 83
Park Clo., Wey. AW58 92
Park Clo., Wind. AO44 61
Park Copse, Dor. BK71 119
Park Corner Dr., Lthd. BB67 110
Park Corner Ms. W. W1 BV38 56
Park Corner Rd., Grav. DC49 81
Park Corner, Wind. AM45 61
Park Cres. Ms. E. W1 BV38 1
Park Cres. Ms. E. W1 BV38 56
Great Portland St.
Park Cres. Ms. W. W1 BV38 1
Park Cres. Ms. W. W1 BV38 56
Park Cres. N3 BS29 38
Park Cres. Rd., Erith CS43 69
Park Cres. W1 BV38 1
Park Cres. W1 BV38 56
Park Cres., B.Wd. BL24 28
Park Cres., Enf. BZ24 30
Park Cres., Erith CS43 69
Park Cres., Har. BH30 36
Park Cres., Hem.H. AZ11 8
Park Cres., Horn. CU33 50
Park Cres., Twick. BG47 74
Park Croft, Edg. BN30 37
Park Ct. N12 BT28 38
Park Ct. SE27 BZ48 77
Park Ct. W4 BN42 65
Park Rd. N.
Park Ct., Harl. CN10 6
Park Ct., Kings.T. BK51 84
Park Ct., Lthd. BF66 111
Church Rd.
Park Ct., N.Mal. BN52 85
Park Ct., Wall. BX56 95
Park Ct., Wem. BL35 46
Park Ct., Wok. AS62 100
Park Dr. Clo. SE7 CK42 68
Park Dr. N21 BZ25 30
Park Dr. NW11 BS33 47
Park Dr. SE7 CK42 68
Park Dr. SW14 BN45 65
Park Dr. W3 BM41 65
Park Dr., Dag. CS34 50
Park Dr., Har. BF33 45
Park Dr., Harrow Weald BH29 36
Park Dr., Long. DC52 90
Park Dr., Pot.B. BS19 20
Park Dr., Rom. CS31 50
Park Dr., Upmin. CX35 51
Park Dr., Wok. AS62 100
Park End NW3 BU35 47
Park End Rd., Rom. CT31 50
Park End, Brom. CG51 88
Park Farm Clo. N2 BT31 47
Park Farm Clo., Pnr. BC32 44
Park Farm Rd., Brom. CJ51 88
Park Farm Rd., Kings.T BL50 75
Park Farm Rd., Upmin. CW35 51
Park Fields, Croy. CD54 87
Park Fields, Harl. CH11 13
Park Gate Gdns. SW14 BN46 75
Park Gate N21 BX26 38
Park Gate SE3 CG45 68
Park Gate W5 BK39 54
Mount Av.
Park Gdns. E10 CE33 48
Park Gdns. NW9 BM31 46
Park Gdns., Erith CS42 69
Park Gdns., Kings.T. BL50 75
Park Grn., Lthd. BF65 102
Park Gro. E15 CH37 58
Park Gro. N11 BW29 38
Park Gro. Rd. E11 CG34 49
Park Gro., Bexh. CS45 69
Park Gro., Brom. CH51 88
Park Gro., Ch.St.G. AR24 25
Park Gro., Edg. BL28 37
Park Hall Rd. N2 BU31 47
Park Hall Rd. SE21 BZ48 77
Park Hall Rd., Reig. BS69 121
Park Hill Clo., Cars. BU56 95
Park Hill Ct. SW17 BU48 76
Beeches Rd.
Park Hill Gdns., Croy. CA55 87
Park Hill Rd.
Park Hill Rd., Brom. CF51 87
Park Hill Rd., Croy. CA55 87
Park Hill Rd., Hem.H. AW13 8
Park Hill Rd., Sev. CW62 108
Park Hill Rd., Sid. CM48 78
Park Hill Rd., Wall. BV57 95
Park Hill Ri., Croy. CA55 87
Park Hill SE23 CB48 77
Park Hill SW4 BW46 76
Park Hill W5 BK39 54
Park Hill, Brom. CK52 88
Park Hill, Cars. BU57 95
Park Hill, Harl. CO 9 6
Park Hill, Loug. CJ25 31
Park Hill, Rich. BL46 75
Park Ho. Dr., Reig. BR71 120
Park Ho. Gdns., Twick. BK46 74
Park Ho. N21 BX26 38
Park Ho. Pass. N6 BV33 47
Park Horsley, Lthd. BC68 110
Park La. Clo. N17 CB29 39
Park La.
Park La. E15 CF37 57
High St.
Park La. N17 CB29 39
Park La. N18 CA27 39
Park La. N9 CA27 39
Park La. W1 BU40 56
Park La. W1 BV40 3
Park La., Chadwell Heath CP32 50
Park La., Brox. CD13 12
Park La., Cars. BV56 95
Park La., Chsnt. CB17 21
Park La., Couls. BW64 104
Park La., Cranford BC43 63
Park La., Croy. BZ55 87
Park La., Guil. AU69 118
Park La., Har. BF34 45
Park La., Harl. CM10 6
Park La., Hayes BB39 53
Park La., Hem.H. AX14 8
Park La., Horn. CU36 59
Park La., Horton AT45 62
Park La., Houns. BC43 63
Park La., Kemsing CX62 108
Park La., Reig. BR71 120
Park La., Rich. BK45 64
Park La., Rom. CT32 50
Park La., S.Ock. CY40 60
Park La., Seal CX64 108
Park La., Sev. CV65 108
Park La., Slou. AQ41 62
Park La., St.Alb. BM15 10
Park La., Sutt. BR57 94
Park La., Swan. CV51 90
Park La., Tedd. BH50 74
Park La., Uxb. AW29 35
Park La., Wal.Cr. CC20 21
Park La., Wem. BL35 46
Park La., Wormley CB14 12
Park Lane Paradise, Chsnt. CB16 21
Park Lane Paradise, Ash. BL62 103
Park Lawn Av., Epsom BM60 94
Park Lawn Rd., Wey. AZ56 92
Park Lawns, Wem. BL35 46
Park Ley Rd., Cat. CC63 105
Park Mans. NW4 BP32 46
Park Mead, Har. BF34 45
Park Mead, Harl. CL10 6
Park Mead, Sid. CO46 79
Park Meadow, Brwd. DB22 33
Park Meadow, Hat. BQ12 10
Park Ms., Hat. BQ11 10
Park Ms., Hmptn. BG49 74
Park Nook Gdns., Enf. BZ22 30
Park Par. NW10 BO37 55
Park Par. W3 BM41 65
Park Par., Pnr. BE29 36
Park Pl. Gdns. W2 BT39 56
Park Place Vill.
Park Pl. SW1 BW40 3
Park Pl. SW1 BW40 56
Park Pl. Vill. W2 BT39 1
Park Pl. Vill. W2 BT39 56
Park Pl. W3 BM42 65
Park Pl. W5 BK40 54
Park Pl., Amer. AP22 25
Park Pl., Hmptn. BG50 74
Park Pl., Mitch. BU52 86
Park Pl., Sev. CS65 107
Bessels Green Rd.
Park Pl., St.Alb. BG17 18
Park Pl., Wem. BL35 46
Park Pl., Wind. AO44 61
Kings Rd.
Park Rd. E. W3 BM41 65
Park Rd. E., Kings.T. BL49 75
Park Rd. E., Uxb. AX37 53
Park Rd. E10 CE33 48
Park Rd. E12 CH33 49
Park Rd. E15 CH37 58
Park Rd. E17 CD32 48
Park Rd. E6 CJ37 58
Park Rd. N. W3 BM41 65
Park Rd. N. W4 BN42 65
Park Rd. N11 BW29 38
Park Rd. N14 BW26 38
Park Rd. N15 BY31 47
Park Rd. N18 CA28 39
Park Rd. N2 BT31 47
Park Rd. N8 BW31 47
Park Rd. NW1 BU38 56
Park Rd. NW10 BN37 55
Park Rd. NW4 BP33 46
Park Rd. NW8 BU38 1
Park Rd. NW8 BU38 56
Park Rd. NW9 BN33 46
Park Rd. SE25 CA52 87
Park Rd. SW19 BT50 76
Park Rd. SW20 BP50 75
Park Rd. W., Kings.T. BL49 75
Park Rd. W4 BN43 65
Park Rd. W7 BH40 54
Park Rd., Amer. AP22 25
Park Rd., Ash. BL62 103
Park Rd., Ashf. AZ49 73
Park Rd., Bans. BS61 104
Park Rd., Barn. BR24 28
Park Rd., Beck. CD50 77
Park Rd., Brom. CH51 88
Park Rd., Brwd. DA27 42
Park Rd., Bush. BF25 27
Park Rd., Cat. CA65 105
Park Rd., Chis. CL50 78
Park Rd., Dart. CX47 80
Park Rd., E.Mol. BG52 84
Park Rd., Egh. AT49 72
Park Rd., Enf. CD21 30
Park Rd., Esher BF56 93
Park Rd., Felt. BD49 74
Park Rd., Grav. DG48 81
Park Rd., Grays DD42 71
Park Rd., Guil. AR70 118
Park Rd., Hackbridge BV55 86
Park Rd., Hampton Wick BK51 84
Park Rd., Hayes BB39 53
Park Rd., Hem.H. AX14 8
Park Rd., Hmptn. BF49 74
Park Rd., Hodd. CE12 12
Park Rd., Houns. BF46 74
Park Rd., Ilf. CM34 49
Park Rd., Islw. BJ44 64
Park Rd., Ken. BY61 104
Park Rd., Kings.T. BL49 75
Park Rd., Long. DC52 90
Park Rd., N.Mal. BN52 85
Park Rd., New Barnet BT24 29
Park Rd., Orp. CP53 89
Park Rd., Oxt. CG67 115
Park Rd., Pot.B. BV18 20
Park Rd., Rad. BJ21 27
Park Rd., Red. BU69 121
Park Rd., Rich. BL46 75
Park Rd., Rick. AY26 35
Park Rd., Shep. AZ54 83
Park Rd., Slou. AO37 52
Park Rd., Stai. AW46 73
Park Rd., Sun. BC50 73
Park Rd., Surb. BL53 85
Park Rd., Sutt. BR57 94
Park Rd., Swan. CT52 89
Park Rd., Swans. DC46 81
Park Rd., Tedd. BH50 74
Park Rd., Twick. BK46 74
Park Rd., Uxb. AY36 53
Park Rd., Wal.Cr. CC20 21
Park Rd., Wall. BV56 95
Park Rd., Warl. CG60 97
Park Rd., Wat. BC23 26
Park Rd., Wem. BL36 55
Park Rd., Wok. AS62 100
Park Ri. SE23 CD47 77
St. Germans Rd.
Park Ri., Berk. AP12 7
Park Ri., Har. BH30 36
Park Ri., Lthd. BJ64 102
Park Ridings N8 BY31 47
Park Rise Clo., Lthd. BJ64 102
Park Rise Rd. SE23 CD47 77
Park Row SE10 CF42 67
Park Royal Rd. W3 & NW10 BN38 55
Park Side, Sutt. BR57 94
Park Side, Wey. AW58 92
Park Spring Gro., Iver AT36 52
Park Sq. E NW1 BV38 56
Park Sq. E. NW1 BV38 1
Park Sq. Ms. NW1 BV38 1
Park Sq. Ms. NW1 BV38 56
Park Sq. W. NW1 BV38 1
Park Sq. W. NW1 BV38 56
Park Sq., Esher BF56 93
Park Rd.
Park St. La., St.Alb. BF18 18
Park St. N1 BZ37 57
Park St. SE1 BZ40 57
Park St. W1 BV40 3
Park St. W1 BV40 56
Park St., Berk. AQ12 7
Park St., Colnbrook AU44 62
Park St., Croy. BZ55 87
Park St., Guil. AR71 118
Park St., Hat. BQ12 10
Park St., Slou. AP41 62
Park St., St.Alb. BG16 18
Park St., Tedd. BH50 74
Park St., Wind. AO44 61
Park Ter., Green. DB46 80
Park Ter., Wor.Pk. BP54 85
Park View Cres. N11 BV28 38
Park View Est. E2 CC37 57
Park View Gdns. N22 BY30 38
Dunbar Rd.
Park View Gdns. NW4 BQ32 46
Park View Gdns., Bark. CN37 58
Park View Gdns., Grays DD42 71
Park View Gdns., Ilf. CK31 49
Woodford Av.
Park View Rd. N17 CB31 48
Park View Rd. N3 BS30 38
Park View Rd. NW10 BO35 46
Park View Rd. W5 BL39 55
Park View Rd., Berk. AQ13 7
Park View Rd., Cat. CD64 105
Park View Rd., Pnr. BC29 35
Park View Rd., Sthl. BF40 54
Park View Rd., Well. CO45 69
Park Vill. SE3 CH43 68
Park Vill., Rom. CP32 50
Park Village E. NW1 BV37 1
Park Village E. NW1 BV37 56
Park Village W. NW1 BV37 1
Park Village W. NW1 BV37 56
Park Vista SE10 CF43 67
Park Vw. N21 BX26 38
Park Vw. W3 BN39 55
Park Vw., Hat. BQ11 10
Park Vw., Hodd. CE12 12
Park Vw., Lthd. BF66 111
Park Vw., N.Mal. BO52 85
Park Vw., Pnr. BE30 36
Park Vw., Pot.B. BT20 20
Park Vw., S.Ock. CY40 60
Park Vw., Sev. CP65 107
Park Vw., Wem. BM35 46
Park W. W2 BU39 1
Park W. W2 BU39 56
Park Way N20 BU28 38
Park Way NW11 BR32 46
Park Way, Bex. CT48 79
Park Way, Brwd. DC26 122
Park Way, E.Mol. BF52 84
Park Way, Edg. BM30 37
Park Way, Enf. BY23 29
Park Way, Felt. BC47 73
Park Way, Ilf. CN34 49
Park Way, Lthd. BF65 102
Park Way, Rain. CU38 59
Park Way, Rick. AX26 35
Park Way, Ruis. BC33 44
Park West Pl. W2 BU39 1
Park West Pl. W2 BU39 56
Park Wk. NW3 BU35 47
Park Wk. SW10 BT43 3
Park Wk. SW10 BT43 66
Park Wk., Ash. BL62 103
Rectory La.
Park Wk., Barn. BT24 29
Park Wood Clo., Bans. BQ61 103
Park Wood N20 BU27 38
Park Wood Rd., Bex. CQ47 79
Park Wood Vw., Bans. BQ61 103
Park Works Rd., Red. BX70 121
Park, The N6 BV32 47
Park, The NW11 BS33 47
Park, The SE19 CA50 77
Park, The W5 BK40 54
Park, The, Cars. BU56 95
Park, The, Lthd. BF65 102
Park, The, Sid. CO49 79
Park, The, St.Alb. BJ12 9
Parkcroft Rd. SE12 CG47 78
Parkdale Cres., Wor.Pk. BN55 85
Parkdale N11 BW29 38
Parkdale Rd. SE18 CN42 68
Parke Rd. SW13 BP44 65
Parke Rd., Sun. BC52 83
Parker Av., Til. DH44 71
Parker Clo. E16 CK40 58
Parker St.
Parker Rd., Croy. BZ56 96
Parker Rd., Grays DC42 71
Parker St. E16 CK40 58
Parker St. WC2 BX39 2
Parker St. WC2 BX39 56
Parker St., Wat. BC23 26
Parkers Clo., Ash. BL63 103
Parkers Hill, Ash. BL63 103
Parkers La., Ash. BL63 103
Parkers Row SE1 CA41 67
Parkes Rd., Chig. CN28 40
Parkfield Av. SW14 BO45 65
Parkfield Av., Amer. AO22 25
Parkfield Av., Felt. BC48 73
Parkfield Av., Har. BG30 36
Parkfield Av., Nthlt. BD37 54
Parkfield Av., Uxb. AZ38 53
Parkfield Clo., Edg. BM29 37
Parkfield Clo., Nthlt. BE37 54
Parkfield Cres., Felt. BC48 73
Parkfield Cres., Har. BG30 36
Parkfield Cres., Ruis. BE34 45
Parkfield Dr., Nthlt. BD37 54
Parkfield Gdns., Har. BF31 45
Parkfield Rd. NW10 BP36 55
Parkfield Rd. SE14 CD44 67
Parkfield Rd., Felt. BC48 73
Parkfield Rd., Har. BG34 45
Parkfield Rd., Nthlt. BE37 54
Parkfield Rd., Uxb. AZ34 44
Parkfield St. N1 BY37 2
Parkfield St. N1 BY37 56
Parkfield Way, Brom. CK53 88
Parkfield, Long. DC52 90
Parkfield, Rick. AV24 25
Parkfield, Sev. CW65 108
Parkfields Av. NW9 BN33 46
Parkfields Av. SW20 BP51 85
Parkfields Clo., Cars. BV56 95
Devonshire Rd.
Parkfields Rd., Kings.T. BL49 75
Parkfields SW15 BQ45 65
Parkfields, Welw.G.C. BQ 8 5
Parkgate Av., Barn. BT23 29
Parkgate Clo., Kings.T. BM50 75
Warboys App.
Parkgate Cres., Barn. BT23 29
Parkgate Rd. SW11 BU43 66
Parkgate Rd., Reig. BS71 121
Parkgate Rd., Wall. BV56 95
Parkgate Rd., Wat. BD22 27
Parkham St. SW11 BT44 66
Parkhill Clo., Horn. CV34 51
Parkhill Rd. E4 CF26 39
Parkhill Rd. NW3 BU35 47
Parkhill Rd., Bex. CQ47 79
Parkhill Rd., Epsom BO59 94
Parkhill Wk. NW3 BU35 47
Parkholme Rd. E8 CA36 57
Parkhouse St. SE5 BZ43 67
Parkhurst Gdns., Bex. CQ47 79
Parkhurst Rd. E12 CL35 49
Parkhurst Rd. E17 CD31 48
Parkhurst Rd. N11 BW28 38
Parkhurst Rd. N17 CB30 39
Parkhurst Rd. N22 BX29 38
Parkhurst Rd. N7 BX35 47
Parkhurst Rd., Bex. CR47 79
Parkhurst Rd., Guil. AQ70 118
Parkhurst Rd., Sutt. BT56 95
Parkhurst, Epsom BN58 94
Parkland Av., Rom. CT30 41
Parkland Av., Slou. AR42 62
Parkland Av., Upmin. CX35 51
Parkland Clo., Hodd. CE10 12
Parkland Clo., Sev. CV68 117
Parkland Gdns. SW19 BQ47 75
Inner Park Rd.
Parkland Gro., Ashf. AZ49 73
Parkland Rd. N22 BX30 38
Parkland Rd., Ashf. AZ49 73
Parkland Rd., Wdf.Grn. CH29 40
Parkland Way, Ong. CW18 24
Parkland Wk. N6 BW33 47
Parklands Clo. SW14 BN46 75
Parklands Clo., Chig. CM27 40
Parklands Ct., Houns. BD44 64
Parklands Dr. N3 BR31 46
Parklands Pl., Guil. AT70 118
Parklands Rd. SW16 BV49 76
Parklands Way, Wor.Pk. BO55 85
Grafton Park Rd.
Parklands, Chig. CM27 40
Parklands, Epp. CP18 23
Parklands, Oxt. CG69 115
Parklands, Surb. BL53 85
Parklands, Wal.Abb. CF19 21
Parklands, Wey. AX56 92
Liberty La.
Parklands, Wey. AX57 92
Parklea Clo. NW9 BO30 37
Parkleigh Rd. SW19 BS51 86
Parkleys, Rich. BK49 74
Parkmead Gdns. NW7 BO29 37
Parkmead SW15 BP46 75
Parkmead, Loug. CL25 31
Parkmore Clo., Wdf.Grn. CH28 40
Parkpale La., Bet. BM73 120
Parksend Rd. SW11 BV44 66
Battersea Park Rd.
Parkshot, Rich. BK45 64
Parkside Av. SW19 BQ49 75
Parkside Av., Bexh. CS44 69
Parkside Av., Brom. CK52 88
Parkside Av., Rom. CS31 50
Parkside Av., Til. DG44 71
Parkside Clo., Lthd. BB66 110
Parkside Cres., Surb. BN53 85
Parkside Cross, Bexh. CT44 69
Parkside Dr., Edg. BM27 37
Parkside Dr., Wat. BB23 26
Parkside Est. E9 CC37 57
Parkside Gdns. SW19 BQ49 75
Parkside Gdns., Barn. BU26 38
Parkside Gdns., Couls. BV62 104
Parkside N3 BS30 38
Parkside NW2 BP34 46
Parkside NW7 BO29 37

Parkside Pl., Lthd. BB66 110
Parkside Rd. SW11 BV44 66
Parkside Rd., Belv. CS42 69
Parkside Rd., Houns. BF46 74
Parkside Rd., Nthwd. BB28 35
Parkside SE3 CG43 68
Parkside SW19 BQ47 75
Parkside Ter. N18 BZ28 39
Parkside Way, Har. BF31 45
Parkside, Buck.H. CH27 40
Parkside, Grays DE41 71
Parkside, Hmptn. BG49 74
Parkside, Pot.B. BT19 20
Parkside, Sev. CQ60 98
Parkside, Sid. CO48 79
Parkstead Rd. SW15 BP46 75
Parkstone Av. N18 CA29 39
Parkstone Av., Horn. CW32 51
Parkstone Rd. SE15 CB44 67
Rye La.
Parkthorne Clo., Har. BF32 45
Parkthorne Dr., Har. BF32 45
Parkthorne Rd. SW12 BW47 76
Parkvale Rd. SW6 BR44 65
Parkview Rd. SE9 CL47 78
Parkview Rd., Croy. CB54 87
Parkview Vale, Guil. AU69 118
Parkville Rd. SW6 BR43 65
Parkway Clo., Welw.G.C. BQ 8 5
Parkway Ct., St.Alb. BJ15 9
Drakes Dr.
Parkway Ms., Croy. BV50 76
Park Av.
Parkway N14 BX27 38
Parkway NW1 BV37 1
Parkway NW1 BV37 56
Parkway SW20 BQ52 85
Parkway, Croy. CE58 96
Parkway, Dor. BJ71 119
Parkway, Erith CQ41 69
Parkway, Rom. CT30 41
Parkway, Saw. CQ 6 6
Parkway, The, Cranford BC42 63
Parkway, The, Iver AU37 52
Parkway, Uxb. AZ36 53
Parkway, Wdf.Grn. CJ28 40
Parkway, Welw.G.C. BQ 8 5
Parkway, Wey. BA56 92
Parkwood Av., Esher BG54 84
Parkwood Clo., Hodd. CD13 12
Parkwood Dr., Hem.H. AV13 7
Parkwood Gro., Sun. BC52 83
Parkwood Ms. N6 BV32 47
Wood La.
Parkwood Rd. SW19 BR49 75
Parkwood Rd., Bans. BQ61 103
Parkwood Rd., Islw. BH44 64
Parkwood Rd., Red. BX70 121
Parkwood Rd., West. CK64 106
Parkwood, Beck. CE50 77
Parlaunt Rd., Slou. AT42 62
Parley Dr., Wok. AR62 100
Parliament Hill NW3 BU35 47
Parliament Sq. SW1 BX41 4
Parliament Sq. SW1 BX41 66
Parliament St. SW1 BX41 4
Parliament St. SW1 BX41 66
Parma Cres. SW11 BU45 66
Parmiter St. E2 CB37 57
Parnall Rd., Harl. CM12 13
Parndon Wood Rd., Harl. CM13 13
Parnell Clo., Edg. BM27 37
Parnell Clo., Wat. BB18 17
Parnell Rd. E3 CD37 57
Parnham St. E14 CD39 57
Parolles Rd. N19 BW33 47
Paroma Rd., Belv. CR41 69
Parr Av., Epsom BP58 94
Parr Clo. N9 CB28 39
Parr Clo., Lthd. BH63 102
Parr Ct., Felt. BD49 74
Parr Rd. E6 CJ37 58
Parr Rd., Stan. BK30 36
Parr St. N1 BZ37 2
Parris Cft., Dor. BK73 119
Parrock Av., Grav. DH47 81
Parrock Rd., Grav. DH47 81
Parrock St., Grav. DG46 81
Parrots Clo., Rick. AZ25 26
Parrs Clo., S.Croy. BZ58 94
Parrs Pl., Hmptn. BF50 74
Tudor Rd.
Parry Av. E6 CK39 58
Parry Clo., Epsom BP57 94
Parry Grn., Slou. AS42 62
Parry Pl. SE18 CL42 68
Parry Rd. SE25 CA52 87
Parry St. SW8 BX43 66
Parsifal Rd. NW6 BS35 47
Parsley Gdns., Croy. CC54 87
Primrose La.
Parsloe Rd., Epp. CL14 13
Parsloes Av., Dag. CP35 50
Parson St. NW4 BQ31 46
Parsonage Clo., Dor. BG72 119
Parsonage La.
Parsonage Clo., Hayes BB39 53
Parsonage Clo., Warl. CD61 105
Parsonage Clo., Wat. BB18 17
Parsonage Field, Brwd. DB22 33
Parsonage Gdns., Enf. BZ23 30
Parsonage La., Dor. BG72 119
Parsonage La., Enf. BZ23 30
Parsonage La., Hat. BP15 10
Parsonage La., S.Dnth. CX50 80
Parsonage La., Sid. CQ49 79
Parsonage La., Slou. AO36 52
Parsonage La., Wind. AN44 61
Parsonage Leys, Harl. CN11 13
Parsonage Manorway, Belv. CR43 69
Parsonage Rd., Ch.St.G. AQ27 34
Parsonage Rd., Egh. AR49 72
Parsonage Rd., Grays DB43 70
Parsonage Rd., Hat. BP15 10
Parsonage Rd., Rain. CV37 60
Parsonage Rd., Rick. AX26 35
Parsonage St. E14 CF42 67
Parsons Cres., Edg. BM27 37
Parsons Grn. La. SW6 BS44 66
Parsons Grn. SW6 BS44 66
Parsons Grn., Guil. AR69 109
Parsons Gro., Edg. BM27 37
Parsons Hill SE18 CL41 68
Powis St.
Parsons La., Dart. CU48 79
Parsons Mead, Croy. BY54 86
Parsons Mead, E.Mol. BG52 84
Parsons Pightle, Couls. BY63 104
Parsons Rd. E13 CJ37 58
Parsonsfield Clo., Bans. BQ61 103
Parsonsfield Rd., Bans. BQ61 103
Parthenia Rd. SW6 BS44 66
Parthia Clo., Tad. BP63 103
Partingdale La. NW7 BQ28 37
Partington Clo. N19 BW33 47
Partridge Clo. E16 CJ39 58
Partridge Clo., Bush. BF26 36
Partridge Clo., Chesh. AP17 16
Partridge Dr., Orp. CM55 88
Partridge Grn. SE9 CL48 78
Partridge Knoll, Pur. BY60 96
Partridge Mead, Bans. BQ61 103
Partridge Rd., Harl. CM12 13
Partridge Rd., Hmptn. BF50 74
Partridge Rd., Sid. CN48 78
Partridge Rd., St.Alb. BG11 9
Partridge Sq. E6 CK39 58
Nightingale Way
Partridge Vill., Uxb. AX37 53
Cricket Field Rd.
Partridge Way N22 BX30 38
Partridge Way, Guil. AV69 118
Parvills Rd., Wal.Abb. CF19 21
Parvin St. SW8 BW44 66
Deeley Rd.
Parvis Rd., Wey. AW60 92
Pasadena Clo., Hayes BC41 63
Pascal St. SW8 BW43 66
Pascoe Rd. SE13 CF46 77
Pasfield Clo., Wal.Abb. CF19 21
Parvills Rd.
Pasley Clo. SE17 BZ42 4
Pasley Clo. SE17 BZ42 67
Pasley Rd. SE17 BZ42 67
Pasquier Rd. E17 CD31 48
Passage, The, Rich. BL45 65
The Quadrant
Passey Pl. SE9 CK46 78
Passfield Dr. E14 CE39 57
St. Leonards Rd.
Passfield Path SE28 CO40 59
Booth Clo.
Passfields W14 BR42 65
Passing Alley EC1 BY39 2
St. Johns La.
Passmore Gdns. N11 BW29 38
Passmore St. SW1 BV42 3
Passmore St. SW1 BV42 66
Pastens Rd., Oxt. CJ69 115
Pasteur Clo. NW9 BO30 37
Pasteur Gdns. N18 BY28 38
Paston Clo. E5 CC34 48
Millfields Rd.
Paston Cres. SE12 CH47 78
Paston Rd., Hem.H. AX12 8
Pastor St. SE11 BY42 4
Pastor St. SE11 BY42 66
Pasture Clo., Bush. BG26 36
Pasture Clo., Wem. BJ34 45
Pasture Rd. SE6 CG47 78
Pasture Rd., Dag. CQ35 50
Pasture Rd., Wem. BJ34 45
Pasture, The, St.Alb. BF15 9
Pastures Mead, Uxb. AZ36 53
Hercies Rd.
Pastures, The N20 BR26 37
Pastures, The, Hat. BP13 10
Pastures, The, Hem.H. AV13 7
Pastures, The, Wat. BD26 36
Pastures, The, Welw.G.C. BS 9 5
Pat More La., Walt. BB57 92
Patch, The, Sev. CT64 107
Patcham Ct., Sutt. BT57 95
Patcham Ter. SW8 BV44 66
Pater St. W8 BS41 66
Paternoster Clo., Wal.Abb. CG20 22
Paternoster Hill, Wal.Abb. CG19 22
Paternoster Row EC4 BY39 56
St. Pauls Churchyard
Paternoster Row EC4 BZ39 2
Paternoster Row, Hav. CV26 42
Paternoster Sq. EC4 BY39 2
Paternoster Sq. EC4 BY39 56
Warwick La.
Paterson Rd., Ashf. AX49 73
Pates Manor Dr., Felt. BA47 73
Path, The SW19 BS51 86
Pathfield Rd. SW16 BW50 76
Pathway, The, Rad. BH21 27
Pathway, The, Wat. BD26 36
Pathway, The, Wok. AV66 109
Patience Rd. SW11 BU44 66
Patio Clo. SW4 BW46 76
Patmore Link, Hem.H. BA13 8
Patmore Rd., Wal.Abb. CG20 22
Patmore St. SW8 BW44 66
Patmore Way, Rom. CR28 41
Patmos Rd. SW9 BY43 66
Paton Clo. E3 CE38 57
Paton St. EC1 BZ38 2
Paton St. EC1 BZ38 57
Patricia Ct., Well. CO43 69
Wickham La.
Patricia Dr., Horn. CW33 51
Patricia Gdns., Sutt. BS59 95
Patrick Connolly Gdns. E3 CE38 57
Talwin St.
Patrick Pass. SW11 BU44 66
Winders Rd.
Patrick Rd. E13 CJ38 58
Patrington Clo., Uxb. AX38 53
Patriot Sq. E2 CB37 57
Patriot St. SE6 CE46 77
Patrol Pl. SE6 CE46 77
Patrons Dr., Uxb. AV32 43
Patrons Way, Uxb. AV32 43
Patshull Pl. NW5 BW36 56
Patshull Rd.
Patshull Rd. NW5 BW36 56
Patten All., Rich. BK46 74
Ormond Rd.
Patten Av., Rich. BK46 74
Ormond Rd.
Patten Rd. SW18 BU47 76
Pattenden Rd. SE6 CD47 77
Patterdale Clo., Brom. CG50 78
Patterdale Rd. SE15 CC43 67
Patterdale Rd., Dart. CY47 80
Patterson Ct. SE19 CA50 77
Patterson Ct., Dart. CX46 80
Farnol Rd.
Patterson Rd. SE19 CA50 77
Pattison Rd. NW2 BS34 47
Pattison Wk. SE18 CM42 68
Sandbach Pl.
Paul Clo. E15 CG37 58
Paul St.
Paul Gdns., Croy. CA55 87
Paul St. E15 CF37 57
Paul St. EC2 BZ38 2
Paul St. EC2 BZ38 57
Paulet Rd. SE5 BY44 66
Paulhan Rd., Har. BK31 45
Paulin Dr. N21 BY26 38
Pauline Cres., Twick. BG47 74
Paulins Clo., Orp. CP51 89
Pauls Grn., Wal.Cr. CC20 21
Eleanor Rd.
Pauls La., Hodd. CE12 12
Pauls Pl., Ash. BM62 103
Paultons Sq. SW3 BT43 66
Paultons St. SW3 BT43 66
Old Church St.
Pauntley St. N19 BW33 47
Paved Ct., Rich. BK46 74
King St.
Paveley Dr. SW11 BU43 66
Paveley St. NW8 BU38 1
Paveley St. NW8 BU38 56
Pavement Ms., Rom. CP33 50
Pavement Sq., Croy. CA54 87
Teevan Rd.
Pavement, The SW4 BW45 66
Pavet Clo., Dag. CR36 59
Pavilion Gdns., Stai. AW50 73
Pavilion Rd. E15 CG38 58
Springfield Rd.
Pavilion Rd. SW1 BU41 3
Pavilion Rd. SW1 BU41 66
Pavilion Rd., Ilf. CK33 49
Pavilion St. SW1 BU41 3
Pavilion Ter., Ilf. CN32 49
South Down Cres.
Pavilion Way, Edg. BM29 37
Pavilion Way, Ruis. BD34 45
Pawleyne Clo. SE20 CC50 77
Pawsey Clo. E13 CH37 58
Plashet Rd.
Pawsons Rd., Croy. BZ53 87
Paxford Rd., Wem. BJ34 45
Paxton Av., Slou. AO41 61
Paxton Clo., Rich. BL44 65
Paxton Clo., Walt. BD54 84
Paxton Gdns., Wok. AU59 91
Paxton Pl. SE27 CA49 77
Paxton Rd. N17 CA29 39
Paxton Rd. W4 BO43 65
Paxton Rd., Berk. AR13 7
Paxton Rd., Brom. CH50 78
College Rd.
Paxton Rd., St.Alb. BH14 9
Paxton Ter. SW1 BV42 66
Churchill Gdns. Rd.
Paxton Ter. SW1 BV43 3
Paycock Rd., Harl. CL12 13
Payne Rd. E3 CE38 57
Bow Rd.
Payne St. SE8 CD43 67
Paynes La., Wal.Abb. CF15 12
Paynesfield Av. SW14 BN45 65
Paynesfield Rd., Bush. BH26 36
Paynesfield Rd., West. CJ63 106
Pea La., Berk. AO12 7
Pea La., Upmin. DA36 60
Peabody Av. SW1 BV42 3
Peabody Av. SW1 BV42 66
Peabody Bldgs. SE1 BY40 4
Peabody Bldgs. SE17 BZ42 4
Peabody Bldgs. WC1 BX38 2
Peabody Bldgs. WC1 BX38 56
Peabody Clo. SE10 CE44 67
Devonshire Dr.
Peabody Est. EC1 BZ38 57
Peabody Est. N17 CA30 39
Peabody Est. SE1 BY40 56
Peabody Est. SE24 BY47 76
Peabody Est. SW11 BU45 66
Peabody Est. W6 BQ42 65
Peabody Hill Est. SE21 BZ47 77
Peabody Hill SE21 BY47 76
Peabody Sq. N1 BZ37 2
Peabody Sq. SE1 BY41 4
Peabody Trust SW3 BU43 3
Peabody Trust SW3 BU43 66
Chelsea Manor St.
Peabody Yd. N1 BZ36 57
Greenman St.
Peabody Yd. N1 BZ37 2
Peace Clo. N14 BV25 29
Peace Clo., Wal.Cr. CB18 21
Peace Gro., Wem. BM34 46
Chalkhill Rd.
Peach Cft., Grav. DE48 81
Peach Tree Av., West Dr. AY39 53
Peaches Clo., Sutt. BR57 94
Peachey La., Uxb. AX39 53
Peachum Rd. SE3 CG43 68
Peacock Av., Felt. BA47 73
Peacock Clo., Horn. CW31 51
Peacock Gdns., S.Croy. CD58 96
Peacock St. SE17 BY42 4
Peacock St. SE17 BY42 66
Peacock St., Grav. DH47 81
Peacock Wk. N6 BV33 47
Cholmeley Cres.
Peacock Wk., Dor. BJ72 119
Rose Hill
Peacock Yd. SE17 BY42 4
Peacocks, Harl. CK12 13
Peahen Ct. EC2 CA39 57
Bishopsgate
Peak Clo., Guil. AQ69 118
Peak Hill Av. SE26 CC49 77
Peak Hill Gdns., SE26 CC49 77
Spring Hill
Peak Hill SE26 CC49 77
Peak, The SE26 CC49 77
Peakes La., Chsnt. CA17 21
Peakes Way, Chsnt. CA17 21
Peaketon Av., Ilf. CJ31 49
Peaks Hill Ri., Pur. BX58 95
Peaks Hill, Pur. BW58 95
Peal Gdns. W13 BJ38 54
Peall Rd., Croy. BX53 86
Pear Clo. NW9 BN31 46
Pear Clo. SE14 CD43 67
Southerngate Way
Pear Pl. SE1 BY41 4
Waterloo Rd.
Pear Tree Av., West Dr. AY39 53
Pear Tree Clo., Beac. AO29 34
Pear Tree Clo., Swan. CS51 89
Pear Tree Ct. EC1 BY38 2
Pear Tree Ct. EC1 BY38 56
Pear Tree Mead, Harl. CO12 14
Pear Tree Rd., Ashf. BA49 73
Pear Tree Rd., Wey. AW56 92
Pear Tree St. EC1 BY38 2
Pear Tree St. EC1 BY38 56
Pear Tree Wk., Chsnt. BZ16 21
Pear Trees, Brwd. DE29 122
Pearcefield Av. SE23 CC47 77
Pearcroft Rd. E11 CF34 48
Peardon St. SW8 BV44 66
Silverthorne Rd.
Peareswood Gdns., Stan. BK30 36
Peareswood Rd., Erith CT44 69
Pearfield Rd. SE23 CD48 77
Pearl Clo. E6 CL39 58
Pearl Ct., Wok. AP61 100
Langmans Way
Pearl Rd. E17 CE31 48
Pearl St. E1 CB40 57
Penang St.
Pearle Rd., E.Mol. BF51 84
Pearmain Clo., Shep. AZ53 83
Laleham Rd.
Pearman St. SE1 BY41 4
Pearman St. SE1 BY41 66
Pears Rd., Houns. BG45 64
Pearscroft Ct. SW6 BS44 66
Pearscroft Rd. SW6 BS44 66
Pearson St. E2 CA37 2
Pearson St. E2 CA37 57
Pearsons Av. SE14 CD44 67
Tanners Hill
Peartree Av., Ashf. BA49 73
Peartree Clo., Brwd. DB22 33
Peartree Clo., Erith CS44 69
Peartree Clo., Hem.H. AW13 8
Peartree Clo., Mitch. BU51 86
Peartree Clo., S.Croy. CB60 96
Orchard Rd.
Peartree Clo., S.Ock. DB37 60
Peartree Clo., Welw.G.C. BR 8 5
Peartree Ct., Welw.G.C. BR 8 5
Peartree Gdns., Dag. CO35 50
Peartree Gdns., Rom. CR30 41
Peartree La. E1 CC40 57
Glamis Rd.
Peartree La., Brwd. DB22 33
Peartree La., Welw.G.C. BR 8 5
Peartree Rd., Enf. CA24 30
Peartree Rd., Hem.H. AW13 8
Peary Pl. E2 CC38 57
Kirkwall Pl.
Peascod Pl., Wind. AO44 61
Peascod St.
Peascod St., Wind. AO44 61
Peascroft Rd., Hem.H. AZ15 8
Pease Hill, Sev. DC57 99
Peatmore Av., Wok. AW61 101
Pebble Hill, Lthd. BA70 110
Pebble La., Epsom BL64 103
Pebble La., Lthd. BL65 103
Pebblehill Rd., Bet. BO69 120
Pebblehill Rd., Tad. BO68 112
Pebworth Rd., Har. BJ34 45
Peckarmans Wood SE26 CB48 77
Peckett Sq. N7 BZ35 48
Peckford Pl. SW9 BY44 66
Peckford Yd. SW9 BY44 66
Peckford Pl.
Peckham Gro. SE15 CA43 67
Peckham High St. SE15 CA44 67
Peckham Hill St. SE15 CB43 67
Peckham Park Rd. SE15 CB43 67
Peckham Rd. SE5 & SE15 CA44 67
Peckham Rye SE15 & SE22 CB45 67
Peckham Walk Av., Sev.& Ton. DC67 117
Pecks Hill, Wal.Abb. CG14 13
Peckwater St. Est. NW5 BW35 47
Peckwater St. NW5 BW35 47
Islip St.
Pedlars End., Ong. CU14 14
Pedlars Wk. N7 BX36 56
Pedley Rd., Dag. CP33 50
Pedley St. E1 CA38 2
Pedley St. E1 CA38 57
Pedro St. E5 CC34 48
Pedworth Gdns. SE16 CC42 67
Rotherhithe New Rd.
Peek Cres. SW19 BQ49 75
Peel Clo., Wind. AN45 61
Peel Dr. NW9 BP31 46
Peel Dr., Ilf. CK31 49
Peel Gro. E2 CC37 57
Peel Pl., Ilf. CK30 40
Peel Precinct NW6 BS37 56
Peel Rd. E18 CG30 40
Peel Rd. NW6 BS38 56
Peel Rd. NW9 BP31 46
Peel Rd., Har. BH31 45
Peel Rd., Orp. CM56 97
Peel Rd., Wem. BK34 45
Peel St. W8 BS40 56
Peel Way, Rom. CW30 42
Peel Way, Uxb. AY39 53
Peerage Way, Horn. CW33 51
Peerless St. EC1 BZ38 2
Peerless St. EC1 BZ38 57
Pegamoid Rd. N18 CC27 39
Pegasus Pl. SE11 BY43 66
Clayton St.
Pegasus Rd., Croy. BY57 95
Pegelm Gdns., Horn. CW33 51
Pegg Rd., Houns. BD43 64
Peggotty Waye, Uxb. AZ39 53
Pegley Gdns., SE12 CH48 78
Pegmire La., Wat. BG23 27
Pegrams Rd., Harl. CM12 13
Pegwell St. SE18 CN43 68
Peket Clo., Stai. AV51 82
Pekin Clo. E14 CE39 57
Pekin St.
Pekin St. E14 CE39 57
Peldon Ct., Rich. BL45 65
Peldon Pass., Rich. BL45 65
Sheen Rd.
Peldon Rd., Harl. CL12 13
Peldon Wk. N1 BZ37 57
Popham St.
Pelham Av., Bark. CN37 58
Pelham Clo., SE5 CA45 67
Pelham Cres. SW7 BU42 3
Pelham Cres. SW7 BU42 66
Pelham Ct. SW3 BU42 3
Pelham Ct. SW3 BU42 66
Fulham Rd.
Pelham Ct., Hem.H. BA13 8
Pelham Ct., Stai. AW49 73
Pelham Ct., Welw.G.C. BT 8 5
Pelham Pl. SW7 BT42 3
Pelham Pl. SW7 BU42 66
Pelham Rd. E18 CH31 49
Pelham Rd. N15 CA31 48
Pelham Rd. N22 BY30 38
Pelham Rd. SW19 BS50 76
Pelham Rd., Beck. CC51 87
Pelham Rd., Bexh. CR45 69
Pelham Rd., Grav. DF47 81
Pelham Rd., Ilf. CM34 49
Pelham St. SW7 BT42 3
Pelham St. SW7 BT42 66
Pelham Way, Lthd. BF66 111
Pelhams Clo., Esher BF56 93
Pelhams Wk., Esher BF55 84
Pelhams, The, Wat. BD21 27
Pelican Wk. SW9 BY45 66
Loughborough Pk.
Pelier St. SE17 BZ43 4
Pelier St. SE17 BZ43 67
Pelinore Rd. SE6 CG48 78
Pell St. E1 CB40 57
Pellant Rd. SW6 BR43 65
Pellatt Gro. N22 BY30 38
Pellatt Rd. SE22 CA46 77
Pellerin Rd. N16 CA35 48
Pelling Hill, Wind. AQ47 72
Pelling St. E14 CE39 57
Pellipar Clo. N13 BY27 38
Pellipar Clo. SE18 CK42 68
Hillreach
Pellipar Gdns. SE18 CK42 68
Ogilby St.
Pellipar Rd. SE18 CK42 68
Pells La., Sev. DA59 99
Pelly Rd. E13 CH37 58
Pelter St. E2 CA38 2
Pelter St. E2 CA38 57
Pelton Av., Sutt. BS58 95
Pelton Rd. SE10 CG42 68
Pembar Av. E17 CD31 48
Pember Rd. NW10 BQ38 55
Pemberton Av., Rom. CV31 51
Pemberton Clo., St.Alb. BG15 9
Pemberton Gdns. N19 BW34 47
Pemberton Gdns., Rom. CQ32 50
Pemberton Gdns., Swan. CT51 89
Bonney Way
Pemberton Pl. E8 CB36 57
Mare St.
Pemberton Rd. N4 BY32 47
Pemberton Rd., E.Mol. BG52 84
Pemberton Row EC4 BY39 56
East Harding St.
Pemberton Ter. N19 BW34 47
Pembrey Way, Horn. CV36 60
Pembridge Av., Twick. BE47 74
Pembridge Chase, Hem.H. AT17 16
Pembridge Clo.
Pembridge Clo., Hem.H. AS17 16
Pembridge Cres. W11 BS40 56
Pembridge Gdns. W2 BS40 56
Pembridge La., Hert. BZ13 12
Pembridge Ms. W11 BS40 56
Pembridge Ms. W8 BS43 66
Earls Court Rd.
Pembridge Pl. W2 BS40 56
Pembridge Rd. W11 BS40 56
Pembridge Rd., Hem.H. AT17 16
Pembridge Sq. W2 BS40 56
Pembridge Vill. W11 BS40 56
Pembroke Av., Enf. CB23 30
Pembroke Av., Har. BJ31 45
Pembroke Av., Surb. BM53 85
Pembroke Av., Walt. BD56 93

Pembroke Clo., Bans. BS62 104
Pembroke Clo., Brox. CD15 12
Church La.
Pembroke Clo., Horn. CW31 51
Pembroke Clo., S.at H. CX51 90
Main Rd.
Pembroke Clo., SW1 BV41 3
Pembroke Clo., SW1 BV41 66
Pembroke Dr., Chsnt. BY18 20
Pembroke Gdns. Clo. W8 BS41 66
Pembroke Gdns. W8 BR42 65
Pembroke Gdns., Dag. CR34 50
Pembroke Gdns., Wok. AT62 100
Pembroke Rd.
Pembroke Ms. E3 CD38 57
Morgan St.
Pembroke Ms. N10 BV30 38
Pembroke Rd.
Pembroke Ms. W8 BS41 66
Earls Court Rd.
Pembroke Pl. W8 BS41 66
Pembroke Pl., Edg. BM29 37
Pembroke Pl., Islw. BH44 64
Clifton Rd.
Pembroke Pl., S.at H. CX51 90
Main Rd.
Pembroke Rd. E17 CE32 48
Pembroke Rd. E6 CK39 58
Pembroke Rd. N10 BV30 38
Pembroke Rd. N13 BZ27 39
Pembroke Rd. N15 CA32 48
Pembroke Rd. N8 BX31 47
Pembroke Rd. SE25 CA52 87
Pembroke Rd. W8 BR42 65
Pembroke Rd., Brom. CJ51 88
Pembroke Rd., Erith CS42 69
Pembroke Rd., Grnf. BF38 54
Pembroke Rd., Ilf. CN33 49
Pembroke Rd., Mitch. BV51 86
Pembroke Rd., Nthwd. BA27 35
Pembroke Rd., Ruis. BB33 44
Pembroke Rd., Sev. CU66 116
Pembroke Rd., Wem. BK34 45
Pembroke Rd., Wok. AT62 100
Pembroke Sq. W8 BS41 66
Pembroke St. N1 BX36 2
Pembroke St. N1 BX36 56
Pembroke Studios W8 BR41 65
Pembroke Vills. Rich. BK45 64
Pembroke Vills. W8 BS41 66
Pembroke Way, Hayes BA41 63
Pembroke Wk. W8 BS42 66
Pembroke Vill.
Pembury Av., Wor.Pk. BP54 85
Pembury Clo., Brom. CG54 88
Pembury Clo., Couls. BV60 95
Pembury Cres., Sid. CQ48 79
Pembury Ct., Hayes BA43 63
Pembury Est. E5 CB35 48
Pembury Pl. E5 CB35 48
Pembury Rd. E5 CB35 48
Pembury Rd. N17 CA30 39
Pembury Rd. SE25 CB52 87
Pembury Rd., Bexh. CQ43 69
Pemdevon Rd., Croy. BY54 86
Pemell Clo. E1 CC38 57
Colebert Av.
Pemerich Clo., Hayes BB42 63
Pemsel Ct., Hem.H. AX14 8
Crabtree La.
Pen Dr., Uxb. AV32 43
Penally Pl. N1 BZ37 2
Penally Pl. N1 BZ37 57
Penang St. E1 CB40 57
Penarth St. SE15 CC43 67
Penberth Rd. SE6 CF47 77
Penbury Rd., Sthl. BE42 64
Pencombe Ms. W11 BS40 56
Ledbury Ms. W.
Pencraig Way SE15 CB43 67
Penda Rd., Erith CS43 69
Pendarves Rd. SW20 BQ51 85
Pendas Mead E9 CD35 48
Kings Mead Est.
Pendell Av., Hayes BB43 63
Pendell Rd., Red. BY69 121
Pendennis Clo., Wey. AW60 92
Pendennis Rd. N17 BZ31 48
Pendennis Rd. SW16 BX49 76
Pendennis Rd., Orp. CP55 89
Pendennis Rd., Sev. CU65 107
Penderel Rd., Houns. BF46 74
Penderry Ri. SE6 CF48 77
Penderyn Way N7 BW35 47
Carlton Rd.
Pendle Rd. SW16 BV50 76
Pendlestone Rd. E17 CE32 48
Pendleton Rd., Red. BU71 121
Sandpit Rd.
Pendleton Rd., Reig. & Red. BT72 121
Pendragon Rd., Brom. CG48 78
Pendragon Wk. NW9 BO32 46
Fryent Gro.
Pendrell Rd. SE4 CD44 67
Pendrell St. SE18 CM43 68
Pendula Dr., Hayes BD38 54
Penerley Rd. SE6 CE47 77
Penerley Rd., Rain. CU39 59
Penfold Clo., Croy. BY56 95
Epsom Rd.
Penfold La., Bexh. CP48 79
Penfold Pl. NW1 BU39 1
Penfold Pl. NW1 BU39 56
Penfold Rd. N9 CC26 39
Penfold St. NW1 BT38 56
Penfold St. NW1 & NW8 BT38 1
Penfold St. NW8 BT38 56
Penford Gdns. SE9 CJ45 68
Penford St. SE5 BY44 66
Pengarth Rd., Bex. CP46 79
Penge La. SE20 CC50 77
Penge Rd. E13 CJ37 58
Penge Rd. SE20 CB51 87
Penge Rd. SE25 CB52 87
Pengelly Clo., Chsnt. CB18 21
Burygreen Rd.

Penhall Rd. SE7 CJ42 68
Penhill Rd., Bex. CP47 79
Penhurst Rd., Ilf. CL29 40
Penhurst, Wok. AS60 91
Peninsular Clo., Felt. BA46 73
Penistone Rd. SW16 BX50 76
Penistone Wk., Rom. CV29 42
Okehampton Rd.
Penketh Dr., Har. BG34 45
Penlow Rd., Harl. CM12 13
Penman Clo., St.Alb. BF17 18
Penmon Rd. SE2 CO41 69
Penn Clo., Grnf. BF37 54
Penn Clo., Har. BK31 45
Penn Clo., Rick. AU25 25
Penn Clo., Uxb. AX38 53
Penn Gaskell La., Ger.Cr. AS28 34
Penn Gdns., Chis. CL51 88
Penn Gdns., Rom. CR29 41
Penn La., Bexh. CP46 79
Penn Meadow, Slou. AP37 52
Penn Pl., Rick. AX26 35
Northway
Penn Rd. N7 BX35 47
Penn Rd., Datchet AR44 62
Penn Rd., Ger.Cr. AR30 34
Penn Rd., Rick. AV26 34
Penn Rd., Slou. AO38 52
Penn Rd., St.Alb. BG17 18
Penn Rd., Wat. BC23 26
Penn St. N1 BZ37 2
Penn St. N1 BZ37 57
Penn Way, Rick. AU25 25
Pennack Rd. SE15 CA43 67
Pennant Ms. W8 BS42 66
Pennant Ter. E17 CD30 39
Pennard Rd. W12 BQ41 65
Pennards, The, Sun. BD52 84
Penner Clo. SW19 BR48 75
Victoria Dr.
Pennethorne Clo. E9 CC37 57
Victoria Park Rd.
Pennethorne Rd. SE15 CB43 67
Pennethorpe Clo. E2 CC37 57
Penney Clo., Dart. CV47 80
Pennine Dr. NW2 BQ34 46
Pennine La. NW2 BQ34 46
Pennine Dr.
Pennine Way, Bexh. CT44 69
Pennine Way, Grav. DF48 81
Pennine Way, Hayes BA43 63
Pennine Way, Hem.H. AY12 8
Pennings Av., Guil. AP69 118
Pennington Clo. SE27 BZ49 77
Pennington Clo., Rom. CR28 41
Pennington Dr., Wey. BB55 83
Pennington Rd., Ger.Cr. AR29 34
Pennington St. E1 CB40 57
Penningtons, The, Amer. AP22 25
Penny Clo., Rain. CU38 59
Stirling Clo.
Penny La., Shep. BB54 83
Penny Rd. NW10 BM38 55
Pennycroft, Croy. CC58 96
Pennyfield, Cob. BC60 92
Pennyfields E14 CE40 57
Pennyfields, Brwd. DB28 42
Junction Rd.
Pennylets Grn., Slou. AP36 52
Pennymead Dr., Lthd. BB67 110
Pennymead Ri., Lthd. BB67 110
Pennymead, Harl. CO11 14
Pennymore Wk. W9 BR38 55
Ashmore Rd.
Pennypot La., Wok. AO59 91
Pennyroyal Av. E6 CL39 58
Penpoll Rd. E8 CB36 57
Penpool La., Well. CO45 69
Penrhyn Av. E17 CD30 39
Penrhyn Cres. E17 CE30 39
Penrhyn Cres. SW14 BN45 65
Penrhyn Gdns., Kings.T. BK52 84
Penrhyn Gro. E17 CE30 39
Penrhyn Rd., Kings.T. BL52 85
Penrith Clo. SW15 BR46 75
Penrith Clo., Brom. CE51 87
Albemarle Rd.
Penrith Clo., Red. BU70 121
Penrith Clo., Uxb. AX37 53
High St.
Penrith Cres., Horn. CU35 50
Penrith Rd. N15 BZ32 48
Penrith Rd., Ilf. CN29 40
Penrith Rd., N.Mal. BN52 85
Penrith Rd., Rom. CX29 42
Penrith Rd., Th.Hth. BZ51 87
Penrith St. SW16 BW50 76
Penrose Av., Wat. BE27 36
Penrose Ct., Hem.H. AY11 8
Penrose Gro. SE17 BZ42 4
Penrose Gro. SE17 BZ42 67
Penrose Ho. SE17 BZ42 4
Penrose Ho. SE17 BZ42 67
Penrose Rd., Lthd. BG64 102
Penrose St. SE17 BZ42 4
Penrose St. SE17 BZ42 67
Penry St. SE1 CA42 4
Penry St. SE1 CA42 67
Marcia Rd.
Penryn St. NW1 BW37 1
Penryn St. NW1 BW37 56
Pensbury Pl. SW8 BW44 66
Pensbury St. SW8 BW44 66
Penscroft Gdns., B.Wd. BN24 28
Pensford Av., Rich. BM44 65
Penshurst Av., Sid. CO46 79
Penshurst Clo., Ger.Cr. AR30 34
Penshurst Clo., Sev. CZ57 99
Penshurst Gdns., Edg. BM28 37
Penshurst Grn., Brom. CG53 88
Penshurst Rd. E9 CC36 57
Penshurst Rd. N17 CA29 39
Penshurst Rd., Bexh. CQ44 69
Penshurst Rd., Pot.B. BT19 20
Penshurst Rd., Th.Hth. BY53 86

Penshurst Way, Sutt. BS57 95
Penshurst, Harl. CP 9 6
Pensmead Ter. E4 CF28 39
Mead Cres.
Pensons La., Ong. CU17 23
Penstock Footpath N22 BX31 47
Pentelowe Gdns., Felt. BC46 73
Pentire Clo., Upmin. CZ32 51
Pentire Rd. E17 CF30 39
Pentland Av., Shep. AZ53 83
Pentland Clo. NW11 BR34 46
Pentland Gdns. SW18 BT46 76
St. Annes Hill
Pentland Rd., Bush. BG25 27
Pentland St. SW18 BT46 76
Pentland Way, Uxb. BA34 44
Pentland, Hem.H. AY12 8
Mendip Way
Pentlands Clo., Mitch. BV52 86
Pentley Clo., Welw.G.C. BQ 6 5
Pentley Pk., Welw.G.C. BQ 6 5
Pentlow St. SW15 BQ45 65
Pentlow Way, Buck.H. CK26 40
Pentney Rd. E4 CF26 39
Pretoria Rd.
Pentney Rd. SW12 BW47 76
Pentney Rd. SW19 BR51 85
Midmoor Rd.
Penton Av., Stai. AV50 72
Penton Dr., Chsnt. CC18 21
Penton Gro. N1 BY37 2
Penton Hall Dr., Stai. AW51 83
Penton Hook Rd., Stai. AW51 83
Penton Pl. SE17 BY42 4
Penton Pl. SE17 BY42 66
Penton Rd., Stai. AV50 72
Penton Ri. WC1 BX38 2
Penton Ri. WC1 BX38 56
Penton St. N1 BY37 2
Penton St. N1 BY37 56
Pentonville Rd. N1 BX37 56
Pentonville Rd. N1 BY37 2
Pentreath Av., Guil. AP71 118
Pentrich Av., Enf. CB22 30
Pentridge St. SE15 CA43 67
Pentyre Av. N18 BZ28 39
Penwerris Av., Islw. BG43 64
Penwith Rd. SW18 BS48 76
Penwood End, Wok. AQ64 100
Penwortham Rd. SW16 BV50 76
Penwortham Rd., S.Croy. BA58 96
Penylan Pl., Edg. BM29 37
Penywern Rd. SW5 BS42 66
Penzance Clo., Uxb. AX30 35
Penzance Gdns., Rom. CX29 42
Penzance Pl. W11 BR40 55
Penzance Rd., Rom. CX29 42
Penzance St. W11 BR40 55
Peony Clo., Brwd. DA25 33
Lavender Av.
Peony Gdns. W12 BP40 55
The Curve
Pepler Rd. SE15 CA43 4
Pepler Rd. SE15 CA43 67
Peplins Clo., Hat. BR16 19
Peplins Way, Hat. BR16 19
Peploe Rd. NW6 BQ37 55
Peplow Clo., West Dr. AX40 53
Pepper Alley, Loug. CG23 31
Pepper Clo. E6 CK39 58
Hallywell Cres.
Pepper Hill, Grav. DE48 81
Pepper St. E14 CE41 67
Pepper St. SE1 BZ41 4
Pepper St. SE1 BZ41 67
Peppercroft St., Grav. DG47 81
Peppermint Clo., Croy. BX54 86
Alfriston Av.
Pepys Clo., Ash. BL62 103
Pepys Clo., Dart. CX45 70
Pepys Clo., Grav. DE48 81
Pepys Clo., Slou. AT43 62
Pepys Clo., Til. DH44 71
Pepys Clo., Uxb. AZ35 44
Pepys Cres., Barn. BQ25 28
Pepys Rd. SE14 CC44 67
Pepys Rd. SW20 BQ51 85
Pepys Ri., Orp. CN54 88
Pepys St. EC3 CA40 4
Pepys St. EC3 CA40 57
Perceval Av. NW3 BU35 47
Perch St. E8 CA35 48
Percheron Rd., B.Wd. BN25 28
Percival Ct. N17 CA29 39
High Rd.
Percival Gdns., Rom. CP32 50
Percival Rd. SW14 BN46 75
Percival Rd., Enf. CA24 30
Percival Rd., Felt. BB48 73
Percival Rd., Horn. CV32 51
Percival Rd., Orp. CL55 88
Percival St. EC1 BY38 2
Percival St. EC1 BY38 56
Percival St. SE2 CP41 69
Harrow Manorway
Percival Way, Epsom BN56 94
Percy Av., Ashf. AZ49 73
Percy Bryant Rd., Sun. BB50 73
Percy Cir. WC1 BX38 2
Percy Cir. WC1 BX38 56
Percy Gdns., Enf. CC25 30
Percy Gdns., Hayes BB38 53
Percy Gdns., Islw. BJ45 64
Percy Gdns., Wor.Pk. BN54 85
Percy Ms. W1 BW39 1
Percy Ms. W1 BW39 56
Rathbone Pl.
Percy Pl., Slou. AQ44 62
Percy Rd. E11 CG33 49
Percy Rd. E16 CG38 58
Percy Rd. N12 BT28 38
Percy Rd. N21 BZ26 39
Percy Rd. NW6 BS38 56
Percy Rd. SE20 CC51 87
Percy Rd. SE25 CA53 87
Percy Rd. W12 BP41 65
Percy Rd., Bexh. CQ44 69

Percy Rd., Guil. AQ69 118
Percy Rd., Hmptn. BF50 74
Percy Rd., Ilf. CO33 50
Percy Rd., Islw. BJ45 64
Percy Rd., Mitch. BV54 86
Percy Rd., Rom. CR31 50
Percy Rd., Twick. BF47 74
Percy Rd., Wat. BC24 26
Percy St. W1 BW39 1
Percy St. W1 BW39 56
Percy St. WC1 BX38 2
Percy St., Grays DE43 71
Percy Way, Twick. BG47 74
Percy Yd. WC1 BX38 2
Great Percy St.
Peregrine Clo. NW10 BN36 55
Kingfisher Way
Peregrine Clo., Wat. BE20 18
Peregrine Ct. SW16 BX49 76
Leithcote Gdns.
Peregrine Gdns., Croy. CD55 87
Peregrine Rd., Ilf. CO28 41
Peregrine Rd., Sun. BB51 83
Peregrine Way SW19 BQ50 75
Peregrine Wk., Rain. CU36 59
Heron Flight Av.
Perham Rd. W14 BR42 65
Peridot St. E6 CK39 58
Perifield SE21 BZ47 77
Perimeade Rd., Grnf. BK37 54
Perimeter Rd., Red. BW73 121
Periton Rd. SE9 CJ45 68
Perivale Gdns. W13 BJ38 54
Bellevue Rd.
Perivale Gdns., Wat. BC20 17
Perivale La., Grnf. BJ38 54
Perkins Clo., Wem. BJ35 45
Perkins Ct., Ashf. AY49 73
Fairholme Rd.
Perkins Rd., Ilf. CM32 49
Perkins Rents SW1 BW41 3
Perkins Rents SW1 BW41 66
Old Pye St.
Perkins Sq. SE1 BZ40 4
Porter St.
Perks Clo. SE3 CG45 68
Hurren Clo.
Perpins Rd. SE9 CM46 78
Perram Clo., Brox. CD16 21
Garner Dr.
Perran Clo., Hart. DC52 90
Perran Rd. SW2 BY47 76
Perran Wk., Brent. BL42 65
Burford Rd.
Perren St. NW5 BV36 56
Ryland Rd.
Perrers Rd. W6 BP42 65
Perrin Clo., Ashf. AY49 73
Perrin Rd., Wem. BJ35 45
Perring Est. E3 CE39 57
Perrins Ct. NW3 BT35 47
Hampstead High St.
Perrins La. NW3 BT35 47
Perrins Wk. NW3 BT35 47
Perriors Clo., Chsnt. CB17 21
Adamsfield
Perry Clo., Rain. CS37 59
Perry Clo., Uxb. AZ39 53
Perry Croft, Wind. AM45 61
Perry Garth, Nthlt. BD37 54
Perry Gdns. N9 BZ27 39
Perry Grn., Hem.H. AZ10 8
Perry Gro., Dart. CX45 70
Perry Hall Clo., Orp. CO54 89
Perry Hall Rd., Orp. CN54 88
Perry Hill Est. SE23 CD48 77
Perry Hill SE6 CD48 77
Perry Hill, Wal.Abb. CG15 13
Perry Mead, Bush. BF26 36
Perry Mead, Enf. BY23 29
Perry Rd., Harl. CM12 13
Perry Ri. SE23 CD48 77
Perry Spring, Harl. CP12 14
Perry St. Gdns., Chis. CN50 78
Perry St. Shaw, Chis. CN50 78
Perry St., Chis. CM50 78
Perry St., Dart. CT45 69
Perry St., Grav. DF47 81
Perry Vale SE23 CC48 77
Perry Way, S.Ock. CY40 60
Perryfield La., Ong. CY12 15
Perryfield Way NW9 BO32 46
Perryfield Way, Rich. BJ48 74
Perryhow, Wor.Pk. BO54 85
Perrymans Farm Rd., Ilf. CM32 49
Perrymead St. SW6 BS44 66
Perryn Rd. SE16 CB41 67
Perryn Rd. W3 BN40 55
Perrys La., Orp. CO60 98
Perrys Pl. W1 BW39 1
Perrysfield Rd., Chsnt. CD16 21
Persant Rd. SE6 CG48 78
Perseverance Pl. SW9 BY43 66
Mandela St.
Perseverance Pl., Rich. BL45 65
Kew Rd.
Persfield Clo., Epsom BO58 94
Pershore Clo., Ilf. CL32 49
Pershore Gro., Cars. BT53 86
Pert Clo. N10 BV29 38
Perth Av. NW9 BN33 46
Perth Av., Hayes BD38 54
Perth Clo. SW20 BP51 85
Perth Rd. E10 CD33 48
Perth Rd. E13 CH37 58
Perth Rd. N22 BY30 38
Perth Rd. N4 BY33 47
Perth Rd., Bark. CM37 58
Perth Rd., Beck. CF51 87
Perth Rd., Ilf. CL32 49
Perth Ter., Ilf. CM33 49
Perwell Av., Har. BE33 45
Perwell Ct., Har. BE33 45
Perystreete SE23 CC48 77
Perry Vale
Pescot Hill, Hem.H. AW12 8

Peter Av. NW10 BP36 55
Peter Av., Oxt. CF68 114
Peter St. W1 BW40 3
Peter St. W1 BW40 56
Peterboat Clo. SE10 CG42 68
Peterborough Av., Upmin. CZ33 51
Peterborough Gdns., Ilf. CK33 49
Peterborough Ms. SW6 BS44 66
Peterborough Rd. E10 CF32 48
Peterborough Rd. SW6 BS44 66
Peterborough Rd., Cars. BT53 86
Peterborough Rd., Guil. AP69 118
Peterborough Rd., Har. BH33 45
Peterborough Vill. SW6 BS44 66
Petergate SW11 BT45 66
Peterhill Clo., Ger.Cr. AS28 34
Peterlee Ct., Hem.H. AY11 8
Peters Av., St.Alb. BK16 18
Peters Clo., Stan. BK29 36
Peters Hill EC4 BZ39 57
Carter La.
Peters La. EC1 BY39 2
Peters La. EC1 BY39 56
Cowcross St.
Peters La., Maid. AG43 61
Peters Path SE26 CB49 77
Peters Pl., Berk. AP12 7
Petersfield Av., Rom. CW29 42
Petersfield Av., Slou. AQ40 52
Petersfield Av., Stai. AX49 73
Petersfield Clo. N18 BZ28 39
Petersfield Clo., Rom. CX29 42
Petersfield Cres., Couls. BX61 104
Petersfield Rd. W3 BN41 65
Petersfield Ri. SW15 BP47 75
Petersfield Way, Brwd. DE32 123
Petersham Av., Wey. AY59 92
Petersham Clo., Rich. BK48 74
Petersham Clo., Sutt. BS56 95
Petersham Clo., Wey. AY59 92
Petersham Dr., Orp. CN51 88
Petersham Gdns., Orp. CN51 88
Petersham Dr.
Petersham La. SW7 BT41 3
Petersham La. SW7 BT41 66
Petersham Ms. SW7 BT41 3
Petersham Ms. SW7 BT41 66
Petersham Pl. SW7 BT41 3
Petersham Pl. SW7 BT41 66
Petersham Rd., Rich. BK46 74
Petersham Ter., Croy. BX55 86
Richmond Grn.
Petersham Way, Orp. CO52 89
Peterstone Rd. SE2 CO41 69
Peterstow Clo. SW15 BR48 75
Princes Way
Peterswood, Harl. CM13 13
Petherton Rd. N5 BZ35 48
Petley Rd. W6 BQ43 65
Peto Pl. NW1 BV38 1
Peto Pl. NW1 BV38 56
Peto St. N. E16 CG40 58
Peto St. S. E16 CG40 58
Petre Clo., Brwd. DE32 123
Petridge Rd., Red. BU73 121
Petrie Clo. NW2 BR36 55
Pett St. SE18 CK42 68
Petten Clo., Orp. CP54 89
Petten Gro., Orp. CP54 89
Petters Rd., Ash. BL61 103
Petticoat La. E1 CA39 2
Pettits Boul., Rom. CT30 41
Pettits Clo., Rom. CT30 41
Pettits La. N., Rom. CS30 41
Pettits La., Brwd. DC22 33
Pettits La., Rom. CT30 41
Pettits Pl., Dag. CR35 50
Pettits Rd., Dag. CR35 50
Pettiward Clo. SW15 BQ45 65
Colinette Rd.
Pettley Gdns., Rom. CS32 50
Pettman Cres. SE28 CM41 68
Petts Grove Av., Wem. BK35 45
Petts Hill, Nthlt. BF35 45
Petts La., Shep. AZ52 83
Petts Wood Rd., Orp. CM53 88
Petty France SW1 BW41 3
Petty France SW1 BW41 66
Petty La., Brom. CH51 88
Church Rd.
Petty Ward Clo. SW15 BP45 65
Petworth Clo., Couls. BW63 104
Starrock Rd.
Petworth Clo., Nthlt. BE36 54
Petworth Gdns. SW20 BP52 85
Petworth Gdns., Uxb. BA37 53
Petworth Rd. N12 BU28 38
Petworth Rd., Bexh. CR46 79
Petworth St. SW11 BU44 66
Petworth Way, Horn. CT35 50
Petyt Pl. SW3 BU43 66
Petyward SW3 BU42 3
Petyward SW3 BU42 66
Pevensey Av. N11 BW28 38
Pevensey Av., Enf. BZ23 30
Pevensey Clo., Houns. BG43 64
Pevensey Rd. E7 CG35 49
Pevensey Rd. SW17 BT49 76
Pevensey Rd., Felt. BE47 74
Peveril Dr., Tedd. BG49 74
Pewley Bank, Guil. AS71 118
Pewley Hill, Guil. AR71 118
Pewley Way, Guil. AS71 118
Pewsey Clo. E4 CE28 39
Peyton Pl. SE10 CF43 67
Peytons Cotts., Red. BX69 113
Pheasant Clo., Berk. AR13 7
Pheasant Clo., Pur. BY60 95
Partridge Knoll
Pheasant Hill, Ch.St.G. AR27 34
Pheasant Ri., Chesh. AO20 16
Pheasant Wk., Ger.Cr. AR28 34
Pheasants Way, Rick. AW26 35
Phelips Rd., Harl. CL13 13
Phelp St. SE17 BZ42 67
Phelp St. SE17 BZ43 4

Phelps Clo., Sev. CZ57 99
Phelps Way, Hayes BB42 63
Phene St. SW3 BU43 3
Phene St. SW3 BU43 66
Phil Brown Pl. SW8 BV45 66
Heath Rd.
Philan Way, Rom. CS29 41
Philanthropic Rd., Red. BV71 121
Philbeach Gdns. SW5 BS42 66
Philchurch Pl. E1 CB39 57
Ellen St.
Philchurch St. E1 CB39 57
Ellen St.
Philip Av., Rom. CS33 50
Philip Clo., Brwd. DA25 33
Philip Clo., Rom. CS33 50
Philip Av.
Philip Gdns., Croy. CD55 87
Philip La. N15 BZ31 48
Philip Rd. SE15 CB45 67
Philip Rd., Rain. CT38 59
Philip Rd., Stai. AX50 73
Philipot Path SE9 CK46 78
Philipp St. E13 CH38 58
Philipp Wk. SE15 CB45 67
Philippa Gdns. SE9 CJ46 78
Philippa Way, Grays DG42 71
Philips Way N1 BZ37 2
Phillida Rd., Rom. CX30 42
Phillimore Clo., Rad. BH21 27
Phillimore Gdns. Clo. W8 BS41 66
Phillimore Gdns. NW10 BQ37 55
Phillimore Gdns. W8 BS41 66
Phillimore Pl. W8 BS41 66
Phillimore Pl., Rad. BH21 27
Phillimore Wk. W8 BS41 66
Phillip Av., Swan. CS52 89
Phillipers, Wat. BD21 27
Phillipp St. N1 CA37 2
Phillipp St. N1 CA37 57
Phillips Clo., Dart. CU46 79
Phillips Way, Brom. CH51 88
Lownds Av.
Philpot La. EC3 CA40 4
Philpot La. EC3 CA40 57
Philpot La., Wok. AR59 91
Philpot Path, Ilf. CM34 49
Philpot Sq., Surb. BS45 66
Peterborough Rd.
Philpot St. E1 CB39 57
Philsdon Clo. SW19 BQ47 75
Inner Park Rd.
Phineas Pett Rd. SE9 CK45 68
Phipp St. EC2 CA38 2
Phipp St. EC2 CA38 57
Phipps Bridge Rd. SW19 BT51 86
Phipps Bridge Rd., Mitch. BT52 86
Phipps Hatch La., Enf. BZ22 30
Phipps Ms. SW1 BV42 3
Eccleston Pl.
Phipps Ter. SW19 BT51 86
Palestine Gro.
Phobe Rd., Hem.H. AY12 8
Phoebeth Rd. SE4 CE46 77
Phoenix Clo. E8 CA37 2
Stean St.
Phoenix Clo. E8 CA37 57
Stean St.
Phoenix Clo., Nthwd. BB28 35
Phoenix Clo., W.Wick. CF55 87
Phoenix Dr., Kes. CJ55 88
Phoenix Lane Mans. W6 BQ42 65
Brook Grn.
Phoenix Pl. WC1 BX38 2
Phoenix Pl. WC1 BX38 56
Phoenix Pl., Dart. CV47 80
Phoenix Rd. NW1 BW38 1
Phoenix Rd. NW1 BW38 56
Phoenix Rd. SE20 CC50 77
Phoenix St. WC2 BW39 1
Phoenix St. WC2 BW39 56
Stacey St.
Phoenix Way, Houns. BD43 64
Phygtle, The, Ger.Cr. AS29 34
Phyllis Av., N.Mal. BP53 85
Phyllis Ct. NW3 BS34 47
Piazza, The WC2 BX40 4
Picardy Manorway, Belv. CR41 69
Picardy Rd., Belv. CR42 69
Picardy St., Belv. CR41 69
Piccadilly Cicus W1 BW40 3
Piccadilly Pl. W1 BW40 3
Piccadilly Pl. W1 BW40 56
Piccadilly
Piccadilly W1 BV40 3
Piccadilly W1 BV40 56
Piccotts End La., Hem.H. AX12 8
Piccotts End Rd., Hem.H. AW11 8
Pick Hill, Wal.Abb. CG19 22
Pickard St. EC1 BY38 2
Pickard St. EC1 BY38 56
Moreland St.
Pickering Av. E6 CL37 58
Pickering Ms. W2 BS39 1
Pickering Ms. W2 BS39 56
Bishops Bridge Rd.
Pickering Pl. SW1 BW40 3
St. James St.
Pickering Pl. SW1 BW40 56
St. James St.
Pickering St. N1 BY37 56
Essex Rd.
Picket Cft., Stan. BK30 36
Pickets Clo., Bush. BH26 36
Pickets St. SW12 BV47 76
Picketts Lock La. N9 CC27 39
Picketts, Welw.G.C. BQ6 5
Pickford Clo., Bexh. CQ44 69
Pickford La., Bexh. CQ45 69
Pickford Rd., Bexh. CQ45 69
Pickford Rd., St.Alb. BJ14 9
Sutton Rd.
Pickhurst Grn., Brom. CG54 88
Pickhurst La., Brom. CG54 88
Pickhurst La., W.Wick. CG53 88
Pickhurst Mead., Brom. CG54 88
Pickhurst Pk., Brom. CG53 88
Pickhurst Ri., W.Wick. CF54 87
Pickins Piece, Slou. AT44 62
Pickmoss La., Sev. CU61 107
Pickwick Clo., Houns. BE46 74
Dorney Way
Pickwick Gdns., Grav. DE48 81
Pickwick Ms. N18 CA28 39
Pickwick Pl., Har. BH33 45
Pickwick Rd. SE21 BZ47 77
Pickwick St. SE1 BZ41 4
Pickwick St. SE1 BZ41 67
Pickwick Way, Chis. CM50 78
Dickens Dr.
Pickworth Clo. SW8 BX43 66
Kenchester Clo.
Picquets Way, Bans. BR61 103
Picton Pl. W1 BV39 1
Picton Pl. W1 BV39 56
Picton St. SE5 BZ43 67
Piedmont Rd. SE18 CM42 68
Pield Heath Av., Uxb. AZ38 53
Pield Heath Rd., Uxb. AY38 53
Pier Rd. E16 CL40 58
Pier Rd. Est. E16 CL41 68
Pier Rd., Erith CT43 69
Pier Rd., Felt. BC46 73
Pier Rd., Grav. DF46 81
Pier Rd., Green. DA45 70
High St.
Pier St. E14 CF42 67
Pier Ter. SW18 BS45 66
Jews Row
Pier Way SE28 CM41 68
Pier Wk., Grays DD43 71
Piercing Hill, Epp. CM21 31
Piermont Grn. SE22 CB46 77
Peckham Rye
Piermont Rd. SE22 CB46 77
Upland Rd.
Pierrepoint Rd. W3 BM40 55
Pierrepoint Row Arc. N1 BY37 56
Charlton Pl.
Pierson Rd., Wind. AL44 61
Pigeon La., Hmptn. BF49 74
Pigeonhouse La., Couls. BT66 113
Piggot St. E14 CE39 57
Pike Clo., Brom. CH49 78
Pike Gdns. SE1 BY40 56
Pike Gdns. SE1 BZ40 4
Pike La., Upmin. CZ35 51
Pike Rd. NW7 BN28 37
Ellesmere Av.
Pike Way, Epp. CR17 23
Pikes End, Pnr. BC31 44
Pikes Hill, Epsom BO60 94
Pikestone Clo., Hayes BE38 54
Berrydale Rd.
Pilgrim Clo., Brwd. CZ25 33
Pilgrim Clo., St.Alb. BG17 18
Pilgrim Hill SE27 BZ49 77
Pilgrim Hill, Orp. CQ51 89
Pilgrim St. EC4 BY39 2
Pilgrim St. EC4 BY39 56
Pilgrimage St. SE1 BZ41 4
Pilgrimage St. SE1 BZ41 67
Pilgrims Clo. N13 BX28 38
Pilgrims Clo., Brwd. CZ25 33
Pilgrims Clo., Dor. BJ69 119
Pilgrims Clo., Nthlt. BG35 45
Pilgrims Clo., Wat. BD20 18
Kytes Dr.
Pilgrims Ct. SE3 CH44 68
Pilgrims La. NW3 BT35 47
Pilgrims La., Brwd. CY24 33
Pilgrims La., Cat. BY66 113
Pilgrims La., Grays DB40 60
Pilgrims La., Oxt. CH66 115
Pilgrims Pl. NW3 BT35 47
Hampstead High St.
Pilgrims Rd., Swans. DC45 71
Pilgrims Ri., Barn. BU25 29
Pilgrims Way E., Sev. CV61 108
Pilgrims Way N19 BW33 47
Pilgrims Way W., Sev. CS61 107
Pilgrims Way, BJ69 119
West Humble
Pilgrims Way, Dart. CX47 80
Pilgrims Way, Dor. BG70 119
Pilgrims Way, Dor. BL70 120
& Bet.
Pilgrims Way, Guil. AO73 118
Pilgrims Way, Guil. AR72 118
Pilgrims Way, Reig. BR69 120
Pilgrims Way, S.Croy. CA57 96
Pilgrims Way, Sev. CY61 108
Pilgrims Way, Wem. BM33 46
Pilgrims Way, West. CL65 106
Pilkington Rd. SE15 CB44 67
Pilkington Rd., Orp. CL55 88
Pillions, The, Hayes BA38 53
Pillmans Clo., Sid. CO50 79
Pilot Ind. Est. NW10 BN38 55
Pilots Pl., Grav. DH46 81
East Ter.
Pilsden Clo. SW17 BU48 76
Inner Park Rd.
Piltdown Rd., Wat. BD28 36
Pilton Est., Croy. BY55 86
Pilton Pl. SE17 BZ42 4
Pilton Rd. SW6 BS44 66
Pimlico Rd. SW1 BV42 3
Pimlico Rd. SW1 BV42 66
Pimlico Wk. N1 CA38 2
Pimlico Wk. N1 CA38 57
Pimms Clo., Guil. AT68 109
Pimpernel Way, Rom. CV29 42
Pinceybrook Rd., Harl. CM13 13
Pinchbeck Rd., Orp. CN57 97
Pinchfield, Rick. AU28 34
Pinchin St. E1 CB40 4
Pinchin St. E1 CB40 57
Pincott La., Lthd. AZ68 110
Pincott Rd. SW19 BT50 76
Pincott Rd., Bexh. CR46 79
Pindar Rd., Hodd. CF11 12
Pindock Ms. W9 BS38 1
Pindock Ms. W9 BS38 56
Pine Av. E15 CF35 48
Ashlin Rd.
Pine Av., Grav. DH47 81
Pine Av., W.Wick. CE54 87
Pine Cft., Brwd. DD26 122
Pine Clo. N14 BW26 38
Pine Clo. N19 BW34 47
Hargrave Pk.
Pine Clo., Berk. AQ13 7
Pine Clo., Chsnt. CC17 21
Pine Clo., Ken. BZ62 105
Pine Clo., Stan. BJ28 36
Pine Clo., Swan. CT52 89
Pine Clo., Wey. AW59 92
Pine Clo., Wok. AR61 100
Pine Coombe, Croy. CC56 96
Pine Cres., Brwd. DE25 122
Pine Cres., Cars. BT59 95
Pine Ct., Upmin. CX35 51
Pine Dean, Lthd. BF66 111
Pine Gdns., Ruis. BC33 44
Pine Gdns., Surb. BM53 85
Pine Glade, Orp. CK56 97
Pine Gro. N20 BR26 37
Pine Gro. N4 BX34 47
Pine Gro. SW19 BR49 75
Pine Gro., Bush. BE23 27
Pine Gro., Hat. BS16 20
Pine Gro., St.Alb. BE18 18
Pine Gro., Wey. AZ56 92
Pine Grove Mt., Wey. BA56 92
Pine Hill, Epsom BN61 103
Pine Needles La., Sev. CU65 107
Pine Pl., Bans. BQ60 94
Pine Pl., Hayes BB38 53
Pine Rd. N11 BV27 38
Pine Rd. NW2 BQ35 46
Pine Rd., Wok. AR63 100
Pine Ridge, Cars. BV57 95
Pine St. EC1 BY38 2
Pine St. EC1 BY38 56
Pine Tree Clo., Houns. BC44 63
Pine Tree Hill, Wok. AU61 100
Pine Trees Dr., Uxb. AY35 44
Pine Way, Egh. AQ50 72
Pine Wk. E., Cars. BT59 95
Pine Wk. W., Cars. BT58 95
Pine Wk., BF66 111
Great Bookham
Pine Wk., Bans. BU62 104
Pine Wk., Cat. CA64 105
Pine Wk., Cob. BD60 93
Pine Wk., East Horsley BB67 110
Pine Wk., Surb. BM53 85
Pine Wood, Sun. BC51 83
Pineapple Rd., Amer. AP23 25
Pinecrest Gdns., Orp. CL56 97
Pinecroft Cres., Barn. BR25 28
Hillside Gdns.
Pinecroft, Brwd. DD26 122
Pinecroft, Hem.H. AY15 8
Pinecroft, Pnr. BF29 36
Pinefield Clo. E14 CE40 57
Pinehurst Clo., Tad. BS64 104
Pinehurst Clo., Wat. BB19 17
Pinehurst Wk, Orp. CN54 88
Pinehurst, Sev. CW64 108
Pinelands Clo. SE3 CG43 68
St. Johns Pk.
Pines Av., Enf. CC21 30
Pines Clo., Nthwd. BB29 35
Pines Rd., Brom. CK51 88
Pines, The N14 BW25 29
Chase Rd.
Pines, The, Dor. BJ72 119
South Ter.
Pines, The, Grays DD40 71
Pines, The, Pur. BY60 95
Pines, The, Sun. BC52 83
Pines, The, Wdf.Grn. CH27 40
Pinetree Clo., Ger.Gr. AR29 34
Pinetree Clo., Hem.H. AX13 8
Christchurch Rd.
Pinetree La., Sev. DA66 117
Pineview Clo., Guil. AV73 118
Pinewood Av., Pnr. BF29 36
Pinewood Av., Rain. CU38 59
Pinewood Av., Sev. CV64 108
Pinewood Av., Sid. CN47 78
Pinewood Av., Uxb. AY39 53
Pinewood Av., Wey. AX58 92
Pinewood Clo., B.Wd. BN23 28
Pinewood Clo., Croy. CD55 87
Pinewood Clo., Ger.Cr. AS33 43
Pinewood Clo., Iver AU36 52
Pinewood Clo., Orp. CM54 88
Pinewood Clo., S.le H. DK42 71
Pinewood Clo., St.Alb. BK13 9
Pinewood Clo., Wok. AT61 100
Pinewood Dr., Orp. CM56 97
Pinewood Dr., Stai. AW49 73
Pinewood Gdns., Hem.H. AW13 8
Pinewood Grn., Iver AU36 52
Pinewood Gro. W13 BK39 54
Pinewood Gro., Wey. AW58 92
Pinewood Pk., Wey. AW59 92
Pinewood Rd. SE2 CP43 69
Pinewood Rd., Brom. CH52 88
Pinewood Rd., Felt. BC48 73
Pinewood Rd., Hav. CS28 41
Pinewood Rd., Iver AT36 52
Pinewood Rd., Vir.W. AQ52 82
Pinewood Way, Brwd. DE25 122
Pinewood, Welw.G.C. BR9 5
Pinfold Rd. SW16 BX49 76
Pinfold Rd., Bush. BE23 27
Pinkcoat Clo., Felt. BC48 73
Tanglewood Way
Pinkerton Pl. SW16 BW49 76
Riggindale Rd.
Pinks Hill, Swan. CT53 89
Pinkwell Av., Hayes BA42 63
Pinkwell La., Hayes BA42 63
Pinley Gdns., Dag. CO37 59
Pinn Clo., Uxb. AX39 53
Pinn Way, Ruis. BA33 44
Pinnacle Hill N., Bexh. CR45 69
Pinnacle Hill, Bexh. CR45 69
Pinnacles, Wal.Abb. CG20 22
Pinnate Pl., Welw.G.C. BR10 5
Pinnell Pl. SE9 CJ45 68
Pinnell Rd. SE9 CJ45 68
Pinner Cres., Pnr. BE32 45
Pinner Ct., Pnr. BF31 45
Pinner Grn., Pnr. BD30 36
Pinner Hill Rd., Pnr. BD30 36
Pinner Hill, Pnr. BD30 36
Pinner Park Av., Har. BG30 36
Pinner Park Gdns., Har. BG30 36
Pinner Rd., Nthwd. BB30 35
Pinner Rd., Pnr. BE31 45
Pinner Rd., Wat. BD25 27
Pinner Vw., Har. BG32 45
Pinnicks Av., Grav. DG47 81
Pintail Clo. E6 CK39 58
Swann App.
Pintail Rd., Wdf.Grn. CH29 40
Pinto Clo., B.Wd. BN25 28
Pinto Way SE3 CH45 68
Pioneer Way W12 BP39 55
Piper Clo. N7 BX35 47
Piper Rd., Kings.T. BM52 85
Pipers Clo., Cob. BD61 102
Pipers End, Vir.W. AR52 82
Pipers Gdns., Croy. CD54 87
Pipers Green La., Edg. BL27 37
Pipers Green Rd., West. CO67 116
Pipers Grn. NW9 BN32 46
Pipers La., West. CO67 116
Pipewell Rd., Mitch. BU53 86
Pippbrook Gdns., Dor. BJ71 119
Pippens, Welw.G.C. BR6 5
Pippin Clo., Croy. CO54 87
Pippins Clo., West.Dr. AX41 63
Pippins Ct., Ashf. AZ50 73
Pippins, The, Slou. AS40 52
Pickford Dr.
Piquet Rd. SE20 CC51 87
Pirbright Cres., Croy. CF57 96
Pirbright Rd. SW18 BR47 75
Pirie St. E16 CH40 58
Pirrip Clo., Grav. DK48 81
Pirton Clo., St.Alb. BK11 9
Pishiobury Dr., Saw. CP7 6
Pit Farm Rd., Guil. AT70 118
Pit Head Ms. W1 BV40 3
Pit Wood Grn., Tad. BQ63 103
Pitcairn Clo., Rom. CR31 50
Pitcairn Rd., Mitch. BU50 76
Pitchfont La., Oxt. CH66 115
Pitchford St. E15 CF36 57
Pitfield Cres. SE28 CO40 59
Pitfield Est. N1 CA38 57
Pitfield St. N1 CA38 2
Pitfield St. N1 CA38 57
Pitfield Way NW10 BN36 55
Pitfield Way, Enf. CC23 30
Pitfold Clo. SE12 CH46 78
Pitfold Rd. SE12 CH46 78
Pitlake, Croy. BY55 86
Pitman St. SE5 BZ43 67
Pitmans Field, Harl. CN10 6
Pitsea Pl. E1 CC39 57
Pitsea St.
Pitsea St. E1 CC39 57
Pitsfield, Welw.G.C. BQ6 5
Pitshanger La. W5 BJ38 54
Pitsmead Av., Brom. CH54 88
Pitstone Clo., St.Alb. BK11 9
Highview Gdns.
Pitt Cres. SW19 BS49 76
Pitt Pl., Epsom BO60 94
Pitt Rd., Epsom BO60 94
Pitt Rd., Har. BG34 45
Pitt Rd., Orp. CM56 97
Pitt Rd., Th.Hth. BZ53 87
Pitt St. SE15 CA44 67
Pitt St. W8 BS41 66
Pittman Clo., Brwd. DE28 122
Brentwood Rd.
Pitts Ct. SE1 CA40 4
Braidwood St.
Pitts Head Ms. W1 BV40 56
Pitts Rd., Slou. AO40 61
Pittville Gdns. SE25 CB52 87
Pittwood, Brwd. DD26 122
Pix Farm La., Berk. AT14 7
Pixfield Ct., Brom. CG51 88
Pixham La., Dor. BK70 119
Pixholme Gro., Dor. BK70 119
Pixie Cres., Hem.H. AV14 7
Pixley St. E14 CD39 57
Pixton Way, Croy. CD58 96
Place Farm Rd., Brwd. DA21 33
Place Farm Rd., Red. BZ68 114
Place House La., Couls. BX63 104
Placket Way, Slou. AL40 61
Plain, The, Epp. CP18 23
Plaistow Grn., Brom. CH50 78
Plaistow Gro. E15 CG37 58
Plaistow Gro., Brom. CH50 78
Plaistow La., Brom. CH50 78
Plaistow Park Rd. E13 CH37 58
Plaistow Rd. E15 CG37 58
Plaitford Clo., Rick. AY27 35
Plane Av., Grav. DE47 81
Plane St. SE26 CB48 77
Plane Tree Cres., Felt. BC48 73
Plane Tree Wk. SE19 CA50 77
Central Hill Est.
Planes, The, Cher. AX54 83
Bridge Rd.
Plantagenet Clo., BN56 94
Wor.Pk.
Plantagenet Gdns., Rom. CP33 50
Plantagenet Pl., Rom. CP33 50
Broomfield Rd.
Plantagenet Rd., Barn. BT24 29
Plantain Pl. SE1 BZ41 4
Plantation Dr., Orp. CP54 89
Plantation La., Warl. CD63 105
Plantation Rd., Amer. AP22 25
Plantation Rd., Erith CU44 69
Plantation Rd., Swan. CO50 79
Plantation Way, Amer. AP22 25
Plantation Wk., Hem.H. AW12 8
Plantation, The SE3 CH44 68
Plasel Ct. E13 CH37 58
Plashet Gdns., Brwd. DD28 122
Plashet Gro. E6 CJ36 58
Plashet Rd. E13 CH37 58
Plashetts, Bish. CS7 6
Plassy Rd. SE6 CE47 77
Platford Grn., Horn. CW31 51
Platina St. EC1 BZ38 57
Tabernacle St.
Platina St. EC2 BZ38 2
Plato Rd. SW2 BX45 66
Platt Meadow, Guil. AU69 109
Eustace Rd.
Platt St. NW1 BW37 1
Platt St. NW1 BW37 56
Platt, The SW15 BQ45 65
Platts La. NW3 BS35 47
Platts Rd., Enf. CC23 30
Plawsfield Rd. SE20 CC51 87
Plaxdale Green Rd., Sev. DB59 99
Plaxtol Clo., Brom. CJ51 88
Plaxtol Pl. SE10 CH42 68
Westcombe Hill
Plaxtol Rd., Erith CR43 69
Playfield Av., Rom. CS30 41
Playfield Cres. SE22 CA46 77
Playfield Rd., Edg. BN30 37
Playford Rd. N4 BX34 47
Playgreen Way SE6 CE48 77
Playhouse Yd. EC4 BY39 2
Playhouse Yd. EC4 BY39 56
Pleasance Rd. SW15 BP45 65
Pleasance Rd., Orp. CO51 89
Pleasance, The SW15 BP45 65
Pleasance Rd.
Pleasant Gro., Croy. CD55 87
Pleasant Pl. N1 BY36 2
Pleasant Pl. N1 BY36 56
Pleasant Pl., Har. BG33 45
Pleasant Pl., Walt. BD57 93
Pleasant Rd., Kings.T. BN52 85
Pleasant Ri., Hat. BQ11 10
Pleasant Row NW1 BV37 1
Pleasant Row NW1 BV37 56
Camden High St.
Pleasant Vw. Pl., Orp. CM56 97
Pleasant Vw., Erith CT42 69
Pleasant Way, Wem. BK37 54
Pleasure Pit Rd., Ash. BM62 103
Plender Pl. NW1 BW37 1
Plender Pl. NW1 BW37 56
Plender St.
Plender St. Est. NW1 BW37 56
Plender St. NW1 BW37 1
Plender St. NW1 BW37 56
Pleshey Rd. N7 BW35 47
Plesman Way, Pur. BX57 95
Plevna Cres. N15 CA32 48
Plevna Rd. N9 CB27 39
Plevna Rd., Hmptn. BF51 84
Plevna St. E14 CF41 67
Plevna St. E6 CL40 58
Plevny Clo. N15 BY31 47
Shepstone St.
Pleydell Av. SE19 CA50 77
Pleydell Av. W6 BO42 65
Pleydell Ct. EC4 BZ39 57
Fleet St.
Pleydell St. EC4 BY39 2
Bouverie St.
Plimsoll Clo. E14 CE39 57
Grundy St.
Plimsoll Rd. N4 BY34 47
Plough All. E1 CB40 57
Hermitage Wall
Plough Ct. EC3 BZ40 4
Lombard St.
Plough Est. SE8 CC42 67
Plough Farm Clo., Ruis. BA32 44
Plough Hill, Cuff. BX18 20
Plough La. Clo., Wall. BX56 95
Plough La. SE22 CA46 77
Plough La. SW17 BS49 76
Plough La. SW19 BS49 76
Plough La., Berk. AT11 7
Plough La., Cob. BC62 101
Plough La., Pur. BX58 95
Plough La., Rick. AV20 16
Plough La., Slou. AQ37 52
Plough La., Uxb. AX29 35
Plough La., Wall. BX56 95
Plough Pl. EC4 BY39 2
Plough Pl. EC4 BY39 56
New Fetter La.
Plough Rd. SW11 BT45 66
Plough Rd., Brent. BK43 64
Brent Way
Plough Rd., Epsom BN58 94
Plough Ri., Upmin. CZ33 51
Plough St. E1 CA39 2
Buckle St.
Plough Ter. SW11 BT45 66
Plough Way SE16 CC42 67
Plough Yd. EC2 CA38 2
Plough Yd. EC2 CA38 57
Hearn St.
Ploughlees La., Slou. AP40 52
Ploughmans Clo. NW1 BW37 1
Ploughmans End, BT8 5
Welw.G.C.
Forresters Dr.
Ploughmans End, Islw. BG46 74
Crofters Clo.
Plover Clo., Berk. AR13 7
Plover Clo., Stai. AV48 72
Plover Gdns., Upmin. CZ33 51
Plovers Baron, Brwd. DB21 33
Plovers Mead, Brwd. DB21 33
Plowman Way, Dag. CP33 50
Ployters Rd., Harl. CM13 13
Pluckington Pl., Sthl. BE41 64
Plum Garth, Brent BK42 64
Plum La. SE18 CL43 68
Plumbers Row E1 CB39 2

Plumbers Row E1 CB39 57
Plumbridge St. SE10 CE44 67
Plummer La., Mitch. BU51 86
Plummer Rd. SW4 BW46 76
Plumpton Av., Horn. CW35 51
Plumpton Clo., Nthlt. BF36 54
Plumpton Rd., Hodd. CF11 12
Plumpton Way, Cars. BU55 86
Plumstead Common Rd. SE18 CL43 68
Plumstead High St. SE18 CN42 68
Plumstead Rd. SE18 CL42 68
Plumtree Clo., Wall. BW57 95
Plumtree Ct. EC4 BY39 2
Plumtree Ct. EC4 BY39 56
Shoe La.
Plumtree Mead, Loug. CL24 31
Pluto Ri., Hem.H. AY12 8
Plymouth Dr., Sev. CV65 108
Plymouth Pk., Sev. CV65 108
Plymouth Rd. E16 CH39 58
Plymouth Rd., Brom. CH51 88
Plymouth Wf. E14 CF42 67
Plympton Av. NW6 BR36 55
Plympton Clo., Belv. CQ41 69
Halifield Dr.
Plympton Pl. NW8 BU38 1
Plympton Rd. NW6 BR36 55
Plympton St. NW8 BU38 1
Plympton St. NW8 BU38 56
Plymstock Rd., Well. CP43 69
Pocketsdell La., Hem.H. AR17 16
Pocklington Clo. NW9 BO30 37
Pocock St. SE1 BY41 4
Pocock St. SE1 BY41 66
Pococks La., Eton AP42 62
Podmore Rd. SW18 BT45 66
Poets Corner SW1 BX41 4
Poets Rd., N5 BZ35 48
Poets Way, Har. BH31 45
Point Clo. SE10 CF44 67
Point Hill
Point Hill SE10 CF43 67
Point Pleasant SW18 BS45 66
Point, The, Ruis. BB35 44
Pointalls Clo. N3 BT30 38
Pointer Clo. SE28 CP39 59
Pointers Clo. E14 CE42 67
Pointers Hill, Dor. BG72 119
Pointers Rd., Cob. BA61 101
Poland St. W1 BW39 1
Poland St. W1 BW39 56
Polayn Garth, Welw.G.C. BQ 7 5
Pole Cat Alley, Brom. CG55 88
Pole Hanger La., Hem.H. AV12 7
Pole Hill Rd. E4 CF26 39
Pole Hill Rd., Uxb. AZ38 53
Pole La., Ong. CT12 14
Polebrook Rd. SE3 CJ45 68
Polecroft La. SE6 CD48 77
Poles Hill, Rick. AV20 16
Polesden Gdns. SW20 BP51 85
Polesden La., Wok. AV65 100
Polesden Rd., Dor. BF68 111
Polesden Vw., Lthd. BF67 111
Polesteeple Hill, West. CJ62 106
Polesworth Rd., Dag. CP36 59
Polhill, Sev. CS61 107
Police Station La., Bush. BF26 36
School La.
Police Station Rd., Walt. BD57 93
Pollard Av., Ger.Cr. AV32 43
Pollard Clo. E16 CH40 58
Munday Rd.
Pollard Clo. N7 BX35 47
Pollard Clo., Chig. CO28 41
Pollard Clo., Wind. AQ46 72
Pollard Hatch, Harl. CL12 13
Pollard Rd. N20 BU27 38
Pollard Rd. NW9 BO33 46
The Broadway
Pollard Rd., Mord. BT53 86
Pollard Rd., Wok. AT61 100
Pollard Row E2 CB38 57
Pollard St. E2 CB38 57
Pollard Wk., Sid. CP50 79
Evry Rd.
Pollards Clo., Chsnt. BZ18 21
Pollards Cres. SW16 BX52 86
Pollards Hill E. SW16 BX52 86
Pollards Hill N. SW16 BX52 86
Pollards Hill S. SW16 BX52 86
Pollards Hill W. SW16 BX52 86
Pollards Oak Cres., Oxt. CH69 115
Pollards Oak Rd., Oxt. CH69 115
Pollards Wood Hill, Oxt. CH68 115
Pollards Wood Rd. SW16 BX52 86
Pollards Wood Rd., Oxt. CH69 115
Pollards, Loug. CJ25 31
Pollards, Rick. AU28 34
Pollen St. W1 BV39 1
Pollen St. W1 BW39 56
Hanover St.
Pollicot Clo., St.Alb. BK11 9
Pirton Clo.
Pollitt Dr. NW8 BT38 1
Polls La., Sev. DA60 99
Pollyhaugh, Eyns. CV55 90
Polperro Clo., Orp. CN53 89
Cotswold Ri.
Polsted La., Guil. AO73 118
Polsted Rd. SE6 CD47 77
Polthorne Gro. SE18 CM42 68
Poltimore Ms. W3 BN41 65
Mill Hill Gro.
Poltimore Rd., Guil. AQ71 118
Polworth Rd. SW16 BX49 76
Polygon Ms. W2 BU39 1
Polygon Rd. NW1 BW37 1
Polygon Rd. NW1 BW37 56
Polytechnic St. SE18 CL42 68
Pomell Way E1 CA39 2
Pomeroy Clo., Amer. AO23 25
Pomeroy Cres., Wat. BC21 26
Pomeroy Sq. SE14 CC43 67
Pomeroy St.
Pomeroy St. SE14 CC44 67
Pomfret Rd. SE5 BZ45 67
Flaxman Rd.
Pompadour Clo., Brwd. DB28 42
Queen St.
Pond Cft., Hat. BO12 10
Pond Clo. SE3 CG44 68
Pond Clo., Uxb. AX30 35
Pond Clo., Walt. BB57 92
Pond Cottage La., W.Wick. CE54 87
Pond Cotts. SE21 CA47 77
Pond Grn., Ruis. BB34 44
Pond Hill Gdns., Sutt. BR57 94
Pond Hill, Sutt. BR57 94
Pond Ho. SW3 BU42 3
Pond Ho. SW3 BU42 66
Pond La., Ger.Cr. AQ30 34
Pond La., Sev. CZ66 117
Pond Mead SE21 BZ46 77
Pond Meadow, Guil. AP70 118
Pond Piece, Lthd. BF60 93
Pond Pl. SW3 BU42 3
Pond Pl. SW3 BU42 66
Pond Rd. E15 CG37 58
Pond Rd. SE3 CG44 68
Pond Rd., Egh. AU50 72
Pond Rd., Hem.H. AZ16 17
Pond Rd., Wok. AQ63 100
Pond Sq. N6 BV33 47
Pond St. NW3 BU35 47
Pond Way, Tedd. BK50 74
Pond Wk., Upmin. CZ34 51
Pondcroft, Welw.G.C. BR 8 5
Ponder St. N7 BX36 56
Pondfield Cres., St.Alb. BJ11 9
Pondfield La., Brwd. DD27 122
Pondfield Rd., Brom. CG54 88
Pondfield Rd., Dag. CR35 50
Pondfield Rd., Ken. BY61 104
Pondfield Rd., Orp. CL55 88
Pondfield, Welw.G.C. BS 6 5
Lumbards
Pondside Clo., Hayes BA43 63
Pondwicks Clo., St.Alb. BG14 9
Pondwood Ri., Orp. CN54 88
Ponler St. E1 CB39 57
Ponsard Rd. NW10 BP38 55
Ponsford St. E9 CC36 57
Ponsonby Pl. SW1 BW42 3
Ponsonby Pl. SW1 BW42 66
Ponsonby Rd. SW15 BP47 75
Ponsonby Ter. SW1 BW42 3
Ponsonby Ter. SW1 BW42 66
Pont St. Ms. SW1 BU41 3
Pont St. Ms. SW1 BU41 66
Pont St. SW1 BU41 3
Pont St. SW1 BU41 66
Pontefract Rd., Brom. CG49 78
Ponton Rd. SW8 BW43 66
Pontosie Clo., Sev. CT64 107
Pontypool Pl. SE1 BY41 4
Valentine Pl.
Pontypool Wk., Rom. CV29 42
Saddleworth Rd.
Pony Chase, Cob. BE60 93
Pool Clo., Beck. CE49 77
Pool Clo., E.Mol. BF53 84
Pool Rd., E.Mol. BE53 84
Pool Rd., Har. BG33 45
Poole Clo., Ruis. BB34 44
Poole Court Rd., Houns. BE44 64
Poole Ho., Grays DG41 71
Poole Rd. E9 CC36 57
Poole Rd., Epsom BN57 94
Poole Rd., Horn. CX33 51
Poole Rd., Wok. AS62 100
Poole St. N1 BZ37 2
Poole St. N1 BZ37 57
Poole Way, Hayes BB38 53
Pooles Cotts., Rich. BK48 74
Clifford Rd.
Pooles La. SW10 BT43 66
Lots Rd.
Pooles La., Dag. CQ37 59
Pooles Pk. N4 BY34 47
Pooley Av., Egh. AT49 72
Pooley Green Clo., Egh. AV49 72
Pooley Green Rd., Egh. AT49 72
Pooleys La., Hat. BP15 10
Poolmans Rd., Wind. AL45 61
Poolmans St. SE16 CC41 67
Poolsford Rd. NW9 BO31 46
Poonah St. E1 CC39 57
Hardinge St.
Pootings Rd., Eden. CM70 115
Pope Clo. SW19 BT50 76
Shelley Way
Pope Clo., Felt. BB47 73
Pope Rd., Brom. CJ53 88
Pope St. SE1 CA41 4
Pope St. SE1 CA41 67
Popes Av., Twick. BH48 74
Popes Clo., Amer. AP22 25
Popes Clo., Slou. AT43 62
Popes Dr. N3 BS30 38
Popes Gro., Croy. CD55 87
Popes Gro., Twick. BH48 74
Popes Head All. EC3 BZ39 2
Cornhill
Popes La. W5 BK41 64
Popes La., Oxt. CG70 115
Popes La., Wat. BC22 26
Popes Rd. SW9 BY45 66
Popes Rd., Wat. BB19 17
Popham Clo., Felt. BE48 74
Popham Gdns., Rich. BM45 65
Marksbury Av.
Popham Rd. N1 BZ37 2
Popham Rd. N1 BZ37 57
Popham St. N1 BZ37 2
Popham St. N1 BZ37 57
Essex Rd.
Poplar Av., Amer. AP23 25
Poplar Av., Grav. DH49 81
Poplar Av., Lthd. BJ64 102
Poplar Av., Mitch. BU51 86
Poplar Av., Orp. CL55 88
Poplar Av., Sthl. BF41 64
Poplar Av., West Dr. AY40 53
Poplar Bath St. E14 CE40 57
Lawless St.
Poplar Clo., Ing. DC19 24
Poplar Clo., Pnr. BD30 36
Poplar Clo., Slou. AV44 62
Poplar Clo., Wat. BC19 17
Poplar Cres., Epsom BN57 94
Poplar Ct. SW19 BS49 76
Poplar Dr., Bans. BQ60 94
High Beeches
Poplar Farm Clo., Epsom BN57 94
Poplar Gdns., N.Mal. BN51 85
Poplar Gro. N11 BV29 38
Poplar Gro. W6 BQ41 65
Poplar Gro., N.Mal. BN52 85
Poplar Gro., Wem. BN34 46
Poplar Gro., Wok. AS63 100
Poplar High St. E14 CE40 57
Poplar Mt., Belv. CR42 69
Poplar Pl. SE28 CP40 59
Poplar Pl. W2 BS40 3
Poplar Pl. W2 BS40 56
Poplar Pl., Hayes BC40 53
Poplar Rd. S. SW19 BS52 86
Poplar Rd. SE24 BZ45 67
Poplar Rd. SW19 BS51 86
Poplar Rd., Ashf. BA49 73
Poplar Rd., Guil. AS74 118
Poplar Rd., Lthd. BJ64 102
Poplar Rd., Sutt. BR54 85
Poplar Rd., Uxb. AX35 44
Poplar Row, Epp. CN22 31
Poplar Shaw, Wal.Abb. CG20 22
Poplar St., Rom. CS31 50
Poplar Way, Felt. BC48 73
Poplar Way, Ilf. CM31 49
Poplar Wk. SE24 BZ45 67
Poplar Wk., Croy. BZ54 87
Poplars Av. NW2 BQ36 55
Poplars Av., Hat. BN12 10
Poplars Clo., Hat. BN12 10
Poplars Clo., Ruis. BB33 44
Poplars Rd. E17 CE32 48
Poplars, The N14 BV25 29
Poplars, The, B.Wd. BM23 28
Grove Rd.
Poplars, The, Hem.H. AW14 8
Poplars, The, Rom. CO24 32
Poplars, The, St.Alb. BJ15 9
Poplars, Welw.G.C. BS 7 5
Poppins Ct. EC4 BY39 2
Poppins Ct. EC4 BY39 56
St. Bride St.
Poppleton Rd. E11 CG32 49
Poppy Clo., Brwd. DA25 33
Poppy La., Croy. CC54 87
Poppyfields, Welw.G.C. BT 8 5
Forresters Dr.
Porch Way N20 BU27 38
Porchester Clo. SE5 BZ45 67
Porchester Gdns. Ms. W1 BT39 1
Porchester Gdns. W2 BS40 3
Porchester Gdns. W2 BS40 56
Porchester Mead, Beck. CE50 77
Porchester Ms. W2 BS39 1
Porchester Pl. NW1 BW36 56
Agar Gro.
Porchester Pl. W2 BU39 1
Porchester Pl. W2 BU39 56
Porchester Rd. W2 BS39 1
Porchester Rd. W2 BS39 56
Porchester Rd., Kings.T. BM51 85
Porchester Sq. Ms. W2 BS39 1
Porchester Sq. W2 BS39 1
Porchester Sq. W2 BS39 56
Porchester Ter. N. W2 BS39 1
Porchester Ter. N. W2 BS39 56
Porchester Ter. W2 BT39 56
Porchester Ter. W2 BT40 3
Porchfield Clo., Grav. DH48 81
Porchfield Clo., Sutt. BS58 95
Hulverston Clo.
Porcupine Clo. SE9 CK48 78
Porden Rd. SW2 BX45 66
Porlock Av., Har. BG33 45
Porlock Rd., Enf. CA26 39
Porlock St. SE1 BZ41 4
Porlock St. SE1 BZ41 67
Porrington Clo., Brom. CL51 88
Lubbock Rd.
Port Av., Green. DA46 80
Port Cres. E13 CH38 58
Port Hill, Orp. CO59 98
Portal Clo. SE27 BY48 76
Portal Clo., Ruis. BC35 44
Portal Clo., Uxb. AY36 53
Portbury Clo. SE15 CB44 67
Clayton Rd.
Portchester Clo., Horn. CW32 51
Portcullis Lo. Rd., Enf. BZ24 30
Silver St.
Portelet Rd. E1 CC38 57
Porten Rd. W14 BR41 65
Porter Clo., Grays DB43 70
Porter Rd. E6 CK39 58
Porter St. W1 BU39 1
Porter St. W1 BU39 56
Baker St.
Porters Av., Dag. CO36 59
Porters Clo., Brwd. DA26 42
Greenshaw
Porters Way, West Dr. AY41 63
Porters Wk. E1 CB40 57
Pennington St.
Porters Wood, St.Alb. BH11 9
Porteus Rd. W2 BT39 1
Porteus Rd. W2 BT39 56
Portgate Clo. W9 BR38 55
Ashmore Rd.
Porthcawe Rd. SE26 CD49 77
Porthkerry Av., Well. CO45 69
Portia Way E3 CD38 57
Portinscale Rd. SW15 BR46 75
Portland Av. N16 CA33 48
Portland Av., Grav. DG48 81
Portland Av., N.Mal. BO54 85
Portland Av., Sid. CO46 79
Portland Cres. SE9 CK48 78
Portland Cres., Felt. BA49 73
Portland Cres., Grnf. BF38 54
Portland Cres., Stan. BK30 36
Portland Dr., Chsnt. CB19 21
Portland Dr., Red. BW68 113
Portland Gdns. N4 BY32 47
Portland Gdns., Rom. CP32 50
Portland Gro. SW8 BX44 66
Lansdowne Way
Portland Ms. W1 BW39 1
Darblay St.
Portland Pl. SE25 CB52 87
Portland Rd.
Portland Pl. W1 BV38 1
Portland Pl. W1 BV38 56
Portland Pl., Epsom BO59 94
Portland Rd. N15 CA31 48
Portland Rd. SE25 CB52 87
Portland Rd. SE9 CK48 78
Portland Rd. W11 BR40 55
Portland Rd., Ashf. AY49 73
Portland Rd., Brom. CJ49 78
Portland Rd., Dor. BJ71 119
Portland Rd., Grav. DE46 81
Portland Rd., Grav. DG47 81
Portland Rd., Hayes BB38 53
Portland Rd., Kings.T. BL52 85
Portland Rd., Mitch. BU51 86
Portland Rd., Sthl. BE41 64
Portland Ri. N4 BY33 47
Portland Rise Est. N4 BY33 47
Portland Sq. E1 CB40 57
Vinegar St.
Portland St. SE17 BZ42 4
Portland St. SE17 BZ42 67
Portland St., St.Alb. BG13 9
Portland Ter., Rich. BK45 64
Portley La., Cat. CA64 105
Portley Wood Rd., Cat. CA63 105
Portman Av. SW14 BN45 65
Portman Bldgs. NW1 BU38 1
Portman Bldgs. NW1 BU38 56
Portman Clo. W1 BU39 1
Portman Clo. W1 BU39 56
Portman Clo., Bex. CS47 79
Portman Clo., Bexh. CP45 69
Glynde Rd.
Portman Clo., St.Alb. BK11 9
Portman Dr., Wdf.Grn. CJ30 40
Portman Gdns. NW9 BN30 37
Portman Ms. S. W1 BV39 1
Portman Ms. S. W1 BV39 56
Portman Pl. E2 CC38 57
Portman Rd., Kings.T. BL51 85
Portman Sq. W1 BV39 1
Portman Sq. W1 BV39 56
Portman St. W1 BV39 1
Portman St. W1 BV39 56
Portmeadow Wk. SE2 CP41 69
Portmeers Clo. E17 CD32 48
Lennox Rd.
Portmore Gdns., Rom. CR28 41
Portmore Park Rd., Wey. AY56 92
Portnall Dr., Vir.W. AP53 82
Portnall Rd. W9 BR38 55
Portnall Rd., Vir.W. AP53 82
Portnall Ri., Vir.W. AP53 82
Portnalls Clo., Couls. BV61 104
Portnalls Rd., Couls. BV62 104
Portnalls Ri., Couls. BV61 104
Portnoi Clo., Rom. CS30 41
Portobello Ct. W11 BR40 55
Portobello Ms. W11 BS40 56
Portobello Rd.
Portobello Rd. W10 & W11 BR39 55
Portpool La. EC1 BY39 2
Portpool La. EC1 BY39 56
Portree St. E14 CF39 57
Portsdown Av. NW11 BR32 46
Portsdown, Edg. BM28 37
Portsea Ms. W2 BU39 1
Portsea Ms. W2 BU39 56
Kendal St.
Portsea Pl. W2 BU39 1
Portsea Pl. W2 BU39 56
Kendal St.
Portsea Rd., Til. DH44 71
Portslade Rd. SW8 BW44 66
Portsmouth Av., Surb. BJ54 84
Portsmouth Bldgs. NW1 BU39 56
Portsmouth Rd. SW15 BQ47 75
Portsmouth Rd., Sendmarsh AV66 109
Portsmouth Rd., Esher Common BE58 93
Portsmouth Rd., Hinchley Wood BH55 84
Portsmouth Rd., Cob. BA60 92
Portsmouth Rd., Cob. BC60 92
Portsmouth Rd., Esher BG56 93
Portsmouth Rd., Guil. AR72 118
Portsmouth Rd., Kings.T. BK52 84
Portsmouth Rd., Ripley AW65 101
Portsmouth Rd., Surb. BK52 84
Portsmouth Rd., T.Ditt. BH55 84
Portsmouth Rd., Wisley AZ62 101
Portsmouth St. WC2 BX39 56
Portugal St.
Portsoken St. E1 CA40 4
Portsoken St. E1 CA40 57
Portswood Pl. SW15 BO46 75
Danebury Av.
Portswood SW15 BO46 75
Danebury Av.
Portugal Gdns., Twick. BG48 74
Portugal Rd., Wok. AS61 100
Portugal St. WC2 BX39 2
Portugal St. WC2 BX39 56
Portway Cres., Epsom BP58 94
Portway E15 CG37 58
Portway Gdns. SE18 CJ43 68
Portway, Epsom BP58 94
Post House La., Lthd. BF66 111
Post La., Twick. BG47 74
Post Meadow, Iver AU38 52
Post Office Alley, Hmptn. BF51 84
Thames St.
Post Office App. E7 CH35 49
Post Office Ct. EC3 BY39 2
Lombard St.
Post Office La., Slou. AR39 52
Post Office Way SW8 BW43 66
Postern Grn., Enf. BY24 29
Postfield, Welw.G.C. BS 6 5
Lumbards
Postway Ms., Ilf. CL34 49
Clements Rd.
Potier St. SE1 BZ41 4
Potier St. SE1 BZ41 67
Potkiln La., Beac. AO30 34
Pott St. E2 CB38 57
Bethnal Green Rd.
Potten End, Berk. AT12 7
Potter Clo., Mitch. BV51 86
Potter Heights Clo., Pnr. BC29 35
Potter St. Hill, Pnr. BC29 35
Potter St., Harl. CO11 14
Potter St., Nthwd. BC30 35
Potter St., Pnr. BC30 35
Potterne Clo. SW19 BQ47 75
Castlecombe Dr.
Potters Clo., Croy. CD54 87
Potters Clo., Loug. CK23 31
Potters Cross, Iver AV38 52
Potters Field, Harl. CP12 14
Potters Field, St.Alb. BH11 9
Potters Fields SE1 CA40 4
Potters Fields SE1 CA40 57
Potters Gro., N.Mal. BN52 85
Potters La. SW16 BW50 76
Potters La., B.Wd. BN23 28
Potters La., Barn. BS24 29
Potters La., Guil. AT66 109
Potters La., Wok. AT65 100
Potters Rd., Barn. BS24 29
Potters Way, Reig. BT72 121
Pottery La. W11 BR40 55
Portland Rd.
Pottery Rd., Bex. CS48 79
Whenman Av.
Pottery Rd., Brent. BL43 65
Pottery St. SE16 CB41 67
Wilson Gro.
Pouchen End La., Hem.H. AU14 7
Pouchen Hill La., Hem.H. AU13 7
Poulcott, Stai. AS46 72
Poulett Gdns., Twick. BJ47 74
Poulett Rd. E6 CK37 58
Poulner Way SE15 CA43 67
Poulters Wood, Kes. CJ56 97
Poulton Av., Sutt. BT55 86
Poulton Clo. E8 CB35 48
Spurstowe Ter.
Poultry Av. EC1 BY39 2
Poultry EC2 BZ39 2
Poultry EC2 BZ39 57
Cheapside
Pound Bank Clo., Sev. CZ58 99
Ash Tree Dr.
Pound Clo., Orp. CM55 88
Pound Clo., Surb. BK54 84
Pound Clo., Wal.Abb. CG15 13
Pound Court Dr., Orp. CM55 88
Pound Cres., Lthd. BG64 102
Pound Ct., Ash. BL62 103
The Marld
Pound Field, Wat. BB21 17
Ashfields
Pound La. NW10 BP36 55
Pound La., Knockholt Pound CP61 107
Pound La., Epsom BN59 94
Pound La., Rad. BL20 19
Pound La., Sev. CV65 108
Pound Park Rd. SE7 CJ42 68
Pound Pl. SE9 CL46 78
Pound Pl., Guil. AS73 118
Pound Place Clo., Guil. AS73 118
Pound Rd., Bans. BR62 103
Pound Rd., Cher. AW54 83
Pound St., Cars. BU56 95
Poundfield Gdns., Wok. AU63 100
Poundfield Rd., Loug. CL25 31
Poundwell, Welw.G.C. BS 8 5
Pounsley Rd., Sev. CT64 107
Pountney Rd. SW11 BV45 66
Poverest Rd., Orp. CN53 88
Powder Mill La., Dart. CW48 80
Powder Mill La., Twick. BE47 74
Powderham Ct., Wok. AO62 100
Powdermill La., Wal.Abb. CE20 21
Powell Clo., Edg. BL29 37
Powell Clo., Guil. AP71 118
Powell Gdns., Dag. CR35 50
Powell Rd. E5 CB34 48
Powell Rd., Buck.H. CJ26 40
Powells Clo., Dor. BJ73 119
Powells Wk. W4 BO43 65
Power Rd. W4 BM42 65
Power Road N., Houns. BM42 65
Powers Ct., Twick. BK47 74
Powerscroft Rd. E5 CC35 48
Powerscroft Rd., Sid. CP50 79
Powis Ct., Pot.B. BT20 20
Powis Gdns. NW11 BR33 46
Powis Gdns. W11 BR39 55
Powis Ms. W11 BR39 55
Powis Pl. WC1 BX38 2
Powis Pl. WC1 BX38 56
Powis Rd. E3 CE38 57
Powis Sq. W11 BR39 55
Powis St. SE18 CL41 68
Powis Ter. W11 BR39 55

Powlett Pl. NW1 BV36 56
Harmood St.
Pownall Gdns., Houns. BF45 64
Pownall Rd. E8 CA37 2
Pownall Rd. E8 CA37 57
Pownall Rd., Houns. BF45 64
Powster Rd., Brom. CH49 78
Powys Clo., Bexh. CP43 69
Powys La. N13 BX28 38
Powys La. N14 BX28 38
Poyle Rd., Guil. AS71 118
Poyle Rd., Slou. AV45 62
Poynder Rd., Til. DG44 71
Poynders Ct. SW4 BW46 76
Poynders Gdns. SW4 BW47 76
Poynders Hill, Hem.H. BA14 8
Poynders Rd. SW4 BW46 76
Plummer Rd.
Poynings Clo., Orp. CO55 89
Poynings Rd. N19 BW34 47
Poynings Way W12 BS28 38
Poynings Way, Rom. CW30 42
Poynings, The, Iver AV42 62
Poyntell Cres., Chis. CM50 78
Poynter Rd., Enf. CA25 30
Poynton Rd. N17 CB30 39
Poyntz Rd. SW11 BU44 66
Poyser St. E2 CB37 57
Old Bethnal Green Rd.
Prae Clo., St.Alb. BF13 9
Praed Ms. W2 BT39 1
Praed Ms. W2 BT39 56
Norfolk Pl.
Praed St. W2 BT39 1
Praed St. W2 BT39 56
Praetorian Ct., St.Alb. BG15 9
Pragel St. E13 CJ37 58
Pragnell Rd. SE12 CH48 78
Prague Pl. SW2 BX46 76
Prah Rd. N4 BY34 47
Prairie Clo., Wey. AW55 83
Prairie Rd., Wey. AW55 83
Prairie St. SW8 BV44 66
Pratt Ms. NW1 BW37 1
Pratt Ms. NW1 BW37 56
Pratt St.
Pratt St. NW1 BW37 1
Pratt St. NW1 BW37 56
Pratt Wk. SE11 BX42 4
Pratt Wk. SE11 BX42 66
Pratts La., Walt. BD56 93
Prayle Gro. NW2 BQ33 46
Prebend Gdns. W4 & W6 BO42 65
Prebend St. N1 BZ37 2
Prebend St. N1 BZ37 57
Precinct Rd., Hayes BC40 53
Precinct, The N1 BZ37 2
Precinct, The, E.Mol. BF52 84
Premier Av., Grays DE41 71
Premier Pl. SW15 BQ45 65
Putney High St.
Prendergast Rd. SE3 CG45 68
Prentice Pl., Harl. CP12 14
Prentis Rd. SW16 BW49 76
Prentiss Ct. SE7 CJ42 68
Presburg Rd., N.Mal. BO53 85
Prescelly Pl., Edg. BL30 37
Prescot Rd., Slou. AV44 62
Prescot St. E1 CA40 4
Prescot St. E1 CA40 57
Prescott Av., Orp. CL53 88
Prescott Clo. SW16 BX50 76
Prescott Grn., Loug. CM24 31
Prescott Pl. SW4 BW45 66
Prescott Rd., Chsnt. CD17 21
President Dr. E1 CB40 57
President St. EC1 BZ38 2
Macclesfield Rd.
Press Rd. NW10 BN34 46
Press Rd., Uxb. AX36 53
Pressland St. W10 BR39 55
Kensal Rd.
Prestbury Cres., Bans. BU61 104
Prestbury Ct., Wok. AQ62 100
Muirfield Rd.
Prestbury Rd. E7 CJ36 58
Prestbury Sq. SE9 CK49 78
Prested Rd. SW11 BU45 66
St. Johns Hill
Preston Av. E4 CF29 39
Preston Clo. SE1 CA42 4
Preston Clo. SE1 CA42 67
Preston Clo., Twick. BH48 74
Preston Ct., Shep. AZ53 83
Preston Rd.
Preston Ct., Walt. BD54 84
St. Johns Dr.
Preston Dr. E11 CJ32 49
Preston Dr., Bexh. CP44 69
Preston Dr., Epsom BO57 94
Preston Gdns., Enf. CD22 30
Preston Gdns., Ilf. CK32 49
Preston Gro., Ash. BK62 102
Preston Hill, Chesh. AO18 16
Preston Hill, Har. BL32 46
Preston La., Tad. BQ63 103
Preston Pl. NW2 BP36 55
Preston Pl., Rich. BL46 75
Preston Rd. E11 CG32 49
Preston Rd. SE19 BY50 76
Preston Rd. SW20 BO50 75
Preston Rd., Grav. DF47 81
Preston Rd., Har. BL33 46
Preston Rd., Rom. CV28 42
Preston Rd., Shep. AZ53 83
Preston Rd., Slou. AR40 52
Preston Rd., Wem. BL33 46
Preston Waye, Har. BL33 46
Prestons Rd. E14 CF40 57
Prestons Rd., Brom. CH55 88
Prestwick Clo., Sthl. BE42 64
Prestwick Rd., Wat. BC28 35
Prestwood Av., Har. BJ31 45
Prestwood Clo., Har. BJ31 45
Prestwood Dr., Rom. CS28 41
Prestwood Gdns., Croy. BZ54 87
Queens Rd.
Prestwood St. N1 BZ37 2
Prestwood St. N1 BZ37 57
Wenlock Rd.
Prestwood, Slou. AQ39 52
Pretoria Av. E17 CD31 48
Pretoria Clo. N17 CA29 39
Pretoria Cres. E4 CF26 39
Pretoria Rd. E11 CF33 48
Pretoria Rd. E16 CG38 58
Pretoria Rd. E4 CF26 39
Pretoria Rd. N. N18 CA29 39
Pretoria Rd. N17 CA29 39
Pretoria Rd. N18 CA29 39
Pretoria Rd. SW16 BV50 76
Pretoria Rd., Cher. AV54 82
Pretoria Rd., Ilf. CL35 49
Pretoria Rd., Rom. CS31 50
Pretoria Rd., Wat. BC24 26
Prevost Rd. N11 BV27 38
Prey Heath Clo., Wok. AR65 100
Prey Heath Rd., Wok. AQ65 100
Price Clo. NW7 BR29 37
Price Clo. SE5 BZ45 67
Champion Hill
Price Clo. SW17 BU48 76
Price Clo., Hem.H. AZ13 8
Price Rd., Croy. BY56 95
Price Way, Hmptn. BE50 74
Victors Dr.
Prices La., Reig. BS72 121
Prices St. SE1 BY40 4
Prices St. SE1 BY40 56
Prices Yd. N1 BX37 2
Prices Yd. N1 BX37 56
Caledonian Rd.
Pricklers Hill, Barn. BS25 29
Prickley Wood, Brom. CG54 88
Prideaux Pl. W3 BN40 55
Friars Place La.
Prideaux Pl. WC1 BX38 2
Prideaux Pl. WC1 BX38 56
Prideaux Rd. SW9 BX45 66
Pridham Rd., Th.Hth. BZ52 87
Priest Hill, Egh. & Wind. AR48 72
Priest Wk., Grav. DK48 81
Priestfield Rd. SE23 CD48 77
Priestlands Park Rd., Sid. CN48 78
Priestley Ct., Grays DE42 71
Palmers Dr.
Priestley Gdns., Rom. CO32 50
Priestley Rd., Guil. AO71 118
Priestley Rd., Mitch. BV51 86
Priestley Way E17 CC31 48
Priestley Way NW2 BP33 46
Priests Av., Rom. CS30 41
Priests Br. SW14 BO45 65
Priests Ct. EC2 BZ39 57
Foster La.
Priests Field, Brwd. DE28 122
Priests La., Brwd. DC26 122
Prima Rd. SW9 BY43 66
Primley La., Bish. CS6 6
Primrose Av., Enf. BZ23 30
Primrose Av., Rom. CO33 50
Primrose Clo. SE6 CF49 77
Primrose Clo., Har. BE34 45
Primrose Clo., Hat. BP13 10
Primrose Clo., Hem.H. AV14 7
Campion Rd.
Primrose Ct. E15 CF36 57
Angel La.
Primrose Field, Harl. CN12 13
Primrose Gdns. NW3 BU36 56
Primrose Gdns., Bush. BF26 36
Primrose Gdns., Ruis. BD35 45
Primrose Glen, Horn. CW31 51
Primrose Hill Br. NW8 BU37 1
Primrose Hill Ct. NW3 BU36 56
Primrose Hill EC4 BY39 2
Primrose Hill EC4 BY39 56
Primrose Hill NW3 BU36 56
Primrose Hill Rd. NW3 BU36 1
Primrose Hill Rd. NW3 BU36 56
Primrose Hill, Brwd. DB27 42
Primrose Hill, Kings L. AZ17 17
Primrose Hill, Orp. CN58 97
Primrose La., Croy. CC54 87
Primrose La., Maid. AG43 61
Primrose Path, Chsnt. CB19 21
Primrose Rd. E10 CE33 48
Primrose Rd. E18 CH30 40
Lubbock Rd.
Port Av., Green. DA46 80
Port Cres. E13 CH38 58
Port Hill, Orp. CO59 98
Portal Clo. SE27 BY48 76
Portal Clo., Ruis. BC35 44
Portal Clo., Uxb. AY36 53
Portbury Clo. SE15 CB44 67
Clayton Rd.
Portchester Clo., Horn. CW32 51
Portcullis Lo. Rd., Enf. BZ24 30
Silver St.
Portelet Rd. E1 CC38 57
Porten Rd. W14 BR41 65
Porter Clo., Grays DB43 70
Porter Rd. E6 CK39 58
Porter St. W1 BU39 1
Porter St. W1 BU39 56
Baker St.
Porters Av., Dag. CO36 59
Porters Clo., Brwd. DA26 42
Greenshaw
Porters Way, West Dr. AY41 63
Porters Wk. E1 CB40 57
Pennington St.
Porters Wood, St.Alb. BH11 9
Porteus Rd. W2 BT39 1
Porteus Rd. W2 BT39 56
Portgate Clo. W9 BR38 55
Ashmore Rd.
Porthcawe Rd. SE26 CD49 77
Porthkerry Av., Well. CO45 69
Portia Way E3 CD38 57
Portinscale Rd. SW15 BR46 75
Portland Av. N16 CA33 48
Portland Av., Grav. DG48 81
Portland Av., N.Mal. BO54 85
Portland Av., Sid. CO46 79
Portland Cres. SE9 CK48 78
Portland Cres., Felt. BA49 73
Portland Cres., Grnf. BF38 54
Portland Cres., Stan. BK30 36
Portland Dr., Chsnt. CB19 21
Portland Dr., Red. BW68 113
Portland Gdns. N4 BY32 47
Portland Gdns., Rom. CP32 50
Portland Gro. SW8 BX44 66
Lansdowne Way
Portland Ms. W1 BW39 1
Darblay St.
Portland Pl. SE25 CB52 87
Portland Rd.
Portland Pl. W1 BV38 1
Portland Pl. W1 BV38 56
Portland Pl., Epsom BO59 94
Portland Rd. N15 CA31 48
Portland Rd. SE25 CB52 87
Portland Rd. SE9 CK48 78
Portland Rd. W11 BR40 55
Portland Rd., Ashf. AY49 73
Portland Rd., Brom. CJ49 78
Portland Rd., Dor. BJ71 119
Portland Rd., Grav. DE46 81
Portland Rd., Grav. DG47 81
Portland Rd., Hayes BB38 53
Portland Rd., Kings.T. BL52 85
Portland Rd., Mitch. BU51 86
Portland Rd., Sthl. BE41 64
Portland Ri. N4 BY33 47
Portland Rise Est. N4 BY33 47
Portland Sq. E1 CB40 57
Vinegar St.
Portland St. SE17 BZ42 4
Portland St. SE17 BZ42 67
Portland St., St.Alb. BG13 9
Portland Ter., Rich. BK45 64
Portley La., Cat. CA64 105
Portley Wood Rd., Cat. CA63 105
Portman Av. SW14 BN45 65
Portman Bldgs. NW1 BU38 1
Portman Bldgs. NW1 BU38 56
Portman Clo. W1 BU39 1
Portman Clo. W1 BU39 56
Portman Clo., Bex. CS47 79
Portman Clo., Bexh. CP45 69
Glynde Rd.
Portman Clo., St.Alb. BK11 9
Portman Dr., Wdf.Grn. CJ30 40
Portman Gdns. NW9 BN30 37
Portman Ms. S. W1 BV39 1
Portman Ms. S. W1 BV39 56
Portman Pl. E2 CC38 57
Portman Rd., Kings.T. BL51 85
Portman Sq. W1 BV39 1
Portman Sq. W1 BV39 56
Portman St. W1 BV39 1
Portman St. W1 BV39 56
Portmeadow Wk. SE2 CP41 69
Portmeers Clo. E17 CD32 48
Lennox Rd.
Portmore Gdns., Rom. CR28 41
Portmore Park Rd., Wey. AY56 92
Portnall Dr., Vir.W. AP53 82
Portnall Rd. W9 BR38 55
Portnall Rd., Vir.W. AP53 82
Portnall Ri., Vir.W. AP53 82
Portnalls Clo., Couls. BV61 104
Portnalls Rd., Couls. BV62 104
Portnalls Ri., Couls. BV61 104
Portnoi Clo., Rom. CS30 41
Portobello Ct. W11 BR40 55
Portobello Ms. W11 BS40 56
Portobello Rd.
Portobello Rd. W10 & W11 BR39 55
Portpool La. EC1 BY39 2
Portpool La. EC1 BY39 56
Portree St. E14 CF39 57
Portsdown Av. NW11 BR32 46
Portsdown Av., Edg. BM28 37
Portsea Ms. W2 BU39 1
Portsea Ms. W2 BU39 56
Kendal St.
Portsea Pl. W2 BU39 1
Portsea Pl. W2 BU39 56
Kendal St.
Portsea Rd., Til. DH44 71
Portslade Rd. SW8 BW44 66
Portsmouth Av., Surb. BJ54 84
Portsmouth Bldgs. NW1 BU39 56
Portsmouth Rd. SW15 BQ47 75
Portsmouth Rd., Sendmarsh AV66 109
Portsmouth Rd., Esher Common BE58 93
Portsmouth Rd., Hinchley Wood BH55 84
Portsmouth Rd., Cob. BA60 92
Portsmouth Rd., Cob. BC60 92
Portsmouth Rd., Esher BG56 93
Portsmouth Rd., Guil. AR72 118
Portsmouth Rd., Kings.T. BK52 84
Portsmouth Rd., Ripley AW65 101
Portsmouth Rd., Surb. BK52 84
Portsmouth Rd., T.Ditt. BH55 84
Portsmouth Rd., Wisley AZ62 101
Portsmouth St. WC2 BX39 56
Portugal St.
Portsoken St. E1 CA40 4
Portsoken St. E1 CA40 57
Portswood Pl. SW15 BO46 75
Danebury Av.
Portswood SW15 BO46 75
Danebury Av.
Portugal Gdns., Twick. BG48 74
Portugal Rd., Wok. AS61 100
Portugal St. WC2 BX39 2
Portugal St. WC2 BX39 56
Portway Cres., Epsom BP58 94
Portway E15 CG37 58
Portway Gdns. SE18 CJ43 68
Portway, Epsom BP58 94
Post House La., Lthd. BF66 111
Post La., Twick. BG47 74
Post Meadow, Iver AU38 52
Post Office Alley, Hmptn. BF51 84
Thames St.
Post Office App. E7 CH35 49
Post Office Ct. EC3 BY39 2
Lombard St.
Post Office La., Slou. AR39 52
Post Office Way SW8 BW43 66
Postern Grn., Enf. BY24 29
Postfield, Welw.G.C. BS6 5
Lumbards
Postway Ms., Ilf. CL34 49
Clements Rd.
Potier St. SE1 BZ41 4
Potier St. SE1 BZ41 67
Potkiln La., Beac. AO30 34
Pott St. E2 CB38 57
Bethnal Green Rd.
Potten End, Berk. AT12 7
Potter Clo., Mitch. BV51 86
Potter Heights Clo., Pnr. BC29 35
Potter St. Hill, Pnr. BC29 35
Potter St., Harl. CO11 14
Potter St., Nthwd. BC30 35
Potter St., Pnr. BC30 35
Potterne Clo. SW19 BQ47 75
Castlecombe Dr.
Potters Clo., Croy. CD54 87
Potters Clo., Loug. CK23 31
Potters Cross, Iver AV38 52
Potters Field, Harl. CP12 14
Potters Field, St.Alb. BH11 9
Potters Fields SE1 CA40 4
Potters Fields SE1 CA40 57
Potters Gro., N.Mal. BN52 85
Potters La. SW16 BW50 76
Potters La., B.Wd. BN23 28
Potters La., Barn. BS24 29
Potters La., Guil. AT66 109
Potters La., Wok. AT65 100
Potters Rd., Barn. BS24 29
Potters Way, Reig. BT72 121
Pottery La. W11 BR40 55
Portland Rd.
Pottery Rd., Bex. CS48 79
Whenman Av.
Pottery Rd., Brent. BL43 65
Pottery St. SE16 CB41 67
Wilson Gro.
Pouchen End La., Hem.H. AU14 7
Pouchen Hill La., Hem.H. AU13 7
Poulcott, Stai. AS46 72
Poulett Gdns., Twick. BJ47 74
Poulett Rd. E6 CK37 58
Poulner Way SE15 CA43 67
Poulters Wood, Kes. CJ56 97
Poulton Av., Sutt. BT55 86
Poulton Clo. E8 CB35 48
Spurstowe Ter.
Poultry Av. EC1 BY39 2
Poultry EC2 BZ39 2
Poultry EC2 BZ39 57
Cheapside
Pound Bank Clo., Sev. CZ58 99
Ash Tree Dr.
Pound Clo., Orp. CM55 88
Pound Clo., Surb. BK54 84
Pound Clo., Wal.Abb. CG15 13
Pound Court Dr., Orp. CM55 88
Pound Cres., Lthd. BG64 102
Pound Ct., Ash. BL62 103
The Marld
Pound Field, Wat. BB21 17
Ashfields
Pound La. NW10 BP36 55
Pound La., Knockholt Pound CP61 107
Pound La., Epsom BN59 94
Pound La., Rad. BL20 19
Pound La., Sev. CV65 108
Pound Park Rd. SE7 CJ42 68
Pound Pl. SE9 CL46 78
Pound Pl., Guil. AS73 118
Pound Place Clo., Guil. AS73 118
Pound Rd., Bans. BR62 103
Pound Rd., Cher. AW54 83
Pound St., Cars. BU56 95
Poundfield Gdns., Wok. AU63 100
Poundfield Rd., Loug. CL25 31
Poundwell, Welw.G.C. BS8 5
Pounsley Rd., Sev. CT64 107
Pountney Rd. SW11 BV45 66
Poverest Rd., Orp. CN53 88
Powder Mill La., Dart. CW48 80
Powder Mill La., Twick. BE47 74
Powderham Ct., Wok. AO62 100
Powdermill La., Wal.Abb. CE20 21
Powell Clo., Edg. BL29 37
Powell Clo., Guil. AP71 118
Powell Gdns., Dag. CR35 50
Powell Rd. E5 CB34 48
Powell Rd., Buck.H. CJ26 40
Powells Clo., Dor. BJ73 119
Powells Wk. W4 BO43 65
Power Rd. W4 BM42 65
Power Road N., Houns. BM42 65
Powers Ct., Twick. BK47 74
Powerscroft Rd. E5 CC35 48
Powerscroft Rd., Sid. CP50 79
Powis Ct., Pot.B. BT20 20
Powis Gdns. NW11 BR33 46
Powis Gdns. W11 BR39 55
Powis Ms. W11 BR39 55
Powis Pl. WC1 BX38 2
Powis Pl. WC1 BX38 56
Powis Rd. E3 CE38 57
Powis Sq. W11 BR39 55
Powis St. SE18 CL41 68
Powis Ter. W11 BR39 55
Powlett Pl. NW1 BV36 56
Harmood St.
Pownall Gdns., Houns. BF45 64
Pownall Rd. E8 CA37 2
Pownall Rd. E8 CA37 57
Pownall Rd., Houns. BF45 64
Powster Rd., Brom. CH49 78
Powys Clo., Bexh. CP43 69
Powys La. N13 BX28 38
Powys La. N14 BX28 38
Poyle Rd., Guil. AS71 118
Poyle Rd., Slou. AV45 62
Poynder Rd., Til. DG44 71
Poynders Ct. SW4 BW46 76
Poynders Gdns. SW4 BW47 76
Poynders Hill, Hem.H. BA14 8
Poynders Rd. SW4 BW46 76
Plummer Rd.
Poynings Clo., Orp. CO55 89
Poynings Rd. N19 BW34 47
Poynings Way W12 BS28 38
Poynings Way, Rom. CW30 42
Poynings, The, Iver AV42 62
Poyntell Cres., Chis. CM50 78
Poynter Rd., Enf. CA25 30
Poynton Rd. N17 CB30 39
Poyntz Rd. SW11 BU44 66
Poyser St. E2 CB37 57
Old Bethnal Green Rd.
Prae Clo., St.Alb. BF13 9
Praed Ms. W2 BT39 1
Praed Ms. W2 BT39 56
Norfolk Pl.
Praed St. W2 BT39 1
Praed St. W2 BT39 56
Praetorian Ct., St.Alb. BG15 9
Pragel St. E13 CJ37 58
Pragnell Rd. SE12 CH48 78
Prague Pl. SW2 BX46 76
Prah Rd. N4 BY34 47
Prairie Clo., Wey. AW55 83
Prairie Rd., Wey. AW55 83
Prairie St. SW8 BV44 66
Pratt Ms. NW1 BW37 1
Pratt Ms. NW1 BW37 56
Pratt St.
Pratt St. NW1 BW37 1
Pratt St. NW1 BW37 56
Pratt Wk. SE11 BX42 4
Pratt Wk. SE11 BX42 66
Pratts La., Walt. BD56 93
Prayle Gro. NW2 BQ33 46
Prebend Gdns. W4 & W6 BO42 65
Prebend St. N1 BZ37 2
Prebend St. N1 BZ37 57
Precinct Rd., Hayes BC40 53
Precinct, The N1 BZ37 2
Precinct, The, E.Mol. BF52 84
Premier Av., Grays DE41 71
Premier Pl. SW15 BQ45 65
Putney High St.
Prendergast Rd. SE3 CG45 68
Prentice Pl., Harl. CP12 14
Prentis Rd. SW16 BW49 76
Prentiss Ct. SE7 CJ42 68
Presburg Rd., N.Mal. BO53 85
Prescelly Pl., Edg. BL30 37
Prescot Rd., Slou. AV44 62
Prescot St. E1 CA40 4
Prescot St. E1 CA40 57
Prescott Av., Orp. CL53 88
Prescott Clo. SW16 BX50 76
Prescott Grn., Loug. CM24 31
Prescott Pl. SW4 BW45 66
Prescott Rd., Chsnt. CD17 21
President Dr. E1 CB40 57
President St. EC1 BZ38 2
Macclesfield Rd.
Press Rd. NW10 BN34 46
Press Rd., Uxb. AX36 53
Pressland St. W10 BR39 55
Kensal Rd.
Prestbury Cres., Bans. BU61 104
Prestbury Ct., Wok. AQ62 100
Muirfield Rd.
Prestbury Rd. E7 CJ36 58
Prestbury Sq. SE9 CK49 78
Prested Rd. SW11 BU45 66
St. Johns Hill
Preston Av. E4 CF29 39
Preston Clo. SE1 CA42 4
Preston Clo. SE1 CA42 67
Preston Clo., Twick. BH48 74
Preston Ct., Shep. AZ53 83
Preston Rd.
Preston Ct., Walt. BD54 84
St. Johns Dr.
Preston Dr. E11 CJ32 49
Preston Dr., Bexh. CP44 69
Preston Dr., Epsom BO57 94
Preston Gdns., Enf. CD22 30
Preston Gdns., Ilf. CK32 49
Preston Gro., Ash. BK62 102
Preston Hill, Chesh. AO18 16
Preston Hill, Har. BL32 46
Preston La., Tad. BQ63 103
Preston Pl. NW2 BP36 55
Preston Pl., Rich. BL46 75
Preston Rd. E11 CG32 49
Preston Rd. SE19 BY50 76
Preston Rd. SW20 BO50 75
Preston Rd., Grav. DF47 81
Preston Rd., Har. BL33 46
Preston Rd., Rom. CV28 42
Preston Rd., Shep. AZ53 83
Preston Rd., Slou. AR40 52
Preston Rd., Wem. BL33 46
Preston Waye, Har. BL33 46
Prestons Rd. E14 CF40 57
Prestons Rd., Brom. CH55 88
Prestwick Clo., Sthl. BE42 64
Prestwick Rd., Wat. BC28 35
Prestwood Av., Har. BJ31 45
Prestwood Clo., Har. BJ31 45
Prestwood Dr., Rom. CS28 41
Prestwood Gdns., Croy. BZ54 87
Queens Rd.
Prestwood St. N1 BZ37 2
Prestwood St. N1 BZ37 57
Wenlock Rd.

Prestwood, Slou.	AQ39	52
Pretoria Av. E17	CD31	48
Pretoria Clo. N17	CA29	39
Pretoria Cres. E4	CF26	39
Pretoria Rd. E11	CF33	48
Pretoria Rd. E16	CG38	58
Pretoria Rd. E4	CF26	39
Pretoria Rd. N. N18	CA29	39
Pretoria Rd. N17	CA29	39
Pretoria Rd. N18	CA29	39
Pretoria Rd. SW16	BV50	76
Pretoria Rd., Cher.	AV54	82
Pretoria Rd., Ilf.	CL35	49
Pretoria Rd., Rom.	CS31	50
Pretoria Rd., Wat.	BC24	26
Prevost Rd. N11	BV27	38
Prey Heath Clo., Wok.	AR65	100
Prey Heath Rd., Wok.	AQ65	100
Price Clo. NW7	BR29	37
Price Clo. SE5	BZ45	67
Champion Hill		
Price Clo. SW17	BU48	76
Price Clo., Hem.H.	AZ13	8
Price Rd., Croy.	BY56	95
Price Way, Hmptn.	BE50	74
Victors Dr.		
Prices La., Reig.	BS72	121
Prices St. SE1	**BY40**	**4**
Prices St. SE1	BY40	56
Prices Yd. N1	**BX37**	**2**
Prices Yd. N1	BX37	56
Caledonian Rd.		
Pricklers Hill, Barn.	BS25	29
Prickley Wood, Brom.	CG54	88
Prideaux Pl. W3	BN40	55
Friars Place La.		
Prideaux Pl. WC1	**BX38**	**2**
Prideaux Pl. WC1	BX38	56
Prideaux Rd. SW9	BX45	66
Pridham Rd., Th.Hth.	BZ52	87
Priest Hill, Egh. & Wind.	AR48	72
Priest Wk., Grav.	DK48	81
Priestfield Rd. SE23	CD48	77
Priestlands Park Rd., Sid.	CN48	78
Priestley Ct., Grays	DE42	71
Palmers Dr.		
Priestley Gdns., Rom.	CO32	50
Priestley Rd., Guil.	AO71	118
Priestley Rd., Mitch.	BV51	86
Priestley Way E17	CC31	48
Priestley Way NW2	BP33	46
Priests Av., Rom.	CS30	41
Priests Br. SW14	BO45	65
Priests Ct. EC2	BZ39	57
Foster La.		
Priests Field, Brwd.	DE28	122
Priests La., Brwd.	DC26	122
Prima Rd. SW9	BY43	66
Primley La., Bish.	CS 6	6
Primrose Av., Enf.	BZ23	30
Primrose Av., Rom.	CO33	50
Primrose Clo. SE6	CF49	77
Primrose Clo., Har.	BE34	45
Primrose Clo., Hat.	BP13	10
Primrose Clo., Hem.H.	AV14	7
Campion Rd.		
Primrose Ct. E15	CF36	57
Angel La.		
Primrose Field, Harl.	CN12	13
Primrose Gdns. NW3	BU36	56
Primrose Gdns., Bush.	BF26	36
Primrose Gdns., Ruis.	BD35	45
Primrose Glen, Horn.	CW31	51
Primrose Hill Br. NW8	**BU37**	**1**
Primrose Hill Ct. NW3	BU36	56
Primrose Hill EC4	**BY39**	**2**
Primrose Hill EC4	BY39	56
Primrose Hill NW3	BU36	56
Primrose Hill Rd. NW3	**BU36**	**1**
Primrose Hill Rd. NW3	BU36	56
Primrose Hill, Brwd.	DB27	42
Primrose Hill, Kings L.	AZ17	17
Primrose Hill, Orp.	CN58	97
Primrose La., Croy.	CC54	87
Primrose La., Maid.	AG43	61
Primrose Path, Chsnt.	CB19	21
Primrose Rd. E10	CE33	48
Primrose Rd. E18	CH30	40
Primrose Rd., Walt.	BD56	93
Primrose St. EC2	**CA39**	**2**
Primrose St. EC2	CA39	57
Primrose Way, Wem.	BK37	54
Primula St. W12	BP39	55
Prince Albert Rd. NW1	BU37	56
Prince Albert Rd. NW8	**BU38**	**1**
Prince Albert Rd. NW8	BU38	56
Prince Albert Sq., Red.	BU73	121
Prince Alberts Rd., Wind.	AP43	62
Prince Alberts Wk., Wind.	AP43	62
Prince Arthur Ms. NW3	BT35	47
Perrins La.		
Prince Arthur Rd. NW3	BT35	47
Prince Charles Av., S.Dnth.	CY51	90
Prince Charles Dr. NW4	BQ33	46
Prince Charles Rd. SE3	CG44	68
Prince Charles Way, Wall.	BV55	86
Prince Consort Cotts., Wind.	AO44	61
Prince Consort Dr., Chis.	CM51	88
Prince Consort Rd. SW7	**BT41**	**3**
Prince Consort Rd. SW7	BT41	66
Prince Edward Rd. E9	CD36	57
Prince Edward St., Berk.	AR13	7
Prince George Av. N14	BW24	29
Prince George Rd. N16	CA35	48
Prince George Rd. SW19	BT51	86
Prince Georges Av. SW20	BQ51	85
Prince Henry Rd. SE7	CJ43	68
Prince Imperial Rd., Chis.	CL50	78
Prince Imperial Way SE18	CL43	68
Prince John Rd. SE9	CK46	78
Prince of Wales Clo. NW4	BP31	46
Church Ter.		
Prince of Wales Dr. SW11	BU44	66
Prince of Wales Rd. E16	CJ39	58
Prince of Wales Rd. NW5	BV36	56
Prince of Wales Rd. SE3	CG44	68
Prince of Wales Rd., Sutt.	BT55	86
Prince of Wales Rd., Red.	BY74	121
Prince of Wales Ter. W4	BO42	65
Devonshire Rd.		
Prince of Wales Ter. W8	**BS41**	**3**
Prince of Wales Ter. W8	BS41	66
Prince Philip Av., Grays	DD40	71
Prince Pk., Hem.H.	AW14	8
Prince Rd. SE25	CA53	87
Prince Regent Rd., Houns.	BG45	64
Prince Regents La. E13	CH38	58
Prince Regents La. E16	CJ39	58
Prince Rupert Rd. SE9	CK45	68
Prince St. SE8	CD43	67
Prince St., Wat.	BD24	27
Princedale Rd. W11	BR40	55
Princelet St. E1	**CA39**	**2**
Princelet St. E1	CA39	57
Princes Av. N10	BV31	47
Princes Av. N13	BY28	38
Princes Av. N22	BW30	38
Princes Av. NW9	BM31	46
Princes Av. W3	BM41	65
Princes Av., Cars.	BU57	95
Princes Av., Dart.	CX47	80
Princes Av., Enf.	CD21	30
Princes Av., Grnf.	BF39	54
Princes Av., Orp.	CN53	88
Princes Av., S.Croy.	CB61	105
Princes Av., Surb.	BM54	85
Princes Av., Wat.	BB25	26
Princes Av., Wdf.Grn.	CH28	40
Princes Clo. NW9	BM31	46
Princes Clo. SW4	BW45	66
Old Town		
Princes Clo., Berk.	AQ12	7
Princes Clo., Edg.	BM28	37
Princes Clo., Epp.	CS16	23
Princes Clo., S.Croy.	CB61	105
Princes Clo., Sid.	CP48	79
Princes Clo., Tedd.	BG49	74
Princes Ct., Hem.H.	AW15	8
Roughdown Rd.		
Princes Ct., Wem.	BL35	46
Princes Dr., Har.	BH31	45
Princes Dr., Lthd.	BH59	93
Princes Gate Ct. SW7	**BT41**	**3**
Princes Gate Ct. SW7	BT41	66
Exhibition Rd.		
Princes Gate Ms. SW7	BT41	66
Princes Gate SW7	BT41	3
Princes Gate SW7	BT41	66
Princes Gate, Harl.	CN 9	6
Princes Gdns. Ms. SW7	BT41	3
Princes Gdns. SW7	**BT41**	**3**
Princes Gdns. SW7	BT41	66
Princes Gdns. W3	BM39	55
Princes Gdns. W5	BK38	54
Princes La. N10	BV31	47
Princes Ms. SW7	**BT41**	**3**
Princes Ms. SW7	BT41	66
Exhibition Rd.		
Princes Ms. W2	BS40	56
Princes Par., Pot.B.	BS20	20
High St.		
Princes Park Av. NW11	BR32	46
Princes Park Av., Hayes	BA40	53
Princes Park Cir., Hayes	BA40	53
Princes Park Clo., Hayes	BA40	53
Princes Park La., Hayes	BA40	53
Princes Park Par., Hayes	BA40	53
Princes Pk., Rain.	CU36	59
Princes Pl. W11	BR40	55
Princes Plain, Brom.	CK54	88
Princes Rd. N., Dart.	CU46	79
Princes Rd. N18	CC28	39
Princes Rd. SE20	CC50	77
Princes Rd. SW14	BN45	65
Princes Rd. SW19	BS50	76
Princes Rd. W13	BJ40	54
Mattock La.		
Princes Rd., Ashf.	AY49	73
Princes Rd., Buck.H.	CJ27	40
Princes Rd., Dart.	CU47	79
Princes Rd., Dart.	CY47	80
Princes Rd., Egh.	AS50	72
Princes Rd., Felt.	BB48	73
Princes Rd., Grav.	DG49	81
Princes Rd., Ilf.	CM31	49
Princes Rd., Kew	BL44	65
Princes Rd., Kings.T.	BM50	75
Princes Rd., Navestock	CW23	33
Princes Rd., Red.	BU71	121
Princes Rd., Rich.	BL46	75
Princes Rd., Rom.	CU32	50
Princes Rd., Tedd.	BG49	74
Princes Rd., Wey.	AZ56	92
Princes Ri. SE13	CF44	67
Princes Sq. W2	BS40	56
Princes St. EC2	**BZ39**	**2**
Princes St. EC2	BZ39	57
Princes St. N17	CA29	39
Queen St.		
Princes St. W1	**BV39**	**1**
Princes St. W1	BV39	56
Princes St., Bexh.	CQ45	69
Princes St., Rich.	BL45	65
Princes St., Slou.	AQ41	62
Princes St., Sutt.	BT56	95
Princes Ter. E13	CH37	58
Princes Ter. W3	BN41	65
Church Rd.		
Princes Vw., Dart.	CX47	80
Princes Way SW19	BQ47	75
Princes Way, Brwd.	DD27	122
Princes Way, Buck.H.	CJ27	40
Princes Way, Croy.	BX57	95
Princes Way, Ruis.	BE35	45
Princes Way, W.Wick.	CG56	97
Princesfield Rd., Wal.Abb.	CH20	22
Princess Av. N3	BS30	38
Princess Av., Wem.	BL34	46
Princess Av., Wind.	AN45	61
Princess Cres. N4	BY34	47
Princess Gdns., Wok.	AT61	100
Princess Margaret Rd., S.le H.	DK41	71
Princess Marys Rd., Wey.	AX55	83
Princess May Rd. N16	CA35	48
Princess Ms. NW3	BT35	47
Princess Par., Dag.	CR37	59
Whitebarn La.		
Princess Par., Orp.	CL55	88
Princess Rd. NW1	**BV37**	**1**
Princess Rd. NW1	BV37	56
Princess Rd. NW6	BS37	56
Princess Rd., Croy.	BZ53	87
Princess Rd., Swan.	CU50	79
Princess Rd., Wok.	AT61	100
Princess St. SE1	**BY41**	**4**
Princess St. SE1	BY41	66
Princess St., Grav.	DG46	81
Church St.		
Princess Way, Red.	BU70	121
Princethorpe Rd. SE26	CC49	77
Princeton St. WC1	**BX39**	**2**
Princeton St. WC1	BX39	56
Pring St. W10	BQ40	55
Freston Rd.		
Pringle Gdns. SW16	BW49	76
Printers Way, Harl.	CO 8	6
Printing House La., Hayes	BB41	63
Printing House Yd. E2	CA38	57
Hackney Rd.		
Priolo Rd. SE7	CJ42	68
Prior Av., Sutt.	BT57	95
Prior Boulton St. N1	BY36	56
Compton Rd.		
Prior Chase, Grays	DC42	71
Bersham La.		
Prior Gro., Chesh.	AO18	16
Prior Rd., Ilf.	CL34	49
Prior St. SE10	CF43	67
Prioress Rd. SE27	BY48	76
Prioress St. SE1	BZ41	67
Priors Cft. E17	CD30	39
Priors Cft., Wok.	AT64	100
Priors Clo., Slou.	AQ41	62
Priors Fld., Nthlt.	BE36	54
Arnold Rd.		
Priors Gdns., Ruis.	BD35	45
Priors Mead, Enf.	CA23	30
Priors Mead, Lthd.	BF66	111
Priors Pk., Horn.	CV34	51
Priors Rd., Wind.	AL45	61
Priors Way, Maid.	AG42	61
Priors, The, Ash.	BK63	102
Priorsford Av., Orp.	CO52	89
Priory Av. E17	CE32	48
Priory Av. E4	CD27	39
Priory Av. N8	BW31	47
Priory Av. W4	BO42	65
Priory Av., Harl.	CP 8	6
Priory Av., Orp.	CM53	88
Priory Av., Sutt.	BQ56	94
Priory Av., Uxb.	AX31	44
Priory Av., Wem.	BH35	45
Priory Br. SW14	BO45	65
Priory Clo. E18	CH30	40
Priory Clo. E4	CD27	39
Priory Clo. N14	BV25	29
Priory Clo. N20	BR26	37
Priory Clo. N3	BR30	37
Priory Clo., Beck.	CD52	87
Priory Clo., Brox.	CD15	12
Priory Clo., Brwd.	DA25	33
Priory Clo., Chis.	CK51	88
Priory Clo., Dart.	CV46	80
Priory Clo., Denham	AW34	44
Priory Clo., Dor.	BJ72	119
Harrow Rd. W.		
Priory Clo., Harefield	AX31	44
Priory Clo., Hmptn.	BE51	84
Priory Clo., Hodd.	CE12	12
Priory Clo., Ruis.	BB33	44
Priory Clo., Stan.	BH27	36
Priory Clo., Sudbury	BH35	45
Priory Clo., Sun.	BC50	73
Priory Clo., Wok.	AU60	91
Priory Cotts., Uxb.	AX31	44
Priory Cres. SE10	BZ50	77
Priory Cres., Sutt.	BQ56	94
Priory Cres., Wem.	BJ34	45
Priory Ct. E17	CD30	39
Priory Ct. E6	CJ37	58
Priory Rd.		
Priory Ct. Est. E17	CD30	39
Priory Ct. SW8	BW44	66
Priory Ct., Berk.	AR13	7
Priory Gdns.		
Priory Ct., Harl.	CO12	14
Priory Ct., St.Alb.	BH14	9
Old London Rd.		
Priory Dr. SE2	CP42	69
Priory Dr., Reig.	BS71	121
Priory Dr., Stan.	BH27	36
Priory Field Dr., Edg.	BM28	37
Priory Fields, Farn.	CW54	90
Priory Gdns. N6	BV32	47
Priory Gdns. SW13	BO45	65
Priory Gdns. W5	BL38	55
Priory Gdns., Berk.	AR13	7
Priory Gdns., Dart.	CV46	80
Priory Gdns., Hmptn.	BE50	74
Priory Gdns., Uxb.	AX31	44
Priory Gdns., Walt.	BC55	83
Priory Grn. Est. N1	**BX37**	**2**
Priory Grn. Est. N1	BX37	56
Priory Grn., Stai.	AW49	73
Priory Gro. SW8	BX44	66
Priory Gro., Rom.	CW27	42
Priory Hill, Dart.	CV46	80
Priory Hill, Wem.	BJ35	45
Priory La. SW15	BO46	75
Priory La., E.Mol.	BF52	84
Priory La., Farn.	CW54	90
Priory La., Rich.	BM43	65
Forest Rd.		
Priory Mead, Brwd.	DB21	33
Priory Ms. SW8	BW44	66
Priory Ms., Stai.	AW49	73
Chestnut Manor Clo.		
Priory Par., Wem.	BH35	45
Priory Path, Rom.	CW27	42
Priory Pk. Rd. NW6	BR37	55
Priory Pk. Rd., Wem.	BJ35	45
Priory Pk. SE3	CG45	68
Priory Pl. SW15	BO45	65
Upper Richmond Rd.		
Priory Pl., Dart.	CV46	80
Priory Rd.		
Priory Pl., Walt.	BC55	83
Priory Clo.		
Priory Rd. E6	CJ37	58
Priory Rd. N8	BW31	47
Priory Rd. NW6	BS37	56
Priory Rd. SW19	BT50	76
Priory Rd. W4	BN41	65
Priory Rd., Bark.	CM36	58
Priory Rd., Chess.	BL55	85
Priory Rd., Croy.	BY54	86
Priory Rd., Dart.	CV46	80
Priory Rd., Ger.Cr.	AR31	43
Priory Rd., Hmptn.	BE50	74
Priory Rd., Houns.	BG46	74
Priory Rd., Loug.	CK24	31
Priory Rd., Reig.	BS71	121
Priory Rd., Rich.	BM43	65
Priory Rd., Rom.	CW27	42
Priory Rd., Sutt.	BQ56	94
Priory St. E3	CE38	57
Bromley High St.		
Priory Ter. NW6	**BS37**	**1**
Priory Ter. NW6	BS37	56
Priory Ter., Sun.	BC50	73
Priory Vw., Bush.	BH26	36
Priory Way, Ger.Cr.	AR31	43
Priory Way, Har.	BF31	45
Priory Way, Slou.	AQ43	62
Priory Way, Sthl.	BD41	64
Western Rd.		
Priory Way, West Dr.	AY43	63
Priory Wk. SW10	**BT42**	**3**
Priory Wk. SW10	BT42	66
Priory Wk., St.Alb.	BH15	9
Priory, The SE3	CG45	68
Priory, The, Gdse.	CB69	114
Pritchards Rd. E2	CB37	57
Priter Rd. SE16	**CB41**	**4**
Priter Rd. SE16	CB41	67
St. James Rd.		
Priter Way SE16	**CB41**	**4**
Priter Way SE16	CB41	67
Private Rd., Enf.	BZ25	30
Private Rd., Grav.	DD47	81
Private Rd., S.Ock.	CX41	70
Private Rd., Wal.Cr.	BZ19	21
Probert Rd. SW2	BY45	66
Probyn Rd. SW2	BY48	76
Procter St. WC1	**BX39**	**2**
Procter St. WC1	BX39	56
High Holborn		
Proctor Gdns., Lthd.	BF66	111
Proctors Clo., Felt.	BC47	73
Profumo Rd., Walt.	BD56	93
Progress Way N22	BY30	38
Progress Way, Croy.	BX55	86
Progress Way, Enf.	CB25	30
Promenade App. Rd. W4	BO43	65
Promenade de Verdun, Pur.	BW59	95
Promenade, The W4	BO44	65
Prospect Clo. SE10	CF44	67
Point Hill		
Prospect Clo. SE26	CB49	77
Wells Park Rd.		
Prospect Clo. SW18	BS45	66
Prospect Clo., Belv.	CR42	69
Prospect Clo., Grav.	DH47	81
Prospect Clo., Houns.	BE44	64
Prospect Clo., Ruis.	BD33	45
Prospect Cotts. SW18	BS45	66
Point Pleasant		
Prospect Cres., Twick.	BG46	74
Prospect Hill E17	CE31	48
Prospect La., Egh.	AQ49	72
Prospect Pl. E1	CC40	57
Prospect Pl. N17	CA29	39
Prospect Pl. N2	BT31	47
Prospect Pl. NW2	BR34	46
Prospect Rd.		
Prospect Pl. W4	BN42	65
Chiswick High Rd.		
Prospect Pl., Brom.	CH52	88
Prospect Pl., Epsom	BO60	94
Prospect Pl., Grav.	DH47	81
Prospect Pl., Grays	DD43	71
Prospect Pl., Rom.	CS30	41
Prospect Pl., Stai.	AV49	72
Prospect Rd. E17	CD32	48
Prospect Rd. NW2	BR34	46
Prospect Rd., Barn.	BS24	29
Prospect Rd., Chsnt.	CC18	21
Prospect Rd., Horn.	CW31	51
Prospect Rd., Sev.	CV65	108
Prospect Rd., St.Alb.	BG14	9
Prospect Rd., Surb.	BK53	84
Prospect Rd., Wdf.Grn.	CJ29	40
Prospect Ring N2	BT31	47
Prospect St. SE16	CB41	67
Jamaica Rd.		
Prospect Vale SE18	CK42	68
Prospect Way, Brwd.	DF24	122
Prospero Rd. N19	BW33	47
Prossers, Tad.	BQ64	103
Prothero Gdns. NW4	BP32	46
Protheroe Rd. SW6	BR43	65
Prout Gro. NW10	BO35	46
Prout Rd. E5	CB34	48
Provence St. N1	**BZ37**	**2**
Provence St. N1	BZ37	57
Providence Ct. W1	**BV40**	**3**
Providence Ct. W1	BV40	56
Providence La., Hayes	BA43	63
Providence Pl. Epsom	BO59	94
Providence Pl. N1	**BY37**	**2**
Providence Pl. N1	BY37	56
Upper St.		
Providence Pl., Rom.	CQ30	41
Providence Rd., West Dr.	AY40	53
Providence Row N1	BX37	56
Northdown St.		
Providence St., Green.	DA46	80
Providence Yd. E2	**CA38**	**2**
Columbia Rd.		
Provost Dwellings N1	BZ37	57
Provost Rd. NW3	BU36	56
Provost St. N1	**BZ37**	**2**
Provost St. N1	BZ37	57
Prowse Av., Bush.	BG27	36
Prowse Pl. NW1	BW36	56
Bonny St.		
Pruden Clo. N14	BW27	38
Prune Hill, Egh.	AR50	72
Prusom St. E1	CB40	57
Pryor Clo., Wat.	BB19	17
Pryors, The NW3	BT34	47
Puck La., Wal.Abb.	CF18	21
Puckshill, Wok.	AO62	100
Beechwood Rd.		
Pudding La. EC3	**BZ40**	**4**
Pudding La. EC3	BZ40	57
Pudding La., Chig.	CN26	40
Pudding La., Hem.H.	AW12	8
Pudding La., Sev.	CX64	108
Church Rd.		
Pudding Mill La. E15	CE37	57
Puddle Dock EC4	**BY40**	**4**
Puddle Dock EC4	BY40	56
Upper Thames St.		
Puddledock La., Dart.	CT49	79
Puddledock La., West.	CN70	115
Puers La., Beac.	AP29	34
Pulborough Rd. SW18	BR47	75
Pulborough Way, Houns.	BD45	64
Pulford Rd. N15	BZ32	48
Pulham Av. N2	BT31	47
Puller Rd., Barn.	BR23	28
Puller Rd., Hem.H.	AW14	8
Pulleyns Av. E6	CK38	58
Pulleys Clo., Hem.H.	AV13	7
Pulleys La., Hem.H.	AV12	7
Pullman Ct. SW2	BX47	76
Pullman Gdns. SW15	BQ46	75
Pulross Rd. SW9	BX45	66
Pulteney Clo. E3	CD37	57
Pulteney Rd. E18	CH31	49
Pulteney Ter. N1	**BX37**	**2**
Pulteney Ter. N1	BX37	56
Pulton Rd. SW6	BS43	66
Puma Ct. E1	**CA39**	**2**
Puma Ct. E1	CA39	57
Commercial St.		
Pump Alley, Brent.	BK53	64
High St.		
Pump Hill, Loug.	CK23	31
Pump La., Chesh.	AP20	16
Pump La., Epp.	CL15	13
Pump La., Hayes	BB41	63
Pump La., Orp.	CR56	98
Pump Pail N., Croy.	BZ55	87
Pump Pail S., Croy.	BZ55	87
Pumping Station Rd. W4	BO43	65
Punch Bowl La., Hem.H. & St.Alb.	BA12	8
Punchbowl La., Dor.	BK71	119
Pundersons Gdns. E2	CB38	57
Purbeck Av., N.Mal.	BO53	85
Purbeck Dr. NW2	BQ34	46
Purbeck Dr., Wok.	AS60	91
Purbeck Rd., Horn.	CU33	50
Purberry Gro., Epsom	BO58	94
Purbrock Av., Wat.	BD21	27
Purbrook Clo., Red.	BW67	113
Purbrook Est. SE1	**CA41**	**4**
Purbrook Est. SE1	CA41	67
Purbrook St. SE1	**CA41**	**4**
Purbrook St. SE1	CA41	67
Purcell Clo., B.Wd.	BK23	27
Stainer Rd.		
Purcell Cres. SW6	BR43	65
Purcell Ms. NW10	BO36	55
Suffolk Rd.		
Purcell Rd., Grnf.	BF39	54
Purcell St. N1	**CA37**	**2**
Purcell St. N1	CA37	57
Purcells Av., Edg.	BM28	37
Purcells Clo., Ash.	BL62	103
Purcers Cross Rd. SW6	BR44	65
Purcers Rd. SW6	BR45	65
Purchese St. NW1	**BW37**	**1**
Purchese St. NW1	BW37	56
Purdy St. E3	CE38	57
Purex Rd., Grnf.	BG37	54
Purfleet Arterial Rd., S.Ock.	CX41	70
Purfleet By-pass, S.Ock.	CX42	70
Purfleet Rd., S.Ock.	CX41	70
Purford Grn., Harl.	CO11	14
Purland Clo., Dag.	CQ33	50
Purland Rd. SE28	CN41	68
Purleigh Av., Wdf.Grn.	CK29	40
Purley Av. NW2	BR34	46
Purley Bury Av., Pur.	BZ59	96
Purley Bury Clo., Pur.	BZ59	96
Purley Clo., Ilf.	CL30	40

Purley Ct., Pur. BY58 95
Purley Downs Rd., Pur. BZ58 96
Purley Hill, Pur. BY59 95
Purley Knoll, Pur. BX59 95
Purley Oaks Rd., S.Croy. BZ58 96
Purley Park Rd., Pur. BY58 95
Purley Pl. N1 BY36 56
Islington Park St.
Purley Rd. N9 BZ27 39
Purley Rd., Pur. BY59 95
Purley Rd., S.Croy. BZ57 96
Purley Ri., Pur. BX59 95
Purley Vale, Pur. BY60 95
Purley Way, Croy. BX54 86
Purlieu Way, Epp. CN21 31
Purlings Rd., Bush. BF25 27
Purneys Rd. SE9 CJ45 68
Purrett Rd. SE18 CN42 68
Pursewardens Clo. W13 BK40 54
Pursley Gdns., B.Wd. BM22 28
Pursley Rd. NW7 BP29 37
Purves Rd. NW10 BP38 55
Putney Bridge App. SW6 BR45 65
Putney Bridge Rd. SW15 BR45 65
Putney Bridge Rd. SW18 BS46 76
Putney Common SW15 BQ45 65
Putney Heath La. SW15 BQ46 75
Putney Heath SW15 BP47 75
Putney High St. SW15 BQ45 65
Putney Hill SW15 BQ46 75
Tibbets Ride
Putney Park Av. SW15 BP45 65
Putney Park La. SW15 BP45 65
Putney Rd., Enf. CC21 30
Puttenham Clo., Wat. BD27 36
Putters Cft., Hem.H. AY11 8
Puttocks Clo., Hat. BQ15 10
Puttocks Dr., Hat. BQ15 10
Pycroft Way N9 CB28 39
Pyecombe Cor. N12 BR28 37
Pyenest Rd., Harl. CL12 13
Pyghtle, The, Uxb. AW33 44
Pylbrook Rd., Sutt. BS55 86
Pyle Hill, Guil. AS66 109
Pyle Hill, Wok. AR65 100
Pym Clo., Barn. BT25 29
Pym Pl., Grays DD42 71
Pymers Mead SE21 BZ47 77
Pymmes Clo. N13 BX28 38
Pymmes Clo. N17 CB30 39
Pymmes Gdns. N. N9 CA27 39
Pymmes Gdns. S. N9 CA27 39
Pymmes Green Rd. N11 BV28 38
Pymmes Rd. N13 BX29 38
Pymms Gdns., Barn. BU24 29
Pynchester Clo., Uxb. AZ34 44
Pyne Rd., Surb. BM54 85
Pynestgreen La., Wal.Abb. CH22 31
Pynham Clo. SE2 CO41 69
Pynnacles Clo., Stan. BJ28 36
Pypers Hatch, Harl. CN11 13
Pyrcroft La., Wey. AZ56 92
Hanger Hill
Pyrcroft Rd., Cher. AV54 82
Pyrford Common Rd., Wok. AU61 100
Pyrford Heath, Wok. AV61 100
Pyrford Rd., Wey. AW60 92
Pyrford Rd., Wok. AW61 101
Pyrford Woods Clo., Wok. AV61 100
Pyrford Woods Rd., Wok. AV61 100
Pyrford Woods, Wok. AV61 100
Pyrland Rd. N5 BZ35 48
Pyrland Rd., Rich. BL46 75
Pyrles Grn., Loug. CL23 31
Pyrles La., Loug. CL23 31
Pyrmont Gro. SE27 BY48 76
Pyrmont Rd. W4 BM43 65
Pyrmont Rd., Ilf. CM34 49
High Rd.
Pytchley Cres. SE19 BZ50 77
Pytchley Rd. SE22 CA45 67
Pytt Field, Harl. CO11 14

Q

Quadrangle, The, Welw.G.C. BQ 7 5
Quadrangle, The, Guil. AQ71 118
Quadrant Arc., Rom. CT32 50
Quadrant Clo. NW4 BP32 46
Quadrant Gro. NW5 BU35 47
Quadrant Rd. N1 BZ36 57
Essex Rd.
Quadrant Rd., Rich. BK45 64
Quadrant Rd., Th.Hth. BY52 86
Quadrant, The SE24 BZ46 77
Quadrant, The SW20 BR51 85
Quadrant, The, Bexh. CP43 69
Quadrant, The, Grays CY42 70
Quadrant, The, Rich. BK46 74
Quadrant, The, St.Alb. BJ12 9
Quadrant, The, Sutt. BT57 95
Wellesley Rd.
Quadrant, The, Wey. AZ56 92
Quaggy Wk. SE3 CH45 68
Quail Gdns., S.Croy. CD58 96
Quainton St. NW10 BN34 46
Quaker Clo., Sev. CV65 108
Quaker La., Islw. BJ44 64
Quaker La., Sthl. BF41 64
Quaker La., Wal.Abb. CF20 21
Quaker St. E1 CA38 2
Quaker St. E1 CA38 57
Quakers Clo., Hart. DC52 90
Quakers Course NW9 BO30 37
Quakers Hall La., Sev. CV64 108
Quakers La., Pot.B. BS18 20
Quakers Wk. N21 BZ25 30
Quality Ct. WC2 BY39 56
Chancery La.
Quality Ct. WC2 BY39 2
Quality St., Red. BV67 113
Quantock Clo., Hayes BA43 63
Quantock Clo., Slou. AT42 62
Quantock Clo., St.Alb. BK11 9
Chiltern Rd.
Quantock Gdns. NW2 BQ34 46
Quantock Rd., Bexh. CT44 69
Quantocks, Hem.H. AY12 8
Quarles Clo., Rom. CR29 41
Quarley Way SE15 CA43 67
Quarr Rd., Cars. BT53 86
Quarrendon Rd., Amer. AO23 25
Quarrendon St. SW6 BS44 66
Quarry Clo., Couls. BX61 104
Quarry Clo., Oxt. CG68 115
Quarry Hill Park Rd., Reig. BY69 121
Quarry Hill Rd., Sev. DC64 108
Quarry Hill, Grays DD42 71
Quarry Hill, Sev. CV65 108
Quarry Ms., Grays CX42 70
Fanns Ri.
Quarry Park Rd., Sutt. BR57 94
Quarry Rd. SW18 BT46 76
Quarry Rd., Oxt. CG68 115
Quarry Ri., Sutt. BR57 94
Quarry Spring, Harl. CO11 14
Quarry St., Guil. AR71 118
Quarter Mile La. E10 CE35 48
Quarter Mile La. E15 CE35 48
Quartermaine Av., Wok. AS64 100
Quartermass Clo., Hem.H. AW13 8
Quartermass Rd., Hem.H. AW13 8
Quaves Rd., Slou. AQ41 62
Quay West, Tedd. BJ49 74
Quebec Av., West. CM66 115
Quebec Ms. W1 BU39 1
Quebec Ms. W1 BU39 56
Quebec Rd., Hayes BD39 54
Quebec Rd., Ilf. CL33 49
Quebec Rd., Til. DG44 71
Quebec Sq., West. CM66 115
Quebec Way SE16 CC41 67
Queen Adelaide Rd. SE20 CC50 77
Queen Alexandras Ct. SW19 BR49 75
Queen Anne Av., Brom. CG52 88
Queen Anne Clo., Esher BH58 93
Queen Anne Gate, Bexh. CP45 69
Regency Way
Queen Anne Gate, Bexh. CP45 69
Glynde Rd.
Queen Anne Gdns., Mitch. BU52 86
Queen Anne Ms. W1 BV39 1
Queen Anne Ms. W1 BV39 56
Chandos St.
Queen Anne Rd. E9 CC36 57
Queen Anne St. W1 BV39 1
Queen Anne St. W1 BV39 56
Queen Annes Clo., Twick. BG48 74
Queen Annes Gate SW1 BW41 3
Queen Annes Gate SW1 BW41 66
Queen Annes Gdns. W4 BO41 65
Queen Annes Gdns. W5 BL41 65
Queen Annes Gdns., Enf. CA25 30
Queen Annes Gdns., Lthd. BJ64 102
Upper Fairfield Rd.
Queen Annes Gro. W4 BO41 65
Bedford Rd.
Queen Annes Gro. W5 BL41 65
Queen Annes Gro., Enf. BZ26 39
Queen Annes Pl., Enf. CA25 30
Queen Annes Rd., Wind. AO45 61
Queen Annes Ter., Lthd. BJ64 102
Upper Fairfield Rd.
Queen Annes Wk. WC1 BX39 56
Guilford St.
Queen Caroline Est. W6 BQ42 65
Queen Caroline St. W6 BQ42 65
Queen Clo., Wey. BB57 92
Queen Dale Ct., Wok. AP61 100
Queen Eleanor Clo., Ash. BL63 103
Queen Eleanor Rd., Guil. AP71 118
Queen Elizabeth Gdns., Mord. BS52 86
Hatherleigh Clo.
Queen Elizabeth Pl., Til. DG45 71
Queen Elizabeth Rd. E17 CD31 48
Queen Elizabeth Rd., Kings.T. BL51 85
Queen Elizabeth St. SE1 CA41 4
Queen Elizabeth St. SE1 CA41 67
Queen Elizabeth Way, Wok. AS63 100
Queen Elizabeth Wk. SW13 BP44 65
Queen Elizabeth Wk., Wall. BW56 95
Queen Elizabeths Clo. N16 BZ34 48
Queen Elizabeths Dr. N14 BX26 38
Queen Elizabeths Dr., Croy. CF58 96
Queen Elizabeths Gdns., Croy. CF58 96
Queen Elizabeths Dr
Queen Elizabeths Wk. N16 BZ33 48
Queen Hythe Rd., Guil. AR67 109
Queen Margarets Gro. N1 CA35 48
Queen Mary Av., Mord. BQ53 85
Queen Mary Clo., Rom. CT32 50
Richmond Rd.
Queen Mary Clo., Wok. AU61 100
Queen Mary Rd. SE19 BY50 76
Queen Mary Rd., Shep. BA51 83
Queen Marys Av., Cars. BU57 95
Queen Marys Av., Wat. BB24 26
Queen Marys Dr., Wey. AV58 91
Queen Mothers Dr., Uxb. AV32 43
Queen Sq. WC1 BX38 2
Queen Sq. WC1 BX38 56
Queen St. EC4 BZ40 4
Queen St. EC4 BZ40 57
Queen St. Mayfair W1 BV40 3
Queen St. Mayfair W1 BV40 56
Queen St. N17 CA29 39
Queen St., Bexh. CQ45 69
Queen St., Brwd. DB28 42
Queen St., Cher. AW54 83
Queen St., Croy. BZ55 87
Queen St., Erith CT43 69
Queen St., Grav. DG46 81
Queen St., Kings L. AW19 17
Queen St., Ong. CZ14 15
Queen St., Rom. CS32 50
Queen St., St.Alb. BG13 9
Queen Street Pl. EC4 BZ40 4
Queen Street Pl. EC4 BZ40 57
Queen Victoria Av., Wem. BK36 54
Queen Victoria St. EC4 BY40 4
Queen Victoria St. EC4 BY40 56
Queenborough Gdns., Chis. CM50 78
Queenborough Gdns., Ilf. CL31 49
Queenhill Rd., S.Croy. CB58 96
Queenhithe EC4 BZ40 4
Queenhithe EC4 BZ40 57
Queens Acre, Sutt. BQ57 94
Queens All., Epp. CN19 22
Hemnall St.
Queens Av. N10 BV31 47
Queens Av. N20 BT27 38
Queens Av. N21 BY26 38
Queens Av. N3 BT29 38
Queens Av., Felt. BD49 74
Queens Av., Grnf. BF39 54
Queens Av., Stan. BK31 45
Queens Av., Wat. BB24 26
Queens Av., Wdf.Grn. CH28 40
Queens Av., Wey. AX59 92
Queens Cir. SW11 BV43 66
Queens Clo., Dag. BM28 37
Queens Clo., Tad. BP65 103
Queens Clo., Wind. AQ46 72
Queens Club Gdns. W14 BR43 65
Queens Court Ride, Cob. BC60 92
Queens Cres. NW5 BV36 56
Queens Cres., Rich. BL46 75
Queens Cres., St.Alb. BJ12 9
Queens Ct. NW11 BR32 46
Queens Ct. SE23 CC48 77
Queens Ct. W5 BK39 54
Queens Wk.
Queens Ct., Slou. AP40 52
Queens Rd.
Queens Ct., St.Alb. BJ13 9
Queens Dr. E10 CE33 48
Queens Dr. N4 BY34 47
Queens Dr. W3 BL39 55
Queens Dr., Guil. AQ69 118
Queens Dr., Lthd. BG59 93
Queens Dr., Sev. CV63 108
Queens Dr., Slou. AS37 52
Queens Dr., Surb. BM54 85
Queens Dr., T.Ditt. BJ54 84
Queens Dr., The, Rick. AV26 34
Queens Dr., Wal.Cr. CE20 21
Queens Dr., Wat. BB19 17
Queens Elm Sq. SW3 BT42 3
Queens Elm Sq. SW3 BT42 66
Queens Gate Gdns. SW7 BT41 3
Queens Gate Gdns. SW7 BT41 66
Queens Gate Ms. SW7 BT41 3
Queens Gate Ms. SW7 BT41 66
Queens Gate Pl. Ms. SW7 BT41 3
Queens Gate Pl. Ms. SW7 BT41 66
Queens Gate Pl. SW7 BT41 3
Queens Gate Pl. SW7 BT41 66
Queens Gate SW7 BT41 3
Queens Gate SW7 BT41 66
Queens Gate Ter. SW7 BT41 3
Queens Gate Ter. SW7 BT41 66
Queens Gdns. NW4 BQ32 46
Queens Gdns. W2 BT40 3
Queens Gdns. W2 BT40 56
Queens Gdns. W5 BK38 54
Queens Gdns., Dart. CX47 80
Queens Gdns., Houns. BE44 64
Queens Gdns., Rain. CS37 59
Queens Gdns., Upmin. CZ32 51
Queens Gro. NW8 BT37 1
Queens Gro. NW8 BT37 56
Queens Gro. Rd. E4 CF26 39
Queens Gro. Studios NW8 BT37 1
Queens Head St. N1 BY37 2
Queens Head St. N1 BY37 56
Queens Head Wk., Brox. CD15 12
High Rd.
Queens Head Yd. SE1 BZ40 4
Queens Ho., Tedd. BH50 74
Queens La., Ashf. AY49 73
Clarendon Rd.
Queens Mans. NW4 BP32 46
Queens Mead Rd., Brom. CG51 88
Queens Mkt. E13 CJ37 58
Queens Ms. W2 BS40 3
Queens Ms. W2 BS40 56
Salem Rd.
Queens Parade Clo. N12 BU28 38
Hollyfield Av.
Queens Park Ct. W10 BQ38 55
Queens Park Gdns., Felt. BC48 73
Queens Park Rd., Cat. CA65 105
Queens Park Rd., Rom. CX30 42
Queens Pl., Mord. BS52 86
Queens Pl., Walt. BB56 92
Queens Pl., Wat. BD24 27
Queens Prom., Kings.T. BK52 84
Queens Rd. E11 CF33 48
Queens Rd. E13 CH37 58
Queens Rd. E17 CD32 48
Queens Rd. N11 BX29 38
Queens Rd. N3 BT30 38
Queens Rd. N9 CB27 39
Queens Rd. NW4 BQ32 46
Queens Rd. SE15 CB44 67
Queens Rd. SW14 BN45 65
Queens Rd. SW19 BR50 75
Queens Rd. W. E13 CH37 58
Queens Rd. W5 BL39 55
Queens Rd., Bark. CM36 58
Queens Rd., Barn. BQ24 28
Queens Rd., Beck. CD51 87
Queens Rd., Berk. AQ12 7
Queens Rd., Brom. CH51 88
Queens Rd., Brwd. DB27 42
Queens Rd., Buck.H. CH27 40
Queens Rd., Chis. CL50 78
Queens Rd., Croy. BY53 86
Queens Rd., Datchet AQ43 62
Queens Rd., Egh. AS49 72
Queens Rd., Enf. CA24 30
Queens Rd., Epp. CR16 23
Queens Rd., Erith CT43 69
Queens Rd., Eton AM42 61
Queens Rd., Felt. BC47 73
Queens Rd., Grav. DH48 81
Queens Rd., Guil. AR70 118
Queens Rd., Hayes BB39 53
Queens Rd., Hmptn. BF49 74
Queens Rd., Houns. BF45 64
Queens Rd., Ilf. CM34 49
Queens Rd., Kings.T. BM50 75
Queens Rd., Loug. CK24 31
Queens Rd., Mitch. BT52 86
Queens Rd., Mord. BS52 86
Queens Rd., N.Mal. BO52 85
Queens Rd., Rich. BL47 75
Queens Rd., Slou. AP40 52
Queens Rd., Sthl. BE41 64
Queens Rd., Sutt. BS59 95
Queens Rd., T.Ditt. BH53 84
Queens Rd., Tedd. BH50 74
Queens Rd., Twick. BJ47 74
Queens Rd., Uxb. AX38 53
Queens Rd., Wal.Cr. CD20 21
Queens Rd., Wall. BV56 95
Queens Rd., Walt. BB56 92
Queens Rd., Wat. BD24 27
Queens Rd., Well. CO44 69
Queens Rd., West Dr. AY41 63
Queens Rd., Wey. AZ56 92
Queens Rd., Wind. AO44 61
Queens Rd., Wok. AO62 100
Queens Ri., Rich. BL46 75
Queens Ride SW13 BP45 65
Queens Row SE17 BZ43 4
Queens Row SE17 BZ43 67
Queens Sq, The, Hem.H. AY13 8
Queens Ter. E13 CH37 58
Queens Ter. NW8 BT37 1
Queens Ter. NW8 BT37 56
Queens Ter., Islw. BJ45 64
Queens Ter., Wind. AO45 61
Queens Way, Felt. BD49 74
Queens Way, Rad. BL19 19
Queens Wk. E4 CF26 39
Green Wk.
Queens Wk. NW9 BN34 46
Queens Wk. SW1 BW40 3
Queens Wk. SW1 BW40 56
Queens Wk. W5 BK38 54
Queens Wk., Ashf. AX49 73
Queens Wk., Har. BH31 45
Queens Wk., Ruis. BD34 45
Queens Wood Rd. N10 BV32 47
Queensberry Ms. W. SW7 BT42 3
Queensberry Ms. W. SW7 BT42 66
Queens Gate
Queensberry Pl. SW7 BT42 3
Queensberry Pl. SW7 BT42 66
Queensberry Way SW7 BT42 3
Harrington Rd.
Queensborough Ct. N3 BR31 46
North Circular Rd.
Queensborough Ms. W2 BT40 3
Porchester Ter.
Queensborough Pass. W2 BT40 56
Queensborough Ter.
Queensborough Ter. W2 BS40 3
Queensborough Ter. W2 BT40 56
Queensbridge Ct. E2 CA37 2
Queensbridge Ms., Islw. BH46 74
Queensbridge Pk., Islw. BH46 74
Queensbridge Rd. E2 CA36 57
Queensbridge Rd. E2 CA37 2
Queensbridge Rd. E8 CA36 57
Queensbridge Rd. E8 CA37 2
Queensbury Pl., Rich. BK46 74
Retreat Rd.
Queensbury Rd. NW9 BN33 46
Queensbury Rd., Wem. BL37 55
Queensbury St. N1 BZ36 2
Queensbury St. N1 BZ36 57
Morton Rd.
Queensbury Station Par., Edg. BL31 46
Queenscourt, Wem. BL35 46
Queenscroft Rd. SE9 CJ46 78
Queensdale Cres. W11 BQ40 55
Queensdale Pl. W11 BR40 55
Queensdale Rd. W11 BQ40 55
Queensdale Wk. W11 BR40 55
Queensdown Rd. E5 CB35 48
Queensgate Gdns. SW15 BP45 65
Queensgate Gdns., Chis. CM51 88
Prince Consort Dr.
Queensgate Pl. NW6 BS36 56
Kingsgate Rd.
Queensgate Pl. NW6 BS37 56
Kingsgate Pl.
Queensland Av. N18 BZ29 39
Queensland Av. SW19 BS51 86
Queensland Pl. N7 BY35 47
Queensland Rd.
Queensland Rd. N7 BY35 47
Queensmead Av., Epsom BP58 94
Queensmead NW8 BT37 56
Queensmead, Slou. AQ44 62
Queens Rd.
Queensmere Clo. SW19 BQ48 75
Queensmere Rd. SW19 BQ48 75
Queensmere Rd., Slou. AQ41 62
Queensmere, Slou. AP41 62
Queensmill Rd. SW6 BQ43 65
Queensthorpe Rd. SE26 CC49 77
Queenstown Gdns., Rain. CT38 59
Queenstown Rd. SW8 BV45 66
Queensville Rd. SW12 BW47 76
Queensway N., Walt. BD56 93
Beech Clo.
Queensway NW4 BQ32 46
Queensway S., Walt. BD56 93
Queensway W2 BS39 1
Queensway W2 BS39 56
Queensway, Croy. BX57 95
Queensway, Enf. CB25 30
Queensway, Hat. BP12 10
Queensway, Hem.H. AX13 8
Queensway, Ong. CW16 24
Queensway, Orp. CM53 88
Queensway, Red. BU70 121
Queensway, Sun. BC51 83
Queensway, The, Ger.Cr. AR31 43
Queensway, W.Wick. CG55 83
Queensway, Wal.Cr. CD20 21
Longcroft Dr.
Queensway, Walt. BD56 93
Queenswell Av. N20 BU28 38
Queenswood Av. E17 CF30 39
Queenswood Av., Brwd. DE25 122
Queenswood Av., Hmptn. BF50 74
Queenswood Av., Houns. BE44 64
Queenswood Av., Th.Hth. BY53 86
Queenswood Av., Wall. BW56 95
Queenswood Cres., Wat. BC20 17
Queenswood Ct. SW4 BX46 76
Queenswood Gdns. E11 CH33 49
Queenswood Pk. N3 BR30 37
Queenswood Rd. SE23 CC48 77
Queenswood Rd., Sid. CN46 78
Queenswood Rd., Wok. AO63 100
Quemerford Rd. N7 BX35 47
Quendon Dr., Wal.Abb. CF20 21
Quennel Way, Brwd. DE26 122
Quentin Pl. SE13 CG45 68
Quentin Rd. SE13 CG45 68
Quentin Way, Vir.W. AQ52 82
Quernmore Clo., Brom. CH50 78
Quernmore Rd. N4 BY32 47
Quernmore Rd., Brom. CH50 78
Querrin St. SW6 BT44 66
Quex Ms. NW6 BS37 56
Quex Rd. NW6 BS37 56
Quick Pl. N1 BY37 2
Quick Pl. N1 BY37 56
Essex Rd.
Quick Rd. W4 BO42 65
Quick St. N1 BY37 2
Quick St. N1 BY37 56
Quickbeams, Welw.G.C. BS 6 5
Rowans
Quickberry Pl., Amer. AO23 25
Quickley La., Rick. AU25 25
Quickley Ri., Rick. AU25 25
Quickmoor La., Kings L. AW20 17
Quicks Rd. SW19 BS50 76
Quicksilver Pl. N22 BX30 38
Quickswood NW3 BU36 56
Quickwood Clo., Rick. AV25 25
Quiet Clo., Wey. AW56 92
Quiet Nook, Kes. CJ55 88
Quill Hall La., Amer. AP22 25
Quill La. SW15 BQ45 65
Cardinal Pl.
Quillot, The, Walt. BB56 92
Quilp St. SE1 BZ41 4
Quilp St. SE1 BZ41 67
Redcross Way
Quilter Gdns., Orp. CP54 89
Quilter Rd., Orp. CP54 89
Quilter St. E2 CA38 2
Quilter St. E2 CA38 57
Quinbrookes, Slou. AR39 52
Quince Tree Clo., S.Ock. DB38 60
Quinces Cft., Hem.H. AW12 8
Quincy Rd., Egh. AT49 72
Quinta Dr., Barn. BP25 28
Quintin Clo., Pnr. BC32 44
High Rd., Eastcote
Quinton Av. SW20 BR51 85
Quinton Clo., Beck. CF52 87
Quinton Clo., Houns. BC43 63
Quinton Clo., Wall. BV56 95
Quinton Rd., T.Ditt. BJ54 84
Quinton St. SW18 BT48 76
Quintrell Clo., Wok. AQ62 100
Quixley St. E14 CF40 57
Naval Row
Quorn Rd. SE22 CA45 67

R

Raans Rd., Amer. AP22 25
Rabbit La., Walt. BC57 92
Rabbit Row W8 BS40 56
Kensington Mall
Rabbits Rd. E12 CK35 49
Rabbits Rd., S.Dnth. CZ51 90
Rabbs Mill, Uxb. AX37 53
Rabies Heath Rd., Red. CA70 114
Rabournmead Dr., Nthlt. BE35 45
Raby Rd., N.Mal. BN52 85

Raby St. E14 CD39 57
Raccoon Way, Houns. BD44 64
Rachel Point E5 CB34 48
Downs Est.
Rachels Way, Chesh. AO20 16
Cresswell Rd.
Rack Rd. W3 BM41 65
Rackham Ms. SW16 BW49 76
Westcote Rd.
Racquet Ct. EC4 BY39 56
Fleet St.
Racton Rd. SW6 BS43 66
Radbourne Av. W5 BK42 64
Radbourne Clo. E5 CC35 48
Glyn Rd.
Radbourne Cres. E17 CF31 48
Radbourne Ct. E5 CC35 48
Clapton Park Est.
Radbourne Rd. SW12 BW47 76
Radburn Clo., Harl. CO13 14
Radcliffe Av. NW10 BP37 55
Radcliffe Av., Enf. BZ23 30
Radcliffe Gdns., Cars. BU57 95
Radcliffe Path SW8 BW44 66
St. Rule St.
Radcliffe Rd. N21 BY26 38
Radcliffe Rd., Croy. CA55 87
Radcliffe Rd., Har. BJ30 36
Radcliffe Sq. SW15 BQ46 75
Radcliffe Way, Nthlt. BD38 54
Radcot Av., Slou. AU41 62
Radcot St. SE11 BY42 4
Radcot St. SE11 BY42 66
Raddington Rd. W10 BR39 55
Radfield Way, Sid. CM47 78
Radford Rd. SE13 CF46 77
Radford Way, Bark. CN38 58
Radipole Rd. SW6 BR44 65
Radland Rd. E16 CG39 58
Radlett Av. SE26 CB48 77
Radlett Clo. E7 CH36 58
Radlett La., Rad. BK21 27
Radlett Park Rd., Rad. BJ20 18
Radlett Pl. NW8 BU37 1
Radlett Pl. NW8 BU37 56
Radlett Rd., Aldenham BG22 27
Radlett Rd., St.Alb. BH18 18
Radlett Rd., Wat. BD24 27
Radley Av., Ilf. CO35 50
Radley Ct. SE16 CC41 67
Thame Rd.
Radley Gdns., Har. BL31 46
Radley La. E18 CH30 40
Radley Ms. W8 BS41 66
Radley Rd. N17 CA30 39
Radleys Mead, Dag. CR36 59
Radlix Rd. E10 CE33 48
Radnor Av., Har. BH32 45
Radnor Av., Well. CO46 79
Radnor Clo., Chis. CN50 88
Homewood Cres.
Radnor Clo., Mitch. BX52 86
Radnor Cres., Ilf. CK32 49
Radnor Ct., Red. BU70 121
Linkfield St.
Radnor Gdns., Enf. CA23 30
Radnor Gdns., Twick. BH48 74
Radnor Gro., Uxb. AZ37 53
Charnwood Rd.
Radnor Ho., Twick. BJ48 74
Radnor Ms. W2 BT39 1
Radnor Ms. W2 BT39 56
Radnor Pl. W2 BT39 1
Radnor Pl. W2 BU39 56
Radnor Rd. NW6 BR37 55
Radnor Rd. SE15 CB43 67
Radnor Rd., Har. BG32 45
Radnor Rd., Twick. BH47 74
Radnor Rd., Wey. AZ55 83
Radnor St. EC1 BZ38 2
Radnor St. EC1 BZ38 57
Radnor Ter. SW8 BX43 66
South Lambeth Rd.
Radnor Ter. W14 BR42 65
Radnor Way NW10 BM38 55
Radnor Way, Slou. AS42 62
Radnor Wk. E14 CE42 67
Barnsdale Av.
Radnor Wk. SW3 BU42 3
Radnor Wk. SW3 BU42 66
Radnor Wk., Croy. CD53 87
Radolphs, Tad. BQ64 103
Radstock Av., Har. BJ31 45
Radstock St. SW11 BU43 66
Parkgate Rd.
Radstock Way, Red. BW67 113
Radstone Ct., Wok. AS62 100
Hill View Rd.
Radwell Path, B.Wd. BL23 28
Cromwell Rd.
Raebarn Gdns., Barn. BP25 28
Raeburn Av., Dart. CU46 79
Raeburn Av., Surb. BM54 85
Raeburn Clo. NW11 BS32 47
Raeburn Clo., Kings.T. BK50 74
Lower Teddington Rd.
Raeburn Rd., Edg. BM30 37
Raeburn Rd., Hayes BA37 53
Raeburn Rd., Sid. CN46 78
Raeburn St. SW2 BX45 66
Rafford Way, Brom. CH51 88
Raft Rd. SW18 BS46 76
Rag Hill Clo., West. CK64 106
Rag Hill Rd., West. CJ64 106
Ragge Way, Sev. CW63 108
The Landway
Ragged Hall La., St.Alb. BE15 9
Raggleswood, Chis. CL51 88
Raglan Av., Wal.Cr. CC20 21
Raglan Clo., Houns. BE46 74
Frampton Rd.
Raglan Clo., Reig. BT69 121
Raglan Ct., S.Croy. BY56 95
Raglan Ct., Wem. BL35 46
Raglan Gdns., Wat. BC26 35
Raglan Rd. E17 CF32 48
Raglan Rd. SE18 CL42 68
Raglan Rd., Belv. CQ42 69
Raglan Rd., Brom. CJ52 88
Raglan Rd., Enf. CA26 39
Raglan Rd., Reig. BS69 121
Raglan Rd., Wok. AP62 100
Raglan St. NW5 BV36 56
Raglan Ter., Har. BF35 45
Stroud Gate
Raglan Way, Nthlt. BG36 54
Ragley Clo. W3 BM41 65
Avenue Rd.
Rags La., Chsnt. CA17 21
Ragstone Rd., Slou. AO41 61
Rahn Rd., Epp. CN19 22
Raider Clo., Rom. CR30 41
Raikes La., Dor. BC74 119
Railey Ms. NW5 BW35 47
Leverton St.
Railpit La., Warl. CG61 106
Railshead Rd., Twick. BJ45 64
Richmond Rd.
Railton Rd. SE24 BY45 66
Railway App. SE1 BZ40 4
Railway App. SE1 BZ40 57
Railway App., Cher. AV54 82
Railway App., Har. BH31 45
Railway App., Twick. BJ47 74
Railway App., Wall. BV56 95
Railway Arches SE8 CE43 67
Deptford High St.
Railway Av. SE16 CC41 67
Railway Cotts, St.Alb. BH10 9
Railway Cotts., Hat. BO13 10
Railway Cotts., Ilf. CM29 40
Railway Ms. W10 BR39 55
Ladbroke Gro.
Railway Pass., Tedd. BJ50 74
Clarence Rd.
Railway Pl. SW19 BR50 75
Hartfield Rd.
Railway Pl., Belv. CR41 69
Railway Rd., Tedd. BH49 74
Railway Rd., Wal.Cr. CD20 21
Railway Ri. SE22 CA45 67
Derwent Rd.
Railway Side SW13 BO45 65
White Hart La.
Railway Sq., Brwd. DB27 42
Railway St. N1 BX37 2
Railway St. N1 BX37 56
Railway St., Grav. DD46 81
Railway St., Rom. CP33 50
Railway Ter. SE13 CE46 77
Railway Ter., Felt. BC47 73
Railway Ter., Slou. AP40 52
Railway Ter., Stai. AU49 72
Railway Ter., West. CN66 115
Rainborough Clo. NW10 BN36 55
Rainbow Av. E14 CE42 67
Rainbow Ct., Wok. AP61 100
Langmans Way
Rainbow St. SE5 CA43 67
Raine St. E1 CB40 57
Rainer Clo., Chsnt. CC18 21
Rainham Clo. SE9 CN46 78
Rainham Clo. SW11 BU46 76
Rainham Rd. N., Dag. CR34 50
Rainham Rd. NW10 BQ38 55
Rainham Rd. S., Dag. CR35 50
Rainham Rd., Rain. CT36 59
Rainhill Way E3 CE38 57
Rainsborough Av. SE8 CD42 67
Rainsford Rd. NW10 BM37 55
Rainsford St. W2 BU39 1
Rainsford St. W2 BU39 56
Sale Pl.
Rainsford Way, Horn. CU33 50
Rainton Rd. SE7 CH42 68
Rainville Rd. W6 BQ43 65
Raisins Hill, Pnr. BC31 44
Raith Av. N14 BW27 38
Raleana Rd. E14 CF40 57
Prestons Rd.
Raleigh Av., Hayes BC39 53
Raleigh Av., Wall. BW56 95
Raleigh Clo. NW4 BQ32 46
Raleigh Clo., Erith CU43 69
Frobisher Rd.
Raleigh Clo., Pnr. BD33 45
Raleigh Clo., Ruis. BB34 44
Raleigh Clo., Slou. AN40 61
Raleigh Ct., Beck. CE51 87
Raleigh Ct., Stai. AW49 73
Raleigh Ct., Wall. BV57 95
Raleigh Dr. N20 BU27 38
Raleigh Dr., Esher BG56 93
Raleigh Dr., Surb. BN54 85
Raleigh Gdns., Mitch. BU51 86
Raleigh Ms. N1 BY37 2
Queens Head St.
Raleigh Ms., Orp. CN56 97
Osgood Av.
Raleigh Rd. N8 BY31 47
Raleigh Rd. SE20 CC50 77
Raleigh Rd., Enf. BZ24 30
Raleigh Rd., Felt. BB48 73
Raleigh Rd., Rich. BL45 65
Raleigh Rd., Sthl. BE42 64
Raleigh St. N1 BY37 2
Raleigh St. N1 BY37 56
Raleigh Way N14 BW26 38
Raleigh Way, Felt. BD49 74
Ralliwood Rd., Ash. BM63 103
Ralph St. SE1 BZ41 4
Ralph St. SE1 BZ41 67
Ralston St. SW3 BU42 3
Ralston St. SW3 BU42 66
Tedworth Sq.
Ralston Way, Wat. BD27 36
Ram Gorse, Harl. CL10 6
Ram Pl. E9 CC36 57
Chatham Pl.
Ram St. SW18 BS46 76
Rama Ct., Har. BH34 45
Ramac Way SE7 CH42 68
Rambler Clo. SW16 BW49 76
Rambler La., Slou. AR41 62
Ramblers Way, Welw.G.C. BT8 5
Rambling Way, Berk. AU12 7
Ramilles Clo. SW2 BX46 76
Ramillies Pl. W1 BW39 1
Ramillies Pl. W1 BW39 56
Ramillies Rd. NW7 BO27 37
Ramillies Rd. W4 BN42 65
Ramillies Rd., Sid. CO46 79
Ramillies St. W1 BW39 1
Ramillies St. W1 BW39 56
Great Marlborough St.
Ramney Dr., Enf. CD22 30
Ramorne Clo., Walt. BE56 93
Rampart St. E1 CB39 57
Commercial Rd.
Ramparts, The, St.Alb. BF14 9
Rampayne St. SW1 BW42 3
Rampayne St. SW1 BW42 66
Rampton Clo. E4 CE27 39
Rams Gro., Rom. CQ31 50
Ramsay Clo., Brox. CD14 12
Ramsay Gdns., Rom. CV30 42
Ramsay Pl., Har. BG33 45
West St.
Ramsay Rd. E7 CG35 49
Ramsay Rd. W3 BN41 65
Ramsbury Rd., St.Alb. BH14 9
Ramscroft Clo. N9 CA26 39
Ramsdale Rd. SW17 BV49 76
Ramsden Clo., Orp. CP54 89
Ramsden Rd.
Ramsden Dr., Rom. CR29 41
Ramsden Rd. N11 BU28 38
Ramsden Rd. SW12 BV46 76
Ramsden Rd., Erith CS43 69
Ramsden Rd., Orp. CO54 89
Ramsden Ri., Hem.H. AV14 7
The Foxgloves
Ramsey Clo. NW9 BO32 46
Ramsey Clo., Har. BG35 45
Ramsey Clo., Hat. BT17 20
Ramsey Clo., St.Alb. BJ14 9
Ramsey Ct. N8 BW32 47
Ramsey Rd., Th.Hth. BX53 86
Ramsey St. E2 CB38 2
Ramsey St. E2 CB38 57
Ramsey Way N14 BW26 38
Windsor Ct.
Ramsey Wk. N1 BZ36 57
Marquess Est.
Ramsgate St. E8 CA36 57
Ramsgill App., Ilf. CN31 49
Ramsgill Dr., Ilf. CN32 49
Ramulis Dr., Hayes BE38 54
Ramus Wood Av., Orp. CN56 97
Rancliffe Gdns. SE9 CK45 68
Rancliffe Rd. E6 CK38 58
Randal Cres., Reig. BS71 121
Randall Av. NW2 BO34 46
Randall Clo. SW11 BU44 66
Randall Clo., Erith CS43 69
Randall Clo., Slou. AS42 62
Randall Cres., Lthd. BJ63 102
Randall Dr., Horn. CV35 51
Randall Pl. SE10 CF43 67
Randall Rd. SE11 BX42 4
Randall Rd. SE11 BX42 66
Randall Row SE11 BX42 4
Randall Row SE11 BX42 66
Randalls Dr., Brwd. DF25 122
Randalls Farm La., Lthd. BJ63 102
Randalls Mkt. E14 CE39 57
Ricardo St.
Randalls Park Av., Lthd. BJ63 102
Randalls Park Dr., Lthd. BJ64 102
Randalls Rd., Lthd. BH63 102
Randalls Ride, Hem.H. AY12 8
Randalls Way, Lthd. BJ64 102
Randell Hill Rd., Sev. DC61 108
Battlefields Rd.
Randells Rd. N1 BX37 2
Randells Rd. N1 BX37 56
Randisbourne Gdns. SE6 CE47 77
Bromley Rd.
Randle Rd., Rich. BK49 74
Randles La., Sev. CP60 98
Randlesdown Rd. SE6 CE49 77
Randolph App. E16 CJ39 58
Baxter Rd.
Randolph Av. W9 BS37 1
Randolph Av. W9 BS38 56
Randolph Clo., Bexh. CS45 69
Randolph Clo., Cob. BF61 102
Randolph Clo., Kings.T. BN49 75
Randolph Clo., Wok. AP62 100
Randolph Cres. W9 BT38 1
Randolph Cres. W9 BT38 56
Randolph Gdns. NW6 BS37 56
Randolph Gro., Rom. CP32 50
Donald Dr.
Randolph Ms. W9 BT38 1
Randolph Ms. W9 BT38 56
Randolph Rd. E17 CE32 48
Randolph Rd. W9 BT38 1
Randolph Rd. W9 BT38 56
Randolph Rd., Epsom BO60 94
Randolph Rd., Slou. AS42 62
Randolph Rd., Sthl. BE41 64
Randolph St. NW1 BW36 56
Randon Clo., Har. BF30 36
Ranelagh Av. SW13 BP44 65
Ranelagh Av. SW6 BR45 65
Ranelagh Bri. W2 BS39 1
Ranelagh Bri. W2 BS39 56
Ranelagh Clo., Edg. BM28 37
Ranelagh Dr., Edg. BM28 37
Ranelagh Dr., Twick. BJ45 64
Ranelagh Est. SW15 BQ44 65
Ranelagh Gdns. E11 CJ32 49
Ranelagh Gdns. SW6 BR45 65
Ranelagh Gdns. W4 BN43 65
Grove Park Gdns.
Ranelagh Gdns., Grav. DF47 81
Ranelagh Gdns., Ilf. CK33 49
Ranelagh Gro. SW1 BV42 3
Ranelagh Gro. SW1 BV42 66
Ranelagh Ms. W5 BK41 64
Ranelagh Rd.
Ranelagh Pl., N.Mal. BO53 85
Ranelagh Rd. E11 CG35 49
Ranelagh Rd. E15 CG37 58
Ranelagh Rd. E6 CL37 58
Ranelagh Rd. N17 CA31 48
Ranelagh Rd. N22 BX30 38
Ranelagh Rd. NW10 BO37 55
Ranelagh Rd. SW1 BW42 66
Lupus St.
Ranelagh Rd. W5 BK41 64
Ranelagh Rd., Hem.H. AZ13 8
Ranelagh Rd., Red. BU70 121
Ranelagh Rd., Sthl. BD40 54
Ranelagh Rd., Wem. BK35 45
Ranelagh St. SW1 BW42 3
Ranfurly Rd., Sutt. BS55 86
Range Rd., Grav. DJ47 81
Range Way, Shep. AZ54 83
Rangefield Rd., Brom. CG49 78
Rangemoor Rd. N15 CA32 48
Rangers Rd. E4 CG26 40
Rangers Sq. SE10 CF44 67
Rangeworth Pl., Sid. CN48 78
Priestlands Park Rd.
Rangoon St. EC3 CA39 2
Rangoon St. EC3 CA39 57
Northumberland Alley
Rankin Clo. NW9 BO31 46
Ranleigh Gdns., Bexh. CQ43 69
Ranmere St. SW12 BV47 76
Ranmoor Clo., Har. BG31 45
Ranmoor Gdns., Har. BG31 45
Ranmore Av., Croy. CA55 87
Ranmore Clo., Red. BV69 121
Ranmore Common Rd., Dogkennel Green BD70 119
Ranmore Common Rd., West Humble BH69 119
Ranmore Path, Orp. CO52 89
Ranmore Rd., Couls. BX62 104
Ranmore Rd., Dor. BG70 119
Ranmore Rd., Sutt. BQ58 94
Rannoch Rd. W6 BQ43 65
Rannoch Wk., Hem.H. AX11 8
Rannock Av. NW9 BN33 46
Ranskill Rd., B.Wd. BM23 28
Ransom Clo., Wat. BD26 36
Ransom Rd. SE7 CJ42 68
Ranston Clo., Uxb. AV32 43
Ranston St. NW1 BU39 1
Ranston St. NW1 BU39 56
Rant Meadow, Hem.H. AZ14 8
Ranulf Rd. NW2 BR35 46
Ranworth Clo., Erith CT44 69
Ranworth Clo., Hem.H. AX14 8
Ranworth Rd. N9 CC27 39
Raphael Av., Rom. CT30 41
Raphael Av., Til. DG44 71
Raphael Dr., Wat. BD23 27
Raphael Rd., Grav. DH47 81
Raphael St. SW7 BU41 3
Raphael St. SW7 BU41 66
Rapier Clo., Grays CX42 70
Rasehill Clo., Rick. AX25 26
Rashleigh St. SW8 BV44 66
Rashleigh Way, Hort.K. CY52 90
Rasper Rd. N20 BT27 38
Rastell Av. SW2 BW48 76
Ratcliffe Cross St. E1 CC39 57
Ratcliffe La. E14 CD39 57
Ratcliffe Orchard E1 CC40 57
Ratcliffe Rd. E7 CJ35 49
Ratcliffe Rd., Uxb. AX38 53
Rathbone Mkt. E16 CG39 58
Rathbone Pl. W1 BW39 1
Rathbone Pl. W1 BW39 56
Rathbone Point E5 CB34 48
Downs Est.
Rathbone St. E16 CG39 58
Rathbone St. W1 BW39 1
Rathbone St. W1 BW39 56
Rathcoole Av. N8 BX31 47
Rathcoole Gdns. N8 BX32 47
Rathfern Rd. SE6 CD47 77
Rathgar Av. W13 BJ40 54
Rathgar Clo. N3 BR30 37
Rathgar Clo., Red. BV73 121
Rathlin Wk. N1 BZ36 57
Marquess Est.
Rathlin, Hem.H. AZ14 8
Rathmell Dr. SW4 BW46 76
Rathmore Rd. SE7 CH42 68
Rathmore Rd., Grav. DG47 81
Rats La., Loug. CH22 31
Rattray Rd. SW2 BY45 66
Rattys La., Hodd. CF12 12
Raul Rd. SE15 CB44 67
Ravel Gdns., S.Ock. CY39 60
Ravel Rd., S.Ock. CY39 60
Raveley St. NW5 BW35 47
Raven Clo., Rick. AX26 35
Raven Ct., Hat. BP13 10
Raven Rd. E18 CJ30 40
Raven Row E1 CB39 57
Ravencroft, Grays DG41 71
Alexandra Clo.
Ravendale Rd., Sun. BB51 83
Ravenet St. SW11 BV44 66
Strasburg Rd.
Ravenfield Rd. SW17 BU48 76
Ravenfield Rd., Welw.G.C. BR8 5
Ravenfield, Egh. AR50 72
Ravenhill Rd. E13 CJ37 58
Ravenna Rd. SW15 BQ45 65
Ravenor Park Rd., Grnf. BF38 54
Ravens Clo., Brom. CG51 88
Ravens Clo., Enf. CA23 30
Ravens Clo., Red. BU70 121
Ravens Clo., Wok. AO61 100
Ravens Ct., Sun. BB51 83
Ravens La., Berk. AR13 7
Ravens Mead, Ger.Cr. AS28 34
Ravens Way SE12 CH46 78
Ravensbourne Av., Brom. CF50 77
Ravensbourne Av., Ilf. CL30 40
Ravensbourne Av., Stai. AY47 73
Ravensbourne Cres., Rom. CW31 51
Ravensbourne Est., Brom. CF49 77
Ravensbourne Gdns. W13 BJ39 54
Ravensbourne Gdns., Ilf. CL30 40
Ravensbourne Pk. Cres. SE6 CD47 77
Ravensbourne Pk. SE6 CD47 77
Ravensbourne Rd. SE6 CD47 77
Ravensbourne Rd., Brom. CH52 88
Ravensbourne Rd., Dart. CU45 69
Ravensbourne Rd., Twick. BK46 74
Ravensbury Av., Mord. BT53 86
Ravensbury Gro., Mitch. BT52 86
Ravensbury La., Mitch. BT52 86
Ravensbury Path, Mitch. BT52 86
Ravensbury Rd. SW18 BS48 76
Ravensbury Rd., Orp. CN52 88
Ravensbury Ter. SW18 BS47 76
Ravensbury Rd.
Ravenscar Rd., Brom. CG49 78
Ravenscar Rd., Surb. BL55 85
Ravenscourt Av. W6 BP42 65
Ravenscourt Clo., Horn. CW34 51
Ravenscourt Dr.
Ravenscourt Clo., Ruis. BA33 44
Ravenscourt Dr., Horn. CW34 51
Ravenscourt Gdns. W6 BP42 65
Ravenscourt Gro., Horn. CW34 51
Ravenscourt Pk. W6 BP42 65
Ravenscourt Pl. W6 BP42 65
King St.
Ravenscourt Rd. W6 BP41 65
Ravenscourt Rd., Orp. CO51 89
Ravenscourt Sq. W6 BP41 65
Ravenscraig Rd. N11 BW28 38
Ravenscroft Av. NW11 BR33 46
Ravenscroft Av., Wem. BL33 46
Ravenscroft Clo. E16 CH39 58
Ravenscroft Park Rd., Barn. BQ24 28
Ravenscroft Pk., Barn. BQ24 28
Ravenscroft Rd. E16 CH39 58
Ravenscroft Rd. W4 BN42 65
Ravenscroft Rd., Beck. CC51 87
Ravenscroft Rd., Wey. BA59 92
Ravenscroft St. E2 CA37 2
Ravenscroft St. E2 CA37 57
Ravenscroft, St.Alb. BE21 27
Ravensdale Av. N12 BT28 38
Ravensdale Gdns. SE19 BZ50 77
Ravensdale Rd. N16 CA33 48
Ravensdale Rd., Houns. BE45 64
Ravensdell, Hem.H. AV13 7
Ravensdon St. SE11 BY42 4
Ravensdon St. SE11 BY42 66
Ravensfield Clo., Dag. CP35 50
Ravensfield Gdns., Epsom BO56 94
Ravensfield St. SE11 BY42 66
Ravensfield, Slou. AR41 62
Ravenshaw St. NW6 BR35 46
Ravenshead Clo., S.Croy. CC59 96
Ravenshill, Chis. CL51 88
Ravenshurst Av. NW4 BQ31 46
Ravenslea Rd. SW12 BU47 76
Ravensmead Rd., Brom. CF50 77
Ravensmede Way W4 BO42 65
Ravensmere, Epp. CO19 23
Ravenstone Rd. N8 BY31 47
Ravenstone Rd. NW9 BO32 46
Ravenstone St. SW12 BV47 76
Ravenswold, Ken. BZ61 105
Ravenswood Av., Surb. BL55 85
Ravenswood Av., W.Wick. CF54 87
Ravenswood Clo., Cob. BD61 102
Ravenswood Clo., Croy. BY55 86
Ravenswood Rd.
Ravenswood Clo., Rom. CR28 41
Ravenswood Cres., W.Wick. CF54 87
Ravenswood Cres., Har. BE34 45
Ravenswood Ct., Kings.T. BM50 75
Ravenswood Ct., Wok. AS62 100
Hill View Rd.
Ravenswood Gdns., Islw. BH44 64
Ravenswood Pk., Nthwd. BC29 35
Ravenswood Rd. E17 CE31 48
Ravenswood Rd. SE9 CK48 78
Ravenswood Rd. SW12 BV47 76
Ravenswood Rd., Croy. BY55 86
Ravenswood, Bex. CQ47 79
Ravensworth Rd. NW10 BP38 55
Ravent Rd. SE11 BX42 4
Ravent Rd. SE11 BX42 66
Ravey St. EC2 CA38 2
Ravey St. EC2 CA38 57
Ravine Gro. SE18 CN43 68
Rawchester Clo. SW18 BR47 75
Rawdon Dr., Hodd. CE12 12
Rawhurst Av., Wey. AW57 92
Rawlings Clo., Orp. CN56 97
Rawlings La., Beac. AO27 34
Rawlings St. SW3 BU42 3
Rawlings St. SW3 BU42 66
Rawlins Clo. N3 BR30 37
Rawlins Clo., S.Croy. CD57 96
Rawlinson Ter. N17 CA31 48
Rawnsley Av., Mitch. BU53 86
Rawreth Wk. N1 BZ37 57
Basire St.
Rawson St. SW11 BV44 66
Strasburg Rd.
Rawstone Wk. E13 CH37 58
Rawstorne Pl. EC1 BY38 2
Rawstorne St.
Rawstorne Pl. EC1 BY38 56
Rawstorne St.

Rawstorne St. EC1 BY38 2
Rawstorne St. EC1 BY38 56
Ray Field, Welw.G.C. BQ 6 5
Ray Gdns., Bark. CO37 59
Ray Gdns., Stan. BJ28 36
Ray Lodge Rd., Wdf.Grn. CJ29 40
Ray Rd., E.Mol. BF53 84
Ray Rd., Rom. CR28 41
Ray St. EC1 BY38 2
Ray St. EC1 BY38 56
Ray Wk. N7 BX34 47
Andover Rd.
Raybarn Rd., Hem.H. AW12 8
Rayburn Rd., Horn. CX33 51
Raydean Rd., Barn. BS25 29
Raydon Rd., Chsnt. CC19 21
Theobalds La.
Raydon St. N19 BV34 47
Raydons Gdns., Dag. CQ35 50
Raydons Rd., Dag. CQ35 50
Rayfield Clo., Brom. CK53 88
Rayfield, Epp. CN18 22
Rayford Av. SE12 CG47 78
Rayford Clo., Dart. CV46 80
Rayleas Clo. SE18 CL44 68
Rayleigh Av., Tedd. BH50 74
Rayleigh Clo. N13 BZ27 39
Rayleigh Clo., Brwd. DE25 122
Rayleigh Ct. N22 BZ30 39
Rayleigh Ct., Kings.T. BM51 85
Cambridge Rd.
Rayleigh Rd. N13 BZ27 39
Rayleigh Rd. SW19 BR51 85
Rayleigh Rd., Brwd. DD25 122
Rayleigh Rd., Wdf.Grn. CJ29 40
Rayleigh Ri., S.Croy. CA57 96
Rayley La., Epp. CR15 14
Raymead Av., Th.Hth. BY53 86
Raymead Clo., Loug. CM25 31
Raymead Clo., Lthd. BH64 102
Raymead NW4 BQ31 46
Raymead Way, Lthd. BH64 102
Raymer Clo., St.Alb. BH13 9
Raymere Gdns. SE18 CM43 68
Raymond Av. E18 CG31 49
Raymond Av. W13 BJ41 64
Raymond Bldgs. WC1 BX39 2
Raymond Bldgs. WC1 BX39 56
Raymond Clo. SE26 CC49 77
Raymond Clo., Slou. AV44 62
Raymond Clo., Wat. BA19 17
Raymond Cres., Guil. AP71 118
Raymond Gdns., Chig. CO27 41
Raymond Rd. E13 CJ36 58
Raymond Rd. SW19 BR50 75
Raymond Rd., Beck. CD52 87
Raymond Rd., Ilf. CM33 49
Raymond Rd., Slou. AT42 62
Raymond Way, Esher BJ57 93
Raymonds Clo., Welw.G.C. BR 9 5
Raymonds Plain, Welw.G.C. BR 9 5
Raymouth Rd. SE16 CB42 67
Rayne Ct. E18 CG31 49
Rayner St. E9 CC36 57
Rayners Clo., Slou. AU43 62
Rayners Cres., Nthlt. BC38 53
Rayners Ct., Har. BF33 45
Rayners Gdns., Nthlt. BC38 53
Rayners La., Har. BF33 45
Rayners La., Pnr. BE32 45
Rayners Rd. SW15 BQ46 75
Raynes Av. E11 CJ33 49
Raynham Av. N18 CB29 39
Raynham Rd. N18 CB28 39
Raynham Rd. W6 BP42 65
Raynham Ter. N18 CB28 39
Raynor Clo., Sthl. BE40 54
Raynor Pl. N1 BZ37 2
Raynors Clo., Wem. BK35 45
Raynton Clo., Har. BE33 45
Raynton Clo., Hayes BB38 53
Raynton Dr., Hayes BB38 53
Raynton Rd., Enf. CC22 30
Rays Av. N18 CC28 39
Rays Av., Wind. AM43 61
Rays Hill, Dart. CY53 90
Rays Rd. N18 CB28 39
Rays Rd., W.Wick. CF54 87
Raywood Clo., Hayes BA43 63
Raywood St. SW8 BV44 66
Reachview Clo. NW1 BW37 1
Baynes St.
Read Ct., Wal.Abb. CH20 22
Read Rd., Ash. BK62 102
Read Way, Grav. DH49 81
Reade Wk. NW10 BO36 55
Denbigh Clo.
Readens, The, Bans. BU61 104
Readgold St. W11 BO40 55
Reading Arch Rd., Red. BU70 121
Reading La. E8 CB36 57
Reading Rd., Nthlt. BF35 45
Reading Rd., Sutt. BT56 95
Reading Way NW7 BR28 37
Readings, The, Harl. CN12 13
Readings, The, Rick. AV24 25
Reads Clo., Ilf. CL34 49
Roden St.
Reads Rest La., Tad. BS63 104
Reapers Clo. NW1 BW37 1
Reapers Way, Islw. BG46 74
Reardon Path E1 CB40 57
Reardon St. E1 CB40 57
Reaston St. SE14 CC43 67
Rebecca Ter. SE16 CC41 67
Reckingham Rd., Guil. AQ69 118
Reckitt Rd. W4 BO42 65
Record St. SE15 CC43 67
Recovery St. SW17 BU49 76
Recreation Av., Harold Wood CW35 42
Recreation Av., Rom. CS32 50
Recreation Rd. SE26 CC49 77
Recreation Rd., Brom. CG51 88
Recreation Rd., Guil. AR70 118
Recreation Rd., Sthl. BE42 64
Recreation Way, Mitch. BW52 86
Rector St. N1 BZ37 2
Rector St. N1 BZ37 57
Rectory Chase, Doddinghurst DB22 33
Rectory Chase, Brwd. DB31 51
Rectory Clo. E4 CE27 39
Rectory Clo. E4 CE27 39
Brindwood Rd.
Rectory Clo. N3 BR30 37
Rectory Clo. SW20 BQ52 85
Rectory Clo., Ash. BL63 103
Rectory Clo., Dart. CT45 69
Rectory Clo., Guil. AU69 118
Rectory Clo., Hat. BU12 11
Rectory Clo., Shep. AZ52 83
Rectory Clo., Sid. CO49 79
Rectory Clo., Stan. BJ28 36
Rectory Clo., Surb. BK54 84
Rectory Clo., Wey. AY60 92
Rectory Clo., Wind. AN44 61
Rectory Cres. E11 CJ32 49
Rectory Field Cres. SE7 CJ43 68
Rectory Field, Harl. CL12 13
Rectory Gdns. N8 BX31 47
Rectory Gdns. SW4 BW45 66
Rectory Gro.
Rectory Gdns., Hayes BA42 63
Rectory Gdns., Nthlt. BE37 54
Rectory Gdns., Upmin. CZ34 51
Rectory Grn. La., Bet. BO69 120
Rectory Grn., Beck. CD51 87
Rectory Gro. SW4 BW45 66
Rectory Gro., Croy. BY55 86
Rectory Gro., Hmptn. BE49 74
Rectory La. SW17 BV50 76
Rectory La., Ash. BL62 103
Rectory La., Bans. BU60 95
Rectory La., Berk. AR13 7
Rectory La., Edg. BM29 37
Rectory La., Ightham DB64 108
Rectory La., Kings L. AZ17 17
Rectory La., Loug. CL23 31
Rectory La., Lthd. BE66 111
Rectory La., Rad. BM19 19
Rectory La., Rick. AX26 35
Rectory La., Sev. CV66 117
Rectory La., Sid. CO49 79
Rectory La., Stan. BJ28 36
Rectory La., Surb. BJ54 84
Rectory La., Wall. BW55 86
Rectory La., West. CP65 107
Rectory La., Wey. AY60 92
Rectory Meadow, Grav. DD50 81
Rectory Pk. Av., Nthlt. BE38 54
Rectory Pk., S.Croy. CA60 96
Rectory Pl. SE18 CL42 68
Rectory Rd. E12 CK35 49
Rectory Rd. E17 CE31 48
Rectory Rd. N16 CA34 48
Rectory Rd. SW13 BP44 65
Rectory Rd. W3 BM40 55
Rectory Rd., Beck. CE51 87
Rectory Rd., Couls. BS66 113
Rectory Rd., Dag. CR36 59
Rectory Rd., Grays DE41 71
Rectory Rd., Green. CZ46 80
Church Rd.
Rectory Rd., Hayes BC39 53
Rectory Rd., Houns. BC44 63
Rectory Rd., Kes. CJ57 97
Rectory Rd., Rick. AX26 35
Rectory Rd., Sthl. BE41 64
Rectory Rd., Sutt. BS55 86
Rectory Rd., Swans. DC47 81
Rectory Rd., Til. DH43 71
Rectory Rd., Welw.G.C. BP 6 5
Rectory Rd., West. CK65 106
Rectory Sq. E1 CC39 57
Rectory Way, Uxb. AZ34 44
Rectory Wood, Harl. CM10 6
Reculver Ms. N18 CB28 39
Reculver Rd. SE16 CC42 67
Red Anchor Clo. SW3 BU43 66
Old Church St.
Red Barracks Rd. SE18 CK42 68
Red Bull Yd. EC4 BZ40 57
Upper Thames St.
Red Cedars Rd., Orp. CN54 88
Red Cottage Ms., Slou. AR41 62
London Rd.
Red Cross, Reig. BS70 121
Red Ct., Slou. AP40 52
Stoke Poges La.
Red Hall La., Rick. AY23 26
Red Hill, Chis. CL49 78
Red Hill, Cob. BA61 101
Red House La., Bexh. CP45 69
Red House La., Walt. BC55 83
Red House Rd., Croy. BW53 86
Red La., Dor. BL74 120
Red La., Esher BJ57 93
Red La., Oxt. CH69 115
Red Law Way SE16 CB42 67
Red Leaf Clo., Slou. AS40 52
Pickford Dr.
Red Lion Clo. SE17 BZ42 67
Red Lion Row
Red Lion Clo., Orp. CP53 89
Red Lion Cres., Harl. CP12 14
Red Lion Ct. EC4 BY39 2
Red Lion Ct. EC4 BY39 56
Fleet St.
Red Lion Hill N2 BT30 38
Red Lion La. SE18 CL44 68
Red Lion La., H.Hem. AZ16 17
Red Lion La., Harl. CP12 14
Red Lion La., Rick. AW21 26
Red Lion La., Wok. AP58 91
Red Lion Rd., Surb. BL55 85
Red Lion Rd., Wok. AP58 91
Red Lion Row SE17 BZ43 67
Red Lion Sq. SW18 BS46 76
Hardwicks Way
Red Lion Sq. WC1 BX39 2
Red Lion Sq. WC1 BX39 56
Red Lion Sq., Hmptn. BF51 84
Red Lion St. WC1 BX39 2
Red Lion St. WC1 BX39 56
Theobalds Rd.
Red Lion St., Rich. BK46 74
Red Lion Yd., Wat. BD24 27
Red Lodge Cres., Bex. CS48 79
Red Lodge Gdns., Berk. AQ13 7
Red Lodge Rd., Bex. CS48 79
Red Lodge Rd., W.Wick. CF54 87
Red Oak Clo., Orp. CL55 88
Red Oaks Mead, Epp. CM22 31
Red Pl. W1 BV40 3
Red Pl. W1 BV40 56
Park St.
Red Post Hill SE21 BZ46 67
Red Post Hill SE24 BZ45 67
Red Rd., B.Wd. BL24 28
Red Rd., Bet. BN69 120
Red Rd., Brwd. DA28 42
Red Rose La., Ing. DC18 24
Red St., Grav. DD50 81
Red Willow, Harl. CK12 13
Red Wood Mt., Reig. BS69 121
Redan Pl. W2 BS39 1
Redan Pl. W2 BS39 56
Redan St. W14 BQ41 65
Redan Ter. SE5 BZ44 67
Flaxman Rd.
Redbarn Clo., Pur. BY59 95
Redberry Gro. SE26 CC48 77
Redbourn Rd., Hem.H. AZ11 8
Redbourn Rd., St.Alb. BE12 9
Redbourne Av. N3 BS30 38
Redbridge Gdns. SE5 CA44 67
Dalwood St.
Redbridge La. E., Ilf. CJ32 49
Redbridge La. W., E11 CH32 49
Redburn St. SW3 BU43 3
Redburn St. SW3 BU43 66
Redburn Ter., Enf. CC25 30
South St.
Redbury Clo., Rain. CV39 60
Redcar Clo., Nthlt. BF36 54
Redcar Rd., Rom. CW28 42
Redcar St. SE5 BZ43 67
Redcastle Clo. E1 CC40 57
Redchurch St. E2 CA38 2
Redchurch St. E2 CA38 57
Redcliffe Clo. SW5 BS42 66
Redcliffe Gdns. SW10 BS42 3
Redcliffe Gdns. SW10 BS42 66
Redcliffe Gdns., Ilf. CL33 49
Redcliffe Ms. SW10 BS42 3
Redcliffe Ms. SW10 BS42 66
Redcliffe Pl. SW10 BT43 66
Redcliffe Rd. SW10 BT42 3
Redcliffe Rd. SW10 BT42 66
Redcliffe Sq. SW10 BS42 3
Redcliffe Sq. SW10 BS42 66
Redcliffe St. SW10 BS43 3
Redcliffe St. SW10 BS43 66
Redclose Av., Mord. BS53 86
Redclyffe Rd. E6 CJ37 58
Redcourt, Wok. AU61 100
Redcroft Rd., Sthl. BG40 54
Redcross Pl. SE1 BZ41 4
Redcross Pl. SE1 BZ41 67
Redcross Way
Redcross Way SE1 BZ41 4
Redcross Way SE1 BZ41 67
Redden Court Rd., Horn. CW31 51
Reddings Av., Bush. BF25 27
Reddings Clo. NW7 BO28 37
Reddings, Hem.H. AY14 8
Reddings, The NW7 BO27 37
Reddings, The, B.Wd. BL24 28
Red Rd.
Reddings, Welw.G.C. BQ 7 5
Reddington Clo., S.Croy. CA58 96
Reddington Dr., Slou. AS42 62
Reddins Rd. SE15 CB43 67
Redditch Ct., Hem.H. AY11 8
Reddons Rd., Beck. CD50 77
Reddown Rd., Couls. BW62 104
Reddy Rd., Erith CT43 69
Rede Ct., Wey. AZ55 83
Rede Pl. W2 BS39 56
Redesdale Gdns., Islw. BJ43 64
Redesdale St. SW3 BU42 3
Redesdale St. SW3 BU42 66
Redfern Av., Twick. BF47 74
Redfern Clo., Uxb. AX37 53
Redfern Gdns., Rom. CV30 42
Redfern Rd. NW10 BO36 55
Redfern Rd. SE6 CF47 77
Brownhill Rd.
Redfield La. SW5 BS42 66
Redford Av., Couls. BV60 95
Redford Av., Th.Hth. BX52 86
Redford Av., Wall. BX57 95
Redford Rd., Wind. AL44 61
Redford Way, Uxb. AX36 53
Redford Wk. N1 BZ37 57
Popham St.
Redgate Dr., Brom. CH55 88
Redgate Ter. SW15 BQ46 75
Lytton Gro.
Redgrave Clo. SE25 CA53 87
Redgrave Rd. SW15 BQ45 65
Redhall Clo., Hat. BO14 10
Redhall Dr., Hat. BO14 10
Redheath Clo., Wat. BC20 17
Redhill Dr., Edg. BN30 37
Redhill Rd., Cob. AZ59 92
Redhill St. NW1 BV37 1
Redhill St. NW1 BV37 56
Redhill, Uxb. AU33 43
Redholm Vill. N16 BZ35 48
Winston Rd.
Redhouse Rd., West. CJ64 106
Redington Gdns. NW3 BS35 47
Redington Rd. NW3 BS35 47
Redlands Gdns., E.Mol. BE52 84
Redlands Rd., Enf. CD23 30
Redlands Rd., Sev. CT65 107
Redlands Way SW2 BX47 76
Redlands, Couls. BX61 104
Redlaw Way SE16 CB42 67
Bonamy Est. W.
Redleaf Clo., Belv. CR43 69
Redleaves Av., Ashf. AZ50 73
Redlees Clo., Islw. BJ45 64
Redmans La., Sev. CT57 98
Redmans Pl., Sev. CV66 117
Redmans Rd. E1 CC39 57
Redmead La. E1 CB40 4
Redmead La. E1 CB40 57
Redmead Rd., Hayes BB42 63
Redmore Rd. W6 BP42 65
Redpoll Way, Erith CP41 69
Maran Way
Redrick La., Harl. CN 8 6
Redriff Est. SE16 CD41 67
Redriff Rd. SE16 CC41 67
Redriff Rd., Rom. CR30 41
Redriffe Rd. E13 CG37 58
Redroofs Clo., Beck. CE51 87
The Avenue
Redruth Clo. N22 BX29 38
Redruth Clo., Rom. CW28 42
Redruth Gdns., Rom. CW28 42
Redruth Rd. E9 CC37 57
Redruth Rd., Rom. CW28 42
Redruth Wk., Rom. CW28 42
Redstart Clo. E6 CK39 58
Columbine Av.
Redstart Clo. SE14 CD43 67
Southerngate Way
Redstart Clo., Croy. CF58 96
Redston Rd. N8 BW31 47
Redstone Hill, Red. BV70 121
Redstone Hollow, Red. BV71 121
Redstone Mans., Red. BV70 121
Redstone Pk., Red. BV70 121
Redstone Rd., Red. BV71 121
Redvers Rd. N22 BY30 38
Redvers Rd., Warl. CC62 105
Redvers St. N1 CA38 2
Redwald Rd. E5 CC35 48
Redway Dr., Twick. BG46 74
Redwell La., Sev. DA65 108
Redwing Clo., S.Croy. CC59 96
Redwing Path SE28 CM41 68
Whinchat Rd.
Redwing Ri., Guil. AU69 118
Redwood Clo. N14 BW26 38
The Vale
Redwood Clo. SE16 CD40 57
Redwood Clo., Guil. AU73 118
Redwood Clo., Ken. BZ60 96
Redwood Clo., Uxb. AZ37 53
Redwood Clo., Wat. BD28 36
Redwood Dr., Hem.H. AY14 8
Redwood Gdns., Chig. CO28 41
Redwood Gdns., Slou. AO40 52
Godolphin Rd.
Redwood Ri., B.Wd. BM22 28
Redwood Way, Barn. BQ25 28
Redwood, Egh. AV51 82
Redwoods Clo., Buck.H. CH27 40
Beech La.
Redwoods SW15 BP46 75
Redwoods, Welw.G.C. BQ 5 5
Reece Ms. SW7 BT42 3
Reece Ms. SW7 BT42 66
Reed Av., Orp. CM55 88
Reed Clo. E16 CH39 58
Plymouth Rd.
Reed Clo. SE12 CH46 78
Reed Clo., Iver AV39 52
Dutton Way
Reed Holm Vill. N16 BZ35 48
Reed Pl., Wey. AV60 91
Reed Pond Wk., Rom. CT30 41
Reed Rd. N17 CA30 39
Reedan Clo., St.Alb. BF18 18
Reede Gdns., Dag. CR35 50
Reede Rd., Dag. CR36 59
Reede Way, Dag. CR36 59
Reedham Clo. N15 CB31 48
Reedham Dr., Pur. BX60 95
Reedham Park Av., Pur. BY61 104
Reedham St. SE15 CB44 67
Reeds La., Ton. DC68 117
Reeds Pl. NW1 BW36 56
Rochester Pl.
Reedsfield Rd., Ashf. AZ49 73
Reedworth St. SE11 BY42 4
Reedworth St. SE11 BY42 66
Reenglass Rd., Stan. BK28 36
Rees Gdns., Croy. CA53 87
Rees Rd., Red. BU70 121
High St.
Rees St. N1 BZ37 2
Rees St. N1 BZ37 57
Reesland Clo. E12 CL35 49
Reets Farm Clo. NW9 BO32 46
Reeve Rd., Maid. AG43 61
Reeve Rd., Reig. BT72 121
Reeves Av. NW9 BN33 46
Reeves Clo., Brwd. DA20 24
Reeves Cres., Swan. CS52 89
Reeves La., Harl. CJ13 13
Reeves Ms. W1 BV40 3
Reeves Ms. W1 BV40 56
Reeves Rd. E3 CE38 57
Reeves Rd. SE18 CL43 68
Reform Row N17 CA30 39
Reform St. SW11 BU44 66
Regal Clo. E1 CB39 57
Regal Clo. W5 BK39 54
Regal Cres., Wall. BV55 86
Prince Charles Way
Regal Ct. N18 CA28 39
Regal Field Clo., Guil. AP68 109
Regal La. NW1 BV37 1
Regal La. NW1 BV37 56
Regents Park Rd.
Regal Way, Har. BK32 45
Regan Clo., Guil. AQ68 109
Regan Way N1 CA37 2
Regan Way N1 CA37 57
Regarder Rd., Chig. CO28 41
Regarth Av., Rom. CT32 50
Regency Clo. W5 BL39 55
Regency Clo., Chig. CM28 40
Regency Clo., Hmptn. BE49 74
Regency Clo., Sev. CZ57 99
Regency Ct., Brwd. DB27 42
Crown St.
Regency Ct., Harl. CO12 14
Regency Dr., Ruis. BB33 44
Regency Dr., Wey. AV60 91
Regency Gdns., Horn. CV33 51
Regency Ms. NW10 BO36 55
High Rd.
Regency Ms., Islw. BH46 74
Regency Pl. SW1 BW42 3
Regency St. SW1 BW42 3
Regency St. SW1 BW42 66
Regency Way, Bexh. CP45 69
Regency Wk., Croy. CD53 87
Regency Wk., Rich. BL46 75
The Vineyard
Regent Av., Uxb. AZ36 53
Regent Clo., Grays DE41 71
Regent Clo., Har. BL32 46
Regent Clo., Houns. BC44 63
Regent Clo., St.Alb. BK11 9
Portman Clo.
Regent Clo., Wey. AX58 92
Regent Cres., Red. BU69 121
Linkfield La.
Regent Ct., Slou. AP39 52
Stoke Poges La.
Regent Gdns., Ilf. CO32 50
Regent Ho., Surb. BL53 85
Regent Pl. W1 BW40 3
Regent Pl. W1 BW40 56
Warwick St.
Regent Pl., Croy. CA54 87
Regent Rd. SE24 BY46 76
Regent Rd., Epp. CN18 22
Regent Rd., Surb. BL53 85
Regent Sq. E3 CE38 57
Regent Sq. WC1 BX38 2
Regent Sq. WC1 BX38 56
Regent Sq., Belv. CR42 69
Regent St. NW10 BQ38 55
Kilburn La.
Regent St. SW1 BW40 3
Regent St. SW1 BW40 56
Regent St. W1 BV39 1
Regent St. W1 BV39 56
Regent St. W4 BM42 65
Regent St., Wat. BC22 26
Regents Av. N13 BY28 38
Regents Bridge Gdns. SW8 BX43 66
Regents Clo., Hayes BB39 53
Grange Par.
Regents Clo., Rad. BJ20 18
Regents Clo., S.Croy. CA57 96
Regents Clo., Whyt. CA62 105
Regents Dr., Kes. CJ56 97
Regents Ms. NW8 BT37 1
Regents Park Est. NW1 BV38 1
Regents Park Est. NW1 BV38 56
Regents Park Rd. N3 BR31 46
Regents Park Rd. NW1 BU37 1
Regents Park Rd. NW1 BU37 56
Regents Park Ter. NW1 BU37 1
Regents Park Ter. NW1 BY37 56
Oval Rd.
Regents Pl. SE3 CH44 68
Regents Row E8 CB37 57
Regina Clo., Barn. BQ24 28
Regina Rd. N4 BX33 47
Regina Rd. SE25 CB52 87
Regina Rd. W13 BJ40 54
Regina Rd., Sthl. BE42 64
Reginald Rd. E7 CH36 58
Reginald Rd. SE8 CE43 67
Reginald Rd., Nthwd. BB30 35
Reginald Rd., Rom. CX30 42
Reginald Sq. SE8 CE43 67
Regis Rd. NW5 BV35 47
Regis Way SE17 BY43 66
Regnart Bldgs. NW1 BW38 56
Euston St.
Reid Av., Cat. BZ64 105
Reid Clo., Pnr. BC31 44
Reidhaven Rd. SE18 CN42 68
Reigate Av., Sutt. BS55 86
Reigate Hill Clo., Reig. BS69 121
Reigate Hill Rd., Reig. BS70 121
Reigate Hill, Reig. BS68 113
Reigate Rd., Sidlow Bridge BS74 121
Reigate Rd., Bet. BN70 120
Reigate Rd., Brom. CG48 78
Reigate Rd., Dor. BK71 119
Reigate Rd., Epsom BP58 94
Reigate Rd., Ilf. CN34 49
Reigate Rd., Lthd. BK65 102
Reigate Rd., Reig. BS70 121
Reigate Way, Wall. BX56 95
Reighton Rd. E5 CB34 48
Relay Rd. W12 BQ40 55
Relf Rd. SE15 CB45 67
Relinque Rd. SE26 CD49 77
Porthcawe Rd.
Relko Ct., Epsom BN59 94
Blakeney Clo.
Relko Gdns., Sutt. BT56 95
Sutton Gro.
Relton Ms. SW7 BU41 3
Cheval Pl.
Rembrandt Clo. E14 CF41 67
Amsterdam Rd.
Rembrandt Dr., Grav. DE48 81
Rembrandt Rd. SE13 CG45 68
Rembrandt Rd., Edg. BM30 37
Rembrandt Way, Walt. BC55 83
Remington Rd. E6 CK39 58
Remington Rd. N15 BZ32 48
Remington St. N1 BY37 2
Remington St. N1 BY37 56
Remnant St. WC2 BX39 2

Remnant St. WC2 BX39 56
Kingsway
Remus Rd. E3 CE36 57
Monier Rd.
Rendlesham Av., Rad. BH22 27
Rendlesham Clo., Brom. CJ51 88
Rendlesham Rd. E5 CB35 48
Rendlesham Rd., Enf. BY23 29
Rendlesham Way, Rick. AU25 25
Renforth St. SE16 CC41 67
Renfree Way, Shep. AZ54 83
Renfrew Clo. E6 CL40 58
Renfrew Rd. SE11 BY42 4
Renfrew Rd. SE11 BY42 66
Renfrew Rd., Houns. BD44 64
Renfrew Rd., Kings.T. BN50 75
Renmans, The, Ash. BL61 103
Renmuir St. SW17 BU50 76
Rennell St. SE13 CF45 67
Renness Rd. E17 CD31 47
Rennetts Clo. SE9 CM46 78
Rennetts Wood Rd. SE9 CM46 78
Rennie Clo., Ashf. AX48 73
Rennie St. SE1 BY40 4
Rennie St. SE1 BY40 56
Rennie Ter., Red. BV71 121
Renown Clo., Croy. BY54 86
Renown Clo., Rom. CR30 41
Rensburg Rd. E17 CC32 48
Renters Av. NW4 BQ32 46
Renton Dr., Orp. CP54 89
Renwick Clo., Orp. CP52 89
Renwick Rd., Bark. CO38 59
Repens Way, Hayes BD38 54
Stipularis Dr.
Rephidim St. SE1 BZ41 4
Replingham Rd. SW18 BR47 75
Reporton Rd. SW6 BR43 65
Repository Rd. SE18 CK43 68
Repton Av., Hayes BA42 63
Repton Av., Rom. CU31 50
Repton Av., Wem. BK35 45
Repton Clo., Cars. BU56 95
Repton Ct. E5 CC35 48
Clapton Park Est.
Repton Ct., Beck. CE51 87
Repton Dr., Rom. CU31 50
Repton Gdns., Rom. CU31 50
Repton Grn., St.Alb. BG12 9
Repton Gro., Ilf. CK30 40
Repton Rd., Har. BL31 46
Repton Rd., Orp. CO56 98
Repton St. E14 CD39 57
Repton Way, Rick. AZ25 26
Repulse Clo., Rom. CR30 41
Reservoir Rd. N14 BW25 29
Reservoir Rd. SE4 CD44 67
Reservoir Rd., Loug. CH23 31
Reservoir Rd., Ruis. BA32 44
Resolution Wk. SE18 CK41 68
Venus Rd.
Reson Way, Hem.H. AW14 8
Ressland Clo. E12 CL35 49
Restell Clo. SE3 CG43 68
Reston Clo., B.Wd. BM22 28
Reston Path, B.Wd. BM22 28
Reston Pl. SW7 BT41 3
Reston Pl. SW7 BT41 66
Palace Gate
Restons Cres. SE9 CM46 78
Restormel Clo., Houns. BF46 74
Retcar Clo. N6 BV34 47
Retford Clo., Rom. CX29 42
Retford Path, Rom. CX29 42
Retford Rd., Rom. CX29 42
Retford St. N1 CA38 2
Retingham Way E4 CE27 39
Retreat Clo., Har. BK32 45
Retreat Pl. E9 CC36 57
Retreat Rd., Rich. BK46 74
Retreat Ter., Brent. BK43 64
Brickfield Clo.
Retreat Way, Chig. CO27 41
Retreat, The NW4 BQ31 46
Heading St.
Retreat, The NW9 BN32 46
Retreat, The SE15 CC44 67
Retreat, The SW14 BO45 65
South Worple Way
Retreat, The, Amer. AS23 25
Retreat, The, Brwd. DA26 42
Costead Manor Rd.
Retreat, The, Brwd. DD25 122
Retreat, The, Egh. AR49 72
Retreat, The, Grays DD43 71
Retreat, The, Har. BF33 45
Retreat, The, Maid. AJ43 61
Retreat, The, Orp. CO57 98
Retreat, The, Surb. BL53 85
Retreat, The, Th.Hth. BZ52 87
Retreat, The, Wor.Pk. BP55 85
Rettiward Clo. SW15 BQ45 65
Colinette Rd.
Reubens Rd., Brwd. DD25 122
Reunion Row E1 CB40 57
Pennington St.
Reveley Sq. SE16 CD41 67
Howland Way
Revell Clo., Lthd. BF64 102
Revell Dr., Lthd. BF64 102
Revell Rd., Kings.T. BM51 85
Revell Rd., Sutt. BR57 94
Revell Ri. SE18 CN43 68
Revelon Rd. SE4 CD45 67
Revelstoke Rd. SW18 BR48 75
Reventlow Rd. SE9 CM47 78
Reverdy Rd. SE1 CB42 4
Reverdy Rd. SE1 CB42 67
Reverend Clo., Har. BF34 45
Revesby Rd., Cars. BT53 86
Review Rd. NW2 BO34 46
Review Rd., Dag. CR37 59
Rewell St. SW6 BT43 66
Rewley Rd., Cars. BT53 86
Rex Av., Ashf. AZ50 73
Rex Clo., Rom. CR29 41
Rex Pl. W1 BV40 3
Rex Pl. W1 BV40 56
Reydon Av. E11 CJ32 49
Reynard Clo., Brom. CL52 88
Blackbrook La.
Reynard Dr. SE19 CA50 77
Reynards Way, St.Alb. BE18 18
Reynardson Rd. N17 BZ29 39
Reynolds Av. E12 CL35 49
Reynolds Av., Chess. BL57 94
Reynolds Av., Rom. CP33 50
Reynolds Clo. NW11 BS33 47
Reynolds Clo., Cars. BU54 86
Reynolds Clo., Hem.H. AW13 8
Reynolds Clo., Mitch. BT51 86
Reynolds Cres., St.Alb. BJ11 9
Reynolds Ct. E11 CG34 49
Reynolds Dr., Edg. BL31 46
Reynolds Pl. SE3 CH43 68
Reynolds Pl., Rich. BL46 75
Cambrian Rd.
Reynolds Rd. SE15 CC45 67
Reynolds Rd. W4 BN41 65
Reynolds Rd., Hayes BD38 54
Reynolds Rd., N.Mal. BN54 85
Reynolds Way, Croy. CA56 96
Rheidol Ms. N1 BZ37 2
Rheidol Ter. N1 BY37 2
Rheidol Ter. N1 BY37 56
Rheingold Way, Pur. BX38 95
Rheola Clo. N17 CA30 39
Rhoda St. E2 CA38 2
Rhoda St. E2 CA38 57
Rhodes Av. N22 BW30 38
Rhodes Moorhouse Ct., Mord. BS53 86
Rhodes St. N7 BX35 47
Mackenzie Rd.
Rhodes Street Est. E8 CA36 57
Rhodes Way, Wat. BD23 27
Rhodesia Rd. E11 CF34 48
Rhodesia Rd. SW9 BX44 66
Rhodeswell Rd. E14 CD39 57
Rhododendron Ride, Egh. AP49 72
Rhodrons Av., Chess. BL56 94
Rhondda Gro. E3 CD38 57
Rhyl Rd., Grnf. BH37 54
Rhyl St. NW5 BV36 56
Rhys Av. N11 BW29 38
Rialto Rd., Mitch. BV51 86
Ribble Clo., Wdf.Grn. CJ29 40
Prospect Rd.
Ribbledale, St.Alb. BL17 19
Thamesdale
Ribblesdale Av., Nthlt. BF36 54
Ribblesdale Rd. N8 BX31 47
Ribblesdale Rd. SW16 BV50 76
Ribblesdale Rd., Dart. CY47 80
Ribblesdale, Dor. BJ72 119
Roman Rd.
Ribblesdale, Hem.H. AY12 8
Wharfedale
Ribchester Av., Grnf. BH38 54
Ribston Clo., Brom. CK54 88
Ricardo Path SE28 CP40 59
Byron Clo.
Ricardo Rd., Wind. AQ46 72
Ricardo St. E14 CE39 57
Ricards Rd. SW19 BR49 75
Ricebridge La., Reig. BP72 120
Rich Clo., West. CH62 106
Rich La. SW5 BS42 66
Earls Court Sq.
Rich St. E14 CD40 57
Richard Clo. SE18 CK42 68
Samuel St.
Richard Foster Clo. E17 CD33 48
Verulam Av.
Richard St. E1 CB39 57
Richard St. E16 CH39 58
Richards Av., Rom. CS32 50
Richards Clo., Har. BJ32 45
Richards Clo., Uxb. AZ37 53
Richards Cotts. W3 BN40 55
Churchfield Rd.
Richards Pl. E17 CE31 48
Richards Pl. SW3 BU42 3
Richards Pl. SW3 BU42 66
Richards Rd., Cob. BF60 93
Richardson Clo. E8 CA37 2
Clarissa St.
Richardson Clo. E8 CA37 57
Clarissa St.
Richardson Clo., Hayes BA43 63
Richardson Clo., St.Alb. BL17 19
Richardson Ms. W1 BW39 56
Warren St.
Richardson Pl., St.Alb. BM14 10
Richardson Rd. E15 CG37 58
Richbell Clo., Ash. BK62 102
Richbell Pl. WC1 BX39 56
Emerald St.
Richborne Ter. SW8 BX43 66
Richborough Clo., Orp. CP52 89
Richborough Rd. NW2 BQ35 46
Riches Rd., Ilf. CM34 49
Richfield Rd., Bush. BG26 36
Richford Rd. E15 CG37 58
Richford St. W6 BQ41 65
Richings Way, Iver AV41 62
Richland Av., Couls. BV60 95
Richlands Av., Epsom BP56 94
Richmer Rd., Erith CT43 69
Richmond Av. E4 CF28 39
Richmond Av. N1 BX37 2
Richmond Av. N1 BX37 56
Richmond Av. NW10 BQ36 55
Richmond Av. SW20 BR51 85
Richmond Av., Felt. BB46 73
Richmond Av., Uxb. AZ36 53
Richmond Bldgs. W1 BW39 1
Richmond Bldgs. W1 BW39 56
Dean St.
Richmond Br., Rich. & Twick. BK46 74
Richmond Clo. E17 CD32 48
Richmond Clo., Chsnt. CC18 21
Dewhurst Rd.
Richmond Clo., Epsom BO60 94
Richmond Clo., Lthd. BF65 102
Richmond Cres. E4 CF28 39
Richmond Cres. N1 BX37 2
Richmond Cres. N1 BY37 56
Richmond Cres. N9 CB26 39
Richmond Cres., Slou. AQ40 52
Richmond Cres., Stai. AV49 72
Richmond Ct. N4 BZ32 48
Wiltshire Gdns.
Richmond Ct. SW20 BP51 85
Richmond Rd.
Richmond Ct., Brox. CD13 12
Richmond Ct., Pot.B. BT19 20
Hatfield Rd.
Richmond Dr., Shep. BA53 83
Richmond Dr., Wat. BB23 26
Richmond Gdns. NW4 BP31 46
Richmond Gdns., Har. BH29 36
Richmond Grn., Croy. BX55 86
Richmond Gro. N1 BY36 56
Halton Rd.
Richmond Gro., Surb. BL53 85
Richmond Hill Ct., Rich. BL46 75
Richmond Hill, Rich. BL46 75
Richmond Ms. W1 BW39 56
Dean St.
Richmond Park Rd. SW14 BN46 75
Richmond Park Rd., Kings.T. BL51 85
Richmond Pl. SE18 CM42 68
Richmond Rd. E11 CF34 48
Richmond Rd. E17 CD32 48
Richmond Rd. E4 CF26 39
Richmond Rd. E7 CH35 49
Richmond Rd. E8 CA36 57
Richmond Rd. N11 BX29 38
Richmond Rd. N15 CA32 48
Richmond Rd. N2 BT30 38
Brighton Rd.
Richmond Rd. N3 BT30 38
Chamberlain Rd.
Richmond Rd. SW20 BP51 85
Richmond Rd. W5 BL41 65
Richmond Rd., Barn. BT25 29
Richmond Rd., Couls. BV61 104
Richmond Rd., Croy. BX55 86
Richmond Rd., Grays DE43 71
Richmond Rd., Ilf. CM34 49
Richmond Rd., Islw. BJ45 64
Richmond Rd., Kings.T. BK49 74
Richmond Rd., Pot.B. BT19 20
Richmond Rd., Rom. CT32 50
Richmond Rd., Stai. AV49 72
Richmond Rd., Th.Hth. BY52 86
Richmond Rd., Twick. BJ47 74
Richmond St. E13 CH37 58
Richmond Ter. Ms. SW1 BX41 4
Richmond Ter. Ms. SW1 BX41 66
Parliament St.
Richmond Ter. SW1 BX41 4
Richmond Ter. SW1 BX41 66
Richmond Way E11 CH34 49
Richmond Way W12 BQ41 65
Richmond Way W14 BQ41 65
Richmond Way, Lthd. BF65 102
Richmond Way, Rick. BA24 26
Richmount Gdns. SE3 CH45 68
Rickard Clo. SW2 BX47 76
Rickard Clo., West Dr. AX41 63
Rickards Clo., Surb. BL54 85
Ricketts Hill Rd., West. CJ62 106
Ricketts St. SW6 BS43 66
Rickfield Clo., Hat. BP13 10
Woods Av.
Rickford Hill., Guil. AO66 109
Rickman Cres., Wey. AW55 83
Rickman Hill Rd., Couls. BV62 104
Rickman Hill, Couls. BV62 104
Rickman St. E1 CC38 57
Mantos Rd.
Rickmans La., Slou. AP35 43
Rickmansworth By-pass, Rick. AX26 35
Rickmansworth La., Ger.Cr. AS29 34
Rickmansworth Rd., Nthwd. AZ28 35
Rickmansworth Rd., Amer. AO22 25
Rickmansworth Rd., Pnr. BC30 35
Rickmansworth Rd., Rick. AV24 25
Rickmansworth Rd., Uxb. AX30 35
Rickmansworth Rd., Wat. BB24 26
Ricksons La., Lthd. AZ67 110
Rickthorne Rd. N19 BX34 47
Rickyard Path SE9 CK45 68
Rickyard, Guil. AO70 118
Riddell Park Ms., Enf. BY23 29
Bycullah Rd.
Ridding La., Grnf. BH35 45
Riddings La., Harl. CO13 14
Riddlesdown Av., Pur. BZ59 96
Riddlesdown Rd., Pur. BZ59 96
Riddons Rd. SE12 CJ48 78
Ride, The, Brent. BJ42 64
Ride, The, Enf. CC24 30
Ride, The, Lthd. BB66 110
Rider Clo., Sid. CN46 78
Riders Way, Gdse. CC69 114
Ridgdale St. E3 CE37 57
Ridge Av. N21 BZ26 39
Ridge Av., Dart. CT46 79
Ridge Clo. NW4 BQ30 37
Ridge Clo. NW9 BN31 46
Ridge Clo., Bet. BM72 120
Ridge Clo., Houns. BF45 64
Ridge Clo., Wok. AQ64 100
Ridge Crest, Enf. BX23 29
Ridge Green Clo., Red. BX72 121
Ridge Grn., Red. BX72 121
Ridge Hill NW11 BR33 46
Ridge Hill, Pot.B. BN18 19
Ridge La., Wat. BB21 26
Ridge Langley, S.Croy. CB58 96
Ridge Lea, Hem.H. AV13 7
Ridge Pk., Pur. BW58 95
Ridge Pl. SW4 BW45 66
Ridge Rd. N21 BZ26 39
Ridge Rd. N8 BX32 47
Ridge Rd. NW2 BR34 46
Ridge Rd., Mitch. BV50 76
Ridge Rd., Sutt. BR54 85
Ridge St., Wat. BC22 26
Ridge View Clo., Barn. BQ25 28
Ridge Way SE19 CA50 77
Central Hill Est.
Ridge Way, Dart. CT46 79
Ridge Way, Iver AV40 52
Ridge, The, Bex. CQ47 79
Ridge, The, Cat. CE66 114
Ridge, The, Couls. BX60 95
Ridge, The, Epsom BN62 103
Ridge, The, Orp. CM55 88
Ridge, The, Pur. BW58 95
Ridge, The, Surb. BM53 85
Ridge, The, Twick. BG47 74
Ridge, The, Wok. AT62 100
Ridgebrook Rd. SE3 CJ45 68
Ridgebrook Ter. SE3 CJ45 68
Ridgecroft Clo., Bex. CS47 79
Ridgegate Clo., Reig. BT69 121
Ridgehurst Av., Wat. BB20 17
Ridgelands, Lthd. BG65 102
Ridgemead Rd., Egh. AQ48 72
Ridgemount Av., Couls. BV62 104
Ridgemount Av., Croy. CC55 87
Ridgemount Clo. SE20 CB50 77
Ridgemount End, Ger.Cr. AS28 34
Ridgemount Gdns., Enf. BY23 29
Ridgemount, Guil. AQ71 118
Ridgemount, Wey. BB55 83
Ridges, The, Guil. AR73 118
Ridgeview Rd. N20 BS27 38
Ridgeway Av., Barn. BU25 29
Ridgeway Av., Grav. DG48 81
Ridgeway Clo., Dor. BJ72 119
Ridgeway Rd.
Ridgeway Clo., Lthd. BG60 93
Ridgeway Clo., Wok. AR61 100
Ridgeway Cres., Orp. CN55 88
Ridgeway Crescent Gdns., Orp. CN55 88
Ridgeway Ct., Red. BU71 121
Ridgeway Dr., Brom. CH49 78
Ridgeway Dr., Dor. BJ73 119
Ridgeway E., Sid. CN46 78
Ridgeway Gdns. N6 BW33 47
Hornsey La.
Ridgeway Gdns., Ilf. CK32 49
Ridgeway Gdns., Wok. AR61 100
Ridgeway N14 BX27 38
Ridgeway Rd. E4 CF26 39
Ridgeway Rd. N., Islw. BH43 64
Ridgeway Rd., Dor. BJ72 119
Ridgeway Rd., Islw. BH43 64
Ridgeway Rd., Red. BU70 121
Ridgeway W., Sid. CN46 78
Ridgeway Wk., Nthlt. BE36 54
Ridgeway, Berk. AP13 7
Ridgeway, Brom. CH55 88
Ridgeway, Brwd. DD26 122
Ridgeway, Dart. CZ49 80
Ridgeway, Epsom BN59 94
Ridgeway, Felt. BE48 74
Ridgeway, Grays DF42 71
Ridgeway, Rick. AW26 35
Ridgeway, The E4 CE27 39
Ridgeway, The N11 BU28 38
Ridgeway, The N14 BX27 38
Ridgeway, The N3 BS29 38
Ridgeway, The NW11 BR33 46
Ridgeway, The NW7 BP27 37
Ridgeway, The NW9 BN31 46
Ridgeway, The W3 BM41 65
Ridgeway, The, Harold Wood CW30 42
Ridgeway, The, Amer. AO23 25
Ridgeway, The, Croy. BX55 86
Ridgeway, The, Cuff. BV17 20
Ridgeway, The, Enf. BV21 29
Ridgeway, The, Ger.Cr. AR31 43
Ridgeway, The, Gidea Pk. CU31 50
Ridgeway, The, Guil. AT71 118
Ridgeway, The, Kenton BK32 45
Ridgeway, The, Lthd. BG65 102
Ridgeway, The, N.Harrow BE32 45
Ridgeway, The, Oxshott BG60 93
Ridgeway, The, Pot.B. BU21 29
Ridgeway, The, Rad. BH22 27
Ridgeway, The, Ruis. BC33 44
Ridgeway, The, S.Croy. CA58 96
Ridgeway, The, St.Alb. BJ11 9
Ridgeway, The, Stan. BK29 36
Ridgeway, The, Wat. BB22 26
Ridgeway, Walt. BB54 83
Ridgeway, Wdf.Grn. CJ28 40
Ridgeway, Welw.G.C. BS 8 5
Ridgeway, Wok. AR61 100
Ridgewell Clo. N1 BZ37 57
Basire St.
Ridgewell Clo., Dag. CR37 59
Ridgewell Rd. E16 CJ39 58
Ridgewick Ct., Guil. AS71 118
Chesham Rd.
Ridgmont Gdns., Edg. BN28 37
Ridgmont Rd., St.Alb. BH14 9
Ridgmount Gdns. WC1 BW38 56
Ridgmount Gdns. WC1 BW39 1
Ridgmount Pl. WC1 BW39 1
Ridgmount Rd. SW18 BS46 76
Ridgmount St. WC1 BW39 1
Ridgmount St. WC1 BW39 56
Store St.
Ridgway Clo., Wok. AR61 100
Ridgway Gdns. SW19 BQ50 75
Ridgway Ms. SW19 BR50 75
Ridgway Pl. SW19 BR50 75
Ridgway Rd. SW9 BY45 66
Ridgway SW19 BQ50 75
Ridgway, The, Sutt. BT57 95
Ridgway, Wok. AW61 101
Riding Court Rd., Slou. AR43 62
Riding Hill, S.Croy. CB60 96
Riding House St. W1 BV39 1
Riding House St. W1 BV39 56
Riding La., Ton. & Sev. CY71 117
Riding, The NW11 BR33 46
Golders Green Rd.
Riding, The, Wok. AT60 91
Ridings Av. N21 BY24 29
Ridings La., Wok. AZ65 101
Ridings, The W5 BL38 55
Ridings, The, Amer. AO21 25
Ridings, The, Ash. BK62 102
Ridings, The, Chesh. AR21 25
Ridings, The, Cob. BF59 93
Ridings, The, Epsom BO61 103
Ridings, The, Iver AV42 62
Ridings, The, Loug. CJ24 31
Ridings, The, Lthd. BB66 110
Ridings, The, Reig. BT69 121
Ridings, The, Sun. BC51 83
Ridings, The, Surb. BM53 85
Ridings, The, Tad. BR63 103
Ridings, The, West. CK62 106
Ridings, The, Wey. AV57 91
Ridings, The, Wok. AW65 101
Ridlands Clo., Oxt. CK68 115
Ridlands Gro., Oxt. CK68 115
Ridlands Ri., Oxt. CK68 115
Ridler Rd., Enf. CA22 30
Ridley Av. W13 BJ41 64
Ridley Clo., Brom. CG52 88
Ridley Clo., Rom. CU30 41
Ridley Rd. E7 CJ35 49
Ridley Rd. E8 CA35 48
Ridley Rd. NW10 BP37 55
Ridley Rd. SW19 BS50 76
Ridley Rd., Brom. CG52 88
Ridley Rd., Warl. CC62 105
Ridley Rd., Well. CO44 69
Ridley Several SE3 CH44 68
Blackheath Pk.
Ridout St. SE18 CK42 68
Ridsdale Rd. SE20 CB51 87
Ridsdale Rd., Wok. AQ62 100
Riefield Rd. SE9 CM46 78
Riesco Dr., Croy. CC57 96
Riffel Rd. NW2 BQ35 46
Riffhams, Brwd. DD27 122
Rifle Butts Alley, Epsom BO60 94
Rifle Ct. SE11 BY43 4
Kennington Park Rd.
Rifle Pl. W11 BQ40 55
Rifle St. E14 CE39 57
Rigault Rd. SW6 BR44 65
Rigby Clo., Croy. BY55 86
Rigby Gdns., Grays DG42 71
Rigby La., Hayes BA41 63
Rigby Ms., Ilf. CL34 49
Rigden St. E14 CE39 57
Duff St.
Rigeley Rd. NW10 BP38 55
Rigg App. E10 CC33 48
Riggindale Rd. SW16 BW49 76
Riley Rd. SE1 CA41 4
Riley Rd. SE1 CA41 67
Riley Rd., Enf. CC22 30
Riley St. SW10 BT43 66
Rinaldo Rd. SW12 BV47 76
Ring Clo., Brom. CH50 77
Ring Rd., Hayes BC40 53
Ring Way Rd., St.Alb. BG17 18
Ring, The W2 BT40 3
Ring, The W2 BT40 56
Ringcroft St. N7 BY35 47
Madras Pl.
Ringers Rd., Brom. CH52 88
Ringford Rd. SW18 BR46 75
Ringlestone Clo., AY43 63
West Dr.
Ringlewell Clo., Enf. CB23 30
Bishops Clo.
Ringley Park Av., Reig. BT71 121
Ringley Park Rd., Reig. BT70 121
Ringmer Av. SW6 BR44 65
Ringmer Gdns. N19 BX34 47
Ringmer Pl. N21 BZ25 30
Ringmer Way, Brom. CK53 88
Ringmore Dr., Guil. AU69 118
Ringmore Rd., Walt. BD55 84
Ringmore Ri. SE23 CB47 77
Ringshall Rd., Orp. CO52 89
Ringslade Rd. N22 BX30 38
Ringstead Rd. SE6 CE47 77
Ringstead Rd., Sutt. BT56 95
Ringway N11 BW29 38
Ringway, Sthl. BE42 64
Ringwold Clo., Beck. CD50 77
Aldersmead Rd.
Ringwood Av. N2 BU30 38
Ringwood Av., Croy. BX54 86
Ringwood Av., Horn. CV34 51
Ringwood Av., Orp. CP58 98
Ringwood Av., Red. BU69 121
Ringwood Clo., Pnr. BD31 45
Ringwood Gdns. SW15 BP46 75
Ringwood Rd. E17 CD32 48
Ringwood Way N21 BY26 38
Ringwood Way, Hmptn. BF49 74
Ripley Av., Egh. AS50 72
Ripley By-pass, Wok. AV66 109
Ripley Clo., Brom. CK53 88
Ringmer Way
Ripley Clo., Croy. CF57 96
Ripley Clo., Slou. AS42 62
Ripley Gdns. SW14 BN45 65
Ripley Gdns., Sutt. BT56 95
Ripley La., Lthd. AZ66 110
Ripley La., Wok. AY65 101
Ripley Rd. E16 CJ39 58
Ripley Rd., Belv. CR42 69
Ripley Rd., Enf. BZ22 30
Ripley Rd., Guil. AW67 110
Ripley Rd., Hmptn. BF50 74

Ripley Rd., Ilf.	CN34	49
Ripley Vw., Loug.	CL22	31
Ripley Way, Chsnt.	CB18	21
Ripley Way, Hem.H.	AV13	7
Riplington Ct. SW15	BP47	75
Ripon Clo., Guil.	AP69	118
Ripon Clo., Nthlt.	BF36	54
Ripon Gdns., Chess.	BK56	93
Ripon Gdns., Ilf.	CK32	49
Ripon Rd. N17	BZ31	48
Ripon Rd. N9	CB26	39
Ripon Rd. SE18	CL43	68
Ripon Way, B.Wd.	BN24	28
Ripon Way, St.Alb.	BK11	9
Rippersley Rd., Well.	CO44	69
Ripple Rd., Bark.	CM36	58
Ripplevale Gro. N1	**BX36**	**2**
Ripplevale Gro. N1	BX36	56
Rippolson Rd. SE18	CN42	68
Ripston Rd., Ashf.	BA49	73
Risborough Dr., Wor.Pk.	BP54	85
Risborough St. SE1	**BY41**	**4**
Risborough St. SE1	BY41	66
Risdon St. SE16	CC41	67
Rise Park Boul., Rom.	CT30	41
Rise Park Par., Rom.	CT30	41
Rise, The E11	CH32	49
Rise, The N13	BY28	38
Rise, The NW10	BN35	46
Rise, The NW7	BO29	37
Rise, The, Amer.	AO22	25
Rise, The, B.Wd.	BL25	28
Rise, The, Bex.	CP47	79
Rise, The, Buck.H.	CJ26	40
Rise, The, Couls.	BW60	95
Rise, The, Dart.	CT45	69
Rise, The, Edg.	BM28	37
Rise, The, Epsom	BO58	94
Rise, The, Grav.	DJ49	81
Rise, The, Grnf.	BJ35	45
Rise, The, S.Croy.	CC58	96
Rise, The, Sev.	CV67	117
Rise, The, Sid.	CP47	79
Rise, The, St.Alb.	BG16	18
Rise, The, Tad.	BQ64	103
Fairacres		
Rise, The, Uxb.	AY37	53
Risebridge Chase, Rom.	CT29	41
Risebridge Rd., Rom.	CT30	41
Risedale Clo., Hem.H.	AY15	8
Risedale Hill, Hem.H.	AY15	8
Risedale Rd., Bexh.	CR45	69
Risedale Rd., Hem.H.	AY15	8
Riseldine Rd. SE23	CD46	77
Riseway, Brwd.	DC27	122
Rising Hill Clo., Nthwd.	BA29	35
Risinghill St. N1	**BX37**	**2**
Risinghill St. N1	BX37	56
Risingholme Clo., Bush.	BF26	36
Risingholme Clo., Har.	BH30	36
Risingholme Rd., Har.	BH30	36
Risings, The E17	CF31	48
Risley Av. N17	BZ30	39
Rita Rd. SW8	BX43	66
Ritches Rd. N15	BZ32	48
Ritchie Rd., Croy.	CB53	87
Ritchie St. N1	**BY37**	**2**
Ritchie St. N1	BY37	56
Ritchings Av. E17	CD31	48
Ritcroft Clo., Hem.H.	AZ14	8
Ritcroft Dr., Hem.H.	AZ14	8
Ritcroft St.		
Ritcroft St., Hem.H.	AZ14	8
Ritherdon Rd. SW17	BV48	76
Ritson Rd. E8	CB38	57
Ritter St. SE18	CL43	68
Ritz Ct., Pot.B.	BS19	20
Rivaz Pl. E9	CC36	57
Rivenhall End, Welw.G.C.	BT8	5
Rivenhall Gdns. E18	CG31	49
River Av. N13	BY27	38
River Av., Hodd.	CE11	12
River Av., T.Ditt.	BJ54	84
River Bank N21	BZ26	39
River Bank SE10	CF41	67
River Bank, T.Ditt.	BH52	84
River Barge Clo. E14	CF41	67
Stewart St.		
River Clo. E11	CJ32	49
River Clo., Rain.	CU39	59
River Clo., Ruis.	BB32	44
River Clo., Surb.	BK53	84
River Clo., Wal.Cr.	CE20	21
River Dr., Upmin.	CY32	51
River Front, Enf.	BZ24	30
River Gdns., Cars.	BV55	86
River Gdns., Felt.	BD46	74
River Gdns., Maid.	AH41	61
River Grove Pk., Beck.	CD51	87
River Hill, Sev.	CW68	117
River La., Lthd.	BG64	102
River La., Rich.	BK47	74
River Mead Ct. SW6	BR45	65
Ranelagh Gdns.		
River Meads Av., Twick.	BF48	74
River Meads Est., Twick.	BF48	74
River Nook Clo., Walt.	BD53	84
River Park Gdns., Brom.	CF50	77
River Park Rd. N22	BX30	38
River Pk., Hem.H.	AW14	8
River Pl. N1	**BZ36**	**2**
River Pl. N1	BZ36	57
River Rd., Bark.	CN37	58
River Rd., Brwd.	CZ28	42
River Rd., Buck.H.	CK26	40
River Rd., Stai.	AV51	82
River Reach, Tedd.	BK49	74
Broom Water		
River St. EC1	**BY38**	**2**
River St. EC1	BY38	56
River St., Wind.	AO43	61
River Ter. W6	BQ42	65
Crisp Rd.		
River Ter., Berk.	AQ12	7
River View Gdns. SW13	BP43	65
River View Gdns., Twick.	BH48	74
River Vw., Enf.	BZ24	30
River Vw., Welw.G.C.	BR6	5
River Way SE10	CG41	68
River Way, Epsom	BN56	94
River Way, Loug.	CK25	31
River Way, Twick.	BF48	74
River Wk., Uxb.	AX35	44
River Wk., Walt.	BC53	83
Riverbank, E.Mol.	BH52	84
Rivercourt Rd. W6	BP42	65
Riverdale Dr., Wok.	AS64	100
Riverdale Gdns., Twick.	BK46	74
Riverdale Rd. SE18	CN42	68
Riverdale Rd., Bex.	CQ47	79
Riverdale Rd., Erith	CR42	69
Riverdale Rd., Felt.	BE49	74
Riverdale Rd., Twick.	BK46	74
Riverdale SE13	CF45	67
Riverdell Clo., Cher.	AV54	82
Riverdene Rd., Ilf.	CL34	49
Riverdene, Edg.	BN27	37
Riverfield La., Saw.	CQ5	6
Riverfield Rd., Stai.	AV50	72
Riverhead Clo. E17	CC30	39
Riverholme Dr., Epsom	BN58	94
Rivermead Clo., Tedd.	BJ49	74
Rivermead Clo., Wey.	AX57	92
Rivermead, Wey.	AY60	92
Rivermill, Harl.	CM10	6
Rivermount Gdns., Guil.	AR72	118
Rivermount, Walt.	BB54	83
Riverpark Av., Egh.	AU49	72
Rivers End Rd., Hem.H.	AX15	8
Riversdale Rd. N5	BY34	47
Riversdale Rd., Rom.	CR29	41
Riversdale Rd., Surb.	BJ53	84
Riversdale, Grav.	DF48	81
Riversdell Clo., Cher.	AV54	82
Riversfield Rd., Enf.	CA24	30
Riverside Av., Brox.	CE14	12
Riverside Av., E.Mol.	BG53	84
Riverside Clo. W7	BH38	54
Riverside Clo., Kings L.	AZ18	17
Riverside Clo., Kings.T.	BK52	84
Riverside Clo., Orp.	CP51	89
Riverside Clo., St.Alb.	BH14	9
Riverside Clo., Stai.	AV50	72
Riverside Clo., Wall.	BV55	86
Riverside Dr. W4	BN43	65
Riverside Dr.,	AV49	72
Egham Hythe		
Riverside Dr., Esher	BF56	93
Riverside Dr., Mitch.	BU53	86
Riverside Dr., Rich.	BJ48	74
Riverside Dr., Rick.	AX26	35
Riverside Dr., Stai.	AV51	82
Riverside Gdns. W6	BP42	65
Riverside Gdns., Berk.	AQ12	7
Riverside Gdns., Enf.	BZ23	30
Riverside Gdns., Wem.	BL37	55
Riverside Gdns., Wok.	AT64	100
High St.		
Riverside NW4	BP33	46
Riverside Path, Chsnt.	CC18	21
Riverside Pl., Stai.	AX46	73
Riverside Rd. E15	CF37	57
Riverside Rd. N15	CB32	48
Riverside Rd. SW17	BS49	76
Riverside Rd., Sid.	CQ48	79
Riverside Rd., St.Alb.	BH14	9
Riverside Rd., Stai.	AV50	72
Riverside Rd., Stanwell	AX46	73
Riverside Rd., Walt.	BE56	93
Riverside Rd., Wat.	BC25	26
Riverside SE7	CH41	68
Riverside Way, Dart.	CW46	80
Riverside Way, Uxb.	AW37	53
Riverside Wk. E5	CC34	48
Riverside Wk. SE1	**BX41**	**4**
Riverside Wk. SE1	BX41	66
Riverside Wk., Bex.	CP47	79
Riverside Wk., Dart.	CW48	80
Riverside Wk., Islw.	BH45	64
Riverside, Dor.	BK70	119
Riverside, Eyns.	CV55	90
Riverside, Guil.	AR69	118
Riverside, Runnymede	AT48	72
Riverside, Shep.	BB54	83
Riverside, Stai.	AV51	82
Riverside, Twick.	BJ47	74
Riverside, Wraysbury	AR47	72
Riversmead, Hodd.	CE12	12
Riverton Clo. W9	BR38	55
Riverview Gro. W4	BM43	65
Riverview Pk. SE6	CE48	77
Riverview Rd. W4	BM43	65
Riverview Rd., Epsom	BN56	94
Riverview Rd., Green.	DA46	80
Riverview, Grays	DF42	71
Riverway N13	BY28	38
Riverway, Harl.	CO9	6
Riverway, Stai.	AW51	83
Riverwood La., Chis.	CM51	88
Rivett Drake Rd., Guil.	AQ58	109
Rivey Clo., Wey.	AV60	91
Rivington Av., Wdf.Grn.	CJ30	40
Rivington Cres. NW9	BO29	37
Rivington Ct. NW10	BP37	55
Longstone Av.		
Rivington Pl. EC2	**CA38**	**2**
Rivington St. EC2	**CA38**	**2**
Rivington St. EC2	CA38	57
Rivington Wk. E8	CB37	57
Wilde Clo.		
Rivulet Rd. N17	BZ29	39
Rixon Clo., Slou.	AS39	52
Rixon Ho. SE18	CL43	68
Rixsen Rd. E12	CK35	49
Roach Rd. E3	CE36	57
Roads Pl. N19	BX34	47
Roakes Av., Wey.	AW55	83
Roan St. SE10	CE43	67
Roasthill La., Wind.	AL43	61
Robart House E11	CG33	49
Robarts Clo., Ruis.	BC32	44
Field End Rd.		
Robb Rd., Stan.	BJ29	36
Robbs Clo., Hem.H.	AW12	8
Robe End, Hem.H.	AV12	7
Robert Adam St. W1	BV39	56
Robert Av., St.Alb.	BF15	9
Robert Clo. W9	**BT38**	**1**
Robert Clo. W9	BT38	56
Robert Clo., Chig.	CN28	40
Robert Clo., Pot.B.	BR20	19
Robert Clo., Walt.	BC56	92
Robert Dashwood Way SE17	**BZ42**	**4**
Robert Gentry Ho. W14	BR42	65
Robert Keen Clo. SE15	CB44	67
CicelyRd.		
Robert Lowe Clo. SE14	CC43	67
Robert Ms. NW1	BW38	56
Hampstead Rd.		
Robert Owen Ho. SW6	BQ44	65
Robert Rd., Slou.	AO34	43
Robert St. E16	CL40	58
Robert St. E2	CB37	57
Old Bethnal Green Rd.		
Robert St. NW1	**BV38**	**1**
Robert St. NW1	BV38	56
Robert St. SE18	CM42	68
Robert St. WC2	**BX40**	**4**
Robert St. WC2	BX40	56
Savoy Pl.		
Robert St., Croy.	BZ55	87
High St.		
Roberta St. E2	**CB38**	**2**
Roberta St. E2	CB38	57
Roberton Dr., Brom.	CJ51	88
Roberts Alley W5	BK41	64
Church Gdns.		
Roberts Clo. SE9	CM47	78
Beaverbank Rd.		
Roberts Clo., Rom.	CU30	41
Roberts Clo., Stai.	AX46	73
Park Rd.		
Roberts Clo., Sutt.	BQ57	94
Roberts Clo., West Dr.	AY40	53
Roberts Clo.,Orp.	CP53	89
Sholden Gdns.		
Roberts La., Ger.Cr.	AT28	34
Roberts Ms. SW1	**BV41**	**3**
Lowndes Pl.		
Roberts Pl. EC1	**BY38**	**2**
Bowling Green La.		
Roberts Rd. E17	CE30	39
Roberts Rd. NW7	BR29	37
Roberts Rd., Belv.	CR42	69
Roberts St., Wat.	BD25	27
Roberts Way, Egh.	AR50	72
Roberts Way, Hat.	BO13	10
Roberts Wood Dr.,	AS28	34
Ger.Cr.		
Robertsbridge Rd.,	BT54	86
Cars.		
Robertson Clo., Brox.	CD16	21
Robertson Rd. E15	CF37	57
Robertson St. SW8	BV45	66
Robeson St. E3	CD39	57
Ackroyd Dr.		
Robin Clo. NW7	BO27	37
Robin Clo., Hmptn.	BE49	74
Robin Clo., Rom.	CS29	41
Robin Clo., Wey.	AW56	92
Robin Cres. E6	CJ39	58
Robin Gdns., Red.	BV69	121
Kingfisher Dr.		
Robin Gro. N6	BV34	47
Robin Gro., Brent.	BK43	64
Robin Gro., Har.	BL32	46
Robin Hill Dr., Chis.	CK50	78
Wood Dr.		
Robin Hill, Berk.	AR13	7
St. Edmunds		
Robin Hood Clo., Mitch.	BW52	86
Robin Hood Clo., Slou.	AM40	61
Robin Hood Clo., Wok.	AP62	100
Robin Hood Cres., Wok.	AP62	100
Robin Hood Dr., Bush.	BE23	27
Robin Hood Dr., Har.	BH29	36
Robin Hood Grn., Orp.	CO53	89
Robin Hood La. E14	CF39	57
Robin Hood La. SW15	BO48	75
Robin Hood La., Bexh.	CQ46	79
Robin Hood La., Guil.	AS65	100
Robin Hood La., Hat.	BP12	10
The Common		
Robin Hood La., Mitch.	BW52	86
Robin Hood La., Sutt.	BS56	95
Robin Hood Meadow,	AY11	8
Hem.H.		
Robin Hood Rd. SW19	BO49	75
Robin Hood Rd., Brwd.	DB26	42
Robin Hood Rd., Wok.	AP62	100
Robin Hood Way SW15	BO49	75
Robin Hood Way SW20	BO49	75
Robin Hood Way, Grnf.	BH36	54
Robin Hood Yd. EC1	BY39	56
Leather La.		
Robin Mead, Welw.G.C.	BS6	5
Robin Rd., Hem.H.	AZ14	8
Robin St. SW3	BU42	66
Flood St.		
Robin St. SW3	**BU43**	**3**
Robin Way, Cuff.	BX17	20
Robin Way, Guil.	AQ68	109
Robin Way, Orp.	CO52	89
Robin Way, Stai.	AW48	72
Robina Clo., Bexh.	CP45	69
Brunswick Rd.		
Robinia Av., Grav.	DE47	81
Robinia Clo., Chig.	CN28	40
Robins Clo., Uxb.	AX39	53
Robins Ct. SE12	CJ48	78
Robins Ct., Beck.	CF51	87
Robins Dale, Wok.	AO62	100
Robins Gro., Kes.	CH55	88
Robins La., Epp.	CM21	31
Robins Nest Hill, Hert.	BW11	11
Robins Orchard, Ger.Cr.	AS29	34
Robins Way, Hat.	BO14	10
Robins, The, Brwd.	DB21	33
Robinscroft Ms. SE10	CE44	67
Sparta St.		
Robinsfield, Hem.H.	AW13	8
Robinson Av., Chsnt.	BY17	20
Robinson Cres., Bush.	BG27	36
Robinson Rd. E2	CC37	57
Robinson Rd. SW17	BU50	76
Robinson Rd., Dag.	CR35	50
Robinson St. SW3	BU43	66
Christchurch St.		
Robinsons Clo. W13	BJ39	54
Robinsway, Wal.Abb.	CG20	22
Roundhills		
Robinsway, Walt.	BD56	93
Robinwood Pl. SW15	BN49	75
Robsart St. SW9	BX44	66
Robson Av. NW10	BP36	55
Robson Clo. E6	CK39	58
Linton Gdns.		
Robson Clo., Enf.	BY23	29
Robson Clo., Ger.Cr.	AS28	34
Robson Rd. SE27	BY48	76
Robsons Clo., Chsnt.	CC18	21
Robsons Clo., Wal.Cr.	CC18	21
Robyns Cft., Grav.	DE48	81
Peach Cft.		
Robyns Way, Sev.	CT64	107
Roch Av., Edg.	BL30	37
Rochdale Rd. E17	CE33	48
Rochdale Rd. SE2	CO42	69
Rochdale Way SE8	CD43	67
Idonia St.		
Roche Rd. SW16	BX51	86
Roche Wk., Cars.	BT53	86
Rochelle Clo. SW11	BT45	66
Nantes Clo.		
Rochelle St. E2	**CA38**	**2**
Rochelle St. E2	CA38	57
Swanfield St.		
Rochemont Wk. E8	CA37	57
Broadway Market Est.		
Rochester Av. E13	CJ37	58
Rochester Av., Brom.	CH51	88
Rochester Av., Felt.	BB48	73
Rochester Clo. SW16	BX50	76
Rochester Clo., Enf.	CA23	30
Rochester Clo., Sid.	CO46	79
Rochester Dr., Bex.	CR46	79
Rochester Dr., Pnr.	BD32	45
Rochester Gdns., Croy.	CA55	87
Rochester Gdns., Ilf.	CK33	49
Rochester Ms. NW1	BW36	56
Rochester Rd.		
Rochester Pl. NW1	BW36	56
Rochester Rd. NW1	BW36	56
Rochester Rd., Cars.	BU56	95
Rochester Rd., Dart.	CX47	80
Rochester Rd., Grav.	DJ47	81
Rochester Rd., Nthwd.	BB31	44
Rochester Row SW1	**BW42**	**3**
Rochester Row SW1	BW42	66
Rochester Sq. NW1	BW36	56
Rochester St. SW1	**BW41**	**3**
Rochester St. SW1	BW42	66
Rochester Row		
Rochester Ter. NW1	BW36	56
Rochester Way Relief Rd. SE9	CL45	68
Rochester Way SE3	CJ45	68
Rochester Way SE9	CK45	68
Rochester Way, Dart.	CT47	79
Rochester Way, Rick.	AZ24	26
Rochester Wk., Reig.	BS73	121
Castle Dr.		
Rochford Av., Brwd.	DD25	122
Rochford Av., Loug.	CM24	31
Rochford Av., Rom.	CP32	50
Rochford Av., Wal.Abb.	CF20	21
Rochford Clo. E6	CJ37	58
Boleyn Rd.		
Rochford Clo., Brox.	CD16	21
Rochford Clo., Horn.	CU36	59
Rochford Grn., Loug.	CM24	31
Rochford St. NW5	BU35	47
Rochford Way, Croy.	BX53	86
Rochford Wk. E8	CB36	57
Wilman Gro.		
Rochfords Gdns., Slou.	AR40	52
Rock Av. SW14	BN45	65
South Worple Way		
Rock Gdns., Dag.	CR35	50
Rock Grove Way SE16	CB42	67
Blue Anchor La.		
Rock Hill SE26	CA49	77
Rock Hill, Orp.	CR57	98
Rock La., Dag.	CR36	59
Rock St. N4	BY34	47
Rockbourne Rd. SE23	CC47	77
Rockchase Gdns., Horn.	CW32	51
Rockcliffe Av., Kings L.	AZ18	17
Rockdale Rd., Sev.	CU66	116
Rockells Pl. SE22	CB46	77
Rockfield Clo., Oxt.	CG69	115
Rockfield Rd., Oxt.	CG68	115
Rockford Av., Grnf.	BJ37	54
Rockhall Rd. NW2	BQ35	46
Rockhampton Rd. SE27	BY49	76
Rockhampton Rd.,	BZ57	96
S.Croy.		
Rockingham Av., Horn.	CU32	50
Rockingham Clo. SW15	BO45	65
Rockingham Clo., Uxb.	AX37	53
Rockingham Est. SE1	**BZ41**	**4**
Rockingham Est. SE1	BZ41	67
Rockingham Par., Uxb.	AX36	53
Rockingham Rd., Uxb.	AX37	53
Rockingham St. SE1	**BZ41**	**4**
Rockingham St. SE1	BZ41	67
Rockland Rd. SW15	BR45	65
Rocklands Dr., Stan.	BJ30	36
Rockley Rd. W14	BQ41	65
Rockmead Rd. E9	CC37	57
Rockmount Rd. SE18	CN42	68
Rockmount Rd. SE19	BZ50	77
Rocks La. SW13	BP44	65
Rockshaw Rd., Red.	BW67	113
Rockware Av., Grnf.	BH37	54
Rockways, Barn.	BO25	28
Rockwell Gdns., Dag.	CR35	50
Rockwell Rd., Dag.	CR35	50
Rockwells Ct. SE19	CA49	77
Rockwells Gdns. SE19	CA49	77
Rockwood Gdns.,	CH27	40
Wdf.Grn.		
Whitehall La.		
Rockwood Pl. W12	BQ41	65
Shepherds Bush Grn.		
Rocky La., Reig.	BU67	113
Rocliffe St. N1	**BY37**	**2**
Rocliffe St. N1	BY37	56
Rocombe Cres. SE23	CC47	77
Rocque La. SE3	CG45	68
Rodborough Rd. NW11	BS33	47
Roden Clo., Harl.	CQ9	6
Roden Gdns., Croy.	CA53	87
Roden St. N7	BX34	47
Roden St., Ilf.	CL34	49
Roden Way, Ilf.	CL34	49
Roden St.		
Rodenhurst Rd. SW4	BW46	76
Roderick Rd. NW3	BU35	47
Rodgers Clo., B.Wd.	BK25	27
Roding Av., Wdf.Grn.	CK29	40
Roding Clo., Ong.	CY14	15
Roding Ho., Wdf.Grn.	CK29	40
Roding La. N., Wdf.Grn.	CJ30	40
Roding La. S., Ilf.	CJ31	49
Roding La., Buck.H.	CJ27	40
Roding Ms. E1	CB40	57
Kennet St.		
Roding Rd. E5	CC35	48
Roding Rd. E6	CL39	58
Roding Rd., Loug.	CK25	31
Roding St. E7	CH35	49
Oakhurst Rd.		
Roding Trd. Est., Bark.	CL36	58
Roding Vw., Buck.H.	CJ26	40
Roding Vw., Ong.	CX17	24
Roding Way, Rain.	CV37	60
Briscoe Rd.		
Rodings Clo., Ong.	CY14	15
Ongar Rd.		
Rodings, The, Upmin.	CY32	51
Rodings, The, Wdf.Grn.	CJ29	40
Snakes La.		
Rodmarton St. W1	**BU39**	**1**
Rodmarton St. W1	BU39	56
Rodmell Clo., Hayes	BE38	54
Ditchfield Rd.		
Rodmell Slope N12	BR28	37
Rodmere St. SE10	CG42	68
Rodmill La. SW2	BX47	76
Rodney Av., St.Alb.	BJ14	9
Rodney Clo., Croy.	BY54	86
Rodney Clo., N.Mal.	BO52	85
Rodney Clo., Pnr.	BE33	45
Rodney Clo., Walt.	BD55	84
Rodney Rd.		
Rodney Cres., Hodd.	CE11	12
Rodney Gdns., Pnr.	BC32	44
Rodney Gdns., W.Wick.	CH56	97
Rodney Grn., Walt.	BD55	84
Rodney Rd.		
Rodney Pl. E17	CD30	39
Rodney Pl. SE17	**BZ42**	**4**
Rodney Pl. SE17	BZ42	67
Rodney Pl. SW19	BT51	86
Rodney Rd. E11	CH31	49
Rodney Rd. SE17	**BZ42**	**4**
Rodney Rd. SE17	BZ42	67
Rodney Rd., Mitch.	BU51	86
Rodney Rd., N.Mal.	BO53	85
Rodney Rd., Ong.	CW18	24
Rodney Rd., Twick.	BF46	74
Rodney Rd., Walt.	BC55	83
Rodney St. N1	**BX37**	**2**
Rodney St. N1	BX37	56
Rodney St. SE18	CL41	68
Rodney Way, Guil.	AT70	118
Rodney Way, Rom.	CR30	41
Rodney Way, Slou.	AV44	62
Rodona Rd., Wey.	BA59	92
Rodsley Pl. SE15	CB44	67
Commercial Way		
Rodsley St. SE1	CB43	67
Old Kent Rd.		
Rodway Rd. SW15	BP47	75
Rodwell Clo., Ruis.	BD33	45
Rodwell Pl., Edg.	BM29	37
Rodwell Rd. SE22	CA46	77
Roe End NW9	BN31	46
Roe Fields Clo., Hem.H.	AW15	8
Roe Green Clo., Hat.	BO13	10
Roe Green La., Hat.	BO12	10
Roe Grn. NW9	BN32	46
Roe Hill Clo., Hat.	BO13	10
Roe La. NW9	BM31	46
Roe Way, Wall.	BX57	95
Roebourne Way E16	CL40	58
Pier Rd.		
Roebuck Clo. N17	CA29	39
High Rd.		
Roebuck Clo., Ash.	BL63	103
Roebuck Clo., Felt.	BC49	73
Roebuck Grn., Slou.	AM40	61
Roebuck La., Buck.H.	CJ26	40
Roebuck Rd., Chess.	BM56	94
Roebuck Rd., Ilf.	CO28	41
Roedean Av., Enf.	CC23	30
Roedean Clo., Enf.	CC23	30
Roedean Clo., Orp.	CO56	98
Roedean Cres. SW15	BO46	75
Roehampton Clo. SW15	BP45	65
Roehampton Clo., Grav.	DJ47	81
Roehampton Dr., Chis.	CM50	78
Roehampton Gate SW15	BO46	75
Roehampton High St.	BP47	75
SW15		
Roehampton La. SW15	BP45	65
Roehampton Vale SW15	BO48	75
Roestock Gdns., St.Alb.	BO14	10
Roestock La., St.Alb.	BN15	10
Rofant Rd., Nthwd.	BB29	35
Roffes La., Cat.	BZ66	114
Roffey Clo., Pur.	BY61	104
Roffey St. E14	CF41	67

Roffords Clo., Wok. AQ62 100
Roffords, Wok. AQ62 100
Marston Rd.
Rogate Ho. E5 CB34 48
Downs Est.
Roger Simmons Ct., Lthd. BE65 102
Roger St. WC1 BX38 2
Roger St. WC1 BX38 56
Rogers Clo., Cat. CB64 105
Rogers Clo., Couls. BY62 104
Rogers Ct., Swan. CU52 89
London Rd.
Rogers Gdns., Dag. CR35 50
Rogers La., Slou. AP36 52
Rogers Mead, Gdse. CB69 114
Rogers Rd. E16 CG39 58
Rogers Rd. SW17 BT49 76
Rogers Rd., Dag. CR35 50
Rogers Rd., Grays DE42 71
Rogers Ruff, Nthwd. BA30 35
Rogers Wk. N12 BS27 38
Brook Meadow
Rogers Wood La., Fawk. DA56 99
Rojack Rd. SE23 CC47 77
Roke Clo., Ken. BZ60 96
Roke Lodge Rd., Ken. BY60 95
Roke Rd., Ken. BY61 104
Rokeby Ct., Wok. AP62 100
Rokeby Gdns., Wdf.Grn. CH30 40
Rokeby Pl. SW20 BP50 75
Rokeby Rd. SE4 CD44 67
Rokeby St. E15 CF37 57
Roker Park Av., Uxb. AY35 44
Rokesby Clo., Well. CM44 68
Rokesby Clo., Wem. BK35 45
Rokesby Pl., Wem. BK35 45
Rokesly Av. N8 BX32 47
Roland Gdns. SW7 BT42 3
Roland Gdns. SW7 BT42 66
Roland Gdns., Felt. BE48 74
Roland Ms. E1 CE39 57
Stepney Grn.
Roland Rd. E17 CF32 48
Roland St., St.Alb. BJ13 9
Roland Way SE17 BZ42 4
Roland Way SE17 BZ42 67
Roland Way SW7 BT42 3
Roland Way SW7 BT42 66
Roland Way, Wor.Pk. BO55 85
Roles Gro., Rom. CP31 50
Rolfe Clo., Barn. BU24 29
Rolfe Rd. SE7 CK42 68
Rolinsden Way, Kes. CJ56 97
Roll Gdns., Ilf. CL32 49
Rollesby Rd., Chess. BM57 94
Rollesby Way SE28 CP40 59
Rolleston Av., Orp. CL53 88
Rolleston Clo., Orp. CL54 88
Rolleston Rd., S.Croy. BZ57 96
Rollins St. SE15 CC43 67
Rollit Cres., Houns. BF46 74
Rollit St. N7 BY35 47
Rollo Rd., Swan. CT50 79
Rolls Bldgs. EC4 BY39 2
Rolls Bldgs. EC4 BY39 56
Fetter La.
Rolls Park Av. E4 CE28 39
Rolls Park Rd. E4 CE28 39
Rolls Pass. EC4 BY39 2
Rolls Pass. EC4 BY39 56
Chancery La.
Rolls Rd. SE1 CA42 4
Rolls Rd. SE1 CA42 67
Rollscourt Av. SE24 BZ46 77
Rollswood, Welw.G.C. BR 9 5
Rolt St. SE8 CD43 67
Rolvenden Gdns., Brom. CJ50 78
Rom Cres., Rom. CT33 50
Rom Valley Way, Rom. CT33 50
Roma Rd. E17 CD31 48
Roma Read Clo. SW15 BP47 75
Roman Clo. W3 BM41 65
Roman Clo., Felt. BD46 74
Roman Clo., Green. CZ46 80
Thamesview Clo.
Roman Clo., Rain. CS37 59
Roman Clo., Uxb. AW30 35
Roman Gdns., Kings L. AZ18 17
Roman Rd. E2 CC38 57
Roman Rd. E3 CC38 57
Roman Rd. E6 CK38 58
Roman Rd. N10 BV29 38
Roman Rd. W4 BO42 65
Roman Rd., Dor. BJ72 119
Roman Rd., Epsom BL65 103
Roman Rd., Grav. DE48 81
Roman Rd., Ilf. CL36 58
Roman Rise SE19 BZ50 77
Roman Sq. SE28 CO40 59
Roman St., Hodd. CE11 12
Roman Vale, Harl. CP 8 6
Roman Villa Rd., S.Dnth. CY50 80
Roman Way N7 BX36 56
Roman Way SE15 CC43 67
Clifton Way
Roman Way, Croy. BY55 86
Roman Way, Dart. CT46 79
Roman Way, Enf. CA25 30
Romanhurst Av., Brom. CG52 88
Romanhurst Gdns., Brom. CG52 88
Romans End, St.Alb. BG14 9
Romans Way, Wok. AW61 101
Romany Gdns. E17 CD30 39
McEntee Av.
Romany Gdns., Sutt. BS54 86
Romany Rd., Grav. DF48 81
Romany Rd., Wok. AO60 91
Romany Ri., Orp. CM54 88
Romberg Rd. SW17 BV48 76
Romborough Gdns. SE13 CF46 77
Romborough Way SE13 CE46 77
Romeland Hill, St.Alb. BG13 9
Romeland, St.Alb. CF20 21
Romeland, Wal.Abb. CF20 21
Romero Clo. SW9 BX45 66
Stockwell Rd.
Romero Sq. SE3 CJ45 68
Romeyn Rd. SW16 BX48 76
Romford Cres., Rom. CT33 50
Romford Rd. E12 CG36 58
Romford Rd. E15 CG36 58
Romford Rd. E7 CG36 58
Romford Rd., Chig. CO27 41
Romford Rd., Ong. CW19 24
Romford Rd., Rom. CQ29 41
Romford Rd., S.Ock. CW39 60
Romford St. E1 CY39 57
Romilly Dr., Wat. BE28 36
Romilly Rd. N4 BY34 47
Romilly St. W1 BW40 3
Romilly St. W1 BW40 56
Rommany Rd. SE27 BZ49 77
Romney Chase, Horn. CX32 51
Romney Clo. N17 CB30 39
Romney Clo. NW11 BT33 47
Romney Clo. SE14 CC43 67
Romney Clo., Ashf. BA49 73
Romney Clo., Chess. BL56 94
Romney Clo., Har. BF33 45
Romney Dr., Brom. CJ50 78
Romney Dr., Har. BF33 45
Romney Gdns., Bexh. CQ44 69
Romney Lock Rd., Wind. AP43 62
Romney Rd. SE10 CF43 67
Romney Rd., Hayes BA37 53
Romney Rd., N.Mal. BN53 85
Romney St. SW1 BW41 3
Romney St. SW1 BW41 66
Romola Rd. SE24 BY47 76
Romsey Clo., Orp. CL56 97
Broadwater Gdns.
Romsey Clo., Slou. AS41 62
Romsey Dr., Slou. AO34 43
Romsey Gdns., Dag. CP37 59
Romsey Rd. W13 BJ40 54
Romsey Rd., Dag. CP37 59
Rona Rd. NW3 BV35 47
Rona Wk. N1 BZ36 57
Marquess Est.
Ronald Av. E15 CG38 58
Ronald Clo., Beck. CD52 87
Ronald Rd., Rom. CX30 42
Ronald St. E1 CE39 57
Devonport St.
Ronalds Rd. N5 BY35 47
Ronalds Rd., Brom. CH51 88
Ronaldstone Rd., Sid. CN46 78
Ronart St., Har. BH31 45
Rondu Rd. NW2 BR35 46
Ronelean Rd., Surb. BL55 85
Roneo Cor., Rom. CT33 50
Roneo Link, Horn. CT33 50
Ronfearn Av., Orp. CP53 89
Ronneby Clo., Wey. BB55 83
Ronson Way, Lthd. BJ64 102
Ronver Rd. SE12 CG47 78
Rood La. EC3 CA40 4
Rood La. EC3 CA40 57
Rook Clo., Rain. CU37 59
Rook Dean, Sev. CS64 107
Rook Hill, Cat. BY65 104
Rook La., Cat. BX65 104
Rook Wk. E6 CK39 58
Allhallows Rd.
Rooke Way SE10 CG42 68
Glenister Rd.
Rookeries Clo., Felt. BC48 73
Rookery Clo. NW9 BO32 46
Rookery Clo., Grays DA43 70
The Rookery
Rookery Clo., Lthd. BG65 102
Rookery Cres., Dag. CR36 59
Rookery Ct., Grays DA43 70
The Rookery
Rookery Dr., Chis. CL51 88
Rookery Dr., Dor. BF72 119
Rookery Gdns., Orp. CP53 89
Rookery Hill, Ash. BM62 103
Rookery La., Brom. CJ53 88
Rookery La., Grays DE42 71
Rookery La., Wal.Abb. CF18 21
Rookery Rd. SW4 BW45 66
Rookery Rd., Ing. DB17 24
Rookery Rd., Orp. CK58 97
Rookery Rd., Stai. AW49 73
Rookery Vw., Grays DE42 71
Rookery Way NW9 BO32 46
Rookery Way, Tad. BR67 112
Rookery, The, Dor. BF72 119
Rookery, The, Grays DA43 70
Rookery, The, Wat. BC26 35
Rookesley Rd., Orp. CP54 89
Rookfield Av. N10 BW31 47
Rookfield Clo. N10 BW31 47
Cranmore Way
Rookley Clo., Sutt. BS58 95
Hulverston Clo.
Rooks Hill, Rick. AX24 26
Rooks Hill, Sev. CY68 117
Rooks Hill, Welw.G.C. BQ 8 5
Rooksmead Rd., Sun. BB51 83
Rookstone Rd. SW17 BU49 76
Rookwood Av., Loug. CM24 31
Rookwood Av., N.Mal. BP52 85
Rookwood Av., Wall. BW56 95
Rookwood Clo., Grays DD42 71
Rookwood Clo., Red. BV68 113
Rookwood Ct., Guil. AR72 118
Rookwood Gdns. E4 CG27 40
Whitehall Rd.
Rookwood Gdns., Ilf. CO29 41
Rookwood Gdns., Loug. CM24 31
Rookwood Rd. N16 CA32 48
Roosevelt Way, Dag. CS36 59
Roothill La., Bet. BM73 120
Rope Maker Rd. SE16 CD41 67
Rope St. SE16 CD41 67
Rope Walk Gdns. E1 CB39 57
Commercial Rd.
Rope Wk., Sun. BD52 84
Rope Yard Rails SE18 CL41 68
Ropemaker St. EC2 BZ39 2
Ropemaker St. EC2 BZ39 57
Ropemakers Flds. E14 CD40 57
Roper La. SE1 CA41 4
Roper La. SE1 CA41 67
Roper St. SE9 CK46 78
Roper Way, Mitch. BV51 86
Ropers Av. E4 CE28 39
Ropery St. E3 CD38 57
Ropley St. E2 CB37 2
Ropley St. E2 CB37 57
Shipton St.
Rosa Alba Ms. N5 BZ35 48
Kelross Rd.
Rosa Av., Ashf. AZ49 73
Rosalind Franklin Clo., Guil. AP71 118
Rosaline Rd. SW6 BR43 65
Rosamond St. SE26 CB48 77
Rosary Clo., Houns. BE44 64
Rosary Ct., Pot.B. BS18 20
Rosary Gdns. SW7 BT42 3
Rosary Gdns. SW7 BT42 66
Rosary Gdns., Ashf. AZ49 73
Rosary, The, Egh. AV51 82
Rosavale Rd. SW6 BR43 65
Roscoe St. EC1 BZ38 2
Roscoe St. EC1 BZ38 57
Roscoff Clo., Edg. BM30 37
East Rd.
Rose & Crown Ct. EC2 BZ39 57
Foster La.
Rose & Crown La. W6 BQ42 65
Talgarth Rd.
Rose & Crown Yd. SW1 BW40 3
Rose & Crown Yd. SW1 BW40 56
King St.
Rose Acre, Saw. CP 5 6
Rose Alley SE1 BZ40 4
Rose Alley SE1 BZ40 57
Rose Av. E18 CH30 40
Rose Av., Grav. DJ47 81
Rose Av., Mitch. BU51 86
Rose Av., Mord. BT53 86
Rose Bank SE20 CB50 77
Rose Bank SW6 BQ43 65
Rose Bank, Brwd. DB27 42
Rose Bates Dr. NW9 BM31 46
Rose Briar Clo., Wok. AW61 101
Pyrford Rd.
Rose Cott. W5 BK40 54
Western Rd.
Rose Ct. SE26 CB48 77
Rose Ct., Pnr. BD31 45
Nursery Rd.
Rose Dr., Chesh. AO19 16
Rose End, Wor.Pk. BQ54 85
Rose Garden Clo., Edg. BL29 37
Rose Gdns. W5 BK41 64
Rose Gdns., Felt. BC48 73
Rose Gdns., Sthl. BF38 54
Rose Gdns., Wat. BC25 26
Rose Glen NW9 BN31 46
Rose Glen, Rom. CT33 50
Rose Hill Av., Wok. AR61 100
Rose Hill, Dor. BJ71 119
Rose Hill, Hmptn. BF51 84
Rose Hill, Sutt. BS55 86
Rose La., Rom. CP31 50
Rose La., Wok. AX64 101
Rose Lawn, Bush. BG26 36
Rose Mary Cres., Guil. AP68 109
Rose Mead, Pot.B. BT18 20
Rose St. WC2 BX40 4
Rose St. WC2 BX40 56
Floral St.
Rose St., Grav. DD46 81
Rose Vale, Hodd. CE12 12
Rose Vall., Brwd. DB27 42
Rose Way SE12 CH46 78
Rose Wk., Pur. BW59 95
Rose Wk., Rad. BJ22 27
Rose Wk., St.Alb. BK12 9
Rose Wk., Surb. BM53 85
Rose Wk., W.Wick. CF55 87
Rose Wood Gdns., Wall. BV57 95
Roseacre Clo. W13 BJ39 54
Roseacre Clo., Horn. CW33 51
Roseacre Gdns., Guil. AV73 118
Roseacre Gdns., Welw.G.C. BT 8 5
Sylvan Way
Roseacre Rd., Well. CO45 69
Roseacre, Oxt. CH70 115
Roseary Clo., West Dr. AX42 63
Rosebank Av., Horn. CV35 51
Rosebank Av., Wem. BH35 45
Rosebank Cotts., Wok. AS64 100
Rosebank Gdns. E3 CD37 57
St. Stephens Rd.
Rosebank Gdns. W3 BN39 55
York Rd.
Rosebank Gro. E17 CD31 48
Rosebank Rd. E17 CE32 48
Rosebank Rd. E3 CD37 57
Norman Gro.
Rosebank Rd. W7 BH41 64
Rosebank Vill. E17 CE31 48
High St.
Rosebank Way W3 BN39 55
Rosebank Wk. NW1 BW36 56
Maiden La.
Rosebank Wk. SE18 CK42 68
Samuel St.
Rosebank, Epsom BN60 94
Rosebank, Wal.Abb. CG20 22
Roseberry Av. EC1 BY38 56
Roseberry Clo., Mord. BQ53 85
Roseberry Clo., Upmin. CZ32 51
Roseberry Ct., Wat. BC23 26
Roseberry Gdns., Dart. CV47 80
Roseberry Gdns., Orp. CN55 88
Roseberry Gdns., Upmin. CZ32 51
Roseberry Pl. E8 CA36 57
Roseberry St. SE16 CB42 67
Rosebery Av. E12 CK36 58
Rosebery Av. EC1 BY38 2
Rosebery Av. EC1 BY38 56
Rosebery Av. N17 CB30 39
Rosebery Av., Epsom BO60 94
Rosebery Av., Har. BE35 45
Rosebery Av., N.Mal. BO51 85
Rosebery Av., Sid. CN47 78
Rosebery Av., Th.Hth. BZ51 87
Rosebery Cres., Wok. AS64 100
Rosebery Gdns. N4 BY32 47
Rosebery Gdns. N8 BX32 47
Rosebery Gdns. W13 BJ39 54
Rosebery Gdns., Sutt. BS56 95
Lewis Rd.
Rosebery Ms. N10 BW30 38
Rosebery Rd.
Rosebery Rd. N10 BW30 38
Rosebery Rd. N9 CB27 39
Rosebery Rd. SW2 BX46 76
Rosebery Rd., Bush. BF26 36
Rosebery Rd., Epsom BN63 103
Rosebery Rd., Grays DC43 71
Rosebery Rd., Houns. BG46 74
Rosebery Rd., Kings.T. BM51 85
Rosebery Rd., Sutt. BR57 94
Rosebery Sq., Kings.T. BM51 85
Rosebine Av., Twick. BG47 74
Rosebriar Wk., Wat. BB21 26
Rosebriars, Cat. CA63 105
Salmons La. W.
Rosebrook Vill. E17 CD31 48
High St.
Rosebury Rd. SW6 BS44 66
Rosebury Vale, Ruis. BB33 44
Rosebushes, Epsom BP61 103
Rosecourt Rd., Croy. BX53 86
Rosecroft Av. NW3 BS34 47
Rosecroft Clo., Orp. CP53 89
Rosecroft Dr., Wat. BB22 26
Rosecroft Gdns. NW2 BP34 46
Rosecroft Gdns., Twick. BG47 74
Rosecroft Rd., Sthl. BF38 54
Rosecroft Wk., Pnr. BD32 45
Rosecroft Wk., Wem. BK35 45
Rosedale Av., Chsnt. CA18 21
Rosedale Av., Hayes BA39 53
Rosedale Clo. SE2 CO41 69
Finchale Rd.
Rosedale Clo. W7 BH41 64
Boston Rd.
Rosedale Clo., Dart. CX47 80
Rosedale Clo., St.Alb. BE18 18
Rosedale Clo., Stan. BJ29 36
Rosedale Ct. N5 BY35 47
Leigh Rd.
Rosedale Gdns., Dag. CO36 59
Rosedale Rd. E7 CJ35 49
Rosedale Rd., Dag. CO36 59
Rosedale Rd., Epsom BP56 94
Rosedale Rd., Grays DE42 71
Rosedale Rd., Rich. BL45 65
Rosedale Rd., Rom. CS30 41
Rosedale Way, Chsnt. CB17 21
Rosedale, Ash. BK62 102
Rosedale, Chsnt. CA17 21
Rosedale, Orp. CL55 88
Rosedale, Welw.G.C. BR 6 5
Rosedene Av. SW16 BX48 76
Rosedene Av., Croy. BX54 86
Rosedene Av., Grnf. BF38 54
Rosedene Av., Mord. BS53 86
Rosedene Ct., Dart. CV47 80
Shepherds La.
Rosedene Ct., Ruis. BB33 44
Rosedene Gdns., Ilf. CL31 49
Rosedene NW6 BQ37 55
Rosedene Ter. E10 CE34 48
Rosedew Rd. W6 BQ43 65
Rosefield Gdns. E14 CE40 57
Morant St.
Rosefield Gdns., Cher. AU57 91
Rosefield Rd., Stai. AW49 73
Rosefield, Sev. CU65 107
Rosehart Ms. W11 BS39 56
Westbourne Gro.
Rosehatch Av., Rom. CP31 50
Roseheath Rd., Houns. BE46 74
Roseheath, Hem.H. AV13 7
Rosehill Av., Sutt. BT54 86
Rosehill Clo., Hodd. CD12 12
Rosehill Ct., Slou. AQ41 62
Yew Tree Rd.
Rosehill Farm Meadow, Bans. BS61 104
The Tracery
Rosehill Gdns., Grnf. BH35 45
Rosehill Gdns., Sutt. BS55 86
Rosehill Gdns., Wat. BA19 17
Rosehill Pk. W., Sutt. BS54 86
Rosehill Rd. SW18 BT46 76
Rosehill Rd., West. CJ62 106
Rosehill, Esher BJ57 93
Roseland Clo. N17 BZ29 39
Roselands Av., Hodd. CD11 12
Roseleigh Av. N5 BY35 47
Roseleigh Clo., Twick. BK46 74
Rosemary Av. N3 BS30 38
Rosemary Av. N9 CB26 39
Rosemary Av., E.Mol. BF52 84
Rosemary Av., Enf. BZ23 30
Rosemary Av., Houns. BD44 64
Rosemary Av., Rom. CT31 50
Rosemary Clo., Harl. CP 9 6
Garden Terrace Rd.
Rosemary Clo., Oxt. CH70 115
Holland La.
Rosemary Clo., S.Ock. DB38 60
Rosemary Clo., Uxb. AZ39 53
Rosemary Dr. E14 CF39 57
Coriander Av.
Rosemary Dr., Ilf. CJ32 49
Rosemary Gdns. SW14 BN45 65
Rosemary La.
Rosemary Gdns., Chess. BL56 94
Rosemary Gdns., Dag. CQ33 50
Rosemary La. SW14 BN45 65
Rosemary La., Egh. AT52 82
Rosemary Rd. SE15 CA43 67
Rosemary Rd. SW17 BT48 76
Rosemary Rd., Well. CN44 68
Rosemary St. N1 BZ37 2
Rosemead Av., Felt. BB48 73
Rosemead Av., Mitch. BW52 86
Rosemead Av., Wem. BL35 46
Rosemead Clo., Red. BT71 121
Rosemead Gdns., Brwd. DE24 122
Rosemead NW9 BO33 46
Rosemont Av. N12 BT29 38
Rosemont Ct. W3 BM40 55
Rosemont Rd.
Rosemont Rd. NW3 BT36 56
Rosemont Rd. W3 BM40 55
Rosemont Rd., N.Mal. BN52 85
Rosemont Rd., Rich. BL46 75
Rosemont Rd., Wem. BL37 55
Rosemoor St. SW3 BU42 3
Rosemoor St. SW3 BU42 66
Rosemount Av., Wey. AW60 92
Rosemount Clo., Wdf.Grn. CK29 40
Chapelmount Rd.
Rosemount Dr., Brom. CK52 88
Rosemount Rd. W13 BJ39 54
Rosemount, Harl. CL12 13
Rosenau Cres. SW11 BU44 66
Rosenau Rd. SW11 BU44 66
Rosendale Rd. SE21 BZ47 77
Rosendale Rd. SE24 BZ47 77
Rosendale St. E5 CB34 48
Roseneath Av. N21 BY26 38
Roseneath Clo., Orp. CP57 98
Roseneath Rd. SW11 BV46 76
Roseneath Wk., Enf. BZ24 30
Rosens Wk., Edg. BM27 37
Rosenthal Rd. SE6 CE46 77
Rosenthorpe Rd. SE15 CC46 77
Roserton St. E14 CF41 67
Rosery, The, Croy. CC53 87
Roses La., Wind. AL44 61
Roses, The, Wdf.Grn. CG29 40
Bunches La.
Rosethorn Clo. SW12 BW47 76
Rosetrees, Guil. AT71 118
Rosevale Rd. SW6 BR44 65
Roseveare Rd. SE12 CJ49 78
Roseville Av., Houns. BF46 74
Roseville Rd., Hayes BC42 63
Rosevine Rd. SW20 BQ51 85
Rosewarne Clo., Wok. AQ62 100
Roseway SE21 BZ46 77
Rosewood Av., Grnf. BJ35 45
Rosewood Av., Horn. CU35 50
Rosewood Clo., Sid. CP48 79
Rosewood Ct., Hem.H. AV13 7
The Shrubbery
Rosewood Dr., Enf. BY21 29
Rosewood Dr., Shep. AY53 83
Rosewood Gdns. SE13 CF44 67
Lewisham Rd.
Rosewood Gro., Sutt. BT55 86
Rosewood Sq. W12 BP39 55
Primula St.
Rosewood, Bex. CT49 79
Rosewood, Cars. BT58 95
Bawtree Clo.
Rosher Clo. E15 CF36 57
Rosina St. E9 CC35 48
Roskell Rd. SW15 BQ45 65
Roslin Rd. W3 BM41 65
Roslin Way, Brom. CH49 78
Roslyn Clo., Brox. CD14 12
Roslyn Clo., Mitch. BT51 86
Roslyn Gdns., Rom. CT30 41
Roslyn Ms. N15 BZ32 48
Roslyn Rd.
Roslyn Rd. N15 BZ32 48
Rosmead Rd. W11 BR40 55
Rosoman Pl. EC1 BY38 2
Rosoman St.
Rosoman St. EC1 BY38 2
Rosoman St. EC1 BY38 56
Ross Av. NW7 BR28 37
Ross Av., Dag. CQ34 50
Ross Clo. E4 CF27 39
Ross Clo., Har. BG29 36
Ross Clo., Hat. BP11 10
Ross Clo., Hayes BA42 63
Ross Cres., Wat. BC21 26
Ross Ct. NW1 BU38 1
Ross Ct. SW15 BQ47 75
Ross Par., Wall. BV57 95
Ross Rd. SE25 BZ52 87
Ross Rd., Cob. BD60 93
Ross Rd., Dart. CU46 79
Ross Rd., Twick. BG47 74
Ross Rd., Wall. BW56 95
Ross Way SE9 CK45 68
Ross Way, Nthwd. BB28 35
Rossall Clo., Horn. CU32 50
Rossall Cres. NW10 BL38 55
Rossdale Dr. N9 CC25 30
Rossdale Dr. NW9 BN33 46
Rossdale Rd. SW15 BQ45 65
Rossdale, Sutt. BU56 95
Rosse Ms. SE3 CH44 68
Rossendale St. E5 CB34 48
Rossendale Way NW1 BW36 1
Rossendale Way NW1 BW36 56
Rossgate, Hem.H. AW12 8
Galley Hill
Rossindel Rd., Houns. BF46 74
Rossington Av., B.Wd. BL22 28
Rossington St. E5 CB34 48
Rossiter Clo., Slou. AS42 62
Rossiter Rd. SW12 BV47 76
Rossland Clo., Bexh. CR46 79
Rosslyn Av. E4 CG27 40
Rosslyn Av. SW13 BO45 65
Rosslyn Av., Barn. BU25 29
Rosslyn Av., Dag. CQ33 50
Rosslyn Av., Felt. BC46 73
Rosslyn Av., Rom. CW30 42
Rosslyn Clo., Hayes BA39 53
Rosslyn Clo., W.Wick. CG55 88
Rosslyn Cres. N., Har. BH31 45

Rosslyn Cres. S., Har. BH32 45
Rosslyn Cres., Har. BH31 45
Rosslyn Cres., Wem. BL35 46
Rosslyn Ct., Wok. AQ62 100
St. Johns Rd.
Rosslyn Hill NW3 BT35 47
Rosslyn Ms. NW3 BT35 47
Rosslyn Hill
Rosslyn Park Ms. NW3 BT35 47
Rosslyn Pk., Wey. BA56 92
Rosslyn Rd. E17 CF31 48
Rosslyn Rd., Bark. CM36 58
Rosslyn Rd., Twick. BK46 74
Rosslyn Rd., Wat. BC24 26
Rossmore Rd. NW1 BU38 1
Rossmore Rd. NW1 BU38 56
Rossway Dr., Bush. BG25 27
Rossway La., Berk. AO13 7
Rosswood Gdns., Wall. BW57 95
Rostrevor Av. N15 CA32 48
Rostrevor Gdns., Hayes BB40 53
Rostrevor Gdns., Iver AU37 52
Rostrevor Gdns., Sthl. BE42 64
Rostrevor Ms. SW6 BR44 65
Rostrevor Rd. SW19 BS49 76
Rostrevor Rd. SW6 BR44 65
Roswell Clo., Chsnt. CD18 21
Rotary St. SE1 BY41 4
Rotary St. SE1 BY41 66
Roth Dr., Brwd. DD27 122
Roth Wk. N7 BX34 47
Durham Rd.
Rothbury Av., Rain. CU39 59
Rothbury Gdns., Islw. BJ43 64
Rothbury Rd. E9 CD36 57
Rothbury Wk. N17 CB29 39
Rother Clo., Wat. BD20 18
Rotherfield Rd., Cars. BV56 95
Rotherfield Rd., Enf. CC22 30
Rotherfield St. N1 BZ36 2
Rotherfield St. N1 BZ36 57
Rotherhill Av. SW16 BW50 76
Rotherhithe New Rd. SE16 CB42 67
Rotherhithe Old Rd. SE16 CC42 67
Rotherhithe St. SE16 CB41 67
Rotherhithe Tunnel App. E14 CD40 57
Rothermere Rd., Croy. BX56 95
Rotherwick Hill W5 BL38 55
Rotherwick Rd. NW11 BS33 47
Rotherwood Clo. SW20 BR51 85
Rotherwood Rd. SW15 BQ45 65
Rothery St. N1 BY37 56
Gaskin St.
Rothes Rd., Dor. BJ71 119
Rothesay Av. SW20 BR51 85
Rothesay Av., Grnf. BG36 54
Rothesay Av., Rich. BM45 65
Rothesay Rd. SE25 BZ52 87
Rothsay Rd. E7 CJ36 58
Rothsay St. SE1 CA41 4
Rothsay St. SE1 CA41 67
Rothsay Wk. E14 CE42 67
Charnwood Gdns.
Rothschild Rd. W4 BN41 65
Rothschild St. SE27 BY49 76
Rothwell Gdns., Dag. CP37 59
Rothwell Rd., Dag. CP37 59
Rothwell St. NW1 BU36 56
Rotten Row SE3 CG44 68
Rotten Row SW11 BU43 66
Rotten Row SW7 BT41 3
Rotten Row SW7 BU41 66
Rotterdam Dr. E14 CF41 67
Rouel Rd. SE16 CB42 4
Rouel Rd. SE16 CB41 67
Rougemont Av., Mord. BS53 86
Rough Rd., Wok. AO64 100
Rough Rew, Dor. BJ73 119
Rough Wood Clo., Wat. BB22 26
Roughdown Av., Hem.H. AW15 8
Roughdown Rd., Hem.H. AW15 8
Roughdown Villas Rd., Hem.H. AW15 8
Roughetts La., Red. CA68 114
Roughlands, Wok. AV60 100
Roughs, The, Nthwd. BB27 35
Roughwood La., Ch.St.G. AS26 34
Round Ash Way, Hart. DC53 90
Round Gro., Croy. CC54 87
Round Hill SE26 CB48 77
Round Oak Rd., Wey. AY55 83
Round Way, Egh. AU49 72
Round Wood Rd., Amer. AP22 25
Round Wood Vw., Bans. BQ61 103
Round Wood Way, Bans. BQ61 103
Roundabouts, The, Dor. BE71 119
Roundacre Est. SW19 BQ48 75
Roundaway Rd., Ilf. CK30 40
Roundcroft, Chsnt. CA16 21
Roundhay Clo. SE23 CC48 77
Roundhedge Way, Enf. BX22 29
Roundhill Clo., Wok. AT62 100
Roundhill Dr., Enf. BX24 29
Roundhill Dr., Wok. AT63 100
Roundhill Way, Cob. BF59 93
Roundhill Way, Guil. AP70 118
Roundhills, Wal.Abb. CG20 22
Roundmead Av., Loug. CL24 31
Roundmead Clo., Loug. CL24 31
Roundmoor Dr., Chsnt. CD18 21
Roundtable Rd., Brom. CG48 78
Roundthorne Way, Wok. AP61 100
Roundtree Rd., Wem. BJ35 45
Roundway, The N17 BZ30 39
Roundway, The, Esher BH57 93
Roundway, The, Wat. BB25 26
Roundway, West. CJ61 106
Sunningvale Av.
Roundways, The, Ruis. BB34 44
Roundwood Av., Brwd. DD26 122
Roundwood Clo., Ruis. BA33 44

Roundwood Dr., Welw.G.C. BQ7 5
Roundwood Gro., Brwd. DD26 122
Roundwood Rd. NW10 BO36 55
Roundwood, Chis. CL51 88
Roundwood, Kings L. AY17 17
Rounton Dr., Wat. BB22 26
Rounton Rd. E3 CE38 57
Rounton Rd., Wal.Abb. CG20 22
Roupel Park Est. SW2 BX47 76
Roupell Rd. SW2 BX47 76
Roupell St. SE1 BY40 4
Roupell St. SE1 BY40 56
Rous Rd., Buck.H. CK26 40
Rousden St. NW1 BW36 56
Camden Rd.
Rouse Gdns. SE21 CA49 77
Rousebarn La., Rick. AY22 26
Rousebarn La., Wat. BA24 26
Routh Rd. SW18 BU47 76
Routh St. E6 CK39 58
Rover Av., Ilf. CN29 40
Row Cft., Hem.H. AV14 7
Row Hill St. NW3 BU35 47
Rowallan Rd. SW6 BR43 65
Rowan Av. E4 CD29 39
Rowan Av., Egh. AU49 72
Rowan Clo. SW16 BW51 86
Rowan Clo. W5 BL41 65
Rowan Clo., Bricket Wood BF19 18
Rowan Clo., Guil. AR69 118
Rowan Clo., N.Mal. BO51 85
Rowan Clo., Reig. BT71 121
Rowan Clo., St.Alb. BL13 10
Cranbrook Dr.
Rowan Clo., Wem. BJ34 45
Rowan Cres. SW16 BW51 86
Rowan Cres., Dart. CV47 80
Rowan Ct. SE12 CG47 78
Rowan Dr. NW9 BP31 46
Rowan Dr., Brox. CD16 21
Rowan Gdns. W6 BQ42 65
Bute Gdns.
Rowan Gdns., Croy. CA55 87
Rowan Grn., Brwd. DC27 122
Rowan Grn., Couls. BV64 104
Rowan Grn., Wey. BA56 92
Rowan Pl., Hayes BB40 53
Rowan Rd. SW16 BW51 86
Rowan Rd. W6 BQ42 65
Rowan Rd., Bexh. CQ45 69
Rowan Rd., Brent BJ43 64
Rowan Rd., Swan. CS52 89
Rowan Rd., West Dr. AX42 63
Rowan Way, Rom. CP31 50
Rowan Wk. N19 BW34 47
Bredgar Rd.
Rowan Wk. N2 BT32 47
Rowan Wk. W10 BR38 55
Droop St.
Rowan Wk., Brom. CK55 88
Rowan Wk., Hat. BP14 10
Southdown Rd.
Rowan Wk., Horn. CV31 51
Rowanhurst Dr., Slou. AO35 43
Rowans, The N13 BY27 38
Rowans, The, Ger.Cr. AR31 43
Rowans, The, Hem.H. AW13 8
Rowans, The, Sun. BB49 73
Rowans, The, Wok. AS62 100
Montgomery Rd.
Rowans, Welw.G.C. BS6 5
Rowantree Clo. N21 BZ26 39
Rowantree Rd. N21 BZ26 39
Rowantree Rd., Enf. BY23 29
Rowbarns Way, Lthd. BB68 110
Rowben Clo. N20 BS26 38
Rowberry Clo. SW6 BQ44 65
Rowcross Pl. SE1 CA42 4
Rowcross St.
Rowcross St. SE1 CA42 4
Rowcross St. SE1 CA42 67
Rowdell Rd., Nthlt. BF37 54
Rowden Park Gdns. E4 CE29 39
Rowden Rd.
Rowden Rd. E4 CE29 39
Rowden Rd., Beck. CD51 87
Rowden Rd., Epsom BM56 94
Rowditch La. SW11 BV44 66
Rowdon Av. NW10 BP36 55
Rowdow La., Sev. CV60 99
Rowdow La., Sev. CV61 108
Rowdown Cres., Croy. CF58 96
Rowdowns Rd., Dag. CQ37 59
Rowe Gdns., Bark. CN37 58
Rowe La. E9 CC35 48
Urswick Rd.
Rowe Wk., Har. BF34 45
Rowena Cres. SW11 BU44 66
Rowfant Rd. SW17 BV47 76
Rowhedge, Brwd. DD27 122
Rowhill Rd. E5 CB35 48
Rowhill Rd., Dart. CT50 79
Rowhill, Wey. AV57 91
Rowhurst Av., Lthd. BH62 102
Rowington Clo. W2 BS39 1
Rowington Clo. W2 BS39 56
Rowland Av., Har. BK31 45
Rowland Clo., Wind. AL45 61
Rowland Cres., Chig. CN28 40
Fairview Dr.
Rowland Gro. SE26 CB48 77
Dallas Rd.
Rowland Hill Av. N17 BZ29 39
Rowland Hill St. NW3 BU35 47
Rowland Rd. SW4 BW45 66
Rowland Way SW19 BS51 86
Hayward Clo.
Rowland Way, Ashf. BA50 73
Rowland Wk., Hav. CT27 41
Rowlands Av., Pnr. BF28 36
Rowlands Clo. NW7 BP29 37
Rowlands Clo., Chsnt. CC18 21
Rowlands Fields, Chsnt. CC18 21
Clarendon Rd.
Rowlands Rd., Dag. CQ34 50

Rowlatt Clo., Dart. CV49 80
Rowlatt Dr., St.Alb. BF14 9
Rowlatt Rd., Dart. CV49 80
Rowley Av., Sid. CO47 79
Rowley Clo., Wat. BE25 27
Rowley Clo., Wem. BL36 55
Rowley Gdns. N4 BZ33 48
Rowley Gdns., Chsnt. CC17 21
Davison Dr.
Rowley Green Rd., Barn. BO25 28
Rowley La., B.Wd. BN23 28
Rowley La., Slou. AR37 52
Rowley Mead, Epp. CP16 23
Rowley Rd. N15 BZ32 48
Rowley Ter. NW5 BV36 56
Rowley Way NW8 BS37 56
Rowley Way NW8 BT37 1
Rowlheys Pl., West Dr. AY41 63
Rowlls Rd., Kings.T. BL52 85
Rowney Gdns., Dag. CO36 59
Rowney Gdns., Saw. CP7 6
Rowney Rd., Dag. CO36 59
Rowney Wood, Saw. CP6 6
Rowns Way, Loug. CK24 31
Rowntree Path SE28 CO40 59
MacAuley Way
Rowntree Rd., Twick. BH47 74
Rowse Clo. E15 CF37 57
Rowsley Av. NW4 BQ31 46
Rowstock Gdns. N7 BW35 47
Rowton Rd. SE18 CM43 68
Rowtown, Wey. AV57 91
Roxborough Av., Har. BG33 45
Roxborough Av., Islw. BH43 64
Roxborough Pk., Har. BH33 45
Roxborough Rd., Har. BG32 45
Roxbourne Clo., Nthlt. BE36 54
Arnold Rd.
Roxburgh Av., Upmin. CY35 51
Roxburgh Rd. SE27 BY49 76
Roxburn Way, Ruis. BB34 44
Roxby Pl. SW6 BS43 66
Roxeth Ct., Ashf. AZ49 73
Roxeth Green Av., Har. BF34 45
Roxeth Gro., Har. BF35 45
Roxeth Hill, Har. BG34 45
Roxford Clo., Shep. BB53 83
Roxley Rd. SE13 CE46 77
Roxton Gdns., Croy. CE56 96
Roxwell Clo., Slou. AM40 61
Roxwell Rd. W12 BP41 65
Roxwell Rd., Bark. CO37 59
Roxwell Way, Wdf.Grn. CJ29 40
Roxy Av., Rom. CP33 50
Roy Gdns., Ilf. CN31 49
Roy Gro., Hmptn. BF50 74
Roy Rd., Nthwd. BB29 35
Roy Sq. E14 CD40 57
Royal Arc. W1 BW40 3
Old Bond St.
Royal Av. SW3 BU42 3
Royal Av. SW3 BU42 66
Royal Av., Wal.Cr. CD20 21
Royal Av., Wor.Pk. BO55 85
Royal Cir. SE27 BY48 76
Royal Clo., Ilf. CO33 50
Royal Clo., Uxb. AY39 53
Royal Clo., Wor.Pk. BO55 85
Royal College St. NW1 BW36 1
Royal College St. NW1 BW36 56
Royal Cres. W11 BQ40 55
Royal Cres., Ruis. BE35 45
Royal Ct., Hem.H. AY15 8
Royal Dr., Epsom BP62 103
Royal Exchange Av. EC3 BZ39 2
Finch La.
Royal Exchange Bldgs. EC3 BZ39 2
Royal Exchange Bldgs. EC3 BZ39 57
Cornhill
Royal Hill SE10 CF43 67
Royal Hospital Rd. SW3 BU43 3
Royal Hospital Rd. SW3 BU43 66
Royal La., Uxb. & West Dr. AY38 53
Royal London Ind. Est. NW10 BN37 55
Royal Mint Pl. E1 CA40 57
Royal Mint St.
Royal Mint St. E1 CA40 4
Royal Mint St. E1 CA40 57
Royal Naval Pl. SE14 CD43 67
Hereford Pl.
Royal Oak Ct. N1 CA38 57
Royal Oak Pl. SE22 CB46 77
Royal Oak Rd. E8 CB36 57
Wilton Way
Royal Oak Rd., Bexh. CQ46 79
Royal Oak Rd., Wok. AR62 100
Royal Opera Arc. SW1 BW40 3
Royal Par. SE3 CG44 68
Royal Par. W5 BL38 55
Western Av.
Royal Par., Chis. CM50 78
Royal Parade Ms., Chis. CM50 78
Royal Par.
Royal Pier Ms., Grav. DG46 81
Royal Pier Rd.
Royal Pier Rd., Grav. DG46 81
Royal Pl. SE10 CF43 67
Royal Rd. E16 CJ39 58
Royal Rd. SE17 BY43 66
Royal Rd., Dart. CX49 80
Royal Rd., Sid. CP48 79
Royal Rd., St.Alb. BJ13 9
Royal Rd., Tedd. BG49 74
Royal Route, Wem. BL35 46
Royal St. SE1 BX41 4
Royal St. SE1 BX41 66
Royal Victor Pl. E3 CC37 57
Old Ford Rd.
Royal Wk., Wall. BV55 86
Prince Charles Way
Royalty Ms. W1 BW39 56
Dean St.
Royce Clo., Brox. CD14 12

Roycraft Av., Bark. CN37 58
Roycraft Clo., Bark. CN37 58
Roycroft Clo. E18 CH30 40
Roycroft Clo. SW2 BY47 76
High Trees
Roydene Rd. SE18 CN43 68
Roydon Clo. SW11 BU44 66
Reform St.
Roydon Clo., Loug. CK26 40
Roydon Ct., Hem.H. AZ10 8
Elstree Rd.
Roydon Rd., Harl. CJ10 13
Roydon St. SW11 BV44 66
Royle Clo., Ger.Cr. AS29 34
Royle Clo., Rom. CU32 50
Royle Cres. W13 BJ38 54
Roymount Ct., Twick. BH48 74
Royston Av. E4 CE28 39
Royston Av., Sutt. BT55 86
Royston Av., Wall. BW56 95
Royston Av., Wey. AY60 92
Royston Clo., Houns. BC44 63
Royston Clo., Walt. BC54 83
Royston Ct., Rich. BL44 65
Royston Ct., Surb. BM55 85
Royston Gdns., Ilf. CJ32 49
Royston Gro., Pnr. BE29 36
Royston Park Rd., Pnr. BE29 36
Royston Rd. SE20 CC51 87
Royston Rd., Dart. CT46 79
Royston Rd., Rich. BL46 75
Royston Rd., Rom. CX29 42
Royston Rd., St.Alb. BJ14 9
Royston Rd., Wey. AY59 92
Royston St. E2 CC37 57
Roystons, The, Surb. BM53 85
Rozel Rd. SW4 BW44 66
Rubastic Rd., Sthl. BD41 64
Rubens Rd., Nthlt. BD37 54
Rubens St. SE6 CD48 77
Ruberoid Rd., Enf. CD24 30
Ruby Clo., Slou. AN41 61
Ruby Rd. E17 CE31 48
Ruby St. SE15 CB43 67
Ruckholt Clo. E10 CE34 48
Ruckholt Rd. E10 CE35 48
Rucklers La., Kings L. AW17 17
Ruckles Way, Amer. AO23 25
Station Rd.
Rucklidge Av. NW10 BO37 55
Rudall Cres. NW3 BT35 47
Willoughby Rd.
Rudd St. SE18 CL42 68
Ruddles Way, Wind. AL44 61
Ruden Way, Epsom BP61 103
Rudge Rd., Wey. AV56 91
Rudland Rd., Bexh. CR45 69
Rudloe Rd. SW12 BW47 76
Rudolph Rd. E13 CG37 58
Rudolph Rd. NW6 BS37 56
Rudolph Rd., Bush. BF25 27
Rudwick Clo., Wal.Cr. CD17 21
Ashdown Cres.
Rudyard Gro. NW7 BN29 37
Rue de St. Laurence, Wal.Abb. CF20 21
Quaker La.
Ruffets Wood, Grav. DH50 81
Ruffetts Clo., S.Croy. CB57 96
Ruffetts Way, Tad. BR62 103
Ruffetts, The, S.Croy. CB57 96
Rufford Clo., Har. BJ32 45
Rufford St. N1 BX37 2
Rufford St. N1 BX37 56
Rufus Clo., Ruis. BE34 45
Rufus St. EC1 CA38 57
Old St.
Rufus St. N1 CA38 2
Rugby Av. N9 CA26 39
Rugby Av., Grnf. BG36 54
Rugby Av., Wem. BJ35 45
Rugby Clo., Har. BH31 45
Rugby Gdns., Dag. CP36 59
Rugby La., Sutt. BQ58 94
Rugby Rd. NW9 BM31 46
Rugby Rd. W4 BO41 65
Rugby Rd., Dag. CO36 59
Rugby Rd., Twick. BH46 74
Rugby St. WC1 BX38 2
Rugby St. WC1 BX38 56
Rugby Way, Rick. AZ25 26
Rugg St. E14 CE40 57
Rugged La., Wal.Abb. CJ20 22
Ruggles-Brise Rd., Ashf. AX49 73
Ruislip Clo., Grnf. BF38 54
Ruislip Rd. E. W13 BG38 54
Ruislip Rd. E. W7 BG38 54
Ruislip Rd. E., Grnf. BG38 54
Ruislip Rd., Grnf. BE38 54
Ruislip Rd., Nthlt. BD37 54
Ruislip St. SW17 BU49 76
Rum Clo. E1 CB40 57
Rumania Wk., Grav. DJ48 81
Cervia Way
Rumballs Clo., Hem.H. AZ15 8
Rumballs Rd., Hem.H. AZ15 8
Rumbold Rd. SW6 BS43 66
Rumbold Rd., Hodd. CF11 12
Rumsey Clo., Hmptn. BE50 74
Rumsley Rd. SW9 BX45 66
Runbury Circ. NW9 BN34 46
Runcie Clo., St.Alb. BJ11 9
Runciman Clo., Orp. CP58 98
Runcorn Cres., Hem.H. AY11 8
Runcorn Pl. W11 BR40 55
Rundell Cres. NW4 BP32 46
Rundells, Harl. CO13 14
Runham Rd., Hem.H. AY14 8
Runham St. SE17 BZ42 67
Runn Way E7 CH35 49
Runnelfield, Har. BH34 45
Runnemede Ct., Egh. AT49 72
Runnemede Rd., Egh. AS49 72
Running Horse Yd., Brent. BL43 65
Pottery Rd.
Running Waters, Brwd. DD28 122

Runnymede Clo., Twick. BF46 74
Runnymede Cres. SW16 BW51 86
Runnymede Gdns., Grnf. BG37 54
Runnymede Gdns., Twick. BF46 74
Runnymede Rd., Twick. BF46 74
Runnymede SW19 BT51 86
Runrig Hill, Amer. AP21 25
Runsley, Welw.G.C. BR6 5
Runtley Wood La., Guil. AS66 109
Runton St. N19 BW33 47
Runway, The, Ruis. BD35 45
Rupack St. SE16 CC41 67
St. Mary Church St.
Rupert Av., Wem. BL35 46
Rupert Ct. W1 BW40 3
Rupert St.
Rupert Gdns. SW9 BY44 66
Rupert Rd. N19 BW34 47
Rupert Rd. NW6 BR37 55
Rupert Rd. W4 BO41 65
Rupert Rd., Guil. AQ71 118
Rupert St. W1 BW40 3
Rupert St. W1 BW40 56
Rural Vale, Grav. DF47 81
Rural Way SW16 BV50 76
Rural Way, Red. BV70 121
Ruscoe Dr., Wok. AT62 100
Pembroke Rd.
Ruscoe Rd. E16 CG39 58
Ruscombe Dr., St.Alb. BG16 18
Ruscombe Gdns., Slou. AQ43 62
Ruscombe Way, Felt. BB47 73
Rush Green Gdns., Rom. CS33 50
Rush Green Rd., Rom. CR33 50
Rush Grove St. SE18 CK42 68
Rush Hill Ms. SW11 BV45 66
Rush Hill Rd.
Rush Hill Rd. SW11 BV45 66
Rusham Park Av., Egh. AS50 72
Rusham Rd. SW12 BU46 76
Rusham Rd., Egh. AS50 72
Rushbrook Cres. E17 CD30 39
Rushbrook Rd. SE9 CM48 78
Rushcroft Rd. E4 CE29 39
Rushcroft Rd. SW2 BY45 66
Rushden Clo. SE19 BZ50 77
Rushden Gdns. NW7 BQ29 37
Rushden Gdns., Ilf. CL31 49
Rushdene Av., Barn. BU26 38
Rushdene Clo., Nthlt. BD37 54
Rushdene Cres., Nthlt. BD37 54
Rushdene Gdns., Ilf. CL30 40
Rushdene Rd., Brwd. DB26 42
Rushdene Rd., Pnr. BD32 45
Rushdene SE2 CP41 69
Rushdene Wk., West. CJ62 106
Rushdon Clo., Grays DD41 71
Rushen Wk., Cars. BT54 86
Rushes Mead, Harl. CN12 13
Rushes Mead, Uxb. AX37 53
Rushet Rd., Orp. CO51 89
Rushett Clo., T.Ditt. BJ54 84
Rushett Dr., Dor. BJ73 119
Rushett Gdns., Surb. BJ54 84
Rushett La., Chess. BK59 93
Rushett Rd., T.Ditt. BJ54 84
Rushetts Rd., Reig. BT72 121
Rushetts Rd., Sev. CZ57 99
Rushey Clo., N.Mal. BN52 85
Rushey Grn. SE6 CE47 77
Rushey Hill, Enf. BX24 29
Rushey Mead SE4 CE46 77
Rushfield, Pot.B. BQ20 19
Rushfield, Saw. CQ6 6
Rushford Rd. SE4 CD46 77
Rushgrove Av. NW9 BO32 46
Rushleigh Av., Chsnt. CC18 21
Rushley Clo., Grays DE40 71
Rushley Clo., Kes. CJ56 97
Rushmead Clo., Croy. CA56 96
Rushmead Clo., Edg. BM27 37
Rushmead E2 CB38 57
Florida St.
Rushmead, Rich. BJ48 74
Rushmere Av., Upmin. CY35 51
Rushmere La., Chesh. AQ17 16
Rushmoor Clo., Guil. AP69 118
Rushmoor Clo., Pnr. BC31 44
Rushmoor Clo., Rick. AX27 35
Rushmoor Ct., Wor.Pk. BP55 85
Rushmore Clo., Brom. CK52 88
Rushmore Cres. E5 CC35 48
Rushmore Hill Rd., Sev. CP60 98
Rushmore Hill, Orp. CP58 98
Rushmore Rd. E5 CC35 48
Rusholme Av., Dag. CR34 50
Rusholme Gro. SE19 CA49 77
Rusholme Rd. SW15 BQ46 75
Rushout Av., Har. BJ32 45
Rushton Av., Wat. BC21 26
Rushton St. N1 BZ37 2
Rushton St. N1 BZ37 57
Rushworth Gdns. NW4 BP31 46
Rushworth Rd., Reig. BS70 121
Rushworth St. SE1 BY41 4
Rushworth St. SE1 BY41 66
Rushymead, Sev. CX62 108
Ruskin Av. E12 CK36 58
Ruskin Av., Felt. BB46 73
Ruskin Av., Rich. BM43 65
Ruskin Av., Upmin. CY33 51
Ruskin Av., Wal.Abb. CG20 22
Ruskin Av., Well. CO45 69
Ruskin Clo. NW11 BS32 47
Ruskin Clo., Chsnt. CA16 21
Hammond Street Rd.
Ruskin Dr., Orp. CN55 88
Ruskin Dr., Well. CO45 69
Ruskin Dr., Wor.Pk. BP55 85
Ruskin Gdns. W5 BK38 54
Ruskin Gdns., Har. BL31 46
Ruskin Gdns., Rom. CU30 41
Ruskin Gro., Dart. CX46 80
Ruskin Gro., Well. CO44 69
Ruskin Park Ho. SE5 BZ45 67
Ruskin Rd. N17 CA30 39

Ruskin Rd., Belv.	CR42	69
Ruskin Rd., Cars.	BU56	95
Ruskin Rd., Croy.	BY55	86
Ruskin Rd., Grays	DG42	71
Ruskin Rd., Islw.	BH45	64
Ruskin Rd., Stai.	AV50	72
Ruskin Rd., Sthl.	BE40	54
Ruskin Way SW19	BT51	86
Brangwyn Cres.		
Ruskin Wk. N9	CB27	39
Ruskin Wk. SE24	BZ46	77
Ruskin Wk., Brom.	CK53	88
Rusland Av., Orp.	CM55	88
Rusland Park Rd., Har.	BH31	45
Rusper Clo. NW2	BQ34	46
Rusper Clo., Stan.	BK28	36
Rusper Ct. SW9	BX44	66
Clapham Rd.		
Rusper Rd. N22	BY30	38
Rusper Rd., Dag.	CP36	59
Russelcroft Rd., Welw.G.C.	BQ 7	5
Russell Av. N22	BY30	38
Russell Av., St.Alb.	BG13	9
Russell Clo. NW10	BN36	55
Russell Clo. SE7	CJ43	68
Russell Clo., Amer.	AR23	25
Russell Clo., Beck.	CE52	87
Russell Clo., Bexh.	CR45	69
Russell Clo., Brwd.	DA26	42
Russell Clo., Dart.	CU45	69
Russell Clo., Nthwd.	BA28	35
Russell Clo., Ruis.	BD34	45
Russell Clo., Tad.	BP66	112
Russell Clo., Wok.	AR61	100
Russell Cres., Wat.	BB21	26
Russell Ct. SW1	**BW40**	**3**
Russell Ct. SW1	BW40	56
Cleveland Row		
Russell Ct., Chesh.	AO18	16
Russell Ct., Lthd.	BJ64	102
Russell Ct., St.Alb.	BF18	18
Black Boy Wood		
Russell Dr., Stai.	AX46	73
Russell Gdns. Ms. W14	BR41	65
Russell Gdns. N20	BU27	38
Russell Gdns. NW11	BR32	46
Russell Gdns. W14	BR41	65
Russell Gdns., Rich.	BK48	74
Russell Gdns., West Dr.	AZ43	63
Russell Green Clo., Pur.	BY58	95
Russell Gro. NW7	BO28	37
Russell Gro. SW9	BY43	66
Russell Hill Pl., Pur.	BY59	95
Russell Hill Rd., Pur.	BY58	95
Russell Hill, Pur.	BX58	95
Russell Kerr Clo. W4	BN43	65
Burlington La.		
Russell La. N20	BU27	38
Russell La., Wat.	BA21	26
Russell Mead, Har.	BH29	36
Russell Pl. SE16	CD41	67
Onega Gate		
Russell Pl. SW1	BW42	66
Vauxhall Bridge Rd.		
Russell Pl., Hem.H.	AW15	8
Russell Pl., S.at H.	CX51	90
Russell Rd. E10	CE32	48
Russell Rd. E16	CH39	58
Russell Rd. E17	CD31	48
Russell Rd. E4	CD28	39
Russell Rd. N13	BX29	38
Russell Rd. N15	CA32	48
Russell Rd. N20	BU27	38
Russell Rd. N8	BW32	47
Russell Rd. NW9	BO32	46
Russell Rd. SW19	BS50	76
Russell Rd. W14	BR41	65
Russell Rd., Buck.H.	CH26	40
Russell Rd., Enf.	CA22	30
Russell Rd., Grav.	DH46	81
Russell Rd., Grays	DD42	71
Russell Rd., Mitch.	BU52	86
Russell Rd., Nthlt.	BG35	45
Russell Rd., Nthwd.	BA27	35
Russell Rd., Shep.	AZ54	83
Russell Rd., Til.	DF44	71
Russell Rd., Twick.	BH46	74
Russell Rd., Walt.	BC53	83
Russell Rd., Wok.	AR61	100
Russell Sq. WC1	**BX38**	**2**
Russell Sq. WC1	BX38	56
Russell St. E3	CH37	58
Russell St. WC2	**BX40**	**4**
Russell St. WC2	BX40	56
Russell St., Wind.	AO44	61
Russell Way, Sutt.	BS56	95
Russell Wk., Rich.	BL46	75
Pyrland Rd.		
Russells Footpath SW16	BX49	76
Russells Ride, Chsnt.	CD19	21
Russels, Tad.	BQ64	103
Russet Clo., Stai.	AV46	72
Russet Clo., Uxb.	BA38	53
Russet Clo., Walt.	BE55	84
Broad Clo.		
Russet Cres. N7	BX35	47
Stock Orchard Cres.		
Russet Way SE13	CE44	67
Conington Rd.		
Russet Way, Dor.	BK73	119
Russets Clo., Wok.	AS61	100
Russett Clo., Cat.	CB66	114
Russett Clo., Orp.	CO56	98
Russett Way, Swan.	CS51	89
Russetts, Welw.G.C.	BT 8	5
Russetts Clo. E4	CF28	39
Larkshall Rd.		
Russia Ct. EC2	**BZ39**	**2**
Russia Row		
Russia Dock Rd. SE16	CD40	57
Russia La. E2	CC37	57
Russia Row EC2	**BZ39**	**2**
Russia Row EC2	BZ39	57
Milk St.		
Russington Rd., Shep.	BA53	83
Rust Sq. SE5	BZ43	67

Rusthall Av. W4	BN42	65
Rusthall Clo., Croy.	CC53	87
Rustic Av. SW16	BV50	76
Rustic Clo., Upmin.	CZ33	51
Rustic Pl., Wem.	BK35	45
Rustington Wk., Mord.	BR54	85
Ruston Av., Surb.	BM54	85
Ruston Ms. W11	BR39	55
Ruston St. E3	CD37	57
Rutford Rd. SW16	BX49	76
Ruth Clo., Har.	BL31	46
Ruthen Clo., Epsom	BM60	94
Rutherford Clo., Sutt.	BT57	95
Rutherford St. SW1	**BW42**	**3**
Rutherford Way, Bush.	BG26	36
Rutherford Way, Wem.	BM35	46
Rutherglen Rd. SE2	CO43	69
Rutherland St. SW1	BW42	66
Rutherwick Ri., Couls.	BX62	104
Rutherwyk Rd., Cher.	AV54	82
Rutherwyke Clo., Epsom	BP57	94
Ruthin Clo. NW9	BO32	46
Ruthin Rd. SE3	CH43	68
Ruthven Av., Wal.Cr.	CC20	21
Ruthven St. E9	CC37	57
Lauriston Rd.		
Rutland App., Horn.	CX32	51
Rutland Av., Sid.	CO47	79
Rutland Av., Slou.	AO39	52
Rutland Clo. SW14	BN45	65
Rutland Clo. SW19	BU50	76
Rutland Rd.		
Rutland Clo., Bex.	CP47	79
Rutland Clo., Chess.	BL57	94
Rutland Clo., Dart.	CV46	80
Rutland Clo., Epsom	BN58	94
Rutland Clo., Red.	BU70	121
Rutland Ct. SE5	BZ45	67
Rutland Dr., Horn.	CX32	51
Rutland Dr., Mord.	BR53	85
Rutland Dr., Rich.	BK47	74
Rutland Gate Ms. SW7	**BU41**	**3**
Rutland Gate Ms. SW7	BU41	66
Rutland Gate SW7	**BU41**	**3**
Rutland Gate SW7	BU41	66
Rutland Gate, Belv.	CR42	69
Rutland Gate, Brom.	CG52	88
Rutland Gdns. Ms. SW7	**BU41**	**3**
Rutland Gdns.		
Rutland Gdns. N4	BY32	47
Rutland Gdns. SW7	**BU41**	**3**
Rutland Gdns. SW7	BU41	66
Rutland Gdns. W13	BJ39	54
Rutland Gdns., Croy.	CA56	96
Rutland Gdns., Dag.	CP35	50
Rutland Gdns., Hem.H.	AY13	8
Rutland Gdns., Rich.	BK47	74
Rutland Gro. W6	BP42	65
Rutland Ms. NW8	BS37	56
Rutland Ms. NW8	**BT37**	**1**
Rutland Ms. S. SW7	**BU41**	**3**
Ennismore St.		
Rutland Pk. NW2	BQ36	55
Rutland Pk. SE6	CD48	77
Rutland Pl. EC1	**BY39**	**2**
Charterhouse Sq.		
Rutland Pl., Bush.	BG26	36
The Butts		
Rutland Rd. E11	CH32	49
Rutland Rd. E17	CE32	48
Rutland Rd. E7	CJ36	58
Rutland Rd. E9	CC37	57
Rutland Rd. SW19	BU50	76
Rutland Rd., Har.	BG32	45
Rutland Rd., Hayes	BA42	63
Rutland Rd., Ilf.	CL35	49
Rutland Rd., Sthl.	BF38	54
Rutland Rd., Twick.	BG48	74
Rutland St. SW7	**BU41**	**3**
Rutland St. SW7	BU41	66
Rutland Way, Orp.	CP53	89
Rutland Wk. SE6	CD48	77
Rutley Clo. SE17	BY43	66
Royal Rd.		
Rutlish Rd. SW19	BS51	86
Rutson Rd., Wey.	AY60	92
Rutter Gdns., Mitch.	BT52	86
Rutters Clo., West Dr.	AZ41	63
Ruttesland St. N1	CA37	57
Hoxton St.		
Rutts Ter. SE14	CC44	67
Rutts, The, Bush.	BG26	36
Ruvigny Gdns. SW15	BQ45	65
Ruxbury Rd., Cher.	AU53	82
Ruxley Clo., Epsom	BM56	94
Ruxley Clo., Sid.	CP50	79
Ruxley Cres., Esher	BJ57	93
Ruxley La., Epsom	BM57	94
Ruxley Ms., Epsom	BM56	94
Ruxley Ridge, Esher	BJ57	93
Ruxton Clo., Swan.	CT52	89
Ryan Clo. SE3	CJ45	68
Ryarsh Cres., Orp.	CN56	97
Rycott Path SE22	CB47	77
Lordship La.		
Rycroft Cres., Barn.	BP25	28
Rycroft La., Sev.	CT68	116
Rycroft Way N17	CA31	48
Ryculff Sq. SE3	CG44	68
Rydal Clo. NW4	BR30	37
Rydal Clo., Pur.	BZ60	96
Rydal Cres., Grnf.	BJ37	54
Rydal Dr., Bexh.	CQ44	69
Rydal Dr., W.Wick.	CG55	88
Rydal Gdns. NW9	BO32	46
Rydal Gdns. SW15	BO49	75
Rydal Gdns., Houns.	BF46	74
Rydal Gdns., Wem.	BK33	45
Rydal Rd. SW16	BW49	76
Rydal Way, Egh.	AT50	72
Rydal Way, Enf.	CC25	30
Rydal Way, Ruis.	BD35	45
Ryde Clo., Wok.	AX64	101
Ryde Heron, Wok.	AP62	100
Ryde Pl., Twick.	BK46	74
Ryde Vale Rd. SW12	BV48	76
Ryde, The, Hat.	BQ11	10

Ryde, The, Stai.	AW51	83
Rydens Av., Walt.	BC55	83
Rydens Clo., Walt.	BD55	84
Rydens Gro., Walt.	BD56	93
Rydens Rd., Walt.	BC55	83
Rydens Way, Wok.	AT63	100
Ryder Clo., Brom.	CH49	78
Ryder Clo., Bush.	BF25	27
Ryder Clo., Hem.H.	AT17	16
Ryder Gdns. E6	CL39	58
Ryder Gdns., Rain.	CT36	59
Ryder St. SW1	**BW40**	**3**
Ryder St. SW1	BW40	56
Ryders Av., Hat.	BO13	10
Ryders Ter. NW8	**BT37**	**1**
Ryders Ter. NW8	BT37	56
Rydes Av., Guil.	AP69	118
Rydes Clo., Wok.	AY63	100
Rydes Hill Cres., Guil.	AP68	109
Rydes Hill Rd., Guil.	AP69	118
Rydings, Wind.	AM45	61
Rydon St. N1	**BZ37**	**2**
Rydon St. N1	BZ37	57
St Paul St.		
Rydons Clo. SE9	CK45	68
Rydons La., Couls.	BZ63	105
Rydons Pk., Walt.	BD55	84
Rydons Wood Clo., Couls.	BZ63	105
Rydston Clo. N7	BX36	56
Sutterton St.		
Rye Clo., Bex.	CR46	79
Rye Clo., Guil.	AP69	118
Rye Clo., Horn.	CV35	51
Rye Cres., Orp.	CP54	89
Rye Hill Est. SE15	CC45	67
Rye Hill Pk. SE15	CC45	67
Rye Hill Rd., Epp.	CO15	14
Rye Hill Rd., Harl.	CM13	13
Rye La. SE15	CB44	67
Rye La., Longford	CT63	107
Rye La., Otford	CU61	107
Rye Pass. SE15	CB45	67
Rye Rd. SE15	CC45	67
Rye Rd., Hodd.	CE11	12
Rye Way, Edg.	BL29	37
Rye Wk. SW15	BQ46	75
Rye, The N14	BW26	38
Ryebrook Clo., Lthd.	BJ62	102
Ryebrook Rd., Lthd.	BJ62	102
Ryecotes Mead SE21	CA47	77
Ryecroft Av., Ilf.	CL30	40
Ryecroft Av., Twick.	BF47	74
Ryecroft Clo., Hem.H.	BA14	8
Poynders Hill		
Ryecroft Ct., St.Alb.	BL13	10
Fourways		
Ryecroft Rd. SE13	CF46	77
Ryecroft Rd. SW16	BY50	76
Ryecroft Rd., Orp.	CM53	88
Ryecroft Rd., Sev.	CU61	107
Ryecroft St. SW6	BS44	66
Ryecroft, Harl.	CL11	13
Ryecroft, Hat.	BO13	10
Ryecroft, Wind.	AM45	61
Ryedale SE22	CB46	77
Ryefield Av., Uxb.	AZ36	53
Ryefield Cres., Pnr.	BC30	35
Ryefield Path SW15	BP47	75
Bessborough Rd.		
Ryefield Rd. SE19	BZ50	77
Ryefield Rd., Croy.	CC60	96
Ryefield, Orp.	CP55	89
Ryehill Ct., N.Mal.	BO54	85
Ryeland Clo., West Dr.	AY39	53
Ryelands Clo., Cat.	CA64	105
Ryelands Cres. SE12	CJ46	78
Ryelands Ct., Lthd.	BJ62	102
Kingston Rd.		
Ryelands, Welw.G.C.	BR 9	5
Ryfold Rd. SW19	BS48	76
Ryhope Rd. N11	BW28	38
Rykhill, Grays	DG41	71
Ryland Clo., Felt.	BB49	73
Ryland Rd. NW5	BV36	56
Rylandes Rd. NW2	BP34	46
Rylandes Rd., S.Croy.	CD58	96
Rylett Cres. W12	BO41	65
Rylett Rd. W12	BO41	65
Rylston Rd. N13	BZ27	39
Rylston Rd. SW6	BR43	65
Ryman Ct., Rick.	AU25	25
Stag La.		
Rymer Rd. SW18	BT45	66
Alma Rd.		
Rymer Rd., Croy.	CA54	87
Rymer St. SE24	BY46	76
Rymill Clo., Hem.H.	AT17	16
Rymill St. E16	CL40	58
Rysbrack St. SW3	**BU41**	**3**
Rysbrack St. SW3	BU41	66
Rysted La., West.	CM66	115
Rythe Ct., T.Ditt.	BJ54	84
Rythe Rd., Esher	BH56	93
Ryvers Rd., Slou.	AS41	62

S

Sabah Ct., Ashf.	AZ49	73
Sabbarton St. E16	CG39	58
Victoria Dock Rd.		
Sabella Ct. E3	CE37	57
Mostyn Gro.		
Sabina Rd., Grays	DH42	71
Sabine Rd. SW11	BU45	66
Sabines Rd., Rom.	CV23	33
Sable Clo., Houns.	BD45	64
Sable St. N1	BY36	56
Sach Rd. E5	CB34	48
Sackville Av., Brom.	CH54	88
Sackville Clo., Har.	BG34	45
Sackville Clo., Sev.	CU64	107
Sackville Cres., Rom.	CW30	42
Sackville Est. SW16	BX48	76
Sackville Gdns., Ilf.	CK33	49
Sackville Rd., Dart.	CV48	80
Sackville Rd., Sutt.	BS57	95
Sackville St. W1	**BW40**	**3**
Sackville St. W1	BW40	56
Sackville Way SE22	CB47	77
Wilkie Way		
Sacombe Rd., Hem.H.	AV12	7
Saddington St., Grav.	DH47	81
Saddlers Clo., B.Wd.	BN25	28
Farriers Way		
Saddlers Clo., Pnr.	BF29	36
Saddlers Mead, Harl.	CO11	14
Saddlers Ms., Wem.	BH35	45
The Boltons		
Saddlers Pk., Eyns.	CV55	90
Saddlers Way, Epsom	BN63	103
Saddlescombe Way N12	BS28	38
Saddleworth Rd., Rom.	CV29	42
Saddleworth Sq., Rom.	CV29	42
Sadie St. SE5	BZ44	67
Orpheus St.		
Sadler Clo., Mitch.	BU51	86
Sadlers Clo., Guil.	AU70	118
Sadlers Ride, E.Mol.	BG51	84
Sadlier Rd., St.Alb.	BH14	9
Saffron Clo. NW11	BR32	46
Saffron Clo., Brwd.	DE32	123
Saffron Clo., Hodd.	CD11	12
Saffron Clo., Slou.	AQ44	62
Saffron Hill EC1	BY38	56
Saffron Hill EC1	**BY39**	**2**
Saffron La., Hem.H.	AW13	8
Saffron Platt, Guil.	AQ68	109
Saffron Rd., Rom.	CS30	41
Saffron St. EC1	**BY39**	**2**
Saffron St. EC1	BY39	56
Saffron Hill		
Sage St. E1	CC40	57
Cable St.		
Saigasso Clo. E16	CJ39	58
Royal Rd.		
Sail St. SE11	**BX42**	**4**
Sail St. SE11	BX42	66
Sainfoin Rd. SW17	BV48	76
Sainsbury Rd. SE19	BZ49	77
St. Agathas Dr., Kings.T.	BL50	75
St. Agathas Gro., Cars.	BU54	86
St. Agathas Wk., Kings.T.	BM50	75
Alexandra Rd.		
St. Agnells Ct., Hem.H.	AZ11	8
St. Agnells La., Hem.H.	AY11	8
St. Agnes Clo. E9	CC37	57
Gore Rd.		
St. Agnes Pl. SE11	BY43	66
St. Aidans Rd. SE22	CB46	77
St. Aidans Rd. W13	BJ41	64
St. Aidans Way, Grav.	DJ48	81
St. Albans Av. E6	CK38	58
St. Albans Av. W4	BN42	65
St. Albans Av., Felt.	BD49	74
St. Albans Av., Upmin.	CZ34	51
St. Albans Av., Wey.	AZ55	83
St. Albans Clo. NW11	BS33	47
North End Rd.		
St. Albans Clo., Grav.	DH48	81
St. Albans Cres. N22	BY30	38
St. Albans Cres., Wdf.Grn.	CH29	40
St. Albans Gdns., Grav.	DH48	81
St. Albans Gdns., Tedd.	BJ49	74
St. Albans Gro. W8	**BS41**	**3**
St. Albans Gro. W8	BS41	66
St. Albans Gro., Cars.	BU54	86
St. Albans Hill, Hem.H.	AY15	8
St. Albans La. NW11	BS33	47
West Heath Br.		
St. Albans La., St.Alb.	BC16	17
St. Albans Ms. W2	**BT39**	**1**
St. Albans Ms. W2	BT39	56
Edgware Rd.		
St. Albans Pl. N1	**BY37**	**2**
St. Albans Pl. W1	BY37	56
St. Albans Rd. E., Hat.	BP12	10
St. Albans Rd. NW10	BO37	55
St. Albans Rd. NW5	BV34	47
St. Albans Rd. W., Hat.	BN12	10
St. Albans Rd., Kings.T.	BL50	75
St. Albans Rd., Wdf.Grn.	CH29	40
St. Albans Rd., Barn.	BQ22	28
St. Albans Rd., Dart.	CW47	80
St. Albans Rd., Epp.	CP18	23
St. Albans Rd., Garston	BD20	18
St. Albans Rd., Hat.	BP12	10
St. Albans Rd., Hem.H.	AX14	8
St. Albans Rd., Ilf.	CN33	49
St. Albans Rd., Kings.T.	BL50	75
St. Albans Rd., Pot.B.	BO19	19
St. Albans Rd., Reig.	BS70	121
St. Albans Rd., St.Alb.	BJ11	9
St. Albans Rd., Sutt.	BR56	94
St. Albans Rd., Wat.	BC23	26
St. Albans St. SW1	**BW40**	**3**
St. Albans St. SW1	BW40	56
Jermyn St.		
St. Albans St., Wind.	AO44	61
St. Albans Ter. W6	BR43	65
St. Alfege Rd. SE7	CJ43	68
St. Alphage Ct. NW9	BN31	46
St. Alphage Gdns. EC2	**BZ39**	**2**
St. Alphage Gdns. EC2	BZ39	57
St. Alphage High Wk. EC2	**BZ39**	**2**
St. Alphage Gdns.		
St. Alphege Pass. SE10	CF43	67
Roan St.		
St. Alphege Rd. N9	CC26	39
St. Alphonsus Rd. SW4	BW45	66
St. Amunds Clo. SE6	CE49	77
St. Andrew St. EC4	**BY39**	**2**

St. Andrew St. EC4	BY39	56
St. Andrew St. W14	BR43	65
St. Andrews Av., Horn.	CU35	50
St. Andrews Av., Wem.	BJ35	45
St. Andrews Av., Wind.	AM44	61
St. Andrews Clo. N12	BT28	38
Woodside Av.		
St. Andrews Clo. NW2	BP34	46
St. Andrews Clo., Epp.	CS15	14
St. Andrews Clo., Islw.	BH44	64
St. Andrews Clo., Reig.	BS71	121
St. Marys Rd.		
St. Andrews Clo., Ruis.	BD34	45
St. Andrews Clo., Shep.	BA52	83
St. Andrews Clo., Stai.	AS47	72
St. Andrews Clo., Stan.	BK30	36
St. Andrews Clo., Wind.	AQ46	72
St. Andrews Cres., Wind.	AM44	61
St. Andrews Ct. SW18	BT48	76
Waynflete St.		
St. Andrews Dr., Orp.	CO53	89
St. Andrews Dr., Stan.	BK30	36
St. Andrews Gro. N16	BZ33	48
St. Andrews Hill EC4	BY39	56
St. Andrews Hill EC4	**BY40**	**4**
St. Andrews Ms. N16	CA33	48
Dunsmure Rd.		
St. Andrews Pl. NW1	**BV38**	**1**
St. Andrews Pl. NW1	BV38	56
St. Andrews Pl., Brwd.	DC27	122
St. Andrews Rd. E11	CG32	49
St. Andrews Rd. E13	CH38	58
St. Andrews Rd. E17	CC30	39
St. Andrews Rd. N9	CC26	39
St. Andrews Rd. NW10	BP36	55
St. Andrews Rd. NW11	BR32	46
St. Andrews Rd. NW9	BN33	46
St. Andrews Rd. W14	BR43	65
St. Andrews Rd. W3	BO40	55
St. Andrews Rd. W7	BH41	64
St. Andrews Rd., Cars.	BU55	86
St. Andrews Rd., Couls.	BV61	104
St. Andrews Rd., Croy.	BZ56	96
St. Andrews Rd., Enf.	BZ24	30
St. Andrews Rd., Hem.H.	AX15	8
St. Andrews Rd., Ilf.	CK33	49
St. Andrews Rd., Rom.	CS32	50
St. Andrews Rd., Sid.	CP48	79
St. Andrews Rd., Surb.	BK53	84
St. Andrews Rd., Til.	DF44	71
St. Andrews Rd., Uxb.	AY37	53
St. Andrews Rd., Wat.	BD27	36
St. Andrews Sq. W11	BR39	55
St. Marks Rd.		
St. Andrews Sq., Surb.	BK53	84
St. Andrews Way E3	CE38	57
St. Andrews Way, Oxt.	CK69	115
St. Andrews Way, Slou.	AL40	61
St. Andrews Wk., Cob.	BC61	101
St. Anne St. E14	CD39	57
St. Annes Av., Stai.	AX47	73
St. Annes Clo. N6	BV34	47
St. Annes Clo., Chsnt.	CA17	21
St. Annes Clo., Grays	DD40	71
St. Annes Clo., Wat.	BD28	36
St. Annes Ct. W1	**BW39**	**1**
St. Annes Ct. W1	BW39	56
Wardour St.		
St. Annes Gdns. NW10	BL38	55
St. Annes Pass. E14	CD39	57
Newell St.		
St. Annes Rd. E11	CF34	48
St. Annes Rd., Brwd.	DE23	122
St. Annes Rd., Cher.	AV53	82
St. Annes Rd., St.Alb.	BK17	18
St. Annes Rd., Uxb.	AX31	44
St. Annes Rd., Wem.	BK35	45
St. Annes Row E14	CD39	57
St. Anne St.		
St. Anns Clo., Cher.	AV53	82
St. Anns Cres. SW18	BT46	76
St. Anns Gdns. NW5	BV36	56
Queens Cres.		
St. Anns Hill Rd., Cher.	AU53	82
St. Anns Hill SW18	BS46	76
St. Anns La. SW1	**BW41**	**3**
St. Anns La. SW1	BW41	66
Old Pye St.		
St. Anns Park Rd. SW18	BT46	76
St. Anns Pass. SW13	BO45	65
Cross St.		
St. Anns Rd. N15	BY32	47
St. Anns Rd. N9	CA27	39
St. Anns Rd. SW13	BO44	65
St. Anns Rd. W11	BQ40	55
St. Anns Rd., Cher.	AV53	82
St. Anns Rd., Har.	BH32	45
St. Anns St. SW1	**BW41**	**3**
St. Anns St. SW1	BW41	66
St. Anns St., Bark.	CM37	58
Morley Rd.		
St. Anns Ter. NW8	**BT37**	**1**
St. Anns Ter. NW8	BT37	56
St. Anns Vill. W11	BQ40	55
St. Anns Way, S.Croy.	BY57	95
St. Anns, Bark.	CM37	58
St. Anselms Pl. W1	**BV40**	**3**
St. Anselms Pl. W1	BV40	56
Davies St.		
St. Anselms Rd., Hayes	BB41	63
St. Anthonys Av., Hem.H.	AZ14	8
St. Anthonys Av., Wdf.Grn.	CJ29	40
St. Anthonys Clo. E1	**CB40**	**4**
St. Anthonys Clo. E1	CB40	57
St. Anthonys Clo. SW17	BU48	76
College Gdns.		
St. Anthonys Rd. E7	CH36	58
St. Anthonys Way, Felt.	BB45	63
St. Arvans Clo., Croy.	CA55	87
St. Asaph Rd. SE4	CC45	67
St. Aubyns Av. SW19	BR49	75
St. Aubyns Av., Houns.	BF46	74
St. Aubyns Clo., Orp.	CN55	88
St. Aubyns Gdns., Orp.	CN55	88

St. Aubyns Rd. SE19 CA50 77
St. Audrey Av., Bexh. CR44 69
St. Audreys Clo., Hat. BP13 10
St. Audreys Grn., Welw.G.C. BR8 5
St. Augustine Rd., Grays DG42 71
St. Augustines Av. W5 BL37 55
St. Augustines Av., Wem. BL34 46
St. Augustines Av., S.Croy. BZ57 96
St. Augustines Av., Brom. CK53 88
St. Augustines Clo., Brox. CD13 12
St. Augustines Dr., Brox. CD13 12
St. Augustines Rd. NW1 BW36 56
St. Augustines Rd., Belv. CQ42 69
St. Austell Clo., Edg. BL30 37
St. Austell Rd. SE13 CF44 67
St. Awdrys Rd., Bark. CM36 58
St. Awdrys Wk., Bark. CM36 58
St. Barnabas Clo., Beck. CF51 87
St. Barnabas Rd. E17 CE32 48
St. Barnabas Rd., Mitch. BV50 76
St. Barnabas Rd., Wdf.Grn. CH30 40
St. Barnabas Rd., Sutt. BT56 95
St. Barnabas St. SW1 BV42 3
St. Barnabas St. SW1 BV42 66
St. Barnabas Ter. E9 CC35 48
Wardle St.
St. Barnabas Vill. SW8 BX44 66
Guildford Rd.
St. Bartholomews Clo. SE26 CB49 77
St. Bartholomews Rd. E6 CK37 58
St. Benedicts Av., Grays DJ48 81
St. Benedicts Clo. SW17 BV49 76
Church La.
St. Benets Clo. SW17 BU48 76
College Gdns.
St. Benets Gro., Cars. BT54 86
St. Benets Pl. EC3 BZ40 4
Gracechurch St.
St. Bernards Clo. SE27 BZ49 77
St. Gothard Rd.
St. Bernards Rd. E6 CJ37 58
St. Bernards Rd., St.Alb. BH13 9
St. Bernards Rd., Slou. AR41 62
St. Bernards, Croy. CA55 87
St. Blaise Av., Brom. CH51 88
St. Botolph Rd., Grav. DE48 81
Pepper Hill
St. Botolph Row EC3 CA39 57
Houndsditch
St. Botolph St. EC3 CA39 2
St. Botolph St. EC3 CA39 57
St. Botolphs Av., Sev. CU65 107
St. Botolphs Rd., Sev. CU65 107
St. Brelades Clo., Dor. BJ72 119
St. Bride St. EC4 BY39 2
St. Bride St. EC4 BY39 56
St. Brides Av. EC4 BY39 2
Bride La.
St. Brides Av., Edg. BL30 37
St. Brides Clo., Erith CP41 69
St. Katherines Rd.
St. Brides Pass. EC4 BY39 56
Dorset Ri.
St. Catharines Rd., Brox. CE13 12
St. Catherines Clo. SW17 BU48 76
College Gdns.
St. Catherines Clo., Wok. AR63 100
St. Catherines Cross, Red. CA70 114
St. Catherines Ct. W4 BO42 65
Newton Gro.
St. Catherines Dr. SE14 CC44 67
Kitto Rd.
St. Catherines Dr., Guil. AQ72 118
St. Catherines Est., Wok. AR63 100
St. Catherines Farm Ct., Ruis. BA32 44
Howletts La.
St. Catherines Rd. E4 CE27 39
St. Catherines Rd., Ruis. BA32 44
St. Cecilia Rd., Grays DG42 71
St. Chads Dr., Grav. DJ48 81
St. Chads Gdns., Rom. CQ33 50
St. Chads Pl. WC1 BX38 2
St. Chads Pl. WC1 BX38 56
St. Chads Rd., Rom. CQ32 50
St. Chads Rd., Til. DG44 71
St. Chads St. WC1 BX38 56
St. Charles Pl. W10 BR39 55
Chesterton Rd.
St. Charles Rd., Brwd. DA26 42
St. Charles Sq. W10 BQ39 55
St. Christopher Rd., Uxb. AX39 53
St. Christophers Clo., Islw. BG44 64
St. Christophers Gdns., Th.Hth. BY52 86
Warwick Rd.
St. Christophers Ms., Wall. BW56 95
Bute Rd.
St. Christophers Pl. W1 BV39 1
St. Christophers Pl. W1 BV39 56
Barrett St.
St. Clair Clo., Ilf. CK30 40
St. Clair Clo., Oxt. CF68 114
St. Clair Clo., Reig. BT70 121
St. Clair Dr., Wor.Pk. BP55 85
St. Clair Rd. E13 CH37 58
St. Clairs Rd., Croy. CA55 87
St. Clare St. EC3 CA39 2
St. Clare St. EC3 CA39 57
Minories
St. Clement St. N7 BY36 56
Offord Rd.
St. Clement Way, Uxb. AX39 53
St. Clements Av., Grays DA43 70
St. Clements Ct. EC4 BZ40 4
Clements La.
St. Clements Ct. N7 BY36 56
Arundel Sq.
St. Clements Ct., Grays CX42 70
Thamley
St. Clements Heights SE26 CB48 77
Wells Park Rd.
St. Clements La. WC2 BX39 2
St. Clements La. WC2 BX39 56
Portugal St.
St. Clements Rd., Grays DB43 70
St. Clere Hill Rd., Sev. CY60 99
St. Cloud Rd. SE27 BZ49 77
St. Columbas Clo., Grav. DJ48 81
St. Crispins Clo. NW3 BU35 47
St. Crispins Clo., Sthl. BE39 54
St. Crispins Way, Cher. AU58 91
St. Cross St. EC1 BY39 2
St. Cross St. EC1 BY39 56
St. Cuthberts Gdns., Pnr. BE29 36
Westfield Pk.
St. Cuthberts NW3 BS34 47
St. Cuthberts Rd. N13 BY29 38
St. Cuthberts Rd. NW2 BR36 55
St. Cuthberts Rd., Hodd. CF10 12
St. Cyprians St. SW17 BU49 76
St. David Clo., Uxb. AX39 53
St. Davids Clo., W.Wick. CE54 87
St. Davids Clo., Hem.H. BA14 8
St. Davids Clo., Iver AU37 52
St. Davids Clo., Reig. BT70 121
St. Davids Clo., Wem. BN34 46
St. Davids Cres., Grav. DH49 81
St. Davids Dr., Brox. CD13 12
St. Davids Dr., Edg. BL30 37
St. Davids Pl. NW4 BP33 46
St. Davids Rd., Swan. CT50 79
St. Davids, Pur. BX62 104
St. Denis Rd. SE27 BZ49 77
St. Denys Clo., Wok. AO62 100
St. Dionis Rd. SW6 BR44 65
St. Donatts Rd. SE14 CD44 67
St. Dunstans All. EC3 CA40 57
Idol La.
St. Dunstans Av. W3 BN40 55
St. Dunstans Clo., Hayes BB42 63
St. Dunstans Dr., Grav. DJ49 81
St. Dunstans Gdns. W3 BN40 55
St. Dunstans Av.
St. Dunstans Hill EC3 CA40 4
St. Dunstans Hill EC3 CA40 57
St. Dunstans Hill, Sutt. BR57 94
St. Dunstans La. EC3 CA40 4
St. Dunstans La. EC3 CA40 57
Idol La.
St. Dunstans La., Beck. CF53 87
St. Dunstans Rd. E7 CJ36 58
St. Dunstans Rd. SE25 CA52 87
St. Dunstans Rd. W6 BQ42 65
St. Dunstans Rd. W7 BH41 64
St. Dunstans Rd., Houns. BC44 63
St. Dunstans Rd., Felt. BB48 73
St. Ediths Rd., Sev. CX62 108
St. Edmund Clo. SW17 BU48 76
College Gdns.
St. Edmunds Av., Ruis. BA32 44
St. Edmunds Clo. NW8 BU37 1
St. Edmunds Clo. NW8 BU37 56
St. Edmunds Ter.
St. Edmunds Clo., Erith CP41 69
St. Katherines Rd.
St. Edmunds Dr., Stan. BJ30 36
St. Edmunds La., Twick. BF47 74
St. Edmunds Rd. N9 CB26 39
St. Edmunds Rd., Dart. CX45 70
St. Edmunds Rd., Ilf. CK32 49
St. Edmunds Ter. NW8 BU37 1
St. Edmunds Ter. NW8 BU37 56
St. Edmunds Way, Harl. CP9 6
St. Edmunds, Berk. AR13 7
St. Edwards Clo. NW11 BS32 47
Finchley Rd.
St. Edwards Clo., Croy. CF59 96
St. Edwards Way, Rom. CT31 50
St. Egberts Way E4 CF26 39
St. Elmo Clo., Slou. AO38 52
St. Elmo Cres.
St. Elmo Cres., Slou. AO38 52
St. Elmo Rd. W12 BO40 55
St. Elmos Rd. SE16 CC41 67
St. Erkenwald Rd., Bark. CM37 58
St. Ermins Hill SW1 BW41 66
Broadway
St. Ervans Rd. W10 BR39 55
St. Ethelredas Dr., Hat. BQ12 10
St. Faiths Clo., Enf. BZ23 30
St. Faiths Rd. SE21 BY47 76
St. Fidelis Rd., Erith CS42 69
St. Fillans Rd. SE6 CF47 77
St. Francis Av., Grav. DJ49 81
St. Francis Clo., Pot.B. BT20 20
St. Vincents Way
St. Francis Clo., Orp. CN53 88
St. Francis Clo., Wat. BC26 35
St. Francis Rd. SE22 CA45 67
St. Francis Rd., Erith CS42 69
West St.
St. Francis Rd., Uxb. AV32 43
St. Francis Way, Grays DH42 71
St. Gabriel St. SE11 BY42 4
St. Gabriels Clo. E11 CH33 49
St. Gabriels Rd. NW2 BQ35 46
St. George St. W1 BV39 56
St. George St. W1 BV40 3
St. Georges Av. E7 CH36 58
St. Georges Av. N7 BW35 47
St. Georges Av. NW9 BN31 46
St. Georges Av. W5 BK41 64
St. Georges Av., Grays DE42 71
St. Georges Av., Horn. CW33 51
St. Georges Av., Sthl. BE40 54
St. Georges Av., Wey. AZ57 92
St. Georges Cir. SE1 BY41 4
St. Georges Cir. SE1 BY41 66
St. Georges Clo. NW11 BR32 46
St. Georges Clo., Wem. BJ34 45
St. Georges Clo., Wey. BA56 92
St. Georges Clo., Wind. AM44 61
St. Georges Cres., Grav. DH49 81
St. Georges Ct. E6 CK38 58
St. Georges Ct. SW7 BT41 3
St. Georges Ct. W8 BT41 66
St. Georges Dr. SW1 BV42 3
St. Georges Dr. SW1 BV42 66
St. Georges Dr., Uxb. AY34 44
St. Georges Dr., Wat. BE27 36
St. Georges Est., Amer. AQ23 25
St. Georges Flds. W2 BU39 1
St. Georges Flds. W2 BU39 56
Albion St.
St. Georges Gdns., Surb. BM55 85
Hamilton Av.
St. Georges Gdns., Epsom BO60 94
St. Georges Gro. SW17 BT48 76
St. Georges La. EC3 BZ40 57
Pudding La.
St. Georges Lo., Wey. BA56 92
St. Georges Ms. NW1 BU36 56
Regents Park Rd.
St. Georges Pl., Twick. BJ47 74
Church St.
St. Georges Rd. E10 CF34 48
St. Georges Rd. E7 CH36 58
St. Georges Rd. N13 BX27 38
St. Georges Rd. N21 BX27 38
St. Georges Rd. N9 CB27 39
St. Georges Rd. NW11 BR32 46
St. Georges Rd. SE1 BY41 4
St. Georges Rd. SE1 BY41 66
St. Georges Rd. SW19 BR50 75
St. Georges Rd. W., Brom. CK51 88
St. Georges Rd. W4 BN41 65
St. Georges Rd. W7 BH40 54
St. Georges Rd., Addlestone AX56 92
St. Georges Rd., Kings.T. BM50 75
St. Georges Rd., Beck. CE51 87
St. Georges Rd., Brom. CK51 88
St. Georges Rd., Dag. CQ35 50
St. Georges Rd., Enf. CA22 30
St. Georges Rd., Felt. BD49 74
St. Georges Rd., Hem.H. AX15 8
St. Georges Rd., Ilf. CK33 49
St. Georges Rd., Mitch. BV52 86
St. Georges Rd., Orp. CM53 88
St. Georges Rd., Rich. BL45 65
St. Georges Rd., Sev. CU64 107
St. Georges Rd., Sid. CP50 79
St. Georges Rd., Swan. CT52 89
St. Georges Rd., Twick. BJ46 74
St. Georges Rd., Wall. BV56 95
St. Georges Rd., Wat. BC22 26
St. Georges Rd., Wey. BA57 92
St. Georges Sq. E14 CD40 57
Narrow St.
St. Georges Sq. E7 CH36 58
St. Georges Sq. Ms. SW1 BW42 3
St. Georges Sq. SE8 CD42 67
St. Georges Sq. SW1 BW42 3
St. Georges Sq. SW1 BW42 66
St. Georges Sq., Long. DC52 90
Bramblefield Clo.
St. Georges Ter. NW1 BU36 1
Regents Park Rd.
St. Georges Way SE15 CA43 67
St. Georges Wk., Croy. BZ55 87
St. Gerards Clo. SW4 BW46 76
St. Germans Bungalows SE3 CG44 68
St. Germans Pl. SE3 CH44 68
St. Germans Rd. SE23 CD47 77
St. Giles Av., Dag. CR36 59
St. Giles Av., Pot.B. BP20 19
St. Giles Av., Uxb. BA35 44
St. Giles Cir. W1 BW39 1
St. Giles Cir. WC1 BW39 1
St. Giles Cir. WC2 BW39 1
St. Giles Clo., Dag. CR36 59
St. Giles Clo., Orp. CM56 97
St. Giles Ct. WC2 BW39 1
St. Giles High St. WC2 BW39 1
St. Giles High St. WC2 BW39 56
St. Giles Rd. SE5 CA43 67
St. Gothard Rd. SE27 BZ49 77
St. Gregory Clo., Ruis. BD35 45
St. Gregorys Cres., Grav. DJ48 81
St. Helena Rd. SE16 CC42 67
St. Helena St. WC1 BY38 2
St. Helena Ter., Rich. BK46 74
Friars La.
St. Helens Clo., Uxb. AX39 53
St. Helens Cres. SW16 BX51 86
St. Helens Ct., Epp. CO18 23
St. Helens Ct., Rain. CU38 59
St. Helens Gdns. W10 BQ39 55
St. Helens Pl. EC3 CA39 2
St. Helens Pl. EC3 CA39 57
Bishopsgate
St. Helens Rd. SW16 BX51 86
St. Helens Rd. W13 BJ40 54
Dane Rd.
St. Helens Rd., Erith CP41 69
St. Helens Rd., Ilf. CK32 49
St. Helier Av., Mord. BT54 86
St. Heliers Av., Houns. BF46 74
St. Heliers Rd. E10 CF32 48
St. Hildas Rd., St.Alb. BJ11 9
St. Hildas Av., Ashf. AY49 73
St. Hildas Clo. NW6 BQ36 55
St. Hildas Clo. SW17 BU48 76
St. Hildas Clo., Ashf. AY49 73
St. Hildas Clo., Wok. AO62 100
St. Hildas Rd. SW13 BP43 65
St. Hildas Way, Grav. DJ49 81
St. Huberts Clo., Ger.Cr. AS34 43
St. Huberts La., Ger.Cr. AS34 43
St. Hughs Clo. SW17 BU48 76
College Gdns.
St. Hughs Rd. SE20 CB51 87
Ridsdale Rd.
St. Ives Clo., Welw.G.C. BR5 5
St. Ivians Dr., Rom. CU31 50
St. James Av. E2 CC37 57
St. James Av. N20 BU27 38
St. James Av., Beck. CD52 87
St. James Av., Epsom CO59 94
St. James Av., Ong. CW18 24
St. James Av., Sutt. BS56 95
St. James Clo. N20 BU27 38
St. James Clo. SE18 CM42 68
Congleton Gro.
St. James Clo., Epsom BO60 94
St. James Clo., Ruis. BD34 45
St. James Ct. SW1 BW41 3
Buckingham Gate
St. James Gdns., Wem. BK36 54
St. James La., Green. CZ47 80
St. James Ms. E14 CF41 67
St. James Pass. EC3 CA39 2
Dukes Pl.
St. James Pl., Dart. CV46 80
St. James Pl., Enf. CC25 30
South St.
St. James Rd. E15 CG35 49
St. James Rd. N9 CB27 39
St. James Rd. SE16 CB41 4
St. James Rd., Mitch. BV50 76
St. James Rd., Pur. BY60 95
St. James Rd., Surb. BK53 84
St. James Rd., Sutt. BS56 95
St. James SE14 CD44 67
St. James Ter. NW8 BU37 1
St. James Way, Sid. CQ49 79
St. James Wk. SE15 CA44 67
Sumner Est.
St. James Wk., Iver AV41 62
St. James's Av. W13 BJ40 54
St. James's Av., Grav. DG47 81
St. James's Av., Hmptn. BG49 74
St. James's Clo. SW12 BU48 76
St. James's Dr.
St. James's Clo., N.Mal. BO53 85
St. James's Cotts., Rich. BL46 75
Paradise Rd.
St. James's Cres. SW9 BY45 66
St. James's Dr. SW17 BU47 76
St. James's Gdns. W11 BR40 55
St. James's Gro. SW11 BU44 66
Reform St.
St. James's La. N10 BV31 47
St. James's Mkt. SW1 BW40 3
St. James's Pass. EC3 CA39 57
Dukes Pl.
St. James's Path E17 CD32 48
St. James's Pk., Croy. BZ54 87
St. James's Pl. SW1 BW40 3
St. James's Pl. SW1 BW40 56
St. James's Rd. SE1 CB41 67
St. James's Rd. SE16 CB41 67
St. James's Rd., Kings.T. BK51 84
St. James's Rd., Brwd. DB27 42
St. James's Rd., Cars. BU55 86
St. James's Rd., Chsnt. BZ17 21
St. James's Rd., Croy. BY54 86
St. James's Rd., Grav. DG47 81
St. James's Rd., Hmptn. BF49 74
St. James's Rd., Sev. CU64 107
St. James's Rd., Wat. BC25 26
St. James's Row EC1 BY38 2
St. James's Row EC1 BY38 56
Clerkenwell Clo.
St. James's SE14 CD44 67
St. James's Sq. SW1 BW40 3
St. James's Sq. SW1 BW40 56
St. James's St. E17 CD32 48
St. James's St. SW1 BW40 3
St. James's St. SW1 BW40 56
St. James's St. W6 BQ42 65
St. James's St., Grav. DG46 81
St. James's Ter. Ms. NW8 BU37 1
St. James's Ter. Ms. NW8 BU37 56
St. James's Wk. EC1 BY38 2
St. James's Wk. EC1 BY38 56
Sekforde St.
St. Jeromes Gro., Hayes BA39 53
St. Joans Rd. N9 CA27 39
St. John Fisher Rd., Erith CQ41 69
St. John St. EC1 BY37 56
St. Johns Av. N11 BU28 38
St. Johns Av. NW10 BO37 55
St. Johns Av. SW15 BQ46 75
St. Johns Av., Brwd. DB28 42
St. Johns Av., Epsom BO59 94
St. Johns Av., Harl. CP9 6
St. Johns Av., Lthd. BJ64 102
St. Johns Church Rd. E9 CC35 48
Urswick Rd.
St. Johns Church Rd., Dor. BE73 119
St. Johns Clo., Guil. AQ71 118
St. Johns Clo., Lthd. BK64 102
St. Johns Clo., Pot.B. BT20 20
St. Johns Clo., Rain. CU36 59
St. Johns Clo., Wem. BL35 46
St. Johns Cotts. SE20 CC50 77
Maple Rd.
St. Johns Cotts., Rich. BL45 65
Kew Foot Rd.
St. Johns Cres. SW9 BY45 66
St. Johns Cres., Islw. BH44 64
St. Johns Ct. N4 BY34 47
St. Johns Ct., Buck.H. CJ26 40
St. Johns Ct., Egh. AT49 72
St. Johns Ct., Islw. BH44 64
St. Johns Ct., Nthwd. BB29 35
Murray Rd.
St. Johns Ct., St.Alb. BJ12 9
Beaumont Av.
St. Johns Dr. SW18 BS47 76
St. Johns Dr., Walt. BD54 84
St. Johns Dr., Wind. AM44 61
St. Johns Est. N1 BZ37 57
St. Johns Est. SE1 CA41 4
St. Johns Est. SE1 CA41 67
St. Johns Est. SW11 BT44 66
St. Johns Gdns. W11 BR40 55
St. Johns Gro. N19 BW34 47
St. Johns Gro. SW13 BO44 65
Terrace Gdns.
St. Johns Gro., Rich. BL45 65
Kew Foot Rd.
St. Johns Hill Gro. SW11 BT45 66
St. Johns Hill Rd., Wok. AQ63 100
St. Johns Hill SW11 BT45 66
St. Johns Hill, Couls. BY62 104
St. Johns Hill, Pur. BY61 104
St. Johns Hill, Sev. CV64 108
St. Johns La. EC1 BY38 56
St. Johns La. EC1 BY38 2
St. Johns Ms., Wok. AQ62 100
St. Johns Rd.
St. Johns Par., Sid. CO49 79
St. Johns Pass. SW19 BR50 75
St. Johns Pathway SE23 CC47 77
Devonshire Rd.
St. Johns Pk. SE3 CG43 68
St. Johns Pl. EC1 BY38 2
St. Johns Rd. E16 CH39 58
St. Johns Rd. E17 CE30 39
St. Johns Rd. E4 CE28 39
St. Johns Rd. E6 CK37 58
St. Johns Rd. N15 CA32 48
St. Johns Rd. NW11 BR32 46
St. Johns Rd. SE20 CC50 77
St. Johns Rd. SW11 BU45 66
St. Johns Rd. SW19 BR50 75
St. Johns Rd., Bark. CN37 58
St. Johns Rd., Cars. BU55 86
St. Johns Rd., Croy. BY55 86
Sylverdale Rd.
St. Johns Rd., Dart. CY47 80
St. Johns Rd., Dor. BG72 119
St. Johns Rd., E.Mol. BG52 84
St. Johns Rd., Epp. CN18 22
St. Johns Rd., Erith CS42 69
St. Johns Rd., Felt. BE49 74
St. Johns Rd., Grav. DH47 81
St. Johns Rd., Grays DG42 71
St. Johns Rd., Guil. AQ71 118
St. Johns Rd., Har. BH32 45
St. Johns Rd., Hem.H. AW14 8
St. Johns Rd., Ilf. CM33 49
St. Johns Rd., Islw. BH44 64
St. Johns Rd., Kings.T. BK51 84
St. Johns Rd., Loug. CK23 31
St. Johns Rd., Lthd. BK64 102
St. Johns Rd., N.Mal. BN52 85
St. Johns Rd., Orp. CM53 88
St. Johns Rd., Red. BU71 121
St. Johns Rd., Rich. BL45 65
St. Johns Rd., Rom. CS28 41
St. Johns Rd., Sev. CU64 107
St. Johns Rd., Sid. CO49 79
St. Johns Rd., Slou. AQ40 52
St. Johns Rd., Sthl. BE41 64
St. Johns Rd., Sutt. BS55 86
St. Johns Rd., Uxb. AW37 53
St. Johns Rd., Wat. BC23 26
St. Johns Rd., Well. CO45 69
St. Johns Rd., Wem. BK35 45
St. Johns Rd., Wind. AN44 61
St. Johns Rd., Wok. AQ62 100
St. Johns Ri., Wok. AQ62 100
St. Johns Sq. EC1 BY38 2
St. Johns Sq. EC1 BY38 56
Clerkenwell Rd.
St. Johns St. EC1 BY37 2
St. Johns St. W10 BQ39 55
Harrow Rd.
St. Johns Ter. E7 CH36 58
St. Johns Ter. Rd., Red. BU71 121
St. Johns Ter. SE18 CM43 68
St. Johns Ter. W10 BQ38 55
Harrow Rd.
St. Johns Ter., Enf. BZ22 30
St. Johns Vale SE8 CE44 67
St. Johns Vill. N19 BW34 47
St. Johns Way N19 BW34 47
St. Johns Well La., Berk. AQ12 7
St. Johns Wood Ct. NW8 BT38 1
St. Johns Wood Ct. NW8 BT38 56
St. Johns Wood Rd.
St. Johns Wood High St. NW8 BT37 1
St. Johns Wood High St. NW8 BT37 56
St. Johns Wood Pk. NW8 BT37 1
St. Johns Wood Pk. NW8 BT37 56
St. Johns Wood Rd. NW8 BT38 1
St. Johns Wood Rd. NW8 BT38 56
St. Johns Wood Ter. NW8 BT37 1

St. Johns Wood Ter. NW8 BT37 56
St. Johns, Dor. BK73 119
St. Joseph St. SW8 BV44 66
St. Josephs Clo. W10 BR39 55
Bevington Rd.
St. Josephs Clo., Orp. CN56 97
Stapleton Rd.
St. Josephs Dr., Sthl. BE40 54
St. Josephs Gro. NW4 BP31 46
The Burroughs
St. Josephs Rd. N9 CB26 39
St. Josephs Rd., Wal.Cr. CD20 21
Swanfield Rd.
St. Josephs Vale SE3 CF45 67
St. Jude St. N16 CA35 48
St. Judes Clo., Egh. AR49 72
St. Judes Rd. E2 CB37 57
St. Judes Rd., Egh. AR49 72
St. Julians Clo. SW16 BY49 76
St. Julians Farm Rd. SE27 BY49 76
St. Julians Hill, St.Alb. BG15 9
St. Julians Rd. NW6 BR37 55
St. Julians Rd., St.Alb. BG14 9
St. Julians Rd., Sev. CW68 117
St. Justin Clo., Orp. CP52 89
St. Katharines Prec. NW1 BV37 56
Outer Circle
St. Katharines Way E1 CA40 4
St. Katharines Way E1 CB40 57
St. Katherines Rd., Erith CP41 69
St. Katherines Rd., Cat. CB66 114
St. Katherines Row EC3 CA40 4
St. Katherines Way, Berk. AP11 7
St. Keverne Rd. SE9 CK49 78
St. Kilda Rd. W13 BJ40 54
St. Kilda Rd., Orp. CN54 88
St. Kildas Rd. N16 BZ33 48
St. Kildas Rd., Brwd. DA26 42
St. Kildas Rd., Har. BH32 45
St. Kitts Road Ter. SE19 CA49 77
St. Laurence Dr., Brox. CD15 12
St. Laurences Clo. NW6 BQ37 55
St. Lawrence Clo., Hem.H. AT17 16
St. Lawrence Clo., St.Alb. BE18 18
St. Lawrence Clo., Edg. BL29 37
Whitchurch La.
St. Lawrence Clo., Orp. CP52 89
St. Lawrence Clo., Wat. BB18 17
St. Lawrence Dr., Pnr. BC32 44
St. Lawrence Gdns., Ing. DC19 24
St. Lawrence Rd., Upmin. CY34 51
St. Lawrence St. E14 CF40 57
St. Lawrence Ter. W10 BR39 55
St. Lawrence Way SW9 BY44 66
St. Lawrence Way, St.Alb. BE18 18
St. Lawrence Way, Slou. AQ41 62
St. Lawrence, Rue de, Wal.Abb. CF20 21
John Foxe Pl.
St. Leonards Av. E4 CF29 39
St. Leonards Av., Har. BK32 45
St. Leonards Av., Wind. AO44 61
St. Leonards Clo., Bush. BE24 27
St. Leonards Clo., Well. CO45 69
Hook La.
St. Leonards Cres., St.Alb. BK10 9
St. Leonards Ct. SW14 BN45 65
St. Leonards Rd.
St. Leonards Gdns., Houns. BE44 64
St. Leonards Gdns., Ilf. CM35 49
St. Leonards Hill, Wind. AM45 61
St. Leonards Rd. E14 CE39 57
St. Leonards Rd. NW10 BN38 55
St. Leonards Rd. SW14 BM45 65
St. Leonards Rd. W13 BK40 54
St. Leonards Rd., T.Ditt. BK53 84
St. Leonards Rd., Wal.Abb. CF15 12
St. Leonards Rd., Amer. AP21 25
St. Leonards Rd., Croy. BY55 86
St. Leonards Rd., Epsom BQ63 103
St. Leonards Rd., Esher BH57 93
St. Leonards Rd., Surb. BJ53 84
St. Leonards Rd., Wind. AN45 61
St. Leonards Ri., Orp. CM56 97
St. Leonards Sq. NW5 BV36 56
St. Leonards Sq., Surb. BK53 84
St. Leonards St. E3 CE38 57
St. Leonards Ter. SW3 BU42 3
St. Leonards Ter. SW3 BU42 66
St. Leonards Way, Horn. CU34 50
St. Leonards Wk. SW16 BX50 76
St. Leonards Wk., Iver AV41 62
St. Loo Av. SW3 BU43 3
St. Loo Av. SW3 BU43 66
St. Louis Rd. SE27 BZ49 77
St. Loys Rd. N17 CA30 39
St. Luke Clo., Uxb. AX39 53
St. Lukes Av. SW4 BW45 66
St. Lukes Av., Enf. BZ22 30
St. Lukes Av., Ilf. CL35 49
St. Lukes Clo. EC1 BZ38 2
St. Lukes Clo. EC1 BZ38 57
Old St.
St. Lukes Clo. SE25 CB53 87
St. Lukes Clo., Swan. CS51 89
The Orchard
St. Lukes Ms. W11 BR39 55
St. Lukes Pass., Kings.T. BL51 85
St. Lukes Pl., St.Alb. BJ14 9
St. Lukes Rd. W11 BR39 55
St. Lukes Rd., Uxb. AY36 53
Thompson Rd.
St. Lukes Rd., Whyt. CA62 105
St. Lukes Rd., Wind. AQ46 72
St. Lukes Sq. E16 CG39 58
St. Lukes St. SW3 BU42 3
St. Lukes St. SW3 BU42 66
St. Lukes Yd. W9 BR38 55
St. Malo Av. N9 CC27 39
St. Margarets Av. N15 BY31 47
St. Margarets Av. N20 BT27 38
St. Margarets Av., Ashf. AZ49 73
St. Margarets Av., Har. BG34 45
St. Margarets Av., Sid. CM48 78
St. Margarets Av., Sutt. BR55 85
St. Margarets Av., Uxb. AZ38 53
St. Margarets Clo. EC2 BZ39 2
Lothbury
St. Margarets Clo., Berk. AR13 7
St. Margarets Clo., Iver AU37 52
St. Margarets Clo., Orp. CO55 89
St. Margarets Cres. SW15 BP46 75
St. Margarets Cres., Grav. DJ48 81
St. Margarets Ct. SE1 BZ40 4
St. Margarets Dr., Twick. BJ46 74
St. Margarets Gate, Iver AU37 52
St. Margarets Gro. SE18 CM43 68
St. Margarets Gro., Twick. BJ46 74
St. Margarets Ms. WC2 BX40 4
St. Margarets NW3 BS34 47
St. Margarets Pass. SE13 CG45 68
St. Margarets Path SE18 CM42 68
St. Margarets Pl. SW1 BW41 3
St. Margarets Pl. SW1 BW41 66
Artillery Row
St. Margarets Rd. E12 CJ34 49
St. Margarets Rd. N17 CA31 48
St. Margarets Rd. NW10 BQ38 55
St. Margarets Rd. SE4 CD45 67
St. Margarets Rd. W7 BH41 64
St. Margarets Rd., Twick. BJ45 64
St. Margarets Rd., Couls. BV64 104
St. Margarets Rd., S.Dnth. CZ50 80
St. Margarets Rd., Beck. CC52 87
St. Margarets Rd., Edg. BM28 37
St. Margarets Rd., Grav. DF47 81
Perry St.
St. Margarets Rd., Ruis. BA32 44
St. Margarets Sq. SE4 CD45 67
Adelaide Av.
St. Margarets St. SW1 BX41 4
St. Margarets St. SW1 BX41 66
St. Margarets Ter. SE18 CM42 68
St. Margarets Way, Hem.H. BA13 8
St. Margarets, Bark. CM37 58
St. Margarets, Guil. AS70 118
St. Marks Av., Grav. DF47 81
St. Marks Clo. SE10 CF43 67
Ashburnham Pl.
St. Marks Clo. W11 BQ40 55
Lancaster Rd.
St. Marks Clo., Barn. BS24 29
St. Marks Cres. NW1 BV37 1
St. Marks Cres. NW1 BV37 56
St. Marks Gate E9 CD36 57
St. Marks Gro. SW10 BS43 66
St. Marks Hill, Surb. BL53 85
St. Marks Pl. SW19 BR50 75
Wimbledon Hill Rd.
St. Marks Pl. W11 BR39 55
St. Marks Pl., Wind. AO44 61
St. Marks Rd. SE25 CB52 87
Coventry Rd.
St. Marks Rd. W10 BQ39 55
St. Marks Rd. W11 BR39 55
St. Marks Rd. W5 BL40 55
The Common
St. Marks Rd. W7 BH41 64
St. Marks Rd., Brom. CH52 88
St. Marks Rd., Enf. CA25 30
St. Marks Rd., Epsom BQ62 103
St. Marks Rd., Mitch. BU51 86
St. Marks Rd., Tedd. BJ50 74
St. Marks Rd., Wind. AO44 61
St. Marks Ri. E8 CA35 48
St. Marks Sq. NW1 BV37 1
St. Marks Sq. NW1 BV37 56
Regents Park Rd.
St. Marks St. E1 CA39 2
St. Marthas Av., Wok. AS64 100
St. Martin Clo., Uxb. AX39 53
St. Martins App., Ruis. BB33 44
St. Martins Av. E6 CJ37 58
St. Martins Av., Epsom BO60 94
St. Martins Clo. NW1 BW37 1
St. Martins Clo., West Dr. AX41 63
St. Martins Clo., Brwd. DE26 122
St. Martins Clo., Enf. CB23 30
St. Martins Clo., Epsom BO60 94
St. Martins Clo., Erith CP41 69
St. Helens Rd.
St. Martins Clo., Lthd. BB69 110
St. Martins Clo., Wat. BD28 36
Muirfield Rd.
St. Martins Ct. WC2 BX40 4
St. Martins Ct. WC2 BX40 56
St. Martins La.
St. Martins Ct., Ashf. AX49 73
St. Martins Dr., Eyns. CV56 99
St. Martins Dr., Walt. BD55 84
St. Martins Est. SW2 BY47 76
St. Martins La. WC2 BX40 4
St. Martins La. WC2 BX40 56
St. Martins le Grand EC1 BZ39 2
St. Martins le Grand EC1 BZ39 57
St. Martins Meadow, West. CP65 107
St. Martins Ms. WC2 BX40 56
Adelaide St.
St. Martins Pl. WC2 BX40 4
St. Martins Rd. N9 CB27 39
St. Martins Rd. SW9 BX44 66
St. Martins Rd., West Dr. AX41 63
St. Martins Rd., Dart. CW46 80
St. Martins St. WC2 BW40 3
St. Martins St. WC2 BW40 56
Whitcomb St.
St. Martins Way SW17 BT48 76
St. Mary Abbots Pl. W8 BR41 65
St. Mary Abbots Ter. W14 BR41 65
St. Mary at Hill EC3 CA40 4
St. Mary at Hill EC3 CA40 57
Lower Thames St.
St. Mary Av., Wall. BV55 86
St. Mary Axe EC3 CA39 2
St. Mary Axe EC3 CA39 57
St. Mary Clo. N17 CB30 39
Kemble Rd.
St. Mary Rd. E17 CE32 48
St. Mary St. SE18 CK42 68
St. Marychurch St. SE16 CC41 67
St. Marys App. E12 CK35 49
Church Rd.
St. Marys Av. E11 CH32 49
St. Marys Av. N3 BR30 37
St. Marys Av., Berk. AO12 7
St. Marys Av., Brom. CG52 88
St. Marys Av., Brwd. DD25 122
St. Marys Av., Nthwd. BB28 35
St. Marys Av., Stai. AX47 73
St. Marys Av., Sthl. BF42 64
St. Marys Av., Tedd. BH50 74
St. Marys Clo. E12 CK35 49
Church Rd.
St. Marys Clo., Chess. BL57 94
St. Marys Clo., Epsom BO57 94
St. Marys Clo., Grav. DH48 81
St. Marys Clo., Grays DE43 71
Dock Rd.
St. Marys Clo., Lthd. BG65 102
St. Marys Clo., Orp. CO51 89
St. Marys Clo., Oxt. CG68 115
St. Marys Clo., Stai. AX47 73
St. Marys Clo., Sun. BC52 83
St. Marys Clo., Uxb. AW31 44
St. Marys Clo., Wat. BD24 27
St. Marys Cotts. SW19 BS51 86
St. Marys Rd.
St. Marys Cres. NW4 BP31 46
St. Marys Cres., Hayes BC40 53
St. Marys Cres., Islw. BG43 64
St. Marys Cres., Stai. AX47 73
St. Marys Ct. E6 CK38 58
St. Marys Ct. W5 BK41 64
St. Marys Rd.
St. Marys Dr., Felt. BA47 73
St. Marys Dr., Sev. CT65 107
St. Marys Gdns. SE11 BY42 4
St. Marys Gdns. SE11 BY42 66
St. Marys Grn. N2 BT31 47
Thomas More Way
St. Marys Grn., West. CJ62 106
St. Marys Gro.
St. Marys Gro. N1 BY36 56
St. Marys Gro. SW13 BP45 65
St. Marys Gro. W4 BM43 65
St. Marys Gro., Rich. BL45 65
St. Marys Gro., West. CJ62 106
St. Marys La., West Horndon DC33 123
St. Marys La., Upmin. CX34 51
St. Marys Mans. W2 BT39 1
St. Marys Ms. NW6 BB36 56
Priory Rd.
St. Marys Ms. W2 BT39 56
St. Marys Path N1 BY37 2
St. Marys Path N1 BY37 56
Gaskin St.
St. Marys Pl. SE9 CK46 78
Eltham High St.
St. Marys Rd. E10 CF34 48
St. Marys Rd. E13 CH37 58
St. Marys Rd. N8 BX31 47
High St.
St. Marys Rd. N9 CB26 39
St. Marys Rd. NW10 BO37 55
St. Marys Rd. NW11 BR33 46
St. Marys Rd. SE15 CC44 67
St. Marys Rd. SE25 CA52 87
St. Marys Rd. SW19 BR49 75
St. Marys Rd. W5 BK40 54
St. Marys Rd., Wimbledon SW19 BR49 75
St. Marys Rd., Barn. BU26 38
St. Marys Rd., Bex. CS47 79
St. Marys Rd., Chsnt. CC18 21
St. Marys Rd., Denham AV32 43
St. Marys Rd., E.Mol. BG53 84
St. Marys Rd., Grays DG42 71
St. Marys Rd., Green. CZ45 70
St. Marys Rd., Harefield AW31 44
St. Marys Rd., Hayes BB40 53
St. Marys Rd., Hem.H. AX13 8
St. Marys Rd., Ilf. CM34 49
St. Marys Rd., Long Ditton BK54 84
St. Marys Rd., Lthd. BJ64 102
St. Marys Rd., Merton SW19 BS51 86
St. Marys Rd., Reig. BS71 121
St. Marys Rd., S.Croy. BZ58 96
St. Marys Rd., Slou. AS40 52
St. Marys Rd., Surb. BK53 84
St. Marys Rd., Swan. CS52 89
St. Marys Rd., Wat. BC24 26
St. Marys Rd., Wey. BA56 92
St. Marys Rd., Wok. AR62 100
St. Marys Rd., Wor.Pk. BO55 85
St. Marys Sq. W2 BT39 1
St. Marys Sq. W2 BT39 56
St. Marys Ter.
St. Marys Ter. W2 BT39 1
St. Marys Ter. W2 BT39 56
St. Marys Vw., Har. BK32 45
St. Leonards Av.
St. Marys Way, Ger.Cr. AR30 34
St. Marys Way, Long. DC52 90
St. Marys Way, Wdf.Grn. CL28 40
St. Marys Wk. SE11 BY42 4
St. Marys Wk. SE11 BY42 66
St. Marys Wk., Hayes BB40 53
St. Marys Wk., St.Alb. BJ11 9
St. Marys, Bark. CM37 58
St. Matthew Clo., Uxb. AX39 53
St. Matthew Rd., Red. BU70 121
St. Matthew St. SW1 BW41 3
St. Matthew St. SW1 BW41 66
Old Pye St.
St. Matthews Av., Surb. BL54 85
St. Matthews Clo., Rain. CU36 59
St. Matthews Dr., Brom. CK52 88
St. Matthews Rd. SW2 BX45 66
St. Matthews Rd. W5 BL40 55
The Common
St. Matthews Row E2 CB38 2
St. Matthews Row E2 CB38 57
St. Matthias Clo. NW9 BO32 46
St. Maur Rd. SW6 BR44 65
St. Merryn Clo. SE18 CM43 68
St. Meryl Est., Wat. BE27 36
St. Michaels All. EC3 BZ39 2
Cornhill
St. Michaels All. EC3 BZ39 57
Cornhill
St. Michaels Av. N9 CC26 39
St. Michaels Av., Hem.H. AZ14 8
St. Michaels Av., Wem. BM36 55
St. Michaels Clo. E16 CJ39 58
Long Mark Rd.
St. Michaels Clo. N12 BU28 38
St. Michaels Clo. N3 BR30 37
Hendon La.
St. Michaels Clo., Pot.B. BS18 20
Church Rd.
St. Michaels Clo., Harl. CN10 6
School La.
St. Michaels Clo., Belv. BP41 69
St. Helens Rd.
St. Michaels Clo., Brom. CK52 88
St. Michaels Clo., Walt. BD55 84
St. Michaels Cres., Pnr. BE32 45
St. Michaels Dr., Sev. CV61 108
St. Michaels Gdns. W10 BR39 55
Ladbroke Gro.
St. Michaels Rd. NW2 BQ35 46
St. Michaels Rd. SW9 BX44 66
St. Michaels Rd., Brox. CD13 12
St. Michaels Rd., Ashf. AZ49 73
St. Michaels Rd., Cat. BZ64 105
St. Michaels Rd., Croy. BZ54 87
St. Michaels Rd., Grays DG42 71
St. Michaels Rd., Wall. BW56 95
St. Michaels Rd., Well. CO45 69
St. Michaels Rd., Wok. AU60 91
St. Michaels St. SE8 CD44 67
Tanners Hill
St. Michaels St. W2 BT39 1
St. Michaels St. W2 BT39 56
St. Michaels St., St.Alb. BF13 9
St. Michaels Ter. N22 BX30 38
St. Michaels Vw., Hat. BP11 10
Drovers Way
St. Michaels Way, Pot.B. BS18 20
Church Rd.
St. Mildreds Ct. EC2 BZ39 57
Poultry
St. Mildreds Rd. SE12 CG47 78
St. Mildreds Rd., Guil. AS70 118
St. Monicas Rd., Tad. BR64 103
St. Nazaire Clo., Egh. AU49 72
Mullens Rd.
St. Neots Clo., B.Wd. BM22 28
The Campions
St. Neots Rd., Rom. CW29 42
St. Nicholas Av., Horn. CU34 50
St. Nicholas Av., Lthd. BF66 111
St. Nicholas Clo., Amer. AQ23 25
St. Nicholas Clo., B.Wd. BK25 27
Elstree Hill N.
St. Nicholas Clo., Uxb. AX39 53
St. Nicholas Dr., Shep. AZ54 83
St. Nicholas Glebe SW17 BV49 76
St. Nicholas Gro., Brwd. DE28 122
St. Nicholas Hill, Lthd. BJ64 102
St. Nicholas La., Chis. CK51 88
St. Nicholas Mt., Hem.H. AV13 7
St. Nicholas Rd. SE18 CN42 68
St. Nicholas Rd., T.Ditt. BH53 84
St. Nicholas Rd., Sutt. BS56 95
St. Nicholas St. SE8 CE44 67
Lucas St.
St. Nicholas Way, Sutt. BS56 95
Robin Hood Rd.
St. Norbert Grn. SE4 CD45 67
St. Norbert Rd. SE4 CC46 77
St. Normans Way, Epsom BP58 94
St. Olafs Rd. SW6 BR43 65
St. Olaves Clo., Twick. AV50 72
St. Olaves Ct. EC2 BZ39 2
St. Olaves Est. SE1 CA41 4
St. Olaves Est. SE1 CA41 67
St. Olaves Rd. E6 CL37 58
St. Olaves Wk. SW16 BW51 86
St. Omer Rd., Guil. AT71 118
St. Omer Ridge, Guil. AT71 118
St. Oswalds Pl. SE11 BX42 4
St. Oswalds Pl. SE11 BX42 66
St. Oswalds Rd. SW16 BT51 86
St. Oswulf St. SW1 BW42 3
St. Oswulf St. SW1 BW42 66
Erasmus St.
St. Pancras Ct. N2 BT30 38
St. Pancras Way NW1 BW36 56
St. Pancras Way NW1 BW37 1
St. Patricks Gdns., Grav. DH48 81
St. Patricks Pl., Grays DG42 71
St. Paul Clo., Uxb. AX39 53
St. Paul St. N1 BZ37 2
St. Paul St. N1 BZ37 57
St. Pauls Alley EC4 BY39 56
St. Pauls Churchyard
St. Pauls Av. NW2 BP36 55
St. Pauls Av. SE16 CC40 57
St. Pauls Av., Har. BL32 46
St. Pauls Av., Slou. AP40 52
St. Pauls Churchyard EC4 BY39 2
St. Pauls Churchyard EC4 BY39 56
St. Pauls Clo. SE7 CJ42 68
St. Pauls Clo. W5 BL41 65
St. Pauls Clo., Ashf. BA49 73
St. Pauls Clo., Cars. BU54 86
St. Pauls Clo., Chess. BK56 93
St. Pauls Clo., Hayes BA42 63
St. Pauls Clo., Houns. BE44 64
St. Pauls Clo., S.Ock. CY40 60
St. Pauls Courtyard SE8 CE43 67
Deptford High St.
St. Pauls Cray Est., Chis. CN52 88
St. Pauls Cray Rd., Chis. CM50 78
St. Pauls Cres. NW1 BW36 56
St. Pauls Dr. E15 CF35 48
St. Pauls Est. W14 BQ42 65
St. Pauls Pl. N1 BZ36 57
St. Pauls Pl., S.Ock. CY40 60
St. Pauls Clo.
St. Pauls Pl., St.Alb. BJ13 9
St. Pauls Rd. E., Dor. BJ71 119
St. Pauls Rd. N1 BY36 56
St. Pauls Rd. N17 CB29 39
St. Pauls Rd. W., Dor. BJ72 119
St. Pauls Rd., Bark. CM37 58
St. Pauls Rd., Brent. BK43 64
St. Pauls Rd., Erith CS43 69
St. Pauls Rd., Hem.H. AX13 8
St. Pauls Rd., Rich. BL45 65
St. Pauls Rd., Stai. AU50 72
St. Pauls Rd., Th.Hth. BZ52 87
St. Pauls Rd., Wok. AT62 100
St. Pauls Shrubbery N1 BZ36 57
St. Pauls Sq., Brom. CG51 88
Church Rd.
St. Pauls St. E3 CD39 57
St. Pauls Ter. SE17 BY43 4
St. Pauls Ter. SE17 BY43 66
St. Pauls Way E3 CD39 57
St. Pauls Way N3 BS29 38
St. Pauls Way, Wal.Abb. CF20 21
Rochford Av.
St. Pauls Way, Wat. BD23 27
St. Pauls Wood Hill, Orp. CN51 88
St. Peters Alley EC3 BZ40 4
Gracechurch St.
St. Peters Av. E17 CG31 49
St. Peters Av. E2 CB37 57
St. Peters Clo.
St. Peters Av. N18 CB28 39
St. Peters Av., Ong. CW16 24
St. Peters Clo. E2 CB37 57
St. Peters Clo. SW17 BU48 76
College Gdns.
St. Peters Clo. W5 BK39 54
Regal Clo.
St. Peters Clo., Barn. BP25 28
St. Peters Clo., Bush. BG26 36
St. Peters Clo., Chis. CM50 78
St. Peters Clo., Ger.Cr. AS30 34
St. Peters Clo., Hat. BP12 10
St. Albans Rd.
St. Peters Clo., Ilf. CN31 49
St. Peters Clo., Rick. AW26 35
St. Peters Clo., Ruis. BD34 45
St. Peters Clo., St.Alb. BG13 9
St. Peters Clo., Wind. AQ46 72
St. Peters Clo., Wok. AU63 100
St. Peters Ct. SE3 CG45 68
St. Peters Ct., Ger.Cr. AS30 34
St. Peters Gdns. SE27 BY49 76
St. Peters Gro. W6 BP42 65
St. Peters La., Orp. CO51 89
St. Peters Rd. N9 CB26 39
St. Peters Rd. SW6 BR44 65
Filmer Rd.
St. Peters Rd. W6 BP42 65
St. Peters Rd., Brwd. DA28 42
St. Peters Rd., Croy. BZ56 96
St. Peters Rd., E.Mol. BF52 84
St. Peters Rd., Grays DG42 71
St. Peters Rd., Kings.T. BM51 85
Cambridge Rd.
St. Peters Rd., St.Alb. BH13 9
St. Peters Rd., Stai. AV50 72
St. Peters Rd., Sthl. BF39 54
St. Peters Rd., Twick. BJ46 74
St. Peters Rd., Uxb. AX39 53
St. Peters Rd., Wok. AT63 100
St. Peters Sq. E2 CB37 57
St. Peters Clo.
St. Peters Sq. W6 BP42 65
St. Peters St. Ms. N1 BY37 2
St. Peters St.
St. Peters St. Ms. N1 BY37 56
St. Peters St.
St. Peters St. N1 BY37 2
St. Peters St. N1 BY37 56
St. Peters St., S.Croy. BZ56 96
St. Peters St., St.Alb. BG13 9
St. Peters Ter. SW6 BR43 65
Filmer Rd.
St. Peters Vill. W6 BP42 65

St. Peters Way N1 CA36 57
De Beauvoir Sq.
St. Peters Way W5 BK39 54
St. Peters Way, Cher. AU55 91
St. Peters Way, Hayes BA42 63
St. Peters Way, Rick. AT24 25
St. Petersburgh Ms. W2 BS40 3
St. Petersburgh Ms. W2 BS40 56
St. Petersburgh Pl. W2 BS40 56
St. Philip Sq. SW8 BV44 66
St. Philip St. SW8 BV44 66
St. Philips Av., Wor.Pk. BP55 85
St. Philips Pl. W2 BT39 1
Paddington Grn.
St. Philips Rd. E8 CB36 57
St. Philips Rd., Surb. BK53 84
St. Philips Way N1 BZ37 57
Linton St.
St. Pinnocks Av., Stai. AW51 83
St. Quentin Rd., Well. CN45 68
St. Quintin Av. W10 BQ39 55
St. Quintin Gdns. W10 BQ39 55
St. Quintin Rd. E13 CH37 58
St. Raphaels Way NW10 BN36 55
St. Regis Clo. N10 BV30 38
St. Ronans Clo., Barn. BT22 29
St. Ronans Cres., Wdf.Grn. CH29 40
St. Rule St. SW8 BW44 66
St. Saviours Est. SE1 CA41 67
St. Saviours Rd. SW2 BX46 76
St. Saviours Rd., Croy. BY53 86
St. Silas Pl. NW5 BV36 56
St. Simons Av. SW15 BQ46 75
St. Stephens Av. E17 CF32 48
St. Stephens Av. W12 BP40 55
St. Stephens Av. W13 BJ39 54
St. Stephens Av., St.Alb. BF14 9
St. Stephens Av., Ash. BL61 103
St. Stephens Clo. E17 CE32 48
St. Stephens Clo. NW8 BU37 1
St. Stephens Clo. NW8 BU37 56
St. Stephens Clo., St.Alb. BF15 9
St. Stephens Clo., Grays CX42 70
St. Stephens Clo., Sthl. BF39 54
St. Stephens Cres. W2 BS39 56
St. Stephens Cres., Th.Hth. BY52 86
St. Stephens Cres., Brwd. DD28 122
St. Stephens Gdn. Est. W2 BS39 56
St. Stephens Gdns. SW15 BR46 75
Normanby Clo.
St. Stephens Gdns. W2 BS39 56
St. Stephens Gdns., Twick. BK46 74
St. Stephens Gro. SE13 CF45 67
St. Stephens Hill, St.Alb. BG14 9
St. Stephens Ms. W2 BS39 56
Chepstow Rd.
St. Stephens Pass., Twick. BK46 74
St. Stephens Rd. E17 CE32 48
St. Stephens Rd. E6 CJ36 58
St. Stephens Rd. W13 BJ39 54
St. Stephens Rd., West Dr. AX40 53
St. Stephens Rd., Barn. BQ25 28
St. Stephens Rd., Enf. CC22 30
St. Stephens Rd., Houns. BF46 74
St. Stephens Row EC4 BZ39 57
Walbrook
St. Stephens Ter. SW8 BX43 66
St. Stephens Wk. SW7 BT42 66
Southwell Gdns.
St. Swithins La. EC4 BZ40 4
St. Swithins La. EC4 BZ40 57
St. Swithuns Rd. SE13 CF46 77
St. Teresa Wk., Grays DG42 71
St. Theodores Way, Welw.G.C. BQ 7 5
Wigmores N.
St. Theresas Rd., Felt. BB45 63
St. Thomas Ct., Bex. CR47 79
St. Thomas Dr., Orp. CM54 88
St. Thomas Dr., Pnr. BE30 36
St. Thomas Pl., Grays DE43 71
East Thurrock Rd.
St. Thomas Rd. E16 CH39 58
St. Thomas Rd. N14 BW26 38
St. Thomas Rd., Belv. CS41 69
St. Thomas Rd., Brwd. DB27 42
St. Thomas St. SE1 BZ40 4
St. Thomas St. SE1 BZ40 57
St. Thomas's Av., Grav. DG48 81
St. Thomas's Clo., Wal.Abb. CH20 22
St. Thomas's Dr., Guil. AY69 110
St. Thomas's Gdns. NW5 BV36 56
Queens Cres.
St. Thomas's Gdns., Ilf. CM36 58
St. Thomas's Pl. E9 CC36 57
St. Thomas's Rd. N4 BY34 47
St. Thomas's Rd. NW10 BO37 55
St. Thomas's Rd. W4 BN43 65
St. Thomas's Sq. E9 CB36 57
St. Thomas's Way SW6 BR43 65
St. Ursula Rd., Sthl. BF39 54
St. Ursulas Gro., Pnr. BD32 45
St. Vincent Clo. SE27 BY49 76
Cedar Tree Gro.
St. Vincent Dr., St.Alb. BJ15 9
St. Vincent Est. E14 CD40 57
St. Vincent Rd., Twick. BG46 74
St. Vincent Rd., Walt. BC55 83
St. Vincent St. W1 BV39 1
St. Vincent St. W1 BV39 56
Aybrook St.
St. Vincents Av., Dart. CX46 80
St. Vincents Rd., Dart. CX46 80
St. Vincents Way, Pot.B. BT20 20
St. Wilfrids Clo., Barn. BT25 29
St. Wilfrids Rd.
St. Wilfrids Rd., Barn. BT25 29
St. Winifreds Av. E12 CK35 49
St. Winifreds Clo., Chig. CM28 40
St. Winifreds Rd., Tedd. BJ50 74
St. Winifreds Rd., West. CK62 106
St. Winifreds, Ken. BZ61 105
St. Winifrids Wk. SE17 BY43 66
Lorrimore Rd.
St. Yon Ct., St.Alb. BL13 10
Saints Dr. E7 CJ35 49
Saints Wk., Grays DH42 71
Saints, The, Wat. BD20 18
Sakins Cft., Harl. CN12 13
Saladin Dr., Grays CX42 70
Chieftan Dr.
Salamanca Pl. SE1 BX42 66
Salamanca St.
Salamanca Pl. SE11 BX42 4
Salamanca St. SE1 BX42 66
Salamanca St. SE11 BX42 4
Salamanca St. SE11 BX42 66
Salamons Way, Rain. CT39 59
Salcombe Dr., Mord. BQ54 85
Salcombe Dr., Rom. CQ32 50
Salcombe Gdns. NW7 BQ29 37
Salcombe Rd. E17 CD33 48
Salcombe Rd., Ashf. AY49 73
Salcombe Way, Hayes BB38 53
Salcombe Way, Ruis. BC34 44
Salcot Cres., Croy. CF58 96
Salcote Rd., Grav. DJ49 81
Salcott Rd. SW11 BU46 76
Salcott Rd., Croy. BX55 86
Sale Pl. W2 BU39 1
Sale Pl. W2 BU39 56
Sale St. E2 CB38 2
Sale, The E4 CG28 40
Salehurst Clo., Har. BL32 46
Salehurst Rd. SE4 CD46 77
Salem Pl., Croy. BZ55 87
Salem Rd. W2 BS40 3
Salem Rd. W2 BS40 56
Porchester Gdns.
Salford Rd. SW2 BW47 76
Salhouse Clo. SE28 CP40 59
Rollesby Way
Salisbury Av. N3 BR31 46
Salisbury Av., Bark. CM36 58
Salisbury Av., St.Alb. BJ13 9
Salisbury Av., Sutt. BR57 94
Salisbury Av., Swan. CU52 89
Salisbury Clo. SE17 BZ42 4
Salisbury Clo. SE17 BZ42 67
Chatham St.
Salisbury Clo., Amer. AP23 25
Salisbury Clo., Pot.B. BT19 20
Salisbury Clo., Upmin. CZ34 51
Salisbury Clo., Wor.Pk. BO55 85
Salisbury Cres., Chsnt. CC19 21
Theobalds La.
Salisbury Ct. EC4 BY39 2
Salisbury Ct. EC4 BY39 56
Salisbury Gdns. SW19 BR50 75
Salisbury Gdns., Welw.G.C. BR 8 5
Salisbury Gdns., Buck.H. CJ27 40
Victoria Rd.
Salisbury Pl. SW9 BY43 66
Langton Rd.
Salisbury Pl. W1 BU39 1
Salisbury Pl. W1 BU39 56
Salisbury Plain NW4 BQ32 46
Brent St.
Salisbury Rd. E10 CF34 48
Salisbury Rd. E12 CJ35 49
Salisbury Rd. E17 CF32 48
Salisbury Rd. E4 CE27 39
Salisbury Rd. E7 CH36 58
Salisbury Rd. N22 BY30 38
Salisbury Rd. N4 BY32 47
Salisbury Rd. N9 CB27 39
Salisbury Rd. SE25 CB53 87
Salisbury Rd. SW19 BR50 75
Salisbury Rd. W13 BJ41 64
Salisbury Rd., Welw.G.C. BR 8 5
Salisbury Rd., Bans. BS60 95
Salisbury Rd., Barn. BR24 28
Salisbury Rd., Bex. CR47 79
Salisbury Rd., Brom. CK53 88
Salisbury Rd., Cars. BU57 95
Salisbury Rd., Dag. CR36 59
Salisbury Rd., Dart. CY47 80
Salisbury Rd., Enf. CD22 30
Salisbury Rd., Felt. BD47 74
Salisbury Rd., Gdse. CC69 114
Salisbury Rd., Grav. DF47 81
Salisbury Rd., Grays DE43 71
Salisbury Rd., Har. BG32 45
Salisbury Rd., Hodd. CF11 12
Salisbury Rd., Houns. BD45 64
Salisbury Rd., Ilf. CN34 49
Salisbury Rd., N.Mal. BN52 85
Salisbury Rd., Pnr. BC31 44
Salisbury Rd., Rich. BL45 65
Salisbury Rd., Rom. CU32 50
Salisbury Rd., Sthl. BE42 64
Salisbury Rd., Uxb. AW37 53
Salisbury Rd., Wat BD23 27
Salisbury Rd., Wok. AS63 100
Salisbury Rd., Wor.Pk. BN56 94
Salisbury Sq. EC4 BY39 2
Salisbury Sq. EC4 BY39 56
Salisbury Sq., Hat. BQ12 10
Salisbury St. NW8 BU38 1
Salisbury St. NW8 BU38 56
Salisbury St. W3 BN41 65
Salisbury Ter. SE15 CC45 67
Salisbury Wk. N19 BW34 47
Magdala Rd.
Salix Clo., Sun. BC50 73
Salix Rd., Grays DE43 71
Salmen Rd. E13 CG37 58
Salmon La. E14 CD39 57
Salmon Rd., Belv. CR42 69
Salmon St. E14 CD39 57
Salmon La.
Salmon St. NW9 BM33 46
Salmond Clo., Stan. BJ29 36
Salmonds Gro., Brwd. DE28 122
St. Nicholas Gro.
Salmons La. W., Cat. CA63 105
Salmons La., Whyt. CA63 105
Salmons Rd. N9 CB26 39
Salmons Rd., Chess. BL57 94
Salmons Rd., Lthd. BD68 111
Salomons Rd. E13 CJ39 58
Salop Rd. E17 CC32 48
Salt Box Hill, West. CH60 97
Salt Box Rd., Guil. AP68 109
Salt Hill Av., Slou. AO40 61
Salt Hill Clo., Uxb. AY35 44
Salt Hill Dr., Slou. AO40 61
Salt Hill Way, Slou. AO40 61
Saltash Clo., Sutt. BR56 94
Saltash Rd., Ilf. CM29 40
Saltash Rd., Well. CP44 69
Saltcoats Rd. W4 BO41 65
Greenend Rd.
Saltcroft Clo. NW9 BM33 46
Salter Rd. SE16 CD40 57
Salter St. E14 CE40 57
Salter St. NW10 BP38 55
Salterford Rd. SW17 BV50 76
Salters Clo., Berk. AP12 7
Salters Hall Ct. EC4 BZ40 4
Cannon St.
Salters Hill SE19 BZ49 77
Salters Rd. E17 CF31 48
Salters Rd. W10 BQ38 55
Salterton Rd. N7 BX34 47
Saltford Clo., Erith CT42 69
Saltoun Rd. SW2 BY45 66
Saltram Clo. N15 CA31 48
Saltram Cres. W9 BR38 55
Saltwell St. E14 CE40 57
Saltwood Clo., Orp. CP56 98
Saltwood Gro. SE17 BZ42 4
Salusbury Rd. NW6 BR37 55
Salvador SW17 BU49 76
Salvia Gdns., Grnf. BJ37 54
Salvin Rd. SW15 BQ45 65
Salway Clo., Wdf.Grn. CG29 40
Salway Pl. E15 CF36 57
Broadway
Salway Rd. E15 CF36 57
Salwey Cres., Brox. CD13 12
Sam Bartram Clo. SE7 CJ42 68
Samantha Clo. E17 CD33 48
Samantha Ms., Hav. CT27 41
Sambruck Ms. SE6 CE47 77
Samels Ct. W6 BP42 65
South Black Lion La.
Samford St. NW8 BU38 1
Samian Gate, St.Alb. BE15 9
Samos Clo. SE3 CG43 68
Samos Rd. SE20 CB51 87
Samphire Ct., Grays DE43 71
Salix Rd.
Sampleoak La., Guil. AV73 118
Sampson Av., Barn. BQ25 28
Sampson Clo., Belv. CP41 69
Carrill Way
Sampson St. E1 CB40 57
Samson St. E13 CJ37 58
Samuel Clo. SE18 CK42 68
Samuel St.
Samuel Johnson Clo. SW16 BX49 76
Curtis Field Rd.
Samuel Lewis Bldgs. SE5 BZ44 67
Samuel Lewis Dws. SW6 BS43 66
Vanston Pl.
Samuel Lewis Trust Bldgs. E8 CB35 48
Samuel Lewis Trust Dws. N1 BY36 56
Samuel St. SE18 CK42 68
Sancroft Clo. NW2 BP34 46
Sancroft Rd., Stan. BJ30 36
Sancroft St. SE11 BX42 4
Sancroft St. SE11 BX42 66
Sanctuary Clo., Dart. CV46 80
Sanctuary Clo., Uxb. AX29 35
Sanctuary Rd., Houns. AZ46 73
Beacon Rd.
Sanctuary St. SE1 BZ41 4
Sanctuary St. SE1 BZ41 67
Sanctuary, The SW1 BW41 3
Sanctuary, The, Bex. CP46 79
Sanctuary, The, Mord. BS53 86
Sandal Rd. N18 CB28 39
Sandal Rd., N.Mal. BN53 85
Sandal St. E15 CG37 58
Sandal Wood, Guil. AQ71 118
Sandale Clo. N16 BZ34 48
Stoke Newington St.
Sandall Clo. W5 BL38 55
Sandall Rd. NW5 BW36 56
Sandall Rd. W5 BL38 55
Sandalwood Clo. E1 CD38 57
Solebay St.
Sandalwood Rd., Felt. BC48 73
Sanday Clo., Hem.H. AZ14 8
Sandbach Pl. SE18 CM42 68
Sandbanks Hill, Dart. DA50 80
Sandbourne Av. SW19 BS51 86
Sandbourne Rd. SE4 CD44 67
Sandbrook Clo. NW7 BN29 37
Sunnyvale Gro.
Sandbrook Rd. N16 CA34 48
Sandby Grn. SE9 CK45 68
Sandcliff Rd., Erith CS42 69
Sandcross La., Reig. BR72 120
Sandell St. SE1 BY41 4
Sandell St. SE1 BY41 66
Sandells Av., Ashf. BA49 73
Sanders Clo., Hem.H. AY15 8
Sanders Clo., Hmptn. BG49 74
Sanders Clo., St.Alb. BK17 18
Sanders La., NW7 BQ29 37
Sanders La., Wok. AQ64 100
Sanders Rd., Hem.H. AY15 8
Sanders Way N19 BW33 47
Sussex Way
Sandersfield Gdns., Bans. BS61 104
Sandersfield Rd., Bans. BS61 104
Sanderson Clo. NW5 BV35 47
Highgate Rd.
Sanderson Clo., Brwd. DE32 123
Sanderson Cres., Grnf. BJ37 54
Clausen Way
Sanderstead Av. NW2 BR34 46
Sanderstead Clo. SW4 BW47 76
Sanderstead Court Av., S.Croy. CB60 96
Sanderstead Hill, S.Croy. CA59 96
Sanderstead Rd. E10 CD33 48
Sanderstead Rd., Orp. CO53 89
Sanderstead Rd., S.Croy. BZ57 96
Sandes Pl., Lthd. BJ62 102
Sandfield Gdns., Th.Hth. BY52 86
Sandfield Pass., Th.Hth. BZ52 87
Sandfield Rd., St.Alb. BJ13 9
Sandfield Rd., Th.Hth. BY52 86
Sandfield Ter., Guil. AR71 118
Sandfield, Hat. BP14 10
Sandfields, Wok. AU65 100
Sandford Av. N22 BZ29 39
Sandford Av., Loug. CM24 31
Sandford Clo. E6 CK38 58
Sandford Rd.
Sandford Ct. N16 CA33 48
Sandford La. N16 CA34 48
Brooke Rd.
Sandford Rd. E6 CK38 58
Sandford Rd., Bexh. CQ45 69
Sandford Rd., Brom. CH52 88
Sandford Row SE17 BZ42 67
Sandford St. SW6 BS43 66
Kings Rd.
Sandford Wk. SE14 CC43 67
Sandford St.
Sandgate La. SW18 BU47 76
Sandgate Rd., Well. CP43 69
Sandgate St. SE15 CB43 67
Sandhills Ct., Vir.W. AS53 82
Sandhills La., Vir.W. AS53 82
Sandhills Rd., Reig. BS71 121
Sandhills, Wall. BW56 95
Sandhurst Av., Har. BF32 45
Sandhurst Av., Surb. BM54 85
Sandhurst Clo. NW9 BM31 46
Sandhurst Clo., S.Croy. CA58 96
Sandhurst Ct. SW2 BX45 66
Sandhurst Dr., Ilf. CN35 49
Sandhurst Rd. N9 CC25 30
Sandhurst Rd. NW9 BM31 46
Sandhurst Rd. SE6 CF47 77
Sandhurst Rd., Bex. CP46 79
Sandhurst Rd., Orp. CO55 89
Sandhurst Rd., Sid. CN48 78
Sandhurst Rd., Til. DH44 71
Sandhurst Way, S.Croy. CA57 96
Sandiford Rd., Sutt. BR55 85
Sandiland Cres., Brom. CG55 88
Sandilands La. SW6 BS44 66
Sandilands Rd. SW6 BS44 66
Sandilands, Croy. CB55 87
Sandilands, Sev. CS64 107
Sandison St. SE15 CA45 67
Sandland St. WC1 BX39 2
Sandland St. WC1 BX39 56
Sandlands Gro., Tad. BP65 103
Sandlands Rd., Tad. BP65 103
Sandlewood Av., Cher. AV55 82
Sandling Ri. SE9 CL48 78
Sandlings, The N22 BY30 38
Sandmere Clo., Hem.H. AZ14 8
St. Albans Rd.
Sandmere Rd. SW4 BX45 66
Sandon Clo., Esher BG54 84
Sandon Pl., Ong. CX18 24
Sandon Rd., Chsnt. CC18 21
Sandover Rd. SE5 CA43 4
Sandover Rd. SE5 CA43 67
Sandow Av., Horn. CV34 51
Sandown Av., Dag. CS36 59
Sandown Av., Esher BG56 93
Sandown Clo., Houns. BC44 63
Sandown Cres. Hayes BB41 63
Sandown Ct., Esher BF56 93
Sandown Dr., Cars. BV58 95
Southdown Rd.
Sandown Rd. SE25 CB53 87
Sandown Rd., Couls. BV61 104
Sandown Rd., Esher BG56 93
Sandown Rd., Grav. DH49 81
Sandown Rd., Wat. BD22 27
Sandown Way, Nthlt. BE36 54
Sandpiper Rd., S.Croy. CC59 96
Sandpiper Way, Orp. CP52 89
Sandpipers, The, Grav. DH48 81
Sandpit Cres., St.Alb. BJ12 9
Sandpit Gro., Hert. BV12 11
Sandpit Hall Rd., Wok. AQ59 91
Sandpit La., Brwd. CZ25 33
Sandpit La., St.Alb. BH13 9
Sandpit Pl. SE7 CK42 68
Maryon Rd.
Sandpit Rd., Brom. CG49 78
Sandpit Rd., Dart. CV45 70
Sandpit Rd., Red. BU71 121
Sandpit Rd., Welw.G.C. BR 9 5
Sandpits Head, Guil. AO68 109
Sandpits Rd., Croy. CC56 96
Sandpits Rd., Rich. BK48 74
Sandra Clo. N22 BZ30 39
New Rd.
Sandra Clo., Houns. BF46 74
Sandridge Clo., Har. BH31 45
Sandridge Clo., Hem.H. AZ10 8
Elstree Rd.
Sandridge Ct. N4 BZ34 48
Kings Cres. Est.
Sandridge Rd., St.Alb. BH12 9
Sandridge St. N19 BW34 47
Archway
Sandridgebury La., St.Alb. BH11 9
Sandringham Av. SW20 BR51 85
Sandringham Clo., Enf. CA23 30
Sandringham Clo., Ilf. CM31 49
Sandringham Gdns.
Sandringham Cres., St.Alb. BJ11 9
Sandringham Cres., Har. BF34 45
Sandringham Ct. W9 BT38 1
Sandringham Ct. W9 BT38 56
Sandringham Ct., Har. BF34 45
Sandringham Dr., Ashf. AX49 73
Sandringham Dr., Well. CN44 68
Sandringham Gdns. N12 BT29 38
Sandringham Gdns. N8 BX32 47
Sandringham Gdns., Houns. BC43 63
Sandringham Gdns., Ilf. CM31 49
Sandringham Ms. W5 BK40 54
High St.
Sandringham Rd. E10 CF32 48
Sandringham Rd. E7 CJ35 49
Sandringham Rd. E8 CA35 48
Sandringham Rd. N22 BZ31 48
Sandringham Rd. NW11 BR33 46
Sandringham Rd. NW2 BP36 55
Sandringham Rd., Bark. CN35 49
Sandringham Rd., Brom. CH49 78
Sandringham Rd., Brwd. DA25 33
Sandringham Rd., Houns. AY46 73
Sandringham Rd., Nthlt. BF36 54
Sandringham Rd., Pot.B. BS18 20
Sandringham Rd., Th.Hth. BZ53 87
Sandringham Rd., Wat. BD22 27
Sandringham Rd., Wor.Pk. BP55 85
Sandringham Way, Wal.Cr. CC20 21
Sandrock Pl., Croy. CC56 96
Sandrock Rd. SE13 CE45 67
Sandrock Rd., Dor. BF72 119
Sandroyd Way, Cob. BF60 93
Sands Way, Wdf.Grn. CK29 40
Sandsend La. SW6 BS44 66
Sandstone Pl. N6 BV34 47
Sandstone Rd. SE12 CH48 78
Sandtoft Rd. SE7 CH43 68
Sandway Rd., Orp. CP52 89
Sandway, Orp. CP52 89
Sandwell Cres. NW6 BS35 47
Sumatra Rd.
Sandwich St. WC1 BX38 2
Sandwich St. WC1 BX38 56
Sandy Bank Rd., Grav. DG47 81
Sandy Bury, Orp. CM55 88
Sandy Clo., Twick. BJ47 74
Sandy Clo., Wok. AU62 100
Sandy Dr., Cob. BF59 93
Sandy Dr., Felt. BB47 73
Sandy Hill Av. SE18 CL42 68
Sandy Hill Rd. SE18 CL42 68
Sandy Hill Rd., Wall. BW58 95
Sandy La. Est., Rich. BK48 74
Sandy La. N., Wall. BW56 95
Sandy La. S., Wall. BW58 95
Sandy La., Chadwell St. Mary DG43 71
Sandy La., Bet. BO71 120
Sandy La., Bletchingley BY69 121
Sandy La., Bush. BG24 27
Sandy La., Chobham AP58 91
Sandy La., Cob. BE59 93
Sandy La., Dart. DB48 80
Sandy La., Guil. AO73 118
Sandy La., Har. BL32 46
Sandy La., Ivy Hatch DA66 117
Sandy La., Limpsfield CH67 115
Sandy La., Mitch. BV51 86
Sandy La., Nthwd. BB27 35
Sandy La., Nutfield BW71 121
Sandy La., Orp. CO54 89
Sandy La., Oxt. CF68 114
Sandy La., Rain. CW40 60
Sandy La., Reig. BP71 120
Sandy La., Rich. BK48 74
Sandy La., Send AU65 100
Sandy La., Sev. CV65 108
Sandy La., Sid. CP50 79
Sandy La., St.Pauls Cray CP51 89
Sandy La., Sutt. BR58 94
Sandy La., Tad. BR65 103
Sandy La., Tedd. BJ50 74
Sandy La., Vir.W. AS52 82
Sandy La., Walt. BS53 83
Sandy La., West Thurrock DA42 70
Sandy La., West. CM66 115
Sandy La., Wok. AU61 100
Sandy Lodge La., Nthwd. BB27 35
Sandy Lodge Rd., Rick. AZ27 35
Sandy Lodge Way, Nthwd. BB29 35
Sandy Mead, Maid. AH42 61
Moor End
Sandy Rd., NW3 BS34 47
Sandy Rd., Wey. AW57 92
Sandy Ri., Ger.Cr. AS30 34
Sandy Ridge, Chis. CK50 78
Sandy Way, Cob. BF59 93
Sandy Way, Croy. CD55 87
Sandy Way, Walt. BB54 83
Sandy Way, Wok. AU62 100
Sandycombe Rd., Felt. BC47 73
Sandycombe Rd., Rich. BL45 65
Sandycombe Rd., Twick. BK46 74
Sandycroft Rd., Amer. AR22 25
Sandycroft SE2 CO43 69
Sandyhill Rd., Ilf. CL35 49
Sandymount Av., Stan. BK28 36
Sandys Row E1 CA39 2
Sandys Row E1 CA39 57
Sanfoin End, Hem.H. AZ12 8

Sanford La. N16	CA34	48
High St.		
Sanford St. SE14	CD43	67
Sanford Ter. N16	CA34	48
Sanford Wk. N16	CA34	48
Smalley Rd.		
Sanford Wk. SE14	CD43	67
Coldblow La.		
Sanger Av., Chess.	BL56	94
Sangley Rd. SE25	CA52	87
Sangley Rd. SE6	CE47	77
Sangora Rd. SW11	BT45	66
Strathblaine Rd.		
Sans Wk. EC1	**BY38**	**2**
Sans Wk. EC1	BY38	56
Woodbridge St.		
Sansom Rd. E11	CG34	49
Sansom St. SE5	BZ43	67
Santers La., Pot.B.	BR20	19
Santley St. SW4	BX45	66
Santos Rd. SW18	BS46	76
Santway, The, Stan.	BH28	36
Sanway Clo., Wey.	AY60	92
Sanway Rd., Cob.	AY61	101
Sanway Rd., Wey.	AY60	92
Saperton Wk. SE11	**BX42**	**4**
Sapho Pk., Grav.	DJ49	81
Saphora Clo., Orp.	CM56	97
Sappers Clo., Saw.	CQ 6	6
Sapphire Clo. E6	CL39	58
Sapphire Clo., Dag.	CP33	50
Crystal Way		
Sapphire Rd. SE14	CD42	67
Sara Pk., Grav.	DJ49	81
Saracen Clo., Croy.	BZ53	87
Saracen St. E14	CE39	57
Saracens Head, Hem.H.	AZ13	8
Sarah St. N1	**CA38**	**2**
Sarah St. N1	CA38	57
Saratoga Rd. E5	CC35	48
Sardinia St. WC2	**BX39**	**2**
Sardinia St. WC2	BX39	56
Kingsway		
Sargeant Clo., Uxb.	AX38	53
Sarita Clo., Har.	BG30	36
Sarjant Path SW19	BR48	75
Queensmere Rd.		
Sark Clo., Houns.	BF44	64
Sark Wk. E16	CH39	58
Sarnesfield Rd., Enf.	BZ24	30
Sarratt Av., Hem.H.	AZ10	8
Sarratt La., Rick.	AW23	26
Sarratt Rd., Rick.	AW22	26
Sarre Av., Horn.	CV36	60
Sarre Rd. NW2	BR35	46
Sarre Rd., Orp.	CP53	89
Sarsby Dr., Stai.	AT48	72
Feathers La.		
Sarsen Av., Houns.	BE44	64
Sarsfeld Rd. SW12	BU47	76
Sarsfield Rd., Grnf.	BJ37	54
Sartor Rd. SE15	CC45	67
Sarum Grn., Wey.	BB55	83
Sarum Pl., Hem.H.	AY11	8
Satanita Clo. E16	CJ39	58
Satchell Mead NW9	BO30	37
Satchwell Rd. E2	**CB38**	**2**
Satchwell St. E2	**CB38**	**2**
Saturn Way, Hem.H.	AY12	8
Sauls Grn. E11	CG34	49
Napier Rd.		
Saunders Clo., Grav.	DF48	81
Saunders Copse, Wok.	AQ64	100
Saunders La., Wok.	AP64	100
Saunders Ness Rd. E14	CF42	67
Saunders Rd. SE18	CN42	68
Saunders Rd., Uxb.	AY36	53
Saunders St. SE11	**BX42**	**4**
Saunders St. SE11	BY42	66
Saunders Way SE28	CO40	59
Saunderton Rd., Wem.	BJ35	45
Saunton Av., Hayes	BB43	63
Saunton Rd., Horn.	CU34	50
Savage Gdns. E6	CK39	58
Savage Gdns. EC3	**CA40**	**4**
Savage Gdns. EC3	CA40	57
Savay La., Uxb.	AW32	44
Savernake Rd. N9	CB25	30
Savernake Rd. NW3	BU35	47
Savile Clo., N.Mal.	BO53	85
Savile Gdns., Croy.	CA55	87
Savile Row W1	**BW40**	**3**
Savile Row W1	BW40	56
Savill Gdns. SW20	BP52	85
Saville Cres., Ashf.	BA50	73
Saville Gdns., Croy.	CA55	87
Saville Rd. E16	CK40	58
Saville Rd. W4	BN41	65
Saville Rd., Rom.	CQ32	50
Saville Rd., Twick.	BH47	74
Saville Row, Enf.	CC23	30
Saville Row, Wdf.Grn.	CH29	40
Saviours Est. SE1	**CA41**	**4**
Savona Clo. SW19	BQ50	75
Savona Est. SW8	BW43	66
Savona St. SW8	BW43	66
Savoy Av., Hayes	BB42	63
Savoy Clo. E15	CG37	58
Savoy Clo., Edg.	BM28	37
Savoy Clo., Uxb.	AX30	35
Savoy Ct. WC2	**BX40**	**4**
Savoy Ct. WC2	BX40	56
Strand		
Savoy Hill WC2	**BX40**	**4**
Savoy Pl. WC2	**BX40**	**4**
Savoy Pl. WC2	BX40	56
Savoy Rd., Dart.	CV46	80
Savoy St. WC2	**BX40**	**4**
Savoy St. WC2	BX40	56
Savoy Way WC2	BX40	56
Carting La.		
Savoy Wood, Harl.	CL13	13
Sawells, Brox.	CD14	12
Sawkins Clo. SW19	BQ48	75
Thursley Gdns.		
Sawley Rd. W12	BP40	55
Sawpit La., Guil.	AY69	110
Sawtry Clo., Cars.	BT54	86
Sawyer Clo. N9	CB27	39
Lion Rd.		
Sawyer St. SE1	**BZ41**	**4**
Sawyer St. SE1	BZ41	67
Sawyers Clo., Dag.	CS36	59
Sawyers Clo., Wind.	AM43	61
Sawyers Hall La., Brwd.	DB26	42
Sawyers La., B.Wd.	BJ23	27
Sawyers La., Pot.B.	BQ20	19
Sawyers Lawn W13	BJ39	54
Sawyers Way, Hem.H.	AY13	8
Saxby Rd. SW2	BX47	76
Saxbys Rd., Sev.	CY64	108
Saxham Rd., Bark.	CN37	58
Saxlingham Rd. E4	CF27	39
Saxon Av., Felt.	BE48	74
Saxon Clo., Brwd.	DD27	122
Saxon Clo., Grav.	DE48	81
Saxon Clo., Rom.	CW30	42
Saxon Clo., Slou.	AS41	62
Saxon Clo., Surb.	BK53	84
Saxon Clo., Uxb.	AY39	53
Saxon Ct., B.Wd.	BL23	28
Saxon Dr. W3	BM39	55
Saxon Gdns., Sthl.	BE40	54
Saxon Ho., Felt.	BE48	74
Saxon Pl., Hort.K.	CY53	90
Saxon Rd. E3	CD37	57
Saxon Rd. E6	CK38	58
Saxon Rd. N22	BY30	38
Saxon Rd. SE25	BX53	87
Saxon Rd., Ashf.	BA50	73
Saxon Rd., Brom.	CG50	78
Saxon Rd., Dart.	CW49	80
Saxon Rd., Ilf.	CL36	58
Saxon Rd., Sthl.	BE40	54
Saxon Rd., Walt.	BD55	84
Linley Dr.		
Saxon Rd., Welw.	BP 5	5
Saxon Rd., Wem.	BM34	46
Saxon Way N14	BW25	29
Saxon Way, Reig.	BR70	120
Saxon Way, Wal.Abb.	CF20	21
Saxon Way, West Dr.	AX43	63
Saxon Way, Wind.	AQ46	72
Saxon Wk., Sid.	CP50	79
Cray Rd.		
Saxonbury Av., Sun.	BC51	83
Saxonbury Clo., Mitch.	BT52	86
Saxonbury Gdns., Surb.	BK54	84
Saxons, Tad.	BQ64	103
Saxony Par., Hayes	BA39	53
Saxton Clo. SE13	CF45	67
Saxville Rd., Orp.	CO52	89
Sayer Ct., Wok.	AP62	100
Sayer St. SE17	**BZ42**	**4**
Sayers Clo., Lthd.	BG65	102
Sayers Gdns., Berk.	AQ11	7
Sayers Wk., Rich.	BL47	75
Stafford Pl.		
Sayes Court Est. SE8	CD42	67
Sayes Court Farm Dr., Wey.	AW56	92
Sayes Court Gdns. SE8	CD42	67
Sayes Court Rd., Orp.	CO52	89
Sayes Court St. SE8	CD43	67
Sayes Ct., Wey.	AW56	92
Sayesbury Av., Saw.	CP 5	6
Sayward Clo., Chesh.	AO18	16
Scabharbour Rd., Sev.	CV70	117
Scads Hill Clo., Orp.	CN53	88
Scala St. W1	**BW39**	**1**
Scala St. W1	BW39	56
Scales Rd. N17	CA31	48
Scampston Ms. W10	BQ39	55
Scampton Rd., Houns.	AY46	73
Southampton Rd.		
Scandrett St. E1	CB40	57
Wapping High St.		
Scarba Wk. N1	BZ36	57
Scarborough Clo., Sutt.	BR59	94
Scarborough Clo., West.	CJ62	106
Scarborough Rd. E11	CF33	48
Scarborough Rd. N4	BY33	47
Scarborough Rd. N9	CC26	39
Scarborough St. E1	**CA39**	**2**
Scarborough Way, Slou.	AN41	61
Scarbrook Rd., Croy.	BZ55	87
Scarbrook St., Croy.	BZ55	86
Scarbrook Rd.		
Scarle Rd., Wem.	BK36	54
Scarlet Rd. SE6	CG48	78
Scarlett Clo., Wok.	AP62	100
Scarsbrook Rd. SE3	CJ45	68
Scarsdale Gro. SE5	CA43	67
Neate St.		
Scarsdale Pl. W8	BS41	66
Wrights La.		
Scarsdale Rd. SE5	**CA43**	**4**
Scarsdale Rd., Har.	BG34	45
Scarsdale Vill. W8	BS41	66
Scarth Rd. SW13	BO45	65
Scatterdells La., Kings L.	AV18	16
Scawen Rd. SE8	CD42	67
Scaynes Link N12	BS28	38
Sceaux Est. SE5	CA44	67
Sceptre Rd. E2	CC38	57
Schofield Rd. SE3	CH43	68
Schofield Wk. SE3	CH43	68
Dornbergh Clo.		
Scholars Rd. E4	CF26	39
Scholars Rd. SW12	BW47	76
Scholars Wk., Hat.	BP13	10
Scholefield Rd. N19	BW33	47
Scholes Cres. SW2	BY47	76
School Alley, Twick.	BJ47	74
Bell La.		
School Bell Ms. E3	CD38	57
Arbery Rd.		
School Clo., Guil.	AR69	118
Bellfields Rd.		
School Gdns., Berk.	AT12	7
School Green La., Epp.	CS16	23
School Hill, Red.	BW67	113
School House La., Tedd.	BJ50	74
School La. SE23	CB48	77
Eliot Bank		
School La., Ayot St.Peter	BO 5	5
School La., Beac.	AO29	34
School La., Brwd.	DE29	122
School La., Bush.	BF26	36
School La., Cat.	CA66	114
School La., Ch.St.G.	AQ27	34
School La., Dart.	DB49	80
School La., Dor.	BG72	119
School La., Egh.	AT49	72
School La., Essenden	BU12	11
School La., Ger.Cr.	AR30	34
School La., Guil.	AY69	110
School La., Harl.	CN10	6
School La., Hat.	BQ12	10
School La., Hort.K.	CY52	90
School La., Kings.T.	BK51	84
Park Rd.		
School La., Lthd.	BG65	102
School La., Mickleham	BK67	111
School La., Ong.	CZ10	15
School La., Plaxtol	DC67	117
School La., Pnr.	BE31	45
School La., Seal	CW64	108
School La., Shep.	AZ53	83
School La., Slou.	AQ36	52
School La., St.Alb.	BF19	18
School La., Surb.	BM54	85
School La., Swan.	CU51	89
School La., Tad.	BP66	112
School La., Tewin	BU 6	5
School La., Tilegate Green	CS12	14
School La., W.Horsley	AZ68	110
School La., W.Kingsdown	CZ59	99
School La., Well.	CO45	69
School La., Wey.	AW56	92
School La., Wok.	AZ64	101
School Mead, Wat.	BA19	17
School Pass., Kings.T.	BL51	85
School Pass., Sthl.	BE40	54
School Pl. E1	CB38	57
Buckhurst St.		
School Rd. Av., Hmptn.	BG50	74
School Rd. E12	CK35	49
School Rd. NW10	BN38	55
School Rd. W4	BN42	65
Belmont Rd.		
School Rd., Ashf.	AZ49	73
School Rd., Brwd.	CZ22	33
School Rd., Chis.	CM51	88
School Rd., Dag.	CR37	59
School Rd., E.Mol.	BG52	84
School Rd., Grav.	DH48	81
School Rd., Hmptn.	BG50	74
School Rd., Houns.	BG45	64
School Rd., Kings.T.	BK51	84
Park Rd.		
School Rd., Ong.	CT18	23
School Rd., Pot.B.	BT18	20
School Rd., West Dr.	AX43	63
School Row, Hem.H.	AV14	7
School Way N12	BT28	38
School Way, Dag.	CP34	50
School Wk., Sun.	BC52	83
Schoolbell Ms. E3	CD37	57
Arbery Rd.		
Schoolfield Rd., Grays	DA43	70
Schoolhouse La. E1	CC40	57
Schooner Clo. SE16	CC41	67
Kinburn St.		
Schroder Ct., Egh.	AQ49	72
Schubert Rd. SW15	BR46	75
Schubert Rd., B.Wd.	BK25	27
Scilla Ct., Grays	DE43	71
Scillonian Rd., Guil.	AQ71	118
Sclater St. E1	**CA38**	**2**
Sclater St. E1	CA38	57
Scobie Pl. N16	CA35	48
Amhurst Rd.		
Scoresby St. SE1	**BY40**	**4**
Scoresby St. SE1	BY40	56
Scorton Av., Grnf.	BJ37	54
Scot Gro., Pnr.	BD29	36
Scotch Common W13	BJ39	54
Scoter Clo., Wdf.Grn.	CH29	40
Scotland Bridge Rd., Wey.	AW59	92
Scotland Green Rd. N., Enf.	CC24	30
Scotland Green Rd., Enf.	CC25	30
Scotland Grn. N17	CA30	39
Scotland Pl. SW1	**BX40**	**4**
Great Scotland Yd.		
Scotland Rd., Buck.H.	CJ26	40
Scotney Wk., Horn.	CV35	51
Bonnington Rd.		
Scots Hill Clo., Rick.	AY25	26
Scots Hill, Rick.	AY25	26
Scotscraig, Rad.	BH21	27
Scotsdale Clo., Orp.	CN52	88
Scotsdale Clo., Sutt.	BR57	94
Scotsdale Rd. SE12	CH46	78
Scotshall La., Warl.	CF61	105
Scotswold Wk. N17	CB29	39
Waverley Rd.		
Scotswood Rd. EC1	**BY38**	**2**
St. James's Row		
Scotswood Wk. N17	CB29	39
Northumberland Pk.		
Scott Clo. SW16	BX51	86
Fairview Rd.		
Scott Clo., Epsom	BN56	94
Scott Clo., Guil.	AQ69	118
Scott Clo., West Dr.	AY42	63
Scott Cres., Erith	CT44	69
Scott Cres., Har.	BF33	45
Scott Ellis Gdns. NW8	**BT38**	**1**
Scott Ellis Gdns. NW8	BT38	56
Scott Farm Clo., E.Mol.	BJ54	84
Scott Gdns., Houns.	BD43	64
Scott Lidgett Cres. SE16	**CB41**	**4**
Scott Lidgett Cres. SE16	CB41	67
Scott Rd., Grav.	DH49	81
Scott Rd., Grays	DG42	71
Scott St. E1	CB38	57
Scottes Rd., Dag.	CP33	50
Valence Av.		
Scotts Av., Brom.	CF51	87
Scotts Av., Sun.	BB50	73
Scotts Clo., Horn.	CV35	51
Rye Clo.		
Scotts Clo., Stai.	AX47	73
Scotts Dr., Hmptn.	BF50	74
Scotts Farm Rd., Epsom	BN57	94
Scotts Gro. Clo., Wok.	AO60	91
Scotts Gro. Rd., Wok.	AO60	91
Scotts La., Brom.	CF52	87
Scotts Mill Rd., Rick.	AY25	26
Scotts Rd. E10	CF33	48
Scotts Rd. W12	BP41	65
Scotts Rd., Brom.	CH50	78
Scotts Rd., Sthl.	BD41	64
Scotts Way, Sev.	CT64	107
Scotts Way, Sun.	BB50	73
Scottswood Clo., Bush.	BE23	27
Scottswood Rd., Bush.	BE23	27
Scoulding Rd. E16	CG39	58
Rogers Rd.		
Scout App. NW10	BN35	46
Scout La. SW4	BW45	66
Scout Way NW7	BN28	37
Scovell Cres. SE1	**BZ41**	**4**
Scovell Cres. SE1	BZ41	67
Great Suffolk St.		
Scovell Rd. SE1	**BZ41**	**4**
Scovell Rd. SE1	BZ41	67
Scovell Wk. SE1	BZ41	67
Scovell Rd.		
Scrafton Rd., Ilf.	CL34	49
Scratchers La., Farn.	CY55	90
Scrattons Ter., Bark.	CP37	59
Scriven St. E8	**CA37**	**2**
Scriven St. E8	CA37	57
Scrooby St. SE6	CE46	77
Scrubbits Park Rd., Rad.	BJ21	27
Scrubs La. NW10	BP38	55
Scrubs La. W10	BP39	55
Scrutton Clo. SW12	BW47	76
Scrutton St. EC2	**CA38**	**2**
Scrutton St. EC2	CA38	57
Scudamore La. NW9	BN31	46
Scudders Hill, Fawk.	DA53	90
Scutari Rd. SE22	CB46	77
Scylla Rd. SE15	CB45	67
Scylla Rd., Houns.	AZ46	73
Seaborough Rd., Grays	DH41	71
Seabright St. E2	CB38	57
Bethnal Green Rd.		
Seabrook Dr., W.Wick.	CF55	87
Seabrook Gdns., Rom.	CR33	50
Seabrook Rd., Dag.	CP34	50
Seabrook Rd., Kings L.	BA17	17
Seabrooke Ri., Grays	DD43	71
Seaburn Clo., Rain.	CT38	59
Seacoal La. EC4	**BY39**	**2**
Seacoal La. EC4	BY39	56
Seacourt Rd. SE2	CP41	69
Seacourt Rd., Slou.	AT42	62
Seacroft Gdns., Wat.	BD27	36
Seafield Rd. N11	BW28	38
Seaford Clo., Ruis.	BA34	44
Seaford Rd. E17	CE31	48
Seaford Rd. N15	BZ31	48
Seaford Rd. W13	BJ40	54
Seaford Rd., Enf.	CA24	30
Seaford Rd., Stai.	AX46	73
Sandringham Rd.		
Seaford St. WC1	**BX38**	**2**
Seaford St. WC1	BX38	56
Seaforth Av., N.Mal.	BP53	85
Seaforth Clo., Rom.	CT29	41
Seaforth Cres. N5	BZ35	48
Seaforth Dr., Wal.Cr.	CC20	21
Seaforth Gdns. N21	BX26	38
Seaforth Gdns., Epsom	BO56	94
Seaforth Gdns., Wdf.Grn.	CJ28	40
Seaforth Pl. SW1	**BW41**	**3**
Seaforth Pl. SW1	BW41	66
Buckingham Gate		
Seager Pl. E3	CD39	57
Burdett Rd.		
Seagrave Clo., Wey.	AZ57	92
Seagrave Rd. SW6	BS43	66
Seagry Rd. E11	CH32	49
Seal Chart, Sev.	CY64	108
Seal Dr., Sev.	CW64	108
Seal Hill, Sev.	CX64	108
Seal Hollow Rd., Sev.	CV65	108
Seal Rd., Sev.	CV64	108
Seal St. E8	CA35	48
Sealand Rd., Houns.	AZ46	73
Sealand Wk., Nthlt.	BD38	54
Wayfarer Rd.		
Seale Hill, Reig.	BS71	121
Seaman Clo., St.Alb.	BG16	18
Searches La., Wat.	BC17	17
Searchwood Rd., Warl.	CB62	105
Searle Pl. N4	BX33	47
Evershot Rd.		
Searles Clo. SW11	BU43	66
Searles Rd. SE1	**BZ42**	**4**
Searles Rd. SE1	BZ42	67
Sears St. SE5	BZ43	67
Seasprite Clo., Nthlt.	BD38	54
Seaton Av., Ilf.	CN35	49
Seaton Clo. E13	CH38	58
New Barn St.		
Seaton Clo. SW15	BP47	75
Seaton Clo., Twick.	BG46	74
Seaton Dr., Ashf.	AY48	73
Seaton Gdns., Ruis.	BC34	44
Seaton Pl. NW1	**BW38**	**1**
Seaton Pl. NW1	BW38	56
Seaton Point E5	CB34	48
Downs Est.		
Seaton Rd., Dart.	CU47	79
Seaton Rd., Hayes	BA42	63
Seaton Rd., Hem.H.	AX15	8
Seaton Rd., Mitch.	BU51	86
Seaton Rd., St.Alb.	BK17	18
Seaton Rd., Twick.	BG46	74
Seaton Rd., Well.	CP43	69
Seaton Rd., Wem.	BL37	55
Seaton St. N18	CB28	39
Sebastian Av., Brwd.	DD25	122
Sebastian St. EC1	**BY38**	**2**
Sebastian St. EC1	BY38	56
Sebastopol Rd. N9	CB28	39
Sebbon St. N1	**BY36**	**2**
Sebbon St. N1	BY36	56
Sebert Rd. E7	CH35	49
Sebright Pass. E2	CB37	57
Sebright Rd., Barn.	BQ23	28
Sebright Rd., Hem.H.	AW14	8
Secker Cres., Har.	BG30	36
Secker St. SE1	**BY40**	**4**
Secker St. SE1	BY40	56
Second Av. E12	CK35	49
Second Av. E13	CH38	58
Second Av. E17	CE32	48
Second Av. N18	CC28	39
Second Av. NW4	BQ31	46
Second Av. SW14	BO45	65
Second Av. W10	BR38	55
Second Av. W3	BO40	55
Second Av., Brwd.	DB20	24
Second Av., Dag.	CR37	59
Second Av., Enf.	CA25	30
Second Av., Grays	DA43	70
Second Av., Harl.	CN11	13
Second Av., Hayes	BB40	53
Second Av., Rom.	CP32	50
Second Av., Walt.	BC53	83
Second Av., Wat.	BD21	27
Second Av., Wem.	BK34	45
Second Clo., E.Mol.	BG52	84
Second Cross Rd., Twick.	BG48	74
Second Way, Wem.	BM35	46
Secretan Rd. SE5	**CA42**	**4**
Secretan Rd. SE5	CA42	67
Sedan Way SE17	**CA42**	**4**
Sedan Way SE17	CA42	67
Sedcombe Clo., Sid.	CO49	79
Knoll Rd.		
Sedcote Rd., Enf.	CC25	30
Sedding St. SW1	**BV42**	**3**
Sedding St. SW1	BV42	66
Seddon Rd., Mord.	BT53	86
Sedge Ct., Grays	DE43	71
Sedge Grn., Harl.	CF13	12
Sedgebrook Rd. SE3	CJ44	68
Sedgecombe Av., Har.	BK32	45
Sedgefield Clo., Rom.	CW28	42
Sedgefield Cres., Rom.	CW28	42
Sedgeford Rd. W12	BO40	55
Sedgehill Rd. SE6	CE49	77
Sedgemere Av. N2	BT31	47
Sedgemere Rd. SE2	CP41	69
Sedgemoor Dr., Dag.	CR35	50
Sedgeway SE6	CG47	78
Sedgewick Av., Uxb.	AZ36	53
Sedgewood Clo., Brom.	CG54	88
Sedgmoor Pl. SE5	CA43	67
Sedgwick Rd. E10	CF34	48
Sedgwick St. E9	CC35	48
Sedleigh Rd. SW18	BR46	75
Sedlescombe Rd. SW6	BS43	66
Sedley Gro., Uxb.	AX31	44
Sedley Pl. W1	**BV39**	**1**
Sedley Pl. W1	BV39	56
Oxford St.		
Sedley Ri., Loug.	CK23	31
Sedley, Grav.	DD49	81
Seeley Dr. SE21	CA49	77
Seeleys, Harl.	CP 9	6
Seelig Av. NW9	BP33	46
Seely Rd. SW17	BV50	76
Seer Green La., Beac.	AP29	34
Seer Mead, Beac.	AO29	34
Seething La. EC3	**CA40**	**4**
Seething La. EC3	CA40	57
Seething Wells La., Surb.	BK53	84
Sefton Av. NW7	BN28	37
Sefton Av., Har.	BG30	36
Sefton Clo., Orp.	CN52	88
Sefton Clo., Slou.	AP37	52
Sefton Clo., St.Alb.	BH13	9
Blenheim Rd.		
Sefton Paddock, Slou.	AQ36	52
Sefton Rd., Croy.	CB54	87
Sefton Rd., Epsom	BN58	94
Sefton Rd., Orp.	CN52	88
Sefton St. SW15	BQ45	65
Sefton Way, Uxb.	AX39	53
Segal Clo. SE23	CD47	77
Brockley Pk.		
Sekforde St. EC1	**BY38**	**2**
Sekforde St. EC1	BY38	56
Selah Dr., Swan.	CS51	89
Selan Gdns., Hayes	BC39	53
Selbie Av. NW10	BO35	46
Selborne Av. E12	CL35	49
Selborne Av., Bex.	CQ47	79
Selborne Gdns. NW4	BP31	46
Selborne Gdns., Grnf.	BJ37	54
Selborne Rd. E17	CD32	48
Selborne Rd. N14	BX27	38
Selborne Rd. N22	BX30	38
Selborne Rd. SE5	BZ44	67
Denmark Hill		
Selborne Rd., Croy.	CA55	87
Selborne Rd., Ilf.	CL34	49
Selborne Rd., N.Mal.	BO51	85
Selborne Rd., Sid.	CO49	79
Selbourne Av., Surb.	BL55	85
Selbourne Av., Wey.	AW58	92
Selbourne Clo., Wey.	AW58	92
Selbourne Rd., Guil.	AT69	118
Sutherland Dr.		
Selbourne Sq., Gdse.	CC68	114
Selby Av., St.Alb.	BG13	9

Selby Chase, Ruis. BC34 44
Selby Clo. E6 CK39 58
Linton Gdns.
Selby Clo., Chess. BL57 94
Selby Clo., Chis. CL50 78
Selby Gdns., Sthl. BF38 54
Selby Grn., Cars. BU54 86
Selby Rd. E11 CG34 49
Selby Rd. E13 CH39 58
Selby Rd. N17 CA29 39
Selby Rd. SE20 CB51 87
Selby Rd. W5 BJ38 54
Selby Rd., Ashf. BA50 73
Selby Rd., Cars. BU54 86
Selby St. E1 CB38 57
Selby Wk., Wok. AQ62 100
Wyndham Rd.
Selcroft Rd., Pur. BY59 95
Selden Hill, Hem.H. AX14 8
Selden Rd. SE15 CC44 67
Selden Wk. N7 BX34 47
Durham Rd.
Selhurst Clo., Wok. AS61 100
Selhurst New Rd. SE25 CA53 87
Selhurst Pl. SE25 CA53 87
Selhurst Rd. N9 BZ27 39
Selhurst Rd. SE25 CA53 87
Selinas La., Dag. CQ33 50
Selkirk Dr., Erith CT44 69
Selkirk Rd. SW17 BU49 76
Selkirk Rd., Twick. BG48 74
Sellers Hall Clo. N3 BS29 38
Sellincourt Rd. SW17 BU49 76
Sellindge Clo., Beck. CD50 77
Sellon Ms. SE11 BX42 4
Newport St.
Sellon Ms., SE11 BX42 66
Newport St.
Sellons Av. NW10 BO37 55
Sellwood Dr., Barn. BQ25 28
Selma Ho. W12 BP39 55
Du Cane Rd.
Selsdon Av., S.Croy. BZ57 96
Selsdon Clo., Rom. CS30 41
Selsdon Clo., Surb. BL53 85
Selsdon Cres., S.Croy. CC58 96
Selsdon Park Rd., S.Croy. CC58 96
Selsdon Rd. E11 CH33 49
Selsdon Rd. E13 CJ37 58
Selsdon Rd. NW2 BO34 46
Selsdon Rd. SE27 BY48 76
Selsdon Rd., S.Croy. BZ56 96
Selsdon Rd., Wey. AW59 92
Selsdon Way E14 CE41 67
Selsey Cres., Well. CP44 69
Selsey Pl. N6 CA35 48
Crossway
Selsey St. E14 CE39 57
Selvage La. NW7 BN28 37
Selway Clo., Pnr. BC31 44
Selwood Clo., Stai. AX46 73
Selwood Gdns., Stai. AX46 73
Selwood Pl. SW7 BT42 3
Selwood Pl. SW7 BT42 66
Selwood Rd., Brwd. CZ27 42
Selwood Rd., Chess. BK56 93
Selwood Rd., Croy. CB55 87
Selwood Rd., Sutt. BR54 85
Selwood Rd., Wok. AT63 100
Selwood Ter. SW7 BT42 3
Selwood Ter. SW7 BT42 66
Selworth Clo. E11 CH32 49
Selworthy Rd. SE6 CD48 77
Selwyn Av. E4 CF29 39
Selwyn Av., Hat. BN13 10
Selwyn Av., Ilf. CN32 49
Selwyn Av., Rich. BL45 65
Selwyn Clo., Houns. BE45 64
Cambridge Rd.
Selwyn Cres., Hat. BO12 10
Selwyn Cres., Well. CO45 69
Selwyn Ct. SE3 CG45 68
Selwyn Ct., Edg. BM29 37
Selwyn Dr., Hat. BN12 10
Selwyn Grn., Walt. BD54 84
Cromwell Rd.
Selwyn Pl., Orp. CO52 89
Selwyn Rd. E13 CH37 58
Selwyn Rd. E3 CD37 57
Selwyn Rd. NW10 BN36 55
Selwyn Rd., N.Mal. BN53 85
Selwyn Rd., Til. DF44 71
Selwyn Rd., Walt. BD54 84
St. Johns Dr.
Semaphore Rd., Guil. AS71 118
Semley Pl. SW1 BV42 3
Semley Pl. SW1 BV42 66
Semley Rd. SW16 BX51 86
Semper Clo., Wok. AP62 100
Semper Rd., Grays DH41 71
Semphill Rd., Hem.H. AY15 8
Senate St. SE15 CC44 67
Gibbon Rd.
Senator Wk. SE28 CM41 68
Garrick Dr.
Send Barns La., Wok. AU65 100
Send Clo., Wok. AU65 100
Send Hill Rd., Wok. AU65 100
Send Parade Clo., Wok. AU65 100
Send Rd., Wok. AT65 100
Sendbarns La., Wok. AU65 100
Sendmarsh Rd., Wok. AU65 100
Seneca Rd. SW4 BX45 66
Seneca Rd., Th.Hth. BZ52 87
Senga Rd., Wall. BV54 86
Senhouse Rd., Sutt. BQ55 85
Senior St. W2 BS39 56
Senlac Rd. SE12 CH47 78
Sennen Rd., Enf. CA26 39
Sennen Wk. SE9 CK48 78
Nunnington Clo.
Senrab St. E1 CC39 57
Sentinel Clo., Nthlt. BE38 54
Sentinel Sq. NW4 BQ31 46
Sentis Ct., Nthwd. BB29 35
Carew Rd.
September Way, Stan. BJ29 36
Septimus Pl., Enf. CB25 30
Ermine Side
Sequoia Clo., Bush. BG26 36
Sequoia Gdns., Orp. CN54 88
Sequoia Pk., Pnr. BF29 36
Serbin Clo. E10 CF33 48
Sergeants Green La., Wal.Abb. CJ20 22
Sergehill La., Wat. BC16 17
Serjeants Inn EC4 BY39 2
Lombard La.
Serle St. WC2 BX39 2
Serle St. WC2 BX39 56
Sermon Dr., Swan. CS52 89
Sermon La. EC4 BZ39 57
Carter La.
Serpentine Ct., Sev. CV65 108
Serpentine Rd.
Serpentine Grn., Red. BW68 113
Malmstone Av.
Serpentine Rd. W2 BU40 3
Serpentine Rd. W2 BU40 56
Serpentine Rd., Sev. CV65 108
Service La., Ing. DB19 24
Service Rd. SE13 CF45 67
Service Rd., Brwd. DB27 42
Service Rd., The, Pot.B. BS19 20
Byng Dr.
Service Rd., Wind. AL44 61
Serviden Dr., Brom. CJ51 88
Setchell Rd. SE1 CA42 4
Setchell Rd. SE1 CA42 67
Setchell Way SE1 CA42 4
Seth St. SE16 CC41 67
Swan Rd.
Seton Gdns., Dag. CP36 59
Settle Rd. E13 CH37 58
Settle Rd., Rom. CX28 42
Settles St. E1 CB39 57
Settrington Rd. SW6 BS44 66
Seven Acres, New A.G. DC55 90
Seven Acres, Swan. CS53 89
Seven Arches Rd., Brwd. DB27 42
Seven Arches, New A.G. DC55 90
Seven Dials WC2 BX39 2
Seven Hills Clo., Walt. BB58 92
Seven Hills Rd., Cob. BB59 92
Seven Hills Rd., Iver AT35 43
Seven Hills Rd., Walt. BB57 92
Seven Kings Rd., Ilf. CN33 49
Seven Sisters Rd. N15 BZ33 48
Seven Sisters Rd. N4 BZ33 48
Seven Sisters Rd. N7 BX34 47
Sevenoaks By-pass, Sev. & Ton. CV69 117
Sevenoaks Clo., Bexh. CR45 69
Sevenoaks Clo., Rom. CV28 42
Sevenoaks Rd. SE4 CD46 77
Sevenoaks Rd., Green Street Green CN57 97
Sevenoaks Rd., Orp. CN56 97
Sevenoaks Rd., Otford CU62 107
Sevenoaks Rd., Sev. DA65 108
Sevenoaks Rd., West. CM66 115
Sevenoaks Way, Sid. CO50 79
Seventh Av. E12 CK35 49
Seventh Av., Enf. CB25 30
Seventh Av., Hayes BC40 53
Severalls Av., Chesh. AO18 16
Severn Av., Rom. CU31 50
Severn Cres., Slou. AT43 62
Severn Dr., Enf. CB22 30
Severn Dr., Esher BJ55 84
Severn Dr., Upmin. CY32 51
Severn Dr., Walt. BD55 84
Severn Mead, Hem.H. AY12 8
Severn Rd., S.Ock. CY39 60
Severn Way NW10 BO35 46
Severn Way, Wat. BD20 18
Severnake Clo. E14 CE42 67
Charnwood Gdns.
Severns Field, Epp. CO18 23
Severnvale, St.Alb. BL17 19
Thamesdale
Severus Rd. SW11 BU45 66
Seville St. SW1 BU41 3
Seville St. SW1 BU41 66
Sevington Rd. NW4 BP32 46
Sevington St. W9 BS38 56
Seward Rd. W7 BJ41 64
Seward Rd., Beck. CC51 87
Seward St. EC1 BY38 2
Seward St. EC1 BY38 56
Sewardstone Gdns. E4 CE25 30
Sewardstone Rd. E2 CC37 57
Sewardstone Rd. E4 CE26 39
Sewardstone St. Wal.Abb. CF20 21
Sewardstone Way, Wal.Abb. CF21 30
Sewdley St. E5 CC34 48
Sewell Clo., St.Alb. BL13 10
Sewell Harris Clo., Harl. CN10 6
Minchen Rd.
Sewell Rd. SE2 CO41 69
Sewell St. E13 CH38 58
Sewells, Welw.G.C. BR 6 5
Sextant Av. E14 CF42 67
Sexton Clo., Rain. CT37 59
Sexton Rd., Til. DF44 71
Seymer Rd., Rom. CS31 50
Seymour Av. N17 CB30 39
Seymour Av., Epsom BP58 94
Seymour Av., Mord. BQ53 85
Seymour Clo. EC1 BY38 2
Sekforde St.
Seymour Clo., E.Mol. BG53 84
Seymour Clo., Pnr. BE30 36
Seymour Cres., Hem.H. AY13 8
Seymour Ct. E4 CG27 40
Seymour Ct. N10 BV30 38
Seymour Ct. NW2 BP34 46
Seymour Dr., Brom. CK54 88
Seymour Gdns. SE4 CD45 67
Seymour Gdns., Felt. BD49 74
Seymour Gdns., Ilf. CK33 49
Seymour Gdns., Ruis. BD33 45
Seymour Gdns., Surb. BL53 85
Seymour Gdns., Twick. BJ47 74
Seymour Ms. W1 BV39 1
Seymour Ms. W1 BV39 56
Seymour Pl. SE25 CB52 87
Seymour Pl. W1 BU39 1
Seymour Pl. W1 BU39 56
Seymour Rd. E10 CD33 48
Seymour Rd. E4 CE26 39
Seymour Rd. E6 CJ37 58
Seymour Rd. N3 BS29 38
Seymour Rd. N8 BY32 47
Seymour Rd. N9 CB27 39
Seymour Rd. SW18 BR46 75
Seymour Rd. SW19 BQ48 75
Seymour Rd. W4 BN42 65
Seymour Rd., Berk. AP12 7
Seymour Rd., Cars. BV56 95
Seymour Rd., Ch.St.G. AR28 34
Seymour Rd., E.Mol. BG53 84
Seymour Rd., Grav. DF48 81
Seymour Rd., Hmptn. BG49 74
Seymour Rd., Kings T. BK51 84
Seymour Rd., Mitch. BV54 86
Seymour Rd., Slou. AO41 61
Seymour Rd., St.Alb. BH12 9
Seymour Rd., Til. DF44 71
Seymour St. W1 & W2 BU39 1
Seymour St. W1 BU39 56
Seymour St. W2 BU39 56
Seymour Ter. SE20 CB51 87
Selby Rd.
Seymour Vill. SE20 CB51 87
Seymour Way, Sun. BB50 73
Seymour Wk. SW10 BT42 3
Seymour Wk. SW10 BT42 66
Seymours, Harl. CK12 13
Seymours, Loug. CL23 31
Seyssel St. E14 CF42 67
Shaa Rd. W3 BN40 55
Shacklands Rd., Sev. BR59 98
Shackleford Rd., Wok. AT64 100
Shacklegate La., Tedd. BH49 74
Shackleton Clo. SE23 CB48 77
Featherstone Av.
Shackleton Rd., Slou. AP40 52
Shackleton Rd., Sthl. BE40 54
Shackleton Way, Welw.G.C. BT 8 5
Shackleton Wk., Guil. AP70 118
Humbolt Clo.
Shacklewell Grn. E8 CA35 48
Shacklewell La.
Shacklewell La. E8 CA35 48
Shacklewell Rd. N16 CA35 48
Shacklewell St. E2 CA38 2
Shacklewell St. E2 CA38 57
Shad Thames SE1 CA40 4
Shad Thames SE1 CA40 57
Shadbolt Clo., Wor.Pk. BO55 85
Shadwell Dr., Nthlt. BE38 54
Shadwell Pl. E1 CC40 57
Shady La., Wat. BC23 26
Shadybush Clo., Bush. BG26 36
Shaef Way, Tedd. BJ50 74
Shafter Rd., Dag. CS36 59
Shaftesbury Av. W1 BW40 3
Shaftesbury Av. W1 BW40 56
Shaftesbury Av. WC2 BW40 56
Shaftesbury Av., Barn. BT24 29
Shaftesbury Av., Enf. CC23 30
Shaftesbury Av., Felt. BC46 73
Shaftesbury Av., Har. BF33 45
Shaftesbury Av., Kenton BK32 45
Shaftesbury Av., Sthl. BF42 64
Shaftesbury Cres., Stai. AX50 73
Shaftesbury Ct. N1 BZ37 2
Shaftesbury Ct. N1 BZ37 57
Shaftesbury La., Dart. CX45 70
Shaftesbury Pl. EC1 BZ39 2
Aldersgate St.
Shaftesbury Rd. E10 CE33 48
Shaftesbury Rd. E17 CE32 48
Shaftesbury Rd. E4 CF26 39
Shaftesbury Rd. E7 CJ36 58
Shaftesbury Rd. N18 CA29 39
Shaftesbury Rd. N19 BX33 47
Shaftesbury Rd., Beck. CD51 87
Shaftesbury Rd., Cars. BT54 86
Shaftesbury Rd., Epp. CN18 22
Shaftesbury Rd., Rich. BL45 65
Shaftesbury Rd., Rom. CT32 50
Shaftesbury Rd., Wat. BD24 27
Shaftesbury Rd., Wok. AT62 100
Shaftesbury St. N1 BZ37 2
Shaftesbury St. N1 BZ37 57
Shaftesbury Way, Twick. BH48 74
Shaftesbury Waye, Hayes BD39 54
Shaftesbury, Loug. CJ24 31
Shaftesburys, The, Bark. CM37 58
Shafto Ms. SW1 BU41 3
Shafto Ms. SW1 BU41 66
Cadogan Sq.
Shafton Rd. E9 CC37 57
Shafts Ct. EC3 CA39 2
Shafts Ct. EC3 CA39 57
Shaftsbury Rd., Beck. CD51 87
Croydon Rd.
Shaftsbury Way, Kings L. BA17 17
Shaggy Calf La., Slou. AQ40 52
Shakespeare Av. N11 BW28 38
Shakespeare Av. NW10 BN37 55
Shakespeare Av., Felt. BC46 73
Shakespeare Av., Hayes BC39 53
Shakespeare Av., Til. DG44 71
Shakespeare Cres. NW10 BN37 55
Shakespeare Cres. E12 CK36 58
Shakespeare Dr., Har. BL32 46
Shakespeare Gdns. N2 BU31 47
Shakespeare Ho. N14 BW27 38
Shakespeare Rd. E17 CC30 39
Shakespeare Rd. NW7 BO28 37
Shakespeare Rd. SE24 BY46 76
Shakespeare Rd. W3 BN40 55
Shakespeare Rd. W7 BH40 54
Shakespeare Rd., Bexh. CQ44 69
Shakespeare Rd., Dart. CX45 70
Shakespeare Rd., Rom. CT32 50
Shakespeare Rd., Wey. AX56 92
Shakespeare Sq., Ilf. CM29 40
Shakespeare St., Wat. BC22 26
Shakespeare Way, Felt. BD49 74
Shakespeare Wk. N16 CA35 48
Shakletons, Ong. CX17 24
Shalcomb St. SW10 BT43 66
Shalcross Dr., Chsnt. CD18 21
Shaldon Dr., Mord. BR53 85
Shaldon Dr., Ruis. BD34 45
Shaldon Rd., Edg. BL30 37
Shaldon Way, Walt. BD55 84
Shale Grn., Red. BW68 113
Shalfleet Dr. W10 BQ40 55
Shalford Clo., Orp. CM56 97
Shalford Dr. W10 BQ40 55
Shalford Rd., Guil. AR72 118
Shalimar Gdns. W3 BN40 55
Shalimar Rd. W3 BM40 55
Hereford Rd.
Shallcross Cres., Hat. BO14 10
Shallons Rd. SE9 CL49 78
Shalston Rd. SW14 BM45 65
Shalston Vill., Surb. BL53 85
Shamrock Clo., Lthd. BG64 102
Shamrock Rd., Croy. BX53 86
Shamrock Rd., Grav. DJ47 81
Shamrock St. SW4 BW45 66
Clapham Manor St.
Shamrock Way N14 BV26 38
Shand St. SE1 CA41 4
Shand St. SE1 CA41 67
Shandon Rd. SW4 BW46 76
Shandy St. E1 CC39 57
Shanklin Gdns., Wat. BD28 36
Shanklin Rd. N15 CB31 48
Shanklin Rd. N8 BW32 47
Shanklin Way SE15 CA43 67
Hordle Promenade S.
Shannon Clo., Sthl. BE42 64
Ringway
Shannon Gro. SW9 BX45 66
Shannon Pl. NW3 BU37 1
Mackennal St.
Shannon Pl. NW8 BU37 56
Shannon Way, Beck. CE50 77
Shannon Way, S.Ock. CY40 60
Shantock Hall La., Hem.H. AS18 16
Shantock La., Hem.H. AS18 16
Shap Cres., Cars. BU54 86
Shardcroft Av. SE24 BY46 76
Shardeloes Rd. SE14 CD45 67
Shards Sq. SE15 CB43 67
Sharland Rd., Grav. DH48 81
Sharman Ct., Sid. CO49 79
Carlton Rd.
Sharman St. E14 CE39 57
Broomfield St.
Sharnbrooke Clo., Well. CP45 69
Sharney Av., Slou. AT42 62
Sharon Clo., Epsom BN60 94
Sharon Clo., Lthd. BF65 102
Sharon Clo., Surb. BK54 84
Sharon Gdns. E9 CC37 57
Sharon Rd. W4 BN42 65
Sharon Rd., Enf. CD23 30
Sharp Way, Dart. CW45 70
Sharpe Cft., Harl. CM11 13
Sharpes La., Berk. AT14 7
Sharples Hall St. NW1 BU36 56
Regents Park Rd.
Sharpness Clo., Hayes BE39 54
Kennett Dr.
Sharps La., Ruis. BA33 44
Sharratt St. SE15 CC43 67
Sharsted St. SE17 BY42 4
Sharsted St. SE17 BY42 66
Sharvel La., Nthlt. BC37 53
Shaw Av., Bark. CQ37 59
Shaw Clo. SE28 CO40 59
Shaw Clo., Bush. BH27 36
Shaw Clo., Cher. AU57 91
Shaw Clo., Chsnt. CC17 21
Shaw Clo., Epsom BO59 94
Shaw Clo., S.Croy. CA59 96
Shaw Cres., Brwd. DE24 122
Shaw Cres., S.Croy. CA59 96
Shaw Cres., Til. DG44 71
Shaw Dr., Walt. BD54 84
Shaw Gdns., Bark. CQ37 59
Shaw Rd., Brom. CG48 78
Shaw Rd., Enf. CC23 30
Shaw Rd., West. CJ63 106
Shaw Sq. E17 CD30 39
Shaw Way, Wall. BX57 95
Shawbridge, Harl. CM12 13
Shawbrooke Rd. SE9 CJ46 78
Shawbury Rd. SE22 CA46 77
Shawbury Rd., Grnf. BF38 54
Shawfield Pk., Brom. CJ51 88
Shawfield St. SW3 BU42 3
Shawfield St. SW3 BU42 66
Shawford Ct. SW15 BP47 75
Shawford Rd., Epsom BN57 94
Shawley Cres., Epsom BQ62 103
Shawley Way, Epsom BP62 103
Shawline Cres. E17 CD30 39
Shaws Cotts. SE23 CD48 77
Shaws, The, Welw.G.C. BT 8 5
Shaxton Cres., Croy. CF58 96
Shearing Dr., Cars. BT54 86
Stavordale Rd.
Shearling Way N7 BX36 56
Shearman Rd. SE3 CG45 68
Shears Green Ct., Grav. DG48 81
Shearwood Cres., Dart. CU45 69
Sheaths La., Lthd. BF60 93
Sheaveshill Av. NW9 BO31 46
Sheba St. E1 CA38 2
Sheehy Way, Slou. AQ40 52
Sheen Common Dr., Rich. BM45 65
Sheen Court Rd., Rich. BM45 65
Sheen Ct., Rich. BM45 65
Sheen Gate Gdns. SW14 BN45 65
Sheen Gro. N1 BY37 2
Sheen La. SW14 BN46 75
Sheen Pk., Rich. BL45 65
Sheen Rd., Orp. CN52 88
Sheen Rd., Rich. BL46 75
Sheen Way, Wall. BX56 95
Sheen Wood SW14 BN46 75
Sheendale Rd., Rich. BL45 65
Sheenewood SE26 CB49 77
Sheep Hill, Sev. DB66 117
Sheep La. E8 CB37 57
Sheep Wk., Epsom BN64 103
Sheep Wk., Reig. BP69 120
Sheep Wk., Shep. AY54 83
Sheep Wk., The, Wok. AU62 100
Sheepbarn La., War. CG59 97
Sheepcot Dr., Wat. BD20 18
Sheepcot La., Wat. BC20 17
Sheepcote Clo., Houns. BC43 63
Sheepcote Gdns., Uxb. AV32 43
Denham Green La.
Sheepcote La. SW11 BU44 66
Sheepcote La., Orp. CQ53 89
Sheepcote Rd., Eton AN42 61
Sheepcote Rd., Har. BH32 45
Sheepcote Rd., Hem.H. AY13 8
Sheepcote, Welw.G.C. BS 9 5
Sheepcotes Rd., Rom. CP31 50
Sheepfold La., Amer. AO23 25
Sheepfold Rd., Guil. AP69 118
Sheepfold, Twick. BK47 74
Sheephouse Grn., Dor. BE73 119
Sheephouse La., Dor. BE73 119
Sheephouse Rd., Hem.H. AY14 8
Sheephouse Way, N.Mal. BN54 85
Sheeplands Av., Guil. AU69 118
Sheepwalk La., Lthd. BB70 110
Sheering Lower Rd., Saw. CR 6 6
Sheering Mill La., Saw. CQ 6 6
Sheering Rd., Harl. CP 9 6
Sheerwater Av., Wey. AV60 91
Sheerwater Rd. E16 CJ39 58
Sheerwater Rd., Wey. AV60 91
Sheet Hill, Sev. DC66 117
Sheet St., Wind. AO44 61
Sheet Street Rd., Wind. AO46 61
Sheethanger La., Hem.H. AW15 8
Sheffield Dr., Rom. CX28 42
Sheffield Gdns., Rom. CX28 42
Sheffield Sq. E3 CE37 58
Malmesbury Rd.
Sheffield St. WC2 BX39 2
Sheffield St. WC2 BX39 56
Portugal St.
Sheffield Ter. W8 BS41 66
Shefton Ri., Nthwd. BC29 35
Sheila Clo., Rom. CR29 41
Sheila Rd., Rom. CR29 41
Sheilings, The, Horn. CW32 51
Sheilings, The, Sev. CW63 108
Shelbourne Clo., Pnr. BE31 45
Shelbourne Rd. N17 CB30 39
Shelburne Rd. N7 BX35 47
Shelbury Clo., Sid. CO48 79
Shelbury Rd. SE22 CB46 77
Shelden Ct., Guil. AS71 118
Sheldon Av. N6 BU33 47
Sheldon Av., Ilf. CL30 40
Sheldon Clo. SE12 CH46 78
Sheldon Clo. SE20 CB51 77
Sheldon Clo., Chsnt. CA16 21
Sheldon Clo., Reig. BS71 121
Lymden Gdns.
Sheldon Ct., Guil. AS71 118
Lower Edgeborough Rd.
Sheldon Rd. N18 CA28 39
Sheldon Rd. NW2 BQ35 46
Sheldon Rd., Bexh. CQ44 69
Sheldon Rd., Dag. CQ36 59
Sheldon St., Croy. BZ55 87
Sheldrake Pl. W8 BS41 66
Sheldrick Clo. SW19 BT51 86
Sheldwick Ter., Brom. CK53 88
Shelford Pl. N16 BZ34 48
Shelford Rd., Barn. BQ25 28
Shelford Ri. SE19 CA50 77
Shelgate Rd. SW11 BU46 76
Shell Clo., Brom. CK53 88
Manor Way
Shell Rd. SE13 CE45 67
Shellbank La., Dart. DA49 80
Shelley Av. E12 CK36 58
Shelley Av., Grnf. BG38 54
Shelley Av., Horn. CT34 50
Shelley Clo., Bans. BQ61 103
Shelley Clo., Edg. BM28 37
Shelley Clo., Grnf. BG38 54
Shelley Clo., Hayes BC39 53
Shelley Clo., Nthwd. BB28 35
Shelley Clo., Ong. CW16 24
Shelley Clo., Orp. CN55 88
Shelley Clo., Slou. AT42 62
Shelley Cres., Houns. BD44 64
Shelley Cres., Sthl. BE39 54
Shelley Dr., Well. CN44 68
Shelley Gdns., Wem. BK34 45
Shelley Gro., Loug. CK24 31
Shelley Rd. NW10 BN37 55
Shelley Rd., Brwd. DE26 122
Shelley Rd., Har. BH31 45
Shelley Way SW19 BT50 76
Shelleys La., Sev. CO61 107
Shellfield Clo., Stai. AW46 73
Shellgrove Est. N16 CA35 48
Shellness Rd. E5 CB35 48
Shellow Rd., Ong. DB13 15
Shellwood Dr., Dor. BK73 119
Shellwood Rd. SW11 BU44 66
Shellwood Rd., Reig. BN74 120
Shelmerdine Clo. E3 CE39 57
Shelson Av., Felt. BB48 73

Shelton Av., Warl. CC62 105
Shelton Clo., Guil. AQ68 109
Montgomerie Dr.
Shelton Clo., Warl. CC62 105
Shelton Ct., Slou. AR41 62
St. Bernards Rd.
Shelton Rd. SW19 BS51 86
Shelton St. WC2 BX39 2
Shelton St. WC2 BX39 56
Shelvers Grn., Tad. BQ64 103
Shelvers Spur, Tad. BQ64 103
Shelvers Way, Tad. BQ64 103
Shen Clo., Sev. CV67 117
Shenden Way, Sev. CV67 117
Shenfield Cres., Brwd. DC27 122
Shenfield Gdns., Brwd. DD25 122
Shenfield Grn., Brwd. DD26 122
Shenfield Pl., Brwd. DC26 122
Shenfield Rd., Brwd. DB27 42
Shenfield Rd., Wdf.Grn. CH29 40
Shenfield St. N1 CA37 2
Shenfield St. N1 CA37 57
Shenley Av., Ruis. BB34 44
Shenley Hill, Rad. BJ21 27
Shenley La., St.Alb. BJ16 18
Shenley Rd. SE5 CA44 67
Shenley Rd., B.Wd. BM24 28
Shenley Rd., Dart. CX47 80
Shenley Rd., Hem.H. AZ10 8
Shenley Rd., Houns. BE44 64
Shenley Rd., Rad. BK20 18
Shenstone Clo., Dart. CS45 69
Shenstone Gdns., Rom. CV30 42
Shephard Pl. N1 BZ38 2
Shepherd Mkt. W1 BV40 3
Shepherd Mkt. W1 BV40 56
Shepherd St. W1 BV40 3
Shepherd St. W1 BV40 56
Shepherd St., Grav. DE47 81
Shepherdess Pl. N1 BZ38 57
Shepherdess Wk.
Shepherdess Wk. N1 BZ37 2
Shepherdess Wk. N1 BZ37 57
Shepherds Bush Grn. W12 BQ41 65
Shepherds Bush Mkt. W12 BQ41 65
Shepherds Bush Pl. W12 BQ41 65
Shepherds Bush Rd. W6 BQ42 65
Shepherds Clo. N6 BV32 47
Shepherds Clo., Rom. CP32 50
Shepherds Clo., Shep. AZ53 83
Shepherds Clo., Uxb. AX38 53
Shepherds Grn., Chis. CM50 78
Shepherds Grn., Hem.H. AV14 7
Shepherds Hill, Guil. AQ69 118
Shepherds Hill, Red. BW66 113
Shepherds Hill, Rom. CX30 42
Shepherds Hill. N6 BV32 47
Shepherds La. E9 CC35 48
Shepherds La., Dart. CU47 79
Shepherds La., Guil. AP69 118
Shepherds La., Rick. AU25 25
Shepherds Path NW3 BT35 47
Lyndhurst Ter.
Shepherds Path, Nthlt. BE36 54
Ridgeway Wk.
Shepherds Pl. W1 BV40 56
Lees Pl.
Shepherds Rd., Wat. BB24 26
Shepherds Way, Chesh. AO20 16
Shepherds Way, Guil. AS72 118
Shepherds Way, Hat. BT17 20
Shepherds Way, Rick. AW26 35
Shepherds Way, S.Croy. CC57 96
Shepherds Wk. NW3 BT35 47
Hampstead High St.
Shepherds Wk., Epsom BM64 103
Shepiston La., Hayes AZ42 63
Shepley Clo., Cars. BV55 86
Shepley Clo., Horn. CV35 51
Chevington Way
Shepley Dr., Ascot AO53 82
Shepley End, Ascot AO53 82
Shepley Ms., Enf. CE22 30
Sheppard Clo., Enf. CB22 30
Sheppard Clo., Kings.T. BL52 85
Beaufort Rd.
Sheppard St. E16 CG38 58
Shepparda Clo., St.Alb. BH12 9
Sheppards, Harl. CK12 13
Shepperton Clo., B.Wd. BN23 28
Shepperton Court Dr., Shep. AZ53 83
Shepperton Rd. N1 BZ37 2
Shepperton Rd. N1 BZ37 57
Shepperton Rd., Orp. CM53 88
Shepperton Rd., Shep. AY52 83
Shepperton Rd., Stai. AX52 83
Sheppey Clo., Erith CU43 69
Sheppey Gdns., Dag. CP36 59
Sheppey Rd.
Sheppey Rd., Dag. CO36 59
Sheppey Wk. N1 BZ36 57
Marquess Est.
Sheppeys La., Kings L. BA18 17
Sheppy Pl., Grav. DG47 81
Sherard Rd. SE9 CK46 78
Sheraton Clo., B.Wd. BL25 28
Sheraton Dr., Epsom BN59 94
Sheraton Ms., Wat. BB24 26
Sheraton St. W1 BW39 1
Sheraton St. W1 BW39 56
Wardour St.
Sherborne Av., Enf. CC23 30
Sherborne Av., Sthl. BF42 64
Sherborne Clo., Epsom BQ62 103
Sherborne Gdns. NW9 BM31 46
Sherborne Gdns. W13 BJ39 54
Sherborne Gdns., Rom. CR28 41
Sherborne La. EC4 BZ40 4
Sherborne La. EC4 BZ40 57
King William St.
Sherborne Rd., Chess. BL56 94
Sherborne Rd., Felt. BA47 73
Sherborne Rd., Orp. CN53 88
Sherborne Rd., Sutt. BS55 86
Sherborne St. N1 BZ37 57
Sherborne Wk., Lthd. BK64 102
Windfield
Sherborough Rd. N15 CA32 48
Sherbourne Clo., Sev. CZ57 99
Sherbourne Clo., Slou. AV44 62
Sherbourne Cres., Mord. BU54 86
Sherbourne Dr., Vir.W. AO53 82
Sherbourne Dr., Wind. AM45 61
Sherbourne Ms. N1 BZ37 2
Sherbourne St. N1 BZ37 2
Sherbourne Way, Bexh. CQ45 69
Sherbourne Way, Rick. AZ24 26
Sherbrook Gdns. N21 BY26 38
Sherbrooke Clo., Bexh. CR45 69
Graham Rd.
Sherbrooke Rd. SW6 BR43 65
Shere Av., Sutt. BQ58 94
Shere Clo., Dor. BK73 119
Holmbury Dr.
Shere Rd., Guil. AW70 110
Shere Rd., Ilf. CL32 49
Shere Rd., Lthd. BA71 110
Shere Rd., West Horsley AZ68 110
Shereboro Rd. N15 CA32 48
Ermine Rd.
Sheredan Rd. E4 CF28 39
Sheredes Dr., Hodd. CD13 12
Sherfield Av., Rick. AX27 35
Sherfield Gdns. SW15 BO46 75
Sherfield Rd., Grays DD43 71
Sheridan Clo., Rom. CV29 42
Sheridan Clo., Swan. CT52 89
Sheridan Clo., Uxb. BA38 53
Alpha Rd.
Sheridan Cres., Chis. CL51 88
Penn Gdns.
Sheridan Ct., Dart. CW45 70
Keyes Rd.
Sheridan Ct., Houns. BE46 74
Frampton Rd.
Sheridan Gdns., Har. BK32 45
Sheridan Ms. E11 CH32 49
Woodbine Pl.
Sheridan Pl. SW13 BO44 65
Brookwood Av.
Sheridan Pl., Hmptn. BG51 84
Sheridan Rd. E12 CK35 49
Sheridan Rd. E7 CG34 49
Sheridan Rd. SW19 BR51 85
Sheridan Rd., Belv. CR42 69
Sheridan Rd., Bexh. CQ45 69
Sheridan Rd., Rich. BK48 74
Sheridan Rd., Wat. BD26 36
Sheridan St. E1 CB39 57
Watney St.
Sheridan Ter., Nthlt. BF35 45
Sheridan Way, Beck. CD51 87
Turners Meadow Way
Sheridan Wk. NW11 BS32 47
Sheridan Wk., Cars. BU56 95
Park Hill
Sheridans Rd., Lthd. BG66 111
Sheriff Way, Wat. BC20 17
Sheringham Av. E12 CK35 49
Sheringham Av. N14 BW25 29
Sheringham Av., Felt. BC48 73
Sheringham Av., Rom. CS32 50
Sheringham Av., Twick. BE47 74
Sheringham Dr., Bark. CN35 49
Sheringham Rd. N7 BX36 56
Sheringham Rd. SE10 CC51 87
Sherington Av., Pnr. BF29 36
Sherington Rd. SE7 CH43 68
Sherland Rd., Twick. BH47 74
Sherlies Av., Orp. CN55 88
Sherlock Ms. W1 BU39 1
Sherman Rd., Brom. CH51 88
Sherman Rd., Slou. AP39 52
Shermanbury Pl., Erith CT43 69
Shernbroke Rd., Wal.Abb. CG20 22
Shernells Way SE2 CO42 69
Shernhall St. E17 CF31 48
Sherpa Rd., Houns. AZ46 73
Sherrard Rd. E12 CJ36 58
Sherrard Rd. E7 CJ36 58
Sherrards Park Rd., Welw.G.C. BQ 7 5
Sherrards Way, Barn. BS25 29
Sherrick Green Rd. NW10 BP35 46
Sherriff Rd. NW6 BS36 56
Sherringham Av. N17 CB30 39
Sherrock Gdns. NW4 BP31 46
Sherwin Rd. SE14 CC44 67
Sherwood Av. E18 CH31 49
Sherwood Av. SW16 BW50 76
Sherwood Av., Grnf. BH36 54
Sherwood Av., Hayes BC38 53
Sherwood Av., Pot.B. BR19 19
Sherwood Av., Ruis. BB32 44
Sherwood Av., St.Alb. BJ12 9
Sherwood Clo. SW15 BP45 65
Sherwood Clo. W13 BJ40 54
Sherwood Clo., Bex. CP46 79
Sherwood Clo., Lthd. BG65 102
Sherwood Clo., Slou. AS42 62
Sherwood Clo., Wok. AP62 100
Sherwood Cres., Reig. BS72 121
Sherwood Gdns. E14 CE42 67
Barnsdale Av.
Sherwood Gdns., Bark. CM36 58
Sherwood Park Av., Sid. CO47 79
Sherwood Park Rd., Mitch. BW52 86
Sherwood Park Rd., Sutt. BS56 95
Sherwood Pl., Hem.H. AY11 8
Henry Wells Sq.
Sherwood Rd. NW4 BQ31 46
Sherwood Rd. SW19 BR50 75
Sherwood Rd., Couls. BW61 104
Sherwood Rd., Croy. CH54 87
Sherwood Rd., Har. BG34 45
Sherwood Rd., Hmptn. BG49 74
Sherwood Rd., Ilf. CM31 49
Sherwood Rd., Well. CN44 68
Sherwood St. N20 BT27 38
Sherwood St. W1 BW40 3
Sherwood St. W1 BW40 56
Brewer St.
Sherwood Ter. N20 BT27 38
Sherwood Way, W.Wick. CE55 87
Sherwood, Grays DC40 71
Sherwoods Rd., Wat. BE26 36
Shetland Clo., B.Wd. BN25 28
Percheron Rd.
Shetland Clo., Guil. AT68 109
Weybrook Dr.
Shetland Rd. E3 CD37 57
Shevon Way, Brwd. CZ28 42
Shewins Rd., Wey. BA56 92
St. Marys Rd.
Shey Copse, Wok. AU62 100
Shield Dr., Brent. BJ43 64
Shield Rd., Ashf. BA49 73
Shieldhall St. SE2 CP42 69
Shifford Path SE23 CC48 77
Shilburn Way, Wok., AQ62 100
Shiliber Wk., Chig. CN27 40
Shillibeer Pl. W1 BU39 1
Harcourt St.
Shillingford St. N1 BY36 2
Shillingford St. N1 BY36 56
Cross St.
Shillitoe Av., Pot.B. BQ19 19
Shillitoe Rd. N13 BY28 38
Shimmings, The, Guil. AT70 118
Shinfield St. W12 BQ39 55
Shingle Ct., Wal.Abb. CH20 22
Winters Way
Shinglewell Rd., Erith CR43 69
Shinners Clo. SE25 CB52 87
Stanger Rd.
Ship & Half Moon Pass. SE18 CL41 68
Weston St.
Ship & Mermaid Row SE1 BZ41 4
Weston St.
Ship Alley E1 CB40 57
Wellclose Sq.
Ship Hill, West. CJ64 106
Ship La. SW14 BN45 65
Ship La., S.at H. CV51 90
Ship La., S.Ock. CW40 60
Ship St. SE8 CE44 67
Ship Tavern Pass. EC3 CA39 57
Lime St.
Shipbourne Rd., Sev. & Ton. CY69 117
Shipfield Clo., West. CJ64 106
Shipka Rd. SW12 BV47 76
Shipman Rd. E16 CH39 58
Shipman Rd. SE23 CC48 77
Shipton Clo., Dag. CP34 50
Shipton Rd., Uxb. AY35 44
Shipton St. E2 CA38 2
Shipton St. E2 CA38 57
Shipway Ter. N16 CA34 48
Victorian Rd.
Shipwright Rd. SE16 CD41 67
Shirburn Clo. SE23 CC47 77
Shirbutt St. E14 CE40 57
Shire Clo., Brox. CD16 21
Groom Rd.
Shire La., Ger.Cr. AT27 34
Shire La., Orp. CK57 97
Shire La., Rick. AT25 25
Shirebrook Rd. SE3 CJ45 68
Shirehall Clo. NW4 BQ32 46
Shirehall Gdns. NW4 BQ32 46
Shirehall La. NW4 BQ32 46
Shirehall Pk. NW4 BQ32 46
Shiremeade, B.Wd. BL25 28
Shires House, Wey. AY60 92
Shires, The, Rich. BL49 75
Shirland Ms. W9 BR38 55
Shirland Rd. W9 BS38 55
Shirley Av., Bex. CP47 79
Shirley Av., Cheam BR58 94
Shirley Av., Couls. BY63 104
Shirley Av., Croy. CC54 87
Shirley Av., Red. BU73 121
Shirley Av., Sutt. BT56 95
Shirley Av., Wind. AM44 61
Shirley Church Rd., Croy. CC55 87
Shirley Clo. E17 CE32 48
Addison Rd.
Shirley Clo., Brox. CD15 12
Westlea Rd.
Shirley Clo., Chsnt. CB18 21
Shirley Clo., Dart. CV45 70
Shirley Clo., Houns. BG46 74
Shirley Cres., Beck. CC52 87
Shirley Dr., Houns. BG46 74
Shirley Gdns. W7 BH40 54
Shirley Gdns., Bark. CN36 58
Shirley Gdns., Horn. CV34 51
Shirley Gro. N9 CC26 39
Shirley Gro. SW11 BV45 66
Shirley Heights, Erith CQ45 69
Avenue Rd.
Shirley Hills Rd., Croy. CC56 96
Shirley House Dr. SE7 CJ43 68
Shirley Oak Rd., Croy. CC54 87
Shirley Park Rd., Croy. CB54 87
Shirley Pl., Wok. AO62 100
Shirley Rd. E15 CG36 58
Shirley Rd. W4 BN41 65
Shirley Rd., Croy. CB54 87
Shirley Rd., Enf. BZ24 30
Shirley Rd., Sid. CN48 78
Shirley Rd., St.Alb. BH14 9
Shirley Rd., Wall. BW58 95
Shirley Rd., Wat. BB19 17
Shirley St. E16 CG39 58
Shirley Way, Croy. CD55 87
Shirlock Rd. NW3 BU35 47
Shobden Rd. N17 BZ30 39
Shoe La. EC4 BY39 2
Shoe La. EC4 BY39 56
Shoe La., Harl. CQ11 14
Shoebury Rd. E6 CK36 58
Sholden Gdns., Orp. CP53 89
Shonks Mill Rd., Rom. CU22 32
Shoot Up Hill NW2 BR35 46
Shooters Av., Har. BK31 45
Shooters Dr., Wal.Abb. CG14 13
Shooters Hill Rd. SE18 CF44 67
Shooters Hill Rd. SE3 CF44 67
Shooters Hill SE18 CK44 68
Shooters Hill, Well. CK44 68
Shooters Rd., Enf. BY22 29
Shootersway La., Berk. AP13 7
Shootersway Pk., Berk. AP13 7
Shootersway, Berk. AO12 7
Shoplands, Welw.G.C. BQ 6 5
Shord Hill, Ken. BZ61 105
Shore Clo., Felt. BB47 73
Shore Clo., Hmptn. BE50 74
Stewart Clo.
Shore Gro., Felt. BF48 74
Shore Pl. E9 CC36 57
Shore Rd. E9 CC36 57
Shore, The, Grav. DE46 81
Shorediche Clo., Uxb. AY34 44
Shoreditch High St. E1 CA38 2
Shoreditch High St. E1 CA38 57
Shoreham Clo. SW18 BS46 76
Ram St.
Shoreham Clo., Bex. CP47 79
Stansted Cres.
Shoreham Clo., Croy. CC53 87
Shoreham La., Halstead CQ59 98
Shoreham La., Orp. CR57 98
Shoreham La., Sev. CT64 107
Shoreham Pl., Sev. CU59 98
Shoreham Rd. E., Houns. AY46 73
Shoreham Rd. W., Houns. AY46 73
Shoreham Rd., Orp. CO51 89
Shoreham Rd., Sev. CU59 98
Shoreham St. SW18 BS46 76
Barchard St.
Shoreham Way, Brom. CH53 88
Shorehill La., Sev. CW61 108
Shores Rd., Wok. AS60 91
Shorncliffe Rd. SE1 CA42 4
Shorncliffe Rd. SE1 CA42 67
Shorndean St. SE6 CF47 77
Shorne Clo., Orp. CP52 89
Shorne Clo., Sid. CO46 79
Park Mead
Shornefield Clo., Brom. CL52 88
Shorrolds Rd. SW6 BR43 65
Short Croft, Brwd. CZ22 33
Short Gate N12 BR28 37
Short Hill, Har. BH33 45
High St.
Short La., Oxt. CH69 115
Short La., St.Alb. BE18 18
Short La., Stai. AY47 73
Short Path SE18 CL43 68
Westdale Rd.
Short Rd. E11 CG34 49
Short Rd. E15 CF37 57
Short Rd. W4 BO43 65
Short Rd., Houns. AY46 73
Short St. NW4 BQ31 46
Short St. SE1 BY41 4
Short St. SE1 BY41 66
Short Wall E15 CF38 57
Short Way N12 BU29 38
Short Way SE9 CK45 68
Short Way, Amer. AO22 25
Short Way, Twick. BG47 74
Shortcroft Rd., Epsom BO57 94
Shortcrofts Rd., Dag. CQ36 59
Shorter Av., Brwd. DC26 122
Shorter St. E1 CA40 4
Shortfern, Slou. AR39 52
Knolton Way
Shortland Rd. E10 CE33 48
Shortlands Av., Ong. CW16 24
Shortlands Clo. N18 BZ27 39
Shortlands Gdns., Brom. CG51 88
Shortlands Grn., Welw.G.C. BR 8 5
Shortlands Gro., Brom. CF51 87
Shortlands Ms. W6 BQ42 65
Shortlands Rd., Brom. CF52 87
Shortlands Rd., Kings.T. BL50 75
Shortlands W6 BQ42 65
Shortlands, Hayes BA43 63
Shortmead Dr., Chsnt. CD19 21
Shorts Croft NW9 BM31 46
Shorts Gdns. WC2 BX39 2
Shorts Gdns. WC2 BX39 56
Shorts Rd., Cars. BU56 95
Shortwood Av., Stai. AW48 73
Shotfield, Wall. BV57 95
Shothanger Way, Hem.H. AU16 16
Shott Clo., Sutt. BT56 95
Turnpike La.
Shottendane Rd. SW6 BS44 66
Shottery Clo. SE9 CK48 78
Shottfield Av. SW14 BO45 65
Shouldam St. W1 BU39 1
Shouldam St. W1 BU39 56
Shoulder of Mutton All. E14 CD40 57
Narrow St.
Showers Way, Hayes BC40 53
Shrapnel Clo. SE18 CK43 68
Stadium Rd.
Shrapnel Rd. SE9 CK45 68
Shrewsbury Av. SW14 BN45 65
Shrewsbury Av., Har. BL31 46
Shrewsbury Clo., Surb. BK55 84
Shrewsbury Cres. NW10 BN37 55
Shrewsbury Ho. SW3 BU43 66
Shrewsbury La. SE18 CL44 68
Shrewsbury Ms. W2 BS39 56
Chepstow Rd.
Shrewsbury Rd. E7 CJ35 49
Shrewsbury Rd. N11 BW29 38
Shrewsbury Rd. NW10 BO37 55
Shrewsbury Rd. W2 BS39 56
Shrewsbury Rd., Beck. CD52 87
Shrewsbury Rd., Cars. BU53 86
Shrewsbury Rd., Red. BU70 121
Shrewsbury Wk., Islw. BJ45 64
South St.
Shrewton Rd. SW17 BU50 76
Shroffold Rd., Brom. CG49 78
Shropshire Clo., Mitch. BX52 86
Shropshire Rd. N22 BX29 38
Shroton St. NW1 BU39 1
Shroton St. NW1 BU39 56
Shrubberies, The E18 CH30 40
Shrubberies, The, Chig. CM28 40
Shrubbery Clo. N1 BZ37 2
St. Paul St.
Shrubbery Gdns. N21 BY26 38
Shrubbery Rd. N9 CB27 39
Shrubbery Rd. SW16 BX49 76
Shrubbery Rd., Grav. DH47 81
Shrubbery Rd., S.Dnth. CY51 90
Shrubbery Rd., Sthl. BF40 54
Shrubbery, The, Hem.H. AV13 7
Shrubbery, The, Upmin. CY34 51
Shrubbs Hill, Wok. AQ58 91
Shrubhill Rd., Hem.H. AV14 7
Shrubland Est. E8 CA36 57
Shrubland Gro., Wor.Pk. BQ55 85
Shrubland Rd. E10 CE33 48
Shrubland Rd. E17 CE32 48
Shrubland Rd. E8 CA37 2
Shrubland Rd. E8 CA37 57
Shrubland Rd., Bans. BR61 103
Shrublands Av., Berk. AQ13 7
Shrublands Av., Croy. CE55 87
Shrublands Clo. N20 BT26 38
Shrublands Clo., Chig. CM29 40
Shrublands Rd., Berk. AQ12 7
Shrublands, Hat. BS16 20
Shrublands, The, Pot.B. BR20 19
Shrubs Rd., Rick. AY28 35
Shuna Wk. N1 BZ36 57
Clephane Rd.
Shurland Av., Barn. BT25 29
Shurland Gdns. SE15 CA43 67
Rosemary Rd.
Shurlock Av., Swan. CS51 89
Shurlock Dr., Orp. CM56 97
Broadwater Gdns.
Shuter Sq. W14 BR42 65
Sun Rd.
Shuttle Clo., Sid. CN47 78
Shuttle Rd., Dart. CU45 69
Shuttle St. E1 CA38 57
Buxton St.
Shuttle St. E1 CB38 2
Shuttlemead, Bex. CQ47 79
Shuttleworth Rd. SW11 BU44 66
Sibella Rd. SW4 BW44 66
Sibley Clo., Bexh. CQ46 79
Mount Rd.
Sibley Gro. E12 CK36 58
Sibthorp Rd., Mitch. BU51 86
Sibthorpe Rd. SE12 CH47 78
Sibthorpe Rd., Hat. BQ15 10
Sibton Rd., Cars. BU54 86
Sicilian Av. WC1 BX39 2
Bloomsbury Way.
Sickert Ct. N1 BZ36 57
Sickle Cor., Dag. CR38 59
Sicklefield Clo., Chsnt. CA16 21
Sidbury Av. SW6 BR45 65
Sidbury St. SW6 BR44 65
Sidcup By-pass, Sid. CM48 78
Sidcup High St., Sid. CO49 79
Sidcup Hill Gdns., Sid. CP49 79
Sidcup Hill, Sid. CO49 79
Sidcup Pl., Sid. CO49 79
Sidcup Rd. SE12 CJ47 78
Sidcup Rd. SE9 CJ47 78
Siddons Clo., S.le H. DK41 71
Lower Cres.
Siddons La. NW1 BU38 1
Siddons La. NW1 BU38 56
Siddons Rd. N17 CB30 39
Siddons Rd. SE23 CC48 77
Siddons Rd., Croy. BY55 86
Side Rd. E17 CD32 48
South Gro.
Side Rd., Uxb. AU33 43
Sidewood Rd. SE9 CM47 78
Sidford Clo., Hem.H. AV13 7
Sidford Pl. SE1 BX41 4
Sidford Pl. SE1 BX41 66
Sidings, The E11 CF33 48
Sidings, The, Hat. BO13 10
Crossbrook
Sidmouth Av., Islw. BH44 64
Sidmouth Clo., Wat. BC27 35
Sidmouth Dr., Ruis. BC34 44
Sidmouth Rd. E10 CF34 48
Sidmouth Rd. NW2 BQ36 55
Sidmouth Rd. SE15 CA44 67
Sidmouth Rd., Orp. CO53 89
Sidmouth Rd., Well. CP43 69
Sidmouth St. WC1 BX38 2
Sidmouth St. WC1 BX38 56
Sidney Av. N13 BX28 38
Sidney Elson Way E6 CL38 58
Edwin Av.
Sidney Est. E1 CC39 57
Sidney Gdns., Brent. BK43 64
Boston Manor Rd.
Sidney Gdns., Sev. CV62 108
Sidney Gro. EC1 BY38 56
Wakley St.
Sidney Rd. E7 CH34 49
Sidney Rd. N22 BX29 38
Sidney Rd. SE25 CB53 87
Sidney Rd. SW9 BX44 66
Sidney Rd., Beck. CD51 87
Sidney Rd., Epp. CM21 31
Sidney Rd., Har. BG31 45
Sidney Rd., Sutt. BS56 95
Sidney Rd., Twick. BJ46 74
Sidney Rd., Walt. BC54 83
Sidney Sq. E1 CC39 57
Sidney St. E1 CB39 57
Sidney St., Stai. AW49 73
Sidworth St. E8 CB36 57

Siebert Rd. SE3 CH43 68
Siemens Rd. SE18 CJ41 68
Sifford Pl., Brwd. DB28 42
Blackthorn Way
Sigdon Rd. E8 CB35 48
Sigers, The, Pnr. BC32 44
Sigismund St. SE10 CG41 68
Silas St. Est. NW5 BV36 56
Silbury St. N1 BZ38 2
Silbury St. N1 BZ38 57
East Rd.
Silchester Ct., Th.Hth. BY52 86
Silchester Ms. W10 BQ40 55
Walmer Rd.
Silchester Rd. W10 BQ39 55
Silcote Rd. SE5 CA42 4
Albany Rd.
Silecroft Rd., Bexh. CR44 69
Silesia Bldgs. E8 CB36 57
London La.
Silex St. SE1 BY41 4
Silex St. SE1 BY41 66
Silk Clo. SE12 CH46 78
Silk Mill Rd., Wat. BC26 35
Silk Mills Path SE13 CF44 67
Silk St. EC2 BZ39 2
Silk St. EC2 BZ39 57
Silkfield Rd. NW9 BO32 46
Silkham Rd., Oxt. CF67 114
Silkins, The, Rom. CT30 41
Silkmore La., Lthd. AZ66 110
Silkstream Rd., Edg. BN30 37
Silsden Cres., Ch.St.G. AR27 34
Silsoe Rd. N22 BX30 38
Silver Birch Av. E4 CD29 39
Silver Birch Av., Epp. CQ17 23
Silver Birch Clo. N11 BV29 38
Poplar Gro.
Silver Birch Clo., Dart. CT49 79
Silver Birch Clo., Uxb. AY35 44
Silver Birch Clo., Wey. AV59 91
Silver Birches, Brwd. DD26 122
Silver Clo. SE14 CD43 67
Southerngate Way
Silver Clo., Har. BG29 36
Silver Clo., Sutt. BR56 94
Silver Clo., Tad. BP63 103
Silver Cres. W4 BM42 65
Silver Dell, Wat. BB21 26
Silver Hill, Ch.St.G. AQ27 34
Silver Jubilee Way, Houns. BC44 63
Silver La., Pur. BW59 95
Silver La., W.Wick. CF55 87
Silver Pl. W1 BW40 3
Silver Pl. W1 BW40 56
Lexington St.
Silver Rd. W12 BQ40 55
Silver Rd., Grav. DJ48 81
Silver Spring Clo., Erith CR43 69
Silver St. EC2 BZ39 57
Wood St.
Silver St. N18 BZ28 39
Silver St., Chsnt. BZ18 21
Silver St., Enf. BZ24 30
Silver St., Rom. CO24 32
Silver St., Wal.Abb. CF20 21
Silver Way, Rom. CR31 50
Silver Wk. SE16 CD40 57
Silverbirch Wk. NW3 BU36 56
Maitland Park Vw.
Silvercliffe Gdns., Barn. BU24 29
Silverdale Av., Ilf. CN32 49
Silverdale Av., Lthd. BG60 93
Silverdale Av., Walt. BB55 83
Silverdale Clo. W7 BH40 54
Cherington Rd.
Silverdale Clo., Bet. BM72 120
Silverdale Clo., Har. BE35 45
Silverdale Ct., Stai. AW49 73
Silverdale Dr. SE9 CK48 78
Silverdale Dr., Horn. CU35 50
Silverdale Dr., Sun. BC51 83
Silverdale Gdns., Hayes BC41 63
Silverdale Rd. E4 CF29 39
Silverdale Rd., Bexh. CR44 69
Silverdale Rd., Bush. BE25 27
Silverdale Rd., Hayes BB41 63
Silverdale Rd., Petts Wood CM52 88
Silverdale Rd., St.Mary Cray CO52 89
Silverdale SE26 CC49 77
Silverdale, Enf. BX24 29
Silverdale, Stai. AW49 73
Leacroft
Silverfield, Brox. CD14 12
Silverhall St., Islw. BJ45 64
Silverholme, Har. BL33 46
Silverland St. E16 CK40 58
Silverleigh Rd., Th.Hth. BX52 86
Silverlocke Rd., Grays DE43 71
Silvermere Av., Rom. CR28 41
Silvermere Rd. SE6 CE47 77
Silversmiths Way, Wok. AR62 100
Silverstead La., West. CM64 106
Silverston Way, Stan. BK29 36
Silverstone Clo., Red. BU69 121
Goodwood Rd.
Silverthorn Dr., Hem.H. AZ15 8
Silverthorne Gdns. E4 CE27 39
Silverthorne Rd. SW8 BV44 66
Silverton Rd. W6 BQ43 65
Silvertown By-pass E16 CJ40 58
Silvertown Way E16 CG39 58
Silvertree Clo., Walt. BC55 83
Silvertree La., Grnf. BG38 54
Silvertrees, St.Alb. BE18 18
Silverwood Clo., Beck. CE50 77
Brackley Rd.
Silverwood Clo., Croy. CD58 96
Silverwood Clo., Nthwd. BA30 35
Silvester Rd. SE22 CA46 77
Silvester St. SE1 BZ41 4
Silvester St. SE1 BZ41 67
Silvesters, Harl. CK12 13
Silwood Est. SE16 CC42 67
Silwood St. SE16 CC42 67
Simla Clo. SE14 CD43 67
Chubworthy St.
Simmil Rd., Esher BH56 93
Simmonds Ri., Hem.H. AX14 8
Lamsey Rd.
Simmons Clo. N20 BU27 38
Simmons Clo., Slou. AT42 62
Simmons La. E4 CF27 39
Simmons Pl., Grays DD40 71
Simmons Rd. SE18 CL42 68
Brookhill Rd.
Simmons Way N20 BU27 38
Simms Clo., Cars. BU55 86
Simms Rd. SE1 CB42 4
Simms Rd. SE1 CB42 67
Simnel Rd. SE12 CH47 78
Simon Clo. W11 BS40 56
Portobello Rd.
Simon Dean, Hem.H. AT17 16
Simonds Rd. E10 CE34 48
Simone Clo., Brom. CJ51 88
Simone Dr., Ken. BZ62 105
Simons Clo., Cher. AU57 91
Simons Wk. E15 CF36 57
Alma St.
Simons Wk., Egh. AR50 72
Simplemarsh Rd., Wey. AW56 92
Simpson Dr. W3 BN39 55
Ferguson Dr.
Simpson Rd., Houns. BE46 74
Simpson Rd., Rain. CT36 59
Simpson Rd., Rich. BK49 74
Simpson St. SW11 BU44 66
Simpsons Rd. E14 CE40 57
Simpsons Rd., Brom. CH52 88
Simrose Ct. SW18 BS46 76
Wandsworth High St.
Sims Clo., Rom. CT31 50
Sims Wk. SE3 CG45 68
Lee Rd.
Sinclair Gdns. W14 BQ41 65
Sinclair Gro. NW11 BQ32 46
Sinclair Rd. E4 CD28 39
Sinclair Rd. W14 BQ41 65
Sinclair Way, Dart. CY49 80
Sinclare Clo., Enf. CA23 30
Sincots Rd., Red. BU70 121
Lower Bridge Rd.
Sindall Rd., Grnf. BJ37 54
Sinderby Clo., Brwd. BL23 28
Singapore Rd. W13 BJ40 54
Singer St. EC2 BZ38 2
Singer St. EC2 BZ38 57
Cowper St.
Single St., Orp. CL60 97
Singles Cross La., Sev. CP60 98
Singleton Clo., Croy. BZ54 87
St. Saviours Rd.
Singleton Clo., Horn. CU35 50
Cowdray Way
Singleton Clo., Mitch. BU50 76
Singleton Rd., Dag. CQ35 50
Singleton Scarp N12 BS28 38
Singlewell Rd., Grav. DG48 81
Singret Pl., Uxb. AX38 53
Sinnott Rd. E17 CC30 39
Sion Rd., Twick. BJ47 74
Sipson Clo., West Dr. AZ43 63
Sipson La., West Dr. AZ43 63
Sipson Rd., West Dr. AY41 63
Sipson Way, West Dr. AZ44 63
Sir Alexander Clo. W3 BO40 55
Sir Alexander Rd.
Sir Alexander Rd. W3 BO40 55
Sir Francis Way, Brwd. DA27 42
Sir Theodores Way, Welw.G.C. BQ 7 5
Stonehills
Sir Thomas More Est. SW3 BT43 66
Sirdar Rd. N22 BY31 47
Sirdar Rd. W11 BQ40 55
Sirdar Rd., Mitch. BU50 76
Sirdar Strand, Grav. DJ49 81
Sirus Rd., Nthwd. BC28 35
Sise La. EC4 BZ39 2
Queen Victoria St.
Siskin Clo., B.Wd. BM24 28
Goldfinch Way
Sisley Rd., Bark. CN37 58
Sispara Gdns. SW18 BR46 75
Sissinghurst Rd., Croy. CB54 87
Sisters Av. SW11 BU45 66
Sistova Rd. SW12 BV47 76
Sisulu Pl. SW9 BY45 66
Wiltshire Rd.
Sittingbourne Av., Enf. BZ25 30
Sitwell Gro., Stan. BH28 36
Siverst Clo., Nthlt. BF36 54
Siviter Way, Dag. CR36 59
Siward Rd. N17 BZ30 39
Siward Rd. SW17 BT48 76
Siward Rd., Brom. CH52 88
Six Acres, Hem.H. AZ15 8
Six Bells La., Sev. CV66 117
Sixth Av. E12 CK35 49
Sixth Av. W10 BR38 55
Sixth Av., Enf. CA25 30
Sixth Av., Hayes BB40 53
Sixth Av., Wat. BD21 27
Sixth Cross Rd., Twick. BG48 74
Skardu Rd. NW2 BR35 46
Skarnings Ct., Wal.Abb. CH20 22
Skeena Hill SW18 BR47 75
Skeet Hill La., Orp. CQ54 89
Skeffington Rd. E6 CK37 58
Skelbrook St. SW18 BS48 76
Skelgill Rd. SW15 BR45 65
Skelley Rd. E15 CG36 58
Skelton Clo. E8 CA36 57
Rhodes Dev.
Skelton Rd. E7 CH36 58
Skeltons La. E10 CE33 48
Skelwith Rd. W6 BQ43 65
Skerries Ct., Slou. AT42 62
Blacksmith Row
Sketchley Gdns. SE16 CC42 67
Sketty Rd., Enf. CA24 30
Skibbs La., Orp. CQ56 98
Skid Hill La., War. CG60 97
Skidmore Way, Rick. AY26 35
Skiers St. E15 CF37 57
Skiffington Clo. SW2 BY47 76
Skillet Hill, Wal.Abb. CH21 31
Skimpans Clo., Hat. BQ15 10
Skin Market Pl. SE1 BZ40 4
Skin Market Pl. SE1 BZ40 57
Skinner Ct. E2 CB37 57
Parmiter St.
Skinner Pl. SW1 BV42 66
Bourne St.
Skinner St. EC1 BY38 2
Skinner St. EC1 BY38 56
Skinners La. EC4 BZ40 4
Skinners La., Ash. BK62 102
Skinners La., Garlick Hill EC4 BZ40 57
Queen Victoria St.
Skinners La., Houns. BF44 64
Skips Corner, Epp. CS16 23
Skipsey Av. E6 CK38 58
Skipton Dr., Hayes BA42 63
Skipton St. SE1 BY41 4
Skipton St. SE1 BY41 66
Keyworth St.
Skipworth Rd. E9 CC37 57
Skomer Wk. N1 BZ36 57
Sky Peals Rd., Wdf.Grn. CF30 39
Skylark Rd., Uxb. AU33 43
Skyport Dr., West Dr. AX43 63
Skys Wood Rd., St.Alb. BJ11 9
Slackesbury Hatch, Harl. CL11 13
Slade Ct., Cher. AU57 91
Slade Gdns. SW9 BX44 66
Slade Gdns., Erith CT44 69
Slade Green Rd., Erith CU43 69
Slade Oak La., Ger.Cr. AU31 43
Slade Rd., Cher. AU57 91
Slade Wk. SE5 BZ43 67
Slade, The SE18 CN43 68
Sladebrook Rd. SE3 CJ45 68
Sladedale Rd. SE18 CN42 68
Slades Clo., Enf. BY24 29
Slades Cotts., Chis. CL49 78
Slades Dr., Chis. CM48 78
Slades Gdns., Enf. BY23 29
Slades Hill, Enf. BY24 29
Slades Ri., Enf. BY24 29
Slagrove Pl. SE13 CE46 77
Slaidburn St. SW10 BT43 66
Slaithwaite Rd. SE13 CF45 67
Slaney Pl. N7 BY35 47
Rolitt St.
Slapleys, Wok. AS63 100
Sleaford Grn., Wat. BD27 36
Sleaford St. SW8 BW43 66
Sleap Cross Gdns., St.Alb. BM14 10
Sleapshyde La., St.Alb. BM14 10
Sleath Wk. SW19 BT51 86
Brangwyn Cres.
Sleddale, Hem.H. AY12 8
Wharfedale
Sleepers Farm Rd., Grays DG41 71
Sleets End, Hem.H. AW12 8
Slewins Clo., Horn. CV32 51
Slewins La., Horn. CV32 51
Slievemore Clo. SW4 BW45 66
Voltaire Rd.
Slimmons Dr., St.Alb. BJ11 9
Slines New Rd., Cat. CB63 105
Slines Oaks Rd., Cat. CE64 105
Slingsby Ms. Pl. WC2 BX40 4
Slingsby Pl. WC2 BX40 56
Long Acre
Slipe La., Brox. CD15 12
Slippers Pl. SE16 CB41 67
Slipshatch Rd., Reig. BQ72 120
Slipshoe St., Reig. BR70 120
Sloane Av. SW3 BU42 3
Sloane Av. SW3 BU42 66
Sloane Ct. E. SW3 BV42 3
Sloane Ct. E. SW3 BV42 66
Sloane Ct. W. SW3 BV42 3
Sloane Ct. W. SW3 BV42 66
Sloane Gdns. SW1 BV42 3
Sloane Gdns. SW1 BV42 66
Sloane Gdns., Orp. CM55 88
Sloane Sq. SW1 BU42 3
Sloane Sq. SW1 BU42 66
Sloane Sq., Long. DC52 90
Bramblefield Clo.
Sloane St. SW1 BU41 3
Sloane St. SW1 BU41 66
Sloane Ter. SW1 BU42 3
Sloane Ter. SW1 BV42 66
Sloane Wk., Croy. CD53 87
Sloansway, Welw.G.C. BR 6 5
Slocock Hill, Wok. AR62 100
Slocum Clo. SE28 CP40 59
Woodpecker Rd.
Slough La. NW9 BN32 46
Slough La., Bet. BP69 120
Slough La., Epsom BN66 112
Slough Rd., Eton AO42 61
Slough Rd., Iver AU38 52
Slough Rd., Slou. AP42 62
Sly St. E1 CB39 57
Cannon St. Rd.
Slyfield Grn., Guil. AS68 109
Small Acre, Hem.H. AV13 7
Small Cft., Welw.G.C. BS 7 5
Brooksfield
Small Grains, Fawk. DA55 90
Smallbrook Ms. W2 BT39 1
Smallbrook Ms. W2 BT39 56
Craven Rd.
Smallbury Av., Islw. BH44 64
Smalley Clo. N16 CA34 48
Smalley Rd.
Smalley Rd. N16 CA34 48
Smallford La., St.Alb. BM14 10
Smalls Hill Rd., Reig. BP74 120
Smallwood Rd. SW17 BT49 76
Smardale Rd. SW18 BT46 76
Alma Rd.
Smarden Clo., Belv. CR42 69
Essenden Rd.
Smarden Gro. SE9 CK49 78
Prestbury Sq.
Smart Clo., Rom. CU30 41
Smart St. E2 CC38 57
Smarts Grn., Chsnt. CB17 21
Adamsfield
Smarts Heath La., Wok. AQ65 100
Smarts Heath Rd., Wok. AQ65 100
Smarts La., Loug. CJ24 31
Smarts Pl. N18 CB28 39
Fore St.
Smarts Pl. WC2 BX39 2
Smarts Pl. WC2 BX39 56
Stukeley St.
Smarts Rd., Grav. DG48 81
Smeaton Rd. SW18 BS47 76
Smeaton Rd., Wdf.Grn. CK28 40
Smeaton St. E1 CB40 57
Smedley St. SW4 BW44 66
Smedley St. SW8 BW44 66
Smeed Rd. E3 CE36 57
Smelbury Ter. NW1 BU38 1
Smith Clo. SE16 CC40 57
Smith Hill, Brent. BL43 65
High St.
Smith Rd., Reig. BR72 120
Smith Sq. SW1 BX41 4
Smith Sq. SW1 BX41 66
Smith St. E16 CG40 58
Smith St. SW3 BU42 3
Smith St. SW3 BU42 66
Smith St., Surb. BL53 85
Smith St., Wat. BD24 27
Smith Ter. SW3 BU42 3
Smith Ter. SW3 BU42 66
Smithambottom La., Pur. BW59 95
Smithamdowns Rd., Pur. BW60 95
Smithers, The, Bet. BM71 120
Smithfield St. EC1 BY39 2
Smithfield St. EC1 BY39 56
Smithies Ct. E15 CF35 48
Smithies Rd. SE2 CO42 69
Smiths Cres., St.Alb. BM14 10
Smiths La., Chsnt. BZ16 21
Smiths La., Eden. CM70 115
Smiths La., Wind. AM44 61
Smiths Yd. SW18 BS48 76
Summerley St.
Smithson Rd. N17 BZ30 39
Smithwood Clo. SW19 BR47 75
Smithy Clo., Tad. BR66 112
Smithy La., Tad. BR67 112
Smithy St. E1 CC39 57
Smock Wk., Croy. BZ53 87
Beulah Gro.
Smoke La., Reig. BS71 121
Smokehouse Yd. EC1 BY39 2
St. John St.
Smoothfield, Houns. BF45 64
Smug Oak La., St.Alb. BF18 18
Smugglers Way SW18 BS45 66
Smyrks Rd. SE17 CA42 4
Smyrks Rd. SE17 CA42 67
Smyrna Rd. NW6 BS36 56
Smythe Rd., S.at H. CX51 90
Smythe St. E14 CE40 57
Snag La., Sev. CM59 97
Snakes Hill, Brwd. CY23 33
Snakes La., Wdf.Grn. CH28 40
Snape Spur, Slou. AP39 52
Snaresbrook Dr., Stan. BK28 36
Snaresbrook Rd. E11 CG31 49
Snarsgate St. W10 BQ39 55
Snatts Hill, Oxt. CG68 115
Sneath Av. NW11 BR33 46
Snelling Av., Grav. DF48 81
Snellings Rd., Walt. BD56 93
Snells La., Amer. AQ23 25
Snells Pk. N18 CA29 39
Snells Wood Ct., Amer. AR23 25
Sneyd Rd. NW2 BQ35 46
Snodland Clo., Orp. CL58 97
Snow Hill Cotts., Chesh. AP15 7
Snow Hill EC1 BY39 2
Snow Hill EC1 BY39 56
Snowbury Rd. SW6 BS44 66
Snowden Av., Uxb. AZ37 53
Snowden St. EC2 CA39 2
Snowden St. EC2 CA39 57
Snowdon Clo., Wind. AL45 61
Snowdon Cres., Hayes BA41 63
Snowdon Dr. NW9 BO32 46
Snowdown Clo. SE20 CC51 87
Avenue Rd.
Snowdrop Clo., Hmptn. BF50 74
Gresham Rd.
Snowdrop Path, Rom. CV29 42
Snowerhill Rd., Bet. BO71 120
Snows Fields SE1 BZ41 4
Snows Fields SE1 BZ41 67
Snowshill Rd. E12 CK35 49
Soames Mead, Brwd. DA20 24
Soames St. SE15 CA45 67
Soames Wk., N.Mal. BO51 85
Socket La., Brom. CH53 88
Soham Rd., Enf. CD22 30
Soho Sq. W1 BW39 1
Soho Sq. W1 BW39 56
Soho St. W1 BW39 1
Solander Gdns. Est. E1 CC40 57
Sole Farm Av., Lthd. BE66 111
Sole Farm Clo., Lthd. BE65 102
Sole Farm Rd., Lthd. BE66 111
Solebay St. E1 CD38 57
Solecote, Lthd. BF66 111
Solefelds Rd., Sev. CU67 116
Solent Rd. NW6 BS35 47
Solent Rd., Houns. AY46 73
Soleoak, Sev. CV67 117
Solesbridge Clo., Rick. AV24 25
Solesbridge La., Rick. AV24 25
Soley Ms. WC1 BY38 2
Solid La., Brwd. CZ23 33
Solna Av. SW15 BQ46 75
Solna Rd. N21 BZ26 39
Solomon Hill, Rick. AX26 35
Solomons Pass. SE15 CB45 67
Solomons Ter. N20 BT26 38
Soloms Court Rd., Bans. BT62 104
Solon New Rd. SW4 BX45 66
Solon Rd. SW2 BX45 66
Soloway Clo. E8 CA36 57
Rhodes Dev.
Solway Clo., Houns. BE45 64
Solway Rd. N22 BY30 38
Solway Rd. SE22 CB45 67
Solway, Hem.H. AY12 8
Somaford Gro., Barn. BT25 29
Somali Rd. NW2 BR35 46
Somerby Clo., Brox. CE14 12
Somerby Rd., Bark. CM36 58
Somercoates Clo., Barn. BU24 29
Somerden Rd., Orp. CP54 89
Somerfield Clo., Pnr. BC31 44
Somerfield Clo., Tad. BR63 103
Somerfield Rd. N4 BY34 47
Somerford Est. N16 CA35 48
Somerford Gro. N16 CA35 48
Somerford Gro. N17 CB29 39
Somerford St. E1 CB38 57
Brady St.
Somerford Way SE16 CD41 67
Somerhill Av., Sid. CO47 79
Somerhill Rd., Well. CO44 69
Someries Rd., Hem.H. AV12 7
Somerleyton Pass. SW9 BY45 66
Mayall Rd.
Somerleyton Rd. SW9 BY45 66
Somers Clo. NW1 BW37 1
Somers Clo., Reig. BS70 121
Somers Cres. W2 BU39 1
Somers Cres. W2 BU39 56
Somers Ms. W2 BU39 1
Somers Ms. W2 BU39 56
Radnor Pl.
Somers Pl. SW2 BX47 76
Somers Rd. E17 CD31 48
Somers Rd. SW2 BX46 76
Somers Rd., Hat. BQ15 10
Somers Rd., Reig. BS70 121
Somers Sq., Hat. BQ15 10
Somers Way, Bush. BG26 36
Somersby Gdns., Ilf. CK32 49
Somerset Av. SW20 BP51 85
Somerset Av., Chess. BK56 93
Somerset Av., Well. CN46 78
Somerset Clo., Epsom BN58 94
Hollymoor La.
Somerset Clo., N.Mal. BO53 85
Somerset Clo., Walt. BC56 92
Queens Rd.
Somerset Clo., Wdf.Grn. CH30 40
Harold Rd.
Somerset Est. SW11 BT44 66
Somerset Gdns. N6 BV33 47
Somerset Gdns. SE13 CE44 67
Somerset Gdns. SW16 BX52 86
Somerset Gdns., Horn. CX33 51
Somerset Gdns., Tedd. BH49 74
Somerset Rd. E17 CE32 48
Somerset Rd. N17 CA31 48
Somerset Rd. N18 CA28 39
Somerset Rd. NW4 BQ31 46
Somerset Rd. SW19 BQ48 75
Somerset Rd. W13 BJ40 54
Somerset Rd. W4 BN41 65
Somerset Rd., Barn. BS25 29
Somerset Rd., Brent. BK43 64
Somerset Rd., Dart. CU46 79
Somerset Rd., Enf. CE22 30
Somerset Rd., Har. BG32 45
Somerset Rd., Kings.T. BL51 85
Somerset Rd., Orp. CO54 89
Somerset Rd., Red. BT71 121
Somerset Rd., S.le H. DK41 71
Somerset Rd., Sthl. BE39 54
Somerset Rd., Tedd. BH49 74
Somerset Sq., W14 BR41 65
Somerset Way, Iver AV41 62
Somerset Waye, Houns. BE43 64
Somersham Rd., Bexh. CQ44 69
Somersham, Welw.G.C. BU 8 5
Somerton Av., Rich. BM45 65
Somerton Clo., Pur. BY61 104
Somerton Rd. NW2 BQ34 46
Somerton Rd. SE15 CB45 67
Somertons Clo., Guil. AQ69 118
Somertrees Av. SE12 CH48 78
Somervell Ct., Har. BF35 45
Somervell Rd., Har. BE35 45
Somerville Rd. SE14 CC44 67
Somerville Rd. SE20 CC50 77
Somerville Rd., Cob. BF60 93
Somerville Rd., Dart. CW46 80
Somerville Rd., Eton AO42 61
Somerville Rd., Rom. CP32 50
Sonderburg Rd. N7 BX34 47
Seven Sisters Rd.
Sondes Pl. Dr., Dor. BH71 119
Sondes St. SE17 BZ43 4
Sondes St. SE17 BZ43 67
Sonia Ct., Har. BH32 45
Sonia Gdns. N12 BT28 38
Sonia Gdns. NW10 BO35 46
Sonia Gdns., Houns. BF43 64
Sonnet Wk., West. CJ62 106
Kings Rd.
Sonning Gdns., Hmptn. BE50 74
Sonning Rd. SE25 CB53 87
Soothouse Spring, St.Alb. BH11 9
Sopers Rd., Cuff. BX18 20
Sophia Clo. N7 BX36 56
Mackenzie Rd.
Sophia Rd. E10 CE33 48

Sophia Rd. E16 CH39 58
Sopwell La., St.Alb. BG14 9
Sopwith Av., Chess. BL56 94
Sopwith Clo., West. CJ61 106
Hillcrest Rd.
Sopwith Rd., Houns. BD43 64
Sopwith Way, Kings.T. BL51 85
Kingsgate Rd.
Sorbie Clo., Wey. BA57 92
Sorrel Bank, Croy. CD58 96
Sorrel Clo. SE28 CO40 59
Sorrel Ct., Grays DE43 71
Salix Rd.
Sorrel Way, Grav. DF49 81
Sorrel Wk., Rom. CT31 50
Sorrell Clo. SE14 CD43 67
Southerngate Way
Sorrell Clo. SW9 BY44 66
Myatts Fields Dev.
Sorrell Gdns. E6 CK39 58
Sorrento Rd., Sutt. BS55 86
Sotheby Ms. N5 BY34 47
Sotheby Rd. N5 BY34 47
Sotheran Clo. E8 CB37 2
Sotheran Clo. E8 CB37 57
Sotheron Rd. SW6 BS43 66
Sotheron Rd., Wat. BD24 27
Soudan Rd. SW11 BU44 66
Souldern Rd. W14 BQ41 65
Souldern St., Wat. BC25 26
Sounds Lodge, Swan. CS53 89
South Access Rd. E17 CD33 48
South Acre NW9 BO30 37
South Africa Rd. W12 BP40 55
South Albert Rd., Reig. BR70 120
South App., Nthwd. BA27 35
South Ash Rd., Sev. DB58 99
South Audley St. W1 BV40 3
South Audley St. W1 BV40 56
South Av. E4 CE26 39
South Av. Gdns., Sthl. BE40 54
South Av., Cars. BU57 95
South Av., Egh. AU50 72
South Av., Rich. BM44 65
Sandycombe Rd.
South Av., Sthl. BE40 54
South Bank Lo., Surb. BL53 85
South Bank Rd., Berk. AP12 7
South Bank Ter., Surb. BL53 85
South Bank, Chis. CM49 78
South Bank, Surb. BL53 85
South Bank, West. CM66 115
South Birkbeck Rd. E11 CF34 48
South Black Lion La. W6 BP42 65
South Bolton Gdns. SW5 BS42 3
South Bolton Gdns. SW5 BS42 66
South Border, The, Pur. BX59 95
South Church Ct. N13 BX28 38
Palmerston Cres.
South Circular Rd. SE23 CC47 77
South Circular Rd., Rich. BM43 65
South Clo. N6 BV32 47
South Clo., Barn. BR24 28
South Clo., Bexh. CP45 69
South Clo., Dag. CR37 59
South Clo., Epsom BN58 94
South Clo., Mord. BS53 86
South Clo., Pnr. BE33 45
South Clo., St.Alb. BF16 18
South Clo., Twick. BF48 74
South Clo., West Dr. AY41 63
South Clo., Wok. AR61 100
South Close Grn., Red. BV67 113
South Common Rd., Uxb. AY36 53
South Consort Way, Uxb. AV32 43
South Cottage Dr., Rick. AV25 25
South Cottage Gdns., Rick. AV25 25
South Countess Rd. E17 CD31 48
South Cres. WC1 BW39 1
South Cres. WC1 BW39 56
South Cross Rd., Ilf. CM32 49
South Croxted Rd. SE21 BZ48 77
South Dagenham Rd., Dag. CS36 59
South Dene NW7 BN27 37
South Down Cres., Ilf. CN32 49
South Dr. SW11 BU44 66
South Dr., Bans. BU60 95
South Dr., Brwd. DB28 42
South Dr., Couls. BW61 104
South Dr., Cuff. BX18 20
South Dr., Dor. BK71 119
South Dr., Orp. CN56 97
South Dr., Rom. CV31 51
South Dr., Ruis. BB33 44
South Dr., Sutt. BR58 94
South Dr., Vir.W. AQ54 82
South Ealing Rd. W5 BK41 64
South Eastern Av. N9 CA27 39
South Eaton Pl. SW1 BV42 3
South Eaton Pl. SW1 BV42 66
South Eden Park Rd., Beck. CE53 87
South Edwardes Sq. W8 BR41 65
South Emmwood Clo., Hem.H. AZ13 8
South End Clo. NW3 BU35 47
South End Rd.
South End Grn. NW3 BU35 47
South End Rd. NW3 BU35 47
South End Rd., Rain. CU37 59
South End Row W8 BS41 3
South End Row W8 BS41 66
South End W8 BS41 3
South End W8 BS41 66
St.Albans Gro.
South End, Croy. BZ56 96
South End, Lthd. BF66 111
South Esk Rd. E7 CJ36 58
South Gate, Harl. CM11 13
South Gdns. SW19 BT50 76
South Gipsy Rd., Well. CP45 69
South Glade, The, Bex. CQ47 79
South Grn. NW9 BO29 37
Clayton Field
South Grn., Slou. AP40 52
South Gro. E17 CD32 48
South Gro. N15 BZ32 48
South Gro. N6 BV33 47
South Gro., Cher. AV53 82
South Grove Ho. N6 BV33 47
South Hall Clo., Farn. CW43 90
Eynsford Rd.
South Hall Dr., Rain. CU39 59
South Hill Av., Har. BG34 45
South Hill Gro., Har. BH35 45
South Hill Pk. Gdns. NW3 BU35 47
South Hill Pk. NW3 BU35 47
South Hill Rd., Brom. CG52 88
South Hill Rd., Grav. DH47 81
South Hill Rd., Hem.H. AX13 8
South Hill, Chis. CK50 78
South Hill, Guil. AR71 118
South Island Pl. SW9 BX43 66
South Kent Av., Grav. DE46 81
South La. W., N.Mal. BN52 85
South La., Kings.T. BK52 84
South La., N.Mal. BN52 85
South Lambeth Pl. SW8 BX43 66
South Lambeth Rd.
South Lambeth Rd. SW8 BX43 66
South Ley, Welw.G.C. BR 9 5
South Lodge Av., Mitch. BX52 86
South Lodge Cres., Enf. BW24 29
South Lodge Dr. N14 BW24 29
South Lodge W5 BK40 54
Webster Gdns.
South Mall N9 CB27 39
South Mead NW9 BO30 37
South Mead, Red. BU69 121
South Meadow La., Wind. AO43 61
South Meadows, Wem. BL35 46
Park Lawns
South Mimms By-pass, Pot.B. BO19 19
South Molton La. W1 BV39 1
South Molton La. W1 BV39 56
South Molton Rd. E16 CH39 58
South Molton St. W1 BV39 1
South Molton St. W1 BV39 56
South Moreton Ter. Ms. SW1 BW42 3
South Mundells, Welw.G.C. BR 7 5
South Norwood Hill SE25 CA51 87
South Oak Rd. SW16 BX49 76
South Par. SW3 BT42 3
South Par. SW3 BT42 66
South Par. W4 BN42 65
South Path, Wind. AO44 61
South Pk. Av., Rick. AV25 25
South Pk. Clo., N.Mal. BN52 85
South Pk. Cres. SE6 CG47 78
South Pk. Cres., Ger.Cr. AS31 43
South Pk. Cres., Ilf. CM34 49
South Pk. Ct., Beck. CE50 77
South Pk. Dr., Ger.Cr. AS31 43
South Pk. Dr., Ilf. CN34 49
South Pk. Est. SE16 CB41 67
South Pk. Gdns., Berk. AQ12 7
South Pk. Hill Rd., S.Croy. BZ56 96
South Pk. La., Red. CB71 114
South Pk. Ley Rd., Cat. CC63 105
South Pk. Ms. SW6 BS45 66
South Pk. Rd. SW19 BR50 75
South Pk. Rd., Ilf. CM34 49
South Pk. Ter., Ilf. CM34 49
South Pk. Vw., Ger.Cr. AS31 43
South Pk. Way, Ruis. BD36 54
South Pk., Ger.Cr. AS32 43
South Pk., Sev. CU66 116
South Pl. EC2 BZ39 2
South Pl. EC2 BZ39 57
South Pl. Ms. EC2 BZ39 2
South Pl.
South Pl. Ms. EC2 BZ39 57
South Pl.
South Pl. SW19 BQ50 75
Thornton Rd.
South Pl., Enf. CC25 30
South St.
South Pl., Harl. CO 9 6
South Pl., Surb. BL54 85
South Rd. N9 CB26 39
South Rd. SE23 CC48 77
South Rd. SW19 BT50 76
South Rd. W5 BK42 64
South Rd., St. George's Hill, Wey. AZ58 92
South Rd., Amer. AO21 25
South Rd., Edg. BM30 37
South Rd., Egh. AR50 72
South Rd., Erith CT43 69
South Rd., Felt. BD49 74
South Rd., Guil. AQ69 118
South Rd., Harl. CO 9 6
South Rd., Hmptn. BE50 74
South Rd., Little Heath CP32 50
South Rd., Reig. BS71 121
South Rd., Rick. AU25 25
South Rd., Rom. CQ32 50
South Rd., S.Ock. DB39 60
South Rd., Sthl. BE40 54
South Rd., Twick. BG48 74
South Rd., West Dr. AY41 63
South Rd., Wey. BA56 92
South Rd., Wok. AR61 100
South Ri., Cars. BU58 95
South Ridge, Wey. AZ58 92
South Riding, St.Alb. BF18 18
South Row SE3 CG44 68
South Sea St. SE16 CD41 67
South Side Common SW19 BQ50 75
South Side W6 BO41 65
South Sq. NW11 BS32 47
South Sq. WC1 BY39 2
South St. W1 BV40 3
South St. W1 BV40 56
South St., Brom. CH51 88
South St., Brwd. DB27 42
South St., Dor. BJ72 119
South St., Enf. CC25 30
South St., Epsom BN60 94
South St., Guil. AR71 118
South St., Islw. BJ45 64
South St., Rain. CS37 59
South St., Rom. CT32 50
South St., Stai. AV49 72
South Station App., Red. BX71 121
South Tenter St. E1 CA40 4
South Tenter St. E1 CA40 57
South Ter. SW7 BU42 3
South Ter. SW7 BU42 66
South Ter., Dor. BJ72 119
South Ter., Surb. BL53 85
South Vale SE19 CA50 77
South Vale, Har. BH35 45
South Vill. NW1 BW36 56
South Ville St. W. SW8 BW44 66
Wandsworth Rd.
South Vw. Av. NW10 BO35 46
South Vw. Av., Til. DG44 71
South Vw. Clo., Bex. CQ46 79
South Vw. Ct., Wok. AS62 100
Constitution Hill
South Vw. Dr. E18 CH31 49
South Vw. Rd. N8 BW31 47
South Vw. Rd., Ash. BK63 102
South Vw. Rd., Dart. CV48 80
South Vw. Rd., Ger.Cr. AR31 43
South Vw. Rd., Grays DB43 70
South Vw. Rd., Loug. CK25 31
South Vw. Rd., Pnr. BC29 35
South Vw. Rd., Warl. CB63 105
South Vw., Brom. CJ51 88
South Vw., Dart. CT46 79
South Way N11 BW29 38
South Way N9 CC27 39
South Way, Brom. CH54 88
South Way, Cars. BT58 95
South Way, Croy. CD55 87
South Way, Har. BF31 45
South Way, Wal.Abb. CE21 30
South Way, Wat. BA20 17
South Way, Wem. BL35 46
South Weald Rd., Brwd. DA27 42
South Western Rd., Twick. BJ46 74
South Wharf Rd. W2 BT39 1
South Wharf Rd. W2 BT39 56
South Wk., Hayes BA39 53
South Wk., Reig. BS70 121
South Wk., W.Wick. CG55 88
South Worple Av. SW14 BO45 65
South Worple Way
South Worple Way SW14 BN45 65
Southacre Way, Pnr. BD30 36
Southall La., Houns. BC43 63
Southall Pl. SE1 BZ41 4
Southall Way, Brwd. CZ28 42
Southam St. W10 BR38 55
Southampton Bldgs. WC2 BY39 2
Southampton Bldgs. WC2 BY39 56
Southampton Gdns., Mitch. BX53 86
Southampton Pl. WC1 BX39 2
Southampton Pl. WC1 BX39 56
Southampton Rd. NW5 BU35 47
Southampton Rd., Houns. AY46 73
Southampton Row WC1 BX39 2
Southampton Row WC1 BX39 56
Southampton St. WC2 BX40 4
Southampton St. WC2 BX40 56
Southampton Way SE5 BZ43 67
Southbank, T.Ditt. BJ54 84
Southborough Clo., Surb. BK54 84
Southborough La., Brom. CK53 88
Southborough Rd. E9 CC37 57
Southborough Rd., Brom. CK53 88
Southborough Rd., Surb. BL54 85
Southbourne Av. NW9 BN30 37
Southbourne Clo., Pnr. BE33 45
Southbourne Cres. NW4 BR31 46
Southbourne Gdns. SE12 CH46 78
Southbourne Gdns., Ilf. CM35 49
Southbourne Gdns., Ruis. BC33 44
Southbourne, Brom. CH54 88
Southbridge Pl., Croy. BZ56 96
Southbridge Rd., Croy. BZ55 87
Southbridge Way, Sthl. BE41 64
Southbrook Dr., Chsnt. CC17 21
Southbrook Ms. SE12 CG46 78
Southbrook Rd.
Southbrook Rd. SE12 CG48 78
Southbrook Rd. SW16 BX51 86
Southbrook, Saw. CQ 6 6
Southbury Av., Enf. CB25 30
Southbury Clo., Horn. CV35 51
Southbury Rd., Enf. CA24 30
Southchurch Rd. E6 CK37 58
Southcliffe Dr., Ger.Cr. AS28 34
Southcombe St. W14 BR42 65
Southcote Av., Felt. BB48 73
Southcote Av., Surb. BM54 85
Southcote Beech, Wok. AR61 100
Southcote Rd. E17 CC32 48
Southcote Rd. N19 BW35 47
Southcote Rd. SE25 CB53 87
Southcote Rd., Red. BW68 113
Southcote Rd., S.Croy. CA58 96
Southcote Ri., Ruis. BA33 44
Southcroft Av., W.Wick. CF55 87
Southcroft Av., Well. CN45 68
Southcroft Rd. SW16 BV50 76
Southcroft Rd. SW17 BV50 76
Southcroft Rd., Orp. CN55 88
Southdale, Chig. CM29 40
Southdean Gdns. SW19 BR48 75
Southdene Ct. N11 BW27 38
Pymmes Green Rd.
Southdene, Sev. CQ60 98
Southdown Av. W7 BJ41 64
Southdown Clo. SW20 BQ50 75
Crescent Rd.
Southdown Cres., Har. BF33 45
Southdown Ct., Hat. BP14 10
Southdown Rd.
Southdown Rd. SW20 BQ51 85
Southdown Rd., Cars. BV58 95
Southdown Rd., Cat. CD64 105
Southdown Rd., Hat. BP14 10
Southdown Rd., Horn. CU33 50
Southdown Rd., Walt. BE56 93
Southdowns, S.Dnth. CY51 90
Southend Arterial Rd., Rom. CV30 42
Southend Arterial Rd., Brwd. DA32 51
Southend Clo. SE9 CL46 78
Southend Cres. SE9 CL46 78
Southend La. SE26 CD49 77
Southend La. SE6 CD49 77
Southend Rd. E17 CF30 39
Southend Rd. E18 CH30 40
Southend Rd. E6 CK36 58
Southend Rd., Beck. CE50 77
Southend Rd., Grays DE42 71
Southend Rd., Wdf.Grn. CH30 40
Southern Av. SE25 CA52 87
Southern Av., Felt. BC47 73
Southern Dr., Loug. CK25 31
Southern Gro. E3 CD38 57
Southern Perimeter Rd., Houns. AY46 73
Southern Pl., Swan. CS52 89
Southern Rd. E13 CH37 58
Southern Rd. N2 BU31 47
Southern Row W10 BR38 55
Southern St. N1 BX37 2
Southern St. N1 BX37 56
Southern Way, Harl. CL12 13
Southern Way, Rom. CR32 50
Southerngate Way SE14 CD43 67
Southernhay, Loug. CJ24 31
Southerns La., Couls. BT65 104
Southerton Rd. W6 BQ41 65
Southey Rd. N15 CA32 48
Southey Rd. SW19 BS50 76
Southey Rd. SW9 BY44 66
Southey St. SE20 CC50 77
Southey Wk., Til. DG44 71
Southfield Av., Wat. BD22 27
Southfield Clo., Uxb. AZ38 53
Southfield Clo., Wind. AL42 61
Southfield Gdns., Twick. BH49 74
Southfield Pk., Har. BF31 45
Southfield Pl., Wey. AZ58 92
Southfield Rd. N17 CA30 39
The Avenue
Southfield Rd. W4 BN41 65
Southfield Rd., Chis. CN52 88
Southfield Rd., Enf. CB25 30
Southfield Rd., Hodd. CE11 12
Southfield Rd., Sev. CZ57 99
Southfield Rd., Wal.Cr. CD19 21
Southfield Way, St.Alb. BK12 9
Southfield, Barn. BQ25 28
Southfield, Welw.G.C. BQ 9 5
Southfields Av., Ashf. AZ50 73
Southfields Cotts. W7 BH41 64
Southfields NW4 BP30 37
Southfields Pass. SW18 BS46 76
Southfields Rd.
Southfields Rd. SW18 BS46 76
Southfields Rd., Cat. CE64 105
Southfields, E.Mol. BH53 84
Southfleet Rd., Dart. DA49 80
Southfleet Rd., Grav. DF47 81
Milroy Av.
Southfleet Rd., Orp. CN55 88
Southfleet Rd., Swans. DC47 81
Southgate Av., Felt. BA49 73
Southgate Cir. N14 BW26 38
Southgate Gro. N1 BZ36 2
Southgate Gro. N1 BZ36 57
Southgate Rd. N1 BZ37 2
Southgate Rd. N1 BZ37 57
Southgate Rd., Grays CY42 70
Southgate Rd., Pot.B. BT20 20
Southholme Clo. SE19 CA51 87
Sylvan Hill
Southhill La., Pnr. BC31 44
Southhill Rd., Chis. CK50 78
Southhill St. E14 CE39 57
Chrisp St.
Southland Rd. SE18 CN43 68
Southland Way, Houns. BG46 74
Southlands Av., Orp. CM56 97
Southlands Clo., Pur. BX61 104
Southlands Gro., Brom. CK52 88
Southlands La., Oxt. CE70 114
Southlands Rd., Brom. CJ53 88
Southlands Rd., Uxb. AV35 43
Southlea Rd., Slou. AQ44 62
Southly Clo., Sutt. BS55 86
Southmead Cres., Chsnt. CD18 21
Southmead NW9 BO30 37
Southmead Rd. SW19 BR47 75
Southmead, Epsom BO57 94
Southmont Rd., Esher BH55 84
Southmoor Wk. E9 CD36 57
Trowbridge Est.
Southold Ri. SE9 CK48 78
Southolm St. SW11 BV44 66
Southover N12 BS27 38
Southover, Brom. CH49 78
Southport Rd. SE18 CM42 68
Southridge Pl. SW20 BQ50 75
Southsea Av., Wat. BC24 26
Southsea Rd., Kings.T. BL52 85
Southside, Ger.Cr. AR31 43
Southspring, Sid. CM47 78
Southvale Rd. SE3 CG44 68
Southview Av. NW10 BO35 46
Southview Clo., Chsnt. CA16 21
Southview Clo., Swan. CT52 89
West View Rd.
Southview Cres., Ilf. CL32 49
Southview Dr., Upmin. CX34 51
Southview Gdns., Wall. BW57 95
Southview Rd., Brom. CF49 77
Southview Rd., Cat. CE65 105
Southview Rd., Dart. CV48 80
Southviews, S.Croy. CC58 96
Southville Clo., Epsom BN57 94
Southville Clo., Felt. BB47 73
Southville Cres., Felt. BB47 73
Southville Rd., Felt. BB47 73
Southville Rd., T.Ditt. BJ54 84
Southwark Br. EC4 BZ40 4
Southwark Br. EC4 BZ40 57
Southwark Br. Rd. SE1 BY41 4
Southwark Br. Rd. SE1 BY41 66
Southwark Br. SE1 BZ40 57
Southwark Gro. SE1 BZ40 4
Southwark Gro. SE1 BZ40 57
Southwark Ms. W2 BT39 1
Southwark Pk. Rd. SE16 CA42 4
Southwark Pk. Rd. SE16 CA42 67
Southwark Pl., Brom. CK52 88
St. Georges Rd.
Southwark St. SE1 BY40 4
Southwark St. SE1 BY40 56
Southwater Clo. E14 CD39 57
Southwater Clo., Beck. CE50 77
Southway Clo. W12 BP41 65
Scotts Rd.
Southway N20 BS27 38
Southway NW11 BS32 47
Southway SW20 BQ52 85
Southway, Guil. AP70 118
Southway, Hat. BP14 10
Southway, Wall. BW56 95
Southweald Dr., Wal.Abb. CF19 21
Southwell Av., Nthlt. BF36 54
Southwell Gdns. SW7 BT41 3
Southwell Gdns. SW7 BT41 66
Southwell Grove Rd. E11 CG34 49
Southwell Rd. SE5 BZ45 67
Southwell Rd., Croy. BY53 86
Southwell Rd., Har. BK32 45
Southwest Rd. E11 CF33 48
Southwick Ms. W2 BT39 56
Southwick St.
Southwick Pl. W2 BU39 1
Southwick Pl. W2 BU39 56
Southwick St. W2 BU39 1
Southwick St. W2 BU39 56
Southwold Dr., Bark. CO35 50
Southwold Rd. E5 CB34 48
Southwold Rd., Bex. CR46 79
Southwold Rd., Wat. BD22 27
Southwood Av. N6 BV33 47
Southwood Av., Cher. AU57 91
Southwood Av., Couls. BW61 104
Southwood Av., Kings.T. BN51 85
Southwood Av., Wok. AO62 100
Southwood Clo., Brom. CK52 88
Southwood Clo., Wor.Pk. BQ54 85
Southwood Ct. NW11 BS32 47
Southwood Dr., Surb. BN54 85
Southwood Gdns., Esher BJ55 84
Southwood Gdns., Ilf. CL31 49
Southwood La. N6 BV33 47
Southwood Lawn Rd. N6 BV33 47
Southwood Rd. SE28 CO40 59
Southwood Rd. SE9 CL48 78
Sovereign Clo. E1 CB40 57
Wapping La.
Sovereign Clo. W5 BK39 54
Sovereign Ms. E2 CA37 57
Pearson St.
Sovereign Way, St.Alb. BG13 9
Chequer St.
Sowerby Clo. SE9 CK46 78
Sowrey Av., Rain. CT36 59
Spa Clo. SE25 CA51 87
Spa Dr., Epsom BM60 94
Spa Green Est. EC1 BY38 56
Spa Hill SE19 BZ51 87
Spa Rd. SE16 CA41 4
Spa Rd. SE16 CA41 67
Spaceway, Felt. BC46 73
Spackmans Way, Slou. AO41 61
Spafield St. EC1 BY38 2
Exmouth Mkt.
Spains Hall Rd., Ong. DB13 15
Spalding Rd. NW4 BQ33 46
Spalding Rd. SW17 BV49 76
Spalt Clo., Brwd. DD27 122
Spanby Rd. E3 CE38 57
Spangate SE3 CG45 68
Spaniards Clo. NW11 BT33 47
Spaniards End NW3 BT33 47
Spaniards Rd. NW3 BT34 47
Spanish Pl. W1 BV39 1
Spanish Pl. W1 BV39 56
Spanish Rd. SW18 BT46 76
Spareleaze Hill, Loug. CK25 31
Sparepenny La., Eyns. CV54 90
Sparkbridge Rd., Har. BH31 45
Sparks Clo. W3 BN39 55
Joseph Av.
Sparks Clo., Hmptn. BE50 74
Victors Dr.
Sparricks Row SE1 BZ41 4
Weston Rd.
Sparrow Clo., Hmptn. BE49 74
Sparrow Dr., Orp. CM54 88
Sparrow Farm Dr., Felt. BD47 74
Sparrow Farm Rd., Epsom BP56 94
Sparrow Farm Rd., Felt. BD47 74
Sparrow Farm Dr.
Sparrow Grn., Dag. CR34 50
Sparrows Herne, Bush. BF26 36

Sparrows La. SE9 CM47 78
Sparrows Mead, Red. BV69 121
Kingfisher Dr.
Sparrows Way, Bush. BG26 36
Sparrows Herne
Sparrowswick Ride, St.Alb. BG11 9
Sparsholt Rd. N19 BX33 47
Sparsholt Rd., Bark. CN37 58
Sparta St. SE10 CE44 67
Spear Ms. SW5 BS42 66
Spearman St. SE18 CL43 68
Spearpoint Gdns., Ilf. CN31 49
Spears Rd. N19 BX33 47
Speart La., Houns. BE43 64
Spedan Clo. NW3 BT34 47
Spedan Tower NW3 BS34 47
Speedgate Hill, Fawk. DA55 90
Speedwell Clo., Guil. AU69 109
Speedwell Clo., Hem.H. AV14 7
Campion Rd.
Speedwell Ct., Grays DE43 71
Speedwell St. SE8 CE43 67
Comet St.
Speer Rd., T.Ditt. BH53 84
Speke Hill SE9 CK48 78
Speke Rd., Th.Hth. BZ51 87
Speldhurst Clo., Brom. CG53 88
Speldhurst Rd. E9 CC36 57
Speldhurst Rd. W4 BN41 65
Spellbrook Wk. N1 BZ37 57
Basire St.
Spelman St. E1 CA39 57
Spelman St. E1 CB39 2
Spelthorne Gro., Sun. BB50 73
Spelthorne La., Ashf. BA51 83
Spence Av., Byfleet AY60 92
Spencer Av. N13 BX29 38
Spencer Av., Chsnt. CA16 21
Spencer Av., Hayes BC39 53
Spencer Clo. N3 BS30 38
Spencer Clo. NW10 BL38 55
Spencer Clo., Epsom BO65 103
Spencer Clo., Orp. CN55 88
Spencer Clo., Uxb. AX38 53
Spencer Clo., Wdf.Grn. CJ28 40
Spencer Clo., Wok. AU60 91
Spencer Cres., Upmin. CY33 51
Spencer Ct. NW8 BT37 1
The Lane
Spencer Ct. SW20 BP51 85
Spencer Rd.
Spencer Ct., Rich. BK49 74
Spencer Dr. N2 BT32 47
Spencer Gate, St.Alb. BH12 9
Spencer Gdns. SE9 CK46 78
Spencer Gdns. SW14 BN46 75
Spencer Gdns., Egh. AR49 72
Spencer Hill Rd. SW19 BR50 75
Spencer Hill SW19 BR50 75
Spencer Ms. W6 BR43 65
Greyhound Rd.
Spencer Pass. E3 CB37 57
Dinmont St.
Spencer Pk. SW18 BT46 76
Spencer Pl. SW1 BW41 3
Spencer Pl. SW1 BW41 66
Greycoat Pl.
Spencer Pl., Croy. BZ54 87
Spencer Rd. E17 CF30 39
Spencer Rd. E6 CJ37 58
Spencer Rd. N11 BW28 38
Spencer Rd. N17 CB30 39
Spencer Rd. SW18 BT45 66
Spencer Rd. SW20 BP51 85
Spencer Rd. W3 BN40 55
Spencer Rd. W4 BN43 65
Spencer Rd., Beddington BU54 86
Spencer Rd., Brom. CG50 78
Spencer Rd., Cat. BZ64 105
Spencer Rd., Cob. BC61 101
Spencer Rd., E.Mol. BG53 84
Spencer Rd., Har. BH30 36
Spencer Rd., Ilf. CN33 49
Spencer Rd., Islw. BG44 64
Spencer Rd., Mitch. BV52 86
Spencer Rd., Rain. CS38 59
Spencer Rd., S.Croy. CA56 96
Spencer Rd., Slou. AS42 62
Spencer Rd., Twick. BH48 74
Spencer Rd., Wem. BK34 45
Spencer Ri. NW5 BV34 47
Spencer St. EC1 BY38 2
Spencer St. EC1 BY38 56
Spencer St. SW1 BW41 3
Spencer St., Grav. DG47 81
Spencer St., St.Alb. BG13 9
Spencer St., Sthl. BD41 64
Spencer Wk., Hem.H. AW12 8
Spencer Way, Red. BV73 121
Spencer Wk. NW3 BT35 47
Hampstead High St.
Spencer Wk. SW15 BQ45 65
Spencer Wk., Rick. AW25 26
Spencer Wk., Til. DG44 71
Spencers Cft., Harl. CO12 14
Spenser Av., Wey. AZ58 92
Spenser Cres., Upmin. CY33 51
Spenser Gro. N16 CA35 48
Spenser Rd. SE24 BY46 76
Spenser St. SW1 BW41 66
Spensley Wk. N16 BZ34 48
Speranza St. SE18 CN42 68
Sperling Rd. N17 CA30 39
Spert St. E14 CD40 57
Spey St. E14 CF39 57
Spey Way, Rom. CT29 41
Speyside N14 BW25 29
Spezia Rd. NW10 BP37 55
Spicer Clo. SE5 BY44 66
Spicer Clo., Walt. BD53 84
Spicers Field, Lthd. BG60 93
Spicers St., St.Alb. BG13 9
Spicersfield, Chsnt. CB17 21
Spices Yd., Croy. BZ56 96
South End
Spielman Rd., Dart. CW45 70
Spiers Clo., N.Mal. BO53 85
Spigurnell Rd. N17 BZ30 39
Spikes Bridge Rd., Sthl. BE39 54
Spillbutters, Brwd. DA21 33
Spilsby Clo. NW9 BO30 37
Spilsby Rd., Rom. CV29 42
Spindles, Til. DG43 71
Spindlewood Gdns., Croy. CA55 87
Coombe Rd.
Spindlewoods, Tad. BP65 103
Spindrift Av. E14 CE42 67
Spinel Clo. SE18 CN42 68
Spingate Clo., Horn. CV35 51
Tylers Cres.
Spinnells Rd., Har. BE33 45
Spinners Wk., Wind. AO44 61
Spinney Clo., Cob. BF59 93
Spinney Clo., N.Mal. BO53 85
Spinney Clo., Rain. CT37 59
Spinney Clo., West Dr. AY40 53
Yew Av.
Spinney Dr., Felt. BA47 73
Spinney Gdns. SE19 CA49 77
Spinney Gdns., Dag. CQ35 50
Spinney Hill, Wey. AV56 91
Spinney Oak, Brom. CK51 88
Spinney Way, Sev. CM59 97
Spinney, Slou. AN41 61
Spinney, The N21 BY26 38
Spinney, The SW16 BW48 76
Spinney, The, Barn. BS23 29
Spinney, The, Brox. CD13 12
Glenwood
Spinney, The, Brwd. DE25 122
Spinney, The, Chesh. AO18 16
Spinney, The, Epsom BP63 103
Spinney, The, Guil. AX67 110
Spinney, The, Lthd. BF65 102
Spinney, The, Ong. CX18 24
Spinney, The, Pot.B. BT19 20
Barwood Clo.
Spinney, The, Pur. BY59 95
Spinney, The, Sid. CQ49 79
Spinney, The, Stan. BL28 37
Spinney, The, Sun. BC51 83
Spinney, The, Sutt. BQ56 94
Spinney, The, Swan. CT51 89
Spinney, The, Wat. BC23 26
Spinney, The, Welw.G.C. BR 8 5
Peartree La.
Spinney, The, Wem. BJ34 45
Spinneys, The, Brom. CK51 88
Spinning Wheel Mead, Harl. CO12 14
Spire Clo., Grav. DG47 81
Spring Gro.
Spires, The, Dart. CV48 80
Spirit Quay E1 CB40 57
Vaughan Way
Spital Hth., Dor. BK71 119
Spital La., Brwd. CZ27 42
Spital Sq. E1 CA39 2
Spital Sq. E1 CA39 57
Spital St. E1 CA39 2
Spital St. E1 CA39 57
Spital St., Dart. CV46 80
Spital Yd. E1 CA39 2
Spital Sq.
Spitfire Way, Houns. BD42 64
Spode Wk. NW6 BS36 56
Lymington Rd.
Spondon Rd. N15 CB31 48
Spook Hill, Dor. BJ73 119
Spooner Wk., Wall. BW56 95
Spooners Dr., St.Alb. BG17 18
Sportsbank St. SE6 CF47 77
Spottons Gro. N17 BZ30 39
Spout Hill, Croy. CE56 96
Spout La. N., Stai. AW45 63
Spout La., Stai. AW46 73
Spratt Hall Rd. E11 CH32 49
Spratts Alley, Cher. AV57 91
Spratts La., Cher. AV57 91
Spray St. SE18 CL42 68
Spreighton Rd., E.Mol. BF53 84
Sprimont Pl. SW3 BU42 3
Sprimont Pl. SW3 BU42 66
Spring Av., Egh. AS50 72
Spring Bottom La., Red. BY67 113
Spring Bridge Ms. W5 BK40 54
Spring Bridge Rd.
Spring Bridge Rd. W5 BK40 54
Spring Clo., B.Wd. BM23 28
Spring Clo., Barn. BQ25 28
Spring Clo., Dag. CP33 50
Spring Clo., Uxb. AX30 35
Spring Close La., Sutt. BR57 94
Spring Cott., Surb. BK53 84
St. Leonards Rd.
Spring Crofts, Bush. BF25 27
Spring Ct. Rd., Enf. BY22 29
Spring Ct., Guil. AQ68 109
Spring Ct., Sid. CO48 79
Spring Dr., Pnr. BC32 44
Spring Gdns. N5 BZ35 48
Spring Gdns. SE11 BX42 66
Goding St.
Spring Gdns. SW1 BW40 3
Spring Gdns. SW1 BW40 56
Spring Gdns., Dor. BJ71 119
Spring Gdns., E.Mol. BG53 84
Spring Gdns., Horn. CU35 50
Spring Gdns., Orp. CO57 98
Spring Gdns., Rom. CS32 50
Spring Gdns., Wall. BW56 95
Spring Gdns., Wat. BD21 27
Spring Gdns., Wdf.Grn. CJ29 40
Spring Glen, Hat. BO13 10
Spring Gro. Cres., Houns. BG44 64
Spring Gro. E3 CE37 57
Old Ford Rd.
Spring Gro. Rd., Houns. BF44 64
Spring Gro. Rd., Rich. BL46 75
Spring Gro. W4 BM42 65
Spring Gro., Grav. DG47 81
Spring Gro., Hmptn. BF51 84
Spring Gro., Loug. CJ25 31
Spring Gro., Lthd. BF65 102
Spring Gro., Mitch. BV51 86
Spring Hill E5 CB33 48
Spring Hill SE26 CC49 77
Sydenham Rd.
Spring Hills, Harl. CL10 6
Spring La. E5 CB33 48
Spring La. SE25 CB53 87
Spring La., Hem.H. AW12 8
Spring La., Oxt. CF69 114
Spring La., Sev. DA64 108
Spring La., Slou. AM40 61
Spring Lake, Stan. BJ28 36
Spring Ms. W1 BU39 56
Crawford St.
Spring Park Av., Croy. CC55 87
Spring Park Dr. N4 BZ33 48
Spring Park Dr., Beck. CF51 87
Spring Park Rd., Croy. CC55 87
Spring Pass. SW15 BQ45 65
The Embankment
Spring Pl. NW5 BV35 47
Spring Pond Meadow, Brwd. DB21 33
Spring Rd., Felt. BB48 73
Spring Ri., Egh. AS50 72
Spring Shaw Clo., Sev. CS65 107
Spring St. W2 BT39 1
Spring St. W2 BT39 56
Spring St., Epsom BO58 94
Spring St., Harl. CM 9 6
Spring Vale Clo., Swan. CT50 79
Egerton Av.
Spring Vale, Bexh. CR45 69
Spring Vale, Dart. CV47 80
Spring Vale, Green. DB46 80
Spring Villa Rd., Edg. BM29 37
Spring Wk., Brox. CC14 12
Spring Woods, Vir.W. AQ52 82
Springall St. SE15 CB43 67
Springate Field, Slou. AS41 62
Springbank Av., Horn. CV35 51
Springbank N21 BX25 29
Springbank Rd. SE13 CF46 77
Springbank Wk. NW1 BW36 56
Agar Gro.
Springbourne Ct., Beck. CF51 87
Springclose La., Sutt. BR57 94
Springcopse Rd., Reig. BT71 121
Springcroft Av. N2 BU31 47
Springdale Rd. N16 BZ35 48
Springett Pl., Amer. AP22 25
Springfarm Clo., Rain. CV38 60
Springfield Av. N10 BW31 47
Springfield Av. SW20 BR52 85
Springfield Av., Brwd. DF26 122
Springfield Av., Hmptn. BF50 74
Springfield Av., Swan. CT52 89
Springfield Clo. N12 BS28 38
Springfield Clo., Chesh. AO20 16
Springfield Clo., Ong. CW16 24
Springfield Clo., Pot.B. BT19 20
Springfield Clo., Rick. AZ25 26
Springfield Clo., Stan. BJ27 36
Springfield Clo., Wind. AN44 61
Springfield Clo., Wok. AP62 100
Springfield Dr., Ilf. CM32 49
Springfield E5 CB33 48
Springfield Est. SW8 BW44 66
Springfield Gdns. E5 CB33 48
Springfield Gdns. NW9 BN32 46
Springfield Gdns., W.Wick. CE55 87
Springfield Gdns., Wdf.Grn. CJ29 40
Springfield Gdns., Upmin. CY34 51
Springfield Gdns., Brom. CK52 88
Springfield Gdns., Ruis. BC33 44
Springfield Gro. SE7 CJ43 68
Springfield Gro., Sun. BC51 83
Springfield La. NW6 BS37 56
Springfield La., Wey. AZ56 92
Springfield Meadows, Wey. AZ56 92
Springfield Mt. NW9 BN32 46
Springfield Pk., Maid. AG42 61
Springfield Rd. E15 CG38 58
Springfield Rd. E17 CD32 48
Springfield Rd. E4 CG26 40
Springfield Rd. E6 CK36 58
Springfield Rd. N11 BV28 38
Springfield Rd. N15 CB31 48
Springfield Rd. NW8 BT37 1
Springfield Rd. NW8 BT37 56
Springfield Rd. SE26 CB49 77
Springfield Rd. SW19 BR49 75
Springfield Rd. W7 BH40 54
Springfield Rd., Ashf. AY49 73
Springfield Rd., Berk. AQ12 7
Springfield Rd., Bexh. CR45 69
Springfield Rd., Brom. CK52 88
Springfield Rd., Chesh. AO19 16
Springfield Rd., Chsnt. CD19 21
Springfield Rd., Colney Heath BM13 10
Springfield Rd., Dor. BF72 119
Springfield Rd., Epsom BQ58 94
Springfield Rd., Grays DF40 71
Springfield Rd., Guil. AS71 118
Springfield Rd., Har. BH32 45
Springfield Rd., Hayes BD40 54
Springfield Rd., Hem.H. AY13 8
Springfield Rd., Kings.T. BL52 85
Springfield Rd., Slou. AT43 62
Springfield Rd., St.Alb. BJ14 9
Springfield Rd., Tedd. BJ49 74
Springfield Rd., Th.Hth. BZ51 87
Springfield Rd., Twick. BF47 74
Springfield Rd., Wall. BV56 95
Springfield Rd., Wat. BC20 17
Haines Way
Springfield Rd., Well. CO45 69
Springfield Rd., Wind. AN44 61
Springfield Ri. SE26 CB48 77
Springfield Wk. NW6 BS37 56
Springfield Wk., Orp. CM54 88
Farm Av.
Springfield, Bush. BG26 36
Springfield, Epp. CN19 22
Springfield, Oxt. CF68 114
Springfield, Wal.Abb. CG20 22
Springfields, Brox. CD13 12
Springfields, Welw.G.C. BP 9 5
Springhall La., Saw. CQ 7 6
Springhall Rd., Saw. CQ 6 6
Springhaven Clo., Guil. AT70 118
Springhead Rd., Erith CT43 69
Springhead Rd., Grav. DE48 81
Springhead Rd., Sev. CW62 108
Springhill Clo. SE5 BZ45 67
Springholm Clo., West. CJ62 106
Upper Dr.
Springpond Rd., Dag. CQ35 50
Springrice Rd. SE13 CF46 77
Springs, The, Brox. CD16 21
Springvale Av., Brent. BL42 65
Springvale Est. W14 BR41 65
Springvale Ter. W14 BQ41 65
Springvale Way, Orp. CP52 89
Springwater Clo. SE18 CL44 68
Springwell Av. NW10 BO37 55
Springwell Av., Rick. AW27 35
Springwell Clo. SW16 BX49 76
Springwell Ct., Houns. BD44 64
Springwell La., Rick. AW27 35
Springwell Rd. SW16 BX49 76
Springwell Rd., Houns. BD44 64
Springwood Clo., Uxb. AX30 35
Springwood Cres., Edg. BM27 37
Springwood Way, Rom. CU32 50
Manor Rd.
Springwood Wk., St.Alb. BK12 9
Springwood, Chsnt. CB16 21
Sprowston Ms. E7 CH35 49
Sprowston Rd. E7 CH35 49
Spruce Dale Gdns., Wall. BX58 95
Spruce Hill, Harl. CN13 13
Spruce Hills Rd. E17 CE30 39
Spruce Pk., Brom. CG52 88
Cumberland Rd.
Spruce Rd., West. CK61 106
Acer Rd.
Spruce Way, St.Alb. BF17 18
Sprucedale Clo., Swan. CT51 89
The Spinney
Sprucedale Gdns., Croy. CC56 96
Sprules Rd. SE4 CD44 67
Spur Clo., Rom. CO24 32
Spur Clo., Wat. BA20 17
Fay Grn.
Spur Rd. N15 BZ31 48
Philip La.
Spur Rd. SW1 BW41 3
Spur Rd. SW1 BW41 66
Spur Rd., Bark. CM38 58
Spur Rd., Edg. BL28 37
Spur Rd., Felt. BC46 73
Spur Rd., Islw. BJ43 64
Spur Rd., Orp. CO55 89
Spur Road Est., Edg. BL28 37
Spurfield, E.Mol. BF52 84
Spurgate, Brwd. DD27 122
Spurgeon Av. SE19 BZ51 87
Spurgeon Rd. SE19 BZ51 87
Spurgeon St. SE1 BZ41 4
Spurgeon St. SE1 BZ41 67
Spurling Rd. SE22 CA45 67
Spurling Rd., Dag. CQ36 59
Spurrell Av., Bex. CS49 79
Spurstowe Rd. E8 CB36 57
Cottrill Rd.
Spurstowe Ter. E8 CB35 48
Squadrons App., Horn. CV36 60
Square Rigger Row SW11 BT45 66
York Pl.
Square, The, Berk. AT11 7
Square, The, Cars. BV56 95
Square, The, Guil. AP71 118
Orchard Rd.
Square, The, Ilf. CL33 49
Square, The, Rich. BL45 65
The Quadrant
Square, The, Saw. CQ 6 6
Square, The, Wat. BC22 26
Square, The, Wdf.Grn. CH28 40
Square, The, West Dr. AW44 63
Square, The, West. CJ63 106
Square, The, Wey. BA56 92
Square, The, Wok. AY61 101
Squarey St. SW17 BT48 76
Squerryes Mead, West. CM67 115
Squirel Chase, Hem.H. AV13 7
Squires Bridge Rd., Shep. AY52 83
Squires La. N3 BS30 38
Squires Mt. NW3 BT34 47
East Heath Rd.
Squires Rd., Shep. AZ52 83
Squires Ride, Hem.H. AY10 8
Squires Way, Dart. CS49 79
Squires Wood Dr., Chis. CK50 78
Bullerswood Dr.
Squirrel Clo., Houns. BD45 64
Squirrel Wood, Wey. AW59 92
Squirrels Chase, Grays DG41 71
Hornsby La.
Squirrels Clo. N12 BT28 38
Woodside Av.
Squirrels Clo., Uxb. AZ36 53
Squirrels Grn., Lthd. BF65 102
Squirrels Grn., Wor.Pk. BO55 85
Squirrels Heath Av., Rom. CU31 50
Squirrels Heath La., Rom. CV31 51
Squirrels Heath Rd., Rom. CW31 51
Squirrels La., Buck.H. CJ27 40
Squirrels Ms. W13 BJ40 54
Felix Rd.
Squirrels Way, Epsom BN61 103
Squirrels, The SE13 CF45 67
Squirrels, The, Welw.G.C. BT 8 5
Foresters Dr.
Squirrels, The, Bush. BG25 27
Squirrels, The, Pnr. BE31 45
Squirries St. E2 CB38 2
Squirries St. E2 CB38 57
Stable Clo., Nthlt. BF37 54
Stable Inn Bldgs. WC2 BY39 56
Southampton Bldgs.
Stable La., Beac. AO29 34
Stable Ms. E11 CG33 49
Grove Rd.
Stable Way W10 BQ39 55
Latimer Rd.
Stable Wk. N2 BT30 38
Stable Yard Rd. SW1 BW40 56
Stable Yard Rd. SW1 BW41 3
Stable Yd. SW1 BW41 3
Stable Yd. SW9 BX44 66
Broomgrove Rd.
Stables End, Orp. CM55 88
Stables Ms. SE27 BZ49 77
Elder Rd.
Stables Way SE11 BY42 4
Stables Way SE11 BY42 66
Stables, The, Buck.H. CJ26 40
Stacey Av. N18 CC28 39
Stacey Clo. E10 CF32 48
Halford Rd.
Stacey Clo., Grav. DJ49 81
Stacey St. WC2 BW39 1
Stacey St. WC2 BW39 56
Stack Field, Harl. CO 9 6
Stack La., Hart. DC53 90
Stack Rd., Dart. CY52 90
Stackhouse St. SW3 BU41 3
Stackhouse St. SW3 BU41 66
Pavilion Rd.
Stacklands Clo., Sev. CZ57 99
Stacklands Rd., Welw.G.C. BP 9 5
Stacy Path SE5 BZ43 67
Elmington Est.
Stadium Rd. NW2 BQ33 46
Stadium Rd. SE18 CK43 68
Stadium St. SW10 BT43 66
Stadium Way, Wem. BL35 46
Staff St. EC1 BZ38 2
Staff St. EC1 BZ38 57
Cranwood St.
Staffa Rd. E10 CC33 48
Stafford Av., Horn. CV31 51
Stafford Av., Wall. BX56 95
Stafford Clo. N14 BW25 29
Stafford Clo. NW6 BS38 56
Stafford Clo., Chsnt. CB18 21
Stafford Clo., Sutt. BR57 94
Stafford Cripps Est. EC1 BZ38 57
Stafford Ct. W8 BS41 66
Stafford Dr., Brox. CE13 12
Stafford Ms. NW6 BS38 56
Stafford Pl. SW1 BW41 3
Stafford Pl. SW1 BW41 66
Stafford Pl., Rich. BL47 75
Queens Rd.
Stafford Rd. E3 CD37 57
Stafford Rd. E7 CJ36 58
Stafford Rd. NW6 BS38 56
Stafford Rd., Cat. CA65 105
Stafford Rd., Croy. BX56 95
Stafford Rd., Har. BG30 36
Stafford Rd., N.Mal. BN52 85
Stafford Rd., Ruis. BB35 44
Stafford Rd., Sid. CN49 78
Stafford Rd., Wall. BW57 95
Stafford Sq., Wey. BA56 92
Rosslyn Pk.
Stafford St. W1 BW40 3
Stafford St. W1 BW40 56
Stafford Ter. W8 BS41 66
Stafford Way, Sev. CV67 117
Staffords, Harl. CQ 9 6
Staffordshire St. SE15 CB44 67
Stag Clo., Edg. BM30 37
Stag Green Av., Hat. BQ11 10
Stag La. NW9 BN30 37
Stag La. SW15 BO48 75
Stag La., Buck.H. CH27 40
Stag La., Edg. BN30 37
Stag La., Rick. AU25 25
Stag Leys, Ash. BL63 103
Stag Pl. SW1 BW41 3
Stag Pl. SW1 BW41 66
Stag Ride SW19 BP48 75
Stagbury Av., Couls. BU62 104
Stagbury Clo., Couls. BU63 104
Stagg Hill, Barn. BU21 29
Staggart Grn., Chig. CO29 41
Staghill, Guil. AQ71 118
Stags Way, Islw. BH43 64
Stahlton La., Brwd. DC30 123
Stainash Cres., Stai. AW49 73
Stainbank Rd., Mitch. BV52 86
Stainby Clo., West Dr. AY41 63
Stainby Rd. N15 CA31 48
Stainer Rd., B.Wd. BK22 27
Stainer St. SE1 BZ40 4
Stainer St. SE1 BZ40 57
Staines Av., Sutt. BQ55 85
Staines By-pass, Egh. & Stai. AU48 72
Staines By-pass, Stai. & Ashf. AW49 73
Staines Clo., Cher. AV53 82
Staines La., Cher. AV53 82
Staines Rd. E., Sun. BC50 73
Staines Rd. W., Ashf. & Sun. AZ50 73
Staines Rd., Cher. AV52 82
Staines Rd., Felt. AZ47 73
Staines Rd., Houns. BE45 64
Staines Rd., Ilf. CM35 49
Staines Rd., Stai. AW50 73
Staines Rd., Twick. BF48 74

Staines Rd., Wraysbury AS47 72
Staines Wk., Sid. CP50 79
Evry Rd.
Stainforth Clo., Ashf. BA49 73
Stainforth Rd. E17 CE31 48
Stainforth Rd., Ilf. CM33 49
Staining La. EC2 BZ39 2
Staining La. EC2 BZ39 57
Gresham St.
Stainmore Clo., Chis. CM50 78
Stains Clo., Chsnt. CD17 21
Stainsbury St. E2 CC37 57
Royston St.
Stainsby Pl. E14 CE39 57
Stainsby Rd. E14 CE39 57
Stainton Rd. SE6 CF46 77
Stainton Rd., Enf. CC23 30
Stainton Wk., Wok. AQ62 100
Inglewood
Stairfoot La., Sev. CS64 107
Staithes Way, Tad. BP63 103
Headley Gro.
Stalbridge St. NW1 BU39 1
Staleys Rd., Sev. DC63 108
Stalham St. SE16 CB41 67
Stalisfield Pl., Orp. CL58 97
Stambourne Way SE19 CA50 77
Stambourne Way, W.Wick. CF55 87
Stamford Brook Av. W6 BO41 65
Stamford Brook Rd. W6 BO41 65
Stamford Clo. N15 CB31 48
Stamford Rd.
Stamford Clo., Har. BH29 36
Stamford Clo., Pot.B. BT19 20
Stamford Clo., Sthl. BF40 54
Stamford Ct. W6 BO42 65
Stamford Dr., Brom. CG52 88
Stamford Gdns., Dag. CP36 59
Stamford Green Rd., Epsom BM60 94
Stamford Gro. E. N16 CB33 48
Oldhill St.
Stamford Gro. W. N16 CB33 48
Oldhill St.
Stamford Hill Est. N16 CA33 48
Stamford Hill N16 CA34 48
Stamford Ho. W12 BP41 65
Stamford Rd. E6 CK37 58
Stamford Rd. N1 CA36 57
Stamford Rd. N15 CB32 48
Stamford Rd., Dag. CO37 59
Stamford Rd., Walt. BD55 84
Stamford Rd., Wat. BC23 26
Stamford St. NW8 BT38 56
Stamford St. SE1 BY40 4
Stamford St. SE1 BY40 56
Stamp Pl. E2 CA38 2
Stamp Pl. E2 CA38 57
Stanard Clo. N16 CA33 48
Amhurst Pk.
Stanborough Av., B.Wd. BM22 28
Stanborough Clo., Welw.G.C. BQ 8 5
Stanborough Clo., B.Wd. BM22 28
Stanborough Av.
Stanborough Clo., Hmptn. BE50 74
Stanborough Grn., Welw.G.C. BQ 9 5
Stanborough La., Welw.G.C. BP 9 5
Stanborough Pass. E8 CA36 57
Abbot St.
Stanborough Rd., Welw.G.C. BP 9 5
Stanborough Rd., Islw. BG45 64
Stanbridge Rd. SW15 BQ45 65
Stanbrook Rd. SE2 CO41 69
Stanbrook Rd., Grav. DF47 81
Stanbury Av., Wat. BB22 26
Stanbury Rd. SE15 CB44 67
Stancroft NW9 BO32 46
Standale Gro., Ruis. BA32 44
Standard Pl. EC2 CA38 2
Rivington St.
Standard Rd. NW10 BN38 55
Standard Rd., Belv. CR42 69
Standard Rd., Bexh. CQ45 69
Standard Rd., Enf. CD22 30
Standard Rd., Houns. BE45 64
Standard Rd., Orp. CL58 97
Standen Av., Horn. CW34 51
Standen Rd. SW18 BR47 75
Standfield Gdns., Dag. CR36 59
Standfield Rd., Dag. CR35 50
Standfield, Wat. BB19 17
Standingford, Harl. CL13 13
Standish Rd. W6 BP42 65
Standring Ri., Hem.H. AW15 8
Stane Clo. SW19 BS50 76
Hayward Clo.
Stane Pass SW16 BX49 76
Streatham High Rd.
Stane St., Dor. BJ74 119
Stane St., Lthd. BL66 112
Stane Way SE18 CJ43 68
Staneway, Epsom BP58 94
Stanfield Rd. E3 CD37 57
Stanford Clo., Hmptn. BE50 74
Stanford Clo., Rom. CR32 50
Stanford Clo., Ruis. BA32 44
Stanford Clo., Wdf.Grn. CK28 40
Stanford Ct., Wal.Abb. CH20 22
Stanford Gdns., S.Ock. CZ40 60
Stanford Pl. SE17 CA42 4
Stanford Pl. SE17 CA42 67
Old Kent Rd.
Stanford Rd. N11 BU28 38
Stanford Rd. SW16 BW51 86
Stanford Rd. W8 BS41 3
Stanford Rd. W8 BS41 66
Stanford Rd., Grays DE41 71
Stanford Rivers Rd., Ong. CW19 24
Stanford St. SW1 BW42 3
Stanford St. SW1 BW42 66
Vincent Sq.
Stanford Way SW16 BW51 86
Stangate Cres., B.Wd. BN24 28
Stangate Gdns., Stan. BJ28 36
Stangate Rd., Sev. DC63 108
Stanger Rd. SE15 CB52 87
Stanham Pl., Dart. CU45 69
Stanham Rd., Dart. CU46 79
Stanhope Av. N3 BR31 46
Stanhope Av., Brom. CG54 88
Stanhope Av., Har. BG30 36
Stanhope Bldgs. SE1 BZ41 4
Stanhope Bldgs. SE1 BZ41 67
Redcross Way
Stanhope Clo. SE16 CC41 67
Middleton Dr.
Stanhope Gate W1 BV40 3
Stanhope Gate W1 BV40 56
Stanhope Gdns. N4 BY32 47
Stanhope Gdns. N6 BV32 47
Stanhope Gdns. NW7 BO28 37
Stanhope Gdns. SW7 BT42 3
Stanhope Gdns. SW7 BT42 66
Stanhope Gdns., Dag. CQ34 50
Stanhope Gdns., Ilf. CK33 49
Stanhope Gro., Beck. CD53 87
Stanhope Heath, Stai. AX46 73
Stanhope Ms. E. SW7 BT42 3
Stanhope Ms. E. SW7 BT42 66
Stanhope Gdns.
Stanhope Ms. S. SW7 BT42 3
Stanhope Ms. S. SW7 BT42 66
Gloucester Rd.
Stanhope Ms. W. SW7 BT42 3
Stanhope Ms. W. SW7 BT42 66
Stanhope Park Rd., Grnf. BG38 54
Stanhope Pl. W2 BU39 56
Stanhope Pl. W2 BU40 3
Stanhope Rd. E17 CE32 48
Stanhope Rd. N11 BV28 38
Stanhope Rd. N12 BT28 38
Stanhope Rd. N6 BW32 47
Stanhope Rd., Barn. BQ25 28
Stanhope Rd., Bexh. CQ44 69
Stanhope Rd., Cars. BV57 95
Stanhope Rd., Croy. CA55 87
Stanhope Rd., Dag. CQ34 50
Stanhope Rd., Grnf. BG39 54
Stanhope Rd., Rain. CU37 59
Stanhope Rd., Sid. CO49 79
Stanhope Rd., St.Alb. BH13 9
Stanhope Rd., Swans. DC46 81
Stanhope Row W1 BV40 3
Stanhope St. NW1 BW37 1
Stanhope St. NW1 BW37 56
Stanhope Ter. W2 BT40 3
Stanhope Ter. W2 BT40 56
Stanhope Way, Sev. CS64 107
Stanhope Way, Stai. AX46 73
Stanhopes, Oxt. CH67 115
Stanier Clo. SW5 BR42 65
Aisgill Av.
Stanlake Ms. W12 BQ40 55
Stanlake Vill.
Stanlake Rd. W12 BQ40 55
Stanlake Vill. W12 BQ40 55
Stanley Av., Bark. CN37 58
Stanley Av., Beck. CF51 87
Stanley Av., Dag. CQ33 50
Stanley Av., Grnf. BG37 54
Stanley Av., N.Mal. BP53 85
Stanley Av., Rom. CU31 50
Stanley Av., St.Alb. BF16 18
Stanley Av., Wem. BL36 55
Stanley Clo., Couls. BX62 104
Stanley Clo., Horn. CV34 51
Stanley Clo., Rom. CU31 50
Stanley Clo., Uxb. AX37 53
Stanley Clo., Wem. BL36 55
Stanley Cotts., Slou. AP40 52
Stanley Cres. W11 BR40 55
Stanley Cres., Grav. DH49 81
Stanley Croft Clo., Islw. BG44 64
Thornbury Rd.
Stanley Gardens Ms. W11 BR40 55
Kensington Park Rd.
Stanley Gardens Rd., Tedd. BH49 74
Stanley Gdns. NW2 BQ35 46
Stanley Gdns. SW17 BV50 76
Ashbourne Rd.
Stanley Gdns. W11 BR40 55
Stanley Gdns. W3 BO40 55
Stanley Gdns., B.Wd. BL23 28
Stanley Gdns., S.Croy. CB59 96
Stanley Gdns., Wall. BW57 95
Stanley Grn., Slou. AS42 62
Stanley Gro. SW8 BV44 66
Stanley Gro., Croy. BY53 86
Stanley Hill Av., Amer. AO23 25
Stanley Hill, Amer. AO23 25
Stanley Park Dr., Wem. BL36 55
Stanley Park Rd., Cars. BU57 95
Stanley Pass. NW1 BX37 2
Stanley Pass. NW1 BX37 56
Stanley Pl., Ong. CX18 24
Stanley Rd. E10 CE32 48
Stanley Rd. E12 CK35 49
Stanley Rd. E15 CF37 57
Stanley Rd. E18 CG30 40
Stanley Rd. E4 CF26 39
Stanley Rd. N., Rain. CT37 59
Stanley Rd. N10 BV29 38
Stanley Rd. N11 BW29 38
Stanley Rd. N15 BY31 47
Stanley Rd. N2 BT31 47
Stanley Rd. N9 CA26 39
Stanley Rd. NW9 BP33 46
Stanley Rd. S., Rain. CT37 59
Stanley Rd. SW14 BM45 65
Stanley Rd. SW19 BS50 76
Stanley Rd. W3 BN41 65
Stanley Rd., Ashf. AY49 73
Stanley Rd., Brom. CH52 88
Stanley Rd., Cars. BV57 95
Stanley Rd., Croy. BY54 86
Stanley Rd., Enf. CA24 30
Stanley Rd., Grav. DF47 81
Coopers Rd.
Stanley Rd., Grays DD42 71
Stanley Rd., Har. BG34 45
Stanley Rd., Horn. CV34 51
Stanley Rd., Houns. BG45 64
Stanley Rd., Ilf. CM34 49
Stanley Rd., Mitch. BV50 76
Stanley Rd., Mord. BS52 86
Stanley Rd., Nthwd. BC30 35
Stanley Rd., Orp. CN54 88
Stanley Rd., Ponders End CC25 30
Stanley Rd., Sid. CO48 79
Stanley Rd., Sthl. BE40 54
Stanley Rd., Sutt. BS57 95
Stanley Rd., Swans. DC46 81
Stanley Rd., Twick. BG48 74
Stanley Rd., Wat. BD24 27
Stanley Rd., Wem. BL36 55
Stanley Rd., Wok. AS61 100
Stanley Sq., Cars. BU58 95
Stanley St. E6 CL40 58
Stanley St. SE8 CD43 67
Stanley St., Cat. BZ64 105
Stanley Ter. N19 BX34 47
Kingsdown Rd.
Stanley Way, Orp. CO53 89
Stanley Wood, Amer. AP23 25
Stanleycroft Clo., Islw. BH44 64
Stanmer St. SW11 BU44 66
Stanmore Gdns., Rich. BL45 65
Stanmore Gdns., Sutt. BT55 86
Stanmore Hill, Stan. BJ27 36
Stanmore Pl. NW1 BV37 1
Stanmore Pl. NW1 BV37 56
Arlington Rd.
Stanmore Rd. E11 CG33 49
Stanmore Rd. N15 BY31 47
Stanmore Rd., Belv. CS42 69
Stanmore Rd., Rich. BL45 65
Stanmore Rd., Wat. BC23 26
Stanmore St. N1 BX37 2
Stanmore St. N1 BX37 56
Stanmore Ter., Beck. CE51 87
Stanmore Way, Loug. CL23 31
Stanmount Rd., St.Alb. BF16 18
Stannard Cres. E6 CL39 58
Stannard Rd. E8 CB36 57
Stannary St. SE11 BY43 4
Stannary St. SE11 BY43 66
Stannington Path, B.Wd. BM23 28
Warenford Way
Stansfeld Rd. E16 CJ39 58
Stansfield Rd. SW9 BX45 66
Stansfield Rd., Houns. BC44 63
Stansgate Rd., Dag. CR34 50
Stanstead Clo., Brom. CG53 88
Stanstead Dr., Hodd. CE11 12
Stanstead Gro. SE6 CD47 77
Stanstead Rd.
Stanstead Rd. E11 CH32 49
Stanstead Rd. SE23 CC47 77
Stanstead Rd. SE6 CC47 77
Stanstead Rd., Cat. CA65 105
Stanstead Rd., Hodd. CE11 12
Stanstead Rd., Houns. AY46 73
Stansted Clo., Horn. CV36 60
Stansted Cres., Bex. CP47 79
Stansted La., Sev. DA58 99
Stanswood Gdns. SE5 CA43 67
Sedgmoor Pl.
Stanthorpe Clo. SW16 BX49 76
Stanthorpe Rd. SW16 BX49 76
Stanton Av., Tedd. BH50 74
Stanton Clo., Chig. CN28 40
Tine Rd.
Stanton Clo., Epsom BM56 94
Stanton Clo., Orp. CP54 89
Finucane Dr.
Stanton Clo., St.Alb. BK11 9
Stanton Clo., Wor.Pk. BQ55 85
Stanton Rd. SE26 CD49 77
Stanton Way
Stanton Rd. SW13 BO44 65
Stanton Rd. SW20 BQ51 85
Stanton Rd., Croy. BZ54 87
Stanton Sq. SE26 CD49 77
Stanton Way
Stanton St. SE15 CB44 67
Stanton Way SE26 CD49 77
Stanton Way, Slou. AS42 62
Stantons, Harl. CL11 13
Stanway Ct. N1 CA37 57
Hoxton St.
Stanway Gdns. W3 BM40 55
Stanway Gdns., Edg. BN29 37
Stanway Rd., Wal.Abb. CH20 22
Ninefields
Stanway St. N1 CA37 2
Stanway St. N1 CA37 57
Stanwell Clo., Stai. AX46 73
Stanwell Gdns., Stai. AX46 73
Stanwell Moor Rd., West Dr. AW43 63
Stanwell Moor Rd., Stai. AW48 73
Stanwell New Rd., Stai. AW48 73
Stanwell Rd., Ashf. AY48 73
Stanwell Rd., Felt. AZ47 73
Stanwell Rd., Slou. AT45 62
Stanwick Rd. W14 BR42 65
Stanworth St. SE1 CA41 4
Stanworth St. SE1 CA41 67
Stanwyck Dr., Chig. CM28 40
Stanwyck Gdns., Rom. CU28 41
Stapenhill Rd., Wem. BJ34 45
Staple Clo., Bex. CS48 79
Tile Kiln La.
Staple Hill Rd., Wok. AO57 91
Staple Inn Bldgs. WC2 BY39 2
Staple Inn Bldgs. WC2 BY39 56
Holborn
Staple Inn WC2 BY39 2
Staple La., Guil. AX69 110
Staple St. SE1 BZ41 4
Staple St. SE1 BZ41 67
Staple Tye, Harl. CM12 13
Staplefield Clo. SW2 BX47 76
Staplefield Clo., Pnr. BE29 36
Stapleford Av., Ilf. CN32 49
Stapleford Clo. E4 CF27 39
Stapleford Clo. SW19 BR47 75
Beaumont Rd.
Stapleford Clo., Kings.T. BM52 85
Vincent Rd.
Stapleford Ct., Sev. CT65 107
Stapleford Gdns., Rom. CR29 41
Stapleford Rd., Rom. CR25 32
Stapleford Rd., Wem. BK36 54
Stapleford Tawney Rd., Rom. CS22 32
Stapleford Way, Bark. CO38 59
Bastable Av.
Stapleford, Welw.G.C. BT 8 5
Tempsford
Staplehurst Dr., Reig. BT72 121
Staplehurst Rd. SE13 CF46 77
Staplehurst Rd., Cars. BU57 95
Staplehurst Rd., Reig. BT72 121
Staples Clo. SE16 CD40 57
Staples Cor. NW9 BP33 46
Staples Rd., Loug. CJ24 31
Stapleton Clo., Pot.B. BU19 20
Coopers Lane Rd.
Stapleton Cres., Rain. CU36 59
Stapleton Gdns., Croy. BY56 95
Stapleton Hall Rd. N4 BX33 47
Stapleton Pl., Pot.B. BU19 20
Coopers Lane Rd.
Stapleton Rd. SW17 BV48 76
Stapleton Rd., B.Wd. BM22 28
Stapleton Rd., Bexh. CQ43 69
Stapleton Rd., Orp. CN55 88
Sevenoaks Rd.
Stapley Rd., Belv. CR42 69
Stapley Rd., St.Alb. BG13 9
Stapylton Rd., Barn. BR24 28
Star & Garter Hill, Rich. BL47 75
Star Alley EC3 CA40 4
Fenchurch St.
Star Hill Rd., Sev. CQ61 107
Star Hill, Dart. CT46 79
Star Hill, Wok. AR63 100
Star La. E16 CG38 58
Star La., Couls. BV64 104
Star La., Epp. CO18 23
Star La., Orp. CP52 89
Star La., Wok. AR63 100
College La.
Star Path, Nthlt. BF37 54
Leander Rd.
Star Rd. W14 BR43 65
Star Rd., Islw. BG44 64
Star Rd., Uxb. BA38 53
Star St. E16 CG39 58
Star St. W2 BT39 1
Star St. W2 BT39 56
Star Yd. WC2 BY39 2
Star Yd. WC2 BY39 56
Starboard Av., Green. DA46 80
Starboard Way E14 CE41 67
Tiller St.
Starch House La., Ilf. CM30 40
Starcross St. NW1 BW38 1
Starcross St. NW1 BW38 56
Starfield Rd. W12 BP41 65
Starkleigh Way SE16 CB42 67
Egan Way
Starling Clo., Buck.H. CH26 40
Starling Clo., Pnr. BD31 45
Starling La., Cuff. BX17 20
Starrock La., Couls. BU63 104
Starrock Rd., Couls. BV63 104
Startfield Rd., Slou. AQ41 62
Wellesley Rd.
Starts Clo., Orp. CL55 88
Starts Hill Av., Orp. CL56 97
Starts Hill Rd., Orp. CL56 97
Starts Rd., Orp. CL55 88
Starvecrow Clo., Ton. DB71 117
Starwood Clo., Wey. AX59 92
Starwood Ct., Slou. AR41 62
London Rd.
State Farm Av., Orp. CL56 97
Staten Gdns., Twick. BH47 74
Statham Gro. N16 BZ34 48
Statham Gro. N18 CA28 39
Station App. E., Croy. BZ55 87
Station App. E., Red. BU71 121
Station App. E7 CH35 49
Woodford Rd.
Station App. N., Sid. CO48 79
Station Rd.
Station App. N11 BV28 38
Station App. Rd. W4 BM43 65
Grove Park Rd.
Station App. Rd., Tad. BQ64 103
Station App. Rd., Til. DG45 71
Station App. S., Sid. CO48 79
Station Rd.
Station App. SE26 CC49 77
Station App. SE3 CH45 68
Station App. SW11 BU45 66
St. Johns Hill
Station App. SW6 BR45 65
Station App. W., Red. BU71 121
Station App. W3 BN41 65
Kingswood Rd.
Station App. W7 BH40 54
Station St.
Station App., Denham Golf Club AU33 43
Station App., Waltham Cross CD20 21
Station App., Mottingham SE9 CK47 78
Station App., Elmstead Woods CK50 78
Station App., Ashf. AY49 73
Station App., Bark. CM36 58
Station App., Barnehurst CS44 69
Barnehurst Rd.
Station App., Bex. CR47 79
High St.
Station App., Bexh. CQ44 69
Pickford La.
Station App., Buck.H. CJ28 40
Station App., Cheam BR57 94
Station App., Chelsfield CO56 98
Station App., Chipstead BU62 104
Station App., Chis. CL51 88
Station App., Chsnt. CD18 21
Station App., Couls. BW61 104
Station App., Crayford CT46 79
Station Rd.
Station App., Dart. CW46 80
Station App., Debden CM24 31
Station App., Denham AW33 44
Station App., Dor. BK70 119
Station App., Elm Pk., Horn. CU35 50
Station App., Eltham CK46 78
Station App., Epsom BN60 94
Station App., Ewell E. BP58 94
Station App., Ewell W. BO58 94
Station App., Ger.Cr. AS32 43
Station App., Grays DD43 71
Station App., Grnf. BJ36 54
Station App., Guil. AS71 118
Station App., Har. BH33 45
Station App., Hatch End BE29 36
Station App., Hayes (Middx.) BB41 63
Station App., Hayes (Kent) CG54 88
Station App., Hem.H. AW15 8
Station App., Hinchley Wood BH55 84
Station App., Hmptn. BF51 84
Milton Rd.
Station App., Loug. CK25 31
Station App., Lthd. BB67 110
Station App., Norbiton BM51 85
Station App., Nthwd. BB29 35
Station App., Orp. CN55 88
Station App., Pnr. BE31 45
Station App., Pot.B. BR19 19
Station App., Pur. BY59 95
Whytecliffe Rd.
Station App., Purfleet CX42 70
Station App., Rich. BM44 65
Station App., Rick. AU24 25
Station App., Ruis. BB33 44
Station App., Shep. BA53 83
Station App., Sid. CO48 79
Station App., Southgate N14 BW26 38
Station App., St.Mary Cray CO52 89
Station App., Stai. AW49 73
Station App., Sthl. BE41 64
Station App., Stoneleigh BO56 94
Station App., Sun. BC51 83
Station App., Swan. CT52 89
Station App., Upper Warl. CA62 105
Station App., Vir.W. AR52 82
Station App., Wat. BB24 26
Station App., Well. CO44 69
Station App., Wem. BJ36 54
Station App., West Dr. AY40 53
Station App., Wey. AW59 92
Station App., Wok. AS62 100
Station Av., Cat. CB65 105
Station Av., Ewell W. BO58 94
Station Av., N.Mal. BO52 85
Station Av., Rich. BM44 65
Station Par.
Station Av., Walt. BB56 92
Station Bldgs., Hayes CG54 88
Station Clo. N3 BS30 38
Station Clo., Hat. BR16 19
Station Clo., Hmptn. BF51 84
Station Clo., Pot.B. BR19 19
Station Cres. N15 BZ31 48
Station Cres. SE3 CH42 68
Station Cres., Ashf. AX49 73
Station Cres., Wem. BJ36 54
Station Dr. NW1 BW38 56
Station Est. Rd., Felt. BC47 73
Station Est., Elmers End CC52 87
Station Forecourt NW1 BW38 1
Station Garage Ms. SW16 BW50 76
Estreham Rd.
Station Gdns. W4 BN43 65
Station Gro., Wem. BL36 55
Station Hill, Hayes CH55 88
Station La., Brwd. DE32 123
Station La., Edg. BM29 37
Station La., Horn. CV34 51
Station Par. E11 CH32 49
High St.
Station Par. NW2 BQ36 55
Station Par. W3 BM39 55
Station Par., Horn. CU35 50
Station Par., Sev. CU65 107
Station Par., Uxb. AZ36 53
Station Par., Vir.W. AR52 82
Station Pass. E18 CH30 40
Maybank Rd.
Station Pass. SE15 CB44 67
Asylum Rd.
Station Path, Stai. AV49 72
Station Pl. N4 BY34 47
Station Rd. E., Oxt. CG67 115
Station Rd. E10 CF34 48
Station Rd. E12 CJ35 49
Station Rd. E15 CF36 57
Station Rd. E17 CD32 48
Station Rd. E7 CH35 49
Station Rd. N., Belv. CR41 69
Station Rd. N., Red. BW67 113
Station Rd. N11 BV28 38
Station Rd. N17 CB31 48

Station Rd. N18 CA28 39
Silver St.
Station Rd. N19 BW34 47
Station Rd. N21 BY26 38
Station Rd. N22 BX30 38
Station Rd. N3 BS30 38
Station Rd. NW10 BO37 55
Station Rd. NW4 BP32 46
Station Rd. NW7 BO28 37
Station Rd. S., Red. BW67 113
Station Rd. SE20 CC50 77
Station Rd. SW13 BO44 65
Station Rd. W., Oxt. CG68 115
Station Rd. W5 BL39 55
Station Rd., Bricket Wood BF19 18
Station Rd., Addlestone AX56 92
Station Rd., Amer. AO23 25
Station Rd., Ash. BL62 103
Station Rd., Ashf. AY49 73
Station App.
Station Rd., B.Wd. BM24 28
Station Rd., Barkingside CM31 49
Station Rd., Barn. BS25 29
Station Rd., Belmont BS58 95
Station Rd., Belv. CR41 69
Station Rd., Berk. AR12 7
Station Rd., Bet. BO69 120
Station Rd., Bexh. CQ45 69
Station Rd., Brom. CH51 88
Station Rd., Brox. CD13 12
Station Rd., Cars. BU56 95
Station Rd., Cat. CD64 105
Station Rd., Cher. AV54 82
Station Rd., Chess. BL56 94
Station Rd., Chig. CL27 40
Station Rd., Chingford E4 CF26 39
Station Rd., Claygate BH56 93
Station Rd., Cob. BE62 102
Station Rd., Colney Hth. BM13 10
Station Rd., Crayford CT47 79
Station Rd., Cuff. BX18 20
Station Rd., Dag. CP33 50
Station Rd., Dor. BJ71 119
Station Rd., Dunton Grn. CT63 107
Station Rd., Edg. BM29 37
Station Rd., Egh. AS49 72
Station Rd., Epp. CO19 23
Station Rd., Esher BG55 84
Station Rd., Eyns. CV55 90
Station Rd., Ger.Cr. AS32 43
Station Rd., Gidea Pk., Rom. CU31 50
Station Rd., Green. DA46 80
Station Rd., Guil. AS73 118
Station Rd., Halstead CQ59 98
Station Rd., Hampton Wick BK51 84
Station Rd., Hanwell W7 BH40 54
Station Rd., Har. BH31 45
Station Rd., Harl. CP 8 6
Station Rd., Harold Wood CW30 42
Station Rd., Hat. BQ15 10
Station Rd., Hayes BB42 63
Station Rd., Hem.H. AW14 8
Station Rd., Hmptn. BF51 84
Station Rd., Houns. BF45 64
Station Rd., Ilf. CL34 49
Station Rd., Ken. BZ60 96
Station Rd., Kings L. AZ18 17
Station Rd., Kings.T. BM51 85
Station Rd., Knockholt CQ58 98
Station Rd., Langley AT41 62
Station Rd., Long. DC52 90
Station Rd., Loug. CK24 31
Station Rd., Lthd. BJ64 102
Station Rd., Merstham BW67 113
Station Rd., Motspur Pk. BP53 85
Station Rd., N.Harrow BF32 45
Station Rd., N.Weald CR17 23
Station Rd., Northfleet DD46 81
Station Rd., Norwood Junc. SE25 CA52 87
Station Rd., Orp. CN55 88
Station Rd., Pnr. BE31 45
Station Rd., Poyle AV44 62
Station Rd., Rad. BJ21 27
Station Rd., Red. BU70 121
Station Rd., Rick. AX26 35
Station Rd., Rom. CU31 50
Station Rd., S.Dnth. CX51 90
Station Rd., S.Ock. DB38 60
Station Rd., Saw. CQ 5 6
Station Rd., Shep. BA53 83
Station Rd., Shoreham CU59 98
Station Rd., Shortlands CG51 88
Station Rd., Sid. CO49 79
Station Rd., Southfleet DD49 81
Station Rd., St.Mary Cray CP52 89
Station Rd., Sun. BC50 73
Station Rd., Sutt. BS58 95
Station Rd., Swan. CT52 89
Station Rd., T.Ditt. BH54 84
Station Rd., Tedd. BJ50 74
Station Rd., Til. DJ43 71
Station Rd., Twick. BH47 74
Station Rd., Upmin. CY34 51
Station Rd., Upper Wall. CA62 105
Station Rd., Uxb. AX38 53
Station Rd., W.Croy. BZ54 87
Station Rd., W.Wick. CF54 87
Station Rd., Wal.Cr. CE20 21
Station Rd., Wat. BC23 26
Station Rd., Welw.G.C. BR 5 5
Station Rd., West Byfleet AW59 92
Station Rd., West Dr. AY41 63
Station Rd., West. CO65 107
Station Rd., Whyt. CA62 105
Station Rd., Winchmore Hill N21 BY26 38
Station Rd., Wok. AP59 91
Station Rd., Wraysbury AS46 72
Station Ri. SE27 BY48 76
Norwood Rd.
Station Row, Guil. AS73 118
Station Sq., St. Mary Cray CO52 89
Station Sq., Petts Wood CM53 88
Station St. E15 CF36 57
Station St. E16 CL40 58
Station Ter. NW10 BQ37 55
Station Ter. SE5 BZ44 67
Station Rd.
Station Vill. NW7 BQ29 37
Bittacy Hill
Station Vw., Grnf. BG37 54
Station Way, Roding Vall. CJ28 40
Station Way, Cheam BR57 94
Station Way, Claygate BH57 93
Station Way, St.Alb. BH13 9
Station Way, Welw.G.C. BQ 7 5
Station Yd., Twick. BJ47 74
Staunton Rd., Kings.T. BL50 75
Staunton Rd., Slou. AO39 52
Staunton St. SE8 CD43 67
Stave Yard Rd. SE16 CD40 57
Staveley Clo. E9 CC35 48
Churchill Wk.
Staveley Clo. N7 BX35 47
Penn Rd.
Staveley Clo. SE15 CC44 67
Staveley Gdns. W4 BN44 65
Staveley Rd. W4 BN43 65
Staveley Rd., Ashf. BA50 73
Staveley Way, Wok. AP62 100
Staverton Rd. NW2 BQ36 55
Staverton Rd., Horn. CV32 51
Stavordale Rd. N5 BY35 47
Stavordale Rd., Cars. BT54 86
Stayne End, Vir.W. AQ52 82
Stayners Rd. E1 CC38 57
Stayton Rd., Sutt. BS55 86
Stead St. SE17 BZ42 4
Stead St. SE17 BZ42 67
Steadfast Rd., Kings.T. BK51 84
Steam Farm La., Felt. BB45 63
Stean St. E8 CA37 2
Stean St. E8 CA37 57
Stebbing Way, Bark. CO37 59
Stebondale St. E14 CF42 67
Stedman Clo., Bex. CT48 79
Stedman Clo., Uxb. AZ34 44
Steedman St. SE17 BZ42 4
Steedman St. SE17 BZ42 67
Steeds Rd. N10 BU30 38
Steeds Way, Loug. CK24 31
Steele Rd. E11 CG35 49
Steele Rd. N17 CA31 48
Steele Rd. NW10 BN37 55
Steele Rd. W4 BN41 65
Steele Rd., Islw. BJ45 64
Steeles Ms. NW3 BU36 56
Steeles Rd. NW3 BU36 56
Steels La. E1 CC39 57
Devonport St.
Steels La., Lthd. BF60 93
Steen Way SE22 CA46 77
Dulwich Gro.
Steep Clo., Orp. CN57 97
Steep Hill SW16 BW48 76
Steep Hill, Croy. CA56 96
Steep Hill, Wok. AO57 91
Steeplands, Bush. BF26 36
Steeple Clo. SW19 BR49 75
Steeple Clo. SW6 BR45 65
Steeple Heights Dr., West. CJ62 106
Steeple Way, Brwd. DA22 33
Steeple Wk. N1 BZ37 57
Basire St.
Steeplestone Clo. N18 BZ28 39
Steerforth St. SW18 BS48 76
Steers Mead, Mitch. BU51 86
Steers Way SE16 CD41 67
Stella Rd. SW17 BU50 76
Stelling Rd., Erith CS43 69
Stellman Clo. E5 CB34 48
Stembridge Rd. SE10 CB51 87
Stents La., Cob. BE63 102
Stepgates Mead La., Cher. AW54 83
Stephan Clo. E8 CB37 2
Stephan Clo. E8 CB37 57
Stephen Av., Rain. CU36 59
Stephen Clo., Egh. AU50 72
Stephen Clo., Orp. CN55 88
Stephen Rd., Bexh. CS45 69
Stephen St. W1 BW39 1
Stephen St. W1 BW39 56
Stephendale Rd. SW6 BS45 66
Stephens Clo., Pnr. BD32 45
Stephens Clo., Rom. CV28 42
Stephens Ms. W1 BW39 56
Gresse St.
Stephens Rd. E15 CG37 58
Stephenson Av., Til. DG44 71
Stephenson Dr., Wind. AN43 61
Clewer Court Rd.
Stephenson Rd. W7 BH39 54
Stephenson Rd., Houns. BF47 74
Stephenson St. E16 CG38 58
Stephenson St. NW10 BO38 55
Stephenson Way NW1 BW38 1
Stephenson Way NW1 BW38 56
Stepney Causeway E1 CC39 57
Stepney Green Dws. E1 CC39 57
Stepney Grn. E1 CC39 57
Stepney High St. E1 CC39 57
Stepney Way E1 CB39 57
Sterling Av., Edg. BL28 37
Sterling Av., Wal.Cr. CC20 21
Sterling Rd., Enf. BZ22 30
Sterling St. SW7 BU41 3
Sterling St. SW7 BU41 66
Montpelier Pl.
Sterling Way N18 BZ28 39
Sterndale Rd. W14 BQ41 65
Sterndale Rd., Dart. CW47 80
Sterne St. W12 BQ41 65
Sternhall La. SE15 CB44 67
Sternhold Av. SW2 BW48 76
Sterry Cres., Dag. CR35 50
Sterry Dr., Epsom BO56 94
Sterry Dr., T.Ditt. BH53 84
Sterry Gdns., Dag. CR36 59
Sterry Rd., Bark. CN37 58
Sterry Rd., Dag. CR35 50
Sterry St. SE1 BZ41 4
Sterry St. SE1 BZ41 67
Steucers La. SE23 CD47 77
St. Germans Rd.
Steve Biko La. SE6 CE49 77
Stevedale Rd., Well. CP44 69
Stevenage Cres., B.Wd. BL23 28
Stevenage Rd. E6 CL36 58
Stevenage Rd. SW6 BQ43 65
Stevenage Ri., Hem.H. AY11 8
Stevens Av. E9 CC36 57
Stevens Clo., Beck. CE50 77
Stumps Hill La.
Stevens Clo., Bex. CS49 79
Stevens Clo., Epsom BO60 94
High St.
Stevens Clo., Hmptn. BE49 74
Stevens Cott. NW2 BP36 55
High Rd.
Stevens Grn., Bush. BG26 36
Stevens La., Esher BJ57 93
Stevens Rd., Dag. CO34 50
Stevens St. SE1 CA41 4
Stevens St. SE1 CA41 67
Riley Rd.
Stevens Way, Chig. CN28 40
Stevenson Clo., Erith CU43 69
Stevenson Rd., Slou. AO34 43
Steventon Rd. W12 BO40 55
Stew La. EC4 BZ40 4
High Timber St.
Steward St. E1 CA39 2
Steward St. E1 CA39 57
Stewards Clo., Epp. CO20 23
Stewards Green Rd., Epp. CO20 23
Stewards Wk., Rom. CT32 50
South St.
Stewart Av., Shep. AZ52 83
Stewart Av., Slou. AP39 52
Stewart Clo. NW9 BN32 46
Stewart Clo., Chis. CL49 78
Stewart Clo., Chsnt. CD18 21
Stewart Clo., Hmptn. BE50 74
Stewart Clo., Maid. AH44 61
Stewart Clo., Wat. BB19 17
Stewart Clo., Wok. AP62 100
Nethercote Av.
Stewart Rd. E15 CF35 48
Stewart St. E14 CF41 67
Stewart, Tad. BQ64 103
Stewarts Av., Upmin. CX34 51
Stewarts Gro. SW3 BT42 3
Stewarts La. SW8 BV44 66
Stewarts Rd. SW8 BW44 66
Stewarts Wk. SW3 BU42 66
Stewartsby Clo. N18 BZ28 39
Steyne Rd. W3 BM40 55
Steyning Clo., Ken. BY61 104
Steyning Gro. SE9 CK49 78
Steyning Way, Houns. BD45 64
Steynings Way N12 BS28 38
Steynton Av., Bex. CP48 79
Stickland Rd., Belv. CR42 69
Stickleton Clo., Grnf. BF38 54
Stifford Clays Rd., Grays DC40 71
Stifford Est. E1 CC39 57
Stifford Hill, S.Ock. DB40 60
Stifford Rd., S.Ock. CZ40 60
Stile Hall Gdns. W4 BM42 65
Stile Path, Sun. BC52 83
Stile Rd., Slou. AR41 62
Stilecroft Gdns., Wem. BJ34 45
Stilecroft, Harl. CO12 14
Stiles Clo., Brom. CK53 88
Stillingfleet Rd. SW13 BP43 65
Stillington St. SW1 BW42 3
Stillington St. SW1 BW42 66
Stillness Rd. SE23 CD46 77
Stilton Cres. NW10 BN36 55
Stilton Path, B.Wd. BM22 28
Stapleton Rd.
Stipularis Dr., Hayes BD38 54
Stirling Clo., Bans. BR62 103
Stirling Clo., Rain. CU38 59
Stirling Clo., Uxb. AX38 53
Stirling Clo., Wind. AL44 61
Stirling Dr., Orp. CO56 98
Stirling Rd. E13 CH37 58
Stirling Rd. E17 CD31 48
Stirling Rd. N17 CB30 39
Stirling Rd. N22 BY30 38
Stirling Rd. Path E17 CD31 48
Stirling Rd. SW9 BX44 66
Stirling Rd. W3 BM41 65
Stirling Rd., Har. BH31 45
Stirling Rd., Hayes BC40 53
Stirling Rd., Houns. AY46 73
Southampton Rd.
Stirling Rd., Twick. BF47 74
Stirling St. SW7 BU41 66
Stirling Way, B.Wd. BN25 28
Stirling Way, Croy. BX54 86
Stirling Way, Welw.G.C. BU 8 5
Stirling Wk., Surb. BM53 85
Stites Hill Rd., Cat. BY63 104
Stiven Cres., Har. BE34 45
Stoats Nest Rd., Couls. BX60 95
Stoats Nest Village, Couls. BX61 104
Stock Hill, West. CJ61 106
Stock La., Dart. CV49 80
Stock Orchard Cres. N7 BX35 47
Stock Orchard St. N7 BX35 47
Stock St. E13 CH37 58
Stock St. WC2 BX39 2
Stockbreach Clo., Hat. BP12 10
Stockbreach Rd., Hat. BP12 10
Stockbury Rd., Croy. CC53 87
Stockdale Rd., Dag. CQ34 50
Stockdales Rd., Eton AM42 61
Stockdove Way, Grnf. BH38 54
Stockers Farm Rd., Rick. AX27 35
Stockers La., Wok. AT63 100
Stockfield Av., Hodd. CE11 12
Stockfield Rd. SW16 BX48 76
Stockfield Rd., Esher BH56 93
Stockhams Clo., S.Croy. BZ59 96
Stockholm Rd. SE16 CC42 67
Stockhurst Clo. SW15 BQ45 65
Ashlone Rd.
Stocking La., Bayford BY12 11
Stocking La., Hert. BW11 11
Stockingswater La., Enf. CD24 30
Stockland Rd., Rom. CS32 50
Stockleigh Hall NW8 BU37 1
Stockley Clo., West Dr. AZ41 63
Stockley Farm Rd., West Dr. AZ41 63
Stockley Rd., West Dr. AZ42 63
Stockport Rd. SW16 BW51 86
Stockport Rd., Rick. AU26 34
Stocks La., Brwd. CZ22 33
Stocks Pl. E14 CD40 57
Grenade St.
Stocksfield Rd. E17 CF31 48
Stocksfield, Brwd. CZ22 33
Stockton Gdns. N17 BZ29 39
Stockton Gdns. NW7 BN27 37
Stockton Rd. N17 BZ29 39
Stockton Rd. N18 CB29 39
Stockton Rd., Reig. BS72 121
Stockwell Av. SW9 BX45 66
Stockwell Clo., Brom. CH51 88
Kentish Way
Stockwell Clo., Chsnt. CB17 21
Stockwell Gdns. SW9 BX44 66
Stockwell Grn. SW9 BX44 66
Stockwell La. SW9 BX44 66
Stockwell La., Chsnt. CB17 21
Stockwell Pk. Rd. SW9 BX44 66
Stockwell Pk. SW9 BX45 66
Stockwell Pk. Cres. SW9 BX44 66
Stockwell Rd. SW9 BX44 66
Stockwell St. SE10 CF43 67
Stockwood St. SW11 BT45 66
Plough Rd.
Stocton Clo., Guil. AR70 118
Stocton Rd., Guil. AR70 118
Stodart Rd. SE20 CC51 87
Stofield Gdns. SE9 CJ48 78
Stoford Clo. SW19 BR47 75
Southmead Rd.
Stoke Av., Ilf. CO29 41
Stoke Clo., Cob. BE61 102
Stoke Common Rd., Slou. AQ35 43
Stoke Court Dr., Slou. AP37 52
Stoke Fields, Guil. AR71 118
Stoke Gdns., Slou. AP40 52
Stoke Grn., Slou. AQ38 52
Stoke Gro., Guil. AR71 118
Stoke Fields
Stoke Newington Common N16 CA34 48
Stoke Newington Church St. N16 BZ34 48
Stoke Newington High St. N16 CA34 48
Stoke Newington Rd. N16 CA35 48
Stoke Pl. NW10 BO38 55
Stoke Poges La., Slou. AP40 52
Stoke Rd., Cob. BD61 102
Stoke Rd., Guil. AR70 118
Stoke Rd., Kings.T. BN50 75
Stoke Rd., Rain. CV37 60
Stoke Rd., Slou. AP40 52
Stoke Rd., Walt. BD55 84
Stoke St., Cob. BD61 102
Stoke Wood La., Slou. AP35 43
Stokenchurch St. SW6 BS44 66
Stokes Rd. E6 CK38 58
Stokes Rd., Croy. CC53 87
Stokesay, Slou. AQ40 52
Stokesby Rd., Chess. BL57 94
Stokesheath Rd., Lthd. BG59 93
Stokesley St. W12 BO39 55
Stompits Rd., Maid. AG43 61
Stompond La., Walt. BC55 83
Stoms Path SE6 CE49 77
Stonard Rd. N13 BY27 38
Stonard Rd., Dag. CO35 50
Stonards Hill, Epp. CO18 23
Stonards Hill, Loug. CK25 31
Stondon Pk. SE23 CD46 77
Stondon Rd., Ong. CX18 24
Stondon Wk. E6 CJ37 58
Abbots Rd.
Stone Bldgs. WC2 BX39 2
Stone Bldgs. WC2 BX39 56
Stone Clo., Dag. CQ34 50
Stone Clo., West Dr. AY40 53
Stone Cres., Felt. BB47 73
Westmacott Dr.
Stone Cross Rd., Swan. CS53 89
Stone Cross, Harl. CM10 6
Stone Hall Rd. N21 BX26 38
Stone House Ct. EC3 CA39 57
Houndsditch
Stone Park Av., Beck. CE52 87
Stone Pl. Rd., Green. CZ46 80
Stone Pl., Wor.Pk. BP55 85
Stone Rd., Brom. CG53 88
Stone St., Croy. BY56 95
Stone St., Grav. DG47 81
Stone St., Sev. CY65 108
Stone Street Rd., Sev. CZ66 117
Stone Yard La. E14 CE40 57
Stonebank, Welw.G.C. BQ 8 5
Stonebanks, Walt. BC54 83
Stonebridge Est. E8 CA37 2
Stonebridge Est. E8 CA37 57
Stonebridge Pk. NW10 BN36 55
Stonebridge Rd. N15 CA32 48
Stonebridge Rd., Grav. DD46 81
Stonebridge Way, Wem. BM36 55
Stonechat Sq. E6 CK39 58
Peridot St.
Stonecot Clo., Sutt. BR54 85
Stonecot Hill, Sutt. BR54 85
Stonecourt Way, Green. CZ46 80
Stonecroft Av., Iver AV39 52
Stonecroft Rd., Erith CS43 69
Stonecroft Way, Croy. BX54 86
Stonecrop Rd., Guil. AU69 118
Stonecross Clo., St.Alb. BH12 9
Stonecross Rd., Hat. BP12 10
Stonecross, St.Alb. BH13 9
Stonecutter St. EC4 BY39 2
Stonecutter St. EC4 BY39 56
Shoe La.
Stonefield Clo., Bexh. CR45 69
Stonefield Clo., Ruis. BE35 45
Stonefield St. N1 BY37 2
Stonefield St. N1 BY37 56
Stonefield Way SE7 CJ43 68
Green Bay Rd.
Stonefield Way, Ruis. BE35 45
Stonegate Clo., Orp. CP52 89
Main Rd.
Stonegrove Ct., Edg. BL28 37
Stonegrove Gdns., Edg. BL28 37
Stonegrove, Edg. BL28 37
Stonehall Av., Ilf. CK32 49
Stoneham Rd. E5 CB34 48
Stoneham Rd. N11 BW28 38
Stonehams Hill, Dart. CT45 69
Stonehill Clo. SW14 BN46 75
Stonehill Clo., Lthd. BF66 111
The Garstons
Stonehill Cres., Wok. AS57 91
Stonehill Green Rd., Dart. CS50 79
Stonehill Rd. SW14 BN46 75
Stonehill Rd. W4 BM42 65
Wellesley Rd.
Stonehill Rd., Wok. AR58 91
Stonehills Ct. SE21 CA48 77
Stonehills, Welw.G.C. BQ 7 5
Stonehorse Rd., Enf. CC25 30
Stonehouse Gdns., Cat. CA66 114
Stonehouse La., Grays CZ42 70
Stonehouse La., Sev. CP58 98
Stonehouse Rd., Sev. CP58 98
Stonehouse St. SW4 BW45 66
Stoneings La., Sev. CN62 106
Stonelea Rd., Hem.H. AY14 8
Stoneleigh Av., Enf. CB22 30
Stoneleigh Av., Wor.Pk. BP55 85
Stoneleigh Clo., Wal.Cr. CC20 21
Stoneleigh Cres., Epsom BQ56 94
Stoneleigh Ct., Ilf. CK31 49
Stoneleigh Dr., Hodd. CE10 12
Stoneleigh Pk. Av., Croy. CC53 87
Stoneleigh Pk. Rd., Epsom BO57 94
Stoneleigh Pk., Wey. BA57 92
Stoneleigh Pl. W11 BQ40 55
Stoneleigh Rd. N17 CA31 48
Stoneleigh Rd., Cars. BU54 86
Stoneleigh Rd., Ilf. CK31 49
Stoneleigh Rd., Oxt. CK68 115
Stoneleigh St. W11 BQ40 55
Stoneleigh Ter. N19 BV34 47
Chester Rd.
Stoneleigh, Saw. CQ 5 6
Stonells Rd. SW11 BU46 76
Chatham Rd.
Stonemead, Welw.G.C. BQ 5 5
Stoneness Rd., Grays DA43 70
Stonenest St. N4 BX33 47
Evershot Rd.
Stones Alley, Wat. BC24 26
Stones End St. SE1 BZ41 4
Stones End St. SE1 BZ41 67
Stones La., Dor. BG72 119
Stones Rd., Epsom BO59 94
Stoneswood Rd., Oxt. CH68 115
Stonewood Rd., Erith CT42 69
Stonewood, Dart. DB48 80
Stoney Brook, Guil. AP70 118
Stoney Ct., Welw.G.C. BS 7 5
Stoney Gro., Chesh. AO18 16
Stoney La. EC3 CA39 2
Stoney La. EC3 CA39 57
Stoney La. SE19 CA50 77
Stoney La., Hem.H. AT17 16
Stoney La., Kings L. AV18 16
Stoney Meade, Slou. AN40 61
Stoney St. SE1 BZ40 4
Stoney St. SE1 BZ40 57
Stoneycroft Clo. SE12 CG47 78
Stoneycroft Rd., Wdf.Grn. CK29 40
Stoneycroft, Hem.H. AW13 8
Long Chaulden
Stoneydown Av. E17 CC31 48
Stoneydown E17 CD31 48
Stoneyfield Rd., Couls. BX62 104
Stoneyfields Gdns., Edg. BN28 37
Stoneyfields La., Edg. BN28 37
Stoneylands Ct., Egh. AS49 72
Stoneylands Rd., Egh. AS49 72
Stonny Cft., Ash. BL62 103
Stonor Rd. W14 BR42 65
Stony Hill, Esher BE57 93
Stony La., Amer. AS22 25
Stony La., Ong. CU15 14
Stony Path, Loug. CK23 31
Stonyshotts, Wal.Abb. CG20 22
Stopford Rd. E13 CH37 58
Stopford Rd. SE17 BY42 4
Manor Pl.
Store Gdns., Brwd. DE25 122
Store Rd. E16 CL41 68
Store St. E15 CF35 48
Store St. WC1 BW39 1
Store St. WC1 BW39 56
Storers Quay E14 CF42 67

Storey Rd. E17 CD31 48
Storey Rd. N6 BU32 47
Storey St. E16 CL40 58
Storey St., Hem.H. AX15 8
Storeys Gate SW1 BW41 3
Storeys Gate SW1 BW41 66
Stories Ms. SE5 CA44 67
Stories Rd. SE5 CA45 67
Stork Rd. E7 CG36 58
Storks Rd. SE16 CB41 67
Storksmead Rd., Edg. BO29 37
Stormont Rd. N6 BU33 47
Stormont Rd. SW11 BV45 66
Stormont Way, Chess. BK56 93
Stormount Dr., Hayes BA41 63
Stornaway Strand, Grav. DJ49 81
Stornoway, Hem.H. AZ14 8
Northend
Storr Gdns., Brwd. DE25 122
Storrington Rd., Croy. CA54 87
Stort Mill, Harl. CO8 6
Stortford Rd., Hodd. CE11 12
Story St. N1 BX36 2
Stothard Pl. EC2 CA39 2
Stothard St. E1 CC38 57
Colebert Av.
Stoughton Av., Sutt. BQ56 94
Stoughton Clo. SW15 BP47 75
Bessborough Rd.
Stoughton Rd., Guil. AQ69 118
Stour Av., Sthl. BF41 64
Stour Clo., Kes. CJ56 97
Stour Clo., Slou. AN41 61
Stour Rd. E3 CE36 57
Stour Rd., Dart. CU45 69
Stour Rd., Grays DG42 71
Stour Way, Upmin. CZ32 51
Stourcliffe St. W1 BU39 1
Stourcliffe St. W1 BU39 56
Stourhead Clo. SW19 BQ47 75
Stourhead Gdns. SW20 BP51 85
Stourton Av., Felt. BE49 74
Stovell Rd., Wind. AN43 61
Stow Cres. E17 CD29 39
Stow Ct., Dart. CY47 80
Nursery Clo.
Stow, The, Harl. CN10 6
Stowage, The SE8 CE43 67
Stowe Cres., Ruis. BA32 44
Stowe Gdns. N9 CA26 39
Stowe Pl. N15 CA31 48
Stowe Rd. W12 BP41 65
Stowe Rd., Orp. CO56 98
Stowell Av., Croy. CF58 96
Stowting Rd., Orp. CN56 97
Stox Mead, Har. BG30 36
Stracey Rd. E7 CH35 49
Stracey Rd. NW10 BN37 55
Strachan Pl. SW19 BQ50 75
Stradbroke Dr., Chig. CL29 40
Stradbroke Gro., Buck.H. CJ26 40
Stradbroke Gro., Ilf. CK31 49
Stradbroke Rd. N5 BZ35 48
Balfour Rd.
Stradella Rd. SE24 BZ46 77
Strafford Av., Ilf. CL30 40
Strafford Clo., Pot.B. BS19 20
Strafford Gate
Strafford Gate, Pot.B. BS19 20
Strafford Rd. W3 BN41 65
Bollo Bridge Rd.
Strafford Rd., Barn. BR24 28
Strafford Rd., Houns. BE45 64
Strafford Rd., Twick. BJ47 74
Strafford St. E14 CE41 67
Strahan Rd. E3 CD38 57
Straight Rd., Rom. CU28 41
Straight Rd., Wind. AQ46 72
Straight, The, Sthl. BE41 64
Strait Rd. E16 CK40 58
Straits, The, Wal.Abb. CE19 21
Straitsmouth SE10 CF43 67
Strakers Rd. SE22 CB45 67
Strand Clo., Epsom BN63 103
Strand La. WC2 BX40 4
Strand La. WC2 BX40 56
Temple Pl.
Strand on the Green W4 BM43 65
Strand Pl. N18 CA28 39
Strand School App. W4 BM43 65
Thames Rd.
Strand WC2 BX40 4
Strand WC2 BX40 56
Strandfield Clo. SE18 CN42 68
Strangeways, Wat. BB21 26
Strangways Ter. W14 BR41 65
Melbury Rd.
Stranraer Rd., Houns. AY46 73
Southampton Rd.
Stranraer Way N1 BX36 56
Strasburg Rd. SW11 BV44 66
Stratfield Dr., Brox. CD13 12
Stratfield Park Clo. N21 BY26 38
Stratfield Rd., B.Wd. BL24 28
Stratfield Rd., Slou. AQ41 62
Stratford Av. W8 BS41 66
Stratford Av., Uxb. AY37 53
Stratford Clo., Bark. CO36 59
Stratford Clo., Dag. CS36 59
Stratford Ct., N.Mal. BN52 85
Kingston Rd.
Stratford Gro. SW15 BQ45 65
Stratford Pl. W1 BV39 1
Stratford Pl. W1 BV39 56
Stratford Rd. E13 CG37 58
Stratford Rd. W3 BN41 65
Stratford Rd. W8 BS41 66
Stratford Rd., Hayes BC38 53
Stratford Rd., Sthl. BE42 64
Stratford Rd., Th.Hth. BY52 86
Stratford Rd., Wat. BC23 26
Stratford Vill. NW1 BW36 56
Stratford Way, Hem.H. AW15 8
Stratford Way, St.Alb. BE18 18
Stratford Way, Wat. BB23 26
Strath Ter. SW11 BU45 66
Strathan Clo. SW18 BR46 75
Strathaven Rd. SE12 CH46 78
Strathblaine Rd. SW11 BT45 66
Strathbrook Rd. SW16 BX50 76
Strathcona Av., Lthd. BE67 111
Strathcona Rd., Wem. BK34 45
Strathdale SW16 BX49 76
Strathdon Dr. SW17 BT48 76
Strathearn Av., Hayes BB43 63
Strathearn Av., Twick. BF47 74
Strathearn Pl. W2 BU40 3
Strathearn Pl. W2 BU40 56
Strathearn Rd. SW19 BS49 76
Strathearn Rd., Sutt. BS56 95
Stratheden Rd. SE3 CH44 68
Strathfield Gdns., Bark. CM36 58
Strathleven Rd. SW2 BX45 66
Strathmore Clo., Cat. CA64 105
Strathmore Gdns. N3 BS30 38
Hervey Clo.
Strathmore Gdns. W8 BS40 56
Strathmore Gdns., Edg. BM30 37
Strathmore Gdns., Horn. CT33 50
Strathmore Rd. SW19 BS48 76
Strathmore Rd., Croy. BZ54 87
Strathmore Rd., Tedd. BH49 74
Strathnairn St. SE1 CB42 4
Strathnairn St. SE1 CB42 67
Strathray Gdns. NW3 BU36 56
Strathville Rd. SW18 BS48 76
Strathyre Av. SW16 BX52 86
Stratton Av., Enf. BZ22 30
Stratton Av., Wall. BW58 95
Stratton Chase Dr., Ch.St.G. AQ26 34
Stratton Clo. SW19 BS51 86
Stratton Clo., Bexh. CQ45 69
Stratton Clo., Edg. BL29 37
Stratton Clo., Houns. BF44 64
Stratton Clo., Walt. BD54 84
Stratton Ct., Guil. AQ69 118
Worplesdon Rd.
Stratton Dr., Bark. CN35 49
Stratton Gdns., Sthl. BE39 54
Stratton Rd. SW19 BS51 86
Stratton Rd., Bexh. CQ45 69
Stratton Rd., Rom. CX28 42
Stratton Rd., Sun. BB51 83
Stratton St. W1 BV40 3
Stratton St. W1 BV40 56
Stratton Wk., Rom. CX28 42
Strattondale St. E14 CF41 67
Strauss Rd. W4 BN41 65
Straw Mead, Hat. BP11 10
Strawberry Field, Hat. BP14 10
Strawberry Fields, Swan. CT51 89
Strawberry Hill Clo., Twick. BH48 74
Strawberry Hill Rd., Twick. BH48 74
Strawberry La., Cars. BU55 86
Strawberry Vale N2 BT30 38
Strawberry Vale, Twick. BJ48 74
Strawfields, Welw.G.C. BS7 5
Strayfield Rd., Enf. BY21 29
Streakes Field Rd. NW2 BP33 46
Stream La., Edg. BM28 37
Streamdale SE2 CO43 69
Streamside Clo., Brom. CH52 88
Sandford Rd.
Streamway, Belv. CQ43 69
Streatfeild Av. E6 CK37 58
Streatfeild Rd., Har. BK31 45
Streatfield St. E14 CD39 57
Streatham Clo. SW16 BX48 76
Leigham Court Rd.
Streatham Common N. SW16 BX49 76
Streatham Common S. SW16 BX50 76
Streatham Ct. SW16 BX48 76
Streatham High Rd. SW16 BX49 76
Streatham Hill Est. SW16 BX48 76
Streatham Hill SW2 BX48 76
Streatham Pl. SW2 BX47 76
Streatham Rd. SW16 BU51 86
Streatham Rd., Mitch. BU51 86
Streatham St. WC1 BX39 2
Streatham St. WC1 BX39 56
Streatham Vale SW16 BW51 86
Streathbourne Rd. SW17 BV48 76
Streatley Pl. NW3 BT35 47
Streatley Rd. NW6 BR36 55
Street, The, Ash. BL62 103
Street, The, Bet. BP70 120
Street, The, Bish. CS7 6
Street, The, Dart. CY52 90
Street, The, Effingham BD67 111
Street, The, Guil. AR73 118
Street, The, Ightham DB64 108
Street, The, Kings L. AW19 17
Street, The, Lthd. BG64 102
Street, The, New A.G. DB56 99
Street, The, Ong. CY17 24
Street, The, W.Clandon AW69 110
Street, The, W.Horsley AZ67 110
Streeters Pit Rd., Wall. BW55 86
Streetfield Ms. SE3 CH45 68
Streimer Rd. E15 CF37 57
Strelley Way W3 BO40 55
Stretton Rd., Croy. CA54 87
Stretton Rd., Rich. BK48 74
Stretton Way, B.Wd. BL22 28
Strickland Av., Dart. CW45 70
Strickland Av., Belv. CR42 69
Picardy Rd.
Strickland Row SW18 BT47 76
Strickland St. SE8 CE44 67
Strickland Way, Orp. CM56 97
Stride Rd. E13 CG37 58
Stringer Av., Guil. AR67 109
Stringhams Copse, Wok. AV65 100
Tuckey Gro.
Strode Clo. N10 BV29 38
Strode Rd. E7 CH35 49
Strode Rd. N17 CA30 39
Strode Rd. NW10 BP36 55
Strode Rd. SW6 BR43 65
Strode St., Egh. AT49 72
Strodes Cres., Stai. AX49 73
Stroma Clo., Hem.H. BA14 8
Strone Rd. E12 CJ36 58
Strone Rd. E7 CJ36 58
Strone Way, Hayes BE38 54
Strongbow Cres. SE9 CK46 78
Strongbow Rd. SE9 CK46 78
Strongbridge Clo., Har. BF33 45
Stronsa Rd. W12 BO41 65
Stronsay Clo., Hem.H. AZ14 8
Strood Av., Rom. CS33 50
Stroud Clo., Wind. AL45 61
Stroud Cres. SW15 BP48 75
Stroud Farm Rd., Maid. AG43 61
Stroud Field, Nthlt. BE36 54
Stroud Gate, Har. BF35 45
Stroud Green Gdns., Croy. CC54 87
Stroud Green Rd. N4 BX33 47
Stroud Green Way, Croy. CB54 87
Stroud Rd. SE25 CB53 87
Stroud Rd. SW19 BS48 76
Stroud Way, Ashf. AZ50 73
Stroude Rd., Egh. AT50 72
Stroude Rd., Vir.W. AS52 82
Stroudes Clo., Wor.Pk. BO54 85
Stroudley Wk. E3 CE38 57
Devons Rd.
Stroudwater Pk., Wey. AZ57 92
Stroughton Clo. SE11 BX42 4
Strouts Pl. E2 CA38 2
Strouts Pl. E2 CA38 57
Pelter St.
Strutton Av., Grav. DF48 81
Strutton Ground SW1 BW41 3
Strutton Ground SW1 BW41 66
Strype St. E1 CA39 2
Strype St. E1 CA39 57
Leyden St.
Stuart Av. NW9 BP33 46
Stuart Av. W5 BL40 55
Stuart Av., Brom. CH54 88
Stuart Av., Har. BE34 45
Stuart Av., Walt. BC54 83
Stuart Clo., Brwd. DA25 33
Stuart Clo., Swan. CU51 89
Victoria Hill Rd.
Stuart Clo., Uxb. AZ36 53
Stuart Clo., Wind. AM44 61
Stuart Cres. N22 BX30 38
Stuart Cres., Croy. CD55 87
Stuart Cres., Hayes BA39 53
Stuart Cres., Reig. BS72 121
Stuart Ct., B.Wd. BK25 27
High St. Elstree
Stuart Evans Clo., Well. CP45 69
Stuart Gro., Tedd. BH49 74
Stuart Mantle Way, Erith CS43 69
Stuart Pl., Mitch. BU51 86
Stuart Rd. NW6 BS38 56
Stuart Rd. SE15 CC45 67
Stuart Rd. SW19 BS48 76
Stuart Rd. W3 BN40 55
Stuart Rd., Bark. CN36 58
Dawson Av.
Stuart Rd., Barn. BU26 38
Stuart Rd., Grav. DG46 81
Stuart Rd., Grays DD42 71
Stuart Rd., Har. BH31 45
Stuart Rd., Reig. BS72 121
Stuart Rd., Rich. BJ48 74
Stuart Rd., Th.Hth. BZ52 87
Stuart Rd., Warl. CB63 105
Stuart Rd., Well. CO44 69
Stuart Rd., Welw. BP5 5
Stuart Way, Chsnt. CB19 21
Stuart Way, Stai. AW50 73
Stuart Way, Vir.W. AQ52 82
Stuart Way, Wind. AM44 61
Stubbers La., Upmin. CZ36 60
Stubbings Hall La., Wal.Abb. CF17 21
Stubbs Clo., Dor. BK72 119
Stubbs End Clo., Amer. AP21 25
Stubbs Hill, Dor. BK72 119
Stubbs Hill, Sev. CP60 98
Stubbs La., Tad. BR67 112
Stubbs Way SW19 BT51 86
Brangwyn Cres.
Stubbs Wood, Amer. AP21 25
Stucley Pl. NW1 BV36 1
Stucley Rd., Houns. BG43 64
Stud Grn., Wat. BC19 17
Studd St. N1 BY37 2
Studdridge St. SW6 BS44 66
Studholm St. SE15 CB43 67
Studholme Ct. NW3 BS35 47
Studio Dr., Wem. BM34 46
Empire Way
Studio Way, B.Wd. BN23 28
Studio, The, Bush. BF25 27
Studios Rd., Shep. AZ52 83
Studland Clo., Sid. CN48 78
Studland Rd. SE26 CC49 77
Studland Rd. W7 BG39 54
Studland Rd., Kings.T. BL50 75
Studland Rd., Wey. AY60 92
Studland St. W6 BP42 65
Studley Av. E4 CF29 39
Studley Clo. E5 CD35 48
Studley Ct., Sid. CO49 79
Studley Dr., Ilf. CJ32 49
Studley Grange Rd. W7 BH41 64
Studley Rd. E7 CH36 58
Studley Rd. SW4 BX44 66
Studley Rd., Dag. CP36 59
Stukeley Rd. E7 CH36 58
Stukeley St. WC2 BX39 2
Stukeley St. WC2 BX39 56
Stumble Hill, Ton. DB68 117
Stump Rd., Epp. CP17 23
Stumps Hill La., Beck. CE50 77
Stumps La., Whyt. CA62 105
Sturdy Rd. SE15 CB44 67
Sturge Av. E17 CE30 39
Sturge St. SE1 BZ41 4
Sturge St. SE1 BZ41 67
Sturgeon Rd. SE17 BZ42 4
Sturgeon Rd. SE17 BZ42 67
Sturges Field, Chis. CM50 78
Sturgess Av. NW4 BP33 46
Sturlas Way, Wal.Cr. CC20 21
Sturmer Way N7 BX35 47
Stock Orchard Cres.
Sturrock Clo. N15 BZ31 48
Ida Rd.
Sturry St. E14 CE39 57
Sturt Ct., Guil. AT69 118
Ashbury Cres.
Sturt St. N1 BZ37 2
Sturt St. N1 BZ37 57
Sturts La., Tad. BO67 112
Stutfield St. E1 CB39 57
Styants Bottom Rd., Sev. CZ64 108
Stychens Clo., Red. BZ70 114
Stychens La., Red. BZ69 114
Style Rd., Slou. AR41 62
Stylecroft Rd., Ch.St.G. AR27 34
Styles End, Lthd. BF67 111
Styles Gdns. SW9 BY44 66
Styles Way, Beck. CF52 87
Styventon Pl., Cher. AV54 82
Cowley Av.
Succombs Hill, Warl. CN63 105
Succombs Pl., Warl. CB62 105
View Rd.
Sudbourne Rd. SW2 BX46 76
Sudbrook Gdns., Rich. BK48 74
Sudbrook La., Rich. BL47 75
Sudbrooke Rd. SW12 BU46 76
Sudbury Av., Wem. BK34 45
Sudbury Cft., Wem. BH35 45
Sudbury Court Dr., Har. BH34 45
Sudbury Court Rd., Har. BH34 45
Sudbury Cres., Brom. CH50 78
Sudbury Cres., Wem. BJ35 45
Sudbury Ct. E5 CC35 48
Clapton Park Est.
Sudbury Gdns., Croy. CA55 87
Sudbury Heights Av., Grnf. BH35 45
Sudbury Hill Clo., Wem. BH35 45
Sudbury Hill, Har. BH34 45
Sudbury Par., Wem. BJ35 45
Sudbury Rd., Bark. CN35 49
Sudeley St. N1 BY37 2
Sudeley St. N1 BY37 56
Sudicamps Ct., Wal.Abb. CH20 22
Winters Way
Sudlow Rd. SW18 BS46 76
Sudrey St. SE1 BZ41 4
Sudrey St. SE1 BZ41 67
Suez Av., Grnf. BH37 54
Suez Rd., Enf. CD24 30
Suffield Clo., S.Croy. CC59 96
Suffield Rd. E4 CE28 39
Suffield Rd. N15 CA32 48
Suffield Rd. SE17 BY42 4
Suffield Rd. SE20 CC51 87
Suffolk Clo., B.Wd. BN25 28
Suffolk Clo., St.Alb. BK16 18
Suffolk Ct. E10 CE33 48
Suffolk Ct., Ilf. CN32 49
Suffolk Dr., Guil. AT68 109
Suffolk Gro. SE16 CC42 67
Hawkstone Rd.
Suffolk La. EC4 BZ40 4
Suffolk La. EC4 BZ40 57
Suffolk Park Rd. E17 CD31 48
Suffolk Pl. E17 CD31 48
Suffolk Pl. SW1 BW40 3
Suffolk Pl. SW1 BW40 56
Suffolk St.
Suffolk Rd. E13 CG38 58
Suffolk Rd. N15 BZ32 48
Suffolk Rd. NW10 BO36 55
Suffolk Rd. SE25 CA52 87
Suffolk Rd. SW13 BO43 65
Suffolk Rd., Bark. CM36 58
Suffolk Rd., Dag. CS35 50
Suffolk Rd., Dart. CW46 80
Suffolk Rd., Enf. CB25 30
Suffolk Rd., Grav. DH46 81
Suffolk Rd., Har. BE32 45
Suffolk Rd., Ilf. CN32 49
Suffolk Rd., Pot.B. BR19 19
Suffolk Rd., Sid. CP50 79
Suffolk Rd., Wor.Pk. BO55 85
Suffolk St. E7 CH35 49
Suffolk St. SW1 BW40 3
Suffolk St. SW1 BW40 56
Suffolk Way, Horn. CX31 51
Suffolk Way, Sev. CV66 117
Buckhurst La.
Sugar House La. E15 CF37 57
Sugar La., Berk. AT14 7
Sugar Loaf Wk. E2 CC38 57
Sugden Rd. SW11 BV45 66
Sugden Rd., T.Ditt. BJ54 84
Sugden St. SE5 BZ43 67
Sugden Way, Bark. CN37 58
Sulgrave Rd. W6 BQ41 65
Sulina Rd. SW2 BX47 76
Sulivan Ct. SW6 BS44 66
Sulivan Rd. SW6 BS45 66
Sullivan Av. E16 CJ39 58
Sullivan Clo. SW11 BU45 66
Sullivan Clo., Dart. CU47 79
Sullivan Cres., Uxb. AX30 35
Sullivan Rd. SE11 BY42 66
Brook Dr.
Sullivan Rd., E.Mol. BH52 84
Sullivan Rd., Til. DG44 71
Sullivan Way, Brwd. BK25 27
Sultan Rd. E11 CH31 49
Sultan St. SE5 BZ43 67
Sultan St., Beck. CC51 87
Sumatra Rd. NW6 BS35 47
Sumburgh Rd. SW12 BV46 76
Summer Av., E.Mol. BH53 84
Summer Clo., Lthd. BG65 102
The Green
Summer Court Rd. E1 CC39 57
West Arbour St.
Summer Ct., Hem.H. AX12 8
Townsend
Summer Dale, Welw.G.C. BQ6 5
Summer Gdns., E.Mol. BH53 84
Summer Gro., B.Wd. BK25 27
Summer Hill Vill., Chis. CL51 88
Summer Hill, B.Wd. BM25 28
Hartfield Av.
Summer Hill, Chis. CL51 88
Summer House Rd. N16 CA34 48
Summer Rd., E.Mol. BH53 84
Summer Rd., T.Ditt. BH53 84
Summerfield Av. NW6 BR37 55
Summerfield Clo., St.Alb. BK16 18
Summerfield Clo., Wey. AW56 92
Summerfield La., Surb. BK55 84
Summerfield Rd. W5 BJ38 54
Summerfield Rd., Loug. CJ25 31
Summerfield Rd., Wat. BC21 26
Summerfield St. SE12 CG47 78
Summerfield, Hat. BP14 10
Summerhayes Clo., Wok. AS60 91
Summerhays, Cob. BD60 93
Summerhill Clo., Orp. CN56 97
Summerhill Ct., St.Alb. BH13 9
Avenue Rd.
Summerhill Gro., Enf. CA25 30
Summerhill Rd. N15 BZ31 48
Summerhill Rd., Dart. CV47 80
Summerhill Way, Mitch. BV51 86
Summerhouse Av., Houns. BE44 64
Summerhouse Dr., Bex. CS49 79
Summerhouse Dr., Dart. CS48 79
Summerhouse La., West Dr. AX43 63
Summerhouse La., Uxb. AW29 35
Summerhouse La., Wat. BG23 27
Summerhouse Way, Wat. BB18 17
Summerland Gdns. N10 BV31 47
Muswell Hill Broadway
Summerlands Av. W3 BN40 55
Summerlands Rd., St.Alb. BK11 9
The Ridgeway
Summerlay Clo., Tad. BR63 103
Summerlea, Slou. AN41 61
Summerlee Av. N2 BU31 47
Summerlee Gdns. N2 BU31 47
Summerly Av., Reig. BS70 121
Summerly St. SW18 BS48 76
Summers Clo. NW9 BM33 46
Summers Clo., Sutt. BS57 95
Overton Rd.
Summers Clo., Wey. AZ59 92
Summers La. N12 BT29 38
Summers Row N12 BU29 38
Summers St. EC1 BY38 2
Summers St. EC1 BY38 56
Back Hill
Summersby Rd. N6 BV32 47
Summerstown SW17 BT48 76
Summerswood Clo., Ken. BZ61 105
Longwood Rd.
Summerswood La., B.Wd. BO10 19
Summerton Way SE28 CP39 59
Summertrees, Sun. BC51 83
Summerville Gdns., Sutt. BR57 94
Summerwood Rd., Islw. BH46 74
Summit Av. NW9 BN32 46
Summit Clo. N14 BW27 38
Summit Clo. NW2 BR35 46
Summit Clo. NW9 BN31 46
Summit Clo., Edg. BM29 37
Summit Clo., Wey. AV56 91
Summit Dr., Wdf.Grn. CJ30 40
Summit Est. N16 CB33 48
Summit Rd. E17 CE31 48
Summit Rd., Nthlt. BF36 54
Summit Rd., Pot.B. BR18 19
Summit Way N14 BV27 38
Summit Way SE19 CA50 77
Summit, The, Loug. CK23 31
Sumner Av. SE15 CA44 67
Sumner Rd.
Sumner Bldgs. SE1 BZ40 4
Sumner Bldgs. SE1 BZ40 57
Sumner St.
Sumner Clo., Orp. CM56 97
Isabella Dr.
Sumner Est. SE15 CA44 67
Sumner Gdns., Croy. CY54 86
Sumner Pl. Ms. SW7 BT42 3
Sumner Pl. Ms. SW7 BT42 66
Sumner Pl.
Sumner Pl. SW7 BT42 3
Sumner Pl. SW7 BT42 66
Sumner Rd. SE15 CA43 67
Sumner Rd., Croy. BY54 86
Sumner Rd., Har. BG33 45
Sumner Rd., S.Croy. BY54 86
Sumner St. SE1 BY40 4
Sumner St. SE1 BY40 56
Sumners Farm Clo., Harl. CL13 13
Sumpter Clo. NW3 BT36 56
Sumpter Yd., St.Alb. BG13 9
Sun Alley, Rich. BL45 65
Sun Ct. EC3 BZ39 2
Cornhill
Sun Hill, Fawk. CZ55 90
Sun La. SE3 CH43 68
Sun La., Grav. DH48 81
Sun Pass. SE16 CB41 4
Frean St.
Sun Pass., Wind. AO44 61
Peascod St.
Sun Ray Av., Brwd. DF25 122
Sun Rd. W14 BR42 65

Street	Grid	Page
Sun Rd., Swans.	DC46	81
Sun Sq., Hem.H.	AX13	8
High St.		
Sun St. EC2	**BZ39**	**2**
Sun St. EC2	BZ39	57
Sun St. EC3	**CA39**	**2**
Sun St. Pass. EC2	**CA39**	**2**
Sun St. Pass. EC2	CA39	57
Sun St., Wal.Abb.	CF20	21
Sunbeam Rd. NW10	BN38	55
Sunbury Av. NW7	BN28	37
Sunbury Av. SW14	BN45	65
Sunbury Court Rd., Sun.	BD51	84
Sunbury Cres., Felt.	BB49	73
Ryland Clo.		
Sunbury Gdns. NW7	BN28	37
Sunbury La. SW11	BT44	66
Sunbury La., Walt.	BC53	83
Sunbury Rd., Eton	AO43	61
Sunbury Rd., Felt.	BB48	73
Sunbury Rd., Sutt.	BQ55	85
Sunbury St. SE18	CK41	68
Sunbury Way, Felt.	BD49	74
Suncourt, Erith	CT44	69
Suncroft Pl. SE26	CC48	77
Sundale Av., S.Croy.	CC58	96
Sunderland Av., St.Alb.	BJ13	9
Sunderland Ct. SE22	CB47	77
Sunderland Mt. SE23	CC48	77
Sunderland Rd. SE23	CC48	77
Sunderland Rd. W5	BK41	64
Sunderland Rd., Houns.	AY46	73
Southampton Rd.		
Sunderland Ter. W2	BS39	56
Sunderland Way E12	CJ34	49
Sundew Av. W12	BP40	55
Sundew Ct., Grays	DE43	71
Salix Rd.		
Sundew Rd., Hem.H.	AV14	7
Sundial Av. SE25	CA52	87
Sundon Cres., Vir.W.	AQ53	82
Sundorne Rd. SE7	CH42	68
Sundown Av., S.Croy.	CA59	96
Sundown Pl., Ilf.	CL34	49
Ilford Hill		
Sundown Rd., Ashf.	BA49	73
Sundra Wk. E1	CC38	57
Beaumont Gro.		
Sundridge Av., Brom.	CJ51	88
Sundridge Av., Well.	CM44	68
Sundridge Clo., Dart.	CX46	80
Sundridge Hill, Sev.	CP62	107
Sundridge Ho., Brom.	CH49	78
Sundridge La., Sev.	CO62	107
Sundridge Pl., Croy.	CB54	87
Sundridge Rd.		
Sundridge Rd., Croy.	CA54	87
Sundridge Rd., Sev.	CQ64	107
Sundridge Rd., Wok.	AT63	100
Sunfields Pl. SE3	CH43	68
Sunflower Way, Rom.	CV30	42
Sunkist Way, Pur.	BX58	95
Sunland Av., Bexh.	CQ45	69
Sunleigh Rd., Wem.	BL37	55
Sunley Gdns., Grnf.	BJ37	54
Sunmead Clo., Lthd.	BH64	102
Sunmead Rd., Hem.H.	AX13	8
Sunmead Rd., Sun.	BC52	83
Sunna Gdns., Sun.	BC51	83
Sunning Hill, Grav.	DF48	81
Sunningdale Av. W3	BO39	55
Sunningdale Av., Bark.	CM37	58
Sunningdale Av., Felt.	BE48	74
Sunningdale Av., Rain.	CU38	59
Sunningdale Av., Ruis.	BD33	45
Sunningdale Clo. E6	CK38	58
Ascot Rd.		
Sunningdale Clo., Stan.	BJ29	36
Sunningdale Gdns. NW9	BN32	46
Sunningdale Gdns. W8	BS42	66
Lexham Ms.		
Sunningdale N14	BW28	38
Wilmer Way		
Sunningdale Rd., Brom.	CK52	88
Sunningdale Rd., Rain.	CU36	59
Sunningdale Rd., Sutt.	BR55	85
Sunningfields Cres. NW4	BP30	37
Sunningfields Rd. NW4	BP30	37
Sunninghill Rd. SE13	CE44	67
Sunnings La., Upmin.	CY36	60
Sunningvale Av., West.	CJ61	106
Sunningvale Clo., West.	CJ61	106
Sunny Bank SE25	CB52	87
Sunny Bank, Epsom	BN61	103
Sunny Bank, Warl.	CD62	105
Sunny Cres. NW10	BN36	55
Sunny Gardens Rd. NW4	BP30	37
Sunny Hill NW4	BP31	46
Sunny Hill Rd., Ger.Cr.	AU29	34
Sunny Nook Gdns., S.Croy.	BZ57	96
Selsdon Rd.		
Sunny Rd., The, Enf.	CC23	30
Sunny Ri., Cat.	BZ65	105
Sunny Side, Wal.Abb.	CG14	13
Hoe La.		
Sunny Side, Walt.	BD53	84
Sunny Vw. NW9	BN32	46
Sunny Way N12	BU29	38
Sunnybank Rd., Pot.B.	BS20	20
Sunnycroft Gdns., Upmin.	CZ33	51
Sunnycroft Rd. SE25	CB52	87
Sunnycroft Rd., Houns.	BF44	64
Sunnycroft Rd., Sthl.	BF39	54
Sunnydale Gdns. NW7	BN29	37
Sunnydale Rd. SE12	CH46	78
Sunnydale, Orp.	CL55	88
Sunnydell, St.Alb.	BF16	18
Sunnydene Av. E4	CF28	39
Sunnydene Av., Ruis.	BC33	44
Sunnydene Clo., Rom.	CW29	42
Sunnydene Rd., Pur.	BY60	95
Sunnydene St. SE26	CD49	77
Sunnydene, Wem.	BK36	54
Sunnyfield NW7	BO27	37
Sunnyfield Rd., Chis.	CO52	89
Sunnyfield, Hat.	BQ11	10
Sunnyhill Rd. SW16	BX49	76
Sunnyhill Rd., Hem.H.	AW13	8
Sunnyhurst Clo., Sutt.	BS55	86
Sunnymead Av., Chesh.	AP17	16
Sunnymead Av., Mitch.	BW52	86
Sunnymead Rd. NW9	BN33	46
Sunnymead Rd. SW15	BP46	75
Sunnymede Av., Cars.	BT59	95
Sunnymede Av., Epsom	BO58	94
Sunnymede Dr., Ilf.	CL32	49
Sunnyside Dr. E4	CF26	39
Sunnyside Gdns., Upmin.	CY34	51
Sunnyside NW2	BR34	46
Sunnyside Pass. SW19	BR50	75
Sunnyside Rd. E. N9	CB27	39
Sunnyside Rd. E10	CE33	48
Sunnyside Rd. N. N9	CB27	39
Sunnyside Rd. N19	BW33	47
Sunnyside Rd. S. N9	CA27	39
Sunnyside Rd. W5	BK40	54
Sunnyside Rd., Epp.	CN19	22
Sunnyside Rd., Ilf.	CM34	49
Sunnyside Rd., Tedd.	BG49	74
Sunnyside SW19	BR50	75
Sunray Av. SE24	BZ45	67
Sunray Av., Brom.	CK53	88
Sunray Av., Surb.	BM55	85
Sunray Av., West Dr.	AX41	63
Sunrise Av., Horn.	CV34	51
Sunrise Clo., Felt.	BE48	74
Sunrise Cres., Hem.H.	AY15	8
Sunset Av. E4	CE26	39
Sunset Av., Wdf.Grn.	CG28	40
Sunset Dr., Hav.	CU28	41
Sunset Gdns. SE25	CA51	87
Sunset Rd. SE5	BZ45	67
Sunset Vw., Barn.	BR23	28
Sunshine Way, Mitch.	BU51	86
Sunstone Grn., Red.	BX68	113
Sunwell Clo. SE15	CB44	67
Surbiton Cres., Kings.T.	BL52	85
Surbiton Ct., Surb.	BK53	84
Surbiton Hall Clo., Kings.T.	BL52	85
Surbiton Hill Pk., Surb.	BL53	85
Surbiton Hill Rd., Surb.	BL52	85
Surbiton Park Ter., Kings.T.	BL52	85
Surbiton Rd., Kings.T.	BK52	84
Surlingham Clo. SE28	CP40	59
Surly Hall Wk., Wind.	AM44	61
Surman Cres., Brwd.	DE26	122
Surr St. N7	BX35	47
Surrendale Pl. W9	BS38	56
Surrey Av., Slou.	AO39	52
Surrey Canal Rd. SE15	CC43	67
Surrey Cres. W4	BM42	65
Surrey Dr., Horn.	CX31	51
Surrey Gdns. W4	BM42	65
Chiswick High Rd.		
Surrey Gdns., Lthd.	BB64	101
Surrey Gro. SE17	**CA42**	**4**
Surrey Gro. SE17	CA42	67
Surrey Gro., Sutt.	BT55	86
Surrey La. SW11	BU44	66
Surrey Ms. SE27	CA49	77
Hamilton Rd.		
Surrey Mt. SE23	CB47	77
Surrey Quays Rd. SE16	CC41	67
Surrey Rd. SE15	CC46	77
Surrey Rd., Bark.	CN36	58
Surrey Rd., Dag.	CR35	50
Surrey Rd., Har.	BG32	45
Surrey Rd., W.Wick.	CE54	87
Surrey Row SE1	**BY41**	**4**
Surrey Row SE1	BY41	66
Surrey Sq. SE17	**CA42**	**4**
Surrey Sq. SE17	CA42	67
Surrey St. E13	CH38	58
Surrey St. WC2	**BX40**	**4**
Surrey St. WC2	BX40	56
Temple Pl.		
Surrey St., Croy.	BZ55	87
Surrey Ter. SE17	**CA42**	**4**
Surrey Ter. SE17	CA42	67
Surrey Sq.		
Surrey Water Rd. SE16	CC40	57
Surridge Clo., Rain.	CV38	60
Surridge Gdns. SE19	BZ50	77
Susan Clo., Rom.	CS31	50
Susan Rd. SE3	CH44	68
Susan Wood, Chis.	CL51	88
Susannah St. E14	CE39	57
Sussex Av., Islw.	BH45	64
Sussex Av., Rom.	CW29	42
Sussex Clo. N19	BX34	47
Sussex Clo., Ch.St.G.	AQ27	34
Sussex Clo., Hodd.	CE11	12
Roman St.		
Sussex Clo., Ilf.	CK32	49
Sussex Clo., N.Mal.	BO52	85
Sussex Clo., Reig.	BT71	121
Sussex Clo., Slou.	AQ41	62
Sussex Keep		
Sussex Clo., Twick.	BJ46	74
Cumberland Clo.		
Sussex Cres., Nthlt.	BF36	54
Sussex Gdns. N4	BZ32	48
Rosebery Gdns.		
Sussex Gdns. N6	BU32	47
Sussex Gdns. W2	**BT39**	**1**
Sussex Gdns. W2	BT39	56
Sussex Gdns., Chess.	BK57	93
Sussex Keep, Slou.	AQ41	62
Sussex Ms. E. W2	**BT40**	**3**
Sussex Ms. E. W2	BT40	56
Clifton Pl.		
Sussex Ms. NW1	**BU38**	**1**
Sussex Ms. NW1	BU38	56
Sussex Pl.		
Sussex Ms. W. W2	**BT40**	**3**
Sussex Pl. NW1	**BU38**	**1**
Sussex Pl. NW1	BU38	56
Sussex Pl. W2	**BT39**	**1**
Sussex Pl. W2	BT39	56
Sussex Pl. W6	BQ42	65
Sussex Pl., Erith	CR43	69
Sussex Pl., N.Mal.	BO52	85
Sussex Rd.		
Sussex Pl., Slou.	AQ41	62
Sussex Rd. E6	CL37	58
Sussex Rd. SW9	BT45	66
Sussex Rd., Brwd.	DA28	42
Sussex Rd., Cars.	BU57	95
Sussex Rd., Dart.	CX47	80
Sussex Rd., Erith	CR43	69
Sussex Rd., Har.	BF32	45
Sussex Rd., N.Mal.	BO52	85
Sussex Rd., Orp.	CP53	89
Sussex Rd., S.Croy.	BZ57	96
Sussex Rd., Sid.	CO49	79
Sussex Rd., Sthl.	BD41	64
Sussex Rd., Uxb.	BA35	44
Sussex Rd., W.Wick.	CE54	87
Sussex Rd., Wat.	BC22	26
Sussex Sq. W2	**BT40**	**3**
Sussex Sq. W2	BT40	56
Sussex St. E13	CH38	58
Sussex St. SW1	**BV42**	**3**
Sussex St. SW1	BV42	66
Sussex Way N7	BX34	47
Sussex Way, Barn.	BV25	29
Sussex Way, Uxb.	AV32	43
Sussex Wk. SW9	BY45	66
Sutcliffe Clo. NW11	BS32	47
Sutcliffe Clo., Bush.	BG24	27
Sutcliffe Rd. SE18	CN43	68
Sutcliffe Rd., Well.	CP44	69
Sutherland Av. W13	BJ39	54
Sutherland Av. W9	**BS38**	**1**
Sutherland Av. W9	BS38	56
Sutherland Av., Cuff.	BW17	20
Sutherland Av., Guil.	AS67	109
Sutherland Av., Hayes	BC42	63
Sutherland Av., Orp.	CN53	88
Sutherland Av., Sun.	BB51	83
Sutherland Av., Well.	CN45	68
Sutherland Av., West.	CJ62	106
Sutherland Clo., Barn.	BR24	28
Sutherland Clo., Wey.	BA56	92
Vaillant Rd.		
Sutherland Ct. NW9	BM32	46
Sutherland Ct., Welw.G.C.	BR 7	5
Sutherland Dr. SW19	BT51	86
Brangwyn Cres.		
Sutherland Dr., Guil.	AS69	109
Sutherland Gdns. SW14	BO45	65
Sutherland Gdns., Wor.Pk.	BP54	85
Sutherland Gdns., Sun.	BB51	83
Sutherland Gro. SW18	BR46	75
Sutherland Gro., Tedd.	BH49	74
Sutherland Pl. W2	BS39	56
Sutherland Point E5	CB34	48
Downs Est.		
Sutherland Rd. E17	CC30	39
Sutherland Rd. N17	CB29	39
Sutherland Rd. N9	CB26	39
Sutherland Rd. Path E17	CC31	48
Sutherland Rd.		
Sutherland Rd. W13	BJ39	54
Sutherland Rd. W4	BO43	65
Sutherland Rd., Belv.	CR41	69
Sutherland Rd., Croy.	BY54	86
Sutherland Rd., Sthl.	BE39	54
Sutherland Row SW1	**BV42**	**3**
Sutherland Row SW1	BV42	66
Sutherland St.		
Sutherland Sq. SE17	**BZ42**	**4**
Sutherland Sq. SE17	BZ42	67
Sutherland St. E3	CD37	57
Sutherland St. SW1	**BV42**	**3**
Sutherland St. SW1	BV42	66
Sutherland Way, Cuff.	BW17	20
Sutherland Wk. SE17	**BZ42**	**4**
Sutherland Wk. SE17	BZ42	67
Sutherlands Rd., Enf.	CC25	30
Sutlej Rd. SE7	CJ43	68
Sutterton St. N7	BX36	56
Sutton Av., Slou.	AR41	62
Sutton Av., Wok.	AP63	100
Sutton Clo., Brom.	CE51	87
Albermarle Rd.		
Sutton Clo., Brox.	CD13	12
Sutton Clo., Loug.	CK26	40
Sutton Clo., Pnr.	BC32	44
Sutton Common Rd., Sutt.	BR54	85
Sutton Cres., Barn.	BQ25	28
Sutton Ct. Rd. E13	CJ38	58
Sutton Ct. Rd. W4	BN43	65
Sutton Ct. Rd., Sutt.	BT57	95
Sutton Ct. Rd., Uxb.	AZ37	53
Sutton Ct. W4	BN43	65
Sutton Dene, Houns.	BF44	64
Sutton Dwellings N1	BY36	56
Sutton Dwellings SE8	CC42	67
Sutton Dwellings SW3	**BU42**	**3**
Sutton Dwellings SW3	BU42	66
Sutton Dwellings W10	BQ39	55
Sutton Gdns., Bark.	CN37	58
Felton Rd.		
Sutton Gdns., Croy.	CA53	87
Sutton Gdns., Red.	BW68	113
Sutton Green Rd., Guil.	AS66	109
Sutton Grn., Bark.	CN37	58
Saxham Rd.		
Sutton Gro., Sutt.	BT56	95
Sutton Hall Rd., Houns.	BF43	64
Sutton La. S. W4	BN43	65
Sutton La. W4	BN43	65
Sutton La., Houns.	BE45	64
Sutton La., Slou.	AT43	62
Sutton La., Sutt.	BS59	95
Sutton Model Dws. EC1	**BZ38**	**2**
Sutton Park Rd., Sutt.	BS57	95
Sutton Path, B.Wd.	BM23	28
Sutton Pl. E9	CC35	48
Sutton Pl., Slou.	AT43	62
Sutton Rd. E13	CG38	58
Sutton Rd. E17	CC30	39
Sutton Rd. N10	BV30	38
Sutton Rd., Bark.	CN37	58
Sutton Rd., Houns.	BF44	64
Sutton Rd., St.Alb.	BJ14	9
Sutton Rd., Wat.	BD24	27
Sutton Row W1	**BW39**	**1**
Sutton Row W1	BW39	56
Sutton Sq. E9	CC35	48
Urswick Rd.		
Sutton Sq., Houns.	BE44	64
Sutton St. E1	CC40	57
Sutton Way W10	BQ38	55
Sutton Way, Houns.	BE44	64
Suttons Av., Horn.	CV34	51
Suttons Gdns., Horn.	CV34	51
Suttons La., Horn.	CV35	51
Suttons Parkway, Upmin.	CW35	51
Suttons Way EC1	**BZ38**	**2**
Swabey Rd., Slou.	AT42	62
Swaby Rd. SW18	BT47	76
Swaffham Way N22	BY29	38
Swaffield Rd. SW18	BS47	76
Swaffield Rd., Sev.	CV64	108
Swain Rd., Th.Hth.	BZ53	87
Swains Clo., West Dr.	AY41	63
Swains La. N6	BV34	47
Swains Rd. SW17	BU50	76
Swainson Rd. W3	BO41	65
Swaisland Dr., Dart.	CT46	79
Crayford Rd.		
Swaisland Rd., Dart.	CU46	79
Swakeleys Dr., Uxb.	AZ35	44
Swakeleys Rd., Uxb.	AY35	44
Swale Clo., S.Ock.	CY39	60
Swale Rd., Dart.	CU45	69
Swaledale Rd., Dart.	CY47	80
Swallands Rd. SE6	CE48	77
Swallow Clo. SE14	CC44	67
Swallow Clo., Bush.	BF26	36
Swallow Clo., Rick.	AX26	35
Nightingale Rd.		
Swallow Clo., Stai.	AV49	72
Swallow Ct., Ruis.	BD33	45
Dollis Cres.		
Swallow Dr. NW10	BN36	55
Kingfisher Way		
Swallow Dr., Nthlt.	BE37	54
Hazelmere Rd.		
Swallow End, Welw.G.C.	BR 8	5
Swallow Fields, Welw.G.C.	BR 8	5
Swallow Gdns., Hat.	BP13	10
Swallow La., St.Alb.	BJ15	9
Swallow Pl. W1	**BV39**	**1**
Swallow St. E6	CK39	58
Swallow St. W1	**BW40**	**3**
Swallow St. W1	BW40	56
Piccadilly		
Swallow St., Iver	AU38	52
Swallow Wk., Rain.	CU36	59
Heron Flight Av.		
Swallowdale Est., Iver	AU38	52
Swallowdale La., Hem.H.	AZ12	8
Swallowdale, Iver	AU38	52
Swallowdale, S.Croy.	CC58	96
Swallowfield Rd. SE7	CH42	68
Swallowfield Way, Hayes	BA41	63
Swallowfield, Egh.	AQ50	72
Heronfield		
Swallowfields, Grav.	DF48	81
Hillary Av.		
Swallows, Harl.	CP 9	6
Swallows, The, Welw.G.C.	BR 6	5
Swan & Pike Rd., Enf.	CE22	30
Swan App. E6	CK39	58
Swan Av., Upmin.	CZ33	51
Swan Clo., Croy.	CA54	87
Swan Clo., Felt.	BE49	74
Swan Clo., Orp.	CO52	89
Swan Ct. N20	BT27	38
Swan Ct. SW3	**BU42**	**3**
Swan Ct. SW3	BU42	66
Swan La. EC4	**BZ40**	**4**
Swan La. EC4	BZ40	57
Wharfside		
Swan La. N20	BT27	38
Swan La., Brwd.	CZ22	33
Swan La., Dart.	CT47	79
Swan La., Guil.	AR71	118
Swan La., Wat.	BB24	26
Swan Mead SE1	**CA41**	**4**
Swan Mead SE1	CA41	67
Swan Mill Gdns., Dor.	BK70	119
Swan Ms. SW9	BX44	66
Stockwell Park Rd.		
Swan Paddock, Brwd.	DB27	42
Chestnut Gro.		
Swan Pass. E1	CA40	57
Royal Mint St.		
Swan Pl. SW13	BO44	65
Swan Rd. SE16	CC41	67
Swan Rd. SE7	CJ41	68
Swan Rd., Felt.	BE49	74
Swan Rd., Iver	AV39	52
Swan Rd., Sthl.	BF39	54
Swan Rd., West Dr.	AX41	63
Swan St. SE1	**BZ41**	**4**
Swan St. SE1	BZ41	67
Swan St., Islw.	BJ45	64
Swan Ter., Wind.	AN43	61
Swan Way, Enf.	CC23	30
Swan Wharf EC4	BZ40	57
Wharfside		
Swan Wk. SW3	BU43	66
Swan Wk., Rom.	CT32	50
Swan Yd. N1	BY36	56
Highbury Station Rd.		
Swanage Rd. E4	CF29	39
Swanage Rd. SW18	BT46	76
Swanage Waye, Hayes	BD39	54
Swanbourne Dr., Horn.	CV35	51
Swanbridge Rd., Bexh.	CR44	69
Swandon Way SW18	BS45	66
Swanfield Rd., Wal.Cr.	CD20	21
Swanfield St. E2	**CA38**	**2**
Swanfield St. E2	CA38	57
Swanhill, Welw.G.C.	BS 6	5
Swanland Rd., Hat.	BP16	19
Swanland Rd., Pot.B.	BP20	19
Swanley Bar La., Pot.B.	BS17	20
Swanley By-pass, Swan.	CS52	89
Swanley Cres., Pot.B.	BS18	20
Swanley La., Swan.	CT52	89
Swanley Rd., Well.	CP44	69
Swanley Vill. Rd., Swan.	CU51	89
Swann App. E6	CK39	58
Swanns Meadow, Lthd.	BF66	111
Swans Clo., St.Alb.	BL14	10
Swanscombe Rd. W11	BQ40	55
Swanscombe Rd. W4	BO42	65
Swanscombe St., Swans.	DC46	81
Swansea Rd., Enf.	CC24	30
Swanshope, Loug.	CL23	31
Swansland Gdns. E17	CD30	39
McEntee Av.		
Swanston Path., Wat.	BD27	36
Swanton Gdns. SW19	BQ47	75
Swanton Rd., Erith	CR43	69
Swanwick Clo. SW15	BO47	75
Swanworth La., Dor.	BJ67	111
Swanzy Rd., Sev.	CV63	108
Sward Rd., Orp.	CO53	89
Swaton Rd. E3	CE38	57
Swaylands Rd., Belv.	CR43	69
Swaynes La., Guil.	AV70	118
Swaynesland Rd., Eden.	CK70	115
Sweden Gate SE16	CD41	67
Swedenborg Gdns. E1	CB40	57
Swedenborg St. E1	CB40	57
Sweeney Cres. SE1	**CA41**	**4**
Sweeney Cres. SE1	CA41	67
Sweeps La., Egh.	AS49	72
Sweeps La., Orp.	CP53	89
Sweet Briar Grn. N9	CA27	39
Briary La.		
Sweet Briar Gro. N9	CA27	39
Sweet Briar Wk. N18	CA28	39
Sweet Briar, Welw.G.C.	BS 8	5
Sweetbriar Clo., Hem.H.	AW12	8
Sweetbriar La., Epsom	BN60	94
Sweetcroft La., Uxb.	AY36	53
Sweetenham Wk. SE18	CM42	68
Sandbach Pl.		
Sweetmans Av., Pnr.	BD31	45
Sweets Way N20	BT27	38
Swete St. E13	CH37	58
Sweyn Pl. SE3	CH44	68
Sweyn Rd., Green.	DB46	80
Sweyne Rd., Swans.	DC46	81
Sweyns, Harl.	CP12	14
Swievelands Hill Rd., West.	CH63	106
Swift Clo., Har.	BF34	45
Swift Clo., Hayes	BB39	53
Swift Clo., Upmin.	CZ33	51
Swift Rd., Felt.	BD49	74
Swift Rd., Sthl.	BF41	64
Swift St. SW6	BR44	65
Swiftsden Way, Brom.	CG50	78
Swinborn Ct. SE5	BZ45	67
Basingdon Way		
Swinbourne Gdns., Til.	DG44	71
Swinbrook Rd. W10	BQ38	55
Swinburn Cres., Croy.	CC53	87
Swinburne Rd. SW15	BP45	65
Swinderby Rd., Wem.	BL36	55
Swindon Clo., Ilf.	CN34	49
Salisbury Rd.		
Swindon Clo., Rom.	CW28	42
Swindon Gdns., Rom.	CW28	42
Swindon La., Rom.	CW28	42
Swindon St. W12	BP40	55
Swinfield Clo., Felt.	BE48	74
Swinford Gdns. SW9	BY45	66
Swing Gate La., Berk.	AR14	7
Swingate La. SE18	CN43	68
Swinnerton St. E9	CD35	48
Swinton Clo., Wem.	BM33	46
Swinton Pl. WC1	**BX38**	**2**
Swinton Pl. WC1	BX38	56
Swinton St.		
Swinton St. WC1	**BX38**	**2**
Swinton St. WC1	BX38	56
Swires Shaw, Kes.	BJ56	97
Swiss Av., Wat.	BB24	26
Swiss Clo., Wat.	BB24	26
Swiss Cottage Pl., Loug.	CJ25	31
High Rd.		
Swithland Gdns. SE9	CK49	78
Swyncombe Av. W5	BJ42	64
Sybourn St. E17	CD33	48
Sycamore App., Rick.	BA25	26
Sycamore Av. W5	BK41	64
Sycamore Av., Hat.	BP13	10
Sycamore Av., Hayes	BB40	53
Sycamore Av., Sid.	CN46	78
Sycamore Av., Upmin.	CX34	51
Sycamore Clo. E16	CG38	58
Clarence Rd.		
Sycamore Clo. N9	CB28	39
Sycamore Clo. SE9	CK48	78
Sycamore Clo., Amer.	AO22	25
Sycamore Clo., Barn.	BT25	29
Sycamore Clo., Bush.	BE23	27
Sycamore Clo., Cars.	BU56	95
Sycamore Clo., Ch.St.G.	AQ27	34
Sycamore Clo., Felt.	BC48	73
Sycamore Clo., Grav.	DH47	81
Sycamore Clo., Lthd.	BH64	102
Sycamore Clo., Nthlt.	BE37	54
Sycamore Clo., Wat.	BC21	26
Sycamore Clo., West Dr.	AY40	53
Sycamore Dean, Chesh.	AO17	16
Sycamore Dr., Brwd.	DB26	42
Mayfield Gdns.		
Sycamore Dr., St.Alb.	BG17	18
Sycamore Dr., Swan.	CT32	89
Sycamore Field, Harl.	CL12	13
Sycamore Gdns. W6	BP41	65
Sycamore Gdns., Mitch.	BT51	86
Sycamore Gro. NW9	BN33	46
Sycamore Gro. SE20	CB51	77
Sycamore Gro., N.Mal.	BN52	85

Sycamore Hill N11 BV29 38
Sycamore Rd. SW19 BQ50 75
Sycamore Rd., Amer. AO22 25
Sycamore Rd., Ch.St.G. AQ27 34
Sycamore Rd., Dart. CV47 80
Sycamore Rd., Guil. AR70 118
Sycamore Rd., Rick. BA25 26
Sycamore Rd., Tedd. BK50 74
Sycamore Ri., Bans. BQ60 94
High Beeches
Sycamore Ri., Berk. AR13 7
Sycamore Ri., Ch.St.G. AQ27 34
Sycamore St. EC1 BZ38 57
Baltic St.
Sycamore Way, Th.Hth. BY53 86
Sycamore Wk. W10 BR38 55
Droop St.
Sycamore Wk., Egh. AQ50 72
Sycamore Wk., Ilf. CM31 49
Civic Way
Sycamore Wk., Slou. AS39 52
Sycamores, The, Hem.H. AV15 7
Sycamores, The, Rad. BJ20 18
Sycamores, The, S.Ock. CY40 60
Dacre Av.
Sydenham Av. SE26 CB49 77
Sydenham Hill SE23 CB47 77
Sydenham Hill SE26 CB47 77
Sydenham Park Rd. SE26 CC48 77
Sydenham Pk. SE26 CC49 77
Sydenham Rd. SE26 CC49 77
Sydenham Rd., Croy. BZ54 87
Sydenham Rd., Guil. AR71 118
Sydenham Ri. SE23 CC48 77
Sydmons Ct. SE23 CC47 77
Sydner Ms. N16 CA35 48
Sydner Rd.
Sydner Rd. N16 CA35 48
Sydney Av., Pur. BX59 95
Sydney Clo. SW3 BT42 3
Sydney Clo. SW3 BT42 66
Sydney Cres., Ashf. AZ50 73
Sydney Gro. NW4 BQ32 46
Sydney Gro., Slou. AO39 52
Sydney Ms. Clo. SW7 BT42 66
Sydney Ms. SW3 BT42 3
Sydney Ms. SW3 BT42 66
Sydney Pl. SW7 BT42 3
Sydney Pl. SW7 BU42 66
Sydney Rd. E11 CH32 49
Sydney Rd. N10 BV30 38
Sydney Rd. N8 BY31 47
Sydney Rd. SE2 CP41 69
Sydney Rd. SW20 BQ51 85
Sydney Rd. W13 BJ40 54
Sydney Rd., Bexh. CP45 69
Sydney Rd., Enf. BZ24 30
Sydney Rd., Guil. AS71 118
Sydney Rd., Ilf. CM30 40
Sydney Rd., Rich. BL45 65
Sydney Rd., Sid. CN49 78
Sydney Rd., Tedd. BH49 74
Sydney Rd., Til. DG44 71
Sydney Rd., Wat. BB25 26
Sydney Rd., Wdf.Grn. CH28 40
Sydney Sq. SE15 CB43 67
Latona Rd.
Sydney St. SW3 BT42 3
Sydney St. SW3 BU42 66
Sykecluan, Iver AV41 62
Sykeings, Iver AV41 62
Sylvan Av. N22 BX29 38
Sylvan Av. N3 BS30 38
Sylvan Av. NW7 BO29 37
Sylvan Av., Horn. CW32 51
Sylvan Av., Rom. CQ32 50
Sylvan Clo., Grays DC42 71
Sylvan Clo., Hem.H. AZ14 8
Sylvan Clo., Oxt. CH68 115
Sylvan Clo., S.Croy. CB58 96
Sylvan Clo., Wok. AT62 100
Sylvan Gdns., Surb. BK54 84
Sylvan Gro. SE15 CB43 67
Sylvan Hill SE19 CA51 87
Sylvan Rd. E11 CH32 49
Sylvan Rd. E17 CE32 48
Sylvan Rd. E7 CH36 58
Sylvan Rd. SE19 CA51 87
Sylvan Rd., Ilf. CM34 49
Sylvan Way, Chig. CO27 41
Sylvan Way, Dag. CO34 50
Sylvan Way, Red. BV71 121
Sylvan Way, W.Wick. CG56 97
Sylvan Way, Welw.G.C. BT 8 5
Sylvana Clo., Uxb. AY37 53
Sylvandale, Welw.G.C. BT 8 5
Sylverdale Rd., Croy. BY55 86
Sylverdale Rd., Ken. BY60 95
Sylvester Av., Chis. CK50 78
Sylvester Gdns., Ilf. CO28 41
Sylvester Rd. E17 CD33 48
Sylvester Rd. E8 CB36 57
Sylvester Rd. N2 BT30 38
Sylvester Rd., Wem. BK35 45
Sylvia Av., Brwd. DE27 122
Sylvia Av., Pnr. BE29 36
Sylvia Ct. N1 BZ37 2
Sylvia Ct., Wem. BM36 55
Sylvia Gdns., Wem. BM36 55
Symes Ms. NW1 BW37 1
Symes Ms. NW1 BW37 56
Symonds Clo., Sev. CZ56 99
Symonds Hyde La., Welw.G.C. BN 9 5
Symons St. SW3 BU42 3
Symons St. SW3 BU42 66
Syon Gate Way, Islw. BJ43 64
Syon La.
Syon La., Islw. BH43 64
Syon Park Gdns., Islw. BH43 64
Syracuse Av., Rain. CV38 60
Syringa Ct., Grays DE43 71
Sythwood, Wok. AQ61 100

T

Tabard Gdn. Est. SE1 BZ41 4
Tabard Gdn. Est. SE1 BZ41 67
Tabard St. SE1 BZ41 4
Tabard St. SE1 BZ41 67
Tabarin Way, Epsom BQ61 103
Tabernacle Av. E13 CH38 58
Tabernacle St. EC2 BZ38 2
Tabernacle St. EC2 BZ38 57
Tableer Av. SW4 BW46 76
Tabley Rd. N7 BX35 47
Tabor Gdns., Sutt. BR57 94
Tabor Gro. SW19 BR50 75
Tabor Rd. W6 BP41 65
Tabrums Way, Upmin. CZ33 51
Tachbrook Ms. SW1 BW42 3
Tachbrook Ms. SW1 BW42 66
Longmore St.
Tachbrook Rd., Felt. BB47 73
Tachbrook Rd., Sthl. BD41 64
Tachbrook Rd., Uxb. AX37 53
Tachbrook St. SW1 BW42 3
Tachbrook St. SW1 BW42 66
Tack Ms. SE4 CE45 67
Tadema Rd. SW10 BT43 66
Tadlows Clo., Upmin. CX35 51
Tadmor Clo., Sun. BB52 83
Tadmor St. W12 BQ40 55
Tadorne Rd., Tad. BQ64 103
Tadworth Av., N.Mal. BO53 85
Tadworth Lodge Est., Mitch. BV52 86
Tadworth Par., Horn. CU35 50
Tadworth Rd. NW2 BP34 46
Tadworth St., Tad. BQ65 103
Taeping St. E14 CE42 67
Taffys How, Mitch. BU51 86
Taft Way E3 CE38 57
St. Leonards St.
Tailworth St. E1 CB39 2
Monthope Rd.
Tailworth St. E1 CB39 57
Casson St.
Tait Rd., Croy. CA54 87
Takeley Clo., Rom. CS30 41
Takeley Clo., Wal.Abb. CF20 21
Talacre Rd. NW5 BV36 56
Talbot Av. N2 BT31 47
Talbot Av., Slou. AS41 62
Talbot Av., Wat. BE26 36
Talbot Clo. N15 CA31 48
Talbot Rd.
Talbot Clo., Reig. BS71 121
Lymden Gdns.
Talbot Cres. NW4 BP32 46
Talbot Ct. EC3 BZ40 4
Gracechurch St.
Talbot Ct. EC3 BZ40 57
Gracechurch St.
Talbot Ct., Hem.H. AX14 8
Crabtree La.
Talbot Gdns., Ilf. CO34 50
Talbot Pl. SE3 CG44 68
Talbot Pl., Slou. AR44 62
Talbot Rd. E6 CK37 58
Talbot Rd. E7 CH35 49
Talbot Rd. N15 CA31 48
Talbot Rd. N22 BW30 38
Talbot Rd. N6 BV32 47
Talbot Rd. W11 BR39 55
Talbot Rd. W13 BJ40 54
Talbot Rd. W2 BS39 56
Talbot Rd., Ashf. AY49 73
Talbot Rd., Brom. CH52 88
Talbot Rd., Cars. BV56 95
Talbot Rd., Dag. CQ36 59
Talbot Rd., Har. BH30 36
Talbot Rd., Hat. BP11 10
Talbot Rd., Islw. BJ45 64
Talbot Rd., Rick. AY26 35
Talbot Rd., Sthl. BE42 64
Talbot Rd., Th.Hth. BZ52 87
Talbot Rd., Twick. BH47 74
Talbot Rd., Wem. BK36 54
Talbot Sq. W2 BT39 1
Talbot Sq. W2 BT39 56
Talbot Wk. W11 BQ40 55
Lancaster Rd.
Talbot Yd. SE1 BZ40 4
Talbot Yd. SE1 BZ40 57
Borough High St.
Talbrook, Brwd. CZ27 42
Talents Clo., Dart. CX49 80
Taleworth Clo., Ash. BK63 102
Taleworth Rd., Ash. BK63 102
Talfourd Pl. SE15 CA44 67
Talfourd Rd. SE15 CA44 67
Talgarth Rd. W6 BQ42 65
Talisman Sq. SE26 CB49 77
Talisman Way, Epsom BQ61 103
Talisman Way, Wem. BL34 46
Tall Elms Clo., Brom. CG53 88
Tall Oaks, Amer. AO22 25
Tall Trees SW16 BX52 86
Tall Trees, Slou. AU44 62
Park St.
Tallack Clo., Har. BH29 36
Tallack Rd. E10 CD33 48
Tallents Clo., S.at H. CX50 80
Tallis Gro. SE7 CH43 68
Tallis St. EC4 BY40 4
Tallis St. EC4 BY40 56
Tallis Way, Brwd. BK23 27
Tallon Rd., Brwd. DF25 122
Tally Ho Corner N12 BT28 38
Tally Rd., Oxt. CK69 115
Talma Gdns., Twick. BH46 74
Talma Rd. SW2 BY45 66
Talmage Clo. SE23 CC47 77
Talman Gro., Stan. BK29 36
Talus Clo., Grays CY42 70
Brimfield Rd.
Talwin St. E3 CE38 57
Tamar Clo., Upmin. CZ32 51
Tamar Dr., S.Ock. CY39 60
Tamar Grn., Hem.H. AY11 8
Tamar Sq., Wdf.Grn. CH29 40
Tamar St. SE7 CK42 68
Tamar Way N17 CA31 48
Tamar Way, Slou. AT42 62
Tamarind Clo., Guil. AQ68 109
Tamarind Yd. E1 CB40 57
Asher Way
Tamarisk Clo., St.Alb. BG11 9
New Greens Av.
Tamarisk Rd., S.Ock. DB38 60
Tamarisk Sq. W12 BO40 55
Tamesis Gdns., Wor.Pk. BO55 85
Tamesis Strand, Grav. DJ49 81
Tamian Way, Houns. BD45 64
Tamplin Ms. W9 BS38 56
Warlock Rd.
Tamworth Av., Wdf.Grn. CG29 40
Tamworth Gdns., Pnr. BD30 36
Tamworth La., Mitch. BV51 86
Tamworth Pk., Mitch. BV52 86
Tamworth Pl., Croy. BZ55 87
Tamworth Rd., Croy. BY55 86
Tamworth St. SW6 BS43 66
Tan House La., Brwd. CX24 33
Tancred Rd. N4 BY32 47
Tandridge Dr., Orp. CM54 88
Tandridge Gdns., S.Croy. CA60 96
Tandridge Hill Lane Gdse. CD68 114
Tandridge La., Oxt. CE69 114
Tandridge Rd., Warl. CC63 105
Tanfield Av. NW2 BO35 46
Tanfield Clo., Chsnt. CB17 21
Spicersfield
Tanfield Ct. EC4 BY39 2
Tanfield Rd., Croy. BZ56 96
Tangent Rd., Rom. CV30 42
Tangier La., Eton AO43 61
Tangier Rd., Guil. AT71 118
Tangier Rd., Rich. BM45 65
Tangier Way, Tad. BR62 103
Tangier Wd., Tad. BR62 103
Tanglebury Clo., Brom. CK52 88
Oldfield Rd.
Tangles Clo., Uxb. AZ38 53
Tanglewood Clo., Cher. AQ55 82
Tanglewood Clo., Croy. CC55 87
Tanglewood Clo., Stan. BH27 36
Tanglewood Clo., Wok. AU61 100
Tanglewood Way, Felt. BC48 73
Tangley Gro. SW15 BO46 75
Tangley La., Guil. AP68 109
Tangley Park Rd., Hmptn. BE49 74
Tanglyn Av., Shep. AZ53 83
Tangmere Cres., Horn. CU36 59
Tangmere Gdns., Nthlt. BD37 54
Tangmere Way NW9 BO30 37
Tanhouse Rd., Oxt. CF69 114
Tanhurst Wk. SE2 CP41 69
Alsike Rd.
Tank Hill Rd., Grays CX42 70
Tank La., Grays CX42 70
Tankerfield Pl., St.Alb. BG13 9
Romeland Hill
Tankerton Rd., Surb. BL55 85
Tankerton St. WC1 BX38 2
Tankerton St. WC1 BX38 56
Cromer St.
Tankerville Rd. SW16 BW50 76
Tankridge Rd. NW2 BP34 46
Tanner St. SE1 CA41 4
Tanner St. SE1 CA41 67
Tanner St., Bark. CM36 58
Tanners Clo., Walt. BC53 83
Tanners Dean, Lthd. BK64 102
Tanners End La. N18 CA28 39
Tanners Hill SE8 CD44 67
Tanners Hill, Bet. BM71 120
Tanners Hill, Wat. BB19 17
Tanners La., Ilf. CM31 49
Tanners Wood La., Wat. BB19 17
Tannery Clo., Beck. CC52 87
Tannery Clo., Dag. CR34 50
Tannery La., Wok. AU65 100
Tannery, The, Red. BU70 121
Oakdene Rd.
Tannington Ter. N4 BY34 47
Tannsfield Clo., Hem.H. AY12 8
Tannsfield Rd. SE26 CC49 77
Tannsmore Clo., Hem.H. AY12 8
Tanrides Rd., Orp. CM54 88
Tansley Clo. N7 BW35 47
Hilldrop Rd.
Tanswell Est. SE1 BY41 4
Tanswell Est. SE1 BY41 66
Tanswell St. SE1 BY41 4
Tanswell St. SE1 BY41 66
Tansy Clo. E6 CL39 58
Tansy Clo., Guil. AU69 118
Tansy Clo., Rom. CW29 42
Tansycroft, Welw.G.C. BS 7 5
Tant Av. E16 CG39 58
Tantallon Rd. SW12 BV47 76
Tantony Gro., Rom. CP31 50
Tanworth Clo., Nthwd. BA29 35
Thirlmere Gdns.
Tanys Dell, Harl. CO 9 6
Tanza Rd. NW3 BU35 47
Tapestry Clo., Sutt. BS57 95
Taplow St. N1 BZ37 2
Taplow St. N1 BZ37 57
Tapners Rd., Reig. BO73 120
Tapp St. E1 CB38 57
Tapp Wk. NW2 BQ34 46
Oxgate Gdns.
Tappesfield Rd. SE15 CC45 67
Tapster St., Barn. BR24 28
Tara Pk., Couls. BU63 104
Taransay, Hem.H. AZ14 8
Tarbay La., Wind. AK45 61
Tarbert Rd. SE22 CA46 77
Tarbert Wk. E1 CC39 57
Juniper St.
Target Clo., Felt. BB46 73
Tariff Rd. N17 CB29 39
Tarleton Gdns. SE23 CB48 77
Tarling Clo., Sid. CO48 79
Tarling Est. E1 CB40 57
Tarling Rd. E16 CG39 58
Tarling Rd. N2 BT30 38
Tarling St. E1 CC39 57
Tarmac Way, Houns. AW43 63
Tarn St. SE1 BZ41 4
Tarn St. SE1 BZ41 67
Tarnbank, Enf. BX25 29
Tarnwood Pk. Est. SE9 CK47 78
Tarnwood Pk. SE9 CK47 78
Tarnworth Rd., Rom. CX28 42
Tarpan Way, Brox. CD16 21
Tarragon Dr., Guil. AQ68 109
Tarragon Gro. SE26 CC50 77
Tarrington Clo. SW16 BW49 76
Tarry La. SE8 CD42 67
Yeoman St.
Tartar Rd., Cob. BD60 93
Tarver Rd. SE17 BY42 4
Tarver Rd. SE17 BY42 66
Tarves Way SE10 CE43 67
Tash Pl. N11 BW28 38
Woodland Rd.
Tasker Clo., Hayes BA43 63
Tasker Rd. NW3 BU35 47
Tasker Rd., Grays DG41 71
Tasman Ct., Ashf. BB50 73
Warren Rd.
Tasman Ho., Til. DG44 71
Leicester Rd.
Tasman Rd. SW9 BX45 66
Tasman Wk. E16 CJ39 58
Royal Rd.
Tasmania Ter. N18 BZ29 39
Tasso Rd. W6 BR43 65
Tatam Rd. NW10 BN36 55
Tate Clo., Lthd. BK65 102
Tate Rd. E16 CK40 58
Tate Rd., Ger.Cr. AS28 34
Tate Rd., Sutt. BS56 95
Tatnell Rd. SE23 CD46 77
Tatsfield Approach Rd., West. CH65 106
Tatsfield Av., Wal.Abb. CF15 12
Tatsfield La., West. CK64 106
Tattenham Corner Rd., Epsom BO62 103
Tattenham Cres., Epsom. BP62 103
Tattenham Gro., Epsom BP62 103
Tattenham Way, Tad. BQ62 103
Tattersall Clo. SE9 CK46 78
Tattershall Dr., Hem.H. AZ10 8
Tatum St. SE17 BZ42 4
Tatum St. SE17 BZ42 67
Taunton Av. SW20 BP51 85
Taunton Av., Cat. CA65 105
Taunton Av., Couls. BY63 104
Taunton Av., Houns. BG44 64
Taunton Clo., Bexh. CS44 69
Taunton Clo., Ilf. CN29 40
Wickets Way
Taunton Clo., Sutt. BS54 86
Taunton Dr., Enf. BY24 29
Taunton La., Couls. BY63 104
Taunton Ms. NW1 BU38 1
Taunton Ms. NW1 BU38 56
Gloucester Pl.
Taunton Pl. NW1 BU38 1
Taunton Pl. NW1 BU38 56
Taunton Rd. SE12 CG46 78
Taunton Rd., Grav. DD46 81
Taunton Rd., Grnf. BF37 54
Taunton Rd., Rom. CV28 42
Taunton Vale, Grav. DH48 81
Taunton Way, Stan. BL31 46
Tavern La. SW9 BY44 66
Myatts Fields Dev.
Taverner Sq. N7 BZ35 48
Taverners Clo. W11 BR40 55
Addison Av.
Taverners Way E4 CG26 40
Douglas Rd.
Taverners, Hem.H. AY12 8
Tavistock Av. E17 CC31 48
Tavistock Av., Grnf. BJ37 54
Tavistock Av., St.Alb. BG15 9
Tavistock Clo., Pot.B. BT19 20
Tavistock Clo., Rom. CV30 42
Tavistock Clo., St.Alb. BG15 9
Tavistock Clo., Stai. AX50 73
Shaftesbury Cres.
Tavistock Cres. W11 BR39 55
Tavistock Cres., Mitch. BX52 86
Tavistock Gdns., Ilf. CN35 49
Tavistock Gro., Croy. BZ54 87
Tavistock Ms. E18 CH31 49
Avon Way
Tavistock Pl. N14 BV25 29
Tavistock Pl. WC1 BX38 2
Tavistock Pl. WC1 BX38 56
Tavistock Pl., Ilf. CH31 49
Tavistock Rd. E15 CG36 58
Tavistock Rd. E18 CH31 49
Tavistock Rd. E7 CG35 49
Tavistock Rd. N4 BZ32 48
Tavistock Rd. NW10 BO37 55
Tavistock Rd. W11 BR39 55
Tavistock Rd., Brom. CG52 88
Tavistock Rd., Cars. BT54 86
Tavistock Rd., Croy. BZ54 87
Tavistock Rd., Edg. BL30 37
Tavistock Rd., Uxb. BA35 44
Tavistock Rd., Wat. BD23 27
Tavistock Rd., Well. CP44 69
Tavistock Rd., West Dr. AX40 53
Tavistock Sq. WC1 BW38 1
Tavistock Sq. WC1 BW38 56
Tavistock St. WC2 BX40 4
Tavistock St. WC2 BX40 56
Tavistock Ter. N19 BW34 47
Tavistock Wk., Cars. BY54 86
Taviton St. WC1 BW38 1
Taviton St. WC1 BW38 56
Tavy Br. SE2 CP41 69
Tavy Clo. SE11 BY42 66
White Hart St.
Tawney Common, Epp. CR18 23
Tawney Rd. SE28 CO40 59
Tawneys Rd., Harl. CN12 13
Tawny Av., Upmin. CX35 51
Tawny Clo., Felt. BC48 73
Tawny Way SE16 CC42 67
Tay Way, Rom. CT30 41
Tayben Av., Twick. BH46 74
Taybridge Rd. SW11 BV45 66
Tayburn Clo. E14 CF39 57
St. Leonards Rd.
Tayfield Clo., Uxb. BA34 44
Tayles Hill, Epsom BO58 94
Taylifers, Harl. CL13 13
Taylor Av., Rich. BM44 65
Taylor Clo. N17 CB29 39
Northumberland Pk.
Taylor Clo., Hmptn. BG49 74
Taylor Clo., Orp. CM56 97
Strickland Way
Taylor Clo., Rom. CR29 41
Taylor Clo., St.Alb. BJ11 9
Taylor Rd., Ash. BK62 102
Taylor Rd., Mitch. BU50 76
Taylor Rd., Wall. BV56 95
Taylor St. SE18 CL42 68
Taylors Av., Hodd. CE12 12
Taylors Bldgs. SE18 CL42 68
Spray St.
Taylors Clo., Sid. CN49 78
Taylors Ct. E15 CF35 48
Taylors Grn. W3 BO39 55
Long Dr.
Taylors La. NW10 BO36 55
Taylors La. SE26 CB49 77
Taylors La., Barn. BR23 28
Taylors Rd., Ches. AO18 16
Taymount Grange SE26 CC48 77
Taymount Ri. SE23 CC48 77
Taynton Dr., Red. BW68 113
Tayport Clo. N1 BX36 56
Tayport Clo. N1 BX37 2
Taywood Rd., Nthlt. BE38 54
Teak Clo. SE16 CD40 57
Teal Clo. E16 CJ39 58
Fulmer Rd.
Teal Clo., S.Croy. CC59 96
Teal Dr., Nthwd. BA29 35
Teale St. E2 CB37 57
Tealing Dr., Epsom BN56 94
Teasel Clo., Croy. CC54 87
Teasel Way E15 CG38 58
Memorial Av.
Teather St. SE5 CA43 67
Southampton Way
Teazlewood Pk., Lthd. BJ62 102
Tebworth Rd. N17 CA29 39
Church Rd.
Tedder Clo., Esher BK56 93
Mansfield Rd.
Tedder Clo., Hayes BA43 63
West End La.
Tedder Clo., Ruis. BC35 44
Tedder Clo., Uxb. AY36 53
Tedder Rd., Hem.H. AZ13 8
Tedder Rd., S.Croy. CC57 96
Teddington Clo., Epsom BN58 94
Teddington Pk. Rd., Tedd. BH49 74
Teddington Pk., Tedd. BH49 74
Tedworth Gdns. SW3 BU42 66
Tedworth Sq. SW3 BU42 3
Tedworth Sq. SW3 BU42 66
Tee, The W3 BO39 55
Tees Av., Grnf. BH37 54
Tees Clo., Upmin. CY32 51
Tees Dr., Rom. CV27 42
Teesdale Av., Islw. BJ44 64
Teesdale Clo. E2 CB37 57
Claredale St.
Teesdale Est. E2 CB38 57
Teesdale Gdns., Islw. BJ44 64
Teesdale Rd. Dart. CY47 80
Teesdale Rd. E11 CG32 49
Teesdale St. E2 CB37 57
Teesdale, Hem.H. AY12 8
Teevan Clo., Croy. CB54 87
Teevan Rd., Croy. CB54 87
Teggs La., Wok. AV61 100
Teignmouth Clo. SW4 BW45 66
Teignmouth Clo., Edg. BL30 37
Teignmouth Gdns., Grnf. BJ37 54
Teignmouth Rd. NW2 BQ35 46
Teignmouth Rd., Well. CP44 69
Telcote Way, Ruis. BD33 45
Telegraph Hill NW3 BS34 47
Telegraph La., Esher BJ57 93
Telegraph Ms., Ilf. CO33 50
Eastwood Rd.
Telegraph Rd. SW15 BP46 75
Telegraph St. EC2 BZ39 2
Telegraph St. EC2 BZ39 57
Telemann Sq. SE3 CH45 68
Telephone Pl. SW6 BR43 65
Telferscot Rd. SW12 BW47 76
Telford Av. SW2 BW47 76
Telford Clo. SE19 CA50 77
Aubyns Rd.
Telford Clo., Wat. BD21 27
Telford Ct., St.Alb. BH14 9
Alma Rd.
Telford Dr., Slou. AN41 61
Telford Dr., Walt. BD54 84
Telford Rd. N11 BW29 38
Telford Rd. NW9 BO33 46
The Broadway
Telford Rd. SE9 CM48 78
Telford Rd. W10 BR39 55
Telford Rd., Houns. BF47 74
Telford Rd., St.Alb. BK17 18
Telford Rd., Sthl. BF39 54
Telford Ter. SW1 BW43 3
Telford Ter. SW1 BW43 66
Churchill Gdns. Rd.
Telford Way W3 BO39 55
Telfords Yd. E1 CB40 57
The Highway

Telham Rd. E6 CL37 58
Tell Gro. SE22 CA45 67
Tellisford, Esher BF56 93
Tellson Av. SE18 CJ44 68
Telscombe Clo., Orp. CN55 88
Telston La., Sev. CT62 107
Temeraire St. SE16 CC41 67
Swan Rd.
Temme Av. E15 CG36 58
Temperance St., St.Alb. BG13 9
Temperley Rd. SW12 BV47 76
Tempest Av., Pot.B. BT19 20
Tempest Rd., Egh. AU50 72
Tempest Way, Rain. CU36 59
Templar Dr. SE28 CP39 59
Templar Ho. NW2 BR36 55
Templar Pl., Hmptn. BF50 74
Templar St. SE5 BY44 66
Templars Av. NW11 BR32 46
Templars Cres. N3 BS30 38
Templars Dr., Har. BG29 36
Temple Av. EC4 BY40 4
Temple Av. EC4 BY40 56
Temple Av. N20 BT26 38
Temple Av., Croy. CD55 87
Temple Av., Dag. CR33 50
Temple Bank, Harl. CO 8 6
Temple Bar Rd., Wok. AP63 100
Temple Cft., Ashf. BA50 73
Temple Clo. E11 CG33 49
Wadley Rd.
Temple Clo. N3 BR30 37
Cyprus Rd.
Temple Clo. SE28 CM41 68
Temple Clo., Chsnt. CB19 21
Temple Clo., Wat. BB23 26
Temple Ct., Pot.B. BQ19 19
Temple Field Clo., Wey. AW57 92
Temple Fortune Hill NW11 BS32 47
Temple Fortune La. NW11 BR32 46
Temple Gdns EC4 BY40 4
Middle Temple La.
Temple Gdns EC4 BY40 56
Middle Temple La.
Temple Gdns. NW11 BR32 46
Temple Gdns., Dag. CP34 50
Bennetts Castle La.
Temple Gdns., Rick. AZ28 35
Temple Gdns., Stai. AV51 82
Temple Gro. NW11 BS32 47
Temple Gro., Enf. BY24 29
Temple Hill Sq., Dart. CW46 80
Temple Hill, Dart. CW46 80
Temple La. EC4 BY39 2
Temple La. EC4 BY39 56
Temple Mead Clo., Stan. BJ29 36
Temple Mead, Harl. CH10 13
Temple Mead, Hem.H. AX12 8
Temple Mill La. E15 CE35 48
Temple Mill Rd. E15 CE35 48
Temple Pk., Uxb. AZ38 53
Temple Pl. WC2 BX40 4
Temple Pl. WC2 BX40 56
Temple Rd. E6 CK37 58
Temple Rd. N8 BX31 47
Temple Rd. NW2 BQ35 46
Temple Rd. W4 BN41 65
Temple Rd. W5 BK41 64
Temple Rd., Croy. BZ56 96
Temple Rd., Epsom BN59 94
Temple Rd., Houns. BF45 64
Temple Rd., Rich. BL45 65
Temple Rd., West. CJ61 106
Hillcrest Rd.
Temple Rd., Wind. AO44 61
Temple Sheen Rd. SW14 BM45 65
Temple Sheen SW14 BN45 65
Temple St. E2 CB37 57
Temple Way, Sutt. BT55 86
Temple Wood La., Slou. AO35 43
Temple, The EC4 BY40 4
Temple, The EC4 BY40 56
Templecombe Ms., Wok. AT61 100
Templecombe Rd. E9 CC37 57
Templecombe Way, Mord. BR53 85
Templedene Av., Stai. AW50 73
Templehof Av. NW2 BQ33 46
Templeman Clo., Pur. BY61 104
Templeman Rd. W7 BH39 54
Templemead Clo. W3 BO39 55
Carlisle Av.
Templemere, Wey. BA55 83
Templepan La., Rick. AY22 26
Templer Av., Grays DG42 71
Templer Dr., Grav. DG49 81
Templeton Av. E4 CE27 39
Templeton Clo. SE19 BZ51 87
Templeton Pl. SW5 BS42 66
Templeton Rd. N15 BZ32 48
Templewood Av. NW3 BS34 47
Templewood Gdns. NW3 BS34 47
Templewood W13 BJ39 54
Templewood, Welw.G.C. BQ 6 5
Tempsford Av., B.Wd. BN24 28
Tempsford Clo., Enf. BZ24 30
Gladbeck Way
Tempsford, Welw.G.C. BT 8 5
Temsford Clo., Har. BG30 36
Ten Acre La., Egh. AU51 82
Ten Acre, Wok. AQ62 100
Abercorn Way
Ten Acres, Lthd. BG65 102
The Green
Ten St. EC2 BZ39 57
Tenbury Clo. E7 CJ35 49
Tenbury Ct. SW2 BW47 76
Tenby Av., Har. BJ30 36
Tenby Clo. N15 CA31 48
Tenby Clo., Rom. CQ32 50
Tenby Gdns., Nthlt. BF36 54
Tenby Pl. N1 BX37 2
Tenby Rd. E17 CD32 48
Tenby Rd., Edg. BL30 37
Tenby Rd., Enf. CC24 30
Tenby Rd., Rom. CQ32 50
Tenby Rd., Well. CP44 69
Tench St. E1 CB40 57
Tenchleys La., Oxt. CJ69 115
Tenda Rd. SE16 CB42 67
Tendring Rd., Harl. CM12 13
Tendring Way, Rom. CP32 50
Tenham Av. SW2 BW48 76
Tenham Ter. SW3 BU42 66
Tenison Ct. W1 BW40 3
Tenison Ct. W1 BW40 56
Kingly St.
Tenison Way SE1 BX40 56
Tennand Clo., Chsnt. CA16 21
Tenniel Ct. W2 CJ40 58
Porchester Gdns.
Tennis St. SE1 BZ41 4
Tennis St. SE1 BZ41 67
Tennison Av., B.Wd. BM25 28
Tennison Clo., Couls. BY63 104
Tennison Rd. SE25 CA52 87
Tennison Way SE1 BX40 4
Tennison Way SE1 BX40 56
Tenniswood Rd., Enf. CA23 30
Tennyson Av. E11 CH33 49
Tennyson Av. E12 CK36 58
Tennyson Av. NW9 BN31 46
Tennyson Av., Grays DD41 71
Tennyson Av., N.Mal. BP53 85
Tennyson Av., Twick. BH47 74
Tennyson Av., Wal.Abb. CG20 22
Tennyson Clo., Felt. BC46 73
Tennyson Clo., Well. CN44 68
Tennyson Ct., Rich. BK49 74
Tennyson Rd. E10 CE34 48
Tennyson Rd. E15 CG36 58
Tennyson Rd. E17 CD32 48
Tennyson Rd. NW6 BR37 55
Tennyson Rd. NW7 BP28 37
Tennyson Rd. SE20 CC50 77
Tennyson Rd. SW19 BT50 76
Tennyson Rd. W7 BH40 54
Tennyson Rd., Ashf. AY49 73
Tennyson Rd., Brwd. DE26 122
Tennyson Rd., Dart. CX46 80
Tennyson Rd., Houns. BG44 64
Tennyson Rd., Rom. CU29 41
Tennyson Rd., St.Alb. BF16 18
Tennyson Rd., Well. CN44 68
Shelley Dr.
Tennyson Rd., Wey. AY56 92
Tennyson St. SW8 BV44 66
Tennyson Way, Horn. CU34 50
Tennyson Wk., Grav. DE48 81
Tennyson Wk., Til. DG44 71
Tensing Av., Grav. DF48 81
Tensing Rd., Sthl. BF41 64
Tent St. E1 CB38 57
Tentelow La., Sthl. BF42 64
Tenter Gro. E1 CA39 2
Tenter Gro. E1 CA39 57
Brune St.
Tenterden Clo. NW4 BQ31 46
Tenterden Clo., SE9 CK49 78
Framlingham Cres.
Tenterden Dr. NW4 BQ31 46
Tenterden Gdns. NW4 BQ31 46
Tenterden Gdns., Croy. CB54 87
Tenterden Gro. NW4 BQ31 46
Tenterden Rd. N17 CA29 39
Tenterden Rd., Croy. CB54 87
Tenterden Rd., Dag. CQ34 50
Tenterden St. W1 BV39 1
Tenterden St. W1 BV39 56
Tenzing Rd., Hem.H. AZ13 8
Terborch Way SE22 CA46 77
Dulwich Gro.
Tercel Path, Chig. CO28 41
Terence Clo., Grav. DJ48 81
Teresa Ms. E17 CE31 48
Cairo Rd.
Terling Clo. E11 CG34 49
Terling Rd., Dag. CR34 50
Terling Wk. N1 BZ37 2
Popham St.
Terling Wk. N1 BZ37 57
Popham St.
Terlings, The, Brwd. DA27 42
Kavanagh Rd.
Terminus Pl. SW1 BV41 3
Terminus Pl. SW1 BV41 66
Terminus St., Harl. CM10 6
Tern Gdns., Upmin. CZ33 51
Tern Way, Brwd. CZ28 42
River Rd.
Terrace Gdns. SW13 BO44 65
Terrace Gdns., Wat. BC23 26
Terrace La., Rich. BL46 75
Friars Stile Rd.
Terrace Rd. E13 CH37 58
Terrace Rd. E9 CC36 57
Terrace Rd., Walt. BC54 83
Terrace St., Grav. DG46 81
Terrace Wk., Dag. CQ35 50
Terrace, The N3 BR30 37
Hendon La.
Terrace, The NW6 BS37 56
Terrace, The SW13 BO44 65
Terrace, The W14 BR42 65
Terrace, The, Dor. BK72 119
Terrace, The, Grav. DG46 81
Terrace, The, Kings.T. BK51 84
Church Gro.
Terrace, The, Maid. AH41 61
Terrace, The, Rich. BL46 75
Terrace, The, Sev. CS64 107
Terrace, The, Wey. AY56 92
Terrapin Rd. SW17 BV48 76
Terretts Pl. N1 BY36 2
Terretts Pl. N1 BY36 56
Upper St.
Terrick Rd. N22 BX30 38
Terrick St. W12 BP39 55
Terrilands, Pnr. BE31 45
Terront Rd. N15 BZ32 48
Terry Way, Brom. CH51 88
Church Rd.
Tessa Sanderson Pl. SW8 BV45 66
Heath Rd.
Testard Rd., Guil. AR71 118
Testers Clo., Oxt. CH69 115
Testerton St. W11 BQ40 55
Testerton Wk. W11 BQ40 55
Lancaster Rd.
Testwood Rd., Wind. AL44 61
Tetbury Pl. N1 BY37 2
Tetbury Pl. N1 BY37 56
Upper St.
Tetcott Rd. SW10 BT43 66
Tetherdown N10 BV30 38
Tethys Rd., Hem.H. AY12 8
Tetterby Way SE16 CB42 67
The Bonamy Est. W.
Teversham La. SW8 BX44 66
Teviot Av., S.Ock. CW39 60
Teviot Clo., Well. CO44 69
Stuart Rd.
Teviot St. E14 CF38 57
Tewin Clo., St.Alb. BK11 9
Tewin Ct., Welw.G.C. BR 7 5
Tewin Hill, Welw.G.C. BU 5 5
Tewin Rd., Hem.H. BA13 8
Tewin Rd., Welw.G.C. BR 8 5
Tewkesbury Av. SE23 CB47 77
Tewkesbury Av., Pnr. BE32 45
Tewkesbury Clo. N15 BZ32 48
Tewkesbury Rd.
Tewkesbury Clo., Wey. AX59 92
Tewkesbury Gdns. NW9 BM31 46
Tewkesbury Rd. N15 BZ32 48
Tewkesbury Rd. W13 BJ40 54
Talbot Rd.
Tewkesbury Rd., Cars. BT54 86
Tewkesbury Ter. N11 BW29 38
Tewson Rd. SE18 CN42 68
Teynham Av., Enf. BZ25 30
Teynham Grn., Brom. CH53 88
Teynton Ter. N17 BZ30 39
Thackeray Av. N17 CB30 39
Thackeray Av., Til. DG44 71
Thackeray Clo. SW19 BQ50 75
Thackeray Clo., Uxb. AZ39 53
Thackeray Dr., Rom. CO33 50
Thackeray Rd. E6 CJ37 58
Thackeray Rd. SW8 BV44 66
Thackeray St. W8 BS41 3
Thackeray St. W8 BS41 66
Thackery Clo., Har. BF33 45
Thakeham Clo. SE26 CB49 77
Thakrah Clo. N2 BT30 38
Thalia Clo. SE10 CF43 67
Feathers Pl.
Thalmassing Clo., Brwd. DD27 122
Roth Dr.
Thame Rd. SE16 CC41 67
Thames Av. SW10 BT44 66
Thames Av., Cher. AW52 83
Eastern Av.
Thames Av., Dag. CS38 59
Thames Av., Grnf. BH37 54
Thames Av., Hem.H. AY11 8
Thames Av., Wind. AO43 61
Thames Bank SW14 BN44 65
Thames Clo., Cher. AX54 83
Thames Clo., Hmptn. BF51 84
Thames Clo., Rain. CU39 59
Thames Dr., Grays DG42 71
Thames Dr., Ruis. BA32 44
Thames Mead, Walt. BC53 83
Thames Mead, Wind. AM44 61
Thames Meadow, E.Mol. BF51 84
Thames Pl. E14 CD40 57
Thames Prom., Twick. BJ45 64
Thames Rd. E16 CJ40 58
Thames Rd. W4 BM43 65
Thames Rd., Bark. CN38 58
Thames Rd., Dart. CT44 69
Thames Rd., Grays DD43 71
Thames Rd., Slou. AT42 62
Thames Side, Cher. AX53 83
Thames Side, Kings.T. BK51 84
Thames Side, Stai. AW51 83
Thames Side, Tedd. BK50 74
Thames Side, Wind. AO43 61
Thames St. SE10 CE43 67
Thames St., Hmptn. BF51 84
Thames St., Kings.T. BK51 84
Thames St., Stai. AV49 72
Thames St., Sun. BC52 83
Thames St., Walt. BB54 83
Thames St., Wey. AZ55 83
Thames St., Wind. AO44 61
Thames Vill. W4 BN44 65
Thames Vw. Est., Bark. CN37 58
Thames Vw., Grays DG42 71
Thamesbank Pl. SE28 CP39 59
Thamesdale, St.Alb. BL17 19
Thamesfield Ct., Shep. BA54 83
Russell Rd.
Thamesgate Clo., Rich. BJ49 74
Thameshill Av., Rom. CS30 41
Thameside, Tedd. BK50 74
Thamesmead, Walt. BC53 83
Thamesmere Dr. SE28 CO40 59
Thamesview Clo., Green. CZ46 80
Thamesville Clo., Houns. BF44 64
Lampton Rd.
Thamley, Grays CX42 70
Thane Vill. N7 BX34 47
Thanescroft Gdns., Croy. CA55 87
Thanet Pl., Croy. BZ56 96
Thanet Rd., Bex. CR47 79
Thanet Rd., Erith CT43 69
Thanet St. WC1 BX38 2
Thanet St. WC1 BX38 56
Thanington Ct. SE9 CN46 78
Tharp Rd., Wall. BW56 95
Thatcham Gdns. N20 BT26 38
Thatcher Clo., West Dr. AY41 63
Thatchers Cft., Hem.H. AY11 8
Thatchers Clo., Loug. CM23 31
Mannock Dr.
Thatchers La., Guil. AO67 109
Thatchers Way, Islw. BG46 74
Reapers Way
Thatches Gro., Rom. CQ31 50
Thavies Inn EC1 BY39 2
St. Andrew St.
Thavies Inn EC1 BY39 56
St. Andrew St.
Thaxted Pl. SW20 BQ50 75
Thaxted Rd. SE9 CM48 78
Thaxted Rd., Buck.H. CJ26 40
Thaxted Way, Wal.Abb. CF20 21
Thaxted Wk., Rain. CT37 59
Thaxton Rd. W14 BR43 65
Thayer St. W1 BV39 1
Thayer St. W1 BV39 56
Thayers Farm Rd., Beck. CD51 87
Thaynesfield, Pot.B. BT19 20
Theatre St. SW11 BU45 66
Theberton St. N1 BY37 2
Theberton St. N1 BY37 56
Theed St. SE1 BY40 4
Theed St. SE1 BY40 56
Thelma Clo., Grav. DJ49 81
Thelma Gdns. SE3 CK44 68
Thelma Gdns., Felt. BE48 74
Thelma Gro., Tedd. BJ50 74
Theobald Clo., B.Wd. BL23 28
Theobald St.
Theobald Cres., Har. BF30 36
Theobald Rd. E17 CD33 48
Theobald Rd., Croy. BY55 86
Theobald St. SE1 BZ41 4
Theobald St. SE1 BZ41 67
Theobald St., B.Wd. BL23 28
Theobald St., Rad. BJ21 27
Theobalds Av. N12 BT28 38
Theobalds Av., Grays DE42 71
Theobalds Clo., Cuff. BX18 20
Theobalds Ct. N4 BZ34 48
Kings Cres. Est.
Theobalds La., Chsnt. CB19 21
Theobalds Pk. Rd., Enf. BY21 29
Theobalds Rd. WC1 BX39 2
Theobalds Rd. WC1 BX39 56
Theobalds Rd., Cuff. BX18 20
Theodore Rd. SE13 CF46 77
Thepps Clo., Red. BX72 121
Therapia La., Croy. BW54 86
Therapia La., Croy. BX53 86
Therapia Rd. SE22 CB46 77
Theresa Rd. W6 BP42 65
Theresas Wk., Croy. BZ58 96
Therfield Ct. N4 BZ34 48
Kings Cres. Est.
Therfield Rd., St.Alb. BG12 9
Thermopylae Gate E14 CE42 67
Theseus Wk. N1 BY37 2
Theseus Wk. N1 BY37 56
Nelson Pl.
Thesiger Rd. SE20 CC50 77
Thessaly Rd. SW8 BW43 66
Thetford Clo. N15 CA32 48
Norfolk Av.
Thetford Clo. N22 BY29 38
Thetford Gdns., Dag. CQ37 59
Thetford Rd., Ashf. AY49 73
Thetford Rd., Dag. CP37 59
Thetford Rd., N.Mal. BN53 85
Theydon Ct., Wal.Abb. CH20 22
Abbots Dr.
Theydon Gdns., Rain. CT36 59
Theydon Gro., Epp. CO18 23
Theydon Gro., Wdf.Grn. CJ29 40
Theydon Park Rd., Epp. CN22 31
Theydon Pl., Epp. CN19 22
Theydon Rd. E5 CC34 48
Theydon Rd., Epp. CM20 22
Theydon St. E17 CD33 48
Thicket Cres., Sutt. BT56 95
Thicket Gro. SE19 CB50 77
Anerley Rd.
Thicket Gro., Dag. CP36 59
Thicket Rd. SE20 CB50 77
Thicket Rd., Sutt. BT56 95
Thicket, The, West Dr. AY39 53
Thicketts, Sev. CV65 108
Thickhorne La., Stai. AX50 73
Third Av. E12 CK35 49
Third Av. E13 CH38 58
Third Av. E17 CE32 48
Third Av. W10 BR38 55
Third Av. W3 BO40 55
Third Av., Dag. CR37 59
Third Av., Enf. CA25 30
Third Av., Grays DA43 70
Third Av., Harl. CK11 13
Third Av., Hayes BB40 53
Third Av., Rom. CP32 50
Third Av., Wat. BD21 27
Third Av., Wem. BK34 45
Third Clo., E.Mol. BG52 84
Third Cross Rd., Twick. BG48 74
Third Way, Wem. BM35 46
Thirkleby Clo., Slou. AO40 61
Thirlby Rd., Edg. BN30 37
Thirleby Rd. SW1 BW41 3
Thirleby Rd. SW1 BW41 66
Thirlmere Av., Grnf. BJ38 54
Thirlmere Dr., St.Alb. BJ14 9
Thirlmere Gdns., Nthwd. BA29 35
Thirlmere Gdns., Wem. BK33 45
Thirlmere Rd. N10 BV30 38
Thirlmere Rd. SW16 BW49 76
Thirlmere Rd., Bexh. CS44 69
Thirlmere Ri., Brom. CG50 78
Thirlstane, St.Alb. BH13 9
Lemsford Rd.
Thirsk Clo., Nthlt. BF36 54
Thirsk Rd. SE25 BZ52 87
Thirsk Rd. SW11 BV45 66
Thirsk Rd., B.Wd. BM22 28
Thirsk Rd., Mitch. BV50 76
Thirza Rd., Dart. CW46 80
Thistle Cft., Hem.H. AV14 7
The Foxgloves
Thistle Gro. SW10 BT42 3
Thistle Gro. SW10 BT42 66
Thistle Gro., Welw.G.C. BT 9 5
Thistle Mead, Loug. CL24 31
Thistle Rd., Grav. DJ47 81
Thistle Wood Cres., Croy. CF59 96
Thistlebrook SE2 CP41 69
Thistlecroft Gdns., Stan. BK30 36
Thistlecroft Rd., Walt. BD56 93
Thistlecroft, Hem.H. AW14 8
Thistledene Av., Har. BE34 45
Thistledene Av., Rom. CR28 41
Thistledene, T.Ditt. BH53 84
Thistledene, Wey. AV60 91
Thistledown, Grav. DH50 81
Thistlemead, Chis. CL51 88
Thistles, The, Hem.H. AW13 8
Thistlewaite Rd. E5 CB34 48
Thistlewood Clo. N7 BX34 47
Durham Rd.
Thistleworth Clo., Islw. BG43 64
Thomas a Becket Clo., Wem BH35 45
Thomas Baines Rd. SW11 BT45 66
Thomas Clo., Brwd. DC27 122
Thomas Derby Ct. W11 BR39 55
Thomas Doyle St. SE1 BY41 4
Thomas Doyle St. SE1 BY41 66
London Rd.
Thomas Dr., Grav. DH48 81
Thomas La. SE6 CE47 77
Thomas More St. E1 CB40 4
Thomas More St. E1 CB40 57
Thomas More Way N2 BT31 47
Thomas Rd. E14 CD39 57
Thomas Sims Ct., Horn. CU36 59
South End Rd.
Thomas St. SE18 CL42 68
Thomas Wall Clo., Sutt. BS56 95
Robin Hood La.
Thompson Av. SE5 BZ43 67
Thompson Av., Rich. BM45 65
Thompson Clo., Ilf. CM34 49
Thompson Clo., Slou. AS42 62
Thompson Rd. SE22 CA46 77
Thompson Rd., Dag. CQ34 50
Thompson Rd., Uxb. AY36 53
Thompson Way, Ilf. CM34 49
Thompsons La., Loug. CG23 31
Thomson Cres., Croy. BY54 86
Thomson Rd., Har. BH31 45
Thong La., Grav. DJ49 81
Thong La., Sev. DC64 108
Thoresby St. N1 BZ38 2
Thoresby St. N1 BZ38 57
Thorkhill Gdns., T.Ditt. BJ54 84
Thorkhill Rd., T.Ditt. BJ54 84
Thorley Clo., Wey. AW60 92
Thorley Gdns., Wok. AW60 92
Thorley Rd., Grays DD40 71
Thorn Av., Bush. BG26 36
Thorn Av., Cat. BZ64 105
Thorn Bank, Edg. BM29 37
Thorn Bank, Guil. AQ71 118
Thorn Clo., Brom. CL53 88
Thorn Clo., Nthlt. BE38 54
Thorn La., Rain. CV37 60
Thornaby Clo. N18 CB29 39
Thornaby Gdns. N18 CB29 39
Thornash Clo., Wok. AR61 100
Thornash Rd., Wok. AR61 100
Thornash Way, Wok. AR61 100
Thornbank Clo., Stai. AW46 73
Thornbridge Rd., Iver AU37 52
Thornbury Av., Islw. BG43 64
Thornbury Gdns., B.Wd. BN24 28
Thornbury Rd. SW2 BX46 76
Thornbury Rd., Islw. BG43 64
Thornbury Sq. N6 BW33 47
Thornby Rd. E5 CC34 48
Thorncliffe Rd. SW2 BX46 76
Thorncliffe Rd., Sthl. BE42 64
Thorncombe Rd. SE22 CA46 77
Thorncroft Clo., Couls. BY63 104
Waddington Av.
Thorncroft Dr., Lthd. BJ65 102
Dorking Rd.
Thorncroft Rd., Sutt. BS56 95
Thorncroft St. SW8 BX43 66
Thorncroft, Egh. AR50 72
Thorncroft, Hem.H. AZ14 8
Thorncroft, Horn. CU32 50
Thorndales, Brwd. DB28 42
Thorndean St. SW18 BT48 76
Thorndene Av. N11 BV26 38
Thorndike Clo. SW10 BT43 66
Thorndike St. SW1 BW42 3
Thorndike St. SW1 BW42 66
Thorndon Av., Brwd. DE31 123
Thorndon Clo., Orp. CN51 88
Thorndon Gate, Brwd. DE28 122
Thorndon Gdns., Epsom BO56 94
Thorndon Rd., Orp. CN51 88
Thorndyke Av., Nthlt. BD37 54
Thorne Clo. E11 CG35 49
Thorne Clo. E16 CG39 58
Thorne Clo., Ashf. BA50 73
Thorne Clo., Erith CS43 69
Thorne Pass. SW13 BO44 65
White Hart La.
Thorne Rd. SW8 BX43 66
Thorne St. E16 CG39 58
Thorne St. SW13 BO45 65
Thorneloe Gdns., Croy. BY56 95
Thornes Clo., Beck. CF52 87
Thornet Wood Rd., Brom. CL52 88
Thorney Hedge Rd. W4 BM42 65
Thorney La. N., Iver AV40 52
Thorney La. S., Iver AV41 62
Thorney Mill Rd., Iver AW41 63
Thorney St. SW1 BX42 4
Thorney St. SW1 BX42 66
Thorneycroft Clo., Walt. BD53 84
Thornfield Av. NW7 BR30 37
Thornfield Rd. W12 BP41 65
Thornfield Rd., Bans. BS62 104

Thornford Rd. SE13	CF46	77
Thorngate Rd. W9	BS38	56
Thorngrove Rd. E13	CH37	58
Thornham Gro. E15	CF35	48
Thornham St. SE10	CE43	67
Thornhaugh St. WC1	**BW38**	**1**
Thornhaugh St. WC1	BW38	56
Thornhill Av. SE18	CN43	68
Thornhill Av., Surb.	BL55	85
Thornhill Bridge Wf. N1	**BX37**	**2**
Thornhill Bridge Wf. N1	BX37	56
Caledonian Rd.		
Thornhill Cres. N1	**BX36**	**2**
Thornhill Cres. N1	BX36	56
Thornhill Gdns. E10	CE34	48
Thornhill Gdns., Bark.	CN36	58
Thornhill Gro. N1	**BX36**	**2**
Thornhill Gro. N1	BX36	56
Lofting Rd.		
Thornhill Rd. E10	CE34	48
Thornhill Rd. N1	BY36	56
Thornhill Rd. N1	**BY37**	**2**
Thornhill Rd., Croy.	BZ54	87
Thornhill Rd., Nthwd.	BA28	35
Thornhill Rd., Surb.	BL55	85
Thornhill Rd., Uxb.	AZ35	44
Thornhill Sq. N1	**BX36**	**2**
Thornhill Sq. N1	BX36	56
Thornhill Way, Shep.	AZ53	83
Sheep Wk.		
Thornhill, Epp.	CS16	23
Thornlaw Rd. SE27	BY49	76
Thornley Cr. SW11	BT43	66
Thornley Ct. N17	CB29	39
Thornley Dr., Har.	BF34	45
Thornley Pl. SE10	CG42	68
Caradoc St.		
Thornridge, Brwd.	DA26	42
Greenshaw		
Thorns Meadow, West.	CP65	107
Thornsbeach Rd. SE6	CF47	77
Thornsett Pl. SE20	CB51	87
Thornsett Rd. SE20	CB51	87
Thornsett Rd. SW18	BS47	76
Thornton Av. SW2	BW47	76
Thornton Av. W4	BO42	65
Thornton Av., Croy.	BX53	86
Thornton Av., West Dr.	AY41	63
Thornton Clo., Guil.	AQ69	118
Thornton Clo., West Dr.	AY41	63
Thornton Ct. SW20	BQ53	85
Thornton Dene, Beck.	CE51	87
Thornton Gdns. SW12	BW47	76
Thornton Gro., Pnr.	BF29	36
Thornton Hl. SW19	BR50	75
Thornton Pl. W1	**BU39**	**1**
Thornton Pl. W1	BU39	56
Thornton Rd. E. SW19	BQ50	75
Thornton Rd.		
Thornton Rd. E11	CF34	48
Thornton Rd. SW12	BW47	76
Thornton Rd. SW14	BN45	65
Thornton Rd. SW19	BQ50	75
Thornton Rd., Barn.	BR24	28
Thornton Rd., Belv.	CR42	69
Thornton Rd., Brom.	CH49	78
Thornton Rd., Cars.	BT54	86
Thornton Rd., Croy.	BX54	86
Thornton Rd., Ilf.	CL35	49
Thornton Rd., Pot.B.	BT18	20
Thornton Row, Th.Hth.	BY53	86
Thornton St. SW9	BT44	66
Robsart St.		
Thornton St., St.Alb.	BG13	9
Thornton Way NW11	BS32	47
Thorntons Farm Av., Rom.	CS33	50
Thorntons, Brwd.	DE29	122
Brentwood Rd.		
Thorntree Rd. SE7	CJ42	68
Thornville St. SE8	CE44	67
Thornwood Clo. E18	CH30	40
Thornwood Rd. SE13	CG46	78
Thornwood Rd., Epp.	CO18	23
Thorogood Gdns. E15	CG35	49
Thorogood Way, Rain.	CT37	59
Thorold Clo., S.Croy.	CC58	96
Thorold Rd. N22	BX29	38
Thorold Rd., Ilf.	CL34	49
Thoroughfare, The, Tad.	BP65	103
Thorparch Rd. SW8	BW44	66
Thorpe By-pass, Egh.	AT52	82
Thorpe Clo. SE26	CC49	77
Silverdale		
Thorpe Clo. W10	BR39	55
Cambridge Gdns.		
Thorpe Clo., Croy.	CF59	96
Thorpe Clo., Nthlt.	BE36	54
Thorpe Clo., Orp.	CN55	88
Thorpe Cres. E17	CD30	39
Thorpe Cres., Wat.	BD26	36
Thorpe Hall Ms. W5	BK39	54
Eaton Ri.		
Thorpe Lea Rd., Egh.	AT50	72
Thorpe Lodge, Horn.	CW33	51
Thorpe Rd. E17	CF30	39
Thorpe Rd. E6	CK37	58
Thorpe Rd. E7	CG35	49
Thorpe Rd. N15	CA32	48
Thorpe Rd., Bark.	CM36	58
Thorpe Rd., Cher.	AU52	82
Thorpe Rd., Kings.T.	BL50	75
Thorpe Rd., St.Alb.	BG14	9
Thorpe Rd., Stai.	AU50	72
Thorpe St. E1	**CA39**	**2**
Thorpe St. E1	CA39	57
Wentworth St.		
Thorpebank Rd. W12	BP40	55
Thorpedale Gdns., Ilf.	CL31	49
Thorpedale Rd. N4	BX33	47
Thorpefield Clo., St.Alb.	BK12	9
Thorpehall Rd. E17	CF30	39
Thorpes Clo., Guil.	AQ69	118
Thorpewood Av. SE26	CB48	77
Thorpland Av., Uxb.	BA34	44
Thorsden Clo., Wok.	AS63	100
Thorsden Ct., Wok.	AS62	100
Guildford Rd.		
Thorsden Way SE19	CA49	77
Oaks Av.		
Thorton Cres., Couls.	BX63	104
Thorverton Rd. NW2	BR34	46
Thoydon Rd. E3	CD37	57
Thrale Rd. SW16	BW49	76
Thrale St. SE1	**BZ40**	**4**
Thrale St. SE1	BZ40	57
Thrasher Clo. E8	**CA37**	**2**
Stean St.		
Thrasher Clo. E8	CA37	57
Stean St.		
Thrawl St. E1	**CA39**	**2**
Thrawl St. E1	CA39	57
Threadneedle St. EC2	**BZ39**	**2**
Threadneedle St. EC2	BZ39	57
Three Arch Rd., Red.	BU72	121
Three Cherrytrees La.,	AZ11	8
Hem.H.		
Three Clo. La., Berk.	AR13	7
Three Colts La. E2	CB38	57
Three Colts St. E14	CD39	57
Three Corners, Bexh.	CR44	69
Three Corners, Hem.H.	AZ14	8
Three Gates Rd., Fawk.	DA54	90
Three Gates, Guil.	AU69	118
Three Horseshoes Rd., Harl.	CL12	13
Three Households, Ch.St.G.	AP28	34
Three Kings Ct. EC4	BY39	56
Gough Sq.		
Three Kings Rd., Mitch.	BU52	86
Three Kings Yd. W1	**BV40**	**3**
Three Kings Yd. W1	BV40	56
Three Mill La. E3	CF38	57
Three Nun Ct. EC2	BZ39	57
Aldermanbury		
Three Oak La. SE1	**CA41**	**4**
Three Oak La. SE1	CA41	67
Three Oaks Clo., Uxb.	AY34	44
Three Pears Rd., Guil.	AU70	118
Threshers Pl. W11	BR40	55
Thriffwood SE23	CC48	77
Thrift Farm La., B.Wd.	BN23	28
Thrift Grn., Brwd.	DD27	122
Thrift La., West.	CM62	106
Thrift, The, Dart.	DB48	80
Beacon Dr.		
Thrifts Mead, Epp.	CN22	31
Thriftvale, Guil.	AU69	118
Thrigby Rd., Chess.	BL57	94
Throckmorten Rd. E16	CH39	58
Throgmorton Av. EC2	**BZ39**	**2**
Throgmorton Av. EC2	BZ39	57
Throgmorton St. EC2	**BZ39**	**2**
Throgmorton St. EC2	BZ39	57
Throwley Clo. SE2	CP41	69
Throwley Rd., Sutt.	BS56	95
Throwley Way		
Throwley Way, Sutt.	BS56	95
Thrums, The, Wat.	BC22	26
Thrupp Clo., Mitch.	BV51	86
Thrupps Av., Walt.	BD56	93
Thrupps La., Walt.	BD56	93
Thrush Av., Hat.	BP13	10
Thrush Grn., Rick.	AX26	35
Thrush La., Cuff.	BX17	20
Thrush St. SE17	**BZ42**	**4**
Thrush St. SE17	BZ42	67
Thruxton Way SE15	CA43	67
Thumbswood, Welw.G.C.	BS9	5
Thumpers, Hem.H.	AY12	8
Thundridge Clo., Welw.G.C.	BS8	5
Thurbarn Rd. SE6	CE49	77
Thurburn Way SW19	BT51	86
Phipps Bridge Rd.		
Thurgood Rd., Hodd.	CE11	12
Thurland Rd. SE16	**CB41**	**4**
Thurland Rd. SE16	CB41	67
Thurlastone Par., Shep.	BA53	83
High St.		
Thurlby Clo., Har.	BJ32	45
Gayton Rd.		
Thurlby Clo., Wdf.Grn.	CK28	40
Thurlby Rd. SE27	BY49	76
Thurlby Rd., Wem.	BK36	54
Thurleigh Av. SW12	BV46	76
Thurleigh Rd. SW12	BU46	76
Thurleston Av., Mord.	BR53	85
Thurlestone Av. N12	BU29	38
Thurlestone Rd. SE27	BY48	76
Thurloe Clo. SW7	**BU42**	**3**
Thurloe Clo. SW7	BU42	66
Thurloe Pl. Ms. SW7	**BT42**	**3**
Thurloe Pl. Ms. SW7	BT42	66
Thurloe Pl.		
Thurloe Pl. SW7	**BT42**	**3**
Thurloe Pl. SW7	BT42	66
Thurloe Sq. SW7	**BU42**	**3**
Thurloe Sq. SW7	BU42	66
Thurloe St. SW7	**BT42**	**3**
Thurloe St. SW7	BT42	66
Thurloe Wk., Grays	DD41	71
Thurlow Clo. E4	CE29	39
Higham Station Av.		
Thurlow Ct. SW3	**BU42**	**3**
Thurlow Ct. SW3	BU42	66
Fulham Rd.		
Thurlow Gdns., Ilf.	CN29	40
Thurlow Gdns., Wem.	BK35	45
Thurlow Hill SE21	BZ47	77
Thurlow Park Rd. SE21	BY47	76
Thurlow Rd. NW3	BT35	47
Thurlow Rd. W7	BJ41	64
Elthorne Park Rd.		
Thurlow St. SE17	**BZ42**	**4**
Thurlow St. SE17	BZ42	67
Thurlow Ter. NW5	BU35	47
Thurlston Rd., Ruis.	BC34	44
Thurlstone Av., Ilf.	CN35	49
Thurlstone Clo., Shep.	BA53	83
Thurlstone Rd. SE27	BY48	76
Thurlton Ct., Wok.	AS61	100
Thurnby Ct., Twick.	BH48	74
Thurnham Way, Tad.	BQ63	103
Thurrock Park Way, Grays	DE43	71
Thursby Rd., Wok.	AQ62	100
Thursland Rd., Sid.	CQ49	79
Thursley Cres., Croy.	CF57	96
Thursley Gdns. SW19	BQ48	75
Thursley Rd. SE9	CK48	78
Thurso Clo., Rom.	CX29	42
Thurso St. SW17	BT49	76
Thurstan Rd. SW20	BP50	75
Thurstans, Harl.	CM13	13
Thurston Path, B.Wd.	BL23	28
Linton Av.		
Thurston Rd. SE13	CE44	67
Thurston Rd., Slou.	AP39	52
Thurston Rd., Sthl.	BE39	54
Thurtle Rd. E2	**CA37**	**2**
Thurtle Rd. E2	CA37	57
Thwaite Clo., Erith	CS43	69
Thyair Way N17	CA31	48
Thyer Clo., Orp.	CM56	97
Thyra Gro. N12	BS29	38
Tibbatts Rd. E3	CE38	57
Tibbenham Wk. E13	CG37	58
Tibberton Sq. N1	**BZ36**	**2**
Tibberton Sq. N1	BZ36	57
Popham Rd.		
Tibbets Clo. SW19	BQ47	75
Tibbets Cor. SW19	BQ47	75
Tibbets Ride SW15	BQ47	75
Tibbles Clo., Wat.	BE21	27
Tibbs Hill Rd., West.	BB18	17
Tiber Gdns. N1	**BX37**	**2**
Tiber Gdns. N1	BX37	56
Treaty St.		
Ticehurst Clo., Orp.	CO50	79
Grovelands Rd.		
Ticehurst Rd. SE23	CD48	77
Tichborne Row W2	**BU39**	**1**
Tichborne Row W2	BU39	56
Hyde Park Cres.		
Tichborne Wd., Rick.	AU28	34
Tichmarsh, Epsom	BN58	94
Tickford Clo.SE2	CP41	69
Tidal Basin Rd. E16	CG40	58
Tidenham Gdns., Croy.	CA55	87
Tideswell Rd. SW15	BQ45	65
Tideswell Rd., Croy.	CE55	87
Tideway Clo., Rich.	BJ49	74
Tidey St. E3	CE39	57
Tidford Rd., Well.	CN44	68
Tidys La., Epp.	CO18	23
Tiepigs La., W.Wick.	CG55	88
Tierney Rd. SW2	BX47	76
Tiger Bay SE16	CC41	67
Tiger Way E5	CB35	48
Tilbrook Rd. SE3	CJ45	68
Tilburstow Hill Rd., Gdse.	CC69	114
Tilbury Clo. SE15	CA43	67
Willowbrook Rd.		
Tilbury Clo., Orp.	CO51	89
Tilbury Gdns., Til.	DG45	71
Tilbury Hotel Rd., Til.	DG45	71
Tilbury Mead, Harl.	CO12	14
Tilbury Rd. E10	CF33	48
Tilbury Rd. E6	CK37	58
Tilbury Rd., Brwd.	DF31	123
Tildesley Rd. SW15	BQ46	75
Tile Farm Rd., Orp.	CM55	88
Tile Gate Rd., Harl.	CN12	13
Tile Gate Rd., Ong.	CS13	14
Tile Kiln Clo., Hem.H.	AZ14	8
Tile Kiln Cres., Hem.H.	AZ14	8
Tile Kiln La. N13	BZ28	39
Tile Kiln La. N6	BW33	47
Tile Kiln La., Bex.	CS48	79
Tile Kiln La., Hem.H.	AZ14	8
Tile Kiln La., Uxb.	AZ33	44
Tile Yd. E14	CD39	57
St. Anne St.		
Tilecroft, Welw.G.C.	BQ6	5
Tilehouse Clo., B.Wd.	BL24	28
Tilehouse La., Ger.Cr.	AV30	34
Tilehouse Rd., Guil.	AS72	118
Tilehouse Way, Uxb.	AV33	43
Tilehurst La., Dor. & Bet.	BL72	120
Tilehurst Rd. SW18	BT47	76
Tilehurst Rd., Sutt.	BR56	94
Tilers Way, Reig.	BT72	121
Tileyard Rd. N7	BX36	56
Tilford Av., Croy.	CF58	96
Tilford Gdns. SW19	BQ47	75
Tilia Rd. E5	CB35	48
Till Av., Farn.	CW54	90
Tiller Rd. E14	CE41	67
Tillett Clo. NW10	BN36	55
Tillett Sq. SE16	CD41	67
Howland Way		
Tillett Way E2	**CB38**	**2**
Gosset St.		
Tillett Way E2	CB38	57
Gosset St.		
Tilley La., Epsom	BM65	103
Tillgate Common, Red.	BZ70	114
Tilling Rd. NW2	BQ33	46
Tillingbourne Gdns. N3	BR31	46
Tillingbourne Grn., Orp.	CN52	88
Tillingbourne Rd., Guil.	AS73	118
Tillingbourne Way N3	BR31	46
Tillingbourne Gdns.		
Tillingdown Hill, Cat.	CB64	105
Tillingdown La., Cat.	CB65	105
Tillingham Ct., Wal.Abb.	CH20	22
Tillingham Way N12	BS28	38
Tillman St. E1	CB39	57
Tilloch St. N1	**BX36**	**2**
Carnoustie Dr.		
Tilloch St. N1	BX36	56
Carnoustie Dr.		
Tillotson Rd. N9	CA27	39
Tillotson Rd., Har.	BF29	36
Tillotson Rd., Ilf.	CL33	49
Tillotson St. E1	CC39	57
Tillwicks Rd., Harl.	CO11	14
Tillys La., Stai.	AV49	72
Tilmans Mead, Farn.	CW54	90
Tilney Ct. EC1	**BZ38**	**2**
Tilney Ct. EC1	BZ38	57
Old St.		
Tilney Dr., Buck.H.	CH27	40
Tilney Gdns. N1	BZ36	57
Baxter Rd.		
Tilney Rd., Dag.	CQ36	59
Tilney Rd., Sthl.	BD42	64
Tilney St. W1	**BV40**	**3**
Tilney St. W1	BV40	56
Tilson Gdns. SW2	BW47	76
Tilson Ho. SW2	BX47	76
Tilson La., Wind.	AM42	61
Tilson Rd. N17	CB30	39
Tilstone Av., Eton	AM42	61
Tilstone Clo., Eton	AM42	61
Tilsworth Wk., St.Alb.	BK11	9
Sandringham Cres.		
Tilt Clo., Cob.	BE61	102
Tilt Meadows, Cob.	BE61	102
Tilt Rd., Cob.	BD61	102
Tilton Rd., Sev.	DC63	108
Tilton St. SW6	BR43	65
Tiltwood, The W3	BN40	55
Acacia Rd.		
Tiltyard App. SE9	CK46	78
Timber Clo., Chis.	CL51	88
Timber Clo., Lthd.	BG67	111
Timber Clo., Wok.	AV60	91
Timber Mill Way SW4	BW45	66
Timber Pond Rd. SE16	CC41	67
Timber Ridge, Rick.	AX24	26
Timber Slip Dr., Wall.	BW58	95
Timber St. EC1	**BZ38**	**2**
Timber St. EC1	BZ38	57
Baltic St.		
Timbercroft La. SE18	CN43	68
Timbercroft, Epsom	BN56	94
Timbercroft, Welw.G.C.	BR6	5
Timberdene NW4	BQ30	37
Timberhill Rd., Cat.	CB65	105
Timberland Rd. E1	CB39	57
Watney Market		
Timberling Gdns., Croy.	BZ58	96
White Hill		
Timbertop Rd., West.	CJ62	106
Timberwharf Rd. N16	CB32	48
Times Sq., Sutt.	BS56	95
High St.		
Timothy Clo. SW4	BW46	76
Elms Rd.		
Timperley Gdns., Red.	BU69	121
Timplings Row, Hem.H.	AW12	8
Tims Way, Stai.	AV49	72
Timsbury Wk. SW15	BP47	75
Foxcombe Rd.		
Tindal St. SW9	BY44	66
Tindale Clo., S.Croy.	BZ59	96
Tindall Clo., Rom.	CW30	42
Rosslyn Av.		
Tinderbox Alley SW14	BN45	65
North Worple Way		
Tine Rd., Chig.	CN28	40
Tingeys Top La., Enf.	BY21	29
Tinglefield, Pot.B.	BS18	20
Tinkerpot La., Sev.	CY60	99
Tinkerpot Ri., Sev.	CY60	99
Tinkers La., Wind.	AL44	61
Tinsby Wk. SW15	BP47	75
Alton Rd.		
Tinsley Rd. E1	CC39	57
Tintagel Clo., Epsom	BO60	94
College Rd.		
Tintagel Clo., Hem.H.	AY11	8
Helston Gro.		
Tintagel Cres. SE22	CA45	67
Tintagel Dr., Stan.	BK28	36
Tintagel Gdns. SE22	CA45	67
Oxonian St.		
Tintagel Rd., Orp.	CP55	89
Tintagel Way, Wok.	AT61	100
Tintells La., Lthd.	AZ67	110
Tintern Av. NW9	BM31	46
Tintern Clo. SW15	BR46	75
Tintern Clo. SW19	BT50	76
Tintern Clo., Slou.	AO41	61
Tintern Ct. W13	BJ40	54
Tintern Gdns. N14	BX26	38
Tintern Rd. N22	BZ30	39
Tintern Rd., Cars.	BT54	86
Tintern St. SW4	BX45	66
Tintern Way, Har.	BF33	45
Tinto Rd. E16	CH38	58
Tinworth Ho. SE11	**BX42**	**4**
Tinworth Ho. SE11	BX42	66
Tinworth St.		
Tinworth St. SE11	**BX42**	**4**
Tinworth St. SE11	BX42	66
Tippendell La., St.Alb.	BF16	18
Tippetts Clo., Enf.	BZ23	30
Tipps Cross La., Brwd.	DA20	24
Tipps Cross Mead, Brwd.	DA21	33
Tipthorpe Rd. SW11	BV45	66
Tipton Dr., Croy.	CA56	96
Tiptree Clo. E4	CF27	39
Tiptree Clo., Horn.	CX33	51
Tiptree Cres., Ilf.	CL31	49
Tiptree Dr., Enf.	BZ24	30
Tiptree Rd., Ruis.	BC35	44
Tiree Clo., Hem.H.	AZ14	8
Tirlemont Rd., S.Croy.	BZ57	96
Tirrell Rd., Croy.	BZ53	87
Tisbury Ct. W1	**BW40**	**1**
Rupert St.		
Tisbury Ct. W1	BW40	56
Rupert St.		
Tisbury Rd. SW16	BX51	86
Tisdall Pl. SE17	**BZ42**	**4**
Tisdall Pl. SE17	BZ42	67
Titan Rd., Grays	DD42	71
Orsett Rd.		
Titan Rd., Hem.H.	AY12	8
Titan Way, Grays	DD42	71
Titchfield Rd. NW8	**BU37**	**1**
Titchfield Rd. NW8	BU37	56
Titchfield Rd., Cars.	BT54	86
Titchfield Rd., Enf.	CD22	30
Titchfield Wk., Cars.	BT54	86
Titchwell Rd. SW18	BT47	76
Tite Hill, Egh.	AR49	72
Tite St. SW3	**BU42**	**3**
Tite St. SW3	BU42	66
Tithe Barn Clo., Kings.T.	BL51	85
Birkenhead Av.		
Tithe Barn Clo., St.Alb.	BG15	9
Tithe Barn Dr., Maid.	AJ42	61
Tithe Barn Way, Nthlt.	BC37	53
Tithe Clo. NW7	BP30	37
Tithe Clo., Maid.	AH42	61
Tithe Ct. NW4	BP30	37
Tithe Ct., Slou.	AT42	62
Tithe Farm Av., Har.	BF34	45
Tithe Farm Clo., Har.	BF34	45
Tithe La., Stai.	AT46	72
Tithe Meadow, Vir.W.	AR53	82
Tithe Meadow, Wat.	BA25	26
Tithe Wk. NW7	BP30	37
Tithebarns La., Wok.	AW66	110
Tithelands, Harl.	CK12	13
Tithepit Shaw La., Warl.	CB62	105
Titian Av., Bush.	BH26	36
Titley Clo. E4	CE28	39
Titmus Clo., Uxb.	BA39	53
Titmuss Av. SE28	CO40	59
Titmuss St. W12	BQ41	65
Titsey Hill, Oxt.	CH65	106
Titsey Rd., Oxt.	CH67	115
Tiverton Av., Ilf.	CL31	49
Tiverton Dr. SE9	CM47	78
Tiverton Gro., Rom.	CX28	42
Tiverton Rd. N15	BZ32	48
Tiverton Rd. N18	CA28	39
Tiverton Rd. NW10	BQ37	55
Tiverton Rd., Edg.	BL30	37
Tiverton Rd., Houns.	BF44	64
Tiverton Rd., Pot.B.	BT19	20
Tiverton Rd., Ruis.	BC34	44
Tiverton Rd., Wem.	BL37	55
Tiverton St. SE1	**BZ41**	**4**
Tiverton St. SE1	BZ41	67
Tiverton Way, Chess.	BK56	93
Tivoli Gdns. SE18	CK42	68
Tivoli Rd. N8	BW32	47
Tivoli Rd. SE27	BZ49	77
Tivoli Rd., Houns.	BE45	64
Tivoli Way SE27	BZ49	77
Holderness Way		
Tobacco Quay E1	CB40	57
Wapping La.		
Tobago St. E14	CE41	67
Manilla St.		
Tobin Clo. NW3	BU36	56
Toby La. E1	CD38	57
Solebay St.		
Todd Brook, Harl.	CL11	13
Todd Clo., Rain.	CV38	60
Todds Wk. N7	BX34	47
Andover Rd.		
Toft Av., Grays	DE42	71
Tokenhouse Yd. EC2	**BZ39**	**2**
Tokenhouse Yd. EC2	BZ39	57
Tokyngton Av., Wem.	BL36	55
Toland Sq. SW15	BP46	75
Tolavaddon, Wok.	AQ62	100
Cardingham		
Tolcarne Dr., Pnr.	BC30	35
Toley Av., Wem.	BL33	46
Tolhurst St. SE4	CD45	67
Foxwell St.		
Tollbridge Clo. W10	BR38	55
Kensal Rd.		
Tolldene Clo., Wok.	AP62	100
Tollers La., Coul.	BX63	104
Tollesbury Gdns., Ilf.	CM31	49
Tollet St. E1	CC38	57
Tollgate Av., Red.	BU73	121
Tollgate Clo., Rick.	AV24	25
Tollgate Dr. SE21	CA48	77
Tollgate Gdns. NW6	BS37	56
Tollgate Rd. E16	CJ39	58
Tollgate Rd. E6	CK39	58
Tollgate Rd., Dart.	CY47	80
Tollgate Rd., Dor.	BJ73	119
Tollgate Rd., St.Alb.	BN15	10
Tollgate Rd., Wal.Cr.	CC21	30
Tollgate, Guil.	AU70	118
Tollhouse La., Wall.	BW58	95
Tollhouse Way N19	BW34	47
Tollington Pk. N4	BX34	47
Tollington Pl. N4	BX34	47
Tollington Rd. N7	BX35	47
Tollington Way N7	BX34	47
Tollpit End, Hem.H.	AW12	8
Tolmers Av., Cuff.	BX17	20
Tolmers Gdns., Cuff.	BX18	20
Tolmers Ms., Hert.	BX16	20
Tolmers Rd., Cuff.	BW16	20
Tolmers Sq. NW1	**BW38**	**1**
Tolmers Sq. NW1	BW38	56
Tolpits Clo., Wat.	BB25	26
Tolpits La., Wat.	BA26	35
Tolpuddle St. N1	**BY37**	**2**
Tolpuddle St. N1	BY37	56
Tolsford Rd. E5	CB35	48
Tolson Rd., Islw.	BJ45	64
Tolver Ct., Brwd.	DB27	42
Tower Hill		
Tolverne Rd. SW20	BQ51	85
Tolworth Clo., Surb.	BM54	85
Tolworth Gdns., Rom.	CP32	50
Tolworth Park Rd., Surb.	BL55	85
Tolworth Rd., Surb.	BL55	85
Tolworth Rise N., Surb.	BM54	85
Tolworth Rise S., Surb.	BM54	85
Tom Coombs Clo. SE9	CK45	68
Westhorne Av.		
Tom Cribb Rd. SE28	CM41	68
Tom Mann Clo., Bark.	CN37	58
Tomahawk Gdns., Nthlt.	BD38	54
Javelin Way		

Tomkins Clo., B.Wd.	BK23	27
Organ Hall Rd.		
Tomkyns La., Upmin.	CY30	42
Tomlins Gro. E3	CE38	57
Tomlins Orchard, Bark.	CM37	58
Tomlins Ter. E14	CD39	57
Tomlins Wk. N19	BX34	47
Briset Way		
Tomlinson Clo. E2	**CA38**	**2**
Tomlinson Clo. E2	CA38	57
Tomlinson Clo. W4	BM42	65
Oxford Rd.		
Tomlyns Clo., Brwd.	DF25	122
Tompion Ho. EC1	**BY38**	**2**
Tompion Ho. EC1	BY38	56
Percival St.		
Tompion St. EC1	**BY38**	**2**
Tompion St. EC1	BY38	56
Northampton Sq.		
Toms Cft., Hem.H.	AY14	8
Toms Hill, Rick.	AY21	26
Toms La., Kings L.	AZ18	17
Tomswood Hill, Ilf.	CL29	40
Tomswood Rd., Chig.	CL29	40
Tonbridge & Sevenoaks By-pass, Sev.	CV69	117
Tonbridge Clo., Bans.	BU60	95
Merrymeet		
Tonbridge Cres., Har.	BL31	46
Tonbridge Rd., E.Mol.	BE53	84
Tonbridge Rd., Rom.	CV29	42
Tonbridge Rd., Sev.	CV67	117
Tonbridge Rd., Ton. & Sev.	DB67	117
Tonbridge St. WC1	**BX38**	**2**
Tonbridge St. WC1	BX38	56
Tonbridge Wk. WC1	**BX38**	**2**
Tonbridge St.		
Tonbridge Wk. WC1	BX38	56
Tonbridge St.		
Tonfield Rd., Sutt.	BR54	85
Tonge Clo., Beck.	CE53	87
Tonsley Hill SW18	BS46	76
Tonsley Pl. SW18	BS46	76
Tonsley Rd. SW18	BS46	76
Tonsley St. SW18	BS46	76
Tonstall Rd., Epsom	BN59	94
Tonstall Rd., Mitch.	BV51	86
Tooke Clo., Pnr.	BE30	36
Tooks Ct. EC4	**BY39**	**2**
Tooks Ct. EC4	BY39	56
Cursitor St.		
Toolands Rd., Islw.	BJ44	64
Tooley St. SE1	**BZ40**	**4**
Tooley St. SE1	BZ40	57
Tooley St., Grav.	DE47	81
Toorack Rd., Har.	BG30	36
Toot Hill Rd., Ong.	CT18	23
Tooting Bec Gdns. SW16	BW49	76
Tooting Bec Rd. SW17	BV48	76
Tooting Gro. SW17	BU49	76
Tooting High St. SW17	BU49	76
Toots Wood Rd., Brom.	CG53	88
Tooveys Mill Clo., Kings L.	AZ18	17
Mill La.		
Top Dartford Rd., Swan.	CT50	79
Top Ho. Rise. E4	CF26	39
Top La., Rick.	AV20	16
Top Pk., Beck.	CF53	87
Top Pk., Ger.Cr.	AR32	43
Top Wk., Cat.	CD64	105
Topaz Clo., Slou.	AN40	61
Pearl Gdns.		
Topcliffe Dr., Orp.	CM56	97
Topham Sq. N17	BZ30	39
Topham St. EC1	**BY38**	**2**
Topham St. EC1	BY38	56
Topiary Sq., Rich.	BL45	65
Topland Rd., Ger.Cr.	AR29	34
Toplands Av., S.Ock.	CX40	60
Topley St. SE9	CJ45	68
Topp Wk. NW2	BQ34	46
Topsfield Rd. N8	BX32	47
Topsham Rd. SW17	BU48	76
Tor Gdns. W8	BS41	66
Tor La., Wey.	BA59	92
Tor Rd., Well.	CP44	69
Torbay Rd. NW6	BR36	55
Torbay Rd., Har.	BE34	45
Torbay St. NW1	BV36	56
Hawley Rd.		
Torbridge Clo., Edg.	BL29	37
Torbrook Clo., Bex.	CQ46	79
Torcross Dr. SE23	CC48	77
Torcross Rd., Ruis.	BC34	44
Torin Ct., Egh.	AR49	72
Torland Dr., Lthd.	BG60	93
Tormead Clo., Sutt.	BS57	95
Tormead Rd., Guil.	AS70	118
Tormount Rd. SE18	CN43	68
Toronto Av. E12	CK35	49
Toronto Rd. E11	CF35	48
Toronto Rd., Ilf.	CL33	49
Toronto Rd., Til.	DG44	71
Torquay Gdns., Ilf.	CJ31	49
Torquay St. W2	BS39	56
Harrow Rd.		
Torr Rd. SE20	CC50	77
Torrance Clo., Horn.	CV33	51
Torrance Rd. SE3	CJ44	68
Torrans Wk., Grav.	DJ49	81
Torre Wk., Cars.	BU54	86
Torrens Rd. E15	CG36	58
Torrens Rd. SW2	BX46	76
Torrens Sq. E15	CG36	58
Torrens St. EC1	**BY37**	**2**
Torrens St. N1	BY37	56
Torriano Av. NW5	BW35	47
Torriano Cotts. NW5	BW35	47
Torriano Av.		
Torriano Est. NW1	BW35	47
Torridge Gdns. SE15	CC45	67
Torridge Rd., Slou.	AT43	62
Torridge Rd., Th.Hth.	BY53	86
Torridge Wk., Hem.H.	AY11	8
Torridon Clo., Wok.	AQ62	100
Torridon Rd. SE13	CF47	77
Torridon Rd. SE6	CF47	77
Torrington Av. N12	BT28	38
Torrington Clo. N12	BT28	38
Torrington Pk.		
Torrington Clo., Esher	BH57	93
Torrington Dr., Har.	BF35	45
Torrington Dr., Loug.	CM24	31
Torrington Dr., Pot.B.	BT19	20
Torrington Gdns. N11	BW29	38
Torrington Gdns., Grnf.	BK37	54
Torrington Gdns., Loug.	CM24	31
Torrington Gro. N12	BU28	38
Torrington Pk. N12	BT28	38
Torrington Pl. E1	CB40	57
Torrington Pl. WC1	**BW39**	**1**
Torrington Pl. WC1	BW38	56
Torrington Rd. E18	CH31	49
Torrington Rd., Berk.	AQ13	7
Torrington Rd., Dag.	CQ33	50
Torrington Rd., Esher	BH57	93
Torrington Rd., Grnf.	BK37	54
Torrington Rd., Ruis.	BB34	44
Torrington Sq., Croy.	BZ54	87
Tavistock Gro.		
Torrington Way, Mord.	BS54	86
Torver Rd., Har.	BH31	45
Torver Way, Orp.	CM55	88
Torwood Clo., Berk.	AP13	7
Torwood La., Whyt.	CA63	105
Torwood Rd. SW15	BP46	75
Torworth Rd., B.Wd.	BL22	28
Totham Lo. SW20	BP51	85
Richmond Rd.		
Tothill St. SW1	**BW41**	**3**
Tothill St. SW1	BW41	66
Totnes Rd. E16	CH39	58
Totnes Rd., Well.	CO43	69
Totnes Wk. N2	BT31	47
Tottenhall Rd. N13	BY29	38
Tottenham Court Rd. W1	**BW38**	**1**
Tottenham Court Rd. W1	BW38	56
Tottenham Grn. E. N15	CA31	48
Tottenham Grn. W. N15	CA31	48
Town Hall App.		
Tottenham La. N8	BX32	47
Tottenham Ms. W1	BW39	56
Tottenham St.		
Tottenham Rd. N1	BZ36	57
Tottenham Sq. N1	CA36	57
Tottenham St. W1	**BW39**	**1**
Tottenham St. W1	BW39	56
Totterdown St. SW17	BU49	76
Totteridge Clo. N20	BS27	38
Totteridge Com. N20	BP27	37
Totteridge La. N20	BS27	38
Totteridge Rd., Enf.	CC22	30
Totteridge Village, Barn.	BR26	37
Totternhoe Clo., Har.	BK32	45
Totton Rd., Th.Hth.	BY52	86
Toulmin Dr., St.Alb.	BG11	9
Toulmin St. SE1	**BZ41**	**4**
Toulmin St. SE1	BZ41	67
Toulon St. SE5	BZ43	67
Wyndham Rd.		
Tournay Rd. SW6	BR43	65
Tovey Av., Hodd.	CE11	12
Tovey Clo., Wal.Abb.	CG15	13
Tovil Clo. SE20	CB51	87
Towcester Rd. E3	CE38	57
Tower Bridge App. E1	**CA40**	**4**
Tower Bridge App. E1	CA40	57
Tower Bridge Rd. SE1 & E1	**CA41**	**4**
Tower Bridge Rd. SE1 & E1	CA41	67
Tower Bridge SE1	**CA40**	**4**
Tower Bridge SE1	CA40	57
Tower Centre, Hodd.	CE12	12
Tower Clo. NW3	BT35	47
Lyndhurst Rd.		
Tower Clo. SE20	CB50	77
Tower Clo., Berk.	AQ13	7
Tower Clo., Epp.	CS15	14
Tower Clo., Grav.	DJ49	81
Tower Clo., Ilf.	CM29	40
Tower Clo., Orp.	CN55	88
Tower Clo., Wok.	AR62	100
Tower Ct. N16	CA33	48
Tower Ct., Brwd.	DA27	42
Tower Ct., Ong.	CX18	24
Stanley Pl.		
Tower Gardens Rd. N17	BZ30	39
Tower Gro., Wey.	BB54	83
Tower Hamlets Rd. E17	CE31	48
Tower Hamlets Rd. E7	CG35	49
Tower Hill EC3	**CA40**	**4**
Tower Hill EC3	CA40	57
Tower Hill Rd., Dor.	BJ72	119
Tower Hill, Brwd.	DB27	42
Tower Hill, Dor.	BJ72	119
Tower Hill, Kings L.	AV18	16
Tower La., Reig.	BT68	113
Tower Ms. E17	CE31	48
High St.		
Tower Pl. EC3	**CA40**	**4**
Tower Pl. EC3	CA40	57
Tower Rd. NW10	BP36	55
Tower Rd., Belv.	CS42	69
Tower Rd., Bexh.	CR45	69
Tower Rd., Dart.	CV47	80
Tower Rd., Epp.	CN18	22
Tower Rd., Orp.	CN55	88
Tower Rd., Tad.	BQ65	103
Tower Rd., Twick.	BH48	74
Tower Ri., Rich.	BL45	65
Tower Royal EC4	BZ39	57
Cannon St.		
Tower St. WC2	**BW39**	**1**
Tower St. WC2	BW39	56
Tower Ter. N22	BX30	38
Mayes Rd.		
Tower Vw., Croy.	CD54	87
Towers Av., Uxb.	BA38	53
Towers Pl., Rich.	BL46	75
Eton St.		
Towers Rd., Grays	DE42	71
Towers Rd., Hem.H.	AY13	8
Towers Rd., Pnr.	BE30	36
Towers Rd., Sthl.	BF38	54
Towers Wk., Wey.	AZ57	92
Towers Wood, Dart.	CY51	90
Towers, The, Ken.	BZ61	105
Towerscroft, Eyns.	CW55	90
Towfield Rd., Felt.	BE48	74
Town Court La., Orp.	CM54	88
Town Court Path N4	BZ33	48
Town End Clo., Cat.	CA64	105
Town End High St., Cat.	CA64	105
Town Field La., Ch.St.G.	AR27	34
Town Fields, Hat.	BP12	10
Town Hall App. N15	CA31	48
Town Hall App. N16	CA35	48
Milton Gro.		
Town Hall Av. W4	BN42	65
Town Hall Rd. SW11	BU45	66
Town La., Stai.	AX46	73
Town Meadow, Brent.	BK43	64
Town Quay, Bark.	CL37	58
Town Quay, Stai.	AW52	83
Blacksmiths La.		
Town Rd. N9	CB27	39
Town Tree Rd., Ashf.	AZ49	73
Town Wharf, Islw.	BJ45	64
Town, The, Enf.	BZ24	30
Towncourt Cres., Orp.	CM53	88
Towney Mead, Nthlt.	BE37	54
Townfield Rd., Hayes	BB40	53
Townfield Sq., Hayes	BB40	53
Townfield, Rick.	AX26	35
Townford Rd., Dor.	BJ72	119
Townholm Cres. W7	BH41	64
Townley Ct. E15	CG36	58
Faraday Rd.		
Townley Rd. SE22	CA46	77
Townley Rd., Bexh.	CQ46	79
Townley St. SE17	**BZ42**	**4**
Townley St. SE17	BZ42	67
Townmead Est. SW6	BS45	66
Townmead Rd. SW6	BS45	66
Townmead Rd., Rich.	BM44	65
Townmead Rd., Wal.Abb.	CF20	21
Townmead, Red.	BZ70	114
Townsend Av. N14	BW28	38
Townsend Av., St.Alb.	BH13	9
Townsend Dr., St.Alb.	BG12	9
Townsend Ind. Est. NW10	BN37	55
Townsend La. NW9	BN33	46
Townsend La., Wok.	AT64	100
St. Peters Rd.		
Townsend Rd. N15	CA32	48
Townsend Rd., Ashf.	AY49	73
Townsend Rd., Sthl.	BE40	54
Townsend St. SE17	**BZ42**	**4**
Townsend St. SE17	BZ42	67
Townsend Way, Nthwd.	BB29	35
Townsend, Hem.H.	AX12	8
Townsends Yd. N6	BV33	47
Townshend Est. NW8	**BU37**	**1**
Townshend Est. NW8	BU37	56
Townshend Rd. NW8	**BU37**	**1**
Townshend Rd. NW8	BU37	56
Townshend Rd., Chis.	CL49	78
Townshend Rd., Rich.	BL45	65
Townshend Ter., Rich.	BL45	65
Townshott Clo., Lthd.	BF66	111
Townside, Harl.	CP11	14
Townslow La., Wok.	AX61	101
Townson Av., Nthlt.	BC37	53
Townson Way, Nthlt.	BC37	53
Towpath, Shep.	AY55	83
Towton Rd. SE27	BZ48	77
Toynbec Clo., Chis.	CL49	78
Beechwood Ri.		
Toynbee Rd. SW20	BQ51	85
Toynbee St. E1	**CA39**	**2**
Toynbee St. E1	CA39	57
Toyne Way N6	BU32	47
Gaskell Rd.		
Toys Hill, West.	CO69	116
Tozer Wk., Wind.	AL45	61
Tinkers La.		
Tracery, The, Bans.	BS61	104
Tracey Av. NW2	BP35	46
Tracey St. SE11	BY42	66
Tracious Clo., Wok.	AQ61	100
Tracious La., Wok.	AQ61	100
Tracy Ct., Stan.	BK29	36
Tracyes Rd., Harl.	CO12	14
Tradescant Rd. SW8	BX43	66
Trading Estate Rd. NW10	BN38	55
Trafalgar Av. N17	CA29	39
Trafalgar Av. SE15	**CA42**	**4**
Trafalgar Av. SE15	CA42	67
Trafalgar Av., Brox.	CD14	12
Trafalgar Av., Wor.Pk.	BQ54	85
Trafalgar Ct., Cob.	BC60	92
Trafalgar Dr., Walt.	BC55	83
Trafalgar Gdns. E1	CC39	57
Trafalgar Gro. SE10	CF43	67
Trafalgar Pl. E11	CH31	49
Trafalgar Pl. N18	CB28	39
Trafalgar Rd. SE10	CF43	67
Trafalgar Rd. SW19	BS50	76
Trafalgar Rd., Dart.	CW48	80
Trafalgar Rd., Grav.	DG47	81
Trafalgar Rd., Rain.	CT37	59
Trafalgar Rd., Twick.	BG48	74
Trafalgar Sq. WC2	**BW40**	**3**
Trafalgar Sq. WC2	BW40	56
Trafalgar St. SE17	**BZ42**	**4**
Trafalgar St. SE17	BZ42	67
Trafalgar Ter., Har.	BG33	45
Nelson Rd.		
Trafalgar Way, Croy.	BX55	86
Trafford Clo. E15	CE35	48
Trafford Clo., Ilf.	CN29	40
Trent Bridge Clo.		
Trafford Rd., Th.Hth.	BX53	86
Trahorn St. E1	CB39	57
Wodeham St.		
Tramway Av. E15	CG36	57
Broadway		
Tramway Av. N9	CB26	39
Tramway La. E13	CG36	58
Broadway		
Tramway Path, Mitch.	BU53	86
Tranby Pl. E9	CC35	48
Tranley Ms. NW3	BU35	47
Fleet Rd.		
Tranmere Rd. N9	CA26	39
Tranmere Rd. SW18	BT47	76
Tranmere Rd., Twick.	BF47	74
Tranquil Dale, Bet.	BO69	120
Tranquil Pass. SE3	CG44	68
Tranquil Vale		
Tranquil Ri., Erith	CT42	69
Tranquil Vale SE3	CG44	68
Transay Wk. N1	BZ36	57
Clephane Rd.		
Transept St. NW1	**BU39**	**1**
Transept St. NW1	BU39	56
Transmere Clo., Orp.	CM53	88
Transom Sq. E14	CE42	67
Westferry Rd.		
Transport Av., Brent.	BJ43	64
Tranton Rd. SE16	CB41	67
Trapps La., Chesh.	AO19	16
Trapps La., Chesh.	AO20	16
Traps Hill, Loug.	CK24	31
Traps La., N.Mal.	BO51	85
Trasher Mead, Dor.	BK73	119
Travellers Clo., Hat.	BQ15	10
Travellers La., Hat.	BP13	10
Travellers La., N.Mymms	BQ14	10
Travellers Way, Houns.	BD44	64
Travers Rd. N7	BY34	47
Treacy Clo., Bush.	BG27	36
Treadgold St. W11	BQ40	55
Treadway St. E2	CB37	57
Treadwell Rd., Epsom	BO61	103
Treaty Rd., Houns.	BF45	64
Treaty St. N1	**BX37**	**2**
Treaty St. N1	BX37	56
Trebble Rd., Swans.	DC46	81
Trebeck St. W1	**BV40**	**3**
Trebeck St. W1	BV40	56
Curzon St.		
Trebellan Dr., Hem.H.	AY13	8
Trebovir Rd. SW5	BS42	66
Treby St. E3	CD38	57
Trecastle Way N7	BW35	47
Carleton Rd.		
Tredegar Ms. E3	CD37	57
Tredegar Ter.		
Tredegar Ms. E3	CD38	57
Tredegar Ter.		
Tredegar Rd. E3	CD37	57
Tredegar Rd. N11	BW29	38
Tredegar Rd., Dart.	CU48	79
Tredegar Sq. E3	CD38	57
Tredegar Ter. E3	CD38	57
Trederwen Rd. E8	CB37	57
Tredown Rd. SE26	CC49	77
Tredwell Rd. SE27	BY49	76
Tree Bourne Rd., West.	CJ62	106
Tree Clo., Rich.	BK47	74
Tree Mount Ct., Epsom	BO60	94
Tree Rd. E16	CJ39	58
Tree Tops Clo., Belv.	CQ42	69
Tree Tops Clo., Nthwd.	BA28	35
Tree Tops, Brwd.	DB26	42
Tree Tops, Grav.	DG49	81
Treebys Av., Guil.	AR67	109
Treelands, Dor.	BK73	119
Treen Av. SW13	BO45	65
Treeside Clo., West Dr.	AX42	63
Treeview Clo. SE19	CA51	87
Sylvan Hill		
Treewall Gdns., Brom.	CH49	78
Treeway, Reig.	BS69	121
Trefgarne Rd., Dag.	CR34	50
Trefil Wk. N7	BX35	47
Williamson St.		
Trefoil Rd. SW18	BT46	76
Trefusis Wk., Wat.	BB23	26
Tregaron Av. N8	BX32	47
Tregaron Gdns., N.Mal.	BO52	85
Avenue Rd.		
Tregarth Pl., Wok.	AP62	100
Tregarvon Rd. SW11	BV45	66
Tregelles Rd., Hodd.	CE11	12
Tregenna Av., Har.	BE35	45
Tregenna Clo. N14	BW25	29
Trego Rd. E9	CD36	57
Tregothnan Rd. SW9	BX45	66
Tregunter Rd. SW10	**BS43**	**3**
Tregunter Rd. SW10	BS43	66
Trehaven Par., Reig.	BS72	121
Hornbeam Rd.		
Trehearn Rd., Ilf.	CM29	40
Trehern Rd. SW14	BN45	65
Treherne Ct. SW17	BV49	76
Treherne Rd. SW9	BY44	66
Trehurst St. E5	CD35	48
Trelawn Clo., Cher.	AU57	91
Trelawn Rd. E10	CF34	48
Trelawn Rd. SW2	BY46	76
Trelawney Av., Slou.	AS41	62
Trelawney Est. E9	CC36	57
Trelawney Gro., Wey.	AZ57	92
Elgin Rd.		
Trelawney Rd., Ilf.	CM29	40
Trellis Sq. E3	CE37	58
Malmesbury Sq.		
Treloar Gdns. SE19	BZ50	77
Tremadoc Rd. SW4	BW45	66
Tremaine Clo. SE4	CE44	67
Tremaine Gro., Hem.H.	AY11	8
Tremaine Rd. SE20	CB51	87
Trematon, Tedd.	BK50	74
Tremlett Gro. N19	BW34	47
Tremlett Ms. N19	BW34	47
Junction Rd.		
Trenance Gdns., Ilf.	CO34	50
Trenance, Wok.	AQ62	100
Cardingham		
Trenchard Av., Ruis.	BC35	44
Trenchard Clo., Stan.	BJ29	36
Trenchard Clo., Walt.	BD56	93
Trenchard Ct., Mord.	BS53	86
Trenchard Rd., Maid.	AG43	61
Trenchard St. SE10	CF42	67
Trenches La., Slou.	AT40	52
Trenchold St. SW8	BX43	66
Trenham Dr., Warl.	CC61	105
Trenholme Clo. SE20	CB50	77
Trenholme Rd. SE20	CB50	77
Trenmar Gdns. NW10	BP38	55
Trent Av. W5	BK41	64
Trent Av., Upmin.	CY32	51
Trent Bridge Clo., Ilf.	CN29	40
Trent Gdns. N14	BV25	29
Trent Rd. SW2	BX46	76
Trent Rd., Buck.H.	CH26	40
Trent Rd., Slou.	AT43	62
Trent Way, Hayes	BB37	53
Trent Way, Wor.Pk.	BQ55	85
Trentham Cres., Wok.	AT64	100
Trentham Dr., Orp.	CO53	89
Trentham Rd., Red.	BV71	121
Trentham St. SW18	BS47	76
Trentwood Side, Enf.	BX24	29
Treport St. SW18	BS47	76
Tresco Clo., Brom.	CG50	78
Hillbrow Rd.		
Tresco Gdns., Ilf.	CO34	50
Tresco Rd. SE15	CB45	67
Tresco Rd., Berk.	AP12	7
Trescoe Gdns., Har.	BE33	45
Trescoe Gdns., Rom.	CS28	41
Tresham Cres. NW8	**BU38**	**1**
Tresham Cres. NW8	BU38	56
Tresham Rd., Bark.	CN36	58
Tresham Wk. E9	CC35	48
Churchill Wk.		
Tresilian Sq., Hem.H.	AY11	8
Tresillian Way, Wok.	AQ62	100
Tressell Clo. N1	BY36	56
Sebbon St.		
Tressillian Cres. SE4	CE45	67
Tressillian Rd. SE4	CD45	67
Tresta Wk., Wok.	AQ61	100
Trestis Clo., Hayes	BD39	54
Jollys La.		
Treswell Rd., Dag.	CQ37	59
Tretawn Gdns. NW7	BO28	37
Tretawn Pk. NW7	BO28	37
Trevanion Rd. W14	BR42	65
Treve Av., Har.	BG33	45
Trevelga Way, Hem.H.	AY11	8
Tremaine Gro.		
Trevellance Way, Wat.	BD20	18
Trevelyan Av. E12	CK35	49
Trevelyan Clo., Dart.	CW45	70
Trevelyan Cres., Har.	BL33	46
Trevelyan Gdns. NW10	BQ37	55
Trevelyan Rd. E15	CG35	49
Trevelyan Rd. SW17	BU49	76
Trevelyan Way, Berk.	AQ12	7
Trevelyn Ct., N.Mal.	BO54	85
Trevereux Hill, Oxt.	CK69	115
Treveris St. SE1	**BY40**	**4**
Treveris St. SE1	BY40	56
Bear La.		
Treverton St. W10	BQ38	55
Ladbroke Gro.		
Treville St. SW15	BP47	75
Treviso Rd. SE23	CC47	77
Farren Rd.		
Trevithick Dr., Dart.	CW45	70
Trevithick St. SE8	CE42	67
Watergate St.		
Trevone Gdns., Pnr.	BE32	45
Trevor Clo., Ban.	BT25	29
Trevor Clo., Brom.	CG54	88
Trevor Clo., Islw.	BH46	74
Trevor Clo., Nthlt.	BD37	54
Trevor Clo., Stan.	BH29	36
Trevor Cres., Ruis.	BB35	44
Trevor Ct., Stai.	AW46	73
Horton Rd.		
Trevor Gdns., Edg.	BN30	37
Trevor Gdns., Nthlt.	BD37	54
Trevor Pl. SW7	**BU41**	**3**
Trevor Pl. SW7	BU41	66
Trevor Rd. SW19	BR50	75
Trevor Rd., Edg.	BN30	37
Trevor Rd., Hayes	BB41	63
Trevor Rd., Wdf.Grn.	CH29	40
Trevor Sq. SW7	**BU41**	**3**
Trevor Sq. SW7	BU41	66
Trevor St. SW7	**BU41**	**3**
Trevor St. SW7	BU41	66
Trevose Av., Wey.	AV60	91
Trevose Rd. SE17	CF30	39
Trevose Way, Wat.	BD27	36
Trewenna Dr., Chess.	BK56	93
Hook Rd.		
Trewenna Dr., Pot.B.	BT19	20
Trewince Rd. SW20	BQ51	85
Trewint St. SW18	BT48	76
Trewsbury Rd. SE26	CC49	77
Triandra Way, Hayes	BD39	54
Triangle Ct. E16	CJ39	58
Tollgate Rd.		
Triangle Pl. SW4	BW45	66
Triangle Rd. E8	CB37	57
Triangle, The, Bark.	CM36	58
Park Av.		
Triangle, The, Hmptn.	BG51	84
Triangle, The, Kings.T.	BN51	85
Triangle, Wok.	AR62	100
Trident Gdns., Nthlt.	BD38	54
Jetstar Way		
Trident Rd., Wat.	BB20	17
Trident St. SE16	CC42	67
Trident Way, Sthl.	BC41	63
Triggs Clo., Wok.	AR63	100
Triggs La., Wok.	AR63	100
Trigo Ct., Epsom	BN59	94
Blakeney Clo.		

Trigon Rd. SW8 BX43 66
Trilby Rd. SE23 CC48 77
Trim St. SE14 CD43 67
Trimmer Wk., Brent. BL43 65
Netley Rd.
Trinder Gdns. N19 BX33 47
Trinder Rd. N19 BX33 47
Trinder Rd., Barn. BQ25 28
Trindles Rd., Red. BX71 121
Tring Av. W5 BL40 55
Tring Av., Sthl. BE39 54
Tring Av., Wem. BM36 55
Tring Clo., Ilf. CM32 49
Tring Clo., Rom. CW28 42
Tring Gdns., Rom. CW28 42
Tring Grn., Rom. CW28 42
Tring Rd., Berk. AO11 7
Tring Wk., Rom. CW28 42
Tringham Clo., Cher. AU56 91
Trinidad Gdns., Dag. CS36 59
Trinidad St. E14 CD40 57
Trinity Av. N2 BT31 47
Trinity Av., Enf. CA25 30
Trinity Church Rd. SW13 BP43 65
Trinity Church Sq. SE1 BZ41 4
Trinity Church Sq. SE1 BZ41 67
Trinity Clo. E11 CG34 49
Trinity Clo. NW3 BT35 47
Hampstead High St.
Trinity Clo. SE13 CF45 67
Wisteria Rd.
Trinity Clo. SE7 CJ42 68
Trinity Clo., Brom. CK54 88
Trinity Clo., Houns. BE45 64
Trinity Clo., Nthwd. BB29 35
Trinity Clo., S.Croy. CA58 96
Trinity Clo., Stai. AX46 73
Trinity Cotts., Rich. BL45 65
Trinity Rd.
Trinity Cres. SW17 BU48 76
Trinity Ct. N1 CA37 2
Trinity Ct. N1 CA37 57
Trinity Est. SE8 CD42 67
Trinity Gdns. E16 CG39 58
Trinity Gdns. SW9 BX45 66
Trinity Gro. SE10 CF44 67
Trinity La., Wal.Cr. CD19 21
Trinity Ms. W10 BQ39 55
Cambridge Gdns.
Trinity Ms., Hem.H. BA14 8
Pancake La.
Trinity Pl. EC3 CA40 4
Trinity Sq.
Trinity Pl. EC3 CA40 57
Trinity Sq.
Trinity Pl., Bexh. CQ45 69
Trinity Pl., Wind. AO44 61
Trinity Rd. N2 BT31 47
Trinity Rd. N22 BX29 38
Trinity Rd. SW18 BT46 76
Trinity Rd. SW19 BS50 76
Trinity Rd., Grav. DH47 81
Trinity Rd., Ilf. CM31 49
Trinity Rd., Rich. BL45 65
Trinity Rd., Sthl. BE40 54
Trinity Ri. SW2 BY47 76
Trinity Sq. EC3 CA40 4
Trinity Sq. EC3 CA40 57
Trinity St. E16 CG39 58
Trinity St. SE1 BZ41 4
Trinity St. SE1 BZ41 67
Trinity St., Enf. BZ23 30
Trinity Way W3 BO40 55
Trinity Wk. NW3 BT36 56
College Cres.
Trinity Wk., Hem.H. BA14 8
Pancake La.
Trio Pl. SE1 BZ41 4
Trio Pl. SE1 BZ41 67
Tripps Hill Clo., Ch.St.G. AQ27 34
Tripton Rd., Harl. CN11 13
Tristan Sq. SE3 CG45 68
Tristram Clo. E17 CF31 48
Tristram Rd., Brom. CG49 78
Triton Sq. NW1 BW38 1
Triton Sq. NW1 BW38 56
Triton Way, Hem.H. AY12 8
Tritton Av., Croy. BX56 95
Tritton Rd. SE21 BZ48 77
Trittons, Tad. BQ64 103
Triumph Clo., Hayes BA43 63
Triumph Rd. E6 CK39 58
Trodds La., Guil. AU70 118
Trojan Way, Croy. BX55 86
Trolling Down Hill, Dart. CY48 80
Tronsay Wk. N1 BZ36 57
Marquess Est.
Troon St. E1 CD39 57
Trosley Av., Grav. DG48 81
Trosley Rd., Belv. CR43 69
Trossachs Rd. SE22 CA46 77
Trothy Rd. SE1 CB42 4
Trothy Rd. SE1 CB42 67
Trots La., West. CM67 115
Trotsworth Av., Vir.W. AS52 82
Trott Rd. N10 BU29 38
Trott St. SW11 BT44 66
Trotters Bottom, Barn. BP22 28
Trotters La., Wok. AQ59 91
Trotters Rd., Harl. CO12 14
Trotwood, Brwd. DC26 122
Trotwood, Chig. CM28 40
Troughton Rd. SE7 CH42 68
Trout La., West Dr. AX40 53
Trout Rd., West Dr. AX40 53
Trout Ri., Rick. AW24 26
Troutbeck Rd. SE14 CD44 67
Troutstream Way, Rick. AW24 26
Trouville Rd. SW4 BW46 76
Trowbridge Est. E9 CD35 48
Trowbridge Rd. E9 CD36 57
Trowbridge Rd., Rom. CV29 42
Trowers Way, Red. BV69 121
Trowley Ri., Wat. BB19 17
Trowlock Av., Tedd. BK50 74
Trowlock Way, Tedd. BK50 74
Troy Clo., Tad. BP63 103
Troy Ct. SE18 CL42 68
Troy Ct. W8 BS41 65
Troy Rd. SE19 BZ50 77
Troy Town SE15 CB45 67
Nutbrook St.
Trucks Alley, Swan. CR51 89
Truesdale Dr., Uxb. AX31 44
Truesdale Rd. E6 CK39 58
Trulock Ct. N17 CB29 39
Trulock Rd. N17 CB29 39
Truman Clo., Edg. BM29 37
Pavilion Way
Trumans Rd. N16 CA35 48
Trump St. EC2 BZ39 2
Trump St. EC2 BZ39 57
King St.
Trumper Way, Uxb. AX37 53
Trumpers Way W7 BH41 64
Trumpetshill Rd., Reig. BP71 120
Trumpington Dr., St.Alb. BG15 9
Trumpington Rd. E7 CG35 49
Trumps Green Clo., Vir.W. AS53 82
Trumpsgreen Rd.
Trumps Mill La., Vir.W. AS53 82
Trumpsgreen Av., Vir.W. AR53 82
Trumpsgreen Rd., Vir.W. AR53 82
Trundle St. SE1 BZ41 4
Trundle St. SE1 BZ41 67
Weller St.
Trundlers Way, Bush. BH26 36
Trundleys Rd. SE8 CC42 67
Trundleys Ter. SE8 CC42 67
Truro Gdns., Ilf. CK33 49
Truro Rd. E17 CD31 48
Truro Rd. N22 BX29 38
Truro Rd., Grav. DH48 81
Truro St. NW5 BV36 56
Truro Way, Hayes BB38 53
Truro Wk., Rom. CV29 42
Truslove Rd. SE27 BY49 76
Trussley Rd. W6 BQ41 65
Trust Rd., Wal.Cr. CD20 21
Trustees Way, Uxb. AV32 43
Trustings Clo., Esher BJ57 93
Trustons Gdns., Horn. CU33 50
Trycewell La., Sev. DB64 108
Tryfan Clo., Ilf. CJ32 49
Tryon St. SW3 BU42 3
Tryon St. SW3 BU42 66
Trys Hill, Cher. AT55 82
Tuam Rd. SE18 CM43 68
Tubbenden Clo., Orp. CN55 88
Tubbenden Dr., Orp. CM56 97
Tubbenden La. S., Orp. CM56 97
Tubbenden La., Orp. CM56 97
Tubbs Rd. NW10 BO37 55
Tubs Hill, Sev. CU65 107
Tubwell Rd., Slou. AQ37 52
Tuck Rd., Rain. CU36 59
Tucker Rd., Cher. AU57 91
Tucker St., Wat. BD25 27
Tuckey Gro., Wok. AV65 100
Tuckton Wk. SW15 BO46 75
Tudor Av., Chsnt. CB19 21
Tudor Av., Hmptn. BF50 74
Tudor Av., Rom. CU31 50
Tudor Av., Wat. BD22 27
Tudor Av., Wor.Pk. BP55 85
Tudor Clo. NW3 BU35 47
Tudor Clo. NW7 BP29 37
Tudor Clo. NW9 BN34 46
Tudor Clo. SW2 BX46 76
Tudor Clo., Ashf. AY49 73
Tudor Clo., Bans. BR61 103
Tudor Clo., Brwd. DD25 122
Tudor Clo., Chess. BL56 94
Tudor Clo., Chig. CL28 40
Tudor Clo., Chis. CK51 88
Tudor Clo., Chsnt. CB19 21
Tudor Clo., Cob. BE60 93
Tudor Clo., Couls. BY62 104
Tudor Clo., Dart. CU46 79
Tudor Clo., Hat. BO14 10
Tudor Clo., Lthd. BE65 102
Tudor Clo., Pnr. BC32 44
Tudor Clo., S.Croy. CB61 105
Tudor Clo., Sutt. BQ57 94
Tudor Clo., Wall. BW57 95
Tudor Clo., Wdf.Grn. CH28 40
Tudor Cres., Enf. BZ23 30
Tudor Cres., Ilf. CL29 40
Tudor Cres., Sev. CV61 108
Tudor Ct. N., Wem. BM35 46
Tudor Ct. S., Wem. BM35 46
Tudor Ct. SE9 CK45 68
Tudor Ct., B.Wd. BL23 28
Tudor Ct., Felt. BD49 74
Tudor Ct., Saw. CQ 5 6
West Rd.
Tudor Dr., Kings.T. BK49 74
Tudor Dr., Mord. BQ53 85
Tudor Dr., Rom. CU31 50
Tudor Dr., Sev. CV61 108
Tudor Dr., Walt. BD54 84
Tudor Dr., Wat. BD22 27
Tudor Est. NW10 BM38 55
Tudor Gdns. NW9 BN34 46
Tudor Gdns. SW13 BO45 65
Treen Av.
Tudor Gdns. W3 BM39 55
Tudor Gdns., Rom. CU31 50
Tudor Gdns., Twick. BH47 74
Tudor Gdns., Upmin. CY34 51
Tudor Gdns., W.Wick. CF55 87
Tudor Gro. E9 CC36 57
Tudor Gro. N20 BU27 38
Church Cres.
Tudor Hill, Hem.H. AX14 8
Tudor Manor Gdns., Wat. BD19 18
Tudor Par., Rick. AW26 35
Berry La.
Tudor Pk., Amer. AO22 25
Tudor Pl. W1 BW39 1
Tudor Pl. W1 BW39 56
Gresse St.
Tudor Pl., Mitch. BU50 76
Tudor Rd. E4 CE29 39
Tudor Rd. E6 CJ37 58
Tudor Rd. E9 CB37 57
Tudor Rd. N9 CB26 39
Tudor Rd. SE19 CA50 77
Tudor Rd. SE25 CB53 87
Tudor Rd., Ashf. BA50 73
Tudor Rd., Bark. CN37 58
Tudor Rd., Barn. BS24 29
Tudor Rd., Beck. CE52 87
Tudor Rd., Har. BG30 36
Tudor Rd., Hayes BA39 53
Tudor Rd., Hmptn. BF50 74
Tudor Rd., Houns. BG45 64
Tudor Rd., Kings.T. BM50 75
Tudor Rd., Pnr. BD30 36
Tudor Rd., St.Alb. BH11 9
Tudor Rd., Sthl. BE40 54
Tudor Rd., Welw. BP 5 5
Tudor Ri., Brox. CD14 12
Tudor Sq., Hayes BA39 53
Tudor St. EC4 BY39 56
Tudor St. EC4 BY40 4
Tudor Way N14 BW26 38
Tudor Way W3 BM41 65
Tudor Way, Orp. CM53 88
Tudor Way, Rick. AW26 35
Tudor Way, Uxb. AZ36 53
Tudor Way, Wal.Abb. CF20 21
Tudor Way, West Dr. AY42 63
Tudor Way, Wind. AM44 61
Tudor Well Clo., Stan. BJ28 36
Tudor Wk., Bex. CQ46 79
Tudor Wk., Lthd. BH63 102
Tudor Wk., Wat. BD22 27
Tudor Wk., Wey. AZ55 83
Palace Dr.
Tudway Rd. SE3 CJ45 68
Tufnail Rd., Dart. CW46 80
Tufnell Park Rd. N7 BW35 47
Tufter Rd., Chig. CN28 40
Tufton Gdns., E.Mol. BF51 84
Tufton Rd. E4 CE28 39
Tufton St. SW1 BW41 3
Tufton St. SW1 BW41 66
Tugela Rd., Croy. BZ53 87
Tugela St. SE6 CD48 77
Tugmutton Clo., Orp. CL56 97
Starts Hill Rd.
Tuilerie St. E2 CB37 2
Tuilerie St. E2 CB37 57
Tulip Clo., Brwd. DA25 33
Poppy Clo.
Tulip Clo., Croy. CC54 87
Primrose La.
Tulip Clo., Hmptn. BF50 74
Partridge Rd.
Tulip Clo., Rom. CV29 42
Cloudberry Rd.
Tulip Ct., Pnr. BD31 45
Nursery Rd.
Tulse Clo., Beck. CF52 87
Tulse Hill Est. SW2 BY46 76
Tulse Hill SW2 BY46 76
Tulsemere Rd. SE27 BZ48 77
Tulyar Clo., Tad. BP63 103
Tumber St., Epsom BN66 112
Tumblefield Rd., Sev. DC60 99
Tumbler Rd., Harl. CO11 14
Tumblewood Rd., Bans. BR61 103
Tumbling Bay, Walt. BC53 83
Tummons Gdns. SE25 CA51 87
Tuncombe Rd. N18 CA28 39
Tunfield Rd., Hodd. CE10 12
Tunis Rd. W12 BP40 55
Tunley Rd. NW10 BO37 55
Tunley Rd. SW17 BV47 76
Tunmarsh La. E13 CJ38 58
Tunmers End, Ger.Cr. AR30 34
Tunnel Av. SE10 CG42 68
Tunnel Cotts., Grays DA43 70
The Rookery
Tunnel Gdns. N11 BW29 38
Tunnel Rd. SE16 CC41 67
Church St.
Tunnel Wood Clo., Wat. BB22 26
Tunnel Wood Rd., Wat. BB22 26
Tunnmeade, Harl. CO10 6
Tuns La., Slou. AO40 61
Tunsgate, Guil. AR71 118
Tunstall Av., Ilf. CO29 41
Tunstall Clo., Orp. CN56 97
Tunstall Rd. SW9 BX45 66
Tunstall Rd., Croy. CA54 87
Tunstall Wk., Brent. BK42 64
Ealing Rd.
Tunstock Way, Belv. CQ41 69
Tunworth Clo. NW9 BN32 46
Tunworth Cres. SW15 BO46 75
Tupwood La., Cat. CB66 114
Tupwood Scrubbs Rd., Cat. CB67 114
Turenne Clo. SW18 BT45 66
Turfhouse La., Wok. AP58 91
Turin Rd. N9 CC26 39
Turin St. E2 CB38 2
Turin St. E2 CB38 57
Turkey Oak Clo. SE19 CA51 87
Hamlyn Gdns.
Turkey St., Enf. CB21 30
Turks Clo., Uxb. AZ38 53
Turks Head Ct., Eton AO43 61
High St.
Turks Head Yd. EC1 BY38 56
Turnhill St.
Turks Head Yd. EC1 BY39 2
Turks Row SW3 BU42 3
Turks Row SW3 BU42 66
Turle Rd. N4 BX33 47
Turle Rd. SW16 BW51 86
Turlewray Clo. N4 BX33 47
Turley Clo. E15 CG37 58
Turmore Dale, Welw.G.C. BQ 8 5
Turnagain La. EC4 CM39 58
Farringdon St.
Turnagain La., Dart. CU48 79
Turnage Rd., Dag. CQ33 50
Turnant Rd. N17 BZ30 39
Lordship La.
Turnberry Dr., St.Alb. BE18 18
Turnberry Quay E14 CE41 67
Pepper St.
Turnberry Way, Orp. CM54 88
Turnbull Clo., Green. CZ47 80
Turner Av. N15 CA31 48
Turner Av., Mitch. BU51 86
Turner Av., Twick. BG48 74
Turner Clo. NW11 BS32 47
Turner Clo., Hayes BA37 53
Turner Dr. NW11 BS32 47
Turner Rd. E17 CF31 48
Turner Rd., Bush. BG24 27
Turner Rd., Dart. DA48 80
Turner Rd., Edg. BL30 37
Turner Rd., N.Mal. BN54 85
Turner Rd., Slou. AR41 62
Turner Rd., West. CJ59 97
Turner Sq. N1 CA37 2
Turner Sq. N1 CA37 57
Regan Way
Turner St. E1 CB39 57
Turner St. E16 CG39 58
Turners Alley EC3 CA40 4
Eastcheap
Turners Alley EC3 CA40 57
Eastcheap
Turners Clo., Ong. CW18 24
Turners Gdns., Sev. CV67 117
Turners Hill, Chsnt. CC18 21
Turners Hill, Hem.H. AY14 8
Turners La., Walt. BC57 92
Turners Meadow Way, Beck. CD51 87
Turners Rd. E3 CD39 57
Turners Way NW11 BT33 47
Wildwood Rd.
Turners Way, Croy. BY55 86
Turners Wood Dr., Ch.St.G. AR27 34
Turners Wood NW11 BT33 47
Wildwood Rd.
Turneville Rd. W14 BR43 65
Turney Rd. SE21 BZ47 77
Turneys Orch., Rick. AU25 25
Turnham Green Ter. W4 BO42 65
Turnham Green Terrace Ms. W4 BO42 65
Turnham Green Ter.
Turnham Rd. SE4 CD46 77
Turnmill St. EC1 BY38 56
Turnmill St. EC1 BY39 2
Turnoak Av., Wok. AS63 100
Turnoak La., Wok. AS63 100
Turnoak Pk., Wind. AM45 61
St. Leonards Hill
Turnpike Clo. SE14 CD43 67
Amersham Vale
Turnpike Ct., Bexh. CP45 69
Crook Log
Turnpike Dr., Orp. CP58 98
Turnpike Grn., Hem.H. AY11 8
Turnpike La. N8 BX31 47
Turnpike La., Sutt. BT56 95
Turnpike La., Til. DH42 71
Turnpike La., Uxb. AY37 53
Turnpike Link, Croy. CA55 87
Turnpin La. SE10 CF43 67
King William Wk.
Turnstone Clo. E13 CH38 58
Turnstone Clo., S.Croy. CC58 96
Turnstones, The, Grav. DH48 81
Turnstones, The, Wat. BE21 27
Turp Av., Grays DE41 71
Turpentine La. SW1 BV42 3
Turpentine La. SW1 BV42 66
Sutherland St.
Turpin Av., Rom. CR29 41
Turpin Est. E13 CH37 58
Turpin Rd., Felt. BB46 73
Staines Rd.
Turpin Way N19 BW33 47
Ashbrook Rd.
Turpin Way, Wall. BV57 95
Turpington Clo., Brom. CK54 88
Turpington La., Brom. CK54 88
Turpins La., Wdf.Grn. CK28 40
Turquand St. SE17 BZ42 4
Turquand St. SE17 BZ42 67
Turret Ct., Ong. CX18 24
Turret Gro. SW4 BW45 66
Turton Mkt., Wem. BL35 46
Turton Rd.
Turton Rd., Wem. BL35 46
Turton Way, Slou. AO41 61
Turville Clo., Lthd. BF66 111
Turville St. E2 CA38 2
Turville St. E2 CA38 57
Old Nichol St.
Tuscan Rd. SE18 CM42 68
Tuskar St. SE10 CG42 68
Tustin Est. SE15 CC43 67
Tuttlebee La., Buck H. CH27 40
Tuxford Clo., B.Wd. BL22 28
Twedwell Clo., Brom. CK52 88
Tweed Glen, Rom. CS29 41
Tweed Grn., Rom. CS29 41
Tweed La., Bet. BM72 120
Tweed Rd., Slou. AT43 62
Tweed Way, Rom. CS29 41
Tweedale Ct. E15 CE35 48
Tweedale Gro., Uxb. BA34 44
Tweedale Rd., Cars. BT54 86
Tweedmouth Rd. E13 CH37 58
Tweedy Rd., Brom. CH51 88
Tweenways, Chesh. AP18 16
Twelve Acre Clo., Lthd. BE65 102
Twelve Acres., Welw.G.C. BR 9 5
Twelve Trees Cres. E3 CF38 57
Devas St.
Twelvetrees Cres. E3 CF38 57
Twentyman Clo., Wdf.Grn. CH28 40
Twickenham Br., Rich. BK46 74
Twickenham Br., Twick. BK46 74
Twickenham Clo., Croy. BX55 86
Twickenham Gdns., Grnf. BJ35 45
Twickenham Gdns., Har. BH29 36
Twickenham Rd. E11 CF34 48
Twickenham Rd., Felt. BE48 74
Twickenham Rd., Islw. BJ46 74
Twickenham Rd., Rich. BK45 64
Twickenham Rd., Tedd. BJ49 74
Twigg Clo., Erith CT43 69
Twilley St. SW18 BS47 76
Twinches La., Slou. AN40 61
Twine Ct. E1 CC40 57
Cable St.
Twineham Grn. N12 BS28 38
Twining Av., Twick. BG48 74
Twinn Rd. NW7 BR29 37
Twinoaks, Cob. BF60 93
Twisden Rd. NW5 BV35 47
Twitchells La., Beac. AP29 34
Twitton Bungalows, Sev. CA52 107
Twitton La., Sev. CS61 107
Two Acres, Welw.G.C. BR 9 5
Two Dells La., Chesh. AP16 16
Two Waters Rd., Hem.H. AX15 8
Twybridge Way NW10 BN36 55
Twyford Abbey Rd. NW10 BL38 55
Twyford Av. N2 BU31 47
Twyford Av. W3 BM40 55
Twyford Cres. W3 BM40 55
Twyford Pl. WC2 BX39 2
Twyford Pl. WC2 BX39 56
Kingsway
Twyford Rd., Cars. BT54 86
Twyford Rd., Har. BF33 45
Twyford Rd., Ilf. CM35 49
Twyford Rd., St.Alb. BK11 9
Twyford St. N1 BX37 2
Twyford St. N1 BX37 56
Twysdens Ter., Hat. BQ15 10
Station Rd.
Tyas Rd. E16 CG38 58
Tybalds Est. WC1 BX39 2
Tybenham Rd. SW19 BR52 85
Tyberry Rd., Enf. CB24 30
Tyburn La., Har. BH33 45
Tyburn Way W1 BU40 3
Tyburns, The, Brwd. DE27 122
Tycehurst Gdns., Ilf. CM35 49
Tycehurst Hill, Loug. CK24 31
Tychbourne Dr., Guil. AU69 118
Tydcombe Rd., Warl. CC63 105
Tye Green Village, Harl. CN12 13
Tye La., Epsom BN67 112
Tye La., Orp. CM56 97
Tyers Est. SE1 CA41 4
Tyers Est. SE1 CA41 67
Tyers Gate SE1 CA41 4
Tyers Gate SE1 CA41 67
Tyers St. SE11 BX42 4
Tyers St. SE11 BX42 66
Tyers Ter. SE11 BX42 4
Tyers Ter. SE11 BX42 66
Tyeshurst Clo. SE2 CQ42 69
Tyfield Clo., Chsnt. CC18 21
Tykeswater La., B.Wd. BK23 27
Tyle Grn., Horn. CW31 51
Tyle Pl., Wind. AQ46 72
Tylecroft Rd. SW16 BX51 86
Tylehost, Guil. AQ68 109
Tyler Clo. E2 CA37 2
Tyler Clo. E2 CA37 57
Hows St.
Tyler Gdns., Wey. AX56 92
Tyler Gro., Dart. CW45 70
Tyler St. SE10 CG42 68
Tylers Causeway, Hert. BW14 11
Tylers Clo., Gdse. CB68 114
Tylers Clo., Kings L. AY18 17
Tylers Clo., Loug. CK26 40
Tylers Cres., Horn. CV35 51
Tylers Est. SE1 CA41 67
Tylers Field, Wat. BC19 17
Tylers Gate SE1 CA41 67
Tylers Gate, Har. BL32 46
Tylers Green Rd., Swan. CS53 89
Tylers Hill Rd., Ches. AP18 16
Tylers Rd., Harl. CJ13 13
Tylers Way, Wat. BG24 27
Tylney Av. SE19 CA49 77
Tylney Cft., Harl. CM12 13
Tylney Rd. E7 CJ35 49
Tylney Rd., Brom. CJ51 88
Tylsworth Clo., Amer. AO22 25
King George V Rd.
Tynan Clo., Felt. BC47 73
Tyndale Clo., Dart. CY47 80
Princes Rd.
Tyndale La. N1 BY36 56
Upper St.
Tyndale Ter. N1 BY36 56
Tyndale La.
Tyndall Rd. E10 CF34 48
Tyndall Rd., Well. CN45 68
Tyne Clo., Upmin. CY32 51
Tyne Gdns., S.Ock. CY40 60
Tyne Rd., Ilf. CM34 49
Tyne St. E1 CA39 2
Whitechapel High St.
Tyne St. E1 CA39 57
Old Castle St.
Tynedale Rd., Bet. BM72 120
Tynedale, St.Alb. BL17 19
Thamesdale
Tyneham Rd. SW11 BV44 66
Tynemouth Dr., Enf. CB22 30
Tynemouth Rd. N15 CA31 48
Tynemouth Rd., Mitch. BV50 76
Tynemouth St. SW6 BT44 66
Tynley Gro., Guil. AR67 109
Type St. E2 CC37 57
Tyrawley Rd. SW6 BS44 66
Tyrell Clo., Har. BH35 45

Tyrell Ct., Cars.	BU56	95
Tyrell Gdns., Wind.	AM45	61
Tyrell Ri., Brwd.	DB28	42
Chindits La.		
Tyrells Clo., Upmin.	CX34	51
Tyron Way, Sid.	CN49	78
Tyrone Rd. E6	CK37	58
Tyrrel Way NW9	BO33	46
Tyrrell Av., Well.	CO46	79
Tyrrell Rd. SE22	CB45	67
Tyrrells Hall Clo., Grays	DE42	71
Tyrrells Wood Dr., Lthd.	BL65	103
Tyrwhitt Av., Guil.	AQ68	109
Tyrwhitt Rd. SE4	CE45	67
Tysea Clo., Harl.	CN12	13
Tysea Hill, Rom.	CT26	41
Tysea Rd., Harl.	CN12	13
Tysoe Av., Enf.	CD22	30
Tysoe St. EC1	**BY38**	**2**
Tysoe St. EC1	BY38	56
Tyson Gdns. SE23	CC47	77
Devonshire Rd.		
Tyson Rd. SE23	CC47	77
Tyssen Pl. E8	BT36	56
Ramsgate St.		
Tyssen Pl., S.Ock.	DB37	60
Gidea Clo.		
Tyssen Rd. N16	CA34	48
Stoke Newington High St.		
Tyssen St. E8	CA36	57
Tythebarn Clo., Guil.	AT68	109
Dairymans Wk.		
Tytherton Rd. N19	BW34	47
Tyttenhanger Grn., St.Alb.	BL15	10
Tyttenhanger La., St.Alb.	BK14	9

U

Uamvar St. E14	CE39	57
Uckfield Gro., Mitch.	BV51	86
Uckfield Rd., Enf.	CC22	30
Udall Gdns., Rom.	CR29	41
Udall St. SW1	**BW42**	**3**
Udall St. SW1	BW42	66
Vincent Sq.		
Udney Hall, Tedd.	BJ49	74
Udney Park Rd., Tedd.	BJ50	74
Uffington Rd. NW10	BP37	55
Uffington Rd. SE27	BY49	76
Ufford Clo., Har.	BF29	36
Ufford Rd., Har.	BF29	36
Ufford St. SE1	**BY41**	**4**
Ufford St. SE1	BY41	66
Ufton Gro. N1	BZ36	57
Ufton Rd. N1	**BZ36**	**2**
Ufton Rd. N1	BZ36	57
Ullathorne Rd. SW16	BW49	76
Ulleswater Rd. N14	BX28	38
Ullin St. E14	CF39	57
St. Leonards Rd.		
Ullswater Clo. SW15	BN49	75
Ullswater Clo., Brom.	CG50	78
Ullswater Clo., Hayes	BB37	53
Ullswater Cres. SW15	BN49	75
Ullswater Cres., Couls.	BW61	104
Ullswater Rd. SE27	BY48	76
Ullswater Rd. SW13	BP43	65
Ullswater Rd., Hem.H.	AZ14	8
Ullswater Way, Horn.	CU35	50
Ulstan Clo., Cat.	CE65	105
Ulster Gdns. N13	BZ28	39
Ulster Pl. NW1	BV38	56
Ulundi Rd. SE3	CG43	68
Ulva Rd. SW15	BQ45	65
Ravenna Rd.		
Ulverscroft Rd. SE22	CA46	77
Ulverston Rd. E17	CF30	39
Ulverstone Rd. SE27	BY48	76
Ulwin Av., Wey.	AY60	92
Ulysses Rd. NW6	BR35	46
Umberston St. E1	CB39	57
Umbria St. SW15	BP46	75
Umfreville Rd. N4	BY32	47
Underacres Clo., Hem.H.	AZ13	8
Undercliff Rd. SE13	CE45	67
Underhill Park Rd., Reig.	BS69	121
Underhill Rd. SE22	CB46	77
Underhill St. NW1	**BV37**	**1**
Underhill St. NW1	BV37	56
Camden High St.		
Underhill, Barn.	BS25	29
Underne Av. N14	BV27	38
Underriver House Rd., Sev.	CX68	117
Undershaft EC3	CA39	57
St. Mary Axe		
Undershaw Rd., Brom.	CG48	78
Underwood Rd. E1	**CB38**	**2**
Underwood Rd. E1	CB38	57
Underwood Rd. E4	CE28	39
Underwood Rd., Cat.	CA66	114
Underwood Rd., Wdf.Grn.	CJ29	40
Underwood Row N1	**BZ38**	**2**
Underwood Row N1	BZ38	57
Underwood St. E1	**CB38**	**2**
Underwood St. E1	CB38	57
Underwood Rd.		
Underwood St. N1	**BZ38**	**2**
Underwood St. N1	BZ38	57
Underwood, Croy.	CF57	96
Underwood, The SE9	CK48	78
Undine Rd. E14	CE41	67
Undine St. SW17	BU49	76
Uneeda Dr., Grnf.	BG37	54
Union Cotts. E15	CG36	58
Union Ct. E15	CF37	57
Union Ct. EC2	**CA39**	**2**
Old Broad St.		
Union Ct. EC2	CA39	57
Old Broad St.		
Union Ct., Ilf.	CL34	49
Ilford Hill		
Union Ct., Rich.	BL46	75
Eton St.		
Union Dr. E1	CD38	57
Solebay St.		
Union Gro. SW8	BW44	66
Union La., Islw.	BJ44	64
Park Rd.		
Union Rd. E17	CD32	48
Union Rd. N11	BW29	38
Union Rd. SW8	BW44	66
Union Rd., Brom.	CJ53	88
Union Rd., Croy.	BZ54	87
Union Rd., Nthlt.	BF37	54
Union Rd., Wem.	BL36	55
Union Sq. N1	**BZ37**	**2**
Union Sq. N1	BZ37	57
Union St. E15	CF37	57
Union St. SE1	**BY41**	**4**
Union St. SE1	BY41	66
Union St., Barn.	BR24	28
Union St., Hem.H.	AX13	8
Union St., Kings.T.	BK51	84
Union Wk. E2	**CA38**	**2**
Union Wk. E2	CA38	57
Union Yd. W1	**BV39**	**1**
Dering St.		
Union Yd. W1	BV39	56
Dering St.		
Unity Rd., Enf.	CC22	30
Unity Way SE18	CJ41	68
University Clo. NW9	BO30	37
Rivington Cres.		
University Pl., Erith	CS43	69
Belmont Rd.		
University Rd. SW19	BT50	76
University St. WC1	**BW38**	**1**
University St. WC1	BW38	56
Unwin Av., Felt.	BA46	73
Unwin Clo. SE15	CB43	67
Unwin Rd., Islw.	BH45	64
Upbrook Ms. W2	**BT39**	**1**
Upbrook Ms. W2	BT39	56
Upcerne Rd. SW10	BT43	66
Burnaby St.		
Upchurch Clo. SE20	CB50	77
Woodbine Gro.		
Upcroft Av., Edg.	BN28	37
Upcroft, Wind.	AN45	61
Updale Clo., Pot.B.	BQ20	19
Updale Rd., Sid.	CN49	78
Upfield Rd., W7	BH38	54
Upfield, Croy.	CB55	87
Upfolds Grn., Guil.	AU68	109
Uphall Rd., Ilf.	CL35	49
Upham Park Rd. W4	BO42	65
Uphill Dr. NW7	BO28	37
Uphill Dr. NW9	BN32	46
Uphill Gro. NW7	BO28	37
Uphill Rd. NW7	BO28	37
Upland Court Rd., Rom.	CW30	42
Upland Rd. E13	CG38	58
Upland Rd. SE22	CB46	77
Upland Rd., Bexh.	CQ45	69
Upland Rd., Cat.	CE63	105
Upland Rd., Epp.	CM16	22
Upland Rd., S.Croy.	BZ56	96
Upland Rd., Sutt.	BT57	95
Upland Way, Epsom	BQ62	103
Uplands Av. E17	CC30	39
Uplands Clo. SW14	BM46	75
Uplands Clo., Ger.Cr.	AS33	43
Uplands Clo., Sev.	CT65	107
Uplands Ct. N21	BY26	38
Uplands Dr., Hat.	BS16	20
Uplands End, Wdf.Grn.	CK29	40
Uplands Park Rd., Enf.	BY24	29
Uplands Rd. N8	BX32	47
Uplands Rd., Barn.	BV26	38
Uplands Rd., Brwd.	DC28	122
Uplands Rd., Ken.	BZ61	105
Uplands Rd., Orp.	CO54	89
Uplands Rd., Rom.	CP31	50
Uplands Rd., Wdf.Grn.	CK29	40
Uplands SW16	BY49	76
Uplands Way N21	BY25	29
Uplands Way, Sev.	CT65	107
Uplands, Ash.	BK63	102
Uplands, Beck.	CE51	87
Uplands, Rick.	AY25	26
Uplands, The, Ger.Cr.	AS33	43
Uplands, The, Loug.	CK24	31
Uplands, The, Ruis.	BC33	44
Uplands, The, St.Alb.	BE18	18
Uplands, Welw.G.C.	BQ 6	5
Upminster Rd. N., Rain.	CV38	60
Upminster Rd. S., Rain.	CU38	59
Upminster Rd., Horn.	CW34	51
Upney Clo., Horn.	CV35	51
Tylers Cres.		
Upney La., Bark.	CN35	49
Upnor Way SE17	**CA42**	**4**
Upnor Way SE17	CA42	67
Uppark Dr., Ilf.	CM32	49
Upper Abbey Rd., Belv.	CQ42	69
Upper Addison Gdns. W14	BR41	65
Upper Ashlyns Rd., Berk.	AQ13	7
Upper Austin Lodge Rd., Eyns.	CV56	99
Upper Av., Grays	DF51	81
Upper Bardsey Wk. N1	BZ36	57
Marquess Est.		
Upper Barn, Hem.H.	AY15	8
Upper Belgrave St. SW1	**BV41**	**3**
Upper Belgrave St. SW1	BV41	66
Upper Berenger Wk. SW10	BT43	66
Worlds End		
Upper Berkeley St. W1	**BU39**	**1**
Upper Berkeley St. W1	BU39	56
Upper Beulah Hill SE19	CA51	87
Upper Blantyre Wk. SW10	BT43	66
Worlds End		
Upper Bray Rd., Maid.	AH42	61
Upper Brentwood Rd., Rom.	CV31	51
Upper Bridge Rd., Red.	BU70	121
Upper Brighton Rd., Surb.	BK53	84
Upper Brockley Rd. SE4	CD45	67
Upper Brook St. W1	**BV40**	**3**
Upper Brook St. W1	BV40	56
Upper Butts, Brent.	BK43	64
Upper Caldy Wk. N1	BZ36	57
Marquess Est.		
Upper Camelford Wk. W11	BQ40	55
Lancaster Rd.		
Upper Cavendish Av. N3	BS31	47
Upper Cheyne Row SW3	BU43	66
Upper Church Hill, Green.	CZ46	80
Upper Clapton Rd. E5	CB33	48
Upper Clarendon Wk. W11	BQ40	55
Lancaster Rd.		
Upper Corner Clo., Ch.St.G.	AQ27	34
Upper Cornsland, Brwd.	DB27	42
Upper Court Rd., Cat.	CE65	105
Upper Court Rd., Epsom	BN59	94
Upper Culver Rd., St.Alb.	BH12	9
Upper Dagnal St., St.Alb.	BG13	9
Upper Dartrey Wk. SW10	BT43	66
Worlds End		
Upper Dengie Wk. N1	**BZ37**	**2**
Popham St. Est.		
Upper Dengie Wk. N1	BZ37	57
Popham St.		
Upper Dr., West.	CJ62	106
Upper Drayton Pl., Croy.	BY55	86
Drayton Rd.		
Upper Dunnymans Ms., Bans.	BR60	94
Basing Rd.		
Upper Edgeborough Rd., Guil.	AS71	118
Upper Elmers End Rd., Beck.	CD52	87
Upper End Rd., Beck.	CE53	87
Upper Fairfield Rd., Lthd.	BJ64	102
Upper Farm Rd.	BE52	84
Upper Field Rd., Welw.G.C.	BR 9	5
Upper Fosters NW4	BQ32	46
Upper George St., Chesh.	AO18	16
Upper Green La., Ton.	DB68	117
Upper Green Rd., Welw.G.C.	BU 5	5
Upper Green, Welw.G.C.	BU 5	5
Upper Grenfell Wk. W11	BQ40	55
Lancaster Rd.		
Upper Grn. E., Mitch.	BU51	86
Upper Grn. W., Mitch.	BU51	86
Upper Gro. SE25	CA52	87
Upper Grosvenor St. W1	**BV40**	**3**
Upper Grosvenor St. W1	BV40	56
Upper Grotto Rd., Twick.	BH48	74
Upper Ground SE1	**BY40**	**4**
Upper Ground SE1	BY40	56
Upper Grove Rd., Belv.	CQ43	69
Upper Guildown Rd., Guil.	AQ72	118
Upper Gulland Wk. N1	BZ36	57
Marquess Est.		
Upper Hall Pk., Berk.	AR13	7
Upper Halliford Rd., Shep.	BB52	83
Upper Ham Rd., Rich.	BK49	74
Upper Handa Wk. N1	BZ36	57
Marquess Est.		
Upper Harley St. NW1	**BV38**	**1**
Upper Harley St. NW1	BV38	56
Upper Hawkwell Wk. N1	**BZ37**	**2**
Popham St. Est.		
Upper Hawkwell Wk. N1	BZ37	57
Popham St.		
Upper Heath Rd., St.Alb.	BH12	9
Upper High St., Epsom	BO60	94
Upper Highway, Kings L.	BA19	17
Upper Highway, Wat.	BA20	17
Upper Hill Ri., Rick.	AW25	26
Upper Hill View Rd., Pnr.	BE29	36
Upper Hitch, Wat.	BE27	36
Upper Holly Hill Rd., Belv.	CR42	69
Upper James St. W1	**BW40**	**3**
Upper James St. W1	BW40	56
Beak St.		
Upper John St. W1	**BW40**	**3**
Upper John St. W1	BW40	56
Beak St.		
Upper Lattimore Rd., St.Alb.	BH13	9
Upper Lismore Wk. N1	BZ36	57
Marquess Est.		
Upper Mall W6	BP42	65
Upper Marlborough Rd., St.Alb.	BH13	9
Upper Marsh La., Hodd.	CE12	12
Upper Marsh SE1	**BX41**	**4**
Upper Marsh SE1	BX41	66
Upper Mealines, Harl.	CO12	14
Upper Montagu St. W1	**BU39**	**1**
Upper Montagu St. W1	BU39	56
Upper Mulgrave Rd., Sutt.	BR57	94
Upper North St. E14	CE39	57
Upper Paddock Rd., Wat.	BE25	27
Upper Palace Rd., E.Mol.	BG52	84
Upper Park Rd. N11	BV28	38
Upper Park Rd. NW3	BU35	47
Upper Park Rd., Belv.	CR42	69
Upper Park Rd., Brom.	CH51	88
Upper Park Rd., Kings.T.	BM50	75
Upper Phillimore Gdns. W8	BS41	66
Upper Pillory Downs, Cars.	BV60	95
Upper Pines, Bans.	BU62	104
Upper Pk., Harl.	CL10	6
Upper Pk., Loug.	CJ24	31
Upper Rainham Rd., Horn.	CT33	50
Upper Ramsey Wk. N1	BZ36	57
Marquess Est.		
Upper Rawreth Wk. N1	**BZ37**	**2**
Popham St. Est.		
Upper Rawreth Wk. N1	BZ37	57
Popham St.		
Upper Rd. E13	CH38	58
Upper Rd., Uxb.	AU33	43
Upper Rd., Wall.	BW56	95
Upper Richmond Rd. SW15	BO45	65
Upper Richmond Rd. W., Rich.	BM45	65
Upper Rose Hill, Dor.	BJ72	119
Upper Ryle, Brwd.	DA26	42
Upper Sales, Hem.H.	AV14	7
Upper Sawley Wood, Bans.	BR60	94
Basing Rd.		
Upper Selsdon Rd., S.Croy.	CA57	96
Upper Sheppey Wk. N1	BZ35	57
Marquess Est.		
Upper Sheridan Rd., Belv.	CR42	69
Coleman Rd.		
Upper Shirley Rd., Croy.	CC55	87
Upper Shot, Welw.G.C.	BS 7	5
Upper Shott, Chsnt.	CA16	21
Upper Spring La., Sev.	DA64	108
Upper Sq., Islw.	BJ45	64
Upper St. Martins La. WC2	**BX40**	**4**
Upper St. Martins La. WC2	BX40	56
Long Acre		
Upper St. N1	**BY37**	**2**
Upper St. N1	BY37	56
Upper Staithe W4	BN44	65
Upper Station Rd., Rad.	BJ21	27
Upper Stoneyfield, Harl.	CL11	13
Upper Sunbury Rd., Hmptn.	BE51	84
Upper Sutton La., Houns.	BF44	64
Upper Swaines, Epp.	CN18	22
Upper Tail, Wat.	BE27	36
Upper Talbot Wk. W11	BQ40	55
Lancaster Rd.		
Upper Teddington Rd., Tedd.	BK50	74
Upper Teddington Rd., Kings.T.	BK50	74
Upper Ter. NW3	BT34	47
Upper Thames St. EC4	**BY40**	**4**
Upper Thames St. EC4	BZ40	57
Upper Tollington Pk. N4	BY33	47
Upper Tooting Pk. SW17	BU48	76
Upper Tooting Rd. SW17	BU49	76
Upper Town Rd., Grnf.	BF38	54
Upper Tulse Hill SW2	BX47	76
Upper Vernon Rd., Sutt.	BT36	95
Upper Walthamstow Rd. E17	CF31	48
Upper West St., Reig.	BR70	120
Upper Whistlers Wk. SW10	BT43	66
Worlds End		
Upper Wickham La., Well.	CO45	69
Upper Wimpole St. W1	**BV39**	**1**
Upper Wimpole St. W1	BV39	56
Upper Woburn Pl. WC1	**BW38**	**1**
Upper Woburn Pl. WC1	BW38	56
Upper Wood, Harl.	CK12	13
Upper Woodcote Village, Pur.	BW59	95
Upperton Rd. E. E13	CJ38	58
Upperton Rd. W. E13	CJ38	58
Upperton Rd., Guil.	AR71	118
Upperton Rd., Sid.	CN49	78
Uppingham Av., Stan.	BJ30	36
Upsdell Av. N13	BY29	38
Upshire Rd., Wal.Abb.	CH20	22
Upshot La., Wok.	AV62	100
Upstall St. SE5	BY44	66
Upton Av. E7	CH36	58
Upton Av., St.Alb.	BG13	9
Upton Clo., Bex.	CQ46	79
Upton Clo., Slou.	AP41	62
Upton Clo., St.Alb.	BG16	18
Upton Court Rd., Slou.	AQ41	62
Upton Gdns., Har.	BJ32	45
Upton Gro., Slou.	AP41	62
Upton La. E7	CH37	58
Upton Lodge Clo., Bush.	BG26	36
Upton Park Rd. E7	CH36	58
Upton Pk., Slou.	AP41	62
Upton Rd. N18	CB28	39
Upton Rd. S., Bex.	CQ46	79
Upton Rd. SE18	CM43	68
Upton Rd., Bexh.	CQ45	69
Upton Rd., Houns.	BF45	64
Upton Rd., Slou.	AQ41	62
Upton Rd., Th.Hth.	BZ51	87
Upton Rd., Wat.	BC24	26
Upton, Wok.	AQ62	100
Upway N12	BU29	38
Upway, Ger.Cr.	AS30	34
Upwood Rd. SE12	CG46	78
Upwood Rd. SW16	BX51	86
Uranus Rd., Hem.H.	AY12	8
Urban Av., Horn.	CV34	51
Urlwin St. SE5	BZ43	67
Urlwin Wk. SW9	BT44	66
Myatts Fields Dev.		
Urmston Dr. SW19	BR47	75
Ursula St. SW11	BU44	66
Urswick Gdns., Dag.	CQ36	59
Urswick Rd. E9	CC35	48
Urswick Rd., Dag.	CQ36	59
Usborne Ms. SW8	BX43	66
Usher Rd. E3	CD37	57
Usk Rd. SW11	BT45	66
Usk Rd., S.Ock.	CY39	60
Usk St. E16	CG40	58
Usk St. E2	CC38	57
Utterton Way, Red.	BT72	121
Uvedale Clo., Croy.	CF59	96
Uvedale Cres., Croy.	CF59	96
Uvedale Rd., Dag.	CR34	50
Uvedale Rd., Enf.	BZ25	30
Uvedale Rd., Oxt.	CG68	115
Uverdale Rd. SW10	BT43	66
Uxbridge Cir., Uxb.	AY35	44
Uxbridge Gdns., Felt.	BD48	74
Uxbridge Rd. W12	BP40	55
Uxbridge Rd. W13	BJ40	54
Uxbridge Rd. W3	BJ40	54
Uxbridge Rd. W5	BM40	55
Uxbridge Rd., Felt.	BD48	74
Uxbridge Rd., Hmptn.	BF49	74
Uxbridge Rd., Kings.T.	BK52	84
Uxbridge Rd., Pnr.	BD30	36
Uxbridge Rd., Rick.	AV27	34
Uxbridge Rd., Slou.	AQ41	62
Uxbridge Rd., Slou. & Iver	AS39	52
Uxbridge Rd., Sthl.	BF40	54
Uxbridge Rd., Uxb. & Hayes	AZ38	53
Uxbridge St. W8	BS40	56
Uxendon Cres., Wem.	BL33	46
Uxendon Hill, Wem.	BL33	46

V

Vache La., Ch.St.G.	AR27	34
Vaillant Rd., Wey.	BA56	92
Valan Leas, Brom.	CG52	88
Valance Av. E4	CG26	40
Vale Av., B.Wd.	BM25	28
Vale Clo. N2	BU31	47
Church Vale		
Vale Clo. W9	**BT38**	**1**
Vale Clo. W9	BT38	56
Vale Clo., Brwd.	CZ25	33
Vale Clo., Couls.	BX60	95
Vale Clo., Orp.	CL56	97
Vale Clo., Twick.	BJ48	74
Vale Clo., Wey.	BA55	83
Vale Cotts., Brom.	CH52	88
Vale Cres. SW15	BO49	75
Vale Ct., Wey.	BA55	83
Vale Dr., Barn.	BR24	28
Vale End SE22	CA45	67
Grove Vale		
Vale Farm Rd., Wok.	AS62	100
Vale Gro. N4	BZ33	48
Vale Gro. W3	BN40	55
Vale Gro., Slou.	AP41	62
Vale La. W3	BM39	55
Vale of Heath NW3	BT34	47
East Heath Rd.		
Vale Pl. W14	BQ14	65
Spring Vale Ter.		
Vale Rd. E7	CH36	58
Vale Rd. N., Surb.	BL55	85
Vale Rd. N4	BZ33	48
Vale Rd. S., Surb.	BL55	85
Vale Rd., Brom.	CL51	88
Vale Rd., Bush.	BE25	27
Vale Rd., Chesh.	AO16	16
Vale Rd., Dart.	CU47	79
Vale Rd., Esher	BH58	93
Vale Rd., Grav.	DE47	81
Vale Rd., Mitch.	BW52	86
Vale Rd., Sutt.	BS56	95
Vale Rd., Wey.	BA55	83
Vale Rd., Wind.	AM44	61
Vale Rd., Wor.Pk.	BO55	85
Vale Ri. NW11	BR33	46
Vale Row N5	BY34	47
Gillespie Rd.		
Vale Royal N7	BX36	56
Vale St. SE27	BZ48	77
Vale Ter. N4	BZ32	48
Vale, The N10	BV30	38
Vale, The N14	BW26	38
Vale, The NW11	BQ34	46
Vale, The SW3	**BT43**	**3**
Vale, The SW3	BT43	66
Vale, The W3	BO40	55
Vale, The, Brwd.	DB26	42
Vale, The, Couls.	BW60	95
Vale, The, Croy.	CC55	87
Vale, The, Felt.	BC46	73
Vale, The, Ger.Cr.	AR30	34
Vale, The, Houns.	BE43	64
Vale, The, Ruis.	BD34	45
Vale, The, Sun.	BC50	73
Vale, The, Wdf.Grn.	CH29	40
Valecroft, Pnr.	BE32	45
Valence Av., Dag.	CP33	50
Valence Cir., Dag.	CQ34	50
Valence Dr., Chsnt.	CB17	21
Valence Ho., Dag.	CQ34	50
Valence Rd., Erith	CS43	69
Valence Wood Rd., Dag.	CP34	50
Valencia Rd., Stan.	BK28	36
Valency Clo., Nthwd.	BB28	35
Valentine Av., Bex.	CQ48	79
Valentine Ct. SE23	**CC48**	**77**
Valentine Ct. SE23	CC48	77
Valentine Pl. SE1	**BY41**	**4**
Valentine Pl. SE1	BY41	66
Valentine Rd. E9	CC36	57
Valentine Rd., Har.	BG34	45
Valentine Row SE1	**BY41**	**4**

Valentine Row SE1 BY41 66
Webber St.
Valentine Way, Ch.St.G. AR27 34
Valentines Rd., Ilf. CL33 49
Valentines Way, Rom. CT34 50
Valerian Way E15 CG38 58
Valerie Clo., St.Alb. BJ13 9
Valerie Ct., Bush. BG26 36
Valeswood Rd., Brom. CG49 78
Valetta Gro. E13 CH37 58
Valetta Rd. W3 BO41 65
Valette St. E9 CB36 57
Valiant Clo., Nthlt. BD38 54
Ruislip Rd.
Valiant Clo., Rom. CR30 41
Valiant Way E6 CK39 58
Vallance Rd. E2 CB38 57
Vallance Rd. N22 BW30 38
Vallentin Ct. E17 CF31 48
Vallentin Rd.
Vallentin Rd. E17 CF31 48
Valley Av. N12 BT28 38
Valley Clo., Dart. CT46 79
Valley Clo., Loug. CK25 31
Valley Clo., Pnr. BC30 35
Valley Clo., Wal.Abb. CF19 21
Valley Clo., Wdf.Grn. CH29 40
Valley Dr. NW9 BM32 46
Valley Dr., Grav. DH49 81
Valley Dr., Sev. CU66 116
Valley Fields Cres., Enf. BY23 29
Valley Gdns. SW19 BT50 76
Valley Gdns., Wem. BL36 55
Valley Grn., Hem.H. AZ10 8
Valley Grn., The, Welw.G.C. BQ 7 5
Valley Gro. SE7 CJ42 68
Valley Hill, Loug. CK26 40
Valley Ms., Twick. BJ48 74
Cross Deep
Valley Rd. SW16 BX49 76
Valley Rd., Belv. CR42 69
Valley Rd., Berk. AP12 7
Valley Rd., Brom. CG51 88
Valley Rd., Dart. CT46 79
Valley Rd., Erith CS42 69
Valley Rd., Fawk. DB53 90
Valley Rd., Ken. BZ60 96
Valley Rd., Orp. CO51 89
Valley Rd., Rick. AV25 25
Valley Rd., St.Alb. BH11 9
Valley Rd., Uxb. AY37 53
Valley Rd., Welw.G.C. BP 8 5
Valley Ri., Wat. BC20 17
Valley Side E4 CE27 39
Valley Side, Hem.H. AV13 7
Valley Vw. Gdns., Ken. CA61 105
Valley Vw., Barn. BR25 28
Valley Vw., Chsnt. BZ17 21
Valley Vw., Green. DA46 80
Valley Vw., West. CJ62 106
Valley Way, Ger.Cr. AR32 43
Valley Wk., Croy. CC55 87
Valley Wk., Rick. BA25 26
Valley, The, Guil. AR72 118
Valleyfield Rd. SW16 BX49 76
Valliant Clo., Nthlt. BD38 54
Valliere Rd. NW10 BP38 55
Valliers Wood Rd., Sid. CM47 78
Vallis Way W13 BJ39 54
Vallis Way, Chess. BK56 93
Valmar Rd. SE5 BZ44 67
Valnay St. SW17 BU49 76
Valognes Av. E17 CD30 39
Valonia Gdns. SW18 BR46 75
Vambery Rd. SE18 CM43 68
Van Dyck Av., N.Mal. BN54 85
Vanbrough Cres., Nthlt. BD37 54
Vanbrugh Clo. E16 CJ39 58
Fulmer Rd.
Vanbrugh Clo., Orp. CN54 88
Vanbrugh Dr., Walt. BD53 84
Vanbrugh Fields SE3 CG43 68
Vanbrugh Hill SE10 CG42 68
Vanbrugh Pk. Rd. SE3 CG43 68
Vanbrugh Pk. Rd. W. SE3 CG43 68
Vanbrugh Pk. SE3 CG43 68
Vanbrugh Rd. W4 BN41 65
Vanbrugh Ter. SE3 CG44 68
Vancouver Clo., Epsom BN59 94
Vancouver Cotts., Epsom BN59 94
Vancouver Rd. SE23 CD48 77
Vancouver Rd., Edg. BM29 37
Vancouver Rd., Hayes BC38 53
Vancouver Rd., Rich. BK49 74
Vanda Cres., St.Alb. BH14 9
Vanderbilt Rd. SW18 BS47 76
Vandome Clo. E16 CH39 58
Vandon Pass. SW1 BW41 3
Vandon Pass. SW1 BW41 66
Petty France
Vandon St. SW1 BW41 3
Vandon St. SW1 BW41 66
Vandy St. EC2 CA38 2
Vandy St. EC2 CA38 57
Vandyke Clo. SW15 BQ46 75
Vandyke Clo., Red. BU69 121
Vandyke Cross SE9 CK46 78
Vane Clo. NW3 BT35 47
Vane Clo., Har. BL32 46
Vane St. SW1 BW42 3
Vane St. SW1 BW42 66
Vincent Sq.
Vanessa Clo., Belv. CR42 69
Vanessa Way, Bex. CS48 79
Vanessa Wk., Grav. DJ49 81
Vanguard Clo., Croy. BY54 86
Vanguard Clo., Rom. CR30 41
Vanguard St. SE8 CE44 67
Vanguard Way, Wall. BX57 95
Vanoc Gdns., Brom. CG48 78
Vanquisher Wk., Grav. DJ48 81
Cervia Way
Vansittart Dr., Wind. AN44 61
Vansittart Rd. E7 CG35 49

Vansittart Rd., Wind. AN44 61
Vansittart St. SE14 CD43 67
Bowerman Av.
Vanston Pl. SW6 BS43 66
Vant Rd. SW17 BU49 76
Vantage Rd., Slou. AN41 61
Vantorts Clo., Saw. CQ 6 6
Vantorts Rd., Saw. CQ 6 6
Varcoe Rd. SE16 CB42 67
Varden St. E1 CB39 57
Vardens Rd. SW11 BT45 66
Vardon Clo. W3 BN39 55
Cotton Av.
Vardon Clo., N3 BR30 37
Claremont Pk.
Varley Rd. E16 CH39 58
Varley Way, Mitch. BT51 86
Varna Rd. SW6 BR43 65
Varna Rd., Hmptn. BF51 84
Varndell St. NW1 BV38 1
Varndell St. NW1 BW38 56
Varney Clo., Chsnt. CB17 21
Varney Clo., Hem.H. AV13 7
Varney Rd., Hem.H. AV13 7
Vartry Rd. N15 BZ32 48
Vassall Rd. SW9 BY43 66
Vauban St. SE16 CA41 4
Vauban St. SE16 CA41 67
Vaughan Av. NW4 BP32 46
Vaughan Av. W6 BO42 65
Vaughan Av., Horn. CV35 51
Vaughan Clo., Hmptn. BE49 74
Oak Av.
Vaughan Gdns., Eton AM42 61
Eton Wick Rd.
Vaughan Gdns., Ilf. CK33 49
Vaughan Rd. E15 CG36 58
Vaughan Rd. SE5 BZ44 67
Vaughan Rd., Har. BG33 45
Vaughan Rd., T.Ditt. BJ54 84
Vaughan Rd., Well. CN44 68
Vaughan Way E1 CB40 4
Vaughan Way E1 CB40 57
Vaughan Way, Dor. BJ71 119
Westcott Rd.
Vaughan Williams Clo. SE8 CE43 67
Watsons St.
Vaux Cres., Walt. BC57 92
Vauxhall Br. Rd. SW1 BW41 3
Vauxhall Br. Rd. SW1 BW41 66
Vauxhall Br. SW1 BX42 4
Vauxhall Br. SW1 BX42 66
Vauxhall Clo., Grav. DF47 81
Vauxhall Cross SW8 BX42 4
Vauxhall Cross SW8 BX43 66
Vauxhall Gdns. Est. SE11 BX42 4
Vauxhall Gdns. Est. SE11 BX42 66
Vauxhall Gdns., S.Croy. BZ57 96
Vauxhall Gro. SW8 BX43 4
Vauxhall Gro. SW8 BX43 66
Vauxhall Pl., Dart. CW47 80
Vauxhall Rd., Hem.H. AZ13 8
Vauxhall St. SE11 BX42 4
Vauxhall St. SE11 BX42 66
Vauxhall Wk. SE11 BX42 4
Vauxhall Wk. SE11 BX42 66
Vawdrey Clo. E1 CC38 57
Vectis Gdns. SW17 BV50 76
Vectis Rd.
Vectis Rd. SW17 BV50 76
Veda Rd. SE13 CE45 67
Vega Cres., Nthwd. BB28 35
Vega Rd., Bush. BG26 36
Vegal Cres., Egh. AQ49 72
Velde Way SE22 CA46 77
Dulwich Gro.
Velizy Av., Harl. CM10 6
Vellum Dr., Cars. BU56 95
Venables Clo., Dag. CR35 50
Webbscroft Rd.
Venables St. NW8 BT38 1
Venables St. NW8 BT38 56
Vencourt Pl. W6 BP42 65
King St.
Venetia Rd. N4 BY32 47
Venetia Rd. W5 BK41 64
Venetian Rd. SE5 BZ44 67
Venette Clo., Rain. CU39 59
Venn St. SW4 BW45 66
Venner Rd. SE26 CC49 77
Venners Clo., Bexh. CT44 69
Venour Rd. E3 CD38 57
Maidman St.
Ventnor Av., Stan. BJ30 36
Ventnor Dr. N20 BS27 38
Ventnor Gdns., Bark. CN36 58
Ventnor Rd. SE14 CC43 67
Ventnor Rd., Sutt. BS57 95
Venton Clo., Wok. AQ62 100
Venture Clo., Bex. CQ47 79
Elmwood Dr.
Venue St. E14 CF39 57
Venus Hill, Hem.H. AT19 16
Venus Rd. SE18 CK41 68
Veny Cres., Horn. CV35 51
Ver Rd., St.Alb. BG13 9
Vera Av. N21 BY25 29
Vera Ct., Wat. BD26 36
Vera Lynn Clo. E7 CH35 49
Dames Rd.
Vera Rd. SW6 BR44 65
Verbena Clo., S.Ock. DB39 60
Verbena Gdns. W6 BP42 65
Verdant Ct. SE6 CG47 78
Verdant La. SE6 CG47 78
Verdayne Av., Croy. CC55 87
Verdayne Gdns., Warl. CC61 105
Verderers Rd., Chig. CO28 41
Verdun Rd. SE18 CO43 69
Verdun Rd. SW13 BP43 65
Vereker Clo., Wat. BE19 18
Vere Rd., Loug. CM24 31
Vere St. W1 BV39 1
Vere St. W1 BV39 56

Vereker Dr., Sun. BC52 83
Vereker Rd. W14 BR42 65
Verity Clo. W11 BR40 55
Veritys, Hat. BP12 10
Vermont Rd. SE19 BZ50 77
Vermont Rd. SW18 BS46 76
Vermont Rd., Sutt. BS55 86
Verney Clo., Berk. AP12 7
Verney Gdns., Dag. CQ35 50
Verney Rd. SE16 CB42 67
Verney Rd., Dag. CQ35 50
Verney Rd., Slou. AT42 62
Verney St. NW10 BN34 46
Verney Way SE16 CB42 67
Vernham Rd. SE18 CM43 68
Vernon Av. E12 CK35 49
Vernon Av. SW20 BQ51 85
Vernon Av., Enf. CD21 30
Vernon Av., Wdf.Grn. CH29 40
Vernon Clo., Cher. AU57 91
Vernon Clo., Epsom BN57 94
Vernon Clo., Orp. CO52 89
Vernon Clo., Sev. CZ58 99
Vernon Clo., St.Alb. BG14 9
Vernon Cres., Barn. BV25 29
Vernon Cres., Brwd. DD27 122
Vernon Dr., Stan. BJ30 36
Vernon Dr., Uxb. AX30 35
Vernon Pl. WC1 BX39 2
Vernon Pl. WC1 BX39 56
Bloomsbury Way
Vernon Rd. E11 CG33 49
Vernon Rd. E15 CG36 58
Vernon Rd. E17 CD32 48
Vernon Rd. E3 CD37 57
Vernon Rd. N8 BY31 47
Vernon Rd. SW14 BN45 65
Vernon Rd., Bush. BE25 27
Vernon Rd., Felt. BB48 73
Vernon Rd., Ilf. CN33 49
Vernon Rd., Rom. CS28 41
Vernon Rd., Sutt. BT56 95
Vernon Rd., Swans. DC46 81
Vernon Ri. WC1 BX38 2
Vernon Ri. WC1 BX38 56
Percy Circus
Vernon Ri., Grnf. BG35 45
Vernon Sq. WC1 BX38 2
Vernon Sq. WC1 BX38 56
Penton Ri.
Vernon St. W14 BR42 65
Vernon Way, Guil. AP70 118
Vernon Wk., Tad. BQ63 103
Vernon Yd. W11 BR40 55
Portobello Rd.
Veroan Rd., Bexh. CQ44 69
Verona Clo., Uxb. AX39 53
Verona Dr., Surb. BL55 85
Verona Gdns., Grav. DJ49 81
Verona Rd. E7 CH36 58
Upton La.
Veronica Clo., Rom. CV29 42
Veronica Gdns. SW16 BW51 86
Veronica Rd. SW17 BV48 76
Veronique Gdns., Ilf. CM32 49
Verran Rd. SW12 BV47 76
Balham Gro.
Versailles Rd. SE20 CB50 77
Verulam Av. E17 CD32 48
Verulam Av., Pur. BW59 95
Verulam Bldgs. WC1 BX39 2
Verulam Bldgs. WC1 BX39 56
Grays Inn Rd.
Verulam Clo., Welw.G.C. BR 8 5
Verulam Rd., Grnf. BF38 54
Verulam Rd., St.Alb. BG13 9
Verulam St. EC1 BY39 56
Verulam St. WC1 BY39 2
Verwood Rd., Har. BG30 36
Veryan, Wok. AQ62 100
Vespan Rd. W12 BP41 65
Vesta Av., St.Alb. BG15 9
Vesta Rd. SE4 CD44 67
Vesta Rd., Hem.H. AY12 8
Vestris Rd. SE23 CC48 77
Vestry Ms. SE5 CA44 67
Vestry Rd. E17 CE32 48
Vestry Rd. SE5 CA44 67
Vestry Rd., Sev. CV63 108
Vestry St. N1 BZ38 2
Vestry St. N1 BZ38 57
Vevers Rd., Reig. BT72 121
Vevey St. SE6 CD48 77
Vexil Clo., Grays CY42 70
Brimfield Rd.
Veysey Gdns., Dag. CR34 50
Viaduct Bldgs. EC1 BY39 2
Saffron Hill
Viaduct Bldgs. EC1 BY39 56
Saffron Hill
Viaduct Pl. E2 CB38 57
Viaduct St. E2 CB38 57
Viaduct Way, Welw.G.C. BR 6 5
Viaduct, The E18 CH30 40
Vian Av., Enf. CD21 30
Vian St. SE13 CE45 67
Vibart Gdns. SW2 BX47 76
Vibart Wk. N1 BX37 2
Vibart Wk. N1 BX37 56
Outram St.
Vicarage Av. SE3 CH44 68
Vicarage Av., Egh. AT49 72
Vicarage Clo., Brwd. CZ28 42
Vicarage Clo., Erith CS43 69
Vicarage Clo., Hem.H. AX14 8
Park Rd.
Vicarage Clo., Lthd. BF66 111
Vicarage Clo., Nthlt. BE36 54
Vicarage Clo., Pot.B. BU18 20
Vicarage Clo., Ruis. BA33 44
Vicarage Clo., St.Alb. BG15 9
Vicarage Clo., Tad. BR65 103
Vicarage Cres. SW11 BT44 66
Vicarage Cres., Egh. AT49 72
Vicarage Ct. W8 BS41 66
Vicarage Gate
Vicarage Ct., Egh. AT50 72

Vicarage Ct., Felt. BA47 73
Vicarage Dr. SW14 BN46 75
Vicarage Dr., Bark. CM36 58
Vicarage Dr., Grav. DE46 81
Vicarage Dr., Maid. AH41 61
Vicarage Farm Rd., Houns. BE44 64
Vicarage Fields, Walt. BD53 84
Vicarage Gate W8 BS41 66
Vicarage Gate, Guil. AQ71 118
Vicarage Gdns. SW14 BN46 75
Vicarage Gdns. W8 BS41 66
Vicarage Gate
Vicarage Gdns., Mitch. BU52 86
Vicarage Gro. SE5 BZ44 67
Vicarage La. E15 CG36 58
Vicarage La. E6 CK38 58
Vicarage La., Chig. CM27 40
Vicarage La., Epp. CS15 14
Vicarage La., Epsom BP58 94
Vicarage La., Grav. DK48 81
Vicarage La., Hem.H. AT17 16
Vicarage La., Ilf. CM33 49
Vicarage La., Kings L. AY18 17
Vicarage La., Laleham AX52 83
Vicarage La., Lthd. BJ64 102
Vicarage La., Sev. CS63 107
Vicarage La., Wok. AU66 109
Vicarage La., Wraysbury AS47 72
Vicarage Path N8 BW33 47
Vicarage Pk. SE18 CM42 68
Vicarage Pl., Slou. AQ41 62
Vicarage Rd. E10 CE33 48
Vicarage Rd. E15 CG36 58
Vicarage Rd. N17 CB30 39
Vicarage Rd. NW4 BP32 46
Vicarage Rd. SE18 CM42 68
Vicarage Rd. SW14 BN46 75
Vicarage Rd., Hampton Wick BK51 84
Vicarage Rd., Berk. AT11 7
Vicarage Rd., Bex. CR47 79
Vicarage Rd., Chobham AO59 91
Vicarage Rd., Croy. BY55 86
Vicarage Rd., Dag. CR36 59
Vicarage Rd., Egh. AT50 72
Vicarage Rd., Epp. CP18 23
Vicarage Rd., Horn. CU33 50
Vicarage Rd., Kings.T. BK51 84
Vicarage Rd., Stai. AV48 72
Vicarage Rd., Sun. BB49 73
Vicarage Rd., Sutt. BS56 95
Vicarage Rd., Ted. BJ49 74
Vicarage Rd., Twick. BH48 74
Vicarage Rd., Wat. BC25 26
Vicarage Rd., Wdf.Grn. CK29 40
Vicarage Rd., Whitton BG46 74
Vicarage Rd., Wok. AS64 100
Vicarage Way NW10 BN34 46
Vicarage Way, Ger.Cr. AS32 43
Vicarage Way, Har. BF33 45
Vicarage Wk. SW11 BT44 66
Battersea Church Rd.
Vicarage Wk., Maid. AH41 61
Vicarage Wk., Walt. BC54 83
Vicarage Wood, Harl. CO10 6
Vicars Bridge Clo., Wem. BL37 55
Vicars Clo. E15 CH37 58
Vicars Clo. E2 CC37 57
Pennethorpe Clo.
Vicars Clo., Enf. CA23 30
Vicars Hill SE13 CE45 67
Vicars Moor La. N21 BY26 38
Vicars Oak Rd. SE19 CA50 77
Vicars Rd. NW5 BV35 47
Vicars Wk., Dag. CO34 50
Viceroy Ct. NW8 BU37 1
Viceroy Ct. NW8 BU37 56
Viceroy Rd. SW8 BX44 66
Hartington Rd.
Vickers Rd., Erith CS42 69
Victor App., Horn. CV33 51
Victor Clo., Horn. CV33 51
Abbs Cross Gdns.
Victor Gdns., Horn. CV33 51
Victor Gro., Wem. BL36 55
Victor Rd. NW10 BP38 55
Victor Rd. SE20 CC50 77
Victor Rd., Har. BG31 45
Victor Rd., Tedd. BH49 74
Victor Rd., Wind. AO45 61
Victor Vills. N9 BZ27 39
Victor Wk., Horn. CV33 51
Victoria Arc., Sthl. BE40 54
Victoria Av. E6 CJ37 58
Victoria Av. EC2 CA39 2
Victoria Av. EC2 CA39 57
Bishopsgate
Victoria Av. N3 BR30 37
Victoria Av., Barn. BT24 29
Victoria Av., E.Mol. BF52 84
Victoria Av., Grav. DG47 81
Victoria Av., Grays DE41 71
Victoria Av., Houns. BF46 74
Victoria Av., Rom. CR29 41
Victoria Av., S.Croy. BZ58 96
Victoria Av., Surb. BK54 84
Victoria Av., Uxb. AZ36 53
Victoria Av., Wall. BV55 86
Victoria Av., Wem. BM36 55
Victoria Clo., Barn. BT24 29
Victoria Clo., Grays DE41 71
Victoria Av.
Victoria Clo., Hayes BA39 53
Victoria Clo., Rick. AX26 35
Nightingale Rd.
Victoria Clo., Wey. BA55 83
Victoria Cotts. N10 BV30 38
Victoria Cotts., Rich. BL44 65
Victoria Cres. N15 CA32 48
Victoria Cres. SE19 CA50 77
Victoria Cres. SW19 BR50 75
Victoria Cres., Hayes AW40 53
Victoria Ct. W3 BM41 65
Victoria Ct., Wem. BM36 55
Victoria Dock Rd. E16 CG39 58

Victoria Dr. SW19 BQ47 75
Victoria Dr., S.Dnth. CY51 90
Victoria Embk. SW1 BX41 4
Victoria Embk. SW1 BX41 66
Victoria Gdns. W11 BS40 56
Victoria Gdns., Houns. BE44 64
Victoria Gdns., West. CJ61 106
Victoria Gro. N12 BT28 38
Victoria Gro. W8 BT41 3
Victoria Gro. W8 BT41 66
Victoria Grove Ms. W2 BS40 56
Victoria Hill Rd., Swan. CT51 89
Victoria La., Barn. BR24 28
Victoria La., Hayes BA42 63
Victoria Ms. NW6 BS37 56
Victoria Ms. SW4 BV45 66
Victoria Ri.
Victoria Park Rd. E9 CB37 57
Victoria Park Sq. E2 CC38 57
Victoria Pl., Epsom BO59 94
Victoria Pl., Rich. BK46 74
Victoria Rd. E13 CH37 58
Victoria Rd. E17 CF30 39
Victoria Rd. E18 CH30 40
Victoria Rd. E4 CG26 40
Victoria Rd. N15 CB31 48
Victoria Rd. N18 CA28 39
Victoria Rd. N22 BW30 38
Victoria Rd. N4 BX33 47
Victoria Rd. N9 CA27 39
Victoria Rd. NW10 BN39 55
Victoria Rd. NW4 BQ31 46
Victoria Rd. NW6 BR37 55
Victoria Rd. NW7 BO28 37
Victoria Rd. SW14 BN45 65
Victoria Rd. W3 BN39 55
Victoria Rd. W5 BJ39 54
Victoria Rd. W8 BS41 3
Victoria Rd. W8 BT41 66
Victoria Rd., Addlestone AX56 92
Victoria Rd., Bark. CL36 58
Victoria Rd., Barn. BT24 29
Victoria Rd., Berk. AR13 7
Victoria Rd., Bexh. CR46 79
Victoria Rd., Brom. CJ53 88
Victoria Rd., Brwd. DB28 42
Victoria Rd., Buck.H. CJ27 40
Victoria Rd., Bush. BF26 36
Victoria Rd., Chis. CL49 78
Victoria Rd., Couls. BW61 104
Victoria Rd., Dag. CR35 50
Victoria Rd., Dart. CV46 80
Victoria Rd., Erith CT43 69
Victoria Rd., Eton AM42 61
Victoria Rd., Felt. BC47 73
Victoria Rd., Grav. DF47 81
Victoria Rd., Guil. AS71 118
Victoria Rd., Kings.T. BL51 85
Victoria Rd., Knaphill AO62 100
Victoria Rd., Mitch. BU50 76
Victoria Rd., Red. BV71 121
Victoria Rd., Rom. CT32 50
Victoria Rd., Ruis. BC33 44
Victoria Rd., Sev. CU66 116
Victoria Rd., Sid. CN48 78
Victoria Rd., Slou. AQ40 52
Victoria Rd., Stai. AV48 72
Victoria Rd., Sthl. BE41 64
Victoria Rd., Surb. BK53 84
Victoria Rd., Sutt. BY56 95
Victoria Rd., Tedd. BJ50 74
Victoria Rd., Twick. BJ47 74
Victoria Rd., Uxb. AX36 53
Victoria Rd., Wal.Abb. CF20 21
Victoria Rd., Wat. BC22 26
Victoria Rd., Wey. BA55 83
Victoria Rd., Wok. AS62 100
Victoria Ri. SW4 BV45 66
Victoria Sq. SW1 BU41 3
Victoria Sq. SW1 BV41 66
Beeston Pl.
Victoria St. E15 CG36 58
Victoria St. SW1 BV41 3
Victoria St. SW1 BV41 66
Victoria St., Belv. CQ42 69
Victoria St., Egh. AR50 72
Victoria St., Slou. AL36 62
Victoria St., St.Alb. BG13 9
Victoria St., Wind. AO44 61
Victoria Ter. N4 BY33 47
Victoria Ter., Dor. BJ71 119
Victoria Ter., Har. BG33 45
Victoria Vills., Rich. BL45 65
Victoria Way SE7 CH42 68
Victoria Way, Wey. BA55 83
Victoria Way, Wok. AS62 100
Victorian Gro. N16 CA34 48
Victorian Rd. N16 CA34 48
Victors Cres., Brwd. DD27 122
Victors Dr., Hmptn. BE50 74
Victors Way, Barn. BR24 28
Victory Av., Mord. BT53 86
Victory Park Rd., Wey. AX55 83
Victory Pl. SE16 CD41 67
Victory Pl. SE17 BZ42 4
Victory Pl. SE17 BZ42 67
Victory Pl. SE19 CA50 77
Victory Rd. SW19 BT50 76
Victory Rd., Berk. AQ12 7
Victory Rd., Cher. AW54 83
Victory Rd., Rain. CU37 59
Victory Sq. SE5 BZ43 67
Victory Way, Houns. BD42 64
Victory Way, Rom. CR30 41
Victory Wk. SE8 CE44 67
Ship St.
Vienna Clo., Ilf. CK30 40
Coburg Gdns.
View Clo., Chig. CM28 40
View Clo., Har. BG31 45
View Clo., West. CJ61 106
View Rd. N6 BU33 47
View Rd., Grays DD43 71
View Rd., Pot.B. BT19 20
View, The SE2 CQ42 69
Viewfield Clo., Har. BL33 46
Viewfield Rd. SW18 BR46 75

Viewfield Rd., Bex. CP47 79
Viewland Rd. SE18 CN42 68
Viewlands Av., Sev. CN63 106
Viga Rd. N21 BY25 29
Vigerons Way, Grays DG42 71
Viggory La., Wok. AR61 100
Vigilant Clo. SE26 CB49 77
Vigilant Way, Grav. DJ49 81
Vignoles Rd., Rom. CR33 50
Vigo St. W1 BW40 3
Vigo St. W1 BW40 56
Vigors Cft., Hat. BO13 10
Viking Clo. E3 CD37 57
Selwyn Rd.
Viking Rd., Grav. DE48 81
Viking Rd., Sthl. BE40 54
Viking Way, Brwd. DA25 33
Viking Way, Sev. CZ57 99
Villa Clo., Grav. DK48 81
Villa Ct., Dart. CW48 80
Greenbanks
Villa Rd. SW9 BY45 66
Villa St. SE17 BZ42 4
Villa St. SE17 BZ42 67
Villacourt Rd. SE18 CO43 69
Village Clo. E4 CF28 39
Village Gdns., Epsom BO58 94
Village Grn. Av., West. CK62 106
Village Grn. Rd., Dart. CU45 69
Village Grn. Way, West. CK62 106
Village La., Slou. AO33 43
Village Rd. N3 BR30 37
Village Rd., Egh. AU52 82
Village Rd., Enf. BZ26 39
Village Rd., Uxb. AV34 43
Village Rd., Wind. AK41 61
Village Row, Sutt. BS57 95
Village Way E., Har. BE33 45
Village Way NW10 BN35 46
Village Way SE21 BZ46 77
Village Way, Amer. AR23 25
Village Way, Ashf. AY49 73
Village Way, Beck. CE52 87
Village Way, Pnr. BE33 45
Village Way, S.Croy. CB60 96
Village, The SE7 CJ43 68
Village, The, Ong. DB13 15
Villas Rd. SE18 CM42 68
Villier St., Uxb. AX37 53
Villiers Av., Surb. BL53 85
Villiers Av., Twick. BE47 74
Villiers Clo. E10 CE34 48
Villiers Clo., Surb. BL52 85
Villiers Cres., St.Alb. BK12 9
Villiers Ct. N20 BT26 38
Villiers Path, Surb. BL53 85
Villiers Rd. NW2 BP36 55
Villiers Rd., Beck. CC51 87
Villiers Rd., Islw. BH44 64
Villiers Rd., Kings.T. BL52 85
Villiers Rd., Slou. AO39 52
Villiers Rd., Sthl. BE40 54
Villiers Rd., Wat. BE25 27
Villiers St. WC2 BX40 4
Villiers St. WC2 BX40 56
Vincam Clo., Twick. BF47 74
Vince St. EC1 BZ38 2
Vince St. EC1 BZ38 57
Vincent Av., Cars. BT59 95
Vincent Av., Surb. BM54 85
Vincent Clo. SE16 CD41 67
Vincent Clo., Barn. BS24 29
Vincent Clo., Brom. CH52 88
Vincent Clo., Cher. AV54 82
Vincent Clo., Chsnt. CD17 21
Vincent Clo., Couls. BU63 104
Vincent Clo., Esher BF55 84
Vincent Clo., Ilf. CM29 40
Vincent Clo., Lthd. BF65 102
Vincent Clo., Sid. CN47 79
Valliers Wood Rd.
Vincent Clo., West Dr. AZ43 63
Vincent Ct. NW4 BQ31 46
Vincent Dr., Shep. BB52 83
Vincent Gdns. NW2 BO34 46
Vincent Grn., Couls. BU63 104
Vincent La., Dor. BJ71 119
Vincent Par. N4 BX33 47
Hanley Rd.
Vincent Rd. E4 CF29 39
Vincent Rd. N15 BZ31 48
Vincent Rd. N22 BY30 38
Vincent Rd. SE18 CL42 68
Vincent Rd. W3 BN41 65
Palmerston Rd.
Vincent Rd., Cher. AV54 82
Vincent Rd., Cob. AM52 102
Vincent Rd., Couls. BW61 104
Vincent Rd., Croy. CA54 87
Vincent Rd., Dag. CQ36 59
Vincent Rd., Dor. BJ71 119
Vincent Rd., Houns. BD44 64
Vincent Rd., Islw. BG44 64
Vincent Rd., Kings.T. BM52 85
Vincent Rd., Rain. CV38 60
Vincent Rd., Wem. BL36 55
Vincent Row, Hmptn. BG50 74
Vincent Sq. SW1 BW42 3
Vincent Sq. SW1 BW42 66
Vincent Sq., West. CJ60 97
Vincent St. E16 CG39 58
Vincent St. SW1 BW42 3
Vincent St. SW1 BW42 66
Vincent Ter. N1 BY37 2
Vincent Ter. N1 BY37 56
Vincent Wk., Dor. BJ71 119
Arundel Rd.
Vincents Dr., Dor. BJ72 119
Vincents Path, Nthlt. BE36 54
Arnold Rd.
Vincenzo Clo., Hat. BQ15 10
Vine Av., Sev. CU65 107
Vine Clo., Stai. AW46 73
Vine Clo., Surb. BL53 85
Vine Clo., Sutt. BT55 86
Vine Clo., Welw.G.C. BR 7 5
Vine Clo., West Dr. AZ42 63
Vine Court Rd., Sev. CV65 108
Vine Ct. E1 CB39 57
Vine Ct., Har. BL32 46
Vine Gdns., Ilf. CM35 49
Vine Gro., Uxb. AZ36 53
Vine Hill EC1 BY38 2
Vine Hill EC1 BY38 56
Vine La. SE1 CA40 4
Vine La. SE1 CA40 57
Vine La., Uxb. AY37 53
Vine Pl., Houns. BF45 64
Vine Rd. E15 CG36 58
Vine Rd. N17 CA29 39
Love La.
Vine Rd. SW13 BO45 65
Vine Rd., E.Mol. BG52 84
Vine Rd., Orp. CN57 97
Vine Rd., Slou. AP36 52
Vine Sq. W14 BR42 65
Vine St. EC3 CA39 2
Vine St. EC3 CA39 57
Vine St. W1 BW40 4
Vine St. W1 BW40 56
Swallow St.
Vine St., Rom. CS31 50
Vine St., Uxb. AX37 53
Vine Street Br. EC1 BY38 2
Vine Street Br. EC1 BY38 56
Farringdon Rd.
Vine Way, Brwd. DB26 42
Vine Yard Path SW14 BN45 65
North Worple Way
Vine Yd. SE1 BZ41 4
Vine Yd. SE1 BZ41 67
Sanctuary St.
Vinegar Alley E17 CE31 48
Vinegar St. E1 CB40 57
Vinegar Yd. SE1 CA41 4
St. Thomas St.
Vinegar Yd. SE1 CA41 67
St. Thomas St.
Viner Clo., Walt. BD53 84
Vineries Bank NW7 BP28 37
Vineries Clo., Dag. CR36 59
Heath Way
Vineries Clo., West Dr. AZ43 63
Vineries, The N14 BW25 29
Vineries, The, Enf. CA24 30
Vinery Vills. NW8 BU38 1
Vinery Vills. NW8 BU38 56
Park Rd.
Vines Av. N3 BS30 38
Vines La., Ton. CY70 117
Viney Bank, Croy. CD58 96
Viney Rd. SE13 CE45 67
Vineyard Av. NW7 BR29 37
Vineyard Clo. SE6 CE47 77
Vineyard Hill Rd. SW19 BR49 75
Vineyard Hill, Pot.B. BV18 20
Vineyard Pass., Rich. BL46 75
Vineyard Rd., Felt. BC48 73
Vineyard Rd., Pot.B. BV18 20
Vineyard Row, Kings.T. BK51 84
Vineyard Wk. EC1 BY38 2
Vineyard Wk. EC1 BY38 56
Pine St.
Vineyard, The, Rich. BK46 74
Vineyard, The, Welw.G.C. BR 7 5
Vining St. SW9 BY45 66
Vinlake Av., Uxb. AZ34 44
Vinson Clo., Orp. CO54 89
Vintners Pl. EC4 BZ40 4
Vintners Pl. EC4 BZ40 57
Viola Av. SE2 CO42 69
Viola Av., Felt. BD46 74
Viola Av., Stai. AY47 73
Viola Clo., S.Ock. DB38 60
Viola Sq. W12 BO40 55
Violet Av., Enf. BZ22 30
Violet Av., Uxb. AY39 53
Violet Gdns., Croy. BY56 95
Violet Hill NW8 BT37 1
Violet Hill NW8 BT37 56
Violet La., Croy. BY56 95
Violet Rd. E17 CE32 48
Violet Rd. E18 CH30 40
Violet Rd. E3 CE38 57
Violet St. E2 CB38 57
Three Colts La.
Violet Way, Rick. AX24 26
Virgil Dr., Brox. CD15 12
Virgil Pl. W1 BU39 1
Seymour Pl.
Virgil Pl. W1 BU39 56
Seymour Pl.
Virgil St. SE1 BX41 4
Virgil St. SE1 BX41 66
Virginia Av., Vir.W. AR53 82
Virginia Beeches, Vir.W. AR52 82
Virginia Clo., Ash. BK62 102
Skinners La.
Virginia Clo., N.Mal. BN52 85
Willow Rd.
Virginia Clo., Stai. AX52 83
Blacksmiths La.
Virginia Clo., Wey. BA57 92
Virginia Dr., Vir.W. AR53 82
Virginia Gdns., Ilf. CM30 40
Virginia Rd. E2 CA38 2
Virginia Rd. E2 CA38 57
Virginia Rd., Th.Hth. BY51 86
Virginia St. E1 CB40 57
Virginia Wk. SW2 BX46 76
Beechdale Rd.
Virginia Wk., Grav. DH50 81
Viscount Dr. E6 CK39 58
Viscount Gdns., Wey. AY59 92
Viscount Gro., Nthlt. BD38 54
Wayfarer Rd.
Viscount Rd., Stai. AX47 73
Viscount St. EC1 BZ38 57
Viscount St. EC1 BZ39 2
Viscount Way, Houns. BB45 63
Vista Av., Enf. CC23 30
Vista Dr., Ilf. CJ32 49
Vista Way, Har. BL32 46
Vista, The SE9 CJ46 78
Vista, The, Sid. CN49 78
Langdon Shaw
Vivash Clo., Hayes BB41 63
Vivian Av. NW4 BP32 46
Vivian Av., Wem. BM35 46
Vivian Clo., Wat. BC27 35
Vivian Gdns., Wat. BC26 35
Vivian Gdns., Wem. BM35 46
Vivian Rd. E3 CD37 57
Vivian Sq. SE15 CB45 67
Vivian Way N2 BT32 47
Vivien Clo., Chess. BL57 94
Hunting Gate Dr.
Vivienne Clo., Twick. BK46 74
Voce Rd. SE18 CM43 68
Voewood Clo., N.Mal. BO53 85
Vogan Clo., Reig. BS72 121
Voltaire Rd. SW4 BW45 66
Voltaire Way, Hayes BB40 53
Voluntary Pl. E11 CH32 49
Vorley Rd. N19 BW34 47
Voss Ct. SW16 BX50 76
Voss St. E2 CB38 2
Voss St. E2 CB38 57
Vulcan Clo., Wall. BX57 95
Vulcan Gate, Enf. BY23 29
Uplands Park Rd.
Vulcan Rd. SE4 CD44 67
Vulcan Ter. SE4 CD44 67
Vulcan Way, Croy. CG58 97
Vulcan Way, N7 BX36 56
Vyne, The, Bexh. CR45 69
Vyner Rd. W3 BN40 55
Vyner St. E2 CB37 57
Vyners Way, Uxb. AZ35 44
Vyse Clo., Barn. BQ24 28

W

Waborne Cres., Ruis. BA32 44
Thames Dr.
Wacketts, Chsnt. CB17 21
Wadding St. SE17 BZ42 4
Wadding St. SE17 BZ42 67
Waddington Av., Couls. BY63 104
Waddington Clo., Couls. BY63 104
Waddington Rd. E15 CF35 48
Waddington Rd., St.Alb. BG13 9
Waddington St. E15 CF36 57
Waddington Ter., Bexh. CR46 79
Waddington Way SE19 BZ50 77
Waddon Clo., Croy. BY55 86
Waddon Ct. Rd., Croy. BY56 95
Waddon Ind. Est., Croy. BX56 95
Waddon Marsh Way, Croy. BX54 86
Waddon New Rd., Croy. BY55 86
Waddon Park Av., Croy. BY56 95
Waddon Rd., Croy. BY55 86
Waddon Way, Croy. BY57 95
Wade Ave., Orp. CP54 89
Wade Dr., Slou. AN41 61
Wade Rd. E16 CJ39 58
Leyes Rd.
Wade, The, Welw.G.C. BR 9 5
Wades Gro. N21 BY26 38
Wades Hill N21 BY25 29
Wades La., Tedd. BJ49 74
Wades Pl. E14 CE40 57
Wades, The, Hat. BP14 10
Wadeson St. E2 CB37 57
Wadeville Av., Rom. CQ32 50
Wadeville Clo., Belv. CR43 69
Wadham Av. E17 CE29 39
Wadham Clo., Shep. BA54 83
Wadham Gdns. NW3 BU37 1
Wadham Gdns. NW3 BU37 56
Wadham Gdns., Grnf. BG36 54
Wadham Rd. E17 CE30 39
Wadham Rd. SW15 BR45 65
Wadham Rd., Wat. BB19 17
Wadhurst Clo. SE20 CB51 87
Wadhurst Rd. SW8 BW44 66
Wadhurst Rd. W4 BN41 65
Wadley Clo., Hem.H. AY14 8
Wadley Rd. E11 CG33 49
Wadsworth Clo., Enf. CC25 30
Falcon Rd.
Wadsworth Clo., Grnf. BK37 54
Wadsworth Rd., Grnf. BJ37 54
Wager St. E3 CD38 57
Waggon Clo., Guil. AP70 118
Waggon La. N17 CB29 39
Waggon Ms. N14 BV26 38
Chase Side
Waghorn Rd. E13 CJ37 58
Waghorn Rd., Har. BK31 45
Waghorn St. SE15 CB45 67
Wagner St. SE15 CC43 67
Ilderton Rd.
Wagon Rd., Barn. BS21 29
Wagon Way, Rick. AX24 26
Wagtail Gdns., S.Croy. CC58 96
Waid Clo., Dart. CW46 80
Wain Clo., Pot.B. BS18 20
Wainfleet Av., Rom. CS30 41
Wainford Clo. SW19 BQ47 75
Windlesham Gro.
Wainwright Av., Brwd. DE25 122
Wainwright Gro., Islw. BG45 64
Waite Davies Rd. SE12 CG47 78
Waite St. SE15 CA43 4
Waite St. SE15 CA43 67
Waith St. EC4 BY39 2
Waitham St. EC4 BY39 56
Pilgrim St.
Wake Rd., Loug. CJ22 31
Wakefield Cres., Slou. AP36 52
Wakefield Gdns. SE19 CA50 77
Wakefield Gdns., Ilf. CK32 49
Wakefield Rd. N11 BW28 38
Wakefield Rd. N15 CA32 48
Wakefield Rd., Rich. BK46 74
Wakefield St. E6 CJ37 58
Wakefield St. N18 CB28 39
Wakefield St. WC1 BX38 2
Wakefield St. WC1 BX38 56
Wakefield Wk., Wal.Cr. CD19 21
Downfield Rd.
Wakehams Hill, Pnr. BE31 45
Wakehurst Path, Wok. AU60 91
Wakehurst Rd. SW11 BU46 76
Wakelin Rd. E15 CG37 58
Wakeling Rd. W7 BH39 54
Wakeling St. E14 CD39 57
Wakeman Rd. NW10 BQ38 55
Wakemans Hill Av. NW9 BN32 46
Wakenham St. N1 BZ36 57
Wakerfield Clo., Horn. CW32 51
Wakering Rd., Bark. CM36 58
Wakerley Clo. E6 CK39 58
Truesdale Rd.
Wakley St. EC1 BY38 2
Wakley St. EC1 BY38 56
Walberswick St. SW8 BX43 66
South Lambeth Rd.
Walbrook EC4 BZ40 4
Walbrook EC4 BZ40 57
Walburgh St. E1 CB39 57
Walburton Rd., Pur. BW60 95
Walcorde Av. SE17 BZ42 4
Walcorde Av. SE17 BZ42 67
Browning St.
Walcot Rd., Enf. CD23 30
Walcot Sq. SE11 BY42 4
Walcot Sq. SE11 BY42 66
Walcott St. SW1 BW42 66
Rochester Row
Waldeck Gro. SE27 BY48 76
Waldeck Rd. N15 BY31 47
Waldeck Rd. SW14 BN45 65
Lower Richmond Rd.
Waldeck Rd. W13 BJ39 54
Waldeck Rd. W4 BM43 65
Waldeck Rd., Dart. CW47 80
Waldeck Ter. SW14 BN45 65
Lower Richmond Rd.
Waldegrave Av., Tedd. BH49 74
Waldegrave Gdns., Twick. BH48 74
Waldegrave Gdns., Upmin. CX34 51
Waldegrave Pk., Twick. BH49 74
Waldegrave Rd. N8 BY31 47
Waldegrave Rd. SE19 CA50 77
Waldegrave Rd. W5 BL39 55
Waldegrave Rd., Brom. CK52 88
Waldegrave Rd., Dag. CP34 50
Waldegrave Rd., Twick. BH49 74
Waldegrove, Croy. CA55 87
Selborne Rd.
Waldemar Av. SW6 BR44 65
Waldemar Av. W5 BK40 54
Waldemar Rd. SW19 BS49 76
Walden Av. N13 BZ28 39
Walden Av., Chis. CK49 78
Walden Av., Rain. CS37 59
Walden Clo., Belv. CQ42 69
Walden Gdns., Th.Hth. BX52 86
Walden Pl., Welw.G.C. BQ 7 5
Walden Rd. N17 BZ30 39
Lordship La.
Walden Rd., Chig. CK50 78
Walden Rd., Horn. CV32 51
Walden Rd., Welw.G.C. BQ 7 5
Walden St. E1 CB39 57
New Rd.
Walden Way NW7 BQ29 37
Walden Way, Horn. CV32 51
Walden Way, Ilf. CN29 40
Waldenhurst Rd., Orp. CP54 89
Waldens Clo., Orp. CP54 89
Waldens Park Rd., Wok. AR61 100
Waldens Rd., Orp. CQ54 89
Waldens Rd., Wok. AR62 100
Waldenshaw Rd. SE23 CC47 77
Waldo Clo. SW4 BW46 76
Elms Rd.
Waldo Pl., Mitch. BU50 76
Waldo Rd. NW10 BP38 55
Waldo Rd., Brom. CJ52 88
Waldorf Clo., S.Croy. BY57 95
Waldram Cres. SE23 CC47 77
Waldram Park Rd. SE23 CC47 77
Waldram Pl. SE23 CC47 77
Waldram Cres.
Waldrist Way, Erith CQ41 69
Waldron Gdns., Brom. CF52 87
Waldron Ms. SW3 BU43 66
Old Church St.
Waldron Rd. SW18 BT48 76
Waldron Rd., Har. BH33 45
Waldron Yd., Har. BG34 45
Waldronhyrst, Croy. BY56 95
Waldrons Path, Croy. BY56 95
Waldrons, The, Croy. BY56 95
Waldrons, The, Oxt. CG69 115
Waleran Bldgs. SE1 CA42 67
Old Kent Rd.
Waleran Clo., Stan. BH28 36
Chenduit Way
Walerand Rd. SE13 CF44 67
Wales Av., Cars. BU56 95
Wales Farm Rd. W3 BN39 55
Waley St. E1 CC39 57
Walfield Av. N20 BS26 38
Walford Rd. N16 CA35 48
Walford Rd., Dor. BK73 119
Walford Rd., Uxb. AX37 53
Walfords Clo., Harl. CP 9 6
Walfrey Gdns., Dag. CQ36 59
Walham Gro. SW6 BS43 66
Walham Ri. SW19 BR49 75
Walham Yd. SW6 BS43 66
Walham Gro.
Walk, The, Eton AN42 61
Walk, The, Horn. CW34 51
Walk, The, Oxt. CE70 114
Tanridge La.
Walk, The, Pot.B. BS19 20
Walk, The, Sun. BB50 73
Walkden Rd., Chis. CL49 78
Walker Av., Ong. CY14 15
Walker Clo. SE18 CM42 68
Walker Clo. W7 BH40 54
Walker Clo., Dart. CT45 69
Walker Clo., Hmptn. BE50 74
Fearnley Ct.
Walker Ho. NW1 BW37 1
Walkers Ct. W1 BW40 3
Walkers Ct. W1 BW40 56
Peter St.
Walkerscroft Mead SE21 BZ47 77
Walkfield Dr., Epsom BP62 103
Walkford Way SE15 CA43 67
Walkley Rd., Dart. CU46 79
Walks, The N2 BT31 47
Wall End Rd. E6 CK36 58
Wall St. N1 BZ36 57
Wallace Clo. SE28 CP40 59
Haldane Rd.
Wallace Clo., Shep. BA52 83
Hawthorn Way
Wallace Clo., Uxb. AY37 53
Wallace Cres., Cars. BU56 95
Wallace Fields, Epsom BO59 94
Wallace Gdns., Swans. DB46 80
Milton St.
Wallace Rd. N1 BZ36 57
Wallace Rd., Grays DD41 71
Wallace Wk., Wey. AX56 92
Wallasey Cres., Uxb. AZ34 44
Wallbutton Rd. SE4 CD44 67
Wallcote Av. NW2 BQ33 46
Walled Garden, The, Bet. BN71 120
Wallenger Av., Rom. CU31 50
Waller Dr., Nthwd. BC30 35
Waller La., Cat. CA65 105
Waller Rd. SE14 CC44 67
Wallers Clo., Wdf.Grn. CK29 40
Wallers Hoppit, Loug. CK23 31
Wallers Way, Hodd. CE10 12
Wallflower St. W12 BO40 55
Wallgrave Rd. SW5 BS42 66
Wallgrave Rd. W8 BS43 66
Wallhouse Rd., Erith CU43 69
Wallingford Av. W10 BQ39 55
Wallingford Rd., Uxb. AW38 53
Wallingford Wk., St.Alb. BG15 9
Wallington Clo., Ruis. BA32 44
Wallington Ct., Wall. BV57 95
Wallington Rd., Ilf. CN33 49
Wallington Sq., Wall. BV57 95
Wallis Clo. SW11 BT45 66
Hope St.
Wallis Clo., Dart. CT48 79
Wallis Ct., Slou. AQ41 62
Nixey Clo.
Wallis Pk., Grav. DD46 81
Wallis Rd. E9 CD36 57
Wallis Rd., Sthl. BF39 54
Walliss Cotts. SW2 BX47 76
Wallorton Gdns. SW14 BN45 65
Wallwood Rd. E11 CF33 48
Wallwood St. E14 CD39 57
Wally St. E1 CC38 57
Walm La. NW2 BQ36 55
Walmar Clo., Barn. BT22 29
Walmer Clo., Rom. CR30 41
Walmer Gdns. W13 BJ41 64
Walmer Pl. W1 BU39 1
Walmer Rd. W11 BR40 55
Walmer St. W1 BU39 1
Walmer Pl.
Walmer Ter. SE18 CM42 68
Walmgate Rd., Grnf. BJ37 54
Walmington Fold N12 BS29 38
Walney Wk. N1 BZ36 57
Clephane Rd.
Walnut Av., West Dr. AZ41 63
Walnut Clo. SE8 CD43 67
Clyde St.
Walnut Clo., Cars. BU56 95
Park Hill
Walnut Clo., Epsom BO61 103
Walnut Clo., Hayes BB40 53
Walnut Clo., Ilf. CM31 49
Civic Way
Walnut Clo., St.Alb. BF17 18
Walnut Ct., Welw.G.C. BR 9 5
Walnut Dr., Tad. BR65 103
Walnut Fields, Epsom BO58 94
Walnut Gdns. E15 CF35 48
Ashlin Rd.
Walnut Grn., Bush. BE23 27
Walnut Gro., Bans. BQ60 94
Walnut Gro., Enf. BZ25 30
Walnut Gro., Hem.H. AX13 8
Walnut Gro., Welw.G.C. BR 9 5
Walnut Ms., Sutt. BT57 95
Christchurch Pk.
Walnut Tree Av., Dart. CW48 80
Walnut Tree Clo. SW13 BO44 65
Lonsdale Rd.
Walnut Tree Clo., Bans. BR59 94
Walnut Tree Clo., Chis. CM51 88
Walnut Tree Clo., Chsnt. CC19 21
Turners Hill
Walnut Tree Clo., Guil. AR70 118
Walnut Tree Clo., Hodd. CE12 12
Walnut Tree Cotts. SW19 BR49 75
Church Rd.
Walnut Tree Cres., Saw. CQ 5 6
Walnut Tree La., Wey. AX59 92
Chertsey La.
Walnut Tree Pk., Guil. AR70 118
Walnut Tree Rd. SE10 CG42 68
Walnut Tree Rd., Brent. BL43 65
Walnut Tree Rd., Dag. CQ34 50
Walnut Tree Rd., Erith CT42 69
Walnut Tree Rd., Houns. BE43 64
Walnut Tree Rd., Shep. BA52 83
Walnut Tree Wk. SE11 BY42 4
Walnut Tree Wk. SE11 BY42 66
Walnut Way, Buck.H. CJ27 40

Walnut Way, Ruis. BD36 54
Walnut Way, Swan. CS51 89
Walnuts Rd., Orp. CO54 89
Walpole Av., Couls. BU62 104
Walpole Av., Rich. BL44 65
Walpole Clo. W13 BK41 64
Walpole Clo., Grays DE42 71
Palmer Dr.
Walpole Clo., Pnr. BF29 36
Walpole Cres., Tedd. BH49 74
Walpole Ct., Twick. BH48 74
Walpole Gdns. W4 BN42 65
Walpole Gdns., Twick. BH48 74
Walpole Pk., Wey. AZ57 92
Walpole Pl., Tedd. BH49 74
Walpole Rd. E17 CD31 48
Walpole Rd. E18 CG30 40
Walpole Rd. E6 CJ36 58
Walpole Rd. N17 BZ30 39
Walpole Rd. SW19 BT50 76
Walpole Rd., Brom. CJ53 88
Walpole Rd., Croy. BZ55 87
Walpole Rd., Surb. BL54 85
Walpole Rd., Tedd. BH49 74
Walpole Rd., Twick. BH48 74
Walpole Rd., Wind. AQ47 72
Walpole St. SW3 BU42 3
Walpole St. SW3 BU42 66
Walpole Way, Barn. BQ25 28
Walrond Av., Wem. BL35 46
Walsh Cres., Croy. CG59 97
Walsham Clo. N16 CB33 48
Braydon Rd.
Walsham Clo. SE28 CP40 59
Walsham Rd. SE14 CC44 67
Walsham Rd., Felt. BC47 73
Walshford Way, B.Wd. BM22 28
Walsingham Gdns., Epsom BO56 94
Walsingham Pk., Chis. CM51 88
Walsingham Rd. E5 CB34 48
Walsingham Rd. W13 BJ40 54
Walsingham Rd., Croy. CF58 96
Walsingham Rd., Enf. BZ24 30
Walsingham Rd., Mitch. BU53 86
Walsingham Rd., Orp. CO51 89
Walsingham Way, St.Alb. BK17 18
Walsingham Wk., Belv. CR43 69
Walter St. E2 CC38 57
Walter St., Kings.T. BL51 85
Canbury Pass.
Walter Ter. E1 CC39 57
Walter Wk., Edg. BN29 37
Walters Mead, Ash. BL62 103
Walters Rd. SE25 CA52 87
Walters Rd., Enf. CC25 30
Walters Way SE23 CC46 77
Walters Yd., Brom. CH51 88
Walterton Rd. W9 BR38 55
Waltham Av. NW9 BM32 46
Waltham Av., Guil. AQ68 109
Waltham Av., Hayes BA41 63
Waltham Clo., Dart. CU46 79
Waltham Clo., Orp. CP54 89
Waltham Ct., Har. BF30 36
Waltham Dr., Edg. BM30 37
Waltham Gdns., Enf. CC22 30
Waltham Park Way E17 CE30 39
Waltham Rd., Cars. BT54 86
Waltham Rd., Cat. CB64 105
Waltham Rd., Sthl. BE41 64
Waltham Rd., Wal.Abb. CG16 22
Waltham Rd., Wdf.Grn. CK29 40
Waltham Way E4 CD28 39
Walthamstow Av. E4 CD29 39
Waltheof Av. N17 BZ30 39
Waltheof Gdns. N17 BZ30 39
Walthorne Gdns., Dag. CR36 59
Acre Rd.
Walton Av., Har. BE35 45
Walton Av., N.Mal. BO52 85
Walton Av., Sutt. BR55 85
Walton Bridge Rd., Shep. BA53 83
Walton Clo. E5 CC34 48
Millfields Rd.
Walton Clo. NW2 BP34 46
Walton Clo. SW8 BX43 66
South Lambeth Rd.
Walton Clo., Har. BG31 45
Walton Cres., Har. BE35 45
Walton Ct., Wok. AT61 100
Boundary Rd.
Walton Dr. NW10. BN36 55
Mitchellbrook Way
Walton Dr., Har. BG31 45
Walton Gdns. W3 BM39 55
Walton Gdns., Brwd DE25 122
Walton Gdns., Felt. BB49 73
Walton Gdns., Grnf. BH35 45
Walton Gdns., Wal.Abb. CE20 21
Walton Gdns., Wem. BL34 46
Walton Grn., Croy. CE58 96
Walton La., Shep. BA54 83
Walton La., Wey. AZ55 83
Walton Pk. La., Walt. BD55 84
Walton Pk., Walt. BD55 84
Walton Pl. SW3 BU41 3
Walton Pl. SW3 BU41 66
Walton Rd. E12 CL34 49
Walton Rd. E13 CJ37 58
Walton Rd., Bush. BD24 27
Walton Rd., E.Mol. BE52 84
Walton Rd., Headley BN64 103
Walton Rd., Epsom Downs BO62 103
Walton Rd., Har. BG31 45
Walton Rd., Hodd. CE11 12
Walton Rd., Rom. CQ29 41
Walton Rd., Sid. CO48 79
Walton Rd., Walt. BD53 84
Walton Rd., Wok. AS61 100
Walton St. SW3 BU42 3
Walton St. SW3 BU42 66
Walton St., Enf. BZ23 30
Walton St., St.Alb. BH12 9
Walton St., Tad. BP65 103
Walton Ter. SW8 BX43 66
South Lambeth Rd.
Walton Ter., Wok. AT61 100
Walton Way W3 BM39 55
Walton Way, Mitch. BW52 86
Waltons Hall Rd., S.le H. DK41 71
Walverns Clo., Wat. BD25 27
Walworth Pl. SE17 BZ42 4
Walworth Pl. SE17 BZ42 67
Walworth Rd. SE17 BZ42 4
Walworth Rd. SE17 BZ42 67
Walworth St. SE17 BZ42 67
Walwyn Av., Brom. CJ52 88
Wambrook Clo., Brwd. DE26 122
Wanborough Dr. SW15 BP47 75
Wandle Bank SW19 BT50 76
Wandle Bank, Croy. BX55 86
Wandle Ct. Gdns., Croy. BX55 86
Wandle Ct., Epsom BN56 94
Wandle Park Trd. Est., Croy. BY54 86
Wandle Rd. SW17 BU48 76
Wandle Rd., Croy. BZ55 87
Wandle Rd., Mord. BT52 86
Wandle Rd., Waddon BX55 86
Wandle Rd., Wall. BV55 86
Wandle Side, Croy. BX55 86
Wandle Side, Wall. BV55 86
Wandle Way SW18 BS47 76
Wandle Way, Mitch. BU53 86
Wandon Rd. SW6 BS43 66
Wandsworth Bri. SW6 & SW18 BS45 66
Wandsworth Bridge Rd. SW6 BS44 66
Wandsworth High St. SW18 BS46 76
Wandsworth Plain SW18 BS46 76
Wandsworth Rd. SW8 BV45 66
Wangey Rd., Rom. CP33 50
Wanless Rd. SE24 BZ45 67
Wanley Rd. SE5 BZ45 67
Wanlip Rd. E13 CH38 58
Wannions Clo., Chesh. AQ18 16
Wannock Gdns., Ilf. CL29 40
Wansbeck Rd. E9 CD36 57
Wansbury Way, Swan. CU53 89
Wansey St. SE17 BZ42 4
Wansey St. SE17 BZ42 67
Wansford Clo., Brwd. CZ27 42
Wansford Grn., Wok. AP62 100
Kenton Way
Wansford Pk., B.Wd. BN24 28
Wansford Rd., Wdf.Grn. CJ30 40
Wanstead Clo., Brom. CJ51 88
Wanstead La., Ilf. CJ32 49
Wanstead Pk. Av. E12 CJ33 49
Wanstead Pk. Rd., Ilf. CJ32 49
Wanstead Pl. E11 CH32 49
Wanstead Rd., Brom. CJ51 88
Wansunt Rd., Bex. CS47 79
Wantage Rd. SE12 CG46 78
Wantz La., Rain. CU38 59
Wantz Rd., Dag. CR35 50
Waplings, The, Tad. BP65 103
Wapping Dock St. E1 CB40 57
Cinnamon St.
Wapping High St. E1 CB40 4
Wapping High St. E1 CB40 57
Wapping La. E1 CB40 57
Wapping Wall E1 CC40 57
Wapseys La., Slou. AP32 43
Wapshott Rd., Stai. AV50 72
War Coppice Rd., Cat. BZ67 114
Warbank Clo., Croy. CG58 97
Warbank Cres., Croy. CG58 97
Warbank La., Kings.T. BO50 75
Warbeck Rd. W12 BP40 55
Warberry Rd. N22 BX30 38
Warblers Grn., Cob. BE60 93
Warboys App., Kings.T. BM50 75
Warboys Cres. E4 CF28 39
Warboys Rd., Kings.T. BM50 75
Warburton Clo., Har. BG29 36
Warburton Rd., Twick. BF47 74
Warburton Ter. E17 CE30 39
Ward Av., Grays DD42 71
Ward Clo., Chsnt. CB17 21
Spicersfield
Ward Clo., Erith CS43 69
Ward Gdns., Slou. AM40 61
Ward Hatch, Harl. CO 9 6
Ward La., Warl. CC61 105
Ward Rd. E15 CF37 57
Ward Rd. N19 BW34 47
Ward Royal, Wind. AO44 61
Ward St., Guil. AR71 118
Wardale Clo. SE16 CB41 67
Wardell Clo. NW9 BO29 37
Wardell Field NW9 BO30 37
Warden Av., Har. BE33 45
Warden Av., Rom. CS28 41
Warden Ct., Har. BE33 45
Warden Rd. NW5 BV36 56
Wardens Gro. SE1 BZ40 4
Wardens Gro. SE1 BZ40 57
Wardle St. E9 CC35 48
Wardley St. SW18 BS47 76
Wardo Av. SW6 BR44 65
Wardour Ms. W1 BW39 1
Wardour St. W1 BW39 1
Wardour St. W1 BW39 56
Wardour St. W1 BW40 3
Wardrobe Pl. EC4 BY39 2
Carter La.
Wardrobe Ter. EC4 BY39 2
Addle Hill
Wardrobe, The, Rich. BK46 74
Old Palace Yd.
Wards La., B.Wd. BH23 27
Wards Rd., Ilf. CM33 49
Ware Rd., Hodd. CE10 12
Wareham Clo., Houns. BF45 64
Waremead Rd., Ilf. CL32 49
Warenford Way, B.Wd. BM23 28
Warenne Rd., Lthd. BG64 102
Warescot Clo., Brwd. DA26 42
Warescot Rd., Brwd. DA26 42
Wareside Clo., Welw.G.C. BS 8 5
Waterford Grn.
Wareside, Hem.H. AZ10 8
Warfield Rd. NW10 BQ38 55
Warfield Rd., Felt. BB47 73
Warfield Rd., Hmptn. BF51 84
Wargrave Av. N15 CA32 48
Wargrave Rd., Har. BG34 45
Warham Rd. N4 BY32 47
Warham Rd., Har. BH30 36
Warham Rd., S.Croy. BY56 95
Warham Rd., Sev. CU61 107
Warham St. SW9 BY43 66
Waring Clo., Orp. CN57 97
Waring Dr., Orp. CN57 97
Waring Rd., Sid. CP50 79
Waring St. SE27 BZ49 77
Warington St. E13 CH38 58
Barking Rd.
Warkworth Gdns., Islw. BJ43 64
Warkworth Rd. N17 BZ29 39
Warland Rd. E., Sev. CZ58 99
Warland Rd. SE18 CM43 68
Warland Rd., Sev. CZ58 99
Warley Av., Dag. CQ33 50
Warley Av., Hayes BC39 53
Warley Gap, Brwd. DA29 42
Warley Hall La., Upmin. DC33 123
Warley Hill, Brwd. DA29 42
Warley Mt., Brwd. DB28 42
Warley Par. NW9 BO31 46
Warley Rd. N9 CC27 39
Warley Rd., Brwd. DA29 42
Warley Rd., Hayes BC39 53
Warley Rd., Ilf. CL30 40
Warley Rd., Upmin. CY30 42
Warley Rd., Wdf.Grn. CH29 40
Warley St. E2 CC38 57
Warley St., Brwd. DB32 51
Warley St., Upmin. DB33 51
Warlingham Rd., Th.Hth. BY52 86
Warlock Rd. W9 BR38 55
Warlters Clo. N7 BX35 47
Warlters Ms. N7 BX35 47
Warlters Rd. N7 BX35 47
Warltersville Rd. N19 BX33 47
Warmark Rd., Hem.H. AV12 7
Warming Clo. E5 CC34 48
Denton Way
Warmington Rd. SE24 BZ46 77
Warmington St. E13 CH38 58
Warminster Gdns. SE25 CB51 87
Warminster Rd. SE25 CA51 87
Warminster Sq. SE25 CB51 87
Warminster Way, Mitch. BV51 86
Warndon St. SE16 CC42 67
Warneford Pl., Wat. BE25 27
Warneford Rd., Har. BK31 45
Warneford St. E9 CB37 57
Warner Av., Sutt. BR55 85
Warner Clo. E15 CG35 49
Warner Clo. NW9 BO33 46
Warner Clo., Hayes BA43 63
Warner Clo., Slou. AM40 61
Warner Par., Hayes BA43 63
Warner Pl. E2 CB37 2
Warner Pl. E2 CB37 57
Warner Rd. E17 CD31 48
Warner Rd. N8 BW31 47
Warner Rd. SE5 BZ44 67
Warner Rd., Brom. CG50 78
Warner St. EC1 BY38 2
Warner St. EC1 BY38 56
Warners Av., Hodd. CD13 12
Warners Clo., Wdf.Grn. CH28 40
Warners End Rd., Hem.H. AW13 8
Warners La., Kings.T. BK49 74
Warnford Rd., Orp. CN56 97
Warnham Court Rd., Cars. BU57 95
Warnham Rd. N12 BU28 38
Warnsford Grn., Wok. AP62 100
Kenton Way
Warple Way W3 BO40 55
Warren Av. E10 CF34 48
Warren Av., Brom. CG50 78
Warren Av., Orp. CN56 97
Warren Av., Rich. BM45 65
Warren Av., S.Croy. CC57 96
Warren Av., Sutt. BR58 94
Warren Clo. N9 CC26 39
Warren Clo. SE21 BZ46 77
Warren Clo. SE24 BZ47 77
Rosendale Rd.
Warren Clo., Bexh. CR46 79
Warren Clo., Esher BF56 93
Warren Clo., Hat. BP11 10
Warren Clo., Slou. AS41 62
Warren Clo., Wem. BK34 45
Warren Cres. N9 CA26 39
Warren Ct., Beck. CD50 77
Warren Ct., Chig. CM28 40
Warren Ct., Sev. CV66 117
Warren Ct., Wey. AZ56 92
Heath Rd.
Warren Cutting, Kings.T. BN50 75
Warren Dale, Welw.G.C. BQ 6 5
Warren Dr. N., Surb. BM54 85
Warren Dr. S., Surb. BN54 85
Warren Dr., Grnf. BF38 54
Warren Dr., Horn. CU35 50
Warren Dr., Orp. CO56 98
Warren Dr., Ruis. BD33 45
Warren Dr., Tad. BR64 103
Warren Dr., The E11 CJ33 49
Warren Farm Clo. E11 CJ32 49
Warren Rd.
Warren Field, Epp. CO19 23
Charles St.
Warren Field, Iver AU37 52
Warren Fields, Stan. BK28 36
Warren Gdns. E15 CF35 48
Warren Gdns., Orp. CO56 98
Warren Grn., Hat. BP11 10
Warren Gro., B.Wd. BN24 28
Warren Hill Ho., Loug. CH25 31
Warren Hill, Epsom BN61 103
Warren Hill, Loug. CJ25 31
Warren Ho., Kings.T. BN50 75
Warren La. SE18 CL41 68
Warren La., Brwd. CZ23 33
Warren La., Grays DB42 70
Warren La., Lthd. BG59 93
Warren La., Oxt. CG70 115
Warren La., Stan. BH27 36
Warren La., Wok. AW62 101
Warren Lodge Dr., Tad. BR65 103
Warren Mead, Bans. BQ61 103
Warren Ms. W1 BV38 1
Warren Park Rd., Sutt. BU57 95
Warren Pk., Kings.T. BN50 75
Warren Pk., Warl. CC62 105
Warren Pl. E1 CC39 57
Pitsea St.
Warren Pond Rd. E4 CG26 40
Warren Rd. E10 CF34 48
Warren Rd. E11 CJ32 49
Warren Rd. E4 CF27 39
Warren Rd. NW2 BO34 46
Warren Rd. SW19 BU50 76
Warren Rd., Ashf. BB50 73
Warren Rd., Bans. BQ60 94
Warren Rd., Bexh. CR46 79
Warren Rd., Brom. CH55 88
Warren Rd., Bush. BG26 36
Warren Rd., Croy. CA54 87
Warren Rd., Dart. CW48 80
Warren Rd., Grav. DD49 81
Warren Rd., Guil. AS71 118
Warren Rd., Ilf. CM32 49
Warren Rd., Kings.T. BN50 75
Warren Rd., Orp. CN56 97
Warren Rd., Pur. BY59 95
Warren Rd., Reig. BS70 121
Warren Rd., Sid. CP48 79
Warren Rd., St.Alb. BG15 9
Warren Rd., Twick. BG46 74
Warren Rd., Uxb. AY35 44
Warren Rd., Wey. AW58 92
Warren Ri., N.Mal. BN51 85
Warren St. Ms. W1 BW38 56
Warren St.
Warren St. W1 BV38 1
Warren St. W1 BW38 56
Warren Ter., Rom. CP31 50
Warren Way NW7 BR29 37
Warren Way, Welw.G.C. BR 5 5
Warren Way, Wey. BA56 92
Warren Wk. SE7 CJ43 68
Warren Wood Clo., Brom. CG55 88
Warren Wood Rd., Brom. CG55 88
Warren, The E12 CK35 49
Warren, The, East Horsley BB68 110
Warren, The, Ash. BL63 103
Warren, The, Cars. BT58 95
Warren, The, Ger.Cr. AS30 34
Warren, The, Grav. DH49 81
Warren, The, Hayes BC39 53
Warren, The, Houns. BE43 64
Warren, The, Lthd. BG59 93
Warren, The, Rad. BJ20 18
Warren, The, Tad. BR65 103
Warren, The, Wor.Pk. BN56 94
Warrender Rd. N19 BW34 47
Warrender Rd., Chesh. AP18 16
Warrender Way, Ruis. BC33 44
Warreners La., Wey. BA57 92
Warrenfield Clo., Chsnt. CB19 21
Portland Dr.
Warrengate La., Pot.B. BQ19 19
Warrengate Rd., Hat. BQ17 19
Warrenne Rd., Bet. BN71 120
Warrens Shawe La., Edg. BM26 37
Warrens, The, Hart. DC53 90
Warriner Av., Horn. CV34 51
Warriner Gdns. SW11 BU44 66
Warrington Av., Slou. AO39 52
Warrington Cres. W9 BT38 1
Warrington Cres. W9 BT38 56
Warrington Gdns. W9 BS39 56
Warwick Av.
Warrington Gdns., Horn. CV32 51
Warrington Pl. E14 CF40 57
Yabsley St.
Warrington Rd., Croy. BY55 86
Warrington Rd., Dag. CP34 50
Warrington Rd., Har. BH32 45
Warrington Rd., Rich. BL46 75
The Hermitage
Warrington Spur, Wind. AQ47 72
Warrington Sq., Dag. CP34 50
Warrington St. E13 CH38 58
Warrior Av., Grav. DH49 81
Warrior Rd. SE5 BY43 66
Warrior Sq. E12 CL35 49
Warsaw Clo., Ruis. BC36 53
Warspite Rd. SE18 CK41 68
Warton Rd. E15 CF37 57
Warwick Av. W2 BS38 56
Warwick Av. W9 BS38 1
Warwick Av. W9 BS38 56
Warwick Av., Cuff. BW17 20
Warwick Av., Edg. BM27 37
Warwick Av., Egh. AU51 82
Warwick Av., Har. BE35 45
Warwick Av., Slou. AO38 52
Warwick Av., Stai. AX50 73
Warwick Clo., Barn. BT25 29
Warwick Clo., Bush. BH26 36
Warwick Clo., Cuff. BW17 20
Warwick Clo., Hmptn. BG50 74
Warwick Clo., Orp. CO55 89
Warwick Cres. W2 BT39 1
Warwick Cres. W2 BT39 56
Warwick Cres., Hayes BB38 53
Warwick Ct. SE15 CB44 67
Warwick Ct. WC1 BX39 2
Warwick Ct. WC1 BX39 56
Warwick Ct., Surb. BL55 85
Warwick Deeping Pl., Cher. AU56 91
Warwick Dene W5 BL40 55
Warwick Dr. SW15 BP45 65
Warwick Dr., Chsnt. CC17 21
Warwick Est. W2 BS39 1
Warwick Est. W2 BS39 56
Warwick Gdns. N4 BZ32 48
Warwick Gdns. W14 BR41 65
Warwick Gdns., Ash. BK62 102
Warwick Gdns., Ilf. CL33 49
Warwick Gdns., Rom. CV31 51
Warwick Gdns., T.Ditt. BH53 84
Warwick Gro. E5 CB33 48
Warwick Gro., Surb. BL54 85
Warwick House St. SW1 BW40 3
Warwick House St. SW1 BW40 56
Warwick La. EC4 BY39 2
Warwick La. EC4 BY39 56
Warwick La., Upmin. CW38 60
Warwick La., Wok. AQ63 100
Warwick Pl. Ms. W9 BT39 56
Warwick Pl. N. SW1 BW42 66
Warwick Pl. SW1 BW42 3
Warwick Pl. W5 BK41 64
Warwick Rd.
Warwick Pl. W9 BT39 1
Warwick Pl. W9 BT39 56
Warwick Pl., Grav. DD46 81
Warwick Pl., Uxb. AX36 53
Warwick Rd. E11 CH32 49
Warwick Rd. E12 CK35 49
Warwick Rd. E15 CG36 58
Warwick Rd. E17 CD30 39
Warwick Rd. E4 CE28 39
Warwick Rd. N11 BW29 38
Warwick Rd. N18 CA28 39
Warwick Rd. SE20 CB52 87
Warwick Rd. SW5 BS42 66
Warwick Rd. W14 BR42 65
Warwick Rd. W5 BK41 64
Warwick Rd., Ashf. AY49 73
Warwick Rd., B.Wd. BN24 28
Warwick Rd., Barn. BS24 29
Warwick Rd., Couls. BW60 95
Warwick Rd., Enf. CD22 30
Warwick Rd., Houns. BC45 63
Warwick Rd., Kings.T. BK51 84
Warwick Rd., N.Mal. BN52 85
Warwick Rd., Rain. CV38 60
Warwick Rd., Red. BU70 121
Warwick Rd., Sid. CO49 79
Warwick Rd., St.Alb. BH12 9
Warwick Rd., Sthl. BE41 64
Warwick Rd., Sutt. BT56 95
Warwick Rd., T.Ditt. BH53 84
Warwick Rd., Th.Hth. BY52 86
Warwick Rd., Twick. BH47 74
Warwick Rd., Well. CP45 69
Warwick Rd., West Dr. AY40 53
Warwick Row SW1 BV41 3
Warwick Row SW1 BV41 66
Warwick Sq. EC4 BY39 2
Warwick Sq. EC4 BY39 56
Warwick Sq. Ms. SW1 BW42 3
Warwick Sq. SW1 BW42 3
Warwick Sq. SW1 BW42 66
Warwick St. W1 BW40 3
Warwick St. W1 BW40 56
Warwick Ter. SE18 CM43 68
Warwick Way SW1 BV42 3
Warwick Way SW1 BV42 66
Warwick Way, Rick. BA24 26
Warwick Wold Rd., Red. BY68 113
Warwick Yd. EC1 BZ38 2
Warwicks Bench La., Guil. AS72 118
Warwicks Bench Rd., Guil. AS72 118
Warwicks Bench, Guil. AS72 118
Warwickshire Path SE8 CD43 67
Payne St.
Wash La., Pot.B. BP20 19
Wash Rd., Brwd. DE25 122
Washington Av. E12 CK35 49
Washington Av., Hem.H. AY11 8
Washington Clo., Reig. BS69 121
Washington Dr., Wind. AM45 61
Washington Rd. E18 CG30 40
Washington Rd. E6 CJ36 58
St. Stephens Rd.
Washington Rd. SW13 BP43 65
Washington Rd., Kings.T. BM51 85
Washington Rd., Wor.Pk. BP55 85
Washneys La., Orp. CO60 98
Washpond La., Warl. CF62 105
Wastdale Ms. SE23 CC47 77
Wastdale Rd.
Wastdale Rd. SE23 CC47 77
Wat Tyler Rd. SE10 CF44 67
Watch Mead, Welw.G.C. BS 7 5
Watchfield Ct. W4 BN42 65
Watchgate, Dart. CY49 80
Watchlytes, Welw.G.C. BT 8 5
Watcombe Cotts., Rich. BM43 65
Rushwood Rd.
Watcombe Rd. SE25 CB53 87
Water End Rd., Berk. AT12 7
Water Field, Welw.G.C. BS 7 5
Water Gdns., Stan. BJ29 36
Gordon Av.
Water La. E15 CG36 58
Water La., Berk. AR13 7
Water La., Brwd. CY23 33
Water La., Cob. BE61 102
Water La., Grays CX42 70
Water La., Harl. CK12 13
Water La., Hem.H. AT18 16
Water La., Ilf. CN34 49
Water La., Kings L. AZ18 17
Water La., Kings.T. BK51 84
Water La., Lthd. BD66 111
Water La., Oxt. CH66 115
Water La., Red. BZ69 114

Water La., Rich. BK46 74
Water La., Sev. CT60 98
Water La., Sid. CQ48 79
Water La., Twick. BJ47 74
Water La., Wat. BD24 27
Water Mead, Tad. BP63 103
Water Mill Clo., Rich. BK48 74
Water Mill Way, Felt. BE48 74
Water Mill Way, S.Dnth. CX51 90
Water Rd., Wem. BL37 55
Water St. WC2 BX40 4
Water St. WC2 BY40 56
Maltravers St.
Water St., Kings.T. BL51 85
Canbury Pass.
Water Tower Clo., Uxb. AY35 44
Water Tower Hill, Croy. BZ56 96
Waterbank Rd. SE6 CE48 77
Waterbeach Dr. NW9 BO30 37
Waterbeach Rd., Dag. CP35 50
Waterbeach Rd., Slou. AO39 52
Waterbeach, Welw.G.C. BT 8 5
Waterbrook La. NW4 BQ32 46
Brent Grn.
Watercress Clo., Sev. CV63 108
Watercress Dr.
Watercress Dr., Sev. CV63 108
Watercress Way, Wok. AQ62 100
Watercroft Rd., Sev. CQ58 98
Waterdale Rd. SE2 CO43 69
Waterdale St., Grav. DE48 81
Waterden Clo., Guil. AS71 118
Waterden Rd. E15 CE35 48
Waterden Rd., Guil. AS71 118
Waterend La., St.Alb. BN 7 5
Waterer Gdns., Tad. BR62 103
Waterer Rd. N20 BT27 38
Waterer Ri., Wall. BW57 95
Waterers Ri., Wok. AO62 100
Waterfall Clo. N14 BW27 38
Waterfall Rd.
Waterfall Clo., Vir.W. AQ52 82
Waterfall Cotts. SW19 BT50 76
Waterfall Rd. N11 BV28 38
Waterfall Rd. N14 BV28 38
Waterfall Rd. SW19 BT50 76
Waterfall Ter. SW17 BU50 76
Waterfield Clo. SE28 CO40 59
Waterfield Dr., Warl. CC63 105
Waterfield Gdns. SE25 BZ53 87
Holmesdale
Waterfield Grn., Tad. BP63 103
Waterfield, Tad. BP63 103
Waterfields, Lthd. BJ63 102
Waterford Grn., BS 8 5
Welw.G.C.
Waterford Rd. SW6 BS43 66
Watergate EC4 BY40 4
Watergate EC4 BY40 56
Tudor St.
Watergate St. SE8 CE43 67
Watergate Wk. WC2 BX40 4
Watergate Wk. WC2 BX40 56
Watergate, Wat. BD27 36
Waterhall Av. E4 CG28 40
Waterhead Clo., Erith CT43 69
Waterhouse Clo. E16 CJ39 58
Waterhouse Clo. NW3 BT35 47
Lyndhurst Rd.
Waterhouse Clo. W6 BQ42 65
Great Church La.
Waterhouse La., Ken. BZ63 105
Waterhouse La., Red. CA69 114
Waterhouse La., Tad. BR64 103
Waterhouse Moor, Harl. CN11 13
Waterhouse St., Hem.H. AX13 8
Wateringbury Clo., Orp. CO52 89
Waterloo Bridge SE1 BX40 56
Waterloo Bridge WC2 & SE1 BX40 4
Waterloo Bridge WC2 BX40 56
Waterloo Clo. E9 CC35 48
Waterloo Est. E2 CC37 57
Waterloo Gdns. E2 CC37 57
Waterloo Gdns., Rom. CT32 50
Waterloo Ms. SE5 BZ43 67
Elmington Rd.
Waterloo Pl. NW6 BR36 55
Willesden La.
Waterloo Pl. SW1 BW40 3
Waterloo Pl. SW1 BW40 56
Waterloo Pl., Rich. BL45 65
The Quadrant
Waterloo Pl., Rich. BM43 65
Waterloo Rd. E10 CE33 48
Waterloo Rd. E6 CJ36 58
Waterloo Rd. E7 CG35 49
Wellington Rd.
Waterloo Rd. NW2 BP33 46
Waterloo Rd. SE1 BX40 4
Waterloo Rd. SE1 BX40 56
Waterloo Rd., Brwd. DB26 42
Waterloo Rd., Epsom BN59 94
Waterloo Rd., Ilf. CM30 40
Waterloo Rd., Rom. CT32 50
Waterloo Rd., Sutt. BT56 95
Waterloo Rd., Uxb. AX37 53
Waterloo St. EC1 BZ38 2
Waterloo St. EC1 BZ38 57
Lever St.
Waterloo Ter. N1 BY36 2
Waterloo Ter. N1 BY36 56
Waterloo Wk. E9 CC35 48
Churchill Wk.
Waterlow Ct. NW11 BS33 47
Waterlow Rd. N19 BW33 47
Waterlow Rd., Reig. BT71 121
Waterman Clo., Wat. BC25 26
Waterman St. SW15 BQ45 65
Waterman Way E1 CB40 57
Waterman Way, Epp. CR17 23
Watermans Wk. SE16 CD40 57
Watermead La., Cars. BU53 86
Watermead Rd. SE6 CE49 77
Watermead, Felt. BB47 73
Watermead, Wok. AP61 100
Watermill La. N18 CA28 39
Waterpetty La., Wok. AP58 91
Waters Dr., Rick. AY26 35
Norfolk Rd.
Waters Dr., Stai., AV48 72
Waters Gdns., Dag. CR35 50
Waters Meet, Harl. CL13 13
Waters Rd. SE6 CG48 78
Waters Rd., Kings.T. BM51 85
Waters Side Way, Wok. AQ62 100
Winnington Way
Waters Sq., Kings.T. BM52 85
Watersedge, Epsom BN56 94
Watersfield Way, Edg. BK29 36
Waterside Clo. SE16 CB41 67
Bevington St.
Waterside Clo., Nthlt. BE38 54
Waterside Ms., Guil. AR69 118
Waterside Pl. NW1 BV37 56
Princess Rd.
Waterside Rd., Guil. AR69 118
Waterside Rd., Sthl. BF41 64
Waterside Way SW17 BT49 76
Waterside, Beck. CD51 87
Waterside, Berk. AR13 7
Waterside, Chesh. AO20 16
Waterside, Dart. CT46 79
Waterside, Kings L. AZ18 17
Waterside, St.Alb. BL17 19
Waterside, Uxb. AX39 53
Waterside, Welw.G.C. BS 7 5
Watersmeet Clo., Guil. AT68 109
Cotts Wood Dr.
Waterson Rd., Grays DG42 71
Waterson St. E2 CA38 2
Waterson St. E2 CA38 57
Watersplash Ct., St.Alb. BL17 19
Barnet Rd.
Watersplash La., Hayes BC42 63
Watersplash Rd., Shep. AZ52 83
Watersplash, Houns. BC42 63
Waterton Av., Grav. DJ47 81
Waterway Rd., Lthd. BJ64 102
Waterworks La. E5 CC34 48
Lea Bridge Rd.
Waterworks Rd. SW2 BX46 76
Waterworks Yd., Croy. BZ55 87
Surrey St.
Watery La. SW20 BR51 85
Watery La., Brox. CD16 21
Watery La., Cher. AU54 82
Watery La., Hat. BO13 10
Watery La., Hayes BB42 63
Watery La., High Laver CV11 15
Watery La., Nthlt. BD37 54
Watery La., Sev. CY64 108
Watery La., Sid. CO50 79
Watery La., St.Alb. BK17 18
Watery La., Willingale DA13 15
Watery La., Wok. AO58 91
Wates Way, Mitch. BU53 86
Wateville Rd. N17 BZ30 39
Watford By-pass, B.Wd. BJ26 36
Watford Clo. SW11 BU44 66
Petworth St.
Watford Clo., Guil. AS70 118
Watford Field Rd., Wat. BD25 27
Watford Heath, Wat. BD26 36
Watford Rd. E16 CH39 58
Watford Rd., B.Wd. BK25 27
Watford Rd., Har. BJ33 45
Watford Rd., Kings L. AZ20 17
Watford Rd., Nthwd. BB29 35
Watford Rd., Rad. BH21 27
Watford Rd., Rick. AZ25 26
Watford Rd., St.Alb. BF17 18
Watford Way NW4 BN28 37
Watford Way NW7 BN28 37
Wathen Rd., Dor. BJ71 119
Watkin Rd., Wem. BM34 46
Watkinson Rd. N7 BX36 56
Watling Av., Edg. BN30 37
Watling Clo., Hem.H. AY11 8
Watling Ct. EC4 BZ39 57
Watling St.
Watling Ct., Bush. BK25 27
Watling Farm Clo., Stan. BJ26 36
Watling Gdns. NW2 BR36 55
Watling Knoll, Rad. BH20 18
Watling St. EC4 BZ39 2
Watling St. EC4 BZ39 57
Watling St., B.Wd. BK23 27
Watling St., Bexh. CR45 69
Watling St., Dart. CX47 80
Watling St., Grav. DE48 81
Watling St., Rad. BH19 18
Watling St., St.Alb. BD10 9
Watling Vw., St.Alb. BG15 9
Watlington Gro. SE26 CD49 77
Watlington Rd., Harl. CP 9 6
Watney Mkt. E1 CB39 57
Watney Rd. SW14 BN45 65
Watney St. E1 CB39 57
Watneys Rd., Mitch. BW53 86
Watson Av. E6 CL36 58
Watson Av., Sutt. BR55 85
Watson Clo. N16 BZ35 48
Matthias Rd.
Watson Clo. SW19 BU50 76
Watson Clo., Grays DA43 70
Watson Rd., Dor. BG72 119
Watson St. E13 CH37 58
Watson Way, Grnf. BJ37 54
Sindall Dr.
Watsons Av., St.Alb. BH12 9
Watsons Ms. W1 BU39 56
Crawford Pl.
Watsons Rd. N22 BX30 38
Watsons St. SE8 CD43 67
Watsons Wk., St.Alb. BH14 9
Watsons Yd. NW2 BO34 46
Wattendon Rd., Ken. BY61 104
Wattisfield Rd. E5 CC34 48
Watts Bridge Rd., Erith CT43 69
Watts Cres., Grays CY42 70
Watts Farm Par., Wok. AP58 91
Watts Gro. E3 CE39 57
Watts La., Chis. CL51 88
Watts La., Tad. BQ64 103
Watts La., Tedd. BJ49 74
Watts Mead, Tad. BQ64 103
Watts Rd., T.Ditt. BJ54 84
Watts St. E1 CB40 57
Watts Way SW7 BT41 3
Watts Way SW7 BT41 66
Wauthier Clo. N13 BY28 38
Wavel Ms. N8 BW31 47
Park Av. S.
Wavel Ms. NW6 BS36 56
Wavel Pl. SE26 CA49 77
Sydenham Hill
Wavell Clo., Chsnt. CD17 21
Wavell Dr., Sid. CN46 78
Wavendene Av., Egh. AT50 72
Wavendon Av. W4 BN42 65
Waveney Av. SE15 CB45 67
Waveney Clo. E1 CB40 57
Kennet St.
Waveney, Hem.H. AY11 8
Waverley Av. E17 CF31 48
Waverley Rd.
Waverley Av. E4 CD28 39
Waverley Av., Ken. CA61 105
Waverley Av., Surb. BM53 85
Waverley Av., Sutt. BS55 86
Waverley Av., Twick. BE47 74
Waverley Av., Wem. BL36 55
Waverley Clo. E18 CJ30 40
Waverley Clo., Brom. CJ53 88
Waverley Clo., Hayes BA42 63
Waverley Cres. SE18 CM42 68
Waverley Cres., Rom. CV29 42
Waverley Dr., Cher. AU55 82
Waverley Dr., Vir.W. AQ52 82
Waverley Gdns. E6 CK39 58
Oliver Gdns.
Waverley Gdns. NW10 BL37 55
Waverley Gdns., Bark. CN37 58
Waverley Gdns., Grays DD41 71
Waverley Gdns., Ilf. CM30 40
Waverley Gdns., Nthwd. BC30 35
Waverley Gro. N3 BQ31 46
Waverley Pl. N4 BY33 47
Adolphus Rd.
Waverley Pl. NW8 BT37 1
Waverley Pl. NW8 BT37 56
Waverley Pl., Lthd. BK64 102
Church Rd.
Waverley Rd. E17 CF31 48
Waverley Rd. E18 CJ30 40
Waverley Rd. N17 CA30 39
Waverley Rd. N17 CB29 39
Waverley Rd. N8 BW32 47
Waverley Rd. SE18 CM42 68
Waverley Rd. SE25 CB52 87
Waverley Rd., Cob. BF60 93
Waverley Rd., Enf. BY24 29
Waverley Rd., Epsom BP57 94
Waverley Rd., Har. BE33 45
Waverley Rd., Rain. CU38 59
Waverley Rd., St.Alb. BG12 9
Waverley Rd., Sthl. BF40 54
Waverley Rd., Wey. AZ56 92
Waverley Way, Cars. BU57 95
Waverley Wk. W2 BS39 56
Waverton Rd. SW18 BT47 76
Waverton St. W1 BV40 3
Waverton St. W1 BV40 65
Wavertree Ct. SW2 BX47 76
Wavertree Rd. E18 CH30 40
Wavertree Rd. SW2 BX47 76
Waxhouse Gate, St.Alb. BG13 9
High St.
Waxlow Cres., Sthl. BF39 54
Waxlow Rd. NW10 BN37 55
Waxwell Clo., Pnr. BD30 36
Waxwell La., Pnr. BD30 36
Waxwell Ter. SE1 BX41 4
Waxwell Ter. SE1 BX41 66
Way Side, Kings L. AW18 17
Way Volante, Grav. DJ49 81
Way, The, Reig. BT70 121
Waycross Rd., Upmin. CZ33 51
Waye Av., Houns. BC44 63
Wayfarer Rd., Nthlt. BD38 54
Wayfaring Grn., Grays DC42 71
Curling La.
Wayford St. SW11 BU44 66
Wayland Av. E8 CB35 48
Waylands Clo., Sev. CQ61 107
Waylands Mead, Beck. CE51 87
Waylands, Swan. CT52 89
Waylett Pl. SE27 BY48 76
Waylett Pl., Wem. BK34 45
Waylett Sq. SE27 BY48 76
Wayne Clo., Orp. CN55 88
Wayneflete Av., Croy. BY55 86
Wayneflete Tower Av., BF55 84
Esher
Waynflete Sq. W10 BQ40 55
Waynflete St. SW18 BT48 76
Wayre Rd., Harl. CP 9 6
Wayside Av., Bush. BG25 27
Wayside Av., Horn. CV34 51
Wayside Clo. N14 BW25 29
Wayside Clo., Rom. CT31 50
Wayside Ct., Twick. BK46 74
Wayside Gdns. SE9 CK49 78
Wayside Gro.
Wayside Gdns., Dag. CR35 50
Wayside Gdns., Ger.Cr. AR33 43
Wayside Gro. SE9 CK49 78
Wayside Ms., Ilf. CL32 49
Gaysham Av.
Wayside NW11 BR33 46
Wayside SW14 BN46 75
Wayside, Pot.B. BT20 20
Wayside, The, Hem.H. AZ14 8
Wayville Rd., Dart. CX47 80
Weald Bridge Rd., Epp. CS15 14
Weald Clo., Brom. CK55 88
Weald Clo., Brwd. DA27 42
Weald Clo., Sev. CU70 116
Weald Hall La., Epp. CP16 23
Weald La., Har. BG30 36
Weald Park Way, Brwd. CZ27 42
Weald Rd., Brwd. CX26 42
Weald Rd., Sev. CU67 116
Weald Rd., Uxb. AZ37 53
Weald Ri., Har. BH29 36
Weald Sq. E5 CB34 48
Rossington St.
Weald Way, Cat. CA67 114
Weald Way, Hayes BB38 53
Weald Way, Reig. BT72 121
Weald Way, Rom. CR32 50
Weald, The, Chis. CK50 78
Weald, The, Grav. DF50 81
Wealdstone Rd., Sutt. BR55 85
Wealdwood Gdns., Pnr. BF29 36
High Banks Rd.
Weale Rd. E4 CF27 39
Weall Grn., Wat. BC19 17
Wear Pl. E2 CB38 57
Wear St. E2 CB38 57
Teesdale St.
Weardale Av., Dart. CY47 80
Weardale Gdns., Enf. BZ23 30
Weardale Rd. SE13 CF45 67
Wearside Rd. SE13 CE45 67
Weasdale Ct., Wok. AP61 100
Weatherall Clo., Wey. AW56 92
Weatherley Clo. E3 CD39 57
Weaver St. E1 CB38 2
Weaver St. E1 CB38 57
Weaver Wk. SE27 BY49 76
Weavers Clo., Grav. DG47 81
Weavers Clo., Islw. BH45 64
Weavers La. SE1 CA40 4
Weavers La. SE1 CA40 57
Weavers La., Sev. CV64 108
Weavers Ter. SW6 BS43 66
Micklethwaite Rd.
Weavers Way NW1 BW37 1
Webb Clo., Slou. AR42 62
Webb Est. E5 CB33 48
Webb Gdns. E13 CH38 58
Kelland Rd.
Webb Rd. SE3 CG43 68
Webb St. SE1 CA41 4
Webb St. SE1 CA41 67
Webber Clo., B.Wd. BK25 27
Webber Clo., Erith CU43 69
Webber Row SE1 BY41 4
Webber Row SE1 BY41 66
Webber St. SE1 BY41 4
Webber St. SE1 BY41 66
Webbs Alley, Sev. CV66 117
Webbs Rd. SW11 BU45 66
Webbs Rd., Hayes BC38 53
Webster Clo., Cob. BF60 93
Webster Clo., Uxb. AX38 53
Webster Clo., Wal.Abb. CG20 22
Webster Gdns. W5 BK40 54
Webster Rd. E11 CF34 48
Webster Rd. SE16 CB41 67
Webster Vill. W5 BK40 54
Webster Gdns.
Websters Clo., Wok. AQ63 100
Wedderburn Rd. NW3 BT35 47
Wedderburn Rd., Bark. CM37 58
Wedgewood Clo., Epp. CO18 23
Theydon Clo.
Wedgewood Clo., BA29 35
Nthwd.
Wedgewood Way SE19 BZ50 77
Beulah Hill
Wedgewood Wk. NW6 BS36 56
Lymington Rd.
Wedgewoods, West. CJ64 106
Westmore Rd.
Wedgwood Ms. W1 BW39 1
Greek St.
Wedhey, Harl. CM11 13
Wedlake Clo., Horn. CW33 51
Wedlake St. W10 BR38 55
Kensal Rd.
Wedmore Av., Ilf. CL30 40
Wedmore Gdns. N19 BW34 47
Wedmore Ms. N19 BW34 47
Wedmore St.
Wedmore Rd., Grnf. BG38 54
Wedmore St. N19 BW34 47
Wednesbury Gdns., CW29 42
Rom.
Wednesbury Grn., Rom. CW29 42
Wednesbury Rd., Rom. CW29 42
Weech Rd. NW6 BS35 47
Weedington Rd. NW5 BV35 47
Weedon Clo., Ger.Cr. AQ30 34
Weekes Dr., Slou. AN40 61
Weekley Sq. SW11 BT45 66
Thomas Baines Rd.
Weetman St. SE10 CG41 68
Weigall Rd. SE12 CH46 78
Weighhouse St. W1 BV39 56
Weighhouse St. W1 BV40 3
Weighton Ms. SE20 CB51 87
Weighton Rd.
Weighton Rd. SE20 CB51 87
Weighton Rd., Har. BG30 36
Weimar St. SW15 BR45 65
Weind, The, Epp. CN21 31
Weinhurst Gdns., Sutt. BT56 95
Weint, The, Slou. AU43 62
Weir Hall Av. N18 BZ29 39
Weir Hall Gdns. N18 BZ28 39
Weir Hall Rd. N17 BZ29 39
Weir Hall Rd. N18 BZ29 39
Weir Pl., Stai. AV51 82
Weir Rd. SW12 BW47 76
Weir Rd. SW19 BS49 76
Weir Rd., Bex. CR47 79
Weir Rd., Cher. AW54 83
Weir Rd., Walt. BC53 83
Weirdale Av. N20 BU27 38
Weirs Pass. NW1 BW38 1
Weirs Pass. NW1 BW38 56
Chalton St.
Weiss Rd. SW15 BQ45 65
Welbeck Av., Brom. CH49 78
Welbeck Av., Hayes BC38 53
Welbeck Av., Sid. CO47 79
Welbeck Clo. N12 BT28 38
Welbeck Clo., B.Wd. BM24 28
Welbeck Clo., Epsom BP57 94
Welbeck Clo., N.Mal. BO53 85
Welbeck Rd. E6 CJ38 58
Welbeck Rd., Barn. BT25 29
Welbeck Rd., Cars. BU54 86
Welbeck Rd., Har. BF33 45
Welbeck Rd., Sutt. BT55 86
Welbeck St. W1 BV39 1
Welbeck St. W1 BV39 56
Welbeck Way W1 BV39 1
Welbeck Way W1 BV39 56
Welbeck Wk., Cars. BT54 86
Welbeck Rd.
Welby St. SE5 BY44 66
Welch Pl., Pnr. BC30 35
Welclose St., St.Alb. BG13 9
Welcomes Rd., Ken. BZ61 105
Welcote Dr., Nthwd. BA29 35
Weld Pl. N11 BV28 38
Welden, Slou. AR39 52
Knolton Way
Welders La., Beac. AP29 34
Weldon Clo., Ruis. BC36 53
Weldon Way, Red. BW68 113
Welfare Rd. E15 CG36 58
Welford Clo. E5 CC34 48
Denton Way
Welford Pl. SW19 BR49 75
Welham Clo., Hat. BQ15 10
Welham Ct., Hat. BQ15 10
Dixons Hill Rd.
Welham Manor, Hat. BQ15 10
Welham Rd. SW17 BV49 76
Welhouse Rd., Cars. BU54 86
Well App., Barn. BQ25 28
Well Cft., Hem.H. AW13 8
Well Clo. E1 CB40 57
Well Clo. SW16 BX49 76
Valley Rd.
Well Clo., Ruis. BE34 45
Well Clo., Wok. AR62 100
Well Cottage Clo. E11 CJ32 49
Well Ct. EC4 BZ39 57
Queen St.
Well Ct. NW8 BT37 1
Well Ct. NW8 BT37 56
Well End Rd., B.Wd. BN22 28
Well Field, Hart. DC52 90
Well Garth, Welw.G.C. BR 8 5
Peartree La.
Well Gro. N20 BT26 38
Well Hall Rd. SE9 CK45 68
Well Hill La., Orp. CR57 98
Well Hill Rd., Sev. CS57 98
Well Hill, Orp. CR57 98
Well La. SW14 BN46 75
Well La., Brwd. CZ24 33
Well La., Grays DC40 60
Well La., Harl. CL10 6
Well La., Wok. AR62 100
Well Pass. NW3 BT34 47
Well Path, Wok. AR62 100
Well Rd. NW3 BT34 47
Well Rd., Barn. BQ25 28
Well Rd., Pot.B. BU17 20
Well Rd., Sev. CV62 108
Well Row, Hert. BX12 11
Well St. E15 CG36 58
Well St. E9 CC36 57
Well Way, Epsom BM61 103
Well Wk. NW3 BT35 47
Wellacre Rd., Har. BJ32 45
Wellan Clo., Sid. CO46 79
Welland Clo., Slou. AT43 62
Welland Gdns., Grnf. BH37 54
Welland Ms. E1 CB40 57
Kennet St.
Welland St. SE10 CF43 67
Wellands Clo., Brom. CK51 88
Wellands, Hat. BP11 10
Wellbrook Rd., Orp. CL56 97
Wellbury Ter., Hem.H. BA13 8
Wellclose Sq. E1 CB40 4
Wellclose Sq. E1 CB40 57
Wellclose St. E1 CB40 4
Wellclose Sq.
Wellcome Av., Dart. CW45 70
Wellcroft Clo., BS 9 5
Welw.G.C.
Wellcroft Rd., Slou. AN40 61
Wellcroft Rd., Welw.G.C. BS 9 5
Welldale Rd. SE16 CC42 67
Welldon Cres., Har. BH32 45
Wellen Ri., Hem.H. AY15 8
Weller Clo., Amer. AP22 25
Weller Rd., Amer. AP22 25
Weller St. SE1 BZ41 67
Wellers Clo., West. CM67 115
Wellers Ct. NW1 BX37 2
Wellers Ct. NW1 BX37 56
Wellers Gro., Chsnt. CB17 21
Wellesford Clo., Bans. BR62 103
Wellesley Av. W6 BP41 65
Wellesley Av., Iver AV41 62
Wellesley Av., Nthwd. BB28 35
Wellesley Cres., Pot.B. BR20 19
Wellesley Cres., Twick. BH48 74
Wellesley Ct. Rd., Croy. BZ55 87
Wellesley Gro.
Wellesley Ct. W9 BT38 56
Wellesley Gro., Croy. BZ55 87
Wellesley Path, Slou. AQ41 62
Wellesley Rd.
Wellesley Pl. NW5 BV35 47
Wellesley Rd. E11 CH32 49
Wellesley Rd. E17 CE32 48
Wellesley Rd. N22 BY30 38
Redvers Rd.
Wellesley Rd. NW5 BV35 47
Wellesley Rd. W4 BM42 65
Wellesley Rd., Brwd. DB26 42
Wellesley Rd., Croy. BZ55 87
Wellesley Rd., Har. BH32 45
Wellesley Rd., Ilf. CL34 49

Wellesley Rd., Slou. AQ41 62
Wellesley Rd., Sutt. BT57 95
Wellesley Rd., Twick. BG48 74
Wellesley St. E1 CC39 57
Wellesley, Harl. CL13 13
Welley Av., Stai. AS45 62
Welley Rd., Stai. AS46 72
Wellfarm Rd., Whyt. CB63 105
Wellfield Av. N10 BV31 47
Wellfield Clo., Hat. BP12 10
Wellfield Rd. SW16 BX49 76
Wellfield Rd., Hat. BP11 10
Wellfield Wk. SW16 BX49 76
Wellfields Rd., Loug. CL24 31
Wellfit St. SE24 BY45 66
Hinton Rd.
Wellgarth Gdns., Grnf. BJ36 54
Wellgarth Rd. NW11 BS33 47
Wellgarth, Welw.G.C. BR 8 5
Peartree La.
Wellhouse La., Barn. BQ24 28
Wellhouse La., Bet. BN72 120
Wellhouse Rd., Beck. CD52 87
Welling Way SE9 CM45 68
Welling Way, Well. CM45 68
Wellington Arc. SW1 BV41 66
Wellington Av. E4 CE27 39
Wellington Av. N15 CA32 48
Wellington Av. N9 CB27 39
Wellington Av., Houns. BF46 74
Wellington Av., Pnr. BE30 36
Wellington Av., Sid. CO46 79
Wellington Av., Vir.W. AQ52 82
Wellington Av., Wor.Pk. BQ56 94
Wellington Bldgs. SW1 BV42 3
Wellington Clo. E4 CE27 39
Wellington Av.
Wellington Clo. SE14 CC44 67
Wild Goose Dr.
Wellington Clo. W11 BS39 56
Wellington Clo., Dag. CS36 59
Wellington Clo., Walt. BB54 83
Wellington Cotts, Lthd. BB68 110
Wellington Cres., N.Mal. BN52 85
Wellington Dr., Dag. CS36 59
Wellington Dr., Welw.G.C. BT 8 5
Wellington Gdns. SE7 CJ42 68
Wellington Gdns., Hmptn. BG49 74
Wellington Hill, Loug. CH22 31
Wellington Ms. SE22 CB45 67
Peckham Rye
Wellington Pass. E11 CH32 49
Wellington Rd.
Wellington Pl. N2 BU32 47
Wellington Pl. NW8 BT38 1
Wellington Pl. NW8 BT38 56
Wellington Pl., Brwd. DB28 42
Britannia Rd.
Wellington Rd. E10 CD33 48
Wellington Rd. E11 CH32 49
Wellington Rd. E17 CD31 48
Wellington Rd. E6 CK37 58
Wellington Rd. E7 CG35 49
Wellington Rd. N., Houns. BE45 64
Wellington Rd. NW10 BQ39 55
Wellington Rd. NW8 BT37 1
Wellington Rd. NW8 BT37 56
Wellington Rd. S., Houns. BE45 64
Wellington Rd. SW19 BS48 76
Wellington Rd. W5 BK41 64
Wellington Rd., Ashf. AY49 73
Wellington Rd., Belv. CQ42 69
Wellington Rd., Bex. CP46 79
Wellington Rd., Brom. CJ52 88
Wellington Rd., Cat. BZ64 105
Wellington Rd., Croy. BY54 86
Wellington Rd., Dart. CV46 80
Wellington Rd., Enf. CA25 30
Wellington Rd., Epp. CR17 23
Wellington Rd., Felt. BB46 73
Wellington Rd., Har. BH31 45
Wellington Rd., Hmptn. BG49 74
Wellington Rd., London Colney BK16 18
Wellington Rd., Orp. CO53 89
Wellington Rd., Pnr. BE29 36
Wellington Rd., St.Alb. BJ14 9
Wellington Rd., Til. DG45 71
Wellington Rd., Uxb. AX37 53
Wellington Rd., Wat. BC23 26
Wellington Row E2 CA38 2
Wellington Row E2 CA38 57
Wellington Sq. SW3 BU42 3
Wellington Sq. SW3 BU42 66
Wellington St. SE18 CL42 68
Wellington St. WC2 BX40 4
Wellington St. WC2 BX40 56
Wellington St., Bark. CM37 58
Axe St.
Wellington St., Grav. DH47 81
Wellington St., Slou. AQ41 62
Wellington Ter. E1 CB40 57
Wellington Ter., Har. BG33 45
Wellington Way E3 CE38 57
Wellington Yd., Rich. BK46 74
George St.
Wellingtonia Av., Hav. CS27 41
Wellmeade Dr., Sev. CU67 116
Wellmeadow Rd. SE13 CG46 78
Wellmeadow Rd. SE6 CG46 78
Wellmeadow Rd. W7 BJ42 64
Wellow Wk., Cars. BT54 86
Wells Clo., Lthd. BF65 102
Wells Clo., Nthlt. BD38 54
Yeading La.
Wells Clo., Wind. AN44 61
Wells Cres. SE5 CA43 67
Southampton Way
Wells Dr. NW9 BN33 46
Wells Gdns., Dag. CR35 50
Wells Gdns., Ilf. CK33 49
Wells Gdns., Rain. CT36 59
Wells House Rd. NW10 BO39 55
Wells Ms. W1 BW39 1
Wells Ms. W1 BW39 56
Wells Park Rd. SE26 CB48 77
Wells Pl. W5 BK40 54
Wells Rd. W12 BQ41 65
Wells Rd., Brom. CK51 88
Wells Rd., Epsom BM60 94
Wells Rd., Guil. AU69 118
Wells Ri. NW8 BU37 1
Wells Ri. NW8 BU37 56
Wells St. W1 BW39 1
Wells St. W1 BW39 56
Wells Ter. N4 BY34 47
Wells Way SE5 BZ43 67
Wells Yd. N7 BY35 47
Holloway Rd.
Wells, The N14 BW26 38
Wellside Clo., Barn. BQ24 28
Wellside Gdns. SW14 BN46 75
Wellsmoor Gdns., Brom. CL52 88
Wellsprings Cres., Wem. BM34 46
Wellstead Av. N9 CC26 39
Wellstead Rd. E6 CL37 58
Wellstones, Wat. BC24 26
Market St.
Wellswood Clo., Hem.H. AZ13 8
Wellwood Clo., Couls. BX60 95
Wellwood Rd., Ilf. CO33 50
Welsford Rd. SE1 CB42 4
Welsford St. SE1 CB42 67
Welsh Clo. E13 CH38 58
Welshpool St. E8 CB37 57
Weltje Rd. W6 BP42 65
Welton Rd. SE18 CN43 68
Welwyn Av., Felt. BB46 73
Welwyn Ct., Hem.H. AY11 8
Welwyn St. E2 CC38 57
Globe Rd.
Welwyn Way, Hayes BB38 53
Wembley Hill Rd., Wem. BL34 46
Wembley Park Dr., Wem. BL35 46
Wembley Rd., Hmptn. BF51 84
Wembley Way, Wem. BM36 55
Wemborough Rd., Stan. BK30 36
Wembury Rd. N6 BV33 47
Wemyss Rd. SE3 CG44 68
Wend, The, Couls. BW60 95
Wendela Clo., Wok. AS62 100
Wendela Ct., Har. BH34 45
Wendell Rd. W12 BO41 65
Wendley Dr., Wey. AV58 91
Wendling Rd., Sutt. BT55 86
Wendon St. E3 CD37 37
Wendover Clo., Hayes BD38 54
Kingsash Dr.
Wendover Clo., St.Alb. BK11 9
Wendover Dr., N.Mal. BO53 85
Wendover Pl., Stai. AU49 72
Wendover Rd. NW10 BO37 55
Wendover Rd. SE17 CA42 4
Wendover Rd. SE17 CA42 67
Wendover Rd. SE9 CJ45 68
Wendover Rd., Brom. CH52 88
Wendover Rd., Stai. AU49 72
Wendover Way, Bush. BG25 27
Wendover Way, Horn. CV35 51
Springbank Av.
Wendover Way, Orp. CO53 89
Wendover Way, Well. CO46 79
Wendover Wk. SE17 CA42 4
Wendover Wk. SE17 CA42 67
Wendron Clo., Wok. AQ62 100
Shilburn Way
Wendy Clo., Enf. CA25 30
First Av.
Wendy Cres., Guil. AQ69 118
Wendy Way, Wem. BL37 55
Wenham Gdns., Brwd. DE25 122
Bannister Dr.
Wenlack Clo., Uxb. AW34 44
Wenlock Ct. N1 BZ37 2
Wenlock Edge, Dor. BK72 119
Wenlock Rd. N1 BZ37 2
Wenlock Rd. N1 BZ37 57
Wenlock Rd., Edg. BM29 37
Wenlock St. N1 BZ37 2
Wenlock St. N1 BZ37 57
Wenlocks La., Ing. DB20 24
Wennington Rd. E3 CC37 57
Grove Rd.
Wennington Rd., Rain. CU38 59
Wensley Av., Wdf.Grn. CG29 40
Wensley Clo. SE9 CK46 78
Court Rd.
Wensley Clo., Rom. CR28 41
Wensley Rd. N18 CB29 39
Wensleydale Av., Ilf. CK30 40
Wensleydale Gdns., Hmptn. BF50 74
Wensleydale Pass., Hmptn. BF51 84
Wensleydale Rd., Hmptn. BF50 74
Wensleydale, Hem.H. AY12 8
Wensum Way, Rick. AX26 35
Wentbridge Path, B.Wd. BL22 28
Wentland Clo. SE6 CF48 77
Wentland Rd.
Wentland Rd. SE6 CF48 77
Wentworth Av. N3 BS29 38
Wentworth Av., B.Wd. BL25 28
Wentworth Clo. N3 BS29 38
Wentworth Clo., Ashf. AZ49 73
Reedsfield Rd.
Wentworth Clo., Grav. DG49 81
Chalky Bank
Wentworth Clo., Mord. BS54 86
Wentworth Clo., Orp. CN56 97
Wentworth Clo., Pot.B. BS19 20
Strafford Gate
Wentworth Clo., Surb. BK55 84
Wentworth Clo., Wat. BB22 26
Wentworth Clo., Wok. AW64 101
Wentworth Cotts., Brox. CD14 12
Wentworth Cres. SE15 CB43 67
Wentworth Cres., Hayes BA41 63
Wentworth Dr., Dart. CU46 79
Wentworth Dr., Pnr. BC32 44
Wentworth Dr., Vir.W. AP52 82
Wentworth Gdns. N13 BY28 38
Wentworth Hill, Wem. BL33 46
Wentworth Mkt. E1 CA39 2
New Goulston St.
Wentworth Ms. E3 CD38 57
Eric St.
Wentworth Pk. N3 BS29 38
Wentworth Pl., Grays DE41 71
Wentworth Pl., Stan. BJ29 36
Wentworth Rd. E12 CJ35 49
Wentworth Rd. NW11 BR32 46
Wentworth Rd., Barn. BQ24 28
Wentworth Rd., Croy. BY54 86
Wentworth Rd., Sthl. BD42 64
Wentworth St. E1 CA39 2
Wentworth St. E1 CA39 57
Wentworth Way, Pnr. BD31 45
Wentworth Way, Rain. CU38 59
Wentworth Way, S.Croy. CB60 96
Wenvoe Av., Bexh. CR44 69
Wernbrook St. SE18 CM43 68
Werndee Rd. SE25 CB52 87
Werneth Hall Rd., Ilf. CK31 49
Werrington St. NW1 BW37 1
Werrington St. NW1 BW37 56
Werter Rd. SW15 BR45 65
Wesley Av. NW10 BN38 55
Wesley Av., Houns. BE44 64
Wesley Clo. N7 BX34 47
Wesley Clo. SE17 BY42 4
Wesley Clo., Chsnt. BZ17 21
Wesley Clo., Har. BG34 45
Wesley Clo., Orp. CP52 89
Main Rd.
Wesley Clo., Reig. BR72 120
Wesley Dr., Egh. AT50 72
Wesley Rd. E10 CF33 48
Wesley Rd. NW10 BN37 55
Wesley Rd., Hayes BC40 53
Wesley Sq. W11 BQ39 55
Lancaster Rd.
Wesley St. W1 BV39 56
Weymouth St.
Wesleyan Pl. NW5 BV35 47
Mortimer Ter.
Wessels, Tad. BQ64 103
Wessex Av. SW19 BS52 86
Wessex Bldgs. N19 BW34 47
Wedmore St.
Wessex Clo., Ilf. CN32 49
Wessex Clo., Kings.T. BM51 85
Gloucester Rd.
Wessex Dr., Erith CT44 69
Wessex Dr., Pnr. BE29 36
Wessex Gdns. NW11 BR33 46
Wessex La., Grnf. BG37 54
Wessex Rd., Houns. AW45 63
Wessex St. E2 CC38 57
Wessex Way NW11 BR33 46
West Acres, Amer. AO23 25
West App., Orp. CM53 88
West Arbour St. E1 CC39 57
West Av. E17 CE31 48
West Av. N3 BS29 38
West Av. NW4 BQ32 46
West Av., Hayes BB40 53
West Av., Pnr. BE32 45
West Av., Red. BV73 121
West Av., St.Alb. BF16 18
West Av., Sthl. BE40 54
West Av., Wall. BX56 95
West Av., Wat. BB58 92
West Avenue Rd. E17 CE31 48
West Bank N16 CA33 48
West Bank, Bark. CL37 58
West Bank, Dor. BH72 119
West Bank, Enf. BZ23 30
West Barnes La. SW20 BP52 85
West Barnes La., N.Mal. BP53 85
West Beech Rd. N22 BY31 47
West Brook, Harl. CK12 13
West Burrow Field, Welw.G.C. BQ 9 5
West Central St. WC1 BX39 2
West Central St. WC1 BX39 56
New Oxford St.
West Clo. N9 CA27 39
West Clo., Ashf. AY49 73
West Clo., Barn. BP25 28
West Clo., Cockfosters BV24 29
West Clo., Grnf. BG37 54
West Clo., Hmptn. BE49 74
Oak Av.
West Clo., Hodd. CE11 12
West Clo., Rain. CU38 59
West Clo., Wem. BL33 46
West Common Clo., Ger.Cr. AS32 43
West Common Rd., Brom. CH55 88
West Common Rd., Uxb. AX36 53
West Common, Ger.Cr. AR32 43
West Cotts. NW6 BS35 47
West Cres. Rd., Grav. DG46 81
West Cres., Wind. AM44 61
West Cromwell Rd. SW5 BR42 65
West Cromwell Rd. W14 BR42 65
West Cross Route W11 BQ40 55
West Cross Way, Brent. BJ43 64
West Ct. SE18 CL43 68
Prince Imperial Way
West Ct., Wem. BK34 45
West Dean, Sutt. BR57 94
Park La.
West Dene Way, Wem. BB55 83
West Dene, Sutt. BR57 94
Park La.
West Dr. N8 BW31 47
Redston Rd.
West Dr. SW11 BU43 66
West Dr. SW16 BW49 76
West Dr., Ascot AO53 82
West Dr., Cars. BT58 95
West Dr., Har. BG29 36
West Dr., Sutt. BQ58 94
West Dr., Tad. BQ62 103
West Dr., Vir.W. AO53 82
West Dr., Wat. BC21 26
West Drayton Park Av., West Dr. AY41 63
West Drayton Rd., Uxb. AY39 53
West Drive Gdns., Har. BG29 36
West Eaton Pl. SW1 BV42 3
West Eaton Pl. SW1 BV42 66
West Ella Rd. NW10 BO36 55
West End Av. E10 CF32 48
West End Av., Pnr. BD31 45
West End Ct., Pnr. BD31 45
West End Ct., Slou. AP37 52
West End Gdns., Esher BE56 93
West End Gdns., Nthlt. BD37 54
West End La. NW6 BS35 47
West End La., Barn. BQ24 28
West End La., Esher BE57 93
West End La., Hat. BT12 11
West End La., Hayes BA43 63
West End La., Pnr. BD31 45
West End La., Slou. AP37 52
West End Rd., Brox. CA15 12
West End Rd., Nthlt. BD36 54
West End Rd., Ruis. BB33 44
West End Rd., Sthl. BE40 54
West End, Sev. CW62 108
West End, West. CO66 116
West Farm Av., Ash. BK62 102
West Farm Clo., Ash. BK63 102
West Farm Dr., Ash. BK63 102
West Field SW13 BO45 65
Cross St.
West Gate Ms. W10 BQ38 55
West Row
West Gate W5 BL38 55
West Gate, Harl. CM11 13
West Gdns. E1 CB40 57
West Gdns. SW17 BU50 76
West Gdns., Epsom BO58 94
West Green Rd. N15 BY31 47
West Gro. SE10 CF44 67
West Gro., Walt. BC56 92
West Gro., Wdf.Grn. CJ29 40
West Halkin St. SW1 BV41 3
West Halkin St. SW1 BV41 66
West Hall Ct. N6 BV34 47
West Hall Rd., Rich. BM44 65
West Hallows SE9 CJ47 78
West Ham La. E15 CG36 58
West Hampstead Ms. NW6 BS36 56
West Harding St. EC4 BY39 2
West Harding St. EC4 BY39 56
Fetter La.
West Hatch Manor, Ruis. BB33 44
West Heath Av. NW11 BS33 47
West Heath Clo. NW3 BS34 47
West Heath Clo., Dart. CT46 79
West Heath Rd.
West Heath Ct. NW11 BS33 47
West Heath Dr. NW11 BS33 47
West Heath Gdns. NW3 BS34 47
West Heath La., Sev. CU67 116
West Heath Rd. NW3 BS34 47
West Heath Rd. SE2 CP43 69
West Heath Rd., Dart. CT46 79
West Hendon Bdy. NW9 BP33 46
West Hill Av., Epsom BM60 94
West Hill Bank, Oxt. CF68 114
West Hill Ct. SW18 BR46 75
West Hill Rd.
West Hill Dr., Dart. CV46 80
West Hill Rd. SW18 BR46 75
West Hill Rd., Wok. AR63 100
West Hill Ri., Dart. CV46 80
West Hill SW15 BQ47 75
West Hill SW18 BQ47 75
West Hill Way N20 BS26 38
West Hill, Ash. BL63 103
West Hill, Dart. CV46 80
West Hill, Epsom BN60 94
West Hill, Har. BH34 45
West Hill, Orp. CK59 97
West Hill, S.Croy. CA58 96
West Hill, Wem. BL33 46
West Holme, Erith CS44 69
West House Clo. SW19 BR47 75
West Hyde La., Ger.Cr. AS29 34
West India Dock Rd. E14 CE40 57
West Kent Av., Grav. DE46 81
West Kentish Town Est. NW5 BV35 47
West La. SE16 CB41 67
West La., Dor. BD73 119
West Lodge Av. W3 BM40 55
West Mall W8 BS40 56
West Malling Way, Horn. CV35 51
West Mead, Welw.G.C. BS 9 5
West Mead, Wok. AQ62 100
West Meads, Guil. AP71 118
West Mede, Chig. CM29 40
West Mount Av., Amer. AO23 25
West Ms. N18 CB29 39
West Oak, Beck. CF51 87
West Palace Gdns., Wey. AZ55 83
West Park Av., Rich. BM44 65
West Park Clo., Rom. CQ32 50
West Park Hill, Brwd. DA27 42
West Park Rd., Epsom BL59 94
West Park Rd., Rich. BM44 65
West Pk. SE9 CK48 78
West Pl. SW19 BQ49 75
West Point, Slou. AL40 61
West Poultry Av. EC1 BY39 2
West Poultry Av. EC1 BY39 56
Charterhouse St.
West Quarters W12 BP39 55
Du Cane Rd.
West Ramp, Houns. AZ44 63
West Rd. E15 CG37 58
West Rd. N17 CB29 39
West Rd. SW14 BN45 65
West Rd. SW3 BU42 66
West Rd. SW4 BW46 76
West Rd. W5 BL39 55
West Rd., Barn. BV26 38
West Rd., Berk. AQ12 7
West Rd., Chadwell Heath CQ32 50
West Rd., Chess. BK59 93
West Rd., Felt. BA46 73
West Rd., Guil. AS71 118
West Rd., Harl. CO 9 6
West Rd., Kings.T. BN51 85
West Rd., Reig. BS71 121
West Rd., Rush Green CS33 50
West Rd., S.Ock. DA38 60
West Rd., Saw. CO 5 6
West Rd., West Dr. AY41 63
West Rd., Wey. AZ58 92
West Ridge Clo., Hem.H. AV13 7
West Ridge Gdns., Grnf. BG37 54
West Riding, St.Alb. BE18 18
West Row W10 BQ38 55
West Shaw, Long. DB51 90
West Sheen Vale, Rich. BL45 65
West Side Common SW18 BQ49 75
West Side SW18 BT46 76
West Side, Brox. CD15 12
West Smithfield EC1 BY39 2
West Smithfield EC1 BY39 56
West Sq. SE1 & SE11 BY41 4
West Sq. SE1 & SE11 BY41 66
West Sq. SE18 CK42 68
West Sq., Iver AV39 52
West St. E11 CG34 49
West St. E17 CE32 48
West St. E2 CB37 57
Clare St.
West St. EC2 BZ39 2
West St. EC2 BZ39 57
Moorgate
West St. WC2 BW39 1
West St. WC2 BW39 56
Lichfield St.
West St., Bexh. CQ45 69
West St., Brent. BK43 64
West St., Brom. CH51 88
West St., Cars. BU55 86
West St., Croy. BZ56 96
West St., Dor. BJ71 119
West St., Epsom BN60 94
West St., Erith CS42 69
West St., Ewell BO58 94
West St., Grav. DG46 81
West St., Grays DD43 71
West St., Har. BG33 45
West St., Reig. BR70 120
West St., Sutt. BS56 95
West St., Wat. BC23 26
West Street La., Cars. BU56 95
West Temple Sheen SW14 BM45 65
West Tenter St. E1 CA39 2
West Tenter St. E1 CA40 57
West Thurrock Arterial Rd., Grays DA41 70
West Thurrock Way, Grays CZ42 70
West Towers, Pnr. BD32 45
West Valley Rd., Hem.H. AX16 17
West View Av., Whyt. CA62 105
Station Rd.
West View Dr., Wdf.Grn. CJ30 40
West View Rd., Crockenhill CS53 89
West View Rd., Dart. CW46 80
West View Rd., St.Alb. BG13 9
West View Rd., Swan. CU52 89
West View Rd., Warl. CB63 105
West View Ri., Hem.H. AX13 8
West Vw. NW4 BQ31 46
West Vw., Chesh. AO18 16
West Vw., Felt. BA47 73
West Vw., Loug. CK24 31
West Walk Way, Sutt. BS56 95
Robin Hood Rd.
West Warwick Pl. SW1 BV42 3
West Warwick Pl. SW1 BW42 66
West Way Gdns., Croy. CC55 87
West Way N18 BZ28 39
West Way NW10 BN35 46
West Way, Brwd. DA27 42
West Way, Cars. BT58 95
West Way, Croy. CD55 87
West Way, Edg. BM29 37
West Way, Houns. BE44 64
West Way, Pnr. BD31 45
West Way, Rick. AW26 35
West Way, Ruis. BB33 44
West Way, Sev. CT64 107
West Way, Shep. BA53 83
West Way, W.Wick. CG53 88
West Way, Wal.Abb. CE21 30
West Way, West. CM66 115
West Wk. W5 BL39 55
West Wk., Barn. BV26 38
West Wk., Harl. CM11 13
West Wk., Hayes BC40 53
West Woodside, Bex. CQ47 79
Westacott Clo. N19 BW33 47
Hazelville Rd.
Westacott, Hayes BB39 53
Westacres, Esher BE57 93
Westall Rd., Loug. CL24 31
Westanley Av., Amer. AO23 25
Westbank Rd., Hmptn. BG50 74
Westbere Dr., Stan. BK28 36
Westbere Rd. NW2 BR35 46
Westbourne Av. N9 CB27 39
Eastbournia Av.
Westbourne Av. W3 BN39 55
Westbourne Av., Sutt. BR55 85
Westbourne Bri. W2 BT39 1
Westbourne Bri. W2 BT39 56
Westbourne Clo., Hayes BD38 54
Westbourne Cres. W2 BT40 3
Westbourne Cres. W2 BT40 56
Westbourne Dr. SE23 CC48 77
Westbourne Dr., Brwd. CZ28 42
Westbourne Gdns. W2 BS39 1

Westbourne Gdns. W2 BS39 56
Westbourne Gro. Ter. W2 BS39 1
Westbourne Gro. Ter. W2 BS39 56
Westbourne Gro. W11 BR40 55
Westbourne Gro. W2 BS39 56
Westbourne Grove Ms. W11 BS39 56
Westbourne Gro.
Westbourne Pk. Ms. W2 BS39 1
Westbourne Pk. Ms. W2 BS39 56
Westbourne Gdns.
Westbourne Pk. Pass. W2 BS39 56
Westbourne Pk. Rd. W11 BR39 55
Westbourne Pk. Rd. W2 BR39 55
Westbourne Pk. Vill. W2 BS39 56
Westbourne Pl. N9 CB27 39
Eastbournia Av.
Westbourne Rd. N7 BX36 56
Westbourne Rd. SE26 CC50 77
Westbourne Rd., Bexh. CP43 69
Westbourne Rd., Croy. CA53 87
Westbourne Rd., Felt. BB48 73
Westbourne Rd., Stai. AW50 73
Westbourne Rd., Uxb. AZ38 53
Westbourne St. W2 BT40 3
Westbourne St. W2 BT40 56
Westbourne Ter. Ms. W2 BT39 1
Westbourne Ter. Ms. W2 BT39 56
Westbourne Ter. Rd. W2 BT39 1
Westbourne Ter. Rd. W2 BT39 56
Westbourne Ter. W2 BT39 1
Westbourne Ter. W2 BT39 56
Westbridge Rd. SW11 BT44 66
Westbrook Av., Hmptn. BE50 74
Westbrook Clo., Barn. BT24 29
Westbrook Cres., Barn. BT24 29
Westbrook Dr., Orp. CP54 89
Westbrook Rd. SE3 CH44 68
Westbrook Rd., Houns. BE43 64
Westbrook Rd., Stai. AV49 72
Westbrook Rd., Th.Hth. BZ51 87
Westbrook Sq., Barn. BT24 29
Westbrook, Maid. AJ42 61
Westbrooke Cres., Well. CP45 69
Westbrooke Rd., Sid. CM48 78
Westbrooke Rd., Well. CO45 69
Westbury Av. N22 BY31 47
Westbury Av., Esher BH57 93
Westbury Av., Sthl. BF38 54
Westbury Av., Wem. BL36 55
Westbury Clo., Ruis. BC33 44
Westbury Clo., Shep. AZ53 83
Burchetts Way
Westbury Clo., Whyt. CA62 105
Station App.
Westbury Dr., Brwd. DA27 42
Westbury Gro. N3 BS29 38
Westbury La., Buck.H. CH27 40
Westbury Lodge Clo., Pnr. BD31 45
Westbury Pl., Brent. BK43 64
Hamilton Rd.
Westbury Rd. E17 CD31 48
Westbury Rd. E7 CH35 49
Westbury Rd. N11 BX29 38
Westbury Rd. N12 BS29 38
Westbury Rd. SE20 CC51 87
Westbury Rd. W5 BL39 55
Westbury Rd., Bark. CM37 58
Westbury Rd., Beck. CD52 87
Westbury Rd., Brom. CJ51 88
Westbury Rd., Brwd. DB27 42
Westbury Rd., Buck.H. CJ27 40
Westbury Rd., Croy. BZ53 87
Westbury Rd., Felt. BD47 74
Westbury Rd., Ilf. CK34 49
Westbury Rd., N.Mal. BN52 85
Westbury Rd., Nthwd. BA28 35
Westbury Rd., Wat. BC25 26
Westbury Rd., Wem. BL36 55
Westbury St. SW8 BW44 66
Westbury Ter. E7 CH36 58
Westbury Ter., Upmin. CZ34 51
Westbury Ter., West. CM66 115
Westbush Clo., Hodd. CD10 12
Westcar La., Walt. BC57 92
Westchester Dr. NW4 BQ31 46
Westcombe Av., Croy. BX53 86
Westcombe Ct. SE3 CG43 68
Westcombe Dr., Barn. BS25 29
Westcombe Hill SE3 CH42 68
Westcombe Park Rd. SE3 CG43 68
Westcoombe Av. SW20 BO51 85
Westcote Rd. SW16 BW49 76
Westcote Ri. Ruis. BA33 44
Westcott Clo. N15 CA32 48
Ermine Rd.
Westcott Clo., Brom. CK53 88
Ringmer Way
Westcott Clo., Croy. CE58 96
Westcott Cres. W7 BH39 54
Westcott Rd. SE17 BY43 4
Westcott Rd. SE17 BY43 66
Westcott Rd., Dor. BH72 119
Westcott St., Dor. BF72 119
Westcott Way, Sutt. BQ58 94
Westcott Way, Uxb. AX37 53
Westcott, Welw.G.C. BT7 5
Westcourt Av., Grav. DG48 81
Westcroft Clo. NW2 BR35 46
Westcroft Clo., Enf. CC22 30
Westcroft Est. NW2 BR35 46
Westcroft Gdns., Mord. BR52 85
Westcroft Rd., Cars. BV56 95
Westcroft Sq. W6 BO42 65
Westcroft Way NW2 BR35 46
Westdale Rd. SE18 CL43 68
Westdean Av. SE12 CH47 78
Westdean Clo. SW18 BS46 76
Denton St.
Westdene Dr., Rom. CV28 42
Westdown Rd. E15 CF35 48
Westdown Rd. SE6 CE47 77
Westdown, Lthd. BF67 111
Wested La., Swan. CU54 89
Westerdale Ct. N5 BY35 47
Leigh Rd.
Westerdale Rd. SE10 CH42 68
Westerdale, Hem.H. AY12 8
Westerfield Rd. N15 CA32 48
Westerfolds Clo., Wok. AU62 100
Westergate Rd. SE2 CQ43 69
Westerham Av. N9 BZ27 39
Westerham Clo., Wey. AX57 92
Westerham Dr., Sid. CO46 79
Westerham Rd. E10 CE32 48
Westerham Rd., Kes. CJ58 97
Westerham Rd., Oxt. CG68 115
Westerham Rd., Sev. CR65 107
Westerham Rd., West. CJ60 97
Westerley Cres. SE26 CD49 77
Western Av. NW11 BQ32 46
Western Av. W3 BJ38 54
Western Av. W5 BJ38 54
Western Av., Brwd. DB26 42
Western Av., Cher. AW52 83
Western Av., Dag. CS36 59
Western Av., Denham AX35 44
Western Av., Egh. AT52 82
Western Av., Epp. CN19 22
Western Av., Grnf. BJ38 54
Western Av., Rom. CV30 42
Western Av., Ruis. BC36 53
Western Av., Uxb. BA36 53
Western Cir. W3 BO40 55
Western Clo., Cher. AW52 83
Western Av.
Western Ct. N3 BS29 38
Western Ct. W3 BN39 55
York Rd.
Western Dr., Shep. BA53 83
Western Gdns. W5 BM40 55
Western Gdns., Brwd. DB27 42
Western La. SW12 BV47 76
Western Par., Barn. BS25 29
Western Perimeter Rd., Houns. AW45 63
Western Pl. SE16 CC41 67
Canon Beck Rd.
Western Rd. E13 CJ37 58
Western Rd. E17 CF32 48
Western Rd. N2 BU31 47
Western Rd. N22 BX30 38
Western Rd. NW10 BN38 55
Western Rd. SW19 BT51 86
Western Rd. SW9 BY45 66
Western Rd. W5 BK40 54
Western Rd., Brwd. DB27 42
Western Rd., Epp. CN19 22
Western Rd., Mitch. BT51 86
Western Rd., Rom. CT32 50
Western Rd., Sthl. BD42 64
Western Rd., Sutt. BS56 95
Western Rd., Wal.Abb. CG14 13
Western St. E15 CF36 57
Western Trading Est. NW10 BN38 55
Western Vw., Hayes BB41 63
Western Way SE28 CM41 68
Western Way, Barn. BS25 29
Westernville Gdns., Ilf. CM33 49
Westferry Rd. E14 CE40 57
Westfield Av., S.Croy. BZ60 96
Westfield Av., Wat. BD22 27
Westfield Av., Wok. AS64 100
Westfield Clo., Enf. CD24 30
Westfield Clo., Grav. DH49 81
Westfield Clo., Sutt. BR56 94
Westfield Clo., Wal.Cr. CD19 21
Westfield Ct., St.Alb. BK12 9
Southfield Way
Westfield Dr., Har. BK32 45
Westfield Dr., Lthd. BF64 102
Westfield Gdns., Har. BK31 45
Westfield Gro., Wok. AS63 100
Westfield La., Har. BK31 45
Westfield La., Slou. AR40 52
Westfield N6 BU34 47
Westfield Par., Wey. AX58 92
Westfield Pk., Pnr. BE29 36
Westfield Rd. N8 BX31 47
Westfield Rd. NW7 BN27 37
Westfield Rd. W13 BJ40 54
Westfield Rd., Beck. CD51 87
Westfield Rd., Berk. AP12 7
Westfield Rd., Bexh. CS44 69
Westfield Rd., Croy. BY55 86
Westfield Rd., Dag. CQ35 50
Westfield Rd., Guil. AS68 109
Westfield Rd., Hodd. CD11 12
Westfield Rd., Mitch. BU51 86
Westfield Rd., Surb. BK53 84
Westfield Rd., Sutt. BR56 94
Westfield Rd., Walt. BE54 84
Westfield Rd., Wok. AR64 100
Westfield St. SE18 CJ41 68
Westfield Way, Ruis. BB34 44
Westfield Way, Wok. AS64 100
Westfield Wk., Wal.Cr. CD19 21
Westfield, Ash. BL62 103
Westfield, Harl. CN11 13
Westfield, Hat. BR15 10
Westfield, Loug. CJ25 31
Longfield
Westfield, Reig BS69 121
Westfield, Sev. CV64 108
Westfield, Welw.G.C. BS7 5
Daniells
Westfields Av. SW13 BO45 65
Westfields Rd. W3 BM39 55
Westfields SW13 BO45 65
Westfields, St.Alb. BF15 9
Westgate Ct., Wal.Cr. CC21 30
Holmesdale
Westgate Rd. SE25 CB52 87
Westgate Rd., Beck. CE51 87
Westgate Rd., Dart. CV46 80
Westgate St. E8 CB37 57
Westgate Ter. SW10 BS42 3
Westgate Ter. SW10 BS42 66
Westglade Ct., Har. BK32 45
Westgrove La. SE10 CF44 67
Westhall Park Rd., Warl. CC63 105
Westhall Rd. SE5 BY43 66
Westhall Rd., Warl. CB62 105
Westharold, Swan. CS52 89
Westhay Gdns. SW14 BM46 75
Westhill Clo., Grav. DG47 81
Leith Park Rd.
Westhill Rd., Hodd. CD11 12
Westholm NW11 BS31 47
Westholme Gdns., Ruis. BC33 44
Westholme, Orp. CN54 88
Westhorne Av. SE12 CH47 78
Westhorne Av. SE9 CH47 78
Westhorpe Gdns. NW4 BQ31 46
Westhorpe Rd. SW15 BQ45 65
Westhumble St., Dor. BJ69 119
Westhurst Dr., Chis. CL49 78
Westlake Clo. N13 BY27 38
Westlake Clo., Hayes BE38 54
Lochan Clo.
Westlake Rd., Bex. CP46 79
Blendon Rd.
Westland Av., Horn. CW33 51
Westland Clo., Stai. AX46 73
Douglas Rd.
Westland Clo., Stai. AX46 73
De Havilland Way
Westland Dr., Brom. CG55 88
Westland Dr., Hat. BR17 19
Westland Pl. N1 BZ38 2
Westland Pl. N1 BZ38 57
Westland Rd., Wat. BC23 26
Westland Vw., Grays DD40 71
Westlands Clo., Hayes BC42 63
Westlands Ct., Epsom BN61 103
Dorking Rd.
Westlands Ter. SW12 BW46 76
Gaskarth Rd.
Westlands Way, Oxt. CF67 114
Westlea Av., Wat. BE22 27
Westlea Clo., Brox. CD15 12
Westlea Rd. W7 BJ41 64
Westlea Rd., Brox. CD15 12
Westlea, St.Alb. BM14 10
Westlees Clo., Dor. BK73 119
Westleigh Av. SW15 BP46 75
Westleigh Av., Couls. BV61 104
Westleigh Dr., Brom. CK51 88
Westleigh Gdns., Egh. BM30 37
Westley St. W1 BV39 1
Westley Wood, Welw.G.C. BS7 5
Westlyn Clo., Rain. CV38 60
Westmacott Dr., Felt. BB47 73
Westmead Rd., Sutt. BT56 95
Westmead SW15 BP46 75
Westmead, Epsom BO57 94
Westmead, Ruis. BD35 45
Westmead, Wind. AN45 61
Westmeade Clo., Chsnt. CB18 21
Westmere Dr. NW7 BN27 37
Westmill Ct. N4 BZ34 48
Kings Crescent Est.
Westminster Av., Th.Hth. BY51 86
Westminster Br. Rd. SE1 BX41 4
Westminster Br. Rd. SE1 BX41 66
Westminster Br. SE1 BX41 66
Westminster Br. SW1 BX41 4
Westminster Br. SW1 BX41 66
Westminster Clo., Ilf. CM30 40
Westminster Clo., Tedd. BJ49 74
Cambridge Rd.
Westminster Ct., St.Alb. BG14 9
Westminster Dr. N13 BX28 38
Westminster Gdns., Bark. CN37 58
Westminster Gdns., Ilf. CM30 40
Westminster Ms. W2 BS40 56
Shrewsbury Rd.
Westminster Rd. N9 CB26 39
Westminster Rd. SE17 BZ43 67
Westminster Rd. W7 BH40 54
Westminster Rd., Sutt. BT55 86
Westmoat Clo., Beck. CF50 77
Westmont Rd., Esher BH55 84
Westmoor Gdns., Enf. CC23 30
Westmoor Rd., Enf. CC23 30
Westmoor St. SE7 CJ41 68
Westmore Rd., West. CJ64 106
Westmoreland Av., Horn. CV32 51
Westmoreland Bldgs. EC1 BZ39 2
Westmoreland Bldgs. EC1 BZ39 57
Aldersgate St.
Westmoreland Dr., Sutt. BS57 95
Westmoreland Pl. SW1 BV42 3
Westmoreland Pl. SW1 BV42 66
Westmoreland Pl. W5 BK39 54
Mount Av.
Westmoreland Rd. NW9 BL31 46
Westmoreland Rd. SE17 BZ43 67
Westmoreland Rd., Brom. CG53 88
Westmoreland Rd., Har. BF32 45
Westmoreland St. W1 BV39 1
Westmoreland St. W1 BV39 56
Westmoreland Ter. SW1 BV42 3
Westmoreland Ter. SW1 BV42 66
Westmoreland Way, Mitch. BW52 86
Westmoreland, Epsom BN58 94
Hollymoor La.
Westmorland Av., Well. CN45 68
Westmorland Clo. E12 CJ33 49
Westmorland Clo., Epsom BO58 94
Longmead Rd.
Westmorland Clo., Twick. BJ46 74
Cumberland Clo.
Westmorland Rd. E17 CE32 48
Westmorland Rd. SE17 BZ43 4
Westmorland Rd. SW13 BO44 65
Westmount Rd. SE9 CK44 68
Westmount, Guil. AR71 118
Westoe Rd. N9 CB27 39
Weston Av., E.Mol. BE52 84
Weston Av., Grays CZ42 70
Weston Av., T.Ditt. BH54 84
Weston Av., Wey. AW56 92
Weston Clo., Brwd. DE26 122
Weston Clo., Couls. BX53 104
Weston Ct. N4 BZ34 48
Kings Crescent Est.
Weston Dr., Stan. BJ30 36
Weston Gdns., Islw. BH44 64
Weston Green Rd., T.Ditt. BH54 84
Weston Green Rd., Esher BG54 84
Weston Grn., Dag. CQ35 50
Weston Grn., T.Ditt. BH54 84
Weston Gro., Brom. CG50 78
Weston Gro., Wok. AV61 100
Weston Lea, Lthd. BA66 110
Weston Park Clo., T.Ditt. BH54 84
Weston Pk. N8 BX32 47
Weston Pk., Kings.T. BL51 85
Fairfield W.
Weston Pk., T.Ditt. BH54 84
Weston Rd. W4 BN41 65
Weston Rd., Brom. CG50 78
Weston Rd., Dag. CQ35 50
Weston Rd., Enf. BZ23 30
Weston Rd., Guil. AQ70 109
Weston Rd., T.Ditt. BH54 84
Weston Ri. WC1 BX38 2
Weston Ri. WC1 BX38 56
Weston St. SE1 BZ41 67
Weston Way, Wok. AV61 100
Weston Yd. SE1 BZ41 67
Weston St.
Westover Clo., Sutt. BS58 95
Hulverston Clo.
Westover Hill NW3 BS34 47
Westover Rd. SW18 BT47 76
Westow Hill SE19 CA50 77
Westow St. SE19 CA50 77
Westpole Av., Barn. BV24 29
Westport Rd. E13 CH38 58
Westport St. E1 CC39 57
Westray, Hem.H. AZ14 8
Westrow Dr., Bark. CO35 50
Westrow Gdns., Ilf. CN34 49
Westrow SW15 BQ46 75
Westside NW4 BP30 37
Westview Clo. NW10 BO35 46
Westview Cres. N9 CA26 39
Westview, Hat. BP11 10
Westville Rd. W12 BP41 65
Westville Rd., T.Ditt. BJ54 84
Westward Dr., Amer. AR23 25
Westward Ho., Guil. AS69 118
Westward Rd. E4 CD28 39
Westward Way, Har. BL32 46
Westway Clo. SW20 BP52 85
Westway Gdns., Red. BV69 121
Westway SW20 BP52 85
Westway W10 BQ39 55
Westway W12 BO40 55
Westway, Cat. BZ64 105
Westway, Guil. AP69 118
Westway, Orp. CM53 88
Westways, Epsom BO56 94
Westwell App. SW16 BX50 76
Westwell Rd.
Westwell Clo., Orp. CP54 89
Westwell Rd. SW16 BX50 76
Westwick Clo., Hem.H. BA14 8
Westwick Gdns. W14 BQ41 65
Westwick Gdns., Houns. BC44 63
Westwick Row, Hem.H. BA13 8
Westwood Av. SE19 BZ51 87
Westwood Av., Brwd. DA28 42
Westwood Av., Har. BF35 45
Westwood Av., Wey. AV59 91
Westwood Clo., Amer. AR23 25
Westwood Clo., Brom. CJ51 88
Westwood Clo., Esher BG55 84
Westwood Clo., Pot.B. BS18 20
Westwood Clo., Ruis. AZ32 44
Westwood Gdns. SW13 BO45 65
Westwood Hill SE26 CB49 77
Westwood La., Sid. CO46 79
Westwood La., Well. CN45 68
Westwood Pk. SE23 CB47 77
Westwood Rd. E16 CH40 58
Westwood Rd. SW13 BO45 65
Westwood Rd., Couls. BW62 104
Westwood Rd., Grav. DC50 81
Westwood Rd., Ilf. CN33 49
Westyoke Rd., Fawk. DA55 90
Wetheral Dr., Stan. BJ30 36
Wetherby Clo., Nthlt. BF36 54
Wetherby Gdns. SW5 BS42 3
Wetherby Gdns. SW5 BT42 66
Wetherby Ms. SW5 BS42 3
Wetherby Ms. SW5 BS42 66
Bolton Gdns.
Wetherby Pk., Wey. BB56 92
Wetherby Pl. SW7 BT42 3
Wetherby Pl. SW7 BT42 66
Gloucester Rd.
Wetherby Rd., B.Wd. BL23 28
Wetherby Rd., Enf. BZ22 30
Wetherby Way, Chess. BL57 94
Wetherden St. E17 CD33 48
Wetherell Rd. E9 CC37 57
Wetherill Rd. N10 BV30 38
Wettern Clo., S.Croy. BZ58 96
Purley Oaks Rd.
Wexford Rd. SW12 BU47 76
Wexham Park La., Slou. AR38 52
Wexham Rd., Slou. AQ40 52
Wexham St., Slou. AQ38 52
Wexham Woods, Slou. AR39 52
Wey Av., Cher. AW52 83
Eastern Av.
Wey Barton, Wey. AY60 92
Wey Clo., Wey. AW60 92
Wey Ct., Epsom BN56 94
Wey Ct., Wey. AX58 92
Wey Manor Rd., Wey. AX58 92
Wey Rd., Wey. AY55 83
Wey Side Clo., Wey. AY59 92
Weybank, Wok. AY61 101
Weybourne Pl., S.Croy. BZ58 96
Weybourne St. SW18 BT48 76
Weybridge Pk., Wey. AZ56 92
Weybridge Rd., Th.Hth. BY52 86
Weybridge Rd., Wey. AX55 83
Weybridge St. SW11 BV44 66
Culvert Rd.
Weybrook Dr., Guil. AT68 109
Weydon Clo. SW19 BR47 75
Weydown Clo., Guil. AQ68 109
Weydown La., Guil. AQ68 109
Cumberland Av.
Weyhill Rd. E1 CB39 57
Holly St.
Weylea Av., Guil. AT69 118
Weylond Rd., Dag. CQ34 50
Weyman Rd. SE3 CJ44 68
Weymarks, The N17 BZ29 39
Weymead Clo., Cher. AX54 83
Weymede, Wey. AY59 92
Weymouth Av. NW7 BO28 37
Weymouth Av. W5 BK41 64
Weymouth Ct., Sutt. BS57 95
Weymouth Dr., Hayes BB38 53
Weymouth Ms. W1 BV39 1
Weymouth Ms. W1 BV39 56
Weymouth St. W1 BV39 1
Weymouth St. W1 BV39 56
Weymouth St., Hem.H. AX15 8
Weymouth Ter. E2 CA37 2
Weymouth Ter. E2 CA37 57
Weymouth Wk., Stan. BJ29 36
Weyside Gdns., Guil. AR69 118
Weyside Rd., Guil. AQ70 118
Weystone Rd., Wey. AY56 92
Whadcote St. N4 BY34 47
Whalebone Av., Rom. CQ32 50
Whalebone Ct. EC2 BZ39 2
Copthall Clo.
Whalebone Gro., Rom. CQ32 50
Whalebone La. E15 CG36 58
Whalebone La. N., Rom. CQ29 41
Whalebone La. S., Dag. CQ32 50
Whalebone La. S., Rom. CQ32 50
Whaley Rd., Pot.B. BT20 20
Wharf La., Berk. AO11 7
Wharf La., Rick. AY26 35
Wharf La., Ripley AX62 101
Wharf La., Send AU65 100
Wharf La., Twick. BJ47 74
Wharf Pl. E2 CB37 57
Wharf Rd. E15 CF37 57
Wharf Rd. NW1 BW37 56
Wharf Rd. N1 BZ37 2
Wharf Rd. N1 BZ37 57
Wharf Rd., Brox. CD15 12
Wharf Rd., Brwd. DB27 42
Wharf Rd., Enf. CD25 30
Wharf Rd., Grav. CJ46 81
Wharf Rd., Grays DC43 71
Wharf Rd., Guil. AR70 118
Wharf Rd., Hem.H. AW14 8
Wharf Rd., Stai. AR47 72
Wharf St. E16 CG39 58
Wharfdale Rd. N1 BX37 2
Wharfdale Rd. N1 BX37 56
Wharfedale Ct. E5 CC35 48
Clapton Park Est.
Wharfedale Gdns., Th.Hth. BX52 86
Wharfedale Rd. Dart. CY47 80
Teesdale Rd.
Wharfedale St. SW10 BS42 66
Wharfedale, Hem.H. AY12 8
Wharfside EC4 BZ40 4
Wharfside EC4 BZ40 57
Wharfside Rd. E16 CG39 58
Barking Rd.
Wharley Hook, Harl. CN12 13
Wharncliffe Dr., Sthl. BG40 54
Wharncliffe Gdns. NW8 BT38 1
Wharncliffe Gdns. NW8 BT38 56
St. Johns Wood Rd.
Wharncliffe Gdns. SE25 CA51 87
Wharncliffe Rd. SE25 BZ51 87
Wharncliffe St. E2 CC37 57
Royston St.
Wharton Clo. NW10 BO36 55
Wharton Rd., Brom. CH51 88
Wharton St. WC1 BX38 2
Wharton St. WC1 BX38 56
Whateley Rd. SE20 CC50 77
Whateley Rd. SE22 CA46 77
Whateley Rd., Guil. AQ68 109
Whatley Av. SW20 BQ52 85
Whatman Rd. SE23 CC47 77
Whatmore Clo., Houns. AW46 73
Wheat Barn, Welw.G.C. BS7 5
Wheat Clo., St.Alb. BJ11 9
Wheat Knoll, Ken. BZ61 105
Hayes La.
Wheat Leys, St.Alb. BK12 9
Wheat St. W1 BV39 1
Wheat St. W1 BV39 56
Marylebone St.
Wheatash Rd., Wey. AW55 83
Wheatbutts, The, Eton AM42 61
Common Rd.
Wheatcroft, Chsnt. CB17 21
Wheatfield Way, Kings.T. BL51 85
Wheatfield, Hat. BP12 10
Crop Common
Wheatfields, Enf. CD23 30
Wheathill Rd. SE20 CB51 87
Wheatland Rd., Slou. AQ41 62
Wheatlands Rd. SW17 BV48 76
Wheatlands, Houns. BF43 64
Wheatley Clo. NW4 BP30 37
Wheatley Clo., Saw. CP6 6

Wheatley Clo., Welw.G.C. BS 9 5
Wheatley Cres., Hayes BC40 53
Wheatley Gdns. N9 CA27 39
Wheatley Rd., Islw. BH45 64
Wheatley Rd., Welw.G.C. BR 8 5
Wheatley St. W1 BV39 56
Marylebone St.
Wheatley Terrace Rd., Erith CT43 69
Wheatley Way, Ger.Cr. AS29 34
Wheatsheaf Clo., Cher. AU57 91
Wheatsheaf Clo., Nthlt. BE35 45
Wheatsheaf Clo., Wok. AS61 100
Wheatsheaf Hill, Halstead CQ58 98
Wheatsheaf Hill, Ide Hill CQ69 116
Wheatsheaf La. SW6 BQ43 65
Holyport Rd.
Wheatsheaf La. SW8 BX43 66
Wheatsheaf La., Stai. AV50 72
Wheatsheaf Rd., Rom. CT32 50
Wheatstone Rd. W10 BR39 55
Wheel Farm Dr., Dag. CS34 50
Wheeler Av., Oxt. CF68 114
Wheeler Gdns. N1 BX37 2
Wheelers Clo., Wal.Abb. CG14 13
Wheelers Cross, Bark. CM37 58
Wheelers Dr., Ruis. BA32 44
Wheelers Farm Gdns., Epp. CR16 23
Wheelers La., Bet. BM71 120
Wheelers La., Brwd. CX24 33
Wheelers La., Epsom BM60 94
Wheelers La., Hem.H. AY14 8
Wheelers Orchard, Ger.Cr. AS29 34
Wheelers, Epp. CN18 22
Wheelwright Clo., Bush. BF26 36
Fidler Pl.
Wheelwright St. N7 BX36 56
Whelan Way, Wall. BW55 86
Wheler St. E1 CA38 2
Wheler St. E1 CA38 57
Whellock Rd. W4 BO41 65
Whenman Av., Bex. CS48 79
Whernside Clo. SE28 CP40 59
Wherwell Rd., Guil. AR71 118
Whetstone Clo. N20 BT27 38
Whetstone Pk. WC2 BX39 2
Whetstone Pk. WC2 BX39 56
Gate St.
Whetstone Rd. SE3 CJ44 68
Whewell Rd. N19 BX34 47
Whichcote Gdns., Chesh. AO20 16
Whichcote St. SE1 BY48 56
Mepham St.
Whidborne Clo. SE8 CE44 67
Cliff Ter.
Whidborne St. WC1 BX38 2
Whidborne St. WC1 BX38 56
Whimbrel Clo. SE28 CP40 59
Whinchat Rd. SE28 CM41 68
Whinfell Clo. SW16 BW49 76
Whinfell Way, Grav. DJ49 81
Whinyates Rd. SE9 CK45 68
Whipley Clo., Guil. AT68 109
Weybrook Dr.
Whippendale Clo., Orp. CO51 89
Whippendale Way, Orp. CO51 89
Whippendell Hill, Kings L. AX18 17
Whippendell Rd., Wat. BB25 26
Whipps Cross Rd. E11 CF32 48
Whiskin St. EC1 BY38 2
Whiskin St. EC1 BY38 56
Gloucester Way
Whisper Wood, Rick. AW24 26
Whisperwood Clo., Har. BH29 36
College Hill Rd.
Whistler Gdns., Edg. BL30 37
Whistler St. N5 BY35 47
Whistler Wk. SW10 BT43 66
Worlds End
Whistlers Av. SW11 BT43 66
Whiston Rd. E2 CA37 2
Whiston Rd. E2 CA37 57
Whitakers Way, Loug. CK23 31
Whitbread Clo. N17 CB30 39
Whitbread Rd. SE4 CD45 67
Whitburn Rd. SE13 CE45 67
Whitby Av. NW10 BM38 55
Whitby Av., Brwd. DE29 122
Whitby Clo., West. CH62 106
Whitby Ct. N7 BX35 47
Parkhurst Rd.
Whitby Gdns. NW9 BM31 46
Whitby Gdns., Sutt. BT55 86
Whitby Rd. SE18 CK42 68
Whitby Rd., Har. BG34 45
Whitby Rd., Ruis. BC34 44
Whitby Rd., Slou. AO40 52
Whitby Rd., Sutt. BT55 86
Whitby St. E1 CA38 2
Whitcher Clo. SE14 CD43 67
Chubworthy St.
Whitcher Pl. NW1 BW36 56
Rochester Rd.
Whitchurch Av., Edg. BL29 37
Whitchurch Clo., Edg. BL29 37
Whitchurch Gdns., Edg BL29 37
Whitchurch La., Edg. BK29 36
Whitchurch Rd. W11 BO40 55
Whitchurch Rd., Rom. CV28 42
Whitcomb St. WC2 BW40 3
Whitcomb St. WC2 BW40 56
White Acre NW9 BO30 37
White Adder Way E14 CE42 67
Spindrift Av.
White Av., Grav. DF48 81
White Beam Way, Tad. BP64 103
White Beams, Hat. BP14 10
Southdown Rd.
White Beams, St.Alb. BG17 18
White Bear Clo. NW3 BT35 47
New End Sq.
White Cft., Swan. CT51 89
White Church La. E1 CB39 57
White Church Pass. E1 CB39 2
White Church La.
White City Clo. W12 BQ40 55
South Africa Rd.
White City Est. W12 BP40 55
White City Rd. W12 BP40 55
White Clo., Slou. AO40 61
White Conduit St. N1 BY37 2
White Conduit St. N1 BY37 56
White Craig Clo., Pnr. BF28 36
White Craig Clo., Stan. BL31 46
Everton Dr.
White Cross Row, Rich. BK46 74
Water La.
White Downs, Dor. BC73 119
White Friars, Sev. CU67 116
White Gate Gdns., Har. BH29 36
White Gates Clo., Rick. AZ24 26
White Gates, Warl. CB63 105
White Gdns., Dag. CR36 59
White Hands Clo., Hodd. CD12 12
White Hart Clo., Hayes BA43 63
White Hart Clo., Sev. CV68 117
White Hart Dr., Hem.H. AY14 8
White Hart La. N17 BX30 38
White Hart La. N22 BZ30 39
White Hart La. NW10 BO36 55
Church Rd.
White Hart La. SW13 BO44 65
White Hart La., Brwd. DB27 42
Chestnut Gro.
White Hart La., Hem.H. AS17 16
White Hart La., Rom. CR30 41
White Hart Meadows, Wok. AX64 101
White Hart Rd. SE18 CN42 68
White Hart Rd., Hem.H. AZ14 8
White Hart Rd., Slou. AO41 61
White Hart St. SE11 BY42 4
White Hart St. SE11 BY42 66
White Hart Wood, Sev. CV68 117
White Hart Yd. SE1 BZ40 4
White Hart Yd. SE1 BZ40 57
Borough High St.
White Heart Av., Uxb. BA39 53
White Hedge Dr., St.Alb. BG12 9
White Hill Clo., Chesh. AO18 16
White Hill La., Red. BZ67 114
White Hill Rd., Berk. AQ14 7
White Hill, Berk. AR15 7
White Hill, Chesh. AO18 16
White Hill, Couls. BU65 104
White Hill, Croy. BZ58 96
White Hill, Hem.H. AV14 7
White Hill, Rick. AZ29 35
White Hill, Welw. BP 5 5
White Ho. SW11 BT44 66
White Horse Alley EC1 BY39 56
Cowcross St.
White Horse Dr., Epsom BN60 94
White Horse Dr., Guil. AT70 118
White Horse Hill, Chis. CK49 78
White Horse La. E1 CC38 57
White Horse La., Wok. AX63 101
White Horse Rd. E1 CD39 57
White Horse Rd. E6 CK38 58
White Horse Rd., Wind. AL45 61
White Horse St. W1 BV40 3
White Horse St. W1 BV40 56
White Horse Yd. EC2 BZ39 57
Coleman St.
White House Dr., Stan. BK28 36
White House La., Guil. AR68 109
White House Rd., Sev. CT68 116
White Kennett St. E1 CA39 2
White Kennett St. E1 CA39 57
White Knights Rd., Wey. BA57 92
White Knobs Way, Cat. CB66 114
White La., Guil. AU71 118
White La., Oxt. CH65 106
White Lion Clo., Amer. AQ23 25
White Lion Ct. EC3 BZ39 2
Cornhill
White Lion Hill EC4 BY40 4
White Lion Hill EC4 BY40 56
White Lion Rd., Amer. AP23 25
White Lion Sq., Hat. BP12 10
The Common
White Lion St. EC1 BZ38 2
Fann St.
White Lion St. N1 BY37 2
White Lion St. N1 BY37 56
White Lion St., Hem.H. AX15 8
White Lodge Clo. NW3 BT32 47
White Lodge Clo., Sutt. BT57 95
White Lodge Est. SE19 BZ50 77
White Lyons Rd., Brwd. DB27 42
Kings Rd.
White Orchard N20 BR26 37
White Orchards, Stan. BJ28 36
White Post Field, Saw. CP 6 6
White Post Hill, Farn. CX54 90
White Post La. E9 CD36 57
White Post La. SE13 CE45 67
Overcliff Rd.
White Post St. SE15 CC43 67
White Rd. E15 CG36 58
White Rd., Bet. & Tad. BM70 120
White Rose La., Wok. AS62 100
White Shack La., Wat. AY22 26
White St., Sthl. BD41 64
White Stubbs La., Brox. BZ14 12
White Stubbs La., Hert. BX13 11
White Swan Ms. W4 BO43 65
Bennett St.
White Way, Lthd. BF66 111
White Wood Rd., Berk. AQ13 7
Whiteadder Way E14 CE42 67
Spindrift Av.
Whitear Wk. E15 CF36 57
Whitebarn La., Dag. CR37 59
Whitebeam Av., Brom. CL54 88
Whitebeam Clo. SW9 BX43 66
Whitebeam Tower E17 CD31 48
Oatland Ri.
Whitebridge Clo., Felt. BB46 73
Whitebroom Rd., Hem.H. AV12 7
Whitebutts Rd., Ruis. BD34 45
Whitechapel High St. E1 CA39 2
Whitechapel High St. E1 CA39 57
Whitechapel Rd.
Whitechapel Rd. E1 CB39 2
Whitechapel Rd. E1 CB39 57
Whitechurch La. E1 CB39 2
Whitecote Rd., Sthl. BF39 54
Whitecroft Clo., Beck. CF52 87
Whitecroft Way, Beck. CF53 87
Whitecroft, St.Alb. BJ15 9
Whitecross Pl. EC2 BZ39 2
Whitecross Pl. EC2 BZ39 57
Whitecross St. EC1 BZ38 2
Whitecross St. EC1 BZ38 57
Whitecross St. EC2 BZ39 2
Whitecross St. EC2 BZ39 57
Whitefield Av. NW2 BQ33 46
Whitefield Av., Pur. BY61 104
Whitefield Clo. SW18 BR46 75
Whitefield Clo., Orp. CP52 89
Whitefields Rd., Chsnt. CC17 21
Whitefoot La., Brom. CF49 77
Whitefoot Ter., Brom. CG48 78
Whiteford Rd., Slou. AP39 52
Whitefriars Av., Har. BG30 36
Whitefriars St. EC4 BY39 2
Whitefriars St. EC4 BY39 56
Whitegates Av., Sev. CZ57 99
Whitegates, Wok. AS63 100
Loop Rd.
Whitehall Clo., Chig. CO27 41
Whitehall Clo., Uxb. AX37 53
Whitehall Clo., Wal.Abb. CG14 13
Whitehall Cres., Chess. BK56 93
Whitehall Ct. SW1 BX40 4
Whitehall Ct. SW1 BX40 56
Whitehall E7 CH35 49
Forest St.
Whitehall Farm La., Vir.W. AS52 82
Whitehall Gdns. E4 CG26 40
Whitehall Gdns. SW1 BX40 4
Whitehall Gdns. W3 BM40 55
Whitehall Gdns. W4 BM43 65
Whitehall La., Buck.H. CH27 40
Whitehall La., Egh. AS50 72
Whitehall La., Erith CT44 69
Whitehall La., Grays DE43 71
Whitehall La., Reig. BR72 120
Whitehall La., Stai. AT46 72
Whitehall Park Rd. W4 BM43 65
Whitehall Pk. N19 BW33 47
Whitehall Pl. E7 CH35 49
Kuhn Way
Whitehall Pl. SW1 BX40 4
Whitehall Pl. SW1 BX40 56
Whitehall Rd. E4 CG27 40
Whitehall Rd. W7 BJ41 64
Whitehall Rd., Brom. CJ53 88
Whitehall Rd., Grays DE42 71
Whitehall Rd., Har. BH33 45
Whitehall Rd., Th.Hth. BY53 86
Whitehall Rd., Uxb. AX37 53
Whitehall Rd., Wdf.Grn. CG27 40
Whitehall St. N17 CA29 39
Whitehall SW1 BX40 4
Whitehall SW1 BX40 56
Whitehart Rd., Orp. CO54 89
Whitehart Slip, Brom. CH51 88
Whitehaven Clo., Brom. CH52 88
Whitehaven St. NW8 BU38 1
Whitehaven St. NW8 BU38 56
Whitehaven, Slou. AP40 52
Montague Rd.
Whitehead Clo. SW18 BT47 76
Whitehead Clo., Dart. CV48 80
Whiteheads Gro. SW3 BU42 3
Whiteheads Gro. SW3 BU42 66
Whiteheath Av., Ruis. BA33 44
Whitehill Ct., Berk. AR12 7
Whitehill
Whitehill La., Grav. DH48 81
Whitehill La., Wok. BA65 101
Whitehill Rd., Dart. CU46 79
Whitehill Rd., Grav. DH48 81
Whitehill Rd., Long. DB51 90
Whitehill, Berk. AR12 7
Whitehills Rd., Loug. CL24 31
Whitehorn Gdns., Croy. CB55 87
Whitehorn Gdns., Enf. BZ25 30
Whitehorse La. SE25 BZ52 87
Whitehorse La., St.Alb. BK16 18
Whitehorse Rd., Croy. BZ54 87
Whitehouse Av., B.Wd. BM24 28
Whitehouse Clo., Ger.Cr. AS29 34
Whitehouse Ct. N14 BW27 38
Whitehouse Est. E10 CF32 48
Whitehouse La., Enf. BZ23 30
Whitehouse La., Wat. BC16 17
Whitehouse Way, Iver AU38 52
Whitehouse Way, N14 BV27 38
Whiteland Av., Rick. AT24 25
Whitelands Way, Rom. CV30 42
Whitelands, Brwd. DB21 33
Whiteleaf Rd., Hem.H. AX15 8
Whiteledges W13 BK39 54
Whitelegg Rd. E13 CG37 58
Whiteley Rd. SE19 BZ49 77
Whiteley Way, Felt. BF48 74
Whiteley, Wind. AM43 61
Whiteleys Cotts. W14 BR42 65
Whitemore Rd., Guil. AR68 109
Whiteoak Dr., Beck. CF51 87
Whiteoaks La., Grnf. BG38 54
Whitepost Hill, Red. BU70 121
Whites Av., Ilf. CN32 49
Whites Grounds Est. SE1 CA41 4
Whites Grounds Est. SE1 CA41 67
Whites Grounds SE1 CA41 4
Whites Grounds SE1 CA41 67
Whites La., Slou. AQ43 62
Whites Row E1 CA39 2
Whites Row E1 CA39 57
Whites Sq. SW4 BW45 66
Nelsons Row
Whitestile Rd., Brent. BK42 64
Whitestone La. NW3 BT34 47
Heath St.
Whitestone Wk. NW3 BT34 47
North End Way
Whitestone Wk., Hem.H. AW12 8
Whitethorn Av., Couls. BV61 104
Whitethorn Av., West.Dr. AY40 53
Whitethorn Gdns., Enf. BZ25 30
Whitethorn Gdns., Horn. CV32 51
Whitethorn Pl., West.Dr. AY40 53
Whitethorn Av.
Whitethorn St. E3 CE38 57
Whitethorn, Welw.G.C. BS 8 5
Whitewaits, Harl. CN10 6
Whitewebbs La., Enf. CA21 30
Whitewebbs Rd., Enf. BY21 29
Whitewebbs Way, Orp. CN51 88
Whitewood Cotts., West. CJ63 106
Whitfield Pl. W1 BW38 1
Whitfield Pl. W1 BW38 56
Whitfield St.
Whitfield Rd. E6 CJ36 58
Whitfield Rd. SE3 CF44 67
Whitfield Rd., Bexh. CQ43 69
Whitfield St. W1 BW38 1
Whitfield St. W1 BW38 56
Whitfield Way, Rick. AV26 34
Whitford Gdns., Mitch. BU52 86
Whitgift Av., S.Croy. BY56 95
Whitgift St. SE11 BX42 4
Whitgift St. SE11 BX42 66
Whitgift St., Croy. BZ55 87
Whiting Av., Bark. CL36 58
Whiting Hill Est., Barn. BP25 28
Whitings Rd., Barn. BQ25 28
Whitings Way E6 CL39 58
Whitland Rd., Cars. BT54 86
Whitlars Dr., Kings L. AY17 17
Whitley Clo., Stai. AY46 73
Whitley Rd. N17 CA30 39
Whitley Rd., Hodd. CE11 12
Whitlock Dr. SW18 BR47 75
Whitman Rd. E3 CD38 57
Whitmoor La., Guil. AR66 109
Whitmore Av., Grays DD40 71
Whitmore Clo. N11 BV28 38
High Rd.
Whitmore Est. N1 CA37 2
Whitmore Gdns. NW10 BQ37 55
Whitmore Rd. N1 CA37 2
Whitmore Rd. N1 CA37 57
Whitmore Rd., Beck. CD52 87
Whitmore Rd., Har. BF33 45
Whitmores Clo., Epsom BN61 103
Whitnell Way SW15 BQ46 75
Whitney Av., Ilf. CJ31 49
Whitney Rd. E10 CE33 48
Whitney Wk., Sid. CQ50 79
Maidstone Rd.
Whitstable Clo., Beck. CD51 87
Whitstable Clo., Ruis. BB34 44
Chichester Av.
Whitta Rd. E12 CJ35 49
Whittaker Av., Rich. BK46 74
Whittaker Rd. E6 CJ36 58
Whittaker Rd., Sutt. BR55 85
Whittaker St. SW1 BV42 3
Whittaker St. SW1 BV42 66
Bourne St.
Whittell Gdns. SE26 CC48 77
Whittenham Clo., Slou. AQ40 52
Whittingstall Rd. SW6 BR44 65
Whittingstall Rd., Hodd. CE11 12
Whittington Av. EC3 CA39 2
Leadenhall St.
Whittington Av., Hayes BB39 53
Whittington Ct. N2 BU32 47
Whittington Rd. N22 BX29 38
Whittington Rd., Brwd. DE25 122
Whittington Way, Pnr. BE32 45
Whittle Clo., Sthl. BF39 54
Whittle Rd., Houns. BD43 64
Whittlebury Clo., Cars. BU57 95
Whittlesea Path, Har. BG30 36
Whittlesea Rd., Har. BG29 36
Whittlesey St. SE1 BY40 4
Whittlesey St. SE1 BY40 56
Whitton Av. E., Grnf. BH35 45
Whitton Av. W., Grnf. BF35 45
Whitton Av. W., Nthlt. BF35 45
Whitton Clo., Grnf. BJ36 54
Whitton Dene, Houns. BF46 74
Whitton Dr., Grnf. BJ36 54
Whitton Manor Rd., Islw. BG46 74
Whitton Rd., Houns. BF45 64
Whitton Rd., Twick. BH46 74
Whitton Waye, Houns. BF46 74
Whitton Wk. E3 CE37 58
Whitwell Rd. E13 CH38 58
Whitwell Rd., Wat. BD21 27
Whitworth Rd. SE18 CL43 68
Whitworth Rd. SE25 CA52 87
Whitworth St. SE10 CG42 68
Whopshot Av., Wok. AR61 100
Whopshot Clo., Wok. AR61 100
Whopshot Dr., Wok. AR61 100
Whorlton Rd. SE15 CB45 67
Whybridge Clo., Rain. CT37 59
Whymark Av. N22 BY31 47
Whytecliffe Rd., Pur. BY59 95
Whytecroft, Houns. BD43 64
Whyteleafe Hill, Whyt. CA63 105
Whyteleafe Rd., Cat. CA63 105
Whyteville Rd. E7 CH36 58
Wick La. E3 CD36 57
Wick La., Egh. AP50 72
Wick Rd. E9 CC36 57
Wick Rd., Egh. AQ51 82
Wick Rd., Tedd. BJ50 74
Wickenden Rd., Sev. CV64 108
Wicker St. E1 CB39 57
Wickers Oake SE19 CA49 77
Wickersley Rd. SW11 BV44 66
Wicket Rd., Grnf. BJ38 54
Wicket, The, Croy. CE56 96
Wickets Way, Ilf. CN29 40
Wickford Clo., Rom. CW28 42
Wickford Dr., Rom. CW28 42
Wickford St. E1 CC38 57
Wickford Way E17 CC31 48
Wickham Av., Croy. CD55 87
Wickham Av., Sutt. BQ56 94
Wickham Chase, W.Wick. CF54 87
Wickham Clo., Enf. CB24 30
Wickham Clo., N.Mal. BO53 85
Wickham Clo., Uxb. AX30 35
Wickham Cres., W.Wick. CF55 87
Wickham Ct. Rd., W.Wick. CF55 87
Wickham Field, Sev. CT61 107
Wickham Gdns. SE4 CD45 67
Wickham La. SE2 CO42 69
Wickham La., Egh. AT50 72
Wickham Rd. E4 CF29 39
Wickham Rd. SE4 CD45 67
Wickham Rd., Beck. CE51 87
Wickham Rd., Croy. CC55 87
Wickham Rd., Grays DH41 71
Wickham Rd., Har. BG30 36
Wickham St. SE11 BX42 4
Wickham St. SE11 BX42 66
Wickham St., Well. CN44 68
Wickham Way, Beck. CF52 87
Wickhurst Rd., Sev. CT69 116
Wickliffe Av. N3 BR30 37
Wickliffe Gdns., Wem. BM34 46
Wicklow St. WC1 BX38 2
Wicklow St. WC1 BX38 56
Wicks Clo. SE9 CJ49 78
Dunkery Rd.
Wicks Rd., Rick. AU28 34
Wicksteed Clo., Bex. CS48 79
Wickwood St. SE5 BY44 66
Wid Clo., Brwd. DE25 122
Widdenham Rd. N7 BX35 47
Widdial Grn., Welw.G.C. BS 8 5
Widford Rd.
Widdicombe Av., Har. BE34 45
Widdin St. E15 CF36 57
Wide Gates E1 CA39 2
Wide Way, Mitch. BW52 86
Widecombe Clo., Rom. CV30 42
Widecombe Ct. N2 BT32 47
Widecombe Gdns., Ilf. CK31 49
Widecombe Rd. SE9 CK48 78
Widecombe Way N2 BT32 47
Widecroft Rd., Iver AV39 52
Widegate St. E1 CA39 57
Sandys Row
Widenham Clo., Pnr. BD32 45
Widford Rd., Welw.G.C. BS 8 5
Widford Ter., Hem.H. AZ10 8
Elstree Rd.
Widgeon Way, Wat. BE22 27
Widley Rd. W9 BS38 56
Widmore Dr., Hem.H. AZ12 8
Widmore Lodge Rd., Brom. CJ51 88
Widmore Rd., Brom. CH51 88
Widmore Rd., Uxb. AZ38 53
Widworthy Hayes, Brwd. DD26 122
Wieland Rd., Nthwd. BC29 35
Wigan Ho. E5 CB33 48
Wigeon Path SE28 CM41 68
Whinchat Rd.
Wiggenhall Rd., Wat. BC24 26
Wiggie La., Red. BV69 121
Wiggington Av., Wem. BM36 55
Wiggins La., Rich. BK48 74
Wiggins Mead NW9 BO30 37
Wightman Rd. N4 BY31 47
Wightman Rd. N8 BY31 47
Wigley Bush La., Brwd. CZ27 42
Wigley Rd., Felt. BD48 74
Wigmore Pl. W1 BV39 1
Wigmore Pl. W1 BV39 56
Wigmore Rd., Cars. BT55 86
Wigmore St. W1 BV39 1
Wigmore St. W1 BV39 56
Wigmore Wk., Cars. BT55 86
Wigmores N., Welw.G.C. BQ 7 5
Wigmores S., Welw.G.C. BQ 8 5
Wigram Rd. E11 CJ32 49
Wigram Sq. E17 CF31 48
Wigston Rd. E13 CH38 58
Wigton Gdns., Stan. BL30 37
Wigton Pl. SE11 BY42 66
Milver St.
Wigton Rd. E17 CD30 39
Wigton Rd., Rom. CW28 42
Wigton Way, Rom. CW28 42
Wilberforce Rd. N4 BY34 47
Wilberforce Rd. NW9 BP32 46
Wilberforce Way SW19 BQ50 75
Wilberforce Way, Grav. DH49 81
Wilbraham Pl. SW1 BU42 3
Wilbraham Pl. SW1 BV42 66
Wilbury Av., Sutt. BR58 94
Wilbury Rd., Wok. AR62 100
Wilbury Way N18 BZ28 39
Wilby Ms. W11 BR40 55
Wilby Rd. SE5 BZ44 67
Grove La.
Wilcot Av., Wat. BE26 36
Wilcox Clo., B.Wd. BN23 28
Wilcox Gdns., Shep. AY52 83
Wilcox Pl. SW1 BW41 66
Victoria St.
Wilcox Rd. SW8 BX43 66
Wilcox Rd., Sutt. BS56 95
Brandon Rd.
Wilcox Rd., Tedd. BG49 74
Wild Acres, Wey. AX59 92
Wild Ct. WC2 BX39 2
Wild Ct. WC2 BX39 56
Wild Goose Dr. SE14 CC44 67
Wild Grn. N., Slou. AT42 62
Verney Rd.

Wild Grn. S., Slou. AT42 62
Swabey Rd.
Wild Hatch NW11 BS32 47
Wild Oaks Clo., Nthwd. BB29 35
Wild St. WC2 BX39 2
Wild St. WC2 BX39 56
Wildcroft Dr., Dor. BK73 119
Wildcroft Gdns., Edg. BK29 36
Wildcroft Manor SW15 BQ47 75
Wildcroft Rd.
Wildcroft Rd. SW15 BQ47 75
Wilde Clo. E8 CB37 2
Wilde Clo. E8 CB37 57
Wilde Clo., Til. DH44 71
Coleridge Rd.
Wilde Pl. N13 BY29 38
Medesenge Way
Wilde Pl. SW18 BT47 76
Wilderness Rd., Chis. CL50 78
Wilderness Rd., Guil. AP71 118
Wilderness Rd., Oxt. CG68 115
Wilderness, The, Berk. AR13 7
Wilderness, The, Hmptn. BF49 74
Park Rd.
Wildernesse Av., Sev. CW64 108
Wildernesse Mt., Sev. CV64 108
Wilders Clo., Wok. AR62 100
Wilderton Rd. N16 CA33 48
Wildfell Rd. SE6 CE47 77
Wildhill Rd., Hat. BS14 11
Wilds Rents SE1 BZ41 4
Wilds Rents SE1 CA41 67
Wildwood Av., St.Alb. BE18 18
Wildwood Clo. SE12 CG47 78
Wildwood Clo., Lthd. BB66 110
Wildwood Clo., Wok. AV61 100
Wildwood Ct., Ken. BZ61 105
Hawkhirst Rd.
Wildwood Gro. NW3 BS33 47
North End Rd.
Wildwood Rd. NW11 BT33 47
Wildwood Ri. NW11 BT33 47
Wildwood, Nthwd. BA29 35
Wilford Clo., Enf. BZ24 30
Little Park Gdns.
Wilford Clo., Nthwd. BA29 35
Wilford Rd., Slou. AS42 62
Wilfred Av., Rain. CU39 59
Wilfred Owen Clo. SW19 BT50 76
Tennyson Rd.
Wilfred St. SW1 BW41 3
Wilfred St. SW1 BW41 66
Wilfred St., Wok. AR62 100
Wilfred Turney Est. W6 BQ41 65
Wilfrid Gdns. W3 BN39 55
Wilhelmina Av., Couls. BW63 104
Wilk Pl. N13 BY29 38
Wolves La.
Wilkers Oak SE19 CA49 77
Glebehurst Coppice
Wilkes Rd., Brwd. DE25 122
Wilkes St. E1 CA39 2
Wilkie Way SE22 CB47 77
Wilkin St. Ms. NW5 BV36 56
Wilkin St.
Wilkin St. NW5 BV36 56
Wilkins Clo., Hayes BB42 63
Wilkins Grn. La., St.Alb. BM13 10
Wilkins Grn. La., Hat. BN13 10
Wilkins Way, West. CO65 107
Wilkinson Clo., Dart. CW45 70
Wilkinson Rd. E16 CJ39 58
Wilkinson St. SW8 BX43 66
Wilkinson Way W4 BN41 65
Wilks Pl. N1 CA37 2
Wilks Pl. N1 CA37 57
Hoxton St.
Will Crooks Gdns. SE9 CJ45 68
Willan Rd. N17 BZ30 39
Willan Wall E16 CG40 58
Peto St. N.
Willard Est. SW8 BV45 66
Willcocks Clo., Chess. BL55 85
Willcott Rd. W3 BM40 55
Willenhall Av., Barn. BT25 29
Willenhall Dr., Hayes BB40 53
Willenhall Rd. SE18 CL42 68
Willersley Av., Orp. CM55 88
Willersley Av., Sid. CN47 78
Willersley Clo., Sid. CN47 78
Willes Rd. NW5 BV36 56
Willesden Grn. NW2 BQ36 55
Willesden La. NW2 BQ36 55
Willesden La. NW6 BQ36 55
Willet Way SE16 CB42 67
Egan Way
Willets La., Uxb. AV35 43
Willett Clo., Nthlt. BD38 54
Broomcroft Av.
Willett Clo., Orp. CN53 88
Willett Clo., Th.Hth. BY53 86
Willett Rd., Th.Hth. BY53 86
Willett Way, Orp. CM53 88
Willey Broom La., Cat. BY66 113
Willey Farm La., Cat. BZ66 114
Willey La., Cat. BZ66 114
William Barefoot Dr. SE9 CK49 78
William Bonney Est. SW4 BW45 66
William Booth Rd. SE20 CB51 77
William Carey Way, Har. BH32 45
William Clo., Rom. CS30 41
William Cory Prom., Erith CT42 69
High St.
William Covell Clo., Enf. BX22 29
William Ct., Hem.H. AX15 8
King Edward St.
William Ellis Clo., Wind. AQ46 72
William Gdns. SW15 BP46 75
William Hayne Gdns. Wor.Pk. BQ55 85
William IV St. WC2 BX40 4
William IV St. WC2 BX40 56
William Margrie Clo. SE15 CB44 67
Moncrieff Est.
William Morley Clo. E6 CJ37 58
William Morris Clo. E17 CD31 48
William Morris Ho. W6 BQ43 65
William Ms. SW1 BU41 66
William Ms. SW1 BU41 3
William Parnell Ho. SW6 BS44 66
William Rd. NW1 BV38 1
William Rd. NW1 BV38 56
William Rd. SW19 BR50 75
William Rd., Cat. BZ64 105
William Rd., Guil. AR70 118
William Rd., Sutt. BT56 95
William Russell Ct., Wok. AP62 100
William St. E10 CE32 48
William St. E15 CF36 57
William St. N12 BT28 38
Lodge La.
William St. N17 CA29 39
William St. SW1 BU41 3
William St. SW1 BU41 66
William St., Bark. CM36 58
William St., Berk. AR13 7
William St., Bush. BD24 27
William St., Cars. BU55 86
William St., Grav. DG47 81
William St., Grays DD43 71
William St., Slou. AP40 52
William St., Wind. AO44 61
William Willison Est. SW19 BR47 75
Williams Av. E17 CD30 39
Williams Bldgs. E2 CC38 57
Malcolm Pl.
Williams Gro. N22 BY30 38
Williams La. SW14 BN45 65
Williams La., Mord. BT53 86
Williams Rd. W13 BJ40 54
Williams Rd., Sthl. BE42 64
Williams Ter., Croy. BY57 95
Williams Ter., Well. CN44 68
Williams Way, Rad. BJ21 27
Williams Wk., Guil. AQ68 109
Williamson Clo. SE10 CG42 68
Lenthorpe Rd.
Williamson St. N7 BX35 47
Williamson Way NW7 BR29 37
Willifield Way NW11 BR31 46
Willingale Clo., Wdf.Grn. CJ29 40
Willingale Clo., Brwd. DF25 122
Fairview Av.
Willingale Clo., Loug. CM23 31
Willingale Rd., Willingale DB15 15
Willingale Rd., Fyfield CZ14 15
Willingale Rd., Ing. DC16 24
Willingale Rd., Loug. CM24 31
Willingdon Rd. N22 BY30 38
Willinghall Clo., Wal.Abb. CF19 21
Southweald Dr.
Willingham Clo. NW5 BW35 47
Leighton Rd.
Willingham Ter. NW5 BW35 47
Willingham Way, Kings.T. BM52 85
Willington Ct. E5 CC35 48
Clapton Park Est.
Willington Rd. SW9 BX45 66
Willis Av., Sutt. BU57 95
Willis Clo., Epsom BM60 94
Willis Rd. E15 CG37 58
Willis Rd., Croy. BZ54 87
Willis Rd., Erith CS42 69
Willis St. E14 CE39 57
Willmore End SW19 BS51 86
Willoughby Av., Croy. BX56 95
Willoughby Clo., Brox. CD14 12
Willoughby Ct., St.Alb. BK16 18
Willoughby Dr., Rain. CT36 59
Willoughby Gro. N17 CB29 39
Willoughby La. N17 CB29 39
Willoughby Pk. Rd. N17 CB29 39
Willoughby Rd. N8 BY31 47
Willoughby Rd. NW3 BT35 47
Willoughby Rd., Kings.T. BL51 85
Willoughby Rd., Slou. AT41 62
Willoughby Rd., Twick. BK46 74
Willoughby Way SE7 CH42 68
Willow Av. SW13 BO44 65
Willow Av., Sid. CO46 79
Willow Av., Swan. CT52 89
Willow Av., Uxb. AX35 44
Willow Av., West.Dr. AY40 53
Willow Bank SW6 BR45 65
Willow Bank, Rich. BJ48 74
Willow Bridge Rd. N1 BZ36 57
Willow Clo. W5 BK39 54
Willow Clo., Doddinghurst DB22 33
Willow Clo., Bex. CQ46 79
Willow Clo., Brent. BK43 64
Willow Clo., Brom. CK53 88
Willow Clo., Brwd. DD25 122
Willow Clo., Buck.H. CJ27 40
Willow Clo., Chsnt. CA16 21
Willow Clo., Erith CU44 69
Willow Clo., Horn. CU34 50
Willow Clo., Orp. CO54 89
Willow Clo., Slou. AU43 62
Willow Clo., Wey. AV59 91
Willow Cott. Rd., Cars. BU53 86
Willow Cotts, Rich. BM43 65
Waterloo Pl.
Willow Cres. E., Uxb. AX35 44
Willow Cres. W., Uxb. AX35 44
Willow Cres., St.Alb. BK13 9
Willow Ct., Edg. BL28 37
Willow Dene, Pnr. BD30 36
Willow Dr., Barn. BR24 28
Willow Dr., Maid. AG42 61
Willow Edge, Kings L. AZ18 17
Blackwell Rd.
Willow End N20 BS27 38
Willow End, Surb. BL54 85
Willow Gdns. N16 CA34 48
Cazenove Rd.
Willow Gdns., Houns. BF44 64
Willow Gdns., Ruis. BB34 44
Willow Grn. NW9 BO29 37
Clayton Field
Willow Grn., B.Wd. BN25 28
Ashley Dr.
Willow Grn., Dor. BJ73 119
Willow Gro. E13 CH37 58
Willow Gro., Chis. CL50 78
Willow Gro., Ruis. BB34 44
Willow Gro., Welw.G.C. BQ 5 5
Willow Hayne Dr., Walt. BC54 83
Willow La., Amer. AP24 25
Willow La., Mitch. BU53 86
Willow La., Wat. BC25 26
Willow Mead, Chig. CO27 41
Willow Mt., Croy. CA55 87
Langton Way
Willow Path, Epsom BM60 94
Willow Path, Wal.Abb. CG20 22
Willow Pk., Sev. CA53 107
Willow Pl. SW1 BW42 3
Willow Pl. SW1 BW42 66
Francis St.
Willow Rd. NW3 BT35 47
Willow Rd. W5 BL41 65
Willow Rd., Dart. CV47 80
Willow Rd., Enf. CA24 30
Willow Rd., Erith CU44 69
Willow Rd., N.Mal. BN52 85
Willow Rd., Red. BT71 121
Willow Rd., Rom. CQ32 50
Willow Rd., Slou. AV44 62
Willow Rd., Wall. BV57 95
Willow Side, St.Alb. BL17 19
Willow St. E4 CF26 39
Willow St. EC2 CA38 2
Willow St. EC2 CA38 57
Willow St., Rom. CS31 50
Willow Tree Clo. SW18 BS47 76
Willow Tree Clo., Hayes BD38 54
Willow Tree La., Hayes BD38 54
Willow Tree Wk., Brom. CH51 88
Willow Vale W12 BP40 55
Willow Vale, Chis. CL50 78
Willow Vale, Lthd. BF65 102
Willow Vw. SW19 BT51 86
Palestine Gro.
Willow Way N3 BS29 38
Willow Way SE26 CB48 77
Willow Way SW19 BT51 86
Phipps Bridge Rd.
Willow Way W11 BQ40 55
St. Anns Rd.
Willow Way, Epsom BN57 94
Willow Way, Gdse. CB69 114
Willow Way, Guil. AR68 109
Willow Way, Hat. BO14 10
Willow Way, Hem.H. AW12 8
Willow Way, Pot.B. BS20 20
Willow Way, Rad. BH21 27
Willow Way, Rom. CX29 42
Willow Way, St.Alb. BF17 18
Willow Way, Sun. BC52 83
Willow Way, Twick. BF48 74
Willow Way, Wem. BJ34 45
Willow Way, Wey. AX59 92
Willow Way, Wok. AR64 100
Willow Wk. E17 CD32 48
Willow Wk. N15 BY31 47
Willow Wk. N2 BT30 38
Willow Wk. N21 BX25 29
Willow Wk. SE1 CA42 4
Willow Wk. SE1 CA42 67
Willow Wk., Cher. AW54 83
Willow Wk., Dart. CV45 70
Willow Wk., Egh. AR49 72
Willow Wk., Ilf. CL34 49
Station Rd.
Willow Wk., Orp. CL55 88
Willow Wk., Sutt. BR55 85
Willow Wk., Upmin. CZ33 51
Willow Wood Cres. SE25 CA53 87
Willowbrook Clo., Sthl. BF41 64
Willowbrook Gro. SE15 CA43 67
Willowbrook Rd. SE15 CA43 67
Willowbrook Rd., Stai. AY48 73
Willowbrook, Eton AO42 61
Willowcourt Av., Har. BJ32 45
Willowdene Clo., Twick. BG47 74
Willowdene Ct., Brwd. DB28 42
Warley Mt.
Willowdene N6 BU33 47
Denewood Rd.
Willowdene, Brwd. CZ25 33
Willowdene, Bush. BH26 36
Willowfield, Harl. CM12 13
Willowfield, Saw. CQ 6 6
Springham Rd.
Willowhayne Gdns., Sutt. BQ55 85
Willowherb Wk., Rom. CV29 42
Clematis Clo.
Willowmead Clo. W5 BK38 54
Brentham Way
Willowmead Clo., Wok. AQ61 100
Willowmead, Saw. CQ 6 6
Springhall Rd.
Willowmead, Stai. AW51 83
Willowmere, Esher BG56 93
Willows Av., Mord. BS53 86
Willows Clo., Pnr. BD30 36
Willows Path, Wind. AL44 61
Willows, The, Esher BH57 93
Willows, The, Grays DE43 71
Willows, The, Rick. AW27 35
Uxbridge Rd.
Willows, The, St.Alb. BJ15 9
Willows, The, Wat. BC26 35
Brookside
Willows, The, Wey. AY60 92
Willowtree Clo., Uxb. BA34 44
Wills Cres., Houns. BF46 74
Wills Gro. NW7 BP28 37
Willshaw St. SE14 CE44 67
Willson Rd., Egh. AQ49 72
Willwood Way NW3 BT33 47
North End Rd.
Willy St. WC1 BX39 2
Willy St. WC1 BX39 56
Great Russell St.
Wilman Gro. E8 CB36 57
Wilmar Clo., Hayes BA38 53
Wilmar Clo., Uxb. AX36 53
Wilmar Gdns., W.Wick. CE54 87
Wilmar Way, Sev. CW63 108
The Landway
Wilmer Clo., Kings.T. BL49 75
Wilmer Cres., Kings.T. BL49 75
Wilmer Gdns. N1 CA37 2
Wilmer Gdns. N1 CA37 57
Wilmer Ho., Kings.T. BL49 75
Wilmer Lea Clo. E15 CF36 57
Wilmer Way N14 BW28 38
Wilmerhatch La., Epsom BM62 103
Wilmington Av. W4 BN43 65
Wilmington Av., Orp. CP55 89
Wilmington Court Rd., Dart. CU48 79
Wilmington Gdns., Bark. CM36 58
Wilmington Sq. WC1 BY38 2
Wilmington Sq. WC1 BY38 56
Wilmington St. WC1 BY38 2
Wilmington St. WC1 BY38 56
Wilmot Clo. N2 BT30 38
Wilmot Clo. SE15 CB43 67
Wilmot Grn., Brwd. DA28 42
Wilmot Pl. NW1 BW36 56
Wilmot Pl. W7 BH40 54
Wilmot Rd. E10 CE34 48
Wilmot Rd. N17 BZ31 48
Wilmot Rd., Dart. CU46 79
Wilmot Rd., Pur. BY59 95
Wilmot St. E2 CB38 57
Wilmot Way, Bans. BS60 95
Wilmots Clo., Reig. BT70 121
Wilmount St. SE18 CL42 68
Wilna Rd. SW18 BT47 76
Wilna Yd. SW18 BS47 76
Wilna Rd.
Wilrose Cres. SE2 CO42 69
Wilsham St. W11 BQ40 55
Wilshaw St. SE14 CE44 67
Deptford Bdy.
Wilshere Av., St.Alb. BG15 9
Wilsman Rd., S.Ock. DB37 60
Wilsmere Dr., Har. BH29 36
Wilsmere Dr., Nthlt. BE36 54
Wilson Av., Mitch. BU50 76
Wilson Clo., Dag. CS36 59
Wilson Clo., Wem. BL33 46
Wilson Dr.
Wilson Dr., Cher. AT56 91
Wilson Dr., Wem. BL33 46
Wilson Gdns. Har. BG33 45
Wilson Gro. SE16 CB41 67
Wilson Rd. E6 CJ38 58
Wilson Rd. SE5 BZ44 67
Wilson Rd., Chess. BL57 94
Wilson Rd., Har. BG33 45
Wilson Rd., Ilf. CK33 49
Wilson St. E13 CH37 58
Wilson St. E17 CF32 48
Wilson St. EC2 BZ39 2
Wilson St. EC2 BZ39 57
Wilson St. N21 BY26 38
Wilson Way, Wok. AR61 100
Wilsons Pl. E14 CD39 57
Salmon La.
Wilsons Rd. W6 BQ42 65
Wilsons, Tad. BQ64 103
Wilstone Clo., Hayes BD38 54
Kingsash Dr.
Wilstone Dr., St.Alb. BK11 9
Wilthorne Gdns., Dag. CR36 59
Acre Rd.
Wilton Av. W4 BO42 65
Wilton Clo., West Dr. AX43 63
Hatch La.
Wilton Cres. SW1 BV41 3
Wilton Cres. SW1 BV41 66
Wilton Cres. SW19 BR51 85
Wilton Cres., Wind. AL45 61
Wilton Ct. N10 BV30 38
Wilton Dr., Rom. CS29 41
Wilton Gdns., E.Mol. BF52 84
Wilton Gdns., Walt. BD54 84
Wilton Gro. SW19 BR50 75
Wilton Gro., N.Mal. BO53 85
Wilton La., Beac. AO29 34
Wilton Ms. SW1 BV41 3
Wilton Ms. SW1 BV41 66
Wilton Par., Felt. BC48 73
Wilton Park Ct. SE18 CL43 68
Prince Imperial Rd.
Wilton Pl. SW1 BV41 3
Wilton Pl. SW1 BV41 66
Wilton Pl., Wey. AX58 92
Wilton Rd. N10 BV30 38
Wilton Rd. SE2 CP42 69
Wilton Rd. SW1 BV41 3
Wilton Rd. SW1 BV41 66
Wilton Rd. SW19 BU50 76
Wilton Rd., Barn. BU24 29
Wilton Rd., Houns. BD45 64
Wilton Rd., Ilf. CL35 49
Cecil Rd.
Wilton Rd., Red. BU71 121
Wilton Row SW1 BV41 3
Wilton Row SW1 BV41 66
Wilton Sq. N1 BZ37 2
Wilton Sq. N1 BZ37 57
Wilton St. SW1 BV41 3
Wilton St. SW1 BV41 66
Wilton Ter. SW1 BV41 3
Wilton Ter. SW1 BV41 66
Wilton Vill. N1 BZ37 2
Wilton Way E8 CB36 57
Wilton Yd. W10 BQ40 55
Bard Rd.
Wiltshire Av., Horn. CW31 51
Wiltshire Clo. SW3 BU42 3
Wiltshire Clo. SW3 BU42 66
Wiltshire Gdns., Twick. BG47 74
Wiltshire La., Pnr. BB31 44
Wiltshire Rd. N1 BZ37 2
Wiltshire Rd. N1 BZ37 57
Wiltshire Rd. SW9 BY44 66
Loughborough Rd.
Wiltshire Rd., Orp. CO54 89
Wiltshire Rd., Th.Hth. BY52 86
Wilverley Cres., N.Mal. BO53 85
Wimbart Rd. SW2 BX47 76
Wimbledon Clo. SW20 BQ50 75
Wimbledon Hill Rd. SW19 BR50 75
Wimbledon Park Est. SW19 BR47 75
Wimbledon Park Rd. SW19 BP48 75
Wimbledon Park Rd. SW18 BR48 75
Wimbledon Park Side SW19 BQ48 75
Wimbledon Rd. SW17 BT49 76
Wimbolt St. E2 CB38 2
Wimbolt St. E2 CB38 57
Wimborne Av., Hayes BC39 53
Wimborne Av., Orp. CN52 88
Wimborne Av., Sthl. BF42 64
Wimborne Clo. SE12 CG46 78
Wimborne Clo., Epsom BO60 94
Wimborne Clo., Saw. CP 6 6
Wimborne Clo., Wor.Pk. BQ54 85
Dorchester Rd.
Wimborne Ct. N1 BZ37 2
Wimborne Dr. NW9 BM31 46
Wimborne Dr., Pnr. BD33 45
Wimborne Gdns. W13 BJ39 54
Wimborne Gro., Wat. BB22 26
Wimborne Rd. N17 CA30 39
Wimborne Rd. N9 CB27 39
Wimborne St. N1 BZ37 2
Wimborne Way, Beck. CC52 87
Wimbourne Av., Red. BU73 121
Wimbourne Clo., Buck.H. CH27 40
Wimbourne Ct. N1 BZ37 57
Wimbourne St. N1 BZ37 57
Wimbrel Clo., S.Croy. BZ59 96
Wimpole Clo., Kings.T. BL51 85
Wimpole Ms. W1 BV39 1
Wimpole Ms. W1 BV39 56
Wimpole Rd., West Dr. AX40 53
Wimpole St. W1 BV39 1
Wimpole St. W1 BV39 56
Winans Wk. SW9 BY44 66
Wincanton Cres., Nthlt. BF35 45
Wincanton Gdns., Ilf. CL30 40
Wincanton Rd. SW18 BR47 75
Wincanton Rd., Rom. CV27 42
Winch Dells, Hem.H. AZ15 8
Winchcomb Gdns. SE9 CJ45 68
Winchcombe Rd., Cars. BT54 86
Winchelsea Av., Bexh. CQ43 69
Winchelsea Clo. SW15 BQ46 75
Winchelsea Cres., E.Mol. BG51 84
Winchelsea Rd. E7 CH34 49
Winchelsea Rd. N17 CA31 48
Winchelsea Rd. NW10 BN37 55
Winchelsey Rd., S.Croy. CA57 96
Winchendon Rd. SW6 BR44 65
Winchendon Rd., Tedd. BG49 74
Winchester Av. NW6 BR37 55
Winchester Av. NW9 BM31 46
Winchester Av., Houns. BE43 64
Winchester Av., Upmin. CZ33 51
Winchester Clo. E6 CK39 58
Winchester Clo. SE17 BY42 4
Winchester Clo., Kings.T. BM50 75
Winchester Clo., Brom. CG52 88
Winchester Clo., Enf. CA25 30
Winchester Clo., Esher BF56 93
Winchester Clo., Slou. AV44 62
Rodney Way
Winchester Cres., Grav. DH48 81
Winchester Dr., Pnr. BD32 45
Winchester Gro., Sev. CU65 107
Winchester Ms. NW3 BT36 56
Winchester Rd.
Winchester Pk., Brom. CG52 88
Winchester Pl. E8 CA35 48
Kingsland High St.
Winchester Pl. N6 BV33 47
Winchester Pl. W3 BN41 65
Winchester Rd. E4 CF29 39
Winchester Rd. N6 BV33 47
Winchester Rd. N9 CA26 39
Winchester Rd. NW3 BT36 56
Winchester Rd., Bexh. CP44 69
Winchester Rd., Brom. CG52 88
Winchester Rd., Felt. BE48 74
Winchester Rd., Har. BL31 46
Winchester Rd., Hayes BB43 63
Winchester Rd., Ilf. CM34 49
Winchester Rd., Nthwd. BB31 44
Winchester Rd., Orp. CO56 98
Winchester Rd., Twick. BJ46 74
Winchester Rd., Walt. BC54 83
Winchester St. SW1 BV42 3
Winchester St. SW1 BV42 66
Winchester St. W3 BN41 65
Winchester Way, Rick. AZ25 26
Winchester Wk. SE1 BZ40 4
Winchester Wk. SE1 BZ40 67
Winchet Wk., Croy. CC53 87
Long La.
Winchfield Clo., Har. BK32 45
Winchfield Rd. SE26 CD49 77
Winchfield Way, Rick. AX26 35
Winchmore Hill Rd. N14 BW26 38
Winchmore Hill Rd. N21 BW26 38
Winchstone Clo., Shep. AY52 83
Winckley Clo., Har. BL32 46
Wincott St. SE11 BY42 4
Wincott St. SE11 BY42 66
Wincrofts Dr. SE9 CM45 68

Wind Hill, Ong. CU13 14
Wind Hill, Welw.G.C. BS 7 5
Windborough Rd., Cars. BV57 95
Windermere Av. N3 BS31 47
Windermere Av. NW6 BR37 55
Windermere Av. SW19 BS52 86
Windermere Av., Horn. CU35 50
Windermere Av., Ruis. BD33 45
Windermere Av., St.Alb. BJ14 9
Windermere Av., Wem. BK33 45
Windermere Clo., Dart. CU47 79
Windermere Clo., Egh. AT50 72
Derwent Rd.
Windermere Clo., Hem.H. BA14 8
Windermere Clo., Orp. CL55 88
Grasmere Gdns.
Windermere Clo., Rick. AU25 25
Copmans Wick
Windermere Ct. SW13 BO43 65
Windermere Gdns., Ilf. CK32 49
Windermere Gro., Wem. BK33 45
Windermere Av.
Windermere Rd. N10 BV30 38
Windermere Rd. N19 BW34 47
Holloway Rd.
Windermere Rd. SW15 BO49 75
Windermere Rd. SW16 BW51 86
Windermere Rd. W5 BK41 64
Windermere Rd., Bexh. CS44 69
Windermere Rd., Couls. BX61 104
Windermere Rd., Croy. CA54 87
Windermere Rd., Sthl. BE39 54
Windermere Rd., W.Wick. CG55 88
Windermere Way, Red. BU70 121
Windermere Way, West Dr. AY40 53
Providence Rd.
Winders Rd. SW11 BU44 66
Windfield Clo. SE26 CC49 77
Windfield, Lthd. BJ64 102
Windgates, Guil. AU69 118
Windham Av., Croy. CF58 96
Windham Rd., Rich. BL45 65
Windhover Way, Grav. DJ49 81
Winding Shot, Hem.H. AW13 8
Winding Way, Dag. CP34 50
Winding Way, Har. BH35 45
Windings, The, S.Croy. CA59 96
Windlass Pl. SE8 CD42 67
Windlesham Gro. SW19 BQ47 75
Windlesham Rd. SW19 BQ47 75
Windlesham Rd., Wok. AO58 91
Windley Clo. SE23 CC48 77
Windmill Av., Epsom BO59 94
Windmill Av., St.Alb. BK11 9
Windmill Clo. SE1 CB42 67
Beatrice Rd.
Windmill Clo., Cat. BZ64 105
Coulsdon Rd.
Windmill Clo., Epsom BO59 94
Windmill Clo., Sun. BB50 73
Windmill Clo., Surb. BK54 84
Windmill Clo., Upmin. CX34 51
Windmill Clo., Wal.Abb. CG20 22
Windmill Clo., Wind. AN44 61
Windmill Dr. SW4 BV46 76
Windmill Dr., Kes. CJ56 97
Lakes Rd.
Windmill Dr., Lthd. BK65 102
Windmill Dr., Reig. BT69 121
Windmill Dr., Rick. AY25 26
Windmill End, Epsom BO59 94
Windmill Gdns., Enf. BY23 29
Windmill Gro., Croy. BZ53 87
Queens Rd.
Windmill Hill NW3 BT34 47
Windmill Hill, Enf. BY24 29
Windmill Hill, Kings L. AV19 16
Windmill Hill, Ruis. BB33 44
Windmill La. E15 CF36 57
Windmill La., Barn. BO25 28
Windmill La., Bush. BG26 36
Windmill La., Chsnt. CD18 21
Windmill La., Epsom BO59 94
Windmill La., Grnf. BG38 54
Windmill La., Houns. BH42 64
Windmill La., Sthl. BG40 54
Windmill La., Surb. BJ53 84
Windmill Ms., Brent. BO42 65
Windmill Rd.
Windmill Rd. N18 BZ28 39
Windmill Rd. SW18 BT46 76
Windmill Rd. SW19 BQ48 75
Windmill Rd. W., Sun. BB51 83
Windmill Rd. W4 BO42 65
Windmill Rd. W5 BK42 64
Windmill Rd., Sevenoaks Weald CU70 116
Windmill Rd., Brent. BK42 64
Windmill Rd., Croy. BZ54 87
Windmill Rd., Dag. CQ34 50
Windmill Rd., Fulmer AR35 43
Windmill Rd., Ger.Cr. AR29 34
Windmill Rd., Hem.H. AY13 8
Windmill Rd., Hmptn. BF49 74
Windmill Rd., Mitch. BW53 86
Windmill Rd., Sev. CU68 116
Windmill Rd., Slou. AO40 61
Windmill Rd., Sun. BB51 83
Windmill Row SE11 BY42 4
Windmill Row SE11 BY42 66
Windmill St. W1 BW39 1
Windmill St. W1 BW39 56
Windmill St., Bush. BH26 36
Windmill St., Grav. DG47 81
Windmill Way, Brwd. CZ22 33
Windmill Way, Reig. BT69 121
Windmill Way, Ruis. BB33 44
Windmill Wk. SE1 BY40 4
Windmill Wk. SE1 BY40 56
Windmore Av., Pot.B. BQ19 19
Windover Av. NW9 BN31 46
Windridge Clo., St.Alb. BF15 9
Windridge Rd., St.Alb. BD15 9
Windrose Clo. SE16 CC41 67
Kinburn St.
Windrush Av., Slou. AT42 62
Windrush Clo. SW11 BT45 66
Maysoule Rd.
Windrush Clo. W4 BN44 65
Windrush Clo., Uxb. AY35 44
Windrush La. SE23 CC48 77
Winds End Clo., Hem.H. AZ12 8
Winds Point Dr. SE15 CB43 67
Ethna Rd.
Winds Ridge, Wok. AU66 109
Windsland Ms. W2 BT39 56
London St.
Windsor Av. E17 CD30 39
Windsor Av. SW19 BT51 86
Windsor Av., E.Mol. BF52 84
Windsor Av., Edg. BM28 37
Windsor Av., Grays DD41 71
Windsor Av., N.Mal. BN53 85
Windsor Av., Rick. AW26 35
Windsor Av., Sutt. BR55 85
Windsor Av., Uxb. AZ37 53
Windsor Clo. N3 BR30 37
Windsor Rd.
Windsor Clo. SE27 BZ49 77
Windsor Clo., B.Wd. BM23 28
Windsor Clo., Brent. BJ43 64
Amalgamated Dr.
Windsor Clo., Chis. CL49 78
Windsor Clo., Chsnt. CB18 21
Windsor Clo., Guil. AP71 118
Powell Clo.
Windsor Clo., Har. BF34 45
Windsor Clo., Hem.H. AT17 16
Pembridge Rd.
Windsor Clo., Nthwd. BC30 35
Windsor Clo., Welw.G.C. BP 5 5
Windsor Court Rd., Wok. AP58 91
Windsor Cres., Har. BF35 45
Windsor Cres., Wem. BM34 46
Windsor Ct. N14 BW26 38
Windsor Ct., Sun. BC50 73
Windsor Dr., Ashf. AX49 73
Windsor Dr., Barn. BU25 29
Windsor Dr., Dart. CU46 79
Windsor Dr., Orp. CO57 98
Windsor Gdns. W9 BS39 56
Windsor Gdns., Croy. BX55 86
Richmond Rd.
Windsor Gdns., Hayes BA41 63
Windsor Gro. SE27 BZ49 77
Windsor Ms. SW18 BT47 76
Inman Rd.
Windsor Park Rd., Hayes BB43 63
Windsor Pl. SW1 BW42 3
Windsor Pl. SW1 BW42 66
Francis St.
Windsor Rd. E10 CE34 48
Windsor Rd. E11 CH33 49
Windsor Rd. E4 CE28 39
Chivers Rd.
Windsor Rd. E7 CH35 49
Windsor Rd. N13 BY27 38
Windsor Rd. N17 CB30 39
Windsor Rd. N3 BR30 37
Windsor Rd. N7 BX34 47
Windsor Rd. NW2 BP36 55
Windsor Rd. W5 BK40 54
Windsor Rd., Barn. BQ25 28
Windsor Rd., Bexh. CQ45 69
Windsor Rd., Brwd. DA25 33
Windsor Rd., Dag. CQ34 50
Windsor Rd., Datchet AQ43 62
Windsor Rd., Egh. AR47 72
Windsor Rd., Enf. CC21 30
Windsor Rd., Ger.Cr. AQ35 43
Windsor Rd., Grav. DG48 81
Windsor Rd., Har. BG30 36
Windsor Rd., Horn. CV33 51
Windsor Rd., Houns. BC44 63
Windsor Rd., Ilf. CL35 49
Windsor Rd., Kings.T. BL50 75
Windsor Rd., Maid. AG41 61
Windsor Rd., Rich. BL44 65
Windsor Rd., Sid. CO50 79
Windsor Rd., Slou. AP41 62
Windsor Rd., Stai. AS46 72
Windsor Rd., Sthl. BE41 64
Windsor Rd., Sun. BC50 73
Windsor Rd., Tedd. BG49 74
Windsor Rd., Th.Hth. BY51 86
Windsor Rd., Wat. BD22 27
Windsor Rd., Welw. BP 5 5
Windsor Rd., Wind. AO42 61
Windsor Rd., Wok. AO56 91
Windsor Rd., Wor.Pk. BP55 85
Windsor St. N1 BY37 2
Windsor St. N1 BY37 56
Windsor St., Cher. AW53 83
Windsor St., Uxb. AX36 53
Windsor Ter. N1 BZ38 2
Windsor Ter. N1 BZ38 57
Windsor Way W6 BQ42 65
Windsor Way, Wok. AU61 100
Windsor Wk. SE5 BZ44 67
Windsor Wk., Wey. AZ56 92
Windspoint Dr. SE15 CB43 67
Green Hundred Rd.
Windus Rd. N16 CA33 48
Windus Wk. N16 CA33 48
Alkham Rd.
Windward Clo., Enf. CC21 30
Windy Hill, Brwd. DE26 122
Windy Ridge, Brom. CK51 88
Windyridge Clo. SW19 BQ49 75
Wine Clo. E1 CC40 57
Wine Office Ct. EC4 BY39 2
Wine Office Ct. EC4 BY39 56
Winern Glebe, Wey. AX60 92
Winford Dr., Brox. CD14 12
Winforton St. SE10 CF44 67
Winfrith Rd. SW18 BT47 76
Wing Way, Brwd. DB26 42
Wingate Cres., Croy. BW53 86
Wingate Rd. W6 BP41 65
Wingate Rd., Ilf. CL35 49
Wingate Rd., Sid. CP49 79
Sidcup Hill
Wingate Way, St.Alb. BJ14 9
Wingfield Clo., Brwd. DD27 122
Wingfield Clo., Wey. AW58 92
Wingfield Gdns., Upmin. CZ32 51
Wingfield Ms. SE15 CB45 67
Wingfield St.
Wingfield Rd. E15 CG35 49
Wingfield Rd. E17 CE32 48
Wingfield Rd., Grav. DG47 81
Wingfield Rd., Kings.T. BL50 75
Wingfield St. SE15 CB45 67
Wingfield Way, Ruis. BC35 44
Wingfield, Grays DC42 71
Wingford Rd. SW2 BX46 76
Wingletye La., Horn. CW33 51
Wingmore Rd. SE24 BZ45 67
Wingrave Cres., Brwd. CZ28 42
Wingrave Rd. W6 BQ43 65
Wingrove Rd. SE6 CG48 78
Winifred Av., Horn. CV35 51
Winifred Gro. SW11 BU45 66
Marjorie Gro.
Winifred Rd. SW19 BS51 86
Winifred Rd., Couls. BV61 104
Winifred Rd., Dag. CQ34 50
Winifred Rd., Dart. CU46 79
Winifred Rd., Erith CT42 69
Winifred Rd., Hem.H. AX15 8
Winifred Rd., Hmptn. BF49 74
Winifred St. E16 CK40 58
Winifred Ter. E13 CH37 58
High St.
Winifred Ter., Enf. CA26 39
Winkers Clo., Ger.Cr. AS30 34
Winkers La., Ger.Cr. AS30 34
Winkfield Rd. E13 CH37 58
Winkfield Rd. N22 BY30 38
Winkfield Rd., Wind. AM46 61
Winkley St. E2 CB38 57
Canrobert St.
Winkwell, Hem.H. AU14 7
Winkworth Pl., Bans. BS60 95
Winkworth Rd., Bans. BS60 95
Winlaton Rd., Brom. CF49 77
Winn Common Rd. SE18 CN43 68
Winn Rd. SE12 CH47 78
Winnett St. W1 BW40 3
Wardour St.
Winnings Wk., Nthlt. BE36 54
Arnold Rd.
Winnington Clo. N2 BT32 47
Winnington Rd. N2 BT32 47
Winnington Rd., Enf. CC22 30
Winnington Way, Wok. AQ62 100
Winnock Rd., West Dr. AX40 53
Winns Av. E17 CD31 48
Winns Ms. N15 CA31 48
Grove Park Rd.
Winns Ter. E17 CE30 39
Winsbeach E17 CF31 48
Winscombe Cres. W5 BK38 54
Winscombe St. N19 BV34 47
Winscombe Way, Stan. BJ28 36
Winsford Rd. SE6 CD48 77
Winsford Ter. N18 BZ28 39
Winsham Gro. SW11 BV46 76
Winslade Rd. SW2 BX46 76
Winslade Way SE26 CE47 77
Winsland Ms. W2 BT39 1
Winsland Ms. W2 BT39 56
Winsland St.
Winsland St. W2 BT39 1
Winsland St. W2 BT39 56
Winsley St. W1 BW39 1
Winsley St. W1 BW39 56
Winslow Clo. NW10 BO34 46
Neasden La. N.
Winslow Clo., Pnr. BC32 44
Winslow Rd. W6 BQ43 65
Winslow Way, Felt. BE48 74
Winslow Way, Walt. BD55 84
Winsor Est. W9 BS39 56
Winsor Ter. E6 CL39 58
Winstanley Clo., Cob. BC60 92
Winstanley Rd. SW11 BT45 66
Winstead Gdns., Dag. CS35 50
Winston Av. NW9 BO33 46
Winston Clo., Har. BH29 36
Winston Clo., Rom. CR31 50
Winston Ct., Har. BF29 36
Winston Dr., Cob. BE62 102
Winston Gdns., Berk. AP13 7
Winston Rd. N16 BZ35 48
Winston Way, Ilf. CL34 49
Winston Way, Pot.B. BS20 20
Winston Way, Wok. AT63 100
Winston Wk. W4 BN41 65
Winstone Clo., Rom. CR31 50
Marlborough Rd.
Winstre Rd., B.Wd. BM23 28
Winter Av. E6 CK37 58
Winter Box Wk., Rich. BL46 75
Kings Rd.
Winterbourne Av., Orp. CM55 88
Winterbourne Gro., Wey. BA57 92
Winterbourne Rd. SE6 CD47 77
Winterbourne Rd., Th.Hth. BY52 86
Winterbourne Rd., Dag. CP34 50
Winterbrook Rd. SE24 BZ46 77
Winterdown Gdns., Esher BE57 93
Winterdown Rd., Esher BE57 93
Winterfold Clo. SW19 BR48 75
Wintergreen Clo. E6 CK39 58
Yarrow Cres.
Winterhill Way, Guil. AT68 109
Winters Cft., Grav. DH50 81
Winters Rd., T.Ditt. BJ54 84
Winters Way, Wal.Abb. CH20 22
Winterscroft Rd., Hodd. CD11 12
Wintersells Rd., Wey. AX58 92
Winterstoke Gdns. NW7 BP28 37
Winterstoke Rd. SE6 CD47 77
Winterton Pl. SW10 BT43 3
Winterton Pl. SW10 BT43 66
Winterwell Rd. SW2 BX46 76
Winthorpe Rd. SW15 BR45 65
Winthrop Pl. E1 CB39 57
Winthrop St.
Winthrop St. E1 CB39 57
Winthrop Wk., Wem. BK34 45
Hutchinson Ter.
Winton App., Rick. BA25 26
Winton Av. N11 BW29 38
Winton Clo. N9 CC26 39
Winton Cres., Rick. AZ25 26
Winton Dr., Chsnt. CD18 21
Winton Dr., Rick. AZ25 26
Winton Gdns., Edg. BL29 37
Winton Rd., Orp. CL56 97
Winton Way SW16 BY49 76
Winvale, Slou. AP41 62
Winwood, Slou. AR39 52
Winyatt St. EC1 BY38 56
Wisbeach Rd., Croy. BZ53 87
Wisborough Rd., S.Croy. CA58 96
Wisdons Clo., Dag. CR34 50
Wise La. NW7 BP28 37
Wise La., West Dr. AX41 63
Wise Rd. E15 CF37 57
Wisemans Gdns., Saw. CP 6 6
Wises La., Hat. BQ17 19
Wises La., Sev. DC57 99
Wiseton Rd. SW17 BU47 76
Wishart Rd. SE3 CJ44 68
Wishbone Way, Wok. AP61 100
Wishford Ct., Ash. BL62 103
Wisley La., Wok. AX61 101
Wisley Rd. SW11 BU46 76
Wisley Rd., Orp. CO50 79
Wissants, Harl. CL13 13
Wisteria Clo., Brwd. DB25 33
Lavender Av.
Wisteria Clo., Orp. CL55 88
Wisteria Gdns., Swan. CS51 89
Wisteria Rd. SE13 CF45 67
Witan St. E2 CB38 57
Coventry Rd.
Witches La., Sev. CT65 107
Witchford, Welw.G.C. BT 8 5
Witham Clo., Loug. CK25 31
Witham Rd. SE20 CC52 87
Witham Rd. W13 BJ40 54
Green Man La.
Witham Rd., Dag. CR35 50
Witham Rd., Horn. CU32 50
Witham Rd., Islw. BG44 64
Withens Clo., Orp. CP52 89
Witherby Clo., Croy. CA56 96
Witherfield Way SE16 CB42 67
Egan Way
Witherings, The, Horn. CW32 51
Witherington Rd. N5 BY35 47
Withers Mead NW9 BO30 37
Withers Pl. EC1 BZ38 2
Withers Pl. EC1 BZ38 57
Old St.
Witherston Way SE9 CL48 78
Withey Clo., Wind. AM44 61
Witheygate Av., Stai. AW50 73
Withies, The, Lthd. BJ63 102
Withy La., Ruis. BA32 44
Withy Mead E4 CF27 39
Withybed Corner, Tad. BP65 103
Withycombe Rd. SW19 BQ47 75
Victoria Dr.
Withycroft, Slou. AS39 52
Witley Cres., Croy. CF57 96
Witley Ct., Sthl. BE42 64
Witley Gdns., Sthl. BE42 64
Witley Rd. N19 BW34 47
Holloway Rd.
Witmore Clo. N11 BV28 38
Witney Clo., Pnr. BE29 36
Witney Clo., Uxb. AY35 44
Witney Path SE23 CC48 77
Wittenham Way E4 CF27 39
Wittersham Rd., Brom. CG49 78
Wivenhoe Clo. SE15 CB45 67
Wivenhoe Ct., Houns. BE45 64
Staines Rd.
Wivenhoe Rd., Bark. CO37 59
Wiverton Rd. SE26 CC50 77
Wix Hill, Lthd. AZ68 110
Wix Rd., Dag. CP37 59
Wixs La., SW4 BV45 66
Woburn Av., Epp. CN22 31
Woburn Av., Horn. CU35 50
Woburn Av., Pur. BY59 95
Woburn Clo. SW19 BT50 76
Tintern Clo.
Woburn Clo., Bush. BG25 27
Woburn Pl. WC1 BW38 2
Woburn Pl. WC1 BW38 56
Woburn Rd., Cars. BU54 86
Woburn Rd., Croy. BZ54 87
Woburn Sq. WC1 BW38 1
Woburn Sq. WC1 BW38 56
Woburn Wk. WC1 BW38 1
Woburn Wk. WC1 BW38 56
Wodeham St. E1 CB39 57
Wodeland Av., Guil. AQ71 118
Woffingham Clo., Kings.T. BK51 84
Woffington Clo., Tedd. BK50 74
Upper Teddington Rd.
Wokindon Rd., Grays DG41 71
Woking Clo. SW15 BO45 65
Woking Rd., Guil. AR67 109
Woking Rd., Wey. AV60 91
Wold, The, Cat. CE64 105
Woldham Rd., Brom. CJ52 88
Woldingham Rd., Woldingham CF66 114
Woldingham Rd., Cat. CB63 105
Wolds Dr., Orp. CL56 97
Wolf La., Wind. AL45 61
Wolfe Clo., Brom. CH53 88
Wolfe Clo., Hayes BC38 53
Ayles Rd.
Wolfe Cres. SE16 CC41 67
Canada St.
Wolfe Cres. SE7 CJ42 68
Wolferton Rd. E12 CK35 49
Wolffe Gdns. E15 CG36 58
Wolffram Clo. SE13 CG46 78
Wolfington Rd. SE27 BY49 76
Wolfs Hill, Oxt. CH69 115
Wolfs Row, Oxt. CH68 115
Wolfs Wood, Oxt. CH69 115
Wolftencroft Clo. SW11 BT45 66
Wollaston Clo. SE1 BZ42 4
Wollaston Clo. SE1 BZ42 67
Wolmer Clo., Edg. BM28 37
Wolmer Gdns., Edg. BM27 37
Wolseley Av. SW19 BS48 76
Wolseley Gdns. W4 BM43 65
Wolseley Rd. E7 CH36 58
Wolseley Rd. N22 BX30 38
Wolseley Rd. N8 BW32 47
Wolseley Rd. W4 BN42 65
Wolseley Rd., Har. BH31 45
Wolseley Rd., Mitch. BV54 86
Wolseley Rd., Rom. CS33 50
Wolseley St. SE1 CA41 4
Wolseley St. SE1 CA41 67
Wolsen St. E1 CC39 57
Sidney St.
Wolsey Av. E17 CD31 48
Wolsey Av. E6 CL38 58
Wolsey Av., Chsnt. CB18 21
Wolsey Av., T.Ditt. BH53 84
Wolsey Clo. SW20 BP50 75
Wolsey Clo., Houns. BG46 74
Wolsey Clo., Kings.T. BM51 85
Wolsey Clo., Sthl. BG41 64
Wolsey Clo., Wor.Pk. BO56 94
Wolsey Cres., Croy. CF58 96
Wolsey Cres., Mord. BR54 85
Wolsey Dr., Kings.T. BL49 75
Wolsey Dr., Walt. BD54 84
Wolsey Gdns., Ilf. CL29 40
Wolsey Gro., Edg. BN29 37
Wolsey Gro., Esher BF56 93
Wolsey Ms. NW5 BW36 56
Caversham Rd.
Wolsey Ms., Orp. CN56 97
Osgood Av.
Wolsey Rd. N1 BZ35 48
Wolsey Rd., Ashf. AY49 73
Wolsey Rd., E.Mol. BG52 84
Wolsey Rd., Enf. CB23 30
Wolsey Rd., Esher BF56 93
Wolsey Rd., Hmptn. BF50 74
Wolsey Rd., Nthwd. BA27 35
Wolsey Rd., Sun. BB50 73
Wolsey St. E1 CC39 57
Sidney St.
Wolsey Way, Chess. BM56 94
Wolsey Wk., Wok. AS62 100
Church St. W.
Wolsley Clo., Dart. CT46 79
Wolstonbury N12 BR28 37
Wolvens La., Dor. BF73 119
Wolvercote Rd. SE2 CP41 69
Wolverley St. E2 CB38 57
Bethnal Green Rd.
Wolverton Av., Kings.T. BM51 85
Wolverton Gdns. W5 BL40 55
Wolverton Gdns. W6 BQ42 65
Wolverton Rd., Stan. BK29 36
Wolverton Way N14 BW25 29
Wolves La. N13 BY29 38
Wolves La. N22 BY29 38
Womersley Rd. N8 BX32 47
Wonersh Way, Sutt. BQ58 94
Wonford Clo., Kings.T. BO51 85
Wonford Clo., Tadd. BP66 112
Wonham La., Bet. BO71 120
Wontford Rd., Pur. BY61 104
Wontner Rd. SW17 BU48 76
Wood Av. NW9 BO33 46
Wood Av., Grays CY42 70
Wood Church Dr., Brom. CJ50 78
Wood Clo. E2 CB38 2
Wood Clo. NW9 BN33 46
Wood Clo., Bex. CT48 79
Wood Clo., Har. BG33 45
Wood Clo., Hat. BP12 10
Wood Clo., Wind. AO45 61
Wood Common, Hat. BP11 10
Wood Cres., Hem.H. AX14 8
Wood Dene, Lthd. BG59 93
Wood Dr., Chis. CK50 78
Wood Dr., Sev. CT66 116
Wood End Av., Har. BF35 45
Wood End Clo., Nthlt. BG35 45
Wood End Clo., Slou. AO34 43
Wood End Gdns., Nthlt. BG35 45
Wood End Green Rd., Hayes BA39 53
Wood End La., Nthlt. BF36 54
Wood End Rd., Har. BG35 45
Wood End Way, Nthlt. BG35 45
Wood End, Esher BG55 84
Wood End, Hayes BB39 53
Wood End, Lthd. BK66 111
Wood End, St.Alb. BG17 18
Wood Farm Rd., Hem.H. AY14 8
Wood Gate, Wat. BC20 17
Wood Green Way, Chsnt. CD19 21
Wood La. N6 BV32 47
Wood La. NW9 BN33 46
Wood La. W12 BQ39 55
Wood La., Cat. BZ65 105
Wood La., Dag. CP35 50
Wood La., Dart. CY49 80
Wood La., Horn. CU35 50
Wood La., Islw. BH43 64
Wood La., Iver AU38 52
Wood La., Ong. DC13 15
Wood La., Ruis. BA33 44
Wood La., Slou. AN41 61
Wood La., Stan. BJ27 36
Wood La., Tad. BR62 103
Wood La., Wdf.Grn. CG28 40
Wood La., Wey. BA58 92
Wood La., Wok. AO62 100
Wood Lane Clo., Iver AU38 52

Wood Lane End, Hem.H. AZ13 8
Wood Lodge Gdns., Brom. CK50 78
Wood Lodge La., W.Wick. CF55 87
Wood Meads, Epp. CO18 23
Wood Pond Clo., Beac. AO29 34
Drovers Way
Wood Rd., Sev. CZ57 99
Wood Rd., Shep. AZ52 83
Wood Rd., West. CJ62 106
Wood Ri., Guil. AP69 118
Wood Ri., Pnr. BC32 44
Wood Ride, Barn. BT23 29
Wood Ride, Orp. CM52 88
Wood Riding, Wok. AV61 100
Wood St. E16 CH39 58
Ethel Rd.
Wood St. E17 CF31 48
Wood St. EC2 BZ39 2
Wood St. EC2 BZ39 57
Wood St. W4 BO42 65
Wood St., Barn. BQ24 28
Wood St., Grays DE43 71
Wood St., Kings.T. BK51 84
Wood St., Mitch. BU54 86
Wood St., Red. BW68 113
Wood St., Swan. CV51 90
Wood Vale Est. SE23 CB47 77
Wood Vale N10 BW32 47
Wood Vale SE23 CB47 77
Wood Vale, Hat. BP12 10
Wood Vw., Chess. BK59 93
Wood Vw., Cuff. BW17 20
Wood Vw., Grays DE41 71
Wood Vw., Hem.H. AW12 8
Wood Way, Orp. CL55 88
Wood Way, Sev. CT64 107
Wood Wharf SE10 CF43 67
Wood Yard Clo. NW5 BV35 47
Gillies St.
Wood, The, Surb. BL53 85
Woodall Rd., Enf. CC25 30
Woodbank N12 BS28 38
Woodbank Rd., Brom. CG48 78
Woodbarn Way, Wal.Cr. CD19 21
Woodbastwick Rd. SE26 CC50 77
Woodberry Av. N12 BT29 38
Woodberry Av. N21 BY27 38
Woodberry Av., Har. BF31 45
Woodberry Clo., Sun. BC50 73
Woodberry Cres. N10 BV31 47
Woodberry Down Est. N4 BZ33 48
Woodberry Down N4 BZ33 48
Woodberry Down, Epp. CO17 23
Woodberry Gdns. N12 BT29 38
Woodberry Gro. N12 BT29 38
Woodberry Gro. N4 BZ33 48
Woodberry Gro., Bex. CS48 79
Briar Rd.
Woodberry Way E4 CF26 39
Woodberry Way N12 BT29 38
Woodbine Clo., Harl. CM12 13
Linford End
Woodbine Clo., Twick. BG48 74
Woodbine Clo., Wal.Abb. CJ21 31
Woodbine Gro. SE20 CB50 77
Woodbine Gro., Enf. BZ22 30
Woodbine La., Wor.Pk. BP55 85
Woodbine Pl. E11 CH32 49
Woodbine Rd., Sid. CN47 78
Woodbine Ter. E9 CC36 57
Homerton Ter.
Woodbines Av., Kings.T. BK52 84
Woodborough Rd. SW15 BP45 65
Woodbourne Av. SW16 BW48 76
Woodbourne Clo. SW16 BW48 76
Woodbourne Dr., Esher BH57 93
Woodbourne Gdns., Wall. BV57 95
Woodbridge Av., Lthd. BJ62 102
Woodbridge Clo. N7 BX34 47
Durham Rd.
Woodbridge Clo. NW2 BP34 46
Newfield Ri.
Woodbridge Clo., Rom. CV28 42
Woodbridge Ct., Wdf.Grn. CK29 40
Vicarage Rd.
Woodbridge Gdns., Lthd. BJ62 102
Woodbridge Hill Gdns., Guil. AQ70 118
Woodbridge Hill, Guil. AQ70 118
Woodbridge La., Rom. CV27 42
Woodbridge Meadows, Guil. AQ70 118
Woodbridge Rd., Bark. CN35 49
Woodbridge Rd., Guil. AR70 118
Woodbridge St. EC1 BY38 2
Woodbridge St. EC1 BY38 56
Woodbrook Clo., Wal.Abb. CG20 22
Woodbrook Rd. SE2 CO43 69
Woodburn Clo. NW4 BQ32 46
Woodburn Clo., Uxb. AZ38 53
Aldenham Dr.
Woodbury Clo. E11 CH31 49
Woodbury Clo., Croy. CA55 87
Woodbury Clo., West. CK62 106
Belvedere Rd.
Woodbury Dr., Sutt. BT58 95
Woodbury Hill, Loug. CK23 31
Woodbury Park Rd. W13 BJ38 54
Woodbury Rd. E17 CE31 48
Woodbury Rd., West. CK62 106
Woodbury St. SW17 BU49 76
Woodchester Sq. W2 BS39 56
Woodchurch Clo., Sid. CM48 78
Woodchurch Rd. NW6 BS36 56
Woodclyffe Dr., Chis. CL51 88
Woodcock Dell Av., Har. BK33 45
Woodcock Hill, B.Wd. BM25 28
Woodcock Hill, Har. BK32 45
Woodcock Hill, Rick. AX28 35
Woodcock Hill, St.Alb. BK10 9
Woodcombe Cres. SE23 CC47 77
Woodcote Av. NW7 BQ29 37
Woodcote Av., Horn. CU35 50
Woodcote Av., Th.Hth. BY52 86
Woodcote Av., Wall. BV58 95
Woodcote Clo., Chsnt. CC18 21
Woodcote Clo., Enf. CC25 30
Woodcote Clo., Epsom BN60 94
Woodcote Clo., Kings.T. BL50 75
Woodcote Dr., Pur. BW58 95
Woodcote End, Epsom BN61 103
Woodcote Green Rd., Epsom BN61 103
Woodcote Green Rd., Wall. BW58 95
Woodcote Gro., Cars. BV59 95
Woodcote Grove Rd., Couls. BW61 104
Woodcote Hurst, Epsom BN61 103
Woodcote La., Pur. BW59 95
Woodcote Park Av., Pur. BW59 95
Woodcote Park Rd., Epsom BN61 103
Woodcote Pl. SE27 BY49 76
Woodcote Rd. E11 CH33 49
Woodcote Rd., Epsom BN60 94
Woodcote Rd., Orp. CN54 88
Woodcote Rd., Wall. BV57 95
Woodcote Side, Epsom BM61 103
Woodcote Valley Rd., Pur. BW60 95
Woodcourt Clo., Wal.Cr. CC18 21
Woodcraft Av., Stan. BJ30 36
Woodcrest Rd., Pur. BX60 95
Woodcrest Wk., Reig. BU69 121
Woodcroft Av. NW7 BO29 37
Woodcroft Cres., Grnf. BJ36 54
Woodcroft Cres., Uxb. AZ37 53
Woodcroft N21 BX26 38
Woodcroft Rd., Chesh. AO17 16
Woodcroft Rd., Th.Hth. BY53 86
Woodcroft SE9 CK48 78
Woodcroft, Harl. CM12 13
Woodcutters Av., Grays DE41 71
Woodedge Clo. E4 CG26 40
Forest Side
Woodend Clo., Wok. AQ63 100
Woodend Gdns., Enf. BX24 29
Woodend Pk., Cob. BD61 102
Woodend Rd. E17 CF30 39
Woodend SE19 BZ50 77
Woodend, Sutt. BT55 86
Woodend, The, Wall. BV58 95
Wooder Gdns. E7 CG35 49
Wooderson Clo. SE25 CA52 87
Clifton Rd.
Woodfall Av., Barn. BR25 28
Woodfall Dr., Dart. CT45 69
Woodfall Rd. N4 BY33 47
Woodfall St. SW3 BU42 3
Woodfall St. SW3 BU42 66
Woodfarrs SE5 BZ45 67
Woodfield Av. NW9 BO31 46
Woodfield Av. SW16 BW48 76
Woodfield Av. W5 BK38 54
Woodfield Av., Cars. BV57 95
Woodfield Av., Grav. DG48 81
Woodfield Av., Nthwd. BB28 35
Woodfield Av., Wem. BK34 45
Woodfield Clo. SE19 BZ50 77
Woodfield Clo., Ash. BK62 102
Woodfield Clo., Couls. BW63 104
Woodfield Clo., Red. BU70 121
Woodfield Cres. W5 BK38 54
Woodfield Dr., Barn. BV26 38
Woodfield Dr., Hem.H. BA14 8
Woodfield Dr., Rom. CU31 50
Woodfield Gdns. W9 BR39 55
Woodfield Rd.
Woodfield Gdns., Hem.H. BA14 8
Woodfield Dr.
Woodfield Gdns., N.Mal. BO53 85
Woodfield Gro. SW16 BW48 76
Woodfield Hill, Couls. BV63 104
Woodfield La. SW16 BW48 76
Woodfield La., Ash. BL62 103
Woodfield La., Hat. BT15 11
Woodfield Pl. W9 BR39 55
Woodfield Rd. W5 BK38 54
Woodfield Rd. W9 BR39 55
Woodfield Rd., Ash. BK62 102
Woodfield Rd., Houns. BC44 63
Woodfield Rd., Rad. BJ21 27
Woodfield Rd., T.Ditt. BH55 84
Woodfield Rd., Welw.G.C. BR 8 5
Woodfield Ri., Bush. BG26 36
Woodfield Way N11 BW29 38
Woodfield Way, Horn. CV33 51
Woodfield Way, Red. BU70 121
Woodfield Way, St.Alb. BK12 9
Woodfields, Sev. CS65 107
Woodfields, The, S.Croy. CA59 96
Woodfines, The, Horn. CV32 51
Burntwood Av.
Woodford Av., Ilf. CJ31 49
Woodford Bridge Rd., Ilf. CJ31 49
Woodford Cres., Pnr. BC30 35
Woodford Ct., Wal.Abb. CH20 22
Abbots Dr.
Woodford New Rd. E17 CG31 49
Woodford New Rd. E18 CG31 49
Woodford New Rd., Wdf.Grn. CG31 49
Woodford Pl., Wem. BL33 46
Woodford Rd. E18 CG33 49
Woodford Rd. E7 CH35 49
Woodford Rd., Wat. BD23 27
Woodford Trd. Est. E18 CJ30 40
Woodgate Av., Chess. BK56 93
Woodgate Cres., Nthwd. BC29 35
Woodgavil, Bans. BR61 103
Woodger Clo., Guil. AU69 118
Woodger Rd. W12 BQ41 65
Goldhawk Rd.
Woodgers Gro., Swan. CT51 89
Swanley La.
Woodget Clo. E6 CK39 58
Remington Rd.
Woodgrange Av. N12 BT29 38
Woodgrange Av. W5 BM40 55
Woodgrange Av., Enf. CB25 30
Woodgrange Av., Har. BK32 45
Woodgrange Clo., Har. BK32 45
Woodgrange Gdns., Enf. CB25 30
Woodgrange Rd. E7 CH35 49
Woodgrange Ter., Enf. CB25 30
Woodgreen La., Wal.Abb. CH20 22
Woodgreen Rd., Wal.Abb. CJ20 22
Woodhall Av. SE21 CA48 77
Woodhall Av., Pnr. BE30 36
Woodhall Clo., Uxb. AX35 44
Woodhall Cres., Horn. CW33 51
Woodhall Ct., Welw.G.C. BR 8 5
Woodhall Dr. SE21 CA48 77
Woodhall Dr., Pnr. BD30 36
Woodhall Gate, Pnr. BD29 36
Woodhall La., Hem.H. AY13 8
Woodhall La., Rad. BL21 28
Woodhall La., Wat. BD27 36
Woodhall La., Welw.G.C. BR 8 5
Woodhall Par., Welw.G.C. BR 9 5
Woodhall Rd., Pnr. BD29 36
Woodham Ct. E18 CG31 49
Woodham La., Wey. AV59 91
Woodham La., Wok. AT60 91
Woodham Park Rd., Wey. AV58 91
Woodham Park Way, Wey. AV59 91
Woodham Rd. SE6 CF48 77
Woodham Rd., Wok. AS61 100
Woodham Ri., Wok. AT61 100
Woodham Waye, Wok. AT60 91
Woodhatch Clo. E6 CK39 58
Leamouth Rd.
Woodhatch Rd., Reig. & Red. BT72 121
Woodhatch Spinney, Couls. BX61 104
Woodhaven Gdns., Ilf. CM31 49
Brandville Gdns.
Woodhaw, Egh. AT49 72
Woodhayes Rd. SW19 BQ50 75
Woodhead Dr., Orp. CN55 88
Woodheyes Rd. NW10 BN35 46
Woodhill Av., Ger.Cr. AS32 43
Woodhill Cres., Har. BK32 45
Woodhill SE18 CK41 68
Woodhill, Harl. CN13 13
Woodhill, Wok. AU66 109
Woodhouse Av., Grnf. BH37 54
Woodhouse Clo., Grnf. BH37 54
Woodhouse Clo., Hayes BB41 63
Woodhouse Eaves, Nthwd. BC29 35
Eastbury Av.
Woodhouse Gro. E12 CK36 58
Woodhouse Rd. E11 CG34 49
Woodhouse Rd. N12 BT29 38
Woodhurst Av., Orp. CL53 88
Woodhurst Av., Wat. BD21 27
Woodhurst Dr., Uxb. AV32 43
Woodhurst La., Oxt. CG68 115
Woodhurst Pk., Oxt. CG68 115
Woodhurst Rd. SE2 CO42 69
Woodhurst Rd. W3 BN40 55
Woodhyrst Gdns., Ken. BY61 104
Wooding Gro., Harl. CL11 13
Woodington Clo. SE9 CL46 78
Woodison St. E3 CD38 57
Woodknoll Dr., Brom. CK51 88
Woodland App., Grnf. BJ36 54
Whitton Dr.
Woodland Av., Brwd. DD25 122
Woodland Av., Hem.H. AW14 8
Woodland Av., Slou. AO40 52
Woodland Av., Wind. AM45 61
Woodland Clo. NW9 BN32 46
Woodland Clo., Brwd. DE25 122
Woodland Clo., Epsom BO57 94
Woodland Clo., Lthd. BB67 110
Woodland Clo., Uxb. AZ34 44
Woodland Clo., Wdf.Grn. CH27 40
Woodland Cres. SE10 CG43 68
Woodland Ct., Oxt. CF67 114
Woodland Dr., Lthd. BB67 110
Woodland Dr., St.Alb. BK13 9
Woodland Dr., Wat. BB23 26
Woodland Gdns. N10 BV32 47
Woodland Gdns., Croy. CC59 96
Woodland Gdns., Islw. BH45 64
Woodland Gdns., S.Croy. CC58 96
Woodland Gro. SE10 CG42 68
Woodland Gro., Wey. BA56 92
Woodland Hill SE19 CA50 77
Woodland La., Rick. AU24 25
Woodland Pl., Hem.H. AW14 8
Woodland Rd. E4 CF26 39
Woodland Rd. N11 BV28 38
Woodland Rd. SE19 CA49 77
Woodland Rd., Loug. CK24 31
Woodland Rd., Rick. AU28 34
Woodland Rd., Th.Hth. BY52 86
Woodland Ri. N10 BV31 47
Woodland Ri., Grnf. BJ36 54
Woodland Ri., Oxt. CG68 115
Woodland Ri., Sev. CW65 108
Woodland Ri., Welw.G.C. BQ 7 5
Woodland St. E8 CA36 57
Dalston La.
Woodland Ter. SE18 CK42 68
Woodland Ter. SE7 CK42 68
Woodland Vw., Chesh. AO20 16
Woodland Way N21 BY27 38
Woodland Way NW11 BS32 47
Woodland Way NW7 BO29 37
Woodland Way SE2 CP42 69
Woodland Way, Cat. CA67 114
Woodland Way, Chsnt. BY17 20
Woodland Way, Croy. CD54 87
Woodland Way, Epp. CM21 31
Woodland Way, Mitch. BV50 76
Woodland Way, Mord. BR52 85
Woodland Way, Ong. CW18 24
Woodland Way, Orp. CM52 88
Woodland Way, Pur. BY60 95
Woodland Way, Surb. BM55 85
Woodland Way, Tad. BR64 103
Woodland Way, W.Wick. CE56 96
Woodland Way, Wdf.Grn. CH27 40
Woodland Way, Wey. BA56 92
Woodland Wk. SE10 CG42 68
Woodland Gro.
Woodlands Av. E11 CH33 49
Woodlands Av. N12 BT29 38
Woodlands Av. W3 BM40 55
High St.
Woodlands Av., Berk. AR13 7
Woodlands Av., Horn. CV32 51
Woodlands Av., N.Mal. BN51 85
Woodlands Av., Red. BU71 121
Woodlands Av., Rom. CQ32 50
Woodlands Av., Ruis. BD33 45
Woodlands Av., Sid. CN47 78
Woodlands Av., Wey. AV60 91
Woodlands Av., Wor.Pk. BO55 85
Woodlands Clo. NW11 BR32 46
Woodlands Clo., B.Wd. BM24 28
Woodlands Clo., Brom. CK51 88
Woodlands Clo., Cher. AT58 91
Woodlands Clo., Esher BH57 93
Woodlands Clo., Ger.Cr. AT32 43
Woodlands Clo., Grays DF41 71
Woodlands Clo., Hem.H. AW14 8
Woodlands Clo., Hodd. CE12 12
Woodlands Clo., Swan. CT52 89
Woodlands Clo., Wey. BA56 92
Woodlands Ct., Wok. AS63 100
Constitution Hill
Woodlands Dr., Har. BH29 36
Woodlands Dr., Hodd. CE13 12
Woodlands Dr., Kings L. BA17 17
Woodlands Dr., Sun. BD51 84
Woodlands Dr., Wat. BC23 26
Woodlands Gdns. E17 CG31 49
Woodford New Rd.
Woodlands Gro., Couls. BV62 104
Woodlands Gro., Islw. BH44 64
Woodlands La., Cob. BF62 104
Woodlands Par., Ashf. BA50 73
Hogarth Av.
Woodlands Park Rd. SE10 CG43 68
Woodlands Park Rd. N15 BY32 47
Woodlands Pk., Bex. CS49 79
Woodlands Pk., Guil. AT70 118
Woodlands Pk., Tad. BM69 120
Woodlands Pk., Wey. AV56 91
Woodlands Rd. E., Vir.W. AR52 82
Woodlands Rd. E11 CG34 49
Woodlands Rd. E17 CF31 48
Woodlands Rd. N9 CC26 39
Woodlands Rd. SW13 BO45 65
Woodlands Rd. W., Vir.W. AR52 82
Woodlands Rd., Effingham BE67 111
Woodlands Rd., Bexh. CQ45 69
Woodlands Rd., Brom. CK51 88
Woodlands Rd., Bush. BE25 27
Woodlands Rd., Enf. BZ23 30
Woodlands Rd., Epsom BM61 103
Woodlands Rd., Guil. AR68 109
Woodlands Rd., Har. BH32 45
Woodlands Rd., Harold Wood CX30 42
Woodlands Rd., Hem.H. AZ17 17
Woodlands Rd., Ilf. CM34 49
Woodlands Rd., Islw. BG45 64
Woodlands Rd., Lthd. BG62 102
Woodlands Rd., Orp. CO57 98
Woodlands Rd., Red. BU71 121
Woodlands Rd., Rom. CT31 50
Woodlands Rd., Sthl. BD40 54
Woodlands Rd., Surb. BK54 84
Woodlands Rd., Vir.W. AR52 82
Woodlands Rd., Wey. AV60 91
Woodlands Ri., Swan. CT51 89
Woodlands St. SE13 CF47 77
Woodlands SW20 BQ52 85
Woodlands Way SW15 BR46 75
Woodlands Way, Ash. BM61 103
Woodlands NW11 BR32 46
Woodlands, Har. BF31 45
Woodlands, Hat. BS17 20
Woodlands, Rad. BJ20 18
Woodlands, The N14 BV26 38
Woodlands, The SE13 CF47 77
Woodlands, The SE19 BZ50 77
Woodlands, The, Amer. AO21 25
Woodlands, The, Esher BG55 84
Woodlands, The, Ger.Cr. AS32 43
Woodlands, The, Islw. BH44 64
Woodlands, The, Orp. CO57 98
Woodlands, The, Wall. BV58 95
Woodlands, The, Wind. AM45 61
Nelson Rd.
Woodlawn Clo. SW15 BR46 75
Woodlawn Cres., Twick. BF48 74
Woodlawn Dr., Felt. BD48 74
Woodlawn Gro., Wok. AS61 100
Woodlawn Rd. SW6 BQ43 65
Woodlea Dr., Brom. CG53 88
Woodlea Est., Brom. CG53 88
Woodlea Gro., Nthwd. BA29 35
Woodlea Rd. N16 CA34 48
Woodleigh Av. N12 BU29 38
Woodleigh Gdns. SW16 BX48 76
Woodley Clo. SW17 BU50 76
Woodley Hill, Chesh. AO20 16
Woodley La., Cars. BU55 86
Woodley Rd., Orp. CP55 89
Woodman La. E4 CG25 31
Woodman Path, Chig. CN29 40
Woodman Pl. SE7 CK42 68
Maryon Rd.
Woodman Rd., Brwd. DB28 42
Woodman Rd., Couls. BW61 104
Woodman Rd., Hem.H. AY14 8
Woodman St. E16 CL40 58
Woodmancote Gdns., Wey. AW60 92
Elmstead Rd.
Woodmans Ct., Stan. BL30 37
Woodmans Gro. NW10 BO35 46
Broadfields Way
Woodmans Ms. W12 BP39 55
Woodmansterne La., Bans. BS61 104
Woodmansterne La., Cars. BU59 95
Woodmansterne Rd. SW16 BW50 76
Woodmansterne Rd., Couls. BW61 104
Woodmansterne Rd., Cars. BU58 76
Woodmansterne St., Bans. BU61 104
Woodmere Av., Croy. CC54 87
Woodmere Av., Wat. BD22 27
Woodmere Clo. SW11 BV45 66
Lavender Hill
Woodmere Clo., Croy. CC54 87
Woodmere Gdns., Croy. CC54 87
Woodmere SE9 CK47 78
Woodmere Way, Beck. CF53 87
Woodmount, Swan. CS54 89
Woodnook Rd. SW16 BV49 76
Woodpecker Clo. N9 CB25 30
Woodpecker Clo., Bush. BG26 36
Woodpecker Clo., Cob. BE59 93
Green La.
Woodpecker Mt., Croy. CD58 96
Woodpecker Rd. SE14 CD43 67
Woodpecker Rd. SE28 CP40 59
Woodpecker Way, Wok. AR65 100
Woodplace Clo., Couls. BW63 104
Woodplace La., Couls. BW64 104
Woodquest Av. SE24 BZ46 77
Woodredon Clo., Harl. CH11 13
Woodridden Hill, Wal.Abb. CJ21 31
Woodridge Clo., Enf. BY23 29
Woodridge Way, Nthwd. BB29 35
Woodridings Av., Pnr. BE30 36
Woodridings Clo., Pnr. BE29 36
Woodriffe Rd. E11 CF33 48
Woodrow Av., Hayes BB39 53
Woodrow Clo., Grnf. BJ36 54
Woodrow SE18 CK42 68
Woodruff Av., Guil. AT69 118
Woodrush Clo. SE14 CD43 67
Southerngate Way
Woodrush Way, Rom. CP31 50
Woods Av., Hat. BP12 10
Woods Bldgs. E1 CB39 57
Durward St.
Woods Clo. SE19 CA50 77
Woodland Hill
Woods Ms. W1 BV40 3
Woods Ms. W1 BV40 56
Woods Pl. SE1 CA41 4
Woods Pl. SE1 CA41 67
Woods Rd. SE15 CB44 67
Woods Way, Lthd. BH60 93
Woods, The, Nthwd. BC28 35
Woods, The, Uxb. AZ35 44
Woodseer St. E1 CA39 2
Woodseer St. E1 CA39 57
Woodsford Sq. W14 BR41 65
Woodshire Rd., Dag. CR34 50
Woodshore Clo., Vir.W. AQ53 82
Woodshots Meadow, Wat. BA25 26
Woodside Av. N10 BU32 47
Woodside Av. N12 BS28 38
Woodside Av. N6 BU32 47
Woodside Av. SE25 CB53 87
Woodside Av., Amer. AO21 25
Woodside Av., Chis. CL49 78
Woodside Av., Esher BH54 84
Woodside Av., Walt. BC56 92
Woodside Av., Wem. BL37 55
Woodside Clo., Amer. AO22 25
Woodside Clo., Bexh. CS45 69
Woodside Clo., Brwd. DE25 122
Woodside Clo., Cat. CA65 105
Woodside Clo., Ger.Cr. AS30 34
Woodside Clo., Rain. CV38 60
Woodside Clo., Stan. BJ28 36
Woodside Clo., Surb. BN54 85
Woodside Clo., Wem. BL37 55
Woodside Clo., Wok. AO62 100
Woodside Cres., Sid. CN48 78
Woodside Ct. Rd., Croy. CB54 87
Woodside Dr., Dart. CT49 79
Woodside End, Wem. BL37 55
Woodside Gdns. E4 CE28 39
Woodside Gdns. N17 CA30 39
Woodside Grange Rd. N12 BS28 38
Woodside Grn. SE25 CB53 87
Woodside Gro. N12 BT27 38
Woodside Hill, Ger.Cr. AS30 34
Woodside La. N12 BS27 38
Woodside La., Bex. CP46 79
Woodside La., Hat. BS15 11
Woodside NW11 BS32 47
Woodside Pk. Av. E17 CF32 48
Woodside Pk. Rd. N12 BS28 38
Woodside Pk. SE25 CB53 87
Woodside Pl., Wem. BL37 55
Woodside Rd. E13 CJ38 58
Woodside Rd. N22 BX29 38
Woodside Rd. SE25 CB53 87
Woodside Rd., Welw.G.C. BR 5 5
Woodside Rd., Amer. AO22 25
Woodside Rd., Bexh. CS45 69
Woodside Rd., Brasted CP65 107
Woodside Rd., Brom. CK53 88
Woodside Rd., Cob. BF60 93
Woodside Rd., Guil. AP70 118
Woodside Rd., Kings.T. BL50 75
Woodside Rd., N.Mal. BN51 85

Name	Grid	Page
Woodside Rd., Nthwd.	BB29	35
Woodside Rd., Pur.	BW60	95
Woodside Rd., Sev.	CU65	107
Woodside Rd., Sid.	CN48	78
Woodside Rd., St.Alb.	BE18	18
Woodside Rd., Sutt.	BT55	86
Woodside Rd., Wat.	BC19	17
Woodside Rd., Wdf.Grn.	CH28	40
Woodside SW19	BR50	75
Woodside Vw., Sev.	CR58	98
Woodside Way, Croy.	CC53	87
Woodside Way, Mitch.	BV51	86
Woodside Way, Red.	BV73	121
Woodside Way, Reig.	BV71	121
Woodside Way, Vir.W.	AQ52	82
Woodside, B.Wd.	BL24	28
Woodside, Buck.H.	CJ27	40
Woodside, Chsnt.	CB19	21
Woodside, Epp.	CP16	23
Woodside, Horsley	BA66	110
Woodside, Lthd.	BF64	102
Woodside, Orp.	CO56	98
Woodside, Tad.	BR67	112
Woodside, Wat.	BC22	26
Woodsome Clo., Wey.	BA57	92
Woodsome Rd. NW5	BV34	47
Woodspring Rd. SW19	BR48	75
Woodstead Gro., Edg.	BL29	37
Woodstock Av. NW11	BR33	46
Woodstock Av. W13	BJ41	64
Woodstock Av., Islw.	BJ46	74
Woodstock Av., Rom.	CX28	42
Woodstock Av., Slou.	AR42	62
Woodstock Av., Sthl.	BE38	54
Woodstock Av., Sutt.	BR54	85
Woodstock Clo., Bex.	CQ47	79
Woodstock Clo., Stan.	BL30	37
Woodstock Cres. N9	CB25	30
Woodstock Ct. SE12	CH46	78
Woodstock Dr., Uxb.	AY35	44
Woodstock Gdns., Beck.	CE50	77
Woodstock Gdns., Hayes	BB39	53
Woodstock Gdns., Ilf.	CO34	50
Woodstock Gro. W12	BQ41	65
Woodstock La., Esher	BJ57	93
Woodstock Ms. W1	**BV39**	**1**
Woodstock Rd. E17	CF30	39
Woodstock Rd. E7	CJ36	58
Woodstock Rd. N., St.Alb.	BJ12	9
Woodstock Rd. N4	BY33	47
Woodstock Rd. NW11	BR33	46
Woodstock Rd. S., St.Alb.	BJ13	9
Woodstock Rd. W4	BO42	65
Woodstock Rd., Brox.	CD13	12
Woodstock Rd., Bush.	BH26	36
Woodstock Rd., Cars.	BV56	95
Woodstock Rd., Couls.	BV61	104
Woodstock Rd., Croy.	BZ55	87
Woodstock Rd., Wem.	BL37	55
Woodstock Ri. Sutt.	BR54	85
Woodstock Rd. SE16	CG39	58
Woodstock St. W1	**BV39**	**1**
Woodstock St. W1	BV39	56
Oxford St.		
Woodstock Ter. E14	CE40	57
Woodstock Way, Mitch.	BV51	86
Woodstock, Guil.	AW67	110
Woodstock, Surb.	BK55	84
Woodstone Av., Epsom	BP56	94
Woodsyre Est. SE26	BZ49	77
Woodthorpe Rd., Ashf.	AX50	73
Woodtree Clo. NW4	BQ30	37
Ashley La.		
Woodvale Av. SE25	CA52	87
Woodview Av. E4	CF28	39
Woodview Clo. N4	BY33	47
Woodview Clo., Orp.	CL55	88
Crofton Rd.		
Woodview Clo., S.Croy.	CB60	96
Woodview Clo., Sev.	CZ57	99
Woodview Rd., Swan.	CS51	89
Woodville Clo., SE12	CH46	78
Woodville Clo., Tedd.	BJ49	74
Woodville Ct., Wat.	BC23	26
Woodville Gdns. NW11	BQ33	46
Hendon Way		
Woodville Gdns. W5	BL39	55
Woodville Gdns., Ilf.	CL31	49
Woodville Gdns., Ruis.	BA33	44
Woodville Gro. N16	CA35	48
Woodville Rd.		
Woodville Gro., Well.	CO45	69
Ruskin Rd.		
Woodville Pl., Cat.	BZ64	105
Woodville Rd. E11	CG33	49
Woodville Rd. E17	CD31	48
Woodville Rd. E18	CH30	40
Woodville Rd. N16	CA35	48
Woodville Rd. NW11	BQ33	46
Woodville Rd. NW6	BR37	55
Woodville Rd. W5	BK39	54
Woodville Rd., Barn.	BS24	29
Woodville Rd., Lthd.	BJ63	102
Woodville Rd., Mord.	BS52	86
Woodville Rd., Rich.	BJ48	74
Woodville Rd., Th.Hth.	BZ52	87
Woodville SE3	CH44	68
Woodville St. SE18	CK42	68
Woodward Av. NW4	BP32	46
Woodward Clo., Grays	DD42	71
Woodward Gdns., Dag.	CO36	59
Woodward Rd.		
Woodward Gdns., Stan.	BJ29	36
May Tree La.		
Woodward Heights, Grays	DD42	71
Woodward Clo.		
Woodward Rd., Dag.	CO36	59
Woodward Ter., Green.	CZ46	80
Woodwarde Rd. SE22	CA46	77
Woodwards, Harl.	CM12	13
Woodway Cres., Harl.	BJ32	45
Woodway, Brwd.	DD26	122
Woodway, Guil.	AT70	118
Woodwaye, Wat.	BD26	36
Woodwell St. SW18	BT46	76
North Side		
Woodyard Clo. NW5	BV35	47
Gillies St.		
Woodyard La. SE21	CA47	77
Woodyates Rd. SE12	CG46	78
Wool Rd. SW20	BP50	75
Woolacombe Rd. SE3	CH44	68
Woolacombe Way, Hayes	BB42	63
Woolaston Rd. N4	BY32	47
Wooler St. SE17	**BZ42**	**4**
Wooler St. SE17	BZ42	67
Woolf Clo. SE28	CO40	59
Woolf Wk., Til.	DH44	71
Coleridge Rd.		
Woolhampton Way, Chig.	CO27	41
Woollam Cres., St.Alb.	BG11	9
Woollard St., Wal.Abb.	CF20	21
Woollard Way, Ing.	DC19	24
Woolmans Clo., Brox.	CD14	12
Woolmead Av. NW9	BP33	46
Woolmer Clo., B.Wd.	BM22	28
Woolmer Dr., Hem.H.	BA13	8
Woolmer Gdns. N18	CB29	39
Woolmer Rd. N18	CB28	39
Woolmongers La., Ing.	DA19	24
Woolmore St. E14	CF40	57
Woolnams, Cat.	CA66	114
Woolneigh St. SW6	BS45	66
Woolsey Rd., Hem.H.	AX14	8
Woolstan Clo., Uxb.	AW34	44
Woolstaplers Way SE16	**CB42**	**4**
Woolston Clo. E17	CC30	39
Woolstone Rd. SE23	CD48	77
Woolwich Church St. SE18	CK41	68
Woolwich Common SE18	CL43	68
Woolwich High St. SE18	CK41	68
Woolwich Ind. Est. SE28	CN41	68
Woolwich Manor Way E16	CL40	58
Woolwich New Rd. SE18	CL42	68
Woolwich Rd. SE10	CG42	68
Woolwich Rd. SE2	CP43	69
Woolwich Rd. SE7	CG42	68
Woolwich Rd., Belv.	CP43	69
Woolwich Rd., Bexh.	CR45	69
Wooster Gdns. E14	CF39	57
Woosters Ms., Har.	BG31	45
Fairfield Dr.		
Wooton Dr., Hem.H.	AY11	8
Wooton Rd., Horn.	CV32	51
Wootton Gro. N3	BS30	38
Station Rd.		
Wootton St. SE1	**BY41**	**4**
Wootton St. SE1	BY41	66
Worbeck Rd. SE20	CB51	87
Worcester Av. N17	CB29	39
Worcester Av., Upmin.	CZ34	51
Worcester Clo., Croy.	CD55	87
Worcester Clo., Green.	DA45	70
Worcester Clo., Mitch.	BV51	86
Worcester Cres. NW7	BO27	37
Worcester Cres., Wdf.Grn.	CH28	40
Worcester Ct., Walt.	BD54	84
Worcester Gdns., Wor.Pk.	BO55	85
Worcester Gdns., Grnf.	BG36	54
Worcester Gdns., Ilf.	CK33	49
Worcester Ms. NW6	BS36	56
Lymington Rd.		
Worcester Park Rd., Wor.Pk.	BN55	85
Worcester Pl. EC4	**BZ40**	**4**
Upper Thames St.		
Worcester Rd. E12	CK35	49
Worcester Rd. E17	CC30	39
Worcester Rd. SW19	BR49	75
Worcester Rd., Guil.	AP69	118
Worcester Rd., Hat.	BO12	10
Worcester Rd., Reig.	BS70	121
Worcester Rd., Sutt.	BS57	95
Worcester Rd., Uxb.	AX39	53
Worcesters Av., Enf.	CB22	30
Wordsworth Av. E12	CK36	58
Wordsworth Av. E18	CG31	49
Wordsworth Av., Grnf.	BG38	54
Wordsworth Av., Pur.	BZ61	105
Valley Rd.		
Wordsworth Clo., Rom.	CV30	42
Wordsworth Clo., Til.	DH44	71
Coleridge Rd.		
Wordsworth Dr., Sutt.	BQ56	94
Wordsworth Pl. N8	BY31	47
Alfoxton Av.		
Wordsworth Rd. N16	CA35	48
Wordsworth Rd. SE20	CC50	77
Wordsworth Rd., Har.	BH31	45
Wordsworth Rd., Hmptn.	BE49	74
Wordsworth Rd., Wall.	BW57	95
Wordsworth Rd., Well.	CN44	68
Wordsworth Rd., Wey.	AX56	92
Wordsworth Way, West Dr.	AY42	63
Wordsworth Way, Dart.	CX45	70
Wordsworth Wk. NW11	BS31	47
Worfield St. SW11	BU43	66
Worgan St. SE11	**BX42**	**4**
Worgan St. SE11	BX42	66
Worland Rd. E15	CG36	58
Worlds End La. N21	BX25	29
Worlds End La., Enf.	BX25	29
Worlds End La., Orp.	CN57	97
Worlds End Pass. SW10	BT43	66
Worlds End Pl. SW10	BT43	66
Worlds End		
Worlds End SW10	BT43	66
Worlds End, Cob.	BC60	92
Worley Rd., St.Alb.	BG13	9
Worlidge St. W6	BQ42	65
Worlingham Rd. SE22	CA45	67
Wormholt Est. W12	BO40	55
Wormholt Rd. W12	BP40	55
Wormingford Ct., Wal.Abb.	CH20	22
Ninefields		
Wormley Ct., Wal.Abb.	CH20	22
Winters Way		
Wormley Lodge Clo., Brox.	CD15	12
Wormwood St. EC2	**CA39**	**2**
Wormwood St. EC2	CA39	57
Wornington Rd. W10	BR38	55
Wornington Yd. W10	BR38	55
Wornington Rd.		
Woronzow Rd. NW8	BT37	1
Woronzow Rd. NW8	BT37	56
Worple Av. SW19	BQ50	75
Worple Av., Islw.	BJ46	74
Worple Av., Stai.	AW50	73
Worple Clo., Har.	BE33	45
Worple Rd. Ms. SW19	BR50	75
Worple Rd. SW19	BQ51	85
Worple Rd. SW20	BQ51	85
Worple Rd., Epsom	BN61	103
Worple Rd., Islw.	BJ45	64
Worple Rd., Lthd.	BJ64	102
Worple Rd., Stai.	AW50	73
Worple St. SW14	BN45	65
Worple Way, Har.	BE33	45
Worple Way, Rich.	BL46	75
Worple, The, Stai.	AS46	72
Worplesdon Rd., Guil.	AP67	109
Worrin Rd., Brwd.	DC26	122
Worrin Rd., Brwd.	DC26	122
Worship St. EC2	**BZ38**	**2**
Worship St. EC2	BZ38	57
Worships Hill, Sev.	CT65	107
Worslade Rd. SW17	BT49	76
Worsley Bridge Rd. SE26	CD49	77
Worsley Bridge Rd., Beck.	CD49	77
Worsley Rd. E11	CG35	49
Worsopp Dr. SW4	BW45	66
Worsted Grn., Red.	BW68	113
Worth Gro. SE17	**BZ42**	**4**
Worth Gro. SE17	BZ42	67
Worthfield Clo., Epsom	BN57	94
Worthing Clo. E15	CG37	58
Worthing Rd., Houns.	BE43	64
Worthington Rd., Surb.	BL54	85
Worthydown Ct. SE18	CL43	68
Prince Imperial Rd.		
Wortley Rd. E6	CJ36	58
Wortley Rd., Croy.	BY54	86
Worton Gdns., Islw.	BG44	64
Worton Rd., Islw.	BG45	64
Worton Way, Islw.	BG44	64
Wotton Dr., Dor.	BD73	119
Wotton Grn., Orp.	CP52	89
Wotton Rd. SE8	CD43	67
Wotton Way, Sutt.	BQ58	94
Wouldham Rd. E16	CG39	58
Wouldham Rd., Grays	DC43	71
Wrabness Way, Stai.	AW51	83
Wragby Rd. E11	CG34	49
Wrampling Pl. N9	CB26	39
Croyland Rd.		
Wrangley Ct., Wal.Abb.	CH20	22
Winters Way		
Wrangthorn Wk., Croy.	BY56	95
Epsom Rd.		
Wray Av., Ilf.	CL31	49
Wray Clo., Horn.	CV33	51
Wray Common Rd., Reig.	BT70	121
Wray Cres. N4	BX34	47
Wray La., Reig.	BT68	113
Wray Park Rd., Reig.	BS70	121
Wray Rd., Sutt.	BR58	94
Wrayfield Av., Reig.	BT70	121
Wrayfield Rd., Sutt.	BQ55	85
Wraylands Dr., Reig.	BT69	121
Wrays Way, Hayes	BB38	53
Wraysbury Clo., Houns.	BE46	74
Dorney Way		
Wraysbury Rd., Stai.	AT48	72
Wrekin Rd. SE18	CM43	68
Wren Av. NW2	BQ35	46
Wren Av., Sthl.	BE42	64
Wren Clo. E16	CG39	58
Wren Clo., Orp.	CP52	89
Sandpiper Way		
Wren Clo., S.Croy.	CC58	96
Wren Cres., Bush.	BG26	36
Wren Cres., Wey.	AX56	92
Wren Ct., Slou.	AT41	62
Wren Dr., West Dr.	AX41	63
Wren Gdns., Dag.	CP35	50
Wren Gdns., Horn.	CT33	50
Wren Path SE28	CM41	68
Whinchat Rd.		
Wren Pl., Brwd.	DB27	42
Wren Rd. SE5	BZ44	67
Wren Rd., Dag.	CP35	50
Wren Rd., Sid.	CP49	79
Wren St. WC1	**BX38**	**2**
Wren St. WC1	BX38	56
Grays Inn Rd.		
Wren Wk., Til.	DG44	71
Poynder Rd.		
Wren Wood, Welw.G.C.	BS 7	5
Wrens Av., Ashf.	BA49	73
Wrens Ct., Grays	DF49	81
Henley Deane		
Wrens Hill, Lthd.	BG61	102
Wrensfield, Hem.H.	AW13	8
Wrentham Av. NW10	BQ37	55
Wrenthorpe Rd., Brom.	CG49	78
Wrenwood Way, Pnr.	BC31	44
Wrestlers Clo., Hat.	BQ11	10
Lockley Cres.		
Wrestlers Ct. EC3	**CA39**	**2**
Camomile St.		
Wrexham Rd. E3	CE37	57
Wrexham Rd., Brwd.	CV27	42
Wricklemarsh Rd. SE3	CH44	68
Wrigglesworth St. SE14	CC43	67
Wright Clo., Swans.	DB46	80
Milton St.		
Wright Rd. N1	CA36	57
Pond Rd.		
Wright Rd., Houns.	BD43	64
Wright Sq., Wind.	AL45	61
Wright		
Wright Way, Wind.	AL45	61
Wright		
Wright, Wind.	AL45	61
Wrights Alley SW19	BQ50	75
Wrights Clo., Dag.	CR35	50
Webbscroft Rd.		
Wrights Grn. SW4	BW45	66
Wrights La. W8	BS41	66
Wrights La., Brwd.	DB21	33
Wrights Pl. NW10	BN36	55
Mitchell Way		
Wrights Rd. E3	CD37	57
Wrights Rd. SE25	CA52	87
Wrights Row, Wall.	BV56	95
Wrights Wk. SW14	BN45	65
North Worple Way		
Wrightsbridge Rd., Rom.	CX26	42
Wrigley Clo. E4	CF28	39
The Avenue		
Wriotsley Way, Wey.	AW57	92
Writtle Wk., Rain.	CT37	59
Wrotham Rd. NW1	**BW36**	**1**
Wrotham Rd. NW1	BW36	56
Agar Pl.		
Wrotham Rd. W13	BJ40	54
Mattock La.		
Wrotham Rd., Barn.	BR23	28
Wrotham Rd., Grav.	DF51	81
Wrotham Rd., Well.	CP44	69
Wroths Path, Loug.	CK23	31
Wrottesley Rd. NW10	BP37	55
Wrottesley Rd. SE18	CL43	68
Wroughton Rd. SW11	BU46	76
Wroughton Ter. NW4	BP31	46
Babington Rd.		
Wroxall Rd., Dag.	CP36	59
Wroxham Av., Hem.H.	AX14	8
Wroxham Gdns. N11	BW29	38
Wroxham Gdns., Enf.	BY21	29
Wroxham Gdns., Pot.B.	BQ19	19
Wroxham Rd. SE28	CP40	59
Wroxton Rd. SE15	CB44	67
Wrythe Green Rd., Cars.	BU55	86
Wrythe Grn., Cars.	BU55	86
Wrythe Green Rd.		
Wrythe La., Cars.	BT54	86
Wulfred Way, Sev.	CX62	108
Wulfstan St. W12	BO39	55
Wyatt Clo., Hayes	BC39	53
Wyatt Clo., Nthlt.	BE36	54
Wyatt Clo., Sev.	DC63	108
Wyatt Park Rd. SW2	BX48	76
Wyatt Rd. E7	CH36	58
Wyatt Rd. N5	BZ34	48
Wyatt Rd., Dart.	CT45	69
Wyatt Rd., Stai.	AW49	73
Wyatt Rd., Wind.	AL45	61
Wyatts Clo., Rick.	AW24	26
Wyatts Green La., Brwd.	DB21	33
Wyatts Green Rd., Brwd.	DB21	33
Wyatts Rd., Rick.	AV24	25
Wybert St. NW1	BV38	56
Munster Sq.		
Wyborne Way NW10	BN36	55
Wyburn Av., Barn.	BR24	28
Wych Elm Clo., Horn.	CX32	51
Wych Elm Pass., Kings.T.	BL50	75
Wych Elm Ri., Guil.	AS72	118
Wych Elm, Harl.	CM10	6
Wych Hill La., Wok.	AS63	100
Wych Hill Pk., Wok.	AR63	100
Wych Hill Ri., Wok.	AR63	100
Wych Hill Waye, Wok.	AR63	100
Wych Hill, Wok.	AR63	100
Wyche Gro., S.Croy.	BZ57	96
Wychelms, St.Alb.	BF17	18
Wycherley Clo. SE3	CG43	68
Vanbrugh Park Rd. W.		
Wycherley Cres., Barn.	BS25	29
Wychford Dr., Saw.	CP 6	6
Wychling Clo., Orp.	CP54	89
Wychwood Av., Edg.	BK29	36
Wychwood Av., Th.Hth.	BZ52	87
Wychwood Clo., Edg.	BK29	36
Wychwood End N6	BW33	47
Wychwood Way, Pnr.	CK31	49
Wychwood Way SE19	CA50	77
Central Hill Est.		
Wychwood Way, Edg.	BK29	36
Wyclif St. EC1	**BY38**	**2**
Wyclif St. EC1	BY38	56
Wycliffe Clo., Well.	CN44	68
Wycliffe Gdns., Red.	BW68	113
Wycliffe Rd. SW11	BV44	66
Wycliffe Rd. SW19	BS50	76
Wycliffe Row, Grav.	DF47	81
Alfred St.		
Wycliffe Way, Grav.	DF47	81
Dover Rd. E.		
Wycombe Gdns. NW11	BS34	47
St. Anns Cres.		
Wycombe Pl. SW18	BT46	76
Wycombe Rd. N17	CB30	39
Wycombe Rd., Ilf.	CK32	49
Wycombe Rd., Wem.	BM37	55
Wycombe Way, St.Alb.	BK12	9
Wyddial Grn., Welw.G.C.	BS 8	5
Widford Rd.		
Wydehurst Rd., Croy.	CB54	87
Wydell Clo., Mord.	BQ53	85
Wydeville Manor Rd. SE12	CH49	78
Wye Clo., Ashf.	AZ49	73
Wye Clo., Orp.	CN54	88
Wye Clo., Ruis.	BA32	44
Thames Dr.		
Wye Rd., Grav.	DH48	81
Wye St. SW11	BT44	66
Wye, The, Hem.H.	AZ11	8
Wyedale, St.Alb.	BL17	18
Thamesdale		
Wyeths Rd., Epsom	BO60	94
Wyevale Clo., Pnr.	BC31	44
Wyfields, Ilf.	CL30	40
Wyfold Rd. SW6	BR44	65
Wyhill Wk., Dag.	CS36	59
Wyke Clo., Islw.	BH43	64
Wyke Est. E9	CD36	57
Wyke Gdns. W7	BJ41	64
Wyke Rd. E3	CE36	57
Wyke Rd. SW20	BQ51	85
Wykeham Av., Dag.	CP36	59
Wykeham Av., Horn.	CV32	51
Wykeham Clo., West Dr.	AZ43	63
Wykeham Grn., Dag.	CP36	59
Wykeham Hill, Wem.	BL33	46
Wykeham Rd. NW4	BQ31	46
Wykeham Rd., Guil.	AU70	118
Wykeham Rd., Har.	BJ31	45
Wykeham Ri. N20	BR26	37
Wylchin Clo., Pnr.	BB31	44
Fore St.		
Wyld Way, Wem.	BM36	55
Wyldes Clo. NW11	BT33	47
Wildwood Rd.		
Wyldfield Gdns. N9	CA27	39
Latymer Rd.		
Wyleu St. SE23	CD47	77
Wylie Rd., Sthl.	BF41	64
Wyllen Clo. E1	CC38	57
Wyllyotts Clo., Pot.B.	BR19	19
Wylo Dr., Barn.	BO25	28
Wymering Rd. W9	BS38	56
Wymond St. SW15	BQ45	65
Wynan Rd. E14	CE42	67
Wynaud Ct. N22	BX29	38
Palmerston Rd.		
Wyncham Av., Sid.	CN47	78
Wynchgate N14	BW26	38
Wynchgate N21	BX26	38
Wynchgate, Har.	BH29	37
Wynchlands Cres., St.Alb.	BK13	9
Wyncote Way, S.Croy.	CC58	96
Wyncroft Clo., Brom.	CK52	88
Wyndale Av. NW9	BM32	46
Wyndcliff Rd. SE7	CH42	68
Wyndcroft Clo., Enf.	BY24	29
Wyndham Av., Barn.	BU26	28
Wyndham Av., Cob.	BC60	92
Wyndham Clo., Orp.	CM54	88
Wyndham Clo., Sutt.	BS57	95
Sackville Rd.		
Wyndham Cres. N19	BW34	47
Wyndham Cres., Houns.	BF46	74
Wyndham Est. SE5	BZ43	67
Wyndham Ms. W1	**BU39**	**1**
Wyndham Ms. W1	BU39	56
Upper Montagu St.		
Wyndham Pl. W1	**BU39**	**1**
Wyndham Pl. W1	BU39	56
Wyndham Rd. E6	CJ36	58
Wyndham Rd. SE5	BY43	66
Wyndham Rd. W13	BJ41	64
Wyndham Rd., Kings.T.	BL50	75
Wyndham Rd., Wok.	AQ62	100
Wyndham St. W1	**BU39**	**1**
Wyndham St. W1	BU39	56
Wyndham Yd. W1	**BU39**	**1**
Wyndham Pl.		
Wyneham Rd. SE24	BZ46	77
Wynell Rd. SE23	CC48	77
Wynford Gro., Orp.	CO52	89
Wynford Rd. N1	**BX37**	**2**
Wynford Rd. N1	BX37	56
Wynford Way SE9	CK48	78
Wynlie Gdns., Pnr.	BC30	35
Wynndale Rd. E18	CH30	40
Wynne Rd. SW9	BY44	66
Wynns Av., Sid.	CO46	79
Lyndon Av.		
Wynnstay Gdns. W8	BS41	66
Wynnstow Pk., Oxt.	CG69	115
Wynter St. SW11	BT45	66
Wynton Gdns. SE25	CA52	87
Wynton Gro., Walt.	BC55	83
Wynton Pl. W3	BM39	55
Wynyard Clo., Rick.	AW21	26
Wynyard Ter. SE11	**BX42**	**4**
Wynyard Ter. SE11	BX42	66
Aveline St.		
Wynyatt St. EC1	**BY38**	**2**
Wyre Gro., Edg.	BM27	37
Wyre Gro., Hayes	BC42	63
Wyresdale Cres., Grnf.	BH38	54
Wyte Leaf Clo., Ruis.	BA32	44
Wythburn Pl. W1	**BU39**	**1**
Wythburn Pl. W1	BU39	56
Seymour Pl.		
Wythens Wk. SE9	CL46	78
Southend Cres.		
Wythenshawe Rd., Dag.	CR34	59
Wythes Clo., Brom.	CK51	88
Wythes Rd. E16	CK40	58
Wythfield Rd. SE9	CK46	78
Wyton, Welw.G.C.	BT 8	5
Wyvenhoe Rd., Har.	BG34	45
Wyver St. Alb.	BH13	9
Avenue Rd.		
Wyvern Clo., Dart.	CV47	80
Wyvern Clo., Orp.	CO55	89
Wyvern Rd., Pur.	BY58	95
Wyvil Est. SW8	BX43	66
Wyvil Rd. SW8	BX43	66
Wyvis St. E14	CE39	57

Y

Yabsley St. E14	CF40	57
Yaffle Rd., Wey.	BA58	92
Yalding Clo., Orp.	CP52	89
Yalding Rd. SE16	**CB41**	**4**
Yalding Rd. SE16	CB41	67
Yale Way, Horn.	CU35	50
Yale, Houns.	BE46	74
Yarborough Rd. SW19	BT51	86
Runnymede		
Yard Mead, Stai.	AT48	72
Yardbridge, Sutt.	BS58	95
Hulverston Clo.		
Yardley Clo. E4	CE25	30
Yardley Clo., Reig.	BS69	121
Yardley La. E4	CE25	30
Yardley St. WC1	**BY38**	**2**
Yardley St. WC1	BY38	56
Yarm Clo., Lthd.	BK65	102
Yarm Court Rd., Lthd.	BK65	102
Yarm Way, Lthd.	BK65	102
Yarmouth Cres. N15	CB32	48
Yarmouth Pl. W1	**BV40**	**3**
Yarmouth Pl. W1	BV40	56
Brick St.		
Yarmouth Rd., Wat.	BD22	27
Yarnton Way SE2	CP41	69
Yarnton Way, Erith	CP41	69
Yarrow Cres. E6	CK39	58
Yarrow Field, Wok.	AR65	100
Yarrow Side, Amer.	AQ23	25
Yateley St. SE7	CJ41	68
Yates Ct. NW2	BQ36	55
Yeading Av., Har.	BE34	45
Yeading Gdns., Hayes	BC39	53
Yeading La., Hayes	BC39	53
Yeading La., Nthlt.	BD38	54
Yeading Lane Fork, Hayes	BD38	54
Yeading Wk., Har.	BE32	45
Yeate St. N1	**BZ36**	**2**
Yeate St. N1	BZ36	57
Yeatman Rd. N6	BU32	47
Yeats Clo. SE13	CF44	67
Eliot Pk.		
Yeats Clo., Red.	BT72	121
Yeldham Rd. W6	BQ42	65
Yellowpine Way, Ilf.	CO28	41
Yelverton Clo., Rom.	CV30	42
Neave Cres.		
Yelverton Rd. SW11	BT44	66
Yens, The, Ashf.	AZ49	73
Reedsfield Rd.		
Yenston Clo., Mord.	BS53	86
Yeo St. E3	CE39	57
Yeoman Clo. SE27	BY48	76
Prioress Rd.		
Yeoman Rd., Nthlt.	BE36	54
Yeoman St. SE8	CD42	67
Yeoman Way, Red.	BV73	121
Spencer Way		
Yeomans Acre, Ruis.	BC32	44
Yeomans Meadow, Sev.	CU66	116
Yeomans Ms., Islw.	BG46	74
Yeomans Rd., Hem.H.	AZ10	8
Yeomans Row SW3	**BU41**	**3**
Yeomans Row SW3	BU41	66
Yeomans Way, Enf.	CB23	30
Yeomans Yd. E1	**CA40**	**4**
Chamber St.		
Yeomans Yd. E1	CA40	57
Chamber St.		
Yeomen Way, Ilf.	CM29	40
Yeoveney Clo., Stai.	AU48	72
Yeovil Clo., Orp.	CN55	88
Yerbury Rd. N19	BW34	47
Yester Dr., Chis.	CK50	78
Yester Pk., Chis.	CK50	78
Yester Rd., Chis.	CL50	78
Yevele Way, Horn.	CW33	51
Yew Av., West Dr.	AY40	53
Yew Clo., Buck.H.	CJ27	40
Yew Gro. NW2	BQ35	46
Yew Gro., Welw.G.C.	BT 8	5
Forresters Dr.		
Yew Tree Bottom Rd., Epsom	BP61	103
Yew Tree Clo. N21	BY26	38
Yew Tree Clo. NW1	BY26	38
Yew Tree Clo., Brwd.	DD25	122
Yew Tree Clo., Chesh.	AQ18	16
Yew Tree Clo., Couls.	BU63	104
Yew Tree Clo., Hem.H.	AW14	8
Yew Tree Clo., Sev.	CS65	107
Yew Tree Clo., Well.	CO44	69
Yew Tree Clo., Wor.Pk.	BO54	85
Yew Tree Dr., Cat.	CA66	114
Yew Tree Dr., Guil.	AR68	109
Yew Tree Dr., Hem.H.	AT17	16
Yew Tree Gdns., Rom.	CS32	50
Yew Tree La., Reig.	BS69	121
Yew Tree Rd. W12	BO40	55
Yew Tree Rd., Dor.	BJ70	119
Yew Tree Rd., Uxb.	AY37	53
Yew Tree Wk., Houns.	BE46	74
Yew Tree Wk., Lthd.	BO67	111
Yew Tree Wk., S.Croy.	BZ58	96
Yew Trees, Egh.	AU52	82
Yew Trees, Shep.	AY52	83
Laleham Rd.		
Yew Wk., Har.	BH33	45
Yew Wk., Hodd.	CE12	12
Yewdale Clo., Brom.	CG50	78
Yewfield Rd. NW10	BO36	55
Yewlands Clo., Bans.	BT61	104
Yewlands, Hodd.	CE12	12
Yewlands, Saw.	CQ 6	6
Yews Av., Enf.	CB21	30
Yews, The, Grav.	DH47	81
Yewtree End, St.Alb.	BG17	18
Yewtree Gdns., Epsom	BM61	103
Yewtree La., Dor.	BF69	119
Yewtree Rd., Beck.	CD52	87
Yewtree Wk., Pur.	BZ58	96
Yiewsley By-pass, Uxb. & West Dr.	AZ39	53
Yiewsley Station Rd., West Dr.	AY40	53
Yoakley Rd. N16	CA34	48
Yoke Clo. N7	BX36	56
Yolande Gdns. SE9	CK46	78
Yonge Pk. N4	BY34	47
York Av. SE17	**BZ42**	**4**
Browning St.		
York Av. SE17	BZ42	67
Browning St.		
York Av. SW14	BN46	75
York Av. W7	BH40	54
York Av., Hayes	BA39	53
York Av., Sid.	CN48	78
York Av., Slou.	AO39	52
York Av., Stan.	BJ30	36
York Av., Wind.	AN44	61
York Bldgs. WC2	**BX40**	**4**
York Bldgs. WC2	BX40	56
Watergate Wk.		
York Clo. E6	CK39	58
Boultwood Rd.		
York Clo. SE5	BZ44	67
Lilford Rd.		
York Clo. W7	BH40	54
York Clo., Amer.	AP23	25
York Clo., Brwd.	DC26	122
York Clo., Kings L.	AZ18	17
York Clo., Wey.	AY59	92
York Cres., B.Wd.	BN23	28
York Cres., Loug.	CK24	31
York Ct., Mord.	BS52	86
York Gate N14	BX26	38
York Gate NW1	**BV38**	**1**
York Gate NW1	BV38	56
York Gdns. N18	CB29	39
York Gdns., Walt.	BD55	84
York Gro. SE15	CC44	67
York Hill SE27	BY48	76
York Hill, Loug.	CK24	31
York House Pl. W8	BS41	66
York Ms. Ilf.	CL34	49
York Rd.		
York Ms. NW5	BV35	47
York Pl. SW11	BT45	66
York Pl. W7	BH40	54
York Pl. WC2	**BX40**	**4**
York Pl. WC2	BX40	56
Villiers St.		
York Pl., Grays	DD43	71
York Pl., Ilf.	CL34	49
York Rd.		
York Pl., Wind.	AO44	61
York Rd. E10	CF34	48
York Rd. E17	CC32	48
York Rd. E4	CD28	39
York Rd. E7	CH36	58
York Rd. N11	BW29	38
York Rd. N18	CB29	39
York Rd. N21	BZ26	39
York Rd. NW9	BO32	46
The Broadway		
York Rd. SE1	**BX41**	**4**
York Rd. SE1	BX41	66
York Rd. SW11	BT45	66
York Rd. SW19	BS50	76
York Rd. W3	BN39	55
York Rd. W5	BK41	64
York Rd., Barn.	BT25	29
York Rd., Brent.	BK42	64
York Rd., Brwd.	DC26	122
York Rd., Byfleet	AX59	92
York Rd., Croy.	BY54	86
York Rd., Dart.	CW47	80
York Rd., Epp.	CR17	23
York Rd., Grav.	DH48	81
York Rd., Guil.	AR71	118
York Rd., Houns.	BF45	64
York Rd., Ilf.	CL34	49
York Rd., Kings.T.	BL50	75
York Rd., Northfleet	DE47	81
York Rd., Nthwd.	BC30	35
York Rd., Rain.	CT36	59
York Rd., Rich.	BL46	75
Albert Rd.		
York Rd., S.Croy.	CC58	96
York Rd., St.Alb.	BH13	9
York Rd., Sutt.	BS57	95
York Rd., Tedd.	BH49	74
York Rd., Uxb.	AX36	53
York Rd., Wal.Cr.	CD20	21
York Rd., Wat.	BD25	27
York Rd., West.	CH63	106
York Rd., Wey.	BA56	92
York Rd., Wind.	AN44	61
York Rd., Wok.	AR63	100
York Ri. NW5	BV34	47
York Ri., Orp.	**CN55**	**88**
York Sq. E14	CD39	57
York St. W1	**BU39**	**1**
York St. W1	BU39	56
York St., Bark.	CL37	58
Abbey Rd.		
York St., Mitch.	BV54	86
York St., Twick.	BJ47	74
York Ter. E. NW1	**BV38**	**1**
York Ter. E. NW1	BV38	56
York Ter. W. NW1	**BV38**	**1**
York Ter. W. NW1	BV38	56
York Ter., Enf.	BZ22	30
York Ter., Erith	CS44	69
York Way Ct. N1	**BX37**	**2**
York Way Ct. N1	BX37	56
York Way N1	BW36	56
York Way N1	**BX36**	**2**
York Way N20	BU27	38
York Way N7	BW36	56
York Way, B.Wd.	BN23	28
York Way, Chess.	BL57	94
York Way, Felt.	BE48	74
York Way, Wat.	BD21	27
York Way, Welw.	BP 5	5
Yorke Gdns., Reig.	BS70	121
Yorke Rd., Reig.	BS70	121
Yorke Rd., Rick.	AZ25	26
Yorkland Av., Well.	CN45	68
Yorks Hill, Sev.	CR69	116
Yorkshire Gdns. N18	CB28	39
Yorkshire Grey Pl. NW3	BY35	47
Heath St.		
Yorkshire Rd. E14	CD39	57
Yorkshire Rd., Mitch.	BX53	86
Yorkton St. E2	**CB37**	**2**
Yorkton St. E2	CB37	57
Young Rd. E16	CJ39	58
Young St. W8	**BS41**	**3**
Young St. W8	BS41	66
Young St., Lthd.	BH65	102
Youngfield, Hem.H.	AV13	7
Youngmans Clo., Enf.	BZ23	30
Youngs Bldgs. EC1	**BZ38**	**2**
Youngs Bldgs. EC1	BZ38	57
Old St.		
Youngs Rd., Ilf.	CM32	49
Youngs Ri., Welw.G.C.	BP 8	5
Youngstroat La., Wok.	AS59	91
Yoxley App., Ilf.	CM32	49
Yoxley Dr., Ilf.	CM32	49
Yukon Rd. SW12	BV47	76
Yule Clo., St.Alb.	BE18	18
St. Lawrence Way		
Yuletide Clo. NW10	BO36	55

Z

Zambra Way, Sev.	CW63	108
Zampa Rd. SE16	CC42	67
Zander Ct. E2	CB38	57
St. Peters Clo.		
Zangwill Rd. SE3	CJ44	68
Zealand Av., West Dr.	AX43	63
Zealand Clo. NW2	BQ33	46
Zealand Rd. E3	CD37	57
Zelah Rd., Orp.	CO54	89
Zennor Rd. SW12	BV47	76
Zenoria St. SE22	CA45	67
Zermatt Rd., Th.Hth.	BZ52	87
Zetland St. E14	CE39	57
Zig Zag Rd., Dor.	BK68	111
Zig-Zag Rd., Ken.	BZ61	105
Zig-Zag Rd., Tad.	BL69	120
Zion Pl., Th.Hth.	BZ52	87
Zion Rd., Th.Hth.	BZ52	87
Zion St., Grav.	DG47	81
Zoar St. SE1	**BZ40**	**4**
Zoar St. SE1	BZ40	57
Zoffany St. N19	BW34	47
Ashbrook Rd.		

PERSONAL INFORMATION

NAME AND ADDRESS	TELEPHONE	NOTES
Postcode		
Postcode		
Postcode		
Postcode		
Postcode		
Postcode		
Postcode		
Postcode		
Postcode		
Postcode		
Postcode		

PERSONAL INFORMATION

NAME AND ADDRESS	TELEPHONE	NOTES
Postcode		
Postcode		
Postcode		
Postcode		
Postcode		
Postcode		
Postcode		
Postcode		
Postcode		
Postcode		
Postcode		

PERSONAL INFORMATION

NAME AND ADDRESS	TELEPHONE	NOTES
Postcode		
Postcode		
Postcode		
Postcode		
Postcode		
Postcode		
Postcode		
Postcode		
Postcode		
Postcode		
Postcode		

PERSONAL INFORMATION

NAME AND ADDRESS	TELEPHONE	NOTES
Postcode		
Postcode		
Postcode		
Postcode		
Postcode		
Postcode		
Postcode		
Postcode		
Postcode		
Postcode		
Postcode		

PERSONAL INFORMATION

NAME AND ADDRESS	TELEPHONE	NOTES
Postcode		
Postcode		
Postcode		
Postcode		
Postcode		
Postcode		
Postcode		
Postcode		
Postcode		
Postcode		
Postcode		

PERSONAL INFORMATION

NAME AND ADDRESS	TELEPHONE	NOTES
Postcode		
Postcode		
Postcode		
Postcode		
Postcode		
Postcode		
Postcode		
Postcode		
Postcode		
Postcode		
Postcode		

PERSONAL INFORMATION

NAME AND ADDRESS	TELEPHONE	NOTES
Postcode		
Postcode		
Postcode		
Postcode		
Postcode		
Postcode		
Postcode		
Postcode		
Postcode		
Postcode		
Postcode		

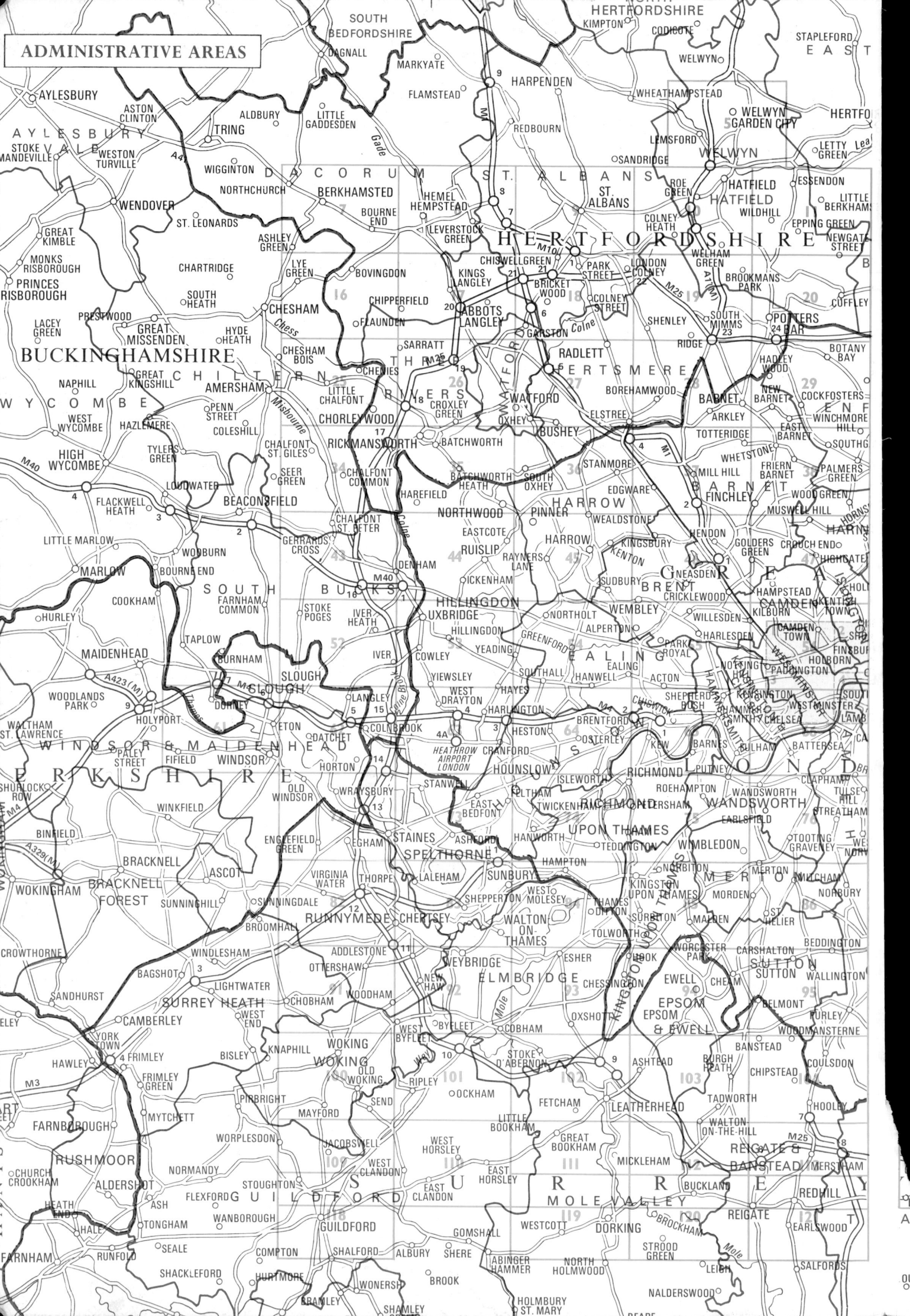

Large scale Central London maps
are numbered 1 to 4

Scale of Miles

0 1 2 3 4 5 6